BIBLIOGRAPHY OF SOUTHERN APPALACHIA

a publication of
THE APPALACHIAN CONSORTIUM, INC.

compiled
by
Appalachian State University
Berea College
Blue Ridge Parkway
East Tennessee State University
Ferrum College
First Tennessee-Virginia Development District
Lees-McRae College
Mars Hill College
U. S. Forest Service
University of North Carolina at Asheville
Warren Wilson College
Western Carolina University
Western North Carolina Historical Association

edited and selectively annotated
by
CHARLOTTE T. ROSS

distributed
by
THE APPALACHIAN CONSORTIUM PRESS
Boone, North Carolina
and
UNIVERSITY OF TENNESSEE PRESS
Knoxville, Tennessee

The Appalachian Consortium was a non-profit educational organization composed of institutions and agencies located in Southern Appalachia. From 1973 to 2004, its members published pioneering works in Appalachian studies documenting the history and cultural heritage of the region. The Appalachian Consortium Press was the first publisher devoted solely to the region and many of the works it published remain seminal in the field to this day.

With funding from the Andrew W. Mellon Foundation and the National Endowment for the Humanities through the Humanities Open Book Program, Appalachian State University has published new paperback and open access digital editions of works from the Appalachian Consortium Press.

www.collections.library.appstate.edu/appconsortiumbooks

ISBN (pbk.: alk. Paper): 978-1-4696-4213-0
ISBN (ebook): 978-1-4696-4215-4

Distributed by the University of North Carolina Press
www.uncpress.org

Entered according to Act of Congress A.D. 1873, by D. Appleton and Co. in the office of the Librarian of Congress, Washington.

Southern Appalachia—circa 1800

INTRODUCTION

For years, a few persistent but isolated scholars and regional institutions, ignored and without support from the larger intellectual community, continuing their work under criticism almost to the point of ridicule, have known that a great wealth of Appalachiana exists, that it's available, that it's significant. What was needed was a synthesis of effort, a unified approach beyond the capability of any one individual or institution. To reach the widespread geographic area the information defined, to bring together in a single compilation the overall volume and diversity of materials, and to build a comprehensive listing from the scarcity of existing holdings in a multitude of individual libraries required a consorted effort of new dimensions.

One group of neo-pioneers seeking to promote regional cooperation and a positive Appalachian consciousness and identity was the Appalachian Consortium, a non-profit, educational organization representing both academic institutions of higher learning and public agencies in the areas of Western North Carolina, East Tennessee, and Southwestern Virginia. In its embryonic stages, before the Consortium's formal incorporation in the early 1970's, the individuals interested in fostering this image were meeting to discuss a common philosophy of purpose and goals on which inter-institutional and inter-agency cooperation could begin. They agreed that one of the first objectives should be the determination of the printed holdings of each potential member and that a union list of regional materials should be prepared. No one at the time anticipated the scope of this five-year project which serves as further evidence of a rich but untapped historical record. It was immediately clear that the project needed to be defined and made manageable. Shortly after the official creation of the Consortium on June 25, 1971, a library committee was formed and the cataloging of materials started in five participating libraries. This effort led to what is now known as the BIBLIOGRAPHY OF SOUTHERN APPALACHIA, which was compiled by the librarians and staffs of eleven institutions and sixty-six other individual contributors. The assembled material was edited and selectively annotated by Charlotte T. Ross of Belk Library, Appalachian State University. What was originally conceived as a listing of perhaps a few hundred holdings in each of five institutions has become a 13,000 entry bibliography, cross-referenced by author and subject, and in addition, includes a separate filmography of Southern Appalachia compiled under the supervision of Professor Robert J. Higgs of East Tennessee State University.

The compilation of the bibliography has worked secondarily to encourage member institutions of the Consortium to increase their Appalachian holdings. In 1970, one particular library had approximately 100–150 books pertaining to the Appalachian Region. Aware suddenly of the bounty, the library began an aggressive three-year campaign of acquisition and increased its holdings from a mere one hundred titles to about 5,000, and today, two years later, boasts a collection of approximately 8,000.

Because response to the initial efforts of the Consortium's member schools was so encouraging, the Consortium decided to enlarge the project and subsequently issued invitations to institutions and regional libraries outside its geographic range. It also sought and received funds from the Rockefeller Foundation to support approximately one-third of the extensive work to follow. This support is gratefully acknowledged along with the contributions of the seventy-seven individuals and institutions who also contributed time, talent and money.

Special appreciation must, however, be given to Berea College for its cooperation in making its Weatherford-Hammond Mountain Collection available. This 53 year-old collection, started by far-sighted President William J. Hutchins in November, 1923, is the oldest and most significant Appalachian Collection in the region, and our bibliographic effort was considerably strengthened by its inclusion. Indeed, many of the rare and original documents in this bibliography can be offered only because of Berea's pioneering effort. It continues to serve as the parent collection from which all other research on Southern Appalachia has come, and this bibliography would have been impossible without the invaluable assistance and encouragement rendered by the faculty and staff of Berea College.

In an effort to avoid unnecessary duplication and inappropriate materials, the Consortium's Library Committee established certain perimeters and criteria. The first major task was to decide on an appropriate definition of "Southern Appalachia" for our specific purpose. Unlike more recent socio-economic definitions, it was decided that the earlier, "pre-pork barrel" geographic demarcations based on elevations would be used. With the exception of topical entries from a few counties in southern Ohio, the central mountains of Pennsylvania, and occasional references to the Appalachians in New York State, the bulk of the entries in this bibliography are derived from a nine-state area. Represented are the entire state of West Virginia, and those areas in eight states referred to by the people of Southern Appalachia as Mountain Maryland, Eastern Kentucky, Western Virginia, East Tennessee, Western North Carolina, Upper South Carolina, North Georgia, and Northern Alabama.

It was further agreed to restrict the bibliography to a listing of books and monographs, and more particularly, books and monographs which pertained to the Southern Appalachian Region. Thus, periodical information has been excluded, as well as non-Appalachian works by Appalachian authors. Outstanding work in compiling a comprehensive bibliography of periodical literature has been undertaken by Dr. Robert F. Munn and the West Virginia University Library staff. Researchers are encouraged to refer to that institution's publications, APPALACHIAN OUTLOOK and APPALACHIAN BIBLIOGRAPHY.

In addition to the holdings of the eleven Consortium members, the card catalogs and shelf lists of the heretofore-mentioned Weatherford-Hammond Collection at Berea College, and those of the Brown Collection at Duke University, the Cherokee Museum and the Cherokee Historical Association Collection in Cherokee, and the Thomas Wolfe Collection and other holdings at Pack Memorial Library in Asheville were used. The collections at Marshall University, the University of Tennessee, the University of North Carolina at Chapel Hill and Asheville, and West Virginia University were also consulted and selectively incorporated into this bibliography.

Once these conventional sources were exhausted, efforts were made to search out largely untapped material housed in the region's small county libraries, local libraries, local historical associations and private collections. This led to extensive correspondence and travel to almost every county in the region; it meant knocking on doors, writing individual authors and county officials, and talking to local residents.

The great quantity of information came as an unexpected but pleasant surprise, for much has been added to the narrative of Appalachia. Never before included in comprehensive works, this record of a people contains hundreds of small monographs, journals, and genealogies never before documented, which occasionally describe the history of Southern Appalachia in more accurate terms than present history records it. Possibilities for a nascent history of Black Appalachians begin to emerge in tentative ways, as the sample entry for this bibliography illustrates. While the Cherokees are the best represented Native Americans in this compilation, researchers will be pleased to discover the large number of other bands of the first Southern Appalachians that are also included.

Without apology, it must be stated that as this bibliography comes off the press it becomes outdated. In fact, this is as planned and was a factor in the method chosen for publication. Through the technological services of Science Press, these entries have become permanently stored in computer memory to stimulate further research and addenda. The Appalachian Consortium welcomes and solicits revisions and additions from all sources. While much has been uncovered, there remains much, much more yet to be discovered. The Consortium alone is responsible for errors and omissions but offers this bibliography in the name of all of its contributors as a research tool not previously available to scholars and academicians within and without the region. We hope that the work will serve as an impetus to individual citizens to look back into their own communities and supplement the on-going inventory. This work is offered not just as a nucleus of library holdings, but as the cumulative culture and heritage of the region. It is a beginning, not an end in itself. While seeking to preserve the work of the past, it encourages new and original work. Perhaps consorted and concerted efforts will help accomplish what has been called the next great task—a definitive and significant history of the Southern Appalachian Region.

F. Borden Mace
Executive Director
The Appalachian Consortium

July 4, 1976

CONTENTS

LOCATOR ABBREVIATIONS AND ADDRESSES

ASU — Appalachian State University
Boone, North Carolina 28607

BC — Berea College
Berea, Kentucky 40403

ETSU — East Tennessee State University
Johnson City, Tennessee 37601

FC — Ferrum College
Ferrum, Virginia 24088

LMC — Lees-McRae College
Banner Elk, North Carolina 28604

MHC — Mars Hill College
Mars Hill, North Carolina 28754

UNCA — University of North Carolina at Asheville
Asheville, North Carolina 28804

WW — Warren Wilson College
Swannanoa, North Carolina 28778

WCU — Western Carolina University
Cullowhee, North Carolina 28723

BIBLIOGRAPHY OF SOUTHERN APPALACHIA

Sample Entry

B6340 ASU BC 1248a

Branham, Levi

My Life and Travels.

Xerox of original.

Dalton, Ga.: A. J. Showalter Co., 1929.

Autobiography of a former slave and later school teacher from Murray County, Georgia. A rare account giving insight into the period during and after the Civil War with commentary on the Ku Klux Klan in Georgia.

1. Biography
2. Appalachian Counties — Georgia — Murray County
3. Appalachian Counties — Tennessee — Marion County
4. Negroes — Appalachia

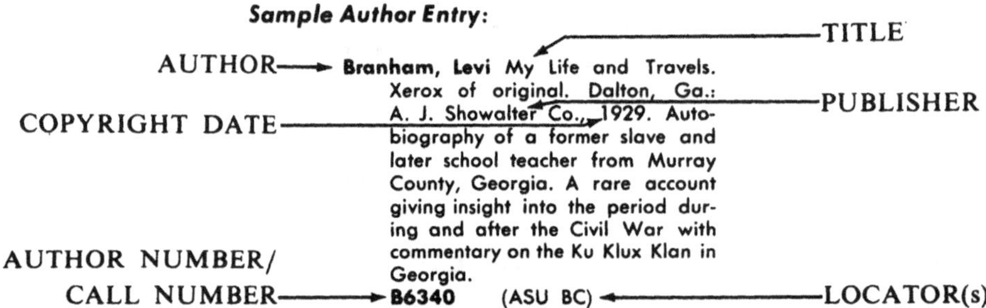

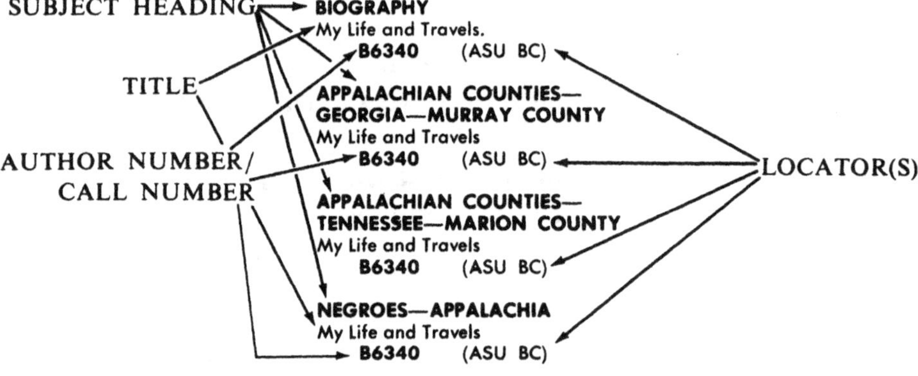

BIBLIOGRAPHY OF SOUTHERN APPALACHIA

Acknowledgements

APPALACHIAN CONSORTIUM LIBRARY COMMITTEE

Robert Balliot, Western Carolina University
Richard Jackson, Lees-McRae College
Elizabeth Shepard, Warren Wilson College
Hal Smith, East Tennessee State University
William Tydeman, Mars Hill College
Dorothea B. Wilburn, Ferrum College
Richard Barker, Appalachian State University, Chairman

PARTICIPATING LIBRARIES

Berea College, Arthur Flandreau
Blue Ridge Parkway, F. Andrew Ketterson, Jr., Historian
Pack Memorial Library, City of Asheville, Kenneth Brown
University of North Carolina at Asheville, Ainsley Whitman

COOPERATING LIBRARIES

Duke University
East Tennessee Historical Association
Marshall University
Roanoke Public Library
University of North Carolina at Chapel Hill
University of Tennessee
University of Virginia
West Virginia University

Special Individual Assistance

Mr. Alfred Baker
Dr. Fred Bentley
Dr. Frank Brown
Mrs. Joan Brown
Mr. and Mrs. G. B. Chiltoskey
Mr. Horton Cooper
Ms. Judy Cornett
Dr. D. P. Culp
Dr. Arthur Derosier, Jr.
Dr. Richard Drake
Ms. Sharon Edwards
Dr. J. Gerald Eller
Ms. Martha Ellison
Mr. Leonard Eury
Dr. H. C. Evans, Jr.
Ms. Sarah Firor
Mrs. Emily Gile
Mrs. Sheri Greene
Dr. Joseph T. Hart
Mrs. Audrey Hartley
Dr. Reuben Holden
Dr. John Hough
Ms. Susan Huffman
Mr. Louis Iglehart
Dr. Harley Jolley
Mr. Loyal Jones
Mr. Ambrose Manning
Mr. Alfred Perrin
Dr. W. H. Plemmons
Mr. Spencer Qualls
Dr. Gerald Roberts
Dr. Harold Frank Robinson
Dr. Carl Ross
Mr. Nick Smith
Mr. George Stephens
Mr. Reuben Teesatuskie
Dr. Willis D. Weatherford
Dr. Herbert W. Wey
Dr. Cratis Williams
Dr. Max Williams
Mrs. Judy Wilson
Ms. Libby Winkler
Ms. Agnes Wise

AUTHOR INDEX

Aandahl, A. R. Soil Survey, Hamblen County, Tennessee. Field Report. 1940. Reprint. Washington: U. S. Department of Agriculture, Plant Industry, Soils, and Agricultural Engineering Bureau, 1946. Contains an excellent map of the county which lists many roads no longer in use.
A10 (ASU)

Abbott, Jane Ludlow Drake Yours for the Asking. Philadelphia: J. B. Lippincott Co., 1943. A Novel: A young minister and his bride find it difficult to adjust to life in the Kentucky Mountains.
A20 (ASU BC)

Abbott, John Stevens Cabot Daniel Boone, Pioneer of Kentucky. New York: Dodd, Mead & Co., 1874.
A30 (ASU)

Daniel Boone, Pioneer of Kentucky. New York: Dodd, Mead and Co., 1898.
A40 (ETSU)

Daniel Boone, the Pioneer of Kentucky. American Pioneers and Patriots. New York: Dodd & Mead, 1872. This is a surprisingly restrained account of the life, travels, heroism and declining fortunes of one of our great pioneers. The largest portion of the book is devoted to Boone's role in the settlement of Kentucky.
A50 (ASU BC)

David Crockett: His Life and Adventures. New York: Dodd & Mead, 1874. A rather extravagant account of the adventures of irrepressible Col. Crockett of East Tennessee.
A60 (ASU ETSU)

Abernethy, Arthur Talmage Moonshine: Being Appalachia's Arabian Nights. Asheville, N. C.: Dixie Pub., 1924. A book of short stories dealing with the world's second oldest profession. Most have Western North Carolina settings.
A70 (ASU LMC)

Abernethy, Thomas Perkins From Frontier to Plantation in Tennessee. Chapel Hill: Univ. of North Carolina, 1932. A history of the culture and politics of Tennessee from the earliest settlement to 1865. Contains much on the East Tennessee mountain region.
A80 (WWC BC)

From Frontier to Plantation in Tennessee: A Study in Frontier Democracy. Southern Historical Publications, no. 12. Univ. of Alabama Press, 1967.
A90 (ASU LMC)

Three Virginia Frontiers. Baton Rouge: Louisiana State Univ. Press, 1940. The second and third of Abernethy's frontiers are the Great Valley of Virginia and that portion of old Virginia which is now the state of Kentucky. Special emphasis is given to settlement patterns.
A100 (ETSU BC)

Three Virginia Frontiers. The Walter Lynwood Fleming Lectures in Southern History. 1940. Reprint. Gloucester, Mass.: Peter Smith, 1962.
A110 (ASU WCU)

Western Lands and the American Revolution. The Univ. of Virginia Institute for Research in the Social Sciences Monograph 25. New York: Appleton, 1937.
A120

Western Lands and the American Revolution. New York: Russell & Russell, 1959. Deals primarily with trans-Appalachian. Excellent section on Vandalia.
A130 (FC BC ASU)

Abrahams, Roger D. Anglo-American Folksong Style. Englewood Cliffs, N. J.: Prentice-Hall, 1968. This is a history of the folksong as an art form. Included are chapters on oral transmission, development of the ballad, stylistic changes, organization of meaning, popular themes, rhythm and meter, and the musical form of folksongs.
A140 (ASU BC)

Absher, Ruby T. Deed Book B-1 Wilkes County, North Carolina. Wilkesboro, N. C.: The Genealogical Society of the "Original" Wilkes County, n.d.
A150

Absher, Ruby T. comp. Land Entry Book, Wilkes County, North Carolina, 1778-1781. North Wilkesboro, N. C.: Genealogical Society of the "Original" Wilkes County, 1971. Contains 18th century land records of Wilkes County, North Carolina.
A160 (ASU)

Absher, Mrs. W. O. Deed Book A-1 Wilkes County, North Carolina. North Wilkesboro, N. C.: The author, n.d.
A170

Absher, Mrs. W. O. see **Absher, Ruby T.**

Abt Associates The Industrialization of Southern Rural Areas: A Study of Industry and Federal Assistance in Small Towns with Recommendations for Future Policy. Boston: The associates, 1968? A study of the feasibility of stemming the tide of out-migration by relocating industries in rural Appalachia.
A180

Achilles, Charles Marvin Cooperative Action on the Educational Problems of Appalachia. Unpublished Paper. n.p.: Appalachian Educational Laboratory, 1969.
A190

Research for Better Schools: A Federal Projects Workshop for Educational Programs in Tennessee and Appalachia. Knoxville: Univ. of Tennessee College of Education, 1971. These discussion papers summarize a workshop conference on the needs of Tennessee educators.
A200

Acid Mine Drainage in Appalachia Message from the President of the United States Transmitting the Appalachian Regional Commission's Report, Acid Mine Drainage in Appalachia, Pursuant to the Provisions of Section 302 (b) of the Appalachian Regional Development Act. Washington: U. S. Govt. Print. Off., 1969. A multi-volume study of the effects of acid mine drainage.
A210 (ASU)

Ackenheil and Associates Geo Systems Evaluation of Pollution Abatement Techniques Applicable to Lost Creek and Brown's Creek Watershed, West Virginia. Washington: Appalachian Regional Commission, 1973. Explores the relative success or failure of various reclamation attempts.
A220 (ASU)

Ackerly, Mary Denham Our Kin. Lynchburg, Va.: J. P. Bell Co., Inc., 1930.
A230

Acklen, Jeanette Tillotson comp. Tennessee Records. Vol. I: TOMBSTONE INSCRIPTIONS AND MANUSCRIPTS, HISTORICAL AND BIOGRAPHICAL. Assisted by K. White, L. W. Bowen, and E. A. Darden. Vol. II. BIBLE RECORDS AND MARRIAGE BONDS. Assisted by E. G. Vaught and others. 2 vols. 1933. Reprint. Baltimore: Genealogical Pub. Co., 1967. An excellent genealogical source for East Tennessee families.
A240 (ASU)

Acuff, J. J. "The Effort and Ability of Grainger County to Support Its Schools." Master's thesis. Univ. of Tennessee, 1955. A survey of school related problems in Grainger Co., Tenn.
A250 (ASU)

Adair, Anthony Garland ed. Heroes of the Alamo: Accounts and Documents. 2nd ed. New York: Exposition Press, 1957. Includes account of the last days of Col. David Crockett of East Tennessee.
A260 (ETSU)

Adair, James Adair's History of the American Indians. Ed. under the auspices of the National Society of Colonial Dames of America in Tennessee. Johnson City, Tenn.: The Watauga Press, 1930. Contains a history of American Indian tribes of the Southeastern United States. Good sections on Cherokee and Catawba Indians.
A270 (BC FC ASU LMC)

Adair's History of the American Indians. 1930. Reprint. Ed. under the auspices of the National Society of Colonial Dames of America in Tennessee. New York: Argonaut Press, 1966.
A280 (WCU)

History of the American Indians. 1930. Reprint. Ed. under the auspices of the National Society of Colonial Dames in America in Tennessee. Johnson City, Tenn.: Blue and Grey Press, 1971.
A290 (ETSU)

The History of the American Indians: Particularly Those Nations Adjoining to the Mississippi, East and West Florida. . . 1775. Reprint. With a new introduction by Robert F. Berkhofer, Jr. New York: Johnson Reprint Co., 1968.
A300 (LMC)

Adair, John comp. Compiled Laws of the Cherokee Nation, Published by Authority of the General Council. Talequah, I. T.: NATIONAL ADVOCATE, 1881.
A310

Compiled Laws of the Cherokee Nation, Published by Authority of the General Council. Reprint. Talequah, Okla.: National Advocate, 1881. This edition is printed in Cherokee.
A320

Adam, Frank The Clans, Septs and Regiments of the Scottish Highlands. Revised by Sir Thomas Innes. 8th ed. Baltimore: Genealogical Pub. Co., 1970. Many of the descendants of these clans live in Appalachia today. A good genealogical source for Scottish surnames.
A330 (ASU)

Adam, James Taylor "A Study of Effect of Government Aid and Other Factors on the Economic Development of Three Selected Areas in Georgia." Master's thesis. Georgia State Univ., 1971.
A340

Adamic, Louis Fighting for Survival: The Bootleg Coal Industry. Huntington: Appalachian Movement Press, 1973. This 41 page booklet appears to be a rewrite of a 1935 article in THE NATION.
A350 (ASU)

Adams, Agatha Boyd Thomas Wolfe, Carolina Student: A Brief Biography. Extension Publication, vol. 15, no. 2. Chapel Hill: Univ. of North Carolina Library, 1950. A biography of Wolfe's formative student days.
A360 (ASU WCU)

Thomas Wolfe: Carolina Student; A Brief Biography. Library Extension Publication, vol. 15, no. 2. 1950. Reprint. Chapel Hill, N. C.: Univ. of North Carolina Library, 1955.
A370 (ASU WCU)

Adams, Elmer Cleveland Walking in the Clouds. Detroit, Mich.: Arnold-Powers, 1939. Describes a hike along that section of the Appalachian trail included in the Great Smoky Mountains National Park.
A380 (ETSU ASU)

Adams, Frank Unearthing Seeds of Fire: The Idea of Highlander. Winston-Salem, N. C.: John F. Blair, 1974.
A390

Adams, Frazier B. Appalachia Revisited: How People Lived Fifty Years Ago. Ashland, Ky.: Economy Printers, 1970. Describes the folklore and customs of Appalachian people during the author's youth in Eastern Kentucky.
A400 (ETSU BC ASU WCU FC LMC)

Adams, Herbert Baxter Thomas Jefferson and the University of Virginia. Contributions to American Educational History, no. 2. Washington: Gov. Print. Off., 1888. Despite all its Old South emphasis, the University is in the Blue Ridge foothills of Albemarle County. This volume also includes sketches of four other Virginia colleges in the Blue Ridge region.
A410 (ASU)

Adams, James Taylor Death in the Dark. Big Laurel, Va.: Adams-Mullins, 1941. A collection of factual ballads of American mine disasters with historical notes.
A420 (BC ASU)

Adams, James Taylor ed. The Cumberland Empire: A Quarterly Review. Big Laurel, Va.: James Taylor Adams, quarterly.
C9410 (BC)

Adams, Lila C. Marriages of Patrick County, 1791-1850. n.p.: n.p., 1972. A resource book on Patrick County, Virginia.
A430

Adams, Paul Jay Mt. LeConte. Knoxville, Tenn.: Holston Print. Co., 1966. Account of the author's life-long love affair with a mountain. Includes accounts of many hiking trips.
A440 (LMC ETSU)

Mt. LeConte. 1966. Reprint. Knoxville, Tenn.: Holston Print. Co., 1968.
A450 (WCU ASU)

Adams, Wayne T. Factors Associated with the Adjustment of Families in Three Low-Income Counties of North Carolina. Raleigh, N. C.: North Carolina State Univ. Press, 1964. Includes one western North Carolina county.
A460 (ASU)

"Factors Associated with the Adjustment of Families in Three Low Income Counties of North Carolina." Master's thesis. North Carolina State Univ., 1964. One western North Carolina county is included in this survey.
A470

Adams, William H. An Economic and Social Survey of Bedford Co., Va. Charlottesville: Univ. of Virginia Extension Series XVIII, No. 2, 1944. Interesting statistics because Bedford is one of Virginia's least populous counties.
A480 (ASU)

Adams, William Henry Davenport Witch, Warlock, and Magician: Historical Sketches of Magic and Witchcraft in England and Scotland. 1889. Reprint. Ann Arbor, Mich.: Gryphon Books, 1971. This volume serves as a delightful introduction to elements of British folklore which are still prevalent in the mountains of Appalachia.
A490 (ASU)

Addington, Hugh M. Encomium for Scott County, Virginia. Nickelsville, Va.: Service Printery, 1951. A panegyric dedicated to Scott County and its mountain folk.
A500

Addington, Luther Foster Indian Stories of Virginia's Last Frontier. Wise, Va.: Historical Society of Southwest Virginia, 1966. Legends of Southwest Virginia and parts of the present state of West Virginia.
A510

The Little Fiddler of Laurel Cove. Illustrated by Jules Gotlieb. 1st ed. Indianapolis, Ind.: Bobbs-Merrill Co., 1960. A children's book describing the efforts of a young brother and sister to attend high school.
A520 (ASU BC)

A Short History of Extreme Southwest Virginia. Big Stone Gap, Va.: Chamber of Commerce, Wise County, Virginia, 1965. A history of Washington, Scott, Lee, Wise, Russell and Dickenson counties.
A530 (ASU LMC)

The Story of Wise County, Virginia. Wise: Centennial Committee and School Board of Wise County, 1956. A short history of Wise County and the Powell Valley includes material on early settlers, Benge's raids, pioneer life, John Fox, Jr., and economic development of the county.
A540 (BC ASU)

Sugar in the Gourd. New York: Bobbs-Merrill, 1961. The story line is based on a favorite mountain fiddle tune. In this story a young girl tries to contribute something special to her family.
A550

Tip Off to Win. New York: Bobbs-Merrill, 1962. A novel from Southwest Virginia about boys and basketball and hot tempered youths.
A560 (BC)

Wise County Geography Supplement. County Geography Supplements, no. 9. Big Stone Gap, Va.: Wise County School Board and Univ. of Virginia, 1928. A nicely illustrated local geography text designed for area school children. Lists landmarks, industries, and points of interest.
A570 (BC)

Addington, Robert M. History of Scott County, Virginia. Kingsport, Tenn.: Kingsport Press, 1932.
A580 (LMC FC ASU BC)

History of Scott County, Virginia. n.p.: n.p., 1932.
A590

Addington, Violet Walters "A Study of Homeschool Contacts and Attitudes toward Participation in Lincoln School, Kingsport, Tennessee." Master's thesis. East Tennessee State College, 1957.
A600 (ETSU)

Ader, Paul Fassett The Leaf Against the Sky. New York: Crown Pub., 1947. Members of a minister's family try to build new lives for themselves in a North Carolina mountain community.
A610 (ASU WCU BC)

Adrosko, Rita J. Natural Dyes and Home Dyeing. U. S. National Museum Bulletin, no. 281. 1968. Reprint. New York: Dover Publications, 1971. A history of dyes and dyeing with instructions.
A620 (BC ASU WCU)

Advisory Panel on Regional Materials of Instruction for the Tennessee Valley Applications of the Common Mooring: Fundamental Principles in the Utilization of Resources. Prepared by Howard P. Emerson, Chairman, Sub-committee on Presentation of the Common Mooring. Knoxville, Tenn.: The committee, 1943.
A630

Agee, J. H. Stroud, James Frank Soil Survey of Shelby County, Alabama. Washington: U. S. Department of Agriculture, Bureau of Soils, 1920.
S8130

Sweet, Arthur T. Soil Survey of Meigs County, Tennessee. Washington: U. S. Department of Agriculture, Bureau of Soils, 1921.
S9570

Agee, James Agee on Film: Five Film Scripts. Foreword by John Houston. n.p.: Beacon Press, 1964. Fine film scripts by Knoxville's well-known author.
A640 (BC ASU)

Agee on Film: Reviews and Comments. Drawings by Tomi Ungerer. n.p.: Beacon Press, 1964.
A650 (ASU)

The Collected Poems of James Agee. Introduction by Robert Fitzgerald. Boston: Houghton Mifflin Co., 1968. These poems, like Agee's best fiction, glow with the mountain idiom that was his heritage.
A660 (ASU WCU ETSU BC)

The Collected Short Prose of James Agee. A memoir by Robert Fitzgerald. Boston: Houghton Mifflin Co., 1968. A post humorous collection of short stories and sketches.
A670 (ASU WCU ETSU BC)

A Death in the Family. New York: McDowell, Obolensky, 1957. This, Agee's strongest book, is a largely autobiographical account of his childhood and his father's death.
A680 (ETSU BC WWC ASU)

A Death in the Family. 1957. Reprint. New York: Grosset & Dunlap, 1967.
A690 (WCU)

Four Early Stories. Collected by Edna Harap. West Branch, Iowa: Cummington Press, 1964.
A700 (ETSU BC)

Letters of James Agee to Father Flye. New York: G. Braziller, 1962.
A710 (BC ETSU ASU)

Letters of James Agee to Father Flye. With a new pref. and previously unpublished letters by Father Flye, 2nd ed. Boston: Houghton Mifflin, 1971.
A720

Let Us Now Praise Famous Men. Boston: Houghton Mifflin Co., 1941. Agee's text and Evan's photographs are combined to produce an unforgetable portrait of the sharecropper in the upland South.
A730 (BC ASU WCU)

Let Us Now Praise Famous Men. 1941. Reprint. Boston: Houghton Mifflin Co., 1960.
A740 (ETSU)

Let Us Now Praise Famous Men. 1941. Reprint. Boston: Houghton Mifflin Co., 1969.
A750 (WCU)

The Morning Watch. 1950. Reprint. Boston: Houghton Mifflin Co., 1951. A touching description of a young boy's early brush with religious expression.
A760 (BC ASU WCU)

Permit Me Voyage. Foreword by Archibald MacLeish. New York: AMS Press, 1971. Agee's first published volume of poems.
A770 (ETSU)

Ahles, Harry E. Radford, Albert E. Atlas of the Vascular Flora of the Carolinas. Raleigh: North Carolina Agricultural Experiment Station, 1965.
R10 (LMC WWC)

Radford, Albert E. Guide to the Vascular Flora of the Carolinas, with Distribution in the Southeastern States. Chapel Hill, N. C.: Book Exchange, 1964.
R20 (LMC WWC)

Radford, Albert E. Manual of the Vascular Flora of the Carolinas. Chapel Hill: Univ. of NORTH Carolina Press, 1968.
R30 (ETSU LMC WWC)

Ahlin, Bjorn "Social and Economic Conditions in Jackson County During the Depression." Master's thesis. Western Carolina Univ., 1971. This thesis illustrates an often quoted truism about the Depression in the Mountains: "It came late and it stayed late."
A780 (WCU)

Ahrens, Pat J. A History of the Musical Careers of Dewitt "Snuffy" Jenkins, Banjoist, and Homer "Pappy" Sherrill, Fiddler. Columbia, S. C.: n.p., 1970.
A790 (LMC)

Ahronholz, Gladys Telleen "Factors Affecting Social Participation in Coal Communities." Microfilm. Master's thesis. West Virginia Univ., 1951. An analysis of social integration in the coal camps. Factors analyzed include: economic status, religion, and kinship networks.
A800 (ASU)

Ainsley, Nancy P. "The Utilization of Community Resources in the Elementary Public Schools of Jackson County." Master's thesis. Western Carolina Univ., 1956.
A810 (WCU)

Akers, Carmen E. "Tuberculosis in Eastern Kentucky." Master's thesis. Univ. of Kentucky, 1951. An analysis of causative factors in the environment: Diet, poor health care, substandard housing, etc. and the incidence of tuberculosis in Eastern Kentucky.
A820 (ASU)

Akers, Elmer "Southern Whites in Detroit." Master's thesis. Univ. of Michigan, 1935. An important early study of the Appalachian migrant and the automobile industry.
A830

Akins, Enos E. "Disciplinary Beliefs and Practices of Selected East Tennessee High School Principals." Master's thesis. Univ. of Tennessee, 1957.
A840

Akins, Richard O. Soil Survey: Dawson, Lumpkin, and White Counties, Georgia. Prepared in cooperation with the Forest Service and the Univ. of Georgia, College of Agriculture, Agricultural Experiment Stations. Washington: U. S. Soil Conservation Service, 1972. Soil survey with maps of three North Georgia counties with heavy mineral deposits.
A850

Alabama, Agricultural Experiment Station, Auburn The Present and Projected Agricultural Economy of the Appalachian Region of Alabama. A report prepared under terms of a contract research project with the Appalachian Regional Commission. J. Homer Blackstone, project leader. Auburn: The station, 1968.
A860 (ASU)

Alabama Appalachian Development Office Appalachian Alabama: Development Plan — 1970. Montgomery: State Appalachian Development Office, 1970.
A870 (ASU)

Alabama Census Returns, 1820: And an Abstract of Federal Census of Alabama, 1830 Alabama, Department of Archives and History, 1944.
A880 (ASU)

Alabama, Department of Archives and History Alabama Census Returns, 1820: And an Abstract of Federal Census of Alabama, 1830. Baltimore: Genealogical Pub. Co., 1971. A good genealogical source for Northern Alabama families many of whom migrated through the Shenandoah, Holston and Tennessee River Valleys.
A890 (ASU)

Alabama Educational Survey Commission Public Education in Alabama. Washington: American Council on Education, 1945. Includes a survey of school systems in Alabama's twenty-eight Appalachian counties.
A900 (ASU)

Alabama, Geological Survey Report. no. 1. 1873. University: The survey, frequency varies. Excellent maps.
A910 (BC)

Alabama State Chamber of Commerce Industrial Alabama, a Directory of Manufacturers. Montgomery: The chamber, 1965.
A920 (ASU)

Alabama, Tri-county Appalachian Regional Health Planning Commission Health Development Plan — 1969, Morgan, Lawrence, Limestone Counties, Alabama. 2 vols. n.p.: The commission, 1969. This report examines a model health plan in rural Northern Alabama.
A930 (ASU)

Health Development Plan — 1970, Morgan, Lawrence, Limestone Counties. 2 vols. n.p.: The commission, 1970.
A940 (ASU)

Regional Health Demonstration Project, Phase 2, Morgan, Lawrence, Limestone Counties, Ala. n.p.: The commission, 1968.
A950 (ASU)

Alabama, University, School of Commerce and Business Administration Manpower Study of Appalachian Alabama. Prepared for Appalachian Regional Commission, under contractual agreement with Auburn Univ. Directed by Robert L. Trewatha. University, Ala.: The univ., 1968. Although Appalachian Alabama has more industry than neighboring states, there is still a poor distribution pattern of job opportunities.
A960

Albemarle County Historical Society, War History Committee Pursuits of War: The People of Charlottesville and Albemarle County, Virginia, in the Second World War. Charlottesville, Va.: The society, 1948. An account of wartime projects conducted by Charlottesville, Albemarle County, and the University of Virginia.
A970 (ASU)

Albert, Anne Roberts Russell County, Virginia Personal Property and Land Tax List . . . n.p.: Privately printed, n.d.
A980

Albert, Ethel Evans History of Five Southern Families. Baltimore: Gateway Press, 1970.
A990

Links With the Past. n.p.: n.p., 1972.
A1000

Alden, George Henry New Governments West of the Alleghenies Before 1780. 1897. Reprint. New York: Arno Press, 1971. Includes accounts of the Vandalia and Transylvania settlements.
A1010 (BC)

State of Franklin. n.p.: n.p., n.d. An account of John Sevier and the men of the Watauga settlements who declared themselves independent of the British colonies and established their own state.
A1020

Alden, John Richard Imperial Management of Indian Affairs in the South 1756-1775. Ph. D. Diss. Univ. of Michigan, 1939.
A1030

John Stuart and the Southern Colonial Frontier. Ann Arbor: Univ. of Michigan Press, 1944.
A1040

John Stuart and the Southern Colonial Frontier: A Study of Indian Relations, War, Trade, and Land Problems in the Southern Wilderness, 1754-1775. Univ. of Michigan Publications. History and Political Science, vol. 15, 1944. Reprint. New York: Gordian Press, 1966. This is the best account I have read of the relationship between the frontiersman and Cherokee, Creek and Catawba nations in the southern mountains.
A1050 (ASU BC FC WCU)

Alderman, John P. comp. Botetourt County, Virginia, 1820 Census. Typescript. Hillsville, Va.: n.d.
A1060

Carroll County, Virginia, 1850 Census. Typescript. Hillsville, Va.: n.d.
A1070

Carroll County, Virginia, 1860 Census. Typescript. Hillsville, Va.: n.d.
A1080

Carroll County, Virginia, 1870 Census. Typescript. Hillsville, Va.: n.d.
A1090

Floyd County, Virginia, 1840 Census. Typescript. Hillsville, Va.: n.d.
A1100

Floyd County, Virginia, 1850 Census. Typescript. Hillsville, Va.: n.d.
A1110

Franklin County, Virginia, 1820 Census. Typescript. Hillsville, Va.: n.d.
A1120

Grayson County, Virginia, Census of 1820, 1830, 1840, 1850. 4 vols. Typescript. Hillsville, Va.: The author, n.d.
A1130

Grayson County Deed Books 1, 2, 3, 4. 4 vols. Typescript. Hillsville, Va.: n.p., n.d.
A1140

Index to Grayson County Deed Books 1-9, Grantee. 1 vol. Typescript. Hillsville, Va.: The author, n.d.
A1150

Index to Grayson County Deed Books 1-9, Grantor. 2 vols. Typescript. Hillsville, Va.: The author, n.d.
A1160

Montgomery County, Virginia, 1820 and 1830 Census. 2 vols. Typescript. Hillsville, Va.: n.d.
A1170

Patrick County, Virginia Census, 1820, 1830, 1840, 1850. Typescript. Hillsville, Va.: The author, n.d.
A1180

Personal Property Tax Lists, Grayson County. Typescript. Hillsville, Va.: The author, n.d.
A1190

Pulaski County, Virginia, 1840 Census. Typescript. Hillsville, Va.: The author, n.d.
A1200

Scott County, Virginia, Census, 1820 and 1830. 2 vols. Typescript. Hillsville, Va.: The author, n.d.
A1210

Wythe County, Virginia, Census, 1810, 1820, 1830, 1840. 4 vols. Typescript. Hillsville, Va.: The author, n.d.
A1220

Alderman, Pat In the Shadow of Big Bald: About the Appalachians and Their People. Illustrated by Edyth Price, Ken Ferguson, Elene Bond. Mars Hill, N. C.: Bald Mountain Development Corp., 1972. Describes life in Union County, Tennessee and Yancey County, North Carolina.
A1230 (ETSU)

One Heroic Hour at Kings Mountain. Erwin, Tenn.: Erwin Pub. Co., 1968. Stresses role of the over-mountain men at the battle of Kings Mountain.
A1240 (BC LMC ASU)

One Heroic Hour at Kings Mountain, October 7, 1780. Erwin: n.p., 1968.
A1250

The Overmountain Men: Early Tennessee History, 1760-1780. Erwin, Tenn.: The Wingreen Co., 1958. Describes exploits of earliest settlers of Tennessee.
A1260 (BC ETSU)

The Overmountain Men: Early Tennessee History, 1760-1795. 1958. Reprint. Johnson City, Tenn.: Overmountain Press, 1970.
A1270 (ASU LMC FC)

The Wonders of the Unakas in Unicoi County. Sponsored by Erwin Business and Professional Women's Club. Erwin, Tenn.: N.P., . Description and tales of the Unaka Mountains.
A1280 (ETSU ASU LMC)

Alderson, William T. ed. Landmarks of Tennessee History. Nashville: Tennessee Historical Society, 1965.
A1290

Aldridge, Duard P. "A Study of the Effect of Participation in Co-curricular Activities on Grades of Male Students at Science Hill High School." Master's Thesis. East Tennessee State Univ., 1966. A Johnson City, Tennessee high school is the subject of this study.
A1300 (ETSU)

Alee, F. Vernon Alee's History of Martensburg and Berkeley Company, West Virginia. Hagerstown, Md.: Mail Pub. Co., 1888.
A1310

Alexander, F. M. The Chattanooga Black Shale, a Possible Future Source of Uranium. Information Circular, no. 1. Nashville: Tennessee Division of Geology, 1953?
A1320 (ETSU)

Alexander, Frank DeWitt Owners and Tenants of Small Farms in the Life of a Selected Community: A Cultural Analysis. Nashville: Joint Universities Library, 1938. Among the factors considered in this study is the impact of the Tennessee Valley Authority on the lives of these farmers. However, the counties studied lie outside the Appalachian region.
A1330

A Rural Community in Time of War: The Valley Community in Rabun County, Georgia. Atlanta: U. S. Department of Agriculture, Bureau of Agricultural Economics, 1945. The study is an attempt to determine how the social structure of the community was changed by the war.
A1340 (BC)

Alexander, Gross History of the Methodist Episcopal Church, South. New York: American Church History Series, 1894.
A1350 (ASU)

Alexander, Holmes Moss American Nabob. New York: Harper & Brothers, 1939. A saga of the evolution of West Virginia as a separate state.
A1360 (BC)

Pen and Politics: The Autobiography of a Working Writer. Morgantown: West Virginia Univ. Library, 1970. The autobiography of a West Virginia journalist.
A1370 (ASU)

Alexander, Marguerite Kirsty's Secrets: A Yearly Round of Scottish Fare. Winston-Salem, N. C.: John F. Blair, 1958. A cookbook of Scottish recipes, designed for North Carolina's many families of Scottish descent.
A1380 (ASU)

Alexander, Michael David "Kentucky State Aid and the Educationally Disadvantaged Child." Ed. D. Diss. Indiana Univ., 1969. Investigates the effectiveness of Kentucky's Foundation Program.
A1390

Alexander, Nancy Here Will I Dwell: The Story of Caldwell County. Salisbury, N. C.: Rowan Print. Co., 1956. History of Caldwell County and its founding families.
A1400 (ASU WCU BC)

Tom Dooley. Lenoir, N. C.: Lenoir News-Topic, 1959. A story of one of North Carolina's most famous crimes.
A1410 (ASU LMC)

Alexander, Nancy comp. Isbell, Robert Lee The World of My Childhood. Lenoir, N. C.: Lenoir News-Topic, 1955.
1970 (ASU LMC)

Alexander, Ted "A Study of the Effect of Participation in Football on the Grades of Students at Bristol, Tennessee, High School." Master's Thesis. East Tennessee State College, 1952.
A1420 (ETSU)

Alexander, Thomas Benjamin Political Reconstruction in Tennessee. Nashville: Vanderbilt Univ. Press, 1950.
A1430

Political Reconstruction in Tennessee. New York: Russell & Russell, 1968. East Tennessee was bitterly divided from the rest of the state by Civil War issues. Political reconstruction was not accomplished until well into this century.
A1440 (BC ASU)

Thomas A. R. Nelson of East Tennessee. Nashville: Tennessee Historical Commission, 1956. Nelson was an orator, politician, and leader of the Whig Party in Tennessee.
A1450 (ASU LMC BC)

Alexander, William C. "An Avifaunal Strip Census on Grandfather Mountain." Master's Thesis. Appalachian State Univ., 1970. A treatise on the birds of Grandfather Mountain.
A1460 (ASU)

Alinsky, Saul David John L. Lewis: An Unauthorized Biography. New York: Putnam, 1949. Contains a fascinating account of the growth of the United Mine Workers.
A1470 (WCU BC)

Allan, William History of the Campaign of General T. J. (Stonewall) Jackson in the Shenandoah Valley of Virginia from Nov. 4, 1861, to June 17, 1862. With full maps of the region and of the battlefields by Jed Hotchkin. Philadelphia: J. B. Lippincott & Co., 1880.
A1480 (ASU)

Alldredge, J. Haden A History of Navigation on the Tennessee River System: An Interpretation of the Economic Influence of This River System on the Tennessee Valley. House Doc. 254, 75th Cong., 1st sess. Washington, D. C.: GPO, 1937.
A1490

Allee, Marjorie Hill The Road to Carolina. New York: Houghton, 1936. A novel of East Tennessee during the Civil War.
A1491 (WWC BC)

Alleghany County Centennial, 1859-1959 County History and Souvenir Booklet. n.p.: n.p., 1959?
A1730

Allen, Arthur Thomas Zonation of the Middle and Upper Ordovician Strata in Northwestern Georgia. Bulletin, no. 66. Atlanta: Georgia Department of Mines, Mining and Geology, 1957.
A1500 (ETSU)

Allen, Arthur Thomas, Jr. Cramer, Howard Ross Annotated Bibliography of Georgia Geology Through 1959. Atlanta: Georgia Department of Mines, Mining and Geology, 1967.
C8500 (ETSU)

Allen, Charles Fletcher Crockett's Life. Illustrated by Frank McKernau. Philadelphia: J. B. Lippincott Co., 1911.
A1510 (ETSU)

David Crockett; Scout, Small Boy, Pilgrim, Mountaineer, Soldier, Bearhunter, and Congressman, Defender of the Alamo. Philadelphia: Lippincott, 1912. Yet another biography of the irrepressible Col. Crockett of East Tennessee.
A1520 (BC)

Allen, Charles W. Historic Greeneville, Tennessee. A City among the Mountains. New York: Moss, 1899.
A1530

Allen, Ira Tom, Jr. "Vocational Preferences of Eighth Grade Students at Ross N. Robinson Junior High School, Kingsport, TENNESSEE, Master's Thesis. East Tennessee State Univ., 1968.
A1540 (ETSU)

Allen, Ivan Earnest The Cherokee Nation: Fort Mountain, Vann House, Chester Inns, New Echota. Atlanta: I. Allen Co., 1958? This pamphlet describes three Cherokee landmarks in Northwest Georgia, the last stronghold of the Nation before 1838 removal. The fourth site, Fort Mountain, in Murray County is a prehistoric ruin.
A1550 (ASU BC)

Allen, J. Sidna Memoirs of J. Sidna Allen, Being a True Narrative of His Life and Early Manhood, the History of the Allen Family, What Happened at Hillsville and His Life at the Penitentiary. Mount Airy, N. C.: F. H. Lamb, 1929. A true and stirring account of the Allen outlaws and their exploits at Hillsville, Carroll County, Virginia.
A1560 (LMC ASU)

Allen, James Lane Aftermath; The Bride of the Mistletoe; A Cathedral Singer; The Choir Invisible; The Doctor's Christmas Eve. . . ; The Emblems of Fidelity; Flute and Violin, and Other Kentucky Tales and Romances; The Heroine in Bronze; A Kentucky Cardinal; The Kentucky Warbler; The Landmark; The Last Christmas Tree; The Mettle of the Pasture; The Reign of Law: A Tale of the Hemp Fields; and Summer in Arcady: A Tale of Nature. n.p.: n.p., n.d. Note: Many of the schools submitting entries for this bibliography included the works of James Lane Allen, the Kentucky novelist. In the judgement of this editor these books are not Appalachian. In the main, their settings are in and around Lexington or points west. However, since so many schools submitted them, a title listing is included.
A1570

Allen, John D. Philip Pendelton Cooke. Chapel Hill: Univ. of North Carolina Press, 1942. Cook spent most of his life in the Great Valley and Blue Ridge sections of Virginia. His best-known work is FROISSART BALLADS, AND OTHER POEMS.
A1580 (BC)

Allen, Judson Boyce ed. Cox, Norman Wade Encylopedia of Southern Baptists. Nashville: Broadman Press, 1958.
C8220 (ASU)

Allen, Martha Norburn Asheville and Land of the Sky. Rev. and enlarged ed. Charlotte, N. C.: Heritage House, 1960. A history of Asheville and the French Broad Country from the time of the Cherokee to twentieth century Asheville.
A1590 (BC ASU WCU LMC MHC)

Allen, Mary Moore North Carolina Sketches and Places. Goldsboro, N. C.: n.p., 1946. Includes sketches of many western North Carolina landmarks.
A1610 (ASU)

Allen, Merritt Parmelee The White Feather. 1st. ed. Illustrated by C. B. Falls. New York: Longmans, Green & Co., 1944. THE WHITE FEATHER is a Civil War story for older boys.
A1600 (BC ASU)

Allen, Penelope Johnson comp. Guide Book of Chattanooga and Vicinity. Chattanooga: USD of 1812, 1935.
A1620

Tennessee Soldiers in the Revolution: A Roster of Soldiers Living During the Revolutionary War in the Counties of Washington and Sullivan. Taken from the Revolutionary Army Accounts of North Carolina. . . Published under the auspices of the Tennessee Society, Daughters of the American Revolution. Bristol, Tenn.: King Printing Co., 1935.
A1630 (ETSU)

Allen, Ronald R. comp. Some Tennessee Rarities. Knoxville, Tenn.: n.p., 1973. A bibliography of rare books from Tennessee.
A1640 (ASU)

Tennessee Books: A Preliminary Guide. Knoxville, Tenn.: n.p., 1969.
A1650 (LMC)

Allen, Roscoe J. "A History and Development of Education in Wilkes County, North Carolina." Master's thesis. Univ. of Tennessee, 1952.
A1660

Allen, T. P. The West Virginia Hills: A Study of the Work of the Presbyterian Church in the United States in the Synod of West Virginia. St. Louis, Mo.: Buxton & Skinner, 1927.
A1670 (ASU)

Allen, V. C. Rhea and Meigs Counties (Tennessee) in the Confederate War. n.p.: n.p., 1908. Sketches of Confederate soldiers from two East Tennessee Counties.
A1680 (ASU BC)

Allen, Vernon The Appalachian Regional Commission, Educational Advisory Committee Interim Report. Ed 021653. Washington: Govt. Print. Off., 197?
A1690

Allen, William Cicero The Annals of Haywood County, North Carolina: Historical, Sociological, Bibliographical, and Genealogical. n.p.: n.p., 1935. Includes accounts of Hazelwood, Clyde, Canton and the Qualla Reservations of the Cherokee.
A1700 (ASU WCU BC)

Centennial of Haywood County and Its County Seat Waynesville, N. C., 1808-1908. Waynesville: Courier, 1908.
A1710

North Carolina History Stories. Richmond: B. F. Johnson Pub. Co., 1901. Includes some Western North Carolina yarns.
A1720 (LMC MHC)

Alley, Felix Eugene Random Thoughts and the Musings of a Mountaineer. 1st ed. Salisbury, N. C.: Rowan Print. Co., 1941. A delightful reminiscence and informal history of Western North Carolina. This unpretentious volume is probably the best source we have on Western North Carolina.
A1740 (BC ASU WCU LMC ETSU)

Allingham, William ed. The Ballad Book. London: Macmillan & Co., 1872. A choice collection of 76 traditional British ballads.
A1750 (BC)

Allison, Elizabeth Kelly Early Southwest Virginia Families. Auburn, Ala.: n.p., 1960.
A1760

Allison, John Dropped Stitches in Tennessee History. Nashville, Tenn.: Marshall & Bruce Co., 1897. Contains much information about Andrew Jackson's exploits as a young hot-tempered lawyer in East Tennessee.
A1770 (ASU BC)

Allison, John ed. Notable Men of Tennessee: Personal and Genealogical with Portraits. 2 vols. Atlanta: Southern Historical Assoc., 1905. Contains personal histories, genealogical records, and portraits of Tennessee notables.
A1780 (ASU)

Allison, Louise B. Early History of Snowville. n.p.: n.p., n.d. Twenty-eight pages with illustrations.
A1790

Allison, Richard C. "Marketing of Lumber Produced by Sawmills in Pennsylvania." Master's thesis. Pennsylvania State Univ., 1960.
A1800

Allison, T. F. P. arr. Gattinger, Augustin The Medicinal Plants of Tennessee Exhibiting Their Commercial Value, with an Analytical Key, Descriptions in Aid of Their Recognition, and Notes Relating to Their Distribution, Time and Mode of Collection, and Preparation for the Drug Market. Nashville: F. M. Paul, 1894.
G610

Allman, Clarence Brent Lewis Wetzel: Indian Fighter. The Life and Times of a Frontier Hero. Original title: The Life and Times of Lewis Wetzel. New York: Devin-Adair Co., 1961. Wetzel was West Virginia's best-known frontiersman, scout, and Indian fighter.
A1810 (ASU BC)

The Mound Builders. Philadelphia: F. A. Davis Co., 1940. Special attention is given to mound builders in West Virginia and the Ohio Valley.
A1820 (BC)

Allred, C. C. Masters, F. N. The Cumberland Plateau in Tennessee. Knoxville: Tennessee Agricultural Experiment Station, Univ. of Tennessee, 1944.
M4140

Allred, Charles E. An Economic Analysis of Farming in Overton County, Tennessee. Knoxville: Department of Agricultural Education, Univ. of Tennessee, 1927.
A1830 (ETSU)

Effects of Industrial Development on Rural Life in Sullivan County, Tennessee. Univ. of Tennessee RECORD, vol. 5, no. 3. Knoxville: Division of Univ. Extension, Univ. of Tennessee, 1928.
A1840

How the Swiss Farmers Operate on the Cumberland Plateau. Knoxville: Agricultural Experiment Station, Univ. of Tennessee, 1937.
A1860

Significant Changes in Agriculture of Cumberland County, Tennessee. Report. Knoxville: Tennessee Agricultural Experiment Station, 1942.
A1870

Significant Changes in Agriculture of Cumberland County, Tennessee. Knoxville: Agricultural Experiment Station, Univ. of Tennessee, 1942.
A1880

Social Factors Associated with Land Class in Overton County, Tennessee. Report. Knoxville: Agricultural Experiment Station, 1940. Examines correlations between land ownership and social activity.
A1890

Allred, Charles E. and others Grundy County, Tennessee, Relief in a Coal Mining Community. Report. Knoxville: Tennessee Agricultural Experiment Station, 1936. A study of social and relief agencies in a Grundy County coal mining community.
A1850

Allred, Rulon Clark The Allred Family in America. 1st ed. Salt Lake City: Wm. R. Bischoff, 1965. This is a common family name in Appalachia.
A1900 (ASU)

Allston, Susan Lowndes Early Sketch of St. John in the Wilderness and Flat Rock, North Carolina. n.p.: n.p., 1964. History of an Episcopal Church at Flat Rock, North Carolina.
A1910 (ASU)

Alonso, William ed. Friedmann, John Regional Development and Planning: A Reader. Cambridge, Mass.: M. I. T. Press, 1964.
F3320 (ASU)

Alpha Phi Alpha Fraternity West Virginia Collegiate Institute. ELOJO (The Eye). Institute, West Virginia: West Virginia Collegiate Institute, 1923. A yearbook of the Alpha Phi Alpha Fraternity.
A1920 (ASU)

Althouse, Ronald Work, Safety, and Life Style Among Southern Appalachian Coal Miners. A Survey of the Men of Standard Mines. Morgantown, W. Va.: Office of Research and Development, Appalachian Center, West Virginia Univ., 1974.
A1930

Work, Safety, and Life Style Among Southern Appalachian Coal Miners: A Survey of the Men of Standard Mines. Morgantown: Office of Research and Development, Appalachian Center, West Virginia Univ., 1974. A case study of miners employed at a mine complex owned by Standard Mines.
A1970 (ASU)

Altsheler, Joseph Alexander The Sword of Antietam: A Story of the Nation's Crisis. Civil War Series. New York: D. Appleton & Co., 1914. This volume of Civil War fiction for young readers is partially set in the Appalachians. Dick Mason and his young friends pursue Stonewall Jackson's troops through the Valley of Virginia.
A1950 (ASU)

The Young Trailers: A Story of Early Kentucky. New York: D. Appleton & Co., 1907. A fictional account of pioneer life in Eastern Kentucky.
A1960 (ASU WCU BC)

Altshells, Joseph Alexander The Rock of Chickamauga: A Story of the Western Crisis. New York: D. Appleton & Co., 1915. A novel based on the life of General George H. Thomas, a Virginia-born Unionist who saved the Union Army at the Battle of Chickamauga.
A1940 (ASU BC)

Alvey, Richard H. Wings Over Kingsport, No. 2: Tennessee's Planned City & Its Industries as Viewed from the Sky in 1938 and 1963. Kingsport, Tenn.: n.p., 1963.
A1980 (ETSU)

Alvord, Clarence Walworth The First Explorations of the Trans-Allegheny Region by the Virginians, 1650-1674. Cleveland: Arthur H. Clark, 1912. Includes excerpts from the journals of Lederer, Batts, and Fallam as well as accounts of the river routes through the mountains.
A1990 (ASU BC)

Ambler, Charles Henry A History of Education in West Virginia, from Early Colonial Times to 1949. Huntington, W. Va.: Standard Print & Pub. Co., 1951.
A2000 (ASU)

A History of West Virginia. . . New York: Prentice-Hall, 1933.
A2010 (BC WCU)

The Makers of West Virginia and Their Work. Huntington, W. Va.: Gentry Brothers, Printers, 1942. A reprint from volume I of Debates and proceedings of the first Constitutional convention of West Virginia, 1861-1863.
A2020

Sectionalism in Virginia from 1776-1861. Reprint, 1910. New York: Russell & Russell, 1964. An account of politics and government in Virginia from the Revolution through the Civil War.
A2030

West Virginia, the Mountain State. Books on History. New York: Prentice-Hall, 1940. This edition was apparently written for the younger reader.
A2040 (ASU ETSU BC)

West Virginia, the Mountain State. 2nd ed. Englewood Cliffs, N. J.: Prentice-Hall, 1958. A general, readable history of the mountain state.
A2050 (ASU WCU ETSU)

West Virginia: Stories and Biographies. New York: Rand McNally, 1937. Designed for use as a textbook in sixth and seventh grade classes.
A2060

Ambrister, Mrs. Floyd L., Jr. comp. Wayland, Mrs. Charles F., Sr. Tombstone Inscriptions and Death Records, Calvary Cemetery, Knoxville, Tennessee, 1869-1967. n.p.: n.p., 1967.
W1640 (ETSU)

American Ancestry: Giving the Name and Descent, in the Male Line, of Americans Whose Ancestors Settled in the United States Previous to the Declaration of Independence, A. D. 1776 Reprint, 1887-99, 12 vols. Baltimore: Genealogical Pub. Co., 1968. Since most Appalachian families are descended from very early emigrants, this volume is a useful research tool.
A2070 (ASU)

American Bible Society Cherokee Bible. (Title in Cherokee). New York: American Bible Society, 1860. Printed in Cherokee with notes in English.
A2080 (ASU)

American Civil Liberties Union The Kentucky Miner's Struggle: The Record of a Year of Lawless Violence. The Only Complete Picture of Events Briefly Told. New York: The union, 1932. This is a partial record of the mine wars in Eastern Kentucky. This horror and its corresponding events in other Appalachian states have been largely disregarded by the press and government agencies. Is this the greatest conspiracy of silence in recent American history?
A2090 (ASU)

American Constitutional Association, Charleston Life in a West Virginia Coal Field. Charleston, W. Va.: The assoc., 1923. A pretty, pretty picture of an idealized coal camp, written in refutation of articles depicting barbarism in the coal fields. Naturally the association was funded by coal operators.
A2100

American Council of Learned Societies Devoted to Humanistic Studies Surnames in the United States Census of 1790; an Analysis of National Origins of the Population. Committee on Linguistics and National Stocks in the Population of the United States. Baltimore: Genealogical Pub. Co., 1969. Forever lays to rest the myth that mountaineers are predominately Scotch-Irish. Numerically, it just isn't so, although the Scotch-Irish tended to absorb other ethnic groups in the mountains.
A2110

American Dialect Society Word-lists from the South. Publications, no. 2. Greensboro, N. C.: The society, 1944. Includes articles on mountain speech by Josiah Combs, H. C. Laughlin, Cratis Williams, and F. C. Hayes.
A2120 (ASU)

American Enterprise Institute for Public Policy Research The Appalachian Regional Development Bill. S3, Sen. Randolph; H.R. 4, Rep. Fallon. Legislative Analysis, 91st Congress, 1st Sess., no. 6. Washington: The institute, 1965.
A2130 (UNCA)

American Forest Products Industries Government Land Acquisition: A Summary of Land Acquisition by Federal, State and Local Governments up to 1964. Washington, D. C.: The author, 1965. Millions of acres of mountain land belong to the state and federal government.
A2140 (LMC)

American Indian Mission Association, Kentucky Minutes, 1834-1852. Microfilm. n.p.: n.p., n.d.
A2150 (WCU)

American Mining Congress Coal Mine Modernization Year Book. 1928. Washington: American Mining Congress, 1928. A sort of official apologia for the abominable lack of mine safety standards in Appalachia.
A2160

American Mountain People Prepared by the Special Publications Division, National Geographic Society. Washington: National Geographic Society, 1973. Discusses America's mountains and the special breed of people who inhabit them.
A2170 (ASU BC)

American Public Welfare Association "Public Welfare and Related Problems in Grundy County, Tennessee." Chicago: Unpublished typescript, 1940.
A2180

American Technical Assistance Corp. An Analysis of the Vista Program and Appalachian Volunteers, Inc. Washington: American Technical Assistance Corp., 1967. Examines successes and failures of the Vista Program in Appalachia, giving reasons for both.
A2190

Ames, Russell Abbott The Story of American Folk Song. New York: Grosset & Dunlap, 1955. This volume is excellent background material on folksongs. It demonstrates the close relationship between historical events and movements and the folk songs which popularize these events.
A2200 (ASU BC)

Amick, Dorothy D. The Methodist Temple of Beckley, West Virginia: A History of Seventy-five Years of Active Organization, 1891-1966. Charleston, W. Va.: Jarrett Print. Co., 1966.
A2210 (ASU)

Ammons, John Outlines of History of French Broad Association and Mars Hill College . . . 1807 to 1907. Raleigh: Edwards & Broughton, n.d.
A2220

Ammons, Nellie Strausbaugh, Perry Daniel Common Seed Plants of the Mid-Appalachian Region. Morgantown, W. Va.: Book Exchange, 1948.
S7820 (ASU BC)

Amsden, Thomas William Geology and Water Resources of Garrett County. Bulletin, no 13. Baltimore: Maryland Department of Geology, Mines and Water Resources, 1954. A geological survey of one of Maryland's three Appalachian Counties.
A2230 (ETSU)

Amyx, Katherine McClure Wedding of the Waters. Detroit: Harlo Press, 1973. Poems from Grassy Creek, Kentucky.
A2240 (BC)

Andarawewa, Asoka B. "An Economic Analysis of Fertility Differentials Among Rural Farm Communities in United States in 1960." Ph. D. Diss. Michigan State Univ., 1964.
A2250

Anderson, Ethel Cassell Nichols and others comps. Draper Families in America. Nashville, Tenn.: Parthenon Press, 1964. The Draper family followed the frontier land grants through the hills and valleys of Appalachia.
A2260 (ASU)

Anderson, Frances Gaines "Leisure Time Interests and Activities of Girls in High School." Master's thesis. West Virginia Univ., 1942. This study uses West Virginia mountain girls as a sample group.
A2270

Anderson, Geneva "A Collection of Ballads and Songs from East Tennessee." Master's thesis. Univ. of North Carolina, 1932.
A2280 (LMC)

Anderson, Isaac A Sermon, Delivered on September 8th, 1813. . . Rogersville: The author, 1814.
A2290

Anderson, Lorena Handbook of Appalachian Materials. Charleston, W. Va.: West Virginia Department of Education, 1971. An immensely useful compilation of West Virginia materials.
A2300

Anderson, Margaret The Children of the South. Foreword by Ralph McGill. New York: Farrar, Straus and Giroux, 1958. Here is a teacher's warm and sensitive account of her Negro students during the integration troubles in Clinton, Anderson County, Tennessee.
A2310

Anderson, Paul F. "The History of Educational Development in Sullivan County, Tennessee." Master's thesis. Univ. of Tennessee, 1936.
A2320

Anderson, Richard A. "An Evaluation of the Physical Education Programs in the High Schools in the Washington County School System." Master's thesis. East Tennessee State Univ., 1971.
A2330 (ETSU)

Anderson, Robert Campbell The Story of Montreat from Its Beginning, 1897-1947. Montreat, N. C.: The author, 1949. A history of Montreat College, Montreat, N. C. and the Presbyterian Mountain Retreat Association there.
A2340 (ASU WCU LMC)

Anderson, Rufus Memoir of Catherine Brown, a Christian Indian of the Cherokee Nation. (Xerox copy of the original.) Boston: Armstrong, & Crocker & Brewster; New York: J. P. Haven, 1825. Catherine was born in present day Wills Valley and her memoir deals primarily with her life and work at Brainerd Mission School for the Cherokee. Both Wills Valley and Brainerd are today suburbs of Chattanooga.
A2350 (ASU BC)

Memoir of Catherine Brown, a Christian Indian of the Cherokee Nation. Rev. ed. Philadelphia, Pa.: Am. Sunday School Union, 1832.
A2360

Anderson, Sherwood Beyond Desire. New York: Liveright, Inc., 1932. The scene is a Southern mill town which is in the process of unionizing. The story appears to be based on the author's experiences in Appalachia.
A2370 (ASU)

The Buck Fever Papers. Charlottesville: Univ. Press of Virginia, 1971. A collection of Anderson's columns in the Smyth County News and/or The Marion Democrat. Anderson lived for several years in the Virginia Blue Ridge country.
A2380 (ASU)

Death in the Woods and Other Stories. New York: Liveright Publishing Corp., 1933. This anthology includes several of Anderson's mountain stories.
A2390

Hello Towns. New York: Liveright, 1929.
A2400 (ASU)

Hello Towns. New York: Appel, 1970. Articles and tales of life in and around Marion, Virginia.
A2410 (LMC ASU)

Kit Brandon: A Portrait. New York: Charles Scribner's Sons, 1936. This portrait of a mountain girl who escapes rural poverty and the degradation of a mill town by becoming a driver for a moonshine magnet has to be Anderson's strongest characterization. Strangely it has received little acclaim.
A2420 (ASU ETSU BC)

Letters; Selected and Edited with an Introduction and Notes by Howard Mumford Jones, in association with Walter B. Rideout. Boston: Little, Brown, 1953. Includes letters from his years in Appalachia.
A2430 (BC ASU)

Anderson, Thomas A. A Description of Hiwassee Old Town. London: n.p., 1842. A description of one of the five major Cherokee towns.
A2440

The Ocoee District, South East Tennessee in the United States of America, Especially the Hundred Thousand Acres, and the Gold Region, with a Sketch of the Character of the People Who Inhabit East Tennessee Generally. London: J. Leath, 1842.
A2450

Anderson, Thomas Dale "The Geography of Christmas Tree Production and Marketing in Anglo-America: With Special Attention to Twelve Counties in Western Pennsylvania." Ph. D. Diss. Univ. of Nebraska, Lincoln, 1966. This dissertation urges the use of tree-farming as an economic alternative in an area where marginal farms are failing.
A2460

Anderson, Walter C. A Method of Appraising Pine Sawtimber in South Carolina. U. S. Forest Service. Station Paper, no. 122. Asheville, N. C.: Southeastern Forest Experiment Station, 1961. Four Appalachian counties of South Carolina are heavily forested.
A2470 (WCU)

Todd, A. S. An Appraisal of Methods for Salvaging Small Sawmill Residues in the Southeast. Asheville, N. C.: Southeastern Forest Experiment Station, 1957.
T8780 (WCU)

Anderson, Walter Wadsley Kill 1, Kill 2. New York: W. Morrow, 1940. Fiction. A mysterious disappearance and a strange memo throw the inhabitants of lodges in the Blue Ridge Mountain into a panic. The drama is enacted against the backdrops of a ridge the Indians call Murder Mountain.
A2480 (BC ASU)

Andress, J. L. Taylor, Arthur Elijah Soil Survey of Clay County, Alabama. Washington: U. S. Department of Agriculture, Bureau of Soils, 1916.
T410

Andrews, Columbus Caldwell County, North Carolina Geography Supplement. Chapel Hill: Univ. of North Carolina, 1927-1928. This supplement includes a new set of maps.
A2490 (ASU)

Andrews, Earnest M. Georgia's Fabulous Treasure Hoards: A Compendium for Rockhounds, Prospectors, and Various Seekers of Gold, Silver, Diamonds, etc., with Known and Historic Locations, . . . Harperville, Ga.: n.p., 1966. A handbook for rockhounds and treasure seekers.
A2500 (MHC)

Andrews, Matthew Page Virginia, the Old Dominion. Richmond, Va.: Dietz Press, 1956. Deals very sparingly with the mountain regions of Virginia.
A2510 (FC BC)

Andrews, Peter Sergeant York: Reluctant Hero. New York: Putnam, 1969. Biography of Alvin York, war-hero from East Tennessee.
A2520 (ETSU)

Andrews, Thomas Gayleon Burchard, Ernest Francis Iron Ore Outcrops of the Red Mountain Formation in Northeast Alabama. University: Alabama Geological Survey, 1947.
B8450 (ETSU)

Angel, Samuel P. Scott, Samuel W. History of the Thirteenth Regiment, Tennessee Volunteer Cavalry, U. S. A., Including a Narrative of the Bridge Burning: The Carter County Rebellion, and the Loyalty, Heroism and Suffering of the Union Men and Women of Carter and Johnson Counties, Tennessee, During the Civil War. Knoxville, Tenn.: The authors, 1903.
S1460 (ASU LMC)

Angle, Eula Ferguson Peter Angle, 1754-1968, and Related Families: Wills, Lee, Mooreman. Richmond: Dietz, 1969.
A2530

Anglin, Frances B. "A Follow-up Study of Graduates of Roane County High School, 1946-55." Master's thesis. Univ. of Tennessee, 1956. This study indicates that those graduates who are most successful in obtaining an education or a well-paying job are those who left Roane County.
A2540

Anglin, Robert A. The Characteristics and Attitudes of Juvenile Delinquents of Kanawha County. Charleston: Proceedings of the West Virginia Academy of Science, 1966.
A2550

Status of the Aging in Kanawha County. Bulletin, Series 48, no. 5. Institute; West Virginia State College, 1961. Predictably, this is a sad little volume about the problems of the aged, in an area which is urbanizing rapidly.
A2560

Anonymous Sharp-Eye; or the Scout's Revenge. London: n.p., 1850. An account of pioneer life in northwestern North Carolina.
A2570

Anscombe, Francis Charles I Have Called You Friends: The Story of Quakerism in North Carolina. Boston: Christopher Pub. House, 1959. Includes accounts of Quaker explorations and settlements in the mountains.
A2580 (ASU)

Anslin, Robert A. The Characteristics and Attitudes of Juvenile Delinquents of Kanawha County, West Virginia. Charleston: Proceedings of the West Virginia Academy of Sciences, 1966.
A2590

Anson, August Bitter Sweet, A Mountain Story. Chicago: Scroll, 1900.
A2600 (LMC)

Anson, Charles P. "A History of the Labor Movement in West Virginia." Ph. D. Diss. Univ. of North Carolina, 1940.
A2610

Anthony, Ivan Blair The Potters O'Skunk Hollow. Boston: B. Humphries, 1947. Here is a classic example of poor taste and bad dialect in mountain fiction. The Potters live well during World War II because Louisa is drawing support checks from all eight of her husbands.
A2620 (BC ASU)

Antone, George Peter, Jr. "Willis Duke Weatherford: An Interpretation of His Work in Race Relations, 1906-1946." Ph. D. Diss. Vanderbilt Univ., 1969. Weatherford was connected with the Blue Ridge Assembly and Black Mountain College in Western North Carolina and with Berea College in Eastern Kentucky. He was the author of a pioneer survey of the Appalachian Region.
A2630 (ASU BC)

Appalachia vol. 1, no. 1, June 1876. Brattleboro, Vt.: Appalachian Mountain Club. A sort of house organ for the Appalachian Mountain Club.
A2640 (ASU)

Appalachia vol. 1, (Appalachian Digest, vol. 1-2.) September, 1967. Washington, D. C.: Appalachian Regional Commission, monthly. The official organ of the Appalachian Regional Commission.
A2650 (ASU MHC LMC)

Appalachia; A Case Study of Regional Business Development, Second Major Business Institute Report, Oct. 19-20, 1966. Athens, Ohio University, College of Business Administration, 1966.
A2660 (BC)

Appalachia Bulletin New series, vol. 1, Apr. 1935. Brattleboro, Vt.: Appalachian Mtn. Club.
A2670 (ASU)

Appalachia Conference on Research in Poverty and Development, Virginia Polytechnic Institute, 1968. Seeking More Effective Means to Overcome Poverty: Proceedings. In cooperation with the Appalachian Regional Commission. Blacksburg: Research and Extension Division, Virginia Polytechnic Institute, 1969.
A2680 (ASU LMC)

Appalachia: An Economic Report — 1970. Trends in Employment, Income and Population Appalachian Regional Commission. Washington: Govt. Print. Off., 1970.
A2681

Appalachia — An Economic Report: Trends in Employment, Income and Population Appalachian Regional Commission. Washington: Appalachian Regional Commission, 1972.
A2683 (ASU)

Appalachia — An Economic Report: Trends in Employment, Income and Population. Supplement Washington: Appalachian Regional Commission, n.d.
A2682 (ASU)

Appalachia Educational Laboratory The Appalachia Preschool Education: A Home-oriented Approach. Charleston, W. Va.: The laboratory, 1970. A report on the use of home-study kits in selected Appalachian communities.
A2690

The Appalachia Preschool Education Program. Folder. Charleston, W. Va.: The laboratory, 1970.
A2700

Directions for Educational Development in Appalachia; Report of an Educational Needs and Feasibility Study Involving the Appalachian Areas of Six States. Charleston, W. Va.: The Laboratory, 1971.
A2710 (ASU)

The Emerging Pattern of Appalachian Regional Development. Charleston, W. Va.: The Laboratory, 1970.
A2720

Quality Education for Appalachia: A prospectus proposing the establishment of a regional educational laboratory. Submitted to the United States Office of Education. . . University Park, Pa.: Pennsylvania State University, 1965.
A2730 (FC)

Appalachia Educational Laboratory, Division of Research and Evaluation Evaluation Report: Early Childhood Education Program, 1969-1970 Field Test. Summary report. Charleston, W. Va.: The laboratory, 1971.
A2740

Appalachia Hand Craft Catalog Oak Ridge, Tenn.: Adroit Print Co., 1974. Booklet describes an area-wide self-help marketing project of Human Economic Appalachian Development (HEAD) Corporation in Berea, Ky. Project is supported by the Commission on Religion in Appalachia.
A2750

Appalachia Kentuckian Bibliography Jackson, Ky., Southeastern Kentucky Regional Library Cooperative, 1974. A bibliography of the cooperative's holdings of: Alice Lloyd College, Hazard Comm. College, Jackson City School Library, LBJ Elem. School Lib. (Jackson, Ky.), Lee County Public Library, Letcher Co. High School Lib., Lees Jr. College Lib., Owsley Co. Pub. Lib., Perry Co. Pub. Lib.
A2760 (BC)

Appalachia Medicine vol. 1-5. -June, 1973. Lexington; Ky.: Appalachian Regional Hospitals, quarterly.
A2770 (ASU)

Appalachia: Opportunity for Progress: Alabama, Kentucky, Maryland, North Carolina, Pennsylvania, Tennessee, Virginia, West Virginia Washington: n.p., 1963.
A2771 (ASU)

Appalachia Region Educational Laboratory Quality Education for Appalachia: A Prospectus Proposing the Establishment of a Regional Education Laboratory. Submitted to U. S. Off. of Education. University Park, Pa., Penn. State Univ., 1965.
A2780 (FC)

Appalachia: A Report, 1964 Appalachian Regional Commission. Washington: Govt. Print. Off., 1964.
A2790 (ASU)

The Appalachian vol. 1, Aug., 1934. Cincinnati: Appalachian Coals, monthly.
A2800

The Appalachian vol. 1, October 9, 1934. Boone, N. C.: Appalachian State Univ., frequency varies.
A2810 (ASU)

Appalachian Adult Basic Education Demonstration Center. Final Report. Morehead, Ky.: Morehead State College, 1969.
A2820

Appalachian Advance vol. 1, October, 1966. Charleston, W. Va.: Appalachia Educational Laboratory, monthly, Oct.-May, except Dec.
A2830 (ETSU BC)

Appalachian and Western North Carolina Railroad Some Facts Concerning the Appalachian and Western North Carolina Railroad. Greensboro, N. C.: Harrison Print. Co., 1924.
A4460 (ASU)

Appalachian Apple Service Annual Report. Martinsburg, W. Va.: The service, n.d.
A2840

Appalachian Basin Ordovician Symposium, Pittsburgh, 1947 Appalachian Basin Ordovician Symposium: Papers Read at the Meeting of the Pittsburgh Geological Society at Pittsburgh, Pa., May 16, 1947, and Published in the Bulletin of the American Assn. of Petroleum Geologists, Aug. 1948. Editorial Committee: John T. Galey, Chairman, and others. Tulsa: American Association of Petroleum Geologists, 1948.
A2850 (BC)

Appalachian Bibliography Compiled for Appalachian Regional Commission. 2 vols., 1967. Morgantown: West Va. Univ. Library, annual. Primarily a listing of articles in current periodicals.
A2860 (ASU ETSU LMC MHC WWC BC)

Appalachian Center, West Virginia University see **West Virginia, University, West Virginia Center for Appalachian Studies and Development**

Appalachian Club Estates, Transylvania County, Brevard, N. C. Asheville: Hackney and Noale, 1913?
A2870

Appalachian Coals, Inc. ACI Bulletin. Cincinnati, 1930.
A2880

ACI experimental 30-day coal consumption forecast. December 1948-April 1949. Cincinnati: 1949. Basic information supplied by U. S. Weather Bureau, Washington, D. C.
A2890

Analysis of Potential Market for ACI Coals in the Production of Gas and Coke. Preliminary report, October, 1934. Cincinnati:
A2900

Coal-weather Forecast. Jan., 1949. Cincinnati: The Co., seasonal. Promotional materials and weather information.
A2910

Design Trends in Boiler Installations in the Pulp & Paper Industry of the South. Industrial Bulletin, 2. Cincinnati: The Co., 1952.
A2920

Forecast. 1949-. Cincinnati: The Co., quarterly. Weather information and promotional materials.
A2930

Fuel Engineering Data. Cincinnati: Appalachian Coals, Inc., Fuel engineering division, 1935. Eight sections, each paged separately.
A2940

Fuels and Hydro Power Used in the Production of Electricity for Public Use in the United States (1933 through 1936). Cincinnati: The Co., 1937.
A2950

Heating Season Weather, 1948-49 Heating Season. Cincinnati: The Co., 1949?
A2960

How to Compare the Heating Values and Costs of Coal, Fuel Oil and Gas. Cincinnati: The Co., 194?.
A2970

Industrial Coal-burning Equipment. Cincinnati: The Co., 1935.
A2980

Miscellaneous Publications. n.p.: n.p., 1937. Unbound pamphlets.
A2990

Residential Heating, Equipment, and Fuel Consumption; Study and Comparison by States, 1940 and 1948. Area - principal A.C.I. marketing states. Cincinnati: n.p., 1949. Cover-title. ---- ---- Solid fuel retailers still have substantial market. Type heating, 1949.
A3000

Southern High-volatile Coals. Cincinnati: Appalachian Coals, 1951. Its Industrial bulletin 1.
A3010

Appalachian Coals, Inc., Fuel Engineering Division Proceedings of the Fuel Engineering Conference Atlanta: Appalachian Coals, 1938.
A3020

Proceedings: General Index of Fuel Engineering Conferences, First Through Twenty-sixth, 1934-1940. Cincinnati: Appalachian Coals, 1943.
A3030

Appalachian Committee for Full Employment Application for Community Organizing Program in the Four Counties of the Upper Kentucky River Area Development Council. Hazard, Ky.: The committee, 1964.
A3040

Appalachian Community Meeting Papers. 1st, Washington, 1966. Bristol, Tenn.: Appalachian Volunteers, 1966?
A3050

Appalachian Data Book Appalachian Regional Commission. vol. 3, Kentucky. 2nd ed. April, 1970. Washington: Govt. Print. Off., 1974.
A3060 (ASU MHC)
Appalachian Regional Commission. vol. 7, North Carolina, 2nd ed. April, 1970. Washington: Gov't Print. Off., 1970.
A3070 (ASU MHC)
Appalachian Regional Commission. vol. 11, Tenn. 2nd ed. April, 1970. Washington: Gov't Print. Off., 1970.
A3080 (MHC ASU)
Appalachian Regional Commission. vol. 12, Virginia. 2nd ed. April, 1970. Washington: Gov't Print. Off., 1970.
A3090 (ASU MHC)

Appalachian Data Book, Summary Volume Appalachian Regional Commission. 2nd ed. Washington: Govt. Print. Off., 1970.
A3100 (ETSU MHC ASU)

Appalachian Digest see **Appalachia**

Appalachian Electric Power Co., Bluefield, W. Va. see **Appalachian Power Co., Bluefield, W. Va.**

Appalachian Exposition Premium List and Prospectus. Knoxville, Tenn.: S. B. Newman, 1910. Records of the 1910 Appalachian Regional Exposition and Fair.
A3110 (LMC)

The Appalachian Finance Association see **Appalachian Financial Review**

Appalachian Financial Review vol. 1, Spring 1966-. Pittsburgh: Appalachian Finance Association, annual.
A3120 (ETSU)

Appalachian Forest Experiment Station, Asheville, N. C. see **U. S. Forest Service. Appalachian Forest Experiment Station, Asheville, N. C.**

Appalachian Geological Society Bulletin. vol. 1, 1949. Charleston: The Society, annual.
A3130 (ASU ETSU LMC)
Fall Meeting of the Appalachian Geological Society and the Pittsburgh Geological Society with the Cooperation of the West Virginia Geological Survey, October 11-12, 1957, at Blackwater Falls State Park: Log of Field Trip. n.p.: n.p., 1957.
A3140 (ETSU)
Silurian Stratigraphy: Central Appalachian Basin. Field conference, April 17-18, 1970. Roanoke, Va.: The society, 1970.
A3150 (ASU)

Appalachian Governors' Conference Meeting, May 8, 1961, the White House. 3d., Washington, 1961. Washington: The conference, 1961.
A3160

Appalachian Hardwood Manufacturers Appalachian Oak in Fine Furniture. 3d. ed. Cincinnati: The Co., 1970.
A3170 (ASU)
Official Grading Rules for Eastern Hemlock Lumber: Conforming to American Lumber Standards Effective November 10, 1950. Cincinnati: The Co., 1950.
A3180

Appalachian Heritage: A Magazine of Appalachian Life and Culture vol. 1, Winter, 1973. Pippa Passes, Ky.: Alice Lloyd College, quarterly.
A3190 (ETSU ASU BC)

Appalachian Institute Committee of the President's Appalachian Regional Commission and the Conference of Appalachian Governors Report of the Appalachian Institute Committee to the Conference of Appalachian Governors and the President's Appalachian Regional Commission. Area Redevelopment Administration Technical Assistance Project, U. S. Department of Commerce. Washington: Govt. Print. Off., 1964.
A3200 (BC ASU)

Appalachian Journal vol. 1-30. 1904-Jan. 1937? (Appalachian Trade Journal, vol. 1-17, no. 1.) Knoxville: n.p., monthly.
A3210

Appalachian Journal vol. 1, 1972. Boone, N. C.: Appalachian State Univ., semiannual. "A Regional Studies Review."
A3220 (ASU ETSU BC)

Appalachian Legal Services Conference, Knoxville, Tenn. 1969 Papers and Proceedings of Appalachian Legal Services Conference, Knoxville, Tenn., July 24-26, 1969. Chicago: National Legal Aid and Defender Association, 1969. Focuses on special legal needs of Appalachia, especially those relating to new government agencies such as the Appalachian Regional Commission.
A3230 (BC)

Appalachian Library and Culture Project Resources of the Appalachian Library and Culture Center, an Annotated Listing of Books, Recordings and Other Media. Cleveland: Cleveland Public Library, 1973.
A3240

Appalachian Lookout vol. 1. 1968. Prestonsburg, Ky.: Appalachian Volunteers, 10 no. a year.
A3250 (BC)

Appalachian Mountain Club Annual Report. Boston: The club, 18-
A3260
Appalachia. vol. 1. no. 1. June 1876. Brattleboro, Vt.: The club, n.d.
A3270
Appalachia Bulletin. vol. 1-28. Nov. 1907-Mar. 1935; new series, vol. 1. Apr. 1935. n.p.: n.p., n.d.
A3280
Suggestions as to Outfit for Tramping and Camping. Boston: The club, 1904.
A3290

Appalachian Mountain Club Bulletin see **Appalachian Bulletin**

Appalachian Mountain Community Center, Penland, N. C. Appalachian Mountain Community Center under the Auspices of the Protestant Episcopal Church. . . Penland, N. C.: n.p., n.d.
A3300

Appalachian Movement Press Literature List, June, 1972. Huntington, W. Va.: The press, 1972.
A3310 (ASU BC)
Pamphlets. irregularly issued. Huntington, W. Va.: The press, 1972.
A3320 (ASU BC)
Songs of Freedom. Huntington, W. Va.: The press, 1972. Eight famous labor songs from Appalachia with histories and arrangements.
A3330

Appalachian National Park Association The Appalachian National Parks; an Analysis of Work Accomplished, November 1899 up to Aug. 30, 1901. Folder compiled by Dr. C. P. Ambler. Asheville: Appalachian National Park Association, 1901.
A3340
Southern Pictures and Pencilings: Official Organ of the Appalachian National Park Association. Asheville: A. H. McQuilkin, 1900.
A3350

Appalachian News Service vol. 1. Jan. 1974. Charleston, W. Va.: n.p., semi-monthly.
A3360 (ASU BC)

Appalachian North Carolina Youth Development Project. Final Report Chapel Hill: North Carolina Internship Office, 1973. A report on a grant to the N. C. Internship office from the Appalachian Regional Commission for 170 youth service-learning internships in western North Carolina.
A3370 (ASU)

Appalachian Notes vol. 1. 1973. Lexington, Ky.: Erasmus Press, quarterly.
A3380 (ASU ETSU BC)

The Appalachian Oral History Project at Lees Junior College, Jackson, Kentucky Recollections. Jackson, Ky.: Lees Junior College, 1972.
A3390

Appalachian Outlook vol. 1. Oct. 1964. Morgantown: West Virginia Univ. Library, quarterly.
A3400 (BC ETSU ASU)

Appalachian People's History Book Text by Suzanne Crowell. Louisville, Ky.: Mountain Education Associates and Southern Conference Education Fund, 1971? A biased but informative version of Appalachia's history.
A3410 (ASU)

Appalachian Poets vol. 1. 1952. (Appalachian Poets Yearbook, 1952-1955.) Kermit, W. Va.: Appalachian Poetry Guild, annual?
A3420

Appalachian Poets Yearbook see **Appalachian Poets**

Appalachian Power Company Report. Roanoke, Va.: The Co., 1939, annual.
A3510

Appalachian Power Company, Bluefield, W. Va. To Bankers Trust Company and F.N.B. Close, Trustees; Trust Deed. New York: n.p., 1913.
A3430
Hydro-electric Power in the Southwest of Virginia. Bluefield, W. Va.: The Co., 1913.
A3440
Order of Business for Real Estate and Rights of Way. Roanoke, Va.: Stone Print. & Mfg. Co., 1927.
A3450
Profitable Boat Manufacturing Opportunities in Virginia. Introductory Report to Boat Manufacturers. Roanoke, Va.: The company's Area Development Department, 1960.
A3460
Safety Hand Book. Issue of July 1, 1928. Roanoke, Va.: Stone Printing and Manufacturing Co.?, 1928.
A3470
The Story of the Reusens Hydro-electric Station, tracing its development over a thirty-year period 1903-1931. Lynchburg, Va.: Appalachian Electric Power Company, 1931.
A3480
United States of America, on the Relation of Oscar L. Chapman, Secretary of the Interior, Petitioner v. Federal Power Commission, Virginia Electric and Power Company, et al. Virginia REA Association, et al. On Writs of Certiorari to the United States Court of Appeals for the Fourth Circuit. Brief for Appalachian Electric Power Company, Intervenor. n.p.: n.p., 1952.
A3490
When Men and Mountains Meet. Bluefield?: The Co., 1966.
A3500

Appalachian Power Company, Roanoke, Va. Appalachian Power Company and the American Electric Power System. Roanoke?: The co., 1962.
A3520

Appalachian Regional Commission Abstract of the New York State Appalachian Program: A Development Plan. n.p.: Office of Planning Coordination, 1968.
A3530
Acid Mine Drainage in Appalachia. Washington, D. C.: The commission, 1969. An economic and engineering study of the effects of acid mine drainage in Appalachia in six volumes.
A3540 (ASU BC)
Annual Report. 1965. Washington: Gov't. Print. Off., annual.
A3550
Appalachia: A Report, 1964. Washington, D. C.: Govt. Print. Off., 1964.
A3560 (LMC ASU WCU ETSU)
Appalachia: An Economic Report — 1970. Trends in Employment, Income and Population. Washington: Govt. Print. Off., 1971.
A3570 (ASU)
Appalachia — An Economic Report: Trends in Employment, Income and Population. Washington, D. C.: Govt. Print. Off., 1972.
A3580 (WCU ASU ETSU)
Appalachia — An Economic Report: Trends in Employment, Income and Population. Supplement. Washington: Govt. Print. Off., 1973.
A3590 (ASU)
Appalachian Data Book. Washington, D. C.: Govt. Print. Off., 1967.
A3600 (ASU ETSU BC)
Appalachian Data Book. 2nd ed. 14 vols. Washington, D. C.: Govt. Print. Off., 1970.
A3610 (MHC BC ETSU ASU)

Appalachian Regional Commission
The Appalachian Experiment, 1965-1970. Washington: Govt. Print. Off., 1972. A Study of the various programs of the Appalachian Regional Commission.
A3620 (ASU)
Appalachian Highlands Recreation Study, Phase I, Inventory and Analysis. Washington, D. C.: Govt. Print. Off., 1968.
A3630 (ASU)
Appalachian North Carolina Youth Development Project, Final Report. Washington: The commission, 1973. Report on a grant from the Commission to the North Carolina Internship office for 170 service-learning internships in Western North Carolina.
A3640 (ASU)
The Appalachian Region: A Statistical Appendix of Comparative Socioeconomic Indicators. ERIC RC003508. Washington, D. C.: The commission, 1968. Factors studied in statistical index include: population; population distribution by age, sex, state and family income; education; distribution of labor force according to educational levels; industry; industrial location; and employment and unemployment patterns.
A3650 (MHC ASU)
Appalachian Research Reports. no. 1. 1966. Washington, D. C.: Govt. Print. Off., issued irregularly. See individual entries.
A3660 (ASU WCU)
Appalachia's Forest Resources: Timber. A task force report on the timber resources of Appalachia. Washington: Govt. Print. Off., 1963.
A3670
At Transition: Executive Director's Semiannual Administrative and Economic Report, July 1-December 31, 1968. Washington: Govt. Print. Off., 1968.
A3680 (ASU)
A Bibliography of Research Studies Produced with Appalachian Regional Development Program Funds. Washington: The commission, 1969.
A3690
Capitalizing on New Development Opportunities along the Baltimore-Cincinnati Appalachian Development Highway: A Staff Recommendation. Appalachian Research Report, no. 11. Washington: Govt. Print. Off., 1968.
A3700 (ASU)
Code. Washington: Govt. Print. Off., 1966.
A3710 (WCU ASU)
Current Regional Reports. Washington: The commission, 1973.
A3720
The Economic Impact of Public Policy on the Appalachian Coal Industry and the Regional Economy. Washington: Govt. Print. Off., n.d.
A3730 (ASU)
Guidelines for Funding Appalachian Projects, Development Districts, and Research. Washington: Govt. Print. Off., 1968.
A3740 (ASU)
Guidelines for Funding Appalachian Projects, Development Districts and Research. Washington: Govt. Print. Off., 1969.
A3750 (ASU)
Manpower Report for the Appalachian Coal Industry. Washington: The commission, 1973. A report on the manpower needs of the coal industry and the current distribution and supply of manpower.
A3760 (ASU)
New Directions: Executive Director's Semi-annual Report, January 1-June 30, 1971. Washington: Govt. Print. Off., 1972?
A3770
Preliminary Analysis for Development of Central Appalachia, Kentucky, Tennessee, Virginia, West Virginia. Appalachian Research Report, no. 8. Washington: Govt. Print. Off., 1969.
A3780
A Program for Simulation of Acid Mine Drainage in a River Basin. Cambridge, Mass.: Meta Systems, Inc., 1969.
A3790 (ASU)
Report. 1965. Washington: Govt. Print. Off., annual.
A3800 (ETSU ASU WCU BC)
A Report on the Identification of Areas of Potential Growth in the Appalachian Region of New York State and a General Development Philosophy for the Region. Albany: New York Appalachian Regional Commission, 1966.
A3810
A Select Bibliography on High Risk Education for Appalachian Youth: Programs and Practices. Washington: Govt. Print. Off., 1969.
A3820
State and Regional Development Plans in Appalachia. Washington: Govt. Print. Off., 1968.
A3830 (ASU)
A Summary Economic Report: Appalachian Region. Washington: Govt. Print. Off., 1971.
A3840 (ASU)
Summary Report. Washington: Govt. Print. Off., 1964.
A3850 (ASU)
Survey of Environmental Education Programs in Colleges and Universities in the Appalachian Region. Washington: The commission, 1972.
A3860 (ASU)
An Urban Development Program for the Big Sandy Area. Lexington, Ky.: Spindletop Research, 1965.
A3870
Updated Investment Guidelines for North Carolina Appalachian Region 1971 to 1975, and A Plan for Public Investment in Appalachian North Carolina, Fiscal 1971. n.p.: n.p., 1971?
A3880

Appalachian Regional Commission, Child Development Staff Federal Programs for Young Children. Washington: Govt. Print. Off., 1970.
A3890 (ASU ETSU)
Programs for Infants and Young Children. 4 vols. Washington: Govt. Print. Off., 1970.
A3900 (ASU ETSU)

Appalachian Regional Commission, Education Advisory Committee Appalachian — Education for Tomorrow. Washington: The Appalachian Regional Commission, 1971.
A3910 (ASU)
Early Childhood Education for Appalachia. Washington: Govt. Print. Off., n.d.
A3920 (ASU)
Interim Report. 1967. Washington: Govt. Print. Off., annual.
A3930 (ASU LMC BC)
Preliminary Report. Washington: Govt. Print. Off., 1967.
A3940
Status of Secondary Vocational Education in Appalachia. Appalachian Research Report, no. 10. Washington: Govt. Print. Off., 1968.
A3950 (ASU LMC)
Summary and Recommendations to the Appalachian Regional Commission: Report I. Cover-title: Appalachia — Education for Tomorrow. Washington: Govt. Print. Off., 1971.
A3960 (ASU)

Appalachian Regional Commission, Health Advisory Committee Report to the Appalachian Regional Commission. Washington: Govt. Print. Off., 1966.
A3970 (ASU)

Appalachian Regional Commission, Youth Development Leadership Program Youth Action and Youth Issues in Appalachia: A Report. Washington: Govt. Print. Off., 1971.
A3980 (ASU)

Appalachian Regional Hospitals Evolution of a Model Rural Non-profit Health Care System, 1963-1973. Lexington, Ky.: n.p., 1973. Taking over the hospitals created by the UMW, the ARH has grown from a chain of hospitals into a modern health care system since 1963.
A3990 (ASU)
A Model Rural Non-profit Health Care System. Lexington, Ky.: The authors, 1971.
A4000 (ASU)

Appalachian Research and Defense Fund Appalachian Research and Defense Fund Public Interest Report. no. 1. Charleston, W. Va.: The fund, 1970.
A4010
Newsletter. no. 1. 1971. Charleston, W. Va.: n.p., n.d. Nine volumes issued ending with winter 72-73.
A4020 (BC)

Appalachian Review vol. 1. Summer 1966. Morgantown: W. Va. Univ., quarterly.
A4030 (ASU ETSU BC)

Appalachian School, Penland, N. C. The Appalachian School. . . Penland, N. C.: The school, 1933.
A4040
The Appalachian School Department of Fireside Industries. Penland, N. C.: n.p., 1936.
A4050
Appalachian School Summer Camp. Penland, N. C.: n.p., n.d.
A4060

The Appalachian South vol. 1. 1965. Charleston, W. Va.: Appalachian Associates, quarterly.
A4070 (ASU ETSU MHC BC)

Appalachian State University, Belk Library The American Indian: A Bibliography. Boone, N. C.: Appalachian State Univ., The Library, 1973.
A4071

Appalachian State University, Boone, N. C. see **North Carolina, Appalachian State University, Boone**

The Appalachian Structural Front in Alabama Guidebook for the Annual Field Trip, no. 7. University: Alabama Geological Society, 1969.
A4080 (ETSU)

Appalachian Structural Seminar, 2nd, Mont Chateau, W. Va., 1971. Appalachian Structures: Origin, Evolution and Possible Potential for New Exploration Frontiers. A seminar, March 3-5, 1971, directed by William H. Kanes. Morgantown: West Virginia Univ. and West Virginia Geological and Economic Survey, 1972.
A4090

Appalachian Studies Center Twigs. vol. 1. June 1965. Pikeville, Ky.: Pikeville College, n.d. Vol. 1-4 published by Hilltop Editons, Pikeville College Press, Pikeville, Ky.
A4100 (ASU)

Appalachian Trade Journal see **Appalachian Journal (1904-1937?)**

Appalachian Trade Union Conference, Charleston, W. Va., 1964 Proceedings, October 12-14, 1964. Indianapolis: Cornelius Print. Co., 1964.
A4110

Appalachian Trail Conference The Appalachian Trail. 6th ed. Pub. no. 5. Washington: The conference, 1950.
A4120
The Appalachian Trail: A Mountain Footpath — A National Scenic Trail. Publication no. 5. 8th ed. Washington: The conference, 1970.
A4130 (LMC ETSU)
The Appalachian Trail. Publication, no. 17. Washington, D. C.: The conference, 1970.
A4140 (ETSU)
The Appalachian Trail: A Footpath Through the Wilderness for More Than 2,000 Miles from Katahdin in Maine to Springer Mountain in Georgia. 12th ed. Publication, no. 17. Washington: The conference, 1963.
A4150 (ASU)
The Appalachian Trail: A Mountain Footpath, a National Scenic Trail. 9th ed. Publication, no. 5. Harpers Ferry, W. Va.: The conference, 1973.
A4160 (ASU)
Appalachian Trail Conference, Undertaking the Appalachian Trail (A Mountain Foot-path from Maine to Georgia. . . . New York: The conference, 1933.
A4170 (ASU)

Appalachian Trail Conference
Guide to the Appalachian Trail in Central and Southwestern Virginia. 5th ed. Washington, D. C.: The conference, 1960.
A4180 (BC LMC ASU)
Guide to the Appalachian Trail in the Great Smokies, the Nantahalas, and Georgia. 1st ed. Publication, no. 23. Washington, D. C.: The conference, 1963.
A4190 (LMC BC)
Guide to the Appalachian Trail in the Great Smokies, the Nantahalas, and Georgia. 2nd ed. Publication, no. 3. Washington: The conference, 1967.
A4200 (ASU BC)
Guide to the Appalachian Trail in the Great Smokies, the Nantahalas, and Georgia. 4th ed. Publication, no. 23. Harpers Ferry, W. Va.: The conference, 1973.
A4210 (ASU)
Guide to the Appalachian Trail in Maine. . . 2nd ed. Washington, D. C.: The conference, 1936.
A4220
Guide to the Appalachian Trail in Maine; the Route of the Appalachian Trail in Maine. . . 3rd ed. Washington, D. C.: The conference, 1938.
A4230
Guide to the Appalachian Trail in Maine. . . 4th ed. Washington, D. C.: The conference, 1942.
A4240
Guide to the Appalachian Trail in the Southern Appalachians. 2nd ed. Publication, no. 8. Washington, D. C.: The conference, 1942.
A4250 (ASU BC)
Guide to the Appalachian Trail in the Southern Appalachians. 3rd ed. Publication, no. 8. Washington, D. C.: The conference, 1950.
A4260 (ASU)
Guide to the Appalachian Trail in the Southern Appalachians. 4th ed. Publication, no. 8. Washington, D. C.: The conference, 1960.
A4270 (ASU)
Guide to the Appalachian Trail in Tennessee and North Carolina, Cherokee, Pisgah, and the Great Smokies. 1st ed. Publication, no. 24. Washington, D. C.: The conference, 1963.
A4280 (LMC)
Guide to the Appalachian Trail in Tennessee and North Carolina: Cherokee, Pisgah, and Great Smokies. 2nd ed. Publication, no. 24. Washington: The conference, 1967.
A4290
Guide to the Appalachian Trail in Tennessee and North Carolina, Cherokee, Pisgah, and Great Smokies. 3rd ed. Publication, no. 24. Washington, D. C.: The conference, 1971.
A4300 (ETSU)
Guide to the Appalachian Trail in Tennessee and North Carolina, Cherokee, Pisgah, and Great Smokies. 4th ed. Publication, no. 24. Harpers Ferry, W. Va.: The conference, 1973.
A4310 (ASU)
Guide to the Southern Appalachians. The Appalachian Trail from Virginia-Tennessee Line to Mt. Oglethorpe, Ga. Publication, no. 8. Washington: The conference, 1937.
A4320 (ASU BC)
Plans for an Appalachian Trail Lean-to. . . 4th ed. Washington: The conference, 1949. Gives a list of shelters along the App. Trail.
A4330 (ASU)
Suggestions for Appalachian Trail Users. 3rd ed. Publication, no. 15. Washington: The conference, 1944.
A4340
Suggestions for Appalachian Trail Users. 4th ed. Publication, no. 15. Washington: The conference, 1949.
A4350
Suggestions for Appalachian Trail Users. 6th ed. Publication, no. 15. Washington: The conference, 1962.
A4360
Trail Manual for the Appalachian Trail. Washington: The conference, 1931.
A4370 (ASU)
Trail Manual for the Appalachian Trail. 3rd ed. Publication, no. 1. Washington: The conference, 1935.
A4380
Trail Manual for the Appalachian Trail. 4th ed. Publication, no. 1. Washington: The conference, 1940.
A4390 (ASU)
Trail Manual for Appalachian Trail. 5th ed. Washington: The conference, 1951.
A4400
Trail Manual for the Appalachian Trail. 6th ed. Washington: The association, 1966.
A4410

Appalachian Trailway News vol. 1. 1939. Washington: Appalachian Trail Conference, quarterly.
A4420 (ASU)

Appalachian Traveling Conference, Kentucky Section Traveling Conference of the Department of Agriculture in the Southern Appalachian Region, Oct. 30-Nov. 4, 1939. Washington: The conference, 1939.
A4430

Appalachian Underground Corrosion Short Course, West Virginia University Proceedings. 1st. 1956. Technical Bulletin. Morgantown: West Virginia Univ., Engineering Experiment Station, annual.
A4440

Appalachian Wage Conference, Coal Operators' Committee Facts about the Bituminous Coal Industry. New York: The conference, 1939.
A4450

Appalachia's People, Problems, Alternatives: An Introductory Social Science Reader Comp. by PARC. 2 vols. Morgantown, W. Va.: People's Appalachian Research Collective, 1971. Although poorly printed and researched, this volume does attempt to represent Appalachia as an example of colonialism whose natural resources are owned by people outside the region.
A4470 (ASU)

Appalshop Appalbrochure, 1971. Whitesburg, Ky.: The author, 1971. A catalog of current media, films and video tapes available from the Appalshop, Whitesburg, Ky.
A4480 (ASU)
Appalbrochure, 1974. Whitesburg, Ky.: The author, 1974.
A4490 (ASU ETSU)

Appell, Darlene Skillern Family History and Genealogy. n.p.: N.P., .
A4510

Applewhite, James ed. Voices from Earth, a Collection of Writings on Environment. Greensboro: Univ. of North Carolina, Greensboro, 1971.
A4500 (ASU)

Arbor and Bird Dog Manual Charleston, W. Va.: Extension Department, College of Agriculture, West Virginia, 1915. Lists forty common birds of West Virginia.
A4520 (BC)

Archambo, Judith P. Rural Child Care Project, 1968-1969 Research Evaluation. vol. I: A Description of the Rural Child Care Project. vol. II: Hypotheses 1-8 Final Report. Frankfort, Ky.: Kentucky Child Welfare Research Foundation, Inc., 1970.
A4530
Rural Child Care Project, 1969-1970 Research Evaluation. Final Report. Frankfort: Kentucky Child Welfare Research Foundation, Inc., 1970. Contains much information on Eastern Kentucky.
A4540

Archer, Cordelia Pearl "History of the Schools of Johnson City, Tennessee, 1868-1950." Master's thesis. East Tennessee State Univ., 1953.
A4550 (ETSU)

Archer, Robert Archer and Silvester Families. 1870. Reprint. Richmond, Va.: William Byrd Press, 1937.
A4560

Ardery, Julia Hoge Spencer comp. Kentucky Records. Early Wills and Marriages Copied from Court House Records by Regents, Historians and the State Historian. Old Bible Records and Tombstone Inscriptions. Records from Barren, Bath, Bourbon Counties. 1926. Reprint. Baltimore, Md.: Genealogical Pub. Co., 1965.
A4570 (BC ASU)

Ardery, Mrs. William Breckenridge see **Ardery, Julia Hoge Spencer**

Arena, Susan P. ed. Kentucky Living Cookbook. Bicentennial Edition. Shelbyville, Ky.: Landmark Community Newspapers, 1974. Contains many recipes from Eastern Kentucky.
A4580

Argo, William V. The 20,000,000,000 a Year Racket of Bootleggers and Liquor-stamp Counterfeiters in Several Southeastern States Is Here Detailed by One of the Men Who Broke It Up. N. Y.: Vantage, 1962. Fully documented, naming names and pinpointing places, the book has the pace and suspense of a thriller.
A4590
No Place for Revenuers. New York: Vantage Press, 1962. An account of the author's experiences as an undercover IRS agent.
A4600 (BC LMC)

Arkle, Thomas Sandstones of West Virginia. Report of Investigations, no. 16. Morgantown: W. Va. Genealogical Survey, 1957.
A4610 (ETSU)

Arlart, Ernest James A Survey of Monogenetic Trematodes from the Gills of Salmo Gairdneri, Salverinus Fontinalis, and Salmo Trutta in Watauga County, North Carolina. Master's thesis. Boone, N. C.: Appalachian State Univ., 1974.
A4620

Armentrout, Walter Wardlaw Employment and Underemployment of Rural People in the Appalachian Area. Morgantown: West Virginia Univ., n.d.
A4630
Rural Development Problems and Prospects in Fayette, Raleigh, and Summers Counties, West Virginia. Morgantown: West Virginia Agricultural Experiment Station, 1960. A study of financial, legal, ecological, and other problems related to development in rural areas.
A4640

Armes, Ethel Marie The Story of Coal and Iron in Alabama. Birmingham: Chamber of Commerce, 1910. A survey of resources and the companies which use them.
A4650 (ASU)

Armes, William Dallam ed. Old English Ballads and Folk Songs. New York: Macmillan, 1904. This 1904 edition lists popular versions, variants and notes for 35 old English ballads.
A4660
LeConte, Joseph The Autobiography of Joseph LeConte. New York: D. Appleton and Co., 1903.
L1270 (BC ASU LMC)

Armfield, Lucille Songs from the Carolina Hills. New York: Doxey's Press, 1901.
A4670

Armitage, Catherine Smith "A Report of a Summer Internship at Buckhorn Children's Center, Buckhorn, Kentucky." Master's thesis. Western Michigan Univ., 1971.
A4680 (ASU)

Armour, Eugene "The Melodic and Rhythmic Characteristics of the Traditional Ballad Variants Found in the Southern Appalachians." Microfilm. Ph. D. Diss. New York Univ., 1961.
A4690 (ASU)

Armour, Robert The Attack upon and Defense of Fort Sanders, Knoxville, Tennessee, November 29, 1863. Read at the states meeting of December 7, 1898. Military Orders of the Loyal Legion of the U. S. Commandery of the District of Columbia. War Papers, 30. Xerox copy of the original. Washington: Govt. Print. Off., 1893.
A4700 (ASU)

Arms, Fred Sevier and others Soil Survey, Adair County, Kentucky. Soil Survey, Series 1961, no. 4. Washington: U. S. Department of Agriculture, Soil Conservation Service, 1964. Adair County is in the foothills of the Appalachians in Eastern Kentucky. Its agricultural potential is greater than that of its more mountainous neighboring counties.
A4710

Armstrong, Anne Wetzell This Day and Time. New York: Alfred A. Knopf, 1930.
A4720 (ASU)

This Day and Time. With a personal reminiscence by David McClellan. 1930. Reprint. Johnson City: Research Advisory Council, East Tennessee State Univ., 1970. A novel about an East Tennessee woman's struggle to earn a living in the early 1920's.
A4730 (BC ETSU ASU)

Armstrong, Randy Cate, Herma The Southern Appalachian Heritage. Boone, N. C.: The Appalachian Consortium, 1974.
C2041

Armstrong, Zella Hamilton County Confederate Soldiers. Chattanooga: Lookout, n.d.
A4740

History of the First Presbyterian Church of Chattanooga. Chattanooga: Lookout, 1945.
A4750

The History of Hamilton County and Chattanooga, Tennessee. Chattanooga, Tenn.: Lookout Pub. Co., 1931.
A4760 (ETSU BC ASU)

The Sevier Family. Chattanooga, Tenn.: Lookout Pub. Co., 1926. A history of Tennessee's first family, the descendants of John Sevier and Valentine Sevier.
A4780 (BC)

Some Tennessee Heroes of the Revolution; Compiled from Pension Statements. Chattanooga: Lookout, 1933.
A4790

Who Discovered America? The Amazing Story of Madoc. Chattanooga: Lookout, 1950. There is a theory that Descendants of this Welsh prince's expedition settled in the Appalachians.
A4800

French, Janie Vreston Collup The Crockett Family and Connecting Lines. Bristol, Tenn.: King Print. Co., 1928.
F3240

French, Janie Preston Collup Davy Crockett and the Crockett Family. Chattanooga: Lookout, 1951.
F3250

Armstrong, Zella comp. Notable Southern Families. 6 vols. Chattanooga, Tenn.: Lookout Pub. Co., 1918-33. An excellent genealogical source.
A4770 (ASU ETSU)

Arndt, Harold H. Wood, Gordon H., Jr. Systematic Jointing in Western Part of Anthracite Region of Eastern Pennsylvania. Washington: U. S. Geological Survey, 1969.
W8510

Arnett, Lizzie 'Mongst the Hills of Kentucky. Illustrated by Tip Saunders. Louisville: R. H. Carothers & Son, 1909. A love story set against the background of Eastern Kentucky events such as picnics, tooth-pulling, fights and bee-keeping.
A4810 (ASU)

Arnold, Dorothy Andora "Some Recent Contributions of the Cherokee Indians of North Carolina to the Crafts of the Southern Highlands." Master's thesis. Univ. of Tennessee, 1952. An excellent study of traditional Cherokee crafts still being produced.
A4820 (ASU ETSU)

Arnold, Jacob Hiram Farm Practices That Increase Crop Yields in Kentucky and Tennessee. Farmers' Bulletin 981. Washington, D. C.: U. S. Govt. Print. Off., 1918. A study of farming methods in the limestone and mountain districts of Kentucky and Tennessee.
A4830 (BC)

Ways of Making Southern Mountain Farms More Productive. Farmers' Bulletin, 905. Washington: U. S. Department of Agriculture, Office of Farm Management, 1918. A practical manual dealing with the special problems of agriculture in mountainous country.
A4840 (ASU BC)

Arnold, Lattye Eunice Aunt Malissa's Memory Jug: Original Folk Stories. New York: Exposition Press, 1962.
A4850 (BC)

Arnold, Thomas Jackson Early Life and Letters of General Thomas J. Jackson, "Stonewall" Jackson. New York: Fleming H. Revell Co., 1916. Jackson was a native of the Valley of Virginia and his most brilliant campaigns were conducted there.
A4860 (ASU)

Arnold, William Erastus A History of Methodism in Kentucky. Louisville, Ky.: The Penticostal Pub. Co., 1936. Includes accounts of circuit riders, camp meetings, and the development of the Pentecostal Holiness sect.
A4870 (BC)

Arnold Zogry Associates A Demonstration Program in Rural Housing: An Area-wide Housing Organization in the Northwest Local Development District. Prepared for the North Carolina State Planning Division, Department of Administration, with the financial assistance of the Appalachian Regional Commission. Raleigh, N. C.: n.p., 1970. Describes a model rural housing project in Northwestern N. C.
A4880

Tri-county Housing: A Multi-county Response to Housing Problems. Prepared for North Carolina State Planning Division, Department of Administration, with the financial assistance of the Appalachian Regional Commission. Raleigh, N. C.: n.p., 1971. Plans for a model housing program in North Carolina's Appalachian Region.
A4890

Arnow, Harriette Louisa Simpson The Dollmaker. New York: Macmillan Co., 1954. A classic novel which deals with the plight of the Appalachian migrant.
A4900 (ETSU BC ASU WCU LMC MHC WWC)

Flowering of the Cumberland. New York: Macmillan Co., 1963. An account of the development of the Cumberland River Valley and plateau.
A4910 (FC BC UNCA WWC ASU WCU LMC MHC)

Hunter's Horn. New York: Macmillan Co., 1949. A novel about a man's obsession with a legendary fox who can't be caught.
A4920 (BC ASU ETSU WCU LMC MHC WWC)

Kentucky Trace: A Novel of the American Revolution. New York: Alfred A. Knopf, Inc., 1974. A fictional account of the settlement of Kentucky.
A4930

Mountain Path. Appalachian Heritage Book. Berea, Ky.: Council of the Southern Mountains, 1963. A novel about a young teacher's life in a feud-haunted valley.
A4940 (ASU WCU MHC ETSU UNCA BC LMC)

Seedtime on the Cumberland. New York: Macmillan Co., 1960. Development and settlement of the Cumberland Valley and Plateau.
A4950 (ETSU FC ASU WCU BC LMC MHC WWC)

Arrington, Ted E. Salesman of Appalachia. New York: Vantage Press, 1966. An account of the life of the salesman in Appalachia and observations on his travels.
A4960

Arrowood, Charles Flinn Thomas Jefferson and Education in a Republic. New York: AMS Press, 1971. Mr. Jefferson's University is in the Blue Ridge foothills and several of his other educational experiments took place in the mountain region.
A4970 (ETSU)

Art Works in Hamilton County Chattanooga: W. H. Parrish, 1895.
A4980

Arthur, John Preston A History of Watauga County, North Carolina. With Sketches of Prominent Families. Written at the request of Roy M. Brown, W. D. Farthing, and others. . . who guaranteed all costs of publication.08511Richmond: Everett Waddey Co., 1915. One of the better Western North Carolina county histories.
A4990 (ASU LMC)

Western North Carolina: A History (from 1730 to 1913). Published by the Edward Buncombe chapter of the Daughters of the American Revolution, of Asheville, N. C. Raleigh, N. C.: Edwards and Broughton Print. Co., 1914.
A5000 (BC ASU UNCA WCU LMC WWC)

Western North Carolina; a History, 1730-1913. 1914. Reprint. Spartanburg, S. C.: Reprint Co., 1973.
A5010 (ETSU ASU LMC)

Arthur, Timothy Shay The History of Kentucky, from Its Earliest Settlement to the Present Time. Cabinet Histories of the States. Philadelphia: Lippincott, Grambo & Co., 1852.
A5020 (BC WCU)

Artman, J. O. Forest Fires and Area Burned, State and Private Lands, Tennessee Valley, 1934-1958. Norris, Tennessee: TVA, 1959.
A5030

Asbury, Francis Francis Asbury in North Carolina. Nashville, Tenn.: Parthenon Press, 1964. The N. C. portions of the journals of Bishop F. Asbury (vols. I and II of the Clark edition.)
A5040 (ASU)

Journal of Rev. Francis Asbury, Bishop of the Methodist Episcopal Church. 3 vols. New York: Lane & Scott, 1852. Asbury was singularly pessimistic about the state of the mountaineer's soul. He seemed to regard his travels in Appalachia as a penance. Often he feared for his life among the rough mountain people.
A5050 (BC)

Journal and Letters. 3 vols. London: Epworth Press and Nashville, Tenn.: Abingdon Press, 1958.
A5060 (ASU BC WWC)

Asbury, Herbert A Methodist Saint. New York: Knopf, 1927. Asbury was one of the earliest circuit riders to come into the mountains.
A5070 (ASU)

Ashby, Bernice M. comp. Shenandoah County, Virginia, Marriage Bonds, 1772-1850. Berryville, Va.: Virginia Book Co., 1967. Excellent genealogical source for families who passed through the Valley regions of Virginia.
A5080 (ASU ETSU)

Ashby, Lowell D. Growth in Employment by County, 1940-1950 and 1950-1960. vol. 5. Southeast. Washington: U. S. Office of Business Economics, Regional Economics Division, 1966. A sad statistical record of Appalachia's loss of population due to lack of employment opportunities.
A5090

Ashe, Samuel A'Court History of North Carolina. 2 vols. Greensboro, N. C.: C. L. Van Noppen, 1908-25. Includes some Western North Carolina information.
A5110 (BC LMC ASU)

History of North Carolina. 1908-25. Reprint. 2 vols. Spartanburg, S. C.: Reprint Co., 1971.
A5120 (WWC UNCA)

Ashe, Samuel A'Court ed. Biographical History of North Carolina from Colonial Times to the Present. 7 vols. Greensboro, N. C.: C. L. Van Noppen, 1905-07. Contains sketches of a few Western North Carolina men.
A5100 (WWC)

Ashe, William Willard The Possibilities of a Maple Sugar Industry in Western North Carolina. North Carolina Geological Survey. Economic Papers, no. 1. Winston-Salem, N. C.: M. I. and J. C. Stewart, 1897.
A5130 (ASU LMC)
Shade Trees for North Carolina. North Carolina Geological and Economics Survey. Bulletin, no. 16. Raleigh, N. C.: E. M. Uzzell and Co., 1908. Identifies all native trees.
A5140 (ASU LMC)
Ayres, Horace Bumer The Southern Appalachian Forests. Washington: Govt. Print. Off., 1905.
A5850 (ASU BC LMC ETSU)
Foster, Harold Day Chestnut Oak in the Southern Appalachians. Washington: Govt. Print. Off., 1908.
F2320 (ASU)
Greeley, William Buckout White Oak in the Southern Appalachians. Washington: U. S. Department of Agriculture, Forest Service, 1911.
G3480 (ASU)
Pinchot, Gifford Timber Trees and Forests of North Carolina. Winston, N. C.: MI & J. C. Stewart, 1897.
P2990 (UNCA ASU WCU LMC)

Asheville, N. C. City Directory. 1896. Asheville, N. C.: Piedmont Directory Co., annual.
A5160

Asheville, N. C. Board of Trade Asheville and Vicinity. "Where the Snowbirds Nest." Asheville, N. C.: The Citizen, 1898-99. Promotional material.
A5150 (BC ASU)

Asheville, N. C., Chamber of Commerce Asheville — Live and Invest in the Land of the Sky. Asheville, N. C.: Inland Press, n.d. Tourist brochure.
A5170 (ASU)
In the Land of the Sky, for Your Year-round Home. Cover title: Asheville, live and invest in the land of the sky. Asheville, N. C.: Chamber of Commerce, n.d.
A5180 (ASU)

Asheville, N. C., Chamber of Commerce, Industrial Department Asheville Handbook: A Condensed Summary of Important Facts and Figures. 1926. Asheville, N. C.: The chamber, annual.
A5190 (LMC)

Asheville, N. C., Juvenile Planning Council Community Action for Social Redevelopment in Asheville and Buncombe County. Asheville, N. C.: n.p., 1962.
A5200 (WWC)

Asheville, N. C., Metropolitan Planning Board A Population and Economic Analysis of the Asheville Metropolitan Area and the Western North Carolina That It Serves. Asheville: The board, 1966.
A5210 (BC)

Ashland, Ky., Centennial Committee A History of Ashland, Kentucky, 1786 to 1954. Ashland, Ky.: Graber Print. Co., 1954.
A5220 (ASU BC)

Ashley, George Hall The Abram Creek-Stony River Coal Field, Northeastern West Virginia. U. S. Geological Survey Bulletin, no. 711-F. Washington: Govt. Print. Off., 1920.
A5230
Geology and Mineral Resources of Part of the Cumberland Gap Coal Field, Kentucky. In cooperation with the Geological Department of Kentucky. U. S. Geological Survey Professional Paper, no. 49. Washington: Govt. Print. Off., 1906.
A5240 (ASU)
Outline Introduction to the Mineral Resources of Tennessee. Nashville: Folk-Keelin Print. Co., 1910. All of Eastern Tennessee contains large concentrations of mineral deposits.
A5250 (ETSU)

Ashton, Horace Exploring the Endless Caverns of New Market, Virginia. New York: Nomad Pub. Co., 1926. A guide book, short history, and promotional brochure.
A5260 (LMC)

Ashton, John A Century of Ballads. Collected, edited and illustrated in facsimile of originals, 1887. Reprint. Detroit: Singing Tree Press, 1968.
A5270 (ASU)
The Devil in Britain and America. 1896. Reprint. Ann Arbor, Mich.: Gryphon Books, 1971. This volume examines the British origins of some common Appalachian superstitions and beliefs.
A5280 (ASU)

Association of American State Geologists Centennial Field Trip. Sponsored by the West Virginia Geological and Economic Survey. Log of Trip, May 5, 8, 9, 1963. n.p.: n.p., 1963.
A5290 (ETSU)

Atalie, Princess see **Unkalunt, Atalie**

Athens "Press" Presents the Story of Niota, Tennessee; Its History, Products, and Services in Words and Pictures Niota: Athens Press, 1961.
A5300

Atkin, Edmond The Appalachian Indian Frontier. The Edmond Atkin Report and Plan of 1755. Introduction by Wilbur R. Jacobs. Lincoln: Univ. of Nebraska Press, 1967. An excellent account of relations between Appalachian settlers and the Indians. Contains records of deeds and treaties and maps of army outposts.
A5310 (ASU BC WCU LMC ETSU)

Atkins, Benjamin Elberfield Extracts from the Diary of Benjamin Elberfield Atkins: A Teacher of the Old School, 1848-1909. Gastonia, N. C.: n.p., 1947. Atkins taught school in Gaston County when mountaineers were beginning to move into the area to work in the textile mills.
A5320 (LMC)

Atkins, Emmet D. comp. Atkins, Benjamin Elberfield Extracts from the Diary of Benjamin Elberfield Atkins: A Teacher of the Old School, 1848-1909. Gastonia, N. C.: n.p., 1947.
A5320 (LMC)

Atkins, James W. comp. Atkins, Benjamin Elberfield Extracts from the Diary of Benjamin Elberfield Atkins: A Teacher of the Old School, 1848-1909. Gastonia, N. C.: n.p., 1947.
A5320 (LMC)

Atkins, Pres ed. When the Trains Came to Norton, Wise County, in Old Virginia in 1891. Norton, Va.: Norton Press, 1941.
A5330 (BC ASU)

Atkins, S. W. Allred, Charles E. An Economic Analysis of Farming in Overton County, Tennessee. Knoxville: Department of Agricultural Education, Univ. of Tennessee, 1927.
A1830 (ETSU)

Atkins, Samuel Wesley "An Economic Analysis of Farming in Overton County, Tennessee." Master's thesis. Univ. of Tennessee, 1927.
A5340
Increasing Incomes Through Farm Adjustments in the Red Soil Area, Eastern Highland Rim of Tennessee. Knoxville: Tennessee Agricultural Experiment Station, 1955. Suggestions for crop rotation and new crop alternatives for marginal farm lands.
A5350 (ASU)

Atkinson, A. A. A Key to Mine Ventilation. Scranton, Pa.: Colliery Engineer Co., 1892. An elementary treatise on the principles of coal mining and mine safety.
A5360 (BC)

Atkinson, C. H. Higbee, Howard William Soil Survey, Huntingdon County, Pennsylvania. Washington: U. S. Department of Agriculture, Bureau of Plant Industry, Soils and Agricultural Engineering, 1944.
H5260

Atkinson, Cuthbert Harry Burke, Richard Thomas Avon Soil Survey of Indiana County, Pennsylvania. Washington: U. S. Bureau of Chemistry and Soils, 1936.
B8700

Atkinson, G. H. Simmons, Charles Shaffer Soil Survey of Wayne County, Pennsylvania. Washington: U. S. Department of Agriculture, Bureau of Chemistry and Soils, 1938.
S3430

Atkinson, George Wesley After the Mountaineers. Wheeling, W.Va.: Fren & Campbell, 1881. A revenue agent's account of some exciting raids.
A5370 (BC)
The West Virginia Pulpit of the Methodist-Episcopal Church. Wheeling, W. Va.: Fren & Campbell, 1883. Includes sermons and sketches of ministers living at the time of publication.
A5380 (BC)

Atkinson, Mary Davis Braxton County, Virginia (Now West Virginia) Marriage Book 1. Fort Worth, Texas: American Reference Pub., 1968. A good genealogical source.
A5390 (ASU)
Doddridge County, Virginia (Now West Virginia) Marriage Book 1: Being a Record of the First Marriage in That County Created in 1845 from Parts of Tyler, Harrison, Lewis, and Ritchie Counties. Fort Worth, Texas: American Reference Pub., 1968.
A5400 (ASU)
Pleasants County, West Virginia, Register of Deaths, 1853 — 1873. Cairo, W. Va.: n.p., 1969.
A5410 (ASU)
Ritchie County, Virginia (now West Virginia) Marriages 1843 — 1853: Minister's Returns — With Notes on the Ancestry and Birth Place of Some of the Earliest Settlers. Fort Worth, Texas: American Reference, Pub., 1968.
A5420 (ASU)
Tyler County, Virginia (Now West Virginia) Marriages, 1815 — 1852. Fort Worth, Texas: American Reference Pub., 1968.
A5430 (ASU)

Atlas of the Church in Appalachia; Administrative Units and Boundaries. Knoxville: Commission on Religion in Appalachia, 1970.
A5440 (BC)

Attwood, Stanley Bearce The Length and Breadth of Maine. "Maine Studies," no. 96. Orono: Univ. of Maine, 1973. We have a tendency to forget that the northern reach of Appalachia is in Maine, but this comprehensive accumulation of data will tell us differently. It gives all basic information about the civil divisions of the state, centers of population, physical features, mountains, flora, and fauna.
A5450

Atwater, Mary Meigs Shuttlecraft Book of American Handweaving. New York: Macmillan, 1947. Includes instructions and patterns.
A5460 . (BC)

Augsburg, Paul Deresco Bob and Alf Taylor: Their Lives and Lectures. The Story of Senator Robert Love Taylor and Governor Alfred Alexander Taylor. Followed by the Most Famous of Their Lectures and Speeches, Including "The Fiddle and the Bow" and "Yankee Doodle" and "Dixie". Morristown, Tenn.: Morristown Book Co., 1925.
A5470 (BC)

Augusta County Va. Chronicles of the Scotch-Irish Settlement in Virginia. By Lyman Chalkley. 3 vols. Rosslyn, Va.: Commonwealth Print. Co., 1912. Traces the Scotch-Irish migration routes down the Great Valley of Virginia.
A5480 (ASU)
Chronicles of the Scotch-Irish Settlement in Virginia, Extracted from the Original Court Records of Augusta County, 1745-1800. 1912. Reprint. 3 vols. Baltimore: Genealogical Pub. Co., 1965.
A5490 (ASU)
First Marriage Records of Augusta County, Virginia, 1785-1813. Transcribed by Betty Robson Pritchard. Verona, Va.: McClure Press, 1970.
A5500 (ASU)

Aull, Edward Early History of Staunton and Beverley Manor in Augusta County, Virginia. Birmingham, Ala.: n.p., 1963.
A5510 (ASU BC)

Ault, Mrs. Jamie Wayland, Mrs. Charles F., Sr. Tombstone Inscriptions and Death Records, Calvary Cemetery, Knoxville, Tennessee, 1869-1967. n.p.: n.p., 1967.
W1640 (ETSU)

Aurand, Harold Wilson "The Anthracite Mine Workers, 1869-1897: A Functional Approach to Labor History." Ph. D. Diss. Pennsylvania State Univ., 1969. An account of labor history in the coal fields before the advent of the United Mine Workers of America.
A5520 (ASU)

From the Molly Maguires to the United Mine Workers: The Social Ecology of an Industrial Union, 1869-1897. Philadelphia: Temple Univ. Press, 1971. An account of the terror in the coal fields. No other U. S. industry has known such anarchy.
A5530 (WCU BC)

Aurbach, Herbert A. "An Empirical Study of the Application of the Folk-urban Typology to the Classification of Social Systems." Microfilm. Ph. D. Diss. Univ. of Kentucky, 1960. This study uses many Appalachian people as examples of persons from a folk-culture.
A5540 (ASU)

Austin, Lou You Are Greater Than You Know. Winchester, Va.: Partnership Foundation, 1955. Sentimental autobiography of a Winchester businessman. Stresses correlation between Christian life and business success.
A5550 (BC)

Austin, Moris E. Soil Survey, Claiborne County, Tennessee. Prepared in cooperation with the Tennessee Agricultural Experiment Station and the Tennessee Valley Authority. Soil Survey Report, Series 1939, no. 5. Washington: U. S. Department of Agriculture, Bureau of Plant Industry, Soils, and Agricultural Engineering, 1948.
A5560 (ASU)

Austin, Neal F. A Biography of Thomas Wolfe. Austin, Texas: Roger Beacham, 1968. A biography of Western North Carolina's greatest literary figure.
A5570 (ASU WCU)

Austin, Reba Hodges My Rose Valley. A Geneva Book. New York: Carlton Press, 1969. A charming children's story with a Western North Carolina setting.
A5580 (ASU)

Austin, Richard C. The Strip Mining of America: An Analysis of Surface Coal Mining and the Environment. New York: Sierra Club, 1971. Deals primarily with Appalachia's ravaged surfaces.
A5590 (ASU)

Austin, Richard Cartwright A Search for Appalachian People. San Francisco: San Anselmo Theological, 1967. Rev. Austin served several years as a Presbyterian minister in Appalachia. Unlike his colleague, Rev. Jack Weller, author of YESTERDAY'S PEOPLE, he sees virtues in the folk culture of the people and hope for the future.
A5600

Austin, Suelle Reece "Dan Tompkins: Mountain Editor." Master's thesis. Western Carolina Univ., 1966.
A5610 (WCU)

Auvil, Myrtle Covered Bridges of West Virginia, Past and Present. Parsons, W. Va.: McClain Print. Co., 1972. Pictures, descriptions, brief histories and exact locations of West Virginia's remaining covered bridges.
A5620 (ASU BC)

Auxier, Sylvia Trent The Grace of the Bough. Dallas, Texas: Royal Pub. Co., 1957. Poems from Appalachia.
A5630 (ASU BC)

Green of a Hundred Springs. Appalachia: Young Publications, 1966. Poems from the hills.
A5640 (ASU BC)

Love-vine. Dallas, Texas: Story Book Press, 1953. Poems from Appalachia.
A5650 (ASU BC)

Meadow-rue. Prairie City, Ill.: Decker Press, 1948. Poems from Appalachia.
A5660 (ASU BC)

No Stranger to the Earth. Mill Valley, Cal.: Wings Press, 1957. Poems from the hills.
A5670 (ASU BC)

With Thorn and Stone. New and Selected Poems. Pikeville, Ky.: Pikeville College Press, 1968. Poems from Appalachia.
A5680 (ASU BC)

Availability for Employment of Rural People in the Upper Monongahela Valley, West Virginia Bulletin no. 639. Morgantown: W. Va. Agricultural Experiment Station, 1956.
A5690

Avant, Julius H. ed. Jones, Houston Gwynne Union List of North Carolina Newspapers, 1751-1900. Raleigh, North Carolina: Department of Archives and History, 1963.
J2360 (LMC)

Avary, Philip H. Smith, Howard C. Soil Survey of Chambers County, Alabama. Washington: U. S. Department of Agriculture, Bureau of Soils, 1911.
S4760

Avary, T. H. Hurst, Lewis Alexander Soil Survey of Calhoun County, Alabama. Washington: U. S. Department of Agriculture, Bureau of Soils, 1910.
H8540

Averill, Esther Daniel Boone. New York: Harper, 1945. Yet another biography of the great frontiersman. This one is appropriate for younger readers.
A5700 (ETSU BC)

Averitt, Paul The Early Grove Gas Field, Scott and Washington Counties, Virginia. Prepared in cooperation with the Geological Survey of the U. S. Department of the Interior. Virginia Geological Survey. Bulletin no. 56. University, Va.: n.p., 1941.
A5710 (ETSU)

Averitt, S. D. Kerr, John Alexander Soil Survey of Garrard County, Kentucky. Washington, D. C.: U. S. Dept. of Agriculture, Bureau of Soils, 1926.
K1640

Avery, Alphonso C. History of the Presbyterian Churches at Quaker Meadows and Morganton, from the Year 1780 to 1913. Raleigh: Edwards, 1913.
A5720

Avery County, N. C. Planning Board Overall Economic Development Program for Avery County. n.p.: Western North Carolina Regional Planning Commission, 1962. Avery County is attempting to avoid the kinds of devastation wreaked on neighboring Watauga, Co. by too rapid, unplanned development.
A5790 (LMC)

Avery, Isaac Erwin Idle Comments. Reprinted in part from the Charlotte Observer. Charlotte, N. C.: The Stone Pub. Co., 1912. Recollections of life in Burke County and other areas of North Carolina.
A5730

Avery, Myron H. ed. Arnold Guyot's Notes on the Geography of the Mountain District of Western North Carolina. Washington: The Appalachian Trail Conference, 1938.
A5740

Avery, Robert Sterling Experiment in Management: Personnel Decentralization in the Tennessee Valley Authority. Knoxville: Univ. of Tennessee Press, 1954. An analysis of practices in personnel administration.
A5750

Experiment in Management: Personnel Decentralization in the Tennessee Valley Authority. Knoxville: Univ. of Tennessee Press, 1954. An attempt to decentralize the massive TVA bureaucracy.
A5760 (ASU LMC)

Greene, Lee Seifert Government in Tennessee. Knoxville: Univ. of Tennessee Press, 1966.
G3810 (BC LMC)

Avery, Robert W. A Community Organizes for Action: A Case Study of the Mon-Yough Region in Pennsylvania. University Park: Pennsylvania State Univ. Institute for Research on Human Resources, 1967. A summary of Monongahela-Youghiogheny Valley Community action program. Includes socio-economic profile of the region.
A5770

Avery, Thomas Eugene Identifying Southern Forest Types on Aerial Photographs. U. S. Forest Service Station Paper, no. 112. Asheville, N. C.: Southeastern Forest Experiment Station, 1960.
A5780 (WCU)

Axelrod, Jim Growing Up Country. Clintwood, Va.: Council of the Southern Mountains, 1973. Essays, poems and stories from the younger generation of mountain youth.
A5800 (BC ASU LMC)

Axelrod, Jim ed. Thoughts of Mother Jones; Compiled from her Writings and Speeches. Huntington: Appalachian Movement Press, 1971. Mother Jones began her career as a union organizer in mid-life and became a legendary figure in the labor movement.
A5810

Jones, Mary Harris Thoughts of Mother Jones: Compiled from Her Writings and Speeches. Huntington, W. Va.: Appalachian Movement Press, 1973.
J2510 (WCU)

Axelson, Frederick R. "The Economics of Strip Coal Mining." Microfilm. Master's thesis. Pennsylvania State College, 1950. A treatise on the dollars and cents rationale for strip-mining.
A5820 (ASU)

Ayars, James Caudill, Rebecca Contrary Jenkins. New York: Holt, Rinehart and Winston, 1969.
C2320 (ASU MHC ETSU BC)

Ayer, Katherine ed. Goodale, Dora Read Mountain Dooryards. Berea, Ky.: Council of the Southern Mountains, 1961.
G2500 (ASU LMC MHC BC)

Ayer, Perley Seeking a People Partnership: Eleven Speeches. ed. by Alfred H. Perrin. Berea, Ky.: Council of the Southern Mountains, 1969. Ayer was executive director of the Council. Under his leadership it knew its best days.
A5830 (ASU LMC MHC WCU BC)

Ayers, Orla L. Griffen, A. M. Soil Survey of Madison County, Kentucky. Washington: U. S. Bureau of Soils, 1907.
G4090

Griffen, A. M. Soil Survey of Upshur County, West Virginia. Washington: U. S. Bureau of Soils, 1914.
G4100

Ayres, Ethel Shuler "A History of Ferrum College — The First Fifty Years, 1913-1963." Master's thesis. Appalachian State Teachers College, 1963. A history of a Methodist Junior College in Franklin County, Virginia.
A5840 (ASU)

Ayres, Horace Bumer The Southern Appalachian Forests. U. S. Geological Survey Professional Paper, no. 37. Washington: Govt. Print. Off., 1905. An exhaustive survey of the forests of the Southern Highlands. Shows private, state and federal holdings.
A5850 (ASU BC LMC ETSU)

Ayres, Nellie F. Ayres Kin and Kin to Kin. Memphis, Tenn.: n.p., 1961.
A5860

Ayrs, Orla L. Soil Survey of Overton County, Tennessee. Field Operations, 1908. Washington: U. S. Department of Agriculture, Bureau of Soils, 1911.
A5880

Ayrs, Orla L. and others Soil Survey of Marion County, Alabama. Field Operations 1908. Washington: U. S. Dept. of Agriculture, Bureau of Soils, 1912.
A5870

Baber, Adin Nancy Hanks, the Destined Mother of a President: The Factual Story of a Pioneer Family as Revealed in an Exhaustive Study of Ancestral History. Hanks Family Historical Series, no. 3. Glendale, Cal.: Arthur H. Clark Co., 1963. Deals with the once widespread rumor that Lincoln was the son of a Swain Co., North Carolina Mountaineer to whom Nancy Hanks was bonded for a short time.
B10 (ASU)

Baby, Raymond S. Webb, William Snyder The Adena People, no. 2. Columbus: Ohio State Univ. Press, 1957.
W2080 (MHC)

Bachman, J. W. Memorial of the Rev. James Park. Nashville: Smith & Lamar, 1912. Park was pastor of the First Presbyterian Church at Knoxville.
B20

Back, Troy L. The Brashear Story: A Family History, Containing a Partial Account of a Family That Has Been in America for Well over Three Hundred Years. n.p.: The authors, 1963. Traces a family that followed the frontier westward finally settling in Eastern Kentucky.
B30 (BC)

Backman, Jules Bituminous Coal Wages, Profits and Productivity. Presented before the Presidential Coal Board. n.p.: Southern Coal Producers Association, 1950. Studies correlations between wages, working conditions, profits and productivity.
B40

Bacon, Daniel D. King, John M. Soil Survey of Transylvania County, North Carolina. Washington: U. S. Soil Conservation Service, 1974.
K2300

Bacon, George Washington Life and Speeches of President Andrew Johnson. Embracing His Early History, Political Career, Speeches, Proclamations, etc. With a Sketch of the Secession Movement, and His Course in Relation Thereto; Also His Policy as President of the United States. London: Bacon, 1865.
B50

Bacon, H. Stuart Immunization Cooperation in Southwest Virginia. Berea, Ky.: Council of the Southern Mountains, 1959. A study of the reception received by health care workers attempting to convince mountain people of the need for immunization.
B60

Bacon, Lenice Ingram American Patchwork Quilts. Photography by Creative Photographers, Boston. New York: Morrow, 1973. A lavishly-illustrated volume of old patchwork patterns with text and instructions.
B70 (ASU)

Bacon, S. R. Austin, Moris E. Soil Survey, Claiborne County, Tennessee. Washington: U. S. Department of Agriculture, Bureau of Plant Industry, Soils, and Agricultural Engineering, 1948.
A5560 (ASU)

Higbee, Howard William Soil Survey, Huntingdon County, Pennsylvania. Washington: U. S. Department of Agriculture, Bureau of Plant Industry, Soils and Agricultural Engineering, 1944.
H5260

Bacon, Samuel Rankin Soil Survey, Montour and Northumberland Counties, Pennsylvania. U. S. Soil Conservation Service Soil Survey, Series 1942, no. 11. Washington: Govt. Print. Off., 1955.
B90

Soil Survey, Union County, Pennsylvania. Prepared in cooperation with the Pennsylvania State College School of Agriculture and Experiment Station. Soil Survey Report, Series 1940, no. 2. Washington: U. S. Department of Agriculture, Bureau of Plant Industry, Soils, and Agricultural Engineering, 1946.
B100

Jurney, Robert Campbell Soil Survey of Davie County, North Carolina. Washington: U. S. Department of Agriculture, Bureau of Chemistry and Soils, 1930.
J2870

Lee, William Daniel Soil Survey of Burke County. Washington: Govt. Print. Off., 1926.
L1430

Lee, William Daniel Soil Survey of Burke County, North Carolina. Washington: U. S. Department of Agriculture, Bureau of Chemistry and Soils, 1930.
L1440

Bacon, Samuel Rankin and others Soil Survey, McMinn County, Tennessee. Correlation by M. J. Edwards. United States Soil Conservation Service, Soil Survey, Series 1948, no. 4. Washington: Govt. Print. Off., 1957.
B80

Bade, William Frederic ed. Muir, John A Thousand-Mile Walk to the Gulf. Boston and New York: Houghton Mifflin Co., 1916.
M8470

Badenhop, M. B. An Economic Survey of the Upper Cumberland Area with a Special Reference to Agriculture. Bulletin, 428. Knoxville: Tennessee Agricultural Experiment Station, 1967.
B110 (ASU)

Bagdikian, Ben H. In the Midst of Plenty: The Poor in America. Boston: Beacon Press, 1964. Three sections of this volume deal with Appalachian people at home or in the cities to which they have migrated.
B120 (BC)

Baggerly, Franklin Clyde The History of the Town of Washington, Virginia, "The First Washington of All." Washington, Va.: Town Council, n.d. Washington is the county seat of Rappahannock Co., Va.
B130 (BC)

Bagnell, Charles Robert, Jr. "Twenty-five Common Mosses of Watauga County, North Carolina." Master's thesis. Appalachian State Univ., 1969.
B140 (ASU)

Bail, Paul T. Rough, Robert L. Cost Study of Pumping Versus Flowing Oil Production from Appalachian Waterfloods. Pittsburgh: U. S. Bureau of Mines, 1960.
R3970

Bailey, Benjamin H. Characteristics of High School Seniors as Related to Subsequent College Attendance. Investigators: Harold A. Gibbard and Stanley O. Ikenberry. Morgantown: W. Va. Univ., Division of Education, 1966. This study is based entirely upon graduates of West Virginia high schools.
B150

Bailey, Betty Butcher "Appalachian Fertility Levels and the Role of Interpersonal Relations." Ph. D. Diss. Florida State University, 1972.
B160

Bailey, Betty W. and others Economic Provisions for Old Age of Rural Families in Five Southern States. Southern Cooperative Series, Bulletin no. 138. Athens: Georgia Agricultural Experiment Station, 1968. Many of the subjects for this study were drawn from the isolated ridges and valleys of Appalachia.
B170

Bailey, Carol "Training for Coal Miners in Cooperation with the Public Schools of Tennessee." Master's thesis. Univ. of Tennessee, 1952.
B180

Bailey, Carolyn Sherwin Stories from an Indian Cave: The Cherokee Cave Builders. Illustrated by Joseph Eugene Dash. Just Right Book. Chicago: A. Whitman & Co., 1924.
B190 (ASU ETSU WCU)

Bailey, Charlotte P. "A Study of the Development of Special Education in Claiborne County." Master's thesis. East Tennessee State College, 1958.
B200 (ETSU)

Bailey, E. Brasher "The Negro in East Tennessee." Master's thesis. New York Univ., 1947.
B210 (ASU)

Bailey, Edgar W. "History of Education of Magoffin County, Kentucky." Master's thesis. Univ. of Kentucky, 1932.
B220

Bailey, Edna Peterson "The Diagnosis and Remediation of Comprehensive Skills of a Sixth-grade Class at Rock Creek School in Erwin, Tennessee." Master's thesis. East Tennessee State College, 1962.
B230 (ETSU)

Bailey, Harold Harris The Birds of Virginia. Lynchburg, Va.: J. P. Bell Co., 1913. With fourteen full page colored plates, one map, and one hundred and eight half-tones taken from nature. Treating one hundred and eighty-five species and subspecies: All the birds that breed within the state.
B240 (ASU)

Bailey, James D. Commanders at King's Mountain. Gaffney, S. C.: E. H. De Camp, 1926.
B250

Some Heroes of the American Revolution. Spartanburg, S. C.: Band and White Printers, 1924.
B260

Bailey, James F. Davies, William Edward West Virginia's Buffalo Creek Flood: A Study of the Hydrology and Engineering Geology. Washington: U. S. Geological Survey, 1972.
D720

Bailey, James L. comp. Tennessee Timber Trees. Nashville: Tennessee Dept. of Conservation and Commerce, 1962.
B270

Bailey, Joan Smith "Southern Appalachian Non-standard Speech in Conflict with the Standard English of the Classroom." Master's thesis. East Tennessee State Univ., 1971.
B280 (ETSU)

Bailey, John Making an Appalachian Dulcimer. London: English Folk Dance & Song Society, 1966. Includes excellent set of instructions with diagrams and specifications.
B290 (LMC BC)

Bailey, John Herbert "Conservation Projects by Community Organizations in Tennessee and Other Southeastern States." Ed. D. Diss. Cornell Univ., 1960.
B300

Bailey, John Marvin Two Supply Cooperatives Serving Low-income Farmers: A Preliminary Analysis in Appalachia. General Report, no. 138. Washington: U. S. Department of Agriculture, Farmer Cooperative Service, 1966.
B310

Bailey, Kenneth K. Southern White Protestantism in the Twentieth Century. New York: Harper & Row, Publishers, 1964.
B320

Bailey, Kenneth P. The Ohio Company of Virginia and the Westward Movement, 1748-1792. Glendale, Cal.: Arthur Clark Co., 1939. A history of the Ohio Company and the settlement of the Trans-Appalachian West.
B330 (BC)

Bailey, Natalie S. "Student Involvement in the Policies of a Junior High School Library — An Experiment." Master's thesis. East Tennessee State Univ., 1971.
B340 (ETSU)

Baily, Francis Journal of a Tour in the Unsettled Parts of North America, in 1796 and 1797. London: Baily, 1856.
B350

The Unsettled Parts of North America in 1796 and 1797. Reprint. Louisville, Ky: Lost Cause, 1959.
B360

Journal of a Tour in the Unsettled Parts of North America in 1796 and 1797. Carbondale: Southern Illinois University Press, 1969.
B370

Baily, Louise Howe Along the Ridges. Asheville, N. C.: Groves Print. Co., 1971. Informal history and recollections of Henderson Co., N. C.
B380 (ASU LMC)

Baily, Waldron The Autobiography of Waldron Baily, New York: Exposition Press, 1958. Baily was a North Carolina author and politician.
B390 (ASU LMC BC)

Heart of the Blue Ridge. New York: W. J. Watt & Co., 1915. A novel idealizing life in the Blue Ridge Mountains.
B400 (ASU WCU LMC BC)

Heart of the Blue Ridge. New York: Grosset & Dunlap, 1915.
B410 (ETSU)

June Gold. New York: W. J. Watt, 1922.
B420 (WCU)

When the Cock Crows. Illustrated by G. W. Gage. New York: Bedford, 1918.
B430 (WCU)

Bain, Grady Lee The Circle's End. Boston: Meador Pub. Co., 1932. A novel. Set in Western North Carolina.
B440

Bainder, Herman C. "Maryland's Reaction to Andrew Johnson, 1865-1868." Master's thesis. Univ. of Maryland, 1949.
B450

Baird, Charles O'Connor "Wood Production Investment Opportunities on the Cumberland Plateau in Tennessee: A Regional Economic Analysis." D. F. Diss. Duke Univ., 1963.
B460

Baird, Charles W. History of the Huguenot Emigration to America. Baltimore, Genealogical Pub. Co., 1966.
B470 (FC)

Baird, Nancy Chappelear Fauquier County, Virginia, Tombstone Inscriptions. n.p.: n.p., 1970.
B480 (ASU)

Baird, Robert Norris "An Application of the Leontief Regional Model: An Input-output Analysis for Eastern Kentucky." Ph. D. Diss. Univ. of Kentucky, 1965.
B490

Baisden, A. M. Jurney, Robert Campbell Soil Survey, Smyth County, Virginia. Washington: U. S. Department of Agriculture, Bureau of Plant Industry, Soils and Agricultural Engineering, 1948.
J2930

Bakeless, John Edwin Daniel Boone. New York: W. Morrow & Co., 1939. Another biography of the famous frontiersman. Much of the volume is devoted to Boone's exploits in Kentucky.
B500 (ASU FC ETSU UNCA BC)

Daniel Boone. 1939. Reprint. New York: William Morrow & Co., 1955.
B510 (ASU WCU)

Daniel Boone. 1939. Reprint. Harrisburg, Pa.: Stackpole Co., 1965.
B520 (ASU MH)

Fighting Frontiersman, the Life of Daniel Boone. Morrow Junior Books. New York: Morrow, 1948.
B530

Fighting Frontiersman, the Life of Daniel Boone. Based on Daniel Boone, Illustrated by Edward Shenton. New York: William Morrow & Co., 1948.
B540 (ASU BC)

Master of the Wilderness: Daniel Boone. New York: Morrow, 1939.
B550

Spies of the Confederacy. Philadelphia, Pa.: Lippincott, 1970.
B560

Baker, Blanche "James Robertson: Frontiersman." Master's thesis. George Peabody College, 1926. James Robertson secured land grants from the Cherokee, fought at King's Mountain and was an early political and military leader.
B570

Baker, Clarence W. Guide Book to Lookout Mountain and a Brief Account of Battles Fought near Chattanooga, Tennessee. Chattanooga: C. W. Baker, 1876.
B580

Baker, Emma Eugene Hall The Master of L'Etrange by Eugene Hall, pseud. Philadelphia: T. B. Peterson, 1886. A novel. A Gothic setting and a tale of lost nobility superimposed on a Western North Carolina novel.
B590

Baker, Mrs. F. Columbia County, Georgia, Early Court Records. Albany, Ga.: Georgia Pioneers, 1967. This is one of three Georgia Counties where settlers waiting for admission into the Cherokee Nation waited while lottery numbers were drawn and the Cherokee removed.
B600 (ASU)

Baker, Jimmy Harold "An Analysis of Curriculum Offerings, Changes and Trends in Five Selected Hamilton County High Schools." Master's thesis. East Tennessee State Univ., 1968.
B610 (ETSU)

Baker, Joe L. Men of Affairs in Knoxville. Knoxville: Knoxville Litho., 1917.
B620

Baker, John A. Geology and Ground-water Resources of the Paintsville Area, Kentucky. U. S. Geological Survey Water-supply Paper, no. 1257. Washington: Govt. Print. Off., 1955.
B630 (ASU)

Baker, Louise Regina Cis Martin: Or, The Furriners in the Tennessee Mountains. Illustrated by F. P. Klix. New York: Eaton & Mains; Cincinnati, Ohio: Curts & Jennings, 1898. In this cliche-ridden novel, a New York family moves to Tennessee to capitalize on the timber boom.
B640 (ASU BC)

Baker, Raymond Campfires Along the Appalachian Trail. New York: Carlton Press, 1971. Account of a 2,000 mile hike along the Appalachian Trail.
B650 (ASU LMC WCU BC)

Baker, Todd "The Office of Knox County Sheriff: An Administrative Study." Master's thesis. Univ. of Tennessee, 1959.
B660

"Politics of Innovation." Ph. D. Diss. Univ. of Tennessee, 1968. A study of 20 demands made in Knoxville and Knox County between 1955-63.
B670

Bakerman, Theodore "Anthracite Coal: A Study in Advanced Industrial Decline." Ph. D. Diss. Univ. of Pennsylvania, 1956. Discusses the declining market for anthracite coal due to strip mining and the nation's shift to other forms of fuel.
B680

Bakersville, North Carolina, Historical Celebration, 1956. Prepared for Citizens, Friends, and Visitors of Mitchell County. n.p., n.d. Promotional brochure on Mitchell County. Locally published for the tourist trade.
B690 (LMC BC)

Baldwin, Agnes Leland First Settlers of South Carolina, 1670-1680. Tricentennial Booklet, no. 1. Columbia: Univ. of South Carolina Press, 1969.
B700 (ASU)

Baldwin, Joseph Glover Party Leaders: Sketches of Thomas Jefferson, Alex'r Hamilton, Andrew Jackson, Henry Clay, John Randolph, of Roanoke, Including Notices of Many Other Distinguished American Statesmen. New York: D. Appleton & Co., 1855. Jefferson and Randolph were from the Virginia Blue Ridge area and Jackson began his law career in Appalachia.
B710 (ASU)

Baldwin, Lloyd, R. Barkan, Barry Picking Poverty's Pocket. Huntington, W. Va.: Appalachian Movement Press, 1972.
B1150

Baldwin, Mark Long, David Daniel Soil Survey of Jackson County, Georgia. Washington: U. S. Dept. of Agriculture, Bureau of Soils, 1915.
L3250

Long, David Daniel Soil Survey of Polk County, Georgia. Washington: U. S. Dept. of Agriculture, Bureau of Soils, 1916.
L3270

Baldwin, Seth Alas Lucinda London: Dennis Archer, 1932. A melodramatic novel of mountain life.
B720

Bales, Vivian D. Ball, Bonnie Sage The Dickenson Families of England and America. n.p.: n.p., 1972.
B740

Ball, Arthur Voices from Vale and Hill. New York: Exposition Press, 1954. A collection of articles on nature, history, and folk-lore in the Ohio River Valley.
B730 (BC)

Ball, Bonnie Sage The Dickenson Families of England and America. n.p.: n.p., 1972.
B740

The Melungeons (Their Origin and Kin). 2nd. ed. n.p.: n.p., 1970. A report on a mysterious ethnic minority centered in Hawkins and Hancock Counties, Tennessee.
B760 (ASU LMC WCU FC BC)

Red Trails and White. New York: Exposition Press, 1955. A biography of Caty Sage and her abduction by Indians reconstructed from family letters and legends.
B770 (BC)

Scott County, Virginia: U. S. Census, 1850. n.p.: n.p., 1963.
B780 (BC ASU)

The Seventh Population Census of the United States for Russell County, Virginia, 1850. n.p.: n.p., 1964.
B790 (BC ASU)

Ball, Bonnie Sage ed. March of the Sages. Radford, Va.: Commonwealth Press, 1967. Extensive (600 pages) history of the Sage family.
B750

Ball, Carleton R. A Study of the Work of the Land-Grant Colleges in the Tennessee Valley Area in Cooperation with the Tennessee Valley Authority. Knoxville: U. S. Dept. of Agriculture and TVA, 1939.
B800

Ball, Clyde L. ed. North Carolina, Laws, Statutes, etc., Indexes North Carolina County Legislation Index: A Complete Listing of the Local or Special Acts Passed by the General Assembly for Each County, 1669-1961. Chapel Hill: Univ. of North Carolina Institute of Government, 1964.
N2440 (LMC)

Ball, Palmer Ray comp. The Ball Family of Southwest Virginia: A Genealogy of Some of the Descendants of Moses Ball of Fairfax County. Compiled from court, Bible and church records and gravestone inscriptions. Big Laurel, Va.: Cumberlandcrafters, 1933.
B810 (ASU)

Ball, Richard Allen "The Southern Appalachian Coal Community: An Explorative Study." Master's thesis. West Virginia Univ., 1960. An exploration of life in one of Appalachia's many coal camps.
B820 (ASU)

Ballance, P. S. ed. North Carolina Index: Guide to North Carolina's Periodical Literature. A Cumulative Author and Subject Index Covering Material in N. C. Publications. . . . Winston-Salem: The Editors, irregular serial supplements.
N2430 (ASU UNCA)

Ballard, Alan Blair Laments of an Egotist. New York: Vantage Press, 1962. Sixty-six "home spun" poems which express inmost thought about life in the mountains.
B830

Ballard, Albert M. A Barbecue Toast. Asheville, N. C.: n.p., 1900. An hilarious and historical narrative poem of topics around Asheville.
B840 (ASU)

Ballard, Helen Houston Geraldine the Sightseeing Cow. Greeneville, Va.: The author, 1969. Geraldine escapes her pasture and goes sightseeing. Fiction for ages 3-8.
B850 (ASU LMC BC)

Ballard, Jones The Long Way Through. Boston: Houghton Mifflin, 1959. A young soldier in a stockade reminisces about his West Virginia childhood and the sense of freedom mountains convey.
B860 (BC)

Ballard, Margaret Byrnside William Ballard: A Genealogical Record of His Descendants in Monroe County. Baltimore?: n.p., 1957.
B870 (BC)

Ballenger, Thomas L. "The Development of Law and Legal Institutions among the Cherokees." Ph. D. Diss. Univ. of Oklahoma, 1938.
B880

Ballentine, Nelle "A Bibliographical Checklist of Knoxville and Memphis Imprints, 1867-1876 with an Introductory Essay on the Knoxville and Memphis Press." Master's thesis. Univ. of Tennessee, 1957.
B890

Bandy, Lewis David "Folklore of Macon County, Tennessee." Master's thesis. George Peabody College, 1940.
B900

Banker, Katherine Thomas A Church Called Bethel. Kingston: n.p., 1968. A Presbyterian church.
B910

Banker, Luke H. "Fort Southwest Point, Tennessee: The Development of a Frontier Post, 1792-1807." Master's thesis. Univ. of Tennessee, 1972.
B920

Banks, Charles Edward The Planters of the Commonwealth. A Study of the Emigrants and Emigration in Colonial Times. To Which Are Added Lists of Passengers to Boston and to the Bay Colony: The Ships Which Brought Them, Their English Homes and the Places of Their Settlement in Massachusetts, 1620-1640. Baltimore, Md.: Genealogical Pub. Co., 1961.
B930 (ASU)

Topographical Dictionary of 2885 English Emigrants to New England, 1620-1650. Indexed by Elijah Ellsworth Brownell. 3rd ed. Baltimore: Genealogical Pub. Co., 1963.
B940 (ASU)

Banks Gabriel Conklyn Back to the Mountains, Autobiography. Morehead, Ky.: n.p., 1964. An author's account of his need to live in the mountains.
B950 (BC)

The End of the Day. 1st ed. New York: Pageant Press, 1966. A romantic tale reminiscent of Romeo and Juliet. Two lovers plight their troth in a Kentucky mountain inn and he goes off to war. A sudden succession of letters produces misunderstanding and leads to two deaths.
B960 (ASU)

The Witch and Cinderella, The Boom-cat Kid and other stories. 1st ed. New York: Greenwich Book Publishers, 1965.
B970 (ASU)

Banks, Nancy Huston The Little Hills. New York: The Macmillan Company, 1905. The story is about a widow of a village minister who has to live with her in-laws in Eastern Kentucky.
B980

The Little Hills. Authorized facsimile made by Xerox University Microfilms, Ann Arbor, Michigan, 1975. New York, London: The Macmillan Co., 1905. Romantic fiction with a mountain setting.
B990 (ASU)

Oldfield: A Kentucky Tale of the Last Century. New York: Macmillan Co., 1902.
B1000 (ASU BC WCU)

Banks, Vera J. Beale, Calvin, L. Characteristics of the United States Population by Farm and Nonfarm Origin. Washington: Economic Research Service, Economic and Statistical Analysis Division, 1964.
B2240

Banks, Vera J. comp. Migration of Farm People: An Annotated Bibliography, 1946-1960. Miscellaneous Publications, 954. Washington: U. S. Economic Research Service, Economic and Statistical Analysis Division, 1963. An invaluable source in an area in which so little data is available.
B1010

Banning, Margaret Culkin I Took My Love to the Country. 1st ed. New York: Harper and Row, 1966. A novel set in the Blue Ridge Mountains of North Carolina. A young couple flee the city to find rejuvenation in the mountains.
B1020 (ASU)

Baratte, John J. Lost State of Franklin. Exhibition catalog, including historical sketch. Johnson City: B. Carroll Reece Memorial Museum, East Tennessee State Univ., 1965. A catalog from the museum's show on the Lost State of Franklin. Descriptive information and illustrations.
B1030 (ETSU)

Barb, John Milliken "Strikes in the Southern West Virginia Coal Fields, 1912-1922." Microfilm. Master's thesis. West Virginia Univ., 1949. A cool dry look at a very hot issue. The terror in the coal fields of West Virginia is one of the least-known issues in American History.
B1040 (ASU)

Barbe, Waitman In the Virginias, Stories and Sketches. Illustrated by John Rettig. Akron, Ohio: Werner Co., 1896. The characters are called mountaineers but they differ little from their flatland neighbors.
B1050 (ASU BC WCU)

Barber, Henry British Family Names: Their Origin and Meaning with Lists of Scandinavian, Frisian, Anglo-Saxon and Norman Names. 1903. Reprint. Baltimore, Md.: Genealogical Pub. Co., 1968. A good genealogical guide to the proportional representation of the various ethnic groups in Appalachia.
B1060 (ASU)

Barber, Lunette and others Our Wildlife Neighbors: Important Game Mammals, Fur Bearers, Upland Game Birds and Fish of North Carolina. n.p.: N. C. Wildlife Resources Commission, n.d.
B1070 (LMC)

Barbery, Willard Sanders Story of the Life of Robert Sayers Sheffey. Bluefield, Va.: Trinity Methodist Church, n. d. A biography of a Methodist circuit rider from Southwestern Virginia.
B1080 (BC)

Barbour, Roger W. Wharton, Mary E. A Guide to the Wildflowers and Ferns of Kentucky. Lexington: Univ. Press of Kentucky, 1971.
W5000 (ASU ETSU WCU BC WWC)

Barbour, Roger William Amphibians and Reptiles of Kentucky. Kentucky Nature Studies, 2. Lexington: Univ. Press of Kentucky, 1971.
B1090 (BC ASU LMC WCU)

Barbour, Roger William and others Kentucky Birds: A Finding Guide. Lexington, Ky.: Univ. Press of Kentucky, 1973.
B1100 (ASU)

Barckman, June B. Rent, Robertalee comp. 1810 Montgomery County Census. n.p.: n.p., 1966.
R1510

Barclay, Frank Hunt "The Natural Vegetation of Johnson County, Tennessee, Past and Present." Ph. D. Diss. Univ. Of Tennessee, 1957.
B1110 (ETSU)

Barclay, Robert Edward Ducktown Back in Raht's Time. Chapel Hill: Univ. of North Carolina Press, 1946. A personal recollection of Tennessee's copper producing area and Eckhardt Raht, local character.
B1120 (BC ASU WCU ETSU)

Bardsley, Charles Wareing Endell A Dictionary of English and Welsh Surnames, with Special American Instances. Rev. for the press by his widow. 1901. Reprint. Baltimore: Genealogical Pub. Co., 1968. An aid in tracing English and Welsh settlers along the Appalachian frontier.
B1130 (ASU)

Baring-Gould, Sabine Family Names and Their Story. 1910. Reprint. Baltimore, Md.: Genealogical Pub. Co., 1968. A genealogical aid.
B1140 (ASU)

Barkan, Barry Picking Poverty's Pocket. Huntington, W. Va.: Appalachian Movement Press, 1972. A diatribe against economic colonialism as embodied in the coal industry.
B1150

Barker, Lawrence Wilbur Mink, Oscar G. Dropout Proneness in Appalachia. Morgantown: Appalachian Center, West Virginia Univ., 1968.
M6180 (ASU)

Mink, Oscar G. Dropout Proneness in Appalachia. Morgantown: Appalachian Center, West Virginia Univ., 1968.
M6190 (ETSU)

Barker, Tommie D. Libraries of the South — A Report on Developments, 1930-1935. Chicago: American Library Association, 1936. Includes a section on library facilities in the Southern Appalachians.
B1160

Barkey, Frederick Allan "The Socialist Party in West Virginia from 1898 to 1920: A Study in Working Class Radicalism." Ph. D. Diss. Univ. of Pittsburgh, 1971.
B1170

Barkley, Anna M. "Local History Stories for the Third Grade Washington and Sullivan Counties, Tennessee." Master's thesis. East Tennessee State College, 1952.
B1180 (ETSU)

Barkovitch, Frank S. "The Kentucky Council on Public Higher Education." Master's thesis. Univ. of Louisville, 1970.
B1190

Barlow, James A. Coal and Coal Mining in West Virginia. Morgantown: West Virginia Geological and Economic Survey, 1974. Describes deep mining, surface mining, coal, the environment, uses of coal, and the future of coal.
B1200

Barlowe, Texie Horton The Hortons of Western North Carolina. Lenoir, N. C.: The author, 1934. Family coat of arms and genealogy of the Horton family with the Genealogy of the Barnabas family to 1600 in Mousley, Leichestershire, England.
B1210

Barmann, Dolly Trammel Fork Creek. Dallas, Texas: Kaleidograph Press, 1952. Verse.
B1220 (BC)

Barnard, Jerald R. The Structure of the Kentucky Economy: An Input-output Study. Report number 1 — Preliminary findings. Lexington: Univ. of Kentucky, Office of Development Services and Business Research, College of Business and Economics, 1969. This study attempts to determine the interrelationships between industries, households and government in the Kentucky economy.
B1230

Barnes, Annie Maria The Ferry Maid of the Chattahoochee: A Story for Girls. Illustrated by Ida Waugh. Philadelphia: Penn. Pub. Co., 1899. Romantic fiction centering upon a shy hill girl.
B1240 (ASU)

Barnes, Bertha Rebecca Boone Cook Book. Illustrated by Darrell Isaacs. Harlan, Ky.: Durham Printing and Offset Co., 1974. Pioneer favorites from Eastern Kentucky.
B1250 (ASU)

Barnes, Carmen Time Lay Asleep. New York: Harper and Brothers, 1946. Saga of an East Tennessee family in the Sequatchie valley. Action centers around South Pittsburgh, Tennessee.
B1260 (BC)

Barnes, Clarence E. "The Pattern and Nature of the Informal and Formal Institutional Contacts Participated in by Residents of New Hill." Master's thesis. West Virginia Univ., 1952.
B1270

Barnes, Florence "An Educational History of Unicoi County, Tennessee." Master's thesis. George Peabody College, 1935.
B1280

Barnes, Joe Man on a Mountain. Birmingham, Ala.: Southern Univ. Press, 1969. A reminiscence of Alabama's mountain lakes region.
B1290 (BC)

Barnes, John "A Case Study of Mingo County Economic Opportunity Commission: The Use of Title II of the Economic Opportunity Act of 1964 in a Rural County in West Virginia." D. S. W. Diss. Univ. of Pennsylvania, 1970.
B1300

Barnes, Raymond P. A History of Roanoke. Radford, Va.: Commonwealth Press, 1968.
B1310 (FC)

Barnes, Ruth A. I Hear America Singing. Chicago: John C. Winston Co., 1937. An anthology of folk poetry.
B1320 (BC)

Barnes, Walter Sunset Views: A Book of Verses. Bradenton, Fla.: The author, 1958.
B1330 (ASU)

Barnett, Lucille "A Study of the Causative Factors for Reading Retardation in the Eighth Grade in the Parkway School." Master's thesis. Appalachian State Teachers College, 1953.
B1350 (ASU)

Barnette, Brenda Freeman "The Establishment of a Remedial Reading Program at Columbus Powell Elementary School, Johnson City, Tennessee, School Year, 1966-1967." Master's thesis. East Tennessee State Univ., 1967.
B1340 (ETSU)

Barney, Richard J. Appalachian Scale Shelter. U. S. Forest Service Research Note, 88. Ogden, Utah: Intermountain Forest and Range Experiment Station, 1962.
B1360

Barnhart, John Donald Valley of Democracy: The Frontier Versus the Plantation in the Ohio Valley, 1755-1818. Bloomington: Indiana Univ. Press, 1953. A well-documented and lucid account of the development of political conflict growing out of the inevitable conflict between planters and yeomen.
B1370 (BC)

Barnitz, Wirt W. Ashton, Horace Exploring the Endless Caverns of New Market, Virginia. New York: Nomad Pub. Co., 1926.
A5260 (LMC)

Barns, William D. "The Granger and Populist Movements in West Virginia, 1873-1914." Ph. D. Diss. West Virginia Univ., 1947.
B1380

The West Virginia State Grange: The First Century, 1873-1973. Morgantown: West Virginia Univ., 1974. Condensed and revision of the author's extensive writings on the history of the West Va. Patrons of Husbandry. Traces the economic and social forces that caused the spread of the organization throughout the Mountain State.
B1390

Barnum, Darold T. The Negro in the Bituminous Coal Mining Industry. Racial Policies of American Industry Report, no. 14. Philadelphia: Industrial Research Unit, Wharton School of Finance and Commerce, Univ. of Pennsylvania, 1970. Records the sad role of the negro in the mines and labor struggles of Appalachia.
B1400 (WCU BC MHC)

Barnum, Frances Courtenay (Baylor) Behind the Blue Ridge: A Homely Narrative. Philadelphia: Lippincott, 1887. A poorly plotted novel about Virginia hill folk.
B1410 (BC ASU)

Behind the Blue Ridge. A Homely Narrative. . . Philadelphia, J. B. Lippincott Co., 1887. A loosely structured novel of the Virginia mountains.
B1411 (ASU)

Barnwell, Mildred Gwin Faces We See. Gastonia, N. C.: The Southern Combed Yarn Spinners Association, 1939. A pictorial survey of mill workers in the Appalachin foothills.
B1420 (ASU BC LMC)

Barr, Leslie Beckwith The Mountain Pine. Dallas, Texas: Triangle Pub. Co., 1962. Poetry from the hills.
B1430 (BC)

Barr, Phyllis Cox "The Melungeons of Newman's Ridge." Master's thesis. East Tennessee State Univ., 1965.
B1440 (ETSU ASU)

Barr, Thomas C., Jr. Caves of Tennessee. Tennessee Geological Survey Bulletin no. 64. Nashville: Tennessee Dept. of Conservation, 1961.
B1450

Barrett, John Gilchrist The Civil War in North Carolina. Chapel Hill: Univ. of North Carolina Press, 1963. Several raids and skirmishes but no major battles were fought in Western N. C. including the last action of the war.
B1460 (UNCA ASU LMC)

Barrett, William Alexander English Folk-songs Collected, Arranged, and Provided with Symphonies and Accompaniments for the Pianoforte. 1891. Reprint. Darby, Pa.: Norwood Editions, 1973. The 1891 edition was published by Novello Press, London.
B1470 (ASU)

Barrus, Ben M. A People Called Cumberland Presbyterians. Foreword by C. Ray Dobbins. Introduction and chapter 16 by Hubert M. Marrow. 1st ed. Memphis, Tenn.: Frontier Press, 1972. The Cumberland Presbyterians Church was a distinctly Appalachian phenomena in that the Presbyterians split over the issue of "Called" ministers versus formally trained ministers following the Great Revival of 1805.
B1480 (BC ASU)

Barry, Ada Loomis Yunini's Story of the Trail of Tears. London: Fudge and Co., 1932. An account of the Cherokee Removal written for the younger reader.
B1490 (ETSU)

Barry, Helen B. "A Study of Special Services in the Schools of Greenville County, South Carolina." Master's thesis. Furman Univ., 1954.
B1500

Barry, Jane The Carolinians. 1st ed. Garden City, N. Y.: Doubleday, 1959. A novel of western Carolina in the time of the American Revolution.
B1510 (ASU WWC)

Barry, Joseph The Strange Story of Harper's Ferry, with Legends of the Surrounding Country. 1903. Reprint. Harper's Ferry, W. Va.: Woman's Club of Harper's Ferry District, 1959. The "Facts" as collected from local residents before events at Harper's Ferry had become the stuff of legend or history.
B1520 (BC)

Barth, Nancy Mueller, Eva Migration into and out of Depressed Areas. Washington: Area Redevelopment Administration, 1964.
M8460

Barthalomew, Marshall Nye, Susannah Mountain Songs of North Carolina. New York: Schirmer, n.d.
N3030

Bartlett, Alex The History of New Providence Church, Maryville, Tennessee. Maryville: College Printing, 1876.
B1530

Bartlett, Frederick Orin Big Laurel. Boston: Houghton Mifflin Co., 1922. A romantic quadrangle envolving a shy mountain maiden, a dashing flatland visitor, a gun-toting swain and a genteel lady.
B1540 (BC ASU LMC)

Bartlett, John Russell Dictionary of Americanisms. A glossary of Words and Phrases Usually Regarded as Peculiar to the United States. 2nd ed. Boston: Little, Brown and Co., 1859. Includes some mountain dialect.
B1550 (ASU)

Barton, Charles T. comp. Botetourt County, Virginia, 1820 Census. Typescript. Troutville, Va.: The author, n.d.
B1560

Barton, J. H. Grieve, W. G. Operations Guide for TVA Forest Nurseries. Norris, Tennessee: TVA, 1960.
G4080

Barton, Lewis N. ed. Russell, William Greenway What I Know about Winchester: Recollections of William Greenway Russell, 1800-1891. Staunton, Va.: McClure Print. Co., 1953.
R4410 (ASU BC)

Barton, William Eleazar Abraham Lincoln, Kentucky Mountaineer: An Address Delivered before the Faculty and Students of Berea College, Berea, Kentucky, Thursday, March 8, 1923. Berea, Ky.: Berea College Press, 1923.
B1570 (ASU BC)

The Autobiography of William E. Barton. Indianapolis: Bobbs-Merrill Co., 1932. Barton was an Eastern Kentucky author and educator.
B1580 (BC)

A Hero in Homespun. A Tale of the Loyal South. Boston: Lamson, Wolffe and Co., 1897. A novel of Eastern Kentuckians and other Appalachian men who leave their mountain fastness to serve in the Civil War.
B1590 (BC ASU)

A Hero in Homespun. A Tale of the Loyal South. New York: D. Appleton and Co., 1901.
B1600

Life in the Hills of Kentucky. Oberlin, Ohio: E. J. Goodrich, 1890. Three tales of the Eastern Kentucky mountains.
B1610 (ASU ETSU LMC BC)

Pine Knot. Indianapolis: Bobbs-Merrill Co., 1932. A poor novel featuring abolition, the Civil War, ghosts, hunting for silver, and school teachers.
B1620 (BC)

Pine Knot. A Story of Kentucky Life. New York: D. Appleton and Co., 1900.
B1630 (ASU)

Sim Galloway's Daughter. Indianapolis: Bobbs-Merrill Co., 1932.
B1640 (BC)

Sim Galloway's Daughter-in-Law. Boston and Chicago: The Pilgrim Press, 1897.
B1650

A Tale of the Cumberland Mountains. The Wind-up of the Big Meetin' on No Business. Oberlin, Ohio: The Oberlin News, 1887.
B1660 (BC ASU)

The Truth about the Trouble at Roundstone. Boston and Chicago: The Pilgrim Press, 1897.
B1670

Truth about the Trouble at Roundstone. Indianapolis: Bobbs-Merrill Co., 1932. Two adults quarrel and a retarded girl drowns. A marvelous public relations piece for Appalachia.
B1680 (BC ASU)

Wind-up of the Big Meetin' on No Business. Indianapolis: Bobbs-Merrill Co., 1932.
B1690 (BC)

Bartram, John Diary of a Journey through the Carolinas, Georgia, and Florida, 1765-66. Philadelphia: American Philosophical Society, 1942. Includes botanical notes from the Southern Appalachians.
B1700 (ASU BC)

Bartram, William Travels. 1791. Reprint. Commentary and an annotated index, by Francis Harper. Naturalist's ed. New Haven, Conn.: Yale Univ. Press, 1958.
B1710 (LMC)

The Travels of William Bartram. 1791. Reprint. New York: Barnes and Noble, 1940. Includes notes from his travels in Appalachia. Much good information about the Cherokee, their folkways and mores.
B1720 (WCU)

The Travels of William Bartram. 1791. Reprint. An American Bookshelf. New York: Dover Pub., 1955.
B1730 (ASU)

Travels through North Carolina and South Carolina, Georgia, East and West Florida. 1792. Reprint. Savannah, Ga.: n.p., 1973. Reprint. "A facsimile of the 1792 London edition. . ."
B1740 (ASU)

Barwick, Robert C. "The Economics of Oil Refining in the Pennsylvania Area." Master's thesis. Pennsylvania State Univ., 1955.
B1750

Bascom, Major Dick The Carpet-bagger in Tennessee. Clarksville: J. Jay Buck, 1869. Reconstruction was less onerous in East Tennessee than in many other areas, because there were no occupying forces.
B1760

Basham, Russell Eugene "A Study of the Intramural Sports Program in George W. Vance Junior High School, Bristol, Tennessee." Master's thesis. East Tennessee State Univ., 1968.
B1770 (ETSU)

Baskervill, William Malone Southern Writers: Biographical and Critical. 2 vols. Nashville: Publishing House of the Methodist Episcopal Church, South, 1897-1903. Includes sketches of mountain authors, but fails to draw a distinction between Appalachian literature and that of the rest of the South.
B1780

Bass, Althea Leah Bierbower Cherokee Messenger. Norman: Univ. of Okla. Press, 1936. Bibliography of Samuel Worchester and his wife, missionaries to the Cherokees from 1825 to 1859.
B1790 (ASU)

Cherokee Messenger. The Civilization of the American Indian, 12. Norman: Univ. of Oklahoma Press, 1936.
B1800 (BC ASU WCU)

Cherokee Messenger. The Civilization of the American Indian, 12. 1936. Reprint. Norman: Univ. of Oklahoma Press, 1968.
B1810 (ASU)

Bassett, Fletcher S. The Folk-lore Manual. Chicago Folk-lore Society Publications, no. 1. 1892. Reprint. Darby, Pa.: Norwood Editions, 1973.
B1820 (ASU)

Bassett, John Spencer The Life of Andrew Jackson. 2 vols. Garden City, N. Y.: Doubleday, 1911. Probably the best single biography of Jackson available.
B1830

The Life of Andrew Jackson. Reprint. 2 vols. New York: Macmillan, 1916, 1925, 1928, 1931. Probably the best single biography of Jackson available.
B1840

The Life of Andrew Jackson. Reprint. 2 vols in 1. Hamden, Conn.: Shoe String, 1967. Probably the best single biography of Jackson available.
B1850

Bassler, Ray Smith The Cement Resources of Virginia, West of the Blue Ridge. Introductory chapter on the materials and manufacture of hydraulic cements by Edwin C. Eckel. Virginia Geological Survey, Bulletin, no. 11-A. Charlottesville, Va.: Univ. of Virginia, 1909.
B1860 (ASU)

Bastin, E. S. The Gold Log Mine, Talladega County, Alabama. U. S. Geological Survey Bulletin, no. 640-I. Washington: Govt. Print. Off., 1917.
B1870

Batch, Donald L. Branson, Branley A. Fishes of the Red River Drainage, Eastern Kentucky. Lexington, Ky.: Univ. Press of Kentucky, 1974.
B6360

Batchelder, Martha The Art of Hooked-rug Making. Peoria, Ill.: Manual Arts Press, 1947.
B1880 (LMC)

Bate, William B. The Dedication of the Chickamauga and Chattanooga National Park. Address of Gen. Wm. B. Bate, One of the Speakers Appointed by the Secretary of War for the Above Occasion, Delivered on September 20, 1895. Nashville: Brandon, 1895.
B1890

Bates, Robert Lee The Story of Smithfield, Jefferson County, West Virginia. New York: Endicott, 1958.
B1900

Batson, Wade T. Wild Flowers in South Carolina. Columbia: Univ. of South Carolina Press, 1964.
B1910 (ASU LMC)

Battaglia, Joseph Charles "The Social and Economic History of Maryville since 1890." Master's thesis. Univ. of Tennessee, 1936.
B1920

Battelle Memorial Institute A Study of Potential State and Local Programs to Stimulate Low- and Moderate-income Housing Construction in Ohio Appalachia. Supplement. n.p.: Ohio Department of Urban Affairs, 1969.
B1930 (ASU)

Batterham, Rose, pseud. see Housekeeper, Mrs. William G.

Battey, George Magruder, Jr. A History of Rome and Floyd County, State of Georgia, United States of America, Including Numerous Incidents of More Than Local Interest from 1540-1922. Atlanta: Webb and Vary Co., 1922.
B1940 (BC ASU)

A History of Rome and Floyd County, State of Georgia, United States of America, Including Numerous Incidents of More Than Local Interest from 1540-1922. 1922. Reprint. Atlanta: Cherokee Publishing Company, 1969.
B1950 (LMC MHC)

Battison, E. J. A Framework for Community Economic Planning Based on the Integration of an Input-output Model and a Linear Programming Model. University Park: Pennsylvania Agricultural Experiment Station, 1969. A systems model for relating economic changes to basic factors input in Appalachia Pennsylvania.
B1960

Battle, J. H. Kentucky: A History of the State. Louisville: F. A. Bettey, 1885. Includes scant information on the eastern region of Kentucky.
B1970

Battle of King's Mountain and Battle of Cowpens. Washington, D. C.: Govt. Print. Off., 1928.
B1980

Battles and Leaders of Civil War 4 vols. N. Y.: Century Co., 1884-1887.
B1990

Bauder, Ward W. Characteristics of Families on Small Farms. Bulletin, no. 644. Lexington: Kentucky Agricultural Experiment Station, 1956. Includes studies of some Appalachian farms.
B2000

Bauer, Fred B. Land of the North Carolina Cherokees. Brevard, N. C.: G. E. Buchanan Printer, 1970.
B2010 (ASU MHC ETSU)

Bauer, Harry C. comp. An Indexed Bibliography of the Tennessee Valley Authority. Various editions covering the period from 1941 to 1942. Knoxville: TVA Information Div., 1941-42.
B2020

Bauer, John Public Organization of Electric Power: Conditions, Policies, and Program. New York: Harper & Brothers, 1949.
B2030

Bauer, William Rudolph The Sineath Family and Affiliated Family Lineages. Columbia, S. C.: R. L. Bryan Co., 1970.
B2040 (ASU)

Baugher, Ruby Dell Kentucky, Yesterday and Today. Evansville, Ind.: Creative Press, 1962. Verse.
B2050 (LMC BC)

Listening Hills. New York: Hobson Book Press, 1947. Verse — Story of D. Boone and early Kentucky.
B2060 (BC)

Baum, Emanuel Lester Coltrane, Robert Irvin An Economic Survey of the Appalachian Region, with Special Reference to Agriculture. Washington: Economic Research Service, U. S. Dept. of Agriculture, 1965.
C6100 (ETSU WCU LMC ASU)

Fuller, Theodore Elwood Employment, Unemployment, and Low Incomes in Appalachia. Washington: U. S. Dept. of Agriculture, Economic Research Service, 1965.
F3760 (LMC ASU)

Baum, Willa K. Oral History for the Local Historical Society, American Assoc. for State and Local History. Nashville: The Conference of California Historical Societies, 1971.
B2070

Baumbach, Ludwig Carl Wilhelm von Briefe aus den Vereinigten Staaten von Nord-amerika in die Heimath, mit besonderer Rucksicht auf deutsche Auswanderer. Cassel: Theodor Fischer, 1851. East Tennessee is strongly recommended for German farmers, although there is no evidence that Baumbach knew the region personally.
B2080

Baumgardner, James Lewis "Andrew Johnson and the Patronage." Ph. D. Diss. Univ. of Tennessee, 1968.
B2090

"Inconsistent Men of Principle: Future Liberal Republicans and the Johnson Administration." Master's thesis. Univ. of Tennessee, 1964.
B2100

Baumgardner, James Travis A Baumgardner Family in America. Austin, Tex.: San Felipe Press, 1970. This book gives records of many Baumgardner families, and has extensive records of those in Wythe County. It contains many illustrations and an excellent section on source material references.
B2110

Baumgras, John E. Configuration of Appalachian Logging Roads. U. S. Forest Service Research Paper, NE-198. Upper Darby, Pa.: Northeastern Forest Experiment Station, 1971. Instant Nostalgia.
B2120

Baxter, Dow Vawter Deterioration of Chestnut in the Southern Appalachians. Technical Bulletin, 257. Washington: U. S. Department of Agriculture, Bureau of Plant Industry, 1931. Records the loss of the native chestnut.
B2130

Bayard, Ferdinand Marie Travels of a Frenchman in Maryland and Virginia with a Description of Philadelphia and Baltimore, in 1791: Or, Travels in the Interior of the United States, to Bath, Winchester, in the Valley of the Shenandoah, etc., During the Summer of 1791. Translated from the 2nd ed., 1798, with introd., notes, and index by Ben C. McCary. Ann Arbor, Mich.: Edwards Brothers, 1950.
B2140

Bayard, Samuel Preston ed. Hill Country Tunes: Instrumental Folk Music of Southwestern Pennsylvania. Memoirs of the American Folklore Society, vol. 39. 1944. Reprint. New York: Kraus Reprint Company, 1969.
B2150 (LMC)

Bayles, Robert E. and others Wood County Deep Well. Well Log, Sample, and Core Description. Description of cores by Leonard D. Harris and Russell R. Flowers. Report of Investigations, no. 14. Morgantown: West Virginia Geological and Economic Survey, 1956.
B2160 (ETSU)

Bayley, William Shirley Deposits of Brown Iron Ores (Brown Hematite) in Western North Carolina. North Carolina Geological Survey Bulletin, no. 31. Raleigh: Edwards and Broughton Print. Co., 1925.
B2170 (ASU LMC WCU UNCA)

General Features of the Brown Hematite Ores of Western North Carolina. U. S. Geological Survey Bulletin, no. 735-F. Washington: Govt. Print. Off., 1923.
B2180 (ASU)

General Features of the Magnetite Ores of Western North Carolina and Eastern Tennessee. U. S. Geological Survey Bulletin, no. 735-G. Washington: Govt. Print. Off., 1923.
B2190 (UNCA ASU)

Geology of the Tate Quadrangle. Georgia Department of Mines, Mining and Geology Bulletin, no. 43. Atlanta: Stein Print. Co., 1928. The Tate Quadrangle contains some of the finest marble and granite deposits in the U. S.
B2200 (ETSU)

Bayley, William Shirley
The Kaolins of North Carolina. Prepared in connection with the U. S. Geological Survey. North Carolina Geological Survey Bulletin, no. 29. Raleigh, N. C.: Edwards and Broughton Pub. Co., 1925.
B2210 (WCU)
Magnetic Iron Ores of East Tennessee and Western North Carolina. Bult. no. 32. Chapel Hill: North Carolina Geological and Economic Survey, 1923.
B2220 (UNCA)

Baylor, Frances Courtenay see **Barnum, Frances Courtenay Baylor**

Beach, Robert F. "Book Extension Services in Eastern Kentucky." Microfilm. Master's thesis. Columbia Univ., 1940.
B2230 (ASU)

Beadles, C. B. Hasty, Allen Henry Soil Survey, Rhea County, Tennessee. Washington: U. S. Department of Agriculture, Bureau of Plant Industry, Soils, and Agricultural Engineering, 1948.
H3390

Beale, Calvin, L. Characteristics of the United States Population by Farm and Nonfarm Origin. Agricultural Economic Report, 66. Washington: Economic Research Service, Economic and Statistical Analysis Division, 1964.
B2240
Recent Population Trends in the United States with Emphasis on Rural Areas. Prepared in cooperation with the Population Research and Training Center, University of Chicago. Agricultural Economic Report, 23. Washington: U. S. Department of Agriculture, Farm Population Branch, 1963.
B2250
Bogue, Donald J. Economic Subregions of the United States. Washington: Govt. Print. Off., 1953.
B5100

Beale, Howard K. The Critical Year: A Study of Andrew Johnson and Reconstruction. New York: Harcourt, 1930.
B2260
The Critical Year: A Study of Andrew Johnson and Reconstruction. Reprint. n.p.: American Classics Series, n.d.
B2270
The Critical Year: A Study of Andrew Johnson and Reconstruction. New York: Ungar, 1958.
B2280

Bealer, Alex W. The Art of Blacksmithing. New York: Funk and Wagnalls, 1969. A nice study of a vanishing occupation.
B2290 (ASU)
Only the Names Remain: The Cherokees and the Trail of Tears. Illustrated by William Sauts Bock. 1st ed. Boston: Little, Brown and Co., 1972. An inaccurate, but touching account of the Removal.
B2300 (ASU BC WCU ETSU)

Bealle, Kathryn S. "An Overview of Special Education Services in the Elizabethton City School with Emphasis on the Homebound Program." Master's thesis. East Tennessee State College, 1957.
B2310 (ETSU)

Beals, Frank Lee Davy Crockett. Illustrated by Jack Merryweather. Chicago: Wheeler Pub. Co., 1941.
B2320 (ETSU)

Beamish, Tony Appalachian Wilderness. New York: Ballantine, 1971.
B2330

Bean, Frank Dawson "The Interrelationships of Organized Religion and Certain Other Community Subsystems in Five Selected Counties of Kentucky with Implications for Educational Administration." Ed. D. Diss. Univ. of Kentucky, 1960. Includes a sample community from Eastern Kentucky.
B2340

Bean, Robert Bennett The Peopling of Virginia. Boston: Chapman and Grimes, Inc., 1928.
B2350 (ASU)
The Peopling of Virginia. Boston: Crescendo, 1969.
B2360 (FC)

Bearden, James H. ed. The Travel Industry in North Carolina. Proceedings of the Governor's Travel Information Conference. Greenville, N. C.: Bureau of Business Research, 1964? Many of North Carolina's travel attractions are in the western portion of the state.
B2370 (LMC)

Bears, Betsy After the Goat Man. New York: Viking Press, 1974. Appalachian fiction.
B2371

Beasley, Paul W. "The Life and Times of Isaac Shelby." Ph. D. Diss. Univ. of Kentucky, 1968.
B2380

Beaty, John O. John Esten Cooke, Virginian. New York: Columbia University Press, 1922. Cooke is a native of the Valley of Virginia. It is the locale for some of his work.
B2390

Beaty, Richard Edward The Blue Ridge Boys; Narrations of Early Actual Mountain Experiences and Humorous Anecdotes of the Shenandoah National Park Section. Front Royal, Va.: R. E. Beaty, 1938.
B2400 (BC)
The Mountain Angels: Trials of the Mountaineers of the Blue Ridge and Shenandoah Valley. Front Royal, Va.: The author, 1928.
B2410 (BC ASU LMC)

Bechtol, Paul Theodore, Jr. "Migration and Economic Opportunity in Tennessee Counties, 1940-1950." Ph. D. Diss. Vanderbilt Univ., 1962. Includes valuable information on Eastern Tennessee Counties.
B2420

Beck, Donald E. Cubic-foot Volume Tables for Yellow-poplar in the South Appalachians. U. S. Forest Service Research Note, SE-16. Asheville, N. C.: Southeastern Forest Experiment Station, 1963.
B2430
Effect of Competition on Survival and Height Growth of Red Oak Seedlings. U. S. Forest Service Research Paper, SE-56. Asheville, N. C.: Southeastern Forest Experiment, 1970.
B2440 (WCU)
Seed Production in Southern Appalachian Oak Stands. U. S. Forest Service Research Note, SE-91. Asheville, N. C.: Southeastern Forest Experiment Station, 1968.
B2450
Yield of Unthinned Yellow-poplar. U. S. Forest Service Research Paper, SE-58. Asheville, N. C.: Southeastern Forest Experiment Station, 1970.
B2460 (WCU)
Smalley, Glendon W. Cubic-foot Volume Table and Point-sampling Factors for White Pine Plantations in Southern Appalachians. New Orleans: Southern Forest Experiment Station, 1971.
S4320

Beck, M. W. Latimer, William James Soil Survey of Kanawha County, West Virginia. Washington: U. S. Department of Agriculture, Bureau of Soils, 1914.
L730

Beck, Samuel E. ed. Chiltoskey, Mary Ulmer ed. Cherokee Cooklore: Preparing Cherokee Foods. Asheville, N. C.: Stephens Press, 1951.
C3870 (ASU LMC MHC WCU)

Becker, Bess McReynolds From the Heart. New York: Exposition Press, 1958. Some sixty poems on a wide range of subjects.
B2470
Men "Pro and Con." Bristol, Va.: Quality Printers, Inc., 1968. Twenty-eight poems about men.
B2480

Becker, Joseph M. In Aid of the Unemployed. Baltimore: Johns Hopkins Press, 1965. A collection of essays on unemployment and the aid programs designed to help the unemployed.
B2490

Beckley Newspaper Corporation Brief History of Beckley, West Virginia. Beckley: n.p., n.d.
B2500 (ASU)

Beckwith, Nancy Stout The Story of Washington Bottom, Wood County, West Virginia. Parkersburg, W. Va.: West Augusta Historical and Genealogical Society, 1953.
B2510 (BC)

Beddow, Elizabeth Russell The Oracle of Moccasin Bend: A Story of Lookout Mountain. New York: Neale Pub. Co., 1903. A novel. Setting is the present-day site of Chattanooga.
B2520 (ASU BC)

Bedinger, Singleton B. Kentuckians, C. S. A. Xerox of the original. Taylor, Texas: Merchants Press, 1965. Most Kentucky mountaineers were pro-Union; there were, however, exceptions and these names are listed in this volume of Kentucky's Confederate Troops.
B2530 (ASU)

Beebe, Burdetta Faye Appalachian Elk. Illustrated by James Ralph Johnson. New York: David McKay Co., 1962. The American elk, or wapite was exterminated in Appalachia by 1855. Fictional Background.
B2540 (ASU)

Beebe, Gilbert Wheeler Contraception and Fertility in the Southern Appalachians. Medical Aspects of Human Fertility Series. Baltimore, Md.: Published for the National Committee on Maternal Health, Inc. by the Williams and Wilkins Co., 1942.
B2550 (BC ASU)
"Contraception and Fertility in the Southern Appalachians." Ph. D. Diss. Columbia Univ., 1943.
B2560
Contraception and Fertility in the Southern Appalachians. 1942. Reprint. Family in America. New York: Arno Press and the New York Times, 1972. The empirical observations concern a sample of 1300 families in Logan County, West Virginia.
B2570 (LMC)

Beene, William Virgil In Retrospect: Reminiscencies (sic) and Observations of a Hamilton County, Tennessee, Retired Teacher. Chattanooga: Target, 1958.
B2580

Beerbower, Ethel Peaslee Through the Years: A History of Methodism in Kingwood, West Virginia. Parkersburg, W. Va.: Banner Print. Co., 1951.
B2590 (ASU)

Beers, Alma Holland Coker, William Chambers The Boletaceae of North Carolina.
C5650 (ASU WWC)

Beers, Howard W. Brown, James Stephen Rural Population Changes in Five Kentucky Mountain Districts, 1943-1946. Lexington: Kentucky Agricultural Experiment Station, University of Kentucky, 1949.
B7200
Galloway, Robert E. Utilization of Rural Manpower in Eastern Kentucky. Lexington: Kentucky Agricultural Experiment Station, 1953.
G180
Heflin, Catherine Urban Adjustments of Rural Migrants: A Study of 297 Families in Lexington, Kentucky, 1942. Lexington: Kentucky Agricultural Experiment Station, Univ. of Kentucky, 1946.
H4310
Williams, Robin M. Attitudes Toward Rural Migration and Family Life in Johnson and Robertson Counties, Kentucky, 1941. Lexington: Kentucky Agricultural Experiment Station, Univ. of Ky., 1943.
W6690

Beers, Howard Wayland Mobility of Rural Population. Bulletin No. 505. Lexington: Kentucky Agricultural Experiment Station, Univ. of Kentucky, 1947.
B2600
People and Resources in Eastern Kentucky. (Bulletin No. 500) Lexington: Kentucky Agricultural Experiment Station, Univ. of Kentucky, 1947.
B2610

Beers, Howard Wayland
Rural People in the City: A Study of the Socio-economic Status of 297 Families in Lexington, Kentucky. Lexington: Kentucky Agricultural Experiment Station, 1945. A number of the migrant families in this study are from the Kentucky mountains.
B2620
Urban Adjustments of Rural Migrants. (Bulletin No. 487.) Lexington: Kentucky Agriculture Experiment Station, Univ. of Kentucky, 1946. A number of mountain families were used in this study.
B2630

Beery, Donald Call of the Mountains. Parsons, W. Va.: McClain Print. Co., 1973. A history of sawmilling and pioneer life for the east central part of West Virginia.
B2640 (BC ASU)

Beesley, Thomas Edward and others Soil Survey, Cocke County, Tennessee. U. S. Soil Conservation Service Soil Survey, Series 1944, no. 4. Washington: Govt. Print. Off., 1955.
B2650

Beg, Mirza Amjad Ali "The Regional Growth Points in Economic Development; A Comparison of West Virginia and West Pakistan." Ph. D. Diss. Univ. of Wisconsin, 1964.
B2660

Beglez, Nancy Strange Lady. Ashland, Ky.: Economy Printers, 1972. A novel about a young girl growing up in the eastern Kentucky Mountains, her life, love and education in a mountain school.
B2670 (BC)

Belcher, J. R. A Brief History of the Athens Methodist Church (1848-1942). Typescript. n.p.: n.p., 1942. History of the Athens Methodist Church in Concord, West Virginia.
B2700

Belcher, John Cheslow Number of Inhabitants of the Southern Appalachians, 1900-1957. Population Data Series, no. 1. Prepared in cooperation with the University of Georgia. Athens, Ga.: Southern Appalachian Studies, 1959.
B2680
Use of Health Care Services and Enrollment in Voluntary Health Insurance in Habersham County, Georgia, 1957. Athens: Georgia Agricultural Experiment Station, 1960.
B2690

Belcher, Margaret Crowder Sunday Shoes. New York: Pageant Press, 1955. A West Virginia mountain patriarch copes with his family, the church, and World War I.
B2710 (BC ASU)

Belden, Henry M. Ass. ed. Duke University, Durham, N. C., Library The Frank C. Brown Collection of North Carolina. Durham: Duke Univ. Press, 1952-64.
D3810 (ASU WCU LMC MHC BC WWC ETSU)

Beldon, H. L. Drake, Jerry A. Soil Survey of Cherokee County, South Carolina. Washington: U. S. Department of Agriculture Bureau of Soils, 1907.
D3230

Belk, George W. Floreen: Or the Story of Mitchell. Charlotte, N. C.: Stone Press, 1916.
B2720

Bell, C. Ritchie Radford, Albert E. Atlas of the Vascular Flora of the Carolinas. Raleigh: North Carolina Agricultural Experiment Station, 1965.
R10 (LMC WWC)
Radford, Albert E. Guide to the Vascular Flora of the Carolinas, with Distribution in the Southeastern States. Chapel Hill, N. C.: Book Exchange, 1964.
R20 (LMC WWC)
Radford, Albert E. Manual of the Vascular Flora of the Carolinas. Chapel Hill: Univ. of North Carolina Press, 1968.
R30 (ETSU LMC WWC)

Bell, Corydon Some Snow for Christmas. Cleveland: n.p., 1947. A children's story about a mountain doctor set in the old Blue Ridge.
B2730 (BC ASU)
John Rattling-Gourd of Big Cove: A Collection of Cherokee Indian Legends. New York: Macmillan Co., 1955. A collection of reasonably authentic Cherokee legends edited for children.
B2740 (ASU WCU LMC WWC)

Bell County Centennial Commission, Inc. The Unfolding of a Century. Pineville, Ky.: Sun Publishing Co., 1967. Promotional and historical booklet prepared for the Bell Co. Centennial.
B2750

Bell, D. Ritchie Justice, William S. Wild Flowers of North Carolina. Chapel Hill: Univ. of North Carolina Press, 1968.
J3020 (ASU LMC WWC ETSU)

Bell, Ed. Fish on the Steeple. New York: Farrar and Rinehart, 1935. A novel of troubled adolescence set in the Blue Ridge foothills.
B2760 (ASU)

Bell, Landon Covington Cumberland parish, Lunenburg County, Virginia, 1746-1816. Vestry book, 1746-1816. Richmond, Va.: The William Byrd Press, Inc., 1930. "At the time of its creation Cumberland parish embraced. . . the territory which is now comprised in the counties of Lunenburg, Mecklenburg, Halifax, Charlotte, Pittsylvania, Henry, Patrick, and Franklin. . . and the greater part of Bedford and Campbell counties, and a part of Appomattox. It was, therefore. . . the parent of: Antrim parish in Halifax County. . . of Cornwall parish. . of St. James parish. . . and others.
B2770 (ASU)
The Golden Anniversary Dinner, February 24, 1940, in Honor of William McClellan Ritter, Founder of W. M. Ritter Lumber Company. Richmond: Garrett and Massie, 1940.
B2780 (WCU)
Lunenburg County, Virginia wills, 1746-1825. Indexed by Lorraine L. Fuller and Jean V. Sipe. Berryville: Virginia Book Co., 1972. During this period Lunenburg County included parts of the present day counties of Patrick, Franklin and Bedford.
B2790 (ASU)

Bell, N. E. Burke, Richard Thomas Avon Soil Survey of St. Clair County, Alabama. Washington: U. S. Dept. of Agriculture, Bureau of Soils, 1920.
B8750

Bell, N. Eric Taylor, Arthur Elijah Soil Survey of Clay County, Alabama. Washington: U. S. Department of Agriculture, Bureau of Soils, 1916.
T410
Waldrop, Charles S. Soil Survey of Jackson County, Alabama. Washington: U. S. Department of Agriculture, Bureau of Soils, 1912.
W200
Waldrop, Charles S. Soil Survey of Marshall County, Alabama. Washington: U. S. Department of Agriculture, Bureau of Soils, 1913.
W210

Bell, Robert ed. Early Ballads, Illustrative of History, Traditions, and Customs: Also Ballads and Songs of the Peasantry of England, Taken Down from Oral Recitation and Transcribed from Private Manuscripts, Rare Broadsides, and Scarce Publications. 1877. Reprint. Detroit, Mich.: Singing Tree Press, 1968. Many of these ballads and customs were carried over to Appalachia.
B2800 (ASU)

Bell, Robert Monroe "The Cost of Administering Criminal Justice in Memphis and Knoxville, Tennessee." Master's thesis. Univ. of Tennessee, 1931. Knox County, Tennessee — County History, Political History and Public Administration.
B2810

Bell, Sadie The Church, the State, and Education in Virginia. 1930. Reprint. American Education: Its Men, Ideas and Institutions. New York: Arno Press, 1969.
B2820 (MHC)

Bell, Thelma Harrington Mountain Boy. New York: Viking Press, 1947. A children's story about a lad growing up in the Southern mountains.
B2830 (LMC)
Snow. Illustrated by Corydon Bell. New York: Viking Press, 1954. A children's story about the best snowfall of the year.
B2840 (ASU)
The Two Worlds of Davy Blount. Illustrated by Corydon Bell. New York: Viking Press, 1962. A story of an heroic young mountain lad.
B2850 (ASU BC)
Yaller-Eye. New York: Viking Press, 1947.
B2860

Bendall, John W. "A Study of the Minnesota Multiphasic Personality Inventory and Its Use in Identification of Acceptable Mine Foremen." Master's thesis. West Virginia Univ., 1955.
B2870

Benet, Laura Caleb's Luck. New York: Grosset and Dunlap, 1942. A picture and story book about a parade and a young mountain boy.
B2880

Benkelman, Olive Porter Scott James and Rachel Holmes Scott. Elk Creek, Va.: n.p., 1971. An attractive genealogical chart record commemorating the 200th anniversary of the importation of James and Rachel Scott.
B2890

Bennecker, Ruth He That Serveth; Twenty-five Years' Adventures in Christian Ministry, George Creswell and Second Church. Knoxville: Second Methodist Church, 1945.
B2900

Bennett, Charles W. "Life and Literary Contributions of Luther Foster Addington, a Southwest Virginia Writer and Educator. Master's thesis. East Tennessee State Univ., 1965.
B2910

Bennett, Clara Willis "A Study of Book Losses During the Period 1965-1969 in the Dobyns-Bennett High School Materials Center, Kingsport, Tennessee." Master's thesis. East Tennessee State Univ., 1970.
B2920 (ETSU)

Bennett, Clemmon A. "History of Education in Gordon County, Georgia." Master's thesis. Univ. of Kentucky, 1932.
B2930

Bennett, Emerson The Bride of the Wilderness. Philadelphia: L. B. Peterson, 1854. A tale of pioneering in Northwestern W. Va. along the Monongahela River.
B2940 (BC)
Ella Barnwell. Cincinnati: U. P. James, 1853. A tale of the settlement of the border county of Kentucky.
B2950 (BC)
The Phantom of the Forest: A Tale of the Dark and Bloody Ground. Author's rev. ed. Xerox copy of the original. Philadelphia: J. E. Potter, 1868. A tale of frontier Kentucky. Action occasionally ranges into the mountains.
B2960 (ASU BC)

Bennett, Frank Burke, Richard Thomas Avon Soil Survey of Rockcastle County, Kentucky Washington: U. S. Dept. of Agriculture, Bureau of Soils, 1911.
B8740

Bennett, H. D. Lessons in Appalachian Forestry. Cincinnati: Appalachian Hardwood Manufacturers, 1950. A text for secondary schools which attempts to explain the role of forestry, lumbering, and logging in Appalachia.
B2970

Bennett, Hugh Hammond Soils of the Shenandoah River Terrace: Revision of Certain Soils in the Albemarle Area, Virginia. Circular, 53. Washington: U. S. Department of Agriculture, Bureau of Soils, 1912.
B2980

Bennett, James D. "Struggle for Power: The Relations between the Tennessee Valley Authority and the Private Power Industry, 1933-1939. Ph. D. Diss. Vanderbilt Univ., 1969.
B2990

Bennett, John Nathan Jennie Wiley, Pioneer: The True Story of a Virginia Frontier Heroine. 1st ed. New York: Exposition Press, 1955.
B3000 (ASU)

Bennett, Wallace R. Report of the Economic Growth of Oak Hill, Correlated With the History of King Coal-Fayette County's First Major Industry. Oak Hill, W. Va.: The author, n.d. Statistical survey of Oak Hill's population, finances, housing and industry.
B3010

Bent, Allen Herbert A Bibliography of the White Mountain. Boston: Pub. for the Appalachian Mountain Club, by Houghton Mifflin Co., 1911.
B3020

Bentley, Blanche S. Sketch of Beersheba Springs: and: Chickamauga Trace. Chattanooga: Lookout, 1928.
B3030

Bentley, Hubert Blair "Andrew Johnson, Governor of Tennessee, 1853-1857." Ph. D. Diss. Univ. of Tennessee, 1972.
B3040

Benton, Robert L. "A Study of McMinn County High School as Determined by Its Graduates." Master's thesis. Univ. of Tennessee, 1952.
B3050

Berea College, Kentucky Berea College, Kentucky, An Interesting History. Approved by the Prudential Committee. Cincinnati, Ohio: Elm Street Print. Co., 1883.
B3060 (ASU)

Favorite Folk Dance Tunes. Berea, Ky.: Council of Southern Mountains, 1968.
B3070 (ASU BC)

1924 Works of Fiction by Southern Appalachian Authors, Or with Southern Appalachian Settings: Mountain Fiction from Addington to Zugsmith. Berea, Ky.: The college, 1972.
B3080 (ASU MHC ETSU BC)

Berea College, Kentucky Appalachian Center Newsletter. vol. 1. 1972. n.p.: n.p., quarterly.
B3090 (BC ASU)

Berea College, Kentucky, Department of Education Evidence of Inequality of Educational Opportunity in Kentucky Mountain Counties. Berea, Ky.: The college, 1953.
B3100 (BC)

Berea College, Kentucky, Rural School Improvement Project. Report, 1953-1957. Lexington: Transylvania Print. Co., 1958.
B3110 (BC ETSU)

Berea, Kentucky, Planning Commission Land Use Plan for the City of Berea, Ky. Berea: Berea Planning Commission, 1965.
B3120 (BC)

Public Improvements for the City of Berea, Ky. Berea: Berea Planning Commission, 1965.
B3130 (BC)

Bergaust, Erik Rocket City U. S. A. from Huntsville, Alabama to the Moon. N. Y.: F. M. Hill Books, 1963.
B3140

Berglund, Abraham and others Labor in the Industrial South: A Survey of Wages and Living Conditions in Three Major Industries of the New Industrial South. Charlottesville, Va.: Institute for Research In the Social Sciences, Univ. of Virginia, 1930.
B3150 (LMC)

Berhard, Karl, Herzog von Sachsen-Weimar-Eisnach Reise sr. Hoheit des Herzogs Bernhard zu Sachsen-Weimar-Eisenach durch Nord-Amerika in den Jahren 1825 und 1826. 2 vols. Weimar: Wilhelm Hoffmann, 1828. Observation on the country around Winchester, Staunton, Natural Bridge, Lexington (Va.), and Charlottesville.
B3190

Berkhofer, Robert F. "Protestant Missionaries to the American Indians, 1789 to 1862." Ph. D. Diss. Cornell Univ., 1960.
B3160

Berkman, Sigmund S. Appalachia, Rebirth of a Nation. Washington: U. S. Department of Labor, Office of Manpower, Automation and Training, 1964.
B3170

Bernert, Eleanor H. Farm Migration, 1940-1945: An Annotated Bibliography. Library List, no. 48. Washington: U. S. Department of Agriculture Library, 1947. A very useful tool in an area in which too little research has been done.
B3180

Berney, William Richardson, Howard Dark of the Moon. New York: Theatre Arts Books, 1957.
R2100 (ASU WCU)

Richardson, Howard Dark of the Moon. London: Heinemann, 1966.
R2110 (ASU)

Richardson, Howard Dark of the Moon. New York: Theatre Arts Books, 1966.
R2120 (LMC MHC)

Richardson, Howard Dark of the Moon. New York: Theatre Arts Books, 1970.
R2130 (ETSU)

Bernheim, Cotthardt Dellmann History of the German Settlements and of the Lutheran Church in North and South Carolina, from the Earliest Period of the Colonization of the Dutch, German and Swiss Settlers to the Close of the First Half of the Recent Century. Xerox of the original. Philadelphia: Lutheran Book Store, 1872.
B3200 (ASU)

Berry, Brian J. L. A Bibliographic Guide to the Economic Regions of the United States. Chicago: Univ. of Chicago, 1963. Includes a condescending survey of Appalachia.
B3210

Berry, Charles A. "Measurement of the Economic Impact of Public Investment of Regional Economic Growth in Appalachia." Ph. D. Diss. Univ. of Cincinnati, 1968.
B3220

Berry, Edward Wilbee Loughlin, Gerald Francis Limestones and Marls of North Carolina. Raleigh: Edwards and Broughton Print. Co., 1921.
L3630 (ASU LMC WCU)

Berry Erick One-string Fiddle. Chicago: Winston, 1939. A story of a little Tennessee mountain boy and his homemade fiddle.
B3230 (LMC)

Berry, Paul C. and others The Future of American Poverty, Some Basic Issues in Evaluating Alternative Anti-poverty Measures. Croton-on-Hudson, N. Y.: Hudson Institute, 1968. Includes a survey of Appalachian poverty.
B3240

Berry Wendall The Memory of Old Jack. New York: Harcourt Brace Jovanovich, Inc. 1974. Jack Beechum was one of the most endearing characters in A PLACE ON EARTH. This volume is about his death, burial and the memories he leaves behind.
B3270 (ASU)

Berry, Wendell Farming: A Hand Book. New York: Harcourt, Brace, Jovanovich, 1970. A handbook on farming by Eastern Kentucky's well-known novelist.
B3250 (WCU ASU)

The Long-legged House. 1st ed. New York: Harcourt, Brace and World, 1969. An eloquent ecological plea for the future of Appalachia.
B3260 (ASU MHC WCU BC)

A Place on Earth. 1st ed. New York: Harcourt, Brace and World, 1967. A novel of a Kentucky foothill town during World War II.
B3280 (ASU LMC BC)

A Place on Earth. New York: Avon Books, 1969. A novel of a Kentucky foothill town during World War II.
B3290 (ASU WCU)

The Unforeseen Wilderness: An Essay on Kentucky's Red River Gorge. Photographs by Gene Meatyard. Lexington: Univ. Press of Kentucky, 1971.
B3300 (ASU BC LMC)

Berryhill, Henry Lee, Jr. Coal Reserves of the Pittsburgh (No. 8) Bed in Belmont County, Ohio. U. S. Geological Survey Circular, no. 363. Washington: Govt. Print. Off., 1955. A survey of coal resources in the Appalachian Counties of Appalachia.
B3310 (ASU)

Bers, Melvin Labor Force Participation in the Pittsburgh Standard Metropolitan Area. Pittsburgh: Regional Planning Association, 1960. An economic survey of the Pittsburgh region.
B3320

Berthy, Howard Phillip Selected Opportunities for Wood Industries Development in West Virginia Through Application of Forest Products Laboratory Research. U. S. Forest Service Research Note, FPL-016. Madison, Wis.: Forest Products Laboratory, 1963. Summarizes forest products research applicable to West Virginia. Includes a bibliography.
B3330

Bertrand, Alvin L. Terry, Geraldine B. The Labor Force Characteristics of Women in Low-Income Rural Areas of the South. n.p.: Southern Cooperative Series, 1966.
T7630

Best, Billy F. "From Existence to Essence; A Conceptual Model for an Appalachian Studies Curriculum." Ed. D. Diss. Univ. of Massachusetts, 1973. Offers clear, logical counterpoint to culturally biased appraisals of mountaineers. He suggests a model Appalachian studies curriculum.
B3340

Best, Irmgard Appalachians Speak Up. Berea, Ky.: The author, 1972. Through a series of interviews, the author has reached a consensus of Appalachian attitudes.
B3350 (BC)

Bethell, Thomas N. Conspiracy in Coal. Huntington, W. Va.: Appalachian Movement Press, n.d. A searing indictment of the coal industry's lack of safety standards and the failure of federal inspectors to report substandard operations.
B3360

The Hurricane Creek Massacre: An Inquiry into the Circumstances Surrounding the Deaths of Thirty-eight Men in a Coal Mine Explosion. Perennial Library, P251. New York: Harper and Row, 1972. A hard-hitting indictment of mine safety standards and the criminal negligence of inspectors.
B3370 (ASU BC LMC WCU MHC)

The Pittston Mentality: Manslaughter on Buffalo Creek. Huntington: Appalachian Movement Press, 1972. An indictment of the corporation responsible for the Buffalo Creek Disaster.
B3380

Bett, Henry The Games of Children, Their Origin and History. London: Methuen and Co., Ltd., 1929. A book of folk and play party games which were popular in Appalachia two generations ago.
B3390 (ASU)

Bettis, Glenn E. "A Proposed Central Supply, Storage, and Technicians' Work Area for the Industrial Education Department of East Tennessee State University." Master's thesis. East Tennessee State Univ., 1967.
B3400 (ETSU)

Betts, Doris The Gentle Insurrection, and Other Stories. New York: Putnam, 1954. Doris Betts, a young North Carolinian, is a writer concerned with serious and perceptive reporting of the Southern small town and Southern people.
B3410 (LMC)

Betts, Edward Chambers Early History of Huntsville, Alabama, 1804-1870. Rev. Montgomery, Ala.: Brown Print. Co., 1916.
B3420 (ASU BC)

Betts, Leonidas Gateway to North Carolina Folklore. Raleigh: School of Education Office of Publications, North Carolina State Univ. at Raleigh, 1974.
B3430

Beverage, Woodrow Wilson Soil Survey, Barbour County, West Virginia. Washington: U. S. Department of Agriculture, Soil Conservation Service, 1968.
B3440

Soil Survey, Marshall County, West Virginia. Soils surveyed by Merrill Kunkle, Joseph D. Ruffner, and John Webb. Correlation by Morris E. Austin. Soil Survey, Series 1957, no. 4. Washington: U. S. Department of Agriculture, Soil Conservation Service, 1960.
B3450

Losche, Craig K. Soil Survey, Tucker County, Part of Northern Randolph County, West Virginia. Washington: U. S. Dept. of Agriculture, Soil Conservation Service, 1967.
L3540

Patton, Boyd J. Soil Survey, Preston County, West Virginia. Washington: Govt. Print. Off., 1959.
P820

Beverett, Andrew J. Perkins, Edward L. Guidelines for an Appalachian Airport System. Washington: Appalachian Regional Commission, 1967.
P2050 (ASU WCU)

Beverly, Frank Monroe Echoes from the Cumberlands, Being Made from His Poems Written During the Last Thirty Years. Strasburg: Shenandoah Pub. House, 1928. Poems, primarily about nature in the Cumberland Mountains.
B3460 (ASU BC)

Beverly, Lucia Bird, Ronald Status of Rural Housing in the United States. Washington: U. S. Economic Research Service, Economic Development Division, 1968.
B4120

Bias, W. B. A Short History of the Wayne Methodist Church. Typescript. n.p.: n.p., n.d. (1846-1960)
B3470

Bible, Bond L. Buck, Roy Clair Educational Attainment among Pennsylvania Rural Youth. University Park: Pennsylvania Agricultural Experiment Station, 1961.
B8200

Bible, Mary Ozelle "The Post-presidential Career of Andrew Johnson." Master's thesis. Univ. of Tennessee, 1936.
B3480

Bibliography of Coal in Kentucky Lexington, Ky.: Univ. of Ky., 1970. Excellent source material on mining in Kentucky.
B3490 (BC)

Bibliography on the Appalachian South, 1973-1974; Books, Records, Pamphlets, Magazines, and Films Clintwood, Va.: Council of the Southern Mtns., 1974.
B3500 (ASU)

Bick, Kenneth F. Geology of the Lexington Quadrangle, Virginia. Charlottesville, 1960.
B3510 (ETSU ASU)

Geology of the Williamsville Quadrangle, Virginia. Report of Investigations, no. 2. Charlottesville: Virginia Division of Mineral Resources, 1962. Includes Highland and Rockbridge Counties.
B3520 (ETSU)

Bickley, George Washington Lafayette History of the Settlement and Indian Wars of Tazewell County, Virginia. Parsons, W. Va.: McClain Print. Co., 1973. Includes sketches of Indians in the county and a sketch of the author's life.
B3530 (FC ASU)

History of the Settlement and Indian Wars of Tazewell County, Va. with added material compiled by J. Allen Neal. Parsons, W. Va.: McClain Print. Co., 1974.
B3540

Biddle, Loureide J. Biddle, William W. The Community Development Process: The Rediscovery of Local Initiative. New York: Holt, Rinehart and Winston, 1965.
B3550

Biddle, William W. The Community Development Process: The Rediscovery of Local Initiative. New York: Holt, Rinehart and Winston, 1965. Report of a successful three year development in an Appalachian county.
B3550

Bidgood, Lee Alvord, Clarence Walworth The First Explorations of the Trans-Allegheny Region by the Virginians, 1650-1674. Cleveland: Arthur H. Clark, 1912.
A1990 (ASU BC)

Bieber, Paul P. Ground-water Features of Berkeley and Jefferson Counties, West Virginia. Prepared by U. S. Geological Survey in cooperation with West Virginia Geological and Economic Survey. Bulletin, no. 21. Morgantown: West Virginia Geological Survey, 1961.
B3560 (ETSU)

Nace, Raymond Lee Ground-water Resources of Harrison County, West Virginia. Morgantown: West Virginia Geological Survey, 1958.
N20 (ETSU)

Biesecker, James E. Stream Quality in Appalachia as Related to Coal-mine Drainage, 1965. Geological Survey, Circular, 526. Washington: Govt. Print. Off., 1966. A frightening analysis of the effects of mine drainage on streams.
B3570 (LMC BC ASU)

Stream Quality in Appalachia as Related to Coal-mine Drainage. U. S. Geological Survey Circular 576. Washington: U. S. Govt. Print. Off., 1966.
B3571

Biggs, Nina Mitchell History of Greenup County, Kentucky. Louisville, Ky.: The authors, 1951.
B3580 (BC)

A Supplementary Edition of a History of Greenup County. New York: Vantage Press, 1962. A supplement to the 1951 edition.
B3590 (ASU BC)

Biggs, Riley O. "Development of Railroad Transportation in East Tennessee during the Reconstruction Period." Master's thesis. Univ. of Tennessee, 1934.
B3600

Biles, James M. "A Study of School Transportation, Roane County, Tennessee." Master's thesis. Univ. of Tennessee, 1961.
B3610

Billings, Henry All Down the Valley. New York: Viking Press, 1952. Some public relations man's idea of a soft sell for the TVA. No mention of lines destroyed, historic sites drowned, or farmlands flooded so that electricity could be piped to distant cities.
B3620 (BC ASU WCU LMC)

Billingsley, G. A. Robinson, W. H. Water Supply of the Birmingham Area, Alabama. Washington: Govt. Print. Off., 1953.
R3340

Bills, Nelson Lawrence "An Input-output Analysis of the Upper South Branch Valley of West Virginia." Master's thesis. West Virginia Univ., 1967. A systems analysis study of a West Virginia community.
B3630

Bills, Robert E. The Incentive Approach to State School Administration: Change in Two Pilot Centers, Mason County, West Virginia, and Doddridge County, West Virginia, 1959-60. Charleston: West Virginia Department of Education, Division of Research and Planning, 1961.
B3640

Billups, Edward W. comp. The Sweet Songster, a Collection of the Most Popular and Approved Songs, Hymns and Ballads. 1854. Reprint. Wayne, W. Va.: Arrowood Brothers, n.d. A popular item throughout Appalachia in the last century. Used to "line out" songs by the song leader, this volume has no music only words.
B3650 (ASU BC WCU)

The Sweet Songster, a Collection of the Most Popular and Approved Songs, Hymns and Ballads n.p.: n.p., n.d.
S9580

Billy Boy Verses selected by Richard Chase. Drawings by Glen Rounds. San Carlos, Cal.: Golden Gate Junior Books, 1966.
B3660 (BC ASU)

Biltmore House and Gardens Asheville, N. C.: Biltmore Estate, 1965. An American castle in Western North Carolina. The grounds of this estate comprised the first school of forestry in the U. S.
B3670 (WCU)

Biltmore Nursery Flowering Trees and Shrubs. Biltmore, N. C.: Biltmore Nursery, 1909. A guide to flowering trees and shrubs by Asheville's most famous nursery.
B3680

Bimba, Anthony The Molly Maguires. New York: International Pub., 1970. A history of a terrorist organization in the Pennsylvania coal fields. Membership was largely Irish.
B3690 (ASU WCU BC)

Bing, William K. Conner, Maynard Calvin An Economic and Social Survey of Patrick County. Charlottesville: Univ. of Va., 1937.
C6680 (BC)

Bingham, Edgar "Land Utilization in the New and Watauga River Basins of North Carolina." Ph. D. Diss. Ohio State Univ., 1954. Explores the rapidly changing land use patterns of Western North Carolina.
B3700 (LMC)

Bingham, R. W. Joe, A Civil War Novel of the Blue Ridge. n.p.: n.p., 1889. No information available.
B3710

Bingham, William Paul "The Growth and Development of Education in Watauga County." Master's thesis. Appalachian State Teachers College, 1950.
B3720 (ASU)

Bining, Arthur C. Pennsylvania's Iron and Steel Industry. Pennsylvania History Studies, no. 5. Gettysburg: Pennsylvania Historical Assoc., 1954.
B3730 (ASU)

Pennsylvania Iron Manufacture in the Eighteenth Century. Clifton, N. J.: Augusta M. Kelley Pub., 1974. A classic in economic history and colonial art and industry.
B3740

Binnicker, Dana Pell Blue Moon Over Cashier's Valley. Charleston: Nelson's Southern Print. and Pub. CO., . Novel with a western North Carolina setting and very standard plot featuring romance, suspense and violence.
B3750

Biographical Directory: Bledsoe County Members of the Tennessee General Assembly, 1796- Nashville: State Library and Archives, 1968. This volume also includes Marion and Sequatchie counties.
B3760

Biographical Directory: Blount County Members of the Tennessee General Assembly, 1796- Nashville: State Library and Archives, 1968.
B3770

Biographical Directory: Bradley County Members of the Tennessee General Assembly, 1796- Nashville: State Library and Archives, 1968. This volume also contains Polk County.
B3780

Biographical Directory: Carter County Members of the Tennessee General Assembly, 1796- Nashville: State Library and Archives, 1968. This volume also contains Johnson and Unicoi counties.
B3790

Biographical Directory: Coffee County Members of the Tennessee General Assembly, 1796- Nashville: State Library and Archives, 1968. This volume also contains Grundy County.
B3800

Biographical Directory: DeKalb County Members of the Tennessee General Assembly, 1796- Nashville: State Library and Archives, 1968. This volume also contains Cannon County.
B3810

Biographical Directory: Fentress County Members of the Tennessee General Assembly, 1796- Nashville: State Library and Archives, 1968. This volume also contains Overton and Pickett counties.
B3820

Biographical Directory: Franklin County Members of the Tennessee General Assembly, 1796- Nashville: State Library and Archives, 1968. This volume also contains Moore County.
B3830

Biographical Directory: Grundy County Members of the Tennessee General Assembly, 1796- Nashville: State Library and Archives, 1968. This volume also contains Coffee County.
B3840

Biographical Directory: Hamilton County Members of the Tennessee General Assembly, 1796- Nashville: State Library and Archives, 1968.
B3850

Biographical Directory: Johnson County Members of the Tennessee General Assembly, 1796- Nashville: State Library and Archives, 1968. This volume also contains Carter and Unicoi counties.
B3860

Biographical Directory: Knox County Members of the Tennessee General Assembly, 1796- Nashville: State Library and Archives, 1968. Knox County, Tennessee-County History, Political History and Public Administration.
B3870

Biographical Directory: Loudon County Members of the Tennessee General Assembly, 1796- Nashville: State Library and Archives, 1968. This volume also contains Monroe County.
B3880

Biographical Directory: McMinn County Members of the Tennessee General Assembly, 1796-
B3910

Biographical Directory: Macon County Members of the Tennessee General Assembly, 1796. Nashville: State Library and Archives, 1968.
B3890

Biographical Directory: Marion County Members of the Tennessee General Assembly, 1796- Nashville: State Library and Archives, 1968. This volume also contains Bledsoe and Sequatchie counties.
B3900

Biographical Directory: Meigs County Members of the Tennessee General Assembly, 1796- This volume also contains Rhea County.
B3920

Biographical Directory: Monroe County Members of the Tennessee Assembly, 1796- Nashville: State Library and Archives, 1968. This volume also contains Loudon County.
B3930

Biographical Directory: Overton County Members of the Tennessee General Assembly, 1796- Nashville: State Library and Archives, 1968. This volume also contains Fentress and Pickett counties.
B3940

Biographical Directory: Pickett County Members of the Tennessee General Assembly, 1796- Nashville: State Library and Archives, 1968. This volume also contains Fentress and Overton counties.
B3950

Biographical Directory: Polk County Members of the Tennessee General Assembly, 1796- Nashville: State Library and Archives, 1968. This volume also contains Bradley County.
B3960

Biographical Directory: Rhea County Members of the Tennessee General Assembly, 1796- Nashville: State Library and Archives, 1968. This volume also contains Meigs County.
B3970

Biographical Directory: Roane County Members of the Tennessee General Assembly, 1796- Nashville: State Library and Archives, 1968.
B3980

Biographical Directory: Sequatchie County Members of the Tennessee General Assembly, 1796- Nashville: State Library and Archives, 1968. This volume also contains Bledsoe and Marion counties.
B3990

Biographical Directory: Smith County Members of the Tennessee General Assembly, 1796- Nashville: State Library and Archives, 1968.
B4000

Biographical Directory: Unicoi County Members of the Tennessee General Assembly, 1796- Nashville: State Library and Archives, 1968. This volume also contains Carter and Johnson counties.
B4010

Biographical Directory: Van Buren County Members of the Tennessee General Assembly, 1796- Nashville: State Library and Archives, 1968. This volume also contains Warren and White counties.
B4020

Biographical Directory: Warren County Members of the Tennessee General Assembly, 1796- Nashville: State Library and Archives, 1968. This volume also contains White and Van Buren counties.
B4030

Biographical Directory: White County Members of the Tennessee General Assembly, 1796- Nashville: State Library and Archives, 1968. This volume also contains Van Buren and Warren counties.
B4040

Biographical Sketches and Short History of Giles, Montgomery, Pulaski, Roanoke, Smyth and Wythe County. Pearisburg, Va.: Painter's Print Shop, 1973.
B4050

Bird, Alan R. Poverty in Areas of the United States. Agricultural Economic Report, 63. Washington: U. S. Economic Research Service, Resource Development Economics Division, 1964. Includes a study of Appalachian Poverty.
B4060

White Americans in Rural Poverty. Agricultural Economic Report, no. 124. Washington: U. S. Department of Agriculture, Economic Research Service, 1967. Includes study of poor Appalachians.
B4070 (ASU)

Bird, Robert Montgomery The Hawks of Hawk Hollow. Philadelphia: Carey, Lee & Blanchard, 1835.
B4080 (BC)

The Hawks of Hawk Hollow. London: Ward and Lock, 1856.
B4090

Peter Pilgrim: Or, A Rambler's Recollections. Xerox copy of the original. 2 vols. Philadelphia: Lea & Blanchard, 1838. Sketches and scenes of travel in Appalachia.
B4100 (ASU)

Bird, Ronald Income Opportunities for Rural Families from Outdoor Recreation Enterprises. Agricultural Economic Report, 68. Washington: Y. S. Economic Research Service, Resource Development Economics Division, 1965. Outdoor recreation and tourism have become a big business in Southern Appalachia, especially in Western North Carolina.
B4110

Status of Rural Housing in the United States. Agricultural Economic Report, 144. Washington: U. S. Economic Research Service, Economic Development Division, 1968. Includes a study of sub-standard housing in Appalachia.
B4120

Bird, Traveller The Path to Snowbird Mountain. New York: Farrar, Straus & Giroux, 1972. An old tale retold by a latter-day Indian raconteur and historian.
B4130 (ETSU)

Tell Them They Lie. Los Angeles, Cal.: Westernlore Pub., 1971. Bird, a lineal descendant of Sequoyah, would have us know that his ancestor was not a kindly man who taught children to read, nor invented a syllabary but was instead a leader of the radical element of the Cherokee nation who lived and died as a renegade.
B4140 (ASU LMC)

Bird, William Earnest Lyrics of a Layman. Greensboro, N. C.: Piedmont Press, 1962. Poems by a Western North Carolina educator.
B4180 (WCU)

Bird, William Ernest The History of Western Carolina College: The Progress of an Idea. Chapel Hill, N. C.: Univ. of North Carolina Press, 1963.
B4160 (BC ASU LMC WCU)

Level Paths: New Songs by the Layman. Asheville, N. C.: Biltmore Press, 1964. Poems by a Western Carolina educator.
B4170 (WCU ASU)

Bird, William Ernest ed. Among the Highlanders Yesterday and Today. (A PAGEANT OF Western North Carolina.) Produced by students of the Cullowhee State Normal School, Cullowhee, N. C., under the auspices of the English, Music and Physical Education Depts. Cullowhee, N. C.: n.p., 1927.
B4150 (ASU WCU)

The Spirit of Western North Carolina: A Pageant. Produced by the students of the Cullowhee State Normal School, Cullowhee, N. C., under the auspices of the English Department. Asheville, N. C.: Jarrett's Press, 1926.
B4190 (WCU LMC)

Birdwell, Bobby T. Soil Resources of Johnson City, Tennessee. Johnson City: Regional Planning Commission, 1963.
B4200 (ETSU)

Birmingham, Alabama, Pioneers Club Early Days in Birmingham. Birmingham: Southern Univ. Press, 1968.
B4210 (BC)

Bishop, Carol and others Vocational and Educational Goals of Rural Youth in Virginia. Bulletin, 568. (Cover title: Educational and Vocational Goals of Rural Youth in Virginia.) Blacksburg: Virginia Agricultural Experiment Station, 1966? Samples for this study were students in the Blacksburg, Virginia area.
B4220

Bishop, John Peale Act of Darkness. 1935. Reprint. An Avon Library Book, NA17. New York: Avon Books, 1967. A violent crime and the subsequent trial bring two families in the Shenandoah Valley into conflict with the heretofore unquestioned code of the Southern gentleman.
B4230 (ASU)

Bishop, R. F. Camerton Slope, a Story of Mining Life. Xerox copy of the original. Cincinnati: Cranston & Curtis; New York: Hunt & Eaton, 1893. A documentary study of life in a mine camp.
B4240 (ASU BC)

Bishop, Robert Safford, Carleton L. America's Quilts and Coverlets. New York: Dutton, 1972.
S80 (ASU)

Bishop, Robert Charles Safford, Carleton L. America's Quilts and Coverlets. New York: Dutton, 1972.
S70 (ASU)

Bishop, William Henry History of Roane County, West Virginia, from the Time of Its Exploration to A. D. 1927. Spencer, W. Va.: The author, 1927. Another good county history from West Virginia. Almost every county in West Virginia has a written history. The Appalachian regions of other states have relatively few.
B4250 (ASU BC)

Bissell, Richard Pike The Monongahela. New York: Rinehart, 1952. A stirring history of the river which brought men and their industries into backwoods Virginia and West Virginia.
B4260 (BC)

Bituminous Coal Research Mine Drainage Abstracts, a Bibliography. n.p.: Pennsylvania Coal Research Board, 1964. And Supplements, 1- 1965-.
B4270 (ASU)

Bivins, John, Jr. Longrifles of North Carolina. Photography by George Shumway. Longrifle Series. York, Pa.: G. Shumway, 1968. A pictorial treatise on early guns, gunsmiths and the role the rifle played in opening the frontier.
B4280 (ASU LMC BC)

The Moravian Potters in North Carolina. Photography by Bradford L. Rauschenberg. Chapel Hill: Univ. of North Carolina Press, 1972. It was the Moravians who began the pottery industry in North Carolina and many of their descendants continue the tradition today. Excellent photographs.
B4290 (LMC)

Bixler, Harold Hench The Superior and Gifted Student Project at Cullowhee, Western Carolina College. Cullowhee, N. C.: n.p., 1964.
B4300 (WCU)

Black, Charles J. History of the First Baptist Church of Kings Mountain, N. C. Kings Mountain: Herald, 1926.
B4310

Black, Doris E. "A Contract Plan of Teaching Fifth Grade at Jefferson Elementary School in Kingsport, Tennessee." Master's thesis. East Tennessee State Univ., 1969.
B4320 (ETSU)

Black, Elizabeth McDonald Scheer, Julian Tweetsie, the Blue Ridge Sidewinder. Charlotte, N. C.: Heritage House, 1958.
S870 (ASU LMC BC)

Black, Mary C. American Folk Painting. New York: Clarkson N. Potter, 1966. Includes the works of a few mountain artists. However, folk art in the mountains usually took some form other than painting.
B4330 (ASU)

Black Mountain Review 1954-57. Reprint. 3 Vols. New York: AMS Press, 1969. During the last three years of its existence, the controversial experimental school at Black Mountain, North Carolina published a very good review dealing primarily with literature and the arts.
B4340 (ASU)

Black, William Henry Wintering Beef Cattle in the Appalachian Region. Circular, 408. Washington: U. S. Department of Agriculture, Bureau of Animal Industry, 1927. A practical handbook for getting cattle through the Appalachian winters in the most economical way.
B4350

Blackhurst, W. E. Afterglow: A Collection of Short Stories and Poems. Parsons, W. Va.: McClain Print. Co., 1972. A collection of stories and poems about the lumbering boom in West Virginia.
B4360 (ASU BC)

Mixed Harvest. Parsons, W. Va.: McClain Print. Co., 1970. Blackhurst's novel of life during his grandmother's day when the first railroad surveyors and lumbermen came to look over West Virginia and plot its devastation.
B4370 (ASU BC)

Of Men and a Mighty Mountain. Parsons, W. Va.: McClain Print. Co., 1965. Loosely plotted novel strung together by having each character living or dead speak of his or her experiences and observations of the hometown during the lumber boom.
B4380 (ASU WCU BC)

Riders of the Flood. 1954. Reprint. Parsons, W. Va.: McClain Print. Co., 1968. A novel of railroads and lumberjacks in the author's native West Virginia.
B4390 (ASU BC)

Sawdust in Your Eyes. Parsons, W. Va.: McClain Print. Co., 1963. A novel of a town called Sawdust Pile which could have been any town during the great, ravishing lumbering years which despoiled the Appalachian Mountains.
B4400 (ASU WCU BC)

Your Train Ride through History: An Authentic History of the Town of Cass and the Great Lumber Empire Which Gave Rise to Your Ride on the Cass Scenic Railroad. Parsons, W. Va.: McClain Print. Co., 1968.
B4410 (ASU BC)

Blackmore, John "A Watershed Development Program for the TVA. Ph. D. Diss. Harvard Univ., 1954.
B4420

Blackmun, Ora A Spire in the Mountains: The Story of 176 Years of a Church and a Town Growing Together, 1794-1969. Asheville, N. C.: First Presbyterian Church, 1970.
B4430 (ASU ETSU UNCA)

Blackstone, J. Homer The Present and Projected Agricultural Economy of the Appalachian Region of Alabama. Auburn, Ala.: Auburn Univ. Agricultural Experiment Station, 1968.
B4440 (ASU)

Blaine, James Cyril Dickson The Industrial Development Program of North Carolina, 1954 to 1962, with Projections to 1970. Research Paper, 13. Chapel Hill: Univ. of North Carolina Graduate School of Business Administration, 1964. Includes projections for bringing more industry into Western North Carolina.
B4450

Blair, Everetta Love "Jesse Stuart and His Work: A Critical Study." Master's thesis. Univ. of South Carolina, 1954. A critical study of Appalachia's best-known author.
B4460 (ASU BC)

Jesse Stuart: His Life and Works. 1st. ed. Columbia: Univ. of South Carolina Press, 1967.
B4470 (ASU BC)

Blair, Reuben M. "Development of Education in Polk County, Tennessee." Master's thesis. Univ. of Tennessee, 1941.
B4480

Blair, Walter Davy Crockett, Frontier Hero; the Truth as He Told It, the Legend as Friends Built It. New York: Coward-McCann, 1955. A defense of Crockett the man versus the legend he left.
B4490

Native American Humor (1800-1900). New York: American Book Co., 1937. Includes work of three mountain humorists.
B4500 (MHC BC)

Blake, Alma Carwile Of Life and Love and Things. Parsons, W. Va.: McClain Print. Co., 1971. Poems from the West Virginia hills.
B4510 (ASU BC)

Blake, Thaddeus C. The Old Log House, a History and Defense of the Cumberland Presbyterian Church. Nashville Tenn.: Cumberland Presbyterian Pub. House, 1897.
B4520 (ASU)

Blakely, Edward James "Toward a Theory of Training People for the War on Poverty — A Qualitative Comparative Study of Three Antipoverty Training Centers." Ed. D. Diss. Univ. of California, Los Angeles, 1971. One of these centers deals with Appalachian poverty.
B4530

Blakely, Hunter B. Religion in Shoes. Birmingham, Ala.: Birmingham Pub. Co., 1967. Biography of J. A. Bryan, Birmingham minister.
B4540 (BC)

Blakemore, John A. Known Descendants of Edward Blakemore, Junior, of Lancaster Co. Virginia. n.p.: n.p., 1963.
B4550

Blakeslee, E. B. Brooks, Fred Ernest Studies of the Codling Moth in the Central Appalachian Region. Washington: U. S. Department of Agriculture, Bureau of Entomology, 1915.
B6920

Blalock, Mary R. Crum "A Survey of the Elementary School Libraries in Washington County, Tennessee." Master's thesis. East Tennessee State Univ., 1967.
B4560 (ETSU)

Bland County Centennial Corporation History of Bland County (Virginia). Radford, Va.: Commonwealth Press, 1961. Promotional material and a history prepared for the county's centennial.
B4570 (ASU BC)

Bland, Edward The Discovery of New Brittaine. Reprint of the London 1651 ed. Ann Arbor: Univ. Microfilms, 1966.
B4580 (ASU BC)

Bland, Frances Moore Stray Leaves from the Hillside. Scottsdale, Pa.: Mennonite Pub. House, 1930. Poems and short stories.
B4590

Bland, Marion F. "Superstitions about Food and Health among Negro Girls in Elementary and Secondary Schools in Marion County, West Virginia." Master's thesis. West Virginia Univ., 1950.
B4600

Blaney, Ralph Phillips, Samuel William Soil Survey of Belmont County, Ohio. Washington: U. S. Department of Agriculture, Bureau of Chemistry and Soils, 1931.
P2620

Phillips, Samuel William Soil Survey of Washington County, Ohio. Washington: U. S. Department of Agriculture, Bureau of Chemistry and Soils, 1930.
P2670

Blankenship, Lela McDowell When Yesterday Was Today. Nashville: Tennessee Bk., 1966. A novel of guerrilla warfare in the Tennessee highlands during the Civil War.
B4610

Burns, Amanda Fiddles in the Cumberlands. New York: Richard R. Smith, 1943.
B9020 (ASU BC)

Blanshard, Paul Labor in the Southern Cotton Mills. New York: New Republic, 1927. Many of these mills were located in the foothills in order to take advantage of cheap labor from the mountains.
B4620

Blanton, Catherine Trouble on Old Smoky. Illustrated by Anne Merriman Peck. Whittlesey House Publications. New York: McGraw-Hill, 1951. The Smoky Mountains are the setting for this adventure story for young people.
B4630 (ETSU)

Blanton, Gladys Shomaker "A Comparative Analysis of Student Teaching Programs in the Elementary Schools at Appalachian State Teachers College." Master's thesis. Appalachian State Teachers College, 1957.
B4640 (ASU)

Blanton, John O. Pre-historic Man in Tennessee. The Problem Solved. A Centennial Booklet. Tracy City: Tracy City News, 1896. This is a period piece and is unreliable at best.
B4650

Blanton, Wyndham Bolling Medicine in Virginia in the Seventeenth Century. Spartanburg, S. C.: Reprint Co. 1973, c1930. Includes a survey of home remedies and folk medicine.
B4660

Blasingame, Ralph Upshaw Library Services in West Virginia, Present and Proposed. Assisted by Thornton J. Ridinger. Charleston, W. Va.: Library Commission, 1965. A survey of West Virginia's ambitious plan for public libraries.
B4670 (ASU)

Blassingame, Wyatt How Davy Crockett Got a Bearskin Coat. Champaign, Ill.: Garrard Pub. Co., 1972. Davey chases his bear in this story for youngsters.
B4680 (ETSU)

Bledsoe, Mary Shadows Slant North. Boston: Lothrop, Lee and Shepard Co., 1937. Avery, Ashe and Watauga Counties North Carolina are the setting for this story. A young girl who leaves college to cope with family emergencies, and becomes a businesswoman.
B4690 (ASU)

Bledsoe, Thomas Or We'll All Hang Separately: The Highlander Idea. Boston: Beacon Press, 1969. An account of the controversial Highlander Folk School at Monteagle and the Highlander Research and Education Center in Knoxville.
B4700 (LMC WWC ETSU BC)

Blee, C. E. Development of the Tennessee River Waterway. American Society of Civil Engineers. Centennial Transactions: n.p., 193.
B4710

Bleeker, Sonia The Cherokee: Indians of the Mountains. Illustrated by Althea Karr. New York: William Morrow and Co., 1952. A sensitive account of the Cherokee and their mountain empire.
B4720 (ASU BC WCU LMC)

Blevins, R. L. Weisenberger, Billy C. Soil Survey, Bath County, Kentucky. Washington: U. S. Soil Conservation Service, 1963.
W2360

Blevins, Robert L. McDonald, Herman Patrick Reconnaissance Soil Survey, Fourteen Counties in Eastern Kentucky. Washington: U. S. Dept. of Agriculture, Soil Conservation Services, 1965.
M1140

Bliss, Russell L. "Teenage Dating Behavior in Two Eastern Kentucky High Schools." Master's thesis. Univ. of Kentucky, 1957.
B4730

Blomquist, Hugo Leander The Grasses of North Carolina. Durham, N. C.: Duke Univ. Press, 1948.
B4740 (ASU BC LMC WWC)

Greene, Wilhelmina F. Flowers of the South, Native and Exotic. Chapel Hill: Univ. of North Carolina Press, 1953.
G3840 (ASU BC)

Bloody Harlan: The Story of Four Miners Serving Life n.p.: n.p., 1937. They dared to organize a union, strike and picket. Here are facts from the court record of the frame-up.
B4750 (BC)

Bloom, Benjamin S. Compensatory Education for Cultural Deprivation. New York: Holt, 1965. Deals, in part, with Appalachia.
B4760

The Blotter Brasstown, N. C.: John C. Campbell Folk School, 19--. Monthly. House organ for the John C. Campbell Folk School.
B4770 (BC)

Blount, Mrs. Godfrey The Story of a Homespun Web. London: J. M. Dent, n.d. A guide to weaving and hand spinning with instructions.
B4780 (BC)

The Blount Mansion Association The Blount Mansion, Built 1792. Knoxville: Knoxville Engr., 1930.
B4790

Blue Ridge Parkway Association The Blue Ridge Parkway: Accommodations and Services. 23d ed. n.p.: The association, 1971-72. Promotional material and information for tourists.
B4800 (ETSU)

Blue Ridge Parkway News vol. 1-, 193-. Roanoke, Va.: Office of the Blue Ridge Parkway, National Park Service, 193-.
B4810

Blue Ridge School for Boys Hendersonville, N. C.: The school, 1936. A catalog for the 1937-38 academic year and a history of the school.
B4820

Bluegrass Unlimited vol. 1- 1966-. Burke, Va.: Bluegrass Unlimited, monthly. The country music journal. Unfortunately bluegrass is becoming more popular than traditional folk music in the mountains.
B4830 (ETSU)

Bluestein, Gene The Voice of the Folk: Folklore and American Literary Theory. Amherst: University of Massachusetts Press, 1972.
B4840 (FC)

Blume, George T. Highlights of Vocational and Educational Goals of Rural Youth in Virginia. Circular No. 1030. Blacksburg: Cooperative Extension Service, Virginia Polytechnic Institute, November, 1966. Blacksburg area youth were used for this study.
B4850

Blumenthal, Walter Hart American Indians Dispossessed: Fraud in Land Cessions Forced Upon the Tribes. Philadelphia: George S. MacManus Co., 1955. Includes accounts of land cessions in Appalachia.
B4860 (ASU)

Blythe, LeGette Alexandriana. Harrisburg, Pa.: Stackpole Sons, 1940. A novel of North Carolina in the Revolution.
B4870 (ASU BC WCU LMC)

Gift from the Hills. Chapel Hill: Univ. of North Carolina Press, 1971. The story of Lucy Morgan and her unique Penland Crafts School.
B4880 (ASU LMC)

James W. Davis, North Carolina Surgeon. Foreword by Johnson J. Hayes. Charlotte, N. C.: William Loftin Pub., 1956. Mountain born doctor beloved by generations of Carolinian's.
B4890 (ASU BC MHC)

Mountain Doctor. Photographs by Bruce Roberts. New York: William Morrow and Co., 1964.
B4900 (ASU BC WCU LMC MHC WWC)

Morgan, Lucy Gift from the Hills: Miss Lucy Morgan's Story of Unique Penland School. Chapel Hill: UNC Press, 1971.
M7630

Sloop, Mary T. Martin Miracle in the Hills. New York: McGraw-Hill, 1953.
S4230 (ASU WCU LMC WWC BC)

Blythe, William LeGette see **Blythe, LeGette**

Bobbitt, James Riley "Educational Values of the Berea College Labor Program." Ph. D. Diss. Indiana Univ., 1961.
B4910 (ASU)

The Impact of Berea College on Student Characteristics. Berea, Ky.: Berea College Press, 1969.
B4920 (BC)

Boccardy, Joseph A. Effects of Surface Mining on Fish and Wildlife in Appalachia, Special Report. U. S. Sport Fisheries and Wildlife Bureau Resource Publications, 65. Washington: Govt. Print. Off., 1968.
B4930

Bodamer, Richard Sebor, Miles The Economic Geography of Tennessee. Nashville: Tennessee State Planning Commission, 1965.
S1600

Boddie, John Bennett Colonial Surry. Baltimore: Genealogical Pub. Co., 1966. A good genealogical source for families who settled Western North Carolina and Eastern Kentucky.
B4940 (ASU BC)

Historical Southern Families. 1957. Reprint. VOLS. Baltimore: Genealogical Pub. Co., 1967.
B4950 (ASU)

Southside Virginia Families. 1955. Reprint. 2 vols. Baltimore: Genealogical Pub. Co., 1966.
B4960 (ASU)

Boehm, Robert Blair "The Civil War in Western Virginia: The Decisive Campaigns of 1861." Ph. D. Diss. Ohio State University, 1957.
B4970

Boesman, William C. Gates, Gary R. A Kentucky Riverlands Development Program. Lexington, Ky.: Spindletop Research, 1965.
G570

Boette, Marie comp. Singa Hipsy Doodle, and Other Folk Songs of West Virginia. Music notes drawn by John Laflin. Illustrated by Marcia Ogilore. Parsons, W. Va.: McClain Print. Co., 1971.
B4980 (ASU ETSU BC)

Bogart, Eva Kate "A Program for Developing Mental and Emotional Health in Third-grade Children at Love Street School, Erwin, Tennessee." Master's thesis. East Tennessee State College, 1951.
B4990 (ETSU)

Bogart, William Henry The Border Boy. Boston: Lee and Shepard, 1884. The Border Boy and how he became the great pioneer of the West: a life of Daniel Boone.
B4991

The Border Boy and How He Became the Great Pioneer of the West; a Life of Daniel Boone. Boston: Lee and Shepard, 1884. Appears to be merely a different edition of the author's Daniel Boone and the Hunters of Kentucky.
B5000 (BC)

Daniel Boone, and the Hunters of Kentucky. New York: Miller, Orton and Mulligan, 1856.
B5010 (ASU)

Daniel Boone, and the Hunters of Kentucky. Boston: Lee and Shepard, 1873.
B5020 (LMC)

Daniel Boone, and the Hunters of Kentucky. New York: C. M. Saxton, 1876.
B5030 (ETSU)

Boger, Lorise C. The Southern Mountaineer in Literature, an Annotated Bibliography. Morgantown: West Virginia Univ. Library, 1964. The book is very nicely annotated, but there are some startling omissions.
B5040 (ETSU ASU LMC BC FC UNCA)

Boggs, Elsie Byrd The Hammers and Allied Families. Harrisonburg, Va.: J. K. Ruebush Co., 1950. Area: Pendleton Co., W. Va. Families: Byrd, Cunningham, Harper, Hinkle, Kile, Meadows, Puddles and Caplingers.
B5050 (BC)

A History of Franklin, the County Seat of Pendleton County, West Virginia. Staunton, Va.: McClure Print. Co., 1960.
B5060 (BC)

Boggs, Martha Frye Jack Crews. New York: G. W. Dillingham, 1899. An ailing railroad man marries a mountain girl and finds himself an outcast, whose life is endangered, in his western North Carolina mountain home.
B5070

Boggs, Rebecca L. The Bleeding Hills of West Virginia. New York: Exposition Press, 1965. A novel of economic colonialism in Appalachia that is almost too realistic to be fiction. Oil, gas, and coal industries are exposed as exploiters of the poor.
B5080 (BC ASU)

Bogie, Donald Wayne Sociocultural Differences Among Three Areas in Kentucky, as Determinants of Educational and Occupational Aspirants and Expectations of Rural Youth. Master's thesis. University of Kentucky, 1971. Eastern Kentucky counties compared to central and western counties.
B5090 (BC)

Bogue, Donald J. Beale, Calvin L. Recent Population Trends in the United States with Emphasis on Rural Areas. Washington: U. S. Department of Agriculture, Farm Population Branch, 1963.
B2250

Economic Subregions of the United States. Washington: Govt. Print. Off., 1953. Includes a study of Appalachia.
B5100

Bohland, James I. "Geographic Analysis of Single Dwelling Settlement in Northeast Georgia." Ph. D. Diss. Univ. of Georgia, 1970.
B5110 (LMC BC ASU)

Bokum, Hermann The Testimony of a Refugee from East Tennessee. Philadelphia: n.p., 1863. The unionists of East Tennessee comprised a very effective guerilla unit and were constantly involved in skirmishes with Confederate Troops.
B5120 (ASU)

Boles, John B. The Great Revival, 1787-1805: The Origins of the Southern Evangelical Mind. Lexington: Univ. Press of Kentucky, 1962. An account of the meeting at Cane Ridge and the extraordinary effect it had on the Southern frontier.
B5130 (ASU BC)

Bollinger, G. A. The Earthquake History of Virginia, 1900-1970. Blacksburg, Va.: Dept. of Geological Sciences, Virginia Polytechnic Institute and State University, 1972.
B5140

Hooper, Margaret G. The Earthquake History of Virginia, 1774 to 1900. Blacksburg: Virginia Polytechnic Institute and State Univ., 1971.
H7140

Bolster, Roy Hale Leighton, Marshall Ora The Relation of the Southern Appalachian Mountains to the Development of Water Power. Washington: Govt. Print. Off., 1908.
L1660 (ASU BC)

Bolte, Mary Dark and Bloodied Ground. Photographs by Mary Eastman. Riverside, Conn.: Chatham Press, 1973. A Kentucky history which deals tangentially with Appalachian Kentucky.
B5150 (ASU)

Bolton, Charles Knowles Scotch Irish Pioneers in Ulster and America. With maps and illustrations by Ethel Stanwood Bolton. . Reprint. Baltimore: Genealogical Pub. Co., 1967. The Appalachians were heavily populated by the Scotch-Irish.
B5170 (ASU)

Bolton, Charles Knowles comp. Marriage Notices, 1785-1794, for the Whole United States, Copied from the Massachusetts Centinel and the Columbian Centinel. 1900. Reprint. Baltimore: Genealogical Pub. Co., 1965.
B5160 (ASU)

Bolton, Ethel Stanwood comp. Immigrants to New England, 1700-1775. 1931. Reprint. Baltimore: Genealogical Pub. Co., 1966. An aid in tracing the many Appalachian families who went from New England ports to Pennsylvania and thence southward along the frontier.
B5180 (ASU)

Bolton, Henry Carrington The Counting-Out Rhymes of Children: Their Antiquity, Origin, and Wide Distribution, A Study in Folk-lore. 1888. Reprint. Detroit: Singing Tree Press, 1969. Just two generations ago these games and rhymes were common in Appalachia.
B5190 (ASU)

Bolton, Ivy Mae Tennessee Outpost. New York: Longmans, Green and Company, 1939. Historical tale for boys and girls about Tennessee when it was claimed by the Spanish. The hero is a sixteen-year-old boy, but a brave girl also has an important part.
B5200

Bolton, Jeanette Bolton, Stanley Black Blood in Kentucky. New York: Vantage Press, 1957.
B5210 (BC)

Bolton, Stanley Black Blood in Kentucky. New York: Vantage Press, 1957. A novel based upon the struggle of miners in southeastern Kentucky to unionize the million dollar coal fields.
B5210 (BC)

Bonar, Ross "The Status of the Secondary School Principal of West Virginia During the Years 1935-36." Master's thesis. West Virginia Univ., 1937.
B5220

Bond, Donovan H. A Half-Century of Nursing in West Virginia: The History of the West Virginia State Nurses' Association 1907-1957. Charleston, W. Va: Jarrett Print. Co., 1957.
B5230 (ASU)

Bond, Octavia Louise Zollicoffer The Family Chronicle and Kinship Book of Maclin, Clack, Cocke, Carter, Taylor, Cross, Gordon and Other Related American Lineages. Nashville, Tenn.: McDaniel Print. Co., 1928.
B5240 (ASU ETSU)

Old Tales Retold: Or, Perils and Adventures of Tennessee Pioneers. Nashville, Tenn.: Vanderbilt Univ. Press, 1941.
B5250 (ASU LMC BC)

Bond, Sirus O. The Light of the Hills: A History of Salem College. Charleston, W. Va.: Educational Foundation, 1960. One of the more interesting institutional histories of West Virginia.
B5260

Bondurant, J. H. Nicholls, W. D. Family Incomes and Land Utilization in Knott County, Kentucky. Lexington: Kentucky Agricultural Experiment Station, Univ. of Kentucky, 1937.
N900

Nicholls, W. D. Farm Management and Family Incomes in Eastern Kentucky. Lexington: Kentucky Agricultural Experiment Station, Univ. of Kentucky, 1946.
N920

Bondurant, John H. Labor Supply and Farm Production on Eastern Kentucky Farms. Lexington: Kentucky Agricultural Experiment Station, 1945. The war drastically changed both the numbers and characteristics of farm workers.
B5270

Bone, Winston Paine History of Cumberland University, 1842-1935. Lebanon, Tenn.: The author, 1935.
B5280 (ASU)

Boner, John Henry Whispering Pines. Winston-Salem, N. C.: John F. Blair, Pub., 1954. Poems from the hills.
B5290 (ASU)

Bonham, Valeria Langeloth Utopia in the Hills. Story of Valeria Home. New York: R. M. McBride, 1948. Lest anyone feel that only the Southern Appalachias got the benefit of mission efforts here is a tale of a New York home.
B5300

Bonner, James Calvin Georgia's Last Frontier: The Development of Carroll County. Athens: Univ. of Georgia Press, 1971. About one-third of Carroll County is in the Appalachian Region.
B5310 (ASU LMC BC)

Bonner, John Wyatt Bibliography of Georgia Authors, 1949-1965. Athens: Univ. of Georgia Press, 1966. A useful tool for finding Georgia's Appalachian authors.
B5320 (BC ASU)

Bonner, Sherwood see **McDowell, Katherine Sherwood Bonner**

Bonser, Howard Jacob Better Farming Practices through Rural Community Organization. Knoxville: Tennessee Agricultural Experiment Station, 1958. A study of rural community improvement clubs in East Tennessee and their impact on farming methods.
B5330

Better Homemaking Practices through Rural Community Organization. Knoxville: Tennessee Agricultural Experiment Station, 1958. A study of rural community organizations in East Tennessee.
B5340

Electricity on Farms and in Rural Homes in the East Tennessee Valley. Knoxville: Tennessee Agricultural Experiment Station, 1951.
B5350

Local Leadership in Rural Communities of Cumberland County, Tennessee. Knoxville: Tennessee Agricultural Experiment Station, Monograph 144, 1958.
B5360

Neighborhoods and Communities of Cumberland County, Tennessee. Knoxville: Agricultural Experiment Station, Univ. of Tennessee, 1941.
B5370

Selective Participation of Farmers and Their Wives in Rural Organization. Knoxville: Tennessee Agricultural Experiment Station, 1957. A study of farm family participation in four East Tennessee counties.
B5380

Booghor, William Fletcher Gleanings of Virginia History. Washington, D. C.: n.p., 1903. This rather informal history contains much information on the western part of the state.
B5390

Booker, Jim Trail to Oklahoma. Illustrated by William Moyers. Nashville: Broadman Press, 1959. A novel of the Cherokee Removal.
B5400 (ASU)

Boone, James W. "The Econometric Forecasting of National Rail Car Requirements for Bituminous Coal." Master's thesis. Pennsylvania State Univ., 1970.
B5410

Boone, Larry M. Changes in Tennessee Agriculture by Counties, 1954-64. Knoxville: Agricultural Experiment Station Bulletin 435, 1967. Explores changes in crops, farming methods, and population.
B5420

Boone, North Carolina Code. Charlottesville, Va.: Mitchie City Publications Co., 1972.
B5430 (ASU)

Boone, North Carolina, Planning Board Land Development Plan. Boone, North Carolina: Boone, North Carolina, 1964.
B5440 (BC ASU)

Land Development Plan. Boone: The board, 1964.
B5450

Boone Trial Herald vol. 1, 1925-. Winston-Salem, N. C.: Boone Trial Herald, 1925-, bi-monthly. Commemorates Daniel Boone Trial.
B5460 (BC)

Boone, Weldon Wesley A History of Botany in West Virginia. Parsons, W. Va.: McClain Print. Co., 1965. A thorough and nicely-annotated study.
B5470 (ASU, ETSU WCU BC)

Booth, Doris Neal "Guidelines for the Cooperating Teachers in Bristol, Virginia, High School." Master's thesis. East Tennessee State Univ., 1966.
B5480 (ETSU)

Booton, John Heiskell Songs and Fantasies. Salem, Va., Sentinel Publishing Co., Roanoke College Annual Staff, 1900.
B5490

Booz, Allen A Study of the Eastern Industrial Coal Market. Prepared for the Office of Coal Research, U. S. Department of the Interior. Washington: The author, 1967.
B5500

Survey of Opportunities to Stimulate Coal Utilization. Submitted to the U. S. Department of Interior, Office of Coal Research. VOLS. Chicago: The company, 1962.
B5510

Booz, Hamilton Booz, Allen A Study of the Eastern Industrial Coal Market. Washington: The author, 1967.
B5500

Booz, Allen Survey of Opportunities to Stimulate Coal Utilization. Chicago: The company, 1962.
B5510

Borger, Louise C. The Southern Mountaineer in Literature. Morgantown, West Virginia University Library, 1964. An excellent listing with brief annotations.
B5520

Borland, Ralph J. The Legal Problems of the Appalachian Area in the Immediate Region of Western North Carolina. Cullowhee, N. C.: Western Carolina University, n.d.
B5530 (LMC)

Born, Kendall Eugene Summary of the Mineral Resources of Tennessee. Nashville: Department of Education, Division of Geology, 1936.
B5540 (ETSU)

Borrelli, Peter Austin, Richard C. The Strip Mining of America: An Analysis of Surface Coal Mining and the Environment. New York: Sierra Club, 1971.
A5590 (ASU)

Boschen, Albert O. Andrew Trayton: A Novel of Modern Life. Richmond, Va.: Clyde W. Saunders and Sons, 1928. A truly horrible novel of a smug young ministerial student come to save the pore mountaineer. The mountain family he encounters might well be guest stars on "The Beverly Hillbillies."
B5550 (ASU)

Bosher, Kate Lee Langley His Friend Miss McFairlane. New York: Harper and Brothers, 1919. A Novel. A young mountain lad unjustly confined in a reformatory is befriended by a society lady.
B5560 (BC ASU)

Bost, Danny Hart "An Investigation of Instructors' and Students' Philosophy of Education with Student Evaluations of Instructors at Blue Ridge Technical Institute During the First Year of Operation." Master's thesis. Appalachian State University, 1971.
B5570 (ASU)

Boswell, George W. ed. 1964 Cox, John Harrington comp. Traditional Ballads and Folk-songs Mainly from West Virginia. n.p.: American Folklore Society, 1964.
C8180 (ASU WCU ETSU BC)

Bosworth, Albert S. A History of Randolph County, West Virginia, from Its Earliest Settlement to the Present Time. Elkins?, W. Va.: n.p., 1916.
B5580 (BC)

Bosworth, J. Allen All the Dark Places. Garden City, N. Y.: Doubleday and Co., Inc., 1968. Fiction pertaining to the cave region in Kentucky.
B5590 (BC ASU)

Bosworth, Karl Andrew Tennessee Valley Country: Rural Government in the Hill Country of Alabama. Publications, 4. Univ.: Univ. of Alabama, Bureau of Public Administration, 1941. An experiment in community planning in northern Alabama.
B5600

Botkin, Benjamin Albert The American Play-party Song. University Studies of the University of Nebraska, vol. 38, nos. 1-4. 1937 Reprint. New York: Frederick Ungar, 1963. Play-parties were popular forms of entertainment in the mountains until the late twenties.
B5610 (ASU)

A Treasury of American Folklore: Stories, Ballads, and Traditions of the People. With a foreword by Carl Sandburg. New York: Crown Pub., 1944. Includes representative Appalachian selections.
B5620 (ASU FC)

Botkin, Benjamin Albert ed. A Treasury of Southern Folklore: Stories, Ballads, Traditions and Folkways. New York: Crown Pub., 1949. Includes representative Appalachian selections.
B5630 (WWC BC FC ETSU WCU)

Bott, Matthias W. "Some Aspects of the Coal Mining Industry in Monongalia County, West Virginia." Master's thesis. W. Va. Univ., 1949.
B5640

Bouldin, Powhatan Home Reminiscences of John Randolph, of Roanoke. Danville, Va.: The author, Richmond, Va.: Clemmitt & Jones, 1878.
B5650 (ASU)

Bousman, Louise Tate Kentucky Coverlets. Louisville, Ky.: Commercial Lithograph Co., 1938. Illustrated book of coverlets; knotted, white on white, patchwork, woven and appliqued.
B5660 (BC)

Bowen, John W. Smith County History. Available at the Tennessee State Library and Archives. n.p.: n.p., n.d. Undistinguished account of Smith County's history.
B5670

Bowen, Robert A. Tall in the Sight of God. Winston-Salem, N. C.: John F. Blair, 1958. Autobiographical fiction about a Negro family from Wilkes Co., N. C.
B5680 (ASU LMC BC)

Bowen, Rosalie Arcuri "The Development of a Prediction Equation for Geometry at Holston Valley High School, Bristol, Tennessee." Master's thesis. East Tenn. State Univ., 1968.
B5690 (ETSU)

Bowen, Zeddie Paul Brachipoda of the Keyser Limestone (Silurian-Devonian) of Maryland and Adjacent Areas. New York: Geological Society of America, 1967.
B5700 (ETSU)

Bowerman, Charles E. Gulick, John Socio-cultural Adaptation of Newcomers to Cities in the Piedmont Industrial Crescent. Chapel Hill: Institute for Research in Social Science, Univ. of North Carolina, 1961.
G4850

Bowers, J. H., Jr. Taylor, Arthur Elijah Soil Survey, Catoosa County, Georgia. Washington: U. S. Department of Agriculture, Bureau of Plant Industry, 1941.
T400

Bowles, Edgar Oliver McMurray, Lynn L. The Talc Deposits of Talledega County, Alabama. University: Alabama Geological Survey, 1941.
M2320 (BC ETSU)

Bowles, Ella Shannon Homespun Handicrafts. Philadelphia: Lippincott Co., 1931. Illustrated, with descriptions and instructions.
B5710 (BC)

Bowles, Gladys K. Bernert, Eleanor H. Farm Migration, 1940-1945: An Annotated Bibliography. Washington: U. S. Department of Agriculture Library, 1947.
B3180

Farm Population: Net Migration from the Rural Farm Population, 1940-1950. (Statistical Bulletin No. 176.) Washington: U. S. Department of Agriculture, June 1956. Statistics from this period reflect the great wartime exodus from Appalachia.
B5720

Net Migration of the Population, 1950-1960 by Age, Sex and Color. Washington: Economic Research Service, U. S. Department of Agriculture, 1965. Excellent source in an area in which too little research has been done.
B5730

Bowles, Isaac A. History of Letcher Co., Ky., Its Political and Economic Growth and Development. Lexington, Ky.: Hurst Print. Co., 1949. Advertising, stories, history and illustrations.
B5740

Bowlick, C. A. "A Study of the Cranberry Ore Belt." Master's thesis. Appalachian State Teachers College, 1955.
B5750 (ASU)

Bowman, Blanche Sappenfield "Study of a Dialect Employed by the People of the Kentucky Mountains and Presented through a Group of Original Short Stories." Master's thesis. Kansas State College of Agriculture and Applied Science, 1940. The dialect is rather poorly presented, but the stories are interesting.
B5760 (ASU)

Bowman, Elizabeth Skaggs Land of High Horizons. Kingsport, Tenn.: Southern Pub., 1938. A panegyric for the Great Smokies.
B5770 (ASU WCU LMC BC ETSU)

Bowman, Mary Jean Communication and Mountain Development: A Summary Report Two East Kentucky Studies. Washington: U. S. Department of Commerce, Economic Development Administration, 1969.
B5780

Resources and People in East Kentucky: Problems and Potentials of a Lagging Economy. Baltimore: Published for Resources for the Future by John Hopkins Press, 1963.
B5790 (ASU WCU LMC ETSU BC)

Plunkett, H. Dudley Elites and Change in the Kentucky Mountains. Lexington: Univ. Press of Kentucky, 1973.
P3260 (ASU MHC WCU BC)

Bowman, Mary Keller Reference Book of Wyoming County History. Parsons, W. Va.: McClain Print. Co., 1965. Another good county history from West Virginia.
B5800 (ASU BC LMC)

Bowman, Mary L. comp. A Bibliography of Kentucky Archaeology. Louisville, Ky.: Archaeological Association, 1933.
B5810

Bowman, Owen "A Study of a Small School in the Mountains of Virginia." Master's thesis. Virginia Polytechnic Institute, 1953.
B5820

Bowron, William M. Hand-Book to the Sequatchie Valley. Nashville: Foster & Webb, 1888. A marvelous period piece; a travel guide to a then little-known valley rich in mineral resources, archeological sites, and folkways.
B5830

Boyce, Everett Robert ed. Hooper, Ben W. The Unwanted Boy: The Autobiography of Governor Ben W. Hooper. Knoxville: Univ. of Tennessee Press, 1963.
H7040 (ASU BC)

Boyd, Charles Rufus Resources of South-west Virginia, Showing the Mineral Deposits of Iron, Coal, Zinc, Copper and Lead. Also, the Staples of the Various Counties, Methods of Transportation Access, etc. New York: John Wiley & Sons, 1881.
B5840 (ASU BC)

Southwest Virginia and Contiguous Territory: Mineral Resources and Railway Facilities, Statistics, Information, Markets for Coke, Fuel, Ores, etc. Wytheville, Va.: n.p., 1891.
B5850 (BC)

Boyd, Cleo Y. Detroit's Southern Whites and the Store Front Church. Detroit: Council of Churches, 1958. Account of down home religion in far-off Detroit.
B5860

Boyd, James Drums. New York: Scribner's, 1925. A novel of a young boy in wartime with an Appalachian setting.
B5870 (MHC)

Drums. New York: Scribner's, 1928.
B5880 (LMC ETSU)

Long Hunt. New York: Charles Scribner's Sons, 1930. A novel of young men on a long hunt with an Appalachian setting.
B5890 (ASU BC ETSU LMC)

Marching On. New York: Charles Scribner's Sons, 1927. This is a story of the South during the Civil War. The hero is in the confederate army, and the action ranges into the Blue Ridge Mountains.
B5900 (ASU BC ETSU WWC)

Boyd, L. The Irvines and Their Kin. Chicago: R. R. Donnelly & Sons Co., 1908.
B5920

Boyd, Lorenz Follow the Butterfly Stream. Nashville: Abingdon Press, 1971. A children's book about butterflies in the mountains on a spring day.
B5910 (ASU)

Boyd, Robert Personal Memoirs. Cincinnati: Methodist Book Concern, 1862. An autobiography of an itinerant Methodist minister in the mountains of Pennsylvania, West Virginia, and Kentucky.
B5930 (BC)

Boyd, Thomas Alexander Simon Girty, the White Savage. New York: Minton, Balch & Co., 1928. A biography of West Virginia's frontier hero. There is scant mention of his turncoat period during the Revolution.
B5940 (ASU)

Boyd, Virlyn A. "Household and Family Composition in Selected Rural Areas of Eleven Kentucky Counties." Master's thesis. Univ. of Ky., 1948. Eight of the selected counties are Appalachian.
B5950

Boyden, Lucile Kirby The Village of Five Lives: The Fontana of the Great Smoky Mountains. Fontana Dam, N. C.: Govt. Services, 1964. An interesting account of the growth of one of the area's best known resorts.
B5960 (ASU BC LMC WCU)

Boyer, Frederick F. Pratt, Joseph Hyde Western North Carolina Facts, Figures, Photographs. Asheville, N. C.: Inland Press, 1925.
P4210 (LMC WCU)

Boyer, Marie L. Early Days: All Souls' Church and Biltmore Village. n.p.: Biltmore, 1933. A history of the church in the village that grew up at the gates of an American Castle, the Biltmore Estate.
B5970

Boyer, Reba Bayless A History of Mars Hill Presbyterian Church, Athens, Tenn. 1823-1973. Athens: The church, 1973. Compiled from session minute books, church rolls, etc.; includes history, short biographical sketches of all ministers and an annotated list of over 2,000 members.
B5980 (ASU)

Marriage Records of McMinn County, Tennessee, 1820-1870. Athens, Tenn.: The author, 1964.
B5990 (ASU BC)

Monroe County Records, 1820-1870. 2 vols. Athens: The author, 1969, 1970.
B6000

Population Schedule of U. S. Census of 1850 for McMinn County, Tennessee. Athens, Tenn.: The author, 1970.
B6020 (ASU)

Boyer, Reba Bayless comp. Wills and Estate Records of McMinn County, Tennessee, 1820-1870. Athens, Tenn.: The author, 1966.
B6030 (ASU BC)

Boyer, Reba Bayless ed. Monroe County, Tennessee: Records, 1820-1870. n.p.: The author, 1969.
B6010 (ASU BC)

Boyer, Richard Owen Labor's Untold Story. 1st ed. New York: Cameron Associates, 1955.
B6040 (ASU)

Boyer, Walter E. Songs along the Mahantongo: Pennsylvania Dutch Folk-songs. Hatboro, Pa.: Folklore Associates, 1964.
B6050 (ASU)

Boykin, Elizabeth Jones The Call of the Mountains. Philadelphia: Dorrance & Co., 1928. A young widow in the Tenn. mountains faces a plethora of legal, financial and personal problems. Justice triumphs.
B6060 (BC)

Boynton, Henry Van Chattanooga and Chickamauga, Reprint of Gen. H. V. Boynton's Letters to the Cincinnati Commercial Gazette, August, 1888. Washington: Gray & Clarkson, Printers, 1888.
B6070 (ASU BC)

The National Military Park, Chickamauga-Chattanooga. An Historical Guide. Rosters of both armies at Chickamauga, pp. 60-87, and at Chattanooga, pp. 140-166. Cincinnati: Clarke, 1895.
B6090

The National Military Park, Chickamauga-Chattanooga: An Historical Guide, with Maps and Illustrations. Cincinnati, Ohio: Robert Clarke Co., 1895.
B6100 (ASU BC)

Boynton, Henry Van comp. Dedication of the Chickamauga and Chattanooga National Military Park, September 18-20, 1895. Report of the Joint Committee to Represent the Congress at the Dedication of the . . . comp. Washington, D. C: Govt. Print. Off., 1896.
B6080 (ASU)

Bozie, Donald Wayne "Sociocultural Differences among Three Areas in Kentucky." Master's thesis. Univ. of Ky., 1971. One of the areas is Eastern Kentucky.
B6110

Brabson, Fay Warrington Andrew Johnson: A Life in Pursuit of the Right Course, 1808-1875. The Seventeenth President of the United States. Durham, N. C.: Seeman Printery, 1972. East Tennessee's only president is the subject.
B6120 (ASU)

Brackeen, Leonard Geoffrey Soil Survey, Colbert County, Alabama. U. S. Bureau of Chemistry and Soils, Soil Survey Report Series 1933, no. 22. Washington: Govt. Print. Off., 1939.
B6130

Brackeen, Leonard Geoffrey and others Soil Survey, Elmore County, Alabama. Prepared in cooperation with the Alabama Department of Agriculture and Industries. Soil Survey, Series 1939, no. 26. Washington: U. S. Soil Conservation Service, 1955.
B6140

Bradford, R. H. Rural Underemployment and Land Use in a Marginal Agricultural Area of West Virginia. Morgantown: W. Va. Agricultural Experiment Station, 1943.
B6150

Bradford, Roark The Three-Headed Angel. 1st ed. New York: Harper & Brothers, 1937. Newlyweds and a feud form the background for this story with a Tennessee ridge setting.
B6160 (ASU BC)

Bradley, Arthur Granville Sketches from Old Virginia. New York: Macmillan, 1897. The two chapters entitled, "The Poor Whites of the Mountains," and "Two Episodes on Rumbling Creek," deal with Virginia's mountain counties in a very cavalier fashion.
B6170 (BC)

Bradley, Frances Sage Rural Children in Selected Counties of North Carolina. 1918 Reprint. Rural Child Welfare Series, no. 2. New York: Negro Univ. Press, 1969. Includes mountain county surveys.
B6180 (ASU BC LMC)

Bradley, Frank H. Geological Report: Coal Creek Mining and Manufacturing Company of Tennessee. New York: David H. Gildersleeve, 1872.
B6190

Bradley, William Aspenwall Old Christmas, and Other Kentucky Tales in Verse. Boston: Houghton Mifflin Co., 1917. Kentucky mountain poems.
B6200 (BC)

Singing Carr and Other Song-ballads of the Cumberlands. New York: A. A. Knopf, 1918.
B6210 (ASU BC)

Bradshaw, Grace Beatrice "Some Phases of the Social and Economic History of Washington County, Tennessee, 1865-1917." Master's thesis. Univ. of Tennessee, 1942.
B6220

"Some Phases of the Social and Economic History of Washington County, Tennessee, 1865-1917." Master's thesis. Univ. of Tennessee, 1942.
B6230 (ETSU)

Brady, Cyrus Townsend Border Fights and Fighters. Garden City, N. Y.: Doubleday, Page & Co., 1913. Contains excellent material on John Sevier, Daniel Boone, the Watauga settlements and the Battle of King's Mountain.
B6240 (BC)

Braley, Silas Alonzo Special Report on an Evaluation of Mine Scaling. Pittsburg: Mellon Institute, 1962.
B6250 (ASU)

Bramer, Henry Conrad "The Economic Aspects of the Water Pollution Abatement Program in the Ohio River Valley." Ph. D. Diss. Univ. of Pittsburgh, 1960.
B6260

Bramlett, Gene A. Economic Development in the Ohio River Valley Region. Prepared for the Kentucky Department of Commerce. Lexington, Ky.: Spindletop Research, 1964.
B6280

Bramlett, Gene A. and others Development Opportunities in Kentucky: Final Report. Prepared for the Kentucky Department of Commerce. 3 vols. Lexington, Ky.: Spindletop Research, 1965.
B6270

Bramlett, Glenn L. Soil Survey, Gordon County, Georgia. Soils surveyed by Glenn L. Bramlett and Howard T. Stoner. Soil Survey, Series 1962, no. 9. Washington: U. S. Department of Agriculture,
B6290

Branch, Carrick B. "A Study of the Trends and Guidelines of Inservice Education Programs in the Carter County Public School System, Carter County, Tennessee." Master's thesis. East Tennessee State Univ., 1969.
B6300 (ETSU)

Brand, Oscar The Ballad Mongers: Rise of the Modern Folk Song. New York: Funk & Wagnalls, 1962.
B6310 (BC)

Brandenberg, David Kentucky Harvest. With introduction by Si Cornell. Cincinnati, Ohio: Kentucky Writers Guild, Harvest Press, 1967. Vignettes taken from antique currency.
B6320 (BC LMC)

Kentucky's Covered Bridges. Cincinnati: Harvest Press, 1968. Pictorial guide to Kentucky's remaining covered bridges. Descriptions. Directions.
B6330

Brandenberg, Phyllis Brandenberg, David Kentucky's Covered Bridges. Cincinnati: Harvest Press, 1968.
B6330

Brandenberg, Phyllis ed. Brandenberg, David Kentucky Harvest. Cincinnati, Ohio: Kentucky Writers Guild, Harvest Press, 1967.
B6320 (BC LMC)

Branham, Levi My Life and Travels. Xerox of original. Dalton, Ga.: A. J. Showalter Co., 1929. Autobiography of a former slave and later school teacher from Murray County, Georgia. A rare account giving insight into the period during and after the Civil War with commentary on the Ku Klux Klan in Georgia.
B6340 (ASU)

Branscome, James Annihilating the Hillbilly: The Appalachians' Struggle with America's Institutions. Huntington: Appalachian Movement Press, n.d. Beautifully articulated article of the struggle to keep the mountaineer from being inundated by our technological society and America's middle class values.
B6350

Branson, Branley A. Fishes of the Red River Drainage, Eastern Kentucky. Lexington, Ky.: Univ. Press of Kentucky, 1974. Reports the ichthyological findings of one survey in a long-term bio-ecological analysis of the Kentucky River drainage.
B6360

Branson, Eugene C. Our Carolina Highlanders. Circular No. 2. Chapel Hill: Univ. of North Carolina, Extension Bureau, 1916. Rather coy and cavalier treatment of mountain people.
B6370 (ASU WCU)

Branson, H. M. Annual Handbook of Knoxville, Tennessee, for the Year 1892. A Concise Statement of the Financial, Commercial and Manufacturing Interests of This City; Its Climate, and the Magnificent Scenery of Its Surroundings; Its Mineral, Marble and Timber Interests, as well as a Complete Memoranda of the Laws of Tennessee, and Other Matters of Interest to Homeseekers and Capitalists. Knoxville: Tribune, 1892.
B6380

Brantley, William Henderson Battle of Horseshoe Bend in Tallapoosa County, Alabama, March 27, 1814. Birmington, Ala.: Southern Univ. Press, 1969.
B6390 (BC)

Brashear, Leon Back, Troy L. The Brashear Story: A Family History, Containing a Partial Account of a Family That Has Been in America for Well over Three Hundred Years. n.p.: The authors, 1963.
B30 (BC)

Brasington, Clayton Furman, Jr. Livestock Auction Markets in the Appalachian Area: Methods and Facilities. Prepared in cooperation with Agricultural Experiment Stations of Virginia and West Virginia. U. S. Department of Agriculture Marketing Research Report, 309. Washington: Agricultural Marketing Service, Marketing Research Division, 1959.
B6400

Brasington, George Furman, Jr. "The McMinn County, Tennessee, Election of August 1, 1946." Master's thesis. Emory Univ., 1948. A pallid account of the Athens, Tennessee War. How could anyone write a dull thesis about a contested election, a gun battle between the entrenched political machine, its imported poll watchers, and the state police? He even fails to mention that the local radio station was strategically located smack in the middle of the shootout and broadcasting line bulletins of the "Athens War" to a startled nation. This one is enough to make you reflect on the circumspection of graduate theses.
B6410 (ASU)

Brearley, William H. Recollections of the East Tennessee Campaign, Battle of Campbell Station, 16th Nov., 1863: Siege of Knoxville, 17th Nov.-5th Dec., 1863. Detroit: Tribune, 1871.
B6420

Breazeale, J. W. M. Life As It Is: Or, Matters and Things in General. 1842. Reprint. Nashville: Charles Elder, 1969. A Tennessee classic.
B6430 (ASU BC ETSU)

Breazeale, Norma J. "Association of Selected Socio-economic Characteristics with Net Migration from Three Kentucky Economic Areas, 1920-1950." Master's thesis. Univ. of Kentucky, 1958. One of the areas is Appalachia.
B6440

Breckinridge, Mary Wide Neighborhoods: A Story of the Frontier Nursing Service. 1st ed. New York: Harper & Row, 1952. Kentucky's Frontier Nursing Service brought health care to the mountains despite incredible odds. Miss Breckinridge started this health care service herself.
B6450 (ASU BC LMC MHC WCU WWC)

Breeding, Clarence H. "Appraisal of Vocational Education in Agriculture in Claiborne County by Business and Professional Leaders." Master's thesis. Univ. of Tennessee, 1959.
B6460

Brennan, Ignatius Mountain State Gleanings. Boston: R. G. Badger, 1911. West Virginia verse.
B6470 (BC)

Brenni, Vito Joseph West Virginia Authors: A Bio-bibliography. Morgantown: West Virginia Library, 1957. A comprehensive listing which was revised in 1968 by Joyce Binder.
B6480

West Virginia Authors: A Bibliography. Morgantown: West Virginia Library Assoc., 1968. A very useful guide to West Virginia authors. Revised edition.
B6490 (BC)

Brent, William Bonney Geology of the Clinchport Quadrangle, Virginia. Report of Investigations, no. 5. Charlottesville: Virginia Division of Mineral Resources, 1963.
B6500 (ETSU)

Brents, John A. The Patriots and Guerrillas of East Tennessee and Kentucky. The Suffering of the Patriots. Also the Experience of the Author as an Officer in the Union Army. Including Sketches of Noted Guerrillas and Distinguished Patriots. New York: The Author, 1863.
B6510

Brewder, E. V. Wenger, Karl Frederick The Relation of Growth to Stand Density in Natural Loblolly Pine Stands. Asheville, N. C.: Southeastern Forest Experiment Station, 1958.
W2820 (WCU)

Brewer, Amanda Meade I Sing of Appalachia: Poems. Appalachia, Va.: Young Pubs., 1967.
B6520 (ASU BC)

Brewer, Earl D. C. Weatherford, Willis Duke Life and Religion in Southern Appalachia, an Interpretation of Selected Data from the Southern Appalachian Studies. New York: Friendship Press, 1962.
W1920 (ASU MHC WCU LMC ETSU WWC BC UNCA)

Brewer, Edward O. Soil Survey, Alleghany County, North Carolina. Prepared in cooperation with the North Carolina Agricultural Experiment Station. Washington: U. S. Soil Conservation Service, 1973.
B6530

Brewer, Mary T. Of Bolder Men (A History of Leslie County). Hyden, Ky.: Leslie County Press, 1970.
B6540 (BC)

Brewer, Robert Water Use by Appalachian Manufacturers, 1964. Prepared with the assistance of Joseph M. Conrad for Office of Appalachian Studies, Corps of Engineers, by Water Industries and Engineering Services Division. Washington: U. S. Department of Commerce, Business and Defense Services Administration, 1967.
B6550

Brice, Douglas The Folk-carol of England. London: Jenkins, 1967. Many of these are still sung in Appalachia today.
B6560 (BC)

Brice, Marshall Moore Conquest of a Valley. Charlottesville: Univ. Press of Virginia, 1965. An account of the Shenandoah Valley Campaign, May through August 1864, and the Battle of Piedmont.
B6570

Daughter of the Stars. Verona, Va.: McClure Press, 1973. Novel about Jean McGreal, Augusta County and adjacent Shenandoah Valley setting.
B6580

The Stonewall Brigade Band. Verona, Va.: McClure Print. Co., 1967. A history of the Confederate Army's Stonewall Brigade Band.
B6590 (ASU BC)

Brickell, John The Natural History of North Carolina. 1973. Reprint. Murfreesboro, Tenn.: Johnson Pub. Co., 1968.
B6600 (ASU BC LMC)

Bridge, Josiah Stratigraphy of the Mascot-Jefferson City Zinc District, Tennessee. Introduction by John Rodgers. U. S. Geological Survey Professional Paper, no. 277. Washington: Govt. Print. Off., 1956.
B6610

Briggs, G. H., Jr. Hunt, C. B. Coal Deposits of Pike County, Kentucky. Washington: Govt. Print. Off., 1937.
H8370

Briggs-Currer, Noel Virginia Settlers and English Adventurers: Abstracts of Wills, 1484-1798, and Legal Proceedings, Relating to Early Virginia Families. 3 vols. in 1. Baltimore: Genealogical Pub. Co., 1970.
B6620 (ASU)

Brigham, Albert Perry From Trail to Railway through the Appalachians. Boston: Ginn & Co., 1907.
B6630 (ASU BC LMC)

From Trail to Railway through the Appalachians. 1907. Reprint. Kennikat Series on Man and His Environment. Port Washington: Kennikat Press, 1970.
B6640 (ETSU MHC)

Bright, Lois Wallace A Legend of Oconaluftee. Spindale, N. C.: Spindale Press, n.d.
B6650 (ASU)

Brimley, C. S. Pearson, Thomas Gilbert Birds of North Carolina. Raleigh, N. C.: Edwards, 1919.
P1380 (WWC)

Brimley, H. H. Pearson, Thomas Gilbert Birds of North Carolina. Raleigh, N. C.: Edwards, 1919.
P1380 (WWC)

Briscoe, Mary E. Archambo, Judith P. Rural Child Care Project, 1968-1969 Research Evaluation. Frankfort, Ky.: Kentucky Child Welfare Research Foundation, Inc., 1970.
A4530

Briscoe, W. Russell Her Walls before Thee Stand: History of the Second Presbyterian Church, 1818-1968. Knoxville: n.p., 1969.
B6660

Bristol, Barbara Rose "An Investigation of the Readability of Textbooks Used in the Intermediate Grades in the Elizabethton, Tennessee, School System." Master's thesis. East Tennessee State Univ., 1971.
B6670 (ETSU)

Bristol, Eng. Bristol and America, a Record of the First Settlers in the Colonies of North America, 1654-1685, Including the Names with Places of Origin of More than 10,000 Servants to Foreign Plantations Who Sailed from the Port of Bristol to Virginia, Maryland, and Other Parts of the Atlantic Coast, and Also to the West Indies from 1654 to 1685. This list is compiled and published from their records by special permission of the Corporation of the city of Bristol, England. With preface by N. Dermont Harding and historical intro. by William Dodgson Bowman. 1929, 1931. Reprint. Baltimore: Genealogical Pub. Co., 1967.
B6680 (ASU)

Bristol Literary Arts Guild, Inc. Anthology '67. Vol. I, No. 1. Bristol, Virginia-Tennessee: Bristol Literary Arts Guild, Inc., 1967. This anthology is a collection of poetry, essays, short stories, articles, children's poems, and stories written by area authors.
B6690

Bristol, Tennessee. Public Schools Course of Study for Elementary Schools, Bristol, Tennessee, Grades 1-6. Prepared by the teachers. Bristol: n.p., 1950.
B6700

New Course of Study; A Teachers Guide for the Elementary Schools of Bristol, Tennessee. . . Published by Bristol Tennessee Board of Education for Bristol Tennessee Public Schools, 1954.
B6710 (ETSU)

Broadfoot, Thomas North Carolina Fiction, 1958-1971: An Annotated Bibliography. Wendell, N. C.: Broadfoot's Bookmark, 1972.
B6720 (ASU)

Broadhead, Mrs. Eva Wilder McGlasson An Earthy Paragon. New York: Harper and Brothers, 1892. Novel. A city girl finds happiness and a husband in the mountains of Kentucky.
B6730 (ASU)

Bound in Shallows. New York: Harper and Brothers, 1897. A story of city folk in a Kentucky mountain lumbering company.
B6740

Broadhurst, Samuel Davis An Introduction to the Topography, Geology, and Mineral Resources of North Carolina. Educational Series, 2. 1962. Reprint. Raleigh: North Carolina Department of Conservation & Development, Division of Mineral Resources, 1965.
B6750 (ETSU)

Brock, George G. Soil Survey, Banks and Stevens Counties, Georgia. Prepared in cooperation with the University of Georgia, College of Agriculture, Agricultural Experiment Station. Washington: U. S. Soil Conservation Service, 1971.
B6760

Brock, Robert Alonzo Documents, Chiefly Unpublished, Relating to the Huguenot Emigration to Virginia and to the Settlement at Manakintown, with an Appendix of Genealogies, Presenting Data of the Fontaine, Maury, Dupuy, Trabue, Marys, Chastain, Cooke, and Other Families. Baltimore: Genealogical Pub. Co., 1966.
B6770 (ASU)

Brock, Samuel M. The Myles Job Mine — A Study of Benefits and Costs of Surface Mining for Coal in Northern West Virginia. Research Series 1. Morgantown: West Virginia Univ. Appalachian Center, Office of Research and Development, 1968.
B6780

Brockman, Charles Raven Adams, Caruthers, Clancy, Neely and Townsend Descendants Composing the Adams, Legerton, Wakefield, Brockmann and Other Twentieth Century Families of the Carolinas. Charlotte, N. C.: n.p., 1950.
B6790 (BC)

Brodin, Pierre Thomas Wolfe Translation by Imogene Riddick. Preface by Richard Walser. Asheville, N. C.: Stephens Press, 1949.
B6800 (ASU WCU)

Broehl, Wayne G., Jr. The Molly Maguires. Cambridge, Mass.: Harvard Univ. Press, 1964. Account of a terrorist organization in the coal fields in the 1860's and 1870's. Much of the information in this volume came from recently opened Pinkerton Agency and Reaching Railroad files.
B6810 (ASU WCU)

Bromme, Traugott Reisen durch die Vereinigten Staaten und Ober-Canada. 3 vols. Baltimore: C. Scheld & Co., 1834-1835. Bromme visited Knoxville and Rogersville in Tennessee; Abingdon, Staunton, Harrisonburg, and Winchester in Virginia. His travels were undertaken to study the possibilities for German immigrants; he preferred the Deep South over Appalachia for German colonization.
B6820

Bronson, Bertrand Harris The Traditional Tunes of the Child Ballads. Princeton: Princeton Univ. Press, 1959. Child remains the best source for ballads and variants from England and Scotland.
B6830 (ASU BC)

Brookes, Stanley C. "An Investigation of the Administrative Duties and Responsibilities of Selected Assistant Principals in Upper East Tennessee." Master's thesis. East Tennessee State Univ., 1967.
B6840 (ETSU)

Brookhart, Mary Bishop A Brief History of the First Congregational Church, Crossville, Tennessee, 1887-1962. Crossville: Chronicle, Pub., 1962.
B6850

Brooks, Alonzo Beecher Forestry and Wood Industries. West Virginia Geological Survey Reports, vol. 5. Morgantown: Acme Pub. Co., 1910.
B6860 (ETSU)

Brooks, Alonzo Beecher
West Virginia Trees. West Virginia University College of Agriculture, Agricultural Experiment Station, bulletin 175. 1920. Reprint. Parsons, W. Va.: McClain Print. Co., 1972.
B6870 (ASU WCU)

Brooks, Bert K. The Bedroom of the Poor. New York, N. Y.: Carlton Press, Inc., 1973. Includes section on Appalachian poverty.
B6880

Brooks, Cora Davis History of Morristown, 1787-1936. Nashville: The Survey, WPA, 1940.
B6890

Brooks, Earle Amos A Descriptive Bibliography of West Virginia Ornithology. Newton Highlands, Mass.: n.p., 1938.
B6900 (BC)

List of the Birds Found in West Virginia. Newton Highlands, Mass.: The author, 1938.
B6910

Brooks, Fred Ernest Studies of the Codling Moth in the Central Appalachian Region. Bulletin, 189. Washington: U. S. Department of Agriculture, Bureau of Entomology, 1915.
B6920

Brooks, Joe F. Blueberries, Production Guide for North Carolina. Extension Circular 474. Reprint. Raleigh, N. C.: Agricultural Extension Service, 1968. Western N. C. has a growing blueberry industry.
B6930 (LMC)

Brooks, Joe F. and others Soil Survey, Carroll and Haralson Counties, Georgia. Prepared in cooperation with the Univ. of Georgia, College of Agriculture, Agricultural Experiment Station. Washington: U. S. Soil Conservation Service, 1971. Only portions of these two counties are mountains.
B6940

Brooks, John R. Report of a Board of Army Officers upon the Claim of Maj. Gen. William Farrar Smith, U. S. V., That He, and Not General Rosecrans, Originated the Plan for the Relief of Chattanooga in October, 1863. Washington, D. C.: Govt. Print. Off., 1901.
B6950 (ASU)

Brooks, Maurice Graham The Appalachians. Boston: Houghton Mifflin Co., 1965. First volume of a series designed to interest North Americans in wild-life, plants and geology of their continent. Explains in a very readable way the natural history of the entire Appalachian range, with some emphasis on West Virginia.
B6960 (ASU WCU LMC MHC FC WWC ETSU BC FC UNCA)

The Life of the Mountains. New York: McGraw-Hill, 1967. Contains much information about the national parks, forests, and reserves and about the ecological balance of the mountains.
B6970 (BC)

Brooks, Michael P. The Dimensions of Poverty in North Carolina. Durham, N. C.: n.p., 1964. Some sections are devoted to poverty in North Carolina's 28 mountain counties.
B6980

Broom, Leonard Speck, Frank Gouldsmith Cherokee Dance and Drama. Berkeley: Univ. of California Press, 1951.
S6090 (ASU WCU ETSU BC)

Brosg'e, William Miller, Ralph L. Geology and Oil Resources of the Jonesville District, Lee County, Virginia. Washington: U. S. Govt. Print. Off., 1954.
M5960

Browder, John Caldwell Nisi Prius. New York: Neale Pub. Co., 1912. A Kentucky lawyer's remeniscenses of his years at the bar. Many Appalachian references.
B6990 (ASU BC)

Browder, Nathaniel C. The Cherokee Indians and Those Who Came After, Notes for a History of Cherokee County, North Carolina, 1835-1860. Hayesville, N. C.: Draft Copy, 1973.
B7000 (ASU)

Brown, Arthur Aladine Lumbering on the Cumberland: A Romance Taken from Life. Cincinnati: Lumber Worker, 1887. A dramatic account of lumbering in the mountains of Tenn. and Ky. The lumberjacks lived a dangerous, adventurous life with its own code and, to some extent, its own language.
B7010 (BC)

Brown, Barbara "Needs and Interests in Family Relationships of a Selected Group of West Virginia Eighth and Ninth Grade Pupils, 1948-1949." Master's thesis. West Virginia Univ., 1949.
B7020

Brown, Beverly Holladay The Mystery of the Wizard Clip. Richmond: Catholic Historical Society, 1949. This W. Va. town is so named because of a recorded case of wizardry in its early days. A priest exorcised the wizard, but the story lived on.
B7030 (ASU)

Brown, Cecil Kenneth Old Roads in Kentucky. Harrodsburg, Ky.: Daniel M. Hutton, 1929. Includes: Wilderness Rd., Indian War tracts, buffalo trails, early road descriptions and customs.
B7040 (ASU BC)

Brown, Charles Edward "The Nolachucky Baptist Association of East Tennessee, 1828-1871." Master's thesis. East Tennessee State Univ., 1971. The Nolachucky Association is one of the oldest in the state.
B7050 (ETSU)

Brown, Dalton Milford "An Educational and Economic Survey of Bledsoe County, Tennessee." Thesis. Univ. of Tennessee, 1926.
B7060

Educational, Economic and Community Survey, Bledsoe County. Knoxville: School of Education, Univ. of Tennessee, 1927.
B7070

Brown, David Buttrick, Daniel S. TSVLVKI SQCLVLV: A Cherokee Spelling Book. Knoxville: Heiskell and Brown, 1819.
B9450

Brown, Dee Alexander Thee Bold Cavaliers. Morgan's 2nd Kentucky Cavalry Raiders. Philadelphia, Pa.: Lippincott, 1959. Morgan's men made four major forays into the mountain region.
B7080

Brown, Douglas MacArthur "Productive Capacity and Economic Growth in West Virginia." Ph. D. Diss. West Virginia Univ., 1969.
B7090

Brown, Douglas Summers The Catawba Indians: The People of the River. Columbia: Univ. of South Carolina Press, 1966. The Catawba tribe inhabited the foothill country of North and South Carolina.
B7100 (ASU)

A History of Lynchburg's Pioneer Quakers and Their Meeting House, 1754-1936. 1st ed. Lynchburg, Va.: J. P. Bell Co., 1936.
B7110 (ASU)

Brown, E. Evan The Economic Development of the Northeast Georgia Commission Area Through Use of Forest Products and Water Resources. Athens, Ga.: Northeast Georgia Planning and Development Commission, 1966.
B7120 (ASU ETSU)

Brown, Frederick Fernando "The Mountain People of the South: A Sociological Study." Microfilm. Ph. D. Diss. Southern Baptist Theological Seminary, 1913. A rather condescending study of mountain people by yet another theologian striken by the plight of us pore mountain folk.
B7130 (WCU)

Brown, Harlan R. A Brief History of Our Early Life and Morgan County, Kentucky. Ashland, Ky.: n.p., 1950. A mixture of autobiography and country history.
B7140 (BC)

In the Foothills of the Cumberland; a History of Eastern Kentucky. Ashland, Ky.: Graber, 1959. Informal history of Eastern Kentucky.
B7150 (BC)

Brown, James Moore The Captives of Abb's Valley. Philadelphia: Presbyterian Board of Publications, 1854. A saga of the Moore family of Tazewell County, who on three different occasions were captured by Indians and taken to Canada.
B7151

The Captives of Abb's Valley, a Legend of Frontier Life. New ed., with introduction, notes and appendices, maps and illustrations, by Robert Bell Woodworth. Xerox copy of the original. Staunton, Va.: McClure Co., 1942.
B7152 (ASU)

Brown, James S. Schwarzweller, Harry K. Social Structure of the Contact Situation, Rural Appalachia and Urban America. Morgantown: West Va. Univ., Appalachian Center, 1969.
S1290

Brown, James Stephen Basic Population Data for the Southern Appalachians by State, Economic Area, and Metropolitan Area. Lexington: Univ. of Kentucky, 1958. A wealth of useful information, well indexed.
B7160

The Changing Kentucky Population: A Summary of Population Data for Counties. Progress Report, 67. Lexington: Kentucky Agricultural Experiment Station, 1958.
B7170

The Family Group in a Kentucky Mountain Farming Community. Bulletin No. 588. Lexington: Kentucky Agricultural Experiment Station, University of Kentucky, June, 1952.
B7180

The Farm Family in a Kentucky Mountain Neighborhood. Bulletin No. 587. Lexington: Kentucky Agricultural Experiment Station, University of Kentucky, August, 1952.
B7190

Rural Population Changes in Five Kentucky Mountain Districts, 1943-1946. Bulletin No. 532. Lexington: Kentucky Agricultural Experiment Station, University of Kentucky, 1949.
B7200

"The Social Organization of an Isolated Kentucky Mountain Neighborhood." Ph. D. Diss. Harvard Univ., 1950. A study of social and kinship networks in the Kentucky mountains.
B7210 (ASU)

Southern Appalachian Population Change, 1960-1970: A First Look at the 1970 Census. n.p.: n.p., 1971?
B7220 (BC)

Schwarzweller, Harry K. Mountain Families in Transition: A Case Study of Appalachian Migration. Univ. Park: Pennsylvania State Univ. Press, 1971.
S1270 (ASU WCU LMC ETSU WWC BC UNCA)

Brown, Jilda J. Publications of the Southeastern Forest Station, 1921-1958. U. S. Forest Service Station Paper, no. 117. Southeastern Forest Experiment Station, 1960.
B7230 (WCU)

Brown, John Mason Daniel Boone: The Opening of the Wilderness. Illustrated by Lee J. Ames. Landmark Books, 21. New York: Random House, 1952.
B7240 (ASU BC)

Brown, John P. Old Frontiers: The Story of the Cherokee Indians from Earliest Times to the Date of their Removal to the West, 1838. Kingsport, Tenn.: Southern Publishers, 1938. Like most histories of the Cherokee this one merges legend with fact.
B7250 (ASU BC ETSU LMC WCU)

Old Frontiers: The Story of the Cherokee Indians from Earliest Times to the Date of Their Removal to the West, 1838. Rpt., First American Frontier Series. New York: Arno, 1971.
B7260

Pioneers of Old Frontiers. With supplements: Pioneer settlers of the Chattanooga area, by Penelope J. Allen, and The story of another pioneer: A brief history of Pioneer Bank. Chattanooga: Pioneer Bank, 1962.
B7270 (ETSU)

Brown, L. A. Higbee, Howard William Soil Survey, Huntingdon County, Pennsylvania. Washington: U. S. Department of Agriculture, Bureau of Plant Industry, Soils and Agricultural Engineering, 1944.
H5260

Simmons, Charles Shaffer Soil Survey of Wayne County, Pennsylvania. Washington: U. S. Department of Agriculture, Bureau of Chemistry and Soils, 1938.
S3430

Brown, Len The Encyclopedia of Country and Western Music. New York: Tower Pub., 1971.
B7280 (WCU)

Brown, Lloyd Arnold Early Maps of the Ohio Valley. Pittsburgh: Univ. of Pittsburgh Press, 1959. Maps, plans and views made by Indians and colonists from 1673 to 1783.
B7290 (BC)

Brown, Londo H. Rights-of-Way for Removal of Natural Resources From West Virginia Land: An Examination of Existing Applicable Law and of Possible Changes Therein. Series no. 1. Office of Research and Development, West Virginia Univ., 1965.
B7300 (ASU)

Brown, Louie A. Dimensions of Change in East Tennessee, Tennessee, the South, and the Nation: A Comparative Analysis. Institute of Regional Studies Monograph, no. 2. Johnson City: East Tennessee State Univ., 1966.
B7310 (ASU ETSU LMC WCU)

Brown, Luie A. Measurements of Poverty in East Tennessee. Monograph, no. 1. Johnson City: Institute of Regional Studies, East Tennessee State Univ., 1965.
B7320 (ASU BC ETSU LMC)

Brown, Marcella Ellis "A Seventh Grade Homeroom Guidance Experiment at Elizabethton Junior High School, Elizabethton, Tennessee." Master's thesis. East Tennessee State College, 1958.
B7330 (ETSU)

Brown, Minnie M. Marsh, C. Paul Facilitative and Inhibitive Factors in Training Program Recruitment Among Rural Negroes. n.p.: n.p., n.d.
M3360

Brown, Nancy Keen A Broken Bondage. Boston: Roxburgh Pub. Co., 1911.
B7340

Brown, O. Lester Blanford Barnard Dougherty, a Man to Match His Mountains. n.p.: n.p., 1963. Biography of the founders of Appalachian State University.
B7350 (ASU)

Brown, Ralph Geron "Family Removal of the Tennessee Valley." Master's thesis. Univ. of Tennessee, 1951. A pallid account of the tragic loss of Tennessee's wild rivers and best farm land.
B7360

Brown, Raphael, pseud. see **Brown, Beverly Holladay**

Brown, Robert M. Brewer, Edward O. Soil Survey, Alleghany County, North Carolina. Washington: U. S. Soil Conservation Service, 1973.
B6530

Brown, Roy Melton Steiner, Jesse Frederick The North Carolina Chain Gang: A Study of County Convict Road Work. Chapel Hill: Univ. of North Carolina Press, 1927.
S6920 (LMC)

Steiner, Jesse Frederick The North Carolina Chain Gang: A Study of County Convict Road Work. Montclair, N. J.: Patterson Smith, 1969.
S6930 (WWC)

Brown, Stuart E., Jr. Annals of Blackwater and the Land of Canaan, 1746-1880. Berryville, Va.: Chesapeake Book Co., 1959.
B7380 (ASU BC)

The Guns of Harpers Ferry. Berryville, Va.: Virginia Book Co., 1968.
B7390 (ASU BC)

Virginia Baron: The Story of Thomas, 6th Lord Fairfax. Berryville, Va.: Chesapeake Book Co., 1965. Lord Fairfax's hldings extended all the way to the Allegheny Mtns. Much of Shenandoah Valley was included in this area.
B7400 (ASU BC)

Pollock, George Freeman Skyland: The Heart of the Shenandoah National Park. n.p.: n.p., 1960.
P3420 (FC BC ASU WCU)

Brown, Stuart E., Jr. comp. Virginia Genealogies: A Trial List of Printed Books and Pamphlets. Berryville, Va.: Virginia Book Co., 1967.
B7410 (ASU)

Brown, Virginia Holmes Greene, Lee Seifert Rescued Earth, a Study of the Public Administration of Natural Resources in Tennessee. Knoxville: Univ. of Tennessee Press, 1948.
G3820 (ASU LMC ETSU)

Brown, Virginia P. Mary Gordon Duffee's Sketches of Alabama. University: Univ. of Alabama Press, 1970.
B7420

Brown, William Griffee History of Nicholas County, West Virginia. Richmond: Dietz Press, 1954. Another good history of a West Virginia County. Proportionally, West Virginia has written histories for more of its counties than any other Appalachia area. Some were begun with WPA funds.
B7430 (ASU BC)

Brown, William Randall Geology and Mineral Resources of the Lynchburg Quadrangle, Virginia. Bulletin, 74. Charlottesville: Virginia Division of Mineral Resources, 1958.
B7440 (ETSU)

Brown, Zenith Jones, pseud. see **Ford, Leslie**

Brownell, Elijah Ellsworth ed. Banks, Charles Edward Topographical Dictionary of 2885 English Emigrants to New England, 1620-1650. Baltimore: Genealogical Pub. Co., 1963.
B940 (ASU)

Browning, Charles Henry Welsh Settlement of Pennsylvania. 1912. Reprint. Baltimore: Genealogical Pub. Co., 1967.
B7450 (ASU)

Browning, Clyde A Bibliography of Dissertations in Geography, 1901-1969. Chapel Hill: Univ. of North Carolina, n.d. A useful index to geologic formations throughout the mountains.
B7460 (LMC)

Browning, Howard Miller "Washington County Court: The Government of a Tennessee Frontier Community." Master's thesis. Vanderbilt Univ., 1938. This county court served as a training ground for many major American political figures.
B7470

Browning, Mary Carmel, Sister Kentucky Authors, a History of Kentucky Literature. Evansdale, Ind.: Keller-Crescent, 1968. A nice tool for ferreting out little-known Eastern Kentucky authors.
B7480 (ASU BC)

Brownlee, Frederick The John C. Campbell Folk School, 1925-1952. Brasstown, N. C.: n.p., 1952? One of the better folk schools, Campbell is still a going concern. Its founder, John C. Campbell, wrote one of the classic books on Appalachia; THE SOUTHERN HIGHLANDER AND HIS HOMELAND.
B7490

Brownlow, William Gannaway Ought American Slavery to be Perpetuated? A Debate between Rev. W. G. Brownlow and Rev. A. Pryne. Held at Philadelphia, September, 1858. Philadelphia: J. B. Lippincott and Co., 1858. Here's Parson Brownlow again in his role as a great unionist, abolitionist, and an orator of national reknown.
B7520 (ASU BC)

Sketches of the Rise, Progress, and Decline of Secession: with a Narrative of Personal Adventure among the Rebels. Philadelphia: George W. Childs; Cincinnati, Ohio: Applegate and Co., 1862. Parson Brownlow was East Tennessee's leading unionist. He became the Reconstruction governor of Tennessee.
B7530 (ASU)

Brownlow, William Gannoway The Great Iron Wheel Examined: Or, Its False Spokes Extracted, and an Exhibition of Elder Graves, Its Builder. Nashville, Tenn.: The author, 1856. A polemic against the established church and some of its leaders. Brownlow, a leading unionist and nationally reknowned orator, had so many causes to expouse and so many enemies to denounce that he established his own press in Jonesboro, so he might be equal to the task.
B7500 (ASU)

Helps to the Study of Presbyterianism. . . . Knoxville: n.p., 1834. One of Brownlow's few restrained works, this appears to be an aid to self-study for Presbyterians.
B7510

Broyles, Bettye J. Second Preliminary Report: The St. Albans Site, Kanawha County, West Virginia, 1964-1968. With appendices by Sigfus Olafson, James A. Barlow, and George E. Snider, Jr. Report of Archeological Investigations, no. 3. Morgantown: West Virginia Geological and Economic Survey, 1971.
B7540 (ASU)

Brubaker, Earl Available for Work: The Pennsylvania Unemployment Compensation Interpretation. Bulletin, no. 61. University Park: Pennsylvania State Univ., Bureau of Business Research, 1958. Describes Pennsylvania's unique interpretation unemployment compensation laws.
B7550

Bruccoli, Matthew-Joseph ed. Davis, Arthur Kyle, Jr. ed. More Traditional Ballads of Virginia: Collected with the Cooperation of Members of the Virginia Folklore Society. Chapel Hill: Univ. of North Carolina Press, 1960.
D790 (ASU FC BC LMC)

Bruce, Dickson D. And They All Sang Hallelujah, Plainfolk Camp-meeting Religion, 1800-1845. Knoxville: University of Tennessee Press, 1974.
B7560 (ASU)

Bruce, Henry Addington Bayley Daniel Boone and the Wilderness Road. New York: The Macmillan Company, 1910. A complete and accurate account of the life of Daniel Boone and his contributions to the military, political, economic, and social aspects of the Western expansion.
B7570 (ASU BC)

Daniel Boone and the Wilderness Road. New York: Macmillan, 1934.
B7580 (ETSU)

Life of General Houston, 1793-1863. Makers of America Series. New York: Dodd, 1891. Houston's boyhood years were spent in Eastern Tennessee. His Cherokee neighbors exerted a lasting influence on him.
B7590

Bruce, Kathleen Virginia Iron Manufacture In the Slave Era. New York: Agustus M. Kelley Publishers, n.d.
B7600

Bruce, Oscar Clayton Soil Survey of Allegany County, Maryland. Prepared in cooperation with the Maryland Geological Survey and the Maryland Agricultural Experiment Station. Field Operations, 1921. Washington: U. S. Department of Agriculture, Bureau of Soils, 1926. Allegany is one of Maryland's three Appalachian counties.
B7610

Bruce, Philip Alexander Economic History of Virginia in the Seventeenth Century. New York: Macmillan, 1896. Economic conditions of people?
B7620 (BC FC)

Bruce, Philip Alexander
Institutional History of Virginia in the Seventeenth Century: An Inquiry into the Religious, Moral, Educational, Legal, Military, and Political Condition of the People Based on Original and Contemporaneous Records. New York: G. P. Putnam's Sons, 1910.
B7630 (ETSU)

Bruce, Thomas Heritage of the Trans-Allegheny Pioneers: Or, Resources of Central West Virginia. Baltimore: Nicholas, Killam, and Moffitt, 1894. A history of the settlement of the great central valley of West Virginia.
B7640 (ASU BC)

Southwest Virginia and Shenandoah Valley. An Inquiry into the Causes of the Rapid Growth and Wonderful Development of Southwest Virginia and Shenandoah Valley, with a History of the Norfolk and Western and Shenandoah Valley Railroads. Richmond: J. L. Hill Pub. Co., 1891.
B7650 (ASU BC FC)

Bruce, William Cabell Below the James, a Plantation Sketch. Boston: Houghton Mifflin Co., 1927. Sketches on Virginia's Social Life and Customs and Plantation life.
B7660 (ASU)

Brucker, Elizabeth C. "A Survey of the Status of the Retired School Teacher in West Virginia." Master's thesis. Marshall College, 1952.
B7670

Bruer, H. L. List of Tennessee Certified Nurseries Collectors of Native Wild Plants and Nursery Dealers for the Season 1967-1968. Nashville: Tennessee Department of Agriculture, 1968.
B7680 (LMC)

Brumbaugh, Gaius Marcus Revolutionary War Records: Vol. I, Virginia. Lancaster, Pa.: Lancaster Press, 1936.
B7690

Revolutionary War Records: Vol. I, Virginia. Virginia Army and Navy Forces with Bounty Land Warrants for Virginia Military Scrip: From Federal and State Archives. 1936. Reprint. Baltimore: Genealogical Pub. Co., 1967.
B7700 (ASU)

Brumit, Robert F. "History of Boone's Creek School, 1851-1958." Master's thesis. East Tennessee State Univ., 1958.
B7710

Brumley, Robert H. "The Applicability of the Industrial Arts Curriculum Project, Construction to the New Junior High Schools in Johnson City." Master's thesis. East Tennessee State Univ., 1972.
B7720 (ETSU)

Brunk, Harry Anthony History of Mennonites in Virginia. vol. 1. Harrisonburg, Va.: H. A. Brunk, 1959.
B7730 (ASU BC FC)

Brunner, Edmund de S. Douglas, H. Paul The Protestant Church as a Social Institution. New York: Harper and Brothers, 1935.
D3130

Brunner, Edmund de Schweinita Church Life in the Rural South: A Study of the Opportunity of Protestantism Based Upon Data From Seventy Counties. Committee on Social and Religions Surveys. Unique Studies of Rural American town, and County Series, vol. 4. New York: George H. Doran Co., 1923. Study includes some Appalachian Counties.
B7740 (ASU BC)

Brush, Frederick Hill Doctor, Tells in Story and Ballads, Tales of the Appalachians. Selingsgrove, Pa.: Susquehanna Univ. Press, 1956.
B7750

Bryan, Daniel The Mountain Muse: Comprising the Adventures of Daniel Boone. And, The Power of Virtuous and Refined Beauty. Harrisonburg, Va.: The author, 1813. A 252 page narrative poem in flowery style praising Boone.
B7760 (ASU BC)

Bryan, Emma Lyon 1860-1865. A Romance of the Valley of Virginia. Harrisonburg, Va.: J. Taliaffero, 1892. Romantic fiction with a Shenandoah Valley setting.
B7770 (ASU BC)

Bryan, Paul Wiebe, A. H. Waterfowl on the Tennessee River Impoundments. Norris, Tenn.: Tennessee Valley Authority, 1950.
W5960

Bryan, Raymond Arthur A History of William Taylor and Sarah Jones and their Descendants. Raleigh, N. C.: Litho Industries, Inc., 1972.
B7780 (UNCA)

Bryant, Bruce Geology of the Grandfather Mountain Window and vicinity, North Carolina and Tennessee. Geological Survey Professional Paper, no. 615. Washington: Govt. Print. Off., 1970.
B7800 (ASU)

Bryant, Bruce Hazelton Geology of the Blowing Rock Quadrangle, N. C. Washington: Govt. Print. Off., 1962.
B7790

Geology of the Linville Quadrangel, North Carolina-Tennessee: A Preliminary Report. Contributions to General Geology Geological Survey, Bulletin, 1121-D. Washington: Govt. Print. Off., 1962.
B7810 (LMC)

Mineral Resources of the Grandfather Mountain Window and Vicinity, North Carolina. Washington: Govt. Print. Off., 1966.
B7820 (ASU)

Bryant, Elizabeth Jean "The Attitudes of Freshmen Female Students Toward Physical Education at Western Carolina University." Master's thesis. Western Carolina University, 1971.
B7830 (WCU)

Bryant, Frank Egbert A History of English Balladry, and Other Studies. 1913. Reprint. n.p.: Folcroft Library Editions, 1970. An excellent history of the popular English ballads. With notes.
B7840 (ASU)

Bryant, Margaret M. Proverbs, and How to Collect Them. Publication, no. 4. Greensboro, N. C.: American Dialect Society, 1945.
B7850 (ASU)

Bryant, William A. "A Brief Survey of Industrial Plants in Kingsport, Tennessee, with Emphasis on the Geographic Location of the Industrial Worker." Master's thesis. East Tennessee State College, 1951.
B7860 (ETSU)

"A Brief Survey of Industrial Plants in Kingsport, Tennessee with Emphasis on the Geographic Location of the Industrial Worker." Master's thesis. East Tennessee State College, 1951.
B7870

Bryson, Anne Dunbar These Friendly Mountains. Asheville: Miller Printing Co., 1937. Promotional and descriptive text on the wonders of the North Carolina mountains.
B7880 (ASU)

Bryson, Herman Jennings The Story of the Geologic Making of North Carolina. Educational Series, no. 1. Raleigh, N. C.: Department of Conservation and Development, 1928.
B7890 (LMC UNCA)

The Buccaneer Vol. 1-. 1937-. Johnson City: East Tennessee State College, annual.
B7900 (ETSU)

Buchan, Peter comp. Ancient Ballads and Songs of the North of Scotland. 2 vols. 1875. Reprint. Norwood, Pa.: Norwood Editions, 1973.
B7910 (ASU)

Gleanings of Scarce Old Ballads, With Explanatory Notes. Reprint of London 1825 ed. Norwood, Pa.: Norwood Editions, 1974.
B7920 (ASU)

Gleanings of Scotch, English, and Irish: Scarce Old Ballads, Chiefly Tragical and Historical. Many of Them Connected with the Localities of Aberdeenshire. 1825. Reprint. Norwood, Pa.: Norwood Editions, 1974.
B7930 (ASU)

Buchanan, Cecil "Municipal Ownership of Public Utilities in Chattanooga, Tennessee." Master's thesis. Louisiana State Univ., 1941.
B7940

Buchanan, David P. "The Relations of the Cherokee Indians with the English in America Prior to 1763." Master's thesis. Univ. of Tennessee, 1923. A sad history of strange negotiations and abortative treaties.
B7950 (ASU)

Buchanan, John A. "A Survey of Labor Requirements in Northern West Virginia Coal Mines in 1957." Master's thesis. West Virginia Univ., 1960.
B7960

Buchanan, Margaret Terry "The Migration of Workers from Tennessee to Michigan." Master's thesis. Vanderbilt Univ., 1940.
B7970 (ASU)

Buchanan, Susie Groce "A Study of the Music Education Program of Watauga County." Master's thesis. Appalachian State Teachers College, 1953.
B7980 (ASU)

Buchanan, W. Wray Keeling, William B. Tourism Development in the Chattahoochee-Flint Area. Athens: Univ. of Georgia, Bureau of Business and Economic Research, 1967.
K430

Buchele, William Recreating the Kentucky Rifle. 2nd ed. York, Pa.: George Shumway, Pub., 1966.
B7990 (ASU BC)

Buck, Charles Neville The Battle Cry. Illustrated by Douglas Duer. New York: W. J. Watt and Co., 1914. A Bryn Mawr graduate moves to the Kentucky mountains to teach school. She becomes involved with a feud leader, helps him in a shootout and feels she must marry him.
B8000 (ASU BC LMC)

The Call of the Cumberlands. Illustrated by Douglas Durer. New York: Grosset and Dunlap, 1913. An artist from the flatlands stumbles onto a full-blown feud in the Kentucky hills, escapes with his life and marries a mountain heroine.
B8010 (ASU WCU LMC BC)

The Code of the Mountains. Illustrated by G. W. Gage. New York: W. J. Watt and Co., 1915. A murderer recently released from the state penitentary, finds himself in a feud, which is finally settled by the Spanish-American War.
B8020 (ASU WCU LMC BC)

Destiny. Illustrated by R. F. Schabelitz. New York: W. J. Watt and Co., 1916. Setting for this story is a barren rocky farm in the White mountains.
B8030 (ASU BC)

Flight to the Hills. Garden City, N. Y.: Doubleday, Page and Co., 1926. A New York actress flees a murder scene and finds peace in the mountains of Kentucky.
B8040 (ASU BC)

Hazard of the Hills. New York: Macauley Company, 1932. A mountain man and a city woman vascillate between Cape Cod and the Kentucky hills.
B8050 (ASU)

Iron Will. Garden City, N. Y.: Doubleday, Page and Co., 1927. A Kentucky born, Harvard-educated lawyer leads a group of mountain men against the dishonest state political machine.
B8060 (ASU BC)

The Key to Yesterday. Illustrated by R. Schabelitz. New York: W. J. Watt and Co., 1910.
B8070 (ASU BC)

Marked Men. New York: Doubleday, Doran and Co., 1929. A mountain lawyer outwits big city detectives and solves the mystery of a millionaire's murder.
B8080

Mountain Justice: A Tale of the Cumberlands. Boston: Houghton Mifflin Co., 1935. A schoolmarm finds a connection between a mountain feud and a murder in an exclusive Louisville club.
B8090 (ASU LMC BC)

Buck, Charles Neville
A Pagan of the Hills. New York: Grosset and Dunlap, 1919. A mountain girl learns the lumbering business.
B8100 (BC)
A Pagan of the Hills. New York: W. J. Watt and Co., 1919.
B8110 (ASU)
The Portal of Dreams. New York: W. J. Watt and Co., 1912.
B8120
The Roof Tree. Illustrated by Lee F. Conrey. Garden City, N. Y.: Doubleday, Page and Co., 1921. A fugitive from Virginia finds refuge, long-lost kin and a ready-made feud in his new home in Kentucky.
B8130 (LMC BC ASU)
The Rouge's Badge. Garden City: Doubleday, Page, 1924. A mountain boy becomes a jockey in the Bluegrass area until his father's murder calls him home for revenge.
B8140
The Tempering. Garden City, N. Y.: Doubleday, Page and Co., 1920. A story of the Kentucky mountains spanning the years between the feud-ridden period of the late nineteenth century and World War I.
B8150 (ASU BC)
When "Bear Cat" Went Dry. Illustrated by George W. Gage. New York: W. J. Watt and Co., 1918. Bear Cat is a drunk who reforms.
B8160 (ASU WCU BC)

Buck, Elizabeth Salmon "An Inquiry into Present Practices in Guidance in Transylvania County High Schools." Master's thesis. Appalachian State University, 1969.
B8170 (ASU)

Buck, James P. "A History of the Library Resources of Putnam County, Tennessee." Master's thesis. Tennessee Polythechnic Institute, 1961.
B8180

Buck, Pearl Once Upon a Christmas. New York: John Day Co., 1972. Includes recollection of her West Virginia childhood.
B8190

Buck, Roy Clair Educational Attainment among Pennsylvania Rural Youth. University Park: Pennsylvania Agricultural Experiment Station, 1961. Appalachian counties were used in this study.
B8200
Formal Participation Patterns in a Central Pennsylvania Rural Community. Progress Report No. 129. University Park: Agricultural Experiment Station, Pennsylvania State University, January, 1955. Explores possible relationships between location and size of homes and social participation.
B8210

Buck, Roy Clark Factors Related to Changes in Social Participation in a Pennsylvania Rural Community. Bulletin No. 582. University Park: Agricultural Experiment Station, Pennsylvania State University, 1954. Factors studied included: Age, income, family cycle, church affiliation and length of residence.
B8220

Buck, William Joseph History of Montgomery County with the Schuylkill Valley: Containing Sketches of all the Townships, Boroughs and Villages, in Said Limits, from the Earliest Period to the Present Time. With an Account of the Indians, the Swedes, and Other Early Settlers, and the Local Events of the Revolution: Besides Notices of the Progress of Population, Improvements, and Manufactures. Norristown, Pa.: E. L. Acker, 1859.
B8230 (ASU)

Buckalew, Marshall The Life of Morris Purdy Shawkey. Charleston, W. Va.: West Virginia Pub. Co., 1941. Shawkey was a West Virginia educator; a school teacher at fifteen he rose through the West Virginia Public school system to become president of Marshall University.
B8240 (ASU BC)

Buckhorn Association, Inc., Brooklyn, N. Y. Buckhorn: The Story of a Christian Enterprise on Squabble Creek in the Mountains of Kentucky. Brooklyn, N. Y.: The assoc., n.d. Promaterial brochure for Witherspoon College, Perry County, Kentucky and Presbyterian Home Missions.
B8250 (BC)

Buckingham, James Silk The Slave States of America. 2 vols. n.p.: London, Paris: Fisher, Son and Co., 1842. This world traveller traveled through eastern Tennessee and western North Carolina and Virginia en route to White Sulphur Springs. He was interested in manners, morals, and social conditions.
B8260

Buckland, Golden T. "A Study of the Needs for an Audio-Visual Education Center at Appalachian State Teachers College." Master's thesis. Appalachian State Teachers College, 1949.
B8270 (ASU)

Buckland, Grace Young "A Survey of the Reading Materials Found in the Homes of the Fourth and Seventh Grade Students of the Elementary Demonstration School, Boone, North Carolina." Master's thesis. Appalachian State Teachers College, 1951.
B8280 (ASU)

Buckland, Roscoe Verne Berea College, Kentucky, Rural School Improvement Project. Report, 1953-1957. Lexington: Transylvania Print. Co., 1958.
B3110 (BC ETSU)

Buckles, Eleanor Valley of Power. New York: Creative Age Press, 1945. An unimaginative novel about the impact of the TVA project on East Tennessee communities.
B8290 (LMC WCU BC ASU)

Buckmaster, Henrietta, pseud. see **Henkle, Henrietta**

Buckner, William Aylette "The Mountains and the Blue Grass: A Comparative Study of County Officials in Kentucky." Ph. D. Diss. Univ. of Kentucky, 1968. It's a pity the author was so restricted in his investigation; the study covers social, educational, and statistical factors. A survey of the relative levels of corruption would have been much more fun.
B8300

Buehler, Katherine Boies Briscoe, W. Russell Her Walls before Thee Stand: History of the Second Presbyterian Church, 1818-1968. Knoxville: n.p., 1969.
B6660

Buehr, Walter Underground Riches: The Story of Mining. Morrow Junior Books. New York: Morrow, 1958. An account of the rapid depletion of the nation's coal reserves. Written for young children (Grades 2-6.)
B8310 (ASU)

Buell, Augustus C. History of Andrew Jackson: Pioneer, Patriot, Soldier, Politician, President. 2 vols. New York: Charles Scribner's Sons, 1904. Portions of Jackson's youth and most of his early legal and military careers were spent in Appalachia.
B8320 (ASU)

Buffington, Albert T. Boyer, Walter E. Songs along the Mahantongo: Pennsylvania Dutch Folk-songs. Hatboro, Pa.: Folklore Associates, 1964.
B6050 (ASU)

Bull, Donald Eugene "The Attitudes of a Selected Group of Community Leaders Concerning Consolidation of Five Rural Elementary Schools in Washington County, Tennessee." Master's thesis. East Tennessee State Univ., 1966.
B8330 (ETSU)

Bullard, Helen Cumberland County's First Hundred Years. Crossville: Cumberland Co. Centennial Committee, 1956. Promotional and historical information.
B8340 (LMC)

Bullard, Todd Hupp "The West Virginia Labor Federation and the West Virginia Legislature, 1957-1961." Ph. D. Diss. Univ. of Pittsburgh, 1964.
B8350

Bullen, Robert Whitefield McDowell County, West Virginia, Library Survey. Charleston: West Virginia Library Commission, 1957.
B8360 (BC)
Survey for Library Development in Fayette and Raleigh Counties, West Virginia. Charleston: West Virginia Library Commission, 1959.
B8370 (BC)

Bulletin n.p.: Appalachian Geological Society, n.d.
B8380

Buncombe County, Economic and Social: A Laboratory Study at the University of North Carolina, Dept. of Rural Social Economics Asheville, N. C.: Central Bank and Trust Co., 1923. In cooperation with A. M. Moser and others.
B8390 (BC)

Bunn, Maude Davis The Genealogy of Marion-Davis Families. Raleigh, N. C.: Edwards and Broughton Co., 1973. A western North Carolina family.
B8400 (ASU)

Burch, Robert Renfroe's Christmas. Illustrated by Rocco Negri. New York: The Viking Press, 1971. A young boy learns the meaning of Christmas in a surprisingly unsentimental Christmas tale set in northern Georgia.
B8410

Burchard, Ernest Francis Iron Ore in the Red Mountain Formation in Greasy Cove, Alabama. U. S. Geological Survey Circular, no. 1. Washington: Govt. Print. Off., 1933.
B8420
Preliminary Report on the Red Iron Ores of East Tennessee, Northeast Alabama, and Northwest Georgia. U. S. Geological Survey Bulletin, no. 540-G. Washington: Govt. Print. Off., 1914.
B8430
The Red Iron Ores of East Tennessee. Nashville: Brandon Print. Co., 1913.
B8440 (BC)
Iron Ore Outcrops of the Red Mountain Formation in Northeast Alabama. Prepared in cooperation with the U. S. Geological Survey. Special Report, 19. University: Alabama Geological Survey, 1947.
B8450 (ETSU)
Iron Ores, Fuels, and Fluxes of the Birmingham District, Alabama. With chapters on the origin of the ores by E. C. Eckel. U. S. Geological Survey Bulletin, no. 400. Washington: Govt. Print. Off., 1910.
B8460
Russellville Brown Iron Ore District, Franklin County, Alabama. With introduction and annotations by Hugh D. Pallister. Bulletin, 70. University: Alabama Geological Survey, 1960.
B8470 (ETSU)

Burchinal, Lee G. ed. Rural Youth in Crises: Facts, Myths, and Social Change. Prepared for the National Committee for Children and Youth. Washington: Welfare Administration, Office of Juvenile Delinquency and Youth Development, 1965. Twenty-seven readings on juvenile delinquency in Appalachia.
B8480

Bureau of Community Service Where Bluegrass and Mountains Meet: A Community Profile of Mt. Sterling and Montgomery County, Kentucky. "Kentucky Community Series," no. 18. Mimeographed. Lexington: Bureau of Community Service, College of Arts and Sciences, University of Kentucky, September 1, 1957.
B8490

Bureau of Cooperative Medicine Medical Care in Selected Areas of the Appalachian Bituminous Coal Fields. New York: The bureau, 1939.
B8500
Medical-Hospital Problems in the Bituminous Coal Mining Areas. American Medical Association: n.p., 1953.
B8510

Bureau of Municipal Research, New York County Government in Virginia. Report on a survey made for the governor and his Committee on Consolidation and Simplification, Jan., 1927. Richmond: D. Bottom, 1928. Includes Appalachian Counties.
B8520

Burford, Arthur E. Annual Field Trip of the Appalachian and Pittsburgh Geological Societies in the Great Valley in West Virginia. Sponsored by the West Virginia Geological and Economic Survey. Thomas Arkle, Jr., Chairman. Log of trip October 16-17, 1964. Morgantown, W. Va.: n.p., 1964?
B8530 (ETSU)

Burford, Roger L. Net Migration for Southern Counties, 1940-1950 and 1950-1960. Research Paper No. 24. Atlanta: Bureau of Business and Economic Research, Georgia State College, 1963.
B8540

Probability Projections of Rates of Net Migration for Southern Counties and Other Applications of Markov Chains. Louisiana Business Bulletin, Vol. 25, no. 1. Baton Rouge: Division of Research, College of Business Administration, Louisiana State University, 1966.
B8550

Burgan, John Long Discovery. New York: Farrar Strauss, 1950. Novel of strife in a small mining town in the Pennsylvania mountains during the 1930's.
B8560

Burges, George A Journal of a Surveying Trip into Western Pennsylvania under Andrew Ellicott in the Year 1795. Mount Pleasant, Mich.: John Cumming, 1965.
B8570 (BC)

Burgess, JoAnne Smith "A Study of the Media Center in the Individualized Instructional Program of Jefferson Elementary School in Kingsport, Tennessee." Master's thesis. East Tennessee State Univ., 1972.
B8580 (ETSU)

Burgess, Louis Virginia Soldiers of 1776. Reprint of 1929 ed. Vol. I and II, 1927, Richmond, Va.: Richmond Press; Vol. III, Spartanburg, S. C.: Reprint Co., 1973.
B8590

Burgner, Goldene F. comp. Kirchen Buch (Church Book) Register, 1815-1828. St. James Lutheran Church, Greene County, Tennessee. Greenville: The authors, 1964.
B8600

Burgner, Marion Keith Population Schedule of the United States Census of 1850 for Sullivan County, Tennessee. Knoxville: Clinchdale Press, 1963.
B8610 (ETSU)

Burk, E. H. Handbook of Smith County. Supplement to the Carthage Post. Carthage: Carthage Post, 1903. Promotional material, brief history and notes on prominent families.
B8620

Burke, Carmel E. "Geographic Factors Influencing the Development of Scott County, Tennessee." Master's thesis. Univ. of Tennessee, 1959.
B8630

Burke, Clyde T. photo. ed. Coleman, John Winston, Jr. ed. Kentucky: A Pictorial History. Lexington: Univ. of Kentucky Press, 1971.
C5780 (ASU)

Burke County, N. C. Board of Education Interdisciplinary Cultural Heritage Program. Supplemented by project addendum. Morganton, N. C.: n.p., 1968.
B8640 (WCU)

Supplement to Annotated Bibliography of Burke County Resource Materials, 1969. Morganton: Burke Co. Board of Education, 1969.
B8650 (ASU)

Burke, Fielding, pseud. see **Dargan, Olive Tilford**

Burke, James Lee To the Bright and Shining Sun. New York: Scribner, 1970. The book's plot centers around the 17-year-old hero, a third generation miner in the Cumberland Mountains of Kentucky.
B8660 (ASU LMC BC)

Burke, R. T. A. Higbee, Howard William Soil Survey, Huntingdon County, Pennsylvania. Washington: U. S. Department of Agriculture, Bureau of Plant Industry, Soils and Agricultural Engineering, 1944.
H5260

Burke, Richard Thomas Avon Soil Survey of Alleghany County, North Carolina. Washington: U. S. Govt. Print. Off., 1917. Good maps.
B8670 (ASU)

Soil Survey of Alleghany County. Washington: Govt. Print. Off., 1917.
B8680

Soil Survey of Washington County, Maryland. Prepared in cooperation with the Maryland Geological Survey and the Maryland Agricultural Experiment Station. Field Operations, 1917. Washington: U. S. Dept. of Agriculture, Bureau of Soils, 1923.
B8690

Soil Survey of Indiana County, Pennsylvania. In cooperation with Pennsylvania State College School of Agriculture and Experiment Station. Soil Survey Report, Series 1931, no. 27. Washington: U. S. Bureau of Chemistry and Soils, 1936.
B8700

Soil Survey of Limestone County, Alabama. Prepared in cooperation with Alabama. Field Operations, 1914. Washington: U. S. Dept. of Agriculture, Bureau of Soils, 1916.
B8710

Soil Survey of Madison County, Alabama. Prepared in cooperation with Alabama. Field Operations, 1911. Washington: U. S. Dept. of Agriculture, Bureau of Soils, 1913.
B8720

Soil Survey of Randolph County, Alabama. Soils Bureau Field Operations, 1911. Washington: Govt. Print. Off., 1912.
B8730

Soil Survey of Rockcastle County, Kentucky Field Operations, 1910. Washington: U. S. Dept. of Agriculture, Bureau of Soils, 1911.
B8740

Soil Survey of St. Clair County, Alabama. Prepared in cooperation with Alabama. Field Operations, 1917. Washington: U. S. Dept. of Agriculture, Bureau of Soils, 1920.
B8750

Hendrickson, Bertram Higbie Soil Survey of Tioga County, Pennsylvania. Washington: U. S. Department of Agriculture, Bureau of Chemistry and Soils, 1934.
H4610

Hendrickson, Bertram Higbie Soil Survey of Wyoming County, Pennsylvania. Washington: U. S. Department of Agriculture, Bureau of Chemistry and Soils, 1934.
H4620

Burke, William The Mineral Springs of Virginia. Richmond, Va.: Morris and Brother, 1851.
B8760

The Mineral Springs of Western Virginia: with Remarks on Their Use, and The Diseases to Which They are Applicable. Boston: Edward Morrill and Son, 1853. As the owner of Red Sulphur Springs, Dr. Burke gives this watering place more attention than others, but virtually all are noted.
B8770

Burkett, Elsie May Staples ed. Historical Review, Rockwood's Centennial Year, 1868-1968. Rockwood: Rockwood Times, 1968.
B8780

Burkhead, Homer Guest's Guide; Points of Interest in Cleveland. Cleveland: n.p., n.d.
B8790

Burleigh, William Grant Mac Day, Crusader; A Story of the Fight for Americanism. n.p.: n.p., 1925. Biography of a federal prohibition agent in West Virginia.
B8800 (BC)

The Man from Buchanan. n.p.: n.p., 1926. The life of Samuel R. Hurley of Buchanan County, a politician.
B8810

The Minstrel of the Mountains. Charleston, W. Va.: Kanawha Valley Pub. Co., 1913. A novel based on the life of John Falsome whose music was known throughout the coal fields of W. Va.
B8820 (BC)

Burleson, Berney ed. Johnson City, Tennessee. Science Hill High School To the Top with the Toppers; the History of Science Hill High School Football, 1920-1970, with Official Team and Individual Statistics. Johnson City: n.p., 1971.
J1550 (ETSU)

Burleson, David Sinclair History of the East Tennessee State College. n.p.: n.p., 1947.
B8830 (ETSU)

Burleson, McBerney East Tennessee State University Football Statistics, 1920-1970. East Tenn. State Univ. Library, Johnson City, Tenn., 1970.
B8840 (ETSU)

Burleson, McBerney comp. East Tennessee State University, Library East Tennessee State University Track and Field School Records, Together with ETSU Field Records for College Meets. Johnson City, Tenn.: East Tennessee State University, 1969-.
E400 (ETSU)

Burleson, Nell P. "The Evolution of Southern Appalachian Culture as Evidenced in Folklore." Master's thesis. East Tenn. State Univ., 1963.
B8850 (ETSU)

Burman, Ben Lucien Everywhere I Roam. Illustrated by Alice Caddy, 1st ed. Garden City, New York: Doubleday, 1949. Story of a mountain family who leave the hills and travel the world over to return disheartened.
B8860 (ASU WCU ETSU BC)

The Four Lives of Mundy Tolliver. New York: Julian Messner, 1953. Mundy leaves the mountains for war work but eventually comes home to Coal Creek, Kentucky.
B8870 (ASU WCU ETSU BC)

Rooster Crows for Day. Illustrated by Alice Caddy. New York: E. P. Dutton and Co., 1945. Kentucky mountain story about a wise foral.
B8880 (ETSU)

Burman, Linda C. The Technique and Variation in an American Fiddle Tune. The John Edwards Memorial Foundations, Inc. Univ. of Calif., Los Angeles, Calif., 1968.
B8890

Burmeister, Walter Frederick Appalachian Water: Maryland, Virginia, West Virginia, Kentucky, North Carolina, Tennessee, Alabama, Georgia, South Carolina, and Florida. 2 vols. Washington, D. C.: Canoe Cruisers Assoc., 1962.
B8900 (LMC)

Burnett, Frances Hodgson In Connection with The De Willoughby Claim. New York: Charles Scribner's Sons, 1899. Tom De Willoughby raises an abandoned child and encounters complications twenty years later.
B8910 (ASU WCU LMC ETSU BC)

Jarl's Daughter: and Other Novelettes. 1881. Reprint. Short Story Index Reprint Series. Freeport, N. Y.: Books for Libraries Press, 1969.
B8920 (ASU ETSU)

Louisiana. New York: Charles Scribner's Sons, 1880. A few days at a fashionable resort cause Louisiana Rogers to be dissatisfied with her mountain environment.
B8930 (ASU BC)

Louisiana. The Pretty Sister of Jose'. Illustrated. New York: C. Scribner's Sons, 1914.
B8940 (ASU LMC WCU)

Surly Tim, and Other Stories. New York: Armstrong, and Co., 1877. Short stories. Some with mountain settings.
B8950 (ASU BC)

Surly Tim, and Other Stories. New York: Charles Scribner's Son, 1905.
B8960 (WCU BC)

Burnett, Frances Hodgson
Surly Tim, and Other Stories. New York: C. Scribner's Sons, 1914.
B8970 (ASU LMC ETSU)

Burnett, Fred M. This Was My Valley. Illustrated by Kenneth Whitsett. Ridgecrest, N. C.: n.p., 1960. Memories of a Western North Carolina valley.
B8980 (ASU WCU LMC WWC UNCA)

Burnett, G. Lafayette Gap o' the Mountains. Knoxville: S. B. Newman, 1939. Thirty odd sketches of mountain life. Good anecdotes.
B8990

Burnett, James Jehu Sketches of Tennessee's Pioneer Baptist Preachers. vol. 1, series 1. Microfilm. Nashville: Marshall and Bruce Co., 1919.
B9000 (WCU)

Burnett, Swan M. The Over Mountain Men: Some Passages from a Page of Neglected History. Washington, D. C.: American Hist. Reg., 1895.
B9010

Burns, Amanda Fiddles in the Cumberlands. New York: Richard R. Smith, 1943. The Civil War diary of Amanda McDowell Burns.
B9020 (ASU BC)

Burns, Annie Walker Abstract of Pensions of North Carolina Soldiers of the Revolution, War of 1812, and Indian Wars. Washington: n.p., 1960.
B9030 (ASU)

Family History Records of Dr. Thomas Walker, First Explorer of Kentucky. Reprint with additions. n.p.: Privately published, n.d.
B9040

Estill County, Kentucky, Record of Abstracts of Pension Papers of Revolutionary Soldiers, War of 1812 and Indian Wars. . . . n.p.: n.p., n.d.
B9050

Hensley Family Records and Allied Families. Washington: n.p., 1965.
B9060

History Records of Harlan County, Kentucky, People. Washington: n.p., 1961.
B9070 (BC)

Memorial Records of Josh Bell County, Kentucky (Adjoining Historical Cumberland Gap, Tennessee), Family Bible Records Given to the United States Census Taken in 1870. Washington: n.p., 1960?
B9080 (BC)

United States Census of Bell County, Kentucky, 1880: Which are Family Bible Records as Given the Census Taker on That Date. Washington: n.p., 1961.
B9100 (BC)

United States Census of Bell Co., Ky., 1890. Washington: Census Bureau, 1961.
B9110

Virginia Genealogies and County Records. vols. I-VII. n.p.: n.p., 1941.
B9120

Burns, Annie Walker comp. Military and Genealogical Records of the Famous Indian Woman; Nancy Ward. . . . Washington, D. C.: n.p., 1957.
B9090

Burns, Inez E. History of Blount County, Tennessee, From War Trail to Landing Strip, 1795-1955. Sponsored by Mary Blount Chapter, D. AR. Maryville: Tenn. Historical Commission, 1957.
B9130 (ASU ETSU BC)

Burns, Inez E. comp. McCown, Mary Hardin Soldiers of the War of 1812 Buried in Tennessee. Johnson City, Tenn.: USD of 1812, 1959.
M670 (ASU)

Burns, J. C. and others Pastures and Grazing Systems for the Mountains of the Mountains of North Carolina. Agricultural Experiment Station Bulletin, no. 437. Raleigh: North Carolina State Univ., 1970.
B9150 (LMC)

Burns, James Anderson The Crucible, A Tale of the Kentucky Feuds. Oneida, Ky.: Oneida Institute, 1928.
B9140 (ASU LMC WWC BC)

Burns, William A. comp. Abstracts of Death and Obituary Notices Gathered from Herald-Tribune, Jonesboro, Tennessee. 4 vols. in 1. Phoenix, Ariz.: n.p., 1967-1973.
B9160 (ETSU)

Burock, Frank P. V. "A Study of the Need for Curricular Changes in Secondary Schools in an Economically Distressed Area of Pennsylvania." Ed. D. Diss. Pennsylvania State Univ., 1956.
B9170

Burrell, Robert G. Wild Water West Virginia: A Paddler's Guide to the White Water Rivers of the Mountain State. Parsons, W. Va.: McClain Print. Co., 1972.
B9180 (ASU BC)

Burrison, John A. "Georgia Jug Makers: A History of Southern Folk Pottery." Ph. D. Diss. University of Penn., 1973. Chapter five is a study of Northern Georgia. Hill and Mountain Potteries.
B9190

Burroughs, Wilbur Greeley The Geography of the Kentucky Knobs. Frankfort: Kentucky Geological Survey, 1926. Illustrated and with maps.
B9200 (BC)

Burt, B. Stanley Apple Handling and Packing in the Appalachian Area. U. S. Dept. of Agriculture Marketing Research Reports, 476. Washington: Agricultural Marketing Service, Transportation and Facilities Research Division, 1961.
B9210

Burt, Jesse Clifton Indians of the Southeast: Then and Now. Nashville: Abingdon Press, 1973. Prepared for the younger reader.
B9220 (BC)

Burt, Katharine Newlin Still Water. Philadelphia: Macrae-Smith Co., 1948. Novel of suspense with the foothills of the Smoky Mountains as background.
B9230 (ASU)

Burt, Struthers The Delectable Mountains. New York: Scribner's, 1927. Novel of southwestern Virginia in the Revolution.
B9240 (LMC ASU)

Burton, Carl D. Satan's Rock. New York: Appleton-Century-Crofts, 1954. Fiction. Young man obsessed with wild young girl who is subject of many local legends.
B9250 (LMC BC)

Burton, J. I. Community Relationships. n.p.: Wise County School Board, 1939. A community study of Norton, Wise County, Virginia.
B9260 (BC)

Burton, Janice H. "The Predictive Value of the Metropolitan Readiness Tests for First Grade Achievement for Selected Groups of Children in the Johnson City, Tennessee, Public Schools." Master's thesis. East Tenn. State Univ., 1971.
B9270 (ETSU)

Burton, Ray Berry "The Financing of Reconstruction in Tennessee." Master's thesis. Univ. of Pennsylvania, 1966.
B9280

Burton, Thomas G. ETSU Collection of Folklore; Folksongs. Johnson City, Tenn.: ETSU Press, 1967.
B9310 (LMC)

Burton, Thomas G. ed. Collection of Folklore: Folksongs. Musical notations and analysis by Annette Wolfaed. Monograph, no. 4. Johnson City: Institute of Regional Studies, East Tennessee State Univ., 1967.
B9290 (ASU LMC WCU ETSU BC)

Collection of Folklore: Folksongs II. Musical notations and analysis by Annette Wolfaed. Johnson City: Institute of Regional Studies, East Tennessee State Univ., 1969.
B9300 (ASU LMC ETSU BC)

A Collection of Folklore by Undergraduate Students of East Tennessee State University Johnson City: East Tennessee State Univ., 1966.
C5920 (ETSU ASU LMC BC)

Bush, Florence Lilian Bush, Isabel Graham Goose Creek Folks: A Story of the Kentucky Mountains. New York: Fleming H. Revell Co., 1912.
B9320 (ETSU BC)

Bush, Isabel Graham Goose Creek Folks: A Story of the Kentucky Mountains. New York: Fleming H. Revell Co., 1912. A story which cheerfuly concludes that mission schools cannot solve mountain problems.
B9320 (ETSU BC)

Bush, Michael E. James Folk Songs of Central West Virginia. vol. 1. Ravenswood, W. Va.: Custom Print. Co., 1969. Forty-four songs with guitar chords and notes.
B9330 (ASU WCU LMC BC)

Bushnell, David Ives, Jr. Evidence of Indian Occupancy in Albemarle County, Virginia. Washington: Smithsonian Inst., 1933.
B9340 (BC)

Tribal Migrations East of the Mississippi. Washington: Smithsonian Inst., 1934.
B9350 (ASU BC)

Bushnell, T. M. O'Neal, Alfred M., Jr. Soil Survey of Fayette County, Alabama. Washington: U. S. Department of Agriculture, Bureau of Soils, 1920.
O700

Bushong, Millard Kessler A History of Jefferson County, West Virginia. Charlestown, W. Va.: Jefferson Pub. Co., 1941.
B9360 (ASU BC)

Old Jube: A Biography of Jubat A. Early from West Point in the 1830's to the Battles of Chancellorsville, Lynchburg, Winchester, and a Wealth of Other Data on the Civil War. Boyce, Va.: C. J. Carrier, 1969.
B9370

Butler, Alan Stem, Thad, Jr. Senator Sam Ervin's Best Stories. Durham, N. C.: Moore Pub. Co., 1974.
S6950 (WCU BC ASU)

Butler, Bion H. Old Bethesda at the Head of Rockfish. Kingsport, Tenn.: n.p., 1933.
B9380 (LMC)

Butler, Donald C. "Analysis of the Values and Value Systems Reported by Students, The General Public, and Educators in a Selected Appalachian Public School District." Ph. D. Diss. Michigan State University, 1973. "Differences were noted between the values of the Appalachian culture and the values of the larger American society." Author also found significant differences between three test groups.
B9390

Butler, Lorine Letcher My Old Kentucky Home. Philadelphia: Dorrance and Co., 1929. Description and travel, and pictures on Kentucky. Much on Eastern Kentucky.
B9400 (BC)

Butler, Mann A History of the Commonwealth of Kentucky. 1834. Reprint. Berea, Ky.: Oscar Rucker, Jr., 1969. Good source for eastern Kentucky information pertaining to the early years.
B9410 (ASU LMC MHC WCU BC)

Butler, Ovid ed. Schenck, Carl Alvin The Biltmore Story: Recollections of the Beginning of Forestry in the United States. St. Paul: American Forest History Foundation, Minnesota Historical Society, 1955.
S880 (ASU WCU BC)

Butt, Herbert Bonser, Howard Jacob Selective Participation of Farmers and Their Wives in Rural Organization. Knoxville: Tennessee Agricultural Experiment Station, 1957.
B5380

Butterfield, Consul Willshire History of the Girty's Being a Concise Account of the Girty Brothers. Cincinnati: R. Clarke and Co., 1890. Biography of West Virginia's famous frontiersmen.
B9420 (BC)

Buttita, Anthony After the Good Gay Times: Asheville — Summer of '35; A Season with F. Scott Fitzgerald. New York: Viking, 1974. Focuses on events surrounding Fitzgerald's stay in Asheville, the society and city of Asheville, the literary world of North Carolina.
B9430

Button, Carl Lloyd "The Rhetoric of Immediacy: Baptist and Methodist Preaching on the Trans-Appalachian Frontier. Ph. D. Diss. Univ. of California, Los Angeles, 1972.
B9440 (ASU BC)

Buttrick, Daniel S. TSVLVKI SQCLVLV: A Cherokee Spelling Book. Knoxville: Heiskell and Brown, 1819.
B9450

Butts, Charles Burchard, Ernest Francis Iron Ores, Fuels, and Fluxes of the Birmingham District, Alabama. Washington: Govt. Print. Off., 1910.
B8460

Coals in the Area between Bon Air and Clifty, Tennessee. U. S. Geological Survey Bulletin, no. 641-k. Washington: Govt. Print. Off., 1917.
B9460

Fensters in the Cumberland Overthrust Block in Southwestern Virginia. Prepared in cooperation with the U. Geological Survey. Bulletin, 28. University: Virginia Geological Survey, 1927.
B9470 (ETSU)

Geology and Mineral Resources of the Crossville Quadrangle, Tennessee. Surveyed in cooperation with the U. S. Geological Survey. Bulletin, 33-D. Nashville: Tenn. Division of Geology, 1925.
B9480 (ETSU)

Geology and Oil Possibilities of the Northern Part of Overton County, Tennessee, and of Adjoining Parts of Clay, Pickett and Fentress Counties. Tenn. State Geological Survey Bulletin, 24. Nashville: Williams Print. Co., 1919.
B9490 (ETSU)

Geology of the Appalachian Valley in Virginia. Prepared in cooperation with the U. S. Geological Survey, Virginia Geological Society Bulletin, 52. 2 vols. Charlottesville: Univ. of Virginia, 1940.
B9500 (ETSU ASU)

Geologic Map of the Appalachian Valley of Virginia with Explanatory Text. Prepared in cooperation with the U. S. Geological Survey. Bulletin, 42. University: Virginia Geological Survey, 1933.
B9510 (ETSU)

Oil and Gas Possibilities at Early Grove, Scott County, Virginia. Charlottesville, Va.: Michie Co., 1927.
B9520 (ETSU)

Butts, Charles ed. International Geological Congress Southern Appalachian Region. Washington: The Congress; 16th Session, 1933.
I880

By the American Indian Historical Society Henry, Jeannette Textbooks and the American Indian. San Francisco: Indian Historian Press, 1970.
H4760 (MHC)

Byar, Thomas Madison "The Student Population in the Institutions of Higher Education in the Southern Appalachian Region, 1933-1958." Ed. D. Diss. Univ. of Tenn., 1959.
B9530 (BETSU)

Byars, Betsy The Summer of the Swans. New York: Viking Press, 1974. Sensitive story of a fourteen year old girl and her mentally retarded brother. Appalachian setting.
B9540

Byers, Tracy Martha Berry: The Sunday Lady of Possum Trot. New York: G. P. Putnam's Sons, 1932.
B9550 (ASU LMC WWC BC)

Martha Berry: The Sunday Lady of Possum Trot. New York: Putnam, 1934.
B9560 (LMC)

Byington, Robert H. ed. Goldstein, Kenneth S. Two Penny Ballads and Four Dollar Whiskey: A Pennsylvania Folklore Miscellany. Hatboro, Pa.: Folklore Associates, 1966.
G2370

Bynum, Curtis Marriage Bonds of Tryon and Lincoln Counties, North Carolina. Asheville: n.p., 1929.
B9570

Marriage Bonds of Tryon and Lincoln Counties, North Carolina. 2nd printing. n.p.: Catawba Co. Hist. Assn., and Lincoln Co. Hist. Assn., 1962.
B9590

Bynum, Curtis comp. Marriage Bonds of Tryon and Lincoln Counties, North Carolina. 1929. Reprint. Newton, N. C. and Lincoln, N. C.: Catawba County Historical Asso.; Lincoln County Historical Assoc., 1962.
B9580 (ASU)

Byrd, Huger Strickland Soil Survey, Oconee County, South Carolina. Soil Survey, Series 1958, no. 25. Washington: U. S. Department of Agriculture, Soil Conservation Service, 1963.
B9600

Soil Survey, Pickens County, South Carolina. Prepared in cooperation with the South Carolina Agricultural Experiment Station. Washington: U. S. Soil Conservation Service, 1972.
B9610

Byrd, William Histories of the Dividing Line Betwixt Virginia and North Carolina. New York: Dover Publications, 1967. Includes descriptions of the foothill counties of both states. Byrd had a very low opinion of the mountain men he encountered.
B9620 (BC FC)

Byrne, J. Holt Country Style: An Anthology of Hillbilly Humor. Charleston, W. Va.: J. Holt Byrne, 1970. Humorous sketches, stories, jokes, anecdotes etc.
B9630 (LMC)

Byrne, Michael Kunkin, Dorothy Appalachians in Cleveland. Cleveland: Institute of Urban Studies, 1972.
K3400 (LMC ASU)

Byrne, William Eston Randolph Tale of the Elk. Charleston: West Virginia Pub. Co., 1940. A story of the Elk Valley in West Virginia.
B9640

Caargill, Oscar Pollock, Thomas Clarke ed. Thomas Wolfe at Washington Square. New York: New York Univ. Press, 1954.
P3440 (WCU ASU)

Cabell, Margaret Couch Sketches and Recollections of Lynchburg, by the Oldest Inhabitant. Richmond: C. H. Wynne, 1858. A warm and rambling reminiscence of bygone days in Lynchburg.
C10 (ASU)

Cadden, Virginia Hinkins The Story of Strasburg. Strasburg: First National Bank, 1961. History of Strasburg with sketches of leading citizens and historic events.
C20 (ASU)

Cady, E. R. Wiebe, A. H. Waterfowl on the Tennessee River Impoundments. Norris, Tenn.: Tennessee Valley Authority, 1950.
W5960

Cain, James M. The Butterfly. 1st ed. New York: Alfred A. Knopf, 1947. A story of incest, fighting, shootings and degeneration in a coal camp on the Kentucky — West Virginia line.
C30 (ASU WCU LMC ETSU BC)

Cain, Stephen R. A Selective Description of a Knox County Mountain Neighborhood. Community Action in Appalachia, Unit 3. Lexington: Univ. of Kentucky, Center for Developmental Change, 1968.
C40

Cain, Stith Malone A History of Our Cain Family of Virginia, Alabama and Tennessee. Whitewater, Wis.: The author, 1970.
C50 (FC)

Caine, Thomas A. Soil Survey of the Wheeling Area, West Virginia. Prepared in cooperation with the West Virginia Geological Survey. Field Operations, 1906. Washington: U. S. Department of Agriculture, Bureau of Soils, 1908.
C70

Caine, Thomas A. and others Soil Survey of the Middlebourne Area, West Virginia. Prepared in cooperation with the West Virginia Geological Survey. Field operations, 1907. Washington: U. S. Department of Agriculture, Bureau of Soils, 1909.
C60

Cairns, John S. List of the Birds of Buncombe County, North Carolina. Weaverville, N. C.: n.p., 1891.
C80 (ASU LMC)

Caisse, Leroi De. Blue Ridge Magic and Other Poems. Asheville: Norman Press, 1960.
C90 (ASU)

Calarie, Edwin P. "A literature Survey of the Effects and Controls of Pneumoconiosis." Master's thesis West Virginia Univ., 1970.
C100

Caldwell, Erskine ed. Callahan, North Smoky Mountain Country. New York: Duell, Sloan and Pearce, 1952.
C320 (ASU WCU LMC ETSU BC)

Caldwell, James A. White, Alvin D. History of the Mount Prospect Graveyard and Cemetery, in Mount Pleasant Township, Washington County, Pennsylvania. Parsons, W. Va.: McClain Print. Co., 1972.
W5300

Caldwell, Janet Taylor There Was Time. New York: Charles Scribner's Sons, 1947. Story of young man trying to become rich in the mountains of Kentucky.
C110

Caldwell, Joshua William Joshua William Caldwell. A Memorial Volume, Containing His Biography, Writings and Addresses. Prepared and edited by a Committee of the Irving Club, Knoxville, Tenn. Nashville: Brandon Print. Co., 1909. Biography and tribute to a Knoxville pioneer, professional man, and author.
C120

Sketches of the Bench and Bar of Tennessee. Knoxville, Tenn.: Ogden Brothers and Co., 1898. Emphasis on East Tennessee. Caldwell was a resident of the Knoxville area.
C130 (ASU)

Caldwell, Kate Livingston Diary of Kate Livingston, 1859-1868. Nashville: WPA, 1938. Biography and county history of Hamblen County, Tennessee.
C140

Caldwell, Mary French Tennessee: The Dangerous Example; Watauga to 1849. Nashville: Aurora Publishers, 1974. In 1774 Lord Dunsmore, then colonial governor of Virginia warned King George III of the dangers inherent in allowing colonists to set up free, independent, and separate governments such as that currently existing in Watauga County. It was, he wrote, "a dangerous example" which might lead to other declarations of independence within the colonies. How fitting that Mary Caldwell's book has been published in time for our nation's bicentennial.
C150 (BC)

The Duck's Back: A Report on Certain Phases of the Socialistic Experiments Conducted by the Federal Government in Tennessee Valley. Nashville: The author, 1952. Author's thesis is that Roosevelt socialism is unlikely to have anymore effect on East Tennessee mountaineers than April showers on a duck's back. Delightful indictment of the TVA.
C160 (BC)

Caldwell, Ray Von The Genealogy of James Caldwell and his Descendants, 1750-1968: With the Intermarried Families of Campbell, Drum, Grice, Jones, Reep, Setzer, Styles, and Williams. Newton, N. C.: Epps Print. Co., 1968.
C170 (ASU)

Caldwell, Taylor The Balance Wheel. New York: Charles Scribner's Sons, 0u51.
C180 (ASU BC)

The Balance Wheel. New York: Pyramid, 1970. Novel of a family fortune built in the armaments trade. The setting is a fictitious town in Western Pennsylvania.
C190 (WCU)

There Was a Time. New York: Charles Scribner's Sons, 1947. Novel. Partially set in Appalachia. Hero tries to bring in an oil well in Eastern Kentucky; fails and returns to New York City.
C200 (ASU BC)

Caldwell, Taylor, pseud. see also Reback, Marcus and Reback, Janet Taylor Caldwell

Caldwell, Walter Coal Company Scrip. Fayetteville, Va.: n.p., 1969. An account of the economic stranglehold exerted over miners by forcing them to trade with the company store.
C210 (ASU)

Caldwell, Willie Walker Donald McElroy, Scotch Irishman. Philadelphia: George W. Jacobs and Co., 1918.
C220 (ASU BC)

Calendar of the Tennessee and King's Mountain Papers of the Draper Collection of the Manuscripts Madison: Wisconsin Hist. Soc., 1929. An account of the role of Tennessee in the American Revolution.
C230

Calfee, Mrs. Berkeley G. Confederate History of Culpepper County. Culpepper, Va.: The author, 1948. Culpepper County in the war between the states, together with a complete roster of the Confederate soldiers from this county.
C240

Calhoun, Harlan M. Twixt North and South. Franklin, W. Va.: McCoy Publishing Co., 1974. A history of the Civil War in Pendleton County, West Virginia.
C250 (ASU)

Calico, Forrest History of Garrard County, Kentucky, and Its Churches. New York: Hobson Book Press, 1947. Well-illustrated county history with emphasis on churches and founding families.
C260 (BC)

A Story of Four Churches and Reminiscences of Poosey Ridge in Madison County, Kentucky. New York: Hobson Book Press, 1946. Churches included are: Gilead Baptist, Cornith Christian, Friendship Church, and history of Salem Church; with Reminiscences of Poosey Ridge.
C270 (BC)

California, University, University at Los Angeles, Library The George Pullen Jackson Collection of Southern Hymnody: A Bibliography. Los Angeles: The library, 1964.
C280 (BC)

Callahan, James Morton History of West Virginia: Old and New, in One Volume. Chicago: American Historical Society, 1923. A concise history of the mountain states.
C290 (LMC BC)

Semi-Centennial History of West Virginia. With Special Articles on Development and Resources. Charleston, W. Va.: Semi-Centennial Commission, 1913.
C300 (ASU ETSU BC)

Callahan, North Daniel Morgan, Ranger of the Revolution. New York: Holt, Rinehart and Winston, 1961. Morgan was a noted frontiersman and explorer and a native, albeit untutored, military genius. His role in the revolution is given the attention it deserves in this volume. His home territory was the area around Winchester, Virginia.
C310 (BC)

Smoky Mountain Country. 1st. ed. American Folkways. New York: Duell, Sloan and Pearce, 1952.
C320 (ASU WCU LMC ETSU BC)

Calmeo, Neville Unto the Hills. A story of the Blue Ridge Mountains. New York: H. Revell Co., 1932. A flatland preacher moves to the Virginia mountains and learns to accept his flock and serve them.
C330

Calvert, William Jonathan, Jr. Saul. Nashville, Tenn.: Blue and Gray Press, 1973. A novel with a rural Alabama (the Anniston — Garlsden area) setting.
C340 (ASU)

Camak, David English Human Gold from Southern Hills, Not a Novel But a Romance of Facts. Greer, S. C.: n.p., 1960. Account of author's lifelong struggle to educate the mountain youths, he found in the mill towns. Included reminiscences of Spartanburg Junior College.
C350 (BC)

June of the Hills: The Junaluska Prize Novel, a Story of the Southern Mountains with Lake Junaluska, N. C., as the Center of Action. Waynesville, N. C.: n.p., 1927. Moralistic fiction from the Carolina Mountains.
C360 (ASU WCU LMC BC)

Cambiaire, Celestin Pierre East Tennessee and Western Virginia Mountain Ballads (The Last Stand of American Pioneer Civilization). London: Mitre Press, 1934.
C370 (ASU BC)

Camblos, Ruth Shopping Round the Mountains. Asheville: The authors, 1972. A guide to tourist spots, outlets, crafts and other things to see and do in Western North Carolina.
C380

Cameron, Eugene Nathan Feldspar Deposits of the Bryson City District, North Carolina. Prepared by Geological Survey, U. S. Department of the Interior, in cooperation with the North Carolina Department of Conservation and Development. Bulletin, No. 62. Raleigh, N. C.: n.p., 1951.
C390 (ASU WCU)

Cameron, John D. Glimpses of a Land of Beauty. Asheville: Cameron and Cushman, n.d. Promotional material in the tourist trade in the Asheville area.
C400

Cameron, Viola Root comp. Emigrants from Scotland to America, 1774-1775. Copied from a Loose Bundle of Treasury Papers in the Public Record Office, London, England. Baltimore: Genealogical Pub. Co., 1965.
C410 (ASU)

Camp, Anthony J. Tracing Your Ancestors. Toyle's Handbook. London: W. and G. Foyle, 1964. A handy how-to book for genealogists.
C420 (ASU)

Camp, Cordelia David Lowry Swain, Governor and University President. Asheville, N. C.: Stephens Press, 1963. Biography of a Western North Carolina statesman, politician, and governor of North Carolina. Contains genealogical and historical sketches.
C430 (ASU WCU LMC)

Governor Vance: A Life for Young People. Asheville, N. C.: Stephens Press, 1961. Biography of North Carolina's only governor from the western, mountainous, part of the state prior to 1973.
C440 (ASU WCU WWC)

Governor Vance, a Life for Young People. Asheville, N. C.: Stephens Press, 1964?.
C450 (LMC)

The Influences of Geography Upon Early North Carolina. Raleigh, N. C.: Carolina Charter Tercentenary Commission, 1963. Explains the role of geography in the settlement, economy, and politics of Western North Carolina.
C460 (ASU LMC WWC)

The Settlement of North Carolina. Cullowhee, N. C. Cordelia Camp, 1942. Describes the settlements of the various regions of North Carolina.
C470 (ASU BC)

Sketches of Burke County. n.p.: n.p., 1954. Historical and biographical sketches of Burke County, North Carolina.
C480 (ASU)

Sketches of Burke County. Morganton: News-Herald, 1954.
C490

The Thought at Midnight: The Story of the Asheville Normal. Asheville, N. C.: The author, 1968. Story of the founding and subsequent years of the Asheville Normal School.
C500 (LMC)

Camp, Wallace Jefferson Soil Survey, Spartanburg County, South Carolina. Washington: U. S. Soil Conservation Service, 1968.
C510

Campbell, Carlos Clinton Birth of a National Park in the Great Smoky Mountains: An Unprecedented Crusade which Created, as a Gift of the People, the Nation's Most Popular Park. Knoxville: Univ. of Tennessee Press, 1960. Description of the enormous efforts of many people from 1920 to 1940 to create the park.
C520 (ASU ETSU WCU MHC WWC BC)

Birth of a National Park in the Great Smoky Mountains; an Unprecedented Crusade Which Created, as a Gift of the People, the Nation's Most Popular Park. rev. ed. Knoxville: Univ. of Tennessee Press, 1970.
C530

Great Smoky Mountains Wildflowers. Enlarged ed. Knoxville: Univ. of Tennessee Press, 1964.
C550 (ASU LMC WCU WWC BC)

Great Smoky Mountains Wildflowers. 3rd ed. Knoxville: Univ. of Tennessee Press, 1970. 175 full color plates with flowers so natural they seem to be alive.
C560 (ETSU BC)

Campbell, Carlos Clinton and others Great Smoky Mountains Wildflowers. Knoxville: Univ. of Tennessee Press, 1962.
C540 (LMC WCU ETSU)

Campbell County, Tenn., 1830 Census n.p.: n.p., n.d. Census data for Campbell County, Tennessee.
C561

Campbell, Evelyn Survival. New York: L. MacVeagh, Dial Press, 1928. Novel. Heroine runs from the horror of a murder trial to the serenity of the Black Mountains of North Carolina seeking peace and renewal. Her involvement with the local people helps to lead her back to life and happiness.
C570 (BC)

Campbell, Floyd Oren "An Examination of the Leisure Activities and Recreational Interests of Students, and Available Equipment and Facilities at Appalachian State Teachers College." Master's thesis. Appalachian State Teachers College, 1957.
C580 (ASU)

Campbell, Harry Modean Elizabeth Madox Roberts, American Novelist. Norman: Univ. of Oklahoma Press, 1956. A critical survey of the life and works of one of Kentucky's greatest novelists.
C590 (BC)

Campbell, J. E. Managing 10,000 Miles of Shoreline. Address Before Knoxville (Tennessee) Technical Society, August 30, 1954. Knoxville, Tennessee: TVA, 1954. This address summarizes the use and administration of reservoir shoreline property and property rights including the land and land rights involved in recreation use and development.
C670

Campbell, James B. "Some Social and Economic Phases of Reconstruction in East Tennessee, 1864-1869." Master's thesis. Univ. of Tennessee, 1946.
C600

Campbell, John Charles From Mountain Cabin to Cotton Mill. Washington: National Child Labor Committee, 1913. Pamphlet. Deals with migration from the mountains to the textile mills that dot the foothill country.
C610

Future of the Church and Independent Schools in Our Southern Highlands. New York: Russell Sage Foundation, 1917. A tract urging support for the more than 200 mountain mission schools supported by 13 denominations in the upland South.
C620 (BC)

The Future of the Church and Independent Schools in our Southern Highlands. New York: Russell Sage Foundation, 1917. Authorized facsimile made by Xerox University Microfilms, Ann Arbor, Michigan, 1975.
C630 (ASU)

Campbell, John Charles
The Southern Highlander and His Homeland. New York: Russell Sage Foundation, 1921. One of the classic works on the Southern Mountains.
C640 (ASU ETSU WWC BC)
The Southern Highlander and His Homeland. Foreword by Rupert B. Vance and an introduction by Henry D. Shapiro, 1921. Reprint. Lexington, Kentucky: Univ. Press, 1969.
C650 (LMC MHC WCU FC)
The Southern Highlander and His Homeland. Spartanburg, S. C.: The Reprint Co., 1973.
C660

Campbell, John Gregorson Superstitions of the Highlands and Islands of Scotland. Xerographic Copy. Cleveland, Ohio: Bell and Howell Co., 1974.
C680

Campbell, Libb Marsh Swing Old Adam. Philadelphia: Dorrance and Co., 1965. Milltown is a mountain community of some two hundred families clustered around a sawmill in the Appalachians. Births, deaths, courtships, weddings, parties, accidents, fights and killings, all play their part in the lives of the mountain people.
C690

Campbell, Lillian Smart "An Individualized Reading Program for Students in Grades 4-7 at Hayter's Gap Elementary School, Fall 1970." Master's thesis. East Tennessee State Univ., 1970.
C700 (ETSU)

Campbell, Marie Cloud-walking. With a Foreword by Olive V. Keliher. Illustrated by John A. Spilman, III. New York: Farrar and Rinehart, 1942.
C710 (ASU WWC BC)
Cloud-walking. 1960. Reprint. Bloomington: Indiana Univ. Press, 1971.
C720 (LMC ETSU WCU BC)
Folks Do Get Born. New York: Rinehart, 1946. Stories of Midwifery in the South.
C730 (BC)
Tales from the Cloud Walking Country. Illustrated by Clare Leighton. Bloomington: Indiana Univ. Press, 1958. Lonely stories and sketches in authentic dialect.
C740 (ASU WCU LMC MHC ETSU BC)

Campbell, Marius Robinson Character of Coal in the Thomas Bed near Harrison, West Virginia. U. S. Geological Survey Bulletin, no. 716-H. Washington: Govt. Print. Off., 1921.
C750
Geology of the Big Stone Gap Coal Field of Virginia and Kentucky. U. S. Geological Survey Bulletin, no. 111. Washington: Govt. Print. Off., 1893.
C760 (BC)

Campbell, Marius Robinson and others The Valley Coal Fields of Virginia. Prepared in cooperation with the U. S. Geological Survey. Virginia Geological Survey Bulletin, 25. Charlottesville: Univ. of Virginia, 1925.
C770 (ETSU)

Campbell, Mary Emily R. The Attitude of Tennesseans toward the Union. -. New York: Vantage Press, 1961
C780 (BC ASU)
Tennessee and the Union, 1847-1861. Ph. D. Diss. Vanderbilt Univ. 1937.
C790
"Tennessee's Attitude toward Secession." Master's thesis. Vanderbilt Univ. 1929.
C800

Campbell, Merrill G. Directions for Education Development in Appalachia: Report of an Educational Need and Feasibility Study Involving the Appalachian Areas of Six States. Charleston, W. Va.: Appalachia Educational Laboratory, 1971.
C810 (BC ASU)

Campbell, Olive Arnold Dame Adjustment to Rural Industrial Change with Special Reference to Mountain Areas. Washington: National Education Association, 1929.
C820
English Folk Songs from the Southern Appalachians, Comprising 122 Songs and Ballads, and 323 Tunes. With an introduction and notes. New York: G. P. Putnam's Sons, 1917.
C830 (ASU LMC WWC BC)
The Life and Work of John Charles Campbell, September 15, 1868-May 2, 1919. Madison, Wisc.: College Print. and Typing Co., 1968. Biography of one of Appalachia's foremost authors and educators. His THE SOUTHERN HIGHLANDER AND HIS HOMELAND is a mountain classic.
C840 (WWC BC)
The Southern Highlands: A selected Bibliography. New York: Russell Sage Foundation Library, 1920. This Bibliography is part of that which Mrs. Campbell included in the edition of her husband's work, The Southern Highlander and His Homeland.
C850
Southern Mountain Schools Maintained by Denominational and Independent Agencies. New York: Russell Sage Foundation, 1929. A plea for support of the various mountain mission schools.
C870

Campbell, Olive Arnold Dame comp. Southern Highland Schools Maintained by Denominational and Independent Agencies. New York: Russell Sage Foundation, 1921. Authorized facsimile made by Xerox University Microfilms, Ann Arbor, Michigan, 1975.
C860 (ASU)

Campbell, Robert Alvord Farm Woodland Management in Southern Appalachians, 8-Year Summary. U. S. Forest Service Station Paper, no. 41. Asheville, N. C.: Southeastern Forest Experiment Station, 1954.
C880
Forest Service Log Grades for Southern Pine. U. S. Forest Service Research Paper, SE-11. Asheville, N. C.: Southeastern Forest Experiment Station, 1964.
C890 (WCU)
A Guide to Grading Features in Southern Pine Logs and Trees. U. S. Forest Service Station Paper, no. 156. Asheville, N. C.: Southeastern Forest Experiment Station, 1962.
C900 (WCU)
Ten Years of Experimental Farm Woodland Management in the Southern Appalachians. U. S. Forest Service Station Paper no. 83. Asheville, N. C.: Southeastern Forest Experiment Station, 1957.
C910 (WCU)
Tree Grades Give Accurate Estimate of Second-Growth Yellow Poplar Values. U. S. Forest Service Station Paper, no. 108. Asheville, N. C.: Southeastern Forest Experiment Station, 1959.
C920 (WCU)

Campbell, Robert F. "A Classification of Mountain Whites." n.p., A Pamphlet reprinted from The Southern Workman, 1901.
C930
Mission Work among the Mountain Whites in Asheville Presbytery, North Carolina. Asheville, N. C.: Citizen Co., 1899.
C940 (BC)

Campbell, Thomas Corwith Freight Rates of West Virginia Wood Products. West Virginia Department of Commerce Economic Development Series, no. 5. West Virginia Univ. Bulletin Series 65, no. 10-11. Morgantown: n.p., 1965.
C950 (ASU)

Campbell, Thomas Jefferson Records of Rhea: A Condensed County History. Dayton, Tenn: Rhea Pub. Co., 1940. Includes account of the famous "monkey" trial.
C960 (ASU BC)
The Upper Tennessee. Chattanooga, Tenn.: The author, 1932. Pen and camera pictures with text describing life and travel on the Tennessee over a 150 year period.
C970 (BC)

Campbell, Will D. Up to Our Steeples in Politics. New York: Paulist Press, 1970. Author laments political involvement of the Church in Appalachia. Says mission of church is "to be" and not "to do."
C990 (WCU BC)

Campbell, Will D. comp. The Failure and the Hope: Essays of Southern Churchmen. Grand Rapids, Mich.: Eerdmans, 1972. A collection of essays on the role of the church in the South. Some attention given to Appalachia.
C980 (WCU ASU BC)

Camping on Mount Mitchell: Information Regarding Good Places for Summer Camps in United States Forests in North Carolina n.p.: Issued by the Southern Railway, 1916.
C1000 (BC)

Cams, W. P., Jr. The Smokeless Coal Fields of West Virginia. Morgantown: West Virginia Univ. 1963. A study of anthracite mines in West Virginia.
C1010 (LMC)

Canaday, Julie Big End of the Horn. Washington: Vantage, 1906.
C1020 (LMC)

Canfield, Clifford R. The Copenhaver Family of Wythe County. Pasadena, Calif.: Privately printed. . Also includes notes on Capp, Neff, Kegley and Leedy families.
C1030
The Descendants of Joseph Samson Hounshell and Mandana Hedrick. Pasadena, Calif., n.p., 1955.
C1040
The Hounshell Family of Southwest Virginia. Frankfurt, Germany. Privately printed. Also includes notes on Lambert and Messersmith families. Replaces and updates and enlarges descendants of Joseph Samson Hounshell and Mandana Hedrick, 1955 by Canfield.
C1050
Rosenbaum Family. Frankfurt, Germany: n.p., 1963.
C1060
Rosenbaum-Rosenbalm Family of Southwest Virginia. Frankfurt, Germany: Privately printed. Also includes notes on Bauman, Rosseler, Sommer, Dill, (Thill), Conradt, Sprecher (Spraker), Copenhaver, Phillippi, Eichelberger and Fox families.
C1070

Cann, Marion Stuart On Skidd's Branch, a Tale of the Kentucky Mountains. Xerox Copy of the Original. Scranton, Pa.: Republican Job Rooms, 1884. A novel of a struggle between a miller/moonshiner and a young revenuer who loves the miller's daughter. Naturally, love and right triumph.
C1080 (ASU BC)

Cannon, Brenda, pseud. see **Moore, Bertha Bella**

Cannon, Elizabeth Rob ed. Vance, Zebulon Baird My Beloved Zebulon; the Correspondence of Zebulon B. Vance and Harriett Newell Espy. Chapel Hill: Univ. of North Carolina Press, 1971.
V100

Cannon, Elizabeth Roberts ed. My Beloved Zebulon. The correspondence of Zebulon Baird Vance and Harriett Neivell Espy. With an introduction by Frances Gray Patton. Chapel Hill: Univ. of North Carolina Press, 1971. Vance was our first Western North Carolina governor.
C1090 (ASU)

Cannon, LeGrand, Jr. Look to the Mountain. New York: Holt, 1942. Long novel about pioneering in the New Hampshire Grants from 1769 to 1777. The chief characters are a young bride and groom who left the settlements to make their home in the wilderness of the Northern Appalachians.
C1100 (LMC)

Cansler, Charles W. Three Generations: The Story of a Colored Family of Eastern Tennessee. Kingsport, Tenn.: Kingsport Press, 1939.
C1110 (ASU LMC BC)

Cantrell, Clyde Hull Southern Literary Culture: A Bibliography of Master's and Doctor's Theses. University: Univ. of Alabama Press, 1955. Lists many Appalachian sources.
C1120 (ASU LMC)

Cantrell, L. Winston, Robert A. Soil Survey of Tuscaloosa County, Alabama. Washington: U. S. Department of Agriculture, Bureau of Soils, 1912.
W7820

Cantrell, Llano Soil Survey of Chilton County, Alabama. Prepared in cooperation with Alabama. Field Operations, 1911. Washington: U. S. Department of Agriculture, Bureau of Soils, 1913.
C1130

Cantrell, Roy My Friends, the Cherokees. Cherokee, N. C.: Howineetah Publications, 1973.
C1140 (MHC)

Canyus, Lucy Josephine The History of Bartow County, Formerly Cass. Cartersville, Ga.: Tribune Pub. Co., 1933. This county changed names after the Civil War because Cass was from Michigan and therefore unfit to have a Georgia county named for him.
C1150 (ASU)

Capers, Henry Dickson The Life and Times of C. G. Memmings. Richmond: Everett Waddey Co., 1893. Biography of a South Carolina Governor who participated in the Blue Ridge Railroad venture.
C1160 (ETSU)

Caperton, Helena L. Legends of Virginia. Richmond: Garrett and Massie, 1931. Legends from Western Virginia.
C1170 (LMC)

Capitalizing on New Development Opportunities along the Baltimore-Cincinnati Appalachian Development Highway: A Staff Recommendation. Washington: Appalachian Regional Commission, n.d. The planners dream of future development along the highway. Little relevance to the people who live there.
C1180

Cappon, Lester Jesse Bibliography of Virginia History Since 1865. Charlottesville: Univ. of Virginia Institute for Research in the Social Sciences, 1930. Marvelous research tool for Western Virginia items.
C1190 (BC FC)

Capps, Claudius Meade Indian Legends and Poems. Dalton, Ga.: A. J. Showalter Co., 1932. Legends of the Cherokee, especially those in the North Georgia and East Tennessee region.
C1200 (ASU)

Carawan, Candie Carawan, Guy Voices from the Mountain. New York: Alfred A. Knopf, 1975.
C1210 (ASU)

Carawan, Guy Voices from the Mountain. New York: Alfred A. Knopf, 1975. This is a fine collection of words, songs, and photographs representing the constant struggle for sustenance, dignity and life that is Appalachia today.
C1210 (ASU)

Carbert, Leslie E. The Impact of State and Local Taxes in North Carolina and the Southeastern States. Raleigh: N. C. Tax Commission, 1956.
C1220 (LMC)

Carden, H. B. Peters, J. T. History of Fayette County, West Virginia. Charleston, W. Va.: Jarrett Print. Co., 1926.
P2310 (ASU)

Carder, Roscoe H. "History of Education in Jackson County, Kentucky." Master's thesis. Univ. of Kentucky, 1937.
C1230

Cardwell, Dudley H. The Newburg of West Virginia. Morgantown: West Virginia Geological and Economic Survey, 1971.
C1240

Carey, Faris Jane Exploring the Mountains of North Carolina. Raleigh, N. C.: Provincial Press, 1972.
C1250 (MHC)

Carleton, David A. "The Economic Geography of the State Industry in Eastern Pennsylvania." Master's thesis. Pennsylvania State College, 1951.
C1260

Carlisle, George William Frederick Howard Travels in America. The Poetry of Pope. Two Lectures Delivered to the Leeds Mechanics' Institution and Literary Society, December 5th and 6th, 1850. New York: G. P. Putnam, 1851. This English gentleman saw no more of Appalachia than White Sulphur Springs.
C1270

Carlisle, Laura Mae comp. Huffard, Grace Thompson comp. My Poetry Book. New York: Holt, Rinehart and Winston, 1956.
H8010 (ASU)

Carlston, Charles William Ground-water Resources of Monongalia County, West Virginia. Prepared by the U. S. Geological Survey in cooperation with the West Virginia Geological and Economic Survey. Bulletin, no. 15. Morgantown: West Virginia Geological and Economic Survey, 1958.
C1280 (ETSU)

Carmer, Carl Lamson Stars Fell on Alabama. New York: Farrar and Rinehart, 1934. Includes account of the author's experiences in Northern Alabama. The author's brief story in this state made an indelible impression on him.
C1290 (BC)

Carnathan, Ralph D. Experiment in Regional Federalism: Implementation of the Appalachian Regional Development Act of 1965 in Georgia, North Carolina, and Tennessee. Ph.D. Diss. University of Tennessee, 1973. History of the Appalachian Regional Development Act, its Administration and Implementation in each of the Three States.
C1300

Carnes, Douglas Status of West Virginia in the Economic Opportunity Program under Public Law 88-452. Charleston: n.p., 1966.
C1310

Carolina Comments vol. 1- 1952-. Raleigh, N. C.: State Department of Archives and History, bimonthly. Each issue generally includes some Western North Carolina Material.
C1320 (ASU)

Carolina Mountaineer The 1916 Pictorial Story of Haywood County. Reprint of a special industrial and resort edition of the Carolina Mountaineer. Waynesville, N. C.: Haywood County Historical Society, n.d.
C1330 (WCU)

Carothers, J. Edward Keepers of the Poor. Cincinnati, Ohio: Joint Commission on Education and Cultivation, Board of Missions of the Methodist Church, 1966.
C1340 (ASU LMC)

Carpenter, Allen North Carolina from Its Glorious Past to the Present. Chicago: Childrens Press, 1965. Children's book of North Carolina history. Profusely illustrated, Section on Appalachia.
C1350 (ASU)

Carpenter, Clarence A. The Best from Almar Farm in Western North Carolina. Illustrated by Constance M. Green. Raleigh, N. C.: The author, 1969.
C1360 (LMC ASU)

Carpenter, E. F. Mountain Lyrics and Sketches. n.p.: n.p., 1940. A poem to the Appalachian Mountains.
C1370 (WCU)

Carpenter, Hugh King's Mountain, an Epic of Revolution: With Historical and Biographical Sketches, and Illustrations. Knoxville: The author, 1936.
C1380 (BC)

Carpenter, J. Raymond Johnson, Hugh A. Exurban Development in Selected Areas of the Appalachian Mountains. Washington: Govt. Print. Off., 1963.
J1790

Carpenter, Mrs. V. K. Seventh Census of the United States, 1850: Fentress County, Tennessee, Free Population Schedules. Fort Worth, Texas: Miran Publishers, 1969.
C1390 (ASU)

Seventh Census of the United States, 1850: Franklin County, Tennessee, Free Population Schedules. Huntsville, Ala.: Century Enterprises, 1970.
C1400 (ASU)

Carpenter, William Henry Arthur, Timothy Shay The History of Kentucky, from Its Earliest Settlement to the Present Time. Philadelphia: Lippincott, Grambo & Co., 1852.
A5020 (BC WCU)

History of Tennessee. Philadelphia: Remsen and Haffelfinger, 1868. Contains a great deal of information on Eastern Tennessee.
C1410

Carr, Howard Ernest Washington College: A Study of an Attempt to Provide Higher Education in Eastern Tennessee. Knoxville: S. B. Newman and Co., 1935. Washington College is reputed to be the second oldest college west of the mountains.
C1420 (ETSU BC)

Carr, Jess The Saint of the Wilderness. Radford, Va.: Commonwealth Press, 1974. A biographical novel depicting the life and works of Robert Sayers Sheffey, Appalachian Minister
C1430 (ASU)

The Second Oldest Profession: An Informal History of Moonshining in America. Englewood Cliffs, N. J.: Prentice-Hall, 1972. Most instances cited are from the Appalachians, particularly Western Virginia.
C1440 (ASU BC)

Carr, Larry Douglas "The Changing Economic Position of Southwest Virginia as Affected by the Coal Industry." Master's thesis. East Tennessee State Univ., 1968.
C1450 (ETSU)

Carr, Maria Graham My Recollections of Rocktown, Now Known as Harrisonburg. Harrisonburg, Va.: F. Stoner, 1959. A touching, personal recollection of the early days of Harrisonburg, Virginia.
C1460 (ASU BC)

Carroll, Bartholomew Rivers ed. Historical Collections of South Carolina. Embracing many rare and valuable pamphlets and other documents, relating to the history of that state from its first discovery to its independence, in the year 1776. 2 vols. New York: Harper and Brothers, 1836.
C1470 (ASU)

Carroll, Dorothy Sedimentary Studies in the Middle River Drainage Basin of the Shenandoah Valley of Virginia. U. S. Geological Survey Professional Paper, no. 314-F. Shorter Contributions to General Geology, 1957. Washington: Govt. Print. Off., 1959.
C1480 (ASU)

Carroll, Latrobe Carroll, Ruth Robinson Beanie. New York: H. Z. Walck, 1953.
C1510 (ASU WWC BC)

Carroll, Ruth Robinson The Christmas Kitten. New York: H. Z. Walck, 1970.
C1520 (MHC)

Carroll, Ruth Robinson The Picnic Bear. New York: H. Z. Walck, 1966.
C1550 (ASU)

Carroll, Ruth Robinson Runaway Pony. New York: H. Z. Walck, 1963.
C1560 (ASU MHC BC)

Carroll, Ruth Robinson Tough Enough. New York: H. Z. Walck, 1954.
C1570 (ASU MHC WWC BC)

Carroll, Ruth Robinson Tough Enough and Sassy. New York: H. Z. Walck, 1958.
C1580 (ASU LMC BC)

Carroll, Ruth Robinson Tough Enough's Indians. n.p.: H. Z. Walck, 1960.
C1590 (ASU LMC ETSU)

Carroll, Ruth Robinson Tough Enough's Pony. New York: H. Z. Walck, 1957.
C1600 (ASU MHC LMC BC)

Carroll, Ruth Robinson Tough Enough's Trip. New York: H. Z. Walck, 1956.
C1610 (ASU MHC LMC BC)

Carroll, Ruth Robinson Tough Enough's Trip. New York: Oxford Univ., 1956.
C1620 (WWC)

Carroll, Otis Ward "Industrial Waste and Human Sewage Pollution within the New River Drainage Basin of Watauga County." Master's thesis. Appalachian State Teachers College, 1964.
C1490 (ASU)

Carroll, Richard R. Structure of Employment in the Area Development Districts of Kentucky, 1960-1970: Analysis and Implications. Ph.D. Diss. University of Kentucky, 1973. Studies find that agriculture and mining are declining, and importance of manufacturing is growing.
C1500

Carroll, Ruth Robinson Beanie. New York: H. Z. Walck, 1953. A Children's story of a too-clever dog in the Western North Carolina Mountains.
C1510 (ASU WWC BC)

The Christmas Kitten. New York: H. Z. Walck, 1970. Western North Carolina is the setting for this story of a Christmas gift.
C1520 (MHC)

From the Appalachians: A Portfolio of Drawings and Paintings. New York: H. Z. Walck, 1964. A folio of mountain drawings and paintings.
C1530 (ASU BC)

Peanut. New York: Oxford Pa.: . Children's Story with a Western North Carolina setting.
C1540

The Picnic Bear. New York: H. Z. Walck, 1966. There's a mountain setting for this children's story about a hungry bear.
C1550 (ASU)

Runaway Pony. New York: H. Z. Walck, 1963. Children's story with a Western North Carolina setting.
C1560 (ASU MHC BC)

Tough Enough. New York: H. Z. Walck, 1954. Mountain setting; animal story.
C1570 (ASU MHC WWC BC)

Tough Enough and Sassy. New York: H. Z. Walck, 1958. Mountain setting; animal story.
C1580 (ASU LMC BC)

Tough Enough's Indians. n.p.: H. Z. Walck, 1960. A dog story for children, set in the Smoky Mountains of North Carolina and Tennessee.
C1590 (ASU LMC ETSU)

Tough Enough's Pony. New York: H. Z. Walck, 1957. A Smoky Mountain setting; pony story.
C1600 (ASU MHC LMC BC)

Tough Enough's Trip. New York: H. Z. Walck, 1956. A Smoky Mountain setting; dog story.
C1610 (ASU MHC LMC BC)

Tough Enough's Trip. New York: Oxford Univ., 1956. A Smoky Mountain setting; dog story.
C1620 (WWC)

Carroll, William M. "Marketing Forest Products in Pennsylvania; a study of Marketing Practices and Pricing Processes at the Farm level for Forest Products in Pennsylvania 1949-1951." Master's thesis. Penn. State College, 1951.
C1630

Carron, Elizabeth Clifton Forge, Virginia. n.p., n.p., n.d.
C1640

Carson and Newman College, Jefferson City, Tenn. An Educational Study of Jefferson County, Tennessee. Made co-operatively by faculty members of Carson-Newman College, County superintendent of instruction, Principals of county schools, school year, 1934-35. Jefferson City: The college book store, 1936.
C1650

Carson-Newman College see **Carson and Newman College, Jefferson City, Tenn.**

Carter, Clyde Cass "Administrations of John Sevier." Master's thesis. Vanderbilt Univ., 1928. Sevier was governor of Tennessee and the state of Franklin.
C1660

Carter County, Tenn., 1830 Census n.p.: n.p., n.d. Census data for Carter County, Tennessee.
C1661

Carter, David Wendel Carter of Tennessee, Including the Taylors: Descendants of Colonel John Carter of Tennessee. Pamphlet ed. Chattanooga: Lookout Pub. Co., 1927.
C1670 (ETSU)

Carter, Ethel Mae Eylar Appell, Darlene Skillern Family History and Genealogy. n.p.: N.P., .
A4510

Carter, Everett C. The Impact of Highway Beautification on the Outdoor Advertising Industry in West Virginia. Sponsored by the West Virginia State Road Commission and the U. S. Department of Transportation, Federal Highway Administration, Bureau of Public Roads. State Road Commission Report, no. 22. Morgantown: West Virginia Univ. Engineering Experiment Station, 1967.
C1680

Carter, Herbert The Boy Scouts in the Blue Ridge: Or Marooned Among the Moonshiners. New York: A. L. Burt Co., 1913. A stirring tale of young men adventuring among the moonshiners of the Blue Ridge.
C1690 (ASU LMC BC)

Carter, James Health and Nutrition in Disadvantage Children. Nashville: Vanderbilt Univ., 1970. Includes references to Appalachian children.
C1700

Carter, John Benjamin Soil Survey, Rappahannock County, Virginia. Field Survey by C. S. Coleman and others. Soil Survey, Series 1958, no. 11. Washington: U. S. Dept. of Agriculture, Soil Conservation Service, 1961.
C1710

Carter, M. Devereux Wood, Gordon H., Jr. Systematic Jointing in Western Part of Anthracite Region of Eastern Pennsylvania. Washington: U. S. Geological Survey, 1969.
W8510

Carter, Mary Nelson North Carolina Sketches: Phases of Life Where the Galax Grows. Chicago: A. C. McClurg and Co., 1900. Seventeen sketches of North Carolina mountaineers. Well done.
C1720 (ASU WCU LMC BC)

Carter, Oliver Reuben Soil Survey, Chambers County, Alabama. Soils surveyed by O. R. Carter and others. Correlation by I. L. Martin. Soil Survey, Series 1956, no. 3. Washington: U. S. Soil Conservation Service, 1959. Good Maps.
C1730

Carter, R. G. "A Study of the Progress of Negro Education in Saint Clair County, Alabama." Master's thesis. Alabama State College, 1953.
C1750

Carter, Randy Canoeing White Water: A Guide Book to the Rivers of Virginia and Eastern West Virginia, The Great Smoky Mountain Area. Warrenton, Va.: The author, 1967.
C1740 (LMC)

Carter, S. Grafton, A. Edwin A Manual of West Virginia's Wood-using Industries, with Directory. Morgantown: Office of Research and Development, Center for Appalachian Studies and Development, West Virginia Univ., 1965.
G3110 (ASU)

Carter, W. R. History of the First Regiment of Tennessee Volunteer Cavalry in the Great War of the Rebellion: With the Armies of the Ohio and Cumberland, under Generals Morgan, Rosecrans, Thomas, Stanley and Wilson, 1862-1865. Knoxville, Tenn.: Gaut-Ogden, 1902. This unit engaged in several campaigns in the mountains.
C1760 (LMC)

Carter, William T., Jr. Soil Survey of the Leesburg, Virginia, Area. Field Operations, 1903. Washington: U. S. Department of Agriculture, Bureau of Soils, 1904.
C1770

Cartmell, Thomas Kemp comp. Shenandoah Valley Pioneers and Their Descendants: A History of Frederick County, Virginia, from Its Formation in 1738 to 1908. Compiled mainly from original records of old Frederick County, now Hampshire, Berkeley, Shenandoah, Jefferson, Hardy, Clarke, Warren, Morgan and Frederick. Indexed edition. Winchester, Va.: Eddy Press Corp., 1909.
C1780 (ASU BC)

Shenandoah Valley Pioneers and Their Descendants: A History of Frederick County, Virginia, from Its Formation in 1738 to 1908. Compiled mainly from original records of old Frederick County, now Hampshire, Berkeley, Shenandoah, Jefferson, Hardy, Clarke, Warren, Morgan and Frederick. 2 vols. Indexed edition. 1909. Reprint. Berryville, Va.: Chesapeake Book Co., 1963.
C1790 (ASU ETSU)

Cartwright, Betty Goff Cook comp. North Carolina Land Grants in Tennessee, 1778-1791. Memphis: J. C. Harper Co., 1958.
C1800 (ETSU BC ASU)

Cartwright, Peter Autobiography of Peter Cartwright, the Backwoods Preacher. Cincinnati: Cranston and Curts, 1856. Cartwright had a long ministry in Pennsylvania, West Va. and other border states.
C1810 (BC)

Caruso, John Anthony The Appalachian Frontier: America's First Surge Westward. Maps by Francis J. Mitchell. Indianapolis: Bobbs-Merrill Co., 1959. Includes: Indians, Wetzel, Crockett, Sovier, the Watauga settlements and the Long Hunters — the most exciting chapter in American History.
C1820 (ASU WCU LMC MHC WWC ETSU BC UNCA)

The Southern Frontier. The American Frontier. Indianapolis: Bobbs-Merrill, Co., 1963. Accounts of adventures and hardship on the Southern Frontier.
C1830 (WCU)

Caruthers, Eli Washington Interesting Revolutionary Incidents: And Sketches of Character, Chiefly in the "Old North State." 2nd series. Philadelphia: Hayes and Zell, 1856.
C1840 (ASU)

Revolutionary Incidents: And Sketches of Character, Chiefly in the "Old North State." Philadelphia: Hayes and Zell, 1854.
C1850 (ASU)

Caruthers, Eugene "An Investigation of the Exceptional Child in the Negro Secondary Schools of East Tennessee." Master's thesis. East Tennessee State College, 1957.
C1860

Caruthers, William Alexander The Knights of the Golden Horse-shoe: A Traditionary Tale of the Cocked Hat Gentry in the Old Dominion. With an introduction by Curtis Carroll Davis, 1845. Reprint. Southern Literary Classics Series. Chapel Hill: Univ. of North Carolina Press, . Va. agents move into frontier through Green Valley over Blue Ridge and fight Indians.
C1870 (WCU ETSU BC)

The Knights of the Horseshoe. "Harper's Franklin Square Library no. 269." New York: Harper and Brothers, 1882.
C1880

Cary, Richard Mary N. Murfree. United States Authors Series, no. 121. New York: Twayne Pub., 1967. A critical study of the life and works of the woman who turned the nation's literary attention toward Appalachia.
C1890 (ASU)

Casdorph, Paul Douglas "Legislative Politics and the Public Schools in West Virginia, 1933-1958: A Twenty-five Year History." Ph. D. Diss. Univ. of Kentucky, 1970.
C1900 (ASU BC)

Case, Dale Edward "Oak Ridge, Tennessee: A Geographic Study." Ph. D. Diss. Univ. of Tenn., 1955.
C1910

Case, Earl Clark "The Valley of East Tennessee: The Adjustment of Industry to Natural Environment." Ph. D. Diss. Univ. of Chicago, 1925. The Tennessee Valley is one of the few places in Appalachia where this adjustment has been possible.
C1920 (LMC)

Case, H. L. Personnel Policy in a Public Agency: The TVA Experience. New York: Harper and Brothers, 1955. This is a book about the development and present status of personnel administration in TVA by a former Director of Personnel.
C1930

Casey, Joseph J. Personal Names in Hening's "Statutes at Large of Virginia" and Shepherd's Continuation. 1896 reprint. Baltimore: Genealogical Pub. Co., 1967.
C1940 (ASU)

Cash, James I. Autobiography and Sermons. Spring City: n.p., 1934. An autobiography with sermons and a history of Polk County, Tenn.
C1950

Caskey, Willie Malvin "The Administration of Governor Andrew Johnson 1853-1857." Master's thesis. George Peabody College, 1928.
C1960

Cassell, Charles Willis ed. History of The Lutheran Church in Virginia and East Tennessee. Strasburg, Va.: Shenandoah Pub. House, 1930.
C1970 (ASU BC FC)

Cassell, William Haller ed. Fugitive Lyrics of John Heiskell Booton. Salem, Va.: Sentinel Pub. Co., 1899.
C1980

Cassidy, Frederic Gomes A Method for Collecting Dialect. With the collaboration of Andrew R. Duckert. Publication, no. 20. Gainesville, Fla.: American Dialect Society, 1953.
C1990 (ASU)

Castanea: The Journal of the Southern Appalachian Botanical Club vol. 1. January, 1936. Morgantown, W. Va.: The club, monthly except June, July, August, September.
C2000 (ETSU UNCA BC)

Castleden, Louise Decatur Otha. Washington, D. C.: New Edition, 1962. Author's sketch of a humble and religious old mountain man who left a lasting impression on her.
C2010 (ASU BC)

A Catalog of the South Birmingham: Oxmoore House, 1974. This catalog is published by the same corporation that publishes Southern Living. Like the Magazine, the book contains a great deal of information on Appalachia.
C2030

Catalogue of the Fine Arts Section of the Appalachian Exposition Knoxville: Newman, 1910. This is a catalogue of the Great Appalachian Fair in Knoxville in 1910. Apparently it was the only area-wide fair of its kind.
C2040 (ASU)

Cate, Herma The Southern Appalachian Heritage. Boone, N. C.: The Appalachian Consortium, 1974. A delightful account of life, manners, customs and conditions in the high mountain valleys of the Appalachians. Reminiscence of life as it was.
C2041

Cates, Alma Lydia "A Study of the Language Arts Program in Grade One of the Carter County School System with Some Suggestions for the Improvement of the Program." Master's thesis. East Tenn. State College, 1959.
C2050 (ETSU)

Cather, Elaine Rittenhouse, Gordon The Texture of Mississippian, Upper Devonian, and Lower Pennsylvanian Sandstones in the Appalachian Basin. Washington: Govt. Print. Off., 1946.
R2530

Rittenhouse, Gordon The Texture of Paleozoic Sandstones and Sandy Limestones in the Appalachian Basin. Washington: Govt. Print. Off., 1946.
R2540

Cather, Willa Sibert Sapphira and the Slave Girl. 1st ed. New York: A. A. Knopf, 1940. Character sketch of a Virginia lady, Sapphira Dodderidge Colbert, of the Loudaun County Dodderidges, who was considered to have married beneath her. Her husband ran the mill in the Blue Ridge frontier town where they went to live. This, Miss Cather's only non-western novel was written from stories her parents told her about their relatives in Virginia.
C2060 (ASU ETSU)

Cathey, Cornelius Oliver Agricultural Developments in North Carolina, 1783-1860. James Sprunt Studies in History and Political Science, vol. 38. Chapel Hill: Univ. of North Carolina Press, 1956.
C2070 (LMC)

Cathey, James H. The Genesis of Lincoln: Truth is Stranger than Fiction. n.p.: The author, 1899. There's a persistent rumor that Lincoln was the son of Abraham Enlon of Swain Co., N. C. to whom Nancy Hanks was once indentured.
C2080 (LMC)

Truth is Stranger than Fiction: Or, the True Genesis of a Wonderful Man. n.p.: n.p., n.d.
C2090 (ASU)

Catholic Education in North Carolina Washington, D. C.: Williams and Heintz, 1958. Catholicism is the fastest growing religion in the Southern Mountains.
C2100 (LMC)

Catlett, Clay Michie An Economic and Social Survey of Augusta County. Univ. of Va. Extension Series, vol. 12, no. 7. Charlottesville: Univ. of Va., 1928.
C2110 (ASU BC)

Caton, Joseph L. Wild Flowers of the Great Smokies and Surrounding Area, a Pictorial Guide. Knoxville, Tenn.: J. L. Caton, 1940. A beautifully illustrated pictorial guide to the flora of the Great Smokies.
C2120 (ASU UNCA)

Catron, Ada Grace Early Records of Lee County, Virginia. vol. 2. n.p.: n.p., 1972. Land and Court Records of Lee County Virginia.
C2130

Tombstone Inscriptions of Lee County, Virginia. Pennington Gap, Va.: The author, 1966.
C2140 (BC)

Catron, Anna Grace The Public Career of David Crockett. Master's thesis. Univ. of Tenn., 1955.
C2150

Catron, Henry Hardy Kettenring Family. Name changed to Catron. Edinburg, Ill.: n.p., 1966. Many Wythe County families included. This replaces the author's Kettenring Family in America, Mt. Pulaski, Ill.: H. J. Wible Print Co., 1955.
C2160

Cattermole, E. G. Famous Frontiersmen, Pioneers and Scouts: The Vanguards of American Civilization. Chicago: W. V. Harrison, Jr., 1886. Includes: Boone, Girty and Wetzel as well as mention of lesser known Appalachian pioneer scouts.
C2170 (BC)

Caudill, Bernice C. Pioneers of Eastern Kentucky, Their Feuds and Settlements. Cincinnati: Creative Printing, 1969. Fascinating account of the people who settled Eastern Kentucky and the routes they took, their fights and towns.
C2180 (ASU)

Caudill, Harry Poverty and Affluence in Appalachia. Huntington: Appalachian Movement Press, n.d.
C2190

Caudill, Harry M. Dark Hills to Westward: The Saga of Jennie Wiley. 1st ed. Atlantic Monthly Press Book. Boston: Little, Brown and Co., 1969. Account of her capture by Indians and subsequent escape.
C2200 (ASU WCU LMC MHC ETSU BC)

My Land is Dying. 1st ed. New York: E. P. Dutton, 1971. Account of the devastation caused by strip-mining by the area's most eloquent ecologist.
C2210 (ASU MHC LMC WCU ETSU BC)

Night Comes to the Cumberlands: A Biography of a Depressed Area. With a foreword by Stewart L. Udall. Atlantic Press Book. Boston: Little, Brown, 1962. Eloquent diatribe on the havoc the coal industry is wrecking on Eastern Kentucky.
C2220 (WWC BC FC)

Night Comes to the Cumberlands: Biography of a Depressed Area. Foreword by Stewart L. Udall. Boston: Little, Brown, 1963. This is Appalachia's most eloquent ecological plea.
C2230 (ASU MHC WCU ETSU FC UNCA)

Night Comes to the Cumberlands: A Biography of a Depressed Area. With a foreword by Stewart L. Udall. Boston: Little, Brown, 1964.
C2240 (LMC)

The Senator from Slaughter County. 1st ed. Boston: Little, Brown, 1973. A fictional account of political conception and economic colonialism in Eastern Kentucky.
C2250 (ASU BC)

Caudill, Morris K. A Poverty Program and the Public Schools. Bureau of School Service Bulletin, vol. 41, no. 2. Lexington: Univ. of Kentucky College of Education, 1968. A look at poverty funds in the public schools. How much actually gets to the schools; how is it spent.
C2260

Caudill, Rebecca Barrie and Daughter. New York: The Viking Press, 1943.
C2270

Barrie and Daughter. Illustrated by Berkeley Williams, Jr. 1943. Reprint. New York: Viking Press, 1967. Setting is author's childhood home in the Southern mountains.
C2280 (ASU ETSU)

The Best-loved Doll. New York: Holt, Rinehart and Winston, 1962. A touching story of a child and a doll in a land where there are few dolls.
C2290 (ETSU)

A Certain Small Shepherd. Illustrated by William Pene DuBois. 1st ed. New York: Holt, Rinehart and Winston, 1965. Tear-jerker about a mute child and a Christmas miracle.
C2300 (ASU LMC WWC ETSU)

Come Along. Illustrated by Ellen Raskin. 1st ed. New York: Holt, Rinehart and Winston, 1969. The glories of the mountains presented in haiku verse.
C2310 (ASU WCU ETSU BC)

Contrary Jenkins. Illustrated by Glen Rounds, 1st ed. New York: Holt, Rinehart and Winston, 1969. A marvelous man who must disagree with any suggestion.
C2320 (ASU MHC ETSU BC)

Did You Carry the Flag Today, Charley? Illustrated by Nancy Grossman, 1st ed. New York: Holt, Rinehart and Winston, 1966. A mountain boy goes off to kindergarten.
C2330 (ASU LMC MHC ETSU WWC BC)

The Far-off Land. New York: Viking Press, 1964. Another what lies over the hills and far-away theme.
C2340 (LMC WCU ASU)

Happy Little Family. Illustrated by Decie Merwin, 1st ed. Philadelphia: J. C. Winston and Co., 1947. Bonnie and Debby are four and six and are from Eastern Kentucky.
C2350 (ASU LMC ETSU BC)

Higgins and the Great Big Scare. New York: Holt, 1960. Higgins learns a lesson about being afraid. Mountain setting.
C2360 (ETSU)

The High Cost of Writing. Cumberland: Southeast Community College, Univ. of Kentucky, 1965. An address about her life and work delivered before Southeast Community College, University of Kentucky, Cumberland, Kentucky.
C2370 (BC)

Caudill, Rebecca
My Appalachia: A Reminiscence. Photographs by Edward Wallowitch, 1st ed. New York: Holt, Rinehart and Winston, 1966. A reminiscence of the mountains before the land strippers came.
C2380 (ASU LMC MHC ETSU WCU FC WWC BC UNCA)
A Pocketful of Cricket. Illustrated by Evaline Ness, 1st. ed. New York: Holt, Rinehart and Winston, 1964. A Tennessee farm boy makes a pet of a cricket.
C2390 (ASU WWC LMC WCU ETSU)
Saturday Cousins. Illustrated by Nancy Woltmate, 1st ed. Philadelphia: Winston, 1953. Games and adventures of six cousins who played together every Saturday, 50 years ago.
C2400 (ASU LMC BC)
Saturday Cousins. 1953. Reprint. New York: Holt, Rinehart and Winston, 1968.
C2410 (ETSU)
Schoolhouse in the Woods. Illustrated by Decie Merwin. New York: Holt, Rinehart and Winston, 1949. A story about a one room mountain school a generation ago.
C2420 (ASU LMC WCU ETSU BC)
Schoolroom in the Parlor. Illustrated by Decie Merwin, 1st. ed. Philadelphia: Winston, 1959. A snowbound mountain family has school in the front parlor.
C2430 (ASU LMC WCU)
Schoolroom in the Parlor. 1959. Reprint. Philadelphia: Winston, 1970.
C2440 (ETSU)
Susan Cornish. New York: Viking Press, 1955. A story of a young teacher's first school in a poor mountain community.
C2450 (WCU ETSU BC)
Susan Cornish. 1955. Reprint. New York: Viking Press, 1966.
C2460 (ASU LMC)
Time for Lisa. New York: T. Nelson, 1959. A Story of a lonely girl who yearns for time and attention.
C2470
Tree of Freedom. Illustrated by Dorothy Bayley Morse. New York: Viking Press, 1947. A teen-aged girl finds herself alone on the frontier during the 18th century.
C2480 (ASU LMC BC)
Tree of Freedom. New York: Viking Press, 1949.
C2490 (ETSU)
Up and Down the River. Illustrated by Decie Merwin, 1st ed. New York: Holt, Rinehart and Winston, 1951. Two children turn salesmen during summer vacation.
C2500 (ASU LMC WCU ETSU BC)
The Wooden Tower. Charlestown: Morris Harvey Publication, 1975. 176 pages of prose, poetry and graphics by mountain authors and artisans.
C2510

Causey, Lawson V. Availability of Ground Water in Talladega County, Alabama: A Reconnaissance. Bulletin, 81. University: Division of Water Resources Geological Survey of Alabama, 1965.
C2520 (ETSU)
Geology and Ground-water Resources of Cherokee County, Alabama: A Reconnaissance. Bulletin, 79. University: Division of Water Resources, Geological Survey of Alabama, 1965.
C2530 (ETSU)
Ground-water Resources of Etowah County, Alabama: A Reconnaissance. Information Series, 25. University: Alabama Geological Survey, 1961.
C2540 (ETSU)
Harris, Hobart B. Interim Report on Ground-water Study in Colbert County, Alabama. University: Alabama Geological Survey, 1960.
H2880 (ETSU)
Miller, J. D., Jr. Geology and Ground-water Resources of Tuscaloosa County, Alabama. University: Alabama Geological Survey, 1958.
M5760 (ETSU)
Warman, James C. Geology and Ground-Water Resources of Calhoun County, Alabama. University: Alabama, Geological Survey, 1962.
W830 (ETSU)

Cauthen, Charles Edward South Carolina Goes to War, 1860-1865. James Sprunt Studies in History and Political Science, vol. 32. Chapel Hill: Univ. of North Carolina Press, 1950.
C2550 (ASU)

Cauthorn, Robert C. Economic Structure of West Virginia. W. Va. Center for App. Studies and Development, W. Va. State Development Plans, Basic Information Series, Report, no. 5. Morgantown: W. Va. Univ. Office of Research and Development, 1967.
C2560

Cavallaro, Joseph A. Froth Floatation Washability Data of Various Appalachian Coals Using Timed Release Analysis Technique. Pittsburgh: Mines Bureau, 1965.
C2570

Cave Research Foundation The Flint Ridge Cave System, Mammoth Cave National Park, Kentucky. Done in cooperation with the National Park Service. Washington: The foundation, 1966.
C2580 (ASU BC)

Cawood, Steven C. A Survey of the Legal Environment of Knox County, Kentucky. Oak Ridge: Oak Ridge Asso. Universities, 1967. Another study of corruption in Eastern Kentucky.
C2590

Caylor, Betty Shearer The Double Head Academy. Louisville: J. M. Gray and Associates, 1971.
C2600 (BC)

Caywood, William Curtis Kentucky Mayor: The Humor and Philosophy of John Edwin Garner. Winchester, Ky.: n.p., 1950.
C2610 (BC)

Census of Pensioners for Revolutionary or Military Services Baltimore: Genealogical Pub. Co., 1967. (1840, 1841).
C2620

Centenary . . . the Story of a Church Chattanooga: n.p., 1962.
C2630

Centennial Anniversary of the First Presbyterian Church of Knoxville, Tennessee, and the Semi-centennial Anniversary of the Ministry of Rev. James Park, D. D., Knoxville, Tennessee, October 11, 1896 Knoxville: Bean, Warters and Gaut, 1897.
C2640

Centennial of Holston Presbytery Celebrated in the Jonesboro Presbyterian Church, Jonesboro, Tennessee, October 18-19, 1926. Greenville: John R. Self, 1927. The Holston Presbytery is the oldest in Tenn.
C2650

Chadsey, Charles E. "The Struggle between President Johnson and the Congress over Reconstruction." Ph. D. Diss. Columbia Univ., 1896.
C2660

Chaffin, Lillie D. Bear Weather. Illustrated by Helga Aichinger. New York: Macmillan, 1968. A mother bear and her cubs enjoy a spring day after hibernation.
C2670 (BC ASU)
Coal: Energy and Crisis. New York: Harvey House, 1974.
C2680
Freeman. New York: Macmillan, 1972. 12 year old Freeman is shocked to learn that his parents are alive and are returning after his father's release from prison.
C2690 (ASU LMC BC)
John Henry McCoy. Illustrated by Emanuel Schongut. New York: Macmillan, 1971. Tired of constant moves, a 10 year old boy tries to find a way for his family to stay in Appalachia.
C2700 (ASU LMC MHC BC)
Lines and Points. Pikeville, Ky.: Pikeville College Press, 1966. Poems from Eastern Kentucky.
C2710 (BC)
A World of Books. Chicago: Childrens Press, 1970. A Kentucky woman speaks of her long struggles to become a writer and teacher.
C2720 (BC)

Chait, William A Survey of the Public Libraries of Asheville and Buncombe County, North Carolina. Chicago: American Library Assoc., 1965.
C2730 (LMC ETSU ASU)

Chalkey, Lyman Chronicles of the Scotch-Irish Settlement in Virginia. Rosslyn, Va.: The Commonwealth Printing Co., 1913. Material extracted from the records of original Augusta Co., Va.
C2740 (BC ASU)

Chalkley, Lyman Augusta County, Va. Chronicles of the Scotch-irish Settlement in Virginia, Extracted from the Original Court Records of Augusta County, 1745-1800. Baltimore: Genealogical Pub. Co., 1965.
A5490 (ASU)

Chalkley, Lyman comp. Chronicles of Scotch-Irish Settlement in Virginia. First published 1912. Vols. Baltimore, Genealogical Pub. Co., 1965.
C2750

Chamberlain, E. Burnham comp. Birds of Southern Appalachians. Southern Region. Washington: U. S. Forest Service, 1968.
C2760

Chambers, Joseph Lenoir The Breed and the Pasture. Charlotte, N. C.: Stone and Barringer Co., 1910. A successful businessman feels a deep-seated longing for the mountains of home, so he returns to the scene of his childhood for a long visit. Setting appears to be Western North Carolina.
C2770 (ASU)

Chambers, Lenoir Stonewall Jackson. 2 vols. New York: W. Morrow, 1959.
C2780 (ASU)

Chambers, Martha T. "A Survey of the Occupational Information Needs of the Ninth Graders of the Elizabethton High School, Elizabethton, Tennessee." Master's thesis. East Tennessee State Univ., 1965.
C2790 (ETSU)

Chambers, Robert comp. Popular Rhymes of Scotland. New ed. London: W. and R. Chambers, 1870. Many of these rhymes were used in the play-party games in the mountains until well into this century.
C2800 (ASU)

Chambers, Vaughn D. "Differences between Negro and Caucasian Students at John Sevier Junior High School, Kingsport, Tennessee." Master's thesis. East Tennessee State Univ., 1968.
C2810 (ETSU)

Chambers, Virginia Anne "Music in Four Kentucky Mountain Settlement Schools." Ph. D. Diss. Univ. of Michigan, 1970. Schools included: Pine Mountain Settlement, Hindman Settlement, Alice Lloyd College, Henderson Settlement School.
C2820 (LMC BC)

Champion, Myra The Lost World of Thomas Wolfe, Thomas Wolfe Home. n.p.: n.p., 1970.
C2830 (LMC MHC ASU)

Champlin, James Early Biography, Travels and Adventures of Rev. James Champlin, Who Was Born Blind; with a Description of the Different Countries through Which He Has Traveled in America, and of the Different Institutions, etc., Visited by Him; Also an Appendix, Which Contains Extracts from Addresses Delivered by Him upon Several Occasions. 2nd ed., rev. Columbus, Ohio: C. Scott's Power Press, 1842. This itinerant Methodist "public exhorter" traveled widely in eastern Tennessee. His handicap limits the value of his observations.
C2840

Chance, Henry Martyn Report on the Mining Methods and Appliances Used in Anthracite Coal Fields. Pennsylvania Geological Survey, 2nd, Report of Progress AC. Harrisburg, Pa.: Board of Commissioner for the Second Geological Survey, 1883. Includes mine laws and a glossary of mining terms.
C2850 (BC)

Chance, Hilda Index to Hungerford and Ellis' History of Susquehanna and Juniata Valleys. Fort Worth, Texas: American Reference Pub., n.d.
C2860 (ASU)

Western Maryland Pioneers: Marriages, Early Settlers, Births and Deaths with Location. 2 vols. Liberty, Pa.: The author, n.d.
C2870 (ASU)

Chancellor, John Miller The Library in the TVA Adult Education Program. Chicago: American Library Association, 1937.
C2880 (ETSU)

Chandler, Helen Deane A Brief Description of the Battle of King's Mountain, "The Turning Point of the American Revolution," Fought in York County, S. C. October 7, 1780. Together the Brief Accounts of Previous Celebrations, Illustrations Showing the Battlefield and Monuments and Interesting Data Concerning 150th Anniversary Celebration To Be Held on the Battleground October 7, 1930. Gastonia, N. C.: Publicity Comm. of the Sesquicentennial Celebration Comm., 1930.
C2890

Chaney, Jim Carolina Country Reader. Durham, N. C.: Moore Pub. Co., 1974.
C2900 (WCU)

Chaney, Rex "An Evaluation of the Community Service or Continuing Education Project: Developing and Stimulating Recreation in Six Counties of Eastern Kentucky." Master's thesis. Morehead State Univ., 1969.
C2910

Chang, Kwang Yue "The Relation of Level of Living to Selected Additional Characteristics of Central Appalachia Rural Families." Master's thesis. Univ. of Tennessee, 1965.
C2920 (ASU)

Chang, Po Shin "History of the Hamilton National Bank of Knoxville." Master's thesis. Univ. of Tenn., 1962.
C2930

Channing, Marion L. The Magic of Spinning. 4th ed. Marion, Mass.: n.p., 1971. Includes information about wool, the spinning wheel, where to get material and instructions on how to spin.
C2940 (ASU WCU)

Chapin, Anna Alice The Eagle's Mate. Illustrated by Douglas Duer. New York: Grosset and Dunlap, 1914. A shy, delicate girl marries into a rugged feuding clan and accepts their way of life.
C2950 (ASU LMC BC)

The Eagle's Mate. New York: W. J. Watt and Co., 1914.
C2960

Mountain Madness. Illustrated by George W. Gage. New York: Grosset and Dunlap, 1917. Unlikely tale of socializing between summer residents at an old West Virginia resort and rough mountaineers who live nearby.
C2970 (ASU BC)

Mountain Madness. New York: W. J. Watt and Co., 1917.
C2980

The Under Trail. Boston: Little, Brown, 1912. Novel of adventure in the Blue Ridge Mountains of Virginia.
C2990

Chapman, Arthur Glenn Minckler, Leon Sherwood Tree Planting in the Central Piedmont, and Southern Appalachian Region. U. S. Department of Agriculture Farmers' Bulletin, no. 1994. Washington: Govt. Print. Off., 1957.
M6130 (WCU)

Chapman, Berlin Basil Education in Anttal West Virginia, 1910-1975. Illustrated by Webster Springs High School. Parson, W. Va.: McClain Printing Co., 1974.
C3000 (ASU)

Chapman, Bob The Whistling Wind and Other Poems. Hazard, Ky.: Don's Printery, 1972.
C3010 (BC)

Chapman, John H., Jr. The Structure of the West Virginia Economy, 1965: A Preliminary Report. Morgantown: Regional Research Institute, West Virginia Univ., 1967.
C3020 (LMC)

Chapman, John S. H. Chapman, Mary Clue of the Faded Dress. New York: D. Appleton-Century Co., 1939.
C3150

Chapman, Mary Eagle Cliff. New York: D. Appleton-Century Co., 1940.
C3160

Chapman, Mary Flood in Glen Hazard. New York: D. Appleton-Century Co., 1939.
C3170 (ASU)

Chapman, Mary Girls of Glen Hazard. New York: D. Appleton-Century Co., 1939.
C3180

Chapman, Mary Marsh Island Mystery. New York: D. Appleton-Century Co., 1936.
C3190

Chapman, Mary Mystery of the Missing Car. New York: D. Appleton-Century Co., 1939.
C3200

Chapman, Mary Rogues on Rid Hill. New York: D. Appleton-Century Co., 1973.
C3210

Chapman, Mary Timber Train. New York: D. Appleton-Century Co., 1933.
C3220

Chapman, John Stanton Higham, and Chapman, Mary see Chapman, Maristan, pseud.

Chapman, Maristan Clue of the Faded Dress. New York: D. Appleton-Century Co., 1938. A mystery story for young people with a Tennessee mountain setting.
C3030 (ASU BC)

Eagle Cliff. New York: Appleton-Century, 1934.
C3040 (WWC ASU)

Glen Hazard. Illustrated by Horace Raymond Bishop. New York: A. A. Knopf, 1933. A rural sheriff searches for a murderer and has some amusing encounters with mountaineers along the way.
C3050 (ASU LMC BC)

The Happy Mountain. New York: Literary Guild of America, 1928.
Wait-still-on-the-Lord Lowe finds big city life is not to his liking and heads home to the hills of Tennessee.
C3060 (ASU BC)

The Happy Mountain. New York: Viking Press, 1928.
C3070 (LMC WCU ETSU WWC)

Homeplace. New York: Viking Press, 1929. A young man inherits a cabin which enables him to ask his girl to marry him.
C3080 (ASU BC ETSU LMC WCU WWC)

Mystery of the Broken Key. New York: Appleton, 1940.
C3090 (WWC)

Rogue's March. Philadelphia: J. B. Lippincott Co., 1949. Fiction centering on the battle of King's Mountain.
C3100 (ASU WCU LMC BC)

The Weather Tree. New York: Viking Press, 1932. An outlander brings new industry and a reformers zeal to Glen Hazard. The natives get restless when he tries to remake the whole town.
C3110 (ETSU ASU WCU LMC BC)

The Weather Tree. New York: Book League of America, 1932.
C3120 (WWC)

Wild Cat Ridge. New York: Appleton-Century, 1932. A novel of mystery and intrigue in the Tennessee mountains.
C3130 (LMC BC)

Wild Cat Ridge. New York: D. Appleton-Century Co., 1932. Mystery story with a mountain setting.
C3140

Chapman, Mary Clue of the Faded Dress. by Maristan Chapman, pseud. New York: D. Appleton-Century Co., 1939. A mystery story with a Tennessee mountain setting.
C3150

Eagle Cliff. by Maristan Chapman, pseud. New York: D. Appleton-Century Co., 1940.
C3160

Flood in Glen Hazard. by Maristan Chapman, pseud. New York: D. Appleton-Century Co., 1939.
C3170 (ASU)

Girls of Glen Hazard. by Maristan Chapman, pseud. New York: D. Appleton-Century Co., 1939. Mystery story written for young girls.
C3180

Marsh Island Mystery. by Maristan Chapman, pseud. New York: D. Appleton-Century Co., 1936.
C3190

Mystery of the Missing Car. by Maristan Chapman, pseud. New York: D. Appleton-Century Co., 1939.
C3200

Rogues on Rid Hill. by Maristan Chapman, pseud. New York: D. Appleton-Century Co., 1973.
C3210

Timber Train. by Maristan Chapman, pseud. New York: D. Appleton-Century Co., 1933.
C3220

Chapman, Mary, and Chapman, John Stanton Higham see Chapman, Maristan, pseud.

Chapman, Mary Lucile "The Influence of Coal in the Big Sandy Valley." Ph. D. Diss. Univ. of Kentucky, 1945.
C3230 (ASU)

Chapman, Thomas C. Wiseman Family. Redwood City, Cal.: n.p., 1967.
C3240 (LMC)

Chappelear, Nancy comp. Early Fauquier County, Virginia, Marriage Bonds, 1759-1854. Washington, D. C.: The authors, 1965.
C3250 (ASU)

Chappell, Fred Dagon. 1st ed. New York: Harcourt, Brace and World, 1968. A young minister inherits a farm in the North Carolina and with it the emotional legacy of his family. He finds that the debts of fast generations are heavy to bear.
C3260 (ASU LMC)

The Gaudy Place. New York: Harcourt, Brace, Jovanovich, 1973. A novel of a young hustler in Asheville, North Carolina.
C3270 (ASU)

The Inkling. 1st ed. New York: Harcourt, Brace and World, 1965. Gothic novel of two disturbed children in a strange mountain family.
C3280 (ASU LMC)

It Is Time, Lord. 1st ed. New York: Atheneum, 1963. A novel of childhood, family quiet, and madness with a western North Carolina setting.
C3290 (ASU)

Chappell, Louis Watson Folk-songs of Roanoke and the Albemarle. Morgantown, W. Va.: Ballad Press, 1939.
C3300 (ASU)

John Henry, a Folklore Study. Jena: Frommannsche Verlag, Walter Biedermann, 1933.
C3310

John Henry: A Folklore Study. Port Washington, N. Y.: Kennikat Press, 1968.
C3320

Chappell, Mary Jane "The Social and Economic Aspects of the Novels of Jesse Stuart." Master's thesis. Vanderbilt Univ., 1959.
C3330 (ASU)

Chappell, Vernon Glenn, Jr. "The Identification and Evaluation of Factors Affecting Economic Growth in the Tennessee Valley Region, 1950-1960." Ph. D. Diss. Univ. of Tennessee, 1970.
C3340

Chappelle, Daniel E. Value Growth of Pine Pulpwood on the George Walton Experimental Forest. U. S. Forest Service Station Paper, no. 140. Asheville, N. C.: Southeast Forest Station, 1962.
C3350 (WCU)

Charle, Edwin George "The Demand for Coal for Power Generation in the Tennessee Valley and the Impact of Changing Demand Patterns on a Supplying Coal Field." Ph. D. Diss. Indiana Univ., 1958.
C3360

Charleston Youth Community, Inc. Action for Appalachian Youth: A Demonstration Program for Kanawha County Youth under the Auspices and Direction of the President's Committee on Juvenile Delinquency and Youth Crime. Charleston: The Committee, 1963.
C3370 (ASU)

Charlesworth, Harold K. Barnard, Jerald R. The Structure of the Kentucky Economy: An Input-output Study. Lexington: Univ. of Kentucky, Office of Development Services and Business Research, College of Business and Economics, 1969.
B1230

Chartier, Barbara "Weaverton — A Study of Culture and Personality in a Southern Mill Town." Master's thesis. Univ. of N. C., 1949.
C3380

Chase, Lewis "Changes in Social and Economic Status of the People in Sullivan County for a Thirty Year Period." Master's thesis. Univ. of Tenn., 1936.
C3390 (ASU)

Chase, Richard Jack and the Three Sillies. Illustrated by Joshua Tolfaed. A Jack tale from Beech Mountain, North Carolina.
C3440 (ASU LMC MHC WCU BC)

Singing Games and Playparty Games. Hullabaloo, and Other Singing Folk Games. Illustrated by Joshua Tolfaed. With six piano settings by Hilton Rufty. 1949. Reprint.
C3490 (ASU MHC BC)

Wicked John and the Devil. Illustrated by Joshua Tolfaed. Boston: Houghton Mifflin, 1951.
C3500 (WCU BC)

Chase, Richard comp. Hullabaloo, and Other Singing Folk Games. Illustrated by Joshua Tolfaed. With six piano settings by Hilton Rufty. Boston: Houghton-Mifflin, 1949.
C3430 (WCU WWC BC)

Chase, Richard ed. American Folk Tales and Songs, and Other Examples of English-American Tradition as Preserved in the Appalachian Mountains and Elsewhere in the United States. Illustrated by Joshua Tolfaed. Music edited with the assistance of Raymond Kane McLain, Annabel Morris Buchanan, and John Powell. New York: New American Library, 1956.
C3400 (ASU WCU LMC BC)

American Folk Tales and Songs, and Other Examples of English-American Tradition as Preserved in the Appalachian Mountains and Elsewhere in the United States. Compiled with introduction and notes. Illustrated by Joshua Tolfaed. Music edited with the assistance of Raymond Kane McLain, Annabel Morris Buchanan and John Powell. . Reprint. New York: Dover Publications, 1971.
C3410 (WWC)

Grandfather Tales: American-English Folk Tales. Illustrated by Berkeley Williams, Jr. Boston: Houghton Mifflin, 1948. American-English folk tales that have been handed down for generations in the North Carolina Mountains.
C3420 (ASU WCU LMC MHC WWC ETSU BC FC)

The Jack Tales. Told by R. M. Ward and his kindred in the Beech Mountain section of western North Carolina and by other descendants of Council Harmon (1803-1896) elsewhere in the southern mountains: With three tales from Wise County, Virginia. Appendix compiled by Herbert Halpert. Illustrated by Berkeley Williams, Jr. Boston: Houghton Mifflin, 1943.
C3450 (ASU LMC MHC WWC WCU ETSU BC)

The Jack Tales. Boston: Houghton-Mifflin Co., 1950.
C3460

Old Songs and Singing Games. Chapel Hill: Univ. of N. C. Press, 1938.
C3470 (ASU WCU BC)

Old Songs and Singing Games. 1938. Reprint. New York: Dover Pub., 1972.
C3480 (LMC)

Chase, Stuart Rich Land, Poor Land; A Study of Waste in the Natural Resources of America. Reprint. New York: AMS, 1969. New York: McGraw-Hill, 1936. Includes study of the TVA.
C3510

Chattanooga Research report. no. 1. n.p.: n.p., 1957.
C3530 (BC)

Chattanooga Chamber of Commerce Chattanooga, Industrial Center of the South. Chattanooga: Chattanooga Community Advertising Assoc., 1929.
C3520

Chattanooga, Tennessee, Sts. Peter and Paul's Parish The Centenary of Sts. Peter and Paul's Parish, Chattanooga, Tenn. The Story of the First One Hundred Years of the Catholic Church in Hamilton County. Chattanooga: The parish, 1952.
C3540

Chavers, Gordon D. Coal Workers' Pneumoconisosis: Workmen's Compensation Treatment and It's Prevention in Kentucky. For the Kentucky Office of Economic Opportunity. Atlanta: Resource Development Internship Project, n.d.
C3550 (ASU)

Checchi and Company Capital Resources in the Central Appalachian Region. Appalachian Research Report, no. 9, appendix C. Washington: The co., 1969.
C3560 (ASU ETSU)

Cheek, Mr. and Mrs. Charles comp. 1850 Census: Wilkes County, North Carolina. Wilkesboro: Genealogical Society of the "Original" Wilkes County, N. C., n.d.
C3570 (ASU)

Cheek, Claude John The Simple Things and Other Poems. Brea, Cal.: The author, 1965.
C3580 (LMC)

Cheek, Curtis Leon "The Singing School and Shapednote Tradition: Residuals in 20th Century American Hymnody." Master's thesis. Microfilm. Univ. of Southern California, 1968.
C3590 (WCU)

Cheek, Donald M. The Population and Economy of Boone, North Carolina. n.p.: N. C. Dept. of Conservation and Development, Division of Community Of Planning, 1963.
C3600 (LMC ASU)

Chen, Kuna "Agriculture Production in Pennsylvania." Master's thesis. Pennsylvania State Univ., 1954.
C3610

Chen, Ping-fan Some Low-alumina Quartzitic Sandstones in West Virginia: A Preliminary Report. Circular, no. 1. Morgantown: W. Va. Geological and Economic Survey, 1965.
C3620 (ETSU)

Cherokee Alphabet Card Cherokee, N. C.: Cherokee Pub., n.d. A card, suitable for framing, with the Cherokee alphabet in color.
C3630 (ASU)

Cherokee Historical Association Unto These Hills: A Drama of the Cherokee People. Souvenir program. Chapel Hill, N. C.: Creative Printers, 1950.
C3650 (WCU ASU)

Cherokee Historical Association, Inc., pub. Oconaluftee Indian Village. Cherokee: The Association, n.d. A beautifully illustrated booklet advertising Cherokee's nicest tourist attraction. The Oconaluftee Indian Village which attempts to recreate village life in the 1750's.
C3640 (ASU)

Cherokee Indian Village. Pigeon Forge, Tennessee These Are My People. Pigeon Forge, Tenn.: Cherokee Indian Village, 1975. A moving history of the tribe and their involvement in the larger events of U. S. history.
C3660

Cherokee Lands. Report Raleigh, N. C.: Holder and Wilson Printers to the State, 1857. Petition of Samuel Tate and others to the N. C. Legislative asking relief from payment of excessive rates for lands acquired from the Cherokee. These rates were the result of a short-lived speculative boom in mountain property.
C3670 (ASU)

Cherokee Nation Constitution and Laws of the Cherokee Nation. Published by authority of the National Council. The revised code of laws as prepared by Messrs. The revised code of laws as prepared by Messrs William P. Boudinot, D. H. Ross, and Joseph A. Scales. St. Louis: R. and T. A. Ennis, 1875.
C3680 (ASU)

Memorial of the Cherokee Indians Residing in North Carolina. Paying the Payment of Their Claims, Agreeably to the 8th and 12th Articles of the Treaty of 1835. Washington: U. S. Senate, 29th Congress, 1st Sess., 1901.
C3690 (ASU)

Reply of the Southern Cherokees to the Memorial of Certain Delegates from the Cherokee Nation. Together with the Message of John Ross, Ex-chief of the Cherokees, and Proceedings of the Council of the "Loyal Cherokees," Relative to the Alliance with the So-called Confederate States. Washington: Government Printing Office, 1834.
C3700

Cherokee Phoenix New Echota, Ga.: Isaach Harris, Printer for the Cherokee Nation, 1828. New Echota, near present day Calhoun, was the last capitol of the Cherokee nation in the East. The Phoenix was printed in both English and Cherokee.
C3710 (ASU)

Cherokee Souvenir Map Cherokee, N. C.: Cherokee Publications, 1973. A colorful guide to attractions in present day Cherokee, the Reservation, and The Smoky Mountains National Park.
C3720 (ASU)

Cherokee Testament New York: American Bible Society, n.d.
C3730 (MHC ASU)

Cherry, Bess Fayne Parlance of Kentucky Backwoods. Louisville, Ky.: Standard Print. Co., 1935. A rather superficial treatment of Kentucky speech patterns. Includes word-lists.
C3740 (BC)

Cherry, Thomas Crittenden Kentucky; The Pioneer State of the West. New York: D. C. Heath and Co., 1923.
C3750

Chesapeake and Ohio Railway Co. Views of Chesapeake and Ohio Railroad Scenery. Portland, Me.: Chisholm Brothers, n.d. This railroad serves West Virginia, Virginia and Kentucky Appalachian Counties.
C3760 (BC)

Chesapeake and Patomac Telephone Co. of West Virginia A Forecast of the Economy of West Virginia and the Effect on Certain Operations of the Chesapeake and Potomac Telephone Company of West Virginia, 1961-1970. Charleston: The Co., 1961.
C3770

Cheshire, Joseph Blount The Church in the Confederate States: A History of the Protestant Episcopal Church in the Confederate States. London: Logmans, Green, 1912.
C3780 (LMC)

Fishers of Men: A Charge to the Clergy of the Jurisdiction of Asheville, by the Bishop of North Carolina. n.p.: n.p., 1896.
C3790 (WCU)

Chesler, Herbert A. Avery, Robert W. A Community Organizes for Action: A Case Study of the Mon-Yough Region in Pennsylvania. University Park: Pennsylvania State Univ. Institute for Research on Human Resources, 1967.
A5770

Chesnel, Paul History of Cavelier de LaSalle, 1643-1687; Explorations in the Valleys of the Ohio, Illinois and Mississippi, taken from his Letters, Reports to King Louis XIV, also the Reports of Several of his Associates, Official Acts and Contemporaneous Documents, New York: Putnam, 1932. Includes descriptions of West Virginia and Kentucky.
C3800

Cheu, Piug-Fau Burford, Arthur E. Annual Field Trip of the Appalachian and Pittsburgh Geological Societies in the Great Valley in West Virginia. Morgantown, W. Va.: n.p., 1964?
B8530 (ETSU)

Cheyney, Edward G. Scott Burton in the Blue Ridge. New York: D. Appleton and Co., 1924. A novel of a young man's adventures in the Blue Ridge County. Appears to have been written for junior high students.
C3810

Child, Francis James Letters on Scottish Ballads from Professor Child to William Walter. Darby, Pa.: Norwood Editions, 1992.
C3840 (ASU)

Child, Francis James ed. The English and Scottish Popular Ballads. New York: Dover Publications, 1965. This is the classic work on English and Scottish ballads.
C3820 (ASU)

The English and Scottish Popular Ballads. 5 vols. in 10. Boston: Houghton Mifflin and Co., 1882-1892.
C3830 (BC)

Child, Sargent B. Checklist of Historical Records Survey Publications: Bibliography of Research Projects Reports. Assistance in checking and arranging by Cyril E. Paquin WPA Technical Series, Research and Records Bibliography, no. 7. Rev. 1943. Reprint. Baltimore: Genealogical Pub. Co., 1969.
C3850 (ASU)

Chilman, Catherine S. Growing Up Poor: An Over-view and Analysis of Child-rearing and Family Life Patterns Associated with Poverty. Division of Research Publication, no. 13. Washington: U. S. Dept. of Health, Education and Welfare, Welfare Administration, 1966. Includes a study of Appalachian families.
C3860

Chiltoskey, Mary Ulmer Cherokee Words with Pictures. Asheville, N. C.: Stephens Press, 1972.
C3880 (ASU LMC BC)

To Make My Bread. Cherokee, N. C.: Museum of Cherokee Indian, 1951.
C3890

Chiltoskey, Mary Ulmer ed. Cherokee Cooklore: Preparing Cherokee Foods. Asheville, N. C.: Stephens Press, 1951.
C3870 (ASU LMC MHC WCU)

Chittick, Victor Lovitt Oakes Ring-tailed Roarers: Tall Tales of the American Frontier, 1830-60. Wood engravings by Lloyd J. Reynolds. Caldwell, Id.: Caxton Printers, 1941.
C3900 (ASU)

Cholakian, Tony Kevork "A Follow-up Study of Twenty-four Dropouts and Twenty-four High School Graduates: Paired at the Seventh Grade Level, North Junior High School, Johnson City, Tennessee, 1953-1962." Master's thesis. East Tennessee State Univ., 1965.
C3910 (ETSU)

Chowan College, Creative Writing Group Southern Home Remedies. Murfrecsboro, N. C.: Johnson Pub. Co., 1968.
C3920 (BC ASU)

Chreitzberg, Abel McKee Early Methodism in the Carolinas. Barbee and Smith, Agents, xerox of original. Nashville: Publishing House of the Methodist Episcopal Church, South, Barbee and Smith, Agents, 1897.
C3930 (ASU BC)

Chrisman, Arthur Bowie Clarke County, 1836-1936. Berryville, Va.: Clarke Courier Press, 1936.
C3940 (ASU)

Christeson, R. P. comp. The Old-time Fiddler's Repertory: 245 Traditional Tunes. Columbia: Univ. of Missouri Press, 1973. Its very different to find printed music for the fiddle; this should become a classic.
C3950 (ASU BC)

Christian, Bolivar Scotch-Irish Settlers in the Valley of Virginia. Alumni address at Washington College, July 1, 1859. Washington and Lee University Historical Papers, no. 3. Baltimore: J. Murphy and Co., 1892.
C3960 (BC)

Christian, Charles Russell The Mountain Bard: A Series of Original Poems. Huntington, W. Va.: Argus Book and Job Off., 1885.
C3970 (BC)

Christiansen, Bobbie Huffman "A Survey of the Reading Interests of Sixth-grade Pupils in Washington County, Tennessee." Master's thesis East Tennessee State Univ., 1967.
C3980 (ETSU)

Christiansen, John R. Informal Social Participation in Five Kentucky Counties. Progress Report no. 43. Lesington: Kentucky Agricultural Experiment Station, Univ. of Ky., 1956. Includes Appalachian Counties.
C3990

Trends in the Number and Distribution of Medical Doctors in Kentucky. Progress Report, 69. Lexington: Ky. Agricultural Experiment Station, 1958.
C4010

Christiansen, John R. and others Social Security and the Farmer in Kentucky. Bulletin, 645. Lexington: Ky. Agricultural Experiment Station, 1958. Survey includes Kentucky's 49 Eastern Counties.
C4000

Christopher, Frederick John Basketry. Dover-Foyle Handbook. New York: Dover Pub., 1953.
C4020 (ASU WCU)

Chun, Leona Hayes Rouse with the Dawn. A Banner Book. Birmingham, Ala.: Banner Press, 1965. Many of these poems are set in the mountains of North Carolina and northern Alabama.
C4030 (ASU)

Church, Martha E. "Some Factors That Have Influenced the Location of the Electric Power Plants in the Greater Pittsburgh Area." Master's thesis. Univ. of Pittsburgh, 1954.
C4040

Church, Mary L. The Hills of Habersham. Clarksville, Ga.: The author, 1962. A history of the North Georgia County from the time of the Cherokee forward.
C4050 (ASU LMC BC)

The Hills of Habersham. Photocopy of the original made by University Microfilms, Ann Arbor, Michigan, 1974. Clarksville, Ga.: The author, 1962.
C4060

Seventy Years in Clarksville Baptist Church. Ann Arbor, Mich.: Edwards Brothers, 1958.
C4070 (ASU)

Church of Jesus Christ of the Latter Day Saints A General Index to a Census of Pensioners for the Revolutionary or Military Service 1840. Prepared by the Genealogical Society of the Church of Jesus Christ of Latter-Day Saints. Baltimore: Genealogical Pub. Co., 1965.
C4080 (ASU)

Churchill, Norma J. Soil Survey, Fulton County, Pennsylvania. Prepared in cooperation with the Pennsylvania State University, College of Agriculture and Agricultural Experiment Station and Pennsylvania Department of Agriculture, State Soil and Water Conservation Commission. Washington: U. S. Soil Conservation Service, 1969.
C4090

Churchill, Winston The Crossing. Illustrated by Sidney Adamson and Lilian Bayliss. New York: Macmillan Co., 1904. A novel of pioneer days in western North Carolina and of a young man's adventures crossing the Blue Ridge.
C4100 (ASU LMC ETSU BC)

The Crossing. Upper Saddle River, N. J.: Liturature House, 1969.
C4110 (WCU)

Ciokolo, Mary "TVA — A Critique of a Regional Plan." Master's thesis. Univ. of Rochester, 1948.
C4130

Cist, Henry Martin The Army of the Cumberland. New York: C. Scribner's Sons, 1882. This unit saw extensive action in Appalachia; they were in campaigns in the mountains of Virginia, Tennessee and Georgia.
C4140

Citizen's Commission to Investigate the Buffalo Creek Disaster Disaster on Buffalo Creek, 1972; Report of the Citizen's Commission Investigation. Charlestown, W. Va.: The commission, 1972. A report on criminal negligence in a mining Commission.
C4160 (BC ASU WCU)

Citizens Committee for Community Planning Survey of Governmental and Voluntary Health, Welfare and Recreation Services in Greater Kanawha Valley. (Community Services Report.) Community Services Report. Charleston: The committee, 1966.
C4170

Citizen's of Inquiry into Hunger and Malnutrition in the United States. Hunger, U. S. A.: A Report. With an introductory comment by Robert F. Kennedy. Boston: Beacon Press, 1969. Includes material on Appalachia.
C4150 (WCU)

City Planning and Zoning Commission, Roanoke, Va. Comprehensive City Plan, Roanoke. Prepared under the direction of City Planning and Zoning Commissions. Roanoke: Stone Printing Co., 1928.
C4180

Claiborne, Nathaniel H. Notes on the War in the South; with Biographical Sketches of the Lives of Montgomery, Jackson, Sevier, the Late Governor Claiborne, and Others. Richmond, Va.: William Ramsay, 1819. Reprint., First American Frontier Series. New York: Arno, 1971.
C4190

Claibourne, William Stirling Roy in the Mountains. New York: E. S. Gorham, 1916. A novel of a young man from the flatlands who goes to southwestern Virginia to work on a railroad and stays to organize an adult education center for mountaineers.
C4200 (ASU)

Clancy, Paul R. Just a Country Lawyer; a Biography of Senator Sam Ervin. Bloomington: Indiana University Press, 1974.
C4210 (ASU BC)

Clapp, Elsie Ripley Community Schools in Action. New York: Viking Press, 1939. Half the volume is devoted to the Arthurdale School, Arthurdale, W. Va.
C4220 (ASU)

Clapp, Gordon Rufus Power Supply in the Development of the Region. Address before the Knoxville (Tennessee) Kiwanis Club, December 4, 1952. Knoxville, Tennessee: TVA, 1952.
C4230

The TVA: An Approach to the Development of a Region. Charles R. Walgreen Foundation Lectures. Chicago: Univ. of Chicago Press, 1955.
C4240 (ASU WWC BC)

The TVA: An Approach to the Development of a Region. New York: Russell, 1971.
C4250

Clark, Betty Jean "A Study of the Reactions of a Representative Group of Students toward Guidance Received While Attending Bristol, Tennessee, High School, 1958-59." Master's thesis. East Tennessee State College, 1961.
C4260 (ETSU)

Clark, Billy C. The Champion of Sourwood Mountain. Illustrated by Harold Eldridge. New York: Putnam, 1966. Children's story with an Eastern Kentucky setting.
C4270 (LMC BC ASU)

Goodbye Kate. Illustrated by Harold Eldridge. New York: Putnam, 1964. A juvenile fiction about a mule and her boy and their many adventures in the Tennessee hill country.
C4280 (ASU BC)

Clark, Billy C.
A Long Row to Hoe. New York: Crowell, 1960. A semi-autobiographical account of childhood in the Eastern Kentucky mountains.
C4290 (ASU BC)
The Mooneyed Hound. New York: Putnam, 1958. Children's story with an Eastern Kentucky setting.
C4300 (BC ASU)
Sourwood Tales: Stories. Illustrated by Harold Eldridge. New York: G. P. Putnam's Sons, 1968. A collection of short stories with an Eastern Kentucky setting.
C4310 (ASU)

Clark, Blanche Henry The Tennessee Yeomen, 1840-1860. Nashville: Vanderbilt Univ. Press, 1942. Certainly, it was hearty, yeoman stock which populated Tennessee's Eastern counties.
C4320 (ASU ETSU)
The Tennessee Yeomen, 1840-1860. 1942. Reprint. New York: Octagon Book, 1971.
C4330 (LMC)

Clark, C. Dunning Captain Paul, the Kentucky Moonshiner; or, the Boy Spy of the Mountains. "Beadle's Half-Dime Library." no. 135. New York: Beadle and Adams, 1880. Poorly-written fiction about moonshiners in the Kentucky mountains.
C4340

Clark, Carroll H. My Grandfather's Diary of the War. McMinnville: n.p., 1963. Relates to the Civil War in Warren Co., Tennessee.
C4350

Clark, David ed. Blue Ridge Facts and Legends. Charlotte, N. C.: Clark Pub. Co., 1955. A collection of odd facts about the mountains and a collection of legends.
C4360 (ASU LMC)

Clark, Donald L. "A Survey of the Guidance Programs in North Carolina Junior Colleges." Master's thesis. Appalachian State Teachers College, 1958. Includes colleges in the state's 28 county mountain region.
C4370 (ASU)

Clark, Dorothy Park, and McMeekin, Isabel McLennan see McMeekin, Clark, pseud.

Clark, Electa Cherokee Chief: The Life of John Ross. New York: Crowell-Collier Press, 1970. A good biography of the Principle chief of the Cherokee Nation during their last years in the East.
C4380 (LMC ETSU)

Clark, Ellery H. The Strength of the Hills: A Story of Andrew Jackson, and of the Pioneers of Tennessee. New York: Thomas Y. Crowell Co., 1929.
C4390 (LMC WWC BC)

Clark, Elmer T. ed. Asbury, Francis Journal and Letters. London: Epworth Press and Nashville, Tenn.: Abingdon Press, 1958.
A5060 (ASU BC WWC)

Clark, Elmer Talmage Methodism in Western North Carolina. Nashville: Parthenon Press, 1966. Includes sketches of ministers and histories of individual churches.
C4410 (ASU WCU LMC MHC)
The Small Sects in America. Rev. ed. New York: Abingdon-Cokesbury Press, 1949. Fascinating descriptions of the small sects which flourish in Appalachia.
C4420 (ASU)
The Small Sects in America. Nashville: Cokesbury Press, 1937.
C4430

Clark, Elmer Talmage and others eds. The Journals and Letters of Francis Asbury. 3 vols. Nashville, Tenn.: Abingdon Press, 1958. Asbury's comments on the mountains and mountaineers were generally negative.
C4400

Clark, Eunice Hicks "A History of Traphill Institute, Wilkes County, North Carolina." Master's thesis. Appalachian State Teachers College, 1954.
C4440 (ASU)

Clark, H. T. "A History of Mountain View School, Wilkes County, North Carolina." Master's thesis. Appalachian State Teachers College, 1954.
C4450 (ASU)

Clark, Henry Scott, pseud. see Cox, Millard F.

Clark, Herbert Leon "Tennessee: A Reluctant Seceder, 1847-1861." Master's thesis. Tennessee State A and I Univ., 1966. East Tennessee was defiantly pro-union throughout the secession debate.
C4460

Clark, Joe Back Home. Kingsport, Tennessee. Kingsport: Kingsport Press, 1965. A pictorial study of Kingsport and Sullivan County, Tennessee.
C4470 (BC ASU)
Tennessee Hill Folk. Essay by Jessee Stuart. Nashville: Vanderbilt Univ. Press, 1972. Lovely photographic essay on the area around the Cumberland Gap during the 1930's. Instant nostalgia for anyone who grew up in the mountains.
C4480 (ASU MHC LMC WCU ETSU BC)

Clark, John T. petitioner Was Rev. J. R. Moffett Murdered? Clark vs. Commonwealth, D. M. No. 43Z, from the Corporation Court of the City of Danville. Richmond: Taylor and Dalton, 1893. An inquiry into one of Virginia's most famous murder trials.
C4490 (ASU)

Clark, Joseph Harold "History of the Knoxville Iron Company." Master's thesis. Univ. of Tennessee, 1948.
C4500

Clark, Michael J. Lazar and Boone Stop Strip Mining Bully to Save Apple Valley and Buttermilk Creek. Huntington, W. Va.: Appalachian Movement Press, Inc., 1973. A cartoon strip for children. Anti-strip mining message.
C4510 (ASU)

Clark, Richard U. The Mountaineers, and Other Poems. Summit, N. J.: n.p., 1903.
C4520 (BC)

Clark, Septima Poinsette Echo in My Soul. New York: Dutton, 1962. Autobiography of a woman educator, and leader in race relations. She recalls the early, turbulent days of Highlander Folk School.
C4530 (BC)

Clark, Thomas Allen "A Study to Present the Status of Industrial Arts in the Five White Carter County, Tennessee, High Schools." Master's thesis. East Tennessee State College, 1956.
C4540 (ETSU)

Clark, Thomas D. assoc. ed. Coleman, John Winston, Jr. ed. Kentucky: A Pictorial History. Lexington: Univ. of Kentucky Press, 1971.
C5780 (ASU)

Clark, Thomas Dionysius A History of Kentucky. History Series. New York: Prentice-Hall, 1937.
C4550 (ASU BC)
The Kentucky. Illustrated by John A. Spelman, III. Rivers of America. New York: Farrar and Rinehart, 1942. A history of the Kentucky River and the people who live along its banks.
C4560 (WWC WCU UNCA)
The Kentucky. Illustrated by John A. Spelman, III. . Reprint. Lexington, Ky.: Henry Clay Press, 1969.
C4570 (ASU UNCA BC)
Kentucky: Land of Contrast. 1st. ed. Regions of America Book. New York: Harper and Row, 1968. Includes material on Eastern Kentucky's 49 Appalachian counties.
C4580 (LMC ASU WCU BC UNCA)
The Rampaging Frontier: Manners and Humors of Pioneer Days in the South and Middle West. Indianapolis: Bobbs-Merrill Co., 1939.
C4590 (ASU)
The Rampaging Frontier: Manners and Humors of Pioneer Days in the South and Middle West. 1939. Reprint. Bloomington: Indiana Univ. Press, 1964.
C4600 (WWC)
Simon Kenton, Kentucky Scout. New York: Rinehart, 1943. Further adventures of Kentucky and West Virginia's famous scout. Little emphasis is given his role in the latter days of the Revolution.
C4610 (BC)
Travels in the New South: A Bibliography. American Exploration and Travel Series, Vol. 36, 2 vols. Norman: Univ. of Oklahoma Press, 1962. This helpful aid lists early explorations and early accounts of travel in the Appalachian region.
C4620
Travels in the Old South: A Bibliography. American Exploration and Travel Series, No. 19. 3 vols. Norman: Univ. of Oklahoma Press, 1956-69.
C4630

Clark, Thomas Henry ed. Appalachian Tectonics. Royal Society of Canada Special Publications, no. 10. Toronto: Univ. of Toronto Press, 1967. A fascinating study of the forces which produced the Appalachians.
C4640 (ASU ETSU LMC WCU)

Clark, Walter Caldwell County, North Carolina in the Great War of 1861-1865. Hickory: Clay, 1910.
C4650

Clark, Walter ed. Histories of the Several Regiments and Battalions from North Carolina in the Great War, 1861-65. Written by members of the respective command. 5 vols. n.p.: State of North Carolina, 1901.
C4660 (LMC)

Clarke, Kenneth W. Uncle Bud Long: The Birth of a Kentucky Folk Legend. Lexington: Univ. Press of Kentucky, 1973.
C4670 (ASU)

Clarke, Mary Washington Jesse Stuart's Kentucky. 1st ed. New York: McGraw-Hill, 1968. An account of the almost mythical Kentucky portrayed in the stories and novels of Jesse Stuart.
C4680 (ASU WCU LMC MHC BC)
Proverb, Proverbial Phrases and Proverbial Comparisons in the Writings of Jesse Stuart. n.p.: n.p., 1962.
C4690

Clarke, Matthew St. Clair ed. Lowrie, Walter ed. American State Papers. Indian Affairs. Washington, D. C.: Gales and Seaton, 1832-34.
L3750

Clarkeson, Rosetta E. Herbs: Their Culture and Uses. New York: Macmillan, 1956. Includes material on folk medicine and the botanical drug industry which still flourishes in Appalachia.
C4700 (LMC)

Clarkson, Roy B. Tumult on the Mountains: Lumbering in West Virginia, 1770-1920. Illustrated by William A. Lunk. Parsons, W. Va.: McClain Print. Co., 1964. A documentary account of the lumbering industry which was once the primary industry in the mountains.
C4710 (ASU LMC WCU MHC BC)

Clary, Martin The Facts About Muscle Shoals. New York: Ocean Pub. Co., 1924. A discussion of the electric power and fertilizer facilities at the TVA's Muscle Shoals plant.
C4720 (LMC)

Claudel, Alice Moser Southern Season. Foreword by Richard Harter Fogle. Pikeville, Ky.: Appalachian Studies Center, Pikeville College, 1972.
C4730 (ASU)

Clavers, Mrs. Mary, pseud. Kirkland, Caroline Matilda A New Home — Who'll Follow? or, Glimpses at Western Life. New York: C. S. Francis, 1839.
K2640

Clay, Alfred Poems for Her. McClain Publishing Co., 1973. Poetry with an Appalachian setting.
C4740

Clay, Cassius Marcellus The Life of Cassius Marcellus Clay. Memoirs, Writings, and Speeches, Showing His Conduct in the Overthrow of American Slavery, the Salvation of the Union, and the Restoration of the Autonomy of the States. In 2 vols. Only vol. 1 published. Cincinnati: J. F. Brennan and Co., 1886. Biographical material on Eastern Kentucky's famous abolitionist, educator and orator.
C4750 (MHC BC)

Clay, Cassius Marcellus
The Meaning of the Past for the Future. Delivered at the Sesquicentennial celebration of the founding of Madison County, Richmond, Ky., October 17, 1937.
C4760 (BC)
Oration before Students and Historical Class of Berea College, Berea, Ky., Oct. 16, 1895. Richmond, Ky.: Pantagraph Job Press, 1896.
C4770 (BC)

Clay County, N. C. Historical Committee Clay County, 1861-1961; Commemorating the One Hundredth Anniversary of the Creating of Clay County, North Carolina. n.p.: n.p., 1961.
C4780

Clay, James C. Kentucky Law on Water. Research Report, no. 25. Frankfort, Ky.: Legislative Research Commission, 1965. A discussion of Kentucky's inadequate laws governing water pollution by acid mine drainage.
C4790

Clay, John Wesley Gunpowder Creek Philosophy. Winston-Salem, N. C.: Clay Print. Co., 1963. Solutions from Wesley's daily column in the Winston-Salem Journal.
C4800 (BC)

Clayton, Claud Franklin . . . Land Utilization in Laurel County, Kentucky. U. S. Dept. of Agriculture. Technical bulletin no. 289. Washington: U. S. Govt. Print. Off., 1932.
C4810 (ASU)
Land Utilization in Laurel County, Kentucky. Prepared in cooperation with the Kentucky Agricultural Experiment Station. Technical Bulletin, 289. Washington: U. S. Department of Agriculture, Bureau of Agricultural Economics, 1932.
C4820 (BC)

Clayton, John Bell The Strangers Were There: Selected Stories. New York: Macmillan, 1957. A selection of finely wrought short stories set in the Virginia foothill country.
C4830 (BC)

Cleaver, Bill Cleaver, Vera Where the Lilies Bloom. Philadelphia: J. B. Lippincott Co., 1969.
C4840 (BC ASU)

Cleaver, Vera Where the Lilies Bloom. Philadelphia: J. B. Lippincott Co., 1969. Children's story about a brave young girl who struggles to keep her family together after they are orphaned.
C4840 (BC ASU)

Cleaves, Freeman Rock of Chickamauga, the Life of General George H. Thomas. 1st ed. Norman: Univ. of Oklahoma Press, 1948. Biography of the Civil War general who rallied the Union Forces at the Battle of Chickamauga.
C4850 (ASU)

Cleland, Charles Leslie Church and Family in Modern Rural Appalachia. Morgantown, W. Va.: Center for Appalachian Studies and Development, 1967.
C4860 (ASU)
Selected Population and Agricultural Statistics for Tennessee Counties. Knoxville: Univ. of Tennessee, Agricultural Experiment Station, 1963. A study of out-migration from rural Tennessee counties.
C4870 (ASU)

Clem, Gladys B. It Happened around Staunton in Virginia. 2nd ed. Staunton, Va.: McClure Print. Co., 1964. Memoirs of life in and around Staunton with historical sketches, and descriptions of some landmarks.
C4880 (ASU)

Clemens, William Montgomery North and South Carolina Marriage Records. n.p.: n.p., 1927 reprinted 1973. This near-legendary work contains a list of almost 7,500 marriages performed in the Carolinas from the earliest colonial days to the time of the Civil War.
C4900
Virginia Wills Before 1799: A Complete Abstract Register of All Names Mentioned in Over Six Hundred Recorded Wills. Copied from the courthouse records of Amherst, Bedford, Campbell, Loudoun, Prince William, and Rockbridge counties. Baltimore: Genealogical Pub. Co., 1973.
C4910 (ETSU)

Clemens, William Montgomery ed. American Marriage Records before 1699. 1926. Reprint. Baltimore: Genealogical Pub. Co., 1967.
C4890 (ASU)

Clement, Maud Carter Frontiers Along the Upper Roanoke River, 1740-1776. Lynchburg: J. P. Bell Co., 1964. A very good history of the Roanoke Valley's early settlement and pioneer families.
C4920

Clemmer, James D. "J. D. Clemmer's Scrapbooks, 1884-1934." Unpublished typescript. Microfilm copy (5 reels) at Tennessee State Library and Archives. n.p.: n.p., n.d. A history of Polk County in possession of the Clemmer family.
C4930

Clemson Agriculture College of South Carolina, Department of Agricultural Economics and Rural Sociology. Survey of Unemployment Compensation Beneficiaries in Anderson, Greenville, Spartanburg Counties, South Carolina. Clemson: The Dept., 1958.
C4940

Clendening, John A. Gillespie, William H. Plant Fossils of West Virginia. Morgantown: West Virginia Geological and Economic Survey, 1966.
G1650 (BC ETSU)
Gillespie, William H. West Virginia Geology, Archaeology, and Pedology: A Bibliography and Index. Morgantown: West Virginia Univ. Library, 1964.
G1660 (BC ETSU)

Cleveland, Catherine Caroline The Great Revival in the West, 1797-1805. Chicago: University of Chicago Press, 1916.
C4950
The Great Revival in the West, 1797-1805. 1916. Reprint. Gloucester, Mass: Peter Smith, 1959. Formal religion gave way to revivalism when it encountered the frontier mind. In a sense, the revivalism movement is an Appalachian Phenomena, for it was here that formal religion met its strongest resistance.
C4960 (ASU)

Cleveland Chamber of Commerce Bradley County, Tennessee. 2 vols. Cleveland: Historical and Pictorial Advertising, 1929. A comprehensive historical and genealogical record of Bradley County Tennessee.
C4970
City and County with a Future: Cleveland, Bradley County, Tennessee. Cleveland: Historical and Pictorial Advertising, 1929.
C4980

Cleveland Public Library John Griswold White Collection. Cleveland: Bell and Howell Company, 1966. A listing of an excellent folklore collection.
C4990
Resources of the Appalachian Library and Culture Center: An Annotated Listing of Books. Cleveland: Cleveland Public Library, 1973.
C5000 (WCU ASU)

Clifford, William B. "Attitudes toward Education and the Schools in a Rural Industrialized County." Master's thesis. West Virginia Univ., 1965.
C5010
Sizer, Leonard M. Rural Industrialization: A Case Study in Educational Values and Attitudes. Morgantown: West Virginia Univ. Agricultural Experiment Station, 1966.
S3810 (ASU)

Clift, Garrett Glenn Kentucky Marriages, 1797-1865. Baltimore: Genealogical Pub. Co., 1966.
C5020 (BC)
Notes on Kentucky Veterans of the War of 1812. Anchorage, Ky.: Borderland Books, 1964.
C5030 (BC)
"Second Census" of Kentucky, 1800: A Private Compiled and Published Enumeration of Tax Payers Appearing in the 79 Manuscript Volumes Extant of Tax Lists of the 42 Counties of Kentucky in Existence in 1800. 1954. Reprint. Baltimore: Genealogical Pub. Co., 1966.
C5040 (ASU BC)

Clift, Garrett Glenn comp. Kentucky Historical Society Kentucky Marriages, 1797-1865. Baltimore: Genealogical Pub. Co.
K1260 (ASU BC)

Climatic Summaries of Resort Areas, Georgia Mountain Areas Washington: U. S. Dept. of Commerce, Environmental Data Service, 1970.
C5050

Clinard, Jones Weston Clinard Looks Back, a Compilation of Short Stories Covering Early Days in Hickory. Hickory, N. C.: Hickory Print. Co., 1962.
C5060 (ASU LMC)

Cline, M. G. Austin, Moris E. Soil Survey, Claiborne County, Tennessee. Washington: U. S. Department of Agriculture, Bureau of Plant Industry, Soils, and Agricultural Engineering, 1948.
A5560 (ASU)

Clingman, Thomas Lanier Measurements of the Black Mountains. n.p.: Gideon Printers, 1856. Elevations for peaks in the Black Mountain range, reprinted from the Asheville Times.
C5070
Selections from the Speeches and Writings of Hon. Thomas L. Clingman, of North Carolina. With Additions and Explanatory Notes. Raleigh, N. C.: J. Nichols, 1877.
C5080 (ASU BC)

Clitherow, Ronald Harper "Extent of Sexual Knowledge, Accumulation of Sexual Information, and Sex Education Attitudes of Undergraduate Students at Appalachian State University." Master's thesis. Appalachian State University, 1971.
C5090 (ASU)

Cloos, Ernst Microtectonics Along the Western Edge of the Blue Ridge, Maryland and Virginia. Baltimore: John Hopkins Press, 1971. Discuss the formations of the smaller mountains and ridges along the Western Blue Ridge.
C5100 (LMC)

Clopper, Edward N. Child Welfare in Kentucky. New York: National Child Labor Commission, 1919. Special attention is given to Eastern Kentucky's coal camps and poorer rural areas.
C5110 (ASU)

Clowes, Molly One-Fourth of Kentucky. Eleven Stories on the Mountains. Reprint. Louisville: Courier-Journal, n.d. These stories are set in Eastern Kentucky's thirty-five mountain counties.
C5120 (BC ASU)

Cloyd, A. D. Genealogy of the Cloyd, Basye and Tapp Families in America. Columbus, Ohio: Champlin Press, 1912.
C5130

Clugston, Katharine Wilderness Road. Garden City, N. Y.: Sun Dial Press, 1941. This history of the Wilderness Road contains biographical material on Boone and good descriptive passages on frontier life in Kentucky.
C5150 (BC)

Clugston, Katherine Wilderness Road. New York: Blue Ribbon Books, Inc., 1937.
C5140 (ASU)

Clyde, N. C. Planning Board Planning for Flood Damage Prevention at Clyde, N. C. Clyde, N. C.: The Board, 1965. Includes flood prevention plans for the Pigeon and Tuckaseegee River Basins.
C5160 (LMC)

Coal Age vol. 1. 1911-. New York: McGraw-Hill Pub. Co., weekly; 1927- monthly. Public relations material sponsored by the major coal companies.
C5170 (BC)
Practical Kinks for Coal Mining Men. New York: Coal Age, 193?
C5180 (BC)
Successful Solutions to Everyday Coal Mining Problems. New York: McGraw-Hill Pub. Co., 1931.
C5190 (BC)
Coal Industry Advisory Committee to Oranco. Mine Drainage Abstracts: A Bibliography. 1966 Supplement. n.p.: n.p., n.d.
C5200 (ASU)
Coal Patrol no. 1- . 197-. Washington: Appalachian Information, irregular.
C5210 (BC)
Coale, Charles B. The Life and Adventures of Wilburn Waters, Early History of Southwest Virginia. Richmond, Va.: G. W. Gary and Co., Steam Book and Job Printers, 1878.
C5220
The Life and Adventures of Wilburn Waters, the Famous Hunter and Trapper of White Top Mountain. Richmond: G. W. Gary and Co., 1878. Waters was a famous hunter and trapper in the southern mountains.
C5230 (BC)
Wilburn Waters History 1812-1879. Richmond, Virginia: n.p., 1878. The life and adventures of the famous hunter and trapper, Wilburn Waters, in the mountains of Virginia, North Carolina, and Tennessee.
C5240
Coates, Harold Wilson Stories of the Kentucky Feuds. Knoxville, Tennessee: Holmes-Darst Coal Corporation, 1923.
C5250
Stories of Kentucky Feuds. Knoxville, Tenn.: Holmes-Darst Coal Corp., 1942.
C5260 (ASU LMC)
Coatsworth, Elizabeth Jane Down Tumbledown Mountain. Illustrated by Aldren Watson. Evanston, Ill.: Row, Peterson and Co., 1958. Children's story with an Appalachia setting.
C5270 (LMC)
Old Whirlwind. Illustrated by Manning DeV. Lee. New York: Macmillan, 1953. A picture story of Davy Crockett's adventures on the Appalachian frontier. Contains several stories about his early years in East Tennessee.
C5280 (ETSU)
Cobb, Alice Lucy "Sect Religion and Social Change in an Isolated Rural Community of Southern Appalachia, with Case Story, "Fruit of the Land"." Microfilm. Ph. D. Diss. Boston Univ., 1965. A study of upper Mutton community in Harlan County, Kentucky.
C5290 (ASU)
Cobb, Ann Kinfolks: Kentucky Mountain Rhymes. Boston: Houghton Mifflin Co., 1922.
C5300 (ASU BC)
Cobb, Clayton W., pseud. see **Patten, J. A.**
Cobb, Donald "The Educational Development of Tyler County, West Virginia." Master's thesis. Marshall College, 1952.
C5310
Cobb, Irene S. "Variance in the Theory and Practice of Attendance Workers in Selected East Tennessee Systems." Master's thesis. Univ. of Tennessee, 1959.
C5320
Cobb, W. B. Dickey, John B. R. Soil Survey of Frederick County, Virginia. Washington: U. S. Department of Agriculture, Bureau of Soils, 1916.
D2180
Cobb, William B. Soil Survey of Caldwell County. Washington: Govt. Print. Off., 1919.
C5330
Soil Survey of Caldwell County, North Carolina. Prepared in cooperation with the North Carolina Department of Agriculture. Field Operations, 1917. Washington: U. S. Department of Agriculture, Bureau of Soils, 1923.
C5340
Cobb, William Vattle Davis, William Anderson Soil Survey of Watauga County, North Carolina. Washington: U. S. Department of Agriculture, Bureau of Chemistry and Soils, 1930.
D1280 (ASU)
Coblentz, Catherine Cate Sequoya. Illustrated by Ralph Ray, Jr. New York: Longmans, Green and Co., 1946.
C5350 (WCU ETSU BC)
Sequoya. New York: McKay, 1962.
C5360 (ASU)
Coccari, Ronald Louis "A Regional Linear Programming Model of the West Virginia Economy." Ph.D. Diss. West Virginia Univ., 1970.
C5370
Cochran, John A. "Collective Bargaining in the Bituminous Coal Industry." Microfilm. Ph. D. Diss. Harvard Univ., 1949.
C5380 (ASU)
Cochran, Samuel Lodge Simon Kenton. Illustrated by Earle H. Tiffany. Strasburg, Va.: Shenandoah Pub. House, 1932. Biography of West Virginia's most famous frontiersman.
C5390 (ASU)
Cocke, Charles Francis Parish Lines, Diocese of Southwestern Virginia. Richmond: Virginia State Library, 1960.
C5400 (ETSU)
Cocke County, Tenn., 1830 Census n.p.: n.p., n.d. Census statistics for Cocke County, Tennessee.
C5401
Cocke, Sarah Johnson Bypaths in Dixie: Folk Tales of the South. New York: E. P. Dutton and Co., 1911. Tales from the upland South.
C5410 (ASU BC)
The Master of the Hills: A Tale of the Georgia Mountains. New York: E. P. Dutton and Co., 1917. Mrs. Johnson's characters seem more like southern gentry than Georgia mountain folk.
C5420 (ASU BC)
Cocke, William J. Johnny Park Talks of Thomas Wolfe. Asheville, N. C.: Inland Press, 1973.
C5430 (ASU LMC)
Cockrill, Elizabeth Bibliography of Tennessee Geology, Soils, Drainage, Forestry, etc. with Subject Index. Tennessee State Geological Survey Bulletin, no. 1, Extract B. Nashville: Folk-Keelin Print. Co., 1911.
C5440 (LMC ETSU)
Cockrum, James Earl "A Study of the Development of Organized Religion in Jefferson County, Tennessee (1785-1950)." Master's thesis. Univ. of Tennessee, 1951.
C5450
Coddington, Keith E. "A Comparison of Intelligence in Students with Mixed and Lateral Dominance in Johnson City Vocational Schools." Master's thesis. East Tennessee State Univ., 1971.
C5460 (ETSU)
"A Comparison of Intelligence in Students with Mixed and Lateral Dominance in Johnson City Vocational Schools." Master's thesis. East Tennessee State Univ., 1971.
C5460 (ETSU)
Coe, David B. Record of the Coe Family and Descendants from 1596-1856. Cincinnati: Standard Pub. Co., 1885.
C5470 (BC)
Coe, Robert H. "Benjamin Hawkins, Indian Agent from 1796-1817." Master's thesis. Univ. of Tennessee, 1926. Hawkins was, perhaps, the best agent the Cherokee ever had.
C5480
Coffey, Horace Marcus The Glass House, a Novel. New York: Business Bourse, 1946. A novel with an Appalachian setting.
C5490 (BC ASU)
Coffin, Tristram Potter The British Traditional Ballad in North America. Rev. ed. Philadelphia: American Folklore Society, 1963.
C5500 (ASU FC)
Coffin, Tristram Potter ed. Indian Tales of North America: An Anthology for the Adult Reader. Bibliographical and Special Series, vol. 13. Philadelphia: American Folklore Society, 1961.
C5510 (ASU)
Coger, William N. "A Study of Administrative and Supervisory Practices of Principals in the Public School System of Jefferson County, Alabama." Master's thesis. Alabama State College, 1954.
C5520
Coggins, James Caswell Abraham Lincoln: A North Carolinian. Asheville, N. C.: Advocate Pub. Co., 1925. Another volume setting forth the oft-repeated theory that Lincoln was the son of Abraham Enlow of Swain County.
C5530 (ASU)
The Eugenics of President Abraham Lincoln: His German-Scotch Ancestry Irrefutably Established from Recently Discovered Documents. Milligan College, Tenn.: Goodwill Press, 1940.
C5540 (ASU)
The Thrones of the Apostles, a Study of the Pentecostal Phenomena. Elizabethton, Tenn.: n.p., 1947. A doctrinal study of the Disciples of Christ and of the growth of the Pentecostal Phenomena.
C5550 (BC)
Coghill, Kenneth L. The Lawmaking Process in West Virginia: A Study in Legislative Ethics. Parsons, W. Va.: McClain Print. Co., 1970.
C5560 (LMC)
Cogswell, Leander Winslow A History of the Eleventh New Hampshire Regiment, Volunteer Infantry in the Rebellion War, 1861-65. . . Chapter V-VII. Concord: Republican Press Association, 1891. This unit participated in several campaigns in the Southern mountains.
C5570
Cohen, Caroline Records of the Myers, Hays and Mordecai Families, 1707-1913. n.p.: n.p., n.d.
C5580
Cohen, David Stephen "They Walk These Hills: A Study of Social Solidarity among the Racially-mixed People of the Ramapo Mountains." Ph.D. Diss. Univ. of Pennsylvania, 1971.
C5590 (ASU)
Cohen, Irwin B. An Economic and Social Survey of Botetourt County." Master's thesis. Univ. of Virginia, 1942.
C5600
Cohen, William Howard The Hill Way Home: Poems from the Appalachian Highlands, Including "A House in the Country, II." Pippa Pass, Ky.: Mountain Press Alice Lloyd College, 1965.
C5610 (LMC BC)
Coincon, J. B. Colonial History of Nelson County, 1734-1807. Amherst, Va.: Amherst Pub. Co., n.d.
C5620 (ASU)
Cokeley, Harlin Rex A Son of the Mountains. Boston: Chapman and Grimes, 1935. A tale of a young man struggling to educate himself in the West Virginia mountains.
C5630
Coker, Robert E. ed. Research and Regional Welfare. Papers presented at a conference on research at the University of North Carolina at Chapel Hill. Chapel Hill: Univ. of North Carolina, 1946. Includes material on welfare in North Carolina's twenty-eight mountain counties.
C5640 (ASU)
Coker, William Chambers The Boletaceae of North Carolina. Chapel Hill: Univ. of North Carolina Press, 1943. An illustrated book of North Carolina's mushrooms.
C5650 (ASU WWC)
The Trees of North Carolina. Chapel Hill, N. C.: W. C. Coker, 1916.
C5660 (ASU)
Trees of the Southeastern States, Including Virginia, North Carolina, South Carolina, Tennessee, Georgia, and Northern Florida. 3rd ed. Chapel Hill: Univ. of North Carolina Press, 1945.
C5670 (ASU BC)
Cole, Charles D. Cumberland Gap, and Other Poems. n.p.: n.p., 1960.
C5680 (BC)

Cole, Charles D.
My Land — My People. n.p.: n.p., 1967. Poems celebrating life in Southeastern Kentucky.
C5690 (BC)

Cole, Lois Dwight Kentucky Cargo. New York: Macmillan, 1939. Poems.
C5700 (BC)

Cole, Lucy W. Kaufman, Harold P. Poverty Programs and Social Mobility. State College: Mississippi State Univ., Social Science Research Center, 1966.
K290

Cole, Mary Cross Cross, John Newton William Cross of Botetourt County, Virginia and His Descendants, 1733-1932. Columbia, Mo.: E. W. Stephens Publishing Co., 1932.
C9080

Cole, Redmond S. Ancestry, Life and Family of Col. William Edmiston of Washington County. n.p.: typescript, 1937.
C5710
Story of Captain Jesse Cox of Johnson Co., Tennessee. Revised by Mrs. Redmond S. Cole, 1958-60. n.p.: The author, 1960.
C5720

Cole, Mrs. Redmond S. ed. Cole, Redmond S. Story of Captain Jesse Cox of Johnson Co., Tennessee. n.p.: The author, 1960.
C5720

Coleman, Clarence Samuel and others Soil Survey, Culpeper County, Virginia. Soil Survey Report, Series 1941, no. 3. Washington: U. S. Bureau of Plant Industry, Soils and Agricultural Engineering, 1952.
C5730

Coleman, Howell F. "An Enrollment Projection for the Estes Elementary School, Anderson, S. C." Master's thesis. Western Carolina University, 1971.
C5740 (WCU)

Coleman, James Plemon and others The Robert Coleman Family, from Virginia to Texas, 1652-1965. Ackerman, Miss.: The author, 1965. A history and genealogy of a western Virginia family.
C5750 (ASU)

Coleman, John Winston, Jr. A Bibliography of Kentucky History. Lexington: Univ. of Kentucky Press, 1949.
C5770 (ASU LMC)

Coleman, John Winston, Jr. ed. Kentucky: A Pictorial History. Lexington: Univ. of Kentucky Press, 1971.
C5780 (ASU)

Coleman, McAlister Men and Coal. New York: Farrar and Rinehart, 1943. A pro-union, pro-Lewis book by a former union spokesman.
C5790 (ASU BC)
Men and Coal. 1943. Reprint. American Labor: From Conspiracy to Collective Bargaining.
C5800 (MHC WCU)

Coleman, Richard Douglas "The Distribution and Relative Abundance of Some Immature Aquatic Insects in Red Fork Creek, Unicoi County, Tennessee." Master's thesis. East Tennessee State Univ., 1967.
C5810 (ETSU)

Coleman, Sara Lindsay The Common Problem. New York: Doubleday, Doran and Company, 1929. A novel of manners overlaid with mystery and set in Western North Carolina.
C5820

Coleman, Thaddeus The Land of the Sky, an Idyl. Asheville, N. C.: Furman's Print., n.d. Paean to the Western North Carolina mountains.
C5830 (LMC ASU)

Coleman, Wilma "Mountain Dialect in North Georgia." Master's thesis. Univ. of Georgia, 1936. This rather superficial study of mountain speech consists primarily of phrases and vocabulary lists.
C5840 (ETSU ASU)

Colemen, James Walter The Molly Maguire Riots: Industrial Conflict in the Pennsylvania Coal Region. 1936. Reprint. American Labor: From Conspiracy to Collective Bargaining.
C5760 (WCU ASU)

Coles, Robert Children of Crisis. 1st ed. 3 vols., An Atlantic Monthly Press Book. Boston: Little, Brown, 1967. Volumes II and III contain major sections on the Southern mountaineers at home, or as migrants to northern cities.
C5850 (WCU ASU)
Dead End School. Illustrated by Norman Rockwell. An Atlantic Monthly Press Book. Boston: Little, Brown, 1968. A sympathetic study of school dropouts in the mountains.
C5860 (ASU)
An Evaluation of the Appalachian Volunteers. Typewritten copy. n.p.: n.p., 1966. Study of the problems encountered by the Appalachian volunteers and some speculations about reasons for the relative failure of the program.
C5870 (BC)
Farewell to the South. 1st ed., An Atlantic Monthly Press Book. Boston: Little, Brown, 1972. Includes material taken from the author's case studies of Appalachia.
C5880 (ASU WCU)
Migrants, Sharecroppers, Mountaineers. Children of Crisis, vol. 2. Boston: Little, Brown, 1971. The Appalachian mountaineers are one of three groups studied in this survey of poor sub-cultures in the South. The author has difficulty distinguishing between mountaineers and other Southerners.
C5890 (BC ASU)
The South Goes North. Children of Crisis, vol. 3. Boston: Little, Brown, 1971. A study of Southern migrants in northern cities.
C5900 (ASU BC)
Wages of Neglect. Chicago: Quadrangle Books, 1969. Includes sections on Appalachian children. Emphasis is on the effects of poverty and neglect on the development of a child's mind and spirit.
C5910 (ASU)

A Collection of Folklore by Undergraduate Students of East Tennessee State University Institute of Regional Studies Monograph, no. 3. Johnson City: East Tennessee State Univ., 1966. Folklore collected primarily in Avery and Watauga counties of North Carolina.
C5920 (ETSU ASU LMC BC)

Collier, Charles R. Influences of Strip Mining on the Hydrologic Environment of Parts of Beaver Creek Basin, Kentucky, 1955-59. Washington: Govt. Print. Off., 1964.
C5930 (BC)

Collier, John Roseanna McCoy: Final Screenplay. Hollywood, Cal.: Ball Script Service Co., 1948. A screenplay of the life of Roseanna McCoy and her role in the Hatfield and McCoy feud.
C5940

Collins, Carvil Emerson The Literary Tradition of the Southern Mountaineer, 1824-1900. Xerox of original. Ph. D. Diss. Univ. of Chicago, 1944.
C5950 (ETSU ASU)
Nineteenth Century Fiction of the Southern Appalachians. n.p.: n.p., 1943.
C5960

Collins, Charlie J. "Study of Industrial Arts Education in Public Secondary Schools of the Southern Appalachian Region." Master's thesis. West Virginia Univ., 1968.
C5970

Collins, Christian C. A Song of the Alleghenies. Johnson City, Tenn.: F. M. Hill Books, 1923.
C5980

Collins, Ernest M. "Political Behavior in Breathitt, Knott, Perry and Leslie Counties, Kentucky." Master's thesis. Univ. of Kentucky, 1940.
C5990

Collins, Frederick Lewis Uncle Sam's Billion-dollar Baby, a Taxpayer Looks at the TVA. New York: G. P. Putnam's Sons, 1945. A realistic look at the waste perpetrated by the TVA.
C6000 (ASU UNCA)

Collins, Louis Historical Collections of Kentucky. 2 vols. Louisville: John P. Norton Company, 1874.
C6010

Collins, Margaret Humes Plenteous Heritage. Philadelphia: Dorrance, 1966.
C6020 (BC)

Collins, Richard H. Collins, Louis Historical Collections of Kentucky. Louisville: John P. Norton Company, 1874.
C6010

Collin's Travelbook of North Carolina Winston-Salem: Collins Co., annual. Many of the travel attractions listed are in the Western, mountainous section of the state.
C6030 (LMC)

Collins, W. D. and others Springs of Virginia. In cooperation with U. S. Geological Survey. Richmond: Division of Purchase and Printing, State Commission of Conservation and Development, Division of Water Resources and Power, 1930.
C6040

Collins, William From the Freedom of the Mountains to the Hurly-burly City. Cincinnati: Cincinnati Inquirer, n.d.
C6050

Collins, William E. Folk Ways and Customs of Old Kentucky. Lexington, Ky.: Uldean W. Johnston, 1971. A book of folklore and folkways collected in the foothill country of Kentucky.
C6060 (ASU BC)

Colonial Records of Virginia Baltimore, Genealogical Publishing Co., 1973.
C6070

Colony, Horatio Free Forester: A Novel of Pioneer Kentucky. Boston: Little, Brown and Co., 1935. A novel about a long-hunter and trapper who crosses the mountains to live among the Shawnee and Wyandottes.
C6080 (ASU LMC WCU BC)

Colton, Henry E. Mountain Scenery: The Scenery of the Mountains of Western North Carolina and Western South Carolina. Raleigh, N. C.: W. L. Pomeroy; Philadelphia: Hayes and Zell, 1859.
C6090 (ASU WCU)

Coltrane, George A. ed. North Carolina, University, Institute of Government County Government in North Carolina. Chapel Hill: The institute, 1968.
N2680 (WWC ASU LMC)

Coltrane, Robert Iroin Pavlick, Anthony Leo Quality of Rural and Urban Housing in the Appalachian Region. Washington: Economic Research Service, Resource Development Economics Division, U. S. Dept. of Agriculture, 1964.
P1050 (LMC)

Coltrane, Robert Irvin An Economic Survey of the Appalachian Region, with Special Reference to Agriculture. Prepared in cooperation with the West Virginia Agricultural Experiment Station Report. Agricultural Economic Report, no. 69. Washington: Economic Research Service, U. S. Dept. of Agriculture, 1965.
C6100 (ETSU WCU LMC ASU)

Combs, Harriette Reynolds The Bubble. Richmond, Virginia: Satterwhite Printing Co., 1965. A collection of twenty-six poems simply but charmingly written.
C6110

Combs, Jerry W. "Population Migration in the State of Tennessee." Master's thesis. Univ. of Tennessee, 1948.
C6120

Combs, Josiah Henry Folksongs of the Southern United States. Publications of the American Folklore Society. Bibliographical and Special Series, vol. 19. Austin: Univ. of Texas Press, 1967.
C6130 (ASU WCU MHC LMC WWC BC FC)
The Kentucky Highlanders from a Native Mountaineers Viewpoint. Lexington, Ky.: J. L. Richardson and Co., 1913.
C6140 (BC ASU)

Combs, Maxine Solow Gauthier "A Study of the Black Mountain Poets." Ph. D. Diss. Univ. Oregon, 1967. Black Mountain college and the surrounding resort area attracted a substantial colony of all types of artists, including poets.
C6150 (WCU)

Cometti, Elizabeth ed. The Thirty-fifth State: Documentary History of Virginia. Morgantown: W. Va. Univ. Library, 1966.
C6160 (ASU LMC BC)

Commission Book of Governor John Sevier, 1796-1801 Nashville: Tenn. Hist. Comm., 1957. Record book of Tennessee's most exciting governor and the fight for statehood.
C6170

Commission on Religion in Appalachia CORA: Our Christian Commitment in Appalachia. Knoxville: The commission, 1971.
C6180

Directory of Appalachian Mission Enterprises. Knoxville, Tenn.: n.p., 1972.
C6190 (BC)

Proceedings: A United Approach to Fulfilling the Church's Mission in Appalachia. Knoxville, Tenn.: The commission, 1966.
C6210 (ASU WCU)

Commission on Religion in Appalachia, Economic and Political Issues Task Force. Strip Mining in Appalachia. Knoxville: Commission on Religion in App., 1970.
C6200

Common Forest Trees of West Virginia Charleston: W. Va. Conservation Commission, n.d.
C6220

Community Research Associates Prelude to Planning in Buncombe County, North Carolina. New York: The Co., 1963.
C6230 (WWC)

Community Service of Clarksburg, W. Va. The Shawnee Trail Program: An Historical Pageant Presented at Clarksburg, W. Va., June 13, and 15, 1923. Clarksburg: The service, 1923. Included an outline of the early history of Harrison County, West Virginia.
C6240 (BC)

Compton, Hannibal Albert A Moonshiner's Folly, and Other Stories. Boston: Roxburgh Pub. Co., 1916. Stories about blockading corn huskings, haints, and mountain religion.
C6250 (BC)

Comstock, Charles Freemasonry in Pioneer Times, White County. Sparta: n.p., 1929.
C6260

Comstock, Harriet Theresa The Man Thou Gavest. Garden City, N. Y.: Doubleday, Page and Co., 1917. A young writer, recovering his health in the Virginia mountains, marries and then abandons a mountain girl. Many years later he works out his guilt by writing a play about her.
C6270 (ASU BC)

The Shield of Silence. Garden City, N. Y.: Doubleday, Page and Co., 1921. Novel about a home for Episcopal sisters in the southern mountains and its effects on four women who live there.
C6280 (ASU BC)

A Son of the Hills. Garden City, N. Y.: Doubleday, Page and Co., 1913. Novel about a young man who wants escape the hopelessness of life in Lost Hollow and chooses education and out as his route of escape. As a successful artist he is able to reflect more favorably on his mountain background.
C6290 (ASU WCU BC)

Comstock, Jim F. Best of Hillbilly: A Prize Collection of 100-proof Writings from Jim Comstock's West Virginia Hillbilly. 1st ed. Anderson, S. C.: Droke House, 1968.
C6300 (ASU MHC WCU LMC BC)

Pa and Ma and Mister Kennedy. Richwood, W. Va.: App. Press, 1965. An account of John Kennedy's West Virginia primary campaign.
C6310 (ASU BC)

Concord College, Athens, W. Va. see **West Virginia, Concord College, Athens**

Condit, D. D. Economic Geology of the Summerfield and Woodsfield Quadrangles, Ohio, with Descriptions of Coal and Other Mineral Resources, Except Oil and Gas. U. S. Geological Survey Bulletin, no. 720. Washington: Govt. Print. Off., 1923.
C6320

Structure of the Berea Oil Sand in the Summerfield Quadrangle, Guernsey, Noble, and Monroe Counties, Ohio. U. S. Geological Survey Bulletin, no. 621-N. Washington: Govt. Print. Off., 1916.
C6330

Condon, Mabel Amanda Green A History of Harlan County. Nashville: Parthenon Press, 1962. An informal but rather good history of Harlan County. Special attention is given to education and religion.
C6340 (BC)

Conference of Governors on Underdeveloped Areas of the Appalachian Region, Lexington, Ky., 1960. Summary. Atlanta: Council of State Governments, Southern Office, 1961?
C6350

Conference of Southern Mountain Workers The Southern Highlands, an Inquiry into their Needs, and Qualifications Desired in Service Workers in the Mountain Country. Asheville, N. C. Inland Press, 1915.
C6360

Conference of Southern Mountain Workers see **Council of Southern Mountain Workers**

Conference of Southern Workers see also **Council of the Southern Mountains**

Conference on Appalachian Development, Princeton, N. J., 1964 Report. Conference organized by the graduate students of the Woodrow Wilson School of Public and International Affairs of Princeton University, March 20-22, 1964. Princeton, N. J.: n.p., 1964.
C6370

Conference on Economic Progress, Washington, D. C. Poverty and Deprivation in the United States: The Plight of Two-fifths of a Nation. Washington: n.p., 1962.
C6380

Conference on Interstate Pollution of North Fork Holston River Report of the Conference, 2D Kingsport, Tennessee, 1962. Kingsport, Tenn.: The Conference, 1962.
C6390

Conference on Low Income Farms Proceedings. Morgantown, W. Va.: W. Va. Univ., Agricultural Experiment Station, 1940. A study of the statis marginal farms.
C6400

Conference on Manpower Requirements and Human Resource Adjustment Papers. (Charlotte, 1964.) ("API Series," no. 15.) Raleigh: Agricultural Policy Institute, State College of Agriculture and Engineering, N. C. Univ., 1965.
C6410

Conference on New Approaches to Strip Mining Proceedings. The Planning Concept. Lexington: Univ. of Kentucky Student Council on Pollution and Environment, 1970.
C6420

Conference on Poverty-in-Plenty — The Poor in Our Affluent Society Poverty in Plenty. Foreword by Sargent Shriver. Contributors: Wilbur J. Cohen and others. Wisdom and Discovery Book. New York: P. J. Kenedy, 1964. Includes sections on poverty in the Appalachian Mountains.
C6430

Conference on Surface Mining, Roanoke, Va., 1964. Surface Mining — Extent and Economic Importance, Impact on Natural Resources, and Proposals for Reclamation of Mined-lands: Proceedings. Chicago: Council of State Governments, 1964.
C6440 (ASU)

Conference on the Application of Engineering Technology to the Problems of Appalachia Draft Paper Discussing the Background of the Problems in Appalachia. Conference at W. Va. Univ., 1965. Morgantown: W. Va. Univ., 1965.
C6450

Conference on Training in Biomathematics, Western Carolina College, 1961 The Cullowhee Conference on Training in Biomathematics: An International Conference Held at Western Carolina College, Cullowhee, North Carolina, August 14-18, 1961. Raleigh: Institute of Statistics, N. C. State College, 1962.
C6460 (WCU)

Conference on Water Resources and Economic Development in the South Papers. (Atlanta, 1964.) ("API Series," no. 15.) Raleigh: Agricultural Policy Institute, State College of Agriculture and Engineering, N. C. Univ., 1965.
C6470 (ASU)

Conference to Identify Broadened Roles for College and Secondary School Industrial Arts Programs in Appalachia and to Plan Pilot Educational Projects, Eastern Ky. State College, 1964 Proceedings. Richmond: The College, 1964.
C6480 (ASU)

Conger, J. T. Taylor, Arthur Elijah Soil Survey, Dade County, Georgia. Washington: U. S. Department of Agriculture, Bureau of Plant Industry, 1942.
T440

Congleton, Betty Carolyn "The Southern Poor Whites 1800-1869, with Particular Reference to Kentucky and Tennessee." Master's thesis. Univ. of Ky., 1948.
C6490 (ASU)

Conklin, J. Douglas Selected South Carolina Economic Data. Columbia: Univ. of S. C., Bureau of Business and Economic Research, 1969.
C6500

Conley, Betty Rutter "An Evaluation of the Elementary School Libraries in Washington County, Virginia." Master's thesis. East Tenn. State Univ., 1966.
C6510 (ETSU)

Conley, James F. Mineral Localities of North Carolina. Information Circular 16. Raleigh: N. C. Dept. of Conservation and Development, 1971. The state's most valuable mineral resources are in the western mountains.
C6520 (ASU)

Conley, Philip Mallory As I See It. Charleston, W. Va.: Education Foundation, 1965. The author's thoughts on success and proper conduct in life. Largely autobiographical.
C6530 (ASU)

Beacon Lights of West Virginia History. Vol. 1. Charleston: W. Va. Pub. Co., 1939.
C6540 (BC)

History of West Virginia Coal Industry. Charleston, W. Va.: Education Foundation, 1960.
C6550 (ASU BC)

The Mountain Murder. Gold and Blue Series, no. 1. Charleston, W. Va.: W. Va. Pub. Co., 1939. A mystery story set in the West Virginia mountains.
C6560 (ASU BC)

Uncle Amos, Politician. 1st ed. Charleston, W. Va.: W. Va. Pub. Co., 1940.
C6570 (ASU BC)

West Virginia: Brief History of the Mountain State. Charleston, W. Va.: n.p., 1963.
C6580 (ASU BC)

West Virginia History. Charleston: n.p., 1975. A very good new history of West Virginia.
C6600

West Virginia Reader, Stories of Early Days. Charleston, W. Va.: Education Foundation, 1970. Delightful stories taken from West Virginia history.
C6610 (ASU ETSU)

West Virginia, Yesterday and Today. Charleston: W. Va. Review Press, 1931. A school text stressing the geography, history, natural resources, industries, and government of the state.
C6620 (BC)

West Virginia, Yesterday and Today. 3rd ed., rev. and rewritten. Charleston, W. Va.: Education Foundation, 1952.
C6630 (ASU)

Conley, Philip Mallory ed. The West Virginia Encyclopedia. 1st ed. Charleston, W. Va.: W. Va. Pub. Co., 1929. An information packed volume of fact and trivia of West Virginia history.
C6590 (LMC BC)

Connelley, William Elsey Eastern Kentucky Papers: The Founding of Harman's Station, with an Account of the Indian Captivity of Mrs. Jennie Wiley and the Exploration and Settlement of the Big Sandy Valley in the Virginia's and Kentucky. To Which Is Affixed a Brief Account of the Connelley Family and Some of Its Collateral and Related Families in America. New York: Torch Press, 1910.
C6640 (ASU)
The Founding of Harman's Station and the Wiley Captivity. Original title: Eastern Kentucky Papers. 1910. Reprint. With four additional chapters by Edward R. Hagelett.
C6650 (BC ASU)

Connelly, Thomas Lawrence Army of the Heartland: The Army of Tennessee, 1861-1862. Baton Rouge: Louisiana State Univ. Press, 1967. The army of Tennessee saw action in the mountain areas of three states.
C6660 (LMC ASU)
Discovering the Appalachians: What to Look for from the Past in the Present along America's Eastern Frontier. Harrisburg, Pa.: Stackpole Books, 1968. A guide to the recreational attractions of the various mountain ranges which comprise the Appalachians.
C6670 (ASU WCU MHC ETSU LMC WWC UNCA BC)

Conner, Maynard Calvin An Economic and Social Survey of Patrick County. Extension Record Extension Series, vol. 31, no. 6. Charlottesville: Univ. of Va., 1937.
C6680 (BC)

Connor, Phyllis Old Timey Recipes. Bluefield, W. Va.: n.p., 1966. Recipes and home remedies from the hills of West Virginia.
C6690 (ASU LMC BC)
Old Timey Recipes. 3rd ed. Bluefield, W. Va.: n.p., 1970.
C6700 (WCU BC)
Old Timey Recipes. Bluefield, W. Va.: n.p., 1973.
C6710 (LMC)

Connor, Robert Diggs Wimberly History of North Carolina. 6 vols. Chicago: Lewis Pub. Co., 1919.
C6720 (LMC)
Makers of North Carolina History. Raleigh, N. C.: Thompson Pub. Co., 1923.
C6730 (LMC)
North Carolina: Rebuilding an Ancient Commonwealth, 1584-1925. 4 vols. Chicago: American Historical Society, 1929.
C6740 (UNCA BC LMC)
Race Elements in the White Population of North Carolina. Studies in North Carolina History, no. 1. Greensboro: Woman's College of the Univ. of N. C., 1933. Deals with the various ethnic groups in North Carolina's population.
C6750 (ASU BC)
Revolutionary Leaders of North Carolina. Studies in North Carolina History, no. 2. Greensboro: North Carolina College for Women, 1930.
C6760 (ASU LMC)
Revolutionary Leaders of North Carolina. 1930. Reprint. Spartanburg, S. C.: Reprint Co., 1971.
C6770 (WWC)

Conrey, G. W. Paschall, Alfred H. Soil Survey, Athens County, Ohio. Washington: U. S. Department of Agriculture, Bureau of Chemistry and Soils, 1938.
P530
Paschall, Alfred H. Soil Survey of Vinton County, Ohio. Washington: U. S. Department of Agriculture, Bureau of Chemistry and Soils, 1938.
P540
Taylor, Arthur Elijah Soil Survey of Adams County, Ohio. Washington: U. S. Department of Agriculture, Bureau of Chemistry and Soils, 1938.
T390

Conrey, Guy Woolard Soil Survey, Scioto County, Ohio. Prepared in cooperation with the Ohio Agricultural Experiment Station. Soil Survey Report, Series 1933, no. 31. Washington: U. S. Dept. of Agriculture, Bureau of Plant Industry, 1940.
C6780

Consolidated Coal Company History of the Consolidated Coal Company. New York: The Company, 1934.
C6790

Conway, Martha Bell ed. The Compacts of Virginia. Richmond, Va.: Commonwealth of Va., 1963. A history of the interstate and boundary agreements of Virginia.
C6800 (FC)

Conway, Robert Traditional Pottery in North Carolina by Bob Conway. Photographed by Ed Gilreath. Waynesville, N. C.: Mountaineer Printers, 1974.
C6810

Cook County, Ill., Department of Public Aid Southern Appalachian Migrant on Public Aid in Cook County. A follow-up study directed by Raymond M. Hilliard. Chicago: The dept., 1964.
C6820 (ASU)
A Study of Families from the Southern Appalachian Region Receiving Public Assistance. Chicago: The dept., 1960.
C6830 (ASU)

Cook, Gerald Wildon The Descendants of Claiborne Howard, Soldier of the American Revolution. 1st ed. Cholon, Vietnam: n.p., 1960, 1961.
C6840 (ASU)

Cook, John Harrison "A Study of the Mill Schools of North Carolina." Ph. D. Diss. Columbia Univ., 1925. Many of the textile mills are located in the foothill country of North Carolina.
C6850

Cook, Katherine M. ed. Gaumnitz, Walter Herbert Education in the Southern Mountains. Washington: Govt. Print. Off., 1938.
G640 (ASU BC)

Cook, Raymond Allen Fire from the Flint: The Amazing Careers of Thomas Dixon. Winston-Salem, N. C.: J.P. Blair, 1968. Biography of the novelist, education and politician from western North Carolina.
C6860 (BC ASU)
Thomas Dixon: His Books and His Career. Unpublished Ph. D. Diss. Emory Univ., 1954. Biography of a North Carolina novelist.
C6870

Cook, Roy Bird The Annals of Pharmacy in West Virginia. Charleston, W. Va.: Barrett Print. Co., 1946.
C6880 (ASU)
Christ Church Methodist, a Historical Sketch, 1804-1961. Charleston, W. Va.: Charleston Print. Co., 1961. History of one of Charleston's oldest Methodist Churches.
C6890 (ASU)
The Family and Early Life of Stonewall Jackson. 4th ed., rev. Charleston, W. Va.: Education Foundation, 1963. Jackson was a native of western Virginia.
C6900 (ASU)
Washington's Western Lands. Strasburg, Va.: Shenandoah Pub. House, 1930. Washington owned land in western Virginia and in what is now West Virginia.
C6910 (ASU)

Cook, Ruth E. "Food Habits of a Selected Group of Pupils in the Wellsbury High School, West Virginia." Master's thesis. West Virginia Univ., 1951.
C6920

Cooke, Addie M. "A History of the Public Library in Murphy, N. C." Master's thesis. Fla. State Univ., 1962.
C6930

Cooke, Dan Boy "Developing a Core Plan in the Seventh and Eighth Grades at Candler Elementary School." Master's thesis. Western Carolina Univ., 1955.
C6940 (WCU)

Cooke, Grace MacGowan The Power and the Glory. New York: Doubleday, 1910. A novel about a Tennessee mountain girl who moves to a nearby textile town. Conditions in the mill are realistically described but the plot is overly romantic.
C6950 (BC)

Cooke, John Esten Fairfax: Or, the Master of Greenway Court. A Chronicle of the Valley of the Shenandoah. New York: Carleton and Co.; London: S. Low, Son and Co., 1868. Novel of frontier life in western Virginia.
C6960 (BC ASU)
The Last of the Foresters: Of Humors on the Border. A Story of the Old Virginia Frontier. New York: Derby and Jackson; Cincinnati: H. W. Derley and Co., 1856. A novel of the western Virginia frontier.
C6970 (ASU BC)
Leather Stocking and Silk. New York: Harper, 1854. The area around Martinsburg West Virginia is the setting for this novel based on the life of hunter John Meyers.
C6980 (BC)
Mohun: Or, The Last Days of Lee and His Paladins. Final Memoirs of a Staff Officer Serving in Virginia. From the MSS. of Colonel Surry, of Eagle's Nest. 1869. Reprint. Americans in Fiction. Ridgewood, N. J.: Gregg Press, 1968.
C6990 (ASU WCU BC)
Stonewall Jackson. New York: G. W. Dillingham Co., 1897. A biography of Appalachian Virginia's greatest general.
C7000 (ASU BC)
Stonewall Jackson and the Old Stonewall Brigade. Charlottesville: Univ. of Virginia Press for the Tracy W. McGregor Library, 1954.
C7010 (ASU BC)

Cooke, John White "Isaac Shelby, 1750-1796." Master's thesis. Vanderbilt Univ., 1959. Shelby was a politician, soldier and leader in the Watauga settlements.
C7030

Cooke, Kennis "A History of Education in Wyoming County, West Virginia." Master's thesis. Marshall College, 1952.
C7040

Cooke, Philip Pendleton Froissart Ballads, and Other Poems. Philadelphia: Carey and Hart, 1847. This volume is the best-known work of this Appalachian Virginia author.
C7050 (BC)

Cooley, Elmer J. The Inside Story of the World Famous Courtroom Tragedy. Charlottesville, Va.: Michie Co., 1961. An eyewitness account of the trail of the Allen outlaws at Hillsville, Virginia.
C7060 (BC)

Coon, Charles Lee The Beginnings of Public Education in North Carolina: A Documentary History, 1790-1840. 2 vols. Raleigh: N. C. Historical Commission, 1908.
C7070 (LMC BC)

Coon, Charles Lee comp. North Carolina Schools and Academies, 1790-1840: A Documentary History. Raleigh, N. C.: Edwards and Broughton, 1915.
C7080 (LMC WWC)

Coop Howard Poems From a Land of Hills. London, Ky.: Kentuckiana Press, 1969. Poems about Heigira, a land of hills at the western tip of the mountains in Kentucky.
C7090 (ASU LMC)

Cooper, A. B. "Exploratory Study of the Views toward Birth Control Services." Master's thesis. Univ. of Tenn., 1966. Some Eastern Tennessee families are used in this study.
C7100

Cooper, Byron Nelson Geology of the Draper Mountain Area, Virginia. Virginia Geological Survey Bulletin, 55. Richmond: Division of Purchase and Print., 1939.
C7110 (ETSU)
The Geology of the Region Between Roanoke and Winchester in the Appalachian Valley of Western Virginia. Baltimore: Johns Hopkins Univ., 1960.
C7120

Cooper, Byron Nelson
Grand Appalachian Field Excursion. Engineering Extension Series. Geological Guidebook, no. 1. Blacksburg: Virginia Polytechnic Institute, 1961. Includes description of Pennsylvania rocks along the West Virginia turnpike.
C7130 (BC)

Cooper, Frank Ocona of the Cherokee Hills. n.p.: The author, 1955.
C7140 (ASU LMC MHC)

Cooper, H. P. Veatch, Jethro O. Soil Survey of Blair County, Pennsylvania. Washington: U. S. Department of Agriculture, Bureau of Soils, 1917.
V490

Cooper, Herston Crossville. Miami, Fla.: Adams Press, 1965. A description of the World War II interment camp in Cumberland County, Tennessee.
C7150

Cooper, Hobart S. "German and Swiss Colonization in Morgan County, Tennessee." Master's thesis. Univ. of Tenn., 1925.
C7160 (ASU)

Cooper, Horton History of Avery County, North Carolina. Asheville, N. C.: Biltmore Press, 1964.
C7170 (ASU LMC WCU BC)

North Carolina Mountain Folklore and Miscellany. Murfreesboro, N. C.: Johnson Pub. Co., 1972.
C7180 (MHC ASU LMC BC)

Cooper, John R. "A Study of Pupil Withdrawal in Ten Secondary Schools of Floyd, Knott, Letcher, and Pike Counties through the School Year of 1932-33."
C7190

Cooper, R. W. Wenger, Karl Frederick The Relation of Growth to Stand Density in Natural Loblolly Pine Stands. Asheville, N. C.: Southeastern Forest Experiment Station, 1958.
W2820 (WCU)

Cooper, Robert Warren Silvical Characteristics of Slash Pine. U. S. Forest Service Station Paper, no. 81. Asheville, N. C.: Southeastern Forest Experiment Station, 1957.
C7200 (WCU)

Cooper, Susan Fenimore ed. William West Skiles: A Sketch of Missionary Life at Valle Crucis in Western North Carolina, 1842-1862. New York: James Pott and Co., 1890.
C7210 (ASU WCU BC)

Skiles, William West A Sketch of Missionary Life at Valle Crucis in Western North Carolina, 1842-1862. New York: James Pott and Co., 1890.
S4010 (LMC)

Cooper, Williamson Lee Stuart Robinson School and Its Work. Nashville: Parthenon Press, 1936. Reverend E. O. Guerrant's Presbyterian mission school in Letcher County, Kentucky.
C7220 (BC)

Cooperative Recreation Service Handy Square-Dance Book. Delaware, Ohio: n.p., 1955. A well-illustrated book giving directions for most American square dances.
C7230 (WCU ASU)

Songs of All Time. 1946. Reprint. Berea, Ky.: Cooperative Recreation Service, 1957.
C7240 (WCU)

Cope, Annis D. "A History of Education in Hawkins County with Special Reference to Rock Hill School." Master's thesis. Univ. of Tenn., 1957.
C7250

Cope, Robert F. The County of Gaston: Two Centuries of a North Carolina Region. With a foreword by William Friday. Gastonia: Gaston County Historical Society, 1961.
C7260 (LMC ASU BC)

Cope, Robert S. Carry Me Back: Slavery and Servitude in Seventeenth Century Virginia. 1st ed. Pikeville, Ky.: Pikeville College Press of the Appalachian Studies Center, 1973.
C7270 (MHC FC ASU)

Copeland, Helen This Snake is Good. Illustrated by Charles W. Walker. New York: Thomas Y. Crowell Co., 1968. A children's story about a pet snake. Appalachian mountain setting.
C7280 (ASU)

Copeland, Lewis C. Estimating Tennessee's Tourist Business. A study for the Tenn. Dept. of Conservation, Division of State Information, by the Bureau of Business Administration, the Univ. of Tenn. and the Institute of Research and Training in the Social Sciences, Vanderbilt Univ., in cooperation with the Tenn. Valley Authority: Study, no. 26. Knoxville: Univ. of Tenn., Bureau of Business Research, 1955.
C7290 (ASU)

Methods for Estimating Income Payments in Counties; a Technical Supplement to County Income Estimates for Seven Southeastern States. Charlottesville, Va.: Bureau of Population and Economic Research, Univ. of Va., 1952.
C7300

Tourists and the Travel Service and Transportation Business in Tennessee, 1948 to 1961, Inclusive, an Economic Analysis. n.p.: Tenn. Division of State Information and Tourist Promotion, 1962.
C7310

Travel Industry in North Carolina. An Economic Survey. Raleigh, N. C., 1959.
C7320

Copeland, Pauline B. "An Evaluation of the Remedial Speech Program in the Johnson City Schools." Master's thesis. E. Tenn. State College, 1952.
C7330 (ETSU)

Copley, Robert W. "The Development of a Management Evaluation System for Community Action Agencies." Master's thesis. Univ. of Louisville, 1970.
C7340

Copp, James H. ed. Our Changing Rural Society — Perspectives and Trends. Ames: Iowa State Univ. Press, 1964.
C7350

Corbett, H. Roger, Jr. Blue Ridge Voyages: One and Two Day River Cruises. Pennsylvania, Maryland, Virginia, West Virginia. 2 vols. in 1. Falls Church, Va.: Blue Ridge Voyageurs, 1965-66.
C7360 (LMC)

Corbin, David The Socialist and Labor Star, Huntington, West Virginia, 1912-1915. Huntington: App. Movement Press, 1971. An account of the strike and lookouts at the Socialist and Labor Star.
C7370 (ASU BC)

Corbin, John B. An Index of State Geological Survey Publications Issued in Series. New York: Scarecrow, 1965.
C7380 (LMC)

Corby, Jane Irenita Simon Kenton, the Scout: A Tale of Frontier Life During the Revolution. New York: Thomas Crowell Co., 1925. This is one of the few biographies of Kenton that deals with his change of loyalties at the end of the Revolution.
C7390 (BC)

Core, Earl Lemley The Monongalia Story, a Bicentennial History. Parson, W. Va.: McClain Printing Co., 1974.
C7400

Morgantown Disciples: A History of the First Christian Church of Morgantown, West Virginia. Parsons, W. Va.: McClain Print. Co., 1960.
C7410 (ASU)

Spring Wild Flowers. Series 58, no. 4-2. Morgantown: W. Va. Univ. Bulletin, 1958.
C7430 (BC)

Vegetation of West Virginia. Parsons, W. Va.: McClain Print. Co., 1966.
C7440 (ASU LMC BC)

Strausbaugh, Perry Daniel Common Seed Plants of the Mid-Appalachian Region. Morgantown, W. Va.: Book Exchange, 1948.
S7820 (ASU BC)

Strausbaugh, Perry Daniel Flora of West Virginia. Morgantown: West Virginia Univ. Press, 1952-1964.
S7830 (ASU)

Core, Earl Lemley and others Plant Life of West Virginia. New York: Scholar's Library, 1960.
C7420 (ETSU)

Core, George ed. Stewart, Randall Regionalism and Beyond: Essays of Randall Stewart. Nashville: Vanderbilt Univ. Press, 1968.
S7340 (ASU)

Corey, Faris Jane Exploring the Mountains of North Carolina. Raleigh, N. C.: Provincial Press, 1972.
C7450 (ASU LMC SCU WCU)

Corgan, D. Leonard A Description of the George Korson Folklore Archine. Compiled by Judith Tiering, Special Collections Librarian. Wilkes-Barre, Pa.: King's College Press, 1973.
C7460 (ASU)

Corkran, David H. The Carolina Indian Frontier. 1st ed. S. C. Tricentennial Commission Booklet, no. 6. Univ. of S. C. Press, 1970.
C7470 (ASU WCU)

The Cherokee Frontier: Conflict and Survival, 1740-62. 1st ed. The Civilization of the Am. Indian Series.
C7480 (LMC WCU BC UNA ASU UNCA)

The Cherokee Frontier; Conflict and Survival, 1740-62. The Civilization of the American Indian Series. Norman: Univ. of Oklahoma Press, 1966.
C7490 (WCU)

The Cherokee Frontier: Conflict and Survival, 1740-62. 1st ed. The Civilization of the American Indian Series. . Reprint. Norman: Univ. of Oklahoma Press, 1967.
C7500 (ASU)

The Creek Frontier, 1540-1783. 1st ed. The Civilization of the American Indian Series, 1962. Reprint. Norman: Univ. of Oklahoma Press, 1967.
C7510 (ASU BC)

Corlsen, Carl, pseud. see **Fey, Arthur Willard**

Corn, James Franklin Farewell the Hills: A Novel of the Eastern Cherokees. New York: Vantage Press, 1971. Set in Western North Carolina, East Tennessee and North Georgia.
C7520 (ASU LMC)

Red Clay and Rattlesnake Springs: A History of the Cherokee Indians of Bradley County, Tennessee. Cleveland, Tenn.: n.p., 1959. Important, and essentially disastrous, councils were held at both these communities in the early 1830's.
C7530 (ASU LMC MHC BC)

Cornell, F. D. A Social and Economic Survey of the Spencer Soil Conservation Area. Morgantown: West Virginia Agricultural Experiment Station, 1936.
C7540

Cornett, Essie Richardson The Cornett Family. N. Y., Vantage Press, 1971.
C7550

Cornett, Lowell "A Proposed Social Studies Curriculum for the Schools of Johnson City, Tennessee." Master's thesis. East Tennessee State Univ., 1971.
C7560 (ETSU)

Cornwell, John Jacob A Mountain Trail: To the Schoolroom, the Editor's Chair, the Lawyer's Office, and the Governorship of West Virginia. Philadelphia: Dorrance and Co., 1939.
C7570 (ASU BC)

Corpening, B. H. Vogenberger, R. A. Method for Determining Public Fire Control Expenditures for Private Lands. Norris, Tenn.: Tennessee Valley Authority, 1957.
V1310

Corron, Elizabeth Hicks Clifton Forge, Virginia: Scenic, Busy, Friendly. Rev. ed. Roanoke, Va.: Stone Printing Co., 1971. Promotional material prepared for the independent city of Clifton Forge.
C7580 (FC)

Corry, Ormond C. Comparative Economic Growth Measures — Population and Personal Income Estimates for Tennessee Counties, 1950 Through 1962. Study, no. 30. Knoxville: Univ. of Tennessee Bureau of Business and Economic Research, 1964. Personal income rose very slowly in Eastern Tennessee.
C7590

Corwin, Euphemia Kipp Unto the Hills; Glimpses of Berea's Outdoors. Cincinnati: Abington Press, n.d.
C7600

Costello, E. J. The Shame That Is Kentucky's The Story of the Harlan Mine War. Huntington, W. Va.: Appalachian Movement Press, 1972.
C7610 (ASU)

Costello, Emily P. "Locating and Providing for Murphy High School's Bright Pupils." Master's thesis. Western Carolina University, 1959.
C7620 (WCU)

Costello, Peter Bauer, John Public Organization of Electric Power: Conditions, Policies, and Program. New York: Harper & Brothers, 1949.
B2030

Costner, Ella V. Barefoot in the Smokies. n.p., 1969.
C7630 (LMC)

Lamp in the Cabin: Poems of the Smokies. Sevierville, Tenn.: Tri-County News, 1967.
C7640 (BC)

Poems of Paradise. New York: Carlton Press, 1968.
C7650 (BC)

Poems of the Smokies. n.p., 1967.
C7660 (LMC)

Song of Life in the Smokies. Maryville, Tenn.: Brazos Press, 1971. An account of life in the Smokies before the advent of the Park.
C7670 (LMC)

Song of Life in the Smokies: Stories of Mine Own People and Sketches of Life as It Was Lived in the Mountains Before the Park Took Over. Maryville, Tenn.: M. R. Mangrum, 1971.
C7680 (ETSU)

Costo, Rupert ed. Henry, Jeannette Textbooks and the American Indian. San Francisco: Indian Historian Press, 1970.
H4760 (MHC)

Cothran, Jean comp. The Whang Doddle; Folk Tales from the Carolinas. Columbia, S. C.: Sandlapper Press, 1972. 21 legends, tall tales, stories of mountaineers, Indians and European Settlers.
C7690 (BC)

Cotterill, Robert S. History of Pioneer Kentucky. Cincinnati, Ohio: Johnson and Hardin, 1917. An excellent history of the pioneer period in Kentucky. Most of the material in this volume was extracted from the Draper and Derret manuscript collections.
C7700 (LMC BC ASU)

The Southern Indians: The Story of the Civilized Tribes Before Removal. The Civilization of the American Indian, 38. Norman: Univ. of Oklahoma Press, 1954.
C7710 (ASU WCU BC)

The Southern Indians: The Story of the Civilized Tribes Before Removal. The Civilization of the American Indian. . Reprint. Norman: Univ. of Oklahoma Press, 1966. This work treats the major tribes of the Southeast from the Colonial Period to the Removal.
C7720 (LMC)

Cotton, James A. and others Soil Survey, Fayette County, Alabama. Soil Survey, Series 1962, no. 4. Washington: U. S. Department of Agriculture, Conservation Service, 1965.
C7730

Cotton, William D. "Appalachian North Carolina: A Political Study, 1860-1889." Ph.D. Diss. Univ. of North Carolina, 1955.
C7740

Couch, Robert Clarence "The Zinc Industry of Jefferson County, Tennessee." Master's thesis. Univ. of Tennessee, 1953.
C7750

Couch, William Terry Culture in the South. Chapel Hill: Univ. of North Carolina Press, 1934. Includes some observations on the Southern mountains.
C7760 (ASU LMC MHC BC)

Coulter, Ellis Merton Auraria: The Story of a Georgia Gold-Mining Town. Athens: Univ. of Georgia Press, 1956. This village, near present-day Dahlonega, was the site of the first gold rush in the United States.
C7770 (ASU BC)

The Civil War and Readjustment in Kentucky. Chapel Hill: Univ. of North Carolina Press, 1926.
C7780 (BC)

A Short History of Georgia. Chapel Hill: Univ. of North Carolina Press, 1933. A text for high school children.
C7800 (LMC BC ASU)

William G. Brownlow, Fighting Parson of the Southern Highlands. Chapel Hill: Univ. of North Carolina Press, 1937. Brownlow was a nationally-known orator and abolitionist.
C7810 (ASU WCU BC)

William G. Brownlow: Fighting Parson of the Southern Highlands. With an introduction of James W. Patton. Tennesseana Editions. Knoxville: Univ. of Tennessee Press, 1971.
C7820 (ETSU)

Coulter, Ellis Merton, ed. A List of the Early Settlers of Georgia. Athens: Univ. of Georgia Press, 1949.
C7790 (ASU)

Coulter, Roy D. "The Negroes of Chattanooga, Tennessee." B.D. thesis. Vanderbilt Univ., 1934.
C7830

Counce, Paul A. "Social and Economic History of Kingsport before 1908." Master's thesis. Univ. of Tennessee, 1939. Sullivan County, Tenn. — County History.
C7840 (ETSU)

Council of Southern Mountain Workers The Southern Highlands: An Inquiry into Their Needs, and Qualifications Desired in Church, Educational, and Social Service Workers in the Mountain Country. n.p.: Conference of Southern Mountain Workers, 1915.
C7960 (BC ASU)

Council of State Governments, Southern Regional Conference, Committee on Economic Development Education for Economic Development — The South's Education and Employment Prospects for the Future. A report. AMS Publications, no. 28. Atlanta: The council, 1964.
C7970

Council of the Southern Mountains Coal: Southwest Virginia's Source of Misery. Berea, Ky.: Council of the Southern Mountains, n.d.
C7850

How to Pay for College, a Complete Guide to Scholarships, Loans and Self-help Opportunities in the Appalachian South. n.p.: The council, 1966.
C7860 (MHC ASU BC)

Mass Meeting Study of the Appalachian South. The Afternoon Program. . . of the Forty-sixth Annual Conference of the Council of the Southern Mountains. Berea: The council, 1958. Processed.
C7870

1973-1974 Bibliography of the Appalachian South: Books, Records, Pamphlets, Magazines, and Films. Berea, Ky.: The council, 1973. A list of materials available through the Council bookstore.
C7880 (ASU ETSU)

Report of Social Welfare Manpower Project for Appalachia, July 15, 1969 to August 31, 1970. Berea, Ky.: The council, 1970. Project directors were Ronan R. Hoffman and Julian Mosley.
C7890 (ASU BC)

A Selection of Books, Magazines and Records on the Appalachian South. n.p.: The council, n.d. A list of materials available through the Council bookstore.
C7900 (MHC ASU)

Songs of All Time. Rev. ed. Berea, Ky.: The council, 1957.
C7910 (ASU ETSU LMC BC)

We Will Stop the Bulldozers. Berea, Ky.: The Council, n.d. A pamphlet describing the work of anti-strip mine organizations in the mountains.
C7920

Council of the Southern Mountains, Health Committee Health Care Services and Facilities in the Southern Appalachian Region. Tuskegee, Ala.: Tuskegee Institute, 1955.
C7930 (BC)

Health Careers in the Appalachian South. Berea, Ky.: The council, 1963.
C7940 (BC)

Council of the Southern Mountains, Mountain Life and Work see Mountain Life and Work

Council of the Southern Mountains. Youth Commission Directory. Berea, Ky.: Council of the Southern Mountains, n.d. A directory of organizations, publications and services available in the Southern Mountains.
C7950 (ASU)

Counts, Charles Common Clay. Photographs by Bill Haddox. Atlanta, Ga.: Droke House Hallux, 1971. Counts is one of the region's best-known potters. He lives near Rising Faun in the North Georgia Mountains.
C7980 (LMC ASU WCU)

Encouraging American Craftsmen. Report of the Interagency Crafts Committee. Washington: Govt. Print. Off., 1972. Encouraging American handcrafts.
C7990 (WCU LMC ASU)

Encouraging American Handcrafts: What Role in Economic Development? Prepared for the U. S. Economic Development Administration. Washington: Govt. Print. Off., 1966.
C8000 (LMC)

Pottery Workshop: A Study in the Making of Pottery from Idea to Finished Form. New York: Macmillan, 1973.
C8010 (WCU)

Couper, William History of Shenandoah Valley. 3 vols. N. Y.: Lewis Historical Publishing Co., 1952. An exhaustive history of Virginia's great valley and its role in the region's development.
C8020

The V. M. I. New Market Cadets. Biographical Sketches of All Members of the Virginia Military Institute Corps of Cadets Who Fought in The Battle of New Market, May 15, 1864. Charlottesville, Va.: Michie Company, 1933.
C8030 (ASU)

Courtner, Edna H. "A Survey of the Guidance Services Available in the Elementary Schools of Johnson County, Tennessee." Master's thesis. East Tennessee State Univ., 1966.
C8040 (ETSU)

The Cousins' Journey; or, Sketches of American Scenery. Boston: L. C. Bowles, 1853. Designed for young people. There are descriptions of Winchester, New Market, Lexington, and Abingdon in Virginia, and of Knoxville, Huntsville, and the Choctaw country on the other side of the mountains.
C8050

Couto, Richard A. Poverty, Politics, and Health Care: An Appalachian Experience. New York: Praeger Publishers, 1975. Material for this volume was collected by extensive interviewing in Floyd County, Kentucky.
C8060 (ASU)

Covert, Hester Lewis "Glass Production Processes of the Kanawha Valley Area." Master's thesis. West Virginia Univ., 1969.
C8070 (ASU)

Covington, Va., Chamber of Commerce Alleghany County, Virginia: Its Resources and Industries. Covington: The chamber, 1907.
C8080 (BC)

Cowan, Anne Bixler, Harold Hench The Superior and Gifted Student Project at Cullowhee, Western Carolina College. Cullowhee, N. C.: n.p., 1964.
B4300 (WCU)

Cowan, Frank An American Story-book. Short Stories from Studies of Life in Southwestern Pennsylvania. Xerox copy of the original. Greensburg, Pa.: n.p., 1881. Stories from frontier life and from the coal and steel towns of Southwestern Pennsylvania.
C8090 (ASU)

Southwestern Pennsylvania in Song and Story. Gettysburg, Pa.: The author, 1878.
C8100

Cowan, Samuel Kinkade Sergeant York and His People. Illustrations from photographs taken especially for this book. New York: Funk and Wagnalls Co., 1922. A biography of the celebrated World War I hero from East Tennessee.
C8110 (WWC ETSU BC)

Sergeant York and His People. 1910. Reprint. New York: Grosset and Dunlap, 1922.
C8120 (ASU LMC FC)

Cowell, Sidney R. Lomax, Alan American Folk Songs and Folklore: A Regional Bibliography. New York: Progressive Education Assoc., 1942.
L3110

Cowhig, James Daniel Age-grade School Progress of Farm and Nonfarm Youth: Agricultural Economic Report, no. 40. Washington: U. S. Department of Agriculture Economic Research Service, 1963. Appalachian youths were used as a control group in this study.
C8130

Cox, Aras B. Foot Prints on The Sands of Time, A History of South-western Virginia and North-western North Carolina. Sparta, N. C.: Star Pub. Co. 1900. A history of the sparsely populated area in the Va.-N. C. border.
C8140 (ASU LMC)

Cox, Cora Rogers "A Study of the Word Recognition Abilities in the Fourth and Sixth Grades of Douglass School, 1957-58, in Kingsport, Tennessee." Master's thesis. East Tennessee State College, 1958.
C8150 (ETSU)

Cox, John Harrington comp. Traditional Ballads and Folk-songs Mainly from West Virginia. Bibliographical and Special Series, vol. 15. n.p.: American Folklore Society, 1964.
C8180 (ASU WCU ETSU BC)

Cox, John Harrington ed. Folk-songs of the South. Collected Under the Auspices of the West Virginia Folk-lore Society. Cambridge, Mass.: Harvard Univ. Press, 1925.
C8160 (ETSU BC FC)

Folk-songs of the South. Collected Under the Auspices of the West Virginia Folk-lore Society. Foreword by Arthur Kyle Davis, Jr. Reprint. Hatboro, Pa.: Folklore Associates, 1963.
C8170 (ASU WCU LMC MHC ETSU)

Cox, Marian Emily Roalfe An Introduction to Folk-lore. New and enlarged ed. Reprint. Detroit: Singing Tree Press, 1968. A handbook for field work in folklore.
C8190 (ASU)

Cox, Millard F. The Legionaries; a Story of the Great Raid. New York: Grosset and Dunlap, 1899. A southern born West Point graduate joins Morgan on his raids through Kentucky and the Ohio Valley. Lone story.
C8200

Cox, Naomi D. Poverty Poems. Charleston, Ill.: Prairie Press Books, 1968.
C8210 (BC)

Cox, Norman Wade Encylopedia of Southern Baptists. 2 vols. Nashville: Broadman Press, 1958.
C8220 (ASU)

Cox, Roy Leonard "The Curriculum of the Senior High School: A Survey of Offerings, Changes and Current Trends in the Southern Appalachian Region." Ed. D. Diss. Univ. of Tennessee, 1961.
C8230

Coyle, D. C. Conservation: An American Story of Conflict and Accomplishment. New Brunswick, N. J.: Rutgers University Press, 1957.
C8240

Coyle, David C. Breakthrough to the Great Society. Dobbs Ferry, N. Y.: Oceana Publications, 1965. Contains a discussion of Appalachian poverty.
C8250

Coyle, David Cushman Land of Hope: The Way of Life in the Tennessee Valley. Evanston, Ill.: Row, 1941.
C8260 (WWC ASU)

Crabb, Alfred Leland A Mockingbird Sang at Chickamauga: A Tale of Embattled Chattanooga. Indianapolis: Bobbs-Merrill Co., 1949. Civil War Fiction
C8270 (ASU WCU WWC)

Peace at Bowling Green. 1st ed. Indianapolis: Bobbs-Merrill Co., 1955. A novel of frontier life in Kentucky. Partially set in the mountains.
C8280 (ASU BC)

Reunion at Chattanooga. New York: Bobbs Merrill, 1950. Fiction with an East Tennessee setting.
C8290

Crabtree, Beth G. North Carolina Governors, 1585-1958: Brief Sketches. Raleigh, N. C.: State Department of Archives and History, 1958. Only two governors during this period were from Western North Carolina.
C8300 (LMC BC)

Crabtree, Lillian Gladys "Songs and Ballads Sung in Overton County, Tennessee a Collection." Master's thesis. George Peabody College, 1936.
C8310

Craddock, Charles Egbert see **Murfree, Mary Noailles**

Craddock, Ernest B. "A Study of the Status of the Elementary Principal of Logan County, West Virginia." Master's thesis. Marshall College, 1954.
C8320

Craft, E. Paul Construction-grade Plywood from Grade 3 Appalachian Oak. U. S. Forest Service Research Paper, NE-163. Upper Darby, Pa.: Northeastern Forest Experiment Station, 1970.
C8330

Craft, James Elliott Wheels on the Mountains. Parsons, W. Va.: McClain Print. Co., 1969. A history of West Virginia's largest transportation system and a biography of the mountain boy who built this bus line.
C8340 (ASU LMC WCU BC)

Crafts Horizon. Crafts of the Southern Highlands 1 vol. unpaged. New York: American Craftsmen's Council, n.d.
C8350 (WCU ASU)

Craghead, Paul "Cost of Operating the Schools in Raleigh County, West Virginia, from 1940-50." Master's thesis. Marshall College, 1952.
C8360

Craig, Edward Marshall ed. Highways and Byways of Appalachia: A Study of the Work of the Synod of Appalachia of the Presbyterian Church in the United States. Kingsport, Tenn.: Kingsport Press, 1927. The Presbyterians were the largest church in the mountains, and their mission efforts in the region were prodigious.
C8370 (ASU LMC BC)

Craig, James Hicklin The Arts and Crafts in North Carolina, 1699-1840. Winston-Salem, N. C.: Museum of Early Southern Decorative Arts, Old Salem, Inc., 1965.
C8380 (ASU LMC MHC BC)

Craig, Lawrence C. King, Philip Burke Geology and Manganese Deposits of Northeastern Tennessee. Nashville: Tennessee Department of Conservation Division of Geology, 1944.
K2410 (ETSU)

Craig, Lillian Kennerly Johnnie Mountain. New York: Doubleday, 1936. Children's story set in the Appalachian Mountains.
C8390 (WWC)

Rev. John Craig, 1709-1774, his Descendants and Allied Families. New Orleans, La.: Accurate Letter Company, 1963.
C8400

The Singing Hills. New York: Crowell, 1951. Light fiction with an Appalachian setting.
C8410 (ASU WCU BC)

Craig, Locke Mitchell's Peak and Dr. Mitchell. Raleigh, N. C.: Edwards and Broughton, 1915. Facts about Mt. Mitchell and the naturalist for whom it was named.
C8420 (ASU LMC)

Craig, Ronald B. Forestry in the Economic Life of Knott County, Kentucky. Lexington: Kentucky Agricultural Experiment Station, 1932.
C8430

Virginia Forest Resources and Industries. U. S. Department of Agriculture Miscellaneous Publication, no. 681. Washington, D. C.: Govt. Print. Off., 1949.
C8440 (LMC)

Craighead, James Geddes Scotch and Irish Seeds in American Soil: The Early History of the Scotch and Irish Churches, and Their Relations to the Presbyterian Church of America. Philadelphia: Presbyterian Board of Publication, 1878. The Scotch-Irish were the largest single ethnic groups to settle in Appalachia.
C8450 (BC)

Crain, Ellen Smoke on the Mountain. New York: Dodd, Mead, 1967.
C8460 (LMC)

Crain, Jim Camping Around the Appalachian Mountains. New York: Random House, Inc., 1975. A comprehensive guide to campsites in Alabama, Georgia, Kentucky, Tennessee, North Carolina, Virginia, and West Virginia.
C8470 (ASU)

Craine, Lyle Eggleston Maryland's Role in Water Resources Development: A Study. College Park: Univ. of Maryland Water Resources Study Committee, 1966.
C8480

Cramblet, Wilbur H. The Christian Church (Disciples of Christ) in West Virginia. St. Louis: Bethany Press, 1971. A history of the development of the Christian Church in West Virginia.
C8490 (BC)

Cramer, Howard Ross Annotated Bibliography of Georgia Geology Through 1959. Geological Survey Bulletin, no. 79. Atlanta: Georgia Department of Mines, Mining and Geology, 1967.
C8500 (ETSU)

Crampton, Charles Ward The Folk Dance Book for Elementary Schools, Class Room, Playground, and Gymnasium. New York: A. S. Barnes, 1913. Includes diagrams and instructions.
C8510 (BC)

Crane, Verner Winslow The Southern Frontier, 1670-1732. Durham, N. C.: Duke Univ. Press, 1928.
C8520 (WCU BC)

The Southern Frontier, 1670-1732. 1929. Reprint. Ann Arbor Books, AA4. Ann Arbor: Univ. of Michigan Press, 1956.
C8530 (ASU LMC FC)

Cranes, Douglas Status of West Virginia in the Economic Opportunity Program Under Public Law 88-452. Charleston: n.p., 1966.
C8540

Cranford, E. Wade Second Awakening. New York: Vantage Press, 1956. A mass murder stuns an isolated mountain town. The sole survivor, a young boy, unravels the horror and the mystery committing his life to an allegorical denouement.
C8550 (BC)

Cranford, Fred B. The Waldenses of Burke County. Illustrated by Jackie Deaton. Valdese, N. C.: Burke County Schools' Graphics and Industrial Communications Students, 1969.
C8560 (ASU WCU LMC)

Craven, Wesley Frank White, Red, and Black: The Seventeenth-century Virginian. Charlottesville: Univ. Press of Virginia, 1971.
C8570 (ETSU)

Crawford, Barbara Ann "Ballad Characteristics in Modern Popular Country Music." Master's thesis. East Tennessee State Univ., 1969.
C8580 (ETSU)

Crawford, Charles Bierne "The Mine War on Cabin Creek and Paint Creek, West Virginia, in 1912-1913." Master's thesis. Univ. of Kentucky, 1939.
C8590 (ASU)

Crawford, Jean Jugtown Pottery: History and Design. Winston-Salem, N. C.: J. F. Blair, 1964.
C8600 (ASU LMC MHC BC)

Crawford, John Reed Stewart, Noah A. The Crash. Asheville, N. C.: Gladiator Productions, 1969.
S7320 (ASU LMC WCU BC)

Crawford, Thomas J. Hurst, Vernon J. Exploration for Mineral Deposits in Haversham County, Georgia. Washington: Govt. Print. Off., 1964.
H8580

Hurst, Vernon J. Exploration for Mineral Deposits in Habersham County, Georgia. Washington: U. S. Area Redevelopment Administration, Dec., 1964.
H8590 (LMC)

Crayon, Porte, pseud. see **Strother, David Hunter**

Credle, Ellis Big Doin's on Razorback Ridge. Nelson, 1956. Children's story with a southern mountain setting.
C8610 (ETSU ASU)

Down Down the Mountain. New York: Nelson and Sons, 1961. Story book for children 5-8.
C8620 (ASU MHC BC)

Johnny and His Mule. Photographs by Charles Townsend. New York: Oxford Univ. Press, 1946. A story of a mountain lad and his best friend, a mule.
C8630 (ETSU ASU)

Tall Tales from the High Hills, and Other Stories. Illustrated by Richard Bennett. New York: T. Nelson, 1957. Twenty folk tales from the Southern mountains.
C8640 (ASU LMC MHC WCU BC)

Creecy, Richard Benbury Grandfather's Tales of North Carolina History. Raleigh, N. C.: Edwards and Broughton, 1901.
C8650 (ASU WCU LMC MHC BC UNCA)

Creek Nation Laws of the Creek Nation. Union of Georgia Library Miscellaneous Publications, no. 1. Athens: Univ. of Georgia Press, 1960.
C8660 (ASU)

Creekmore, Betsey Beeler Arrows to Atoms, The Story of East Tennessee. Knoxville: Univ. of Tennessee Press, 1959. A history of East Tennessee from the days of the Cherokee to those of atomic energy.
C8670 (ASU LMC ETSU BC)

Knoxville. 2nd ed. Knoxville.: Univ. of Tennessee Press, 1967. History of Knoxville, Tennessee.
C8680 (ASU ETSU BC)

Creekmore, Pollyanna ed. Population Schedule of the U. S. Census of 1850 (Seventh Census) for Sevier County, Tennessee. Knoxville: The authors, 1953.
C8690 (ETSU BC)

Tennessee Marriage Records. 3 vols. Knoxville: Clinchdale Press, 1958-.
C8700 (ETSU)

Cressler, Charles W. Geology and Ground-water Resources of Catoosa County, Georgia. Geological Survey Information Circular, 28. Georgia Department of Mines, Mining and Geology, 1963.
C8710 (ETSU)

Geology and Ground-water Resources of the Paleozoic Rock Area, Chattooga County, Georgia. Information Circular, 27. Atlanta: Georgia Department of Mines, Mining and Geology, 1964.
C8720 (ETSU)

Geology and Ground-water Resources of Walker County, Georgia. Information Circular, 29. Atlanta: Georgia Department of Mines, Mining and Geology, 1964.
C8730 (ETSU)

Creswell, J. B. Brief Historical Sketch of the Village of Bearden. Knoxville: Newman, 1899.
C8740 —

Crick, Herbert W. "History of Education in Pike County Kentucky." Master's thesis. Univ. of Kentucky, 1930.
C8750

Crickard, Madeline W. comp. Index to 1810 Virginia Census. Parsons: West Virginia, McClain Printing Co., 1971.
C8760

Crickmay, Geoffrey William Geology of the Crystalline Rocks of Georgia. Bulletin, 58. Atlanta: Georgia Department of Mines, Mining and Geology, 1952.
C8770 (ETSU)

Crider, Albert Foster The Fire Clays and Fire Clay Industries of the Olive Hill and Ashland Districts of Northeastern Kentucky. 4th series, vol. 1, pt. 2. Frankfort: Kentucky Geological Survey, 1913. This area of Kentucky traditionally had many small pottery factories and other clay-based industries.
C8780 (BC)

Crim, Matt In Beaver Cove and Elsewhere. New York: Charles L. Webster and Co., 1892. Miss Crim's North Georgia stories are remarkable for their excellent characterizations and dialect.
C8790 (ASU BC)

Crisman, Rev. E. B. Origin and Doctrines of the Cumberland Presbyterian Church. St. Louis: Pevin and Smith, 1877. The Cumberland Presbyterians separated from the Presbyterian Church over issues predicated on frontier life and values.
C8800

Critical Issues in Public Finance in an Underdeveloped Region: The West Virginia Case Proceedings of a conference sponsored by the Office of Research and Development Center for Appalachian Studies and Development, West Virginia University, in cooperation with the College of Business and Economics, West Virginia University and the West Virginia State Department of Commerce, May 25-27, 1969. Morgantown: West Virginia Univ., 1971.
C8810 (ASU WCU BC)

Crittenden, Charles Christopher North Carolina Newspapers before 1790. Sprunt Studies, vol. 20, no. 1. Chapel Hill: Univ. of North Carolina Press, 1928.
C8820 (LMC)

Crittenden, Charles Christopher ed. 100 Years, 100 Men: 1871-1971. Raleigh, N. C.: Edwards and Broughton, 1971.
C8830 (ASU)

Crittenden, Edward B. The Entwined Lives of Miss Gabrielle Austin, Daughter of the Late Rev. Ellis C. Austin, and of Redmond, the Outlaw Leader of the North Carolina "Moonshiners". Philadelphia: Barclay and Co., 1880. Fantastic tale of a minister's daughter falsely accused of a crime and vindicated by an infamous outlaw.
C8840 (BC)

Crittenden, Henry Temple comp. The Comp'ny: The Story of the Surry, Sussex and Southampton Railway and the Surry Lumber Company. Parsons, W. Va.: McClain Print. Co., 1967.
C8850 (ASU LMC BC)

Crittendeu, Charles Christopher ed. Historical Records Survey, North Carolina The Historical Records of North Carolina. Raleigh: The North Carolina Historical Commission, 1938.
H5730 (ASU LMC BC)

Crocker, C. D. Gorman, John Loyd Soil Survey, Berkeley County, West Virginia. Washington: U. S. Department of Agriculture, Soil Conservation Service, 1966.
G2770

Crockett, David An Account of Col. Crockett's Tour to the North and Down East, in the Year of Our Lord One Thousand Eight Hundred and Thirty-four. His Object Being to Examine the Grand Manufacturing Establishments of the Country; and Also to Find Out the Condition of Its Literature and Morals, the Extent of Its Commerce, and the Practical Operation of "The Experiment." Written by Himself. Reprint. Philadelphia, Pa.: E. L. Carey and A. Hart, 1835.
C8860

An Account of Col. Crockett's Tour to the North and Down East, in the Year of Our Lord One Thousand Eight Hundred and Thirty-four. His Object Being to Examine the Grand Manufacturing Establishment of the Country; and Also to Find Out the Condition of Its Literature and Morals, the Extent of Its Commerce, and the Practical Operation of "The Experiment." Written by Himself. Reprint. Boston: Ticknor, 1835.
C8870

An Account of Col. Crockett's Tour to the North and Down East, in the Year of Our Lord One Thousand Eight Hundred and Thirty-four. His Objective Being to Examine the Grand Manufacturing Establishments of the Country; and Also to Find Out the Condition of Its Literature and Morals, the Extent of Its Commerce, and the Practical Operation of "The Experiment." Written by Himself. Reprint. New York: Graham, 1848.
C8880

The Adventures of Davy Crockett: Told Mostly by Himself. Illustrated by John W. Thomason, Jr. New York: Charles Scribner's Sons, 1934.
C8890 (ASU)

The Adventures of Davy Crockett, Told Mostly by Himself. New York: Scribners, 1934, 1955, 1958.
C8900

The Autobiography of David Crockett. New York: C. Scribner's Sons, 1923.
C8910 (ETSU)

The Autobiography of David Crockett. The Modern Student's Library. New York: Scribners, 1923.
C8920

The Crockett Almanacks. Nashville Series, 1835-1838. Chicago: Caxton Club, 1955.
C8930

The Crockett Tavern and Pioneer Museum. Unpaged pamphlet. Morristown: n.p., n.d. A guide to a museum and tavern near Crockett's birthplace in Eastern Tennessee.
C8940

Davy Crockett's Own Story as Written by Himself; the Autobiography of America's Great Folk Hero. Illustrations Milton Glaser. New York: Citadel, 1955. A collection of Crockett's autobiographical works.
C8950

Life of Col. Crockett, Written by Himself. Philadelphia: G. G. Evans, 1859.
C8960 (ETSU)

Life of David Crockett. New York: Lovell, Coryell and Co., n.d. Biography of the famous frontiersman from East Tennessee.
C8970 (ETSU)

Life of David Crockett. Philadelphia: T. K. and P. G. Collins, 1836.
C8980 (ETSU)

Life of David Crockett, the Original Humorist and Irrepressible Backwoodsman: Comprising His Early History; His Bear Hunting and Other Adventures. His Services in the Creek War. His Electioneering Speeches and Career in Congress. With His Triumphal Tour Through the Northern States, and Services in the Texas War. To Which Is Added an Account of His Glorious Death at the Alamo while Fighting in Defence of Texan Independence. Philadelphia: Porter and Coates, 1865.
C8990 (ASU)

Life of David Crockett, the Original Humorist and Irrepressible Backwoodsman, Comprising His Early History: His Bear Hunting and Other Adventures, His Services in the Creek War. His Electioneering Speeches and Career in Congress. With His Triumphal Tour Through the Northern States and Services in the Texan War. To Which Is Added an Account of His Glorious Death at the Alamo while Fighting in Defence of Texan Independence. Philadelphia: John E. Potter and Co., 1865.
C9000 (ASU BC)

Crockett, David
Life of David Crockett, the Original Humorist and Irrepressible Backwoodsman: Comprising His Early History; His Bear Hunting and Other Adventures; His Services in the Creek War; His Electioneering Speeches and Career in Congress with His Triumphal Tour Through the Northern States, and Services in the Texan War. To Which Is Added an Account of His Glorious Death at the Alamo while Fighting in Defence of Texan Independence. . . Dallas: Talty and Wiley, 1890.
C9010 (ASU)
A Narrative of the Life of David Crockett of the State of Tennessee. Facsimile edition with annotations and introduction by James A. Shackelford and Stanley J. Folmsbee. Knoxville: University of Tennessee Press, 1973. This edition rejects much spurious material that has appeared in various editions since the original appeared in 1834.
C9020 (ASU)
A Narrative of the Life of David Crockett of the State of Tennessee. 1834. Reprint. A facsimile edition with annotations and an introduction by James A. Shackford and Stanley J. Folmshee. Tennesseana editions. Knoxville: Univ. of Tennessee Press, 1973.
C9030 (ASU MHC)
A Narrative of the Life of David Crockett of the State of Tennessee. Philadelphia, Pa.: E. L. Carey and A. Hart, 1834. Reprint. Tennesseana Editions, with an introduction and annotations by James A. Shackford and Stanley J. Folmsbee. Knoxville: Univ. of Tennessee Press, 1973. Many reprints of this "Genuine" autobiography were published in 1834-36; the title was usually combined with other works supposedly written by Crockett.
C9040
A Narrative of the Life of David Crockett, Written by Himself. Philadelphia: E. L. Carey and A. Hart; Baltimore: Carey, Hart and Co., 1834.
C9050 (ETSU)
The Sayings of Davy Crockett in His Own Language. n.p.: Larry Miles, 1938. Includes some of the more outrageous sayings of Tennessee's irrepressible frontiersman.
C9060 (ASU)

Crockett, M. H., Sr. ed. Adair, Anthony Garland ed. Heroes of the Alamo: Accounts and Documents. New York: Exposition Press, 1957.
A260 (ETSU)

Croft, Malcolm Swann, Maurice Edward Soil Survey of Winston County, Alabama. Washington: U. S. Department of Agriculture, Bureau of Chemistry and Soils, 1937.
S9450

Croft, Mark G. Geology and Ground-water Resources of Dade County, Georgia. Information Circular, 26. Atlanta: Georgia Department of Mines, Mining and Geology, 1964.
C9070 (ETSU)

Croom, C. W. Goldston, Eugene Frizzell Soil Survey, Jackson County, North Carolina. Washington: U. S. Bureau of Plant Industry, Soils, and Agricultural Engineering, 1948.
G2410
Goldston, Eugene Frizzell Soil Survey, Madison County, North Carolina. Washington: U. S. Department of Agriculture, Bureau of Plant Industry, 1942.
G2430
Perkins, Samuel Oscar Soil Survey, Henderson County, North Carolina. Washington: U. S. Department of Agriculture, Bureau of Plant Industry, Soils, and Agricultural Engineering, 1943.
P2100
Perkins, Samuel Oscar Soil Survey, Transylvania County, North Carolina. Washington: U. S. Department of Agriculture, Bureau of Plant Industry, Soils, and Agricultural Engineering, 1948.
P2130

Crosby, Marian K. comp. Burgner, Goldene F. comp. Kirchen Buch (Church Book) Register, 1815-1828. St. James Lutheran Church, Greene County, Tennessee. Greenville: The authors, 1964.
B8600

Cross, John Newton William Cross of Botetourt County, Virginia and His Descendants, 1733-1932. Columbia, Mo.: E. W. Stephens Publishing Co., 1932.
C9080

Cross, Jonathan Five Years in the Alleghanies. New York: American Tract Society, 1863. Narrative of an early tour of the Alleghanies; a treasure trove of social commentary and candid observations.
C9090 (ASU BC)

Cross, Luther L. "A Study of Scott County, Tennessee, and Oneida Independent School District Finances." Master's thesis. East Tennessee State College, 1961.
C9100

Cross Reference Directory, Greater Asheville and Vicinity: Hendersonville, Canton, Waynesville, Brevard. Independence, Kansas: City Publishing Co., 1970-.
C9110 (UNCA)

Cross, Tom Peete Witchcraft in North Carolina. Studies in Philology. Chapel Hill: Univ. of North Carolina, 1919. A general work with few special references to Western North Carolina's 28 mountain counties.
C9120 (LMC)

Crossely, D. A. Gist, Clayton S. The Litter Arthropod Community in a Southern Appalachian Hardwood Forest: Numbers, Biomass and Mineral Element Content. Logan, Utah: Utah State Univ. Ecology Center, 1973.
G1850

Crouch, John Historical Sketches of Wilkes County. Wilkesboro: J. Crouch, 1902. Sketches collected and written for the fiftieth anniversary edition of the Journal Patriot.
C9130 (ASU)

Crouch, Stella E. Carselowey Story of the Cherokee Indians, and the Trial of Tears, Battle of Cabin Creek, Alloting of Lands: Personal Interviews of Famous People. Vinita, Okla.: n.p., 1967.
C9140 (MHC WCU)

Crouch, William Ward "Missionary Activities among the Cherokee Indians, 1757-1838." Master's thesis. Univ. of Tennessee, 1932.
C9150

Crouse, A. L. Historical Sketches of Alexander County. Hickory: Crouse and Son, 1905. A history of Alexander County with special emphasis on the Civil War, Taylorsville and Moravian Falls.
C9160

Crowden, John Joseph "Alienation Among Low-income People in Appalachia." Ph.D. Diss. Univ. of Kentucky, 1970. A very thorough study of social interaction and alienation among Appalachia's poor.
C9170 (LMC ASU)

Crowe, Dan Willard "An Analysis of the Industrial Potential of Carter County, Tennessee." Master's thesis. East Tennessee State College, 1960.
C9180 (ETSU)

Crowe, Martin, Jay "The Occupational Adaptation of a Selected Group of Eastern Kentuckians in Southern Ohio." Ph. D. Diss. Univ. of Kentucky, 1964. A study of the sad plight of the modern migrant in Cincinnati and other Ohio cities.
C9190

Crowe, Richard G. "Economic Education in Kentucky Public Secondary Schools." Master's thesis. Morehead State Univ., 1969.
C9200

Crowe, Ruth Amis "Educational and Vocational Choices of the 1960 Graduates of Dobyns-Bennett High School, Kingsport, Tennessee." Master's thesis. East Tennessee State Univ., 1967. A follow-up study of the career choices of the class of 1960.
C9210 (ETSU)

Crowell, Suzanne Appalachian People's History Book. Louisville, Ky.: Mountain Education Associates, 1971. This text published by the Southern Conference Educational Fund concentrates on the sort of history you didn't learn in school. Interesting, but a little over-laden with propaganda.
C9220 (ASU FC WCU ETSU)

Crowson, Shirley Bremson "A Comparative Analysis of Three Evaluation Procedures Used with Kindergarten Pupils at Southside Elementary School, Johnson City, Tennessee." Master's thesis. East Tennessee State Univ., 1970.
C9230 (ETSU)

Crozier, Ethelred W. The White-Caps: A History of the Organization in Sevier County. Knoxville: The author, 1899. History of lawless factionalism in Sevier County of the 1890's. Actually, the white-cap movement was rather wide-spread throughout Southern Appalachia.
C9240
The White-Caps: A History of the Organization in Sevier County. Rev. ed. Knoxville: n.p., 1937. History of lawless factionalism in Sevier County of the 1890's. Actually, the white-cap movement was rather wide-spread throughout Southern Appalachia.
C9250
The White-Caps: A History of the Organization in Sevier County. Sevierville: Brazos, 1963. History of lawless factionalism in Sevier County of the 1890's, Actually, the white-cap movement was rather wide-spread throughout Southern Appalachia.
C9260

Crozier, William Armstrong Virginia Colonial Militia, 1651-1776. Baltimore, Southern Book Co., 1954 (1905).
C9310

Crozier, William Armstrong ed. Crozier's General Armory: A Registry of American Families Entitled to Coat Armor. 1904. Reprint. Baltimore: Genealogical Pub. Co., 1966.
C9270 (ASU)
Early Virginia Marriages. 1907. Reprint. Virginia County Records, vol. 4. Baltimore: Southern Book Co., 1953.
C9280 (ASU)
Early Virginia Marriages. 1907. Reprint. Virginia County Records, vol. 4. Baltimore: Genealogical Pub. Co., 1968.
C9290 (ASU)
A Key to Southern Pedigrees, Being a Comprehensive Guide to the Colonial Ancestry of Families in the States of Virginia, Maryland, Georgia, North Carolina, South Carolina, Kentucky, Tennessee, West Virginia and Alabama. 2d. ed. Virginia County Record Publications, vol. 8. Baltimore: Southern Book Co., 1953.
C9300 (ASU)
Virginia Colonial Militia, 1651-1776. 1905. Reprint. Baltimore: Genealogical Pub. Co., 1965.
C9320 (ASU)
Virginia Heraldica, Being a Registry of Virginia Gentry Entitled to Coat Armor with Genealogical Notes of the Families. 1908. Reprint. Baltimore: Genealogical Pub. Co., 1965.
C9330 (ASU)

Crum, Mason The Story of Lake Junaluska. Greensboro, N. C.: Piedmont Press, 1950. Lake Junaluska is the Methodist Convention center and retreat for Southeastern conferences. The center, near Waynesville, North Carolina is named for a Cherokee Chief.
C9340 (BC)

Crumine, Boyd Virginia Court Records in Southwestern Pennsylvania. Records of the District of West Augusta and Ohio and Yohogania Counties, Virginia, 1775-1780. Indexed by Inez Walden Maier. Excerpted from Annals of the Carnegie Museum, vol. I-III, 1902-1905. n.p.: n.p., n.d.
C9350

Crush, Charles W. The Montgomery County Story, 1776-1957. Christiansburg, Va.: n.p., 1957. Montgomery County records, militia lists, Confederate companies, and photographs are included.
C9360 (ASU)

Crutcher, T. P. Spurrier with the Wildcats and Moonshiners. Xerox of the original. Nashville, Tenn.: Univ. Press, 1892. Fancifully embroidered tale about revenue agents and illicit distillers.
C9370 (ASU BC)

Crymes, Joseph Thomas Sociological Aspects of Poverty, a Bibliography. Columbus: Ohio University School of Social Work, 1964. Includes a good selection of entries pertaining to Appalachia.
C9380

Csorba, J. J. Johnson, Hugh A. Private Outdoor Recreation Enterprises in Rural Appalachia. Washington: Govt. Print. Off., 1969.
J1800

Cubby, Edwin Albert "The Transformation of the Tug and Guyandot Valleys: Economic Development and Social Change in West Virginia, 1888-1921." Ph. D. Diss. Syracuse University, 1962.
C9390

Culin, Stewart Games of the North American Indians. 24th Annual Report of the Bureau of American Ethnology to the Secretary of the Smithsonian Institute. 1902-03. Washington, D. C.: Govt. Print. Off., 1907. Includes games of the Cherokee, Catawba and Shawnee.
C9400 (LMC)

Culver, David W. Brown, E. Evan The Economic Development of the Northeast Georgia Commission Area Through Use of Forest Products and Water Resources. Athens, Ga.: Northeast Georgia Planning and Development Commission, 1966.
B7120 (ASU ETSU)

The Cumberland Empire: A Quarterly Review. vol. 1-5. 1932-1933. Big Laurel, Va.: James Taylor Adams, quarterly.
C9410 (BC)

Cumberland Gap: Its Geographical and Commercial Features and Importance as a Railroad Centre. New York: Fleming, Brewster, n.d.
C9420

Cumberland Presbyterian Church. Alabama Synod. Historical Contributions. no. 1- 1904-. Montgomery, Ala.: n.p., irregularly issued. The Cumberland Presbyterian Church developed as a natural consequence of conflicts between traditional Presbyterianism and mountain or frontier culture.
C9430

Cumberland, Robert A. Profits from Pruning Appalachian White Pine. U. S. Forest Service Station Paper, 65. Asheville, N. C.: Southeastern Forest Experiment Station, 1956.
C9440

Cumberlands Hiking Club, Chattanooga Outdoors in the Cumberlands. Chattanooga, Tenn.: Chattanooga Community Assoc., 1933.
C9450 (BC)

Cumming, William P. Rights, Douglas LeTell The Discoveries of John Lederer. Charlottesville: Univ. of Virginia Press, 1958.
R2330 (ASU LMC)

Cumming, William Patterson North Carolina in Maps. Raleigh, N. C.: State Department of Archives and History, 1966. Includes maps of North Carolina's 28 mountain counties.
C9460 (ASU WCU)

The Southeast in Early Maps with an Annotated Check List of Printed and Manuscript Regional and Local Maps of Southeastern North America during the Colonial Period. Chapel Hill: Univ. of North Carolina Press, 1962.
C9470 (ASU LMC)

Cummings, Edward Marmaduke of Tennessee. Illustrated by Frank E. Schoonover. Chicago: A. C. McClurg and Co., 1914. This sentimental novel has more overtones of the deep South than of its East Tennessee setting.
C9480 (ASU BC)

Cundiff, Ruby Ethel comp. List of Books and Related Materials About Virginia for use of Schools. compiled under the direction of Ruby Ethel Cundiff by students in L. L.S. 81-82. Harrisonburg, Va.: Madison College, 1950.
C9490

Cunningham, A. B. Dresser, Davis The Great Yant Mystery. N. Y.: Detective Club, 1943.
D3410

Cunningham, Addie J. "What Progress in Health Has Been Made among the Negro Youths of the Elementary School Age for the Past Ten Years in Talladega County, Alabama." Master's thesis. Alabama State College, 1952.
C9500

Cunningham, Albert Benjamin The Affair at the Boat Landing. 1st ed. New York: E. P. Dutton and Co., 1943. Mystery novel with an Appalachian setting.
C9510 (ASU BC)

The Bancock Murder Case. New York: Dutton, 1942. Mystery with a mountain setting.
C9520

The Cane-patch Mystery. 1st ed. New York: E. P. Dutton and Co., 1944. A mountain mystery.
C9530 (ASU BC)

Death at "the Bottoms." New York: Dutton, 1942. Yet another mountain mystery.
C9540

Death Haunts the Dark Lane. New York: Dutton, 1948. A mountain mystery story.
C9550 (ASU)

Death Rides a Sorrel Horse. 1st ed. New York: E. P. Dutton and Co., 1946. Mountain mystery.
C9560 (ASU BC)

Death Visits the Apple Hole. New York: Dutton, 1946. Mountain mystery.
C9570 (ASU)

The Great Yant Mystery. New York: Dutton, 1943.
C9580

The Hunter is the Hunted. 1st ed. Guilt Edged mysteries. New York: E. P. Dutton and Co., 1950.
C9590 (ASU BC)

The Killer Watches the Manhunt. New York: Dutton, 1950.
C9600

The Manse at Barren Rocks. New York: George H. Doran Co., 1918. A mystery story with a West Virginia setting.
C9610 (ASU BC)

Murder at Deer Lick. New York: E. P. Dutton and Co., 1939. A mountain mystery.
C9620 (BC)

Murder at the Schoolhouse. New York: Dutton, 1940. A mountain mystery.
C9630

Murder Before Midnight. 1st ed. New York: E. P. Dutton and Co., 1945. A mystery novel with a mountain setting.
C9640 (ASU BC)

Murder Without Weapons. 1st ed. Guilt Edged mystery. New York: E. P. Dutton and Co., 1949.
C9650 (ASU BC)

One Man Must Die. 1st ed. New York: E. P. Dutton and Co., 1946. A mountain mystery.
C9660 (ASU BC)

Singing Mountains. New York: George H. Doran Co., 1919. A sequel to The Manse at Barren Rocks.
C9670 (ASU BC)

Skeleton in the Closet. 1st ed. Guilt edged mystery. New York: E. P. Dutton and Co., 1951. A mountain mystery.
C9680 (ASU BC)

Strait is the Gait. New York: Dutton, 1946.
C9690

The Strange Death of Manny Square. New York: E. P. Dutton and Co., 1941. A mountain mystery.
C9700 (BC)

Strange Return. 1st ed. Guilt edged mystery. New York: E. P. Dutton and Co., 1952. A mountain setting.
C9710 (ASU BC)

Who Killed Pretty Becky Low? 1st ed. Guilt edged mystery. New York: E. P. Dutton and Co., 1951.
C9720 (ASU BC)

Cunningham, Allan Traditional Tales of the English and Scottish Peasantry. London: Taylor and Hessy, 1882.
C9730

Traditional Tales of the English and Scottish Peasantry, Vol. I. Published on demand by University Microfilms. Ann Arbor, Michigan: University Microfilms, 1975.
C9740

Traditional Tales of the English and Scottish Peasantry, Vol. II. Published on demand by University Microfilms. Ann Arbor, Michigan: University microfilms, 1975.
C9750

Cunningham, Earl Harold "Religious Concerns of Southern Appalachian Migrants in a North Central City." Ph. D. Diss. Boston Univ., 1962.
C9760

Cunningham, Everett W. Jewell, Malcom Edwin Kentucky Politics. Lexington: Univ. of Kentucky Press, 1968.
J820 (ASU BC)

Cunningham, Raymon "Current and Future Needs for Vocational Education in Jackson County, West Virginia." Master's thesis. West Virginia Univ., 1967.
C9770

Cunningham, Shirley Hubbard "A Descriptive Study of the Science Fair at Robinson Junior High School, Kingsport, Tennessee, and in Orange County, Florida, for 1960-1962." Master's thesis. East Tennessee State College, 1962.
C9780 (ETSU)

Cunningham, William The Real Book about Daniel Boone. Garden City, N. Y.: Garden City Books, 1952. This volume attempts to dispel some of the myths about Boone.
C9790 (BC)

Cunyus, Lucy Josephine The History of Bartow County, Formerly Cass. Easley, S. C.: Genealogical Reprints, 197? A very good local history. The name change referred to in the title is an outgrowth of Civil War hostilities.
C9800 (BC ASU)

Cuppett, Donald G. Air-drying Practices in Central Appalachians. U. S. Forest Service Research Paper, NE-56. Upper Darby, Pa.: Northeastern Forest Experiment Station, 1966.
C9820

Cuppk, Albert M. A History of Methodism in Rockbridge County, Virginia. n.p.: n.p., 195?
C9810 (BC)

Curcie, Charles Peter "Merger of Local Government: Case Study, Washington County and Bristol, Virginia, 1971." Master's thesis. East Tennessee State Univ., 1971.
C9830 (ETSU)

Curle, Lawrence Duke Soil Survey, Yadkin County, North Carolina. Fieldwork by J. D. Roberts and others. Soil Survey, Series 1959, no. 16. Washington: U. S. Department of Agriculture, Soil Conservation Service, 1962.
C9840

Curry, Jane Louise Beneath the Hill. New York: McGraw Hill, 1974. A 4th grade to Jr. High book in which youngsters encounter the evils of strip-mining.
C9850

Curry, R. Bruce Hoffman, Glenn J. Annotated Bibliography on Slope Stability of Strip Mine Soil Banks. Wooster: Ohio Agricultural Experiment Station, 1964.
H6250 (ASU)

Hoffman, Glenn J. Slope Stability of Coal Strip Mine Spoil Banks. Wooster: Ohio Agricultural Experiment Station, 1964.
H6260 (ASU)

Curry, Richard Orr "A House Divided: A Study of Statehood Politics and the Copperhead Movement in West Virginia During the Civil War." Ph.D. Diss. University of Pennsylvania, 1961.
C9860

Curry, Richard Orr
A House Divided: A Study of Statehood Politics and the Copperhead Movement in West Virginia. Pittsburgh: Univ. of Pittsburgh Press, 1964.
C9870 (WCU ETSU ASU BC)

Curtis, Claude Davis Three Quarters of a Century at Martha Washington College. Bristol: King Print. Co., 1928. History of a former girls' school in Abingdon, Va.
C9880 (ASU)

Curtis, Edna Earl "Some Types of County and City Library Services to Schools in Tennessee." Master's thesis. East Tennessee State College, 1953.
C9890 (ETSU)

Curtis, Jennie K. "Art Handbook for Elementary Teachers of Elizabethton City Schools, Elizabethton, Tennessee." Master's thesis. East Tennessee State College, 1956.
C9900 (ETSU)

Curtis, M. A. Botany: Containing a Catalogue of the Indigenous and Naturalized Plants of the State. Geological and Natural History Survey of North Carolina, part 3. Raleigh, N. C.: Institution for the Deaf and Dumb and the Blind, 1867.
C9910 (LMC ASU)

The Shrubs and Woody Vines of North Carolina. A reprint from Geological and Natural History Survey, Part III, 1860. Bulletin, no. 46. Raleigh, N. C.: Department of Conservation, 1945.
C9920 (LMC)

Curtis, Mary Barnett Early East Tennessee Tax Lists. A compiled list of residents of the area covered for which there is no (sic) census records prior to 1830. These lists are composed of names of those people who appear on tax lists or petitions for the early 1800's. Fort Worth, Tex.: Arrow Print. Co., 1964.
C9930 (ASU)

Petitions of Anderson County Tennessee. Fort Worth, Texas: American Reference Pub. Co., n.d. Reprint of a petition to the General Assembly of Tennessee asking that Anderson County be created from what was then Knox County. Includes names of petitioners.
C9940 (ASU)

Curtis, W. A. Smith, C. D. A Brief History of Macon County, North Carolina. Franklin, N. C.: Franklin Press, 1905.
S4430

Cushman, Joseph Augustine Loughlin, Gerald Francis Limestones and Marls of North Carolina. Raleigh: Edwards and Broughton Print. Co., 1921.
L3630 (ASU LMC WCU)

Cushman, Rebecca Swing Your Mountain Gal, Sketches of Life in the Southern Highlands. Boston: Houghton Mifflin, 1934. Fairly accurate sketches of mountain life with good renditions of the dialect.
C9950 (ASU WCU LMC MHC BC)

Cushman, Walter S. Cameron, John D. Glimpses of a Land of Beauty. Asheville: Cameron and Cushman, n.d.
C400

Cushwa, Charles T. Forest Recreation: Estimated and Predictions in the North River Area, George Washington National Forest, Virginia. Bulletin, 558. Blacksburg: Virginia Agricultural Experiment Station, 1965.
C9960

Cutlip, Ralph V. The Hickory Grew Tall. New York: Exposition Press, 1970. A novel of pioneer life in the Appalachian Mountains and one man's vision.
C9970

Cutten, George Barton The Silversmiths of North Carolina. Raleigh, N. C.: State Department of Archives and History, 1948. Many of the silversmiths are in the Western, mountainous, part of the state.
C9980 (ASU)

Cutten, George Burton The Silversmiths of Virginia. Richmond: Dietz Press, 1972.
C9990 (FC BC)

Dabney, Charles William Universal Education in the South. Chapel Hill: Univ. of North Carolina Press, 1936. Includes some discussion of educators in the mountains. However, the definitive work in educational movements in the mountains has yet to be done.
D10 (WWC BC)

Dabney, Joseph Earl Mountain Spirits, a Chronicle of Corn Whiskey from King James Ulster Plantation to America's Appalachians and the Moonshine Life. New York: Scribner, 1974.
D20 (BC ASU)

Dabney, Virginius Virginia, The New Dominion. 1st ed. Garden City, N. Y.: Doubleday, 1971. Scant mention of life in the western mountains of Virginia.
D30 (FC BC)

Dahir, James Region Building: Community Development Lessons from the Tennessee Valley. 1st ed. New York: Harper, 1955.
D40 (ASU)

Dahle, Robert D. "A Preliminary Economic Evaluation of the Corey Creek Watershed." Master's thesis. Pennsylvania State Univ., 1956.
D50

Dale, Edward Everett Cherokee Cavaliers: Forty Years of Cherokee History as Told in the Correspondence of the Ridge — Watie — Boudinot Family. 1st ed. Norman: Univ. of Oklahoma Press, 1939. Three prominent interrelated families reveal, in their letters, contemporary attitudes toward the issues that split in the Cherokee nation in the 1830's.
D60 (ASU WCU LMC BC)

Dandridge, Danske Bedinger American Prisoners of the Revolution. 1911. Reprint. Baltimore: Genealogical Pub. Co., 1967. A list of captured Continentals.
D70 (ASU)

George Michael Bedinger: A Kentucky Pioneer. Charlottesville, Va.: Michie Co., 1909.
D80 (ASU)

Daneker, Jerome G. The Romance of Georgia Marble. Baltimore: Thomsen-Ellie Co., 1927.
D90 (ASU BC)

Danford, Harry Edmund The Trail of the Gray Dragoon. New York: H. Vinal, 1928. A love story of a fiery rebel girl, a Yankee soldier, and an old inn on the Kanawha turnpike on Ganley Mountain in West Virginia.
D100 (ASU)

The West Virginian. New York: Harold Vinal, 1926. A novel of coal camp labor difficulties set in Mingo and Pocahontas counties, West Virginia.
D110 (BC)

Daniel, Ella Mae Hunger: A Tragedy of North Carolina Farm Folk. n.p.: n.p., n.d. Drama about mountain people ekeing out a marginal existence on a rocky farm.
D120

Daniel, J. R. V. ed. Hornbook of Virginia History. Richmond, Va.: Division of History of the Virginia Department of Conservation and Development, n.d.
D130

Daniel, James Walter The Girl in Checks: Or, The Mystery of the Mountain Cabin. Nashville: Pub. House of the M. E. Church, South, 1890. A Mystery story with a mountain setting and religious overtones.
D140 (ASU BC)

Daniel, John S., Jr. "Special Warfare in Middle Tennessee and Surrounding Areas, 1861-62." Master's thesis. Univ. of Tennessee, 1971. Includes accounts of the Coleman Scouts and other guerrilla activity in East Tennessee.
D150

Daniels, Freeman, Junior "The Mountain People of Virginia: Their Nature and Their Needs." Master's thesis. Univ. of Virginia, 1925.
D160 (ASU)

"The Mountain People of Virginia: Their Nature and Their Needs." Microfilm. Master's thesis. Univ. of Virginia, 1925.
D170 (ASU)

Daniels, Jonathan A Southerner Discovers the South. New York: Macmillan Co., 1938. Includes sections on the mountain South.
D180 (ASU BC FC)

Tar Heels. New York: Dodd, 1941. Includes sections on Western North Carolina.
D190 (LMC BC)

Thomas Wolfe: October Recollections. Columbia, S. C.: Bostick & Thornley, 1961. Contains some seldom-told Wolfe anecdotes.
D200 (ASU)

Daniels, Ophelia Cope "Formative Years of Johnson City, Tennessee, 1885-1890: A Social History." Master's thesis. Tennessee Agricultural & Industrial State College, 1947.
D210 (ETSU)

Daniels, Robert Norman Furman University, a History. Greenville, S. C.: Furman Univ., 1951.
D220 (WCU)

Daniels, W. M. comp. Should We Have More TVA's? (The Reference Shelf, vol. 22, no. 2.) New York: H. W. Wilson Co., 1950.
D230

Danielson, V. A. Waste Disposal Costs at Two Coal Mines in Kentucky and Alabama. Information circular, 8406. Washington: W. S. Bureau of Mines, 1969.
D240

Danley, Robert A. Population Estimates for Kentucky Counties and Economic Area, July 1, 1958. Lexington: Kentucky Agricultural Experiment Station, 1959.
D250 (ASU)

Dargan, Olive Tilford Call Home the Heart. New York: Longmans, Green & Co., 1932. A young mountain woman goes to a mill village and is exposed to unions and communism. Although she is a natural leader in these moments she yearns for her mountains and returns to her family.
D260 (ASU BC)

From My Highest Hill; Carolina Mountain Folks. Photographs by Bayard Wootten. Rev. ed. Reprint. (Original title: Highland annals.) Philadelphia: J. B. Lippincott Co., 1941. Eight stories of mountain people by social propagandist Dargan.
D270 (ASU WCU BC UNCA)

Highland Annals. New York: C. Scribner's Sons, 1925. Original edition and title of FROM MY HIGHEST HILL.
D280 (ASU WCU LMC ETSU UNCA BC)

Innocent Bigamy, and Other Stories. Winston-Salem, N. C.: J. F. Blair, 1962. Short stories set primarily in the North Carolina mountains.
D290 (ASU WCU LMC BC)

Lords and Lovers, and Other Dramas. New York: C. Scribner's Sons, 1906.
D300 (ASU BC)

The Mortal Gods, and Other Plays. N. Y.: Scribner, 1912.
D310 (UNCA WCU)

Path, Flower, and Other Verses. London: J. M. Dent & Sons; New York: C. Scribner's Sons, 1914.
D320 (ASU BC)

Semiranis, and Other Plays. N. Y.: Scribner, 1909.
D330 (BC)

The Spotted Hawk. Winston-Salem, N. C.: J. F. Blair, 1958. Short stories by one of North Carolina's prominent mountain authors.
D340 (ASU WCU BC UNCA)

A Stone Came Rolling. 1st ed. New York: International Pub., 1935. This sequel to CALL HOME THE HEART brings the heroine and her family down from the mountains to fight evil in the mill villages.
D350 (ASU BC WCU LMC)

A Stone Came Rolling. By Fielding Burke, pseud. New York: Longmans, Green and Co., 1935.
D360

D'Armand, Roscoe Carlisle D. C. Armond Family in America. Knoxville, Tenn.: n.p., 1954.
D370

D'Armand, Roscoe Carlisle comp. Knox County, Tenn., Marriage Records. Knoxville, Tenn.: Family Record Society, 1970.
D380 (ETSU)

Darnell, Elias A Journal Containing an Accurate and Interesting Account of the Hardships, Suffering, Battles, Defeat, and Captivity of Those Heroic Kentucky Volunteers and Regulars, Commanded by General Winchester, in the Years 1812-13. Also, Two Narratives by Men That Were Wounded in the Battles on the River Raisen, and Taken Captive by the Indians. Philadelphia: Lippincott, Grambo, & Co., 1854.
D390 (ASU BC)

Darnell, Harold L. "A Study of the Problems of Sixth Grade Students in Selected Schools of Scott County, Virginia." Master's thesis. East Tennessee State College, 1957.
D400

Darrah, Lawrence B. Economic Study of Land Utilization in Schuyler County, N. Y. Ithaca: Cornell Agriculture Experiment Station, 1942.
D410

Darrison, Marquerite Porter ed. A Handweaver's Source Book; A Selection of 224 Patterns from the Laura M. Allen Collection. Swarthmore, Pa.: n.p., 1953.
D1300

Darst, Henry Jackson The Darsts of Virginia: A Chronicle of Ten Generations in the Old Dominion. Williamsburg, Va.: n.p., 1972.
D420

Darter, Oscar H. The Darter-Tarter Family. Illus., indexed. Richmond: Garrett & Massie, 1965. Includes Wythe County families.
D430

Daubeny, Charles Giles Bridle Journal of a Tour through the United States and Canada, Made during the Years 1937-38. Oxford: Printed by T. Combe, Printers to the University, for private circulation only, 1843. This British naturalist visited the Virginia springs and vicinity.
D440

Dauenheimer, Anne R. "Some Correlates of Alienation Among Southern Appalachians." Master's thesis. West Virginia Univ., 1967. An excellent study of difficulties encountered by Appalachian people in relating to the larger U. S. society.
D450 (ASU)

Daugherty, James Henry Daniel Boone. New York: Viking Press, 1939. This biography with excellent drawings won the 1940 Newberry Award for children's literature.
D460 (MHC ETSU UNCA)

Daniel Boone. 1939. Reprint. New York: Viking Press, 1940.
D470 (ASU)

Daughters of the American Revolution, Georgia. Historical Collections of the Georgia Chapters. 1932. Reprint. 4 vols. Vidalia, Ga.: Genealogical Reprints, 1967.
D480 (ASU)

Daughters of the American Revolution, Kentucky. Hazard Chapter. History of Perry County, Ky. Hazard, Ky.: The chapter, 1933. Interesting but rather superficial study of Perry County, Kentucky.
D490

History of Perry County, Kentucky. Reprint. Hazard: Hazard Chapter DAR, 1953.
D500 (BC)

Daughters of the American Revolution Lineage Books. Roster of the Virginia Daughters of the American Revolution. vols 91 through 166. rev. ed. Richmond: Garrett & Massie, 1959.
D510

Daughters of the American Revolution Magazine vol. 1. July, 1892. Washington: National Society, n.d.
D520 (ASU)

Daughters of the American Revolution; North Carolina. Roster of Soldiers from North Carolina in the American Revolution, with an Appendix Containing a Collection of Miscellaneous Records. 1932. Reprint. Baltimore: Genealogical Pub. Co., 1967.
D530 (ASU)

Daughters of the American Revolution Patriot Index. Washington: National Society D.A.R., 1967.
D540

Daughters of the American Revolution, Pennsylvania, Pittsburgh Chapter. Fort Duquesne and Fort Pitt. Early Names of Pittsburgh Streets. Pittsburgh: Eichbaum Press, 1899.
D550 (ASU)

Daughters of the American Revolution, Tennessee. Beloved Landmarks of Loudon County, Tennessee. Loudon: Hiwassee Chap., DAR, 1962.
D560 (BC)

Daughters of the American Revolution, Tennessee, Lydia Russell Bean Chapter, Knoxville. Benton County, Tennessee, Marriages, 1832-1957. From records originally copied from the Benton County court records, by Mr. G. B. Holladay, and published in the CAMDEN CHRONICLE, Camden, Tenn., January through May, 1959. Knoxville, Tenn.: n.p., 1962.
D570 (ASU)

Daughters of Colonial Wars, Kentucky. Kentucky Pioneers and Their Descendants. 1951. Reprint. Baltimore: Genealogical Pub. Co., 1967.
D580 (ASU BC)

Davenport, Fredrick Morgan Primitive Traits in Religious Revivals. New York: Macmillan Co., 1906. Describes some of the more interesting abberations of Appalachia's smaller sects.
D590

Davey, Frankland Wilmot "Theory and Practice in the Black Mountain Poets Duncan, Olson, and Creeley." Ph. D. Diss. Microfilm. Univ. of Southern California, 1968. Black Mountain College, now defunct, once served as the nucleus for a flourishing artist colony.
D600 (WCU)

David, Boileau Bacon, Samuel Rankin Soil Survey, Union County, Pennsylvania. Washington: U. S. Department of Agriculture, Bureau of Plant Industry, Soils, and Agricultural Engineering, 1946.
B100

David, John Peter "Earnings, Health, Safety, and Welfare of Bituminous Coal Miners Since the Encouragement of Mechanization by the United Mine Workers of America." Ph. D. Diss. West Virginia Univ., 1972.
D610

Davids, Richard D. The Man Who Moved a Mountain. Philadelphia: Fortress Press, 1970. Account of the ministry of Rev. Bob Childress in the mountains of Southwestern Virginia.
D620 (ASU FC BC)

Davidson, Donald The Tennessee. Rivers of America. 2 vols. New York: Rinehart & Co., 1946-48. A moving lyrical history of the river and the people who settled along it.
D630 (ASU WCU LMC MHC UNCA BC)

Davidson, Dwight M. Loomis, Charles P. Standards of Living of the Residents of Seven Rural Resettlement Communities. Washington, D. C.: n.p., 1938.
L3440

Davidson, Dwight M., Jr. Standards of Living in Six Virginia Counties. Prepared in cooperation with the Agricultural Economics Bureau, the Work Projects Administration, and Virginia Polytechnic Institute. Social Research Report, 15. Washington: Farm Security Administration, 1940. Wythe and Rockbridge counties are included in this study.
D640

Davidson, Grace Gillam comp. Wilkes County. Early Records of Georgia, vol. 1-2. . Reprint. VOLS. IN . Vidalia, Ga.: S. E. Lucas, 1968.
D650 (ASU)

Davidson, J. D. A Curiosity in Chancery. Lexington, Va.: The author, n.d. A description of a court case from Rockbridge County, Virginia which had far-reaching political implications.
D660

Davidson, Mrs. Josephine Martin Josie M. Davidson, Her Life and Work, by Herself. Prestonsburgh, Ky.: Mrs. A. J. Davidson, 1922. Autobiography of a Kentucky mountain woman who grew up during Civil War and Reconstruction.
D670 (BC)

Davidson, Mary Frances The Dye-Pot. Gatlinburg, Tenn.: The author, 1974. Excellent handbook for natural dyes and dyeing.
D680

Davidson, Paul Colwell Burrell, Robert G. Wild Water West Virginia: A Paddler's Guide to the White Water Rivers of the Mountain State. Parsons, W. Va.: McClain Print. Co., 1972.
B9180 (ASU BC)

Davidson, Roger Harry "The Depressed Area Controversy; A Study in the Politics of American Business." Microfilm. Ph. D. Diss. Columbia Univ., 1963. Includes material on Appalachian counties.
D690 (ASU)

Davidson, S. F. Cobb, William B. Soil Survey of Caldwell County. Washington: Govt. Print. Off., 1919.
C5330

Cobb, William B. Soil Survey of Caldwell County, North Carolina. Washington: U. S. Department of Agriculture, Bureau of Soils, 1923.
C5340

Jurney, Robert Campbell Soil Survey of Cherokee County, North Carolina. Washington: U. S. Department of Agriculture, Bureau of Soils, 1926.
J2860 (ASU)

Perkins, Samuel Oscar Soil Survey, Henderson County, North Carolina. Washington: U. S. Department of Agriculture, Bureau of Plant Industry, Soils, and Agricultural Engineering, 1943.
P2100

Davidson, Samuel Fred Goldston, Eugene Frizzell Soil Survey, Madison County, North Carolina. Washington: U. S. Department of Agriculture, Bureau of Plant Industry, 1942.
G2430

Jurney, Robert Campbell Soil Survey of Rutherford County, North Carolina.
J2910

Lee, William Daniel Soil Survey, Yadkin County, North Carolina. Washington: U. S. Department of Agriculture, Bureau of Chemistry and Soils, 1928.
L1450

Davidson, Theodore Fulton Reminiscences and Traditions of Western North Carolina. Asheville: Service Print. Co., n.d. A happy collection of memoirs from the western North Carolina mountains.
D700

Davies, William Edward Caverns of West Virginia. Reports, vol. 19-A. Reprinted with supplement. Morgantown: West Virginia Geological Survey, 1965.
D710 (ETSU)

West Virginia's Buffalo Creek Flood: A Study of the Hydrology and Engineering Geology. Circular, 667. Washington: U. S. Geological Survey, 1972. Account of recent criminal negligence in the West Virginia coal country.
D720

Daviess, Maria Thompson The Melting of Molly. Illustrated by R. M. Crosby. Indianapolis: Bobbs-Merrill Co., 1912. A novel of romance and, would you believe, dieting set in Eastern Tennessee.
D730 (ASU)

Over Paradise Ridge: A Romance. New York: Harper & Brothers, 1915. Romantic fiction with an Eastern Tennessee setting.
D740 (ASU BC)

The Davis and Elkins Historical Magazine vol. 1, no. 1. May 1948. Elkins, W. Va.: Davis and Elkins College, 1948.
D750 (BC)

Davis, Arthur Kyle, Jr. Folk-songs of Virginia, a Descriptive Index and Classification of Material. Collected under the auspices of the Virginia Folklore Society. Durham, N. C.: Duke Univ. Press, 1949. A classic volume in the field of American folk songs.
D770 (ASU LMC FC BC)

Folk-songs of Virginia, a Descriptive Index and Classification of Material. Collected under the auspices of the Virginia Folklore Society. Reprint. New York: AMS Press, 1965.
D780 (ETSU)

Traditional Ballads of Virginia. Cambridge: Harvard University Press, 1929.
D800

Virginia War Agencies Selective Draft and Volunteers. Source Vol. IV. Richmond, Va.: Virginia War History Commission, 1926.
D830

Virginia War History in Newspaper Clippings. Source Vol. II. Richmond, Va.: Virginia War History Commission, 1924.
D840

Virginia War Letters and Diaries and Editorials. Source Vol. III. Richmond, Va.: Virginia War History Commission, 1925.
D850

Davis, Arthur Kyle, Jr. ed. Folksongs of Virginia. Durham, N. C.: Duke Univ., 1949.
D760 (ASU)

More Traditional Ballads of Virginia: Collected with the Cooperation of Members of the Virginia Folklore Society. Chapel Hill: Univ. of North Carolina Press, 1960.
D790 (ASU FC BC LMC)

Traditional Ballads of Virginia. Harvard Univ. Press, 1929.
D801 (ASU)

Traditional Ballads of Virginia: Collected Under the Auspices of the Virginia Folk-lore Society. 1929. Reprint. Charlottesville: Univ. Press of Virginia, 1957.
D810 (LMC FC BC)

Traditional Ballads of Virginia: Collected Under the Auspices of the Virginia Folklore Society. 1929. Reprint. Charlottesville: Univ. Press of Virginia, 1969.
D820 (WCU ETSU ASU)

Virginians of Distinguished Service in World War. Source Vol. I. Richmond, Va.: Virginia War History Commission, 1923.
D860

Davis, Burke Jeb Stuart, the Last Cavalier. Maps by Rafall D. Palacios. New York: Rinehart, 1957. An excellent biography with descriptions of major campaigns.
D870 (ASU)

They Called Him Stonewall: A Life of Lt. General T. J. Jackson, C. S. A. New York: Rinehart, 1954. An excellent biography of Appalachian Virginia's most famous military man.
D880 (ASU BC)

Davis, Caroline Heath comp. Rutherford County, North Carolina, Abstracts of Wills, 1779-1822. Rutherfordton, N. C.: The author, 1972.
D890 (ASU)

Davis, Carolyn I. "A Study of Health Instruction in Selected High Schools in Washington County, Tennessee." Master's thesis. East Tennessee State Univ., 1969.
D900 (ETSU)

Davis, Charles Elton "Theodore Roosevelt, Franklin Historian." Master's thesis. Kansas State Univ., 1961. A study of Roosevelt's excellent but little-known history of the state of Franklin.
D910

Davis, Charles V. "A Study of the Vocational Guidance Now Provided to Non-college Bound Students in East Tennessee High Schools." Master's thesis. Tennessee Technical Univ., 1968.
D920

Davis, Claude J. Issues of Constitutional Revision in West Virginia. Morgantown: West Va. Univ., 1966.
D930

Davis, Claude J. and others West Virginia State and Local Government. Bulletin Series 63, no 12-5. Morgantown: Bureau for Government Research, West Virginia Univ., 1963.
D940 (ETSU BC)

Davis, Curtis Carroll Chronicle of the Cavaliers: A Life of the Virginia Novelist, Dr. William A. Caruthers. Richmond: Dietz Press, 1953. Although Caruthers never created very sympathetic or believable mountain characters, he did use mountain settings in some of his works.
D950 (WCU ASU)

Davis, Darrell Haug Geography of the Mountains of Eastern Kentucky. Ky. Geological Survey no. 18. Frankfort, Ky.: n.p., 1924. Descriptions, elevations and histories of the Kentucky Cumberlands and other ranges are contained in this informative volume.
D960 (BC ASU)

Davis, Dorothy History of Harrison County, West Virginia. Clarksburg, Va.: American Association of University Women, 1970. Another very good history from West Virginia. This state has a written history for almost every county.
D970 (BC ASU)

Davis, Dudley H. The Kingdom Gained and Other Poems. Richmond: B. F. Johnson Pub. Co., 1896. Poems, some with mountain settings or themes.
D980 (BC)

Davis, Eliza Timberlake ed. Frederick County, Virginia, Marriages, 1771-1825. Baltimore: Genealogical Pub. Co., 1973. Excellent resource material on one of Virginia's earliest settled mountain counties.
D990 (ASU ETSU)

Davis, Harold Lenoir Beulah Land. New York: W. Morrow, 1949. A novel about a young Cherokee girl from Crowtown in Western North Carolina and her adventures during the Civil War and the westward movement.
D1000 (ASU BC WCU)

Davis, Haze A. "The Study of the Four High Schools in Claiborne County, Tennessee." Master's thesis. Univ. of Tennessee, 1957.
D1010

Davis, Hester A. "Social Interaction and Kinship in Big Cove Community, Cherokee, N. C." Master's thesis. Univ. of North Carolina, 1957. An excellent study of social and kinship patterns on the Cherokee Reservation.
D1020 (ASU)

"Social Interaction and Kinship in Big Cove Community, Cherokee, N. C." Microfilm. Master's thesis. Univ. of North Carolina, 1957.
D1030 (ASU)

Davis, Hubert J. Christmas in the Mountains, Southwest Virginia Christmas Customs and Their Origins. Illustrated by Carolee Jackson. Murfreesboro, N. C.: Johnson Pub. Co., 1972. The most complete volume I know on the many and varied Christmas customs of the Southern mountains.
D1040 (ASU BC FC)

'Pon my Honor, Hit's the Truth; Tall Tales from the Mountains. Murfreesboro, N. C.: Johnson Pub. Co., 1973. A delightful collection of mountain humor and tall tales.
D1050 (BC)

Davis, Innis C. and others A Bibliography of West Virginia. Two parts. Charleston, West Virginia: Charleston Print. Co. for the West Virginia Department of Archives and History, 1939.
D1060

Davis, J. L. The Mountain Preacher. Cincinnati, Ohio: F. L. Roure, 1909. The author's experiences as a minister in the Southern mountains are told in dialect.
D1070 (BC)

Davis, J. Lee Bits of History and Legends Around and About the Natural Bridge of Virginia, 1730-1950. Lynchburg, Va.: Brown-Morrison Co., Ind., 1949. A fascinating booklet of facts and lore pertaining to Western Virginia's oldest travel attraction.
D1080 (ASU)

Bits of History and Legends around and about the Natural Bridge of Virginia from 1730-1950. Lynchburgh: Natural Bridge of Va., 1950.
D1090 (BC)

Tompkins, Edmund Pendleton The Natural Bridge and Its Historical Surroundings. Natural Bridge, Va.: Natural Bridge of Va., 1939.
T8880 (ASU FC BC)

Davis, James H. A Social Study of the Colored Population of Knoxville, Tennessee. Knoxville: n.p., 1926.
D1100

"A Study of Seven School Communities of Hawkins County, Tennessee." Master's thesis. Univ. of Tennessee, 1937. This study includes different economic, ethnic and educational levels in the test communities.
D1110

Davis, Joe F. Bonser, Howard Jacob Electricity on Farms and in Rural Homes in the East Tennessee Valley. Knoxville: Tennessee Agricultural Experiment Station, 1951.
B5350

Davis, John D. "A Study of the Applied Psychology Classes for Sophomores and Juniors at Appalachian State Teachers College." Master's thesis. Appalachian State Teachers College, 1955.
D1120 (ASU)

Davis, Julia Legacy of Love. New York: Harcourt, Brace, 1961. Autobiography of an eventful childhood divided between two sets of grandparents — The intellectual Davises of Clarksburg, W. Va. and the lively, eclectic McDonalds of the Shenandoah Valley of Virginia.
D1130

The Shenandoah. The Rivers of America. New York: Farrar & Rinehart, 1945. A beautifully-written history of the river and the people who live along its shores.
D1140 (ASU BC FC)

A Valley and a Song; the Story of the Shenandoah River. N. Y.: Holt, Rinehart and Winston, 1963. This volume stresses the role of the Shenandoah in our country's westward movement, folklore and folksong. Written for the younger reader.
D1150 (BC ASU)

Davis, Julia Lavinia "A Study of Visually-handicapped Children in the Eighth Grade of Boone High School." Master's thesis. Appalachian State Teachers College, 1950.
D1160 (ASU)

Davis, Lloyd ed. The Public University in Its Second Century Morgantown: Office of Research and Development, West Virginia Center for Appalachian Studies and Development, West Virginia Univ., 1967.
P4830

Davis, Mack Parker "Problem of the Public School Principals in East Tennessee." Ed. D. Diss. Univ. of Tennessee, 1954.
D1170 (ETSU)

Davis, Rebecca Harding Kent Hampden. New York: Charles Scribner's Sons, 1892. A story of young Kent Hampden's growing up years in Wheeling, West Virginia. Virtue is, of course, rewarded.
D1180 (BC ASU)

Life in the Iron Mills: Or, The Korl Woman. 1st ed. Feminist Press Reprint. Series, no. 1. New York: Feminist Press, 1972. An account of life in the iron mills of Pennsylvania.
D1190 (ASU)

Silhouettes of American Life. New York: Scribner, 1892. Contains six sketches from the Southern mountains.
D1200 (ETSU ASU)

Silhouettes of American Life. 1892. Reprint. American Short Story Reprint Series, vol. 9. New York: Garrett Press, 1968.
D1210 (ASU BC ETSU)

Waiting for the Verdict. New York: Sheldon and Company, 1868. Local color. A mystery novel with a mountain setting.
D1220

Davis, Samuel Hoffman Separated by Mountains. Philadelphia: Dorrance & Co., 1933. A Civil War novel set in Virginia and West Virginia. Young David Hart, the mountaineer hero of the piece represents accurately the divided sentiments of mountaineers in Southern states.
D1230 (ASU)

Davis, Susan Lawrence Authentic History of Ku Klux Klan, 1865-1877. New York: The author, 1924. Despite the fact that the abolition movement in the U. S. started in Appalachia and most mountaineers were pro-Union, there was some Ku Klux activity in the mountains.
D1240 (LMC)

Davis, Virgil H. "Coordination of Anti-poverty Programs in Chattanooga." Master's thesis. Middle Tennessee State Univ., 1971.
D1250

Davis, William Anderson Soil Survey, Stokes County, North Carolina. Prepared in cooperation with the North Carolina Department of Agriculture and the North Carolina Agricultural Experiment Station. Soil Survey Report, Series 1934, no. 20. Washington: U. S. Department of Agriculture, Bureau of Plant Industry, 1940.
D1260 (ASU)

Soil Survey of Surry County, North Carolina. Prepared in cooperation with the North Carolina Department of Agriculture and the North Carolina Agricultural Experiment Station. Soil Survey Report, Series 1932, no. 20. Washington: U. S. Department of Agriculture, Bureau of Chemistry and Soils, 1937.
D1270

Soil Survey of Watauga County, North Carolina. Prepared in cooperation with the North Carolina Department of Agriculture and the North Carolina Agricultural Experiment Station. Soil Survey Report, 1928, Series, no. 1. Washington: U. S. Department of Agriculture, Bureau of Chemistry and Soils, 1930.
D1280 (ASU)

Devereux, Robert Eddins Soil Survey of Macon County, North Carolina. Washington: U. S. Department of Agriculture, Bureau of Chemistry and Soils, 1933.
D1970

Goldston, Eugene Frizzell Soil Survey, Jackson County, North Carolina. Washington: U. S. Bureau of Plant Industry, Soils, and Agricultural Engineering, 1948.
G2410

Goldston, Eugene Frizzell Soil Survey, Madison County, North Carolina. Washington: U. S. Department of Agriculture, Bureau of Plant Industry, 1942.
G2430

Jurney, Robert Campbell Soil Survey of Cherokee County, North Carolina. Washington: U. S. Department of Agriculture, Bureau of Soils, 1926.
J2860 (ASU)

Jurney, Robert Campbell Soil Survey of Rutherford County, North Carolina.
J2910

Davison, Marguerite Porter A Handweaver's Pattern Book. Rev. ed. Layout and live illustrations drawn by Charles C. Dengler. Photographs by E. Fletcher Brown. Swarthmore, Pa.: The author, 1950. This very thorough guide to handweaving contains 345 threading directions and a wide range of traditional patterns.
D1290 (ASU BC)

Pennsylvania German Home Weaving. Plymouth Meeting, Pa.: Mrs. C. N. Keyser, 1947. Another of Mrs. Porter's excellent guidebooks with patterns and clear instructions.
D1310

Dawley, Thomas Robinson, Jr. The Child That Toileth Not: The Story of a Government Investigation. New York: Gracie Pub. Co., 1912. This expose on child labor includes material on the textile mills in the Southern mountains.
D1320 (ASU BC)

Dawson, Amelia Cate East Tennessee Kinsman. Seaford, Del.: n.p., 1962.
D1330

Dawson, Ann Three Steps. N. Y.: Vantage Press, 1961. Young Eddie Mullins leaves his home on the French Broad River in North Carolina for a well-paying job in Chicago. There he must learn to deal with harsh realities and an uncaring world. His younger brother is corrupted by moneyed outsiders.
D1340 (BC ASU)

Dawson, Fielding The Black Mountain Book. New York: Groton Press, 1970. An exciting history of the controversial and non-conformist Black Mountain College at Black Mountain, North Carolina.
D1350

Dawson, George W. "Problem Survey of the Elementary and High School at Crum, West Virginia." Master's thesis. Marshall College, 1952.
D1360

Dawson, Laura Leslie Banner Shepherd Monroe Dugger: A Critical Biography. Master's thesis. Univ. of North Carolina, 1973.
D1370 (LMC ASU)

Daxey, Charles T. Marshall, Edward In Old Kentucky. New York: G. W. Dillingham Co., 1910.
M3430 (ETSU BC ASU)

Day, D. L. "Impact of World War II on Juvenile Delinquency in Knox County, Tennessee." Master's thesis. Univ. of Tennessee, 1948.
D1380

Day, Edith Eleanor The Girl of Luna's Creek. Petersburg, W. Va.: Great Court Press, 1949. Narrative poem about a young girl's encounter with a fairy who represents the spirit of the mountains.
D1390 (BC)

Day, John F. Bloody Ground. 1st ed. Garden City, N. Y.: Doubleday, Doran & Co., 1941. An unusual volume full of anecdotes, folklore and sociological commentary on the author's native eastern Kentucky.
D1400 (ASU LMC BC)

Dayton Human Relations Commission Southern Appalachian Migration. Dayton, Ohio: The commission, 1966. A sad look at the alienation experienced by Appalachians who migrate to northern cities.
D1410

Dayton, Ruth Neeson Woods Greenbrier Pioneers and Their Homes. Charleston, W. Va.: West Virginia Pub. Co., 1942.
D1420

Lewisburg Landmarks. Illustrated by Naomi S. Hostermau. Charleston, W. Va.: Education Foundation, 1957.
D1430 (ASU BC)

Pioneers and Their Homes on Upper Kanawha. Illustrated by Naomi S. Hosterman. Map by Ashton Woodman Reniers. Charleston, W. Va.: West Virginia Pub. Co., 1947.
D1440 (ASU BC)

Dayton, Ruth Woods ed. Hall, James Edmond The Diary of a Confederate Soldier: James E. Hall. Lewisburg, W. Va.: n.p., 1961.
H760 (ASU)

de Lys, Claudin A Treasury of American Superstition. New York: Philosophical Library, 1948.
D1770

Deal, Borden Dunbar's Cove. New York: Scribner, 1957.
D1450 (ASU WCU BC)

Dunbar's Cove. London: Hutchinson & Co., 1958. This, perhaps Deal's best novel, is a powerful story of a mountain man's struggle to save his valley from the TVA. Old Matthew Dunbar is one of the strongest characterizations in Appalachian fiction.
D1460 (ASU)

The Insolent Breed. New York: Scribner, 1959. A fiddlin' fool moves into a valley where the pious have forbidden music at religious services and stays to win converts to that good 'ole mountain music.
D1470 (ASU BC)

Walk Through the Valley. New York: Scribner, 1956. Another of Deal's strong novels featuring mountain people in conflict with outside values.
D1480 (ASU BC)

Deal, Loyse Youth see **Deal, Borden**

Dean, A. F. Observations from a Peak in Lumpkin: Or, the Writings of W. Ba. Townsend, Editor, The Dahlonega Nugget. Atlanta: Oglethorpe Univ. Press, 1936. Delightful nuggets from an old time, folksy Georgia mountain paper.
D1490 (ASU)

Dean, Benjamin Hawkins Skull Mountain. New York: Doubleday, Doran and Co., 1941. A mystery novel with a North Carolina mountain setting.
D1500

Dean, Loyd Larsh Creech and Joseph Wynn Family Tree. Morehead, Ky.: n.p., 1964.
D1510 (BC)

Dean, Stuart Burford, Arthur E. Annual Field Trip of the Appalachian and Pittsburgh Geological Societies in the Great Valley in West Virginia. Morgantown, W. Va.: n.p., 1964?
B8530 (ETSU)

Dearmer, Percy and others The Oxford Book of Carols. 1928. Reprint. New York: Oxford Univ. Press, 1964. Many of these same carols are sung in the Southern Mountains today.
D1520 (LMC)

Deaver, R. Map of the Cherokee County, 1837. Washington: Corps of Engineers, War Dept., 1838. Excellent map of the constricted Cherokee Nation just before the 1838 removal.
D1530

Debar, J. H. Dess The West Virginia Handbook and Immigrant's Guide. Parkersburg, W. Va.: Gibbens Bros. Printers, 1870.
D1540

Debusman, Paul Marshall "Social Factors Affecting Selected Southern Baptist Churches in the Southern Appalachian Region of the United States." Microfilm. Ph. D. Diss. Southern Baptist Theological Seminary, 1962.
D1550 (WCU ASU)

DeCarlo, Vincent R. "The Net Direct Economic Effect of the University of Tennessee on the City of Knoxville and on Knox County Resulting from the Expansion of the Knoxville Campus since 1962." Master's thesis. Univ. of Tennessee, 1969.
D1560

Deckard, Percy Edward Genealogy of the Deckard Family. Ptttsburgh, Pa.: Pittsburgh Print. Co., 1932.
D1570

Decker, Elmer History of Knox County, Kentucky (1674-1941). n.p.: n.p., n.d. A very interesting short history of one of Kentucky's lesser-known Appalachian counties.
D1580 (BC)

Dedmond, Francis B. Lengthened Shadows: A History of Gardner-Webb College, 1907-1956. This small private church-related college is located in Cleveland Co., North Carolina.
D1590 (ASU)

Deegan, Paul J. ed. Fitch, Robert Beck Grandfather's Land: We Are Mountain People. Mankate, Minn.: Creative Educational Society, 1972.
F1310 (WCU)

Deeter, Earl B. Soil Survey of Mercer County, Pennsylvania. Prepared in cooperation with Pennsylvania State College. Field Operations, 1917. Washington: U. S. Department of Agriculture, Bureau of Soils, 1919.
D1600

Deffenbaugh, Walter Sylvanus Schools in the Bituminous Coal Regions of the Appalachian Mountains. Bulletin, 21. Washington: Bureau of Education, 1920.
D1610

DeGering, Etta Wilderness Wife: The Story of Rebecca Bryan Boone. Illustrated by Ursula Koering. New York: D. McKay Co., 1966. A biography of the woman who married adventure and followed it westward all her life.
D1620 (ASU MHC WCU BC)

DeGruyter, Julius Allan The Kanawha Spectator. Charleston, W. Va.: n.p., 1953. A County Historical paper full of wit, wisdom and local news.
D1630

DeHass, Wills History of the Early Settlement and Indian Wars of Western Virginia: Embracing an Account of the Various Expeditions in the West, Previous to 1795. Also, Biographical Sketches of Distinguished Actors in Our Border Wars. Wheeling, W. Va.: H. Hoblitzell; Philadelphia: King & Baird, 1851.
D1640 (ASU BC)

History of the Early Settlement and Indian Wars of Western Virginia: Embracing an Account of the Various Expeditions in the West Previous to 1795. Also, Biographical Sketches of Co. Ebenezer Zane. . . and other Distinguished Actors in our Border Wars. 1851. Reprint. Parsons, W. Va.: McClain Print. Co., 1960.
D1650 (ASU LMC FC)

De Jarnette, D. L. Webb, W. S. An Archeological Survey of Rickwick Basin in the Adjacent Portions of the States of Alabama, Mississippi, and Tennessee. Washington: Govt. Print. Off., 1942.
W2070

DeJong, Gordon F. Appalachian Fertility Decline: A Demographic and Sociological Analysis. Lexington: Univ. of Kentucky Press, 1968. An interesting study, however, the sociological analysis appears to be primarily speculative.
D1660 (ASU WCU LMC ETSU BC UNCA)

Fertility Data for the Southern Appalachian Region. (KAES-RS22.) Lexington: Department of Rural Sociology, Kentucky Agricultural Experiment Station, Univ. of Kentucky, July, 1963.
D1670

"Human Fertility in the Southern Appalachian Region: Some Demographic and Sociological Aspects." Ph. D. Diss. Univ. of Kentucky, 1963.
D1680 (ASU)

Is Out-migration from Appalachia Declining? Paper presented at Rural Sociological Meeting, San Francisco, Cal., August 28-31, 1969. (ERIC RC 003586) Washington: U. S. Dept. of Health, Education, and Welfare. Office of Education, 1968.
D1690 (ASU)

The Population of Kentucky: Changes in the Number of Inhabitants, 1950-1960. Bulletin no. 675. Lexington: Kentucky Agricultural Experiment Station, Univ. of Kentucky, December, 1961. A study of the population shift from rural to urban areas in Kentucky.
D1700

Delaney, A. Otis Geologic-Map of the Adult Quadrangle, Northeastern Kentucky. Washington: U. S. Geological Survey, 1973.
D1710

DeLeon, Thomas Cooper Juny: Or, Only One Girl's Story. A Romance of the Society Crust — Upper and Under. Mobile, Ala.: Gossip Print. Co., 1890. A mountain girl finds her entry into high society to be an awkward and heart-rending process.
D1720 (ASU)

Della-Bianca, Lino Beck, Donald E. Yield of Unthinned Yellow-poplar. Asheville, N. C.: Southeastern Forest Experiment Station, 1970.
B2460 (WCU)

Intensive Cleaning Increases Sapling Growth and Browse Production in Southern Appalachians. U. S. Forest Service Research Note, SE-110. Asheville, N. C.: Southeastern Forest Experiment Station, 1969.
D1730

Delozier, Robert Campbell "Public School Enrollment Prediction for the Southern Appalachian Region." Master's thesis. Univ. of Tennessee, 1959.
D1740

Delp, Lester Charles "A Proposed Nongraded Primary Organization for Central School: Bristol, Tennessee." Master's thesis. East Tennessee State Univ., 1966.
D1750 (ETSU)

Deluca, Donald R. "Patterns of Development and Net Migration, 1960-1970: A Study of West Virginia Counties." Master's thesis. West Virginia Univ., 1971. A study of rural to urban migration blend in the state of West Virginia.
D1760

Demarest, D. F. Pepper, J. F. Geology of the Bedford Shale and Berea Sandstone in the Appalachian Basin. Washington: Govt. Print. Off., 1954.
P2000

Demarest, Phyllis Gordon The Wilderness Brigade. New York: Doubleday and Co., 1957. A historical novel about the Civil War in North Carolina. A Union soldier, escaping from a Confederate prison camp, is rescued by Southerners, gets caught up in family tribulations, and ends by marrying the lady of the manor. Set in the foothill country of North Carolina with the military action ranging into the mountains.
D1780

Demetriades, Despina Gus "A Study to Identify Some Personality Characteristics of Freshmen Academic Underachievers at Appalachian State University." Master's thesis. Appalachian State University, 1967.
D1790 (ASU)

DeMond, Robert Orley The Loyalists in North Carolina during the Revolution. 1940. Reprint. Hamden, Conn.: Archon Books, 1964. Very few loyalists were found in the western counties.
D1800 (ASU LMC)

De Morgan, A. ed. Baily, Francis Journal of a Tour in the Unsettled Parts of North America, in 1796 and 1797. London: Baily, 1856.
B350

Dennis, Earle Sale Marriage Bonds of Bedford County, Virginia 1755-1800. Richmond: Dennis & Smith, 1932.
D1810 (ASU FC)

Dennison, John M. Stratigraphy of Onesquethaw Stage of Devonian in West Virginia and Bordering States. Bulletin, no. 22. Morgantown: West Virginia Geological Survey, 1961.
D1820 (ETSU)

Structure of Devonian Strata along Allegheny Front from Corriganville, Maryland, to Spruce Knob, West Virginia. Bulletin, no. 24. Charlestown: West Virginia Geological Survey, 1963.
D1830 (ETSU)

Dent, Thomas Lee Ludlow on the Kanawha. New York: Comet Press Books, 1959. An orphan girl in the West Virginia hills discovers she is the long-lost granddaughter of a wealthy business woman. A West Virginia setting.
D1840 (ASU BC)

Depass, Rudolph Earl "Analysis of the Market Structure of the Fluid Milk Industry in Pennsylvania." Master's thesis. Pennsylvania State Univ., 1961.
D1850

Depew, E. Douglas Land of Waterfalls: A Portfolio of Exclusive Lithographs Suitable for Framing. Asheville, N. C.: Stephens Press, 1954. Pictorial guide to Western North Carolina's many water-falls.
D1860 (WCU)

Derden, J. H. Rogers, Reese F. Soil Survey of Jackson County, Tennessee. Washington: U. S. Department of Agriculture, Bureau of Soils, 1915.
R3570

DeRosier, Arthur H. comp. Through the South with a Union Soldier. Johnson City, Tenn.: ETSU, Research Advisory Council, 1969. A collection of 140 letters, written September 29, 1862-May 2, 1865, by A. A. and C. L. Dunham privates in the 129th Illinois Regt. Both brothers saw action in the Southern Mountains.
D1870

Derrick, Bruce B. Soil Survey of Cambria County, Pennsylvania. Prepared in cooperation with the Pennsylvania State College of Agriculture and Experiment Station. Field Operations, 1915. Washington: U. S. Department of Agriculture, Bureau of Soils, 1917.
D1880

Derthick, Lawrence G. "The Indian Boundary Line in the Southern District of British North America, 1763-1779." Master's thesis. Univ. of Tennessee, 1930. The 1763 Proclamation Line followed the Blue Ridge Mountains' Crest.
D1890

Deschamps, Alfred J. "Land Use in Powell County, Kentucky." Master's thesis. Univ. of Kentucky, 1954. A study of changing land use patterns in a county which was once primarily agricultural.
D1900

DeTurk, David A. The American Folk Scene; Dimensions of the Folksong Revival. N. Y.: Dell Pub. Co., 1967.
D1910 (BC)

Deurbrouck, A. W. Survey of Sulfur Reduction in Appalachian Coals by Stage Crushing. Based on work done in cooperation with Public Health Service, Health, Education, and Welfare Department. U. S. Mines Bureau Information Circular, 8282. Pittsburgh: Mines Bureau, 1966.
D1920

Development Planning Associated, Inc. Industrial and Commercial Potentials and Site and Project Analysis in Braxton, Clay and Nicholas Counties, West Virginia. San Francisco: n.p., 1965.
D1930

Devereaux, Robert Eddins Jurney, Robert Campbell Soil Survey of Augusta County, Virginia. Washington: U. S. Department of Agriculture, Bureau of Chemistry and Soils, 1937.
J2850

Jurney, Robert Campbell Soil Survey of Rockbridge County, Virginia. Washington: U. S. Department of Agriculture, Bureau of Chemistry and Soils, 1934.
J2900

Devereux, Robert Eddins Davis, William Anderson Soil Survey of Watauga County, North Carolina. Washington: U. S. Department of Agriculture, Bureau of Chemistry and Soils, 1930.
D1280 (ASU)

Soil Survey, Albemarle County, Virginia. Prepared in cooperation with the Virginia Agricultural Experiment Station. Soil Survey Report, Series 1935, no. 14. Washington: U. S. Department of Agriculture, Bureau of Plant Industry, 1940.
D1940

Soil Survey of Grayson County, Virginia. Prepared in cooperation with the Virginia Agricultural Experiment Station. Soil Survey Report, Series 1930, no. 19. Washington: U. S. Department of Agriculture, Bureau of Chemistry and Soils, 1934.
D1950

Soil Survey of Macon County, North Carolina. Prepared in cooperation with the North Carolina Department of Agriculture and the North Carolina Agricultural Experiment Station. Soil Survey Report, Series 1929, no. 16. Washington: U. S. Department of Agriculture, Bureau of Chemistry and Soils, 1933.
D1970

Obenshain, S. S. Soil Survey, Russell County, Virginia. Washington: U. S. Department of Agriculture, Bureau of Plant Industry, Soils, and Agricultural Engineering, 1945.
O100 (BC)

Devereux, Robert Eddins and others Soil Survey of Macon County. Washington: Govt. Print. Off., 1929. Contains a map.
D1960

Deveron, Hugh A Rosary of the Ridges. Burnsville, N. C.: Edwards Print., 1919. Poetry from the hills of Ottaray and Yancey and Mitchell Counties, North Carolina.
D1980 (ASU)

Devis, Innis C. and others A Bibliography of West Virginia. Two parts. Charleston, W. Va.: Charleston Printing Co. for the West Virginia Department of Archives and History, 1939.
D1990

De Vorsey, Louis, Jr. The Indian-Boundary in the Southern Colonies, 1763-1775. 1961. Reprint. Chapel Hill: Univ. of North Carolina, 1966. The proclamation line prohibiting settlement of Indian lands ran almost exactly down the Blue Ridge.
D2000 (ASU WCU LMC BC)

Dewees, Francis Percival The Molly Maguires. The Origin, Growth, and Character of the Organization. Philadelphia: J. B. Lippincott & Co., 1877. A fascinating and fairly sympathetic history of the band of Irish terrorists who controlled the coal fields of Pennsylvania for two decades.
D2010 (ASU WCU)

Dewey, Maybelle Jones Push the Button: The Chronicle of a Professor's Wife. Atlanta: Tupper & Love, 1951. Biography of a Cartersville, Georgia woman and her life as wife of the director of the Emory Glee Club.
D2020 (ASU)

DeWitt, David M. The Impeachment and Trial of Andrew Johnson, Seventeenth President of the United States; a History. New York: Macmillan, 1903.
D2030

The Impeachment and Trial of Andrew Johnson, Seventeenth President of the United States; a History. Reprint, Introduction Stanley I. Kutler. Madison: State Hist. Soc. of Wisconsin, 1967.
D2040

DeWitt, Wallace, Jr. Age of Bedford Shale, Berea Sandstone, and Sunbury Shale in the Appalachian and Michigan Basins, Pennsylvania, Ohio, and Michigan. U. S. Geological Survey Bulletin, 1294-G. Contributions to Stratigraphy. Washington: Govt. Print. Off., 1970.
D2050

Pepper, J. F. Geology of the Bedford Shale and Berea Sandstone in the Appalachian Basin. Washington: Govt. Print. Off., 1954.
P2000

Dexter, O. P. A Genealogical Cross Index of the Four Volumes of the Genealogical Dictionary of James Savage. Xerox copy of the original. New York: The author, 1884.
D2060 (ASU)

Diamond, Michael Jay "The Negro and Organized Labor as Voting Blocs in Tennessee, 1960-1964." Master's thesis. Univ. of Tennessee, 1965. Contains scant references to Appalachian Counties.
D2070

Dick, Everett Newton The Dixie Frontier, a Social History of the Southern Frontier from the First Transmontane Beginnings to the Civil War. New York: A. A. Knopf, 1948.
D2080 (ASU MHC)

Dickens, Roy Selman "The Pisgah Culture and Its Place in the Prehistory of the Southern Appalachians." Microfilm. Ph. D. Diss. Univ. of North Carolina, 1970. A very thorough study of a unique prehistoric tribe which dwelt in what is now Haywood County, North Carolina.
D2090 (ASU WWC WCU)

Dickenson County, Va. Diamond Jubilee Commission "Meet Virginia's Baby"; a Brief Pictorial History of Dickenson County. Clintwood, Va.: The commission, 1955. A fascinating blend of history, legend, folklore, tall tales and sketches of the counties leading families and industries.
D2100 (BC ASU)

Dickerman, G. S. The Mountain People in Eastern Kentucky. Berea, Ky.: Berea College, n.d.
D2110

Dickerson, Florence Smith Dickerson and Walden Families. Richmond: Dietz Press, 1961.
D2120 (ASU)

The James Stewart Family of Early Augusta County, Virginia, and Descendants, 1740-1960. n.p.: The author, n.d.
D2130 (ASU)

Dickey, James Buckdancer's Choice: Poems by James Dickey. 1st ed. Wesleyan Poetry Program. Middletown, Conn.: Wesleyan Univ. Press, 1965. This slim volume contains much of Dickey's best work. It was written before fame and vulgarity corrupted him.
D2140 (ASU)

Deliverance. Boston: Houghton Mifflin, 1970. In terms of plot, movement, characterization, and strong lyrical descriptive passages this should have been a great novel. It failed because the author destroyed the credibility of his mountain characters by the addition of false stereotypes and the most unlikely sort of pornography.
D2150 (ASU WCU)

Deliverance. New York: Dell Pub. Co., 1970.
D2160 (ASU)

Poems, 1957-1967. 1st ed. Middletown, Conn.: Wesleyan Univ. Press, 1967.
D2170 (ASU)

Dickey, John B. R. Soil Survey of Frederick County, Virginia. Field Operations, 1914. Washington: U. S. Department of Agriculture, Bureau of Soils, 1916.
D2180

Dickfore, Marie Hessian Soldiers in the American Revolution: Records of Their Marriages and Baptisms of Children in America Performed by the Rev. G. C. Coster, 1776-1783, Chaplain of Two Hessian Regiments. Cincinnati: D. J. Krehbiel Co., 1959.
D2190 (ASU)

Dickinson, John N. ed. Andrew Johnson, 1808-1875. Chronology-Documents-Bibliographical Aids. Dobbs Ferry, N. Y.: Oceana Publications, 1970.
D2200 (ASU)

Dickinson, Meriwether Blair "A Lexicographical Study of the Vocabulary of Greenup County, Kentucky, Set Forth in Jesse Stuart's "Beyond Dark Hills"." Master's thesis. Univ. of Virginia, 1941. An interesting study. However the author gives insufficient weight to the fact Stuart's youth was spent outside the mountains and his speech is not necessarily that of Greenup County.
D2210 (ASU)

Dickson, John "The Judicial History of the Cherokee Nation from 1721 to 1835." Ph. D. Diss. Univ. of Oklahoma, 1964. A very good study of the superior legal system of the Cherokee Nation prior to the Removal.
D2220

Dickson, Lura D. Great Smokies: Wonderland for Boys and Girls. Illustrated by Bill Chapman. Gems of Our Nation. Seymour, Ind.: Dickson's, 1968. An illustrated guide to the wonders of the Great Smokies written especially for children.
D2230 (ASU)

Dickson, R. I. Ulster Emigration to Colonial America, 1718-1775. Ulster-Scot Historical Series, no. 1. London: Routledge & Kegan Paul, 1966. Above 40 percent of the Appalachian families are of Scotch-Irish descent.
D2240 (ASU)

Dickson, Sallie O'Hear Howard McPhlinn. A Story for Boys. Richmond, Va.: The Presbyterian Committee of Publication, 1897. A novel of mountain people who appear unaccountably receptive to Presbyterian propaganda. Faith triumphs over evil.
D2250

Reuben Dalton, Preacher: A Sequel to "The Story of Marthy." Richmond, Va.: The Presbyterian Committee of Publication, 1900. Preacher Reuben and his wife Marthy attempt to lead their unfortunate North Carolina mountain parishioners toward God and progress. Very sentimental and condescending.
D2260

The Story of Marthy. Richmond, Va.: The Presbyterian Committee of Publication, 1898. A sentimental story of a young minister's wife in the North Carolina mountains.
D2270

Diddle, W. H. West Virginia Gems: Songs for the Revival and Social Prayer Meeting. Pennsboro, W. Va.: Parkersburg Pub. Society, U. B. C.; Singer's Glen, Va.: J. Fund's Sons, printers, 1870.
D2280

Diegel, Howard E. "Application of Unitization to the Pennsylvania Crude Oil Industry." Master's thesis. Pennsylvania State Univ., 1961.
D2290

Diehl, George West Old Oxford and Her Families. Verona, Va.: McClure Print. Co., 1971.
D2300

The Reverend Samuel Houston. Verona, Va.: McClure Press, 1970. Biography of a Rockbridge County, Virginia minister.
D2310 (BC)

Diehl, James A. "A Proposed Program of Public Relations for the Schools of Mason County, West Virginia." Master's thesis. Ohio Univ., 1954.
D2320

Diehl, William D. "Farm-nonfarm Migration in the Southeast: A Costs-returns Analysis." Ph. D. Diss. North Carolina State College, 1965. A study of out migration from rural areas and its implications for the economy. Appalachian Counties are included in the survey.
D2330

Dietrich, Richard Vincent Geology and Mineral Resources of Floyd County of the Blue Ridge Upland, Southwestern Virginia. Engineering Experiment Station Series, no. 134. Bulletin, vol. 52, no. 12. Blacksburg: Virginia Polytechnic Institute, 1959. Virginia's largest mineral deposits are in the western mountain counties.
D2340 (ETSU)

Geology and Virginia. Charlottesville: Univ. Press of Virginia, 1970.
D2350 (ETSU)

Virginia Mineral Localities. Revised ed. Blacksburg: Virginia Polytechnic Institute, 1960. Many of the state's more valuable mineral deposits are in Western Virginia.
D2360 (ETSU)

Digges, George A. comp. Buncombe County, North Carolina, Grantee Deed Index. 2 vols. Asheville: Miller (c1927).
D2370

Buncombe County, North Carolina, Grantor Deed Index. 3 vols. Asheville: Miller (c1926).
D2380

Digges, George A., Jr. Historical Facts Concerning Buncombe County Government. Asheville: Biltmore Press, 1935.
D2390 (WCU LMC)

Dill, Henry W., Jr. Johnson, Hugh A. Exurban Development in Selected Areas of the Appalachian Mountains. Washington: Govt. Print. Off., 1963.
J1790

Dillard, Annie Pilgrim at Tinker Creek. New York: Harper's Magazine Press, 1974. A moving account of one woman's sojourn among the natural beauty of the Blue Ridge Mountains near Roanoke, Virginia.
D2400 (BC ASU)

Pilgrim at Tinker Creek. New York: Harper and Row, 1974.
D2410 (ASU)

Diller, J. S. Peridotite of Elliott County, Kentucky. U. S. Geological Survey Bulletin, no. 38. Washington: Govt. Print. Off., 1887.
D2420

Dillin, John Grace Wolfe The Kentucky Rifle: A Study of the Origin and Development of a Purely American Type of Firearm, Together with Accurate Historical Data Concerning Early Colonial Gunsmiths and Profusely Illustrated with Photographic Reproduction of Their Finest Work. Washington: National Rifle Association of America, 1924.
D2430 (LMC BC)

The Kentucky Rifle. 5th ed. Longrifle Series. York, Pa.: G. Shumway, 1967.
D2440 (ASU MHC BC)

Dillman, Buddy Leroy "Local Government Social Overhead Expenditures and Economic Growth in the Appalachian Region." Ph. D. Diss. North Carolina State Univ., 1967. This disturbing survey implies that little can or will be done to change existing patterns.
D2450

Dillow, Nola M. "The Qualifications and Instructional Program of 100 Elementary Geography Teachers in Northeast Tennessee." Master's thesis. East Tennessee State College, 1952.
D2460

Dills, Gary G. "Macroinvertebrate Community Structure as an Indicator of Acid Mine Pollution." Ph. D. Diss. Univ. of Alabama, 1973. Discusses a new method of testing water purity.
D2470

d'Invilliers, E. V. McCreath, Andrew Smith New River Cripple Creek Mineral Region of Virginia. Harrisburg, Pa.: Harrisburg Pub. Co., 1887.
M940

Direction vol. 1-, 1966. Johnson City, Tenn.: First Tennessee-Virginia Development District, 9 issues yearly.
D2480 (ETSU)

Directions vol. 1-, Summer/Fall, 1972-. Asheville, N. C.: Compass Publications, quarterly.
D2490 (ASU)

Directory of Community Services for Asheville and Buncombe County, North Carolina Asheville, N. C.: Information and Referral Service and the Social Planning Division of the United Fund of Asheville and Buncombe County, Inc., 1972.
D2500 (UNCA)

A Directory of Representative Business and Professional Men of Augusta Co., and Staunton, Va. Staunton: Rohrer and Diamond, 1899.
D2510 (ASU)

Dishner, Ernest K. "A Study of the Reading Abilities of the Economically Deprived Students in the Fourth, Fifth, and Sixth Grades at Stratton Elementary School." Master's thesis. East Tennessee State Univ., 1966.
D2520 (ETSU)

Divita, Charles, Jr. "Adult Basic Education: A Study of the Backgrounds, Characteristics, Aspirations, and Attitudes of Undereducated Adults in West Virginia." Master's thesis. Marshall Univ., 1969. A sad little volume dealing with one of Appalachia's most formidable problems.
D2530

Dixon, Hertha "A Survey of the Library Facilities in the Negro Schools of Tuscaloosa County, Alabama." Master's thesis. Alabama State College, 1952. This Survey concludes that the library facilities are inadequate.
D2540

Dixon, Margaret Collins Denny Vann, Elizabeth Chapman Denny Virginia's First German Colony. Richmond: n.p., 1961.
V350 (ASU FC)

Dixon, Thomas The Black Hood. New York: D. Appleton and Co., 1924. Reconstruction fiction set in the North Carolina foothills.
D2550 (ASU)

The Clansman: An Historical Romance of the Ku Klux Klan. Illustrated by Arthur I. Keller. Reprint. Americans in Fiction. Ridgewood, N. J.: Gregg Press, 1967.
D2560 (ASU)

The Traitor: A Story of the Fall of the Invisible Empire. Illustrated by C. D. Williams. New York: Doubleday, Page and Co., 1907. A Reconstruction fiction set in the North Carolina foothills.
D2570 (ASU)

The Traitor: A Story of the Fall of the Invisible Empire. New York: Grosset and Dunlap, 1907. A Reconstruction fiction set in the North Carolina foothills.
D2580 (ETSU)

Dixon, Thomas W. The Rise and Fall of Alderson, West Virginia. Alderson, W. Va.: n.p., 1967. An account of the growth and decline of a one industry W. Va. town.
D2590 (ASU BC)

Doane, C. F. Cheesemaking Brings Prosperity to Farmers of Southern Mountains. Washington: U. S. Dept. of Agriculture, 1917.
D2600 (ASU)

Dober, Virginia Darlene "An Analysis of the Social Life and Customs of the Southern Appalachians as Reflected in Selected Children's Books." Master's thesis. Univ. of North Carolina, 1956.
D2610 (ASU)

"An Analysis of the Social Life and Customs of the Southern Appalachians as Reflected in Selected Children's Books." Master's thesis. Microfilm. Univ. of North Carolina, 1956.
D2620 (ASU)

Dobson, Wayne W. "Some Phases of the Congressional Career of Andrew Johnson." Master's thesis. East Tennessee State Univ., 1952.
D2630

Dodd, James Harvey A History of Production in the Iron and Steel Industry in the Southern Appalachian States. Ph. D. Diss. George Peabody College for Teachers, 1928.
D2640

Doddridge, Joseph Logan. The Last of the Race of Shikellemus, Chief of the Cayuga Nation. A Dramatic Piece. To Which Is Added, the Dialogue of the Backwoodsman and the Dandy, First Recited at the Buffaloe Seminary. July the 1st 1821. 1823. Reprint. Parsons, W. Va.: McClain Print. Co., 1971.
D2650 (ASU BC)

Notes on the Settlement and Indian Wars of the Western Parts of Virginia and Pennsylvania from 1763 to 1783. Together with a Review of the State of Society and Manners of the First Settlers of the Western Country. With a memoir of the author by his daughter, Narcissa Doddridge. Republished. 1912. Reprint. Parsons, W. Va.: McClain, Print. Co., 1960.
D2660 (ASU BC FC)

Notes on the Settlements and Indian of the Western Parts of Virginia and Pennsylvania from 1763 to 1783, Inclusive. Albany, N. Y.: J. Munsell, 1876.
D2670 (ETSU BC)

Dodds, G. S. Van Liere, Edward J. History of Medical Education in West Va. Morgantown: W. Va. Univ. Library, 1965.
V320

Dodge, Emma Florence History of Pleasant Hill; a History of Pleasant Hill Academy and Who's Who of Alumni. Kingsport: Kingsport Press, 1938.
D2680 (BC)

Dodge, J. R. West Virginia: Its Farms and Forest, Mines and Oil Wells, with a Glimpse of Its Scenery, a Photograph of Its Population, and an Exhibit of Its Industrial Statistics. Philadelphia: Lippincott, 1865.
D2690 (BC)

Dodge, Louis Rosy. New York: Charles Scribner's Sons, 1919. A tangled plot about innocent convicts, assumed identities, a war hero with a draft dodger's name and the mountain lass who loves the one and shields the other.
D2700

Dodge, Richard L. "Factors Influencing the Development of the Broadway Shopping Center at Knoxville, Tennessee." Master's thesis. Univ. of Tennessee, 1958.
D2710

Dodrill, Charles Tunis Heritage of a Pioneer, Being the Story of William (English Bill Doddridge) Dodrill and His Wife, Rebecca (Lewis) Daugherty, Their Family, the Times in Which They Lived, and a Genealogy. Huntington, W. Va.: The author, 1967.
D2720 (ASU)

Dodrill, William Christian Moccasin Tracks, and Other Imprints. Charleston, W. Va.: Lovett Print. Co., 1915. A collection of sketches most of which relate to early history of Webster County, West Virginia.
D2730 (BC)

Moccasin Tracks and Other Imprints. Parsons: McClain Print. Co., 1974.
D2740 (ASU)

Dodson, Chester Lee Geology and Ground-water Resources of Morgan County, Alabama. With a section on the chemical quality of the water by James C. Warman. Prepared by the U. S. Geological Survey in cooperation with the Morgan County Board of Revenue and Control, the City of Decatur and the Geological Survey of Alabama. Bulletin, 76. Univ.: Alabama Geological Survey, 1965.
D2750 (ETSU)

Geology and Ground-water Resources of the Murphy Area, North Carolina. North Carolina Division of Ground Water Bulletin, no. 13. Raleigh: n.p., 1968.
D2760 (WCU)

Interim Report on the Geology and Groundwater Resources of Morgan County, Alabama. Prepared by the U. S. Geological Survey in cooperation with Morgan County Board of Revenue and Control and the Geological Survey of Alabama. Information Series, 24. Univ.: Alabama Geological Survey, 1961.
D2770 (ETSU)

Dodson, J. D. and others An Economic Adjustment Study of Dairy Farms in Western North Carolina. Economics Information Report, no. 22. Raleigh: North Carolina State Univ., Dept. of Economics, 1971.
D2780 (LMC)

Dodson, L. S. Loomis, Charles P. Standards of Living in Four Southern Appalachian Mountain Counties. Farm Security Administration Social Research Report, no. 10. Washington: U. S. Dept. of Agriculture, 1938.
L3430 (LMC ASU BC)

Dodson, Linden Seymour Living Conditions and Population Migration in Four Appalachian Counties. Prepared in cooperation with the Bureau of Agricultural Economics. Social Research Report, 3. Washington: U. S. Farm Security Administration, 1937.
D2790

Doggett, Frank A. Dipped in Sky; a Study of Percy MacKaye's "Kentucky Mountain Cycle." N. Y.: Longmans, Green and Co., 1930.
D2800 (BC)

Doherty, William Thomas Conley, Philip Mallory West Virginia History. Charleston: n.p., 1975.
C6600

Berkeley County, U. S. A.: A Bicentennial History of a Virginia and West Virginia County, 1772-1972. Parsons, W. Va.: McClain Print. Co., 1972.
D2810 (ASU BC)

Doliante, J. Sharon Johnson Genealogical Serendipity. Alexandria, Va.: n.p., 1965.
D2820

Doll, W. L. Smith, R. C. Water Resources of the Wheeling-Steubenville Area, West Virginia and Ohio. Washington: Govt. Print. Off., 1955.
S4960

Doll, Warwick L. Water Resources of Kanawha County, West Virginia. Prepared by the U. S. Geological Survey in cooperation with the County Court of Kanawha County, W. Va. Bulletin, no. 20. Morgantown: West Virginia Geological and Economic Survey, 1960.
D2830 (ETSU)

Dollars for Duke Power; Hell for Harlan County. Clintwood, Va.: n.p., 1974. A pamphlet describing the effect of the Brookside Miner's Strike on Harlan County.
D2840

Dolsen, Hildegarde The Great Oildarado; the Gaudy and Turbulent Years of the First Oil Rush: Pennsylvania, 1859-1880. N. Y.: Random, 1959.
D2850

Dombrowski, Alfred Warne, Alice E. An Economic Survey of Clinton Co., Pa. University Park: Penn. State Univ., Bureau of Business Research, 1958.
W840

Donaldson, Alan C. Burford, Arthur E. Annual Field Trip of the Appalachian and Pittsburgh Geological Societies in the Great Valley in West Virginia. Morgantown, W. Va.: n.p., 1964?
B8530 (ETSU)

Donaldson, Martha McComb, Thomas M. Knoxville-Knox County Consolidation and the County and City School Systems. Knoxville: Univ. of Tennessee. Bureau of Business Research, 1958.
M510

Donaldson, Thomas ed. Eastern Band of Cherokees in North Carolina. Washington, D. C.: U. S. Census Office, 1892. The 1892 census of the Cherokee Indians of North Carolina.
D2860

Donaway, Wayland F. Scotch-Irish of Colonial Pennsylvania. Chapel Hill: Univ. of North Carolina Press, 1944.
D2870

Donnelly, Clarence Shirley Notable Mine Disasters of Fayette County, West Virginia. n.p.: Fayette County Historical Society, 1951. Taken from official reports of West Virginia Department of Mines.
D2880 (BC)

Donnelly, Shirley The Hatfield-McCoy Feud Reader. Parsons, W. Va.: McClain Print. Co., 1971.
D2890 (ASU BC)

History of Oak Hill, West Virginia. Charleston, W. Va.: Jarrett Print. Co., 1953. Very incomplete historical notes on Fayette County's largest early settlement.
D2900

Donohew, Lewis Impacts of Educational Change Efforts in Appalachia. Las Cruces, N. M.: ERIC Clearinghouse on Rural Education and Small Schools, 1970. An overly optimistic view of changes in mountain education.
D2910 (ETSU)

Dooley, G. B. Smiles and Tears. Lawrenceburg, Tenn.: n.p., 1925?
D2920 (ASU)

Doolittle, Warren T. Site Index Curves for Natural Stands of White Pine in the Southern Appalachians. U. S. Forest Service Research Note, 141. Asheville, N. C.: Southeastern Forest Experiment Station, 1960.
D2930

Doran, Edwina B. "Folklore in White County, Tennessee." Ph. D. Diss. George Peabody College for Teachers, 1969. An excellent study of the folklore of one Eastern Tennessee County.
D2940

Dorman, Coy "Manufacturing in the West Central Knoxville Area." Master's thesis. Univ. of Tennessee, 1959.
D2950

Dorman, John Frederick comp. Virginia Revolutionary Pension Applications. 16 vols. Abstracted by author. Washington, D. C.: Privately published, 1971.
D2960

Dornbusch, C. E. Regimental Publications and Personal Narratives of the Civil War. A Checklist. New York: Public Library, 1961. This comprehensive guide includes items relating to the war in the mountains.
D2970 (LMC)

Dorrance, Mrs. Ethel Arnold Smith Flames of the Blue Ridge. New York: Macaulay Co., 1919. Would you believe a temperance novel set in the Blue Ridge? The city-bred drunk reforms and wins the love of his shy mountain maiden.
D2980 (ASU LMC BC)

Dorrance, James Dorrance, Mrs. Ethel Arnold Smith Flames of the Blue Ridge. New York: Macaulay Co., 1919.
D2980 (ASU LMC BC)

Dorris, Jonathan Truman A Glimpse at Historic Madison County and Richmond, Kentucky. Richmond, Ky.: Richmond Daily Register Co., 1934.
D3000 (BC)

Glimpses of Historic Madison County, Ky. Nashville: Williams Print. Co., 1955.
D3010

Old Cane Springs; a Story of the War Between the States in Madison County, Kentucky. Louisville: The Standard Print. Co., 1936.
D3020 (BC)

Pardon and Amnesty under Lincoln and Johnson; the Restoration of the Confederates to Their Rights and Privileges, 1861-1898. Introd. J. G. Randall. Chapel Hill: Univ. of North Carolina Press, 1953.
D3030

Dorris, Jonathan Truman ed. Five Decades of Progress: Eastern Kentucky State College, 1906-1957. Eastern Kentucky. Richmond: n.p., 1957. An interesting history. However it will still leave you wondering why Eastern Kentucky is located near the bluegrass and only 30 miles from the University of Kentucky.
D2990 (ASU)

Dorson, Richard Mercer America in Legend: Folklore from the Colonial Period to the Present. New York: Pantheon Books, 1973. Includes some Appalachian items.
D3040 (FC)

Buying the Wind: Regional Folklore in the United States. Chicago: Univ. of Chicago Press, 1964. Appalachia is one of seven regions covered in this volume.
D3050 (ASU WWC LMC BC)

Dorson, Richard Mercer ed. Davy Crockett: American Comic Legend. New York: Spiral, 1939. Selections from The Crockett Almanacks (1835-56.)
D3060 (ASU)

Dos Passos, John Adventures of a Young Man. Boston: Houghton, Mifflin, 1938. In one section of the novel the hero tries to assist in unionizing coal miners in the Southern mountains. Scenes and people are well drawn.
D3070 (ASU)

Adventures of a Young Man. New York: Harcourt, Brace and Co., 1938.
D3080

Dotson, Benny Rogers "A Population Study of the Appalachian Members of the Freshman Class at Morehead (Kentucky) State University, 1967-1968." Ed. D. Diss. n.p.: Indiana Univ., 1969.
D3090

Dotson, John Andrew "The Public School in the Mining Community." Master's thesis. n.p.: Univ. of Kentucky, 1931. A heart-rending look at the general failure of public schools to reach coal camp youngsters.
D3100

Dougherty, John J. "A Study of Fatal Roof Fall Accidents in Bituminous Coal Mines." Master's thesis. n.p.: West Virginia Univ., 1971.
D3110 (LMC)

Doughty, Richard M. Krochmal, Arnold Guide to Medicinal Plants of Appalachia. Upper Darby, Pa.: Northeastern Forest Experiment Station, 1969.
K3230 (BC)

Krochmal, Arnold A Guide to Medicinal Plants of Appalachia. Washington: U. S. Forest Service, 1971.
K3240 (ASU ETSU LMC)

Douglas, Byrd Steamboatin' on the Cumberland. Nashville: Tennessee Book Co., 1961. Includes information pertaining to the half dozen Eastern Kentucky counties through which the river passes.
D3120 (BC ASU ETSU)

Douglas, H. Paul The Protestant Church as a Social Institution. New York: Harper and Brothers, 1935.
D3130

Douglas, Harlan P. Christian Reconstruction in the South. Boston: Pilgrim Press, 1909.
D3140

Douglas, P. B. Jurney, Robert Campbell Soil Survey, Smyth County, Virginia. Washington: U. S. Department of Agriculture, Bureau of Plant Industry, Soils and Agricultural Engineering, 1948.
J2930

Porter, Hobart Clarke Soil Survey, Tazewell County, Virginia. Washington: U. S. Department of Agriculture, Bureau of Plant Industry, Soils, and Agricultural Engineering, 1948.
P3660

Douglas, William The Douglas Register, Being a Detailed Record of Births, Marriages, and Deaths, Together with Other Interesting Notes, as Kept by the Rev. William Douglas from 1750 to 1797; an Index of Goochland Wills Notes on the French-Huguenot Refugees Who Lived in Manakin-town. Transcribed by W. Mas Jones. . Reprint. Baltimore: Genealogical Pub. Co., 1966.
D3150 (ASU)

Dowd, Clement Life of Zebulon B. Vance. Charlotte N. C.: Observer Print. and Pub. House, 1897. Vance is one of three governors ever to come from the western part of the state. He was governor during the Civil War.
D3160 (ASU LMC BC)

Downey, Fairfax Davis Storming of the Gateway: Chattanooga, 1863. New York: D. McKay Co., 1960. A fast-paced account of the exciting campaigns at Missionary Ridge, Chattanooga, and Chickamauga.
D3170 (WCU BC ASU)

Downey, James Cecil "The Music of American Revivalism." Microfilm. Ph. D. Diss. Tulane Univ., 1968. A history of revival music from Cane Ridge to the present.
D3180 (WCU)

Downing, H. T. Malmberg, Glenn Thomas Geology and Ground-water Resources of Madison County, Alabama. University: Alabama Geological Survey, 1957.
M2890 (ETSU)

Downum, James Monroe Lays of Life from the Southern Appalachians. n.p.: The author, n.d.
D3190 (ASU LMC)

Doyle, D. V. Evaluating Appalachian Woods for Highway Posts. U. S. Forest Service Research Paper FPL-111. Madison, Wis.: Forest Products Laboratory, 1969.
D3200

Doyle, H. N. Lainhart, William S. Pneumoconiosis in Appalachian Bituminous Coal Miners. Washington: Bureau of Occupational Safety and Health, 1969.
L150

Drake, Chad ed. Goodale, Dora Read Mountain Dooryards. Berea, Ky.: Council of the Southern Mountains, 1961.
G2500 (ASU LMC MHC BC)

Drake, Charles D. ed. Drake, Daniel Pioneer Life in Kentucky, a Series of Reminiscential Letters from Daniel Drake . . . to His Children. Cincinnati, R. Clarke and Co., 1970.
D3220 (ASU)

Drake, Daniel Pioneer Life in Kentucky, 1785-1800. Edited from the original ms. with introductory comments and a biographical sketch by Emmet Field Horine. New York: H. Schuman, 1948.
D3210 (ASU ETSU BC)

Pioneer Life in Kentucky, a Series of Reminiscential Letters from Daniel Drake . . . to His Children. With notes by his son, Charles D. Drake. Cincinnati, R. Clarke and Co., 1970.
D3220 (ASU)

Drake, Jerry A. Soil Survey of Cherokee County, South Carolina. Field Operations, 1905. Washington: U. S. Department of Agriculture Bureau of Soils, 1907.
D3230

Drake, Richard Bryant The Appalachian South: An Historical Bibliography. Berea, Ky.: Berea College, 1962. A five page annotated list of historical materials.
D3250

Appalachian Volunteer Reader. Berea, Ky.: n.p., 1966. A curriculum developed for the Appalachian Volunteers and the cooperating public schools within the region.
D3260 (BC)

An Outline History of Appalachian America. Berea, Ky.: n.p., 1960. An excellent chronological guide to the major events in Appalachian history.
D3270 (BC ASU)

Drake, Richard Bryant ed. An Appalachian Reader. 2 vols. Berea, Ky.: n.p., 1970. A very good introductory text for Appalachian Studies programs.
D3240 (WCU MHC FC BC ASU)

Drake, William Earle Higher Education in North Carolina before 1860. A Reflection Book. New York: Carlton Press, 1964. There was, of course, more education in the mountains prior to 1860 than for the next twenty years thereafter.
D3280 (LMC)

Drane, Brent S. The Mineral Industry in North Carolina from 1918-1923. Economic Paper, no. 55. Raleigh, N. C.: Geological and Economic Survey, 1925. Many of the state's richer mineral resources are in Western North Carolina.
D3290 (LMC)

Draper, Lyman Copeland Kings Mountain and Its Heroes. Baltimore: Genealogical Pub. Co., 1966.
D3300

King's Mountain and Its Heroes: History of the Battle of King's Mountain. Reprint. . Nashville: Blue and Gray, 1971.
D3310 (LMC)

King's Mountain and Its Heroes: History of the Battle of King's Mountain, October 7th, 1780, and the Events Which Led to It. Cincinnati: P. G. Thomson, 1881.
D3320 (BC ASU)

King's Mountain and Its Heroes: History of the Battle of King's Mountain, October 7th, 1780, and the Events Which Led to It. Reprint. New York: Dauber and Pine, 1929. A definitive account of this Revolutionary War battle in which a substantial number of Tennesseans participated.
D3330

King's Mountain and Its Heroes: History of the Battle of King's Mountain, October 7th, 1780, and the Events Which Led to It. 1881. Reprint. Marietta, Ga.: Continental Book Co., 1954.
D3340 (ASU LMC)

King's Mountain and Its Heroes: History of the Battle of King's Mountain, October 7th, 1780, and the Events Which Led to It. Reprint, North Carolina Heritage Series, vol. 5. Spartanburg, S. C.: Reprint Co., 1967. A definitive account of this Revolutionary War battle in which a substantial number of Tennesseans participated.
D3350

Draper, R. C. "Early History of Jackson County, Tennessee." Gainesboro: Jackson County Sentinel, 1928-29. Published as a series of newspaper articles.
D3360

Draper, Sam L. A Winner on Satin's Doorstep. Chicago: Blindfall Press, 1971. A true story of two Kentucky mountain youths who were born in poverty, became unruly and incorrigible and died in the electric chair.
D3370 (BC)

Draughon, Wallace R. North Carolina Genealogical Reference: Research Guide for All Genealogists Both Amateur and Professional. 2d ed. Durham, N. C.: n.p., 1966.
D3380 (ASU LMC)

Drayton, John Memoirs of the American Revolution, from Its Commencement to the Year 1776, Inclusive: As Relating to the State of South Carolina. And Occasionally Refering to the States of North Carolina and Georgia. 2 vols. (sic) Xerox copy of the original. Charleston, S. C.: A. E. Miller, 1821.
D3390 (ASU)

Drennen, C. W. Stratigraphy and Structure of Outcropping Pre-Selma Coastal Plain Beds of Fayette and Lamar Counties, Alabama. U. S. Geological Survey Circular, no. 267. Washington: Govt. Print. Off., 1953.
D3400 (ASU)

Drennen, Charles W. Paulson, Quentin Frank Ground-water Resources and Geology of Tuscaloosa County, Alabama. Univ.: Alabama Geological Survey, 1962.
P1030 (ETSU)

Dresser, Davis see Cunningham, A. B.

Dresser, Davis The Great Yant Mystery. N. Y.: Detective Club, 1943.
D3410

A Taste for Violence. Brett Holliday, pseud. New York: Dodd, Mead and Co., 1949.
D3420

Dressler, Muriel Appalachia, My Land. Charleston, W. Va.: Morris Harvey College, 1973. Mrs. Dressler is one of Appalachia's finest and most representative poets.
D3430

Drewes, George, Jr. Phillips, Samuel William Soil Survey of Belmont County, Ohio. Washington: U. S. Department of Agriculture, Bureau of Chemistry and Soils, 1931.
P2620

Phillips, Samuel William Soil Survey of Washington County, Ohio. Washington: U. S. Department of Agriculture, Bureau of Chemistry and Soils, 1930.
P2670

Drexel Enterprises, Inc. Sixty Years of Progress in the Making of Fine Furniture, 1903-1963. Haarlam, Holland: Joh. Enscbede en Zonen?, 1963.
D3440 (ASU LMC)

Driscoll, L. S. Kern, E. E. An Inventory of Human and Physical Resources of Cherokee, Dekalb, Jackson, and Marshall Counties, Alabama. Auburn, Ala.: Auburn Univ. Agricultural Experiment Station, 1966.
K1590 (ASU)

Driver, Carl Samuel John Sevier: Pioneer of the Old Southwest. Ph. D. Diss. Vanderbilt Univ., 1929. An excellent biography of Tennessee's greatest leader.
D3450

John Sevier: Pioneer of the Old Southwest. Ph. D. Diss. Nashville: n.p., 1929. An excellent biography of Tennessee's greatest leader.
D3460

John Sevier: Pioneer of the Old Southwest. Chapel Hill: Univ. of North Carolina Press, 1932.
D3470 (ASU LMC BC)

Driver, Harold Edson Indians of North America. Chicago: Univ. of Chicago Press, 1961.
D3480 (ASU)

Droke, Anna Scott At the Foot of No-man. Cincinnati: Monfort and Co., 1906. A family saga of the Mc Donoughs who have mountains in their blood and, generation after generation, find they must return to the hills.
D3490 (BC)

Dromgoole, Will Allen Cinch, and Other Stories: Tales of Tennessee. Boston: D. Estes and Co., 1898. Miss Dromgoole's stories often deal with the hard lot of women in the mountains.
D3500 (ASU ETSU BC)

Harum-scarum Joe. Illustrated by Louis Meynelle. Young of Heart Series, vol. 17. Boston: D. Estes and Co., 1899. The plot is dull and the hero unconvincing.
D3510 (ASU)

The Heart of Old Hickory and Other Stories of Tennessee. With preface by B. O. Flower. 2nd ed. Boston: Arena Pub. Co., 1895.
D3520 (ASU BC)

The Heart of Old Hickory, and Other Stories of Tennessee. With preface by B. O. Flower. 1895. Reprint. Short Story Index Reprint Series. Freeport, N. Y.: Books for Libraries Press, 1970. This volume of Tennessee stories contains one excellent mountain story "Fiddling his Way to Fame."
D3530 (ETSU WWC BC ASU)

Hero-chums. Boston: Estes and Lauriat, 1898. A children's tale from the Tennessee hills.
D3540 (ASU BC)

The Island of Beautiful Things: A Romance of the South. Illustrated in color from paintings by Edmund H. Garrett. Boston: L. C. Page and Co., 1912.
D3550 (ASU BC)

A Moonshiner's Són. Philadelphia: Penn. Pub. Co., 1898.
D3560 (ASU)

A Moonshiner's Son. Illustrated by F. A. Carter. Philadelphia: Penn. Pub. Co., 1925. A poor boy gets an education and makes his way upward, and piously, in the world.
D3570 (WCU LMC BC)

Rare Old Chums. Illustrated by Etheldred B. Barry. Boston: D. Estes and Co., 1898.
D3580 (ASU BC)

The Sunny Side of the Cumberland: A Story of the Mountains. Philadelphia: J. B. Lippincott Co., 1886. A group of outlanders come to view the Tennessee scenery and the quaint folk who live thereabouts.
D3590 (ETSU BC)

The Valley Path. Boston: Estes and Lauriat, 1898.
D3600 (ASU BC)

Drosdoff, Matthew Miller, John T. Soil Survey, Hall County, Georgia. Washington: U. S. Department of Agriculture, Bureau of Plant Industry, 1941.
M5850 (ASU)

Droze, Wilmon Henry High Dams and Slack Water: TVA Rebuilds a River. Baton Rouge: Louisiana State Univ. Press, 1965. A discussion of navigation on the TVA waterway system.
D3610 (ASU WCU LMC BC)

"Tennessee River Navigation; Government and Private Enterprise Since 1932." Ph. D. Diss. Nashville, Tennessee: Vanderbilt Univ., 1960.
D3620

Drugge, Sten Erik "Economic Inventory and Value Added Estimates of the Natural Resources of a Watershed Region Located in the Appalachian Highland Area of Ohio." Ph. D. Diss. Ohio State Univ., 1964.
D3630

Drury, Doris Marie "A Study of the Literature on Accidents in Coal Mines of the United States with Comparisons of the Records in Other Coal-producing Countries." Ph. D. Diss. Indiana Univ., 1965. The U. S. has the poorest mine safety record of any major coal producing region.
D3640

Duberman, Martin Black Mountain: An Exploration in Community. New York: E. P. Dutton and Co., 1972. A controversial history of a controversial college which closed in 1957. The school attracted many people proficient in the arts and literature.
D3650 (ASU WWC BC)

Dudding, Earl Endicott The Trail of the Dead Years. . . Huntington, W. Va.: Prisoners Relief Society, 1933.
D3660

Dudley, Harold J. ed. Hale, John Peter Trans-Allegheny Pioneers. . . . Raleigh, N. C.: Dorreth Print. Co., 1971.
H360 (ETSU)

Duerr, William Allen "The Economic Problems of Forestry in the Appalachian Region." Ph. D. Diss. Harvard Univ., 1945.
D3670

The Economic Problems of Forestry in the Appalachian Region. Harvard Economic Studies, vol. 84. Cambridge, Mass.: Harvard Univ. Press, 1949.
D3680 (ASU LMC BC)

Duff, Frank "Government in an Eastern Kentucky Coal Field County." Master's thesis. Univ. of Kentucky, 1950. A rather bland thesis that might easily have been developed into an expose.
D3690 (ASU)

Duffee, Mary Gordon Sketches of Alabama, Being an Account of the Journey from Tuscaloosa to Blount Springs through Jefferson County on the Old Stage Roads, Now First Published in Book Form. Prepared for the press, with introduction and notes, by Virginia Pounds Brown and Jane Porter Nabers. Illustrated with advertisements from the Jones Valley TIMES of 1854. Univ.: Univ. of Alabama Press, 1970.
D3700 (ASU)

Duffus, Robert Luther The Valley and Its People, a Portrait of TVA. Illustrations by the Graphics Department of the Tennessee Valley Authority. New York: A. A. Knopf, 1944. Unconvincing, saccharine pro-TVA propaganda.
D3710 (ASU LMC BC)

Duggan, W. L. Facts about Sevier County. Sevierville: n.p., 1910.
D3720

Dugger, Shepherd Monroe The Balsam Groves of the Grandfather Mountain: A Tale of the Western North Carolina Mountains. Together with information relating to the section and its hotels, also a table showing the height of important mountains, etc.
D3730 (ASU WCU LMC BC)

The Balsam Groves of the Grandfather Mountain. Banner Elk, North Carolina: S. M. Dugger, 1907.
D3740

Romance of the Siamese twins, a Thrilling Story of a Cherokee Indian Family. Burnsville, N. C.: Edwards Print. Co., 1936. There is some question as to whether the twins were actually Cherokee.
D3750

The War Trails of the Blue Ridge, Containing an Authentic Description of the Battle of King's Mountain, the Incidents Leading up to and the Echoes of the Aftermath of This Epochal Engagement, and Other Stories Whose Scenes Are Laid in the Blue Ridge. Banner Elk, N. C.: The author, 1932.
D3760 (BC ASU LMC)

Duggins, A. C. Lest We Forget. First Baptist Church, Greenville, Tenn., 1871-1960. Kingsport, Tenn.: Kingsport Press, 1960.
D3770 (BC)

Duggins, A. C. comp. Burgner, Goldene F. comp. Kirchen Buch (Church Book) Register, 1815-1828. St. James Lutheran Church, Greene County, Tennessee. Greenville: The authors, 1964.
B8600

Duke, Basil Wilson History of Morgan's Cavalry. Cincinnati: Miami Print., 1867. Morgan made three major raids in the Appalachian region.
D3780

History of Morgan's Cavalry. Reprint. Civil War Centennial Series. Bloomington: Indiana Univ. Press, 1960. Morgan made three major raids in the Appalachian region.
D3790

History of Morgan's Cavalry. Reprint. Millwood, N. Y.: Kraus, 1968. Morgan made three major raids in the Appalachian region.
D3800

Duke University, Durham, N. C., Library The Frank C. Brown Collection of North Carolina. Collected by Dr. Frank C. Brown during the years 1912-1934, in collaboration with the North Carolina Folklore Society. Wood engravings by Claire Leighton. 7 vols. Durham: Duke Univ. Press, 1952-64.
D3810 (ASU WCU LMC MHC BC WWC ETSU)

Dula, Mary Susannah "The Growth of a Community Centered Curriculum at Wilkes Central High School, 1952-1960." Master's thesis. Appalachian State Teachers College, 1961.
D3820 (ASU)

Dulaney, Ben Bane An Economic and Social Survey of Washington County. University of Virginia Record. Extension Series, vol. no. 6. Charlottesville: Univ. of Virginia, 1932.
D3830 (ASU BC)

Dumond, Dwight L. The Secession Movement, 1860-1861. Ph. D. Diss. Univ. of Michigan, 1929. The majority of mountain counties were pro-union. Much of Appalachia's partisan politics today grows out of Civil War feuds.
D3840

The Secession Movement, 1860-1861. New York: Macmillan, 1931. The majority of mountain counties were pro-union. Much of Appalachia's partisan politics today grows out of Civil War feuds.
D3850

The Secession Movement, 1860-1861. Reprint. Westport, Conn.: Greenwood, 1931. The majority of mountain counties were pro-union. Much of Appalachia's partisan politics today grows out of Civil War feuds.
D3860

The Seccession Movement, 1860-1861. Reprint. New York: Octagon, 1963. The majority of mountain counties were pro-union. Much of Appalachia's partisan politics today grows out of Civil War feuds.
D3870

Dunaway, Wayland F. The Scotch-Irish of Colonial Pennsylvania. Chapel Hill: The Univ. of N. C. Press, 1944. More than 40 of the original settlers of the Appalachians were Scotch-Irish and many of them emigrated to Pennsylvania.
D3880

Dunbar, Anthony Our Land Too. New York: Pantheon Books, 1971. About half of the book deals with Dunbar's experiences in Appalachia. His thesis is that black and white minorities are oppressed by the same enemies.
D3890 (ASU BC WCU)

Dunbar, Paul Laurence The Heart of Happy Hollow. 1904. Reprint. Short Story Index Reprint Series. Freeport, N. Y.: Books for Libraries Press, 1970. A book of short stories featuring Negro characters somewhere in the Upland South.
D3900

Duncan, Budd L. Boyer, Reba Bayless A History of Mars Hill Presbyterian Church, Athens, Tenn. 1823-1973. Athens: The church, 1973.
B5980 (ASU)

Duncan, Georgia Elizabeth Samanthy Billins of Hangin' Dog. Atlanta: Mutual Publishing Co., 1905. A novel featuring quaintly drawn characters, a pat plot and a western North Carolina and North Georgia setting.
D3910

Duncan, Katherine McKinstry The History of Marshall County, Alabama. vol. 1. Albertville, Ala.: Thompson Print., 1969. A very thorough first volume of a projected series on Marshall County, Alabama.
D3920 (ASU BC)

Duncan, Norvin C. Pictorial History of the Episcopal Church in North Carolina, 1701-1964. Asheville, N. C.: n.p., 1965. Includes many interesting and historic churches and missions in the mountains.
D3930 (LMC)

Duncan, Otis Dudley Social Stratification in a Pennsylvania Rural Community. (Bulletin No. 543.) University Park: Pennsylvania Agricultural Experiment Station, Pennsylvania State University, 1951. Property ownership, church attendance and income level were used as variables.
D3940

Dunkelberger, J. E. Kern, E. E. An Inventory of Human and Physical Resources of Cherokee Dekalb, Jackson, and Marshall Counties, Alabama. Auburn, Ala.: Auburn Univ. Agricultural Experiment Station, 1966.
K1590 (ASU)

Dunlap, Boutwell Augusta County, Virginia, in the History of the U. S. Frankfort, Ky.: State Historical Society, 1918. An attempt to place Augusta County events in the larger perspective of world events.
D3950 (BC)

Dunlap, W. C. Life of S. Miller Willis Atlanta: Constitution Pub. Co., 1892. Autobiography of a fire-baptized lay evangelist who traveled and preached all over these mountains.
D3960 (BC)

Dunmire, D. E. Kurtenacker, R. S. Appalachian Hardwoods for Pallets, Laboratory Evaluation. Madison, Wis.: Forest Products Laboratory, 1967.
K3430

Dunn, Billy Gean "West Virginia Higher Education Long-range Enrollment and Operating Budget Projections." Ph. D. Diss. West Virginia Univ., 1965.
D3970

Dunn, Mrs. M. H. see Dunn, Shirley

Dunn, Millard Charles Foothills: Poems. N. Y.: Exposition Press, 1960.
D3980 (BC)

Dunn, Shirley comp. Early Lincoln County History. n.p.: n.p., n.d. An abbreviated history of the county compiled primarily from land records, deeds, and marriage books.
D3990 (ASU BC)

Dunnagan, Macon R. The Red Strings Baseball Team of Yadkin County, N. C., 1896-1902. New Bern: Dunn, 1956. History of a famous and hilarious baseball team.
D4000

Dunne, George Harold ed. Conference on Poverty-in-Plenty — The Poor in Our Affluent Society Poverty in Plenty. New York: P. J. Kenedy, 1964.
C6430

Dunning, William A. A Little More Light on Andrew Johnson. Reprint from Massachusetts Hist. Soc. Proceedings, Nov. 1905. Cambridge, Mass.: J. Wilson, 1905.
D4010

Dunson, Josh Anthology of American Folk Music. Interviews with Moses Asch and Frank Walker. New York: Oak Publications, 1973.
D4020 (ASU BC)

Raim, Ethel ed. Grass Roots Harmony. New York: Oak Publications, 1968.
R120 (LMC)

Dupont, H. A. Campaign of 1864 in the Valley of Virginia and the Expedition to Lynchburg. New York: C. J. Carrier, 1925. Includes battles of New Market, Lynchburg, Berryville, Winchester, Fisher's Hill and Cedar Creek.
D4030

DuPuy, Edward L. Artisans of the Appalachians. Text by Emma Weaver. Asheville, N. C.: Miller Print. Co., 1967. This volume preserves in words and pictures the dying arts and crafts of the mountains.
D4040 (ASU WCU LMC MHC WWC BC)

Durham, Francis M. Dubose Heyward: The Southern as Artist. Unpublished doctoral dissertation, Columbia Univ., 1953. Heyward wrote one highly successful mountain novel, Angel.
D4050

Durham, Gertrude "Public Education in Tennessee during the Reconstruction Period." Master's thesis. Univ. of Tennessee, 1936. In point of fact there was very little public education in the mountain counties until the 1880's.
D4060

Durisch, L. L. Upon Its Own Resources: Conservation and State Administration. University, Alabama: University of Alabama Press, 1951.
D4070

Durloo, Leslie H., Jr. Hack, John Tilton Geology of Luray Caverns, Virginia. Charlottesville: Virginia Division of Mineral Resources, 1962.
H80 (ETSU FC)

Durr, R. N. Conrey, Guy Woolard Soil Survey, Scioto County, Ohio. Washington: U. S. Dept. of Agriculture, Bureau of Plant Industry, 1940.
C6780

Durr, William H. "The Status of School Board Members of West Virginia." Master's thesis. West Virginia Univ., 1940.
D4080

Durrett, Harold L. "A Validation Study of a Psychological Test Battery for Selection of Joy Ripper-type Continuous Miner Operators." Master's thesis. West Virginia Univ., 1960.
D4090

Durrett, Reuben T. John Filson, the First Historian of Kentucky: An Account of His Life and Writings. Louisville: Filson Club, 1884.
D4100 (LMC)

Dutton, William Sherman Stay on, Stranger: An Extraordinary Story of the Kentucky Mountains. New York: Farrar, Straus, and Young, 1954. An account of Miss Alice Lloyd's mission school on Coney Creek which grew to become Alice Lloyd College.
D4110 (ASU LMC WWC BC)

Duty, Elaine T. "An Annotated Bibliography of Books by Southwest Virginia Authors." Master's thesis. East Tennessee State Univ., 1968.
D4120 (ETSU ASU)

Dwight, Allan pseud. see **Cole, Lois Dwight**

Dwyer, Lynn E. "The Social Backgrounds of Scientists and Engineers in Oak Ridge, Tennessee, and Huntsville, Alabama." Master's thesis. Univ. of Tennessee, 1972.
D4130

Dyck, Robert G. Statewide Development Planning for West Virginia — A Prospectus for Implementation Under Provisions of Section 701 of the Housing Act of 1954. Morgantown: West Virginia Center for Appalachian Studies and Development, Office of Research and Development, 1964.
D4140

Dye, Harold Eldon The Prophet of Little Cane Creek. Madison, N. J.: Drew Theological Seminary, 1947.
D4150

The Prophet of Little Cane Creek. The Church in Its Community Rural. Atlanta: Home Mission Board, Southern Baptist Convention, 1949. Moralistic fiction with a mountain setting.
D4160 (WCU)

Dye, William Milburn Highlights and Travels of a Southern Highlander. Reserve Pension Fund, Holston Conference Methodist Church, 1941. Journals of a Methodist Circuit Rider.
D4170 (ASU)

Dyer, Diana Smith Before I Sleep. New York: Pageant Press, 1958. Romance set against background of a coal mine strike. Romance bridges the gap between miners and owners.
D4180 (BC)

Dykeman, Wilma The Border States: Kentucky, North Carolina, Tennessee, Virginia, West Virginia. New York: Time-Life Books, 1968.
D4190 (BC ASU LMC WWC ETSU)

The Far Family. 1st ed. New York: Holt, Rinehart and Winston, 1966. A fine novel about a far-flung family which returns to the mountains for a family crisis and finds that old ties bind fast and the land is in their blood.
D4200 (ASU LMC MHC WWC ETSU BC)

The French Broad. Illustrated by Douglas Gorstine. Knoxville: Univ. of Tennessee Press, 1955. An account of the river and the people who live along it. Lyrically written.
D4210 (WWC BC)

The French Broad. 1955. Reprint. Knoxville: Univ. of Tennessee Press, 1965.
D4220 (ASU ETSU WCU LMC MHC BC)

Look to This Day. 1st ed. New York: Holt, Rinehart and Winston, 1968. Dawn over the southern mountains brings waves of memories to the author.
D4230 (ASU LMC MHC WWC ETSU)

Neither Black nor White. New York: Rinehart (1957). A discussion of race relations in the South, including Appalachia.
D4240 (ASU WWC ETSU BC)

Prophet of Plenty: The First Ninety Years of W. D. Weatherford. 1st ed. Knoxville: Univ. of Tennessee Press, 1966. Biography of Berea's famous president who focused attention on the southern mountains.
D4250 (ASU WCU LMC MHC ETSU FC WWC BC)

Return the Innocent Earth. 1st ed. New York: Holt, Rinehart, and Winston, 1973. Novel of a giant canning corporation with midwestern offices and East Tennessee farms. Classic clash between agrarian and corporate values.
D4260 (ASU WWC MHC ETSU BC)

Seeds of Southern Change: The Life of Will Alexander. Chicago: Univ. of Chicago Press, 1962.
D4270 (WWC WCU MHC ETSU)

Southern Appalachian Books: An Annotated, Selected Bibliography. Knoxville: Univ. of Tennessee, 1971.
D4280 (WWC BC)

The Tall Woman. New York: Holt, Rinehart and Winston, 1962. A classic mountain novel of a strong woman who brings her family and community through the war, Reconstruction and poverty while imparting idealistic values to her children.
D4290 (ASU LMC MHC WWC ETSU BC)

Too Many People, Too Little Love. New York: Holt, Rinehart and Winston, 1974. Only tangentially Appalachian, this is a documentary on the consequences of lack of family planning among the poor.
D4300

Dykes, Archie Reece "A Study of Public School Finance in the Southern Appalachian Region." Ed. D. Diss. Univ. of Tennessee, 1959.
D4310

"What the Patrons of Hawkins County Schools Think about Their Schools." Master's thesis. East Tennessee State College, 1956.
D4320 (ETSU)

Dykes, Mack E. "The Effect of Team Teaching on Academic Achievement, John Sevier Junior High School, Kingsport, Tennessee." Master's thesis. East Tennessee State Univ., 1968.
D4330 (ETSU)

Eads, Lawrence Henry "A Proposed Curriculum for Consolidated High Schools in Washington County, Tennessee." Master's thesis. East Tennessee State Univ., 1967.
E10 (ETSU)

Eads, Ora Wilbert "The History of Banking in Watauga County, North Carolina." Master's thesis. Appalachian State Teachers College, 1966.
E20 (ASU)

Eagan, Gerald V. Minimum Land Requirements for Specified Levels of Farm Income in the Eastern Highland Rim of Tennessee. Knoxville: Tennessee Agricultural Experiment Station, 1969.
E30

Early History of McMinn County from the Time It Was Organized to the Year 1887 Athens: Herald, n.d.
E40

Early, Margaret Abigail Holt comp. Holt-Bennett Family History. Parsons, W. Va.: McClain Print. Co., 1974.
E50 (ASU)

Early, Ruth Hairston Campbell Chronicles and Family Sketches, Embracing the History of Campbell County, Virginia, 1782-1926. n.p.: n.p., n.d.
E60 (ASU BC)

East Tennessee Education Association, Research Committee Research Bulletin. vol. 1- , 1940-. Lenoir City, Tenn.: V. L. Adams, annual?
E70 (ETSU)

East Tennessee: Historical and Biographical Illustrated. Chattanooga: A. D. Smith and Co., 1893. A vanity press item giving biographies of prominent citizens and genealogies of leading families.
E80 (ETSU)

East Tennessee Historical Society Early History of Carter County. Knoxville: East Tennessee Historical Society, 1972. A rather thorough history of Carter County from 1760-1861.
E90

Index to Marriages 1792-1900. Knoxville: The Society, 1970.
E100

Marriages 1795-1865. Knoxville: East Tennessee Historical Society, 1971.
E110

Marriages 1796-1837. Knoxville: East Tennessee Historical Society, 1971.
E120

Marriages 1796-1850. Knoxville: East Tennessee Historical Society, 1971.
E130

East Tennessee Historical Society, Knoxville Publications. . . . no. 1. Knoxville, Tenn.: The society, 1929-.
E140 (ASU WCU ETSU BC)

East Tennessee Historical Society, Knoxville, Knox County History Committee The French Broad-Holston Country: A History of Knox County, Tennessee. Knoxville: The society, 1946.
E150 (ASU BC)

East Tennessee Land Company Two Years of Harriman, Tennessee. Established by the East Tennessee Land Company, February 26, 1890. New York: South Pub. Co., 1892? An interesting study of a land company which was influential in the area around Cumberland Gap.
E160 (ASU BC)

East Tennessee State College Bulletin. vol. 1-14, 1911-1925 as East Tennessee state normal, Bulletin. vol. 15-34, 1925-1944 as East Tennessee State Teachers College, Bulletin. Johnson City, Tenn.: n.p., 1911.
E180 (ETSU)

Scrap Book. 1911-1948. VOLS. Johnson City: East Tennessee Normal School (later The college), Irregular.
E190 (ETSU)

Teacher Preparation Programs. Johnson City: The college, 1955.
E200 (ETSU)

Teacher Preparation Programs, East Tennessee State College. Johnson City, Tenn.: The college, 1955.
E210 (ETSU)

East Tennessee State College, Alumni Association Alumni Quarterly. vol. 1- 1935-. Johnson City: The college, quarterly.
E220 (ETSU)

East Tennessee State College, Bookstore Master Booklist. Johnson City, Tenn.: East Tennessee State Univ., 19--.
E230 (ETSU)

East Tennessee State College, Dean's Office The Dean Says. n.p.: n.p., 1950.
E240 (ETSU)

East Tennessee State College, Economic Education Work Conference Report. 1st- 1955-. Johnson City: The college, n.d.
E250 (ETSU)

East Tennessee State College, Graduate Division Manual on Thesis Writing. 1st ed. Johnson City: The college, 1951.
E260 (ETSU)

East Tennessee State College, Graduate School. Abstracts of Theses Done at East Tennessee State College, Graduate School, by Candidates for the Master of Arts Degree during 1950-. Johnson City: The college, 1950-.
E270 (ETSU)

Complete List of Master's Theses in the Graduate School . . . For Degrees Awarded, Through August 1960-. n.p.: n.p., n.d.
E280

Complete List of Master's Theses in the Graduate School . . . For Degrees Awarded, Through August 1960-. n.p.: n.p., n.d.
E290 (ETSU)

East Tennessee State College, Library Audio-visual Materials at East Tennessee State College in the Teaching Aids Laboratory: Films, Filmstrips, Disc Recordings, Tape Recordings, Framed Pictures. Johnson City, Tenn.: East Tennessee State College, 1963.
E300 (ETSU)

East Tennessee State College, Library Educational Films and Filmstrips; East Tennessee State College Collection. . . . 2 vols. Johnson City, Tenn.: The college, 1951-54.
E310 (ETSU)

Library handbook. . . . Johnson City, Tenn.: Sherrod Library, ETSU, .
E320 (ETSU)

East Tennessee State College, Steering Committee on General Education Report. Johnson City: The college, 1960.
E330 (ETSU)

East Tennessee State Teachers College The Buccaneer, 1937-. Vol. 1-. Published by the senior class of the East Tennessee State Teachers College. . . . Johnson City, Tenn.: ETSTC, 1937-.
E170

East Tennessee State University Bulletin. (Catalog issue) vol. 1- 1911-. n.p.: n.p., n.d.
E340 (ETSU)

East Tennessee State University Basketball Press Guide. --. n.p.: n.p., n.d.
E350 (ETSU)

The Role and Scope of East Tennessee State University, a Report Submitted to the Tennessee Higher Education Commission, June 1968. Johnson City: The University, 1968.
E360 (ETSU)

East Tennessee State University, Audio-Visual Center Film Catalog. Johnson City, Tenn.: n.p., 1964.
E370 (ETSU)

Subject Index to Films Available at the Audio-Visual Center. Johnson City, Tenn.: n.p., n.d.
E380 (ETSU)

East Tennessee State University, Department of Journalism The ETSU Journalist. Vol. 1- March, 1969-. Johnson City, Tenn.: n.p., n.d.
E390 (ETSU)

East Tennessee State University, Johnson City, Tenn. see Tennessee, East Tennessee State University, Johnson City

East Tennessee State University, Library East Tennessee State University Track and Field School Records, Together with ETSU Field Records for College Meets. Johnson City, Tenn.: East Tennessee State University, 1969-.
E400 (ETSU)

East Tennessee State University, Library, Instructional Materials Center Catalog of Films and Filmstrips, by Subject (and) by Title. Revised January 1973. 1 vol. (unpaged) 28 cm. Johnson City, Tennessee: The Univ., 1973.
E410 (ETSU)

Catalog of films, by Subject (and) by Title. Rev. March 1971. Johnson City, Tenn.: n.p., 1971.
E420 (ETSU)

Catalog of Filmstrips, by Subject (and) by Title. Rev. January 1973. VOL. (unpaged) 28 cm. Johnson City, Tenn.: n.p., 1973.
E430 (ETSU)

Resources: Recordings and Cassettes. Johnson City, Tenn.: ETSU, 1973.
E440 (ETSU)

East Tennessee State University, Library, Teaching Aids Laboratory Film Catalog. Johnson City, Tenn.: n.p., 1967.
E450 (ETSU)

East Tennessee State University, School Public Relations Workshop Newsletter. vol. 1, no. 1; Sept. 1964. 1 no. n.p.: n.p., n.d.
E460 (ETSU)

East Tennessee, Virginia and Georgia Railroad Company Guide to the Summer Resorts and Watering Places of East Tennessee. Memphis: The Co., 1879.
E470

Eastern Band of Cherokee Indians Eastern Cherokees of North Carolina; a Collection of Eight Reports and Memorials. Washington: Govt. Print. Off., 1868-1902.
E480

Eastern Band of Cherokee Indians. Planning Board Bibliography; the Eastern Band of Cherokee Indians. Raleigh: N. C. Dept. of Natural and Economic Resources, Division of Community Services, 1974.
E490

The Eastern Cherokees: How They Live Today, Their History Knoxville, Tenn.: J. L. Caton, 1937.
E500 (ASU)

The Eastern Cherokees: Their History, How They Live Today Knoxville, Tenn.: J. L. Caton, 1937.
E510 (ASU)

Eastern Kentucky Regional Planning Commission A Decade of Action for Progress in Kentucky. Hazard, Ky.: Eastern Kentucky Regional Planning Commission, 1960.
E520 (ASU)

Program 60, 1960-70; a Decade of Action for Progress in Eastern Kentucky. Hazard: The commission, 1960.
E530 (BC)

Eastern West Virginia Research and Development Center Annual Report for 1964. Shepherdstown, W. Va.: Shepherd College, 1965.
E540

Eastman, Fred Unfinished Business of the Presbyterian Church in America. Prepared under the direction of the Board of Home Missions of the Presbyterian Church in the U. S. A., the Woman's Board of Home Missions, the Board of Publication and Sabbath School Work, the Board of Missions for Freedom. Philadelphia: Westminster Press, 1921.
E550 (ASU)

Eaton, Allen Hendershott Handicrafts of the Southern Highlands: With an Account of the Rural Handicraft Movement in the United States and Suggestions for the Wider Use of Handicrafts in Adult Education and in Recreation. Containing fifty-eight illustrations from photographs taken for the work by Doris Ulmann. New York: Russell Sage Foundation, 1937. The classic work on Appalachian arts and crafts.
E560 (ASU WCU LMC MHC WWC ETSU BC)

Eaton, Miriam Boyd "A History of the Cherokee Indians, 1763-1776." Master's thesis. Univ. of Tennessee: n.p., 1928. A fascinating history of the Cherokee during one of their most active periods of political disputes.
E570 (ASU)

Eaton, Rachael Caroline John Ross and the Cherokee Indians. Menasha, Wis.: Banta Press, 1914.
E580 (ASU)

John Ross and the Cherokee Indians. Ph. D. Diss. Univ. of Chicago, 1919.
E590 (ASU)

John Ross and the Cherokee Indians. Muskogee, Okla.: Star Printery, 1921. A biography of the last strong chief of the Cherokee nation before the Removal.
E600 (ASU BC)

Eavenson, Howard Nicholas Coal Through the Ages. New York: American Inst. of Mining, 1935.
E610 (BC)

Ebaugh, Laura Smith Bridging the Gap. A Guide to Early Greenville, South Carolina. Greenville, S. C.: Greenville County Events — S. C. Tricentennial, 1970. An interesting history of an Appalachian city with very little Appalachian flavor.
E620 (ASU)

Ebbs, Eloise Buckner Carolina Mountain Breezes. Asheville, N. C.: Miller Press, 1929. Tales, yarns and descriptive material on the western North Carolina mountains.
E630 (ASU)

Ebel, Bernard Hughes Insects Affecting Seed Production of Slash and Longleaf Pines: Their Identification and Biological Annotation. U. S. Forest Service Research Paper SE6. Asheville, N. C. Southeastern Forest Experiment Station, 1963.
E640 (WCU)

Eberling, Ernest Jacob Manpower and Employment Trends in Tennessee. Lexington: Kentucky Agricultural Experiment Station, 1959. Another glimpse at the reasons people are leaving the farms for industry.
E650

Ebert, Lucy Timothy Corn Stories; as Told by Uncle Dave Arnold of Knobley Farm. n.p.: n.p., n.d. A delightful series of folktales from Hardy Co., West Virginia.
E660

Eby, James Brian The Geology and Mineral Resources of Wise County and the Coal-bearing Portion of Scott County, Virginia. With chapters by M. R. Campbell and G. W. Stose. Prepared in cooperation with the U. S. Geological Survey. With a chapter on the forests of Wise County, Virginia, by Fred C. Pederson. Prepared in cooperation with the Office of State Forester. Virginia Geological Survey Bulletin, no. 24. Charlottesville: Univ. of Virginia, 1923.
E670 (ETSU ASU)

Echoes from the East Tennessee Historical Society vol. 1- . . Knoxville: East Tennessee Historical Society, quarterly.
E680 (ETSU)

Echoes of West Virginia. A Magazine of Representative Verse vol. 1- 1949-. Huntington, W. Va.: The Magazine, 1949-.
E690

Eckard, Miles R. A Comprehensive Study of the Academic Characteristics and Success Patterns of North Carolina Community College Transfer Students and Native Students of Appalachian State University. Master's thesis. North Carolina State, 1971.
E700

Eckenrode, Hamilton James List of the Colonial Soldiers of Virginia. Richmond, Va.: Virginia State Library, Department of Archives and History, 1917.
E710 (ASU)

The Political History of Virginia During the Reconstruction. Gloucester, Mass.: P. Smith, 1966 (1904). Many mountain counties were pro-union during the war and suffered for it during and after Reconstruction.
E720

The Revolution in Virginia. Boston: Houghton Mifflin, 1916.
E730 (LMC FC)

Separation of Church and State in Virginia; A Study in the Development of the Revolution. Richmond: Davis Bottom, 1910. Many Scotch-Irish people who migrated down the Great Valley of Virginia and later fetched up in the mountains because Colonial Virginia's mandatory tax to support the Anglican Church was offensive to them. This relationship between church and state was one factor in the events leading to Virginia's entry into the Revolution.
E740

Eckert, Allan W. The Court-martial of Daniel Boone: A Novel. 1st ed. Boston: Little, Brown and Co., 1973. Another fictionalized account of Boone's life written for the younger reader.
E750 (ASU BC)

Eckert, Allen W. The Frontiersmen. New York: Little Brown, 1967. Includes a section on Appalachian frontiersmen, explorers, scouts.
E760

Eckley, Wilton Harriette Arrow. N. Y.: Twayne Publishers, 1974. Biography and critical study of one of Appalachia's leading authors.
E770 (BC)

Economic Development of the Upper French Broad Area; Summary of Needs and Opportunities, Resources, the Regional Economy (by) N. C. Dept. of Water Resources, Tennessee Valley Authority, and Western North Carolina Regional Planning Commission. Raleigh, N. C.: Dept. of Agricultural Economics, 1964.
E780 (ASU)

The Economic Impact of TVA Based on a series of lectures presented at a symposium in 1964. Knoxville: Univ. of Tennessee Press, 1967.
E790 (ASU LMC WCU BC UNCA)

Economic Opportunity Council, Inc., Cumberland Valley Area Selected Demographic Studies, Knox Co., Ky. Barbourville, Ky.: The council, 1967? Study of population patterns in Knox County, Kentucky.
E800

Economic Study of the Origin and Management of Beef Cattle and Other Types of Farmers in Russell County Charlottesville: Va. Ag. Experiment Station, 1941.
V550

Eddy, Daniel Clarke Heroine of the Missionary Enterprize. Boston: Ticknor, Reed and Fields, 1850. Appalachia attracted almost as many missionaries as Africa during the 19th century.
E810 (BC)

Edens, Marion A. "An Analysis of Educational Qualifications and Methods of Selection of School Board Members in the First Congressional District of Tennessee." Master's thesis. East Tennessee State Univ., 1970.
E820 (ETSU)

Edgar, Betsy Jordan The McNeel Family Records: Descendants of Pioneer John McNeel and Martha Davis of Pocahontas County, West Virginia, 1765-1967. Parson, W. Va.: McClain Print. Co., 1967.
E830 (ASU)

Our House. Parsons, W. Va.: McClain Print. Co., 1972. A description of the author's life in the birth place of Pearl S. Buck.
E840 (ASU)

We Live with the Wheel Chair. Parsons, W. Va.: McClain Print. Co., 1970. Account of family life with a disabled husband and a warm family life in an historic home.
E860 (ASU)

Edgar, Betsy Jordan comp. Pocahontas County Cooking Yesterday and Today. Parsons, W. Va.: McClain Print. Co., 1973. A collection of recipes used by pioneers. Directions for selecting wild game and wild plants.
E850

Edington, John F. comp. A Church Census of the 134 Churches in the City of Knoxville, Tennessee as of Date January 31, 1925. Knoxville: Southside, 1925.
E870

Editors of Time-Life Books Dykeman, Wilma The Border States: Kentucky, North Carolina, Tennessee, Virginia, West Virginia. New York: Time-Life Books, 1968.
D4190 (BC ASU LMC WWC ETSU)

Edmunds, Murrell Earthenware, a Group of Stories. Lynchburg, Va.: Little Bookshop, 1930. Excellent short stories, some with mountain settings.
E880 (ASU)

Red, White and Black: Twelve Stories of the South. New York: Backerman, 1945. Excellent short stories some with Appalachian settings.
E890 (ASU BC)

Edmunds, Pocahontas Wight Tar Heels Track the Century: Andrew Johnson, Z. B. Vance, M. W. Ransom, C. B. Aycock, O. Henry, J. B. Duke, W. H. Page, F. M. Simmons, Josephus Daniels, Thomas Wolfe. Raleigh, N. C.: Edwards and Broughton Co., 1966.
E900 (WCU ETSU ASU)

Edmundson, R. S. Industrial Limestones and Dolomites in Va.: James River District West of the Blue Ridge. Charlottesville: Univ. of Va., Agricultural Experiment Station, n.d.
E910

Educating the Disadvantaged vol. 1- 1968/69-. New York: AMS Press, annual. Includes material on Appalachian children and their special educational needs.
E920

Education Advisory Committee, The Appalachian Regional Commission Appalachia, Education for Tomorrow. Washington: The Appalachian Regional Commission, 1971.
E930

The Status of Secondary Vocational Education in Appalachia. Research Report No. 10. Washington: The committee, 1968.
E940

Education for Mountaineers in the 70's; School-Community Understanding and Cooperation Morgantown: West Virginia University College of Human Resources and Education, 1969.
E950

Edwards, Allen David Garnett, William Edward Virginia's Marginal Population — A Study in Rural Poverty. Blacksburg: Virginia Agricultural Experiment Station, 1941.
G420 (BC)

Edwards, Bobby Gale Glimpses of Historical Wayne County, Kentucky. Lexington, Ky.: Thoroughbred Press, 1970.
E960 (ASU BC)

Edwards, Charles Thomas Tales of the Blue Ridge. New York: Exposition Press, 1970. A delightful group of tales, folklore, and fiction from the Blue Ridge.
E970 (LMC ASU BC)

Edwards, Dorothy E. "The Dialect of the Southern Highlander as Recorded in North Carolina Novels." Master's thesis. Univ. Rochester, 1935.
E980 (ASU)

Edwards, Evelyn L. "The Reading Habits of 200 Adults in Kingsport, Tennessee." Master's thesis. East Tennessee State College, 1956.
E990

Edwards, Everett Eugene References on the Handicrafts of the Southern Highlands. Washington: United States Department of Agriculture. Bureau of Agricultural Economics, 1934.
E1000 (BC)

References on the Mountaineers of the Southern Appalachians. Washington, D. C.: U. S. Department of Agriculture, 1935.
E1010

References on the Mountaineers of the Southern Appalachians. U. S. Department of Agriculture Library Bibliographical Contributions, no. 28. Washington: Govt. Print. Off., 1935.
E1020 (BC ETSU LMC ASU)

Edwards, Georgie Hortense Historic Sketches of the Edwards and Todd Families and Their Descendants, 1523-1895. 1894. Reprint. Lexington: Univ. of Kentucky, 1964.
E1030 (ASU)

Edwards, Harry Stillwell The Marbeau Cousins. Mason, Ga.: J. W. Burke Co., 1897. Romantic turn-of-the-century fiction with a few scenes set in the mountains.
E1040 (ASU BC)

Two Runaways, and Other Stories. New York: Century Co., 1889. Short stories, some with mountain settings.
E1050 (ASU BC)

Edwards, John Ellis The Log Meeting-house, and the McIlhanys. Nashville: Southern Methodist Pub. House, 1884.
E1060 (ASU)

Edwards, Jonathan The Life of Rev. David Brainerd, Chiefly Extracted from His Diary, Somewhat Abridged, Embracing, in the Chronological Order, Brainerds Public Journal. New York: American Tract Society, n.d. (1749?).
E1070 (LMC)

Edwards, Lawrence "The Baptists of Tennessee: With Particular Attention to the Primitive Baptist of East Tennessee." Master's thesis. Univ. of Tennessee, 1940.
E1080 (LMC)

Gravel in My Shoe. Montevallo, Ala.: Times Print. Co., 1963. Folklore, humor and ghost stories from the mountains.
E1090 (ASU WCU LHC MHC ETSU BC)

Old Speedwell Families. Montevallo, Ala.: n.p., 1955.
E1110

School at Speedwell. n.p.: n.p., 1958. Reminiscences of author's youth in Northern Alabama.
E1120

Speedwell Sketches. 2nd ed. Boston: B. Humphries, 1951. Memoirs of childhood and school days in Northern Alabama.
E1130 (ASU BC)

Edwards, Lawrence ed. Minutes of Davis Creek Church, 1897-1907. Montevallo, Ala.: Times Printing, 1968. History of a Baptist Church in Claiborne Co., Tenn.
E1100

Edwards, Martha L. "Government Patronage of Indian Missions." Ph. D. Diss. Univ. of Wisconsin, 1916.
E1140

Edwards, Max J. and others Soil Survey, Greene County, Tennessee. U. S. Soil Conservation Service Soil Survey, Series 1947, no. 7. Washington: Govt. Print. Off., 1958.
E1150

Edwards, Norman Fayne "The State Employment Service in Appalachian Kentucky." Ph. D. Diss. The Univ. of Kentucky, 1969.
E1160

Edwards, Pat A Bibliography of Appalachian Children's and Young People's Books. Berea, Ky.: Berea College Appalachian Center, 1973. A useful and extensive annotated listing of books on the region appropriate for children and young people.
E1170

Edwards, Rapha Olga Jones "The Connection" in East Tennessee. Washington College, Tenn.: Pioneer Printers, 1969. One of the most interesting volumes of genealogy ever to come out of East Tennessee.
E1180 (ASU BC)

Descendants of East Tennessee Pioneers. Gatlinburg: n.p., 1963.
E1190 (ASU)

Edwards, Virgil L. The Appalachian Mountain Log Book. Burnsville, N. C.: Edwards Printing Co., 1957.
E1200

Edwards, William Seymour Coals and Coke of W. Va.; a Handbook of the Coals and Cokes of the Great Kanawah, New River, Flat Top, and Adjacent Coal Districts in W. Va. Cincinnati: Clarke, 1892.
E1210 (BC)

Eelking, Max Von The German Allied Troops in the North American War of Independence, 1776-1783. Translated and abridged from the German by J. G. Rosengarten. 1893. Reprint. Baltimore: Genealogical Pub. Co., 1969.
E1220 (ASU)

Egerton, Cecil Baker "A History of the First Baptist Church of Knoxville, Tennessee." Master's thesis. Univ. of Tennessee, 1960.
E1230

Eggan, Frederick R. ed. Social Anthropology of North American Tribes. Chicago: Univ. of Chicago Press, 1937. Includes section on the Eastern Cherokee social organization.
E1240

Eggers, Mrs. Daisy Williams A Survey of Speech Education in Selected North Carolina High Schools. Master's thesis. App. State Teachers College, 1953. This survey includes sixty-eight schools in twenty-one western North Carolina counties.
E1250 (ASU)

Eggers, Herman B. The First Baptist Church at Boone, North Carolina: A History. n.p.: n.p., 1969.
E1260 (ASU LMC)

Eggleston, George Cary Camp Venture; a Story of the Virginia Mountains. Boston: Lothrop, 1901. Romantic turn of the century novel with poorly drawn characterizations of mountain people.
E1270 (ETSU ASU)

Irene of the Mountains; a Romance of old Virgina. Boston: Lothrop, Lee, and Shepard, 1909. A novel of politics and mountaineer-makes-good-in-society.
E1280 (ASU BC)

A Man of Honor. New York: Orange Judd Co., 1873. Romantic fiction partially set in the valley of Virginia.
E1290 (ASU BC)

Egle, William Linn, John Blair Persons Naturalized in the Province in Pennsylvania, 1740-1773. Baltimore: Genealogical Pub. Co., 1967.
L2650 (ASU)

Egle, William Henry Pennsylvania Genealogies: Chiefly Scotch Irish and German. 1886. Reprint. Baltimore: Genealogical Pub. Co., 1969.
E1310 (ASU)

Egle, William Henry ed. Names of Foreigners Who Took the Oath of Allegiance to the Province and State of Pennsylvania, 1727-1775, with the Foreign Arrivals, 1786-1808. 1892. Reprint.
E1300 (ASU)

Ehle, John The Journey of August King. 1st ed. New York: Harper and Row, 1971. A western North Carolina farmer circa 1850 risks life, property and reputation to save an escaping slave girl. Western North Carolina setting.
E1320 (ASU WCU LMC BC)

The Land Breakers. New York: Popular Library, 1964.
E1330 (ASU BC)

The Land Breakers. 1st ed. New York: Harper and Row, 1964. A powerful novel of pioneer life in western North Carolina.
E1340 (ASU WCU LMC MHC ETSU BC)

Lion on the Hearth. 1st ed. New York: Harper, 1961. Novel of a western North Carolina mercantile family.
E1350 (ASU WCU LMC BC)

Move Over, Mountain. 1957. Novel of pioneer life in the western North Carolina Mountains.
E1360 (ASU WCU LMC BC)

The Road. 1st ed. New York: Harper and Row, 1967. A novel about the building of a railroad through the rugged North Carolina mountains. Includes realistic descriptions of the building of the Swannanoa tunnel.
E1370 (ASU WCU LMC ETSU BC)

Time of Drums: A Novel. 1st ed. New York: Harper and Row, 1970. A novel of mountain men caught up in the Civil War.
E1380 (ASU WCU LMC MHC BC)

Eilert, John W. A Profile and Economic Impact Analysis of Four Cumberland Gap Counties. Prepared for, and with, the National Park Service. Memphis: Bureau of Business and Economic Research, Tennessee, State Univ., 1968.
E1390

Eisenberg, Larry Eisenbert, Helen And Promenade All. Berea, Ky.: Council of the Southern Mountains, 1968.
E1400

Eisenberg, William Edward The Lutheran Church in Virginia, 1717-1962. Lynchburg, Va.: J. P. Bell Co., 1967. Material on Churches in Wythe and surrounding counties, photographs, preachers, schools, etc.
E1420 (FC)

The First Hundred Years of Roanoke College, 1842-1952. Salem, Va.: Trustees of Roanoke College, 1942. History of a small private school in the Valley of Virginia.
E1430

Eisenbert, Helen And Promenade All. Berea, Ky.: Council of the Southern Mountains, 1968. Instruction for the most popular square dances.
E1400

Eisenbert, William Edward This Heritage. Story of Lutheran Beginnings in Lower Shenandoah Valley and of Grace Church, Winchester. Boyce, Va.: Carr Publishing Co., 1954.
E1410

Ejlali, Majid "An Assessment of Needs and Guidelines for Development of an Industrial Ceramics Program." Master's thesis. East Tennessee State Univ., 1967.
E1440 (ETSU)

Eke, Paul A. Peck, Millard Economic Utilization of Marginal Lands in Nicholas and Webster Counties, West Virginia. Washington: U. S. Department of Agriculture, 1932.
P1540

Elabert, Ethel Evans Albert, Anne Roberts Russell County, Virginia Personal Property and Land Tax List . . . n.p.: Privately printed, n.d.
A980

Elam, Shelby S. Kentucky through Thick and Thin. Lexington, Ky.: Southside Press, 1955.
E1450

Elder, Alma Echoes from the Hills, A Novel. New York: Exposition Press, 1950.
E1460 (ETSU BC)

Elder, Joe A. Soil Survey, Loudon County, Tennessee. Soil Survey, Series 1958, no. 2. Washington: U. S. Department of Agriculture, Soil Conservation Service, 1961.
E1480

Soil Survey, Marion County, Tennessee. Correlation by Lester E. Edom. U. S. Soil Conservation Service, Soil Survey, Series 1950, no. 2. Washington: Govt. Print. Off., 1958.
E1490

Elder, Joe A. and others Soil Survey, Blount County, Tennessee. Correlation by Max J. Edwards. Soil Survey, Series 1953, no. 7. Washington: U. S. Department of Agriculture, Soil Conservation Service, 1959.
E1470

Soil Survey, Washington County, Tennessee. U. S. Soil Conservation Service Soil Survey, Series. 1948, no. 5. Washington: Govt. Print. Off., 1958.
E1500

Eldridge, Robert L. A History of the First Methodist Church in Livingston, Tennessee, Established 1836. Livingston: Enterprise, 1962.
E1510

Eldridge, Robert L. A History of the First Methodist Church in Livingston, Tennessee, Established 1836. Livingston: Enterprise, 1962.
E1510

Eleazer, Carolyn "Political Attitudes of the Poor — An Inquiry into Their Position on a Liberal-Conservative Continuum." Master's thesis. Univ. of Tenn., 1966. An interesting but inconclusive study of the politics of the poor.
E1520

Eliason, Mary Easter Story. n.p.: Annie Emery Flinn Library, 1971:
E1530 (LMC)

Wendy's Halloween Ride: Witch Shadows. Buies Creek, N. C.: The author, 1971.
E1540 (LMC)

Eliason, Norman Ellsworth Tarheel Talk: An Historical Study of the English Language in North Carolina to 1860. Chapel Hill: Univ. of N. C. Press, 1956.
E1550 (ASU LMC MHC ETSU)

Elizabethton, Tenn. Helping Our Children Grow. Elizabethton: Board of Education, 1952.
E1560 (ETSU)

The Elkhorn Review "From the Heart of the Hills." vol. 1. 1935. Ernine, Ky.: n.p., n.d.
E1570

Elkins, Ada Mae Thirty-eight years in the Parsonage: The Fruitful Career of the Reverend Opie Eldridge in the Methodist Ministry of Rural and Urban West Virginia-Perceptively Recounted by His Wife and Fellow Worker. New York: William-Frederick Press, 1960.
E1580 (ASU)

Elkins, John E. "History of Education of Lawrence County, Kentucky." Master's thesis. Univ. of Ky., 1936.
E1590

Elledge, Barry Ward The Impact of Appalachain State University on the Economy of Watauga County. Boone, N. C.: The author, 1971.
E1600 (ASU)

Elledge, Charles Cowles "Eliminations from the Class of 1950 in the Marion High School." Master's thesis. Appalachian State Teachers College, 1951.
E1610 (ASU)

Ellenburg, Fred Carroll A History of Reidville Private High Schools, Reidville, South Carolina. Master's thesis. Appalachian State Teachers College, 1963.
E1620 (ASU)

Eller, Oliver Eugene, Jr. "The Role of the Bristol, Virginia, Elementary School Principals in Classroom Visitation." Master's thesis. East Tenn. State Univ., 1969.
E1630 (ETSU)

Eller, Thomas R., Jr. The Dissent of Commissioner Thomas R. Eller, Jr., in the Nantahala Power and Light Company Transfer Case. n.p.: N. C. Consumer Committee for Low-Cost Power, 1962. Records of a price dispute over electric power from western North Carolina plants.
E1640 (WCU)

Ellington, Charles Linwood "The Sacred Harp Tradition of the South: Its Origin and Evolution. Microfilm. Ph. D. Diss. Fla. State Univ., 1969. Sacred harp music and its shape note songbooks were widespread throughout the Appalachian region.
E1650 (WCU)

Elliott, Carl comp. Annals of Northwest Alabama. 2 vols. Tuscaloosa, Ala.: Privately Printed, 1958.
E1660

Annals of Northwest Alabama Vol. III; Including a Reprint of the 1856 Nelson F. Smith's History of Pickens County, Alabama. Northport, Ala.: Heritage Press, 1965.
E1670

Elliott, Katherine Blackwell comp. Marriage Records, 1749-1840, Cumberland County, Virginia. South Hill, Va.: n.p., 1969.
E1680 (ASU)

Elliott, Nova J. "The Personal Characteristics, Social Background, and Academic Achievements of Forty Non-Promoted Pupils at Kennburg School." Master's thesis. East Tenn. State College, 1961.
E1690 (ETSU)

Elliott, Sarah Barnwell The Durket Sperret. New York: Henry Holt and Co., 1898. A novel about two cousins who alternately fight and consider marriage. Poor use of dialect and idiom.
E1700 (ASU)

An Incident, and Other Happenings. Illustrated by W. T. Smedley. 1899. Reprint. Short Story Index Reprint Series. Freeport, N. Y.: Books for Libraries Press, 1969. Rather sketchy mountain fiction with poorly defined characters.
E1710 (WCU BC)

Jerry, a Novel. New York: Holt, 1891. A melodramatic and unbelievable story of the redemption of a young mountain lad.
E1720 (LMC BC)

Sam Houston. Beacon Biographies of Eminent Americans Series. Boston: Small, Maynard, 1900, 1917. Houston's youth was spent in East Tennessee.
E1730

Elliott, William The Southern Appalachian Forest Reserve. Washington: U. S. Forest Service, 1902.
E1740

Ellis, Daniel Thrilling Adventures of Daniel Ellis, the Great Union Guide of East Tennessee, for a Period of Nearly Four Years During the Great Southern Rebellion. Containing a short biography of the author. New York: Harper and Brothers, 1867.
E1750 (ASU LMC BC)

Thrilling Adventures of Daniel Ellis, the Great Union Guide of East Tennessee, for a Period of Nearly Four Years during the Great Southern Rebellion. Written by Himself. Containing a Short Biography of the Author. Black Heritage Library Collection. Freeport, N. Y.: Bks. for Libraries, 1972.
E1760

Ellis, Edward Sylvester The Last Trail. Philadelphia: Porter and Coates, 1889. Fictionalized account of frontier life on the Appalachian frontier.
E1770

The Life and Times of Col. Daniel Boone, Hunter, Soldier, and Pioneer. With sketches of Simon Kenton, Lewis Wetzel, and other leaders in the settlements of the West. Alta Edition.
E1780 (ETSU BC FC ASU WCU LMC)

The Life and Times of Col. Daniel Boone, the Hunter of Kentucky, with Sketches of His Contemporaries: Narrative of St. Clair's Defeat. Mrs. Merrill's Adventures, etc. Beadle's Dime Biographical Library, no. 2. New York: Beadle and Co., 1860.
E1790 (ASU BC)

Ellis, Edward Sylvester
Life of Colonel David Crockett: Comprising His Adventures as Backwoodsman and Hunter; His Services as Soldier and Scout in the Creek War; His Electioneering Canvasses; His Career as Congressman; His Tour through the Northern States; and His Services and Death in the Texan War of Independence. To Which Are Added, Sketches of General Sam Houston, General Santa Anna, Rezin P. and Colonel James Bowie. Philadelphia, Pa.: Parter and Coates, 1884.
E1800 (ASU)
Logan the Mingo; a Story of the Frontier. N. Y.: Dutton, 1902. A fictionalized account of life of one of Appalachia's most famous Indian Chiefs.
E1810

Ellis, James Tandy Kentucky Stories. Lexington: Richardson Co., 1909. Includes some mountain stories.
E1820
Tang of the South Stories. Kingsport, Tenn.: F. M. Hill, 1924. Includes an Appalachian character.
E1830

Ellis, Lowell "A Proposed Course of Study in Electronics for Johnson City Vocational School's Evening Program." Master's thesis. East Tenn. State College, 1959.
E1840 (ETSU)

Ellis, Ruby Haskins comp. Jenkins, Ida Powell comp. Lineage Book of the National Society of Daughters of American Colonists. Washington: Judd and Detweiler Inc. Press, 1929.
J640

Ellis, Shirley Rose "A Study of the Title I Reading Program During the 1966-68 School Years in Carter County, Tennessee." Master's thesis. East Tenn. State Univ., 1970.
E1850 (ETSU)

Ellison, Kate Henson "Dealing with Problem Children in the Mabel Elementary School." Master's thesis. App. State Teachers College, 1953.
E1860 (ASU)

Ellyson, W. J. Soil Survey, Wood and Wirt Counties, West Virginia. Prepared in cooperation with the W. Va. Agricultural Experiment Station. Washington: U. S. Soil Conservation Service, 1970.
E1870

Elrod, Henry J. "Educational Development of Oconee County, South Carolina." Master's thesis. Univ. of S. C., 1934.
E1880

Ely, William The Big Sandy Valley: A History of the People and Country from the Earliest Settlement to the Present Time. 1887. Reprint. Baltimore: Genealogical Pub. Co., 1969. An interesting and eminently readable account of the history of the river and valley which shaped so much of Kentucky's history.
E1890 (ASU)

Embree, Elihu The Emancipator. 1820. Reprint. Nashville: B. H. Murphy, 1932. The emancipation movement in the United States began in East Tennessee. The Emancipator, Embree's third and most popular publication was the focus for the emancipation movement.
E1900 (ASU)

The Emeralds of North Carolina; a Book for the Rockhound, the gemnologist, the Serious Collector or the Person who enjoys reading North Carolina History. n.p.: n.p., n.d.
E1910

Emerson, Frederick B. Tennessee Valley Wildlife: An Outlook for the Year 2000. Norris: Div. of Forestry Development, TVA, 1968.
E1920

Emery, Anne Mountain Laurel. New York: G. P. Putnam's Sons, 1948. Poems from the hills.
E1930 (LMC ETSU BC)

Emgels, Richard A. Changing Patterns of Fertility in Tennessee, 1960-1970. Knoxville: Center for Economic Research and Business, Univ. of Tenn., 1972.
E1940

Emmet, Boris Labor Relations in the Fairmont, West Virginia, Bituminous Coal Field. U. S. Bureau of Labor Statistics Bulletin, Miscellaneous Series no. 361. Washington: Govt. Print. Off., 1924.
E1950 (ASU)

Emmons, W. F. Palo, G. P. Tennessee Valley Authority's Bull Run Steam Plant. Knoxville, Tenn.: TVA, 1963.
P130

Emmons, W. H. Geology and Ore Deposits of the Ducktown Mining District, Tennessee. With the collaboration of Arthur Keith. U. S. Geological Survey Professional Paper, no. 139. Washington: Govt. Print. Off., 1926.
E1960 (ASU BC)

Emrich, Duncan Folklore on the American Land. 1st ed. Boston: Little, Brown, 1972. General folklore volume with few special references to Appalachia.
E1970 (ASU BC MHC)
The HodgePodge Book, An Almanac of American Folklore. New York: Four Winds Press, 1972.
E1980
The Nonsense Book of Riddles, Rhymes, Tongue Twisters, Puzzles and Jokes from American Folklore. Illustrated by I. B. Ohlsson. New York: Four Winds Press, 1970.
E1990 (ASU BC)

Engineering Economic Study of Mine Drainage Control Techniques, Appendix B to Acid Mine Drainage in Appalachia. Pittsburgh, Pa.: Cyrus Rice and Co., 1969.
E2000

Engle, Winfield S. H. The Meechor Engle Family History and Genealogy. Lima, Ohio: The author, 1940.
E2010 (BC)

Englund, K. J. Geology and Coal Resources of the Cannel City Quadrangle, Kentucky. U. S. Geological Survey Bulletin, 1020-A. (General title: Geology of the Cannel City Area, Kentucky.) Washington: Govt. Print. Off., 1955.
E2020

Enroth, Ronald M. "Patterns of Response to Rural Medical Practice and Rural Life in Eastern Kentucky." Ph. D. Diss. Univ. of Ky., 1967.
E2030

Enslow, Ella Harlow, Alvin Schoolhouses in the Foothills. New York: Simon and Schuster, 1937.
H2370

Enslow, Ella, pseud. see **Murray, Lena Davis**

Enterline, P. E. Lainhart, William S. Pneumoconiosis in Appalachian Bituminous Coal Miners. Washington: Bureau of Occupational Safety and Health, 1969.
L150

Enterprise Publishing Company Resources and Enterprises of Upper East Tennessee: Johnson City, Jonesboro, Greenville, Rogersville, Morristown, Watauga, Tennessee. Franklin, Territory South of the Ohio. Knoxville: n.p., 1885. An excellent source book on upper East Tennessee history.
E2040 (ETSU)

Environmental Quality Systems Determination of Estimated Mean Mine Water, Quantity and Quality from Imperfect Data and Historical Records. Washington: App. Regional Commission, 1973.
E2050 (ASU)

Episcopal Female Institute, Winchester, Va. Announcement. 1874/75. Baltimore: A. Hoen and Co., annual?
E2060 (ASU)

Epley, Irwin B. Elder, Joe A. Soil Survey, Marion County, Tennessee. Washington: Govt. Print. Off., 1958.
E1490

Epperson, Terry Elmer, Jr. "The Boones Creek Community, Some Geographical Aspects." Master's thesis. Univ. of Ky., 1952.
E2070 (ETSU)
"Geographic Factors Influencing the Manufactural Industries of Upper East Tennessee." Ph. D. Diss. Univ. of Tenn., 1960.
E2080 (LMC)

Eppes, Allan, pseud. see **Wright, Allen Eppes**

Epstein, Beryl Epstein, Samuel The Andrews Raid; or, The Great Locomotive Chase, April 12, 1862. New York: Coward-McCann, 1956.
E2090

Epstein, Samuel The Andrews Raid; or, The Great Locomotive Chase, April 12, 1862. New York: Coward-McCann, 1956. An exciting account of the great locomotive chase between Big Shanty and Chattanooga.
E2090

Equality of Educational Opportunity for Children of Appalachia. Pikeville, Ky.: Pikeville College, 1968.
E2100

Ernst, Harry W. The Primary that Made a President: West Virginia, 1960. Eagleton Institute Cases in Practical Politics, no. 26. New York: McGraw-Hill, 1962. An account of John Kennedy's West Virginia primary and the beginnings of the war on poverty.
E2110 (ASU)

Erskine, Emma Payne A Girl of the Blue Ridge. Boston: Little, Brown and Co., 1915. Three plots in one carry the reader through pathos, mystery, revenge and the corning of industry and missionaries.
E2120 (ASU)
The Girl of the Blue Ridge. New York: A. L. Burt Co., 1915.
E2130 (BC ASU LMC)
The Mountain Girl. Illustrated by J. Duncan Gleason. Boston: Little, Brown and Co., 1912. Backwoods North Carolina mountain girl marries a British peer and makes an amazing adjustment to society.
E2140 (ASU LMC BC)
When the Gates Lift up Their Heads: A Story of the Seventies. Boston: Little, Brown and Co., 1901. More moralistic fiction with a western North Carolina setting.
E2150 (ASU)

Erskine, Harlan Mercer Flood of August 4-5, 1943, in Central West Virginia, with a Summary of Flood Stages and Discharges in West Virginia. U. S. Geological Survey Water-supply Paper, no. 1134-A. Notable Local Floods of 1942-43. Washington: Govt. Print. Off., 1951.
E2160 (ASU)
Surface Water Supply of West Virginia. Prepared in cooperation with the U. S. Geological Survey. Bulletin, no. 5. Morgantown: W. Va. Geological Survey, 1942.
E2170 (ETSU)

Ervin, Sara Sullivan South Carolinians in the Revolution. With service records and miscellaneous data, also abstracts of wills, Lauren County (Ninety-Six District) 1775-1855. 1949. Reprint. Baltimore: Genealogical Pub. Co., 1965.
E2180 (ASU)

Erwin, Robert B. Burford, Arthur E. Annual Field Trip of the Appalachian and Pittsburgh Geological Societies in the Great Valley in West Virginia. Morgantown, W. Va.: n.p., 1964?
B8530 (ETSU)
Chen, Ping-fan Some Low-alumina Quartizitic Sandstones in West Virginia: A Preliminary Report. Morgantown: W. Va. Geological and Economic Survey, 1965.
C3620 (ETSU)
Publications of West Virginia Geological Survey. Morgantown: W. Va. Geological Survey, 1971.
E2190 (ASU)

Erwin, William Yancey Wanetka, and Other Poems. Lexington, Ky.: J. E. Hughes, 1909. Poems from the Kentucky hill country.
E2200 (ASU)

Eschmeyer, R. W. Fish and Fishing in TVA Impoundments. Nashville, Tenn.: Tenn. Dept. of Conservation, 1950.
E2210

Eshleman, Henry Frank Historic Background and Annals of the Swiss and German Pioneer Settlers of Southeastern Pennsylvania, and of Their Remote Ancestors from the Middle of the Dark Ages down to the Time of the Revolutionary War. 1917. Reprint. An authentic history, from original sources. With particular reference to the German-Swiss Mennonites or Anabaptists, the Amish, and other non-resistant sects.
E2220 (ASU)

Eskew, Harry Lee "Shape Note Hymnody in the Shenandoah Valley, 1816-1860." Microfilm. Ph. D. Diss. Tulane Univ., 1966. A fine study of Christian Harmony and shape-note singing.
E2230 (WCU)

Essary, John Thurman Tennessee Mountaineers in Type: A Collection of Stories. New York: Cochrane Pub. Co., 1910. Short stories from the mountains. Essary's speciality is the character sketch.
E2240 (ASU BC)

Estepp, James D. A Brief History of Johnson City, Tennessee. Johnson City: Centennial Commission, 1969. A history of upper East Tennessee's largest city.
E2250 (ETSU)

Eubanks, David Lawson "Dr. J. G. M. Ramsey of East Tennessee: A Career of Public Service." Ph. D. Diss. Univ. of Tenn., 1965.
E2260

Eusebia Presbyterian Church, Blount County, Tennessee: Eusebia Church History Maryville: n.p., 1924.
E2270

Evans, Augusta Jane see **Wilson, Augusta Jane Evans**

Evans, Bob Clyde "A Comparison of Certain Factors Related to Dropouts and Potential Dropouts in South Junior High School." Master's thesis. East Tenn. State Univ., 1964.
E2280 (ETSU)

Evans, Clement Anselm ed. Confederate Military History: A Library of Confederate States History. Written by distinguished men of the South. 12 vols. Atlanta: Confederate Pub. Co., 1899.
E2290 (ASU)

Evans, Harriet Catherine The Pine Ridge Feud. St. Louis: Concordea Pub. House, 1930.
E2300

Evans, Homer Clark "The Nature of Competition among Apple Processors in the Appalachian Area." Ph. D. Diss. Univ. of Minnesota, 1956.
E2310

Some Effects of Price and Income Support Programs on Marginal Farms. Morgantown: West Virginia Agricultural Experiment Station, 1961.
E2320

Evans, Lewis K. Pioneer History of Greene County, Pennsylvania. Waynesburg, Pa.: Waynesburg, Republican, 1941. Green County Pennsylvania was one of the major migration routes into the mountains.
E2340 (ASU)

Evans, Mona "David Crockett: An Interpretation." Master's thesis. Vanderbilt Univ., 1924.
E2350

Evans, Sidney Horance "Analysis of Costs and Benefits from Commuting for Employment among Core and Satellite Communities in the Appalachian Region of Ohio." Ph. D. Diss. Oklahoma State Univ., 1967.
E2360

Evans, Sylvester Hassel "Written Board of Education Policies for Unicoi County, Tennessee." Master's thesis. East Tenn. State Univ., 1964.
E2370 (ETSU)

Evans, T. C. Wenger, Karl Frederick The Relation of Growth to Stand Density in Natural Loblolly Pine Stands. Asheville, N. C.: Southeastern Forest Experiment Station, 1958.
W2820 (WCU)

Evans, Walker Agee, James Let Us Now Praise Famous Men. Boston: Houghton Mifflin Co., 1941.
A730 (BC ASU WCU)

Agee, James Let Us Now Praise Famous Men. Boston: Houghton Mifflin Co., 1960.
A740 (ETSU)

Agee, James Let Us Now Praise Famous Men. Boston: Houghton Mifflin Co., 1969.
A750 (WCU)

Evans, William J. The Development of Kentucky's Handicraft Industry. Prepared for the Kentucky Dept. of Commerce. Lexington, Ky.: Spindletop Research, 1963.
E2380

Everett, Edward Account of the Fund for the Relief of East Tennessee; with a Complete List of Contributors. Boston: Little, 1864.
E2390

Everinden, William L. "The Professional Status of Teachers in the Southern Appalachian Region." Master's thesis. Univ. of Tenn., 1960
E2400

Everton, George B., Sr. ed. The Handy Book for Genealogists. 6th ed., revised and enlarged. Logan, Utah: Everton Pub., 1971.
E2410 (ASU)

Ewan, Joseph John Banister and His Natural History of Virginia, 1678-1692. Urbana: Univ. of Ill. Press, 1970.
E2420 (LMC)

Ewell, Leighton History of Coffee County, Tennessee. Manchester: Doak, 1936.
E2430

Ewen, Cecil Henry L.'Estrange A History of Surnames of the British Isles: A Concise Account of the Origin, Evolution, Etymology, and Legal Status. 1931. Reprint. Baltimore: Genealogical Pub. Co., 1968.
E2440 (ASU)

Exchanging Cultural Values; A Study of Newcomers in Columbus, Ohio Public Schools. Columbus: n.p., 1964.
E2450 (ASU)

Exline, Edouard Evartt Maxwell, Phillip Herbert Valhalla in the Smokies. Cleveland: G. A. Exline, 1938.
M4580 (ETSU ASU BC)

Exum, Helen McDonald Helen Exum's Chattanooga Cook Book. 1st ed. Chattanooga, Tenn.: Chattanooga News — Free Press, 1970.
E2460 (ASU)

Fabricant, Ruth A. "Regional Labor Markets and Migration: An Analysis of Gross Migration in the United States, 1955-1960." Ph. D. Diss. Univ. of California: Berkeley, 1967.
F10

Fairbairn, Charlotte Judd Historic Harpers Ferry in Jefferson Co., W. Va. Ranson, W. Va.: Whitney and White, 19--.
F20 (BC)

The Washington Homes of Jefferson County, West Virginia. Illustrated by William D. Eubank. Ranson, W. Va.: Whitney and White, n.d. George Washington's westernmost homes have been loving restored.
F30 (WCU)

Fairbairn, James comp. Fairbairn's Book of Crests of the Families of Great Britain and Ireland. 4th ed., revised and enlarged. 1905. Reprint. 2 vols. in 1. Baltimore: Heraldic Book Co., 1968. Most Appalachian families came from Scotland, Ireland, England and Wales.
F40 (ASU)

Fairchild, Edward Henry Berea College, Ky. Cincinnati: Elm St. Print., 1883. Appears to have been originally written as an address or speech for some special occasion.
F50

Fairmont, W. Va. High School. J. O. Watson Class Marion County in the Making. Baltimore: Press of Meyer and Thalheimer, 1917. A surprizingly good student written history of the county.
F60 (BC)

Fallows, Arthur Journal. Reprint of the text as edited by David I. Bushnell, Jr., in his "Discoveries beyond the Appalachian Mountains in September 1671," published in American Anthropologist, new series, vol. 9, 1907. March of America Facsimile Microfilms, Series, no. 33. Ann Arbor, Mich.: Univ., 1966.
F70 (LMC ETSU ASU)

Famous Labor Songs from Appalachia. 2 vols. Huntington, W. Va.: Appalachian Movement Press, 1970.
F80 (ASU)

Fannin, Allen Handspinning: Art and Technique. New York: Van Nostrand Reinhold, 1970. One of the best "how to" books on the art of spinning.
F90 (LMC)

Fansler, Homer Floyd History of Tucker County, West Virginia. Parsons, W. Va.: McClain Print. Co., 1962. Another good county history from West Virginia.
F100 (LMC ASU BC)

Fantus Company, Fantus Area Research Division Industrial Location Research Studies. Reprint of reports prepared for the Appalachian Regional Commission. 4 vols. Appalachian Research Report, no. 4-7. New York: The Co., 1966.
F110 (ASU WCU)

Farber, David J. Apprenticeship and Economic Change. Washington: D. S. Department of Labor, Bureau of Apprenticeship and Training, 1964.
F120

Faris, John Thomson Nolichucky Jack. Illustrated by D. Cammerota. Philadelphia: J. B. Lippincott, 1927. Biography of John Sevier written for the younger reader.
F130 (ASU LMC ETSU)

Roaming the Eastern Mountains. N. Y.: Farrar and Reinhart, 1932.
F140 (ASU BC)

Seeing the Sunny South. Philadelphia: J. B. Lippincott Co., 1921. Includes sketches of the upland South.
F150 (ASU LMC BC)

Farish, Hunter Dickinson The Circuit Rider Dismounts: A Social History of Southern Methodism, 1865-1900. Richmond: Dietz Press, 1938. An account of the church's adaptations to the changes in 35 years of mountain life.
F160 (ASU BC)

Farley, G. M. Schneider, Norris F. Betty Zane, Heroine of Fort Henry. Williamsport, Md.: Zane Grey Collector, 1970.
S1010 (ASU)

Farley, Jessee Kelso Jr. Twelve Generations of Farleys. Chicago: Press of Albin O. Horn Co., 1943.
F170

Farm Policy Review Conference Papers. 1st-. 1960-. Sponsored with the North Carolina State College, Agricultural Policy Institute. Ames?: Iowa State Univ., Center for Agricultural and Economic Development, annual. (Each year has a distinctive title.) Includes brief mention of North Carolina mountain problems.
F180

Farmer, Fawn "Available Material in Knox County for Enriching the Teaching of Tennessee History." Master's thesis. East Tennessee State College, 1952.
F190 (ETSU)

Farmers Advocate Print Military Operations in Jefferson County, Virginia and West Virginia, 1861-1865. n.p.: n.p., n.d.
F200

Farnham, Thomas J. Powell, William Stevens The Regulators in North Carolina: A Documentary History, 1759-1776. Raleigh, N. C.: State Dept. of Archives and History, 1971.
P4030 (ASU)

Farnsworth, Charles H. Folk-songs, Chanteys and Singing Games. New York: H. W. Gray Co., n.d.
F210 (ASU LMC BC)

Farnsworth, Floyd F. The Man on Horseback; a Story of Life Among W. Va. Hills. Charleston, W. Va.: Tribune Print. Co., 1921. Biography of a missionary doctor in the West Virginia mountains.
F220 (BC)

The Saga of the Country Doctor Among the W. Va. Hills. Milton, W. Va.: n.p., 1940.
F230 (BC)

Farrar, Emmie (Ferguson) Old Virginia Houses. 2 vols. Illustrated with photos. by Harry Bagby and others. New York: Hastings House, 1955.
F240 (FC)

Farrow, Mary Cloyd Howe A Way of Life in Virginia at the Turn of the Century. Photographs and bibliography. Greenville, S. C.: The author, 1972. Memoirs of the author's life in Pulaski County, Virginia. Howe family history, especially Haven B. Howe.
F250

Farthing, Benjamin Walter The Philosophy of a Partriarch. n.p.: Piedmont Press, 1967. Maxims, poems, family history and memoirs from Watauga County, North Carolina.
F260 (ASU BC)

Fast, Howard Melvin Power: A Novel. 1st ed. Garden City, N. Y.: Doubleday, 1962. A novel of labor struggles in West Virginia in the 1920's.
F270 (ASU BC)

The Tall Hunter. Illustrated by Fafaello Busoni. 1st ed. New York: Harper Brothers, 1942. Fiction. West Virginia setting.
F280 (ASU BC)

Fast, Richard E. The History and Government of West Virginia. Morgantown: Acme Publishing Co., 1901.
F290 (BC)

Faulkner, Charles Herman "Archaeological Investigations in the Tims Ford Reservation, Tennessee, 1966." Master's thesis. Univ. of Tennessee, 1968.
F300 (ETSU)

The Excavation and Interpretation of the Old Stone Fort, Coffee County, Tennessee. n.p.: n.p., 1967.
F310 (ASU)

Excavations in Nickajack Reservoir: Season I. Knoxville, Tenn.: n.p., 1965.
F320 (ETSU)

The Old Stone Fort: Exploring an Archaeological Mystery. University of Tennessee Study in Anthropology. Knoxville: Univ. of Tennessee Press, 1968.
F330 (ASU LMC BC)

Faulkner, Nancy The Secret of the Simple Code. Garden City, N. J.: Doubleday, 1965. A lame boy finds two friends in the southern mountains and shares an adventure with them.
F340

Fauquier County Bicentennial Committee Fauquier County Va., 1759-1959. Warrenton, Va.: Fauquier County Bicentennial Committee and the Board of Supervisors, 1959.
F350 (ASU)

Faust, Albert Bernhardt Lists of Swiss Emigrants in the Eighteenth Century to the American Colonies. 2 vol. 1920-25. Reprint. Baltimore: Genealogical Pub. Co., 1968.
F360 (ASU)

Faust, Albert Nernhardt German Element in the United States. 2 vols. Boston: Houghton Mifflin Co., Riverside Press, Cambridge, 1909.
F370

Favour, Alpheus Hoyt Old Bill Williams, Mountain Man. New ed. Norman: Univ. of Oklahoma Press, 1962.
F380 (ASU)

Fawcett, Joseph W. Journal of Jos. W. Fawcett. With an introduction by Eugene D. Rigney. Chillicothe, Ohio: David K. Webb, Private Press, 1944. Diary of his trip in 1840 down the Ohio and Mississippi Rivers to Gulf of Mexico and up the Atlantic Coast to Boston. Includes descriptions of West Virginia.
F390 (ASU)

Fayette Co. Development Corp. Professional Overall Economic Development for Fayette Co., West Virginia. Fayetteville: the corporation, 1961.
F400

Fazzaro, Charles J. Puzzuoli, David A. Development of Tele-lecture and Associated Media Systems for the Improvement of Nursing Education in West Virginia. Morgantown: West Virginia Univ., 1971.
P4950

Puzzuoli, David A. Project Era: A Three Year Study of a Follow Through Program. A Longitudinal Study of the Monongalia County Follow Through Program. Morgantown: Monongalia Co. Board of Education, 1970.
P4960

Featherstonhaugh, George William A Canoe Voyage up the Minnay Sotor; with an Account of the Lead and Copper Deposits in Wisconsin; of the Gold Region in the Cherokee Country: and Sketches of Popular Manners. 2 vols. London: R. Bentley, 1847.
F410

A Canoe Voyage up the Minnay Sotor; with an Account of the Lead and Copper Deposits in Wisconsin; of the Gold Region in the Cherokee Country: and Sketches of Popular Manners. 2 vols. Reprint. St. Paul: Minnesota Hist. Soc., 1970.
F420

Excursion through the Slave States, from Washington on the Potomac to the Frontier of Mexico; with Sketches of Popular Manners and Geological Notices. 2 vols. London: J. Murray, 1844. This British traveller started his journey to Appalachia at White Sulphur Springs and went to Blountville, Tenn., via Fincastle, Wytheville, Abingdon, and Saltville. He describes taverns (at Wytheville and Blountville), the salt works at Saltville.
F430 (ASU LMC)

Federal Writers' Project These are our Lives; as Told by the People and Written by Members of the Federal Writers' Project of the Works Progress Administration in North Carolina, Tennessee, and Georgia. Chapel Hill: Univ. of North Carolina Press, 1939.
F440 (FC ASU)

Federal Writers' Project see **Writers' Program**

Federal Writers' Project. North Carolina. . . . North Carolina, a Guide to the Old North State. Chapel Hill: Univ. of North Carolina Press, 1939.
F450 (WWC ASU UNCA)

Federal Writers' Project of the Work Projects Administration. American Guide Series. Breathitt: A Guide to the Feud Country. Northport, New York: Bacon, Percy and Daggett, 1941.
F460

Kentucky: A Guide to the Blue Grass State. New York: Harcourt, Brace and Co., 1939. Includes some Eastern Kentucky material.
F470

Tennessee: A Guide to the State. New York: The Viking Press, 1939.
F480

Virginia: A Guide to the Old Dominion. New York: Oxford Univ. Press, 1940.
F490

Federation Employment and Guidance Service, New York, Library A Guide to Resources for Anti-poverty Programs: A Selected Bibliography. New York: The service, 1965.
F500 (ASU)

Federation of Communities in Service Discovery, Expression, Communication: An Arts Approach to the Problems of Appalachia. Big Stone Gap, Va.: The Federation, 1969.
F510

Fee, John Gregg Autobiography of John G. Fee, Berea, Kentucky. Chicago: National Christian Association, 1891. Autobiography of mountain minister, educator and founder of Berea College.
F520 (ASU BC)

Fee, William I. Bringing in the Sheaves; Gleanings from Harvest Fields in Ohio, Ky., and W. Va. Cincinnati: Cranston and Curtis, 1896.
F530

Felix, Linda Daybreak on Cranberry Ridge. Berea, Ky.: Council of the Southern mountains, 1974. A study of two West Virginia mountain families.
F540 (ASU)

Fellows, Alice Laurel, a Novel. 1st ed. New York: Harcourt, Brace, 1950. A novel of family intrigue set in the foothill country of Virginia.
F550 (ASU)

Felming, Arklie Lee "Economic Set-up of the Cumberland Homesteads, Crossville, Tennessee." Master's thesis. George Peabody College, 1941.
F1450

Felton, Harold W. John Henry and His Hammer. New York: Alfred Knopf, 1950. West Virginia's most famous folk tale retold.
F560

Felton, Rebecca Latimer Country Life in Georgia in the Days of My Youth. Atlanta: Index Print. Co., 1919. She was the first woman in United States Congress.
F570

Fendlosa, Mary McNeil Christopher Laird. New York: Dodd, Mead, 1919. A tale of inter-marriage between landed lowland gentry and hill folk in Virginia.
F580

Fenton, John H. Politics in the Border States. New Orleans: Hauser, 1957. A fascinating study of the entriguing politics of the upland South.
F590 (UNCA ASU)

Fenton, William N. ed. Symposium on Cherokee and Iroquois Culture, Washington, D. C., 1958 Papers. Washington: Govt. Print. Off., 1961.
S97.70 (ETSU WCU BC)

Ferger, Edward Guide to Chattanooga, Lookout Mountain and Chickamauga National Military Park. Chattanooga: Ferger and Taylor, 1895.
F600

Ferguson, Herman White King, Philip Burke Geology and Manganese Deposits of Northeastern Tennessee. Nashville: Tennessee Department of Conservation Division of Geology, 1944.
K2410 (ETSU)

King, Philip Burke Geology of Northeasternmost Tennessee with a Section on the Description of the Basement Rocks by Warren Hamilton. Washington: Govt. Print. Off., 1959.
K2420 (ETSU)

Ferguson, Leland Greer "South Appalachian Mississippian." Ph. D. Diss. Univ. of North Carolina, 1971. An attempt to find correlations between Appalachia and Eudora Welty's northeastern Mississippi people.
F610 (WCU BC)

Ferguson, Nieta H. "A Transitional English Program for Crockett High School, Washington County, Tennessee." Master's thesis. East Tennessee State Univ., 1971.
F620 (ETSU)

Ferguson, Roland H. The Timber Resources of West Virginia. U. S. Forest Service Resource Bulletin, NE-2. Upper Darby, Pa.: Northeastern Forest Experiment Station, 1964.
F630 (ASU)

The Timber Resources of Pennsylvania. U. S. Forest Service Resource Bulletin, NE-8. Upper Darby, Pa.: Northeastern Forest Experiment Station, 1968.
F640 (ASU)

Ferguson, Russell J. Early Western Pennsylvania Politics. Pittsburgh: Univ. of Pittsburgh Press, 1938.
F650

Ferguson, Thomas Wiley Home on the Yadkin. New ed. Winston-Salem, N. C.: Clay Print. Co., 1957.
F660 (ASU BC)

Springboard to Optimism Versus Majoring in the Minors: A Dozen Books in One. Hickory, N. C.: Hickory Print. Co., 1967. Memoirs of author's youth in North Carolina foothills.
F670 (ASU)

Ferman, Louis A. Job Development for the Hard-to-employ. A joint publication of the Institute of Labor and Industrial Relations (University of Michigan-Wayne State University) and the West Virginia University Center for Appalachian Studies and Development. Policy Papers in Human Resources and Industrial Relations, no. 11. Ann Arbor, Mich.?: n.p., 1969.
F680 (ETSU)

Ferman, Louis A. ed. Poverty in America. Ann Arbor: Univ. of Michigan Press, 1965. Includes discussion of Appalachian poverty.
F690

Fernstrom, John R. A Community Attack on Chronic Unemployment: Hazleton, Pennsylvania, a Case Study. Community Development Series, no. 1. Washington: U. S. Office of Area Development, 1960.
F700

Ferree, Miles Joseph Ineson, Frank Avery The Anthracite Forest Region, a Problem Area. Washington: Govt. Print. Off., 1948.
I760 (ASU)

Ferris, George Titus comp. Our Native Land: Or, Glances at American Scenery and Places, with Sketches of Life and Adventure. New York: D. Appleton and Co., 1882.
F710 (ASU)

Fertig, James Walter The Secession and Reconstruction of Tennessee. . . . Chicago: Univ. of Chicago Press, 1898. No state in the union was more bitterly divided by the war than Tennessee.
F720 (ASU LMC)

Fessler, Donald R. The Challenge: Motivating the Poor. Blacksburg: Cooperative Extension Service, Virginia Polytechnic Institute, December, 1965.
F730

Fetherling, Dale Mother Jones, the Miners' Angel: A Portrait. Carbondale: Southern Illinois Press, 1974. An unconvincing biography of Mother Jones.
F740 (ASU MHC)

Fetterman, John Stinking Creek. 1st ed. New York: Dutton, 1967. An in-depth study of the social life and customs of Knox County, Kentucky.
F750 (ASU WCU LMC ETSU WWC BC FC UNCA)

Fey, Arthur Willard Buried Black Treasure: The Story of Pennsylvania Anthracite. Dansville, N. Y.: F. A. Owen Pub. Co., 1954.
F760 (ASU)

Field, Hope Stormy Present. New York: E. P. Dutton and Co., 1942. Romantic fiction set in the West Virginia hills. Book abounds with recipes and home cures.
F770 (ASU BC)

Field, Leslie A. ed. Thomas Wolfe: Three Decades of Criticism. New York: New York Univ. Press, 1968.
F780 (ASU WCU BC UNCA)

Field, Thomas P. Recent Home Construction in Two Appalachian Counties. n.p.: n.p., 1968. Compares Clay and Knox Counties in Kentucky.
F790

Field, Thomas Warren An Essay towards an Indian Bibliography: Being a Catalog of Books Relating to the History, Antiquities, Languages, Customs, Religion, Wars, Literature, and Origin of the American Indians, in the Library of Thomas W. Field. With biographical and historical notes, and synopses of the contents of some of the works best known. 1873. Reprint. Detroit: Gale Research Co., 1967.
F800 (LMC BC)

Fields, Ellis M. "A Discriminative Study of Trends and Innovations: Modern Educational Concepts and Their Application to the Norton, Virginia, City Schools." Master's thesis. East Tennessee State Univ., 1965.
F810 (ETSU)

Fields, Jeff A Cry of Angels. 1st ed. N. Y.: Atheneum, 1974. A novel of the North Georgia marble country.
F820 (ASU)

Fields, Nancy Addington, Luther Foster Wise County Geography Supplement. Big Stone Gap, Va.: Wise County School Board and Univ. of Virginia, 1928.
A570 (BC)

Fifth Avenue Baptist Church, Huntington, W. Va. Diamond Jubilee. Fifth Avenue Baptist Church. Huntington: The Church, n.d.
F830

Filler, Louis The Removal of the Cherokee Nation: Manifest Destiny or National Dishonor? Problems in American Civilization. Boston: Heath, 1962.
F840 (WCU UNCA FC)

Filson, John The Adventures of Colonel Daniel Boone, formerly a Hunter: Containing a Narrative of the Wars of Kentucky, with the Discovery, Purchase, and Settlement of Kentucky, and the Piankashaw Council, 1784, and Territory of North American Indians, and the Rights Land in Kentucky. A new edition with numerous folding maps and illustrations. Xenia, Ohio: Old Chelicothe Press, 1968.
F850 (BC ASU LMC)

The Discovery and Settlement of Kentucky. 1784. Reprint. March of America Facsimile Series, no. 50. Ann Arbor, Mich.: University Microfilms, 1966.
F860 (LMC ETSU BC)

The Discovery, Settlement, and Present State of Kentucky. Introd. by William H. Masterson. New York: Corinth Books, 1962.
F870 (UNCA)

The Discovery, Settlement, and Present State of Kentucky. 1784. Reprint. American Experience Series. New York: Corinth Books, 1962.
F880 (ASU)

Kentucky and the Adventures of Col. Daniel Boone. Louisville, Ky.: JPP. Morton and Co., 1934. (facsimile of 1784)
F890

Finch, Floyd William "A Study of School Leavers at the Patterson School for Boys, Caldwell County, North Carolina." Master's thesis. Appalachian State University, 1968.
F900 (ASU)

Finchum, Bernice S. "A Survey of Selected Characteristics of the Washington County, Tennessee, School Teacher." Master's thesis. East Tennessee State Univ., 1969.
F910 (ETSU)

Finchum, George A. "Washington County Court, 1796-1836." Master's thesis. East Tennessee State Univ., 1959.
F920 (ETSU)

Finck, William John ed. Cassell, Charles Willis ed. History of The Lutheran Church in Virginia and East Tennessee. Strasburg, Va.: Shenandoah Pub. House, 1930.
C1970 (ASU BC FC)

Findley, Benjamin F. "A Case Study of the Effects of Automation on Employment in a West Virginia Continuous Process Industry." Master's thesis. West Virginia Univ., 1969.
F930

Finer, Herman T. V. A. Lessons for International Application. Montreal: International Labour Office, 1944.
F940

The T. V. A. Lessons for International Application. International Labour Office Studies and Reports, Series B, no. 37. New York: Da Capo, 1972.
F950

Fink, Miriam L. "Some Phases of the Social and Economic History of Jonesboro, Tennessee, prior to the Civil War." Master's thesis. Univ. of Tennessee, 1934. Jonesboro is the oldest town in Tennessee.
F960

Fink, Paul M. Bits of Mountain Speech Gathered Between 1910 and 1965 along the Mountains Bordering North Carolina and Tennessee. Boone, N. C.: Appalachian Consortium Press, 1974.
F970 (ASU)

Fink, Paul Mathes Jonesborough: The First Century of Tennessee's First Town. Publication, no. 394. Johnson City: Tennessee State Planning Commission, 1972. Well-written history of the oldest settlement in Tennessee.
F980 (ETSU ASU BC)

Jonesborough: The First Century of Tennessee's First Town. Springfield, Va.: National Technical Information Service, 1972.
F990 (ASU)

That's Why They Call It . . . the Names and Lore of the Great Smokies. Jonesboro, Tenn.: n.p., 1956.
F1000 (WCU ETSU BC ASU)

That's Why They Call It . . . the Names and Lore of the Great Smokies. Jones, Tenn.: The author, 1964.
F1010 (ASU LMC)

Finlayson, John L. Shinnston tornado. N. Y. Hobson Bk. Press, 1946. (W. Va.) Account of the 1944 tornado which nearly destroyed Shinnston, W. Va.
F1020

Finley, Joseph E. The Corrupt Kingdom: The Rise and Fall of the United Mine Workers. New York: Simon and Schuster, Inc., 1973.
F1030

Finley, Ruth E. Old Patchwork Quilts and the Women Who Made Them. Philadelphia: J. B. Lippincott Co., 1929.
F1040 (BC)

Finn, Raymond F. Ten Years of Strip-mine Forestation Research in Ohio. U. S. Forest Service Technical Paper, 153. Columbus, Ohio: Central States Forest Experiment Station, 1958.
F1050

Finney, Raymond A. "History of Private Educational Institutions of Franklin County, Tennessee." Master's thesis. Univ. of Tennessee, 1939.
F1060

Firestone, Clark Barnaby Bubbling Waters. 1st ed. New York: Robert M. McBride and Co., 1938. A history of health resorts, watering places, spas etc. in the Southern mountains.
F1070 (ASU LMC BC)

Sycamore Shores. 1st ed. New York: National Travel Club, 1936. Recollections of many trips along the Ohio River in West Virginia.
F1080 (ASU)

First Baptist Church, Rogersville, Tennessee. Diamond Anniversary, 1890-1965 Rogersville: n.p., 1965.
F1090

First Marriage Record of Augusta County, 1785-1813 Published by the Col. Thomas Hughart Chapter, D.A.R. Staunton, Va.: McClure Pub. Co., n.d.
F1100

First Presbyterian Church, 1845-1945, Marion, North Carolina Marion: n.p., 1945.
F1110

Fish, Frederic F. A Catalog of the Inland Fishing Waters in North Carolina. Raleigh, N. C.: Division of Inland Fisheries, 1968. Includes guides to mountain trout streams.
F1120 (LMC)

Fishburne, Elliot Guthree Catlett, Clay Michie An Economic and Social Survey of Augusta County. Charlottesville: Univ. of Va., 1928.
C2110 (ASU BC)

Fisher, Charles Adam Central Pennsylvania Marriages, 1700-1896. Reprint of the 1946 ed. published in Selinsgrove, Pa. Baltimore: Genealogical Pub. Co., 1974.
F1130 (ASU)

Central Pennsylvania Marriages, 1700-1896. Baltimore: Genealogical Pub. Co., Inc., 1974. A record of marriages that took place in Central Pennsylvania which served as a great migration route for the Appalachians.
F1140 (ASU)

Probate and Orphans Court Records of Snyder County, Pennsylvania. Baltimore: Genealogical Pub. Co., 1974. More than 10,000 entries.
F1150

Fisher, Charles Adam
Wills and Administrations of Northumberland County. Baltimore: Genealogical Pub. Co., 1974.
F1160

Fisher, George W. ed. Studies of Appalachian Geology: Central and Southern New York: Interscience Publishers, 1970.
S8790 (ETSU WWC ASU)

Fisher, George W. ed. and others Studies of Appalachian Geology: Central and Southern. New York: Interscience Pubs., 1970.
F1170 (ASU LMC ETSU)

Fisher, Glenn Luce and others Soil Survey, Carbon County, Pennsylvania. Soil Survey, Series 1959, no. 14. Washington: U. S. Department of Agriculture, Soil Conservation Service, 1962.
F1180

Fisher, Lee Fire in the Hills, the Story of Parson Frakes and the Henderson Settlement. Inroduction by Billy Graham. Nashville: Abingdon Press, 1971.
F1190 (ASU LMC BC)

Fisher, Ronald M. The Appalachian Trail. Photographed by Dick Durrauce, II. Foreword by Benton Mackaye. Washington: National Geographic Society, 1972.
F1200 (BC ASU FC WWC ETSU MHC)

Fisher, Vardis Thomas Wolfe as I Knew Him, and Other Essays. Denver: Alan Swallow, 1963.
F1210 (BC ASU UNCA WCU)

Fisher, Waldo E. "Economic Consequences of the Seven-hour Day and Wage Changes in the Bituminous Coal Industry." Ph. D. Diss. Univ. of Pennsylvania, 1939.
F1220

Wage Rates and Working Time in the Bituminous Coal Industry, 1912-1922. Philadelphia: U.q. Pa. Press, 1932.
F1230 (BC)

Fishman, Betty G. Economic Effects of Internal Migration: An Exploratory Study, Substantive Report. Morgantown: Bureau of Business Research, West Virginia Univ., 1968? A study of West Virginia's farm to town trend.
F1240

Fishman, Leo Employment Changes in West Virginia, 1948-1958. Business and Economic Studies, vol. 7, no. 3. Morgantown, W. Va.: West Virginia Univ., 1961.
F1250 (ASU)

Fishman, Leo ed. Poverty and Affluence. New Haven: Yale University Press, 1966. Includes discussion of Appalachian poverty.
F1260

Fiske, Horace Spencer Provincial Types in American Fiction. New York: Chautauqua Press, 1903. Includes some mountain characterizations.
F1270 (ASU)

Fiske, John The Dutch and Quaker Colonies in America. Houghton, Mifflin and Co., 1899.
F1280 (ASU)

Old Virginia and Her Neighbours. 2 vols. Boston: Houghton Mifflin and Co., 1901.
F1290 (ASU MHC)

Fitch, J. C. Allred, Charles E. Effects of Industrial Development on Rural Life in Sullivan County, Tennessee. Knoxville: Division of Univ. Extension, Univ. of Tennessee, 1928.
A1840

Fitch, Lynn Fitch, Robert Beck Grandfather's Land: We Are Mountain People. Mankate, Minn.: Creative Educational Society, 1972.
F1310 (WCU)

Fitch, Michael Hendrick The Chattanooga Campaign, with Especial Reference to Wisconsin's Participation Therein. Original Paper, no. 4. Madison: Wisconsin History Commission, 1911.
F1300 (ASU BC)

Fitch, Robert Beck Grandfather's Land: We Are Mountain People. Mankate, Minn.: Creative Educational Society, 1972.
F1310 (WCU)

Fitch, William Edward The Origin, Rise and Downfall of the State of Franklin under Her First and Only Governor, John Sevier. Publications of the New York Society of the Founders and Patriots of America, vol. 25. New York: The society, 1910.
F1320

Fitzgerald, Mary Newman The Cherokee. Bryson City, N. C.: Bryson City Times, 1937.
F1330 (BC)

The Cherokee and His Smoky Mountain Legends. 3d ed. Asheville, N. C.: Stephens Press, 1946.
F1340 (ASU ETSU BC)

The Cherokees, 1540-1937. Knoxville, Tenn.: n.p., 1927.
F1350 (ASU UNCA)

The Cherokees. Knoxville: Coleman, 1937.
F1360

Fitzgerald, Robert ed. Agee, James The Collected Poems of James Agee. Boston: Houghton Mifflin Co., 1968.
A660 (ASU WCU ETSU BC)

Agee, James The Collected Short Prose of James Agee. Boston: Houghton Mifflin Co., 1968.
A670 (ASU WCU ETSU BC)

Fitzsimmons, Roxie Cross One Hundred Years of Methodism, the History of St. John's Methodist Church, New Martinsville, W. Va. New Martinsville: The church, 1956.
F1370

Fitzwater, A. J. A Brief History of the Musical Movement or Stream, Which was Started in Mountain Valley (Now Singers Glen, Va.) in the Early Part of the Nineteenth Century by Joseph Funk.
F1380 (ASU FC)

Flanigen, George J. The Centenary of St. Peter and St. Paul's Parish, Chattanooga, Tennessee. The Story of the First 100 Years of the Catholic Church in Hamilton County. Chattanooga: St. Peter and St. Paul's Parish, 1952.
F1390

Flannagan, Roy The Forest Cavalier: A Romance of America's First Frontier and of Bacon's Rebellion. 1st ed. Indianapolis: Bobbs-Merrill Co., 1952. A fictional account of trans-montane settlements and Bacon's Rebellion.
F1400 (ASU BC)

Fleer, Jack D. North Carolina Politics: An Introduction. Chapel Hill: Univ. of North Carolina Press, 1968.
F1410 (LMC)

Fleet, Beverley Virginia Colonial Abstracts Vol. XXXIV, Washington County Marriage Register, 1782-1820. Baltimore: Genealogical Pub. Co., 1961.
F1420

Fleischmann, Glen The Cherokee Removal, 1838: An Entire Indian Nation Is Forced Out of Its Homeland. A Focus Book. New York: Franklin Watts, 1971. Actually thousands of Cherokees remained in Appalachia.
F1430 (ASU BC WCU ETSU)

While Rivers Flow. New York: Macmillan Co., 1963. Fictional account of Cherokee political difficulties.
F1440 (ASU BC)

Fleming, Helen Parr The Parr Family: Allied Families — Holden, Hutchinson, Moore, Jolly, Franks, Sheets, et al. Parsons, W. Va.: McClain Print. Co., 1968.
F1460 (ASU)

Fleming, Jo Lee James D. Vaughan, Music Publisher, Lawrenceberg, Tennessee, 1912-1964. Microfilm. Sm. D. thesis. Union Theological Seminary, 1972.
F1470 (WCU)

Fleming, Robert Sketch of the Life of Elder Humphrey, Baptist Missionary to the Cherokee Indians. Philadelphia, Pa.: King and Baird, 1852. Established missions at Spring Place Georgia and near present-day Chattanooga, Tennessee.
F1480

Fleming, Vivian Minor Campaigns of the Army of Northern Virginia, Including the Jackson Valley Campaign, 1861-1865. Richmond: William Byrd Press, 1928. Another laudatory history of Jackson Valley Campaign.
F1490 (ASU)

Fletcher, A. J. The Story of a Mountain Missionary: Rev. James Floyd Fletcher, 1858-1946. Raleigh, N. C.: The author, 1966. The mountains of western North Carolina, especially Ashe County, still have the imprint of Fletcher's unique theological interpretations.
F1500 (ASU)

Fletcher, Alice C. Indian Story and Song from North America. Boston: Small Maynard and Co., n.d.
F1510 (FC)

Fletcher, Arthur Lloyd Ashe County: A History. Jefferson, N. C.: Ashe County Research Association, 1963. A rather good local history of this county which once served as a gateway west.
F1520 (ASU WCU)

Fletcher, J. F. A History of the Ashe County, North Carolina, and New River, Virginia, Baptist Associations. Raleigh, N. C.: Commercial Print. Co., 1935.
F1530 (ASU)

Fliegel, Frederick C. The Low-Income Farmer in a Changing Society. (Bulletin No. 731.) University Park: Pennsylvania Agricultural Experiment Station, Pennsylvania State University, March, 1966. A study of subsistence farmers in Fayette County, Pennsylvania.
F1540

Flint, Carl R. comp. and ed. Graham, William Franklin The Quotable Billy Graham. Anderson, S. C.: Droke House, 1966.
G3160 (WCU)

Flint, Russell F. Fluvial Sediment in the Salem Fork Watershed, West Virginia. Prepared in cooperation with the Soil Conservation Service. Administrative Report. Columbus, Ohio: U. S. Geological Survey, Water Resources Division, 1970.
F1550

Flint, Timothy Biographical Memoir of Daniel Boone, the First Settler of Kentucky: Interspersed with Incidents in the Early Annals of the Country. 1833. Reprint. Cincinnati: G. Conclin, 1841.
F1560 (ASU BC)

Biographical Memoir of Daniel Boone, the First Settler of Kentucky: Interspersed with Incidents in the Early Annals of the Country. 1833. Reprint. Edited for the modern reader by James K. Folsom. The Masterworks of Literature Series. New Haven: College and Univ. Press, 1967.
F1570 (ETSU WCU)

The Life and Adventures of Daniel Boone, the First Settler of Kentucky. Cincinnati: U. P. James, 1868.
F1580 (ETSU)

Flohr, G. D. Sermons and Essays. Baltimore: John Murphy, 1840.
F1590

Flory, John A. Growth and Labor Characteristics of Manufacturing Industries. Area Redevelopment Bookshelf of Community Aids. Washington: U. S. Area Redevelopment Administration, 1964. A survey of correlations between industrial growth and labor characteristics. Some data from Appalachia.
F1600

Flowers, Russell R. A Subsurface Study of the Greenbrier Limestone in West Virginia. Report of Investigations, no. 15. Morgantown: West Virginia Geological and Economic Survey, 1956.
F1610 (ETSU ASU)

Flowers, William Lucas, Jr. "The Community Action Movement in North Carolina." Master's thesis. North Carolina State, 1970.
F1620 (LMC)

Floyd, Charles Frederick "Public Policy for Depressed Areas with Special Reference to North Carolina." Ph. D. Diss. Univ. of North Carolina, 1966. Study focuses on several western North Carolina counties.
F1630

Floyd, Nicholas Jackson Biographical Genealogies of the Virginia-Kentucky Floyd Families, with Notes of Some Collateral Branches. Baltimore: Williams & Wilkins Co., 1912.
F1640 (ASU)

Flynn, Elizabeth Gurley The Alderson Story; my Life as a Political Prisoner. N. Y.: International Publishers, 1972, 1963. (Anderson, W. Va.) Biography of a prisoner in the Federal Penitentiary for Women in Alderson, W. Va.
F1650

Fogg, Gordon Pickeral, John Julian An Economic and Social Survey of Frederick County.
P2840 (ASU LMC)

Foley, Helen S. comp. First Marriage Records, 1838-1850, Barbour County, Alabama. Fort Worth, Texas: American Reference Pub., 1969.
F1660 (ASU)

Marriage Records, 1850, Barbour County, Alabama. Fort Worth, Texas: American Reference Pubs., 1969.
F1670 (ASU)

Folger, John K. Migration and Level of Living in the Tennessee Valley. Ph. D. Diss. Univ. of North Carolina, 1951.
F1680

Folk Songs of the Southern Appalachians as Sung by Jean Ritchie: 77 Traditional Songs, Tunes, and Ballads from the Singing of Jean Ritchie and the Ritchie Family, with Guitar Chords and Notes on the Songs. Foreword by Alan Lomax. New York: Oak Pubs., 1965.
F1690 (ASU BC WCU WWC LMC ETSU FC)

Folmsbee, Stanley John Blount College and East Tennessee College, 1794-1840: The First Predecessors of the University of Tennessee. Knoxville: Univ. of Tennessee, 1946. Histories of the two colleges which merged to form the University of East Tennessee which later became the University of Tennessee.
F1700 (ETSU)

East Tennessee University, 1840-1879, Predecessor of the University of Tennessee. University of Tennessee Record, vol. 62, no. 3. Knoxville: Univ. of Tennessee Record, 1959. A predecessor of the University of Tennessee.
F1710 (ASU)

The Founding of Knoxville. Knoxville: East Tennessee Historical Society, 1941. A truly delightful history of the early days of one of our regions largest cities.
F1720 (ETSU)

A Narrative of the Life of David Crockett of the State of Tennessee. Knoxville: Univ. of Tenn. Press, 1970.
F1730

Sectionalism and Internal Improvements in Tennessee, 1796-1845. Knoxville: n.p., 1939. Much of the text is devoted to East Tennessee.
F1740 (WWC ASU)

Tennessee; a Short History (by) Stanley J. Folmsbee, Robert E. Corlew and Enloch L. Mitchell. A condensation and revision of vol. 1-2 of the author's History of Tennessee published in 1960. Knoxville: Univ. of Tennessee Press, 1969.
F1750 (LMC ASU BC)

Folsom, Montgomery M. Scraps of Songs and Southern Scenes: A Collection of Humorous and Pathetic Poems and Descriptive Sketches of Plantation Life in the Backwoods of Georgia. Atlanta: C. P. Byrd, 1889. Includes some mention of life in Georgia's upland counties.
F1760 (ASU)

Foner, Philip Coal Creek Rebellion. Huntington, W. Va.: Appalachian Movement Press, Inc., 1973. The story of coal miners at Coal Creek, East Tennessee in the late 1800's. They went on strike to protest the convict labor system in the mines.
F1770 (ASU)

Fonner, R. F. Ellyson, W. J. Soil Survey, Wood and Wirt Counties, West Virginia. Washington: U. S. Soil Conservation Service, 1970.
E1870

Fontana Village, N. C. Annual Fontana Conservation Roundup Proceedings. Fontana Village, N. C.: n.p., 1960? annual. (Each vol. has a distinctive title.)
F1780 (WCU)

Foote, William Henry Sketches of North Carolina, Historical and Biographical, Illustrative of the Principles of a Portion of Her Early Settlers. 3rd ed. 1846. Reprint. Raleigh, N. C.: H. J. Dudley for the Committee on Historical Matters of the Synod of North Carolina, Presbyterian Church in the U. S., 1965.
F1790 (ASU LMC)

Sketches of North Carolina, Historical and Biographical, Illustrative of the Principles of a Portion of Her Early Settlers. New York: Robert Carter, 1846.
F1800 (MHC BC)

Sketches of Virginia. Richmond, Va.: John Knox Press, 1850.
F1810

Sketches of Virginia Historical and Biographical. vol. I. Philadelphia, Pa.: William S. Martin, 1850.
F1820

Sketches of Virginia Historical and Biographical. 2nd series, 2nd ed. rev. Philadelphia, Pa.: J. P. Lippincott & Co., 1856.
F1830

Sketches of Virginia: Historical and Biographical, First Series. New ed. Richmond: John Knox Press, 1966.
F1840 (LMC UNCA)

Forbes, John Joseph Vincent Coal Losses of Tennessee. Prepared by the Bureau of Mines, Department of the Interior, for the U. S. Coal Commission. Nashville: n.p., 1925.
F1850 (ETSU)

Forbes-Lindsay, Charles Harcourt Ainslee Daniel Boone, Backwoodsman. Philadelphia: Lippincott, 1908.
F1860

Ford, Anne Davy Crockett. Illustrated by Leonard Vosburg. New York: Putnam, 1961.
F1870 (ETSU)

Ford, Bonnie Willis The Story of the Penland Weavers. n.p.: n.p., 1941.
F1880 (ASU BC)

Ford, Daniel Heath "Some Geographical Aspects of the Poultry Processing Industry in North Carolina." Master's thesis. Appalachian State Univ., 1969. This industry is heavily concentrated in the foothill counties of North Carolina.
F1890 (ASU)

Ford, Ernest Jennings This is My Story: This is My Song. Englewood Cliffs, N. J.: Prentice-Hall, 1963. Biography of "Tennessee Ernie" Ford.
F1900 (BC)

Ford, Evelyn Meek "Enriching the Curriculum of South Side School, Johnson City, Tennessee, by Parent Participation." Master's thesis. East Tennessee State College, 1956.
F1910 (ETSU)

Ford, Henry Jones The Scotch-Irish in America. Princeton: Princeton Univ. Press, 1915.
F1920

The Scotch-Irish in America. 1915. Reprint. Hamden, Conn.: Archon Books, 1966. The Scotch-Irish were the Predominate group in early mountain settlement.
F1930 (ASU)

Ford, Jean I'll Walk to the Mountain. New York: Greenburg, 1936. A Greenwich Village girl hitch-hikes to the Tennessee mountains to try a new lifestyle.
F1940 (ASU)

Ford, Jesse Hill The Liberation of Lord Byron Jones. 1st ed. An Atlantic Monthly Press Book. Boston: Little, Brown, 1965. A novel of violence and racial tension set in the foothill country of Tennessee.
F1950 (ASU WCU ETSU BC)

Mountains of Gilead, a Novel. 1st ed. An Atlantic Monthly Press Book. Boston: Little, Brown, 1961. The mountains in this case are Indian mounds in flatland Tennessee, but the people are not far removed from mountain characterizations.
F1960 (BC ASU ETSU)

Ford, Leslie Burn Forever. New York: Popular Library, 1963. Young lovers are caught in a web of violence, murder and intrigue in the Tennessee Valley.
F1970 (ASU BC)

Ford, Robert Vagabond Songs and Ballads of Scotland. Paisley and London: A. Gardner, 1899.
F1980 (ASU)

Ford, Thomas R. Christiansen, John R. Trends in the Number and Distribution of Medical Doctors in Kentucky. Lexington: Ky. Agricultural Experiment Station, 1958.
C4010

Employment Problems of the Eastern Kentucky Mountain People. Hearing before the Special Committee on Unemployment Problems, United States Senate. Washington: U. S. Govt. Print. Off., 1960.
F1990

Health and Demography in Kentucky. Lexington: Univ. of Kentucky, 1964.
F2000 (LMC BC)

Ford, Thomas R. ed. The Southern Appalachian Region: A Survey. Lexington: Univ. of Kentucky Press, 1962. At the time of its publication, this book was hailed as a mountain classic. Interesting but dated.
F2010

Southern Appalachian Studies, Berea, Ky. The Southern Appalachian Region; A Survey. Lexington: Univ. of Kentucky Press, 1962.
S5670 (BC ASU UNCA FC)

Southern Appalachian Studies, Berea, Ky. The Southern Appalachian Region. Lexington: Univ. of Kentucky Press, 1967.
S5680 (ASU ETSU FC LMC MHC WCU WWC BC)

Foreman, Carolyn Thomas Indian Women Chiefs. Muskogee (?), Okla.: n.p., 1954. A good account of Nancy Ward, Cherokee chief, is included.
F2020 (MHC ASU)

Indians Abroad, 1493-1938. The Civilization of the American Indian Series. Norman: Univ. of Oklahoma Press, 1943. The story of Indians taken to Europe and other parts of the world by the white man from the time of Columbus, including the 18th-century trips to England by Overhill Cherokee leaders.
F2030

Foreman, Grant The Five Civilized Tribes. Introductory note by John R. Swanton. 1st ed. Reprint. The Civilization of the American Indian. Norman: Univ. of Oklahoma Press, 1966.
F2040 (WCU BC)

The Five Civilized Tribes. The Civilization of the American Indian Series. Intro. John R. Swanton. Univ. of Oklahoma Press, 1934.
F2050

The Five Civilized Tribes. The Civilization of the American Indian Series. Intro. John R. Swanton. Univ. of Oklahoma Press, 1971.
F2060

Indian Removal: The Emigration of the Five Civilized Tribes of Indians. New ed. Civilization of the American Indian. Norman: Univ. of Oklahoma Press, 1953.
F2070 (ASU BC LMC WCU)

Sequoyah. Norman: Univ. of Oklahoma Press, 1938.
F2080 (BC UNCA WCU ETSU)

Sequoyah. The Civilization of the American Indian Series, vol. 16. Norman: Univ. of Oklahoma Press, 1959. The best biography of this Cherokee who gave his people their first syllabary. However, he did not invent it.
F2090 (ASU)

Foreman, Grant
Sequoyah. 1st ed. 1938. Reprint. The Civilization of the American Indian, vol. 16. Norman: Univ. of Oklahoma Press, 1970.
F2100 (ASU LMC)

Foreman, Ulysses Grant see Foreman, Grant

Forest City, N. C. First Baptist Church The First Baptist Church of Forest City, N. C. Forest City, N. C.: Forest City Courier, 1939.
F2110 (BC)

Forest, Herman Silva Jessie's Children. New York: Vantage Press, 1959. A memoir of hiking in the Great Smokies and of family experiences there.
F2120 (LMC)

Forest Improvement Measures for the Southern Appalachians, with a List of Selected References Appalachian Forest Experiment Station. U. S. D. A. Technical Bulletin 476. Washington: Govt. Print. Off., 1935.
F2130

Forest Products Laboratory, Madison, Wis.
Suitability of Appalachian Woods for Sanitary Tissue and Toweling. U. S. Forest Service Research Paper, FPL-66. Madison: Laboratory, 1966.
F2140

Forman, Mary Douglass Fundaburk ed.
Fundaburk, Emma Lila Sun Circles and Human Hands: The Southeastern Indians Art and Industries. Luverne, Ala.: n.p., 1957.
F3830 (ASU MHC WCU BC)

Forrest, Williams Trail of Tears. New York: Crown Pub., 1959. Novel of the 1838 Cherokee Removal to Oklahoma.
F2150 (WCU BC)

Fort, John Porter God in the Straw Pen, a Novel. New York: Dodd, Mead & Co., 1931. Novel of a hell-raising North Georgia revival camp meeting. Tidy plot.
F2160 (ASU WCU BC)

Make Way for the Great. Nashville: Benson Print. Co., 1950. Accounts of great men who grew up in Tennessee. There was a popular saying in my grandmother's day, "There were giants in the earth in East Tennessee in the old days."
F2170 (ETSU BC)

Stone Dougherty. New York: Dodd, Mead & Co., 1929. Romantic fiction with a mountain setting.
F2180 (BC)

Fortney, Harvey C. History of Worthington, West Virginia, and Surrounding Communities. Parsons, W. Va.: McClain Print. Co., 1968. A very good community history.
F2190 (ASU)

Fortune, Alonzo Willard The Disciples in Kentucky. Lexington, Ky.: Convention of the Christian Churches in Kentucky, 1932.
F2200 (BC)

Fortune, Crawford Economic Base Study and Survey of Basic Services. Atlanta: Resource Development Internship Project, Southern Regional Board, 1969.
F2210

Economic Base Study and Survey of Basic Services for the Hiwassee River Watershed Development Association. Atlanta: Resource Development Internship Project, Southern Regional Education Board, n.d.
F2220 (BC)

Foscue, Edwin Jay Gatlinburg, Gateway to the Great Smokies. American Resort Series no. 1. Dallas: Southern Methodist Univ. Press, 1946. A brief history of the community.
F2230

Fosdick, Lucian John The French Blood in America. New York: F. H. Revell Co., 1906.
F2240 (ASU)

Foss, George Abrahams, Roger D. Anglo-American Folksong Style. Englewood Cliffs, N. J.: Prentice-Hall, 1968.
A140 (ASU BC)

Foster, Clementine R. "A Critical Study of Negro Education in Cleveland County, North Carolina, from 1944 to 1954." Master's thesis. North Carolina College, 1958.
F2250 (ASU)

Foster, G. Allen Impeached: The President Who Almost Lost His Job. New York: Criterion, 1964.
F2260

Foster, George Everett Reminiscences of Travel in Cherokee Lands. An Address Delivered before the Ladies' Missionary Society of the Ithaca, New York, Congregational Church, 1898. Ithaca, N. Y.: Democrat Press, 1899.
F2270

Se-quo-yah; the American Cadmus and Modern Moses. A Complete Biography of the Greatest of Redmen, around Whose Wonderful Life Has Been Woven the Manners, Customs and Beliefs of the Early Cherokees, Together with a Recital of Their Wrongs and Wonderful Progress toward Civilization. Illus. Miss C. S. Robbins. Philadelphia, Pa.: Off. of the Indian Rights Assoc., 1885. More fiction and sermonizing than biography.
F2280

Se-quo-yah; the American Cadmus and Modern Moses. A Complete Biography of the Greatest of Redmen, around Whose Wonderful Life Has Been Woven the Manners, Customs and Beliefs of the Early Cherokees, Together with a Recital of their Wrongs and Wonderful Progress toward Civilization. Illus. Miss C. S. Robbins. Reprint. Tahlequah, N. C.: Stone, 1885. More fiction and sermonizing than biography.
F2290

Se-quo-yah; the American Cadmus and Modern Moses. A Complete Biography of the Greatest of Redmen, around Whose Wonderful Life Has Been Woven the Manners, Customs and Beliefs of the Early Cherokees, Together with a Recital of Their Wrongs and Wonderful Progress toward Civilization. Illus. Miss C. S. Robbins. Reprint. New York: B. Franklin, 1971. More fiction and sermonizing than biography.
F2300

Story of the Cherokee Bible. An Address, with Additional nal and Explanatory Notes, Delivered before the Meeting of the Ladies' Missionary Society of the First Congregational Church, Ithaca, N. Y., Feb. 5, 1897. Cherokee History Series. Enl. 2nd ed. Ithaca, N. Y.: Democrat Press, 1899. With this is bound Foster's REMINISCENCES OF TRAVEL IN CHEROKEE LANDS.
F2310

Foster, Harold Day Chestnut Oak in the Southern Appalachians. U. S. Forest Service Circular, 135. Washington: Govt. Print. Off., 1908.
F2320 (ASU)

Foster, John Wells Prehistoric Races of the United States of America. 6th ed. Chicago: S. D. Griggs & Co.; London: Truibner & Co., 1887. Includes accounts of mound builders and other mountain races.
F2330 (ASU)

Foster, Lillian comp. Andrew Johnson, President of the United States: His Life and Speeches. New York: Richardson, 1866.
F2340 (ASU)

Foster, Ruel Ehon Jesse Stuart. Twayne's United States Authors Series. New York: Twayne Pubs., 1968.
F2350 (ASU LMC WCU BC)

Fothergill, Augusta Bridgland Middleton Virginia Tax Payers, 1782-87: Other Than Those Published by the United States Census Bureau. 1940. Reprint. Baltimore: Genealogical Pub. Co., 1966.
F2360 (ASU)

Fothergill, Gerald Emigrants from England, 1773-1776. Baltimore: Genealogical Pub. Co., 1964.
F2370 (ASU)

A List of Emigrant Ministers to America, 1690-1811. 1904. Reprint. Baltimore: Genealogical Pub. Co., 1965.
F2380 (ASU)

Foulke, Roy A. Foulke Family, one branch descended from James Ffookes. Bronxville, N. Y.: n.p., 1972.
F2390

Fowler, David C. A Literary History of the Popular Ballad. Durham, N. C.: Duke Univ. Press, 1968. An impressive work of ballad scholarship.
F2400 (BC ASU)

Fowler, Earl D. Taylor, Arthur Elijah Soil Survey of Adams County, Ohio. Washington: U. S. Department of Agriculture, Bureau of Chemistry and Soils, 1938.
T390

Fowler, Gary L. Up Here and Down Home: Appalachians in Cities. Cincinnati: Urban Appalachian Council, n.d. Discusses the problems of the migrants in the cities.
F2410 (ASU)

Fowler, Ila (Earle) Capt. John Fowler of Virginia and Kentucky; Patriot, Soldier, Pioneer, Statesman, Land Baron, and Civic Leader. Cynthiana, Ky.: The Hobson Press, 1942.
F2430 (BC)

Fowler, Ila Earle comp. Daughters of Colonial Wars, Kentucky. Kentucky Pioneers and Their Descendants. Baltimore: Genealogical Pub. Co., 1967.
D580 (ASU BC)

Fowler, James Alexander Memoirs. 6 vols. Knoxville: Unpublished typescript, n.d.
F2420

Fowler, Walter "An Educational, Economic and Community Survey of White County, Tennessee." Master's thesis. Univ. of Tennessee, 1932.
F2440

Fowler, William Joseph "History of Roane County, Tennessee, 1860-1870." Master's thesis. Univ. of Tennessee, 1964. Roane County was practically torn asunder by the divided loyalties engendered by the Civil War.
F2450

Fowler, William W. Woman on the American Frontier. Hartford: Scranton, 1881. Includes accounts of women crossing the mountains.
F2460

Fox, Charles J. and others Soil Survey, Bradley County, Tennessee Correlation by L. E. Odom. U. S. Soil Conservation Service, Soil Survey, Series 1951, no. 2. Washington: Govt. Print. Off., 1958.
F2470

Soil Survey, Franklin County, Tennessee Correlation by L. E. Odom. U. S. Soil Conservation Service, Soil Survey, Series 1949, no. 8. Washington: Govt. Print. Off., 1958.
F2480

Fox, Genevieve May Cynthia of Bee Tree Hollow. Illustrated by Farrest W. Orr. Boston: Little, 1948.
F2490 (ETSU ASU)

Lona of Hollybrush Creek. Boston: Little, Brown and Co., 1935.
F2500 (ASU)

Mountain Girl. Illustrated by Forrest W. Orr. Boston: Little, 1932.
F2510 (ETSU BC ASU)

Mountain Girl Comes Home. Illustrated by Forrest W. Orr. Boston: Little, Brown & Co., 1934.
F2520 (ASU BC)

Fox, George Edmund Social and Economic Trends in Tennessee and Their Implications for Education. Johnson City: East Tennessee State College, 1957.
F2530 (ETSU)

Fox, Heisal M. Fortney, Harvey C. History of Worthington, West Virginia, and Surrounding Communities. Parsons, W. Va.: McClain Print. Co., 1968.
F2190 (ASU)

Fox, John, Jr. Blue-grass and Rhododendron: Out-doors in Old Kentucky. New York: C. Scribner's Sons, 1901. A tale of the mountains and the bluegrass.
F2540 (ASU BC)

Blue-grass and Rhododendron: Out-doors in Old Kentucky. New York: Scribner, 1910.
F2550 (LMC)

Christmas Eve on Lonesome. New York: Charles Scribner's Sons, 1920.
F2560 (WWC)

Christmas Eve on Lonesome and Other Stories. New York: C. Scribner's Sons, 1904. Overly sentimental mountain tale that was enormously popular in its day.
F2570 (BC ASU WCU LMC ETSU)

Fox, John, Jr.
Christmas Eve on Lonesome, "Hell-fer-sartin," and Other Stories. Illustrated by F. C. Yohn, A. I. Keller and others. New York: Scribner's, 1909. Short stories with Kentucky mountain settings.
F2580 (MHC BC)
Crittenden: A Kentucky Story of Love and War. New York: C. Scribner's Sons, 1900. Stereotypical mountaineers move across a set stage in a too-pat plot.
F2590 (ASU WCU LMC BMC BC)
A Cumberland Vendetta. New York: Charles Scribner's Sons, 1908.
F2600
A Cumberland Vendetta: A Novel. New York: Harper & Brothers, 1910. More feuding mountaineers.
F2610 (ASU)
A Cumberland Vendetta and Other Stories. New York: Harper & Brothers, 1896. Four stories,primarily about feuds.
F2620 (ETSU BC)
A Cumberland Vendetta, and Other Stories. 1895. Reprint. Short Story Index Reprint Series. Freeport, N. Y.: Books for Libraries Press, 1970.
F2630 (WCU)
Erskine Dale, Pioneer. Illustrated by F. C. Yohn. New York: C. Scribner's Sons, 1920. Romantic, moralistic fiction with a Kentucky mountain setting.
F2640 (ASU LMC ETSU)
The Heart of the Hills. Illustrated by F. C. Yohn. New York: C. Scribner's Sons, 1913. A novel of feuds, fatched-on flatlanders, young love and fierce pride and loyalties. The good guys win.
F2650 (ASU WCU LMC ETSU BC)
"Hell-fer-sartain" and Other Stories. New York: Harper, 1897. Ten humorous and sentimental stories which fail to shed any light on the complex characteristics of the mountaineer.
F2660 (LMC ETSU BC)
Hell for Sartain and Other Stories. New York: Charles Scribner's Sons, 1906.
F2670 (ASU)
"Hell for Sartain" and Other Stories. New York: Charles Scribner's Sons, 1914.
F2680 (ASU)
"Hell fer Sartain" and Other Stories. 1897. Reprint. The American Short Story Series, vol. 14. New York: Garrett Press, 1969.
F2690 (ASU)
In Happy Valley. Illustrated by F. C. Yohn. New York: C. Scribner's Sons, 1917. Ten more humorous stories. Unfortunately, the mountaineer comes off looking slightly ridiculous. Fox never caught the elusive mountain character.
F2700 (ASU LMC ETSU)
The Kentuckians. New York: Charles Scribner's Sons, 1909.
F2710
The Kentuckians: A Knight of the Cumberland. Illustrated by W. T. Smedley and F. C. Yohn. New York: C. Scribner's Sons, 1909. Two novels bound together.
F2720 (ASU WCU LMC ETSU)
The Kentuckians: A Knight of the Cumberland. New York: Scribner's, 1912.
F2730 (WWC)
A Knight of the Cumberland. Illustrated by F. C. Yohn. New York: C. Scribner's Sons, 1906. Two traveling city gals stumble across an unlikely mountain fracas and wind up at an affair resembling a medieval joust.
F2740 (ASU LMC ETSU BC)
The Kentuckians: A Novel. Illustrated by W. T. Smedley. New York: Harper, 1898. A mountain legislator pines for a bluegrass lady of quality and eventually wins her heart and hand.
F2750 (WCU BC)
The Little Shepherd of Kingdom Come. Illustrated by F. C. Yohn. New York: C. Scribner's Sons, 1903.
F2760 (WCU UNCA BC)
The Little Shepherd of Kingdom Come. Illustrated by F. C. Yohn. New York: Scribner, 1906.
F2770 (LMC)
The Little Shepherd of Kingdom Come. Illustrated by F. C. Yohn. New York: Grosset & Dunlap, 1920.
F2780 (MHC)
The Little Shepherd of Kingdom Come. New York: Grosset and Dunlap, 1931. Chad, an orphan and the "little Shepherd" finds a home with the mountaineer Turners. A trip to Lexington with the Turners is the beginning of a new life for him. He reaches manhood, finds love, solves the mystery of his birth, and fights on the side of the Union during the Civil War. Typical Fox ending.
F2790
The Little Shepherd of Kingdom Come. Illustrated by F. C. Yohn. New York: Grosset & Dunlap, 1931.
F2800 (ASU)
The Little Shepherd of Kingdom Come. Illustrated by N. C. Wyeth. New York: C. Scribner's Sons, 1931.
F2810 (ASU ETSU)
A Mountain Europa. New York: Charles Scribner's Sons, 1899.
F2820
A Mountain Europa. New York: Charles Scribner's Sons, 1909. Three stories are contained in this book: "A Mountain Europa." "A Cumberland Vendetta," and "The Last Stetson." The first story has the theme of the "furrener" coming to the hills and falling in love. The last two stories are concerned with feuding.
F2830
A Mountain Europa. New York: Charles Scribner's Sons, 1914.
F2840 (ASU BC)
A Mountain Europa. A Cumberland Vendetta. The Last Stetson. Illustrated by F. C. Yohn and Louis Loeb. New York: C. Scribner's Sons, 1909.
F2850 (WCU ETSU MHC BC)
A Mountain Europa. A Cumberland Vendetta. The Last Stetson. Illustrated by F. C. Yohn and Louis Loeb. New York: Scribner, 1911.
F2860 (LMC)
A Mountain Europa. A Cumberland Vendetta. The Last Stetson. Illustrated by F. C. Yohn and Louis Loeb. New York: Scribner, 1915.
F2870 (LMC)
A Purple Rhododendron and Other Stories. Appalachia, Va.: Young Publication, 1967. A posthumous collection of Fox's short stories.
F2880 (ASU ETSU BC)
The Southern Mountaineer. New York: Scribners, 1901. Fox's attempt to describe the mountaineers around him. Differs very little from his fiction.
F2890
The Trail of the Lonesome Pine. New York: Charles Scribner's Sons, 1908.
F2900
The Trail of the Lonesome Pine. New York: C. Scribner's Sons, 1909. A love affair between a mountain girl and an outlander results in her being sent out of the mountains to acquire some polish. When she returns, naturally, she suffers from divided loyalties.
F2910 (ASU WCU LMC MHC BC)
The Trail of the Lonesome Pine. Illustrated with scenes from the photoplay, a Paramount picture. New York: Grosset & Dunlap, 1923, 1936.
F2920 (WCU)
The Trail of the Lonesome Pine. New York: C. Scribner's Sons, 1931.
F2930 (ETSU)
The Trail of the Lonesome Pine. New York: Grosset & Dunlap, 1936.
F2940 (WCU)

Fox, Stephen Eugene "A Study of Vocational Education at the Elizabethton, Tennessee, Area Vocational-Technical School." Master's thesis. East Tennessee State Univ., 1973.
F2950 (ETSU)

Foxfire vol. 1- 1967- Rabun Gap, Nacooche School, Ga.: Southern Highlands Literary Fund, quarterly. An enormously popular periodical written and edited by high school students. Their primary sources are taped interviews with local people.
F2960 (ASU ETSU BC)

The Foxfire Book: Hog Dressing, Log Cabin Building, Mountain Crafts and Foods, Planting by the Signs, Snake Lore, Hunting Tales, Faith Healing, Moonshining, and Other Affairs of Plain Living Introduction by Eliot Wigginton. 1st ed. Garden City, N. Y.: Doubleday, 1972.
F2970 (ASU WWC MHC ETSU BC FC)

Foxfire 2: Ghost Stories, Spring Wild Plant Foods, Spinning and Weaving, Midwifing, Burial Customs, Corn Shuckin's, Wagon Making and More Affairs of Plain Living Garden City, N. Y.: Anchor Press, 1973.
F2980 (WWC ASU BC FC)

Foy, Bernard L. A Bibliography for the T.V.A. Program. Knoxville: Technical Library, Tennessee Valley Authority, 1966. A quite comprehensive 73 page listing of materials on the TVA.
F2990

Foy, Bernard L. comp. Bauer, Harry C. comp. An Indexed Bibliography of the Tennessee Valley Authority. Knoxville: TVA Information Div., 1941-42.
B2020
The TVA Program: A Bibliography. Knoxville: TVA Information Div., 1943-1968. Various editions covering the period from 1943 to 1968.
F3000

Foye, G. Gibson Emory and Henry's Contribution to the Development of Democracy. Address to the Washington County Historical Society, Bulletin no. 16. Abingdon, Va.: n.p., December 1947.
F3010

Foyles, Edward J. The Genealogy about Mills Springs, Monticello Quadrangle, Kentucky. New York: American Museum of National History, 1921.
F3020 (BC)

France, Irene Bolton "A Program of Library Instruction for the Ninth Grade Pupils at Jonesboro High School." Master's thesis. East Tennessee State College, 1956. Jonesboro is the oldest town in Tennessee, yet its school system is one of the most innovative in the state.
F3030 (ETSU)

Francis, Elesabeth Wheeler Lost Links: New Recordings of Old Data from Many States. Nashville, Tenn.: McQuiddy Print. Co., 1945.
F3040 (ASU)

Francis, G. S. Obenshain, S. S. Soil Survey, Russell County, Virginia. Washington: U. S. Department of Agriculture, Bureau of Plant Industry, Soils, and Agricultural Engineering, 1945.
O100 (BC)

Francis, Phillip Seventy Years in the Coal Mines. Manuscript. n.p.: n.p., 1943? Personal memoir of a lifetime in the mines of Kentucky and Tennessee.
F3050 (BC)

Frank, Bernard Peck, Millard Economic Utilization of Marginal Lands in Nicholas and Webster Counties, West Virginia. Washington: U. S. Department of Agriculture, 1932.
P1540

Frank, Robert M. "Pennsylvania Markets for Primary Forest Products." Master's thesis. Pennsylvania State Univ., 1956.
F3060

Franklin, James Rutherford In the Path of the Storm. New York: E. P. Dutton & Co., 1927. A college youth working his way through school by selling pots and pans is stranded with a mountain moonshining family and later suspected of informing on the illegal operation.
F3070 (ASU BC LMC)

Frantz, Mabel Goode Full Many a Name; the Story of Sam Davis, Scout and Spy, C. S. A. Jackson, Tenn.: McCowat-Mercer Press, 1961.
F3080

Frawley, Margaret L. Surface Mined Areas: Control and Reclamation of Environmental Damage; a Bibliography. Washington: U. S. Dept. of Interior, Office of Library Services, 1971.
F3090 (ASU)

Frayser, Anne Rebecca Finch Mission. Richmond: Dietz Press, 1951. An account of the Protestant Episcopal Church's Missions in Virginia.
F3100 (ASU LMC BC)

Frazier, Anne A. "A Critical Analysis of the Counselor's Role in Blountville Junior High School." Master's thesis. East Tennessee State Univ., 1969.
F3110 (ETSU)

Frazier, Chalmer "History of Education of Floyd County, Kentucky." Master's thesis. Univ. of Kentucky, 1939. A very interesting study of the role of education in one of Kentucky's most controversial counties.
F3120

Frazier, Evelyn McD Hunting Your Ancestors in South Carolina: A Guide for Amateur Genealogists. Watterboro, S. C.: Florentine Press, 1969.
F3130 (ASU)

Frazier, Thomas R. The Underside of American History: Other Readings Since 1865. n.p.: n.p., n.d. Volume II is dedicated to Myles Horton and the Highlander idea. It contains a great deal of information on the Appalachian Region.
F3140

Freedman, Ronald "Recent Migration into Chicago." Ph. D. Diss. Univ. of Chicago, 1948. Many of the migrants are from the Appalachians. The author is sensitive and literate and the volume is quite readable for a dissertation.
F3150

Recent Migration into Chicago. Chicago: Univ. of Chicago Press, 1950.
F3160

Freel, Margaret Walker Our Heritage, the People of Cherokee County, North Carolina, 1540-1955. Asheville, N. C.: Miller Print. Co., 1956. One of western North Carolina's better county histories.
F3170 (ASU WCU BC)

Freeman, Berry B. Bechtler's Gold. Spindale, N. C.: Spindale Press, 1958. Interesting phamplet about the discovery of gold in Rutherford County, North Carolina.
F3180

Freeman, John F. A Guide to Manuscripts relating to the American Indian in the library of the American Philosophical Society. Memoirs, vol. 65. Philadelphia: American Philosophical Society, 1966.
F3190 (ASU MHC)

Freeman, Louise Barton Regional Subsurface Stratigraphy of the Cambrian and Ordovician in Kentucky and Vicinity. University of Kentucky Geological Survey, Series 9, Bulletin, no. 12. 1953. Reprint. Lexington: n.p., 1960.
F3200 (ETSU)

Freeman, Richard B. Segal, Martin Economic Redevelopment Research: Population, Labor Force and Unemployment in Chronically Depressed Areas. Washington: Area Redevelopment Administration, 1964.
S1730

French, Evelyn Jackson Mountain Ballads. n.p.: n.p., n.d. Typewritten copy with notes.
F3210 (BC)

French, Jack, Jr. "Segration Patterns in a Coal Camp." Master's thesis. West Virginia Univ., 1953. A study of isolates and other forms of social segregation and alienation in a West Virginia coal camp.
F3220 (ASU)

French, Jack Phillip "Evaluation of Reading in the Bristol, Virginia, Schools with a Suggested Corrective Program." Master's thesis. East Tennessee State Univ., 1971.
F3230 (ETSU)

French, Janie Preston Collup Davy Crockett and the Crockett Family. Chattanooga: Lookout, 1951.
F3250

Notable Southern Families. The Doak Family. Chattanooga, Tenn.: Lookout Publishing Co., 1933.
F3260

French, Janie Vreston Collup The Crockett Family and Connecting Lines. (Notable Southern Families, vol. 5.) Bristol, Tenn.: King Print. Co., 1928. Contains almost one hundred pages of original court records pertaining to the Crockett family. Index not complete.
F3240

Frenchburg Reporter; a Voice from the Mountain Schools of W. G. M. S. vol. 1, 1931. Frenchburg, Ky.: Frenchburg Schools, 1931. An account of the work of the United Presbyterian Church.
F3270 (BC)

Freund, Virginia ed. Strachey, William The History of Travel Into Virginia Britania (1612). London: Hakluyt Society, 1953.
S7730 (ASU)

Freytag, Ethel A History of Morgan County, Tennessee. Wartburg, Tenn.: Specialty Print. Co., 1971. Contains reprints of early records and good genealogical information.
F3280 (ASU BC)

Fridell, Guy What Is It About Virginia? Richmond, Virginia: The Dietz Press, Inc., 1966.
F3290

Fridley, H. M. Vessel, A. J. Soil Survey, Greenbrier County, West Virginia. Washington: U. S. Dept. of Agriculture, Bureau of Plant Industry, 1941.
V580

Williams, Blonnie Hugh Soil Survey of Hardy and Pendleton Counties, West Virginia. Washington: U. S. Department of Agriculture, Bureau of Chemistry and Soils, 1934.
W6430

Williams, Blonnie Hugh Soil Survey of Pocahontas County, West Virginia. Washington: U. S. Department of Agriculture, Bureau of Chemistry and Soils, 1938.
W6440

Williams, Blonnie Hugh Soil Survey of Randolph County, West Virginia. Washington: U. S. Department of Agriculture, Bureau of Chemistry and Soils, 1936.
W6450

Fridley, Harry Marion The Geomorphic History of the New Kanawha River System. Report of Investigations, no. 7. Morgantown: West Virginia Geological & Economic Survey, 1950. The New River is reputedly the first or second oldest in the world.
F3300 (ETSU)

Friedl, Joseph J. "History of Education in McDowell County, West Virginia." Master's thesis. Univ. of Kentucky, 1940.
F3310

Friedmann, John Regional Development and Planning: A Reader. Cambridge, Mass.: M. I. T. Press, 1964. A hand book for community action and anti-poverty groups.
F3320 (ASU)

Friedmann, John R. The Spatial Structure of Economic Development in the Tennessee Valley. (Research Paper No. 39.) Chicago: Department of Geography, University of Chicago, 1955.
F3330 (BC)

Friend, Llerena Sam Houston, the Great Designer. Austin: Univ. of Texas Press, 1954, 1969. Houston's youth was spent in East Tennessee.
F3340

Friend, Robert C. and others Giles County, 1806-1956, a Brief History. Pearisburg, Va.: Giles County Chamber of Commerce, n.d. One of a very few published sources on Giles County.
F3350

Friermood, Elizabeth Hamilton Ballad of Calamity Creek. 1st ed. Garden City, N. Y.: Doubleday, 1962. Humorous tale with a mountain setting.
F3360 (ASU BC)

Fries, Adelaide Lisetta The Moravians in Georgia, 1735-1740. 1905. Reprint. Baltimore: Genealogical Pub. Co., 1967. The Moravians were the first missionaries in the Cherokee Nation of Georgia.
F3370 (ASU)

The Road to Salem. Chapel Hill: Univ. of North Carolina Press, 1944. Contains occassional references to the mountain settlements.
F3390 (ASU LMC)

Some Moravian Heroes. Bethlehem, Pa.: Comenius Press, 1936.
F3400 (ASU)

Fries, Adelaide Lisetta ed. Records of the Moravians in North Carolina. ? vols. Raleigh: Edwards & Broughton Print. Co., 1922. At one time the Moravians had a number of churches in the western mountains of N. C.
F3380 (ASU LMC MHC)

Frings, Ketti Look Homeward, Angel: A Play Based on the Novel by Thomas Wolfe. With introduction by Edward C. Aswell. New York: Scribner, 1958.
F3410 (ASU BC)

Frisch, Isadore "Twentieth Century Development of the Coal Mining Industry in Eastern Kentucky and Its Influence upon the Political Behavior of This Area." Master's thesis. Microfilm. Univ. of Kentucky, 1938. A fascinating topic which proved too large for this one thesis.
F3420 (ASU)

Friscia, August Blake "Industrial Retardation and Economic Growth: A Case Study of Secular and Structural Change in the United States, 1920-1960." Ph. D. Diss. New York Univ., 1970.
F3430

Fritz, Arah Miller Crabtrees of Southwest Virginia. Pecos, Texas: Hawks Printing Co., 1965.
F3440

Frizzell, Izora Waters Edwards, Rapha Olga Jones "The Connection" in East Tennessee. Washington College, Tenn.: Pioneer Printers, 1969.
E1180 (ASU BC)

Froelicb, Albert J. Geological Map of the Balkan Quadrangle, Bell and Harlan Counties, Kentucky. Washington: U. S. Geological Survey, 1973.
F3450 (BC)

From the Hills Charleston, W. Va.: MHC Publications, Morris Harvey College, 1972-. Formed by uniting STORIES FROM THE HILLS, ed. Barbara Yeager and POEMS FROM THE HILLS, ed. Bill Plumley.
F3460 (ASU BC)

Frome, Michael Strangers in High Places: The Story of the Great Smoky Mountains. Maps by Stephen Kraft. Garden City, N. Y.: Doubleday, 1966. A story of the near-war between Tennessee and North Carolina over the location of the Great Smoky Mountains National Park.
F3470 (ASU WCU LMC MHC FC ETSU BC)

Virginia. New York: Coward-McCann, Inc., 1966.
F3480 (ASU)

Whose Woods These Are: The Story of the National Forests. 1st ed. Garden City, N. Y.: Doubleday, 1962.
F3490 (MHC)

Frontier Nursing Service, Inc. Quarterly Bulletin. vol. 1, no. 1-. Lexington, Ky.: Frontier Nursing Services, Inc., 1926.
F3500 (ASU BC)

Thirty Years Onward. Frontier N. S., 1925-1955. Lexington: Frontier Nursing Service, 1955.
F3510 (BC ASU)

Today, Yesterday and Tomorrow. n.p.: n.p., 1963.
F3520 (BC)

Frost, John Border Wars of the West. Auburn, N. Y.: Derby and Miller, 1853. Includes material on Pennsylvania, Virginia, Kentucky, and Tennessee.
F3530 (BC)

Frost, Norman A Statistical Study of the Public Schools of the Southern Appalachian Mountains. Bulletin 11, 1915; no. 636. Washington: U. S. Bureau of Education, 1915.
F3540 (ASU BC)

Frost, Ralph Walter "A History, of the Cherokee Indians of the Tennessee Region from 1783-1794." Master's thesis. Univ. of Tennessee, 1925.
F3550 (ASU)

Frost, William Goodell Berea College from Servitude to Service, Being the Old South Lectures on the History and Work of the Negro. Boston: American Unitarian Assoc., 1905.
F3560 (BC)

For the Mountains, an Autobiography. New York: Fleming H. Revell Co., 1937. Autobiography of a Berea College president who dedicated himself to the Southern Mountains.
F3570 (ASU LMC BC)

Frothingham, Earl Hazeltine Timber Growing and Logging Practice in the Southern Appalachian Region. U. S. Department of Agriculture Technical Bulletin, 250. Washington: Govt. Print. Off., 1931. A study of reforestation, forest practices, and management.
F3580 (BC ASU)

Frothingham, Robert The Pioneer: A Biography. N. Y.: The Knickerbocker Press, 1920. A biography of Albert E. Humphrey born on the frontier near Sissonville, West Virginia. He became a wealthy coal and iron magnate in Appalachia.
F3590 (BC)

Fry, Joshua The Fry and Jefferson Map of Virginia and Maryland. Charlottesville: Univ. Press of Virginia, 1950.
F3600 (FC)

Fry, Mary A. A. Tennessee Centennial Poem. A Synopsis of the History of Tennessee from Its Earliest Settlement on Watauga to the Present Time, with Short Biographies of Her Most Prominent Men. Chattanooga, Tenn.: The author, 1896.
F3610 (ASU)

Frye, Garland Varney "Job Opportunities for High School Graduates in the Manufacturing Industries in Washington County, Tennessee." Master's thesis. East Tennessee State Univ., 1969.
F3620 (ETSU)

Fulknier, Virginia comp. Dear Annie: A Collection of Letters, 1860-1886. Art work by Patrick H. Schell, Jr. Parsons, W. Va.: McClain Print. Co., 1969. Civil War letters from a soldier to his wife.
F3640 (ASU)

Fulks, James Billy "A Proposed Master of Arts in Teaching Program for East Tennessee State University." Master's thesis. East Tennessee State Univ., 1967.
F3650 (ETSU)

Fuller, Edwin Wiley The Angel in the Cloud: With Memoir and Portrait of the Author, and Additional Poems. 3d ed. New York: E. J. Hale & Son, 1878.
F3660 (ASU)

The Angel in the Cloud. n.p.: n.p., 1907.
F3670 (ASU)

Fuller, G. L. Miller, John T. Soil Survey, Hall County, Georgia. Washington: U. S. Department of Agriculture, Bureau of Plant Industry, 1941.
M5850 (ASU)

Fuller, Glenn Loren Soil Survey of Bartow County, Georgia. Prepared in cooperation with the Georgia State College of Agriculture. Soil Survey Report, Series 1926, no. 11. Washington: U. S. Department of Agriculture, Bureau of Chemistry and Soils, 1930.
F3680

Fuller, Hugh Eckel "Joseph Ketron and His Kingsley Seminary, Sullivan County, Tennessee." Master's thesis. East Tennessee State Univ., 1953.
F3690 (ASU)

Fuller, Justin "History of the Tennessee Coal, Iron, and Railroad Company, 1852-1907." Ph. D. Diss. University of North Carolina, 1966.
F3700

Fuller, R. V. A Study of the Physical Education Problems as Found In Negro Schools in East Tennessee." Master's thesis. Tennessee Agricultural and Industrial University, 1956.
F3710

Fuller, Ruby Jewell. A Study of Library Services in Some Southwest Virginia Schools." Master's thesis. East Tennessee State Univ., 1963.
F3720 (ETSU)

Fuller, Stephen Souther "The Appalachian Experiment: Growth or Development." Ph. D. Diss. Cornell Univ., 1969. Explores the impact, or lack of it, of the War on Poverty's infusion of money during the 1960's.
F3730

Fuller, Theodore Elwood "An Analysis of the Spatial Structure of Manufacturing in the Appalachian Region Between 1950-1960." Microfilm. Ph. D. Diss. Pennsylvania State Univ., 1966.
F3740 (ASU)

Employment in Appalachia: Trends and Prospects. Agricultural Economic Report, no. 134. ERIC RC 002 964. Washington: Economic Research Service, U. S. Department of Agriculture, 1968.
F3750 (ASU)

Employment, Unemployment, and Low Incomes in Appalachia. In cooperation with the Pennsylvania State University College of Agriculture, Agricultural Experiment Station. Agricultural Economic Report, no. 73. Washington: U. S. Dept. of Agriculture, Economic Research Service, 1965.
F3760 (LMC ASU)

Fulmer, John L. Development Potentials For Kentucky Counties With Related Statistics Lexington: Bureau of Business Research, College of Business and Economics, Univ. of Kentucky.
F3770

Fulmer, John Leonard Kentucky Employment Trends from 1951 to 1963 with Projections to 1965-1975. Lexington: Bureau of Business Research, Univ. of Kentucky, 1965.
F3780

Kentucky Employment Trends from 1951 to 1963, with Projections to 1965-75. Lexington: Univ. of Kentucky, Bureau of Business Research, 1965.
F3790

Fulton, Eleanore Jane An Index to the Will Books and Interstate Records of Lancaster County, Pennsylvania, 1729-1850, with an Historical Sketch and Classified Bibliography. Lancaster, Pa.: Intelligencer Print. Co., 1936.
F3800 (ASU)

Fulton, Maurice Garland Southern Life in Southern Literature. Boston: Ginn and Co., 1917. Scant mention of Appalachian literature.
F3810

Fundaburk, Emma Lila Sun Circles and Human Hands: The Southeastern Indians Art and Industries. Luverne, Ala.: n.p., 1957.
F3830 (ASU MHC WCU BC)

Fundaburk, Emma Lila ed. Southeastern Indians: Life Portraits: A Catalogue of Pictures, 1564-1860. Luverne, Ala.: n.p., 1958.
F3820 (MHC BC)

Funk, David T. A Revised Bibliography of Strip Mine Reclamation. U. S. Department of Agriculture, Forest Service, Miscellaneous Release 35. Washington: U. S. Govt. Print. Off., 1962.
F3840 (ASU)

Funkhouser, William Delbert Ancient Life in Kentucky: A Brief Presentation of the Paleontological Succession in Kentucky Coupled with a Systematic Outline of the Archaeology of the Commonwealth. Illustrated with one hundred and seventy-six original photographs and diagrams. Series 6, Geologic Reports, vol. 34. Frankfort: Kentucky Geological Survey, 1928.
F3850 (ASU BC)

Ancient Life in Kentucky: A Brief Presentation of the Paleontological Succession in Kentucky Coupled with a Systematic Outline of the Archaeology of the Commonwealth. Illustrated with one hundred and seventy-six original photographs, maps, and diagrams. Series 6, Geologic Reports, vol. 34. 1928. Reprint. Berea, Ky.: Kentucke Imprints, 1972.
F3860 (WCU MHC BC)

Furches, John Frank The Furches Folks. Clemmons, N. C.: The author, 1971.
F3870 (ASU)

A Genealogical Resume of "The Furches Folks." Clemmons, N. C.: The author, n.d.
F3880 (ASU)

Furman, Lucy The Glass Window; a Story of the Kentucky Mountains. Boston: Little, Brown and Co., 1929.
F3890

The Glass Window: A Story of the Quare Woman. Boston: Little, Brown & Co., 1925. A novel about the founding of the Hindman Settlement School.
F3900 (ASU LMC BC)

The Lonesome Road. Boston: Little, Brown & Co., 1928. The grandson of a hard-shell Baptist preacher wanders into the big world then decides to return home.
F3910 (WWC)

Lonesome Road. Boston: Little, Brown and Co., 1927.
F3920

The Lonesome Road. Boston: Little, Brown & Co., 1937.
F3930 (ASU LMC)

Mothering on Perilous. Illustrated by Mary Lane. New York: Macmillan Co., 1913. A settlement school worker finds her students incomprehensible and they must learn to adjust to her.
F3940 (ASU BC)

Mothering on Perilous. New York: The Macmillan Co., 1914.
F3950

The Quare Women. Boston: Atlantic Monthly Press, 1923. A group of early female social workers camp out in Knott Co., Ky. Feuds and humor predominate.
F3960 (BC WWC)

Quare Women. Boston: Little, Brown and Co., 1937.
F3970

The Quare Women: A Story of the Kentucky Mountains. Boston: Little, Brown & Co., 1937.
F3980 (ASU LMC BC)

Sight to the Blind: A Story. With an introduction by Ida Tarbell. New York: Macmillan Co., 1914. Missionaries arrange to convert a woman by having cataracts removed from her eyes.
F3990 (ASU LMC BC)

Furman University. Greenville, S. C. The Furman Bulletin, New Series. vol. 1. Greenville, S. C.: Furman Univ., 1951.
F4000

Furr, William R. Tomorrow Achieved, a Novel. Kansas City, Mo.: Chapman Publishers, 1946. Young Dusty Lanier journey's from Hyden to Hazard to work in mines. He finds job and romance.
F4010 (ASU BC)

Fuson, Henry Harvey Ballads of the Kentucky Highland. London: Mitre Press, 1931.
F4020 (ASU LMC ETSU BC)

History of Bell County, Kentucky. New York: Hobson Book Press, 1947. Interesting history of Josh Bell County and the Gaparea.
F4030 (BC)

History of the Fuson Family. London: Mitre Press, 1932. Native to Harlan and Bell Counties, Ky.
F4040 (BC)

Chant the Mountains. Louisville: Standard Print. Co., 1945. A verse about the Kentucky mountains.
F4050 (BC)

Just from Kentucky. Louisville: J. P. Morton & Co., 1925. Poems from the Kentucky hills.
F4060 (BC)

Fuson, Henry Harvey
The Pinnacle and Other Kentucky Mountain Poems. Louisville, Ky.: J. P. Morton & Co., 1921. Poems from the Kentucky hills.
F4070 (ASU BC)
The Strange Shape. Louisville: Standard Print. Co., 1946.
F4080 (BC)

Fussell, Kenneth Eugene Soil Survey, Marshall County, Alabama. Soils surveyed by K. E. Fussell and others. Correlation by I. L. Martin. U. S. Soil Conservation Service, Soil Survey, Series 1956, no. 2. Washington: Govt. Print. Off., 1959.
F4090

Gabbard, Eugene Field "History of Education in Owsley County, Kentucky." Master's thesis. Univ. of Kentucky, 1939.
G10 (BC)
Notes from the History of Education in Owsley County. Master's thesis. Univ. of Kentucky, 1939.
G20

Gabel, Hortense West Virginia Housing. A Consultant's Report to the Governor's Task Force on Housing and the West Virginia State Development Plan. West Virginia State Development Plan, Program Development Series, Working Paper, no. 3. Morgantown: Office of Research and Development, West Virginia Center for Appalachian Studies and Development, West Virginia Univ., 1967.
G30

Gable, William Russell "The Tennessee Valley Authority and Its Relation to Private Enterprise." Master's thesis. Louisiana State Univ., 1949.
G40

Gableman, John W. Uranium in the Appalachian Mobile Belt. U. S. Atomic Energy Commission Research and Development Report, RME-4107. Washington: Govt. Print. Off., 1968.
G50 (LMC)

Gabriel, Ralph Henry Elias Boudinot, Cherokee, and His America. Norman: Univ. of Oklahoma Press, 1941. A biography of a Cherokee leader who exemplified American Protestantism confronting not only a race problem, but also one of adjustment between two radically different cultures.
G60 (ASU BC UNCA)

Gaby, L. I. Forced Air Drying of Southern Pine Lumber. U. S. Forest Service Station Paper, no. 121. Asheville, N. C.: Southeastern Forest Experiment Station, 1961.
G70 (WCU)

Gaddis, Haxwell Pierson Foot-prints of an Itinerant. Cincinnati: Methodist Book Concern, 1855. At various times during his career with the Cincinnati Conference of the Methodist Episcopal Church, Gaddis visited several of the Virginia springs and gives considerable attention to them.
G80

Gage, Wilson, pseud. see Steele, Mary Q.

Gahr, David The Face of Folk Music. Text by Robert Shelton. 1st ed. New York: Citadel Press, 1968.
G90 (ASU)

Gainer, Patrick W. The West Virginia Centennial Book of One Hundred Songs, 1863-1963; Patriotic Songs, Folk Songs and Hymns. Morgantown, W. Va.: n.p., 1963. Some of the hymns have shape note notations.
G100

Gaither, Gene A. Akins, Richard O. Soil Survey: Dawson, Lumpkin, and White Counties, Georgia. Washington: U. S. Soil Conservation Service, 1972.
A850

Galbraith, Vivian Hunter An Introduction to the Use of the Public Records. 1934. Reprint. London: Oxford Univ. Press, 1952. A good research tool for searching out ships records of those who emigrated to America.
G110 (ASU)

Galbreath, Paul M. Maryland Water Law: Water Laws and Legal Principles Affecting the Use of Water in Maryland. College Park: Water Sources Study Committee, Univ. of Maryland, 1965. Maryland has three Appalachian counties from which a number of rivers rise.
G120

Gale, Thomas H. The Wonder of the Nineteenth Century, Rock Oil in Pennsylvania and Elsewhere. Erie, Pa.: Sloan & Griffith, 1860.
G130 (ASU)

Gallatin, M. H. Austin, Moris E. Soil Survey, Claiborne County, Tennessee. Washington: U. S. Department of Agriculture, Bureau of Plant Industry, Soils, and Agricultural Engineering, 1948.
A5560 (ASU)

Gallimore, Leonard R. "An Inspection of Standardized Test Results in the Schools of Bath County, Virginia." Master's thesis. East Tennessee State College, 1962.
G140 (ETSU)

Galloway, Carl Wilson This is My Country: A Book of Poetry. Graham, N. C.: n.p., 1959. Poems praising the western North Carolina mountain country.
G150 (ASU)

Galloway, Robert E. Part-time Farming in Eastern Kentucky. Bulletin, 646. Lexington: Kentucky Agricultural Experiment Station, 1956. Study shows that even marginal farmers who must take jobs in industry prefer to think of themselves as farmers.
G160
Rural Manpower in Eastern Kentucky: A Study of Under-Employment among Rural Workers in Economic Area Eight. Bulletin no. 627. Lexington: Kentucky Agricultural Experiment Station, Univ. of Kentucky, 1955.
G170
Utilization of Rural Manpower in Eastern Kentucky. Lexington: Kentucky Agricultural Experiment Station, 1953.
G180

Galt, W. I. Deeter, Earl B. Soil Survey of Mercer County, Pennsylvania. Washington: U. S. Department of Agriculture, Bureau of Soils, 1919.
D1600

Gamble, Hays B. Glass, Janet H. A Regional Economic Study of Cameron County, Pennsylvania. University Park: Pennsylvania State Univ., 1967.
G2050 (ASU)

Gamble, Hays Bentley The Economic Structure of Sullivan County, Pennsylvania. University Park: Pennsylvania State Univ., College of Agriculture, Agricultural Experiment Station, 1967.
G190 (ASU)
"Equating Timber and Wildlife Values and Returns to the Farm Resource Base in Sullivan County, Pennsylvania." Master's thesis. Pennsylvania State Univ., 1962.
G200
The Impact of Interchange Development on the Economy of Clinton County. Research Report, no. 10. University Park, Pa.: Institute for Research on Land and Water Resources, 1966.
G210
"An Input-output Model Incorporating Impact Analysis to Evaluate the Resources and Economy of a Rural Appalachian Community." Ph. D. Diss. Pennsylvania State Univ., 1966.
G220

Gamble, Margaret Elizabeth "The Heritage and Folk Music of Cades Cove, Tennessee." Master's thesis. Univ. of Southern California, 1947. A nicely-done study of the heritage of Cades Cove collected just before the final government evictions.
G230 (LMC)

Gandee, Lee R. Strange Experience: The Autobiography of a Hexenmeister. Englewood Cliffs, N. J.: Prentice-Hall, 1971. Autobiography of a West Virginia clairvoyant.
G240 (LMC)

Ganier, Albert F. A Distributional List of the Birds of Tennessee. Nashville: Tennessee Dept. of Game and Fish, 1933.
G250

Gannett, Henry Dictionary of Altitude in the U. S. Washington: Govt. Print. Off., 1906.
G260
A Gazetteer of West Virginia. U. S. Geological Survey Bulletin, no. 233. Washington: Govt. Print. Off., 1904. Lists place names for post villages, towns, counties, mountains, and rivers.
G270 (BC ASU)

Gardner, Annie Cofield "Social Organization and Community Solidarity in Painttown, Cherokee, North Carolina." Master's thesis. Univ. of North Carolina, 1958. A very good study of kinship and social patterns on the Cherokee reservation.
G280 (ETSU ASU)

Gardner, Caroline Clever Country: Kentucky Mountain Trails. N. Y.: F. H. Revell, 1931.
G290 (LMC BC)

Gardner Gidley & Associates Master Plan for Recreation and Parks: Jackson County, North Carolina. Winston-Salem: n.p., 1969.
G300 (WCU)

Gardner, Jeanne A Grain of Mustard. New York: Trident Press, 1969. Autobiography of the clairvoyant and prophet from Elkins, West Virginia.
G310

Gardner, R. M. Palo, G. P. Tennessee Valley Authority's Bull Run Steam Plant. Knoxville, Tenn.: TVA, 1963.
P130

Gardner, Rufus L. The Courthouse Tragedy at Hillsville, Va. Mt. Airy, N. C.: Reliable Print. Co., 1962. This book is based on newspaper articles, courthouse records, and last statements by Claud Allen and his father Floyd Allen, who requested before being electrocuted that this information be passed on to the public.
G320 (ASU)

Garland, Matilda Pierce "Effect of Consolidation on Johnson County School, Johnson City, Tennessee." Master's thesis. East Tennessee State College, 1956.
G330 (ETSU)

Garner, Edward Dixon For All the Lost and Lonely. Published with the assistance of Lena Mearle Shull Endowment. Old North State Poets, Series 1, no. 3. Raleigh: Poetry Council of North Carolina, 1965.
G340 (LMC ASU WCU)
Sketchbook from Hell. Durham, N. C.: Moore Pub. Co., 1974?
G350 (WCU)
When Men and Mountains Meet. n.p.: Green Leaf Publishers, 1969.
G360 (WCU LMC MHC ASU)

Garner, Isaac Leonard "A Study of Certain Phases of the Educational and Economic Conditions of Marion County, Tennessee." Master's thesis. Univ. of Tennessee, 1930.
G370

Garner, Thomas E. The Igneous Rocks of Pendleton County, West Virginia. Report of Investigations, no. 12. Morgantown: West Virginia Geological and Economic Survey, 1956.
G380 (ETSU)

Garnett, William Edward A Social Study of the Blacksburg Community. Bulletin, 299. Blacksburg: Virginia Agricultural Experiment Station, 1935.
G390 (ASU)
The Virginia Rural Church and Related Influences, 1900-1950. Bulletin, 479. Blacksburg: Virginia Agricultural Experiment Station, 1957.
G400
Virginia Rural Youth Adjustments. Bulletin, 405. Blacksburg: Virginia Agricultural Experiment Station, 1947.
G410

Garnett, William Edward
Virginia's Marginal Population — A Study in Rural Poverty. A report on official project 465-31-3-139 conducted under the auspices of the Works Progress Administration. Bulletin, 335. Blacksburg: Virginia Agricultural Experiment Station, 1941.
G420 (BC)

Garrett, Jill K. A History of Florence, Alabama, with 1850 Census of Lauderdale County. Columbia, Tenn.: The author, 1968. Not quite all of Lauderdale County is in the region and Florence is on the very edge.
G430 (ASU)

Garrett, Lawrence D. Physical Suitability of Appalachian Hardwood Sawlogs for Sawed Timbers. U. S. Forest Service Research Note, NE-121. Upper Darby, Pa.: Northeastern Forest Experiment Station, 1970.
G440

Garrett, Mitchell Bennett Horse and Buggy Days on Hatchet Creek. Montgomery: Univ. of Alabama Press, 1957. An informative and entertaining history of upper Alabama.
G450 (ASU BC)

Garrett, William Robertson History of the South Carolina Cession, and the Northern Boundary of Tennessee. Nashville: Southern Methodist Pub. House, 1884. A strip of land 12 miles wide, 400 miles long and south of present boundary of Tennessee. A Tennessee, Georgia, North Carolina, and South Carolina dispute still continues although a settlement was reached further west in Mississippi and Alabama.
G460 (ETSU BC)

Garriott, William Campbell, Jr. "The Effects of Environment on Public Planning: The Case of Appalachian Planning in Tennessee." Master's thesis. Vanderbilt Univ., 1969. A sad tale of too-little, too-late in terms of public concern and effective legislation to save the environment.
G470 (LMC)

Garrison, Charles B. comp. Non-federal Aid for Community Development Projects in Kentucky. Lexington, Ky.: Spindletop Research, 1964. Includes material on programs in Eastern Kentucky.
G480

Garrison, Winfred Ernest Religion Follows the Frontier; a History of the Disciples of Christ. New York: Harper, 1931.
G490 (BC)

Garst, William Tell Our Garst Family in America. 1st ed. Kansas City, Mo.: Brown-White Lowell Press, 1950.
G500

Garth, John Hill Man. New York: Pyramid Books, 1960. A powerful novel of violence and desire in the Kentucky mountains.
G510 (BC)

Garvey, Edward B. Appalachian Hiker: Adventure of a Lifetime. Oakton, Va.: Appalachian Books, 1971. A very readable account of a back-packing trip along the 2,000 mile Appalachian Trail.
G520 (BC ASU WCU ETSU)

Garvey, K. F. "A Descriptive Study of Patients Accepted for Service During a Three-month Period at Psychiatric Service Clinic in Norton, Virginia." Master's thesis. Univ. of Tennessee, 1956.
G530

Gaskins, Morris M. A Lighthouse in the Wilderness. Albany, Ky.: Clear Fork Baptist Church, 1972. History of the Clear Fork Baptist Church in Albany Kentucky.
G540 (BC)

Gasque, Jim Hunting and Fishing in the Great Smokies. 1st ed. Borzai Books for Sportsmen. New York: A. A. Knopf, 1948.
G550 (BC UNCA ASU WCU LMC)

Gaston, Arthur George Green Power, the Successful Way of A. G. Gaston. Birmingham, Ala.: Southern Univ. Press, 1968. Success story of a Birmingham businessman and civic leader.
G560

Gates, Gary R. A Kentucky Riverlands Development Program. Prepared for the Kentucky Department of Commerce. Lexington, Ky.: Spindletop Research, 1965.
G570

Leslie, J. D. Management of Kentucky Natural Resources. Lexington, Ky.: Spindletop Research, 1965.
L1900

Gates, Margaret Haynes "Fact and Fiction in the Early Biographies of David Crockett." Master's thesis. Univ. of Illinois, 1929. A fascinating and much needed study of the interwoven fact and legend surrounding Crockett.
G580

Gatewood, William B., Jr. Preachers, Pedagogues and Politicians: The Evolution Controversy in North Carolina, 1920-1927. Chapel Hill: Univ. of North Carolina Press, 1966.
G590 (WCU WWC)

Gath see **Townsend, George Alfred**

Gattinger, Augustin The Flora of Tennessee and a Philosophy of Botany, Respectfully Dedicated to the Citizens of Tennessee. Nashville: Gospel Advocate, 1901.
G600

The Medicinal Plants of Tennessee Exhibiting Their Commercial Value, with an Analytical Key, Descriptions in Aid of Their Recognition, and Notes Relating to Their Distribution, Time and Mode of Collection, and Preparation for the Drug Market. Nashville: F. M. Paul, 1894.
G610

The Tennessee Flora: With Special Reference to the Flora of Nashville. Phaenogams and Vascular Crytogams. Nashville: The author, 1887.
G620

Gault, Thomas G. "Rural Land Use in Franklin County, Tennessee." Ed. D. Diss. George Peabody College for Teachers, 1959.
G630

Gaumnitz, Walter Herbert Education in the Southern Mountains. Rev. by Katherine M. Cook. Office of Education Bulletin 1937, no. 26. Washington: Govt. Print. Off., 1938. A review of the many educational phenomena in Appalachia.
G640 (ASU BC)

Good References on Educational Problems of the Southern Highlands. Washington: U. S. Dept. of the Interior, 1936.
G650

Gaut, John M. Cumberland: The Story of a Name. Nashville: Cumberland Presbyterian Pub. House, 1903. More than any other church, the Cumberland Presbyterian Church can be said to be an Appalachian phenomena.
G660 (BC)

Gavett, Thomas William Migration and Changes in the Quality of the Labor Force. Business and Economic Studies, vol. 10, no. 2. Also, Bulletin, Series 67, no. 7-1. Morgantown: West Virginia Univ., Bureau of Business Research, 1967.
G670 (ETSU)

The Unemployed in West Virginia. Business and Economic Studies, vol. 8, no. 1. Also, Bulletin, Series 62, no. 12-2. Morgantown: Bureau of Business Research, College of Commerce, West Virginia Univ., 1962.
G680 (ASU)

Wage Differentials in West Virginia. Business and Economic Studies, vol. 7, no. 4. Bulletin Series 61, no. 12-1. Morgantown: Bureau of Business Research, College of Commerce, West Virginia Univ., 1961.
G690

Gavin, Alsa Franklin "Beginnings: A History of the Founding of Churches in Transylvania County, 1795-1865." Master's thesis. Western Carolina Univ., 1970.
G700 (WCU)

Gazaway, Rena The Longest Mile. 1st ed. Garden City, N. Y.: Doubleday, 1969. A sensitive but depressing book about the author's experiences with Appalachian families.
G710 (ASU WCU LMC ETSU FC BC WWC)

Gearing, Frederick O. Priest and Warriors: Social Structures for Cherokee Politics in the 18th Century. Memoir 93, vol. 64, no. 5. Menasha, Wis.: American Anthropological Assoc., 1962.
G720 (ASU ETSU BC)

Gearreald, T. N. Morgan, E. L. Farmer Cooperation in Southwest Virginia. Blacksburg: Virginia Agricultural Experiment Station, 1941.
M7500 (ASU)

Gedney, Frederick G. Shenandoah; or The Horizon's Bar. A Story of the War. New York: J. S. Ogilne, 1890. Civil War fiction set in the Shenandoah Valley.
G730

Gee, Wilson ed. Catlett, Clay Michie An Economic and Social Survey of Augusta County. Charlottesville: Univ. of Va., 1928.
C2110 (ASU BC)

Gee, Wilson Parham An Economic and Social Survey of Albemarle County. Berryville, Va.: Virginia Book Co., 1922.
G740

Geib, W. J. Wilder, Henry Jason Soil Survey of the Pikeville Area, Tennessee. Washington: U. S. Dept. of Agriculture, Bureau of Soils, 1904.
W6130

Geiger, James E. "Suburban Opposition to Annexation: Case Study Bristol, Virginia, 1972." Master's thesis. East Tennessee State Univ., 1972.
G750 (ETSU)

Geisler, Adalene "An Economic Study of Old Age Pensions with Special Reference to Seven Upper East Tennessee Counties." Master's thesis. East Tennessee State College, 1953.
G760

Genealogical Society of Pennsylvania Palatine Church Visitations, 1609. Publications, Special Number. Philadelphia (?): The society, 1930.
G780 (ASU)

Genealogical Society of the Original Wilkes County Will Books, Wilkes County, North Carolina. Projected series of which the following have been published: vol. 1, 1778-1811. vol. 2, 1811-1848. Wilkesboro, N. C.: n.p., 1970.
G770

General Index to Census of Pensioners, 1840. Prepared by the Genealogical Society of the Church of Jesus Christ of Latter-Day Saints, Salt Lake City, Utah. Baltimore: Genealogical Pub. Co., 1965.
G790

Genth, Friedrich August Ludwig Karl Wilhelm The Minerals and Mineral Localities of North Carolina. Being Chapter 1, vol. 2 of the Geology of North Carolina. Reprinted by order of the Board of Agriculture. Raleigh: P. M. Hale, 1885. Most of these localities are in western North Carolina.
G800 (ASU)

Gentry, James A., Jr. Blaine, James Cyril Dickson The Industrial Development Program of North Carolina, 1954 to 1962, with Projections to 1970. Chapel Hill: Univ. of North Carolina Graduate School of Business Administration, 1964.
B4450

Gentry, Linnell A History and Encyclopedia of Country, Western, and Gospel Music. Nashville: Clairmont Corp., 1969.
G810 (ASU)

Gentry, Winalee One More River to Cross. Philadelphia: Westminster Press, 1955. Wife's account of bushland's experiences in gas and oil fields of East Kentucky.
G820 (BC)

Geological Society of Kentucky Itinerary: Some Stratigraphic and Structural Features of the Middlesboro Basin. Road log for field conference, Geological Society of Kentucky and Appalachian Geological Society. Field trip, 1957. Lexington, Ky.: The society, 1957.
G830 (ETSU)

Geological Society of Kentucky
Selected Features of the Kentucky Fluorspar District and the Barkley Dam Site. Annual Spring meeting of the society. Field trip, 1962. Published in cooperation with Kentucky Geological Survey. Lexington, Ky.: The society, 1962.
G840 (ETSU)

George, Francis The Only Nancy. A Tale of the Kentucky Mountains. New York and London: Fleming H. Revell Co., 1917. Mountain lass discovers love and a heretofore unsuspected aristocratic background all in one short season.
G850

George, Francis, pseud. see Robertson, George Francis

George, Jean Craighead The Moon of the Bears. Illustrated by Mac Shepard. The Thirteen Moons. New York: Crowell, 1967. An animal tale for children about a family of bears in the East Tennessee mountains.
G860 (ETSU)

George, John R. Biesecker, James E. Stream Quality in Appalachia as Related to Coal-mine Drainage, 1965. Washington: Govt. Print. Off., 1966.
B3570 (LMC BC ASU)

George, Kochuparampel Mammen "Association of Selected Economic Factors with Net Migration Rates in the Southern Appalachian Region, 1935-1937." Master's thesis. Univ. of Kentucky, 1961.
G870

George, S. R. Biesecker, James E. Stream Quality in Appalachia as Related to Coal-mine Drainage. Washington: U. S. Govt. Print. Off., 1966.
B3571

Georgia Board of Education Georgia: A Guide to Its Towns and Countryside. 1st ed. 1940. Reprint. American Guide Series. St. Clair Shores, Mich.: Somerset, 1973. The Georgia mountains have many scenic attractions.
G880 (MHC)

Georgia. Department of Archives and History
Georgia's Roster of the Revolution. 1920. Reprint. Baltimore: Genealogical Pub. Co., 1967.
G890 (ASU)

Georgia, Department of Industry and Trade, Research Division Developing Georgia, a Statistical Study. Atlanta: The division, 1965.
G900

Georgia. Department of Mines, Mining and Geology. Publications on the Geology and Mineral Resources of Georgia. n.p.: n.p., n.d.
G910 (ETSU)

Short Contributions to the Geology, Geography, and Archaeology of Georgia. Bulletin, no. 56, 60,- Atlanta: n.p., 1950-.
G920 (ETSU)

The Georgia Genealogical Magazine No. 1- . July, 1961- . Index, numbers 1-46, 1961-1972. Homerville, Ga.: n.p., quarterly.
G930 (ASU)

Georgia Genealogical Reprints The Third and Fourth or 1820 and 1821 Land Lotteries of Georgia. Easley, S. C.: Georgia Genealogical Reprints and Southern Historical Press, 1973.
G940 (ASU)

Georgia Historical Society Index to United States Census of Georgia for 1820. Compiled under the auspices of the Georgia Historical Society. 2nd ed. With additions and corrections by Mrs. Eugene A. Stanley. Baltimore: Genealogical Pub. Co., 1969.
G950 (ASU)

Georgia Manufacturers, Producers-Processors. Atlanta: Georgia Department of Commerce, 1951- .
G960

Georgia Pioneers Century of Columbia County, Georgia, Wills, 1790-1890. Albany, Ga.: The author, 1966.
G970 (ASU)

Columbia County, Georgia, Early Court Records. Albany, Ga.: Georgia Pioneers, 1967. Columbia County served as a sort of holding pen for families waiting to get into the Cherokee Nation lottery lands.
G980 (ASU)

Columbia County, Georgia: Early Marriage Records. Albany, Ga.: The author, 1966.
G990 (ASU)

The Georgia Review vol. 1- . 1947- . Athens: Univ. of Georgia, quarterly.
G1000 (MHC)

Georgia. State Engineering Experiment Station, Atlanta. Highlights of the Economy of the Georgia Mountains Area. Atlanta: State Experiment Station, 1964.
G1010 (BC ASU)

Georgia, State Geologist The Paleozoic Group: The Geology of Ten Counties of Northwestern Georgia. Atlanta: G. W. Harrison, 1893. Unfortunately many of these promising sites have been or are slated to be inundated by the TVA.
G1020 (BC ASU)

Georgia. University. Department of English
Thomas Wolfe and the Glass of Time. Athens: Univ. of Georgia Press, 1974.
G1030 (ETSU ASU)

Geo-Technical Service Sugar Creek Resettlement Area, Leslie County, Kentucky. A Report of a Conference on Planned Relocation, New Housing and Local Employment in Eastern Kentucky, 1966. n.p.: The conference, 1966.
G1040

Gerrard, Louise Burr "Impact of a Federal Grant-in-aid Program on an Economically Depressed, Rural State: A Case Study of Mental Health Programs in West Virginia." Ph. D. Diss. Columbia Univ., 1969.
G1050

Gersmehl, Phillip Joel "A Geographic Approach to a Vegetation Problem: The Case of the Southern Appalachian Grassy Balds." Ph. D. Diss. Univ. of Georgia, 1970. A very nice dissertation but the Cherokee explanation for the balds is far more interesting.
G1060 (BC ASU)

Gerson, Noel Bertram The Cumberland Rifles. 1st ed. Garden City, N. Y.: Doubleday, 1952. Historical fiction set in the Cumberland during the Revolution.
G1070 (ASU BC)

Franklin, America's "Lost State." America in the Making. New York: Crowell-Collier Press, 1968. Novel based on the life of John Sevier and the State of Franklin.
G1080 (ASU ETSU)

The Yankee from Tennessee. 1st ed. Garden City, N. Y.: Doubleday, 1960. Historical fiction about Andrew Johnson.
G1090 (ASU ETSU BC)

Gerstel, Eva "Health, Education, and Income as Correlates of Demand for Hospital Care in the Southern Mountains." Master's thesis. North Carolina State College, 1963. As might be expected, there is a negative correlation between low income and education and those who seek medical aid.
G1100

Getis, Arthur "A Geographical Analysis of the Rail Freight Shipments of Pennsylvania." Master's thesis. Pennsylvania State Univ., 1958. The mountainous regions have fewer railroads and higher freight rates.
G1110

Gettys, William Goldston, Eugene Frizzell Soil Survey, Graham County, North Carolina. Washington: Govt. Print. Off., 1953.
G2390

Goldston, Eugene Frizzell Soil Survey, Macon County, North Carolina. Washington: Govt. Print. Off., 1956.
G2420

Perkins, Samuel Oscar Soil Survey, Cherokee County, North Carolina. Washington: Govt. Print. Off., 1951.
P2070

Perkins, Samuel Oscar Soil Survey, Clay County, North Carolina. Washington: U. S. Department of Agriculture, Bureau of Plant Industry, 1941.
P2080

Perkins, Samuel Oscar Soil Survey, Henderson County, North Carolina. Washington: U. S. Department of Agriculture, Bureau of Plant Industry, Soils, and Agricultural Engineering, 1943.
P2100

Perkins, Samuel Oscar Soil Survey, Mitchell County, North Carolina. Washington: U. S. Bureau of Plant Industry, Soils, and Agricultural Engineering, 1952.
P2110

Perkins, Samuel Oscar Soil Survey, Swain County, North Carolina. Washington: U. S. Department of Agriculture, Bureau of Plant Industry, Soils, and Agricultural Engineering, 1947.
P2120

Perkins, Samuel Oscar Soil Survey, Transylvania County, North Carolina. Washington: U. S. Department of Agriculture, Bureau of Plant Industry, Soils, and Agricultural Engineering, 1948.
P2130

Perkins, Samuel Oscar Yancey County, North Carolina. Washington: U. S. Bureau of Plant Industry, Soils and Agricultural Engineering, 1952.
P2140

Ghei, Deebak Rigsby, Michael Spirit Happy. Brevard?, N. C.: The Loom Press, 1974.
R2340

Ghormley, Hugh William The Church's Distinctive Challenge in Southern Appalachia. Master's thesis. Lexington, Ky.: Lexington Theological Seminary, 1966. At one time there were almost as many missionaries sent south to Appalachia as to Africa.
G1120 (BC)

Gibbard, Harold A. "Habitat-economy-society, a Frame of Reference Applied to Southern Appalachian Coal Country." Master's thesis. West Virginia Univ., 1961.
G1130

Gibbons, William Futhey Those Black Diamond Men: A Tale of the Anthrax Valley. New York: F. H. Revell Co., 1902.
G1140 (BC ASU)

Gibbs, Carter B. Tree Diameter, Poor Indicator of Age in West Virginia Hardwoods. U. S. Forest Service Research Note, NE-11. Upper Darby, Pa.: Northeastern Forest Experiment Station, 1963.
G1150

Gibson, Ernest Willis "The Economic History of Boyd County, Kentucky." Microfilm. Master's thesis. Univ. of Kentucky, 1929.
G1160 (ASU)

Gibson, Jeremy Sumner Wycherley comp. Wills and Where to Find Them. Baltimore: Genealogical Pub. Co., Inc., 1974.
G1170 (ASU)

Gibson, Vivian L. "A Study of Voluntary Withdrawals from McHenry and Five Feeder Schools in Floyd County, Georgia." Master's thesis. Univ. of Alabama, 1952.
G1180

Gibson, William Lloyd, Jr. Economic Land Classification of Pulaski County. Bulletin, 398. Blacksburg: Virginia Agricultural Experiment, Station, 1946.
G1190

Gielow, Martha Sawyer The Light on the Hill: A Romance of the Southern Mountains. New York: Fleming H. Revell Co., 1915. A story of romance and politics and attempts to bring civilization to the mountains.
G1200 (BC ASU LMC)

Mammy's Reminiscences, and Other Sketches. New York: A. S. Barnes and Co., 1898. A series of sketches about mountain life and manners.
G1210 (ASU BC)

Mountain Pageant of Historic Tableaux and Symbolic Figures: The Story of a People Lost in the Appalachians for Nearly Two Hundred Years. Washington: Southern Industrial Educational Assoc., n.d. Sweetly nonsensical pageant which purports to represent Appalachian history.
G1220 (LMC)

Gielow, Martha Sawyer
Old Andy, the Moonshiner. Washington: W. F. Roberts Co., 1909. Old Andy sends his granddaughter to the mission school with money saved from distilling. He's caught; a good lawyer gets him off and books solicits funds for the Southern Industrial Education Association.
G1230 (LMC ASU BC)
Uncle Sam. New York: Fleming H. Revell Co., 1913. Another sentimental story about mountain people who are variously characterized.
G1240 (ASU BC LMC)
The Whispering Fairy: Constructive Stories for Children. Los Angeles: J. F. Rowny Press, 1923.
G1250 (LMC)

Gieseman, Raymond W. Underemployment Concept, Way to Measure Need for Economic Development in Appalachia. Economic Research Service, Department of Agriculture, Series, 347. Washington: Govt. Print. Off., 1967. In this study need for economic development is tied directly to unemployment patterns.
G1260

Giffin, Philip E. Annotated Bibliography on Industrial Concentration and Firm Diversification in the Bitumonous Coal Industry with Special Reference to the Southeastern United States, 1950-1970. Knoxville: Appalachian Resources Project at the University of Tennessee, 1972. A thirty-one page compilation drawn mainly from periodical literature.
G1270

Gilbert, John F. Crossties Over Saluda. Raleigh: Crossties Press, 1971.
G1280

Gilbert, John F. ed. Crossties through Carolina. Raleigh: Helios Press, 1969.
G1290 (ASU LMC MHC)

Gilbert, Vernon Collis "Vegetation of the Grassy Balds of the Great Smoky Mountains." Master's thesis. Univ. of Tennessee, 1954.
G1300

Gilbert, William Harlan The Cherokees of North Carolina. Washington: Smithsonian Institution, Annual Report, 1956.
G1310

Gilbert, William Harlan, Jr. The Eastern Cherokees. Univ. of Chicago, 1934. Smithsonian Institution, Bureau of American Ethnology Anthropoligical Papers no. 23. Ph. D. Diss. Washington, D. C.: GPO, 1943.
G1320

Gilbreath, Allie Lou Felton ed. Research in the Language Arts at East Tennessee State College. Sponsored by the Research Council and the Graduate School. 1 vol. Johnson City: East Tennessee State College Press, 1962.
G1330 (ETSU)

Giles, Albert William The Geology and Coal Resources of Dickenson County, Virginia. Virginia Geological Survey Bulletin, no. 21. Charlottesville: Univ. of Virginia, 1921.
G1340 (ETSU)
The Geology and Coal Resources of the Coal-bearing Portion of Lee County, Virginia. Prepared in cooperation with the U. S. Geological Survey. With a chapter on the forests of Lee County, Virginia, by Harry Lee Baker. Prepared in cooperation with the Office of State Forester, Virginia Geological Survey Bulletin, no. 26. Charlottesville: Univ. of Virginia Press, 1925.
G1350 (LMC ETSU)

Giles, Henry E. Around Our House. Boston: Houghton Mifflin, 1971. Memoirs of family life in the home of these Appalachian novelists.
G1360 (BC)
Harbin's Ridge. Boston: Houghton Mifflin, 1951. Two well-drawn characters, sons legitimate and illegitimate, make this a warm and sensitive novel of mountain life.
G1370 (BC ASU WCU LMC WWC)
A Little Better Than Plumb: The Biography of a House. Illustrated by Pansy Wilcoxson Phillips. Boston: Houghton Mifflin, 1963. A tale of life in the home of two Appalachian families.
G1380 (BC ASU ETSU)

Giles, Jack McCormick "Small Mammals of Washington and Unicoi Counties, Tennessee." Master's thesis. East Tennessee State Univ., 1969.
G1390 (ETSU)

Giles, Janice Holt Giles, Henry E. A Little Better Than Plumb: The Biography of a House. Boston: Houghton Mifflin, 1963.
G1380 (BC ASU ETSU)
40 Acres and No Mule. Philadelphia: Westminster Press, 1952. Autobiographical novel of life in the Kentucky hills.
G1400 (ETSU BC)
40 Acres and No Mule. 2nd ed., with a new prologue by the author. Boston: Houghton Mifflin, 1967.
G1410 (ASU WWC)
The Believers. Boston: Houghton Mifflin, 1957. Novel set in Eastern Kentucky's ridge country.
G1420 (BC ASU WCU ETSU)
The Enduring Hills. Philadelphia: Westminster Press, 1950. This was Miss Giles first novel. It is autobiographical in that the main character, Hod, is brought home to the hills by his outland wife, Mary who knows he'll never be happy away from the mountains.
G1430 (BC ASU WCU LMC WWC)
The Enduring Hills. 2nd ed., new foreword by the author. Boston: Houghton Mifflin, 1971.
G1440 (WCU)
The Great Adventure: A Novel. Boston: Houghton Mifflin, 1966. Fiction with a mountain setting. Reflects the pioneering spirit accurately.
G1450 (BC ASU ETSU)
Hannah Fowler. Boston: Houghton Mifflin, 1956. Hannah is an Eastern Kentucky heroine with surprising resources.
G1460 (ASU WCU ETSU BC)
The Kentuckians. Boston: Houghton Mifflin, 1953. Novel of pioneer life in Eastern Kentucky.
G1470 (BC ASU WCU MHC LMC)
The Land Beyond the Mountains. Boston: Houghton Mifflin, 1958. Another of Miss Giles' well-crafted stories with Kentucky mountain characters.
G1480 (BC ASU WCU)
Miss Willie. Philadelphia: Westminster Press, 1951. Mary Pierce's Aunt Willie comes to the Kentucky mountains to teach school and mix her flatland culture with that of her mountain students.
G1490 (BC)
Miss Willie. Chicago: Peoples Book Club, 1951.
G1500 (BC WWC)
Miss Willie. Greenwich, Conn.: Fawcett Crest Book, 1972.
G1510 (LMC)
The Plum Thicket. Boston: Houghton-Mifflin, 1954. Tales from the Plum Grove hills.
G1520
Run Me a River. Boston: Houghton Mifflin, 1964. More Kentucky mountain fiction from the prolific Miss Giles.
G1530 (BC ASU ETSU)
Savanna. Boston: Houghton Mifflin, 1961. A surprising mountain heroine brings this book to life.
G1540 (ASU BC WCU)
Shady Grove: A Novel. Boston: Houghton Mifflin, 1968. This novel of frontier Kentucky in the Break Neck area takes its title, appropriately enough, from an old mountain fiddle tune.
G1550 (ASU BC WCU LMC MHC ETSU)
Six-Horse Hitch: A Novel. Boston: Houghton Mifflin, 1969. A folksy sort of novel from the Plum Thicket area of Kentucky.
G1560 (ASU BC)
Tara's Healing. Philadelphia: Westminster Press, 1951.
G1570 (ASU WWC BC)
Tara's Healing. Philadelphia: Westminster Press, 1952. Hood's old army buddy broken in spirit comes to the mountains for a cure and saves the community from an epidemic.
G1580

Gilfillan, Harriett Woodbridge I Went to Pit College. New York: Literary Guild, 1934. Autobiography of college life in the strife-torn Pittsburgh of the 1930's.
G1590

Gilham, William Manual of Instruction for the Volunteers and Militia of the Confederate States. Richmond: West & Johnston, 1861.
G1600 (LMC)

Gill, George Creswell Beyond the Bluegrass; A Kentucky Novel. New York: Neale Pub. Co., 1908. Novel of a land company and the coming of a railroad in eastern Kentucky. Much praise for mountain folk.
G1610

Gill, L. S. Baxter, Dow Vawter Deterioration of Chestnut in the Southern Appalachians. Washington: U. S. Department of Agriculture, Bureau of Plant Industry, 1931.
B2130

Gillenwater, Mack H. "Cultural and Historical Geography of Mining Settlements in the Pocahontas Coal Fields of Southern West Virginia, 1880 to 1930." Ph. D. Diss. Univ. of Tennessee, 1972.
G1620

Gillespie, William H. A Compilation of the Edible Wild Plants of W. Va. N. Y.: Scholar's Library, 1959. Yes, you can live off the land and this book even makes it all sound appealing.
G1630
A Guide to the Common Fossils Plants of W. Va. Morganton, W. Va.: Geological and Economic Survey. Educational Series, 1960.
G1640
Plant Fossils of West Virginia. Revised edition. Educational Series. 1960. Reprint. (Original title: A Guide to the Common Fossil Plants of West Virginia.) Morgantown: West Virginia Geological and Economic Survey, 1966.
G1650 (BC ETSU)
West Virginia Geology, Archaeology, and Pedology: A Bibliography and Index. Archaeological references compiled by Edward V. McMichael. Soils references compiled by Willem A. van Eck. West Virginia Univ. Bulletin. Morgantown: West Virginia Univ. Library, 1964.
G1660 (BC ETSU)

Gillett, Mary Bugles at the Border. Illustrated by Bruce Tucker. Winston-Salem, N. C.: J. F. Blair, 1968. Revolutionary War novel about a North Carolina boy who participates in the Battle of King's Mountain.
G1670 (ASU WCU BC)

Gilman, Caroline The Poetry of Traveling in the United States. With additional sketches by a few friends. And a week among autographs by Rev. S. Gilman. New York: Coleman, 1838. Section II includes many Appalachian sketches.
G1680 (LMC BC)

Gilman, Glenn Human Relations in the Industrial Southeast, a Study of the Textile Industry. Chapel Hill: Univ. of North Carolina Press, 1956. Many of the textile plants are located in the foothill country and draw their cheap labor from the mountains.
G1690 (BC)

Gilmer, George Rockingham Sketches of Some of the First Settlers of Upper Georgia, of the Cherokees, and the Author. 1926. Reprint. With an added index. Baltimore: Genealogical Pub. Co., 1965.
G1700 (ASU BC LMC)
Sketches of Some of the First Settlers of Upper Georgia, of the Cherokees, and the Author. 1926. Reprint. With an added index. Baltimore: Genealogical Pub. Co., 1970.
G1710 (ETSU)

Gilmer, Gertrude Cordelia Checklist of Southern Periodicals to 1861. Useful Reference Series, no. 49. Boston: F. W. Faxon Co., 1934.
G1720 (LMC)

Gilmore, James Roberts The Advance-Guard of Western Civilization. New York: F. M. Hill, 1888. Biography of James Robertson, land-speculation and common wealth builder, arch-rival of Sevier.
G1730

Among the Pines: Or, South in Secession-time. Detroit: Negro History Press, 1862.
G1740 (WCU MHC)

John Sevier as a Commonwealth-builder. A Sequel to The Rear-guard of the Revolution. New York: D. Appleton & Co., 1887. Biography of Sevier and the history of the State of Franklin.
G1750 (ASU WCU LMC BC)

A Mountain-White Heroine. New York and Chicago: Belford, Clarke and Co., 1889. Romantic fiction with a mountain setting complete with violence, moonshine, feuds and mountain laurel.
G1760

My Southern Friends. New York: Carlton, 1868. Scant reference to the mountains.
G1770 (BC WCU)

On the Border. Boston: Lee & Shepard, 1867. A tale of Indians and colonists engaged in disputes along the Appalachian frontier.
G1780 (ASU WCU BC)

The Rear-guard of the Revolution. New York: D. Appleton & Co., 1886.
G1790 (BC LMC)

Gilpatrick, Delbert Harold Jeffersonian Democracy in North Carolina, 1789-1816. Studies in History, Economics and Public Law, no. 344. New York: Columbia Univ. Press, 1931.
G1800 (LMC)

Gilpin, Pete Bascom Lamar Lunsford, "Minstrel of the Appalachians." His Ballads and His Folk Songs, His Mountain Square Dancing. Ashevillle, N. C.: Stephens Press, 1966. Mr. Lunsford's work in preserving the heritage of the mountains was invaluable. All of us will miss him.
G1810 (ASU UNCA WCU LMC WWC MHC)

Gilreath, Ed Traditional Pottery in North Carolina. Waynesville, N. C.: Mountaineer, 1974. The aim of this publication is to offer samples of some of the finest pottery -past and present-made in the state. . . intended only as a sampler; not a complete pictorial survey.
G1820

Ginger, Ray Six Days or Forever? Tennessee v. John Thomas Scopes. Boston: Beacon Press, 1958. An account of the 1925 legal circus at Dayton.
G1830 (ASU BC)

Giovanni, Nikki Gemini. n.p.: n.p., n.d. An autobiography picturing life in Knoxville and Nashville.
G1840

Gist, Clayton S. The Litter Arthropod Community in a Southern Appalachian Hardwood Forest: Numbers, Biomass and Mineral Element Content. Logan, Utah: Utah State Univ. Ecology Center, 1973. This study was conducted in the Nantahalas.
G1850

Gitlin, Todd Uptown: Poor Whites in Chicago. 1st ed. New York: Harper & Row, 1970. Two white writers who helped organize JOIN discuss the problems of the mountaineer in the cities.
G1860 (ASU BC)

Gittings, John G. West Virginia Lyrics. Morgantown: Acme Pub. Co., 1902.
G1870 (ASU)

Giuseppi, Montague Spencer ed. Naturalizations of Foreign Protestants in the American and West Indian Colonies, (Pursuant to Statute 13 George 2, c. 7). 1921. Reprint. Baltimore: Genealogical Pub. Co., 1969.
G1880 (ASU)

Givan, Francis P. "Indian Affairs in the Southern Department, 1763-1785." Master's thesis. Univ. of Louisville, 1956.
G1890

Givens, Charles G. All Cats Are Gray. Indianapolis: Bobbs-Merrill Co., 1937. A well-written tale about a young East Tennessee lawyer and an old unsolved mystery.
G1900 (BC ASU LMC)

The Devil Takes a Hill Town. Indianapolis: Bobbs-Merrill Co., 1939. A fantasy about a self-made preacher and his encounter with God. They decide government money has ruined the local people and God floods the valley washing everyone to Glory, only to find that the WPA has already set up offices.
G1910 (ASU BC)

The Doctor's Pills Are Stardust. Indianapolis: Bobbs-Merrill Co., 1938. A well-written tale of a dying town in the coal and iron region of East Tennessee. The local doctor tries to find a way to save the town.
G1920 (ASU BC)

Givens, Dorothy Hall A Givens-Hall Family History from Pre-Revolutionary Times to 1970. . . Radford, Va.: Commonwealth Press, 1971. Although most of the volume is on Givens and Hall families, several allied branches are given in some detail. Covers mostly Giles-Pulaski areas.
G1930

Givens, Larry Kenneth "Annexation: A Case Study of Supporting and Opposing Factions in Johnson City, Tennessee." Master's thesis. East Tennessee State Univ., 1971.
G1940 (ETSU)

Givhan, Mercer A. "Factors Contributing to the Educational Development of the Negro Schools in the Jefferson County (Alabama) School System, 1945-51." Master's thesis. Alabama State College, 1952.
G1950

Gladden, Sanford Charles The Durst and Darst Families of America, with Discussions of Some Forty Related Families. Boulder, Colo.: Johnson Pub. Co., 1969. Many families of Pulaski County.
G1960

Glasgow, Ellen Anderson Gholson Barren Ground. New York: Doubleday, Page and Co., 1925.
G1970

Barren Ground. Garden City, N. Y.: Doubleday, Doran & Co., 1926. A sensitive novel of a strange and lovely girl in the Knob Hill country of Kentucky.
G1980 (MHC)

Barren Ground. 1933. Reprint. American Century Series, 5-14. New York: Sagamore Press, 1957.
G1990 (ASU)

The Battle-ground. New York: Doubleday, Page & Co., 1902. A novel of rugged life in the Appalachians. Battles rage and peace is rare and precious.
G2000 (ETSU)

The Battle-ground. New York: Doubleday, Page & Co., 1903.
G2010 (ASU)

Vein of Iron. 1st ed. New York: Harcourt, Brace & Co., 1935. Another Glasgow novel about the descendants of Appalachian pioneers.
G2020 (ASU MHC ETSU)

Glasgow, Maude The Scotch-Irish in Northern Ireland and in the American Colonies. New York: G. P. Putnam's Sons, 1936.
G2030 (ASU)

Glass, Daniel "A Study of the Causes of Drop-outs and Irregular Attendance among Boys in the Four Negro High Schools of Talledega County, Alabama." Master's thesis. Tuskegee Institute, 1953.
G2040

Glass, Janet H. A Regional Economic Study of Cameron County, Pennsylvania. Institute for Research on Land and Water Resources Research Publication, 53. University Park: Pennsylvania State Univ., 1967.
G2050 (ASU)

Glass, Paul Songs of Hill and Mountain Folk, Ballads, Historical Songs, Folk Songs. Arranged for voice and piano with guitar chords. Simplified instructions on styling and strumming and chart of basic guitar chords. New York: Grosset & Dunlap, 1967.
G2060 (BC ASU)

Glassie, Henry Leach, MacEdward A Guide for Collectors of Oral Traditions. n.p.: Penn. Historical and Museum Commission, 1968.
L1150

Glassie, Henry H. Folksongs and Their Makers. Bowling Green, Ohio: Bowling Green Univ., Popular Press, 1970.
G2070 (ASU MHC BC)

Pattern in the Material Folk Culture of the Eastern United States. Monographs in Folklore and Folklife, no. 1. Philadelphia: Univ. of Pennsylvania Press, 1969. The classic work on artisans and material.
G2080 (ASU BC WCU LMC FC)

Glazner, John Frank Geography of the Great Appalachian Valley of Alabama. Jacksonville, Ala.: n.p., 1938.
G2090 (BC ASU)

Gleeson, Patrick Language and Culture. Columbus, Ohio: E. C. Merrill, 1968. Contains an excellent article on mountain speech by Cratis D. Williams.
G2100 (ASU BC)

Gleeson, Paul comp. Archaeological Investigations in the Tellico Reservoir: Interim Report, 1970. Contributions by Howard Earnest and others. Knoxville: Univ. of Tennessee, Department of Anthropology, 1971.
G2110 (ASU ETSU)

Glenn, Alfonso Greer "A Survey of Public Education in Watauga County, North Carolina." Master's thesis. Univ. of North Carolina, 1932.
G2120 (ASU)

Glenn, Leonidas Chalmers Ashley, George Hall Geology and Mineral Resources of Part of the Cumberland Gap Coal Field, Kentucky. Washington: Govt. Print. Off., 1906.
A5240 (ASU)

Denudation and Erosion in the Southern Appalachian Region and the Monongehela Basin. U. S. Geological Survey Professional Paper, no. 72. Washington: Govt. Print. Off., 1911.
G2130 (ASU ETSU)

The Northern Tennessee Coal Field. Nashville: n.p., 1925.
G2140 (ETSU)

Glenn, Max E. ed. Appalachia in Transition. St. Louis: Bethany Press, 1970. The twelve chapters were prepared by people familiar with the region's problems and hopeful for its future.
G2150 (ASU WCU LMC MHC ETSU FC BC)

Glenn, Thomas Allen Merion in the Welsh Tract, With Sketches of the Townships of Haverford and Padner. Historical and genealogical collections concerning the Welsh Barony in the Province of Pennsylvania, settled by the Cymric Quakers in 1682. 1896. Reprint. Baltimore: Genealogical Pub. Co., 1970.
G2170 (ASU)

Welsh Founders of Pennsylvania. 1911-1913. Reprint. Baltimore: Genealogical Pub. Co., 1970.
G2180 (ASU)

Glenn, Thomas Allen comp. AList of Some American Genealogies Which Have Been Printed in Book Form. 1897. Reprint. Baltimore: Genealogical Pub. Co., 1969.
G2160 (ASU)

Globetti, Gerald Development and Application of a Level-of-living Scale for White, Open Country Families, Both Farm and Non-farm in the Southeast. Sociology and Rural Life Series, no. 16. State College: Mississippi State Univ. Agricultural Experiment Station, 1966. Study includes Appalachian counties.
G2190

Glover, Julia Lestarjette Unto the Hills. Columbus, Ohio: Wartburg Press, 1941.
G2200 (ASU)

Glover, Lynn Stratigraphy and Uranium Content of the Chattanooga Shale in Northeastern Alabama, Northwestern Georgia, and Eastern Tennessee. U. S. Geological Survey Bulletin, no. 1087-E. Contributions to the Geology of Uranium, 1958. Washington: Govt. Print. Off., 1959.
G2210

Gobbel, Luther Lafayette Church-state Relationships in Education in North Carolina since 1776. Durham, N. C.: Duke Univ. Press, 1938.
G2220 (LMC)

Godsey, Edwin Cabin Fever. Chapel Hill: Univ. of North Carolina Press, 1967. Thirty-two poems written with versatility of form and moods.
G2230

Godshalk, Rolfe F. ed. Newport. Newport: Cliftan Club, 1970.
G2240

Goerch, Carl comp. Down Home. 1st ed. Raleigh: Edwards & Broughton Co., 1943. Memoirs of a North Carolina childhood. Some references to the mountains.
G2250 (ASU)

Goff, Mrs. Jessie A History of the First Methodist Church. Keyser, W. Va.: The church, 1963.
G2260

Goff, Kenneth James "An Investigation of the Factors Causing Absenteeism at Blountville High School." Master's thesis. East Tennessee State College, 1957.
G2270 (ETSU)

Gohdes, C. B. The Lily of Carlisle: a Story of the Days of Cromwell and Blake. The Parson of the S. Fork; a Story of W. Va. Hills. Columbus, O. Lutheran BK Concern, 1913. Two books bound together. The second has an Appalachian setting.
G2280

Goho, Curtis D. Characteristics of Factory-grade Hardwood Logs Delivered to Appalachian Sawmills. U. S. Forest Service Research Paper, NE-166. Upper Darby, Pa.: Northeastern Forest Experiment Station, 1970.
G2290

Goke, A. E. Obenshain, S. S. Soil Survey, Russell County, Virginia. Washington: U. S. Department of Agriculture, Bureau of Plant Industry, Soils, and Agricultural Engineering, 1945.
O100 (BC)

Goke, Alvin William Soil Survey of Mercer County, West Virginia. In cooperation with the West Virginia Geological Survey. Soil Survey Report, Series 1923, no. 9. Washington: U. S. Department of Agriculture, Bureau of Chemistry and Soils, 1928.
G2300

Golatz, Helmut J. Readings in Pennsylvania Economic Growth. University Park: Pennsylvania State Univ., Center for Continuing Liberal Education, 1965.
G2310

Gold, Charles Edward "A Study of the Gospel Song." Microfilm. Master's thesis. Univ. of Southern California, 1953.
G2320 (WCU)

Gold, Thomas Daniel History of Clarke County, Virginia, and Its Connection with the War between the States, with Illustrations of Colonial Homes and of Confederate Officers. Sketches by H. C. Sommerville and others. Indexed edition. Berryville, Va.: Chesapeake Book Co., 1962.
G2330 (BC ASU LMC)

Gold, W. D. The County of Smith. 1903. Reprint. Livingston: n.p., 1968. Newspaper articles made into a scrapbook.
G2340

Golden, Charles Edward "A Survey of the Causes of Absences in the Public School System of White County and Sparta, Tennessee." Master's thesis. George Peabody College for Teachers, 1954.
G2350

Goldfarb, Larry S. Perkins, Edward L. Guidelines for an Appalachian Airport System. Washington: Appalachian Regional Commission, 1967.
P2050 (ASU WCU)

Goldstein, Kenneth S. A Guide for Field Workers in Folklore. Preface by Hamish Henderson. Hatboro, Pa.: Folklore Associates, 1964. A useful tool for oral history interviewers.
G2360 (BC ASU)

Two Penny Ballads and Four Dollar Whiskey: A Pennsylvania Folklore Miscellany. Published for the Pennsylvania Folklore Society. Hatboro, Pa.: Folklore Associates, 1966.
G2370

Goldston, E. F. Robinson, Glenn Hugh Soil Survey, Avery County, North Carolina. Washington: U. S. Soil Conservation Service, 1955.
R3290

Goldston, Eugene Frizzell Davis, William Anderson Soil Survey, Stokes County, North Carolina. Washington: U. S. Department of Agriculture, Bureau of Plant Industry, 1940.
D1260 (ASU)

Davis, William Anderson Soil Survey of Surry County, North Carolina. Washington: U. S. Department of Agriculture, Bureau of Chemistry and Soils, 1937.
D1270

Devereux, Robert Eddins Soil Survey of Macon County, North Carolina. Washington: U. S. Department of Agriculture, Bureau of Chemistry and Soils, 1933.
D1970

Soil Survey, Graham County, North Carolina. Rev. by G. H. Robinson and R. C. Jurney. U. S. Soil Conservation Service, Soil Survey Report, Series 1942, no. 1. Washington: Govt. Print. Off., 1953.
G2390

Soil Survey, Jackson County, North Carolina. In cooperation with the North Carolina Agricultural Experiment Station and the Tennessee Valley Authority. Soil Survey Report, Series 1938, no. 19. Washington: U. S. Bureau of Plant Industry, Soils, and Agricultural Engineering, 1948.
G2410

Soil Survey, Macon County, North Carolina. Rev. by R. C. Jurney. U. S. Soil Conservation Service, Soil Survey, Series 1944, no. 6. Washington: Govt. Print. Off., 1956.
G2420

Soil Survey, Madison County, North Carolina. In cooperation with the North Carolina Department of Agriculture, North Carolina Agricultural Experiment Station and the Tennessee Valley Authority. Soil Survey Report, Series 1936, no. 19. Washington: U. S. Department of Agriculture, Bureau of Plant Industry, 1942.
G2430

Perkins, Samuel Oscar Soil Survey, Clay County, North Carolina. Washington: U. S. Department of Agriculture, Bureau of Plant Industry, 1941.
P2080

Perkins, Samuel Oscar Soil Survey, Henderson County, North Carolina. Washington: U. S. Department of Agriculture, Bureau of Plant Industry, Soils, and Agricultural Engineering, 1943.
P2100

Perkins, Samuel Oscar Soil Survey, Transylvania County, North Carolina. Washington: U. S. Department of Agriculture, Bureau of Plant Industry, Soils, and Agricultural Engineering, 1948.
P2130

Goldston, Eugene Frizzell and others Soil Survey, Buncombe County, North Carolina. U. S. Soil Conservation Service, Soil Survey, Series 1942, no. 6. Washington: Govt. Print. Off., 1954.
G2380

Soil Survey, Haywood County, North Carolina. Rev. by R. C. Jurney. U. S. Soil Conservation Service, Soil Survey, Series 1940, no. 11. Washington: Govt. Print. Off., 1954.
G2400

Goldthwaite, Eaton D. ed. Giles County, 1806-1956. Typescript. Pearisburg, Va.: Giles County Chamber of Commerce, 1956. A brief history of Giles County, Virginia, gives accounts of the churches, schools, industries, newspapers and public utilities.
G2440

Goldthwaite, Eaton K. ed. Friend, Robert C. and others Giles County, 1806-1956, a Brief History. Pearisburg, Va.: Giles County Chamber of Commerce, n.d.
F3350

Gomme, George Laurence Ethnology in Folklore. Modern Science Series. New York: D. Appleton and Co., 1892.
G2450 (ASU)

Gooch, Ernest D. Changes in the Market Movement of Kentucky Livestock. Lexington: Kentucky Agricultural Experiment Station, 1960.
G2460

Good, Daniel B. "Industrial Parks in East Tennessee: Characteristics and Effectiveness in Attracting Manufacturing." Ph. D. Diss. University of Tennessee, 1973.
G2470

Good, Paul The American Serfs. New York: Ballantine Books, 1968. Sub-title: A Report on poverty in the rural South. Explains the failure of the war on poverty in Appalachia and other parts of the rural South.
G2480 (ASU)

The American Serfs. New York: Putnam, 1968.
G2490 (WCU)

Goodale, Dora Read Mountain Dooryards. Illustrated by Mary Rogers. 2d ed. Berea, Ky.: Council of the Southern Mountains, 1961.
G2500 (ASU LMC MHC BC)

Goode, James B. The Whistel and the Wind. 1st ed. Frankfore, Ky.: Whippoorwill Press, 1972. Poetry, mostly about Harlan County, Kentucky.
G2510 (ASU LMC MHC BC)

Goodlett, John C. Hack, John Tilton Geomorphology and Forest Ecology of the Mountain Region in the Central Appalachians. Washington: Govt. Print. Off., 1960.
H90

Goodlett, Mildred W. The History of Travelors Rest. n.p.: The author, 1966. History of a South Carolina Community.
G2520 (ASU)

Goodman, K. V. Roberts, Wallace Soil Survey, Hamilton County, Tennessee. Washington: U. S. Department of Agriculture, Bureau of Plant Industry, Soils, and Agricultural Engineering, 1947.
R3100

Goodman, Kenneth Veryl Soil Survey, Potter County Pennsylvania. U. S. Soil Conservation Service Soil Survey, Series 1953, no. 2. Washington: Govt. Print. Off., 1958.
G2530

Hendrickson, Bertram Higbie Soil Survey of Tioga County, Pennsylvania. Washington: U. S. Department of Agriculture, Bureau of Chemistry and Soils, 1934.
H4610

Hendrickson, Bertram Higbie Soil Survey of Wyoming County, Pennsylvania. Washington: U. S. Department of Agriculture, Bureau of Chemistry and Soils, 1934.
H4620

Goodman, Leonard H. The Economic Needs of Neighborhood Youth Corps Enrollees. Final Report. Submitted to the U. S. Office of Manpower Research. Washington: Bureau of Social Science Research, 1969.
G2540

Goodman, William M. The First Exposition of Conservation and its Builders; an Official History of the National Conservation Exposition, Held at Knoxville, Tenn. in 1913 and of its Forerunner, the Appalachian Expositions of 1910-1911, Embracing a Review of the Conservation Movement in the U. S. from its Inception the Present Time. Knoxville: Press of Knoxville Lithographing Co., 1914.
G2550

Goodman, William M.
Souvenir History of Knoxville. Knoxville: Knoxville Engraving Co., 1908.
G2560 (BC)

Goodman, William M. ed. Souvenir History of Knoxville, the Marble City and Great Jobbing Market. Its Importance as a Manufacturing Center. . . . Knoxville: Knoxville Engr., 1907.
G2570

Goodpasture, Albert V. Life of Jefferson Dillard Goodpasture with Genealogy of the Family of James Goodpasture by his Sons. Nashville, Tenn.: Cumberland Presbyterian Publishing House, 1897.
G2580

Overton County Address of Albert V. Goodpasture Delivered at Livingston, Tennessee, July 4, 1876. Nashville: Cumberland Presbyterian Pub. House, 1877.
G2590

Overton County Address of Albert V. Goodpasture Delivered at Livingston, Tennessee, July 4, 1876. 1877. Reprint. Nashville: B. C. Goodpasture, 1954.
G2600

Goodpasture, W. H. Goodpasture, Albert V. Life of Jefferson Dillard Goodpasture with Genealogy of the Family of James Goodpasture by his Sons. Nashville, Tenn.: Cumberland Presbyterian Publishing House, 1897.
G2580

Goodrich, Frances Louisa Mountain Homespun. Amasa Stone Mother Memorial Publication Fund. New Haven: Yale Univ. Press, 1931. A classic work on weaving, with patterns and instructions.
G2610 (ASU WCU LMC MHC ETSU BC WWC)

Goodspeed's History of Tennessee: Containing Historical and Biographical Sketches of Thirty East Tennessee Counties 1887. Reprint. Nashville: C. and R. Elder Booksellers, 1972.
G2620 (ASU BC)

Goodwin, John R. Twenty Feet from Glory: From the Land of Ford to the Land of Canaan. Illustrated by O. D. Hagedorn. Morgantown, W. Va.: n.p., 1970. An account of a disastrous balloon accident in West Virginia.
G2630 (ASU BC)

Goodwin, Maud Wilder The Colonial Cavalier: Or, Southern Life Before the Revolution. Illustrated by Harry Edwards. New York: Lovell, Coryell and Co., 1894. Scant reference to the mountain country.
G2640 (LMC)

Goolrick, John T. Fredericksburg, Virginia. Its Homes and History, the Battlefields and the Rappahanrock Valley. Fredericksburg: J. A. Brown, 1934.
G2650

Gordon, Armistead Churchill In the Picturesque Shenandoah Valley. Introduction by Phillip Alexander Bruce. Richmond: Garrett and Massie, 1930.
G2660 (ASU BC)

Men and Events: Chapters of Virginia History. Staunton, Va.: McClure Co., 1923.
G2670 (LMC)

Gordon, C. H. Marble Deposits of East Tennessee: Occurrence and Distribution. Constitution and adaptations of the Holston marbles by T. N. Dale. Technology of marble quarrying by Oliver Bowles. Bulletin, no. 28. Nashville: Division of Geology, 1924.
G2680 (LMC)

Gordon, Caroline The Forest of the South. New York: C. Scribner's Sons, 1945. A novel of mountain life in frontier Virginia.
G2690 (ASU BC WWC)

Green Centuries. New York: Charles Scribner's Sons, 1941. Fiction from the Virginia hills, beautifully written but outside the usual trend of Appalachian fiction.
G2700

Green Centuries. 1941. Reprint. New York: Cooper Square Pub., 1971. A novel dealing with the westward movement across the mountains from Virginia to Kentucky.
G2710 (WCU BC)

Gordon, George Jacob Intergovernment Relations in the Tennessee Valley. Master's thesis. Syracuse Univ.: n.p., 1971.
G2720

Gordon, Jan On Wandering Wheels, Through Roadside Camps from Maine to Georgia in an Old Sedan Car. New York: Dodd, Mead and Co., 1928. Describes camping experiences in the Appalachian mountains.
G2730

Gordon, Kenneth Frederick "Labor Market Adjustments in a Depressed Area." Ph. D. Diss. Univ. of Rochester, 1967. The area examined is Wilkes-Barre-Hazleton, Pennsylvania.
G2740

Gore, James Howard My Mother's Story. Philadelphia: Judson Press, 1923. Biography of Mrs. Sidney Sophia Gore and her childhood and later life in Appalachia.
G2750 (BC)

Gore, Nina L. "The Development of a Plan for Parent Education for the Speech Handicapped Children in Overton County, Tennessee." Master's thesis. Univ. of Tennessee, 1955.
G2760

Gorman, John Loyd Soil Survey, Berkeley County, West Virginia. Soil Survey, Series 1960, no. 30. Washington: U. S. Department of Agriculture, Soil Conservation Service, 1966.
G2770

Soil Survey, Jackson and Mason Counties, West Virginia. Fieldwork by James B. Rayburn and others. Soil Survey, Series 1957, no. 11. Washington: U. S. Department of Agriculture, Soil Conservation Service, 1961.
G2790

Soil Survey, Monroe County, West Virginia. Soil Survey, Series 1960, no. 23. Washington: U. S. Department of Agriculture, Soil Conservation Service, 1965.
G2800

Gorman, John Loyd and others Soil Survey, Greenbrier County, West Virginia. Prepared in cooperation with the West Virginia Agricultural Experiment Station. Washington: U. S. Soil Conservation Service, 1972.
G2780

Gorr, Robert Lathrop "An Analysis of the Tennessee Valley Authority." Master's thesis. Univ. of Iowa, 1936.
G2810

Gose, George B. The Groseclose Family History. typescript. n.p.: n.p., n.d.
G2820

Pioneers of the Virginia Bluegrass (And Their Descendants). Blacusburg, Va.: n.p., 1964. In addition to the Gose Family, includes Peery, Groseclose, Repass, Brown, and other Wythe County names.
G2830

Gott, John K. History of Long Branch Baptist Church, Faquier County, Virginia. Richmond: Williams Print. Co., 1967.
G2840

Gott, John Kenneth comp. Chappelear, Nancy comp. Early Fauquier County, Virginia, Marriage Bonds, 1759-1854. Washington, D. C.: The authors, 1965.
C3250 (ASU)

Gottlieb, David Adolescent Behavior in Urban Areas: A Bibliographic Review and Discussion of the Literature. New York: Free Press of Glencoe, 1963. Includes references to Appalachian migrant children.
G2850

Understanding Children of Poverty. Foundation of Education Series. Chicago: Science Research Associates, 1967. Includes references to Appalachian children.
G2860 (WCU BC)

Gottman, Jean Virginia at Mid-century. New York: Henry Holt, 1955.
G2870 (FC BC)

Gottmann, Jean Virginia in our Century. Charlottesville: Univ. Press of Virginia, 1969.
G2880 (BC FC)

Gouin, Ellen Ammerman The Development Index for 60 Counties in Central Appalachia. Prepared for the Commission on Religion in Appalachia in cooperation with the Dept. of Agriculture. Univ. of Tenn. Knoxville: Commission on Religion in Appalachia, 1972.
G2890 (ASU BC)

Goulding, Francis Robert Sal-o-quah; or, Boy-life Among the Cherokees. Macon: J. W. Burlie and Co., 1870. A novel of a boy's adventures among the Cherokee.
G2900

. . . Sal-o-quah; or, Boy-life Among the Cherokees. Philadelphia: Claxton, Remsen and Haffelfinger, 1870. A novel of a boy's adventures among the Cherokees.
G2910

Govan, Christine West, Emmy Danger down River. New York: Viking Press, 1972.
W3010 (ASU LMC)

Govan, Christine Noble Rachel Jackson: Tennessee Girl. 1st ed. Indianapolis: Bobbs-Merrill Co., 1955.
G2920 (BC LMC ETSU)

Sweet Opossum Valley. Illustrated by Manning de V. Lee. Boston: Houghton Mifflin Co., 1940. An overly-cute mountain story with a too trite plot.
G2930 (ASU WWC BC)

Those Plummer Children. Boston: Houghton Mifflin Co., 1934. Children's fiction with a mountain setting.
G2940 (ETSU)

Govan, Gilbert Eaton The Chattanooga Country, 1540-1951: From Tomahawks to TVA. 1st ed. New York: Dutton, 1952. A history of the development of Chattanooga and the surrounding area.
G2950 (ASU LMC MHC ETSU BC)

The Chattanooga Country, 1540-1962: From Tomahawks to TVA. Revised ed. Chapel Hill: Univ. of North Carolina Press, 1963.
G2960 (WCU)

The University of Chattanooga: Sixty Years. Chattanooga: Univ. of Chattanooga, 1947. An excellent history of the formative years of the university.
G2970 (ASU WCU ETSU BC)

Governor's Conference on Appalachian Development, Asheville-Biltmore College, 1968. Proceedings. Compiled by State Planning Task Force, Division of the North Carolina Dept. of Administration. Raleigh, 1968.
G2980 (ASU BC)

Gowen, Emmett Dark Moon of March. Indianapolis: Bobbs-Merrill Co., 1933. A dreary tale of a tenant farmer who leaves the mountains, becomes a moonshiner, gets caught, serves time and returns to the hills and an uncertain future.
G2990 (ASU BC)

Mountain Born. Indianapolis: Bobbs-Merrill Co., 1930. A fiddler named Fate courts a lass called Nearer My God to Thee.
G3000 (WWC BC ASU)

Mountain Born. Indianapolis: Bobbs-Merrill Co., 1932.
G3010 (ASU)

Old Hell. Illustrated by Howard Simon. Blue Seal Books, no. 4.
G3020 (ASU WCU BC)

Old Hell. New Yorn Age, 1938. The author draws a distinction between the poor-whites of this novel and the usual sturdy mountain people of his fiction.
G3030

Gowing, Mary C. Virginia Beyond the Blue Ridge; a Pictorial Survey of Western Virginia. Va.: Commonwealth Press, 1974.
G3040 (ASU)

Gracie, Archibald The Truth about Chickamauga. Boston: Houghton Mifflin Co., 1911. A controversial account of the battle of Chickamauga.
G3050 (ASU)

Grady, James T. ed. and comp. The City of Knoxville, Tennessee and Vicinity and Their Resources. Knoxville: Knoxville Bd. of Trade, 1906.
G3060

Grady, Jamie Ault Bowens of Virginia and Tennessee; Descendants of John Bowen and Lily McIlhaney. Knoxville, Tenn.: n.p., 1969.
G3070

Tombstone Inscriptions and Death Records, Calvary. Macedonia Cemetery, Knoxville, Tennessee, 1851-1967. Baptismal Records, 1846-1870, Immaculate Conception Church, Knoxville, Tennessee. Knoxville: n.p., 1969.
G3080 (ETSU)

Graebner, William Sievers "Coal Mining Safety: National Solutions in the Progressive Period." Ph. D. Diss. Univ. of Illinois, Urbana-Champaign, 1970.
G3090

Graf, LeRoy P. ed. The Papers of Andrew Johnson. 3 vols. to date. Knoxville: Univ. of Tennessee Press, 1967-. Vol. 1 (1967), 1822-51; vol. 2 (1970), 1852-57; vol. 3 (1972), 1858-60. The First 3 volumes of a projected 10 volume series bring Johnson from the obscurity of his tailor shop to the verge of national attention as a Southerner defending the Union.
G3100

Grafton, A. Edwin A Manual of West Virginia's Wood-using Industries, with Directory. Bulletin Series 66, no. 3-1. Morgantown: Office of Research and Development, Center for Appalachian Studies and Development, West Virginia Univ., 1965.
G3110 (ASU)

Graham County Centennial, 1872-1972 Robbinsville: Hilton Business Equipment Co., 1972.
G3120 (ASU LMC)

Graham, James Robert The Planting of the Presbyterian Church in Northern Virginia, Prior to the Organization of Winchester Presbytery, December 4, 1794. Winchester, Va.: George F. Norton Pub. Co., 1904.
G3130 (ASU BC LMC)

Graham, Margaret Collier Stories of the Foot-hills. 1895. Reprint. Freeport, N. Y.: Books for Libraries Pres, 1969.
G3140 (ASU)

Graham, Paul H. Horn, Allen F. Opportunities for Forest-Based Industries in Pennsylvania: A Manual for the Development of Pennsylvania's Wood Using Industries. Washington: U. S. Area Development Administration, 1965.
H7160

Graham, William Franklin The Faith of Billy Graham. Introduction by Cort. R. Flint. 1st ed. Anderson, S. C.: Droke House, 1968.
G3150 (WCU)

The Quotable Billy Graham. 1st ed. Anderson, S. C.: Droke House, 1966.
G3160 (WCU)

Grainger County, Tenn., 1830 Census n.p.: n.p., n.d. Census statistics for Grainger County, Tennessee.
G3170

Gramley, Dale I. A Study of Water Pollution Control in the Textile Industry of North Carolina. Water Resources Research Institute Report, no. 21. Chapel Hill: Univ. of North Carolina, 1970.
G3180 (LMC)

Grammer, Norma Rutledge Marriage Record of Washington County, Tennessee, 1787-1840. n.p.: n.p., n.d.
G3190 (ETSU)

Marriage Records of Washington County, Tennessee, 1787-1840. Baltimore: Genealogical Print. Co., 1975.
G3200 (ASU)

Grandview Student Body Association Old Grandview: Grandview Normal Institute, Grandview, Tennessee, 1884-1919: A History. Grandview: The Assoc., 1966.
G3210

Grant, Anne Mae Vicar Essays on the Superstitions of the Higlanders of Scotland. Norwood, Pa.: Norwood Editions, 1973. Many of the same superstitions are found in Appalachia today.
G3220

Grant, Henry Lee Grant's West Virginia Illustrated. Oakland, Md.: Grant, 1901. Fifty illustrations of scenic beauty, natural resources and industry.
G3230

Grant, Howard B. The Presbyterian Church at Philippi, West Virginia. n.p.: n.p., n.d.
G3240

Grant, Isabel Frances Highland Folk Ways. London: Routledge and Paul, 1961. The same practices are still common in Appalachia today.
G3250 (ASU)

Grant, John L. "Behavioral Premises in the Culture of Conservative Eastern Cherokee Indians." Master's thesis. Univ. of North Carolina, 1957.
G3260 (ASU)

Grant, Willard Huntington Field Excursion: Stone Mountain — Lithonia District. Geological Society of America Southeastern Section Guidebook, no. 2. Atlanta: Georgia Department of Mines, Mining and Geology, 1962.
G3270 (ETSU)

Grasett, K. Complete Guide to Hand Spinning, Teasing, Carding, Spinning. Illustrated. London: London School of Weaving, 195-.
G3280 (ASU)

Graton, L. C. Reconnaissance of Some Gold and Tin Deposits of the Southern Appalachians. With notes on the Dahlonega Mines b by Waldemar Lindgren. U. S. Geological Survey Bulletin, no. 293. Washington: Govt. Print. Off., 1906.
G3290

Gravatt, George Flippo Chestnut Blight in the Southern Appalachians. Circular, 370. Washington: U. S. Department of Agriculture, Bureau of Plant Industry, 1926.
G3300

Graves, James Robinson The Great Iron Wheel: Or, Republicanism Backwards and Christianity Reversed. In a series of letters addressed to J. Soule, senior bishop of the M. F. Church, South. 9th ed. Nashville: Graves, Marks and Rutland, 1855.
G3310 (ASU)

Gray, A. J. The Tennessee River Valley; a Case Study. Washington, D. C.: Housing and Home Finance Agency, 1960.
G3320

Gray, Adonis Lyle Brackeen, Leonard Geoffrey Soil Survey, Colbert County, Alabama. Washington: Govt. Print. Off., 1939.
B6130

Gray, Edna One Woman's Life. The Steppings of Faith. Edna Gray's Story. Atlanta: Franklin Print. and Pub. Co., 1898.
G3330 (ASU BC)

Gray, Ernest E. "An Assessment of Why Part-time Under-graduates Are Enrolled at the Kingsport University Center." Master's thesis. East Tennessee State Univ., 1973.
G3340 (ETSU)

Gray, Idyl Dial ed. Azure-lure, a Romance of the Mountains: Souvenir of Asheville and Western North Carolina. Asheville, N. C.: Advocate Pub. Co., 1924.
G3350 (ASU BC WCU LMC WWC UNCA)

Gray, John Thompson A Kentucky Chronicle. N. Y.: Neale Co., 1906. "Among the Virginia emigrants to the Falls, was Reginald Thornton, a stately, kindly gentleman of the old school." He established himself at Last Lands, a few miles from the Falls, and it is the life of his children, his grandchildren, their friends and enemies that makes up this chronicle which is "more than a romance, it is a wisdom book."
G3360

Gray, L. C. and others U. S. Dept. of Agriculture Economic and Social Problems and Conditions of the Southern Appalachians. Washington: Govt. Print. Off., 1935.
U2490

Gray, Lewis Cecil Economic and Social Problems and Conditions of the Southern Appalachians. U. S. Department of Agriculture, Miscellaneous Publication, no. 205. Washington: U. S. Govt. Print. Off., 1935.
G3370

History of Agriculture in the Southern United States to 1860. Assisted by Ester Katherine Thompson, with an introductory note by Henry Charles Taylor. 2 vols. Publication, no. 430. Also, Contributions to American Economic History, 7. Washington: Carnegie Institution of Washington, 1933.
G3380 (BC MHC)

Gray, Minnie Dills A History of Dillsboro, North Carolina. Asheville, N. C.: Stephens Press, 1959.
G3390 (WCU)

Gray, Randal Lockhart The Wonderful Shenandoah Valley. Staunton, Va.: R. L. Gray, 1932.
G3400

Gray, Robert The McGavock Family. A Genealogical History of James McGavock and His Descendants from 1760-1903. Richmond: W. E. Jones, 1903.
G3410 (ASU)

McGavock Family, a Genealogical History of James McGavock and his Descendants, 1760-1903. (first pub. 1903). Petersburg, Va.: Plummer Print. Co., 1961.
G3420

Great Smoky Mountains National Park Denver: Kistler Graphics, 1968.
G3440 (ASU)

The Great Smoky Mountains National Park, Tennessee and North Carolina Knoxville: Great Smoky Mtns. Pub., 1928.
G3450 (ASU)

Great Smoky Mountains Natural History Association Mountain Makin's in the Smokies: A Cookbook. Asheville, N. C.: Stephens Press, 1957.
G3430 (LMC)

Greater Knoxville Illustrated. A Glance at Her History, a Review of Her Commerce. . . Nashville: n.p., 1910.
G3460

Greater Western N. C. Association for 1913 "The Land of the Sky." Asheville: Inland Press, 1913. Promotional material in the Asheville area.
G3470

Greeley, William Buckout White Oak in the Southern Appalachians. Circular, 105. 1907. Reprint. Washington: U. S. Department of Agriculture, Forest Service, 1911.
G3480 (ASU)

Green, Archie Aunt Molly Jackson Memorial Issue. Excerpted from KENTUCKY FOLKLORE RECORD. Urbana: Univ. of Illinois, n.d.
G3490

Only a Miner: Studies in Recorded Coalmining Songs. Music in American Life. Urbana: Univ. of Illinois Press, 1972. A very erudite study, of the recorded songs from the coalfields.
G3500 (ASU LMC MHC WCU BC)

"Recorded American Coal Mining Songs." Ph. D. Diss. Univ. of Pennsylvania, 1969.
G3510

Green, Bennett Wood Word-book of Virginia Folk-speech. Richmond: W. E. Jones, 1899. The classic work of mountain speech and dialect.
G3520 (ASU LMC BC)

Word-book of Virginia Folk-speech. Richmond: Wm. Ellis Jones' Sons, 1912.
G3530 (ETSU)

Green, Charlotte Hilton Birds of the South: Permanent and Winter Birds Commonly Found in Gardens, Fields, and Woods. Chapel Hill: Univ. of North Carolina Press, 1933.
G3540 (ASU BC UNCA)

Trees of the South. Chapel Hill: Univ. of North Carolina Press, 1939.
G3550 (ASU BC)

Green, Clarence Jasper An Analysis of the Real Cost of TVA Power. Original and Supplemental Reports. Washington, D. C.: U. S. Chamber of Commerce, 1948.
G3560

Green, John P. comp. Abstracts of Deeds, Rutherford County, North Carolina, Volumes A-D. Dallas, Tex.: Family Heritage, 1968.
G3570

Green, John Webb Bench and Bar of Knox County, Tennessee. Knoxville: Archer and Smith, 1947.
G3580 (BC)

Green, Lewis W. And Scatter the Proud. Winston-Salem, N. C.: John F. Blair, 1969. Short stories and a novella centering around incidents along the Blue Ridge Parkway.
G3590 (ASU LMC WWC BC)

Green, Margaret Defender of the Constitution: Andrew Johnson. New York: Messner, 1962.
G3600

Green, Mary Honeysuckle Hill; a Hillbilly Makes the Grade. New York: Exposition Press, 1961. A shotgun wedding, conquest of big city society, a divorce and a return to the hills complete this trite plot.
G3610

Green, Nathan Sparks from a Blacklog. St. Louis: Cumberland Presbyterian Pub. House, 1891.
G3620

Green, Paul Wilderness Road; a Parable for Modern Times. New York: Samuel French, 1956.
G3630

Wilderness Road: A Symphonic Outdoor Drama. New York: French, 1956.
G3640 (WCU BC ASU)

Green, Raleigh Travers comp. Genealogical and Historical Notes on Culpepper County, Virginia. Embracing a rev. and enlarged ed. of Dr. Philip Slaughter's History of St. Mark's Parish. 1900. Reprint. Baltimore: Regional Pub. Co., 1964.
G3650 (ASU)

Green, Sylvia Patchwork for Beginners. New York: Watson-Guptill, 1972. Excellent instructions and illustrations.
G3660 (ASU)

Green, T. C. Taylor, Arthur Elijah Soil Survey of Adams County, Ohio. Washington: U. S. Department of Agriculture, Bureau of Chemistry and Soils, 1938.
T390

Green, Thomas Marshall Historic Families of Kentucky, with Special Reference to Stocks Immediately Derived from the Valley of Virginia. 1889. Reprint. Baltimore: Regional Pub. Co., 1964.
G3670 (ASU MHC BC)

Green, William F. "An Edited Collection of Beech Mountain Folksongs." Master's thesis. East Tennessee State Univ., 1968. Songs collected in Avery and Watauga Counties, North Carolina.
G3680 (ETSU)

Greenbrier County, 160th Anniversary, 1778-1938, Historical Booklet Charleston, W. Va.: n.p., 1938.
G3690

Greenbrier Historical Society The Journal of the Greenbrier Historical Society. Lewisburg, W. Va.: The society, 1968.
G3700 (ASU)

Greene, Carla I Want to Be Coal Miner. Illus. by Audrey Williamson. Chicago: Childrens Press, 1957.
G3710

Greene County Teacher's Workshop. May 28-June 1, 1951. Greenville, Tenn.: n.p., 1951.
G3720 (ETSU)

Greene, Earle R. and others Birds of Georgia: A Preliminary Check-list and Bibliography of Georgia Ornithology. With a historical narrative by Eugene E. Murphey. Georgia Ornithological Society Occasional Publication, no. 2. Athens: Univ. of Georgia Press, 1945.
G3730 (ASU)

Greene, Earle R. comp. Greene, Earle R. and others Birds of Georgia: A Preliminary Check-list and Bibliography of Georgia Ornithology. Athens: Univ. of Georgia Press, 1945.
G3730 (ASU)

Greene, Evarts Boutell Provinical America, 1690-1740. New York: Harper and Brothers, 1905. Includes material on the great Appalachian barrier.
G3740

Greene, Homer The Blind Brother: A Story of the Pennsylvania Coal Mines. New York: T. Y. Crowell and Co., 1887. A novel of the Pennsylvania mining country.
G3750 (ASU BC)

Coal and Coal Mines. N. Y.: Houghton, Mifflin, 1891.
G3760 (BC)

Coal and Coal Mines. Boston: Houghton Mifflin, 1928.
G3770 (ASU)

Greene, Ivery C. A Disastrous Flood, a True and Fascinating Story. Lenoir, N. C.: Smith Print. Co., 1964. An account of the 1940 flood in Watauga County, North Carolina.
G3780 (ASU LMC)

Greene, John W. Forgotten Trails. Erwin, Tenn.: Erwin Pub. Co., 1971. Stories of the Cherokee Indians in North Carolina and Tennessee.
G3790

Greene, Katherine Glass Winchester, Virginia, and Its Beginnings, 1743-1814: From Its Founding by Colonel James Wood to the Close of the Life of His Son, Brigadier General and Governor James Wood. With the Publication for the first Time of Valuable Manuscripts, relics of their long Tenure of Public offices. Strasburg, Va.: Shenandoah Pub. House, 1926.
G3800 (ASU BC)

Greene, Lee Seifert Government in Tennessee. 2d ed. Knoxville: Univ. of Tennessee Press, 1966.
G3810 (BC LMC)

Rescued Earth, a Study of the Public Administration of Natural Resources in Tennessee. Knoxville: Univ. of Tennessee Press, 1948.
G3820 (ASU LMC ETSU)

Greene, Nanci Lewis Nance; a Story of Kentucky Feuds. Chicago: F. T. Neely, 1893. Romance and feuds are closely interwoven in this novel of young lovers from opposing factions of bitter feud.
G3830

Greene, Wilhelmina F. Flowers of the South, Native and Exotic. Chapel Hill: Univ. of North Carolina Press, 1953.
G3840 (ASU BC)

Greenlee, J. A. When I Was a Boy. Charleston, W. Va.: Greenlee Brothers, 1963. Memoirs of a West Virginia childhood.
G3850 (ASU)

Greenslade, Rush V. "The Economic Effects of Collective Bargaining in Bituminous Coal Mining." Ph. D. Diss. Univ. of Chicago, 1953.
G3860

Greenville County, S. C. Community Council Greenville's Big Idea. Greenville, S. C.: The council, 1950.
G3870 (ETSU)

Greenway, John American Folksongs of Protest. Philadelphia: University of Penn. Press, 1953.
G3880

Greenwood, Elma L. How Churches Fight Poverty, 60 Successful Local Projects. New York: Friendship Press, 1968. Some of the cases studies are Appalachian Church groups.
G3890 (ASU LMC WCU)

Greer, Archie Foner, Philip Coal Creek Rebellion. Huntington, W. Va.: Appalachian Movement Press, Inc., 1973.
F1770 (ASU)

Greer, George Cabell Early Virginia Immigrants, 1623-1666. Baltimore: Genealogical Pub. Co., 1960.
G3900 (ASU FC)

Greer-Petrie, Cordia Angeline Doin' Society. Louisville: Angeline Pub. Co., 1923. A stereotypical mountain matron expresses amazement at the wonders of modern civilization and manages to make all mountaineers seem ridiculous.
G3910 (BC)

Angeline Hittin' on High. Louisville: Angeline Pub. Co., 1925. This one is siller than the last.
G3920 (BC)

Angeline of the Hill Country. Illustrated by Carle Michel Boog. New York: Thomas Y. Crowell Co., 1925. More stereotypical nonsense.
G3930 (ASU WCU BC)

Angeline Steppin' Out. Louisville: Angeline Pub. Co., 1923. More of Angeline's antics.
G3940 (BC)

Gregg, Margaret Clark, Michael J. Lazar and Boone Stop Strip Mining Bully to Save Apple Valley and Buttermilk Creek. Huntington, W. Va.: Appalachian Movement Press, Inc., 1973.
C4510 (ASU)

Gregg, Polly "Change in Attitude toward the Indian As the Frontier Line Advanced." Master's thesis. East Tennessee State Univ., 1954.
G3950

Gregg, Shelah F. "An Inservice Program to Promote the Use of the John S. Battle High School Media Center Based on a Study of Faculty Attitudes Toward the Use of Instructional Materials and the Media Services Rendered." Master's thesis. East Tennessee State Univ., 1973.
G3960 (ETSU)

Gregory, Horace ed. The Portable Sherwood Anderson. New York: The Viking Press, 1949. Includes material from his decade in Appalachia.
G3970

Gregory, Jack Cherokee Hymns. Fayetteville, Ark.: Indian Heritage Assoc., n.d.
G3980 (ASU)

Sam Houston with the Cherokees, 1829-1833. Austin: Univ. of Texas Press, 1967.
G3990 (ASU WCU MHC)

Gregory, Jack ed. Starr's History of the Cherokee Indians. Fayetteville, Ark.: Indian Heritage Assoc., 1967.
G4000 (BC ASU)

Starr, Emmet History of the Cherokee Indians. Fayetteville, Ark.: Indian Heritage Assoc., 1967.
S6670 (ASU BC ETSU WCU)

Gregory, Madeline T. "A Survey of Special Education Services in Washington, Carter and Sullivan Counties, Tennessee." Master's thesis. East Tennessee State College, 1955.
G4010

Gregory, Paul W. Abstract of Reddies River Church Membership. n.p.: n.p., n.d.
G4020

Grellet, Stephen Memoirs of the Life and Gospel Labours of Stephen Grellet. 2 vols. Philadelphia: H. Longstreth, 1860. Memoirs of a long ministry in Appalachia.
G4030 (ASU)

Greve, Jeanette S. The Story of Gatlinburg. Strasburg, Va.: Shenandoah Pub. House, 1931.
G4040

Grey, Katharine A Little Leaven. Philadelphia: Lippincott, 1922. Mountain lass marries out-lander but fails to adjust to his world. Many years later, when she has acquired education and fame, they are reunited.
G4050 (WCU ASU)

Grice, Darrell G. Soil Survey, Mercer County, Pennsylvania. Prepared in cooperation with the Pennsylvania State University Agricultural Experiment Station. Washington: U. S. Soil Conservation Service, 1971.
G4060

Grider, George Wrobel, Sylvia Isaac Shelby Kentucky's First Governor and Hero of Three Wars. Danville, Ky.: The Cumberland Press, 1974.
W9780

Gridley, Marion Eleanor ed. Indians of Today. 3rd ed. Chicago: n.p., 1960.
G4070 (MHC)

Grieve, W. G. Operations Guide for TVA Forest Nurseries. Norris, Tennessee: TVA, 1960.
G4080

Griffen, A. M. Soil Survey of Madison County, Kentucky. Field Operations, 1905. Washington: U. S. Bureau of Soils, 1907.
G4090

Soil Survey of Upshur County, West Virginia. Field Operations, 1905. Washington: U. S. Bureau of Soils, 1914.
G4100

Griffin, Clarence W. Centennial History of Pleasant Grove Methodist Church, 1838-1938. Forest City, N. C.: Pleasant Grove Centennial Committee, 1938.
G4110 (ASU BC)

Essays on North Carolina History. Forest City, N. C.: Forest City Courier, 1951. Includes commentary on western North Carolina.
G4120 (ASU LMC)

History of Old Tryon and Rutherford Counties, North Carolina, 1730-1936. Asheville, N. C.: Miller Print. Co., 1937.
G4130 (ASU BC WCU)

History of Rutherford County, 1937-1951. n.p.: Inland Press, 1952.
G4140 (WCU LMC BC)

Public Officials of Rutherford County, N. C. 1779-1934: With Introductory Sketches of Orgin and Development of Various County Offices, and Public and Local Laws Governing Same.
G4150 (ASU BC)

Revolutionary Service of Col. John Walker & Family and Memoirs of Hon. Felix Walker. Forest City, N. C.: Forest City Courier, 1930.
G4160 (BC)

Western North Carolina Sketches. Forest City, N. C.: Forest City Courier, 1941.
G4180 (ASU BC WCU LMC MHC)

Griffin, James Bennett ed. Archaeology of Eastern United States. Chicago: Univ. of Chicago Press, 1952.
G4190 (WCU)

Griffin, Richard W. Newspaper History of a Town: A History of Danville, Kentucky. Danville: Danville Advocate-Messenger and the Kentucky Advocate, 1965.
G4200 (ASU)

Griffin, Dr. Roscoe Report of a Workshop on the Southern Mountaineer in Cincinnati. Cincinnati, Ohio: The Cincinnati Human Relations Commission, 1971.
G4210 (ASU)

Griffin, William W. comp. Greene, Earle R. and others Birds of Georgia: A Preliminary Check-list and Bibliography of Georgia Ornithology. Athens: Univ. of Georgia Press, 1945.
G3730 (ASU)

Griffis, Robert J. Bristol-Kingsport Metropolitan Area Projections and Economic Base Analysis. Richmond, Va.: Division of Planning, 1967.
G4220

Griffith, Henrietta Mae "A History of Religious Education in the Kentucky Mountains." Master's thesis. Asbury Theological Seminary, 1950. There were many mission schools and missionaries in the Kentucky mountains.
G4230 (ASU)

Griffitts, W. R. Part 5, Shelby-Hickory District, North Carolina. Part 6, Outlying Deposits in North Carolina. Professional Paper 248-D. Washington: U. S. Geological Survey, Government Print. Office, 1953.
G4240

Grigsby, Shaw Earl Rural Social Organization of Frederick County, Maryland. College Park: Maryland Agricultural Experiment Station, 1949.
G4250

Grime, John Harvey Recollections of a Long Life. Lebanon: n.p., 1930.
G4260

Grimsley, George Perry Iron Ores, Salt and Sandstones. West Virginia Geological Survey Reports, vol. 4. Morgantown: Acme Pub. Co., 1909.
G4270 (ETSU)

Jefferson, Berkeley, and Morgan Counties. County Reports. Wheeling: West Virginia Geological Survey, 1916.
G4280 (ETSU)

Grindstaff, A. B. "A Survey of the Flowering Plants and Ferns on the Forge Hill, Carter County, Tennessee." Master's thesis. East Tennessee State College, 1956.
G4290 (ETSU)

Grindstaff, Dana R. "A Study of the Program of Vocational Rehabilitation in Carter County, Tennessee." Master's thesis. East Tennessee State College, 1953.
G4300

Grinnell, George Bird ed. Hunting and Conservation: The Book of the Boone and Crockett Club. New Haven, Conn.: Yale Univ. Press, 1925.
G4310 (ETSU)

Grisso, Robert D. Elements of Success in Marketing Appalachian Apples. Blacksburg: Virginia Agricultural Experiment Station, 1959.
G4320

Griswold, W. M. Descriptive List of Novels and Tales Dealing with American Country Life. Cambridge, Mass.: W. M. Griswold, 1890. Occasional references to Appalachia.
G4330

Griswold, W. T. Geology of Oil and Gas Fields in Steubenville, Burgettstown, and Claysville Quadrangles, Ohio, W. Va., and Pa. U. S. Geological Survey Bulletin, no. 318. Washington: Govt. Print. Off., 1907.
G4340

Grizzell, Mary Frances "A Historical Survey of Education in Warren County, Tennessee." Master's thesis. Tennessee Technological Univ., 1964.
G4360

Groene, Bertram H. Tracing your Civil War Ancestor. Winston-Salem, N. C.: J. F. Blair, 1973.
G4370 (ASU)

Gronseth, Elbert E. "The Reaction of Presbyterian Ministers in the Knoxville Area to Specific Questions Concerning Ministerial Counseling." Master's thesis. Univ. of Tennessee, 1961.
G4380

Groome, Harry Connelly Fauquier during the Proprietorship: A Chronicle of the Colonization and Organization of a Northern Neck County. 1927. Reprint. Baltimore: Regional Pub. Co., 1969.
G4390 (ASU)

Gross, Maxine Tipton "A Study of Special Classes for Educable Mentally Handicapped Children." Master's thesis. East Tennessee State Univ., 1969.
G4400 (ETSU)

Gross, Novice Hendrix "A Proposed Method of Instruction Based on the British Infant and Primary Schools for First and Second Year Students at East Side Elementary School." Master's thesis. East Tennessee State Univ., 1971.
G4410 (ETSU)

Gross, W. E. Mann, Charles J. Soil Survey of Bedford County, Pennsylvania. Washington: U. S. Dept. of Agriculture, Bureau of Soils, 1913.
M3130

Gross, William F. "A Study of Underachieving Academically Talented Students in a Knox County School." Master's thesis. Univ. of Tennessee, 1961.
G4420

Grosscup, Ben S. Zeigler, Wilbur Gleason The Heart of the Alleghanies: Or, Western North Carolina. Comprising Its Topography, History, Resources, People, Narratives, Incidents, and Pictures of Travel, Adventures in Hunting and Fishing and Legends of Its Wildernesses. Raleigh, N. C.: A. Williams and Co.; Cleveland: W. W. Williams, 1883.
Z40 (ASU LMC WCU BC ETSU)

Grosser, Charles F. Helping Youth: A Study of Six Community Organization Programs. JD Publication, 1006. Washington: U. S. Office of Juvenile Delinquency and Youth Development, Social and Rehabilitation Service, 1968. Study includes Appalachian communities.
G4430

Grossman, D. A. The Appalachian Region: A Preliminary Analysis of Economic and Population Trends in an Eleven State Problem Area. Atlanta: Council of State Governments, 1960.
G4440

Grove, J. G. This Is My Story. Commerce, Tex.: n.p., 1966.
G4450

Grove Park Inn In the Land of the Sky, Grove Park Inn. Asheville, N. C.: Grove Park Inn, n.d. Promotional material on the inn and the Asheville area.
G4460 (ASU)

Grover, N. C. The Floods of March, 1936, Part 3, Potomac, James, and Upper Ohio Rivers. With a section on the weather associated with the floods of March, 1936, by Stephen Lichtblau. U. S. Geological Survey Water-supply Paper, no. 800. Washington: Govt. Print. Off., 1937.
G4470

Floods of Ohio and Mississippi Rivers, January-February, 1937. With a section on the Flood deposits of the Ohio River, January-February, 1937, by G. R. Mansfield. U. S. Geological Survey Water-supply Paper, no. 838. Washington: Govt. Print. Off., 1938.
G4480

Surface Water Supply of the New-Kanawha River Basin, West Virginia, and North Carolina. U. S. Geological Survey Water-supply Paper, no. 536. Washington: Govt. Print. Off., 1925.
G4490

Grubb, Davis The Barefoot Man. New York: Simon & Schuster, 1971. A powerful novel of the West Virginia coalfields during the depression.
G4500 (ASU WCU MHC BC)

A Dream of Kings. New York: Scribners, 1955. A story of a young girl, Cathie and her "dream of kings.' Tom, the man who loves her joins the army in the Civil War, returns during the last weeks of defeat (this is in West Virginia) to find Cathie is still lost in her dream and he can not save her.
G4510 (LMC WWC BC ASU)

Fools' Parade. An NAL Book. New York: World Pub. Co., 1969. Powerful and dramatic novel set in the West Virginia mining country.
G4520 (ASU LMC)

The Night of the Hunter. 1st ed. New York: Harper, 1953. Classic story of good and evil told through the adventures of two Appalachian children.
G4530 (ASU WCU BC)

Shadow of My Brother. New York: Holt, Rinehart & Winston, 1966. A novel of racial violence set in the southern mountains.
G4540 (WCU BC ASU)

A Tree Full of Stars. New York: Scribner, 1965. Fiction with an Appalachian setting.
G4550

Twelve Tales of Suspense and the Supernatural. Greenwich, Conn.: Fawcett Pub., 1964. Short fiction with mountain settings and supernatural.
G4560 (LMC BC)

The Voices of Glory. New York: Scribner, 1962. More superb mountain fiction with a West Virginia setting.
G4570 (BC ASU WCU LMC)

The Watchman. N. Y.: Scribner, 1961. West Virginia fiction.
G4580

Grubb, Kenneth "A Study of Teacher and Parent Opinion of McMinn County High School, Athens, Tennessee." Master's thesis. Univ. of Tennessee, 1961.
G4590

Grubb, Robert G. Grice, Darrell G. Soil Survey, Mercer County, Pennsylvania. Washington: U. S. Soil Conservation Service, 1971.
G4060

Grubbs, David Harold "City-county Consolidation Attempts in Nashville and Knoxville, Tennessee." Ph. D. Diss. Univ. of Pennsylvania, 1961.
G4600

Guerrant, Edward Owings The Gatherers: The Gospel among the Highlanders. Richmond: Onward Press, 1910.
G4610 (ASU LMC)

The Gospel of the Lilies. Boston: Sherman Finch & Co., 1912.
G4620 (BC)

Guerrant, Grace Owings McAllister, James Gray Edward O. Guerrant: Apostle to the Southern Highlanders. Richmond: Richmond Press, 1950.
M40 (LMC BC ASU)

Guerry, Alexander Men and Vision: The Secret of Yesterday's Success, the Formula for Tomorrow's. A Brief History of the Chattanooga Medicine Company. N. Y.: Newcomen Society in North America, 1963.
G4630 (ETSU)

Guide to Gatlinburg: Authentic Information About Gatlinburg and the Great Smoky Mountains 1st ed., 1939. Gatlinburg, Tenn.: Gatlinburg News, annual.
G4640 (ASU)

Guide to the Appalachian Trail in Central and South-western Virginia 5th ed. n.p.: Appalachian Trail Conference, n.d.
G4650

Guide to the Appalachian Trail in Tennessee and North Carolina, Cherokee, Pisgah, and Great Smokies 1st ed. n.p.: Appalachian Trail Conference, n.d.
G4720

Guide to the Appalachian Trail in Tennessee and North Carolina, Cherokee, Pisgah, and Great Smokies 2nd ed. n.p.: Appalachian Trail Conference, n.d.
G4730

Guide to the Appalachian Trail in Tennessee and North Carolina, Cherokee, Pisgah, and Great Smokies 3rd ed. n.p.: Appalachian Trail Conference, n.d.
G4740

Guide to the Appalachian Trail in Tennessee and North Carolina, Cherokee, Pisgah, and Great Smokies 4th ed. n.p.: Appalachian Trail Conference, n.d.
G4750

Guide to the Appalachian Trail in the Great Smokies, the Nantahalas, and Georgia 1st ed. n.p.: Appalachian Trail Conference, n.d.
G4660

Guide to the Appalachian Trail in the Great Smokies, the Nantahalas, and Georgia 2nd ed. n.p.: Appalachian Trail Conference, n.d.
G4670

Guide to the Appalachian Trail in the Great Smokies, the Nantahalas, and Georgia 4th ed. n.p.: Appalachian Trail Conference, n.d.
G4680

Guide to the Appalachian Trail in the Southern Appalachians 2nd ed. n.p.: Appalachian Trail Conference, n.d.
G4690

Guide to the Appalachian Trail in the Southern Appalachians 3rd ed. n.p.: Appalachian Trail Conference, n.d.
G4700

Guide to the Appalachian Trail in the Southern Appalachians 4th ed. n.p.: Appalachian Trail Conference, n.d.
G4710

Guide to the Southern Appalachians. The Appalachian Trail from Virginia-Tennessee Line to Mt. Oglethorpe, Ga. n.p.: Appalachian Trail Conference, n.d.
G4760

Guidebook to Contrast in Style of Deformation of the Southern and Central Appalachians of Virginia Blacksburg: VPI Dept. of Geological Sciences, 1971.
G4770

Guidelines for Funding Appalachian Projects, Development Districts, and Research n.p.: Appalachian Regional Commission, n.d.
G4780

Guild, Josephus Conn Old Times in Tennessee, with Historical, Personal, and Political Scraps and Sketches. Nashville: Tavel, Eastman and Howell, 1878.
G4790 (ASU)

A Report on Coal Lands Lying in Bledsoe County. Nashville: n.p., 1887.
G4800

Guilday, John E. Biological and Archaeological Analysis of Bones from a 17th Century Indian Village (46 PU 31), Putnam County, West Virginia. Report of Archeological Investigations, no. 4. Morgantown: W. Va. Geological and Economic Survey, 1971.
G4810 (ASU)

Guines, Mary M. "An Identification of Social-personal Problems in Two Selected Junior High Schools: Implications for Guidance Services." Master's thesis. Univ. of Tenn., 1961.
G4820

Guinn, Lorraine Jones "Diversions in East Tennessee, 1920-25." Master's thesis. East Tennessee State Univ., 1966.
G4830 (ETSU)

Gulick, John Cherokees at the Crossroads. Institute for Research in Social Science Monographs. Chapel Hill: Univ. of North Carolina, 1960.
G4840 (ASU BC WCU LMC WWC ETSU)

Socio-cultural Adaptation of Newcomers to Cities in the Piedmont Industrial Crescent. With an appendix on social stratification in Greensboro. An Urban Studies Research Paper. Chapel Hill: Institute for Research in Social Science, Univ. of North Carolina, 1961. Includes Appalachian migrants.
G4850

Gulick, John ed. Symposium on Cherokee and Iroquois Culture, Washington, D. C., 1958 Papers. Washington: Govt. Print. Off., 1961.
S9770 (ETSU WCU BC)

Gullett, George Preble "A Study of Glass and Paper Recycling in Johnson City, Tennessee." Master's thesis. East Tennessee State Univ., 1972.
G4860 (ETSU)

Gullick, Guy A. Greenville County, Economic and Social. Bulletin 102. Columbia, S. C.: Univ. of S. C., 1921.
G4870

Greenville County, Economic and Social. Assisted by J. S. Meares and J. O. Williams. Bulletin, 102. Columbia: Univ. of South Carolina, 1921.
G4880

Gulliver, Lucile Daniel Boone. True Stories of Great Americans. New York: Macmillan Co., 1930.
G4890 (ASU BC)

Gummere, Francis Barton Old English Ballads. Boston: Ginn and Co., 1894.
G4900 (BC)

Gunther, John Story of TVA. New York: Harper and Brother, 1951.
G4910

The Story of TVA. New York: Harper, 1953. Pro-TVA propaganda.
G4920

Guppy, Henry Brougham Homes of Family Names in Great Britain. 1890. Reprint. Baltimore: Genealogical Pub. Co., 1968.
G4930 (ASU)

Gutheim, Frederick Albert The Potomac. Illustrated by Mitchell Jamieson. New York: Rinehart, 1949.
G4940 (FC)

Guthrie, Alfred Bertram, Jr. Big Sky. New York: Sloane, 1947. Review: Novel of the opening of the American West, during the years 1830 to 1843. It is the story of the primitive life of the frontier with its dirt savagery and Indians. The hero is Boone Caudill, a Kentucky boy, who tried to kill his vicious father, then stole his gun and set out for the West.
G4950 (WCU WWC BC)

The Blue Hen's Chick: A Life in Context. 1st ed. New York: McGraw-Hill, 1965.
G4960 (WCU)

Guthrie, Charles Snow Riddles from the Cumberland Valley. Introduction by William Hugh Jansen. Bowling Green: Kentucky Folklore Society, 1973.
G4970 (ASU)

Guthrie, Ellen Emma Old Scottish Customs, Local and General. London: Hamilton, Adams & Co., 1885.
G4980 (ASU)

Guthrie, Thomas F. "The Development of Education in Rhea County, Tennessee." Master's thesis. Univ. of Tennessee, 1961.
G4990

Guttmann, Allen ed. Filler, Louis The Removal of the Cherokee Nation: Manifest Destiny or National Dishonor? Boston: Heath, 1962.
F840 (WCU UNCA FC)

Guyot, Arnold Henry Measurements of Points in North Carolina and Tennessee. Aiken, S. C.: Schofield School Press, 1890.
G5000

Notes on the Geography of the Mountain District of Western North Carolina. Appalachian Trail Conference Publication no. 10. n.p.: The conference, 1938.
G5010

Gwathmey, John Hastings Historical Register of Virginians in the Revolution. Richmond, Va.: Dietz Press, 1938.
G5020 (ASU)

Twelve Virginia Counties Where Western Migration Began. Richmond, Va.: Dietz Press, 1937.
G5030

Haagen, Victor B. The Pictorial History of Huntsville, 1805-1865. Huntsville, Ala.: n.p., 1963. At this time Huntsville was just another sleepy southern town, and so it remained until Redstone Arsenal was installed.
H10 (BC)

Haas, Ben The Last Valley. New York: Simon & Schuster, 1966. Powerful story of North Carolina mountain family's fight against eminent domain, the state political machine, and a power company.
H20 (BC ASU LMC MHC)

Look Away, Look Away: A Novel. New York: Simon & Schuster, 1964. Tale of a North Carolina mountain dynasty.
H30 (ASU WCU)

Haas, Raymond M. An Analysis of Some Selected Characteristics of Cabin Vacationists in West Virginia State Parks and Forests in 1961. Morgantown: West Virginia Univ., Office of Research and Development of the West Virginia Center for Appalachian Studies and Development, 1963.
H40 (ASU)

Economic Impact of the Mountain State Art and Craft Fair, Ripley, West Virginia, 1964. Morgantown: West Virginia Univ. Bureau of Business Research, 1965.
H50

The Manufacture of Hardwood Dimension Stock in West Virginia, a Feasibility Study. Morgantown: Bureau of Business Research, West Virginia Univ., 1967.
H60 (ASU)

West Virginia Travel and Tourism Study — The Potential Market. Morgantown: W. Va. Univ., Bureau of Business Research, 1968.
H70

Schmidt, T. William West Virginia Travel and Tourism Study: An Evaluation. Morgantown: West Virginia Univ., Bureau of Business Research, 1965.
S960

Haber, Alan ed. Ferman, Louis A. ed. Poverty in America. Ann Arbor: Univ. of Michigan Press, 1965.
F690

Hack, John Tilton Geology of Luray Caverns, Virginia. Report of Investigations, 3. Charlottesville: Virginia Division of Mineral Resources, 1962.
H80 (ETSU FC)

Hack, John Tilton
Geomorphology and Forest Ecology of the Mountain Region in the Central Appalachians. Prepared in cooperation with Harvard Forest, Harvard University. U. S. Geological Survey Professional Paper, no. 347. Washington: Govt. Print. Off., 1960.
H90
Intrenched Meanders of the North Fork of the Shenandoah River, Virginia. U. S. Geological Survey Professional Paper, no. 35-A. Shorter Contributions to General Geology, 1959. Washington: Govt. Print. Off., 1959.
H100

Hackamack, Lawrence C. "Cooperation-conflict in Labor Management: A Study of Contrasting Cases (Women's Garment Industry and Bituminous Coal Industry)." Ph. D. Diss. Univ. of Iowa, 1956. Coal and textiles are the two largest industries in the Southern Appalachians.
H110

Hackensmith, Charles William Out of Time and Tide: The Evolution of Education in Kentucky (the Beginnings Through the 1930's). Lexington: Univ. of Kentucky, 1970. Includes accounts of some of the more bizarre educational innovations in the mountain missions.
H120 (ETSU)

Hacker, Stanley E. Early School Leavers in Kentucky. Lexington: Bureau of School Service, Univ. of Kentucky, 1953.
H130

Hackley, Woodford B. The Little Fork Rangers: A Sketch of Company "D," Fourth Virginia Cavalry. Richmond: Press of the Dietz Print. Co., 1927. This regiment saw action in several mountain campaigns.
H140 (ASU)

Haden, Ben Kingsport, Tennessee — a Modern American City Developed through Industry. Kingsport: Kingsport Rotary Club, 1963.
H150

Hadley, Jarvis B. Geology of the Eastern Great Smoky Mountains, North Carolina and Tennessee. Geological Survey Professional Paper, no. 349-B. Washington: Govt. Print. Off., 1963.
H160 (LMC ASU)
Preliminary Report on Corundum Deposits in the Buck Creek Peridotite, Clay County, North Carolina. U. S. Geological Survey Bulletin, no. 948-E. Strategic Minerals Investigations, 1945. Washington: Govt. Print. Off., 1949.
H170 (ASU)

Hadley, Jarvis B. ed. Studies of Appalachian Geology: Northern and Maritime New York: Interscience Publishers, 1968.
S8800 (ASU ETSU UNCA)

Hadley, Jarvis Bardwell King, Philip Burke Geology of the Great Smoky Mountains National Park, Tennessee and North Carolina. Washington: U. S. Department of the Interior Geological Survey, 1968.
K2450 (ETSU)

Hagan, Francis J. A Mountain Exile: The Story of a Kentucky Feud. Cincinnati: S. Rosenthal and Co., 1899. A flatlander wanders into mountain country, causes trouble but eventually finds peace.
H180

Hagan, Jane Gray The Story of Danville. New York: Stratford House, 1950. A history of Danville, Virginia.
H190 (ASU)

Hagenstein, Perry Reginald "The Location Decision for Primary Wood-using Industries in the Northern Appalachians." Ph. D. Diss. Univ. of Michigan, 1963.
H200
Location Decision for Wood-using Industries in Northern Appalachians. U. S. Forest Service Research Paper, NE-16. Upper Darby, Pa.: Northeastern Forest Experiment Station, 1964.
H210

Hagey, King Albert The Hagey Families in America and the Dulaney Family. Bristol, Tenn.: King Print. Co., 1951.
H220

Hagey, William Anderson Hagey, King Albert The Hagey Families in America and the Dulaney Family. Bristol, Tenn.: King Print. Co., 1951.
H220

Hagood, Beatrice S. "The Use of the Case Method in the Study of Juvenile Delinquency in Johnson City." Master's thesis. East Tennessee State Univ., 1964.
H230 (ETSU)

Hagood, Margaret J. "Mothers of the South: A Population Study of Native White Women of Childbearing Age of the Southeast." Ph. D. Diss. Univ. of North Carolina, 1938.
H240

Hagy, James W. Castle's Woods 1769-1799, Frontier Virginia Settlement. Master's thesis. East Tennessee State, 1966.
H250
Castle's Woods: Frontier Virginia Settlement, 1779-1799. Abingdon, Virginia: Washington County Technical School, 1967. This was the first and most important settlement in what is now Russell County.
H260

Hahn, George W. ed. The Catawba Soldier of the Civil War. A Sketch of Every Soldier from Catawba County, North Carolina, with the Photograph, Biographical Sketch, and Reminiscence of Many of Them, Together with a sketch of Catawba County from 1860 to 1911. Hickory, N. C.: Clay Print. Co., 1911. At this time Catawba included sections of mountain counties.
H270 (ASU)

Hahn, William P. "The Leisure Time Activities and Interests of the Boys of Spencer High School." Master's thesis. West Virginia Univ., 1939.
H280

Hailey, O. L. History of the Baptists of Tennessee. Microfilm. n.p.: n.p., n.d.
H290 (WCU)

Haille, Ann Byrne "History of the Development of Education prior to 1900 in Jackson County, Tennessee." Master's thesis. Tennessee Technological Univ., 1961.
H300

Haiman, Miecislaus Polish Pioneers of Virginia and Kentucky with Notes on Genealogy of the Sadowski Family. Chicago: Polish R. C. Union of America, 1937.
H310 (BC)

Halderman, Daisy Sherman History of Methodism in the South Branch Valley. Moorefield, W. Va.: n.p., 1950.
H320

Hale, Carl W. The Contributions of Local Subsidies to the Economic Development of West Virginia, 1956-1966. Economic Development Series, no. 12. Also, Bulletin, Series 69, no. 7-7. Morgantown: Bureau of Business Research, College of Commerce, and Office of Research and Development, West Virginia Center for Appalachian Studies and Development, West Virginia Univ., 1969.
H330 (ASU)

Hale, J. W. ed. Autobiography of "Old Claib Jones." Hazard, Ky.: Hazard Bk. Co., 1915. (Jones, James Claybourn) Autobiography of a famous Kentucky mountain man, a hunter and trapper and a man with a reputation for violence.
H370

Hale, John Peter Daniel Boone. Some Facts and Incidents Not Hitherto Published. His Ten or Twelve Years' Residence in Kanawha County, Near Charleston, West Virginia. Wheeling: L. Baker & Co., 188?
H340 (ASU BC)
Trans-Allegheny Pioneers. 2nd ed. Charleston, W. Va.: Kanawha Valley Pub. Co., 1931.
H350 (ASU)
Trans-Allegheny Pioneers. . . . 3rd ed. Raleigh, N. C.: Dorreth Print. Co., 1971.
H360 (ETSU)
Trans-Allegheny Pioneers: Historical Sketches of the First White Settlements West of the Alleghenies 1784 and After. Wonderful Experiences of Hardships and Heroism of Those Who First Braved the Dangers of the Inhospitable Wilderness, and the Savage Tribes That Then Inhabited It. Cincinnati: Graphic Press, 1886.
H380 (ASU BC)

Hale, Jonathan D. Champ Ferguson: A Sketch of the War in East Tennessee Detailing Some of the Awful Murders on the Border and Describing One of the Leading Spirits of the Rebellion. Cincinnati: n.p., 1862.
H390

Hale, Laura Virginia Four Valiant Years in the Lower Shenandoah Valley 1861-1865. Strasburg: Shenandoah Publishing House, 1968.
H400 (ASU)

Hale, Nathan Scott "A Nutrition Survey of Some Eleventh Grade Students in Washington County, Tennessee." Master's thesis. East Tennessee State College, 1957.
H410 (ETSU)

Hale, Peter M. comp. The Woods and Timbers of North Carolina. A compilation from the botanical and geological reports of Drs. Curtis, Emmons and Kerr; to which are added information obtained from the Census Bureau and accurate reports from the several counties. New York: E. J. Hale & Son, 1883.
H440 (ASU LMC)
Woods and Timbers of North Carolina. Raleigh, N. C.: The author, 1883. Extensive botanical notes and maps.
H450 (BC)

Hale, Peter M. ed. In the Coal and Iron Counties of North Carolina. Raleigh, N. C.: P. M. Hale; New York: E. J. Hale, 1883.
H420 (LMC WCU)
In the Coal and Iron Counties of North Carolina. New York: E. J. Hale & Son, 1883. Contains census and geological reports and sketches and maps of fifty-six counties.
H430 (BC ASU)

Hale, Wade H. "The Scope of Religious Education in the Secondary Schools of Greenville County, South Carolina." Master's thesis. Furman Univ., 1958.
H460

Hale, William Thomas The Backward Trail; Stories of the Indians and Tennessee Pioneers. Nashville, Tenn.: Cumberland Press, 1899.
H470
Early History of Warren County. McMinnville, Tenn.: Standard Print. Co., 1930.
H480 (ASU BC ETSU)
History of DeKalb County, Tennessee. Nashville: P. Hunter, 1915.
H490
History of DeKalb County, Tennessee. 1915. Reprint. McMinnville, Tenn.: Ben Lemond Press, 1969.
H500 (ASU BC)
True Stories of Jamestown and Its Environs. Nashville: Methodist Pub. House, 1907.
H510

Haley, Elliot Clarke and others An Economic and Social Survey of Warren County. Virginia County Survey Series, 26. Charlottesville: Univ. of Virginia, 1943.
H520 (ASU)

Haley, Nancy Marlene "Cry Aloud and Spare Not; the Formative Years of Brownlow's WHIG, 1839-1841." Master's thesis. Univ. of Tennessee, 1966.
H530

Halfacre, R. Gordon Carolina Landscape Plants. Raleigh, N. C.: Sparks, 1971.
H540 (LMC)

Halik, Constance "The Tennessee Valley Authority: An Examination of Its Historical Background and of Some of the Major Controversies in Which It Has Been Involved." Master's thesis. Univ. of Rochester, 1947.
H550

Hall, Arleen S. My Sunrise. Dallas: Rozat Pub. Co., 1957. Poems from the Southern muntains.
H560 (BC)

Hall, C. W. Three Score Years and Ten. Cincinnati: Elm Street Print. Co., 1884.
H570 (ETSU)

Hall, Carl Mitchell Jenny Wiley Country. Kingsport, Tenn.: Kingsport Press, 1972. Describes Kentucky's Jennie Wiley State Park.
H580

Hall, Carrie A. The Romance of the Patchwork Quilt in America: In Three Parts. Pt. I. History and Quilt Patches. Pt. II. Quilts and Quilting — Antique and Modern. Pt. III. Quilting and Quilt Designs, by Rose G. Kretsinger. Photographs by Mary Ellen Everhard. 1935. Reprint. New York: Bonanza Books, n.d.
H590 (ASU BC)

Hall, Clifton R. Andrew Johnson: Military Governor of Tennessee. Ph. D. Diss. Princeton Univ., 1914. An attempt to depict the personality of Andrew Johnson from 1862 to 1865. Hall views Johnson's experience in reconstructing his own state as good training for his work at the national level.
H600 (BC ASU)

Andrew Johnson: Military Governor of tennessee. Princeton: Princeton Univ. Press, 1916. An attempt to depict the personality of Andrew Johnson from 1862 to 1865. Hall views Johnson's experience in reconstructing his own state as good training for his work at the national level.
H610 (BC ASU)

Hall, Donald C. "Employer Reaction to Retraining in the Clarksburg, West Virginia Labor Market Area." Master's thesis. West Virginia Univ., 1964.
H620

Hall, Eliza Calvert see Obenchain, Eliza Caroline Calvert

Hall, Esther Greenacre The Here to Yonder Girl. New York: Macmillan Co., 1937. Tassie Tyler, a young girl in the Kentucky mountains, finds a way to get an education and make her dreams come true.
H630 (ASU BC)

Up Creek and Down Creek. Illustrated by Anna Parker Braune. New York: Junior Literary Guild & Random House, 1936. A collection of short stories about Kentucky mountain children.
H640 (WCU LMC BC)

Hall, Esther May "An Improved Language Arts Program for a Selected Third Grade at Thomas Jefferson School, Kingsport, Tennessee." Master's thesis. East Tennessee State College, 1961.
H650 (ETSU)

Hall, G. M. Ground Water in the Ordovician Rocks near Woodstock, Virginia. U. S. Geological Survey Water. Supply Paper, no. 596-C. Washington: Govt. Print. Off., 1928.
H660

Hall, Granville Davisson Daughter of the Elm. A Tale of Western Virginia Before the War. Chicago: Mayer and Miller, 1899. Romantic novel set in the Blue Ridge Mountains of Virginia.
H670

Daughter of the Elm: A Tale of Western Virginia before the War. Chicago: The author, 1907.
H680 (LMC BC)

Daughter of the Elm: A Tale of Western Virginia before the War. Chicago: Mayer & Miller, 1913.
H690 (ASU)

The Rending of Virginia; a History. Chicago: Mayer and Miller, 1901.
H700 (BC)

The Two Virginias: Gensis of Old and New; a Romance of American History; State Sovereignty, Phantom of a Stupendous Folly. Chicago: Mayer & Miller, 1915.
H710 (BC)

Hall, J. W. "Tales of the Mountains" A Complete Directory of the Eastern Kentucky Coalfields with Extracts from the Geological Reports, Forestry, Oil Development, Education, Superstitions, and Religion of the Mountains. Lexington: Hazard Book Co., 1922.
H730

Hall, J. W. ed. Autobiography of "Old Claib Jones." Lexington: Hazard Bk. Co., 1915. Autobiography of James Clayborn Jones famous Kentucky mountain man.
H720

Hall, James The Harpe's Head. Philadelphia: Key & Biddle, 1833. A Kentucky legend partially set in eastern Kentucky.
H740 (BC)

Tales of the Border. 1835. Reprint. Upper Saddle River, N. J.: Literature House, 1970. A collection of stories of frontier life in trans-Allegheny west.
H750 (WCU BC)

Hall, James Edmond The Diary of a Confederate Soldier: James E. Hall. Lewisburg, W. Va.: n.p., 1961. Diary of a West Virginia soldier who fought in several mountain campaigns.
H760 (ASU)

Hall, Joseph Sargent The Phonetics of Great Smoky Mountain Speech. American Speech, Reprints and Monographs, no. 4. New York: King's Crown Press, 1942.
G790 (ASU ETSU)

Mountain Speech in the Great Smokies. Washington: U. S. Govt. Print. Off., 1941.
H770 (BC)

The Phonetics of Great Smoky Mountain Speech. Ph. D. Diss. Columbia Univ., 1941.
H780

Smoky Mountain Folks and Their Lore. Asheville, N. C.: Great Smoky Mountains Natural History Assoc., 1960.
H810 (BC ASU WCU LMC MHC)

Smoky Mountain Folks and Their Lore. 1960. Reprint. Asheville, N. C.: Great Smoky Mountains Natural History Assoc., 1964.
H820 (ETSU)

Hall, Joseph Sargent ed. Sayings from Old Smoky, Some Traditional Phrases, Expressions, and Sentences Heard in the Great Smoky Mountains and Nearby Areas: An Introduction to a Southern Mountain Dialect. Asheville, N. C.: Cataloochee Press, 1972.
H800 (ASU BC LMC MHC)

Hall, Lester Ray "A Comparison of Special Characteristics of College Bound Seniors and Non-college Seniors from Virginia High School, Bristol, Virginia." Master's thesis. East Tennessee State Univ., 1966.
H830 (ETSU)

Hall, Louise Fortune A History of Damascus. Abingdon, Va.: The John Anderson Press, 1950. This is the story of one hundred and fifty-seven years of life in the town now known as Damascus. Early families were the Wrights, the Hands, the Rambos, the Larimers and the Wideners, descendants of whom are still living on Damascus lands.
H840

Hall, Mary Boilin' n Bakin' in Boogar Hollow. Lindale, Ga.: Country Originals, 1971.
H850 (BC ASU)

Hall, Maxy Reddick Leighton, Marshall Ora The Relation of the Southern Appalachian Mountains to the Development of Water Power. Washington: Govt. Print. Off., 1908.
L1660 (ASU BC)

Hall, Mitchel Johnson County, Kentucky: A History of the County, and Genealogy of Its People up to the Year 1927. 2 vols. Louisville, Ky.: Standard Press, 1928.
H860 (ASU BC)

Hall, Paul M. The Musical Million: A Study and Analysis of the Periodical Promoting Music Reading through Shape Notes in North America from 1870 to 1914. Ph. D. Diss. Catholic Univ., 1970.
H870 (WCU)

Hall, Rufus Clifford Preliminary Study of Forest Conditions in Tennessee. Nashville: McQuiddy Prrint. Co., 1910.
H880 (ETSU)

Hall, Samuel Carter The Book of British Ballads. London: Putnam, 1888.
H890 (BC)

Hall, Septimius Genealogy of Thomas Hall, His Children and Grandchildren. With added notes, pictures and documents on the Halls, Rogers, and other early settlers of Volga, Barbour County, West Virginia by Tasker H. Williams. Parsons, W. Va.: McClain Print. Co., 1967.
H900 (ASU)

Hall, William F. "A History of Carson-Newman College." Master's thesis. Microfilm. Univ. of Tennessee, 1956.
H910 (WCU)

Hall, William Logan Waning Hardwood Supply and the Appalachian Forests. Washington: U. S. Dept. of Agriculture, Forest Service Circular 116, 1907.
H920

Halley, Harry John "An Analysis and Evaluation of the OEO National Antipoverty Planning Process." D. B. A. Diss. George Washington Univ., 1971. The author seems genuinely surprised that the War on Poverty was lost in Appalachia.
H930

Halley, Robert A. Dr. Augustin Gattinger: The Pioneer Botanist of Tennessee. Nashville: Cumberland, 1904. Includes survey of Eastern Tennessee flora and fauna.
H940

Halliburton Services Development of an Economic/Environmental Plan for Dents Run Watershed, West Virginia. Washington: Appalachian Regional Commission, 1973.
H950 (ASU)

Halls, Lowell K. Atlas of Southern Forest Game. New Orleans: U. S. Southern Forest Experiment Station, 1971.
H960 (ASU)

Halperin, Bernard Seymour "Andrew Johnson, the Radicals, and the Negro, 1865-1866." Ph. D. Diss. Berkeley: Univ. of California, 1966.
H970

Halpert, Herbert ed. 1939 Cox, John Harrington comp. Traditional Ballads and Folk-songs Mainly from West Virginia. n.p.: American Folklore Society, 1964.
C8180 (ASU WCU ETSU BC)

Halsey, Don Peters Historic and Heroic Lynchburg. Lynchburg, Va.: J. P. Bell Co., 1935. A fascinating warmly-written history of one of western Virginia's more interesting cities.
H980 (ASU)

Halterman, Daisy Sherman History of Methodism in the South Branch Valley. Moorfield, W. Va.: n.p., 1950. With original poems and pen drawings by the author.
H990 (BC)

Ham, Tom Give Us This Valley. Chicago: Sears Readers Club, 1952. An account of a mountain family's struggle to win and hold a mountain valley.
H1000 (BC ASU)

Give Us This Valley. New York: Macmillan Co., 1952.
H1010

Hamby, Robert P. History of Meridian Baptist Church. Old Sevierville Pike, Knoxville, Tennessee: Church Directory and Church Roll in Celebration of the Seventy-sixth Anniversary. Knoxville: n.p., 1950.
H1020

Hamelman, Paul W. Prospects and Problems for the Manufacture of Laminated Timber in West Virginia. Morgantown: West Virginia Univ., 1964.
H1030

Hamer and Co. Associates Economy of Western North Carolina. Atlanta, Ga.: n.p., 1961.
H1040

Hamer, Philip M. Fort Loudoun on the Little Tennessee. Raleigh, N. C.: Edwards & Broughton, 1925. This historic fort will soon be flooded by the TVA.
H1050 (ASU)

Hamer, Philip M. ed. Tennessee, a History, 1673-1932. 4 vols. New York: American Historical Society, 1933.
H1060 (LMC)

Hamilton, Alice M. A Doctor's Pilgrimage. Harrogate: Cumberland Gap Hotel and Park, 1892.
H1070

Hamilton, Betsy, pseud. see Moore, Idora McClellan

Hamilton, C. H. Hay, Donald G. Acceptance of Voluntary Health Insurance in Four Rural Communities of Haywood County, North Carolina. Raleigh: North Carolina Agricultural Experiment Station, 1954.
H3790

Hamilton, C. Horace Perry, Josef H. 1980 Population Projections for North Carolina Counties, with 1950, 1960 and 1970 Population by Age Groups. Raleigh: North Carolina Division of Community Planning, 1964.
P2240

Hamilton, Charles ed. Cry of the Thunderbird: The American Indian's Own Story. New York: Macmillan, 1950.
H1080 (MHC)

Hamilton, Charles Horace Health and Health Services in the Southern Appalachians, a Source Book. Progress Report, RS-35. Raleigh: Southern Appalachian Studies and the North Carolina Agricultural Experiment Station, 1959.
H1090 (ASU ETSU)

Hamilton County, Tennessee. Public Schools The Hamilton County Course of Study. n.p.: n.p., 1926.
H1100 (ETSU)

Hamilton, Emory L. Frontier Forts along the Clinch, Powell and Holston. n.p.: Typescript, n.d.
H1130 (BC)

Hamilton, J. G. de Roulhac Party Politics in North Carolina, 1835-1960. James Sprunt Studies, vol. 15, no. 1-2. Chapel Hill: Univ. of North Carolina Press, 1916.
H1140 (LMC)

Hamilton, John Taylor History of the Moravian Church: The Renewed Unitas Fratrum, 1722-1957. (Original title: A History of the Church Known as the Moravian Church.) Maps drawn by Fred Bles. 1900. Reprint. Bethlehem, Pa.: Interprovincial Board of Christian Education Moravian Church in America, 1967.
H1150 (ASU)

Hamilton, Joseph G. de Roulhac Life of Andrew Johnson, Seventeenth President of the United States. Greenville: Brown, 1928, 1930.
H1160

Hamilton, Kate The Parson's Proxy. Boston: Houghton Mifflin & Co., 1896. Religion acquires some strange trappings on the Kentucky frontier. A young man devotes himself to God and finds unexpected aid and rewards.
H1170 (BC)

Hamilton, Kenneth G. ed. Records of the Moravians in North Carolina. Raleigh: State Dept. of Archives and History, 1969.
H1180 (ASU)

Hamilton, Kenneth Gardiner Hamilton, John Taylor History of the Moravian Church: The Renewed Unitas Fratrum, 1722-1957. Bethlehem, Pa.: Interprovincial Board of Christian Education Moravian Church in America, 1967.
H1150 (ASU)

Hamilton, Lillian Opal Zeb Harkins. New York: Vantage, 1952. Schoolteacher Zeb takes rapidly to the mountains' charms including moonshine, friendly folk and a sweetheart.
H1190

Hamilton, Michael Ministry to the Southern Mountaineer. A Report of the Research Work Done by the Church of the Advent in the Neighborhood of Walnut Hills, Cincinnati, Ohio, from August, 1955, to August, 1958. Cincinnati: n.p., 1958. (Processed).
H1200

Hamilton, Sally W. ed. Our County Origins. n.p.: n.p., 1940.
H1210 (FC)

Hamilton, Warren Geology of the Richardson Cove and Jones Cove Quadrangles, Tennessee. U. S. Geological Survey Professional Paper, 349-A. Washington: Govt. Print. Off., 1961.
H1220 (LMC)

Hamilton-Edwards, Gerald K. In Search of British Ancestry. 3rd ed. Baltimore: Genealogical Pub. Co., 1974.
H1110

In Search of Scottish Ancestry Baltimore: Genealogical Pub. Co., 1974.
H1120 (ASU)

Hamlett, James Clifton "Long-lots in Washington County, Tennessee, with Reference to Past and Present Land-holding Shapes." Master's thesis. East Tennessee State College, 1962.
H1230 (ETSU)

Hamlin, Charles Hughes They Went Thataway. 3 vol. in one. Baltimore: Genealogical Pub. Co., 1974. Designed to assist researchers in the difficult problem of finding the area from which or into which the ancestor moved.
H1240

Virginia Ancestors and Adventurers. Richmond, Va.: n.p., 1967. This new collection of genealogical vignettes derives from predominantly miscellaneous records and documents.
H1250

Hamm, Kathleen Appalachian Regional Commission Appalachia — An Economic Report: Trends in Employment, Income and Population. Supplement. Washington: Govt. Print. Off., 1973.
A3590 (ASU)

Hammer and Company Associates The Economy of Metropolitan Knoxville. A Study Focused on the Economic Base and Potentials of Knoxville and Knox County. Washington, D.C.: Metro. Planning Comm. of Knoxville and Knox County, 1962.
H1260 (ETSU)

The Economy of Western North Carolina. Prepared for the WNC Regional Planning Commission, August 25, 1961. Atlanta: The Co., 1961.
H1270 (LMC UNCA)

Hammer, Greene, Siler Associates Investment Guidelines for the North Carolina Appalachian Region. Prepared for State of North Carolina, N. C. Dept. of Administration and Appalachian Regional Commission. Washington: n.p., 1967.
H1280 (WCU WWC ASU)

Investment Guidelines for the North Carolina Appalachian Region. Prepared for the State of North Carolina, North Carolina Department of Administration and Appalachia Regional Commission. Washington: n.p., 1967.
H1290 (WWC)

Manpower Education in the North Carolina Appalachian Region. Prepared for State Planning Task Force, Department of Administration, Raleigh, North Carolina. Washington: n.p., 1968.
H1300 (ASU WWC LMC)

Manpower Education in the North Carolina Appalachian Region. Prepared for North Carolina Planning Task Force Dept. of Administration. Washington: The company, 1968.
H1310 (LMC ASU WWC)

Manpower Education in the North Carolina Appalachian Region. Atlanta: State Planning Task Force, 1971.
H1320 (ASU)

Hammill, Anne Natural Resource Special Districts in Appalachia: Review of Enabling Laws. U. S. Department of Agriculture Economic Service Series, 444. Washington: Govt. Print. Off., 1970.
H1330

Hammond, Harriot Milton Aunt Bet, the Story of a Long Life: A Memoir of Elizabeth S. W. Taylor. Biographical sketch of Miss Hammond and an appendix by Anne Middleton Holmes. 2nd ed. Winchester, Va.: Handley Library, 1927.
H1340 (ASU BC LMC)

Hamner, Earl, Jr. Fifty Roads to Town, a Novel. New York: Random House, 1953. Fictional account of a young boy's growing up years in the Blue Ridge mountains of Virginia and an encounter with a traveling preacher.
H1350 (ASU BC)

The Homecoming: A Novel about Spencer's Mountain. 1st ed. New York: Random House, 1970. A Christmas novel about Hamner's youth in Virginia.
H1360 (BC FC ASU LMC WWC ETSU)

Spencer's Mountain. New York: Dial Press, 1961. A novel of a Blue Ridge family who yearn for education for their children.
H1370 (BC ASU WWC)

Hampton, Ann M. "Proposed Curriculum for Sequential Concept Development in Language Arts for Upper East Tennessee Exemplary Kindergarten Project." Master's thesis. East Tennessee State Univ., 1971.
H1380 (ETSU)

Hamrick, George R. ed. History of First Baptist Church of Shelby, North Carolina. Shelby: The Church, 1969.
H1390

Hamrick, Hubert Founding in America of the Hamrick (Hamerick) Family by Hans George Hamerick in the Year 1731 at the Port of Philadelphia, Pa. n.p.: The author, n.d.
H1400 (ASU)

Hamsley, Bob Morrison, John The Real David Crockett: A Short, Authentic, Illustrated, History of Tennessee's Famous Hunter, Frontiersman, Soldier, Legislator, Statesman, Patriot, and Hero of the Alamo, Colonel David Crockett. Lawrenceburg: n.p., 1955.
M7930

Hancock County, Tennessee. Comprehensive Overall Economic Development Program Association Report. n.p.: The assoc., 1963.
H1410 (ETSU)

Hancock, Mrs. Floyd ed. Ryan, Arthur Frank ed. Historical Forts and Houses in Knoxville and Nearby Vicinity. Knoxville: Knox Co. Libr., 1962.
R4450

Hancock, Harry L. "A Study of School Transportation, Bradley County, Tennessee." Master's thesis. Univ. of Tennessee, 1953.
H1420

Hancock, Mary A. Menace on the Mountain. Illustrated by H. Tom Hall. Philadelphia: Macrae Smith, 1968. A novel about union sympathizers in western North Carolina during the Civil War.
H1430 (BC ASU LMC WCU)

Hanczaryk, Edwin W. The Labor Force in West Virginia — A Study of Its Growth and Characteristics. ("Business and Economic Studies," vol. 3, no. 4.) Morgantown: West Virginia Univ., 1954.
H1440

Hand, Wayland D. American Folk Legend. Berkeley: Univ. of California Press, 1971.
H1450

Hanes, Frank Borden Abel Anders. New York: Farrar, Straus & Young, 1951. A mountain epic in verse.
H1460 (BC)

Hanes, John K. Powell, Jules V. Costs of Marketing Appalachian Apples. Washington: Agricultural Marketing Service, Marketing Research Division, 1959.
P3950

Haney, Glenn P. Silvical Characteristics of Southern Red Oak. U. S. Forest Service Station Paper, no. 106. Asheville, N. C.: Southeastern Forest Experiment Station, 1959.
H1480 (WCU)

Haney, Glenn P. comp. A Revised Shortleaf Pine Bibliography. U. S. Forest Service Station Paper, no. 155. Asheville, N. C.: Southeastern Forest Experiment Station, 1962.
H1470 (WCU)

Haney, William Henry The Mountain People of Kentucky. An Account of Present Conditions with the Attitude of the People toward Improvement. Cincinnati: Rossler Brothers, 1906.
H1490 (ASU BC)

Hankins, Thomas D. Berry, Brian J. L. A Bibliographic Guide to the Economic Regions of the United States. Chicago: Univ. of Chicago, 1963.
B3210

Hanlon, Russell W. Men of Affairs in Knoxville. Knoxville: Journal & Tribune, 1921. Publication of Who's Who in Knoxville.
H1500

Hanna, Charles Augustus Ohio Valley Genealogies, Relating Chiefly to Families in Harrison, Belmont and Jefferson Counties, Ohio, and Washington, Westmoreland, and Fayette Counties, Pennsylvania. 1900. Reprint. Baltimore: Genealogical Pub. Co., 1972.
H1510 (ASU BC)

The Scotch-Irish: Or, the Scot in North Britain, North Ireland, and North America. 2 vols. New York: G. P. Putnam's Sons, 1902.
H1520 (ASU BC)

The Scotch-Irish: Or, The Scot in North Britain, North Ireland, and North America. 2 vols. 1902. Reprint. Baltimore: Genealogical Pub. Co., 1968.
H1530 (ASU BC)

The Wilderness Trail: Or, The Ventures and Adventures of the Pennsylvania Traders on the Allegheny Path, with Some New Annals of the Old West, and the Records of Some Strong Men and Some Bad Ones. With eighty maps and illustrations. 2 vols. New York: G. P. Putnam's Sons, 1911.
H1540 (ASU BC)

Hanna, Edwin B. The Integration of Locality Groups in an Eastern Kentucky County. (Bulletin no. 640.) Lexington: Kentucky Agricultural Experiment Station, Univ. of Kentucky, 1956.
H1550

Hanna, Margaret "Drain of Talent out of Georgia and South Carolina." Master's thesis. Kent State Univ., 1957. Includes surveys of mountain counties in both states.
H1560 (ASU)

Hannah, David Hardgrave Archaeological Excavations on Virginius Island, Harpers Ferry National Historic Park, 1966-1968. Prepared for the U. S. National Park Service. Harpers Ferry: Harpers Ferry Job Corps Civilian Conservation Center, 1969.
H1570

Hannah, Howard M. Confederate Action in Franklin County, Tennessee. Sewanee: Franklin Co. Civil War Centennial Comm., 1963.
H1580

Hannum, Alberta Pierson The Gods and One. 1st ed. New York: Duel, Sloan & Pierce, 1941. A young mountain girl and her illegitimate child join an extended family of man, three wives and thirty some odd children.
H1590 (ASU BC)

The Hills Step Lightly. New York: W. Morrow & Co., 1934. This life story of an unusual mountain women is packed with bits of mountain folklore. Western North Carolina setting.
H1600 (ASU ETSU BC)

Look Back with Love: A Recollection of the Blue Ridge. New York: Vanguard Press, 1969. Memories of Mrs. Hannum's years in Avery County, North Carolina.
H1610 (ASU WCU LMC MHC ETSU FC WWC BC)

Thursday April. New York: Harper, 1931. Novel of a young girl in Avery County, North Carolina who is saved from early marriage and given an opportunity for schooling.
H1630 (WCU ASU)

Thursday April. New York and London: Harper and Brothers, 1931.
H1640

Hannum, Alverta Pierson Roseanna McCoy. New York: Henry Holt & Co., 1947. A fictional account of the Hatfield-McCoy feud.
H1620 (BC ASU)

Hansbrough, Thomas ed. Southern Forests and Southern People. Baton Rouge: Louisiana State Univ., 1963.
H1650 (LMC)

Hansell, J. E. Hill-Billy Bill; a Biography of Hon. J. Will Taylor of Tennessee. LaFolette, Tenn.: The LaFolette Press, 1932.
H1660 (BC)

Hansen, James C. Appalachian Students and Guidance. Guidance Monograph Series, 6. New York: Houghton Mifflin, 1971.
H1670 (ASU BC WCU MHC ETSU)

Hansen, Marcus Lee The Atlantic Migration, 1607-1860: A History of the Continuing Settlement of the United States. Foreword by Arthur M. Schlesinger. Introduction to the Torchbook edition by Oscar Haudling. Harper Torchbook, 1052. New York: Harper, 1961.
H1680 (ASU)

Hansen, Niles M. A Review of the Appalachian Regional Commission Program. Austin: Univ. of Texas, 1969.
H1690 (ASU)

Hansen, Robert P. Rites of Summer. New York: Morrow, 1961. Romantic fiction set in modern day Appalachia.
H1700 (ASU BC)

Hansen, Viola Karen "Factors That Influence Young Couples to Stay on the Farm in Adair County, Kentucky: Some Social and Economic Factors That Influence Young Couples to Stay on the Farm in a Low-income County in Kentucky." Ph. D. Diss. Columbia Univ., 1962.
H1710

Hanson, Ivan Hammill, Anne Natural Resource Special Districts in Appalachia: Review of Enabling Laws. Washington: Govt. Print. Off., 1970.
H1330

Hanson, Raus McDill Virginia Place Names: Derivations, Historical Uses. Verona, Va.: McClure Press, 1969.
H1720 (ASU BC FC)

Hanten, Edward W. "An Analysis of the Industrial Potential of Johnstown, Pennsylvania." Master's thesis. Univ. of Pittsburgh, 1958. Not unexpectedly, water-power was a major consideration in this study.
H1730

Harbaugh, Thomas Chalmers Middletown Valley in Song and Story. n.p.: n.p., 1910. Stories and poems celebrating life and legends in the Middletown Valley of Kentucky.
H1740 (BC)

Harbaugh, William Henry Lawyer's Lawyer; the Life of John W. Davis. New York: Oxford Univ. Press, 1973.
H1750 (ASU BC)

Harben, Will Nathaniel Abner Daniel. New York: A. L. Burt Co., 1902. A delightful yarn about such turn of the century improvements as the coming of the railroad in Murray County, Georgia. Abner's dry wit and wry wisdom are used as counterpoint in this series of novels.
H1760 (ASU)

Abner Daniel. New York and London: Harper and Brothers, 1903.
H1770

Ann Boyd. New York: Harper & Brothers, 1903.
H1780 (ETSU)

Ann Boyd. New York and London: Harper and Brothers, 1906. A novel of romance and courage in the face of social conventions. This one is set in the lower end of Murray County.
H1790

Ann Boyd: A Novel. New York: A. L. Burt Co., 1906.
H1800 (ASU BC)

The Cottage of Delight: A Novel. New York: Harper & Brothers, 1919. A novel of young love set in what appears to be the Spring Place Community of Murray County, Georgia.
H1810 (ASU BC)

The Desired Woman. New York and London: Harper and Brothers, 1913. A comedy of manners set in Spring Place and the nearby metropolis of Dalton.
H1820

The Desired Woman. New York: A. L. Burt Co., 1913.
H1830 (ASU BC)

The Divine Event. New York: A. L. Burt Co., 1920. More romantic fiction from Murray and Whitfield counties.
H1840 (ASU BC)

Dixie Hart. New York: Harper & Brothers, 1910. Brave young tom-boyish Dixie holds her family together and catches the man of her dreams.
H1850 (ASU BC)

The Georgians: A Novel. New York: Harper & Brothers, 1904. Another novel of Murray County, Georgia featuring encounters between mountaineers, poor farmers and town folk. The clever mountain man is often the hero.
H1860 (ASU BC)

Gilbert Neal: A Novel. New York: Harper & Brothers, 1908. Gilbert is a hard-working lad from the Ramhurst community of Murray County who overcomes poverty and social stigma to become a leading merchant.
H1870 (ASU BC)

The Hills of Refuge: A Novel. New York: Harper & Brothers, 1918. A novel about the mountains of Murray County and the refuge they represent to a confused lad who has encountered trouble in the cities.
H1880 (ASU BC)

The Inner Law: A Novel. New York: Harper & Brothers, 1915. A novel about the wages of sin and the effects of conscience.
H1890 (ASU ETSU BC)

Jane Dawson: A Novel. New York: Harper & Brothers, 1911. Jane is another poor lass from the southern end of Murray County who triumphs over adversity.
H1900 (ASU)

Mam' Linda: A Novel. Illustrated by F. B. Masters. New York: Harper & Brothers, 1907. A novel about a negro woman in Spring Place and an ugly little racial incident which transpires there.
H1910 (ASU ETSU BC)

The New Clarion. New York and London: Harper and Brothers, 1914. A novel about an attempt to launch a new business venture in Murray and Whitfield counties.
H1920

The New Clarion. New York: A. L. Burt Co., 1914.
H1930 (ASU BC)

Northern Georgia Sketches. Chicago: A. C. McClurg & Co., 1900. A series of short fiction of which "Trundle's Crisis," and "The Convict's Return" are the best.
H1940 (ASU WCU LMC)

Northern Georgia Sketches. Freeport, N. Y.: Books for Libraries Press, 1970.
H1950 (ETSU)

Paul Rundel: A Novel. New York: Harper & Brothers, 1912. This novel about an outlander is a departure from Harben's usual formula for fiction.
H1960 (ASU BC)

Pole Baker. New York and London: Harper and Brothers, 1905.
H1970

Pole Baker: A Novel. New York: A. L. Burt Co., 1905. Another Murray County novel. Pole, the mountaineer, and Abner, his valley farmer counterpart, are based at least in part upon the exploits of my great-grandfather.
H1980 (ASU LMC BC)

The Redemption of Kenneth Galt. New York: A. L. Burt Co., 1909. Pore' Kenneth has sinned against church and family and is sowing the fields around Dennis Mill with bitterness until love softens him and the minister does the rest.
H1990 (BC)

The Redemption of Kenneth Galt. New York: Harper and Brothers, 1911.
H2000

Second Choice. New York: A. L. Burt & Company, 1916. The moral of this one seems to be that second choices have a way of working out for the best.
H2010 (ASU BC)

Second Choice. New York: Harper & Brothers, 1916.
H2020 (ETSU)

Harben, Will Nathaniel
The Triumph: A Novel. New York: Harper & Brothers, 1917. Another North Georgia novel with many outland scenes and characters.
H2030 (ASU BC)
Westerfelt. New York and London: Harper and Brothers, 1901. An attempt to contrast gentility and mountain characteristics. Actually, Harben seems to have preferred the yeoman farmer.
H2040

Harbison, T. G. A Preliminary Check-list of the Ligneous Flora of the Highland Region, North Carolina. Highlands, N. C.: Highlands Museum & Biological Laboratory, 1931.
H2050 (ASU)

Hardeman, William D. Geologic Map of Tennessee. Assisted by Robert A. Miller and George D. Swingle. Nashville: Tennessee, Division of Geology, 1966.
H2060 (ETSU)

Harden, John William The Devil's Tramping Ground, and Other North Carolina Mystery Stories. Illustrated by Mary Lindsay McAlister. Chapel Hill: Univ. of North Carolina Press, 1949. A collection of strange occurrences in the old North State. Many from the mountain region.
H2070 (ASU LMC MHC BC)
Tar Heel Ghosts. Illustrated by Lindsay McAlister. Chapel Hill: Univ. of North Carolina Press, 1954.
H2080 (ASU BC LMC MHC ETSU)

Hardert, Ronald Albert "Social Structural Factors Influencing the Urbanization of Appalachian Hill Emigrants in an Urban Ghetto." Ph. D. Diss. Indiana Univ., 1967.
H2090

Hardesty, Kenneth Legge Songs of the Woods Poet. Parsons, W. Va.: McClain Print. Co., 1969.
H2100 (ASU BC)

Hardesty's Historical and Geographical Encyclopedia VIRGINIA ED. N. Y.: H. H. Hardesty and Co. Publishers, 1884, with notes by R. A. Brock. Includes Wythe and Smyth County biographies.
H2110

Hardin, Gail The Road from West Virginia. Chicago: Children's Press, 1970. Coalminer's daughter and school dropout tells about factory jobs which made her value a high school diploma.
H2120 (ASU BC LMC)

Hardin, James W. North Carolina Drug Plants of Commercial Value. Bulletin, no. 418. Raleigh: Agricultural Experiment Station, 1962. Wilcox Drug Company in Boone, North Carolina is the largest botanical drug company left in the mountains.
H2130 (ASU LMC UNCA)
Poisonous Plants of North Carolina. Bulletin, no. 414. Raleigh: Agricultural Experiment Station, 1961.
H2140 (LMC)

Hardin, John E. "A Study of the Physical Education Programs of the High Schools in Carter County, Tennessee." Master's thesis. East Tennessee State College, 1961.
H2150 (ETSU)

Harding, Arthur Robert Ginseng and Other Medicinal Plants; a Book of Valuable Information for Growers as well as Collectors of Medicinal Roots, Barks, Leaves, etc. Columbus, O.: A. R. Harding Pub. Co., 1908.
H2160

Hardison, Robinson B. Soil Survey of Ashe County, North Carolina. Prepared in cooperation with the North Carolina Department of Agriculture. Field Operations, 1912. Washington: U. S. Department of Agriculture, Bureau of Soils, 1914.
H2170

Hardy, Earl Souvenir Views of the Beautiful Blowing Rock Region. Twelve photographs. Lenoir, N. C.: n.p., n.d.
H2180

Hardy, Lucina Elizabeth An Album of Historical Memories. Chatata-Tasso, Bradley County, Tennessee, 1830-1961. n.p.: n.p., n.d. Includes memories before the Cherokee removal.
H2190

Hardy, Stella Pickett Colonial Families of the Southern States of America: A History and Genealogy of Colonial Families Who Settled in the Colonies Prior to the Revolution. 2nd ed. with revisions and additions by the author. 1958. Reprint. Baltimore: Genealogical Pub. Co., 1965.
H2200 (ASU)

Hare, Charles E. Heck, Edward Timmel Appalachian Connate Water. Charleston: West Virginia Geological Survey, 1964.
H4290 (ETSU)
Price, Paul Holland Salt Brines of West Virginia. Morgantown: West Virginia Geological Survey, 1937.
P4560 (ETSU)

Hargrove, Jack B. "A Comparative Study of School Dropouts from 1945-50 in Holt Junior High School and Jaylorville Junior High School, Tuscaloosa County, Alabama." Master's thesis. Alabama State College, 1952.
H2210

Hargrove, Michael Brutus "Economic Development of Areas Contiguous to Multipurpose Reservoirs: The Kentucky-Tennessee Experience." Ph. D. Diss. Univ. of Kentucky, 1971.
H2220 (BC)

Harker, Timothy L. Economic Stability and Growth Potential, Fairmont, W. Va. Oak Ridge, Tenn.: Oak Ridge Associated Universities, 1967.
H2230

Harkins, Joe R. Surface Water Resources of Calhoun County, Alabama. With a section on quality of water, by Rodney G. Grantham. Circular, 33. University: Alabama Geological Survey, 1965.
H2240 (ETSU)

Harkness, David James Abraham Lincoln and the Cumberland Gap. Knoxville: Univ. of Tennessee, 1959.
H2250 (ASU ETSU)
Literary Profiles of the Southern States: A Manual for Schools and Clubs. News-letter, vol. 32, no. 1. Knoxville: Division of University Extension, Univ. of Tennessee, 1953. Includes Appalachian authors.
H2280 (ASU)
Tennessee and Virginia, the Mountain Empire. Knoxville: Univ. of Tennessee, 1970.
H2290 (ETSU)

Harkness, David James comp. Kentucky and Tennessee, Twin Centers of Interest. Extension Series, vol. 41, no. 1. Knoxville: Univ. of Tennessee, 1966.
H2260 (ASU BC)
Legends and Lore, Southern Indians, Flowers, Holidays. News-letter, vol. 40, no. 2. Knoxville: Univ. of Tennessee, 1961.
H2270 (ASU)

Harkrader, Charles J. Witness to an Epoch: Personal Inventory of the Experiences and Impressions of a Man of Varied Interests. Kingsport, Tenn.: The author, 1965.
H2300 (LMC)

Harlan County, Ky., School Survey Council Harlan County Schools Have Problems. Lexington: Bureau of School Service, College of Education, Univ. of Kentucky, 1961.
H2310 (ASU)

Harlan Miners Speak n.p.: Harcourt, Brace & Company, 1932. The classic work on mine wars, union struggles, and labor troubles in the mountains.
H2320

Harless, N. R. "A Study of School Transportation, Blount County, Tennessee." Master's thesis. Univ. of Tennessee, 1959.
H2330

Harless, Rod The Hillbillys, a Book for Children. Illustrated by Dan Cutler. Huntington, W. Va.: Appalachian Movement Press, 1970. An attempt to help mountain youngsters understand their heritage.
H2340 (ASU)
The West Virginia Establishment. Huntington, W. Va.: Appalachian Movement Press, 1971.
H2350 (ASU)

Harlin, William Vernon and others Soil Survey, Calhoun County, Alabama. Report by William V. Harlin and E. A. Perry. Soil Survey, Series 1958, no. 9. Washington: U. S. Department of Agriculture, Soil Conservation Service, 1961.
H2360

Harlow, Alvin Schoolhouses in the Foothills. New York: Simon and Schuster, 1937.
H2370

Harman, B. H. Dan Georgen of the Divided House. A Geneva Book. New York: Carlton Press, 1965. A novel of a boy who grew up in the Blue Ridge in an atmosphere of superstition and later lived in the midwest. He chose to return to the mountains.
H2380 (ASU LMC)
Malinda of the Blue Ridge. A Geneva Book. New York: Carlton Press, 1964. Children's fiction with a mountain setting.
H2390 (ASU LMC)

Harman, John Newton Harman Genealogy (Southern Branch), with Biographical Sketches, 1700-1924. Richmond, Va.: W. C. Hill Print. Co., 1925.
H2410

Harman, William Times Gone By. Blowing Rock, N. C.: The author, 1973. Recollection of life in western North Carolina.
H2420

Harmeling, Mary Bernadette "Social and Cultural Links in the Urban and Occupational Adjustment of Southern Appalachian Migrants." Ph. D. Diss. Fordham University, 1969.
H2430

Harmon, John Newton Annals of Tazewell County, Virginia from 1800 to 1922. Richmond, Va.: W. C. Hill Print. Co., 1922-25. Pt. 1 - Court records. Pt. 2 - Republication of Bickley's History of the settlement and Indian Wars of Tazewell Co. - 1852.
H2400 (BC ASU)

Harmon, Milton Slow Creek. Parsons, W. Va.: McClain Print. Co., 1969.
H2440 (ASU)

Harmon, Roy Lee Hillbilly Ballads. Beckley, W. Va.: Beckley Newspapers Corp., 1938.
H2450
Rhymes of a Mountaineer. Detroit: Harlo, 1968.
H2460 (ASU)
Rhymes of a Mountaineer; the Best of Roy Lee Harmon. Detroit: Harlo Press, 1968.
H2470 (BC)

Harms, William R. Spacing-environmental Relationships in a Slash Pine Plantation. U. S. Forest Service Research Paper, no. 150. Asheville, N. C.: Southeastern Forest Experiment Station, 1962.
H2480 (WCU)

Harned, Joseph Edward Wild Flowers of the Alleghanies. Oakland, Md.: Sencell Print. Co., 1936.
H2490 (BC)

Harner, Warren Bartlett Hill Saga. Sherperdstown, W. Va.: n.p., 1936.
H2500

Harnsberger, Thomas K. The Geology and Coal Resources of the Coal-bearing Portion of Tazewell County, Virginia. Prepared in cooperation with the U. S. Geological Survey. Virginia Geological Survey Bulletin, no. 19.
H2510 (ETSU)

Harold, Kathleen E. "A Study of a Group of Drop-outs of the Greenville High School." Master's thesis. East Tennessee State College, 1952.
H2520

Harper, Francis ed. Bartram, William Travels. New Haven, Conn.: Yale Univ. Press, 1958.
B1710 (LMC)

Harper, George W. F. Reminiscences of Caldwell County, N. C., in the Great War of 1861-65. Lenoir: n.p., 1913.
H2530

Harper, Roland McMillan . . . Natural Resources of the Tenn. Valley Region in Alabama. Ala. Geological Survey, special report 17. Tuscaloosa: Univ. of Ala., 1942.
H2540 (BC)

Harpine, J. William Lindamood Family History. n.p.: n.p., n.d.
H2550

Harpster, John W. ed. Pen Pictures of Early Western Pennsylvania. Maps and illustrations by Harvey Cushman. Western Pennsylvania Historical Survey. Pittsburgh: Univ. of Pittsburgh Press, 1938.
H2560 (ASU)

Harrah, D. D. Wilson, L. Craig School-community Improvement, a Report of the Greenbrier County Program. New York: World Book Co., 1959.
W7360 (ASU WCU)

Harrell, Isaac Samuel Loyalism in Virginia: Chapters in the Economic History of the Revolution. 1926. Reprint. New York: AMS Press, 1965.
H2570 (ASU LMC)

Harrelson, Martha Langston Lemert, Benjamin Franklin North Carolina Geography: A Study of How We Live in North Carolina. Oklahoma City: Harlow Pub. Corp., 1954.
L1710 (LMC ASU)

Harrigan, Terrence D. The Changing Economy of Claiborne County, Tennessee. Oak Ridge, Tenn.: Oak Ridge Associated Universities, 1966.
H2580

Harrill, Bob E. "A Study of the Practices and Techniques Used by Principals and Teachers in the McMinn County Schools to Improve School Attendance." Master's thesis. Univ. of Tennessee, 1958.
H2590

Harrill, L. R. Memories of 4-H. Raleigh: North Carolina State Univ. Print. Shop, 1967.
H2600 (ASU)

Harrington, Mark Raymond Cherokee and Earlier Remains on Upper Tennessee River. New York: Heye Foundation, 1922.
H2610 (BC LMC)

Harrington, Michael The Other America: Poverty in the United States. New York: Macmillan, 1962. References to Appalachian Poverty.
H2620 (MHC BC)

Harris, Bernice Kelly Hearthstones, a Novel of the Roanoke River Country in North Carolina. 1st ed. Garden City, N. Y.: Doubleday, 1948. A novel of pioneer life in western North Carolina.
H2630 (WCU)

Janey Jeems. 1st ed. Garden City, N. Y.: Doubleday and Co., 1946. A couple with a houseful of children live on a subsistence farm in the western North Carolina mountains. Much about religion and superstitions.
H2640 (ASU WCU BC)

Harris, Bernice Kelly ed. Southern Home Remedies. By the Creative Writing Group of Chowan College. Murfreesboro, N. C.: Johnson Pub. Co., 1968.
H2650 (AASU LMC)

Harris, Corra May White A Circuit Rider's Widow. Illustrated by Walter H. Everett. Garden City, N. Y.: Doubleday, Page and Co., 1916. A North Georgia author writes about her experiences as a Methodist minister's wife. Semi-autobiographical novel.
H2660 (ASU WCU BC)

A Circuit Rider's Wife. Illustrated by William H. Everett. Philadelphia: Henry Altemus Co., 1910. Semi-autobiographical novel of her experiences as a Methodist minister's wife.
H2670 (ASU BC LMC WCU)

The Co-citizens. Illustrated by Hanson Booth. Garden City, N. Y.: Doubleday, Page and Co., 1915. One of North Georgia's early woman's liberation novels.
H2680 (ASU BC)

Eve's Second Husband. Philadelphia: Henry Altemus Co., 1911. Auto-biographical fiction from the North Georgia hills.
H2690 (ASU)

Flapper Anne. New York: Grosset and Dunlap, 1926. Fiction with a North Georgia setting.
H2700 (ASU)

The Happy Pilgrimage. Boston: Houghton Mifflin Co., 1927. Religious novel partially set in the mountains.
H2710 (ASU BC)

In Search of a Husband. New York: Grosset and Dunlap, 1913. Fiction partially set in North Georgia.
H2720 (ASU)

My Book and Heart. Illustrated by Frederick Greiger. Boston: Houghton Mifflin Co., 1924. Autobiographical memoirs of a feminist, minister's wife, and novelist.
H2730 (ASU BC)

My Son. New York: George H. Doran Co., 1921. Autobiography of the author's son.
H2740 (ASU BC)

The Recording Angel. Illustrated by W. H Everett. Garden City, N. Y.: Doubleday, Page and Co., 1912. Religious fiction.
H2750 (ASU BC)

Harris, Credo Sunlight Patch. Boston: Small, Maynard and Co., 1915. A mountain man attends Miss Jane's settlement school in the Kentucky mountains in an attempt to live up to his late wife's expectations.
H2760 (BC)

Harris, Evelyn L. K. From Humble Beginnings; West Virginia State Federation of Labor, 1903-1957. Charleston: Charleston, W. Va. Labor History Pub. Fund, 1960.
H2770 (BC)

Harris, Gene G. Smoke on Old Thunderhead. Illustrated by Don Harris. Winston-Salem, N. C.: J. F. Blair, 1962. A boy, a witch and a black bear are caught in a fire in the Great Smoky Mountains.
H2780 (ASU BC LMC)

Harris, George E. "The Drain of Talent out of Kentucky." Master's thesis. Kent State Univ., 1956.
H2790

Harris, George Washington High Times and Hard Times: Sketches and Tales. Introductory essays by M. Thomas Inge. Illustrated by Mary Alice Bahler. Nashville: Vanderbilt Univ. Press, 1967.
H2800 (ASU BC)

The Lovingood Papers. Athens, Tennessee, Sut. Society. vol. 1-. 1962-. Athens, Tenn.: Tenn. Wesleyan College, 1962-.
H2810

Sut Lovingood. Introduction to Brom Weber. New York: Grove Press, 1954.
H2820 (ASU)

Sut Lovingood. Yarns Spun by a "Nat'ral Born Durn'd Fool." Warped and Wove for Public Wear. New York: Dick and Fitzgerald, 1867.
H2830 (ASU BC ETSU)

Sut Lovingood's Yarns. Edited for the modern reader by M. Thomas Inge. Masterworks of Literature Series. New Haven, Conn.: College and Univ. Press, 1966.
H2840 (ASU WWC)

Harris, Gertrude Manna: Foods of the Frontier. Illustrated by Heidi Palmer. San Francisco: 101 Productions, 1972. A guide to survival in the wilderness.
H2850 (ASU WCU)

Harris, H. "Two Famous Kentucky Feuds and Their Causes." Master's thesis. Kent State Univ., 1956.
H2860

Harris, Hobart B. Geology and Ground-water Resources of Colbert County, Alabama. Prepared by the U. S. Geological Survey in cooperation with the Colbert County Board of Revenue, the City of Tuscumbia and the Geological Survey of Alabama. County Report, 10. University: Alabama Geological Survey, 1963.
H2870 (ETSU)

Interim Report on Ground-water Study in Colbert County, Alabama. Prepared by the U. S. Geological Survey in cooperation with the Colbert County Board of Revenue and the Geological Survey of Alabama. Information Series, 20. University: Alabama Geological Survey, 1960.
H2880 (ETSU)

Springs in Colbert and Lauderdale Counties, Alabama. Prepared by the U. S. Geological Survey in cooperation with the Boards of Revenue of Colbert and Lauderdale Counties and the Geological Survey of Alabama. Information Series, 10. University: Alabama Geological Survey, 1957.
H2890 (ETSU)

Harris, Isabella Deas "Charles Egbert Craddock as an Interpreter of Mountain Life." Master's thesis. Duke University, 1933.
H2900

"Charles Egbert Craddock as an Interpreter of Mountain Life." Microfilm. Master's thesis. Duke Univ., 1933.
H2910 (ASU)

"The Southern Mountaineer in American Fiction, 1824-1910." Ph. D. Diss. Duke Univ., 1948.
H2920 (ASU ETSU)

Harris, James Coffee Cave Spring and Van's Valley. Cave Spring, Ga.: n.p., 1927. This warm water large spring and lake were sacred to the Cherokee.
H2930 (LMC)

Harris, Joel Chandler Balaam and His Master, and Other Sketches and Stories. 1891. Reprint. Short Story Index Reprint Series. Freeport, N. Y.: Books for Libraries Press, 1969. Two mountain sketches are included in the collection.
H2940 (WCU)

Joel Chandler Harris, Editor and Essayist: Miscellaneous Literary, Political and Social Writings. Chapel Hill: Univ. of North Carolina, 1931. Harris wrote several mountain sketches with surprisingly good dialect.
H2950 (WCU)

Mingo. 1884. Reprint. Upper Saddle River, N. J.: Literature House, 1970.
H2960 (WCU)

Mingo and Other Sketches. New York: McKinley, 1884. Includes one mountain sketch, "At Teague Potect's."
H2970 (WWC)

Mingo and Other Sketches in Black and White. 1884. Reprint. Short Story Index Reprint Series. Freeport, N. Y.: Books for Libraries Press, 1970.
H2980 (WCU)

Harris, Julia Collier Florida Harris, Joel Chandler Joel Chandler Harris, Editor and Essayist: Miscellaneous Literary, Political and Social Writings. Chapel Hill: Univ. of North Carolina, 1931.
H2950 (WCU)

Harris, Mrs. L. H. see **Harris, Corra May White**

Harris, Luther Calvin "An Educational Survey of Coal Creek Community, Anderson County, Tennessee." Master's thesis. Univ. of Tennessee, 1932.
H2990

Harris, Meriel Daniel "Two Famous Kentucky Feuds and Their Causes." Master's thesis. Univ. of Kentucky, 1940.
H3000 (ASU)

"Two Famous Kentucky Feuds and Their Causes." Microfilm. Master's thesis. Univ. of Kentucky, 1940.
H3010 (ASU)

Harris, Oscar J. "An Investigation of Some Needs for Expansion of Vocational Education in Monogalia, Preston and Taylor Counties, West Virginia." Master's thesis. West Virginia Univ., 1966.
H3020

Harris, Wiley F., Jr. Dodson, Chester Lee Geology and Ground-water Resources of Morgan County, Alabama. Univ.: Alabama Geological Survey, 1965.
D2750 (ETSU)

Dodson, Chester Lee Interim Report on the Geology and Groundwater Resources of Morgan County, Alabama. Univ.: Alabama Geological Survey, 1961.
D2770 (ETSU)

Harris, Wiley F., Jr.
Geology and Ground-water Resources of Lawrence County, Alabama: A Reconnaissance. Prepared by the U. S. Geological Survey in cooperation with the Geological Survey of Alabama. Bulletin, 78. University: Alabama Geological Survey, 1965.
H3030 (ETSU)
McMaster, William M. General Geology and Ground-water Resources of Limestone County, Alabama: A Reconnaissance. University: Alabama Geological Survey, 1963.
M2170 (ETSU)

Harrison, Clifford Marion Social Types in Southern Prose Fiction. Ph. D. Diss. Univ. of Virginia, 1921. Does a very poor job of identifying the mountaineer as a distinctive fictional type.
H3040

Harrison, Constance C. A Son of the Old Dominion. New York, Boston and London: Lamson, Wolffe and Company, 1897. Action of the novel ranges into the mountains.
H3050

Harrison, Henry Surnames of the United Kingdom: A Concise Etymological Dictionary. Assisted by Gyda Pulling Harrison. 1912. Reprint. 2 vols. in 1. Baltimore: Genealogical Pub. Co., 1969.
H3060 (ASU)

Harrison, James A. ed. Poe, Edgar Allan "A Tale of the Ragged Mountains" in The Complete Works of Edgar Allan Poe. New York: Thomas Y. Crowell and Co., 1902.
P3280 (ASU ETSU)

Harrison, John Houston Settlers by the Long Grey Trail, Some Pioneers to Old Augusta County, Virginia, and Their Descendants, of the Family of Harrison and Allied Lines. Dayton, Va.: Joseph K. Ruebush Co., 1935.
H3070 (ASU BC)

Harrison, Paul M. Authority and Power in the Free Church Tradition: A Social Case Study of the American Baptist Convention. Princeton: Princeton University Press, 1959.
H3080

Harrison, Virginia M. The Fear and the Guilt. New York: Ace, 1954. Lurid fiction with an eastern Kentucky setting.
H3090
Heat Lightening. New York: Ace, 1954. This novel manages to make everyone in eastern Kentucky sound like a degenerate.
H3100 (ASU)
The Mating Call. New York: Ace, 1954. Lurid, degenerate novel set in eastern Kentucky.
H3110

Harrisonburg, Virginia: Diary of a Citizen from May 9, 1862-August 22, 1864, Local Events during the Civil War. Harrisonburg, Va.: E. R. Grymes Heneberger, 1961.
H3120 (ASU)

Harriss, Frances Latham Lawson, John History of North Carolina, Containing the Exact Description and Natural History of That Country, Together with the Present State Thereof, and a Journal of a Thousand Miles Traveled Through Several Nations of Indians, Giving a Particular Account of Their Customs, Manners, Etc., Etc. Richmond: Garrett and Massie, 1952.
L970 (LMC MHC BC)

Harriss, Frances Latham ed. Lawson, John History of North Carolina, Containing the Exact Description and Natural History of that Country, Together with the Present State Thereof, and a Journal of a Thousand Miles Traveled through Several Nations of Indians, Giving a Particular Account of Their Customs, Manners, Etc., Etc. Richmond: Garrett and Massie, 1951 and 1960.
L980 (UNCA)

Harry, P. Map of the Cherokee Territory. Corps of Engineers, War Department. Washington: Government Printing Office, 1837.
H3130

Harshaw, Lou The Rubies of Cowee Valley, Franklin, N. C. and other Native Gem and Mineral Locations in Macon County, N. C. Asheville, N. C.: Hexagon Co., 1973.
H3140 (ASU)

Harshbarger, Richard B. "The Coal Buying Policies: Effects on Prices and Method of Mining in Supplying States." Ph. D. Diss. Indiana Univ., 1964.
H3150

Hart, Freeman Hansford The Valley of Virginia in the American Revolution, 1763-1789. Chapel Hill: Univ. of North Carolina Press, 1946.
H3160 (ASU BC FC)

Hart, George Trimble, George R., Jr. Appraisal of Early Reproduction After Cutting in Northern Appalachian Hardwood Stands. Upper Darby, Pa.: Northeastern Forest Experiment Station, 1961.
T9290

Hart, Joseph K. Education for an Age of Power: The TVA Poses a Problem. New York: Harper and Brothers, 1935. At last, a book that recognizes that the TVA has caused a great many problems.
H3170 (ASU)

Hartford, Ellis Ford Emphasizing Values in Five Kentucky Schools. With contributions from Willa F. Harmon, Robert Woosley, and Metta Woosely. College of Education Bureau of school service bulletin, vol. 26, no. 4. Lexington: Univ. of Kentucky, 1954.
H3180 (ASU)

Hartley, Cecil B. The Life of Daniel Boone, the Founder of the State of Kentucky. With an introduction by G. Mercer Adorm. New York: A. L. Burt Co., 1902.
H3190 (ASU)
Life of Daniel Boone, the Great Western Hunter and Pioneer, Comprising an Account of His Early History, His Daring and Remarkable Career as the First Settler of Kentucky. To Which is Added His Autobiography Complete as Dictated by Himself. New York: American, 1865.
H3200 (WCU BC ETSU)
Life of Daniel Boone, the Great Western Hunter and Pioneer, Comprising an Account of His Early History, His Daring and Remarkable Career as the First Settler of Kentucky. To Which Is Added His Autobiography Complete as Dictated by Himself. Philadelphia: J. E. Potter, 1865.
H3210 (ASU BC ETSU)

Hartley, Loyde Hobart "Sectarianism and Social Participation: A Study of the Relationship between Religious Attitudes and Involvement in Voluntary Organizations in Seventy-two Churches in the Southern Appalachian Mountains." Ph. D. Diss. Emory Univ., 1968.
H3220 (LMC)

Hartley, Rachel Augusta Brett "Ananias Davisson: Southern Tune Book Compiler (1780-1857)." Ph. D. Diss. Univ. of Michigan, 1972.
H3230

Hartman, Vladimir E. "A Cultural Study of a Mountain Community in Western North Carolina." Ph. D. Diss. Univ. of North Carolina, 1957.
H3240 (ASU)
"A Cultural Study of Mountain Community in Western North Carolina." Microfilm. Ph. D. Diss. Univ. of North Carolina, 1957.
H3250 (ASU)

Hartsog, E. R. Hooky Cop Saga: Frustrations and Rewards of an Attendance Officer in Appalachia. Illustrated by William F. Rexrode. Parsons, W. Va.: McClain Print. Co., 1967.
H3260 (ASU BC)

Harvey, Katherine A. The Best-dressed Miners: Life and Labor in the Maryland Coal Region, 1835-1910. Ithaca, N. Y.: Cornell Univ. Press, 1969. The earliest coal mining in the United States took place in Western Maryland. Miners were relatively well-off.
H3270 (ASU)
"The Coal Miners of Western Maryland." Ph. D. Diss. American University, 1962.
H3280

Harvey, Stella Mowbray Tales of the Civil War Era. Crossville: Chronicle Pub., 1963. Publication of this volume was sponsored by the Cumberland County Civil War Centennial Committee.
H3290

Harvill, Alton McCaleb Spring Flora of Virginia. Parsons, W. Va.: McClain Print. Co., 1970.
H3300 (ASU BC LMC)

Harville, Thomas J. "Team Teaching at Douglas School, Elizabethton, Carter County, Tennessee." Master's thesis. East Tennessee State Univ., 1964.
H3310 (ETSU)

Harwell, Richard Barksdale ed. Cooke, John Esten Stonewall Jackson and the Old Stonewall Brigade. Charlottesville: Univ. of Virginia Press for the Tracy W. McGregor Library, 1954.
C7010 (ASU BC)
Proceedings of the County Committees, 1774-1776, The Committees of Safety of Westmoreland and Fincastle. Richmond: Virginia State Library, 1956. Discusses and compares the two sets of Resolutions and includes the minutes of the Fincastle County Committee of Safety, and the Resolutions themselves. Fincastle's activities centered at the Lead Mines, now Wythe County.
H3320

Harwood, Herbert H., Jr. Blue Ridge Trolley. The Hagerstown and Frederick Railway. San Marino, Cal. Golden West Books, 1970.
H3330 (ASU)

Hash, Judith Haws "A History of the First Presbyterian Church of Jonesboro, Tennessee." Master's thesis. East Tennessee State Univ., 1965. Jonesboro is the oldest town in Tennessee.
H3340 (ETSU)

Hash, Lewis J. Hunter, Charles Eugene Halloysite Deposits of Western North Carolina. Raleigh: North Carolina Department of Conservation & Development, 1949.
H8410 (ETSU WCU)

Hashe, Mary Dell "Professional Characteristics of the Master's Degree Graduates of East Tennessee State University." Master's thesis. East Tennessee State Univ., 1965.
H3350 (ETSU)

Haskins, Ralph W. ed. Graf, LeRoy P. ed. The Papers of Andrew Johnson. Knoxville: Univ. of Tennessee Press, 1967-.
G3100

Hassall, Harry Sharp A History of Concord Presbyterian Church, Concord, Tennessee. Knoxville: Letter Shop, 1963.
H3360

Hassell, Bluford Leslie "An Administrative and Educational Survey of the Schools of Campbell County, Tennessee." Master's thesis. Univ. of Tennessee, 1933.
H3370

Hastings, Earl L. Lamont, W. E. Resource and Beneficiation Studies of Copperbearing Pyrite Ore, Pyriton, Clay County, Alabama. Univ.: Alabama Geological Survey, 1964.
L240 (ETSU)

Hasty, Allen Henry Soil Survey, Limestone County, Alabama. U. S. Soil Conservation Service, Soil Survey, Series 1941, no. 5. Washington: Govt. Print. Off., 1953.
H3380
Soil Survey, Rhea County, Tennessee. Prepared in cooperation with the Tennessee Agricultural Experiment Station and the Tennessee Valley Authority. Soil Survey Report Series 1940, no. 3. Washington: U. S. Department of Agriculture, Bureau of Plant Industry, Soils, and Agricultural Engineering, 1948.
H3390

Hatcher, Harlan Patterns of Wolfpen. Indianapolis: Bobbs-Merrill Company, 1934. Novel about an educated, valley family which has been in Eastern Kentucky since 1790. Mountain but refined.
H3400

Hatcher, Orie Lathan ed. A Mountain School: A Study Made by the Southern Woman's Educational Alliance and Kennarock Training School. Richmond: Garrett and Massie, 1930.
H3410 (WWC BC)

Hatfield, Craig Bond Stratigraphy and Paleoecology of the Saluda Formation (Cincinnation) in Indiana, Ohio, and Kentucky. Special Paper, no. 95. Regional Studies. Boulder, Colo.: Geological Society of America, 1968.
H3420 (ETSU)

Hatfield, Emmanuel Stories of Hatfield, the Pioneer. New Albany, Ind.: Ledger Co., 1889.
H3430

Stories of Hatfield, the Pioneer; embracing a detailed account of His Experience in the Wilderness of East Tennessee, Kentucky, and Southern Indiana. New Albany, Ind.: Ledger Co., Printers and binders, 1890.
H3440 (BC)

Hatfield, G. Elliott The Hatields. Revised by Leonard Roberts and Henry P. Scalf. Stanville, Ky.: Big Sandy Valley Historical Society, 1974. A low-keyed history of the controversial feuding family.
H3450 (ASU)

Hatfield, Gilbert Harris. "A Study of Rural Cooperative Organizations in Overton County, Tennessee." Master's thesis. Univ. of Tennessee, 1929.
H3460

Hatfield, James Monroe "A History and Educational Survey of Putnam County, Tennessee." Master's thesis. Univ. of Tennessee, 1937.
H3470

Hatfield, Lawrence D. The True Story of the Hatfield and McCoy Feud. Charleston, W. Va.: Jarett, 1944. A history of the feud written by a descendant of one of the principals.
H3480 (BC)

Hatfield, William F. Beverage, Woodrow Wilson Soil Survey, Barbour County, West Virginia. Washington: U. S. Department of Agriculture, Soil Conservation Service, 1968.
B3440

Soil Survey, Jefferson County, West Virginia. Prepared in with the West Virginia Agricultural Experiment Station. Washington: U. S. Soil Conservation Service, 1973.
H3490

Hathaway, J. R. B. ed. The North Carolina Historical and Genealogical Register
N2400 (ASU)

Hatmaker, Arthur J. "A Study for a Guidance Program at Jonesville High School, Jonesville, Virginia." Master's thesis. East Tennessee State Univ., 1967.
H3500 (ETSU)

Haught, Oscar L. Coal and Coal Mining in West Virginia. Rev. ed. Educational Series. Morgantown: West Virginia Geological and Economic Survey, 1964. Propaganda for the coal industry.
H3510 (ASU BC ETSU)

Geology of Oil and Gas. Circular, 3. Morgantown: West Virginia Geological and Economic Survey, 1965.
H3520 (ETSU)

Oil and Gas in Southern West Virginia. Bulletin, no. 17. Morgantown: West Virginia Geological and Economic Survey, 1959.
H3530 (ETSU)

Oil and Gas in West Virginia. Educational Series. Morgantown: West Virginia Geological and Economic Survey, 1964.
H3540 (ETSU)

Oil and Gas Report and Map of Doddridge and Harrison Counties, West Virginia. Bulletin, no. 16. Morgantown: West Virginia Geological Survey, 1959.
H3550 (ETSU)

Oil and Gas Report and Map of Lewis and Gilmer Counties, West Virginia. Bulletin, no. 18. Morgantown: West Virginia Geological and Economic Survey, 1960.
H3560 (ETSU)

Oil and Gas Report and Map of Marshall, Wetzel, and Tyler Counties, West Virginia. Bulletin, no. 12. Morgantown: West Virginia Geological Survey, 1955.
H3570 (ETSU)

Oil and Gas Report and Map of Monongalia, Marion, and Taylor Counties, West Virginia. Bulletin, no. 13. Morgantown: West Virginia Geological Survey, 1956.
H3580 (ETSU)

Oil and Gas Report and Map of Pleasants, Wood, and Ritchie Counties, West Virginia. Bulletin, no. 11. Morgantown: West Virginia Geological Survey, 1955.
H3590 (ETSU)

Oil and Gas Report on Barbour and Upshur Counties, West Virginia. Bulletin, 31. Charleston: West Virginia Geological and Economic Survey, 1965.
H3600 (ETSU)

Oil and Gas Report on Braxton and Clay Counties, West Virginia. Bulletin, 29. Charleston: West Virginia Geological and Economic Survey, 1964.
H3610 (ETSU)

Oil and Gas Report on Kanawha County, West Virginia. Bulletin, no. 19. Morgantown: West Virginia Geological and Economic Survey, 1960.
H3620 (ETSU)

West Virginia's Oil and Gas Lubricants and Fuels. Bulletin, 26. Charleston: West Virginia Geological and Economic Survey, 1964.
H3630 (ETSU)

Haught, Thomas William West Virginia Wesleyan College, First 50 Years, 1890-1940. Buckhannon, W. Va.: The college, 1940.
H3640

Haun, Mildred "Cocke County Ballads and Songs." Microfilm. Master's thesis. Vanderbilt Univ., 1937.
H3650 (ASU)

The Hawk's Done Gone. Indianapolis: Bobbs-Merrill Company, 1940. Twenty-three stories covering one family's lore, songs, tales and legends in Hamblen County, Tennessee from pioneer days to 1940. Beautifully done.
H3660

The Hawk's Done Gone And Other Stories. 1940. Reprint. Nashville: Vanderbilt Univ. Press, 1968.
H3670 (ASU BC WCU LMC WWC)

Hauser, Robert E. Geological Society of Kentucky Itinerary: Some Stratigraphic and Structural Features of the Middlesboro Basin. Lexington, Ky.: The society, 1957.
G830 (ETSU)

Hauser, William Patrick "An Analysis of Occupational Conditions in Selected Shops and Laboratories at East Tennessee State University." Master's thesis. East Tennessee State Univ., 1972.
H3680 (ETSU)

Hawk, Ruth Lillian "A Study of an Enriched Language Arts Program for Third Grade Students at Fairmont School." Master's thesis. East Tennessee State Univ., 1968.
H3690 (ETSU)

Hawkins, Caroline A. Cherokee Legends and Myths: Appendix to "Junaluska." Roanoke, Va.: Hammond's Print. and Litho. Works, 1916.
H3700 (LMC)

Junaluska at the Battle of Horse Shoe Bend: True Story of the Cherokee Chief. Roanoke, Va.: Press of the Stone Print. Co., 1916.
H3710 (LMC)

Hawkins, Dean pseud. Dean, Benjamin Hawkins Skull Mountain. New York: Doubleday, Doran and Co., 1941.
D1500

Hawks, Francis Lister Adventures of Daniel Boone, the Kentucky Rifleman. New York: Appleton, 1843-4.
H3720 (BC)

History of North Carolina. 2 vols. North Carolina Heritage Series, no. 2-3. 1857-58. Reprint. Spartanburg, S. C.: Reprint Co., 1961. Not much emphasis on the western counties.
H3730 (LMC MHC)

Hawks, Wills Moonshine Strategy, and Other Stories. Baltimore: I and Ottenheimer, 1906. Short stories, some with mountain settings.
H3740 (BC)

Hawley, Marion H. Income and Population in Alabama. 3rd ed. Bureau of Business Research Printed Series, no. 27. (Original title: Personal Income in Alabama Counties Since 1939.) University: Univ. of Alabama, 1960.
H3750 (ASU)

Personal Income in Alabama Counties since 1939. Rev. Printed Series, 25. University: Bureau of Business Research, School of Commerce and Business Administration, Univ. of Alabama, 1959.
H3760 (ASU)

Hawn, Ashley T. "The Lenoir City Company, An Attempt in Community Development." Master's thesis. Univ. of Tennessee, 1940.
H3770

Hawthorne, Frances Hughston "A Survey of Reading Readiness and Reading Achievement of City Kindergarten and Non-kindergarten Children in the First Grades in Elizabethton, Tennessee." Master's thesis. East Tennessee State Univ., 1969.
H3780 (ETSU)

Hay, Donald G. Acceptance of Voluntary Health Insurance in Four Rural Communities of Haywood County, North Carolina. Raleigh: North Carolina Agricultural Experiment Station, 1954.
H3790

Hay, Gertrude Sloan ed. Daughters of the American Revolution; North Carolina. Roster of Soldiers from North Carolina in the American Revolution, with an Appendix Containing a Collection of Miscellaneous Records. Baltimore: Genealogical Pub. Co., 1967.
D530 (ASU)

Hay, James, Jr. The Bellamy Case. New York: Dodd, Mead and Co., 1925. Mystery tale set in the North Carolina mountains near Asheville.
H3800 (ASU)

The Hidden Women. New York: Dodd, Mead and Co., 1929. Mystery yarn with a mountain setting.
H3810 (BC)

The Winning Clue. New York: Dodd, Mead and Co., 1919. Mountain mystery set in Asheville, North Carolina.
H3820 (ASU BC)

Hayden, Horace Edwin Virginia Genealogies: A Genealogy of the Glassell Family of Scotland and Virginia, Also of the Families of Ball, Brown, Bryan, Conway, Daniel, Ewell, Holladay, Lewis, Littlepage, Nioncure, Peyton, Robinson, Scott, Taylor, Wallace and Others of Virginia and Maryland. Baltimore: Southern Book Co., 1959.
H3830 (ASU)

Hayes, Adam A. "The Background, Education, and Experience of Teachers in Rutherford County, N. C." Master's thesis. Furman University, 1954.
H3840

Hayes, Carl N. Neighbor against Neighbor, Brother against Brother; Greene County in the Civil War. Greeneville: The author, 1966.
H3850

Hayes, Charles The Hanging of "Bad Tom" Smith and the Events Leading to his Hanging. Whitesburg, Ky.: Eagle Print. Co., 1969. Includes an account of the French and Eversole feud and other Breathitt County troubles.
H3860 (BC)

Hayes, Charles Willard Physiography of the Chattanooga District in Tenn., Georgia, and Ala. 1899. Washington: Govt. Print. Off., 1899.
H3870

The Southern Appalachians. n.p.: National Geographic Society Monographs, No. 10, 1895.
H3880

The Southern Appalachians. Cincinnati: American Book Co., 1895.
H3890 (ASU BC)

Hayes, Clair Wallace The Boy Troopers Among the Wild Mountaineers. New York: A. L. Burt Company, 1922. Fiction contrived to liken mountain folk to barbarians.
H3900 (BC)

Hayes, Harold L. "The Settlement Pattern of Upper East Tennessee." Master's thesis. East Tennessee State Univ., 1966. A fascinating study of the early settlement of the Watauga Country.
H3910 (ETSU)

Hayes, Irene comp. What's Cooking in Kentucky? Rev. 1st ed. Louisville, Ky.: V. G. Reed and Sons, 1970.
H3920 (ASU BC WCU)

Hayes, Johnson J. The Land of Wilkes. Wilkesboro, N. C.: Wilkes County Historical Society, 1962. A very good county history.
H3930 (ASU WCU LMC BC)

Hayhurst, Donald E. Employment Security in West Virginia. Morgantown: Bureau of Government Research, West Virginia University, 1966.
H3940

Haymond, Bruce Borderland Echoes, a W. Va. Story. Boston: Roxburgh, 1921.
H3950 (BC ASU)

Haymond, Henry History of Harrison County. Morgantown, W. Va.: Acne Pub. Co., 1973.
H3960 (ASU)

Hays, Bentley G. "Equating Timber and Wildlife Values and Returns to the Farm Resources Base in Sullivan County, Pennsylvania." Master's thesis. Pennsylvania State Univ., 1962.
H3970

Hays, Brooks Vogel, H. D. TVA Revenue Bond Financing Presented by the Board of Directors, Tennessee Valley Authority. New York: Municipal Forum of New York, 1960.
V1290

Hays, D. Sanger, S. F. The Olive Branch of Peace and Good Will to Men: Anti-war History of the Brethren and Mennonites, the Peace People of the South, During the Civil War, 1861-1865. Elgin, Ill.: Brethren Pub. House, 1907.
S440 (ASU)

Hays, Nancy Margaret "A Proposed Course in Ceramics for the Fine Arts Department of East Tennessee State College." Master's thesis. East Tennessee State College, 1960.
H3980 (ETSU)

Hays, Willard Murrell "Andrew Johnson's Reputation: A Study of Changing Interpretations." Master's thesis. Univ. of Tennessee, 1958.
H3990

Hays, Wilma Pitchford Highland Halloween. New York: Coward-McCann, 1962.
H4000 (LMC)

Haywood, Charles A Bibliography of North American Folklore and Folksong. 2nd rev. ed. 2 vols. New York: Dover Pub., 1961.
H4010 (ASU WWC)

Haywood County Planning Board Land Use Plan, Haywood County, N. C. Waynesville, N. C.: The author, 1962.
H4020 (LMC)

Haywood, John The Civil and Political History of the State of Tennessee, from Its Earliest Settlement up to the Year 1796: Including the Boundaries of the State. 1823. Reprint. Knoxville, Tenn.: Tenase Co., 1969.
H4030 (ASU WCU LMC MHC BC)

The First American Frontier: Civil and Political History of the State of Tennessee from Its Earliest Settlement up to the Year 1796. New York: Arno Press, 1971.
H4040 (LMC)

The Natural and Aboriginal History of Tennessee, up to the First Settlements Therein by the White People in the Year 1768. Including archaeological, geological, and historical annotations bringing the ancient account into focus with present day knowledge, and an introductory sketch of the author by Mary U. Rothrock. Jackson, Tenn.: McCowat-Mercer Press, 1959.
H4050 (ASU ETSU BC)

Haywood, Marshall Delancey Builders of the Old North State: Selected Sketches. Raleigh: The compiler, 1968.
H4060 (LMC)

Lives of the Bishops of North Carolina from the Establishment of the Episcopate in that State down to the Division of the Diocese. Raleigh: A. Williams Co., 1910.
H4070 (LMC)

Haywood, Mattie Bailey comp. Haywood, Marshall Delancey Builders of the Old North State: Selected Sketches. Raleigh: The compiler, 1968.
H4060 (LMC)

Haywood, William Dudley Bill Haywood's Book: The Autobiography of William D. Haywood. New York: International Pubs., 1929. Haywood was founder of the IWW and organized some strikes in Appalachia.
H4080 (ASU WCU)

Hazard, Kentucky. Chamber of Commerce Industrial Resources, Hazard, Kentucky. Frankfort, Ky.: Chamber of Commerce, 1966.
H4090

Hazard, Lucy Lockwood The Frontier in American Literature. New York: The Thomas Y. Crowell Co., 1927. Discusses some Appalachian books.
H4100

Head, James William History and Comprehensive Description of Loudoun County, Virginia. Washington: Park View Press, 1908.
H4110 (ASU BC)

Headden, Damon Headden, Harmon Clay Conservation of Wildlife and Forests in Tennessee. Kingsport, Tenn.: Southern Pubs., 1936.
H4120 (ETSU BC)

Headden Harmon Clay Conservation of Wildlife and Forests in Tennessee. Nashville: McQuiddy, 1941.
H4130

Headden, Harmon Clay Conservation of Wildlife and Forests in Tennessee. Kingsport, Tenn.: Southern Pubs., 1936.
H4120 (ETSU BC)

Conservation of Wildlife and Forests in Tennessee. Reprint. Nashville: McQuiddy, 1941.
H4130

Headlee, Alvah John Washington Germanium in Coals of West Virginia. Report of Investigations, no. 8. Morgantown: West Virginia Geological & Economic Survey, 1951.
H4140 (ETSU)

Permeability, Porosity, Oil, and Water Content of Natural Gas Reservoirs, Kanawha-Jackson and Campbells Creek Oriskany Fields. West Virginia Geological Survey Bulletin, no. 8. Morgantown, W. Va.: Morgantown Print. & Bind. Co., 1945.
H4150 (ETSU)

Price, Paul Holland Physical and Chemical Properties of Natural Gas of West Virginia. Morgantown: West Virginia Geological Survey, 1937.
P4540 (ETSU)

Headrick, Warren B. "A Study of the Physical Plants of Blount County High Schools." Master's thesis. Univ. of Tennessee, 1952.
H4160

Heads of Families at the First Census, 1790 Baltimore: Genealogical Pub. Co., 1966.
H4170

Heald, Milton T. Lithification of Sandstones in West Virginia. Bulletin, 30. Charleston: West Virginia Geological & Economic Survey, 1965.
H4180 (ETSU)

Hearn, Williamson Edward Soil Survey of Gaston County, North Carolina. Washington, D. C.: U. S. Govt. Print. Off., 1911. Gaston County borders on the mountain region and is populated primarily by mountaineers who work in the textile mills.
H4190 (ASU)

Soil Survey of Henderson County, North Carolina. Prepared in cooperation with the North Carolina Department of Agriculture. Field Operations, 1907. Washington: U. S. Department of Agriculture, Bureau of Soils, 1909.
H4200

Soil Survey of Transylvania County, North Carolina. Prepared in cooperation with the North Carolina Department of Agriculture. Field Operation, 1906. Washington: U. S. Department of Agriculture, Bureau of Soils, 1908.
H4210

Soil Survey of Transylvania County. Washington: Govt. Print. Off., 1907.
H4220

Heaster, Emmett Limericks and Lyrics from My Rhododendron Thicket. Parsons, W. Va.: McClain Print. Co., 1973.
H4230 (ASU)

Heath, Emily P. "A Study of the Relationship Existing Between Amount of Education Completed by White and Negro Head of Households in Floyd County." Master's thesis. Univ. of Georgia, 1948.
H4240

Heath, Milton S., Jr. Flood Damage Prevention in North Carolina. Raleigh: North Carolina Department of Water Resources, 1963. Many of the states disastrous floods occur in the mountains.
H4250 (LMC)

Heatwole, Cornelius Jacob A History of Education in Virginia. N. Y.: Macmillan Co., 1916.
H4260 (ETSU FC)

Heavener, U. S. A. German New River Settlement, Virginia. n.p.: n.p., 1929? Church, court, and family records of several families of Montgomery County near Blacksburg.
H4270 (ASU FC)

Hebson, Ann The Lattiner Legend. N. Y.: Macmillan, 1961. A family saga set against a Civil War background.
H4280 (LMC BC)

Heck, Edward Timmel Appalachian Connate Water. Bulletin, 200. Charleston: West Virginia Geological Survey, 1964.
H4290 (ETSU)

Price, Paul Holland Greenbrier County. Wheeling: West Virginia Geological Survey, 1939.
P4530 (LMC ETSU)

Heebink, T. B. Kurtenacker, R. S. Appalachian Hardwoods for Pallets, Laboratory Evaluation. Madison, Wis.: Forest Products Laboratory, 1967.
K3430

Heer, Clarence Income and Wages in the South. Chapel Hill: Univ. of North Carolina Press, 1930.
H4300 (LMC)

Heflin, Catherine Urban Adjustments of Rural Migrants: A Study of 297 Families in Lexington, Kentucky, 1942. (Bulletin No. 487.) Lexington: Kentucky Agricultural Experiment Station, Univ. of Kentucky, 1946.
H4310

Heflin, Catherine P. Beers, Howard Wayland People and Resources in Eastern Kentucky. Lexington: Kentucky Agricultural Experiment Station, Univ. of Kentucky, 1947.
B2610

Beers, Howard Wayland Rural People in the City: A Study of the Socio-economic Status of 297 Families in Lexington, Kentucky. Lexington: Kentucky Agricultural Experiment Station, 1945.
B2620

Beers, Howard Wayland Urban Adjustments of Rural Migrants. Lexington: Kentucky Agriculture Experiment Station, Univ. of Kentucky, 1946.
B2630

Hein, Polly W. Keeling, William B. Tourism Development in the Chattahoochee-Flint Area. Athens: Univ. of Georgia, Bureau of Business and Economic Research, 1967.
K430

Heinemann, Charles Brunk comp. First Census of Kentucky, 1790. 1940. Reprint. Baltimore: Genealogical Pub. Co., 1965.
H4320 (ASU BC UNCA)

Heiskill, Samuel Gordon Andrew Jackson and Early Tennessee History. Nashville: Ambrose Print. Co., 1918. Jackson began his legal career in Jonesboro, Tennessee.
H4330

Heitman, Francis Bernard Historical Register of Officers of the Continental Army During the War of the Revolution, April, 1775 to December, 1783. New, rev. and enlarged ed. with addenda by Robert H. Kelby, 1932. 1914. Reprint. Baltimore: Genealogical Pub. Co., 1967.
H4340 (ASU)

Helms, David Mack A Study of Ohio Appalachian and Non-Appalachian Public Secondary School Teacher's Attitudes Towards Selected Aspects of Training and Experience. Master's thesis. Ohio Univ., 1971. Univ. Microfilms, 1973.
H4350

Helmut, Jan Daisy's Fanny. N. Y.: Vantage Press, 1951. A raw and violent tale of feuds, fights, and moonshine-making in the hills of Tennessee.
H4360 (BC)

Helmut, Jan pseud. Sherman, Katharine Daisy's Fanny. New York: Vantage, 1951.
S2920

Helmut, Jan, pseud. see also **Sherman, Katherine**

Helper, Hinton A. Asheville, Western North Carolina, Nature's Trundle-Bed of Recuperation for Tourist and Health-beds. N. Y.: South Pub. Co., 1886.
H4370

Helton, Roy Addison Lonesome Water. N. Y.: Harper & Brothers, 1930. Hauntingly beautiful poems about life in the mountains.
H4380 (BC)

Nitchey Tilley. N. Y.: Harper and Brothers, 1934. In a remote North Carolina mountain cove a boy is reared without contact with the outside world. When his mentor dies, he must make his own way into the big world.
H4390

Nitchey Tilley, a Novel. 1st ed. N. Y.: Harper & Brothers, 1943.
H4400 (ASU BC)

Helvey, J. D. Rainfall Interception by Hardwood Forest Litter in Southern Appalachians. U. S. Forest Service Research Paper, SE-8. Asheville, N. C.: Southeastern Forest Experiment Station, 1964.
H4410 (WCU)

Hemphill, William Edwin and others Albemarle County Historical Society, War History Committee Pursuits of War: The People of Charlottesville and Albemarle County, Virginia, in the Second World War. Charlottesville, Va.: The society, 1948.
A970 (ASU)

Henderson, Archibald The Conquest of the Old Southwest: The Romantic Story of the Early Pioneers into Virginia, the Carolinas, Tennessee, and Kentucky, 1740-1790. N. Y.: Century Co., 1920.
H4420 (ASU WCU LMC BC)

Dr. Thomas Walker and The Loyal Company of Virginia. Reprinted from Proceedings of the American Antiquarian Society. Worcester, Mass.: n.p., 1931.
H4430

North Carolina: The Old North State and the New. 5 vols. Chicago: Lewis Pub. Co., 1941.
H4440 (UNCA LMC)

The Transylvania Company and the Founding of Henderson, Ky. Henderson, Ky.: n.p., 1929. This land company was instrumental in the settlement of Kentucky.
H4450 (ASU)

Henderson, Daniel MacIntyre Boone of the Wilderness: A Tale of Pioneer Adventures and Achievement in "The Dark and Bloody Ground." N. Y.: E. P. Dutton & Co., 1921.
H4460 (ASU BC)

Henderson, George Survivals in Belief Among the Celts. Glasgow: J. Maclehose and Sons, 1911.
H4470

Henderson, George Francis Robert Stonewall Jackson and the American Civil War. 2 vols. London: Longmans, Green & Co., 1927.
H4480 (ASU BC)

Henderson, Harold Alpheus Adjustments of Rural Resources Use and Characteristics to Economic Growth. Knoxville: Univ. of Tennessee, Agricultural Experiment Station, 1963.
H4490 (ASU)

"Economic Progress and Resource Adjustments of Rural Households is the Upper East Tennessee Valley." Microfilm. Ph. D. Diss. Purdue Univ., 1962.
H4500 (ASU)

Income Differences of Rural People in the Upper East Tennessee Valley. (Bulletin No. 365.) Knoxville: Tennessee Agricultural Experiment Station, Univ. of Tennessee, August, 1963.
H4510 (ASU)

Resources and Incomes of Rural Upper East Tennessee People, a Progress Report of a Study of the Economic Status and Opportunities of Rural People. Knoxville: Univ. of Tennessee Agricultural Experiment Station, 1960.
H4520 (ASU BC)

Henderson, Helen Ruth A Curriculum Study in a Mountain District. Contributions to Education, no. 732. N. Y.: Teachers College, Columbia Univ., 1937. This study took place in Buchanan County, Virginia.
H4530 (ASU ETSU BC)

Henderson, Lawson Pinckney, III. Windsongs. Mount Airy, N. C.: The author, 1969.
H4540 (ASU)

Henderson, Moffitt Sinclair A Long, Long Day for November. Charlotte: Delmar Co., 1972. Well-written historical fiction about Revolutionary days in western North Carolina.
H4550 (ASU)

Henderson, William A. "Nolachucky Jack." (Gov. John Sevier.) Lecture of Wm. A. Henderson, to the Board of Trade of the City of Knoxville, January 7th, 1873. Knoxville, Tenn.: Printed at the Press and Herald Steam Book and Job Office, 1873.
H4560

Hendersonville, N. C., Etowah Baptist Church Minutes and Records, Feb., 1917-Dec. 25, 1960. Microfilm, 3 reels. Nashville: Historical Commission, Southern Baptist Convention, 1960.
H4570 (WCU)

Hendersonville, N. C., Planning Board A Study of the Hendersonville Central Business District. n.p.: The board, 1965?
H4580 (LMC)

Hendricks, Garland A. Appalachian Shepherd: A Story of Religion in the Southern Appalachians. Foreword by Dr. W. D. Weatherford. Atlanta: Spiritural Life Publishers, 1965.
H4590 (BC ASU LMC ETSU FC WWC)

Hendricks, William C. ed. Bundle of Troubles, and Other Tarheel Tales. Durham, N. C.: Duke Univ. Press, 1943.
H4600

Hendrickson, Bertram Higbie Soil Survey of Tioga County, Pennsylvania. In cooperation with the Pennsylvania State College, School of Agriculture and Experiment Station. Soil Survey Report, Series 1929, no. 30. Washington: U. S. Department of Agriculture, Bureau of Chemistry and Soils, 1934.
H4610

Soil Survey of Wyoming County, Pennsylvania. In cooperation with the Pennsylvania State College, School of Agriculture and Experiment Station. Soil Survey Report, Series 1929, no. 34. Washington: U. S. Department of Agriculture, Bureau of Chemistry and Soils, 1934.
H4620

Hendrix, David B. Smoky Mountain Square Dances. Ann Arbor, Mich.: Edwards Brothers, Inc., 1941.
H4630 (ASU)

Henkel, Alice American Medicinal Barks. U. S. Department of Agriculture Bureau of Plant Industry Bulletin, no. 139. Washington: Govt. Print. Off., 1909.
H4640 (ASU)

American Medicinal Leaves and Herbs. U. S. Department of Agriculture Bureau of Plant Industry Bulletin, no. 219. Washington: Govt. Print. Off., 1911.
H4650 (ASU)

Henkel, Elon Oseander ed. Cassell, Charles Willis ed. History of The Lutheran Church in Virginia and East Tennessee. Strasburg, Va.: Shenandoah Pub. House, 1930.
C1970 (ASU BC FC)

Henkel, Henrietta Deep River. 1st ed. N. Y.: Book Find Club, 1944. A novel of romance with a North Georgia mountain setting.
H4660 (ASU BC)

Henley, John C. This Is Birmingham. Birmingham, Ala.: Southern Univ. Press, 1960. The story of the founding and growth of the city.
H4670 (BC)

Hennen, Dorothy T. Hennen's Choice: A Compilation of the Descendents of Matthew Hennen (1752-1839). Parsons, W. Va.: McClain Print. Co., 1970.
H4680 (ASU)

Hennen, Earl M. "A Study of the Effects of Foreign Imports on the Hand-blown and Hand-pressed Glass Industry in the United States, Especially in Ohio, Pennsylvania, and West Virginia from 1948-1958." Master's thesis. Virginia Polytechnic Institute, 1959.
H4690

Hennen, Ray Vernon Braxton and Clay Counties. Aided in the field by Robert M. Gawthorp. Wheeling: West Virginia Geological Survey, 1917.
H4700 (ASU)

Fayette County. Assisted by D. Dee Teets, Jr. Assisted in Office by Rietz Courtney Tucker and A. M. Hagan. West Virginia Geological Survey. Wheeling, W. Va.: Wheeling News Litho. Co., 1919.
H4710 (ETSU)

Wirt, Roane and Calhoun Counties. West Virginia Geological Survey County Reports. Morgantown, W. Va.: Acme Pub. Co., 1911.
H4720 (ETSU)

Wyoming and McDowell Counties. Aided by Robert M. Gawthrop. County Reports. Wheeling: West Virginia Geological Survey, 1915.
H4730 (ETSU)

Henri, Florette King's Mountain. Garden City, N. Y.: Doubleday, 1950. A novel about the Tennessee mountain men in the Battle of King's Mountain.
H4740 (ASU BC)

Henry, E. F. Jurney, Robert Campbell Soil Survey, Smyth County, Virginia. Washington: U. S. Department of Agriculture, Bureau of Plant Industry, Soils and Agricultural Engineering, 1948.
J2930

Porter, Hobart Clarke Soil Survey, Tazewell County, Virginia. Washington: U. S. Department of Agriculture, Bureau of Plant Industry, Soils, and Agricultural Engineering, 1948.
P3660

Henry, J. Milton "The Tennessee Conservatives and Secession, 1847-61." Ph. D. Diss. Univ. of Chicago, 1951. The conservatives were mostly mountain men.
H4750

Henry, Jeannette Textbooks and the American Indian. San Francisco: Indian Historian Press, 1970.
H4760 (MHC)

Henry, Jim Gordon "Child-rearing Practices in Mountain Country, Kentucky." Ph. D. Diss. Univ. of Kentucky, 1970.
H4770 (LMC)

Henry, Mellinger Edward Bibliography for the Study of American Folk Songs with Many Titles from Other Lands. London: The Mitre Press, 1937.
H4780

Henry, Mellinger Edward
Songs Sung in the Southern Appalachians. London: Mitre Press, 1934.
H4800 (BC)
Still More Ballads and Folk-songs from the Southern Highlands. Authorized facsimile. Cleveland, Ohio: Micro Photo Division, Bell and Howell Co., 1974.
H4810

Henry, Mellinger Edward ed. Folk-songs from the Southern Highlands. 1st ed. N. Y.: J. J. Augustin, 1938.
H4790 (ASU LMC MHC ETSU BC)

Henry, Ruby Addison The First West. Nashville: Aurora Publishers, 1972. Describes the great Appalachian barrier.
H4820 (ASU WCU MHC ETSU BC)

Henry, Thomas R. Sherman, Mandel Hollow Folk. New York: Thomas Y. Crowell Co., 1933.
S2940 (BC LMC ETSU WWC)
Sherman, Mandel Hollow Folk. Berryville, Va.: Virginia Book Co., 1973.
S2950 (ASU)

Henschel, A. Lainhart, William S. Pneumoconiosis in Appalachian Bituminous Coal Miners. Washington: Bureau of Occupational Safety and Health, 1969.
L150

Henshaw, William Wade comp. Encyclopedia of American Quaker Genealogy. (Vol. VI, Virginia). Ann Arbor, Mich.: Edwards Brothers Printers, 1950.
H4830

Hensley, J. L. Rise and Progress of the Church of the United Brethren in Christ of West Virginia. n.p.: n.p., 1886.
H4840

Hensley, J. L., M. d. The Rise and Progress of the United Brethren in Christ in West Virginia. n.p.: n.p., n.d.
H4850 (BC ASU)

Henson, Paul Lost Silver Mines and Buried Treasures of Kentucky. Louisville: United Christian Print. Service, 1972.
H4860 (BC)

Henty, George Alfred True to the Old Flag: A Tale of the American War of Independence. N. Y.: A. L. Burt, 1896? Partially set in the mountains.
H4870 (ASU)

Hepting, George H. Decay in Merchantable Oak, Yellow Poplar, and Basswood in the Appalachian Region. Washington: U. S. Dept. of Agriculture, Plant Industry Bureau, 1937.
H4880

Herbert, Hilary Abner and others Why the Solid South? or, Reconstruction and its Results. Baltimore: R. H. Woodward & Co., 1890. Many Appalachian counties had aligned themselves with the Union.
H4890 (ASU)

Hergesheimer, Joseph The Limestone Tree. N. Y.: Grosset & Dunlap, 1931. Fiction with a mountain setting.
H4900 (ASU WCU BC)
Mountain Blood, a Novel. N. Y.: Mitchell Kennerley, 1915. A mountain stage driver marries a wealthy woman but the marriage does not work out.
H4910 (ASU BC)
Tol'able David. N. Y.: A. A. Knopf, 1923. A mountain tale with too much emphasis on coincidence and dialect.
H4920 (BC)

Herndon, G. Melvin William Tatham and the Culture of Tobacco: Including a Facsimile Reprint of an Historical and Practical Essay on the Culture and Commerce of Tobacco by William Tatham.
H4930

Heroes and Hunters of the West; Comprising Sketches and Adventures of Boone, Kenton, Brady. . . . Philadelphia: Crawford, n.d.
H4940 (BC ASU)

Herrick, Allyn Marsh Grading and Measuring Hickory Trees, Logs, and Products. Hickory Task Force Report, no. 7. Asheville, N. C.: Southeastern Forest Experiment Station, 1958.
H4950 (WCU)

Herrick, Huldah, pseud. see **Ober, Sarah Endicott**

Herrick, Owne W. A Look at Kentucky's Lumber Industry. U. S. Forest Service Research Paper, NE-63. Upper Darby, Pa.: Northeastern Forest Experiment Station, 1967.
H4960 (BC)

Herrin, Eric "Development of a Course in Fractions for Johnson City Vocational School." Master's thesis. East Tennessee State College, 1951.
H4970 (ETSU)

Herring, Harriet L. Passing of the Mill Village. Chapel Hill: Univ. of North Carolina Press, 1949. Many textile mills are located in the foothill counties of Appalachia.
H4980
Welfare Work in Mill Villages, the Story of Extra-mill Activities in North Carolina. Chapel Hill: Univ. of North Carolina, 1929.
H4990 (WWC)
Simpson, George Lee Western North Carolina Associated Communities. Cherokee, N. C.: Cherokee Historical Association, 1956.
S3610 (WCU)

Herrmann, Leo Anthony Geology of the Stone Mountain-Lithonia District, Georgia. Bulletin, no. 61. Atlanta: Georgia Geological Survey, 1954.
H5000 (ETSU)

Herron, Phillip R. "The Use of Inquiry Learning in Teaching Early Tennessee History." Master's thesis. East Tennessee State Univ., 1971.
H5010 (ETSU)

Herron, Richard W. "The Southern Indians as a Factor in the Relations of Spain and the U. S., 1783-1795." Master's thesis. Univ. of Cincinnati, 1938.
H5020

Hersh, Alan "The Development of the Iron Industry in East Tennessee." Master's thesis. Univ. of Tennessee, 1958.
H5030 (ASU)

Hersh, D. M. Weisenberger, Billy C. Soil Survey, Bath County, Kentucky. Washington: U. S. Soil Conservation Service, 1963.
W2360

Hershey, Robert E. Limestone and Dolomite Resources of Tennessee. Bulletin, 65. Nashville: Tennessee Division of Geology, 1963.
H5040 (ETSU)

Herzog, George ed. Cox, John Harrington comp. Traditional Ballads and Folk-songs Mainly from West Virginia. n.p.: American Folklore Society, 1964.
C8180 (ASU WCU ETSU BC)

Hesler, Lexemuel Ray Mushrooms of the Great Smokies: A Field Guide to Some Mushrooms and Their Relatives. Knoxville: Univ. of Tennessee Press, 1960.
H5050 (ASU WHC LMC UNCA BC WWC)
Some Mushrooms of Eastern Tennessee. I. Amanitas. Extension Series, vol. 6, no. 5. Knoxville: Univ. of Tennessee Record, 1930.
H5060 (ASU)

Hess, Albert Luther Leyden, Dennis R. Personal Income in West Virginia Counties by Type and Magnitude, 1960-1963: A Pilot Study. Morgantown: Bureau of Business and Research, College of Commerce, and Office of Research and Development of the West Virginia Center for Appalachian Studies and Development, West Virginia Univ., 1966.
L2410 (ASU)

Hess, Effie A. ed. Sites, Carrie B. A History of the Town of Dayton, Virginia. Dayton, Va.: Dayton Women's Club, 1962.
S3760 (ASU BC)

Hess, J. W. ed. Struggle in the Coal Fields. The Autobiography of Fred Mooney, Secretary-Treasurer, District 17, United Mine Workers of America. Morganton: W. Va. Univ. Library, 1967. Mooney participated in the West Virginia labor struggles.
H5070 (ASU)

Hesseltine, William B. ed. Ramsey, James Gettys McGready Autobiography and Letters. Nashville: Tennessee Historical Commission, 1954.
R260 (ASU BC)

Hesseltine, William Best The South in American History. History Series. 1936. Reprint. (Original title: A History of the South, 1607-1936.) N. Y.: Prentice-Hall, 1943. Scant mention of Appalachia.
H5090 (LMC FC)

Hesseltine, William Best ed. Dr. J. G. Ramsey: Autobiography and Letters. Nashville: Tennessee Historical Commission, 1954. Autobiography of an early Tennessee historian and professional man.
H5080 (ASU LMC)

Hester, Bertha B. Thickety Bush: A Drama in Three Acts. N. Y.: Carleton Press, 1967. A drama with a mountain setting.
H5100 (WCU WWC)

Hester, Jack Hills, Hollers and Hickory Flats. N. Y.: T. Gans Sons, Printers, 1942. A hilarious and surprisingly accurate account of everyday life and adventures in the Southern Mountains.
H5110 (BC)

Hevener, John Watts "A New Deal for Harlan: The Roosevelt Labor Policies in a Kentucky Coal Field, 1931-1939." Ph. D. Diss. Ohio State Univ., 1971. An interesting account of one of two times this administration investigated labor troubles in Appalachia.
H5120 (BC)

Hewett, D. F. Possibilities for Manganese Ore on Certain Undeveloped Tracts in the Shenandoah Valley, Virginia. U. S. Geological Survey Bulletin, no. 660-J. Washington: Govt. Print. Off., 1918.
H5130

Heye, George Gustav Certain Mounds in Haywood County, North Carolina. Contributions from the Museum, vol. 5, no. 3. N. Y.: Museum of the American Indian, Heye Foundation, 1919.
H5140 (ASU)

Heyl, Allen V. Jolly, Janice L. Mercury and Other Trace Elements in Sphalerite and Wallrocks from Central Kentucky, Tennessee, and Appalachian Zinc Districts. Washington: U. S. Geological Survey, 1968.
J2250

Heyward, Du Bose Skylines and Horizons. N. Y.: Macmillan Co., 1924. Lyrical descriptions of the mountain country of western North Carolina.
H5160 (ASU LMC BC)

Heywood, Du Bose Angel. N. Y.: George H. Doran Co., 1926. A sensitive novel of a young mountain girl forced into an unfortunate marriage.
H5150 (ASU ETSU BC)

Hiatt, Ellen O. M. Sequatchie Valley, a Historical Sketch. Photographs by Marguerite Hiatt. Nashville: Methodist Pub. House, 1916.
H5170

Hibbard, Clarence Addison ed. Stories of the South, Old and New. With an introduction, biographical notes and bibliography. Univ. of N. C. Press, 1931. Scant mention of the mountains.
H5180 (ASU BC WWC)

Hickerson, Thomas Felix Echoes of Happy Valley: Letters and Diaries, Family Life in the South, Civil War History. Chapel Hill, N. C.: Bull's Head Bookshop, 1962.
H5190 (ASU LMC BC)
Happy Valley, History and Genealogy. Chapel Hill, N. C.: The author, 1940.
H5200 (ASU)

Hicks, Billy C. Martin, Joe Allen The Economics of Using Low-Quality Hardwoods for Producing Charcoal in Tennessee. Knoxville: Univ. of Tennessee, Agriculture Experiment Station, 1964.
M3700

Hicks, Glenda "The Forgotten Sons: North Carolinans in the Union Army." Master's thesis. Appalachian State Univ., 1968. Many mountaineers were Union soldiers.
H5210 (ASU)

Hicks, Marie Leach "The Hepatic Flora of Watauga County, North Carolina." Master's thesis. Appalachian State Teachers College, 1964.
H5220 (ASU)

Hicks, Nannie Lee Community Historical Sketches in Knox County, Tennessee: Corryton — Harbison's Cross Roads — Smithwood. Community Historical Sketches, no. 1. Knoxville: Knox Co. Lib., 1958.
H5230

Historic Treasure Spots of Knox County, Tennessee. Knoxville: Simon Harris Chapter, Daughters of the American Revolution, 1964.
H5240 (ETSU BC)

The John Adair Section of Knox County, Tennessee. Knoxville: n.p., 1968.
H5250

Higbee, Howard William Soil Survey, Huntingdon County, Pennsylvania. Prepared in cooperation with the Pennsylvania State College, School of Agriculture and Experiment Station. Soil Survey Report Series 1934, no. 27. Washington: U. S. Department of Agriculture, Bureau of Plant Industry, Soils and Agricultural Engineering, 1944.
H5260

Moon, J. W. Soil Survey, Jefferson County, Tennessee. Washington: U. S. Department of Agriculture, Bureau of Plant Industry, 1941.
M6630

Higgins, Hazel Briggs "The Diagnosis and Remediation of Difficulties in Arithmetical Skills of a Seventh-grade Class at Rock Creek School in Erwin, Tennessee." Master's thesis. East Tennessee State Univ., 1966.
H5270 (ETSU)

High, Fred Waynesburg, Prosperous and Beautiful, a Souvenir Pictorial Story of the Biggest and Best Little City in Pennsylvania. . . . Wanyesburg, Pennsylvania: Green County Historical Society, 1973.
H5280

High Schools, Gaston County, N. C.; a Southern Cotton Mill Town Charlotte, N. C.: Observer Print. House, 1908.
H5290 (ASU)

Highlander Folk School The Story of an Educational Center for Working People. n.p.: n.p., n.d.
H5310

Highlander Folk School, Monteagle, Tenn. Annual Report. n.p.: n.p., 1951-.
H5300

Hilbert, Archer Butler Boone's Wilderness Road. Historic Highways of America, Vol. 6. Cleveland: Arthur H. Clark Co., 1903.
H5320

Hilbish, Florence M. A. Tales of a Frontier Preacher. N. Y.: Pageant, 1959. Memoirs of a frontier preacher who served long years in the mountains.
H5330

Hildreth, Arthur L. A Brief History of New Market and Vicinity. The Battle of New Market Centennial, May 15, 1864-1964. New Market, Va.: Henkel Press, 1964. One of the most tragic campaigns of the entire war.
H5340 (ASU)

Hill, Alonzo F. The White Rocks; or The Robbers Den; a Tragedy of the Mountains. Morgantown, W. Va.: Morgantown Print. and Binding Co., 1925. Fact turned to legend and later to fiction.
H5350 (BC)

Hill, Daniel Harvey Bethel to Sharpsbury. 2 vols. Raleigh, N. C.: Edwards & Broughton Co., 1926.
H5360 (ASU LMC)

Young People's History of North Carolina. Raleigh, N. C.: Williams, 1916.
H5370 (LMC WWC)

Hill, Emory Akers "The Design and Preparation of a Proposal for Federal Aid for the Education of Children from Low Income Families in Damascus Elementary School, Washington County, Virginia." Master's thesis. East Tennessee State Univ., 1966.
H5380 (ETSU)

Hill (Eric) Associates Johnson City, Tennessee, Population and Economic Base Study. 2 vols. in 1. Atlanta: Johnson City Regional Planning Comm., 1964-65.
H5390

Hill, George Canning Daniel Boone: The Pioneer of Kentucky. N. Y.: Lippincott, 1859.
H5400

Life and Adventures of Daniel Boone, the Pioneer of Kentucky. N. Y.: Hurst & Co., n.d.
H5410 (ASU BC)

Hill, Howard L. The Herbert Walters Story. 2 vols. Morristown: Morristown Print., 1963-66.
H5420

Hill, J. J. comp. Old Cherokee Families: "Old Families and Their Genealogy" . . . with a Comprehensive Index. Norman: Univ. of Oklahoma Press, 1968.
H5430

Hill, Jack Kenneth "Social and Economic Implications of Strip Mining in Harrison County, W. Va." Master's thesis. Ohio State Univ., 1965.
H5440

Hill, James Edwin "The Strawberry Industry of the Hilly and Mountainous Regions of Tennessee." Master's thesis. Univ. of Tennessee, 1959.
H5450 (ASU)

Hill, James Otto "Sewanee a Unique Community." Master's thesis. Middle Tennessee State Univ., 1952.
H5460

Hill, Louise Biles History of Mt. Zion Methodist Episcopal Church 4, South of Mount Zion, Warren County, Tenn., 1809-1930. McMinnville: Standard, 1930.
H5470

Hill, Samuel S. Southern Churches in Crisis. 1st ed. N. Y.: Holt, Rinehart, & Winston, 1967.
H5480 (WCU WWC)

Hill, West T. The Theatre in Early Kentucky, 1790-1820. Lexington: Univ. Press of Kentucky, 1971. Very few performances were given in the mountains.
H5490 (BC)

Hill, William Laurie The Master of the Red Buck and the Bay Doe: A Story of Whig and Tory Warfare in North Carolina in 1781-83. Charlotte, N. C.: Stone Pub. Co., 1913. Action ranges into the mountains.
H5500 (LMC)

Hillard, George Stillman Life and Campaigns of George B. McClellan, Major-General U. S. Army. Philadelphia: J. B. Lippincott & Co., 1865. Includes some information about campaigns in the Valley of Virginia.
H5510 (ASU)

Hillbilly Cookin' by the Tates Thorn Hill, Tenn.: F. Tate, 1968.
H5520

Hillery, George A. Population Growth in Kentucky, 1820-1960. (Bulletin No. 705.) Lexington: Kentucky Agricultural Experiment Station, Univ. of Kentucky, 1966.
H5530

Hillis, Florence Elliott comp. and ed. Daughters of the American Revolution, Tennessee, Lydia Russell Bean Chapter, Knoxville. Benton County, Tennessee, Marriages, 1832-1957. Knoxville, Tenn.: n.p., 1962.
D570 (ASU)

Hilmon, J. B. Plants of the Caloosa Experimental Range. U. S. Forest Service Research Paper, SE-12. Asheville, N. C.: Southeastern Forest Experiment Station, 1964.
H5540 (WCU)

Hind, James Fox "The History of Transportation Advertising, 1850-1956, and a Study of Its Importance in Knoxville, Tennessee." Master's thesis. Univ. of Tennessee, 1958.
H5550

Hinde, H. K. The Shenandoah National Park Travelogue; an Official Illustrated Guide Book for the First Great Nat'l Park of the East. Luray, Va.: Shenandoah Nat'l Park, 1937.
H5560

Hinebaugh, Margaret H. "History of Education of Marion County, West Virginia." Master's thesis. West Virginia Univ., 1940.
H5570

Hines, Chet How to Make and Play the Dulcimore. An Early American Society Book. Harrisburg, Pa.: Stackpole Books, 1973. An excellent book of directions and instructions for the traditional Appalachian instrument.
H5580 (WCU ASU BC)

Hines, Lois Davidson Lynch Families of the Southern States. n.p.: Dorothy Ford Wulfeck privately printed, 1966.
H5590

Hinke, William John ed. Strassburger, Ralph Beaver Pennsylvania German Pioneers: A Publication of the Original Lists of Arrivals in the Port of Philadelphia from 1727 to 1808. Norristown, Pa.: Pennsylvania German Society, 1934.
S7790 (ASU)

Strassburger, Ralph Beaver Pennsylvania German Pioneers: A Publication of the Original Lists of Arrivals in the Port of Philadelphia from 1727 to 1808. Baltimore: Genealogical Pub. Co., 1966.
S7800 (ASU)

Hinkle, Jerry W. "Fish Fauna Diversity as an Indication of Pollution Stress in Streams." Master's thesis. East Tennessee State Univ., 1972.
H5600 (ETSU)

Hinkley, Julian Wisner A Narrative of Service With the Third Wisconsin Infantry. Original Papers, no. 7. Madison: Wisconsin History Commission, 1912. This unit saw action in the Appalachian mountains.
H5610 (ASU)

Hinricks, Albert Ford "The United Mine Workers of America and the Non-Union Coal Fields." Ph. D. Diss. Columbia Univ., 1923.
H5620

Hinsen, Herbert G. Floods on Small Streams in North Carolina: Probable Magnitude and Frequency. Prepared in cooperation with the North Carolina State Highway Commission. Circular, 517. Washington: U. S. Geological Survey, 1965, 1966.
H5630 (LMC)

Hinshaw, William Wade Encyclopedia of American Quaker genealogy. 2 vol. 1936-1938. Reprint. Baltimore: Genealogical Pub. Co., 1969-.
H5640 (ASU)

Hinton, Bruce "Significant Factors Influencing Quality and Success of Supervised Farming Programs of Vocational Agriculture Students in Seven Schools of East Tennessee." Master's thesis. Univ. of Tennessee, 1958.
H5650

Hirsch, Arthur Henry The Huguenots of Colonial South Carolina. 1928. Reprint. Hamden, Conn.: Archon Books, 1962.
H5660 (ASU)

Hirsch, Herbert "Political Socialization in Appalachia: An Inquiry into the Process of Political Learning in an American Sub-Culture." Ph. D. Diss. The Univ. of Kentucky, 1968.
H5670

Hirsch, Nathaniel David Mithron An Experimental Study of the East Kentucky Mountaineers: A Study in Heredity and Environment. Genetic Psychology Monographs, vol. 3, no. 3. n.p.: Clark Univ., 1928.
H5680 (ETSU BC ASU)

Hislop, Alexander The Proverbs of Scotland. N. Y.: Norwood Editions, 1868.
H5690 (ASU)

Historical Highlights of Elliott County, 1869-1969 Sandy Hook, Ky.: Elliott Centennial Committee, 1969.
H5700

Historical, Pictorial, Fraternal Souvenir of Knoxville, Tennessee Knoxville: n.p., 1903.
H5710

Historical Records Survey, Maryland Inventory of the County and Town Archives of Maryland. Prepared by the Historical Records Survey, Division of Women's and professional projects, work progress administration. no. 21. Baltimore: The Historical Records Survey, 1937. Three Maryland counties are in the Appalachian region.
H5720 (ASU)

Historical Records Survey, North Carolina The Historical Records of North Carolina. With a preface by Luther H. Evans. 3 vols. Raleigh: The North Carolina Historical Commission, 1938.
H5730 (ASU LMC BC)
Index to Moore's Roster of North Carolina Troops in the War Between the States. 15 reels. Raleigh: North Carolina Department of Archives and History, 1958.
H5740 (ASU)
Introduction to the County Records of North Carolina, Including the General Introduction to the Historical Records of North Carolina. Raleigh: North Carolina Historical Commission, 1938.
H5750 (ASU)

Historical Records Survey, Tennessee Directory of Churches, Missions, and Religious Institutions of Tennessee, no. 33. Hamilton County. Nashville: The Survey, WPA, 1940.
H5760
Directory of Churches, Missions, and Religious Institutions of Tennessee, no. 47. Knox County. Nashville: The Survey, WPA, 1941.
H5770
Directory of Churches, Missions, and Religious Institutions of Tennessee, no. 90. Washington County. Nashville: The Survey, WPA, 1942.
H5780
Guide to Depositories of Manuscript Collection in Tennessee. Nashville: The Survey, 1940.
H5790 (ETSU)
Inventory of the County Archives of Tennessee: Anderson County. Nashville: The Survey, WPA, 1941.
H5800
Inventory of the County Archives of Tennessee: Blount County. Nashville: The Survey, WPA, 1941.
H5810
Inventory of the County Archives of Tennessee: Bradley County. Nashville: The Survey, WPA, 1941.
H5820
Inventory of the County Archives of Tennessee: Hamilton County, Tennessee. Nashville: The Survey, WPA, 1937.
H5830
Inventory of the County Archives of Tennessee: Knox County. Nashville: The Survey, WPA, 1941.
H5840
Inventory of the County Archives of Tennessee: Loudon County. Nashville: The Survey, WPA, 1941.
H5850
Inventory of the County Archives of Tennessee. Nashville: The Survey, 19-.
H5860 (ETSU)
Inventory of the County Archives of Tennessee: Sullivan County. Nashville: The Survey, WPA, 1942.
H5870
List of Tennessee Imprints, 1793-1840, in Tennessee Libraries. Nashville: The Survey, 1941.
H5880 (ETSU)
Summary of Special Legislation Relating to the Government of Sullivan County. 19 leaves. Nashville: The Survey, WPA, 1940.
H5890
Tennessee Records of Roane County Marriage Records, 1801-1838. Nashville: The Survey, 1939.
H5900 (ETSU)

Historical Records Survey, Tennessee. Works Projects Administration Transcription of the County Archives of Tennessee: Minutes of the County Court of Knox County (Book No. 0") 1792-95. Division of Community Service Programs, Work Projects Administration. Nashville, Tenn.: Historical Records Survey, 1941.
H5910 (ASU)

Historical Records Survey, West Virginia A Check List of West Virginia Imprints, 1791-1830. American Imprints Inventory, the WPA Historical Records Survey Program, Division of Professional and Service Projects, no. 14. 1940. Reprint. New York: Kraus Reprint, 1964.
H5930 (ETSU BC)
W. Va. Co. Formations and Boundary Changes. Charleston, W. Va.: Hist. Records Survey, 1938.
H5940 (BC)

Historical Records Survey, Works Progress Administration Historical Records Survey of County Archives of West Virginia. Charleston, W. Va.: The Historical Records Survey, 1937. This is only one of a number of WPA-Historical Records Survey listings focusing on state and local areas, many of which relate to the Appalachian region.
H5920

Historical Society of Southwest Virginia Historical Sketches of Southwest Virginia. Wise, Va.: The Society, 1965-.
H5950

Historical Society of Washington County, Virginia Publications of the Historical Society of Washington County, Virginia. Abingdon: The Society, n.d. This book is composed of eighteen addresses that were delivered before the Historical Society of Washington County, Virginia, by various people at various times. The addresses are concerned with outstanding people, places, and events of the town of Abingdon and of Washington County, Virginia.
H5960

History and Illustrations of Knoxville, Tennessee Knoxville: n.p., 1896, 1900.
H5970

History of Andersonville Baptist Church and Andersonville Institute Knoxville: Coleman's, 1966.
H5980

A History of Etowah County, Alabama Gadsen: Etowah Co. Centennial Committee, 1968.
H5990

History of Humphreys Memorial United Methodist Church, Charleston, W. Va. Charleston: The Church, 1973.
H6000

History of North Carolina 6 vols. Chicago: Lewis Pub. Co., 1919.
H6010 (MHC)

History of the Knoxville Public Schools Knoxville: Dept. of Secondary Educ., 1953.
H6020

History of the Smith Run Methodist Church, Lewis County, Virginia from 1832 to 1952 n.p.: n.p., 1952. A five page typescript including history of the establishment of the church, copies of deeds, list of curcuit riders, and some church records and minutes.
H6030

Hitchcock, Mrs. Caroline (Hanks) Nancy Hanks, the Story of Abe Lincoln's Mother. N. Y.: n.p., 1899. Nancy Hanks was an indentured servant in Swain Co., North Carolina.
H6040

Hite, James Cleveland "The Short-run Supply of Industrial Labour in Four Rural Areas of the Southeast, 1949-1964." Ph. D. Diss. Clemson Univ., 1966. The survey includes one Appalachian Area.
H6050

Hite, Mary Elizabeth My Rappahannock Storybook. Richmond: Dietz Press, 1950. Stories from western Virginia.
H6060 (BC ASU)

Hobbs, Samuel Huntington, Jr. North Carolina: An Economic and Social Profile. Chapel Hill: Univ. of North Carolina Press, 1958.
H6070 (LMC BC)
North Carolina, Economic and Social. Chapel Hill: Univ. of North Carolina, 1930.
H6080 (WWC LMC BC UNCA)

Hobday, Victor Carr Sparks at the Grassroots; Municipal Distribution of TVA Electricity in Tennessee. Ph. D. Diss. Syracuse Univ., 1966.
H6090
Sparks at the Grassroots, Municipal Distributions of TVA Electricity in Tennessee. Knoxville: Univ. of Tennessee Press, 1969.
H6100 (ASU WCU LMC BC)

Hobson, Leo Guy "The Agricultural, Cooperative and Rural Electrification Activities of the Tennessee Valley Authority, and the Work of the Farm Credit Administration in the Tennessee River Basin." Ph. D. Diss. Cornell Univ., 1936.
H6110

Hochstrasser, Donald Lee "Possum Ridge Farmers: A Study in Cultural Change." Microfilm. Ph. D. Diss. Univ. of Oregon, 1963. A study of an isolated Appalachian community in transition.
H6120 (ASU)

Hodge, Clarence Lewis The Tennessee Valley Authority: A National Experiment in Regionalism. Washington: American Univ. Press, 1938.
H6130 (LMC BC)
The Tennessee Valley Authority: A National Experiment in Regionalism. 1938. Reprint. N. Y.: Russell & Russell, 1968.
H6140 (ASU)

Hodge, David C. Hutchison, Robert S. An Economic Survey of Blount County, Tennessee, a Study of Resources and Industrial Potentials. Knoxville: Bureau of Business Research, Univ. of Tennessee, 1957.
H8720

Hodge, James Michall Coals of the North Fork of the Ky. River in Perry and Portions of Breathitt & Knott Co. Ky. Washington: U. S. Geological Survey, 1918.
H6150

Hodge, Joyce W. "Community Correlates of Crime and Law Enforcement Activities in Northwestern North Carolina." Master's thesis. Appalachian State Univ., 1972.
H6160 (ASU)

Hodges, Charles Sasnette Diseases in Southeastern Forest Nurseries and Their Control. U. S. Forest Service Station Paper, no. 142. Asheville, N. C.: Southeastern Forest Experiment Station, 1962.
H6170 (WCU)

Hodges, Sidney Cecil "Handicrafts in Sevier County, Tennessee." Master's thesis. Univ. of Tennessee, 1951.
H6180 (ASU)

Hodgin, David Reid The Ballad of Tall Tom Wolfe. Boone, N. C.: n.p., 1950.
H6190 (ASU)

Hodgson, Adam Letters from North America Written During a Tour in the United States and Canada. 2 vols. London and Edinburgh: Hurst, Robinson and Co., A. Constable and Co., 1824. One of the earliest travelogues mentioning Appalachia.
H6200

Hodgson, Richard S. ed. In Quiet Ways: George H. Mead, the Man and the Company. Dayton, Ohio: Mead Corp., 1970.
H6210 (LMC)

Hodson, Ivan Conrey, Guy Woolard Soil Survey, Scioto County, Ohio. Washington: U. S. Dept. of Agriculture, Bureau of Plant Industry, 1940.
C6780 ()

Hoffer, Frank William Presbyterian Churches of Roanoke, Virginia. Roanoke, Va.: Economic Print. Co., 1937?
H6220 (ASU BC)

Hoffer, Isaac Genealogy of Matthias Hoffer (Huffard) and his Descendants in the United States of America. Republished with additions by Paul P. Huffard. N. Y.: Paul P. Huffard, 1945.
H6231

Hoffer, Isaac comp. Genealogy of Matthias Hoffer (Huffard) and his Descendants in the United States of America. Mt. Joy, Pa.: J. R. Hoffer, 1868.
H6230

Hoffman, Charles Fenno A Winter in the West. By a New Yorker. 2 vols. N. Y.: Harper, 1835. Hoffman travelled from Lexington, apparently via the Wilderness Road, to Cumberland Gap, thence to Tazewell (Tenn.), Pearisburg, and White Sulphur Springs, on his return trip from the west. He was keenly observant of the natural beauties of the region and he gives a detailed account of a homestead and its family in Clay County, Kentucky.
H6240

Hoffman, Glenn J. Annotated Bibliography on Slope Stability of Strip Mine Soil Banks. Wooster: Ohio Agricultural Experiment Station, 1964.
H6250 (ASU)

Slope Stability of Coal Strip Mine Spoil Banks. Final report on State project 231: Reclamation and use of strip mined land in Ohio. Subproject 4: Factors influencing structual stability of spoils. Prepared in cooperation with the Central States Forest Experiment Station, U. S. Department of Agriculture. Wooster: Ohio Agricultural Experiment Station, 1964.
H6260 (ASU)

Hoffman, Laban Miles Our Kin. Charlotte, N. C.: Queen City Print. Co., 1915.
H6270

Hoffman, Marie E. Lindy Loyd, a Tale of the Mountains. Boston: Marshall Jones Co., 1920. A tale of thwarted love, mystery and estrangement set in the Tennessee Mountains.
H6280 (BC ASU)

Hoffman, N. March Follow-up Study of MDTA E. and D. Project at Bluefield State College. Washington: Bureau of Social Science, Research, 1967.
H6290

Hoffman, Richard L. ed. Holt, Perry C. ed. The Distributional History of the Biota of the Southern Appalachians. Charlottesville: University Press of Virginia, 1974.
H6940

Hoffman, Ronan R. Report of a Social Welfare Manpower Project for Appalachia, July 15, 1969 to August 31, 1990. Berea, Ky.: Council of the Southern Mountains, 1990.
H6300 (BC ASU)

Hoffman, William The Dark Mountains. N. Y.: Garden City, 1963. A mystery story with a mountain setting.
H6310 (BC)

A Walk to the River. Garden City, N. Y.: Doubleday & Co., 1970. A fiction with a mountain setting.
H6320 (WCU)

Hoffman, William S. Andrew Jackson and North Carolina Politics. (James Sprunt Studies in History and Political Science vol. 40). Chapel Hill: Univ. of N. C. Press, 1958.
H6330 (LMC)

Hoffsommer, Harold Grigsby, Shaw Earl Rural Social Organization of Frederick County, Maryland. College Park: Maryland Agricultural Experiment Station, 1949.
G4250

Hofstetter, Arthur N. "Analysis and Projection of Population and School Enrollment in Harrison County." Master's thesis. Morgantown, W. Va. Univ., 1965.
H6340

The Need for a New Perspective of the School Plant and School Organization in Taylor County. Morgantown, W. Va.: W. Va. Univ., 1965.
H6350

A Survey of Attitudes and Opinions of Preston County Voters. Morgantown: W. Va. Univ., 1964.
H6360

Hogan, Leo Francis "A Proposed Course of Study for General Shop in the John Sevier Junior High School." Master's thesis. East Tennessee State College, 1955.
H6370 (ETSU)

Hogan, William G. The Effect of Workmen's Compensation on the Logging and Sawmilling Industries in the Northeast. Morgantown: W. Va. Univ., Office of Research and Development, 1971.
H6380

Hoge, Arista ed. The First Presbyterian Church, Staunton, Virginia. Staunton, Va.: Press of Caldwell Sites Co., 1908.
H6390 (ASU BC)

Hogg, Dorothy Hall, Mary Boilin' n Bakin' in Boogar Hollow. Lindale, Ga.: Country Originals, 1971.
H850 (BC ASU)

Hogue, Albert Ross Davy Crockett and Others in Fentress County Who Have Given the County a Prominent Place in History. Jamestown, Tenn.: n.p., 1955.
H6400 (ETSU BC)

History of Fentress County, Tennessee, the Old Home of Mark Twain's Ancestors. Nashville: Williams, 1916, 1920.
H6410

Mark Twain's Obedstown and Knobs of Tennessee; a History of Jamestown and Fentress County, Tennessee. Jamestown: Cumberland, 1951.
H6420

One Hundred Years in the Cumberland Mountains along the Continental Line. McMinnville, Tenn.: Standard Print. Co., 1933.
H6430 (ETSU ASU)

Holcombe, Julia Irene "Southern Mountain Folk Songs for American Schools." Master's thesis. Eastman School of Music, Univ. of Rochester, 1941.
H6440 (ASU)

Holcombe, Ransome "The Textile Strikes in Marion, North Carolina, 1929: A Challenge to the New South." Master's thesis. East Tennessee State Univ., 1971.
H6450 (ETSU)

Holcombe, William Frederic Bulletin of the Virginia State Library: Index to Mrs. Cabell's "Sketches and Recollections of Lynchburg." Richmond, Va.: Superintendent of Public Printing, 1920.
H6460 (ASU)

Holden, Anna and others Clinton, Tennessee: A Tentative Description and Analysis of the School Desegregation Crisis. New York: Anti-Defamation League, 1957.
H6470

Holden, Katherine C. "A Survey of the Qualification of Some Teachers of the Educable Mentally Retarded in East Tennessee." Master's thesis. East Tennessee State Univ., 1969.
H6480 (ETSU)

Holden, Patricia Padgett "An Archaeological Survey of Transylvania County, North Carolina." Ph. D. Diss. Univ. of North Carolina, 1966.
H6490 (WCU)

Hollan, Clay Genealogy of Hollon and Related Families. Chicago: The author, 1958. Genealogy of an Eastern Kentucky family.
H6500

Holland, Carl W. "Educational Facilities and Economic Development of Bristol, 1930-1950." Master's thesis. East Tennessee State Univ., 1956.
H6510

"Educational Facilities and Economic Development of Bristol, 1930-1950." Master's thesis. East Tennessee State College, 1956.
H6520 (ETSU)

Holland, Cecil Fletcher Morgan and His Raiders: A Biography of the Confederate General. New York: Macmillan, 1942. This favorable treatment confines itself to John Hunt Morgan's activities as leader of cavalry raiders during the Civil War. Holland, working largely from previously untouched materials, depicts his subject as one of the most popular figures of the Confederacy.
H6530

Holland, Charles T. Current and Proposed Regulations and Legislation on Water Pollution Concerning Appalachian Industries. Morgantown: W. Va. Univ., Coal Research Bureau, 1969.
H6540

Research, Education and Mine Personnel Safety in W. Va. Morgantown, W. Va.: W. Va. Univ., Coal Research Bureau, 1969.
H6550 (BC)

Holland, Charlton Gilmore An Archaeological Survey of Southwest Virginia. Smithsonian Contributions to Anthropology, no. 12. Washington: Smithsonian Institution Press, 1970.
H6560 (ASU WCU ETSU BC)

Holland, Collen J. "The Tribal Voice of a People in Transition." Ph. D. Diss. Univ. of Minnesota, 1956.
H6570

Holland, W. J. The Educational Needs of Appalachia. An address delivered at the commencement of the West Virginia University. Morgantown: Acme Print. Co., 1901.
H6580

Hollander, Nanci Gitlin, Todd Uptown: Poor Whites in Chicago. New York: Harper & Row, 1970.
G1860 (ASU BC)

Hollandsworth, Genevieve Youth Recreation in the Coal Mining Towns of West Virginia. Morgantown: W. Va. Univ., 1942.
H6590

Hollenbeck, Ronald P. Ceramic Evaluation of Clays and Shales of East Tennessee. Nashville: Division of Geology, 1969.
H6600 (ETSU)

Raw Materials for Lightweight Aggregate in Appalachian Region, Alabama and Georgia. U. S. Mines Bureau Report of Investigations, 7244. Pittsburgh: Mines Bureau, 1969.
H6610

Shales for Lightweight Aggregate in Appalachian Region, Kentucky and Tennessee. U. S. Mines Bureau Report of Investigation, 7129. Pittsburgh: Mines Bureau, 1968.
H6620

Holley, Marie E. "A Study of Absenteeism in the Tazewell County One Room Negro Elementary Schools." Master's thesis. Ohio State Univ., 1954.
H6630

Holliday, Carl A History of Southern Literature. Washington, D. C.: Neale Pub. Co., 1906. Scant mention of Appalachian fiction.
H6640

Holliday, Robert Kelvin Tests of Faith. Oak Hill, W. Va.: Fayette Tribune, 1966.
H6650 (ASU BC)

Holling, Clancy The Book of Indians. Illus. by H. C. and Lucille Holling. New York: The Platt & Munk Co., Inc. 1935. A volume of Indian lore.
H6660 (ASU MHC)

Hollings, Ernest F. The Case Against Hunger: A Demand for a National Policy. New York: Cowles Book Co., 1970. Some mention of Appalachian poverty and that of other minorities.
H6670

Hollingsworth, Jesse Gentry History of Surry County, or, Annals of Northwest North Carolina. Greensboro, N. C.: W. H. Fisher Co., 1935.
H6680 (LMC ASU WCU BC)

History of Surry County, or, Annals of Northwest North Carolina. Mt. Airy, N. C.: J. G. Hollingsworth, 1935.
H6690

Hollon, Clay Genealogy of Hollon and Related Families. Chicago: The author, 1950. An Eastern Kentucky family.
H6700

Genealogy of Hollon and Related Families: Early Settlers of Eastern Ky. and Their Descendants. Chicago: n.p., 1958.
H6710

Holloway, James Y. Campbell, Will D. Up to Our Steeples in Politics. New York: Paulist Press, 1970.
C990 (WCU BC)

Holloway, Roland F. Five Months in the Old North State. Chicago: The author, 1914.
H6720 (ASU BC)

Holly, John Fred The Economy of Greeneville, Tennessee; a Study of the Information and Data Related to the Greeneville, Tennessee, Economic Community. Bureau of Research, College of Business Administration Study no. 21. Knoxville: Univ. of Tennessee, 1950.
H6730

"The Social and Economic Effects Produced upon Small Towns by Rapid Industrialization." Master's thesis. Univ. of Tennessee, 1938. Elizabethton is described in this study.
H6740

"The Social and Economic Effects Produced upon Small Towns by Rapid Industrialization." Master's thesis. Univ. of Tennessee, 1938. Includes Kingsport.
H7650

Holman, Clarence Hugh Thomas Wolfe. Pamphlets on American Writers, no. 6. Minneapolis: Univ. of Minnesota Press, 1960.
H6760 (ASU UNCA)

Three Modes of Modern Southern Fiction: Ellen Glasgow, William Faulkner, Thomas Wolfe. Mercer University Lamar Memorial Lectures, no. 9. Athens: Univ. of Georgia Press, 1966.
H6770 (ASU MHC)

The World of Thomas Wolfe. A Scribner Research Anthology. New York: Scribner, 1962.
H6780 (ASU WCU MHC UNCA)

Holmes, Alexander Pen and Politics, the Autobiography of a Working Writer. n.p.: n.p., n.d. Autobiography of a working writer from West Virginia.
H6790

Holmes, Dorothy P. Child, Sargent B. Checklist of Historical Records Survey Publications: Bibliography of Research Projects Reports. Baltimore: Genealogical Pub. Co., 1969.
C3850 (ASU)

Holmes, Jack E. Structure of County Government in Tennessee. n.p.: n.p., n.d.
H6800

Holmes, Jimmy A. Tourist and Recreation Facility Survey of Nine Counties in Southeastern Kentucky. Oak Ridge, Tenn.: Oak Ridge Associated Universities, 1966.
H6810

Holmes, John Simcox Common Forest Trees of North Carolina: How to Know Them. A Pocket Manual. 4th ed. Raleigh: North Carolina Department of Conservation & Development, 1929.
H6820 (LMC)

Common Forest Trees of North Carolina: How to Know Them. A Pocket Manual. 5th ed. Raleigh: North Carolina Department of Conservation & Development, 1944.
H6830 (LMC ASU)

Forest Conditions in Western North Carolina. In cooperation with the U. S. Forest Service. North Carolina Geological Survey Bulletin, no. 23. Raleigh: Edwards and Broughton Print. Co., 1911.
H6840 (ASU WCU LMC UNCA)

Organization of Co-operative Forest Fire Protective Areas in North Carolina. Being the proceedings of the Special Conference on forest fire protection held as part of the Conference on forestry and nature study, Montreat, N. C., July 8, 1915. North Carolina Geological & Economic Survey Economic Paper, no. 42. Raleigh: E. M. Uzzell & Co., 1915.
H6850 (ASU)

Holmes, John Simcox comp. Proceedings of Second Annual Convention of the North Carolina Forestry Association Held at Raleigh, North Carolina, February 21, 1912. Forest fires in North Carolina during 1911. Suggested forestry legislation. North Carolina Geological & Economic Survey Economic Paper, no. 25. Raleigh: Edwards & Broughton Print. Co., 1912.
H6860 (ASU)

Holmes, Mary Hull Holmes Family History. n.p.: n.p., 1964.
H6870

Holmes, Mary Jane Rose Mather. New York: G. W. Carleton and Co., 1868. Sentimental fiction with a mountain setting.
H6880

Holmes, William Henry Aboriginal Pottery of the Eastern United States. Washington: U. S. Bureau of American Ethnology, 1903.
H6890

Handbook of Aboriginal American Antiquities. Part I, the Lithic industires. Nashville: Blue and Gray Press, 1972.
H6900 (LMC)

Holt, Andrew David The Struggle for a State System of Public Schools in Tennessee, 1903-1936. Contributions to Education, no. 753. New York: Teacher's College, Columbia Univ., 1938.
H6910 (ETSU)

Holt, C. L. Seventy Years in the Cumberlands. n.p.: n.p., 1970.
H6920

Holt, Felix Dan'l Boone Kissed Me. 1st ed. New York: Dutton, 1954. Juvenile book based on frontier life in Kentucky.
H6930 (ASU)

Holt, Janice Giles, Henry E. Around Our House. Boston: Houghton Mifflin, 1971.
G1360 (BC)

Holt, Perry C. ed. The Distributional History of the Biota of the Southern Appalachians. Charlottesville: University Press of Virginia, 1974. Three parts. A comprehensive review of the vertebrates, flora and vertebrates found in the Southern Appalachians.
H6940

Holteman, Harvey Azure-Lure: A Romance of the Mountains. Asheville: n.p., 1924. Promotional material about Western North Carolina disguised as fiction.
H6950

Holthouser, Julia McNeely "Community Resources of Tryon, North Carolina." Master's thesis. Western Carolina State Teachers College, 1959.
H6960 (WCU)

Holyfield, Frank The Southern Mountains, a Collection of Drawings. Chapel Hill: Univ. of North Carolina Press, 1973. A lovely collection of drawings many from Madison County, North Carolina.
H6970 (ASU BC)

Home Demonstration Club, Asheville, N. C. Good Victuals from the Mountains. Asheville: Inland Press, 1951.
H6980

Homecoming, First Presbyterian Church, Knoxville, Tennessee, 1796-1925 Knoxville: n.p., 1925.
H6990

Hood, Flora Mae Pink Puppy. Illustrated by James Spanfeller. New York: Putnam, 1967. Children's story with a mountain setting.
H7000 (ASU)

Hood, Frazer ed. If Ye Know These Things: The Presbyterian Task in North Carolina. Charlotte, N. C.: Presbyterian Standard Pub. Co., 1927.
H7010 (LMC)

Hood, John O. History of the Chilhowee Baptist Association. n.p.: n.p., n.d. This association is located in Blount County.
H7020

Hooker, Elizabeth Robbins Religion in the Highlands: Native Churches and Missionary Enterprises in the Southern Appalachian Area. Section on missionary and philanthropic schools by Fannie Wyche Dunn. New York: Home Missions Council, 1933.
H7030 (WWC ASU BC)

Hooks, W. Gary ed. The Appalachian Structural Front in Alabama University: Alabama Geological Society, 1969.
A4080 (ETSU)

Hooper, Ben W. The Unwanted Boy: The Autobiography of Governor Ben W. Hooper. Knoxville: Univ. of Tennessee Press, 1963. This Tennessee governor was born amid scandal in Newport and spent the first eight years of his life roaming East Tennessee while his mother looked for work. After a year in Knoxville orphanage he was acknowledged by his father and reared in Newport.
H7040 (ASU BC)

Hooper, James E. Land-use in Clay County. Cullowhee, N. C.: Western Carolina Univ., n.d.
H7050 (LMC)

Hooper, Johnson Jones Some Adventures of Capt. Simon Suggs. 1848. Reprint. Upper Saddle River, N. J.: Gregg House, 1970. Ribald tales from the frontier, including upper Georgia, Alabama, and Tennessee.
H7060 (ASU)

Hooper, Margaret G. The Earthquake History of Virginia, 1774 to 1900. Blacksburg: Virginia Polytechnic Institute and State Univ., 1971.
H7140

Hooper, Ralph M. McGee, Charles E. Regeneration After Clearcutting in the Southern Appalachians. Asheville, N. C.: Southeastern Forest Experiment Station, 1970.
M1390 (LMC)

Olson, David F., Jr. Early Survival and Growth of Planted Northern Red Oak in Southern Appalachians. Asheville, N. C.: Southeastern Forest Experiment Station, 1968.
O630

Hoos, Ida Russakoff Retraining the Work Force, an Analysis of Current Experience. Berkeley: Univ. of California Press, 1967.
H7070

Hoover, Hazel Marie "A Survey of the Study Habits of the Freshman Class of 1959-1960 at Appalachian State Teachers College." Master's thesis. Appalachian State Teachers College, 1960.
H7080 (ASU)

Hopkins, Arthur Moonshine; a One Act Play. New York: S. French, 1921. A mountain melodrama.
H7090 (BC)

Hopkins, Samuel The Youth of the Old Dominion. Boston: J. P. Jewett & Co.; New York: Sheldon, Blakeman & Co., 1856.
H7100 (ASU)

Hopkins, T. C. Western Maryland Mine Drainage Survey, 1962-65. Annapolis: Md. Dept. of Water Resources, 1965.
H7110

Hopkins, Walter Lee Hopkins of Virginia and Related Families. Richmond: J. W. Ferguson & Sons, 1931.
H7120

Leftwich-Turner Families of Virginia and Their Connections. Richmond: J. W. Ferguson & Sons, 1931.
H7130

Hopper, Margaret G. Bollinger, G. A. The Earthquake History of Virginia, 1900-1970. Blacksburg, Va.: Dept. of Geological Sciences, Virginia Polytechnic Institute and State University, 1972.
B5140

Hopson, C. F. Report of C. F. Hopson, M. D., Director, Bureau of Negro Welfare and Statistics of the State of West Virginia to Governor Clarence W. Meadows, 1945-46. Charleston, W. Va.: Jarrett Print. Co., 1946.
H7150 (ASU)

Horn, Allen F. Opportunities for Forest-Based Industries in Pennsylvania: A Manual for the Development of Pennsylvania's Wood Using Industries. Washington: U. S. Area Development Administration, 1965.
H7160

Horn, Dorothy D. Sing to Me of Heaven: A Study of Folk and Early American Materials in Three Old Harp Books. Gainesville: Univ. of Florida Press, 1970.
H7170 (ASU BC)

Horn in the West. Scrapbooks, 1954- . Vol. 54 cm. n.p.: n.p., n.d. Includes advertisements, newspaper clippings, photographes, and programs relating to the Horn in the West outdoor drama.
H7180 (ASU)

Horn, Stanley Fitzgerald This Fascinating Lumber Business. New York: Bobbs-Merrill, 1943.
H7190 (ASU)

The Army of Tennessee: A Military History. 1st ed. Indianapolis: Bobbs-Merrill Co., 1941.
H7200 (ASU)

Invisible Empire: The Story of the Ku Klux Klan, 1866-1871. Boston: Houghton, 1939. The author's premise is that the Klan, in its early stages, was designed to preserve some degree of law and order in the South after the War.
H7210

Invisible Empire: The Story of the Ku Klux Klan, 1866-1871. American Historical Series no. 47. New York: Haskell, 1969. The author's premise is that the Klan, in its early stages, was designed to preserve some degree of law and order in the South after the War.
H7211

Invisible Empire: The Story of the Ku Klux Klan, 1866-1871. Cos Cob, Conn.: Edwards, 1969. The author's premise is that the Klan, in its early stages, was designed to preserve some degree of law and order in the South after the War.
H7212

Invisible Empire: The Story of the Ku Klux Klan, 1866-1871. New York: Gordon, 1969. The author's premise is that the Klan, in its early stages, was designed to preserve some degree of law and order in the South after the War.
H7213

Invisible Empire: The Story of the Ku Klux Klan, 1866-1871. 2nd enl. ed., Criminology, Law Enforcement, and Social Problems Series no. 81. Montclair, N. J.: Patterson Smith, 1969. The author's premise is that the Klan, in its early stages, was designed to preserve some degree of law and order in the South after the War.
H7214

Tennessee's War: 1861-1865, Described by Participants. Nashville: Civil War Centennial Commission, 1965.
H7220 (BC ASU)

Hornbeck, Betty Dutton Upshur Brothers of the Blue and the Gray. Parsons, W. Va.: McClain Print. Co., 1967.
H7230 (ASU)

Horner, Junius M. Southern Appalachian Highlanders of Western North Carolina. Asheville, N. C.: n.p., 1927.
H7240

Hornsby, Henry Lonesome Valley. New York: W. Sloane Associates, 1949. A mountain orphan lad goes to school, comes home to the hills, and never overcomes his basic loneliness.
H7250 (ASU LMC BC ETSU)

Horry County, S. C., Historical Society 1880 Census of Horry County, South Carolina. Charleston, S. C.: Walker, Evans, & Cogswell, 1970. Horry County was one of the migration routes into the mountains.
H7260 (ASU)

Horsley, Reginald The Blue Balloon, a Tale of the Shenandoah Valley. New York: E. P. Dutton Co., 1896. A fantastic tale of western Virginia in the last century.
H7270

Horsman, Reginald Expansion and American Indian Policy, 1783-1812. East Lansing: Michigan State Univ. Press, 1967. Horsman describes the tension between the nation's desire to expand because of population pressure, strategic reasons, and growing nationalism, and a genuine desire to treat the Indian fairly according to the developing national tradition. Unfortunately this fairness did not extend to the Cherokee.
H7280

Horton, A. H. Grover, N. C. Surface Water Supply of the New-Kanawha River Basin, West Virginia, and North Carolina. Washington: Govt. Print. Off., 1925.
G4490

The Ohio Valley Flood of March-April, 1913, Including Comparisons with Some Earlier Floods. U. S. Geological Survey Water-supply Paper, no. 334. Washington: Govt. Print. Off., 1913.
H7290

Horton, Albert Howard Leighton, Marshall Ora The Relation of the Southern Appalachian Mountains to Inland Water Navigation. Washington: Govt. Print. Off., 1908.
L1650 (BC ASU)

Horton, Clyde Gibson "Tennessee Valley Authority Legislation." Master's thesis. George Peabody College, 1938.
H7300

Horton, F. O. O'Neal, Alfred M., Jr. Soil Survey of Fayette County, Alabama. Washington: U. S. Department of Agriculture, Bureau of Soils, 1920.
O700

Horton, Frazier Robert "Negro Life in Watauga County." Bachelor's thesis. Agricultural and Technical College of North Carolina, 1942.
H7310 (ASU)

Horton, Myles Adams, Frank Unearthing Seeds of Fire: The Idea of Highlander. Winston-Salem, N. C.: John F. Blair, 1974.
A390

Horwitz, Elinor Lander Mountain People, Mountain Crafts. Photographs by Joshua Horwitz and Anthony Horwitz. New York: J. B. Lippincott Co., 1974.
H7320 (ASU)

Hoskins, Homer Arthur Heck, Edward Timmel Appalachian Connate Water. Charleston: West Virginia Geological Survey, 1964.
H4290 (ETSU)

Martens, James Hart Curry Dolomite Zone at Base of Greenbrier Limestone (Big Lime). Morgantown: West Virginia Geological and Economic Survey, 1948.
M3520 (ETSU)

Price, Paul Holland Salt Brines of West Virginia. Morgantown: West Virginia Geological Survey, 1937.
P4560 (ETSU)

Price, Paul Holland Springs of West Virginia. Morgantown: West Virginia Geological Survey, 1936.
P4570 (ETSU)

Hoss, Hugh F. Knoxville: Commercial and Industrial Survey of Knoxville, Tennessee. Knoxville: n.p., 1939.
H7330

Hoss, May Dikeman The Pike. New York: Appleton-Century-Crofts, 1954. A mountain family is embroiled in legal troubles. Hugh, the son home from the army, fights to reconcile two lifestyles.
H7340 (LMC BC WCU)

Hosterman, James L. Burke, Richard Thomas Avon Soil Survey of Indiana County, Pennsylvania. Washington: U. S. Bureau of Chemistry and Soils, 1936.
B8700

Hostetler, John A. Participation in the Rural Church. (Paper no. 1762.) State College: Pennsylvania Agricultural Experiment Station, Pennsylvania State College, October, 1952. Study includes Pennsylvania's Appalachian counties.
H7350

Hotten, John Camden ed. The Original Lists of Persons of Quality, Emigrants, Religious Exiles, Political Rebels, Serving Men Sold for a Term of Years, Apprentices, Children Stolen, Maidens Pressed, and Others, Who Went from Great Britain to the American Plantations, 1600-1700. With their ages, the localities where they formerly lived in the mother country, the names of the ships in which they embarked, and other interesting particulars. From mss. preserved in the State Paper Dept. of Her Majesty's Public Record Office, England. 1874. Reprint. Baltimore: Genealogical Pub. Co., 1968.
H7360 (ASU BC)

Hougen, Richard Torgor Cooking with Hougen. New York: Abingdon Press, 1960. Recipes from Berea's famous Boone Tavern.
H7370 (ASU)

Look No Further. Illustrated by Robert D. Bigelow. 1955. Reprint. New York: Abingdon Press, 1958.
H7380 (ASU)

More Hougen Favorites. Nashville: Parthenon Press, 1971.
H7390 (ASU)

Hough, Emerson The Way Out, a Story of the Cumberland Today. New York: Grosset & Dunlap, 1918. Dave Joslin leaves the hills to gain an education and returns to help his people turn from backward practices.
H7400 (ASU BC)

Hough, Van Ness D. Photogeologic Techniques Applied to the Mapping of Rock Joints. Report of Investigations, no. 19. Morgantown: West Virginia Geological Economic Survey, 1960.
H7410 (ETSU)

Hough, Walter S. Braddock's Road Through the Virginia Colony. Winchester, Va.: Winchester-Frederick County Historical Society, 1970.
H7420 (ASU)

Houk, Eloise Andrews "A Five-year Study of an Educable Mentally Retarded Class in Keystone School, Johnson City, Tennessee." Master's thesis. East Tennessee State College, 1961.
H7430 (ETSU)

House, Floyd Nelson Fort Lewis: A Community in Transition. Univ. of Virginia, Institute for Research in Social Sciences, 1930.
H7450

House, Floyd Nelson and others Fort Lewis: A Community in Transition. Transition. A report based on a study made by the Community League of Fort Lewis, Roanoke County, Virginia. Under the auspices of the Cooperative Education Association of Virginia, with technical assistance by the School of Sociology of the University of Virginia. Univ. of Virginia Institute for Research in the Social Sciences, 1930.
H7440 (FC)

Fort Lewis: A Community in Transition. Charlottesville, Va.: Michie Co., 1930.
H7460

House, Ray A Handful of Stars 1st ed. Louisville, Ky.: Touchstone Pub. Co., 1970. Autobiographical fiction by a native mountaineer who has succeeded in the outside world but still values the mountain way of life.
H7470 (ASU MHC BC)

Housekeeper, Mrs. William G. Pleasure Piece. 1st ed. New York: Harper & Brothers, 1935. After her father dies young Celie fights her way through Gothic situations to a city in the valley where she finds her lover and her long-lost mother.
H7480 (ASU BC)

Housing in Appalachia, the Future in Public-Private Collaborations. Morgantown: W. Va. Univ. Office of Research and Development, 1969.
H7490

Houston, Margaret D. "A Language Arts Program for a Fourth Grade of Culturally Deprived Pupils." Master's thesis. East Tennessee State Univ., 1964.
H7500 (ETSU)

Houston, Martha Lou comp. Indexes to the Country Wills of South Carolina. Baltimore: Genealogical Pub. Co., 1964.
H7510 (ASU)

600 Revolutionary Soldiers Living in Georgia in 1827-8. Athens, Ga.: Heritage Papers, 1965.
H7520 (ASU)

Houston, Sam M. "TVA, a Study in Policy Formation." Ph. D. Diss. Univ. of Iowa, 1942.
H7530

Houts, Paul G. "An Educational, Economic, and Community Survey of Blount County, Tennessee." Master's thesis. Univ. of Tennessee, 1928.
H7540

Hovey, Horace Carter Celebrated American Caverns. Cincinnati: R. Clarke, 1882. Many of the nation's most famous caves and caverns are in the Appalachian region.
H7550

Celebrated American Caverns, Especially Mammoth, Wyandot, and Luray. Cincinnati: R. Clarke & Co., 1882.
H7560

Mammoth Cave of Kentucky . . . with an Account of Colossal Cave. Louisville: J. P. Morton & Co., 1889.
H7570

Howard, Elizabeth Metzger Before the Sun Goes Down. 1st ed. Garden City, N. Y.: Doubleday & Co., 1946. Melodramatic fiction with a mountain setting.
H7580 (ASU)

Howard, Herbert Allen "External Diseconomies of Bituminous Coal Surface Mining — A Case Study of Eastern Kentucky, 1960-1967." Ph. D. Diss. Indiana Univ., 1969.
H7590

Howard, Hugh A. "The Economic History of Knox County." Master's thesis. Univ. of Kentucky, 1937.
H7600

Howard, James Edward "Migration Patterns of Residents in a High In-Migration County, Hamblen County, Tennessee." Master's thesis. Univ. of Tennessee, 1969.
H7610

Howard, Montice B. "A Study of the Use of Student Library Assistants in the Secondary Schools of East Tennessee." Master's thesis. East Tennessee State College, 1958.
H7620

Howard, O. O. The Feuds in the Cumberland Mountains. Louisville: Independent, 1904.
H7630

Howard, Quentin R. Down a Dusty Road. Pikeville, Ky.: Hilltop Editions, Pikeville College Press, 1967. Personal recollections of day to day life in the Kentucky hill country.
H7640 (BC ASU)

Howard, Quenton R. ed. Wind Pikeville, Ky.: n.p., 3 times a year.
W7640 (BC)

Howard, T. Levron "Federal Payments in Lieu of Taxation with Emphasis on the Program of the Tennessee Valley Authority." Ph. D. Diss. Univ. of Wisconsin, 1943.
H7650

The TVA and Economic Security in the South. Southern Policy Papers, no. 7. Chapel Hill: Univ. of North Carolina Press, 1936.
H7660 (ASU WCU LMC)

Howard, Waldorf Vivian Authority in the TVA Land. Kansas City, Mo.: F. Glenn Pub. Co., 1948.
H7670 (ASU LMC BC)

Howe, Daniel Dunbar Listen to the Mockingbird. Boyce, Va.: Carr Pub. Co., Inc., 1961. A story of the life and times of a pioneer Virginia family from the Shenandoah Valley who moves into Pulaski, Montgomery and Giles counties. Brief accounts of the wars from the American Revolution through 1945 are given. Approximately the last one hundred pages contain the genealogies of the Howe, Hoge, DeJarnette, Haven and Patton families.
H7680

Listen to the Mockingbird; The Life and Times of a Pioneer Virginia Family. Boyce, Va.: Carr Pub. Co., 1961.
H7690

Lovely Mount Tavern: The Birth of a City, and Something of the Early New River Settlers. Reprinted by the New River Historical Society. Boyce, Va.: Carr Pub. Co., 1963. Radford and vicinity.
H7700

Howe, Henry Historical Collections of Virginia . . . Charleston: South Carolina, Babcock & Co., 1845.
H7710

Historical Collections of Virginia. 1845. Reprint. Baltimore: Genealogical Pub. Co., 1969.
H7720

Howell, Joseph C. Birds of Knox County. Knoxville: Univ. of Tennessee, 1970.
H7730

Howes, R. M. People's Shorelines. Address before Tennessee Public Power Association, Nashville, Tennessee, April 15-18, 1958. Knoxville, Tenn.: TVA, 1958.
H7740

Planning for Recreation Use of Impounded Waters — TVA Experience. Knoxville, Tenn.: TVA, 1956. Paper before Conference on Recreation Use of Impounded Water, December 13, 1956, Berkeley, California.
H7750

Howse, Nathaniel Roosevelt "Political Activities of the Republican Party in the State of Tennessee, 1860-1870." Master's thesis. Tennessee State A & I Univ., 1951.
H7760

Hoyle, Columbus A. comp. Panorama of Progress: Jackson County Centennial. Sylva: Jackson Co. Centennial Celebration Executive Committee, 1951.
H7780

Hoyt, Edwin Palmer Your National Parks: Great Smoky Mountains. New York: Putnam, 1965.
H7790 (ETSU)

Hubbard, E. H. Swann, Maurice Edward Soil Survey, Roane County, Tennessee. Washington: U. S. Department of Agriculture, Bureau of Plant Industry, 1942.
S9440

Hubbard, Edgar Harvey Soil Survey, Grainger County, Tennessee. Soil Survey Report Series 1940, no. 4. Washington: U. S. Department of Agriculture, Bureau of Plant Industry, Soils and Agricultural Engineering, 1948.
H7810

Hubbard, Edgar Harvey and others Soil Survey, Cumberland County, Tennessee. Soil Survey Report, Series 1938, no. 25. Washington: U. S. Bureau of Plant Industry, Soils, & Agricultural Engineering, 1950.
H7800

Hubbard, Harlan Payne Hollow. New York: The Book Organization, n.d. Mystery story with a mountain setting.
H7820

Hubbard, Margaret Ann The History Limb. N. Y.: The Macmillan Co., 1942. A novel of John Sevier and the Watauga settlements.
H7830 (BC ASU)

Hubbard, Preston J. Origins of the TVA; the Muscle Shoals Controversy, 1920-1932. Ph. D. Diss. Vanderbilt Univ., 1955. This work presents the political and economic origins of the TVA through examining the struggle for control for the Tennessee River system from 1920 to 1932. The focal point of this struggle was at Muscle Shoals. Hubbard concludes that TVA owes its existence to a small number of Progressives in the Congress led by Sen. George Norris.
H7840

Origins of the TVA; The Muscle Shoals Controversy, 1920-1932. Nashville: Vanderbilt Univ. Press, 1961.
H7850 (ASU LMC WCU)

Origins of the TVA; the Muscle Shoals Controversy, 1920-1932. 1955. Reprint. New York: Norton, 1968. This work presents the political and economic origins of the TVA through examining the struggle for control of the Tennessee River system from 1920 to 1932. The focal point of this struggle was at Muscle Shoals. Hubbard concludes that TVA owes its existence to a small number of Progressives in the Congress led by Sen. George Norris.
H7860

Hubert, Archer Butler Boone's Wilderness Road. Cleveland: A. H. Clark Co., 1903.
H7870 (ETSU BC)

Huckleberry Poems; Poems Written about the Mountains and Huckleberry Mountain Workshop Camp at Hendersonville, N. C. n.p.: n.p., n.d.
H7880

Hudden, William P. History of the Hebron Lutheran Church, Madison Co., Va. New Market, Va.: Hankel and Co., 1907.
H7890 (BC)

Huddle, J. W. Oil and Gas Wells Drilled in Southwestern Virginia before 1950. U. S. Geological Survey Bulletin, no. 1027-L. Contributions to Economic Geology, 1955. Washington: Govt. Print. Off., 1956.
H7900 (ASU)

Huddle, Lula May Huddle, W. D. History of the Descendants of John Hottel. Strasburg, Va.: Shenandoah Publishing House, 1930.
H7910

Huddle, W. D. History of the Descendants of John Hottel. Strasburg, Va.: Shenandoah Publishing House, 1930.
H7910

Huddleston, Edwin Glenn The Claybrooks. New York: Macmillan Co., 1951. An East Tennessee girl leaves the crumbling family home to find adventure.
H7920 (ASU WCU BC)

Huddleston, George comp. Huddleston Family Tables. Concord, N. H.: Rumford Press, 1933.
H7930

Huddleston, Tim History of Pickett Co., Tenn. Collegedale, Tenn.: College Press, 1973.
H7940

Pioneer Families of Pickett County, Tennessee. Collegedale: College Press, 1968.
H7950

Hudson, C. Donald "Augusta County, Virginia: A Study of Patterns." Master's thesis. Univ. of Chicago, 1934.
H7960 (LMC)

"Augusta County, Virginia: A Study of Patterns." Microfilm. Master's thesis. Univ. of Chicago, 1934.
H7970 (ASU)

Hudson, Charles M. The Catawba Nation. Monographs, no. 18. Athens: Univ. of Georgia Press, 1970.
H7980 (LMC)

Hudson, John C. Beale, Calvin, L. Characteristics of the United States Population by Farm and Nonfarm Origin. Washington: Economic Research Service, Economic and Statistical Analysis Division, 1964.
B2240

Hudson, Monie Taras, Michael Andrew Seasoning and Preservative Treatment of Hickory Crossties. Asheville, N. C.: Southeastern Forest Experiment Station, 1959.
T240 (WCU)

Hudson, Robert P. Songs of the Cumberlands. Nashville, Tenn.: CR and HH Harch Pub., 1887. A series of poems descriptive of scenes and incidents among the Cumberlands.
H7990 (BC)

Huff, Jane Whom the Lord Loveth; the Story of James A. Huff. N. Y.: McGraw Hill, 1961. A wife's account of her brief and happy marriage to a young, and seriously ill, minister from East Tennessee.
H8000 (BC)

Huff, Judith M. Johnson, Hugh A. Private Outdoor Recreation Enterprises in Rural Appalachia. Washington: Govt. Print. Off., 1969.
J1800

Hufford, Grace Thompson comp. My Poetry Book. New York: Holt, Rinehart and Winston, 1956. This is an extensive anthology of modern verse for boys and girls. The selections are classed under such headings as "At Our House." "When It's Time to Play," "Going Places," "My Birds," "My Flowers," etc. Miss Carlisle lives in Wytheville, Virginia.
H8010 (ASU)

Huggins, Edith Warren In All Its Glory. New York: Philadelphia & Dorrance, 1945. North Carolina fiction. The action of the novel ranges into the mountains.
H8020

Huggins, Maloy A. A History of North Carolina Baptists, 1727-1932. Raleigh: The General Board Baptist State Convention of N. C., 1967.
H8030 (LMC)

Hughart, Col. Thomas, Chapter Daughter of the American Revolution comp. Augusta County, Va. First Marriage Records of Augusta County, Virginia, 1785-1813. Verona, Va.: McClure Press, 1970.
A5500 (ASU)

Hughes, Ann A Handbook and Resource Guide for New Craft Groups. Knoxville: Commission on Religion in Appalachia, 1972.
H8040

Hughes, Arizona Houston Aunt Zona's Web. As told to Thomas C. Chapman. Gastonia, N. C.: Publications Engineers, & Consultants, 1962. Memoirs of a life in Appalachia filled with laughs, lore and advice.
H8050 (ASU LMC)

Hughes, Frank G. "A Study of the School Buildings of McMinn County." Master's thesis. Univ. of Tennessee, 1958.
H8060

Hughes, Hatcher Hell-bent for Heaven, a Play in Three Acts. 1st ed. Harper's Modern Plays. New York: Harper & Brothers, 1924. Pulitzer prize winning drama with a Watauga County, North Carolina setting.
H8070 (ASU LMC ETSU BC)

Ruint; a Folk Comedy in Four Acts. New York: Harper, 1925. A comedy about a shotgun wedding. The mountaineers are made to look ridiculous.
H8080

Hughes, Josiah Pioneer West Virginia. Charleston, W. Va.: The author, 1932. Appears to have been written for school children. Gives genealogies of pioneer families.
H8090 (ASU)

Hughes, Nicholas Collin Hendersonville in Civil War Times. Hendersonville, N. C.: Blue Ridge Speciality Printing, 1936.
H8100

Hughes, Ralph H. Fertilization of Young Slash Pine in a Cultivated Plantation. U. S. Forest Service Station Paper, no. 148. Asheville, N. C.: Southeastern Forest Experiment Station, 1962.
H8110 (WCU)

Hughes, Roscoe Durall Exploring Virginia's Human Resources. Charlottesville: Univ. Press of Virginia, 1965.
H8120 (ASU BC)

Hughes, Thomas Rugby, Tennessee, Being Some Account of the Settlement Founded on the Cumberland Plateau by the Board of Aid to Land Ownership, Ltd. London: Macmillan, 1881.
H8130 (LMC BC)

Hughes, Thomas P., Jr. Pittsylvania County, Virginia Abstracts of Wills, 1768-1800. n.p.: n.p., 1956.
H8140

Hughson, Walter The Church's Mission to the Mountaineers of the South. Hartford, Conn.: Church Missions Pub. Co., 1908.
H8150

Huheey, James E. Amphibians and Reptiles of Great Smoky Mountains National Park. Knoxville: Univ. of Tennessee Press, 1967, 1972.
H8160 (UNCA ASU LMC WCU BC)

Huhta, James K. Powell, William Stevens The Regulators in North Carolina: A Documentary History, 1759-1776. Raleigh, N. C.: State Dept. of Archives and History, 1971.
P4030 (ASU)

Hulbert, Archer Butler Soil: Its Influence on the History of the United States, with Special Reference to Migration and the Scientific Study of Local History. 1930. Reprint. New York: Russell & Russell, 1969.
H8170 (ASU)

Hull, C. H. J. Bibliography of Maryland Water Resources Data. Baltimore: n.p., 1962.
H8180

Hull, Cordell The Memoirs of Cordell Hull. New York: Macmillan Co., 1948. Hull was born in Overton County, Tennessee, educated at Cumberland College.
H8190 (ASU)

Hull, Vernam Taylor, Archer A Collection of Irish Riddles. Los Angeles: Univ. of California Press, 1955.
T380 (FC)

Hull, William I. William Penn and the Dutch Quaker Migration to Pennsylvania. 1935. Reprint. Baltimore: Genealogical Pub. Co., 1970.
H8200 (ASU)

Hulme, Francis Pledger Come Up the Valley: Ballads and Poems. Illustrated by Rafaello Busoni. New Brunswick: Rutgers Univ. Press, 1949.
H8210 (ASU BC WWC)

Human, William D. "A Study of Preparatory to Cooperative Development of Board of Education Policies for Morgan County, Tennessee." Master's thesis. Univ. of Tennessee, 1954.
H8220

Humbert, R. L. Industrial Survey. Blacksburg, Va. Blacksburg: Engineering Extension Division, V. P. I., 1928-30. For the following counties: Bland, Buchanan, Carroll, Craig, Dickenson, Floyd, Giles, Grayson, Lee, Pulaski, Russell, Scott, Smyth, Tazewell, Washington, Wise, Wythe, Wythe reprint, Bedford. And the following cities: City of Radford and Montgomery County, Wytheville.
H8230

Industrial Survey, Bland County, Virginia. Blacksburg: Engineering Extension Division, Virginia Polytechnic Institute, 1930.
H8240

Industrial Survey, Wytheville, Virginia. Blacksburg: Engineering Extension Division, Virginia Polytechnic Institute, 1928.
H8250 (ASU)

Hume, Brit Death and the Mines: Rebellion and Murder in the United Mine Workers. New York: Grossman, 1971. Account of the degradation, violence and ineffectiveness of the United Mine Workers in the past two decades.
H8260 (ASU BC LMC WCU)

Humes, Thomas William Historical Discourse of St. John's Church, Knoxville, Tennessee. Knoxville: n.p., 1886.
H8270

The Loyal Mountaineers of Tennessee. Knoxville: Ogden Brothers & Co., 1888. Almost all of East Tennessee remained loyal to the Union.
H8280 (ASU BC LMC)

Hummel, B. L. Davidson, Dwight M., Jr. Standards of Living in Six Virginia Counties. Washington: Farm Security Administration, 1940.
D640

Hummel, Ray D. ed. Southeastern Broadsides Before 1877. Sponsored by the Association of Southeastern Research Libraries. Publications, no. 33. Richmond: Virginia State Library, 1971.
H8290 (ASU)

Humphrey, Hubert H. War on Poverty. New York: McGraw-Hill, 1964. Some discussion of the failure of the war on poverty in Appalachia and the reasons for that failure.
H8300

Humphrey, Inez Faith From the Prairies to the Mountains; Memories Especially of Illinois and Eastern Kentucky. N. Y.: Exposition Press, 1968.
H8310

Humphreys, Flynn G. "The Status and Problems of the Ministry in Knox County." Master's thesis. Univ. of Tennessee, 1936.
H8320

Humphreys, Gertrude Adventures in Good Living. West Virginia Extension Homemakers Council. Parsons, W. Va. McClain Print. Co., 1972.
H8330 (ASU BC)

Humphreys, Samuel H. "Learning Opportunities in Science in Six Public Schools in Upper East Tennessee." Master's thesis. East Tennessee State Univ., 1968.
H8340 (ETSU)

Hunnicutt, Samuel J. Twenty Years of Hunting and Fishing in the Great Smoky Mountains. Knoxville: Newman, 1926.
H3850

Twenty Years of Hunting and Fishing in the Great Smoky Mountains. 1926. Reprint. Maryville: n.p., 1951.
H8360

Hunt, C. B. Coal Deposits of Pike County, Kentucky. U. S. Geological Survey Bulletin, no. 876. Washington: Govt. Print. Off., 1937.
H8370

Hunt, Walter Bernard The Golden Book of Indian Crafts and Lore. New York: Simon & Schuster, 1954.
H8380 (MHC)

Hunter, Catherine H. "A History of Higher Education in Franklin County, Tennessee." Master's thesis. Univ. of Tennessee, 1940.
H8390

Hunter, Charles Eugene Forsterite Olivine Deposits of North Carolina and Georgia. Published in cooperation with TVA. Bulletin, no. 47. Raleigh: North Carolina Department of Conservation & Development, 1941.
H8400 (ETSU WCU)

Halloysite Deposits of Western North Carolina. Bulletin, no. 58. Raleigh: North Carolina Department of Conservation & Development, 1949.
H8410 (ETSU WCU)

Hunter, Cyrus Lee Sketches of Western North Carolina, Historical and Biographical, Illustrating Principally the Revolutionary Period of Mecklenburg, Rowan, Lincoln, and Adjoining Counties. Raleigh, N. C.: Raleigh News Steam Job Print., 1877.
H8420 (ASU BC WCU)

Sketches of Western North Carolina, Historical and Biographical, Illustrating Principally the Revolutionary Period of Mecklenburg, Rowan, Lincoln and Adjoining Counties, Accompanied with Miscellaneous Information, Much of It Never Before Published. Reprint. Baltimore: Regional Pub. Co., 1970.
H8430 (ASU LMC ETSU)

Hunter, Edgar F. "A History of Yancey Collegiate Institute." Master's thesis. Appalachian State Teachers College, 1952.
H8440 (ASU)

Hunter, George George Hunter's Map of the Cherokee Country and the Paths Thereto in 1730. Comments by A. S. Salley, Jr. South Carolina Historical Commission Bulletin, no. 4. Columbia, S. C.: State Co., 1917.
H8450 (WCU)

Hunter, Kermit Unto These Hills: A Drama of the Cherokee. 1950. Reprint. Chapel Hill: Univ. of North Carolina Press, 1950.
H8460 (ASU MHC ETSU)

Hunter, Richard G. Chen, Ping-fan Some Low-alumina Quartizitic Sandstones in West Virginia: A Preliminary Report. Morgantown: W. Va. Geological and Economic Survey, 1965.
C3620 (ETSU)

Renton, John J. A Simple Technique for the Determination of Weight Per Cent of Calcite and Dolomite in Carbonate Rocks. Morgantown: West Virginia Geological & Economic Survey, 1965.
R1530 (ETSU)

Tallon, Walter A. High-alumina Clays of West Virginia. Morgantown: West Virginia Geological and Economic Survey, 1959.
T120 (ETSU)

Hunter, Richard Glenn Arkle, Thomas Sandstones of West Virginia. Morgantown: W. Va. Genealogical Survey, 1957.
A4610 (ETSU)

Headlee, Alvah John Washington Germanium in Coals of West Virginia. Morgantown: West Virginia Geological & Economic Survey, 1951.
H4140 (ETSU)

Spectrographic Chemical Analysis. Report of Investigations, no. 5. Morgantown: West Virginia Geological & Economic Survey, 1948.
H8470 (ETSU)

Hunter, William M. Missa Appalachia. Logan, W. Va.: Trinity Episcopal Church, 1964. Moralistic fiction about the West Virginia hills.
H8480

Huntington, W. Va. Board of Park Commissioners Huntington's Park System and Recreational Facilities. Huntington: Standard Print. & Pub. Co., 1942.
H8490

Huntley, Troy Charles "A Curriculum Analysis of the Undergraduate Professional Preparation Program in Health and Physical Education at Western Carolina University." Master's thesis. Western Carolina Univ., 1970.
H8500 (WCU)

Hupp, John Cox Down in West Virginia and Other Poems. New York: Hubson Book Press, 1946.
H8510

Hurlburt, J. S. History of the Rebellion in Bradley County, East Tennessee. Indianapolis: Downey & Brause, 1866.
H8520

Hurley, Edward R. and Associates A Plan for Development of Ohio Appalachia. Columbus: Ohio Department of Urban Affairs, n.d.
H8530 (ASU)

Hurst, Lewis Alexander Soil Survey of Calhoun County, Alabama. Prepared in cooperation with Alabama. Field Operations, 1908. Washington: U. S. Department of Agriculture, Bureau of Soils, 1910.
H8540

Hurst, Otis C. "Trends in the Social Studies in Eighty Tennessee High Schools, 1931-1952." Master's thesis. East Tennessee State College, 1952.
H8550

Hurst, Samuel Need The Mountains Redeemed; the Romance of the Mountains, a True Story of Life and Love in Southwest Virginia, Interwoven with an Exposition of her Mountain Life and the Weird Religion of the Mountains, Embracing Scores of Humorous, Ridiculous, Laughable, and Tragic Stories, Episodes, and Incidents and the Religious, Moral, Educational, Industrial and Political Redemption of the Mountains. Illus. by S. N. Hurst, Jr. Appalachia, Va.: Hurst and Co., 1929.
H8560

Hurst, Thomas E. "Tennessee Coal Mining and Marketing Trends." Master's thesis. East Tennessee State College, 1951.
H8570 (ETSU)

Hurst, Vernon J. Exploration for Mineral Deposits in Haversham County, Georgia. Washington: Govt. Print. Off., 1964.
H8580

Exploration for Mineral Deposits in Habersham County, Georgia. Prepared in cooperation with the Habersham County Redevelopment Corporation and Institute of Community and Area Development. Washington: U. S. Area Redevelopment Administration, Dec., 1964.
H8590 (LMC)

Exploration for Mineral Deposits in White County, Georgia. Washington: Govt. Print. Off., 1965.
H8600 (LMC)

Field Excursion: Ocoee Metasediments: North Central Georgia and Southeast Tennessee. Geological Society of America Southeastern Section Guidebook, no. 3. Atlanta: Georgia Department of Mines, Mining & Geology, 1962.
H8610 (ETSU)

The Geology and Mineralogy of Graves Mountain, Georgia. Bulletin, no. 68. Atlanta: Georgia Department of Mines, Mining & Geology, 1959.
H8620 (ETSU)

Stratigraphy, Structure, Mineral Resources of the Mineral Bluff Quadrangle, Georgia. Bulletin, no. 63. Atlanta: Georgia Department of Mines, Mining & Geology, 1955.
H8630 (ETSU)

Hurt, A. B. "Educational Development of Ashe County." Master's thesis. Univ. of North Carolina, 1929.
H8640

Hurt, Helen Jones "The Home Visitation Program of the Bristol, Tennessee, Schools, 1948-1969." Master's thesis. East Tennessee State Univ., 1969.
H8650 (ETSU)

Hurt, Samuel S. "Gentlemen, I ain't a-goin'." Roanoke, Va.: Stone Print. and Manufacturing Co., 1913. An account of the Hillsville, Virginia courthouse tragedy and the Allen family's role in the feud.
H8660

Hustvedt, Sigurd Bernhard Ballad Books and Ballad Men: Raids and Rescues in Britain, America, and the Scandinavian North Since 1800. Cambridge, Mass.: Harvard Univ. Press, 1930.
H8670 (ASU BC)

Hutchens, Paul Yesterday's Rain. Grand Rapids, Mich.: Wm. B. Eerdmans Pub. Co., 1938. Melodramatic fiction with a mountain setting.
H8680 (ASU LMC WCU BC)

Hutchens, Ross E. Hidden Valley of the Smokies. New York: Dodd, 1971. Deep in the Great Smoky Mountains lies a valley known to few people. It is a place of primitive beauty and it is here that naturalist-photographer Ross Hutchins takes the reader.
H8690

Hidden Valley of the Smokies: With a Naturalist in the Great Smoky Mountains. Illustrated with photographs by the author. New York: Dodd, Mead & Co., 1971.
H8700 (ASU LMC MHC WWC BC WCU ETSU)

Hutchins, Francis Stephenson Berea College: The Telescope and the Spade. Newcomen Address. New York: Newcomen Society in North America, 1963.
H8710 (ASU)

Hutchison, Robert S. An Economic Survey of Blount County, Tennessee, a Study of Resources and Industrial Potentials. Knoxville: Bureau of Business Research, Univ. of Tennessee, 1957.
H8720

Migration and Industrial Development in Tennessee. Nashville: Legislative Council, 1958.
H8730

Hutson, A. C., Jr. "The Coal Miner's Insurrections, 1891-1892." Master's thesis. Univ. of Tennessee, 1933.
H8740 (ASU)

Hutson, William F. Campbell, Carlos Clinton and others Great Smoky Mountains Wildflowers. Knoxville: Univ. of Tennessee Press, 1962.
C540 (LMC WCU ETSU)

Campbell, Carlos Clinton Great Smoky Mountains Wildflowers. Knoxville: Univ. of Tennessee Press, 1964.
C550 (ASU LMC WCU WWC BC)

Huxley, Julian Sorell TVA, Adventure in Planning. Cheam, Surrey, England: Architectural Press, 1943.
H8750

TVA, Adventure in Planning. London: Reader's Union, 1945.
H8760

Huyck, Earl E. Page, William J., Jr. Appalachia: Realities of Deprivation. Washington: U. S. Department of Health, Education and Welfare, 1964.
P60

Hyams, C. The Flora of North Carolina from Ranunculaceae to Salviniaceae. Bulletin, no. 164. Raleigh: North Carolina College, 1899.
H8770 (LMC)

Hyatt, Rebecca Dougherty Marthy Lou's Kiverlid. Morristown, Tenn.: Triangle Press, 1937. Both a story and a book of weaving instructions.
H8780

"Marthy Lou's Kiverlid," a Sketch of Mountain Life. Morristown, Tenn.: Triangle Press, 1937.
H8790 (ASU)

"Marthy Lou's Kiverlid," a Sketch of Mountain Life. 2nd ed. Morristown, Tenn.: Morrison Print. Co., 1963.
H8800 (ASU)

Hyde, Victor A. "A Geographical Survey of Knoxville, Tennessee." Master's thesis. Univ. of Tennessee, 1939.
H8810

Hyder, Carroll "A Follow-up Study of Graduates in Industrial Technology at East Tennessee State University, 1962 Through 1967." Master's thesis. East Tennessee State Univ., 1967.
H8820 (ETSU)

Hyder, Jane "An Evaluation of the Changes in Reading Achievement Effected by a Federal Project in the Bristol, Tennessee, Elementary Schools." Master's thesis. East Tennessee State Univ., 1968.
H8830 (ETSU)

Iacopi, Robert L. Look to the Mountain Top. San Jose, Calif.: Gousha Publications, 1972. Addresses, essays and lectures — many about Indians, including the Cherokee.
I10

Iannone, Ron "School Ain't No Way . . ." Appalachian Consciousness. Parsons, W. Va.: McClain Print. Co., 1972. A marvelous book which explains how the public schools fail the Appalachian child. This should be mandatory reading for the region's teachers.
I20 (ASU LMC MHC WCU BC)

Ickis, Marguerite The Standard Book of Quilt Making and Collecting. N. Y.: Dover, 1959. This classic work on American quilts is a must for regional differences in traditional patterns.
I30 (ASU BC)

Weaving as a Hobby. New York: Sterling Pub. Co., 1968. Includes patterns, instructions for warping your loom and illustrations that are easily deciphered.
I40 (BC ASU)

Ilsen, Isa Maud Chimney Rock Anthology. Asheville: Hackney Press, 1921. An anthology of poetry and fiction from the scenic highlands near Asheville.
I50

Images No. 1-. 1970-. vol. illus. Asheville: Univ. of North Carolina, irregular.
I60 (BC UNCA)

Imlay, Gilbert A Topographical Description of the Western Territory of North America. 3 vols. New York: Samuel Campbell, 1793. This three volume work may have been the first to depict the Appalachian man as a hero. Imlay's novel expands upon this rustic hero theme.
I70

A Topographical Description of the Western Territory of North America. 3rd ed. 1797. Reprint. New York: Johnson Reprint Co., 1968.
I80 (LMC ETSU BC)

A Topographical Description of the Western Territory of North America. 3rd ed. 1797. Reprint. Reprints of Economic Classics. New York: Augustus M. Kelley, 1969.
I90 (LMC)

Impact of Mine Drainage on Recreation and Stream Ecology. Appendices E and F to Acid Mine Drainage in Appalachia Appendix E prepared by Robert R. Nathan Associates. Washington: Appalachian Regional Commission, 1969.
I100 (ASU)

Impact of Mine Drainage Pollution on Industrial Water Users in Appalachia; Appendix A to Acid Mine Drainage in Appalachia Report Prepared by Battelle Memorial Institute. Washington: Appalachian Regional Commission, 1969.
I110 (ASU)

Impacts of Mine Drainage Pollution on Location Decisions of Manufacturing Industry in Appalachia; Appendix D to Acid Mine Drainage in Appalachia Prepared by Fantus Co., Inc. Washington: Appalachian Regional Commission, 1969.
I120 (ASU)

Incidence and Formation of Mine Drainage Pollution in Appalachia; Appendix C to Acid Mine Drainage in Appalachia Prepared by the Office of Appalachian Studies. n.p.: Army Corps of Engineers, 1969.
I130 (ASU)

Index of the Rolls of Honor (Ancestor's Index) in the Lineage books of the National Society of the Daughters of the American Revolution (1916-1940). Four volumes in two. Baltimore: Genealogical Pub. Co., 1972. Contains more than 25,000 names of servicemen.
1150

Index to American Genealogies: And to Genealogical Materials Contained in All Works as Town Histories, County Histories, Local Histories, Historical Society Publications, Biographies, Historical Periodicals, and Kindred Works Originally published by Joel Munsell's Sons. 5th ed. with Supplement. 1900, 1908. Reprint. Baltimore: Genealogical Pub. Co., 1967.
1160 (ASU)

Index to Marshall Wingfield's "Marriage Bonds of Franklin County, Virginia 1786-1858" Berryville, Va.: Virginia Book Co., n.d.
1180 (FC)

Index to Revolutionary War Pension Applications Washington, D. C.: National Genealogical Society, 1966.
1140

Index to the Andrew Johnson Papers Washington: Govt. Print. Off., 1963.
1170

The Indian Advocate, January, 1846-1855 Microfilm. Washington: Library of Congress Photo-Duplication Service, 1955. Includes material on the Cherokee.
1190 (WCU)

Industrial Directory of South Carolina Columbia, S. C.: State Development Board, 1950-.
1210

Industrial Directory of the Commonwealth of Pennsylvania Harrisburg, Pa.: Pennsylvania State Development Board, 1913-.
1200

Industrial Education Association for Southern Mountaineers Statement of Conditions 1930. n.p.: n.p., 1931.
1220

Industrial Resources Survey, Kentucky Frankfort, Ky.: Department of Economic Development, 1950-. Study includes the following areas: Richmond; Rockcastle Co.; Russell Co.; Russellville; Russellville — Logan County; Salyersville; Somerset; Stanford; Vanceburg; Vanceburg — Tollesboro; West Liberty; Whitesbury; and Williamsburg.
1230

Industrial Resources Survey, Kentucky Frankfort, Ky.: Department of Economic Development, 1952-. Study includes the following areas: Barbourville, Bath County, Bell County, Berea, Burkesville, Burnside Compton, Carter County, Catlettsburg, Columbia, Corbin, Cumberland, Elkhorn City, Frankfort, Grayson, Greenup County, Harlan, Hazard, Hinaman, Hyden, Irvine-Ravenna, Jackson, Jackson County, Knott County, Lancaster, Lee County, Liberty, Livingston, London, Louisa, McCreary, McKee, Martin, Middlesboro, Morehead, Mt. Olivet, Mt. Vernon, Ohio County, Olive Hill, Owingsville, Paintsville, Pike County, Pikeville, Pineville, Powell County, Prestonburg, and Pulaski.
1240

Industrial Resources Survey, Kentucky. Bath County, Kentucky Frankfort: Kentucky Department of Commerce, 1970.
1250

Industrial Resources Survey, Kentucky. Bell Co., Kentucky Frankfort: Kentucky Department of Commerce, 1969.
1260

Industrial Resources Survey, Kentucky. Berry, Kentucky Frankfort: Kentucky Department of Economic Development, 195-.
1270

Industrial Resources Survey, Kentucky. Burkesville, Kentucky Frankfort: Department of Economic Development, 1950.
1280

Industrial Resources Survey, Kentucky. Burnside, Kentucky Frankfort: Dept. of Economic Development, 195-.
1290

Industrial Resources Survey, Kentucky. Campton, Kentucky Frankfort: Department of Economic Development, 195-.
1300

Industrial Resources Survey, Kentucky. Carter Co. Frankfort: Kentucky Department of Economic Development, 195-.
1310

Industrial Resources Survey, Kentucky. Catlettsburg, Kentucky Frankfort: Kentucky Department of Economic Development, 195-.
1320

Industrial Resources Survey, Kentucky. Columbia, Kentucky Frankfort: Department of Economic Development, 195-.
1330

Industrial Resources Survey, Kentucky. Corbin, Kentucky Frankfort: Kentucky Department of Economic Development, 195-.
1340

Industrial Resources Survey, Kentucky. Cumberland, Kentucky Frankfort: Kentucky Department of Economic Development, 195-.
1350

Industrial Resources Survey, Kentucky. Elkhorn, Kentucky Frankfort: Kentucky Department of Economic Development, 195-.
1360

Industrial Resources Survey, Kentucky. Greenup Co. Frankfort: Kentucky Department of Economic Development, 195-.
1370

Industrial Resources Survey, Kentucky. Harlan, Kentucky Frankfort: Kentucky Department of Economic Development, 195-.
1380

Industrial Resources Survey, Kentucky. Hazard, Kentucky Frankfort: Kentucky Department of Economic Development, 195-.
1390

Industrial Resources Survey, Kentucky. Hindman, Kentucky Frankfort: Kentucky Department of Economic Development, 195-.
1400

Industrial Resources Survey, Kentucky. Hyden, Kentucky Frankfort: Kentucky Department of Economic Development, 195-.
1410

Industrial Resources Survey, Kentucky. Irvine Ravenne, Kentucky Frankfort: Dept. of Economic Development, 195-.
1420

Industrial Resources Survey, Kentucky. Jackson Co. Frankfort: Kentucky Department of Commerce, 1969.
1440

Industrial Resources Survey, Kentucky. Jackson, Kentucky Frankfort: Kentucky Department of Economic Development, 195-.
1430

Industrial Resources Survey, Kentucky. Knott Co. Frankfort: Kentucky Department of Economic Development, n.d.
1450

Industrial Resources Survey, Kentucky. Lancaster, Kentucky Frankfort: Department of Economic Development, 195-.
1460

Industrial Resources Survey, Kentucky. Lee Co. Frankfort, Ky.: Dept. of Economic Development, 195-.
1470

Industrial Resources Survey, Kentucky. Liberty, Kentucky Frankfort: Department of Economic Development, 195-.
1480

Industrial Resources Survey, Kentucky. Livingston, Kentucky Frankfort: Department of Economic Development, 195-.
1490

Industrial Resources Survey, Kentucky. London, Kentucky Frankfort: Kentucky Department of Economic Development, 195-.
1500

Industrial Resources Survey, Kentucky. Louisa, Kentucky Frankfort: Kentucky Department of Economic Development, 195-.
1510

Industrial Resources Survey, Kentucky. McCreary, Kentucky Frankfort: Kentucky Department of Economic Development, 195-.
1520

Industrial Resources Survey, Kentucky. Manchester, Kentucky Frankfort: Kentucky Department of Economic Development, 195-.
1530

Industrial Resources Survey, Kentucky. Martin, Kentucky Frankfort: Department of Economic Development, 195-.
1540

Industrial Resources Survey, Kentucky. Middlesboro, Kentucky Frankfort: Kentucky Department of Economic Development, 195-.
1550

Industrial Resources Survey, Kentucky. Monticello, Kentucky Frankfort: Department of Economic Development, 195-.
1560

Industrial Resources Survey, Kentucky. Morehead, Kentucky Frankfort: Kentucky Department of Economic Development, 195-.
1570

Industrial Resources Survey, Kentucky. Mt. Vernon, Kentucky Frankfort: Department of Economic Development, 195-.
1580

Industrial Resources Survey, Kentucky. Olive Hill, Kentucky Frankfort: Department of Economic Development, 195-.
1590

Industrial Resources Survey, Kentucky. Owingsville, Kentucky Frankfort: Department of Economic Development, 195-.
1600

Industrial Resources Survey, Kentucky. Paintsville, Kentucky Frankfort: Department of Economic Development, 195-.
1610

Industrial Resources Survey, Kentucky. Pike Co. Frankfort: Kentucky Department of Commerce, 1970.
1620

Industrial Resources Survey, Kentucky. Pikeville, Kentucky Frankfort: Kentucky Department of Economic Development, 195-.
1630

Industrial Resources Survey, Kentucky. Pineville, Kentucky Frankfort: Kentucky Department of Economic Development, 195-.
1640

Industrial Resources Survey, Kentucky. Powell Co. Frankfort: Kentucky Department of Economic Development, n.d.
1650

Industrial Resources Survey, Kentucky. Prestonburg, Kentucky Frankfort: Kentucky Department of Economic Development, 195-.
1660

Industrial Resources Survey, Kentucky. Pulaski Co. Frankfort: Kentucky Department of Commerce, 1970.
1670

Industrial Resources Survey, Kentucky. Richmond, Kentucky Frankfort: Kentucky Department of Economic Development, 195-.
1680

Industrial Resources Survey, Kentucky. Rockcastle Co. Frankfort: Kentucky Dept. of Commerce, 1966.
1690

Industrial Resources Survey, Kentucky. Russell Co. Frankfort: Kentucky Dept. of Economic Development, 195-.
1700

Industrial Resources Survey, Kentucky. Somerset, Kentucky Frankfort: Department of Economic Development, 195-.
1710

Industrial Resources Survey, Kentucky. Vanceburg-Tollesboro, Kentucky Frankfort: Kentucky Department of Commerce, 1969.
1720

Industrial Resources Survey, Virginia Blacksburg, Va.: Engineering Extension Division of Virginia Polytechnic Institute, 1920-. Survey includes: Lee County and Scott County.
1730

Industrial Review: Big Sandy and Kentucky Reviews. Coal — Oil — Gas Paintsville, Ky.: Paintsville Herald, n.d.
1740

Industrial Workers of the World Songs of the Workers to Fan the Flames of Discontent. Chicago: The Workers, 1973. Includes folk and labor songs from the Appalachian region.
I750 (ASU)

Ineson, Frank Avery The Anthracite Forest Region, a Problem Area. U. S. Department of Agriculture Miscellaneous Publication, no. 648. Washington: Govt. Print. Off., 1948.
I760 (ASU)

Ingalls, Fay The Valley Road. Illustrated by Margaret Lowengrund. Cleveland: World Pub. Co., 1949. Includes descriptive material on Hot Springs, and Warm Springs, Virginia.
I770 (ASU BC FC)

Inge, Della Addington, Luther Foster Wise County Geography Supplement. Big Stone Gap, Va.: Wise County School Board and Univ. of Virginia, 1928.
A570 (BC)

Inge, M. Thomas ed. Harris, George Washington High Times and Hard Times: Sketches and Tales. Nashville: Vanderbilt Univ. Press, 1967.
H2800 (ASU BC)

Ingersoll, Ernest To the Shenandoah and Beyond: The Chronicle of a Leisurely Journey through the Uplands of Virginia and Tennessee, Sketching Their Scenery, Noting Their Legends, Portraying Social and Material Progress, and Explaining Routes of Travel. New York: Leve & Alden, 1885.
I780

Ingles, Andrew Lewis ed. Steel, Roberta Ingles Escape From Indian Captivity. The Story of Mary Draper Ingles and Son Thomas Ingles. Radford, Va.: Commonwealth Press, n.d.
S6740

Ingram, Bowen Light as the Morning. Boston: Houghton Mifflin, 1954. A young boy agonizes over the impending loss of a beautiful valley to the Tennessee Valley Authority.
I790 (ETSU BC ASU)

Milbry. New York: Crown Pub., 1972. A novel with a mountain setting but no convincingly Appalachian characters.
I800 (LMC BC)

Ingram, Henry R. "Study of Factors Causing Potential Drop-outs to Remain in the Mitchell County, North Carolina, High Schools." Master's thesis. East Tennessee State College, 1959.
I810

Ingram, Milton J. "A History of Negro Education in Wilkes County, North Carolina." Master's thesis. North Carolina Agricultural and Technical College, 1954.
I820

Inman, Buis T. Bird, Ronald Income Opportunities for Rural Families from Outdoor Recreation Enterprises. Washington: Y. S. Economic Research Service, Resource Development Economics Division, 1965.
B4110

Inman, E. ed. Stories of Hatfield the Pioneer . . . His Experiences in the Wilderness of East Tennessee, Kentucky and South Indiana. New Albany, Ind.: G. Fishback, 1889, 1890.
I830

Inman, Mrs. W. H. Rudicil, Rowland K. Historic Hamblen, 1870-1970. Morristown: Morristown Print. Co., 1970.
R4210

Innes, Thomas C. "A Study of Some Problems of Eighth Grade Students of John Sevier Junior High School, Kingsport, Tennessee." Master's thesis. East Tennessee State College, 1957.
I840 (ETSU)

Innis, Pauline B. Gold in the Blue Ridge: The True Story of the Beale Treasure. Washington: R. B. Luce, 1973. Documentary fiction about two million dollars in gold supposedly hidden near the Peaks of Otter in southwestern Virginia.
I850 (ASU LMC)

Innis, Walter Dean Innis, Pauline B. Gold in the Blue Ridge: The True Story of the Beale Treasure. Washington: R. B. Luce, 1973.
I850 (ASU LMC)

Inservice Education for Case Workers in Home Management Improvement for Welfare Recipient Families in Ten Eastern Kentucky Counties Annual Report, 1969-70. Morehead, Ky.: Department of Home Economics, Morehead State Univ., 1970.
I860

Institute for Rural America Poverty, Rural Poverty and Minority Groups Living in Rural Poverty, an Annotated Bibliography. Lexington, Ky.: Spindletop Research, 1969.
I870

Inter-League Survey Committee for the Ohio River Basin The Ohio River Basin. Washington: League of Women Voters Education Fund, 1964.
I890

International Geological Congress Southern Appalachian Region. Washington: The Congress; 16th Session, 1933. This pamphlet seems to be intended more as a guidebook for excursions than a geologic report.
I880

Interstate Commission on the Potomac River Basin Appalachia Meets the Potomac. Washington: The Commission, 1966.
I900

Potomac River Basin Directory. Bethesda, Md.: The Commission, 1974. Includes federal, state, county, city and local action groups.
I910

Investigation Mine Survey of a Small Watershed; a Field Investigation to Locate and Define Unknown Hidden Drift Mine Openings in the Brown's Creek Watershed of West Ford River in W. Va. Washington: Govt. Print. Off., n.d.
I920

Irelan, Lola M. ed. Low-income Life Styles. Publication, 14. Washington: U. S. Welfare Administration, Division of Research, 1966. Includes a discussion of rural Appalachian poverty.
I930

Ireland, Robert M. The County Courts in Antebellum Kentucky. Lexington: Univ. Press of Kentucky, 1972. Includes material about Kentucky's 49 Appalachian counties.
I940 (BC WWC)

Irwin, Frank E. "A Study of School Transportation, Anderson County, Tennessee." Master's thesis. Univ. of Tennessee, 1958.
I950

Isaac, Paul E. Prohibition and Politics: Turbulent Decades in Tennessee, 1885-1920. Knoxville: Univ. of Tennessee Press, 1965. Includes some material on the East Tennessee whiskey industry.
I960 (ASU LMC)

Isaacs, I. J. comp. The City of Bristol, Virginia-Tennessee, Its Interests and Industries; Compiled under the Auspices of the Board of Trade. Also a Series of Comprehensive Sketches of Representative Business Enterprises. Bristol: King, 1915.
I990

Isaacs, Neil D. Maddux, Rachel Fiction Into Film: A Walk in the Spring Rain. Knoxville: Univ. of Tennessee Press, 1970.
M2710 (ASU)

Isbell, Robert Lee The World of My Childhood. Illustrated by Marjorie Talton. Lenoir, N. C.: Lenoir News-Topic, 1955. Memories of life in a western North Carolina county.
I970 (ASU LMC)

Israel, Marion Louise Cherokees. Illustrated by Harry Timmins. Look, Read, Learn. Chicago: Melmont Pubs., 1961. A children's text on the Cherokee tribe. Profusely illustrated.
I980 (MHC)

Issack, Thomas S. Thompson, James H. Factors Influencing Plant Location in West Virginia, 1945-1956. Morgantown: Bureau of Business Research, West Va. Univ., 1956.
T8210

Iverson, Evan A. Greene, Lee Seifert Rescued Earth, a Study of the Public Administration of Natural Resources in Tennessee. Knoxville: Univ. of Tennessee Press, 1948.
G3820 (ASU LMC ETSU)

Ives, Edward D. Glassie, Henry H. Folksongs and Their Makers. Bowling Green, Ohio: Bowling Green Univ., Popular Press, 1970.
G2070 (ASU MHC BC)

Ives, L. Silliman The Trials of a Mind in the Progress to Catholicism: A Letter to His Old Friends. Boston: Patrick Donahoe, 1854. These letters reflect both personal soul-searching and the status of and attitudes toward Catholicism in the mountain region in the 1850's.
I1000 (LMC)

Ivey, George Franks Loom-fixing and Weaving; A Book for All Who Are Interested in Such Matters. Hickory, N. C.: The author, 1901. A handyman's guide to basic loom repair, maintenance, warping and weaving.
I1010

Ivey, J. B. Robinson, W. H. Water Supply of the Birmingham Area, Alabama. Washington: Govt. Print. Off., 1953.
R3340

Izard, Ralph Stead "West Virginia's Program of State Publicity." Master's thesis. West Virginia Univ., 1962.
I1020

Jack, George S. History of Roanoke Co. Roanoke: Stone Print., 1912. Includes historical material on the city, the county, and the Norfolk and Western Railroad.
J10 (BC)

Jackson, Allen Keith "Religious Beliefs and Social Status: A Study of the Relationships between Religious Beliefs and Social Status Levels in Sixty-one Churches of the Southern Appalachian Mountains." Microfilm. Ph. D. Diss. Emory Univ., 1960.
J20 (ASU)

Jackson County, North Carolina. Committee on Appraising Outdoor Recreation Potential Outdoor Recreation Potential Appraisal. Sylva, N. C.: The committee, 1971.
J30 (WCU)

Jackson, George Pullen White and Negro Spirituals, Their Life Span and Kinship, Tracing 200 Years of Untrammeled Song Making and Singing Among Our Country Folk, with 116 Songs as Sung by Both Races. New York: J. J. Augustin, 1944.
J90 (ASU BC)

White Spirituals in the Southern Uplands. Chapel Hill: Univ. of North Carolina Press, 1933.
J100

White Spirituals in the Southern Uplands: The Story of the Fascola Folk, Their Songs, Singings, and "Buckwheat Notes". 1933. Reprint. Hatboro, Pa.: Folklore Associates, 1964.
J110 (ASU BC WCU ETSU LMC MHC)

White Spirituals in the Southern Uplands: The Story of the Fasola Folk, Their Songs, Singings, and "Buckwheat Notes". 1933. Reprint. Dover Books, T1425.
J120 (ETSU WWC)

Jackson, George Pullen ed. Another Sheaf of White Spirituals. Gainesville: Univ. of Florida Press, 1952.
J40 (ASU LMC)

Down-east Spirituals, and Others: Three Hundred Songs Supplementary to the Author's Spiritual Folk-songs of Early America. New York: J. J. Augustin, 1943.
J50 (ASU)

Spiritual Folk-songs of Early America: Two Hundred and Fifty Tunes and Texts with an Introduction and Notes. New York: J. J. Augustin, 1937.
J60 (ASU)

Spiritual Folk-songs of Early America: Two Hundred and Fifty Tunes and Texts with an Introduction and Notes. 1937. Reprint. New York: Dover Publications, 1964.
J70 (ASU WCU LMC BC)

Jackson, George Pullen ed.
The Story of The Sacred Harp, 1844-1944, a Book of Religious Folk Songs as an American Institution. Nashville: Vanderbilt Univ. Press, 1944.
J80 (LMC WCU MHC BC ASU)

Jackson, George T. and others Soil Survey, Putnam County, Tennessee. Soil Survey, Series 1960, no. 7. Washington: U. S. Department of Agriculture, Soil Conservation Service, 1963.
J130
Soil Survey, Warren County, Tennessee. Washington: U. S. Soil Conservation Service, 1967.
J140

Jackson, H. J. Horton, A. H. The Ohio Valley Flood of March-April, 1913, Including Comparisons with Some Earlier Floods. Washington: Govt. Print. Off., 1913.
H7290

Jackson, Helen F. "The German Swiss Settlers at Gruetli, Tennessee." Master's thesis. Vanderbilt Univ., 1933.
J150 (ASU)

Jackson, James E. Hughes, Ralph H. Fertilization of Young Slash Pine in a Cultivated Plantation. Asheville, N. C.: Southeastern Forest Experiment Station, 1962.
H8110 (WCU)

Jackson, Luther Porter Free Negro Labor and Property Holding in Virginia, 1830-1860. New York: D. Appleton-Century Co., 1942.
J160 (ETSU)

Jackson, Minnie L. "A History of the Development of Schools for Negroes in Walker County, Georgia." Master's thesis. Tennessee Agriculture and Industrial State Univ., 1958.
J170

Jackson, Ralph F. "Bituminous Coal Open Pit Mining in Clarion County, Pennsylvania." Master's thesis. Univ. of Pittsburgh, 1959.
J180

Jackson, Robert Montgomery Smith The Mountain. Philadelphia: Lippincott, 1860. Fiction with an unspecified mountain setting.
J190 (LMC BC)

Jackson, Ward B. "The History of Education of Boyd County, Kentucky." Master's thesis. Univ. of Kentucky, 1932.
J200

Jacob, John Jeremiah A Biographical Sketch on the Life of the Late Captain Michael Cresap. Intro. by Otis K. Rice. 1866. Reprint. Parsons, W. Va.: McClain Print. Co., 1971. Biography of an Indian fighter, controversial military man, and Appalachian Scout.
J210

Jacobs, Lucile Frizzell Duck River Valley in Tennessee and Its Pioneers. n.p.: n.p., 1968. A warm, rambling and very readable family chronicle from East Tennessee.
J220 (ASU)

Jacobs, Marion Lee Index of Plants of North Carolina With Reputed Medicinal Uses. n.p.: n.p., 1958. Primarily a list of plants from the western North Carolina Mountains, an area which provides a large percentage of the nation's raw botanical drugs.
J230 (WWC)

Jacobs, Wilbur R. ed. Atkin, Edmond The Appalachian Indian Frontier. The Edmond Atkin Report and Plan of 1755. Lincoln: Univ. of Nebraska Press, 1967.
A5310 (ASU BC WCU LMC ETSU)
The Appalachian Indian Frontier: The Edmond Atkin Report and Plan of 1755. Columbia: Carolina University of South Carolina Press, 1954. A carefully edited and indexed edition of Atkins' advice to the British Board of Trade regarding the expansion of British autonomy immediately prior to the French and Indian War.
J240
Indians of the Southern Colonial Frontier; The Edmond (Edmund) Atkin Report and Plan of 1755. Lincoln: Univ. of Nebraska Press, 1967.
J250

Jacobsen, E. T. Huddle, J. W. Oil and Gas Wells Drilled in Southwestern Virginia before 1950. Washington: Govt. Print. Off., 1956.
H7900 (ASU)

Jacobus, Donald Lines Genealogy As Pastime and Profession. Introduction by Milton Rubincam. 1930. Reprint. Baltimore: Genealogical Pub. Co., 1968.
J260 (ASU)
Index to Genealogical Periodicals. 3 vols. 1932, 1948, 1964. Reprint. Baltimore: Genealogical Pub. Co., 1963-1969.
J270 (ASU)

Jahoda, Gloria Delilah's Mountain. Boston: Houghton Mifflin, 1963. Novel set in southwestern Virginia's Clinch Valley during the period of Indian wars. Contains some good descriptive passages on frontier life.
J280 (ETSU ASU WCU BC)

Jalliffe, John Chattanooga. Cincinnati: Wrighton and Co., 1858. Descriptive material designed to attract industry and tourists to the area.
J290

James, Bessie Rowland Six Feet Six, the Heroic Story of Sam Houston. Illustrated with woodcuts by Lowell Balcom. 1st ed. Indianapolis: Bobbs-Merrill Co., 1931. Houston's early years were spent in east Tennessee.
J300 (ASU)

James, Charles M. "Measuring Productivity in Coal Mining: A Case Study of Multiple Input Measurement at the County Level in Pennsylvania." Ph. D. Diss. Univ. of Pennsylvania, 1952.
J310

James, Edgar The Allen Outlaws: A Complete History of Their Lives and Exploits, Concluding with the Hillsville Courthouse Tragedy. Baltimore: Phoenix Pub. Co., 1912.
J320 (ASU BC)

James, Garland Ewing "A Study of the Procedures Used for the Recruitment, Selection, and Assignment of Professional Personnel in Six Selected East Tennessee School Systems." Master's thesis. East Tennessee State Univ., 1969.
J330 (ETSU)

James, George Wharton Indian Basketry. Pasadena, Calif.: The author, 1902. Includes a section on Cherokee basketry.
J340

James, Harlean Romance of the National Parks. New York: Macmillan Co., 1939. This history of the national park system includes material on the many parks along the Appalachian mountain range.
J350 (ASU)

James, Marquis James, Bessie Rowland Six Feet Six, the Heroic Story of Sam Houston. Indianapolis: Bobbs-Merrill Co., 1931.
J300 (ASU)
The Raven, a Biography of Sam Houston. New York: Blue Ribbon Books, 1929.
J360

Jameson, Gladys Vee Sweet Rivers of Song: A Book of Traditional Songs From the Southern Appalachian Mountain Region. Berea, Ky.: Berea College, 1967. A fine collection of old favorites from the southern mountains. Music arranged by Gladys Jameson.
J370 (ASU MHC WCU BC)
Wake and Sing: A Miniature Anthology of the Music of Appalachian America. New York: Broadcast Music, 1955. A small but fairly representative anthology of hill country music.
J380 (WWC BC ASU)

Janney, Samuel Macpherson Memoirs of Samuel M. Janney; Late of Lincoln, Loudoun Co., Va. Philadelphia: Friends Bk. Association, 1890. Biography of a Quaker minister who lived and worked in western Virginia.
J390

Jansma, J. Dean Battison, E. J. A Framework for Community Economic Planning Based on the Integration of an Input-output Model and a Linear Programming Model. University Park: Pennsylvania Agricultural Experiment Station, 1969.
B1960

Janssen, Raymond Ellsworth Earth Science, A Handbook on the Geology of West Virginia. Clarksburg, W. Va.: West Virginia Educational Marketeers, 1973.
J400

Jaquish, Orin W. Grice, Darrell G. Soil Survey, Mercer County, Pennsylvania. Washington: U. S. Soil Conservation Service, 1971.
G4060

Jarrell, Hampton M. William Gilmore Simms: Realistic Romancer. Ph. D. Diss. Duke University, 1932. Despite the title, Simm's Appalachian fiction is hardly realistic.
J410

Jarrett, Robert Frank Back Home and Other Poems. Being a Collection of Poems. Asheville, N. C.: Inland Press, 1911. A book of poems with western North Carolina settings.
J420 (LMC)
Occoneechee, the Maid of the Mystic Lake. New York: Shakespeare Press, 1916.
J430 (ASU WCU)
Occoneechee, the Maid of the Mystic Lake. Atlanta: n.p., 1946.
J440 (UNCA LMC)

Jarrett, Tim W. Sluder, Earl Ray Tests on Direct Seeding of Oak in Piedmont and Southern Appalachians of North Carolina. Asheville, N. C.: Southeastern Forest Experiment Station, 1961.
S4250 (WCU)

Jarvis, James Allen "Factors Influencing Political Behavior in Bell, Clay, Knox, and Whitley Counties." Master's thesis. Univ. of Kentucky, 1948.
J450 (ASU)

Jasper, Mary Katherine "Social Value of Settlement Schools in the Kentucky Mountains." Microfilm. Master's thesis. Univ. of Kentucky, 1930. A rather saccharin account of the supposed social value of the Kentucky settlement schools.
J460 (ASU)

Jaworek, Walter Gibson "The Use and Interchangeability of Fuels in Pennsylvania." Ph. D. Diss. Pennsylvania State Univ., 1960. Deals with oil, gas, and coal industries of Pennsylvania.
J470

Jeffers, Jack A Photographic Documentary of the Blue Ridge Mountains. Lyndhurst, Va.: The author, 1973. A lovely photographic essay on Virginia's Blue Ridge range.
J480 (LMC)

Jefferson County Camp, United Confederate Veterans Military Operations in Jefferson Co., Virginia and West Virginia, 1861-65. n.p.: Whitney and White, 1960.
J490 (ASU)

Jefferson, Peter Fry, Joshua The Fry and Jefferson Map of Virginia and Maryland. Charlottesville: Univ. Press of Virginia, 1950.
F3600 (FC)

Jefferson, Thomas Notes on the State of Virginia. Boston: Lilly and Wait, 1832. Includes commentary on the potential of Virginia's western counties.
J500 (ASU)
Notes on the State of Virginia. New York: Harper and Row, 1964.
J510 (FC)

Jefferys, Grady Gilbert, John F. Crossties Over Saluda. Raleigh: Crossties Press, 1971.
G1280
Easy to Follow Directions on How to Get Lost in the Land of the Sky. Asheville, N. C.: Miller Print. Co., n.d. A humorous guide to the mountain regions near Asheville.
J580 (WCU)

Jeffords, Russell MacGregor Ground-water Conditions along the Ohio Valley at Parkersburg, West Virginia. Bulletin, no. 10. Morgantown: West Virginia Geological Survey, 1945.
J520 (ETSU)

Jeffrey, Arthur David "An Economic Analysis of Idle Farm Land, Potter County, Pennsylvania, 1953." Ph. D. Diss. Pennsylvania State Univ., 1956.
J530

Jeffrey, Betty Educational and Vocational Goals of Rural Youth and Their Parents in Tennessee. Bulletin no. 399. Knoxville: Tennessee Agricultural Experiment Station, Univ. of Tennessee, 1966. Deals primarily with Eastern Tennessee counties.
J540 (ASU)

Jeffreys, Alois Waldo Tuning and Playing the Appalachian Dulcimer. Waynesboro, Va.: n.p., 1958. A handbook for beginning dulcimer players.
J550 (ASU LMC)

Tuning and Playing the Appalachian Dulcimer. Staunton, Va.: The author, 1958.
J560 (BC)

Tuning and Playing the Appalachian Dulcimer. Staunton, Va.: n.p., 1964.
J570 (WCU)

Jemison, George Meredith "The Effect of Basal Wounding By Forest Fires on the Diameter Growth of Some Southern Appalachian Hardwoods." Ph. D. Diss. Duke University, 1942.
J590

Timber Stand Improvement in the Southern Appalachian Region. Washington: U. S. Dept. of Agriculture, 1949.
J600

Jenkins, Brenda J. "The Effect of the Physical Activity Program on the Strength Development of Freshmen at Appalachian State Teachers College." Master's thesis. Appalachian State Teachers College, 1963.
J610 (ASU)

Jenkins, Clifford T. Floods in Tennessee; Magnitude and Frequency. Nashville: Tennessee Dept. of Highways, 1960.
J620

Jenkins, Clifton Hubbard, Edgar Harvey Soil Survey, Grainger County, Tennessee. Washington: U. S. Department of Agriculture, Bureau of Plant Industry, Soils and Agricultural Engineering, 1948.
H7810

Rudolph, Foster Soil Survey, Carter County, Tennessee. Washington: U. S. Soil Conservation Service, 1953.
R4220

Jenkins, George "The History of Watauga Academy of Butler, Tennessee." Master's thesis. Appalachian State Teachers College, 1950. An interesting study of a Johnson County, Tennessee institution which seems fairly representative of the 1880-1915 academy movement.
J630 (ASU)

Jenkins, Ida Powell comp. Lineage Book of the National Society of Daughters of American Colonists. Washington: Judd and Detweiler Inc. Press, 1929.
J640

Jenkins, John Sitwell Life and Public Services of General Andrew Jackson. New York: Miller, Orton, and Mulligan, 1856.
J650

Jenkins, Mark Rev. Calvary Church Episcopal, where City and County Meet to Worship God; A Historical Sketch of Calvary Episcopal Church. Fletcher, N. C.: Calvary Episcopal Church, 1959.
J660

Jenkins, William J. Mountain Rhythms: Or, Poems of a Mountaineer. Raleigh, N. C.: Commercial Print. Co., 1922.
J670 (ASU)

Jennings, Edith Gasteiger "A Multilevel Approach to Reading for One Section of a Sixth Grade Class in Keystone Elementary School Year, 1965-1966." Master's thesis. East Tennessee State Univ., 1966.
J680 (ETSU)

Jennings, Ruby Brugh Botetourt County, Virginia, 1850 Census. 2 vols. Roanoke, Va.: Privately Printed, 1974.
J690

Jensen, Harold R. A General Picture of Commercial Agriculture in Eastern Kentucky. Lexington: Kentucky Agriculture Experiment Station, 1957.
J700

Jensen, Henry W. The Little Seeds of Christmas and Other Stories. Swannanoa, N. C.: International Relations Club, Warren Wilson College, 1964. Short stories with a western North Carolina setting.
J710 (WWC)

Jensen, Richard E. Archeological Survey of the Rowlesburg Reservoir Area, West Virginia. Report of Archeological Investigations, no. 2. Morgantown: West Virginia Geological and Economic Survey, 1970.
J720 (ASU)

Jesse Stuart, the Man: Poet, Novelist, Short Story Writer, Educator Ashland, Ky.: Economy Printers, 1968.
S8620

Jessee, R. W. Bacon, H. Stuart Immunization Cooperation in Southwest Virginia. Berea, Ky.: Council of the Southern Mountains, 1959.
B60

Jessey, Gary D. Letcher County's Pine Mountain Caves. Cromona, Ky.: Superior Print. and Pub. Co., 1973. Descriptive material, maps and illustrations about Letcher County's extensive caves.
J730 (BC)

Jeter, Virginia Lockhart "Elements of Local Color in the Prose Fiction of Jesse Stuart." Master's thesis. East Tennessee State College, 1956.
J740 (ASU)

Jewell, Aurelia M. Loudoun Co., Virginia, Marriage bonds, 1762-1850. Berryville: Chesapeake Bk. Co., 1962. Includes maps of early Loundoun County.
J750 (ASU)

Jewell, James William Kentucky Days. Lexington, Ky.: Lang Co., 1950. Memoirs of a Kentucky childhood.
J760 (ETSU)

Kentucky Mountain Melodies. Lexington: Lang Co., 1950. A collection of Kentucky hill country favorites with musical arrangements.
J770

Melee; or Woman in Command. Mimeographed copy. Lexington: Lang Co., 1951.
J780 (BC)

My Kentucky; Plain Verse of a Mountain Man from Old Kentucky. Mimeographed copy. Lexington: n.p., n.d.
J790 (BC)

"A Proposed Certification Plan for Kentucky Teachers Through Credentials, a Complete Investigation and a Comprehensive Examination in Major Fields." New York: Hobson Book Press, 1947.
J800 (LMC BC)

Walking Bear of Silvermine Mountain. Lexington: Lang Co., 1950. An Indian legend from the Kentucky hills.
J810

Jewell, Malcom Edwin Kentucky Politics. Lexington: Univ. of Kentucky Press, 1968.
J820 (ASU BC)

Jillson, Willard Rouse Bibliography of Clark Co., Kentucky. Frankfort: Roberts Print. Co., 1963.
J830

Bibliography of Elliott Co., Ky. Frankfort: Perry Pub. Co., 1958.
J840

Bibliography of Floyd Co., Ky. Frankfort: Perry Pub. Co., 1956.
J850

Bibliography of Knox Co., Ky. Frankfort: Perry Pub. Co., 1958.
J860

Bibliography of Lawrence Co., Ky. Frankfort: Roberts Print. Co., 1969.
J870

Bibliography of Licking River Valley in Ky. Frankfort: Roberts Print. Co., 1968.
J880

Bibliography of Madison Co., Ky. Frankfort: Perry Pub. Co., 1964.
J890

Bibliography of Menifee Co., Ky. Frankfort: Roberts Print. Co., 1967.
J900

Bibliography of Powell Co., Ky. Frankfort: Perry Pub. Co., 1961.
J910

Bibliography of Pulaski Co., Ky. Frankfort: Roberts Pub. Co., 1954.
J920

Bibliography of the Big Sandy Valley. Frankfort: Perry Pub. Co., 1960. Since the Big Sandy was host to Kentucky's early extractive industries, this bibliography includes some interesting facts.
J930

Bibliography of the Cumberland River Valley. Frankfort: Perry Pub. Co., 1960.
J940

A Bibliography of the Mineral Resources of Kentucky. Frankfort: Roberts Print. Co., 1966.
J950

The Big Sandy Valley: A Regional History Prior to the Year 1850. Boone Day Address, 1922, Kentucky State Historical Society. Louisville, Ky.: J. P. Morgan and Co., 1923.
J960 (ASU BC)

The Big Sandy Valley: A Regional History Prior to the Year 1850. Boone Day address, 1922, Kentucky State Historical Society. 1923. Reprint. With a new foreword by the author. Baltimore: Regional Pub. Co., 1970.
J970 (MHC)

The Boone Narrative. Louisville, Ky.: Standard Print., 1932. This Boone family narrative contains a great deal of material on Kentucky.
J980 (LMC)

The Coal Industry in Kentucky. Frankfort: The State Journal Co., 1922.
J990

The Coal Industry in Kentucky. Frankfort: Kentucky Geological Survey.
J1000

Daniel Boone in Kentucky. Frankfort: State Journal Co., 1939.
J1010

Geology and Coal of Stinking Creek. Frankfort: Dept. of Geology and Forestry, 1919.
J1020

The Geology and Mineral Resources of Kentucky: A Brief Description of the Physiography, Stratigraphy, Areal and Structural Geology, and Mineral Resources of Each of the Counties Comprising the Commonwealth. Illustrated with two hundred and fifty-one photographs, maps and diagrams. Geologic Reports, series 6, vol. 17. Frankfort: Kentucky Geological Survey, 1928.
J1030 (ETSU)

Geology of a New Oil Pool in Casey Co., Ky. Frankfort: Roberts Print. Co., 1967.
J1040

Geology of Clark Co., Ky. Frankfort: Roberts Print. Co., 1969.
J1050

Geology of Pickett Co., Tenn. Frankfort: Roberts Print. Co., 1948.
J1070

Geology of Cumberland Co., Kentucky. n.p.: n.p., 1951.
J1070

Geology of Powell Co., Ky. Frankfort: Roberts Print. Co., 1969.
J1080

Geology of the Area Around Powell Co., Ky. Frankfort: Roberts Print. Co., 1963.
J1090

Geology of the Glencairn and Pine Ridge Faults. Frankfort: Roberts Print. Co., 1965.
J1100

Geology of the Goose Creek Dome. Frankfort: Perry Pub. Co., 1960.
J1110

Bibliography of the Green River Valley. Frankfort: Perry Pub. Co., 1968.
J1120

Geology of the Meadow Anticline. Frankfort: Roberts Print. Co., 1954.
J1130

Geology of the Mica Dome in Clark Co., Ky. Frankfort: Roberts Print. Co., 1963.
J1140

Geology of the Nimtonville Dome in Casey Co., Ky. Frankfort: Roberts Print. Co., 1962.
J1150

Jillson, Willard Rouse
The Kentucky Land Grants: A Systematic Index to the Land Grants Recorded in the State Land Office at Frankfort, Kentucky, 1782-1924. 1925. Reprint. Baltimore: Genealogical Pub. Co., 1971.
J1160 (ASU)
Natural Gas in Eastern Ky. Louisville: Standard Print. Co., 1937.
J1170
Oil Domes of Ashland. Des Moines: Geological Pub. Co., 1926.
J1180
Old Kentucky Entries and Deeds. A Complex Index to All of the Earliest Land Entries, Military Warrants, Deeds and Wills of the Commonwealth of Kentucky. 1926. Reprint. Baltimore: Genealogical Pub. Co., 1969.
J1190 (ASU MHC)
Red River Iron Works. Frankfort: Roberts, 1964.
J1200
The Rose Hill Oil Pool. Frankfort: Roberts Print. Co., 1947.
J1210
A Tour Downstream. Frankfort: Perry Pub. Co., 1959.
J1220

Jitodai, Ted Terua "Migration, Mobility and Social Participation." Ph. D. Diss. Univ. of Michigan, 1963.
J1230

Joel Munsell's Sons comp. Index to American Genealogies: And to Genealogical Materials Contained in All Works as Town Histories, County Histories, Local Histories, Historical Society Publications, Biographies, Historical Periodicals, and Kindred Works Baltimore: Genealogical Pub. Co., 1967.
I160 (ASU)

John, Bruce M. Appalachia: Problems and Solutions. n.p.: Association of Southern Agricultural Workers, Agricultural Economics and Rural Sociology Sections, 1965.
J1240 (ASU)

John, M. E. Forces Influencing Rural Life. Bulletin no. 388. University Park: Pennsylvania Agricultural Experiment Station, Pennsylvania State Univ., 1940. Study uses mountain counties in central Pennsylvania.
J1250

Johns, Patricia The Violent Years. New York: Hastings House, 1962. Biography of the Controversial scout, frontiersman and soldier from West Virginia.
J1260 (BC)

Johnson, Allen Monroe "A Study of Reasons Why Freshmen Drop Out of Appalachian State Teachers College." Master's thesis. Appalachian State Teachers College, 1953.
J1270 (ASU)

Johnson, Andrew Speeches of Andrew Johnson, President of the United States. Boston: Little, Brown, 1865.
J1280
Speeches of Andrew Johnson, President of the United States. New York: B. Franklin, 1968.
J1290 (ASU)

Johnson, Augusta Phillips A Century of Wayne County, Kentucky, 1800-1900. Louisville, Ky.: Standard Print. Co., 1939.
J1300 (ASU BC)

Johnson, Charles A. A Narrative History of Wise County, Virginia. Norton, Va.: Norton Press, 1938. An informal but informative history of Wise County from its earliest settlement to date.
J1310 (LMC ASU)

Johnson, Charles Albert The Frontier Camp Meeting. Dallas: Southern Methodist Univ. Press, 1955. Deals with the camp meeting phenomena from the Great Revival of 1805 to the present. In many regards the revivalism movement may be considered an Appalachian phenomena.
J1320 (WWC)

Johnson, Charles Spurgeon and others Statistical Atlas of Southern Counties Listing and Analysis of Socio-economic Indices of 1104 Southern Counties. Chapel Hill: Univ. of North Carolina Press, 1941. Contains valuable statistical material on Appalachian Counties.
J1330 (ASU LMC MHC BC)

Johnson City Area Industrial Commission Industrial Advantages of the Johnson City Area. Johnson City, Tenn.: The commission, 1970.
J1340 (ETSU)

Johnson City. East Tennessee State Normal School Curriculum for the Observation and Practice School. Nashville: State Board of Education, 1914.
J1350 (ETSU)

Johnson City High School, Senior Class, 1924. The Wataugan Annual. Johnson City, Tenn.: Union, 1924.
J1360 (ETSU)

Johnson City, Tennessee Annual Report . . . for Fiscal Year Ended June 30, 1944-. Johnson City, Tenn.: The City, 1944-.
J1370 (ETSU)
Annual Report . . . for Fiscal Year Ended June 30, 1944-. Johnson City, Tenn.: The city, 1944-.
J1380 (ETSU)
Code. Rochester, N. Y.: Lawyers Co-operative Pub. Co., 1951. Also, 1956 Supplement.
J1390 (ETSU)
The Code of the City of Johnson City, Tennessee: The Chart and the General Ordinances of the City, Published by Order of the Board of Commissioners. Charlottesville, Va.: Michie City Pub. Co., 1964.
J1400 (ETSU)
Zoning Ordinance for the City of Johnson City, Tennessee. Johnson City: n.p., 1963.
J1410 (ETSU)

Johnson City, Tennessee. Chamber of Commerce Map of Johnson City, Washington County, Tennessee. Johnson City: Chamber of Commerce, 1961.
J1420 (ETSU)
Newsletter. vol. 1- 19--. n.p.: n.p., Frequency varies.
J1430 (ETSU)

Johnson City, Tennessee. First Methodist Church Directory of First Methodist Church, November 1, 1950. . . Johnson City: The church, 1950.
J1440 (ETSU)

Johnson City, Tennessee. North Junior High School and the Southern Association of Colleges and Secondary Schools. Secondary Commission. Evaluation Report, North Junior High School, Johnson City, Tennessee. Mimeographed copy. Johnson City: The Ass'n, 1965.
J1450 (ETSU)

Johnson City, Tennessee. Office of Civil Defense Washington County-Johnson City Civil Defense Operational Survival Plan. Johnson City: Office of Civil Defense, 1961.
J1460 (ETSU)

Johnson City, Tennessee. Public Schools. Learning, Resources, and Service Center Manual for Receiving and Processing Instructional Materials. Revised by Opal Johnson, Processor. Johnson City, Tenn.: The author, 1970.
J1470 (ETSU)

Johnson City, Tennessee, Regional Planning Commission Johnson City Shopping Center District Regulations. Johnson City: The commission, 1964.
J1480 (ETSU)
Johnson City, Tennessee: Population and Economic Base Study. Prepared by Eric Hall Associates for the City of Johnson City, Tennessee, and the Johnson City Regional Planning Commission. 3 vols. in 1. Atlanta: n.p., 1964-65.
J1490 (ETSU)
Johnson City's Community Facilities. Johnson City: The commission, 1962.
J1500 (ETSU)
Land Use Analysis. Johnson City: The commission, 1965.
J1510 (ETSU)
Land Use Plan. Johnson City: The commission, 1965?
J1520 (ETSU)
Neighborhood Analyses. 2 vols. in 1. Johnson City: The commission, 1962.
J1530 (ETSU)
Subdivision Regulations of Johnson City Regional Planning Commission. Adopted November 12, 1957. Prepared with the assistance of Upper East Tennessee Office, Tennessee State Planning Commission. n.p.: n.p., 1957.
J1540 (ETSU)

Johnson City, Tennessee. Science Hill High School To the Top with the Toppers; the History of Science Hill High School Football, 1920-1970, with Official Team and Individual Statistics. Johnson City: n.p., 1971.
J1550 (ETSU)

Johnson City, Tennessee. Science Hill High School and the Southern Association of Colleges and Secondary Schools. Secondary Commission. Evaluative Study Made in Science Hill High School, Johnson City, Tennessee . . . March 4-8, 1951. Mimeographed. Johnson City: The commission, 1951.
J1570 (ETSU)

Johnson City, Tennessee. South Junior High School and the Southern Association of Colleges and Secondary Schools. Secondary Commission. Evaluative Study of South Junior High School, Johnson City, Tennessee; Completed by the Visiting Committee March 15-18, 1965. . . Johnson City, Tenn.: The Ass'n, 1965.
J1560 (ETSU)

Johnson, Clifton Highways and Byways of the South. New York: Macmillan, 1904. Contains descriptive material on the mountain regions of eight southern states.
J1580 (BC LMC)

Johnson County, Tennessee, Comprehensive Overall Economic Development Program Report. Johnson County: Development Committee, 1963.
J1590 (ETSU)

Johnson, Cyrus M. Mountain Families in Poverty. Mimeographed. Lexington: Departments of Sociology and Rural Sociology, in cooperation with the Social Research Service, and the Kentucky Agricultural Experiment Station, University of Kentucky, May, 1965.
J1600

Johnson, D. H. Appalachian Rivers. New York: Hafner, n.d. Comprehensive listing and descriptive material on the region's rivers.
J1610

Johnson, Douglas ed. Quinn, Bernard Atlas of the Church in Appalachia, Administrative Units and Boundaries. Knoxville, Tenn.: Commission on Religion in Appalachia, 1970.
Q180 (ASU)

Johnson, Douglas W. The Commission on Religion in Appalachia, Inc.; a Case Study. New York: National Council of the Churches of Christ, 1971. An evaluation of CORA's many regional projects.
J1620 (BC ASU)

Johnson, Douglas Wilson Stream Sculpture on the Atlantic Slope: A Study in the Evolution of Appalachian Rivers. 1931. Reprint. Columbia Geomorphic Studies. New York: Hafner Pub. Co., 1967.
J1630 (ASU LMC ETSU)

Johnson, Edward A. "Compulsory and Flexible Retirement Policies and Practices; An Analysis of West Virginia Industrial Patterns." Master's thesis. West Virginia Univ., 1970.
J1640

Johnson, Eileen Jayne "A Survey of the Problems of Freshmen-Student Nurses at Memorial Hospital and a Proposed Guidance Program." Master's thesis. East Tennessee State College, 1952.
J1650 (ETSU)

Johnson, Elmer D. Thomas Wolfe: A Checklist. Kent, Ohio: Kent State Univ. Press, 1970.
J1670 (ASU)

Johnson, Elmer D.
Of Time and Thomas Wolfe: A Bibliography with a Character Index of His Works. New York: Scarecrow Press, 1959.
J1680 (ASU UNCA)

Johnson, Elmer D. ed. A Checklist of Southwest Virginia Newspapers, 1800-1974. Compiled by Dept. of History, Radford College. Radford, Va.: Dept. of History, Radford College, 1974.
J1660

Johnson, Emily Davis, Innis C. and others A Bibliography of West Virginia. Charleston, West Virginia: Charleston Print. Co. for the West Virginia Department of Archives and History, 1939.
D1060

Devis, Innis C. and others A Bibliography of West Virginia. Charleston, W. Va.: Charleston Printing Co. for the West Virginia Department of Archives and History, 1939.
D1990

Johnson, Frances Nelson A Five Year Follow-up Study of Graduates of Asheville-Buncombe Technical Institute, 1966-67 through 1970-71. Master's thesis. Appalachian State University, 1974.
J1690 (ASU)

Johnson, Frank A. The White Pole Meeting House, Hillsboro, West Virginia. Franklin, W. Va.: n.p., 1963.
J1700 (ASU BC)

Johnson, Frank Roy How and Why Stories in Carolina Folklore. Spartanburg: Johnson Reprint, 1971. Includes some western North Carolina tales.
J1720 (LMC)

The Tuscaroras: Mythology, Medicine, Culture. 2 vols. Murfreesboro, N. C.: Johnson Pub. Co., 1967.
J1730 (ASU LMC)

Witches and Demons in History and Folklore. Murfreesboro, N. C.: Johnson Pub. Co., 1969. Tales of the supernatural collected primarily in North Carolina.
J1740 (LMC)

Johnson, Frank Roy ed. How and Why: Stories in Carolina Folklore. Murfreesboro, N. C.: Johnson Pub. Co., 1971. Includes some western North Carolina tales.
J1710 (WCU)

Johnson, Gerald W. An Honorable Titan: A Biographical Study of Adolph S. Ochs. New York: Harper, 1946. Ochs was a Chattanooga journalist who later controlled the NEW YORK TIMES.
J1750

Johnson, Gerald White Randolph of Roanoke: A Political Fantastic. New York: Minton, Balch and Co., 1929. Biography of John Randolph politician and statesman.
J1760 (ASU)

Johnson, Gerald Wolblet "West Virginia Politics: A Socio-Cultural Analysis of Political Participation." Ph. D. Diss. Univ. of Tennessee, 1970.
J1770

Johnson, Guy B. John Henry: Track Down a Negro Legend. Chapel Hill: Univ. of North Carolina Press, 1929. An intriguing account of a researcher's attempt to validate the legend of John Henry.
J1780

Johnson, Hugh A. Exurban Development in Selected Areas of the Appalachian Mountains. U. S. Department of Agriculture Resource Development Economics Division, Economic Research Service Series, 111. Washington: Govt. Print. Off., 1963.
J1790

Private Outdoor Recreation Enterprises in Rural Appalachia. U. S. Department of Agriculture Economic Research Service Series, 429. Washington: Govt. Print. Off., 1969.
J1800

Johnson, Jack Dempsey "Economic Factors Affecting Cattle Prices at Appalachian Auctions." Ph. D. Diss. Iowa State Univ., 1958.
J1810

Johnson, James Gibson Southern Fiction Prior to 1860: An Attempt at a First Hand Bibliography. 1909. Reprint. New York: Johnson Reprint Corp., 1967.
J1820 (ASU)

Southern Fiction Prior to 1860: An Attempt at a First-hand Bibliography. 1909. Reprint. New York: Phaeton Press, 1968. Includes early Appalachian fiction.
J1830 (MHC)

Johnson, James Pearce "A "New Deal" for Soft Coal: The Attempted Revitalization of the Bituminous Coal Industry under the New Deal." Ph. D. Diss. Columbia Univ., 1968.
J1840

Johnson, James Ralph Lost on Hawk Mountain. New York: Follett Pub. Co., 1954. Children's adventure story with an Appalachian setting.
J1850 (ASU)

Johnson, John Lang "Distribution of Income Payments to Individuals in Kentucky Counties by Amount, by Type, and by Size: 1950." Ph. D. Diss. Univ. of Kentucky, 1954. Eastern Kentucky income levels are noticeably lower than those of non-mountainous areas of the state.
J1860

Income in Kentucky: County Distributions by Amount, by Type, and by Size. Lexington: Univ. of Kentucky Press, 1955.
J1870 (LMC BC)

Johnson, Katherine Baker The Knox County Missionary Baptists 1786-1945. Typescript. n.p.: n.p., 1946.
J1880

Johnson, Opal ed. Johnson City, Tennessee. Public Schools. Learning, Resources, and Service Center Manual for Receiving and Processing Instructional Materials. Johnson City, Tenn.: The author, 1970.
J1470 (ETSU)

Johnson, Pamela Hansford The Art of Thomas Wolfe. 1948. Reprint. (Original title: Hungry Gulliver.) New York: Scribner, 1963.
J1890 (ASU WCU)

Thomas Wolfe: A Critical Study. London: W. Heinemann, 1947.
J1900 (ASU WCU BC)

Johnson, Patricia Givens James Patton and the Appalachian Colonists. Verona, Va.: McClure Press, 1973. A well-documented work on the activities of James Patton and his trans-montane settlements.
J1910 (ASU)

Johnson, Paul M. "Integration in West Virginia Since 1954." Microfilm. Master's thesis. West Virginia Wesleyan College, 1959.
J1920 (ASU)

Johnson, Reginald Brimley Popular British Ballads, Ancient and Modern. London: J. M. Dent and Co., 1894.
J1930

Johnson, Roy L. "A Study of Reorganization of Attendance Centers in Hawkins County, Tennessee." Master's thesis. Univ. of Tennessee, 1955.
J1940

Johnson, Victor M. "A Study of the Drop-outs from the Bristol, Tennessee, School Systems in Grades 8-12 from 1946 to 1951." Master's thesis. Univ. of Tennessee, 1952.
J1950

Johnson, William Perry ed. Draughon, Wallace R. North Carolina Genealogical Reference: Research Guide for All Genealogists Both Amateur and Professional. Durham, N. C.: n.p., 1966.
D3380 (ASU LMC)

Index to North Carolina Wills, 1663-1900. 3 vols. Raleigh, N. C.: The author, n.d.
J1960 (ASU)

The North Carolinian . . . A Quarterly Journal of Genealogy and History. n.p.: n.p., 1955--.
J1970 (ASU)

Johnston, Annie Fellows Georgina's Service Stars. Illustrated by Thelma Gooch. New York: Britton Pub. Co., 1918. Sentimental fiction with an East Tennessee setting.
J1980 (WCU)

In League with Israel; a Tale of the Chattanooga Conference. Nashville: Pub. House of the Methodist Episcopal Church South, 1896. Novel about the Epworth League in the Chattanooga area.
J1990

The Little Colonel's Knight Comes Riding. Illustrated by Etheldred B. Barry. Boston: L. C. Page and Co. Romantic fiction in which the mountain setting is almost incidental.
J2000 (ASU BC)

Johnston, Coy Kelley William Johnston of Isle of Wight County, Virginia, and His Descendants, 1648-1964: A Genealogical Study of One Branch of the Family in the South. West Hartford, Conn.: The authors, 1965.
J2010 (ASU)

Johnston, David Emmons A History of Middle New River Settlements and Contiguous Territory. Huntington, W. Va.: Standard Print. and Pub. Co., 1906. An early history of the territory which was formerly a part of Augusta, Fincastle, Montgomery, Greenbrier, Wythe, Monroe, Tazewell and Giles Counties.
J2020 (ASU FC)

Johnston, Frances Benjamin The Early Architecture of North Carolina: A Pictorial Survey. Architectural history by Thomas Tileston Waterman. Foreword by Leicester B. Holland. Chapel Hill: Univ. of North Carolina Press, 1947.
J2030 (ASU MHC LMC)

Johnston, Frontis W. ed. Vance, Zebulon Baird Papers. Raleigh: N. C. State Department of Archives and History, 1963.
V110 (ASU LMC)

Johnston, Hugh B. Johnston, Coy Kelley William Johnston of Isle of Wight County, Virginia, and His Descendants, 1648-1964: A Genealogical Study of One Branch of the Family in the South. West Hartford, Conn.: The authors, 1965.
J2010 (ASU)

Johnston, I. H. Birds of West Virginia, Their Economic Value and Aesthetic Beauty. Charleston: State Department of Agriculture, 1923.
J2040 (ASU)

Johnston, Joseph Eggleston Narrative of Military Operations, Directed, During the Late War Between the States. New York: D. Appleton and Co., 1874. General Johnston a native of Appalachian Virginia led several brilliant campaigns in the southern mountains. His campaign from Chattanooga to Kennesaw Mountain is a military classic. Both Sherman and Grant considered him the best general in the Civil War.
J2050 (ASU)

Johnston, Josiah Stoddard First Explorations of Kentucky Doctor Thomas Walker's Journal, of an Exploration of Kentucky in 1750, Being the First Record of a White Man's Visit to the Interior of that Territory . . . Also Colonel Christopher Gist's Journal, of a Tour through Ohio and Kentucky in 1751. . . Louisville: John P. Morton, 1898.
J2060

Johnston, Mary Audrey. Illustrated by F. C. Yohn. Boston: Houghton Mifflin and Co., 1902. Novel of life on the Appalachian frontier.
J2070 (ASU BC WCU ETSU)

Cease Firing. Illustrated by N. C. Wyeth. Boston: Houghton Mifflin Co., 1912. Fiction partially set in the Appalachian mountains.
J2080 (ASU WWC BC)

The Great Valley. Boston: Little, Brown and Co., 1926. Novel of pioneer life in western Virginia, East Tennessee, and Kentucky.
J2090 (ASU BC)

Hagar. Boston: Houghton Mifflin, 1913. Novel partially set in the Appalachian mountains.
J2100 (WCU)

Hunting Shirt. Boston: Little, Brown and Co., 1931. Novel of pioneer life in the mountains.
J2110 (BC ASU WWC ETSU)

Lewis Rand. Illustrated by F. C. Yohn. Boston: Houghton Mifflin Co., 1908. Mountain fiction.
J2120 (ASU BC ETSU WCU)

Johnston, Mary
The Long Roll. Illustrated by N. C. Wyeth. Boston: Houghton Mifflin, 1911. Novel partially set in the Appalachian mountains.
J2130 (ASU WWC)
Sir Mortimer, a Novel. New York: Harper and Brothers, 1904. Romantic fiction with a mountain backdrop.
J2140 (ASU BC)

Johnston, P. M. Ground-water Supplies in Shale and Sandstone in Fairfax, Loudoun, and Prince William Counties, Virginia. U. S. Geological Survey Circular, no. 424. Washington: Govt. Print. Off., 1960.
J2150

Johnston, Richard Malcolm Mr. Absalom Billingslea, and Other Georgia Folk. 1887. Reprint. Short Story Index Reprint Series. Freeport, N. Y.: Books for Libraries Press, 1970. Includes some sketches from the area around Cartersville.
J2160 (WCU)

Johnston, Ross B. comp. West Virginia Estate Settlements (1753-1850). Texas: American Reference Publishers, 1969.
J2170 (ASU)

Johnston, William Drumm, Jr. Physical Divisions of Northern Alabama. Prepared in cooperation with the U. S. Geological Survey. Bulletin, no. 38. University: Alabama Geological Survey, 1930.
J2180 (ETSU)

Johnstone, Herrick The Secret Shot, or the Rivals of Misty Mount, A Romance of the Old North State. New York: Frank Starr and Co., 1874. Fiction with a western North Carolina setting.
J2190

Joint Commission on Education and Cultivation ed. Jones, Wayne Marshall A Pocket Full of Change: Methodist Ministries in the New Appalachia. Cincinnati: Board of Missions, The Methodist Church, n.d.
J2630

Joint Committee of Hopewell Friends Hopewell Friends History, 1734-1934, Frederick County, Virginia: Records of Hopewell Monthly Meetings and Meetings Reporting to Hopewell. Strasburg, Va.: Shenandoah Pub. House, 1936. Two hundred years of history and genealogy compiled from official records and published by a joint committee of Hopewell Friends assisted by John W. Wayland.
J2200 (ASU)

Joint Committee on North Carolina Literature and Bibliography of the North Carolina English Teachers Association and the North Carolina Library Association North Carolina Fiction, 1734-1957: An Annotated Bibliography. Chapel Hill: University of North Carolina Library, 1958.
J2210 (ASU MHC)

Jolley, Harley E. The Blue Ridge Parkway. 1st ed. Knoxville: Univ. of Tennessee Press, 1969. The definitive work on the Blue Ridge Parkway.
J2220 (BC ASU LMC WCU WWC FC ETSU)
"The Blue Ridge Parkway: Origins and Early Development." Ph. D. Diss. Florida State University, 1964.
J2230

Jolliffe, John Chattanooga. Cincinnati: Anderson, Gates and Wright, 1858. Fiction with an East Tennessee setting.
J2240

Jolly, Janice L. Mercury and Other Trace Elements in Sphalerite and Wallrocks from Central Kentucky, Tennessee, and Appalachian Zinc Districts. Bulletin, 1252-F. Contributions to Economic Geology. Washington: U. S. Geological Survey, 1968.
J2250

Jonas, Anna I. ed. International Geological Congress Southern Appalachian Region. Washington: The Congress; 16th Session, 1933.
I880

Jones, A. R. Vogel, H. D. TVA Revenue Bond Financing Presented by the Board of Directors, Tennessee Valley Authority. New York: Municipal Forum of New York, 1960.
V1290

Jones, Abraham "The Status of the Negro Teachers in Blount, Cullman, DeKalb, and Marshall Counties, Alabama 1952-53." Master's thesis. Alabama State College, 1954.
J2260

Jones, Alexander The Cymry of '76: Or, Welshmen and Their Descendants of the American Revolution. An address with an appendix, containing notes, sketches, and nomenclature of the Cymbri. To which is added a letter on eminent Welshmen, by Samuel Jenkins; and a brief sketch of St. David's Benevolent Society. 2nd ed. 1855. Reprint. Baltimore: Genealogical Pub. Co., 1968.
J2270 (ASU)

Jones, Chapin Common Forest Trees of Tennessee: How to Know Them, a Pocket Manual. 6th ed. Nashville: U. S. Department of Agriculture, Forest Service, 1922.
J2280 (LMC)
Common Forest Trees of Virginia: A Pocket Manual Describing Their Most Important Characteristics. Forestry Publication, no. 26. Charlottesville: Virginia State Conservation and Development Commission, 1928.
J2290 (BC LMC)

Jones, Clarence Fielden Semple, Ellen Churchill American History and Its Geographic Conditions. New York: Russell and Russell Co., 1968.
S1860 (ASU MHC)

Jones, Erma Lee "A Preliminary Edition of a Reading Test For Use With Disadvantaged Children in the Primary Grades of the Southern Appalachian Region." Master's thesis. East Tennessee State Univ., 1971.
J2300 (ETSU)

Jones, Frank Anderson "The Incidence of Social Diseases among Negroes in Chattanooga, Tennessee, and the Educational Implications." Master's thesis. Fisk Univ., 1944.
J2310

Jones, Gilmer Andrew Songs from the Hills. Franklin, N. C.: n.p., 1950.
J2320 (WCU)

Jones, Gwyn Welsh Legends and Folk-Tales. Illustrated by Joan Kiddell-Monroe. Oxford Myths and Legends. New York: Henry Z. Walck, 1955. Many of these motifs are still found in Appalachia.
J2330 (ASU)

Jones, Houston Gwynne For History's Sake: The Preservation and Publication of North Carolina History, 1663-1903. Chapel Hill: Univ. of North Carolina Press, 1966.
J2340 (BC LMC ASU MHC)
Union List of North Carolina Newspapers, 1751-1900. Raleigh, North Carolina: Department of Archives and History, 1963.
J2360 (LMC)

Jones, Houston Gwynne ed. North Carolina's Local Records Program. Cedar Rapids, Iowa: Torch Press, 1961.
J2350 (ASU)

Jones, Hugh The Present State of Virginia; from Whence Is Inferred a Short View of Maryland and North Carolina. Chapel Hill, N. C.: Univ. of North Carolina Press, 1956.
J2370 (FC)

Jones, James Athearn Traditions of the North American Indians. 2nd ed. 1830. Reprint. 3 vols. in 1. Upper Saddle River, N. J.: Literature House/Gregg Press, 1970.
J2380 (LMC)

Jones, James Claybourn Autobiography of "Old Claib Jones." Hazard, Ky.: Hazard Bk. Co., 1915. The remarkable story of a legendary fighting man from the Eastern Kentucky hills.
J2390

Jones, James G. "A Survey of ESEA Title 1 Equipment and Its Extended Usage in Carter County, Tennessee." Master's thesis. East Tennessee State Univ., 1969.
J2400 (ETSU)

Jones, James Sawyer Life of Andrew Johnson; Seventeenth President of the United States. Greeneville, Tenn.: East Tennessee Pub. Co., 1901. Biography of East Tennessee's only United States president.
J2410

Jones, Joseph Explorations of the Aboriginal Remains of Tennessee. Smithsonian Contributions to Knowledge, vol. 22, article 2. Also, Smithsonian Publication, 259.
J2420 (ASU BC)

Jones, Joseph Seawell A Defence of the Revolutionary History of the State of North Carolina from the Aspersions of Mr. Jefferson. Boston: C. Bowen; Raleigh, N. C.: Turner & Hughes, 1834. Mr. Jefferson objected to North Carolina's Mecklenburg Declaration and other claims to early involvement in the Revolution.
J2430 (ASU BC)

Jones, Laura Sage Sage, Clara McCormack Early Records, Hampshire County Virginia, Now West Virginia, Including at the Start Most of Known Va. Aside from Augusta District. Baltimore: Genealogical Pub. Co., 1969.
S130 (BC ASU)

Jones, Leslie "An Experimental and Field Study of North Georgia Mountaineers." Microfilm. Master's thesis. Univ. of Georgia, 1934.
J2440 (ASU)

Jones, Lewis Wade Johnson, Charles Spurgeon and others Statistical Atlas of Southern Counties Listing and Analysis of Socio-economic Indices of 1104 Southern Counties. Chapel Hill: Univ. of North Carolina Press, 1941.
J1330 (ASU LMC MHC BC)

Jones, Mabel J. "Regional English of the Former Inhabitants of Cades Cove in the Great Smoky Mountains." Ph. D. Diss. Univ. of Tennessee, 1973. Cades Cove was purchased by the National Park Service and all its native population were moved out.
J2450

Jones, Madison A Buried Land, a Novel. New York: Viking Press, 1963. A novel set in the TVA country of Eastern Tennessee.
J2460 (BC ASU LMC WCU ETSU)
An Exile. New York: Viking Press, 1967. A novel with an Eastern Tennessee setting.
J2470 (BC ASU WCU ETSU)
Forest of the Night. 1st ed. New York: Harcourt, Brace, 1960. A novel with an Eastern Tennessee setting.
J2480 (BC ASU LMC ETSU)
The Innocent. 1st ed. New York: Harcourt, Brace, 1957. East Tennessee fiction.
J2490 (ASU LMC WCU ETSU BC)

Jones, Mary Harris Thoughts of Mother Jones: Compiled from Her Writings and Speeches. Huntington, W. Va.: Appalachian Movement Press, 1973.
J2510 (WCU)

Jones, Mary Harris ed. Autobiography of Mother Jones. Introduction by Clarence Darrow. 1925. Reprint. American labor from conspiracy to collective bargaining. New York: Arco & New York Times, 1969. Biography of Appalachia's famous union organizer in the coal fields with accounts of her participation in the region's mine wars and strikes.
J2500 (BC LMC ASU WCU MHC)

Jones, Michael Owen "Chairmaking in Appalachia: A Study in Style and Creative Imagination in American Folk Art." Ph. D. Diss. Indiana Univ., 1969. A monumental two volume work on one of the region's oldest handicrafts.
J2520 (ASU)

Jones, Oleona My Colorful Days. Boston: Christopher, 1940. Autobiography of the author's years as a social worker and teacher among underprivileged mountain folks.
J2530

Jones, Ora L. Peculiarities of the Appalachian Mountaineers: A Summary of Legends, Traditions, Signs, and Superstitions That Are Almost Forgotten. Detroit: Harlo Press, 1967.
J2540 (BC ASU LMC WCU ETSU MHC)

Jones, Pearl Eggars Shirley. New York: Greenwich Book Publishers, 1959. A romantic fiction partially set in the southern mountains.
J2550

Jones, Perry "A Historical Study of the European Wild Boar in North Carolina." Master's thesis. Appalachian State Teachers College, 1957.
J2560 (ASU)

Jones, Reece A. "A Geographical Survey of Morgan County, Tennessee." Master's thesis. Univ. of Tennessee, 1940.
J2570

Jones, Russell Bradley Uncle Sandy. Dalton, Ga.: A. J. Showalter Co., 1946. Tales of a North Georgia eccentric as cultivated by her family and friends.
J2580 (ASU)

Jones, Samuel Porter Sermons, Wise and Witty: By Rev. Sam P. Jones, the Mountain Evangelist. New York: Cheap Pub. Co., 1885.
J2590 (ASU)

Jones, Stephen Collins The Hamrick Generation, Being a Genealogy of the Hamrick Family. Raleigh, N. C.: Edwards and Broughton Print. Co., 1920.
J2600 (ASU)

Jones, Uriah James Simon Girty, the Outlaw. Harrisburg, Pa.: Anrand Press, 1931. Includes biographical sketches and notes. This is one of a very few non-romanticized biographies of Girty.
J2610

Jones, Virgil Carrington The Hatfields and the McCoys. Chapel Hill: Univ. of North Carolina Press, 1948. A realistic account of the famous Kentucky feud.
J2620 (BC ASU LMC WCU WWC)

Jones, W. Mac ed. Douglas, William The Douglas Register, Being a Detailed Record of Births, Marriages, and Deaths, Together with Other Interesting Notes, as Kept by the Rev. William Douglas from 1750 to 1797; an Index of Goochland Wills Notes on the French-Huguenot Refugees Who Lived in Manakin-town. Baltimore: Genealogical Pub. Co., 1966.
D3150 (ASU)

Jones, Wayne Marshall A Pocket Full of Change: Methodist Ministries in the New Appalachia. Prepared by the Joint Commission on Education and Cultivation. Cincinnati: Board of Missions, The Methodist Church, n.d.
J2630

Jones, Weimar My Affair with a Weekly. Winston Salem, N. C.: J. B. Blair, 1960. An account of life with a western North Carolina newspaper.
J2640 (ASU LMC MHC BC)

Jones, William "Environmental School Sanitation of an Eastern Kentucky County." Master's thesis. Univ. of Kentucky, 1954.
J2650

Jones, William B. Methodism in Bedford County; a Study Made by William B. Jones with Recommendations by C. Ralph Arthur. n.p.: Virginia Conference of the Methodist Church, Commission on Town and County Work, 1953.
J2660 (FC)

Jones, William Emmett Soil Survey, Cherokee County, South Carolina. Soils surveyed by R. L. Bishop and others. Soil Survey, Series 1958, no. 19. Washington: U. S. Department of Agriculture, Soil Conservation Service, 1962.
J2670

Jonesboro, Tenn. Jonesboro High School and the Southern Association of Colleges and Secondary Schools. Secondary Commission Evaluative Study; Made in Jonesboro High School, Jonesboro, Tennessee . . . Completed by the Visiting Committee April 8-11, 1957. . . Mimeographed. Jonesboro, Tenn.: The Assn., 1957.
J2680 (ETSU)

Jonesville Methodist Church, Woman's Society of Christian Service Jonesville Cook Book. Jonesville, Va.: First Methodist Church, October 1, 1964. This cookbook contains recipes donated by members of the Woman's Society of Christian Service and their friends. Some are recipes handed from generation to generation; others are new.
J2690

Jordan, Bruce C. "A Study of the School Transportation Problem in Grainger County, Tennessee." Master's thesis. Univ. of Tennessee, 1961.
J2700

Jordan, Dan H. and others Soil Survey, Cherokee, Gilmer, and Pickens Counties, Georgia. Prepared in cooperation with the University of Georgia, College of Agriculture, Agricultural Experiment Station. Washington: U. S. Soil Conservation Service, 1973.
J2710

Jordan, David Starr Your Family Tree. 1929. Reprint. Baltimore: Genealogical Pub. Co., 1968.
J2720 (ASU)

Jordan, James D. Underwood, Evelyn comp. CRISIS: Addresses Delivered at the Spring Symposium, Mars Hill College, 1967, 1968. Mars Hill, N. C.: Mars Hill College, n.d.
U70 (WCU)

Jordan, Thomas The Campaigns of Lieut.-Gen. N. B. Forrest, and of Forrest's Cavalry. 1868. Reprint. Dayton, Ohio: Morningside Bookshop, 1973. Includes accounts of Forrest's brilliant use of the mountain terrain in his calvary raids.
J2740 (ASU)

Jordan-Smith, Paul The Road I Came. Caldwell, Idaho: The Caxton Printers, Ltd., 1960. One man's chronicle dealing with the area from the Upper Valley of Virginia to the Redwood Groves of California.
J2730

Joseph, J. S. Headlee, Alvah John Washington Permeability, Porosity, Oil, and Water Content of Natural Gas Reservoirs, Kanawha-Jackson and Campbells Creek Oriskany Fields. Morgantown, W. Va.: Morgantown Print. & Bind. Co., 1945.
H4150 (ETSU)

Joss, Alexander Economic Study of Land Utilization in Chautaugua County, New York. Ithaca: Cornell Agricultural Experiment Station, 1939.
J2750

Economic Study of Land Utilization in Otsego County, New York. Ithaca: Cornell Univ. Agricultural Experiment Station, 1943.
J2760

Journal of the Alleghenies Spring 1963-. Pittsburgh, Pa.: Council of the Alleghenies, quarterly 1963-67, annual 1968.
J2770

Joyner, Charles W. Folk Song in South Carolina. 1st ed. South Carolina Tricentennial Booklet, no. 9. Columbia: Univ. of South Carolina Press, 1971.
J2780 (WCU)

Joyner, Judith Rebecca "Treatment of Pupil Misbehavior by Textbooks Used in Undergraduate Education Courses at Appalachian State Teachers College." Master's thesis. Appalachian State Teachers College, 1957.
J2790 (ASU)

Judson, John C. Jack and Jill Go Up a Hill. With a "thirteen-year-old's" version by Mary Elizabeth Judson. Gatlinburg, Tenn.: Little Pigeon Press of the Gatlinburg News, 1940. A mountaineer's version of an English nursery rhyme.
J2800 (ASU)

Judy, Elvin Lycurgus History of Grant and Hardy Counties, West Virginia. Charleston, W. Va.: Charleston Print. Co., 1951.
J2810 (ASU)

Julian Price Memorial Park Blue Ridge Parkway. Greensboro, N. C.: Jefferson Standard Life Insurance Co., 1971.
J2820 (ETSU LMC)

Junior Service League of Johnson City, Tenn. Smoky Mountain Magic; a Superb View of Treasured Recipes. Greenville, Miss.: Democrat Print. Co., 1960.
J2830 (LMC)

Junker, Buford H. Johnson, Charles Spurgeon and others Statistical Atlas of Southern Counties Listing and Analysis of Socio-economic Indices of 1104 Southern Counties. Chapel Hill: Univ. of North Carolina Press, 1941.
J1330 (ASU LMC MHC BC)

Jurney, Mrs. James A. (Josephine Ramsey Jurney) 79 Families of Washington County. 21 Pedigree charts, typescript. n.p.: n.p., n.d.
J2840

Jurney, Robert Campbell Soil Survey of Augusta County, Virginia. In cooperation with the Virginia Agricultural Experiment Station. Soil Survey Report, Series 1932, no. 13. Washington: U. S. Department of Agriculture, Bureau of Chemistry and Soils, 1937.
J2850

Soil Survey of Cherokee County, North Carolina. Prepared in cooperation with the North Carolina Department of Agriculture and the North Carolina Agricultural Experiment Station. Field Operations, 1921. Washington: U. S. Department of Agriculture, Bureau of Soils, 1926.
J2860 (ASU)

Soil Survey of Davie County, North Carolina. In cooperation with the North Carolina Department of Agriculture and the North Carolina Agricultural Experiment Station. Soil Survey Report, Series 1927, no. 5. Washington: U. S. Department of Agriculture, Bureau of Chemistry and Soils, 1930.
J2870

Soil Survey, Lee County, Virginia. U. S. Soil Conservation Service, Soil Survey, Series 1939, no. 17. Washington: Govt. Print. Off., 1953.
J2890

Soil Survey of Rockbridge County, Virginia. In cooperation with the Virginia Agricultural Experiment Station. Soil Survey Report, Series 1931, no. 4. Washington: U. S. Department of Agriculture, Bureau of Chemistry and Soils, 1934.
J2900

Soil Survey of Rutherford County, North Carolina. In cooperation with the North Carolina Department of Agriculture and the North Carolina Agricultural Experiment Station. Soil Survey Report, Series 1924, no. 5.9511Washington: U. S. Department of Agriculture, Bureau of Chemistry and Soils, 1928.
J2910

Soil Survey, Scott County, Virginia. U. S. Bureau of Plant Industry, Soils, and Agricultural Engineering, Soil Survey Report, Series 1939, no. 13. Washington: Govt. Print. Off., 1951.
J2920

Soil Survey, Smyth County, Virginia. Prepared in cooperation with the Virginia Agricultural Experiment Station and the Tennessee Valley Authority. Soil Survey Report Series 1938, no. 16. Washington: U. S. Department of Agriculture, Bureau of Plant Industry, Soils and Agricultural Engineering, 1948.
J2930

Soil Survey of Wilkes County, North Carolina. Prepared in cooperation with the North Carolina Department of Agriculture. Field Operations, 1918. Washington: U. S. Department of Agriculture, Bureau of Soils, 1921.
J2950

Obenshain, S. S. Soil Survey, Russell County, Virginia. Washington: U. S. Department of Agriculture, Bureau of Plant Industry, Soils, and Agricultural Engineering, 1945.
O100 (BC)

Porter, Hobart Clarke Soil Survey, Tazewell County, Virginia. Washington: U. S. Department of Agriculture, Bureau of Plant Industry, Soils, and Agricultural Engineering, 1948.
P3660

Jurney, Robert Campbell and others Soil Survey of Haywood County, North Carolina. Prepared in cooperation with the North Carolina Department of Agriculture and the North Carolina Agricultural Experiment Station. Field Operations, 1922. Washington: U. S. Department of Agriculture, Bureau of Soils, 1928.
J2880

Soil Survey, Washington County, Virginia. In cooperation with the Virginia Agricultural Experiment Station and the Tennessee Valley Authority. Soil Survey Report, Series 1937, no. 14. Washington: U. S. Department of Agriculture, Bureau of Plant Industry, Soils, and Agricultural Engineering, 1945.
J2940

Justice, Dewey J. "A Study of the Opinions of the Various Classes of People Toward Pike County's Medical Facilities." Master's thesis. Univ. of Kentucky, 1958.
J2960

Justice, Ralph The Ghost of the Gugan. Boston: Bruce Humphries, 1948. Mystery story about a young man who comes home to West Virginia in answer to father's deathbed plea.
J2970 (BC)

Justice, William M. A Man and a Woman and God. Pikesville, Ky.: The author, 1939. Love sonnets from Eastern Kentucky.
J2980 (BC)

Take Time to Stroll. Pikesville, Ky.: The author, 1965. Poetry from Eastern Kentucky.
J2990

Tears and Laughter and Other Poems. Berea, Ky.: Berea College Press, 1934.
J3000

This Way Lies Peace. Pikeville, Ky.: The author, 1957.
J3010

Justice, William S. Wild Flowers of North Carolina. Chapel Hill: Univ. of North Carolina Press, 1968.
J3020 (ASU LMC WWC ETSU)

Justus, May Big Log Mountain. New York: Henry Holt, 1958. Young people's fiction with an Appalachian setting.
J3030 (LMC ASU)

Children of the Great Smoky Mountains. 1st ed. New York: Dutton, 1952. Sixteen stories from the Smokies.
J3040 (WCU ETSU)

Children of the Great Smoky Mountains. Illustrated by Robert Henneberger. New York: Dutton, 1967.
J3050 (ASU LMC MHC)

The Complete Peddler's Pack: Games, Songs, Rhymes, and Riddles from Mountain Folklore. Illustrated by Jean Tamburine. Knoxville: Univ. of Tennessee Press, 1967.
J3060 (ASU WCU LMC MHC WWC ETSU FC)

Eben and the Rattlesnake. Champaign, Ill.: Garrard Pub. Co., 1969. Children's story with a mountain setting.
J3070 (ETSU)

Here Comes Mary Ellen. Philadelphia: J. B. Lippincott Co., 1940. Children's fiction with a mountain setting.
J3080 (ETSU)

Holidays in No-End Hollow. Illustrated by Vivian Berger. Champaign, Ill.: Garrard Pub. Co., 1970. Four short stories tell how Thanksgiving, Christmas, a housewarming, and a school's birthday are celebrated in Tennessee's Great Smoky Mountains.
J3090

Holidays in No-End Hollow. Illustrated by Vivian Berger. A Reading Shelf Book. Champaign, Ill.: Garrard Pub. Co., 1970.
J3100 (BC ETSU)

Honey Jane. Garden City, N. Y.: Doubleday, Doran and Co., 1935. Children's fiction with a Smoky Mountain setting.
J3110 (ETSU)

House in No-End Hollow. Illustrated by Erick Berry. New York: Doubleday, 1938.
J3120 (ETSU WWC ASU)

Hurrah for Jerry Jake. Chicago: A. Whitman and Co., 1945. Children's fiction set in the Smoky Mountains.
J3130 (ETSU)

It happened in No-End Hollow. Champaign, Ill.: Garrard Pub. Co., 1969. Smoky Mountain setting.
J3140

Jerry Jake Carries On. Chicago: A. Whitman and Co., 1943. Mountain setting.
J3150 (ETSU ASU)

Jumping Johnny Outwits Skedaddle. Illustrated by Raymond Burns. Champaign, Ill.: Garrard Pub. Co., 1971.
J3160

Lester and His Hound Pup. Illustrated by Joan Balfour Payne. New York: Hastings House, 1960.
J3170 (ASU LMC)

Lizzie. Chicago: A. Whitman and Co., 1944.
J3180 (ETSU ASU)

Luck for Little Lihu. New York: Aladdin, 1950.
J3190 (ETSU ASU)

Lucky Penny. 1st ed. New York: Aladdin Books, 1951.
J3200 (ETSU ASU)

The Mail Wagon Mystery. Chicago: A. Whitman, 1940.
J3210 (ASU WWC ETSU)

New Boy in School. Illustrated by Joan Balfour Payne. New York: Hastings House, 1963.
J3220 (LMC MHC WCU ASU)

A New Home for Billy. New York: Hastings House, 1966.
J3230 (LMC ASU)

The Other Side of the Mountain. Illustrated by Berkeley Williams. New York: Hastings House, 1957.
J3240 (ASU LMC WCU)

Peddler's Pack. 1st ed. New York: Holt, 1957.
J3250 (ETSU ASU)

Peter Pocket and His Pickle Pup. Illustrated by Jean Tamburine. New York: Holt, 1953.
J3260 (ETSU)

Sammy. Illustrated by Christine Chrisholm. Chicago: A. Whitman, 1946.
J3270 (ETSU ASU)

Smoky Mountain Sampler: Stories. Illustrated by Jean Tamburine. New York: Abingdon, 1962.
J3280 (ASU LMC MHC)

Step Along and Jerry Jake. Chicago: A. Whitman and Co., 1942.
J3290 (ETSU ASU)

Surprise for Perky Pup. Illustrated by Mimi Korach. Champaign, Ill.: Garrard Pub. Co., 1971.
J3300

Surprise for Peter Pocket. Illustrated by Jean Tamburine. 1st ed. Holt Books for Young People. New York: Holt, 1955.
J3310 (ASU LMC)

Tales from Near-side and Far. Drawings by Herman B. Vestal. Champaign, Ill.: Garrard Pub. Co., 1970. Four stories set in Tennessee's Great Smoky Mountains tell about a troublesome pup, a peddler named Step-Along, a pet mule, and a boy who knew how to use his legs.
J3320

Tale of a Pig. Adaptation of an American folk song. New York: Abingdon, 1963.
J3330 (LMC ASU)

Then Came Mr. Billy Barker. Illustrated by Joan Balfour Payne. New York: Hastings House, 1959.
J3340 (ASU LMC WCU)

Toby Has a Dog. Chicago: A. Whitman and Co., 1949.
J3350 (ETSU)

Use Your Head, Hildy. Illustrated by Jean Tamburine. 1st ed. New York: Holt, 1956.
J3360 (ASU LMC ETSU)

Winds a Blowing. Illustrated by Jean Tamburine. New York: Abingdon Press, 1961.
J3370 (ASU LMC)

You're Sure Silly, Billy. Illustrated by Herman Vestal. Champaign, Ill.: Garrard Pub. Co., 1972.
J3380 (ASU)

Jyams, Charles Walter The Flora of North Carolina from Ranunculaceae to Salviniaceae. The North Carolina College of Agriculture and Mechanic Arts, Agricultural Experiment Station. Bulletin no. 164. Raleigh, N. C.: n.p., 1899.
J3390 (ASU)

Kahn, Edward A. "The Carter Family: A Reflection of Changes in Society." Microfilm. Ph. D. Diss. Univ. of California, Los Angeles, 1970. A study of a musical mountain family who became country and western stars.
K10 (WCU)

Kahn, Kathy Hillbilly Women. Photographs by Al Clayton. Migrant photographs by Frank Blechman, Jr. 1st ed. Garden City, N. Y.: Doubleday, 1973. This book is permeated by the biases of the social activist, and the women chosen for study are not representative mountain women.
K20 (ASU BC UNCA)

Kahn, Si Readings About Appalachia: A Guide to Pamphlets and Periodicals. Mineral Bluff, Ga.: Cut Cane Associates, 1971.
K50

Kahn, Si Who Speaks for Appalachia 1972? Mineral Bluff, Ga.: Cut Cane Associates, 1972.
K60 (ASU)

Kahn, Si The Forest Service and Appalachia. n.p.: John Hay Whitney Foundation, 1974. The United States Forest Service owns vast tracts of tax-exempt land in the Appalwchian Mountains.
K30 (ASU)

How People Get Power: Organizing Oppressed Communities Get Action. N. Y.: McGraw-Hill, 1970. A do-it-yourself handbook for community action agencies in the Southern mountains.
K40 (WCU ASU)

Readings About Appalachia: A Guide to Pamphlets and Periodicals. Mineral Bluff, Ga.: Cut Cane Associates, 1971. A four page listing of inexpensive materials which deal with regional problems.
K50

Who Speaks for Appalachia 1972? Mineral Bluff, Ga.: Cut Cane Associates, 1972.
K60 (ASU)

Kains, Maurice G. Ginseng, Its Cultivation, Harvesting, Marketing and Market Value: With a Short Account of Its History and Botany. New York: Orange Judd Co., 1902. A study of the highest priced botanical drug grown in the Southern mountains.
K70 (WWC)

Kaminkow, Jack A List of Emigrants from England to America, 1718-1759. Baltimore: Magna Charta Book Co., 1966.
K80 (ASU)

Kaminkow, Marion Kaminkow, Jack A List of Emigrants from England to America, 1718-1759. Baltimore: Magna Charta Book Co., 1966.
K80 (ASU)

Kan, Lincoln Shiao Hing "A Historical Study of the Relationship Between the Watauga Democrat and Appalachian State Teachers College." Master's thesis. Appalachian State Teachers College, 1961.
K90 (ASU)

Kanawha River Basin Coordinating Committee Kanawha River: Comprehensive Basin Study. Charleston: n.p., 1971.
K100 (ASU)

Kanawha Welfare Council Our Troubled Children. Charleston, W. Va.: The Council, 1957.
K110

Kane, Harnett Thomas The Gallant Mrs. Stonewall: A Novel Based on the Lives of General and Mrs. Stonewall Jackson. 1st ed. Garden City, N. Y.: Doubleday, 1957. Partially set in the southern mountains.
K120 (MHC)

Gone Are the Days: An Illustrated History of the Old South. 1st ed. N. Y.: Dutton, 1960. Scant mention of the mountain region.
K130 (MHC)

Kane, Harnett Thomas
Miracle in the Mountains. With Inez Henry. 1st ed. Garden City, N. Y.: Doubleday, 1956. The story of a rural mountain health center, school, and hospital in Avery County, North Carolina.
K140 (ASU LMC MHC WCU WWC FC BC)
The Southern Christmas Book: The Full Story from Earliest Times to Present. People, Customs, Conviviality, Carols, Cooking. New York: D. McKay Co., 1958.
K150 (MHC)

Kane, John T. Engineering and the Future of Appalachia. Frankfort, Ky.: n.p., 1963.
K160

Kanner, Leo Folklore of the Teeth. New York: Macmillan Co., 1928. This whole volume is devoted to superstitions and folklore of teeth, both human and animal.
K170 (ASU)

Kaplan, Berton H. Blue Ridge: An Appalachian Community in Transition. Bulletin, series 71, no. 7-2. Morgantown: Office of Research and Development, Appalachian Center, West Virginia Univ., 1971. This study of an isolated western North Carolina community proposes that the mountains should join the modern world.
K180 (ASU WCU FC ETSU BC)
"Social Change, Adaptive Problems, and Health in a Mountain Community." Microfilm. Master's thesis. Univ. of North Carolina, 1962. This study of an isolated western North Carolina community could serve as a blueprint for the destruction of mountain culture.
K190 (LMC ASU)

Kaplan, Sylvan J. ed. Appalachia Conference on Research in Poverty and Development, Virginia Polytechnic Institute, 1968. Seeking More Effective Means to Overcome Poverty: Proceedings. Blacksburg: Research and Extension Division, Virginia Polytechnic Institute, 1969.
A2680 (ASU LMC)
Seeking More Effective Means to Overcome Poverty. Washington: Research and Extension Division Virginia Polytechnical Institute, in cooperation with the Appalachian Regional Commission, 1969.
K200 (ASU)

Kappa, Mary Ann "A Survey of Programs Offered for the Academically Talented Students at Dobyns-Bennett High School, Kingsport, Tennessee, and the Resulting Implications for the School Library." Master's thesis. East Tennessee State Univ., 1966.
K210 (ETSU)

Karaska, Gerald James "The Pattern of Settlements in the Southern and Middle Anthracite Region of Pennsylvania." Ph. D. Diss. Pennsylvania State Univ., 1962. A study of the extent to which the coal industry has determined settlement patterns in West Virginia.
K220

Karpeles, Maud Cecil Sharp: His Life and Work. Chicago: Univ. of Chicago Press, 1967. Biography of one of Appalachia's most famous folklorists, musicologists, and ballad collector.
K230 (BC ASU LMC)

Karpeles, Maud comp. Sharp, Cecil James Eighty English Folk Songs from the Southern Appalachians. Cambridge: Massachusetts Institute of Technology Press, 1968.
S2300 (WCU ASU BC ETSU)

Karpeles, Maud ed. Sharp, Cecil James comp. English Folk Songs from the Southern Appalachians, Comprising 273 Songs and Ballads with 968 Tunes, Including 39 Tunes Contributed by Olive Dame Campbell. London: Oxford Univ. Press, H. Milford, 1932.
S2310 (ASU)
Sharp, Cecil James English Folk Songs from the Southern Appalachians. London: Oxford Univ. Press, H. Milford, 1932.
S2320 (ASU WWC FC)
Sharp, Cecil James comp. English Folk Songs from the Southern Appalachians. London: Oxford Univ. Press, 1966.
S2340 (ASU WCU LMC MHC)

Katz, F. J. Hewett, D. F. Possibilities for Manganese Ore on Certain Undeveloped Tracts in the Shenandoah Valley, Virginia. Washington: Govt. Print. Off., 1918.
H5130

Kauffman, Henry J. The Pennsylvania-Kentucky Rifle. Harrisburg, Pa.: Stackpole Books, 1960. An interesting treatise on the development of the frontier rifle.
K240 (BC LMC ASU)

Kaufman, Harold F. Participation in Organized Activities in Selected Kentucky Localities. Bulletin 528. Lexington: Kentucky Agricultural Experiment Station, 1949.
K250
Religious Organization in Kentucky. Lexington: Kentucky Agricultural Experiment Station, 1948.
K260
Rural Churches in Kentucky, 1947. Bulletin no. 530. Lexington: Kentucky Agricultural Experiment Station, Univ. of Kentucky, 1949.
K270
Social Changes and Their Implications for Southern Agriculture. Series no. 11. State College: Mississippi Agricultural Experiment Station, Mississippi State Univ., August, 1959. Includes statistics on the mountain regions of six Appalachian states.
K280

Kaufman, Harold P. Poverty Programs and Social Mobility. State College: Mississippi State Univ., Social Science Research Center, 1966. Examines poverty programs in the rural south including Appalachian states.
K290

Kaufmann, Jacob Joseph ed. Golatz, Helmut J. Readings in Pennsylvania Economic Growth. University Park: Pennsylvania State Univ., Center for Continuing Liberal Education, 1965.
G2310

Kavanagh, Michael J. Preliminary Over-all Economic Development Program for the North-western Pennsylvania Redevelopment Area. Greenville: Northwestern Pennsylvania Conference for Economic Development, 1961.
K300

Kaylor, Peter Cline Abstract of Land Grant Surveys, 1761-1791. Assisted by George Warren Chappelaer. Dayton, Va.: Shenandoah Press, 1938.
K310 (ASU)

Kearfoot, Clarence Baker Highland Mills. New York: Vantage Press, 1970.
K320

Kearfoot, Robert R. Kerfoot, Kearfoot and Allied Families in America. n.p.: n.p., 1948.
K330

Kearins, Jack J. Yankee Revenooer. Durham, N. C.: Moore Pub. Co., 1969. A stereotypical revenue agent meets and learns to understand the mountaineers.
K340 (ASU LMC)

Keats, Ezra J. John Henry: An American Legend. New York: Pantheon, 1965. A 28 page version of the legend of John Henry and his mighty hammer.
K350

Kee, William D. "Water Data for Industrial Site Development, Monongahela Valley, West Virginia." Master's thesis. West Virginia Univ., 1964.
K360

Keebler, Alleen Smith "Problems of Beginning Teachers in Washington County, Tennessee." Master's thesis. East Tennessee State College, 1955.
K370 (ETSU)

Keech, James Maynard Workmen's Compensation in North Carolina, 1929-1940. Publications. Durham, N. C.: Duke Univ. Press, 1942.
K380 (LMC)

Keeler, Robert W. "An Archaeological Survey of the Upper Catawba River Valley." Honors Essay, Dept. of Anthropology, Univ., of North Carolina, 1971.
K390
"An Archaeological Survey of the Upper Catawba River Valley." Honors Essay, Dept. of Anthropology, Univ. of North Carolina, 1971.
K400

Keeling, William B. The Georgia Travel Industry, 1960-1963. Athens, Ga.: Univ. of Georgia, Bureau of Business and Economic Research, 1965. Includes material on the Georgia mountain resort area.
K410
A Study of Out-of-State Requests for Travel Information from the State of Georgia. Athens: Univ. of Georgia, Bureau of Business Research, 1962. Includes requests for information on the North Georgia mountains.
K420
Tourism Development in the Chattahoochee-Flint Area. Athens: Univ. of Georgia, Bureau of Business and Economic Research, 1967. The Chattahoochee rises in the North Georgia mountains.
K430

Keesecker, Guy L. ed. Marriage Records of Berkeley County, Virginia, for the Period of 1781-1854, Located at Berkeley County Court House, Martinsburg, West Virginia. Martinsburg?, W. Va.: n.p., 1969.
K440 (ETSU)

Kegley, Charles Guido My Life's History. Bristol: Doak Print. Co., 1959.
K450

Kegley, F. B. St. John's Evangelical Lutheran Church, Wythe County, Virginia, Its Pastors and Their Records 1800-1924. n.p.: privately published, 1961.
K460

Kegley, Frederick Bittle Kegley's Virginia Frontier: The Beginning of the Southwest. The Roanoke of Colonial Days, 1740-1783. Introduction by Samuel M. Wilson. Roanoke, Va.: Southwest Virginia Historical Society, 1938. Focuses on the Roanoke area, frontier Virginia through 1760, the French and Indian War, and Botetourt County.
K470 (ASU ETSU FC BC)

Kegley, Marietta McWane Chuckles to Brighten the Day. Bristol: Doak Print. Co., 1960.
K480
History and Genealogy, Dudley, 1406-1956 and McWane, 1796-1956. n.p.: Privately Printed, 1956.
K490
. . . History (and) Genealogy, Kegley, 1760-1959 and Grubb, 1743-1959. n.p.: Privately Printed, 1959.
K500
My Memoirs and Autobiography. Bristol: Doak Print. Co., 1959.
K501

Kegley, Mary B. Kegley, F. B. St. John's Evangelical Lutheran Church, Wythe County, Virginia, Its Pastors and Their Records 1800-1924. n.p.: privately published, 1961.
K460
New River Tithables, 1770-73. Roanoke: Copy Cat, 1972. Contains tithes and taxes for seven western Virginia counties.
K510
Tax List of Montgomery County, Virginia, 1782. Roanoke, Va.: Copy Cat, 1974. Lists all males over 21, personal property, and land tax records for Wythe, Pulaski, Giles, Grayson, Carroll, Bland, Floyd, Smythe, and Tazewell Counties.
K520

Keim, Phyllis R. "Minimum Wages in Pennsylvania." Master's thesis. Pennsylvania State College, 1952.
K530

Keister, E. E. Strasburg, Virginia and the Keister Family. Strasburg, Va.: Shenandoah Pub. House, 1972.
K540

Keith, Arthur Tin Resources of the King's Mountain District, North Carolina and South Carolina. U. S. Geological Survey Bulletin, no. 660-D. Washington: Govt. Print. Off., 1918.
K550

Keith, Arthur
Topography and Geology of the Southern Appalachians. Washington: Govt. Print. Off., 1902.
K560

Keller, Allan Thunder at Harper's Ferry. Englewood Cliffs, N. J.: Prentice-Hall, 1958. A romanticized account of Harper's Ferry's role in the American Civil War.
K570 (ASU)

Keller, Alvin "Bituminous Coal Strip Mines; Some Financing Considerations." Master's thesis. University of Pittsburgh, 1951.
K580

Keller, Luther Jensen, Harold R. A General Picture of Commercial Agriculture in Eastern Kentucky. Lexington: Kentucky Agriculture Experiment Station, 1957.
J700

Keller, Luther H. Eagan, Gerald V. Minimum Land Requirements for Specified Levels of Farm Income in the Eastern Highland Rim of Tennessee. Knoxville: Tennessee Agricultural Experiment Station, 1969.
E30

Kelley, Julielma M. Biographical Record of Daniel and Mary (Jackson) Williams — Early Kentucky Pioneers, 1752-1898. 1898. Reprint. Lexington: Univ. of Kentucky, 1964.
K590 (ASU)

Kelley, Paul Achilles, Charles Marvin Research for Better Schools: A Federal Projects Workshop for Educational Programs in Tennessee and Appalachia. Knoxville: Univ. of Tennessee College of Education, 1971.
A200

Kellner, Ester Lewis, Clarence Cry to the Hills. Garden City, N.Y.: Doubleday, 1966.
L2090 (BC LMC ASU)

Kellner, Esther Moonshine: Its History and Folklore. Indianapolis: Bobbs-Merrill, 1971. Emphasizes the ties between the Irish whisky industry and moonshine industry in the Southern mountains.
K600 (BC ASU LMC WCU MHC)

Kellogg, Louise Phelps ed. Thwaites, Reuben Gold ed. Documentary History of Dunmore's War, 1774. Madison, Wis.: Wisconsin Historical Society, 1905.
T8510

Thwaites, Reuben Gold ed. Frontier Defense on Upper Ohio, 1777-1778. Madison, Wis.: Wisconsin Historical Society, 1912.
T8520

Thwaites, Reuben Gold ed. Revolution on the Upper Ohio, 1775-1777. Madison, Wis.: Wisconsin Historical Society, 1908.
T8530

Kellogg, Remington Cetothere Skeletons from the Miocene Choptank Formation of Maryland and Virginia. Washington: Smithsonian Institution Press, 1969.
K610 (ETSU)

Kellogg, Sanford Cobb The Shenandoah Valley and Virginia, 1861 to 1865: A War Study. New York: Neale Pub. Co., 1903.
K620 (ASU BC)

Kelly, Donovan B. Davies, William Edward West Virginia's Buffalo Creek Flood: A Study of the Hydrology and Engineering Geology. Washington: U. S. Geological Survey, 1972.
D720

Kelly, Eleanor Mercein Kildares of Storm. New York: The Century Co., 1916. Novel in which the mountain characters and setting are tangential to the plot.
K630

The Mansion House. New York: Century Co., 1925. Novel partially set in Appalachia and featuring one memorable Appalachian character.
K640 (ASU BC)

Mixed Company. New York: Harper, 1936. A group of short stories from the Cumberland mountains.
K650

Kelly, J. A. Burk(e) Family of Southwest Virginia in Valley. Copied with permission of Mrs. John Boswell. Haverford, Pa.: n.p., 1944.
K660

Kelly, Mary Hope Betsy's Descendants. The Descendants of Thomas Jefferson Duff and his wife Ann Elizabeth (Betsy) Spraker Ketron. n.p.: n.p., 1966.
K670

Kelly, Paul Historic Fort Loudoun. Vonore, Tenn.: Fort Loudoun Assoc., 1958. Unfortunately the recently restored fort is in danger of being flooded by the TVA.
K680

Historic Fort Loudoun. Vonore: Fort Loudoun Assoc., 1961.
K690

Kemp, Harry Talton "An Investigation of Elementary Guidance in Pickens County." Master's thesis. Appalachian State Univ., 1967.
K700 (ASU)

Kemp, J. F. The Deposits of Copper — Ores at Ducktown Tenn. n.p.: n.p., n.d.
K710

Kemp, Oliver Wilderness Homes. New York: The Outing Pub. Co., 1908. Includes descriptions of frontier homes in mountain regions of eastern America.
K720

Kendrick, M. A. Lainhart, William S. Pneumoconiosis in Appalachian Bituminous Coal Miners. Washington: Bureau of Occupational Safety and Health, 1969.
L150

Kenna, Edward Benninghaus Songs of the Open Air and Other Poems. Charleston, W. Va.: Tribune Print. Co., 1912. Poems from the West Virginia hills.
K730 (BC)

Kennedy, Harold "A History of St. Andrew's School." Master's thesis. Middle Tennessee State Univ., 1952.
K740

Kennedy, John Pendleton The Blackwater Chronicle; A Narrative of an Expedition into the Land of Canaan. New York: Redfield, 1853. An account of a trip into the wilderness of Randolph County, Virginia in 1851.
K750 (BC ASU)

Horse-shoe Robinson. With an introduction, chronology, and bibliography, by Ernest E. Leisy. American Fiction Series. New York: American Book Company, 1937. Partially set in the Appalachian Mountains.
K760 (WCU ASU)

Horse-shoe Robinson: A Tale of the Tory Ascendency. New York: American Book Co., 1957.
K770 (ETSU)

Horse-shoe Robinson: A Tale of the Tory Ascendency in South Carolina, in 1780. New York: A. L. Burt Co., 1928. This Revolutionary War novel includes forays into the Appalachians.
K780 (MHC BC)

Kennedy, Ralph Emerson An Economic and Social Survey of Wise County. Record Extension Series, vol. 12, no. 11, also, Virginia County Surveys, 11. Charlottesville: Univ. of Virginia, 1928.
K790 (ASU BC)

Kennedy, Richard S. The Window of Memory: The Literary Career of Thomas Wolfe. Chapel Hill: Univ. of North Carolina Press, 1962.
K800 (BC UNCA ASU WCU)

Kennerly, Billie Weyrick Tenn. Grainger Co., Marriage Bonds and Licenses. Houston, Tex.: n.p., 1964.
K810

Kennerly, Wesley Travis The Battle of Fort Sanders. An Address Delivered November 28th, 1814 . . . at the Unveiling and Dedication of the Monument Erected by the Knoxville Chapter, United Daughters of the Confederacy, to the Memory of the Confederate Soldiers Who Lost Their Lives during the Siege of Knoxville, Tennessee, November 29, 1863. Knoxville: Breen, 1914.
K820

Kennesaw Mountain National Battlefield Park, Ga. S/N 2405-0120. Washington: Govt. Print. Off., n.d.
K830

Kenney, A. E. The Geography of West Virginia. Chicago: Werner School Book Co., 1896.
K840

Kenny, Hamill Thomas West Va. Place Names. Piedmont, W. Va.: Place Name Press, 1945. Includes names of streams, villages, towns and mountains.
K850

Kent, D. F. Techniques Used in Mine-water Problems of the East Tennessee Zinc District. U. S. Geological Survey Circular, no. 71. Washington: Govt. Print. Off., 1950.
K860 (ASU)

Kent, Deane F. Rodgers, John Stratigraphic Section at Lee Valley, Hawkins County, Tennessee. Nashville: Tennessee Department of Conservation, Division of Geology, 1948.
R3400 (ETSU)

Kent, William B. History of Saltville, Virginia. Radford, Virginia: Commonwealth Press, 1955. History of a community famous for its salt mines since frontier days.
K870

Kent, William H. An Analysis of Appalachian State Coal Mine Health and Safety and Workmen's Compensation Programs: Recommendations for Improvement. A report to the Appalachian Regional Commission. State College, Pa.: n.p., 1973.
K880 (ASU)

Kenton, Edna Simon Kenton: His Life and Period. New York: Doubleday, 1930. Biography of the famous West Virginia frontiersman, scout and sometimes traitor.
K890 (ASU)

Kentucky, Adjutant-General's Office Kentucky Soldiers of the War of 1812. Original title: Report of the Adjutant General of the state of Kentucky: Soldiers of the War of 1812. 1891. Reprint. With an added index compiled by Minnie S. Wilder, 1931, and a new introduction by B. Glenn Clift. Baltimore: Genealogical Pub. Co., 1969.
K900 (ASU)

Kentucky Agricultural and Industrial Development Board Economic Data on Eastern Kentucky Coal Fields. Frankfort: The board, 1956.
K910

Kentucky Agricultural Experiment Station Circular. No. 1-. Frankfort: Ky. Agricultural Experiment Station, n.d.
K920

Farm Population Changes in Eastern Kentucky. Lexington: Ky. Agricultural Experiment Station, 1943.
K930

Tables Showing Components of Population Change and Percent Due to Net Migration for State Economic Areas, Metropolitan Areas, and Counties, Southern Appalachians, 1950-1960. Lexington: Kentucky Agricultural Experiment Station, University of Kentucky, 1960.
K940

Utilization of Rural Manpower in Eastern Kentucky. Lexington: Ky. Agricultural Experiment Station, 1953. A study of Kentucky's economic area no. 8.
K950

Kentucky Ancestors vol. 1-., 1965-. Frankfort: Kentucky Historical Society.
K960

Kentucky Birds: A Finding Guide Kentucky Nature Studies, 3. Lexington: Univ. Press of Kentucky, 1973.
K970 (ASU WCU)

Kentucky Commission on Human Rights Kentucky's Black Heritage. Frankfort: n.p., 1971.
K980 (BC ETSU)

Kentucky Commission on Law Enforcement and Crime Prevention Delinquency in Kentucky. Frankfort: The Commission, 1967.
K990

Kentucky Conference on Youth, Louisville, 1963 Dropouts and Jobs: The Report of the Kentucky Conference on Youth, August 22-23, 1963. Frankfort: Kentucky Commission on Children and Youth, 1963?
K1000

Kentucky, Department of Commerce Commonwealth and Community: The Kentucky Program of State Assistance for Community Improvement. Frankfort?: The department, 1964?
K1010

Industrial Resources: Northern Kentucky. In cooperation with the Northern Kentucky Chamber of Commerce. n.p.: Kentucky Department of Commerce, 1971.
K1020 (ASU)

Kentucky, Department of Commerce, Economic Research Division Resources for Industry. 6 vols. Frankfort: The division, 1962-64.
K1030 (ASU)

Kentucky, Department of Commerce, Research Division Frankfort: The division, 1966.
K1040 (ETSU ASU)

Natural Resources of Kentucky. Frankfort: The division, 1967.
K1050 (ETSU ASU)

Kentucky, Department of Economic Development Action Programs for Eastern Kentucky: Final Report of the Kentucky Flood Rehabilitation Study. Frankfort: The department, 1957.
K1060 (BC ASU)

Eastern Kentucky Economic Atlas. Frankfort: Kentucky Department of Economic Development, October, 1958.
K1070

Kentucky, Department of Education History of Education in Kentucky. Frankfort: The department, 1914.
K1090 (ETSU ASU)

Youth Education and the Economic Opportunity Act of 1964: Some Indications of Need for Broad-based School and Community Action Programs for Kentucky Youth with Implications for Federal Assistance Programs. Frankfort?: The department, 1964. Special emphasis on poor Appalachian counties.
K1100

Kentucky, Department of Education. Division of Research Educational Attainment of the Adult Population in the Forty-four County Appalachian Region of Kentucky. Frankfort: The division, 1964.
K1080 (ASU)

Kentucky, Department of Mines and Minerals Annual Report, 1885-1919. Frankfort: The department, 1885-1919.
K1110

Kentucky, Department of Mines and Minerals: Geological Division Directory of Kentucky Mineral Operators. Lexington: State Dept. of Mines and Minerals, 1935.
K1120

Kentucky, Department of Natural Resources Strip Mining in Kentucky. n.p.: The department, 1965.
K1130 (BC ASU)

Kentucky, Division of Community Planning and Development Existing Land Use Analysis, Leslie County, Kentucky. Frankfort: The Division, 1967. Land use analysis for Hyden and Leslie Counties, Kentucky.
K1140

Harlan County, Existing Land Use Analysis. Harlan-Harlan County Major Thoroughfare Plan. Frankfort: The Division, 1967.
K1150

Pikeville, Kentucky, Neighborhood Analysis. Frankfort: The Division, 1966.
K1160

Kentucky, Division of Planning and Development Population-Economic Study, Harlan-Harlan County, Kentucky. Frankfort: The Division, 1966.
K1170

Kentucky, Division of Reclamation Surface Mining and Reclamation in Kentucky. Frankfort: n.p., 1972.
K1180

Kentucky, Division of the Budget Federal Aid in Kentucky. Frankfort: The Division, 1962.
K1190

Kentucky, Division of Tourism and Travel Promotion Travel in Kentucky. Frankfort: The Division, Annual.
K1200

Kentucky, Eastern Kentucky State College, Richmond Five Decades of Progress. Richmond: The College, 1957. Written by faculty members.
K1210

Kentucky Folklore Record Vol. 1-, 1955. Bowling Green: Kentucky Folklore Society, quarterly.
K1220 (ASU ETSU BC)

Kentucky General Assembly. House of Representatives Articles of Impeachment Against John A. Duff, Surveyor of Perry Co. Frankfort: The Assembly, 1847.
K1230

Kentucky General Assembly. Joint Legislative Committee on UnAmerican Activities Hearings Held at Pikeville. Pikeville: The Committee, 1968.
K1240

Kentucky, Geological Survey . . . Geological Map of Kentucky. Presented in Colors, Showing Oil, Gas, Coal, Fluorspar, and Asphalt Fields; and Other Mineral Resources and Geologic Data Including Faults, Folds, Sections, Elevations, and Physiographic Divisions of the Commonwealth. Series, no. 6. Frankfort: Kentucky Geological Survey, 1929.
K1250

Kentucky Historical Society Kentucky Marriages, 1797-1865. Baltimore: Genealogical Pub. Co.
K1260 (ASU BC)

Kentucky Illiteracy Commission Moonlight School Courses of Study. Frankfort: Commission, 1918.
K1270

Kentucky Land Office A Calendar of the Warrants for Land in Kentucky Granted for Service in the French and Indian War. Abstracted by Philip Fall Taylor. 1917. Reprint. Baltimore: Genealogical Pub. Co., 1967.
K1280 (BC ASU)

Kentucky Legislative Research Commission Strip Mining. Frankfort: The Commission, 1954.
K1290

Kentucky Mining Institute Coal Mining Reference Book. Reprinted by Oklahoma State Department of Vocational and Technical Education, 1970. Frankfort: Kentucky Mining Institute, 1958.
K1300

Proceedings. vol. 1- annual. Lexington, Ky.: n.p., 1940?
K1310

Kentucky Mountain Club Yearbook. Lexington, Ky.: The Club, 1929.
K1320

Kentucky Mountain Missions. v. 1- 1930- Frakes, Ky.: Kentucky Mountain Missions of the Methodist Episcopal Church, 1930. v. monthly. Monthly news letter published in the interest of our missionary work in the Kentucky mountains.
K1330

Kentucky, University, Bureau of Business Research Analysis of Manufacturing Employment Trends in Kentucky Counties, 1960-64, and Their Economic Significance. John Leonard Fulmer, director. Lexington: The Bureau, 1966. Includes statistics for Kentucky's forty-nine mountain counties.
K1340

Analysis of Occupational Trends in Kentucky from 1950 to 1960, with Projections to 1975. John Leonard Fulmer, director. Lexington: The Bureau, 1965. Includes statistics for the mountain counties.
K1350

Development Potentials for Kentucky Counties with Related Statistics. John L. Fulmer, director. Lexington: The Bureau, 1966.
K1360 (ASU)

Kentucky Tourist Preferences. Lexington: The Bureau, 1962. Includes material on the mountain resort areas.
K1370

Kentucky, University, Center for Developmental Change Community Action in Appalachia: An Appraisal of the "War on Poverty" in a Rural Setting of Southeastern Kentucky. 13 vols. Lexington: Univ. of Kentucky, Bureau of School Service, 1968.
K1380

Kentucky, University, College of Agriculture and Home Economics Appalachian Resource Development Project, Submitted to the Kellogg Foundation. Lexington: The College, 1960.
K1390

Kentucky, University, Department of Agriculture New Towns for the Appalachian Regions: A Case Study Located in Eastern Kentucky. Under the auspices of the Kentucky Research Foundation. Lexington: The Univ., 1960.
K1400

Kentucky, University, Geological Survey Bibliography of Coal in Kentucky. Series X, Special Publications, 19. Lexington: The Survey, 1970.
K1410

Kentucky, University, Social Research Service Basic Population Data for the Southern Appalachians. Southern Appalachian Series: Report no. 1. Lexington: The University, 1958.
K1420

Kentucky Water Resources, 1965 Frankfort: Kentucky Dept. of Natural Resources, 1965.
K1430

Kentucky Writing Morehead, Ky.: Morehead State College Press, 1954.
K1440

Kentucky's Resources: Their Development and Use Rev. ed. Prepared under the direction of a core committee appointed by the Commissioner of Conservation and the Superintendent of Public Instruction. Preface by W. Paul Street. Bulletin of the Bureau of School Service, vol. 31, no. 2. Lexington: Univ. of Kentucky, 1958.
K1450 (ETSU ASU)

Kephart, Horace Camping and Woodcraft: A Handbook for Vacation Campers and for Travelers in the Wilderness. New ed. 1917. Reprint. New York: Macmillan Co., 1967. The author also wrote OUR SOUTHERN HIGHLANDERS, the first book which attempted to portray the southern highlands.
K1460 (ASU)

The Cherokees of the Smoky Mountains. Silver Spring, Md.: Westland Print. Co., 1971.
K1470 (WCU ASU)

The Cherokees of the Smoky Mountains: A Little Band That Has Stood Against the White Tide for Three Hundred Years. Ithaca, N. Y.: Atkinson Press, 1936. Kephart lived and worked with the Cherokee for many years.
K1480 (ASU MHC UNCA)

Our Southern Highlanders. New York: Outing Pub. Co., 1913.
K1490 (ETSU BC ASU)

Our Southern Highlanders: Narrative of Adventure in the Southern Appalachians and a Study of the Life Among the Mountaineers. New York: Macmillan Co., 1921.
K1500 (BC ASU)

Our Southern Highlanders: Narrative of Adventure in the Southern Appalachians and a Study of the Life Among the Mountaineers. New and enlarged ed. New York: Macmillan Co., 1922.
K1510 (ASU WCU LMC)

Our Southern Highlanders: Narrative of Adventure in the Southern Appalachians and a Study of the Life Among the Mountaineers. New and enlarged ed. New York: Macmillan Co., 1926.
K1520 (ASU)

Our Southern Highlanders: A Narrative of Adventure in the Southern Appalachians and a Study of Life Among the Mountaineers. 1922. Reprint. New York: Macmillan Co., 1936.
K1530 (WWC)

Kephart, Horace
Our Southern Highlanders: A Narrative of Adventure in the Southern Appalachians and a Study of the Life Among the Mountaineers. Rev. ed. 1941. Reprint. New York: Macmillan Co., 1967.
K1540 (FC)

Kercheval, Samuel A History of the Valley of Virginia. 4th ed., rev. ed. and extended by John Walter Wayland, the author, and new notes added by Oren Frederic Morton, the editor. Strasburg, Va.: Shenandoah Pub. Co., 1925.
K1550 (ASU BC)
History of the Valley of Virginia. 2nd ed. rev. Woodstock, Va.: John Gatewood Printer, 1850.
K1560
History of the Valley of Virginia. 3rd ed. Woodstock, Va.: W. N. Grabill Power Press, 1902.
K1570

Kerhoff, Jennie Ann Old Homes of Page County, Virginia. Luray, Va.: Lauck and Co., Inc., 1962.
K1580

Kern, E. E. An Inventory of Human and Physical Resources of Cherokee, Dekalb, Jackson, and Marshall Counties, Alabama. Auburn, Ala.: Auburn Univ. Agricultural Experiment Station, 1966.
K1590 (ASU)

Kern, Ethel Kelley M. The Trail of the Three Notched Road. Silhouette sketches by Margaret Eugenie Kern. Richmond: William Byrd Press, 1929. Novel with a Cumberland Mountain setting.
K1600 (BC)

Kernodle, Michael Wilson, John M. Summary of Ground Water Data for Tennessee, Through May 1971. n.p.: State of Tennessee Department of Conservation Division of Water Resources, 1970.
W7350 (LMC)

Kerns, Carole Smithers "High-interest, Low-vocabulary Original Prose and Poetry for Teenagers in Southern Appalachia." Master's thesis. East Tennessee State University, 1970.
K1610 (ETSU)

Kerr, Dewey Winston "An Analysis of the Relationship of Religious Commitment and Alienation Among High School Students of Bristol, Tennessee." Master's thesis. East Tennessee State University, 1971.
K1620 (ETSU)

Kerr, John Alexander Soil Survey of Fayette County, West Virginia. In cooperation with the West Virginia Geological Survey. Field Operations, 1919. Washington, D. C.: U. S. Dept. of Agriculture, Bureau of Soils, 1921.
K1630
Soil Survey of Garrard County, Kentucky. Prepared in cooperation with the Kentucky Agricultural Experiment Station. Field Operations, 1921. Washington, D. C.: U. S. Dept. of Agriculture, Bureau of Soils, 1926.
K1640
Soil Survey of Monroe County, West Virginia. In cooperation with the West Virginia Geological Survey. Soil Survey Report, series 1925, no. 15. Washington, D. C.: U. S. Dept. of Agriculture, Bureau of Chemistry and Soils, 1930.
K1650
Soil Survey of Summers County, West Virginia. In cooperation with the West Virginia Geological Survey. Soil Survey Report, series 1924, no. 21. Washington, D. C.: U. S. Dept. of Agriculture, Bureau of Chemistry and Soils, 1929.
K1660

Kerr, W. C. Report of the Geographical Survey of North Carolina: Physical Geography, Resume, Economical Geology. Raleigh, N. C.: Turner, 1875.
K1670 (LMC ASU)

Kerr, Washington Caruthers Genth, Friedrich August Ludwig Karl Wilhelm The Minerals and Mineral Localities of North Carolina. Raleigh: P. M. Hale, 1885.
G800 (ASU)

Kershaw, Joseph A. Government Against Poverty. Washington, D. C.: Brooking's Institution, 1970.
K1680

Kerwood, Robert V. "Effects of Urbanization on Vocational Agriculture in Jackson County, West Virginia." Master's thesis. West Virginia Univ., 1963.
K1690

Kesler, T. L. Geology and Mineral Deposits of the Cartersville District, Georgia. U. S. Geological Survey Professional Paper, no. 224. Washington, D. C.: Govt. Print. Off., 1950.
K1700

Kesner, Mernie Bibliography for Appalachian Studies. Berea, Ky.: Berea College Appalachian Center, 1973. A listing of books, tapes, periodicals, and pamphlets for high school libraries.
K1710

Kester, Vaughan The Prodigal Judge. Illustrated by M. Leone Bracker. Indianapolis: Bobbs-Merrill Co., 1911. Fictional account of an actual event in the southern hills.
K1720 (BC ASU LMC WCU)

Keun, Odette A Foreigner Looks at the TVA. 1st ed. New York: Longmans, Green and Co., 1937. A too, too rosy picture of America's largest socialist experiment.
K1730 (BC ASU WWC)

Key, Alexander Cherokee Boy. Philadelphia: Westminster Press, 1957. Juvenile fiction about a young boy growing up on the Cherokee reservation.
K1750 (ASU BC)
Escape to Witch Mountain. Illustrated by Leon B. Wisdom, Jr. Philadelphia: Westminster Press, 1968. Science fiction tale in which two children seek their former home in Western North Carolina mountains.
K1760 (ASU)
The Forgotten Door. Philadelphia: Westminster Press, 1965. A boy from another planet falls to earth in Western North Carolina and uses supernatural powers.
K1770
With Daniel Boone on the Caroliny Trail. Philadelphia: John C. Winston Co., 1941. A novel of frontier and pioneer life in North Carolina.
K1780 (ASU LMC WCU ETSU BC)

Keyes, Charles A. Parson of the Hills. New York: Vantage Press, 1956. Biographical material on North Carolina's famous Parson of the Hills.
K1790

Keys, Bernelle Mitchell "The Enriched Curriculum as a Means of Meeting the Emotional and Social Needs of First Grade Children in Washington County." Master's thesis. East Tennessee State College, 1952.
K1800 (ETSU)

Keys, Lucy Lowery Hoyt The Wahnenauhi Manuscripts: Historical Sketches of the Cherokees, Together with Some of Their Customs, Traditions, and Superstitions. Introduction by Jack Frederick Kilpatrick. U. S. Bureau of American Ethnology Bulletin, no. 196. Washington: Govt. Print. Off., 1966.
K1810 (WCU)

Keys, Robert Kenneth "Some Problems Concerning the Relations of Administrators and Beginning Teachers in the Washington County School System, 1955-1956." Master's thesis. East Tennessee State College, 1957.
K1820 (ETSU)

Keys, William G. "Editorial Attitudes of West Virginia Newspapers toward School and Education." Master's thesis. West Virginia Univ., 1937.
K1830

Keyserling, Leon Poverty and Deprivation in the United States. Washington: Conference on Economic Progress, 1962. Includes material on rural Appalachia.
K1840

Keystone Folklore Quarterly vol. 1- . 1956- . Lewisburg, Pa.: n.p., quarterly.
K1850 (ETSU)

Keystone Trails Association Guide to the Appalachian Trail in Pennsylvania: From the Maryland Line to the Delaware Water Gap---222.4 Miles. Appendix describing 13 other trails maintained by member clubs of K. T. A. 2nd ed. Concordville, Pa.: The assoc., 1970.
K1860 (ETSU)

Kidd, Paul E. "Governmental Assistance to Industrial Development in West Virginia." Master's thesis. West Virginia Univ., 1958.
K1870

Kidd, Robert H. Mountain Stories. Grafton, W. Va.: Grafton Press, 1931. A collection of short stories from the hills of West Virginia.
K1880

Kiddle, Mary White, Lamar Highlights of the Economy of the Georgia Mountains Area. Atlanta: Industrial Development Division, Engineering Experiment Station, Georgia Institute of Technology, 1964.
W5510

Kidwell, J. H. Silver Fleece, a Tale of the Swift Mines of Old Kentucky. New York: Avondale Press, 1927. A tale of the fabulous Silver Fleece mines in Kentucky.
K1890 (LMC BC)

Killebrew, Joseph Buckner The Grasses of Tennessee: Including Cereals and Forage Plants. Nashville: American Co., 1878.
K1900 (BC ASU LMC)
Knoxville as an Iron Center. Nashville: Eastman and Howell, 1880.
K1910
Tennessee: Its Agricultural and Mineral Wealth, With an Appendix Showing the Extent, Value and Accessibility of its Ores, With Analyses of the Same. Nashville: Tavel, Eastman, and Howell, 1877.
K1920 (ASU LMC)
Warren County, Its Organization, Scenery, Resources and Representative Men. Nashville: Union and American, 1871.
K1930
Safford, James Merrill The Elements of the Geology of Tennessee. Nashville: Ambrose and Bostelman, 1904.
S90 (ASU LMC BC)

Killian, Lewis M. "Southern White Laborers in Chicago's West Side." Microfilm. Ph. D. Diss. Univ. of Chicago, 1950. Describes the fate of the hillbilly worker in Chicago's hillbilly ghetto.
K1940 (ASU)

Killion, Ronald G. A Treasury of Georgia Folk-lore. Illustrated by Maureen O'Leary. Atlanta: Cherokee Pub. Co., 1972. Includes material from Georgia's thirty-five mountain counties.
K1950 (BC ASU MHC ETSU)

Kilpatrick, Anna Gritts Chronicles of Wolftown: Social Documents of the North Carolina Cherokees, 1850-1862. U. S. Bureau of American Ethnology Bulletin, no. 196. Also, Anthropological Papers, no. 75. Washington: Govt. Print. Off., 1966.
K1960 (WCU ASU)
Kilpatrick, Jack Frederick Eastern Cherokee Folktales: Reconstructed from the Field Notes of Frans M. Olbrechts. Washington: Govt. Print. Off., 1966.
K1970 (WCU ASU)
Kilpatrick, Jack Frederick Friends of Thunder, Folktales of the Oklahoma Cherokees. Dallas: Southern Methodist Univ. Press, 1964.
K1980 (ASU)
Kilpatrick, Jack Frederick Notebook of a Cherokee Shaman. Washington: Smithsonian Institution Press, 1970.
K2000 (WCU ETSU UNCA ASU)
Kilpatrick, Jack Frederick Run Toward the Nightland: Magic of the Oklahoma Cherokees. Dallas: Southern Methodist Univ. Press, 1967.
K2010 (LMC MHC)
Kilpatrick, Jack Frederick Walk in Your Soul: Love Incantations of the Oklahoma Cherokees. Dallas: Southern Methodist Univ. Press, 1965.
K2030 (LMC)

Kilpatrick, Anna Gritts ed. Kilpatrick, Jack Frederick New Echota Letters: Contributions of Samuel A. Worcester to the Cherokee Phoenix. Dallas: Southern Methodist Univ. Press, 1968.
K1990 (WCU LMC MHC ASU)
Kilpatrick, Jack Frederick The Shadow of the Sequoyah: Social Documents of the Cherokees, 1862-1964. Norman: Univ. of Oklahoma Press, 1965.
K2020 (BC ASU WCU LMC ETSU)

Kilpatrick, Jack Frederick Kilpatrick, Anna Gritts Chronicles of Wolftown: Social Documents of the North Carolina Cherokees, 1850-1862. Washington: Govt. Print. Off., 1966.
K1960 (WCU ASU)
Eastern Cherokee Folktales: Reconstructed from the Field Notes of Frans M. Olbrechts. U. S. Bureau of American Ethnology Bulletin, no. 1. Also, Anthropological Papers, no. 80. Washington: Govt. Print. Off., 1966.
K1970 (WCU ASU)
Friends of Thunder, Folktales of the Oklahoma Cherokees. Dallas: Southern Methodist Univ. Press, 1964. Tales collected in Oklahoma from survivors and descendants of those who were in the "Trail of Tears" removal.
K1980 (ASU)
New Echota Letters: Contributions of Samuel A. Worcester to the Cherokee Phoenix. Dallas: Southern Methodist Univ. Press, 1968. New Echota near present-day Calhoun, Georgia was the last eastern capital of the Eastern Cherokee. The Phoenix was the Cherokee language newspaper.
K1990 (WCU LMC MHC ASU)
Notebook of a Cherokee Shaman. Smithsonian Contributions to Anthropology, vol. 2, no. 6. Washington: Smithsonian Institution Press, 1970.
K2000 (WCU ETSU UNCA ASU)
Run Toward the Nightland: Magic of the Oklahoma Cherokees. Dallas: Southern Methodist Univ. Press, 1967.
K2010 (LMC MHC)
The Shadow of the Sequoyah: Social Documents of the Cherokees, 1862-1964. 1st ed. Civilization of the American Indian Series. Norman: Univ. of Oklahoma Press, 1965.
K2020 (BC ASU WCU LMC ETSU)
Walk in Your Soul: Love Incantations of the Oklahoma Cherokees. Dallas: Southern Methodist Univ. Press, 1965.
K2030 (LMC)

Kilpatrick, Jack Frederick ed. Keys, Lucy Lowery Hoyt The Wahnenauhi Manuscripts: Historical Sketches of the Cherokees, Together with Some of Their Customs, Traditions, and Superstitions. Washington: Govt. Print. Off., 1966.
K1810 (WCU)

Kim, Byong-suh "Religiosity as Related to Social Factors and Modes of Social Institutional Behavior in the Southern Appalachian Region." Ph. D. Diss. Emory Univ., 1968.
K2040 (LMC ASU)

Kim, Ungsoo "Measuring and Analyzing the Impact of Employment Generation Benefits of a Public Water Resource Development Project in Appalachia." Ph. D. Diss. The Catholic Univ. of America, 1972.
K2050

Kimball, Sarah Louise Jordan, David Starr Your Family Tree. Baltimore: Genealogical Pub. Co., 1968.
J2720 (ASU)

Kimel, Doris Elizabeth "A Study of the Changing Role of the Music Specialist in the North Carolina Elementary Schools, 1950-1957." Master's thesis. Appalachian State Teachers College, 1958. Includes data on the twenty-eight mountain counties.
K2060 (ASU)

Kimery, Greer Jackson "Return Jonathan Meigs, Cherokee Indian Agent, 1801-1823." Master's thesis. Univ. of Tennessee, 1948.
K2070

Kimmel, Donald C. "Agriculture Development in the Pittsburgh District." Ph. D. Diss. Pennsylvania State Univ., 1950.
K2080

Kimsey, William Warren "The Chattanooga Region as a Plant Site for the Nylon Industry." Master's thesis. East Tennessee State College, 1952.
K2090 (ETSU)

Kimzey, Herbert Bennett Habersham County, Georgia, Genealogical Records. Cornelia, Ga.: The author, 1969.
K2100 (ASU)

Kimzey, Herbert Bennett comp. Rabun County, Georgia, Records. Cornelia, Ga.: The author, 1971. Contents.- Part 1. The 1830 census, family heads only listed. -Part 2. The 1850 census, showing name, age and sex of all residents of county and the state of birth of family head and wife.
K2110 (ASU)

Kinard, J. D. Farm Business Study of the Six Mile Area of Pickens County, 1940. n.p.: South Carolina Agricultural Experiment Station, 1942.
K2120 (ASU)

Kincaid, Bradley ed. Favorite Mountain Ballads and Old Time Songs. n.p.: n.p., 1928.
K2130

Kincaid, Robert L. The Wilderness Road. Harrogate: Lincoln Memorial Univ. Press, 1955.
K2170

Kincaid, Robert Lee A Boy Finds a College. Harrogate, Tenn.: privately pub., 1955. President Kincaid's sentimental tale of young man who discovers Lincoln Memorial University. Supposedly based on fact.
K2140
Jinny and Jim. Harrogate, Tenn.: Lincoln Memorial Univ., 1941. A mountain tale by the president of Lincoln Memorial University. Supposedly based on actual characters from Kincaid's family.
K2150 (ASU)
The Wilderness Road. 1st ed. New York: Bobbs-Merrill, 1947.
K2160 (BC WCU WWC ETSU)
The Wilderness Road. 3rd ed. Middlesboro, Ky.: n.p., 1966.
K2180 (ASU LMC)

Kinder, Chuck Snakehunter. New York: Alfred A. Knopf, 1973. Adventure story with a mountain setting.
K2190 (ASU LMC)

Kinder, Don R. "Secession and Civil War in Jefferson County, Tennessee, 1860-1865." Master's thesis. East Tennessee State Univ., 1973.
K2200 (ETSU)

Kindig, Joe Thoughts on the Kentucky Rifle in its Golden Age. New York: Bonanza, 1964.
K2210 (ASU)

King, Beverly Country and Bluegrass Dobro. 2nd ed. 2 vols. in 1. Revere, Pa.: n.p., 1973.
K2220 (WCU)

King, Carl W. "A Study of a Labor Unions of the Textile Industry in the Southern Appalachian Piedmont." Master's thesis. East Tennessee State Univ., 1969.
K2230 (ETSU)

King, Charles Norman Holt: A Story of the Army of the Cumberland. Illustrated by John Huybers and Seymour M. Stone. New York: G. W. Dillingham Co., 1901.
K2240 (BC ASU)

King, E. J. comp. White, Benjamin Franklin The Sacred Harp. Nashville: Broadman Press, 1968.
W5310 (WCU ASU)

King, Edward The Great South: A Record of Journeys. Illustrated by J. Wells Champney. 1875. Reprint. 2 vols. New York: Burt Franklin, 1969.
K2250 (LMC)
The Great South: A Record of Journeys in Louisiana, Texas, the Indian Territory, Missouri, Arkansas, Mississippi, Alabama, Georgia, Florida, South Carolina, North Carolina, Kentucky, Tennessee, Virginia, West Virginia, and Maryland. Illustrated by J. Wells Champney. Hartford, Conn.: American Pub. Co., 1875.
K2260 (ASU BC)

King, Elisha Sterling The Wild Rose of Cherokee, or Nancy Ward, "The Pocahontas of the West." A Story of the Early Exploration, Occupancy, and Settlement of the State of Tennessee. A Romance Founded on and Interwoven With History. Nashville: Univ. Press, 1895.
K2270 (LMC BC)
The Wild Rose of Cherokee: Or, Nancy Ward, "The Pocahontas of the West", a Story of the Early Exploration, Occupancy and Settlement of the State of Tennessee. A Romance, Founded on and Interwoven with History. Etowah, Tenn.: Myrtle K. Tatum, 1938.
K2280 (BC ASU)

King, Howard M. "What Citizens of Sullivan County Know about Their Schools." Master's thesis. East Tennessee State College, 1952.
K2290

King, John M. Soil Survey of Transylvania County, North Carolina. Washington: U. S. Soil Conservation Service, 1974.
K2300

King, Joseph Leonard, Jr. Dr. William George Bagby: A Study of Virginian Literature 1850-1880. New York: Columbia Univ. Press, 1927.
K2310
Dr. George William Bagby: A Study of Virginia Literature, 1850-1880. 1927. Reprint. New York: AMS Press, 1966.
K2320 (ASU)

King, Judson Conservation Fight from Theodore Roosevelt to the Tennessee Valley Authority. Washington: Public Affairs Press, 1959.
K2330
Legislative History of Muscle Shoals. Knoxville, Tenn.: Tennessee Valley Authority, 1936.
K2340
TVA Labor Relations Policy at Work; Successful Cooperation Between Public Power and Organized Labor in the Public Interest. Revised ed. Washington: National Popular Government League, April 19, 1940.
K2350

King, Junie Estelle Stewart Abstract of Early Kentucky Wills and Inventories, Copied From Original and Recorded Wills and Inventories. 1933. Reprint. Baltimore: Genealogical Pub. Co., 1961.
K2360 (BC ASU)
Abstracts of Wills, Inventories, and Administrations Accounts of Frederick County, Virginia. Includes some notes on early settlers; Frederic Rentals, 1746 Land Holders 1750; Cemetery Inscriptions; and Survey Warrants. Berryville, Va.: Virginia Book Co., n.d.
K2370

King, Louis Eugene "Negro Life in a Rural Community." Ph. D. Diss. Columbia Univ., 1951.
K2380

King, Marie Halbert Cabin in the Valley. Asheville: Stephens Press, 1969. Fiction with a western North Carolina setting.
K2390
Forgotten Valleys. Asheville: Stephens Press, 1958. Fiction with a western North Carolina setting.
K2400

King, Philip Burke Geology and Manganese Deposits of Northeastern Tennessee. Bulletin, 52. Nashville: Tennessee Department of Conservation Division of Geology, 1944.
K2410 (ETSU)
Geology of Northeasternmost Tennessee with a Section on the Description of the Basement Rocks by Warren Hamilton. U. S. Geological Survey Profession Paper, 311. Washington: Govt. Print. Off., 1959.
K2420 (ETSU)

King, Philip Burke
Geology of the Central Great Smoky Mountains, Tennessee. Geological Survey Professional Paper, no. 349-C. 2 vols. Washington: Govt. Print. Off., 1964.
K2430 (ASU LMC)
Geology of the Elkton Area, Virginia. U. S. Geological Survey Professional Paper, no. 230. Washington: Govt. Print. Off., 1950, 1954.
K2440
Geology of the Great Smoky Mountains National Park, Tennessee and North Carolina. Professional Paper, 587. Washington: U. S. Department of the Interior Geological Survey, 1968.
K2450 (ETSU)
Manganese Deposits of the Elkton Area, Virginia. U. S. Geological Survey Bulletin, no. 940-B. Washington: Govt. Print. Off., 1943.
K2460

King, Spencer Bidwell Selective Service in North Carolina in World War II. Chapel Hill: Univ. of North Carolina Press, 1949.
K2470 (LMC)

King, W. M. History of First Settlers of Cow Run. n.p.: W. M. King, Typescript, 1953. Cow Run is located in Jackson County, Union District, West Virginia. The History includes: History of first settlers of Cow Run; History of the parents of the children that went to old log Antioch schoolhouse; Antioch, The log schoolhouse on the hill; The Old Cherry Grove Church; The way people lived in my childhood days; Late-settlers in Antioch district; and a poem THE BACKWOODSMAN.
K2480

King, Warren R. Water Resources of Tennessee: Being A Compilation of Existing Data Pertaining to the Surface Waters of Tennessee and Their Utilization. Bulletin, no. 34. Nashville: Division of Geology, 1925.
K2490 (LMC)

King's Mountain National Military Park, South Carolina S/N 2405-0172. Washington: Govt. Print. Off., n.d.
K2500

Kingsport Press Kingsport Book of Type Faces. 3 vols. New York: n.p., n.d.
K2510 (ETSU)
A Way of Life, Our Home in the Southern Appalachians. Kingsport, Tenn.: The press, 1973.
K2520 (BC ETSU)

Kingsport, Tennessee. John Sevier Junior High School "Flexible Scheduling in Secondary Schools." Master's thesis. East Tennessee State University, 1968.
K2530 (ETSU)

Kingsport, Tennessee. Public Schools New Dimensions in Mathematics for the Elementary Schools in Kingsport, Tennessee. Kingsport, Tenn.: n.p., 1966.
K2540 (ETSU)

Kingsport, Tennessee. Rotary Club Kingsport, the Planned Industrial City. (Original title: Kingsport, city of industries, schools, churches and homes.) Kingsport: The club, 1946.
K2550 (ETSU)
Kingsport, Tennessee, a Modern American City — Developed through Industry. Kingsport: The club, 1962.
K2560 (LMC ETSU)
Kingsport, the Planned Industrial City. (Original title: Kingsport, city of industries, schools, churches and homes.) Kingsport: The club, 1951.
K2570 (ETSU ASU)

Kingston, Marion A Folk Song Chapbook. Chapbook, no. 4. Beloit, Wis.: Beloit Poetry Journal, 1955.
K2580 (LMC)

Kinicely, Howard "Characteristics of Mobile Workers in a Rural Industrialized Community." Master's thesis. West Virginia Univ., 1960.
K2600

Kinkel, Arthur R., Jr. The Ore Knob Copper Deposit, North Carolina, and Other Massive Sulfide Deposits of the Appalachians. Washington: Govt. Print. Off., 1967.
K2590 (LMC)

Kinnaird, James Brown Historical Sketches of Lancaster and Garrard County, 1796-1924. n.p.: n.p., 1924.
K2610

Kinnear, Duncan Lyle The First 100 Years: A History of Virginia Polytechnic Institute and State University. Illustrations, index, and bibliography. Blacksburg: Polytechnic Institute Educational Foundation, 1972.
K2620

Kirk, Charles H. ed. History of the Fifteenth Pennsylvania Volunteer Cavalry: Which Was Recruited and Known as the Anderson Cavalry in the Rebellion of 1861-1865. Philadelphia: Historical Committee, 1906.
K2630 (LMC)

Kirke, Edmund pseud. Gilmore, James Roberts A Mountain-White Heroine. New York and Chicago: Belford, Clarke and Co., 1889.
G1760

Kirke, Edmund, pseud. see **Gilmore, James Roberts**

Kirkland, Caroline Matilda A New Home — Who'll Follow? or, Glimpses at Western Life. New York: C. S. Francis, 1839. Fiction partially set in the mountains.
K2640

Kirkland, W. M. Where the Star Still Shines. n.p.: n.p., n.d.
K2650 (LMC)

Kirkpatrick, Perl Ellis "Carter County's Greatest Need in the Homebound Program of Services for Exceptional Children, 1952-54." Master's thesis. East Tennessee State College, 1954.
K2660 (ETSU)

Kiser, James L., Jr. A Study of Judicial Procedures on the Cherokee Indian Reservation. Cullowhee: Western Carolina Univ., 1970.
K2670 (LMC ASU)

Kistner, Joyce Allison "The Third-grade Social Studies Program in Bristol, Virginia, 1969-70." Master's thesis. East Tennessee State Univ., 1970.
K2680 (ETSU)

Klein, Edward L. "An Analysis of the Christmas Tree Industry in Pennsylvania." Master's thesis. Pennsylvania State Univ., 1961.
K2690

Klein, Maury History of the Louisville and Nashville Railroad. New York: Macmillan, 1972. The L and N was one of Appalachia's most significant corporation from the founding of Birmingham, Alabama, through the opening of the Elkhorn Field in 1910. This railroad continues to be one of the region's main carriers.
K2700

Klindt, Thomas Harold "Development of Procedures for Quantifying and Assessing the Economic Well-being of Rural Areas." Ph. D. Diss. Univ. of Kentucky, 1971.
K2710

Klingberg, Frank J. Old Sherry, Portrait of a Virginia Family (Wysors). Richmond, Va.: Garrett and Massie, 1938.
K2720

Knapp, Daniel Scouting the War on Poverty: Social Reform Politics in the Kennedy Administration. Lexington, Mass.: Heath Lexington Books, 1971.
K2740

Knapp, David The Confederate Horsemen. New York: Vantage, 1966.
K2730

Knapp, George L. A Young Volunteer With Old Hickory. Illustrated by Leslie Crump. New York: Dodd, Mead, and Co., 1929. Fictional account of young man's adventures with Andy Jackson.
K2750 (ASU BC)

Kneberg, Madeline Lewis, Thomas McDowell Nelson The First Tennesseans; an Interpretation of Tennessee Prehistory. Knoxville: Dept. of Anthropology, Univ. of Tennessee, 1955.
L2260
Lewis, Thomas McDowell Nelson The Prehistory of the Chickamauga Basin in Tennessee, a Preview. Knoxville: Dept. of Anthropology, Univ. of Tennessee, 1941.
L2280

Knechtel, M. M. Manganese Deposits of the Lyndhurst-Vesuvius District, Augusta and Rockbridge Counties, Virginia. U. S. Geological Survey Bulletin, no. 940-F. Washington: Govt. Print. Off., 1944.
K2760

Knight, Edgar Wallace ed. A Documentary History of Education in the South before 1860. 5 vols. Chapel Hill: Univ. of North Carolina Press, 1949-53. Tangentially Appalachian.
K2770 (WWC)

Knight, Herbert A. Virginia's Timber, 1966. U. S. Forest Service Resource Bulletin, SE-8. Asheville, N. C.: Southeastern Forest Experiment Station, 1967.
K2780 (LMC)

Knight, Howard Vernon Scenic and Historic Old Virginia and Eastern National Parks. Asheville, N. C., and Richmond: Southern Park and Playgrounds, 1930.
K2790 (WCU)

Knight, Lucian Lamar Stone Mountain: Or, the Lay of the Gray Minstrel. An Epic Poem in Twenty-four Parts, Commemorative of the South's Confederate, Pre-Historic, Colonial, Revolutionary, and World War Days, to Which Are Added a Number of Other Poems, Patriotic, Humorous, and Occasional, Besides a Few Prose Selections. Atlanta: Johnson-Dallas Co., 1923.
K2800 (ASU)

Knight, Lusian Lamar comp. Georgia. Department of Archives and History Georgia's Roster of the Revolution. Baltimore: Genealogical Pub. Co., 1967.
G890 (ASU)

Knight, Mazie M. "A History of the Secondary Schools of Cocke County, Tennessee." Master's thesis. Univ. of Tennessee, 1952.
K2810

Knittle, Walter Allen Early Eighteenth Century Palatine Emigration: A British Government Redemptioner Project to Manufacture Naval Stores. 1937. Reprint. Baltimore: Genealogical Pub. Co., 1965. Many of these settlers left the coast and slipped over the mountain wall in search of land.
K2820 (ASU)

Knott, Sarah Gertrude A Gatherin'; Ky. Lore of Mt. Music, Songs, and Dances. Frankfort: Ky. Council of the Performing Arts and Ky. Dept. of Commerce, 1963.
K2830

Knowles, Clifton Dixon "A Study of the Motor Ability of a Selected Number of Boys at the Appalachian Elementary School During the 1959-1960 School Year." Master's thesis. Appalachian State Teachers College, 1960.
K2840 (ASU)

Knowlson, Thomas Sharper The Origins of Popular Superstitions and Customs. 1910. Reprint. Detroit: Gale Research Co., 1968. Deals with the Celtic origins of Appalachian customs, superstitions and folklore.
K2850 (ASU)

Knox County in the World War: 1917-1918-1919 Knoxville: Knoxville Litho., 1919.
K2860

Knox, Joe Little Benders. 1st ed. Philadelphia: Lippincott, 1952. A book of short stories including several set in the western North Carolina mountains.
K2870 (BC ASU WCU)

Knox, John Ballenger The People of Tennessee: A Study of Population Trends. Prepared for the Bureau for Sociological Research with the assistance of Jerry W. Combs, Jr., and others. With an introduction by William E. Cole. Knoxville: Univ. of Tennessee Press, 1949.
K2880 (BC ASU WCU)

The Knoxville Chalkboard vol. 1- . 1961- . Knoxville: Knoxville Teachers League, monthly.
K2890 (ETSU)

Knoxville District Dietetic Association The Knoxville Area Diet Manual. Knoxville: The assoc., 1967.
K2900 (ETSU)

Knoxville, Tennessee, Public Schools The Other Children: A Seatwork Activities Bulletin. New York: Harper and Row, 1960.
K2910 (ETSU)

Knoxville, Tennessee, the Queen City of the Mountains Knoxville: Knoxville Board of Trade, 1909.
K2920

Knutson, Robert Look at Mine-timber Market in the Appalachian Bituminous Coal Region. U. S. Forest Service Research Paper, NE-147. Upper Darby, Pa.: Northeastern Forest Experiment Station, 1970.
K2930

Koch, ? Up the Big Mountain. Birmingham, Ala.: Title Books, n.d. Children's adventure story set in the southern Appalachians.
K2940

Koch, Frederick Henry ed. Carolina Folk-plays. Introduction. Foreword by Paul Green. Illustrated from photographs of the original productions of the plays. 3rd ed. New York: H. Holt and Co., 1928.
K2960 (LMC)

Kochenderfer, James N. Erosion Control on Logging Roads in the Appalachians. U. S. Forest Service Research Paper, NE-158. Upper Darby, Pa.: Northeastern Forest Experiment Station, 1970.
K2970 (ASU LMC)

Kock, Frederick Henry ed. Carolina Folk-Plays. Introduction on folk-play making. Illustrated from photographs of the original productions of the plays. New York: H. Holt and Co., 1922. Includes some mountain material.
K2950 (ASU BC)

Kolb, F. W. Lewis, Henry Guy Soil Survey of Cleburne County, Alabama. Washington: U. S. Department of Agriculture, Bureau of Soils, 1915.
L2170

Kollmorgen, Walter Martin The German Settlement in Cullman County, Alabama: An Agricultural Island in the Cotton Belt. Washington: Department of Agriculture, Bureau of Agricultural Economics, 1941.
K2980 (BC)

The German-Swiss in Franklin County, Tennessee: A Study of the Significance of Cultural Considerations in Farming Enterprises. Washington: U. S. Dept. of Agriculture, Bureau of Agricultural Economics, 1940.
K2990 (ASU BC)

Koon, William Henry "Folk Songs of Watauga." Ph. D. Diss. Univ. of Georgia, 1966.
K3000

Koontz, Louis Knott The Virginia Frontier, 1754-1763. Xerox copy of the original. Baltimore: Johns Hopkins Press, 1925.
K3010 (ASU BC)

Kopas, Frank A. Soil Survey, Fayette County, Pennsylvania. Prepared in cooperation with the Pennsylvania State University, Agricultural Experiment Station and Agricultural Extension Service, and Pennsylvania Department of Agriculture, State Soil and Water Conservation Commission. Washington: U. S. Soil Conservation Service, 1973.
K3020

Kornbluh, Joyce L. ed. Ferman, Louis A. ed. Poverty in America. Ann Arbor: Univ. of Michigan Press, 1965.
F690

Korson, George Gershon Black Land, the Way of Life in the Coal Fields. Evanston, Ill.: Row, Peterson, 1941.
K3030

Black Rock: Mining Folklore of the Pennsylvania Dutch. 1st ed. Baltimore: Johns Hopkins Press, 1960.
K3040 (ASU)

Coal Dust on the Fiddle: Songs and Stories of the Bituminous Industry. Foreword by John Greenway. Hatboro, Pa.: Folklore Associates, 1965. The foremost source on coal miner's songs.
K3050 (ASU LMC WCU BC)

Minstrels of the Mine Patch: Songs and Stories of the Anthracite Industry. Foreword by Archie Green. 1938. Reprint. Hatboro, Pa.: Folklore Associates, 1964.
K3060 (ASU LMC MHC BC)

Pennsylvania Songs and Legends. Philadelphia: Univ. of Pennsylvania Press, 1949.
K3070

Korstian, Clarence Ferdinand The Economic Development of the Furniture Industry of the South and Its Future Dependence Upon Forestry. Raleigh: North Carolina Department of Conservation and Development, 1926.
K3080 (LMC)

Kozee, William Carlos Early Families of Eastern and Southeastern Kentucky and Their Descendants. 1961. Reprint. Baltimore: Genealogical Pub. Co., 1973.
K3090 (ASU)

Pioneer Families of Eastern and Southeastern Kentucky. 1957. Reprint. Baltimore: Genealogical Pub. Co., 1973.
K3100 (ASU BC)

Kozsuch, Mildred Spaulding "A Study of the Use of Periodicals Received by the Dobyns-Bennett Senior High School Materials Center, Kingsport, Tennessee." Master's thesis. East Tennessee State Univ., 1969.
K3110 (ETSU)

Kraft, John Christian Morphologic and Systematic Relationships of Some Middle Ordovician Ostracoda. New York: n.p., 1962.
K3120 (ETSU)

Kramer, Loren W. Settlement Institutions in Southern Appalachia. Mineographed. n.p.: Atlantic Resource Project, Southern Regional Education Board, 1969.
K3130

Krassen, Miles Appalachian Fiddle. New York: Oak Publications, 1973. Contains old fiddle favorites and hard-to-find printed music for fiddlers.
K3140

Kraus, John F. The Olustee Arboretum Performance of 67 Species of Forest Trees. U. S. Forest Service Research Paper, no. SE-4. Asheville, N. C.: Southeastern Forest Experiment Station, 1963.
K3150 (WCU)

Kraus, Richard Folk Dancing. New York: The Macmillan Co., 1962.
K3160 (FC ASU)

Krause, Mary Lou "An Experimental Study of the Effect of an Individualized Reading Program on Third, Fourth, and Fifth Grade Students in the Thomas Jefferson School, Kingsport, Tennessee." Master's thesis. East Tennessee State Univ., 1966.
K3170 (ETSU)

Krebs, Charles E. Cabell, Wayne and Lincoln Counties. Wheeling: West Virginia Geological Survey, 1913.
K3180 (ETSU ASU)

Krebs, F. J. Harris, Evelyn L. K. From Humble Beginnings; West Virginia State Federation of Labor, 1903-1957. Charleston: Charleston, W. Va. Labor History Pub. Fund, 1960.
H2770 (BC)

Krebs, Frank J. Where there is Faith; The Morris Harvey College Story, 1888-1970. Charleston: The college, 1974.
K3190

Krebs, Friedrich Emigrants From the Palatinate to the American Colonies in the 18th Century. Introduction by Milton Rubincam. Special Study, no. 1. Norristown: Pennsylvania German Society, 1953.
K3200 (ASU)

Krechniak, Helen Bullard Cumberland County's First Hundred Years. Crossville, Tenn.: Centennial Committee, 1956.
K3210 (ASU ETSU LMC BC)

Krechniak, Joseph M. Bullard, Helen Cumberland County's First Hundred Years. Crossville: Cumberland Co. Centennial Committee, 1956.
B8340 (LMC)

Krechniak, Joseph Marshall Krechniak, Helen Bullard Cumberland County's First Hundred Years. Crossville, Tenn.: Centennial Committee, 1956.
K3210 (ASU ETSU LMC BC)

Kretsch, Jack Louis "Influence of Reservoir Projects on Land Values." Ph. D. Diss. Harvard Univ., 1963.
K3220

Krochmal, Arnold Guide to Medicinal Plants of Appalachia. Forest Service Research Paper, NE-138. Upper Darby, Pa.: Northeastern Forest Experiment Station, 1969.
K3230 (BC)

A Guide to Medicinal Plants of Appalachia. Washington: U. S. Forest Service, 1971.
K3240 (ASU ETSU LMC)

Kroll, Harry Harrison The Cabin in the Cotton. New York: R. Long and R. R. Smith, 1931. This Kroll novel, unlike his others, is only tangentially Appalachian.
K3250 (ASU BC)

Darker Grows the Valley. 1st ed. Indianapolis: Bobbs-Merrill Co., 1947. A saga of Tennessee's Clinch family from pioneer days to the coming of the TVA. A magnificent drama of eighteenth century values in conflict with the federal government.
K3260 (ASU LMC ETSU BC)

The Mountain Singer. New York: William Morrow and Co., 1928. A mountain boy finds his identity through music.
K3270 (BC ASU)

My Heart's in the Hills. Philadelphia: Westminster Press, 1956. A novel celebrating Kroll's love for the mountains.
K3280 (ASU BC)

The Rider on the Bronze Horse. New York: Bobbs-Merrill, 1942. Novel in which mountain characters and settings are incidental to the action of the novel.
K3290

The Smouldering Fire. New York: Ace Co., 1955. A novel based on the Breathitt County feuds.
K3300

Summer Gold. Philadelphia: Westminster Press, 1955. Only tangentially Appalachian.
K3310 (BC)

Their Ancient Grudge. 1st ed. Indianapolis: Bobbs-Merrill Co., 1946. A finely wrought novel based on the Hatfield-McCoy feud.
K3320 (ASU ETSU BC)

Three Brothers and Seven Daddies. New York: R. Long and R. R. Smith, 1932. Superstition flourishes in the shadow of Three Brothers and Seven Daddies until a young couple trapped in a cave are forced to apply logic to their superstition.
K3330 (ASU LMC BC)

Kruegel, David Leo "Metropolitan Dominance and the Diffusion of Human Fertility Patterns, Kentucky, 1939-65." Ph. D. Diss. Univ. of Kentucky, 1968.
K3340

Projected Kentucky Population Growth by Age, Sex, and Color Groups: 1960 to 1970. Bulletin no. 703. Lexington: Kentucky Agricultural Experiment Station, University of Kentucky, 1965.
K3350

Krueger, Daniel W. Wind Directions for Prescribed Burning in Southeastern United States. U. S. Forest Service Station Paper, no. 131. Asheville, N. C.: Southeastern Forest Experiment Station, 1961.
K3360 (WCU)

Kuhaida, Andrew Jerome, Jr. "Debris Avalanching as a Natural Hazard in the Southern Appalachians: A Case Study of the Davis Creek Watershed, Virginia." Master's thesis. East Tennessee State Univ., 1971.
K3370 (ETSU)

Kuhns, Levi Oscar The German and Swiss Settlements of Colonial Pennsylvania: A Study of the So-called Pennsylvania Dutch. New York: Abingdon Press, 1914.
K3380 (ASU)

Kull, Donald C. Budget Administration in the Tennessee Valley Authority. Master's thesis. Univ. of Minnesota, and Knoxville: Univ. of Tennessee Record, May 1948. A study sponsored by the Bureau of Research of the College of Business Administration and the Bureau of Public Administration, University of Tennessee.
K3390

Kunkin, Dorothy Appalachians in Cleveland. Cleveland: Institute of Urban Studies, 1972. A study of "Over-the-Rhine," a Cleveland ghetto for mountaineers.
K3400 (LMC ASU)

Kunkle, W. M. Ellyson, W. J. Soil Survey, Wood and Wirt Counties, West Virginia. Washington: U. S. Soil Conservation Service, 1970.
E1870

Kunz, George Frederick History of the Gems Found in North Carolina. Bulletin, no. 12. Raleigh: North Carolina Geological and Economic Survey, 1907.
K3410 (LMC)

Kupferer, Harriet J. The "Principal People", 1960: A Study of Cultural and Social Groups of the Eastern Cherokee. U. S. Bureau of American Ethnology Bulletin, no. 196. Also, Anthropological Papers, no. 78. Washington: Govt. Print. Off., 1966.
K3420 (WCU)

Kurtenacker, R. S. Appalachian Hardwoods for Pallets, Laboratory Evaluation. U. S. Forest Service Research Paper, FPL-76. Madison, Wis.: Forest Products Laboratory, 1967.
K3430

Kutsche, Rudolph Paul, Jr. "A Rorschach Comparison of Adult Male Personality in Big Cove, Cherokee, North Carolina, and "Henry's Branch', Kentucky." Ph. D. Diss. Univ. of Pennsylvania, 1961. A study of personality differentials between adult males in two isolated mountain communities.
K3440

Kuvlesky, William Peter "The Non-attainment of Adolescents' Occupational Aspirations: A Longitudinal Study of Rural Pennsylvania Males." Ph. D. Diss. Pennsylvania State Univ., 1965. Survey covers a number of mountain counties in Pennsylvania.
K3450

Kyger, M. E. Smith, Elmer L. The Pennsylvania Germans of the Shenandoah Valley. Allentown, Pa.: The Folklore Association, 1964.
S4620 (ASU)

Kyle, John H. The Building of TVA, an Illustrated History. 1st ed. Baton Rouge: Louisiana State Univ., 1958.
K3460 (ASU WCU LMC BC)

La Barre, Weston They Shall Take Up Serpents: Psychology of the Southern Snake-handling Cult. Minneapolis: Univ. of Minnesota Press, 1962. A documentary account of the Southern snake-handlers.
L10 (BC ASU WCU WWC)

They Shall Take Up Serpents: Psychology of the Southern Snake-handling Cult. New York: Schocken Books, 1962.
L20 (ASU)

Lacey, Anna Elizabeth "A Guidance Program for Elizabethton High School." Master's thesis. East Tennessee State College, 1957.
L30 (ETSU)

Lacy, Ann K. "A Survey of Physical Education Programs for Educable Mentally Retarded Students in Tennessee Public Elementary Schools." Master's thesis. East Tennessee State Univ., 1971.
L40 (ETSU)

Lacy, Dan ed. Historical Records Survey, North Carolina The Historical Records of North Carolina. Raleigh: The North Carolina Historical Commission, 1938.
H5730 (ASU LMC BC)

Lacy, Eric Russell "Sectionalism in East Tennessee, 1796 to 1861." Ph. D. Diss. Univ. of Georgia, 1963.
L50

Vanquished Volunteers: East Tennessee Sectionalism From Statehood to Secession. Johnson City: East Tennessee State Univ. Press, 1965.
L60 (LMC ETSU BC)

Ladd, H. S. Manganese Deposits of the Sweet Springs District, West Virginia and Virginia. U. S. Geological Survey, no. 940-G. Washington: Govt. Print. Off., 1944.
L70

Ladd, Robert A. "The Development of Education in Roane County, Tennessee." Master's thesis. Univ. of Tennessee, 1958.
L80

Ladd, William Mueller, Eva Migration into and out of Depressed Areas. Washington: Area Redevelopment Administration, 1964.
M8460

Lael, Ralph I. The Brown Mountain Lights. n.p.: The author, 1965. A nonsensical space fantasy written as an explanation of the Brown Mountain Lights, an ancient and mysterious North Carolina phenomena.
L90 (ASU LMC)

Lafky, John Delmar "Tennessee Valley Authority 1933 to 1960: An Investigation of Progress." Master's thesis. Univ. of Texas, 1960.
L100

Laing, James T. The Drain of Talent Out of the Virginias. Morgantown: West Virginia Academy of Science, 1938.
L110

A Further Note on the Drain of Talent Out of the Virginias. Morgantown: West Virginia Academy of Science, 1939.
L120

"The Negro Miner in West Virginia." Ph. D. Diss. Ohio State Univ., 1933.
L130

Lainhart, William S. Pneumoconiosis in Appalachian Bituminous Coal Miners. Washington: Bureau of Occupational Safety and Health, 1969.
L150

Lainhart, William S. and others Pneumoconiosis in Appalachian Bituminous Coal Miners. Public Health Service Publication, no. 2000. Washington: U. S. Bureau of Occupational Health and Safety, Consumer Protection and Environmental Health Service, 1969. A study of the major health problem in coal fields.
L140 (ASU)

Lair, John Renfro Valley; Then and Now. n.p.: n.p., 1957. A study of Renfro Valley's contributions to country music and dance.
L160

Lamar, Ralph E. "Fundamentalism and Selected Social Factors in the Southern Appalachian Region." Microfilm. Master's thesis. Univ. of Kentucky, 1962.
L170 (ASU)

Lambert, Darwin Seymour The Earthman Story, Starring Shenandoah Skyline. 1st ed. Shenandoah Natural History Association Bulletin, no. 6. An Exposition Banner Book. New York: Exposition Press, 1972. Focuses attention on the social, recreational and conservational roles of the Skyline.
L180 (BC ASU MHC)

Lambert, H. D. Burke, Richard Thomas Avon Soil Survey of Alleghany County. Washington: Govt. Print. Off., 1917.
B8680

Lambert, Oscar Doane West Virginia and its Government. Boston: Heath, 1951.
L190

Lambert, Stella Wilson Along Came the Other Girl; a Story of Love and Adventure in Pre-Revolutionary Virginia. New York: American Press, 1961. Romantic fiction from frontier Virginia.
L200

Lambert, Walter Holmes, Jack E. Structure of County Government in Tennessee. n.p.: n.p., n.d.
H6800

Lambert, Walter N. Governments in Knox County. Knoxville: Univ. of Tennessee, 1965.
L210 (ETSU)

Lambie, Joseph T. From Mine to Market: The History of Coal Transportation on the Norfolk and Western Railway. Graduate School of Business Administration. Business History Series. New York: New York Univ. Press, 1954.
L220 (ASU BC)

"The Norfolk and Western Railroad, 1881-1896: A Study in Coal Transportation." Ph. D. Diss. Harvard Univ., 1948.
L230

Lamont, W. E. Resource and Beneficiation Studies of Copperbearing Pyrite Ore, Pyriton, Clay County, Alabama. Circular, 27. Univ.: Alabama Geological Survey, 1964.
L240 (ETSU)

Lancaster, Bruce Night March. 1st ed. Boston: Little, Brown, 1958. Novel with an Appalachian setting and a wartime backdrop.
L250 (ASU BC WCU)

No Bugles Tonight. 1st ed. Boston: Little, Brown, 1948. Action-packed novel with a wartime Appalachian setting.
L260 (ASU)

Lancaster, John L. Personal Income Estimates for Virginia Counties and Cities, 1955. Charlottesville: Univ. of Va., Bureau of Population and Economic Research, 1958. Includes western Virginia towns and counties.
L270

"Some Economic Aspects of the Changes in Towns County Agriculture during the Period, 1934-1950." Master's thesis. Univ. of Georgia, 1952.
L280

Lancour, Harold A Bibliography of Ship Passenger Lists, 1538-1825: Being a Guide to Published Lists of Early Immigrants to North America. 3rd ed. Revised and enlarged by Richard J. Wolfe. With a list of passenger arrival records in the National Archives by Frank E. Bridger. New York: New York Public Library, 1963.
L290 (ASU)

"Land of the Sky" and The Great Smoky Mountains National Park Asheville, N. C.: Great Smoky Mountains Pub. Co., 1929.
L300 (UNCA ASU)

Landmarks; a Pictorial History of DeKalb Co., Ala. n.p.: Landmarks of DeKalb Co., Inc., 1971.
L310

Landrum, John Belton O'Neall Colonial and Revolutionary History of Upper South Carolina, Embracing for the Most Part the Primitive and Colonial History of the Territory Comprising the Original County of Spartanburg with a General Review of the Entire Military Operations in the Upper Portion of South Carolina and Portions of North Carolina. 1897. Reprint. South Carolina Heritage Series, no. 1. Spartanburg, S. C.: Reprint Co., 1959.
L320 (ASU WCU LMC BC)

Colonial and Revolutionary History of Upper South Carolina. 1897. Reprint. Spartanburg, S. C.: Reprint Co., 1971.
L330 (LMC)

History of Spartanburg County: Embracing an Account of Many Important Events, and Biographical Sketches of Statesmen, Divines and Other Public Men. 1900. Reprint. South Carolina Heritage Series, no. 2. Spartanburg, S. C. Reprint Co., 1960.
L340 (ASU BC)

Lane, Billy Joe "Some Factors Affecting School Attendance as a Family Problem, as Revealed by a Comparison of Two Groups of Families in Washington County, Tennessee, 1951-1952." Master's thesis. East Tennessee State College, 1952.
L350 (ETSU)

Lane, Charles Franklin "Physiography of the Grassy Cove District, Cumberland County, Tennessee." Ph. D. Diss. Northwestern Univ., 1952.
L360 (LMC)

Lane, Rose Wilder Hill-billy. New York: Grosset and Dunlap, 1926. A humorous but derogatory novel about mountaineers.
L370 (ASU BC)

Lane, Winthrop David Civil War in West Virginia: A Story of the Industrial Conflict in the Coal Mines. With an introduction by John R. Commons. 1921. Reprint. The Freeman Pamphlets. New York: Arno Press, 1969.
L380 (ASU BC)

Laney, F. B. Emmons, W. H. Geology and Ore Deposits of the Ducktown Mining District, Tennessee. Washington: Govt. Print. Off., 1926.
E1960 (ASU BC)

Laney, Francis Baker Bibliography of North Carolina Geology, Mineralogy, and Geography, with a List of Maps. North Carolina Geological Survey Bulletin, no. 18. Raleigh: E. M. Uzzell and Co., 1909.
L390 (ASU LMC WWC ETSU)

The Geology and Ore Deposits of the Virgilina District of Virginia and North Carolina. North Carolina Department of Conservation and Development Bulletin, no. 26. Also, Virginia Geological Survey Bulletin, 14. Lynchburg, Va.: J. P. Bell, 1917.
L400 (ETSU ASU)

The Gold Hill Mining District of North Carolina. North Carolina Department of Conservation and Development Bulletin, no. 21. Raleigh: Edwards and Broughton Print Co., 1910.
L410 (LMC ETSU)

Laney, R. L. Dodson, Chester Lee Geology and Ground-water Resources of the Murphy Area, North Carolina. Raleigh: n.p., 1968.
D2760 (WCU)

Lang, Theodore F. Loyal W. Va. from 1861 to 1865. Baltimore: Deutsch Pub. Co., 1895.
L420

Langley, John Wesley They Tried to Crucify Me; or, the Smokescreen of the Cumberlands. Pikesville, Ky.: The author, 1929. Biography of a man falsely accused and publicly abused on hearsay evidence.
L430

Langman, R. C. Appalachian Kentucky, an Exploited Region. Selected Studies in the United States. Toronto: McGraw-Hill Ryerson, 1971. Deals with absentee ownership of Kentucky's natural resources.
L440 (ETSU)

Langstaff, John comp. Langstaff, Nancy comp. Jim Along, Josie; a Collection of Folk Songs and Singing Games for Young Children. New York: Harcourt, Brace, Jovanovich, Inc., 1970.
L470 (ASU)

Langstaff, John M. Hi Ho The Rattlin' Hog and other Folk Songs for Group Singing. Selected by John Langstaff. Piano settings by John Edmunds and others. Guitar chords suggested by Happy Traum. Illustrated by Robin Jacques. N. Y.: Harcourt, Brace, and World, 1969. Not primarily Appalachian.
L450

The Swapping Boy. Illustrated by Beth and Joe Krush. 1st ed. New York: Harcourt, Brace, 1960. Mountain folk songs arranged for children.
L460 (ASU)

Langstaff, Nancy comp. Jim Along, Josie; a Collection of Folk Songs and Singing Games for Young Children. Piano arrangement by Seymour Berah. Guitar chords by Happy Traum. Illustrated by Jan Pienkowski. New York: Harcourt, Brace, Jovanovich, Inc., 1970.
L470 (ASU)

Lanham, Robert Eugene "The West Virginia Statehouse Democratic Machine; Structure, Function and Process." Master's thesis. Claremont College, 1971.
L480

Lanier, Ruby Jeanne "Blanford Barnard Dougherty: Mountain Educator." Ed. D. Diss. Duke Univ., 1971.
L490 (ASU)

Blanford Barnard Dougherty, Mountain Educator. Durham, N. C.: Duke Univ. Press, 1974.
L500 (ASU)

Lanier, Sidney The Centennial Edition of the Works of Sidney Lanier. 10 vols. Baltimore: Johns Hopkins Press, 1945. Lanier wrote one novel and several poems about the mountains.
L510 (MHC)

Tiger-lilies: A Novel. New York: Hurd and Houghton, 1867.
L520 (ASU)

Tiger-lilies: A Novel. Introduction by Richard Harwell. Southern Literary Series. Chapel Hill: Univ. of North Carolina Press, 1969. A romantic Civil War novel in the florid German tradition set in Pike County, Tennessee. Cain and Gorn Smallin are realistically drawn mountain characters.
L530 (ASU ETSU)

Lankford, Jesse R. "The Campaign for a National Park in Western North Carolina, 1885-1940." Master's thesis. Western Carolina Univ., 1973.
L540 (WCU)

Lanman, Charles Adventures in the Wilds of the United States and British American Provinces. Appendix by Campbell Hardy. 2 vols. Philadelphia: John W. Moore, 1856. Includes descriptions of travel in Appalachia.
L550 (LMC)

Letters from the Allegheny Mountains. New York: Putnam, 1849. The record of a trip from Dahlonega, Georgia to Harper's Ferry, West Virginia.
L560 (LMC ASU BC)

Lansing, Elizabeth Carleton Hubbard Rider on the Mountains. New York: Crowell, 1949. A Boston society girl volunteers for a tour of duty with Kentucky's Frontier Nursing Service. As she proves herself, she becomes sympathetic to the mountain folks.
L570

Shoot for a Mule. New York: Thomas Y. Crowell Co., 1951. A story of youth, poverty and ambition set in the Cumberland mountains.
L580

Lansinger, Sarah Lucille "A Distributive Education Program for Washington County, Tennessee, High Schools Based on an Occupational Survey of the County." Master's thesis. East Tennessee State Univ., 1965.
L590 (ETSU)

Lantz, Herman R. People of Coal Town. With the assistance of J. C. McCrary. New York: Columbia Univ. Press, 1958. A haunting description of life in an Appalachian coal camp.
L600 (ASU BC WWC WCU)

People of Coal Town. Carbondale: Southern Ill. Univ. Press, 1971.
L610 (LMC)

Lapham, Jesse Erwin Soil Survey of the Asheville, North Carolina, Area. Field Operations, 1903. Washington: U. S. Department of Agriculture, Bureau of Soils, 1904.
L620

Lapsley, Robert A., Jr. Home Mission Investments. Richmond: John Knox Press, 1946.
L630 (LMC)

Large, Mary Harriott The Twelfth Juror. Boston: C. M. Clark Pub. Co., 1908. A young man, reared outside the mountains returns home to find himself elected foreman of a jury in the trial of a mountain man for an unusual murder.
L640 (BC ASU)

Larsen, Christian L. South Carolina's Natural Resources: A Study in Public Administration. Columbia: Univ. of South Carolina Press, 1947.
L650 (ASU)

Lart, Charles Edmund Huguenot Pedigrees. 1924-48. Reprint. 2 vols. in 1. Baltimore: Genealogical Pub. Co., 1967.
L660 (ASU)

Lathrop, Frank H. The Old Naturalist's Notebook: Wild Flowers of the Appalachian. Asheville, N. C.: Asheville-Biltmore Botanical Gardens, 1968.
L670 (UNCA ASU)

Latimer, Elizabeth Wormeley Our Cousin Veronica; or, Scenes and Adventures over the Blue Ridge. New York: Bunce and Brothers, 1855. Period fiction in which stereotypical mountaineers move across a set stage.
L680

Latimer, Ira S., Jr. Gillespie, William H. Plant Fossils of West Virginia. Morgantown: West Virginia Geological and Economic Survey, 1966.
G1650 (BC ETSU)

Latimer, William James Soil Survey of Barbour and Upshur Counties, West Virginia. Prepared in cooperation with the West Virginia Geological Survey. Field Operations, 1917. Washington: U. S. Department of Agriculture, Bureau of Soils, 1923.
L690

Soil Survey of Boone County, West Virginia. In cooperation with the West Virginia Geological Survey. Field Operations, 1913. Washington: U. S. Department of Agriculture, Bureau of Soils, 1915.
L700

Soil Survey of Braxton and Clay Counties, West Virginia. Prepared in cooperation with the West Virginia Geological Survey. Field Operations, 1918. Washington: U. S. Department of Agriculture, Bureau of Soils, 1920.
L710

Soil Survey of Jefferson, Berkeley, and Morgan Counties, West Virginia. Prepared in cooperation with the West Virginia Geological Survey. Field Operations, 1916. Washington: U. S. Department of Agriculture, Bureau of Soils, 1921.
L720

Soil Survey of Kanawha County, West Virginia. Prepared in cooperation with the West Virginia Geological Survey. Field Operations, 1912. Washington: U. S. Department of Agriculture, Bureau of Soils, 1914.
L730

Soil Survey of Lewis and Gilmer Counties, West Virginia. Prepared in cooperation with the West Virginia Geological Survey. Field Operations, 1915. Washington: U. S. Department of Agriculture, Bureau of Soils, 1917.
L740

Soil Survey of Logan and Mingo Counties, West Virginia. In cooperation with the West Virginia Geological Survey. Field Operations, 1913. Washington: U. S. Department of Agriculture, Bureau of Soils, 1915.
L750

Soil Survey of McDowell and Wyoming Counties, West Virginia. Prepared in cooperation with the West Virginia Geological Survey. Field Operations, 1914. Washington: U. S. Department of Agriculture, Bureau of Soils, 1916.
L760

Soil Survey of Preston County, West Virginia. Prepared in cooperation with the West Virginia Geological Survey. Field Operations, 1912. Washington: U. S. Department of Agriculture, Bureau of Soils, 1914.
L770

Soil Survey of Raleigh County, West Virginia. Prepared in cooperation with the West Virginia Geological Survey. Field Operations, 1914. Washington: U. S. Department of Agriculture, Bureau of Soils, 1916.
L780

Soil Survey of the Huntington Area, West Virginia. In cooperation with the West Virginia Geological Survey. Field Operations, 1911. Washington: U. S. Department of Agriculture, Bureau of Soils, 1912.
L800

Latimer, William James
Soil Survey of the Point Pleasant, West Virginia, Area. Prepared in cooperation with the West Virginia Geological Survey. Field Operations, 1910. Washington: U. S. Department of Agriculture, Bureau of Soils, 1911.
L810
Soil Survey of the Spencer, West Virginia, Area. Prepared in cooperation with the West Virginia Geological Survey. Field Operations, 1909. Washington: U. S. Department of Agriculture, Bureau of Soils, 1910.
L820
McLendon, Willie E. Soil Survey of Oconee County, South Carolina. Washington: U. S, Department of Agriculture, Bureau of Soils, 1909.
M2060
Meeker, Fred N. Soil Survey of the Parkersburg Area, West Virginia. Washington: U. S. Department of Agriculture, Bureau of Soils, 1909.
M4920
Winston, Robert A. Soil Survey of Tuscaloosa County, Alabama. Washington: U. S. Department of Agriculture, Bureau of Soils, 1912.
W7820

Latimer, William James and others Soil Survey of Spartanburg County, South Carolina. Field Operations, 1921. Washington: U. S. Department of Agriculture, Bureau of Soils, 1926.
L790

Laughrun, Clark Jan "A Study of the Blue Ridge Job Corps Center." Master's thesis. East Tennessee State Univ., 1969.
L830 (ETSU)

Lauritzen, Mrs. J. R. Some Sketches from My Life, Written for My 80th Birthday, May 1, 1910. Knoxville: n.p., 1910.
L840

Law, Alton Dennis "Types, Quantities and Destinations of West Virginia's Manufactured Exports, an Exploratory Study." Master's thesis. West Virginia Univ., 1964.
L850

Law, Harry Lavegia A Brief Geography of Tennessee. Clarksville, Tenn.: Queen City Book Co., 1949.
L860 (ASU)

Lawhon, William T. "Radial Growth and Wood Density of White Pine in Relation to Coal-Derived Environmental Pollutants." Ph. D. Diss. Univ. of Tennessee, 1973. Study concludes pine density was affected but not radial growth.
L870

Lawless, Ray McKinley Folksingers and Folksongs in America. New York: Duell, Sloan and Co., 1960.
L880 (BC)
Folksingers and Folksongs in America: A Handbook of Biography, Bibliography, and Discography. Illustrated from paintings by Thomas Hart Benton and others and from designs in Steuben glass. New rev. ed. with special supplement. New York: Duell, Sloan and Pearce, 1965.
L890 (ASU WWC BC)

Lawrence, Elizabeth L. A Southern Garden: A Handbook for the Middle South. Rev. ed. 1942. Reprint. Chapel Hill: Univ. of North Carolina Press, 1967.
L900 (ASU)

Lawrence, Mildred Walk a Rocky Road. New York: Harcourt, Brace, Jovanovich, 1971. An Appalachian girl who can't afford to go to college finds an unexpected opportunity to open up the gates of her small insular world.
L910 (LMC)

Lawritis, Eve-Malle ed. Appalachian Legal Services Conference, Knoxville, Tenn. 1969 Papers and Proceedings of Appalachian Legal Services Conference, Knoxville, Tenn., July 24-26, 1969. Chicago: National Legal Aid and Defender Association, 1969.
A3230 (BC)

Laws, George Malcolm American Balladry from British Broadsides: A Guide for Students and Collectors of Traditional Song. Bibliographical and Special Series, vol. 8. Philadelphia: American Folklore Society, 1957.
L920 (BC ASU)
Native American Balladry, a Descriptive Study and a Bibliographical Syllabus. Rev. ed. Philadelphia: American Folklore Society, 1964.
L930 (FC)

Laws of the Cherokee Nation: Adopted by the Council at Various Periods, 1808-1835. Printed for the Benefit of the Nation. Tahlequah, N. C.: Cherokee Advocate, 1852.
L940

Lawson, Ernest Marshall Awakening. Of Cumberland County on the Last Fifty Years. Burkesville, Ky.: Cumberland County Pub. Co., 1973.
L950 (ASU BC)

Lawson, Inez R. Kingsport, Tennessee. John Sevier Junior High School "Flexible Scheduling in Secondary Schools." East Tennessee State University, 1968.
K2530 (ETSU)
"Flexible Scheduling in Secondary Schools." Master's thesis. East Tennessee State Univ., 1968.
L960 (ETSU)

Lawson, John History of North Carolina, Containing the Exact Description and Natural History of That Country, Together with the Present State Thereof, and a Journal of a Thousand Miles Traveled Through Several Nations of Indians, Giving a Particular Account of Their Customs, Manners, Etc., Etc. 1709. Reprint. 2nd ed. (Original title: A New Voyage to Carolina.) Richmond: Garrett and Massie, 1952.
L970 (LMC MHC BC)
History of North Carolina, Containing the Exact Description and Natural History of that Country, Together with the Present State Thereof, and a Journal of a Thousand Miles Traveled through Several Nations of Indians, Giving a Particular Account of Their Customs, Manners, Etc., Etc. London: Printed for W. Taylor at the Ship, and F. Baker at the Black Boy, in Pater-Noster Row, 1714. 3rd ed. Richmond: Garrett and Massie, 1951 and 1960.
L980 (UNCA)
History of North Carolina, Containing the Exact Description and Natural History of That Country, Together with the Present State Thereof and a Journal of a Thousand Miles Traveled Through Several Nations of Indians, Giving Particular Account of Their Customs, Manners, Etc. 1709. Reprint. Richmond: Garrett and Massie, 1960.
L990 (WWC ASU)
A New Voyage to Carolina. 1709. Reprint. March of America Facsimile Series, no. 35. Ann Arbor: Univ. Microfilms, 1966.
L1000 (LMC ETSU)
A New Voyage to Carolina. Chapel Hill: Univ. of North Carolina Press, 1967.
L1010 (UNCA)

Lawson, Laura Bennett Leonora, A Tale of the Great Smokies. New York: Neale Pub. Co., 1904. An abandoned woman stumbles into Asheville and dies of childbirth and grief. The daughter discovers this at the death of her stepmother and sets out to avenge her mother. By the time she discovers her father, her anger has burned itself out.
L1020

Lawson, Michael Edwin "A Program of Visual Instruction for Use in Teaching the Location of Major Resources in the East Tennessee State University Library." Master's thesis. East Tennessee State Univ., 1969.
L1030 (ETSU)

Lawson, W. B. The Hatfield-McCoy Feud. New York: Street and Smith, 1898. A romanticized version of the Hatfield-McCoy feud.
L1040
The Hatfield-McCoy Vendetta. New York: Street and Smith, 1894. An account of forty years of feuding along the Kentucky-West Virginia line.
L1050

Lawton, Mrs. James M. comp. Family Names of Huguenot Refugees to America. Baltimore: Genealogical Pub. Co., 1963.
L1060 (ASU)

Lay, Elery Arnold "An Industrial and Commercial History of the Tri-cities in Tennessee." Ed. D. Diss. George Peabody College for Teachers, 1960.
L1070

Laycock, George Big Nick: The Story of a Remarkable Black Bear. Illustrated by Nancy Grossman. 1st ed. New York: W. W. Norton, 1967. A big black bear with a colorful personality roams the Appalachians.
L1080 (ASU BC)
The Diligent Destroyers. 1st ed. Garden City, N. Y.: Doubleday, 1970. An attack on agencies and industries who are destroying our environment.
L1090 (ASU WCU)

Layne, Ora Sequatchie County: History and Development. Dunlap: The author, 1969.
L1100

Layne, Raymond Lee Descendants of Isham Lane. Madison Co., Ky.: Valley Station, Ky., 1966. Saga and genealogy of one of Kentucky's pioneer families.
L1110

Lazenby, Mary Elinor comp. Catawba Frontier, 1775-1781: Memories of Pensioners. Washington: The author, 1950.
L1120 (ASU BC)

Leach, MacEdward The Ballad Book. New York: Harper, 1955.
L1130 (ASU)
The Ballad Book. New York: A. S. Barnes, 196-.
L1140 (WCU)
A Guide for Collectors of Oral Traditions. n.p.: Penn. Historical and Museum Commission, 1968.
L1150

Leach, Maria God Had a Dog: Folklore of the Dog. New Brunswick, N. J.: Rutgers Univ. Press, 1961.
L1160 (ASU)
How the People Sang the Mountains Up: How and Why Stories. Illustrated by Glen Rounds. New York: Viking Press, 1967.
L1170 (ASU)
The Rainbow Book of American Folk Tales and Legends. Illustrated by Marc Simon. 1st ed. Cleveland: World Pub. Co., 1958.
L1180 (ASU FC)

League of Women Voters, Boone, N. C. Handbook of Watauga County. Boone, N. C.: The league, 1967.
L1190 (ASU LMC)
This is Our Town: Boone, N. C. Boone, N. C.: The league, 1964.
L1200 (LMC ASU)

League of Women Voters, Kingsport, Tenn. A Survey of Social Services in the Greater Kingsport Area. Kingsport, Tenn.: The league, 1948.
L1210 (ETSU)

Leather Stocking and Silk; or Hunter John Meyers and His Times New York: Harper and Brothers, 1854.
L1220

Leatherman, Martin Conrey, Guy Woolard Soil Survey, Scioto County, Ohio. Washington: U. S. Dept. of Agriculture, Bureau of Plant Industry, 1940.
C6780 ()

Leavell, Frank Hartwell "The Literary Career of Jesse Stuart." Microfilm. Ph. D. Diss. Vanderbilt Univ., 1965.
L1230 (ASU)

Leavitt, Mrs. Sturgis Ellens ed. Stories and Poems From the Old North State. Durham, N. C.: Seeman, 1923.
L1240 (LMC)

Leavy, Thomas A. "Agricultural Regions of Clarion County, Pennsylvania." Master's thesis. Pennsylvania State Univ., 1952.
L1250

Lebus, William F., Jr. Economic Data on Eastern Kentucky Coal Field. Frankfort: The author, 1956.
L1260

LeConte, Joseph The Autobiography of Joseph LeConte. New York: D. Appleton and Co., 1903. Mt. LeConte was named for this early explorer.
L1270 (BC ASU LMC)

Lederer, John The Discoveries of John Lederer. 1672. Reprint. March of America Facsimile Series, no. 25. Ann Arbor: Univ. Microfilms, 1966.
L1280 (LMC)

The Discoveries of John Lederer, in Three Several Marches From Virginia, to the West of Carolina, and Other Parts of the Continent: Begun in March 1669, and Ended in September 1670. Together with a general map of the whole territory which he traversed. Collected and translated out of Latine from his discourse and writings, by Sir William Talbot, baronet. 1672. Reprint. Rochester, N. Y.: G. P. Humphrey, 1902.
L1290 (ASU FC BC)

The Discoveries of John Lederer, with Unpublished Letters By and About Lederer to Governor John Winthrop, Jr. 1792. Reprint. An Essay on the Indians of Lederer's Discoveries by Douglas L. Rights and William Patterson Cummings. Edited with notes by William Patterson Cummings. Charlottesville: Univ. of Virginia Press, 1958.
L1300 (ASU WCU ETSU)

Lee, Betty Arrowood "A Study of the Academic Achievement of Kindergarten and Non-kindergarten Children in a Rural School in Appalachia." Master's thesis. East Tennessee State Univ., 1972.
L1310 (ETSU)

Lee, Chi Yuen "The Impact of TVA on Agriculture." Master's thesis. Univ. of Tennessee, 1949.
L1320

Lee, Enoch Lawrence Indian Wars In North Carolina, 1663-1763. Raleigh, N. C.: Carolina Charter Tercentenary Commission, 1963.
L1330 (ASU LMC ETSU WWC BC UNCA)

Lee, George Taylor A Virginia Feud: The Story of a Mountain Lassie. New York: Neale Pub. Co., 1908. A young surveyor meets a mountain girl and finds it difficult to be accepted by her family.
L1340 (ASU BC)

Lee, Howard Burton Bloodletting in Appalachia: The Story of West Virginia's Four Major Mine Wars and Other Thrilling Incidents of Its Coal Fields. Morgantown: West Virginia Univ., 1969.
L1350 (ASU WCU LMC BC MHC)

The Burning Springs, and Other Tales of the Little Kanawha. Morgantown: West Virginia Univ., 1968.
L1360 (ASU BC)

My Appalachia: Pipestem State Park Today and Yesterday. Parsons, W. Va.: McClain Print. Co., 1971.
L1370 (ASU BC ETSU LMC)

Lee, Jesse Memoir of the Rev. Jesse Lee. With Extracts From His Journals. 1823. Reprint. New York: Arno Press, 1969.
L1380 (ASU FC)

Lee, K. Y. Geologic Map of the Maulden Quadrangle, Southeastern Kentucky. Washington, D. C.: Geological Survey, 1974.
L1390

Lee, Lewey K. "An Analysis of Particulate Pollution in Johnson City and Rural Washington County, Tennessee." Master's thesis. East Tennessee State Univ., 1971.
L1400 (ETSU)

Lee, Marguerite du Pont Virginia Ghosts. Rev. ed. Berryville, Va.: Virginia Book Co., 1966. Some of these tales are set in the Virginia mountains.
L1410 (FC ASU BC)

Lee, Mary Law "The Influence of Geography on the Growth of Chattanooga Industries." Master's thesis. Vanderbilt Univ., 1931.
L1420

Lee, W. D. Jurney, Robert Campbell Soil Survey of Cherokee County, North Carolina. Washington: U. S. Department of Agriculture, Bureau of Soils, 1926.
J2860 (ASU)

Lee, William Daniel Jurney, Robert Campbell Soil Survey of Rutherford County, North Carolina.
J2910

Soil Survey of Burke County. Washington: Govt. Print. Off., 1926.
L1430

Soil Survey of Burke County, North Carolina. In cooperation with the North Carolina Department of Agriculture and the North Carolina Agricultural Experiment Station. Soil Survey Report, Series 1926, no. 22. Washington: U. S. Department of Agriculture, Bureau of Chemistry and Soils, 1930.
L1440

Soil Survey, Yadkin County, North Carolina. In cooperation with the North Carolina Department of Agriculture and the North Carolina Agricultural Experiment Station. Soil Survey Report, Series 1924, no. 1. Washington: U. S. Department of Agriculture, Bureau of Chemistry and Soils, 1928.
L1450

Lee, William E. Haiku and Tanka. Penacook, N. H.: Sunburst Anthology Press, 1973. Lee is a Watauga County, North Carolina poet.
L1460 (ASU)

Leeder, Joseph A. Thomas, Jeannette Bell The Singin' Gatherin': Tunes From the Southern Appalachians. New York: Silver Burdett Co., 1939.
T7940 (UNCA BC ETSU ASU)

Thomas, Jeannette Bell The Singin' Gatherin': Tunes From the Southern Appalachians. New York: Silver Burdett, 1939.
T7950 (LMC BC)

Leeper, Louise South "Development of a Comprehension Skills Program for the Primary Educable Mentally Retarded Class in Kingsport, Tennessee." Master's thesis. East Tennessee State Univ., 1966.
L1470 (ETSU)

Lees-McRae College, Banner Elk, N. C. Report on Its Institutional Self-study for the Commission on Colleges and Universities, Southern Association, 1962-63. Banner Elk, N. C.: The college, 1964.
L1480 (LMC)

LeFevre, Laura Zenobia Stoke of Brier Hill. Cleveland, Tenn.: Pathway Press, 1962. A rather Southern interpretation of the mountain country.
L1490 (BC)

Leffard, Warren Lee "Employment Opportunities and Training Needs for Technicians in the Metalworking Manufacturing Industries of the Central Ohio Valley with Projections through 1975." Ed. D. Diss. Univ. of Missouri, Columbia, 1968.
L1500

Lefferts, Walter The Taming of the Tennessee: Continued Study Units in Geographic Backgrounds. Philadelphia: Davis, 1941.
L1510

Lefler, Hugh Talmage A Guide to the Study and Reading of North Carolina History. Chapel Hill: Univ. of North Carolina Press, 1955.
L1520 (LMC)

A Guide to the Study and Reading of North Carolina History. Rev. ed. Chapel Hill: Univ. of North Carolina Press, 1963.
L1530 (UNCA ASU)

A Guide to the Study and Reading of North Carolina History. 3rd ed. Chapel Hill: Univ. of North Carolina Press, 1969.
L1540 (LMC)

History of North Carolina. 4 vols. New York: Lewis Historical Pub. Co., 1956.
L1550 (BC LMC UNCA)

North Carolina, the History of a Southern State. Chapel Hill: Univ. of North Carolina Press, 1954.
L1570 (UNCA WWC)

North Carolina, the History of a Southern State. Rev. ed. Chapel Hill: Univ. of North Carolina Press, 1963.
L1580 (BC FC ASU LMC)

Lefler, Hugh Talmage ed. North Carolina History Told by Contemporaries. Chapel Hill: Univ. of North Carolina Press, 1934.
L1560 (BC LMC WWC)

Leftwich, Nina Two Hundred Years at Muscle Shoals Being an Authentic History of Colbert County, 1700-1900. Tuscumbia, Ala.: n.p., 1935.
L1590

Leftwich, Rodney L. Arts and Crafts of the Cherokee. Cullowhee, N. C.: Land-of-the-Sky Press, 1970.
L1600 (UNCA ASU WCU LMC ETSU BC)

Legislative Work Conference on Southern Regional Education Technical-Vocational Education and the Community College. Williamsburg, Va.: Proceedings of the Thirteen Annual Conference, 1964.
L1610

Lehman, John William Changing Sawmill Industry; a Status Report on 58 Circular Sawmills in the Tennessee Valley, 1950-60. Norris, Tenn.: TVA, 1961.
L1620

Products from Hickory Bolts. Hickory Task Force Report, no. 6. Asheville, N. C.: Southeastern Forest Experiment Station, 1958.
L1630 (WCU)

Leibel, Irene Hope Look Back Into Your Mighty Ancestors. Lincoln, Nebr.: n.p., n.d.
L1640

Leidheiser, Henry, Jr. ed. Hughes, Roscoe Durall Exploring Virginia's Human Resources. Charlottesville: Univ. Press of Virginia, 1965.
H8120 (ASU BC)

Leighton, Marshall Ora The Relation of the Southern Appalachian Mountains to Inland Water Navigation. U. S. Forest Service Circular, 143. Washington: Govt. Print. Off., 1908.
L1650 (BC ASU)

The Relation of the Southern Appalachian Mountains to the Development of Water Power. U. S. Forest Service Circular, 144. Washington: Govt. Print. Off., 1908.
L1660 (ASU BC)

Leighty, Ralph G. Porter, Hobart Clarke Soil Survey, Tazewell County, Virginia. Washington: U. S. Department of Agriculture, Bureau of Plant Industry, Soils, and Agricultural Engineering, 1948.
P3660

Leighty, W. J. Robinson, Glenn Hugh Soil Survey, Avery County, North Carolina. Washington: U. S. Soil Conservation Service, 1955.
R3290

Leighty, Willis Jay and others Soil Survey, Watauga County, North Carolina. U. S. Soil Conservation Service, Soil Survey, Series 1944, no. 5. Washington: Govt. Print. Off., 1958.
L1670

Leininger, Mary "The Regionalist Movement in the Cumberland." Master's thesis. Ohio State Univ., 1942. An account of the brief literary regionalistic movement in Appalachia and its few political implications.
L1680 (ASU)

Leisy, Ernest E. ed. Kennedy, John Pendleton Horse-shoe Robinson. New York: American Book Company, 1937.
K760 (WCU ASU)

Lemaster, Jimmie Ray "Jesse Stuart: Kentucky's Chronicler-poet." Ph. D. Diss. Bowling Green State Univ., 1970.
L1690

Lemert, Benjamin Franklin The Cotton Textile Industry of the Southern Appalachian Piedmont. Chapel Hill: Univ. of North Carolina Press, 1933.
L1700 (BC ASU ETSU)

Lemert, Benjamin Franklin
North Carolina Geography: A Study of How We Live in North Carolina. Oklahoma City: Harlow Pub. Corp., 1954. Includes material on the 28 western counties.
L1710 (LMC ASU)

Lemmon, Robert E. "Geology of the Bat Cave and Fuitland Quadrangles and the Origin of the Henderson Gneiss, Western North Carolina." Ph. D. Diss. Univ. of North Carolina, 1973. The first detailed study of Henderson County's remarkable geologic formations.
L1720

Lemmon, Sarah McCullah ed. Haywood, Marshall Delancey Builders of the Old North State: Selected Sketches. Raleigh: The compiler, 1968.
H4060 (LMC)

Lemmon, Sarah McCulloh Frustrated Patriots: North Carolina and the War of 1812. Chapel Hill: Univ. of North Carolina Press, 1973.
L1730 (MHC)

Lemond, Thomas Addison "The Good Government League and Polk County Politics, 1946-1965." Master's thesis. Vanderbilt Univ., 1970. Polk County has one of bloodiest, most entrenched and most patriarchal political machines in America.
L1740

Lemons, James "A Study of the Working Relationships of the Agriculture Extension Service and the Vocational Agriculture Program in East Tennessee." Master's thesis. Univ. of Tennessee, 1958.
L1750

Lenoir, N. C., Chamber of Commerce The Lenoir-Blowing Rock Wonderland. Lenoir, N. C.: The chamber, 1926. Promotional material on the Lenoir-Blowing Rock Tourist attractions.
L1760 (ASU)

Lenoir, William B. History of Sweetwater Valley. Sweetwater: The author, 1916.
L1770

Lenski, Lois Blue Ridge Billy. New York: J. B. Lippincott Co., 1946. Story of a barefoot boy in the remote coves of the North Carolina mountains.
L1780 (ASU LMC MHC BC WCU ETSU)

Coal Camp Girl. New York: Lippincott, 1959. An autobiographical story of a young girl's life in a West Virginia coal camp.
L1790 (WCU ETSU BC)

Lentz, Fred W. "A Study of the Educational Facilities of the Public Schools of Alexander County, North Carolina." Master's thesis. Univ. of North Carolina, 1951.
L1800

Leonard, Elmore The Moonshine War. Garden City, N. Y.: Doubleday, 1969. Realistic fiction about the mountains' oldest industry.
L1810 (LMC)

Leonard, Henry C. Pigeon Cove and Vicinity. n.p.: n.p., n.d. An account of a remote cove taken over by the Blue Ridge Parkway.
L1820

Leonard, Jacob C. History of Catawba College, Formerly Located at Newton, Now at Salisbury, N. C. n.p.: Trustees of Catawba College, 1927.
L1830 (ASU)

Leoprapai, Boonlert "Mobility and Economic Progress in the Tennessee Valley Region: 1957-65." Ph. D. Diss. Univ. of Massachusetts, 1971.
L1840

Lepawsky, Albert State Planning and Economic Development in the South. NPC Committee of the South, Report no. 4. Washington: National Planning Association, 1949.
L1850

LeRay, Nelson L. Employment and Underemployment in Rural People: Low Income Groups in Arkansas, Maryland, and West Virginia. no. 43-109. Washington: Agricultural Research Service, U. S. Department of Agriculture, December, 1959.
L1860

Lerning, John Young Experiences of a Circuit Rider. New York: Methodist Book Concern, 1932. The personal experiences of a young Methodist circuit rider.
L1870

Lesch, Alma Vegetable Dyeing: 151 Color Recipes for Dyeing Yarns and Fabrics with Natural Materials. New York: Watson-Guptill Publications, 1970. A comprehensive guidebook for making dyes from natural materials.
L1880 (ASU)

Lesh, F. R. Shearin, A. E. Soil Survey, Pickens County, South Carolina. Washington: U. S. Department of Agriculture, Bureau of Plant Industry, Soils, and Agricultural Engineering, 1943.
S2570

Lesley, J. Peter Manual of Coal and Its Topography. Philadelphia: Lippincott, 1856.
L1890

Leslie, J. D. Management of Kentucky Natural Resources. Lexington, Ky.: Spindletop Research, 1965. The general conclusion is that natural resources are poorly managed.
L1900

Lessing, Peter and others, eds. Appalachian Structural Seminar, 2nd, Mont Chateau, W. Va., 1971. Appalachian Structures: Origin, Evolution and Possible Potential for New Exploration Frontiers. Morgantown: West Virginia Univ. and West Virginia Geological and Economic Survey, 1972.
A4090

Lester, James G. Allen, Arthur Thomas Zonation of the Middle and Upper Ordovician Strata in Northwestern Georgia. Atlanta: Georgia Department of Mines, Mining and Geology, 1957.
A1500 (ETSU)

Lester, James George Cramer, Howard Ross Annotated Bibliography of Georgia Geology Through 1959. Atlanta: Georgia Department of Mines, Mining and Geology, 1967.
C8500 (ETSU)

Lester, William Stewart The Transylvania Colony. Spencer, Ind.: S. R. Guard & Co., 1935. An interesting history of the land company which drew settlers into the mountain wilderness.
L1910 (BC ASU)

Lesure, Frank G. Mica Deposits of the Blue Ridge in North Carolina. U. S. Geological Survey Professional Paper, 577. Washington: Govt. Print. Off., 1968.
L1920 (LMC)

Lett, W. L. Tharp, William Edgar Soil Survey of Bibb County, Alabama. Washington: U. S. Department of Agriculture, Bureau of Soils, 1910.
T7660

Tharp, William Edward Soil Survey of Cullman County, Alabama. Washington: U. S. Department of Agriculture, Bureau of Soils, 1910.
T7670

Leubke, B. H. and others Types of Farming in Tennessee. Bulletin no. 169. Knoxville: Tennessee Agricultural Experiment Station, University of Tennessee, 1939. Includes survey of Tennessee's mountain counties.
L1930

Leuthold, Frank O. Population Changes in Tennessee since 1930. Bulletin no. 403. Knoxville: Tennessee Agricultural Experiment Station, University of Tennessee, 1966.
L1940

LeVan, Donald C. Catalog of Oil and Gas Wells in Well Sample Repository on August 1, 1959. Charlottesville: Univ. of Virginia, 1962.
L1950

Directory of the Mineral Industry in Virginia, 1966. Charlottesville: Virginia Division of Mineral Resources, 1966.
L1960

Wells Drilled for Oil and Gas in Virginia Prior to 1962. Charlottesville: Univ. of Virginia, 1962.
L1970 (ETSU)

Leverett, Frank The Pleistocene of Northern Kentucky, a Regional Reconnaissance Study of the Physical Effects of Glaciation Within the Commonwealth. Preface by T. C. Chamberlin. Presented with four separate geological papers by Stephen Sargent Visher, Arle H. Sutton, James (sic, Joseph) K. Roberts, and Arnim Kohl Lobeck. Illustrated with sixteen photographs, maps, and diagrams. Series 6, Geological Reports, vol. 31. Frankfort: Kentucky Geological Survey, 1929.
L1980 (ETSU)

Levin, Melvin R. Grossman, D. A. The Appalachian Region: A Preliminary Analysis of Economic and Population Trends in an Eleven State Problem Area. Atlanta: Council of State Governments, 1960.
G4440

Levine, Daniel Settle "Economic Development in Appalachia." Ph. D. Diss. Northwestern Univ., 1971.
L1990 (BC ASU)

Levine, Louis The Potential for Human Resources and Economic Growth in a Declining Local Community; A Socioeconomic Study of the Johnstown, Penn. Economy. Univ. Park: Institute for Research on Human Resources, Penn. State Univ., 1969.
L2000

Levitan, Sar A. Federal Aid to Depressed Areas — An Evaluation of the Area Redevelopment Association. Baltimore: Johns Hopkins Press, 1964.
L2010 (BC)

The Great Society's Poor Law, a New Approach to Poverty. Baltimore: Johns Hopkins Press, 1969.
L2020

Programs in Aid of the Poor. Kalamazoo, Mich.: Upjohn Institute, 1965.
L2030

Programs in Aid of the Poor for the 1970's. Baltimore: Johns Hopkins Press, 1969.
L2040

Levy, Charles "School Desegregation in Warren County, Virginia, During 1958-1960; A Study in the Mobilization of Restraints." Master's thesis. Univ. of Chicago, 1961.
L2050

Lewis, Alfred Allan The Mountain Artisans Quilting Book. New York: Macmillan, 1973. A description of the Renaissance of the mountain folk art of quilting in West Virginia.
L2060 (BC ASU LMC)

Lewis, Alfred Henry When Men Grew Tall: Or, The Story of Andrew Jackson. New York: D. Appleton & Co., 1907. Novel based on the life of Andrew Jackson.
L2070 (ASU)

Lewis, Arthur H. Lament for the Molly Maquires. New York: Pocket Books, 1969. A nostalgic look at the Irishmen who ruled America's coal fields for two generations.
L2080

Lewis, Clarence Cry to the Hills. 1st ed. Garden City, N.Y.: Doubleday, 1966. Moralistic fiction with a mountain setting.
L2090 (BC LMC ASU)

Lewis, Claudia Louise Children of the Cumberland. Photographs by William T. Buttrick, Jr. New York: Columbia Univ. Press, 1946. An educator and sociologist takes a realistic look at "backward" mountain children.
L2100 (BC ASU LMC WCU WWC)

Children of the Cumberland. Photographs by William Butterick, Jr. Xerox copy of the original. New York: Columbia Univ. Press, 1946.
L2110 (ASU)

Lewis County Development Committee Overall Economic Development Program. Weston, W. Va.: The Committee, 1962.
L2120

Lewis, David Parks "Single and Multi-region Intersectoral Plows Analysis: An Examination of the Rows-only Approach with Applications to the Tennessee Economy." Ph. D. Diss. Univ. of Tennessee, 1968. Study includes Eastern Tennessee.
L2130

Lewis, Don L. "The Status of Geography Teaching in the Schools of Carter County, Tennessee." Master's thesis. East Tennessee State College, 1955.
L2140 (ETSU)

Lewis, Helen Matthews "Occupational Roles and Family Roles: A Study of Coal Mining Families in the Southern Appalachians." Ph. D. Diss. Univ. of Kentucky, 1970.
L2150

Lewis, Henry Guy Soil Survey of Cleburne County, Alabama. Prepared in cooperation with Alabama. Field Operations, 1913. Washington: U. S. Department of Agriculture, Bureau of Soils, 1915.
L2170

Soil Survey of Lawrence County, Alabama. Prepared in cooperation with Alabama. Field Operations, 1914. Washington: U. S. Department of Agriculture, Bureau of Soils, 1916.
L2180

Lewis, Henry Guy and others Soil Survey of Carroll County, Georgia. Prepared in cooperation with the Georgia State College of Agriculture. Field Operations, 1921. Washington: U. S. Department of Agriculture, Bureau of Soils, 1926. About one-third of Carroll County falls within the Appalachian region.
L2160

Lewis, John New Hope; or, The Rescue. A Tale of the Great Kanawha. New York: Bunce, 1855. Young Kate is rescued from hostile Indians.
L2190 (ASU)

Young Kate; or, The Rescue. A Tale of the Great Kanawha. Two volumes in one. New York: Harper and Brothers, 1844.
L2200

Lewis, Joseph Volney Corundum and the Basic Magnesian Rocks of Western North Carolina. North Carolina Geological Survey Bulletin, no. 11. Winston-Salem: M. I. & J. C. Stewart, 1896.
L2210 (WCU)

Pratt, Joseph Hyde Corundum and the Peridotites of Western North Carolina. Raleigh, N. C.: Geological Survey, 1904.
P4220 (ASU WCU LMC)

Lewis, Madeline Kneberg Lewis, Thomas McDowell Nelson Eva, an Archaic Site. Knoxville: Univ. of Tennessee Press, 1961.
L2250 (BC ASU WCU ETSU)

Lewis, Thomas McDowell Nelson Hiwassee Island, an Archaeological Account of Four Tennessee Indian Peoples. Knoxville: Univ. of Tennessee Press, 1946.
L2270 (ETSU ASU WCU LMC BC)

Lewis, Thomas McDowell Nelson Tribes That Slumber: Indian Times in the Tennessee Region. Knoxville: Univ. of Tennessee Press, 1958.
L2290 (ASU LMC WCU MHC BC)

Lewis, Thomas McDowell Nelson Tribes That Slumber: Indians of the Tennessee Region. Knoxville: Univ. of Tennessee Press, 1970.
L2300 (ETSU)

Lewis, Ruth Fretwell "The Southern Mountaineer in Fiction." Master's thesis. Univ. of Virginia, 1929.
L2220 (ASU)

Lewis, Sinclair Cheap and Contented Labor; the Picture of a Southern Mill Town in 1929. New York: United Feature Syndicate, Inc., 1929. (Marion, N. C.) This syndicated feature shows the changes which overcome Lewis during his early encounters in Appalachia. Western North Carolina and Eastern Kentucky events caused him to "drop out" of mainstream life and move to Appalachia.
L2230

Lewis, Thomas McDowell Nelson Annotations Pertaining to Prehistoric Research in Tennessee. Knoxville: Dept. of Anthropology, Univ. of Tennessee, 1937. Cherokee and other Indians of Tennessee, and early inhabitants are listed.
L2240

Eva, an Archaic Site. Study in Anthropology. Knoxville: Univ. of Tennessee Press, 1961. A fascinating study of an ancient Tennessee site.
L2250 (BC ASU WCU ETSU)

The First Tennesseans; an Interpretation of Tennessee Prehistory. Knoxville: Dept. of Anthropology, Univ. of Tennessee, 1955. This publication was revised and enlarged and issued as TRIBES THAT SLUMBER, which described the Cherokee and four other Indians of Tennessee.
L2260

Hiwassee Island, an Archaeological Account of Four Tennessee Indian Peoples. Partially based on field reports by Charles H. Nash. Knoxville: Univ. of Tennessee Press, 1946.
L2270 (ETSU ASU WCU LMC BC)

The Prehistory of the Chickamauga Basin in Tennessee, a Preview. Knoxville: Dept. of Anthropology, Univ. of Tennessee, 1941. Various pagings.
L2280

Tribes That Slumber: Indian Times in the Tennessee Region. Knoxville: Univ. of Tennessee Press, 1958. The archaeologists' report on four primitive tribes of Tennessee.
L2290 (ASU LMC WCU MHC BC)

Tribes That Slumber: Indians of the Tennessee Region. 1958. Reprint. Knoxville: Univ. of Tennessee Press, 1970.
L2300 (ETSU)

Lewis, Virgil Anson First Biennial Report of the Department of Archives and History of the state of West Virginia. Charleston: The Tribune Print. Co., 1906.
L2310 (ASU)

History and Government of West Virginia. New century ed. State Government Series. New York: American Book Co., 1912.
L2320 (ASU)

History and Government of West Virginia. New century ed. State Government Series. New York: American Book Co., 1922.
L2330 (WCU)

History of the Battle of Point Pleasant. Charleston, W. Va.: Tribune Print. Co., 1909. An account of Lord Dunsmore's expedition against the Indians at the mouth of the Kanawha River. Theodore Roosevelt describes this as one of the most decisive battles in the winning of the West.
L2340 (BC ASU)

History of West Virginia In two parts. Philadelphia: Hubbard Brothers, 1889.
L2350 (BC ASU)

The Soldiery of West Virginia in the French and Indian War, Lord Dunmore's War, The Whiskey Insurrection, The Second War with England, The War with Mexico, and Addenda Relating to West Virginians in the Civil War. 1911. Reprint. Baltimore: Genealogical Pub. Co., 1967.
L2370 (ASU)

Third Biennial Report of the Department of Archives and History of the State of West Virginia. Charleston: The News-Mail Co., 1911.
L2380 (ASU)

Lewis, Virgil Anson ed. How West Virginia was Made. Proceedings of the First Convention of the People of North-western Virginia at Wheeling, May 13, 14 and 15, 1861, and the Journal of the Second Convention of the People of Northwestern Virginia at Wheeling, which Assembled, June 11th 1861. With appendixes and an introduction, annotations and addenda, by Virgil A. Lewis. Charleston, W. Va.: News-Mail Co., Public Printer, 1909. Records transcribed from the "Daily Intelligencer" of Wheeling.
L2360 (ASU)

Lewis, W. W. Obenshain, S. S. Soil Survey, Russell County, Virginia. Washington: U. S. Department of Agriculture, Bureau of Plant Industry, Soils, and Agricultural Engineering, 1945.
O100 (BC)

Lewisburg, Tennessee. Planning Commission Planning for Flood Damage Prevention. Lewisburg, Tennessee: The commission, 1956.
L2390

Leyburn, James Graham The Scotch-Irish: A Social History. Chapel Hill: Univ. of North Carolina Press, 1962. An interesting but nearly-mouthed account of the influence of the Scotch-Irish.
L2400 (ASU BC)

Leyden, Dennis R. Personal Income in West Virginia Counties by Type and Magnitude, 1960-1963: A Pilot Study. Business and Economic Studies, vol. 10, no. 1. Also, Bulletin, Series 66, no. 12-3. Morgantown: Bureau of Business and Research, College of Commerce, and Office of Research and Development of the West Virginia Center for Appalachian Studies and Development, West Virginia Univ., 1966.
L2410 (ASU)

Licensed Beverage Industries The Incredible Moonshine Menace. New York: The author, 1967. Alas, now and here's a book with no appreciation of what was once a great art form.
L2420 (ASU)

Moonshine: Public Enemy. New York: The author, n.d.
L2430 (ASU)

Lilienthal, David Eli The Journals of David E. Lilienthal. New York: Harper, 1964-71. Lilienthal was a pioneer in the development of the Tennessee Valley Authority.
L2440

TVA: Democracy on the March. 1st ed. New York: Harper & Brothers, 1944.
L2450 (BC WCU LMC MHC)

TVA: Democracy on the March. 20th anniversary ed. New York: Harper, 1953.
L2460 (ASU MHC WWC BC UNCA)

Lillard, Richard G. The Great Forest. New York: Knopf, 1948. Fiction partially set in Appalachia.
L2470 (LMC)

Lillard, Roy G. "A Brief History of the First Baptist Church (Ocoee Baptist Church), Benton, Tennessee, 1836-1959." Benton: Unpublished typescript, 1964. About 50 pages. In possession of author.
L2480

"The Ocoee Lodge no. 212, F & A. M., Benton, Tennessee." Benton: Unpublished typescript, 1963. About 10 pages. In possession of author.
L2490

"Some Aspects of Polk County Politics." Benton: Unpublished typescript, 1962. About 50 pages. In possession of author.
L2500

Lilley, Lee Reaching for Reality. Bluefield, W. Va.: The author, 1965. The 13 characters in this group of related stories search for their own identities and differ in their perceptions of reality.
L2510 (BC)

Linback, Neal G. Atlas of Alabama. Montgomery: State Printers, n.d. A state atlas with 130, 2 color and 4 color maps, tables, graphs, illustrations, and 52 short essays.
L2520

Lincoln Memorial University. Harrogate, Tenn. The Living Memorial to Lincoln. Cumberland Gap, Tenn.: LMU, n.d. This small university in the Cumberland Gap is a memorial to Lincoln.
L2530

Lincoln Memorial University, Harrogate, Tennessee Lincoln Memorial University. "Sine Qua Non." Why It Is, Why It Should Be, Why It Must Be, Why It Is America's Hope. Harrogate, Tenn.: Lincoln Memorial Univ., n.d.
L2551 (BC)

The Living Memorial to Lincoln. Cumberland Gap, Tenn.: Lincoln Memorial Univ., n.d.
L2552 (BC)

Lindell, Gary R. Marketing West Virginia Lumber to Manufacturers in Other States. U. S. Forest Service Research Paper, NE-35. Upper Darby, Pa.: Northeastern Forest Experiment Station, 1965.
L2540

Lindsay, Marie Batterham The First Shearing. Richmond: Whittet & Shapperson, 1904. Moralistic fiction set in the Blue Ridge Mountains.
L2550 (ASU)

Lindsey, Thomas H. Lindsey's Guidebook to Western North Carolina. Asheville, N. C.: The Randolph-Kerr Print. Co., 1890.
L2560

Lindsley, John Berrien ed. The Military Annals of Tennessee: Confederate. First Series. Embracing a Review of Military Operations with Regimental Histories and Memorial Rolls Compiled from Original and Official Sources. Nashville, Tenn.: J. M. Lindsley, 1886.
L2570 (LMC)

Lindstrom, David B. ed. Kaplan, Sylvan J. ed. Seeking More Effective Means to Overcome Poverty. Washington: Research and Extension Division Virginia Polytechnical Institute, in cooperation with the Appalachian Regional Commission, 1969.
K200 (ASU)

Lindstrom, David E. ed. Appalachia Conference on Research in Poverty and Development, Virginia Polytechnic Institute, 1968. Seeking More Effective Means to Overcome Poverty: Proceedings. Blacksburg: Research and Extension Division, Virginia Polytechnic Institute, 1969.
A2680 (ASU LMC)

Lineberry, Mildred Memoirs of Burkes Garden and Tazewell County. n.p.: n.p., n.d.
L2580

Lingar, Charles S. "A Study of the Influence of Certain Personal and Other Factors on the Number of Observed Unsafe Acts and Injuries Sustained by Employees of Kingsport Power Company." Master's thesis. East Tennessee State Univ., 1964.
L2590 (ETSU)

Linger, Margaret Virginia "French Creek Community." Master's thesis. West Virginia Univ., 1934. Sociological study of an Appalachian community.
L2600 (ASU)

Lingley, Charles Ramsdell The Transition in Virginia from Colony to Commonwealth. Studies in History, Economics and Public Law, No. 96. New York: Columbia Univ. Press, 1910.
L2610 (LMC)

Link, A. D. A Planner's Reference Guide Relating to Socioeconomic Factors Within Appalachia as Applied to Public Education. Las Cruces, N. M.: ERIC Clearinghouse on Rural Education and Small Schools, 1970.
L2620 (ETSU)

Link, Gertrude Bible "A History of Marion County." Master's thesis. Middle Tennessee State Univ., 1953.
L2630

Linkous, Carlos T. "The Development of a Community Water Supply to Serve a Rural Area of Southern Appalachia." Master's thesis. East Tennessee State Univ., 1972.
L2640 (ETSU)

Linn, John Blair Persons Naturalized in the Province in Pennsylvania, 1740-1773. Baltimore: Genealogical Pub. Co., 1967.
L2650 (ASU)

Record of Pennsylvania Marriages, Prior to 1810. Baltimore: Genealogical Pub. Co., 1968. Includes marriage, church and military records.
L2660 (ASU)

Linn, John Blair ed. Record of Pennsylvania Marriages, Prior to 1810. 1880-90. Reprint. 2 vols. Pennsylvania Archives, 2nd Series, vol. 13-19. Baltimore: Genealogical Pub. Co., 1968.
L2670 (ASU)

Linney, Romulus Heathen Valley. New York: Antheneum, 1962. Sensational novel about an Episcopal bishop's attempts to tame the savage mountain people of Valle Crucis, North Carolina. One of the saddest portraits ever painted of mountain life.
L2680 (ASU LMC WCU)

Slowly, By Thy Hand Unfurled. 1st ed. New York: Harcourt, Brace and World, 1965. Novel partially set in Linney's Watauga County, North Carolina homeland. Southern gothic mountain style.
L2690 (ASU)

The Sorrows of Frederick: A Play. 1st ed. New York: Harcourt, Brace and World, 1966. Not Appalachian; but a surprising number of mountain phrases and attitudes are present.
L2700 (ASU)

Linzey, Alicia W. Mammals of the Great Smoky Mountains National Park. 1st ed. Knoxville: Univ. of Tennessee, 1971. A listing of mammals from the Eastern U. S.'s largest park. Beautifully illustrated with a text that flows well.
L2710 (WCU WWC ASU LMC)

Mammals of Great Smoky Mountains National Park. Knoxville: Univ. of Tennessee Press, 1972.
L2720 (BC)

Linzey, Donald W. Linzey, Alicia W. Mammals of the Great Smoky Mountains National Park. Knoxville: Univ. of Tennessee, 1971.
L2710 (WCU WWC ASU LMC)

Linzey, Alicia W. Mammals of Great Smoky Mountains National Park. Knoxville: Univ. of Tennessee Press, 1972.
L2720 (BC)

Lipscombe, George A. Vocational Agricultural Instruction for Adult Farmer Classes in Preston County. Morgantown: West Virginia Univ., 1963.
L2730

Lisenby, William Foy "An Administrative History of Public Programs for Dependent Children in North Carolina, Virginia, Tennessee, and Kentucky, 1900-1942." Ph. D. Diss. Vanderbilt Univ., 1962. Includes children from the poorer mountain counties of each state.
L2740

List of North Carolina Land Grants in Tennessee, 1778-1791 1 reel. 35mm. Microfilm. Washington: National Archives, 1944.
L2750 (WCU ASU)

List of Pensioners on the Roll, January 1, 1883 5 vols. Baltimore: Genealogical Pub. Co., 1970 (1883).
L2760

List of References on the Mountain Whites Washington: Library of Congress, 1935. An incomplete, biased and foolish attempt at a bibliography on "us pore barefoot hillbillies."
L2770 (ASU MHC)

Litsey, Edwin Carlile A Maid of the Kentucky Hills. Chicago: Browne and Howell Co., 1913. Romantic fiction burdened with a victorian style. True love triumphs and mountain speech is effectively presented.
L2780 (ASU)

Stones for Bread. Caldwell, Idaho: Caxton Printers, 1940. A tale of two brothers and their lives of hunger, poverty, despair, and terror in Desolate Valley.
L2790 (BC)

Little, Arthur D., Inc. Teachers in Appalachia. Appalachian Research Report, no. 12. Washington: n.p., 1970. Prepared for the Appalachian Regional Commission.
L2810 (ASU ETSU MHC)

Little, Arthur, Inc. Project Economic Study of the Ohio River Basin. Cambridge, Mass.: n.p., 1964.
L2800

Little, Elvin Wesley "A Study to Determine the Major Causes of Withdrawal from Science Hill High School During the 1965-1966 School Year." Master's thesis. East Tennessee State Univ., 1967.
L2820 (ETSU)

The Little Mohee: An Appalachian Ballad. Illustrated by Joanna Troughton New York: E. P. Dutton, 1971. One of the region's most popular ballads.
L2830 (BC ASU ETSU)

The Little Smith Barn: A Story of the Triangular Plot Now Called Pritchard Park Asheville, N. C.: n.p., 1947.
L2840

Littleton, Gary L. A Survey of Low-Cost Housing in Carter County, Kentucky. Oak Ridge, Tenn.: Oak Ridge Associated Universities, 1966.
L2850 (ASU)

Litton, Gaston Dale, Edward Everett Cherokee Cavaliers: Forty Years of Cherokee History as Told in the Correspondence of the Ridge — Watie — Boudinot Family. Norman: Univ. of Oklahoma Press, 1939.
D60 (ASU WCU LMC BC)

Litton Industries, Economic Development Division A Preliminary Analysis for an Economic Development Plan for the Appalachian Region. Washington: Appalachian Regional Commission, 1965.
L2860

Livaditis, Nicholas John "A Comparison of Tennessee's Revenue Potential, Utilization, Tax Burden, and Educational Effort with Selected States." Ed. D. Diss. East Tennessee State Univ., 1972. Much emphasis on Appalachian counties.
L2870 (ETSU)

Lively, Robert A. Fiction Fights the Civil War: An Unfinished Chapter in the Literary History of the American People. Chapel Hill: Univ. of North Carolina Press, 1957. Many mountain novels are included.
L2880 (ASU)

Livengood, Joseph Michael "Vascular Flora of the Sim's Pond Area." Master's thesis. Appalachian State Univ., 1972.
L2890 (ASU)

Liverpool List of Emigrants to America from Liverpool, 1697-1707. Transcribed by Elizabeth French. Baltimore: Genealogical Pub. Co., 1962.
L2900 (ASU)

Livesay, Elizabeth Ann Geology of the Mammoth Cave National Park Area. Rev. by Preston McGrain. Kentucky Geological Survey Series 10, Special publication 7. Revision of Series 9, Special publication 2. Lexington: Univ. of Kentucky, 1962.
L2910 (ETSU ASU)

Livesay, Glenn Q. "A Study of Public School Finance in Hancock County, Tennessee." Master's thesis. Univ. of Tennessee, 1954.
L2920

Livingood, James W. Raulston, J. Leonard Sequatchie: A Story of the Southern Cumberlands. Knoxville: Univ. of Tennessee Press, 1974.
R540 (ASU)

Livingood, James Weston Govan, Gilbert Eaton The Chattanooga Country, 1540-1951: From Tomahawks to TVA. New York: Dutton, 1952.
G2950 (ASU LMC MHC ETSU BC)

Govan, Gilbert Eaton The Chattanooga Country, 1540-1962: From Tomahawks to TVA. Chapel Hill: Univ. of North Carolina Press, 1963.
G2960 (WCU)

Govan, Gilbert Eaton The University of Chattanooga: Sixty Years. Chattanooga: Univ. of Chattanooga, 1947.
G2970 (ASU WCU ETSU BC)

Livingston Academy, Class of 1951 Echoes from the Foothills. Livingston: n.p., 1951.
L2930

Livingston, Inex Baisden "School Attendance in Harlan County, Kentucky, 1948-1954." Master's thesis. Ohio State Univ., 1956.
L2940

Livingston, William J. "Coal Miners and Religion." Master's thesis. Union Theological Seminary, 1951. Shows no significant difference due to occupation.
L2950

Lloyd, Emma Rouse Clasping Hands with Generations Past. Cincinnati: Private Printing (Wiesen-Hart Press), 1932.
L2960

Lloyd, John Uri Felix Moses, the Beloved Jew of Stringtown on the Pike. Illustrated by J. Augustus Knapp. Cincinnati: Caxton Press, 1930. Short Stories.
L2970 (ASU BC)

Lloyd, John Uri
Our Willie: A Folklore Story of the Gunpowder Creek and Hills, Boone County, Kentucky. Cincinnati: J. G. Kidd and Son, 1934. Short Stories.
L2980 (ASU WCU)
Red Head. Illustrated by Reginald B. Birch. New York: Dodd, Mead and Co., 1903. A tale of the Red-head — Holcomb feud.
L2990 (BC ASU WCU LMC ETSU)
Stringtown on the Pike: A Tale of Northernmost Kentucky. New York: Dodd, Mead and Co., 1900. More about the Red-head feud. Short Stories.
L3000 (BC LMC ETSU ASU WCU)
Warwick of the Knobs: A Story of Stringtown County, Kentucky. New York: Dodd, Mead and Co., 1901. Photographic illustrations of Knob County.
L3010 (ASU LMC WCU ETSU)

Lloyd, Ralph Walde Maryville College: A History of 150 Years, 1819-1969. Maryville, Tenn.: Maryville College Press, 1969.
L3020 (ETSU WWC ASU)

Lockard, E. Kidd "The Temperance Movement in West Virginia." Master's thesis. West Virginia Univ., 1960. 'Nigh onto a teetotal failure.
L3030

Locke, Jerry "The Politics of Legislative Reapportionment in Tennessee, 1962." Master's thesis. Univ. of Tennessee, 1963.
L3040

Lockwood, Green and Co. Report of Industrial Survey of Florence, Alabama, and Muscle Shoals District. Florence, Ala.: Chamber of Commerce, 1925.
L3050 (ASU)

Logan, Frenise A. The Negro in North Carolina, 1876-1894. Chapel Hill: Univ. of North Carolina Press, 1964.
L3060 (LMC)

Logan, John Henry A History of the Upper Country of South Carolina. Charleston, S. C.: S. G. Courtenay, 1859. Includes South Carolina's six mountain counties.
L3070 (LMC BC)
A History of the Upper Country of South Carolina: From the Earliest Periods to the Close of the War of Independence. vol. 1. 1859 Reprint. South Carolina Heritage Series, no. 5. Spartanburg, S. C.: Reprint Co., 1960.
L3080 (ASU WCU LMC)

Logan, William Hugh A Peddlar's Pack of Ballads and Songs. Detroit: Singing Tree Press, 1968.
L3090 (ASU BC)

Logue, Calvin McLeod Ralph McGill, Editor and Publisher. Durham, N. C.: Moore Pub. Co., 1969. Biography of an East Tennessee journalist who attained national prominence.
L3100 (ASU)

Lomask, Milton Andrew Johnson: President on Trial. New York: Farrar, Straus, 1960.
L3120 (MHC ASU BC)

Lomax, Alan American Folk Songs and Folklore: A Regional Bibliography. New York: Progressive Education Assoc., 1942.
L3110

Lomax, Alan comp. Hard Hitting Songs for Hard Hit People: American Folk Songs of the Depression and the Labor Movement of the 1930's. Notes on the songs by Woody Guthrie. Music transcribed and edited by Pete Seeger. New York: Oak Publications, 1967.
L3140 (BC ASU MHC LMC)
Lomax, John Avery American Ballads and Folk Songs. New York: Macmillan Co., 1934.
L3160 (LMC BC FC)
Lomax, John Avery American Ballads and Folk Songs. New York: Macmillan Co., 1967.
L3170 (WCU ASU)
Lomax, John Avery Folk Song U. S. A., the 111 Best American Ballads. New York: New American Library, 1966.
L3180 (WCU FC ASU)
Lomax, John Avery Our Singing Country: A Second Volume of American Ballads and Folk Songs. New York: Macmillan Co., 1941.
L3190 (WCU BC)

Lomax, Alan ed. The Folk Songs of North America, in the English Language. Melodies and guitar chords transcribed by Peggy Seeger with one-hundred piano arrangements by Matyas Seiber and Don Banks. Illustrated by Michael Leonard. Editorial assistant Shirley Collins. Garden City, N. Y.: Doubleday, 1960.
L3130 (WCU ASU)

Lomax, John Avery Adventures of a Ballad Hunter. Illustrated by Ken Chamberlain. New York: Hafner Co., 1947.
L3150 (ASU BC)
American Ballads and Folk Songs. With a foreword by George Lyman Kittredge. New York: Macmillan Co., 1934.
L3160 (LMC BC FC)
American Ballads and Folk Songs. With a foreword by George Lyman Kittredge. 1934 Reprint. New York: Macmillan Co., 1967.
L3170 (WCU ASU)
Folk Song U. S. A., the 111 Best American Ballads. 1947 Reprint. A Signet Book. New York: New American Library, 1966.
L3180 (WCU FC ASU)
Our Singing Country: A Second Volume of American Ballads and Folk Songs. Ruth Crawford Seeger, music ed. New York: Macmillan Co., 1941.
L3190 (WCU BC)

London, Martha H. "An Analysis of the Types of Retardation in the Elementary Departments of Five Negro Union Schools in Rural Cleveland County." Master's thesis. North Carolina Agriculture and Technical College, 1952.
L3200

Long, Alton Blanton "An Economic and Educational Survey of Rogersville Community." Master's thesis. Univ. of Tennessee, 1940.
L3210

Long Bob of Kentucky By the author of "Zeke Sternum". New York: George Munro, 1866. A once popular dime novel of frontier life.
L3220

Long, David Daniel Soil Survey of Floyd County, Georgia. Prepared in cooperation with the Georgia State College of Agriculture. Field Operations, 1917. Washington: U. S. Dept. of Agriculture, Bureau of Soils, 1923.
L3230
Soil Survey of Jackson County, Georgia. Washington: U. S. Dept. of Agriculture, 1915.
L3240
Soil Survey of Jackson County, Georgia. Prepared in cooperation with the Georgia State College of Agriculture. Washington: U. S. Dept. of Agriculture, Bureau of Soils, 1915.
L3250
Soil Survey of Madison County, Georgia. Prepared in cooperation with the Georgia State College of Agriculture. Washington: U. S. Dept. of Agriculture, Bureau of Soils, 1921.
L3260
Soil Survey of Polk County, Georgia. Prepared in cooperation with the Georgia State College of Agriculture. Washington: U. S. Dept. of Agriculture, Bureau of Soils, 1916.
L3270
Soil Survey of Rabun County, Georgia. In cooperation with the Georgia State College of Agriculture. Washington: U. S. Dept. of Agriculture, Bureau of Soils, 1924.
L3280
Mangum, Adolphus W. Soil Survey of Chattooga County, Georgia. Washington: U. S. Dept. of Agriculture, Bureau of Soils, 1913.
M3030

Long, Howard Kingsport: A Romance of Industry. Kingsport, Tenn.: Sevier Press, 1928.
L3290 (BC ASU ETSU)

Long, Millard Fillmore "The Price of Coal: A Study of the Policies of the National Coal Board." Ph. D. Diss. Univ. of Chicago, 1961.
L3300

Long, R. S. Higbee, Howard William Soil Survey, Huntingdon County, Pennsylvania. Washington: U. S. Department of Agriculture, Bureau of Plant Industry, Soils and Agricultural Engineering, 1944.
H5260

Long, Richard A. "Socioeconomic Factors Which May Affect Part Time Farmer Education in Butler County, Pennsylvania." Master's thesis. West Virginia Univ., 1970.
L3310

Longstreet, Augustus Baldwin Georgia Scenes. New York: Harper and Brothers, 1835. Many sketches from Northern Georgia.
L3320 (ASU)
Georgia Scenes: Characters, Incidents, etc., in the First Half Century of the Republic. Introduction by B. R. McElderry, Jr. American Century Series, S-24. New York: Sagamore Press, 1957.
L3330 (ASU)
Georgia Scenes: Characters, Incidents, etc., in the First Half Century of the Republic. Introduction by B. R. McElderry, Jr. American Century Series, S-24. 1957 Reprint. Gloucester, Mass.: Peter Smith, 1970.
L3340 (ASU)

Lonsdale, Richard E. Atlas of North Carolina. Assisted by John B. Cile and others. Chapel Hill: Univ. of North Carolina Press, 1967.
L3350 (ASU LMC UNCA)

Lontz, Mary Belle Early Assessment Records: Union County and Northumberland County. Milton, Pa.: n.p., 1966.
L3360 (ASU)
Index to History of Northumberland, Huntingdon, Mifflin, Centre, Union, Columbia, Juanita, and Clinton Counties, Pennsylvania. 1847 Reprint. Milton, Pa.: The author, n.d.
L3370 (ASU)
Tombstone Inscriptions of Union County, Pennsylvania. n.p.: The author, 1967.
L3380 (ASU)
Union County, Pennsylvania, 1865-1965. Milton, Pa.: n.p., 1966.
L3390 (ASU)

Looff, David H. Appalachia's Children: The Challenge of Mental Health. Lexington: Univ. Press of Kentucky, 1971.
L3400 (ASU WCU ETSU LMC MHC WWC BC)

Lookabill, Robert E. "A Survey of Withdrawals from Mullins High School in 1954-1958." Master's thesis. West Virginia Univ., 1960.
L3410

Loomis, Charles P. Social Relationships and Institutions in Seven Rural Communities. United States Farm Security Administration Social Research Report no. 18. Includes Cumberland County. Washington, D. C.: n.p., 1940.
L3420
Standards of Living in Four Southern Appalachian Mountain Counties. Farm Security Administration Social Research Report, no. 10. Washington: U. S. Dept. of Agriculture, 1938.
L3430 (LMC ASU BC)
Standards of Living of the Residents of Seven Rural Resettlement Communities. United States Farm Security Administration Social Research Report, no. 11. Washington, D. C.: n.p., 1938.
L3440

Looney, Louisa Preston Tennessee Sketches. Chicago: A. C. McClurg and Co., 1901. Includes some East Tennessee sketches.
L3450 (ASU ETSU BC)

Lorant, Stefan ed. Pittsburg: The Story of an American City. With contributions by Henry Steele Commager and others. 1st ed. Garden City, N. Y.: Doubleday, 1964.
L3460 (ASU)

Lord, G. William The Blue Ridge Parkway Guide. Washington: National Park Service, 1969.
L3470 (LMC ASU)

Lord, Gerald D. "Federal Centralization versus Local Values: A Case Study of Federal-Local Relations in the Knoxville-Knox County Community Action Committee." Master's thesis. Univ. of Tennessee, 1969.
L3480

Lord, James H. An Economic Profile of Tucker County, West Virginia. Morgantown, W. Va.: Bureau of Business Research, West Virginia Univ., 1967.
L3490 (ASU)

Lord, May Carleton On a High Hill. Winston-Salem, N. C.: John F. Blair, 1973.
L3500 (ASU)

Lord, Sharon Burmeister "Self-concepts of Appalachian Children: A Comparative Study of Economically Poor and Economically Disadvantaged Children Using the Piers-Harris Self-concept Inventory." Master's thesis. Indiana Univ., 1970.
L3510 (LMC ASU)

Lord, William George The Blue Ridge Parkway Guide. 4 vols. Asheville, N. C.: Stephens Press, 1959-1963.
L3520 (BC LMC ASU WCU)

Lorentz, Jeffrey Lane "An Evaluation of the Tennessee Valley Authority Manpower Training and Development Demonstration Project." Ed. D. Diss. Univ. of Tennessee, 1971.
L3530 (ASU BC)

Losche, Craig K. Soil Survey, Tucker County, Part of Northern Randolph County, West Virginia. Washington: U. S. Dept. of Agriculture, Soil Conservation Service, 1967.
L3540

The Lost Children of the Alleghanies: Found by a Dream: A True Story with a Moral Philadelphia: W. P. Zimmerman, 1856. Romantic and moralistic nineteenth century fiction.
L3550

Lothrop, Laura Egerton "A History of the Webb School of Knoxville, Tennessee." Master's thesis. Univ. of Tennessee, 1972.
L3560

Lotti, Thomas Silvical Characteristics of Cherrybark Oak. U. S. Forest Service Station Paper, no. 88. Asheville: Southeastern Forest Experiment Station, 1957.
L3570 (WCU)

Silvical Characteristics of Shumard Oak. U. S. Forest Service Station Paper, no. 113. Asheville, N. C.: Southeastern Forest Experiment Station, 1960.
L3580 (WCU)

Silvical Characteristics of Swamp Chestnut Oak. U. S. Forest Service Station Paper, no. 110. Asheville, N. C.: Southeastern Experiment Station, 1960.
L3590 (WCU)

Wenger, Karl Frederick The Relation of Growth to Stand Density in Natural Loblolly Pine Stands. Asheville, N. C.: Southeastern Forest Experiment Station, 1958.
W2820 (WCU)

Loudoun Co., Va. Civil War Centennial Commission Loudoun County and the Civil War: A History and Guide. Leesburg: n.p., 1961.
L3600

Lough, Glenn D. Now and Long Ago, a History of the Marion County Area. n.p.: n.p., 1969. A really interesting and readable county history.
L3610 (ASU)

Loughead, Leo V., Jr. "A Survey of Guidance Activities in the Public Secondary Schools of Tennessee." Master's thesis. East Tennessee State Univ., 1968.
L3620 (ETSU)

Loughlin, Gerald Francis Limestones and Marls of North Carolina. North Carolina Geological Survey Bulletin, no. 28. Raleigh: Edwards and Broughton Print. Co., 1921.
L3630 (ASU LMC WCU)

Loughry, F. G. Paschall, Alfred H. Soil Survey, Athens County, Ohio. Washington: U. S. Department of Agriculture, Bureau of Chemistry and Soils, 1938.
P530

Paschall, Alfred H. Soil Survey of Vinton County, Ohio. Washington: U. S. Department of Agriculture, Bureau of Chemistry and Soils, 1938.
P540

Lounsbury, Clarence Burke, Richard Thomas Avon Soil Survey of Rockcastle County, Kentucky Washington: U. S. Dept. of Agriculture, Bureau of Soils, 1911.
B8740

Love, Gary Leslie "A Study of Factors Related to the Entrophication of Boone Reservoir, Tennessee." Master's thesis. East Tennessee State Univ., 1972.
L3640 (ETSU)

Love, Jolee Love's Valley. Nashville: Ambrose, 1954. Memoirs of life in Dekalb County, Tennessee.
L3650

Love, Theodore R. and others Soil Survey, Coffee County, Tennessee. Correlation by J. H. Winsor. Soil Survey Series 1950, no. 5. Washington: U. S. Dept. of Agriculture, Soil Conservation Service, 1956.
L3660

Loving, Robert S. Double Destiny: The Story of Bristol, Tennessee-Virginia. Bristol, Tenn.: King Print. Co., 1955.
L3670 (LMC ETSU)

Double Destiny: The Story of Bristol, Tennessee-Virginia. 2nd ed. Bristol, Tenn.: King Print. Co., 1956.
L3680 (ASU)

Lovingood, Paul Evans, Jr. "The Asheville Basin of North Carolina: A Study in Highland Agricultural Land Use." Ph. D. Diss. Univ. of North Carolina, 1963.
L3690 (LMC ASU)

Low Income Farms in West Virginia, A Symposium Morgantown: West Virginia Agricultural Experiment Station, 1938.
L3740

Lowdermilk, William Harrison History of Cumberland (Maryland), From the Time of the Indian Town, Caiuctucus, in 1728, Up to the Present Day, Embracing an Account of Washington's First Campaign, and the Battle of Fort Necessity, Together with a History of Braddock's Expedition. Washington: J. Anglim, 1878.
L3700 (ASU)

Lowe, Cornelia "Initiating the Rural Library Program in Towns and Union Counties, Georgia." Master's thesis. Univ. of Georgia, 1948.
L3710

Lowe, Patricia L. "The Reactions of the Students of the Jonesboro, Tennessee, Middle School to Newbery Book Award Winners." Master's thesis. East Tennessee State Univ., 1972.
L3720 (ETSU)

Lowe, R. B. Sawyer, W. K. Electrical and Hydraulic Flow Properties of Appalachian Petroleum Reservoir Rocks. Pittsburgh: Mines Bureau, 1971.
S610

Lower, Mark Antony English Surnames. An Essay on Family Nomenclature, Historical, Etymological, and Humorous. With several illustrative appendices. 2 vols. 1875 Reprint. Detroit: Gale Research Co., 1968.
L3730 (ASU)

Lowrie, Walter ed. American State Papers. Indian Affairs. 2 vols. Washington, D. C.: Gales and Seaton, 1832-34. These volumes contain much primary material relating to the government's relations with various Indian tribal groups between 1789 and 1814.
L3750

Lowry, R. E. Organization for Watershed Planning in the Public Interest. Knoxville, Tenn.: n.p., 1959. Paper presented at Symposium on the Economics of Watershed Planning.
L3760

Lowther, Minnie Kendall Blennerhassett Island in Romance and Tragedy; the Authentic Story of Blennerhassett Island, with the Burr Episode Entwined about it; the Romance and Mystery of the Blannerhassetts; Burr under Footlights and Shadows; Tragedy of Theodosia Burr. Parsons, W. Va.: McClain Print. Co., 1974. Blennerhassett was a privately owned island in the Ohio River.
L3770

Lowther, Russell D. Laughter and Tears in the Mountains. Huntington, W. Va.: Cook Print. Co., 1968.
L3780 (ASU BC)

Lubin, Isador Miner's Wages and the Cost of Coal: An Inquiry into the Wages System in the Bituminous Coal Industry. New York: McGraw-Hill Book Co., 1924.
L3790

Lucas, Joseph Richard "The Competitive Position of Bituminous Coal in the Utility Markets of the Northeast." Ph. D. Diss. Columbia Univ., 1965.
L3800

Lucas, Rex Archibald Men in Crisis: A Study of a Mine Disaster. New York: Basic Books, 1969.
L3810

"Social Behavior under Conditions of Extreme Stress: A Study of Miners Entrapped by a Coal Mine Disaster." Ph. D. Diss. Columbia Univ., 1967.
L3820

Lucas, Silas Emmett, Jr. Index to the Headright and Bounty Grants of Georgia, 1759-1909. Vidalia: Georgia Genealogical Reprints, 1970.
L3830 (ASU)

The Second or 1807 Land Lottery of Georgia. Vidalia: Georgia Genealogical Reprints, 1968.
L3840 (ASU)

Supplement to the History of the Dodson-Dotson Family of Southwest Virginia. Swainsboro, Ga.: n.p., 1966.
L3850 (ASU)

Lucas, Silas Emmett, Jr. ed. The Georgia Genealogical Magazine Homerville, Ga.: n.p., quarterly.
G930 (ASU)

Lucas, Wavie Harman Births in Court Records of Montgomery County, Virginia, 1853-1871. n.p.: n.p., 1972.
L3860

Lucke, John B. McCue, John Bruce Limestones of West Virginia. Parkersburg, W. Va.: Scholl Print. Co., 1939.
M960 (ASU ETSU)

Lucke, John Becker Bibliography and Index of West Virginia Geology and Natural Resources to July 1, 1937. Bulletin 4. Morgantown: West Virginia Geological Survey, 1937.
L3870 (ETSU)

Luden, Heinrich ed. Berhard, Karl, Herzog von Sachsen-Weimar-Eisnach Reise sr. Hoheit des Herzogs Bernhard zu Sachsen-Weimar-Eisenach durch Nord-Amerika in den Jahren 1825 und 1826. Weimar: Wilhelm Hoffmann, 1828.
B3190

Ludlum, John Charles The Geology of Cacapon State Park, West Virginia. Morgantown: West Virginia Geological Survey, 1951.
L3880 (ETSU)

The Geology of Hawks Nest State Park, West Virginia. State Park Series, Bulletin, No. 1. Morgantown: West Virginia Geological Survey, 1951.
L3890 (ETSU)

The Geology of Lost River State Park, West Virginia. State Park Series, Bulletin, No. 3. Morgantown: West Virginia Geological Survey, 1952.
L3900 (ETSU)

The Geology of Watoga and Droop Mountain Battlefield State Parks, West Virginia. State Park Series, Bulletin, No. 4. Morgantown: West Virginia Geological and Economic Survey, 1954.
L3910 (ETSU)

Ludlum, John Charles
"Inside Down Under Australia and New Zealand Development Characteristics Compared to West Virginia as a Part of the Appalachian Highlands, U. S. A." Master's thesis. West Virginia Univ., 1965.
L3920

Luebke, B. H. Martin, Joe Allen Types of Farming in Tennessee. Knoxville: Univ. of Tennessee, Agriculture Experiment Station, 1960.
M3710 (ASU)

Luihn, Sigurd Allan "A Critical Study of the Physical Education Undergraduate Curriculum at Appalachian State Teachers College." Master's thesis. Appalachian State Teachers College, 1962.
L3930 (ASU)

Lumer, Hyman Poverty — Its Roots and the Future. New York: Internationals Publishers, 1965.
L3940

Lumpkin, Ben Gray Folk Songs on Records. Denver: Alan Swallow, 1950.
L3950 (ASU)

Lumpkin, Grace To Make My Bread. New York: Macaulay Co., 1932. Proletariat novel about mountain people's problems in the foothill textile mills. Poverty, drama, violence and a well drawn plot make this a superior novel.
L3960 (ASU BC)

Lumpkin, Wilson The Removal of the Cherokee Indians from Georgia. 1907. Reprint. 2 vols. in 1. New York: Arno Press, 1969. Including his speeches in the U. S. Congress on the Indian question, as representative and senator of Georgia, and later as U. S. Commissioner to the Cherokees, 1827-1841, together with a sketch of his life and conduct while holding many public offices under the government of Georgia and the U. S., prior to 1827, and after 1841.
L3970 (ASU LMC BC)

Lunsford, Bascom Lamar It's Fun to Square Dance: Southern Appalachian Calls and Figures. Asheville, N. C.: n.p., n.d.
L3980

30 and 1 Folksongs from the Southern Mountains. Chicago: Carl Fischer, 1929. Lunsford was one of the old-time ballad collectors and founder of one of the better mountain music festivals.
L3990 (ASU BC)

Lunsford, Hugh The Law of Hemlock Mountain. New York: Grosset and Dunlap, 1920. A confused novel in which two antagonists from the Philippines meet in Kentucky mountains. Right triumphs as the good guy gets the job, the girl, and redeems his reputation.
L4000 (BC ASU)

Luther, Edward T. The Coal Industry of Tennessee. Information Circular, no. 10. Nashville: Tennessee Division of Geology, 1960.
L4010 (ETSU)

The Coal Reserves of Tennessee. Bulletin, 63. Nashville: Tennessee Division of Geology, 1959.
L4020 (ETSU)

Lutheran Church The Proceedings of a Special Conference Held in Madison County, Virginia, in the Lutheran Congregation of Said County, on the 14th Day of September, 1817, and the Subsequent Days. n.p.: n.p., n.d.
L4030 (ASU)

Luttrell, Laura F. comp. Calvin Morgan McClung Historical Collection. n.p.: n.p., n.d.
L4040

Lyback, Johanna R. M. Indian Legends. n.p.: Lyons and Carnahan, 1925.
L4050 (LMC)

Lyle, Thomas ed. Ancient Ballads and Songs, Chiefly from Tradition, Manuscripts, and Scarce Works. 1827. Reprint. Norwood, Pa.: Norwood Editions, 1973.
L4060 (ASU)

Lyman, Webb S. Carter, William T., Jr. Soil Survey of the Leesburg, Virginia, Area. Washington: U. S. Department of Agriculture, Bureau of Soils, 1904.
C1770

Soil Survey of Etowah County, Alabama. Prepared in cooperation with Alabama. Field Operations, 1908. Washington: U. S. Dept. of Agriculture, Bureau of Soils, 1910.
L4070

McLendon, Willie E. Soil Survey of Grainger County, Tennessee. Washington: U. S. Department of Agriculture, Bureau of Soils, 1908.
M2050

Lynch, Lawrence K. Evans, William J. The Development of Kentucky's Handicraft Industry. Lexington, Ky.: Spindletop Research, 1963.
E2380

Lynchburg, Virginia, Chamber of Commerce
Lynchburg in Old Virginia, the City of Industry and Opportunity. Lynchburg, Va.: Brown-Morrison Co., n.d.
L4080 (ASU)

Lynde, Francis Battles of Chattanooga and Vicinity. Chattanooga: Chattanooga Community Assoc., 1930.
L4090

Chickamauga and Chattanooga National Military Park with Narratives of the Battles of Chickamauga, Lookout Mountain and Missionary Ridge. Chattanooga: Birchmore, 1895.
L4100

Lynn View School Elizabethon, Tenn. Helping Our Children Grow. Elizabethon: Board of Education, 1952.
E1560 (ETSU)

Lyon, Walter W., Jr. Carter, Everett C. The Impact of Highway Beautification on the Outdoor Advertising Industry in West Virginia. Morgantown: West Virginia Univ. Engineering Experiment Station, 1967.
C1680

Lyons, Edward Francis "Industrial Organization of the Appalachian Hardwood Lumber Using Industry." Ph. D. Diss. Virginia Polytechnic Institute and State Univ., 1969.
L4110

Lytle, Andrew Nelson Bedford Forrest and His Critter Company. Rev. ed. New York: McDowell, Obolensky, 1960.
L4120 (ASU)

The Long Night 1st ed. Indianapolis: Bobbs-Merrill Co., 1936.
L4130 (ASU)

The Velvet Horn. New York: McDowell, Obolensky, 1957.
L4140 (ASU WCU ETSU BC)

Lytle, Leonard The Descendants of John Little of Botetourt and Rockbridge Counties, Virginia. n.p.: n.p., 1960.
L4150

M. T. ed. The Washington Randolphs and Their Friends: Extracts from the Diary of a Lady of Old Virginia, Selected and Edited by T. M. Lynchburg, Va.: J. P. Bell Co., Inc., 1915.
M10 (ASU)

Maben, Charlotte Romance of the Cumberlands. New York: Vantage Press, 1953. Story of a Cumberland Mountain family in West Virginia which is plagued by poverty and a greedy neighbor who had done them out of everything worth having for generations by legal trickery.
M20 (LMC BC ASU)

McAdams, Mrs. Harry Kenneth comp. Kentucky Pioneer and Court Records: Abstracts of Early Wills, Deeds, and Marriages from Court Houses and Records of Old Bibles, Churches, Grave Yards and Cemeteries. Baltimore: Genealogical Pub. Co., 1967.
M30 (ASU)

McAllister, James Gray Edward O. Guerrant: Apostle to the Southern Highlanders. Richmond: Richmond Press, 1950. Guerrant was among the best known and best loved of the Presbyterian missionaries to the Southern Highlands.
M40 (LMC BC ASU)

Sketch of Captain Thompson McAllister, Co. A, 27th Virginia Regiment. Petersburg, Va.: Fenn and Owen, 1896. The story of Thompson McAllister — His life and military exploits. Areas in which story takes place: Cumberland County, Lost Creek Valley, parts of Pennsylvania, and parts of Virginia.
M50 (ASU)

McAllister, Jean Graham A Brief History of Bath County, Virginia. Under the auspices of the county school board and the board of supervisors of the county. Staunton, Va.: McClure Co., 1920. Short and informal history of Bath County, Virginia, with family sketches and accounts of historic spots within the county.
M60 (ASU)

McAllister, John Merriwether Genealogies of the Lewis and Kindred Families. Columbia, Mo.: E. W. Stephens Pub. Co., 1906.
M70

McAllister, Joseph Thompson Historical Sketches of Virginia. Salem, Va.: Salem Print. and Pub. Co., 1908. A descriptive history of Virginia which includes much information on the mountain region.
M80

Historical Sketches of Virginia, Hot Springs, Warm Sulphur Springs and Bath County. Salem, Va.: Salem Print. and Pub. Co., 1908. History and descriptions of the famous spas of Bath County.
M90 (BC)

Virginia Militia in the Revolutionary War: McAllister's Data. Hot Springs, Va.: McAllister Pub. Co., 1913. A list of militiamen from Montgomery County with an indexed list of all Virginia militiamen who received pensions as of 1835.
M100 (ASU)

McAteer, Davitt Bethell, Thomas N. The Pittston Mentality: Manslaughter on Buffalo Creek. Huntington: Appalachian Movement Press, 1972.
B3380

McAteer, James Davitt Coal Mine Health and Safety; the Case of West Virginia. Foreword by Ralph Nader. Afterword by Arnold Miller. New York: Praeger, 1973.
M110 (BC)

Coal Mining Health and Safety in West Virginia. Morgantown, W. Va.: n.p., 1970. A revealing look at some of the frightening conditions in West Virginia mines.
M120

McAvoy, Rogers "An Analysis of Achievement, Motivational, and Perceptual Variables Between High School Seniors Who Do and Do Not Attend College." Ph. D. Diss. Indiana Univ., 1967. West Virginia high school seniors were used as a sample for this study.
M130

McBride, George Adams "A Plan Formulation Methodology for the Appalachian Development Highway System." Ph. D. Diss. Univ. of North Carolina, 1969. A case study of Corridor K which runs from Sylva, North Carolina to the Tennessee line. The author feels the highway planners did not discriminate among beneficiaries and possible contributors to the investment.
M140

McBride, Nancy S. Gordon Kinship. Verona, Va.: McClure Print. Co., 1973.
M150

McBride, Robert M. ed. More Landmarks of Tennessee History. Nashville: Tennessee Historical Society, 1969. A descriptive history of Tennessee which cites major historic sites.
M160 (ASU LMC)

McCabe, James D., Jr. Planting the Wilderness: Or, The Pioneer Boys: A Story of Frontier Life. The Frontier Series. Boston: Lee and Shepard, 1869. A fast-moving novel of life on the trans-Appalachian frontier.
M170 (BC)

McCabe, Nicholas Other Fires: The Story of Tsali. Kingsport, Tenn.: Southern Publishing, 1940. A fictional account of Tsali's sacrifice and the roundup of the Cherokee.
M180 (WWC BC)

McCague, James The Cumberland. River of America Series. New York: Holt, 1973. A history of the Cumberland River and the effect it had upon the settlement and development of Kentucky and Tennessee, including some Appalachian areas in both states.
M190 (LMC)

McCall, Edith S. Cumberland Gap and Trails West. Chicago: Childrens Press, 1961. An illustrated children's history of the westward movement, its major trails, and the geographical and historical reasons for their locations.
M200 (BC)

McCall, Ettie Tidwell Roster of Revolutionary Soldiers in Georgia. 2 vols. 1941. Reprint. Baltimore: Genealogical Pub. Co., 1968. Since the Georgia records were destroyed in both Washington and in the state's capitol, these records are invaluable sources.
M210 (ASU)

McCall, Mrs. Howard H. see McCall, Ettie Tidewell

McCall, William A. Cherokees and Pioneers. Asheville, N. C.: Stephens Press, 1952. Explore the ever changing relationships between the Cherokee and the settlers.
M220 (ASU LMC)

McCalley, Henry Report on the Coal Measures of the Plateau Region of Alabama. Montgomery, Ala.: Smith, Alfred and Co., 1891. Includes good maps of the coal fields in the area around Blount County.
M230 (BC)

McCampbell, Vera Cleo "An Educational Survey of the Elementary Schools of Grundy County, Tennessee." Master's thesis. Univ. of Tennessee, 1935.
M240

McCann, Glenn C. A Study of Farm Families and Their Level of Living Income Patterns in Watauga County, North Carolina. Rural Adjustment Studies, Progrêss Report Rs-39. Raleigh: Dept. of Rural Sociology, Univ. of North Carolina, 1961. Watauga County is more prosperous than many other Appalachian counties.
M250 (ASU)

McCarthy, Cormac Appalachian Gothic. New York: Random, n.d. A collection of sketches and short fiction by one of the region's foremost authors.
M270 (ASU)

Child of God. n.p.: n.p., n.d. Novel of depravity, replete with psychological insights and the author's effective use of an East Tennessee background.
M280 (ASU)

The Orchard Keeper. New York: Random House, 1965. A drifter and a Tennessee hill man meet and mingle their destinies in the Green Fly Inn in a hollow not too far from Knoxville. Violence and a fastpaced story.
M290 (ASU WCU LMC ETSU BC)

Outer Dark. New York: Random House, 1968. A gothic novel of a child born in incest in a mountain cabin, abandoned by his father/uncle and rescued by a passing tinker. Suspicious, the mother investigates and at last tries to claim her child.
M300 (ASU LMC ETSU BC)

McCarty, Harold H. The Geographic Basis of American Economic Life. New York: Harper, 1940. Touches briefly on the relationship between geography, isolation and the economic conditions in the mountains.
M310 (ASU)

McCary, Ben Clyde Bibliography of the Virginia Indians. Richmond: Archeological Society of Va., 1946. Includes references to the Indians of the mountains. Excellent resource.
M320 (FC)

Indians in Seventeenth Century Virginia. Historical Booklet, no. 18. Williamsburg, Va.: 350 Anniversary Celebration Corp., 1957. Excellent resource material.
M330 (ASU)

McCauley, Orris D. Forestry Returns Evaluated for Uneven-aged Management in Two Appalachian Woodlots. U. S. Forest Service Research Paper, NE-244. Upper Darby, Pa.: Northeastern Forest Experiment Station, 1972.
M340

Sawmill Practices and Problems in Appalachian Hill Country of Ohio and Kentucky. U. S. Forest Service Research Paper, NE-80. Upper Darby, Pa.: Northeastern Forest Experiment Station, 1967.
M350

Value Added by Sawmilling in Appalachian Hill Country of Ohio and Kentucky. Forest Service Research Note, NE-67. Upper Darby, Pa.: Northeastern Forest Experiment Station, 1967.
M360

McClain, Walter Stephen A History of Putnam County. Cookville, Tenn.: Q. Dyer and Co., 1925. Informative history of Putnam County, Tennessee. Chapter eight appears to have been written by Quimby Dyer, the publisher.
M370

McClellan, George Brinton Report on the Organization and Campaigns of the Army of the Potomac: To Which Is Added an Account of the Campaign in Western Virginia, with Plans of Battlefields. New York: Sheldon and Co., 1864. Detailed maps and description of the campaign in Appalachian Virginia.
M380 (ETSU)

McClellan, Henry Brainerd The Life and Campaigns of Major General J. E. B. Stuart, Commander of the Calvary of the Army of Northern Virginia. Boston: Houghton Mifflin and Co., 1885. Stuart campaigned extensively in the mountains.
M390

McClelland, Margaret G. pseud. see McClelland, Mary Greenaway

McClelland, Mary Greenaway Burkett's Lock. New York: Cassell and Co., 1886. Frontier fiction partially set in the mountains.
M410 (ASU)

Jean Montioth. New York: Henry Holt and Co., 1887. Mountain fiction featuring some very good character sketches.
M420 (ASU)

Oblivion: An Episode. New York: H. Holt and Co., 1885. In the North Carolina mountains a flooded river strands a lovely outland lady and her child. The child drowns; the mother loses memory and her English and reverts to her native French. The mountain folk take her in and eventually she marries one.
M430 (ETSU BC)

McClendon, James B. Bone and Striffen. 1st ed. Nashville: Blue and Gray Press, 1972. This story is set in a hilly section of Alabama, a land of small farms and poor, rocky soil in the nineteen hundreds.
M440 (ASU)

McCloskey, Robert Sawyer; Ruth Journey Cake, Ho! New York: The Viking Press, 1970.
S600 (ASU)

McCluen, Marilyn N. Roane County, Tennessee: Abstracts of Estate Book "A" 1801-1824. Rockwood: n.p., 1965.
M450 (ASU)

McClung, James Wilson Historical Significance of Rockbridge County, Virginia. Staunton, Va.: McClure Co., 1939. Lists natural features, historic houses, and important events of the past.
M460 (BC)

McClung, John Alexander Sketches of Western Adventure: Containing an Account of the Most Interesting Incidents Connected with the Settlement of the West, from 1755 to 1794. Louisville, Ky.: R. H. Collins and Co., 1879.
M470 (ETSU BC)

McClure, Virginia Clay "The Settlement of the Kentucky Appalachian Highlands." Microfilm. Ph. D. Diss. Univ. of Kentucky, 1934. Fascinating account of the settlement of the mountains, giving migration routes and ethnic background for many of the settlers.
M480 (ASU BC)

McComas, B. B. Marriage Records of Kanawha County, West Virginia 1816-1850. Parsons, W. Va.: McClain Print. Co., 1972.
M490

McComas, E. W. Relative Merits of Producing Creep-fed, Feeder, and Lot-Fattened Clones in the Appalachian Region. Washington: U. S. Dept. of Agriculture, Animal Industry Bureau, 1938.
M500

McComb, Thomas M. Knoxville-Knox County Consolidation and the County and City School Systems. Knoxville: Univ. of Tennessee. Bureau of Business Research, 1958.
M510

McConnell, Catherine S. High on a Windy Hill. Bristol, Tenn.: The King Printing Co., 1968. The inscriptions in this book were copied from tombstones, located in three hundred and thirty-three cemeteries in Washington County, Virginia.
M520 (ASU)

Sanders Saga. Verona, Va.: McClure Press, 1972. Indexed, well-documented, includes photographs, maps, and sketches, not only of Sanders families of Wythe County, but of forty-six allied families.
M530

McConnell, John Preston Who Am I? A Brief Sketch of the McConnell and Related Families in Southwest Virginia. East Radford, Va.: n.p., 1929.
M540 (ASU)

McConnell, Lela Grace Faith Victorious in the Kentucky Mountains. Winna Lake, Ind.: Light and Life Press, 1946. Account of a 22 year ministry in the mountains of Kentucky.
M550 (BC)

Faith Victorious in the Kentucky Mountains. Berne, Ind.: Light and Hope Publishing, 1950.
M560

Hitherto and Henceforth in the Kentucky Mountains. Lawson, Ky.: n.p., n.d. Account of 25 years of the Mountain Holiness Association in the Kentucky mountains.
M570 (BC)

The Pauline Ministry in the Kentucky Mountains: Or, A Brief Account of the Kentucky Mountain Holiness Association. Louisville, Ky.: Pentecostal Pub. Co., 1942.
M580 (ASU LMC BC)

McConnell, Thomas Calvin "A Survey of Industrial Arts Students at Dobyns-Bennett High School, 1950-1955." Master's thesis. East Tennessee State College, 1956.
M590 (ETSU)

McCorkle, William Alexander The Recollections of Fifty Years of West Virginia. New York: G. P. Putnam's Sons, 1928. A lawyer's recollections of fifty years of growth and change in his state.
M600 (BC ASU)

The White Sulphur Springs: The Traditions, History, and Social Life of the Greenbriar, White Sulphur Springs. New York: Neale Pub. Co., 1916. History of the famous resort and spa.
M610 (ASU BC)

McCormick, Allen "Development of the Coal Industry of Grundy County, Tennessee." Master's thesis. George Peabody College, 1934.
M620

McCormick, Kyle The New-Kanawha River and the Mind War of West Virginia. Charleston, W. Va.: Mathews Print., 1959. Account of yet another mine war in West Virginia. The river was an important source of transportation.
M630 (BC)

The Story of Mercer County. Charleston, W. Va.: Charleston Print. Co., 1957. Another excellent county history from West Virginia.
M640 (BC ASU)

McCown, Mary Hardin 100th Anniversary History and Directory, 1871-1971, First Christian Church, Johnson City, Tennessee. Johnson City: n.p., 1971.
M650

McCown, Mary Hardin
Brief Chronological History of Johnson City, Tennessee and Three Suggested Historical Tours of the Johnson City Area. Johnson City, Tenn.: Chamber of Commerce, 1963.
M660 (BC LMC ETSU ASU)
Soldiers of the War of 1812 Buried in Tennessee. Johnson City, Tenn.: USD of 1812, 1959.
M670 (ASU)

McCown, Mary Hardin ed. Washington County, Tennessee, Records. Johnson City, Tenn.: n.p., 1964.
M680 (ETSU ASU)
Washington County, Tennessee, Records, Transcribed by Mary Hardin McCown. Vol. 1, Washington County Lists of Taxables, 1778-1801, ed. Nancy E. Jones Stickley and Inez Burns. Johnson City, Tenn.: privately printed, 1964.
M690

McCoy, Freida The Tempter's Harvest. Findley, Ohio: Ellisonia, Manse of the Muses, 1954. Poems from the hills.
M700
Till the Frost. Pikeville, Ky.: n.p., 1952. Appalachian poetry.
M710

McCoy, George William Battle of Asheville. Publication, no. 1. Asheville, N. C.: Buncombe County Confederate Centennial Committee, 1965? A minor battle in the closing days of the war.
M720 (ASU LMC UNCA)
A Bibliography for the Great Smoky Mountains. Asheville, N. C.: n.p., 1932.
M730
A Brief History of the Great Smoky Mountains National Park Movement in North Carolina. Asheville, N. C.: Inland Press, 1940.
M740
The First Presbyterian Church, Asheville, North Carolina, 1794-1951. Asheville, N. C.: Miller Print. Co., 1951.
M750
Guide to the Great Smoky Mountains National Park. 1st ed. Asheville, N. C.: Inland Press, 1933.
M760 (WCU)

McCoy, George William comp. Official Data on Western North Carolina's 223 Highest Mountain Peaks. Asheville, N. C.: Asheville Citizens-Times Co., 1946. A marvelous store of information on the western mountains.
M770 (WCU)

McCoy, Homer Claude "The Rise of Education and the Decline of Feudal Tendencies in the Tug River Valley of West Virginia and Kentucky in Relation to the Hatfield and McCoy Feud." Master's thesis. Marshall College, 1950. Written by one of the McCoy kinsmen.
M780 (ASU)

McCoy, Isaac History of Baptist Indian Missions: Embracing Remarks of the Former and Present Condition of the Aboriginal Tribes. Their Settlement Within the Indian Territory, and Their Future Prospects. Microfilm. Washington: H. and S. Raynor, 1840.
M790 (WCU)

McCoy, John L. Bird, Alan R. White Americans in Rural Poverty. Washington: U. S. Department of Agriculture, Economic Research Service, 1967.
B4070 (ASU)

McCoy, John Pleasant Big as Life. New York: Harper and Brothers, 1950. A wealthy widower becomes infatuated with Flossie Sowers, forty years his junior. His daughter is horrified; his housekeeper remembers another romance. It is a story of a family who stands together.
M800 (LMC BC ASU)
The Secret Doorways. New York: Weybright and Talley, 1971. A tale of life and love and terror in a coal town on the Cumberland River.
M810
Swing the Big-eyed Rabbit. Philadelphia: Blakiston Co., 1944. A shy mountain boy is accepted as a student at the newly established mission school. He has a great desire for knowledge but life at the school proves almost too real. Temptation in the form of seductive Millie Darnell, the teacher he idolizes, almost brings his dream to an end.
M820 (ASU LMC ETSU BC)

McCoy, Lola Love Tom Wolfe's "Dixieland." Asheville, N. C.: Stephans Press, 1949. Asheville and environs, the south of Thomas Wolfe.
M830 (ASU WCU)

McCoy, Lottie "History of Education in Harlan County, Kentucky." Master's thesis. Univ. of Kentucky, 1936.
M840

McCoy, Truda The Tempter's Harvest. Pikeville, Ky.: n.p., 1954. Poems.
M850
Till the Frost. Pikeville, Ky.: n.p., 1952.
M860 (ASU BC)

McCoy, William Joseph "The Tennessee Political System: The Relationship of the Socioeconomic Environment to Political Processes and Policy Outputs." Ph. D. Diss. Univ. of Tennessee, 1970. Draws some interesting conclusions about depressed areas in East Tennessee.
M870

McCracken, Dennis W. "A Study of Serum Protein Variation in Peromyscus Maniculatus Nubiterrae Rhoads at Six Attitudinal Habitats on Roan Mountain, Carter County, Tennessee, and Mitchell County, North Carolina." Master's thesis. East Tennessee State Univ., 1972.
M880 (ETSU)

McCracken, George Englert The Welcome Claimants Proved, Disproved and Doubtful with an Account of Their Descendants. With a foreword by Walter Lee Sheppard, Jr. Welcome Society of Pennsylvania Publications, no. 2. Baltimore: Genealogical Pub. Co., 1970. The Welcome was one of William Penn's first emigrant ships to come to Pennsylvania.
M890 (ASU)

McCrady, Edward The History of South Carolina in the Revolution, 1775-1780. Xerox copy of the original. New York: Macmillan Co., 1901. Information on the campaign which included Kings Mountain and Cowpens.
M900 (ASU)

McCrary, Mary Jane The Goodly Heritage: A History of St. Phillips Church of Brevard, N. C., and of St. Pauls in the Diocese of Western Carolina. Kennesaw, Ga.: Continental Book Co., 1959.
M910 (WCU BC)

McCraw, Thomas K. TVA and the Power Fight. New York: Lippincott, 1971. Recounts the various struggles of the TVA in establishing their vast bureacracy.
M920 (LMC BC)

McCreath, Andrew Smith The Mineral Wealth of Virginia Tributary to the Lines of the Norfolk and Western and Shenandoah Valley Railroad Companies. Harrisburg, Pa.: L. S. Hart, Printer and Binder, 1884.
M930 (BC)
New River Cripple Creek Mineral Region of Virginia. Harrisburg, Pa.: Harrisburg Pub. Co., 1887.
M940

McCue, John Bruce Limestones of West Virginia. West Virginia Geological Survey Reports, vol. 12. Parkersburg, W. Va.: Scholl Print. Co., 1939.
M960 (ASU ETSU)

McCue, John Bruce and others Clays of West Virginia. Reports, vol. 18. Morgantown: West Virginia Geological Survey, 1948.
M950 (ETSU)

McCulloch, Delia A. Pioneers of Mason County, West Virginia. Charleston, W. Va.: J. B. F. Yoak, 1910.
M970

McCulloch, Jack D. "A Study of the Status of Rural Teachers in East Tennessee." Master's thesis. East Tennessee State College, 1951. Examines academic background, certification and experience of rural teachers in East Tennessee.
M980 (ETSU)

McculIoh, Judith Hillbilly Records and Tune Transcriptions. Los Angeles: The John Edwards Memorial Foundation, Univ. of California, 1967.
M990
Some Child Ballads on Hillbilly Records. Los Angeles: The John Edwards Memorial Foundation, 1966.
M1000

McCurdy, Howard E., Jr.
"Centralization-decentralization in a Context of Intergovernmental Relations: A Study of Selected Federal Projects in Appalachia." Ph. D. Diss. Cornell Univ., 1969.
M1010

McCurry, Bertha Moore Black Top. Grand Rapids, Mich.: Wm. B. Eerdmans Pub. Co., 1956. The mountain community resents the coming of a road that threatens to isolate their best land.
M1020 (WCU BC ASU)
On Silver Creek Knob. Chicago: Moody Institute Press, 1939. Two youngsters orphaned by a tornado go to the mountains to live on a great uncle's abandoned farm, renew their courage, and plan their lives.
M1021 (BC)
Strength of the Hills. Chicago: Moody Press, 1952. A young physician, Mark Murray, returns wounded from World War II and finds himself identifying through time and space and by coincidence and intuition with his great grandparents to come to the hills to escape the war and dreamed of rearing a doctor.
M1030 (BC)

McCurry, Betsey pseud. see **McCurry, Bertha Moore**

McCurry, John Gordon The Social Harp. 1855. Reprint. Edited by Daniel W. Patterson and John F. Garst. Athens: Univ. of Georgia Press, 1973. The most popular of the shape-note songsters which were used all through these mountains until very recent times.
M1040 (ASU BC)

McDade, Frank E. "History of Education in Logan County, West Virginia." Master's thesis. Univ. of Kentucky, 1941.
M1050

McDaniel, Harold W. History of Forestdale Evangelical United Brethren Church. Knoxville: The Church, 1956.
M1060

McDaniel, Susie Blaylock Official History of Catoosa County, Georgia, 1853-1953. Dalton, Ga.: Gregory Print. and Office Supply, 1953.
M1070 (ASU LMC BC)

McDonald Associates Evaluation of Timber Development Organization. Reprint of a report prepared for the Appalachian Regional Commission. Appalachian Research Report, no. 1. Washington: n.p., 1966.
M1080 (ASU WCU)
A Forest Industry Processing and Marketing Complex for Eastern Kentucky. Prepared for the U. S. Area Redevelopment Administration. Washington: Govt. Print. Off., April, 1963, i. e. 1964.
M1090 (LMC)

McDonald, Benjamin Wilburn History of the Cumberland Presbyterian Church. 4th ed. Nashville, Tenn.: Board of publication of Cumberland Presbyterian Church, 1888.
M1100

McDonald Cornelia Peake A Diary with Reminiscences of the War and Refugee Life in the Shenandoah Valley, 1860-1865. Annotated and supplemented by Hunter McDonald. Nashville: Cullom and Ghertner Co., 1935.
M1110 (ASU LMC)

McDonald, David John Coal and Unionism: A History of the American Coal Miners Unions. Indianapolis, Ind.: Cornelius Print. Co., 1939.
M1120 (BC ASU)

McDonald, Everett The Red Debt. New York: G. W. Dillingham Co., 1916. A novel about a feud in the highlands of Kentucky, replete with moonshiners, churches, and an aura of fiefdom.
M1130 (BC)

McDonald, H. P. Weisenberger, Billy C. Soil Survey, Elliott County, Kentucky. Washington: U. S. Soil Conservation Service, 1965.
W2390

McDonald, Herman Patrick Reconnaissance Soil Survey, Fourteen Counties in Eastern Kentucky. Soil Survey, Series 1962, no. 1. Washington: U. S. Dept. of Agriculture, Soil Conservation Services, 1965.
M1140

McDonald, Lois Southern Mill Hills, a Study of Social and Economic Forces in Certain Textile Mill Villages. New York: Alex L. Hillman, 1928. Includes villages in the foothills of Appalachia.
M1150 (ASU WWC)

McDonald, Patrick A Collection of Highland Vocal Airs. 1784. Reprint. Norwood, Pa.: Norwood Editions, 1973. Many of these are still sung in Appalachia.
M1160 (ASU)

McDonnold, B. W. History of the Cumberland Presbyterian Church. 2nd ed. Nashville: Cumberland Presbyterian Church, 1888. The Cumberland Presbyterian Church is truly an Appalachian phenomena.
M1170 (ASU BC)

History of the Cumberland Presbyterian Church. 4th ed. Nashville: Board of Publication of the Cumberland Presbyterian Church, 1899.
M1180 (ASU)

McDowell, Flora Folk Dances of Tennessee; Folk Customs and Old Play Party Games of the Caney Fork Valley. Delaware, Ohio: Cooperative Recreation Service, n.d.
M1190 (ASU)

Folk Dances of Tennessee; Old Play Party Games of the Caney Fork Valley. n.p.: Edward Brothers, Inc., 1938.
M1200 (BC ASU)

McDowell, Katherine Sherwood Bonner Dialect Tales. New York: Harper and Brothers, 1883. Some of the best renditions of mountain speech found in Appalachian literature.
M1210 (BC ASU ETSU)

McDowell, L. L. Songs of the Old Camp Ground. Ann Arbor, Mich.: n.p., 1937. Religious songs of the Tennessee hill country.
M1220 (BC ASU)

McDowell, Lucien McDowell, Flora Folk Dances of Tennessee; Folk Customs and Old Play Party Games of the Caney Fork Valley. Delaware, Ohio: Cooperative Recreation Service, n.d.
M1190 (ASU)

McDowell, Flora Folk Dances of Tennessee; Old Play Party Games of the Caney Fork Valley. n.p.: Edward Brothers, Inc., 1938.
M1200 (BC ASU)

McDowell, Robert C. Geologic Map of the Sardis Quadrangle, Northwestern Kentucky. Washington: U. S. Geological Survey, 1973.
M1230 (BC)

McDowell, Sam Surname Index to the 1850 Federal Population Census of Kentucky. n.p.: The author, n.d. Index includes Clay, Clinton, Crittenden, and Cumberland Counties.
M1240

Surname Index to the 1850 Federal Population Census of Kentucky. n.p.: n.p., n.d. Index includes: Grayson, Green, Greenup, and Hancock.
M1250

McDowell, William L., Jr. ed. Documents Relating to Indian Affairs, 1754-1756. Colonial Records of South Carolina, series 2. Columbia: Univ. of South Carolina Press, 1970. Includes some Cherokee information.
M1260 (LMC)

McElderry, Bruce Robert Thomas Wolfe. United States Authors Series, 50. New York: Twayne Publishers, 1964.
M1270 (ASU WCU UNCA)

McEldowney, John C. History of Wetzel County, West Virginia. n.p.: n.p., 1901.
M1280 (BC)

McElroy, Don D. "A Comparative Analysis of the Results of the Kraus-Weber Test for Minimum Muscular Fitness in Four of the Elementary Schools of Johnson City, Tennessee." Master's thesis. East Tennessee State College, 1957.
M1290

McElroy, Lucy Cleaver Juletty: A Story of Old Kentucky. New York: T. Y. Crowell and Co., 1901. Romantic tale of a mountain girl and a young revenue agent.
M1300 (ASU BC)

McFall, Pearl Smith It Happened in Pickens County. Pickens, S. C.: Sentinel Press, 1959. Informal history of Pickens County, South Carolina.
M1310 (ASU BC)

The Keowee River and Cherokee Background. n.p.: n.p., 1966. A history of the Keowee River and the Cherokees who once lived along it.
M1320 (BC)

McFarlan, Arthur Crane Some Old Chester Problems — Correlations Along the Eastern Belt of Outcrop. Series 9, Bulletin, no. 20. Lexington: Kentucky Geological Survey, 1956.
M1330 (ETSU)

McFarland, Berty Sketches of Early Watauga. Illustrated by Peggy Polson. Boone, N. C.: American Association of University Women, 1973. Sketches of historic homes and buildings in Watauga County.
M1340 (ASU)

McFarland, Robert W. The Surrender of Cumberland Gap. Columbus, Ohio: Smythe, 1898.
M1350

McFarlane, James The Coal Regions of America. New York: D. Appleton and Co., 1873. Discusses topography, geology and development of the coal regions of America.
M1360

McGann, Agnes Geraldine, Sister Nativism in Kentucky in 1860. Ph. D. Diss. Catholic Univ. of America, 1944. Study traces nativism — anti-foreign, anti-Catholic social and political movement in Kentucky prior to the Civil War.
M1370 (ASU)

McGee, Bluford Bartlett The Country Youth: Autobiography of B. B. McGee. North Wilkesboro, N. C.: Pearson Pub. Co., 1964. Recollections of life in Wilkes County, North Carolina with an introduction by James Larkin Pearson.
M1380 (ASU)

McGee, Charles E. Regeneration After Clearcutting in the Southern Appalachians. U. S. Forest Service Research Paper, SE-70. Asheville, N. C.: Southeastern Forest Experiment Station, 1970.
M1390 (LMC)

Regeneration in Southern Appalachian Oak Stands. U. S. Forest Service Research Note, SE-72. Asheville, N. C.: Southeastern Forest Experiment Station, 1967.
M1400

McGee, Gentry Richard A History of Tennessee from 1663 to 1905. For use in schools. New York: American Book Co., 1899. The portions devoted to the earlier years contain much information on East Tennessee.
M1410 (ASU BC)

A History of Tennessee from 1663 to 1930. Revised and enlarged by C. J. Ijams. 1930. Reprint. Nashville: Charles Elder, 1971.
M1420 (ASU)

McGee, Ivan Clair "The Identification and Analysis of Agricultural Occupations in Seventeen Pennsylvania Counties." Ed. D. Diss. Pennsylvania State Univ., 1965. A careful study of farm tasks in Appalachian Pennsylvania.
M1430

McGee, Leroy Randolph Income and Employment in the Southeast: A Study of Cyclical Behavior. Lexington: Univ. of Kentucky Press, 1967. Includes information relative to Appalachian counties.
M1440 (ASU BC)

McGee, Thomas D'Arcy A History of the Irish Settlers in North America, from the Earliest Period to the Census of 1850. 6th ed. Boston: Patrick Donahoe, 1855.
M1450 (ASU)

McGehee, Thomasine Cobb Journey Proud. New York: Macmillan Co., 1939. Romantic fiction set in the Cumberland Mountains.
M1460 (ASU)

McGhee, Lucy Kate comp. Cherokee and Creek Indians. Returns a Property Left in Tennessee and Georgia, 1838. n.p.: n.p., n.d.
M1470

Historical Records of East Tennessee. Jefferson County, Dandridge Edition. 2 vols. Washington, D. C.: n.p., 1954.
M1480

Southwest Virginia Historical Records, Census of 1810, Wytheville, Wythe County edition. n.p.: n.p., n.d. Wythe county history in census and other records.
M1490

McGhee, Maxie B. "Socioeconomic Characteristics of Young Farmers Enrolled in Vocational Agriculture Classes in West Virginia." Master's thesis. West Virginia Univ., 1970.
M1500

McGill, John For Which the First Was Made. Boston: Qualls, Hood and Co., 1974. John McGill, veteran newsman, has written a novel about his native Carter County, Kentucky, incorporating much local tradition. Especially fascinating is the story of Matthew Sellers, who wanted to be the first man to fly an airplane. A vigilante group known as The Regulators recalls some of the violence that has plagued the region in the past.
M1510

McGill, Josephine comp. Folk-songs of the Kentucky Mountains. New York: Boosey and Co., 1917. Twenty traditional ballads and other English folk-songs, notated from the singing of the Kentucky mountain people. Introductory note by H. E. Krehbiel.
M1520 (ASU WCU BC)

McGill, Nettie Pauline The Welfare of Children in Bituminous Coal Mining Communities in West Virginia. Publication, no. 117. Washington: U. S. Dept. of Labor, Children's Bureau, 1923.
M1530 (ASU)

McGill, William M. Caverns of Virginia. University, Va.: State Commission on Conservation and Development, 1933. Description of and directions to the caves and caverns of Virginia.
M1540 (LMC)

Outline of the Mineral Resources of Virginia. Bulletin, no. 47, Educational Series, no. 3. Richmond: Virginia Geological Survey, 1936.
M1550 (LMC)

McGowan, Alice Judith of the Cumberlands. Illustrated by George Wright. New York: G. P. Putnam's Sons, 1908. A romantic novel with lovely Roan Mountain, Tennessee, as a backdrop.
M1560 (ASU)

The Sword in the Mountains. New York: Grosset and Dunlap, 1910. A civil war novel with a mountain setting.
M1570 (ASU BC)

The Sword in the Mountains. New York and London: G. P. Putnam's Sons, 1910.
M1580

The Wiving of Lance Cleaverage. New York: G. P. Putnam's Sons, 1909. Two wild spirits wed, flont tradition, separate, and reunite when Lance is charged with murder.
M1590 (BC)

McGowan, Daniel A. "Measurement of Personal Wealth in Centre County, Pennsylvania." Ph. D. Diss. Pennsylvania State Univ., 1973.
M1600

McGraw, Thomas K. Morgan vs. Lilienthal: The Feud within the TVA. Chicago: Loyola Univ. Press, 1970. Internecine strife during the early days of TVA which resulted in Mr. Arthur F. Morgan's resignation from a TVA directorship.
M1610

"TVA and the Power Fight, 1933-1939." Ph. D. Diss. Univ. of Wisconsin, 1970.
M1620

McGregor, James Clyde The Disruption of Virginia. New York: Macmillan Co., 1922. The beginnings of West Virginia history.
M1630 (BC ASU ETSU)

McGrew, Ellen Z. North Carolina Census Records, 1784-1900. Raleigh: North Carolina State Dept. of Archives and History, 1967.
M1640

McGuffey, Charles D. ed. Chattanooga and Her Battlefields. Chattanooga: MacGowan-Cooke, 1912.
M1650

Standard History of Chattanooga, Tennessee, with Full Outline of the Early Settlement, Pioneer Life, Indian History and General and Particular History of the City to the Close of the Year 1910. Knoxville: Crew and Dorey, 1911.
M1660

McGuire, Edna Daniel Boone. Chicago: Wheeler Pub. Co., 1945.
M1670 (ETSU)

McIlhany, Hugh Milton Some Virginia Families Being Genealogies of the Kinney, Stribling, Trout, McIlhany, Milton, Rogers, Tate, Snickers, Taylor, McCormick, and other Families of Virginia. Baltimore: Genealogical Pub. Co., 1962.
M1710 (ASU)

McIlwaine, H. R. ed. Journals of the Council of the State of Virginia. 4 vols. Virginia State Library, 1931.
M1680

McIlwaine, Shields The Southern Poor-white from Lubberland to Tobacco Road. Norman: Univ. of Oklahoma Press, 1939. Draws a useful distinction between the mountaineer and the poor white.
M1690 (ASU)

The Southern Poor-white from Lubberland to Tobacco Road. 1939. Reprint. New York: Cooper Square Pub., 1970.
M1700 (LMC)

McIntyre, C. L. Soil Survey: Dawson, Lumpkin, and White Counties, Georgia. Washington: U. S. Dept. of Agriculture, 1972.
M1720

Robertson, Stanley M. Soil Survey, Habersham County, Georgia. Washington: U. S. Soil Conservation Service, 1963.
R3190

McIntyre, John Thomas In Kentucky with Daniel Boone. Philadelphia: The Penn Pub. Co., 1913.
M1730 (ASU)

McJunkin, Frederick E. Water Resources of Virginia. Blacksburg: Virginia Polytechnic Institute, 1966. Appalachian Virginia's water resources are listed.
M1740

McKaye, Percy The Gobbler of God: A Poem of the Southern Appalachians. New York: Longmans, Green and Co., 1928.
M1750 (LMC WCU BC)

Kentucky Mountain Fantasies: Three Short Plays for an Appalachian Theatre. Illustrated by Arvia MacKaye. New York: Longmans, Green and Co., 1928. Three humorous plays with mountain folk getting the best of city folk.
M1760 (ASU BC)

Kentucky Mountain Fantasies: Three Short Plays for an Appalachian Theatre. 1928. Reprint. New York: Samuel French, 1933.
M1770 (LMC)

Tall Tales of the Kentucky Mountains. New York: George H. Doran Co., 1926. Sol Shell travels the hills telling tales for his board. A sort of mountain minstrel.
M1780 (ASU WCU LMC BC)

This Fine Pretty World: A Comedy of the Kentucky Mountains. New York: Macmillan Co., 1924. Marital shenanigans. Gilly Maggot wants a child and his wife is past child-bearing age.
M1790 (ASU LMC ETSU BC)

Weathergoose-wool. Illustrated by Arvia MacKaye. London: Longmans, Green and Co., 1929. Tales leaning toward the supernatural.
M1800 (ASU LMC BC)

McKee, Ella F. Plumed Depths. Lynchburg, Va.: Coleman and Bradley, 1956. God, trees, weather and people come and go in these eighty poems.
M1810

McKee, George Wilson The McKees of Virginia and Kentucky. n.p.: n.p., 1890.
M1820

McKellar, William H. "Churvallic's Chronicle of Franklin County, Tennessee." Unpublished typescript, n.d.
M1830

McKelvie, Martha Groves Belonging: A Nostalgic Look at Appalachia. Illustrated by Emily Touraine. Philadelphia: Franklin Pub. Co., 1954 or 5.
M1840 (LMC)

McKenney, Thomas Lorraine Memoirs, Official and Personal; with Sketches of Travels among the Northern and Southern Indians; Embracing a War Excursion, and Descriptions of Scenes along the Western Borders. 2 vols. New York: Paine and Burgess, 1846. As an official of the Bureau of Indian Affairs, McKenney conferred with the Chickasaws, Choctaws, and Cherokees about their removal across the Mississippi.
M1850

McKenzie, Helen R. West Virginia Housing, Considerations for Planning and Programming. Charleston: West Virginia Department of Commerce, 1967.
M1860

McKim, C. R. Fifty Year History of the Monongahela National Forest. Elkins, W. Va.: n.p., 1970.
M1870

McKim, Ruby Short One Hundred and One Patchwork Patterns: Quilt Name Stories, Cutting Designs, Material Suggestions, Yardage Estimates, Definite Instructions for Every Step of Quilt Making. Rev. ed. New York: Dover Publications, 1962. One of the clearest books of instructions available.
M1880 (ASU WCU BC)

McKinney, Ernest Lee "A Follow-up Study of the 1959-1963 Graduates of Langston High School, Johnson City, Tennessee." Master's thesis. East Tennessee State Univ., 1964.
M1890 (ETSU)

McKinney, Gordon Bartlett "Mountain Republicanism, 1876-1900." Ph. D. Diss. Northwestern Univ., 1971. The fierce mountain republicanism that was the heritage of the Civil War and Reconstruction is well documented in this study.
M1900

McKinney, John C. The South in Continuity and Change. Durham, N. C.: Duke Univ. Press, 1965. Some selections of this study are applicable to the mountains.
M1910 (BC FC)

McKinney, Lavonia "Factors Affecting the Health and Educational Growth of Elementary Pupils in Three Selected Schools of Jefferson County, Alabama." Master's thesis. Alabama State College, 1952.
M1920

McKinney, Zeyland G. "The County Farm Life Schools of North Carolina." Master's thesis. Appalachian State Teachers College, 1953.
M1930 (ASU)

McKitrick, Eric L. Andrew Johnson and Reconstruction. Chicago: Univ. of Chicago Press, 1960. A sensitive study of the U. S. President who inherited the most difficult conditions that have ever gone with that office.
M1940 (ASU)

McKnight, Charles Captain Jack, the Scout: Or, the Indian Wars about Old Fort Duquesne, an Historical Novel. Illustrated. Philadelphia: John C. Winston Co., 1873. A stirring novel of frontier life in the Trans-Appalachian West.
M1950 (ASU BC)

Old Fort Duquesne: Or, Captain Jack, the Scout. An Historical Novel with Copious Notes. Pittsburgh: Peoples Monthly Pub. Co., 1873. A different edition and title, but the same novel as the preceding entry.
M1960 (ASU)

McKoy, Harry Brent Simon Kenton as Soldier, Scout, and Citizen: An Address Delivered Wednesday, August 19, 1936 at the Blue Licks Battlefield State Park, Robertson County, Kentucky on the Occasion of the Celebration of the Battle of the Blue Licks and Commemoration of the Centenary of the Death of General Simon Kenton. Lexington: n.p., 1936.
M1970

McLain, Nelson Wylie The Forgotten Region. Chicago: Ram's Horn Print., 1897. At head of the title: "Appalachian America," appears to be a plea for Berea College and other mission efforts in the Southern mountains.
M1990 (BC)

McLean, John Patterson An Epitome of the Superstitions of the Highlanders of Scotland. Microphoto copy. Cleveland: Bell and Howell Co., 1974.
M2000

A Historical Account of the Settlements of Scotch Highlanders in America Prior to the Peace of 1783: Together with Notices of Highland Regiments and Biographical Sketches. Baltimore: Genealogical Pub. Co., 1968. Many Scots eventually settled in Appalachia; the earlier arrivals were noted for their acceptance into the Cherokee nation.
M2010 (ASU)

McLean, Patricia "Human Resources Available to the Schools of Washington County, Tennessee." Master's thesis. East Tennessee State Univ., 1969.
M2020 (ETSU)

McLendon, Willie E. Soil Survey of Coffee County, Tennessee. Field Operations, 1908. Washington: U. S. Department of Agriculture, Bureau of Soils, 1910.
M2030

Soil Survey of Franklin County, Georgia. Field Operations, 1909.
M2040

Soil Survey of Grainger County, Tennessee. Field Operations, 1906. Washington: U. S. Department of Agriculture, Bureau of Soils, 1908.
M2050

Soil Survey of Oconee County, South Carolina. Field Operations, 1907. Washington: U. S. Department of Agriculture, Bureau of Soils, 1909.
M2060

Soil Survey of Walker County, Georgia. Field Operations, 1910. Washington: U. S. Department of Agriculture, Bureau of Soils, 1911.
M2070

McLeod, John Angus From These Stones: Mars Hill College, 1856-1968. Mars Hill, N. C.: Mars Hill College, 1968.
M2080 (LMC WCU WWC)

From These Stones: Mars Hill College, the First Hundred Years. Mars Hill, N. C.: Mars Hill College, 1955. A well written history of this Madison County College.
M2090 (ASU WCU BC)

"The Southern Highlands in Prose Fiction." Master's thesis. Univ. of North Carolina, 1930. An interesting but incomplete study of mountain fiction.
M2100 (ASU WCU)

McLeod, William Christie The American Indian Frontier. The History of Civilization Historical Ethnology. New York: A. A. Knopf, 1928. Includes maps of the Indian holdings from the seventeenth century foreward.
M2110 (ASU)

McLinden, John J. "An Historical Study of the Growth of Commercial Television in West Virginia." Master's thesis. West Virginia Univ., 1967.
M2120

McLysaght, Edward A Guide to Irish Surnames. 2nd ed. rev. and enlarged. Dublin: Helicon, 1965. There are literally thousands of Irish surnames in Appalachia.
M2130 (ASU)

More Irish Families. Galway, Ireland: O'Gorman, Ltd., 1960.
M2140 (ASU)

Supplement to Irish Families. Baltimore: Genealogical Book Co., 1964.
M2150 (ASU)

McMahon, Blanche C. Sevier County, Tennessee. Fifth Census. Knoxville, Tenn.: n.p., 1956.
M2160

McMaster, William M. General Geology and Ground-water Resources of Limestone County, Alabama: A Reconnaissance. County Report, 11. University: Alabama Geological Survey, 1963.
M2170 (ETSU)

McMechen, James H. Legends of the Ohio Valley. Wheeling: West Virginia Print. Co., 1887. Stirring tales of pioneers and Indians in early West Virginia.
M2180 (BC ASU)

McMeekin, Clark Old Kentucky Country. 1st ed. American Folkways. New York: Duell, Sloan and Pearce, 1957.
M2190 (ASU LMC WWC BC UNCA)

Tyrone of Kentucky. New York: Appleton-Century-Crofts, 1954. Returning to his ravaged Kentucky farm with an attractive Alabama bride, David Tyrone, a Confederate soldier, strives to wrest a living from the soil and to resolve the strained relationship with his former fiancee in a novel of conflicting loyalties during the Reconstruction.
M2200 (WCU)

McMeekin, Isabel McLennan The Bronze Hunter. Philadelphia: Dorrance and Co., 1935. Poems from Kentucky.
M2210

Journey Cake. New York: J. Messner, 1942. Juba, a free colored woman, in the Yadkin Valley of North Carolina takes her dead mistress's children over the mountains to Kentucky to join their father.
M2220 (BC)

Juba's New Moon. Illustrated by Nicholas Panesis. New York, J. Messner, 1944. Another story of the invincible Juba and the youngsters she guards in the wilds of Kentucky.
M2230 (ASU WCU BC)

Melodies and Mountaineers. Boston: Stratford Co., 1921.
M2240 (ASU)

McMeekin, Isabel McLennan, and Clark, Dorothy Park see McMeekin, Clark pseud.

McMichael, Edward V. Archeological Survey of Nicholas County, West Virginia. Archeological Series, no. 1. Morgantown: West Virginia Geological and Economic Survey, 1965.
M2250 (ASU)

Excavation of the Murad Mound, Kanawha County, West Virginia, and an Analysis of Kanawha Valley Mounds. Report of Archeological Investigations, no. 1. Morgantown: West Virginia Geological and Economic Survey, 1969.
M2260 (ASU)

Introduction to West Virginia Archeology. Illustrated by Bettye J. Broyles and Paul W. Queen. 2nd ed. rev. Educational Series. Morgantown: West Virginia Geological and Economic Survey, 1968.
M2270 (ASU)

Introduction to West Virginia Archeology. Morgantown: West Virginia Geological and Economic Survey, 1969.
M2280

McMillan, Homer "Unfinished Tasks" of the Southern Presbyterian Church. Richmond: Presbyterian Committee of Publication, 1922. One chapter devoted to unfinished tasks in Appalachia.
M2290

McMullen, Robert B. History of the First Presbyterian Church in Knoxville, Tennessee. Knoxville: John B. G. Kinsloe, 1855.
M2300

McMurray, Lynn L. The Talc Deposits of Talledega County, Alabama. Circular, no. 16. University: Alabama Geological Survey, 1941.
M2320 (BC ETSU)

McMurry, Charles Alexander Chattanooga: Its History and Geography. Morristown, Tenn.: Globe Book Co., 1923. A very thorough account of the development of Chattanooga.
M2310 (BC ETSU)

McMurry, Richard M. The Road Past Kennesaw: The Atlanta Campaign of 1864. Foreword by Bell I. Wiley. Washington: U. S. National Park Service, 1972. Kennesaw Mountain was the site of the last battle in General Joe Johnson's brilliant mountain campaign from Chickamauga to Kennesaw.
M2330

McNair, James Birtley comp. McNair, McNear, and McNeir Genealogies. Chicago: The author, 1923.
M2340 (ASU)

McNamara, Mary C. "Glory" of the Hills. Covington, Ky.: Mary C. McNamara, 1930. A dull and unbelievable novel of a mountain beauty, government geologists, a campaign to get mountain men into the war, education and, of course, love.
M2350 (BC)

McNeer, May Yonge The Story of the Southern Highlands. Illustrated by Cornelius High DeWitt. New York: Harper and Brothers, 1945. A sensitive text and beautiful illustrations interpret the mountains for the younger reader.
M2360 (ASU MHC LMC ETSU BC WWC WCU)

McNeil, Norman L. ed. Lumpkin, Ben Gray Folk Songs on Records. Denver: Alan Swallow, 1950.
L3950 (ASU)

McNeill, Douglas The Last Forest; Tales of the Allegheny Woods. New York: Forteeny's, 1940. A tale of the trans-Appalachian West.
M2370

McNeill, George Douglas Tales of Pocahontas County. Marlington, W. Va.: n.p., 1958.
M2380

McNeill, Louise From a Dark Mountain, Lyrics from the Production of Louise McNeill's Premiere Reading. Charleston, W. Va.: Morris Harvey Publications, 1972.
M2390 (ASU)

Gauley Mountain. 1st ed. New York: Harcourt, Brace and Co., 1939. One of the most marvelous books of poetry from the Appalachians. The whole history of her West Virginia home and its marvelous characters is here in verse.
M2400 (ASU LMC BC)

Mountain White. Dallas: Kaleidoscope Pubs., 1931. More great poetry from West Virginia's best-loved poet.
M2410

Paradox Hill from Appalachia to Lunar Shore. Morgantown: West Virginia Univ. Library, 1972.
M2420 (ASU)

McNeill, Robert H. Historical Address . . . in Celebration of the Founding of Beaver Creek Baptist Church, Wilkes County. The church, 1949.
M2430

McNelley, Pat ed. The First 40 Years: John C. Campbell Folk School. Atlanta: McNelley-Rudd Print. Service, 1966. A history of one of the region's most successful folk schools.
M2440 (ASU LMC MHC BC)

McNutt, Robert Britton and others Soil Survey, Cullman County, Alabama. Report by R. B. McNutt and E. A. Perry. Soil Survey, Series 1959, no. 9. Washington: U. S. Department of Agriculture, Soil Conservation Service, 1962.
M2450

McNutt, Samuel H. "Evaluation of the Collection of the Solid Waste in Bristol, Virginia, with a Consideration for the Proposed Annexation Area." Master's thesis. East Tennessee State Univ., 1971.
M2460 (ETSU)

McPherson, Ruth McNeil "A Follow-up Study of the Physics Students at Science Hill High School from 1944-1955." Master's thesis. East Tennessee State College, 1956.
M2470 (ETSU)

McQueen, David Raymond "A Determination of Ambient Air Concentrations of Sulfur Dioxide in Elizabethton, Tennessee." Master's thesis. East Tennessee State Univ., 1971.
M2480 (ETSU)

McRay, Sybil Wood comp. Hall County, Georgia, 1819-1839, Marriages. Gainesville, Ga.: The author, 1968. During this period Hall County was the last Georgia County on the frontier — to the north and west lay the Cherokee Nation.
M2490 (ASU)

Tombstone Inscriptions of Hall County, Georgia. Gainesville, Ga.: n.p., 1971.
M2500 (ASU)

McSpadden, J. Walker Storm Center. New York: Dodd, Mead and Co., 1947. A novel of the life of Andrew Johnson.
M2510 (BC)

McSpadden, Lynn Four and Twenty Songs for the Mountain Dulcimer. Music transcribed by Dorothy French. Mountain View, Ark.: Dulcimer Shoppe, 1970.
M2520 (ASU BC)

McTeer, Will A. History of New Providence Presbyterian Church, Maryville, Tennessee, 1786-1921. Maryville, Tenn.: n.p., 1921. History of the oldest Presbyterian Church in Maryville.
M2530 (ETSU)

McVaugh, Rogers Ferns of Georgia. Athens: Univ. of Georgia Press, 1951. Includes mountain varieties.
M2550 (LMC)

McVey, Frank Le Rond The Gates Open Slowly: A History of Education in Kentucky. Lexington: Univ. of Kentucky Press, 1949. Includes some discussion of educational phenomena in the mountains.
M2560 (BC LMC)

McWhiney, H. Grady "The Ordeal of Command: Bragg before Chickamauga." Ph. D. Diss. Columbia Univ., 1960.
M2540

McWhirter, Millie Hushed Were the Hills. Nashville: Abingdon Press, 1969. A widow and her two daughters move from the city to the Tennessee hills during the depression.
M2570 (ASU LMC ETSU MHC WCU BC)

McWhorter, John Camillus The Scout of the Buckongehanon: An Historical Romance of the Western Virginia Border, 1764-1782. Boston: Christopher Pub. House, 1927. Stirring novel of frontier West Virginia.
M2580 (ASU WCU BC)

McWhorter, Lucullus Virgil The Border Settlements of Northwestern Virginia from 1768-1795. Hamilton, Ohio: Republican Pub. Co., 1915. Includes notes on Indian raids, the lives of the scouts and anecdotes.
M2590 (BC)

McWhorter, Minnie S. History of Henry McWhorter Family of New Jersey and West Virginia. Charleston, W. Va.: Charleston Print. Co., 1948. The McWhorter family is found all through the mountains from West Virginia to Alabama.
M2600 (ASU)

McBride, Robert M. ed. Alderson, William T. ed. Landmarks of Tennessee History. Nashville: Tennessee Historical Society, 1965.
A1290

McCall, H. F. Burke, Richard Thomas Avon Soil Survey of Washington County, Maryland. Washington: U. S. Dept. of Agriculture, Bureau of Soils, 1923.
B8690

McCall, Sidney pseud. Fendlosa, Mary McNeil Christopher Laird. New York: Dodd, Mead, 1919.
F580

McCary, Ben C. ed. Bayard, Ferdinand Marie Travels of a Frenchman in Maryland and Virginia with a Description of Philadelphia and Baltimore, in 1791: Or, Travels in the Interior of the United States, to Bath, Winchester, in the Valley of the Shenandoah, etc., During the Summer of 1791. Ann Arbor, Mich.: Edwards Brothers, 1950.
B2140

McCauley, Orris D. Whitaker, James C. Costs and Returns for Hardwood Lumber Production in Appalachian Region of Kentucky and Ohio. Upper Darby, Pa.: Northeastern Forest Experiment Station, 1966.
W5260

McClay, Ben Harris ed. Harris, George Washington The Lovingood Papers. Athens, Tenn.: Tenn. Wesleyan College, 1962-.
H2810

McClure, Joe P. Knight, Herbert A. Virginia's Timber, 1966. Asheville, N. C.: Southeastern Forest Experiment Station, 1967.
K2780 (LMC)

McComás, F. W. Snidow, Francis Arthur An Economic and Social Survey of Giles County. Charlottesville: Univ. of Va. Extension Division, 1927.
S5250

McCue, John B. Price, Paul Holland Salt Brines of West Virginia. Morgantown: West Virginia Geological Survey, 1937.
P4560 (ETSU)

McCue, John Bruce Price, Paul Holland Springs of West Virginia. Morgantown: West Virginia Geological Survey, 1936.
P4570 (ETSU)

McDowell, F. N. Vanatta, Earl Steere Soil Survey of Cleveland County, North Carolina. Washington: U. S. Department of Agriculture, Bureau of Soils, 1918.
V40

McFarland, Betty Polson, Peggy Sketches of Early Watauga. Boone, N. C.: American Assoc. of University Women, Boone Branch, 1973.
P3460

McGehee, A. C. Burke, Richard Thomas Avon Soil Survey of Randolph County, Alabama. Washington: Govt. Print. Off., 1912.
B8730

Winston, Robert A. Soil Survey of Tuscaloosa County, Alabama. Washington: U. S. Department of Agriculture, Bureau of Soils, 1912.
W7820

McGinnes, Byrd S. Cushwa, Charles T. Forest Recreation: Estimated and Predictions in the North River Area, George Washington National Forest, Virginia. Blacksburg: Virginia Agricultural Experiment Station, 1965.
C9960

Machir, Delores Genealogical History of the Descendants of Machir of Scotland. Mt. Pleasant, W. Va.: Mattox Print. Service, 1964. Based on material compiled by Marchirs and Machir descendants and by Mae R. Crummel and James L. Pyles, both of whom married descendants.
M2610 (ASU)

Machir, Violette Somerville Machir, Delores Genealogical History of the Descendants of Machir of Scotland. Mt. Pleasant, W. Va.: Mattox Print. Service, 1964.
M2610 (ASU)

Machir, Violette Somerville comp. The Somerville Family and Descendants, 1789-1963. Greenville, Ill.: Naco Print. Co., 1963.
M2620 (ASU)

McIntyre, C. L. Akins, Richard O. Soil Survey: Dawson, Lumpkin, and White Counties, Georgia. Washington: U. S. Soil Conservation Service, 1972.
A850

McIntyre, Julian H. Brewer, Edward O. Soil Survey, Alleghany County, North Carolina. Washington: U. S. Soil Conservation Service, 1973.
B6530

McKee, J. M. Shaw, Charles Frederick Reconnaissance Soil Survey of Northeastern Pennsylvania. Washington: U. S. Department of Agriculture, Bureau of Soils, 1913.
S2470

Mackey, Lila Thrasher "The Social and Educational Aspects of the Tennessee Valley Authority." Master's thesis. George Peabody College, 1937.
M2630

McMahon, Blanche C. Creekmore, Pollyanna ed. Population Schedule of the U. S. Census of 1850 (Seventh Census) for Sevier County, Tennessee. Knoxville: The authors, 1953.
C8690 (ETSU BC)

McMaster, William M. Harris, Wiley F., Jr. Geology and Ground-water Resources of Lawrence County, Alabama: A Reconnaissance. University: Alabama Geological Survey, 1965.
H3030 (ETSU)

McNeilly, J. H. Bachman, J. W. Memorial of the Rev. James Park. Nashville: Smith & Lamar, 1912.
B20

MacNider, G. M. Hearn, Williamson Edward Soil Survey of Henderson County, North Carolina. Washington: U. S. Department of Agriculture, Bureau of Soils, 1909.
H4200

Hearn, Williamson Edward Soil Survey of Transylvania County, North Carolina. Washington: U. S. Department of Agriculture, Bureau of Soils, 1908.
H4210

Hearn, Williamson Edward Soil Survey of Transylvania County. Washington: Govt. Print. Off., 1907.
H4220

Macon County Home Demonstration Clubs Favorite Recipes. n.p.: n.p., n.d. Everything from chitlins to twice stewed possum.
M2640

Macon, Hershal L. Campbell, Carlos Clinton and others Great Smoky Mountains Wildflowers. Knoxville: Univ. of Tennessee Press, 1962.
C540 (LMC WCU ETSU)

Campbell, Carlos Clinton Great Smoky Mountains Wildflowers. Knoxville: Univ. of Tennessee Press, 1964.
C550 (ASU LMC WCU WWC BC)

McProud, Margaret Milam Fritz, Arah Miller Crabtrees of Southwest Virginia. Pecos, Texas: Hawks Printing Co., 1965.
F3440

McTuown, Ruth Shannon, Jasper Berry Presidential Politics in Kentucky, 1824-1948: A Compilation of Election Statistics and an Analysis of Political Behavior. Lexington: Bureau of Government Research, College of Arts and Sciences, Univ. of Kentucky, 1950.
S2230 (LMC)

Madden, David Bijou, A Novel. New York: Crown Publishers, 1974. A novel of a declining Appalachian town, a growing boy and the town's entertainment center and hotel.
M2650

Cassandra Singing: A Novel. New York: Crown Pub. Co., 1969. A novel of modern Kentucky with poverty, trouble, sickness, motorcycle culture, and through it all, somehow, Cassandra singing.
M2660 (ASU BC)

Rediscoveries: Informdl Essays in Which Well-known Novelists Rediscover Neglected Works of Fiction by One of Their Favorite Authors. Edited with an introduction by David Madden. New York: Crown Publishers, 1971. Three chapters deal with Appalachian writers.
M2670 (ASU)

Madden, Nancy Sawyer Sevier Sevier, Cora Bales Sevier Family History, with the Collected Letters of Gen. John Sevier, First Governor of Tennessee and 28 Collateral Family Lineages. Washington: Kaufman Print. Co., 1961.
S2030 (ASU ETSU MHC BC)

Maddocks, Durward Swing Your Partners: A Guide to Modern Country Dancing. Brattleboro, Vt.: Stephen Daye Press, 1964.
M2680

Maddox, Kathryn ed. In West Virginia, It Is Working: One Teacher Education Center in Action. Washington: Teacher Education, 1972. A study of the Kanawha County multi-institutional teacher education center.
M2690 (WCU BC ASU)

Maddox, Rufus Sherrill Common Forest Trees of Tennessee, How to Know Them; a Pocket Manual. Nashville, Tenn.: Dept. of Conservation, 1922.
M2700

Maddux, Rachel Fiction Into Film: A Walk in the Spring Rain. Knoxville: Univ. of Tennessee Press, 1970. An Appalachian novel is connected into film.
M2710 (ASU)

Madison County Industrial Commission We Look Unto These Hills and See Them Not As Obstacles But As Opportunities. n.p.: n.p., n.d. Madison County, North Carolina looks to the future.
M2720 (LMC)

Madison County Newsweek vol. 1. Richmond, Ky.: 1970. A newspaper with a mountain emphasis.
M2730

Madison, Monroe Bolling Drug Plants of Western North Carolina. n.p.: n.p., n.d. Western North Carolina is a leading center in the botanical drug trade.
M2740 (WCU ASU)

The Magazine of Albemarle County History vol. 1 — 1940. Charlottesville, Va.: Albemarle County Historical Society, annual.
M2750 (ASU)

Magazine of History — Biography Randolph County Historical Society, 1926.
M2760

Maggard, Ella Weep for the Dawn. New York: Carlton Press, 1969. After their father's death, two children are reclaimed by the mother they have never known.
M2770 (ASU WCU BC)

Magill, Mary Tucker History of Virginia, for the Use of Schools. 6th ed. Lynchburg, Va.: J. P. Bell, 1882. Virginia history text for children.
M2780 (LMC)

The Holcombes. A Story of Virginia Homelife. Philadelphia: J. B. Lippincott and Co., 1871. The children in a Blue Ridge mountain family are apprehensive about having a stepmother.
M2790 (ASU BC)

Magruder, James Mosby, Jr. comp. Index of Maryland Colonial Wills, 1634-1777, in the Hall of Records, Annapolis, Maryland. Reprinted with additions and a new introduction by Louise E. Magruder. 3 vols. in 1. Baltimore: Genealogical Pub. Co., 1967.
M2800 (ASU)

Magruder's Maryland Colonial Abstracts: Wills, Accounts and Inventories, 1772-1777. 1934-1939. Reprint. With a new introduction by Louise E. Magruder. 5 vols. in 1. Baltimore: Genealogical Pub. Co., 1968.
M2810 (ASU)

Mahan, Paul E. Smoky Mountain Wines. New York: Arco Pub. Co., 1973.
M2820 (ASU)

Maher, Stuart Wilder Hershey, Robert E. Limestone and Dolomite Resources of Tennessee. Nashville: Tennessee Division of Geology, 1963.
H5040 (ETSU)

Mahoney, James W. The Cherokee Physician . . . As Given by Richard Foreman. Chattanooga: J. M. Edney, 1846.
M2830

Maidment, James A New Book of Old Ballads. Edinburg: n.p., 1891. Songs still sung in the southern mountains.
M2840

Mairs, Oscar L. McMichael, Edward V. Excavation of the Murad Mound, Kanawha County, West Virginia, and an Analysis of Kanawha Valley Mounds. Morgantown: West Virginia Geological and Economic Survey, 1969.
M2260 (ASU)

Malcolm, Gerald C. "A Study of the Effect of Individualization on Achievement in Language Arts at North Side Elementary School." Master's thesis. East Tennessee State Univ., 1970.
M2850 (ETSU)

Maldonado, Ray F. Kiser, James L., Jr. A Study of Judicial Procedures on the Cherokee Indian Reservation. Cullowhee: Western Carolina Univ., 1970.
K2670 (LMC ASU)

Malesky, Gaynelle S. Green Autumn. Francestown, N. H.: Golden Quill Press, 1967. Fifty-one poems of farm and mining life.
M2860 (BC)

Mallison, Sam Thomas The Great Wildcatter. Charleston: Education Foundation of West Virginia, 1953. Biography of West Virginia's greatest oil magnate.
M2870 (ASU BC)

Let's Set a Spell. Charleston, W. Va.: Education Foundation, 1962. Tales from West Virginia.
M2880 (ASU)

Malmberg, Glenn Thomas Geology and Ground-water Resources of Madison County, Alabama. County Report, 3. University: Alabama Geological Survey, 1957.
M2890 (ETSU)

Malnak, Julian "The Appalachian Regional Development Act of 1965." D. P. A. Diss. New York Univ., 1968. An analysis of the Appalachian Regional Development Act and the Commission.
M2900

Malone, Bill C. Country Music U. S. A.: A Fifty-year History. Publications of the American Folklore Society Memoir Series, vol. 54. Austin: Univ. of Texas Press, 1968.
M2910 (FC ASU)

Malone, Henry Thompson Cherokees of the Old South: A People in Transition. Athens: Univ. of Georgia Press, 1956.
M2920 (UNCA ASU WCU LMC BC ETSU)

The Early Nineteenth Century Missionaries in the Cherokee Country. n.p.: n.p., n.d.
M2930

"A Social History of the Eastern Cherokee Indians from the Revolution to the Removal." Microfilm. Ph. D. Diss. Emory Univ., 1952.
M2940 (WCU ASU)

Malone, Howard D. "A History of Education in Jefferson County, Tennessee." Master's thesis. Univ. of Tennessee, 1955.
M2950

Malone, Joseph S. Sons of Vengeance. New York: F. H. Revell, 1903. A tale of feuding and fighting in the Cumberland highlands of Tennessee and Kentucky.
M2960 (BC ASU)

Maloney, Forrest B. The Rural Land Use of Washington County, Tennessee. Knoxville: Univ. of Tennessee, 1956.
M2970

Management and Economic Research Inc. Guidelines for an Appalachian Airport System. Research Report No. 3. Washington: Appalachian Regional Commission, 1966.
M2980

Manarin, Louis H. ed. North Carolina Troops, 1861-1865, a Roster. 2 vols. Raleigh, N. C.: State Dept. of Archives and History, 1966.
M2990 (ASU LMC)

Mangalam, J. J. Schwarzweller, Harry K. Mountain Families in Transition: A Case Study of Appalachian Migration. Univ. Park: Pennsylvania State Univ. Press, 1971.
S1270 (ASU WCU LMC ETSU WWC BC UNCA)

Mangalam, Joseph J. Human Migration: A Guide to Migration Literature in English, 1955-1962. Lexington: Univ. of Kentucky Press, 1968. Includes material on Appalachian migrants.
M3000

Mangrum, Claude Thomas "The Drain of Talent Out of North Carolina and Tennessee." Master's thesis. Kent State Univ., 1958. Mountain counties often lose their most promising students. Few of the educated come home again to live.
M3010 (ASU)

Mangum, Adolphus W. Soil Survey of the Campobello Area, South Carolina. Field Operations, 1903. Washington: Dept. of Agriculture, Bureau of Soils, 1904.
M3020

Soil Survey of Chattooga County, Georgia. Prepared in cooperation with the Georgia State College of Agriculture, Field Operations, 1912. Washington: U. S. Dept. of Agriculture, Bureau of Soils, 1913. Maps.
M3030

Mangum, Charles Staples The Legal Status of the Tenant Farmer in the Southeast. Chapel Hill: Univ. of North Carolina Press, 1952.
M3040 (LMC)

Mangus, A. R. Subsequent Movement of Kentucky Hill Families Relocated as Farm Laborers in Ohio. Columbus: Ohio State Univ. and Ohio Agriculture Experiment Station, 1943.
M3050 (ASU)

Mank, Russell W., Jr. "Senator Kenneth D. McKellar and the Tennessee Valley Authority, 1933-1944." Master's thesis. Univ. of Maryland, 1964.
M3060

Mankin, Virginia T. The Crowning Event and Other Stories. Philadelphia: Dorrance and Co., 1953. Stories of rowdy and funloving mountain folk centered in and around West Virginia.
M3070 (ASU)

A Mountain Code and Other Stories. Philadelphia: Dorrance and Co., 1938. Humorous stories of West Virginia mountain folk.
M3080 (ASU)

Manley, Joe F. Fishing in the Great Smoky Mountains National Park and Adjacent Waters. Gatlinburg, Tenn.: author, 1938.
M3090

Manley, Louise Southern Literature from 1579-1895. Richmond, Va.: B. F. Johnson Pub. Co., 1895. Includes Appalachian items.
M3100

Manly, Marline Kentucky Kate; or, The Moonshiners' League. "Log Cabin Library," No. 366. New York: Street and Smith, 1896. A Kentucky mountain moonshine tale complete with a lovely heroine.
M3110

Mann, Cathrine Cleek comp. Marriage Record "A', Floyd County, Georgia, 1834-1848. Cedar Bluff, Ala.: Mannsford, 1970.
M3120 (ASU)

Mann, Charles J. Soil Survey of Bedford County, Pennsylvania. Prepared in cooperation with the Pennsylvania State College School of Agriculture and Experiment Station. Field Operations, 1911. Washington: U. S. Dept. of Agriculture, Bureau of Soils, 1913.
M3130

Manning, Ambrose N. ed. Burton, Thomas G. ed. Collection of Folklore: Folksongs. Johnson City: Institute of Regional Studies, East Tennessee State Univ., 1967.
B9290 (ASU LMC WCU ETSU BC)

Burton, Thomas G. ed. Collection of Folklore: Folksongs II. Johnson City: Institute of Regional Studies, East Tennessee State Univ., 1969.
B9300 (ASU LMC ETSU BC)

A Collection of Folklore by Undergraduate Students of East Tennessee State University Johnson City: East Tennessee State Univ., 1966.
C5920 (ETSU ASU LMC BC)

Mannis, Martha A. "A Study Designed for the Attitudes of the Negro Teachers of Bedford County, Virginia Toward In-Service Teacher Education." Master's thesis. North Carolina Agricultural and Technical College, 1954.
M3140

Manpower Development and Training Project A Report of the Findings of a Demonstration Retraining Project for Long Term Unemployed Persons in a Rural Appalachian Mountain Area. Bluefield, W. Va.: Bluefield State College, 1965.
M3150 (ASU)

Mansfield, George Rogers Origin of the Brown Mountain Light in North Carolina. Washington: U. S. Geological Survey (Circular 646), 1971.
M3160 (ASU)

Manual and Directory of the First Methodist Episcopal Church, Huntington, West Virginia Huntington: The church, n.d.
M3170

Manufacturing and Mercantile Resources of Knoxville, Tennessee Knoxville: n.p., 1882.
M3180

Marcher, Melvin V. Tuscaloosa Formation in Tennessee. Report of Investigations, no. 17. Nashville: Tennessee Division of Geology, 1962.
M3190 (ETSU)

Marcy, W. L. Surveys of the Tennessee River. Washington: Govt. Print. Off., 1846.
M3200

Marden, D. W. Wilpolt, R. H. Geology and Oil and Gas Possibilities of Upper Mississippian Rocks of Southwestern Virginia, Southern West Virginia, and Eastern Kentucky. Washington: Govt. Print. Off., 1959.
W7060 (ASU)

Marion County Regional Planning Commission Public Administration Study: Marion County, Tennessee. Chattanooga: The Commission, 1973.
M3210

Marion County Teachers Association History of Marion County, Alabama. n.p.: The Association, 1959.
M3220

Marion County, Tennessee, 1830 Census n.p.: n.p., n.d. Census data for Marion County, Tennessee.
M3230

Marion, Leonard M. "A Guidance Program for the Schools of Hawkins County." Master's thesis. Univ. of Tennessee, 1959.
M3240

Maris, Alan H. "Severity of Malocclusion Found in Children of Appalachian Heritage Compared with Children of Non-Appalachian Heritage." Master's thesis. West Virginia Univ., 1971.
M3250

Marius, Richard The Coming of Rain. 1st ed. New York: Knopf, 1969. A novel of Eastern Tennessee in the 1880's. The shadows of the war and Reconstruction still lie on the land.
M3260 (WCU ETSU BC)

Markey, Gene That Far Paradise. New York: David McKay Co., 1960. A novel of the Kensal family and all their retinue traveling through the Virginia mountains to the Ohio and downriver to Kentucky in 1794.
M3270 (BC)

Markey, Mabel Lee Biggs, Nina Mitchell History of Greenup County, Kentucky. Louisville, Ky.: The authors, 1951.
B3580 (BC)

Biggs, Nina Mitchell A Supplementary Edition of a History of Greenup County. New York: Vantage Press, 1962.
B3590 (ASU BC)

Marler, Martha Griffis Kentucky Jane. San Antonio: Naylor, 1962. Autobiographical sketches from the life of a young mountain girl.
M3280

Marler, Mike comp. "Name Index to (Hale's) History of DeKalb County, Tennessee." Nashville: Unpublished typescript, 1971.
M3290

Marlin, Lloyd Garrison The History of Cherokee County. Atlanta: Walter B. Brown Pub. Co., n.d. A rather nice, informal, history of Cherokee County, Georgia.
M3300 (BC)

Marnin, Gene Vestige of Valor. New York: Vantage Press, 1973.
M3310 (BC)

Marriage Records, Warren County, Tennessee, 1852-1900 McMinnville, Tenn.: Womack Print. Co., 1965.
M3320 (ASU)

Marriages, Births and Deaths from Virginia and East Tennessee Lutheran Church in America Records Prepared by the General James Breckinridge Chapter, D. A. R., Roanoke, Virginia, Typescript. Roanoke: Breckinridge Chapter, D. A. R., 1969.
M3330

Marriott, Alice Lee Sequoyah: Leader of the Cherokees. Illustrated by Bob Riger. Landmark Books. New York: Random House, 1956. A fictional account of Sequoyah; bears little resemblance to actual events.
M3340 (ASU LMC BC)

Marschner, Francis Joseph Rural Population Density in the Southern Appalachians. U. S. Department of Agriculture Miscellaneous Publications, no. 367. Washington: U. S. Govt. Print. Off., 1940.
M3350 (ASU)

Marsh, C. Paul Facilitative and Inhibitive Factors in Training Program Recruitment Among Rural Negroes. n.p.: n.p., n.d.
M3360

Mason, Marie Migration Within Kentucky. Lexington: Univ. of Kentucky, Agriculture Experiment Station, 1954.
M3990

Marsh, Kenneth Frederick Historic Flat Rock: Where the Old South Lingers. Text by Blanche Marsh. 1st ed. Asheville, N. C.: Biltmore Press, 1961. Description of the interesting past of Flat Rock, North Carolina.
M3370 (ASU LMC BC)

Marsh, Owen T. Reconnaissance of the Ground-water Resources in the Waynesville Area, North Carolina. Chemical quality of water section by R. L. Laney. Ground-water Bulletin, no. 8. Raleigh: North Carolina Dept. of Water Resources, 1966.
M3380 (LMC WCU)

Marsh, Ruby Kenan Keepers of Memories: Biographical Sketches of Confederate Widows Living in North Carolina, 1861-1961, Plus Other Related Features. Asheboro, N. C.: n.p., 1965. A few of these ladies were from Western North Carolina.
M3390 (MHC)

Marshall, Bernard G. Old Hickory's Prisoner: A Tale of the Second War for Independence. New York: D. Appleton and Co., 1925. A novel of the Civil War in Appalachia.
M3400 (ASU)

Marshall, Catherine Wood Christy. New York: McGraw-Hill, 1967. A young girl accepts a teaching post in the remote mountains of East Tennessee and finds love and a vocation among the mountaineers.
M3410 (ASU LMC MHC ETSU WCU WWC BC)

Marshall College, Huntington, West Virginia One Hundred Years of Marshall College. Huntington: The college, 1937. An account of the centennial celebration and a history of the college.
M3420 (BC)

Marshall, Edward In Old Kentucky. New York: G. W. Dillingham Co., 1910. A story based on Charles Dazey's play of the bluegrass and the mountains.
M3430 (ETSU BC ASU)

Marshall, Humphrey The History of Kentucky. 1812. Reprint. Berea, Ky.: Oscar Rucker, Jr., 1971.
M3440 (MHC BC)

Marshall, Martha A Golden Book of the History and Tradition of Bristol, Tennessee, High School, 1915-1965. n.p.: n.p., n.d.
M3450 (ETSU)

Marshall, Peter D. "Imperial Regulation of American Indian Affairs 1763-1774." Ph. D. Diss. Yale Univ., 1959.
M3460

Marshall, R. P. Gravatt, George Flippo Chestnut Blight in the Southern Appalachians. Washington: U. S. Department of Agriculture, Bureau of Plant Industry, 1926.
G3300

Marshall, Richard Moon Burke, Richard Thomas Avon Soil Survey of Indiana County, Pennsylvania. Washington: U. S. Bureau of Chemistry and Soils, 1936.
B8700

Marshall, Robert K. Julia Gwynn. New York: Duell, Sloan and Pearce, 1952. A gothic tale of murder and family secrets. An aging Julia Gwynn comes out of seclusion to help her nephew who is on trial for his life. She is still the first lady of Tatesboro.
M3470 (WCU BC)

Little Squire Jim. 1st ed. New York: Duell, Sloan and Pearce, 1949. The boy-loves-teacher tale is set against a backdrop of murder and the supernatural in the North Carolina mountains.
M3480 (ETSU BC)

Marston, Wendell G. "The Problems of Unemployment in a Depressed Area." Master's thesis. Virginia Polytechnic Institute, 1962. A study of unemployment in Beckley, West Virginia.
M3490

Martel Methodist Church, 1795-1962 n.p.: The Church, n.d.
M3500

Martens, James Hart Curry Dolomite Zone at Base of Greenbrier Limestone (Big Lime). Report of Investigations, no. 4. Morgantown: West Virginia Geological and Economic Survey, 1948.
M3520 (ETSU)

Petrology and Correlation of Deep-well Sections in West Virginia and Adjacent States. West Virginia Geological Survey Reports, vol. 11. Morgantown: Morgantown Print. and Binding Co., 1939.
M3530 (ETSU)

Possibility of Shaft Mining of Greenbrier Limestone. Report of Investigations, no. 6. Morgantown: West Virginia Geological and Economic Survey, 1948.
M3540 (ETSU)

Rock Salt Deposits of West Virginia. Bulletin, no. 7. Morgantown: West Virginia Geological Survey, 1943.
M3550 (ETSU)

Sulphate Minerals in West Virginia. Bulletin, 25. Charleston: West Virginia Geological and Economic Survey, 1963.
M3560 (ETSU)

Well-sample Records. West Virginia Geological Survey Reports, vol. 17. Charleston: Jarrett Print. Co., 1945.
M3570 (ETSU)

Martin, Arlee "History of the Development of Negro Public Schools in Bradley County, Tennessee, 1931-1951." Master's thesis. Tennessee Agricultural and Industrial Univ., 1952.
M3580

Martin, Charlene E. "Pupil Transportation in Pickett County, Tennessee." Master's thesis. Tennessee Polytechnic Institute, 1961.
M3590

Martin, Christopher see Hoyt, Edwin Palmer

Martin, Harold H. Ralph McGill, Reporter. Boston: Little Brown, 1973. This book is a labor of love by a colleague who worked with Ralph McGill on the Atlanta Constitution for thirty years. McGill became one of the great Southern liberal voices in the 1950's and 1960's by an unusual route that began in East Tennessee, then took him through sports writing with the NASHVILLE BANNER and the CONSTITUTION, and finally to his influential editorship.
M3500

Ralph McGill, Reporter. Boston: Little Brown, 1973. This book is a labor of love by a colleague who worked with Ralph McGill on the Atlanta Constitution for thirty years. McGill became one of the great Southern liberal voices in the 1950's and 1960's by an unusual route that began in east Tennessee, then took him through sports writing with the NASHVILLE BANNER and the CONSTITUTION, and finally to his influential editorship.
M3600

Martin, Isaac Patton A Minister in the Tennessee Valley. Nashville: Parthenon Press, 1954. Account of a 67 year ministry in the Tennessee Valley.
M3610 (BC)

Church Street Methodists, Children of Francis Asbury: A History of Church Street Methodist Church. Knoxville, Tennessee, 1816-1947. Knoxville: Methodist Hist. Soc. of Holston Conference, 1947.
M3620

Methodism in Holston. Knoxville: Methodist Hist. Soc. of Holston Conference, 1945.
M3630

A Minister in the Tennessee Valley for Sixty Seven Years. Knoxville: Parthenon Press, 1954.
M3640

Martin, James E., Jr. Irrigation Arrangements in Buncombe County, North County, North Carolina; a Report of an Irrigation Survey in Buncombe County, Conducted in the Summer of 1962. Chapel Hill: Institute of Government, Univ. of N. C., 1963.
M3650 (LMC)

Irrigation Arrangements in Henderson County, North Carolina; a Report of an Irrigation Survey in Henderson County, Conducted in the Summer of 1962. Chapel Hill: Institute of Government, Univ. of N. C., 1963.
M3660 (LMC)

Irrigation Arrangements in Transylvania County, North Carolina; a Report of an Irrigation Survey in Transylvania County, Conducted in the Summer of 1962. Chapel Hill: Institute of Government, Univ. of N. C., 1963.
M3670 (LMC)

Martin, James O. Soil Survey of the Lock Haven, Pennsylvania, Area. Field Operations, 1903. Washington: U. S. Department of Agriculture, Bureau of Soils, 1904.
M3680

Soil Survey of the Lock Haven, Pennsylvania, Area. Washington: U. S. Dept. of Agriculture, Bureau of Soils, 1904.
M3690

Martin, Joe Allen The Economics of Using Low-Quality Hardwoods for Producing Charcoal in Tennessee. Bulletin 375. Knoxville: Univ. of Tennessee, Agriculture Experiment Station, 1964.
M3700

Types of Farming in Tennessee. Bulletin, 311. Knoxville: Univ. of Tennessee, Agriculture Experiment Station, 1960.
M3710 (ASU)

Martin, John R. Berryman Brown of Roanoke County, Virginia and Clinton Dade and Ozark Counties, Missouri. n.p.: n.p., 1957. Compares life in the Ozarks and the Appalachians.
M3720

Martin, LeRoy A. A History of Tennessee Wesleyan College. n.p.: Louis Ginsburg, n.d.
M3730

Martin, LeRoy Albert A History of Tennessee Wesleyan College, 1857-1957. Athens? Tenn.: n.p., 1957. A history of a Methodist College in Athens, Tennessee.
M3740 (WCU ASU)

Martin, Patricia Miles Daniel Boone. Illustrated by Glen Dines. A See and Read Beginning to Read Biography. New York: Putnam, 1965.
M3750 (ASU)

Martin, Peggy O. "A Team Teaching Approach to Reading in the Fourth Grade at Dickson Elementary School in Kingsport, Tennessee, 1964-1965." Master's thesis. East Tennessee State Univ., 1966.
M3760 (ETSU)

Martin, Robert Lewis "The Sequatchie Valley, Tennessee, a Study in Land Utilization." Ph. D. Diss. George Peabody College, 1941.
M3770

Martin, Roscoe C. ed. The First Twenty Years. University: Univ. of Alabama Press, and Knoxville: Univ. of Tennessee Press, 1956. An authoritative review of Tennessee Valley Authority's many activities.
M3780

Martin, Roscoe Coleman ed. TVA TVA: The First Twenty Years. A Staff Report. Univ. of Alabama Press, 1956.
T3790 (ASU WCU LMC)

TVA TVA: The First Twenty Years; A Staff Report. Univ., Ala.: Univ. of Alabama Press, 1956.
T3800 (UNCA)

Martindale, Donald L. Silvical Characteristics of Sweetgum. U. S. Forest Service Station Paper, no. 90. Asheville, N. C.: Southeastern Forest Experiment Station, 1958.
M3790 (WCU)

Martindale, Mrs. J. W. Cheek, Mr. and Mrs. Charles comp. 1850 Census: Wilkes County, North Carolina. Wilkesboro: Genealogical Society of the "Original" Wilkes County, N. C., n.d.
C3570 (ASU)

Martineau, Harriet Retrospect of Western Travel. New York: Harper and Brothers, 1838. This widely read English writer covered the South rather extensively, but in Appalachia she saw only White Sulphur and Hot Springs and the Natural Bridge of Virginia.
M3800

Martinez, Corinne Coffee County from Arrowheads to Rockets: A History of Coffee County, Tennessee. Tullahoma: Coffee Co. Conservation Bd., 1969.
M3590

Coffee County from Arrowheads to Rockets; a History of Coffee County, Tennessee. Tullahoma: Coffee Co. Conservation Bd., 1969.
M3810

Coffee County: From Arrowheads to Rockets. A History of Coffee County, Tennessee. Tullahoma, Tenn.: Coffee Co. Conservation Bd., 1969.
M3820 (ETSU)

Martinson, H. M. Effectiveness of Apprentice Training in the Tennessee Valley Authority. Master's thesis. Univ. of Tennessee, 1949.
M3830

Martinson, Vince Leonard An Appalachian Valley. n.p.: n.p., 1964. Observations about nature during the various seasons of the year in travels throughout western North Carolina.
M3840 (ASU)

An Appalachian Valley. n.p.: n.p., 1964. Observations about nature during the various seasons of the year in travels throughout Western North Carolina.
M3840 (ASU)

Mary Sharp College Club of Nashville, Tennessee Dr. Z. C. Graves and the Mary Sharp College, 1850-1896. Nashville: Baptist Board of Pub., 1926.
M3850

Maryland, Department of Economic Development The Appalachian Region: A Preliminary Analysis of Economic and Population Trends in an Eleven State Problem Area. Annapolis: The department, 1960.
M3860 (BC)

Directory of Maryland Manufacturers. Annapolis: Department of Economic Development, 1965.
M3870

Fact Sheet on Appalachian Maryland — Garrett, Alleghany, and Washington Counties.
M3880

Occupational Outlook for Washington County. Baltimore: Department of Employment Security, 1966.
M3890

Maryland, Department of Geology, Mines and Water Resources Alleghany County. Baltimore: Johns Hopkins Press, 1900. Survey of mineral and water resources.
M3900 (ETSU)

The Physical Features of Washington County. Baltimore: n.p., 1951.
M3910 (ETSU)

Maryland, Executive Department Copy of a Correspondence Between Governor Thomas, of Maryland, and Governor Tazewell, of Virginia, in Relation to the Unsettled Divisional Boundary Lines Between the Two States. Annapolis: Jeremiah Hughes, 1835.
M3920 (ASU)

Maryland, University School of Law Legal Problems of Coal Mine Reclamation: Study in Maryland, Ohio, Pennsylvania, and West Virginia. Project directors: Everett F. Goldberg and Garrett Power. Water Pollution Control Research Series. Washington: U. S. Environmental Protection Agency, 1972.
M3930 (BC)

Maryville College Students "Social Survey of Blount County, Tennessee." Maryville: Unpublished typescript, 1930.
M3940

Masa, George McCoy, George William Guide to the Great Smoky Mountains National Park. Asheville, N. C.: Inland Press, 1933.
M760 (WCU)

Maser, Frederick E. The Dramatic Story of Early American Methodism. New York: Abingdon Press, 1965.
M3950 (ASU)

Masney, S. ed. Tennessee Poetry Journal vol. 1-4, 1967-1971 Martin, Tenn.: n.p., 1967-1971.
T1790

Mason, Charles Dwight "A Survey of the Training and Experience of Secondary Principals in Five Upper East Tennessee Counties." Master's thesis. East Tennessee State College, 1957.
M3960 (ETSU)

Mason, D. D. Porter, Hobart Clarke Soil Survey, Tazewell County, Virginia. Washington: U. S. Department of Agriculture, Bureau of Plant Industry, Soils, and Agricultural Engineering, 1948.
P3660

Mason, Francis Van Wyck see Mason, Van Wyck

Mason, Harrison D. Locust Bloom. Pittsburgh: Cramer Print. and Pub. Co., 1924. Stories and descriptions of the Ohio River Valley with verses.
M3970 (BC)

Mason, Kathryn Harrod James Harrod of Kentucky. Southern Biography Series. Baton Rouge: Louisiana State Univ. Press, 1951. One of the Kentucky's earliest settlers and pioneers.
M3980 (ASU)

Mason, Marie Migration Within Kentucky. Lexington: Univ. of Kentucky, Agriculture Experiment Station, 1954.
M3990

Rural Family Health in a Selected County in Kentucky. Lexington: Univ. of Kentucky, Agriculture Experiment Station, 1949. Powell County, Kentucky is the subject of this study.
M4000

Mason, Miriam Evangeline Daniel Boone: Wilderness Trailblazer. Illustrated by Harve Stein. Piper Books. Boston: Houghton Mifflin, 1961.
M4010 (ASU ETSU)

Mason, Pearl E. "Some Employment Opportunities of the Vocational Agriculture Trainees of Gilmer County." Master's thesis. West Virginia Univ., 1964.
M4020

Mason, Robert Lindsay The Lure of the Great Smokies. Boston: Houghton, 1927.
M4030

The Lure of the Great Smokies. Boston: Houghton Mifflin Co., 1927.
M4040 (ASU LMC WCU ETSU WWC BC)

Mason, Van Wyck Hang My Wreath. Center Books Edition. New York: Wilfred Funk, 1941. A Civil War novel partially set in Appalachia.
M4050 (ASU)

Massachusetts Infantry, 35th Regt., 1862-65 History of the Thirty-fifth Regiment Massachusetts Volunteers, 1862-1865. With a roster. By a committee of the regimental association. Boston: Mills, Knight and Co., 1884.
M4060

Massachusetts Infantry, 36th Regt., 1862-1865 History of the Thirty-sixth Regiment Massachusetts Volunteers, 1862-1865. By a committee of the regiment. Boston: Rockwell and Churchill, 1884.
M4070 (ASU)

Massay, Glenn Frank "Coal Consolidation: Profile of the Fairmont Field of Northern West Virginia, 1852-1903." Ph. D. Diss. West Virginia Univ., 1970.
M4080

"Coal Consolidation: Profile of the Fairmont Field of Northern West Virginia, 1852-1903." Ph. D. Diss. West Virginia Univ., 1970.
M4090

Massengill, Samuel Evans The Massengills, Massengales and Variants 1472-1931. Bristol, Tenn.: n.p., 1931.
M4100

The Massengills, Massengales and Variants 1472-1931. Bristol, Tenn.: King Print. Co., 1931.
M4110

Massey, A. B. The Ferns and Fern Allies of Virginia. Bulletin, vol. 37, no. 7. Blacksburg: Virginia Polytechnic Institute, 1944.
M4120 (LMC)

Massie, Joseph L. Blazer and Ashland Oil; a Study in Management. Lexington: Univ. of Kentucky Press, 1960.
M4130

Masters, F. N. The Cumberland Plateau in Tennessee. Bulletin no. 192. Knoxville: Tennessee Agricultural Experiment Station, Univ. of Tennessee, 1944.
M4140

Masters, Gil Sissy, She's Coming Sunday. Kingwood, W. Va.: n.p., 1969. Youngsters book based on a favorite singing game from the Appalachians.
M4150

Masters, Roxie A. The Valley of the Long Hunters. Parsons, W. Va.: McClain Print. Co., 1969. A history of early Tennessee explorers in the bountiful Tennessee Valley.
M4160 (ASU LMC ETSU BC)

Masterson, Clara Estelle "A History of Knoxville Journalism." Master's thesis. George Peabody College, 1933.
M4170

Masterson, William Henry William Blount. Baton Rouge: Louisiana State Univ. Press, 1954. Biography of early Tennessee politician.
M4180 (BC ETSU)

Matacia, Louis J., Jr. Corbett, H. Roger, Jr. Blue Ridge Voyages: One and Two Day River Cruises. Pennsylvania, Maryland, Virginia, West Virginia. Falls Church, Va.: Blue Ridge Voyageurs, 1965-66.
C7360 (LMC)

Matheny, Emma Robertson comp. 1850 Census of Highland County, Virginia. n.p.: The author, 1966.
M4190

Matheny, H. E. Major General Thomas Maley Harris, A Member of the Military Commission That Tried the President Abraham Lincoln Assassination Conspirators, and Roster of the 10th West Virginia Volunteer Infantry Regiment, 1861-1865. Parsons, W. Va.: McClain Print. Co., 1963.
M4200 (ASU BC)

Mather, William A. Hostetler, John A. Participation in the Rural Church. State College: Pennsylvania Agricultural Experiment Station, Pennsylvania State College, October, 1952.
H7350

Mathes, Charles Hodge Tall Tales from Old Smoky. Kingsport, Tenn.: Southern Pubs., 1952.
M4210 (ASU LMC BC ETSU)

Mathes, Wileta "A Study of Problems of Junior High School Students of Johnson City, Tennessee." Master's thesis. East Tennessee State College, 1953.
M4220 (ETSU)

Matheson, James Reed, Andrew A Narrative of the Visit to the American Churches, by the Deputation from the Congregational Union of England and Wales. London: Jackson and Walford, 1835.
R1010

Matheson, Robert Edwin Special Report on Surnames in Ireland. Together with Varieties and Synonyms of Surnames and Christian Names in Ireland. 1901, 1909. Reprint. 2 vols. in 1. Baltimore: Genealogical Pub. Co., 1968.
M4230 (ASU)

Mathews, A. A. L. Marble Prospects in Giles County, Virginia, with a section on Petrography of Marbles by Arthur A. Pegan. Virginia Commission on Conservation and Development. Virginia Geological Survey Bulletin no. 40. Charlottesville: Univ. of Virginia, 1934.
M4240

Mathis, Willie H. "A Survey to Determine the Need of Trade and Industrial Education in Warren County, Tennessee." Master's thesis. Univ. of Tennessee, 1961.
M4250

Matteson, Maurice Beech Mountain Folk-Songs and Ballads. New York: Schirmer, 1936. Collected in Watauga County, North Carolina.
M4260

Matthews, Earle Dwight Soil Survey, Washington County, Maryland. Survey by Boyd D. Gilbert and others. Soil Survey, Series 1959, no. 17. Washington: U. S. Department of Agriculture, Soil Conservation Service, 1962.
M4270

Matthews, Elmora Messer Neighbor and Kin: Life in a Tennessee Ridge Community. Nashville: Vanderbilt Univ. Press, 1965, i. e. 1966. Sociological study of an isolated hill community in Tennessee.
M4280 (ASU WCU LMC BC WWC FC UNCA)

Matthews, Etta Lane Over the Blue Wall. Illustrated by James Dougherty. Chapel Hill: Univ. of North Carolina Press, 1937.
M4290 (BC ASU LMC ETSU WCU)

Matthews, Fred D. History of Sevier County, Tennessee. Knoxville: East Tennessee Historical Society, n.d.
M4300

Matthews, Joseph Carson, Jr. Human Resources in the Economy of the Upper French Broad Area. Raleigh: North Carolina State Univ., 1965.
M4310 (LMC)

Matthews, Martin Taylor Experience-worlds of Mountain People: Institutional Efficiency in Appalachian Village and Hinterland Communities. Contributions to Education, no. 700. New York: Teachers College, Columbia Univ., 1937.
M4320 (ETSU WWC BC)

Experience-worlds of Mountain People: Institutional Efficiency in Appalachian Village and Hinterland Communities. Contributions to Education, no. 700. 1937. Reprint. New York: AMS Press, 1972.
M4330 (ASU)

Matthews, Riley Kingston "A Survey of Recreational Music Activities Available to the General College Student in Georgia, North Carolina, South Carolina and Tennessee." Master's thesis. Appalachian State Teachers College, 1961.
M4340 (ASU)

Matthews, S. A. comp. Kentucky Mountain Square Dancing Running Set. London: English Folk Dance and Song Society, 1969.
M4350 (ASU)

Matthews, Thomas Edwin General James Robertson, Father of Tennessee. Nashville: Parthenon Press, 1934. Robertson was a leader of the Watauga Settlements and the Overmountain men; a politician and land surveyor.
M4360 (ETSU ASU)

Matzek, B. L. Hubbard, Edgar Harvey Soil Survey, Grainger County, Tennessee. Washington: U. S. Department of Agriculture, Bureau of Plant Industry, Soils and Agricultural Engineering, 1948.
H7810

Rudolph, Foster Soil Survey, Carter County, Tennessee. Washington: U. S. Soil Conservation Service, 1953.
R4220

Matzek, B. L. and others Soil Survey, Sullivan County, Tennessee. U. S. Soil Conservation Service, Soil Survey Reports, Series 1944, no. 2. Washington: Govt. Print. Off., 1953.
M4370

Maughan, Edwin K. Geologic Map of Part of the Rose Hill Quadrangle, Harlan County, Kentucky. Washington: U. S. Geological Survey, 1973.
M4380 (ASU)

Maughan, William ed. A Guide to Forestry Activities in North Carolina, South Carolina, and Tennessee. Asheville, N. C.: Asheville Section, Society of American Foresters, 1939.
M4390 (ETSU LMC)

Maupin, Juanita "A Study of Living Conditions in the Pittman Center Community, 1934-1935." Master's thesis. Univ. of Tennessee, 1936.
M4400

Maurer, B. B. Mountain Heritage, Mountain State Art and Craft Fair Cedar Lakes. Ripley, W. Va.: Morgantown Print. and Binding Co., 1974.
M4420

Photiadis, John Community Size and Social Attributes in West Virginia. Morgantown: West Virginia Univ., n.d.
P2730 (WCU ASU)

Photiadis, John Religion in an Appalachian State. Morgantown: West Virginia Univ., n.d.
P2740

Maurer, B. B. ed. Mountain Heritage. Ripley, W. Va.: Mountain State Art and Craft Fair, 1974.
M4410

Maurer, Beryl Flake "The Rural Church and Organized Community Activity, a Study of Church-community Relations in Two East Tennessee Communities." Master's thesis. Univ. of Tennessee, 1953.
M4430

Maurer, David W. Kentucky Moonshine. Lexington: Univ. Press. of Kentucky, 1974.
M4440

Maurice, George H. Daniel Boone in North Carolina. 2d ed. rev., and enlarged. (Original title: On the Trail of Daniel Boone in North Carolina.) Eagle Springs, N. C.: Ballingtoy, 1959.
M4450 (ASU LMC WCU BC)

On the Trail of Daniel Boone in North Carolina. Eagle Springs, N. C.: The author, 1955.
M4460 (ASU)

Maury, Matthew Fontaine The Resources of the Coal Field of the Upper Kanawha, with a Sketch of the Iron Belt of Virginia, Setting Forth Some of Their Markets and Means of Development. Baltimore: Sherwood and Co., 1873.
M4470 (ASU)

The Resources of the Coal Field of the Upper Kanawha, with a Sketch of the Iron Belt of Virginia, Setting Forth Some of Their Markets and Means of Development. Baltimore: Sherwood and Co., 1873.
M4480

Maxwell, Ann History of Tucker County, West Virginia. Kingswood, W. Va.: Preston Pub. Co., 1884. Another interesting county history from West Virginia.
M4490

Maxwell, Henry V. Chilhowee, a Legend of the Great Smoky Mountains. Illustrated by Clara T. Gresham. Knoxville, Tenn.: S. B. Newman Co., 1897. The legend of Chilhowee's ghost in verse.
M4500 (LMC BC)

Maxwell, Hu Fast, Richard E. The History and Government of West Virginia. Morgantown: Acme Publishing Co., 1901.
F290 (BC)

The History of Barbour County, West Virginia, from Its Earliest Exploration and Settlement to the Present Time. 1899. Reprint. Parsons, W. Va.: McClain Print. Co., 1968.
M4510 (ASU ETSU)

History of Hampshire County, West Virginia, from Its Earliest Settlement to the Present. Morgantown: A. B. Boughner, 1897.
M4520

History of Hampshire County, West Virginia, from Its Earliest Settlement to the Present. 1897. Reprint. Parsons, W. Va.: McClain Print. Co., 1972.
M4530 (ASU)

The History of Randolph County, West Virginia, from Its Earliest Settlement to the Present, Embracing Records of All the Leading Families, Reminiscences and Traditions. 1898. Reprint. Parsons, W. Va.: McClain Print. Co., 1961.
M4540 (ASU)

History of Tucker County, West Virginia, from the Earliest Explorations and Settlements to the Present Time: With Biographical Sketches of More Than Two Hundred and Fifty of the Leading Men, and a Full Appendix of Official and Electional History. Also, an Account of the Rivers, Forests and Caves of the County. Illustrated with twenty-eight phototypes of noted persons. Kingswood, W. Va.: Preston Pub. Co., 1884.
M4550 (ASU)

Jonathan Fish and His Neighbors. Morgantown, W. Va.: Acme Pub. Co., 1902. Fine short stories; sketches of West Virginia characters.
M4560 (BC)

Miller, Thomas Condit West Virginia and Its People. New York: Lewis Historical Pub. Co., 1913.
M6010

Maxwell, Kathleen A. Mountain Echoes, a Book of Poetic Reflections. Galax, Va.: Gazette Press, 1973.
M4570 (ASU)

Maxwell, Phillip Herbert Valhalla in the Smokies. Cleveland: G. A. Exline, 1938. A paean for the Great Smokies.
M4580 (ETSU ASU BC)

May, Earl Chapin Principio to Wheeling. New York: Harper and Brothers, 1945. A history of the iron and steel industry in West Virginia from 1715-1945.
M4590 (BC)

May, Emma Wells History of the First Methodist Church Prestonsburg, Ky. Prestonsburg, Ky.: n.p., n.d.
M4600

Mayhall, Jane Cousin to Human. 1st ed. New York: Harcourt, Brace, 1960. A comic novel from the northern Alabama hills.
M4610 (ASU)

Maynadier, Gustaves B. Wilder, Henry Jason Reconnaissance Soil Survey of Northwestern Pennsylvania. Washington: U. S. Dept. of Agriculture, Bureau of Soils, 1910.
W6120

Maynor, Theodore R. "A Historical Analysis of Student Drop-outs in the Negro Schools for Bibb County, Alabama." Master's thesis. Alabama State College, 1954.
M4620

Mayor's Friendly Relations Committee Report of a Workshop on the Southern Mountaineer in Cincinnati, April 29, 1954. Cincinnati: Human Relations Commission, 1971.
C4120 (ASU BC)

Mays, Lee Cain. n.p.: Naylor, 1969.
M4630

Call of the Hills. n.p.: Naylor, 1971.
M4640

Child of the Hills. Philadelphia: Dorrance, 1953.
M4650

Echoes from the Hills. Philadelphia: Dorrance, 1957.
M4660

Epic of Creation. n.p.: Naylor, 1965.
M4670

Philosophy of the Hills. n.p.: Naylor, 1968.
M4680

Ramble in the Hills. n.p.: Naylor, 1969.
M4690

The Return to the Hills. Philadelphia: Dorrance, 1955.
M4700

Mazek, Warren F. "The Efficacy of the Labor Migration with Special Emphasis on Depressed Areas." Ph. D. Diss. Univ. of Pittsburgh, 1965.
M4710

Mazzei, Frank J. "A Study of the Factors Influencing Job-satisfaction among Factory Workers of Clarksburg, West Virginia, and Coal Miners of Morgantown, West Virginia." Master's thesis. West Virginia Univ., 1951.
M4720

McCants, Elliot Crayton In the Red Hills: A Story of the Carolina Country. New York: Doubleday, Page and Co., 1904. Story of upper Carolina Country.
M260 (ASU)

Mead, Edward Campbell Historic Homes of the South-west Mountains, Virginia. With twenty-three illustrations and a map. Philadelphia: J. B. Lippincott Co., 1899.
M4730 (ASU BC ETSU LMC)

Mead, Everard Kidder ed. Chrisman, Arthur Bowie Clarke County, 1836-1936. Berryville, Va.: Clarke Courier Press, 1936.
C3940 (ASU)

Mead, Martha Elizabeth Norburn Asheville, in Land of the Sky. Richmond: Dietz Press, 1942. Illustrated, well-written pertaining to Asheville and the surrounding area.
M4740 (ASU WCU LMC WWC UNCA)

Meade, Bishop Old Churches, Ministers and Families of Virginia. 2 vols. Philadelphia, Pa.: J. B. Lippincott Co., 1857.
M4750

Meade, Everard Kidder Frederick Parrish, Virginia, 1744-1780. Winchester, Va.: Pifer Print. Co., 1947. Accounts of churches, chapels, ministers and vestries. With early maps.
M4760 (BC)

Meade, William Old Churches, Ministers, and Families of Virginia. 1857. Reprint. With digested index and genealogical guide compiled by Jennings Cropper Wise. Baltimore: Genealogical Pub. Co., 1966.
M4770 (ASU)

Meadowcroft, Enid LaMonte On Indian Trails with Daniel Boone. New York: Crowell, 1945. Adventure tale of the Trans-Appalachian West.
M4780 (ETSU)

On Indian Trails with Daniel Boone. New York: Crowell, 1947.
M4790 (ETSU)

The Story of Andrew Jackson. Illustrated by David Hendrickson. Signature Books. New York: Grosset and Dunlap, 1953. Novel of Andy Jackson, set partially during his early day in Appalachia.
M4800 (ASU BC)

The Story of Davy Crockett. Illustrated by Charles B. Falls. Signature Books. New York: Grosset and Dunlap, 1952. Novel of the exploits of the irrepressible Mr. Crockett.
M4810 (ASU BC ETSU WCU)

Medal of Honor Recipients, 1863-1973 Washington, D. C.: Govt. Print. Off., 1973.
M4820

Medford, W. Clark The Early History of Haywood County. Waynesville, N. C.: The author, 1961. History of Haywood County and Waynesville, North Carolina.
M4830 (LMC WCU)

Finis and Farewell. Illustrated by Helen Medford Cartwright. Waynesville, N. C.: Miller Print., 1969. Describes social life and customs in Haywood County.
M4840 (ASU BC LMC WCU)

Great Smoky Mountain Stories and Sun over Ol' Starlin. Waynesville, N. C.: The author, 1966.
M4850 (LMC WCU)

Haywood's Heritage and Finest Hour. Asheville, N. C.: Daniels Graphics, 1971.
M4860 (ASU BC WCU)

Land o' the Sky; History, Stories, Sketches. Asheville, N. C.: Miller Print. Co., 1965. About the Asheville, Buncombe, Haywood, Madison County areas.
M4870 (ASU BC LMC WCU UNCA)

The Middle History of Haywood County, with Story Supplement. Waynesville, N. C.: The author, 1968. History, sketches and stories from Haywood County.
M4880 (BC LMC WCU)

Mountain People, Mountain Times. Waynesville, N. C.: The author, 1963. Sketches of mountain people in and around Haywood County.
M4890 (BC LMC WCU)

R. A. Sentelle, Educator, Preacher, Public Servant. n.p.: n.p., n.d. Biography of a mountain educator and preacher in Western North Carolina.
M4900 (LMC)

Meeker, Mrs. A. M. Eliza Ross; or, Illustrated Guide of Lookout Mountain. Atlanta: Franklin, 1870.
M4910

Meeker, F. N. Lapham, Jesse Erwin Soil Survey of the Asheville, North Carolina, Area. Washington: U. S. Department of Agriculture, Bureau of Soils, 1904.
L620

Latimer, William James Soil Survey of the Spencer, West Virginia, Area. Washington: U. S. Department of Agriculture, Bureau of Soils, 1910.
L820

Smith, William G. Soil Survey of Blount County, Alabama. Washington: U. S. Department of Agriculture, Bureau of Soils, 1914.
S5180

Meeker, Fred N. Soil Survey of the Parkersburg Area, West Virginia. Prepared in cooperation with the West Virginia Geological Survey. Field Operations, 1908. Washington: U. S. Department of Agriculture, Bureau of Soils, 1909.
M4920

Soil Survey of Meigs County, Ohio. Prepared in cooperation with the Ohio Agricultural Experiment Station. Field Operations, 1906. Washington: U. S. Department of Agriculture, Bureau of Soils, 1908.
M4930

Meeker, Stella Colby The Parson's Mountaineers. New York: Frederick H. Hitchcock, 1927. Sentimental fiction about a preacher's supposed influence in an isolated mountain community.
M4940 (BC)

The Valley People. Terre Haute, Ind.: Viquesney Co., 1920. Stereotypical and uninspired novel stressing differences between native mountaineers and outlanders.
M4950 (BC)

Meeks, Carl Garnett "Resources for Physical Recreation in the Tennessee Valley Authority Region." Ed. D. Diss. Teachers College, Columbia Univ., 1953.
M4960

Meet Virginia's Baby Pictorial History of Dickenson County, Virginia, 1880-1955 Clintwood, Va.: n.p., 1955.
M4970

Meigs, Cornelia Lynde Call of the Mountain. Illustrated by James Daugherty. Boston: Little, Brown and Co., 1940. Nostalgic novel of life in the northern Appalachians.
M4980 (ASU)

Meine, Franklin J. ed. Crockett, David The Crockett Almanacks. Nashville Series, 1835-1838. Chicago: Caxton Club, 1955.
C8930

Meissner, Hanna H. ed. Poverty in the Affluent Society. New York: Harper and Row, 1966. A collection of reprints and unpublished materials on the history of poverty in the United States. Some mention of Appalachian poverty as a separate concern.
M4990

Melbo, Irving Robert Our Country's National Parks. 2 vols. Indianapolis: Bobbs-Merrill Co., 1941. Includes material on the many national parks within the Appalachian region.
M5000 (ASU)

Mellen, George F. ed. Rule, William ed. Standard History of Knoxville, Tennessee, with Full Outline of the Natural Advantages, Early Settlement, Territorial Government, Indian Troubles and General and Particular History of the City Down to the Present Time. Chicago: Lewis, 1900.
R4280

Melton, Robert W., Company Digest of Information About Transylvania County, North Carolina, Containing Information of General Interest to Commercial and Industrial Businesses. Brevard, N. C.: n.p., 1968. Promotional material and descriptive and historical facts about the county.
M5010 (WCU)

Memminger, Edward Read Historical Sketch of Flat Rock. Asheville: Stephens Press, 1954.
M5040 (ASU)

An Historical Sketch of Flat Rock . . . Flat Rock, N. C.: Privately published by his daughter, Mrs. Walter M. Norment, 1954.
M5050 (ASU)

Memoir of John Arch, a Cherokee Young Man, from Communications of Missionaries in the Cherokee Nation 4th ed. Boston: Massachusetts Sabbath School Society, 1838.
M5020 (ASU)

Memoranda of the Preston family Lexington: Univ. of Kentucky, 1963.
M5030 (ASU)

Memory Days, in Which the Shenandoah Valley Is Seen in Retrospection, with Glimpses of School Days and the Life of Virginia People n.p.: Neale Pub. Co., 1908.
P1080

Mendel, Joseph J. Forestry Accomplishments in Southeastern Ohio under the U. S. Agricultural Conservation Program, 1957-64. U. S. Forest Service Research Paper, NE-65. Upper Darby, Pa.: Northeastern Forest Experiment Station, 1967.
M5060

Mental Health in Appalachia. A Report of a Conference in Bethesda, Md., July 13-14, 1964 Washington: U. S. Dept. of Health, Education, and Welfare, 1965.
M5070

Mercer, J. C. Taylor, Arthur Elijah Soil Survey, Catoosa County, Georgia. Washington: U. S. Department of Agriculture, Bureau of Plant Industry, 1941.
T400

Mercer, J. C.
Taylor, Arthur Elijah Soil Survey, Dade County, Georgia. Washington: U. S. Department of Agriculture, Bureau of Plant Industry, 1942.
T440

Mercer, Julia "North Georgia Life in the Fiction of Will N. Harben." Master's thesis. Duke Univ., 1938. Harben's novels are set in Murray and Whitfield counties.
M5080

Merchant, Jane Halfway Up the Sky. n.p.: n.p., n.d. Poems from the hills.
M5100

Mereness, Newton Dennison ed. Travels in the American Colonies. Edited under the Auspices of the National Society of the Colonial Dames of America. New York: Antiquarian Press, 1961. One of the earlier traveler's observations on the mountain South.
M5090 (ASU BC)

Merinar, Elmer K. "A Study of the Status of the Elementary School Principal of West Virginia." Master's thesis. West Virginia Univ., 1953.
M5110

Merkel, Edward P. Hydraulic Spray Applications of Insecticides for the Control of Slash Pine Cone and Seed Insects. U. S. Forest Service Research Paper, SE-9. Asheville, N. C.: Southeastern Forest Experiment Station, 1964.
M5120 (WCU)

Merrens, Harry Roy Colonial North Carolina in the Eighteenth Century: A Study in Historical Geography. Chapel Hill: Univ. of North Carolina Press, 1964.
M5130 (UNCA LMC)

Merriam, Lucius Salisbury Higher Education in Tennessee. Washington: Govt. Print. Off., 1893.
M5140 (ETSU)

Merrill, William McKinley "Economics of the Southern Smokeless Coals." Ph. D. Diss. Univ. of Illinois, Urbana-Champaign, 1953.
M5150

Merritt, Frank Early History of Carter County, 1760-1861. Knoxville: East Tennessee Historical Society, 1950.
M5160 (ASU ETSU LMC)

Mertie, J. B., Jr. Quartz Crystal Deposits of Southwestern Virginia and Western North Carolina. U. S. Geological Survey Bulletin, 1072-D. Contributions to Economic Geology, 1957. Washington: Govt. Print. Off., 1959.
M5170

Mertins, Herman, Jr. West Virginia Budgeting: Problems and Possibilities. Morgantown: West Virginia Univ., Bureau of Government Research, 1971.
M5180

Message from the President of the U. S. Transmitting a Report of the Secretary of Agriculture in Relation to the Forests, Rivers, and Mountains of the Southern Appalachian Region Washington: Govt. Print. Off., 1902.
M5190 (ASU)

Metcalf, Paul C. Will West. Highlands, N. C.: Jonathan Williams, 1956. Cherokee history is interwoven in this tale of an Indian baseball player who makes his way west.
M5200

Methodist Episcopal Church, Southern Conferences. Western North Carolina Journal of the Western North Carolina Annual Conference . . . 1890-. n.p.: n.p., n.d.
M5210 (WCU)

Metropolitan Charter Commission. Knoxville and Knox County, Tenn. Proposed Metropolitan Government Charter for Knoxville and Knox County, Tennessee, 1959. n.p.: n.p., n.d.
M5220

Metz, Louis John Haney, Glenn P. Silvical Characteristics of Southern Red Oak. Asheville, N. C.: Southeastern Forest Experiment Station, 1959.
H1480 (WCU)

Metzler, W. H. Porter, Ward F. Availability for Employment of Rural People in the Upper Monongahela Valley. Morgantown: W. Va. Univ., 1956.
P3700

Metzler, William H. Employment and Underemployment of Rural People in the Upper Monongahela Valley, West Virginia. Bulletin No. 404. Morgantown: West Virginia Agricultural Experiment Station, West Virginia Univ., June, 1957.
M5230

Meyer, Duane The Highland Scots of North Carolina. A condensed version. Raleigh, N. C.: Tercentenary Commission, 1963.
M5240 (LMC BC)

Meyer, Duane Gilbert The Highland Scots of North Carolina, 1732-1776. Chapel Hill: Univ. of North Carolina Press, 1961. Focuses on the circumstances of emigration and politics after arrival.
M5250 (ASU LMC WWC)

Meyer, H. B. List of References on the Mountain Whites. Bulletin No. 633. Washington, D. C.: Library of Congress Division of Bibliography, 1922.
M5260

Meyer, Simon ed. One Hundred Years: An Anthology — Charleston Jewry. Charleston, W. Va.: Jones Print. Co., 1972.
M5270 (ASU)

Meyers, June ed. Bibliography of the Eastern Band of Cherokee Indians. Raleigh, N. C.: Dept. of Natural and Economic Resources, Division of Community Services, 1974.
M5280

Meyers, Robert Cornelius V. Life and Adventures of Lewis Wetzel. Philadelphia: John E. Potter, n.d. Wetzel was considered one of the greatest scouts and Indian fighters in our history.
M5290 (BC)

Meyertons, Carl Theile Triassic Formations of the Danville Basin. Report of Investigations, 6. Charlottesville: Virginia Division of Mineral Resources, 1963.
M5300 (ETSU)

Michalek, Daniel D. "Fan-like Features and Related Periglacial Phenomena of the Southern Blue Ridge." Microfilm. Ph. D. Diss. Univ. of North Carolina, 1967.
M5310 (WCU)

Michalik, Benjamin A. "The Decline of Anthracite, 1913-1955." Ph. D. Diss. Fordham Univ., 1957.
M5320

Michaux, Francois Andre Travels to the West of the Allegheny Mountains . . . London: Barnard and Sultzer, 1805.
M5330 (ASU BC)

Michaux, R. R. Sketches of Life in North Carolina. Culler, N. C.: W. C. Phillips, 1894. Includes material on the western portions of the state.
M5340

Mickley, Minnie F. Genealogy of the Mickley Family of America. Mickleys, Pa.: n.p., 1893.
M5350

Middleton, Elmon Harlan County, Kentucky. Big Laurel: J. T. Adams, 1934.
M5360 (BC)

Miernyk, William H. Appalachian Development: The Long-run View. Ann Arbor, Mich.: Poverty and Human Resources Abstracts, 1967. The author is looking down the years at the human and physical resources of Appalachia.
M5370 (LMC)

Appalachian Future, the Economic Challenge. Morgantown: Center for Appalachian Studies and Development, 1968.
M5380

Stimulating Regional Economic Development with an Input-Output Model. Morgantown: West Virginia Univ., Regional Research Institute, 1968.
M5390

Stimulating Regional Economic Development. An Interindustry Analysis of West Virginia Economy. Morgantown: West Virginia Univ., Regional Research Institute, 1969.
M5400

The Structure of the West Virginia Economy in 1975, a Preliminary Forecast. Morgantown: West Virginia Univ., Regional Research Institute, 1968.
M5410

Milam, Thomas Riley "An Individualized Reading Program for a Fifth Grade Group of Students at Andrew Johnson School, Kingsport, Tennessee." Master's thesis. East Tennessee State Univ., 1963.
M5420 (ETSU)

Miles, Emma Bell Our Southern Birds. Morristown, Tenn.: Globe Book Co., 1922. Lists and describes Southern birds, their habits and habitats.
M5430 (ASU BC)

The Spirit of the Mountains. New York: J. Pott and Co., 1905. A description of mountain life, customs and culture.
M5440 (ASU BC WCU)

Strains from a Dulcimore. Atlanta: E. Hartsock, Bozart Press, 1930. Mountain poetry — some of excellent quality.
M5450 (BC)

Miles, Miska Gertrude's Pocket. Illustrated by Emily McCully. 1st ed. Boston: Little, Brown, 1970.
M5460 (ASU BC LMC ETSU)

Hoagie's Rifle-Gun. Illustrated by John Schoenberr. 1st ed. An Atlantic Monthly Press Book. Boston: Little, Brown, 1970. Story of a young boy's hunting trips and the unexpected trouble he encounters.
M5470 (ASU BC LMC)

Milici, Robert C. Stratigraphy of the Chickamauga Supergroup in Its Type Area. Report of Investigations, no. 24. Nashville: Tennessee Division of Geology, 1969.
M5480 (ETSU)

Military Operations in Jefferson County Virginia (and West Virginia) 1861-1865 n.p.: Farmers' Advocate Printers, 1911.
M5490

Millen, Eli Moffatt Bethel. Garden City, N. Y.: Doubleday, Doran and Co., 1929. The story of a Kentucky mountain preacher who struggles to keep his church from the clutches of a millionaire landowner.
M5500 (ASU BC LMC)

Miller, Mrs. Alex M. Daintie's Cruel Rivals. Cleveland: George Munro, 1898.
M5510 (BC)

Lynette's Wedding. New York: Strut and Smith Corp., 1896.
M5520 (BC)

The Pearl and the Ruby. New York: George Munro's Sons, 1884.
M5530 (BC)

Miller, Allen Guivere As Once I Passed This Way. Boston: The Meador Pub. Co., 1935. Verse from the hills.
M5540

Miller, B. R. Kern, E. E. An Inventory of Human and Physical Resources of Cherokee Dekalb, Jackson, and Marshall Counties, Alabama. Auburn, Ala.: Auburn Univ. Agricultural Experiment Station, 1966.
K1590 (ASU)

Miller, Barbara Martin "A Comparison of Socio-economic Status and Art Interest of Two Sixth Grade Groups in Washington County, Tennessee." Master's thesis. East Tennessee State Univ., 1971.
M5550 (ETSU)

Miller, Caroline Lamb in His Bosom. New York: Grosset, 1933. Pulitzer prize novel of family in the foothill country of Georgia.
M5560 (ASU WWC)

Lamb in His Bosom. 1st ed. New York: Harper Brothers, 1933.
M5570 (ASU)

Miller, David Reed The Red Swan's Neck: A Tale of the North Carolina Mountains. Boston: Sherman, French and Co., 1911. A picturesque tale of the North Carolina mountains during and immediately following the Civil War.
M5580

Miller, Delmas Ferguson "A Survey of the Public Relations Programs of West Virginia High Schools." Master's thesis. West Virginia Univ., 1934.
M5590

Miller, Edna Lucille "A Study of Folklore in Watauga County, North Carolina." Master's thesis. George Peabody College for Teachers, 1938.
M5600 (LMC)

Miller, Ernest C. Pennsylvania's Oil Industry. Rev. ed. Gettysburg, Pa.: Historical Assoc., 1959.
M5610

Miller, Francis Pickens Man from the Valley: Memoirs of a 20th-Century Virginian. Chapel Hill: Univ. of North Carolina Press, 1971.
M5620 (ASU)

Miller, Harold W. "Characteristics of Mining and Nonmining Psychiatric Patients." Master's thesis. West Virginia Univ., 1960.
M5630

Miller, Harvey J. News from Pigeon Roost. Rabun Gap, Ga.: The Foxfire Press, 1975. This North Carolina and East Tennessee ridge community is analyzed in depth by Miller, the country correspondent with the rare faculty for catching his neighbors on paper.
M5640 (ASU)

Miller, Heather Ross The Edge of the Woods. New York: Atheneum, 1964. A woman in the Uwharrie mountains of North Carolina searches her past as she fights for sanity.
M5650 (ASU)

Tenants of the House. New York: Harcourt, Brace and World, 1966. This volume is made up of fourteen brief accounts of the people and events of Johnsboro, a small, backward North Carolina aluminium-smelting town. No Appalachian focus.
M5660 (WCU BC)

The Wind Southerly. New York: Harcourt, Brace and World, 1967.
M5670

Miller, Helen A Proposed Regional Library for Wood, Pleasants, Tyler, and Wetzel Counties. n.p.: n.p., 1960.
M5710

Miller, Helen Topping After the Glory. New York: Appleton-Century-Crofts, 1958. A novel of Reconstruction Days in Tennessee. Partially set in the mountains.
M5680 (ASU BC ETSU)

Hawk in the Wind. New York: D. Appleton Century Co., 1938. A strong mountain woman runs a pulp mill in the mountains of North Carolina.
M5690 (ASU BC)

Horns of Capricorn. New York: Appleton, 1950. A romantic story of North Carolina at the turn of the century when the tobacco business was beginning to boom. Not Appalachian in content or setting.
M5700 (BC ETSU WCU WWC)

Sharon. Philadelphia: Penn Pub. Co., 1931. A plane falls from the sky, bringing Sharon's drifting day to an end. She marries and begins supporting five people with mountain ingenuity.
M5720 (ASU)

Slow Dies the Thunder. 1st ed. Indianapolis: Bobbs-Merrill, 1955. Fiction with a Revolutionary War background. Set partially in the mountains.
M5730 (ASU BC ETSU)

The Sound of Chariots: A Novel of John Sevier and the State of Franklin. 1st ed. Indianapolis: Bobbs-Merrill Co., 1947.
M5740 (ASU BC ETSU WCU)

Splendor of Eagles. Philadelphia: Penn Pub. Co., 1935. Romantic fiction about a new bride. Partially set in the mountains of Western North Carolina and Eastern Tennessee.
M5750

Miller, J. D. Paulson, Quentin Frank Ground-water Resources and Geology of Tuscaloosa County, Alabama. Univ.: Alabama Geological Survey, 1962.
P1030 (ETSU)

Miller, J. D., Jr. Geology and Ground-water Resources of Tuscaloosa County, Alabama. Prepared by the U. S. Geological Survey in cooperation with the Tuscaloosa County Board of Revenue and the Geological Survey of Alabama. Information Series, 14. University: Alabama Geological Survey, 1958.
M5760 (ETSU)

Ground-water in the Vicinity of Bryce State Hospital, Tuscaloosa County, Alabama. Prepared by the U. S. Geological Survey in cooperation with Alabama State Hospitals and Partlow State Schools and the Geological Survey of Alabama. Information Series, 12. University: Alabama Geological Survey, 1958.
M5770 (ETSU)

Miller, J. T. Taylor, Arthur Elijah Soil Survey of Adams County, Ohio. Washington: U. S. Department of Agriculture, Bureau of Chemistry and Soils, 1938.
T390

Miller, James Henry History of Summers County from the Earliest Settlement to the Present Time. Parsons, W. Va.: McClain Print. Co., 1970.
M5780 (ASU)

Miller, James R. "School Transportation Costs in Unicoi County: A Comparison of Publicly-owned and Privately-owned Systems." Master's thesis. East Tennessee State Univ., 1965.
M5790 (ETSU)

Miller, Jim Wayne Copperhead Cane, Poems. Nashville, Tenn.: R. M. Allen, 1964. Great poetry from the hills. Miller, a native of western North Carolina was educated in Kentucky and Tennessee.
M5800 (ASU BC)

Dialogue with a Dead Man. Athens: University of Georgia Press, 1974. A native son's tribute to his grandfather and his region. Miller is without contest, the finest Appalachian poet of the generation.
M5810 (ASU BC)

A List of Magazines, Journals, Small Presses, Newspapers, etc. of Interest to Students of Appalachia. Berea, Ky.: Berea College, 1973. A listing of thirty-five periodicals, small presses, etc.
M5820

The More Things Change, the More They Stay the Same. Kentucky Poets Series, vol. 1. Frankfort, Ky.: Whippoorwill Press, 1971.
M5830 (ASU BC LMC)

Published Works of Cratis Williams. Berea, Ky.: Berea College, 1974.
M5840 (ASU BC)

Miller, John T. Soil Survey, Hall County, Georgia. Prepared in cooperation with the University of Georgia College of Agriculture. Soil Survey Report, Series, 1937, no. 2. Washington: U. S. Department of Agriculture, Bureau of Plant Industry, 1941.
M5850 (ASU)

Miller, John T. and others Soil Survey, Towns County, Georgia. U. S. Soil Conservation Service, Soil Survey, Series 1939, no. 16. Washington: Govt. Print. Off., 1954.
M5860

Soil Survey, Union County, Georgia. Soil Survey Report, Series 1938, no. 28. Washington: U. S. Bureau of Plant Industry, Soils and Agricultural Engineering, 1950.
M5870

Miller, Joseph Lyon The Descendants of Capt. Thomas Carter. Harrisonburg, Va.: C. J. Carrier Co., 1972. Includes a section on southwest Virginia Carters of Scott County.
M5880

Miller, L. F. TVA Lakes as a Fishery and Wildlife Asset. Norris, Tenn.: TVA Fish and Game Branch, 1959.
M5890

Miller, Leonard P. Education in Buncombe County, 1793-1965. Asheville, N. C.: n.p., 1965.
M5900

Miller, Lewis Sketches and Chronicles: The Reflections of a Nineteenth Century Pennsylvania German Folk Artist. York, Pa.: The Historical Society of York County, 1966.
M5910 (FC)

Miller, Martin A. "Farm-level Demand Analysis of the Appalachian Fresh Apple Industry." Master's thesis. West Virginia Univ., 1970.
M5920

Miller, Marvin G. The Hills and Home. Parsons, W. Va.: McClain Print. Co., 1971. Poems. Very Good.
M5930 (ASU)

Miller, Mary L. Community Analysis and Program Planning, Big Caney Valley, Kentucky. Oak Ridge: Associated Universities, 1966.
M5940

Miller, Nora Girl in the Rural Family. Chapel Hill: Univ. of North Carolina Press, 1935. Child from an Appalachian mill town is used in this study.
M5950 (ASU BC)

Miller, Ralph L. Geology and Oil Resources of the Jonesville District, Lee County, Virginia. Washington: U. S. Govt. Print. Off., 1954. Prepared in cooperation with the Virginia Geological Survey.
M5960

Miller, Robert W. Zeller, Frederick A. Problems of Community Action in Appalachia. Morgantown: West Virginia Univ., Appalachian Center, Office of Research and Development, 1968.
Z70

Miller, Robert W. ed. Approaches to University Extension Work with the Rural Disadvantaged: Description and Analysis of a Pilot Effort. Morgantown: West Virginia Center for Appalachian Studies and Development West Virginia Univ., 1972.
M5970

Miller, Robert Wilbur ed. Zeller, Frederick Anthony Manpower Development in Appalachia: An Approach to Unemployment. New York: Praeger, 1968.
Z80 (UNCA ASU LMC ETSU)

Miller, Russell Allen "Mercury Pollution in Fish in Boone Reservoir, Tennessee." Master's thesis. East Tennessee State Univ., 1971.
M5980 (ETSU)

Miller, Sampson Newton Annals of Webster County, West Virginia. Webster Springs, W. Va.: n.p., 1969.
M5990

Miller, Stanley "The United Mine Workers: A Study of How Trade Union Policy Relates to Technological Change." Ph. D. Diss. Univ. of Wisconsin, 1957.
M6000

Miller, Thomas Condit West Virginia and Its People. New York: Lewis Historical Pub. Co., 1913.
M6010

Miller, Tracey R. "Investigation of the Regional English of Unicoi County, Tennessee." Ph. D. Diss. University of Tennessee, 1973. Focuses on the older citizens with little formal education.
M6020

Miller, Virgil Thomas "Geographic Factors Affecting Manufacturers of Durable Goods in Johnson City, Tennessee." Master's thesis. East Tennessee State College, 1951.
M6030 (ETSU)

Milligan, Jack A. "A Comparison of the Personal and Economic Characteristics of the Mobile and Immobile." Master's thesis. West Virginia Univ., 1960.
M6040

Milling, Chapman James Red Carolinians. Photographs by Dr. Bruce Mayne and others. Chapel Hill: Univ. of North Carolina Press, 1940.
M6050 (ASU BC WCU)

Milling, Chapman Jarves Red Carolinians. 1940. Reprint. Columbia: Univ. of South Carolina Press, 1969.
M6060 (LMC)

Mills, Anita U. Radomski, Alexander L. Family Income and Related Characteristics Among Low-Income Counties and States. Washington: Division of Research, Welfare Administration, U. S. Department of Health, Education and Welfare, 1964.
R40

Mills, Josephine J. "An Investigation of the Reading Interest of the Junior High School Students in Greenville, Tennessee." Master's thesis. East Tennessee State College, 1954.
M6070

Mills, Mary Hampton Be Ye Begger or King. Asheville, N. C.: Advocate Pub. Co., 1925. No copy available for examination. Reputedly Appalachian in setting.
M6080

Mills, Oma H. Sommerville, Geraldine David Rawson Ancestors and Descendants. n.p.: n.p., 1974.
S5460 (ASU)

Mills, Robert L. "A Method of Measuring the Financial Ability of Kentucky School Districts to Support an Educational Program." Master's thesis. Univ. of Kentucky, 1951.
M6090

Millspaugh, Charles Frederick Part 1: The Living Flora of West Virginia. Part 2: The Fossil Flora of West Virginia. West Virginia Geological Survey Reports, vol. 5-A. Wheeling: Wheeling News Litho. Co., 1913.
M6100 (ETSU)

Milne, Terry Crain, Jim Camping Around the Appalachian Mountains. New York: Random House, Inc., 1975.
C8470 (ASU)

Milton, Charles Subsurface "Basement" Rocks of Georgia. Washington: U. S. Geological Survey, n.d.
M6110 (ETSU ASU)

Milton, George Fort The Age of Hate: Andrew Johnson and the Radicals. New York: Coward-McCann, 1930.
M6120 (ASU)

Minckler, Leon Sherwood Tree Planting in the Central Piedmont, and Southern Appalachian Region. U. S. Department of Agriculture Farmers' Bulletin, no. 1994. Washington: Govt. Print. Off., 1957.
M6130 (WCU)

Mine Drainage Abstracts, a Bibliography Bituminous Coal Research: n.p., n.d.
M6140

Miner, William Harvey Daniel Boone. New York: B. Franklin, 1970. An exhaustive study of sources on Daniel Boone.
M6160 (ASU BC ETSU)

Mineral Resources of the Appalachian Region Washington: U. S. Geological Survey, 1968.
M6170 (ASU)

The Miner's Voice vol. 1-, 1970. Morgantown, W. Va.: Fund for the future, monthly.
M6150 (BC)

Mink, Oscar G. Dropout Proneness in Appalachia. Research Series, 3. ERIC RC 003132. Morgantown: Appalachian Center, West Virginia Univ., 1968.
M6180 (ASU)

Dropout Proneness in Appalachia. Research Series, 3. Morgantown: Appalachian Center, West Virginia Univ., 1968.
M6190 (ETSU)

Minnick, Howard Edward "A Search for a Meaningful Program in Mathematics for the Slow Learner in the Seventh Grade in the Bristol, Tennessee, City Schools." Master's thesis. East Tennessee State Univ., 1971.
M6200 (ETSU)

Mischaikov, Michael K. Postwar Changes in the Export Markets for American Coal: A Study in the Industry Response to Variations in Foreign Demand. West Virginia University Business and Economic Studies, vol. 9, no. 3. Also, Bulletin, Series 65, no. 7-1. Morgantown: Bureau of Business Research, College of Commerce, 1965.
M6210 (ASU)

Miser, H. D. Hewett, D. F. Possibilities for Manganese Ore on Certain Undeveloped Tracts in the Shenandoah Valley, Virginia. Washington: Govt. Print. Off., 1918.
H5130

Miser, Hugh Dinsmore Mineral Resources of the Waynesboro Quadrangle, Tennessee. Bulletin, no. 26. Nashville: Tennessee Geological Survey, 1921.
M6220 (ETSU)

Mish, Mary Vernon Jonathan Hager, Founder of Hagerstown, Maryland. Hagerstown, Md.: Stouffer Print. Co., 1962.
M6230

Missionary District of Asheville (Episcopal). Woman's Auxiliary to the Board of Missions Annual Report. n.p.: n.p., 1913-.
M6240 (LMC)

Mitchell, Beulah "A Study of the Life and Works of Jesse Stuart." Master's thesis. East Texas State Teachers College, 1952. A critical study of the works of Kentucky's best-known writer.
M6250 (ASU)

Mitchell, Carrie "An Analysis of the Possibilities for Local Support of Education in Pickett County, Tennessee." Master's thesis. Tennessee Polytechnic, 1959.
M6270

Mitchell, Cleophus H. "A Study of the Changes in the Educational Levels of the Negro Teachers in Jefferson County, Alabama, 1930-50." Master's thesis. Fisk Univ., 1952.
M6280

Mitchell County, N. C., Board of Education Discovering Mitchell County, 1939-40: A Cooperative Study Made by the Teachers and Pupils of Mitchell County. Bakersville, N. C.: The Board, 1940. A descriptive history of Mitchell County, North Carolina.
M6290 (ASU)

Mitchell, Elisha Diary of a Geological Tour by Dr. Elisha Mitchell in 1827 and 1828. With introduction and notes by Dr. Kemp Plummer Battle. James Sprunt Historical Monograph, no. 6. Chapel Hill: Univ. of North Carolina, 1905. Mitchell took copious scientific notes throughout the Appalachians. He was attempting to measure the altitude of the highest peak in the Appalachians when he fell to his death. The mountain was named for him.
M6300 (ASU BC LMC)

Mitchell, Fred E. Fading Hi-lights Relating to the Birth and Growth of the Swannanoa Valley in Western North Carolina, 1845-1960. Aiken, S. C.: The author, 1962. Relates incidents from the history of the Swannanoa Valley. Much about the gap as a way west and about the famous tunnel.
M6310 (ASU)

Mitchell, Harry E. The Mitchell-Doak Group. n.p.: n.p., 1966.
M6320

Mitchell, Howard W. The Hammered Dulcimer — How to Make and Play It. n.p.: n.p., n.d. A book and record set with diagrams, instructions, photograph and music.
M6330

The Mountain Dulcimer. n.p.: n.p., n.d. Detailed instruction book with record on how to make and play a mountain dulcimer.
M6340

Mitchell, Langdon Edwyn Love in the Backwoods. New York: Harper and Brothers, 1897. Two stories of frontier West Virginia where love does not quite conquer all.
M6350 (BC)

Mitchell, R. L., Jr. "Fifty Years Ago, a History of Overton County, Tennessee, Around the Year 1850." Livingston, Tenn.: The Enterprise, 1931-32. A scrapbook of articles printed in the Livingston Enterprise, 1931-32.
M6360

Mitcholl, Broadus Frederick Law Olmsted: A Critic of the Old South. Baltimore: The Johns Hopkins Press, 1924. Olmsted made several trips into the Southern mountains.
M6260

Miyakawa, Tetsuo Scott Protestants and Pioneers; Individualism and Conformity on the American Frontier. Chicago: Univ. of Chicago Press, 1964.
M6370

Mize, Jessie comp. Richardson, Marian M. 1832 Cherokee Land Lottery: Index to Revolutionary Soldiers, Their Widows and Orphans Who Were Fortunate Drawers. Danielsville, Ga.: Heritage Papers, 1969.
R2150 (ASU WCU)

Mock, Asenath Birchfiel "An Analysis of the Errors in Word Recognition Made by Pupils of One Section Each of the Second Through Sixth Grades of Lynn Avenue School, 1956-57, in Elizabethton, Tennessee." Master's thesis. East Tennessee State College, 1957.
M6380 (ETSU)

Mockler, William Emmett Morgan West Virginia Surnames, the Pioneers. Parsons, W. Va.: McClain Print. Co., 1973. First published for the W. Va. Dialect Society in 1956.
M6390 (ASU)

Moffett, Lee Water Powered Mills of Fauquier County Virginia. Warrington, Va.: The author, 1973. Descriptions photographs, short histories and locations.
M6400 (ASU)

Moffett, Thomas Clinton The American Indian on the New Trail: The Red Man of the United States and the Christian Gospel. New York: Missionary Education Movement of the United States and Canada, 1914.
M6410 (ASU)

Moffitt, James William "A History of the Early Baptist Missions Among the Five Civilized Tribes." Microfilm. Ph. D. Diss. Univ. of Oklahoma, 1946.
M6420 (WCU)

Moffitt, Polly Byrd "An Experimental Program in Grouping for Third Grade at Fairmont School, Johnson City, Tennessee." Master's thesis. East Tennessee State Univ., 1970.
M6430 (ETSU)

Moffitt, William C. and others Soil Survey: DeKalb County, Tennessee. Prepared in cooperation with the Tennessee Agricultural Station. Washington: Soil Conservation Service, 1972.
M6440

Mogen, C. A. Hasty, Allen Henry Soil Survey, Rhea County, Tennessee. Washington: U. S. Department of Agriculture, Bureau of Plant Industry, Soils, and Agricultural Engineering, 1948.
H3390

Roberts, Wallace Soil Survey, Hamilton County, Tennessee. Washington: U. S. Department of Agriculture, Bureau of Plant Industry, Soils, and Agricultural Engineering, 1947.
R3100

Monhollow, Jimmie Ray "The Farmers Home Administration and Agricultural Poverty in Tennessee." Ph. D. Diss. Vanderbilt Univ., 1964. Analyzes contributions of the FHA to improvement of low-income farmers.
M6450

Monongahela Power Company Timber Inventory and Wood Manufacturing Opportunities in the Northern and Central West Virginia Region. Fairmont, W. Va.: n.p., 1967.
M6460

Monongahela River Mine Drainage Remedial Project and Advisory Work Group Handbook of Pollution Control Costs in Mine Drainage Management. Washington: U. S. Federal Water Pollution Control Administration, 1966, i.e. 1967.
M6470

The Monongalia Historical Society The 175th Anniversary of the Formation of Monongalia County, West Virginia, and Other Relative Historical Data. Morgantown, W. Va.: The society, 1954.
M6480 (ASU)

Monroe, Muriel B. Howell, Joseph C. Birds of Knox County. Knoxville: Univ. of Tennessee, 1970.
H7730

Montague, Margaret Prescott Deep Channel. Boston: Atlantic Monthly Press, 1923. Novel of life in the Southern Appalachians.
M6490 (ASU)

In Calvert's Valley. New York: Baker and Taylor Co., 1908. Story centers on a townsman, but West Virginia mountains and mountaineers provide backdrop.
M6500

Montague, Margaret Prescott
Linda. Boston: Houghton Mifflin Co., 1912. Wild, nature-loving Linda is forced to marry a local sawyer. Complications: Linda's pregnant and his presumably dead wife turns up. Linda flees, bears child, and returns to her husband as he lies dying.
M6510 (ASU BC)
The Poet, Miss Kate and I. Illustrated by George W. Hood. New York: Baker and Taylor Co., 1905. A novel of city folk in an Allegheny resort area.
M6520 (ASU BC)
The Sowing of Alderson Cree. New York: Baker and Taylor Co., 1907. Cree sows hatred, revenge, and a desire to commit murder in the heart of son David. Circumstances intervene to save David and right triumphs.
M6530 (ASU BC)
Uncle Sam of Freedom Ridge. Garden City, N. Y.: Doubleday, 1920. His only son is killed in the war and Sam finds his patriotic fervor fading. In the end he commits suicide.
M6540 (BC)
Up Eel River. Illustrated by Martha Bensley Bruere. New York: Macmillan Co., 1928. A lumber camp on Eel River provides backdrop for this series of folk tales.
M6550 (ASU BC LMC WCU)

Montell, William Lynwood The Saga of Coe Ridge: A Study in Oral History. 1st ed. Knoxville: Univ. of Tennessee Press, 1970. An outstanding example of oral history from the Cumberland Ridge country.
M6560 (ASU BC ETSU LMC WCU WWC)

Montgomery, Charles "Community Uses of Public School Buildings in West Virginia." Master's thesis. West Virginia Univ., 1934.
M6570

Montgomery, Ernest Brimer "Some Factors Affecting Retardation in the Six High Schools of Washington County." Master's thesis. East Tennessee State College, 1952.
M6580 (ETSU)

Montgomery, James Elmer "Three Appalachian Communities: Cultural Differentials as They Affect Levels of Living and Population Pressure." Microfilm. Ph. D. Diss. Vanderbilt Univ., 1945. Social history of three Appalachian communities.
M6590 (ASU)
"Two Resettlement Communities on the Cumberland Plateau." Master's thesis. Vanderbilt Univ., 1941. Includes Cumberland Homesteads.
M6600

Montgomery, John F. Wilson, L. Craig School-community Improvement, a Report of the Greenbrier County Program. New York: World Book Co., 1959.
W7360 (ASU WCU)

Montgomery, William John Theory and Practice of Mine Ventilation. Columbus, Ohio: The Jeffrey Manufacturing Co., 1936. Certainly, in Appalachia, there is a wide gap between theory and practice.
M6610

Moody, Minnie Hite Long Meadows. New York: The Macmillan Co., 1941. Historical novel partially set in Western Virginia.
M6620 (ASU)

Moon, J. W. Soil Survey, Jefferson County, Tennessee. Prepared in cooperation with the Tennessee Agricultural Experiment Station, Soil Survey Report, Series 1935, no. 20. Washington: U. S. Department of Agriculture, Bureau of Plant Industry, 1941.
M6630

Mooney, Charles N. Latimer, William James Soil Survey of Braxton and Clay Counties, West Virginia. Washington: U. S. Department of Agriculture, Bureau of Soils, 1920.
L710
Latimer, William James Soil Survey of the Point Pleasant, West Virginia, Area. Washington: U. S. Department of Agriculture, Bureau of Soils, 1911.
L810
Soil Survey of the Albemarle Area, Virginia. Washington: U. S. Dept. of Agriculture, 1903.
M6640
Soil Survey of the Bedford Area, Virginia. Washington: U. S. Dept. of Agriculture, 1902.
M6650
Soil Survey of Centre County, Pennsylvania. Washington: U. S. Dept. of Agriculture, 1910.
M6660
Soil Survey of Clarksburg Area, West Virginia. Washington: U. S. Dept. of Agriculture, 1912.
M6670
Soil Survey of the Greenville Area, Tennessee. Washington: U. S. Dept. of Agriculture, 1905.
M6680
Soil Survey of the Morgantown, West Virginia Area. Washington: U. S. Dept. of Agriculture, 1912.
M6690
Soil Survey of Talladega County, Alabama. Washington: U. S. Dept. of Agriculture, 1909.
M6700

Mooney, Charles W. Soil Survey of Webster County, West Virginia. Washington: U. S. Dept. of Agriculture, 1920.
M6710

Mooney, Fred Struggle in the Coal Fields: The Autobiography of Fred Mooney. Edited by J. W. Hess. Morgantown: West Virginia Univ. Library, 1967.
M6720 (ASU BC WCU)

Mooney, James The Aboriginal Population of America North of Mexico. Smithsonian Miscellaneous Collections, vol. 80, no. 7. Washington, D. C.: Smithsonian Institution, 1928. Contains some mention of the Cherokee and other Indians of the mountains.
M6730
Cherokee Animal Tales. Edited from his Myths of the Cherokee, with an introduction by George F. Scheer. Illustrated by Robert Frankenberg. New York: Holiday House, 1968.
M6740 (ASU)
Myths of the Cherokee. Nineteenth annual report, 1897-98. Washington: U. S. Bureau of American Ethnology, 1900. Includes a glossary of Cherokee words.
M6750 (ASU LMC)
Myths of the Cherokee. 1900. Reprint. Landmarks in Anthropology. New York: Johnson Reprint Corp., 1970. The best book published on the Cherokee.
M6760 (ASU BC WCU)
Myths of the Cherokee. 1900. Reprint. St. Clair Shores, Mich.: Scholarly Press, 1970.
M6770 (ASU ETSU WWC)
Myths of the Cherokee and Sacred Formulas of the Cherokee. Nashville: Charles and Elder, 1972.
M6780 (ASU LMC)
The Sacred Formulas of the Cherokees. Extract from the seventh annual report of the Bureau of American Ethnology. Washington: Govt. Print. Off., 1891.
M6790 (WCU ASU)
The Swimmer Manuscript, Cherokee Sacred Formulas and Medicinal Prescriptions. Washington: Govt. Print. Off., 1932.
M6800 (ETSU)

Mooney, Mary Sue "An Intimate Study of Mary Noailles Murfree, Charles Egbert Craddock." Microfilm. Master's thesis. George Peabody College for Teachers, 1928.
M6810 (ASU)

Moore, Alvin Edward History of Hardy County of the Borderland. Parsons, W. Va.: McClain Print. Co., 1963.
M6820 (ASU BC)

Moore, Arthur K. The Frontier Mind: A Cultural Analysis of the Kentucky Frontiersman. Lexington: Univ. of Kentucky Press, 1959.
M6850

Moore, Arthur Keister The Frontier Mind: A Cultural Analysis of the Kentucky Frontiersman. Lexington: Univ. of Kentucky Press, 1957. Includes bibliographies.
M6830 (ASU BC ETSU UNCA)
The Frontier Mind. 1957. Reprint. McGraw-Hill Paperbacks. New York: McGraw-Hill, 1963.
M6840 (ASU WCU)

Moore, Bertha Belle see also **Cannon, Brenda pseud.**

Moore, Bertha Belle As by Fire. Grand Rapids, Mich.: Eerdmans Pub. Co., 1939. Moralistic fiction for youths. Set in Western North Carolina.
M6860 (ASU)
Autumn on Breezy Hill. Grand Rapids, Mich.: Zondervan Pub. Co., 1956. Moralistic fiction for the younger reader. Set in Western North Carolina.
M6870 (ASU)
Blacktop. Grand Rapids, Mich.: Eerdmans, 1956. This novel, written for young adults, presents a stereotypical plot. The mountaineers are fighting progress. Rather than resolve this conflict, the author lets love conquer all.
M6880 (ASU)
Dan and Jack Find a Pal. Chicago: Moody Press, 1955. Children's fiction partially set in western North Carolina.
M6890 (ASU)
Doctor Happy. Grand Rapids, Mich.: Eerdmans, 1938. Children's fiction.
M6900 (ASU)
Eyes Unto the Hills. Grand Rapids, Mich.: Eerdmans, 1951. Western North Carolina fiction for the younger reader.
M6910 (ASU)
The Girl of the Listening Heart. Grand Rapids, Mich.: Eerdmans, 1937. North Carolina fiction for youths.
M6920
The Healing Hills. Findley, Ohio: Fundamental Truth, Pub., 1941. Moralistic fiction set in western North Carolina.
M6930 (ASU)
The Jolly J's Have a Reunion. Chicago: Moody Press, 1952.
M6940 (ASU)
The Jolly J's Make Decisions. Chicago: Moody Press, 1951. Set in western North Carolina.
M6950 (ASU)
The Jolly J's of Silver Creek. Chicago: Moody Press, 1949.
M6960 (ASU)
Joy Shop Stories. Springfield, Mo.: Gospel Pub. Co., 1929.
M6970 (ASU)
Laborers Together. Grand Rapids, Mich.: Eerdmans, 1952. North Carolina fiction.
M6980
On Silver Creek Knob. Chicago: Moody Institute Press, 1939. Children's fiction from western North Carolina.
M6990 (ASU BC)
Ordered Steps. Grand Rapids: William B. Eerdmans Pub. Co., 1937. Partially set in western North Carolina.
M7000
Silver Creek's Camp Jolly. Chicago: Moody Press, 1954. North Carolina fiction.
M7010 (ASU)
Spring on Breezy Hill. Grand Rapids, Mich.: Zondervan, 1952.
M7020 (ASU)
Strength of the Hills. Chicago: Moody, 1952. Moralistic fiction set in western North Carolina.
M7030 (ASU)
These, My People. Grand Rapids, Mich.: Eerdmans, 1942. North Carolina fiction.
M7040
The Touch of Polly Tucker. Grand Rapids, Mich.: Eerdmans, 1952. Moralistic fiction for youths.
M7050 (ASU)
The Triplets Go to Camp. Grand Rapids, Mich.: Eerdmans, 1955.
M7060

Moore, Caroline T. ed. Abstracts of the Wills of the State of South Carolina, 1740-1760. Columbia, S. C.: R. L. Bryan Co., 1964.
M7070 (ASU)

Moore, Clarence Bloomfield Aboriginal Sites on Tennessee River. Philadelphia, Pa.: The author, 1915.
M7080

Moore, Dean W. Washington's Woods: A History of Ravenswood and Jackson County, West Virginia. 1st ed. Parsons, W. Va.: McClain Print. Co., 1971.
M7090 (ASU)

Moore, Donald Lee Wey, Adelaide Smoky Mountain Ballads. New York: n.p., 1949.
W4980

Moore, Edward Alexander The Story of a Cannoneer, under Stonewall Jackson, in Which Is Told the Part Taken by the Rockbridge Artillery in the Army of Northern Virginia. With introductions by Capt. Robert E. Lee, Jr., and Hon. Henry St. George Tucker. Illustrated by portraits. 2nd ed. Lynchburg, Va.: J. P. Bell Co., 1910.
M7100 (ASU)

Moore, Elizabeth Fox John Fox, Jr.: Personal and Family Letters and Papers. Lexington, Ky.: n.p., 1955.
M7110

Moore, Elwood James "The Effects of a Physical Education Program on the Motor Skills of Selected Severely Retarded Children in Johnson City, Tennessee." Master's thesis. East Tennessee State Univ., 1973.
M7120 (ETSU)

Moore, Ethel Sivley Francis, Elesabeth Wheeler Lost Links: New Recordings of Old Data from Many States. Nashville, Tenn.: McQuiddy Print. Co., 1945.
F3040 (ASU)

Moore, Frank ed. Songs and Ballads of the Southern People, 1861-1865. 1886. Reprint. New York: Burt Franklin, 1971.
M7130 (ASU)

Moore, George Ellis A Banner in the Hills: West Virginia's Statehood. New York: Appleton-Century-Crofts, 1963.
M7140 (ASU BC WCU)

"West Virginia and the Civil War, 1861-1863." Ph. D. Diss. West Virginia University, 1957.
M7150

Moore, Gerald K. Harris, Hobart B. Geology and Ground-water Resources of Colbert County, Alabama. University: Alabama Geological Survey, 1963.
H2870 (ETSU)

Harris, Hobart B. Interim Report on Ground-water Study in Colbert County, Alabama. University: Alabama Geological Survey, 1960.
H2880 (ETSU)

Moore, Grace You're Only Human Once. 1st ed. Garden City, N. Y.: Doubleday, Doran and Co., 1944. Life story of an Appalachian musician.
M7160 (ASU)

Moore, Helen K. Pioneer Superstitions; Old-timey Signs and Sayings. High Point, N. C.: Hutcraft, 1969.
M7170 (ASU BC)

Moore, Ida L. Like a River Flowing. New York: Doubleday, Doran and Co., 1941. Pioneer story of life in the North Carolina mountain country from ante bellum days to the turn of the century.
M7180 (ASU)

Moore, Idora McClellan Southern Character Sketches. Richmond: Dietz Press, 1937. Part I includes tales of northern Alabama hill folk.
M7190 (ASU WCU)

Moore, J. A. Planning for Flood Damage Prevention. Special Report no. 35. Atlanta, Ga.: Engineering Experiment Station, Georgia Institute of Technology, June 1958.
M7200

Moore, J. R. Jurney, Robert Campbell Soil Survey, Smyth County, Virginia. Washington: U. S. Department of Agriculture, Bureau of Plant Industry, Soils and Agricultural Engineering, 1948.
J2930

Schmidt-Bleek, F. Benefit/Cost Approach to Decision Making: The Dilemma with Coal Production. Knoxville: Univ. of Tennessee, The Appalachian Resources Project, 1973.
S970 (ASU)

Schmidt-Bleek, F. K. Statement on Benefit/Cost Evaluation of Strip Mining in Appalachia. Knoxville: Univ. of Tennessee Appalachian Resources Project, 1973.
S980 (ASU)

Moore, James C. "An Analysis of the New Deal Subsistence Homesteads Program in Cumberland County, Tennessee." Master's thesis. Tennessee Technological Univ., 1967.
M7210

Moore, John Monroe The South To-day. Richmond: Presbyterian Committee of Publication, 1916. Contains a great deal of information on the Presbyterian Home Mission Society's efforts.
M7220 (LMC)

Moore, John R. Strip Mining and the Three E's. Report, no. 19. Knoxville: Univ. of Tennessee, Appalachian Resources Project, 1973.
M7240 (ASU)

Moore, John R. ed. The Economic Impact of TVA Knoxville: Univ. of Tennessee Press, 1967.
E790 (ASU LMC WCU BC UNCA)

The Economic Impact of TVA. Knoxville: Univ. of Tennessee Press, 1967. Eight Specialists assess TVA's first 30 years.
M7230

Moore, John Trotwood The Bishop of Cottontown: A Story of the Southern Cotton Mills. Illustrated by the Kinneys. Nashville: Cokesbury Press, 1906. Some of his observations were drawn from Appalachian mill towns.
M7250 (ASU BC)

Hearts of Hickory: A Story of Andrew Jackson and the War of 1812. Nashville: Cokesbury Press, 1926. Novel of Andy Jackson and the War of 1812. Jackson was a long-time resident of Appalachia.
M7260 (ASU BC WCU)

Hearts of Hickory: A Story of Andrew Jackson and the War of 1812. New York: Grosset, 1926.
M7270 (ETSU)

Jack Ballington, Forester. Illustrated by George Gibbs. Philadelphia: John C. Winston Co., 1911. Tangentially Appalachian.
M7280 (ASU)

Songs and Stories from Tennessee. Chicago: J. C. Bauer, 1897.
M7290 (UNCA)

A Summer Hymnal, a Romance of Tennessee. Philadelphia: Henry T. Coates and Co., 1901. Period fiction set in Eastern Tennessee.
M7300 (ASU BC ETSU)

Moore, John W. History of North Carolina: From the Earliest Discoveries to the Present Time. 2 vols. Raleigh, N. C.: Alfred Williams, 1880. Good source on Western North Carolina.
M7310 (LMC)

Roster of North Carolina Troops: In the War Between the States. 4 vols. Raleigh, N. C.: Ashe and Gatling, 1882.
M7320 (LMC)

Moore, Lilian Daniel Boone. New York: Random House, 1955.
M7330

Moore, Martha Kiser "The Appalachia of Wilma Dykeman's Fiction." Master's thesis. East Tennessee State Univ., 1975.
M7340

Moore, Terry A. "The Phytoecology of Boone Fork Sphagnum Bog." Master's thesis. Appalachian State Univ., 1972.
M7350 (ASU)

Moore, William H. "Rockwood: A Prototype of the New South." Master's thesis. Univ. of Tennessee, 1965.
M7360

Moorehead, Warren King Exploration of the Etowah Site in Georgia. New Haven, Conn.: Yale Univ. Press, 1932.
M7370 (ASU)

Morais, Herbert M. Boyer, Richard Owen Labor's Untold Story. New York: Cameron Associates, 1955.
B6040 (ASU)

Morefield, Ada Honea "A Program of Folk Songs Used to Enrich and Implement the Social Studies Program in Grades Four, Five and Six at North Side School, Johnson City, Tennessee." Master's thesis. East Tennessee State College, 1958.
M7380 (ETSU)

Morehead, James Turner An Address in Commemoration of the First Settlement of Kentucky. Frankfort, Ky.: A. G. Hodges, 1840.
M7390

Morehead State University, Morehead, Ky. Bulletin of Applied Linguistics. vol. 1. n.p.: n.p., 1966 — Irregular.
M7400

Morehead State University. School of Applied Sciences and Technology Employment Opportunities and Usable Agricultural Skills in Non-Farm Agricultural Occupations in Appalachia. Morehead: The University, 1965.
M7410

Morehouse, Kathleen Moore Rain on the Just. New York: L. Furman, 1936. A gothic plot involves Least Dolly Allen in a pack of troubles in the Brushy Mountain of North Carolina. Well-written.
M7420 (ASU)

Moretz, Arlie E. Versatile Verse. New York: Vantage Press, 1971.
M7430 (ASU)

Morgan, Arthur E. Log of the TVA. New York: Survey Associates, 1936.
M7440

The Making of the TVA. n.p.: n.p., n.d. Personal account of TVA's early years by its first director. Contacts with Franklin D. Roosevelt are included.
M7450

Morgan, Charles McKinley "An Educational Survey of Carter County, Tennessee." Master's thesis. Univ. of Tennessee, 1936.
M7460

Morgan, Charles Thomas Flickering Light. Berea, Ky.: Berea College Press, 1943. Promotional literature about Berea College.
M7470 (BC WWC)

The Fruit of This Tree: The Story of a Great American College and Its Contribution to the Education of a Changing World. With an introduction by Bruce Barton. Berea, Ky.: Berea College, 1946.
M7480 (ASU BC)

Morgan, Clarita H. Edward Morgan 1751-1884, Pioneer Minister in Southwest, Virginia. Radford, Va.: n.p., 1973. Includes biographical sketch of Rev. Edward Morgan, who served in Pulaski and Giles Counties, and his sons Edward Jr. and Francis Asbury Morgan who lived in Pulaski County.
M7490

Morgan, E. L. Farmer Cooperation in Southwest Virginia. Prepared with the cooperation of the Tennessee Valley Authority. Bulletin, 331. Blacksburg: Virginia Agricultural Experiment Station, 1941.
M7500 (ASU)

Morgan, Edith Wenger Stories My Father Told Us. Berryville, Va.: Virginia Book Co., n.d. Stories from western Virginia.
M7510 (ASU)

Morgan, Fred T. comp. Ghost Tales of the Uwharries. Illustrated by Virginia Ingram. Winston-Salem, N. C.: J. F. Blair, 1968.
M7520 (ASU WCU)

Morgan, French A History and Genealogy of the Family of Col. Morgan the First White Settler of the State of West Virginia. Parsons, W. Va.: McClain Print. Co., 1966.
M7530 (ASU)

Morgan, George Hallenbrooke comp. Annals, Comprising Memoirs, Incidents and Statistics of Harrisburg, from the Period of Its First Settlement. Harrisburg, Pa.: G. A. Brooks, 1858.
M7540 (ASU)

Morgan, Hazel Smith ed. Morgan, Kelly Pioneer Families of Clay County, Kentucky. Manchester, Ky.: n.p., 1970.
M7600 (ASU BC)

Morgan, J. W. Souvenir of the 125th Anniversary of the Greenbriar Baptist Church (1781-1906), Alderson, West Virginia. Huntington, W. Va.: Swan Pub. Co., 1907.
M7550 (ASU)

Morgan, Jackson Kindred David Morgan (ca. 1779-1857) and His Descendants. Danielsville, Ga.: Heritage Papers, 1971.
M7560

Morgan, Jesse W. "Excess Levies and School Bond Issues in Wyoming County (West Virginia) from 1933-1951." Master's thesis. Marshall College, 1952.
M7570

Morgan, John G. Charleston 175. Based on a series of stories in the Charleston Gazette. Charleston, W. Va.: Charleston Gazette, 1970. Celebration of 175 years of the city on the river.
M7580 (ASU)

West Virginia Governors. Charleston, W. Va.: Newspaper Agency Corp., 1960. Lists all governors of the mountain state. Includes biographical sketches.
M7590

Morgan, Kelly Pioneer Families of Clay County, Kentucky. 1st ed. Manchester, Ky.: n.p., 1970.
M7600 (ASU BC)

Morgan, Le Berta H. ed. Staub School. A Brief History of Its First Fifty Years' Service to the Community. Knoxville: Staub PTA, 1947.
M7610

Morgan, Lucy Gift from the Hills: Miss Lucy Morgan's Story of Her Unique Penland School. With LeGette Blythe. 1st ed. Story of the Penland School of Handicrafts.
M7620 (ASU BC ETSU FC WCU WWC)

Gift from the Hills: Miss Lucy Morgan's Story of Unique Penland School. Enl. ed. Chapel Hill: UNC Press, 1971.
M7630

Morgan, Lucy G. Finding His World: The Story of Arthur E. Morgan. Yellow Springs, Ohio: Kahoe, 1927.
M7640

Morgan, Norma D. "A Study of the Factors Influencing the Election of Home Economics at Clyde A. Erwin High School." Master's thesis. Western Carolina University, 1962.
M7650 (WCU)

Morgan, Robert Zirconia Poems. Northwood Narrows, N. H.: Lillabulero Press, 1969.
M7660 (LMC)

Morgan, Stella Embree Again the River. New York: Thomas Y. Crowell Co., 1939. Three times the river washes away Jasper Morton's house. In the first two floods he loses his wife and two daughters. Now, alone and deranged he battles the river for the last time.
M7670 (ASU LMC)

Morgan, W. L. "Improving School Attendance in Six White Elementary Schools in Polk County, Georgia." Master's thesis. Univ. of Georgia, 1949.
M7680

Moricle, Clay Wesley "A Study of Ninth-grade Science Students in Phase Two at John Sevier Junior High School, Kingsport, Tennessee, 1967-1968." Master's thesis. East Tennessee State Univ., 1968.
M7690 (ETSU)

Morland, John K. Millways of Kent. Chapel Hill: Univ. of North Carolina Press, 1958. The report of a social anthropologist's one-year sojourn among the cotton mill workers of a Piedmont Crescent town of about 4,000 people. The Piedmont Crescent encompasses Virginia, the Carolinas, Northern Georgia, and Northern Alabama. Textile mills seem to have sprung up most often in the Blue Ridge foothills.
M7700

Morley, Margaret Warner The Carolina Mountains. Boston: Houghton Mifflin Co., 1913. An inviting survey of the author's beloved mountains.
M7710 (ASU BC LMC MHC WCU WWC)

The Carolina Mountains. Boston: Houghton Mifflin Co., 1913.
M7720 (UNCA)

Morony, Ives Guy "Attitude of Coal Miners toward Union and Coal Industry." Master's thesis. West Virginia Univ., 1959.
M7730 (ASU)

Morrell, David First Blood. New York: J. B. Lippincott Co., 1972. A drifter, thrice warned to leave an Eastern Kentucky town refuses to do so. The situation escalates into a manhunt with state and local police chasing Rambo, the drifter, an excellent guerilla warrior, in the hills. Very bloody.
M7740 (BC)

Morrill, Maurice B. Simpson, George Lee Western North Carolina Associated Communities. Cherokee, N. C.: Cherokee Historical Association, 1956.
S3610 (WCU)

Morris, Byron T. A Charge to Keep; History of the First Baptist Church of Kenova, West Virginia. Parsons, W. Va.: McClain Print. Co., 1971.
M7750 (ASU)

Morris, D. R. Stephen. n.p.: n.p., 19--. Futuristic novel of an urban boy captured by Appalachian guerrillas in the year 2000.
M7760 (ASU)

Morris, Eastin Eastin Morris' Tennessee Gazetteer, 1834, and Matthew Rhea's Map of the State of Tennessee, 1832. Edited by Robert M. McBride and Owen Meredith. With an introd. by Mary U. Rothrock. Nashville: Gazetteer Press, 1971.
M7770 (ASU)

The Tennessee Gazetteer, or Topographical Dictionary: Containing a Description of the Several Counties, Towns, Etc. To which is prefixed a general description of the state and a condensed history from the earliest settlements down to the convention in 1834. With an appendix, containing a list of the practising attorneys at law in each country: Principal officers of the general and state governments. Times of holding courts: and other valuable tables. Nashville: W. H. Hunt and Co., 1834.
M7780 (ASU BC)

Morris, Homer Lawrence The Plight of the Bituminous Coal Miner. Philadelphia: Univ. of Pennsylvania Press, 1934.
M7790 (ASU BC)

Morris, Jerry W. "Aesthetic Attitudes and Values of Selected Appalachian Youths." Ph. D. Diss. Pennsylvania State Univ., 1973. This study of the personality characteristics of Appalachian students refutes some of the triter stereotypes.
M7800

Morris, Margaret Logan Irvins, Doaks, Logans and McCampbells of Virginia and Kentucky. n.p.: n.p., 1916.
M7810

Morris, Robert G. Outdoor Recreation Potential in West Virginia's Eastern Panhandle. Morgantown, W. Va.: U. S. Soil Conservation Service, Potomac Headquarters, 1972.
M7820

Morris, Robert Lee Opie Read, American Humorist, 1852-1939. 1st ed. New York: Helios Books, 1965. Read was an Appalachian novelist.
M7830 (BC WCU)

Morris, Samuel Leslie At Our Own Door: A Study of Home Missions with Special Reference to the South and West. 2nd ed. New York: Revell, 1904.
M7840 (BC LMC)

The Romance of Home Missions. Home Mission Study. Richmond: Presbyterians Committee of Publication, 1924.
M7850 (ASU LMC)

Morris, Thomas John "The Coal Camp: A Pattern of Limited Community Life." Master's thesis. West Virginia Univ., 1950.
M7860 (ASU)

Morris, W. R. Folklore of the Blue Ridge Mountains and Early Settlers. 3 vols. Fancy Gap, Va.: n.p., 1953-. Very strange. Folklore in this instance includes overtures of Sunday Schools, court records an obsession with lineage, character sketches, historic happenings, and descriptions of settlements in the Blue Ridge. Vol. 3, Part 2 has cover title: "Did God Approve Mixing of the Races?"
M7870

Morrison, Alice Marie "Selected Children's Fiction with a Contemporary Setting in the Mountains of Kentucky and North Carolina." Master's thesis. Univ. of North Carolina, Chapel Hill, 1973. An excellent study of contemporary Appalachian fiction for children.
M7880 (ASU)

Morrison, Charles The Fairfax Line, a Profile in History and Geography. Our Potomac Heritage. Parsons, W. Va.: McClain Print. Co., 1970.
M7890 (ASU)

An Outline of the Maryland Boundary Disputes and Related Events. Parsons, W. Va.: McClain Print. Co., 1974.
M7900 (ASU)

Wappatomaka: A Survey of the History and Geography of the South Branch Valley. Parsons, W. Va.: McClain Print. Co., 1971.
M7910 (ASU)

Morrison, Hal "A Study of the Effect of Participation in Athletics on the Grades of Students at East Tennessee State College." Master's thesis. East Tennessee State College, 1955.
M7920 (ETSU)

Morrison, John The Real David Crockett: A Short, Authentic, Illustrated, History of Tennessee's Famous Hunter, Frontiersman, Soldier, Legislator, Statesman, Patriot, and Hero of the Alamo, Colonel David Crockett. Lawrenceburg: n.p., 1955.
M7930

Morrison, Okey J. The Slaughter of the PfostGreen Family of Jackson County, West Virginia. Cincinnati: Gibson and Sons Co., 1898. A History of the Tragedy, with a Notice of the Early Settlers of Jackson County, a Sketch of the Family and John F. Morgan.
M7940 (ASU)

Morrison, Sarah Elizabeth Chilhowee Boys. New York: T. Y. Crowell and Co., 1893. Fiction for young boys. Appalachian mountain setting.
M7950 (ASU)

Morristown Centennial Corporation Morristown Centennial, 1855-1955. The authors: n.p., 1955.
M7960

Morristown, Tennessee, Centennial Celebration Centennial Souvenir Program, 1855-1955: An Historical Pageant of Davy Crockett's Home Town, "Arrows to Atoms." n.p.: n.p., n.d. Promotional material and historical sketches.
M7970 (ETSU)

Morristown, Tennessee, First Methodist Church A Century of Service: The Story of First Methodist Church, Morristown, Tennessee, 1852-1952. Morristown, Tenn.: n.p., 1952.
M7980 (ETSU)

Morristown, Tennessee, High School Senior Class, 1917 The Itakha Annual. Knoxville: Lithrographing Co., 1917.
M7990 (ETSU)

Morton, J. Blair History of the Presbytery of Kanawha, 1895-1956. Charleston, W. Va.: Jarrett Print. Co., 1956.
M8000 (ASU)

Morton, Joseph W. ed. Sparks from the Camp Fire: Or, Tales of the Old Veterans, A Photograph of Our Old Life. Philadelphia: Keystone Pub., 1890. Thrilling stories of heroic Civil War deeds as re-told today around the modern camp fire.
M8010 (LMC)

Morton, Oren Frederic Annals of Bath County, Virginia. Staunton, Va.: The McClure Co., Inc., 1917.
M8020 (BC)
Annals of Bath County, Virginia. 1917. Reprint. Bridgewater, Va.: C. J. Carrier Co., 1970.
M8030 (ASU)
A Centennial History of Alleghany County, Virginia. Dayton, Va.: J. K. Ruebrush Co., 1923.
M8040 (BC)
A Centennial History of Alleghany County, Virginia. 1923. Reprint. Bridgewater, Va.: C. J. Carrier Co., 1970.
M8050 (ASU)
A Handbook of Highland County, and a Supplement to Pendleton and Highland History. Monterey: The Highland Recorder, 1922.
M8060
A History of Highland County, Virginia. 1911. Reprint. Baltimore: Regional Pub. Co., 1969.
M8070 (ASU BC)
A History of Highland County, Virginia. 1911. Reprint. With a new index. Baltimore: Regional Pub. Co., 1972.
M8080 (ASU)
A History of Monroe County, W. Va. Baltimore: Regional Pub. Co., 1974.
M8090 (BC)
A History of Pendleton County, W. Va. Baltimore: Regional Pub. Co., 1974.
M8100 (ASU BC)
A History of Rockbridge County, Virginia. Staunton, Va.: McClure Co., 1920.
M8110 (ASU BC WCU)
Land of the Laurel: A Story of the Alleghenies. Morgantown, W. Va.: Acme Pub. Co., 1903. A sound historical novel giving good descriptions of the day-to-day life in the Alleghenies.
M8120 (ASU BC ETSU)
The Story of Daniel Boone. Hot Springs, Va.: McAllister Pub. Co., 1913.
M8130 (ASU BC)
The Story of Winchester in Virginia, the Oldest Town in the Shenandoah Valley. Strasburg, Va.: Shenandoah Pub. House, 1925.
M8140 (ASU BC ETSU WCU)
Winning or Losing? A Story of the West Virginia Hills. Kingwood, W. Va.: The author, 1901. Farm and social life are well depicted in this novel of Northern West Virginia.
M8150 (BC)

Mory, Samuel A. History of Coal Mining in Laurel County, Kentucky, 1920-1944. London, Ky.: Sentinel-Echo, 1944.
M8160

Mosby, Robert H. "Chief Causes of Non-attendance in the Schools of McDowell County, West Virginia." Master's thesis. Univ. of Kentucky, 1940.
M8170

Mosel, Tad All the Way Home. New York: Avon Books, 1963. A dramatization of James Agee's novel, A Death in the Family.
M8180 (ASU BC)

Mosely, Elizabeth Robards Wilkie, Katherine Elliott Frontier Nurse: Mary Breckenridge. New York: Messner, 1969.
W6290 (ASU LMC BC)

Moser, Artus M. ed. Buncombe County, Economic and Social. A laboratory study at the University of North Carolina, Department of Rural Social Economics, by A. M. Moser and others. Asheville, N. C.: Central Bank and Trust Co., 1923.
M8190

Moser, Artus Monroe Western North Carolina: A History. Prospectus of 3 vol. work. New York: Lewis Historical Pub. Co., n.d.
M8210 (ASU)

Moser, Artus Monroe ed. Buncombe County: Economic and Social. Asheville, N. C.: Central Bank and Trust Co., 1923. A survey of the resources of Buncombe County.
M8200 (ASU BC LMC)

Moser, Mabel Y. Resources for the Study of Appalachia: A Bibliography. Berea, Ky.: Berea College Appalachian Center, 1974. Thirty-two page listing of resources — books, recordings, films, filmstrips and slides — available to college and curriculum libraries.
M8220

Moses H. Cone Memorial Park, Blue Ridge Parkway Washington: National Park Service, 1971. Brochure.
M8230 (ASU ETSU)

Moss, J. Joel West Virginia and Her Population. (Bulletin No. 103.) Morgantown: West Virginia Agricultural Experiment Station, West Virginia University, 1957.
M8240

Moss, Paul Little Church of the Valley (Moss Baptist Church), in the Shadow of the Potrock. Dallas, Tex.: Mathis Van Nort, (c1949).
M8250

Moss, Paul T. The Rock Was Free. Philadelphia: Dorrance and Co., 1945. Poorly defined novel of western North Carolina.
M8260
The Shadow of the Potrock. Dallas: Southwest Press, 1932. A rather disjointed novel with a western North Carolina setting.
M8270

Moss, William Paul comp. The Moss Family: William Paul Moss, Thaddeus Augustus Moss, Amanda Holden Moss, Howell Moss, Crestus Howell Moss, Henry Moss, Their Families and Progenitors. Odessa, Texas: n.p., 1964. Moss families from this branch of the tree are found in all states of the Southern Appalachians.
M8280 (ASU)

Motsinger, Linda Ann "A Proposed Individualized Primary Mathematics Program for Holston Heights Elementary School, Bristol, Tennessee." Master's thesis. East Tennessee State Univ., 1970.
M8290 (ETSU)

Mott, Glen Ford Push Boat. Huntington, W. Va.: Franklin Print. Co., 1941. Story of an orphan lad who builds a business empire out of a sack of medicinal plants and a flat-boat.
M8300 (ASU)

Mott, Pearle G. History of Davis and Canaan Valley. Parsons, W. Va.: McClain Print. Co., 1972.
M8310 (ASU)

Mottern, Eulah Blanche "A Simplified Library Program for the Elementary Schools of Carter County, Tennessee." Master's thesis. East Tennessee State College, 1959.
M8320 (ETSU)

Moultrie, William Memoirs of the American Revolution, So Far as It Is Related to the States of North and South Carolina, and Georgia. 1802. Reprint. 2 vols. New York: Arno Press, 1968.
M8330 (ASU)

Mount Torry Mining Company, Augusta Co., Va. Report. Winchester, Va.: The Company, 1889.
M8340

The Mountain Eagle vol. 1-, 19--. Whitesburg, Ky.: Tom Gish, ed., Weekly paper. One of the best weeklies in Appalachia.
M8350

The Mountain Educator Official organ of the Kentucky Mountain Schools, vol. 1-, 1903-. London, Ky.: Wyatt and Baldwin, Publishers, n.d.
M8360

Mountain Life and Work vol. 1-, 1925-. Berea, Ky.: Council of the Southern Mountains, quarterly. Title and frequency vary through the years. Issued from Clintwood, Va. 1973-.
M8370 (ASU ETSU MHC BC)

Mountain Living vol. 1-, 1970-. Franklin, N. C.: Community Newspapers, quarterly.
M8380 (ASU BC ETSU)

Mountain Milestones Penland, N. C.: Penland School of Handicrafts, 19--. Frequency varies.
M8390

Mountain Review vol. 1-, Sept. 1974-. Whitesburg, Ky.: Appalshop Inc., v. illus. quarterly.
M8400

Mountain Sentinal, The Mountaineers Own Magazine vol. 1-, 1937-. Relief, Ky.: Donald and Webb, ed., monthly.
M8410

Mountain Trails: An Amateur Journal of the Cumberlands vol. 1-, 1936-. Whitesburg, Ky.: Bennett Adams, 1936-.
M8420

Mowbray, Azilee H. "Development of Adoption Practices in East Tennessee." Master's thesis. East Tennessee State College, 1953.
M8430

Moyer, Egbert "The Status of Public Relations Activities in the Secondary Schools of Greene County, Tennessee." Master's thesis. East Tennessee State College, 1956.
M8440

Mozier, W. S. Conrey, Guy Woolard Soil Survey, Scioto County, Ohio. Washington: U. S. Dept. of Agriculture, Bureau of Plant Industry, 1940.
C6780

Mudge, Baden P. Buck, Roy Clair Formal Participation Patterns in a Central Pennsylvania Rural Community. University Park: Agricultural Experiment Station, Pennsylvania State University, January, 1955.
B8210

Muelhof, William E. "An Evaluation of the Pension Plans in the Anthracite Coal Industry." Master's thesis. Pennsylvania State Univ., 1959.
M8450

Mueller, Eva Migration into and out of Depressed Areas. (Economic Redevelopment Research.) Washington: Area Redevelopment Administration, 1964.
M8460

Muir, John A Thousand-Mile Walk to the Gulf. Boston and New York: Houghton Mifflin Co., 1916. Interesting commentary on the Appalachian region of several southern states.
M8470

Muir, Willa Living with Ballads. New York: Oxford University Press, 1965.
M8480 (ASU FC)

Mulkearn, Lois A Traveler's Guide to Historic Western Pennsylvania. Pittsburgh: University of Pittsburgh Press, 1954.
M8490 (ASU)

Mull, J. Alex Mountain Yarns, Legends, and Lore. Illustrated by R. L. Patton. Banner Elk, N. C.: Pudding Stone Press, n.d.
M8500 (ASU LMC)

Mull, Larry W. Everybody Square Dances: In the Southern Appalachians: The Story of Folk Dancing and Mountain Music as Enjoyed by Natives and Visitors in the Southern Highlands. Asheville, N. C.: n.p., 1948.
M8510 (ASU WCU)
Scenic Western North Carolina, a Vacation Guide to the Highlands. New York: William-Frederick Press, 1946.
M8520 (ASU)

Mullenax, Foster G. "Mass Media Use Patterns and Interests Among West Virginia Rural Non-farm Families of Low Socio-economic Status." Master's thesis. West Virginia Univ., 1968.
M8530

Muller, Herbert Joseph Thomas Wolfe. The Makers of Modern Literature. Norfolk, Conn.: New Directions Books, 1947.
M8540 (ASU UNCA)

Mullikan, Trumans An Analysis of School District Organization in Greenville County, South Carolina. Master's thesis. Furman University, 1952.
M8550

Mullins, Isla May The Boy from Hollow Hut. Chicago: Fleming H. Revell, 1911. The Kentucky mountains are the background for this conventional story of a boy growing up, going off to settlement school, finding love and fortune.
M8560 (BC)

Mullins, Marion Day Grammer, Norma Rutledge Marriage Records of Washington County, Tennessee, 1787-1840. Baltimore: Genealogical Print. Co., 1975.
G3200 (ASU)

Mullins, Marion Day comp. Grammer, Norma Rutledge Marriage Record of Washington County, Tennessee, 1787-1840. n.p.: n.p., n.d.
G3190 (ETSU)

Munford, Beverly B. Virginia's Attitude Toward Slavery and Secession. New York: Longmans, Green, 1909.
M8570 (FC LMC)

Munn, M. J. Griswold, W. T. Geology of Oil and Gas Fields in Steubenville, Burgettstown, and Claysville Quadrangles, Ohio, W. Va., and Pa. Washington: Govt. Print. Off., 1907.
G4340

The Menifee Gas Field and the Ragland Oil Field, Kentucky. U. S. Geological Survey Bulletin, no. 531-A. Washington: Govt. Print. Off., 1913.
M8580

Reconnaissance of Oil and Gas Fields in Wayne and McCreary Counties, Kentucky. U. S. Geological Survey Bulletin, no. 579. Washington: Govt. Print. Off., 1914.
M8590

Munn, Robert F. Appalachian Bibliography. 2 vols. Morgantown: West Virginia University Library, 1968. Listing of periodical articles and books according to subject, revised, 1970.
M8600 (ASU BC)

The Coal Industry in America: A Bibliography and Guide to Studies. Morgantown: West Virginia University Library, 1965. The most extensive listing of coal resources and mining in the United States.
M8610 (ASU BC)

Index to the Press of the Kanawha Valley, 1855-1865. Morgantown: West Virginia Univ. Library, 1963.
M8620 (BC)

Index to West Virginiana. Charleston, W. Va.: Education Foundation, 1960. An index to published material dealing with West Virginia.
M8630 (ASU BC)

The Southern Appalachians: A Bibliography and Guide to Studies. Morgantown: West Virginia University Library, 1961. Excellent source for current periodical literature on Appalachia.
M8640 (ASU BC LMC ETSU WCU UNCA)

The Southern Mountaineer: A Bibliography and Guide to Studies. Morgantown: West Virginia University Library, 1961. Since its publication this bibliography has been the standard regional listing.
M8650 (ASU BC)

Strip Mining, an Annotated Bibliography. Morgantown: West Virginia University Library, 1973.
M8660 (ASU BC)

Munro, John Miller "Transportation Investment and Depressed Regions: The Case of Appalachia." D. B. A. Diss. Indiana Univ., 1966. An exhaustive study of the relationship between isolation and poverty.
M8670 (ASU LMC)

Munyan, A. C. Hunt, C. B. Coal Deposits of Pike County, Kentucky. Washington: Govt. Print. Off., 1937.
H8370

Munyan, Arthur Claude Geology and Mineral Resources of the Dalton Quadrangle, Georgia-Tennessee. Bulletin, no. 57. Atlanta: Georgia Department of Mines, Mining and Geology, 1951.
M8680 (ASU ETSU)

Munzer, Martha E. Pockets of Hope: Studies of Land and People. New York: Knopf, 1967. The author has taken five economically depressed areas in the United States and shown how the residents are getting together and lifting themselves out of despair and poverty. She covers the mined-out coal fields around Wilkes-Barre, Pennsylvania and the Johnson Creek watershed in Tennessee.
M8690

Valley of Vision: The TVA Years. New York: Knopf, 1969. A volume of total praise, no reservations, for the Tennessee Valley Authority.
M8700 (ASU BC)

Murdock, Louise S. Almetta of Gabriel's Run. New York: Meridian Press, 1917. The residents of Gabriel's Run, Kentucky take misfortune in stride, take in orphans like Almetta and get on with the business of living. Good illustrations of mountain fatalism.
M8710 (BC)

Murfree, Mary Noailles The Amulet: A Novel. New York: Macmillan Co., 1906. Novel of an English girl in the Cherokee country of the Smoky Mountains at the end of the Seven Years War.
M8720 (ASU BC)

The Bushwhackers, and Other Stories. Chicago: H. S. Stone and Co., 1899. Contains three short stories of the Tennessee hill folk.
M8730 (ASU BC LMC)

The Bushwhackers, and Other Stories. Freeport, N. Y.: Books for Libraries Press, 1969.
M8740 (ASU ETSU)

The Despot of Broomsedge Cove. Boston: Houghton, Mifflin and Co., 1889. A local election causes strife between kin and friend, religion and politics. The sinner reforms and gets the girl.
M8750 (ASU BC ETSU LMC)

Down the Ravine, a Story. Boston: Houghton, Mifflin and Co., 1885. A tale of the quest for gold and trouble over a disputed land grant in East Tennessee.
M8760 (ASU BC ETSU LMC)

The Frontiersmen. Boston: Houghton Mifflin Co., 1904. A tale of pioneers, Cherokee, and British troops in the Great Smokies.
M8770 (ASU BC WCU)

His Vanished Star. Boston: Houghton, Mifflin and Co., 1894. An outlander building a hotel in the remote mountains of Tennessee is thwarted by the natives.
M8780 (ASU BC ETSU LMC)

In the Clouds, a Story. Boston: Houghton Mifflin and Co., 1887. A moonshining troublemaker is in and out of trouble with the law.
M8790 (ASU BC ETSU LMC)

In the "Stranger People's" Country: A Novel. New York: Harper and Brothers, 1891. An archeologist wanders into country inhabited by strange, rough, but appealing people.
M8800 (ASU BC ETSU LMC)

In the Tennessee Mountains. 7th ed. Boston: Houghton Mifflin and Co., 1885.
M8810 (LMC)

In the Tennessee Mountains. 13th ed. Boston: Houghton Mifflin and Co., 1884. A group of short stories that began the trend toward mountain fiction.
M8820 (ASU BC)

In the Tennessee Mountains. 16th ed. Boston: Houghton Mifflin and Co., 1886.
M8830 (ASU BC)

In the Tennessee Mountains. New York: Houghton, 1887.
M8840 (LMC)

In the Tennessee Mountains. 23d ed. Boston: Houghton Mifflin, 1893.
M8850 (ASU LMC)

In the Tennessee Mountains. Boston: Houghton Mifflin Co., 1912.
M8860 (ETSU LMC)

In the Tennessee Mountains. 1884. Reprint. Americans in fiction. Ridgewood, N. J.: Gregg Press, 1968.
M8870 (WCU)

In the Tennessee Mountains. With an introduction by Nathalia Wright. Tennesseana Editions. Knoxville: Univ. of Tennessee, 1970.
M8880 (LMC MHC)

The Juggler. Boston: Houghton Mifflin and Co., 1897. A man returns to the mountains after a long absence during which he has become a juggler. The natives fear he is in league with the devil.
M8890 (ASU BC ETSU LMC)

The Mystery of Witch-Face Mountain and Other Stories. Boston: Houghton Mifflin and Co., 1895. A group of stories about fairs, elections and a mystery.
M8900 (ASU BC ETSU LMC)

The Mystery of Witch-Face Mountain, and Other Stories. American Short Story Series, vol. 72. New York: Garrett Press, 1969.
M8910 (WCU)

The Ordeal: A Mountain Romance of Tennessee. Philadelphia: J. B. Lippincott Co., 1912. More Cherokees and outlanders than mountaineers in this story.
M8920 (ASU BC ETSU)

The Phantoms of the Foot-bridge, and Other Stories. New York: Harper and Brothers, 1895. Short stories.
M8930 (ASU BC ETSU WCU)

The Prophet of the Great Smoky Mountains. Boston: Houghton Mifflin Co., 1885. A man taken by religion gains a reputation for prophecy and tries to influence the outcome of an election.
M8940 (ASU BC)

The Prophet of the Great Smoky Mountains. Boston: Houghton Mifflin Co., 1892.
M8950 (ASU BC LMC WCU)

The Prophet of the Great Smoky Mountains. Boston: Houghton Mifflin Co., 1913.
M8960 (ETSU WCU WWC)

The Raid of the Guerilla, and Other Stories. Illustrated by W. Herbert Dunton and Remintion Schuyler. Philadelphia: J. B. Lippincott Co., 1912. Ten short stories of the Chilhowee country.
M8970 (ASU WWC)

The Raid of the Guerilla, and Other Stories. Illustrated by W. Herbert Dunton and Remington Schyler. Short Story Index. Reprint Series. Freeport, N. Y.: Books for Libraries Press, 1971.
M8980 (ETSU WCU)

A Spectre of Power. Boston: Houghton Mifflin and Co., 1903. A curious Cherokee girl brings grief to the town of Great Tellico and to her nation.
M8990 (ASU BC WCU)

The Storm Centre: A Novel. New York: Macmillan Co., 1905. Story of a man living on the Tennessee River in Southern Tennessee.
M9000 (ASU LMC)

The Story of Keedon Bluffs. Boston: Houghton Mifflin and Co., 1888. A rumor of a treasure hidden beneath the bluffs during the war leads to tragedy.
M9010 (ASU BC ETSU LMC)

The Story of Old Fort Loudon. New York: Macmillan Co., 1899. A novel of the seige and battle of Fort Loudon on the Little Tennessee.
M9020 (ASU BC)

The Story of Old Fort Loudon. 1899. Reprint. Upper Saddle River, N. J.: Literature House, 1970.
M9030 (WCU)

Where the Battle Was Fought: A Novel. Boston: Houghton Mifflin Co., 1884. Novel of a battle and the haunting of the battlefield.
M9040 (ASU)

The Windfall. New York: Duffield, 1907. A sideshow comes to the Tennessee hill country bringing confusion, distrust and death to a moonshining family.
M9050 (ASU BC)

The Young Mountaineers: Short Stories. Illustrated by Malcolm Faser. 1897. Reprint. Short Story Index Reprint Series. Freeport, N. Y.: Books for Libraries Press, 1969. Ten short stories.
M9060 (ASU BC WCU ETSU)

Murfree, Mary Noailles
Parks, Edd Winfield Charles Egbert Craddock. Chapel Hill: Univ. of North Carolina Press, 1941.
P340 (ASU)

Murless, Dick Hiker's Guide to the Smokies. San Francisco: Sierra Club, 1973.
M9070 (ASU LMC WCU)

Murphy, Ottis The Knox County Economic Opportunity Council Anti-Poverty Arts and Crafts. n.p.: n.p., 1968. The project was an unqualified success with all socio-economic groups working together.
M9080

Murray, Doris Lewis "Materials for Teaching Social Studies in a Selected Fifth Grade at Asbury School, Johnson City, Tennessee, 1956-57." Master's thesis. East Tennessee State College, 1957.
M9090 (ETSU)

Murray, Kenneth Down to Earth People of Appalachia. Foreward by Ambrose Manning, afterward by Helen Lewis. Boone, N. C.: Appalachian Consortium Press, 1974. Photographic essay of the plainer folk of Appalachia.
M9100

Murray, Lena Davis Schoolhouse in the Foothills. In collaboration with Alvin Fay Harlow. Illustrated by Thomas Benton. New York: Simon and Schuster, 1935. This book is a "must" for any basic Appalachian Studies reading list. It is a warm and sensitive account of a teacher's experiences in the Tennessee foothills.
M9110 (ASU BC ETSU WWC)

Murray, Thomas Edward Chattanooga, The Mountain City. Chattanooga: The Chattanooga and Tenn. River Power Co., 1906.
M9120 (BC)

Murry, Howard Salt O'Life. With reproductions of the author's water colors. Winston-Salem, N. C.: J. F. Blair, 1961. Proverbs and tales from Western North Carolina.
M9130 (ASU BC LMC WCU)

Muscle Shoals Commission Muscle Shoals: A Plan for the Use of the United States Properties on the Tennessee River by Private Industry for the Manufacture of Fertilizers and Other Useful Products. Washington: Govt. Print. Off., 1931.
M9140 (BC)

Muse, William V. ed. Business and Economic Problems in Appalachia. Athens: Ohio Univ., 1968. A survey of the region's economic status and the reasons for this.
M9150 (ASU LMC)

Musick, G. C. Genealogy of the Musick Family and Some Kindred Lines. Hinton, W. Va.: Bluestone Print. Co., 1964.
M9160

Musick, Ruth Ann Ballads, Folk Songs and Folk Tales from West Virginia. Morgantown: West Virginia Univ. Library, 1960.
M9170 (ASU BC)

Green Hills of Magic, West Virginia Folk Tales from Europe. Illustrated by Archie L. Musick. Lexington: Univ. Press of Kentucky, 1970. Folktales brought to West Virginia by European immigrants.
M9180 (ASU BC LMC WCU)

The Telltale Lilac Bush, and Other West Virginia Ghost Tales. Lexington: Univ. of Kentucky Press, 1965.
M9190 (ASU BC ETSU LMC WCU)

Musmann, Michael A. Black Fury. New York: Fountainhead Pub., 1966. A novel of a young couple in a Pennsylvania Coal Town during the 1925-28 strike and the attempt to organize the UMW.
M9200 (BC)

Musser, Carl Wilson Economic and Social Aspects of Negro Slavery in Wythe County, Virginia, 1790-1860. Master's thesis. Columbian College, George Washington University, 1958.
M9210

Musser, John J. Description of the Physical Environment and of Strip-mining Operations in Parts of the Beaver Creek Basin, Kentucky. Prepared in cooperation with Kentucky and with Federal agencies. U. S. Geological Survey Professional Papers, 427-A. Hydrologic Influence of Strip Mining. Washington: Govt. Print. Off., 1963.
M9220

Mutzenberg, Charles Gustavus Kentucky's Famous Feuds and Tragedies. New York: R. F. Fenno and Co., 1971. An account of Kentucky's feuds and vendettas.
M9230

Myer, William Edward Indian Trails of the Southeast. Nashville: Blue and Gray Press, 1971. Excellent maps of trails and tribal boundaries.
M9240 (ASU FC LMC)

Myers, Albert Cook Immigration of the Irish Quakers into Pennsylvania 1682-1750: With Their Early History in Ireland. Swarthmore, Pa.: The author, 1902. Many of these Irish families eventually settled in Appalachia.
M9250 (ASU)

Irish Quaker Arrivals to Pennsylvania, 1682-1750: List of Certificates of Removal from Ireland, Received at the Monthly Meetings of Friends in Pennsylvania, 1682-1750. With genealogical notes from Friends' records of Ireland and Pennsylvania, genealogies, county histories, and other books and manuscripts. Excerpted from his Irish Quakers into Pennsylvania, 1682-1750. Baltimore: Genealogical Pub. Co., 1964.
M9260 (ASU)

Quaker Arrivals at Philadelphia, 1682-1750: Being a List of Certificates of Removal Received at Philadelphia Monthly Meeting of Friends. 2nd ed. Baltimore, Md.: Southern Book Co., 1957.
M9270 (ASU)

Myers, Elisabeth P. Angel of Appalachia: Martha Berry. New York: Messner, 1968.
M9280 (ASU MHC)

Myers, Grace Funk "Them Missionary Women;" or Work in the Southern Mountains. Hillsdale, Mich.: n.p., 1911.
M9290

Myers, Jerry C. "What the Patrons of the Elementary School of Bristol, Tennessee, Think About Their Schools." Master's thesis. East Tennessee State College, 1957.
M9300 (ETSU)

Myers, Raymond E. The Zollie Tree. Louisville: Falcon Club Press, 1964. Biography of General Felix Zallicoffer, CSA. who was in charge of an Eastern Kentucky Campaign near Somerset.
M9310 (BC)

Myers, Sylvester Myers' History of West Virginia. Wheeling, W. Va.: Wheeling News Lithograph Co., 1915.
M9320 (BC)

Myers, Will S. and others Kentucky Income Payments by Counties, 1939, 1947, 1950 and 1951. Lexington: University of Kentucky, Bureau of Business Research, 1953. Shows discrepancies between Eastern Kentucky counties and those of the more prosperous bluegrass area.
M9330

Myint, Thelma D. Goodman, Leonard H. The Economic Needs of Neighborhood Youth Corps Enrollees. Final Report. Washington: Bureau of Social Science Research, 1969.
G2540

Mylin, Barbara Kendig Fulton, Eleanore Jane An Index to the Will Books and Interstate Records of Lancaster County, Pennsylvania, 1729-1850, with an Historical Sketch and Classified Bibliography. Lancaster, Pa.: Intelligencer Print. Co., 1936.
F3800 (ASU)

N. A. S. A. West Virginia Conference to Explore Ways in which Space Science and Technology Might be Applied to the Development of West Virginia's Industry and Educational Institutions, 1964. Washington: Govt. Print. Off., 1964.
N10

N. C. Div. of Archives and History Artistry in Quilts. Nov. 10, 1974-Jan. 19, 1975 North Carolina Museum of History, Raleigh. Raleigh: N. C. Division of Archives and History, 1974. This instructive and colorfully illustrated brochure was used during the exhibition.
N2010 (ASU)

Nabers, Jane P. Brown, Virginia P. Mary Gordon Duffee's Sketches of Alabama. University: Univ. of Alabama Press, 1970.
B7420

Nace, Raymond Lee Ground-water Resources of Harrison County, West Virginia. Prepared by the U. S. Geological Survey. Bulletin, no. 14. Morgantown: West Virginia Geological Survey, 1958.
N20 (ETSU)

Nadal, Ehrman Syme A Virginian Village, and Other Papers: Together with Some Autobiographical Notes. 1917. Reprint, Essay Index Reprint Series. Freeport, N. Y.: Books for Libraries Press, 1968. The story is about a Virginia mountain village. Book covers Southern literature, a horse-fair pilgrimage, impressions of Lincoln, impressions of Lowell, contrasts of English and American scenery, Cumberland Gap, Lincoln and Stanton, and Virginia women.
N30 (WCU)

Naegele, Orville D. Dennison, John M. Structure of Devonian Strata along Allegheny Front from Corriganville, Maryland, to Spruce Knob, West Virginia. Charlestown: West Virginia Geological Survey, 1963.
D1830 (ETSU)

Nafziger, Alyce J. Analysis of Attitudes Relative to Education in the Appalachian Region. Las Cruces, N. M.: ERIC Clearinghouse on Rural Education and Small Schools, 1971.
N40 (ASU ETSU)

Nankivel, J. R. History and Times of Mars Hill Presbyterian Church, 1823-1923. Athens: Session Bd., n.d.
N50

Napier, John T. The Selected Poetry and Prose of John T. Napier. Edited and introduced by David Lee Rubin. Pikeville, Ky.: Appalachian Studies Center of Pikeville College, 1972. Appalachian poems.
N60 (ASU BC)

Napier, Patrick E. Kentucky Mountain Square Dancing. n.p.: The author, n.d. With historical notes, calls, diagrams and written directions.
N70 (ASU BC LMC)

Napier, Teddy L. The Impact of Water Resources Development upon Local Rural Communities: Adjustment Factors to Rapid Change. Ph. D. Diss. Ohio State Univ., 1971. Two Wayne County, West Virginia and one Guernsey County, Ohio Counties were used in the study.
N80

Narratives of Captivity among the Indians of North America; A List of Books and Manuscripts on this Subject in the Edward E. Ayer Collection of the Newberry Library Ann Arbor, Mich.: Gryphon Books, 1971. Includes accounts of several famous Appalachian captivities.
N90 (ASU)

Nash, Howard P., Jr. Andrew Johnson: Congress and Reconstruction. Rutherford, N. J.: Fairleigh Dickinson Univ. Press, 1972. A brief survey of the principal congressional struggles of Southern Appalachia's only President.
N100

Nash, Leonidas Lydwell Recollections and Observations During a Ministry in the North Carolina Conference, Methodist Episcopal Church, South, of Forty-three Years. Introduction by Rev. R. H. Bennett. Raleigh, N. C.: Mutual Pub. Co., 1916. Describes a town of duty in one of Western North Carolina's conferences.
N110 (ASU)

Nathan (Robert R.) Associates, Washington, D. C. Recreation as an Industry in Appalachia. Prepared for the Appalachian Regional Commission. Appalachian Research Report, no. 2. Washington: n.p., 1966.
N120 (ASU WCU)

National Child Labor Committee, New York Child Welfare in Kentucky: An Inquiry. For the Kentucky Child Labor Association and the State Board of Health, under the direction of Edward N. Clopper. New York: The committee, 1919. This report led to changes in the child labor market of Kentucky.
N130 (ASU BC)

National Committee for the Defense of Political Prisoners Harlan Miners Speak: Report on Terrorism in the Kentucky Coal Fields. New York: Harcourt, Brace, and Co., 1932. This famous committee included Theodore Dreiser, Lester Cohen, Sherwood Anderson and others.
N140 (ASU BC)

Harlan Miners Speak: Report on Terrorism in the Kentucky Coal Fields. 1932. Reprint. Civil Liberties in American History. New York: Da Cape Press, 1970.
N150 (ASU LMC WCU)

National Conference on Medicine and the Federal Coal Mine Safety Act of 1969, Washington, D. C., 1970 Papers and Proceedings. Washington: The Conference, 1970.
N160

National Council of the Churches of Christ in the United States of America Churches and Church Membership in the United States ("Series B," Nos. 1-4; "Series C," Nos. 32-35, 37-38, 40-43.) New York: National Council of the Churches of Christ in the United States of America, 1956-1957. The Church of Christ is rapidly gaining membership in Appalachia.
N170

National Education Association of the United States Carter County, Kentucky; A Study of an Unconscionable Combination of Politics and Education. Washington: The Association, 1963. What this report doesn't stress is that Carter is no worse than many other mountain counties.
N180

The Mountains Are Moving. Sixth NEA National Conference on Human Rights in Education. Equality of Educational Opportunity for Children of Appalachia. Washington, D. C.: National Education Association, 1968.
N190 (ASU)

National Forests in North Carolina: From the Mountains to the Sea Asheville, N. C.: Southeastern Forest Experiment Station, 1970. Much of Western North Carolina is owned by the federal government.
N200 (WCU)

National Forests in the Southern Appalachians Washington: U. S. Dept. of Agriculture, Forest Service, 1940.
N210

National Industrial Conference Board The Tax Problem in West Virginia. New York: National Ind. Conference Board, Inc., 1925.
N220

National Institute of Mental Health see **U. S. National Institute of Mental Health**

National NEA Conference on Human Rights in Education, 6th, Pikeville College, Pikeville, Ky., 1968 Conference Report: Equality of Educational Opportunity for Children of Appalachia. Washington: National Education Association, 1969.
N230 (ASU)

National Planning Association. Center for Economic Projections Joint Reports. ("National-Regional Economic Projections Series.") Washington, D. C.: 1963--. Includes projections for the Appalachian Region.
N240

State Population, Net Migration, Labor Force and Industry Employment Trends to 1975. ("Regional Economic Projection Series," No. 65-I.) Washington, D. C.: n.p., 1965.
N250

The Natural Bridge of Virginia and Its Environs, 1890 n.p.: n.p., n.d. Historical and promotional pamphlet on the Natural Bridge Region.
N260

Nave, Robert Tipton "A History of the Iron Industry in Carter County to 1860." Master's thesis. East Tennessee State College, 1953.
N270 (ETSU)

Neal, Carl B. The Beaver Pond Neals of Virginia. n.p.: n.p., 1965.
N280

The Donnelly-Barry-Butler Families and Their Kin-folks of Johnson Co., Tennessee. Olympia, Wash.: n.p., 1958.
N290

Leonard Shoun and his Wife Barbara Slemp Shoun of Johnson Co., Tennessee. n.p.: n.p., 1957.
N300

The McQueen Family of Johnson Co., Tennessee. n.p.: n.p., 1958.
N310

Wills Family of Johnson County, Tennessee. n.p.: n.p., 1960.
N320

Neal, J. Allen comp. Bickley, George Washington Lafayette History of the Settlement and Indian Wars of Tazewell County, Va. with added material compiled by J. Allen Neal. Parsons, W. Va.: McClain Print. Co., 1974.
B3540

Neal, John Randolph Disunion and Restoration in Tennessee.... Ph. D. Diss. Columbia Univ., 1899.
N330

Disunion and Restoration in Tennessee.... New York: Knickerbocker, 1899.
N340

Nearing, Scott Anthracite: An Instance of Natural Resource Monopoly. Philadelphia: John C. Winston Co., 1915.
N350 (ASU LMC)

Neel, Marvin H. The Word-Book of a Backwoodsman. Ceres, Va.: Backwoods Press, 1957.
N360

Neel, William Trent Neel-Dickson Genealogy. Unpublished typescript, revised to January 1949.
N370

Neher, Evelyn Four-Harness Huck. n.p.: n.p., n.d. Book contains 42 pages for the handweaver, including photographs of handwoven samples, with theory, drafts and weaving directions.
N380

Inkle. n.p.: n.p., n.d. A book about weaving, looms ancient and modern. Over 100 photos.
N390

Neighbors, Kyle comp. The Lima Shays on the Greenbrier, Cheat and Elk Railroad Co. Parsons, W. Va.: McClain Print. Co., 1969.
N400 (ASU)

Nelsen, Anne K. Nelsen, Hart M. Bibliography on Appalachia: A Guide to Studies Dealing with Appalachia in General and Including Rural and Urban Working Class Attitudes Toward Change.
N420 (ASU BC ETSU LMC WCU MHC)

Nelsen, Hart M. Bibliography on Appalachia: A Guide to Studies Dealing with Appalachia in General and Including Rural and Urban Working Class Attitudes Toward Change. Bowling Green: Western Kentucky Univ., 1967. ERIC 002 932.
N430 (ASU)

Nelsen, Hart M. The Appalachian Presbyterian: Some Rural-Urban Differences, a Preliminary Report. Research Bulletin, no. 5. Bowling Green: Western Kentucky Univ., College of Commerce, Office of Research and Service, 1968. ERIC RC 002852.
N410 (ASU BC MHC)

Bibliography on Appalachia: A Guide to Studies Dealing with Appalachia in General and Including Rural and Urban Working Class Attitudes Toward Change. Research Bulletin, no. 4.
N420 (ASU BC ETSU LMC WCU MHC)

Bibliography on Appalachia: A Guide to Studies Dealing with Appalachia in General and Including Rural and Urban Working Class Attitudes Toward Change. Research Bulletin, no. 4. Bowling Green: Western Kentucky Univ., 1967. ERIC 002 932.
N430 (ASU)

A Comparison of Religious Groupings in Appalachia. Bowling Green: Western Kentucky Univ., Office of Research and Services, 1968. Compares Presbyterian, Episcopal, Church of God, and Holiness Denominations.
N440 (ASU)

A Review of the Literature Pertaining to Appalachia; Stressing Attitudes to Social Change and Religious and Educational Orientations; A Working Paper for the Boards of Christian Education of the United Presbyterian Church in the U. S. Unpublished Typescript. n.p., 1967.
N450 (BC)

Nelson, Arnold E. Haven in the Hardwood: The History of Pickens, West Virginia. Parsons, W. Va.: McClain Print. Co., 1971.
N460 (ASU)

Nelson, Donald E. Marketing of Lumber Through Retail Outlets in W. Va. Morgantown, W. Va.: Univ. Agricultural Experiment Station, 1964.
N470

Nelson, Douglas R. "The Life and Works of Lamar Stringfield, 1897-1959." Microfilm. Ph. D. Diss. Univ. of North Carolina, 1971. One of North Carolina's most beloved musician/composers.
N480 (ASU WCU)

Nelson, James Poyntz Claudius Crozet: His Story of the Four Tunnels in the Blue Ridge Region of Virginia. Richmond: Mitchell and Hotchkins, 1917. The tunnels were constructed for the Chesapeake and Ohio Railway.
N490 (BC)

Nelson, Joseph Backwoods Teacher. 1st ed. Philadelphia: J. B. Lippincott Co., 1949. The story of a schoolteacher in the Backwoods of the Appalachian Mountains.
N500 (ASU)

Nelson, Lucretia D. "Distribution of Tardigrades on Roan Mountain, Tennessee - North Carolina." Ph. D. Diss. Univ. of Tenn., 1973.
N510

Nelson, Robert Allen A Program for the Improvement of Instruction in Spelling in the High Schools of Rutherford County. Master's thesis. Appalachian State Univ., 1958.
N520 (ASU)

Nelson, Rosemary Smith Nelson, Arnold E. Haven in the Hardwood: The History of Pickens, West Virginia. Parsons, W. Va.: McClain Print. Co., 1971.
N460 (ASU)

Nelson, Thomas Charles Decorative Plants of Appalachia: A Source of Income. Agriculture Information Bulletin, no. 342. Washington: Govt. Print. Off., 1970.
N530 (ASU ETSU LMC)

Silvical Characteristics of Bitternut Hickory. U. S. Forest Service Station Paper, no. 111. Asheville, N. C.: Southeastern Forest Experiment Station, 1960.
N540 (WCU)

Silvical Characteristics of the Commercial Hickories. In cooperation with Southeastern Forest Experiment Station. Hickory Task Force Report, no. 10. Asheville, N. C.: n.p., 1965.
N550 (WCU)

Silvical Characteristics of Mockernut Hickory. U. S. Forest Service Station Paper, no. 105. Asheville, N. C.: Southeastern Forest Experiment Station, 1959.
N560 (WCU)

Silvical Characteristics of Shagbark Hickory. U. S. Forest Service Station Paper, no. 135. Asheville, N. C.: Southeastern Forest Experiment Station, 1961.
N570 (WCU)

Nelson, Vincent E. Geological Society of Kentucky Itinerary: Some Stratigraphic and Structural Features of the Middlesboro Basin. Lexington, Ky.: The society, 1957.
G830 (ETSU)

Nelson, Wilbur Armistead Butts, Charles Geology and Mineral Resources of the Crossville Quadrangle, Tennessee. Nashville: Tenn. Division of Geology, 1925.
B9480 (ETSU)

The Southern Tennessee Coal Field Included in Bledsoe, Cumberland, Franklin, Grundy, Rhea, Sequatchie, Van Buren, Warren, and White Counties. Bulletin, 33. Nashville: Tennessee Division of Geology, 1925.
N580 (ETSU)

Nesius, Ernest J. The Rural Society in Transition. Public Affairs Series, no. 3. Morgantown: Office of Research and Development, Virginia Center for Appalachian Studies and Development, West Virginia Univ., 1966.
N590 (ASU)

Neskaug, Selmer R. "Agricultural and Social Aspects of the Swiss Settlement in Grundy County, Tennessee." Master's thesis. Univ. of Tennessee, 1936.
N600

Nesselroad, Paul Emmett "Optimum Farm Organizations for a Portion of the Appalachian Plateau." Ph. D. Diss. Pennsylvania State Univ., 1969.
N610

Netherton, Nan Templeman, Eleanor Lee (Reading) Northern Virginia Heritage; a Pictorial Compilation of the Historic Sites and Homes in the Counties of Arlington, Fairfax, Loudoun, Fauquier, Prince William and Stafford, and the Cities of Alexandria and Fredericksburg, by Eleanor Lee Templeman and Nan Netherton. Arlington, Va.: Privately published by E. L. Templeman, 1966.
T860 (BC)

Nettl, Bruno An Introduction to Folk Music in the United States. Detroit: Wayne State Univ. Press, 1962.
N620 (BC)

Neuman, Robert B. Geology of the Western Great Smoky Mountains, Tennessee. U. S. Geological Survey Professional Paper, no. 349-D. Washington: Govt. Print. Off., 1965.
N630 (ASU LMC)

Middle Ordovician Rocks of the Tellico-Sevier Belt, Eastern Tennessee. U. S. Geological Survey Professional Paper, no. 274-F. Shorter Contributions to General Geology, 1955. Washington: Govt. Print. Off., 1955.
N640

Neuman, Robert Ballin King, Philip Burke Geology of the Great Smoky Mountains National Park, Tennessee and North Carolina. Washington: U. S. Department of the Interior Geological Survey, 1968.
K2450 (ETSU)

Neuner, E. J. Financial and Operating Characteristics of the Municipal and Cooperative Distributors of T.V.A. Power. College of Business Administration, Bureau of Research Study no. 20. Knoxville, Tenn.: Division of Univ. Extension, Univ. of Tennessee, May 1949.
N650

New Bethel Presbyterian Church The New Bethel Sesquicentennial 1782-1932. Bristol: King, 1932.
N660

New York, New Jersey Trail Conference Guide to the Appalachian Trail in New York and New Jersey. 7th ed. n.p.: Walker Pub. Co., 1972.
N680 (ASU)

New York. Office of Planning and Coordination New York State Appalachian Development Plan; A Twenty Year Plan for the Fourteen Counties of the New York Appalachian Region. Albany: Office of Planning and Coordination, 1971.
N700

New York (State), Office of Planning Coordination, Cartographic Section The Appalachian Region of New York State: An Atlas of Natural and Cultural Resources. Albany: The office, 1969.
N690 (ETSU)

Newberry, Elizabeth "Civil War Anecdotes and Legends of Chattanooga." Master's thesis. George Peabody College, 1928.
N710

Newcomb, W. H. The First Methodist Episcopal Church, Huntington, West Virginia. n.p.: n.p., n.d.
N670 (ASU)

Newcome, Roy Ground-water Resources of the Cumberland Plateau in Tennessee. Nashville, State of Tennessee, Dept. of Conservation, Division of Water Resources, 1958.
N720 (BC)

Newcomer, Christopher Armour Cole's Cavalry: or, Three Years in the Saddle in the Shenandoah Valley. Baltimore: Cushing and Co., 1895.
N730 (ASU)

Newell, Herbert Moses History of Fayette County, Alabama. Fayette, Ala.: Newell Offset Print., 1960.
N750 (ASU BC)

Newell, William Wells Games and Songs of American Children, Collected and Compared. With a new introduction and index by Carl Withers. Dover Books, 354. New York: Dover Publications, 1963.
N760 (ASU BC)

Newhouse, Joseph Labor Costs in the Bituminous Coal Industry. Morgantown: W. Va. Univ., 1971.
N740

Newman, Harry Wright comp. Maryland Revolutionary Records: Data Obtained from 3,050 Pension Claims and Bounty Land Applications, Including 1,000 Marriages of Maryland Soldiers and a List of 1,200 Proved Services of Soldiers and Patriots of Other States. 1938. Reprint. Baltimore: Genealogical Pub. Co., 1967.
N770 (ASU)

Newman, Leonard S. Gorman, John Loyd Soil Survey, Monroe County, West Virginia. Washington: U. S. Department of Agriculture, Soil Conservation Service, 1965.
G2800

Newman, Monroe Brubaker, Earl Available for Work: The Pennsylvania Unemployment Compensation Interpretation. University Park: Pennsylvania State Univ., Bureau of Business Research, 1958.
B7550

Newman, Monroe Oscar The Political Economy of Appalachia; A Case Study in Regional Integration. Lexington, Mass.: Lexington Books, 1972.
N780 (BC WWC ASU ETSU MHC WCU)

News Letter vol. 1- . Winter, 1972- Berea, Ky.: Appalachian Center, Berea College, quarterly.
N790 (ASU)

Newsfocus: AEL. A Semi-monthly Report on Developments at the Appalachian Educational Laboratory vol. 1- . 1966?-. Charleston, W. Va.: Appalachian Educational Laboratory, semimonthly.
N800 (ASU BC ETSU)

Newsome, Albert Ray Lefler, Hugh Talmage North Carolina, the History of a Southern State. Chapel Hill: Univ. of North Carolina Press, 1963.
L1580 (BC FC ASU LMC)

Newsome, Albert Ray ed. Records of Emigrants from England and Scotland to North Carolina, 1774-1775. Raleigh, N. C.: Dept. of Archives and History, 1962.
N810 (ASU)

Newton, J. H. History of the Pan-handle. Wheeling, W. Va.: J. A. Caldwell, 1879. Includes histories of Brooke, Marshall and Hancock Counties, West Virginia.
N820 (BC)

Nicely, Billy K. "A Study of the Reorganization of the Attendance Centers of the Grainger County School System." Master's thesis. Univ. of Tennessee, 1959.
N830

Nicholls, Leland L. ed. North Carolina, Appalachian State University, Boone Proceedings of the Third Annual Workshop on the Third Annual Workshop on the Planning and Utilization of Leisure Resources, March 18-19. Boone: The Univ., 1974.
N1620 (ASU)

Nicholls, Leland L. ed. Planning a Tourist Recreation Region for the Age of Leisure. Printed by Planning and Land Use Education Program, Appalachian State Univ., 1974. Proceedings of the Third Annual Workshop on the Planning and Utilization of Leisure Resources. Appalachian State University.
N890 (ASU)

Nicholls, W. D. Bondurant, John H. Labor Supply and Farm Production on Eastern Kentucky Farms. Lexington: Kentucky Agricultural Experiment Station, 1945.
B5270

Clayton, Claud Franklin . . . Land Utilization in Laurel County, Kentucky. Washington: U. S. Govt. Print. Off., 1932.
C4810 (ASU)

Clayton, Claud Franklin Land Utilization in Laurel County, Kentucky. Washington: U. S. Department of Agriculture, Bureau of Agricultural Economics, 1932.
C4820 (BC)

Family Incomes and Land Utilization in Knott County, Kentucky. Bulletin no. 375. Lexington: Kentucky Agricultural Experiment Station, Univ. of Kentucky, 1937.
N900

Family Incomes and Land Utilization in Knott County, Kentucky. Lexington: Kentucky Agriculture Experiment Station, Univ. of Kentucky, 1946.
N910

Farm Management and Family Incomes in Eastern Kentucky. Bulletin no. 491. Lexington: Kentucky Agricultural Experiment Station, Univ. of Kentucky, 1946.
N920

Nichols, Beverley A Book of Old Ballads. London: Hutchinson and Co., 1934.
N840 (BC)

A Book of Old Ballads. London: Hutchinson and Co., 1934. Selected chiefly from Percy's Reliques.
N850

Nichols, Earl "An Analysis of Putnam County's Ability to Support Education Based on a Study and Comparison of Assessed Value to Real Value of Property." Master's thesis. Tennessee Polytechnic, 1959.
N860

Nichols, Joseph Van Devanter Legends of Loudoun Valley. With an introduction by John Eisenhard. Leesburgh, Va.: Potomac Press, 1961.
N870 (ASU)

Loudoun Valley Legends. Purcellville?, Va.: n.p., 1955. Stories from the Loudoun Valley and Loudoun County, Virginia dealing with the life and times of the people.
N880 (BC)

Nicholson, Cregoe D. P. Some Early Emigrants to America, Also, Early Emigrants to America from Liverpool, abstracted by Reginal Sharpe France. Baltimore: Genealogical Pub. Co., 1965.
N930 (ASU)

Nicholson, Meredith The Cavalier of Tennessee. Indianapolis: Bobbs-Merrill Co., 1928. Novel of Andy Jackson, early chapters are set in and around Jonesboro, where he was lawyer and judge.
N940 (ASU BC)

Nickell, William Lynn Stacy, Helen Price Selections from Morgan County History: Sesquicentennial Volume. West Liberty, Ky.: n.p., 1972?
S6420 (ASU)

Nickels, Henry C. "An Evaluation of the Impact of the Vocational Education Act of 1963 on Agricultural Education in the Blue Ridge Area of Southwestern Virginia." Master's thesis. East Tennessee State Univ., 1968.
N950 (ETSU)

Nicklin, Philip Holbrook Letters Descriptive of the Virginia Springs: the Roads Leading Thereto and the Doings Thereat. Collected and annotated by Peregrine Prolix. Philadelphia: H. S. Tanner, 1835. Nicklin visited Charlottesville, Staunton, Rock-Fish Gap, Warm Springs, White Sulphur, Salt Sulphur, Red Sulphur, Gray Sulphur, Sweet Springs, and Hot Springs.
N960

Nicks, Roy Sullivan "City-county Separation in Tennessee, a Case Study of Kingsport and Sullivan County." Master's thesis. Univ. of Tennessee, 1957.
N970

Nicolls, William Jasper The Story of American Coals. Philadelphia: J. B. Lippincott Co., 1897. Account of the role of coal in the development of the nation.
N980 (BC)

Niederer, Frances J. Hollins College; an Illustrated History. Charlottesville: Univ. Press of Virginia, 1972. Hollins' history is followed sympathetically from the conversion of the resort at Botetourt Springs in 1842 through the Civil War and Reconstruction trials and the generous gift of John Hollins in 1910 to the present time.
N990

Nielsen, Ralph Leighton "Socio-Economic Readjustment of Farm Families Displaced by the TVA Land Purchase in the Norris Area." Master's thesis. Univ. of Tennessee, 1940.
N1000

Niemi, Esther Personen "A Study of Commercial Banking in Two Economically Depressed Cities: Youngstown, Ohio, and Wheeling, West Virginia, 1951-1967." Ph. D. Diss. Case Western Reserve Univ., 1969.
N1010

Nienburg, Bertha Marie Potential Earning Power of Southern Mountaineer Handicraft. Bulletin, 128. Washington: U. S. Department of Labor, Women's Bureau, 1935.
N1020 (BC)

Niles, John Jacob The Ballad Book. New York: Bramhall House, 1961.
N1040 (ASU ETSU)

The Ballad Book. Illustrated by William Barss. 1961. Reprint. New York: Dover, 1970.
N1050 (ASU WCU)

Folk Ballads for Young Actors. Illustrated by Lee Ames. New York: Holt, Rinehart and Winston, 1962. (Also, phonodisc.)
N1080 (ASU BC)

Folk Carols for Young Actors. Illustrated by Lee Ames. New York: Holt, Rinehart and Winston, 1962. (Also, phonodisc.)
N1090 (ASU)

Seven Kentucky Mountain Tunes. New York: G. Schirmer, 1928. Niles collected these songs from Marion Kerby.
N1110 (BC)

Ten Christmas Carols from the Southern Appalachian Mountains. New York: G. Schirmer, 1935. Arranged for piano accompaniment.
N1130 (ASU BC)

Niles, John Jacob comp. The Ballad Book. Illustrated by William Barss. Boston: Houghton Mifflin, 1961. More than 100 of best Americans ballads from Britain. Includes bibliography.
N1030 (ASU BC FC LMC MHC)

Ballads, Carols, and Tragic Legends from the Southern Appalachian Mountains. American Folk-song Series, set 18. New York: G. Schirmer, 1937.
N1060 (ASU ETSU LMC)

Ballads, Lovesongs, and Tragic Legends from the Southern Appalachian Mountains. American Folk-song Series, set 20. New York: G. Schirmer, 1938.
N1070 (ASU)

More Songs of the Hill-folk: Ten Ballads and Tragic Legends from Kentucky, Virginia, Tennessee, North Carolina, and Georgia. American Folk-song Series, set 17.
N1100 (ASU ETSU)

Niles, John Jacob ed. Songs of the Hill-folk: Twelve Ballads from Kentucky, Virginia, and North Carolina. American Folk-song Series, set 14. New York: G. Schirmer, 1934.
N1120 (ASU BC ETSU LMC)

Nisbet, Alice Send Me An Angel. Chapel Hill: Univ. of North Carolina Press, 1946. Novel about a young girl struggling to manage a plantation in the foothill country of western North Carolina.
N1140 (ASU)

Nitze, Henry Benjamin Charles Gold Deposits of North Carolina. North Carolina Geological Survey Bulletin, no. 3. Winston-Salem: M.I. and J.C. Stewart, 1896. Some of these deposits were in western North Carolina.
N1150 (LMC)

Gold Mining in North Carolina and Adjacent South Appalachian Regions. North Carolina Geological Survey Bulletin, no. 1. Raleigh, N. C.: G. V. Barnes, 1897.
N1160 (ASU WCU LMC)

. . . Iron Ores of North Carolina; A Preliminary Report. Raleigh: J. Daniels, State Printer and Binder, 1893.
N1170 (ASU UNCA)

Monazite, and Monazite Deposits in North Carolina. North Carolina Geological Survey Bulletin, no. 9. Winston-Salem: M.I. and J.C. Stewart, 1895. Some of these deposits are in the western Carolina mountains.
N1180 (WCU)

Nix, Harold L. Opportunities for and Limitations of Social and Economic Adjustments in an Alabama Rural County. Auburn: Alabama Agriculture Experiment Station, 1962. County used in study is Fayette County, Alabama.
N1190

Nixon, Alfred History of Daniel's Evangelical Lutheran & Reformed Churches, Lincoln Co., N. C. Reprinted. n.p.: Lincoln Co. Hist. Assn., 1969. An illustrated history of Lincoln County's Lutheran and Reformed Churches.
N1200

Nixon, H. C. Tennessee Valley, a Recreation Domain. Vanderbilt Univ. Institute of Research and Training in the Social Sciences. Paper no. 9. Nashville, Tenn.: Vanderbilt Univ. Press, June 1945.
N1230

Nixon, Herman Clarence Lower Piedmont Country. American Folkways. New York: Duell, Sloan and Pearce, 1946.
N1210 (ASU BC ETSU LMC WCU)

Possum Trot, Rural Community, South. Norman: Univ. of Oklahoma Press, 1941. Study of an isolated northeast Alabama hill town.
N1220 (ASU BC WCU)

Nixon, Joseph R. The German Settlers in Lincoln County and Western North Carolina. Sprunt Studies, vol. 11, no. 2. Chapel Hill: Univ. of North Carolina Press, 1912.
N1240 (LMC)

Nixon, Phyllis Jones A Glossary of Virginia Words. With a preface by Hans Kurath. The secretary's report. Publication, no. 5. Greensboro? N. C.: American Dialect Society, 1946.
N1250 (ASU)

Noad, Frederick M. The Guitar Songbook. London: Collier-Mcmillan, 1969. Includes guitar instruction and arrangement.
N1260

Noble, Charles Hollister see **Noble, Hollister**

Noble, Cora M. Memories. Boston: Christopher Pub. House, 1964. Memories of a childhood in Breathitt County and of many years as a court clerk in that same county.
N1270 (BC)

Noble, E. L. Bloody Breathitt. 2 vols. Jackson, Ky.: Jackson Times Print. Co., 1936-38. An account of the history of Breathitt County and its famous feuds.
N1280 (BC)

Noble, Hollister Woman with a Sword: The Biographical Novel of Anna Ella Carroll of Maryland. 1st ed. Garden City, N. Y.: Doubleday, 1948. A novel of the Civil War in the Mountains.
N1290 (ASU BC WCU)

Noble, Louis Legrand The Lady Angeline: A Lay of the Appalachians. New York: Sheldon, Blakeman and Co., 1856. Mountain ballads and poetry.
N1300 (BC)

Noble, Lucinda Ann "Structural Analysis of Mothers' Attitudes toward Child Rearing in Four Communities in Appalachia." Ph. D. Diss. Univ. of North Carolina, Greensboro, 1969.
N1310

Noe, Cotton Lincoln and Twenty Other Poems. n.p.: n.p., 1922. Many of the "other poems," have southern mountain settings.
N1320 (BC)

Tip Sams of Kentucky. Lexington: Univ. of Kentucky Press, 1947. A collection of poems from Appalachia. Replete with hill country characters.
N1330 (BC)

Tip Sams Again. Lexington: Univ. of Kentucky Press, 1947. A collection of poems from Appalachia. Replete with hill country characters.
N1330 (BC)

The Valleys of Parnassus; A Selection From the Poetry of J. T. Cotton Noe. Louisville, Ky.: J. P. Morton and Co., Inc., 1935.
N1350

Noel, Lois Purcell Cumberland Falls, Kentucky. n.p.: n.p., n.d. Description and historical notes of the Cumberland Falls area.
N1360

Nolan, Robert L. Rural and Appalachian Health. Springfield, Ill.: Charles C. Thomas, 1973. Focuses on rural health generally, and Appalachian health particularly as examples of health problems. Includes recommendations for legislative changes.
N1370 (ASU)

Nolan, Robert L. ed. Rural and Appalachian Health Springfield, Ill.: Thomas, 1973.
R4310 (ASU BC)

Noland, S. Will Makes a Way. Nashville: Pub. House of the M. E. Church South, 1889. Autobiography of a Methodist minister.
N1380 (BC)

Nolland, Cecil F. ed. Duke, Basil Wilson History of Morgan's Cavalry. Bloomington: Indiana Univ. Press, 1960.
D3790

Norbeck, Mildred E. The Lure of the Hills: A Tale of Life in the Mountains of Kentucky. Cincinnati: Revivalist Press, 1931. A novel of adventure in the mountains of Kentucky.
N1390 (BC ASU)

Norburn, Martha Elizabeth The Influence of the Physiographic Features of Western North Carolina on the Settlement and Development of the Region. Ph. D. Diss. Chapel Hill, 1932. Important dissertation that attempts to document the relationship between the physiographic features of the southern Appalachia and the character of its people.
N1400 (ASU)

Norfolk and Western Railway, Industrial and Shippers Guide Comp. by Agricultural and Industrial Department N & W. Railway. Roanoke, Va.: The Railway, 1916. Contains good material on western Virginia's economy.
N1410

Norman, Gurney Divine Right's Trip: A Folktale. New York: Dial Press, 1972. A tale of boy's trip, in a Day-Glo painted van, from the hippie world of California to his boyhood home in eastern Kentucky. Wild.
N1420 (ASU)

Norman, Jacque B. Appalachian Regional Hospitals. Frankfort: Kentucky Legislative Research Commission, 1966.
N1430

Norman, Victor Louis Chattooga Griffin. Boston: Stratford, 1924. A maudlin tale from the Blue Ridge Mountains. Right triumphs over all.
N1440 (LMC BC ASU)

Norona, Delf Moundsville's Mammoth Mound. Moundsville: West Virginia Archeological Society, 1954.
N1450

West Virginia Imprints, 1790-1863. Moundsville, W. Va.: Library Association, 1958.
N1460

Wheeling: A West Virginia Place Name of Indian Origin. Moundsville, W. Va.: West Virginia Archeological Society, 1958. Maps, statistics, historical sketches and a good bibliography.
N1470 (ASU)

Norona, Delf ed. Upper Ohio Valley Pioneer Moundsville, W. Va.: Delf Norona, quarterly.
U4170

Norris, Hoke All the Kingdoms of Earth, a Novel. New York: Simon and Schuster, 1956. A novel of a flood and other disasters in the foothill country of North Carolina.
N1480 (BC ASU WCU)

Norris, J. E. ed. History of the Lower Shenandoah Valley: Counties of Frederick, Berkeley, Jefferson, and Clarke. Chicago: A. Warner and Co., 1890.
N1490 (ASU BC)

Norris, Roy K. "The Agricultural Needs of Claiborne County, Tennessee." Master's thesis. Univ. of Tennessee, 1965.
N1500

Norris, Tenn. Watershed Dept. Multiple-use on Norris Watershed. Norris: Tenn. Dept. of Conservation and Commerce, 1962.
N1510

Norris Women's Fellowship Cumberland Cook Book. Norris, Tenn.: Norris Women's Fellowship, 1964.
N1520

The North Carolina Almanac and State Industrial Guide. 1950/51- Raleigh, N. C.: Almanac Pub. Co., biennial. References to western North Carolina are, in large measure, references to extractive industries, agricultural industries, and crafts or tourism.
N1530 (LMC ASU UNCA)

North Carolina, Appalachian State Teachers College Singing Light. Boone, N. C.: The college, 1966.
N1560

North Carolina, Appalachian State Teachers College, Boone Faculty Publications. no. 1- . 1957-. Boone: The college, annual.
N1540 (BC ASU LMC ETSU)

Folk Arts Workshop. 1960-. Boone: The college, annual.
N1550 (ASU)

North Carolina, Appalachian State University College Bulletin. Boone, N. C. vol. 1-, 1910-. Boone, N. C.: n.p., irregular.
N1570 (ASU)

North Carolina, Appalachian State University, Belk Library The American Indian: A Bibliography. Boone, N. C.: The Univ., 1973.
N1580

North Carolina, Appalachian State University, Boone Dedication: B. B. Dougherty Administration Building. Boone: The Univ.'s Mountaineer Print. Shop, Industrial Arts Department, 1968.
N1590 (ASU)

Institutional Self-study for the Southern Association of Colleges and Schools. Boone: The Univ., 1971.
N1600 (ASU)

President's Annual Report to the Board of Trustees for the Year Ending June 30, 1969. Boone: The Univ., 1969.
N1610 (ASU)

Proceedings of the Third Annual Workshop on the Planning and Utilization of Leisure Resources, March 18-19. Boone: The Univ., 1974.
N1620 (ASU)

A Proposal for the Institution of Programs Leading to the Bachelor of Arts and the Bachelor of Science Degrees Not Requiring Professional Preparation for Teaching at Appalachian State Teachers College. Boone, N. C.: The college, 1965.
N1630 (ASU)

North Carolina, Appalachian State University, Boone, The Faculty A Self-evaluation Report Submitted to the National Council for Accreditation of Teacher Education. Boone, N. C.: The college, 1962.
N1640 (ASU)

A Self Study Report Submitted to the Southern Association of Colleges and Schools. Boone, N. C.: The college, 1962.
N1650 (ASU)

North Carolina Arts Council The Arts in North Carolina, 1967. Raleigh, N. C.: The council, 1967.
N1660 (LMC)

North Carolina Baptist Association Tuckaseigee Minutes, 1829-1857. Microfilm. Cullowhee, N. C.: E. H. Stillwell, 1929. This Baptist Conference is named for the river which geographically defines it.
N1670 (WCU)

North Carolina Basic County Data V. I Alamance - Jackson. V. II Johnston - Yancey. Raleigh, N. C.: State Planning Board, 1946. Good source of general and statistical information on North Carolina's twenty-eight western counties.
N1680 (ASU LMC)

North Carolina, Board of Health Biennial report. Raleigh, N. C.: pagination varies.
N1690 (ASU LMC)

A History of the North Carolina State Board of Health, 1877-1925. Raleigh: The board, 1966.
N1700 (LMC)

North Carolina, Board of Higher Education Higher Education in North Carolina, 1969-71: Report. Raleigh, N. C.: The board, 1972.
N1710 (LMC ASU)

North Carolina, Civil Defense Agency Watauga County Reception and Care Plan. Watauga County: n.p., n.d. Provisions for contemporary disasters.
N1720 (ASU)

North Carolina Club Contemporary Industrial Processes. Yearbook, 1929-30. Also, Extension Bulletin, vol. 10, no. 2. Chapel Hill: Univ. of North Carolina Press, 1930. Contains a brief discussion of western North Carolina limited to mining, crafts, tourism and agriculture.
N1730 (LMC)

Home and Farm Ownership. Yearbook, 1921-22. Also, Extension Bulletin, vol. 2, no. 9. Chapel Hill: Univ. of North Carolina Press, 1923. Contains limited material on western North Carolina.
N1740 (LMC)

North Carolina: Resources, Advantages, and Opportunities. Yearbook, 1915-16. Also, UNC Record, no. 140. Extension Series, no. 17. Durham: Seeman Printery, 1916.
N1750 (LMC ASU)

State Reconstruction Studies. UNC Record, no. 184. Also, Extension Series, no. 41. Chapel Hill: Univ. of North Carolina, 1921. Western North Carolina had been primarily union territory; thus it fared badly after the War.
N1760 (LMC ASU)

Studies in Taxation. Yearbook, 1927-28. Also, Extension Bulletin, vol. 8, no. 8. Chapel Hill: Univ. of North Carolina Press, 1928. Interesting because the 1928, or pre-tourist, tax base for western North Carolina is so different from today's.
N1770 (LMC)

North Carolina, College of the City of Asheville The Asheville Archive, College of the City of Asheville, N. C. City archives of the library of this college which later became Asheville - Biltmore College. College, n.d.
N1780

North Carolina, Council of Civil Defense Jackson County: Operational Survival Plan. Sylva?: The council, 1962.
N1790 (WCU)

North Carolina, Department of Agriculture North Carolina and Its Resources. Raleigh: J.I. and J.C. Stewart, 1896. At this time western North Carolina's economy was almost entirely agricultural.
N1810 (ASU BC UNCA)

North Carolina: Land of Opportunity. Raleigh: The department, 1923.
N1820 (LMC)

A Sketch of North Carolina. Charleston, S. C.: Lucas-Richardson Co., n.d.
N1830 (ASU LMC)

North Carolina, Department of Archives and History The Formation of the North Carolina Counties, 1663-1943. Raleigh: The department, 1950.
N1840 (WWC)

The North Carolina Census of Wilkes County, 1787. Copied from the original in the state archives. Raleigh, N. C.: Genealogical Society of the "Original" Wilkes County, n.d. Parts of five counties were originally contained within the boundaries of Wilkes county.
N1860 (ASU)

North Carolina Newspapers on Microfilm. 2nd ed. Raleigh: The department, 1963. A checklist of early North Carolina newspapers available on microfilm.
N1870 (ASU LMC)

State Census of North Carolina, 1784-1787. Transcribed and indexed by Alvaretta Kenan Register. 2nd ed., rev. Norfolk, Va.: n.p., 1971.
N1880 (ASU)

State Census of North Carolina, 1784-1787. Transcribed and indexed by Alvaretta Kenan Register. 2nd ed., rev. 1971. Reprint. Baltimore: Genealogical Pub. Co., 1973.
N1890 (ASU)

Watauga County Records: Bonds, Court Records, Estates Records, Land Records, Military and Pension Records, Tax and Fiscal Records and Wills. Microfilm. Raleigh: The department, 1972.
N1900 (ASU)

North Carolina, Department of Community Colleges Educational Guide: Technical Institutes/Community Colleges. Raleigh: Board of Education, 1969.
N1910 (LMC)

North Carolina, Department of Conservation and Development Chromite Deposits of North Carolina: Geology and Mining. Raleigh: Department of Conservation and Development, 1942.
N1920

Common Forest Trees of North Carolina, How to Know Them. A pocket manual prepared by John Simcox Holmes. 6th ed. Raleigh: The department, 1953.
N1930 (ASU UNCA)

A Directory of the Principal Mineral Producers of North Carolina. By William F. Wilson. Raleigh: The department, 1965.
N1940 (ASU ETSU)

The Shrubs and Woody Vines of North Carolina. Raleigh: The department, n.d.
N1970 (ASU)

North Carolina, Department of Public Instruction, Division of Professional Services Report to State Evaluation Committee on Western Carolina University by the Visitation Committee Oct. 1821, 1964. Raleigh: n.p., 1964.
N1990 (ASU WCU)

North Carolina, Department of Water and Air Resources. Board of Water and Air Resources. State of North Carolina North Carolina Water Plan Progress Report, Chapter 44; the Appalachian Region in North Carolina. Raleigh: The department, 1970. Deals with the 28 county mountain area of North Carolina.
N2000 (ASU)

North Carolina. Dept. of Administration Directory of Services Available to Industry from the State of North Carolina. Raleigh: The Department, 1968.
N1800 (UNCA)

North Carolina, Dept. of Archives and History Guide to North Carolina Historical Highway Markers. Raleigh: The department, 1964.
N1850 (ASU)

North Carolina, Dept. of Conservation and Development North Carolina: A Good Place to Live. . . . Issued by the state of North Carolina, Department of Conservation and Development, Wade H. Phillips, Director. Raleigh: Observer Print. House, Inc., 1928.
N1950 (UNCA)

Sawmills and Lumber Production for 26 Counties in Western North Carolina, 1959. Raleigh: The department, 1959.
N1960

North Carolina, Dept. of Local Affairs. Division of Community Planning. Western Area. Community Facilities Plan. Brevard, N. C. Brevard: The department, 1970.
N1980

North Carolina, Division of Community Planning Community Facilities Plan: Brevard, N. C. Raleigh: Division of Community Planning, 1970.
N2020

Community Facilities Plan and Public Improvements Program: Glen Alpine, North Carolina. Raleigh: Division of Community Planning, 1968.
N2030 (WCU)

Community Facilities Plan & Public Improvements Program: Valdese, North Carolina. Raleigh: Division of Community Planning, 1968.
N2040 (WCU)

Land Development Plan for Black Mountain, N. C. Raleigh: Division of Community Planning, 1970.
N2050 (WCU)

Land Development Plan: Boone, North Carolina. Raleigh: Division of Community Planning, 1964.
N2060 (WCU ASU)

Land Development Plan: Burnsville, N. C. Raleigh: n.p., n.d.
N2070 (WCU)

Land Potential Study: Madison County, North Carolina. Raleigh: Division of Community Planning, 1970.
N2080 (WCU)

Land Potential Study & Land Development Plan: Wilkes County, North Carolina. Raleigh: Division of Community Planning, 1968.
N2090 (ASU WCU)

Land Use Survey & Analysis and Land Development Plan: Glen Alpine, North Carolina. Raleigh: Division of Community Planning, 1967.
N2100 (WCU)

Land Use Survey and Analysis and Land Development Plan: Valdese, North Carolina. Raleigh: Division of Community Planning, n.d.
N2110 (WCU)

Neighborhood Analysis: Brevard, N. C. Raleigh: Division of Community Planning, 1970.
N2120 (LMC WCU ASU)

Neighborhood Analysis: Valdese, North Carolina. Raleigh: Division of Community Planning
N2130 (ASU WCU)

Personal Income Statistics for North Carolina Counties, 1949-1959. Raleigh: n.p., 1963. Of special interest is the discrepancy between piedmont and mountain counties.
N2140

Population and Economy: Marshall, N.C. Raleigh: Division of Community Planning, 1969.
N2150 (ASU WCU)

Population and Economy: Valdese, North Carolina. Raleigh: Division of Community Planning, 1967.
N2160 (WCU)

Public Facilities Plan: Wilkes County, North Carolina. Raleigh: Division of Community Planning, 1968.
N2170 (ASU WCU)

Watauga County Land Development Plan. Greensboro, N. C.: Division of Community Planning, 1971. Cover title: Land Development Plan, Watauga, North Carolina.
N2180 (ASU)

Zoning Ordinance: Boone, N. C. n.p.: The author, 1965.
N2190 (LMC ASU)

Zoning Ordinance of the W. Kerr Scott Reservoir Area, Wilkes County, N. C. n.p.: The author, 1964.
N2200 (ASU)

Zoning Ordinance: Wilkes County, North Carolina. Raleigh: The division, 1969.
N2210 (ASU WCU)

North Carolina, Division of Mineral Resources The Mining Industry in North Carolina. Economic Paper. Raleigh: E.M. Uzzell and Co., 1900-.
N2220 (ASU UNCA ETSU LMC)

North Carolina, Education Association, Jackson County Unit Jackson County Public Schools, 1853-1954. n.p.: n.p., 1954.
N2230 (WCU)

North Carolina, Employment Security Commission Area Manpower Review: Asheville Standard Metropolitan Statistical Area — Buncombe County. Asheville, N. C.: The commission, 1973.
N2240 (ASU WWC)

Smaller Communities Program: Manpower Resources Report — Avery County. Raleigh: The commission, 1965.
N2250 (WCU)

North Carolina, Employment Security Commission. Job Market Research Center Measuring Unemployment in Small Rural Labor Areas: Report on a Household Survey Conducted in Alleghany County, N. C., 1969. Raleigh: The commission, 1969.
N2260

North Carolina Folklore. vol. 1-, 1948-. Chapel Hill: Univ. of North Carolina, semiannual.
N2270 (BC ASU ETSU MHC)

North Carolina Folklore Society Folklore Studies in Honor of Arthur Palmer Hudson. Chapel Hill: n.p., 1965.
N2280 (ASU LMC)

North Carolina Fund Characteristics of Households in Areas Served by the W. A. M. Y. Community Action Program. Durham: N. C. Fund, 1966.
N2290 (ASU)

The Dimensions of Poverty in North Carolina. n.p.: The North Carolina Fund, 1963.
N2300 (ASU)

North Carolina Genealogy. v. 1-, 1955-. Raleigh, N. C.: n.p., quarterly.
N2350

North Carolina General Assembly Cherokee Lands, Report. Document no. 34, Session 1856-7. Raleigh, N. C.: Holder and Wilson Printers to the State, 1857. Petition of Samuel Tate and others to the North Carolina Legislature asking relief from payment of excessive rates for lands acquired from the Cherokee. These rates were the result of a short-lived speculative boom in mountain property.
N2360

North Carolina, Geological and Economic Survey Altitudes in North Carolina. Bulletin, no. 27. Raleigh: Edwards and Broughton Print. Co., 1917.
N2310 (ASU LMC WCU)

. . . Altitudes in North Carolina, comp. by the North Carolina Geological and Economic Survey. Raleigh: Edwards and Broughton Print. Co., 1917.
N2320 (ASU UNCA)

Biennial Report of the State Geologist: 1919-1920. Raleigh, N. C.: Edwards and Broughton, 1921.
N2330 (ASU LMC)

Report of the State Geologist and Director. 1891-92 - 1923-24. Raleigh: The survey, 1924.
N2340 (ASU UNCA)

North Carolina Good Roads Association Road Maps and Tour Book of Western North Carolina. Chapel Hill: The assoc., 1916.
N2370 (BC ASU LMC)

North Carolina Higher-Court Records 2 vols. Raleigh, N. C.: State Dept. of Archives and History, 1968-71.
N2380 (ASU UNCA)

The North Carolina Historical and Genealogical Register vol. 1-3 January, 1900-July, 1903.
N2400 (ASU)

North Carolina Historical Commission Literary and Historical Activities of North Carolina, 1900-1905. Raleigh: E. M. Uzzell Co., 1907.
N2390 (LMC WWC ASU)

North Carolina Historical Review vol. 1-, January 1924-. Raleigh, N. C.: N. C. Historical Commission, 1924-.
N2410

The North Carolina Historical Review. . . . vol. 1-, 1924-. Raleigh: North Carolina Historical Commission, quarterly.
N2420 (BC ASU)

North Carolina Index: Guide to North Carolina's Periodical Literature A Cumulative Author and Subject Index Covering Material in N. C. Publications. . . . Winston-Salem: The Editors, irregular serial supplements.
N2430 (ASU UNCA)

North Carolina, Laws, Statutes, etc., Indexes North Carolina County Legislation Index: A Complete Listing of the Local or Special Acts Passed by the General Assembly for Each County, 1669-1961. (Also, Supplement, 1966.) Chapel Hill: Univ. of North Carolina Institute of Government, 1964.
N2440 (LMC)

North Carolina Library Commission Libraries in North Carolina. Raleigh: North Carolina Library Association, 1948.
N2450 (WWC)

North Carolina Lives: The Tar Heel Who's Who A reference edition recording the biographies of contemporary leaders in North Carolina with special emphasis on their achievements in making it one of America's greatest states. Written and prepared under the supervision of William Stevens Powell. Hopkinsville, Ky.: Historical Record Association, 1962.
N2460 (LMC)

North Carolina Museum of History, Raleigh Artistry in Quilts. Raleigh, N. C.: N. C. Museum of History, 1974. The colorfully illustrated brochure prepared for this quilt exhibition was jointly sponsored by the museum and the North Carolina Department of Archives and History.
N2470 (ASU)

North Carolina, Office of State Planning The Southern Highlands Mountain Resources Management Plan. Raleigh: Office of State Planning, n.d.
N2480

North Carolina Parks Commission Complete Report (of the Commission Created to Establish a National Park in the Great Smoky Mountains) Submitted to Governor Clyde R. Hoey, Dec. 31, 1939. Report compiled for the commission by Albert H. Blake. Raleigh?: The commission, 1939.
N2490 (LMC WCU)

North Carolina Plan for Emergency Management of Resources Chapel Hill: Office of Emergency Planning, Institute of Government, 196-?-.
N2500

North Carolina Poetry Society A Time for Poetry: An Anthology. Winston-Salem: J. F. Blair, 1966.
N2510 (LMC)

North Carolina, Presbyterian Church in the U. S. Our Mountain Work. Weaverville, N. C.: The Church, 1953-1959. Issued irregularly.
N2520

North Carolina Rural Electrification Authority Directory of Electric Agencies Serving Rural North Carolina. Raleigh: The authority, 1970.
N2530 (LMC)

North Carolina, Secretary of State Abstract of North Carolina Wills, Compiled from Original and Recorded Wills in the Office of the Secretary of State by J. Bryan Grimes, Secretary of State. Published under authority of the trustees of the public libraries. Raleigh: E.M. Uzzell and Co., 1910.
N2540 (ASU BC)

North Carolina, Secretary of State
Abstract of North Carolina Wills, Compiled from Original and Recorded Wills in the Office of the Secretary of State by J. Bryan Grimes. 1910. Reprint. Baltimore: Genealogical Pub. Co., 1967.
N2550 (ASU BC)
North Carolina Manual 1874-19. Raleigh: n.p., 1874-19--. A reliable source of raw data concerning western Carolina for the past 101 years.
N2560 (ASU LMC)
North Carolina Wills and Inventories, Copied from Original and Recorded Wills and Inventories in the Office of the Secretary of State by J. Bryan Grimes. 1912. Reprint. Baltimore: Genealogical Pub. Co., 1967.
N2570 (ASU)

North Carolina State Board of Health Biennial Report. Raleigh, N. C.: n.p., pagination varies.
N2580 (LMC)

North Carolina State College, Raleigh see **North Carolina, University, State College of Agriculture and Engineering, Raleigh**

North Carolina, State Dept. of Archives and History Guide to Civil War Records in the N. C. State Archives. Raleigh: n.p., 1966.
N2590
Guide to Private Manuscript Collections in the North Carolina State Archives. Prepared by Beth G. Crabtree (archivist). Raleigh: The department, 1964.
N2600 (ASU)

North Carolina, State Education Commission Report: Education in North Carolina, Today and Tomorrow. Raleigh: United Forces for Education, 1948.
N2610 (LMC BC)

North Carolina, State Planning Board North Carolina Basic County Data. Comp. and pub. by N. C. Planning Board, 2 vol. Raleigh, N. C.: The board, 1946.
N2620 (LMC)

North Carolina, State Planning Task Force Water Resource Needs for Selected Development Corridors in Appalachian North Carolina. Rummel, Klepper and Kahl, Consulting Engineers, 9 vols. Raleigh, N. C.: The Task Force, 1970. Projects growth for western North Carolina cities and related developments. Apparently based on the Appalachian Regional Commissions corridor development theory.
N2630 (ASU)

North Carolina, State Stream Sanitation Committee, Survey Report, Raleigh The Watauga River Basin: A Survey of Existing Pollution in the Watauga River Basin Together with Recommended Classification of Its Waters, 1960-1962. Pollution Survey Report, no. 15. Raleigh: North Carolina State Department of Water Resources, Division of Stream Sanitation and Hydrology, 1962.
N2640 (ASU)

North Carolina, University, Buncombe County Club Buncombe County: Economic and Social. Chapel Hill: The club, 1923.
N2670 (ASU)

North Carolina, University, Institute of Government County Government in North Carolina. By Robert G. Byrd and others. 2 vols. Chapel Hill: The institute, 1968.
N2680 (WWC ASU LMC)

North Carolina, University of North Carolina at Asheville Ecological Effects of Hot Water Discharge by an Electric Power Generating Plant. n.p.: The univ., 1971.
N2660 (ASU UNCA)

North Carolina, University of North Carolina, at Asheville Biosystem Character of the Pigeon River in the Primary State of Recovery n.p.: Univ. of N. C., 1973. "A report submitted by undergraduate students at the University of North Carolina at Asheville under the National Science Foundation Student-Originated Studies Program, Grant GY-10780."
N2650 (ASU UNCA)

North Carolina, University, State College of Agriculture and Engineering, Raleigh, Department of Agricultural Economics Economic Development of the Upper French Broad Area: Summary of Needs and Opportunities, Resources, the Regional Economy. By the North Carolina Department of Water Resources, Tennessee Valley Authority, and Western North Carolina Regional Planning Commission. 2 vols. Raleigh, N. C.: Department of Agricultural Economics, 1964.
N2690 (ASU)

North Carolina, Western Carolina University, Cullowhee A Faculty Handbook of Western Carolina University. Cullowhee, N. C.: The univ., annually.
N2700 (WCU)
Regional Sketches. Western Carolina Univ., Bulletin, vol. 15, no. 6, Dec., 1937. Cullowhee: The univ., 1937.
N2710 (WCU)
A Report on Studies and Investigations Dealing with a Prospective Expanded Program of Service by Western Carolina Univ. Cullowhee: The univ., 1952.
N2720 (WCU)
Teacher Education Programs: A Self-study Report to Division of Professional Services, State Department of Public Instruction. Cullowhee: The college, 1964.
N2730 (WCU ASU)
Views. Cullowhee State Normal School. Asheville: Advocate Pub. Co., n.d.
N2740 (ASU WCU)

North Carolina, Western Carolina University, Cullowhee, School of Education and Psychology College Preparatory Program for Visually Impaired Students: A Cooperative Program Between the North Carolina Commission for the Blind and Western Carolina University. n.p.: n.p., 1967?
N2750 (WCU)

North Carolina, Western Carolina University, Cullowhee, Steering Committee Institutional Self Study Report, 1963. Cullowhee: The college, 1963.
N2760 (WCU)
Teacher Education Report to National Council for Accreditation of Teacher Education. Cullowhee: The college, 1964.
N2770 (WCU)

North Carolina, Western Carolina University, Cullowhee, Where from Here Committee Horizon 1980: Report of the Special Committee "Which Way From Here" Appointed by President Paul A. Reid, Sept. 3, 1965. Cullowhee: The college, 1966.
N2780 (WCU)

North Carolina: Western Highlands and Great Smoky Mtns., National Park Miller Print. Co.: n.p., n.d. Map.
N2790 (MHC ASU)

North Wilkesboro, North Carolina Public Improvement Program and Capital Improvement Budget. n.p.: The author, 1967.
N2810 (LMC)

North Wilkesboro's Commerce Bureaus, Inc. North Wilkesboro, Wilkes County, N. C.: Key to the Blue Ridge Parkway. n.p.: The author, 1938?
N2800 (ASU LMC)

Northam, Ray M. Factors Influencing Recent Industrial Growth in Northeastern Georgia. Athens, Ga.: Institute of Community and Area Development, 1962.
N2820 (ASU)

Northwest Planning Council for Crime Deterrence Toward a Safer Society: Five Year Proposal. Boone, N. C.: Appalachian State Univ., 1970?
N2830 (ASU LMC)

Norton, Egbert "History of Education in Rockcastle, Kentucky." Master's thesis. Univ. of Kentucky, 1932.
N2840 (BC)

Norton, Frank Henry The Days of Daniel Boone. New York: American News Co., 1883.
N2850 (ETSU)
The Days of Daniel Boone: A Romance of the "Dark and Bloody Ground". New York: New York Pub. Co., 1882. Novel of pioneer Kentucky.
N2860 (LMC ASU BC)

Norum Organum 6 New Haven, Conn.: n.p., n.d. Is in large part devoted to the problems of Kentucky and Appalachia.
N2920

Norwood, Charles W. comp. The Chickamauga and Chattanooga Campaign and Battle-fields. A Chronological Historic Guide, August 16-November 25, 1863. Chattanooga: Connelly, 1898.
N2870

Norwood, Hayden The Marble Man's Wife, Thomas Wolfe's Mother. New York: C. Scribner's Sons, 1947.
N2880 (ASU WCU BC UNCA)

Norwood, William Howard comp. "General" John Norwood and Related Lines. In cooperation with James Harvey Norwood, Sr. Dallas, Tx.: Trumpet Press, 1964.
N2890 (ASU)

Noss, Marie G. Books on the Southern Mountain Area That Contain Certain Religions or Sections on Religion, 1947-55. Berea, Ky.: Berea College, 1955. Contains eighty titles on mountain religious movements.
N2900 (BC)

Nourse, Paul Francis "The Opinions of Certain Groups Toward Teaching the Bible in Unicoi County High School." Master's thesis. East Tennessee State College, 1952.
N2910 (ETSU)

Nowell, Elizabeth Thomas Wolfe, a Biography. 1st ed. Garden City, N. Y.: Doubleday, 1960.
N2930 (BC ASU WCU UNCA)

Nuckolls, Benjamin Floyd Pioneer Settlers of Grayson County, Virginia. Bristol, Tenn.: King Print. Co., 1914.
N2940 (ASU)

Nuckolls, Bertha The First Virginia Nuckolls and Kindred. Boston, Mass.: Thomas Todd Co., 1960.
N2950

Nugent, Nell Marion Cavaliers and Pioneers: Abstracts of Virginia Land Patents and Grants, 1623-1666. Introduction by Robert Armistead Stewart. 2nd ed. Baltimore: Genealogical Pub. Co., 1963.
N2960 (ASU)

Nugent, Tom Death at Buffalo Creek: The 1972 West Virginia Flood Disaster. New York: W. W. Norton, 1973.
N2970 (BC LMC ASU)

Null, Marion Michael The Forgotten Pioneer: The Life of Davy Crockett. New York: Vantage, 1954. It's quite unlikely one could ever forget the flambouyant Mr. Crockett since his biographers seem endless.
N2980 (ASU ETSU)

Nunburg, Bertha M. Potential Earning Power of Southern Mountaineer Handicrafts. Washington: Govt. Print. Off., 1935. For years this study was considered overly optimistic; however, statistics on craftsmen in recent years seem to support her contention that a decent living could be had from marketing crafts.
N2990

Nuttall, John Trees Above the Coal Below. San Diego: Neyenesch Printers, 1961.
N3000

Nutter, T. comp. Thomas, West Virginia: History, Progress, and Development, 1906. 1906. Reprint. Parsons, W. Va.: McClain Print. Co., 1968.
N3010 (ASU)

Nyden, Paul The Coal Miner's Struggle in Eastern Kentucky. Huntington, W. Va.: Appalachian Movement Press, 1972.
N3020 (ASU)

Nye, Susannah Mountain Songs of North Carolina. New York: Schirmer, n.d. This delightful book contains texts, notations, and music for favorite tunes from the Carolina mountains.
N3030

Nygaard, Norman E. Bishop on Horseback. Grand Rapids, Mich.: Zondervan Pub. House, 1962. Another biography of the circuit-riding bishop who thought serving in Appalachia was his personal penance.
N3040 (BC)

Nyland, Keith Ryan "Doctor Thomas Walker (1715-1794): Explorer, Physician, Surveyor, and Planter of Virginia and Kentucky." Ph. D. Diss. Ohio State Univ., 1971.
N3050 (BC)

Oak Ridge Association Universities, Resource Development Office A Report of Student Internships in Resource Development, & Legal Services Development. Oak Ridge: Associated Universities, 1967.
O10

Oakes, George W. Ochs Chattanooga and Hamilton County, Tennessee. Chattanooga: Tennessee Centennial Exposition Comm., 1897.
O20

Oakley, Wiley Roamin' with the Roamin' Men of the Smoky Mountains. Gatlinburg, Tenn.: Little Pigeon Press of the Gatlinburg News, 1940. A delightful tribute to the Smokies from the men who know them best.
O30 (ASU LMC BC)

Obenchain, Eliza Caroline Calvert Aunt Jane of Kentucky. Illustrated by Beulah Strong. Boston: Little, Brown and Co., 1908. A collection of Kentucky short stories; some with mountain settings.
O40 (ASU)

Aunt Jane of Kentucky. Illustrated by Beulah Strong. 1907. Reprint. Boston: Little, Brown, 1909.
O50 (WCU)

A Book of Handwoven Coverlets. Rutland, Va.: C. E. Tuttle Co., 1966. Numerous illustrations, diagrams, plates and instructions.
O60 (BC)

The Land of Long Ago. Illustrated by G. Patrick Nelson and Beulah Strong. Boston: Little, Brown and Co., 1909.
O70 (BC WCU ASU)

To Love and to Cherish. Boston: Little, Brown and Co., 1911. Reub Ward, leading gubernatorial candidate withdraws from the race because his mountain wife can't adjust to society.
O80 (BC)

Sally Ann's Experience. Illustrated by G. Patrick Nelson and Theodore B. Haphood. Boston: Little, Brown and Co., 1910. Short story separately published. May also be found in AUNT JANE OF KENTUCKY.
O90 (ASU BC)

Obenshain, S. S. Soil Survey, Russell County, Virginia. Prepared in cooperation with the Virginia Agricultural Experiment Station and the Tennessee Valley Authority. Soil Survey Report, Series 1936, no. 21. Washington: U. S. Department of Agriculture, Bureau of Plant Industry, Soils, and Agricultural Engineering, 1945.
O100 (BC)

Obenshain, Samuel Shockley Jurney, Robert Campbell and others Soil Survey, Washington County, Virginia. Washington: U. S. Department of Agriculture, Bureau of Plant Industry, Soils, and Agricultural Engineering, 1945.
J2940

Ober, Sarah Endicott Ginsey Kreider. Boston: Pilgrim Press, 1900. When the folks on Possum Trot finally get a teacher, its a "blab" school for he cannot reach. They rebel, he leaves kidnapping young Ginsey for evil purposes. A native boy returns to Possum Trot to set up a school. The people are scandalized by what he's learned "outside" and lynch him. The young folk rally, Ginsey returns and enlightment begins to creep into the mountains.
O110 (ASU)

Oberholser, Harry Church The Mammals and Summer Birds of Western North Carolina. Biltmore, N. C.: Biltmore Forest School, 1905.
O120

O'Brien, Bonylin Carson The Anxious Seat. New York: Carlton Press, 1971. A novel of life in Cat Valley and peril to Tallie who goes to the big world and is a long time coming home.
O130 (BC)

O'Brien, Michael A. ed. Corpus Genealogiarum Hiberniae. Dublin: Dublin Institute for Advanced Studies, 1962-. Excellent genealogical source on the Irish in America.
O140 (ASU)

O'Brien, Michael Joseph ed. The Irish in America: Immigration, Land, Probate, Administrations, Birth, Marriage, and Burial Records of the Irish in America in and about the Eighteenth Century. Baltimore: Genealogical Pub. Co., 1965.
O150 (ASU)

O'Brien, Warren S. Adventures along the Cumberland. New York: Vantage Press, 1963. Account of many adventures and stirring days along the river.
O160 (BC)

O'Connell, Jeremiah Joseph Catholicity in the Carolinas and Georgia: Leaves of Its History. New York: D. and J. Sadlier and Co., 1879. Catholicity is rapidly growing in the mountains.
O170 (BC ASU WCU LMC)

O'Connor, Jean Smith The Quiet Hills. Philadelphia: Dorrance and Co., 1963. Contemporary poems from the hills.
O180 (BC)

O'Connor, Richard Thomas, Rock of Chickamauga. 1st ed. New York: Prentice-Hall, 1948. Biography of General George Thomas hero of Chickamauga.
O190 (ASU)

O'Dell, Ruth Webb Over the Misty Blue Hills: The Story of Cocke County, Tennessee. Newport: n.p., 1951. An excellent local history.
O200

Odell, Samuel Robert "The First Hundred Days of the New Deal in Upper East Tennessee." Master's thesis. East Tennessee State Univ., 1966. What a fascinating topic. Background material for a whole host of "WPA Roosevelt" stories.
O210 (ETSU)

Oder, Charles Rollin Lorain Geology of the Mascot-Jefferson City Zinc District, Tennessee. Report of Investigations, no. 12. Nashville: Tennessee Division of Geology, 1961.
O220 (ETSU)

Odom, J. N. Austin, Moris E. Soil Survey, Claiborne County, Tennessee. Washington: U. S. Department of Agriculture, Bureau of Plant Industry, Soils, and Agricultural Engineering, 1948.
A5560 (ASU)

Odom, L. E. Soil Survey, Johnson County, Tennessee. Survey by Ralph G. Leighty and others. U. S. Soil Conservation Service, Soil Survey, Series 1946, no. 2. Washington: Govt. Print. Off., 1956.
O270 (BC ASU)

Soil Survey, Sevier County, Tennessee. Survey by E. H. Hubbard and others. U. S. Soil Conservation Service, Soil Survey, Series 1945, no. 1. Washington: Govt. Print. Off., 1956.
O280

O'Donnell, James H. Southern Indians in the American Revolution. Knoxville: Univ. of Tennessee Press, 1973.
O230 (ASU)

Odum, Eugene P. comp. Greene, Earle R. and others Birds of Georgia: A Preliminary Check-list and Bibliography of Georgia Ornithology. Athens: Univ. of Georgia Press, 1945.
G3730 (ASU)

Odum, Howard W. American Regionalism. New York: Henry Holt and Co., 1938. Good discussion of the Appalachian region as separate from the rest of the south.
O240

Odum, Howard Washington Southern Regions of the United States. For the Southern Regional Committee of the Social Science Research Council. Chapel Hill: Univ. of North Carolina Press, 1936. Good information on the Appalachians.
O250 (BC LMC MHC WWC)

The Way of the South: Toward the Regional Balance of America. New York: Macmillan, 1947. Is the South homogenous? Could Appalachia ever be?
O260 (ASU LMC BC)

Oertel, John Frederick Moonshine. Macon, Ga.: J. W. Burke Co., 1926. Novel, North Carolina mountain setting story is sympathetic to those the author calls "real" moonshiners — men who had pride in their work, made a fine product for honest profit and never considered that the state or federal government should have the slightest interest in what he did with his corn. It was his inalienable right to do a little blockading.
O290

Oertel, Julia Adelaide Hand in Hand Through the Happy Valley. Brooklyn: Church Charity Foundation, 1881. Novel set in western North Carolina's legendary Happy Valley.
O300

Office of Evaluation and Management Improvement Catalog of ARC Section 302B. Research and Demonstration Projects. n.p.: n.p., n.d.
O310 (ASU)

Official Booklet of Grainger County, Tennessee Rutledge: Progressive Club, 1926.
O320

Official Souvenir and History, Sesquicentennial Celebration, Knoxville, August 28 through September 1, 1941 Knoxville: n.p., 1941.
O330

Ogburn, Charleton Winespring Mountain. New York: Morrow, 1973. A well-to-do young man is sent to the coal mines to learn the business from the bottom up. A naturalist at heart, he begins a successful campaign to save Winespring Mountains.
O340 (BC ASU)

Ogburn, Dorothy Death on the Mountain. Boston: Little, Brown and Co., 1931. Mystery story with a western North Carolina setting.
O350

Ogletree, James R. Appalachian Schools — A Case of Consistency. Lexington: College of Education, Univ. of Kentucky, 1962.
O360 (ASU)

Ohio, Department of Urban Affairs A Summary of a Study of Potential State and Local Programs to Stimulate Low and Moderate-income Housing Construction in Ohio Appalachia. Columbus: The department, 1970.
O370 (ASU)

Ohio, Development Department A Development Program for the Ohio Valley Region. Columbus: Development Department, n.d.
O380

Ohio, Legislative Service Committee Comparative State Strip Mining and Reclamation Laws. Columbus: Legislative Service Committee, 1965.
O390

The Ohio River Atlas Cincinnati: Picture Marine Pub. Co., 1954. Includes a collection of maps of the river from 1713 to 1954.
O400

Ohio River Basin Survey Coordinating Committee Ohio River Basin: Comprehensive Survey, Main Report. 14 vols. Cincinnati: U. S. Army Engineer Division, 1969.
O410 (ASU)

Ohio River Survey — 1819, Commissioner's Report on Shoals in the Ohio River in 1819, Ohio, Kentucky, Virginia (now West Virginia) and Indiana n.p.: n.p., 1819. A report on obstructions to navigation in Ohio waters.
O420

Ohio University, Athens, Center for Economic Opportunity Appalachia: A Case Study of Regional Business Development. Athens: Major Business Institute Report, 1966.
O430

Ohio Valley Health Service Foundation Ohio Appalachia Health Development Plan, 1970. Athens: The foundation, 1970. A comprehensive plan for improving health care services within the region.
O440 (ASU)

Ohlin, Peter H. Agee. 1st ed. New York: I. Obolensky, 1966. A critical study of the life and works of James Agee.
O450 (WCU)

Okun, Milt Something to Sing About. New York: Collier Books, 1970. The favorite songs of America's leading folk artists.
O460 (BC)

Old First Church, Synod of Appalachia, Presbytery of Knoxville Knoxville: n.p., 1942.
O470

Old Greenfield Church, West Virginia, Copy of Marriage Register of Rev. John Alderson, Jr., 1776-1798. n.p.: n.p., n.d.
O480 (ASU)

Old Hickory vol. 1-11. 1919-1929. Johnson City: East Tennessee State Normal School, 1919-.
O490 (ETSU)

Old Time Music no. 1-, Summer, 1971-. London, Ky.: n.p., quarterly.
O500

Olds, Fred A. An Abstract of North Carolina Wills from about 1760 to about 1800. Supplementing Grimes' Abstract of North Carolina wills, 1663 to 1760. Oxford, N. C.: "The Orphan's Friend", 1925.
O510 (BC ASU)

An Abstract of North Carolina Wills from about 1760 to about 1800. Supplementing Grimes' Abstract of North Carolina wills, 1663 to 1760. 1925. Reprint. Baltimore: Genealogical Pub. Co., 1965.
O520 (BC ASU)

Story of the Counties of North Carolina, with Other Data. As printed in The Orphans' Friend and Masonic Journal. Oxford, N. C.: Press of Oxford Orphanage, n.d. Includes sketches of the twenty-eight western counties.
O530 (ASU)

Oleham, Edythe Virginia Appalachia, Resource Unit. n.p.: n.p., n.d.
O540 (ASU)

Olive, Dame Campbell Sharp, Cecil James Folk Songs from the Southern Appalachians. London: Oxford Univ. Press, 1917.
S2290 (ASU BC)

Oliver, James Dale "Shifts in Land Use in the Appalachian Region of Virginia." Ph. D. Diss. Virginia Polytechnic Institute and State Univ., 1971.
O550 (LMC ASU)

Oliver, John Recreation Grows Up in the Tennessee Valley. Address before Knoxville Tourist Bureau Annual Meeting, June 16, 1952. Knoxville, Tenn.: Tennessee Valley Authority, 1952.
O560

Oliver, K. M. Porter, Hobart Clarke Soil Survey, Tazewell County, Virginia. Washington: U. S. Department of Agriculture, Bureau of Plant Industry, Soils, and Agricultural Engineering, 1948.
P3660

Oliverio, Jean E. comp. Footprints in the Soil and Reflections on the Water: Conservation in West Virginia. Condensed for publication by William H. Gillespie. Parsons, W. Va.: McClain Print. Co., 1972.
O570 (ASU)

Olmsted, Frederick Law A Journey in the Back Country. Our Slave States, 3. New York: Mason Brothers, 1860. Includes an early description of Appalachia and its people.
O580 (ASU LMC)

A Journey in the Back Country. 1860. Reprint. With a new introduction by Clement Eaton. New York: Schocken Books, 1970.
O590 (LMC)

A Journey in the Back Country. 1860. Reprint. Williamstown, Mass.: Corner House Pub., 1972.
O600 (BC LMC)

Olmsted, Stanley At Top of Tobin. New York: Dial Press, 1926. Except for an emphasis on funerals this novel of North Carolina mountain life has a rather clear plot. Mollie Donbrook wants to leave the mountains and raise her young son in Florida where the living is easier, in the end they return to the mountains.
O610 (BC LMC)

Olsen, Evelyn Guard Indian Blood. Parsons, W. Va.: McClain Print. Co., 1967. A history of the Allegheny Indians living along the Youghiogheny River in Pennsylvania.
O620 (ASU)

Olson, David F., Jr. Beck, Donald E. Seed Production in Southern Appalachian Oak Stands. Asheville, N. C.: Southeastern Forest Experiment Station, 1968.
B2450

Early Survival and Growth of Planted Northern Red Oak in Southern Appalachians. Forest Service Research Note, SE-89. Asheville, N. C.: Southeastern Forest Experiment Station, 1968.
O630

Sluder, Earl Ray Tests on Direct Seeding of Oak in Piedmont and Southern Appalachians of North Carolina. Asheville, N. C.: Southeastern Forest Experiment Station, 1961.
S4250 (WCU)

Olson, E. F. Vogenberger, R. A. Method for Determining Public Fire Control Expenditures for Private Lands. Norris, Tenn.: Tennessee Valley Authority, 1957.
V1310

Olson, J. C. Griffitts, W. R. Part 5, Shelby-Hickory District, North Carolina. Part 6, Outlying Deposits in North Carolina. Washington: U. S. Geological Survey, Government Print. Office, 1953.
G4240

Olson, Jerry Chipman Pegmatites of the Cashiers and Zirconia Districts, North Carolina. Bulletin, no. 64. Raleigh: North Carolina Department of Conservation and Development, Division of Mineral Resources, 1952.
O650 (ETSU ASU)

Olson, Jerry Chipman and others Mica Deposits of the Franklin-Sylva District, North Carolina. Bulletin, no. 49. Raleigh: North Carolina Department of Conservation and Development, 1946.
O640 (ASU WCU ETSU)

O'Meara, Walter Daughters of the Country: The Women of the Fur Traders and Mountain Men. 1st ed. New York: Harcourt, Brace and World, 1968. This is an account of the racial and sexual confrontation of the Indian women and the white men on our frontiers.
O660 (WCU)

One Hundred and Fifty Selected Views of Chattanooga, Lookout Mountain, Chickamauga and Chattanooga National Military Park, National Cemetery, and Missionary Ridge Lookout Mountain, Tenn.: Rollins and Linn, 190-?
O670

One Hundred and Fifty Years of American Quilts Lawrence: U. of Kansas Museum of Art, 1973. Booklet prepared for an exhibition at the university museum.
O680 (ASU)

One Man's Cravin' Pine Mountain: Pine Mountain Settlement School, 1945. A biography of the founder, William Creech, of the Pine Mountain Settlement School.
O690

O'Neal, A. M., Jr. Burke, Richard Thomas Avon Soil Survey of Limestone County, Alabama. Washington: U. S. Dept. of Agriculture, Bureau of Soils, 1916.
B8710

Burke, Richard Thomas Avon Soil Survey of Madison County, Alabama. Washington: U. S. Dept. of Agriculture, Bureau of Soils, 1913.
B8720

Veatch, Jethro O. Soil Survey of Walker County, Alabama. Washington: U. S. Department of Agriculture, Bureau of Soils, 1916.
V500

O'Neal, Alfred M., Jr. Soil Survey of Fayette County, Alabama. Prepared in cooperation with Alabama. Field Operations, 1917. Washington: U. S. Department of Agriculture, Bureau of Soils, 1920.
O700

O'Neal, William B. Architecture in Virginia: An Official Guide to Four Centuries of Building in the Old Dominion. 1st ed. New York: Walker, 1968. Includes many old homes from the Shenandoah Valley.
O710 (ASU)

The Oneida Mountaineer v. 1. Oneida, Ky.: n.p., 1915 — Monthly.
O750

O'Neill, Charles Wild Train; the Story of Andrews Raiders. New York: Hastings House, 1956. An account of the great train robbery of the Civil War. Action confined to the mountain areas of north Georgia.
O720

O'Neill, Charles Kendall Wild Train: The Story of the Andrews Raiders. New York: Random House, 1956. Account of the capture of a Confederate Train by a band of Union Raiders. Setting is the north Georgia mountains.
O730 (ASU ETSU)

O'Neill, Dave The Life and Times of a Mountaineer Game Warden. Ft. Pierce, Fla.: n.p., 1971. A fantastic account of people, moonshine and politics in Wise County, Virginia.
O740

Operation Coal and the Southern Student Committee (V.P.I.) Coal, Southwest Virginia's Source of Misery. Printed by the Council of the Southern Mountains. Clintwood, Va.: The council, 1974. Facts about coal, history, economy, miners and coal as a future.
O760 (ASU)

Ord, John ed. The Bothy Songs & Ballads of Aberdeen, Banff & Moray, Angus and the Mearns. With a foreword by Robert S. Raib. Paisley, Great Britain: A. Gardner, 1930. Many still sung in the Southern Mountains.
O770 (ASU)

Ordway, Richard John Geology of the Buffalo Mountain-Cherokee Mountain Area, Northeastern Tennessee. Report of Investigations, no. 9. Nashville: Tennessee Division of Geology, 1959.
O780 (ETSU ASU)

The Ore Knob Copper Deposit North Carolina, and other Massive Sulfide Deposits of the Appalachians Geological Survey Professional Paper 558. Washington: Govt. Print. Off., n.d.
O790

Oriel, Steven S. Geology and Mineral Resources of the Hot Springs Window, Madison County, North Carolina. Bulletin, no. 60. Raleigh: North Carolina Department of Conservation and Development, 1950.
O800 (ASU WCU ETSU)

Ormond, Jesse Marvin The Country Church in North Carolina: A Study of the Country Church of North Carolina in Relation to the Material Progress of the State. Durham: Duke Univ. Press, 1931.
O810 (ASU WCU LMC WWC)

Ormsby, Virginia H. Mountain Magic for Rosy. New York: Crown Publishers, 1969. Granny's magic solves a problem for a guitar-playing girl in the North Carolina mountains.
O820

Ornduff, Peggy Josephine "An Improved Language Arts Program for a Selected Third Grade at Henry Johnson School in Johnson City, Tennessee." Master's thesis. East Tennessee State College, 1959.
O830 (ETSU)

Orr, Helen Allison The History of the Emory and Henry College Library, 1839-1954. Master's thesis. East Tennessee State Univ., 1955. The development of the library at Emory and Henry College is told from its beginning in 1839 to 1954.
O840

Orr, Thomas B. "A Follow-up of 1952 Graduates of Logan High School, Logan, West Virginia." Master's thesis. Marshall College, 1953.
O850

Ortiz-Garcia, Angel Luis "Andrew Johnson's Veto of the First Reconstruction Act." Ph. D. Diss. Carnegie-Mellon Univ., 1970.
O860

Orvedal, A. C. Jurney, Robert Campbell Soil Survey, Smyth County, Virginia. Washington: U. S. Department of Agriculture, Bureau of Plant Industry, Soils and Agricultural Engineering, 1948.
J2930

Obenshain, S. S. Soil Survey, Russell County, Virginia. Washington: U. S. Department of Agriculture, Bureau of Plant Industry, Soils, and Agricultural Engineering, 1945.
O100 (BC)

Osborn, Hampton A Collection of Poems. Clintwood, Va.: n.p., n.d.
O870

Osborn, Scott Compton "A Study and Contrast of the Kentucky Mountaineer and the Bluegrass Aristocrat in the Works of John Fox, Jr." Master's thesis. Univ. of Kentucky, 1939.
O880 (ASU)

Osborne, Barron M. "A Study of the Factors Affecting the Holding Power of High Schools in a Certain Mountainous Rural County." Master's thesis. Virginia Polytechnic Institute, 1961.
O890

Osborne, James T. "Community Use of School Resources in Cherokee County, North Carolina, as Compared with a National Trend." Master's thesis. Univ. of North Carolina, 1950.
O900

O'Shaughnessy, Marjorie ed. Christopher, Frederick John Basketry. New York: Dover Pub., 1953.
C4020 (ASU WCU)

Otis, James The Boy Spies at the Defense of Fort Henry, a Story of Wheeling Creek in 1777. New York: A. L. Burt Co., 1900. Children's adventure story set in and around the present city of Wheeling, West Virginia.
O910 (ASU BC)

Hannah of Kentucky, a Story of the Wilderness Road. New York: American Book Co., 1912. Children's story featuring a young girl's hazardous crossing of the Blue Ridge and Appalachian mountains on the road to Kentucky.
O920 (ASU BC)

Ott, Glena Kreis Freytag, Ethel A History of Morgan County, Tennessee. Wartburg, Tenn.: Specialty Print. Co., 1971.
F3280 (ASU BC)

Otwell, William J. Hurst, Vernon J. Exploration for Mineral Deposits in White County, Georgia. Washington: Govt. Print. Off., 1965.
H8600 (LMC)

Our Mountain Work v. 1. Weaverville, N. C.: Home Missions Committee of Asheville Presbytery, 1930.
O930

Overbeck, Robert M. Amsden, Thomas William Geology and Water Resources of Garrett County. Baltimore: Maryland Department of Geology, Mines and Water Resources, 1954.
A2230 (ETSU)

Overbey, W. K., Jr. Rough, Robert L. Lithologic Descriptions of Appalachian Area Oil-producing Formations. Washington: U. S. Bureau of Mines, 1970.
R3980

Overbey, William K. Oil and Gas Report on Jackson, Mason, and Putnam Counties, West Virginia. Bulletin, no. 23. Morgantown: West Virginia Geological and Economic Survey, 1961.
O940 (ETSU)

Overton, Walter Bruce "An Educational, Economic, and Community Survey of Jackson County, Tennessee." Master's thesis. Univ. of Tennessee, 1927.
O950

Owen, Marguerite Muscle Shoals and the Public Welfare. Washington: National League of Women Voters, 1929.
O960

The Tennessee Valley Authority. New York: Praeger, 1973.
O970

Owen, Pauline "A Comparison of Parents and Teachers Viewpoints Relative to Teacher Competencies in Johnson City, Tennessee." Master's thesis. Tennessee Agricultural and Industrial Univ., 1952.
O980

Owen, Thomas M. comp. Revolutionary Soldiers in Alabama: Being a List of Names, Compiled from Authentic Sources, of Soldiers of the American Revolution, Who Resided in the State of Alabama. 1911. Reprint. Baltimore: Genealogical Pub. Co., 1967.
O990 (ASU)

Owens, Ivan C. Easton-Avery Community History, 1963. Parsons, W. Va.: McClain Print. Co., 1964.
O1000 (ASU)

Owens, Susie L. The Union League of America: Political Activities in Tennessee, the Carolinas, and Virginia, 1865-1870. New York: New York Univ., 1947.
O1010

Owsley, Agnes Grace "An Evaluation of the Library Proficiencies of Freshmen at Appalachian State Teachers College, 1953-54." Master's thesis. Appalachian State Teachers College, 1954.
O1020 (ASU)

Oxford, Jeaner Arguile Dr. John McLeod Oxford, 1841-1928; A Sketch of His Life. Taylorsville, N. C.: n.p., 1930. Biography written by his son.
O1030 (ASU)

Oxmoor House A Catalogue of the South. Birmingham, Ala.: Oxmoor House, 1974. Includes a goodly number of references to the southern Appalachians.
O1040 (ASU)

Oyler, Merton D. Community and Neighborhood Groupings in Knott County, Kentucky. Lexington: Kentucky Agricultural Experiment Station, 1936.
O1050

Fertility Rates and Migration of Kentucky's Population, 1920-1940. Lexington: Kentucky Agricultural Experiment Station, 1944.
O1060 (ASU)

Natural Increase and Migration of Kentucky's Population, 1920-1935. Lexington: Kentucky Agricultural Experiment Station, 1939.
O1070 (ASU)

Neighborhood Standing and Population Changes in Johnson and Robertson Counties. Bulletin no. 523. Lexington: Kentucky Agricultural Experiment Station, Univ. of Kentucky, 1948.
O1080

Pace, E. S. Smith, Howard C. Soil Survey of Jefferson County, Alabama. Washington: U. S. Dept. of Agriculture, Bureau of Soils, 1910.
S4770

Pace, Herbert E. 50 Years Ago Around Saluda, N. C. Saluda: n.p., 1957.
P10

Pace, Mildred Mastin Home Is Where the Heart Is. New York: McGraw-Hill Book Co., 1954. Brady's father leaves her with a well-off family to work her way. She learns to live on her own and take happiness where she can find it.
P20

Pachence, Anthony M. Krueger, Daniel W. Wind Directions for Prescribed Burning in Southeastern United States. Asheville, N. C.: Southeastern Forest Experiment Station, 1961.
K3360 (WCU)

Pack, Devota Parrish Lucas, Wavie Harman Births in Court Records of Montgomery County, Virginia, 1853-1871. n.p.: n.p., 1972.
L3860

Page, Elizabeth Wilderness Adventure. New York: Rinehart and Co., 1946.
P30 (ASU)

Page, Myra With Sun in Our Blood. New York: Citadel Press, 1950. Taking a stranger in out of a storm proves to be the beginning of an adventure for Dolly and her brother and sisters.
P40 (ASU)

Page, Thomas Nelson Red Rock: A Chronicle of Reconstruction. New York: C. Scribner's Sons, 1898. This novel of post-war Virginia is partially set in western Virginia's hill country.
P50 (ASU)

Page, William J., Jr. Appalachia: Realities of Deprivation. Washington: U. S. Department of Health, Education and Welfare, 1964.
P60

Pageant of East Tennessee Commemorating the Sesquicentennial of Greene County at Greeneville, August 18, 1933 Greeneville: n.p., 1933. Souvenir program of the Greene County, Tennessee Historical pageant.
P70

Paine, Dorothy Charlotte A Maid of the Mountains. Philadelphia: George W. Jacobs, 1906. More fiction in which the mountain setting seems almost incidental. Poor use of several minor characters who might have been memorable.
P80

The Paintsville Herald. Special Issue, Industrial Review: Big Sandy and Kentucky Rivers. Coal-oil-gas Paintsville, Ky.: The Herald, n.d.
P90

Palmer, Abram Smythe Folk-etymology, a Dictionary of Verbal Corruptions or Words Perverted in Form or Meaning by False Derivation or Mistaken Analogy. 1882. Reprint. New York: Johnson Reprint Co., 1969.
P100 (ASU)

Palmer, Frederick A. "Westerners at Home: Comments of French and British Travelers on Life in the West, 1800-1840." Ph. D. Diss. Univ. of Illinois, 1948. The term "west" at this time in American history included Appalachia.
P110

Palmer, Susan Tate Thomas Hope of Tennessee, 1757-1820, House Carpenter and Joiner. Knoxville: Privately printed, 1972. A biography and a county history of Knox County, Tennessee.
P120

Palo, G. P. Tennessee Valley Authority's Bull Run Steam Plant. Knoxville, Tenn.: TVA, 1963.
P130

Palowitch, E. P. Deurbrouck, A. W. Survey of Sulfur Reduction in Appalachian Coals by Stage Crushing. Pittsburgh: Mines Bureau, 1966.
D1920

Pamplin, Lily May The Scamps of Bucksnort: Memories of a Nineteenth-century Childhood in Rural Tennessee. 1st ed. New York: Exposition Press, 1962. Memoirs of life in the foothills of Tennessee.
P140 (ASU)

Panorama of progress: Jackson County Centennial, Sylva, North Carolina, September 2-8, 1951 Sylva, N. C.: Herald Pub. Co., 1951.
P150 (WCU)

Papers on the Stratigraphy and Mine Geology of the Kingsport and Mascot Formations (lower Ordovician) of East Tennessee Prepared in cooperation with the Society of Economic Geologists and the University of Tennessee Department of Geology. Report of Investigations, no. 23. Nashville: Tennessee Division of Geology, 1969.
P160 (ETSU)

Parent's Study Group Elizabethon, Tenn. Helping Our Children Grow. Elizabethon: Board of Education, 1952.
E1560 (ETSU)

Parham, Louis L. Chattanooga, Tennessee; Hamilton County, and Lookout Mountain. An Epitome of Chattanooga from Her Early Days Down to the Present; Hamilton County, Its Soil, Climate, Area, Population, Wealth, etc. Lookout Mountain, Its Battlefield, Beauties, Climate, and Other Attractions. Chattanooga: The author, 1876. A history and reminiscence of Hamilton County, Tennessee.
P170

Parish, Peggy Let's Be Early Settlers with Daniel Boone. New York: Harper and Row, 1967. Children's book of frontier life.
P180 (ASU ETSU)

Park, James The Fiftieth Anniversary of the Rogersville Synodical College. McMinnville: Standard, 1899. A brief history of the college and of Hawkins County, Tennessee.
P190

History of the First Presbyterian Church in Knoxville, Tennessee. Knoxville: Ramage, 1876.
P200

Parker, George Martin Nathaniel The Mountain Massacre. Bluefield, W. Va.: Country Life, 1930. Story of the Allen family and the tragedy at Hillsville Courthouse.
P210 (ASU)

Parker, Haywood "Folklore of the North Carolina Mountaineers." Unpublished paper. Asheville: Pen and Plate Club, 1906.
P240

Parker, Helen M. Fruitful Year. n.p.: The author, 1971. Hill country poetry.
P220 (ETSU)

Parker, J. K., Jr. "A Study of the Needs, Growth, and Development of the Presbyterian Church of Boone, N. C." Master's thesis. Appalachian State Teachers College, 1955.
P230 (ASU)

Parker, James Peele Hemlock Twigs and Balsam Sprigs. Black Mountain, N. C.: Black Mountain Printery, 1921.
P250 (ASU)

Parker, Joanne M. Donohew, Lewis Impacts of Educational Change Efforts in Appalachia. Las Cruces, N. M.: ERIC Clearinghouse on Rural Education and Small Schools, 1970.
D2910 (ETSU)

Parker, John Mason Residual Kaolin Deposits of the Spruce Pine District, North Carolina. Prepared by the U. S. Geological Survey. Bulletin, no. 43. Raleigh: North Carolina Department of Conservation and Development Division of Mineral Resources, 1946.
P260 (ETSU)

Parker, Lula Eastman Jeter Ackerly, Mary Denham Our Kin. Lynchburg, Va.: J. P. Bell Co., Inc., 1930.
A230

Parker, Lula Jeter History of Bedford County, Virginia. Bedford: Bedford Democrat, 1954.
P270 (FC)

Parker, Marian Mountain Mating. 1st ed. New York: Pageant Press, 1954. A very poor novel of a group of degenerates at the foot of Grandfather Mountain.
P280 (BC ASU WCU LMC MHC)

Parker, Mattie Erma Edwards ed. North Carolina Higher-Court Records Raleigh, N. C.: State Dept. of Archives and History, 1968-71.
N2380 (ASU UNCA)

Parker, Thomas V. "Relations of the United States Government with the Cherokee Tribe." Ph. D. Diss. New York Univ., 1906. With general history of the Cherokee.
P300

Parker, Thomas Valentine The Cherokee Indians, with Special Reference to Their Relations with the United States Government. Grafton Historical Series. New York: Grafton Press, 1907. Includes general historical background on the Cherokee.
P290 (ETSU ASU WCU LMC)

Parker, W. Gordon Two Boys in the Blue Ridge. Boston: D. Estes and Co., 1901. Two young boys face an ordeal in the mountains and gain maturity from it.
P310 (ASU)

Parker, William Blake Soil Survey, Randolph County, Alabama. Field survey by William B. Parker and others. Washington: U. S. Department of Agriculture, Soil Conservation Service, 1967.
P320

Parks, Aileen Wells Davy Crockett, Young Rifleman. Indianapolis: Bobbs-Merrill Co., 1949. Novel of the young Davy Crockett and his exploits in east Tennessee.
P330 (ETSU)

Parks, Edd Winfield Charles Egbert Craddock. Chapel Hill: Univ. of North Carolina Press, 1941. This is perhaps the best of the studies of Miss Murfree and her work.
P340 (ASU)

Parks, Ina Ruth "Teaching Exceptional Children in the Fifth Grade of Lincoln Elementary School — Kingsport, Tennessee." Master's thesis. East Tennessee State College, 1951.
P350 (ETSU)

Parks, James R. "A Follow-up Study of Attitudes of Sullivan County High School Seniors toward the Church." Master's thesis. East Tennessee State College, 1953. In this county a very high percentage of young people continued to attend church after leaving home.
P360

Parks, Joseph H. The Story of Tennessee. Oklahoma City, Okla.: Harlow Pub. Co., 1958. Children's history of Tennessee.
P370 (LMC)

Parks, Leighton Turnpikes and Dirt Roads. New York: C. Scribners Sons, 1927. Biography of David Clough, dealing primarily with his boyhood in the Valley of Virginia during the Civil War.
P380

Parlier, Gertrude Dana and others Albemarle County Historical Society, War History Committee Pursuits of War: The People of Charlottesville and Albemarle County, Virginia, in the Second World War. Charlottesville, Va.: The society, 1948.
A970 (ASU)

Parman, Guy D. "Geographic Factors in the Land Use of Greene County, Tennessee." Master's thesis. East Tennessee State College, 1954.
P390

Parris, John A. The Cherokee Story. Asheville, N. C.: Stephens Press, 1950. History and sketches of the Cherokee. Many reprinted from Parris' daily column in the Asheville paper.
P400 (UNCA ASU WCU ETSU)

My Mountains, My People. Native flower sketches by Dorothy Luxton Parris. Asheville, N. C.: Citizen-Times Pub. Co., 1957. Sketches of life in the Carolina mountains.
P410 (ASU WWC UNCA)

Mountain Bred. Native flower sketches by Dorothy Luxton Parris. Asheville, N. C.: Citizen-Times Pub. Co., 1967. Sketches of life in the Carolina mountains.
P420 (ASU LMC MHC WCU WWC)

Roaming the Mountains with John Parris. Asheville, N. C.: Citizen-Times Pub. Co., 1955. More sketches of mountain folk and their lives.
P430 (ASU WCU LMC MHC ETSU WWC)

These Storied Mountains. Native flower sketches by Dorothy Luxton Parris. Asheville, N. C.: Citizen-Times Pub. Co., 1972. Stories from the mountains.
P440 (ASU ETSU MHC WCU WWC)

Parrish, Earl L. "Land Utilization in Roane County, Tennessee." Master's thesis. Univ. of Tennessee, 1951. Roane County is still primarily agriculture and local groups are hoping to avoid the blight of tourism.
P450

Parrish, Paul H. Soil Survey, Columbia County, Pennsylvania. Soils surveyed by Paul H. Parrish and others. Washington: U. S. Department of Agriculture, Soil Conservation Service, 1967.
P460

Parson Browndow and the Unionists of East Tennessee, With a Sketch of His Life New York: Beadle's Dime Series, 1862. Overstated and poorly written biography of the region's famous orator and abolitionist.
P470

Parson Brownlow's Book see **Sketches of the Rise, Progress and Decline of Secession**

Parsons, Rhey Boyd "Teacher Education in Tennessee." Ph. D. Diss. Univ. of Chicago, 1935.
P480 (ETSU)

Partadiredja, Atje "Helvetia, West Virginia: A Study of Pioneer Development and Community Survival in Appalachia." Ph. D. Diss. The Univ. of Wisconsin, 1966.
P490

"Helvetia, West Virginia: A Study of Pioneer Development and Community Survival in the Appalachia." Ph. D. Diss. Univ. of Wisconsin, 1966.
P500

Partin, Robert Love "The Secession Movement in Tennessee." Ph. D. Diss. George Peabody College, 1935. More than any other mountain state, Tennessee was bitterly divided by the War.
P510

Parton, Mary Field ed. Jones, Mary Harris ed. Autobiography of Mother Jones. New York: Arco & New York Times, 1969.
J2500 (BC LMC ASU WCU MHC)

Autobiography of Mother Jones. New York: Arno and The New York Times, 1969. Mother Jones joined the union struggle at age fifty and gave nearly fifty years to the cause.
P520 (ASU)

Paschall, A. H. Conrey, Guy Woolard Soil Survey, Scioto County, Ohio. Washington: U. S. Dept. of Agriculture, Bureau of Plant Industry, 1940.
C6780

Phillips, Samuel William Soil Survey of Belmont County, Ohio. Washington: U. S. Department of Agriculture, Bureau of Chemistry and Soils, 1931.
P2620

Phillips, Samuel William Soil Survey of Washington County, Ohio. Washington: U. S. Department of Agriculture, Bureau of Chemistry and Soils, 1930.
P2670

Paschall, Alfred H. Soil Survey, Athens County, Ohio. Prepared in cooperation with the Ohio Agricultural Experiment Station. Soil Survey Report, Series 1932, no. 32. Washington: U. S. Department of Agriculture, Bureau of Chemistry and Soils, 1938.
P530

Soil Survey of Vinton County, Ohio. Prepared in cooperation with the Ohio Agricultural Experiment Station. Soil Survey Report, Series 1933, no. 21. Washington: U. S. Department of Agriculture, Bureau of Chemistry and Soils, 1938.
P540

Pasour, E. C., Jr. Production, Marketing, and Prices of North Carolina Apples, 1947-1963. Agricultural Economics Information Series, no. 117. Raleigh: North Carolina State Univ., 1965.
P550 (LMC)

Passano, Eleanor Phillips An Index of the Source Records of Maryland: Genealogical, Bibliographical, Historical. 1940. Reprint. With a new introduction by W. Filby. Baltimore: Genealogical Pub. Co., 1967.
P560 (ASU)

Passow, A. Harry ed. Work Conference on Curriculum and Teaching in Depressed Urban Areas, 1962 Education in Depressed Areas. n.p.: Teachers College, Columbia University, 1963.
W9170

The Past, Present, and Future of Chattanooga, Tennessee, the Industrial Center of the South Chattanooga: Times, 1885. A history of Chattanooga and Hamilton County, Tennessee, with lists of industries and opportunities.
P570

Pasto, J. K. Gorman, John Loyd Soil Survey, Berkeley County, West Virginia. Washington: U. S. Department of Agriculture, Soil Conservation Service, 1966.
G2770

Patric, James H. Deforestation Effects on Soil Moisture, Streamflow, and Water Balance in Central Appalachians. U. S. Forest Service Research Paper, NE-259. Upper Darby, Pa.: Northeastern Forest Experiment Station, 1973.
P580

Patrick, A. L. Derrick, Bruce B. Soil Survey of Cambria County, Pennsylvania. Washington: U. S. Department of Agriculture, Bureau of Soils, 1917.
D1880 ()

Patrick, Austin L. Higbee, Howard William Soil Survey, Huntingdon County, Pennsylvania. Washington: U. S. Department of Agriculture, Bureau of Plant Industry, Soils and Agricultural Engineering, 1944.
H5260

Patrick, Austin L. and others Soil Survey of Morgan County, Alabama. Prepared in cooperation with Alabama. Field Operations, 1918. Washington: U. S. Department of Agriculture, Bureau of Soils, 1921.
P590

Patrick, Walton R. Cantrell, Clyde Hull Southern Literary Culture: A Bibliography of Master's and Doctor's Theses. University: Univ. of Alabama Press, 1955.
C1120 (ASU LMC)

Patten, Cartter Signal Mountain and Walden's Ridge. Chattanooga: The author, 1961. A history of two ridges in Hamilton County, Tennessee.
P600

Patten, Z. C. So Firm a Foundation. Chattanooga: The author, 1968.
P640

Patten, Elizabeth Bryan History of Summertown, Walden's Ridge, Tennessee. Chattanooga: The author, 1959. 20 leaves. History of a resort in Hamilton County, Tennessee.
P610

Patten, J. A. The Mountaineer Detective. A Thrilling Tale of the Moonshiners. Secret Service Series, no. 16. New York: Street and Smith, 1889. A story of violence and moonshine in the Southern mountains.
P620 (ASU)

Patten, Marjorie The Arts Workshop of Rural America: A Study of the Rural Arts Program of the Agricultural Extension Service. New York: Columbia Univ., Press, 1937.
P630 (LMC)

Patten, Z. C. So Firm a Foundation. Chattanooga: The author, 1968. A history of the Civil War era in Hamilton County, Tennessee.
P640

Patterson, Caleb Perry The Negro in Tennessee, 1790-1865. New York: Negro Universities Press, 1922. Some mention of the Negro in the mountains.
P650 (LMC)

Patterson, Charles Paint Creek Miner. Huntington, W. Va.: Appalachian Movement Press, n.d. Famous labor songs from the Paint Creek incident.
P660

Patterson, Dean Charles "A Study of Two Areas for Future Supermarket Location in Johnson City, Tennessee." Master's thesis. East Tennessee State Univ., 1968.
P670 (ETSU)

Patterson, G. W. Devereux, Robert Eddins Soil Survey of Grayson County, Virginia. Washington: U. S. Department of Agriculture, Bureau of Chemistry and Soils, 1934.
D1950

Classification of Land Ownership in Bedford Co., Virginia. Charlottesville: Virginia Agricultural Experiment Station, 1958.
P680

Economic Land Classification of Augusta Co., Virginia. Charlottesville: Virginia Agricultural Experiment Station, 1945.
P690

Economic Land Classification of Botetourt Co., Virginia. Charlottesville: Virginia Agricultural Experiment Station, 1945.
P700

Economic Land Classification of Carroll County, Virginia. Charlottesville: Virginia Agricultural Experiment Station, 1950.
P710

Economic Land Classification of Clarke Co., Va. Charlottesville: Virginia Agricultural Experiment Station, 1952.
P720

Economic Land Classification of Culpeper Co., Va. Charlottesville: Virginia Agricultural Experiment Station, 1945.
P730

Economic Land Classification of Grayson Co., Va. Charlottesville: Virginia Agricultural Experiment Station, 1946.
P740

Economic Land Classification of Greene Co., Va. Charlottesville: Virginia Agricultural Experiment Station, 1945.
P750

Economic Land Classification of Loudoun Co., Va. Charlottesville: Virginia Agricultural Experiment Station, 1946.
P760

Economic Land Classification of Shenandoah County, Va. Charlottesville: Virginia Agricultural Experiment Station, 1951.
P770

Economic Land Classification of Smyth Co., Va. Charlottesville: Virginia Agricultural Experiment Station, 1951.
P780

Economic Land Classification of Wythe Co., Va. Charlottesville: Virginia Agricultural Experiment Station, 1949.
P790

Patterson, Robert A Narrative of the Campaign in the Valley of the Shenandoah in 1861. Philadelphia: Sherman and Co., 1865.
P800 (ASU)

Patteson, G. W. Jurney, Robert Campbell Soil Survey of Augusta County, Virginia. Washington: U. S. Department of Agriculture, Bureau of Chemistry and Soils, 1937.
J2850

Patton, Abel "Har Lampkins"; A Narrative of Mountain Life, On the Borders of the Two Virginians. New York: Abbey Press, 1901. Novel. Harry Lampkins teaches his first school on the West Virginia border where every new teacher must fight. The reader is apt to side with the schoolboys.
P810

Patton, Boyd J. Beverage, Woodrow Wilson Soil Survey, Marshall County, West Virginia. Washington: U. S. Department of Agriculture, Soil Conservation Service, 1960.
B3450

Soil Survey, Preston County, West Virginia. Fieldwork by David C. Taylor and others. Correlation by Arnold J. Baur. U. S. Soil Conservation Service Soil Survey, Series 1954, no. 3. Washington: Govt. Print. Off., 1959.
P820

Patton, James Biography of James Patton. Asheville: n.p., 186-. Biography of a land speculator who settled in the original Wilkes County.
P830

Patton, James Welch Unionism and Reconstruction in Tennessee, 1860-1869. 1934. Reprint. Gloucester, Mass.: P. Smith, 1966. Tennessee was the only southern state to escape military reconstruction.
P840 (ASU WCU)

Patton, Janet Whitney "The State Development Planning Process: Implementation of the Appalachian Regional Development Act of 1965 in West Virginia." Ph. D. Diss. Univ. of California, Berkeley, 1970.
P850

Patton, Sadie S. Buncombe to Mecklenburg: Speculation Lands. Forest City: Western N. C. Hist. Assn., 1955.
P860

Ghost Stories and Legends of the Mountains. Hendersonville, N. C.: Blue Ridge Specialty Printers, 1935.
P870

Patton, Sadie Smathers A Condensed History of Flat Rock (the Little Charleston of the Mountains). Asheville, N. C.: Church Print. Co., 1961.
P880 (ASU WCU LMC)

The Kingdom of the Happy Land. Asheville, N. C.: Stephens Press, 1957. History of an all black community on the North Carolina/South Carolina boundary. Founded by refugees after the Civil War, this commune had a king and queen.
P890 (ASU LMC)

Sketches of Polk County History. Hendersonville? N. C.: n.p., 1950.
P900 (ASU WCU LMC)

St. James Episcopal Church: Book of Memory, 1843-1950. n.p.: Western North Carolina Historical Assoc., 1953.
P910 (ASU)

Smathers from Yadkin Valley to Pigeon River: Smathers and Agner Families. Henderson, N. C.: Stephens Press, 1954.
P920 (ASU)

Short Stories and Legends of the Mountains. Hendersonville, N. C.: Blue Ridge Specialty Printers, 1935. Stories based on authentic mountain legends.
P930

The Story of Henderson County. Asheville, N. C.: Miller Print. Co., 1947.
P940 (ASU WCU LMC)

The Story of Henderson County. Asheville: Miller, 1947.
P950

Patton, William P. "Those Who Enroll for Vocational Agriculture in West Virginia, Considering Certain Scholastic Achievements and Some Background Factors." Master's thesis. West Virginia Univ., 1965.
P960

Patty, John C. Life of Lucius B. Compton. Cincinnati: Revivalist Press, 1941. Biography of a mountain evangelist.
P970

Paulding, James Kirke The Backwoodsman. Philadelphia: M. Thomas, 1818. Long narrative poem.
P980

Pauley, James H. "Early North Carolina Migrations into the Tennessee Country, 1768-1782: A Study in Historical Demography." Master's thesis. Middle Tennessee State Univ., 1969.
P990

Paulic, Anthony Lou Towards Solving the Low-Income Problem of Small Farmers in the Appalachian Area. Morgantown: West Virginia Univ. Agricultural Station, 1964.
P1010

Paulick, Anthony Leo "An Analysis of the Effects of Federal Farm Programs on Incomes of Appalachian Farmers." Ph. D. Diss. Univ. of Minnesota, 1963.
P1000

Paulsen, Kathryn comp. Witches' Potions and Spells. With decorations by Maggie Jarvis. Mount Vernon, N. Y.: Peter Pauper Press, 1971.
P1020 (ASU)

Paulson, Quentin Frank Ground-water Resources and Geology of Tuscaloosa County, Alabama. Prepared by the U. S. Geological Survey in ccoperation with the Tuscaloosa County Board of Revenue and the Geological Survey of Alabama. County Report, 6. Univ.: Alabama Geological Survey, 1962.
P1030 (ETSU)

Pavlick, Anthony Leo "An Analysis of the Effects of Federal Farm Programs on Incomes of Appalachian Farmers." Ph. D. Diss. Univ. of Minnesota, 1963.
P1040 (LMC)

Quality of Rural and Urban Housing in the Appalachian Region. Agricultural Economics Report, no. 52. Washington: Economic Research Service, Resource Development Economics Division, U. S. Dept. of Agriculture, 1964.
P1050 (LMC)

Towards Solving the Low-income Problem of Small Farmers in the Appalachian Area. Morgantown: West Virginia Univ. Agricultural Experiment Station, 1964.
P1060 (LMC)

Paxson, Frederic Logan History of the American Frontier, 1763-1893. Students's ed. Boston: Houghton Mifflin Co., 1924.
P1070 (ASU BC)

Paxton, Tom Ramblin' Boy, and Other Songs. Original drawing by Agnes Frieseu. Cover design by Ronald Clyne. Music edited by Milt Okum. New York: Oak Publications, 1965.
P1090 (ASU)

Paye, Burrall "A Political History of Morristown and Hamblen County, Tennessee." Master's thesis. Univ. of Tennessee, 1965. A history of politics and life in Hamblen County, Tennessee.
P1100

Payne, Joe G. "A Study of the Physical Education Program at the Junior High School, Johnson City, Tennessee." Master's thesis. East Tennessee State College, 1959.
P1110 (ETSU)

Payne, John Howard John Howard Payne to His Countrymen. Edited with an introduction by Clemeus DeBaillove. Miscellanea Publications. Athens: Univ. of Georgia Press, 1961. Includes accounts of his sojourn with the Cherokee and his imprisonment in Spring Place, Georgia.
P1120 (WCU)

Payne, John Howard, Jr. "A Vegetational Analysis of the Rattlesnake Ridge Area of Unaka Mountain, Unicoi County, Tennessee." Master's thesis. East Tennessee State Univ., 1966.
P1130 (ETSU)

Payton, Jacob S. ed. Asbury, Francis Journal and Letters. London: Epworth Press and Nashville, Tenn.: Abingdon Press, 1958.
A5060 (ASU BC WWC)

Peabody Coal Co. Peabody Atlas. Chicago: n.p., 1906. Atlas of coal resources and mines in the United States.
P1140 (BC)

Peace, Richard R. Geology and Ground-water Resources of Franklin County, Alabama: A Reconnaissance. Prepared by the U. S. Geological Survey. Bulletin, 72. Univ.: Alabama Geological Survey, 1963.
P1150 (ETSU)

Peacock, Mary Thomas The Circuit Rider and Those Who Followed. Sketches of Methodist Churches Organized before 1860 in the Chattanooga Area with Special Reference to Centenary. Chattanooga: Hudson, 1957. A history of Methodism in the Chattanooga Valley.
P1160

Peak, Texarado McKnight The McKnight Families and Their Descendants: Also the Wallace and Alexander Families. Austin, Texas: The author, 1965.
P1170 (ASU)

The McKnight Family and Their Descendants, Also the Wallaces, Alexander and English Families. 3rd ed. Austin, Texas: The author, 1969.
P1180 (ASU)

Peake, C. Rex Roan Mountain. Bakersville, N. C.: Roan View Gift Shop, 1964. Tribute to a beautiful mountain, formed for its rhododendron.
P1190 (LMC)

Peake, Ora Brooks A History of the United States Indian Factory System, 1795-1822. n.p.: n.p., n.d. History of a systematized trading system with the Indians.
P1200

Pearce, Albert "The Growth and Overdevelopment of the Kentucky Coal Industry, 1912-1929." Microfilm. Master's thesis. Univ. of Kentucky, 1930.
P1210 (ASU)

Pearce, John E. The Superfluous People of Hazard, Kentucky. Hazard, Ky.: The author, 1963. Tongue in cheek discussion of migration, the population of a coal town, coal industry problems, and city services.
P1220

Pearce, Kearney C. ed. Isbell, Robert Lee The World of My Childhood. Lenoir, N. C.: Lenoir News-Topic, 1955.
I970 (ASU LMC)

Pearl, Minnie Christmas at Grinder's Switch. New York: Abingdon, 1963. An hilarious account of Christmas in the Tennessee Mountains.
P1230 (LMC)

Pearman, Jack Richard "A Survey of the Vascular Plants of the Sinking Creek Area of Carter County, Tennessee." Master's thesis. East Tennessee State College, 1956.
P1240 (ETSU)

Pearsall, Marion Little Smoky Ridge: The Natural History of a Southern Appalachian Neighborhood. Univ.: Univ. of Alabama Press, 1959. Sociological and anthropological study of a Tennessee community.
P1250 (ASU WCU LMC MHC ETSU WWC FC UNCA)

"Some Aspects of Culture Change in A Mountain Neighborhood of East Tennessee." Ph. D. Diss. The Univ. of California, Berkeley, 1951.
P1260 (ASU)

Pearse, John Teach Yourself Appalachian Dulcimer. London: Folk Dance and Song Society, 1966.
P1270

Pearson, Cora Wallace The Double Standard. North Wilkesboro, N. C.: Pearson Pub. Co., 1966. Novel of a western North Carolina girl who leaves home in disgrace because of her pregnancy.
P1280

Pearson, Edmund Lester Queer Books. Garden City, N. Y.: Doubleday, Doran and Co., 1928. Includes some of the horrors written about the mountains, including Dugger's BALSAM GROVES OF GRANDFATHER MOUNTAIN.
P1290 (ASU LMC)

Pearson, James Larkin Castle Gates (a Book of Poems) Through Which the Knowing Ones Are Admitted into Some of My Castles in Spain. Moravian Falls, N. C.: Pearson Print. Co., 1908. Larkin is a western North Carolina poet and poet laureate of North Carolina.
P1300 (ASU)

Early Harvest: The First Experimental Poems of a Self-taught Farm Boy. Guilford College, N. C.: Pearson Pub. Co., 1952.
P1310 (ASU)

Fifty Acres, and Other Poems. Wilkesboro, N. C.: Pearson Pub. Co., 1933.
P1320 (ASU)

My Fingers and My Toes. Complete Poems of James Larkin Pearson. Compiled and promoted by Wilkes Community College. Nashville: Ingram Book Co., 1971.
P1330 (ASU LMC)

Pearson's Poems. Boomer, N. C.: The author, 1924. A boomer, in mountain parlance, is a squirrel. In this instance the place name speaks volumes about the poet.
P1340 (ASU)

Plowed Ground, Humorous and Dialect Poems. Guilford College, N. C.: Pearson Pub. Co., 1949.
P1350 (ASU)

Selected Poems. Edited with an introduction by Walter Blackstock. Old North State Poets, series 1, no. 1. Charlotte, N. C.: McNally, 1960.
P1360 (ASU LMC)

Pearson, Linda S. "Youth Involvement in Swain County." Master's thesis. Western Carolina Univ., n.d.
P1370 (LMC)

Pearson, Thomas Gilbert Birds of North Carolina. Raleigh, N. C.: Edwards, 1919.
P1380 (WWC)

Birds of North Carolina. Revised by David L. Wray and Harry T. Davis. Raleigh, N. C.: Bynum Print. Co., 1959.
P1390 (ASU WWC)

Peattie, Donald Culross American Heartwood. Illustrated by David Hendrickson. Boston: Houghton, 1949.
P1400 (WCU)

Journey into America. Illustrated by Lynd Ward. Boston: Houghton, 1943. Includes accounts of western North Carolina and other mountain areas.
P1410 (WCU)

Pearson's Falls Glen: Its Story, Its Flora, Its Birds. Tryon, N. C.: Tryon Garden Club, 1962. Account of a western North Carolina resort area.
P1420 (WWC)

Up Country. A Story of the Vanguard. New York: D. Appleton and Co., 1928. A novel of a young girl's journey from England to her new home in the Blue Ridge Mountains.
P1430 (ASU)

Peattie, Elia Wilkinson Annie Laurie and Azalea. Chicago: Reilly and Britten, 1913. Novel about two western North Carolina girls.
P1440

Azalea's Silver Web. Chicago: Reilly and Britten, 1915. Novel about a western North Carolina mountain girl.
P1450

Azalea: The Story of a Girl in the Blue Ridge Mountains. Illustrated by Hazel Roberts. Chicago: Reilly and Britton Co., 1912. Touching story of the Blue Ridge Mountains.
P1460 (ASU WCU)

A Mountain Woman. 1896. Reprint. Freeport, N. Y.: Books for Libraries Press, 1969. A sensitive character study of a mountain woman.
P1470 (ASU)

The Shape of Fear, and Other Ghostly Tales. Short Story Index Reprint Series. Freeport, N. Y.: Books for Libraries Press, 1969.
P1480 (WCU)

The Wander Weed. Chicago: Charles H. Sergel and Co., 1923. Eight plays; some with mountain background.
P1490

Peattie, Louise R. Peattie, Donald Culross Up Country. A Story of the Vanguard. New York: D. Appleton and Co., 1928.
P1430 (ASU)

Peattie, Roderick ed. The Great Smokies and the Blue Ridge: The Story of the Southern Appalachians. The contributors: Edward S. Drake, Ralph Erskine, Alberta Pierson Hannum and others. American Mountain Series, vol. 1. New York: Vanguard Press, 1943. A well-written account of life and travel in the Southern Appalachians.
P1500 (WCU ASU LMC ETSU MHC WWC)

Peck, Elizabeth Sinclair Berea's First Century, 1855-1955. Lexington: Univ. of Kentucky Press, 1955.
P1510 (ASU LMC)

Nurses in Time. Berea, Ky.: Berea College, 1963. Developments in nursing education at Berea College 1898-1963.
P1520

Tibb's Flooders. New York: House of Field, 1941. A tale of the Ohio River Flood of 1937.
P1530

Peck, Millard Economic Utilization of Marginal Lands in Nicholas and Webster Counties, West Virginia. Contribution from the Bureau of Agricultural Economics in cooperation with the West Virginia Agricultural Experiment Station. Technical Bulletin, no. 303. Washington: U. S. Department of Agriculture, 1932.
P1540

Peck, Samuel Minturn Alabama Sketches. Chicago: A. C. McClurg and Co., 1902. Some sketches of the mountain regions.
P1550 (ASU)

Pectol, Loretta L. "A Speech Improvement Program in Kindergarten of the Johnson City, Tennessee, Public School System." Master's thesis. East Tennessee State Univ., 1969.
P1560 (ETSU)

Pederson, Fred C. The Forests of the Valley Coal Fields of Virginia. Charlottesville, Va.: Univ. of Va., 1925.
P1570

Peel, Alfreda Marion Witch in the Mill. Richmond: Dietz Press, 1947. A tale of the supernatural.
P1580 (ASU LMC FC)

Peele, W. J. comp. Historical and Literary Activities in North Carolina, 1900-1905. Goldsboro, N. C.: Nash Brothers, 1904.
P1590 (LMC)

Peirce, Neal R. The Border South, States; People, Politics, and Power in the Five States of the Border South. New York: W. W. Norton and Co., Inc., 1975.
P1600

Peithmann, Irvin M. Red Men of Fire, a History of the Cherokee Indians. With a foreword by N. B. Johnson. Springfield, Ill.: C. C. Thomas, 1964.
P1610 (LMC MHC)

Pelton, Mabell Shippie Clarke see Smith, Mabell Shippie Clarke

Pelton, Robert W. Snake Handlers: God-Fearers? or, Fanatics? Nashville: T. Nelson, 1974.
P1620

Pemberton, Olson "Educational, Economic and Community Survey of Scott County, Tennessee." Master's thesis. Univ. of Tennessee, 1934.
P1630

Pen and Plate Club, Asheville, N. C. The Pen and Plate Club of Asheville, North Carolina. 1904-1929. Asheville, North Carolina: The Inland Press, 1929. Club sponsors programs on regional literature and history.
P1640 (ASU)

Pence, Joe Allen "A Study of Some Differentiating Characteristics of Dropouts and Graduates of Lamar and Jonesboro High Schools." Master's thesis. East Tennessee State Univ., 1969.
P1650 (ETSU)

Pendexter, Hugh Red Belts. Garden City, N. Y.: Doubleday, Page and Co., 1920. A novel of the trans-Appalachian settlements of the 18th century.
P1660 (ASU WCU BC)

Pendleton, Lee Indian Massacres in Montgomery County, 1775-1776; Drapers Meadow Massacre Retold. Also, Fort Vause and Its Traditions. Christiansburg, Va.: n.p., 1968.
P1670

Pendleton, Lewis Beauregard Corona of the Nantahalas, A Romance. New York: The Merriam Co., 1895. A fantastic tale of fancy folk lost and rediscovered in the Nantahala Gorge.
P1680

Pendleton, William C. History of Tazewell County and Southwest Virginia 1748-1920. Richmond: W. C. Hill Print. Co., 1920. A very well-written county history.
P1690 (ASU ETSU LMC)

Political History of Appalachian Virginia 1776-1927. Dayton, Va.: The Shenandoah Press, 1927. Author believes the most deadly peril is political corruption.
P1700 (ASU WCU ETSU LMC)

Penhallegon, William James Building Sandstones of Northern Alabama. Published in cooperation with the Tennessee Valley Authority. Survey, 1940. Circular, no. 13. Univ.: Alabama Geological Survey, 1940.
P1710 (ETSU)

Penland School of Handicraft, Penland, N. C. Catalog. Penland: The school, 1962. Penland is one of the more famous schools of handicrafts in the Southern Highlands.
P1720 (ETSU)

Penley, Larry Howard "A Baptist People and the Events Leading to the Formation of the Three Forks Association." Master's thesis. Appalachian State Teachers College, 1964. The Three Forks Association is the oldest Baptist association in the North Carolina mountains.
P1730 (ASU)

Pennell, Joseph Stanley The History of Rome Hanks and Kindred Matters. New York: C. Scribner's Sons, 1944. The story of a Carolina mountaineer's adventures in the larger world.
P1740 (ASU)

Pennington, Lee Appalachia, My Sorrow: A Play for Voice. Middletown? Ky.: n.p., 1971. Pennington's attempt to capture Appalachia's voices. Excellent poetry.
P1750 (ASU)

April Poems. Brooklyn: Poetry Preview, 1970. Fine poetry from the hills.
P1760

The Dark Hills of Jesse Stuart: A Consideration of Symbolism and Vision in the Novels of Jesse Stuart. Cincinnati: Kentucky Writers Guild, Harvest Press, 1967. Excellent volume of criticism of Stuart's work in symbolism by a Kentucky author.
P1770 (LMC)

Scenes from a Southern Road. Smithtown, N. Y.: J.R.D. Pub. Co., 1969.
P1780 (LMC ASU)

Pennsylvania Archives Muster Rolls of the Pennsylvania Volunteers in the War of 1812-1814. 1890. Reprint. Excerpted. Baltimore: Genealogical Pub. Co., 1967.
P1790 (ASU)

Pennsylvania, Bituminous Coal Research see Bituminous Coal Research

Pennsylvania, Department of Mines and Mineral Industries Operation Scarlift, the After-Effects of Over 100 Years of Coal Mining In Pennsylvania and Current Programs to Combat Them. Harrisburg: Dept. of Mines and Mineral Industries, 1967.
P1800

Pennsylvania, Division of Sanitary Engineering Water Pollution Control In the Monongahela River Basin. Harrisburg: Division of Sanitary Engineering, 1963.
P1810

Pennsylvania, Economic Development Council of North-eastern Pennsylvania Overall Economic Development Program for the Counties of Carbon, Lackawanna, Luzerne, Monroe, Pike, Schuylkill, Wayne, in the Northeastern Pennsylvania Economic Development District. Wilkes-Barre, Pa.: The council, 1967.
P1820 (ASU)

Pennsylvania, General Assembly, Joint State Government Commission Coal in Pennsylvania, Recent Developments and Prospects. Harrisburg: Joint State Government Commission, 1963.
P1830

Pennsylvania, Geological Survey Bituminous Coal Fields in Pennsylvania. 4 vols. Harrisburg: Pa. Geological Survey, 1925.
P1840

Pennsylvania, State Planning Board Capability of Local Government in the Stroudsburg Area, Monroe County. A study prepared under the auspices of the Appalachian Regional Commission. Wilkes Barre: Pennsylvania Economy League, 1969.
P1850 (ASU)

An Economic Background for Regional Planning in the Anthracite Counties. Harrisburg: The board, 1952.
P1860

Pennsylvania Appalachian Development Plan. Prepared to meet the requirements of the Appalachian Regional Commission. Harrisburg: The board, 1968.
P1870 (ASU WCU)

Pennsylvania Appalachian Development Plan: Revision for 1970. Harrisburg, Pa.: Dept. of Commerce, 1969.
P1880 (ASU)

A Rationale for Public Investment in Appalachia Pennsylvania: An Interim Statement. Prepared by the board as advisor to the Pennsylvania state member on the Appalachian Regional Commission. Harrisburg: The board, 1966.
P1890

Pennsylvania, Topographical and Geological Survey Commission Geologic Map of Southwest Pennsylvania. Harrisburg: W. S. Ray, 1914. A really fine topographical map. You can find headwaters for each little creek, compare relative elevations and get a feel for the countryside.
P1900

Pension List of 1818 1820. Reprint. Baltimore: Southern Book Co., 1955.
P1910

Pension List of 1818 Washington: Gales and Seaton, 1820.
P1920

Pension Roll of 1835 4 vols. Baltimore: Genealogical Pub. Co., 1968.
P1930

Pensioners of the Revolutionary War Struck off the Roll, with added Index to States Baltimore: Genealogical Pub. Co., 1969.
P1940

Pentecost, Percy M. "A Corporate History of Knoxville, Tennessee, before 1860." Master's thesis. Vanderbilt Univ., 1946.
P1950

People's Appalachia vol. 1-, March, 1970-. Morgantown, W. Va.: People's Appalachia Research Collective, irregular.
P1960 (ASU BC)

Peoples Appalachian Research Collective Appalachia's People, Problems, Alternatives. vol. 1-. Morgantown, W. Va.: The collective, 1971-. Part V, "Resources," is an issue-oriented collection of general titles, films and resources people.
P1970 (BC ASU)

Appalachia's People, Problems, Alternatives; an Introductory Social Science Reader. Morgantown: The collective, 1971-.
P1980 (BC ASU)

Peplies, Robert Waldemar "Occupance Formation Concept: A Case Study of the Asheville Basin." Ph. D. Diss. Univ. of Georgia, 1968.
P1990 (LMC)

Pepper, J. F. Geology of the Bedford Shale and Berea Sandstone in the Appalachian Basin. U. S. Geological Survey Professional Paper, no. 259. Washington: Govt. Print. Off., 1954.
P2000

Pepper, Nellie Whan The Young Mrs. Blennerhasset: A Novel of Early Days in West Virginia. New York: Exposition Press, 1964. A novel of the Burr conspiracy in West Virginia.
P2010

Percy, Alfred Old Place Names. Madison Heights, Va.: Percy Press, 1950. Includes place names from the west central and Blue Ridge areas of Virginia.
P2020

Perdue, Mabel J. "The Relation of the Hot Lunch Program to the Progress of Pupils in the Deep Water School, West Virginia." Master's thesis. Marshall College, 1952.
P2030

Perkins, David Cullen The Use of Hostile Verbs by Male Committed Youthful Offenders. Master's thesis. Appalachian State Univ., 1972. The subjects for this study were inmates at the Watauga Prison Camp, Boone, North Carolina.
P2040 (ASU)

Perkins, Edward L. Guidelines for an Appalachian Airport System. Phase II of a two-part study prepared for the Appalachian Regional Commission by Management and Economics Research Incorporated, Palo Alto, Cal. Appalachian Research Report, no. 3. Washington: Appalachian Regional Commission, 1967.
P2050 (ASU WCU)

Perkins, Robert Burford, Arthur E. Annual Field Trip of the Appalachian and Pittsburgh Geological Societies in the Great Valley in West Virginia. Morgantown, W. Va.: n.p., 1964?
B8530 (ETSU)

Perkins, S. O. Hardison, Robinson B. Soil Survey of Ashe County, North Carolina. Washington: U. S. Department of Agriculture, Bureau of Soils, 1914.
H2170

Jurney, Robert Campbell Soil Survey of Wilkes County, North Carolina. Washington: U. S. Department of Agriculture, Bureau of Soils, 1921.
J2950

Perkins, Samuel Oscar Soil Survey, Cherokee County, North Carolina. U. S. Bureau of Plant Industry, Soils, and Agricultural Engineering Soil Survey Report, Series 1941, no. 2. Washington: Govt. Print. Off., 1951.
P2070

Soil Survey, Clay County, North Carolina. Prepared in cooperation with the North Carolina Department of Agriculture and the North Carolina Agricultural Experiment Station Soil Survey Report, Series 1935, no. 19. Washington: U. S. Department of Agriculture, Bureau of Plant Industry, 1941.
P2080

Soil Survey, Henderson County, North Carolina. Prepared in cooperation with the North Carolina Department of Agriculture and the North Carolina Agricultural Experiment Station. Soil Survey Report, Series 1937, no. 9. Washington: U. S. Department of Agriculture, Bureau of Plant Industry, Soils, and Agricultural Engineering, 1943.
P2100

Soil Survey, Mitchell County, North Carolina. Soil Survey Report, Series 1939, no. 14. Washington: U. S. Bureau of Plant Industry, Soils, and Agricultural Engineering, 1952.
P2110

Soil Survey, Swain County, North Carolina. Prepared in cooperation with the North Carolina Department of Agriculture, the North Carolina Agricultural Experiment Station, and the Tennessee Valley Authority. Soil Survey Report, Series 1937, no. 18. Washington: U. S. Department of Agriculture, Bureau of Plant Industry, Soils, and Agricultural Engineering, 1947.
P2120

Soil Survey, Transylvania County, North Carolina. Prepared in cooperation with the North Carolina Agricultural Experiment Station and the Tennessee Valley Authority. Soil Survey Report, Series 1938, no. 17. Washington: U. S. Department of Agriculture, Bureau of Plant Industry, Soils, and Agricultural Engineering, 1948.
P2130

Yancey County, North Carolina. Soil Survey Report, Series 1939, no. 15. Washington: U. S. Bureau of Plant Industry, Soils and Agricultural Engineering, 1952.
P2140

Perkins, Samuel Oscar and others Soil Survey of Buncombe County, North Carolina. Prepared in cooperation with the North Carolina Department of Agriculture and State Agricultural Experiment Station. Field Operations, 1920. Washington: U. S. Department of Agriculture, Bureau of Soils, 1923.
P2060

Soil Survey of Greene County, Pennsylvania. Prepared in cooperation with the Pennsylvania State College School of Agriculture and Experiment Station, and the Pennsylvania Department of Internal Affairs, Bureau of Topographic and Geological Survey. Field Operations, 1921. Washington: U. S. Department of Agriculture, Bureau of Soils, 1925.
P2090

Perrin, Alfred H. From Bishop Percy (1765) to John Jacob Niles (1974): 340 Books of Ballads and Songs in the Berea College Collection. Berea, Ky.: Hutchins Library of Berea College, 1974.
P2150 (BC ASU)

Mountain Fiction From Addington to Zugsmith: 924 Works of Fiction by Southern Appalachian Authors, Or With Southern Appalachian Settings. Berea, Ky.: Hutchins Library of Berea College, 1972. An updated reissue of Perrin's 1970 listing of mountain fiction.
P2160

A Shelf List of More than 760 Works of Fiction. Berea, Ky.: Hutchins Library of Berea College, 1970.
P2170

Perrin, Alfred H. ed. Ayer, Perley Seeking a People Partnership: Eleven Speeches. Berea, Ky.: Council of the Southern Mountains, 1969.
A5830 (ASU LMC MHC WCU BC)

Perrin, Richard K. A Survey of Beef Production Patterns in the Mountains and Piedmont of North Carolina. Economics Information Report, no. 27. Raleigh: North Carolina State Univ., Department of Economics, 1972.
P2180 (LMC)

Perry, Catherine "Life of John Sevier." Master's thesis. Vanderbilt Univ., 1923. Biography of Sevier with special attention to land speculation and politics.
P2190

Perry, Dick Reflections of Jesse Stuart on a Land of Many Moods. 1st ed. New York: McGraw-Hill, 1971.
P2200 (BC ASU WCU LMC MHC)

Perry, E. A. Carter, Oliver Reuben Soil Survey, Chambers County, Alabama. Washington: U. S. Soil Conservation Service, 1959.
C1730

Fussell, Kenneth Eugene Soil Survey, Marshall County, Alabama. Washington: Govt. Print. Off., 1959.
F4090

Perry, H. H. Jurney, Robert Campbell Soil Survey, Smyth County, Virginia. Washington: U. S. Department of Agriculture, Bureau of Plant Industry, Soils and Agricultural Engineering, 1948.
J2930

Perry, H. H. and others Soil Survey, Wise County, Virginia. Revised by R. C. Jurney. Soil Survey, Series 1940, no. 12. Washington: U. S. Soil Conservation Service, 1954.
P2210

Perry, Henry Wacaster "A Sampling of the Folklore of Carter County, Tennessee." Master's thesis. George Peabody College, 1938.
P2220

Perry, Huey "They'll Cut Off Your Project": A Mingo County Chronicle. New York: Praeger Pubs., 1972. Perry is an organizer who helps people set up and run their own projects.
P2230 (ASU MHC WCU WWC)

Perry, Josef H. 1980 Population Projections for North Carolina Counties, with 1950, 1960 and 1970 Population by Age Groups. Raleigh: North Carolina Division of Community Planning, 1964.
P2240

Perry, L. Seat Weaving. 3rd ed. Peoria, Ill.: Chas. A. Bennett Co., Inc., Pubs., 1940. Originally published 1917. This is a classic work on caning and seat weaving.
P2250

Perry, Lester Forty Years Mountain Politics, 1930-1970. Parsons, W. Va.: McClain Print. Co., 1971. A West Virginia legislator details political corruption in his state.
P2260 (ASU LMC MHC WCU)

Perry, Octavia J. My Head's High From Proudness. Winston-Salem, N. C.: John F. Blair, 1963. Account of a Negro man's search for pride and independence in the mountains of North Carolina and Virginia.
P2270 (ASU)

Perry, Vernon F. "The Labor Struggle at Wilder, Tennessee." Master's thesis. Vanderbilt Univ., 1934. A violent labor struggle in a mountain industry.
P2280 (ASU)

Perry, Wilbur Don A History of Birmingham-Southern College, 1856-1931. Nashville: Methodist Pub. House, 1931.
P2290

Peterkins, George William A History and Record of the Protestant Episcopal Church in the Diocese of West Virginia. Charleston, W. Va.: Tribune Co., 1902.
P2300

Peters, J. T. History of Fayette County, West Virginia. Charleston, W. Va.: Jarrett Print. Co., 1926.
P2310 (ASU)

Peterson, Arthur G. Historical Study of Prices Received by Producers of Farm Products in Virginia, 1801-1927. Virginia Polytechnic Institute Technical Bulletin, no. 37. Richmond: Virginia Agricultural Experiment Station, 1928.
P2320 (LMC)

Peterson, Bill Coaltown Revisited: An Appalachian Notebook. Chicago: Regnery, 1972. A sad, powerfully-written expose of the land where the war on poverty was lost to an entrenched bureaucracy.
P2330 (ASU LMC ETSU WCU WWC BC)

Peterson, Clarence Stewart Consolidated Bibliography of County Histories in Fifty States in 1961, Consolidated 1935-1961. 2nd ed. 1961. Reprint. Baltimore: Genealogical Pub. Co., 1963.
P2340 (ASU)

Known Military Dead During the American Revolutionary War, 1775-1783. 1959. Reprint. Baltimore: Genealogical Pub. Co., 1967.
P2350 (ASU)

Peterson, David Bruce "The Factors Affecting Absenteeism in the Sixth, Seventh, and Eighth Grades at Barnes Elementary School, Washington County, Tennessee." Master's thesis. East Tennessee State Univ., 1969.
P2360 (ETSU)

Peterson, Elmer Theodore Big Dam Foolishness; the Problem of Modern Flood Control and Water Storage. Introd. Paul B. Sears. New York: Devin-Adair, 1954.
P2370

Peterson, Gene B. Sharpe, Laurie M. The Cleveland Southern In-Migrant Study; an Overview. Washington: Bureau of Social Science Research Inc., 1967.
S2440

Peterson, John M. Copeland, Lewis C. Estimating Tennessee's Tourist Business. Knoxville: Univ. of Tenn., Bureau of Business Research, 1955.
C7290 (ASU)

Peterson, M. J. Kinard, J. D. Farm Business Study of the Six Mile Area of Pickens County, 1940. n.p.: South Carolina Agricultural Experiment Station, 1942.
K2120 (ASU)

Peterson, Z. R. comp. Greene County, Tennessee: Early Marriage Bonds, 1782-1820. Typed for the Public Library of Fort Wayne, Allen County, Indiana. n.p.: n.p., n.d.
P2380

Peto, Florence American Quilts and Coverlets; A History of a Charming Native Art. New York: Chanticleer Press, n.d. Includes a manual of instruction.
P2390

Petracek, Ruth Woods Wallace, Cousin Clues. n.p.: n.p., 1973.
P2400

Petrey, K. D. ed. Tomorrow's People, a Storm in Harlan, Kentucky. In facsimile with a foreword by Jesse Stuart. Composed and compiled by the Writing of Poetry Class, University of Kentucky, Southeast Community College, Cumberland, Kentucky. Cincinnati: Kentucky Writers' Guild, Harvest Press, 1968. The book of poems, TOMORROW'S PEOPLE did indeed cause a storm in Harlan County.
P2410 (LMC)

Petro, James H. Soil Survey, Ross County, Ohio. Fieldwork by James H. Petro and others. Washington: U. S. Soil Conservation Service, 1967.
P2430

Petro, James H. and others Soil Survey, Fauquier County, Virginia. Soil Survey, Series 1944, no. 7. Washington: U. S. Soil Conservation Service, 1956.
P2420

Petro, Sylvester The Kingsport Strike. New Rochelle, N. Y.: Arlington House, 1967. Refers to labor difficulties at the Kingsport Press.
P2440 (ASU LMC BC)

Pettit, Florence Harvey How to Make Whirligigs and Whimmy Diddles and Other American Folkcraft Objects. New York: Crowell, 1972. A lovely, lucid, illustrated book of instructions.
P2450

Peyton, Elsie Mae Comin' Through the Gap. Burlington, Ky.: Pen and Hoe Press, 1953. About the Cumberland Gap and other scenic or historic places in Kentucky.
P2460

Peyton, Green Rain on the Mountain. Boston: Little, Brown and Co., 1934. Novel set in western Virginia. The countryside seems to be as much as a protagonist as the major characters.
P2470

Peyton, John Lewis The Adventures of My Grandfather. New limited ed. With an introduction and Peyton family genealogy by Bernard Peyton Chamberlain. Charlottesville, Va.: John Peyton Memorial Assoc. and Allen Co., 1963.
P2480 (ASU)

History of Augusta County, Virginia. 2nd ed. Containing a revised and enlarged index by Charles R. Carrier. Bridgewater, Va.: n.p., 1953.
P2490 (ASU)

Memoir of John Howe Peyton, in the Sketches of His Contemporaries, Together with Some of His Public and Private Letters, etc., Also a Sketch of Ann M. Peyton. Staunton, Va.: A. B. Blackburn and Co., 1894.
P2500 (ASU)

Phalen, W. C. Economic Geology of the Kenova Quadrangle, Kentucky, Ohio, and West Virginia. U. S. Geological Survey Bulletin, no. 349. Washington: Govt. Print. Off., 1908.
P2510

Pharr, R. F. LeVan, Donald C. Directory of the Mineral Industry in Virginia, 1966. Charlottesville: Virginia Division of Mineral Resources, 1966.
L1960

Phelan, James History of Tennessee: The Making of a State. (Xerox copy of the original, ASU) Boston: Houghton, Mifflin Co., 1888.
P2520 (ASU LMC BC)

Phelan, Mary Kay Martha Berry. New York: Crowell, 1972. Biography of the founder of a school for mountain children which has become a college.
P2530

Pheythyon, Harry The Rock Dust Remedy for Coal Mine Explosions; An Open Letter to the Operators in the 27th Bituminous District of Pennsylvania. Belle Vernon, Pa.: Belle Vernon Agency, 1926.
P2810

Philadelphia, Mayor's Office Record of Indentures of Individuals Bound Out As Apprentices, Servants and of German and other Redemptioneers in the Office of the Mayor of Philadelphia.
P2540

Philips, Claude S. "The Influence of the Baptist Church on Knoxville Government." Master's thesis. Univ. of Tennessee, 1950. A history of the Baptist Church in Knox County, Tennessee.
P2580

Phillippe, M. M. Jurney, Robert Campbell Soil Survey, Smyth County, Virginia. Washington: U. S. Department of Agriculture, Bureau of Plant Industry, Soils and Agricultural Engineering, 1948.
J2930

Phillips Academy, Andover, Massachusetts, Dept. of Archaeology Etowah Papers New Haven, Conn.: Yale Univ. Press, 1932. Archaeological expedition papers from the Etowah Mounds excavation near Cartersville, Georgia.
P2550

Phillips, Alexander Lacy Call of the Home Land; A Study of Home Missions. Richmond: Presbyterian Pub. Committee, 1906.
P2560

Phillips, C. D. Gooch, Ernest D. Changes in the Market Movement of Kentucky Livestock. Lexington: Kentucky Agricultural Experiment Station, 1960.
G2460

Phillips, Charles A Memoir of the Rev. Elisha Mitchell, D. D., Late Professor of Chemistry, Mineralogy and Geology in the University of North Carolina: Together with the Tributes of Respect to His Memory, by Various Public Meetings and Literary Associations, and the Addresses Delivered at the Re-interment of His Remains. By Rt. Rev. James H. Otey. Chapel Hill, N. C.: J. M. Henderson, 1858.
P2570 (ASU LMC)

Phillips, G. Howard Ohio Appalachia Regional Community Study. Columbus: Ohio State Univ., Agricultural Research and Development Center, 1968.
P2590 (ASU)

Phillips, James Monroe "The Attitudes of Students and Parents Toward the Division of Morristown, Tenn., High School." Master's thesis. East Tennessee State Univ., 1969.
P2600 (ETSU)

Phillips, Karen ed. Oxmoor House A Catalogue of the South. Birmingham, Ala.: Oxmoor House, 1974.
O1040 (ASU)

Phillips, Peggy Ann The Effect of Modern Dance Upon Strength and Flexibility in Selected College Students. Master's thesis. Appalachian State Teachers College, 1964. The subjects for this study were physical education majors at Appalachian State Teachers College, Boone, North Carolina.
P2610 (ASU)

Phillips, Perry Anderson, Lorena Handbook of Appalachian Materials. Charleston, W. Va.: West Virginia Department of Education, 1971.
A2300

Phillips, Samuel William Soil Survey of Belmont County, Ohio. Prepared in cooperation with the Ohio Agricultural Experiment Station. Soil Survey Report, Series 1927, no. 17. Washington: U. S. Department of Agriculture, Bureau of Chemistry and Soils, 1931.
P2620

Soil Survey: Fannin County, Georgia. Prepared in cooperation with the Georgia State College of Agriculture. Soil Survey Report, Series 1923, no. 7. Washington: U. S. Department of Agriculture, Bureau of Soils, 1928.
P2630

Soil Survey of Grant and Mineral Counties, West Virginia. Prepared in cooperation with the West Virginia Geological Survey. Field Operations, 1922. Washington: U. S. Department of Agriculture, Bureau of Soils, 1926.
P2640

Soil Survey of Nicholas County, West Virginia. Prepared in cooperation with the West Virginia Geological Survey. Field Operations, 1920. Washington: U. S. Department of Agriculture, Bureau of Soils, 1922.
P2650

Soil Survey of Tucker County, West Virginia. Prepared in cooperation with the West Virginia Geological Survey. Field Operations, 1921. Washington: U. S. Department of Agriculture, Bureau of Soils, 1925.
P2660

Soil Survey of Washington County, Ohio. Prepared in cooperation with the Ohio Agricultural Experiment Station. Soil Survey Report, Series 1926, no. 19. Washington: U. S. Department of Agriculture, Bureau of Chemistry and Soils, 1930.
P2670

Phillips, Thomas Elwood "A Study of Noise Levels at the College of Health Building in East Tennessee State University." Master's thesis. East Tennessee State Univ., 1972.
P2680 (ETSU)

Phillips, Ulrich Bonnell Life and Labor in the Old South. Boston: Little, Brown, 1949. Tangential segments on mountain life.
P2690 (LMC BC FC)

Phillips, William Battle Iron Making in Alabama. Geological Survey of Alabama: Univ. of Alabama, 1912.
P2700 (ASU)

Phlegar, Cornelia Ellen Backman Descendants of Samuel Bachman and wife Rachel Owen. Radford, Va.: Commonwealth Press, 1970.
P2710

Photiadis, John Changes in the Rural Southern Appalachian Community. (ETIC RC 003 131) Morgantown: Appalachian Center, West Virginia Univ. Library, 1969.
P2720 (ASU)

Community Size and Social Attributes in West Virginia. Morgantown: West Virginia Univ., n.d.
P2730 (WCU ASU)

Religion in an Appalachian State. Morgantown: West Virginia Univ., n.d.
P2740

Photiadis, John D. Change in Rural Appalachia: Implications for Action Programs. Philadelphia: Univ. of Pennsylvania Press, 1971.
P2750 (FC LMC WCU ETSU ASU BC)

Improving County School Systems in West Virginia, The School Bond Issues and Its Management. Morgantown: W. Va. Univ., App. Center, 1968.
P2760

Migration and Occupational Adjustment of West Virginians in the City. Morgantown: W. Va. Univ., Appalachian Center, 1974.
P2770

Rural Southern Appalachia and Mass Society, and Overview. Charleston, W. Va.: Center for Appalachian Studies and Development, 1967.
P2780 (ASU LMC)

Selected Social and Sociopsychological Characteristics of West Virginians in Their Own State and in Cleveland, Ohio. 2 vols. Appalachian Center Research Report, 3. Morgantown: West Virginia Univ., 1970.
P2790 (ETSU)

West Virginians in Their Own State and In Cleveland, Ohio. Morgantown: West Virginia Univ., n.d.
P2800 (ASU)

Pickel, Eugene "A History of Roane County to 1860." Master's thesis. Univ. of Tennessee, 1971. A history of pre-war Roane County, Tennessee.
P2820

Pickens, Nell Dry Ridge: Some of Its History, Some of Its People. n.p.: Weaverville: 1962. A survey of a Buncombe County, North Carolina community's legends, lore, and history.
P2830 (LMC ASU)

Pickeral, John Julian An Economic and Social Survey of Frederick County. Record. Extension Series, vol. 15, no. 2. Also Virginia County Surveys, 15.
P2840 (ASU LMC)

Pidgin, Charles Felton Blennerhassett: Or, The Degrees of Fate. A Romance Founded Upon Events in American History. Illustrated by Charles H. Stephens. 4th ed. Boston: C. M. Clark Pub. Co., 1901. A novel of West Virginia and the Burr Conspiracy.
P2850 (ASU WCU WWC BC)

Pieper, Mary G. "Church Organization in Bradley County, Tennessee, in 1950." Master's thesis. Univ. of Tennessee, 1952.
P2860

Pierce, C. I. Sawyer, W. K. Electrical and Hydraulic Flow Properties of Appalachian Petroleum Reservoir Rocks. Pittsburgh: Mines Bureau, 1971.
S610

Slagle, Franklin D. Densities and Porosities of Core Samples from Wells in Appalachian Oilfields. Pittsburgh: Mines Bureau, 1967.
S4130

Pierce, Harvey Cushman Seven Pierce Families. Strasburg, Va.: Shenandoah Pubs., 1936.
P2870

Pierce, Helen M. Warne, Alice E. An Economic Survey of Clinton Co., Pa. University Park: Penn. State Univ., Bureau of Business Research, 1958.
W840

Warne, Alice E. An Economic Survey of Monroe County, Conducted by the Bureau of Business Research, College of Business Administration, Penn. State Univ. in Cooperation with Pocono Mountains Chamber of Commerce, Stroudsburg, Pa. Univ. Park: Penn. State Univ., Bureau of Business Research, 1959.
W850

Pierce, Laurence Barry Surface Water in Tuscaloosa County, Alabama. County Report, 9. Univ.: Alabama Geological Survey, 1962.
P2880 (ETSU)

Pierce, Lloyd Franklin Fox, George Edmund Social and Economic Trends in Tennessee and Their Implications for Education. Johnson City: East Tennessee State College, 1957.
F2530 (ETSU)

Pierce, Mack W. "A Program for Mentally Retarded, Elizabethton City Schools." Master's thesis. East Tennessee State College, 1955.
P2890 (ETSU)

Piers, Maria Coles, Robert Wages of Neglect. Chicago: Quadrangle Books, 1969.
C5910 (ASU)

Pierson, Edna Church The Witch of Turner's Bald. Kingsport, Tenn.: Quickway Print. Center, 1971. A novel with a hint of the supernatural.
P2900 (ASU)

Pifer, Albert Donald The Daughter of the Smokies. Punta Gorda, Fla.: Eternal Light Press, 1966. Novel of a young girl in the Smokies.
P2910 (ASU)

Pike County, Kentucky, Health Department Annual Report. no. 1-, 1926-. n.p.: The department, annual.
P2920 (BC)

Pikl, I. James Copeland, Lewis C. Estimating Tennessee's Tourist Business. Knoxville: Univ. of Tenn., Bureau of Business Research, 1955.
C7290 (ASU)

Pilcher, George William Samuel Davies: Apostle of Dissent in Colonial Virginia. 1st ed. Knoxville: Univ. of Tennessee Press, 1971. Davies was an apostle of the Great Awakening although he was a Presbyterian. He was a moving force in providing Virginia's Negroes with churches or ministers.
P2930 (ASU)

Pilcher, Louis The Story of Hazard, Kentucky. Hazard: Hazard Herald, 1913. Promotional, historical and descriptive material on the city of Hazard.
P2940 (BC)

The Story of Jackson City (Breathitt County). Lexington, Ky.: Beckner Print. Co., 1914. Promotional and historical material on Jackson City and Breathitt County. Includes scant mention of "Bloody Breathitt's" troubled years.
P2950 (BC)

Pilcher, Mary Campbell Historical Sketches of Campbell, Pilcher and Kindred Families. Nashville, Tenn.: n.p., 1911.
P2960

Pinchot, Gifford Biltmore Forest: The Property of Mr. George W. Vanderbilt, and Account of its Treatment, and the Results of the First Year's Work. 1893. Reprint. American Environmental Studies. New York: Arno Press, 1970. Site of first Forestry School in the United States.
P2970 (LMC UNCA ASU)

Breaking New Ground. New York: Harcourt, 1947. An account of the development of the nation's first school of forestry.
P2980 (LMC BC)

Timber Trees and Forests of North Carolina. North Carolina Geological Survey Bulletin, no. 6. Winston, N. C.: MI & J. C. Stewart, 1897.
P2990 (UNCA ASU WCU LMC)

Pinckney, Cathey Ryan, Irene (Granny) Granny's Hillbilly Cookbook. Englewood Cliff, N. J.: Prentice-Hall, 1966.
R4470 (ASU BC)

Pine Mountain Settlement School, Pine Mountain, Harlan County, Kentucky Pine Mountain Bulletin. Pine Mountain: The school, n.d.
P3010 (BC)

Pine Mountain Settlement School, Pine Mountain, Harlan County, Kentucky, Guidance Institute Findings of the Pine Mountain Guidance Institute. Pine Mountain, Ky.: The institute, 1939.
P3000 (BC)

Pine Ridge Booster vol. 1-, 1924-. Pine Ridge, Ky.: Alvin Drew School, 7 issues a year.
P3020

Pinkerton, Allan The Molly Maguires and the Detectives. New York: Dover, 1973. An account of the relationship of the famed Pinkerton detectives, leading strikebreakers in the coal fields, and the Irish-dominated sect which brought terror to the Pennsylvania coal fields in an attempt to improve miners' pay and conditions.
P3030

Pinkett, Harold Thomas Gifford Pinchot: Private and Public Forester. Urbana: Univ. of Illinois Press, 1970.
P3040 (WCU LMC)

Pinkston, O. Estelle "A Projection for the Future Needs and Potentials of the Kingsport Center of East Tennessee State University." Master's thesis. East Tennessee State Univ., 1963.
P3050 (ETSU)

Pinnell, Lois M. French Creek Presbyterian Church: A Memorial to the 150 Years of Service of the French Creek Presbyterian Church. Parsons, W. Va.: McClain Print. Co., 1971.
P3060 (ASU)

Pino, Pietro "A Study of Academic Achievement of Band Students and Non-band Students, Blountville High School (1964-1967)." Master's thesis. East Tennessee State Univ., 1968.
P3070 (ETSU)

Piquet, John A. ed. Kingsport, City of Industries, Schools, Churches and Homes. Kingsport: Kingsport Rotary Club, 1937. History of Kingsport and Sullivan County, Tennessee.
P3080

Kingsport, the Planned Industrial City. Kingsport: Kingsport Rotary Club, 1946. History of Kingsport and Sullivan County, Tennessee.
P3090

Pitcher, June D. "Occupational Status and Reasons for Leaving the State of West Virginia." Master's thesis. West Virginia Univ., 1955.
P3100

Pittard, Mabel Baxter "The Coleman Scouts." Master's thesis. Middle Tennessee State Univ., 1953.
P3120

Pittard, Pen L. Alexander County's Confederates. Taylorsville, N. C.: n.p., 1960.
P3110

Prologue: a History of Alexander County, North Carolina. Taylorsville, N. C.: n.p., 1958.
P3130

Pittenger, William Daring and Suffering: A History of the Andrews Railroad Raid into Georgia in 1862. (Other titles: Capturing a Locomotive; The Great Locomotive Chase.) New York: War Pub. Co., 1887. Account of the exciting chase through the North Georgia mountains during a Civil War raid.
P3140 (ASU WCU)

The Great Locomotive Chase: A History of the Andrews Railroad into Georgia in 1862. 4th ed. (Other titles: Daring and Suffering; Capturing a Locomotive.) Philadelphia: Penn Pub. Co., 1893.
P3150 (ETSU)

Pitts, James E. Fulmer, John Leonard Kentucky Employment Trends from 1951 to 1963 with Projections to 1965-1975. Lexington: Bureau of Business Research, Univ. of Kentucky, 1965.
F3780

Fulmer, John Leonard Kentucky Employment Trends from 1951 to 1963, with Projections to 1965-75. Lexington: Univ. of Kentucky, Bureau of Business Research, 1965.
F3790

Pitts, John Abram Personal and Professional Reminiscences of an Old Lawyer. Kingsport: Southern, 1930. First published as weekly articles in the Nashville CITIZEN APPEAL, beginning in June, 1929.
P3160

Pittsburgh Geological Society Tectonics and Cambrianordovician Stratigraphy in the Central Appalachians of Pennsylvania. Guide book. Field conference, Sept. 19-21, 1963. Also sponsored by Appalachian Geological Society. Pittsburgh: The society, 1963. An interesting and readable account of the formation of the Central Appalachian mountains.
P3170 (ETSU)

Pittsburgh, Regional Planning Association Employment Trends in the Pittsburgh Metropolitan Area. Pittsburgh: Regional Planning Association, 1960.
P3180

Pittsburgh, University of Center for Regional Economic Studies Appalachian Regional Data Book, 1964. Pittsburgh: Center for Reg. Econ. Studies, 1964.
P3190

Pittston Mentality Huntington, W. Va.: Appalachian Movement Press, 1970. A 26 page indictment of the alleged policies and deeds of the Pittston Coal Company.
P3200

Plan of a Memorial for President James Monroe at "Oak Hill," Loudoun County, Virginia n.p.: n.p., n.d. Contains related papers and extracts.
P3210

Platt, Charles Malcolm 1855-1895 How Old Man Corn Held Possession. New York: Current Literature Pub. Co., 1894. A feud, a faulty land title, and a mountain farm figure in this story of the North Carolina hills.
P3220

Platt, Loula Roberts Queen of Appalachia Cook Book. n.p.: n.p., n.d.
P3230

The Pleasant Hill Baptist Church Constituted February 7, 1851, Centennial, Historical Sketch, 1851-1951 n.p.: n.p., 1951.
P3240

Ploch, Louis A. Buck, Roy Clark Factors Related to Changes in Social Participation in a Pennsylvania Rural Community. University Park: Agricultural Experiment Station, Pennsylvania State University, 1954.
B8220

Plumley, William Anderson, Lorena Handbook of Appalachian Materials. Charleston, W. Va.: West Virginia Department of Education, 1971.
A2300

Poems From the Hills. 1970- Charleston, W. Va.: Morris Harvey College, annual.
P3320

Plumley, William comp. Poems From the Hills, 1971. Charleston, W. Va.: MHC Publications, 1970 — v. annual. Great poetry from the Appalachian Region.
P3250 (ASU BC)

Plunkett, H. Dudley Bowman, Mary Jean Communication and Mountain Development: A Summary Report Two East Kentucky Studies. Washington: U. S. Department of Commerce, Economic Development Administration, 1969.
B5780

Elites and Change in the Kentucky Mountains. Lexington: Univ. Press of Kentucky, 1973. A study of hill folk responding to the encroachment of modern civilization.
P3260 (ASU MHC WCU BC)

Poate, Ernest M. The Trouble at Pinelands: A Detective Story. New York: Chelsea House, 1922. Suspense novel with a mountain setting.
P3270

Poe, Edgar Allan "A Tale of the Ragged Mountains" in The Complete Works of Edgar Allan Poe. New York: Thomas Y. Crowell and Co., 1902. Mystery story with Virginia's Ragged Mountains as a setting.
P3280 (ASU ETSU)

Poe, Nan Trantham Beautiful Upon the Mountains, the Story of a Kentucky Missionary. Roanoke, Va.: The author, 1952. Novel. Kentucky mountain mission setting. Trite plot and predictable ending.
P3290 (ASU)

Poe, Orlando M. Personal Recollections of the Occupation of East Tennessee and the Defense of Knoxville. n.p.: n.p., n.d. History of Knoxville during the Civil War and Reconstruction.
P3300

Poem no. 1-, 1967-. Huntsville, Ala.: Literary Guild, 3 times a year.
P3310

Poems From the Hills. 1970- Charleston, W. Va.: Morris Harvey College, annual.
P3320

Poetry Council of North Carolina Bay Leaves. no. 1-, 1952-. Raleigh: Poetry Council of North Carolina, n.d.
P3330 (ASU)

Pohlman, G. G. Patton, Boyd J. Soil Survey, Preston County, West Virginia. Washington: Govt. Print. Off., 1959.
P820

Polansky, Norman Albert Roots of Fertility. San Francisco: Jossey-Bass, 1972. Study of child abuse and social handicrafts in Appalachia.
P3340

Polk County Centennial Commission, Inc. Polk County Centennial: Souvenir Historical Booklet. Tryon, N. C.: The commission, 1955. A 32 page paean to Polk County, North Carolina on its one hundredth anniversary.
P3350

Polk County Historical Society Studies in Polk County History. no. 1, 1965. Benton: Polk Co. Hist. Soc., 1965.
P3360 (ASU BC)

Polk, Kenneth Knapp, Daniel Scouting the War on Poverty: Social Reform Politics in the Kennedy Administration. Lexington, Mass.: Heath Lexington Books, 1971.
K2740

Polk, William Tannahill Southern Accent: From Uncle Remus to Oak Ridge. New York: William Morrow, 1953. Scant mention of Appalachia despite the proper names in the title. Harris did some interesting early dialect work in the North Georgia mountains.
P3370 (LMC WWC BC)

Pollack, Barbara The Collectors: Dr. Claribel and Miss Etta Cone. With a portrait by Gertrude Stein. 1st ed. Indianapolis: Bobbs-Merrill, 1962. Claribel and Etta were sisters of industrialist Moses Cone. The family's interest in the arts is yet reflected at the Cone Craft Center on the Blue Ridge Parkway.
P3400 (ASU)

Pollard, Edward Albert The Virginia Tourist. Sketches of the Springs and Mountains of Virginia: Containing an Exposition of Fields for the Tourist in Virginia, Natural Beauties and Wonders of the State: Also Accounts of Its Mineral Springs. And a Medical Guide to the Use of the Waters, Etc., Etc. Illustrated by engravings from actual sketches. Philadelphia: J. B. Lippincott and Co., 1870.
P3380 (ASU BC)

Pollard, Edward Bagby Paul Judson: A Story of the Kentucky Mountains. Louisville: Baptist Argus, 1905. Mountain boy goes to a Baptist college and spends the rest of his life spreading the word and enjoying the rewards of the just.
P3390

Polley, Robert L. ed. America's Folk Art. Waukesha, Wis.: Country Beautiful Corp., 1971. Unfortunately little attention was paid to the southern mountains during the early years of folk art study. This book rectifies the error by the inclusion of some mountain artisans.
P3410 (ASU)

Pollock, George Freeman Skyland: The Heart of the Shenandoah National Park. With a foreword by Harry F. Byrd. n.p.: n.p., 1960.
P3420 (FC BC ASU WCU)

Pollock, Norman J. Outcomes of Vocational Retraining in West Virginia. Morgantown: West Va. Univ., 1965.
P3430

Pollock, Thomas Clarke ed. Thomas Wolfe at Washington Square. New York: New York Univ. Press, 1954. Western North Carolina's most famous author.
P3440 (WCU ASU)

Polsky, Thomas The Cudgel. New York: Dutton, 1950. The mountain setting is almost entirely incidental to the stock mystery plot.
P3450

Polson, Peggy Sketches of Early Watauga. Boone, N. C.: American Assoc. of University Women, Boone Branch, 1973. A book of beautifully executed sketches of Watauga's historic structures. Historical notes included.
P3460

Pomeroy, Kenneth Brownridge North Carolina Lands: Ownership, Use, and Management of Forest and Related Lands. Land Ownership Series. Washington: American Forestry Assoc., 1964.
P3470 (ASU LMC BC WCU UNCA)

Pond, George Edward The Shenandoah in 1864. New York: Scribners, 1883. Discusses the Shenandoah Valley Civil War Campaign in 1864, prior campaigns in the Valley, and the problems and prospects of the inhabitants as the war ended.
P3480 (BC)

Pool, Maria Louise Against Human Nature. New York: Harper, 1895. A New England spinster travels to North Carolina mountains to care for her friends' orphaned daughter until the girl marries and leaves the mountains. Two cultures clash humorously.
P3490 (BC ASU)

Dally. New York: Harper, 1891. Dally, an untutored mountain girl, goes north to live with a Massachusetts widow. Cultures clash.
P3500 (BC ASU)

In Buncombe County. Chicago: H. S. Stone & Co., 1896. Two northern ladies are scandalized by the North Carolina mountaineers in the Asheville, Buncombe County area.
P3510 (BC ASU LMC WCU)

The Red-bridge Neighborhood, A Novel. New York: Harper, 1898. More fiction about North Carolina mountain folk.
P3520 (LMC BC)

Poole, Ernest Nurses on Horseback. New York: Macmillan Co., 1932. An account of the Frontier Nursing Service and its impact on rural eastern Kentucky.
P3530 (ASU ETSU LMC BC WWC)

Poore, Benjamin P. ed. Trial of Andrew Johnson, President of the United States, before the Senate of the United States, on Impeachment by the House of Representatives for High Crimes and Misdemeanors. Rpt., Law, Politics, and History Series. 3 vols. in 2. New York: Da Capo, 1970. A complete transcript of the proceedings.
P3570

Poovey, Ruth Royal The Burke County Gold Rush. Prepared in conjunction with the Burke County Cultural Heritage Project, Title III, ESEA, 1967. n.p.: n.p., n.d.
P3540 (LMC)

Pope, Adelynne Hiller "Prelude to TVA: The Wadsworth-Kahn Bill, 1919-1921." Master's thesis. Trinity Univ., 1966.
P3550

Pope, Liston Millhand and Preachers, a Study of Gastonia. Yale Studies in Religious Education, 15. New York: Oxford Univ. Press, 1942. Gastonia, North Carolina is a mill town in the foothills of North Carolina. Many mountaineers relocated there were involved in the labor strikes.
P3560 (MHC)

Pope, Tilda Jones Jones, Erma Lee "A Preliminary Edition of a Reading Test For Use With Disadvantaged Children in the Primary Grades of the Southern Appalachian Region." East Tennessee State Univ., 1971.
J2300 (ETSU)

Population Schedule of the United States Census of 1850 (Seventh Census) for Warren County, Tennessee McMinnville: Womack, 1958.
P3580

Porcher, Francis Peyre Resources of the Southern Fields and Forests, Medical, Economical, and Agricultural. Being Also a Medical Botany of the Confederate States. 1863. Reprint. New York: Arno Press, 1970.
P3590 (LMC BC)

Porter, E. Russell When Cultures Meet. Cincinnati: Mayor's Friendly Relations Committee, 1962. Discussion of cultural clash between mountaineer and urbanite.
P3620 (BC ASU)

Porter, Eliot Appalachian Wilderness: The Great Smoky Mountains. Natural and human history by Edward Abbey. Epilogue by Harry M. Caudill. 1st ed. New York: E. P. Dutton and Co., 1970.
P3600 (UNCA BC ASU WCU ETSU)

Appalachian Wilderness: The Great Smoky Mountains. Natural and human history by Edward Abbey. Epilogue by Harry M. Caudill. New York: Dutton, 1973. A beautiful book of natural history mixed with a sad history of a hardy people.
P3610 (ASU BC)

Porter, Estelle Rawl " "They Are a Curious and Most Native Stock." The Southern Mountaineer in the Short-story." Master's thesis. Winthrop College, 1945.
P3630 (ASU)

Porter, H. C. Obenshain, S. S. Soil Survey, Russell County, Virginia. Washington: U. S. Department of Agriculture, Bureau of Plant Industry, Soils, and Agricultural Engineering, 1945.
O100 (BC)

Porter, Hobart Clarke Soil Survey, Tazewell County, Virginia. Prepared in cooperation with the Virginia Agricultural Experiment Station and the Tennessee Valley Authority. Soil Survey Report, Series 1938, no. 18. Washington: U. S. Department of Agriculture, Bureau of Plant Industry, Soils, and Agricultural Engineering, 1948.
P3660

Swann, Maurice Edward Soil Survey, Roane County, Tennessee. Washington: U. S. Department of Agriculture, Bureau of Plant Industry, 1942.
S9440

Porter, Hobart Clarke and others Soil Survey, Bland County, Virginia. Rev. by R. C. Jurney. Soil Survey, Series 1940, no. 15. Washington: U. S. Soil Conservation Service, 1954.
P3640

Soil Survey, Loudoun County, Virginia. Correlation by W. E. Hearn and W. S. Ligon. Soil Survey, Series 1951, no. 8. Washington: U. S. Soil Conservation Service, 1960.
P3650

Porter, Mary Colkey The Southern Highlanders of America. Pittsburgh: Women's General Missionary Society, n.d. Another missionary looks at the "pore mountaineer."
P3670 (BC ASU)

Porter, Nannie Francisco Blacks and Other Families. Richmond: The author, 1954.
P3680 (ASU)

Porter, Sara Lindsay C. The Common Problem. New York: Doubleday, 1929. A novel of human problems in the western North Carolina mountains.
P3690

Porter, Ward F. Availability for Employment of Rural People in the Upper Monongahela Valley. Morgantown: W. Va. Univ., 1956.
P3700

Elk Garden, West Virginia: A Reconnaissance Survey of a Problem Town. Bulletin no. 355-T. Morgantown: West Virginia Agricultural Experiment Station, West Virginia Univ., 1952.
P3710

Porter, William Sidney The Complete Works of O. Henry. New York: Doubleday, Doran and Co., 1923. Author has written five excellent short stories with mountain settings.
P3720

Posey, Thomas E. "The Labor Movement in West Virginia, 1900-1948." Ph. D. Diss. The Univ. of Wisconsin, 1946.
P3730

Posey, Walter Brownlow Frontier Mission: A History of Religion West of the Southern Appalachians to 1861. Lexington: Univ. of Kentucky Press, 1966.
P3740 (BC WWC)

The Presbyterian Church in the Old Southwest, 1778-1838. Richmond: John Knox Press, 1952. The term "Old Southwest" includes portions of Appalachia in Georgia, Tennessee and Alabama.
P3750 (BC LMC)

Religious Strife on the Southern Frontier. Walter Lynwood Fleming Lectures in Southern History. Baton Rouge: Louisiana State Univ. Press, 1965. Fascinating account of strife between religious sects.
P3760 (ASU LMC BC)

Possett, Emanuel Anthony Dictionary of Weaves; a Collection of All Weaves from Four to Nine Harness. Philadelphia: Textile Pub. Co., n.d. Two thousand weaves with directions for implementation.
P3770 (BC)

Post, Melville Davisson Dwellers in the Hills. New York: Putnam, 1901. Allegorical fiction about life in the southern mountains.
P3780

The Mountain Schoolteacher. New York: D. Appleton and Co., 1922. In a heavy-handed allegory, a teacher is killed by a mountain mob after a Christ-like life of service.
P3790 (ASU BC)

Uncle Abner, Master of Mysteries. New York: D. Appleton and Co., 1937. Mystery story with mountain setting.
P3800 (ASU BC)

Potentials for Expanding Agriculture Business in the Tennessee Valley Region n.p.: National Fertilizer Development Center, 1969.
P3810

Potomac Appalachian Trail Club, Washington, D. C. Guide to Paths in the Blue Ridge: The Appalachian Trail and Side Trails in Southern Pennsylvania, Maryland, and Virginia. Washington: The club, 1941.
P3820 (ASU)

Guide to Paths in the Blue Ridge: The Appalachian Trail and Side Trails in Southern Pennsylvania, Maryland, and Virginia. Washington: The club, 1950.
P3830 (ASU)

Guide to the Appalachian Trail and Side Trails in the Shenandoah National Park. 7th ed. (Previous titles: Guide to paths in the Blue Ridge; Guide to trails in the Shenandoah National Park.) Washington: The club, 1970.
P3840 (ETSU)

Guide to the Appalachian Trail: From the Susquehanna River to the Shenandoah National Park. 7th ed. Washington: The club, 1970.
P3850 (WCU ETSU LMC)

Guide to the Appalachian Trail in Central and Southwestern Virginia. 5th ed. Washington: The club, 1960.
P3860

Guide to the Appalachian Trail: Susquehanna River to the Shenandoah National Park. 5th ed. Washington: The club, 1960.
P3870

Guide to Trails in the Shenandoah National Park: The Appalachian Trail and Side Trails. 5th ed. Washington: The club, 1959.
P3880

Hiking, Camping, Mountaineering and Trailclearing Equipment. 7th ed. Washington: The club, 1950.
P3890 (ASU)

Pottery Collector's Newsletter vol. 1-, Oct., 1971-. Asheville, N. C.: n.p., monthly.
P3900 (BC)

Potts, J. Manning ed. Asbury, Francis Journal and Letters. London: Epworth Press and Nashville, Tenn.: Abingdon Press, 1958.
A5060 (ASU BC WWC)

Pound, Merritt B. Benjamin Hawkins, Indian Agent. Athens: Univ. of Georgia Press, 1951. Hawkins was one of the few fair-minded Indian Agents. His death in 1812 precipitated trouble with the Indians.
P3910

Poundstone, Sally "A Plan for Regional Library Development in Eastern Kentucky." Master's thesis. Univ. of Kentucky, 1955.
P3920

Powell, Hobart L. "A Comparative Study of the Relationship Between ACT Composite Scores and GPA of Washington County Students at East Tennessee State University, 1965-66." Master's thesis. East Tennessee State Univ., 1967.
P3940 (ETSU)

Powell, James Curtis "Farm Taxation and County Government in Overton, Clay and Pickett Counties, Tennessee." Master's thesis. Univ. of Tennessee, 1930.
P3930

Powell, Jules V. Costs of Marketing Appalachian Apples. U. S. Department of Agriculture Marketing Research Report, 300. Washington: Agricultural Marketing Service, Marketing Research Division, 1959.
P3950

Powell, Levi M. Who Are These Mountain People? An Intimate Historical Account of Southern Appalachia. 1st ed. An Exposition-Lochinvar Book. New York: Exposition Press, 1966. Intimate historical account of Appalachia.
P3960 (ASU WCU LMC ETSU MHC BC)

Powell, Scott History of Marshall County, from Forest to Hill. A Story of the Early Settlement and Development of Marshall County, W. Va., with Incidents of Early Life and Roster of Soldiers of the Several Wars, with Other Matters of Interest. Moundsville, W. Va.: n.p., 1925.
P3970 (BC ASU)

Powell, William S. Joint Committee on North Carolina Literature and Bibliography of the North Carolina English Teachers Association and the North Carolina Library Association North Carolina Fiction, 1734-1957: An Annotated Bibliography. Chapel Hill: University of North Carolina Library, 1958.
J2210 (ASU MHC)

Powell, William S. ed. Crittenden, Charles Christopher ed. 100 Years, 100 Men: 1871-1971. Raleigh, N. C.: Edwards and Broughton, 1971.
C8830 (ASU)

Powell, William Stevens The North Carolina Gazetteer. Chapel Hill: Univ. of North Carolina Press, 1968.
P4010 (BC ASU LMC MHC UNCA)

North Carolina: A Students' Guide to Localized History. Localized History Series. New York: Bureau of Publications, Teachers College, Columbia Univ., 1965.
P4020 (LMC WCU)

The Regulators in North Carolina: A Documentary History, 1759-1776. Raleigh, N. C.: State Dept. of Archives and History, 1971.
P4030 (ASU)

Powell, William Stevens comp. North Carolina County Histories: A Bibliography. Raleigh, N. C.: State Department of Archives and History, 1954.
P3980 (MHC)

North Carolina County Histories: A Bibliography. Library Studies, no. 1. Chapel Hill: Univ. of North Carolina Library, 1958.
P3990 (ASU)

Powell, William Stevens ed. North Carolina Fiction 1734-1957: An Annotated Bibliography. Chapel Hill: Univ. of North Carolina Press, 1958. Contains a review giving content, locality and an evaluation of each book.
P4000 (ASU MHC)

Power, F. Ray The School Law of West Virginia. Charleston, W. Va.: Jarrett Print. Co., 1939.
P4040 (ASU)

Power, W. Robert Field Excursion: The Georgia Marble District. Geological Society of America, Southeastern Section Guidebook, no. 1. Atlanta: Georgia Department of Mines, Mining and Geology, 1962.
P4050 (ETSU)

Powers, Caleb My Own Story: An Account of the Conditions in Kentucky Leading to the Assassination of William Goobel, Who Was Declared Governor of the State, and My Indictment and Conviction on the Charge of Complicity in His Murder. Illustrated from photographs. Indianapolis: Bobbs-Merrill Co., 1905.
P4060 (ASU)

Powers, Frederick William In the Shadow of the Cumberlands; a Story of Kentucky Mountain Life. Columbus, Ohio: Champlin Print. Co., 1904. A Tennessee moonshiner has a host of troubles. He dies and the pious daughter and the revenuer.
P4070

Powers, Nick Hall, Mary Boilin' n Bakin' in Boogar Hollow. Lindale, Ga.: Country Originals, 1971.
H850 (BC ASU)

Barefoot in Boogar Hollow; Yesterday's Sayings to Live by Today. Lindale, Ga.: Country Originals, 1971.
P4080 (BC LMC ASU)

Powers, Ozelle S. "A History of Education in McMinn County, Tennessee." Master's thesis. Univ. of Tennessee, 1950.
P4090

Powers, Wilann Hall, Mary Boilin' n Bakin' in Boogar Hollow. Lindale, Ga.: Country Originals, 1971.
H850 (BC ASU)

Powers, Nick Barefoot in Boogar Hollow; Yesterday's Sayings to Live by Today. Lindale, Ga.: Country Originals, 1971.
P4080 (BC LMC ASU)

Prater, Otto "Economic History of White County, Tennessee." Master's thesis. George Peabody College, 1932. A history of business and industry in White County, Tennessee.
P4100

Pratt, Audree Webb "Unicoi County Court: 1876-1918." Master's thesis. East Tennessee State College, 1960.
P4110 (ETSU)

Pratt, C. W. "The History and Development of Education in Knox County, Tennessee." Master's thesis. Univ. of Tennessee, 1959.
P4120

Pratt, D. C. Clinch Mountain Gems. Bristol, Tenn.: The King Print. Co., 1963. The poems in this collection reflect the writer's thoughts about God, friendship, home and habits.
P4130

Country Voices. Bristol, Tenn.: The King Print. Co., 1960. The fifty-two poems in this collection are concerned with home and country life.
P4140

Russell County. Bristol, Tenn.: The King Print. Co., 1968. This is a record of the development of Russell County, Virginia.
P4150

Elk Garden Tales. Bristol, Tenn.: The King Print. Co., 1968. A collection of twelve stories that are told repeatedly by the people of the Elk Garden area of Russell County, Virginia about strange phenomena.
P4160

Exploring with Verses. Bristol, Tenn.: Preston Print. Co., 1971.
P4170 (LMC)

Russell County, Virginia's Bluegrass Empire. Bristol: King Pub. Co., 1968. History of Russell County, Virginia with descriptions of interesting features.
P4180 (ASU)

Pratt, Joseph H. Zircon, Monazite and Other Minerals Used in Production of Chemical Compounds Employed in the Manufacture of Lighting Apparatus. Bulletin no. 25. Raleigh: North Carolina Geological and Economic Survey, 1916.
P4190 (LMC)

Pratt, Joseph Hyde Talc and Pyrophyllite Deposits in North Carolina. North Carolina Geological Survey Economic Papers, no. 3. Raleigh, N. C.: E. M. Uzzell, 1900.
P4200 (ASU)

Western North Carolina Facts, Figures, Photographs. Asheville, N. C.: Inland Press, 1925. A guide to western North Carolina's attractions, resources, and industries.
P4210 (LMC WCU)

Corundum and the Peridotites of Western North Carolina. Report, vol. 1. Raleigh, N. C.: Geological Survey, 1904.
P4220 (ASU WCU LMC)

The Tin Deposits of the Carolinas. North Carolina Geological Survey Bulletin, no. 19. Raleigh, N. C.: E. M. Uzzell and Co., public printers and binders, 1904.
P4230 (WCU)

Pratt, L. J. The Unfortunate Mountain Girl: A Collection of Miscellanies in Prose and Verse. Middlebury, Vt.: Register and Job Office, 1854.
P4240 (LMC)

Pratt, Wilburn J. Bramlett, Gene A. Economic Development in the Ohio River Valley Region. Lexington, Ky.: Spindletop Research, 1964.
B6280

Street, James A. Ohio River Valley Population: Trends and Projections, 1930-1970. Lexington, Ky.: Spindletop Research, 1963.
S7850

Preble, John W. Land of Canaan. Plain Tales from the Mountains of West Virginia. Parsons, W. Va.: McClain Print. Co., 1960. Eight stories from the West Virginia hills.
P4250 (ETSU BC)

Land of Canaan: Plain Tales from the Mountains of West Virginia. Parsons, W. Va.: McClain Print. Co., 1965.
P4260 (ASU)

The Sinks of Gandy Creek. Parsons, W. Va.: McClain Print. Co., 1969.
P4270 (ASU BC WCU)

Precambrian-Paleozoic Appalachian Problems Bulletin, no. 80. Atlanta: Georgia Department of Mines, Mining and Geology, 1969.
P4280 (ETSU)

Pree, H. L., Jr. Public and Industrial Water Supplies of the Jackson Purchase Region, Kentucky. U. S. Geological Survey Circular, no. 287. Washington: Govt. Print. Off., 1953.
P4290

Prentice, Harry The Slate-picker: Story of a Boy's Life in the Coal Mines. New York: A. L. Burt, 1892. A depressingly realistic novel of a young boy's life in the coal mines of Pennsylvania.
P4300 (WCU BC)

Presbyterian Committee of Publication Pioneer Presbyterianism in Tennessee; Addresses Delivered at the Tennessee Exposition on Presbyterian Day, Oct. 28, 1897. Richmond, Va.: Whittet and Shepperson, 1898.
P4310 (ASU)

Presgraves, James S. Smyth County Families and History. Pulaski, Va.: B. D. Smith Print. Co., 1974.
P4320

Presgraves, James S. ed. Wythe County Chapters. Pulaski, Va.: B. D. Smith and Bros., Printers, 1972. This new publication is a gathering of material from scarce, rare, or out-of-print sources about Wythe County. Indexes more than 3700 entries on a variety of topics.
P4330 (ASU)

President's Appalachian Regional Commission Appalachia. Washington: Govt. Print. Off., 1964. A report on resources in the Appalachian Region.
P4340 (ASU)

President's Commission of Income Maintenance Programs Poverty Amid Plenty: The American Paradox. n.p.: Govt. Print. Off., 1969. One segment is on Appalachian poverty.
P4350 (MHC)

Preslar, Charles J. ed. A History of Catawba County. Salisbury: Rowan, 1954. Catawba is a foothill county which serves six mountain counties in western North Carolina.
P4360

Presley, James Scopes, John Thomas Center of the Storm: Memoirs of John T. Scopes. New York: Holt, Rinehart and Winston, 1967.
R1340 (ASU WCU)

Pressey, H. A. Hydrography of the Southern Appalachian Region. 2 parts. U. S. Geological Survey Water-supply Paper, nos. 62-3. Washington: Govt. Print. Off., 1902.
P4370

Preston and Virginia Papers of the Draper Collection of Manuscripts Calendar Series, vol. 1. Madison: Wisconsin State Historical Society, 1915.
P4380

Preston, Dennis Richard "Bituminous Coal Mining Vocabulary of the Eastern United States: A Pilot Study in the Collecting of Geographically Distributed Occupational Vocabulary." Ph. D. Diss. Univ. of Wisconsin, 1969. A fascinating study of the private language of the coal miner.
P4390

Preston (E. S.) and Associates Highway Accessibility Study for the Appalachian Development Highway System. Prepared for the Appalachian Regional Commission. Columbus, Ohio: The co., 1968. In general, access has been poorly planned.
P4400

Highway Transportation and Appalachian Development: The Impact and Costs of the Appalachian Development Highway System Appalachian Research Report, no. 13. Columbus? Ohio: The co., 1970. Poor planning has reserved the impact of the corridor in Appalachia.
P4410 (ETSU LMS ASU)

Preston, George Riley Thomas Wolfe, a Bibliography. New York: C. S. Boesen, 1943.
P4420 (BC ASU)

Preston, Nelly C. Paths of Glory. Richmond, Va.: Whittet and Shepperson, 1961. A tale of Elizabeth, sister of Patrick Henry and wife of William Campbell and William Russell who were prominent in the activities on the Virginia frontier prior to 1790.
P4430

Preston, Thomas Wilson Historical Sketches of the Holston Valleys. Holston Historical Library, 1. Kingsport, Tenn.: Kingsport Press, 1926. Sketches of the folk, homes, historic sites, and past events of the Holston Valley.
P4440 (ASU WCU LMC ETSU BC)

The Story of Bristol. Bristol: King Print. Co., 1941. A history of the growth of the city and a glimpse of its future.
P4450 (ETSU ASU)

Prestonburg, Ky. Chamber of Commerce Industrial Resources, Prestonburg, Kentucky. Prestonburg: Chamber of Commerce, 1958. Promotional material designed for potential investors.
P4460

Preys, Louisen Rosalie Dear Teacher. Boston: Mead Pub. Co., 1942. The hilarious story of an old maid teacher in a West Virginia college town. Many adventures.
P4470 (BC)

Preysz, Louisen Rosalie Larning. Boston: Mead Pub. Co., 1939. A tale of an old maid school teacher in the West Virginia mountains. Surprisingly good dialect.
P4480

Price, Edith Ballinger My Lady Lee. New York: Greenberg Pubs., 1925. The story of a blind girl from the southern mountains and the life she finds in a northern institution for the blind.
P4490 (BC)

Price, G. C. Porter, Hobart Clarke Soil Survey, Tazewell County, Virginia. Washington: U. S. Department of Agriculture, Bureau of Plant Industry, Soils, and Agricultural Engineering, 1948.
P3660

Price, Henry R. Melungeons: The Vanishing Colony of Newman's Ridge. Sneedville, Tenn.: Hancock County Drama Assoc., 1971.
P4500 (ETSU)

Price, Olive M. Snifty. Philadelphia: Westminster, 1957. Children's fiction set in western North Carolina.
P4510

Price, Overton Westfeldt Practical Forestry in the Southern Appalachians. Washington: U. S. Department of Agriculture, Division of Forestry, 1901.
P4520

Price, Patricia Ann Corry, Ormond C. Comparative Economic Growth Measures — Population and Personal Income Estimates for Tennessee Counties, 1950 Through 1962. Knoxville: Univ. of Tennessee Bureau of Business and Economic Research, 1964.
C7590

Price, Paul Holland Greenbrier County. Wheeling: West Virginia Geological Survey, 1939.
P4530 (LMC ETSU)

Physical and Chemical Properties of Natural Gas of West Virginia. Reports, vol. 9. Morgantown: West Virginia Geological Survey, 1937.
P4540 (ETSU)

Pocahontas County. West Virginia Geological Survey County Reports. Wheeling, W. Va.: Wheeling News Litho. Co., 1929.
P4550 (ETSU)

Salt Brines of West Virginia. Reports, vol. 8. Morgantown: West Virginia Geological Survey, 1937.
P4560 (ETSU)

Springs of West Virginia. Reports, vol. 6. Morgantown: West Virginia Geological Survey, 1936.
P4570 (ETSU)

Tilton, John Littlefield Hampshire and Hardy Counties. Morgantown, W. Va.: Morgantown Print. and Bind. Co., 1927.
T8670 (ETSU)

Price, Paul Holland
Tilton, John Littlefield Pendleton County. Wheeling, W. Va.: Wheeling News Litho. Co., 1927.
T8680 (ETSU)

Price, Richard Nye Holston Methodism. From Its Origin to the Present Time. 5 vols. Nashville, Tenn.: Dallas, Texas: Pub. House of the M. E. Church, South, 1903-13.
P4580 (BC ASU)

Price, Rolland Ernest Rutherford County: Economic and Social. Durham, N. C.: Seeman Printery, 1918.
P4590 (ASU)

Price, W. E., Jr. Geology and Ground-water Resources of the Prestonburg Quadrangle, Kentucky. U. S. Geological Survey Water-supply Paper, no. 1359. Washington: Govt. Print. Off., 1956.
P4600

Price, Walter L. ed. and comp. Johnson City, Tennessee Code. Rochester, N. Y.: Lawyers Co-operative Pub. Co., 1951. Also, 1956 Supplement.
J1390 (ETSU)

Price, Walter Willard Sing. O Mountaineer Parsons, W. Va.: McClain Print. Co., 1963.
P4610 (BC ASU LMC)

Price, William B. Tales and Lore of the Mountaineer. Salem, W. Va.: Quest Pub. Co., 1963. Tales and folklore from the West Virginia mountains.
P4620 (BC)

Price, William Thomas Historical Sketches of Pocahontas County, West Virginia. Marlington, W. Va.: Price Brothers, 1901. A very good county history.
P4630 (BC ASU)

Without Script or Purse: Or, The Mountain Evangelist. Louisville: The author, 1883. Biography of George O. Barnes, the mountain evangelist.
P4640 (BC)

Prichard, Armstead Mead comp. Allied Families of Read, Corbin, Luttrell, Bywaters. Starting from Culpeper County, Virginia, Their Descendants Are Now Planted in Every State Westward to the Pacific. My Wife's Kin. Staunton, Va.: McClure Co., 1930.
P4650 (ASU)

Prickett, James McChesney A Bit O' Sunshine. Bristol, Tenn.: King Print. Co., 1928.
P4660

Princess Atalie see Unkalunt, Atalie

Pritchett, Charles Herman The Tennessee Valley Authority, a Study in Public Administration. Chapel Hill: Univ. of North Carolina Press, 1943.
P4670 (BC ASU WCU)

Probst, H. Claude This An' That. Grundy, Va.: Virginia Mountaineer, n.d. A variety of articles, poetry, and family meditations published in the Virginia Mountaineer, a weekly county newspaper.
P4680

Proceedings of the Annual Meeting of Washington County Bar Association, January 27, 1941. Abingdon, Va.: The assoc., 1941.
P4690

A Progress Report on the Allegheny Highlands Project, July-Dec., 1970- Morgantown: West Virginia Univ., 1970-
P4700 (BC)

Progressive Knoxville: A Pictorial Review of the City, 1903-1904 2 vols. Knoxville: Russell Harrison, 1904. A general history of the early settlement of Knox County, Tennessee.
P4710

Projections of Population and Labor Force; Tennessee, Regions and Counties: 1975-2000 Knoxville: Univ. of Tennessee Center for Business and Economic Research, 1972.
P4720

The Prospector's Guide: Showing the Resources and Advantages of East Tennessee, and of Her Central and Largest City, Knoxville, Tennessee Knoxville: W. T. Ragsdale, 1888?. A list of resources of Knox County, Tennessee.
P4730

Prosser, Julian Branson Two City Managers in Asheville, North Carolina: Politics, Administration and Policy Formulation. Master's thesis. Univ. of North Carolina, 1972.
P4740 (UNCA)

Proudfout, Merrill Diary of a Sit-in. Chapel Hill: Univ. of North Carolina Press, 1962. Account of a sit-in in Knox County, Tennessee.
P4750 (WCU ETSU)

Prouty, Chilton Eaton Lower Middle Ordovician of Southwest Virginia and Northeast Tennessee. n.p.: n.p., 1946.
P4760 (ETSU)

Prouty, William Frederick Geology and Mineral Resources of Clay County, with Special Reference to the Graphite Industry. County Report, 1. Univ.: Alabama Geological Survey, 1923.
P4770 (ETSU)

Tilton, John Littlefield Hampshire and Hardy Counties. Morgantown, W. Va.: Morgantown Print. and Bind. Co., 1927.
T8670 (ETSU)

Tilton, John Littlefield Pendleton County. Wheeling, W. Va.: Wheeling News Litho. Co., 1927.
T8680 (ETSU)

Prucha, Francis Paul American Indian Policy in the Formative Years, the Indian Trade and Intercourse Acts, 1780-1834. Cambridge, Mass.: Harvard Univ. Press, 1962.
P4780 (BC ASU)

The Sword of the Republic: The United States Army on the Frontier, 1783-1846. Wars of the United States. New York: Macmillan, 1969.
P4790 (ASU)

Pruett, James A Selective Music Bibliography from the Period 1663-1763. Raleigh: Carolina Charter Tercentenary Commission, 1962.
P4800 (LMC)

Pryne, Abram Brownlow, William Gannaway Ought American Slavery to be Perpetuated? A Debate between Rev. W. G. Brownlow and Rev. A. Pryne. Held at Philadelphia, September, 1858. Philadelphia: J. B. Lippincott and Co., 1858.
B7520 (ASU BC)

Pryor, Elinor The Double Man. New York: Norton, 1957. Set in western North Carolina.
P4810

Pryor, J. P. Jordan, Thomas The Campaigns of Lieut.-Gen. N. B. Forrest, and of Forrest's Cavalry. Dayton, Ohio: Morningside Bookshop, 1973.
J2740 (ASU)

Public Education in Harlan County, Kentucky Bulletin of the Bureau of School Service, Vol. XX, no. 2. Lexington: Univ. of Kentucky, 1947.
P4820

The Public University in Its Second Century Papers presented to a symposium sponsored by the State Visiting Committee of the West Virginia Center for Appalachian Studies and Development. Public Affairs Series, no. 5. Morgantown: Office of Research and Development, West Virginia Center for Appalachian Studies and Development, West Virginia Univ., 1967.
P4830

Puckle, Bertram S. Funeral Customs, Their Origin and Development. 1926. Reprint. Detroit: Singing Tree Press, 1968.
P4840 (ASU)

Pugh, Edwin V. Mulkearn, Lois A Traveler's Guide to Historic Western Pennsylvania. Pittsburgh: University of Pittsburgh Press, 1954.
M8490 (ASU)

Pugh, Maud Capon Valley. 2 vols. Capon Bridge, W. Va.: n.p., 1946-1948. A general history of Hampshire County, West Virginia and its people. Family records and sketches.
P4850 (BC)

Purcell, James S., Jr. "The Southern Poor White in Fiction." Unpublished M. A. Thesis. Duke Univ., 1938. Refers to mountain people slightenly.
P4860

Purdy, Ralph D. Wilson, L. Craig School-community Improvement, a Report of the Greenbrier County Program. New York: World Book Co., 1959.
W7360 (ASU WCU)

Purnell, Elizabeth Wilkins John Gamp: Or, Coves and Cliffs of the Cumberlands. A story of the early days of the monteagle Sunday School Assembly. Nashville: Gospel Advocate Pub. Co., 1901. Fiction with Monteagle Assembly as its setting.
P4870 (LMC BC)

Pursell, Donald E. Selected Demographic Aspects of the West Virginia Economy, 1950-1975: Estimates and Projections of Migration and Population. Business and Economic Studies, vol. 11, no. 3. Also, West Virginia University Bulletin, Series 69, no. 8-13. Morgantown: West Virginia Univ., Bureau of Business Research, 1969.
P4880 (ETSU BC)

Purslow, Frank comp. The Foggy Dew; More English Folk Songs from the Hammond and Gardiner Manuscripts. London: E. F. D. S. Publications, 1974.
P4890 (ASU)

Pusey, William Allen The Wilderness Road to Kentucky. New York: George H. Doran Co., 1921. Excellent maps and illustrations. What a pity the road cannot by properly marked in other states.
P4900

Putnam, John F. The Plucked Dulcimer of the Southern Mountains. Berea, Ky.: Council of the Southern Mountains, 1957.
P4910 (ASU BC)

The Plucked Dulcimer and How to Play It. Photographs by Howard A. Matthews. Artwork by Robert F. Connor. Berea, Ky.: Council of the Southern Mountains, 1961. Excellent book of instructions with illustrations, simple melodies and a history of the instrument.
P4920 (WCU ASU BC)

The Plucked Dulcimer and How to Play It. Photographs by Howard A. Matthews, Art work by Robert F. Connor. Rev. ed. Berea, Ky.: Council of the Southern Mountains, 1964.
P4930 (ASU LMC MHC)

Puzzuoli, David A. Educational Renaissance in Appalachia; an Evaluation. Morgantown: Ed. Research & Field Service, W. Va. Univ., 1968.
P4940

Development of Tele-lecture and Associated Media Systems for the Improvement of Nursing Education in West Virginia. Morgantown: West Virginia Univ., 1971.
P4950

Project Era: A Three Year Study of a Follow Through Program. A Longitudinal Study of the Monongalia County Follow Through Program. Morgantown: Monongalia Co. Board of Education, 1970.
P4960

Pyle, Ernest T. (Ernie) Gatlinburg and the Great Smokies. Gatlinburg: Mountain Press, 1951. A history and description of Sevier County, Tennessee.
P4970

Qazilbash, A. Husain "A Dialect Survey of the Appalachian Region." Ph. D. Diss. Florida State Univ., 1971. There are some strangely discordant notes in this study. To the native's ears it sounds rather superficial.
Q10 (LMC ASU)

A Dialect Survey of the Appalachian Region. Atlanta: National Center for Educational Research and Development. (Regional Research Program), Region 4, 1971.
Q20 (BC)

Quackenbush, Robert Go Tell Aunt Rhody. New York: Lippincott, 1973. The folktale, the music, the silly goose, and a host of colorful illustrations dominate this excellent and unusual children's book.
Q30 (ASU)

Quality Education for Appalachia: A Prospectus Proposing the Establishment of a Regional Educational Laboratory Sponsored by school systems, state departments of education, institutions of higher learning and other educationally related agencies in Kentucky, Ohio, Pennsylvania, Tennessee, Virginia and West Virginia. n.p.: n.p., 1965.
Q40

Qualls, Daniel "History of Education in Carter County, Kentucky." Master's thesis. Univ. of Kentucky, 1931.
Q50

"A Quantitative Study of the Subalpine Forests of Roan and Bald Mountains in the Southern Appalachians." Master's thesis. East Tenn. State Univ., 1969.
C2020 (ETSU)

Quarles, Edwin Latham Booton, John Heiskell Songs and Fantasies. Salem, Va., Sentinel Publishing Co., Roanoke College Annual Staff, 1900.
B5490

Quarles, Garland R. The Churches of Winchester, Virginia: A Brief History of Those Established Prior to 1825. Winchester: The author, 1960.
Q60

George Washington and Winchester, Virginia 1748-1758; A Decade of Preparation for Responsibilities to Come. Winchester, Va.: C. J. Carrier, 1974.
Q70 (ASU)

The Schools of Winchester, Virginia. Winchester: The author, 1964.
Q80

The Story of One Hundred Old Homes in Winchester, Virginia. Winchester: The author, 1967. Tribute to Winchester's historic past.
Q90

The Streets of Winchester, Virginia: The Origin and Significance of Their Names. Winchester: The author, n.d. The names read like a history of early America, especially Virginia and the westward movement into the mountains.
Q100

Quarles, Garland R. ed. Russell, William Greenway What I Know about Winchester: Recollections of William Greenway Russell, 1800-1891. Staunton, Va.: McClure Print. Co., 1953.
R4410 (ASU BC)

Quarles, Mary Ann "A Comparison of Some Aspects of Family Life Between Two Areas of Leslie Co., Kentucky." Master's thesis. Univ. of Kentucky, 1952.
Q110

Quarles, Royce W. "A Study of the Economically and Educationally Deprived Students of Bristol, Virginia, Junior High School." Master's thesis. East Tennessee State Univ., 1967.
Q120 (ETSU)

Queener, Verton Madison "The Republican Party in East Tennessee, 1865-1900." Ph. D. Diss. Indiana Univ., 1941. East Tennessee was as bitterly divided by the war as was Virginia. The history of the Republican party 1865-1900 reflected the harsh realities of the war.
Q130

Query, Joy M. Neale "A Cultural Comparison of Schizophrenia in Mountain Rural and Metropolitan Kentucky." Ph. D. Diss. The Univ. of Kentucky, 1961.
Q140

Quesinberry, Ronald A. Conklin, J. Douglas Selected South Carolina Economic Data. Columbia: Univ. of S. C., Bureau of Business and Economic Research, 1969.
C6500

Quigley, Michael J. April Is the Cruelest Month. Dubuque: Kendall/Hunt Pub. Co., 1969. A novel of coal mines, itinerant preachers, and out-migration from West Virginia. Very confused plot.
Q150 (BC)

Quillen, Bess Bradley In the East Kentucky Hills. Philadelphia: Dorrance & Co., 1970.
Q160 (ASU WCU ETSU LMC)

Quincy, Harold C. "Coordination of Physical Education and Community Recreation in Ashe, Avery, and Watauga Counties." Master's thesis. Appalachian State Teachers College, 1948.
Q170 (ASU)

Quinn, Bernard Atlas of the Church in Appalachia, Administrative Units and Boundaries. Knoxville, Tenn.: Commission on Religion in Appalachia, 1970. Useful atlas with clearly drawn districts and boundaries.
Q180 (ASU)

Quinsenberry, Anderson Chenault Kentucky in the War of 1812. 1915. Reprint. With an added preface by G. G. Clift and an added index supplied by the Kentucky Historical Society. Baltimore: Genealogical Pub. Co., 1969.
Q190 (ASU MHC)

Quisenberry, Anderson Chenault The Life and Times of Hon. Humphrey Marshall. 1892. Reprint. Berea, Ky.: Oscar Rucker, Jr., 1971. Marshall was the author of the first systematic history of Kentucky. Much on early Kentucky politics.
Q200 (LMC BC MHC)

Quisenberry, Anderson Chenault comp. Revolutionary Soldiers in Kentucky, Containing a Roll of the Officers of Virginia Line Who Received Land Bounties: A Roll of the Revolutionary Pensioners in Kentucky. A List of the Illinois Regiment Who Served Under George Rogers Clark in the Northwest Campaign, Also a Roster of the Virginia Navy. Baltimore: Southern Book Co., 1959.
Q210 (ASU BC)

Radford, Albert E. Atlas of the Vascular Flora of the Carolinas. Technical Bulletin, no. 165. Raleigh: North Carolina Agricultural Experiment Station, 1965.
R10 (LMC WWC)

Guide to the Vascular Flora of the Carolinas, with Distribution in the Southeastern States. Chapel Hill, N. C.: Book Exchange, 1964.
R20 (LMC WWC)

Manual of the Vascular Flora of the Carolinas. Chapel Hill: Univ. of North Carolina Press, 1968.
R30 (ETSU LMC WWC)

Radomski, Alexander L. Family Income and Related Characteristics Among Low-Income Counties and States. (Welfare Research Report No. 1.) Washington: Division of Research, Welfare Administration, U. S. Department of Health, Education and Welfare, 1964. Includes data on Appalachia.
R40

Ragan, Rev. O. G. History of Lewis County, Kentucky. 1st ed. Cincinnati: Press of Jennings and Graham, n.d.
R50

Ragan, Samuel Talmadge The Tree in the Far Pasture. Winston-Salem, N. C.: J. F. Blair, 1964.
R60 (ASU)

Raggs, Spottsylvania Pokeberry Hills, Hollers and Hickory Flats. n.p.: n.p., n.d. Humorous tales from the hills expressed in verse and prose.
R70

Ragle, Harold E. The Bastins of Casey, Lincoln, and Pulaski County, Kentucky. Liberty, Ky.: Casey County News, 1968.
R80 (BC)

The Blacks of Casey and Pulaski County, Kentucky, and of Kansas. Liberty, Ky.: Casey County News, 1969.
R90 (BC)

The Carmans of Casey County, Kentucky. Casey, Ky.: Casey County News, 1969.
R100

The Ragles of Pennsylvania, Virginia, Kentucky, and Kansas. Liberty, Ky.: The author, 1971.
R110

Raim, Ethel ed. Dunson, Josh Anthology of American Folk Music. New York: Oak Publications, 1973.
D4020 (ASU BC)

Grass Roots Harmony. New York: Oak Publications, 1968.
R120 (LMC)

Raine, James Watt The Land of Saddle-bags: A Study of the Mountain People of Appalachia. New York: Published jointly by Council of Women for Home Missions and Missionary Education Movement of the United States and Canada, 1924. Generally considered a "mountain classic," it is an account of life in eastern Kentucky in the 1920's.
R130 (BC ASU ETSU WWC)

The Land of Saddle-bags: A Study of the Mountain People of Appalachia. 1924. Reprint. Detroit: Singing Tree Press, 1969.
R140 (LMC MHC WCU)

Mountain Ballads for Social Singing. Berea, Ky.: Berea College Press, 1923. Music collected by Cecil J. Sharpe.
R150 (BC)

Saddlebag Folk: The Way of Life in the Kentucky Mountains. The Way of Life Series. Evanston, Ill.: Row, Peterson and Co., 1942. Depicts life in the Kentucky mountains.
R160 (BC ASU LMC ETSU)

Raines, Carroll C. "A Study of School Transportation, Hawkins County, Tennessee." Master's thesis. Univ. of Tennessee, 1954.
R170

Rakestraw, Isaac K. "Negro Education in Cocke County." Master's thesis. Univ. of Tennessee, 1956.
R180 .

Ralston, Frances "History of Education in Letcher County, Kentucky." Master's thesis. Univ. of Kentucky, 1939.
R190

Ramey, James M. "Factors Influencing Social Status, Social Participation in the Elementary School of Crum, West Virginia." Master's thesis. Marshall College, 1953.
R200

Ramey, Lee Oly "An Inquiry into the Life of Jesse Stuart as Related to His Literary Development and a Critical Study of His Works." Master's thesis. Ohio Univ., 1941. A study of the life and literature of Jesse Stuart. Kentucky's best known author.
R210 (ASU)

Ramey, Shirley A. Cleveland County, North Carolina, Marriages, 1851-1868. Lattimore: n.p., 1971.
R220

Ramsay, John American Potters and Pottery. New York: Tudor Pub. Co., 1947. Appalachia has had many fine potteries though few are still producing today.
R230 (BC)

Ramsey, Charles E. Gottlieb, David Understanding Children of Poverty. Chicago: Science Research Associates, 1967.
G2860 (WCU BC)

Ramsey, James Gettys McGready The Annals of Tennessee to the End of the Eighteenth Century: Comprising Its Settlement, as the Watauga Association, from 1769 to 1777. A Part of North Carolina, from 1777 to 1784: The State of Franklin, from 1784-1788. A Part of North Carolina, from 1788-1790: The Territory of the U. States, South of the Ohio, from 1790 to 1796. The State of Tennessee, from 1796 to 1800. Philadelphia: Lippincott, Grambo and Co., 1853. A classic volume on Tennessee history. Earliest information deals almost exclusively with eastern Tennessee.
R240 (ASU BC)

The Annals of Tennessee to the End of the Eighteenth Century: Comprising Its Settlement, as the Watauga Association, from 1769 to 1777. A Part of North Carolina, from 1777 to 1784: The State of Franklin, from 1784-1788. A Part of North Carolina, from 1788-1790: The Territory of the U. States, South of the Ohio, from 1790 to 1796. The State of Tennessee, from 1796 to 1800. 1853. Reprint. Kingsport, Tenn.: Kingsport Press, 1926.
R250 (ASU LMC WCU)

Ramsey, James Gettys McGready
Autobiography and Letters. Nashville: Tennessee Historical Commission, 1954. Letters and autobiography of one of Tennessee's finest historians.
R260 (ASU BC)
History of Lebanon Presbyterian Church, "In the Fork," Five Miles East of Knoxville. Knoxville: Archer and Smith, 1918; 1952.
R270
Tales of the Revolution, by a Young Gentleman of Tennessee. Nashville: Hunt, Tardiff, 1833.
R280

Ramsey, Joyce Education in Appalachia as Depicted in Major Periodicals. Berea, Ky.: Berea College Appalachian Center, 1973. An annotated bibliography.
R290

Ramsey, Ralph J. Brown, James Stephen The Changing Kentucky Population: A Summary of Population Data for Counties. Lexington: Kentucky Agricultural Experiment Station, 1958.
B7170
Forms and Scope of Poverty in Kentucky. ("Resource Development Series, No. 10.") Lexington: Cooperative Extension Service, Univ. of Kentucky, 1967. Includes data on Appalachian counties.
R300

Ramsey, Robert W. Carolina Cradle: Settlement of the Northwest Carolina Frontier, 1747-1762. Chapel Hill: Univ. of North Carolina Press, 1964. Traces migration routes of the westward movement.
R310 (BC LMC ASU)

Ramsey, Thomas R., Jr. The Battle of Kingsport. Illustrated by Georgia P. Neely. Kingsport, Tenn.: Kingsport Press, 1972.
R320 (ASU ETSU)
The Raid, East Tennessee, Western N. Carolina, Southwest Virginia. Kingsport, Tenn.: n.p., 1973.
R330 (ASU)

Ranck, George Washington Boonesborough: Its Founding, Pioneer Struggles, Indian Experiences, Transylvania Days and Revolutionary Annals. With full historical notes and appendix. Filson Cleo Publications, no. 16. Louisville, Ky.: J. P. Morton and Co., 1901.
R340 (BC ASU LMC)
Boonesborough: Its Founding, Pioneer Struggles, Indian Experiences, Transylvania Days and Revolutionary Annals. 1901. Reprint. The First American Frontier. New York: Arno Press and New York Times, 1971.
R350 (ASU WCU ETSU)
"The Traveling Church": An Account of the Baptist Exodus from Virginia to Kentucky in 1781, under the Leadership of Rev. Lewis Craig and Capt. William Ellis. With historical notes. n.p.: n.p., 1910. Offers some explanations for the phenomenal success of the Baptists on the frontier.
R360 (BC)

Rand, James Hall North Carolina Indians. James Sprunt Historical Publication, vol. 12, no. 1. Chapel Hill: Univ. of North Carolina Press, 1900-.
R370 (WCU)
The North Carolina Indians. James Sprunt Historical Publications, vol. 12, no. 2. Chapel Hill: Univ. of North Carolina, 1913. The Indians of North Carolina and their relations with the settlers.
R380 (ASU LMC BC)

Rand, McNally & Co. Indexed County and Railroad Pocket Map and Shipper's Guide of West Virginia. Chicago: The co., 1904. A marvelous source for West Virginia historians. Good map. Contains many routes no longer in use.
R390 (BC)

Randolph, Corliss Fitz A History of Seventh Day Baptist in West Virginia Including the Woodbridgetown and Salemville Churches in Pennsylvania and the Shrewbury Church in New Jersey. Plainfield, N. J.: American Sabbath Tract Society, 1905.
R400 (BC)

Randolph County Historical Society, Elkins, W. Va. Magazine of History — Biography. Elkins: Randolph Co. Hist. Soc., 1924-. annual.
R410

Randolph, John H. "The Revival of the Folk Arts in West Virginia." Master's thesis. West Virginia Univ., 1970.
R420 (ASU LMC)

Randolph-Macon Woman's College, Lynchburg, Va. Randolph-Macon Prose and Verse, a Collection of Undergraduate Writings. Charlottesville, Va.: Michie Co., 1946.
R430 (ASU)

Rankin, G. C. The Story of My Life: Or, More Than a Half Century as I Have Lived It and Seen It Lived. Nashville, Tenn.: Smith & Lamar, 1912. Life of a Methodist circuit-rider in East Tennessee during the Civil War; his years in the Holston Conference, at Hiwassee College, in Knoxville, Chattanooga and Asheville.
R440 (BC LMC)

Rankin, Hugh F. North Carolina in the American Revolution. Raleigh: State Dept. of Archives and History, 1959. Some action took place in the western part of the state.
R450 (ASU LMC)

Ranney, W. P. Expected Returns from Selected Specialized Farming Systems in the Northern Highland Rim Area of Tennessee. Knoxville: Univ. of Tennessee, Agricultural Experiment Station, 1963.
R460 (ASU)

Ransmeier, Joseph Sirera The Tennessee Valley Authority: A Case Study in the Economics of Multiple Purpose Stream Planning. Xerox copy of the original. Nashville: Vanderbilt Univ. Press, 1942.
R470 (ASU BC UNCA)

Ranson, James Morris "The Life and Career of General James Robertson." Master's thesis. Univ. of Tennessee, 1966. A history of the Watauga Association, Indian land purchases, frontier Washington County, State of Franklin, Revolutionary War and other exploits of James Robertson, pioneer.
R480

Raper, J. R. Without Shelter: The Early Career of Ellen Glasgow. Southern Literary Studies. Baton Rouge: Louisiana State Univ. Press, 1971. Some of Miss Glasgow's works are tangentially Appalachian.
R490 (ASU)

Raphael, David L. Gamble, Hays Bentley The Impact of Interchange Development on the Economy of Clinton County. University Park, Pa.: Institute for Research on Land and Water Resources, 1966.
G210

Rasetti, Franco Upper Cambrian Trilobite Faunas of Northeastern Tennessee. Miscellaneous Collections, vol. 148, no. 3; Publication, 4598. Washington: Smithsonian Institution, 1965.
R500 (LMC)

Raskopf, B. D. Production and Marketing of Hatching Eggs in Tennessee. Knoxville: Univ. of Tenn., Agricultural Experiment Station, 1957.
R510

Rasnick, Rose H. "Guidance in the Selection of Elective Courses for the Students of Tennessee High School." Master's thesis. East Tennessee State College, 1956.
R520 (ETSU)

Ratcliffe, Bill Welsh, Stanley Flowers of the Mountain Country. 1975 Deals with Some of the More Representative of Both Conspicuous and Inconspicuous Types. n.p.: n.p., n.d.
W2780

Ratliff, Frank, Jr. Humor among These Hills. Philadelphia: Dorrance, 1971. A verse portrait of humor and pride and simplicity.
R530 (ASU LMC MHC WCU)

Raulston, J. Leonard Sequatchie: A Story of the Southern Cumberlands. Knoxville: Univ. of Tennessee Press, 1974. One of the best local histories of the year. Surely this will win an award from the American Association of State and Local History.
R540 (ASU)

Rawlings, Mary The Albemarle of Other Days. Charlottesville, Va.: Michie Co., 1925. A history of Albemarle County.
R550 (LMC ASU)

Ray, Charles E. The Great Smoky Mountains National Park. Asheville: North Carolina National Park Commission, 1926. Revised edition of the Commission's popular booklet on the Smokies.
R560 (ASU)

Ray, Herman "An Economic, Educational, and Social Survey of Franklin County, Tennessee." Master's thesis. Univ. of Tennessee, 1937.
R570 (ASU)

Ray, Lenoir Postmarks: A History of Henderson County, North Carolina, 1787-1968. Chicago: Adams Press, 1970. A history of Henderson County and its postal service.
R580 (BC ASU ETSU LMC)

Ray, Worth Stickley "Early Days in Monroe County, Tennessee." Austin, Tex.: Unpublished typescript, 1943. An unpublished history of Monroe County, Tennessee.
R590
The Lost Tribes of North Carolina. Where Did They Come from? Where Did They Go? Austin, Texas: The author, 1947. A history, the flood of migrants who passed through North Carolina on the way west.
R620 (ASU)
Ray's Index and Digest to Hathaway's North Carolina Historical and Genealogical Register. With genealogical notes and annotations. n.p.: n.p., 1971.
R630
Tennessee Cousins: A History of Tennessee People. Baltimore: Genealogical Pub. Co., 1966. A history of Tennessee's families, their routes of migration and their descendants.
R640 (BC ASU WCU)

Ray, Worth Stickley comp. Index and Digest to Hathaway's North Carolina Historical and Genealogical Register, with Genealogical Notes and Annotations. Baltimore: Southern Book Co., 1956. (Published also as Part I of the author's The Lost Tribes of North Carolina.)
R600 (ASU)
Index and Digest to Hathaway's North Carolina Historical and Genealogical Register. With genealogical notes and annotations. 1956. Reprint. Baltimore: Genealogical Pub. Co., 1971.
R610 (ASU)

Raya, Florence Pepper comp. The History of the Pepper Family in America and Allied Lines. Fort Madison, Iowa: The Evening Democrat Co., 1973. This volume includes many branches of Peppers in America, one of these being the Montgomery County Kentucky branch.
R650

Rayburn, James B. Gorman, John Loyd Soil Survey, Jackson and Mason Counties, West Virginia. Washington: U. S. Department of Agriculture, Soil Conservation Service, 1961.
G2790

Raymond, Charles Jud. Boston: Houghton Mifflin, 1968. Account of a spoiled city boy whose father takes him to the Smokies for a summer of roughing it.
R660 (ASU)
Up from Appalachia. Chicago: Follett Pub. Co., 1966. Novel of an Appalachian family transplanted to Chicago.
R670 (ASU LMC MHC ETSU)

Raymond, Richard D. The Myth of the Appalachian Brain Drain: A Case Study of West Virginia. Morgantown: West Virginia Univ. Library, 1972. The thesis is that all our native talent does not leave the region.
R680 (BC ASU WCU)

Rayner, Emma Visiting the Sin: A Tale of Mountain Life in Kentucky and Tennessee. Boston: Small, Maynard and Co., 1900. A girl relies on superstition and Biblical direction to learn what caused her father's disappearance and death. She plots her revenge.
R690 (BC ASU)

Rayner, Kenneth Life and Times of Andrew Johnson, Seventeenth President of the United States. New York: Appleton, 1866.
R700

Raynolds, Robert Thomas Wolfe: Memoir of a Friendship. Austin: Univ. of Texas Press, 1965.
R710 (ASU WCU UNCA)

Read, Opie Percival The Captain's Romance, or, Tales of the Backwoods. New York: F. Tennyson Neely, 1896. Five short stories with mountain settings.
R720 (ASU BC)

The Jucklins: A Novel. Chicago: Laird and Lee, 1896. A boy from northern Alabama goes to North Carolina to teach school, woo the daughter of the Jucklin House, and bargain for mica rights in the western Carolina hills.
R730 (BC ASU WCU ETSU)

Odd Folks. Neely's Popular Library, no. 93. New York: F. T. Neely, 1897. A group of character sketches of Tennessee and Kentucky hill people.
R740 (BC ASU WCU)

Old Lim Jucklin. New York: Doubleday, Page and Co., 1905. The philosophy and humor of a North Carolina character and self-styled wit.
R750 (ETSU)

The Starbucks: A New Novel. Chicago: Laird and Lee, 1902. A poorly written novel of east Tennessee during Reconstruction.
R760 (ASU BC)

A Tennessee Judge: A Novel. Library of Choice Fiction, no. 68. Chicago: Laird and Lee, 1893.
R770 (ASU ETSU)

The Waters of Caney Fork: A Romance of Tennessee. Chicago: Rand McNally and Co., 1898. Novel set in the East Tennessee hills.
R780 (ASU ETSU)

Read, Opie Percival 1852-1939 The Wives of the Prophet: A Novel. Chicago: Laird and Lee, 1894. A world-weary lawyer stumbles into an isolated cone and soon convinces its fanatical religious leaders he is a prophet. He has fine wives and all else he could desire until the charade is uncovered. Then he is subjected to a ritualistic murder.
R790 (ASU)

Read, Thomas Buchanan The Wagoner of the Alleghenies: A Poem of the Days of Seventy-six. Philadelphia: Lippincott, 1865. Verse portrait of a revolutionary hero.
R800 (BC)

Reade, Ernest H. Power, W. Robert Field Excursion: The Georgia Marble District. Atlanta: Georgia Department of Mines, Mining and Geology, 1962.
P4050 (ETSU)

Real Estate Research Corporation Economic Analysis and Feasibility Study of Proposed Transient Facilities at East River Mountain, Mercer County, West Virginia. Chicago: The corporation, n.d.
R810

Reback, Janet Taylor Caldwell see Caldwell, Taylor

Reback, Marcus see Caldwell, Taylor

Reber, Clara Smith Tapestry of Time. Charleston, Ill.: Prairie Press Books, 1968. Hill country poems.
R820

Record of Pennsylvania Marriages Prior to 1810 Baltimore: Genealogical Pub. Co., 1968. Since so many Appalachian settlers passed through Pennsylvania in the late 17th century, this is an excellent source.
R830 (ASU)

Red Clay Reader Charlotte, N. C.: Southern Review, 1964-. annually.
R840 (ASU)

Redd, Callie G. "An Examination of the Negro Character in Selected Fiction by White East Tennessee Writers." Master's thesis. East Tennessee State Univ., 1972.
R850 (ETSU)

Redding, Tracy W. The Call of the Smokies. Philadelphia: Dorrance and Co., 1967. Poems with the lure of the Smokies in them.
R860 (BC LMC WCU)

Reddy, Anne Waller West Virginia Revolutionary Ancestors Whose Services Were Non-military and Whose Names, Therefore, Do Not Appear in Revolutionary Indexes of Soldiers and Sailors. An index from Manuscript Public Claims of the Revolutionary War in the Virginia State Library. Baltimore: Genealogical Pub. Co., 1963.
R870 (ASU)

Redford, A. H. Western Cavaliers, Embracing the History of the Methodist Episcopal Church in Kentucky from 1832 to 1844. Nashville, Tenn.: Southern Methodist Pub. House, 1876. Pioneers of Methodism in Tennessee.
R880 (ASU)

Redgrove, Herbert Stanley Bygone Beliefs, Being a Series of Excursions in the Byways of Thought. London: W. Rider and Son, 1920.
R890 (ASU)

Redington, Robert J. Appalachian Mountain Elevations. Washington: Appalachian Trail Conference, 1970. A useful guide to the Appalachians.
R900 (ASU LMC ETSU WCU)

Redwing, Morris Partisan Rate; or, A Stirring Story of the Battle of Mill Springs. "The War Library; Original stories of adventure in the War for the Union." no. 363. New York: Novelist Pub. Co., 1839. Mountain novel set against the backdrop of the Revolution.
R910

Ree, Rev. Stephen ed. Gordon Ballads. Reprinted from vol. 2 of the 1903-07 ed. of the HOUSE OF GORDON, edited by J. M. Bulloch, printed for the New Spalding Club, Aberdeen, Scotland which was issued as no. 26 and 33 of the New Spalding Club Publications. Norwood, Pa.: Norwood Editions, 1974.
R920 (ASU)

Reece, Brazilla Carroll The Courageous Commoner, a Biography of Andrew Johnson. Charleston, W. Va.: Educational Foundation, 1962. Yet another history of East Tennessee's only United States President.
R930 (BC)

Reece, Byron Herbert Ballad of the Bones. New York: E. P. Dutton, 1936. Great poetry from the mountains of northwestern Georgia. Based on folklore and folk motifs.
R940

Better a Dinner of Herbs. 1st ed. A gothic novel of the North Georgia hills.
R950 (ASU)

Bow Down in Jericho. New York: E. P. Dutton, 1950. A selection of ballads with Biblical themes taken from the folklore of the Appalachian mountains.
R960

The Hawk and the Sun. 1st ed. New York: Dutton, 1955. Another chilling tale from the North Georgia hills. This one features violence between the races.
R970

The Season of Flesh. New York: Dutton, 1955. Mountain poetry.
R980 (LMC BC)

A Song of Joy, and Other Poems. New York: E. P. Dutton, 1952. Poems drawn from North Georgia's rich heritage of folk poetry.
R990

Reece, Edna Bray The Brays of Fisher River. Jonesville, N. C.: The author, 1970.
R1000 (ASU)

Reed, A. J. Doane, C. F. Cheesemaking Brings Prosperity to Farmers of Southern Mountains. Washington: U. S. Dept. of Agriculture, 1917.
D2600 (ASU)

Reed, Andrew A Narrative of the Visit to the American Churches, by the Deputation from the Congregational Union of England and Wales. 2 vols. London: Jackson and Walford, 1835. The deputies went from Kentucky to Virginia via Charleston, Lexington and Staunton. They found little support for their church in Appalachia.
R1010

Reed, Carroll E. English Archaisms in Pennsylvania German. A word-list from the Appalachians and the Piedmont area of North Carolina, by Zeta C. Davison. The secretary's report. Publication, no. 19. n.p.: American Dialect Society, 1953.
R1020 (ASU)

Reed, Clyde M. "Business Education in the Kingsport Area High Schools: An Evaluation of Their Business Graduates." Master's thesis. East Tennessee State Univ., 1963.
R1030 (ETSU)

Reed, Frances Frye "The Cyclone of Rye Cove: The Event, the Folklore, the Song." Master's thesis. East Tennessee State Univ., 1971. A fantastic tale of an actual occurrence in eastern Tennessee and an account of its transition to legend and song.
R1040 (ETSU)

Reed, Franklin Weld Report on an Examination of a Forest Tract in Western North Carolina. U. S. Bureau of Forestry Bulletin, no. 60. Washington: Govt. Print. Off., 1905.
R1050 (ASU LMC)

Reed, Gerard Alexander "The Ross-Watie Conflict: Factionalism in the Cherokee Nation, 1839-1865." Ph. D. Diss. Univ. of Oklahoma, 1967. History of factionalism in the Cherokee Nation.
R1060

Reed, Ida Lillard My Life Story. n.p.: The author, 1912. Biography of a West Virginia churchwoman. Memories of her West Virginia childhood , etc.
R1070 (BC)

Songs of the Hills. Boston: Meador Pub. Co., 1940. Poetry set to music to serve as hymns.
R1080 (ASU)

Reed, Jacqueline The Morningside of the Hill. New York: Dodd, Mead and Co., 1960. A young girl living with her grandparents in the foothills of the Cumberlands suddenly receives a legacy.
R1090 (BC)

Reed, John C., Jr. Bryant, Bruce Geology of the Grandfather Mountain Window and Vicinity, North Carolina and Tennessee. Washington: Govt. Print. Off., 1970.
B7800 (ASU)

Geology of the Linville Falls Quadrangle, North Carolina. Geological Survey Bulletin, 1161-B. Contributions to General Geology. Washington: Govt. Print. Off., 1964.
R1100 (ASU)

Reed, Louis Warning in Appalachia: A Study of Wirt County, West Virginia. Morgantown: West Virginia Univ. Library, 1967. This Wirt County study raises questions of population control, care for the aged, economic problems and the effect of changing morality on life in the hills.
R1110 (BC ASU WCU LMC MHC)

Reed, Rufus M. The Green Bough. Appalachia, Va.: Young Publications, 1969. Hill country poems.
R1120 (BC)

Lyrics of Life and the Great Outdoors. New York: Pageant Press, 1953. Mostly about Southwest Virginia.
R1130 (BC)

Reed, Samuel R. The Vicksburg Campaign, and the Battles about Chattanooga under the Command of General U. S. Grant in 1862-63; an Historical Review. Cincinnati: R. Clarke, 1882.
R1140

Reeds, Chester Albert The Endless Caverns of the Shenandoah Valley. New York: Department of Geology, American Museum of Natural History, 1925.
R1150 (BC)

The Natural Bridge of Virginia and Its Environs. New York: Nomad Pub. Co., 1927.
R1160

Reeve, Felix A. East Tennessee in the War of the Rebellion. And Read at the Stated Meeting of December 3, 1902. Xerox copy of the original. Military Order of the Loyal Legion of the U. S. Commandery of the District of Columbia War Papers, 44. Washington: n.p., 1902. East Tennessee was more fiercely divided by the war than were other Appalachian areas.
R1170 (ASU)

Reeve, Jewell B. Climb the Hills of Gordon: Stories of Gordon County and Calhoun, Georgia. Calhoun, Ga.: The author, 1962. Good county history.
R1180 (LMC ASU BC)

A Whimsical Collection. New York: Vantage Press, 1968. Sketches of Gordon County, Georgia and its hills and characters.
R1190

Reeves, Eleanor Baker A Country Doctor Goes to Town. Galax, Va.: Gazette Press, 1966. Biography of an Ashe County (North Carolina) boy who moves to Galax, Virginia and founds a Medical Center. Written by his daughter.
R1200 (ASU)

Reeves, J. Gottlieb, David Adolescent Behavior in Urban Areas: A Bibliographic Review and Discussion of the Literature. New York: Free Press of Glencoe, 1963.
G2850

Reeves, John E. "Population Trends and Other Factors Influencing the Voting Habits of the Cumberland Valley Region of Southeast Kentucky." Master's thesis. Univ. of Kentucky, 1938.
R1210

Reeves, Paschal Thomas Wolfe's Albatross: Race and Nationality in America. Athens: Univ. of Georgia Press, 1968.
R1230 (BC ASU WCU UNCA)

Reeves, Paschal comp. The Merrill Studies in Look Homeward, Angel. Charles E. Merrill Studies. Columbus, Ohio: Merrill, 1970.
R1220 (ASU WCU)

Reeves, Paschal ed. Georgia. University. Department of English Thomas Wolfe and the Glass of Time. Athens: Univ. of Georgia Press, 1974.
G1030 (ETSU ASU)

Thomas Wolfe and the Glass of Time. Athens: Univ. of Georgia Press, 1971. Proceedings of a symposium held April 10-12, 1969, sponsored by the Dept. of English and the College of Arts and Sciences, University of Georgia. Includes bibliographical references.
R1240 (ETSU ASU WCU BC)

Reeves, William T. "A History of Haywood County." Master's thesis. Duke Univ., 1937.
R1250 (ASU)

Reger, David Bright Barbour and Upshur Counties and Western Portion of Randolph County. Assisted by D. Dee Teets, Jr. With introduction by Israel Charles Chite, on deep well borings, and Charles Edwin Van Orstrand, on deep well temperatures. West Virginia Geological Survey County Reports and Maps. Wheeling, W. Va.: Wheeling News Litho. Co., 1918.
R1260 (ASU ETSU)

The Cheat Mountain Coal Field of Randolph County, West Virginia. Bulletin, no. 3. Morgantown: West Virginia Geological Survey, 1928.
R1270 (ASU ETSU)

Mercer, Monroe, and Summers Counties. Assisted by Paul Holland Price. Wheeling: West Virginia Geological Survey, 1926.
R1280 (ASU ETSU)

Mineral and Grant Counties. Assisted by Rietz Courtney Tucker. West Virginia Geological Survey. Morgantown, W. Va.: Morgantown Print. & Bind. Co., 1924.
R1290 (ASU ETSU)

Nicholas County. Assisted in field by William Armstrong Price. Assisted in office by Rietz Courtney Tucker and James Donaldson Sisler. West Virginia Geological Survey County Reports. Wheeling, W. Va.: Wheeling News Litho. Co., 1921.
R1300 (ASU ETSU)

Randolph County. West Virginia Geological Survey. Morgantown: West Virginia Univ., 1931.
R1310 (ASU ETSU)

Tucker County. Assisted in field by William Armstrong Price, and in office by Rietz Courtney Tucker. West Virginia Geological Survey. Wheeling, W. Va.: Wheeling News Litho. Co., 1923.
R1320 (ASU LMC ETSU)

Regional Air Pollution Control Agency An Emission Survey and Ambient Air Quality Data of Buncombe, Haywood, Henderson Counties and the City of Asheville. n.p.: n.p., n.d.
R1330 (WCU)

Register, Alvaretta K. State Census of North Carolina 1784-1787. Raleigh: The author, n.d.
R1340

Rehder, Jessie Clifford Remembrance Way. New York: Putnam, 1956. A disturbed adult recalls a summer at a camp in the North Carolina mountains.
R1350 (ASU)

Reichel, Levin Theodore The Moravians in North Carolina. An authentic history. 1857. Reprint. Baltimore: Genealogical Pub. Co., 1968. The Moravians were among the earliest explorers of western North Carolina.
R1360 (ASU LMC)

Reichert, Alfred Charles Egbert Craddock and die Amerikanische Short Story. Leipsig: Sturm and Koppe, 1912.
R1370

Reichert, Stanley Orville Manganese Resources of East Tennessee. Nashville: n.p., 1942.
R1380 (ETSU)

Reid, Albert Clayton Tales from Cabin Creek. Raleigh, N. C.: Edwards and Broughton, 1967.
R1390 (ASU)

Reid, Christian pseud. see **Tiernan, Frances Christine Fisher**

Reid, H. Extra South. Susquehanna, Pa.: Starrucca Valley Publications, 1964. This is book number 1038 of a first edition limited to 2,000 copies.
R1400 (ASU)

Reid, John Phillip A Law of Blood: The Primitive Law of the Cherokee Nation. New York: New York Univ. Press, 1970.
R1410 (LMC BC UNCA)

Reilly, J. S. Knoxville, Past, Present and Future. n.p.: The author, 1884. Discusses the General History and Early Settlement of Knox County, Tennessee.
R1420

Reilly, John P. "An Analysis of Faculty and Administrative Attitudes Toward Teacher Corps Interns in Carter County, Tennessee." Master's thesis. East Tennessee State Univ., 1969.
R1430 (ETSU)

Rejected or Suspended Applications for Revolutionary War Pensions with an Added Index to the States Baltimore: Genealogical Pub. Co., 1969.
R1440

Relating Denominational Theology to Appalachia Berea, Ky.: Spiritual Life Commission, Council of the Southern Mountains, 197-.
R1450 (BC)

Remembrances: Watauga Academy, Appalachian School, Appalachian State Normal School, Appalachian State Teachers College, Appalachian State University Compiled by Tom Corbitt and William R. Dunlap for the seventy-fifth anniversary of Appalachian State University. Boone, N. C.: The univ., 1974.
R1460 (ASU)

Reniers, Perceval The Springs of Virginia: Life, Love and Death at the Waters, 1775-1900. Chapel Hill: Univ. of North Carolina Press, 1941.
R1470 (ASU FC)

Rennick, G. E. and others Demonstration of Safety Plugging of Oil Wells Penetrating Appalachian Coal Mines. Based on work done in cooperation with Christopher Coal Co., Division of Consolidation Coal Co. Technical Progress Report, 56. Washington: U. S. Bureau of Mines, Coal Mine Health & Safety Research Program, 1972.
R1480

Renshaw, James F. Silvical Characteristics of Yellow-poplar. U. S. Forest Service Station Paper, no. 89. Asheville: Southeastern Forest Experiment Station, 1958.
R1490 (WCU)

Silvical Characteristics of White Basswood. U. S. Forest Service Station Paper, no. 136. Asheville, N. C.: Southeastern Forest Experiment Station, 1961.
R1500 (WCU)

Rent, Robertalee comp. 1810 Montgomery County Census. n.p.: n.p., 1966.
R1510

Renton, John J. A Pressure Chamber for the Impregnation of Porous Rock Specimens. Circular, no. 5. Morgantown: West Virginia Geological & Economic Survey, 1967.
R1520 (ETSU)

A Simple Technique for the Determination of Weight Per Cent of Calcite and Dolomite in Carbonate Rocks. Circular, no. 2. Morgantown: West Virginia Geological & Economic Survey, 1965.
R1530 (ETSU)

Report to the Congress on the Unified Development of the Tennessee River System Knoxville: TVA, 1936.
R1540

Reported Sexual Behavior and Attitudes of Appalachian State University Students; a Comparison of Freshmen Girls and Their Upperclass Sisters Master's thesis. Appalachian State University, 1974.
K1740 (ASU)

Reprint of Official Register of Land Lottery of Georgia, 1827 Baltimore: Genealogical Pub. Co., 1967. Since Georgia records were destroyed by fire in both the national and state capitals, these land lotteries provide one of the best indexes to the settlement of North Georgia Counties.
R1550 (ASU)

Rettie, James C. The Population and Employment Outlook for the Anthracite Region of Pennsylvania. Philadelphia: U. S. Forest Service, Northeast Forest Experiment Station, 1945.
R1560

The Reviewer vol. 1-5; Feb. 15, 1921-Oct. 1925. Richmond, 1921-24. Chapel Hill: Univ. of North Carolina Press, 1925. Carries an occasional Appalachian item.
R1570 (ASU)

Revill, Janie comp. A Compilation of the Original Lists of Protestant Immigrants to South Carolina, 1763-1773. 1939. Reprint. Baltimore: Genealogical Pub. Co., 1968. Many of these families settled in Appalachia.
R1580 (ASU)

Copy of the Original Index Book, Showing the Revolutionary Claims Filed in South Carolina Between August, 20, 1783, and August 31, 1786. Kept by James McCall. Baltimore: Genealogical Pub. Co., 1969.
R1590 (ASU)

Revitt, Paul Joseph The George Pullen Jackson Collection of Southern Hymnody: A Bibliography. Los Angeles: Univ. of California at Los Angeles Library, 1964.
R1600

Rewis, Millard His New Creation; a History of Greene Memorial Methodist Church (1859-1959), from Methodism's Earliest Days in the Roanoke Valley. Roanoke: Art Printing, 1959.
R1610 (FC)

Rexroad, Carl Buckner and others The Silurian Formations of East-central Kentucky and Adjacent Ohio. Prepared in cooperation with the Indiana Geological Survey. Kentucky Geological Survey Series 10, Bulletin 2. Lexington: Univ. of Kentucky College of Arts & Sciences, 1965.
R1620 (ETSU)

Rexrode, William F. Rexrode Art: Sketches from the Hills of West Virginia. Parsons, W. Va.: McClain Print. Co., 1966.
R1630 (ASU)

Reynolds, Buford Greene County Cemeteries, from Earliest Dates to 1970-1971. n.p.: n.p., 1971.
R1640 (ASU ETSU)

Reynolds, Cora Addington, Luther Foster Wise County Geography Supplement. Big Stone Gap, Va.: Wise County School Board and Univ. of Virginia, 1928.
A570 (BC)

Reynolds, Donald E. Editors Make War: Southern Newspapers in the Secession Crisis. Ph. D. Diss. Tulane Univ., 1965. Nashville: Vanderbilt Univ. Press, 1966, 1970. Includes Appalachian Unionist Papers and references to earlier mountain abolitionist papers.
R1650

Reynolds, Hughes The Coosa River Valley from DeSoto to Hydroelectric Power. Cynthiana, Ky.: Hobson Book Press, 1944. A history of the Coosa River Valley from Spanish Explorers to the Tennessee Valley Authority.
R1660 (ASU)

Reynolds, J. J. The Allen Gang. Baltimore: I. & M. Ottenheimer, 1912. A graphic account of the tragedy at Hillsville Courthouse, Hillsville, Virginia.
R1670 (LMC BC ASU)

Reynolds, James E. "Anxiety in Coal Miners." Master's thesis. West Virginia Univ., 1957. One of the few looks at the psychological effects of life in the mines.
R1680

Reynolds, M. M. Shelter, Charles Milestones of West Virginia History...Some Events of Importance in the Development of the Mountain State. Parsons, W. Va.: McClain Print. Co., 1963.
S2660

Reynolds, Michael M. "A Bibliographic Center in the West Virginia Region: An Analysis of Present Needs and Future Directions." Microfilm. Ph. D. Diss. Univ. of Michigan, 1964. A marvelous idea, but one unlikely to develop.
R1690 (ASU)

Forests and Forestry in West Virginia, a Bibliography. Morgantown: W. Va. Univ. Library, 1963.
R1700

Shetler, Charles Milestones of West Virginia History: Some Events of Importance in the Development of the Mountain State. Parsons, W. Va.: McClain Print. Co., 1966.
S3020 (ASU)

Reynolds, Noah M. History of the Feuds of the Mountain Parts of Eastern Kentucky, Lives of Noah and John Reynolds. Whitesburg, Ky.: Eagles Print. Co., n.d.
R1710 (ASU LMC BC)

Reynolds, Roy Lee "A Study of Parent-child Relationships in Greene County, Tennessee." Master's thesis. East Tennessee State College, 1951.
R1720 (ETSU)

Reynolds, Ruth Allen "A Proposed Health Instruction Program for Upper Elementary Grades Adaptable to Carter County." Master's thesis. East Tennessee State College, 1956.
R1730 (ETSU)

Reynolds, Thurlow Weed Born of the Mountains. n.p.: n.p., 1964. Delightful volume of manners and maxims from the hills. Includes personal reminiscences from the author's childhood.
R1740 (ASU WCU LMC)

Cherokee and Creek. Highlands, N. C.: The author, 1966.
R1750 (ASU LMC)

High Lands. Highlands, N. C.: n.p., 1964. Stories of the Carolina mountains and memoirs of a childhood spent there.
R1760 (ASU LMC WCU)

The Southern Appalachian Region: Hitherto Untold Stories. 2 vols. Highlands, N. C.: The author, 1966.
R1770 (ASU LMC)

Rhawn, Heister G. Sturm, Harry Price Rimfire, His Life Story and Selections From His Own Writings. A Study of the Typical Mountaineer, Eli (Rimfire) Hamrick. Parsons, W. Va.: McClain Print. Co., 1967.
S8920 (ASU BC)

Rhea, Caroline McQueen "Sketches and Legends of Upper East Tennessee." Master's thesis. George Peabody College for Teachers, 1932. An excellent thesis chock full of tales from the Holston Valley County.
R1780 (LMC ASU)

Rhea County, Tenn. 1830 Census n.p.: n.p., n.d. Census statistics for Rhea County, Tennessee.
R1790

Rhinehart, Joe P. ed. The Webster Cookbook. Raleigh: Edwards and Broughton Co., 1974. Cookbook from the Webster Community, School, and Restoration Project near Sylva, North Carolina.
R1800

Rhoades, Verne H. Ice Storms in the Southern Appalachian Mountains. With note on the preceding by William Willard Ashe. Washington: U. S. Department of Agriculture, Weather Bureau, 1918.
R1810

Rhode Island School of Design, Providence, Museum of Art Mountain Artisans: An Exhibit of Patchwork and Quilting, Appalachia. Photographs, films and collected music by John Cohen. Providence: The school, 1970.
R1820 (BC)

The Rhododendron vol. 1, no. 1- . 1922- . Boone, N. C.: Appalachian State Univ., annual.
R1830 (ASU)

Rhoton, Thomas Foster "A Brief History of Franklin County, Tennessee." Master's thesis. Univ. of Tennessee, 1941.
R1840

Rhudy, Chelsea Laws "A Reading Improvement Program Developed by a Classroom Teacher for a Selected Seventh-grade Group at Elizabethton Junior High School." Master's thesis. East Tennessee State College, 1957.
R1850 (ETSU)

Rhymes of a Mountaineer Detroit: Harlo, 1968.
R1860

Rhyne, Edwin Hoffman "Political Leadership and Social Structure in a Rural County." Microfilm. Master's thesis. Univ. of North Carolina, 1950. A mountain county was used for the study.
R1870 (ASU)

Rhyne, Jennings J. Some Southern Cotton Mill Workers and Their Villages. Chapel Hill: Univ. of North Carolina, 1930. Many mill villages are located in the Appalachian foothills.
R1880 (WWC ASU)

Rice, Alvin H. The Shenandoah Pottery. Illustrated with photographs from the collection of the author (Rice?) Strasburg, Va.: Shenandoah Pub. House, 1929. A list of early potteries in the valley.
R1890 (ASU BC)

Rice, Charles L. Geologic Map of the Jenkins West Quadrangle, Kentucky-Virginia. Washington, D. C.: U. S. Geological Survey, 1973.
R1900

Geologic Map of the Whitesburg Quadrangle, Kentucky-Virginia, and Part of the Flat Gap Quadrangle, Letcher County, Ky. Washington: U. S. Geological Survey, 1973.
R1910

Rice, Charles Scott Steinmetz, Rollin C. Vanishing Crafts and Their Craftsmen. New Brunswick, N. J.: Rutgers Univ. Press, 1959.
S6940 (ASU)

Rice, DeLong "Old Limber": Or, The Tale of the Taylors. Nashville: McQuiddy Print. Co., 1921. A fanciful tale of Bob and Sef Taylor's rivalry being resolved by making the dog governor.
R1930 (ASU)

Rice, DeLong ed. Governor Bob Taylor's Tales. Nashville, Tenn.: DeLong Rice and Co., 1896. Includes such favorites as "The Fiddle and the Bow" and "The Paradise of Fools."
R1920

Rice, James Phillips "Taxation and Assessment of Coal, Gas and Oil with Special Reference to Western Pennsylvania, Eastern Ohio and Northern West Virginia." Ph. D. Diss. Univ. of Pittsburgh, 1957.
R1940

Rice, Laban Lacy A Mountain Idyll. Nashville: Baird Ward Press, 1921. An idyllic tale in flowery prose. The heroine is pure, right triumphs in the end.
R1950 (WCU BC ASU)

Rice, Lawrence K. "History of Education in Breathitt County, Kentucky." Master's thesis. Univ. of Kentucky, 1933.
R1960

Rice, Otis K. The Allegheny Frontier: West Virginia Beginnings, 1730-1830. Lexington: Univ. Press of Kentucky, 1970. An excellent interpretative history of the role of the first frontier in our country's westward expansion.
R1970 (ASU WCU LMC ETSU MHC WWC BC FC UNCA)

Teacher's Manual for West Virginia: The State and Its People. Grade 8. Parsons, W. Va.: McClain Print. Co., 1972.
R1980

West Virginia: The State and Its People. Parsons, W. Va.: McClain Print. Co., 1972.
R1990 (ASU)

Rice, Otis Kermit "Frontier West Virginia: Some Aspects of Its Political, Social, and Economic Development." Ph. D. Diss. The Univ. of Kentucky, 1961.
R2000 (ASU)

Rich, Mark Some Churches of Coal Mining Communities of West Virginia. Sponsored by the West Virginia Council of Churches and the Committee for Cooperative Field Research. New York: n.p., 1951.
R2010

Richards, John Adair A History of Bath County, Kentucky. Yuma, Ariz.: Southwest Printers, 1961.
R2020 (BC)

Richards, Thomas Addison Tallulah and Jocassee, or, Romances of Southern Landscape, and Other Tales. Charleston, S. C.: Walker, Richards and Co., 1852. As a landscape painter Richards did many scenes of rivers and mountains, some inspired by the hill country of South Carolina and Georgia. There are intimations of mountain scenery in these tales.
R2030

Richards, William Carey Georgia Illustrated in a Series of Views, Embracing Natural Scenery and Public Edifices, Engraved on Steel by Rawdon, Wright, Hatch and Smillie, from Sketches Made Expressly for This Work by T. Addison Richards. Accompanied by Historical and Topographical Sketches, by Our Own Writers. Penfield, Ga.: W. & W. C. Richards, 1842. There are descriptions of "The Rock Mountain," "The Falls of Tallulah," "The Falls of Towaliga," and "The Lover's Leap" with sketches.
R2040

Richardson, Charles H. "A History of Municipal Government in Knoxville since 1911." Master's thesis. Univ. of Tennessee, 1945.
R2050

Richardson, Ethel Park comp. American Mountain Songs. Edited and arranged by Sigmund Spaeth. New York: Greenberg, 1955.
R2060 (ETSU BC ASU)

American Mountain Songs. Edited and arranged by Sigmund Spaeth. 1955. Reprint. New York: Greenburg, 1956.
R2070 (ASU ETSU WCU BC)

Richardson, Frank From Sunrise to Sunset, Reminiscence of Bristol, Tennessee. Bristol: King Print. Co., 1910. Memoirs of a Methodist minister from east Tennessee.
R2080 (BC)

Richardson, Hiram K. Memoirs of Berea. Berea, Ky.: Berea College, 1940.
R2090 (BC)

Richardson, Howard Dark of the Moon. The Drama Library. New York: Theatre Arts Books, 1957. One of our better mountain dramas.
R2100 (ASU WCU)

Dark of the Moon. The Drama Library. London: Heinemann, 1966.
R2110 (ASU)

Dark of the Moon. Rev. ed. New York: Theatre Arts Books, 1966.
R2120 (LMC MHC)

Dark of the Moon. Rev. ed., 1966. Reprint. New York: Theatre Arts Books, 1970.
R2130 (ETSU)

Richardson, James R. Snakes and the Devil. New York: Vantage Press, 1959. A novel of the serpent-handling cults in Appalachia.
R2140

Richardson, Joy W. Roback, Selwyn S. The Effects of Acid Mine Drainage on Aquatic Insects. Philadelphia: Academy of Natural Sciences of Philadelphia, 1969.
R2630 (ASU)

Richardson, Marian M. 1832 Cherokee Land Lottery: Index to Revolutionary Soldiers, Their Widows and Orphans Who Were Fortunate Drawers. Danielsville, Ga.: Heritage Papers, 1969.
R2150 (ASU WCU)

Richardson, Vokes From Cedar Mountain: A Collection of Stories from the Large American Novel, Cedar Mountain. New York: Vantage Press, 1963. A fine collection of stories excerpted from the author's forthcoming novel. Most have Eastern Tennessee settings and are rich in the language and lore of the mountains.
R2160 (ASU)

Richey, Ish Kentucky Literature 1784-1963. Tompkinsville, Ky.: Monroe County Press, 1963. A review of 179 years of Kentucky literature, with bibliography.
R2170 (BC)

Richter, Conrad The Grandfathers. New York: Knopf, 1964. A novel about a young girl growing up in the mountains of Maryland searching for the identity of her father and grandfather.
R2180

Rickels, Milton George Washington Harris. New York: Twayne, 1965. Appalachia's foremost early humorist. Harris' Tennessee tales had a national audience.
R2190 (BC)

Rickert, Edith Ancient English Christmas Carols. New York: Duffield and Co., 1915.
R2200 (FC)

Ricketts, James E. Oder, Charles Rollin Lorain Geology of the Mascot-Jefferson City Zinc District, Tennessee. Nashville: Tennessee Division of Geology, 1961.
O220 (ETSU)

Rico-Velasco, Jesus Antonio "Immigrants from the Appalachian Region to the City of Columbus, Ohio: A Case Study." Master's thesis. Ohio State Univ., 1969. A study of the trauma inflicted on the Appalachian migrant to the big-city ghetto.
R2210 (BC)

Riddel, Frank Stephen "Related Aspects of the Social and Economic Problems, Cultural Transitions and Educational System of Rural Appalachia: An Analysis Based on the Concept of Scale." Ph. D. Diss. Ohio State Univ., 1971.
R2220 (BC)

Riddle, Almeda A Singer and Her Songs. Baton Rouge: LSU Press, 1970. Miss Riddle is noted for her renditions of traditional ballads.
R2230 (BC)

Ridenour, George L. "The Development of Public Education in Campbell County, Tennessee." Master's thesis. Univ. of Tennessee, 1950.
R2240

The Land of the Lake: A History of Campbell County, Tennessee. LaFollette: LaFollette Pub., 1941. An informative and informal history of Campbell County, Tennessee.
R2250

Ridgecrest Baptist Assembly, Ridgecrest, N. C. Day Book, Sept., 1907-Aug. 24, 1909. Microfilm. Ridgecrest, N. C.: n.p., 1907-1909. The mountain assembly and retreat of the Southern Baptists.
R2260 (WCU)

Minutes, 1909-1931. Microfilm. Ridgecrest, N. C.: n.p., n.d.
R2270 (WCU)

Ridgely, Joseph Vincent William Gilmore Simms. New York: Grossett and Dunlap, 1962. Simms wrote several novels with Appalachian settings.
R2280 (BC)

Ridgeway, Florence Holmes Corwin, Euphemia Kipp Unto the Hills; Glimpses of Berea's Outdoors. Cincinnati: Abington Press, n.d.
C7600

A Charge to Keep; Narratives and Episodes Devoted to the Women Who Helped Build a Place for Worship and for Learning on the Berea Ridge. Typescript. Berea: Berea Woman's Club, 1954.
R2290 (BC)

Ries, Heinrich Clay Deposits and Clay Industry in North Carolina, a Preliminary Report. North Carolina Geological Survey Bulletin, no. 13. Raleigh: G. V. Barnes, 1897.
R2300 (WCU)

Riggs, F. E. ed. Tolley, G. S. Economics of Watershed Planning Sponsored by the Southeast Land Tenure Research Committee, the Farm Foundation, and the Tennessee Valley Authority. Ames, Iowa: State Univ. Press, 1961.
T8820

Rights, Douglas LeTell The American Indian in North Carolina. Durham, N. C.: Duke Univ. Press, 1947.
R2310 (WCU)

The American Indian in North Carolina. 2nd ed. Winston-Salem, N. C.: J. F. Blair, 1957.
R2320 (ASU WCU LMC ETSU UNCA BC)

The Discoveries of John Lederer. Charlottesville: Univ. of Virginia Press, 1958.
R2330 (ASU LMC)

Rigsby, Michael Spirit Happy. Brevard?, N. C.: The Loom Press, 1974.
R2340

Ripley, Thomas H. Cushwa, Charles T. Forest Recreation: Estimated and Predictions in the North River Area, George Washington National Forest, Virginia. Blacksburg: Virginia Agricultural Experiment Station, 1965.
C9960

Recreation Impact on Southern Appalachian Campgrounds and Picnic Sites. U. S. Forest Service Station Paper, no. 153. Asheville, N. C.: Southeastern Forest Experiment Station, 1962.
R2350 (WCU)

Risley, Eleanor de a Vergne Doss The Road to Wildcat: A Tale of Southern Mountaineering. Boston: Little, Brown, and Co., 1930. Stories of a flatland couple traveling through the mountains of Appalachia.
R2360 (BC ASU LMC)

Risser, Hubert E. "The Economics of the Coal Industry." Master's thesis. Univ. of Kansas, 1958.
R2370

Ritchie, Andrew Jackson The Rabun Industrial School and Mountain Extension Work Among the Mountain Whites. Atlanta: n.p., 1906. This has become the Rabun Gap Nachoochee Valley School of FOXFIRE fame.
R2380

Sketches of Rabun County History, 1819-1948. 1948. Reprint. Clayton, Ga.: The author, 1959. Stories and historical sketches of Rabun County history.
R2390 (BC ASU LMC)

Ritchie, Frank T., Jr. Robertson, Stanley M. Soil Survey, Habersham County, Georgia. Washington: U. S. Soil Conservation Service, 1963.
R3190

Ritchie, Jean Apple Seeds and Soda Straws: Some Love Charms and Legends. Illustrated by Don Bolagnese. New York: H. Z. Walck, 1965.
R2400 (ASU)

Celebration of Life, Her Songs, Her Poems. New York: Geordie Music Pub., 1969.
R2410 (ASU)

Celebration of Life: Her Songs, Her Poems. New York: Geordie Music Pub., 1971.
R2420 (LMC)

The Dulcimer Book, Being a Book about the Three-stringed Appalachian Dulcimer, Including Some Ways of Tuning and Playing: Some Recollections in Its Local History in Perry and Knott Counties, Kentucky. Some Observations on the Probable Origins of the Instrument in the Old Countries of Europe: And with Words and Music for Some Sixteen Songs from the Ritchie Family of Kentucky. New York: Oak Pub., 1964.
R2430 (ASU BC ETSU LMC WCU)

The Dulcimer Book, Being a Book about the Three-stringed Appalachian Dulcimer, Including Some Ways of Tuning and Playing: Some Recollections in Its Local History in Perry and Knott Counties, Kentucky. Some Observations on the Probable Origins of the Instrument in the Old Countries of Europe: With Plentiful Photographic Illustrations and Drawings. And with Words and Music for Some Sixteen Songs from the Ritchie Family of Kentucky. New York: Oak Pub., 1972.
R2440 (ASU)

Folk Songs of the Southern Appalachian As Sung by Jean Ritchie. New York: Oak Pub., 1965.
R2450 (WWC)

Folk Songs of the Southern Appalachians; As Sung by Jean Ritchie. New York: Oak Pub., 1965.
R2460 (LMC WWC ETSU)

Singing Family of the Cumberlands. Illustrated by Maurice Sendak. New York: Oxford Univ. Press, 1955.
R2490 (ASU MHC WWC BC)

Singing Family of the Cumberlands. Illustrated by Maurice Sendak. 1955. Reprint. New York: Oak Publications, 1963.
R2500 (ASU WCU LMC)

The Swapping Song Book. Photographs by George Pickow. Piano arrangements by A. K. Fossner and Edward Tripp. New York: Oxford Univ. Press, 1952.
R2510 (BC ASU LMC)

Ritchie, Jean comp. Jean Ritchie's Swapping Song Book. Photographs by George Pickow. Piano arrangements by A. K. Fossner and Edward Tripp. New York: H. Z. Walck, 1964.
R2480 (ASU WCU)

Ritchie, Jean ed. A Garland of Mountain Song: Songs from the Repertoire of the Ritchie Family of Viper, Kentucky. With piano accompaniment by Hally Wood Gordon. Produced under the supervision of Milton Rettenberg. New York: Broadcast Music, 1953.
R2470 (ASU WWC)

Ritt, Leonard Gilbert "Presidential Voting Patterns in Appalachia: An Analysis of the Relationship Between Turnout, Partisan Change, and Selected Socioeconomic Variables." Ph. D. Diss. Univ. of Tennessee, 1967.
R2520

Rittenhouse, Gordon The Texture of Mississippian, Upper Devonian, and Lower Pennsylvanian Sandstones in the Appalachian Basin. U. S. Geological Survey Special Publication. Washington: Govt. Print. Off., 1946.
R2530

The Texture of Paleozoic Sandstones and Sandy Limestones in the Appalachian Basin. U. S. Geological Survey Special Publication. Washington: Govt. Print. Off., 1946.
R2540

Ritter, (W. M.) Lumber Company The Romance of Appalachian Hardwood Lumber: 1890 — Fifty Years of Service — 1940. Richmond: Garrett and Massie, 1940.
R2550 (BC ASU WCU LMC)

Rittgers, Fred Henry "A Geographical Survey of Blount County, Tennessee." Master's thesis. Univ. of Tennessee, 1941.
R2560

Rivers, William James A Sketch of the History of South Carolina to the Close of the Proprietary Government by the Revolution of 1719. With an appendix containing many valuable records hitherto unpublished. Xerox copy of the original. Charleston, S. C.: McCarter & Co., 1856.
R2580 (ASU)

Rives, Amelie Tanis, the Sang-Digger. New York: Town Topics Pub. Co., 1893. A surveyor in the mountains meets a strange woman who digs ginseng for a living.
R2570

Rives, Amelie pseud. see also **Troubetzkoy, Amelie Rives Chandler**

Rivkin/Carson Priority Determination Procedure for the Selection of Pollution Abatement Projects in the Monongahela River Basin. With Arthur W. Edwards Associates. Washington: Appalachian Regional Commission, 1972.
R2590 (ASU)

Rizk, Estelle Smith No More Muffled Hoofbeats. Philadelphia: Dorrance, 1960.
R2600 (ASU)

Roanoke Story of County and City Compiled by Workers of Writers Program of W.P.A. in Virginia. American Guide Series. Sponsored by School Board of Roanoke City, and School Board of Roanoke County. 1942. Roanoke: The board, 1942.
R2610

Roanoke Valley Historical Society Journal. vol. 1-, 1964-. Roanoke, Va.: The society, n.d.
R2620 (BC ETSU)

Roback, Selwyn S. The Effects of Acid Mine Drainage on Aquatic Insects. Philadelphia: Academy of Natural Sciences of Philadelphia, 1969.
R2630 (ASU)

Roberson, Zera Hall Public School Education in Buncombe County, 1935-1969. Asheville, N. C.: Miller Print. Co., 1969.
R2640 (WCU)

Robert, Joseph Clarke The Tobacco Kingdom: Plantation, Market, and Factory in Virginia and North Carolina, 1800-1860. 1938. Reprint. Gloucester, Mass.: P. Smith, 1965.
R2650 (ASU)

Robert, O. R. Amsden, Thomas William Geology and Water Resources of Garrett County. Baltimore: Maryland Department of Geology, Mines and Water Resources, 1954.
A2230 (ETSU)

Roberts, Bruce The Carolina Gold Rush. 1st ed. Charlotte, N. C.: McNally and Loftin, 1971. Gold Fields in North Carolina included Burke County and other western areas.
R2660 (ASU MHC ETSU)

The Goodliest Land — North Carolina. New York: Doubleday, 1973. Western North Carolina is allotted adequate coverage. Beautifully illustrated.
R2680 (ASU LMC)

Harper's Ferry in Pictures. Text by W. J. McNally. Charlotte, N. C.: McNally & Loftin, 1963.
R2690 (ASU WCU)

Sense of Discovery: The Mountain. Richmond, Va.: John Knox Press, 1969. A beautifully illustrated book about the mountains, a small girl and a stranger in buckskin.
R2700 (ASU LMC BC WCU)

Where Time Stood Still: A Portrait of Appalachia. New York: Crowell-Collier Press, 1970. Pictorial study of Appalachia; its culture and its people.
R2710 (ASU UNCA BC WCU MHC ETSU FC LMC WWC)

Roberts, Nancy This Haunted Land. Charlotte, N. C.: McNally and Loftin, 1970.
R3040 (ASU MHC BC)

Roberts, Nancy This Haunted Land. Charlotte, N. C.: McNally and Loftin, 1973.
R3050 (LMC)

Roberts, Nancy Sense of Discovery: The Mountain. Richmond: John Knox Press, 1969.
R3060 (ASU LMC WCU BC)

Roberts, Bruce ed. The Face of North Carolina. With text by Dick Gorrell. Foreword by Paul Green. Charlotte, N. C.: McNally & Loftin, 1962.
R2670 (ASU LMC UNCA)

Roberts, Dorothy James The Mountain Journey. New York: D. Appleton-Century Co., 1947. Story of childbirth and a harrowing journey through a West Virginia storm to seek medical aid.
R2720 (ASU)

Roberts, Elizabeth Madox Black Is My Truelove's Hair. New York: Viking Press, 1938. A novel of love and betrayal in the Kentucky mountains.
R2730 (ASU LMC ETSU WCU BC)

A Buried Treasure. New York: Literary Guild, 1931. Set in the foothill country of the Appalachians.
R2740 (ASU LMC WCU ETSU)

The Great Meadow. New York: Viking Press, 1930. A novel of frontier life and the journey over the mountains to Kentucky.
R2750 (ASU LMC ETSU BC WWC)

The Haunted Mirror. New York: The Viking Press, 1932. Stories with a mountain setting, notable for the fluid quality of mountain speech.
R2760

The Haunted Mirror; Stories. New York: Viking, 1932. Stories with a mountain setting and excellent use of the haunting cadence of mountain speech.
R2770

He Sent Forth a Raven. New York: Viking Press, 1935.
R2780 (ASU)

He Sent Forth a Raven. New York: Popular Library, 1963.
R2790 (ETSU)

My Heart and My Flesh, a Novel. New York: Viking Press, 1927.
R2800 (ASU ETSU WCU)

Not by Strange Gods; Stories. New York: Viking, 1941. A group of stories with a Kentucky hill setting.
R2810

Song in the Meadow: Poems. New York: Viking Press, 1940.
R2820 (ASU)

The Time of Man. New York: Viking Press, 1926. The Chesser family migrates from the mountains to pick tobacco in the south.
R2830 (ETSU LMC WCU WWC BC)

The Time of Man, a Novel. With wood engravings by Clare Leighton. New York: Viking Press, 1945.
R2840 (WCU)

The Time of Man, a Novel. Introduction by Robert Penn Warren. With wood engravings by Clare Leighton. Compass Books, C103. New York: Viking Press, 1963.
R2850 (ASU)

Roberts, Elliot One River — Seven States: TVA-State Relations in the Development of the Tennessee River. Record Extension Series, vol. 31, no. 1. Knoxville: Bureau of Public Administration, Univ. of Tennessee, 1955.
R2860 (ASU WCU LMC BC)

Roberts, Ellis Wynn "A History of Land Subsistence and Its Consequences Caused by the Mining of Anthracite Coal in Luzerne County, Pennsylvania." Ph. D. Diss. New York Univ., 1948.
R2870

Roberts, Ina Wear Edwards, Rapha Olga Jones Descendants of East Tennessee Pioneers. Gatlinburg: n.p., 1963.
E1190 (ASU)

Roberts, John Bennett "A Role Definition of Secondary School Assistant Principals in Washington County, Virginia." Master's thesis. East Tennessee State Univ., 1966.
R2880 (ETSU)

Roberts, Joseph Kent Annotated Geological Bibliography of Virginia. Published by the Alderman Library. Univ. of Virginia Bibliographical Series, no. 2. Richmond: Dietz Press, 1942.
R2890 (ETSU)

Roberts, Leon Ward 1912- The Tales and Songs of the Couch Family. Lexington: Univ. of Kentucky Press, 1959. This is the family from whom Mr. Roberts has collected much of his published folklore.
R2900

Roberts, Leonard ed. Hatfield, G. Elliott The Hatfields. Stanville, Ky.: Big Sandy Valley Historical Society, 1974.
H3450 (ASU)

Roberts, Leonard W. Folk Tales of the Southern Mountains. Berea, Ky.: Council of the Southern Mountains, 1958.
R2910 (ASU MHC)

I Bought Me a Dog, and Other Folktales from the Southern Mountains. Berea, Ky.: Council of Southern Mountain Workers, 1954. One dozen authentic folk stories from Appalachia.
R2920 (ASU WCU LMC MHC ETSU BC)

Sang Branch Settler, Folksongs and Tales of a Kentucky Mountain Family. Austin: Univ. of Texas Press, 1974.
R2950 (ASU)

Up Cutshin and Down Greasy: Folkways of a Kentucky Family. Lexington: Univ. of Kentucky Press, 1959.
R2990 (ASU WCU LMC ETSU BC UNCA)

Roberts, Leonard W. comp. Nippy and the Yankee Doodle, and More Folk Tales from the Southern Mountains. 1st ed. Berea, Ky.: Council of the Southern Mountains, 1958.
R2930 (ASU LMC ETSU BC)

Old Greasybeard: Tales from the Cumberland Gap. Illustrated by Leonard Epstein. Detroit: Folklore Associates, 1969. Includes animal, hero, giant, humorous and tall tales.
R2940 (ASU WCU ETSU LMC WWC MHC BC FC)

Roberts, Leonard W. ed. South from Hell-fer-Sartin: Kentucky Mountain Folk Tales. Lexington: Univ. of Kentucky Press, 1955. Collection of folk tales, some from Europe with an Appalachian flavor.
R2960 (ASU WCU MHC BC)

South from Hell-fer-Sartin: Kentucky Mountain Folk Tales. Lexington: Univ. of Kentucky, 1964.
R2970 (LMC MHC ETSU WWC)

South from Hell-fer-Sartin: Kentucky Mountain Folk Tales. 1955. Reprint. First Appalachian Heritage Edition. Berea, Ky.: Council of the Southern Mountains, 1964.
R2980 (ETSU)

Roberts, Lydia Jane The Nutrition and Care of Children in a Mountain County of Kentucky. Publication, 110. Washington: U. S. Department of Labor, Children's Bureau, 1922.
R3000

Roberts, Nancy Roberts, Bruce The Goodliest Land — North Carolina. New York: Doubleday, 1973.
R2680 (ASU LMC)

Roberts, Bruce Sense of Discovery: The Mountain. Richmond, Va.: John Knox Press, 1969.
R2700 (ASU LMC BC WCU)

Roberts, Bruce Where Time Stood Still: A Portrait of Appalachia. New York: Crowell-Collier Press, 1970.
R2710 (ASU UNCA BC WCU MHC ETSU FC LMC WWC)

Ghosts of the Carolinas. With photographs by Bruce Roberts. Foreword by Legette Blythe. Charlotte, N. C.: McNally and Loftin, 1962. A few of the stories are from the mountains.
R3010 (ASU LMC MHC BC)

Ghosts of the Carolinas. With photographs by Bruce Roberts. Foreword by Legette Blythe. 2nd ed. Charlotte, N. C.: McNally and Loftin, 1967.
R3020 (ASU)

Roberts, Nancy
An Illustrated Guide to Ghosts and Mysterious Occurrences in the Old North State. Photographs by Bruce Roberts. Charlotte, N. C.: Old Heritage House, 1959.
R3030 (ASU LMC)
This Haunted Land. 1st ed. A Southern Living Edition. Charlotte, N. C.: McNally and Loftin, 1970.
R3040 (ASU MHC BC)
This Haunted Land. Charlotte, N. C.: McNally and Loftin, 1973.
R3050 (LMC)
Sense of Discovery: The Mountain. Richmond: John Knox Press, 1969. A young girl meets a stranger in buckskin who shows her the wonders of the mountain.
R3060 (ASU LMC WCU BC)

Roberts, Peter Anthracite Coal Communities. New York: Macmillan, 1904. A study of the demography, social, educational and moral life of the coal region.
R3070 (BC)

Roberts, Roy L. Some Postwar Rural Trends in Kentucky, North Carolina, Tennessee, Virginia, and West Virginia. Washington: U. S. Bureau of Agricultural Economics, 1946.
R3080

Roberts, Ruby Altizer Emera Altizer and His Descendants. n.p.: n.p., n.d.
R3090

Roberts, Wallace Moon, J. W. Soil Survey, Jefferson County, Tennessee. Washington: U. S. Department of Agriculture, Bureau of Plant Industry, 1941.
M6630
Soil Survey, Hamilton County, Tennessee. Prepared in cooperation with the Tennessee Agricultural Experiment Station and the Tennessee Valley Authority. Soil Survey Report, Series 1937, no. 22. Washington: U. S. Department of Agriculture, Bureau of Plant Industry, Soils, and Agricultural Engineering, 1947.
R3100
Swann, Maurice Edward Soil Survey, Roane County, Tennessee. Washington: U. S. Department of Agriculture, Bureau of Plant Industry, 1942.
S9440

Roberts, Wallace and others Soil Survey, Knox County, Tennessee. Soil Survey, Series 1942, no. 10. Washington: U. S. Soil Conservation Service, 1955.
R3110

Robertson, Archibald Thomas Slow Train to Yesterday, a Last Glance at the Local. Illustrated by F. Stoobel. Boston: Houghton Mifflin Co., 1945. Railroading in the mountains.
R3120 (ASU LMC BC)

Robertson, George F. A Small Boy's Recollections of the Civil War (War Between the States) Clover, S. C.: The author, 1932.
R3130 (ASU)
A Small Boy's Recollections of the Civil War. Charlotte, N. C.: Standard Print. Co., 1932.
R3140

Robertson, George Francis The Only Nancy. Mount Holly, N. C.: Lowell Pub. Co., 1917.
R3150 (LMC ASU)

Robertson, James Rood Petitions of the Early Inhabitants of Kentucky to the General Assembly of Virginia, 1769. Louisville, Ky.: John P. Morton and Co. Inc., Printers to the Filson Club, 1914.
R3160

Robertson, Seonaid Mairi Dyes from Plants. New York: Van Nostrand Reinhold, 1973.
R3170 (ASU)

Robertson, Stanley M. Soil Survey, Forsyth County, Georgia. Soils surveyed by S. M. Robertson and others. Correlation by A. H. Hasty. Soil Survey, Series 1956, no. 12. Washington: U. S. Soil Conservation Service, 1960.
R3180
Soil Survey, Habersham County, Georgia. Field Survey by Stanley M. Robertson and others. Soil Survey, Series 1959, no. 27. Washington: U. S. Soil Conservation Service, 1963.
R3190

Robinette, Frank L. "What the Eighth Grade Patrons of Scott County Think about Their Schools." Master's thesis. East Tennessee State College, 1957.
R3200

Robinette, Reba "Specific Techniques Used to Improve the Reading of Three Groups of Children in the Eighth Grade at Robinson Jr. High School in Kingsport, Tennessee." Master's thesis. East Tennessee State College, 1958.
R3210 (ETSU)

Robins, Edwards With Thomas in Tennessee. Philadelphia: G. W. Jacobs and Co., 1903. Thomas was the hero of the East Tennessee campaign and saved the day at Chickamauga.
R3220

Robinson, Daniel Merritt Bob Taylor and the Agrarian Revolt in Tennessee. Chapel Hill: Univ. of North Carolina, 1935.
R3230

Robinson, Donald H. Camper's and Hiker's Guide to the Blue Ridge Parkway. Riverside, Conn.: Chatham Press, 1971.
R3240 (ASU LMC ETSU FC WCU BC)

Robinson, Eliot Harlow The Man from Smiling Pass: Or, The Honorable Abe Blount. Illustrated by H. Weston Taylor. New York: A. L. Burt Co., 1924. Young man urges reforms in the mountain, gets elected to Congress and gets the girl.
R3250 (ASU BC)
"Smiles," a Rose of the Cumberlands. Illustrated by H. Weston Taylor. Boston: Page Co., 1919. A novel of life, love and medicine in the mountains.
R3260 (ASU WCU BC)
Smiling Pass: Being a Further Account of the Career of "Smiles," a Rose of the Cumberlands. Illustrated by John Goss. New York: A. L. Burt Co., 1921. A continuation of SMILES. The young nurse, Rose comes home from the war.
R3270 (ASU)

Robinson, George O. The Oak Ridge Story: The Saga of a People Who Share in History. Kingsport, Tenn.: Southern Pubs., 1950.
R3280 (ASU WCU BC)

Robinson, Glenn Hugh Soil Survey, Avery County, North Carolina. Soil Survey, Series 1946, no. 1. Washington: U. S. Soil Conservation Service, 1955.
R3290

Robinson, John Hovey Daniel Boone: Or, The Pioneers of Kentucky. Boston: G. W. Studley, 185?. A fictional account of the exploits of Daniel Boone.
R3300 (BC)

Robinson, Luther We Made Peace with Polio. Nashville: Broadman Press, 1960.
R3310 (ASU)

Robinson, Marie "Public Information and the Community Action Programs of the War on Poverty: The First Three Years." Master's thesis. American Univ., 1970.
R3320

Robinson, Nelson Holmes, Jack E. Structure of County Government in Tennessee. n.p.: n.p., n.d.
H6800

Robinson, Tully M. Occurrence and Availability of Ground Water in Ohio County, West Virginia. Prepared by the U. S. Geological Survey. Bulletin, 27. Charleston: West Virginia Geological and Economic Survey, 1964.
R3330 (ETSU)

Robinson, W. H. Water Supply of the Birmingham Area, Alabama. U. S. Geological Survey Circular, no. 254. Washington: Govt. Print. Off., 1953.
R3340

Robnett, Elizabeth Parham "A History of Bledsoe County, Tennessee: 1807-1957." Ed. S. Diss. George Peabody College, 1957.
R3350

Rockbridge Historical Society Proceedings of the Rockbridge Historical Society. Lexington, Va.: The society, 1941-.
R3360 (BC ASU)

Rockingham, Harrisonburg Civil War Centennial Commission Civil War Action in Rockingham County, Virginia, 1861-1865. Harrisonburg: The author, 1964.
R3370 (ASU LMC)

Rodgers, John King, Philip Burke Geology and Manganese Deposits of Northeastern Tennessee. Nashville: Tennessee Department of Conservation Division of Geology, 1944.
K2410 (ETSU)
Geology and Mineral Deposits of Bumpass Cove, Unicoi and Washington Counties, Tennessee. Bulletin, 54. Nashville: Tennessee Department of Conservation, Division of Geology, 1948.
R3390 (ETSU)
Stratigraphic Section at Lee Valley, Hawkins County, Tennessee. Bulletin, 55. Nashville: Tennessee Department of Conservation, Division of Geology, 1948.
R3400 (ETSU)
The Tectonics of the Appalachians. New York: Wiley — Interscience, 1970. Tectonics, according to Mr. Webster, has to do with the formation of mountains.
R3410 (LMC ETSU WWC)

Rodgers, John comp. Geologic Map of East Tennessee. Prepared in cooperation with U. S. Dept. of Interior Geological Survey. Bulletin, 58, pt. 2. Nashville: Tennessee Department of Conservation, Division of Geology, 1952.
R3380 (ETSU)

Roger's Asheville Photogravures. New York: Alber-type Co., 1895.
R3590 (BC)

Rogers, Elizabeth E. Daddy's Pearl and Other Stories. Philadelphia: J. M. Rogers, 1898. Kentucky mountain stories from a Berea author.
R3420 (BC)
How Jack Went to College. Berea, Ky.: Students' Job Print., 1895. Story of a boy's efforts to go to college; at Berea, of course.
R3430 (BC)

Rogers, Elizabeth Embree Biny's Choice. Berea: Berea College Print. Dept., 1895. Sabina chooses a husband with educational ambitions.
R3440 (BC)
Sarepty's Schoolin'; the Tale of a Mountain Maid Who Hungered for Knowledge. Berea, Ky.: Berea College Print. Dept., n.d.
R3450 (BC)

Rogers, Evelyn Focus on Franklin County. Winchester: n.p., 1966.
R3460

Rogers, George Adventures of Elder Triptolemus Tub. Boston: Abel Tompkins, 1867. A novel of religious experience.
R3470 (WCU)

Rogers, James R. Cane Ridge Meeting-house. To Which Is Appended the Autobiography of B. W. Stone and a Sketch of David Purviance. Cincinnati: Standard Pub. Co., 1910. The Great Revival Movement started at Cane Ridge in Kentucky.
R3480 (BC ASU)

Rogers, Jesse Littleton The Civil War Battles of Chickamauga and Chattanooga. Chattanooga: Andrews, 1942.
R3490

Rogers, John A. R. Birth of Berea College; a Story of Providence. Philadelphia: n.p., 1903.
R3500 (BC ASU)

Rogers, John Almanza Rowley Birth of Berea College: A Story of Providence. With an introduction by Hamilton Wright Mabie. Philadelphia: Coates, 1903, Facsimile, 1970 edition.
R3510 (MHC)

Rogers, Katherine V. "A Description of Government in Gordon, Clark and Paulding Counties, Georgia." Master's thesis. Univ. of Ga., 1941.
R3520

Rogers, Lettie Hamlett Birthright. New York: Simon and Schuster, 1957. A novel about segregation in a Burke County, North Carolina town. A young school teacher takes a stand on the rare problem and sets off a chain of reactions leading to her dismissal.
R3530 (ASU)

Rogers, Louis Leroy "Problem Analysis Study of Selected Freshmen Students at Appalachian State Teachers College." Ed. D. Diss. Univ. of Tennessee, 1959.
R3540 (ASU)

Rogers, Lucille Light from Many Candles: A History of Pioneer Women in Education in Tennessee. Published by XI State, Delta Kappa Gamma. Nashville: McQuiddy Print. Co., 1960.
R3550 (ETSU)

Rogers, Reese F. Soil Survey of Jackson County, Tennessee. Washington: U. S. Dept. of Agriculture, 1915.
R3560

Soil Survey of Jackson County, Tennessee. Prepared in cooperation with the Tennessee Geological Survey. Field Operations, 1913. Washington: U. S. Department of Agriculture, Bureau of Soils, 1915.
R3570

Rogers, Thomas O., Jr. "The Economic Impact of Recreation Resort Development on the Local Economy: A Case Study of Avery County, North Carolina." Master's thesis. Univ. of Tennessee, 1973.
R3580 (LMC)

Rogers, Tommy W. Wilbur, George L. Internal Migration in the United States 1958 to 1964: A List of References. State College: Mississippi Agricultural Experiment Station, Mississippi State Univ., 1965.
W6080

Rogers, William Warren Ward, Robert David Labor Revolt in Alabama: The Great Strike of 1894. University: Univ. of Alabama Press, 1965.
W770 (WCU BC)

Rohrbaugh, Lewis Bunker Rohrback Genealogy. Philadelphia, Pa.: Dando-Schaff Print. and Pub. Co., 1970.
R3600

Rojankovsky, Fedor Daniel Boone. Paris: Domino Press, 1931. Biography of Boone the hunter, pioneer, land speculator, and Indian trader.
R3610 (BC)

Rolfe, Mary A. Our National Parks. Book One. Chicago: Sanborn and Co.; 1927.
R3620 (ASU LMC BC)

Roller, David Charles "The Republican Party of North Carolina: 1900 to 1916." Ph. D. Diss. Duke Univ., 1965. Western North Carolina, the traditional strong-hold of Republicanism, was held accountable for Civil War sins and did not begin to recover from that handicap until after 1916.
R3630

Rollins, Kathleen Impassioned Foothills. New York: William Godwin, 1937. Romantic fiction set in western North Carolina.
R3640

Love's Tapestry. New York: Arcadia House, 1935. Romantic fiction with a western North Carolina setting.
R3650

Rolston, Frances "History of Education in Letcher County, Kentucky." Master's thesis. Univ. of Kentucky, 1939.
R3660

Romagnoli, Alfonso Louis "Worker Education in West Virginia: A Study in Union-University Cooperation." Microfilm. Master's thesis. West Virginia Univ., 1957.
R3670 (ASU)

Romaine, William B. Story of Sam Davis. Pulaski: Pulaski Citizen, 1928.
R3680

Roncker, Robert The Southern Appalachian Migrant. Cincinnati: n.p., 1959. An important early treatise on the problems of the Southern Appalachian mountaineer in the cities.
R3690

Roosevelt, Theodore The Winning of the West. 4 vols. New York: G. P. Putnam's Sons, 1889-96. Early volumes devoted to America's first frontier — the Appalachians. The author recognized the strategic importance of the mountains and the battles fought there.
R3700 (ASU)

Root, A. S. Mangum, Adolphus W. Soil Survey of the Campobello Area, South Carolina. Washington: Dept. of Agriculture, Bureau of Soils, 1904.
M3020

Roper, Marilyn Elizabeth "A Survey of Vocabulary Weaknesses of 417 Freshmen at East Tennessee State University." Master's thesis. East Tennessee State Univ., 1964.
R3710 (ETSU)

Roper, Rosalie "An Analysis of Youth Centers for White Youth in Three Tennessee Cities: Johnson City, Elizabethton and Kingsport." Master's thesis. East Tennessee State College, 1958.
R3720 (ETSU)

Rorabargh, James D. John R. Rohrbach (Rohrabaugh) 1728-1821: Descendants and Marriage Connections. 2 vols. Parsons, W. Va.: McClain Print. Co., 1966-1970.
R3730 (ASU)

Rosa, Bray Roberts, Ruby Altizer Emera Altizer and His Descendants. n.p.: n.p., n.d.
R3090

Rose, Boyd B. Brown, E. Evan The Economic Development of the Northeast Georgia Commission Area Through Use of Forest Products and Water Resources. Athens, Ga.: Northeast Georgia Planning and Development Commission, 1966.
B7120 (ASU ETSU)

Rose, Joseph A. How to Be Successful. Parsons, W. Va.: McClain Print. Co., 1972. A smug little autobiographical volume describing one mountain boy's success. Stuffed with maxims.
R3740

Rose, Mary Glenn "Jesse Stuart: Pioneer Writer of the Kentucky Hills." Microfilm. Master's thesis. George Peabody College for Teachers, 1938.
R3750 (ASU)

Rosenbaum, Art Old-time Mountain Banjo: An Instruction Method for Playing the Old-time Five-string Mountain Banjo Based on the Styles of Traditional Banjo-pickers. New York: Oak Publications, 1968. One of the finest volumes available for the mountain banjo.
R3760 (WCU ASU BC)

Rosenberg, Bruce A. The Art of the American Folk Preacher. New York: Oxford Press, 1970. A grand tribute to the camp-meeting revivalist.
R3770 (BC)

The Folksongs of Virginia. Charlottesville: Univ. Press of Va., 1969.
R3780 (FC)

Ross, Charles C. ed. Story of Rotherwood, from the Autobiography of Rev. Frederick A. Ross. Knoxville: Bean, Warters, 1923. History of Rotherwood in Sullivan County, Tennessee.
R3790

Ross, Clarence Samuel Occurrence and Origin of the Titanium Deposits of Nelson and Amherst Counties, Virginia. U. S. Geological Survey Professional Paper, no. 198. Washington: Govt. Print. Off., 1941.
R3800

Origin of the Copper Deposits of the Ducktown Type in the Southern Appalachian Region. U. S. Geological Survey Professional Paper, no. 179. Washington: Govt. Print. Off., 1935.
R3810 (ETSU ASU)

Ross, Edmund Gibson History of the Impeachment of Andrew Johnson, President of the United States, by the House of Representatives, and His Trial by the Senate, for High Crimes and Misdemeanors in Office, 1868. 1896. Reprint. New York: Burt Franklin, n.d.
R3820 (ASU)

Ross, Ernest Lafayette "An Educational Study of Bradley County, Tennessee." Master's thesis. Univ. of Tennessee, 1940.
R3830

Historical Cemetery Records of Bradley County, Tennessee. 2 vols. Cleveland, Tenn.: n.p., 1973.
R3840 (ETSU)

Ross, Fred E. Jackson Mahaffey, a Novel. Boston: Houghton Mifflin, 1951. A well-written novel of the North Carolina foothill country. Speech patterns are very close to those of mountain speech.
R3850 (ASU)

Ross, James W. "An Analysis of the Relationship Between the Anxiety Level and the Academic Performance of Freshmen at East Tennessee State University for the Year 1965." Master's thesis. East Tennessee State Univ., 1967.
R3860 (ETSU)

Ross, L. M. ed. North Carolina Index: Guide to North Carolina's Periodical Literature A Cumulative Author and Subject Index Covering Material in N. C. Publications. . . . Winston-Salem: The Editors, irregular serial supplements.
N2430 (ASU UNCA)

Ross, Malcolm Harrison The Machine Age in the Hills. New York: Macmillan Co., 1933. Progress by machine comes into the hills. Areas discussed agriculture, textile industry, mining, and spinning mills.
R3870 (ASU LMC BC WWC ETSU)

Ross, W. G. Shaw, Charles Frederick Reconnaissance Soil Survey of Northeastern Pennsylvania. Washington: U. S. Department of Agriculture, Bureau of Soils, 1913.
S2470

Ross, William P. Indian Territory. Washington, D. C.: Gibson Brothers, Printers, 1874. Remarks in opposition to the bill to organize the territory of Oklahoma, by William P. Ross, principal chief of the Cherokee Nation, before the Committee on Territories of the House of Representatives.
R3880 (ASU)

Roth, Elmer R. Heart Rots of Appalachian Hardwoods. U. S. Forest Service Forest Pest Leaflet, 38. Washington: Govt. Print. Off., 1959.
R3890

Roth, William V., Jr. The Appalachian Regional Development Program. Washington: Appalachian Regional Commission, n.d.
R3900 (ASU)

Rothblatt, Donald N. Regional Planning: The Appalachian Experience. Lexington, Mass.: Heath Lexington Books, 1971. An examination of the Appalachian Regional Commission. Concludes that Appalachian people were not represented in the decision making.
R3910 (ASU WCU WWC LMC)

Rothery, Agnes New Roads in Old Virginia. Rev. ed. Boston: Houghton Mifflin, 1937.
R3920 (LMC)

Rothrock, Howard Eugene Geology and Coal Resources of the Northeast Part of the Coosa Coal Field, St. Clair County, Alabama. Prepared by the U. S. Geological Survey in cooperation with the Geological Survey of Alabama. Bulletin, 61. University: Univ. of Alabama, 1949.
R3930 (ETSU)

Rothrock, Mary U. comp. Luttrell, Laura F. comp. Calvin Morgan McClung Historical Collection. n.p.: n.p., n.d.
L4040

Rothrock, Mary U. ed. Haywood, John The Natural and Aboriginal History of Tennessee, up to the First Settlements Therein by the White People in the Year 1768. Jackson, Tenn.: McCowat-Mercer Press, 1959.
H4050 (ASU ETSU BC)

Rothrock, Mary Utopia ed. The French-Broad Holston Country: A History of Knox County, Tennessee. Knoxville, Tenn.: East Tennessee Historical Society, 1946.
R3940 (LMC BC)

Rothrock, Mary Utopia ed.
The French Broad-Holston Country: A History of Knox County, Tennessee. By the Knox County History Committee, East Tennessee Historical Society. 1946. Reprint. Knoxville: East Tennessee Historical Society, 1972.
R3950 (ETSU)

Rothwell, R. P. Report on Stone Hill Copper Mines and Works, Cleburne County, Alabama. Washington: Off. of Engineering and Mining, 1877.
R3960 (ASU)

Rough, Robert L. Cost Study of Pumping Versus Flowing Oil Production from Appalachian Waterfloods. Report of Investigations, 5558. Pittsburgh: U. S. Bureau of Mines, 1960.
R3970

Lithologic Descriptions of Appalachian Area Oil-producing Formations. Information Circular, 8473. Washington: U. S. Bureau of Mines, 1970.
R3980

Rotary Coring of Appalachian Area Oil-producing Formations with Mud or Air. U. S. Mines Bureau Report of Investigations, 7238. Pittsburgh: Mines Bureau, 1969.
R3990

Rourke, Constance Mayfield American Humor: Study of the National Character. New York: Harcourt, Brace and Co., 1931. Scant attention paid to rough mountain wit.
R4000 (MHC)

Davy Crockett. New York: Harcourt, Brace and Co., 1934. Gives less attention to the sensational and more attention to the solid character of the man than most other Crockett biographers.
R4010 (ETSU BC)

Davy Crockett. Illustrated by James MacDonald. Introduction and study guides by Geraldine Murphy. School ed. New York: Harcourt, Brace, 1955.
R4020 (ASU)

Rouse, Elaine Burdett "Union Economic Politics and Union Discipline in the Bituminous Wage Dispute of 1949-1950." Microfilm. Master's thesis. West Virginia Univ., 1953.
R4030 (ASU)

Rouse, W. L. Nicholls, W. D. Family Incomes and Land Utilization in Knott County, Kentucky. Lexington: Kentucky Agriculture Experiment Station, Univ. of Kentucky, 1946.
N910

Rovetch, Warren Program Budgeting for Planners; A Case Study of Appalachia With Projections Through 1985. New York: Praeger Pubs., 1974. Analyzes the Appalachian Regional Commission's program budget.
R4040

Rovit, Earl H. Herald to Chaos: The Novels of Elizabeth Madox Roberts. Lexington: Univ. of Kentucky Press, 1960. Many of her novels are set in western Virginia and eastern Kentucky.
R4050 (ASU BC)

Rowan, Thomas Black Earth. New York: Hillman-Curl, 1935. Novel of the coal, oil and gas industries of Appalachia. Set primarily in northern Alabama.
R4060 (ASU)

Stormy Road. New York: Ives-Washburn, 1934. A nere-do-well mountain family moves to a valley town and becomes very like the white trash around them. Message is that mountain people lose their values and culture in industrial towns.
R4070

Rowell, Adelaide On Jordan's Stormy Banks: A Novel of Sam Davis, the Confederate Scout. Indianapolis: Bobbs-Merrill, 1948.
R4080

Rowell, John W. Yankee Cavalrymen: Through the Civil War with the Ninth Pennsylvania Cavalry. Knoxville: Univ. of Tennessee Press, 1971. Two enlisted men's diaries describe the cavalry raids of this unit in Tennessee.
R4090

Rowland, Joseph M. Bright Angel Trail. Richmond: Richmond Press, 1926. Saccharine fiction with a North Carolina setting and some light but effective humor.
R4100 (ASU)

The Hill Billies. Nashville: Cokesbury Press, 1924. A novel about North Carolina hill folk during World War I. Old Tom's trip to New York to meet his hero son would have made a fine vehicle for a Ma and Pa Kettle film.
R4110 (ASU BC)

Rowland, Joseph Medley Blue Ridge Breezes. Richmond: Appeals Press, 1920. Description of life in the Blue Ridge by a Methodist minister. The twin brothers were based on real people and the Cleveland incident actually happened.
R4120 (LMC FC WCU BC)

Blue Ridge Breezes. Nashville: M. E. Church, South, 1927.
R4130 (ASU BC)

Roy, Andrew A History of the Coal Miners of the United States. Columbus, Ohio: J. L. Trauger Print. Co., 1907.
R4140 (BC)

Royall, Mrs. Anne Newport Sketches of History, Life, and Manners in the United States. By a Traveller. New Haven: The author, 1826. Mrs. Royall travelled on horseback from Alabama, through Knoxville and East Tennessee to the Virginia springs.
R4150

Royall, Margaret Shaw Andrew Johnson — Presidential Scapegoat. New York: Exposition Press, 1958.
R4160 (BC)

Royce, Charles C. "The Cherokee Nation of Indians." Fifth Annual Report of the Bureau of Ethnology to the Secretary of the Smithsonian Institution, 1883-84. Washington, D. C.: Govt. Print. Off., 1887. A general history of the Cherokee Nation.
R4170 (UNCA ASU)

Rubin, Louis Decimus Thomas Wolfe: The Weather of His Youth. Baton Rouge: Louisiana State Univ. Press, 1955.
R4190 (UNCA ASU WCU BC)

Rubin, Louis Decimus ed. Thomas Wolfe; a Collection of Critical Essays. Englewood Cliffs, N. J.: Prentice-Hall, 1973.
R4180 (UNCA)

Rubincam, Milton ed. Krebs, Friedrich Emigrants From the Palatinate to the American Colonies in the 18th Century. Norristown: Pennsylvania German Society, 1953.
K3200 (ASU)

Rucker, Maud Applegate West Virginia, Her Land, Her People, Her Traditions, Her Resources. New York: W. Neale, 1930.
R4200 (BC)

Rudicil, Rowland K. Historic Hamblen, 1870-1970. Morristown: Morristown Print. Co., 1970. A history of Hamblen County, Tennessee.
R4210

Rudolph, Foster Austin, Moris E. Soil Survey, Claiborne County, Tennessee. Washington: U. S. Department of Agriculture, Bureau of Plant Industry, Soils, and Agricultural Engineering, 1948.
A5560 (ASU)

Moon, J. W. Soil Survey, Jefferson County, Tennessee. Washington: U. S. Department of Agriculture, Bureau of Plant Industry, 1941.
M6630

Soil Survey, Carter County, Tennessee. Rev. by L. E. Odom. Soil Survey, Series 1942, no. 4. Washington: U. S. Soil Conservation Service, 1953.
R4220

Rudolph, Foster and others Soil Survey, Norris Area, Tennessee. Rev. by L. E. Odom. Soil Survey, Series 1939, no. 19. Washington: U. S. Soil Conservation Service, 1953.
R4230

Rudolph, L. C. Francis Asbury. Nashville: Abingdon Press, 1966. Asbury regarded the time he spent in the mountains as his personal penance to the Lord. He was afraid of both the land and the mountaineers.
R4240 (ASU WWC BC)

Ruffin, Beverly Augusta Parish, Virginia, 1738-1780. Verona, Va.: McClure Press, 1970.
R4250 (ASU BC)

Ruffner, Henry Address to the People of West Virginia: Shewing That Slavery Is Injurious to the Public Welfare, and That It May Be Gradually Abolished, Without Detriment to the Rights and Interests of Slaveholders. 1857. Reprint. Bridgewater, Va.: Green Bookman, 1933.
R4260 (ASU BC)

Ruggles, Alice McGuffey Morrill The Story of the McGuffeys. New York: American Book Co., 1950. The McGuffey reader series came from an Appalachian family.
R4270 (ASU BC)

Rule, William ed. Standard History of Knoxville, Tennessee, with Full Outline of the Natural Advantages, Early Settlement, Territorial Government, Indian Troubles and General and Particular History of the City Down to the Present Time. Chicago: Lewis, 1900. A General History of the Early Settlement of Knox County, Tennessee.
R4280

Runyan, Nicholas Patterson A Quaker Scout. New York: The Abbey Press, 1900. A novel of a Quaker lad in frontier Appalachia.
R4290

Ruperti, George comp. Tribbeko, John Lists of Germans From the Palatinate Who Came to England in 1709. Baltimore: Genealogical Pub. Co., 1965.
T9270 (ASU)

Rupp, Israel Daniel A Collection of Upwards of Thirty Thousand Names of German, Swiss, Dutch, French, and Other Immigrants in Pennsylvania from 1727 to 1776. 2nd rev. and enlarged ed. With an added index. Baltimore: Genealogical Pub. Co., 1965.
R4300 (ASU)

Rural and Appalachian Health With a foreword by Edward M. Kennedy. Papers presented at a conference at Mont Chateau, W. Va., June 6-8, 1971, under the sponsorship of the Division of Public Health and Preventive Medicine, School of Medicine, West Virginia, University. Springfield, Ill.: Thomas, 1973.
R4310 (ASU BC)

Rush, John DeWitt "Relation of Land Base Quality to the Agricultural Economy of Knox County, Tennessee." Master's thesis. Univ. of Tennessee, 1940. An Economic History of Knox County, Tennessee.
R4320

Ruskin, Gertrude McDavis John Ross, Chief of an Eagle Race. Chattanooga: John Ross House Assoc., 1963. Ross was the principal chief of the Cherokee Nation at the time of their removal to Oklahoma.
R4330 (ASU)

Russel, Dean The TVA Idea. Irvington on Hudson, N. Y.: Foundation for Economic Education, 1949.
R4340 (BC)

Russell, Elizabeth Henry Campbell Paths of Glory: A Simple Tale of a Faring Bride, Elizabeth, Sister of Patrick Henry. By Nelly C. Preston. Richmond: Whittet and Shepperson, 1961. Fictional account of the life of Beth Henry and her two marriages on the Appalachian frontier.
R4350 (ASU)

Russell, James Snakes and the Devil. New York: Vantage Press, 1959. A novel of the snake-handling cults.
R4360 (LMC)

Russell, James pseud. see **Richardson, James**

Russell, Jerry Sutton, Willis A. The Social Dimensions of Kentucky Counties: Data and Rankings of the State's 120 Counties on Each of 81 Characteristics. Lexington: Bureau of Community Service, Univ. of Kentucky, 1964.
S9360

Russell, John Henderson The Free Negro in Virginia, 1619-1865. 1913. Reprint. New York: Negro Universities Press, 1969.
R4370 (ETSU FC)

Russell, Mattie "William Holland Thomas, White Chief of the North Carolina Cherokees." Ph. D. Diss. Duke Univ., 1956.
R4380

Russell, Phillips North Carolina in the Revolutionary War. Charlotte, N. C.: Heritage Printers, 1965.
R4390 (ASU LMC)

Russell Sage Foundation Southern Mountain Schools Maintained by Denominational and Independent Agencies. New York: Russell Sage Foundation, 1929.
R4400 (LMC)

Russell, William Greenway What I Know about Winchester: Recollections of William Greenway Russell, 1800-1891. Reprinted from the Winchester News by Winchester-Frederick County Historical Society. Staunton, Va.: McClure Print. Co., 1953.
R4410 (ASU BC)

Rust Engineering Study The Appalachian Thruway Study. Pittsburg: n.p., 1969. A study of the Appalachian Regional Commission's grandiose scheme to shuttle people through or out of the mountains without providing enough access to allow local people to use the thing.
R4420

Rutherford County, North Carolina, Marriage Bonds Typed by the Genealogical Society of Utah. Salt Lake City: The society, 1943.
R4430 (ASU)

Rutledge, William E., Jr. An Illustrated History of Yadkin County, 1850-1965. Yadkinville, N. C.: The author, 1965.
R4440 (ASU)

Rutman, Gilbert L. Pursell, Donald E. Selected Demographic Aspects of the West Virginia Economy, 1950-1975: Estimates and Projections of Migration and Population. Morgantown: West Virginia Univ., Bureau of Business Research, 1969.
P4880 (ETSU BC)

Ryan, Arthur Frank ed. Historical Forts and Houses in Knoxville and Nearby Vicinity. Knoxville: Knox Co. Libr., 1962. Historical structures and places in Knox County, Tennessee.
R4450

Ryan, Grace Laura comp. Dances of Our Pioneers. Music arrangements by Robert T. Benford. Illustrated by Brooks Emerson. 1926. Reprint. (Original title: Music for Dances of Our Pioneers.) New York: A. S. Barnes and Co., 1939.
R4460 (ASU BC)

Ryan, Irene (Granny) Granny's Hillbilly Cookbook. Illustrated by Bob Bugg. Englewood Cliff, N. J.: Prentice-Hall, 1966. From "The Beverly Hillbillies" TV show.
R4470 (ASU BC)

Ryan, Marah Told in the Hills. New York: Rand, McNally and Co., 1905. Tales from the southern mountains.
R4490

Ryan, Marah Ellis Martin A Pagan of the Alleghanies. Chicago: Rand, McNally and Co., 1891. Romantic and adventurous fiction with a mountain setting.
R4480 (ASU BC)

Ryan, William Blaming the Victim. 1st ed. New York: Pantheon Books, 1971. Shows the national tendency to blame the poor for their plight. References to Appalachia.
R4500 (WCU BC ASU)

Ryder, C. J. The Debt of Our Country to the American Highlanders During the War. New York: Central office of American Missionary Association, n.d.
R4510

Ryland, Garnett The Baptists of Virginia, 1699-1926. Richmond: Baptist Board of Missions and Education, 1955.
R4520 (BC)

Ryssel, Fritz Heinrich Thomas Wolfe. New York: Ungar, 1972.
R4530 (UNCA)

Rywell, Martin comp. Tennessee Cookbook, More Than 300 Tasty Tennessee Recipes. Harriman, Tenn.: Pioneer Press, 1952.
R4540 (ASU)

Saalbach, William Frederick "United States Bituminous Coal Markets — Trends Since 1920, and Prospects to 1975." Ph. D. Diss. Univ. of Pittsburgh, 1960. Apparently the 1974-75 energy crisis was not forseen by any of the long-range forecasters for the coal industry.
S10

Sabbard, Eugene "History of Education in Owsley County, Kentucky." Master's thesis. Univ. of Kentucky, 1939.
S20

Sabin, Edwin Legrand In the Ranks of Old Hickory, When with the Western Riflemen in Defense Against from Within and Without, Young and Old of All Degrees United Under Andrew Jackson to Make the Republic's Borders Safe. Illustrated by Frank Eltonhead. Trail Blazers Series. Philadelphia: J. B. Lippincott Co., 1927. The Cherokee fought with Jackson in his wars against the other tribes.
S30 (ETSU ASU BC)

Saddler, Gordon Taliaferro "The Appalachian Regional Commission: Selected Aspects of Institutions and Processes and Their Relationship to Natural and Human Resources Development." Ph. D. Diss. West Virginia Univ., 1969.
S40

Sadove, Abraham H. "Transport Improvement and the Appalachian Barrier: A Case Study in Economic Innovation." Ph. D. Diss. Harvard Univ., 1950. A very lucid study of the lack of transportation and its effect on the social isolation and economic depression of Appalachia.
S50 (ASU)

Saffell, William Thomas Roberts Records of the Revolutionary War. 3rd ed. 1894. Reprint. With index to Saffell's list of Virginia soldiers in the Revolution, by J. T. McAllister, 1913. Baltimore: Genealogical Pub. Co., 1969.
S60 (ASU)

Safford, Carleton L. America's Quilts and Coverlets. 1st ed. New York: Dutton, 1972.
S70 (ASU)

America's Quilts and Coverlets. New York: Dutton, 1972.
S80 (ASU)

Safford, James Merrill The Elements of the Geology of Tennessee. Prepared for the use of the schools of Tennessee, and for all persons seeking a knowledge of the resources of the state. Nashville: Ambrose and Bostelman, 1904.
S90 (ASU LMC BC)

Geological Reconnaissance of the State, Tennessee. Nashville: G. C. Torbett and Co., 1856. Safford was one of Tennessee's most productive early geologists.
S100 (ASU)

Geology of Tennessee. Nashville: S. C. Mercer, 1869.
S110 (ETSU)

The Saga of a City; Lynchburg, Virginia. 1786-1936 Lynchburg: n.p., 1936.
S120

Sage, Clara McCormack Early Records, Hampshire County Virginia, Now West Virginia, Including at the Start Most of Known Va. Aside from Augusta District. 1939. Reprint. Baltimore: Genealogical Pub. Co., 1969.
S130 (BC ASU)

Sager, William Herman Haley, Elliot Clarke and others An Economic and Social Survey of Warren County. Charlottesville: Univ. of Virginia, 1943.
H520 (ASU)

Saijo, Albert The Backpacker. A Pocket-size Manual Which Deals with All Aspects of Backpacking. Covers Equipment, Food, Getting Organized for Your Trip, and Takes the Reader on a Sample Trip Through the Mountains. San Francisco: 101 Productions, 1972.
S140

Saileau, John M. Tenn. Valley Land and Its Changing Use. Muscle Shoals, Ala.: National Fertilizer Development Center, 1966.
S150

Saint Agnes Church, Franklin, N. C., The First Fifty Years . . . 1888-1938 Franklin: n.p., 1938.
S160

Saint Cloud, Virgil Pioneer Blood. Raleigh, N. C.: Edwards and Broughton Co., 1948.
S170 (ASU)

Saint James Church, Knoxville, Tennessee Knoxville: n.p., 1929. A social and cultural history of Episcopal, religious groups.
S180

Saint James' Episcopal Church, Hendersonville, N. C., 1863-1963 Hendersonville: n.p., 1963.
S190

Salamanca, J. The Lost Country: A Novel. New York: Simon and Schuster, 1958. A novel of a strange pioneer family in the Blue Ridge Mountains of Virginia.
S200 (ASU BC)

Salem Home Sunday School A Brief History of the Moravian Church. Raleigh, N. C.: Edwards and Broughton Print. Co., 1909. The Moravians had many early missions and settlements in the mountains. Especially among the Cherokee.
S210 (ASU)

Salisbury, John W. Geology and Mineral Resources of the Northwest Quarter of the Cohutta Mountain Quadrangle. Bulletin, no. 71. Atlanta: Georgia Department of Mines, Mining and Geology, 1961.
S220 (ETSU)

Salo, Lawr V. ed. Archaeological Investigations in the Tellico Reservoir, Tennessee, 1967-1968: An Interim Report. Contributions by Duane H. King and other. Knoxville: Dept. of Anthropology, Univ. of Tennessee, 1969.
S230 (ASU)

Sames, James Walter comp. Four Steps West. Versailles, Ky.: n.p., 1971. A history of the dividing line between Virginia and North Carolina, Kentucky, and Tennessee. Informative, but Sames is not part of a William Byrd.
S240 (ETSU ASU)

Sams, W. C. Hasty, Allen Henry Soil Survey, Rhea County, Tennessee. Washington: U. S. Department of Agriculture, Bureau of Plant Industry, Soils, and Agricultural Engineering, 1948.
H3390

Samuels, Harriet Brockman ed. Loudoun County, Virginia, Past and Present. Princeton, N. J.: Graphic Arts Press, 1940.
S250 (ASU)

Sanborn, Ruth Burr These Are My People. New York: The Thomas Y. Crowell Co., 1941. Miss Sanborn writes of country people whose traditions stem directly from the early English settlers and generations of independent pioneers. The story is about a young Southern physician, torn between the wealthy patients his fiancee brought him and the sturdy back country people who really love him.
S260 (ASU)

Sandburg, Carl The American Songbag. New York: Harcourt, Brace and Co., 1927.
S270 (FC)

Sandburg, Helga The Wheel of Earth. New York: McDowell, Obolensky, 1958. A novel of farm life, love and hope set in the hill country of Kentucky.
S280 (ASU WCU BC)

The Wizard's Child. New York: Dial Press, 1967. A novel of a strange girl-child in an unspecified setting in the Appalachians.
S290 (ASU WCU LMC)

Sanders, Albert N. Botanical Gardening in Greenville. Greenville, S. C.: Furman Univ., 1962.
S300 (BC ASU)

Sanders, Charles H. "An Educational and Economic Survey of Pickett County, Tennessee." Master's thesis. Univ. of Tennessee, 1924. A Pickett County, Tennessee history.
S310

Sanders, Charles Wesley Hill-bred Barton's Code, a Western Story. New York: Chelsea House, 1925. A novel of a hill man whose code will not allow him to stand still for a legal investigation. He fights and runs and takes a long time to clear his name.
S320 (ASU BC)

Sanders, David B. "Transportation and Trade Areas; Analysis of Morgantown, Fairmont, and Clarksburg." Master's thesis. West Virginia Univ., 1968.
S330 (ASU)

Sanders, John L. Maps of North Carolina Congressional Districts, 1789-1960, and State Senatorial Districts and Apportionment of State Representatives, 1776-1960. Prepared for the General Assembly of North Carolina. Chapel Hill: Institute of Government, Univ. of North Carolina, 1961.
S340 (BC WWC)

Sanders, Retta E. "A Survey of Boone County (West Virginia) School Buildings." Master's thesis. Marshall College, 1952.
S350

Sanders, Robert Stuart An Historical Sketch of Springfield Presbyterian Church, Bath County, Kentucky. Frankfort: Roberts Print. Co., 1954.
S360 (BC)

Sanders, Ronald L. Kentucky Personal Income, 1961. Lexington: Bureau of Business Research, Univ. of Kentucky, 1963. Gives statistics by counties. Good data on Appalachian counties.
S370

Sanders, Walter R. The Scherer Family of Montgomery County, Illinois. Litchfield, Ill.: The author, 1945. Family settled originally in the mountains of West Virginia.
S380 (ASU)

Sanderson, Esther Sharp County Scott and Its Mountain Folk. Huntsville, Tenn.: The author, 1958. A well-written, very interesting county history. Good social commentary and depictions of mountain life.
S390 (ASU LMC WCU BC)

Sandlin, Moselle Stack adapter Underwood, Thomas Bryan adapter Cherokee Legends and the Trail of Tears. Asheville, N. C.: Stephens Press, 1956.
U80 (ASU LMC MHC WCU)

Sandmann, Leo Joseph "Social Effects of the Mining Industry in Eastern Kentucky." Master's thesis. Univ. of Kentucky, 1915. An excellent study of the correlations between mining and a community's social activities.
S400 (ASU)

Sanford, E. T. Blount College and the Univ. of Tennessee. Knoxville: Univ. of Tenn., 1894. Describes the beginnings of the University of Tennessee.
S410 (ASU BC ETSU)

Sanford, Thomas H., Jr. Gound-water Levels in Madison County, Alabama, July 1956 to July 1959. Prepared by the U. S. Geological Survey in cooperation with the Madison County Board of Commissioners and the Geological Survey of Alabama. Information Series, 22. Univ.: Alabama Geological Survey, 1960.
S420 (ETSU)

Ground Water in Marshall County, Alabama: A Reconnaissance. Prepared in cooperation with the U. S. Geological Survey. Bulletin, 85. Univ.: Geological Survey of Alabama, Division of Water Resources, 1966.
S430 (ASU ETSU)

Sanger, S. F. The Olive Branch of Peace and Good Will to Men: Anti-war History of the Brethren and Mennonites, the Peace People of the South, During the Civil War, 1861-1865. Elgin, Ill.: Brethren Pub. House, 1907.
S440 (ASU)

Sartain, James Alfred History of Walker Co., Ga. Dalton: A. J. Showalter Co., 1932. Includes family sketches of early settlers.
S450 (ASU BC)

History of Walker County, Georgia. LaFayette, Ga.: A. M. Mathews, 1972-.
S460 (ASU)

Satterfield, M. H. Soil and Sky; the Development and Use of Tennessee Valley Resources. Knoxville: Bureau of Public Administration, University of Tennessee, 1950.
S470

Saucier, J. R. Taras, Michael Andrew Wood Density Surveys of the Minor Species of Yellow Pine in the Eastern United States: Pt. I — Spruce Pine (Pinus Glabra Walt.). Asheville, N. C.: Southeastern Forest Experiment Station, 1970.
T250 (WCU)

Sauerlender, Owen H. Gamble, Hays Bentley The Impact of Interchange Development on the Economy of Clinton County. University Park, Pa.: Institute for Research on Land and Water Resources, 1966.
G210

Saunders, James Edmonds Early Settlers of Alabama. With notes and genealogies by his granddaughter Elizabeth Saunders Blair Stubbs, 1899. Reprint. 2 parts in 1. Baltimore: Genealogical Pub. Co., 1969.
S480 (ASU BC)

Saunders, Robert J. The Spatial Concentration of Industry in Appalachia: An Analysis of the Potential for Import Substitution. With the assistance of Edmund Rollo. Foreword by William H. Miernyk. Prepared for the Appalachian Regional Commission. Appalachian Research Report, no. 9, appendix B. Morgantown: Regional Research Institute, West Virginia Univ., 1969.
S490 (ASU ETSU)

Saupart, Sylavnia Stories of W. Va. for Boys and Girls. Charleston, W. Va.: Jarrett Print. Co., 1937.
S500

Savage, Henry, Jr. Lost Heritage. New York: William Morrow, 1970. This book surveys the travels and writings of seven Colonial, pre-Audubon naturalists: John Lawson, Mark Catesby, John and William Bartram, Andre and Francois Andre Michaux, and Alexander Wilson.
S510 (LMC)

Savage, James Everett History of Methodism in Montgomery County. Mount Sterling, Ky.: Mount Sterling Advocate, 1939.
S520 (ASU)

Savage, John Life and Public Service of Andrew Johnson. n.p.: Derby and Miller, 1866. A very sympathetic portrait of Johnson's background and his troubled years.
S530

Savage, John H. The Life of John H. Savage: Citizen, Soldier, Lawyer, Congressman. Nashville: The author, 1903. Savage was from Warren County, Tennessee.
S540 (LMC)

Save Our Cumberland Mountains, Inc. Facts about Strip Mining. Lake City, Tenn.: The organization, 1974. A seven page question and answer series about strip-mining.
S560

Save the Children Federation Report on the School Sponsored Program, Appalachian Area. Mimeoprinted. n.p.: n.p., 1955.
S550

Savoldi, Gloria Root Tenn. Boy. Philadelphia: Westminster, 1972. Novel of a lad living alone in a remote cabin in the Smokies during the closing days of the Civil War.
S570 (BC ASU)

Saward, Frederick Edward The Coal Trade, a Compendium of Valuable Information Relative to Coal Production, Prices, Transportation, etc., at Home and Abroad. New York: n.p., 1881. Saward did not foresee the troubles in the Appalachian coal fields.
S580 (BC)

Sawyer, Harriet Adams Souvenir of Asheville or the Sky-land. St. Louis: Nixon-Jones Print. Co., 1892. Promotional and descriptive material on the area around Asheville.
S590 (ASU WCU BC)

Sawyer, Ruth Journey Cake, Ho New York: The Viking Press, 1970. Humorous and informative children's book concerning a trip into the mountains.
S600 (ASU)

Sawyer, W. K. Electrical and Hydraulic Flow Properties of Appalachian Petroleum Reservoir Rocks. U. S. Mines Bureau Report of Investigations, 7519. Pittsburgh: Mines Bureau, 1971.
S610

Saye, Albert B. ed. Coulter, Ellis Merton ed. A List of the Early Settlers of Georgia. Athens: Univ. of Georgia Press, 1949.
C7790 (ASU)

Saylor, Lettie Cradle Valley. New York: Hobson Book Press, 1946. A bleak novel of life in a Kentucky valley torn by a feud that started over a pumpkin. Living, dying, love, marriage nothing arouses the people from their lethargy except the feud.
S620 (BC ASU)

Saylor, Lettie Hoskins Brick Without Straw, a Story of Kentucky Mountain Life. Cincinnati: Hobon Press, Inc., 1843. A mountain girl from a family so large it's running out of names, struggles through the eighth grade by age seventeen. She marries a rich man and becomes an authoress.
S630 (ASU BC)

Saylor, Roger B. An Economic Survey of Indiana County, Pennsylvania. State College: Penn. State College, Bureau of Business Research, 1959.
S640

An Economic Survey of Northumberland County, Pennsylvania. State College: Penn. State College, Bureau of Business Research, 1949.
S650

An Economic Survey of Venango County, Pennsylvania. State College: Penn. State College, Bureau of Business Research, 1950.
S660

Saylor, Roger B. and others Fayette County, Pennsylvania; An Economic Survey. Univ. Park: Penn. State Univ., Bureau of Business Research, 1957.
S670

Scalf, Henry P. ed. Hatfield, G. Elliott The Hatfields. Stanville, Ky.: Big Sandy Valley Historical Society, 1974.
H3450 (ASU)

Scalf, Henry Preston Four Men of the Cumberlands: Big Ed Hall, Devil John Wright, Dr. M. B. Taylor, Bad Talt Hall. Prestonburg, Ky.: The author, 1958. Seems most of Kentucky's heroes are violent men.
S680 (ASU BC)

Historic Floyd, 1890-1950. Prestonburg, Ky.: Floyd Co. Sesquicentennial, 1950. Promotional and historical material on Prestonburg and Floyd County.
S690

Kentucky's Last Frontier. Foreword by Thomas D. Clark. 1st ed. Chicago: Adams Press, 1966.
S700 (MHC BC)

Kentucky's Last Frontier. Prestonburg, Ky.: The author, 1966.
S710 (ASU LMC)

Mountain Kinsmen Ride; a Story of the James Family. Prestonburg, Ky.: The author, 1956. The infamous James brothers are descended from a Floyd County, Kentucky family.
S720

Scarborough, Dorothy A Song Catcher in Southern Mountains: American Folk Songs of British Ancestry. New York: Columbia Univ. Press, 1937. A classic in ballad scholarship.
S730 (ASU WCU ETSU WWC BC)

A Song Catcher in Southern Mountains: American Folk Songs of British Ancestry. 1937. Reprint. New York: AMS Press, 1966.
S740 (ASU LMC ETSU)

Scarbrough, George Tellico Blue. New York: E. P. Dutton & Co., 1949. Mountain poetry.
S750 (BC)

Schaare, C. Richard The Life of Daniel Boone in Picture and Story. New York: Cupples and Leon, 1934. A biography designed for the younger reader.
S760

Schacter, Harry W. Kentucky on the March. Foreword by Niark F. Ethridge. 1st ed. New York: Harper, 1949.
S770 (ASU BC)

Schaefer, Donald Fred "A Quantitative Description and Analysis of the Growth of the Pennsylvania Anthracite Coal Industry, 1820 to 1865." Ph. D. Diss. Univ. of North Carolina, 1967.
S780

Schaeffer, John Randolph From Baltimore to Charleston. Gormania, W. Va.: n.p., 1906.
S790

Schaff, Walter R. "The Growth and Development of Education in Caldwell County." Master's thesis. Univ. of North Carolina, 1926.
S800 (ASU)

Schaie, Klaus Warner The 1965 Head Start Psychological Screening Program; Final Report on the Data Analysis Conducted Under a Contract Between the West Virginia Office of Economic Opportunity and West Virginia University. Morgantown: Human Resources Research Institute, West Virginia Univ., 1967.
S810 (ASU)

Schanz, John Schenck, George E. The Economic Importance of the Coal Industry to Pennsylvania. Univ. Park: Penn. State Univ., Dept. of Mineral Economics, 1967.
S910

Schaper, William August Sectionalism and Representation in South Carolina. Xerox copy of the original. Washington: Govt. Print. Off., 1901. Includes material on South Carolina's six Appalachian counties.
S820 (ASU BC)

Scharf, John Thomas History of Western Maryland. Philadelphia: L. H. Everts, 1882. Includes history of Maryland's three mountain counties.
S830 (ETSU)

History of Western Maryland: Being a History of Frederick, Montgomery, Carroll, Washington, Allegany, and Garrett Counties from the Earliest Period to the Present Day. Including Biographical Sketches of Their Representative Men. 2 vols. 1882. Reprint. Baltimore: Regional Pub. Co., 1968.
S840 (ASU)

Scharf, Paula S. "The Reading Interests of Students as Revealed in a Study of an Individualized Reading Program at Pond Gap School, Knoxville, Tennessee." Master's thesis. Univ. of Tennessee, 1961.
S850

Schauinger, J. Herman Cathedrals in the Wilderness. Milwaukee: Bruce Pub. Co., 1952. Biography of the priest who established first Catholic church west of the Allegheny Mountains.
S860 (BC)

Scheer, Julian Tweetsie, the Blue Ridge Sidewinder. Illustrated by Lee Kalbe. 1st ed. Charlotte, N. C.: Heritage House, 1958. A history of the East Tennessee and Western North Carolina Railroad.
S870 (ASU LMC BC)

Schenck, Carl Alvin The Biltmore Story: Recollections of the Beginning of Forestry in the United States. St. Paul: American Forest History Foundation, Minnesota Historical Society, 1955. Site of first forestry school in the United States.
S880 (ASU WCU BC)

Birth of Forestry in America, Biltmore Forest School, 1898-1913. Santa Cruz, Calif.: Forest History Society and the Appalachian Consortium, 1974.
S890 (ASU)

Schenck, David North Carolina. 1780-81. Being a History of the Invasion of the Carolinas by the British Army Under Lord Cornwallis in 1780-81, with the Particular Design of Showing the Part Borne by North Carolina in That Struggle for Liberty and Independence, and to Correct Some of the Errors of History in Regard to That State and Its People. Raleigh: Edwards and Broughton, 1889.
S900 (ASU LMC)

Schenck, George E. The Economic Importance of the Coal Industry to Pennsylvania. Univ. Park: Penn. State Univ., Dept. of Mineral Economics, 1967.
S910

Schenk, Paul The Colony Bernstadt in Laurel County, Kentucky. London, Ky.: The Sentinel-Echo, 1940. Report on a colony of Swiss farmers who came to Kentucky in 1860.
S920

Schildt, John W. Drums Along the Antietam. Parsons, W. Va.: McClain Print. Co., 1972. A history of the Antietam Valley from its Pennsylvania hill source to Antietam Furnace on the Potomac. Few areas are so rich in history.
S930 (MHC ASU)

Schindall, Henry Let the Spring Come. New York: Appleton-Century-Crofts, 1953. A novel of the American Revolution which includes a trek across the mountains of Virginia to Pittsburgh.
S940 (ETSU BC ASU)

Schlee, John S. Hurst, Vernon J. Field Excursion: Ocoee Metasediments: North Central Georgia and Southeast Tennessee. Atlanta: Georgia Department of Mines, Mining & Geology, 1962.
H8610 (ETSU)

Schlesinger, Arthur M. ed. Hansen, Marcus Lee The Atlantic Migration, 1607-1860: A History of the Continuing Settlement of the United States. New York: Harper, 1961.
H1680 (ASU)

Schloss, Bert P. A Human Relations Study — The Southern White In-Migrant. Chicago: Commission on Human Relations, 1957.
S950

Schmidt, J. William Haas, Raymond M. West Virginia Travel and Tourism Study — The Potential Market. Morgantown: W. Va. Univ., Bureau of Business Research, 1968.
H70

Schmidt, T. William West Virginia Travel and Tourism Study: An Evaluation. Morgantown: West Virginia Univ., Bureau of Business Research, 1965.
S960

Schmidt-Bleek, F. Benefit/Cost Approach to Decision Making: The Dilemma with Coal Production. Supported by National Science Foundation. Knoxville: Univ. of Tennessee, The Appalachian Resources Project, 1973.
S970 (ASU)

Schmidt-Bleek, F. K. Moore, John R. Strip Mining and the Three E's. Knoxville: Univ. of Tennessee, Appalachian Resources Project, 1973.
M7240 (ASU)

Statement on Benefit/Cost Evaluation of Strip Mining in Appalachia. Prepared for the U. S. House of Representatives, Committee on Interior and Insular Affairs, Subcommittee on the Environment and Subcommittee on Mines and Mining. Knoxville: Univ. of Tennessee Appalachian Resources Project, 1973.
S980 (ASU)

Schmitt, Leonard R. "Recreational Habits of Rural Youth in Selected Communities of Hamilton County, Tennessee." Master's thesis. Univ. of Tennessee, 1949.
S990

Schnacke, Dick American Folk Toys: 85 American Folk Toys and How to Make Them. New York: Putnam, 1973.
S1000 (ASU)

Schneider, Norris F. Betty Zane, Heroine of Fort Henry. Williamsport, Md.: Zane Grey Collector, 1970. Partially set in the Appalachian Mountains.
S1010 (ASU)

Schneider, William Joseph Water Resources of the Appalachian Region, Pa. to Ala. Washington: U. S. Geological Survey, 1965. Includes extensive maps.
S1020

Schneiderman, Leonard "The Culture of Poverty — A Study of the Value-orientation Preferences of the Chronically Impoverished." Ph. D. Diss. Univ. of Minnesota, 1963. Contains references to Appalachian poverty.
S1030

Schnell, R. L. Harvesting Pine Pulpwood in the Tennessee Valley. Norris, Tenn.: Tennessee Valley Authority, 1961.
S1040

Scholtz, Carl The Story of Glen Rogers, W. Va. Charleston: Raleigh-Wyoming Coal Co., 1933. Story of Glen Rogers, West Virginia a coal town. Good propaganda for the industry.
S1050 (BC)

Schopf, Johann David Travels in the Confederation, 1783-1784. Translated and edited from the German by Alfred James Morrison. 2 vols. 1911. Reprint. New York: Bergman, 1968. Includes early report of life in the mountains by a European traveler.
S1060 (ASU)

Schrader, F. C. Stose, G. W. Manganese Deposits of East Tennessee. Washington: Govt. Print. Off., 1923.
S7660

Schrader, F. F. Flood of July 5, 1939, in Eastern Kentucky. U. S. Geological Survey Water-supply Paper, no. 967-C. Notable Local Floods of 1939, Part 2. Washington: Govt. Print. Off., 1945.
S1070

Schreiner-Yantis, Netti Supplement to 1810 Census of Virginia. Springfield, Va.: n.p., 1971.
S1110

Schreiner-Yantis, Netti comp. 1800 Tax Lists and Abstracts of Deeds (1796-1800) of Wythe County, Virginia. Springfield, Va.: n.p., 1971. Lists those white males over sixteen who paid personal property tax in 1800. Deeds are abstracted in an attempt to locate the residence of the taxpayer. Map, index.
S1090

Montgomery County, Virginia Circa 1790. Springfield, Va.: n.p., 1972. A comprehensive study, including the 1769 tax lists, abstracts of over eight hundred land surveys, and data concerning migration. Map of the area included.
S1100

Schreiner-Yantis, Netti ed. Archives of the Pioneers of Tazewell County. Springfield, Va.: Privately printed, 1973. Index contains original records from the Tazewell County courthouse. Includes: Orders of court, wills, marriages, militia records, land records, tax lists, records of the descendants of the pioneers of Tazewell County.
S1080

Schretter, Howard A. The Georgia Mountains: A View of Its Resources, Problems, and Potentials. Athens: Institute of Community and Area Development, Univ. of Georgia, 1964.
S1120 (ASU LMC)

Schrey, Frank J. "Forest Products Marketing from Public Lands in Pennsylvania." Master's thesis. Pennsylvania State Univ., 1957.
S1130

Schrier, Arnold Ireland and the American Emigration, 1850-1900. Minneapolis: Univ. of Minnesota Press, 1958.
S1140 (ASU)

Schultz, Katherine E. McChesneys of Virginia. Annville, Pa.: n.p., n.d.
S1150

Schultz, Vincent et al. Statewide Wildlife Survey of Tennessee, a Study of the Land, Wildlife, Farmer, Hunter and Trapper; Final Report of Work Accomplished with Federal Aid to Wildlife Restoration Funds Under Pittman-Robertson Project no. W-16-R. Nashville: Tennessee Game and Fish Commission, 1954.
S1160

Schulz, William F. Conservation Law and Administration: A Case Study of Law and Resource Use in Pennsylvania. New York: Ronald Press, 1953. Like most conservation case studies this one leaves you frustrated. Will the laws ever be enforced?
S1170

Schumacher, G. J. Whiford, L. A. A Manual of the Fresh-Water Algae in North Carolina. Raleigh: North Carolina Agricultural Experiment Station, 1968.
W5740 (LMC)

Schuricht, Herrman History of the German Element in Virginia. Baltimore, Md.: Theo Kroh and Sons Printers, 1898.
S1180

Schusler, William Kenneth "The Economic Position of Railroad Commuter Service in the Pittsburgh District — Its History, Present and Future. Ph. D. Diss. Univ. of Pittsburgh, 1958.
S1190

Schuster, Richard The Selfish and the Strong. New York: Random House, 1958. A novel of the Civil War and love and politics in the Big Sandy Region of Kentucky.
S1200

Schwab, Glenn O. Hoffman, Glenn J. Annotated Bibliography on Slope Stability of Strip Mine Soil Banks. Wooster: Ohio Agricultural Experiment Station, 1964.
H6250 (ASU)

Hoffman, Glenn J. Slope Stability of Coal Strip Mine Spoil Banks. Wooster: Ohio Agricultural Experiment Station, 1964.
H6260 (ASU)

Schwab, W. G. The Forests of Tazewell County, Virginia. Charlottesville: Univ. of Virginia, Va. Geological Commission, 1917.
S1210

Schwartz, Douglas Wright Conceptions of Kentucky Prehistory: A Case Study in the History of Archeology. Studies in Anthropology, no. 6. Lexington: Univ. of Kentucky Press, 1968.
S1220 (ASU BC)

Schwartz, Jerome L. Nolan, Robert L. Rural and Appalachian Health. Springfield, Ill.: Charles C. Thomas, 1973.
N1370 (ASU)

Schwartz, Jerome L. ed. Rural and Appalachian Health Springfield, Ill.: Thomas, 1973.
R4310 (ASU BC)

Schwarze, Edmund History of the Moravian Missions Among Southern Indian Tribes of the United States. Bethlehem, Penn.: Times Pub. Co., Printers, 1923.
S1230 (BC UNCA)

Schwarzweller, Harry K. Education, Migration and Economic Life Chances of Male Entrants to the Labor Force from a Low Income Rural Area. Lexington: Agricultural Experiment Station, 1964.
S1240 (ASU)

Career Placement and Economic Life Chances of Young Men from Eastern Kentucky. ERIC EC 004 030 Lexington: Agricultural Experiment Station, Univ. of Kentucky, 1964.
S1250 (ASU)

Family Ties, Migration, and Transitional Adjustment of Young Men from Eastern Kentucky. Bulletin no. 691. Lexington: Kentucky Agricultural Experiment Station, Univ. of Kentucky in cooperation with the Economic Research Service, U. S. Department of Agriculture, May, 1964.
S1260

Mountain Families in Transition: A Case Study of Appalachian Migration. Univ. Park: Pennsylvania State Univ. Press, 1971.
S1270 (ASU WCU LMC ETSU WWC BC UNCA)

Research Design, Field Work Procedures, and Data Collection Problems in a Follow-Up . Study of Young Men from Eastern Kentucky. RS21. Lexington: Rural Sociology Department, Univ. of Kentucky, May, 1963.
S1280

Social Structure of the Contact Situation, Rural Appalachia and Urban America. Morgantown: West Va. Univ., Appalachian Center, 1969.
S1290

Sociocultural Factors in the Career. Aspirations and Plans of Rural Kentucky High School Seniors. Lexington: Kentucky Agricultural Experiment Station, 1960.
S1300

Sociocultural Origins and Migration Patterns of Young Men from Eastern Kentucky. Lexington: Kentucky Agricultural Experiment Station, 1963.
S1310

Schwarzweller, Harry K. ed. Photiadis, John D. Change in Rural Appalachia: Implications for Action Programs. Philadelphia: Univ. of Pennsylvania Press, 1971.
P2750 (FC LMC WCU ETSU ASU BC)

Schweiker, William F. Health, Welfare, and Housing Needs of the Aged in Berkeley County, West Virginia. Morgantown: W. Va. Univ., 1969.
S1320

Schwendeman, Joseph R. "A Study of Woodworking Industry of the Eastern Mountains and Coal Field Region of Kentucky." Master's thesis. Univ. of Kentucky, 1957.
S1330

Scofield, Kendrick ed. Dillin, John Grace Wolfe The Kentucky Rifle. York, Pa.: G. Shumway, 1967.
D2440 (ASU MHC BC)

Scopes, John Thomas Center of the Storm: Memoirs of John T. Scopes. 1st ed. New York: Holt, Rinehart and Winston, 1967. Scopes was a young teacher who agreed to the trial because he had no job for the summer. By August of 1925 he was a national celebrity.
R1340 (ASU WCU)

The World's Most Famous Court Trial, Tennessee Evolution Case: A Complete Stenographic Report of the Famous Court Test of the Tennessee Anti-evolution Act, at Dayton, July 10 to 21, 1925, Including Speeches and Arguments of Attorneys. Cincinnati: National Book Co., 1925. Scopes published this stenographic report a few months after he was convicted for teaching evolution.
R1350 (ASU BC)

Scott, Edith The Story of Two Chairs. Bristol: King Print. Co., n.d. A story of two chippendale chairs which made the journey from England to Mecklenburg County, North Carolina and across the mountains into East Tennessee with the Ramsey and McReady families.
S1360 (BC)

Scott, Evelyn Parrott Links That Bind. 1st ed. 2 vols. Sudan, Tex.: Sudan Beacon-News, 1967.
S1370 (ASU)

Scott, Evelyn Background in Tennessee. New York: R. M. McBride and Co., 1937. Social life and customs in Tennessee.
S1380 (ASU)

Scott, Evelyn D. Witch Perkins. New York: Henry Holt and Co., 1929. A young girl in a Kentucky mountain town is convinced that the woman who moves in next door is a witch.
S1390 (BC)

Scott, George H. "A Study of the United Mine Workers of America Welfare and Retirement Fund." Master's thesis. West Virginia Univ., 1951.
S1400

Scott, Harold ed. English Song Book. New York: R. M. McBride and Co., 1926. Songs collected, edited and introduced by Harold Scott.
S1410

Scott, James A. "An Interpretation of the Distribution of Crops and Livestock in East Tennessee as Reported by the 1950 Census." Master's thesis. East Tennessee State College, 1953.
S1420 (ETSU)

Scott, John H., Jr. "Pikeville, Market Center of the Upper Sequatchie Valley." Master's thesis. Univ. of Tennessee, 1951.
S1430

Scott, Nancy N. ed. A Memoir of Hugh Lawson White, Judge of the Supreme Court of Tennessee, Member of the Senate of the United States, Etc., Etc. With selections from his speeches and correspondence. Philadelphia: J. B. Lippincott, 1856. Biography of a prominent East Tennessee lawyer and judge.
S1440 (ASU BC)

Scott, Otto J. The Exception; The Story of the Ashland Oil and Refining Co. New York: McGraw, 1968.
S1450

Scott, Samuel W. History of the Thirteenth Regiment, Tennessee Volunteer Cavalry, U. S. A., Including a Narrative of the Bridge Burning: The Carter County Rebellion, and the Loyalty, Heroism and Suffering of the Union Men and Women of Carter and Johnson Counties, Tennessee, During the Civil War. Knoxville, Tenn.: The authors, 1903.
S1460 (ASU LMC)

Scott, W. W. Annals of Caldwell County. Lenoir: News-Topic, 1930.
S1470

"Promotion of the Recreational Use of State Forests, with Special Reference to Pennsylvania." Master's thesis. Univ. of Pennsylvania, 1951.
S1480

Scottina, Joseph P. Kavanagh, Michael J. Preliminary Over-all Economic Development Program for the North-western Pennsylvania Redevelopment Area. Greenville: Northwestern Pennsylvania Conference for Economic Development, 1961.
K300

Scruggs, Earl Earl Scruggs and the 5-string Banjo. New York: Peer International Corp., 1968.
S1490 (WCU BC)

Scully, Carleton Leslie, J. D. Management of Kentucky Natural Resources. Lexington, Ky.: Spindletop Research, 1965.
L1900

Seals, Monroe History of White County. n.p.: n.p., 1935.
S1500

Seamen, Richard M. "An Analysis of Federative Patterns in Social Organization with a Field Study of the Council of Southern Mountain Workers." Ph. D. Diss. Northwestern Univ., 1947.
S1510 (BC)

Sears, Joseph Hamblen Tennessee Printers, 1791-1945: A Review of Printing History from Roulstone's First Press to Printers of the Present. Kingsport, Tenn.: Kingsport Press, 1945.
S1520 (ASU BC)

Seaton, Dorothy B. "Socio-economic Status of Teachers in Kingsport, Tennessee, 1968-1969." Master's thesis. East Tennessee State Univ., 1970.
S1530 (ETSU)

Seaver, Jesse Montgomery The Harris Genealogy. Philadelphia: American Historical Genealogical Society, n.d.
S1540 (ASU)

Seay, Hilton A. "A Study of the Attitudes Toward Modern Mathematics of Secondary Mathematics Teachers in Upper East Tennessee." Master's thesis. East Tennessee State Univ., 1970.
S1550 (ETSU)

Seay, Maurice F. Adult Education, a Part of a Total Educational Program. A Description of the Educational and Training Program of the Tennessee Valley Authority. Lexington: Univ. of Kentucky, 1912.
S1560

Seay, Maurice F. ed. Adult Education, a Part of a Total Educational Program. A Description of the Educational and Training Program of the Tennessee Valley Authority. Lexington, Ky.: Univ. of Ky., 1938.
S1570 (ASU)

Seay, Maurice Farris Elementary Education in Two Communities of the Tennessee Valley: A Description of the Wilson Dam and Gilbertsville Schools. Lexington: Univ. of Kentucky, 1942.
S1580 (ETSU)

Seay, Ruth A. With Reference to Appalachia. Dexter, Mich.: Michigan Institutional Survey and Consulting Service, n.d.
S1590 (ASU)

Sebor, Miles The Economic Geography of Tennessee. Nashville: Tennessee State Planning Commission, 1965. Special section on Appalachian Tennessee.
S1600

Secession: Or, Prose in Rhyme. A Poem by an East Tennessean Philadelphia: S. T. Logan, 1864. A narrative poem of East Tennessee during and shortly before the Civil War.
S1610 (BC)

Seckar, Alveva West Virginia and the Captains of Industry: State Politics and the Origins of Modern Appalachia, 1880-1913. Morgantown: West Virginia Univ., 1974.
S1620

Zuska of the Burning Hills. New York: Oxford Univ. Press, 1952. Zuska, a little girl in an impoverished family in a West Virginia coal town stumbles on a secret which helps her family. Sweet but not trite.
S1630 (BC ASU)

Secrist, Mark H. Zinc Deposits of East Tennessee. Bulletin, no. 31. Nashville, Tenn.: Division of Geology, 1924.
S1640 (LMC)

See, Margielea Stonestree The Banner Floats On and Other Poems. Foreword by Vincent Godfrey Burns. Washington: New World Books, 1971.
S1650 (ASU)

See, Margielea Stonestreet Noon Shouts. Parsons, W. Va.: McClain Print. Co., 1969.
S1660 (ASU)

Seeber, Raymond Clifford "A History of Anderson County, Tennessee." Master's thesis. Univ. of Tennessee, 1928.
S1670

Seebohm, Benjamin ed. Grellet, Stephen Memoirs of the Life and Gospel Labours of Stephen Grellet. Philadelphia: H. Longstreth, 1860.
G4030 (ASU)

Seeger, Peter How to Play the 5-String Banjo: A Manual for Beginners. 3rd ed. rev. Beacon, N. Y.: The author, 1962.
S1680 (ASU LMC)

The Incomplete Folksinger. New York: Simon and Schuster, 1972.
S1690

Seeger, Ruth Porter Crawford American Folk Songs for Christmas. Illustrated by Barbara Cooney. Garden City, N. Y.: Doubleday, 1953.
S1700 (ASU)

Seeman, Elizabeth In the Arms of the Mountain: An Intimate Journal of the Great Smokies. Illustrated by Glen H. Rounds. New York: Crown Pub., 1961. A volume of praise for the Smokies: Natural history, history, and description.
S1710 (ASU WCU LMC ETSU BC)

Seeman, Ernest What's Next? Huntington, W. Va.: Appalachian Movement Press, 1951. A study of American capitalism as seen from the wilderness of East Tennessee.
S1720 (ASU)

Segal, Martin Economic Redevelopment Research: Population, Labor Force and Unemployment in Chronically Depressed Areas. Washington: Area Redevelopment Administration, 1964. Study includes Appalachia.
S1730

Seggar, John F. "Social-psychological Adjustment of Kentucky Mountain Migrants in Urbanized Industrial Areas of Southern Ohio." Master's thesis. Univ. of Kentucky, 1964.
S1740 (ASU)

Seifert, Elizabeth Hillbilly Doctor. Philadelphia: Blakiston Co., 1945.
S1750 (ASU BC)

Seifert, Shirley Never No More, a Novel. Philadelphia: Lippincott, 1964. Fictional account of the life of Daniel and Rebecca Boone.
S1760 (ASU WCU BC)

Seighworth, K. J. Initial Forest Management in the Tennessee Valley. Norris, Tenn.: TVA, 1961.
S1770

Selden, Samuel Frederick Henry Koch: Pioneer Playmaker. A Brief Biography. Chapel Hill: Univ. of North Carolina Press, 1954. Koch is the author of several of the outdoor dramas performed in and written about the Southern Mountains.
S1780 (LMC)

Self, Margaret Cabell Red Clay Country. 1st ed. New York: Harper and Brothers, 1936. Fiction set in the mountainous part of Virginia.
S1790 (ASU)

Seligman, Ben B. Poverty as a Public Issue. New York: Free Press, 1965. A selection of essays on poverty; some on Appalachia.
S1800 (BC)

Sells, Cecil O. "A Study of Pupil Transportation in Polk County, Tennessee." Master's thesis. Tennessee Polytechnic Institute, 1959.
S1810

Selznick, Philip TVA and the Grass Roots. Berkeley: Univ. of California Press, 1949. A study of the organization, not to mention the vast bureaucracy, of the Tennessee Valley Authority's public relations.
S1820 (WWC BC)

Selznick, Phillip TVA and the Grass Roots: A Study in the Sociology of Formal Organization. 1949. Reprint. New preface by the author. Harper Torchbooks. The Academy Library, TB 1230L. New York: Harper and Row, 1966.
S1830 (ASU LMC MHC UNCA)

Semicentennial History of First Methodist Church, Forest City, N. C., 1889-1939 Forest City: Semi-centennial Committee First Methodist Church of Forest City, 1939.
G4170 (BC)

Semones, James King "An Analysis and Evaluation of High School Sociology as Taught in Southern Appalachia." Master's thesis. East Tennessee State Univ., 1972.
S1840 (ETSU)

Semple, Ellen C. American History and Its Geographic Conditions. Boston and New York: Houghton Mifflin Co., 1903. Discusses the role of geography in the preservation of Appalachia's traditions.
S1850 (BC)

Semple, Ellen Churchill American History and Its Geographic Conditions. Rev. 1933. Reprint. New York: Russell and Russell Co., 1968.
S1860 (ASU MHC)

Semple, Robert B. History of the Rise and Progress of the Baptists in Virginia. Richmond: The author, 1810.
S1870 (LMC BC)

Seneker, Stanley Archibald "An Economic Analysis of Competition Between the Tennessee Valley Authority and Private Power." Master's thesis. Univ. of Pennsylvania, 1957.
S1880

Senour, Faunt Le Roy Morgan and His Captors. Cincinnati: C. F. Vent and Co., 1865. Morgan made several raids in the Appalachian region.
S1890 (ASU)

Sensing, Thurman Champ Ferguson, Confederate Guerilla. Nashville: Vanderbilt Univ. Press, 1942.
S1900

The Sentinel-Echo Laurel County, Kentucky. London, Ky.: Sentinel-Echo, 1954. Reprints of the jubilee edition of the Sentinel-Echo. Sketches of Laurel County history and early settlers.
S1910

Sequoya Cherokee Indian New Testament. New York: American Bible Society, 1860. Elias Boudinet, not Sequoya, was responsible for this translation of the Bible.
S1920 (LMC ASU)

Sergeant, John Select Speeches of John Sergeant, of Pennsylvania (1818-1828). Philadelphia: E. L. Carey and A. Hart, 1832. Includes a plea for the Cherokee Nation given before the Supreme Court, 1831.
S1930 (ASU)

Serna, Edgar Barr Making a State, Formation of West Virginia. Charleston: State of W. Va., 1956. A history of the division of West Virginia from Virginia.
S1940

Settel, T. S. ed. and comp. Graham, William Franklin The Faith of Billy Graham. Anderson, S. C.: Droke House, 1968.
G3150 (WCU)

Setters, Jillson see **Thomas, Jean**

Settle, Mary Lee Fight Night on a Sweet Saturday, a Novel. New York: Viking Press, 1964. The third novel in Settle's marvelous trilogy of West Virginia. A strong novel of the legacy of a coal baron's grandchildren, murder, love, and rediscovery of lost kin and lost values.
S1950 (ASU WCU BC)

Know Nothing. New York: Viking Press, 1960. A novel of West Virginia's own brand of frontier life and politics. The second novel of Settle's trilogy.
S1960 (ASU WCU)

O Beulah Land, a Novel. New York: Viking Press, 1956. The first novel of the trilogy treats the discovery of the Kanawha Valley and introduces the McCarkle family, pioneers and dreamers.
S1970 (ASU LMC WCU)

O Beulah Land. 1956. Reprint. New York: Ballantine Books, 1965. Miss Settle is a first rate novelist; her acclaim is long overdue.
S1980 (WWC)

The Scopes Trial: The State of Tennessee v. John Thomas Scopes. New York: F. Watts, 1972. The first completely truthful account of the Scopes trial. Miss Settle shows us how the local merchants' scheme to "put Dayton on the map" got out of hand.
S1990 (ASU)

Setzler, Frank M. Peachtree Mound and Village Site, Cherokee County, North Carolina. Bureau of American Ethnology Bulletin, no. 131. Washington: Govt. Print. Off., 1941.
S2000 (ASU LMC UNCA)

Sever, Charles W. Geology and Ground-water Resources of Crystalline Rocks, Dawson County, Georgia. Prepared in cooperation with the U. S. Geological Survey. Information Circular, 30. Atlanta: Georgia Department of Mines, Mining and Geology, 1964.
S2010 (ASU ETSU)

Severn, William In Lincoln's Footsteps; the Life of Andrew Johnson. New York: Washburn, 1966. Biography of Andrew Johnson written for children.
S2020

Sevier, Cora Bales Sevier Family History, with the Collected Letters of Gen. John Sevier, First Governor of Tennessee and 28 Collateral Family Lineages. Washington: Kaufman Print. Co., 1961. Genealogy of Tennessee's first family. Letters relate to the state of Franklin.
S2030 (ASU ETSU MHC BC)

Seward, Harry M. Scenes and Information about Rockwood, Tennessee, in the Heart of the Great Tennessee Valley Development. Rockwood: Rockwood Times, 1935. This Tennessee Valley Authority propaganda piece includes a Roane County, Tennessee, history.
S2040

Sewell, David Oliver "Training the Poor: A Benefit-cost Analysis of Vocational Instruction in the United States Antipoverty Program." Ph. D. Diss. Duke Univ., 1971. Study included some western North Carolina counties.
S2050

Sexton, Carlie Old Fashioned Quilts. Wheaton, Ill.: n.p., 1928. An illustrated book of patterns and instructions some patterns seldom seen today.
S2060

Sexton, Oswell S. "A History of Education in Scott County, Tennessee." Master's thesis. Univ. of Tennessee, 1951.
S2070

Sexton, Robert Fenimore "Kentucky Politics and Society: 1919-1932." Ph. D. Diss. Univ. Microfilms, 1971. Mentions political corruption in eastern Kentucky and the conditions which cause it.
S2080 (BC)

Sexton, Thomas Anvil to the Pulpit. Knoxville: S. B. Newman and Co., 1906. Biography of the blacksmith preacher of the Appalachian frontier.
S2090 (BC)

Seymour, Charles M., Company A History of 100 Years of St. Johns Episcopal Church in Knoxville, Tenn. Knoxville: Vestry of St. John's Parish, 1947. Includes a history of Knoxville during the Civil War and Reconstruction.
S2100

Seymour, Digby Gordon Divided Loyalties: Fort Sanders and the Civil War in East Tennessee. 1st ed. Knoxville: Univ. of Tennessee Press, 1963. A history of Knoxville and Knox County during the Civil War and Reconstructions.
S2110 (BC ETSU)

Seymour, Flora Warren Smith Daniel Boone, Pioneer. New York: Century Co., 1931. Yet another biography of Boone. No distinguishing features.
S2120 (ASU)

Shackelford, Nevyle Wildflowers of Kentucky. Lexington: Univ. of Ky., College of Agriculture, Cooperative Extension Service, 1970. A book of the folklore and romance of Kentucky wild flowers.
S2130 (BC)

Shackford, James Atkins "The Autobiography of David Crockett: An Annotated Edition." 2 vols. Ph. D. Diss. Vanderbilt Univ., 1948. Shackford's introduction and notes became the foundation for the 1973 Shackford-Folmsbee edition of A NARRATIVE OF THE LIFE OF DAVID CROCKETT. This dissertation was the basis for the best biography of David Crockett.
S2140 (ASU)

Shackford, James Atkins ed. David Crockett, the Man and the Legend. Chapel Hill: Univ. of North Carolina Press, 1956. Features less of the sensational and more of the actual accomplishments and character of Crockett.
S2150 (ASU ETSU BC)

Shafer, Holly M. "Why Pupils Drop Out of School Before Finishing the Grades in the Rural Schools of West Virginia." Master's thesis. West Virginia Univ., 1929.
S2160

Shafron, Isaac "The Relationship Between the Structure of the Transportation Network and the Economic Development of West Virginia." Master's thesis. West Virginia Univ., 1967. Clearly illustrates the primary economic problem of Appalachia; poor transportation which results in poor or indifferent marketing practices.
S2170

Shah, Robin Chandulal "What Lessons India Can Learn from the Tennessee Valley Authority." Master's thesis. Univ. of Pennsylvania, 1958.
S2180

Shaler, Nathaniel Southgate Kentucky: A Pioneer Commonwealth. American Commonwealths Series. Boston: Houghton Mifflin, 1884.
S2190 (LMC BC ASU)

Kentucky: A Pioneer Commonwealth. American Commonwealths Series. Boston: Houghton, 1893.
S2200 (WWC)

Kentucky; a Pioneer Commonwealth. New York: Houghton, Mifflin and Co., 1912.
S2210

Shanks, Royal Eastman Summer Key to Tennessee Trees. 1950. Reprint. Contribution from the Department of Botany, New Series, no. 124. Knoxville: Univ. of Tennessee Press, 1963.
S2220 (ASU LMC BC)

Shannon, Jasper Berry Presidential Politics in Kentucky, 1824-1948: A Compilation of Election Statistics and an Analysis of Political Behavior. Studies in Political Behavior, no. 1. Lexington: Bureau of Government Research, College of Arts and Sciences, Univ. of Kentucky, 1950.
S2230 (LMC)

Shannondale Presbyterian Church Historical Committee Seventy-Five Years: Shannondale Presbyterian Church, Knoxville, Tennessee, 1886-1961. Knoxville: n.p., 1962.
S2240

Shapiro, Henry David "A Strange Land and Peculiar People: The Discovery of Appalachia, 1870-1920." Microfilm. Ph. D. Diss. Rutgers Univ., 1966.
S2250 (ASU LMC)

Shapiro, Irwin Yankee Thunder: The Legendary Life of Davy Crockett. New York: J. Messner, 1944.
S2260 (ASU ETSU)

Sharp, Aaron J. Campbell, Carlos Clinton and others Great Smoky Mountains Wildflowers. Knoxville: Univ. of Tennessee Press, 1962.
C540 (LMC WCU ETSU)

Campbell, Carlos Clinton Great Smoky Mountains Wildflowers. Knoxville: Univ. of Tennessee Press, 1964.
C550 (ASU LMC WCU WWC BC)

Sharp, Aaron John Shanks, Royal Eastman Summer Key to Tennessee Trees. Knoxville: Univ. of Tennessee Press, 1963.
S2220 (ASU LMC BC)

Sharp, Cecil J. Farnsworth, Charles H. Folk-songs, Chanteys and Singing Games. New York: H. W. Gray Co., n.d.
F210 (ASU LMC BC)

Sharp, Cecil James American-English Folk Songs, Collected in the Southern Appalachians. Boston: G. Schirmer, 1918.
S2270 (ASU)

Folk Songs from the Southern Appalachians. London: Oxford Univ. Press, 1917.
S2290 (ASU BC)

Eighty English Folk Songs from the Southern Appalachians. Cambridge: Massachusetts Institute of Technology Press, 1968.
S2300 (WCU ASU BC ETSU)

English Folk Songs from the Southern Appalachians. Comprising two hundred and seventy-three songs and ballads with nine hundred and sixty-eight tunes. Including thirty-nine tunes contributed by Olive Dame Campbell. 2 vols. London: Oxford Univ. Press, H. Milford, 1932.
S2320 (ASU WWC FC)

The Idiom of the People. New York: The Macmillan Co., 1958. English traditional verse with notes from the manuscripts of Cecil J. Sharp.
S2350 (ASU BC)

Sharp, Cecil James arranger Nursery Songs from the Appalachian Mountains. Illustrated by Ester B. MacKinnow. 2 vols. London: Novello and Co., 1923.
S2360 (ASU BC LMC)

Sharp, Cecil James comp. The Country Dance Book. London: Novelle and Co., 1934.
S2280 (ASU BC)

English Folk Songs from the Southern Appalachians, Comprising 273 Songs and Ballads with 968 Tunes, Including 39 Tunes Contributed by Olive Dame Campbell. 1st ed. London: Oxford Univ. Press, H. Milford, 1932.
S2310 (ASU)

English Folk Songs from the Southern Appalachians. 2 vols. in 1. New York: Oxford Univ. Press, 1960.
S2330 (ETSU)

English Folk Songs from the Southern Appalachians. Comprising two hundred and seventy-three songs and ballads with nine hundred and sixty-eight tunes, including thirty-nine tunes contributed by Olive Dame Campbell. 2 vols. 1932. Reprint. London: Oxford Univ. Press, 1966.
S2340 (ASU WCU LMC MHC)

Sharp, Cecil James ed. Campbell, Olive Arnold Dame English Folk Songs from the Southern Appalachians, Comprising 122 Songs and Ballads, and 323 Tunes. New York: G. P. Putnam's Sons, 1917.
C830 (ASU LMC WWC BC)

Sharp, John McClure Recollections of Hearsays of Athens, Fifty Years and Beyond. Athens, Tenn.: The author, 1933. An informal history of McMinn County, Tennessee.
S2370

Sharp, Karl Wayne "A Study of Debt History in Carter County, Tennessee, 1892-1952." Master's thesis. Univ. of Tennessee, 1952.
S2380

Sharpe, Bill A New Geography of North Carolina. 4 vols. Raleigh, N. C.: Sharpe Pub. Co., 1954.
S2390 (ASU LMC BC UNCA)

Tar on My Heels, a Press Agent's Notebook. Photographs by John Hemmer. Winston-Salem, N. C.: Tar Heels, 1946.
S2410 (ASU LMC BC)

Sharpe, Bill ed. North Carolina: A Description by Counties. Compiled by the Division of Advertising and News, North Carolina Department of Conservation and Development. Raleigh, N. C.: Warren, 1948.
S2400 (LMC)

Sharpe, J. Ed Cherokee Fun and Learn Book Play and Color as You Learn About the Cherokee Indian People. Illustrated by Shirley Simmons. Cherokee, N. C.: Cherokee Publications, 1970.
S2420 (ASU)

The Cherokees, Past and Present: An Authentic Guide of the Cherokee People. Illustrated by Shirley Simmons. Cherokee, N. C.: Cherokee Publications, 1970.
S2430 (ASU BC WWC)

Sharpe, Laurie M. The Cleveland Southern In-Migrant Study; an Overview. Washington: Bureau of Social Science Research Inc., 1967.
S2440

Shaver, Hazel G. The Origins and Characteristics of Folk Art in West Virginia. Master's thesis. West Va. Univ., 1964.
S2450

Shaver, Jesse Milton Ferns of Tennessee, with the Fern Allies Excluded. Nashville: George Peabody College for Teachers, 1954.
S2460 (WWC)

Shaw, C. F. Wilder, Henry Jason Reconnaissance Soil Survey of Northwestern Pennsylvania. Washington: U. S. Dept. of Agriculture, Bureau of Soils, 1910.
W6120

Shaw, Charles Frederick Reconnaissance Soil Survey of Northeastern Pennsylvania. Prepared in cooperation with the Pennsylvania State College School of Agriculture and Experiment Station. Field Operations, 1911. Washington: U. S. Department of Agriculture, Bureau of Soils, 1913.
S2470

Shaw, E. W. The Irvine Oil Field, Estill County, Kentucky. U. S. Geological Survey Bulletin, no. 661-D. Washington: Govt. Print. Off., 1918.
S2480

Shaw, Helen L. The British Administration of the Southern Indians, 1756-1783. Lancaster, Pa.: Lancaster Press, 1931. History of Cherokee and other Indians of Tennessee.
S2490

Shaw, James The Scotch-Irish in History as Master Builders of Empires, States, Churches, Schools and Civilization. New York: Eaton and Mains, 1899.
S2500 (ASU BC)

Shaw, Ronald E. Andrew Jackson, 1767-1845: Chronology, Documents, Bibliographical Aids. Dobbs Ferry, N. Y.: Oceana, 1969. Research tools for the study of Andrew Jackson. Grades 9-12.
S2510

Shaw, Wilene pseud. Harrison, Virginia M. The Fear and the Guilt. New York: Ace, 1954.
H3090

Harrison, Virginia M. Heat Lightening. New York: Ace, 1954.
H3100 (ASU)

Harrison, Virginia M. The Mating Call. New York: Ace, 1954.
H3110

Shawe, Fred R. Geologic Map of the Stanford Quadrangle, Boyle and Lincoln Counties, Kentucky. Washington: U. S. Geological Survey, 1974.
S2520

Shawkey, Morris Purdy West Virginia: A Book of Geography, History, and Industry. Boston: Ginn, 1922.
S2530 (WCU)

West Virginia, in History, Life, Literature and Industry. New York: The Lewis Pub. Co., 1928.
S2540

Shearer, Hardin David "The History and Educational Influence of Douglas School, Elizabethton, Tennessee, 1900-1965." Master's thesis. East Tennessee State Univ., 1968.
S2550 (ETSU)

Shearer, Henry K. "The Economic Effects of the Original Section of the Pennsylvania Turnpike on Adjacent Areas." Ph. D. Diss. Univ. of Pennsylvania, 1955.
S2560

Shearin, A. E. Soil Survey, Pickens County, South Carolina. Prepared in cooperation with the South Carolina Agricultural Experiment Station. Soil Survey Report, Series 1937, no. 7. Washington: U. S. Department of Agriculture, Bureau of Plant Industry, Soils, and Agricultural Engineering, 1943.
S2570

Shearin, Hubert Gibson British Ballads in the Cumberland Mountains. Sewanee, Tenn.: Univ. of the South Press, n.d. Originally appeared in Sewanee Review July, 1911.
S2580

A Syllabus of Kentucky Folk-Songs. Lexington: Transylvania Print. Co., 1911.
S2590

Sheehan, Bernard W. Seeds of Extinction: Jeffersonian Philanthropy and the American Indian. Chapel Hill: Pub. for the Institute of Early American History & Culture at Williamsburg, Va., by the Univ. of North Carolina Press, 1973.
S2600 (MHC)

Sheeler, John Reuben "The Negro in West Virginia Before 1900." Ph. D. Diss. West Virginia Univ., 1954.
S2610

Sheffey, Nola B. Zubovic, Peter Distribution of Minor Elements in Coals of Appalachian Region. Washington: U. S. Geological Survey, 1966.
Z150

Sheffy, John P. Handbook of Smyth County, Virginia. n.p.: Board of Supervisors, 1907.
S2620

Shell, Sherman Leroy "A Follow-up of Industrial Arts Graduates of East Tennessee State College from 1930 to 1953." Master's thesis. East Tennessee State College, 1958.
S2630 (ETSU)

Shellans, Herbert comp. Folk Songs of the Blue Ridge Mountains: 50 Traditional Songs as Sung by the People of the Blue Ridge Mountains Country. With notes on the people and the music. New York: Oak Publications, 1968.
S2640 (ASU ETSU LMC MHC WCU BC)

Shellhammer, Kenneth L. Miernyk, William H. Stimulating Regional Economic Development with an Input-Output Model. Morgantown: West Virginia Univ., Regional Research Institute, 1968.
M5390

Miernyk, William H. The Structure of the West Virginia Economy in 1975, a Preliminary Forecast. Morgantown: West Virginia Univ., Regional Research Institute, 1968.
M5410

Shelor, Susan Jefferson Pioneers and Their Coat of Arms of Floyd County: Genealogies of Prominent Early Settlers of the Blue Ridge Plateau of Virginia. Winston-Salem, N. C.: Hunter Pub. Co., 1961.
S2650 (ASU FC)

Shelter, Charles Milestones of West Virginia History...Some Events of Importance in the Development of the Mountain State. Parsons, W. Va.: McClain Print. Co., 1963.
S2660

W. Va. Civil War Literature. Morgantown: W. Va. Univ. Library, 1963.
S2670

Shelton, Barrett Decatur Story. Knoxville, Tenn.: TVA, 1949. Account of a valley town's transformation after the Tennessee Valley Authority programs arrived.
S2680

Shelton, Farrar V. Gibson, William Lloyd, Jr. Economic Land Classification of Pulaski County. Blacksburg: Virginia Agricultural Experiment, Station, 1946.
G1190

Shelton, Ferne Colonial Holiday Treats, Special Recipes. High Point, N. C.: Hutcraft, 1971.
S2690 (ASU BC)

Pioneer Comforts and Kitchen Remedies. Old Timey Highland Secrets from the Blue Ridge and Great Smoky Mountains.
S2730 (MHC ASU BC WCU)

Pioneer Superstitions: Old-timey Signs and Sayings. High Point, N. C.: Hutcraft, 1969.
S2760 (ASU LMC WCU)

Shelton, Ferne ed. Colonial Kitchen Herbs and Remedies: Garden and Kitchen Secrets from Early America. High Point, N. C.: Hutcraft, 1970.
S2700 (ASU LMC)

Colonial Treasure Cookbook. High Point, N. C.: Hutcraft, 1970.
S2710 (ASU)

Pioneer Beauty Secrets: Old and New Cosmetics from the Kitchen, Garden and Insect Control. High Point, N. C.: Hutcraft, 1966.
S2720 (ASU LMC)

Pioneer Cookbook, Favorite Campfire and Kitchen Recipes from Early America. High Point, N. C.: Hutcraft, 1971.
S2740 (ASU BC)

Pioneer Proverbs: Wit and Wisdom from Early America. Collected by Mary Turner. High Point, N. C.: Hutcraft, 1971.
S2750 (ASU WCU)

Southern Appalachian Mountain Cookbook: Rare Time-tested Recipes from the Blue Ridge and Great Smoky Mountains. High Point, N. C.: Hutcraft, 1964.
S2770 (ASU LMC BC)

Turner, Mary comp. Pioneer Proverbs; Wit and Wisdom From Early America. High Point, N. C.: Hutcraft, 1971.
T9830

Shelton, Robert The Country Music Story: A Picture History of Country and Western Music. Photographs by Burt Goldblatt. Indianapolis: Bobbs-Merrill Co., 1966.
S2780 (ASU WCU)

Shelton, Tom "Trends and Needs of the Washington County, Tennessee, Schools, 1948-1966." Master's thesis. East Tennessee State College, 1954.
S2790 (ETSU)

Sheppard, Mrs. Edwin Gold or Guilt. Philadelphia: J. A. Moore, 1877. Novel. Mystery story with a mountain setting and a too-pat ending.
S2800 (ASU)

Sheppard, Muriel Earley Cabins in the Laurel. Illustrated by Bayard Wootten. 1935. Reprint. Chapel Hill: Univ. of North Carolina Press, 1965.
S2820 (FC ASU)

Cloud by Day: The Story of Coal and Coke People. Chapel Hill: Univ. of North Carolina Press, 1947.
S2830 (ASU LMC BC)

Sheppard, Muriel Early Cabins in the Laurel. Illustrated by Bayard Wootten. Chapel Hill: Univ. of North Carolina Press, 1935. A mountain classic. An account of life in the Doe River Valley, North Carolina.
S2810 (ASU MHC LMC WCU ETSU WWC BC FC UNCA)

Sheppard, Walter Lee comp. Passengers and Ships Prior to 1684. Reprints of Articles With Corrections, Additions, and New Materials, by Marion R. Balderston, Hannah Benner Roach and Walter Lee Sheppard, Jr. Reprints of related material by Francis James Dallet, Morgan Bunting and L. Taylor Dickson. Publications of the Welcome Society of Pennsylvania, no. 1. Baltimore: Genealogical Pub. Co., 1970.
S2840 (ASU)

Shepperson, Wilbur Stanley Samuel Roberts: A Welsh Colonizer in Civil War Tennessee. Knoxville: Univ. of Tennessee Press, 1961.
S2850 (ASU)

Sherard, Hoyt Soil Survey: Franklin County, Alabama. Tuscaloosa: Ala. Ag. Exp. Station, 1965.
S2860

Sherard, Hoyt and others Soil Survey, Lawrence County, Alabama. Correlation by Max J. Edwards. Soil Survey, Series 1949, no. 10. Washington: U. S. Soil Conservation Service, 1959.
S2870

Soil Survey, Morgan County, Alabama. Soil Survey, Series 1944, no. 10. Washington: U. S. Soil Conservation Service, 1958.
S2880

Sherburne, James Hacey Miller: A Novel. Boston: Houghton Mifflin, 1971. A story of a young man at Berea who is a staunch abolitionist and must side against his southern family and neighbors in the war.
S2890 (BC LMC ASU)

Stand like Men. Boston: Houghton Mifflin Co., 1973. A novel of the struggle for unions in the mines of Harlan County. Action centers on "Yellow Dog" Mine and on the Hord family who first settled on Dead Dog Branch.
S2900 (BC)

The Way to Fort Pillow: A Novel. Boston: Houghton Mifflin, 1972. Berea, an abolitionist college, is closed by a pro-slavery mob and Hacey Miller a young teacher at the college rides with the Union against the wishes of his Bluegrass family.
S2910 (LMC ASU BC WCU ETSU)

Sherman, Katharine Daisy's Fanny. New York: Vantage, 1951. A middle man in the moonshine business begins courting the daughter of one of his suppliers. The young girl is only twelve years old; in disgust and fear she turns to a Negro boy for love. Situation degenerates rapidly.
S2920

Sherman, Mandel The Development of Attitudes. New York: Payne Fund, 1933. Has implications for Appalachian people facing rapid social change.
S2930

Hollow Folk. Xerox copy of the original - LMC. New York: Thomas Y. Crowell Co., 1933. Considered a mountain classic. This is a social survey of an isolated community about to be displaced by a highway. Sound, if depressing, social commentary.
S2940 (BC LMC ETSU WWC)

Hollow Folk. 1933. Reprint. Berryville, Va.: Virginia Book Co., 1973.
S2950 (ASU)

Sherrill, William Lander Annals of Lincoln County, North Carolina: Containing Interesting and Authentic Facts of Lincoln County History through the Years 1749 to 1937. Charlotte, N. C.: Observer Print. House, 1937.
S2960 (ASU)

Sherwood, Ada Simpson Hungering for the Hills and Other Poems. Philadelphia: Dorrance, 1947.
S2970

Sherwood, George American Colonists in English Records: A Guide to Direct References in Authentic Records, Passenger Lists Not in "Hotten". 2 vols. in 1. 1932-33. Reprint. Baltimore: Genealogical Pub. Co., 1969.
S2980 (ASU)

Shetler, Charles Guide to Manuscripts and Archives in the West Va. Collection, by Charles Shetler. West Va. Univ. Library. West Va. Collection. Morgantown: West Va. Univ. Library, 1958.
S2990 (BC)

Guide to the Study of West Virginia History. Morgantown: West Virginia Univ. Library, 1960.
S3010 (BC)

Milestones of West Virginia History: Some Events of Importance in the Development of the Mountain State. Parsons, W. Va.: McClain Print. Co., 1966.
S3020 (ASU)

West Virginia Civil War Literature. Morgantown: West Virginia Univ. Library, 1963.
S3030

Shetler, Charles
West Virginia Civil War Literature; An Annotated Bibliography. Morgantown: W. Va. Univ. Library, 1963.
S3040

Shetler, Charles W. Guide to the Study of West Virginia History. Morgantown: Virginia Univ. Library, 1960.
S3000

Shetrone, Henry Clyde The Mound-Builders; a Reconstruction of the Life of a Prehistoric American Race, through Exploration and Interpretation of Their Earth Mounds, Their Burials, and Their Cultural Remains. 1930. Reprint. Port Washington, N. Y.: Kennikat, 1964.
S3050

Shifflett, Frances Elaine Eocene Stratigraphy and Foraminifera of the Aquia Formation. Bulletin, 3. Baltimore: Maryland Department of Geology, Mines and Water Resources, 1948.
S3060 (ETSU)

Shinedling, Abraham Isaac West Virginia Jewry: Origins and History, 1850-1958. Philadelphia: M. Jacobs, 1963.
S3070 (ASU LMC)

Shipley, Gertrude G. comp. Centennial Celebration of Island Home Baptist Church, Knoxville, Tennessee, October 2, 1960 - December 11, 1960. Knoxville: Coleman, 1960. Includes a history of the church's first hundred years.
S3080

Shipp, Albert Micajah The History of Methodism in South Carolina. Xerox copy of the original. Nashville: Southern Methodist Pub. House, 1883.
S3090 (ASU BC)

Shirley, Franklin Ray Zebulon Vance, Tarheel Spokesman. Charlotte, N. C.: McNally and Loftin, 1962. Vance was North Carolina's first mountain governor; his term encompassed the Civil War and Secession years.
S3100 (ASU)

Zebulon Vance, Tarheel Spokesman. 1962. Reprint. Charlotte, N. C.: McNally and Loftin, 1963.
S3110 (LMC)

Shoemaker, Henry Wharton Juniata Memories: Legends Collected in Central Pennsylvania. Philadelphia: J. J. McVey, 1916.
S3120

More Allegheny Episodes: Legends and Traditions, Old and New. Altoona, Pa.: Mountain City Press, Times Tribune Co., 1964.
S3130

Penn's Grandest Cavern: The History, Legends and Description of Penn's Cave in Centre County, Pennsylvania. Altoona, Pa.: Altoona Tribune Press, 1914.
S3140

Scotch-Irish and English Proverbs and Sayings of the West Branch Valley of Central Pennsylvania. An address at the Rotary Club, Milton, Pa., June 6, 1927. Reading, Pa.: Reading Eagle Press, 1927.
S3150 (ASU)

South Mountain Sketches, Folk Tales, and Legends Collected in the Mountains of Southern Pennsylvania. Altoona, Pa.: Times Tribune Co., 1920.
S3160 (ASU)

Shore, John W. "Community Appearance Commissions in North Carolina." Master's thesis. Appalachian State Univ., 1972. Shore used Western North Carolina Counties for his study.
S3170 (ASU)

Shores, H. H. Fuller, Glenn Loren Soil Survey of Bartow County, Georgia. Washington: U. S. Department of Agriculture, Bureau of Chemistry and Soils, 1930.
F3680

Short, Eirian Introducing Quilting. New York: Charles Scribner's Sons, 1974.
S3180 (ASU)

Shoup, Charles S. A Bibliography of the Zoology of Tennessee and Tennessee Valley Region. Oak Ridge, Tenn.: U. S. Atomic Energy Commission, 1974.
S3190 (ASU BC)

Showalter, Noah Daniel Atlas of Rockingham County, Virginia. Assisted by Homer B. Vance. Map of Harrisonburg by William G. Myers. Editorial assistants, John W. Wayland and John S. Flory. Harrisonburg, Va.: The author, 1939.
S3200 (ASU)

Shriner, Charles H. History of Murray County. By Charles H. Shriner. n.p.: n.p., 1911. Contains valuable information about this county formed from the Cherokee nation in 1838.
S3210

History of Murray County. Spring Place, Ga.: n.p., 1911. Interesting history of a mountain county created from the Cherokee Nation in 1838.
S3220 (ASU)

Shryock, Richard Harrison Georgia and the Union in 1850. Durham, N. C.: Duke Univ. Press, 1926. Several mountain counties in Georgia remained loyal to the Union throughout the War.
S3230 (MHC)

Shulkcum, Edward Devereux, Robert Eddins Soil Survey, Albemarle County, Virginia. Washington: U. S. Department of Agriculture, Bureau of Plant Industry, 1940.
D1940

Jurney, Robert Campbell Soil Survey of Augusta County, Virginia. Washington: U. S. Department of Agriculture, Bureau of Chemistry and Soils, 1937.
J2850

Jurney, Robert Campbell Soil Survey of Rockbridge County, Virginia. Washington: U. S. Department of Agriculture, Bureau of Chemistry and Soils, 1934.
J2900

Jurney, Robert Campbell Soil Survey, Smyth County, Virginia. Washington: U. S. Department of Agriculture, Bureau of Plant Industry, Soils and Agricultural Engineering, 1948.
J2930

Jurney, Robert Campbell and others Soil Survey, Washington County, Virginia. Washington: U. S. Department of Agriculture, Bureau of Plant Industry, Soils, and Agricultural Engineering, 1945.
J2940

Shull, Lena Meare Fire on the Mountain. Verse Craft Series. Atlanta: Banner Press, 1955.
S3240 (ASU WCU)

Night Is Always Kind. Dallas, Texas: Kaleidograph Press, 1948.
S3250 (ASU WCU)

Red Leaf Carols. Old North State Poets, series 1, no. 2. Dexter, Mo.: Candor Press, 1961.
S3260 (ASU WCU LMC)

Shull, Peg Children of Appalachia. New York: J. Messner, 1969. A book designed for children and about the life of children in southeastern Kentucky. Author use a composite of families to put across a realistic portrait of life in present day Appalachia.
S3270 (ASU ETSU MHC BC)

Shumate, Samuel B. Ball, Bonnie Sage Scott County, Virginia: U. S. Census, 1850. n.p.: n.p., 1963.
B780 (BC ASU)

Shumate, William H. Petro, James H. Soil Survey, Ross County, Ohio. Washington: U. S. Soil Conservation Service, 1967.
P2430

Shupe, Jane Little "A Survey of Comprehension Weaknesses of 417 East Tennessee State University Freshmen." Master's thesis. East Tennessee State Univ., 1964.
S3280 (ETSU)

Siegmeister, Elie ed. The Music Lover's Handbook. New York: W. Morrow and Co., 1943.
S3290 (ASU)

Siehl, George H. comp. The Issues Related to Surface Mining; a Summary Review, with Selected Readings. Washington: Govt. Print. Off., 1971.
S3300 (WCU)

Silberberg, Elliot D. Celluloid Muse: A Critical Study of James Agee. Ph. D. Diss. Univ. of Wisconsin, 1973. This discussion of Knoxville's James Agee includes poetry, fiction, movie scripts and journalism.
S3310

Siler, David W. comp. The Eastern Cherokees: A Census of the Cherokee Nation in North Carolina, Tennessee, Alabama, and Georgia in 1851. Preface by Fred B. Kniffen. Cottonport, La.: Polyanthos, 1972. Thousands of Cherokees did not move westward on the Trail of Tears, but were exempted for family or occupational reasons.
S3320 (BC ASU)

Siler, James Hayden A History of Jellico, Tennessee, Containing Historical Information on Campbell County, Tennessee and Whitley County, Kentucky. Jellico: n.p., 1938.
S3330

Siler, Margaret R. Cherokee Indian Lore and Smoky Mountain Stories. Bryson City, N. C.: Bryson City Times, 1938. A delightful book of legends, lore and wisdom from the Qualla Reservation.
S3340 (ASU BC)

Cherokee Indian Lore and Smoky Mountains Stories. 1938. Reprint. Bryson City, N. C.: Bryson City Times, 1939.
S3350 (ETSU)

Siler, R. W., Jr. Flood Problems and Their Solution Through Urban Planning Programs. Nashville, Tenn.: Tennessee State Planning Commission, 1955.
S3360

Sill, James B. Historical Sketches of Churches in the Diocese of Western North Carolina Episcopal Church. Asheville, N. C.: Church of the Redeemer, 1955. Sketches of all the Episcopal Churches in North Carolina's mountain region.
S3370 (LMC WCU BC)

Silliphant, Stirling Maddux, Rachel Fiction Into Film: A Walk in the Spring Rain. Knoxville: Univ. of Tennessee Press, 1970.
M2710 (ASU)

Silverman, Jerry Beginning the Folk Guitar, an Instructional Manual. New York: Oak Publications, 1964. A clearly written manual of instruction for beginning guitarists.
S3380 (ASU)

Silverman, Jerry ed. Folk Blues: 110 American Folk Blues. With a chart of basic guitar chord fingering patterns and a full biography and discographer. New York: Macmillan, 1958.
S3390 (ASU)

Silverstone, Naomi ed. Appalachian Regional Commission, Child Development Staff Programs for Infants and Young Children. Washington: Govt. Print. Off., 1970.
A3900 (ASU ETSU)

Silvester, Guy Alwin "A Comparative Analysis of the Felt Need Pattern of the Personality Structure in Rural Appalachia and Suburban America." Master's thesis. East Tennessee State Univ., 1969. An amazingly mature analysis of the psychology of alienation as applied to Appalachian people.
S3400 (ETSU)

Simmendiger, Ulrich B. True and Authentic Register of Persons Still Living, by God's Grace, Who in the Year 1709, under the Wonderful Providence of the Lord, Journeyed from Germany to America or New World, and There Seek Their Piece of Bread at Various Places, Reported with Joy to All Admirers, Especially to Their Families and Close Friends. Translated from the German by Herman F. Vesper. 1934. Reprint. Baltimore: Genealogical Pub. Co., 1966.
S3410 (ASU)

Simmons, Anne Bird, Ronald Status of Rural Housing in the United States. Washington: U. S. Economic Research Service, Economic Development Division, 1968.
B4120

Simmons, C. S. Shearin, A. E. Soil Survey, Pickens County, South Carolina. Washington: U. S. Department of Agriculture, Bureau of Plant Industry, Soils, and Agricultural Engineering, 1943.
S2570

Simmons, Charles Shaffer Burke, Richard Thomas Avon Soil Survey of Indiana County, Pennsylvania. Washington: U. S. Bureau of Chemistry and Soils, 1936.
B8700

Soil Survey of Wayne County, Pennsylvania. Prepared in cooperation with the Pennsylvania State College School of Agriculture and Experiment Station. Soil Survey Report, Series 1932, no. 25. Washington: U. S. Department of Agriculture, Bureau of Chemistry and Soils, 1938.
S3430

Simmons, Corinne John Uri Lloyd: His Life and Works, 1849-1936. Cincinnati: The author, 1972. Biography of a scientist, author and philanthropist. Author of several books on eastern Kentucky.
S3440

Simmons, John Benjamin History of the Public Schools of White County, Georgia 1870 Thru 1938. n.p.: n.p., 1938. Primarily sketches of teachers past and present.
S3450 (BC)

Simmons, Wilhelmina "Community Concept of Juvenile Court Function in Knox County, Tennessee." Master's thesis. Univ. of Tennessee, 1961.
S3460

Simms, William Gilmore Charlemont: Or, the Pride of the Village. A Tale of Kentucky. Border Romances. Chicago: Donohue, Henneberry and Co., 1890. A tale of warfare, Indians and romance in backwoods Kentucky. The action ranges into the Kentucky mountains.
S3470 (ASU)

Charlemont: Or, The Pride of the Village, a Tale of Kentucky. New York: AMS Press, 1970.
S3480 (ETSU)

Guy Rivers: A Tale of Georgia. Atlanta: The Martin and Hoyt Co., n.d. A tale of warfare, scouting, love and betrayal in upcountry Georgia. Simms describes the noble mountaineer in his best purple prose.
S3490

Guy Rivers: A Tale of Georgia. Border Romances. Chicago: Belford, Clarke, and Co., 1888.
S3500 (ASU BC)

Guy Rivers: A Tale of Georgia. 1885. Reprint. New York: AMS Press, 1970.
S3510 (ASU ETSU)

The Scout: Or, The Black Riders of Congaree. 1854. Reprint. Americans in Fiction. Ridgewood, N. J.: Gregg Press, 1968. Revolutionary War fiction in which the action occasionally ranges into the mountains.
S3520 (ASU WCU ETSU)

Voltmeier, or The Mountain Men: A Tale of the Old North State. n.p.: Serialized in THE WESTERN WORLD, 1869. A novel of North Carolina during the Revolutionary War. The Mountain Men are the heroes.
S3530 (ASU)

The Wigwam and the Cabin. Chicago: Belford, Clarke, and Co., 1888. A romance of the backcountry. Some of the action takes place in the Appalachians. More purple prose.
S3540 (ASU)

The Wigwam and the Cabin. Life in America. Ridgewood, N. J.: Gregg Press, 1968.
S3550 (WCU LMC)

Woodcraft: Or, Hawks About the Dovecote A Story of the South at the Close of the Revolution. Rev. ed. 1856. Reprint. Americans in Fiction. Ridgewood, N. J.: Gregg Press, 1968. A novel of the Revolution in South Carolina. Some of the action takes place in the mountains.
S3560 (ASU WCU ETSU)

The Writings of William Gilmore Simms, Centennial Edition. Introduction and Explanatory notes by Donald Davidson and Mary C. Simms Oliphant. Text established by James B. Meriwether. Contents Vol. I.: VOLTMEIER; or, THE MOUNTAIN MEN. Columbia: Univ. of South Carolina Press, 1969.
S3570 (ASU)

Simon, Charlie May Hogue Younger Brother, a Cherokee Indian Tale. New York: E. P. Dutton and Co., 1942.
S3575 (ETSU)

Simpkins, Francis B. The South Old and New. New York: Alfred A. Knopf, 1947. Contains scant information on the mountain south.
S3580 (BC)

Simpson, Donval Riley "An Investigation of the Arithmetical Disabilities of Beginning Ninth Grade Pupils in Appalachian High School." Master's thesis. Appalachian State Teachers College, 1957.
S3590 (ASU)

Simpson, Dorothy Taylor "An Ecological Survey of Flat Rock Mountain." Master's thesis. Appalachian State Teachers College, 1958. Ecological study of one western North Carolina mountain.
S3600 (ASU)

Simpson, George Lee Western North Carolina Associated Communities. Cherokee, N. C.: Cherokee Historical Association, 1956.
S3610 (WCU)

Simpson, James History of the Cross Creek Graveyard and Cross Creek Cemetery. Originally compiled in 1894 by James Simpson, revised and prepared for publication by Alvin D. White. Parsons, West Va.: McClain Print. Co., 1969.
S3620

History of the Cross Creek Graveyard and Cross Creek Cemetery. Parsons, W. Va.: McClain Print. Co., 1969.
S3630

Simpson-Poffenbarger, Livia Nye Battle of Point Pleasant . . . Point Pleasant, W. Va.: State Gazette Pubs., 1909. Contains biographical sketches of the men who participated.
S3640

Sims, Carlton C. "County Government in Tennessee." Ph. D. Diss. Univ. of Chicago, 1930. Some interesting commentary on political practices in East Tennessee. However, considering the publication date, this should have been much more of an expose. The author was too timid.
S3650 (BC)

Sims, Edgar B. Indexes to Land Grants in West Virginia. Charleston, W. Va.: Rose City Press, 1952.
S3660 (ASU)

Sims, Edgar Barr Making a State; Formation of West Virginia, Including Maps, Illustrations, Plats, Grants and the Acts of the Virginia Assembly and the Legislature of West Virginia Creating the Counties. Charleston: State of West Virginia, 1956.
S3670 (BC)

Sims, Marion McCamy Memo. to Timothy Sheldon. Philadelphia: J. B. Lippincott Co., 1938. Novel in the form of a long letter from Lynn Sheldon to her husband. On a vacation in the North Carolina mountains Lynn meets a man she would like to marry and writes a letter to her husband telling him of her plans.
S3680 (ASU)

Simulating Regional Economic Development; an Interindustry Analysis of the West Virginia Economy Lexington, Mass.: D. C. Heath, 1970.
S3690 (UNCA)

Sinclair, Upton B. King Coal. 1917. Reprint. Pasadena, Cal.: n.p., 1930. A novel of the coal industry in Pennsylvania and neighboring states. Like all of Sinclair's work, this book makes a strong sociological statement about life in the coal camps and the unions.
S3700 (ETSU)

Singer, Louis C. Glass, Paul Songs of Hill and Mountain Folk, Ballads, Historical Songs, Folk Songs. New York: Grosset & Dunlap, 1967.
G2060 (BC ASU)

Singh, Ghaguan Krishna Modernization and Diffusion of Innovations in a Rural Appalachia County; General Systems Analysis. Ph. D. Diss. Univ. of Kentucky, 1970.
S3710 (BC)

Singh, Har Swarup "Evaluation of Alternative Income Opportunities For Farm Operations in Macon County, North Carolina." Ph. D. Diss. North Carolina State Univ., 1959.
S3720 (LMC)

Sipe, F. Henry Surveying Rural Property Boundary Lines in West Virginia: A Guide For Surveyors, Attorneys, Landowners, and Others. Parsons, W. Va.: McClain Print. Co., 1965.
S3730 (LMC)

Sister, Janice Call Christopher Call's Family of Preston County, West Virginia 1741-1973. Parsons, W. Va.: McClain Print. Co., 1973.
S3740

Sistler, Byron 1830 Census, East Tennessee. Transcribed and indexed by Byron Sistler. Evanston, Ill.: n.p., 1969.
S3750

Sites, Carrie B. A History of the Town of Dayton, Virginia. Dayton, Va.: Dayton Women's Club, 1962. A history of a small town in Rockingham County, Virginia.
S3760 (ASU BC)

Sitterson, Joseph Carlyle The Secession Movement in North Carolina. James Sprunt Studies in History and Political Science, vol. 23, no. 2. Chapel Hill: Univ. of North Carolina Press, 1939. Mountain counties were opposed to Secession.
S3770 (LMC)

Sizer, Leonard M. County Study Data Book: Measures of Social Change in West Virginia. Bulletin no. 464. Morgantown: West Virginia Agricultural Experiment Station, West Virginia Univ., 1961.
S3780

Population Changes in West Virginia 1900-1950. Morgantown: W. Va. Agricultural Experiment Station, 1957.
S3800

Rural Industrialization: A Case Study in Educational Values and Attitudes. Morgantown: West Virginia Univ. Agricultural Experiment Station, 1966.
S3810 (ASU)

Sizer, Leonard M. and others The Learning Experiences of Youth Groups: A Study of 4-H Clubs in Barbour County, West Virginia. Morgantown: W. Va. Univ. Agricultural Experiment Station, 1959.
S3790

Skaggs, Marvin Lucian North Carolina Boundary Disputes Involving Her Southern Line. James Sprunt Studies in History and Political Science, vol. 25, no. 1. Chapel Hill: Univ. of North Carolina Press, 1941. Disputed territory includes North Carolina's southwestern mountain counties.
S3820 (ASU LMC)

Skaggs, Mevill Maguire The Folk of Southern Fiction. Athens: Univ. of Georgia Press, 1972. This book was a great disappointment. It fails to differentiate the mountain man from other southern types and does not recognize Appalachian fiction as a separate literary entity. However, some attention is given to the formation of the mountain stereotype.
S3830 (ASU)

Skean, Marion Holcomb Circle Left Folk Play of the Kentucky Mountains. Homeplace, Ky.: E. C. Robinson Mountain Foundation, 1939. A nice round-up of old favorites.
S3840 (ASU LMC BC)

Skelly and Loy/Zollman Associates Preparation of Plans and Specifications for Pollution Abatement Activities in Cherry Creek Watershed, Maryland. Washington: Appalachian Regional Commission, 1973.
S3850 (ASU)

"Sketches of Pioneer Medical Doctors of Cocke County." n.p.: unpublished typescript, 1968.
S3860

Skeyhill, Thomas John Sergeant York, Last of the Long Hunters. Philadelphia: John C. Winston Co., 1930.
S3880 (ASU BC)

Skeyhill, Thomas John ed. Sergeant York, His Own Life Story and War Diary. Garden City, N. Y.: Doubleday, Doran, and Co., 1928.
S3870 (ASU ETSU LMC)

Skidmore, Hobert Douglas Disturb Not Our Dreams. Boston: Houghton Mifflin Co., 1947.
S3890 (ASU BC)

O Careless Love. 1st ed. Garden City, N. Y.: Doubleday, 1949. The simultaneous arrival of a wise but innocent mountain girl and a drought prove too much for the village of felicity.
S3900 (ASU)

The Years Are Even, a Novel. New York: Random House, 1952.
S3910 (ASU)

Skidmore, Hubert Hawk's Nest. New York: Doubleday, Doran and Co., 1941. The Great Depression brings an influx of outlanders into West Virginia to blast a tunnel through a mountain. Confusion and trouble follow.
S3920 (BC ASU)

Heaven Came So Near. Garden City, N. Y.: Doubleday, Doran and Co., 1938. Ben Cutlip, unable to adjust to the brutality of the lumber camp, takes to the hills. His mind is unable to cope with other people; he grows stranger and more aloof and at last confesses to a murder he saw in a vision.
S3930 (ASU LMC BC)

Hill Doctor. Illustrated by Benton Spruance. New York: Doubleday, Doran and Co., 1940. A young doctor returns to his mountain homeland and finds himself in conflict with the local midwife and the lumber company which is the only area industry.
S3940 (ASU WCU BC)

Hill Lawyer. Garden City, N. Y.: Doubleday, Doran and Co., 1945. A young lawyer comes to Stoney Fork to help the mountaineers save their land from lumber and mining companies which are trying to force the locals to sell by devious means.
S3950 (BC LMC)

Hill Lawyer. Illustrated by Richard Bennett. Garden City, N. Y.: Doubleday, Doran and Co., 1950.
S3960 (ASU)

I Will Lift Up Mine Eyes. Garden City, N. Y.: Book League of America, 1936. Memorable story of the disintegration of the Cutlip's strong family ties when they leave the hills and move to a lumber town. Powerful novel of the mountaineer versus industrialization.
S3970 (BC ASU)

I Will Lift Up Mine Eyes. Garden City, N. Y.: Doubleday, Doran, 1936.
S3980 (LMC)

River Rising Illustrated by Benton Spruance. New York: Doubleday, Doran and Co., 1939. Novel of York Allen, a teacher trying to earn money for medical school. He has difficulty with the lumber camp families until his heroic action saves some mill property.
S3990 (ASU LMC)

Skidmore, Owings, & Merrill Co. Report to the Atomic Energy Commission on the Master Plan, Oak Ridge, Tennessee. Oak Ridge: The Co., 1948.
S4000 (ASU)

Skiles, William West A Sketch of Missionary Life at Valle Crucis in Western North Carolina, 1842-1862. New York: James Pott and Co., 1890. A description of a harsh and generally unrewarding ministry at an isolated Episcopal Mission in Western North Carolina.
S4010 (LMC)

Skinner, Charles Montgomery Myths & Legends of Our Own Land. 2 vols. Detroit: Singing Tree Press, 1969.
S4020 (ASU)

Skinner, Constance Lindsay Becky Landers; Frontier Warrior. New York: The Macmillan Co., 1926. Novel of a young girl on the Kentucky frontier who has become the provider for her family. Action moves in and out of the mountain area as she associates with famous scouts and warriors.
S4030 (BC)

Pioneers of the Old Southwest. Chronicles of America Series. New Haven: Yale Univ. Press, 1920.
S4040 (LMC)

Pioneers of the Old Southwest: A Chronicle of the Dark and Bloody Ground. Chronicles of America Series, vol. 18. Abraham Lincoln edition. New Haven: Yale Univ. Press, 1919. The term "old southwest" encompasses parts of Appalachia.
S4050 (ASU)

Pioneers of the Old Southwest: A Chronicle of the Dark and Bloody Ground. Chronicles of America Series, vol. 18. New Haven: Yale Univ. Press, 1921.
S4060 (ETSU)

Silent Scot, Frontier Scout. New York: Coward McCann, 1925.
S4070

Silent Scott, Frontier Scout. New York: Macmillan, 1940. Novel of a North Carolina mountain boy who is captured by the British but escapes to become a famous scout. Much about the Cherokee and Sevier's Overmountain Men.
S4080 (WWC BC)

Skinner, George W. comp. Pennsylvania at Chickamauga and Chattanooga: Ceremonies at the Dedication of the Monuments Erected by the Commonwealth of Pennsylvania to Mark the Positions of the Pennsylvania Commands Engaged in the Battles. n.p.: Wm. Stanley Ray, 1900.
S4090 (ASU)

Skordas, Gust The Early Settlers of Maryland: An Index to Names of Immigrants Compiled from Records of Land Patents, 1633-1680, in the Hall of Records, Annapolis, Maryland. Foreword by Morris L. Radoff. Baltimore: Genealogical Pub. Co., 1968.
S4100 (ASU)

Skyland, Situated on High Plateau in the Blue Ridge Near Grand Old Stony Man Peak, Overlooking Famous Shenandoah Valley, 4,000 Feet in the Blue Washington: Judd and Detweiler, 1917.
S4110 (ASU)

Slaats, Gary ed. Religious News Press in Appalachia, 1971. A Directory of News Periodicals of . . . all Members of the Commission on Religion in Appalachia. . . Knoxville: Commission on Religion in Appalachia, 1971.
S4120 (ASU BC)

Slack, Larry J. Wilder, Hugh B. Summary of Data on Chemical Quality of Streams of North Carolina, 1943-67: Quality of Surface Waters of North Carolina. Washington: Govt. Print. Off., 1971.
W6140 (LMC)

Slagle, Franklin D. Densities and Porosities of Core Samples from Wells in Appalachian Oilfields. U. S. Mines Bureau Information Circular, 8330. Pittsburgh: Mines Bureau, 1967.
S4130

Slaughter, Philip A History of Bristol Parish, Va.; With Genealogies of Families Connected Therewith, and Historical Illustrations. 2nd ed. Richmond: J. W. Randolph & English, 1879.
S4140 (ASU BC)

The Knights of the Golden Horseshoe from the History of St. Mark's Parish. Baltimore: Innes and Co., 1877.
S4160

Slaughter, Phillip A History of St. Mark's Parish, Culpeper County, Va., With Notes of Old Churches and Old Families and Illustrations of the Manners and Customs of the Olden Time. Baltimore: Innes and Co., 1877.
S4150 (ASU)

Slaughter, Turbit H. The Water Resources of Allegany and Washington Counties. Prepared in cooperation with the U. S. Geological Survey. Bulletin, no. 24. Baltimore: Maryland Department of Geology, Mines and Water Resources, 1962.
S4170 (ETSU)

Slavin, Richard H. The Pressed and Blown Glassware Industry. Morgantown: Bureau of Business Research, College of Commerce, West Virginia Univ., 1963.
S4180 (ASU)

Slay, James Linwood "A History of Bradley County, Tennessee, to 1861." Master's thesis. Univ. of Tennessee, 1967. A short history of Bradley County, Tennessee and the city of Cleveland.
S4190

Slemp, C. Bascom comp. Addresses of Famous Southwestern Virginians. Bristol: The King Print. Co., 1939.
S4200

Slonaker, Arthur Gordon A History of Shepherd College, Shepherdstown, West Virginia. Parsons, W. Va.: McClain Print. Co., 1967.
S4210 (ASU BC)

Slonaker, Robert Ray "A Curriculum in Agricultural Education for Two Consolidated High Schools in Washington County, Tennessee." Master's thesis. East Tennessee State Univ., 1969.
S4220 (ETSU)

Sloop, Mary T. Martin Miracle in the Hills. New York: McGraw-Hill, 1953. Account of the growth of Crossnore: school, mission, village and hospital.
S4230 (ASU WCU LMC WWC BC)

Sluder, Earl Ray Exploratory Studies on Chemical Control of Unwanted Hardwoods in Southern Appalachians. U. S. Forest Service Research Note, 165. Asheville, N. C.: Southeastern Forest Experiment Station, 1961.
S4240

Tests on Direct Seeding of Oak in Piedmont and Southern Appalachians of North Carolina. U. S. Forest Service Station Paper, 134. Asheville, N. C.: Southeastern Forest Experiment Station, 1961.
S4250 (WCU)

"Variation in Wood Specific Gravity of Yellow-poplar (Liriodendron tulipfera L.) and Its Relationship to Environmental Conditions in the Southern Appalachians." Ph. D. Diss. North Carolina State Univ., 1970.
S4260 (LMC)

A White Pine Provenance Study in the Southern Appalachians. U. S. Forest Service Station Paper, SE-2. Asheville, N. C.: Southeastern Forest Experiment Station, 1963.
S4270 (WCU)

White Pine Provenance Study in the Southern Appalachians. U. S. Forest Service Station Paper, SE-2. Asheville, N. C.: Southeastern Forest Experiment Station, 1963.
S4280 (ASU)

Sluss, Emily "A Comparative Study of Twenty-five Children Who Attended Project Head Start and Twenty-five Children Who Did Not: Paired at the First-grade Level in the Jonesboro Elementary School, Jonesboro, Tennessee, 1965-1966." Master's thesis. East Tennessee State Univ., 1966.
S4290 (ETSU)

Small, John Kunkel Ferns in the Southeastern States. Descriptions of the Fern Plants Growing Naturally in the States South of the Virginia-Kentucky State Line and East of the Mississippi River. Illustrated by Ruth Sinclair George. Lancaster, Pa.: Science Press Print. Co., 1938.
S4300 (ASU BC)

Manual of the Southeastern Flora; Being Descriptions of the Seed Plants Growing in Florida, Alabama, Mississippi, Eastern Louisiana, Tennessee, North Carolina, South Carolina and Georgia. New York: Hafner Pub. Co., 1972.
S4310

Smalley, Glendon W. Cubic-foot Volume Table and Point-sampling Factors for White Pine Plantations in Southern Appalachians. U. S. Forest Service Research Note SO-118. New Orleans: Southern Forest Experiment Station, 1971.
S4320

Smalling, Landon H. Middlesboro and Before Middlesboro Was. Middlesboro, Ky.: The author, 1924.
S4330

Smalling, Sam, Jr. "The Social, Economic, Cultural, Religious and Family Educational Backgrounds of Recent Dropouts from Bristol, Tennessee, High School." Master's thesis East Tennessee State Univ., 1963.
S4340 (ETSU)

Smallwood, Johnny B., Jr. "George W. Norris and the Concept of a Planned Region." Ph. D. Diss. Univ. of North Carolina, 1963.
S4350

Smathers, George Henry The History of Land Titles in Western North Carolina: With Supplement. Asheville, N. C.: Miller Print. Co., 1938.
S4360 (ASU LMC WCU UNCA)

Smelcer, Buna "A Study of Financing a Program for Education in Sevier County, Tennessee." Master's thesis. Univ. of Tennessee, 1956.
S4370

Smeltzer, Wallace Guy The Story of Methodism in the Pittsburgh Region. Freeport, Pa.: Allegheny-Kiski Print. Co., 1958.
S4390 (ASU)

Smeltzer, Wallace Guy ed. Methodism in Western Pennsylvania, 1784-1968. An Historical Records Volume. Little Valley, N. Y.: Straight Pub. Co., 1969.
S4380 (ASU)

Smiley, David L. Lion of White Hall: The Life of Cassius M. Clay. 1962. Reprint. Gloucester, Mass.: P. Smith, 1969. Biography of the great orator from Madison County, Kentucky.
S4400 (MHC)

Smith, A. M. Bruce, Oscar Clayton Soil Survey of Allegany County, Maryland. Washington: U. S. Department of Agriculture, Bureau of Soils, 1926.
B7610

Smith, Abbot Emerson Colonists in Bondage: White Servitude and Convict Labor in America, 1607-1776. Chapel Hill: Pub. for the Institute of Early American History and Culture at Williamsburg, Va., by the Univ. of North Carolina Press, 1947.
S4410 (ASU)

Colonists in Bondage: White Servitude and Convict Labor in America, 1607-1776. Glouchester, Mass.: P. Smith, 1965.
S4420 (ASU)

Smith, C. D. A Brief History of Macon County, North Carolina. Franklin, N. C.: Franklin Press, 1905. Includes promotional material and colorful tales from this well-known stronghold of mountain ways.
S4430

Smith, Charles C. Down by the Riverside. n.p.: Typescript, 1971. Autobiographical sketch of life in eastern Kentucky; an attempt to catch the flavor of times gone by. Typescript is basis for a forthcoming book.
S4440

Smith, Charles Forster Reminiscences and Sketches. Nashville, Tenn.: Publishing House of the M. E. Church, South, Smith and Lamar, Agents, 1908.
S4450 (ASU)

Smith, Charles G. "A Social and Economic Survey of Pickett County." Master's thesis. Vanderbilt Univ., 1928.
S4460

Smith, Charles Henry Bill Arp (pseud.) So Called, a Side Show of the Southern Side of the Civil War. New York: Metropolitan Record Office, 1866. Resuming his column after the War, Smith said, "I killed at least as many of them as they did of me."
S4470 (ASU)

Bill Arp: From the Uncivil War to Date, 1861-1903. Atlanta: The Byrd Print. Co., 1903. Smith's columns written for the Rome (Georgia) and Atlanta newspapers had a wide following. As Bill Arp, he became North Georgia's foremost humorist. Excellent use of mountain characters and dialect.
S4480 (ASU)

Bill Arp's Peace Papers. 1873. Reprint. Upper Saddle River, N. J.: Literature House, 1969. Bill Arp was a well known humorist from the North Georgia mountains. He wrote for the Rome, Cartersville and Atlanta papers.
S4490 (ASU)

Smith, Daniel A Short Description of the Tennessee Government, or The Territory of the United States South of the River Ohio, to Accompany and Explain a Map of That Country. Philadelphia: Mathew Carey, 1793.
S4500 (BC ASU)

Smith, Dennis K. "The Economic Structure and Growth of the Pennsylvania Economy: 1956-1966." Ph. D. Diss. Pennsylvania State Univ., 1970.
S4510

Smith, Dick W. "Economic Levels of Forage and Grain Production on Dairy Farms in East Tennessee." Master's thesis. Univ. of Tennessee, 1956.
S4520

Smith, E. Marvin History of Summersville Normal School, Summersville, West Virginia, 1893-1914. Charleston, W. Va.: Jarrett Print. Co., 1966.
S4530 (ASU)

Smith, Earl The Daniel Boone Story. n.p.: n.p., 1965. Yet another biography of Boone. No distinguishing features.
S4540 (BC)

Smith, Ed M. "History of Educational Development in Jackson County, Tennessee, 1800 to 1950." Master's thesis. Tennessee Technological Univ., 1967.
S4550

Smith, Edith Hutchins Drought, and Other North Carolina Yarns. Illustrated by Elizabeth Toth Spencer. Winston-Salem, N. C.: J. F. Blair, 1955. Some with mountain settings.
S4560 (LMC ASU)

Smith, Edward Conrad The Borderland in the Civil War. New York: McMillan, 1927. Smith's definition of the borderland includes West Virginia and Eastern Kentucky.
S4570

Smith, Eldon D. "Migration and Adjustment Experiences of Rural Migrant Workers in Indianapolis." Ph. D. Diss. Univ. of Wisconsin, 1954. Many of these migrants come from the Appalachian Region.
S4580

Smith, Elizabeth V. "An Accounting Study of the Educational Progress of Knoxville Negro Pupils Over a Sixteen-year Period." Master's thesis. Univ. of Tennessee, 1959.
S4590

Smith, Elizabeth Virginia Descendants of Samuel Miller, John Detrick, John and Mary Snell of Rockingham County, Virginia. Kingston, Pa.: n.p., 1943.
S4600

Smith, Elmer L. The Pennsylvania Germans of the Shenandoah Valley. Allentown, Pa.: The Folklore Association, 1964.
S4620 (ASU)

Shenandoah Valley Cooking; Recipes and Kitchen Lore. Lebanon, Pa.: Applied Arts Pubs., 1970.
S4630 (FC)

Stewart, John An Occult Remedy Manuscript from Pendleton County, West Virginia. n.p.: Madison College, 1964.
S7300

Smith, Elmer L. comp. Arts and Crafts of the Shenandoah Valley. Published for the Shenandoah Valley Folklore. Witmer, Pa.: Applied Arts, 1968.
S4610 (ASU BC FC)

Smith, Mrs. Enoch, Sr. see **Smith, Lilly**

Smith, Ethel Wheeler ed. Washington County, Tennessee, Marriages and Wills. Transcribed from the original bonds and licenses at the county courthouse, Jonesboro. Johnson City, Tenn.: Parrish Print., 1961-.
S4640 (ETSU)

Smith, Evelyn Futch North Carolina Palatine-Germans (Futch Family). Jacksonville, Fla.: The author, n.d.
S4660 (ASU)

Smith, Evelyn Futch comp. Charn Cuimhne to Our Scots of North Carolina. Jacksonville, Fla.: The author, 1969.
S4650 (ASU)

Smith, Frank E. The Politics of Conservation. rev. ed., New York: Harper, 1971. New York: Pantheon, 1966.
S4670

Smith, Frank H. The Appalachian Square Dance. With Rolf E. Hovey. Sketches by Mary Rogers. Photographs by Doris Ulmann and Mattson Studio. Berea, Ky.: Berea College, 1955.
S4680 (ASU MHC LMC WCU BC)

Smith, Fred Neil Shelton, Tom "Trends and Needs of the Washington County, Tennessee, Schools, 1948-1966." East Tennessee State College, 1954.
S2790 (ETSU)

Smith, G. Hobart "An Economic, Social and Educational Survey of Campbell County, Tennessee." Master's thesis. Univ. of Tennessee, 1934.
S4690

Smith, George Gilman The Story of Georgia and the Georgia People, 1732 to 1860. 2nd ed. 1901. Reprint. Baltimore: Genealogical Pub. Co., 1968. Includes good information on the mountain counties.
S4700 (ASU FC BC)

Smith, Gerald Wayne Nathan Goff, Jr., a Biography: With Some Account of Guy Despard Goff and Brazilla Carroll Reece. Charleston, W. Va.: Education Foundation, 1959.
S4710 (ASU)

Smith, H. C. Stroud, James Frank Soil Survey of Shelby County, Alabama. Washington: U. S. Department of Agriculture, Bureau of Soils, 1920.
S8130

Watkins, William Isaac Soil Survey of Greenville County, South Carolina. Washington: U. S. Department of Agriculture, Bureau of Soils, 1924.
W1480

Smith, H. M. Phillips, Samuel William Soil Survey of Washington County, Ohio. Washington: U. S. Department of Agriculture, Bureau of Chemistry and Soils, 1930.
P2670

Smith, Harvey L. Society and Health in a Mountain Community: A Working Paper. Mimeographed. Chapel Hill: Institute for Research in Social Science, Univ. of North Carolina, 1961.
S4720 (ASU)

Smith, Helen Louise Niles, John Jacob Folk Ballads for Young Actors. New York: Holt, Rinehart and Winston, 1962. (Also, phonodisc.)
N1080 (ASU BC)

Niles, John Jacob Folk Carols for Young Actors. New York: Holt, Rinehart and Winston, 1962. (Also, phonodisc.)
N1090 (ASU)

Smith, Henry Clay Epicormic Branching on 8 Species of Appalachian Hardwoods. U. S. Forest Service Research Note, NE-53. Upper Darby, Pa.: Northeastern Forest Experiment Station, 1966.
S4730

Trimble, George R., Jr. What Happens to Living Cull Trees Left After Heavy Cutting in Mixed Hardwood Stands? Upper Darby, Pa.: Northeastern Forest Experiment Station, 1963.
T9340

Smith, Hilda Neff From the Alps to the Appalachians (Neff Families). Arlington, Va.: R. W. Beatty Ltd., 1967.
S4740

Smith, Homer H. Memoirs. Blountville, Tenn.: n.p., 1948. Recollections of life in upper East Tennessee.
S4750 (ETSU)

Smith, Howard C. Soil Survey of Chambers County, Alabama. Prepared in cooperation with Alabama. Field Operations, 1909. Washington: U. S. Department of Agriculture, Bureau of Soils, 1911.
S4760

Soil Survey of Jefferson County, Alabama. Washington: U. S. Dept. of Agriculture, Bureau of Soils, 1910.
S4770

Smith, Hugh M. The Fishes of North Carolina. vol. 2. Raleigh: North Carolina Geological and Economic Survey, 1907.
S4780 (LMC)

Smith, Hugh M. ed. North Carolina Geological and Economic Survey. The Fishes of North Carolina. Raleigh, N. C.: North Carolina Geological and Economic Survey, 1907.
S4790

Smith, J. Gray A Brief Historical, Statistical and Descriptive Review of East Tennessee, United States of America: Developing Its Immense Agricultural, Mining and Manufacturing Advantages, with Remarks to Emigrants. Accompanied with a Map & Lithographed Sketch of a Tennessee Farm, Mansion House, and Buildings. London: J. Leath, 1842. Smith strongly recommends eastern Tennessee to immigrants. He quotes J. S. Buckingham's detailed description of the region.
S4800

Smith, James Clenton "The Economic Impact of the University of Tennessee upon Metropolitan Knoxville." Master's thesis. Univ. of Tennessee, 1964.
S4810

Smith, James F. comp. The Cherokee Land Lottery. New York: Harper and Row, 1838. Because of the destruction of Georgia's records by fire in both national and state capitols, these land lotteries are among the best sources for tracing people through Georgia.
S4820 (LMC ETSU ASU BC)

The Cherokee Land Lottery. 1838. Reprint. Vidalia: Georgia Genealogical Reprints, 1968.
S4830 (ETSU)

The Cherokee Land Lottery, Containing a Numerical List of the Names of the Fortunate Drawers in Said Lottery, With an Engraved Map of Each District. 1838. Reprint. With a new index and map of original Cherokee County. Baltimore: Genealogical Pub. Co., 1969.
S4840 (ASU WCU BC)

Smith, James William Milici, Robert C. Stratigraphy of the Chickamauga Supergroup in Its Type Area. Nashville: Tennessee Division of Geology, 1969.
M5480 (ETSU)

Smith, Jane E. Dennis, Earle Sale Marriage Bonds of Bedford County, Virginia 1755-1800. Richmond: Dennis & Smith, 1932.
D1810 (ASU FC)

Smith, Jean Wesley The Mountaineers: Or, Bottled Sunshine for Blue Mondays. Nashville: M. E. Church, South, 1902. Observations on life in the southern mountains. Mostly accurate and sympathetic; never maudlin or glib.
S4850 (ASU BC)

Smith, John Lawrence Blackwater Country. Parsons, W. Va.: McClain Print. Co., 1972. A descriptive account of the beauty and natural features of Tucker County, West Virginia.
S4860 (ASU WCU MHC BC)

The Potomac Naturalist: The Natural History of the Headwaters of the Historic Potomac. Parsons, W. Va.: McClain Print. Co., 1968.
S4870 (ASU BC)

Smith, Larry Joe Duncan, Katherine McKinstry The History of Marshall County, Alabama. Albertville, Ala.: Thompson Print., 1969.
D3920 (ASU BC)

Smith, Lees "Rural Leadership in Roane County, Tennessee." Master's thesis. Univ. of Tennessee, 1942.
S4880

Smith, Lilly Call of the Big Eastatoe. Columbia, S. C.: State Print. Co., 1970. An autobiographical novel of life in the South Carolina mountains. Excellent descriptions of rural and family life.
S4890 (LMC ASU)

Smith, Mabell Shippie Clarke A Tar-Heel Baron. Illustrated by Edward Stratton Holloway. Philadelphia: J. B. Lippincott Co., 1903. A German baron living in poverty in the North Carolina mountains is found by his brother and sweetheart. All misunderstandings are resolved and everyone lives happily everafter.
S4900 (ASU WCU BC)

A Tar-Heel Baron. Philadelphia: J. B. Lippincott Co., 1908. Novel of life in the foothill country of North Carolina.
S4910 (ASU)

Smith, Mariwyn McClain . . . And Live Forever. A compilation of Senior Citizens articles for THE PARSONS ADVOCATE. Parsons, W. Va.: McClain Print. Co., 1974.
S4920 (ASU)

Smith, Nancy Roberts "The Teaching of French, Grades 3-6, Lincoln School, Kingsport, Tennessee, 1965-1966." Master's thesis. East Tennessee State Univ., 1966.
S4930 (ETSU)

Smith, Nena S. "The Relationship between Reading Capacity and Reading Achievement of One Hundred and Twenty-three Third Grade Children of Morrison and Hamblen County, Tennessee." Master's thesis. Tennessee Agricultural and Industrial Univ., 1952.
S4940

Smith, Ozella Nelson, Arnold E. Haven in the Hardwood: The History of Pickens, West Virginia. Parsons, W. Va.: McClain Print. Co., 1971.
N460 (ASU)

Smith, Presley Alexander Lycurgus Boyhood Memories of Fauquier. Richmond: Old Dominion Press, 1926.
S4950 (ASU)

Smith, R. C. Water Resources of the Wheeling-Steubenville Area, West Virginia and Ohio. U. S. Geological Survey Circular, no. 340. Washington: Govt. Print. Off., 1955.
S4960

Smith, R. L. Hendrickson, Bertram Higbie Soil Survey of Tioga County, Pennsylvania. Washington: U. S. Department of Agriculture, Bureau of Chemistry and Soils, 1934.
H4610

Hendrickson, Bertram Higbie Soil Survey of Wyoming County, Pennsylvania. Washington: U. S. Department of Agriculture, Bureau of Chemistry and Soils, 1934.
H4620

Smith, R. P. Experiences in Mountain Mission Work. Richmond: Presbyterian Committee of Publication, 1931.
S4970 (ASU WWC)

Smith, Reed South Carolina Ballads: With a Study of the Traditional Ballad Today. 1928. Reprint. Spartanburg, S. C.: Reprint Co., 1972.
S4990 (ASU BC)

The Traditional Ballad and Its South Carolina Survivals. Bulletin, no. 162. Columbia: Univ. of South Carolina Extension Division, 1925.
S5000 (LMC)

Smith, Reed ed. American Anthology of Old-world Ballads. Settings by Hilton Rufty. New York: J. Fischer and Brothers, 1973.
S4980 (ASU)

Smith, Richard C. Human Crisis in the Kingdom of Coal. New York: Friendship Press, 1952.
S5010 (ASU BC)

Human Crisis in the Kingdom of Coal. New York: Friendship Press, 1952. The author is a former director of the Mountaineer Mission near Morgantown, West Virginia.
S5020

Smith, Richard Wellington The Phosphate Resources of Tennessee. Bulletin, no. 48. Nashville: Tennessee Department of Conservation, Division of Geology, 1940.
S5030 (ETSU)

Smith, Robert Cullen Stringfield, Victor Timothy Relation of Geology to Drainage, Floods, and Landslides in the Petersburg Area, West Virginia. Morgantown: West Virginia Geological and Economic Survey, 1956.
S8030 (ETSU)

Smith, Robert L. "Basic Industrial Resources of the Altoona, Pennsylvania, Area." Master's thesis. Pennsylvania State College, 1949.
S5040

Smith, Rosalyn Atkinson "Emerson Etheridge as a Candidate in the Tennessee Gubernatorial Election of 1867." Master's thesis. Univ. of Tennessee, 1969.
S5060

Smith, Ross Reminiscences of an Old-Timer. n.p.: Privately printed, 1930. Memoirs of a senior citizen from Washington County, Tennessee.
S5050

Smith, Sam B. Tennessee History, a Bibliography. Knoxville: Univ. of Tennessee Press, 1974. An excellent resource for Tennessee researchers.
S5070 (ASU)

Smith, Virginia Norre "Folk-hymns of the Southland." Microfilm. Master's thesis. Union Theological Seminary, 1948. Some variants of old favorites, but she really added very little that could be found in previously published sources.
S5080 (WCU)

Smith, Warren B. White Servitude in Colonial South Carolina. Columbia: Univ. of South Carolina Press, 1961.
S5090 (ASU)

Smith, Wesley G. An Inventory of Land and Its Use in the Tennessee Valley. Muscle Shoals, Ala.: Tennessee Valley Authority, 1966.
S5100

Level of Education and Estimated Rate of School Dropout in the Tennessee Valley. Muscle Shoals, Ala.: Tennessee Valley Authority, 1967.
S5110 (ASU)

Movement of Labor Between Farm and Non Farm Sectors and Multiple Jobholding by Farm Operators in the Tennessee Valley. Muscle Shoals, Ala.: Tennessee Valley Authority, 1967.
S5120

Smith, Wil J. Zeller, Frederick A. Economic Development in West Virginia. Morgantown: West Virginia Univ., Office of Research and Development, 1968.
Z60

Smith, Wil J. ed. Critical Issues in Public Finance in an Underdeveloped Region: The West Virginia Case Morgantown: West Virginia Univ., 1971.
C8810 (ASU WCU BC)

Smith (Wilbur) and Associates Parking Program, Central Business District, Johnson City, Tennessee. Prepared for the city of Johnson City, Tennessee. New Haven, Conn.: The co., 1959.
S5130 (ETSU)

Traffic and Parking, Johnson City, Tennessee. Prepared for Tennessee Department of Highways and city of Johnson City in cooperation with U. S. Department of Commerce Bureau of Public Roads. New Haven, Conn.: The co., 1959.
S5140 (ETSU)

Smith, William Dale The Lost Children of the Alleghanies. Philadelphia: W. P. Zimmerman, n.d.
S5150 (ASU)

A Multitude of Men. New York: Simon and Schuster, 1959. A novel of love and death and work in a West Virginia steel mill. Two major characters Vera Mae and her brother Dudley are very powerfully drawn. Set against the backdrop of a labor strike.
S5160 (BC)

Smith, William Farrar From Chattanooga to Petersburg Under Generals Grant and Butler: A Contribution to the History of the War, and a Personal Vindication. Boston: Houghton Mifflin and Co., 1893. Includes some battles in the mountain regions.
S5170 (ASU)

Smith, William G. Soil Survey of Blount County, Alabama. Field Operations, 1905. Washington: U. S. Department of Agriculture, Bureau of Soils, 1914.
S5180

Soil Survey of Colbert County, Alabama. Prepared in cooperation with Alabama. Field Operations, 1908. Washington: U. S. Department of Agriculture, Bureau of Soils, 1909.
S5190

Smith, William Robert Lee Charles Lewis Cocke, Founder of Hollins College. Boston: Richard G. Badger, The Gorham Press, 1921.
S5200

The Story of the Cherokees. Cleveland, Tenn.: Church of God Pub. House, 1928. A rather maudlin account of the Cherokee Removal with a general history of the Cherokee.
S5210

Smith, William Winfred ed. Dudding, Earl Endicott The Trail of the Dead Years. . . Huntington, W. Va.: Prisoners Relief Society, 1933.
D3660

Smithwick, J. W. P. Ornithology of North Carolina: A List of the Birds of N. C. with Notes on Each Species. Bulletin, no. 144. Raleigh: North Carolina Agricultural Experiment Station, 1897.
S5220 (LMC)

Smoky Mountain Cultural Arts Development Association Confrontation with the Arts: The Arts in Education — What? For Whom? How? A Symposium Held at Western Carolina University, March 6-7, 1969. Sylva, N. C.: The assoc., 1967.
S5230 (ASU WCU)

Snell, Ruth Freeman "Diagnosis and Remediation of Difficulties in Arithmetic in Fifth Grade at West Side School, Elizabethton, Tennessee, 1956-57." Master's thesis. East Tennessee State College, 1957.
S5240 (ETSU)

Snidow, Francis Arthur An Economic and Social Survey of Giles County. Charlottesville: Univ. of Va. Extension Division, 1927.
S5250

Snitzler, James R. Transportation of Apples in the Appalachian Belt, 1952-53. Washington: U. S. Department of Agriculture, Agricultural Marketing Service, 1954.
S5260

Snodgrass, Billy Broten "Written Board of Education Policies for Hawkins County, Tennessee." Master's thesis. East Tennessee State Univ., 1970.
S5270 (ETSU)

Snow, Dorothea J. A Sight of Everything. Illustrated by Vee Guthrie. Boston: Houghton Mifflin, 1963. Purdie is certain that he has too many brothers and sisters. He can never have anything of his own. Southern mountain setting.
S5280 (ASU)

Snow, John Allen Fisher's River Scenes, Reproduced from the Original. n.p.: The author, 1958. Hilarious sketches of life along the river. Some of the best dialect in all of Appalachian Literature.
S5290 (LMC WCU ASU BC)

Snyder, Ann E. On the Watauga and the Cumberland. Nashville: M. E. Church, South, Pub. House, 1895.
S5300 (LMC)

Snyder, Frank G. ed. Symposium on Mineral Resources of the Southeastern United States, University of Tennessee, 1949 Proceedings. Knoxville: Univ. of Tennessee Press, 1950.
S9780 (ASU BC)

Snyder, J. M. Watkins, William Isaac Soil Survey of Greenville County, South Carolina. Washington: U. S. Department of Agriculture, Bureau of Soils, 1924.
W1480

Snyder, Joseph Buchanan History of the Family Snyder (Schneider) (Snider). St. Lewis: St. Louis Law Print. Co., 1940. Family originated in Whitley County, Kentucky.
S5310

Snyder, Joseph M. and others Soil Survey of Garrett County, Maryland. Prepared in cooperation with the Maryland Geological Survey and the Maryland Agricultural Experiment Station. Field Operations, 1922. Washington: U. S. Department of Agriculture, Bureau of Soils, 1926.
S5320

Snyder, Opal "History of the Great Smoky Mountains National Park." Master's thesis. George Peabody College, 1935.
S5330

Snyder, William U. Thomas Wolfe: Ulysses and Narcissus. 1971. Reprint. Athens: Ohio Univ. Press, 1972.
S5340 (ASU)

Social Register of Knoxville & East Tenn., 1934 Asheville, N. C.: Blue Book Co. of N. Y., 1934.
S5350

Society for the Advancement of Management Financial Control System of the Tennessee Valley Authority. Revised ed. Federal Fiscal Series. Study no. 1. Washington: American Univ. Press, 1945.
S5390

Society of American Foresters, Washington, D. C., Appalachian Section Cumulated Index for Proceedings of the Society of American Foresters, Volumes 1-11, May 1905-1916. Forestry Quarterly, Volumes 1-14. October, 1902 - December, 1916 Journal of Forestry, Volumes 15-27, January 1917-December, 1929. Washington: The society, 1930.
S5360 (ASU)

Society of Colonial Wars, Kentucky Yearbook of the Society of Colonial Wars in the Commonwealth of Kentucky. n.p.: The society, 1895-.
S5380 (ETSU)

Society of the Army of the Tennessee Report of the Proceedings. Cincinnati: n.p., 1896, 1906.
S5370 (LMC)

Soileau, John M. Tenn. Valley Land and Its Changing Use. Muscle Shoals, Ala.: National Fertilizer Development Center, 1966.
S5400

Solberg, Erling Day Suggestion for Planning and Zoning in Appalachia. Agricultural Economic Report, 330. Washington: U. S. Department of Agriculture, Economic Research Service, 1964.
S5410

Solie, Richard John "Job Retraining under the Area Development Act: The Campbell, Claiborne Counties (Tennessee) Case." Ph. D. Diss. Univ. of Tennessee, 1965.
S5420

Solomon, Ben Hiker's Guide. Leisure League Little Book, no. 15. New York: Leisure League of America, 1934. A handy book of advice for hikers.
S5430 (ASU)

Somers, Gerald G. "Grievance Settlement in Coal Mining." Master's thesis. West Va. Univ., 1956.
S5440

Mobility of Chemical Workers in a Coal Mining Area. Morgantown: West Virginia Univ., 1954.
S5450

Sommerville, Geraldine David Rawson Ancestors and Descendants. n.p.: n.p., 1974.
S5460 (ASU)

David Rawson: Ancestors and Descendants, 1636-1974. By Geraldine Sommerville and Oma H. Mills. Parsons, W. Va.: McClain Print. Co., 1974.
S5470

Sondley, Foster Alexander Asheville and Buncombe County. Genesis of Buncombe County, by Theodore F. Davidson. Asheville, N. C.: Citizen Co., 1922.
S5480 (WCU BC)

Early Settlement of Western North Carolina. Asheville: n.p., n.d.
S5490

A History of Buncombe County, North Carolina. 2 vols. Asheville, N. C.: Advocate Print. Co., 1930.
S5500 (ASU WCU LMC BC)

The Indian's Curse; a Legend of the Cherokees. Asheville: n.p., n.d.
S5510 (UNCA ASU)

Songs of Freedom, Famous Labor Songs from Appalachia Huntington, W. Va.: Appalachian Movement Press, n.d.
S5520 (ASU)

Sorrel, G. Moxley Recollections of a Confederate Staff Officer. With Introduction by Senator John W. Daniel. New York: Neale Pub. Co., 1905.
S5530 (LMC)

Sossamon, Leroy Backside of Heaven: Selected Verse From Bystander in the Smoky Mountain Times. Bryson City, N. C.: Village Press, 1957. Poems from and about Swain County, North Carolina.
S5540 (WCU BC UNCA)

Falling Sky. Bryson City, N. C.: Village Press, 1961.
S5550 (WCU)

Soupart, Sylvia Stories of W. Va. for Boys & Girls. Charleston, W. Va.: Jarrett Print. Co., 1937.
S5560

South Carolina, Appalachian Region Health Policy and Planning Council Health Development Plan — 1970. 4 vols. Greenville, S. C.: The council, 1970.
S5570 (ASU)

South Carolina, Department of Agriculture South Carolina: A Handbook. Columbia, S. C.: Clemson College, 1927. Includes discussions of the six mountain counties.
S5580 (LMC)

South Pittsburg on the Tennessee River, Marion County, Tennessee n.p.: Privately printed, 1887.
S5590

South, Stanley A. Indians in North Carolina. Raleigh: N. C. State Department of Archives and History, 1959.
S5600 (ASU WCU MHC BC UNCA)

Southeastern Kentucky Health Resources Development, Technical Assistance Services Southeastern Kentucky Regional Health Demonstration Project. Frankfort, Ky.: Area Development Office, 1967. Appendix also issued in 1967.
S5610 (ASU)

Southeastern Kentucky Regional Health Demonstration Project. Appendix, 1967. Frankfort, Ky.: Area Development Office, 1967.
S5620 (ASU)

Southeastern Kentucky Regional Health Demonstration Health Development Plan for Year, 1968-69. Lexington: The demonstration, 1968.
S5630 (ASU)

Southeastern Kentucky Regional Health Demonstration Project. Health Development Plan for Year 1969-70. By Kentucky River Comprehensive Health Planning Council and Cumberland Valley Comprehensive Health Planning Council. Lexington, Ky.: The demonstration, 1969.
S5640 (ASU)

Southern Appalachia Power Conference Proceedings. 1st, 1922-. Knoxville, Tenn.: The conference, annual-.
S5650

Southern Appalachian National Park Commission see **U. S. Southern Appalachian National Park Commission**

Southern Appalachian Studies Health & Health Service in the Southern Appalachians, a Source Book. Progress report, RS-35. Raleigh, N. C.: N. C. Agricultural Experiment Station, Dept. of Rural Sociology, 1959.
S5660

Southern Appalachian Studies, Berea, Ky. The Southern Appalachian Region; A Survey. Contributors: Rupert B. Vance and others. Lexington: Univ. of Kentucky Press, 1962.
S5670 (BC ASU UNCA FC)
The Southern Appalachian Region. Contributors: Rupert B. Vance and others. Lexington: Univ. of Kentucky Press, 1967.
S5680 (ASU ETSU FC LMC MHC WCU WWC BC)

Southern Association of Colleges and Secondary Schools, Secondary Commission Evaluation of the East Ridge High School, Chattanooga, Tennessee; Completed by the visiting Committee March 5-9, 1962. . . . Mimeographed. Chattanooga, Tenn.: The ass'n., 1962.
S5690
Evaluative study made in Chattanooga High School, Chattanooga, Tennessee; completed by Visiting Committee March 12-16, 1950. Mimeographed. Chattanooga, Tenn.: The ass'n., n.d.
S5700

Southern Education Reporting Service Southern Schools: Progress and Problems. Prepared by staff members and associates of (the) Service. Nashville: The service, 1959.
S5710 (WWC)

Southern Educational Board Educational Conditions in the Southern Appalachians. Knoxville: Southern Educational Board, 1902.
S5720

Southern Folklore Quarterly vol. 1-, 1937. Jacksonville, Fla.: H. and W. Drew Co., quarterly.
S5730 (ASU BC)

Southern Highland Handicraft Guild Crafts in the Southern Highlands. Asheville, N. C.: The guild, 1958.
S5750 (BC ASU)
Crafts in the Southern Highlands. Berea, Ky.: Council of the Southern Mountains, 1968.
S5760
Highland Highlights. v. I, no. 1-, 1942. Mimeographed. n.p.: n.p., n.d.
S5765 (BC)

The Southern Highlander v. II, 1907. Rome, Ga.: Berry College, 1907, monthly.
S5770

The Southern Highlands Asheville, N. C.: News of the Asheville Public Libraries, 1963.
S5780 (MHC)

Southern Indian Studies vol. 1, 1949. Chapel Hill, N. C.: Archaeological Society of North Carolina, annual.
S5790 (ASU)

Southern Newspapers Publishers' Association Catalogue, Southern Newspaper Library. . . . Chattanooga, Tenn.: The ass'n., 1954.
S5800

Southern Postcard Company Sixty-four Selected Views of Western North Carolina, "The Land of the Sky, America's Beauty Spot". Asheville, N. C.: The co., n.d.
S5810 (ASU)

Southern Pulpwood Production Issues by the U. S. Southern Forest Experiment Station in cooperation with the Southern Pulpwood Conservation Association. Asheville, N. C.: Southeastern Forest Experiment Station, annual.
S5820 (WCU)

Southern Railway Camping on Mount Mitchell, Information Regarding Good Places for Summer Camps in United States Forests in North Carolina. n.p.: The railway, 1916.
S5830 (ASU)
Community Life in Western North Carolina. n.p.: The railway, n.d.
S5840 (ASU)

Southern Railway Company The Floods of July 1916: How the Southern Railway Organization Met an Emergency. Washington: The co., 1917.
S5850 (ASU LMC)
The Land of the Sky, Western North Carolina. n.p.: The co., 1914.
S5860 (LMC)

Southern Regional Council Hungry Children: Special Report. Atlanta: The council, 1967.
S5870 (ETSU)

Southern Regional Education Board. Resource Development Project Basic Health Needs and Resources in the Upper Hiwassee Development Association Area. Atlanta: Southern Regional Education Board, 1967.
S5880 (WCU)

Southern West Virginia Economic Development Corporation Coal, The Curse and the Key: Overall Economic Development Program for the Southern West Virginia Economic Development District. n.p.: n.p., 1968.
S5890

Southworth, Emma Dorothy Eliza Nevitte Fallen Pride; or the Mountain Girl's Love. Philadelphia: T. B. Peterson and Brothers, 1968. Romantic nonsense which peoples the mountains with gentry who take pity on the natives.
S5900 (BC)
The Prince of Darkness, a Romance of the Blue Ridge. Philadelphia: T. B. Peterson and Brothers, 1869. A very romantic, very silly tale of good and evil, love and pride in the Blue Ridge Mountains. Mrs. Southworth's fine gentry seem out of place.
S5910

Souvenir Supplement. Sparta Exposition, January, 1902 Sparta: n.p., 1902.
S5920

Spaeth, David Hollingsworth Application of Current Utilization Research to the Kentucky Coal Industry. Prepared for the Kentucky Department of Commerce. Lexington, Ky.: Spindletop Research, 1963.
S5930
The Economic Viability of the Small Underground Coal Mine. . . . Lexington, Ky.: Spindletop Research Center, 1962.
S5940

Spaeth, Sigmund Gottfried Read 'Em and Weep: The Songs You Forgot to Remember. Garden City, N. Y.: Doubleday, Page and Co., 1927.
S5950 (ASU)

Spalding, Arthur Whitefield The Hills o' Ca'liny. Takoma Park, Washington, N. C.: Review and Herald Pub. Assoc., 1921. Observations on life in the North Carolina mountains.
S5960 (ASU LMC)
The Men of the Mountains: The Story of the Southern Mountaineer and His Kin of the Piedmont. With an Account of Some of the Agencies of Progress among Them. Nashville: Southern Pub. Assoc., 1915.
S5970 (ASU ETSU LMC)

Spalding, Henry Stanislaus The Sheriff of the Beech Fork: A Story of Kentucky. New York: Benziger Brothers, 1903. A novel of 20th century Kentucky. Rivers to navigate, troubles to overcome and romance as the reward.
S5980 (ASU BC)

Spalding, S. J. The Old Mill on the Withrose. New York: Benziger Brothers, 1910. A novel of northeastern Kentucky. Romance with a mountain background.
S5990 (BC)

Sparks, Doris Brenda "The History of Patterson School, Caldwell County, North Carolina." Master's thesis. Appalachian State Teachers College, 1961. A history of one of the few private preparatory schools in western North Carolina.
S6000 (ASU)

Sparks, Jared Daniel Boone. The Library of American Biography. Boston: Charles C. Little and James Brown, 1847. Another biography of Daniel Boone, this one has more anecdotes than most others.
S6010

Sparks, Robert ed. Cumberlands Hiking Club, Chattanooga Outdoors in the Cumberlands. Chattanooga, Tenn.: Chattanooga Community Assoc., 1933.
C9450 (BC)

Spaulding, Irving A. Mobility and Fertility Rates of Rural Families in Johnson County, Kentucky, 1918-1941. Lexington: Ky. Ag. Exp. Sta., 1943.
S6020

Spaulding, Willard M., Jr. Boccardy, Joseph A. Effects of Surface Mining on Fish and Wildlife in Appalachia, Special Report. Washington: Govt. Print. Off., 1968.
B4930 ()

Spearman, Walter North Carolina Writers. Chapel Hill: Univ. of North Carolina Press, 1949.
S6030 (LMC)
North Carolina Writers. Chapel Hill: Univ. of North Carolina, 1953.
S6040 (LMC)

Spears, Woodridge "Elizabeth M. Roberts: A Biographical and Critical Study." Ph. D. Diss. Univ. of Kentucky, 1955.
S6050 (ASU)
The Feudalist. New York: The Fine Editions Press, 1946.
S6060 (BC)
River Island. Morehead, Ky.: Morehead State College Press, 1963.
S6070 (BC)

Speck, Frank Gouldsmith Catawba Texts. Contributions to Anthropology, vol. 24. New York: Columbia Univ. Press, 1934.
S6080 (LMC BC)
Cherokee Dance and Drama. In collaboration with Will West Long. Berkeley: Univ. of California Press, 1951.
S6090 (ASU WCU ETSU BC)
. . . Decorative Art and Basketry of the Cherokee. Milwaukee, Wis.: Bulletin of the Public Museum of the City of Milwaukee. v. 2. no. 2 July 27, 1920.
S6100 (ASU)

Speece, Conrad The Mountaineer, A New Edition. Collected essays from a newspaper, the local REPUBLICAN FARMER. Staunton, Va.: Isaac Collett, 1823.
S6110

Speed, Thomas The Wilderness Road: a Description of the Routes of Travel by Which the Pioneers and Early Settlers First Came to Kentucky. 1886. Reprint. Filson Club Publications, no. 2. Burt Franklin Research and Source Work Series, 761. American Class in History and Social Science, 193.
S6120 (ASU FC LMC BC)

Spelman, John A., III At Home in the Hills: Glimpses of Harlan County, Kentucky, through the Media of the Linoleum Block and the Woodcut. Pine Mountain, Ky.: Pine Mountain Print Shop, 1939.
S6130 (LMC BC)

Spence, Joe Edd "The Public Career of Andrew Jackson Graves." Master's thesis. Univ. of Tennessee, 1967. Graves was a Democratic political leader in Knox County in the 1920s.
S6140

Spence, Thomas Hugh The Historical Foundation and Its Treasures. Rev. ed. Montreat, N. C.: Historical Foundations Publications, 1960. The Historical Foundation of the Presbyterian and Reformed Churches is in Montreat, North Carolina in the Appalachian Mountains.
S6150

Spencer, Gary F. "West Virginia's Appalachia Participation." Master's thesis. West Virginia Univ., 1970.
S6160

Spencer, Herbert W. Methodism in Jackson and Breathitt County, Kentucky. n.p.: n.p., 1964.
S6170

Spiceweed, Simon Junaluskie, the Cherokee; a Story of the War. Salisbury, N. C.: J. Bruner, 1865. No copy of this volume has ever been found.
S6180

Spillane, William Henry "Comparative Study of Related Health Fertility Attitudes and Behavior of Families Residing in a Poverty Area." Ph. D. Diss. Univ. of Pittsburgh, 1971. An Appalachian county is used in this study.
S6190

Spillman, Claude O. "The Relationship of the Economic Production of Farmers of the Southern Appalachian Region to Certain Social Factors." Master's thesis. Univ. of Kentucky, 1939.
S6200 (ASU)

Spindletop Research Commonwealth of Kentucky Planning Inventory. Comprehensive State Planning Series, Doc. B-2. Prepared for the Kentucky Program Development Office. Lexington, Ky.: The co., 1969. Includes plans for the Appalachian counties.
S6210

Commonwealth of Kentucky Program Planning Communication & Coordination (P2C2): A Preliminary System Design. Comprehensive State Planning Series, Doc. C-1. Frankfort, Ky.: Kentucky Program Development Office, 1970.
S6220

Goals, Objectives, and Policies. Prepared for the Kentucky Program Development Office. Comprehensive State Planning Series, Doc. G-1. Lexington, Ky.: The co., 1969.
S6230

Kentucky Public Library Inventory and Projected Needs. Prepared for the Kentucky Program Development Office. Comprehensive State Planning Series, Doc. B-1. Lexington, Ky.: The co., 1969.
S6240

A Model for Sequencing Public Investment Programs and Allocating Multiprogram Benefits. Prepared for the Army Corps of Engineers Office of Appalachian Studies. 3 vols. Lexington, Ky.: The co., 1967.
S6250

An Urban Development Program for the Big Sandy Area. Prepared for the Kentucky Program Development Office and the Appalachian Regional Commission. Lexington, Ky.: The co., 1968.
S6260 (ASU)

Spinelli, Michael Ambrose "A Definition of the Economic Subregions of Appalachia Using Factor Analysis." Ph. D. Diss. West Virginia Univ., 1971.
S6270

Spivak, John Louis The Devil's Brigade: The Story of the Hatfield-McCoy Feud. New York: Brewer and Warren, 1930.
S6280 (ASU WCU BC)

A Man in His Time. New York: Horizon Press, 1967. As a journalist, Spivak is best known for his coverage of mine wars and labor disputes in the Appalachians.
S6290 (ASU)

Spoden, Muriel Clark Kingsport, Tennessee: Historical Map of Long Island of the Holston. Kingsport: n.p., 1969.
S6300

Sponaugle, William Clay Biographies of Southwest Virginians. 2 vols. n.p.: n.p., n.d.
S6310

Sprague, William C. Davy Crockett. True Stories of Great Americans Series. New York: Macmillan, 1915.
S6320

Davy Crockett. New York: MacMillan, 1929.
S6330 (WWC)

Spraker, Ella Hazel comp. The Boone Family; a Genealogical History of the Descendants of George and Mary Boone Who Came to America in 1717, Containing Many Unpublished Bits of Early Kentucky History. . . . Baltimore: Genealogical Pub. Co., Inc., 1974.
S6340 (ASU)

Spratt, Barnett Toppy and the Circuit Rider. Salisbury, N. C.: J. Bruner, 1865. No copy available.
S6350

Spring City High School Alumni Association Spring City High School, 1912-1962, Golden Anniversary Celebration, May 12, 1962. Collegedale: College Press, 1962. A history of a high school in Rhea County, Tennessee.
S6360

Springman, Charles ed. North Carolina by North Carolinians: A Photographic Exhibition Sponsored By the North Carolina Arts Council: The People, Places and Things of One State as Seen by the People Who Know It Best — Those Who Live Here. n.p.: North Carolina Arts Council, n.d. Much information on western North Carolina and its scenic spots.
S6370 (LMC)

Springs, Katherine Wooten The Squires of Springfield. Charlotte, N. C.: W. Loftin, 1965.
S6380 (ASU)

Spunders, Fred B. Wise, James O. Optimum Farm Organizations and Area Production Patterns for the Upper Hiwassee Watershed Area. Athens: Georgia Agricultural Experiment Station, 1969.
W7870

Spurrier, Joseph L. Spurrier With the Wildcats and Moonshiners. Nashville, Tenn.: n.p., 1892. Stories of moonshiners and mountain life told by a revenuer.
S6390 (ASU BC)

Squire, Joseph Report on the Cálaba Coal Field. Alabama Geological Survey. Montgomery: Brown Print. Co., 1890.
S6400

Stackpole, Edward James Sheridan in the Shenandoah: Jubal Early's Nemesis. Maps by Wilbur S. Nye. Illustrated from the Keau Archives. 1st ed. Civil War Centennial Series. Harrisburg, Pa.: Stackpole Co., 1961.
S6410 (ASU)

Stacy, Helen Price Selections from Morgan County History: Sesquicentennial Volume. West Liberty, Ky.: n.p., 1972?
S6420 (ASU)

Stadnichenko, Taisia Zubovic, Peter Distribution of Minor Elements in Coals of Appalachian Region. Washington: U. S. Geological Survey, 1966.
Z150

Staff of Quote comp. and ed. Graham, William Franklin The Quotable Billy Graham. Anderson, S. C.: Droke House, 1966.
G3160 (WCU)

Stafford, Emily Ann "A Study of Readiness Needs of the First Grade Children at Henry Johnson School, 1952-1953." Master's thesis. East Tennessee State College, 1953.
S6430 (ETSU)

Stagg, Brian L. Deer Lodge, Tennessee, Its Little-Known History. Oak Ridge: The author, 1964. History of a small community in Morgan County, Tennessee.
S6440

Stahurski, Edward J. "A Study of Buyers on the Allegheny County Farmer's Market, Pittsburgh, Pennsylvania, 1946." Master's thesis. Pennsylvania State College, 1947.
S6450

Stallard, John Junior "A Comparative Study of Twenty Business Trainees of the Gate City, Virginia, MDTA Program with Twenty Business Graduates of the Washington County, Virginia, Technical School." Master's thesis. East Tennessee State Univ., 1968.
S6460 (ETSU)

Stallings, Constance Murlless, Dick Hiker's Guide to the Smokies. San Francisco: Sierra Club, 1973.
M9070 (ASU LMC WCU)

Stallings, James L. and others Resources of the Upper South Branch Valley, West Virginia. Morgantown: West Va. Univ. Ag. Exp. Station, 1967.
S6470

Stallworth, Anne Nall This Time Next Year. New York: Vanguard Press, 1971. A very good first novel about a young girl's life in northwestern Alabama in the 1930's.
S6480 (ASU BC)

Stambaugh, Samuel C. A Faithful History of the Cherokee Tribe of Indians from the Period of Our First Intercourse with Them, Down to the Present Time. The Reasons and Considerations Which Produced a Separation of the Tribe at an Early Period; Organizing a Nation East and a Nation West of the Mississippi River. With a Full Exposition of the Causes Which Led to Their Subsequent Division into Three Parties, and Involved Them in Their Present Deplorable Condition, and of the Nature and Extent of Their Present Claims. Washington, D. C.: J. E. Dow, 1846.
S6490

Stanard, Mary Newton The Story of Virginia's First Century. Philadelphia: Lippincott, 1928.
S6500 (LMC)

Stanard, William Glover comp. Some Emigrants to Virginia. Memoranda in regard to several hundred emigrants to Virginia during the Colonial Period whose parentage is shown or former residence indicated by authentic records. Richmond: W. E. Jones' Sons, 1911.
S6510 (ASU)

Some Emigrants to Virginia. Memoranda in regard to several hundred emigrants to Virginia during the Colonial Period whose parentage is shown or former residence indicated by authentic records. 2nd ed. 1915. Reprint. Baltimore: Genealogical Pub. Co., 1964.
S6520 (ASU)

Stanberry, Thomas W. "The Economic Status of Knox County Teachers." Master's thesis. Univ. of Tenn., 1959.
S6530

Standefer, Jewel B. comp. Hughes, Thomas P., Jr. Pittsylvania County, Virginia Abstracts of Wills, 1768-1800. n.p.: n.p., 1956.
H8140

Standish, Hal Fred Fearnot in West Virginia. New York: Frank Tousey, 1903. A novel of a brave young West Virginia boy who helps the revenue agents during a moonshine raid.
S6540

Stanley, Isaac Newton "An Educational and Economic Survey of Monroe County, Tennessee." Master's thesis. Univ. of Tennessee, 1926.
S6550

Stanley, James A. "The Development of Secondary Education in Watauga County, North Carolina." Master's thesis. Univ. of North Carolina, 1940.
S6560

Stanley, Lawrence L. Ghost Stories from the Southern Mountains. Cashiers, N. C.: n.p., 1971. A series of ghost stories most of them from north Georgia.
S6570 (ASU)

A Rough Road in a Good Land. Rabun Gap, Ga.: Craft House, 1971. Account of the author's growing up years in North Georgia. Good information on rural life during the Depression.
S6580 (ASU)

Stapleton, Ammon Memorials of the Huguenots in America, with Special Reference to Their Emigration to Pennsylvania. Baltimore: Genealogical Pub. Co., 1969.
S6590 (ASU)

Stapleton, Pat Report on Appalachian Culture Preschool Curriculum Project. Greensboro: Univ. of N. C., Center for Leadership for Child Care, 1973. This study done in cooperation with Licking Valley Community Action Program and Kentucky Rural Child Care.
S6600 (ASU)

Starkey, Marion Lena The Cherokee Nation. New York: A. A. Knopf, 1946. One of the better histories of the Cherokee.
S6610 (ASU LMC ETSU BC)

Starnes, Carl Edward "A Study of a Possible Plan for Further School Consolidation in Hawkins County." Master's thesis. East Tennessee State College, 1956.
S6620 (ETSU)

Starnes, John Morris "A Study of Twenty Superior Students at Ketron High School." Master's thesis. East Tennessee State Univ., 1964.
S6630 (ETSU)

Starr, Donald H. "The Educational Progress of the Negro Schools in Cherokee County, Alabama, from 1930-1950." Master's thesis. Alabama State College, 1952.
S6640

Starr, Emmet Cherokees "West," 1794-1839. Oklahoma City: Warden, 1921.
S6650

Early History of the Cherokees: Embracing Aboriginal Customs, Religion, Laws, Folklore and Civilization. Claremore, Okla.: n.p., 1917.
S6660

Starr, Emmet
History of the Cherokee Indians. Indian Heritage Edition. Fayetteville, Ark.: Indian Heritage Assoc., 1967.
S6670 (ASU BC ETSU WCU)
History of the Cherokee Indians and Their Legends and Folk Lore. 1921. Reprint. New York: Kraus Reprint Co., 1969.
S6680 (ASU LMC)
Old Cherokee Families: Old Families and Their Genealogy. Reprinted from History of the Cherokee Indians and their legends and folklore. With comprehensive index compiled by James Julian Hill. Norman: Univ. of Oklahoma Foundation, 1968.
S6690 (WCU MHC)

Staton, Willis A Colorful Career of a Miraculous Mountaineer: A Glimpse into the Life of a Remarkable Character. Johnson City, Tenn.: Christian Craft, 1965.
S6700 (ASU)

Stead, F. W. Manganese and Quartzite Deposits in the Lick Mountain Region of Wythe Co. n.p.: n.p., 1943.
S6710

Stearns, Richard G. Marcher, Melvin V. Tuscaloosa Formation in Tennessee. Nashville: Tennessee Division of Geology, 1962.
M3190 (ETSU)

Stearns, Richard Gordon The Cumberland Plateau Overthrust and Geology of the Crab Orchard Mountains Area, Tennessee. Bulletin, 60. Nashville: Tennessee Division of Geology, 1954.
S6720 (ETSU)
Pennsylvanian Rocks of the Southern Appalachians. Nashville: n.p., 1962.
S6730 (ETSU)

Steel, Robert V. P. see also **Thomas, Lately pseud**

Steel, Roberta Ingles Escape From Indian Captivity. The Story of Mary Draper Ingles and Son Thomas Ingles. Radford, Va.: Commonwealth Press, n.d.
S6740

Steele, Glenn . . . Maternity and Infant Care in a Mountain County in Georgia. Washington, D. C.: U. S. Dept. of Labor, Children's Bureau. Bureau pub. No. 120, Govt. Print. Off., 1923.
S6750 (BC)

Steele, J. G. Paschall, Alfred H. Soil Survey, Athens County, Ohio. Washington: U. S. Department of Agriculture, Bureau of Chemistry and Soils, 1938.
P530
Paschall, Alfred H. Soil Survey of Vinton County, Ohio. Washington: U. S. Department of Agriculture, Bureau of Chemistry and Soils, 1938.
P540
Phillips, Samuel William Soil Survey of Belmont County, Ohio. Washington: U. S. Department of Agriculture, Bureau of Chemistry and Soils, 1931.
P2620

Steele, Mary Q. The Secret of Fiery Gorge. Illustrated by Mary Stevens. 1st ed. Cleveland: World Pub. Co., 1960. Exciting tale about a brother and sister who vacation in the western North Carolina mountains and solve a local mystery.
S6760 (ASU)

Steele, Robert V. P. The First President Johnson: The Three Lives of the Seventeenth President of the United States of America. New York: Morrow, 1968.
S6770

Steele, William O. Daniel Boone's Echo. Illustrated by Nicolas. 1st ed. New York: Harcourt, Brace, 1957. Daniel recruits a boy called Aaron to go to Kentucky with him and come back to tell the folks there is nothing to fear. In this way Boone can persuade settlers to go to Kentucky.
S6780 (ASU BC)
The Far Frontier. New York: Harcourt, Brace and Co., 1959. Another of Steele's well-researched novels of frontier life. Partially set in the mountains.
S6790 (BC)
Flaming Arrows. New York: Harcourt, Brace, 1957. Novel of frontier life in the Trans-Alleghany west. Plenty of Indians and all manner of chances for a boy to grow up. General setting: eastern Kentucky.
S6800 (WCU BC)
John Sevier, Boy Pioneer. Indianapolis: Bobbs Merrill, 1953. Novel of John Sevier who pioneered in the Watauga country and grew up to become governor of the state of Franklin and the state of Tennessee.
S6810 (BC)
The Lone Hunt. New York: Harcourt, Brace and World, 1956. A young man faces his first hunt alone and matures in the process.
S6820 (BC)
The Old Wilderness Road: An American Journey. New York: Harcourt, Brace and World, 1968. A novel of the Wilderness Road and the four men who hacked it from the wilderness: Thomas Walker, Elisha Wallen, Daniel Boone, and John Filson.
S6830 (WCU BC ETSU)
Over-Mountain Boy. New York: Aladdin Books, 1951. This over-mountain boy seems to be a miniature of the legendary over-mountain men who defeated the British at Kings Mountain.
S6840
The Perilous Road. New York: Harcourt, Brace and Co., 1958. Novel of frontier life and the westward movement.
S6850
The Story of Daniel Boone. Illustrated by Warren Baumgartner. Signature Books, 15. New York: Grosset and Dunlap, 1954. A fictionalized account of the life and exploits of Daniel Boone.
S6860 (ASU BC)
Tomahawks and Trouble. New York: Harcourt, Brace and Co., 1955. A novel of the frontier, youth, and Indian troubles in the Cumberland mountains.
S6870 (BC)
Triple Trouble for Hound Dog Zip. Champaign, Ill.: Gerrard Pub. Co., 1972.
S6880
Wilderness Journey. Illustrated by Paul Goldone. 1st ed. New York: Harcourt, Brace and Co., 1953. A journey across the Great Appalachian barrier is the subject of this novel.
S6890 (ASU WCU BC)
Winter Danger. New York: Harcourt, Brace and Co., 1954. Novel of a young boy on his first winter hunting trip in the Cumberlands.
S6900 (WCU BC)

Stein, John G. Hamilton County, Economic and Social: A Laboratory Study in the Department of Agricultural Economics Under the Direction of Professor C. E. Allred. Knoxville: Dept. of Agricultural Economics, Univ. of Tennessee, 1925.
S6910

Steiner, Jesse Frederick The North Carolina Chain Gang: A Study of County Convict Road Work. Chapel Hill: Univ. of North Carolina Press, 1927. Includes reports from the twenty-eight mountain counties.
S6920 (LMC)
The North Carolina Chain Gang: A Study of County Convict Road Work. 1927. Reprint. Montclair, N. J.: Patterson Smith, 1969.
S6930 (WWC)

Steinmetz, Rollin C. Vanishing Crafts and Their Craftsmen. Xerox copy of the original. New Brunswick, N. J.: Rutgers Univ. Press, 1959.
S6940 (ASU)

Stem, Thad, Jr. Senator Sam Ervin's Best Stories. Durham, N. C.: Moore Pub. Co., 1974. Tales from Senator Sam the mountain man. He hails from Morganton, Burke County, North Carolina.
S6950 (WCU BC ASU)

Stephens, Dan V. Peter Stephens and Some of his Descendants, 1690-1935. Fremont, Neb.: Hammond and Stephen Co., 1936. A Virginia family which has branches in the midwest.
S6960

Stephens, Dan V. ed. Stephens Family Genealogies. rev. ed. Fremont, Neb.: Hammond and Stephens Co., 1940.
S6970

Stephens, Erwin D. Nubbins From Fodderstack Ridge. Yanceyville, N. C.: Hyco Press, 1966. Earthy humor and crackerbarrel philosophy from western North Carolina.
S6980 (ASU)

Stephens, George Gilpin, Pete Bascom Lamar Lunsford, "Minstrel of the Appalachians." His Ballads and His Folk Songs, His Mountain Square Dancing. Ashevillle, N. C.: Stephens Press, 1966.
G1810 (ASU UNCA WCU LMC WWC MHC)

Stephens, George M. Lunsford, Bascom Lamar It's Fun to Square Dance: Southern Appalachian Calls and Figures. Asheville, N. C.: n.p., n.d.
L3980

Stephens, George Myers The Smokies Guide. Illustrated by Burnley Weaver. Asheville, N. C.: Stephens Press, 1941. An illustrated guide to the attractions of the Great Smoky Mountains.
S6990 (BC ASU WCU)
The Smokies Guide. Rev. ed. Asheville, N. C.: Stephens Press, 1962.
S7000 (LMC)
William Bartram's Venture into the Cherokee Country, 1775. Asheville, N. C.: Stephens Press, 1967. An account of the great naturalist's stay among the Cherokee.
S7010 (LMC WCU)

Stephens, Julius Harold Echoes From the Hills: Tall Tales From Tennessee. Ohio: The author, 1966. A delightful group of whoppers from the Tennessee hills.
S7020 (LMC BC)
Echoes of a Passing Era (Down Memories Lane). Fairborn, Ohio: The author, 1971. Memories of an Appalachian childhood combined with a lament for a passing culture.
S7030 (LMC BC)

Stephens, M. E. Swann, Maurice Edward Soil Survey of Winston County, Alabama. Washington: U. S. Department of Agriculture, Bureau of Chemistry and Soils, 1937.
S9450

Stephens, Mary Jo Witch of the Cumberlands. Boston: Houghton Mifflin, 1974. An old woman prophesies that three children would come to Devil's Mountain. When they do the old mystery of a mine disaster is unraveled.
S7040

Stephenson, J. W. Phillips, Samuel William Soil Survey: Fannin County, Georgia. Washington: U. S. Department of Agriculture, Bureau of Soils, 1928.
P2630

Stephenson, John B. Shiloh: A Mountain Community. Lexington: Univ. of Kentucky Press, 1968. A report on changes which have taken place in an isolated mountain community since 1940. The move toward the mainstream of American culture has begun.
S7050 (ASU ETSU FC LMC UNCA WCU WWC BC)

Stephenson, John Bell Patterns of Adaptation in a Changing Mountain Community; Stress and Health. Ph. D. Diss. Univ. of North Carolina, 1967.
S7060 (BC)

Stephenson, Mattie Rountree comp. Historical Sketch of Sinking Spring Presbyterian Church of Abingdon, Virginia. n.p.: n.p., 1948. Rev. Charles Cummings answers the call of the Sinking Spring and Ebbing Spring Churches and becomes the first pastor west of the Allegheny Mountains. A succession of pastors follow, and the church grows under their leadership.
S7070

Steputis, Walter J. Beverage, Woodrow Wilson Soil Survey, Barbour County, West Virginia. Washington: U. S. Department of Agriculture, Soil Conservation Service, 1968.
B3440

Steputis, Walter James and others Soil Survey, Clinton County, Pennsylvania. Washington: U. S. Soil Conservation Service, 1966.
S7080

Stern, Ernest George Nails and Spikes in Hickory. Hickory Task Force Report, no. 9. Asheville, N. C.: Southeastern Forest Experiment Station, 1964.
S7090 (WCU)

Sterner, T. E. Laboratory Investigation of In Situ Combustion Process for Recovering Pennsylvania Grade Crude Oil. U. S. Bureau of Mines Report of Investigations, no. 7044. Pittsburgh: Bureau of Mines, 1967.
S7100

Sterrett, D. B. Keith, Arthur Tin Resources of the King's Mountain District, North Carolina and South Carolina. Washington: Govt. Print. Off., 1918.
K550

Sterrett, Douglas Bovard Pratt, Joseph Hyde The Tin Deposits of the Carolinas. Raleigh, N. C.: E. M. Uzzell and Co., public printers and binders, 1904.
P4230 (WCU)

Stevens, Bernice A. A Weavin' Woman. Gatlinburg, Tenn.: Buckhorn Press, 1971. Account of one woman's obsession with weaving. Illustrated, with instructions.
S7110 (LMC)

Stevens, Edmund H. and others Soil Survey, Lycoming County, Pennsylvania. Prepared in cooperation with the Pennsylvania State College, School of Agriculture and Experiment Station. Soil Survey Report, Series 1923, no. 32. Washington: U. S. Department of Agriculture, Bureau of Chemistry and Soils, 1928.
S7120

Stevens, G. C. Grover, N. C. Surface Water Supply of the New-Kanawha River Basin, West Virginia, and North Carolina. Washington: Govt. Print. Off., 1925.
G4490

Stevens, G. R. An Economic and Social Survey of Roanoke County. Charlottesville: n.p., 1930.
S7130

Stevens, William Anvil of Adversity: Biography of Furniture Pioneer. New York: Popular Library, 1968. Biography of the founder of the Broyhill furniture empire in western North Carolina.
S7140 (ASU WCU BC)

Stevens, William Oliver The Shenandoah and Its Byways. New York: Dodd, Mead and Co., 1941. Descriptive and promotional volume on the Shenandoah Valley of Virginia.
S7150 (ASU BC)

Stevenson, Augusta Daniel Boone, Boy Hunter. New York: Bobbs-Merrill Co., 1943. Biography of Daniel Boone. Concentrates primarily on his younger period.
S7160 (ETSU)

Daniel Boone, Boy Hunter. Illustrated by Robert Doremus. Childhood of Famous Americans. Indianapolis: Bobbs-Merrill, 1961.
S7170 (ASU)

Stevenson, B. F. Cumberland Gap. A paper read before the Ohio Commandery of the Loyal Legion of the United States. Cincinnati: H. C. Sherick and Co., 1885.
S7180

Stevenson, George James 1924- Increase in Excellence, a History of Emory and Henry College. New York: Appleton-Century-Crofts, 1963. Emory and Henry is the oldest college in southwest Virginia. A Methodist institution with a history of regional services.
S7190 (ASU BC)

Stevenson, George Washington North Carolina Local History: A Select Bibliography. Raleigh: Office of Archives and History, North Carolina Dept. of Art, Culture, and History, 1972.
S7200 (ASU)

Stevenson, Richard Clugston, Katherine Wilderness Road. New York: Blue Ribbon Books, Inc., 1937.
C5140 (ASU)

Clugston, Katharine Wilderness Road. Garden City, N. Y.: Sun Dial Press, 1941.
C5150 (BC)

Stevic, Richard R. Hansen, James C. Appalachian Students and Guidance. New York: Houghton Mifflin, 1971.
H1670 (ASU BC WCU MHC ETSU)

Steward, Davenport They Had a Glory. Atlanta: Tupper and Love, 1952. A novel of frontier life and the westward movement. Includes vivid account of crossing the Cumberlands and settling Kentucky.
S7210 (ASU BC)

Rainbow Road. Atlanta: Tupper and Love, 1953. A novel about the settlement of North Georgia and the great gold rush there.
S7220 (ASU BC)

Steward, Donald D. Employment, Income and Resources of Rural Families of Southeastern Ohio. Research Bulletin No. 886. Wooster: Ohio Agricultural Experiment Station, June, 1961.
S7230

Steward, Guy H. A Touch of Charisma; a History of the 4-H Club Program in West Virginia. Morgantown: n.p., 1969. A history of William H. Kendrick and the 4-H Club movement in West Virginia.
S7240

Stewart, Acie "A Study of Students Dropping Out of Wyoming County, West Virginia, High Schools for the 1950-51 School Term." Master's thesis. Marshall College, 1952.
S7250

Stewart, Albert The Untoward Hills. Morehead, Ky.: Morehead State College Press, 1962. Poems from eastern Kentucky.
S7260 (BC)

Stewart, Cora W. Moonlight Schools for the Emancipation of Adult Illiterates. New York: Dutton, 1922. A study of Kentucky's unique "moonlight" schools, a movement toward adult education in the Kentucky mountains.
S7270 (BC)

Stewart, Mrs. Frank Ross Cherokee Country History, 1836-1956. 2 vols. Centre, Ala.: n.p., 1958-.
S7280 (ASU BC)

Stewart, Guy H. Guiding Principles for Rural Development in West Virginia. Morgantown: n.p., 1963.
S7290

Stewart, J. G. Smith, Elmer L. The Pennsylvania Germans of the Shenandoah Valley. Allentown, Pa.: The Folklore Association, 1964.
S4620 (ASU)

Stewart, John An Occult Remedy Manuscript from Pendleton County, West Virginia. n.p.: Madison College, 1964. Manuscript of folk and occult remedies collected by a Madison County professor and his class.
S7300

Stewart, John Stephen "The Use of Locational Analysis in the Determination of School Sites: A Case Example, Carter County, Tennessee." Master's thesis. East Tennessee State Univ., 1969.
S7310 (ETSU)

Stewart, Noah A. The Crash. Asheville, N. C.: Gladiator Productions, 1969.
S7320 (ASU LMC WCU BC)

Stewart, Paul D. New Small Business in a Redevelopment Coal Area in West Virginia. Washington: Small Business Administration, 1962.
S7330

Stewart, Randall Regionalism and Beyond: Essays of Randall Stewart. Nashville: Vanderbilt Univ. Press, 1968. Includes discussion of Appalachia, as a regional concept.
S7340 (ASU)

Stickles, Arndt M. East Tennessee, Chickamauga, Chattanooga. Chapter 13 of Simon Bolivar Buckner, Borderland Knight. Chapel Hill: UNC Press, 1940.
S7350 (ASU)

Still, James Hounds on the Mountain. New York: Viking Press, 1937. An excellent volume of poetry by one of Appalachia's finest authors.
S7360 (ETSU BC)

Hounds on the Mountain. 1937. Reprint. New York: Viking Press, 1939.
S7370 (ASU)

Hounds on the Mountain. 1937. Reprint. Lexington, Ky.: Anvil Press, 1965.
S7380 (WWC)

On Troublesome Creek. New York: Viking Press, 1941.
S7390 (ASU UNCA)

River of Earth. New York: Viking Press, 1940. One of the strongest novels ever to come out of Appalachia. Still's story of life in the coal camps will haunt you.
S7400 (BC ASU UNCA)

River of Earth. 1940. Reprint. New York: Popular Library, 1968.
S7410 (LMC ETSU)

River of Earth. 1940. Reprint. New York: Popular Library, 1970.
S7420 (WCU)

Way Down Yonder on Troublesome Creek: Appalachian Riddles and Rusties. New York: G. P. Putnam's Songs, 1974. A collection of riddles and humor from Appalachian Kentucky.
S7430 (BC ASU)

Stillwell, Edgar Herman Notes on the History of Western North Carolina. Cullowhee, N. C.: Cullowhee State Normal School, 1927.
S7440 (WCU)

Stimson, Frederic Jesup Sentimental Calendar, Being Twelve Funny Stories. 1886. Reprint. Short Story Index Reprint Series. Freeport, N. Y.: Books for Libraries Press, 1969. Two of the twelve stories have mountain settings.
S7450 (ASU WCU)

Stine, O. C. A Case Study of Six Central West Virginia Counties of the Interrelationships of Factors Leading to Persistence of Low Incomes and Unemployment with Corrective Suggestions. Morgantown: West Va. Univ., Dept. of Agricultural Economics, 1966.
S7460

Stirling, James Letters from the Slave States. London: J. W. Parker and Son, 1857. In his investigation of slavery, Stirling, visited only Knoxville in one Appalachian region.
S7470

Stith, Lee Street "Rural Leadership in Roane County, Tennessee." Master's thesis. Univ. of Tennessee, 1942.
S7480 (ASU)

Stockton, Ernest L. History Excursions into Tennessee, Its Early Heritage. Kingsport, Tenn.: Newcomen Society, American Branch, 1941.
S7490 (LMC)

Stokeley, James Dykeman, Wilma The Border States: Kentucky, North Carolina, Tennessee, Virginia, West Virginia. New York: Time-Life Books, 1968.
D4190 (BC ASU LMC WWC ETSU)

Stokely, James Dykeman, Wilma Neither Black nor White. New York: Rinehart (1957).
D4240 (ASU WWC ETSU BC)

Dykeman, Wilma Seeds of Southern Change: The Life of Will Alexander. Chicago: Univ. of Chicago Press, 1962.
D4270 (WWC WCU MHC ETSU)

Stokely, Janie May Jones Years of Harvest, Poems and Tales from the Smoky Foothills, 1924-1964. Newport, Tenn.: n.p., 1964. A treasure-trove of tales, lore and poems from the Smokies.
S7500 (BC LMC WCU)

Stone, Barton Warren The Biography of Eld. Barton Warren Stone, Written by Himself. With Additions and Reflections, by John Rogers. 1847. Reprint. Religion in America, Series II. New York: Arno Press, 1972.
S7510 (ASU)

Stone, Harold A. and others City Manager Government in Kingsport. Chicago: Public Administration Service, 1940.
S7520

Stone, Paul S. Change in Agricultural and Economic Trends in North Carolina; Information by Area Development Associations and Counties. Circular no. 454. Raleigh: North Carolina Agricultural Extension Service, 1964. Includes information on twenty-eight mountain counties.
S7530

Stone, Richard Wellington Coal Resources of the Russell Fork Basin in Kentucky and Virginia. U. S. Geological Survey Bulletin, no. 348. Washington: Govt. Print. Off., 1908.
S7540

Stone, William Curtis "Historical Sketches of Clay County, Tennessee." Nashville: Unpublished typescript, 1962.
S7550

Stoneback, Harry Robert "The Hillfolk Tradition and Images of the Hillfolk in American Fiction Since 1926." Ph. D. Diss. Vanderbilt Univ., 1970.
S7560 (LMC BC)

Stonebreaker, Jack D. Potassium-Argon Geochronology of the Brevard Fault, Southern Appalachians. Ph. D. Diss. Florida State Univ., 1973. This process of age-dating was used in a tectonic study of the fault which runs along the North Carolina/Tennessee line and into northern Alabama.
S7570

Stonehouse, Merlin John Wesley North and the Reform Frontier. Minneapolis: Univ. of Minnesota Press, 1965. A history of reconstruction in Appalachia.
S7580

"Lincoln's Carpetbagger, J. W. North." Ph. D. Diss. Univ. of California at Los Angeles, 1961.
S7590

Stoner, Robert Douthat A Seed-bed of the Republic, a Study of the Pioneers in the Upper (Southern) Valley of Virginia. Roanoke: Roanoke Historical Society, 1962.
S7600 (FC BC)

A Seed-bed of the Republic: A Study of the Pioneers in the Upper (Southern) Valley of Virginia. Sponsored by the Roanoke Historical Society. Kingsport, Tenn.: Kingsport Press, 1962.
S7610 (ASU)

Stoney, William S. Historical Sketch of Grace Church, Morganton, North Carolina. Morganton, N. C.: The author, 1935.
S7620 (ASU)

Storey, Theodore G. Wendel, George W. Seasonal Moisture Fluctuations in Four Species of Pocosin Vegetation. Asheville, N. C.: Southeastern Forest Experiment Station, 1962.
W2800 (WCU)

Stories From the Hills Charleston, W. Va.: Morris Harvey College Publications, 1970-, annual.
S7630

Story, Margaret E. "The Status of Eighth Grade Social Science in Washington County, Tennessee, 1960-61." Master's thesis. East Tennessee State College, 1962.
S7640 (ETSU)

The Story of Strasburg, and Other Historical Articles as Published in the Bicentennial Edition of the Northern Virginia Daily, September 20, 1961 Strasburg, Va.: First Nat'l Bank, 1961.
S7650

Stose, G. W. Hewett, D. F. Possibilities for Manganese Ore on Certain Undeveloped Tracts in the Shenandoah Valley, Virginia. Washington: Govt. Print. Off., 1918.
H5130

Manganese Deposits of East Tennessee. U. S. Geological Survey Bulletin, no. 737. Washington: Govt. Print. Off., 1923.
S7660

Phosphate Deposits in Southwestern Virginia. U. S. Geological Survey Bulletin, no. 540-L. Washington: Govt. Print. Off., 1914.
S7670

Stoss, G. W. ed. International Geological Congress Southern Appalachian Region. Washington: The Congress; 16th Session, 1933.
I880

Stoudt, John Baer Rice, Alvin H. The Shenandoah Pottery. Strasburg, Va.: Shenandoah Pub. House, 1929.
R1890 (ASU BC)

Stout, Chester T. "A Study of the Program of Pupil Transportation in Johnson County, Tennessee." Master's thesis. East Tennessee State College, 1962.
S7680 (ETSU)

Stout, Larry "An Overview of Federal Programs and Their Impacts on Appalachia." Master's thesis. Las Cruces: New Mexico State Univ., 1971.
S7690

Stout, Ralph E. "What Citizens of Carter County Know about Their Schools." Master's thesis. East Tennessee State College, 1953.
S7700 (ETSU)

Stover, John F. The Railroads of the South, 1865-1900: A Study in Finance and Control. Chapel Hill: Univ. of North Carolina Press, 1955.
S7710 (LMC BC)

Stover, Virginia Hendrix Angels in the Mountains. Birmingham: n.p., 1957.
S7720

Strachey, William The History of Travel Into Virginia Britania (1612). Works, 2nd series, no. 103. London: Hakluyt Society, 1953.
S7730 (ASU)

Strack, Charles Miller "Agricultural Changes in the TVA Area, 1930-1945." Ph. D. Diss. Univ. of Iowa, 1950.
S7740

Stradley, William Bascom "Local Ability to Support Education in Monroe County, Tennessee." Master's thesis. Univ. of Tennessee, 1955.
S7750

"A Study of Local Sources of Local Government Agencies in Twenty-three Selected Tennessee Counties." Ed. D. Diss. Univ. of Tennessee, 1958. Includes some Appalachian counties.
S7760

Strange, Robert Eoneguski, or the Cherokee Chief: A Tale of Past Wars, by an American. Washington, D. C.: Frank Taylor, 1839.
S7770

Eoneguski: Or, the Cherokee Chief (1839). 2 vols. Foreword by Richard Walser. Facsimile ed. Charlotte, N. C.: McNally, 1960.
S7780 (ASU LMC MHC WCU BC)

Strassburger, Ralph Beaver Pennsylvania German Pioneers: A Publication of the Original Lists of Arrivals in the Port of Philadelphia from 1727 to 1808. 3 vols. Proceedings, vols. 42-44. Norristown, Pa.: Pennsylvania German Society, 1934.
S7790 (ASU)

Pennsylvania German Pioneers: A Publication of the Original Lists of Arrivals in the Port of Philadelphia from 1727 to 1808. 1934. Reprint. 2 vols. Baltimore: Genealogical Pub. Co., 1966.
S7800 (ASU)

Stratemeyer, Edward With Boone on the Frontier, or The Pioneer Boys of Old Kentucky. New York: Grosset and Dunlap, 1903. Fictional account of young boys on the Kentucky frontier.
S7810

Stratton, Garland Smith, R. C. Water Resources of the Wheeling-Steubenville Area, West Virginia and Ohio. Washington: Govt. Print. Off., 1955.
S4960

Strausbaugh, Perry Daniel Common Seed Plants of the Mid-Appalachian Region. Morgantown, W. Va.: Book Exchange, 1948.
S7820 (ASU BC)

Flora of West Virginia. 4 vols. Bulletin, Series 52, no. 12-2; Series 53, no. 12-1. Morgantown: West Virginia Univ. Press, 1952-1964.
S7830 (ASU)

Streaker, Margaret M. see Tamarack

Street, Eugene "The Influence of Community Pressure Groups on School Principals in Carter County." Master's thesis. East Tennessee State College, 1960.
S7840 (ETSU)

Street, James A. Ohio River Valley Population: Trends and Projections, 1930-1970. Prepared for the Kentucky Department of Commerce. Lexington, Ky.: Spindletop Research, 1963.
S7850

Street, James Howell Pride of Possession. 1st ed. New York: Lippincott, 1960. A novel about hunting wild boars in the Great Smoky Mountains.
S7860 (ASU)

Street, Julia Montgomery Drover's Gold. New York: Dodd, Mead, 1961. An adventure tale about herding stock down the Buncombe turnpike wagon road.
S7870

Moccasin Tracks. Illustrated by Frank Kramer. New York: Dodd, Mead, 1958. An adventure tale about an Indian boy and his white friend in the western North Carolina mountains in 1821.
S7880 (ASU)

Street, Paul Vocational Rehabilitation Needs and Resources in Eastern Kentucky. Lexington: Bureau of School Service, Univ. of Ky., 1967.
S7890

Streleski, Nelda comp. Washington County, Tenn., 1830 Federal Census. n.p.: n.p., n.d.
S7900 (ASU)

Stribling, Thomas Sigismund Bright Metal. Garden City, N. Y.: Doubleday, Doran and Co., 1928. A Greenwich Village bride goes home to the hills of Tennessee with her husband and becomes interested in folkways and local politics.
S7910 (ASU LMC ETSU)

The Sound Wagon. 1st ed. Garden City, N. Y.: Doubleday, Doran and Co., 1935. Dramatic tale of the war and its aftermath, personal fortunes and the means by which they were acquired in the mountains of northern Alabama.
S7920 (ASU)

The Store. Garden City, N. Y.: Doubleday, Doran and Co., 1932. Another Stribling tale set in the Alabama mountains.
S7930 (ASU)

Teeftallow. Garden City, N. Y.: Doubleday, Page and Co., 1926. An east Tennessee irontown is the setting for this tale of strife and lynchings.
S7940 (ASU WCU ETSU)

Unfinished Cathedral. Garden City, N. Y.: Doubleday, Doran and Co., 1934. A novel about Florence, Alabama, its churches, schools, libraries, hospitals and its old cotton economy.
S7950 (ASU)

Strickland, L. J. Moon, J. W. Soil Survey, Jefferson County, Tennessee. Washington: U. S. Department of Agriculture, Bureau of Plant Industry, 1941.
M6630

Strickland, Reba Carolyn Religion and the State in Georgia in the Eighteenth Century. 1940. Reprint. New York: AMS Press, 1967.
S7960 (WCU)

Strickland, Rennard Gregory, Jack Cherokee Hymns. Fayetteville, Ark.: Indian Heritage Assoc., n.d.
G3980 (ASU)

Gregory, Jack Sam Houston with the Cherokees, 1829-1833. Austin: Univ. of Texas Press, 1967.
G3990 (ASU WCU MHC)

Strickland, Rennard ed. Starr, Emmet History of the Cherokee Indians. Fayetteville, Ark.: Indian Heritage Assoc., 1967.
S6670 (ASU BC ETSU WCU)

Strickland, W. P. The Life of Jacob Gruder. New York: Carlton and Porter, 1860. Account of the long life and ministry of Jacob Gruder. Many years were spent as an itinerant preacher in East Kentucky, West Virginia and other mountain areas.
S7970 (BC)

Strickler, Harry Miller Massanutten, Settled by the Pennsylvania Pilgrim, 1726: The First White Settlement in the Shenandoah Valley. Strasburg, Va.: Shenandoah Pub. House, 1924.
S7980 (ASU BC)

Strickler, Harry Miller
Old Tenth Legion Marriages; Marriages in Rockingham Co., Va. from 1778 to 1816. Dayton, Va.: J. K. Ruebush Co., 1928.
S7990
A Short History of Page County, Virginia. Richmond, Va.: The Dietz Press, 1952.
S8000 (BC)
Tenth Legion Tithables, Rockingham Division, Rockingham County, Virginia, Tithables for 1792. Luray, Va.: The author, 1930.
S8010

Strike, W. W. Stroud, James Frank Soil Survey of Franklin County, Alabama. Washington: U. S. Department of Agriculture, Bureau of Chemistry and Soils, 1932.
S8120

Stringfield, Lamar comp. Lunsford, Bascom Lamar 30 and 1 Folksongs from the Southern Mountains. Chicago: Carl Fischer, 1929.
L3990 (ASU BC)

Stringfield, Margaret The Cherokee in Romance, Tragedy, and Song in the Great Smokies. Waynesville, N. C.: n.p., 1946.
S8020 (ETSU)

Stringfield, Victor Timothy Relation of Geology to Drainage, Floods, and Landslides in the Petersburg Area, West Virginia. Report of Investigations, no. 13. Morgantown: West Virginia Geological and Economic Survey, 1956.
S8030 (ETSU)

Stripling, R. R. ed. Knight, Howard Vernon Scenic and Historic Old Virginia and Eastern National Parks. Asheville, N. C., and Richmond: Southern Park and Playgrounds, 1930.
K2790 (WCU)

Strip-Mining in Virginia: The 1974 Record and the Facts. Blacksburg, Va.: Operation Coal, 1974.
S8040 (ASU)

The Stripping of Appalachia: A Citizen's Reference Book Washington, D. C.: Center for Science in the Public Interest, 1972.
S8050

Strodtbeck, Fred "Migration from Kentucky: A Study of Intervening Opportunities." Microfilm. Master's thesis. Indiana Univ., 1942.
S8070 (ASU)

Strong, Edna R. "A Sociological Analysis of Ecology, Structure and Processes in a Virginia Coal Mining Community." Master's thesis. Louisiana State Univ., 1943.
S8080

Strong, Jason Rolfe The Starlight of the Hills; A Romance of the Kentucky Mountains. New York: Frederick Pustet Co., 1923. Poorly written tale of Catholic Missions in eastern Kentucky.
S8090

Strong, Paschal Neilson Behind the Great Smokies. Illustrated by Herman Fay, Jr. Boston: Little, Brown and Co., 1937. Makes good use of the Smokies backdrop and of the mountains as protagonists.
S8100 (ASU)

Strother, David Hunter The Old South Illustrated. Edited with an introduction by Cecil D. Eby, Jr. Chapel Hill: Univ. of North Carolina Press, 1959. Some beautiful illustration from the mountain south.
S8060 (ASU BC)
Virginia Illustrated: Containing a Visit to the Virginian Canaan, and the Adventures of Porte Crayon and His Cousins. New York: Harper and Brothers, 1857.
S8110 (ASU BC)

Stroud, J. F. Lewis, Henry Guy Soil Survey of Lawrence County, Alabama. Washington: U. S. Department of Agriculture, Bureau of Soils, 1916.
L2180
Taylor, Arthur Elijah Soil Survey of Coosa County, Alabama. Washington: U. S. Department of Agriculture, Bureau of Chemistry and Soils, 1933.
T430
Veatch, Jethro O. Soil Survey of Walker County, Alabama. Washington: U. S. Department of Agriculture, Bureau of Soils, 1916.
V500

Stroud, James Frank Soil Survey of Franklin County, Alabama. Prepared in cooperation with the Alabama Department of Agriculture and Industries. Soil Survey Report, Series 1927, no. 30. Washington: U. S. Department of Agriculture, Bureau of Chemistry and Soils, 1932.
S8120
Soil Survey of Shelby County, Alabama. Prepared in cooperation with Alabama. Field Operations, 1917. Washington: U. S. Department of Agriculture, Bureau of Soils, 1920.
S8130

Stroud, James Frank and others Soil Survey of Cherokee County, Alabama. Prepared in cooperation with the Alabama Department of Agriculture and Industries. Soil Survey Report, Series 1924, no. 2. Washington: U. S. Department of Agriculture, Bureau of Chemistry and Soils, 1928.
S8140

Stroup, Robert H. Economic Impact of Secondary Road Improvements. Lexington: Univ. of Kentucky, 1963.
S8150

Structure of the Berea Oil Sand in the Flushing Quadrangle, Harrison, Belmont, and Guernsey Counties, Ohio U. S. Geological Survey Bulletin, no. 346. Washington: Govt. Print. Off., 1908.
G4350

Strunk, Flonnie Shoemaker "A Study of Pupil Transportation in Scott County, Tennessee." Master's thesis. Univ. of Tennessee, 1956.
S8160

Stryker, Lloyd P. Andrew Johnson; a Study in Courage. 1971. Reprint. New York: Macmillan, 1929, 1930, 1936. The author describes Johnson as being in the tradition of Lincoln and embracing his program of compassion and reconciliation for the South. Stryker's villains are the Radicals in Congress who blocked Johnson's efforts and ultimately attempted to impeach him.
S8170 (ASU)

Stuart, Jane Eyes of the Mole. Sauk City, Wis.: Stanton and Lee Pub., 1967. Appalachian poetry.
S8180 (BC)
Passerman's Hollow. New York: McGraw-Hill, 1974. A Gothic novel of an area barely recognizable as the mountain south.
S8190 (BC ASU)
A Year's Harvest. Bel Air, Md.: Landmark House, 1957.
S8200 (BC)
Yellowhawk. New York: McGraw-Hill, 1973. A novel of the mountain south, yet very unlike her father's work. Gothic elements in this tale of schoolchildren.
S8210 (BC ASU)

Stuart, Jesse Album of Destiny. New York: Dutton, 1944.
S8220 (LMC WCU ETSU)
Andy Finds a Way. Illustrated by Robert Henneberger. New York: McGraw-Hill, 1961.
S8230 (ASU BC)
Autumn Lovesong: A Celebration of Love's Fulfillment. Kansas City, Mo.: Hallmark, 1971.
S8240 (ETSU ASU)
The Beatinest Boy. Illustrated by Robert Henneberger. New York: McGraw-Hill, 1953. A Christmas tale of mountain children.
S8250 (ASU LMC ETSU WWC WCU MHC)
Beyond Dark Hills: A Personal Story. Illustrated by Ishmael. 1st ed. New York: McGraw-Hill, 1938. This story done for an English class at Vanderbilt started Stuart on his writing career.
S8260 (ASU LMC)
Beyond Dark Hills: A Personal Story. Illustrated by Ishmael. 1938. Reprint. New York: McGraw-Hill, 1972.
S8270 (ETSU WCU)
Clearing in the Sky and Other Stories. New York: McGraw-Hill, 1950. Collection of mountain stories.
S8280 (ETSU ASU)
Come Back to the Farm. 1st ed. New York: McGraw-Hill, 1971. A collection of stories about superstitions, humor, and love of the land.
S8290 (ASU LMC MHC WCU ETSU FC BC)
Come, Gentle Spring. 1st ed. New York: McGraw-Hill, 1969. A group of stories about the War, country doctoring, and mountain life.
S8300 (ASU LMC MHC WCU ETSU BC UNCA)
Come to My Tomorrowland. 1st ed. Nashville: Aurora Pubs., 1971. A young girl crippled by polio feels a special attachment for a deer with a broken hip.
S8310 (LMC ASU WCU MHC ETSU BC)
Daughter of the Legend. 1st ed. New York: McGraw-Hill, 1965. A tale of love between a young outlander and a beautiful melungeon girl.
S8320 (ASU MHC LMC WCU WWC ETSU BC UNCA)
Dawn of Remembered Spring. New York: McGraw-Hill, 1972. Short stories and poems, mostly about animals.
S8330 (ASU WCU LMC ETSU)
Foretaste of Glory. New York: E. P. Dutton and Co., 1946.
S8340 (ASU WCU BC)
God's Oddling: The Story of Mick Stuart, My Father. 1st ed. New York: McGraw-Hill, 1960.
S8350 (ASU MHC WCU ETSU BC)
The Good Spirit of Laurel Ridge. New York: McGraw-Hill, 1953. Theopolis Akers is a mite upset when his citified daughter starts keeping company with a ghost.
S8360 (ASU ETSU BC)
Harvest of Youth. Berea, Ky.: Council of the Southern Mountains, 1964.
S8370 (ASU WCU LMC ETSU BC)
Head o' W-Hollow. 1st ed. New York: E. P. Dutton and Co., 1936. Short stories set in a valley so steep the sun doesn't hit 'til midday.
S8380 (ASU)
Head o' W-Hollow. Short Story Index Reprint Series. Freeport, N. Y.: Books for Libraries Press, 1971.
S8390 (WCU ETSU)
Hie to the Hunters. Study materials by J. Arthur Ferner. High School ed. New York: Whittlesey House, 1950. Dog poisoners and barn burners are causing trouble in the Plum Grove hills. Plenty of fox hunts.
S8400 (ASU WCU LMC MHC ETSU BC)
Hold April: New Poems. Illustrated by Walter Ferro. 1st ed. New York: McGraw-Hill, 1962.
S8410 (ASU WCU LMC ETSU BC)
Huey, the Engineer. St. Helena, Calif.: J. E. Beard, 1930.
S8420
A Jesse Stuart Harvest. New York: Dell Pub. Co., 1965.
S8430 (FC BC ASU)
A Jesse Stuart Reader: Stories and Poems. Foreword by Max Bogert. Commentary and questions by Ella De Mers. New York: McGraw-Hill, 1963.
S8440 (ASU WCU BC ETSU)
Kentucky Is My Land. Poems. 1st ed. New York: Dutton, 1952.
S8450 (ASU ETSU BC)
The Land beyond the River. New York: McGraw-Hill, 1973.
S8460 (LMC MHC WCU ETSU BC)
Man with a Bull-tongue Plow. 1st ed. New York: E. P. Dutton and Co., 1934.
S8470 (ASU WCU BC UNCA)
Man With a Bull-tongue Plow. New rev. ed. Dutton Everyman Paperback, D32. New York: Dutton, 1959.
S8480 (WCU ETSU ASU)

Stuart, Jesse
Men of the Mountains. 1st ed. New York: E. P. Dutton and Co., 1941. Short stories illustrating some of the grotesque and pathetic elements of mountain life.
S8490 (ASU WWC BC)
Mongrel Mettle, the Autobiography of a Dog. New York: Books, Inc., 1944. Autobiography of a dog.
S8500 (LMC WCU UNCA ETSU BC)
Mr. Gallion's School. 1st ed. New York: McGraw-Hill, 1967. A novel based on Stuart's experiences as a principal and teacher.
S8510 (ASU WCU MHC LMC WWC ETSU BC UNCA)
My Land Has a Voice. New York: McGraw-Hill, 1966. Short stories about Tennessee and Kentucky. The Grandma and Grandpa introduced here are hilarious characters.
S8520 (ASU MHC WCU LMC WWC ETSU FC UNCA)
Old Ben. Illustrated by Richard Cuffari. New York: McGraw-Hill, 1970. Tale of a snake who befriends a young boy.
S8530 (ASU LMC ETSU BC)
A Penny's Worth of Character. Illustrated by Robert Henneberger. New York: McGraw-Hill, 1954. A young boy learns a lesson in honesty.
S8540 (ASU LMC MHC WCU ETSU BC)
Plowshare in Heaven: Stories. 1st ed. New York: McGraw-Hill, 1958. Twenty-one stories of the Kentucky hills.
S8550 (ASU WCU MHC WWC ETSU BC)
Red Mule. Illustrated by Robert Henneberger. New York: Whittlesey House, 1955.
S8560 (ASU LMC MHC ETSU BC)
A Ride with Huey, the Engineer. Illustrated by Robert Henneberger. New York: McGraw-Hill, 1966.
S8570 (ASU LMC ETSU BC)
The Rightful Owner. Illustrated by Robert Henneberger. New York: McGraw-Hill, 1960.
S8580 (ASU LMC ETSU BC)
The Rightful Owner. Eau Claire, Wis.: E. M. Hale Co., 1960.
S8590 (WCU)
Save Every Lamb. Illustrated by Jean George. 1st ed. New York: McGraw-Hill, 1964. Short stories, primarily about farm life and animals.
S8600 (ASU WCU MHC ETSU BC)
Stories by Jesse Stuart. Adapted by Laurence Swinburne. Illustrated by Ferd Sondern, Ira Hauders Associates. New York: McGraw-Hill Book Co., 1968.
S8610 (ASU LMC WCU BC)
Tales from the Plum Grove Hills. New York: E. P. Dutton and Co., 1946. A lovely group of stories from Stuart's best-loved place.
S8630 (ASU FC ETSU)
Taps for Private Tussie. New York: Dutton, 1943. The Tussie's collect $10,000 when kin is killed in the war. Relatives descend until there are forty-six in the house and the money runs out.
S8640 (ETSU BC)
Taps for Private Tussie. Illustrated by Thomas Hart Benton. 1943. Reprint. New York: World Pub. Co., 1969.
S8650 (ASU WCU LMC MHC UNCA)
32 Votes before Breakfast: Politics at the Grass Roots, as Seen in Short Stories. New York: McGraw-Hill Book Co., 1974. Stories of mountain politics.
S8660 (ASU BC)
The Thread That Runs So True. New York: C. Scribner's Sons, 1949. Stuart experiences a 17 year old teacher in Lonesome Valley.
S8670 (ASU MHC LMC WCU WWC BC)
The Thread That Runs So True. New York: Scribner, 1958.
S8680 (ETSU UNCA)
Tim, a Story. 1939. Reprint. Cincinnati: Kentucky Writer's Guild and Harvest Press, 1968.
S8690 (ASU LMC BC ETSU)
To Teach, to Love. New York: World Pub. Co., 1970. Stuart's second autobiography about his experiences as a teacher.
S8700 (ASU MHC WWC UNCA ETSU BC)
Trees of Heaven. Illustrated by Woodi Ishmael. New York: E. P. Dutton and Co., 1940. A novel of the rapid deterioration of the Bushman family when they're forced off the land they love but do not own.
S8710 (ASU WCU WWC ETSU BC)
The Year of My Rebirth. Illustrated by Barry Martin. New York: McGraw-Hill, 1956. Account of his heart-attack and recovery.
S8720 (ASU ETSU BC)

Stuart, John Memoir of Indian Wars, and Other Occurrences. Presented to the Virginia Historical and Philosophical Society, by Chas. A. Stuart. 1833. Reprint. With an introd. by Otis K. Rice. Parsons, W. Va.: Reprinted by McClain Print. Co., 1971.
S8730 (ASU)
A Sketch of the Cherokee and Choctaw Indians. Little Rock: Woodruff and Pew, 1837.
S8740

Stubbs, Elizabeth Saunders Blair Early Settlers of Alabama. Baltimore: Genealogical Pub. Co., 1969.
S8750

Stuckey, Jasper Leonidas North Carolina: Its Geology and Mineral Resources. Raleigh: North Carolina Department of Conservation and Development, 1965.
S8760 (LMC WWC ETSU UNCA)
Pyrophyllite Deposits in North Carolina. Bulletin, 80. Raleigh: North Carolina Department of Conservation and Development, 1967.
S8770 (ETSU)

Stucky, J. A. and others Trachoma in Eastern Kentucky. Chicago: American Medical Association, 1913.
S8780

Studies in Polk County History no. 1-, 1965-. Benton, Tenn.: Polk County Historical Society, n.d.
S8810 (ETSU)

Studies of Appalachian Geology: Central and Southern New York: Interscience Publishers, 1970.
S8790 (ETSU WWC ASU)

Studies of Appalachian Geology: Northern and Maritime New York: Interscience Publishers, 1968.
S8800 (ASU ETSU UNCA)

"A Study of Speech Education as It Relates to the Science Hill High School Program." Master's thesis. East Tennessee State College, 1956.
H7770 (ETSU)

"A Study of Twenty Parents in Carter County, Tennessee, Selected as the Best Partners-in-instruction." Master's thesis. East Tenn. State College, 1952.
E2330 (ETSU)

Stull, William Morris Haley, Elliot Clarke and others An Economic and Social Survey of Warren County. Charlottesville: Univ. of Virginia, 1943.
H520 (ASU)

Stump, Roy J. The Effects of School Bus Transportation upon the Achievement of Students in Calhoun County, High School. Master's thesis. West Va. Univ., 1942.
S8820

Stupka, Arthur Huheey, James E. Amphibians and Reptiles of Great Smoky Mountains National Park. Knoxville: Univ. of Tennessee Press, 1967, 1972.
H8160 (UNCA ASU LMC WCU BC)
Birds of the Smokies. Illustrated by Dolores Roberson. Gatlinburg, Tenn.: Buckhorn Press, 1972.
S8830 (LMC)
Great Smoky Mountains National Park, North Carolina and Tennessee. U. S. National Park Service Natural History Handbook Series, no. 5. Washington: Govt. Print. Off., 1960.
S8840 (ASU LMC WCU ETSU)
Notes on the Birds of Great Smoky Mountains National Park. Knoxville: Univ. of Tennessee Press, 1963. Observations of more than 200 species based on 25 years of field work.
S8850 (ASU WCU LMC WWC UNCA BC)
Notes on the Birds of Great Smoky Mountains National Park. Knoxville: Univ. of Tennessee Press, 1968.
S8860 (UNCA)
Trees, Shrubs, and Woody Vines of Great Smoky Mountains National Park. Knoxville: Univ. of Tennessee Press, 1964. The detailed notes are based on the observations of many years.
S8870 (ASU WCU LMC WWC UNCA)
Trees, Shrubs, and Woody Vines of Great Smoky Mountains National Park. Knoxville: Univ. of Tennessee Press, 1968.
S8880
Wildflowers in Color. With the assistance of Donald H. Robinson. 1st ed. New York: Harper and Row, 1965.
S8890 (ASU ETSU UNCA)

Sturgill, Roy L. Crimes, Criminals and Characters of the Cumberlands and Southwest Virginia. Bristol, Va.: Quality Printers, 1970.
S8900

Sturgis, Dudley C. "Standard of Living and Migration of 136 Farm Families in Overton County, Tennessee." Master's thesis. Univ. of Tennessee, 1936.
S8910

Sturm, Harry Price Rimfire, His Life Story and Selections From His Own Writings. A Study of the Typical Mountaineer, Eli (Rimfire) Hamrick. Parsons, W. Va.: McClain Print. Co., 1967. Musings of a mountaineer on the subject of mountaineers.
S8920 (ASU BC)

Stutler, Boyd B. Conley, Philip Mallory West Virginia, Yesterday and Today. Charleston: W. Va. Review Press, 1931.
C6620 (BC)
Conley, Philip Mallory West Virginia, Yesterday and Today. Charleston, W. Va.: Education Foundation, 1952.
C6630 (ASU)

Stutler, Boyd Blynn The Kinnan Massacre. Parsons, W. Va.: McClain Print. Co., 1969. An account of the family massacred by Indians and of the sufferings of Mary Kinnan who was taken captive.
S8930 (ASU BC)
West Virginia in the Civil War. 2nd ed. Charleston, W. Va.: Education Foundation, 1963.
S8940 (ASU BC)

"A Suggested Plan of Consolidation of the Schools of Greene County, Tennessee." Master's thesis. East Tennessee State College, 1958.
F3630

Sullins, D. Recollections of an Old Man. Seventy Years in Dixie. Bristol, Tenn.: King Print. Co., 1910.
S8950

Sullivan, James R. Chickamauga and Chattanooga Battlefields; Chickamauga and Chattanooga National Military Park, Georgia-Tennessee. Washington: National Park Service, 1956.
S8960

Sullivan, John Wentworth The Geology of the Sand Lookout Mountain Area, Northwest Georgia. Information Circular, 15. Atlanta: Georgia Department of Natural Resources Division of Mines, Mining and Geology, 1942.
S8970 (ETSU)

Sulzer, Elmer Griffith Ghost Railroads of Kentucky. Indianapolis: Vane A. Jones Co., 1967. Now that the lumber companies, loggers, and small mines have gone, there are many abandoned railroad beds in Eastern Kentucky.
S8980 (BC)
Twenty-five Kentucky Folk Ballads. Lexington: Transylvania Print. Co. Inc., 1936.
S8990 (BC)

Summers, Festus P. Ambler, Charles Henry West Virginia, the Mountain State. Englewood Cliffs, N. J.: Prentice-Hall, 1958.
A2050 (ASU WCU ETSU)

Summers, Festus P.
Cometti, Elizabeth ed. The Thirty-fifth State: Documentary History of Virginia. Morgantown: W. Va. Univ. Library, 1966.
C6160 (ASU LMC BC)
Borderland Confederate. Pittsburgh: Univ. of Pittsburgh Press, 1962.
S9000

Summers, George W. The Mountain State. Charleston, W. Va.: Moses W. Donnally, 1893. A description of the natural resources of West Virginia.
S9010
Pages from the Past. Charleston, W. Va.: Charleston Journal, 1953. Includes recollections and tales of Old Timers, incidents of early history of West Virginia or that part of Virginia which is now West Virginia.
S9020 (BC)

Summers, Hollis Spurgeon Someone Else; Sixteen Poems About Other Children. Philadelphia: Lippincott, 1962. Eastern Kentucky poems.
S9040

Summers, Hollis Spurgeon ed. Kentucky Story, a Collection of Short Stories. Lexington: Univ. of Kentucky Press, 1954. A collection of stories from Kentucky writers or about Kentucky.
S9030 (ASU BC)

Summers, Lewis Preston Annals of Southwest Virginia, 1769-1800. Abingdon, Va.: The author, 1929. History of Southwest Virginia including legends, lore, sketches of early settlers etc.
S9050 (ASU BC FC ETSU)
History of Southwest Virginia, 1746-1786, Washington County, 1777-1870. Richmond: J. L. Hill Print. Co., 1903. Early history of Washington County and Southwest Virginia from the Revolution to Reconstruction.
S9060 (ASU BC ETSU)
History of Southwest Virginia, 1746-1786, Washington County, 1777-1870. 1903. Reprint. Baltimore: Genealogical Pub. Co., 1966.
S9070 (ASU LMC FC ETSU)
History of Southwest Virginia, 1746-1786, Washington County, 1777-1870. 1903. Reprint. Baltimore: Regional Pub. Co., 1971.
S9080 (ASU ETSU)

Sumsion, Carlton T. Geology and Ground-water of the Morganton Area, North Carolina. Ground Water Bulletin, no. 12. Raleigh: North Carolina Division of Ground Water, 1967.
S9090 (WCU)

Surface, Bill Poisoned Ivy. New York: Coward, McCann and Geoghegan, Inc., 1968.
S9100

Surface, William The Hollow. New York: Coward-McCann, 1971. A sociological study of an isolated mountain hollow: family life, occupations, recreation, social interaction etc.
S9110 (WWC ASU LMC ETSU BC)

Surry of Eagle's Nest: Or, the Memoirs of a Staff-officer Serving in Virginia Edited from the MSS. of Colonel Surry. 1866. Reprint. Ridgewood, N. J.: Gregg Press, 1968.
C7020 (ASU WCU BC)

Survey Staff for the Study of West Virginia Public Schools Public Higher Education in West Virginia. Charleston, W. Va.: The staff, 1956.
S9120 (ASU)

Survey, Union County Univ. of Tennessee Record Extension Series, Vol. 1, no. 2. Knoxville: Div. of Univ. Extension Univ. of Tennessee, 1924.
S9130

Surveys and Research Corporation Appalachian Highway Corridor D-E Impact Study. Final Report. Washington: Surveys and Research Corporation, 1968.
S9140

Sutherland, Elihu Jasper Dickenson County in War Time; a Community History. n.p.: n.p., n.d. A brief account of Dickenson County during the First World War.
S9150
Folk Games from Frying Pan Creek in Dickenson County, Virginia. n.p.: n.p., n.d.
S9160
In Lonesome Cove. New York: Exposition Press, 1951. The Tennessee Valley is the background for this collection of poems. Dialect poems, nature poems, and poems commemorating great events are included.
S9170 (ASU)
In Lonesome Cove: Poems from TVA-land. New York: Exposition Press, 1951.
S9180 (ASU)
Meet Virginia's Baby: A Brief Pictorial History of Dickenson County, Virginia, from Its Formation in 1880 to 1955, with Stress on Pioneer Background. Clintwood, Va.: The author, 1955.
S9200 (ASU LMC BC)
Richard D. B. Sutherland; An Early Leader of Education in Sandy Basin. Clintwood, Va.: The author, 1935.
S9220
Russell Co., Va. Census of 1820. Clintwood, Va.: The author, 1940.
S9230
Sand Lick Primitive Baptist Church; The First Hundred Years, 1837-1937. Richmond, Va.: The author, 1938.
S9240
Some Sandy Basin Characters. Clintwood, Va.: Elihu Jasper Sutherland, 1962. These articles tell of the most striking activities of a few prominent leaders of Sandy Basin. They recount the ways people made a living for their own families, the ways they served others.
S9250
The Sunken Star. Columbia, S. C.: Cary Print. Co., 1917.
S9260 (BC)

Sutherland, Elihu Jasper ed. Meet Virginia's Baby. n.p.: Dickenson County Diamond Jubilee Publication, 1955. A pictorial history of Dickenson County, Virginia. Includes history, the resources, progress, and unsolved problems of Virginia's youngest county.
S9190
Regular Primitive Baptist Washington District Association. Elon College, N. C.: The Primitive Baptist Pub. House, 1952. Included is a short history of the Washington District Association and information on the beliefs and practices of the Primitive Baptist Church.
S9210

Sutherland, Herbert M. Tall Tales of the Devils Apron. Radford, Va.: Commonwealth Press, 1970.
S9270 (LMC BC FC)

Sutherland, J. H. T. Sutherland, Elihu Jasper Dickenson County in War Time; a Community History. n.p.: n.p., n.d.
S9150

Suttle, James H. Carter, Everett C. The Impact of Highway Beautification on the Outdoor Advertising Industry in West Virginia. Morgantown: West Virginia Univ. Engineering Experiment Station, 1967.
C1680
"The Economic Impact of Highway Beautification on the Outdoor Advertising Industry in West Virginia." Master's thesis. West Virginia Univ., 1967.
S9280

Suttlemyre, Charles Greer "Gold Mining in North Carolina: 1799-1860." Master's thesis. Western Carolina Univ., 1970.
S9290 (WCU)

Sutton, Ann The Appalachian Trail; Wilderness on the Doorstep. Foreword by Stewart L. Udall. Philadelphia: Lippincott, 1967.
S9300 (ASU)
The Appalachian Trail: Wilderness on the Doorstep. Foreword by Stewart L. Udall. 1st ed. Philadelphia: Lippincott, 1967.
S9310 (ASU WCU LMC ETSU FC WWC UNCA BC)

Sutton, John Davison History of Braxton County and Central West Virginia. 1919. Reprint. Parsons, W. Va.: McClain Print. Co., 1967.
S9320 (ASU BC)

Sutton, Jurt Hubert "A Follow-up of the Fifth Year Graduates of the Department of Administration and School Personnel." Master's thesis. Western Carolina Univ., 1971.
S9330 (WCU)

Sutton, Margaret Jemima, Daughter of Daniel Boone. New York: Scribner, 1942. Biography of the brave Boone daughter who survived capture by Indians and other harrowing adventures on the frontier.
S9340

Sutton, Myron Sutton, Ann The Appalachian Trail; Wilderness on the Doorstep. Philadelphia: Lippincott, 1967.
S9300 (ASU)
Sutton, Ann The Appalachian Trail: Wilderness on the Doorstep. Philadelphia: Lippincott, 1967.
S9310 (ASU WCU LMC ETSU FC WWC UNCA BC)

Sutton, Rita Kennedy Early Osbornes and Alleys, With Notes on Allied Families. Wise, Va.: Historical Society of Southwest Virginia, 1973. Indexed. Includes records on all the Osbornes of Clinch and New Rivers and Alleys of the Clinch.
S9350 (BC)

Sutton, Willis A. The Social Dimensions of Kentucky Counties: Data and Rankings of the State's 120 Counties on Each of 81 Characteristics. Kentucky Community Series, no. 29. Lexington: Bureau of Community Service, Univ. of Kentucky, 1964.
S9360

Svenson, Henry Tennessee Wildflowers. Nashville: Division of Information, Tennessee Dept. of Conservation, 1964.
S9370

Swain County Chamber of Commerce A National Park in the Great Smoky Mountains. Bryson City, N. C.: Swain Co. Chamber of Commerce, 1925. Promotional material supporting the North Carolina location of the park and touting the advantages of Swain County.
S9380

Swain, George F. and others Papers on the Waterpower in North Carolina, a Preliminary Report. Bulletin, no. 8. Raleigh: North Carolina Geological Survey, 1899.
S9390 (LMC)

Swain, George T. Facts About the Two Armed Marches on Logan. Charleston, W. Va.: Ace Enterprises, 1962. One sided view of the two young wars in the Logan County Coal Fields.
S9400 (ASU BC)
The Incomparable Don Chafin. Charleston, W. Va.: Jones Print. Co., 1962. Lauds the sheriff who used strikebreakers, state and federal troops on the Kanawha Valley Miners.
S9410 (BC ASU)
Princess Aracoma, Beautiful Story of the Comely Daughter of Chief Cornstalk, Great Sachem of the Shawnee Tribe of Indians Who Was Born Near Point Pleasant, Married a "Pale-face", Migrated to the Guyan Valley and There Met a Tragic Fate at the Hands of the White Man. Charleston, W. Va.: Ace Enterprises, n.d.
S9420 (ASU)
The True Facts about the Famous Hatfield-McCoy Feud. Charleston, W. Va.: Ace Enterprises, 1962. All Swain's books of "facts" have the ring of zealotry. He should have been around for the Crusades.
S9430 (ASU BC)

Swann, Maurice E. Austin, Moris E. Soil Survey, Claiborne County, Tennessee. Washington: U. S. Department of Agriculture, Bureau of Plant Industry, Soils, and Agricultural Engineering, 1948.
A5560 (ASU)

Swann, Maurice Edward Soil Survey, Roane County, Tennessee. Prepared in cooperation with the Tennessee Agricultural Experiment Station and the Tennessee Valley Authority. Soil Survey Report, Series 1936, no. 15. Washington: U. S. Department of Agriculture, Bureau of Plant Industry, 1942.
S9440

Swann, Maurice Edward
Soil Survey of Winston County, Alabama. Prepared in cooperation with the Alabama Department of Agriculture and Industries. Soil Survey Report, Series 1932, no. 12. Washington: U. S. Department of Agriculture, Bureau of Chemistry and Soils, 1937.
S9450
Vessel, A. J. Soil Survey, Greenbrier County, West Virginia. Washington: U. S. Dept. of Agriculture, Bureau of Plant Industry, 1941.
V580

Swanson, Neil Harmon The First Rebel; Being a Lost Chapter of Our History on a True Narrative of America's First Uprising Against English Military Authority and An Account of the First Fighting Between Armed Colonists and British Regulars. Together with a Biography of Colonel James Smith. . . Recounted from Contemporary Documents by Neil H. Swanson. New York: Farrar and Rinehart, 1937.
S9460 (BC)

Swanton, John R. The Indians of the Southeastern United States. Smithsonian Institution Bureau of American Ethnology Bulletin 137. Washington, D. C.: Govt. Print. Off., 1946.
S9490 (BC)
The Indian Tribes of North America. Smithsonian Institution Bureau of American Ethnology Bulletin 145. Washington, D. C.: Govt. Print. Off., 1952.
S9520 (FC)

Swanton, John R. ed. Final Report of the United States De Soto Expedition Commission. House Ex. Doc. 71, 76th Cong., 1st sess. Washington, D. C.: Govt. Print. Off., 1939. Apparently De Soto visited the mountains of Georgia, Tennessee, and North Carolina.
S9480

Swanton, John Reed Early History of the Creek Indians and Their Neighbor. Smithsonian Institute Publication, no. 73. Washington: Govt. Print. Off., 1922.
S9470 (LMC)
The Indians of the Southeastern United States. Xerox copy of the original. U. S. Bureau of American Ethnology Bulletin, 137. Washington: Govt. Print. Off., 1946.
S9500 (ASU)
The Indians of the Southeastern United States. 1946. Reprint. Grosse Pointe, Mich.: Scholarly Press, 1969.
S9510 (LMC WCU)

Sweeny, Lenora Higginbotham Amherst County, Virginia, in the Revolution: Including Extracts from the "Lost Order Book", 1773-1782. Lynchburg, Va.: J. P. Bell, 1951.
S9530 (ASU)
Marriage Records of Amherst County, Virginia, 1815-1821, and Subscription for Building St. Mark's Church, Amherst Co., Virginia. Lynchburg, Va.: n.p., 1961.
S9540 (ASU)

Sweeny, William Montgomery Wills of Rappahannock Co., Va., 1656-1692. Lynchburg, Va.: The author, 1947.
S9560 (ASU BC)

Sweeny, William Montgomery comp. Marriage Bonds and Other Marriage Records of Amherst County, Virginia, 1763-1800. Lynchburg, Va.: J. P. Bell Co., 1937.
S9550 (ASU)

Sweet, Arthur T. Soil Survey of Meigs County, Tennessee. Prepared in cooperation with the Tennessee Geological Survey. Field Operations, 1919. Washington: U. S. Department of Agriculture, Bureau of Soils, 1921.
S9570

The Sweet Songster, a Collection of the Most Popular and Approved Songs, Hymns and Ballads n.p.: n.p., n.d. Widely sung in Appalachia as in all of the South.
S9580

Sweet, William Warren Methodism in American History. New York: The Methodist Book Concern, 1933.
S9600 (BC FC)
Religion in Colonial America. New York: Charles Scribner's Sons, 1942.
S9630 (MHC FC)
Religion in the Development of American Culture, 1795-1840. 1952. Reprint. Gloucester, Mass.: P. Smith, 1963. You can't study the American Frontier without reading this book.
S9640 (ASU)
Revivalism in America. New York: n.p., 1944. In a sense the Great Revival of the early 1800's was an Appalachian phenomena. That's where culture and formality hit the frontier spirit head on, and lost.
S9650

Sweet, William Warren ed. The Baptists, a Collection of Source Material, General Introduction by Shirley Jackson Chase. Religion on the American Frontier, 1783-1840. vol. 1. 1936. Reprint. New York: Cooper Square Pubs., 1964. Ever wanted to know how the Baptists got such a toehold on frontier religion even though the Methodists and Presbyterians were trying harder? Read Mr. Sweet's account of their expansion.
S9590 (ASU BC)
The Methodists, a Collection of Source Materials. Religion on the American Frontier, 1783-1840. vol. 4, 1946. Reprint. New York: Cooper Square Pubs., 1964.
S9610 (ASU)
The Presbyterians, a Collection of Source Materials. Religion on the American Frontier, 1783-1840. vol. 2. 1936. Reprint. New York: Cooper Square Pubs., 1964.
S9620 (ASU BC)

Sweeten, Charles Hugh "Tennessee Municipalities and TVA Power." Master's thesis. Univ. of Tennessee, 1966.
S9660

Swenson, Gustavus Adolphus and others Soil Survey, De Kalb County, Alabama. Correlation by M. J. Edwards. Soil Survey, Series 1951, no. 3. Washington: U. S. Soil Conservation Service, 1958.
S9670
Soil Survey, Jackson County, Alabama. Soil Survey, Series 1941, no. 8. Washington: U. S. Soil Conservation Service, 1954.
S9680
Soil Survey, Madison County, Alabama. Soil Survey, Series 1947, no. 3. Washington: U. S. Soil Conservation Service, 1958.
S9690

Swiggett, Howard The Rebel Raider, a Life of John Hunt Morgan. 1st ed. Indianapolis: Bobbs-Merrill Co., 1934. Morgan, who knew the mountains well, made four major raids within Appalachia and used the mountains as an escape route numerous times.
S9700 (BC ASU)

Swingle, George D. Geology, Mineral Resources, and Ground Water of the Cleveland Area, Tennessee. Prepared in cooperation with the U. S. Geological Survey. Bulletin, 61. Nashville: Tennessee Division of Geology, 1959.
S9710 (ETSU)

Swisher, Basil G. S. "A Survey of the Attitudes of Women in Monongalia County, West Virginia, toward the Use of Contraceptives." Master's thesis. West Virginia Univ., 1970.
S9720

Swisher, Howard Llewellyn Maxwell, Hu History of Hampshire County, West Virginia, from Its Earliest Settlement to the Present. Parsons, W. Va.: McClain Print. Co., 1972.
M4530 (ASU)

Swope, Paul W. "Pupil Transportation in W. Va., 1934-55." Master's thesis. Marshall College, 1957.
S9730

Sykes, Robert H. Proud Heritage of West Virginia. New Brunswick, N. J.: Standard Press, 1974.
S9740

Sylva Planning Board Population and Economy: Sylva, N. C. Sylva, N. C.: The board, 1963.
S9750 (LMC)

Sylvester, Letitia Vertrees My Kentucky Cousins. Boston: Christopher Pub. House, 1933. Collection of short stories about Kentucky. Most have mountain settings and the author's understanding of mountain culture is a pleasant surprise.
S9760 (ASU BC)

Sylvester, Mrs. S. A. see **Sylvester, Letitia Vertrees**

Symposium on Cherokee and Iroquois Culture, Washington, D. C., 1958 Papers. U. S. Bureau of American Ethnology Bulletin, no. 180. Washington: Govt. Print. Off., 1961. The Cherokee once belonged to the Iroquois Nation but differences waxed and similarities waned.
S9770 (ETSU WCU BC)

Symposium on Mineral Resources of the Southeastern United States, University of Tennessee, 1949 Proceedings. Contributions by Charles H. Behre, Jr. and others. Knoxville: Univ. of Tennessee Press, 1950.
S9780 (ASU BC)

System Development Corporation Appalachia Project Staff A Report to the Area-Redevelopment Administration; U. S. Department of Commerce on a Model for an Appalachian Regional Commission. Falls Church, Va.: The corporation, 1964. A modern fairy tale, come true.
S9790

Szwed, John F. Glassie, Henry H. Folksongs and Their Makers. Bowling Green, Ohio: Bowling Green Univ., Popular Press, 1970.
G2070 (ASU MHC BC)

Tabb, Marion F. Petro, James H. Soil Survey, Ross County, Ohio. Washington: U. S. Soil Conservation Service, 1967.
P2430

Tabb, William Kenneth "A Recursive Programing Model of Resource Allocation and Technological Change in the United States Bituminous Coal Industry." Ph. D. Diss. Univ. of Wisconsin, 1968.
T10

Tableland Trails vol. 1-, Spring 1953-. Oakland, Md.: Tableland Trails, 1953-. A magazine devoted to the history, folklore and cultural interests of Pennsylvania, Maryland, and West Virginia.
T20

Taglauer, James R. "The History of Lutheran Elementary Education in Catawba County." Master's thesis. Appalachian State Teachers College, 1961.
T30

Tailby, G. W., Jr. Caine, Thomas A. Soil Survey of the Wheeling Area, West Virginia. Washington: U. S. Department of Agriculture, Bureau of Soils, 1908.
C70 ()
Meeker, Fred N. Soil Survey of Meigs County, Ohio. Washington: U. S. Department of Agriculture, Bureau of Soils, 1908.
M4930

Talbert, Charles Gano Benjamin Logan, Kentucky Frontiersman. Lexington: Univ. of Kentucky Press, 1962. Biography of one of Kentucky's pioneer explorers and land speculators, who led a life of public service.
T40 (WCU BC)

Taliaferro, Harden E. Carolina Humor: Sketches. Foreword by David K. Jackson. Richmond: Dietz Press, 1938. These western North Carolina sketches are notable for their humor and excellent dialect.
T50 (ASU)
Fisher's River Scenes. 1859. Reprint. n.p.: J. A. Snow, 1958.
T60 (ASU)
Fisher's River (North Carolina) Scenes and Characters by "Skitt Who Was Raised Thar." New York: Harper and Brothers, 1859. If you could read only one book as an example of Appalachian humor and dialect, this should be it.
T70 (ETSU BC)

Talley, William M. Talley's Kentucky Papers. Fort Worth, Texas: Arrow Print Co., 1966. Primarily court records, registers of birth etc. from Eastern Kentucky.
T80 (BC)

Talley, William M.
Talley's Northeastern Kentucky Papers. Fort Worth, Texas: American Reference Publishers, 1971.
T90

Tallman, Marjorie Dictionary of American Folklore. New York: Philosophical Library, 1959.
T100 (ASU)

Tallon, Walter A. High-alumina Clays of West Virginia. Report of Investigations, no. 17. Morgantown: West Virginia Geological and Economic Survey, 1959.
T120 (ETSU)

Talmadge, John Erwin Rebecca Latimer Felton, Nine Stormy Decades. Athens: Univ. of Georgia Press, 1960. Becky Felton was the first woman to serve in the United States Congress. She was a controversial figure in North Georgia (Bartow County) for most of her ninety odd years, for she was an early feminist and a natural born character.
T110 (ASU)

Tamaracke Taming the Savage River. Parsons, W. Va.: McClain Print. Co., 1968. Man triumphs over a river with the aid of modern technology.
T130 (ASU BC)

Tams, W. P. The Smokeless Coal Fields of West Virginia: A Brief History. Morgantown: West Virginia Univ. Library, 1963.
T140 (BC ETSU ASU WCU)

Tandy, Laura Boulton McAllister, John Merriwether Genealogies of the Lewis and Kindred Families. Columbia, Mo.: E. W. Stephens Pub. Co., 1906.
M70

Taney, Mary Florence Kentucky Pioneer Women. Columbian Poems and Prose Sketches. Cincinnati: Press of R. Clarke and Co., 1893.
T150 (BC)

Tangerman, Elmer John Whittling and Woodcarving. 1936. Reprint. New York: Dover Publications, 1962.
T160 (ASU)

Tankel, Phillip "Bloody" Harlan, 1931-1938; an Appalachian Coal County in the Thirties. Unpublished Paper. Columbia Univ.: n.p., 1968.
T170

Tankersley, Charles W. Genealogy of the Tankersley Family in the United States. 1895. Reprint. Atlanta: Rachel Peeples Rogers, 1950.
T180 (ASU)

Tapp, Hambleton ed. The Register of the Kentucky Historical Society. Published quarterly by the Ky. Historical Society Old State House. Frankfort, Ky.: Kentucky Historical Society, 1973-, quarterly.
T200 (BC)

Tappan, George L. Andrew Johnson — Not Guilty. New York: Comet, 1954.
T210

Taras, Michael Andrew Circular Slide Rule for Calculating Wood Moisture Content. U. S. Forest Service Station Paper, no. 125. Asheville, N. C.: Southeastern Forest Experiment Station, 1961.
T220 (WCU)

A Comparison of Increment Core Sampling Methods For Estimating Tree Specific Gravity. U. S. Forest Service Research Paper, SE-7. Asheville, N. C.: Southeastern Forest Experiment Station, 1963.
T230 (WCU)

Seasoning and Preservative Treatment of Hickory Crossties. Hickory Task Force Report, no. 8. Asheville, N. C.: Southeastern Forest Experiment Station, 1959.
T240 (WCU)

Wood Density Surveys of the Minor Species of Yellow Pine in the Eastern United States: Pt. I — Spruce Pine (Pinus Glabra Walt.). Rev. ed. U. S. Forest Service Research Paper, SE-34. Asheville, N. C.: Southeastern Forest Experiment Station, 1970.
T250 (WCU)

Tarleton, Fiswoode Bloody Ground: A Cycle of the Southern Hills. New York: L. MacVeagh, Dial Press, 1929. This group of stories set in an Eastern Kentucky town deals with the tendency of hill men toward violence.
T260 (ASU LMC BC ETSU)

Some Trust in Chariots. New York: L. MacVeagh, Dial Press, 1930. A settlement school in Eastern Kentucky is burned because of the mountaineer's aversion to accepting either charity or advice from outlanders. A realistic portrayal of the delicate balance between the mountaineer and the mission schools.
T270 (ASU LMC BC ETSU)

Tarrant, Eastham The Wild Riders of the First Kentucky Cavalry. A History of the Regiment in the First Great War of the Rebellion. 1861-1865. Telling of its origin and organization: A description of the material of which it was composed. Its rapid and severe marches, hard service, and fierce conflicts. A regimental roster. Prison life, adventures, and escapes. Published by a committee of the regiment. 1894. Reprint. Lexington, Ky.: Henry Clay Press, 1969.
T280 (ASU)

Tarver, James D. Bowles, Gladys K. Net Migration of the Population, 1950-1960 by Age, Sex and Color. Washington: Economic Research Service, U. S. Department of Agriculture, 1965.
B5730

Tate, Ferrell Hillbilly Cookin' by the Tates. Thorn Hill, Tenn.: Clinch Mountain Lookout, 1968. Receipts for such favorites as squirrel and dumplings and yellowroot tea.
T290 (ASU)

Tate, Leland B. An Economic and Social Survey of Russell County. Charlottesville: Univ. of Va., School of Rural Social Economics, 1931.
T300 (BC)

Lebanon, A Virginia Community. Bulletin 352. Charlottesville: Univ. of Va. Ag. Exp. Station, 1943. A social and economic study of a Southwest Virginia town.
T310

Tate, Luke E. History of Pickens Co. Atlanta: W. W. Brown Pub. Co., 1935.
T320 (ASU)

Tate, Ray J. Soil Survey: Gwinnett County, Georgia. Athens: Univ. of Ga. Agricultural Experiment Station, 1967.
T330

Tate, William Questions and Answers for American Mine Examinations. Scranton, Pa.: The Colliery Engineer Co., 1897.
T340 (BC)

Tatum, Georgia Lee Disloyalty in the Confederacy. 1934. Reprint. New York: AMS Press, 1970. Most of the mountaineers sympathized with the Union. Many enlisted in the Union Army, and some mountain counties seceded from their Confederate states. Of these, Dade County, Georgia and Winston County, Alabama were the last to reunite with their state governments.
T350 (BC LMC)

Taussig, Harry A. Folk-style Autoharp; an Instruction Method for Playing the Autoharp and Accompanying Folk Songs. New York: Oak Publications, 1967.
T360 (ASU)

Taylor, Alfred Alexander Taylor, James Patton Life and Career of Senator Robert Love Taylor (Our Bob) by His Three Surviving Brothers. Nashville: Bob Taylor Pub. Co., 1913.
T580 (ASU)

Taylor, Alfred Heber "Jesse Stuart and the Short Story." Master's thesis. Vanderbilt Univ., 1949.
T370 (ASU)

Taylor, Archer A Collection of Irish Riddles. Los Angeles: Univ. of California Press, 1955. Irish riddlers, maxims, blessings, sayings and curses are still found in North Georgia and other Appalachian areas.
T380 (FC)

Taylor, Arthur Elijah Soil Survey of Adams County, Ohio. Prepared in cooperation with the Ohio Agricultural Experiment Station. Soil Survey Report, Series 1932, no. 29. Washington: U. S. Department of Agriculture, Bureau of Chemistry and Soils, 1938.
T390

Soil Survey, Catoosa County, Georgia. Prepared in cooperation with the Univ. of Georgia College of Agriculture. Soil Survey Report, Series 1937, no. 4. Washington: U. S. Department of Agriculture, Bureau of Plant Industry, 1941.
T400

Soil Survey of Clay County, Alabama. Prepared in cooperation with Alabama. Field Operations, 1915. Washington: U. S. Department of Agriculture, Bureau of Soils, 1916.
T410

Soil Survey of Coosa County, Alabama. Prepared in cooperation with the Alabama Department of Agriculture and Industries. Soil Survey Report, Series 1929, no. 18. Washington: U. S. Department of Agriculture, Bureau of Chemistry and Soils, 1933.
T430

Soil Survey, Dade County, Georgia. Prepared in cooperation with the Univ. of Georgia College of Agriculture. Soil Survey Report, Series 1936, no. 20. Washington: U. S. Department of Agriculture, Bureau of Plant Industry, 1942.
T440

Taylor, Arthur Elijah and others Soil Survey: Clermont County, Ohio. Prepared in cooperation with the Ohio Agricultural Experiment Station. Soil Survey Report, Series 1923, no. 22. Washington: U. S. Department of Agriculture, Bureau of Chemistry and Soils, 1928.
T420

Taylor, Benjamin Franklin Mission Ridge and Lookout Mountain, With Pictures of Life in Camp and Field. New York: D. Appleton and Co., 1872.
T450 (ASU)

Taylor, Bob Lectures and Best Literary Productions of Bob Taylor. Nashville: Bob Taylor Pub. Co., 1913. Lectures and literary output from one half of East Tennessee's Bob and Alf Taylor political circus.
T460 (ASU)

Taylor, Bonnie Kate "Determining the Most Effective Method by Which the Children in Each of Three Groups in the First Grade at South Side School, Carter County, Tennessee, Learn to Recognize Words." Master's thesis. East Tennessee State College, 1959.
T470 (ETSU)

Taylor, Charlotte "A Tentative Health Instruction Program for the Secondary Schools of Carter County, Tennessee." Master's thesis. East Tennessee State College, 1956.
T480 (ETSU)

Taylor, Daniel Benjamin "An Assessment of the Characteristics, Education, and Training of Public School Superintendents in Southern Appalachia and in West Virginia." Ph. D. Diss. West Virginia Univ., 1965.
T490

Taylor, David Bacon, Samuel Rankin Soil Survey, Montour and Northumberland Counties, Pennsylvania. Washington: Govt. Print. Off., 1955.
B90

Taylor, David Clarence and others Soil Survey, Westmoreland County, Pennsylvania. Washington: U. S. Soil Conservation Service, 1968.
T500

Taylor, Dee F. Stamper Tract Prescribed Burn. U. S. Forest Service Research Paper, SE-14. Asheville, N. C.: Southeastern Forest Experiment Station, 1964.
T510 (WCU)

Taylor, Mrs. F. H. Apple and Doughhead Dollmaking: Clothes Patterns Included. Mountain Home, Ark.: n.p., 1968.
T520 (WCU)

Taylor, Mrs. Feamster Rudicil, Rowland K. Historic Hamblen, 1870-1970. Morristown: Morristown Print. Co., 1970.
R4210

Taylor, George Braxton Virginia Baptist Ministers, Fourth Series. Foreword by Edgar Young Mullius. Lynchburg, Va.: J. P. Bell Co., 1913. Biographical sketches of Baptist ministers.
T530 (LMC)

Taylor, Halsey P. "The Short Stories of Jesse Stuart." Master's thesis. Univ. of Southern California, 1952.
T540 (ASU)

Taylor, Helen "A Survey of Innovative Practices in East Tennessee Secondary Schools." Master's thesis. East Tennessee State Univ., 1970.
T550 (ETSU)

Taylor, Hugh Lawson Taylor, James Patton Life and Career of Senator Robert Love Taylor (Our Bob) by His Three Surviving Brothers. Nashville: Bob Taylor Pub. Co., 1913.
T580 (ASU)

Taylor, James Barnett Virginia Baptist Ministers. Philadelphia: J. B. Lippincott and Co., 1859. Sketches of the lives of Baptist ministers.
T560 (ASU)

Taylor, James M. "Teachers Attitudes Toward Their Profession in Greenville County, South Carolina." Master's thesis. Furman Univ., 1952.
T570

Taylor, James Patton Life and Career of Senator Robert Love Taylor (Our Bob) by His Three Surviving Brothers. Nashville: Bob Taylor Pub. Co., 1913. Biography of the famous orator, politician and writer from East Tennessee.
T580 (ASU)

Taylor, Jerome Gregg "The Public Career of Joseph Alexander Mabry." Master's thesis. Univ. of Tennessee, 1968. Mabry was editor of the Knoxville Whig.
T590

Taylor, John M. "History of Education in Laurel County, Kentucky." Master's thesis. Univ. of Kentucky, 1932.
T600

Taylor, John Stuart Sixteenth South Carolina Regiment, CSA, From Greenville, S. C. Greenville, S. C.: The author, 1964.
T610 (ASU)

Taylor, Joyce Ann The Cherokees and the Great Smoky Mountains. Newland, N. C.: Avery Journal, 1965. Stories of Cherokee history, legends and lore.
T620 (LMC)

Taylor, Linda Leslie, J. D. Management of Kentucky Natural Resources. Lexington, Ky.: Spindletop Research, 1965.
L1900

Taylor, Mildred History of Wayne County, West Virginia. n.p.: n.p., 1963.
T630 (ASU)

Taylor, N. Relief for East Tennessee. Meeting at Cooper Institute, Thursday evening, March 10, 1864. Address of Hon. N. G. Taylor (late Representative from East Tennessee.) Reported by A. F. Washburton, stenographer. New York: Wm. C. Bryant, 1864.
T640 (BC)

Taylor, Oliver Historic Sullivan: A History of Sullivan County, Tennessee, with Brief Biographies of the Makers of History. Bristol, Tenn.: King Print. Co., 1909.
T650 (ASU ETSU BC)

Historic Sullivan: A History of Sullivan County, Tennessee, With Brief Biographies of the Makers of History. 1909. Reprint. Blountville, Tenn.: Burmar Books, 1971.
T660 (ASU)

Historic Sullivan: A History of Sullivan County, Tennessee, With Brief Biographies of the Makers of History. Nashville: Charles Elder, 1971. A good county history prepared under difficult circumstances. The written records of the county were burned during the battle of Blountville, 1863.
T670

Taylor, Ouvy Wilburn Early Tennessee Baptists, 1769-1832. Nashville: Tennessee Baptist Convention, 1957.
T680 (ASU)

Taylor, Paul F. "Coal and Conflict: The U.M.W.A. in Harlan County, 1931-1939." Ph. D. Diss. The Univ. of Kentucky, 1969.
T690 (BC ASU)

Taylor, R. Quintard White Sulphur Springs, a Brief History. n.p.: n.p., 1923.
T700 (ASU)

Taylor, Richard Cowling Statistics of Coal. The Geographical and Geological Distribution of Mineral Combustibles or Fossils Fuel, Including, Also, Notices and Localities of the Various Mineral Bituminous Substances, Employed in Arts and Manufactures...Embracing, From Official Reports of the Great Coal-Producing Countries, the Respective Amounts of Their Production, Consumption and Commercial Distribution, in All Parts of the World; Together With Their Prices, Tariffs, Duties and International Regulations... Philadelphia: J. W. Moore, 1848.
T710 (BC)

Taylor, Robert Love Echoes: Centennial and Other Notable Speeches, Lectures, and Stories. Nashville: S. B. Williamson and Co., 1899.
T720 (ASU)

Mainstreams of Mountain Thought; Attitudes of Selected Figures in the Heart of the Appalachian South. Univ. Microfilms, 1973. Ph. D. Diss. Univ. of Tenn., 1971.
T730 (ASU)

Memorial Addresses Delivered in the Senate and the House of Representatives of the United States. Washington: Govt. Print. Off., 1913.
T740 (ASU)

Taylor, Sarah M. "A Study of the Factors Which Might Affect Achievements in Reading in the First Grade of Anderson School, Bristol, Tennessee." Master's thesis. East Tennessee State Univ., 1963.
T750 (ETSU)

Taylor, Welford Dunaway ed. Anderson, Sherwood The Buck Fever Papers. Charlottesville: Univ. Press of Virginia, 1971.
A2380 (ASU)

Taylor, William Thomas "The Development of a Middle School Program for the Morristown City School System, Morristown, Tennessee." Master's thesis. East Tennessee State Univ., 1969.
T760 (ETSU)

Tazelaar, James E. Geologic Map of the Evarts Quadrangle and Part of the Hubbard Springs Quadrangle, Southeastern Kentucky and Virginia. Washington: U. S. Geological Survey, 1974.
T770 (BC)

Teachers and Pupils of Mitchell County Discovering Mitchell County. Bakersville, N. C.: County Board of Education, 1939-1940. A fifty-nine page guide to Mitchell County history compiled by the public schools of the county.
T780

Teachers Training Class. Burnsville, N. C. History and Geography of Yancey County. Burnsville: The class, 1930.
T790 (ASU)

Teale, Edwin Way North With the Spring: A Naturalist's Record of a 17,000 Mile Journey With the North-American Spring. 1951. Reprint. New York: Dodd, Mead, 1957.
T800 (ASU LMC)

Tebbals, Alma Owens A History of Pulaski Co., Kentucky. Bagdad, Ky.: G. O. Moore, 1952.
T810

Tedrow, N. P. Higbee, Howard William Soil Survey, Huntingdon County, Pennsylvania. Washington: U. S. Department of Agriculture, Bureau of Plant Industry, Soils and Agricultural Engineering, 1944.
H5260

Teets, D. Dee, Jr. Krebs, Charles E. Cabell, Wayne and Lincoln Counties. Wheeling: West Virginia Geological Survey, 1913.
K3180 (ETSU ASU)

Temple, Oliver Perry East Tennessee and the Civil War. Cincinnati: The R. Clarke Co., 1899.
T820 (ASU)

East Tennessee and the Civil War. 1899. Reprint. The Black Heritage Library Collection. Freeport, N. Y.: Books for Libraries Press, 1971. The best history of the violence and hatred begun during the Civil War and evident in Tennessee politics yet.
T830 (ETSU)

East Tennessee and the Civil War. 1899. Reprint. Knoxville: Burmar Books, 1972.
T840 (ASU ETSU)

John Sevier, Citizen, Soldier, Legislator, Governor, Statesman. Knoxville, Tenn.: Zi-Po Press, 1910.
T850 (ETSU)

Templeman, Eleanor Lee (Reading) Northern Virginia Heritage; a Pictorial Compilation of the Historic Sites and Homes in the Counties of Arlington, Fairfax, Loudoun, Fauquier, Prince William and Stafford, and the Cities of Alexandria and Fredericksburg, by Eleanor Lee Templeman and Nan Netherton. 1st ed. Arlington, Va.: Privately published by E. L. Templeman, 1966.
T860 (BC)

Teng, Hai Chuan "Marble Deposits and Marble Industry of the Knoxville Area." Master's thesis. Univ. of Tennessee, 1948. Economic and county history of Knox County, Tennessee.
T870

Tennent, Gaillard S. Medicine in Buncombe County Down to 1885, Historical and Biographical Sketches. Asheville: Stephens Press, 1906.
T880

Tennessee. Agricultural Experiment Station Bulletin. no. 1-. Knoxville: Univ. of Tenn., n.d.
T890 (BC)

Rural Research Series. Monograph no. 1-. Knoxville: Univ. of Tenn., irregular.
T900

Tennessee and Kings Mountain Papers of the Draper Collection of Manuscripts Calendar Series Vol. III. Madison, Wis.: Wisconsin Historical Society, 1929.
T1550

Tennessee. Annual Report of the State Geologist Nashville: State Geologist, n.d.
T910 (LMC)

Tennessee Archaeologist vol. 1-, 1944-. Knoxville: Tennessee Archaeological Society, 1944-.
T920 (ETSU)

Tennessee Archeologist Ten Years of the Tennessee Archaeologist: Selected Subjects. Chattanooga, Tenn.: J. B. Graham, 1954.
T930 (ETSU)

Tennessee, Board of Entomology Annual Report of the State Entomologist and Plant Pathologist. Knoxville: The board, annual.
T940 (ETSU)

Tennessee, Civil War Centennial Commission Tennesseans in the Civil War: A Military History of Confederate and Union Units with Available Rosters of Personnel. Nashville: The commission, 1964.
T950 (ASU)

Tennessee, Commission on Youth Guidance Report to the Governor and Members of the General Assembly (81st) State of Tennessee. Nashville: The commission, 1959.
T960 (ETSU)

Report to Honorable Frank G. Clement, Governor, and Members of the 80th General Assembly, State of Tennessee. Nashville: The commission, 1956.
T970 (ETSU)

Tennessee County Inventory. Nashville: The commission, 1959.
T980 (ETSU)

Tennessee, Department of Agriculture Agricultural Trends in Tennessee: A Record of Crop and Livestock Statistics, 1866-1947. Nashville: The Department and the U. S. Department of Agriculture, Bureau of Agricultural Economics, 1948-.
T990 (ETSU)

Tennessee, Department of Agriculture
Makers of Millions, Not for Themselves But for You: Stories of Tennesseans whose Accomplishments for Agriculture Brought Renown to Their State and Caused an Appreciating and Benefited Public to Propose Their Admission to the Tennessee Agricultural Hall of Fame. 1st ed. Nashville: The department, 1951.
T1000 (ASU)

Tennessee, Department of Agriculture, Bureau of Agriculture, Statistics and Mines Mineral and Agricultural Resources of the Portion of Tennessee Along the Cincinnati Southern and Knoxville and Ohio Railroads. Nashville: Tavel, Eastman, and Howell, 1876.
T1010 (ASU)

Tennessee, Department of Conservation Division of Geology Bulletin. Nashville: The division, n.d.
T1020

Tennessee Fishing Waters, Featuring TVA Lakes. Nashville: State of Tennessee, 1948.
T1040

Tennessee, Department of Conservation and Commerce, Education Service "Some Tennessee Trees — a Simple, Illustrated Key." Nashville: Unpublished typescript, 1966.
T1070

Tennessee, Department of Conservation, Division of Geology see also **Tennessee, Division of Geology**

Tennessee, Department of Conservation, Division of Information Tennessee: A Guide to the State. American Guide Series. 1939. Reprint. St. Clair Shores, Mich.: Somerset, 1973.
T1030 (MHC)

Tennessee, Department of Conservation, Division of State Information The Tennessee Scene. Nashville: n.p., 1947.
T1050

Tennessee, Department of Conservation, Educational Service Forest Trees and Forest Facts of Tennessee. Nashville: The department, 1946.
T1060 (ETSU)

Tennessee, Department of Education Bradley County Schools Survey Report. Nashville: State of Tennessee, 1966.
T1080

Campbell County School Survey. Nashville: State of Tennessee, 1962.
T1090

Grainger County Schools Survey Report. Nashville: State of Tennessee, 1965.
T1100

A Guide for Developing and Evaluating Language Arts Courses of Study, Grades 1-12. Johnson City: East Tennessee State College, 1956.
T1110 (ETSU)

Jefferson County Survey Report. Nashville: State of Tennessee, 1965. Relates to the schools of the county.
T1120

Report of the Survey of the Schools of Blount County, Tennessee, for School Year, 1934-1935. Nashville: The department, 1935.
T1130 (ETSU)

Washington County Survey Report. Directed by T. Wesley Pickell. Nashville: The department, 1964.
T1140 (ETSU)

Tennessee, Department of Education, Division of Geology The Magnetic Iron Ore of East Tennessee and Western North Carolina. Bulletin no. 29. Nashville: Dept. of Education, 1923.
T1150

The Valley of East Tennessee. Bulletin no. 36. Nashville: Dept. of Education, 1925.
T1160

Tennessee, Department of Education, Division of Geology see also **Tennessee, Division of Geology**

Tennessee, Department of Employment Security A Study of the Chattanooga Labor Market Area. Nashville: The department's Research and Statistics Section, 1963-.
T1170 (ETSU)

Tennessee, Department of Employment Security, Research and Statistics Section Population and Labor Force Characteristics of Tennessee Counties. Nashville: The department, 1963.
T1180

Tennessee Employment Statistics, 1939-1964. Nashville: The department, 1965.
T1190

Tennessee Manpower: Current Trend and Future Projections. Nashville: The department, 1967.
T1200

Tennessee, Department of Finance and Administration Tennessee — Its Resources and Economy — The Tennessee Economy — Vol. I. Nashville: The department, 1965.
T1210

Tennessee, Department of Highways, Research and Planning Division Johnson City Transportation Study: Major Route Plan. Traffic Operation Study and Parking Study. Nashville: The division, 1968.
T1220 (ETSU)

Tennessee, Department of Public Health, Stream Pollution Control Division Stream Pollution Control In The Upper Cumberland River Basin, 1965. Nashville: The department, 1965.
T1230

Tennessee, Division of Forestry The Horseshoe Properties Forest Management Demonstration. Nashville: The department, 1956.
T1240

Tennessee, Division of Geology Administrative Report of State Geological Survey, 1910-1923-1924. 7 vols. Bulletins, 4, 15, 18, 23, 25, 27, 35. Nashville: The division, 1911-25.
T1250 (ETSU)

Bulletin. no. 1-, 1910-. Nashville: The division, irregular.
T1260 (ETSU)

Geologic Maps and Mineral Resources Summary. Prepared in cooperation with the U. S. Geological Survey and Tennessee Valley Authority. Nashville: The division, 1962-.
T1270 (ETSU)

Geology and Barite Deposits of the Del Rio District, Cocke County, Tennessee. A real geology by Herman W. Ferguson. Economic geology by Willard Brownell Jewell. Bulletin, 57. Nashville: The department, 1951.
T1280 (ETSU)

Tennessee, Division of Mines Report on Mineral Resources of Tenn. Nashville: Rich Print. Co., annual.
T1290

Tennessee, Division of Water Resources Interagency Report on Water Resource Activities in Tennessee. Nashville: The department, 1962.
T1300

Tennessee, East Tennessee State College, Johnson City Curriculum Improvement Conference. Grades 1-12. July 15-29, 1954. Johnson City: The college, 1954.
T1310 (ETSU)

Instructional Leadership Conference, June 25-July 13, 1951. Johnson City: The college, 1951.
T1320 (ETSU)

Tennessee, East Tennessee State Normal School, Johnson City Curriculum for the Observation and Practice School. n.p.: State Board of Education, 1914.
T1330 (ETSU)

Tennessee, East Tennessee State University, Johnson City The Role and Scope of East Tennessee State University. A report submitted to the Tennessee Higher Education Commission, June, 1968. Johnson City: The univ., 1968.
T1350 (ETSU)

Tennessee, East Tennessee University, Johnson City Bulletin. vol. 1-, 1911-. Johnson City: The univ., annual.
T1340 (ETSU)

Tennessee Farm and Home Science. Progress Report no. 1-, 1952-. Knoxville: Univ. of Tennessee Agricultural Experiment Station, quarterly?
T1360 (ETSU)

Tennessee Federal Free Population Census, 1830 n.p.: n.p., n.d. A partial census of 24 East Tennessee counties.
T1370

Tennessee Folklore Society Bulletin. vol. 1-, 1935-. Maryville: The society, quarterly.
T1380 (ETSU)

Tennessee, Game and Fish Commission Amphibians and Reptiles of Tennessee. Nashville: State of Tennessee, 1965.
T1390 (ASU)

Tennessee General Assembly Joint Legislative Committee Report on the Great Smoky Mountains and Other Areas for a National or State Park. Nashville: State of Tennessee, 1925.
T1400

Tennessee, General Assembly, House of Representatives House Journal, 1861-62, of the First Session of the Thirty-Fourth General Assembly of the State of Tennessee, Which Convened at Nashville, on the First Monday in October, A. D. 1861, and Adjourned in Memphis, March 20, 1862. Preface by Robert Hiram White. Nashville: Tennessee Historical Commission, 1957.
T1410 (ASU)

Tennessee, General Assembly, Legislative Council Committee Migration and Industrial Development in Tennessee. Nashville: The committee, 1958.
T1420

Public Education in Tennessee, Grades 1-12: A Report to the Education Survey Subcommittee. Submitted Nov. 18, 1957, by James E. Gibbs, director of the study. Nashville: The committee, 1957.
T1430

Public Library Service Study: Final Report. Nashville: The committee, 1960.
T1440

Study on Automobile Junk Yard and Highway Beautification 1964; A Final Report. Nashville: The committee, 1964.
T1450

Study on the Coal Industry. Nashville: The committee, 1964.
T1460 (ASU)

Tennessee, Governor Messages of the Governors of Tennessee. By Robert Hiram White. Nashville: Tennessee Historical Commission, 1952.
T1470 (ASU)

Tennessee, Governor, 1796-1801 (Sevier) Commission Book, 1796-1801. Nashville: Tennessee Historical Commission, 1957. Records from one of Tennessee's earliest administration.
T1490 (ASU ETSU)

Tennessee, Governor (Clement) A Report to the President of the United States on the Tennessee Valley Authority, October 8, 1953. Nashville, Tenn.: n.p., 1953. Governor Clement's statement for former President Eisenhower dealt with the economic development of the Tennessee Valley as a result of the Tennessee Valley Authority. Particular emphasis was placed on the cooperation which exists between Tennessee Valley Authority and the state and local governments.
T1480

Tennessee, Historical Commission The Blount Journal, 1790-1796. Knoxville: Univ. of Tenn. Press, 1955.
T1500

Tenn. Historical Markers. Nashville: The commission, 1958.
T1510

Tennessee Old and New. Sesquicentennial. 1796-1946. Also sponsored by the Tennessee Historical Society. 2 vols. Kingsport, Tenn.: Kingsport Press, 1946.
T1520 (ASU LMC)

Tennessee, Historical Commission
Three Pioneer Tennessee Documents: Donelson's Journal, Cumberland Compact, Minutes of Cumberland Court. Nashville, Tenn.: The Tennessee Historical Commission, 1964.
T1530 (ASU)

Tennessee, Historical Society Landmarks of Tennessee History. Nashville: The society, 1965.
T1540

Tennessee, Labor Council Labor and TVA; Collective Bargaining Under Government Operation of a Public Utility and an Analysis of the Benefits to All the People of the Integrated Development of a River Basin. Nashville: The council, 1956.
T1560

Tennessee, Laws and Statues Private Acts of Anderson County, 1801-1956. Nashville: Tenn. General Assembly, 1956.
T1570

Tennessee Legislative Council Committee
Tennessee's Water Resources and Related Lands. Submitted August 22, 1962, by David H. Grubbs. Nashville: The committee, 1962.
T1580

Tennessee Libraries vol. 1-7, no. 2, June, 1931-September, 1947. Knoxville: Tennessee Library Assoc., n.d.
T1590 (ETSU)

Tennessee, Nat see **Winston, Nat Taylor**

Tennessee, Office of Urban and Federal Affairs, Appalachian Division Tennessee Appalachian Development Plan, 1969-1970. Report submitted to the Appalachian Regional Commission, and annual supplements. Nashville: The office, 1969.
T1600 (ASU)

Tennessee, Planning Commission Comprehensive Plan for Development: Kentucky Reservoir Region. Nashville: The commission, 1964.
T1610 (ETSU)

An Economic Survey of the Tri-Counties Region of Upper East Tennessee. Prepared by Bristol, Tennessee, Regional Planning Commission and others assisted by the Upper East Tennessee Office of the Tennessee State Planning Commission. Nashville: The commission, 1956.
T1620 (ETSU)

Flood Problems and Their Solution Through Urban Planning Programs. Publication no. 262. Nashville, Tenn.: The commission, 1955.
T1630

Local Planning in Tennessee, 1956-57. Publication no. 280. Nashville: The commission, 1957.
T1640

Melton Hill Reservoir, Comprehensive Plan for Land Use Development. Publication no. 310. Nashville: The commission, 1960.
T1650

A Plan for Development-Nicka Jack Reservoir Area. Also by Marion County Planning Commission in cooperation with Tennessee Valley Authority. Publication no. 335. Nashville: The commission, 1965.
T1660 (ASU LMC)

Policy Conclusions, Problems and Opportunities. Nashville: The commission, 1967.
T1670

Population, Labor Force, and Employment Projections and Interpretations. Nashville: The commission, 1967.
T1680

A Proposed Plan for Development: Sevier County, Tennessee. Nashville: n.p., 1964.
T1690

Reservoir Shore Line Development in Tennessee; a Study of Problems and Opportunities. Nashville: State of Tennessee, 1958.
T1700

Resource Inventory and Analysis of Tennessee Appalachia. Publication no. 355. Nashville: The commission, 1967.
T1710 (ETSU)

Tennessee Resources — Agriculture, Forestry, and Minerals. Nashville: The commission, 1967.
T1720 (ETSU)

The Tennessee River Gorge, Its Scenic Preservation; a Report to the 1961 General Assembly. State Planning Office Publication no. 311. Nashville: n.p., 1961.
T1730

Towers of Power Back Industrial Opportunities in Tennessee, First Public Power State. Nashville: State of Tennessee, 1944.
T1740

Tennessee, Planning Commission, Upper East Tennessee Office Historic District Plan: Jonesborough, Tennessee. Prepared for the Jonesboro Regional Planning Commission. Publication no. 395. Johnson City: The commission, 1972.
T1750

Tennessee, Planning Committee for the White House Conference on Children and Youth Tennessee's Children and Youth. A report to the Honorable Buford Ellington, Governor, State of Tennessee. Nashville: Tennessee Commission on Youth Guidance, 1960.
T1760 (ETSU)

Tennessee, Planning Office, Nashville Appalachian Regional Development Act, 1965-; Rationale and Model for Application in Tennessee. Nashville: State Planning Office, 1965.
T1770

Report on First Year's Activities in the Appalachian Development Program. Publication no. 4. Nashville: The office, 1966.
T1780 (LMC)

Tennessee Poetry Journal vol. 1-4, 1967-1971 Martin, Tenn.: n.p., 1967-1971.
T1790

Tennessee, Research and Statistics Division, Department of Employment Security Population and Labor Force Characteristics of Tennessee Counties. Nashville: The dept., 1963.
T1800

Tennessee, Secondary School Athletic Association Directory of Member Schools. Trenton, Tenn.: The assoc., 1963-.
T1810 (ETSU)

Tennessee, Secretary of State Tennessee Blue Book. Nashville: Secretary of State, annual.
T1820 (LMC)

Tennessee State Library and Archives Guide to the Use of Genealogical Materials in the Tenn. State Library and Archives. Nashville: The library, 1964.
T1830

"Inventory of Bledsoe County Records." Unpublished typescript. Nashville: State Library and Archives, 1964-.
T1840

"Inventory of Blount County Records." Unpublished typescript. Nashville: State Library and Archives, 1964.
T1850

"Inventory of Carter County Records." Unpublished typescript. Nashville: State Library and Archives, 1964.
T1860

"Inventory of Coffee County Records." Unpublished typescript. Nashville: State Library and Archives, 1964.
T1870

"Inventory of Cumberland County Records." Unpublished typescript. Nashville: State Library and Archives, 1964.
T1880

"Inventory of DeKalb County Records." Unpublished typescript. Nashville: State Library and Archives, 1964.
T1890

"Inventory of Franklin County Records." Unpublished typescript. Nashville: State Library and Archives, 1964.
T1900

"Inventory of Grundy County Records." Unpublished typescript. Nashville: State Library and Archives, 1964.
T1910

"Inventory of Loudon County Records." Unpublished typescript. Nashville: State Library and Archives, 1964.
T1920

"Inventory of McMinn County Records." Unpublished typescript. Nashville: State Library and Archives, 1964.
T1930

"Inventory of Marion County Records." Unpublished typescript. Nashville: State Library and Archives, 1964.
T1940

"Inventory of Meigs County Records." Unpublished typescript. Nashville: State Library and Archives, 1964.
T1950

"Inventory of Polk County Records." Unpublished typescript. Nashville: State Library and Archives, 1964.
T1960

"Inventory of Rhea County Records." Unpublished typescript. Nashville: State Library and Archives, 1964.
T1970

"Inventory of Roane County Records." Unpublished typescript. Nashville: State Library and Archives, 1964.
T1980

"Inventory of Sequatchie County Records." Unpublished typescript. Nashville: State Library and Archives, 1964.
T1990

"Inventory of Smith County Records." Unpublished typescript. Nashville: State Library and Archives, 1964.
T2000

"Inventory of Van Buren County Records." Unpublished typescript. Nashville: State Library and Archives, 1964.
T2010

"Inventory of Warren County Records." Unpublished typescript. Nashville: State Library and Archives, 1964.
T2020

"Inventory of Washington County Records." Unpublished typescript. Nashville: State Library and Archives, 1964.
T2030

"Inventory of White County Records." Unpublished typescript. Nashville: State Library and Archives, 1964.
T2040

A Study of the Community of La Follette, Tenn. Nashville: State of Tenn., 1957.
T2050

Tennessee State Library and Archives, Nashville, Manuscript Division Cherokee Collection. Registers, no. 11. Nashville: The library, 1966.
T2060 (LMC WCU ETSU)

Highlander Folk School Audio Collection. Nashville: The library, 1964.
T2070 (ETSU)

Highlander Folk School Manuscript Records Collection, 1932-1966. Registers, no. 9. Nashville: The library, 1968.
T2080 (LMC)

Tennessee, State University, Memphis, Bureau of Business and Economic Research Southeast Tennessee Region Profile and Policies. Project director: John W. Eilert. Research assistant: Sue Magargel. Prepared for the Tennessee State Planning Office. Memphis: The bureau, 1967.
T2090

The Lower Cumberland Region: A Study of Its Population, Economic Base and Potential. Project director: John W. Eilert. Research Assistants: Eugene Gregory and Sue Magargel. Prepared for the Tennessee State Planning Office. Memphis: The bureau, 1967.
T2100 (ETSU)

The Upper Cumberland Economy. Project director: John W. Eilert. Research assistants: Sue Magargel, Eugene Gregory, and Robert West. Prepared for the Tennessee State Planning Office. Memphis: The bureau, 1967.
T2110 (ETSU)

Tennessee, Stream Pollution Control Division Stream Pollution Control in the Upper Cumberland River Basin, 1964. Nashville: Stream Pollution Control Board, 1965.
T2120 (ETSU)

Tennessee, Taxpayers Association A Report of the Survey of the Finances and Management of Greene County, Tennessee. Nashville: The assoc., 1934.
T2130 (ETSU)

A Report of the Survey of the Finances and Management of the Government of Knox County, Tennessee. Prepared for the county court of Knox County. Nashville: The assoc., 1934.
T2140 (ETSU)

A Report of the Survey of the Finances and Management of the Government of Washington County, Tennessee. Prepared for the county court of Washington County. Nashville: The assoc., 1934.
T2150 (ETSU)

A Report of the Survey of the Management and Finances of the Government of Hamilton County. Nashville: The assoc., 1934.
T2160 (ETSU)

Tennessee, University The University of Tennessee Sesqui-Centennial, 1794-1944. Knoxville: The Univ. of Tennessee, 1945.
T2170 (ASU)

Tennessee, University, Agricultural Extension Service Building a Better Tennessee Through Rural Community Improvement. Publ. 321. By Almon J. Sims. Knoxville: Tennessee Agricultural Exp. Station, 1950.
T2180

Tennessee, University, Department of Geography A Geographical Analysis of Selected Ski Resorts in the Southeastern United States. Leland L. Nicholls, principal researcher. Knoxville: The univ., 1972.
T2190 (ASU)

Tennessee, University, Division of Extension East Tennessee University 1840-1879. Knoxville: Univ. of Tennessee, 1959.
T2200

Institute of Regional Development of the Southeast. Knoxville: Univ. of Tenn., Division of Extension, 1949.
T2210

One River, Seven States. By Elliott Roberts. Knoxville: Univ. of Tenn., Division of Extension, 1949.
T2220

Valley of Tomorrow, the TVA and Agriculture. Knoxville: Univ. of Tenn., 1952.
T2230

Tennessee, University, Library University of Tennessee Library Lectures. no. 1-, 1949-. Knoxville: Univ. of Tennessee, Division of Univ. Extension, irregular.
T2240 (ASU)

TVA Annual Report. 1935-. Washington: Govt. Print. Off., annual.
T2250 (ASU WCU LMC BC)

Annual Report of the Distributors of TVA Power, 1937-Date. Chattanooga: Tennessee Valley Authority, 1937.
T2260

An Appraisal of Coal Strip Mining. Knoxville: Tennessee Valley Authority, February 1963.
T2270 (BC)

Articles of Agreement Between the Tennessee Valley Authority and the Salary Policy Employee Panel. Negotiated December 5, 1950. Reprinted with Revisions through May 1, 1952 and, February 4, 1955. n.p.: Tennessee Valley Authority, 1958.
T2280

Articles of Agreement . . . Negotiated December 5, 1950. Revisions Through February 4, 1955. Knoxville: Tennessee Valley Authority, 1955.
T2290

Atlas Finding List of the Tennessee Valley Region. The Tennessee Valley Area and Adjacent Districts in Alabama, Arkansas, Georgia, Illinois, Kentucky, Mississippi, Missouri, North Carolina, South Carolina, Tennessee, Virginia and West Virginia. Knoxville: Tennessee Valley Authority, 1968.
T2300

Atlas of the Tennessee Valley Region. pt. 1. Knoxville: Tennessee Valley Authority, 1936.
T2310

Basic Data on TVA and Its Revenue Bond Financing. Knoxville: Tennessee Valley Authority, 1960.
T2320 (ASU)

Bear Creek Watershed, Summary of Resources. Knoxville: Tennessee Valley Authority, 1962.
T2330

A Bibliography for the TVA Program. Knoxville: Tennessee Valley Authority, Technical Library, 1963.
T2340 (ASU BC LMC)

A Bibliography for the TVA Program. Knoxville: Technical Library, Tennessee Valley Authority, 1964.
T2350 (ASU)

A Bibliography for the TVA Program. Knoxville: Technical Library, Tennessee Valley Authority, 1968.
T2360 (LMC)

The Bull Run Steam Plant; a Report on the Planning, Design, Construction, Costs, and First Power Operations of the Initial One-Unit Plant. Knoxville: Tennessee Valley Authority, 1967.
T2370

Chattanooga Flood Control Problem. 76th Congress, House Document no. 91. Washington: Govt. Print. Off., 1939.
T2380

. . . Chemical Engineering Report, no. 1. Wilson Dam, Ala.: Tennessee Valley Authority, 1942.
T2390

The Cherokee Project, a Comprehensive Report on the Planning, Design, Construction, and Initial Operations of the Cherokee Project. Washington: Govt. Print. Off., 1946.
T2400

. . . The Chickamauga Project, a Comprehensive Report on the Planning, Design, Construction, and Initial Operations of the Chickamauga Project. . . . Knoxville: Tennessee Valley Authority, 1942.
T2410

Clinch-Powell Valley; Summary of Resources. Knoxville: Tennessee Valley Authority, 1963.
T2420

Coal Reserves in Portions of Butler, Edmonson, Grayson, Muhlenberg, Ohio, and Warren Counties, Kentucky. Lexington: College of Arts and Sciences, Univ. of Kentucky, 1963.
T2430

The Colbert Steam Plant; a Report on the Planning, Design, Construction, Costs, and First Power Operations of the Initial Four-Unit Plant. Knoxville: Tennessee Valley Authority, 1963.
T2440

Comparison of Coal-Fired and Nuclear Power Plants for the TVA System. Chattanooga: Tennessee Valley Authority, 1966.
T2450

. . . A Compilation of the More Important Congressional Acts, Treaties, Presidential Messages, Judicial Decisions, and Official Reports and Documents Having to do with the Control Conservation, and Utilization of Water Resources. Prepared by Francis W. Laurent. Knoxville: Tennessee Valley Authority, 1938.
T2460

. . . Communication from Tennessee Valley Authority. Message from the President of the United States, transmitting a copy of a communication from the Tennessee Valley Authority. . . . Washington: Govt. Print. Off., 1934.
T2470

Concrete Production and Control, Tennessee Valley Authority Projects. Washington: Govt. Print. Off., 1947.
T2480

The Cost of Distributing Power, Knoxville, Tennessee. A report on the first year of operation with Tennessee Valley Authority rates. Knoxville: Tennessee Valley Authority, 1939.
T2490

. . . County Government and Administration in the Tennessee Valley States. Issued by Tennessee Valley Authority, Knoxville, Tenn., July 1940. Washington: Govt. Print. Off., 1940.
T2500

Design of TVA Projects. Washington: Govt. Print. Off., 1952.
T2510

Development of the Tennessee Valley. Knoxville: Tennessee Valley Authority, 1935.
T2520

The Development of the Tennessee Valley. Washington: Govt. Print. Off., 1936.
T2530

The Douglas Project; a Comprehensive Report on the Planning, Design, Construction, and Initial Operations of the Douglas Project. Washington: Govt. Print. Off., 1949.
T2540

. . . Drawings for the Chickamauga Project. . . . Knoxville: Tennessee Valley Authority, 1941.
T2550

. . . Drawings for the Guntersville Project. . . . Knoxville: Tennessee Valley Authority, 1940.
T2560

Economic Development of the Upper French Broad Area by North Carolina State and the Tennessee Valley Authority. Knoxville? Tenn.: Tennessee Valley Authority, 1964.
T2570 (LMC)

Electrical Demonstration Branch Electricity in Dairying. Chattanooga: Tennessee Valley Authority, n.d.
T2580

Elk River Watershed; Summary of Resources. Knoxville: Tennessee Valley Authority, 1962.
T2590

Engineering Geology and Mineral Resources of the Tennessee Valley Authority Region. By E. C. Eckel. Geologic Bulletin no. 1. Knoxville: Tennessee Valley Authority, 1934.
T2600

. . . Engineering Geology of the Tennessee River System. . . . Knoxville: Tennessee Valley Authority, 1940.
T2610

Evaluation of Forestry Opportunities on Farms in the Beech River Watershed. By Tennessee Valley Authority in cooperation with the Univ. of Tennessee, June, 1965. Norris, Tenn.: Tennessee Valley Authority, 1965.
T2620

Extent of Recreation Development and Use of TVA Lakes and Actual Lake Frontage Property. Knoxville: Tennessee Valley Authority, 1947. Contains tabulations showing kinds and extent of recreation development and use reservoir and accumulated totals from 1947 to date.
T2630

Facts About Major TVA Dams. Knoxville: Tennessee Valley Authority, 1962.
T2640

Facts About TVA Operations. Knoxville: Tennessee Valley Authority, 1956.
T2650

Facts About TVA Operations. Knoxville, Tenn.: Tennessee Valley Authority, 1964.
T2660

Facts About TVA Steam Plants. Knoxville: Tennessee Valley Authority, 1963.
T2670

Fertilizer Science and the American Farmer — the Research and Education Programs of the Tennessee Valley Authority. Knoxville: Tennessee Valley Authority, 1957.
T2680

Fertilizer Science and the American Farmer — the Research and Education Programs of the Tennessee Valley Authority. Knoxville: Tennessee Valley Authority, 1964.
T2690

Fifty Inches of Rain. A Story of Land and Water Conservation. Washington: Govt. Print. Off., 1939.
T2700 (BC)

. . . Financial Statements. . . . Report of the comptroller to the Board of directors. Knoxville: Tennessee Valley Authority, 1940.
T2710

TVA

Fish and Fishing, Fort Loudoun Reservoir. Unpublished Folder. Norris: Tennessee Valley Authority, 1962.
T2720

Flood Problems and Management in the Tennessee River Basin. Washington: Govt. Print. Off., 1960.
T2730

Floods and Flood Control. Knoxville, Tenn.: Tennessee Valley Authority, 1964.
T2740

Floods on the Tuckaseigee River and Deep Creek in Vicinity of Bryson City, North Carolina. Knoxville: Tennessee Valley Authority, 1960.
T2750

Floods on Watauga and Doe Rivers in Vicinity of Elizabethton, Tennessee. Knoxville: Tennessee Valley Authority, 1957.
T2760

The Fontana Project: A Comprehensive Report on the Planning, Design, Construction, and Initial Operations of the Fontana Project. Technical Report, no. 12. Washington, D. C.: Govt. Print. Off., 1950.
T2770 (WCU)

Forest Inventory Statistics for Buncombe County, North Carolina. Norris, Tenn.: Tennessee Valley Authority, 1956.
T2780

Forest Products Industry Notes, no. 1. Norris: Tennessee Valley Authority Division of Forestry Relations, annual.
T2790 (BC)

Forests and Human Welfare. Washington: Govt. Print. Off., 1940.
T2800

Forestry Bulletin, no. 1. Mimeographed. Norris, Tenn.: n.p., 1937.
T2810 (BC)

The Fort Loudoun Project; a Comprehensive Report on the Planning, Design, Construction, and Initial Operations of the Fort Loudoun Project. Washington: Govt. Print. Off., 1949.
T2820

General Agreement Between the Tennessee Valley Authority and the Tennessee Valley Trades and Labor Council. Chattanooga: Adams Litho, 1957.
T2830

General Outline of Chemical Engineering Activities. 2nd rev. ed. Muscle Shoals, Ala.: Tennessee Valley Authority, 1965.
T2840

Geology and Foundation Treatment, Tennessee Valley Authority Projects. Technical Report, no. 22. Washington: Govt. Print. Off., 1949.
T2850 (ETSU)

The Guntersville Project. A Comprehensive Report on the Planning, Design, Construction, and Initial Operations of the Guntersville Project . . . Knoxville: Tennessee Valley Authority, 1941. Includes bibliographies.
T2860 (BC)

A History of Navigation of the Tennessee River System; an Interpretation of the Economic Influence of this River System on the Tennessee Valley. Message From the President of the United States Transmitting a Survey Entitled "A History of Navigation on the Tennessee River and Its Tributaries." (75th Cong., 1st sess. House Doc. 254.) Washington: Govt. Print. Off., 1937.
T2870 (BC ASU)

The Hiwassee Valley Projects. Washington: Govt. Print. Off., 1946-48.
T2880

How Cheap Electricity Pays Its Way. TVA. Washington: Govt. Print. Off., 1938.
T2890

. . . Hydraulic Data Activities of the Tennessee Valley Authority . . . Knoxville, Tenn.: Tennessee Valley Authority, 1939.
T2900

Hydrology of Small Watersheds in Relation to Various Crop Covers and Soil Characteristics. A Pictorial Brochure. Cooperative Research Project in Western North Carolina. Knoxville, Tenn.: Tennessee Valley Authority, 1960.
T2910

Industrial Development in the TVA Area During 1965. Knoxville: Tennessee Valley Authority, 1966.
T2920

Initial Forest Management in the Tennessee Valley. By Kenneth J. Seigworth chief, Forest Development Branch and James H. Barton forester. Chicago: Tennessee Valley Authority, 1961.
T2930

. . . Injunctions in Cases Involving Acts of Congress. Letter from the Chairman of the Tennessee Valley Authority Transmitting, in Response to Senate Resolution no. 82, Certain Information Concerning Injunctions or Judgments Issued or Rendered by Federal Courts Since March 4, 1933, in Cases Involving Acts of Congress. . . . Washington: Govt. Print. Off., 1937.
T2940

Interterritorial Freight Rate Problem of the United States. (75th Congress, House Document no. 264.) Washington: Govt. Print. Off., 1937. The problem of discriminatory freight rates affecting the South is discussed, and possible solutions are suggested. Two additional Tennessee Valley Authority studies have been made of this problem.
T2950

. . . Investment of the Tennessee Valley Authority in Wilson, Norris, and Wheeler Projects. Letter from the Chairman of the Board of the Tennessee Valley Authority Transmitting a Report on the Investment and the Allocation of the Investment of the Authority in the Wilson, Norris, and Wheeler-Projects, Pursuant to Section 14 of the Tennessee Valley Authority Act of 1933 . . . Washington: Govt. Print. Off., 1938.
T2960

Is the Tennessee Valley Favored in Federal Expenditures? Prepared by Government Relations and Economics Staff. Knoxville: Tennessee Valley Authority, 1955.
T2970 (BC)

The Johnsonville Steam Plant; a Comprehensive Report on the Planning, Design, Construction, Costs, and First Power Operations of the Initial Six-Unit Plant. Knoxville: Tennessee Valley Authority, 1959.
T2980

The Kentucky Project; a Comprehensive Report on the Planning, Design, Construction and Initial Operations of the Kentucky Project. Washington: Govt. Print. Off., 1951.
T2990

Knoxville and Vicinity, Tennessee. 1953. Washington: U. S. Geological Survey, 1956.
T3000

The Land Between the Lakes; A Demonstration in Recreation Resource Development; Revised Concept Statement. Knoxville: Tennessee Valley Authority, 1964.
T3010

Lower Hiwassee Valley; Summary of Resources. Knoxville: Tennessee Valley Authority, 1963.
T3020

Management Services Report. no. 1-. n.p.: n.p., 1942.
T3030

The Melton Hill Project; a Report on the Planning, Design, Construction, Initial Operations, and Costs. Knoxville: Tennessee Valley Authority, 1966.
T3040

Municipal and Cooperative Distributors of TVA Power; Annual Report. Knoxville: Tennessee Valley Authority, annual.
T3050

Municipalities (Electric Departments Only) and Cooperatives Purchasing Power from Tennessee Valley Authority. Financial Statements for the Fiscal Year Ended June 30, 1940; a Report from the Comptroller to the Directors of Tennessee Valley Authority. Knoxville: Tennessee Valley Authority, 1940.
T3060

Nature's Constant Gift, a Report on the Water Resource of the Tennessee Valley. Knoxville: Tennessee Valley Authority, 1963.
T3070 (BC ASU)

Nature's Constant Gift; a Report on the Water Resource of the Tennessee Valley. Knoxville: Tennessee Valley Authority, 1963.
T3080

Nature's Constant Gift; a Report on the Water Resource of the Tennessee Valley. Knoxville: Tennessee Valley Authority, 6.
T3090

Navigation and Economic Growth: Tennessee River Experience; a Report. Knoxville: Tennessee Valley Authority, 1966.
T3100

Non-Urban Outdoor Recreation, an Analysis of Its Functions, Forms, and Types of Areas. Knoxville: Tennessee Valley Authority, Division of Land Planning and Housing, Recreation and Conservation Section, 1935.
T3110

Norris Dam . . . Washington: Govt. Print. Off., 1936.
T3120

. . . The Norris Project, A Comprehensive Report on the Planning, Design, Construction, and Initial Operations of the Tennessee Valley Authority's First Water Control Project . . . Washington: Govt. Print. Off., 1940.
T3130

Operation of TVA Reservoirs, Annual 1963. Knoxville, Tenn.: Tennessee Valley Authority, 1964.
T3140

Outdoor Recreation for a Growing Nation; TVA's Experience With Man-Made Reservoirs. Knoxville: Tennessee Valley Authority, 1961.
T3150

The Paradise Steam Plant; a Report on the Planning, Design, Construction, Costs, and First Power Operations of the Initial Two-Unit Plant. Knoxville: Tennessee Valley Authority, 1964.
T3160

Parker Branch; an Experiment in Appalachian Agriculture, 1953-1962. n.p.: Tennessee Valley Authority and North Carolina State of the Univ. of North Carolina at Raleigh, 1964.
T3170

Parker Branch Research Watershed; Project Report, 1953-1962. Knoxville: Tennessee Valley Authority, 1963.
T3180

Personnel Administration in TVA; the Experience of 14 Years. Knoxville: Tennessee Valley Authority, 1947.
T3190

Pickwick Landing Dam on the Tennessee River. Tennessee Valley Authority, Engineering and Construction Departments. n.p.: Tennessee Valley Authority, 1935.
T3200

. . . The Pickwick Landing Project, a Comprehensive Report on the Planning, Design, Construction, and Initial Operations of the Pickwick Landing Project . . . Washington: Govt. Print. Off., 1941.
T3210

. . . Plant Nutrient Losses in the Tennessee River System. Knoxville: Tennessee Valley Authority, 1943.
T3220

Plant Trees — Grow Jobs; Reforest 7 States in 7 Years. Knoxville, Tenn.: Tennessee Valley Authority, 1962.
T3230 (ASU)

Power Annual Report. 1960-. Knoxville: Tennessee Valley Authority, 1960-.
T3240

TVA

Preliminary Report: Floods on Scott Creek in Vicinity of Sylva, North Carolina. Knoxville: Tennessee Valley Authority, 1966.
T3250

Profile of a Region; Some Characteristics and General Trends, Tennessee Valley States. n.p.: Tennessee Valley Authority, Government Relations and Economics Staff, 1958.
T3260

A Program for Reducing the National Flood Damage Potential. Knoxville: Tennessee Valley Authority, 1958.
T3270

Program for Reducing the National Flood Damage Potential. Committee on Public Works, United States Senate. Washington: Govt. Print. Off., 1959.
T3280

Progress in Seven States. TVA Now. Washington: Govt. Print. Off., 1944.
T3290

Progress in the Valley, TVA, 1947. Washington: Govt. Print. Off., 1947.
T3300

A Quality Environment in the Tennessee Valley. Knoxville: Tennessee Valley Authority, 1969.
T3310

Recreation Areas on TVA Lakes. Knoxville: Tennessee Valley Authority, 1954.
T3320

Recreation Areas on TVA Lakes. n.p.: Tennessee Valley Authority, 1966.
T3330

. . . Recreation Development of the Tennessee River System. Knoxville: Tennessee Valley Authority, 1940.
T3340

Recreational Development of the Southern Highlands Region, A Study of the Use and Control of Scenic and Recreational Resources. Tennessee Valley Authority. Department of Regional Planning Studies, 1938. Knoxville: Tennessee Valley Authority, 1938.
T3350 (ASU)

. . . Regionalized Freight Rates: Barrier to National Productiveness. Message from the President of the United States, Transmitting a Report of the Tennessee Valley Authority Entitled "Regionalized Freight Rates: Barrier to National Productiveness". . . Washington: Govt. Print. Off., 1943.
T3360

Report. Knoxville: Tennessee Valley Authority, annual.
T3370

. . . Report on the Physiographic, Economic, and Other Relationships Between the Tennessee and Cumberland Rivers and Between Their Drainage Areas. Message from the President of the United States, Transmitting Report Entitled "The Physiographic, Economic, and Other Relationships Between the Tennessee and Cumberland Rivers and Between Their Drainage Areas" . . . Washington: Govt. Print. Off., 1945.
T3380

Report on Scientific Research Projects. Knoxville, Tenn.: Tennessee Valley Authority, n.d.
T3390

Report to the Congress on the Unified Development of the Tennessee River System. Knoxville: The authority, 1936.
T3400 (ASU)

Report to the Nation from the Tennessee Valley Authority on Its First Twenty-Five Years. Knoxville: Tennessee Valley Authority, 1958.
T3410

River Traffic and Industrial Growth. Knoxville: Tennessee Valley Authority, 1954.
T3420

River Traffic and Industrial Growth. Knoxville: Tennessee Valley Authority, 1959.
T3430

River Traffic and Industrial Growth. Knoxville: Tennessee Valley Authority, 1963.
T3440

River Traffic and Industrial Growth. Knoxville: Tennessee Valley Authority, 1964.
T3450

The Scenic Resources of the Tennessee Valley. A descriptive and pictorial inventory. Department of Regional Studies, Knoxville, Tennessee. Washington: Govt. Print. Off., 1938.
T3460 (ASU LMC FC)

Sequatchie Valley; Summary of Resources. Knoxville: Tennessee Valley Authority, 1963.
T3470

Short History of the Tennessee Valley Authority, 1933-1963. Knoxville: Tennessee Valley Authority, 1964.
T3480

Soil . . . People, and Fertilizer Technology. Washington: Govt. Print. Off., 1959.
T3490

Southwest Virginia: Lee, Scott, Wise Counties, Summary of Resources. Knoxville, Tenn.: Tennessee Valley Authority, 1964.
T3500 (ASU BC)

Southwest Virginia, Lee, Scott, Wise Counties; Summary of Resources. Knoxville: Tennessee Valley Authority, 1964.
T3510

. . . Statistical Bulletin no. 1-. Chattanooga, Tenn.: Tennessee Valley Authority, 1934.
T3520

A Study of Methods Used in Measurement and Analysis of Sediment Loads in Streams. Planned and Conducted Jointly by Tennessee Valley Authority, Corps of Engineers, Department of Agriculture, Geological Survey, Bureau of Reclamation, Indian Service, and Iowa Institute of Hydraulic Research. Report no. 1-. Iowa City, Iowa.: St. Paul Engineer District sub-office, Hydraulic laboratory, Univ. of Iowa, 1940.
T3530

A Study of Methods Used in Measurement and Analysis of Sediment Loads in Streams, Planned and Conducted Jointly by Tennessee Valley Authority. Report D, progress report: comparative field tests on suspended-sediment samplers as of January 1946. Minneapolis: Project Offices of Cooperating Agencies, 1957.
T3540

Summary of Resources. Knoxville: Tennessee Valley Authority, 1965.
T3550

Summary of Resources Tributary Area Development Program. Knoxville, Tenn.: Tennessee Valley Authority, 1964.
T3560

Survey of Electrical Appliances in the Homes and Farms of the TVA Area. Chattanooga, Tenn.: Tennessee Valley Authority, 1955.
T3570

Surveying, Mapping and Related Engineering. Washington: Govt. Print. Off., 1951.
T3580

Systematic Farm Planning in Relation to Water Resources at Parker Branch Pilot Tributary Watershed. Knoxville, Tenn.: North Carolina State College in cooperation with the Tennessee Valley Authority, 1956.
T3590

. . . Technical Report no. 1. Washington: Govt. Print. Off., 1940.
T3600

. . . A Technical Review of the Chickamauga Project . . . St. Louis: John S. Swift Co., Inc., 1940.
T3610

. . . A Technical Review of the Guntersville Project. Knoxville: Tennessee Valley Authority, 1939.
T3620

. . . A Technical Review of the Hiwassee Project . . . Knoxville: Tennessee Valley Authority, 1940.
T3630

. . . A Technical Review of the Norris Project. Knoxville: Tennessee Valley Authority, 1937.
T3640

. . . A Technical Review of the Pickwick Landing Project . . . Knoxville: Tennessee Valley Authority, 1939.
T3650

. . . A Technical Review of the Wheeler Project. Knoxville: Tennessee Valley Authority, 1938.
T3660

The Tellico Project of the TVA. Knoxville: Tennessee Valley Authority, 1965, 1966.
T3670

Tennessee River History. Knoxville, Tenn.: Tennessee Valley Authority, 1963. Based on the paper "Development of the Tennessee River Waterway," by C. E. Blee, before the American Society of Civil Engineers centennial meeting in Chicago, Illinois, September 12, 1952.
T3680

Tennessee River Navigation. Knoxville, Tenn.: Tennessee Valley Authority, June, 1953.
T3690

The Tennessee River Navigation System; History, Development, and Operation. Knoxville: Tennessee Valley Authority, 1964.
T3700

The Tennessee River Waterway. (a multiple-purpose project) Knoxville: Tennessee Valley Authority, 1963.
T3710

The Tennessee Valley Authority. Washington: Govt. Print. Off., 1934.
T3720

Tennessee Valley Authority. Washington: Govt. Print. Off., 1940. Annual reports, with varying titles, of Tennessee Valley Authority to Congress.
T3730

Tennessee Valley Authority, 1933-1937. Washington: Govt. Print. Off., 1937.
T3740

TVA and the River. Knoxville, Tenn.: Tennessee Valley Authority, 1962. Based on an address by LeRoy Engstrom at a joint meeting of the Engineers Club of Western North Carolina and Greenville Section of A.S.M.E., in Asheville, North Carolina, on November 19, 1951. Data revised and brought up to date in March 1962.
T3750

TVA Dams; the Twenty Major Dams Built by the Tennessee Valley Authority and Wilson Dam. Prepared for the Sixth International Congress of the International Commission on Large Dams. Knoxville, Tenn.: n.p., 1958.
T3760

TVA Electricity Rates, A Statement of Facts. Washington: Govt. Print. Off., 1935.
T3770

Tennessee Valley Authority Facts Book; Norris, Wheeler and Wilson Projects . . . n.p.: n.p., 1934.
T3780

TVA: The First Twenty Years. A Staff Report. Univ. of Alabama Press, 1956.
T3790 (ASU WCU LMC)

TVA: The First Twenty Years; A Staff Report. Univ., Ala.: Univ. of Alabama Press, 1956.
T3800 (UNCA)

TVA Flood Control. Revised. Knoxville?: n.p., 1960.
T3810

TVA Flood Control; New Concepts. Knoxville, Tenn.: Tennessee Valley Authority, 1963.
T3820

TVA's Influence on Electric Rates. Knoxville: Tennessee Valley Authority, 1965.
T3830

TVA — a National Asset. Knoxville, Tenn.: Tennessee Valley Authority, 1958.
T3840

TVA Power, 1966. Knoxville: Tennessee Valley Authority, 1966.
T3850

TVA Power — 1963/64. Chattanooga, Tenn.: Tennessee Valley Authority, 1964.
T3860

TVA; A River Controlled. Washington: Govt. Print. Off., 1958.
T3870

TVA River Traffic and Industrial Growth. Rev. ed. Knoxville: Tennessee Valley Authority, 1963.
T3880

TVA Tames the River. Knoxville: Tennessee Valley Authority, 1964.
T3890

TVA

TVA Today, 1965. Knoxville, Tenn.: Tennessee Valley Authority, 1965.
T3900

TVA 25th Anniversary; Progress Thru Resource Development, A Report to the Nation from the Tennessee Valley Authority on Its First Twenty-Five Years, 1933-1958. n.p.: n.p., 1958.
T3910

TVA, Its Work and Accomplishments. Washington: Govt. Print. Off., 1940.
T3920

TVA, The Valley of Light, 1933-1963. Washington: Govt. Print. Off., 1964. "Contains the principle text of the Tennessee Valley Authority's Annual Report to the President and the Congress . . . 1963."
T3930

TVA's Coal-Buying Program. Knoxville, Tenn.: Tennessee Valley Authority, April 11, 1956.
T3940

TVA's Influence on Electric Rates. Knoxville, Tenn.: Tennessee Valley Authority, 1959.
T3950

General Agreement . . . and Supplementary Schedules. Negotiated August 6, 1940, Revised 1961-62. Knoxville, Tenn.: Tennessee Valley Authority, 1940, 1961-62. One volume covers annual employment and one volume covers hourly employment.
T3960

Tennessee Valley Authority Act, May 18, 1933 with Amendments. Washington: Govt. Print. Off., 1959.
T3961

The Tennessee Valley Region; Population Changes, 1950-1955. n.p.: Tennessee Valley Authority, Government Relations and Economics Staff, 1956.
T3970

Tennessee Valley Resources; Their Development and Use. Knoxville: Tennessee Valley Authority, 1947.
T3980

To Keep the Water in the Rivers and the Soil on the Land . . . Washington: Govt. Print. Off., 1938.
T3990

Tributary Area Development Activities; Selected List of Reports and Publications. 1963. Knoxville, Tenn.: Tennessee Valley Authority, 1963.
T4000

Tributary Area Development in the Tennessee Valley. Knoxville, Tenn.: Tennessee Valley Authority, April 1963.
T4010

Upper Duck River Valley; Summary of Resources. Knoxville, Tenn.: Tennessee Valley Authority, 1965. This volume incorporates information gathered by the Upper Duck River Development Association.
T4020

Upper Hiwassee Valley: Summary of Resources. Knoxville, Tenn.: Tennessee Valley Authority, 1965. Based on information gathered by the Upper Hiwassee Watershed Development Association.
T4030

The Upper Holston Projects: Watauga, South Holston, Boone, and Fort Patrick Henry; a Comprehensive Report on the Planning, Design, Construction, Initial Operations, and Costs of Four Hydro Projects in the Holston Basin at the Eastern Tip of Tennessee. Improvement of the minor Wilbur project . . included as an appendix. Washington: Govt. Print. Off., 1958.
T4040

The Valley is Paying off, TVA 1949. Washington: Govt. Print. Off., 1949.
T4050

Valley With a Future, TVA in the Sixties. Knoxville, Tenn.: Tennessee Valley Authority, 1962.
T4060

. . . Value of Flood Height Reduction from TVA Reservoirs to the Alluvial Valley of the Lower Mississippi River . . . Washington: Govt. Print. Off., 1939.
T4070

The Watts Bar Steam Plant; a Comprehensive Report on the Planning, Design, Construction, and Initial Operation of the Watts Bar Steam Plant. Washington: Govt. Print. Off., 1949.
T4080

. . . The Wheeler Project, A Comprehensive Report on the Planning, Design, Construction, and Initial Operations of the Wheeler Project . . . Washington: Govt. Print. Off., 1940.
T4090

Working With Areas of Special Need, With Examples From the Beech River Watershed. n.p.: n.p., 1953.
T4100

Working with Areas of Special Need, with Examples from the Beech River Watershed. Knoxville, Tenn.: Tennessee Valley Authority, 1955.
T4110

Working with TVA. Knoxville: n.p., 1952.
T4120

The Yellow Creek Port Project. Knoxville: Tennessee Valley Authority, 1968.
T4130

Agricultural Economics Branch Census of Agriculture for the 125 Tennessee Valley Watershed Counties. Computed from state census reports. Wilson Dam, Ala.: Tennessee Valley Authority, 1963.
T4140

Central Joint Cooperative Committee Teamwork: the Cooperative Program of the Tennessee Valley Trades and Labor Council and the Tennessee Valley Authority. Knoxville: Tennessee Valley Authority, 1960.
T4150

Central Joint Cooperative Conference Goals of the Cooperative Program. By L. J. Van Mol, E. A. Shelley, A. R. Carson, and W. G. Clark. Knoxville: Tennessee Valley Authority, 1961. These addresses were presented at the 12th Annual Valley-wide Meeting of Union-Management Cooperative Conferences, Gatlinburg, Tennessee, April 13-14, 1961.
T4160

Commerce Dept. Cheaper Transportation via the Tennessee River. By the Commerce Dept., River Transportation Division. Knoxville: Tennessee Valley Authority, Commerce Dept., 1946.
T4170

Commerce Series. Knoxville: Tennessee Valley Authority, 1942.
T4180

Electric Poultry Equipment for the Farm. Prepared by D. E. Washburn, assistant agricultural engineer. Knoxville: Agricultural Engineering Development Division, Commerce Dept., Tennessee Valley Authority, 1942.
T4190

. . . The Initial Phase of Public-Use Terminal Development at Chattanooga, Tennessee. Prepared by C. T. Barker, Chief, River Transportation Division, and A. D. Spottswood, Chief, Transportation and Industrial Economics Division. Knoxville: Tennessee Valley Authority, Commerce Dept., 1940.
T4200

Pumps and Plumbing for the Farmstead. Prepared by G. E. Henderson, Associate Agricultural Engineer in cooperation with Jane A. Roberts, Associate Specialist in Home Electrification. Illustrator, L. H. Poole. Agricultural Engineering Development Division, Commerce Dept., Tennessee Valley Authority, Nov. 1940. Washington: Govt. Print. Off., 1948.
T4210

Report. Knoxville: Tennessee Valley Authority, The Dept., annual.
T4220

Rural Electrification; Lessons for Boys' Groups. Prepared by D. E. Washburn . . . Illustrator, L. H. Poole . . . Knoxville: Agricultural Engineering Development Division, Commerce Dept., Tennessee Valley Authority, 1941.
T4230

. . . Supplemental Phases of the Interterritorial Freight Rate Problem of the United States. Message from the President of the United States. Tennessee Valley Authority, Commerce department, J. Haden Allredge, director. Transportation and industrial economics division, John H. Goff, chief. Knoxville: Tennessee Valley Authority, 1939.
T4240

Comptroller Financial Statements for the Fiscal Years Ended June 20, 1938-Date. Knoxville: Tennessee Valley Authority, annual.
T4250

Municipalities (Electric Departments Only) and Cooperatives, Purchasing Power from Tennessee Valley Authority. Financial Statements for the Fiscal Years Ended June 30, 1938-Date. Knoxville: Tennessee Valley Authority, annual.
T4260

Dept. of Electricity . . . Statistical Bulletin no. 1. Chattanooga: Tennessee Valley Authority, 1934.
T4270

Dept. of Regional Planning Studies County Government and Administration in the Tennessee Valley States. Issued by Tennessee Valley Authority, Knoxville, Tennessee, July 1940. Washington: Govt. Print. Off., 1940.
T4280

Recreational Development of the Southern Highlands Region; A Study of the Use and Control of Scenic and Recreational Resources. Knoxville: Tennessee Valley Authority, 1938.
T4290 (LMC)

Report of the Project on Research in Agriculture and Industrial Development in the Tennessee Valley Region. Knoxville: Tennessee Valley Authority, n.d.
T4300

The Scenic Resources of the Tennessee Valley; A Descriptive and Pictorial Inventory. Prepared by the Tennessee Valley Authority, Department of Regional Planning Studies, Knoxville, Tennessee. Washington: Govt. Print. Off., 1938.
T4310

TVA Demountable Houses for Defense Workers; a Report. Knoxville: Tennessee Valley Authority, 1941.
T4320

Dept. of Regional Planning, Social and Economic Research Division Social and Economic Characteristics of Six Tennessee Valley Reservoir Areas. Knoxville: Tennessee Valley Authority, 1940.
T4330 (BC)

Division of Agricultural Development Fertilizer Trends. Wilson Dam, Ala.: Tennessee Valley Authority, Division of Agricultural Development, 1962.
T4340

Southern Bulk Blending Conference, Jan. 21-23, 1963. Knoxville: Tennessee Valley Authority, 1963.
T4350

Division of Agricultural Relations Bulk-Blending — An Innovation in Fertilizer Marketing. Knoxville: Tennessee Valley Authority, 1958.
T4360

Changing Agriculture of the Tennessee Valley. Research in Agricultural Development in the Tennessee Valley Region, Report no. 3. Knoxville, Tenn.: Tennessee Valley Authority, 1954.
T4370

Do Fertilizer Education and Services Pay? By John R. Douglas, Jr. Knoxville: Tennessee Valley Authority, 1956.
T4380

Fertilizer Summary Data. Knoxville: Tennessee Valley Authority, The Division, 1958.
T4390

Fertilizer Summary Data. Knoxville: Tennessee Valley Authority, 1959.
T4400

Division of Agricultural Relations
Fertilizer, One Key to Better Land Use. Summary of Distributor Demonstration Program for TVA Fertilizers, Fiscal Year 1955. Knoxville: Tennessee Valley Authority, Division of Agricultural Relations, 1957.
T4410
Fertilizer Trends. Wilson Dam, Ala.: Division of Agricultural Development, Tennessee Valley Authority, 1962.
T4420
Fertilizer Trends; the Scope of TVA's Fertilizer Activities. Prepared by John N. Mahan, Fred D. Lyon and John R. Douglas, Jr. Knoxville: Tennessee Valley Authority, The Division, 1956.
T4430
Fertilizer Trends; the Scope of TVA's Fertilizer Activities. Knoxville: Tennessee Valley Authority, The division, 1958.
T4440
Fertilizer Trends; the Scope of TVA's Fertilizer Activities. Prepared by John R. Douglas and others. Rev. ed. Knoxville: Tennessee Valley Authority, The division, 1960.
T4450
Food at the Grass Roots; the Nation's Stake in Soil Minerals. Knoxville: Tennessee Valley Authority, 1947.
T4460
Income Levels in the Upper Tennessee Valley: A Comparative Analysis. Knoxville: Tennessee Valley Authority, 1957.
T4470
Interpreting Results of Irrigation Experiments; a Progress Report. Knoxville: Tennessee Valley Authority, 1958.
T4480
The Occurrence of Drought in the Tennessee Valley. Knoxville: Tennessee Valley Authority, Division of Agricultural Relations, Agricultural Economics Branch, Division of Water Control Planning, Hydraulic Data Branch, 1958.
T4490
Plant Nutrient Consumption by States and Geographic Areas. Knoxville: Tennessee Valley Authority, Division of Agricultural Relations, 1958.
T4500
Problems and Suggested Programs for Low-Income Farmers with Special Reference to the Tennessee Valley. By Arthur B. Mackie and E. S. Baum. Knoxville: Tennessee Valley Authority, 1959.
T4510
Problems of Underemployed Rural People. By Stephen C. Smith. Knoxville: Tennessee Valley Authority, 1955.
T4520
Progress Through Cooperative Research on Fertilizer Evaluations; a Report of TVA Soils and Fertilizer Research Branch for the Period July 1957 Through June 1960. Wilson Dam, Ala.: Tennessee Valley Authority, The division, 1960.
T4530
Report. Knoxville: Tennessee Valley Authority, The division, annual.
T4540
Research Contributes to More Efficient Use of Fertilizers. A Report of Progress of the Soils and Fertilizers, Fertilizer Research Branch. Knoxville: Tennessee Valley Authority, 1957.
T4550
Test-Demonstration Farms and the Spread of Improved Farm Practices in Southwest Virginia. By John Blackmore, R. M. Dimit, and E. L. Baum. Knoxville, Tenn.: Tennessee Valley Authority, 1955.
T4560
U. S. Plant Nutrient Consumption. Prepared by John R. Douglas, Jr., and Robert D. Grisso. Wilson Dam, Ala.: Tennessee Valley Authority, 1961.
T4570
Use of Linear Programming Technique to Compute Least-Cost Bulk-Blended Fertilizers. Knoxville: Tennessee Valley Authority, 1960.
T4580

Division of Forestry Forest Conditions in Monroe County, Tennessee. Knoxville: Tennessee Valley Authority, 1935.
T4590
Division of Forestry Development Annual Report, 1963. Norris, Tenn.: Tennessee Valley Authority, Division of Forestry Development, 1963.
T4600
The Changing Sawmill Industry; a Status Report on 58 Circular Sawmills in the Tennessee Valley, 1950-1960. By John W. Lehman. Norris: Tennessee Valley Authority, 1961.
T4610
Comparative Data for Additional Hardwood Pulp and Paper Mills in the Tennessee Valley. Norris: Tennessee Valley Authority, 1961.
T4620
Comparative Results of Circular Sawmill Surveys in the Tennessee Valley, 1950 and 1955. Norris, Tenn.: Tennessee Valley Authority, 1956.
T4630
A Demonstration of Watershed Protective Logging, Mars Hill Municipal Watershed, Madison County, North Carolina. Norris, Tenn.: Tennessee Valley Authority, 1960.
T4640
Development of Forests — Fish — Wildlife in the Tennessee Valley. Annual Report for 1962. Norris: Tennessee Valley Authority, 1962.
T4650
Evaluation of Forestry Opportunities on Farms in the Beech River Watershed. In cooperation with the Univ. of Tennessee. Norris, Tenn.: The division, Tennessee Valley Authority, 1965.
T4660 (ETSU)
Fish and Wildlife in the Tennessee Valley. Norris: Tennessee Valley Authority, Division of Forestry Relations, 1950.
T4670
Forest Inventory Statistics for Fannin County, Georgia. Norris, Tenn.: Tennessee Valley Authority, 1959.
T4680
Forest Inventory Statistics — Holston River Tributary Area, East Tennessee and Southwest Virginia. Norris: Tennessee Valley Authority, The division, 1963.
T4690
Forest Inventory Statistics for Towns County, Georgia. Norris, Tenn.: Tennessee Valley Authority, The division, 1959.
T4700
Forest Inventory Statistics for Union County, Georgia. Norris, Tenn.: Tennessee Valley Authority, 1960.
T4710
Forest Inventory Statistics for Walker County, Georgia. Norris, Tenn.: Tennessee Valley Authority, The division, 1958.
T4720
Forest Inventory Statistics for Whitfield County, Georgia. Norris, Tenn.: Tennessee Valley Authority, 1958.
T4730
Forest Resources and Industries in the Tennessee Valley. Norris, Tenn.: The division, 1966.
T4740 (ETSU)
Forest Resources of the Beech River Watershed. Norris, Tenn.: Tennessee Valley Authority, 1953.
T4750
Furniture Industry Expansion in the Tennessee Valley. Norris, Tenn.: Tennessee Valley Authority, 1963.
T4760
Hardwood-Logging Methods and Costs in the Tennessee Valley. Norris, Tenn.: Tennessee Valley Authority, 1960.
T4770
Hardwood Utilization Centers: Their Potential for the Tennessee Valley. Norris, Tenn.: The division, 1964.
T4780 (ASU)

Influence of Woodland and Owner Characteristics of Forest Management. Report no. 217-56. Knoxville: Tennessee Valley Authority, 1956.
T4790
Laminated Lumber From Low-Grade Hardwoods by the Continuous Glue Press Process. Norris, Tenn.: n.p., 1949.
T4800
Multiple-Use of Norris Watershed. Norris, Tenn.: Tennessee Valley Authority, 1962.
T4810
North Georgia Forest Industry Outlook. n.p.: Tennessee Valley Authority, 1966.
T4820
Operations Manual for TVA Forest Nurseries. Norris, Tenn.: Tennessee Valley Authority, 1954.
T4830
Pine Pulpmill Possibilities, North Alabama. Norris, Tenn.: Tennessee Valley Authority, 1964.
T4840
Private Forest Management in the Tennessee Valley. Norris, Tenn.: Tennessee Valley Authority, Division of Forestry Relations, 1954.
T4850
Publications Available for General Distribution. Norris, Tenn.: Tennessee Valley Authority, 1963.
T4860
Status of the Forest Resource in the Tennessee Valley — 1950. Norris, Tenn.: Tennessee Valley Authority, 1953.
T4870
Technical Note. no. 1, July 31, 1940-. Norris, Tenn.: Tennessee Valley Authority, Issued irregularly.
T4880
TVA and Forestry. Norris, Tenn.: Tennessee Valley Authority, Division of Forestry Relations, 1955.
T4890
TVA and Forestry. Norris, Tenn.: Tennessee Valley Authority, 1962.
T4900
TVA and Forestry. Knoxville: Tennessee Valley Authority, 1967.
T4910
Twenty Years of Fire Records for State and Private Forest Lands in the Tennessee Valley. Norris, Tenn.: Tennessee Valley Authority, Division of Forestry Relations, 1954.
T4920
Why Invest in Forest Land? Some Forest Owners Give Their Answers. Norris, Tenn.: Tennessee Valley Authority, 1962.
T4930
Division of Forestry Relations Annual Report. Norris, Tenn.: Tennessee Valley Authority, 1946.
T4940
Design and Operation of Open-Tank Timber Treating Plants. By E. M. Conway and R. L. Schnell. Norris, Tenn.: Tennessee Valley Authority, 1953.
T4950
Farm Forestry Planning Through Linear Programming. By Arthur J. Coutu and Birger W. Ellertsen. Norris, Tenn.: Tennessee Valley Authority, 1960.
T4960
Forest Resource Trends in the Tennessee Valley. Norris, Tenn.: Tennessee Valley Authority, 1961.
T4970
Guide to Selection of Superior Loblolly, Shortleaf and Virginia Pine in the Tennessee Valley. Prepared by Thomas G. Zarger. Norris, Tenn.: Tennessee Valley Authority, 1958.
T4980
Inventorying Forest Properties; Suggested Standard Procedure and Specifications for Use in the Tennessee Valley. Norris, Tenn.: Tennessee Valley Authority, 1956.
T4990
Operations Guide for TVA Forest Nurseries. By William G. Grieve and James H. Barton. Norris? Tenn.: Tennessee Valley Authority, 1960.
T5000

Division of Forestry Relations
Private Forest Management Trends in the Tennessee Valley. Norris, Tenn.: Tennessee Valley Authority, 1961.
T5010
Quality-Control in Circular Sawmill Operation . . . Report by W. W. King, Staff Forester. Norris, Tenn.: Tennessee Valley Authority, 1959.
T5020
Reforestation Estimates for the Tennessee Valley. Norris, Tenn.: Tennessee Valley Authority, 1957.
T5030
Report: A Record of Activities and Accomplishments. Norris? Tenn.: The division, n.d.
T5040
Sawmill Facts; First Step Toward Good Management. Norris, Tenn.: Tennessee Valley Authority, 1951.
T5050
A Survey of Pulpwood Dealers in the Tennessee Valley . . . Norris, Tenn.: Tennessee Valley Authority, 1958.
T5060
TVA Fish and Game Activities. Norris, Tenn.: Tennessee Valley Authority, 1959.
T5070
Utilizing Pine Sawmill Residue for Pulp Chips. Report prepared by John W. Lehman. Norris, Tenn.: Tennessee Valley Authority, 1958.
T5080
Legal Dept. . . . A Compilation of the More Important Congressional Acts, Treaties, Presidential Messages, Judicial Decisions, and Official Reports and Documents Having to do with the Control, Conservation, and Utilization of Water Resources. Prepared by Francis W. Laurent. Knoxville: Tennessee Valley Authority, 1938.
T5090
Division of Navigation Development Benefit-Cost Analysis for Water Resource Projects: A Selected Annotated Bibliography. Knoxville: Tennessee Valley Authority, 1967.
T5100
Benefit-Cost Analysis for Water Resource Projects; a Selected Annotated Bibliography. By Hubert Hinote. Rev. ed. Knoxville: Center for Business and Economic Research. Univ. of Tennessee, 1969.
T5110
Major Freight Terminals on the Tennessee River Waterway. Knoxville, Tenn.: Tennessee Valley Authority, 1963.
T5120
Navigation Charts, Tennessee River Waterway, Paducah, Kentucky to Knoxville, Tennessee; Showing Underwater Conditions, Navigation Channels and Aids and Adjacent Shore Planimetry. Knoxville: Tennessee Valley Authority, 1963.
T5130
The Tennessee River Navigation System: History, Development, and Operation. Knoxville: Tennessee Valley Authority, 1964.
T5140
Division of Property and Supply Land Acquisition in TVA. An Analysis of TVA Land Acquisition, Land Management, and Family Relocation Procedures as They Could Relate to the Missouri Valley Development. Statements Presented Before the Select Subcommittee on Real Property Acquisition of the Committee on Public Works. Chattanooga, Tenn.: Tennessee Valley Authority, 1963.
T5150
Division of Regional Studies The Barge Grain Case — Its Significance to the Tennessee Valley and the Southeast. Knoxville: Tennessee Valley Authority, 1951.
T5160
Comparative Data on Farm Income and Employment, 1929-51. Research in Agricultural and Industrial Development in the Tennessee Valley Region, Report no. 1. Knoxville: Tennessee Valley Authority, 1953.
T5170
Differentials in Farm Income and Employment in the Tennessee Valley Region Counties. Research in Agricultural and Industrial Development in the Tennessee Valley Region Report no. 2. Knoxville: Tennessee Valley Authority, 1953.
T5180
Local Government Services and Industrial Development in the Southeast. Knoxville: Tennessee Valley Authority, n.d. A joint statement by the state universities of the Valley States and Tennessee Valley Authority.
T5190
The Tennessee Valley Region: Highlights of Growth and Change; Historical Perspectives, Recent Trends. Knoxville: Tennessee Valley Authority, 1968.
T5200
Regional Studies Staff The Image of Asheville. n.p.: Tennessee Valley Authority, 1968.
T5210 (LMC)
Division of Reservoir Properties Annual Report, 1958 and 1959. Knoxville: Tennessee Valley Authority, 1959.
T5220
Public Grounds Maintenance Handbook. By H. S. Conover, landscape architect, Site Planning Section, Division of Reservoir Properties. Knoxville: Tennessee Valley Authority, 1953.
T5230
Division of Engineering and Construction Engineering Data. 2 vol. Technical Monograph no. 55. Knoxville: Tennessee Valley Authority, 1954-1955.
T5240
Measurements of the Structural Behavior at Fontana Dam. Technical Monograph no. 69. Knoxville, Tenn.: Tennessee Valley Authority, 1953.
T5250
Measurements of the Structural Behavior of Norris and Hiwassee Dams. Technical Monograph no. 67. Knoxville, Tenn.: Tennessee Valley Authority, 1950.
T5260
Fish and Wildlife Branch Fish and Wildlife, Valuable Natural Resources. Norris, Tenn.: Tennessee Valley Authority, 1963-64.
T5270
Forest Economics Section Crosstie Industry Facts for the Tennessee Valley Counties. By William H. Ogden, staff forester. Norris: Tennessee Valley Authority, Division of Forestry Relations, 1949.
T5280
Statistical Summary of Forest-Products Industries in the Tennessee Valley. By Walter P. Smith. Norris: Tennessee Valley Authority, Division of Forestry Relations, 1949.
T5290
Government Relations and Economics Staff Manufacturing Employment in the Tennessee Valley Region. Knoxville: Tennessee Valley Authority, 1961.
T5300
Manufacturing Structure and Change in the Tennessee Valley Region, 1959-1963. Knoxville, Tenn.: Tennessee Valley Authority, 1964.
T5310
Tennessee Valley Authority Program: The Role of the States and Their Political Subdivisions. Prepared for Israel Congress, International Union of Local Authorities, Tel Aviv, November 14-16, 1960. Knoxville, Tenn.: Tennessee Valley Authority, 1960.
T5320
The Tennessee Valley Region: Important Features and Recent Trends. Knoxville: Tennessee Valley Authority, 1956.
T5330
Health and Safety Dept. . . . Community Health and Safety Series no. 1. Chattanooga, Tenn.: Tennessee Valley Authority, Health and Safety Dept., 1941.
T5340
Full-Scale Study of Dispersion of Stack Gases; a Summary Report. Tennessee Valley Authority, Division of Health and Safety, and Public Health Service, Division of Air Pollution. Chattanooga: Tennessee Valley Authority, The dept., 1964.
T5350
Malaria and Its Control in the Tennessee Valley. 1st ed. Prepared by the staff of the health and safety department, Tennessee Valley Authority, as source material in popular health instruction directed to the prevention and control of malaria. Chattanooga, Tenn.: Tennessee Valley Authority, 1941.
T5360
Malaria and Its Control in the Tennessee Valley. 2nd ed. Prepared by the staff of the health and safety department, Tennessee Valley Authority, as source material in popular health instruction directed to the prevention and control of malaria. Chattanooga, Tenn.: Tennessee Valley Authority, 1942.
T5370
Malaria Control: 1. How the Community Can Help. An Office of War Information Reprint of the Tennessee Valley Authority Booklet. Malaria: The Story of an Individual Problem and a Community Problem. Chattanooga: Tennessee Valley Authority, 1941.
T5380
Malaria Control in the Tennessee Valley. Chattanooga, Tenn.: Tennessee Valley Authority, 1960.
T5390
Malaria, the Story of an Individual Problem and a Community Problem. Chattanooga: Tennessee Valley Authority, 1941.
T5400
Prediction of Stream Reaeration Rates. Chattanooga, Tenn.: Tennessee Valley Authority, 1962.
T5410
Quality of Water in Chickamauga Reservoir. Prepared by Stream Sanitation Staff. Chattanooga: Tennessee Valley Authority, 1964.
T5420
Report. Chattanooga: Tennessee Valley Authority, annual.
T5430
Significant Developments in TVA's Malaria Control Program Through 1947. Tennessee Valley Authority Health and Safety Dept., Malaria Control Division. n.p.: Tennessee Valley Authority, 1948.
T5440
Stream Sanitation in the Tennessee Valley. Chattanooga, Tenn.: Tennessee Valley Authority, 1952.
T5450
Studies of the Pollution of the Tennessee River System. By G. R. Scott, sanitary engineer. Chattanooga, Tenn.: Tennessee Valley Authority, 1941-45.
T5460
Studies of the Pollution of the Tennessee River System. By G. R. Scott. New York: Arno, 1970.
T5470
Surface Water Quality in the Chestuee Creek Watershed. Chattanooga: Tennessee Valley Authority, 1953.
T5480
Surface Water Quality in the Chestuee Creek Watershed. Chattanooga: Tennessee Valley Authority, 1953.
T5490
TVA; the Health of a Region. Knoxville, Tenn.: Tennessee Valley Authority, 1961.
T5500
Vector Control and Water Resource Development — The Experience of TVA. By O. M. Derryberry and F. E. Gartrell. Chattanooga, Tenn.: Tennessee Valley Authority, 1960.
T5510
Hydraulic Data Branch Boone Project, Hydraulic Model Studies. Technical Monograph no. 74. Knoxville: Tennessee Valley Authority, 1954.
T5520

Hydraulic Data Branch
Flood on Piney River, November 18-19, 1957 in the Vicinity of Spring City, Tenn. Knoxville, Tenn.: Tennessee Valley Authority, 1961.
T5530

Fontana Project Hydraulic Model Studies. Technical Monograph no. 68. Knoxville, Tenn.: Tennessee Valley Authority, 1953.
T5540

Influences of Reforestation and Erosion Control Upon the Hydrology of the Pine Tree Branch Watershed 1941 to 1950. Knoxville, Tenn.: Tennessee Valley Authority, 1955.
T5550

Tennessee and Cumberland Valley Reservoirs Level Storage Tables and Profile Storage Charts. Knoxville, Tenn.: Tennessee Valley Authority, 1960.
T5560

Industry Division Agricultural-Industrial Survey of Anderson County, Tennessee. Knoxville: Tennessee Valley Authority, 1934.
T5570

Agricultural-Industrial Survey of Bledsoe County. Knoxville: Tennessee Valley Authority, 1934.
T5580

Agricultural-Industrial Survey of Carter County. Knoxville: Tennessee Valley Authority, 1934.
T5590

Agricultural-Industrial Survey of Cocke County. Knoxville: Tennessee Valley Authority, 1934.
T5600

Agricultural-Industrial Survey of Coffee County. Knoxville: Tennessee Valley Authority, 1934.
T5610

Agricultural-Industrial Survey of Cumberland County. Knoxville: Tennessee Valley Authority, 1935.
T5620

Agricultural-Industrial Survey of Fentress County. Knoxville: Tennessee Valley Authority, 1934.
T5630

Agricultural-Industrial Survey of Franklin County, Tennessee. Knoxville: Tennessee Valley Authority, 1934.
T5640

Agricultural-Industrial Survey of Grainger County. Knoxville: Tennessee Valley Authority, 1934.
T5650

Agricultural-Industrial Survey of Greene County, Tennessee. Knoxville: Tennessee Valley Authority, 1934.
T5660

Agricultural-Industrial Survey of Hamblen County, Tennessee. Knoxville: Tennessee Valley Authority, 1935.
T5670

Agricultural-Industrial Survey of Johnson County, Tennessee. Knoxville: Tennessee Valley Authority, 1934.
T5680

Agricultural-Industrial Survey of Loudon County, Tennessee. Knoxville: Tennessee Valley Authority, 1935.
T5690

Agricultural-Industrial Survey of McMinn County, Tennessee. Knoxville: Tennessee Valley Authority, 1934.
T5700

Agricultural-Industrial Survey of Marion County, Tennessee. 2 vols. Knoxville: Tennessee Valley Authority, 1934.
T5710

Agricultural-Industrial Survey of Meigs County, Tennessee. Knoxville: Tennessee Valley Authority, 1934.
T5720

Agricultural-Industrial Survey of Monroe County, Tennessee. Knoxville: Tennessee Valley Authority, 1934.
T5730

Agricultural-Industrial Survey of Morgan County, Tennessee. Knoxville: Tennessee Valley Authority, 1935.
T5740

Agricultural-Industrial Survey of Polk County, Tennessee. Knoxville: Tennessee Valley Authority, 1935.
T5750

Agricultural-Industrial Survey of Rhea County. Knoxville: Tennessee Valley Authority, 1934.
T5760

Agricultural-Industrial Survey of Sevier County. Knoxville: Tennessee Valley Authority, 1934.
T5770

Agricultural-Industrial Survey of Sullivan County. Knoxville: Tennessee Valley Authority, 1934.
T5780

Agricultural-Industrial Survey of Washington County, Tennessee. Knoxville: Tennessee Valley Authority, 1934.
T5790

Agricultural-Industrial Survey of White County. Knoxville: Tennessee Valley Authority, 1934.
T5800

Agricultural-Industrial Survey of Unicoi County. Knoxville: Tennessee Valley Authority, 1934.
T5810

Industrial Economics Branch Defense Expansion in the Tennessee Valley Region. Knoxville, Tenn.: Tennessee Valley Authority, 1952.
T5820

Land Planning and Housing Division Atlas of the Tennessee Valley Region. Submitted by G. Donald Hudson, chief, Land Classification Section Division of Land Planning and Housing, Tennessee Valley Authority. Knoxville: Tennessee Valley Authority, 1936.
T5830

A Cartographic Summary of United States Census Data, 1930, Tennessee Valley and Surrounding Area by Land Classification Section, Land Planning and Housing Division, Tennessee Valley Authority. Submitted by G. Donald Hudson, chief of section. Knoxville: Tennessee Valley Authority, 1936.
T5840

Houses at Norris, Tennessee; a Review of Costs. Submitted by Louis Grandgent. Knoxville: Tennessee Valley Authority, 1936.
T5850

The Rural Land Classification Program; a Summary of Techniques and Uses Submitted by G. Donald Hudson, Chief, Land Classification Section, Division of Land Planning and Housing, Tennessee Valley Authority. Knoxville: Tennessee Valley Authority, 1935.
T5860

The Three Major Physical Divisions of the Upper Tennessee Basin. By Land Classification Section, Land Planning and Housing Division. Submitted by G. Donald Hudson, chief of section. Knoxville: Tennessee Valley Authority, 1936.
T5870

Library . . . A Bibliography of the Tennessee Valley Authority. Prepared by Harry C. Bauer, technical librarian. Knoxville: Tennessee Valley Authority, 1935.
T5880

A Bibliography for the TVA Program. Knoxville: Tennessee Valley Authority, 1952.
T5890

. . . A Chronology of the Tennessee Valley Authority. Compiled by Harry C. Bauer, technical librarian. Knoxville: Tennessee Valley Authority, 1936.
T5900

Congressional Hearings, Reports, and Documents Relating to TVA. 1933-. Knoxville: Tennessee Valley Authority, n.d.
T5910

Flood Damage Prevention; an Indexed Bibliography. Knoxville: Tennessee Valley Authority, 1963.
T5920

Flood Damage Prevention; an Indexed Bibliography. Knoxville: Tennessee Valley Authority, 1964.
T5930

Flood Damage Prevention; an Indexed Bibliography. 4th ed. Knoxville: Tennessee Valley Authority, 1966.
T5940

Flood Damage Prevention; an Indexed Bibliography. 5th ed. Knoxville: Tennessee Valley Authority, 1967.
T5950

Flood Damage Prevention; an Indexed Bibliography. 6th ed. Knoxville: Tennessee Valley Authority, 1969.
T5960

. . . Government Corporations, a Selected List of References, September 15, 1945. Knoxville: Tennessee Valley Authority, 1945.
T5970

. . . An Indexed Bibliography of the Tennessee Valley Authority, Compiled by Harry C. Bauer, Technical Librarian. Knoxville: Tennessee Valley Authority, 1936.
T5980

. . . Payments in Lieu of Taxes, a Selected List of References, January 2, 1946. Knoxville: Tennessee Valley Authority, 1946.
T5990

Personnel Administration in TVA; a Selected List of References. Rev. December 1, 1951. Knoxville: Tennessee Valley Authority, 1952.
T6000

. . . Regional Authority Developments, a Selected List of References, Including Legislative Bills Introduced in Congress, 1933-1945. Knoxville: Tennessee Valley Authority, 1946.
T6010

. . . A Selected List of Books, Theses, and Pamphlets on TVA, Compiled by Ernest I. Miller, Reference Librarian. Knoxville: Tennessee Valley Authority, 1940.
T6020

. . . A Selected List of Books and Pamphlets on TVA. January 1, 1945. Knoxville: Tennessee Valley Authority, 1945.
T6030

. . . A Selected List of Books, Theses, and Pamphlets on TVA. Compiled by Ernest I. Miller, reference librarian. Knoxville: Tennessee Valley Authority, 1941.
T6040

. . . A Selected List of Books, Theses, and Pamphlets on TVA. Compiled by Bernard L. Foy, acting technical librarian. Knoxville: Tennessee Valley Authority, 1942.
T6050

The TVA Program; a Bibliography of Selected Readings, Prepared by the Training and Educational Relations Staff of the Personnel Dept. and the Staff of the Technical Library. Knoxville: Tennessee Valley Authority, 1946.
T6060

The TVA Program; a Bibliography of Selected Readings, Compiled by Bernard L. Foy, Technical Librarian. Knoxville: Tennessee Valley Authority, 1950.
T6070

The TVA Program; a Bibliography of Selected Readings, Compiled by Bernard L. Foy, Technical Librarian. Rev. Sept. 1, 1951. Knoxville: Tennessee Valley Authority, 1951.
T6080

TVA, Symbol of Valley Resource Development; a Digest and Selected Bibliography of Information. Knoxville: Tennessee Valley Authority, 1961.
T6090

TVA as a Symbol of Resource Development in Many Countries; a Digest and Selected Bibliography of Information. Knoxville: Tennessee Valley Authority, 1952.
T6100

Office of Chemical Engineering, Chemical Engineering Reports Agglomeration of Phosphate Fines for Furnace Use. Compiled by E. I. Stout. Washington: Govt. Print. Off., 1950.
T6110

Analytical Index of Chemical Engineering Publications Patents and Reports. Compiled by E. L. Newman and L. D. Copeland. Washington: Govt. Print. Off., 1954.
T6120

Chemical Engineering Bulletins. Wilson Dam, Ala.: Tennessee Valley Authority, 1952. Issued irregularly.
T6130

Office of Chemical Engineering, Chemical Engineering Reports
Chemical Engineering Reports. Washington: Govt. Print. Off., 1949.
T6140
Development of Processes for Production of Calcium Metaphosphate Fertilizer. Compiled by J. C. Brosheer. Washington: Govt. Print. Off., 1953.
T6150
Development of Processes for Production of Concentrated Superphosphate. Compiled by G. L. Bridger. Washington: Govt. Print. Off., 1949.
T6160
Development of Processes for Production of Fused Tricalcium Phosphate. Compiled by J. C. Brosheer and T. P. Hignett. Washington: Govt. Print. Off., 1953.
T6170
Development of Processes and Equipment for Production of Phosphoric Acid. Compiled by M. M. Striplin, Jr. Washington: Govt. Print. Off., 1949.
T6180
General Outline of Chemical Engineering Activities. By H. A. Curtis, Revised ed., 1949. Washington: Govt. Print. Off., 1949.
T6190
Phosphorus; Properties of the Element and Some of Its Compounds. Compiled by Thad D. Farr. Washington: Govt. Print. Off., 1950.
T6200
Preparation of Research and Engineering Reports. By M. A. Tschantre. Wilson Dam, Ala.: Tennessee Valley Authority, 1950.
T6210
Production of Elemental Phosphorus by the Electric — Furnace Method. Compiled by R. B. Burts and J. C. Barber. Washington: Govt. Print. Off., 1952.
T6220
TVA Chemical Plant and National Defense. Wilson Dam, Ala.: Tennessee Valley Authority, 1955.
T6230
Office of Chief Engineer The Colbert Steam Plant; a Report on the Planning, Design, Construction, Costs, and First Power Operations of the Initial Four-Unit Plant. Knoxville: Tennessee Valley Authority, 1963.
T6240
Construction Plant for TVA Projects. Tennessee Valley Authority, Divisions of Engineering and Construction. Knoxville: Tennessee Valley Authority, 1957.
T6250
Drawings for the Appalachian Project. Knoxville: Tennessee Valley Authority, 1947.
T6260
Drawings for the Boone Project by Tennessee Valley Authority, Divisions of Engineering and Construction. Knoxville: Tennessee Valley Authority, 1957.
T6270
Drawings for the Chatuge and Nottely Projects by the Tennessee Valley Authority, Engineering and Construction Departments. Knoxville: Tennessee Valley Authority, 1946.
T6280
Drawings for the Cherokee Project by the Tennessee Valley Authority, Engineering and Construction Departments. Knoxville: Tennessee Valley Authority, 1947.
T6290
Drawings for the Fontana Project. Knoxville: Tennessee Valley Authority, 1948.
T6300
Drawings for the Fort Loudoun Project by the Tennessee Valley Authority, Divisions of Engineering and Construction. Knoxville: Tennessee Valley Authority, 1950.
T6310
Drawings for the Hiwassee Project. Knoxville: Tennessee Valley Authority, 1941.
T6320
Drawings for the Johnsonville Steam Plant. By Tennessee Valley Authority, Divisions of Engineering and Construction. Knoxville: Tennessee Valley Authority, 1955.
T6330
Drawings for the Kentucky Project. By the Tennessee Valley Authority, Divisions of Engineering and Construction. Knoxville: Tennessee Valley Authority, 1949.
T6340
Drawings for the Ocoee no. 3 Project. Knoxville: Tennessee Valley Authority, 1947.
T6350
. . . Drawings for the Pickwick Landing Project . . . Knoxville: Tennessee Valley Authority, 1939.
T6360
Drawings for the South Holston Project. By Tennessee Valley Authority, Division of Engineering and Construction. Knoxville: Tennessee Valley Authority, 6.
T6370
Drawings for the Watauga and Wilbur Projects. By the Tennessee Valley Authority, Division of Engineering and Construction. Knoxville: Tennessee Valley Authority, 1955.
T6380
Drawings for the Watts Bar Project. By the Tennessee Valley Authority, Engineering and Construction Department. Knoxville: Tennessee Valley Authority, 1948.
T6390
. . . Drawings for the Wheeler Project . . . Knoxville: Tennessee Valley Authority, 1939.
T6400
Engineering Data. Tennessee Valley Authority Projects. Knoxville: Tennessee Valley Authority, 1948.
T6410
Engineering Data. Knoxville: Tennessee Valley Authority, 1955.
T6420
Instructions for Scale Checking Aerial Photographs. By George D. Whitmore, principal cadastral engineer. Washington: Tennessee Valley Authority, 1942.
T6430
Measurements of the Structural Behavior at Fontana Dam. By the Tennessee Valley Authority, Division of Engineering and Construction. Knoxville: Tennessee Valley Authority, 1953.
T6440
Measurements of the Structural Behavior of Norris and Hiwassee Dams. By the Tennessee Valley Authority, Division of Engineering and Construction. Knoxville: Tennessee Valley Authority, 1950.
T6450
Pickwick Landing Dam on the Tennessee River. Knoxville: Tennessee Valley Authority, Engineering and Construction Department, 1935.
T6460
. . . Plans and Specifications for the Norris Dam . . . Knoxville: Tennessee Valley Authority, 1938.
T6470
Plans and Specifications for the Norris Dam. 2nd ed. Knoxville: Tennessee Valley Authority, 1946.
T6480
Office of Engineering Design and Construction The Bull Run Steam Plant; a Report on the Planning, Design, Construction, Costs, and First Power Operations of the Initial One-Unit Plant. Knoxville: Tennessee Valley Authority, 1967.
T6490
The Kingston Steam Plant; a Report on the Planning, Design, Construction, Costs, and First Power Operations. Knoxville: Tennessee Valley Authority, 1965.
T6500
The Melton Hill Project; a Report on the Planning, Design, Construction, Initial Operations, and Costs. Knoxville: Tennessee Valley Authority, 1966.
T6510
The Paradise Steam Plant; a Report on the Planning, Design, Construction, Costs, and First Power Operations of the Initial Two-Unit Plant. Knoxville: Tennessee Valley Authority, 1964.
T6520
Engineering Laboratory Research in the Fields of Civil Engineering, Mechanical Engineering, Instrumentation. 1965/66-. Norris, Tenn.: Tennessee Valley Authority, 1966.
T6530
Office of Health and Environmental Science Annual Report. 1969/70-. Chattanooga: Tennessee Valley Authority, 1970.
T6540
Office of General Manager, Division of Property and Supply Scheduling and Disposal of Records, Prepared by Office Methods Staff. Knoxville: Tennessee Valley Authority, 1949.
T6550
Division of Power Transmission System of Tennessee Valley Authority. Tennessee Valley Authority, Division of Power, January 1951. Washington: Govt. Print. Off., 1951.
T6560
Division of Power Marketing Electricity Sales Statistics, Monthly Report no. 1. Chattanooga, Tenn.: Tennessee Valley Authority, 1935-Date.
T6570
Industrial Development in the TVA Area During 1962. Chattanooga: Tennessee Valley Authority, 1963.
T6580
Division of Power Supply Report on the Plateau Coal Field of Alabama. By Reynold Q. Shotts. Chattanooga: Tennessee Valley Authority, 1953.
T6590
Report on the Reserves of Coal in a Part of the Warrier Coal Field of Alabama. By Reynold Q. Shotts. Chattanooga: Tennessee Valley Authority, September, 1953.
T6600
Electrical Development Branch Electricity and Your Farm; a Manual for Instruction on the Practical Uses and Application of Electricity in Rural Areas. Chattanooga: Tennessee Valley Authority, n.d.
T6610
Office of Power Comparison of Coal-Fired and Nuclear Power Plants for the TVA System. Chattanooga: Tennessee Valley Authority, 1966.
T6620
Fire Protection Manual. Chattanooga: Tennessee Valley Authority, 1963.
T6630
Rate Reductions by the Distributors of TVA Power. Chattanooga: Tennessee Valley Authority, 1956.
T6640
Rate Reductions by the Distributors of TVA Power. Chattanooga: Tennessee Valley Authority, 1957.
T6650
TVA Power. 1953-. Chattanooga: Tennessee Valley Authority, 1953.
T6660
TVA Power and Taxes. Chattanooga: Tennessee Valley Authority, 1959.
T6670
TVA Power and Taxes. Knoxville: Tennessee Valley Authority, 1965.
T6680
Office of Power, Division of Power Marketing Industrial Development in the TVA Area, 1955-Date. Chattanooga: Tennessee Valley Authority, annual.
T6690
Office of Power, Division of Power Utilization Electricity Sales Statistics. Chattanooga: Tennessee Valley Authority, annual.
T6700
Industrial Development in the TVA Area. 1958-. Chattanooga: Tennessee Valley Authority, 1958-.
T6710
All-Electric Schools . . . in the Tennessee Valley. A Special Report on the Growing Use of Electricity in Modern Schools. 2nd ed. Chattanooga, Tenn.: n.p., n.d.
T6720

Office Service Branch File Audit Handbook. Chattanooga: Tennessee Valley Authority, 1956.
T6730

File Operation Handbook. Chattanooga: Tennessee Valley Authority, 1962.
T6740

Records Management in TVA. Revised edition. Chattanooga: Tennessee Valley Authority, 1956.
T6750

Records Retention and Disposal Handbook. Revised edition. Chattanooga: Tennessee Valley Authority, 1961.
T6760

Secretarial Handbook. Revised edition. Chattanooga: Tennessee Valley Authority, 1960.
T6770

. . . **Personnel Dept.** Administration and Standards of Apprenticeship of the Tennessee Valley Authority. Knoxville: Tennessee Valley Authority, 1961.
T6780

Development of Salary Policy Employee Panel (Documentation). Knoxville, Tenn.: Tennessee Valley Authority, 1953.
T6790

Documentation of TVA Apprenticeship Program. Knoxville, Tenn.: Tennessee Valley Authority, 1952.
T6800

Effectiveness of Apprentice Training in TVA. Knoxville: Tennessee Valley Authority, 1951.
T6810

Group Participation in Personnel Administration in the Tennessee Valley Authority. n.p.: Tennessee Valley Authority, 1957.
T6820

Management Guide for Handling Grievances of Employees, Represented by the Salary Policy Employee Panel. Knoxville: Tennessee Valley Authority, 1966.
T6830

Report. n.p.: Tennessee Valley Authority, annual.
T6840

TVA Employment Policy and Methods for Salary Policy Jobs. 2nd ed. Knoxville: Tennessee Valley Authority, 1959.
T6850

TVA and Engineering: Electrical, Civil, Mechanical, Chemical, Architectural, Nuclear, Fuels. Knoxville: Tennessee Valley Authority, 1961.
T6860

TVA Labor Relations, 1933-1953. Knoxville: Tennessee Valley Authority, 1953.
T6870

Valley of Opportunity; Tennessee Valley Authority, 1963-1964. Knoxville: Tennessee Valley Authority, 1964.
T6880

. . . **Technical Library** A Bibliography for the TVA Program. Knoxville: Tennessee Valley Authority, 1957.
T6890

Flood Damage Prevention; An Indexed Bibliography. Knoxville: Tennessee Valley Authority, 1964.
T6900

TVA as a Symbol of Resource Development in Many Countries. Knoxville: Tennessee Valley Authority, 1961.
T6910

Water Control Planning Dept. Boone Project Hydraulic Model Studies. Knoxville: Tennessee Valley Authority, 1954.
T6920

. . . Flood Control for Upper French Broad River and Tributaries; a Preliminary Report. Knoxville, Tenn.: Tennessee Valley Authority, 1942.
T6930

Flood of August 24-25, 1961: Upper French Broad River Basin. Knoxville: Tennessee Valley Authority, 1961.
T6940

Flood on Piney River, November 18-19, 1957, in Vicinity of Spring City, Tennessee. Knoxville: Tennessee Valley Authority, 1961.
T6950

Floods of March 1963 in Tennessee River Basin. Knoxville, Tenn.: Tennessee Valley Authority, 1964.
T6960

Floods on Beaver Creek, in Vicinity of Bristol, Virginia-Tennessee. Knoxville: Tennessee Valley Authority, 1959.
T6970

Floods on Brush Creek in Vicinity of Johnson City, Tennessee. Knoxville, Tenn.: Tennessee Valley Authority, 1959.
T6980

Floods on Cheoah River and Tributary Creeks in Vicinity of Robbinsville, North Carolina. Knoxville: Tennessee Valley Authority, 1969.
T6990

Floods on Clinch River, in Vicinity of Clinton, Tennessee. Flood history to May 1, 1956. Maximum flood of reasonable regional expectancy. Knoxville: Tennessee Valley Authority, 1956.
T7000

Floods on Elk River and Norris Creek, in Vicinity of Fayetteville, Tennessee. Knoxville: Tennessee Valley Authority, 1960.
T7010

Floods on Elk River in Vicinity of Fayetteville, Tennessee. Knoxville: Tennessee Valley Authority, 1961. "Original report . . . issued in October 1954 and revised in May 1957. A supplement was issued in November 1960. This edition of the report incorporates and brings up to date this previously published material.
T7020

Floods on French Broad and Davidson Rivers and King, Nicholson, and Tucker Creeks in Vicinity of Brevard, North Carolina. Knoxville: Tennessee Valley Authority, 1964.
T7030

Floods on French Broad and Swannanoa Rivers, in Vicinity of Asheville, North Carolina. Knoxville: Tennessee Valley Authority, 1960.
T7040

Floods on French Broad River and Spring Creek in Vicinity of Hot Springs, North Carolina. Knoxville: Tennessee Valley Authority, 1960.
T7050

Floods on French Broad River in the Vicinity of Marshall, N. C. Knoxville: Tennessee Valley Authority, 1960.
T7060

Floods on Hiwassee River, Valley River, and Peachtree Creek in Vicinity of Murphy, N C. Revision of May, 1961. Knoxville: Tennessee Valley Authority, 1961.
T7070

Floods on Little Pigeon and West Fork Little Pigeon in the Vicinity of Sevierville, Tenn. Knoxville: Tennessee Valley Authority, 1958.
T7080

Floods on Little Tennessee River, Cullasaja River, and Cartoogechave Creek in Vicinity of Franklin, North Carolina. Knoxville: Tennessee Valley Authority, 1963.
T7090

Floods on Nolichucky River and North and South Indian Creeks in Vicinity of Erwin, Tennessee. Knoxville, Tenn.: Tennessee Valley Authority, 1967.
T7100

Floods on North Chickamauga, Mountain, and Lookout Creeks, in Vicinity of Chattanooga, Tennessee. Knoxville: Tennessee Valley Authority, 1961.
T7110

Floods on North Toe River and Beaver and Grassy Creeks in Vicinity of Spruce Pine, North Carolina. Knoxville, Tenn.: Tennessee Valley Authority, 1963.
T7120

Floods on Oconaluftee and Tuckaseigee Rivers and Soco Creek in Vicinity of Cherokee, North Carolina. Knoxville, Tenn.: Tennessee Valley Authority, 1956.
T7130

Floods on Oostanaula Creek, in Vicinity of Athens, Tennessee. Knoxville: Tennessee Valley Authority, 1956.
T7140

Floods on Oostanaula Creek in Vicinity of Athens, Tenn. Knoxville: Tennessee Valley Authority, 1957.
T7150

Floods on Powell River and South Fork Powell River in Vicinity of Big Stone Gap, Virginia. Knoxville, Tenn.: Tennessee Valley Authority, 1956.
T7160

Floods on Powell River and South Fork Powell River in Vicinity of Big Stone Gap, Virginia. Knoxville, Tenn.: Tennessee Valley Authority, 1960.
T7170

Floods on Reedy Creek in Vicinity of Kingsport, Tennessee. Supplement. Knoxville, Tenn.: Tennessee Valley Authority, 1956.
T7180

Floods on Richland Creek and Tributary Streams in Vicinity of Waynesville and Hazelwood, North Carolina. Knoxville, Tenn.: n.p., 1970.
T7190

Floods on Rock Creek, West Fork and North Fork, in Vicinity of Tullahoma, Tennessee. Knoxville: Tennessee Valley Authority, 1960.
T7200

Floods on South Mouse Creek in Vicinity of Cleveland, Tennessee. Edition of April, 1969. Knoxville, Tenn.: Tennessee Valley Authority, 1969.
T7210

Floods on Streams in Vicinity of Newport, Tennessee. Knoxville, Tenn.: Tennessee Valley Authority, 1968.
T7220

Floods on Streams in Vicinity of Paris, Tennessee. Knoxville, Tenn.: Tennessee Valley Authority, 1969.
T7230

Floods on Swannanoa River and Beetree Creek in Vicinity of Swannanoa, North Carolina. Knoxville, Tenn.: Tennessee Valley Authority, 1963.
T7240

Floods on Swannanoa River and Flat Creek in Vicinity of Black Mountain and Montreat, North Carolina. Knoxville, Tenn.: Tennessee Valley Authority, 1962.
T7250

Floods on Tennessee River and Battle Creek, in Vicinity of South Pittsburg and Richard City, Tennessee. Knoxville: Tennessee Valley Authority, 1960.
T7260

Floods on the Tennessee River and Cypress and Cox Creeks in Vicinity of Florence, Alabama. Knoxville, Tenn.: Tennessee Valley Authority, 1956.
T7270

Floods on Tennessee River in Vicinity of Tri-Counties Alabama (Lawrence, Limestone, Morgan.) Knoxville: Tennessee Valley Authority, 1961.
T7280

Floods on Tennessee River, Little Tennessee River, and Town and Muddy Creeks in Vicinity of Lenoir City, Tennessee. Knoxville: Tennessee Valley Authority, 1964.
T7290

Floods on Toccoa-Ocoee River and Fightingtown Creek, in Vicinity of McCaysville, Ga. — Copperhill, Tenn. Knoxville, Tenn.: Tennessee Valley Authority, 1958.
T7300

Floods on Valley River, Tatham Creek, and Junaluska Creek in Vicinity of Andrews, North Carolina. Knoxville, Tenn.: Tennessee Valley Authority, 1965.
T7310

Floods on Yellow Creek in Vicinity of Burnsville, Mississippi. Knoxville, Tenn.: Tennessee Valley Authority, 1960.
T7320

Fontana Project; Hydraulic Model Studies. Knoxville: Tennessee Valley Authority, 1953.
T7330

Forest Cover Improvement Influences Upon Hydrologic Characteristics of White Hollow Watershed, 1935-1958. Knoxville: Tennessee Valley Authority, 1961.
T7340

Water Control Planning Dept.
Fort Patrick Henry Project: Hydraulic Model Studies. Knoxville: Tennessee Valley Authority, 1960.
T7350

Geologic Bulletin no. 1-10. Knoxville: Tennessee Valley Authority, 1934-1938.
T7360

High and Low Flows and Flow Duration at Stream Gages in North Carolina in Tennessee River Basin. Knoxville: Tennessee Valley Authority, 1959.
T7370

How Topographic Maps are Made. Knoxville: Tennessee Valley Authority, 1952.
T7380

How Topographic Maps Are Made. 2nd ed. Knoxville: Tennessee Valley Authority, 1965.
T7390

. . . Hydraulic Data Activities of the Tennessee Valley Authority . . . Knoxville, Tenn.: Tennessee Valley Authority, n.d.
T7400

Hydraulic Model Investigations of Lock Filling and Emptying Systems. Knoxville: Tennessee Valley Authority, 1947.
T7410

Industrial Water Supplies of the Tennessee Valley Region. By Tennessee Valley Authority, Division of Water Control Planning, Division of Health and Safety and Division of Regional Studies. Knoxville: Tennessee Valley Authority, 1948.
T7420

Influences of Reforestation and Erosion Control Upon the Hydrology of the Pine Tree Branch Watershed 1941 to 1950. Knoxville: n.p., 1955.
T7430

Major Freight Terminals on the Tennessee River Waterway. Knoxville: n.p., 1968.
T7440

Maps and Surveys. Chattanooga, Tenn.: Division of Water Control Planning, Maps and Surveys Branch, Tennessee Valley Authority, 1966.
T7450

Navigation Charts: Tennessee River. Knoxville, Tenn.: n.p., 1946.
T7460

Navigation Charts Tennessee River Reservoirs: Paducah, Kentucky to Knoxville, Tennessee, Showing Underwater Conditions, Navigation Channels and Aids and Adjacent Shore Planimetry. Knoxville: n.p., 1960.
T7470

Precipitation in Tennessee River Basin Annual. Knoxville: n.p., 1936.
T7480

Recreation Maps — Tennessee Valley Lakes. Knoxville: n.p., 1962.
T7490

Reforestation and Erosion Control Influences Upon the Hydrology of the Pine Tree Branch Watershed 1941 to 1960. Knoxville: n.p., 1962.
T7500

Report on Initial Phases, Chestuee Watershed Project. Prepared by A. S. Fry and staff. Knoxville: n.p., 1945.
T7510

. . . Technical Monograph . . . no. 1. Knoxville, Tenn.: n.p., 1941.
T7520

The Watts Bar Project on the Tennessee River. By T. B. Parker, chief engineer. Knoxville: n.p., 1938.
T7530

Watershed Development An Analysis of the Parker Branch Watershed Project, 1953 Through 1959: A Progress Report. North Carolina State College in Cooperation with the Tennessee Valley Authority. Knoxville, Tenn.: Tennessee Valley Authority, 1960.
T7540

Bear Creek Watershed; Summary of Resources. Knoxville, Tenn.: Tennessee Valley Authority, 1962.
T7550

Clinch-Powell Valley; Summary of Resources. Knoxville, Tenn.: Tennessee Valley Authority, 1963.
T7560

Tennessee Valley Public Power Association Answers to Questions That Are Frequently Asked About TVA. Chattanooga, Tenn.: n.p., 1962.
T7580

Tennessee Valley Public Power Association. Underground Residential Distribution Committee Underground Residential Distribution. Chattanooga, Tenn.: n.p., 1966.
T7570

Terango, Larry Development and Learning of Language and Speech: A Brief Synopsis. Johnson City, Tenn.: Johnson City Public Schools, Division of Special Education, Learning and Resources Center, 1969. Includes references to mountain speech as a learning disability or a problem in the development of proper language patterns.
T7590 (ETSU)

Terees, John K. From Laurel Hill to Siler's Bog. 1st ed. New York: Knopf, 1969.
T7600 (ETSU)

Terrell, Issac Long Old Houses in Rockingham County, 1750-1850. Verona: McClure Press, 1970.
T7610 (ASU WCU)

Territory of the United States, South of the River Ohio. Governor, 1790-1796 (Blount) The Blount Journal, 1790-1796: The Proceedings of Government Over the Territory of the United States of America, South of the River Ohio. Nashville: Benson Print. Co., 1955.
T7620 (ASU)

Terry, Geraldine B. The Labor Force Characteristics of Women in Low-Income Rural Areas of the South. n.p.: Southern Cooperative Series, 1966. Includes data from several mountain counties.
T7630

Testerman, Violet M. "A Comparative Study of Certain Personality Traits Between Female Physical Education Majors and Non-Majors at Appalachian State University." Master's thesis. Appalachian State Univ., 1972.
T7640 (ASU)

Tharin, Robert Seymour Symmes Arbitrary Arrests in the South: Or, Scenes From the Experiences of an Alabama Unionist. New York: Negro Universities Press, 1969. Some mention of Alabama mountain areas. Tharin's people, like many mountain families, were pro-union during the war. Tharin, himself, is known today as "the mountain abolitionist."
T7650 (WCU)

Tharp, W. E. Swann, Maurice Edward Soil Survey of Winston County, Alabama. Washington: U. S. Department of Agriculture, Bureau of Chemistry and Soils, 1937.
S9450

Taylor, Arthur Elijah Soil Survey of Adams County, Ohio. Washington: U. S. Department of Agriculture, Bureau of Chemistry and Soils, 1938.
T390

Tharp, William Edgar Soil Survey of Bibb County, Alabama. Prepared in cooperation with Alabama. Field Operations, 1908. Washington: U. S. Department of Agriculture, Bureau of Soils, 1910.
T7660

Tharp, William Edward Soil Survey of Cullman County, Alabama. Prepared in cooperation with Alabama. Field Operations, 1908. Washington: U. S. Department of Agriculture, Bureau of Soils, 1910.
T7670

Thayer, Donald Clifton "A Study of the Effects of the Elementary-Secondary Education Act of 1965 Upon Education at Greendale Elementary School." Master's thesis. East Tennessee State Univ., 1966.
T7680 (ETSU)

Thede, Marion The Fiddle Book: The Comprehensive Book on American Folk Music, Fiddlin, and Fiddle Styles Including More Than 150 Traditional Fiddle Tunes Compiled From Country Fiddlers. New York: Oak Publications, 1967. Includes instructions on bowings, standard tunings, old songs, accessories and the transition from violin to fiddle.
T7690 (ASU)

Thiel, Robert Ellis "Kenneth D. McKellar and the Politics of the Tennessee Valley Authority, 1941-1946." Master's thesis. Univ. of Virginia, 1967.
T7700

Thiessen, Reinhardt et. al. Oil Shales of Kentucky. Frankfort: Kentucky Geological Survey, 1925.
T7710

Thiselton-Dyer, Thomas Firminger The Folk-lore of Plants. 1899. Reprint. Detroit: Singing Tree Press, 1968. Includes folk remedies, lists of medicinal plants, and superstitions regarding planting, growing, and harvesting.
T7720 (ASU)

Thoenen, Eugene David History of the Oil and Gas Industry in West Virginia. Charleston, W. Va.: Education Foundation, 1964.
T7730 (ASU BC)

Thom, William Taylor Petroleum and Coal; the Keys to the Future. Princeton: Princeton Univ. Press, 1929. Mr. Thom was a prophet as well as an early student of Appalachia. He foresaw some of the troubles we've known in 1974-75.
T7740 (BC)

The Struggle for Religious Freedom in Virginia by the Baptists. New York: Johnson Reprint Co., 1973. Religion in Appalachia has never had a peaceful history.
T7750 (ASU)

Thomas, A. Carlin Wise, James O. Optimum Farm Organizations and Area Production Patterns for the Upper Hiwassee Watershed Area. Athens: Georgia Agricultural Experiment Station, 1969.
W7870

Thomas, Clarence General Turner Ashby, the Centaur of the South: A Military Sketch. Winchester, Va.: Eddy Press Corp., 1907.
T7760 (ASU)

Thomas, Cyrus The Cherokees in Pre-Columbian Times. Fact and Theory Papers. New York: Hodges, 1890. Who built the strange fortifications like those at Fort Mountain in Georgia or the Mounds in Tennessee, North Carolina and Georgia? Were they really Cherokee?
T7770 (BC LMC)

"The Cherokees Probably Mound Builders." Fifth Annual Report of the Bureau of Ethnology to the Secretary of the Smithsonian Institution, 1833-84. Washington, D. C.: Govt. Print. Off., 1887.
T7780

Thomas, Daniel Lindsey Kentucky Superstitions. Princeton, N. J.: Princeton Univ. Press, 1920. A truly marvelous book of the things we've almost forgotten.
T7790 (ASU BC)

Thomas, David Nolan "Early History of the North Carolina Furniture Industry, 1880-1921." Ph. D. Diss. Univ. of North Carolina, 1964.
T7800

Thomas, Dora Lair Echoes from the Kentucky Hills. n.p.: n.p., n.d. Personal and descriptive poems.
T7810

Thomas, George Roger Poverty in the Nonmetropolitan South. Lexington: Lexington Books, 1972. Some references to Appalachia are included although there is no distinction made between mountain economic problems and those of other rural areas.
T7820 (WWC)

Thomas, Gerald D. "An Attitudinal Study of Sunday Closing Laws in Johnson City, Tennessee: A Contribution to the "Interest-group" (Conflict) Model of Law." Master's thesis. East Tennessee State Univ., 1972.
T7830 (ETSU)

Thomas, Helen Webb "A Survey of Library Services in the County Schools of Sullivan County, Tennessee." Master's thesis. East Tennessee State Univ., 1958.
T7840 (ETSU)

Thomas, Howard The Singing Hills. 1st ed. Prospect, N. Y.: Prospect Books, 1965.
T7850 (ASU)

Thomas, James F. "The History of the First Baptist Church of Jonesboro, Tennessee." Master's thesis. East Tennessee State Univ., 1955. This church was one of the earliest Baptist churches in Tennessee. Jonesboro is Tennessee's oldest town.
T7860 (ETSU)

Thomas, James Walter History of Allegany County, Maryland. Includes a biographical and genealogical record of representative families, prepared from data obtained from original sources of information. 1923. Reprint. 2 vols. Baltimore: Regional Pub. Co., 1969.
T7870 (ASU)

Thomas, Jean see **Thomas, Jeannette Bell**

Thomas, Jeannette Bell Ballad Makin' in the Mountains of Kentucky. Music arranged by Walter Kob. New York: Oak Publications, 1964. Complete with arrangements and notations for some of the old favorites.
T7880 (ASU WCU LMC ETSU BC)

Big Sandy. New York: H. Holt and Co., 1940. A tale well-told of a river, a valley and its people.
T7890 (ASU BC)

Blue Ridge Country. American Folkways. New York: Duell, Sloan and Pearce, 1942. A description of life in the Blue Ridge mountains. Pleasant and fairly accurate.
T7900 (FC WWC ETSU BC ASU)

Blue Ridge Country. 1942. Reprint. New York: Duell, Sloan and Pearce, 1960.
T7910 (ASU WCU LMC)

Devil's Ditties, Being Stories of the Kentucky Mountain People, Told by Jean Thomas, With the Songs They Sing. Chicago: W. W. Hatfield, 1931. These tales and songs from the Kentucky hills include expurgated versions of the devil's ditties popular in the early 1900's.
T7920 (ASU BC)

The Singin' Fiddler of Lost Hope Hollow. 1st ed. New York: E. P. Dutton and Co., 1938. There are those who say that Jilson Settlers was part of a musical hoax: neither blind nor from Last Hope Hollow. At any rate, it's an interesting book.
T7930 (LMC ASU ETSU BC)

The Singin' Gatherin': Tunes From the Southern Appalachians. Complete ed. New York: Silver Burdett Co., 1939.
T7940 (UNCA BC ETSU ASU)

The Singin' Gatherin': Tunes From the Southern Appalachians. Student's ed. New York: Silver Burdett, 1939.
T7950 (LMC BC)

The Sun Shines Bright. New York: Prentice-Hall, 1940. Autobiography of Jean Thomas, court stenographer, musician extraordinare, and ballad collector.
T7960 (ASU WCU LMC ETSU BC)

The Traipsin' Woman. New York: E. P. Dutton and Co., 1933. Account of Miss Thomas' experiences as a traveling court stenographer in Eastern Kentucky. She has some marvelous insights into the mountain culture.
T7970 (ASU WWC BC)

Thomas, Jerry Bruce "Coal Country: The Rise of the Southern Smokeless Coal Industry and Its Effect on Area Development." Ph. D. Diss. Univ. of North Carolina, 1971.
T7980

Thomas, Lately see also **Robert V. P. Steele**

Thomas, Lately pseud. The First President Johnson: The Three Lives of the Seventeenth President of the United States of America. New York: Morrow, 1968. A well-written biography in three sections. Sympathetic in tone and notable for the author's cognizances of the effect of Johnson's mountain background on his character.
T7990 (ASU)

Thomas, Lucy Blayney Thomas, Daniel Lindsey Kentucky Superstitions. Princeton, N. J.: Princeton Univ. Press, 1920.
T7790 (ASU BC)

Thomas, Maude Morgan Black Diamonds. Illustrated by Robert Elliot Kinsley. Yesterday and Today Series. New York: T. Nelson and Sons, 1941.
T8000 (ASU)

Thomas, Mei Grannies's Remedies. American ed. 1965. Reprint. New York: J. H. Heineman, 1967. A volume to help us remember all those horrible-tasting tonics and remedies we grew up with. Now scientists are saying most old home remedies have positive curative effects. Granny knew that.
T8010 (ASU)

Thomas, Richard G. "Southern Appalachian State Newspapers' Treatment of the Antipoverty and Appalachia Acts." Master's thesis. American Univ., 1967. Interesting topic, but the author makes poor use of his data. Many social and political overtones are ignored.
T8020

Thomas, Roy Edwin comp. Popular Folk Dictionary of Ozarks Talk. Little Rock, Ark.: Dox Books, 1972. Dr. Thomas is now a professor at Appalachian State. He maintains, correctly I think, that there is little difference between Ozark and Appalachian dialect and idiom.
T8030 (ASU)

Thomas, W. E. and others Soil Survey, Carroll County, Virginia. Washington: U. S. Soil Conservation Service, 1967.
T8040

Thomas, Walter "The Drop-Out Problem in Harris High School, Spruce Pine, North Carolina." Master's thesis. Appalachian State Teachers College, 1956.
T8050 (ASU)

Thomas, Walter B. "A Survey of Educational Facilities in Cherokee County, North Carolina." Master's thesis. Univ. of North Carolina, 1948.
T8060 (ASU)

Thomas, William H. Explanation of the Fund Held in Trust By the United States For the North Carolina Cherokees. Washington: L. Towers, 1858. Interesting account of the establishment of the reservation. This is the only reservation in the United States which was privately donated rather than established by the government. Later the government took over the reservation and now manages the Cherokee trust fund.
T8070 (ASU)

Thomas, William Roscoe Life Among the Hills and Mountains of Kentucky. Louisville: Standard Print. Co., 1926. Interesting observations on the mountaineers of Kentucky by an outlander who lived among them for many years. Commentary on resources and industry and social and economic conditions.
T8080 (ASU BC)

Thomason, John Williams Jeb Stuart. New York: Scribner, 1930. Jeb Stuart was born in the mountains of Virginia and he used his knowledge of the terrain to advantage many times during the war. This biography captures his larger than life image and leadership qualities. Well researched; beautifully written.
T8090

Thomason, Ronald E. Grafton, A. Edwin A Manual of West Virginia's Wood-using Industries, with Directory. Morgantown: Office of Research and Development, Center for Appalachian Studies and Development, West Virginia Univ., 1965.
G3110 (ASU)

Thomasson, Lillian Franklin "Education in Swain County, North Carolina." Master's thesis. Univ. of North Carolina, 1939.
T8100

Swain County: Early History and Educational Development. Bryson City, N. C.: n.p., 1965.
T8110 (ASU WCU LMC)

Thompson, Adele Eugenia Brave Heart Elizabeth; a Story of the Ohio Frontier. Boston: Lee and Shepard, 1902. A novel about Betty Zane of Wheeling, West Virginia and the Ohio River frontier country. Courage and goodness triumph.
T8120 (ASU BC)

Thompson, Algernon D. Thompson, Lawrence Sidney The Kentucky Novel. Lexington: Univ. of Kentucky Press, 1953.
T8240 (ASU)

Thompson, Anthony D. Tribal Enrollment of the Eastern Band of Cherokee Indians, Cherokee, North Carolina. Cullowhee, N. C.: Western Carolina Univ., 1970.
T8130 (LMC WCU)

Thompson, Bradford F. History of the 112th Regiment of Illinois Volunteer Infantry, in the Great War of the Rebellion, 1862-1865. Toulon, Ill.: Printed at the Stark County News Office, 1885. This regiment was action in the South mountains.
T8140 (ASU)

Thompson, Edgar T. ed. McKinney, John C. The South in Continuity and Change. Durham, N. C.: Duke Univ. Press, 1965.
M1910 (BC FC)

Thompson, Ernest Trice Presbyterian Missions in the Southern United States. Richmond: Presbyterian Committee of Publications, 1934. The Presbyterians sent more missionaries south to help the "pore mountaineer" than any other denomination.
T8150 (LMC)

Presbyterians in the South. Richmond: John Knox Press, 1963. The Presbyterians were among the first missionaries on the Appalachian frontier, and they kept up the good fight until well into this century.
T8160 (WWC BC)

Thompson, Henry Dewey Drainage Evolution in the Appalachians of Pennsylvania. New York: Academy of Sciences, 1949.
T8170 (ETSU)

Thompson, Holland From the Cotton Field to the Cotton Mill: A Study of the Industrial Transition in North Carolina. New York: Macmillan Co., 1906. Many textile mills located in the foothills and used cheap mountain labor. The damage done to the mountaineer in the transition from freedom and individualism to an automated cipher is incalculable.
T8180 (LMC)

Thompson, J. J. A History of the Feud Between the Hill and Evans Parties of Garrard County, Ky. Cincinnati: U. P. James, 1854. This was one of the most exciting and least understood of Kentucky's bloody feuds. At one time it involved nearly eighty men.
T8190 (ASU BC)

Thompson, James H. The Changing Markets for West Virginia Coal 1951-1963. Morgantown: Bureau of Business Research, West Virginia Univ., 1964.
T8200

Factors Influencing Plant Location in West Virginia, 1945-1956. Morgantown: Bureau of Business Research, West Va. Univ., 1956.
T8210

Labor Market Areas for Manufacturing Plants in West Virginia. Morgantown: Bureau of Business Research, West Va. Univ., 1955.
T8220

Significant Trends in the West Virginia Coal Industry, 1900-1957. Morgantown: West Virginia Univ., n.d.
T8230 (ASU)

Thompson, Lawrence S. assoc. ed. Coleman, John Winston, Jr. ed. Kentucky: A Pictorial History. Lexington: Univ. of Kentucky Press, 1971.
C5780 (ASU)

Thompson, Lawrence Sidney The Kentucky Novel. Lexington: Univ. of Kentucky Press, 1953.
T8240 (ASU)

Kentucky Tradition. Hamden, Conn.: Shoe String Press, 1956. This history of the state and its traditions seems to lack a cohesive central theme.
T8250 (ASU)

Thompson, Mary Lou "An Analysis of the Homebound Program for Exceptional Children in Unicoi County." Master's thesis. East Tennessee State College, 1957.
T8260 (ETSU)

Thompson, Maurice At Love's Extremes. New York: Cassell and Co., 1885. A traveling Englishman finds an old friend in a mountain cabin in Alabama. The host's daughter is in love with the young English boarder, but not until he realizes his cruel English lady is unattainable does he turn to Milly and Sand Mountain for consolation.
T8270 (BC)

Stories of the Cherokee Hills. Boston and New York: Houghton Mifflin Co., 1898. Stories and sketches of the Cherokee country; North Georgia, Eastern Tennessee, and North Alabama.
T8280 (BC WCU)

The Witchery of Archery. With an added chapter by Will Henry Thompson. Edited by Robert Potter Elmer. Pinehurst ed. Pinehurst, N. C.: Archers Co., 1928.
T8290 (ASU)

Thompson, Noble R. "A Geographic Appraisal of Union County, Tennessee." Master's thesis. Univ. of Tennessee, 1965.
T8300

Thompson, Rhodes Voices from Cane Ridge. St. Louis, Mo.: Bethany Press, 1954. Although Cane Ridge is just outside the mountain region, the revivalism movement in the United States was an Appalachian phenomenon. Here, in the mountain, frontier culture met and clashed with the too formal religion of the East. It was the mountaineer who caused established religion to despair and brought on the revival movement.
T8310 (BC)

Thompson, S. F. History of Alleghany County. n.p.: n.p., 1912.
T8320

Thompson, Samuel Hunter The Highlanders of the South. New York: Eaton and Mains; Cincinnati: Jennings and Graham, 1910. Observations on the East Tennessee mountaineers by an outlander. Commentary on social life, customs, the economy, and the characteristics of the mountaineer.
T8330 (ASU ETSU BC LMC)

Thompson, Wesley Sylvester The Free State of Winston: A History of Winston County, Alabama. Winfield, Ala.: Pareil Press, 1968. Winston County was sympathetic to the Union cause and seceded from the state of Alabama.
T8340 (ASU)

Thorn, Joe Oic-? Science Fiction. Parsons, W. Va.: McClain Print. Co., 1971. A science fiction novel set in the Appalachia of the future.
T8350 (ASU)

Thornborough, Laura pseud. see Thornburgh, Laura

Thornburgh, Laura The Great Smoky Mountains. Illustrated by Vivian Moir. New York: Thomas Y. Crowell Co., 1937. A loving description of the Great Smoky Mountains and the National Park.
T8360 (ASU WCU LMC WWC UNCA)

The Great Smoky Mountains. Illustrated by Vivian Moir. Rev. and enlarged ed. New York: Thomas Y. Crowell Co., 1942.
T8370 (WCU LMC BC ETSU)

The Great Smoky Mountains. Illustrated by Vivian Moir. Rev. and enlarged ed. 1942. Reprint. Knoxville: Univ. of Tennessee Press, 1962.
T8380 (ETSU)

Thorndyke, George Howard The Witch's Castle. Knoxville, Tenn.: Life and Letters Co., 1903.
T8390 (ASU)

Thornton, G. D. Taylor, Arthur Elijah Soil Survey, Catoosa County, Georgia. Washington: U. S. Department of Agriculture, Bureau of Plant Industry, 1941.
T400

Taylor, Arthur Elijah Soil Survey, Dade County, Georgia. Washington: U. S. Department of Agriculture, Bureau of Plant Industry, 1942.
T440

Thornton, Mable Harvey Pioneers of Roane County, Tennessee, 1801-1830. Rockwood, Tenn.: n.p., 1965. Source materials include tax lists, muster rolls, election lists, and petitions.
T8400 (ETSU)

Thornton, Marcellus Eugene My "Budie" and I. New York: F. Tennyson Neely, 1899. Romantic fiction about a North Carolina coal baron.
T8410 (ASU)

Thornton, Mary Lindsay A Bibliography of North Carolina, 1589-1955. Chapel Hill: Univ. of North Carolina Press, 1958.
T8420 (LMC UNCA ASU)

Official Publications of the Colony and State of North Carolina, 1749-1939, a Bibliography. Chapel Hill: Univ. of North Carolina Press, 1954.
T8430 (ASU LMC)

Thrasher, James Arvin "An Educational Survey of Unicoi County, Tennessee." Master's thesis. Univ. of Tennessee, 1932.
T8440

Three Fork Baptist Church Minutes. Three Fork Baptist Church, 1790-1895. Raleigh: North Carolina State Department of Archives and History, 1952. This is the oldest Baptist Association in the North Carolina mountains.
T8450 (ASU)

Thrift, Minton Lee, Jesse Memoir of the Rev. Jesse Lee. With Extracts From His Journals. New York: Arno Press, 1969.
L1380 (ASU FC)

Thruston, Gates P. The Antiquities of Tennessee and the Adjacent States, and the State of Aboriginal Society in the Scale of Civilization Represented by Them. Cincinnati: Robert Clarke, 1890.
T8460 (LMC ASU)

Thurmond, Walter R. The Logan Coal Field of West Virginia: A Brief History. Morgantown: West Virginia Univ. Library, 1964.
T8470 (ASU ETSU WCU)

Thurston, Mynna The Washingtons and Their Colonial Homes in W. Va. Charleston: Jefferson Pub. Co., n.d.
T8480 (BC)

Thwaites, Reuben Gold Daniel Boone. New York: D. Appleton and Co., 1902. Another Boone biography with ponderous style and too many interjections.
T8490 (ETSU BC)

Daniel Boone. 1902. Reprint. Appleton's Life Histories Series. New York: D. Appleton and Co., 1926.
T8500 (ASU)

Thwaites, Reuben Gold ed. Documentary History of Dunmore's War, 1774. Madison, Wis.: Wisconsin Historical Society, 1905.
T8510

Frontier Defense on Upper Ohio, 1777-1778. Draper Series, Vol. III. Madison, Wis.: Wisconsin Historical Society, 1912.
T8520

Revolution on the Upper Ohio, 1775-1777. Draper Series, Vol. II. Madison, Wis.: Wisconsin Historical Society, 1908.
T8530

Withers Chronicles of Border Warfare. Cincinnati: Robert Clark Co., 1895.
T8540

Tibbals, Alma Owens A History of Pulaski County, Kentucky. Bagdad, Ky.: G. O. Moore, 1952.
T8550

Tidball, Mary Langdon Barbara's Vagaries. New York: Harper and Brothers, 1886. A North Carolina mountain girl from the French Broad country finds herself in society, and society is overwhelmed by her.
T8560 (WCU BC)

Tidwell, James Nathan ed. A Treasury of American Folk Humor; a Rare Collection of Laughter, Tall Tales, Jests and Other Gems of Merriment of the American People. New York: Crown Pubs., 1956.
T8570 (FC)

Tiernan, Frances Christine Fisher Bonny Kate. A Novel. Library of American Fiction, no. 1. New York: D. Appleton and Co., 1881. A stylized novel of manners with a mountain setting.
T8580 (ASU)

His Victory. Notre Dame, Ind.: Ave Maria Press, 1887. Moralistic fiction with a mountain setting.
T8590

The Land of the Sky; or Adventures in Mountain By-Ways. New York: D. Appleton and Co., 1875. Romantic fiction set in western North Carolina.
T8600

"The Land of the Sky": Or, Adventures in Mountain By-Ways. New York: Appleton, 1882.
T8610 (LMC)

The Land of the Sky: Or, Adventures in Mountain By-Ways. New York: Appleton, 1900.
T8620 (LMC)

"The Land of the Sky": Or, Adventures in Mountain Byways. New York: D. Appleton kd Co., 1907.
T8630

A Little Maid of Arcady. Philadelphia: H. L. Kilner and Co., 1893. Western North Carolina setting.
T8640

A Summer Idyl. New York: Appleton, 1878. Western North Carolina fiction.
T8650

Tight, W. G. Drainage Modifications in Southeastern Ohio and Adjacent Parts of West Virginia and Kentucky. U. S. Geological Survey Professional Paper, no. 13. Washington: Govt. Print. Off., 1903.
T8660

Tigue, William B. Reilly, John P. "An Analysis of Faculty and Administrative Attitudes Toward Teacher Corps Interns in Carter County, Tennessee." East Tennessee State Univ., 1969.
R1430 (ETSU)

Tilton, John Littlefield Hampshire and Hardy Counties. West Virginia Geological Survey County Reports. Morgantown, W. Va.: Morgantown Print. and Bind. Co., 1927.
T8670 (ETSU)

Pendleton County. West Virginia Geological Survey. Wheeling, W. Va.: Wheeling News Litho. Co., 1927.
T8680 (ETSU)

Timberlake, Henry Lieut. Henry Timberlake's Memoirs, 1756-1765. With annotation, introduction and index by Samuel Cole Williams. Johnson City, Tenn.: Watauga Press, 1927.
T8690 (BC ETSU)

Lieut. Henry Timberlake's Memoirs, 1756-1765, With Annotation, Introduction and Index. By Samuel Cole Williams. 1927. Reprint. New York: Arno Press, 1971.
T8700 (ASU WCU LMC)

Memoirs, 1756-1765. With Annotation, Introduction and index by Samuel Cole Williams. 1927. Reprint. Marietta, Ga.: Continental Book Co., 1948.
T8710 (ETSU ASU WCU)

Tinsley, Bob Depew, E. Douglas Land of Waterfalls: A Portfolio of Exclusive Lithographs Suitable for Framing. Asheville, N. C.: Stephens Press, 1954.
D1860 (WCU)

Tippett, James Sterling Schools for a Growing Democracy. In collaboration with the Committee of the Parker School District, Greenville, S. C. New York: Ginn and Co., 1936.
T8720 (ETSU)

Tipple, Ezra Squier Frances Asbury, the Prophet of the Long Road. New York: Methodist Book Concern, 1916.
T8730 (ASU)

The Heart of Asbury's Journal. New York: Earon and Mains, 1904.
T8740

Tipton, Alice Stevens comp. Favorite Recipes of the John C. Campbell Folk School. Edited by Oris Cantrell. Brasstown, N. C.: John C. Campbell Folk School, 1971.
T8750 (BC WCU ASU)

Titler, George J. Hell in Harlan. Beckley, W. Va.: BJW Printers, 1972? Memoirs of the United Mine Workers.
T8760 (WCU)

Titus, Warren Irving John Fox, Jr. New York: Twayne, 1971. Biography of one of Kentucky's most famous novelists. Fox pioneered in popularizing Appalachia as a subject for fiction.
T8770

Todd, A. S. An Appraisal of Methods for Salvaging Small Sawmill Residues in the Southeast. U. S. Forest Service Station Paper, no. 84. Asheville, N. C.: Southeastern Forest Experiment Station, 1957.
T8780 (WCU)

Todd, Joseph Archer The Blue Ridge Parkway: A Poem. Gatlinburg, Tenn.: W. M. Cline, 1971. A paean to the Blue Ridge Parkway.
T8790 (WCU)

Toewe, E. Clayton Geology of the Leesburg Quadrangle, Virginia. Report of Investigations, 11. Charlottesville: Virginia Division of Mineral Resources, 1966.
T8800 (ETSU)

Tollett, Daniel Joseph "An Analysis of the Continuing Consultant Program and the Development of a Profile of Schools in the Tennessee Appalachia Educational Cooperative." Ed. D. Diss. Univ. of Tennessee, 1971.
T8810

Tolley, G. S. Economics of Watershed Planning Sponsored by the Southeast Land Tenure Research Committee, the Farm Foundation, and the Tennessee Valley Authority. Ames, Iowa: State Univ. Press, 1961.
T8820

Tomlinson, Everett Titsworth Scouting with Daniel Boone. American Scouting Series. Garden City, N. Y.: Doubleday, Page and Co., 1914.
T8830 (ASU LMC BC)

Tomlinson, W. F. Biography of the State Officers and Members of the General Assembly of North Carolina, 1893, Other Interesting Facts. Raleigh, N. C.: Edwards and Broughton, 1893.
T8840 (ASU LMC)

Tomorrow's People, a Storm in Harlan, Kentucky Facsimile with a foreword by Jesse Stuart. Ed. by K. D. Petrey. Cincinnati: Harvest Press, 1968. These poems written in Lee Pennington's class at Southeast Community College, Cumberland, Kentucky literally created a storm in Harlan County.
T8850 (BC)

Tompkins, Dorothy C. Poverty in the U. S. During the Sixties, a Bibliography. Berkeley: Univ. of California, 1970. Lists numerous entries on Appalachian poverty.
T8860 (BC)

Tompkins, Dorothy L. (Campbell) Culver Strip Mining for Coal. Berkeley: Institute of Governmental Studies, Univ. of California, 1973.
T8870 (BC)

Tompkins, Edmund Pendleton The Natural Bridge and Its Historical Surroundings. Natural Bridge, Va.: Natural Bridge of Va., 1939.
T8880 (ASU FC BC)

Rockbridge County, Virginia. Richmond, Va.: Whittet and Shepperson, 1952. An informal history of Rockbridge County, Virginia.
T8890

Tompkins, Jerry R. ed. D-Days at Dayton: Reflections on the Scopes Trial. Baton Rouge: Louisiana State Univ. Press, 1965. An account of the circus sponsored by the town of Dayton in 1925.
T8900 (ASU BC)

Toomery, Glen A. The Romance of a Sesquicentennial, The Dumplin Creek Baptist Church of Christ, Jefferson County, Tennessee, Organized 1797. n.p.: n.p., 1947.
T8910 (BC)

Toone, Betty L. Appalachia: The Mountains, the Place, and the People. Illustrated with photographs by Joyce Hoffman. A First Book. New York: F. Watts, 1972. Geographical and historical background legends and life of the people today.
T8920 (ASU LMC MHC BC ETSU)

Torlone, William D. "A Cost Analysis of Methods of Salvaging Logging Residue in Appalachia." Master's thesis. West Virginia Univ., 1968.
T8930

Torpey, Dorothy Margaret Hallowed Heritage: The Life of Virginia. Richmond, Va.: Whittlet and Shepperson, 1961.
T8940 (FC BC)

Torrence, Clayton Virginia Wills and Administrations, 1632-1800: An Index of Wills Recorded in Local Courts of Virginia, 1632-1800, and of Administrations of Estates Shown by Inventories of the Estates of Intestates Recorded in Will (and Other) Books of Local Courts, 1632-1800. 1930. Reprint. Baltimore: Genealogical Pub. Co., 1972.
T8950 (ASU BC)

Torrence, Robert M. Colonel "Davey" Crockett. Washington, D. C.: N. Fagan, 1956.
T8960

Torrey, Bradford Spring Notes From Tennessee. Boston: Riverside Press, 1896.
T8970 (LMC BC)

A World of Green Hills: Observation of Nature and Human Nature in the Blue Ridge. Boston: Houghton, Mifflin and Co., 1898.
T8980 (ASU LMC BC)

Totten, Henry Rolaud Coker, William Chambers The Trees of North Carolina. Chapel Hill, N. C.: W. C. Coker, 1916.
C5660 (ASU)

Coker, William Chambers Trees of the Southeastern States, Including Virginia, North Carolina, South Carolina, Tennessee, Georgia, and Northern Florida. Chapel Hill: Univ. of North Carolina Press, 1945.
C5670 (ASU BC)

Toulmin, Harry A Description of Kentucky in North America: To Which Are Prefixed Miscellaneous Observations Respecting the United States. 1792. Reprint. Edited by Thomas D. Clark. Lexington: Univ. of Kentucky Press, 1945.
T8990 (ASU LMC)

The Western Country in 1793: Reports on Kentucky and Virginia. Edited by Marion Finliag and Godfrey Davies. 1st ed. San Marino, Cal.: n.p., 1948.
T9000 (ASU BC ETSU)

Tourgee, Albion Winegar Bricks Without Straw: A Novel. Americans in Fiction. Ridgewood, N. J.: Gregg Press, 1967. Deals with the question of race in the South. Not specifically Appalachian.
T9010 (WCU BC ETSU)

A Fool's Errand, by One of the Fools: The Famous Romance of American History. New, enlarged and illustrated ed. To which is added by the same author, Part II. The invisible empire: A concise review of the epoch on which the tale is based. With many thrilling personal narratives and startling facts of life at the South never before narrated for the general reader. New York: Fords, Howard and Hulbert, 1880. Deals with the question of race in the South. Not specifically Appalachian.
T9020 (WCU BC)

A Fool's Errand: A Novel of the South During Reconstruction. New York: Harper, 1966.
T9030 (WWC)

The Invisible Empire: A Concise Review of the Epoch, With Many Thrilling Personal Narratives and Startling Facts of Life at the South, Never Before Narrated for the General Reader, All Fully Authenticated. Also published as Part II of A Fool's errand. 1880. Reprint. Americans in Fiction. Ridgewood, N. J.: Gregg Press, 1968. Deals with the question of race in the South. Not specifically Appalachian.
T9040 (WCU)

A Royal Gentleman: A Novel. Original title: Toinette. 1874. Reprint. Americans in Fiction. Ridgewood, N. J.: Gregg Press, 1967.
T9050 (WCU)

Tousey, Sanford Davy Crockett: Hero of the Alamo. Chicago: A. Whitman, 1948. Crockett was born and reared in East Tennessee.
T9060 (ETSU)

Towe, Stuart Baker, Joe L. Men of Affairs in Knoxville. Knoxville: Knoxville Litho., 1917.
B620

Townsend, Mrs. F. L. see **Townsend, Metta Folger**

Townsend, George Alfred Katy of Catoctin: Or, The Chain-Breakers, a National Romance. New ed., with an introduction by Harold R. Manakee. Cambridge, Md.: Tidewater Pubs., 1959. Romantic fiction with a vaguely Appalachian milieu.
T9070 (ASU WCU BC WCU)

Townsend, John Wilson Kentucky in American Letters, 1784-1912. WITH AN INTRODUCTION BY James Lane Allen. 2 vols. Cedar Rapids, Iowa: Torch Press, 1913.
T9080 (ASU BC)

Richard Hickman Menefee. New York: Neale Pub. Co., 1907. Biography of a lawyer-journalist from Owensville, Kentucky.
T9090 (BC)

Townsend, Metta Folger In the Nantahalas: A Novel. New York: Broadway Pub. Co., 1910. A western North Carolina girl leaves the mountains for an education.
T9100 (LMC BC ASU WCU)

Townsend, Wm. B. F. Observations from a Peak in Lumpkin. Atlanta: Oglethorpe Univ. Press, 1936. Collected writings of the longtime editor of the DAHLONEGA NUGGET, one of North Georgia's finest county newspapers.
T9110 (BC ASU)

Tracy, Don Street, James Howell Pride of Possession. New York: Lippincott, 1960.
S7860 (ASU)

Cherokee. New York: Dial Press, 1957. Young people's fiction about the mountain-based Cherokee.
T9120 (LMC BC WCU MHC)

Traffic Planning Associates A Preliminary Major Highway Plan, A Part of the Georgia Mountains Region Development Program. Atlanta: Traffic Planning Associates, n.d.
T9130

Tragos vol. L-, 1970-. Williamsburg, Ky.: Cumberland College, n.d.
T9140 (BC)

Training Corporation of America Training Program for Auxiliary Health and Education Personnel in Nine Counties of Southern West Virginia. Washington: Appalachian Regional Commission, 1968.
T9150 (ASU)

Transallegheny Historical Magazine vol. 1-, 1901-. Morgantown: Transallegheny Historical Society, n.d.
T9160 (BC)

Transylvania Historical Commission 1861-1961, Transylvania County Centennial: Historical Souvenir Program. n.p.: n.p., 1961.
T9170

Treacy, M. F. Prelude to Yorktown: The Southern Campaign of Nathanael Greene, 1780-1781. Chapel Hill: Univ. of North Carolina Press, 1963. Greene campaigned in the foothill country of North Carolina and his forays ranged as far north as the Dan River in Virginia.
T9180 (ASU)

Treaties Between the United States and the Cherokee Nation From 1785 Tahlequah, N. C.: n.p., 1870. A sad volume documenting the official betrayal of the Cherokee.
T9190

Tremble, Stella Craft The Crystal Prison. New York: American Poets Free Press, 1959.
T9200 (BC)

The Silver Chain. Sambornville, N. H.: Wake-Brook Press, 1953.
T9210 (BC)

Tremble, Stella Craft
Thorns and Thistledown. New York: Comet Press Books, 1954.
T9220 (BC)
Wind in the Reed. Boston: Bruce Humphries, 1957.
T9230 (BC)

Trent, William P. William Gilmore Simms. American Men of Letters Series. Boston: Houghton, Mifflin and Co., 1892.
T9240 (ASU)

The Trial of Floyd Allen, April 30, 1912, at Wytheville, Va. Reported by Morris and Hart (Shorthand Reporters), 3 vols. typescript. Roanoke, Va.: n.p., 1912. Transcript of the trial of one of the famous "Allen outlaws" of the Hillsville Courthouse tragedy.
T9250 (BC)

Tribbeko, John Lists of Germans From the Palatinate Who Came to England in 1709. Baltimore: Genealogical Pub. Co., 1965.
T9270 (ASU)

Tri-Cities Arts Council, Johnson City, Tennessee KIOSK. no. 1-, 1967-. Johnson City: The council, quarterly. Quarterly magazine of the Johnson City, Kingsport, Bristol Arts Council.
T9260 (ETSU)

Trimble, David B. Southwest Virginia Families. San Antonio: n.p., 1974.
T9280

Trimble, George R., Jr. McCauley, Orris D. Forestry Returns Evaluated for Uneven-aged Management in Two Appalachian Woodlots. Upper Darby, Pa.: Northeastern Forest Experiment Station, 1972.
M340
Appraisal of Early Reproduction After Cutting in Northern Appalachian Hardwood Stands. U. S. Forest Service Station Paper, 162. Upper Darby, Pa.: Northeastern Forest Experiment Station, 1961.
T9290
Diameter Increase in Second-Growth Appalachian Hardwood Stands, Comparison of Species. Forest Service Research Note, NE-75. Upper Darby, Pa.: Northeastern Forest Experiment Station, 1967.
T9300
Growth of Appalachian Hardwoods as Affected by Site and Residual Stand Density. Forest Service Research Paper, NE-98. Upper Darby, Pa.: Northeastern Forest Experiment Station, 1968.
T9310
Regeneration of Central Appalachian Hardwoods with Emphasis on the Effects of Site Quality and Harvesting Practice. Upper Darby, Pa.: Northeastern Forest Experiment Station, 1973.
T9320
Reproduction 7 Years After Seed-Tree Harvest Cutting in Appalachian Hardwoods. U. S. Forest Service Research Paper, NE-223. Upper Darby, Pa.: Northeastern Forest Experiment Station, 1972.
T9330
What Happens to Living Cull Trees Left After Heavy Cutting in Mixed Hardwood Stands? U. S. Forest Service Research Note, NE-12. Upper Darby, Pa.: Northeastern Forest Experiment Station, 1963.
T9340
Wendel, George W. Early Reproduction After Seed-tree Harvest Cuttings in Appalachian Hardwoods. Upper Darby, Pa.: Northeastern Forest Experiment Station, 1968.
W2790

Trimble, J. Green "Recollections of Breathitt." Jackson: Kentucky Jackson Times Print., 1915. A note on the card indicates that the Berea copy of this rare item is one of three in Kentucky.
T9350 (BC)

Trimble, John Farley Trimble Families of America. Parsons, W. Va.: McClain Print. Co., 1973.
T9360

Trinity Episcopal Church, Woman's Auxiliary Good Cooking in Asheville. Asheville: The auxiliary, n.d.
T9370

Triplett, Frank Conquering the Wilderness: Or, New Pictorial History of the Life and Times of the Pioneer Heroes and Heroines of America. With 200 Portraits from life, and engravings from designs by Nast, Dailey, and other eminent artists. New York: N. D. Thompson and Co., 1883.
T9380 (ASU BC)

Tristate Southern Highlands Study Southern Highlands Mountain Resources Management Plan, Vols. I and II. Atlanta: Georgia Dept. of Natural Resources, N. C. Dept. of Admin., S. C. Dept. of Parks, Recreation, and Tourism, 1974.
T9390

Tritschler, Donald C. Health and Sanitation Needs and Resources, Bradley County, Tennessee. Oak Ridge, Tenn.: Oak Ridge Associated Univ., 1966.
T9400

Triumphant Faith in the Kentucky Hills; Answers to Prayers in the Mountains of Kentucky n.p.: Kentucky Mountains Holiness Assoc., 1942-43.
T9410

Trogdon, W. F. Trogdon Family History. Miami, Fla.: The author, 1926.
T9420 (ASU)

Trosper, Ernest Melvin "The Driving Habits and Experiences of One Hundred Graduates of Tennessee High School, Bristol." Master's thesis. East Tennessee State Univ., 1968.
T9430 (ETSU)

Troubetzkoy, Amelie Rives Chandler Virginia of Virginia: A Story. New York: Harper and Brothers, 1888.
T9450 (LMC)

Troubetzkoy, Amelie Rives Chanler Tanis, the Sang-Digger. New York: Town Popics Pub. Co., 1893. Tale of a ginseng digger who has a profound impact on the life of a surveyor who is visiting the southern mountains.
T9440 (ASU)

Troughton, Joanna The Little Mohee, an Appalachian Ballad. New York: E. P. Dutton and Co., 1970. A ballad concerning the romance of an Indian woman and a man from the Old World. Written and illustrated for children.
T9460

Troutman, Richard Laverne "The Social and Economic Structure of Kentucky Agriculture, 1850-1860." Ph. D. Diss. Univ. of Kentucky, 1958.
T9470

Trouy, Lucien C. "Charles Egbert Craddock and the Southern Mountains and Mountaineers." Master's thesis. Catholic Univ. of America, 1932.
T9480 (ASU)

Trowbridge, John Townsend Cudjo's Cave. Boston: Lothrop, Lee and Shepard Co., 1891. Expounds the legend of a cave in the Cumberland Gap.
T9490 (ASU ETSU)

Troxel, Thomas H. Legion of the Lost Mine; Stories of the Cumberland. n.p.: Comet Press Books, 1958.
T9500

Truesdell, Fred L. "The Development of Negro Education in Rutherford County, North Carolina." Master's thesis. North Carolina Agricultural and Technical College, 1954.
T9510

Truett, Randle Bond Trade and Travel Around the Southern Appalachians Before 1830. Chapel Hill: Univ. of North Carolina, 1935.
T9520 (ASU LMC)

Truex, Everett Palmer "A Comparative Analysis of Per Capita Income and Related Factors in North Carolina Counties and the United States for Selected Years From 1939 to 1954." Ph. D. Diss. Univ. of North Carolina, 1961.
T9530

Tryon, N. C., League of Women Voters Know Our County: People, Places, and Facts. A Survey of Polk County in Western North Carolina. Tryon, N. C.: The league, 1960.
T9540 (WCU)

Tryon, N. C., Town Planning Board Proposed Development Plan, Tryon, N. C., Central Business District. Tryon, N. C.: The board, 1966.
T9550 (LMC)

Tryon Riding and Hunt Club, Tryon, N. C. Souvenir Edition, 20th Anniversary Block House Races. Complete History. Tryon: The club, 1966.
T9560

Tsai, Cha-Houy An Annotated Bibliography of Water Resource Papers Pertaining to West Virginia. Morgantown: n.p., 1963.
T9570

Tucker, Beverley The Partisan Leader. 1836. Reprint. New York: Rudd and Carleton, 1861. Partially set in Virginia's mountain region.
T9580

Tucker, George The Valley of Shenandoah; Or, Memoirs of the Graysons. 2 vols. New York: Charles Riley, 1824.
T9590
The Valley of Shenandoah: Or, Memoirs of the Graysons. Introduction by Donald R. Noble, Jr. Chapel Hill: Univ. of North Carolina Press, 1970.
T9600 (ASU ETSU WWC)

Tucker, Glenn Chickamauga: Bloody Battle in the West. Maps by Dorothy Thomas Tucker. 1st ed. Indianapolis: Bobbs-Merrill, 1961.
T9610 (ASU MHC)
Front Rank. Illustrated by Bill Ballard. Raleigh: North Carolina Confederate Centennial Commission, 1962.
T9620 (LMC)
Tecumseh: Vision of Glory. 1st ed. Indianapolis: Bobbs-Merrill, 1956. Biographical history of Tecumseh, chief of the Shawnee nation.
T9630 (ASU)
Zeb Vance: Champion of Personal Freedom. 1965. Reprint. Indianapolis: Bobbs-Merrill, 1966. Vance was governor of North Carolina during the Civil War.
T9640 (ASU WCU UNCA)

Tucker, Nathaniel Beverley The Partisan Leader. Edited, with an introduction, by Carl Bridenbaugh. American Oleserta. New York: A. A. Knopf, 1933.
T9650 (ASU)
The Partisan Leader. Upper Saddle River, N. J.: Gregg Press, 1968.
T9660 (ETSU)

Tucker, Rietz Courtney Tilton, John Littlefield Hampshire and Hardy Counties. Morgantown, W. Va.: Morgantown Print. and Bind. Co., 1927.
T8670 (ETSU)
Deep-well Records. West Virginia Geological Survey, Reports, vol. 7. Huntington, W. Va.: Gentry Brothers Print. Co., 1936.
T9670 (ETSU)
Summarized Records of Deep Wells. West Virginia Geological Survey Reports, vol. 16. Charleston, W. Va.: Charleston Print. Co., 1943.
T9680 (ETSU)

Tudiver, Neil "Why Aid Doesn't Help: Organizing for Community Economic Development in Central Appalachia." Ph. D. Diss. Univ. of Michigan, 1973. Gives reasons for the futility of current aid programs.
T9690

Tuley, William Floyd The Tuley Family Memoirs; an Historical, Biographical and Genealogical Story of the Tuleys and the Floyd Family Connection in Virginia, Kentucky, and Indiana. New Albany, Ind.: W. J. Hedden, Printer, 1906.
T9700

Tunis, John Roberts Highpockets. New York: W. Morrow, 1948.
T9710 (ASU)
Son of the Valley. New York: W. Morrow, 1949.
T9720 (ASU ETSU)

Turkle, Brinton The Fiddler of High Lonesome. New York: Viking Press, 1968.
T9730 (LMC ASU WCU)

Turman, Nora Miller The Girl in the Rural Family. Chapel Hill: Univ. of North Carolina Press, 1935. Includes sketches of a western North Carolina family.
T9740 (ASU)

Turnbull, Andrew Thomas Wolfe. 1967. Reprint. New York: Scribner, 1968.
T9750 (ASU WCU UNCA)

Turner, Byron J. "What Parents in Two Lewis County Communities Think About the Transportation of Their Children to a Consolidated School." Master's thesis. W. Va. Univ., 1940.
T9760

Turner, Edward Raymond The New Market Campaign, May, 1864. Richmond: Whittet and Shepperson, 1912. An account of the Civil War campaign involving cadets from Virginia Military Academy.
T9770 (ASU)

Turner, Ella May ed. Stories and Verse of West Virginia. Rev. With a foreword by Waitman Barbe. Scottdale, Pa.: The Mennonite Pub. House, 1925. Includes bibliography and biographical sketches.
T9780

Turner, Fitzhugh ed. Nichols, Joseph Van Devanter Legends of Loudoun Valley. Leesburgh, Va.: Potomac Press, 1961.
N870 (ASU)

Turner, Francis Marion Life of General John Sevier. New York: Neale Pub. Co., 1910. Sevier was a frontier general and governor of the State of Franklin and Tennessee.
T9790 (ASU)

Turner, Frederick Jackson The Frontier in American History. 1921. Reprint. New York: Holt and Co., 1923. An analysis of the role of the frontier in American history. Written with erudition, insight and humor.
T9800 (MHC)

The Frontier in American History. Foreword by Ray Allen Billington. 1921. Reprint. New York: Holt, Rinehart and Winston, 1962.
T9810 (ASU)

Rise of the New West, 1819-1829. New York: Harper and Brothers, 1906. Author's thesis is that democracy was born on the frontier.
T9820

Turner, Mary comp. Pioneer Proverbs; Wit and Wisdom From Early America. High Point, N. C.: Hutcraft, 1971.
T9830

Turner, Virginia Casey Cat Claws and Tree Bark. Pikeville, Ky.: Appalachian Studies Center, Pikeville College, 1972.
T9840 (ASU)

Turney, Salley F. Street, James A. Ohio River Valley Population: Trends and Projections, 1930-1970. Lexington, Ky.: Spindletop Research, 1963.
S7850

Turney, Sally F. Gates, Gary R. A Kentucky Riverlands Development Program. Lexington, Ky.: Spindletop Research, 1965.
G570

Turpin, John W. King, John M. Soil Survey of Transylvania County, North Carolina. Washington: U. S. Soil Conservation Service, 1974.
K2300

Tuskegee Institute, Rural Life Council Report to Council of the Southern Mountains on Health Care Services and Facilities in the Southern Appalachian Region. Tuskegee: The council, 1955.
T9850 (ETSU)

Tuttle, Louise Jennings Acres of Beauty. New York: Fortuny's, 1936. Romantic fiction set in western North Carolina.
T9860

Twigs 1-, 1965-. Pikeville, Ky.: Hilltop Editions, Pikeville College Press, n.d.
T9870

Twin-State Development Association Upper Little Tennessee River Region: Summary of Resources. Knoxville, Tenn.: Tennessee Valley Authority, 1968.
T9880 (WWC)

Two Years of Harriman, Tennessee. Established by the East Tennessee Land Company, February 26, 1890 New York: South, 1892. Harriman is a Roane County, Tennessee community which was once the center of a booming land development company.
T9890

Tyer, James Hasty, Allen Henry Soil Survey, Rhea County, Tennessee. Washington: U. S. Department of Agriculture, Bureau of Plant Industry, Soils, and Agricultural Engineering, 1948.
H3390

Roberts, Wallace Soil Survey, Hamilton County, Tennessee. Washington: U. S. Department of Agriculture, Bureau of Plant Industry, Soils, and Agricultural Engineering, 1947.
R3100

Tyler, James Hoge The Family of Hoge — Genealogy. Greensboro, N. C.: Joseph J. Stone and Co., 1927.
T9900

Tyler, Lyon G. Men of Mark in Virginia. 5 vols. Washington, D. C.: Men of Mark Pub. Co., 1906.
T9910

Tyler, Lyon Gardiner The Letters and Times of the Tylers. 3 vols. Richmond, Va.: Whittet and Shepperson, 1884-96.
T9920 (ASU)

Tyrrell, M. E. Hollenbeck, Ronald P. Raw Materials for Lightweight Aggregate in Appalachian Region, Alabama and Georgia. Pittsburgh: Mines Bureau, 1969.
H6610

Hollenbeck, Ronald P. Shales for Lightweight Aggregate in Appalachian Region, Kentucky and Tennessee. Pittsburgh: Mines Bureau, 1968.
H6620

Tyson, Lawrence Davis Tennessee's Part in the Revolution: Address at Valley Forge, at the Presentation of the Tennessee State Flag and Inauguration of Tennessee Sunday, April 24, 1927. Valley Forge, Pa.: Tennessee Soc. of Colonial Dames, 1927.
T9930

UCLA Conference on American Folk Legend, 1969 American Folk Legends; a Symposium. Edited, with a pref., by Wayland D. Hand. Berkeley: Univ. of California Press, 1971.
U10 (FC)

Udall, Stewart and others Look to the Mountaintop. n.p.: n.p., n.d. Includes material on the Cherokee Indians' history, culture and relations with the United States Government.
U20

Ullom, Judith Folklore of the North American Indians. Washington: Library of Congress, 1969.
U30 (LMC)

Ulmann, Doris The Appalachian Photographs of Doris Ulmann. Remembrance by John Jacob Niles. Penland, N. C.: The Jargon Society, 1971. A marvelous collection of character studies done in the 1920's with a plate glass camera. Miss Ulmann's photographs are devoid of sentimentality.
U40 (ASU LMC ETSU FC MHC WCU WWC BC)

Ulmer, Mary see **Chiltoskey, Mary Ulmer**

Umberger, Arthur D. Umberger Family Chart. Aldan, Pa.: n.p., 1956.
U50

The Umberger (Umbarger) Family Chart. 2nd ed. Aldan, Pa.: n.p., 1971. Includes charts and biographies of Umbergers in Pennsylvania and Virginia.
U60

Underwood, Evelyn comp. CRISIS: Addresses Delivered at the Spring Symposium, Mars Hill College, 1967, 1968. Mars Hill, N. C.: Mars Hill College, n.d.
U70 (WCU)

Underwood, Thomas Bryan adapter Cherokee Legends and the Trail of Tears. From the nineteenth annual report of the Bureau of American Ethnology. The John Burnett version of Cherokee removal courtesy of The Museum of the Cherokee Indian. Illustrated by Amanda Crowe. Asheville, N. C.: Stephens Press, 1956.
U80 (ASU LMC MHC WCU)

Legends of the Ancient Cherokee. Asheville: Stephens Press, 1956.
U90

The Story of the Cherokee People. Illustrated by Jacob Anchutin. Knoxville, Tenn.: Newman Print. Co., 1961.
U100 (ASU LMC MHC BC)

The Story of the Cherokee People. Illustrated by Jacob Anchutin. Knoxville, Tenn.: S. B. Newman Print. Co., 1967.
U110 (WCU)

Unicoi County, Tennessee, Unicoi County Redevelopment Committee Overall Economic Development Program for Unicoi County, Tennessee. n.p.: The committee, 1962.
U120 (ETSU)

Union Trust and Deposit Company, Parkersburg, W. Va. The Parkersburg Story. 1st ed. Parkersburg, W. Va.: The bank, 1953.
U130 (ASU)

U. S. Agricultural Research Service, Animal Husbandry Research Division Family Chicken Flock for Appalachia. Leaflet, 541. Washington: Govt. Print. Off., 1966.
U140

U. S. Agricultural Research Service, Crops Research Division Growing Vegetables in Appalachian Region. Information from the Division's publications and from consultation with county agricultural agents and staff members of State agencies of the Appalachian region. U. S. Department of Agriculture House and Garden Bulletin, no. 116. Washington: Govt. Print. Off., 1966.
U150

U. S. Appalachian Regional Commission see **Appalachian Regional Commission**

U. S. Appalachian Regional Commission Appalachian Data Book. 1 vol. (loose-leaf). Washington: n.p., 1967. Includes bibliography.
U160 (UNCA)

U. S. Area Redevelopment Administration Appraisal of ARA Program to Date and Its Relationship to Economic Opportunity and Appalachia Programs, Address by William L. Batt, Jr., Administrator, Area Redevelopment Administration, Department of Commerce, before Association of State Planning and Development Agencies, Washington, D. C., May 26, 1964. Washington: Govt. Print. Off., 1964.
U170

A forest industry processing and marketing complex for eastern Kentucky. Washington, D. C.: n.p., 1963.
U180 (BC)

Opportunities for Economic Development in Mingo County, West Virginia. ARA Field Report. Washington: Govt. Print. Off., 1964.
U190

Recreation & Tourism Develop. Through Federal Programs. Washington: Govt. Print. Off., 1965.
U200

U. S. Area Redevelopment Administration, Office of Planning and Recreation Information Sources for Locating Industrial Prospects. Washington: Govt. Print. Off., 1964.
U210

U. S. Army Corps of Engineers "Big South Fork, Cumberland River (Kentucky-Tennessee), Interagency Field Task Group Report." n.p.: unpublished typescript, 1969.
U220

Big South Fork, Cumberland River, Kentucky and Tennessee. Interagency report to Committee on Public Works, United States Senate, by U. S. Army Corps of Engineers, U. S. Department of the Interior of U. S. Department of Agriculture. Washington: Govt. Print. Off., 1970.
U230 (ETSU)

U. S. Army, Corps of Engineers
Big South Fork, Cumberland River, Kentucky and Tennessee. Interagency report to Committee on Public Works, United States Senate, by U. S. Army Corps of Engineers, U. S. Dept. of the Interior and U. S. Dept. of Agriculture. Washington: Govt. Print. Off., 1970.
U240
Dev. of Water Resources in Appalachia. Cincinnati: n.p., 1969.
U250
Development of Water Resources in Appalachia: Report of the Secretary of the Army. Based on Studies Prepared by the Office of Appalachian Studies. Washington: Govt. Print. Off., 1971.
U260
Flood plain information Lenoir, North Carolina; Lower Creek, Blair Fork, Long Branch. Prepared by the Corps of Engineers, U. S. Army. Charleston, S. C.: n.p., 1970.
U270
Flood plain information, Morganton, North Carolina. Charleston, S. C.: District, U. S. Army Corps of Engineers, 1969.
U280
Interim Study Report on Upper Licking River Basin, Kentucky. Louisville: U. S. Army Engineer District, 1967.
U290 (BC)
Ohio River Basin, Grayson reservoir, Little Sandy River, Kentucky design memorandum no. 3A preliminary master plan. Huntington, W. Va.: U. S. Army Engineer District, 1964.
U300 (BC)
Potomac River Basin Report: Summary. Baltimore: U. S. Army Engineer District, North Atlantic Division, 1963.
U310
Water Resources Dev. by the U. S. Army Corps of Engineers. Cincinnati: n.p., 1965.
U320

U. S. Army War College, Washington, D. C., Historical Section Historical Statements Concerning the Battle of Kings Mountain and the Battle of the Cowpens, South Carolina. 70th Congress, 1st session, House, Document 328. Washington: Govt. Print. Off., 1928.
U330 (ASU)

U. S. Bureau of Agricultural Economics Economic and Social Problems and Conditions of the Southern Appalachians. By the Bureau of Agricultural Economics, Bureau of Home Economics, and Forest Service, in cooperation with the Office of Education, U. S. Department of Interior and the Agricultural Experiment Stations of Tennessee, Virginia, West Virginia, and Kentucky. Miscellaneous Publication, no. 205. Washington: Govt. Print. Off., 1935.
U340 (ETSU ASU BC)
Economic and Social Problems and Conditions of the Southern Appalachians. By the Bureau of Agricultural Economics, Bureau of Home Economics, and Forest Service, in cooperation with the Office of Education, U. S. Department of Interior and the Agricultural Experiment Stations of Tennessee, Virginia, West Virginia, and Kentucky. Miscellaneous Publication, no. 205. 1935. Reprint. New York: Johnson Reprint Corp., 1970.
U350 (ASU ETSU WCU WWC)
Economic and Social Problems and Conditions of the Southern Appalachians. Bureau of Agricultural Economics, Bureau of Home Economics, and Forest Service in cooperation with the Office of Education, U. S. Department of Interior and the Agricultural Experiment Stations of Tennessee, Virginia, West Virginia, and Kentucky. Washington: Govt. Print. Off., 1935.
U360 (ASU)
Economic and Social Problems and Conditions of the Southern Appalachians. Bureau of Agricultural Economics, Bureau of Home Economics, and Forest Service, in cooperation with the Office of Education, U. S. Dept. of Interior and the agricultural experiment stations of Tennessee, Virginia, West Virginia, and Kentucky. New York: Johnson Reprint Corp., 1970.
U370

U. S. Bureau of American Ethnology Annual Report of the Secretary of the Smithsonian Institution, 1879-80. Washington: Govt. Print. Off., 1879.
U380
Anthropological Papers. no. 1. (Smithsonian Institution, Bureau of American Ethnology, Bulletin 119.) Washington: Govt. Print. Off., 1938.
U390 (BC)
Bulletin. no. 1 - 200. 200 vols. Washington: Govt. Print. Off., 1887-1971.
U400 (WCU)
Fifth Annual Report of the Bureau of Ethnology to the Secretary of the Smithsonian Institution, 1883-84. By J. W. Powell, director. Washington: Govt. Print. Off., 1887.
U410 (ASU)
Index to Bulletins 1-100 of the Bureau of American Ethnology; with index to Contributions to North American ethnology. Introductions, and miscellaneous publications, by Biren Bonnerjea. Washington: Govt. Print. Off., 1963.
U420 (WCU)
Reports. Washington: Govt. Print. Off., 1879-80.
U430 (BC)
Seventh annual report of the Bureau of Ethnology to the secretary of the Smithsonian Institution, 1885-86. By J. W. Powell, Director. Washington: Govt. Print. Off., 1891.
U440 (ASU)

U. S. Bureau of Apprenticeship Report on Apprentice Training Program of the Tennessee Valley Authority. Washington: Apprentice-Training Service, 1947.
U450

U. S. Bureau of the Census Census of Population: 1960. The Eighteenth Decennial Census of the United States. Washington: Bureau, 1961.
U460
Fifteenth Census of the United States: 1930. Washington: Govt. Print. Off., 1930.
U470 (BC)
Government in Georgia. Prepared under the supervision of Allen D. Manvel. Census of Governments, 1962, vol. 7, no. 10. Washington: Govt. Print. Off., 1965.
U480 (LMC)
Government in Kentucky. Prepared under the supervision of Allen D. Manvel. Census of Governments, 1962, vol. 7, no. 17. Washington: Govt. Print. Off., 1965.
U490 (LMC)
Government in North Carolina. Prepared under the supervision of Allen D. Manvel. Census of Governments, 1962, vol. 7, no. 33. Washington: Govt. Print. Off., 1965.
U500 (LMC)
Government in Virginia. Prepared under the supervision of Allen D. Manvel. Census of Governments, 1962, vol. 7, no. 46. Washington: Govt. Print. Off., 1965.
U510 (LMC)
United States census 1850 for Knox County, Tennessee. Copied, arr. and indexed by Laura Elizabeth Luttrell. Knoxville: East Tennessee Historical Society, 1949.
U520

U. S. Bureau of the Census, 1st Census, 1790 Heads of Families at the First Census of the United States Taken in the Year 1790: Maryland. 1907. Reprint. Baltimore: Genealogical Pub. Co., 1965.
U530 (ASU)
Heads of Families at the First Census of the United States Taken in the Year 1790: North Carolina. 1908. Reprint. Baltimore: Genealogical Pub. Co., 1966.
U540 (ASU)
Heads of Families at the First Census of the United States Taken in the Year 1790: North Carolina. 1908. Reprint. Spartanburg, S. C.: Reprint Co., n.d.
U550 (LMC)
Heads of Families at the First Census of the United States taken in the Year 1790: North Carolina. Baltimore: Genealogical Pub. Co., 1966.
U560 (ASU UNCA)
Heads of Families at the First Census of the United States Taken in the Year 1790: Pennsylvania. 1908. Reprint. Baltimore: Genealogical Pub. Co., 1966.
U570 (ASU)
Heads of Families at the First Census of the United States Taken in the Year 1790: Records of the State Enumerations, 1782 to 1785, Virginia. 1908. Reprint. Virginia Heritage Series, no. 1. Spartanburg, S. C.: Reprint Co., 1968.
U580 (ASU LMC)
Heads of Families at the First Census of the United States Taken in the Year 1790: South Carolina. 1908. Reprint. Baltimore: Genealogical Pub. Co., 1966.
U590 (ASU)
Heads of Families at the First Census of the United States Taken in the Year 1790: South Carolina. 1908. Reprint. Spartanburg, S. C.: Reprint Co., 1968.
U600 (ASU LMC)
Population Schedules, North Carolina. 2 reels. Washington: National Archives, Microfilm Publications, 1959.
U610 (ASU)

U. S. Bureau of the Census, 2nd Census, 1800 Population Schedules, North Carolina. 6 reels. Washington: National Archives, Microfilm Publications, 1961.
U620 (ASU)

U. S. Bureau of the Census, 3rd Census, 1810 Population Schedules, North Carolina. 6 reels. Washington: National Archives, Microfilm Publications, 1957.
U630 (ASU)

U. S. Bureau of the Census, 4th Census, 1820 Population Schedules, North Carolina. 6 reels. Washington: National Archives, Microfilm Publications, 1958.
U640 (ASU)

U. S. Bureau of the Census, 5th Census, 1830 1830 Census, Tennessee. Transcribed and indexed by Byron Sistler. 3 vols. Evanston, Ill.: n.p., 1969.
U650 (ASU ETSU)
Index to the 1830 Census of Georgia. Compiled by Alvaretta Kenav Register. Baltimore: Genealogical Pub. Co., 1974.
U660 (ASU)
Population Schedules, North Carolina. 8 reels. Washington: National Archives, Microfilm Publications, 1944.
U670 (ASU)

U. S. Bureau of the Census, 6th Census, 1840 A Census of Pensioners for Revolutionary or Military Services, with Their Names, Ages, and Places of Residence, as Returned by the Marshals of the Several Judicial Districts, under the Act for Taking the Sixth Census in 1840. 1840. Reprint. Baltimore: Genealogical Pub. Co., 1967.
U680 (ASU)
Population Schedules, North Carolina. 21 reels. Washington: National Archives, Microfilm Publications, 1967.
U690 (ASU)

U. S. Bureau of the Census, 7th Census, 1850 Coffee County, Tennessee, 1850 Census. Transcribed by Deane Porch. Franklin, Tenn.: Mrs. Clyde Lynch, 1969.
U700 (ETSU)
Fentress County, Tennessee, Free Population Schedules. Transcribed by Mrs. V. K. Carpenter. Fort Worth, Texas: Miran Pubs., 1969.
U710 (ASU)

U. S. Bureau of the Census, 7th Census, 1850
Population Schedules, North Carolina. 38 reels. Washington: National Archives, Microfilm Publications, 1963.
U720 (ASU)
Population Schedule of the U. S. Census of 1850 (Seventh Census) for McMinn County, Tennessee. Transcribed by Reba Bayless Boyer. Athens, Tenn.: McMinn County Chapter, East Tennessee Historical Society, 1961.
U730 (ASU)
Population Schedule of the United States Census of 1850 (Seventh Census) for Warren County, Tennessee. Transcribed from a microfilm copy of the original. McMinnville, Tenn.: Womack Print. Co., 1958.
U740 (ETSU)
The Seventh Population Census of the U. S. for Russell County, Va., 1850. Washington: Govt. Print. Off., 1850.
U750
The Seventh Population Census of the United States for Russell County, Virginia, 1850. Compiled by Bonnie Sage Ball and Ada Grace Catron. Haysi? Va.: n.p., 1964.
U760
Tennessee Population Schedule of the United States Census of 1850, Meigs County. Transcribed by Agnes Maddux. n.p.: n.p., n.d.
U770 (ASU)
United States Census 1850 for Knox County, Tennessee. Copied, arranged, and indexed by Laura Elizabeth Luttrell. Knoxville: East Tennessee Historical Society, 1949.
U780 (ETSU)

U. S. Bureau of the Census, 8th Census, 1860
Population Schedules, North Carolina. 42 reels. Washington: National Archives, Microfilm Publications, 1967.
U790 (ASU)

U. S. Bureau of the Census, 9th Census, 1870
Population Schedules, North Carolina. 46 reels. Washington: National Archives, Microfilm Publications, 1965.
U800 (ASU)

U. S. Bureau of the Census, 10th Census, 1880
Index to the 1880 Population Schedules, North Carolina. 79 reels. Washington: National Archives, Microfilm Publications, 1962.
U810 (ASU)
Population Schedules, North Carolina. 39 reels. Washington: National Archives, Microfilm Publications, n.d.
U820 (ASU)

U. S. Bureau of the Census, 11th Census, 1890
Eastern Band of Cherokees of North Carolina. By Thomas Donaldson. Eleventh Census of the United States, Extra Census Bulletin. Washington: The bureau, 1892.
U830 (WCU)
Special Schedules Enumerating Union Veterans and Widows of Union Veterans of the Civil War, North Carolina. Washington: National Archives, Microfilm Publications, 1948.
U840 (ASU)

U. S. Bureau of the Census, 19th Census, 1970
Selected Rural Counties in Appalachia. 1970 census of population and housing: Employment profiles of selected low-income areas, PHC (3)-70. Prepared by the Demographic Surveys Division. Washington: Govt. Print. Off., 1972.
U850
Selected Rural Counties in Appalachia. Washington: Govt. Print. Off., 1972.
U860

U. S. Bureau of Chemistry and Soils Soil Survey of Blount County, Tenn. Washington: U. S. Dept. of Agr., 1959.
U870 (BC)
Soil Survey of Bradley Co., Tenn. Washington: Dept. of Agriculture, 1958.
U880 (BC)
Soil Survey of Carter Co., Tenn. Washington: Dept. of Agriculture, 1958.
U890
Soil Survey of Claiborne Co., Tenn. Washington: Dept. of Agriculture, 1948.
U900 (BC)
Soil Survey of Cumberland Co., Tenn. Washington: Dept. of Agriculture, 1950.
U910 (BC)
Soil Survey of Cumberland Co., Tenn. Washington: Dept. of Agriculture, 1958.
U920
Soil Survey of Grainger Co., Tenn. Washington: Dept. of Agriculture, 1948.
U930 (BC)
Soil Survey of Grainger Co., Tenn. Washington: Dept. of Agriculture, 1958.
U940
Soil Survey of Hamblen Co., Tenn. Washington: Dept. of Agriculture, 1946.
U950 (BC)
Soil Survey of Hamilton Co., Tenn. Washington: Dept. of Agriculture, 1947.
U960 (BC)
Soil Survey of Hamilton Co., Tenn. Washington: Dept. of Agriculture, 1958.
U970
Soil Survey of Jefferson Co., Tenn. Washington: Dept. of Agriculture, 1941.
U980 (BC)
Soil Survey of Jefferson Co., Tenn. Washington: Dept. of Agriculture, 1958.
U990
Soil Survey of Johnson Co., Tenn. Washington: Dept. of Agriculture, 1956.
U1000 (BC)
Soil Survey of Johnson Co., Tenn. Washington: Dept. of Agriculture, 1958.
U1010
Soil Survey of Knox Co., Tenn. Washington: Dept. of Agriculture, 1955.
U1020 (BC)
Soil Survey of Knox Co., Tenn. Washington: Dept. of Agriculture, 1958.
U1030
Soil Survey of Marion Co., Tenn. Washington: Dept. of Agriculture, 1958.
U1040
Soil Survey of Marion Co., Tenn. Washington: Dept. of Agriculture, 1958.
U1050 (BC)
Soil Survey of McMinn Co., Tenn. Washington: Dept. of Agriculture, 1957.
U1060 (BC)
Soil Survey of Norris Area, Tenn. Washington: Dept. of Agriculture, 1958.
U1070
Soil Survey of Norris Area, Tenn. Washington: Dept. of Agriculture, 1953.
U1080 (BC)
Soil Survey of Rhea Co., Tenn. Washington: Dept. of Agriculture, 1948.
U1090 (BC)
Soil Survey of Rhea Co., Tenn. Washington: Dept. of Agriculture, 1958.
U1100
Soil Survey of Roane Co., Tenn. Washington: Dept. of Agriculture, 1942.
U1110 (BC)
Soil Survey of Roane Co., Tenn. Washington: Dept. of Agriculture, 1958.
U1120
Soil Survey of Sevier Co., Tenn. Washington: Dept. of Agriculture, 1956.
U1130 (BC)
Soil Survey of Sevier Co., Tenn. Washington: Dept. of Agriculture, 1958.
U1140
Soil Survey of Sullivan Co., Tenn. Washington: Dept. of Agriculture, 1953.
U1150 (BC)
Soil Survey of Sullivan Co., Tennessee. Washington: Dept. of Agriculture, 1958.
U1160
Soil Survey of Washington Co., Tennessee. Washington: Dept. of Agriculture, 1958.
U1170 (BC)

U. S. Bureau of Economic Security Family Characteristics of the Long-term Unemployed: A Report on a Study of Claimants under the Temporary Extended Unemployment Compensation Program, 1961-1962. BES, no. U-207-2. Washington: Govt. Print. Off., 1963.
U1180

U. S. Bureau of Education Bulletin. no. 1. n.p.: Bureau of Education, 1913.
U1190 (BC)
Bulletin. 1915. no. 1. n.p.: Bureau of Education, n.d. A statistical study of the public schools of the southern Appalachian Mountains.
U1200 (BC)

U. S. Bureau of Employment Security Bituminous Coal Mining: Labor Market Developments. Prepared by James Woodrow Higgins. Industry Manpower Surveys, no. 106. Washington: Govt. Print. Off., 1963.
U1210

U. S. Bureau of Indian Affairs Census Roll, 1835, of the Cherokee Indians East of the Mississippi. Index to the roll. Microfilm. Washington: National Archives, 1960.
U1220 (ETSU)
Indians of North Carolina. Washington: Govt. Print. Off., 1966.
U1230 (ASU)
Indians of North Carolina. Washington: Govt. Print. Off., 1972.
U1240 (ASU)
Letters Received by the Office of Indian Affairs, 1824-81: Southern Superintendency, 1851-1856. 7 reels. Washington: National Archives, 1958.
U1300 (WCU)

U. S. Bureau of Indian Affairs. Branch of Plant Management. Field Technical Office Rates study for water supply and sewage disposal at Cherokee Indian Agency, Cherokee, North Carolina. Littleton, Colo.: n.p., 1968.
U1250
Report on water and sewerage facilities at Cherokee and Soco Valley, North Carolina. Littleton, Colo.: n.p., 1968. At head of title: Engineering study for the Eastern Band of Cherokee Indians, Cherokee, North Carolina.
U1260

U. S. Bureau of Indian Affairs, Cherokee Agency
Letters Received by the Office of Indian Affairs, 1824-81: Cherokee Reserves, 1828-1850. 2 reels. Washington: National Archives, 1959.
U1270 (WCU)
Letters Received by the Office of Indian Affairs, 1824-81: Cherokee Emigration, 1828-1854. 4 reels. Washington: National Archives, 1959.
U1280 (WCU)
Records of the Cherokee Indian Agency in Tennessee, 1801-1835. 14 reels. Washington: National Archives and Records Services, 1952.
U1310 (WCU)

U. S. Bureau of Indian Affairs, Cherokee Agency (East) Letters Received by the Office of Indian Affairs, 1824-81: Cherokee Agency (East), 1824-36. 6 reels. Washington: National Archives, 1959.
U1290 (WCU)

U. S. Bureau of Labor Statistics Area Wage Survey: The Birmingham, Alabama, Metropolitan Area. April, 1966- Bulletin. (Supersedes in part the Bureau's Occupational wage survey.) Washington: Govt. Print. Off., Annual.
U1320
Area Wage Survey: The Charleston, West Virginia, Metropolitan Area. April, 1966- Bulletin (Supersedes in part the Bureau's Occupational wage survey.) Washington: Govt. Print. Off., annual.
U1330
Area Wage Survey: The Chattanooga, Tennessee-Georgia, Metropolitan Area. September, 1965- . Bulletin, no. 1465-7. (Supersedes in part the Bureau's Occupational wage survey.) Washington: Govt. Print. Off., annual.
U1340
Area Wage Survey: The Greenville, South Carolina, Metropolitan Area. May, 1966- Bulletin. (Supersedes in part the Bureau's Occupational Wage survey.) Washington: Govt. Print. Off., annual.
U1350
Area Wage Survey: The Huntsville, Alabama, metropolitan area. Washington: Govt. Print. Off., n.d.
U1360

U. S. Bureau of Labor Statistics
Area Wage Survey: The Pittsburgh, Pennsylvania, Metropolitan Area. January, 1966- . Bulletin. (Supersedes in part the Bureau's Occupational wage survey.) Washington: Govt. Print. Off., annual.
U1370

Area Wage Survey: The Scranton, Pennsylvania, Metropolitan Area. August, 1965- . Bulletin, no. 1465-3. (Supersedes in part the Bureau's Occupation wage survey.) Washington: Govt. Print. Off., annual.
U1380

Hours and earnings in anthracite and bituminous coal mining. Anthracite — January, 1922, bituminous — winter of 1921-22. July, 1922. Washington: Govt. Print. Off., 1922.
U1390

Impact of the war on the Huntsville Area, Madison County, Alabama; working notebook for use by local groups studying recent economic developments and formulating plans for the post-war period. Washington: U. S. Dept. of Labor, Bureau of Labor Statistics, Employment and Occupational Outlook Branch, Postwar Division, 1943.
U1400

Wage Chronology: Bituminous Coal Mines, 1933/66-. (Supplements in the Bureau's Monthly Labor Review.) Washington: Govt. Print. Off., n.d.
U1410

U. S. Bureau of Mines Bulletin 1. Washington: Govt. Print. Off., 1910.
U1420

List of publications, Bureau of Mines. Supplement...1923/33-1935/36; 1937/38-. Washington: Govt. Print. Off., 1933.
U1430

List of publications, Bureau of Mines. Washington: Govt. Print. Off., n.d.
U1440

List of publications, Bureau of Mines. Supplement. Washington: Govt. Print. Off., n.d.
U1450

Miners' Circular. no. 1, 1910. Washington: Govt. Print. Off., irregular.
U1460

Miners' Circular. no. 1, 1910-. Washington: Govt. Print. Off., irregular publication.
U1470

Mining and Mineral Operations in the United States; a Visitor's Guide. By Staff, Bureau of Mines, area mineral resources offices. Washington: Govt. Print. Off., 1967.
U1480

Story about Fighting Mine Fires in Abandoned Coal Workings, Mine Fire Control Project in Appalachia. Washington: Govt. Print. Off., 1967.
U1490

Story of Operation Backfill, Mine Subsidence Project in Appalachia. Joint project with the Pennsylvania Department of Mines and Mineral Industries, 1964.
U1500

U. S. Bureau of Outdoor Recreation A Report on Outdoor Recreation Demand, Supply, and Needs in Appalachia. Prepared for the Appalachian Regional Commission. Washington: Govt. Print. Off., 1967.
U1510

Tour. & Recreation Potential E. Ky. Washington: U. S. Area Red. Admin., 1963.
U1520

Tourist and Recreation Potential: Eastern Panhandle Area, West Virginia (Grant, Hardy, Hampshire, Mineral, and Morgan Counties). Prepared for the U. S. Area Redevelopment Administration. Washington: Govt. Print. Off., 1964.
U1530

Tourist and Recreation Potential: Lewis Smith Lake (Cullman, Walker and Winston Counties, Alabama). Prepared by the Area Analysis Staff, Division of Planning and Surveys of the Bureau in cooperation with the Area Redevelopment Administration. Washington?: The bureau, 1963.
U1540 (LMC)

Tourist and Recreation Potential: Upper Cumberland Lakes Area of Tennessee (Clay, Dekalb, Jackson, Overton, Pickett, Smith, and Warren Counties). Prepared for Area Redevelopment Administration by James N. Lowe and others. Washington: Govt. Print. Off., 1965.
U1550

Tourist and Recreation Potential: Western North Carolina. Area analysis staff report prepared for the U. S. Area Redevelopment Administration. Washington: Govt. Print. Off., 1964.
U1560

U. S. Bureau of Public Roads Remarks by Lawrence Jones, Deputy Federal Highway Administrator. Prepared for Delivery at Groundbreaking Ceremonies for Appalachian Development Highway at Isom, Kentucky, July 6, 1965. Washington: Govt. Print. Off., 1965.
U1570

U. S. Business and Defense Services Administration Water Used by Appalachian Manufacturers, 1964. Prepared for the Office of Appalachian Studies, Corps of Engineers, by the Water Industries and Engineering Services Division, Business and Defense Services Administration, U. S. Dept. of Commerce. Washington: Govt. Print. Off., n.d.
U1580

Water used by Appalachian Manufacturers, 1964.
U1590

U. S. Census Office see U. S. Bureau of the Census

U. S. Children's Bureau Bureau publication No. 120 Steete, Glenn. Maternity and infant care in a mountain county in Georgia. n.p.: n.p., 1923.
U1600

The Nutrition and Care of Children in a Mountain County in Kentucky. By Lydia Roberts. Washington: Govt. Print. Off., 1922.
U1610

U. S. Coal Mines Administration A medical survey of the bituminous-coal industry. Report of the Coal mines administration. Washington: Govt. Print. Off., 1947.
U1620

U. S. Commission on Civil Rights, North Carolina Advisory Committee Equal Protection of the Laws in North Carolina. Report of the N. C. Advisory Committee to the U. S. Commission on Civil Rights. Washington: Govt. Print. Off., 1959-62.
U1630 (LMC)

U. S. Congress. House Report. The committee on Indian Affairs, to which Was Referred the Petition of Joseph Brown. House of Representatives, Report no. 175, 23rd Congress, 1st session, Jan. 14, 1834. Washington: Govt. Print. Off., 1834.
U1640

U. S. Congress. House. Ad Hoc Subcommittee on Appalachia Appalachian regional development act, 1967. Hearings, Ninetieth Congress, first session, on H. R. 4446, and related bills. Washington: Govt. Print. Off., 1967.
U1650

U. S. Congress. House. Committee on Indian Affairs Indians, Cherokees. May 26, 1840. (26th Cong. 1st sess. House, Doc. no. 222.) Washington, D. C.: n.p., 1840.
U1660

U. S. Congress. House. Committee on Public Works Appalachian Regional Development Act of 1965. Report to accompany S. 3. Washington: Govt. Print. Off., 1965.
U1670

Appalachian Regional Development Act, 1967. Washington: Govt. Print. Off., 1967.
U1680

Tennessee Valley Authority Financing. Hearings, 85th Cong., 1st sess., on H. R. 3236 and H. R. 4266. Washington: Govt. Print. Off., 1957.
U1690

Tennessee Valley Authority. Hearings, 86th Cong., 1st sess., on H. R. 3460 and H. R. 3461. March 10-11, 1959. Washington: Govt. Print. Off., 1959.
U1700

U. S. Congress. House of Representatives, Public Lands Committee National parks in southern Appalachian Mountains. Hearings on H. R. 11980, to provide for securing of lands in southern Appalachian Mountains for perpetual reservation as national parks. n.p.: n.p., n.d.
U1710

U. S. Congress. Joint Committee on Labor-Management Relations Labor-Management Relations in TVA. 81st Cong., 1st Sess., S. Rept. 372. Washington: Govt. Print. Off., 1949.
U1740

U. S. Congress. Joint Committee to Investigate Tennessee Valley Authority Investigation of the Tennessee Valley Authority. Hearings before the Joint Committee 75th Cong. 3rd sess. Washington: Govt. Print. Off., 1939.
U1720

Investigation of the TVA. 75th Congress, 3rd Session, pursuant to public resolution No. 83. Washington: Govt. Print. Off., 1939.
U1730

U. S. Congress. Senate Committee on Education and Labor W. Va. Coal Fields. Washington: Govt. Print. Off., 1921.
U1750

U. S. Congress. Senate Committee on Interstate Commerce Conditions in the Coal Fields of Penn., W. Va., and Ohio. Washington: Govt. Print. Off., 1928.
U1760

U. S. Congress. Senate Committee on Public Works Amending the TVA Act. Hearings, 85th Cong., 1st sess., on S. 1855, S. 1869, S. 1986, and S. 2145. Washington: Govt. Print. Off., 1957.
U1770

Revenue Bond Financing by TVA. Hearings, 86th Cong., 1st sess., on S. 931 and H. R. 3460. June 9-10, 1959. Washington: Govt. Print. Off., 1959.
U1780

Tennessee Valley Authority Financing. Hearings, 84th Cong., 1st sess., on S. 2373; a Bill to Amend the Tennessee Valley Authority Act of 1933. July 21, 22, and 27, 1955. Washington: Govt. Print. Off., 1955.
U1790

U. S. Congress. Senate Committee on Unemployment Problems Unemployment problems. Hearings, Eighty-sixth Cong., 1st sess., on S. Res. 196. Dec. 10, 11, and 14, 1959. Washington: Govt. Print. Off., 1966.
U1800

U. S. Congress. Senate. Select Committee on National Water Resources Water Resources Activities in the United States. Flood Problems and Management in the Tennessee River Basin. (86th Cong., 1st Sess., Committee Print no. 16). Washington: Govt. Print. Off., 1960.
U1810

U. S. Congress (21st), 1st Session, 1829-1830 Speeches on the Passage of the Bill for the Removal of the Indians, Delivered in the Congress of the U. S., April and May, 1830. Boston: Perkins and Marvin; New York: J. Leavitt, 1830.
U1820 (ETSU)

U. S. Congress (29th) Cherokee Indians. 1st Sess Senate Dec. 408; June 25, 1846. n.p.: n.p., n.d.
U1830

U. S. Congress (53rd), 3rd Session, 1894-1895 Memorial addresses on the life and character of Zebulon Baird Vance. Late a senator from North Carolina delivered in the Senate and House of Representatives, Fifty-third Congress, third session. Washington: Govt. Print. Off., 1895.
U1840 (UNCA)

U. S. Congress (56th), Senate Appalachian Mountains. Memorial of Appalachian National Park Association urging establishment of national park in Southern Appalachian region; presented by Mr. Pritchard Jan. 4, 1900. (S doc. 58) n.p.: n.p., n.d.
U1850

Preliminary report of investigations upon forest of Southern Appalachian region. With view to establishment of national park or forest reserve Jan. 16, 1901. (S. doc. 93.) n.p.: n.p., n.d.
U1860

Forest Reservations and Protection of Game Committee. Report favoring S. 5518, for national forest reserve Southern Appalachian Mountains, Feb. 12, 1901. n.p.: n.p., n.d.
U1870

U. S. Congress (57th), Senate The Timber Resources of W. Va. Senate Doc. 33, 87th Congress, 1st sess., 1961. n.p.: n.p., n.d.
U1880

U. S. Congress (61st), 3rd Session, 1910-1911 Walter P. Brownlow. (Late a representative from Tennessee) Memorial addresses delivered in the House of Representatives and the Senate of the United States, Sixty-first Congress, third session. Proceedings in the Senate, December 6, 1910. Proceedings in the House, February 19, 1911. Compiled under the direction of the Joint Committee on printing. Walter P. Brownlow. . . Memorial addresses. . . . Washington: Govt. Print. Off., 1911.
U1890

U. S. Congress (62nd), 3rd Session, 1912-1913 Robert Love Taylor. (Late a senator from Tennessee) Memorial addresses delivered in the Senate and House of Representatives of the United States, Sixty-second Congress, third session. Proceedings in the Senate February 8, 1913. Proceedings in the House February 23, 1913. Prepared under the direction of the Joint Committee on printing. Washington: Govt. Print. Off., 1913.
U1900

U. S. Congress (64th) Statue of Zebulon Baird Vance, Erected Statuary Hall of the United States Capitol by the State of North Carolina. Washington: Govt. Print. Off., 1917.
U1910 (ASU WCU)

U. S. Congress (76th), House Memorial Services Held in the House of Representatives of the United States, Together with Remarks Presented in Eulogy of James Willis Taylor, Late Representative from Tennessee. Washington: Govt. Print. Off., 1941.
U1920 (ASU)

U. S. Congress (81st), Senate, Committee on Labor and Public Welfare Causes of Unemployment in Coal and Other Specified Industries. Report Pursuant to S. Res. 274 with Supplemental View of Mr. Taft. Washington: Govt. Print. Off., 1950.
U1930

U. S. Congress (85th), House, Committee on Interior and Insular Affairs Hearings before the Special Subcommittee on Coal Research on Establishment of Research and Development Program for the Coal Industry. 2 vols. Washington: Govt. Print. Off., 1957.
U1940

U. S. Congress (87th), Senate Printing as Senate Document Information Relative to the Timber Resources and National Forests of West Virginia. Report from the committee on Rules and Administration to Accompany S. Res. 137, June 14, 1961. Washington: Govt. Print. Off., 1961.
U1950

U. S. Congress (88th), House Consideration of H. R. 11946. Report to Accompany H. Res. 861, Aug. 20, 1964. Washington: Govt. Print. Off., 1964.
U1960

U. S. Congress (88th), House, Committee on Public Works Appalachian Regional Development Act of 1964. Hearings before the Ad Hoc Subcommittee on Appalachian Regional Development of the Committee on Public Works on H. R. 11065 and H. R. 11066, May 5-June 11, 1964, to Provide Public Works and Economic Development Programs and the Planning and Coordination Needed to Assist in the Development of the Appalachian Region. Washington: Govt. Print. Off., 1964.
U1970

Appalachian Regional Development Act of 1964: Report to Accompany H. R. 11946, July 31, 1964. Washington: Govt. Print. Off., 1964.
U1980

Appalachian Regional Development Act of 1965: Report to Accompany S. 3, February 17, 1965. Washington: Govt. Print. Off., 1965.
U1990

Section-by-section Analysis of H. R. 11065 and H. R. 11066: Appalachian Regional Development Act of 1964 as Submitted in Draft to the Committee, April 29, 1964. Washington: Govt. Print. Off., 1964.
U2020

U. S. Congress (88th), Senate Proposed Appropriation for Appalachian Regional Commission, Fiscal Year 1965. Sept. 29, 1964. Washington: Govt. Print. Off., 1964.
U2030

U. S. Congress (88th), Senate, Committee on Labor and Public Welfare, Subcommittee on Poverty War on Poverty: The Economic Opportunity Act of 1964. A Compilation of Materials Relevant to S. 2642, Prepared for the Select Subcommittee, July 23, 1964. Washington: Govt. Print. Off., 1964.
U2040

U. S. Congress (88th), Senate, Committee on Public Works Appalachian Regional Development Act of 1964. Report Together with Minority Views to Accompany S. 2782, Aug. 13, 1964. Washington: Govt. Print. Off., 1964.
U2000

Appalachian Regional Development Act of 1964. Hearings on S. 2782, a Bill to Provide Public Works and Economic Development Programs and the Planning Coordination Needed to Assist in the Development of the Appalachian Region, June 22-26, 1964. Washington: Govt. Print. Off., 1964.
U2010

U. S. Congress (89th), House Authorizing Printing of Additional Copies of Hearings by Committee on Public Works on Appalachian Regional Development Act of 1965. Report from Committee on House Administration to Accompany H. Res. 724. June 2, 1966. Washington: Govt. Print. Off., 1966.
U2050

Authorizing Printing of Additional Copies of Committee Print 1 of Committee on Public Works on Section-by-section Analysis of H. R. 4, Appalachian Regional Development Act of 1965, and Difference between H. R. 4 (89th Cong.), and H. R. 11946 (88th Cong.) as Reported to House of Representatives and S. 2782 (88th Cong.) as Passed by Senate. Report from Committee on House Administration to Accompany H. Res. 722. June 2, 1966. Washington: Govt. Print. Off., 1966.
U2060

Supplemental Estimates of Appropriations for Various Agencies for Fiscal Year 1965 to Finance Appalachian Regional Development Act of 1965. Mar. 15, 1965. Washington: Govt. Print. Off., 1965.
U2070

U. S. Congress (89th), House, Committee on Agriculture Establishment of Mount Rogers National Recreation Area in Virginia. Report from the Committee to Accompany H. R. 10366, August 31, 1965. Washington: Govt. Print. Off., 1965.
U2080

Establishment of Spruce Knob-Seneca Rocks National Recreation Area in West Virginia. Report from the Committee to Accompany H. R. 10330, August 31, 1965. Washington: Govt. Print. Off., 1965.
U2090

U. S. Congress (89th), House, Committee on Education and Labor Examination of the War on Poverty Program. Hearings before the Subcommittee on the War on Poverty Program, April 12-30, 1965. Washington: Govt. Print. Off., 1965.
U2100

U. S. Congress (89th), House, Committee on Public Works Appalachian Regional Development Act of 1965: Report to Accompany S. 3. Washington: Govt. Print. Off., 1965.
U2110 (ETSU)

Highlights of Appalachian Regional Development Act of 1965, Mar. 10, 1965. Washington: Govt. Print. Off., 1965.
U2120

Section-by-section Analysis of H. R. 4: Appalachian Regional Development Act of 1965, and Differences between H. R. 4 (89th Congress) and H. R. 11946 (88th Congress), as Reported to the House of Representatives, and S. 2782 (88th Congress) as Passed by the Senate. Washington: Govt. Print. Off., 1965.
U2130

U. S. Congress (89th), House, Committee on Public Works, Ad Hoc Subcommittee on Appalachia Appalachian Regional Development Act of 1965. Hearings on H. R. 4 and S. 3, February 3-5, 1965. Washington: Govt. Print. Off., 1965.
U2140

U. S. Congress (89th), Senate Authorizing Printing for Use of Committee on Public Works of Additional Copies of Its Hearings on Appalachian Regional Development Act of 1965 (S.3). Report from Committee on Rules and Administration to Accompany S. Res. 208. Feb. 16, 1966. Washington: Govt. Print. Off., 1966.
U2150

U. S. Congress (89th), Senate, Committee on Interior and Insular Affairs, Subcommittee on Parks and Recreation The Appalachian Trail. Hearing on S. 622, September 16, 1965. Washington: Govt. Print. Off., 1965.
U2160 (LMC)

U. S. Congress (89th), Senate, Committee on Public Works Appalachian Regional Development Act of 1965. Hearings on S. 3, January 19 and 21, 1965. Washington: Govt. Print. Off., 1965.
U2170

Appalachian Regional Development Act of 1965: Report, Together with Individual Views, to Accompany S. 3, January 27, 1965. Washington: Govt. Print. Off., 1965.
U2180

U. S. Congress (90th), House Appalachian Regional Development Act, 1965, Communication from President of United States Transmitting Recommendation that Congress Extend Appalachian Regional Development Act of 1965. Jan. 23, 1967. Washington: Govt. Print. Off., 1967.
U2190

Appalachian Regional Development Act Amendments of 1967. Conference Report to Accompany S. 602. Sept. 26, 1967. Washington: Govt. Print. Off., 1967.
U2200

U. S. Congress (90th), House, Committee on Public Works Appalachian Regional Development Act Amendments of 1967, and Amendments to Public Works and Economic Development Act of 1965. Report with Additional, Minority, Supplemental, and Separate Views, on S. 602. August 8, 1967.
U2210

Appalachian Regional Development Act, 1967. Hearings on H. R. 4446 and Related Bills, May 9-July 12, 1967. Washington: Govt. Print. Off., 1967.
U2220 (ASU ETSU)

U. S. Congress (90th), Senate, Committee on Interior and Insular Affairs Nationwide System of Trails. Hearings before the Committee on S. 827, March 15 and 16, 1967. Washington: Govt. Print. Off., 1967.
U2230 (LMC)

U. S. Congress (90th), Senate, Committee on Public Works Nomination of Joe W. Fleming II to be Federal Co-chairman of the Appalachian Regional Commission Hearing, Feb. 7, 1967. Washington: Govt. Print. Off., 1967.
U2240

Nomination of Meriwether Lewis Clark Tyler to be Alternate Federal Co-chairman of the Appalachian Regional Commission. Hearing, March 21, 1968. Washington: Govt. Print. Off., 1968.
U2250

Revising and Extending Appalachian Regional Development Act of 1965, and Amending Title 5 to Public Works and Economic Development Act of 1965. Report Together with Supplemental Views, to Accompany S. 602. April 6, 1967. Washington: Govt. Print. Off., 1967.
U2260

U. S. Congress (90th), Senate, Special Subcommittee on Economic Development Appalachian Regional Development Act Amendments of 1967 Hearings on S. 602, Jan. 24-Feb. 3, 1967. Washington: Govt. Print. Off., 1967.
U2270 (ASU)

U. S. Congress (91st), House, Committee on Education and Labor Federal Coal Mine Health and Safety Act of 1969. Report Together with Minority, Supplemental, and Separate Views from the Committee to Accompany H. R. 13950, October 13, 1969. Washington: Govt. Print. Off., 1969.
U2280

Legislative History: Federal Coal Mine Health and Safety Act. Washington: Govt. Print. Off., 1970.
U2290

U. S. Congress (91st), House, Committee on Education and Labor, General Subcommittee on Labor Coal Mine Health and Safety. Hearings before the Subcommittee on H. R. 4047, H. R. 4295, and H. R. 7976, March 4-May 1, 1969. Washington: Govt. Print. Off., 1969.
U2300

U. S. Congress (91st), House, Committee on Public Works Appalachian and Regional Action Planning Commissions. Report. Together with Supplemental Views to Accompany H. R. 4018: June 30, 1969. Washington: Govt. Print. Off., 1969.
U2310

U. S. Congress (91st), Senate, Committee on Appropriations Independent Offices and Department of Housing and Urban Development Appropriations for Fiscal Year 1970. Hearings before the Subcommittee on H. R. 12307. Pt. 1: Appalachian Regional Commission, Appalachian Regional Development Programs (Funds Appropriated to President), Civil Defense, Department of Defense, Civil Service Commission, Commission on Executive, Legislative, and Judicial Salaries, Disaster Relief (Funds Appropriated to President), Emergency Health and Welfare Activities, DHEW, Federal Communications Commission, Federal Home Loan Bank Board, Federal Power Commission, Federal Trade Commission, General Services Administration, National Aeronautics and Space Administration National Aeronautics and Space Council, National Science Foundation, Office of Emergency Preparedness, Office of Science and Technology, Renegotiation Board, Securities and Exchange Commission, Selective Service System, Veterans Administration, Testimony of Members of Congress, Other Interested Individuals and Organizations. Washington: Govt. Print. Off., 1969.
U2320

U. S. Congress (91st), Senate, Committee on Labor and Public Welfare Federal Coal Mine Health and Safety Act of 1969. Report from the Committee Together with Individual Views to Accompany S. 2917, September 17, 1969. Washington: Govt. Print. Off., 1969.
U2330

U. S. Congress (91st), Senate, Committee on Labor and Public Welfare, Subcommittee on Labor Coal Mine Health and Safety. Hearings before the Subcommittee on S. 355, S. 467, S. 1094, S. 1178, S. 1300, and S. 1907, February 27-May 2, 1969. 5 pts. Washington: Govt. Print. Off., 1969.
U2340

U. S. Congress (91st), Senate, Committee on Public Works Nominations of Federal Cochairmen of Regional Economic Development Commissions. Hearing on Nominations of John B. Waters, Jr., to be Federal Cochairman of the Appalachian Regional Commission, W. Donald Brewer to be Federal Cochairman of the Four Corners Regional Commission, G. Fred Steele to be Federal Cochairman of the Coastal Plains Regional Commission, Stewart Lamprey to be Federal Cochairman of the New England Regional Commission, and E. L. Stewart to be Federal Cochairman of the Ozarks Regional Commission, March 25, 1969. Washington: Govt. Print. Off., 1960.
U2350

Nomination of Orville H. Lerch for Alternative Cochairman, Appalachian Regional Commission. Hearing, July 15, 1969. Washington: Govt. Print. Off., 1969.
U2360

Regional Economic Development Legislation. Extension and Revision of Appalachian Regional Development Act of 1965, as Amended, and of Titles 1-5 of Public Works and Economic Development Act of 1965, as Amended. Report to Accompany S. 1072. Washington: Govt. Print. Off., 1969.
U2370

U. S. Congress (92nd), House Public Works Acceleration Act. Public Works and Economic Development Act, Appalachian Regional Development Act Extensions. Conference Report to Accompany S. 575, June 2, 1971. Washington: Govt. Print. Off., 1971.
U2380

U. S. Congress (92nd), House, Committee on Public Works Public Works Acceleration Act. Public Works and Economic Development Act, and Appalachian Regional Development Act Extensions Report with Minority and supplemental Views, 92d Congress, 1st session, on H. R. 5376, March 29, 1971. Washington: Govt. Print. Off., 1971.
U2390

Public Works and Economic Development Act and Appalachian Regional Development Act Extensions. Report to Accompany H. R. 9922, July 21, 1971. Washington: Govt. Print. Off., 1971.
U2400

U. S. Congress (92nd), House, Committee on Public Works, Subcommittee on Flood Control and Internal Development Appalachian Regional Development Act Amendments of 1971. Hearings on H. R. 5376 and Related Bills, March 15-17, 1971. Washington: Govt. Print. Off., 1971.
U2410

U. S. Congress (92nd), Senate Public Works Acceleration Act. Public Works and Economic Development Act, and Appalachian Regional Development Act Extensions. Conference Report to Accompany S. 575, June 1, 1971. Washington: Govt. Print. Off., 1971.
U2420

U. S. Congress (92nd), Senate, Committee on Labor and Public Welfare, Subcommittee on Labor Buffalo Creek (W. Va.) Disaster, 1972. Hearings before the Subcommittee. 2 pts. Washington: Govt. Print. Off., 1972.
U2430

U. S. Congress (92nd), Senate, Committee on Public Works Appalachian Airports. Hearing on Development of Regional Airports for Purpose of Improving Transportation and Passenger Safety, March 2, 1971. Washington: Govt. Print. Off., 1971.
U2440

Appalachian Regional Development Act Amendments of 1971. Report Together with Individual Views to Accompany S. 575, March 9, 1971. Washington: Govt. Print. Off., 1971.
U2450

Public Works and Economic Development Act and Appalachian Regional Development Act Extensions. Report to Accompany S. 2317, July 20, 1971. Washington: Govt. Print. Off., 1971.
U2460

Watershed Work Plan for Little Bigby Creek Watershed, Maury County, Tennessee. Report of the Soil Conservation Service, Department of Agriculture, in Accordance with Public Law 83-566, April, 1971. Washington: Govt. Print. Off., 1971.
U2470

U. S. Congress (92nd), Senate, Committee on Public Works, Subcommittee on Economic Development Appalachian Regional Development Act of 1971. Hearings on S. 575, February 8-10, 1971. Washington: Govt. Print. Off., 1971.
U2480

U. S. Department of Agriculture, Agricultural Research Service see **U. S. Agricultural Research Service**

U. S. Dept. of Agriculture Economic and Social Problems and Conditions of the Southern Appalachians. Washington: Govt. Print. Off., 1935.
U2490

Living Conditions and Population Migration in Four Appalachian Counties. Washington, D. C.: Dept. of Agric., 1937.
U2500 (BC)

Message From the President of the United States Transmitting a Report of the Secretary of Agriculture in Relation to the Forests, Rivers, and Mountains of the Southern Appalachian Region. December 19, 1901. Read, referred to the Committee of forest reservations and the protection of game and ordered to be printed. Washington: Govt. Print. Off., 1902.
U2510 (UNCA ASU ETSU)

References on the Mountaineers of the Southern Appalachians. Washington: Govt. Print. Off., n.d.
U2520

Report on an Examination of a Forest Tract in Western North Carolina. Washington: Govt. Print. Off., 1905.
U2530

Report of the Secretary of Agriculture on the Southern Appalachian and White Mountain Watersheds. Commercial Importance, Area, Condition, Advisability of the Purchase for National Forests, and Probable Cost. Washington: Govt. Print. Off., 1908.
U2540 (BC)

Rural Recreation Enterprises for Profit: An Aid to Rural Areas Development. Agriculture Information Bulletin, 277. Washington: Govt. Print. Off., 1963.
U2550

Standards of Living in Four Southern Appalachian Mountain Counties. By C. P. Loomis and L. S. Dodson. Washington, D. C.: Dept. of Agriculture, 1938.
U2560 (BC)

U. S. Dept. of Agriculture, Agricultural Stabilization and Conservation Service Appalachian land stabilization and conservation program, program results from inception through Dec. 31, 1968. Prepared by Data Division. n.p.: n.p., n.d.
U2565

U. S. Dept. of Agriculture, Bureau of Agricultural Economics Crop Production Practices, Labor, Power, and Materials, by Operation: Sec. 3, Appalachian, Southeast, and Mississippi Delta. FM Series, 92. Washington: Govt. Print. Off., 1953.
U2570

U. S. Dept. of Agriculture, Crop Reporting Board 1967 Regional Summary of Fruit Tree Surveys, Selected Appalachian States. Prepared in cooperation with State Departments of Agriculture and Matching Funds Program, Consumer and Marketing Service. Statistical Reporting Service, 13. Washington: Govt. Print. Off., 1968.
U2580

U. S. Dept. of Agriculture, Economic Research Service Employment, Unemployment, and Low Incomes in Appalachia. Agricultural Economic Report no. 73. n.p.: n.p., n.d.
U2590

An Economic Survey of the Appalachian Region, with special reference to Agriculture. Washington, D. C.: Govt. Print. Off., 1955.
U2600

Suggestions for Planning and Zoning in Appalachia. Washington: Govt. Print. Off., 1967.
U2610 (LMC)

U. S. Dept. of Agriculture, Farmer's Bulletin Ways of Making Southern Mountain Farms More Productive. Farm Practices That Increase Crop Yield in Ky. and Tenn. n.p.: n.p., 1918.
U2620

U. S. Dept. of Agriculture, Forest Service see **U. S. Forest Service**

U. S. Dept. of Agriculture, Soil Conservation Service see **U. S. Soil Conservation Service**

U. S. Dept. of Agriculture, Technical Bulletin no. 1 Family Living in Knott County, Ky. Washington: Govt. Print. Co., 1937.
U2640

Land Utilization in Laurel County, Ky. Washington: Govt. Print. Off., 1932.
U2650

Timber Growing and Logging Practice in the Southern Appalachian Region. Washington: Govt. Print. Off., 1931.
U2660

U. S. Dept. of the Army Development of Water Resources in Appalachia. The Department of the Army, Office of Appalachian Studies, Corps of Engineers. Cincinnati: U. S. Army Corps of Engineers, 1969.
U2670 (ASU)

Environmental Study of Logan, McDowell, and Mingo Counties, West Virginia and Pike County, Kentucky. Prepared for Huntington District, U. S. Corps of Engineers. Columbus, Ohio: Battelle Memorial Institute, 1967.
U2680 (ASU)

U. S. Dept. of Commerce ARA Field Report, Opportunities for Economic Development in Mingo County, W. Va. Washington: Govt. Print. Off., n.d.
U2690

U. S. Dept. of Commerce, Area Redevelopment Administration see **U. S. Area Redevelopment Administration**

U. S. Dept. of Commerce, Bureau of Public Roads see **U. S. Bureau of Public Roads**

U. S. Dept. of Commerce, Economic Development Administration Economic Development, Project Activity Supplement. Includes approved projects assisted under authority of Public Works and Economic Development Act of 1965 and Appalachian Regional Development Act of 1965 that were announced up to Dec. 1, 1966, but not previously listed in economic development. Washington: Govt. Print. Off., 1967.
U2700

Regional Economic Development in the United States. Series of papers presented for Working Party no. 6 of the Industry Committee, Policies for Regional Development, Organization for Economic Cooperation and Development. Washington: Govt. Print. Off., 1967.
U2710

U. S. Dept. of Commerce, Office of Secretary Address by Secretary of Commerce Luther H. Hodges, Prepared for Delivery at 50th Anniversary Observance, Ferrum Junior College, Ferrum, Virginia, May 15, 1964. Washington: Govt. Print. Off., 1964.
U2720

Address by Secretary of Commerce Luther H. Hodges, Prepared for Delivery at Western Carolina College Commencement, Cullowhee, North Carolina, May 24, 1964. Washington: Govt. Print. Off., 1964.
U2730

U. S. Dept. of Health, Education and Welfare, 1971 Conference in the Matter of Pollution of the Interstate Waters of the Monongahela Pines. Washington: Govt. Print. Off., 1963.
U2740

U. S. Dept. of Health, Education and Welfare, Public Health Service Consumer Protection and Environmental Health Service HEW's Eight-point Program to Combat Coal Miners' Pneumoconiosis. Remarks by Charles C. Johnson, Jr., Administrator, for presentation at a session on dust control and health, American Mining Congress, Pittsburgh, Pa., May 5, 1969. Washington: Govt. Print. Off., 1969.
U2750

U. S. Dept. of Housing and Urban Development Appalachian Housing Assistance. HUD Handbooks. Washington: Govt. Print. Off., 1968.
U2760

U. S. Dept. of Indian Affairs The Eastern Cherokees: A Census of the Cherokee Nation in North Carolina, Tennessee, Alabama, and Georgia in 1851. Compiled by David W. Siler, Special Agent. Pref. by Fred B. Kniffen. Cottonport, La.: Polyanthos, 1972. Despite the "Trail of Tears" forced removal many Cherokee families remained in these four states.
U2770

U. S. Dept. of the Interior The Nation's River. Official Report on the Potomac from the Department, with Recommendations for Action by the Federal Interdepartmental Task Force on the Potomac. Washington: Govt. Print. Off., 1968.
U2780

Natural Resources of West Virginia, the Mountain State. Washington: Govt. Print. Off., 1964.
U2790 (ASU)

Origin of the Copper Deposits of the Ducktown Type in the Southern Appalachian Region. Washington: Govt. Print. Off., 1935.
U2800 (ASU)

Potomac Valley, Model of Scenic and Recreational Values: A Preliminary Report of the Joint Federal-State Planning Team on Landscape and Recreation, Potomac Valley. Washington: Govt. Print. Off., 1966.
U2810

Study of the Strip and Surface Mining in Appalachia; an Interim Report to the Appalachian Regional Commission. Washington: Govt. Print. Off., 1966.
U2820 (BC)

Surface Mining and our Environment; a Special Report to the Nation. Washington: Govt. Print. Off., 1967.
U2830 (BC)

Rejected or Suspended Applications for Revolutionary War Pensions. Baltimore: Genealogical Pub. Co., 1969.
U2840 (ASU)

U. S. Dept. of the Interior, Bureau of Indian Affairs see **U. S. Bureau of Indian Affairs**

U. S. Dept. of the Interior, Coal Mines Administration A Medical Survey of the Bituminous-coal Industry. Report. Washington: Govt. Print. Off., 1947.
U2850 (LMC)

U. S. Dept. of the Interior, Division of Information Natural Resources of West Virginia, the Mountain State. Washington: Govt. Print. Off., 1964.
U2860

U. S. Dept. of the Interior, Geological Survey Topographic Maps. Arlington, Va.: Distribution Section, U. S. Geological Survey, n.d. The Charles Sherrod Library of East Tennessee State University has in its holdings the complete collection of topographic maps. Inclusive are those of the Appalachian region.
U2870 (ETSU)

U. S. Dept. of the Interior, National Park Service Arnold Guyot, First to Measure the Peaks of the Appalachians. Washington: The author, 1938.
U2880 (BC)

U. S. Dept. of the Interior, National Park Service see **U. S. National Park Service**

U. S. Dept. of the Interior, Secretary Shenandoah and Other National Parks; Letter from Sec'y of Interior Transmitting Information as to Boundaries and Areas of Shenandoah and Other National Parks. Washington: Govt. Print. Off., 1926.
U2890

U. S. Dept. of the Interior, Southern Appalachian National Park Commission see **U. S. Southern Appalachian National Park Commission**

U. S. Dept. of Labor Appalachia — Rebirth of a Region. Washington: Govt. Print. Off., n.d.
U2900 (ETSU)

U. S. Federal Power Commission Report on Review of Allocations of Costs of the Multiple-Purpose Water Control System in the Tennessee River Basin, as Determined by the Tennessee Valley Authority and Approved by the President Under the Provisions of the TVA Act of 1933 as Amended. Washington: FPC, 1949.
U2910

U. S. Forest Service Nantahala National Forest, Georgia, North Carolina, South Carolina. By Frederick William Wiese. Washington: Govt. Print. Off., 1936.
U2920 (WCU)

National Forests of the Southern Appalachians. Washington: Govt. Print. Off., 1923.
U2930

National Forests of the Southern Appalachians. Help Banish Fire from our Appalachian Forests. Washington: Govt. Print. Off., 1929.
U2940

Progress Report on a Study of Forest Conditions in Kentucky. Frankfort, Ky.: Frankfort Print. Co., 1909.
U2950 (BC)

Purchase of Land under the Weeks Law in the Southern Appalachian and White Mountains. Washington: Govt. Print. Off., 1911.
U2960

Purchase of Land under the Weeks Law in the Southern Appalachian and White Mountains Rev. ed. Washington: Govt. Print. Off., 1913.
U2970

Special Forest Products for Profit, Self-Help Suggestions for Rural Areas Development. Washington: Govt. Print. Off., 1963.
U2980

Timber in North Carolina. Forest Resource Report, no. 15. Washington: Govt. Print. Off., 1959.
U2990 (WCU)

Watauga Lake recreation areas, Cherokee National Forest, Tennessee. Cleveland, Tenn.: n.p., n.d.
U3000

U. S. Forest Service, Appalachian Forest Experiment Station Measures for Stand Improvement in Southern Appalachian Forests with List of Selected References. Washington: U. S. Forest Experiment, 1933.
U3010

U. S. Forest Service, Appalachian Forest Experiment Station, Asheville, N. C. Annual Report and Program. n.p.: n.p., n.d.
U3020 (BC)

U. S. Forest Service, Berea Forest Research Center, Berea, Ky. Strip Mining Reclamation in Appalachia. Berea, Ky.: Berea Forest Research Center, 1971.
U3030

U. S. Forest Service, Southeastern Forest Experiment Station, Asheville, N. C. Annual Report and Program. 1st - 1921/1922. n.p.: n.p., n.d.
U3040

U. S. Forest Service, Southern Region Joyce Kilmer Memorial Forest in the Nantahala National Forest. North Carolina: n.p., 1968.
U3050

U. S. General Accounting Office Highway Program Shows Limited Progress toward Increasing Accessibility to and through Appalachia: Report to the Congress on the Appalachian Regional Commission by the Comptroller General of the United States. Washington: Govt. Print. Off., 1971.
U3060

Opportunities for Improving Administration of Federal Program of Aid to Educationally Deprived Children in West Virginia, Office of Education, Department of Health, Education, and Welfare. Washington: Govt. Print. Off., 1970.
U3070

Report on the Audit of Tennessee Valley Authority. Washington: Govt. Print. Off., n.d.
U3080

U. S. Geological Survey Appalachian Region as Designated by the Appalachian Regional Commission, 1965. Washington: Govt. Print. Off., 1956.
U3090

Asheville Folio, North Carolina — Tennessee. Geologic Atlas of the United States, no. 116. Washington: The survey, 1904.
U3100 (WCU)

Chemical character of surface waters of Kentucky, 1949-1951. By William L. Lamar district chemist and Leslie B. Laird. Frankfort: Agricultural and Industrial Development Board of Kentucky, 1953.
U3110

Coal deposits of Pike Co., Ky. Bulletin no. 876. n.p.: n.p., n.d.
U3120

Cranberry Folio, North Carolina — Tennessee. Geological Atlas of the U. S., no. 90. Washington: The survey, 1903.
U3130 (WCU)

Geology of the Spruce Pine District: Avery, Mitchell, and Yancey Counties, North Carolina. By Donald A. Brobst. Washington: Govt. Print. Off., 1962.
U3130 (ASU)

Floods in Youghiogheny and Kiskiminetas River Basins, Pennsylvania and Maryland, Frequency and Magnitude. Circular, no. 204. Washington: Govt. Print. Off., 1952.
U3140

Geology of Big Stone Gap. Bulletin no. 111.
U3150

Geology & ground water resources in the Paintsville Area, Ky., 1955. Water-supply papers no. 1-1257.
U3160

Geology and Mineral Resources of part of the Cumberland Gap coal field, Ky., 1906. Professional Papers, 1. Washington: Govt. Print. Off., 1902.
U3170

Geology & ore deposits of the Ducktown mining district, Tenn., 1926. Professional papers, 1-139. Washington: Govt. Print. Off., 1902.
U3180

Greenville Folio, Tennessee — North Carolina. Geologic Atlas of the U. S., no. 118. Washington: The survey, 1905.
U3200 (WCU)

Inundation & erosion in the Appalachian region. Professional papers. Washington: Govt. Print. Off., 1902.
U3210

Knoxville Folio, Tennessee — North Carolina. Geologic Atlas of the United States, no. 16. Washington: The survey, 1895.
U3220 (WCU)

Manganese deposits of the Lyndhurst-Vesuvius district, Augusta & Rockbridge Co., Va., 1943. Bulletin no. 940F. n.p., n.p., n.d.
U3230

Manganese deposits of the Flat Top & Round Mtn district, Bland & Giles Co., Va., 1944. Bulletin no. 940H. n.p.: n.p., n.d.
U3240

Mineral Resources of the Appalachian Region: A Compilation of Information on the Mineral Resources, Mineral Industry, and Geology of the Appalachian Region. Also sponsored by the U. S. Bureau of Mines. Geological Professional Paper, 580. Washington: Govt. Print. Off., 1968.
U3250 (ASU LMC ETSU)

Mount Mitchell Folio, North Carolina — Tennessee. Geologic Atlas of the U. S., no. 124. Washington: The survey, 1905.
U3260 (WCU)

Nantahala Folio, North Carolina — Tennessee. Geologic Atlas of the United States, no. 143. Washington: The survey, 1907.
U3270 (WCU)

Oil & gas wells drilled in southwest Va., before 1950. Bulletin no. 1027L. n.p.: n.p., n.d.
U3280

Origin of Copper deposits S. Appal. Region. n.p.: Ken Crawford Books, 1935.
U3290

Pisgah Folio, North Carolina — South Carolina. Geologic Atlas of the United States, no. 147. Washington: The survey, 1907.
U3300 (WCU)

Surface water of the U. S. 1953; Cumberland and Tenn. River Basin. Water-supply papers no. 1-1276. n.p.: n.p., n.d.
U3310 (U)

Possibilities for Manganese ore or certain undeveloped tracks in Shenandoah Valley, Va., 1918. Bulletin 1-660J. n.p.: n.p., n.d.
U3310

Professional papers, 1, 37, 49, 198, 72, 139. Washington: Govt. Print. Off., 1902.
U3320 (BC)

Roan Mountain Folio, Tennessee — North Carolina. Geologic Atlas of the United States, no. 151. Washington: The survey, 1907.
U3330 (WCU)

Soil Maps. Cleveland County, Caldwell County, and Lincoln County. n.p.: Dept. of Agriculture, Bureau of Soils, n.d.
U3340

Soil Survey of the Mt. Mitchell Area. n.p.: n.p., n.d.
U3350

Soil Surveys Alleghany County, Gaston County, Transylvania County. n.p.: n.p., n.d.
U3360

The Southern Appalachian Forest. Professional papers, 1-37. Washington: Govt. Print. Off., 1902.
U3370

Titanium deposits of Nelson and Amherst Co., in Va. Professional papers, 1-198. Washington: Govt. Print. Off., 1902.
U3390

Water supply paper, no. 1. Washington: Govt. Print. Off., 1896.
U3400

U. S. Geological Survey, Division of Water Resources The Ohio River Basin Except the Cumberland and Tennessee River Basins. Water-supply Paper, 1725. Pt. 3-A, Compilation of Records of Surface Waters of the United States, October, 1950-September, 1960. Washington: Govt. Print. Off., 1964.
U3410

U. S. Geological Survey, Water-supply papers Geology and ground water resources in the Paintsville area, Ky. 1955, Surface water of the U. S. 1953; Cumberland and Tenn. River Basin. n.p.: n.p., n.d.
U3420

U. S. Government Document Acid Mine Drainage in Appalachia. 3 vols. Washington, D. C.: Govt. Print. Off., 1969.
U3430 (ASU)

U. S. House of Representatives, Committee on Education and Labor Examination of the War on Poverty Program. Hearings before the Sub-committee on the War on Poverty Program, 89th Congress, 1st Session, April 12-30, 1965. n.p.: n.p., n.d.
U3440

Poverty in the United States. 88th Congress, 2nd Session, April, 1964. n.p.: n.p., n.d.
U3450

U. S. Laws, Statutes, etc. An act to provide public work and economic development programs and the planning and coordination needed to assist in development of the Appalachian Region. (Public law 89-1, 89th Cong. 53, Mar. 9, 1965) Washington: Govt. Print. Off., 1965.
U3460

An act to provide public work & economic development programs & the planning & coordination needed to assist in development of the App. Region. (Public law 89-1, 89th Cong., S 3, Mar. 9, 1965) Washington: Govt. Print. Off., 1965.
U3470

Economic Development Acts: Pt. 1, Public Law 90-103, Title 1, Appalachian Regional Development Act Amendments of 1967, Title 2, Amendments to Public Works and Economic Development Act of 1965. Pt. 1, Section-by-section Analysis of Title 1, Appalachian Regional Development Act of 1967, Appalachian Regional Development Act of 1965, as Amended, Pt. 3, Section-by-section Analysis of Title 2 Amendments to Public Works and Economic Development Act of 1965, Public Works and Economic Development Act of 1965, as Amended. Printed for the use of the Committee on Public Works, 90th Congress, 1st session. Washington: Govt. Print. Off., 1967.
U3480

Economic Development Programs under the Jurisdiction of the Committee of Public Works, Pt. 1, 1971 Amendments to Public Works and Economic Development Act of 1965 and Appalachian Regional Development Act of 1965. Pt. 2, Public Works and Economic Development Act of 1965, as Amended. Pt. 3, Appalachian Regional Development Act of 1965 as Amended, December, 1971, 92nd Congress. Washington: Govt. Print. Off., 1971.
U3490

H. R. 8947, Act Making Appropriations for Public Works for Water and Power Development, Including Corps of Engineers — Civil, Bureau of Reclamation, Bonneville Power Administration and Other Power Agencies of the Department of Interior, Appalachian Regional Development Programs, Federal Power Commission, Tennessee Valley Authority, Atomic Energy Commission, and Related Independent Agencies and Commissions for Fiscal Year Ending June 30, 1974, and for Other Purposes. Approved August 16, 1973. Washington: Govt. Print. Off., 1973.
U3500

H. R. 10090, Act Making Appropriations for Public Works for Water and Power Development, Including Corps of Engineers, Civil, Bureau of Reclamation, Bonneville Power Administration, and Other Power Agencies of Department of Interior, Appalachian Regional Commission, Federal Power Commission, Tennessee Valley Authority, Atomic Energy Commission, and Related Independent Agencies and Commissions for Fiscal Year 1972, and for Other Purposes. Approved Oct. 5, 1971. Washington: Govt. Print. Off., 1971.
U3510

H. R. 15586, Act Making Appropriations for Public Works for Water and Power Development, Including Corps of Engineers — Civil, Bureau of Reclamation, Bonneville Power Administration, and Other Power Agencies of the Department of Interior, Appalachian Regional Development Programs, Federal Power Commission, Tennessee Valley Authority, Atomic Energy Commission, and Related Independent Agencies and Commissions for Fiscal Year 1973, and for Other Purposes. Approved August 25, 1972. Washington: Govt. Print. Off., 1972.
U3520

U. S. Laws, Statutes, etc.
S. 3, Act to Provide Public Works and Economic Development Programs and Planning and Coordination Needed to Assist in Development of Appalachian Region. Approved Mar. 9, 1965. Washington: Govt. Print. Off., 1965.
U3530 (ETSU)
S. 7, Act to Provide for the Establishment of Spruce Knob-Seneca Rocks National Recreation Area in West Virginia, and for Other Purposes. Approved September 28, 1965. Washington: Govt. Print. Off., 1965.
U3540
S. 602, Act to revise and extend Appalachian Regional Development Act of 1965, and to amend Public Works and Economic Development Act of 1965. Approved October 11, 1967. Washington: Govt. Print. Off., 1967.
U3550
S. 2317, Act to Extend Public Works and Economic Development Act of 1965 and Appalachian Regional Development Act of 1965. Approved Aug. 5, 1971. Washington: Govt. Print. Off., 1971.
U3560 (ETSU)
Tennessee Valley Authority Act: Public no. 17-73d Congress, 1st Session (H. R. 5081) May 18, 1933, 48 Stat. 58 . . . as Amended by Public Resolution, no. 88-76th Congress, 3d Session (H. J. Res. 544) June 26, 1940. Washington: Govt. Print. Off., 1941.
U3570

U. S. Library of Congress Check-list of Recorded Songs. n.p.: n.p., n.d.
U3580
West Virginia, the Centennial of Statehood, 1863-1963. An exhibition in the Library of Congress, Washington, D. C., December 12, 1963, to December 11, 1964. State Exhibition Catalogs, 20. Washington: Govt. Print. Off., 1964.
U3590 (ETSU)

U. S. Library of Congress, Legislative Reference Service Valley Authorities. Public Affairs Abstracts, V. II, No. 3. Washington: unp., 1951.
U3600

U. S. Library of Congress, Legislative Reference Service, Economics Division Should the Federal Government Establish a National Program of Public Work for the Unemployed? Selected Excerpts and References Relating to the National College Debate Topic, 1964-65. 88th Congress, House, Document, no. 92. Washington: Govt. Print. Off., 1964.
U3610

U. S. Library of Congress, Music Division, Archive of Folk Song A bibliography of hammered and plucked (Appalachian or mountain) dulcimers and related instruments. Washington, D. C.: Library of Congress, n.d.
U3620

U. S. National Advisory Commission on Rural Poverty The people left behind; a report by the President's National Advisory Commission on Rural Poverty. Washington: Govt. Print. Off., 1967.
U3630

U. S. National Air Pollution Control Administration Kanawha Valley Air Pollution Study. Prepared with the West Virginia Air Pollution Control Commission, Publication APTD Series, 70-1. Raleigh, N. C.: The administration's office of Technical Information and Publications, 1970.
U3640

U. S. National Clearinghouse for Mental Health Information A Selective Bibliography of Writings on Poverty in the United States. Bethesda, Md.: U. S. National Institutes of Health, 1964.
U3650

U. S. National Institute of Mental Health Mental Health in Appalachia: Problems and Prospects in the Central Highlands. A report based on a conference sponsored by the National Institute of Mental Health held in Bethesda, Maryland, July 13-14, 1964. Prepared by Public Information Section. Public Health Service Publication, no. 1375. Washington: Govt. Print. Off., 1965.
U3660 (LMC)
Mental Health in Appalachia. A Report of a Conference in Bethesda, Md., July 13-14, 1964. n.p.: Dept. of HEW, 1965.
U3670

U. S. National Park Service The Allegheny Parkway, West Virginia, Virginia, Kentucky: Report to the Congress of the U. S. Prepared in cooperation with the Bureau of Public Roads. Washington: Govt. Print. Off., 1964.
U3680
Appalachian National Scenic Trail. Washington: Govt. Print. Off., 1973.
U3690
Chickamauga-Chattanooga National Military Park. Tennessee. Georgia. n.p.: n.p., n.d.
U3700
Feasibility Study for Development of a New River Gorge National Parkway Virginia and West Virginia. Washington: n.p., 1963.
U3710
Great Smoky Mountains National Park. North Carolina-Tennessee. The Land and its People. n.p.: n.p., n.d.
U3720
Great Smoky Mountains National Park. North Carolina-Tennessee. The Land and its People. n.p.: n.p., n.d.
U3730

U. S. National Science Foundation Scientific Information Activities of Federal Agencies: Tennessee Valley Authority. Washington: Govt. Print. Off., 1960.
U3740

U. S. Northeastern Forest Experiment Station The Forest Products Marketing Laboratory at Princeton, West Virginia, Research Facility of the Northeastern Forest Experiment Station. Upper Darby, Pa.: Forest Service, 1963.
U3750

U. S. Office of Economic Opportunity A Nation Aroused, 1st Annual Report. Washington: Govt. Print. Off., 1965.
U3760
Poverty Program Information, as of January 1, 1966. 2 vols. Washington: Govt. Print. Off., 1966.
U3770
VISTA Services Urban Ghetto, Rural America, Appalachia, Migrant Worker, American Indian, Mentally Handicapped, Job Corps. Prepared by Community Relations Division, VISTA. Washington: Govt. Print. Off., 1967.
U3780
War on Poverty Projects, March 31, 1965. Washington: Govt. Print. Off., 1965.
U3790
War on Poverty Projects, April 30, 1965. Washington: Govt. Print. Off., 1965.
U3800

U. S. Office of Economic Opportunity, Community Action Program Strengthening Labor's Role in the War on Poverty: Labor Leadership for Community Action in Appalachia. Report of CAP 66-9205 to the Office of E. O. Morgantown, W. Va.: Univ. App. Center, Inst. for Labor Studies, 1967.
U3810
Strengthening labor's role in the War on Poverty: labor leadership training for community action in Appalachia; a report of CAP 66-9205 to the Office of Economic Opportunity, by Frederick A. Zeller, Project Director; Robert W. Miller, Associate Project Director. Morgantown: West Virginia Univ. App. Center, Institute for Labor Studies, 1967.
U3820

U. S. Office of Education Bulletin. n.p.: n.p., n.d.
U3830

U. S. President (Franklin D. Roosevelt) Muscle Shoals Development Message from the President of the U. S. Transmitting a Request for Legislation to Create a Tennessee Valley Authority. 73rd Congress, 1st session House Doc. 15. Washington: Govt. Print. Off., 1933.
U3840

U. S. President's Appalachian Regional Commission
see **App. Regional Commission**

U. S. President's National Advisory Commission on Rural Poverty Rural Poverty in the United States. Washington: Govt. Print. Off., 1968.
U3850

U. S. President's Water Resources Policy Commission Report, V. 2: Ten Rivers in America's Future. Washington: Govt. Print. Off., 1950.
U3860
The Tennessee River Basin. V. 2, In the Commission's Report. Washington: Govt. Print. Off., 1950.
U3870

U. S. Public Health Service Malaria Control on Impounded Water. By the United States Public Health Service and Tennessee Valley Authority, Health and Safety Department. Washington: Govt. Print. Off., 1947.
U3880
Mental Health in Appalachia, Problems and Prospects in the Central Highlands. Publication no. 1375. Bethesda, Md.: n.p., 1965.
U3890
Report on Coosa River System, Georgia-Alabama. Cincinnati: Public Health Service, Robert A. Taft Sanitary Engineering Center, 1963.
U3900

U. S. Secretary of War Revolutionary pensioners; a transcript of the pension list of the United States for 1813. Baltimore: Southern Book Co., 1959.
U3910 (ASU)

U. S. Soil Conservation Service An Appraisal of Potentials for Outdoor Recreational Development in Fort Worth. Prepared in cooperation with Tennessee Game and Fish Commission and others. n.p.: n.p., n.d.
U3920
Cumberland Plateau and Mountains and Southern Appalachian Ridges and Valley of Alabama, Georgia, and Tennessee. Soil Survey Interpretations for Woodlands, Progress Report, W-LL. Fort Worth, Texas: The service, 1969.
U3930
Soil Survey, Watauga County, North Carolina. Washington, D. C.: Govt. Print. Off., 1958.
U3940
Watershed Work plan. Fort Worth, Texas: n.p., 1971.
U3950
Watershed Work Plan . . . Eighteen Mile Creek Watershed, Pickens and Anderson Counties, South Carolina. Fort Worth, Texas: n.p., 1971.
U3960
Watershed Work Plan; Mill Creek Watershed, Jackson and Roane Counties, West Virginia. Prepared under the authority of the Watershed Protection and Flood Prevention. n.p.: n.p., 1969.
U3970 (ASU)

U. S. Southeastern Forest Experiment Station, Asheville, N. C. Forest Survey Release. Asheville, N. C.: n.p., 1939.
U3980
Improvements at Coweeta. Asheville: n.p., 1964.
U3990
Research Information Digest; Recent Publications of the Southeastern Forest Experiment Station. Asheville: n.p., semi-annual.
U4000
1963 Research at the Southeastern Forest Experiment Station. Asheville: The station, 1963.
U4010 (WCU)

U. S. Southern Appalachian National Park Commission Final Report of the Southern Appalachian National Park Commission to the Secretary of the Interior, June 30, 1931. Washington: Govt. Print. Off., 1931.
U4020 (ASU)

U. S. Supreme Court Opinion of the Supreme Court of the U. S. at the Jan. Term, 1832. Delivered by Chief Justice Marshall; together with the opinion of Justice McLeon in the case of Samuel A. Worcester vs. the state of Georgia. Washington: Gates and Seaton, 1832.
U4030

U. S. War Dept. Letter from the Secretary of War in reply to the resolution of the House of Representatives of the 23d ultimo, respecting the interference of any officer or agent of the Government with the Cherokee Indians in the formation of a government for the regulation of their own internal affairs. Washington, D. C.: Blair and Rives, 1840.
U4040

The Pension List of 1818-1819. Orig. Publ. as Letter from the Secretary of War, transmitting a Report of the Names, Rank, and Line of every person placed on the Pension List, etc. n.p.: n.p., 1955.
U4050

Pensioners of Revolutionary War struck off the roll; with an added index to States. Baltimore: Genealogical Pub. Co., 1969.
U4060 (ASU)

Revolutionary Pensioners of 1818. n.p.: n.p., 1959.
U4070

U. S. Work Projects Administration Guide to civilian organizations . . . Louisville, Ky.: n.p., 1942.
U4100

U. S. Work Projects Administration, Federal Writer's Project see Writers' Program

U. S. Works Progress Administration Federal Writer's Project. Historical Records Survey. Louisville, Ky.: The Historical Records Survey, 19-- Inventory of the county archives of Kentucky.
U4080

U. S. Works Progress Administration. Historical Records Survey American Imprints Inventory. n.p.: The WPA historical records survey project, 19--
U4090

University of Tennessee, Bureau of Public Administration Greeneville's Government; a Study of the Organization and Administration of the Government of Greeneville, Tennessee. Knoxville: Univ. of Tennessee, 1950.
U4110

University of Virginia Record, Extension Service An Economic and Social Survey of Virginia Counties. Charlottesville: Univ. of Virginia, 1922-1925. Includes Appalachian counties.
U4120 (FC)

Unkalunt, Atalie The Earth Speaks. New York: Fleming H. Revell Co., 1940.
U4130 (ASU)

Unto the Hills; Glimpses of Berea's Outdoors Compiled by Euphemia Kipp Corwin and Florence Holmes Ridgway. Cincinnati: Printed for the authors by the Abingdon Press, n.d.
U4140

Updated Investment Guidelines for North Carolina Appalachian Region 1971 to 1975, and A Plan for Public Investment in Appalachian North Carolina, Fiscal 1971 Washington: Appalachian Regional Commission, 1972.
U4150

Upper East Tennessee Regional Planning Commission Industrial Site Survey of Carter County, Sullivan County, and Washington County. Nashville: Tenn. State Planning Commission, 1959.
U4160

Upper Ohio Valley Pioneer Moundsville, W. Va.: Delf Norona, quarterly.
U4170

Upshur County Development Committee Overall Economic Development Program for Upshur County, West Virginia. Buckhannon, W. Va.: The committee, 1962.
U4180

Urban America Kentucky Housing Fund: A Housing Proposal for the Commonwealth of Kentucky. Prospectus and Final Report to the Appalachian Regional Commission. Washington: n.p., 1968.
U4190

West Virginia Housing Development Fund: A Housing Proposal for the State of West Virginia. Prospectus and Final Report. Report to the Appalachian Regional Commission. Washington: n.p., 1968.
U4200

The Urban Experience and Folk Tradition Edited by Americo Paredes and Ellen J. Stelcert. Published for the American Folklore Society. Austin: Univ. of Texas Press, 1971.
U4210 (ASU LMC)

URS Research Company Recreation Potential in the Appalachian Highlands: A Market Analysis. Reprint of a report prepared for the Appalachian Regional Commission. Appalachian Research Report, no. 14. San Mateo, Cal.: The co., 1971.
U4220 (ASU)

Use of Health Care Services and Enrollment in Voluntary Health Insurance in Habersham County, Georgia, 1957 n.p.: n.p., n.d.
U4230

Ussery, Clyde Cate, Herma The Southern Appalachian Heritage. Boone, N. C.: The Appalachian Consortium, 1974.
C2041

Vail, Robert W. G. The Voice of the Old Frontier. Philadelphia: Univ. of Pennsylvania Press, 1950.
V10

Val Baker, Denys ed. Voyage; an Anthology of Selected Stories by Mary Lavin, Rhys Davies, James Hanley and Others. London: Sylvan Press, 1945. Includes some mountain items.
V20

Valdese, North Carolina Subdivision Regulations, Valdese, N. C., Adopted April 3, 1967. n.p.: The author, n.d. Valdese and the surrounding areas of Burke County were settled by Waldensians. Their community is unique and attractive.
V30 (LMC)

Vanatta, E. S. Taylor, Arthur Elijah Soil Survey of Clay County, Alabama. Washington: U. S. Department of Agriculture, Bureau of Soils, 1916.
T410

Vanatta, Earl Steere Soil Survey of Cleveland County, North Carolina. Prepared in cooperation with the North Carolina Department of Agriculture. Field Operations, 1916. Washington: U. S. Department of Agriculture, Bureau of Soils, 1918.
V40

Van Benthuysen, Robert N., Jr. "The Sequent Occupance of Tellico Plains, Tennessee." Master's thesis. Univ. of Tennessee, 1951. A Monroe County, Tennessee demographic study.
V50

Van Borries, J. W. The Coal Fields of Perry Co., Ky. Paper presented to the annual meeting Ky. Mining Institute, Pinesville, Ky. May 4, 1915. Pineville: n.p., 1915.
V60

Vance, Carl T., Jr. "A Consultative Conference in Science for Elementary Teachers in Bristol, Virginia, 1955-56." Master's thesis. East Tennessee State College, 1956.
V70 (ETSU)

Vance, Carl Taylor "A Study of High Schools in Hawkins County, Tennessee." Master's thesis. George Peabody College, 1922.
V80

Vance, Rupert Bayless Human Geography of the South: A Study in Regional Resources and Human Adequacy. 2nd ed., Social Series. Chapel Hill: Univ. of North Carolina Press, 1935.
V90 (ASU LMC WWC MHC)

Vance, Zebulon Baird My Beloved Zebulon; the Correspondence of Zebulon B. Vance and Harriett Newell Espy. With an introd. by Frances Gray Patton. Chapel Hill: Univ. of North Carolina Press, 1971. Vance was North Carolina's Civil War governor.
V100

Papers. Raleigh: N. C. State Department of Archives and History, 1963.
V110 (ASU LMC)

Repeal of Civil Service Law. Speech of Hon. Zebulon B. Vance of North Carolina, Delivered in the United States Senate, Wednesday, March 31, 1886. Washington: R. O. Polkinhorn and Son, 1886.
V120 (ASU)

The Scattered Nation. New York: M. Schnitzer, 1916.
V130 (ASU WCU)

The Tariff and the Farmers: Speech of Hon. Z. B. Vance, of North Carolina, on the McKinley Tariff Bill in the Senate of the United States, Friday, 25, 1890. Washington: n.p., 1890.
V140 (ASU)

VanCleve, Dorothy "The History of the First Presbyterian Church of Bristol, Tennessee." Master's thesis. East Tennessee State College, 1959.
V150 (ETSU)

Van Der Beets, Richard comp. Held Captive by the Indians: Selected Narrative, 1642-1836. 1st ed. Knoxville: Univ. of Tennessee Press, 1973.
V170 (ASU MHC)

Van Der Beets, Richard ed. Held Captive by Indians: Selected Narratives, 1642-1836. Knoxville: Univ. of Tennessee Press, 1973. The eighteen narratives give insight into Indian-white relations in Appalachia.
V160 (ASU MHC)

Van der Horst, Brian Folk Music in America. New York: F. Watts, 1972.
V180

Vanderwerth, W. C. Indian Oratory: Famous Speeches by Noted Indian Chieftains. Norman: Univ. of Oklahoma Press, 1971.
V190 (LMC)

Van Devanter, J. N. History of the Augusta Church, from 1737 to 1900. Staunton, Va.: Ross Print. Co., 1900.
V200 (ASU)

Van Doren, Mark ed. Bartram, William The Travels of William Bartram. New York: Barnes and Noble, 1940.
B1720 (WCU)

Bartram, William The Travels of William Bartram. An American Bookshelf. New York: Dover Pub., 1955.
B1730 (ASU)

Van Every, Dale The Captive Witch. New York: J. Messner, 1951.
V210 (ASU)

A Company of Heroes. New York: Wm. Morrow and Co., 1962. A history of the American frontier from 1775-1783.
V220

Disinherited: The Lost Birthright of the American Indian. New York: Morrow, 1966.
V230 (WCU ETSU MHC UNCA)

Forth to the Wilderness: The First American Frontier, 1754-1774. A Menton Book. New York: New American Library, 1962.
V240 (ASU)

Men of the Western Waters; a Second Look at the First Americans. Boston: Houghton, 1956. Includes bibliography.
V250

Our Country Then: Tales of Our First Frontier. 1st ed. New York: Holt, 1958.
V260 (ASU)

The Trembling Earth. New York: J. Messner, 1953.
V270 (ASU)

Van Hook, Joseph Orlando The Kentucky Story. Chattanooga, Tenn.: Harlow Pub. Corp., 1959.
V280

Van Horn, Earl C. Talc Deposits of the Murphy Marble Belt. Prepared and published in cooperation with the Tennessee Valley Authority. Bulletin, no. 56. Raleigh: N. C. Department of Conservation and Development, 1948.
V290 (WCU)

Van Horne, Thomas B. History of the Army of the Cumberland, Its Organization, Campaigns, and Battles; Written at the Request of Maj.-Gen. George H. Thomas, Chiefly from his Private Military Journal and Official and Other Documents Furnished by Him. Illus. with campaign and battle maps comp. by Edward Ruger. n.p.: Robert Clarke and Co., 1875.
V300

Vankirk, Fred Public Facility Location Determinations and Impact of New Highway Investment on Accessibility Changes in a Specified Subregion of W. Va. Morgantown: W. Va. Univ. Office of Research and Development, 1969.
V310

Van Liere, Edward J. History of Medical Education in West Va. Morgantown: W. Va. Univ. Library, 1965.
V320

Van Liere, Edward Jerald Early Teachers in W. Va. Univ. School of Medicine, 1869-1922. Morgantown: W. Va. Univ. Library, 1968.
V330

Van Loon, Elizabeth The Shadow of Hampton Mead. Philadelphia: T. B. Peterson, 1878.
V340

Vann, Elizabeth Chapman Denny Virginia's First German Colony. Richmond: n.p., 1961.
V350 (ASU FC)

Van Noppen, Ina Faye Woestemeyer see also **Woestemeyer, Ina Faye**

Van Noppen, Ina Woestemeyer Stoneman's Last Raid. Raleigh, N. C.: North Carolina State College, 1961.
V360

Stoneman's Last Raid. Raleigh, N. C.: n.p., 1961.
V370 (ASU LMC WCU)

Western North Carolina Since the Civil War. Boone, N. C.: Appalachian Consortium Press, 1973.
V380 (ASU WWC ETSU)

Van Noppen, John James Daniel Boone, Backwoodsman: The Green Woods Were His Portion. Boone, N. C.: Appalachian Press, 1966.
V390 (ASU WCU LMC MHC)

Van Noppen, John J. Van Noppen, Ina Woestemeyer Western North Carolina Since the Civil War. Boone, N. C.: Appalachian Consortium Press, 1973.
V380 (ASU WWC ETSU)

Van Noppen, John James Daniel Boone, Backwoodsman: The Green Woods Were His Portion. Boone, N. C.: Appalachian Press, 1966.
V390 (ASU WCU LMC MHC)

Vann Wagenen, Jared The Golden Age of Homespun. Illustrated by Erwin H. Austin. Ithaca: Cornell Univ. Press, 1953.
V400 (ASU)

Van Sickle, Charles C. Forest Industries in Appalachian Counties of Tennessee. U. S. Forest Service Resources Bulletin, SO-8. New Orleans: Southern Forest Experiment Station, 1967.
V410

Van Sickle, John Valentine Planning for the South, an Inquiry into the Economics of Regionalism. Nashville: Vanderbilt Univ. Press, 1943.
V420 (ASU)

Vantage Point no. 1-, 1973-. Knoxville, Tenn.: Commission on Religion in Appalachia, n.d.
V430

Van Veen, Ted Rhododendrons in America. Portland, Ore.: Sweeny, Kirst and Dimm., 1969.
V440 (ASU)

Vargha, Louis A. Stroup, Robert H. Economic Impact of Secondary Road Improvements. Lexington: Univ. of Kentucky, 1963.
S8150

Vaughn, Lawrence M. Just the Little Story of Cumberland Gap. Middlesboro, Ky.: Middlesboro Chamber of Commerce, 1927.
V450

Vaughn, William Hutchinson "Robert Jefferson Breckinridge as an Educational Administrator." Master's thesis. George Peabody College for Teachers, 1937.
V460 (ETSU)

Vaught, Edgar S. Partial History of the Vaught Family. Oklahoma City, Okla.: n.p., 1950.
V470

Veal, Cora T. "The Development of Education in Monroe County, Tennessee." Master's thesis. Univ. of Tennessee, 1958.
V480

Veatch, Jethro O. Soil Survey of Blair County, Pennsylvania. Prepared in cooperation with the Pennsylvania State College, School of Agriculture and Experiment Station. Field Operations, 1915. Washington: U. S. Department of Agriculture, Bureau of Soils, 1917.
V490

Soil Survey of Walker County, Alabama. Prepared in cooperation with Alabama. Field Operations, 1915. Washington: U. S. Department of Agriculture, Bureau of Soils, 1916.
V500

Vecsey, George One Sunset a Week, the Story of a Coal Miner . . . . New York: Saturday Review Press, E. P. Dutton and Co., Inc., 1974.
V510 (ASU)

Veech, James The Monongahela of Old: Or, Historical Sketches of South-Western Pennsylvania to the Year 1800. Parsons, W. Va.: McClain Print. Co., 1971.
V520 (ASU)

Verhoeff, Mary The Kentucky Mountains, Transportation and Commerce, 1750-1911: A Study in the Economic History of a Coal Field. Filson Club Publications, no. 26. Louisville: J. P. Morton and Co., 1911.
V530 (ASU WCU BC)

. . . The Kentucky River Navigation. Louisville, Ky.: John P. Morton and Co., 1917.
V540

Vernon, J. J. and others Study of the Organization and Management of Farmers in Grayson County, Va. Charlottesville: Va. Agricultural Experiment Station, 1936.
V560

Verve vol. 1-, Fall 1970. Boone, N. C.: Appalachian State Univ., Student Development, quarterly.
V570 (ASU)

Vessel, A. J. Austin, Moris E. Soil Survey, Claiborne County, Tennessee. Washington: U. S. Department of Agriculture, Bureau of Plant Industry, Soils, and Agricultural Engineering, 1948.
A5560 (ASU)

Perkins, Samuel Oscar Soil Survey, Henderson County, North Carolina. Washington: U. S. Department of Agriculture, Bureau of Plant Industry, Soils, and Agricultural Engineering, 1943.
P2100

Soil Survey, Greenbrier County, West Virginia. Prepared in cooperation with the West Virginia Geological Survey and the West Virginia Agricultural Experiment Station. Soil Survey Report, Series 1937, no. 3. Washington: U. S. Dept. of Agriculture, Bureau of Plant Industry, 1941.
V580

Vibhatakarasa, Jin "The Tennessee Valley Authority: Administrative Development of the Last Two Decades, 1940-1960." Master's thesis. Duke Univ., 1961.
V590

Vick, Shirley M. "A Comparative Study of Changes in Selected Personality Variables in Guidance and Counseling Majors as Compared with Reading Majors at Appalachian State University, 1967-68 Academic Year." Master's thesis. Appalachian State Univ., 1968.
V600 (ASU)

Vickery, Dorothy Scovil Hollins College, 1842-1942; an Historical Sketch, Being an Account of the Principal Developments in the One-Hundred-Year History of Hollins College. Hollins College, Va.: Hollins College, 1942.
V610 (BC)

Vimmerstedt, John P. Doolittle, Warren T. Site Index Curves for Natural Stands of White Pine in the Southern Appalachians. Asheville, N. C.: Southeastern Forest Experiment Station, 1960.
D2930 ()

Southern Appalachian White Pine Plantations, Site, Volume, and Yield. U. S. Forest Service Station Paper, 149. Asheville, N. C.: Southeastern Forest Experiment Station, 1962.
V620 (WCU)

Vincent, Bert Bert Vincent's Strolling, Being Sort of a Side-Glance at the Little Odds and Ends of Life in These Parts. Knoxville: W. L. Warters, 1940. Vincent was a feature writer for the Knoxville News-Sentinel.
V630

The Best Stories of Bert Vincent, ed. Willard Yarbrough. Maryville: Brazos, 1968.
V640

More of the Best Stories of Bert Vincent. Maryville: Brazos, 1970.
V650

Vines, Howell This Green Thicket World. Boston: Little, Brown and Co., 1934.
V660 (ASU)

Vinson, Lacy W. "A Study of the Ability of Cocke County to Support Its Schools." Master's thesis. Univ. of Tennessee, 1957.
V670

Virginia, Agricultural Experiment Station Bulletin. Blacksburg, Va.: n.p., 1926.
V680 (BC)

Virginia, Auditor of Public Accounts A List of Lands and Lots Returned as Delinquent, in Grayson County, Va. n.p.: n.p., n.d.
V690 (BC)

Virginia, Board of Immigration Virginia: A Geographical and Political Summary, Embracing a Description of the State, Its Geology, Soils, Minerals and Climate; Its Animal and Vegetable Productions; Manufacturing and Commercial Facilities; Religious and Educational Advantages; Internal Improvements, and Form of Government. Richmond: The author, 1870.
V700 (BC)

Virginia, Commission on Constitutional Government Federal Grants-in-Aid; a Comprehensive Analysis of Federal Grants-in-Aid to All the States, with a Detailed Analysis of Programs in Effect in Each City and County of Virginia. Richmond: The commission, 1961.
V710 (BC)

Virginia Conservation Commission State Historical Markers of Virginia. 5th ed., Edited by the Division of History and Archeology. Richmond: Division of Publicity and Advertising, 1941.
V720

Virginia, County Court (Franklin County) An Old Virginia Court: Being a Transcript of the Records of the First Court of Franklin County, Virginia, 1786-1789, with Biographies of the Justices and Stories of Famous Cases. Transcribed, annotated, glossarized and indexed by Marshall Wingfield. Memphis: West Tennessee Historical Society, 1948.
V730 (ASU ETSU)

Virginia, Department of Conservation and Development A Hornbook of Virginia History. Compiled and edited by James Randolph Vivian Daniel. Richmond: The department's division of history, 1949.
V760 (ASU)

Virginia, Dept. of Agriculture and Immigration Virginia. Pub. by the Department of Agriculture and Immigration of the State of Virginia by Geo. W. Koiner, Commissioner, Richmond. Richmond: D. Bottom, Superintendent of Public Print., 1926.
V740 (BC)

Virginia, Dept. of Conservation and Development, Division of Industrial Development Manufacturing Plants in Va. Established Since 1940, Listed by Counties and Independent Cities. Richmond: The dept., 1958.
V790

Virginia Dept. of Conservation and Development, Division of Water Resources Bulletin. Surface and Water Supply of Va. New, Big Sandy, and Tenn. River Basins, 1942-1950. Richmond: The dept., n.d.
V750 (BC)

Virginia, Dept. of Conservation and Economic Development Industrial Sites and Economic Data. Richmond: The dept., 1960. Describes industrial sites and economic data of Tazewell County, Virginia.
V770 (BC)

Industrial Sites and Economic Data, Botetourt County, Virginia. Richmond: The dept., 1960.
V780

Virginia, Dept. of Highways, Div. of Traffic and Planning Travel Survey of Out-of-State Passenger Cars Using Highways in Virginia. Richmond: The dept., 1964.
V800

Virginia, Division of Industrial Development Economic Data. Richmond: The division, n.d.
V810 (BC)

Virginia, Division of Industrial Development and Planning Projections and Economic Base Analysis: Bristol-Kingsport Metropolitan Area Including the City of Bristol, Virginia, and the Counties of Washington, Virginia, and Sullivan, Tennessee. Richmond: The division, 1967.
V820

Virginia, Division of Mineral Resources Bulletin. Charlottesville: The division, n.d.
V830 (BC)

Virginia, Division of Water Resources New River Basin Comprehensive Water Resources Plan. Richmond: The division, 1967.
V840

Virginia; an Economic Profile Richmond, Va.: Federal Reserve Bank of Richmond, 1962.
V850 (BC)

Virginia, Employment Commission Labor Supply Survey of Bristol, Virginia-Tennessee. Prepared by the Research, Statistics, and Information Division. Richmond: The Commission, 1964.
V860 (ETSU)

Labor Supply Survey of New River Valley. Prepared by Research, Statistics and Information Division, Virginia Employment Commission. Richmond: The commission, 1963.
V870 (ASU)

Labor Supply Survey of Northern Shenandoah Valley. Prepared by Research, Statistics, and Information Division. Richmond: The commission, 1963.
V880 (ASU)

Redevelopment Manpower Report for the Norton-Big Stone Gap Area. Richmond: The commission, 1964.
V890 (ASU)

Virginia, Geological Commission, Office of the State Forester Bulletin. Charlottesville, Va.: Univ. of Virginia, 19--.
V900 (BC)

Virginia, Geological Survey Bulletin. Richmond: n.p., n.d.
V910

The Clay and Shales of Va. West of the Blue Ridge. Bulletin no. 20. Richmond: The survey, 1920.
V920

Contributions to Virginia Geology. Bulletin, no. 46. Richmond: The survey, 1936.
V930 (LMC)

Fensters in the Cumberland Over Thrust in Southwest Va. Bulletin no. 28. Richmond: The survey, 1927.
V940

Geology and Coal Resources of Buchanan Co., Va. Bulletin no. 18. Richmond: The survey, 1918.
V950

The Geology and Coal Resources of the Coal-Bearing Portion of Tazewell Co., Va. Bulletin no. 19. Richmond: The survey, 1919.
V960

The Geology and Coal Resources of Dickenson Co., Va. Bulletin no. 21. Richmond: The survey, 1921.
V970

Geology and Mineral Resources of Wise Co. and Coal Bearing Portions of Scott Co., Va. with a Chapter on the Forest of Wise Co. Bulletin no. 24. Richmond: The survey, 1923.
V980

Guidebook, Field Conference of Pennsylvania Geologists, Virginia — 1938. Compiled by Arthur Charles Beva, with the Collaboration of Charles Butts, Frank M. Swartz, Anna I. Jonas, A. S. Furcon, Earl A. Trager and Joseph K. Roberts. Guide Leaflet no. 1. Univ., Va.: The survey, 1938.
V990 (ETSU)

Marble Prospects in Giles Co., Va. Bulletin no. 40. Richmond: The survey, n.d.
V1000

Oil and Gas Possibilities at Early Grove, in Scott Co., Va. Bulletin 27. Richmond: The survey, 1927.
V1010

Reprint Series. no. 1-, 1937-. Univ., Va.: The survey, irregular.
V1020 (ETSU)

Zinc and Lead Region of Southwestern Va. Bulletin no. 43. Richmond: The survey, 1935.
V1030

Virginia, Guide to the Old Dominion Compiled by the Writers Program of the W.P.A. in Virginia. American Guide Series. New York: Oxford Univ. Press, 1940.
V1040

Virginia Highway Historical Markers: The Tourist Guide Book of Virginia Featuring the Inscriptions on the Official Markers Along the Historic and Romantic Highways of the Mother State. Strasburg, Va.: Shanandoah Pub. House, n.d.
V1050 (BC)

Virginia, Historical Collections, New Series vols 1 through 11. 1882-1892. Richmond, Va.: William Ellis Jones Printer, n.d.
V1060

The Virginia Historical Register, and Literary Companion Ed. by William Maxwell. 1. 1-6, Jan. 1848-Oct. 1853. Richmond: Printed for the Proprietor by Macfarlane and Ferguson, 1848-53.
V1070 (BC)

Virginia, Laws, Statutes, etc. Acts of the General Assembly, Passed at the Extra Session, Held May Sixth, 1862, at the City of Wheeling. Wheeling: Printed at the Dail Press book and job office, 1862. An act giving the consent of the legislature of Virginia to the formation West Virginia.
V1080 (BC)

The Code of Virginia: With the Declaration of Independence and Constitution of the U. S.: And the Declaration of Rights and Constitution of Virginia. Richmond: Wm. F. Ritchie, 1849.
V1090 (LMC)

Virginia Local History: A Bibliography Richmond, Va.: State Library, 1971.
V1100 (LMC)

The Virginia Magazine of History and Biography Published quarterly by the Virginia Historical Society. Richmond, Va.: The Society, 1893.
V1110 (BC)

Virginia Military Institute, Lexington Official Register, 1910-1911. Lexington, Va.: The institute, n.d.
V1120 (ASU)

Virginia Minerals vol. 1-, 1955. Charlottesville, Va.: Division of Mineral Resources, n.d.
V1130 (BC)

Virginia, Outdoor Recreation Study Commission Va's Common Wealth, a Study at Va.'s Outdoor Recreation Resources. Richmond: The survey, 1965.
V1140

Virginia, Polytechnic Institute, Blacksburg Bulletin. Engineering Experiment Station series, no. 1. n.p.: n.p., n.d.
V1150 (BC)

Virginia, Economic and Civic. Prepared in the Virginia Polytechnic Institute in collaboration with the Virginia State Chamber of Commerce. Edited for the Virginia state chamber of commerce by Clarence W. Newman. Richmond: Whittet & Shepperson, 1933.
V1160 (BC)

Virginia, Secretary of the Commonwealth Report. Richmond: n.p., annual.
V1170 (BC)

Virginia, State Library, Richmond A Bibliography of Virginia, Part 1. Containing the Titles of Books in the Virginia State Library which Relate to Virginia and Virginians, the Titles of Those Books Written by Virginians, and of those Printed in Virginia but not including the Titles of the Official Editions of the Laws, of the Journals of the Legislative Bodies, of the Reports of Administrative Officers, and other published official documents. By Earl G. Swem, Assistant Librarian. Richmond: Sup't of Public Print., 1916.
V1180

Virginia, State Library, Richmond, Department of Archives and History List of the Colonial Soldiers of Virginia. Special report for 1913. 1961. Reprint. Baltimore: Genealogical Pub. Co., 1965.
V1190 (ASU)

Virginia Travel Study Committee Travel in Virginia, Its Economic Significance. Richmond: Advisory Council on the Virginia Economy, 1967.
V1200

Virginia, University The University of Virginia Record . . . . Charlottesville: The Univ., irregular.
V1210 (BC)

Virginia, University, Bureau of Population and Economic Research Personal income estimates for Virginia counties and cities, 1957 and 1958, by John Littlepage Lancaster. Charlottesville: Univ. of Virginia, 1961.
V1220 (BC)

Virginia, University, Library The Folksongs of Virginia: A Checklist of the WPA Holdings, Alderman Library University of Virginia. By Bruce A. Rosenberg. Charlottesville: Univ. Press of Virginia, 1969.
V1230 (ETSU ASU LMC)

Virginia, University School of Rural Social Economics An Economic and Social Survey of Warren Co. Charlottesville, Va.: Univ. of Va., 1943.
V1240 (BC ASU)

Virkus, Frederick Adams ed. The Abridged Compendium of American Genealogy: First Families of America, a Genealogical Encyclopedia of the United States. Under the direction of Albert Nelson Marquis. 1925-42. Reprint. 5 vols. Baltimore: Genealogical Pub. Co., 1968.
V1250 (ASU)

Immigrant Ancestors: A List of 2,500 Immigrants to America Before 1750. Baltimore: Genealogical Pub. Co., 1963.
V1260 (ASU)

Immigrants to America Before 1750: An Alphabetical List of Immigrants to the Colonies Before 1750, Compiled from Official and Other Records. Baltimore: Genealogical Pub. Co., 1965.
V1270 (ASU)

Vlachos, P. G. "The Structure and Polarization of Economic Activity in the Appalachian Region." Ph. D. Diss. Univ. of Cincinnati, 1969.
V1280 (LMC)

Vogel, H. D. TVA Revenue Bond Financing Presented by the Board of Directors, Tennessee Valley Authority. Speech before the Municipal Forum of New York, May 12, 1960. New York: Municipal Forum of New York, 1960.
V1290

Vogel, John This Happened in the Hills of Kentucky. Grand Rapids, Mich.: Zondervan Pub. House, 1952. Vogel founded the Galilean Children's Home in Corbin, Kentucky.
V1300 (ASU LMC)

Vogenberger, R. A. Method for Determining Public Fire Control Expenditures for Private Lands. Prepared in Cooperation with North Carolina Department of Conservation and Development and the TVA Division of Forestry Relations. Norris, Tenn.: Tennessee Valley Authority, 1957.
V1310

Voice of the Hills vol. 1, no. 1 ceased pub. after 1st issue, April 1970. Richwood, W. Va.: Mountaineer Hall of Fame, n.d. The voice of the Mountaineer Hall of Fame.
V1320 (BC)

Voigt, Marry Raymond History of Concordia College, Conover, North Carolina. Master's thesis. Appalachian State Teachers College, 1951.
V1330 (ASU)

Vollmer, Lula The Hill Between; a Folk Play in Three Acts. Prepared by Nathaniel E. Reeid. New York: Longmans, Green and Co., 1937. A slow-moving drama about a mountain born doctor and his outland wife who returned to the hills.
V1340

Moonshine and Honeysuckle; a Play in Three Acts. New York: French, 1934. A farcical drama of strife and feuds in the southern mountains.
V1350

Sun-up; a Play in Three Acts. New York: Brentano's Pubs., 1924. A drama of World War 1 volunteers and a deserter set in the southern mountains.
V1360 (ETSU ASU)

Sun-up: A Play in Three Acts. New York: Coward-McCann, 1933.
V1370 (ASU LMC)

Voorhees, Lillian W. The Brown Thrush; Anthology of Verse by Negro Students, Talladega College, Tougaloo College. Edited by Lillian W. Voorhees and Robert W. O'Brien. Bryn Athyn, Penn.: Lawson-Roberts, 1932.
V1380 (BC)

W. F. Stallard ed. The Elkhorn Review "From the Heart of the Hills." Ernine, Ky.: n.p., n.d.
E1570

Wachovia Bank and Trust Company North Carolina County Data. Raleigh: Wachovia Bank and Trust Co., 1968.
W10

Waddell, Joseph A. Annals of Augusta County, Virginia, 1726-1871. 2nd ed. rev. Staunton: C. Russell Caldwell Pub., 1902.
W20

Waddell, Joseph Addison Annals of Augusta County, Virginia, with Reminiscences and a Diary of the War, 1861-1865, and a Chapter on Reconstruction. Richmond: Wm. E. Jones, 1886.
W30 (LMC BC ASU)

Wade, Carlson Natural and Folk Remedies. Foreword by H. W. Holderby. New York: Parker Pub. Co., 1970.
W40 (ASU LMC WCU BC)

Wade, Forest C. Cry of the Eagle: History and Legends of the Cherokee Indians and Their Buried Treasures. Cumming, Ga.: n.p., 1969.
W50 (ASU WCU BC)

Wade, William Frankly Speaking: A Concoction of Humorous, Serious, and Satirical Verses. Beckley, W. Va.: n.p., 1936.
W60 (ASU)

Wadleigh, Francis R. A List of Books and Other Sources of Information Regarding Coal and Coal Products. Washington: W. F. Roberts, 1935.
W70

Wager, Paul Woodford County Government and Administration in North Carolina. Chapel Hill: Univ. of North Carolina, 1928.
W80 (LMC BC)

Waggoner, George C. What Kentuckians Ought to Know about the State Game and Fish Commission . . . . Frankfort, Ky.: Kentucky Game and Fish Commission, 1926.
W90 (BC)

Wagner, A. J. TVA Power System. Address before the Electric League of Chattanooga, May 19, 1964. Knoxville, Tenn.: Tennessee Valley Authority, 1964.
W100

Wagner, Leopold Manners, Customs, and Observances: Their Origins and Signification. 1894. Reprint. Detroit: Gale Research Co., 1968.
W110 (ASU)

Wagstaff, Henry McGilbert Federalism in North Carolina. James Sprunt Studies, vol. 9, no. 2. Chapel Hill: Univ. of North Carolina Press, 1910.
W120 (LMC)

Wiley Buck and Other Stories. Chapel Hill: Univ. of North Carolina Press, 1953.
W130 (LMC)

Wagstaff, Thomas "Andrew Johnson and the National Union Movement." Ph. D. Diss. Univ. of Wisconsin, 1967. Helped make Johnson a national political figure.
W140

Wahl, Kenneth D. Ground Water in the Vicinity of Bryce Hospital, Negro Colony, Tuscaloosa County, Alabama. Prepared by the U. S. Geological Survey in cooperation with the Alabama State Hospitals and the Geological Survey of Alabama. Circular, 25. Univ.: Alabama Geological Survey, 1965.
W150 (ETSU)

Wahlenberg, W. G. Technique for Hand Planting of Forest Trees on Southern Appalachians. U. S. Forest Service, Station Paper, no. 12. Asheville, N. C.: Southeastern Forest Experiment Station, 1951.
W160

Wahlgreu, Harold E. Taras, Michael Andrew A Comparison of Increment Core Sampling Methods For Estimating Tree Specific Gravity. Asheville, N. C.: Southeastern Forest Experiment Station, 1963.
T230 (WCU)

Wakefield, Donald S. A Technical Assistance Program for the Upper Cumberlands of Tennessee. Cookeville, Tenn.: Technological Univ. Upper Cumberland Economic and Resources Development Center., 1968.
W170

Wakefield, Eleanor Ely Folk Dancing in America. New York: J. L. Pratt, 1966. Includes Appalachian folk dances.
W180 (BC)

Wakefield, Nancy comp. Gleeson, Patrick Language and Culture. Columbus, Ohio: E. C. Merrill, 1968.
G2100 (ASU BC)

Waldman, Emerson Beckoning Ridge. Illustrated by James Reid. New York: Henry Holt and Co., 1940.
W190 (ASU)

Waldrop, C. S. Lewis, Henry Guy Soil Survey of Cleburne County, Alabama. Washington: U. S. Department of Agriculture, Bureau of Soils, 1915.
L2170

Lyman, Webb S. Soil Survey of Etowah County, Alabama. Washington: U. S. Dept. of Agriculture, Bureau of Soils, 1910.
L4070

Smith, William G. Soil Survey of Colbert County, Alabama. Washington: U. S. Department of Agriculture, Bureau of Soils, 1909.
S5190

Waldrop, Charles S. Soil Survey of Jackson County, Alabama. Prepared in cooperation with Alabama. Field Operations, 1911. Washington: U. S. Department of Agriculture, Bureau of Soils, 1912.
W200

Soil Survey of Marshall County, Alabama. Prepared in cooperation with Alabama. Field Operations, 1911. Washington: U. S. Department of Agriculture, Bureau of Soils, 1913.
W210

Soil Survey of Putnam County, Tennessee. Prepared in cooperation with the Tennessee Geological Survey. Field Operations, 1912. Washington: U. S. Department of Agriculture, Bureau of Soils, 1914.
W220

Wales, G. Indian Battles, Murders, Sieges and Forays in the South-west. Nashville: n.p., 1853. Cherokees and other Indians of Tennessee. General History of the Cherokees.
W230

Walker, Anne Kendrick Russell Co. in Retrospect. Richmond, Va.: Deitz Press, 1950.
W240 (BC)

Walker, Charles R. Steeltown, an Industrial Case History of the Conflict between Progress and Security. New York: Harper, 1950. An excellent study of social conditions in a Pennsylvania steel town.
W250

Walker, Earnest "Characteristics of School Board Members of Selected Upper East Tennessee School Districts." Master's thesis. East Tennessee State Univ., 1969.
W260 (ETSU)

Walker, Edith C. "Folk Elements in the Fiction of James Still." Master's thesis. Western Kentucky Univ., 1969. Still is one of Appalachias popular authors. His RIVER OF EARTH is a classic.
W270 (ASU)

Walker, Etta Belle Willis, Carrie Hunter Legends of the Skyline Drive and the Great Valley of Virginia. Richmond: Dietz Press, 1937.
W7000 (ASU WCU LMC BC)

Walker, Frank H. Geological Society of Kentucky Itinerary: Some Stratigraphic and Structural Features of the Middlesboro Basin. Lexington, Ky.: The society, 1957.
G830 (ETSU)

McFarlan, Arthur Crane Some Old Chester Problems — Correlations Along the Eastern Belt of Outcrop. Lexington: Kentucky Geological Survey, 1956.
M1330 (ETSU)

Walker, Hugh Tennessee Tales. Nashville: Aurora Pubs., 1970.
W280 (ASU LMC ETSU BC)

Walker, Lewis Meriwether, Jr. An Economic and Social Survey of Alleghany County. Record, Extension Series, vol. 20, no. 7. Charlottesville: Univ. of Virginia, 1936.
W290 (ASU BC)

Walker, Robert S. Chattanooga, Its History and Growth. Chattanooga: Chattanooga Community Assoc., 1930.
W300

The Chickamauga Dam and Its Environs. Chattanooga: Andrews, 1949.
W310

This is Chattanooga. Chattanooga: Andrews, 1949.
W320

Walker, Robert Sparks As the Indians Left It: The Story of the Chattanooga Audubon Society and Its Elise Chapin Wildlife Sanctuary. Chattanooga, Tenn.: C. C. Hudson, 1955.
W330 (ASU MHC)

Lookout, the Story of a Mountain. Kingsport, Tenn.: Southern Pubs., 1941.
W340 (LMC BC)

Torchlights to the Cherokee: The Brainerd Mission. New York: Macmillan Co., 1931.
W350 (ASU ETSU BC)

Walker, Samuel Turence V. Powderly, "Labor Mayor", Workingmen's Politics in Scranton, Pennsylvania, 1870-1884. Ph. D. Diss. Ohio State Univ., 1973.
W360

Walker, Thomas Doctor Walker's Diary of Exploration, 1750; with Will Subjoined. 5th ed. Barbourville, Ky.: Advocate Pub. Co., 1950.
W370 (BC)

Journal of an Exploration in the Spring of the Year 1750. Boston: Little, 1888.
W380

Kentucky's First House; the Journal of Dr. Thomas Walker. Barbourville, Ky.: Advocate Pub. Co., 1940.
W390

Walker, W. H. Pree, H. L., Jr. Public and Industrial Water Supplies of the Jackson Purchase Region, Kentucky. Washington: Govt. Print. Off., 1953.
P4290

Walker, William McJunkin, Frederick E. Water Resources of Virginia. Blacksburg: Virginia Polytechnic Institute, 1966.
M1740

The Southern Harmony Songbook . . . . New York: Hastings House, 1939. A very popular shape-note songbook.
W410 (BC)

Walker, William comp. The Southern Harmony. 1854. Reprint. Edited by Glenn C. Wilcox. First line index by Charles L. Atkins. Los Angeles: Pro Musicamericana, 1966. A very popular shape-note songbook.
W400 (WCU)

Walker, William Edward John Eston Cooke: A Critical Biography. Unpublished doctoral diss. Vanderbilt Univ., 1957.
W420

Walker, William R. Industrial Water Use in North Carolina. Chapel Hill: U.N.C. Institute of Government, 1964.
W430

Walker, Woods Walker Fox Hounds. Cynthiana, Ky.: The Hobson Book Press, 1945. National fox hounds that are famous in Appalachian Hunting Clubs.
W440 (BC)

Walker, Zeddie "An Educational Survey of Grundy County, Tennessee." Master's thesis. Univ. of Tennessee, 1952.
W450

Wall, Sara T. History of the Church of the Redeemer, Shelby, N. C., 1858-1958. Shelby: n.p., 1958.
W460

Wallace, George S. Huntington (West Virginia) Through Seventy Five Years. Huntington, W. Va.: Anderson Newcomb Co., 1947.
W470

Wallace, H. A. Weisenberger, Billy C. Soil Survey, Elliott County, Kentucky. Washington: U. S. Soil Conservation Service, 1965.
W2390

Wallace, Louis D. Tennessee, Department of Agriculture Makers of Millions, Not for Themselves But for You: Stories of Tennesseans whose Accomplishments for Agriculture Brought Renown to Their State and Caused an Appreciating and Benefited Public to Propose Their Admission to the Tennessee Agricultural Hall of Fame. Nashville: The department, 1951.
T1000 (ASU)

Wallace, Richard S. West Virginia — An Economic Profile. Richmond: Federal Reserve Bank of Richmond, 1964.
W480

Wallen, Clarence Monroe Gena of the Appalachians. New York: Cochrane Pub. Co., 1910.
W490 (BC ASU ETSU)

Waller, Charles T. comp. Killion, Ronald G. A Treasury of Georgia Folk-lore. Atlanta: Cherokee Pub. Co., 1972.
K1950 (BC ASU MHC ETSU)

Waller, Eugene C. "A Survey of the Church and Independent Schools and Colleges of the Southern Appalachians." Master's thesis. Univ. of Tennessee, 1931.
W500

Waller, James Flint West of Suez. Verona, Va.: McClure Press, 1970. A collection of widely varied tales, including some of the local history of Virginia, specifically of Rockenbridge and Augusta Counties.
W510 (ASU BC)

Waller, Mary Ella Deep in the Hearts of Men. Boston: Little, Brown, and Co., 1924.
W520 (BC)

The Woodcarver of Olympus. Boston: Little, Brown and Co., 1904.
W530 (ASU)

Wallo, Joseph Appalachian Dulcimer Plans. Washington, D. C.: n.p., 1969. Plans for building your own instrument.
W540

Walls, David S. Appalachia in the Sixties: Decade of Reawakening. Lexington: Univ. Press of Kentucky, 1972.
W550 (ASU LMC WWC WCU MHC ETSU BC UNCA)

Walls, Norah Spencer Looking Back. New York: Exposition Press, 1959.
W560 (BC)

Walser, Richard Betts, Leonidas Gateway to North Carolina Folklore. Raleigh: School of Education Office of Publications, North Carolina State Univ. at Raleigh, 1974.
B3430

Walser, Richard Gaither Literary North Carolina. Raleigh: North Carolina State Department of Archives and History, 1970.
W580 (ASU BC)

Thomas Wolfe: An Introduction and Interpretation. New York: Barnes and Noble, 1961.
W630 (UNCA ASU WCU BC)

Walser, Richard Gaither ed. The Enigma of Thomas Wolfe: Biographical and Critical Selections. Cambridge, Mass.: Harvard Univ. Press, 1953.
W570 (ASU WCU)

The North Carolina Miscellany. Illustrated by Paul Gray. Chapel Hill: Univ. of North Carolina Press, 1962.
W590 (LMC ASU)

North Carolina Poetry. Rev. ed. Richmond: Garrett and Massie, 1951.
W600 (LMC BC)

North Carolina in the Short Story. Chapel Hill: Univ. of North Carolina Press, 1948.
W610 (LMC BC)

Short Stories from the Old North State. Chapel Hill: Univ. of North Carolina Press, 1959.
W620 (ASU LMC WWC)

Walters, Joe Parks "The Marble Industry of the Knoxville Area." Master's thesis. Univ. of Tennessee, 1958.
W640

Walters, Roy N. A Study of Private Secondary Schools in Southeastern Kentucky. Nashville: George Peabody College for Teachers, 1957.
W650

"Survey and Sociological Study of 25 Weekly Newspapers in Eastern Kentucky." Microfilm. Master's thesis. Univ. of Kentucky, 1936.
W660 (ASU)

Walters, Russell S. Krochmal, Arnold Guide to Medicinal Plants of Appalachia. Upper Darby, Pa.: Northeastern Forest Experiment Station, 1969.
K3230 (BC)

Krochmal, Arnold A Guide to Medicinal Plants of Appalachia. Washington: U. S. Forest Service, 1971.
K3240 (ASU ETSU LMC)

Walthall, John A. COPENA: A Tennessee Valley Middle Woodland Culture. Ph. D. Diss. Univ. of North Carolina, 1973. The story of a number of woodland burial mound sites in Northern Alabama.
W670

Walton, Mrs. M. L. Vale of Shenandoah and Other Poems. Snow Hill, Md.: The People Print., n.d.
W680 (ASU)

Walton, Thomas G. Sketches of the Pioneers in Burke County History. n.p.: n.p., 1961.
W690

Wampler, Charles W. My Grandfather, My Grandchildren, and Me: An Autobiography of Charles W. Wampler. Harrisonburg, Va.: Shenandoah Press, 1968.
W700 (ASU)

WAMY Community Action, Inc. A Profile of Community Problems: Watauga, Avery, Mitchell, Yancey Counties. Compiled for WAMY Community Action, Inc. by the North Carolina Fund. n.p.: n.p., n.d.
W710

Warburton, Amber A. Guidance in a Rural-Indust. Comm., Harlan Co., a Ky. Coal Mining District, Plans. Washington: Nat. E. Assoc., 1954.
W720

Ward, Francis Ehl "A Historical Study of the ET&WNC Narrow Gauge Railroad." Master's thesis. Appalachian State Teachers College, 1958.
W730 (ASU)

Ward, George Gordon The Annals of Upper Georgia Centered in Gilmer County. Carrollton, Ga.: Thomasson Print. and Office Equipment Co., 1965.
W740 (ASU LMC)

Ward, John William Andrew Jackson, Symbol for an Age. New York: Oxford Univ. Press, 1955.
W750 (ASU)

Ward, Joseph Marshall "A Proposal for the Two-Dimensional Design Course at Virginia Intermont College, Bristol, Virginia." Master's thesis. East Tennessee State Univ., 1965.
W760 (ETSU)

Ward, Robert David Labor Revolt in Alabama: The Great Strike of 1894. Southern Historical Publication, no. 9. University: Univ. of Alabama Press, 1965.
W770 (WCU BC)

Wardell, Morris L. A Political History of the Cherokee Nation, 1838-1907. Civilization of the American Indian, 17. Norman: Univ. of Oklahoma Press, 1938.
W780 (ASU LMC)

Wardron, Holman D. With Pen and Camera Thro the "Land of the Sky": Western North Carolina and the Asheville Plateau. 10th ed. Portland, Me.: Chesholm Brothers, 1911.
W790 (ASU)

Ware, Charles Crossfield North Carolina Disciples of Christ. St. Louis, Mo.: Christian Board of Publications, 1927.
W800 (BC)

Warfield, Ethelbert Dudley Kentucky Resolutions of 1798. 2nd ed. New York: n.p., 1894.
W810 (BC)

Waring, Antonio J. ed. Creek Nation Laws of the Creek Nation. Athens: Univ. of Georgia Press, 1960.
C8660 (ASU)

Warman, James C. Geology and Ground-Water Resources of Calhoun County, Alabama. Prepared by the U. S. Geological Survey in cooperation with the Calhoun County Board of Commissioners, the City of Anniston, and the Geological Survey of Alabama. County Report, 7. University: Alabama, Geological Survey, 1962.
W830 (ETSU)

Warman, James C. and others Geology and Ground-Water Resources of Calhoun County, Alabama: An Interim Report. Prepared by the U. S. Geological Survey in cooperation with the Calhoun County Board of Commissioners, the City of Anniston, and the Geological Survey of Alabama. Information Series, 17. University: Alabama Geological Survey, 1960.
W820 (ETSU)

Warne, Alice E. An Economic Survey of Clinton Co., Pa. University Park: Penn. State Univ., Bureau of Business Research, 1958.
W840

An Economic Survey of Monroe County, Conducted by the Bureau of Business Research, College of Business Administration, Penn. State Univ. in Cooperation with Pocono Mountains Chamber of Commerce, Stroudsburg, Pa. Univ. Park: Penn. State Univ., Bureau of Business Research, 1959.
W850

Warner, Charles Dudley On Horseback: A Tour In Virginia, North Carolina and Tennessee. With Notes of Travel in Mexico and California. Boston: Houghton, 1888. Early sociological comments and observations.
W860 (BC)

On Horseback: A Tour in Virginia, North Carolina, and Tennessee. With Notes of Travel in Mexico and California. Boston: Houghton, Mifflin and Co., 1892. Early sociological comments and observations.
W870 (ASU WCU LMC)

Warner, Charles Willard Hoskins Road to Revolution; Virginia's Rebels from Bacon to Jefferson, 1676-1776. Richmond: Garrett and Massie, 1961.
W880

Warner, John W. Hatfield, William F. Soil Survey, Jefferson County, West Virginia. Washington: U. S. Soil Conservation Service, 1973.
H3490

Warner, Larkin Bruce "The Economics of the Transportation of Ohio Coal." Ph. D. Diss. Indiana Univ., 1961.
W890

Warner, Paul L. An Economic and Social Survey of Clarke County. Charlottesville: n.p., 1925.
W900

Warre, LA Lincoln's Parentage Childhood. Bartlesville, Okla.: Borderland Books, n.d.
W960

Warren, Charles B. A Paraphrase of Seven Days. Huntington, W. Va.: Huntington Poetry Guild, 1944.
W910 (BC)

Warren County Civil War Centennial Commission Observance, Battle of Front Royal Virginia, May 19-20, 1962. n.p.: The commission, 1962.
W920 (LMC)

Warren, Harlow Beckley, U.S.A. Beckley, W. Va.: n.p., 1955-63.
W930 (BC)

Warren, Harold F. A Right Good People. Boone, N. C.: Appalachian Consortium Press, 1974. Sketches and pictures of mountain people from a feature writer for THE CHARLOTTE OBSERVER. The writing is warm and sensitive and the pictures are classics from the archives of Doris Ulmann, Warren Brunner, Kenneth Murray, Joe Clark and the author.
W940 (ASU)

Warren, Julie B. The People Govern North Carolina. Raleigh, N. C.: Warren, 1946.
W950 (WWC)

Warren, Robert B. Soil Survey of Meigs County, Tenn. Washington, D. C.: U. S. Dept. of Agriculture Soil Conserv. Service, 1974.
W970

Warren, Robert Penn The Cave. New York: Random House, 1959. Set in the Cumberland Region of Kentucky.
W980 (ETSU BC)

Warren, William Robinson The Life and Labors of Archibald McLean. St. Louis, Mo.: Published for United Christian Missionary Society by the Bethany Press, 1923.
W990 (BC)

Washburn, Benjamin Earle A Country Doctor in the South Mountains. Illustrated by John Pike. Asheville, N. C.: Stephens Press, 1955. A biography of a rural North Carolina doctor in Rutherford County.
W1000 (ASU LMC MHC BC).

Rutherford County and Its Hospital. Spindale, N. C.: Spindale Press, 1960.
W1010 (BC)

Washburn, Claude Carlos The Green Arch. New York: Albert and Charles Boni, 1925.
W1020

Washington Center for Metropolitan Studies A Selective Bibliography of Writings on Poverty in the United States. Bethesda, Md.: National Institute of Health, 1964.
W1030

Washington College, Washington College, Tenn. Bulletin. vol. 1. Washington College, Tenn.: Washington College, 19--.
W1040 (BC)

Washington County, Tennessee, Board of Education School Board Policies. Jonesboro, Tenn.: The board, n.d.
W1050 (ETSU)

Washington County, Tennessee, Council of Home Demonstration Clubs Favorite Recipes: A Collection of Favorite Recipes of Home Demonstration Club Women of Washington County. n.p.: The council, 1952.
W1060 (ETSU)

Washington County, Virginia, Historical Society Publications. Abingdon, Va.: The society, n.d.
W1070 (ASU LMC ETSU)

Washington, George The Journal of Major George Washington. Ann Arbor, Mich.: Univ. Microfilms, 1966. As a young militia officer, Washington spent much time on the frontier.
W1080

Washington, Mary Louise "The Folklore of the Cumberlands as Reflected in the Writings of Jesse Stuart." Ph. D. Diss. Univ. of Pennsylvania, 1960.
W1090

Watauga County — Administrator's Bonds 1873-1911 Microfilm. Raleigh: Dept. of Art, Culture and History, 1873-1911.
W1100 (ASU)

Watauga County — Appointment of Administrators and Guardians 1873-1926 Microfilm. Raleigh: Dept. of Art, Culture and History, 1873-1926.
W1110 (ASU)

Watauga County — Appointment of Receivers 1910-1920 Microfilm. Raleigh: Dept. of Art, Culture and History, 1910-1920.
W1120 (ASU)

Watauga County — Apprentice Bonds, 1874-1906 Microfilm. Raleigh: Dept. of Art, Culture and History, 1874-1906.
W1130 (ASU)

Watauga County — Armed Forces Discharges 1922-1957 Microfilm. Raleigh: Dept. of Art, Culture and History, 1922-1957.
W1140 (ASU)

Watauga County — Cross Index to Wills 1873-1969 Microfilm. Raleigh: Dept. of Art, Culture and History, 1873-1969.
W1150 (ASU)

Watauga County — Index to Administrators and Executers 1873-1968 Microfilm. Raleigh: Dept. of Art, Culture and History, 1873-1968.
W1160 (ASU)

Watauga County — Index to Guardians 1873-1968 Microfilm. Raleigh: Dept. of Art, Culture and History, 1873-1968.
W1170 (ASU)

Watauga County — Index to Real Estate Coveyances, Grantees 1872-1969 Microfilm. Raleigh: Dept. of Art, Culture and History, 1872-1969.
W1180 (ASU)

Watauga County — Index to Vital Statistics, 1914-1969 Microfilm. Raleigh: Dept. of Art, Culture and History, n.d.
W1190 (ASU)

Watauga County — Inheritance Tax Records, 1920-1969 Microfilm. Raleigh: Dept. of Art, Culture and History, 1920-1969.
W1200 (ASU)

Watauga County — Marriage Registers, 1873-1969 Microfilm. Raleigh: Dept. of Art, Culture and History, 1873-1969.
W1210 (ASU)

Watauga County, N. C., Board of Education Alleghany, Ashe, Watauga Planning Project for Handicapped Children, ESEA Title III. Boone, N. C.: The board, 1969.
W1360 (WCU)

Watauga County — Record of Accounts 1873-1968 Microfilm. Raleigh: Dept. of Art, Culture and History, 1873-1968.
W1220 (ASU)

Watauga County — Record of Administrators 1911-1968 Microfilm. Raleigh: Dept. of Art, Culture and History, 1911-1968.
W1230 (ASU)

Watauga County — Record of Deeds 1882-1958 Microfilm. Raleigh: Dept. of Art, Culture and History, 1882-1958.
W1240 (ASU)

Watauga County — Record of Elections 1878-1968 Microfilm. Raleigh: Dept. of Art, Culture and History, 1878-1968.
W1250 (ASU)

Watauga County — Record of Executors 1925-1968 Microfilm. Raleigh: Dept. of Art, Culture and History, 1925-1968.
W1260 (ASU)

Watauga County — Record of Guardians 1911-1968 Microfilm. Raleigh: Dept. of Art, Culture and History, 1911-1968.
W1270 (ASU)

Watauga County — Record of Resales 1922-1968 Microfilm. Raleigh: Dept. of Art, Culture and History, 1922-1968.
W1280 (ASU)

Watauga County — Record of Settlements 1873-1968 Microfilm. Raleigh: Dept. of Art, Culture and History, 1873-1968.
W1290 (ASU)

Watauga County — Record of Surveys, 1904-1953 Microfilm. Raleigh: Dept. of Art, Culture and History, 1904-1953.
W1300 (ASU)

Watauga County — Record of Wills, 1902-1968 Microfilm. Raleigh: Dept. of Art, Culture and History, 1902-1968.
W1310 (ASU)

Watauga County — Superior Court Minutes 1873-1959 Microfilm. Raleigh: Dept. of Art, Culture and History, 1873-1959.
W1320 (ASU)

Watauga County — Tax Lists, 1918-1921 Microfilm. Raleigh: Dept. of Art, Culture and History, 1918-1921.
W1330 (ASU)

Watauga County — Tax Scrolls 1888-1926 Microfilm. Raleigh: Dept. of Art, Culture and History, 1888-1926.
W1340 (ASU)

Watauga County — Trust Funds and Accounts for Indigent Children 1915-1960 Microfilm. Raleigh: Dept. of Art, Culture and History, 1915-1960.
W1350 (ASU)

Watauga Historical Association Watauga: "The Dangerous Example." The Story of Sycamore Shoals. In cooperation with the Tennessee Historical Commission and East Tennessee State University. Johnson City: East Tennessee State Univ. Press, 1963.
W1370 (ETSU)

Watauga Review vol. 1, Fall, 1962. Johnson City: East Tennessee State Univ., irregular.
W1380 (ETSU)

The Watauga Spinnerette vol. 1. Elizabethton, Tenn.: North American Rayon Corp. and American Bemberg Division, Beaunit Mills, monthly.
W1390 (ETSU)

Water Development Coordinating Committee for Appalachia Minutes of the Meeting. no. 1-, Sept., 1965. Asheville, N. C.: The committee, n.d.
W1400 (ETSU LMC)

Minutes of the meeting. no. 1, Sept., 1965. Asheville: n.p., n.d.
W1410 (ETSU)

Water, Linda Crussell "A Study of the Cooperative Vocational Education Program at Boones Creek High School." Master's thesis. East Tennessee State Univ., 1970.
W1430 (ETSU)

Waters, Henry Fitz-Gilbert Genealogical Gleanings in England: Abstracts of Wills Relating to Early American Families, with Genealogical Notes and Pedigrees Constructed from the Wills and from Other Records. With the addition of Genealogical gleanings in England (new series) A-Anyon. 2 vols. 1901, 1907. Reprint. Baltimore: Genealogical Pub. Co., 1969.
W1420 (ASU)

Watkins, Charles Hubert Watkins, Floyd C. Yesterday in the Hills. Chicago: Quadrangle Books, 1963.
W1450 (ASU LMC ETSU BC)

Watkins, Floyd C. Thomas Wolfe's Characters: Portraits from Life. 1st ed. Norman: Univ. of Oklahoma Press, 1957.
W1440 (ASU WCU BC UNCA)

Yesterday in the Hills. Chicago: Quadrangle Books, 1963. An Emory University professor and his father recollect tales and tell of Ball Ground in North Georgia.
W1450 (ASU LMC ETSU BC)

Watkins, Grace Virginia "A Study of Selected Fifth Grade Children in Lincoln School, Kingsport, Tennessee." Master's thesis. East Tennessee State College, 1951.
W1460 (ETSU)

Watkins, Samuel R. "Co. Aytch," Maury Grays, First Tennessee Regiment: Or, A Side Show of the Big Show. (original title: 1861 vs. 1882: "Co. Aytch" ...) Introduction by Bill Irvin Wiley. 1882. Reprint. Jackson, Tenn.: McCowat-Mercer Press, 1952.
W1470 (ASU)

Watkins, William Isaac Soil Survey of Greenville County, South Carolina. Field Operations, 1921. Washington: U. S. Department of Agriculture, Bureau of Soils, 1924.
W1480

Watkins, Willie Moss comp. The men, women, events, institutions, and lore of Casey Co., Kentucky. Louisville: Standard Print. Co., 1939.
W1490 (BC)

Watlington, Patricia The Partisan Spirit: Kentucky Politics, 1779-1792. New York: Atheneum, 1972.
W1500 (WWC BC)

Watson, Doc comp. The Songs of Doc Watson. New York: Oak Publications, 1971. Collected favorites of a Watauga County, North Carolina musician and folk singer.
W1510 (ASU WCU)

Watson, Henry Clay Six nights in a Block house. New York: Hust and Co., n.d. Exploits of Daniel Boone.
W1520 (BC)

Watson, Joan "The Library in the Literature Program at Daniel Boone High School, Washington County, Tennessee." Master's thesis. East Tennessee State Univ., 1972.
W1530 (ETSU)

Watson, Judge "The Economic and Cultural Development of Eastern Kentucky from 1900 to the Present." Ph. D. Diss. Indiana Univ., 1963.
W1540 (ASU)

Watson, Thomas Leonard Lead and Zinc Deposits in Virginia. Virginia Department of Agriculture and Immigration, Geological Survey of Virginia, Geological Series Bulletin no. 1. n.p.: Board of Agriculture and Immigration, 1905.
W1550

. . . Mineral Resources of Virginia. Lynchburg, Va.: J. P. Bell Co., Printers and Binders, 1907.
W1560 (LMC)

Watson, Thomas Shelby The Silent Riders. WAKY Radio Documentary. Louisville, Ky.: Beechmont Press, 1971.
W1570 (BC)

Watt, Homer Andrew Wolfe, Thomas The Correspondence of Thomas Wolfe and Homer Andrew Watt. New York: New York Univ. Press, 1954.
W8400 (ASU WCU ETSU)

Watts, George B. The Waldenses of Valdese. Valdese, N. C.: The author, 1965. The story of a unique community settled by immigrants from Northern Italy.
W1580 (LMC WCU)

Watts, Sue E. Some Appalachian Short Stories: A Bibliography. Berea, Ky.: Berea College Appalachian Center, 1973. An evaluation of regional short stories appropriate for junior high school.
W1590

Watts, W. C. Pittard, Pen L. Alexander County's Confederates. Taylorsville, N. C.: n.p., 1960.
P3110

Facts and Events of the Watts Family. Taylorsville: Taylorsville Business Forms, n.d. A sketch of the life and ancestry of the Watts, Jones' and Echerds' of what is now Alexander County.
W1600 (ASU)

Watts, William Courtney Chronicles of a Kentucky Settlement. n.p.: Putnam, 1897.
W1610 (BC)

Way, Frederick The Allegheny. New York: Farrar and Rinehart, 1942. Story of the Allegheny River.
W1620 (BC)

Wayland, Mrs. Charles F., Sr. Abstract of Wills, 1792-1835. Knoxville: East Tenn. Hist. Soc., n.d.
W1630

Tombstone Inscriptions and Death Records, Calvary Cemetery, Knoxville, Tennessee, 1869-1967. n.p.: n.p., 1967.
W1640 (ETSU)

Wayland, John W. A Bird's Eye View of the Shenandoah Valley with Map. Staunton, Va.: McClure Co., Inc., n.d. A pictorial review of the Shenandoah Valley.
W1650

Facts and Fiction in Virginia History. n.p.: n.p., 1929.
W1660

A History of Shenandoah County, Virginia. 2nd ed. Containing the addition of two chapters, and an addition to the Bibliography not found in the first edition. Strasburg, Va.: C. J. Carrier, 1969.
W1670

Scenic and Historical Guide to the Shenandoah Valley. Petersburg, Va.: Louis Ginsberg, n.d.
W1680

Stonewall Jackson's Way. An outline of Jackson's military movements in 1861, 1862 and 1863, with special emphasis on his brilliant campaign in the Shenandoah Valley in the spring and summer of 1862. Verona, Va.: C. J. Carrier, n.d.
W1690

Twenty-Five Chapters on the Shenandoah Valley. Strasburg: Shenandoah Pub. House Inc., 1957.
W1700 (BC)

Virginia Valley Records. Baltimore: Genealogical Pub. Co., 1973.
W1710

The Washingtons and Their Homes. Virginia Homes include "Mount Vernon," "Audley," "Clifton," "Fairfield," "Rising Sun Tavern," and many others. An appendix contains biographical sketches of over 400 Washingtons. Berryville, Va.: C. J. Carrier, n.d.
W1720

Wayland, John Walter The Bowmans, a Pioneering Family in Virginia, Kentucky and the Northwest Territory. Staunton, Va.: Press of the McClure Co., 1943.
W1730 (ASU BC)

German Element of the Shenandoah Valley of Virginia. Charlottesville, Va.: Michie Co. Printers, 1907.
W1740 (BC)

The German Element of the Shenandoah Valley of Virginia. Bridgewater, Va.: C. J. Carrier Co., 1964.
W1750 (ASU)

Historic Harrisonburg. Staunton, Va.: McClure Print. Co., 1949.
W1760 (ASU BC)

Historic Homes of Northern Virginia and the Eastern Panhandle of West Virginia. Staunton, Va.: McClure Co., 1937.
W1770 (ASU)

A History of Rockingham County, Virginia. Dayton, Va.: Ruebush Elkins Co., 1912.
W1780 (ASU BC)

A History of Shenandoah County, Virginia. 1927. Reprint. Strassburg, Va.: Shenandoah Pub. Co., 1969.
W1790 (ASU BC)

A History of Shenandoah County, Virginia (1969) Strasburg, Va.: Shenandoah Pub. House, 1969.
W1800

Scenic and Historical Guide to the Shenandoah Valley: A Handbook of Useful Information for Tourists and Students. 3rd ed., rev. and enlarged. Dayton, Va.: J. K. Ruebush Co., 1923.
W1820 (WCU)

Sidney Lanier at Rockingham Springs. Dayton, Va.: Ruebush-Elkins Co., 1912.
W1840 (BC)

The Valley Turnpike, Winchester to Staunton, and Other Roads. Publications, vol. 6. Winchester, Va.: Winchester-Frederick County Historical Society, 1967.
W1850 (ASU BC)

Wayland, John Walter comp. The Shenandoah Valley in History and Literature. Harrison, Va.: n.p., 1909.
W1830 (ASU)

Wayland, John Walter ed. Men of Mark and Representative Citizens of Harrisonburg and Rockingham County, Virginia. Va.: McClure Co., 1943.
W1810 (ASU BC)

Virginia Valley Records: Genealogical and Historical Materials of Rockingham County, Virginia, and Related Regions. Special contributors: David A. Heatwole and others. 1930. Reprint. Baltimore: Genealogical Pub. Co., 1965.
W1860 (ASU BC)

Waynick, Capus North Carolina Roads and Their Builders. Raleigh, N. C.: Superior Stone Co., 1952.
W1870 (ASU LMC)

Weals, Vic Hillbilly Dictionary, and Enlightening Collection of Mountain Expressions. Gatlinburg, Tenn.: n.p., n.d.
W1880 (ASU)

Wear, Pat Weatherfield and others Teacher Education in Service. By James R. Ogletree, Fred Edmonds, and Pat W. Wear. Bulletin, vol. 35, no. 2. Lexington: Univ. of Kentucky, 1962.
W1890 (BC)

Weatherford, Willis Duke Life and Religion in Southern Appalachia, an Interpretation of Selected Data from the Southern Appalachian Studies. New York: Friendship Press, 1962. A classic study of Appalachian religious beliefs and customs.
W1920 (ASU MHC WCU LMC ETSU WWC BC UNCA)

Pioneers of Destiny: The Romance of the Appalachian People. Birmingham: Vulcan Press, 1955. Romantic view of the Appalachian people.
W1930 (LMC BC)

Weatherford, Willis Duke ed. Educational Opportunities in the Appalachian Mountains. Published under the auspices of the Berea Centennial Committee. Berea, Ky.: Berea College, 1955.
W1900 (ASU LMC WWC BC)

The Goals of Higher Education. By Harold Taylor and others. Cambridge: Harvard Univ. Press, 1960.
W1910 (BC)

Religion in the Appalachian Mountains: A Symposium. Berea, Ky.: Berea College, 1955.
W1940 (ASU BC)

Weathers, Lee Beam The Living Past of Cleveland County, a History. Shelby, N. C.: Star Pub. Co., 1956.
W1950 (ASU)

Weaver, C. E. Illustrated Johnson City, Tennessee. Under the auspices of the Johnson City Chamber of Commerce. Illustrated Cities Series. n.p.: The author, 1915?
W1960 (ETSU)

Weaver, Charles E. Students in Appalachia. Presented at the Education-Business Relations Program Planning Work Shop at Concord College, Athens, West Virginia, May 12, 1971. Columbus: Ohio State Department of Education, 1971.
W1970 (ETSU)

Weaver, Emma Crafts in the Southern Highlands. Asheville: Southern Highland Handicraft Guild, 1958.
W1980

Weaver, John Downing Wind Before Rain. New York: Macmillan Co., 1942. North Carolina mountain novel.
W1990 (ASU LMC BC)

Weaver, Mary One Hundred Years: A Story of the First Baptist Church, Clinton, Tennessee. Clinton: Clinton Courier-News, 1940.
W2000

Weaver, Pearl Meno The Tribe of Jacob: The Descendants of the Reverend Jacob Weaver of Reems Creek, North Carolina, 1786-1868, and Elizabeth Siler Weaver. Weaverville, N. C.: n.p., 1962.
W2010

Weaver, Ward Hang My Wreath. New York: n.p., 1941. Romantic fiction set in Civil War Virginia.
W2020

Weaver, Ward pseud. see **Mason, Van Wyck**

Webb, Charles A. Fifty-eight Years in Asheville. Asheville, N. C.: Asheville Citizen-Times Co., 1948.
W2030 (UNCA)
Mount Mitchell and Dr. Elisha Mitchell. Asheville: Citizen-Times Co., 1956.
W2040
Webb, George Willis "The Resources of the Cumberland Plateau as Exemplified by Cumberland County, Tennessee: A Geographic Analysis." Ph. D. Diss. Univ. of Tennessee, 1956.
W2050
Webb, Ross Allan Benjamin Helm Bristow, Border State Politician. Lexington: Univ. Press of Kentucky, 1969.
W2060 (BC)
Webb, W. S. An Archeological Survey of Rickwick Basin in the Adjacent Portions of the States of Alabama, Mississippi, and Tennessee. Smithsonian Inst. Bureau of Amer. Ethnology, Bulletin 129. Washington: Govt. Print. Off., 1942.
W2070
Webb, William Snyder Funkhouser, William Delbert Ancient Life in Kentucky: A Brief Presentation of the Paleontological Succession in Kentucky Coupled with a Systematic Outline of the Archaeology of the Commonwealth. Frankfort: Kentucky Geological Survey, 1928.
F3850 (ASU BC)
Funkhouser, William Delbert Ancient Life in Kentucky: A Brief Presentation of the Paleontological Succession in Kentucky Coupled with a Systematic Outline of the Archaeology of the Commonwealth. Berea, Ky.: Kentucke Imprints, 1972.
F3860 (WCU MHC BC)
The Adena People, no. 2. With chapters by Charles E. Snow and Robert M. Goslin. In cooperation with the Ohio Historical Society. Columbus: Ohio State Univ. Press, 1957.
W2080 (MHC)
An Archaeological Survey of Guntersville Basin on the Tennessee River in Northern Alabama. Lexington: Univ. of Kentucky Press, 1951.
W2090 (LMC BC)
An Archaeological Survey of the Norris Basin in Eastern Tennessee. Smithsonian Institute Bureau of American Ethnology. Bulletin no. 118. Washington: Govt. Print. Off., 1938.
W2100 (BC)
Indian Knoll. Introd. to the new ed. by Howard D. Winters. 1946. Reprint. Knoxville, Tenn.: Univ. of Tenn. Press, 1974.
W2110
Weber, Brom ed. Harris, George Washington Sut Lovingood. New York: Grove Press, 1954.
H2820 (ASU)
Weber, Julia My Country School Diary. New York: Harper and Bros., 1946.
W2120 (BC)
Webster, Larry Chavers, Gordon D. Coal Workers' Pneumoconisosis: Workmen's Compensation Treatment and Its Prevention in Kentucky. Atlanta: Resource Development Internship Project, n.d.
C3550 (ASU)
Webster, Marie Daugherty Quilts: Their Story and How to Make Them. New York: Tudor Pub. Co., 1915.
W2130 (ASU)
Quilts: Their Story and How to Make Them. Garden City, N. Y.: Doubleday, Page, 1916.
W2140 (BC)
Webster, Ronald C. Hill Country Poems. Parsons, W. Va.: McClain Print. Co., 1970.
W2150 (ASU LMC BC)
Webster, Susie McCarver Historic City, Chattanooga; Containing Views and Descriptive Matter of Historic Points of Interest, Scenery, Pictures of Old and New Buildings, Leading Men, etc., All Artistically and Pleasingly Intermingled. Chattanooga: McGowan-Cooke, 1915.
W2160
Wechsler, James Arthur Labor Baron, a Portrait of John L. Lewis. New York: W. Morrow and Co., 1944.
W2170 (BC)
Wechter, Nell Wise Betsy Dowdy's Ride. Winston-Salem: J. F. Blair, 1960.
W2180
Weddle, Ethel Harsbarger Alvin C. York, Young Marksman. Indianapolis: Bobbs-Merrill, 1967. The story of a young mountain man who becomes the leading hero of World War One.
W2190 (ETSU)
Weddle, Warren F. "A Suggested Plan for Developing a More Effective Community Music Program in Johnson City." Master's thesis. East Tennessee State College, 1954.
W2200 (ETSU)
Weed, W. H. Copper Deposits of the Appalachian States. U. S. Geological Survey Bulletin, no. 455. Washington: Govt. Print. Off., 1911.
W2210
Weeden, Howard Shadows on the Wall: The Life and Works of Howard Weeden. Northport, Ala: Colonial Press, 1962.
W2220 (BC)
Weedfall, Robert O. Climate, Weather and Coal Mine Explosions; with a Meteorological Review of the Farmington Disaster. Morgantown: West Va. Univ. Engineering Experiment Station, 1970.
W2230
Weekley, Wm. Marion Twenty Years on Horseback. Dayton, Ohio: United Brethren Pub. House, 1907. The story of a Circuit Rider.
W2240 (BC)
Weeks, J. D. The Potomac and Roaring Creek Coal Fields in West Virginia. n.p.: n.p., 1894. Geographic and geological summary of one of the major coal areas in the Appalachian Mountains.
W2260
Weeks, J. Devereux Dates of Origin of Virginia Counties and Municipalities. Charlottesville: Institute of Government, Univ. of Virginia, 1967.
W2250
Weeks, Stephen Beauregard . . . Church and State in North Carolina. Baltimore: The Johns Hopkins Press, 1893.
W2270 (BC)
The Religious Development in the Province of North Carolina. Johns Hopkins Univ. Studies. Baltimore: Johns Hopkins Press, 1892.
W2280 (LMC WWC UNCA)
Weiner, Robert S. "The Location and Distribution of the Glass Industry of Ohio, Pennsylvania, and West Virginia." Master's thesis. Univ. of Pittsburgh, 1949.
W2290
Weir, Donald E. A Guidance Program for McMinn County High School. Knoxville: Univ. of Tenn., 1959.
W2300
Weir, Gordon Whitney Geologic Map of the McKee Quadrangle, Jackson and Owsley Counties, Ky. Washington, D. C.: U. S. Geological Survey, 1973.
W2310 (BC)
Geological Map of Paint Lick Quadrangle. USGS. n.p.: n.p., 1969.
W2320 (BC)
Weir, Howard Laurie The Dialect of the Southern Highlands. n.p.: n.p., 1922.
W2330 (BC)
In the Land of Mudholes and Mountains; a Story of Three Years' Missionary Work in the Cumberland Mountains. n.p.: n.p., 1921.
W2340 (BC)
Weisbrod, Burton A. ed. The Economics of Poverty, an American Paradox. Englewood Cliffs, N. J.: Prentice-Hall, 1965.
W2350
Weisenberger, Billy C. Soil Survey, Bath County, Kentucky. Soil Survey, Series 1959, no. 30. Washington: U. S. Soil Conservation Service, 1963.
W2360
Soil Survey, Bath County, Kentucky. By B. C. Weisenberger, R. L. Blevins, and D. M. Hersh. Washington: U. S. Dept. of Agriculture, Soil Conservation Service, 1963.
W2370
Soil Survey, Elliott County, Kentucky. By Billy C. Weisenberger, H. P. McDonald, and H. A. Wallace. Washington: U. S. Dept. of Agriculture, Soil Conservation Service, 1965.
W2380
Soil Survey, Elliott County, Kentucky. Soil Survey, Series 1961, no. 18. Washington: U. S. Soil Conservation Service, 1965.
W2390
Weiser, Frederick S. ed. The Weiser Family. Conrad Weiser Family Association. Mechanicsburg, Pa.: Center Square Press, 1960.
W2400
Weisgerber, Pius "Characteristics of Low Income Rural Families Related to Expenditure and Consumption Patterns: An Analysis of Rural Poverty for Public Program Purposes." Ph. D. Diss. Michigan State Univ., 1966.
W2410
Weiss, Leah The Story of Why and How the Leah Weiss Relief Kitchen Became a Landmark in Cincinnati. Cincinnati: n.p., 195?.
W2420 (BC)
Weiss, Raymond B. A Scenic Guide to the Monongahela National Forest. Parsons, W. Va.: McClain Print. Co., 1969.
W2430 (LMC ASU WCU BC)
Weisser, Anne Teague "The Paradox of the Mountains: A Study of the Influences on Thomas Wolfe." Master's thesis. West Virginia Univ., 1969.
W2440 (LMC)
Weitzell, E. C. Bradford, R. H. Rural Underemployment and Land Use in a Marginal Agricultural Area of West Virginia. Morgantown: W. Va. Agricultural Experiment Station, 1943.
B6150
Certain Econ-Aspects of Agriculture in Jackson Co. Soil Conservation Area. n.p.: n.p., 1939.
W2450
Forest-Land Utilization in Nicholas and Webster Co., W. Va. n.p.: W. Va. Agric. Exp. Station, 1943.
W2460
Welch, Jack History of Hancock Co., Va. and W. Va. n.p.: Wheeling News Print. & Litto Co., 1963.
W2470 (BC)
Weller, Jack E. A Profile of the Appalachian Family. Morgantown: West Va. Univ. Cooperative Extension Service, 1968.
W2480
Yesterday's People: Life in Contemporary Appalachia. Lexington: Univ. of Kentucky Press, 1965. This controversial book suggests that Appalachian culture should be repudiated and all our youngsters incorporated into modern society. In recent years Mr. Weller's position has ameliorated somewhat.
W2490 (UNCA ASU WCU MHC LMC ETSU WWC FC BC)
Welles, G. M. Moon, J. W. Soil Survey, Jefferson County, Tennessee. Washington: U. S. Department of Agriculture, Bureau of Plant Industry, 1941.
M6630
Wellman, Manly Wade Cope, Robert F. The County of Gaston: Two Centuries of a North Carolina Region. Gastonia: Gaston County Historical Society, 1961.
C7260 (LMC ASU BC)
Battle at Bear Paw Gap. New York: Washburn, 1966. A story for children about Indian attacks on the settlers in the North Carolina mountains in the late 18th century.
W2500 (ASU)
Battle for King's Mountain. New York: Washburn, 1962. A young patriot leads the continentals to a group of Tories at King's Mountain.
W2510 (ASU LMC)

Wellman, Manly Wade
Clash on the Catawba. New York: Washburn, 1962. A young patriot is captured by the British while fighting near the Catawba River.
W2520 (ASU)
Dead and Gone: Classic Crimes of North Carolina. Chapel Hill: Univ. of North Carolina Press, 1954.
W2530 (LMC BC)
Harpers Ferry, Prize of War. Charlotte, N. C.: McNally, 1960. A popular history written for the young reader.
W2540 (ASU)
The Kingdom of Madison, a Southern Mountain Fastness and Its People. By Manly Wade Wellman, with drawing by Frank Holyfield. Chapel Hill: Univ. of North Carolina Press, 1973.
W2550
The Kingdom of Madison, a Southern Mountain Fastness and Its People. Chapel Hill: Univ. of North Carolina Press, 1973.
W2560 (ASU LMC WWC WCU MHC BC)
Lights over Skeleton Ridge. New York: Ines Washburn, 1957.
W2570
The Master of Scare Hollow. New York: Washburn, 1964. A suspense and adventure story set in western North Carolina.
W2580 (ASU WCU BC)
Mountain Feud. New York: Washburn, 1969. The story of a feud between two mountain families in North Carolina.
W2590 (ASU MHC BC)
Mystery at Bear Paw Gap. New York: Washburn, 1965. Late 18th century North Carolina mountain settlers are frightened by an unknown beast.
W2600 (ASU)
The South Fork Rangers. New York: Washburn, 1963. During the American Revolution North Carolina patriots unite against the tories.
W2610 (MHC)
The Specter of Bear Paw Gap. New York: I. Washburn, 1966. Story of North Carolina mountain settler in 1792 who hears rumors of Indian demons.
W2620 (WCU BC)
Who Fears the Devil? Sauk City, Wisc.: Arkham House, 1963. Several of these eleven short stories are set in western North Carolina.
W2630 (LMC)

Wells, Bertram Whittier The Natural Gardens of North Carolina, with Keys and Descriptions of the Herbaceous Wild Flowers Found Therein. Chapel Hill: Univ. of North Carolina Press, 1932.
W2640 (ASU WWC)
The Natural Gardens of North Carolina, with Keys and Descriptions of the Herbaceous Wild Flowers Found Therein. 1932. Reprint. Chapel Hill: Univ. of North Carolina Press, 1967.
W2650 (ASU ETSU LMC)
The Remarkable Flora of the Great Smoky Mountains. Asheville: Inland Press, n.d.
W2660

Wells, Donald Theodore "The TVA Tributary Area Development Program." Ph. D. Diss. Univ. of Alabama, 1963.
W2670
The TVA Tributary Area Development Program. Bureau of Public Administration Publications, 64. University: Univ. of Alabama, 1964.
W2680 (LMC BC)

Wells, Emma H. M. The History of Roane County, Tennessee, 1801-1870. Chattanooga: Lookout Pub., 1927.
W2690

Wells, Emma Helm Middleton The History of Roane County, Tennessee, 1801-1870. Chattanooga, Tenn.: Lookout Pub. Co., 1927.
W2700 (ASU LMC ETSU BC)

Wells, Evelyn Kendrick The Ballad Tree, a Study of British and American Ballads, Their Folklore, Verse and Music, Together with Sixty Traditional Ballads and Their Tunes. New York: Ronald Press Co., 1950.
W2710 (BC)

Wells, J. K. A Short History of Paintsville and Johnson County. Paintsville, Ky.: Paintsville Herald, 1962.
W2720 (ASU BC)

Wells, Jane F. "Study of Thought Relating to Strip Mining in the Commonwealth of Kentucky." Ph. D. Diss. Indiana Univ., 1973. A comparison of attitudes of proponents and opponents of strip mining.
W2730

Wells, Joseph William The Big Wells Family. Louisville: Standard Print. Co., 1957.
W2740 (BC)
History of Cumberland County. Louisville: Standard Print. Co., 1947.
W2750 (ASU BC)

Wells, Robert Dial Soil Survey, Douglas County, Georgia. Assisted by C. L. McIntyre and Frank T. Ritchie, Jr. Soil Survey, Series 1959, no. 1. Washington: U. S. Soil Conservation Service, 1961.
W2760

Wells, Ruth Marguerite "Andrew Johnson, Senator from Tennessee, 1857-1862." Master's thesis. Univ. of Pennsylvania, 1933.
W2770

Welsh, Stanley Flowers of the Mountain Country. 1975 Deals with Some of the More Representative of Both Conspicuous and Inconspicuous Types. n.p.: n.p., n.d.
W2780

Wendel, G. W. Taylor, Dee F. Stamper Tract Prescribed Burn. Asheville, N. C.: Southeastern Forest Experiment Station, 1964.
T510 (WCU)

Wendel, George W. Early Reproduction After Seed-tree Harvest Cuttings in Appalachian Hardwoods. Forest Service Research Paper, NE-99. Upper Darby, Pa.: Northeastern Forest Experiment Station, 1968.
W2790
Seasonal Moisture Fluctuations in Four Species of Pocosin Vegetation. U. S. Forest Service Station Paper, no. 147. Asheville, N. C.: Southeastern Forest Experiment Station, 1962.
W2800 (WCU)

Wendorff, Ruth How to Make Cornhusk Dolls. New York: Arco, 1973. Instructions for using cornhusk to make a variety of dolls, animals, flowers, and other accessories. Gives suggestions for using these objects for decorating or for money-making projects.
W2810

Wenger, Karl Frederick The Relation of Growth to Stand Density in Natural Loblolly Pine Stands. U. S. Forest Service Station Paper, no. 97. Asheville, N. C.: Southeastern Forest Experiment Station, 1958.
W2820 (WCU)
Silvical Characteristics of Loblolly Pine. U. S. Forest Service Station Paper, no. 98. Asheville, N. C. Southeastern Forest Experiment Station, 1958.
W2830 (WCU)

Wengert, Norman I. Valley of Tomorrow: The TVA and Agriculture. Record Extension Series, vol. 28, no. 1. Knoxville: Bureau of Public Information, Univ. of Tennessee, 1952.
W2840 (ASU LMC WCU ETSU BC)

Werstein, Irving Labor's Defiant Lady: The Story of Mother Jones. Women of America. New York: Crowell, 1969.
W2850 (ASU)

Wertenbaker, Green Peyton Rain on the Mountain. Boston: Little, Brown, and Co., 1934.
W2860 (BC)

Wertman, W. T. Sterner, T. E. Laboratory Investigation of In Situ Combustion Process for Recovering Pennsylvania Grade Crude Oil. Pittsburgh: Bureau of Mines, 1967.
S7100
Cable-tool Coring with Oil-base Mud in Appalachian Oilfields. Report of Investigations, 5424. Pittsburgh: U. S. Bureau of Mines, 1958.
W2870

Weslager, Clinton Alfred The Log Cabin in America: From Pioneer Days to the Present. New Brunswick, N. J.: Rutgers Univ. Press, 1969.
W2880 (ASU WCU BC)

Wesley, G. R. Hunt, C. B. Coal Deposits of Pike County, Kentucky. Washington: Govt. Print. Off., 1937.
H8370

Wessells, Katherine Tyler The Golden Song Book. New York: Simon and Schuster, 1945.
W2890 (BC)

Wessenauer, G. O. Necessity for a Load Building Program. In American Public Power Association. Proceedings, 1959. Washington, D. C.: n.p., 1959.
W2900
Problems on a Large Power System with Large Generating Units. In Sixth World Power Conference, Melbourne, October 20-27, 1962. Paper no. 82. n.p.: n.p., 1962.
W2910

West, Don Clods of Southern Earth. New York: Boni and Gaer, 1946.
W2920 (BC)
Freedom on the Mountains. Huntington, W. Va.: The Appalachian Movement Press, Inc., 1973. Excerpts from a manuscript on Southern Mountain History which describes abolitionism in the region.
W2930
O Mountaineers A Collection of Poems. Huntington, W. Va.: Appalachian Press, 1974.
W2940 (ASU BC)
People's Cultural Heritage in Appalachia. Huntington, W. Va.: The Appalachian Movement Press, Inc., n.d.
W2950
The Road Is Rocky: A Collection of Poems. New York: New Christian Books, n.d.
W2960 (LMC BC)
Robert Rharin: Biography of a Mountain Abolitionist. Huntington, W. Va.: Appalachian Movement Press, 1970.
W2970 (LMC)
Romantic Appalachia; Or Poverty Pays If You Aren't Poor. Pipestem, W. Va.: The author, 1970.
W2980
Southern Mountain Folk Traditions: And the Folksong "Stars" Syndrome. Huntington, W. Va.: Appalachian Movement Press, n.d.
W2990 (ASU LMC)
A Time for Anger: Poems Selected from. . . . Huntington, W. Va.: Appalachian Movement Press, 1970.
W3000 (ASU LMC)

West, Emmy Danger down River. New York: Viking Press, 1972. Adventure of a young boy on the Tennessee frontier in 1810.
W3010 (ASU LMC)

West, John Foster Appalachian Dawn. Durham, N. C.: Moore Pub., 1973. Novel of life in Wilkes County, North Carolina.
W3020 (ASU LMC WCU)
The Ballad of Tom Dula: The Documented Story Behind the Murder of Laura Foster and the Trials and Execution of Tom Dula. Durham, N. C.: Moore Pub. Co., 1970. The true story behind the Ballad of Tom Dula.
W3030 (ASU BC)
This Proud Land. Charlotte/Santa Barbara: McNally and Loftin Publishers, 1974. THIS PROUD LAND is fittingly described by the author as "a beautifully prejudiced book in favor of what was best and still is best of the Blue Ridge Mountains."
W3040
This Proud Land: The Blue Ridge Mountains. By John Foster West and Bruce Roberts. Charlotte: McNally and Loftin, 1974.
W3050
Time Was. New York: Random House, 1965. Life in the mountains of Wilkes County, North Carolina, 1904-1918.
W3060 (ASU LMC)

West, John Foster
Up Ego 1st ed. New York: Payton Paul Pub. Co., 1951.
W3070 (ASU)

West, John W. Sketches of Our Mountain Pioneers. Lynchburg, Va.: n.p., 1939.
W3080 (BC)

West, L. R. Harris, Hobart B. Geology and Ground-water Resources of Colbert County, Alabama. University: Alabama Geological Survey, 1963.
H2870 (ETSU)

West, Lewis R. Sanford, Thomas H., Jr. Gound-water Levels in Madison County, Alabama, July 1956 to July 1959. Univ.: Alabama Geological Survey, 1960.
S420 (ETSU)

West, Nora R. "School Failure in Relation to Delinquency, Scott County, Tennessee." Master's thesis. Univ. of Tennessee, 1961.
W3090

West, Robert Frederick Alexander Campbell and Natural Religion. New Haven: Yale Univ. Press, 1948.
W3100 (BC)

West, Roy Andre "The Songs of the Mountaineers." Master's thesis. George Peabody College for Teachers, 1922.
W3110 (ASU)

West Virginia, Agricultural Experiment Station Bulletin. West Virginia: Agricultural Experiment Station, n.d.
W3130 (BC)

West Virginia Agriculture and Forestry vol. 1 — Winter, 1969-. Supersedes Science Serves your Home and Farm. Morgantown: West Virginia Univ., College of Agriculture, quarterly.
W3140 (ETSU)

West Virginia Blue Book Charleston: Jarrett Print. Co., 1916.
W3160 (ETSU ASU)

West Virginia Blue Book (Formerly West Virginia Legislative Handbook and Manual and Official Register) Compiled and edited by the clerk of the Senate, West Virginia State Legislature. vols. 23. Charleston, W. Va.: Jarrett Print. Co., 1916.
W3170 (ASU ETSU)

West Virginia Board of Centennial Managers Resources of West Virginia. Wheeling: The Register Co., 1876.
W3180

West Virginia Board of Education Look into These Hills. n.p.: n.p., n.d.
W3190

West Virginia, Bureau of Negro Welfare and Statistics Report 1922. Charleston: The bureau, annual.
W3200 (ETSU)

West Virginia Centennial Commission W. Va. in color. Parkersburg: N. Am. Color Press, 1963.
W3210 (BC)

West Virginia Centennial Committee on Folklore The W. Va. Centennial Book of One Hundred Songs: 1863-1963; Patriotic Songs, Folk Songs, and Hymns. Morgantown: P. W. Gainer, 1963.
W3220 (BC)

West Virginia Chamber of Commerce Retail Trading Areas in W. Va. Charleston: The author, 1965.
W3230

W. Va. Personal Income and Retail Sales by Counties, 1948-1965. Charleston: The author, 1966.
W3240

West Virginia Coal Association W. Va. Coal Facts, 1971. Charleston: The author, 1971.
W3250

West Virginia Coal Mining Institute Proceedings. 1st. Charleston, W. Va.: n.p., 19--.
W3260 (BC)

West Virginia Commission of Aging The Older West Virginian. Charleston: The author, 1964.
W3270

West Virginia Community Planning Association Community Planning Newsletter. Charleston, W. Va.: n.p., 1963.
W3280

West Virginia, Concord College, Athens, Center for Economic Action Utilizing a College's Resources to Provide Technical Assistance to Business Firms in Southern West Virginia: A Report on the Concord College Center for Economic Action, July 1, 1963, Through June 30, 1966. Athens, W. Va.: The center, 1967.
W3290

West Virginia Conservation vol. 1. Charleston: Conservation Commission, monthly.
W3300 (BC)

West Virginia Constitutional Convention Debates and Proceedings. n.p.: n.p., n.d.
W3310 (BC)

West Virginia, Council on Schoolhouse Construction Standards for Schoolhouse Construction Approved by the State Board of Education. Charleston: Division of Schoolhouse Planning, State Department of Education, 1945.
W3320 (ETSU)

West Virginia, Department of Archives and History Biennial Report. Charleston: W. Va. Dept. of Archives and History, 1905.
W3330 (BC)

Short Title Check-list of West Virginia State Publications. 1947/48-. Charlesrleston: The department, annual.
W3340 (ETSU)

West Virginia, Department of Commerce An Economic Atlas for West Virginia. Charleston:: The author, 1965.
W3350

West Virginia, Department of Natural Resources Wonderful West Virginia. Charleston, W. Va.: Department of Natural Resources, n.d.
W3600 (ETSU ASU)

West Virginia, Dept. of Commerce Economic Profiles of West Virginia Counties. Charleston: n.p., n.d.
W3360

Functional Program Planning for the State of W. Va. Charleston: The author, 1967.
W3370

West Virginia Economic Outlook, 1967-1972. Charleston: n.p., 1967.
W3380

West Virginia Manufacturing Directory, 1962. Charleston: The Department, 1962.
W3390 (BC)

W. Va. Redevelopment Plan for Webster County. Charleston: n.p., 1961.
W3400

West Virginia, Dept. of Commerce, Planning and Research Div. West Virginia Economic Outlook 1965-1966. Charleston: n.p., 1965.
W3410

West Virginia, Dept. of Education Bulletin. West Virginia: Dept. of Education, n.d.
W3420 (BC)

West Virginia, Dept. of Employment Security Experimental Rural Area Program. Charleston: n.p., 1964.
W3430

Manpower Requirement of Training Needs. Charleston: n.p., 1958.
W3440

A Study of the Manpower Resources of Braxton, Clay, Lewis, Nicholas, Upshur, and Webster Counties. Charleston: n.p., 1961.
W3450

W. Va. Labor Force. Charleston: n.p., 1960.
W3460

West Virginia Labor Force. Charleston: n.p., 1960.
W3470

Work Force, Employment, Unemployment, 1958. Charleston: n.p., 1966.
W3480

West Virginia, Dept. of Employment Security Research and Statistics Div. Boone County Household Survey. Charleston: n.p., 1971.
W3490

Labor Supply Survey. Charleston: n.p., 1963.
W3500

Personal and Economic Characteristics of the Insured Unemployed. Charleston: n.p., 1961.
W3510

West Central West Virginia Area Manpower Requirements Survey to 1972. Charleston: n.p., 1967.
W3520

West Virginia, Dept. of Finance and Admin. Budget Div. Digest of Programs Containing Federal Funds in W. Va. Charleston: n.p., 1964.
W3530

West Virginia, Dept. of Free Schools Biennial Report. Charleston: Tribune Print. Co., biennial.
W3540 (ETSU)

History of Education in West Virginia. Charleston: Tribune Print. Co., 1904.
W3550 (ASU)

West Virginia, Dept. of Health Report. Charleston: Dept. of Health, 19--.
W3560 (BC)

West Virginia, Dept. of Natural Resources Common Forest Trees of West Virginia: How to Know Them. A pocket manual, rev. by Earl Lemley Core and Roland Lee Guthrie. 6th ed. Charleston: The department, 1968.
W3570 (ASU)

Forest Trees of West Virginia. n.p.: n.p., n.d.
W3580

Wonderful West Virginia. Information and Education Division State Department of Natural Resources State Capitol. Charleston, W. Va.: n.p., n.d.
W3590

West Virginia, Div. of Water Resources A Design for a W. Va. Water Resources Plan. Ann Arbor, Mich: Technology for Planning Center, 1967.
W3610

West Virginia Elementary Principals' Association Year Book. 1st-, 1935-. Charleston: The association, annual.
W3620 (ETSU)

West Virginia Folklore Fairmont: West Virginia Folklore Society, n.d.
W3630 (BC)

West Virginia, Geological Survey Barbour and Upshur Counties. . . . n.p.: n.p., 1918.
W3640 (ETSU)

Bulletin. no. 1, 1901. Morgantown: The survey, irregular.
W3650 (ETSU)

Cabell, Wayne and Lincoln Counties. By C. E. Krebs, assistant geologist, and D. D. Teets, Jr., field assistant, I. C. White, state geologist, Wheeling, 1913. n.p.: n.p., n.d.
W3660 (ETSU)

Characteristics of Minable Coals of West Virginia. 2 vols. Reports, vol. 13-13A. Morgantown: The survey, 1940-55.
W3670 (ETSU)

County Report, no. 1. 1911. Morgantown: The survey, irregular.
W3680 (ETSU)

County Reports and Maps. Pleasants, Wood and Ritchie Counties, W. Va.: n.p., 1910.
W3690 (BC)

Fayette County. By Ray V. Hennen, assistant geologist, assisted by D. D. Teets, Jr., field assistant, assisted in office by R. C. Tucker and A. M. Hagan. . . . Wheeling, W. Va.: Wheeling News Litho. Co., 1919.
W3700 (ETSU)

Geology and Economic Resources of the Ohio River Valley in West Virginia. Reports, vol. 22. Morgantown: The survey, 1956.
W3710 (ETSU)

Greenbrier County. By Paul H. Price, state geologist and E. T. Heck, assistant geologist. Wheeling: n.p., 1939.
W3720 (ETSU)

Hampshire and Hardy Counties. By John L. Tilton, William F. Prouty, R. C. Tucker and Paul H. Price. Morgantown: Morgantown Print. and Bind. Co., 1927.
W3730 (ETSU)

Jefferson, Berkeley, and Morgan Counties. By G. P. Grimsley, assistant geologist. I. C. White, state geologist. Wheeling: The survey, 1916.
W3740 (ETSU)

Log of Appalachian Geological Society Field Trip. June 20, 1953: Elkins, West Virginia, to Clifton Forge, Virginia, June 21, 1953. Clifton Forge, Virginia, to White Sulphur Springs, West Virginia. Morgantown: The survey, 1953.
W3750 (ETSU)

West Virginia, Geological Survey
Logan and Mingo County. County reports and maps. Wheeling: The survey, 1914.
W3760 (BC)
Mercer, Monroe, and Summers Counties. By David B. Reger, assistant geologist, assisted by Paul H. Price. Wheeling: The survey, 1926.
W3770 (ETSU)
Mineral and Grant Counties. By David B. Reger assisted by B. B. Tucker. Morgantown: Morgantown Print. and Bind. Co., 1924.
W3780 (ETSU)
Nicholas County. By David B. Reger, assistant geologist assisted in field by W. Armstrong Price, paleontologist, assisted in office by R. C. Tucker and James D. Sisler. I. C. White, state geologist. Wheeling: Wheeling News Litho Co., 1921.
W3790 (ETSU)
Oil and Gas Report and Map of Doddridge and Harrison Counties, West Virginia. By Oscar L. Haught, petroleum geologist. Morgantown: State of West Virginia Geological and Economic Survey, 1959.
W3800 (ETSU)
Oil and Gas Report and Map of Marshall, Wetzel, and Tyler Counties, West Virginia. By Oscar L. Haught, petroleum geologist. Morgantown: State of West Virginia Geological and Economic Survey, 1955.
W3810 (ETSU)
Oil and Gas Report and Map of Monongalia, Marion, and Taylor Counties, West Virginia. By Oscar L. Haught, petroleum geologist. Morgantown: State of West Virginia Geological and Economic Survey, 1956.
W3820 (ETSU)
Oil and Gas Report and Map of Pleasants, Wood and Ritchie Counties, West Virginia. By Oscar L. Haught, petroleum geologist. Morgantown: State of West Virginia Geological and Economic Survey, 1955.
W3830 (ETSU)
Pendleton County. County reports and maps. Wheeling: The survey, 1927.
W3840 (BC)
Pocahontas County. County reports and maps. Wheeling: The survey, 1929.
W3850 (BC)
'Randolph County. By David B. Reger, associate geologist. Morgantown: West Virginia Univ., 1931.
W3860 (ETSU)
Report of Investigations. no. 1-. 1947-. Morgantown: The survey, irregular.
W3870 (ETSU)
Reports. no. 1-. 1899-. Morgantown: The survey, irregular.
W3880 (ETSU)
Salt Brines of West Virginia. By Paul H. Price, state geologist, Charles E. Hare, assistant geologist, J. B. McCue, chief chemist, Homer A. Hoskins, chemist. Morgantown: The survey, 1937.
W3890 (ETSU)
State Park Series. Bulletin. no. 1-, 1951-. Morgantown: The survey, irregular.
W3900 (ETSU)
Tucker County. By David B. Reger, assistant geologist; assisted in field by W. Armstrong Price, and in office by R. C. Tucker. Wheeling: Wheeling News Litho. Co., 1923.
W3910 (ETSU)
The West Virginia Geological and Economic Survey: Its Accomplishments and Outlook. Reports, vol. 23. Morgantown: The survey, 1963.
W3920 (ETSU)
Wirt, Roane and Calhoun Counties. By Ray V. Hennen, assistant geologist. I. C. White, State geologist. Morgantown: Acme Pub. Co., 1911.
W3930 (ETSU)
Wyoming and McDowell Counties. By Ray V. Hennen, assistant geologist, aided by Robert M. Gawthrop, field assistant, I. C. White, state geologist. Wheeling: The survey, 1915.
W3940 (ETSU)

West Virginia Governor State Papers and Public Addresses. By James W. Harris, Jr. Charleston, W. Va.: Jarrett Pub. Co., 1937.
W3950
State papers and public addresses of Clarence Watson Meadows. Charleston, W. Va.: Jarrett Print. Co., 1950.
W3960
State Papers and Public Addresses of Homer Adams Holt, Twentieth Governor of West Virginia, January 18, 1937 to January 13, 1941. Compiled and annotated by William E. Hughes. Charleston, W. Va.: Jarrett Print. Co., 1942.
W3970
State Papers and Public Addresses of Okey L. Patterson, E. Rosalind Carroll Funk. Charleston, W. Va.: West Virginia State Department of Archives and History, 1953.
W3980
State Papers and Public Addresses of William C. Marland, Twenty-Fourth Governor of the State of West Virginia, 1953-1957. Charleston, W. Va.: West Virginia Dept. of Archives and History, 1953.
W3990

West Virginia Governor's Council of Economic Advisors The Condition and Prospects of the West Virginia Economy. Wheeling: The agency, 1963.
W4000

West Virginia, Governor's Economic Opportunity Agency Status of West Virginia in the Economic Opportunity Program under Public Law 88-452. Edited by Douglas Gene Carnes. Charleston: The agency, 1966.
W4010

West Virginia Governor's Task Force on Housing Homes for Mountaineers. Charleston: The agency, 1966.
W4020
Homes for Mountaineers. Charleston: The agency, 1966.
W4030

West Virginia Heritage Foundation West Virginia Heritage. vol. 1-, 1967-. Richwood, W. Va.: The foundation, annual.
W4040 (ASU BC)

West Virginia Hillbilly vol. 1-, 1956. Richmond, W. Va.: n.p., weekly.
W4050 (BC)

West Virginia Historic Commission West Virginia Highway Markers, Historic, Prehistoric, Scenic, Geologic. Beckley, W. Va.: The commission, 1967.
W4060 (ASU)

West Virginia History; a Quarterly Magazine Charleston, W. Va.: State Department of Archives and History, 1939.
W4070 (UNCA ETSU)

West Virginia Human Rights Commission A Survey of Negroes Employed by the State of West Virginia. Charleston: n.p., 1964.
W4080

West Virginia Illustrated vol. 1-, 19--. St. Albans: Bold Enterprises Corp., monthly.
W4090 (BC)

West Virginia, Industrial Development Division West Virginia: Economic Profile. Charleston: The agency, 1971.
W4100

West Virginia Labor Force vol. 1-, May, 1960. Charleston, W. Va.: Dept. of Employment Security.
W4110 (BC)

West Virginia, Laws, Statutes, etc. The School Law of West Virginia. Charleston: n.p., 1915.
W4130 (BC)
The School Law of West Virginia. Charleston: Jarrett Print. Co., 1943.
W4140 (BC)
School Laws of West Virginia. Reprinted from Michie's West Virginia Code of 1949, and 1953 cumulative supplement. Charlottesville, Va.: Michie Co., 1954.
W4150 (ETSU)
The School Law of West Va. and Opinions of the Attorney-General and Decisions of the State Superintendent of Free Schools. Charleston: W. E. Forsyth, Public Printer, 1897.
W4160 (BC)
Acts of the Legislature of West Virginia at Its First Session, Commencing June 20th, 1863. Wheeling: J. F. M'Dermoot, 1863.
W4120 (BC)

West Virginia, Legislative Interim Committee A Survey of the Educational Programs of the West Virginia Public Schools. Charleston: The agency, 1957.
W4170 (BC)
A Survey of the Educational Programs of the W. Va. Public Schools. Charleston: The agency, 1957.
W4180

West Virginia, Legislature, Interim Committee to Study Problems of Government A Digest of a Report of a Survey of Public Education in the State of West Virginia. Charleston: The committee, 1945.
W4190 (BC)

West Virginia, Legislature, Joint Committee on Government and Finance A New Plan for the Allocation of State Aid for Schools; Report by the Joint Committee on Gov. and Finance and the Commission on Interstate Cooperation. Charleston: Joint Committee on Gov. and Finance, 1952.
W4200
A Study of State Institutions of Higher Education. Charleston: The joint committee, 1957.
W4210 (BC)

West Virginia Libraries vol. 1. Microfilm. Morgantown: West Virginia Library Assoc., quarterly.
W4220 (ETSU)

West Virginia, Manufacturing Directory Charleston, W. Va.: Dept. of Planning, Commerce, Research Div. Charleston: The agency, 1960.
W4230

West Virginia Mining Institute Proceedings. Charleston: n.p., annual.
W4240

West Virginia Review vol. 1-, 1923. Charleston: Conley-Teter Pub. Co., monthly.
W4250 (BC)

West Virginia Rural Areas Development Committee Horizon Committee on Capital and Finance — Capital and Finance for Development. Morgantown: The agency, 1964.
W4260
Horizon Committee on Human Resources. The Development of W. Va.'s Human Resources. Morgantown: The agency, 1965.
W4270
Horizon Committee on Natural Resources. The Development of W. Va.'s Natural Resources. Morgantown: The agency, 1964.
W4280

West Virginia Secretary of State Manual of the state of West Virginia. Charleston: n.p., n.d.
W4290 (BC)

West Virginia, State Board of Centennial Managers Resources of West Virginia. Wheeling: The Register Co., 1876.
W4300 (BC)

West Virginia, State Board of Education Survey of Education in West Virginia. 4 vols. n.p.: The board, 1928-29.
W4310 (ETSU)

West Virginia, State Board of Education, Division of Vocational Education Guidance Services Reference Manual of Occupational Information Materials. Guidance Manual, no. 1. Charleston, W. Va.: The board, 1948.
W4320

West Virginia, State Dept. of Education A Catalog of Educational Change in West Virginia. Charleston: The dept., 1963.
W4330 (BC)
History of Education in West Virginia. Charleston: Tribune Print. Co., 1904.
W4340 (BC)
The History of Education in W. Va. Rev. ed. Charleston: Tribune Print. Co., 1907.
W4350 (BC)

West Virginia, State Dept. of Education, Division of Research An Administrative Survey of the Public Schools of Boone County, West Va. Charleston, W. Va.: West Va. State Dept. of Education, Division of Research, 1934.
W4360 (BC)

West Virginia State Dept. of Free Schools Superintendent of Free Schools Biennial Report of the State Superintendent of Free Schools of West Va. Two years ending June 20, 1920. By M. P. Shawkey, State Sup. Charleston: Tribune Print. Co., n.d.
W4370

West Virginia State Gazetteer and Business Directory vol. 1-, 1878-. Detroit: R. L. Polk, biennial.
W4380 (BC)

West Virginia, State Ornithologist Birds of West Virginia. Charleston: State Dept. of Agriculture, 1923.
W4390 (BC)

West Virginia, State Road Commission Annual Report. Charleston: The commission, 1919.
W4400 (BC)

General Highway Maps. West Virginia: State Road Commission, 1954.
W4410 (BC)

West Virginia Historic and Scenic Highway Markers. Charleston, W. Va.: West Virginia, State Road Commission, 1937.
W4420 (BC)

West Virginia, State Superintendent of Free Schools Biennial Report of the State Superintendent of Free Schools of West Virginia. Two years ending June 30, 1920. By M. P. Shawkey, State Superintendent. Charleston: Tribune Print. Co., n.d.
W4430 (ETSU)

West Virginia Statistical Handbook Morgantown: West Virginia Univ., 1974. A comprehensive reference work.
W4440

West Virginia Statistical Handbook, 1974 Edition If you want the real facts about West Virginia, this is the hottest source. It contains chapters on population, health, education, forests, mining, trade, banking, climate, and much more. Useful, clear, up-to-date. n.p.: n.p., n.d.
W4460

West Virginia Statistical Handbook Bureau of Business Research Morgantown: W. Va. Univ., 1965.
W4450

West Virginia, Superintendent of Schools The History of Education in West Va. Rev. ed. Charleston: Tribune Print. Co., 1907.
W4470 (BC)

West Virginia Tax Commissioner Biennial Report. 1st. Charleston: West Va. Tax Commissioner, 1906.
W4480 (BC)

West Virginia University Business and Economic Studies. vol. 1. n.p.: n.p., n.d.
W4490 (BC)

Publications of the Faculty and Staff, West Va. University, 1960-1969. Morgantown: West Va. Univ., 1970.
W4500 (BC)

West Virginia, University, Appalachian Center see **West Virginia, University, West Virginia Center for Appalachian Studies and development**

West Virginia University, Board of Governors Annual Report of the Board of Governors . . . 1st — July 1, 1972/Oct. 1, 1932. Morgantown, W. Va.: West Va. Univ., 1932.
W4510 (BC)

West Virginia University, Bureau of Business Research Economic Development Series, no. 1. West Virginia Univ.: Bureau of Business Research, n.d.
W4520 (BC)

West Virginia University, Center for App. Studies and Development An Informal Series Covering Agric. Econ., in Its Broadest Sense. Morgantown: The agency, 1962.
W4530

Pilot Project, App. Center, W. Va. Univ., Youhger Youth Science Camp, Aug. 2-7, 1964. Morgantown: West Va. Univ., 1965.
W4540

West Virginia University, Center for App. Studies and Development, Office of Research and Development State Legislation Governing Planning and Land — Use Control and the Value of Planning and Controls in Fostering Highway Detection and Economic Development with Particular Reference to W. Va. and Bordering States. Morgantown: n.p., 1966.
W4550

West Virginia University Conference on Poverty Amid Affluence, 1965 Poverty Amid Affluence: Papers. Edited by Lee Fishman. New Haven: Yale Univ. Press, 1966.
W4560 (ETSU WCU BC)

West Virginia University, Div. of Documents Report of the Archives of the Division of Documents. First — 1935/36. Morgantown, W. Va.: Pub. by Univ., 1936.
W4570 (BC)

West Virginia University, Human Resources Research Institute An Evaluation of the Impact of the Community Action Program Upon Poverty Conditions in McDowell Co. Morgantown: The agency, 1967.
W4580

West Virginia, University, Kanawha Valley Graduate Center Professional Development Lectures. Nitro: The center, 1970.
W4590 (ASU)

Seminar and Conference Reports and Proceedings Series. Nitro: The center, 1970.
W4600 (ASU)

West Virginia, University, Library The Development of a Bibliographic Center in the West Virginia Region: Final Report, 1966. Morgantown: The library, 1966.
W4610 (ASU)

West Virginia, University, Library, West Virginia Collection Guide to Manuscripts and Archives in the West Virginia Collection. Bulletin, Series 53, no. 10-1, Series 65, no. 12-1. Morgantown: The library, 1958.
W4620 (ASU ETSU BC)

West Virginia University Magazine vol. 1-, Spring, 1969. Morgantown: The univ., quarterly.
W4630 (ETSU BC ASU)

West Virginia University, Office of Research and Development Man and His Community, A 100th Anniversary Symposium. Morgantown: West Va. Univ., Office of Research and Development, 1969.
W4640

West Virginia University, West Virginia Center for App. Studies and Development Information Series. no. 1. n.p.: n.p., 1969.
W4650

Public Affairs Series. no. 1, 1965. n.p.: n.p., n.d.
W4660

Research Report. n.p.: n.p., 1969.
W4670

Research Series. n.p.: n.p., 1968.
W4680 (BC)

Work Stoppages and the Grievance Procedure in the Appalachian Coal Industry. By Keith Dix and others. Under contract to the Appalachian Regional Commission. Morgantown: The univ., 1972.
W4690 (ASU)

Work Stoppages and the Grievance Procedure in the Appalachian Coal Industry. By Keith Dix and others. Morgantown, W. Va.: Univ. Appalachian Center, Institute for Labor Studies, n.d.
W4700

Work Stoppages and the Grievance Procedure in the Appalachian Coal Industry. By Keith Dix and others under contract to the Appalachian Regional Commission. Morgantown: The univ., 1972.
W4710 (ASU)

Approaches to University Extension Work with the Rural Disadvantaged: Description and Analysis of a Pilot Effort. By Robert W. Miller and others. Morgantown: The agency, 1972.
W4720

Approaches to University Extension Work with the Rural Disadvantaged: Description and Analysis of a Pilot Effort. By Robert W. Miller and others. Bulletin Series 72, no. 3-3. Morgantown: The center, 1972.
W4730 (ASU)

Bulletin Series. Morgantown: The univ., 1968.
W4740

Conference Papers Series. Morgantown: The univ., 1968.
W4750 (BC)

Information Series. no. 1. Morgantown: The univ., 1969.
W4760 (BC)

Public Affairs Series. no. 1. Morgantown: The univ., 1965.
W4770 (BC)

Public Affairs Series. no. 1. Morgantown: The univ., 1965.
W4780

Research Report. Morgantown: The univ., 1969.
W4790 (BC)

Research Series. Morgantown: The univ., 1968.
W4800

West Virginia Work Trade Mission West Virginia Business Dev. Opportunities. Charleston: The agency, 1964.
W4810

West, William Benjamin America's Greatest Dam, Muscle Shoals, Alabama: Description and Pictorial Illustration of Muscle Shoals. 2nd ed., rev. New York: F. E. Cooper, 1925.
W4815 (ASU)

Westcott, Thompson Names of Persons Who Took the Oath of Allegiance to the State of Pennsylvania between the Years 1888 and 1789 with a History of the "Test Laws" of Pennsylvania. 1865. Reprint. Baltimore: Genealogical Pub. Co., 1965. Excellent research tool. Includes a brief history of the loyalty oaths, test laws, and naturalization laws of Pennsylvania.
W4820 (ASU)

Westerfield, Hargis For Crossing Wide Waters. N. Montpelier, Vt.: The Driftwind Press, 1943.
W4830 (BC)

Give a Man Courage. N. Montpelier, Vt.: The Driftwind Press, 1942.
W4840 (BC)

Western Carolina College see **North Carolina, Western Carolina College, Cullowhee**

Western Carolina College Faculty Studies. Cullowhee: The college, annual.
W4850 (WCU)

Western Carolina University, Cullowhee Journal of Education. Cullowhee, N. C.: n.p., 1969.
W4860

Western Carolina University, Cullowhee, N. C. see **North Carolina, Western Carolina University, Cullowhee**

Western North Carolina: Historical and Biographical Charlotte, N. C.: A. D. Smith and Co., 1890. Includes large portraits with many of the biographical sketches.
W4870 (ASU)

Western North Carolina Library Association Union List of Periodicals in Libraries of Western North Carolina Library Association. n.p.: n.p., 1971.
W4880 (ASU)

Western North Carolina Library Club Union List of Periodicals in Libraries of Western North Carolina. Asheville, N. C.: The club, 1964.
W4890 (LMC)

Western North Carolina R. R. Scenery: "Land of the Sky." n.p.: n.p., n.d.
W4940 (BC)

Western North Carolina Regional Planning Commission The economy of Haywood County. Waynesville: The author, 1963.
W4900

Population and economy of Andrews, N. C. Andrews: The author, 1964.
W4910

Population and economy of Henderson County. Hendersonville, N. C.: The author, 1965.
W4920 (LMC)

Today and Tomorrow, Murphy, North Carolina. n.p.: The author, 1964.
W4930 (LMC)

Western Virginia Black Lung Association Newsletter. vol. 1. Charleston, W. Va.: Black Lung Assoc., 19--.
W4945 (BC)

Weston, George Melville Poor Whites of the South. Washington: Buell and Blancherd, 1856. Mountain people are descended from altogether different stock than that of the poor white. However this distinction has been a difficult one for authors through the years. For further elucidation on this subject see Cratis D. Williams dissertation, "The Southern Mountaineer in Fact and Fiction." New York University, 1960.
W4950

Wetmore, Alexander New Race of Song Sparrows from the Appalachian Region. Washington: Smithsonian Institution, 1936. Concentrates on new folk artists and ballad collectors.
W4960

Wetmore, Susannah Mountain Songs of North Carolina. New York: Schirmer, 1926.
W4970 (BC)

Wey, Adelaide Smoky Mountain Ballads. New York: n.p., 1949.
W4980

Wey, Jean Jensen "A Study of the Freshmen Placement Tests Given at Appalachian State Teachers College as a Basis for Determining Their Effective Use as a Screening Device." Master's thesis. Appalachian State Teachers College, 1958.
W4990 (ASU)

Wharton, Mary E. A Guide to the Wildflowers and Ferns of Kentucky. Kentucky Nature Series, 1. Lexington: Univ. Press of Kentucky, 1971. More than 500 photographs help the reader to identify 800 wildflowers and ferns.
W5000 (ASU ETSU WCU BC WWC)

Trees and Shrubs of Kentucky. Lexington: Univ. of Kentucky Press, 1973.
W5010 (BC)

Wharton, May Cravath Doctor Woman of the Cumberlands: The Autobiography of May Cravath Wharton, M. D. Pleasant Hill, Tenn.: Uplands, 1953. A woman doctor's recollections of her life and practice in the Cumberland mountains. Deeply moving.
W5020 (ASU LMC WWC BC)

Doctor Woman of the Cumberlands; the Autobiography of May Cravath Wharton, M. D. 1953. Reprint. Pleasant Hill, Tenn.: Uplands, 1972.
W5030 (LMC WCU)

Wheaton, Mabel Wolfe Thomas Wolfe and His Family. With LeGette Blythe. 1st ed. Garden City, N. Y.: Doubleday, 1961. Explores the rich family background and the many characters who influenced Wolfe's boyhood. Also presents some interesting observations on "Dixieland."
W5040 (ASU WCU BC UNCA)

Wheeler, Arville White Squaw: The True Story of Jennie Wiley. Illustrated by True Bengtz. Boston: Heath, 1958. An exciting account of the life and captivity of Jennie Wiley.
W5050 (ASU ETSU)

White Squaw: The True Story of Jennie Wiley. Illustrated by True Bengtz. 1958. Reprint. n.p.: Eastern Kentucky Pubs., 1962.
W5060 (MHC)

Wheeler, Billy Edd The Billy Edd Wheeler Song Book. New York: Quartet Music and Bexhill Music Corp., 1962-1968.
W5070 (WWC)

Song of a Woods Colt: Poetry. 1st ed. Anderson, S. C.: Drake House, 1969. Poems of humor and goodwill, courage and protest, hate and love.
W5080 (LMC ASU MHC BC)

Twenty-Five Great Folk Songs. n.p.: Hansen Pubs., 1964.
W5090 (BC)

Wheeler, Mrs. Candace (Thurber) Home Industries and Domestic Weavings. New York: Associate Artists, n.d.
W5100

Wheeler, Jesse Harrison, Jr. "Land Use in Greenbrier County, West Virginia." Ph.D. Diss. Univ. of Chicago, 1951.
W5110 (BC)

Wheeler, John Hill Historical Sketches of North Carolina, from 1584 to 1851. Comp. from original records, official documents, and traditional statements. Philadelphia: Lippincott, Grambo and Co., 1851. Contains biographical sketches of successful men.
W5120 (UNCA)

Historical Sketches of North Carolina from 1584 to 1851. 1851. Reprint. With a foreword by Magnolia McKay Shuford. 2 vols. New York: F. H. Hitchcock, 1925.
W5130 (ASU LMC)

Historical Sketches of North Carolina from 1584 to 1851 Compiled from Original Records, Official Documents, and Traditional Statements, with Biographical Sketches of Her Distinguished Statesmen, Jurists, Lawyers, Soldiers, Divines, etc. 2 vols. in 1. Baltimore: Regional Pub. Co., 1964.
W5140 (LMC BC)

Reminiscences and Memoirs of North Carolina and Eminent North Carolinians. Baltimore: Genealogical Pub. Co., 1966.
W5150 (UNCA BC ASU)

Wheeler, Mary Kentucky Mountain Folk-Songs. The Words and Melodies Collected by M. Wheeler, the Pianoforte Accompaniments by Clara G. Bridge. With an intro. by Edgar Stillman-Kelley. Boston, Mass.: The Boston Music Co., 1937.
W5160

Wheeling College Selected Archeological and Historical Sites in West Virginia; Preliminary Plan for Development. Wheeling, W. Va.: Wheeling College, 1965.
W5170

Wheelwright, Jere H. Gentlemen, Hush New York: Scribner, 91948.
W5180 (BC ETSU)

Wheelwright, Jere Hungerford Kentucky Stand. New York: Scribner, 1951.
W5190 (ASU LMC ETSU WCU BC)

Whelan, Paul A. "Unconventional Warfare in East Tennessee, 1861-1865." Master's thesis. Univ. of Tennessee, 1963. A history of the guerilla warfare, Coleman Scouts, and other Cavalry Raiders in East Tennessee.
W5200

Where Bluegrass and Mountains Meet. A Community Profile of Mt. Sterling and Montgomery County, Ky. Sept. 1, 1957. Lexington, Ky.: Univ. of Ky., n.d. Montgomery is not usually considered a mountain county.
W5210 (BC)

Whetstone, George W. Doll, Warwick L. Water Resources of Kanawha County, West Virginia. Morgantown: West Virginia Geological and Economic Survey, 1960.
D2830 (ETSU)

Whetzel, Virgil L. "Reservoir Impacts on Economic Activity, Land Use and Land Values in Appalachia." Master's thesis. West Virginia Univ., 1969.
W5220

Whiford, L. A. A Manual of the Fresh-Water Algae in North Carolina. Technical Bulletin, no. 186. Raleigh: North Carolina Agricultural Experiment Station, 1968.
W5740 (LMC)

Whisnant, David E. What Has Been Done . . . Missionaries, Planners, and Developers. n.p.: n.p., n.d.
W5230

Whisner, Will Caspar Mark Ellis, or Unsolved Problems: A Story for the Present Day. Morgantown, W. Va.: Acme Pub. Co., 1899. Period fiction with an emphasis on adventure and a moral lesson.
W5240 (ASU)

Whitaker, Fees History of Corporal Fees Whitaker: Kentucky Mountain Life. Louisville: Standard Print. Co., 1918. A history of Letcher County, Kentucky written from an autobiographical and very biased point of view.
W5250 (ASU LMC BC)

Whitaker, James C. Costs and Returns for Hardwood Lumber Production in Appalachian Region of Kentucky and Ohio. U. S. Forest Service Research Paper, NE-55. Upper Darby, Pa.: Northeastern Forest Experiment Station, 1966.
W5260

Whitaker, R. H. Incidents and Anecdotes. Raleigh, N. C.: Edwards & Broughton, 1905. Some of these North Carolina incidents and anecdotes have western North Carolina settings or characters.
W5270 (LMC)

Whitaker, Sarah G. "A History of Livingston Academy from 1909 through 1947." Master's thesis. Tennessee Technological Univ., 1964.
W5280

Whitaker, Walter Clariborne A Round Robin, the Southern Highlands and Highlanders. Harford: Church Mission Pub. Co., 1916. An account of mission work in the southern mountains.
W5290 (BC)

White, Alvin D. History of the Mount Prospect Graveyard and Cemetery, in Mount Pleasant Township, Washington County, Pennsylvania. Parsons, W. Va.: McClain Print. Co., 1972.
W5300

White, Benjamin Franklin The Sacred Harp. 3rd ed., 1859. Facsimile. Including as a historical introduction The Story of the Sacred Harp by George Pullen Jackson. Nashville: Broadman Press, 1968. The most famous of the Christian Harmony songbooks used in mountain religious services.
W5310 (WCU ASU)

White, Benjamin U. "The Climatology of the Southern Blue Ridge Mountains." Master's thesis. Univ. of North Carolina, 1951.
W5320 (LMC)

White, Buchanan The Rural School Teacher: Or, A Double West Virginia Love Story. New York: Broadway Pub. Co., 1909. A suspenseful thriller of the dime novel variety. Right triumphs.
W5330 (BC)

White, Campbell The Northern Appalachian Coal Field. n.p.: n.p., 1902. No copy available for examination.
W5340

White Caps and Blue Bills Knoxville, Tenn.: Seviere Pub. & Distrib. Co., 1937. A treatise on two types vigilante groups active in the southern mountains.
W5350 (BC)

White, Charles Lincoln A Century of Faith. Boston: Pub. for the Amer. Baptist Home Mission Society by the Judson Press, 1932.
W5360 (BC)

White, D. H., Jr. Danielson, V. A. Waste Disposal Costs at Two Coal Mines in Kentucky and Alabama. Washington: W. S. Bureau of Mines, 1969.
D240 ()

White, David Millspaugh, Charles Frederick Part 1: The Living Flora of West Virginia. Part 2: The Fossil Flora of West Virginia. Wheeling: Wheeling News Litho. Co., 1913.
M6100 (ETSU)

Lower Pennsylvanian Species of Mariopteris, Eremopteris, Diplothmema, and Aneimities from the Appalachian Region. Assembled and edited by C. B. Read. U. S. Geological Survey Professional Paper, no. 197-C. Shorter Contributions to General Geology, 1941-42. Washington: Govt. Print. Off., 1943.
W5370

White, Edwin E. Highland Heritage: The Southern Mountains and the Nation. New York: Friendship Press, 1937.
W5380

White, Edwin Elverton Highland Heritage: The Southern Mountains and the Nation. New York: Friendship Press, 1937.
W5390 (ASU LMC BC WWC)

White, Elizabeth "Development of the Bituminous Coal Mining Industry in Logan County, West Virginia." Master's thesis. Marshall College, 1956.
W5400

White, George Historical Collections of Georgia: Containing the Most Interesting Facts, Traditions, Biographical Sketches, Anecdotes, etc., Relating to Its History and Antiquities, from Its First Settlement to the Present Time. Compiled from original records and official documents. Illustrated by nearly one hundred engravings. 1855. Reprint. Baltimore: Genealogical Pub. Co., 1969.
W5410 (ASU BC)

Statistics of the State of Georgia. Savannah: Williams, 1849.
W5420 (BC)

White, H. M. The McClanahans. Roanoke, Va.: Stone Print. Co., 1894.
W5430

White, Hazeltine White, Campbell The Northern Appalachian Coal Field. n.p.: n.p., 1902.
W5340

White, Helen From the Mountain. Memphis: Memphis State Univ. Press, 1972. An account of the lives of Miss Paula Snelling and Miss Lillian Smith and their North Georgia Review and other literary endeavors in Georgia's upcountry.
W5440 (ASU BC)

White, Israel Charles Levels Above Tide. True Meridians. Report on Coal. West Virginia Geological Survey, Reports, vol. 2. Morgantown: Morgantown Post Co., 1903.
W5450 (ETSU)

Levels. Coal Analyses. West Virginia Geological Survey Bulletin, 2. Morgantown: Acme Pub. Co., 1910.
W5460 (ETSU)

Stratigraphy of the Bituminous Coal Field of Pennsylvania, Ohio, and West Virginia. U. S. Geological Survey Bulletin, no. 65. Washington: Govt. Print. Off., 1891.
W5470

Supplementary Coal Report. West Virginia Geological Survey Reports, vol. 2A. Wheeling: Press of Wheeling News Litho. Co., 1908.
W5480 (ETSU)

White, Katherine Keogh The Kings Mountain Men: The Story of the Battle, with Sketches of the American Soldiers Who Took Part. 1924. Reprint. Baltimore: Genealogical Pub. Co., 1966.
W5490 (ASU)

The King's Mountain Men, the Story of the Battle, with Sketches of the American Soldiers Who Took Part. Dayton, Va.: Joseph K. Ruebush, 1924.
W5500 (BC)

White, Lamar Highlights of the Economy of the Georgia Mountains Area. Atlanta: Industrial Development Division, Engineering Experiment Station, Georgia Institute of Technology, 1964.
W5510

White, M. L. A History of the Life of Amos Owens, the Noted Blockader, of Cherry Mountain, North Carolina. Shelby, N. C.: Cleveland Star Job Print., n.d.
W5520 (LMC)

White, Moses Art Work of Knoxville, with Sketch of Knoxville. Chicago: W. H. Parish, 1895.
W5530

White, Nelle Rhea The Bradfords of Virginia in the Revolutionary War, and Their Kin. Richmond: Whittet and Shepperson, 1932.
W5540 (ASU)

White, Newman Ivey General ed. Duke University, Durham, N. C., Library The Frank C. Brown Collection of North Carolina. Durham: Duke Univ. Press, 1952-64.
D3810 (ASU WCU LMC MHC BC WWC ETSU)

White, R. H. Development of the Tennessee State Educational Organization, 1796-1929. Kingsport, Tenn.: Southern Pub., 1929.
W5550 (ETSU BC)

White, Rita Rothgeb Papa's Diary. Luray, Va.: n.p., 1961. Memoirs of the 19th Century in Virginia's Shenandoah Valley.
W5560 (BC)

White, Robert Hiram Tennessee: Its Growth and Progress. Rev. ed. Nashville, Tenn.: n.p., 1947.
W5570 (BC)

White, Stewart Edward Daniel Boone: Wilderness Scout. Illustrated by James Daugherty. Garden City, N. Y.: Doubleday and Co., 1922.
W5580 (ETSU ASU BC)

Daniel Boone; Wilderness Scout. Garden City, N. Y.: Doubleday, Doran, 1929.
W5590 (BC)

Daniel Boone, Wilderness Scout. Garden City, N. Y.: Sun Dial Press, 1937.
W5600 (ETSU)

Daniel Boone: Wilderness Scout. The Life Story and True Adventure of the Great Hunter, Long Knife, Who First Blazed the Wilderness Trail Through the Indian Country to Kentucky. Illustrated by James Daugherty. Garden City, N. Y.: Doubleday, Page and Co., 1926.
W5610 (ASU)

White, Thomas Edward "Development and Operation of the Welfare and Retirement Fund in the Bituminous Coal Industry." Ph. D. Diss. Univ. of Pittsburgh, 1954.
W5620

White, W. S. The Bauxite Deposits of Floyd, Bartow, and Polk Counties of Northwest Georgia. U. S. Geological Survey Circular, no. 193. Washington: Govt. Print. Off., 1952.
W5630

White, Walter S. ed. Studies of Appalachian Geology: Northern and Maritime New York: Interscience Publishers, 1968.
S8800 (ASU ETSU UNCA)

White, William E. A History of Alexander County, North Carolina. Taylorsville: Alexander Co., Hist. Co., 1947. History of a football county in North Carolina. Alexander County's Civil War days are especially interesting.
W5640

Whitehead, Mrs. Raymond H. Genealogical History of Original Murray County. Atlanta, Ga.: The author, 1972. An excellent source for finding families who moved west with the Cherokee land grant.
W5650

Whiteman, Ruth H. "Food Habits of a Sample of University High School Students." Master's thesis. West Virginia Univ., 1952.
W5660

Whitener, Daniel Jay Daniel Boone Wagon Train. Boone, N. C.: n.p., 1964. This promotional material for the annual wagon train also includes Whitener's brief history of Watauga County, and sketches of the founding families. Wagon route follows the Boone Trail.
W5670 (ASU)

History of Watauga County: A Souvenir of Watauga Centennial. Boone, N. C.: Watauga Centennial, 1949. A history of the county, its early exploration and its leading families.
W5680 (ASU WCU LMC ETSU)

Local History — How to Find and Write It. Asheville, N. C.: Western North Carolina Historical Assoc., 1955. Pamphlet discusses possible projects in the local history of western North Carolina as well as local history methodology.
W5690 (ASU)

Prohibition in North Carolina, 1715-1945. James Sprunt Studies, vol. 27. Chapel Hill: Univ. of North Carolina Press, 1946. Some mention of the moonshine industry in western North Carolina.
W5700 (LMC)

Whitfield County, Georgia, History Commission Official History of Whitfield County, Georgia. Dalton, Ga.: A. J. Showalter Co., 1936. Whitfield county was formed from original Murray County, Georgia.
W5710 (BC)

Whitfield, Fred E. Growing Christmas Trees in North Carolina. n.p.: North Carolina Agricultural Extension Service, 1968.
W5720 (WCU)

Whitfield, Vallie Jo Fox Whitfield History and Genealogy of Tennessee. Walnut Creek, Cal.: n.p., 1964. Genealogy of the influencial Whitfield family of early East Tennessee.
W5730 (ASU)

Whitlatch, George Isaac Smith, Richard Wellington The Phosphate Resources of Tennessee. Nashville: Tennessee Department of Conservation, Division of Geology, 1940.
S5030 (ETSU)

Whitlatch, George Isaac ed. Industrial Resources of Tennessee. Rev. ed. 5 vols. Nashville: Tennessee State Planning Commission, 1948.
W5750 (ETSU)

Whitley, Edythe J. R. Sam Davis, Hero of the Confederacy, 1842-1863, Coleman's Scouts. Nashville: Blue and Gray Press, 1971. Biography of famous Civil War Scout and raider in East Tennessee.
W5760

Whitley, Edythe Johns Rucker Tennessee Genealogical Records: Overton County. Nashville: n.p., 1967.
W5770 (BC)

Whitlow, Jane Davis "A Comparative Study of the Science Achievement of Fifth and Sixth Grades in Bristol, Tennessee, 1958-1962." Master's thesis. East Tennessee State Univ., 1963.
W5780 (ETSU)

Whitman, J. A. Historical Facts About Churches of Wythe County. Wytheville, Va.: Southwest Virginia Enterprise, 1939.
W5790

The Iron Industry of Wythe County from 1792. Wytheville, Va.: Southwest Virginia Enterprise, 1942. Wythe County produces iron ores. The forges, furnaces, and foundaries have played an important part in the development of the county.
W5800 (ASU BC)

Whitman, John C. "Cost Estimating Model for Identifying Gross Dollar Needs for West Virginia Highways." Master's thesis. West Virginia Univ., 1971.
W5810

Whitman, Robert H. "Development of the Health Program for Negroes in Franklin County, Tennessee from 1940-1953." Master's thesis. Tennessee Agricultural and Industrial Univ., 1953.
W5820

Whitman, Willson David Lilienthal, Public Servant in a Power Age. New York: Holt and Co., 1948. Biography of a Tennessee Valley Authority man.
W5830 (BC)

God's Valley: People and Power Along the Tennessee River. New York: Viking Press, 1939.
W5840 (ASU WWC BC)

Whitney, Gertrude Cookeville in Retrospect. Dallas: n.p., 1943. A history of Putnam County, Tennessee and the city of Cookeville.
W5850

Whitney, Milton Soils of the Appalachian Mountain and Plateau Province. Bulletin, 78. Washington: U. S. Dept. of Agriculture, Bureau of Soils, 1911.
W5860

Whitsitt, William Heth Life and Times of Judge Caleb Wallace, Some Time a Justice of the Court of Appeals of the State of Ky. Louisville: M. P. Morton and Co., Printers, 1888. Biography of an eastern Kentucky jurist.
W5870 (BC)

Whitson, Philip L. "An Analysis and Basis for Curriculum Revision Concerning the Drafting Program at East Tennessee State University." Master's thesis. East Tennessee State Univ., 1968.
W5880 (ETSU)

Whittaker, Alto ed. and comp. Comstock, Jim F. Best of Hillbilly: A Prize Collection of 100-proof Writings from Jim Comstock's West Virginia Hillbilly. Anderson, S. C.: Droke House, 1968.
C6300 (ASU MHC WCU LMC BC)

Whittaker, James C. McCauley, Orris D. Sawmill Practices and Problems in Appalachian Hill Country of Ohio and Kentucky. Upper Darby, Pa.: Northeastern Forest Experiment Station, 1967.
M350

McCauley, Orris D. Value Added by Sawmilling in Appalachian Hill Country of Ohio and Kentucky. Upper Darby, Pa.: Northeastern Forest Experiment Station, 1967.
M360

Whittaker, Otto Best of Hillbilly. Anderson, S. C.: Droke House, 1968. A collection of the best writings from James Comstock's WEST VA. HILLBILLY.
W5890 (ASU LMC)

Whittenburg, Robert L. Torrence, Robert M. Colonel "Davey" Crockett. Washington, D. C.: N. Fagan, 1956.
T8960

Whitter, Joida Abstracts of Bedford County, Virginia Wills, Inventories and Accounts 1754-1787. n.p.: The author, 1969.
W5900 (FC)

Whittlesay, Susan VISTA: Challenge in Poverty. New York: Coward-McCann, 1970. A history of the VISTA volunteers and their role in the War on Poverty. Contains information about VISTA efforts and problems in the Southern Mountains.
W5910

Whittlesey, Charles War Memoranda: Cheat River to the Tennessee, 1861-1862. Cleveland: W. W. Williams, 1884. Memories of the Civil War in the mountains — from the Cheat River to the Tennessee.
W5920 (BC)

W-Hollow Harvest, a Magazine for Jesse Stuart Buffs vol. 1. Cincinnati: n.p., 1965.
W5930 (BC)

Who's Who in East Tennessee State College Johnson City: The college, 1949.
W5940 (ETSU)

Wichmann, Patricia Guion Christ Church, Episcopal, Rugby, Tennessee, a Short History. Rugby, Tenn.: n.p., 1959.
W5950 (BC)

Wiebe, A. H. Waterfowl on the Tennessee River Impoundments. Norris, Tenn.: Tennessee Valley Authority, 1950.
W5960

Wiech, Edward A. The American Miners Association: A Record of the Origin of Coal Miners' Unions in the United States. New York: Russell Sage Foundation, 1940.
W5970 (ASU)

Wieck, Edward A. The Miners' Case and the Public Interest: A Documented Chronology. Research materials from the Russell Sage Foundation Department of Industrial Studies. New York: Russell Sage Foundation, 1947.
W5980

Preventing Fatal Explosions in Coal Mines: A Study of Recent Major Disasters in the United States as Accompaniments of Technological Change. New York: Russell Sage Foundation, 1942.
W5990

Wiggington, Eliot Foxfire 2: Ghost Stories, Spring Wild Plant Foods, Spinning and Weaving, Midwifing, Burial Customs, Corn Shuckin's, Wagon Making and More Affairs of Plain Living. Edited with an introduction by Eliot Wiggington. Garden City, N. Y.: Anchor Press/Doubleday, 1973.
W6030 (FC ASU BC)

Wiggington, Eliot ed. Foxfire. vol. 1. Rabun Gap, Ga.: n.p., 1967.
W6010 (FC LMC BC WWC ASU WCU ETSU)

The Foxfire Book: Hog Dressing; Log Cabin Building; Mountain Crafts and Foods; Planting by the Signs; Snake Lore, Hunting Tales, Faith Healing; Moonshining; and Other Affairs of Plain Living. Edited with an introd. by Eliot Wiggington. 1st ed. Garden City, N. Y.: Doubleday, 1972.
W6020 (FC ASU BC)

Foxfire 3: Animal Care, Banjos and Dulcimers, Hide Tanning, Summer and Fall Wildplant Foods, Butter Churns, Ginseng, and Still More Affairs of Plain Living. Garden City: Anchor Press/Doubleday, 1975.
W6040 (ASU)

Wigginton, Brooks Elliot Trees and Shrubs for the Southeast. Athens: Univ. of Georgia Press, 1963.
W6000 (BC)

Wigginton, Eliot ed. The Foxfire Book: Hog Dressing, Log Cabin Building, Mountain Crafts and Foods, Planting by the Signs, Snake Lore, Hunting Tales, Faith Healing, Moonshining, and Other Affairs of Plain Living Garden City, N. Y.: Doubleday, 1972.
F2970 (ASU WWC MHC ETSU BC FC)

Wight, Edward A. Wilson, Louis Round County Library Service in the South. Chicago: Univ. of Chicago Press, 1935.
W7390 (BC)

Wikstrom, Thomas N. West Virginia Graduate Research Studies in Education, 1894-1965: A Bibliographical Listing. Prepared under the direction of William K. Hamilton. Charleston: West Virginia Dept. of Education, 1965.
W6050 (ETSU)

Wilbanks, Thomas J. "Socio-cultural Factors and Economic Development in West Central Appalachia." Master's thesis. Trinity Univ., 1960.
W6060

Wilber, George L. Kaufman, Harold F. Social Changes and Their Implications for Southern Agriculture. State College: Mississippi Agricultural Experiment Station, Mississippi State Univ., August, 1959.
K280

Wilborn, Elizabeth W. The North Carolina Historical Almanack, Being a Collection of Notable Events That Have Befallen People and Places in Our Great State. Rev. Raleigh: State Dept. of Archives and History, 1962.
W6070 (ASU BC)

Wilbur, George L. Internal Migration in the United States 1958 to 1964: A List of References. Sociology and Rural Life Series, no. 15. State College: Mississippi Agricultural Experiment Station, Mississippi State Univ., 1965.
W6080

Wilbur, Robert L. The Leguminous Plants of North Carolina. Bulletin, no. 151. Raleigh: N. C. Agricultural Station, 1963.
W6090 (LMC)

Wilburn, Hiram C. Cherokee Landmarks Around the Great Smokies. Asheville, N. C.: Stephens Press, 1966.
W6100 (LMC)

Wildasin, Frances W. "An Analysis of Problems of Eighth and Ninth Grade Students in the Junior High School of Johnson City, Tennessee." Master's thesis. East Tennessee State College, 1952.
W6110 (ETSU)

Wilder, Charles G. Webb, William Snyder An Archaeological Survey of Guntersville Basin on the Tennessee River in Northern Alabama. Lexington: Univ. of Kentucky Press, 1951.
W2090 (LMC BC)

Wilder, Henry Jason Reconnaissance Soil Survey of Northwestern Pennsylvania. Prepared in cooperation with the Pennsylvania State College Agricultural Experiment Station, Field Operations, 1908. Washington: U. S. Dept. of Agriculture, Bureau of Soils, 1910.
W6120

Soil Survey of the Pikeville Area, Tennessee. Field Operations, 1903. Washington: U. S. Dept. of Agriculture, Bureau of Soils, 1904.
W6130

Wilder, Hugh B. Summary of Data on Chemical Quality of Streams of North Carolina, 1943-67: Quality of Surface Waters of North Carolina. Prepared in cooperation with the N. C. Department of Water and Air Resources. U. S. Geological Survey Water-supply Paper, 1895-B. Washington: Govt. Print. Off., 1971.
W6140 (LMC)

Wilder, Minnie S. comp. Kentucky Soldiers of the War of 1812. Baltimore, Md.: Genealogical Pub. Co., 1812.
W6150

Wilder, Robert Mr. G. Strings Along. New York: Putnam's, 1944. Appalachian setting.
W6160 (LMC)

Wilder, William Murtha Wilder and Some Connecting (Especially Some Ware) Families in Southeast United States of America. Columbus, Ga.: Columbus Office Supply Co., 1969.
W6170

Wildlife Resources Commission, State of N. C. Tar Heel Wildlife. By Wm. L. Hamnett and David C. Thornton. Raleigh: The Comm., 1953.
W6180 (LMC)

Wiley, Richard Sim Greene and Tom the Tinker's Men. Philadelphia: John C. Winston Co., 1907.
W6190 (BC)

Wiley, Ruth Smith "Language Experience Approach to Remedial Reading: Fourth Grade, Dunbar School, 1965-66." Master's thesis. East Tennessee State Univ., 1967.
W6200 (ETSU)

Wiley, Samuel T. History of Preston County (West Virginia). 1882. Index by Harold F. Powell. Parsons, W. Va.: McClain Print. Co., 1971.
W6210 (ASU)

History of Preston County (West Virginia). Assisted by A. W. Frederick. 1882. Reprint. Parsons, W. Va.: McClain Print. Co., 1968. A truly good and relatively early county history from West Virginia.
W6220 (ASU BC)

Wilfong, Harry Dean "A Cross-Validation Study of a Mining Foreman Selection He Devised from the Minnesota Multiphasic Personality Inventory." Master's thesis. West Virginia Univ., 1957.
W6230

Wilgus, D. K. Combs, Josiah Henry Folksongs of the Southern United States. Austin: Univ. of Texas Press, 1967.
C6130 (ASU WCU MHC LMC WWC BC FC)

Country-Western Music and the Urban Hillbilly. Los Angeles: Univ. of California, 1970. Reprinted from the JOURNAL OF AMERICAN FOLKLORE April - June, 1970.
W6240 (ASU)

Wilgus, Donald Knight Anglo-American Folksong Scholarship Since 1898. New Brunswick, N. J.: Rutgers Univ. Press, 1959.
W6250 (BC)

Wilhelm, E. J., Jr. The Blue Ridge: Man and Nature in Shenandoah National Park and Blue Ridge Parkway. Charlottesville: Univ. of Virginia, 1968.
W6260 (WCU LMC)

Wilkens, Henry A. J. Nitze, Henry Benjamin Charles Gold Mining in North Carolina and Adjacent South Appalachian Regions. Raleigh, N. C.: G. V. Barnes, 1897.
N1160 (ASU WCU LMC)

Wilkes County, N. C., Board of Education Identifying and Organizing for Individual Needs: An Evaluation. Wilkesboro, N. C.: n.p., 1969.
W6270 (WCU ASU)

Wilkie, Katherine Elliott Daniel Boone: Taming the Wilds. New York: Scholastic Book Service, 1961.
W6280 (BC)

Frontier Nurse: Mary Breckenridge. New York: Messner, 1969.
W6290 (ASU LMC BC)

John Sevier, Son of Tennessee. New York: J. Messner, 1958.
W6300 (ETSU)

John Sevier, Son of Tennessee. 1958. Reprint. New York: Julian Messner, 1966.
W6310 (LMC)

Wilkie, Richard W. Playing Lead Dulcimer. 2nd ed. Albany, N. Y.: Three City Press, 1972.
W6320 (ASU)

Wilkins, Thurman Cherokee Tragedy: The Story of the Ridge Family and the Decimation of a People. New York: Macmillan, 1970.
W6330 (ASU WCU LMC BC UNCA)

Wilkinson, Kenneth P. Kaufman, Harold P. Poverty Programs and Social Mobility. State College: Mississippi State Univ., Social Science Research Center, 1966.
K290

Wilkinson, Sylvia Cale. New York: Avon, 1972.
W6340 (ASU)

Wilkinson, T. L. Doyle, D. V. Evaluating Appalachian Woods for Highway Posts. Madison, Wis.: Forest Products Laboratory, 1969.
D3200

Wilkinson, W. E. Burke, Richard Thomas Avon Soil Survey of Randolph County, Alabama. Washington: Govt. Print. Off., 1912.
B8730

Cantrell, Llano Soil Survey of Chilton County, Alabama. Washington: U. S. Department of Agriculture, Bureau of Soils, 1913.
C1130

Winston, Robert A. Soil Survey of Tuscaloosa County, Alabama. Washington: U. S. Department of Agriculture, Bureau of Soils, 1912.
W7820

Willeford, Mary Bristow "Income and Health in Remote Rural Areas: A Study of Four Hundred Families in Leslie County, Kentucky." Ph. D. Diss. Columbia Univ., 1932.
W6350

Income and Health in Remote Rural Areas; a Study of 400 Families in Leslie County, Ky. New York City: n.p., 1932.
W6360 (BC)

Willey, William Patrick An Inside View of the Formation of the State of West Virginia, with Character Sketches of the Pioneers in that Movement. Wheeling, W. Va.: News Pub. Co., 1901.
W6370 (BC)

William, Ellis R. "Contacts of Negroes and Whites in Morgantown." Master's thesis. West Virginia Univ., 1952.
W6380

Williams, A. ed. Doddridge, Joseph Notes on the Settlements and Indian Wars of the Western Parts of Virginia and Pennsylvania from 1763 to 1783, Inclusive. Albany, N. Y.: J. Munsell, 1876.
D2670 (ETSU BC)

Williams, A. J. A Confederate History of Polk County, Tennessee, 1860-1866. Nashville: McQuiddy, 1923. Polk County was about half Union, half Confederate.
W6390

Williams, B. H. Stroud, James Frank Soil Survey of Franklin County, Alabama. Washington: U. S. Department of Agriculture, Bureau of Chemistry and Soils, 1932.
S8120

Williams, Ben Ames Hostile Valley. New York: E. P. Dutton and Co., 1934.
W6400 (ASU)

Williams, Bertha L. "A Survey of School Library Facilities and Services in Four Selected High Schools in Jefferson County, Alabama." Master's thesis. Alabama State College, 1954.
W6410

Williams, Blonnie Hugh Devereux, Robert Eddins Soil Survey, Albemarle County, Virginia. Washington: U. S. Department of Agriculture, Bureau of Plant Industry, 1940.
D1940

Soil Survey of Hampshire County, West Virginia. Prepared in cooperation with the West Virginia Geological Survey. Soil Survey Report, Series 1927, no. 9. Washington: U. S. Department of Agriculture, Bureau of Chemistry and Soils, 1931.
W6420

Soil Survey of Hardy and Pendleton Counties, West Virginia. Prepared in cooperation with the West Virginia Geological Survey and the West Virginia Agricultural Experiment Station. Soil Survey Report, Series, 1930, no. 14. Washington: U. S. Department of Agriculture, Bureau of Chemistry and Soils, 1934.
W6430

Soil Survey of Pocahontas County, West Virginia. Prepared in cooperation with the West Virginia Geological Survey and the West Virginia Agricultural Experiment Station. Soil Survey Report, Series 1933, no. 14. Washington: U. S. Department of Agriculture, Bureau of Chemistry and Soils, 1938.
W6440

Soil Survey of Randolph County, West Virginia. Prepared in cooperation with the West Virginia Geological Survey and the West Virginia Agricultural Experiment Station. Soil Survey Report, Series 1931, no. Washington: U. S. Department of Agriculture, Bureau of Chemistry and Soils, 1936.
W6450

Williams, Coral "Legends and Stories of White County, Tennessee." Master's thesis. George Peabody College, 1930.
W6460

Williams, Cratis Dearl "Ballads and Songs of Eastern Kentucky." Master's thesis. Univ. of Kentucky, 1937. An excellent source on Kentucky ballads. Includes some very rare variants.
W6470

A Selected Bibliography: The Southern Mountaineer in Fact and Fiction. Bibliography for his dessertation. n.p.: ASU Library, n.d.
W6480 (ASU MHC)

"The Southern Mountaineer in Fact and Fiction." Xerox of the original 3 vols. Ph. D. Diss. New York Univ., 1961. The classic work on mountain literature; an exhaustive study of books published prior to 1960.
W6490 (ASU MHC ETSU WWC BC)

Williams, David G. Mertins, Herman, Jr. West Virginia Budgeting: Problems and Possibilities. Morgantown: West Virginia Univ., Bureau of Government Research, 1971.
M5180

Williams, Dorcas A. "Food Habits of the Pupils in Monongahela and Dunbar (West Virginia) High School Whose Parents are Engaged in Coal Mining." Master's thesis. West Virginia Univ., 1952.
W6500

Williams, Drew B. "A Study of Pupil Transportation in Hancock, Tennessee." Master's thesis. Univ. of Tennessee, 1953.
W6510

Williams, Ethel W. Know Your Ancesters: A Guide to Genealogical Research. Rutland, Vt.: C. E. Tuttle Co., 1961.
W6520 (ASU)

Williams, Faith Moors and others Family Living in Knott County, Kentucky. U. S. Department of Agriculture Technical Bulletin, no. 576. Washington: Govt. Print. Off., 1937.
W6530 (BC)

Williams, G. Croft Social Problems of South Carolina. Columbia, S. C.: State Co., 1928. Scant mention of Appalachian counties.
W6540 (LMC)

Williams, George Walton ed. Davis, Arthur Kyle, Jr. ed. More Traditional Ballads of Virginia: Collected with the Cooperation of Members of the Virginia Folklore Society. Chapel Hill: Univ. of North Carolina Press, 1960.
D790 (ASU FC BC LMC)

Williams, Harold F. "A Comparison of Sources and Expenditures of the Funds Raised by the Schools and Organizations in Carter County with the School Budget of 1960-61." Master's thesis. East Tennessee State College, 1962.
W6550 (ETSU)

Williams, Harrison Legends of Loudoun: An Account of the History and Homes of a Border County of Virginia's Northern Neck. Richmond: Garrett and Massie, 1938.
W6560 (ASU BC)

Williams, Hiram Preston "A Comparative Study of Tendencies and Motivational Factors of Students from Various Academic Departments Who Vandalize Library Materials at Appalachian State University." Master's thesis. Appalachian State Univ., 1971.
W6570 (ASU)

Williams, Iolo A. English Folk Song and Dance. London: Longmans Green and Co., 1935. Variants of the English folk songs and dances can still be found in the Southern Mountains.
W6580

Williams, James Earl "The Industrial Development Policy of the Tennessee Valley Authority for the Period 1933-1950." Master's thesis. Univ. of Tennessee, 1950.
W6590

Williams, Jerry J. The Incidence of Poverty — Social and Economic Conditions in Tennessee. Nashville: Tennessee State Planning Commission, 1965.
W6600

Williams, Jerry Phillip "An Ecological Study of Some Small Mammals of Horse Cove, Washington County, Tennessee." Master's thesis. East Tennessee State Univ., 1963.
W6610 (ETSU)

Williams, John Alexander "Davis and Elkins of West Virginia: Businessmen in Politics." Ph. D. Diss. Yale Univ., 1967.
W6620

Williams, John Augustus Life of Elder John Smith. Nashville: Gospel Advocate Co., 1956. Life of a mountain minister and missionary in the central Appalachians.
W6630 (BC)

Williams, Jonathan Blues and Roots, Rue and Bluets: A Garland for the Appalachians. Photographs by Nicholas Dean. New York: Grossman, 1971. A remarkable book which captures the grandeur, wit, humor, courage and pathos of mountain life in the concrete images of meter and photograph. This man writes poetry as he hears it in the speech of others.
W6640 (ASU LMC BC)

An Ear in Bartram's Tree: Selected Poems, 1957-1967. Chapel Hill: Univ. of North Carolina Press, 1969. Title refers to William Bartram, the Naturalist, whose journals of trips in the Appalachians this poet has studied.
W6650 (LMC BC)

The Loco Logodaedalist in Situ: Selected Poems, 1968-70. New York: Cape Goliard Press, 1972. Poetry, not restricted to Appalachia.
W6660 (LMC)

Williams, Pearl D. "The Development of a Statement of Written Policies for the Roane County Tennessee Board of Education." Master's thesis. East Tennessee State Univ., 1958.
W6670

Williams, Raymond "A Study of Pupil Achievement in the Nongraded John F. Hay Elementary School in Morristown, Tennessee." Master's thesis. East Tennessee State Univ., 1971.
W6680 (ETSU)

Williams, Robin M. Attitudes Toward Rural Migration and Family Life in Johnson and Robertson Counties, Kentucky, 1941. Bulletin no. 452. Lexington: Kentucky Agricultural Experiment Station, Univ. of Ky., 1943.
W6690

Williams, Ruth McKibben "The History of the Soil Conservation Service in Watauga County, North Carolina." Master's thesis. Appalachian State Univ., 1961.
W6700 (ASU)

Williams, Samuel Cole Adair, James Adair's History of the American Indians. Johnson City, Tenn.: The Watauga Press, 1930.
A270 (BC FC ASU LMC)

Adair, James Adair's History of the American Indians. New York: Argonaut Press, 1966.
A280 (WCU)

Adair, James History of the American Indians. Johnson City, Tenn.: Blue and Grey Press, 1971.
A290 (ETSU)

Williams, Samuel Cole
The Baptists of Tennessee. 2 vols. in 1. Kingsport, Tenn.: Southern Pubs., 1930.
W6710 (ASU)
Dawn of Tennessee Valley and Tennessee History. Johnson City, Tenn.: Watauga Press, 1937. Widely acclaimed history of Tennessee. To be used in conjunction with the author's early travels in the Tennessee Country.
W6720 (ASU LMC BC)
Early Travels in the Tennessee County, 1540-1800. 1928. Reprint. Nashville: Franklin Book Reprints, 1970.
W6730 (ETSU)
History of Codification in Tennessee. Johnson City, Tenn.: Watauga Press, 1932.
W6750 (ETSU)
History of Johnson City and Its Environs. Johnson City, Tenn.: Watauga Press, 1940.
W6760 (ASU LMC ETSU BC)
History of Johnson City and Its Environs. 1940. Reprint. Johnson City, Tenn.: Watauga Press, 1954.
W6770 (ETSU)
History of the Lost State of Franklin. Johnson City, Tenn.: Watauga Press, 1924. The first of Judge William's works on Tennessee history.
W6780 (ASU MHC BC)
History of the Lost State of Franklin. Johnson City, Tenn.: The Watauga Press, 1933.
W6790
History of the Lost State of Franklin. Rev. ed. New York: Press of the Pioneers, 1933.
W6800 (LMC WCU ETSU ASU)
History of the Lost State of Franklin. 1924. Reprint. Nashville: Franklin Book Reprints, 1970.
W6810 (ETSU)
History of the Lost State of Franklin. Knoxville: Tenase, 1970. Illustrates that a movement toward separate statehood existed on all frontiers in the 1780's but was achieved only by the State of Franklin.
W6820
Tennessee During the Revolutionary War. Nashville: Tennessee Historical Commission, 1944. The most dramatic event in Tennessee's Revolutionary History was the march of the Overmountain Men from Sycamore Shoals to Kings Mountain and their subsequent victory there.
W6840 (ASU BC)
William Tatham, Wataugan. 2nd, rev. and limited ed. Johnson City, Tenn.: Watauga Press, 1947.
W6850 (ETSU ASU WCU BC)

Williams, Samuel Cole ed. Early Travels in the Tennessee Country, 1540-1800: With Introductions, Annotations and Index. Johnson City, Tenn.: Watauga Press, 1928. Extracts from the writings of early travelers.
W6740 (ASU LMC BC)
Lieutenant Henry Timberlake's Memoirs 1756-1765. 1927. Reprint. Marietta, Ga.: Continental Book Co., 1948. Timberlake's memoirs offer insight into early relations between the British, the colonists, and the Indians, especially the Cherokee.
W6830

Williams, Stanley B. "Disorganization and Delinquency in Three Coal Communities." Microfilm. Master's thesis. West Virginia Univ., 1954.
W6860 (ASU)

Williams, Thomas John Chew Thomas, James Walter History of Allegany County, Maryland. Baltimore: Regional Pub. Co., 1969.
T7870 (ASU)
The History of Washington County, Maryland, from the Earliest Settlements to the Present Time, Including a History of Hagerstown. To this is added a biographical record of representative families prepared from data obtained from original sources of information. 1906. Reprint. 2 vols. Baltimore: Regional Pub. Co., 1968.
W6870 (ASU)

Williams, Vinnie Greenbones. New York: Viking Press, 1967. Setting is the North Georgia mountain region.
W6880 (ASU)
Walk Egypt. New York: Viking Press, 1960. A tale of a strange and lonely woman in the North Georgia hills who finds love and laughter only to lose them again.
W6890 (ASU WCU LMC BC)

Williams, W. D. Whittle Springs Hotel and Golf and Country Club. Knoxville: n.p., 1911. History of a Knox County, Tennessee resort.
W6900

Williams, W. T. History of Ravenna, Kentucky. n.p.: n.p., 1956.
W6910 (BC)

Williams, York Wayland "An Economic Evaluation of the Power Program of the Tennessee Valley Authority." Master's thesis. Univ. of Colorado, 1961.
W6920

Williamson, A. D. Huddle, J. W. Oil and Gas Wells Drilled in Southwestern Virginia before 1950. Washington: Govt. Print. Off., 1956.
H7900 (ASU)

Williamson, Hugh The History of North Carolina. 2 vols. 1812. Reprint. Spartanburg, S. C.: Reprint Co., 1973.
W6930 (ASU LMC BC)

Williamson, Jack A. "Experimental Preschool Intervention in the Appalachian Home." Ph. D. Diss. Univ. of Kentucky, 1970.
W6940

Williamson, John Ferns of Ky; with Full-page Etchings and Wood Cuts. Louisville: J. P. Norton, 1878.
W6950 (BC)

Williamson, Malcome J. Nelson, Thomas Charles Decorative Plants of Appalachia: A Source of Income. Washington: Govt. Print. Off., 1970.
N530 (ASU ETSU LMC)

Williamson, Margaretta A. Bradley, Frances Sage Rural Children in Selected Counties of North Carolina. New York: Negro Univ. Press, 1969.
B6180 (ASU BC LMC)

Williamson, W. H. "A History of Polk County." Benton: Unpublished typescript, n.d.
W6960

Willis, Bailey The Mechanics of Appalachian Structure. Washington: Govt. Print. Off., 1894.
W6970
The Northern Appalachians. National Geographic Monograph, no. 6. New York: American Book Co., 1895.
W6980 (BC)

Willis, Byrd Charles Willis Family of Virginia. Richmond: Whittet and Shepperson, n.d.
W6990

Willis, Carrie Hunter Legends of the Skyline Drive and the Great Valley of Virginia. Richmond: Dietz Press, 1937.
W7000 (ASU WCU LMC BC)
Legends of the Skyline Drive and the Great Valley of Va. Richmond, Va.: The Dietz Press, 1940.
W7010 (BC)

Willis, Richard Henry Willis, Byrd Charles Willis Family of Virginia. Richmond: Whittet and Shepperson, n.d.
W6990

Willis, Roger Lee "A Study of Cooperative Education in Relation to the Industrial Technology Program of East Tennessee State University." Master's thesis. East Tennessee State Univ., 1972.
W7020 (ETSU)

Willis, Virginia G. "The Planning of Art Facilities for Dobyns-Bennett High School, Kingsport, Tennessee." Master's thesis. East Tennessee State Univ., 1966.
W7030 (ETSU)

Willoughby, Charles C. The Virginia Indians in the Seventeenth Century. Reprinted from AMERICAN ANTHROPOLOGIST, vol. 9, no. 1. Lancaster, Pa.: New Era Print. Co., 1907.
W7040 (ASU)

Wilmoth, Benton M. Ground Water in Mason and Putnam Counties, West Virginia. Prepared by the U. S. Geological Survey. Bulletin, no. 32. Morgantown: West Virginia Geological & Economic Survey, 1966.
W7050 (ETSU)

Wilmoth, Benton M., Jr. Doll, Warwick L. Water Resources of Kanawha County, West Virginia. Morgantown: West Virginia Geological and Economic Survey, 1960.
D2830 (ETSU)

Wilpolt, R. H. Geology and Oil and Gas Possibilities of Upper Mississippian Rocks of Southwestern Virginia, Southern West Virginia, and Eastern Kentucky. U. S. Geological Survey Bulletin, no. 1072-K. Contributions to Economic Geology, 1957. Washington: Govt. Print. Off., 1959.
W7060 (ASU)

Wilson, A. Frederick ed. Songs of the University of Virginia. New York: Hinds, Noble and Eldredge, 1906.
W7070 (ASU)

Wilson, Augusta Jane Evans Saint Elmo, a Novel. New York: Grosset and Dunlap, 1896.
W7080 (ASU)
A Speckled Bird. New York: G. W. Dillingham Co., 1902.
W7090 (ASU)

Wilson, Barto G. comp. Knoxville Negro. Knoxville: n.p., 1929.
W7100

Wilson, Charles Morrow Backwoods America. Illustrated by Bayard Wootten. Chapel Hill: Univ. of North Carolina Press, 1934. Although there is more about the Ozarks than the Appalachians some observations on the frontier character and the circumstances of frontier life apply to Appalachia.
W7110 (ASU LMC BC)
The Landscape of Rural Poverty: Corn Bread and Creek Water. New York: H. Holt, 1940.
W7120 (BC)

Wilson, Charles William, Jr. Annotated Bibliography of the Geology of Tennessee Through December, 1950. Bulletin, 59. Nashville: Tennessee Department of Conservation Division of Geology, 1953.
W7130 (ETSU)
Annotated Bibliography of the Geology of Tennessee, January, 1951, Through December, 1960. A supplement to Bulletin 59. Bulletin, 67. Nashville: Tennessee Division of Geology, 1965.
W7140 (ETSU)
Guidebook to Geology Along Tennessee Highways. Report of Investigations, no. 5. Nashville: Tennessee Division of Geology, 1958.
W7150 (ETSU)

Wilson, Clyde Our Bed Is Green. New York: Robert O. Ballou, 1934. A superbly told tale which offers a variation of the Montague-Capulet theme. Set in Watauga County, North Carolina.
W7160

Wilson, David Nature's Pantry; 100 Wild Edible Plants Alphabetically Listed, Each with Full Description, Food Preparation and Folk Medicinal Properties. 1st ed. Virginia Beach, Va.: L. House, 1972.
W7170 (BC)

Wilson, Dell B. The Grandfather and the Globe. Vignettes by Donald R. Baker. Banner Elk, N. C.: Pudding Stone Press, 1969. A well-documented novel set in Civil War era Watauga, Avery, and Caldwell Counties, North Carolina.
W7180 (ASU LMC WWC BC)

Wilson, Eddie W. Camp, Cordelia The Settlement of North Carolina. Cullowhee, N. C. Cordelia Camp, 1942.
C470 (ASU BC)

Wilson, Edwin B. Current and Proposed Regulations and Legislation on Air Pollution Concerning the Appalachian Coal Industry. Morgantown: West Virginia Univ. Coal Research Bureau, 1969.
W7190

Wilson, Everett Broomall America's Vanishing Folkways. New York: A. S. Barnes, 1965.
W7200 (MHC)

Wilson, Frank E. The Hill Billy Kid. Chicago & New York: Rand McNally and Co., 1927. This novel of Night Riders and tobacco wars in Kentucky has a mountain setting but few mountaineers.
W7210 (BC)

Wilson, Gearl D. "The Achievement of Selected Economically Deprived Secondary School Male Athletes as Related to Non-athletes in Blount County, Tennessee, Schools." Master's thesis. East Tennessee State Univ., 1970.
W7220 (ETSU)

Wilson, George Pickett Instructions to Collectors of Dialect. Publication, no. 1. Greensboro, N. C.: American Dialect Society, 1944.
W7230 (ASU)

Wilson, Goodridge Smyth County History and Traditions. Published in connection with the centennial celebration of Smyth County, Virginia, 1932. Kingsport, Tenn.: Kingsport Press, 1932.
W7240 (ASU BC)

Wilson, Gordon Fidelity Folks. Cynthiana, Ky.: Hobson Book Press, 1946.
W7250 (WWC)

Folklore of the Mammoth Cave Region. Ed. by Lawrence S. Thompson. Bowling Green, Ky.: Ky. Folklore Society, 1968.
W7260 (BC)

Wilson, Gregory The Valley of Time. 1st ed. Garden City, N. Y.: Doubleday, 1967. Western North Carolina setting.
W7270 (LMC)

Wilson, Harry Robert arr. Sing and Dance: Folk Songs and Dances Including American Play-party Games. Dance directions prepared by Beatrice A. Hunt, music arranged by Harry Robert Wilson, illustrations by Conura Melder Collier. Chicago: Hall and McCreary, 1945.
W7280 (BC)

Wilson, Hilda Louise "A Study of Relevant Community Resources for Elementary Classes (Grade 4-6) in Walhalla, S. C." Master's thesis. Western Carolina Univ., 1970.
W7290 (WCU)

Wilson, Howard McKnight The Lexington Presbytery Heritage. Verona, Va.: McClure, 1971. The Upper Shenandoah Valley is included in the Lexington Presbytery.
W7300 (BC)

The Lexington Presbytery Heritage; the Presbytery of Lexington and Its Churches in the Synod of Virginia, Presbyterian Church in the United States. Verona, Va.: McClure Press, 1971.
W7310

The Tinkling Spring, Headwater of Freedom: A Study of the Church and Her People, 1732-1952. Fisherville, Va.: Tinkling Spring and Hermitage Presbyterian Churches, 1954.
W7320 (ASU BC)

Wilson, John E. "The Allegheny-Monongahela Flood Control Program and Its Benefits to Metropolitan Pittsburgh." Master's thesis. Univ. of Pittsburgh, 1952.
W7330

Wilson, John M. Ground Water Resources and Geology of Cumberland County, Tennessee. Nashville: Tennessee Department of Conservation Division of Water Resources, 1965.
W7340 (LMC)

Summary of Ground Water Data for Tennessee, Through May 1971. Publication no. 6. n.p.: State of Tennessee Department of Conservation Division of Water Resources, 1970.
W7350 (LMC)

Wilson, L. Craig School-community Improvement, a Report of the Greenbrier County Program. New York: World Book Co., 1959.
W7360 (ASU WCU)

Wilson, Leon This Boy Cody. Illustrated by Ursula Koering. New York: Watts, 1950.
W7370 (ASU ETSU)

This Boy Cody and His Friends. Illustrated by Ursula Koering. New York: F. Watts, 1952.
W7380 (ASU ETSU)

Wilson, Louis Round County Library Service in the South. Chicago: Univ. of Chicago Press, 1935.
W7390 (BC)

Wilson, Mary Allison "The Symphony Orchestra of Kingsport, Tennessee." Master's thesis. East Tennessee State Univ., 1964.
W7400 (ETSU)

Wilson, Maud The A. K. Wilson Family: Abraham Key Wilson and Mary Jane Wilson, Their Descendants and Their Ancestors. n.p.: OSU Cooperative Association, 1961.
W7410 (BC)

Wilson, Minter Towther The Happy Years. Boston: Christopher Pub. House, 1954. Autobiographical sketches from Judge Wilson's mountain childhood.
W7420

Wilson, Neill Compton The Nine Brides and Granny Hite. New York: Morrow, 1952. Fourteen stories featuring Granny Hite's expert meddling.
W7430 (ASU BC)

Wilson, Robert O. "A Survey of Co-curricular Programs in the Five High Schools of Carter County, Tennessee." Master's thesis. East Tennessee State College, 1957.
W7440 (ETSU)

Wilson, Ross H. "A Study of Secondary Schools of Morgan County." Master's thesis. Univ. of Tennessee, 1941.
W7450

Wilson, Samuel M. Virginia Revolutionary Land Bounty Warrants. Baltimore: Southern Book Co., 1953.
W7460

Wilson, Samuel MacKay comp. Catalogue of Revolutionary Soldiers and Sailors of the Commonwealth of Va.; to Whom Land Bounty Warrants were Granted. . . . Baltimore: Southern Elk Co., 1953.
W7470 (BC)

Catalogue of Revolutionary Soldiers and Sailors of the Commonwealth of Virginia to Whom Land Bounty Warrants Were Granted by Virginia for Military Services in the War for Independence. Compiled from official records in the Kentucky State Land Office at Frankfort, Kentucky. 1913. Reprint. Baltimore: Genealogical Pub. Co., 1967.
W7480 (ASU)

Wilson, Samuel Tyndale A Century of Maryville College, 1819-1919, a Story of Altruism. Maryville, Tenn.: Directors of Maryville College, 1916.
W7490 (ASU BC)

Chronicles of Maryville College: A Story of Altruism. Maryville, Tenn.: Directors of Maryville College, 1935.
W7500 (ASU ETSU BC)

Isaac Anderson, Founder and First President of Maryville College. Maryville, Tenn.: Kindred of Dr. Anderson, 1932.
W7510 (BC)

The Southern Mountaineers. New York: Presbyterian Home Missions, Literature Department, 1906. An important early work which helped to focus attention on social conditions and the mountain culture.
W7520 (ASU ETSU MHC WWC BC)

The Southern Mountaineers. 4th ed. New York: Presbyterian Home Missions, Literature Department, 1914.
W7530 (ASU LMC)

Wilson, Vesta M. "Diagnosis and Remediation of Reading and Personality Problems of a Second Level First Grade at Valley Pike School, Sullivan County, Tennessee." Master's thesis. East Tennessee State College, 1961.
W7540

Wimberly, C. F. The Lost Trail: A Story of the Kentucky Mountains. Louisville: Pentecostal Pub. Co., n.d.
W7550 (BC)

Wimberly, Lowry Charles Folklore in the English and Scottish Ballads. 1928. Reprint. New York: Dover Publications, 1965.
W7560 (ASU FC)

Wimer, David C. Derrick, Bruce B. Soil Survey of Cambria County, Pennsylvania. Washington: U. S. Department of Agriculture, Bureau of Soils, 1917.
D1880

Winchester-Frederick County Civil War Centennial Commission Civil War Battles in Winchester and Frederick County, Virginia, 1861-1865. Boyce, Va.: Carr Pub. Co., 1960.
W7570 (BC ASU LMC)

Winchester-Frederick County Historical Society Diaries, Letters and Recollections of the War Between the States. Winchester, Va.: The Society, n.d.
W7580

Gravestone Inscriptions: From 61 Graveyards in Frederick County and the Counties That Were Once a Part of Frederick County and Includes the Inscriptions from the "Old Lutheran and German Reform Graves" in Mt. Hebron Cemetery. Boyce, Va.: Carr Pub. Co., 1960
W7590 (ASU)

2200 Gravestone Inscriptions from Winchester and Frederick County, Virginia (Death Dates Range from 1700's to Early 1900's). Indexed. Boyce, Va.: Carr Pub. Co., 1960.
W7600 (ASU)

Winchester, Va., Fire Department Souvenir. Winchester, Va.: Enterprise Print. Co., 1897.
W7610 (ASU)

Winchester, Va., Historical Society Annual Papers. vol. 1- . 1931-. Winchester, Va.: The Society, annual.
W7620 (ASU)

Winchester, Va., Ordinances, etc. The Code of the City of Winchester, Virginia, 1947. The Charter of the City and the General Ordinances of the City, Enacted as a Whole May 6, 1947, Effective May 6, 1947. Published by order of the Common Council. Charlottesville, Va.: Michie City Pubs. Co., 1947.
W7630 (ASU)

Wind vol. 1- . Spring, 1971-. Pikeville, Ky.: n.p., 3 times a year.
W7640 (BC)

Windham, Gerald O. "Socio-economic Status and Formal Social Participation of Rural Migrant Families in Pittsburgh." Ph. D. Diss. Pennsylvania State Univ., 1960.
W7650

Windy Cove Church, Millboro Springs, Va. A History of Windy Cove Church, Millboro Springs, Virginia, 1929-1949. Including a biography of Rev. Alexander Craighead, the founder of Windy Cove Church in the year 1749. Millboro Springs, Va.: The congregation, 1949.
W7660 (ASU)

Wine, Cecil J. Michael Miller Family. Radford, Va.: Commonwealth Press, 1964.
W7670

Wine, John M. Christian Wine Family. n.p.: n.p., 1960.
W7690

Wine, Jacob David The Wine Family in America, Section 3. Boyce, Va.: Carr Pub. Co., 1961.
W7680

Wine, John M. Christian Wine Family. n.p.: n.p., 1960.
W7690

Wing, Fred Edward "James Still: An Inquiry into the Intrinsic Value of the Works of a Regional Writer." Ed. D. Diss. Colorado State College, 1969. James Still's RIVER OF EARTH is considered one of the finest and most representative Appalachian novels ever published.
W7700 (LMC)

Winger, Sarah Elizabeth B. "The Genesis of TVA." Ph. D. Diss. Univ. of Wisconsin, 1959.
W7710

Winger, Virginia Camblos, Ruth Shopping Round the Mountains. Asheville: The authors, 1972.
C380

Wingfield, Marshall Franklin County, Virginia, a History. Berryville, Va.: Chesapeake Book Co., 1964.
W7720 (ASU BC FC)

Wingfield, Marshall
Hills of Home. Memphis, Tenn.: A R. Taylor Co., 1938.
W7730
Marriage Bonds of Franklin County, Virginia, 1786-1858, Transcribed from the Original Records. Memphis: West Tennessee Historical Society, 1939.
W7740 (ASU BC)
Pioneer Families of Franklin County, Virginia. Berryville, Va.: Chesapeake Book Co., 1964.
W7750 (ASU BC FC)

Wink, Anna T. Housing Conditions in Rural Pennsylvania. Univ. Park: Pa. Agricultural Experiment Station, 1945. Includes data from Pennsylvania's Appalachian Counties.
W7760

Winkle, Karl Franklin "An Occupational Survey of Selected Industries in the Kingsport Area of Sullivan County, Tennessee." Master's thesis. East Tennessee State Univ., 1967.
W7770 (ETSU)

Winser, Justin The Westward Movement. Boston: Houghton, Mifflin and Co., 1897. Includes commentary on the Appalachian frontier.
W7790 (BC)

Winslow, Anne The Frontier Nursing Service. Washington, D. C.: Committee on the Costs of Medical Care, 1932. A study of Eastern Kentucky's famed Frontier Nursing Service.
W7780 (BC)

Winstanley pseud. see **Coleman, Thaddeus**

Winston, Nat Taylor All Good Times. Berea, Ky.: The Council of the Southern Mountains, n.d.
W7800 (BC)
Hit Haint the Fish. Kingsport, Tenn.: Southern Pub., 1949.
W7810 (LMC BC)

Winston, R. A. Deeter, Earl B. Soil Survey of Mercer County, Pennsylvania. Washington: U. S. Department of Agriculture, Bureau of Soils, 1919.
D1600

Winston, Robert A. Soil Survey of Tuscaloosa County, Alabama. Prepared in cooperation with Alabama. Field Operations, 1911. Washington: U. S. Department of Agriculture, Bureau of Soils, 1912.
W7820

Winston, Robert W. Andrew Johnson, Plebian and Patriot. New York: Holt, 1928.
W7830 (ASU)

Winston, Robert Watson It's a Far Cry. New York: H. Holt and Co., 1937. Autobiography.
W7840 (WCU)

Wisconsin State Historical Society Calendar of the Tennessee and King's Mountain Papers of the Draper Collection of Manuscripts. Madison, Wis.: The society, 1929.
W7850 (LMC)

Wise, Charles C., Jr. The Appalachian Center of West Virginia University. Chapel Hill, N. C.: Association of Governing Boards, 1964.
W7860

Wise, James O. Optimum Farm Organizations and Area Production Patterns for the Upper Hiwassee Watershed Area. Athens: Georgia Agricultural Experiment Station, 1969.
W7870

Wise, Jennings Cropper The Military History of the Virginia Military Institute from 1839 to 1865. With appendix, maps, and illustrations. Lynchburg, Va.: J. P. Bell Co., 1915. Includes account of the VMI cadets in the Battle of New Market.
W7880 (ASU)
Wise's Digested Index and Genealogical Guide to Bishop Meade's Old Churches, Ministers and Families of Virginia. Richmond, Va.: n.p., 1910.
W7890

Wise, John Sergeant Diomed: The Life, Travels, and Observations of a Dog. Illustrated by J. Linton Chapman. Boston: Lamson, Wolffe and Co., 1897.
W7900 (ASU)
The End of an Era. Boston: Houghton, Mifflin and Co., 1899.
W7910 (BC)

With the Colors from Hawkins County: 1917-1918-1919. Pressmen's Home: Dunwoody and Reed, 1920.
W7920

Witham, Rose Adelaide ed. English and Scottish Popular Ballads. n.p.: Houghton, 1909. These ballads are still sung in the Southern Mountains.
W7930 (BC)

Withers, Alexander Scott Chronicles of Border Warfare; or, A History of the Settlement by the Whites, of Northwestern Va., and . . . . 1st ed. Clarksburg, Va.: Published by Joseph Israel, 1831.
W7940 (BC)
Chronicles of Border Warfare; or, A History of the Settlement by the Whites, of Northwestern Virginia, and of the Indian Wars and Massacres, in That Section of the State. With reflections, anecdotes. A new ed., edited and annotated by R. G. Thwaites. With the addition of a memoir of the author and several illustrative notes by L. C. Draper. Cincinnati: R. Clarke Co., 1895.
W7950 (ASU ETSU WCU BC)
Chronicles of Border Warfare: or, A History of the Settlement by the Whites, of Northwestern Virginia, and of the Indian Wars and Massacres, in That Section of the State. With reflections, anecdotes. A new ed., edited and annotated by R. G. Thwaites. With the addition of a memoir of the author and several illustrative notes by L. C. Draper. 1895. Reprint. Parsons, W. Va.: McClain Print. Co., 1961.
W7960 (ASU UNCA)

Withington, Alfreda Bosworth Mine Eyes Have Seen: A Woman Doctor's Saga. New York: Dutton, 1941. Biography of a woman doctor in the Southern Mountains.
W7970 (WWC BC)

Withoft, Mabel Swartz Oak and Laurel. Nashville: Sunday School Board of the Southern Baptist Convention, 1923.
W7980 (ASU BC)

Witzel, William T. "The Resources and Industries of the New River Drainage Basin in West Virginia." Master's thesis. Univ. of Tennessee, 1957.
W7990

Woestemeyer, Ina Faye see also **Van Noppen, Ina Faye Woestemeyer**

Woestemeyer, Ina Faye ed. The Westward Movement: A Book of Readings on Our Changing Frontiers. With the editorial collaboration of J. Montgomery Gambrill. New York: Appleton-Century Co., 1939.
W8000 (ASU)

Wofford, Robie Tip of the Toe. Illustrated by Gin Hughey. Atlanta: The author, 1969.
W8010 (LMC)

Wohlford, Marguerite "A Survey of Reading Achievement of First Grade Pupils in Unicoi County." Master's thesis. East Tennessee State College, 1962.
W8020 (ETSU)

Wolcott, Sibyl D. Crest on the Wave. Lexington, Ky.: The author, 1889.
W8030 (BC)

Wolfe Co., Ky., Womans' Club Champion Early and Modern History of Wolfe County. Campton, Ky.: n.p., 1958.
W8035 (ASU BC)

Wolfe, Julia Elizabeth Thomas Wolfe's Letters to His Mother. New York: Charles Scribner's Sons, 1943.
W8040 (ASU WCU)

Wolfe, Thomas The Correspondence of Thomas Wolfe and Homer Andrew Watt. Edited by Oscar Cargill and Thomas Clark Pollock. New York: New York Univ. Press, 1954.
W8050 (UNCA ASU BC)
The Face of a Nation: Poetical Passages from the Writings of Thomas Wolfe. Illustrated by Edward Shenton. New York: Literary Guild of American, n.d.
W8060 (ASU WCU BC ETSU)
From Death to Morning. New York: C. Scribner's Sons, 1935.
W8070 (ASU WCU LMC MHC BC UNCA ETSU)
The Hills Beyond. New York: Harper and Brothers, 1935.
W8080 (WWC)
The Hills Beyond. With a note on Thomas Wolfe by Edward C. Aswell. 1st ed. New York: Harper and Brothers, 1941.
W8090 (ASU WCU MHC ETSU BC)
The Hills Beyond. New York: Lion Books, 1955.
W8100 (UNCA ASU)
Letters. Collected and edited, with an introd. and explanatory text, by Elizabeth Nowell. New York: Scribner, 1956.
W8110 (UNCA)
The Letters of Thomas Wolfe. Collected and edited, with an introduction and explanatory text, by Elizabeth Nowell. New York: C. Scribner's Sons, 1956.
W8120 (ASU WCU ETSU BC)
The Letters of Thomas Wolfe to His Mother. Newly edited from the original manuscripts by Clarence Hugh Holman and Sue Field Ross. Chapel Hill: Univ. of North Carolina Press, 1968.
W8130 (UNCA ASU WCU ETSU BC)
Look Homeward, Angel; a Story of the Buried Life. New York: C. Scribner's Sons, 1929.
W8140 (MHC BC UNCA)
Look Homeward, Angel: A Story of the Buried Life. New York: Modern Library, 1929.
W8150 (WWC)
Look Homeward, Angel: A Story of the Buried Life. Modern Library of the World's Best Books. New York: Modern Library, 1934.
W8160 (WCU)
Look Homeward, Angel: A Story of the Buried Life. Illustrated by Douglas W. Gorsline. With an introduction by Maxwell E. Perkins. Modern Standard Authors. New York: Scribner, 1952.
W8170 (WCU)
Look Homeward, Angel: A Story of the Buried Life. With an introduction by Maxwell E. Perkins. 1929. Reprint. New York: Scribner's, 1957.
W8180 (LMC WCU MHC ETSU)
The Lost Boy. New York: Harper and Row, 1965.
W8190 (BC)
The Lost World of Thomas Wolfe. Prepared by Myra Champion. Selections from Look Homeward, Angel. Asheville, N. C.: Thomas Wolfe Memorial, 1970.
W8200 (ASU WCU ETSU BC UNCA)
Mannerhouse, a Play in a Prologue and Three Acts. New York: Harper, 1948.
W8210 (ASU WCU ETSU BC)
The Mountains: A Play in One Act. The Mountains: A Drama in Three Acts and a Prologue. Edited, with an introduction, by Pat M. Ryan. Chapel Hill: Univ. of North Carolina Press, 1970.
W8220 (ASU WCU ETSU LMC MHC BC UNCA)
The Notebooks of Thomas Wolfe. Edited by Richard S. Kennedy and Paschal Reeves. 2 vols. Chapel Hill: Univ. of North Carolina Press, 1970.
W8230 (UNCA BC WCU ETSU ASU)
Of Time and the River: A Legend of Man's Hunger in His Youth. New York: C. Scribner's Sons, 1935.
W8240 (ASU WCU BC UNCA WWC)
Of Time and the River: A Legend of Man's Hunger in His Youth. Garden City, N. Y.: Sun Dial Press, 1944.
W8250 (ETSU)
The Portable Thomas Wolfe. Edited by Maxwell David Geismar. Viking Portable Library. New York: Viking Press, 1946.
W8260 (WCU ETSU)
Short Novels. Edited, with an introduction and notes, by C. Hugh Holman. New York: Scribner, 1961.
W8270 (UNCA ASU WCU WWC ETSU)
A Stone, a Leaf, a Door: Poems. Selected and arranged in verse by John S. Barnes. 1969. Reprint. New York: C. Scribner's Sons, 1971.
W8280 (ETSU)

Wolfe, Thomas
A Stone, a Leaf, a Door: Poems by Thomas Wolfe. Selected and arranged in verse by John S. Barnes. With a foreword by Louis Untermeyer. New York: C. Scribner's
W8290 (UNCA ASU WCU BC)
The Story of a Novel. New York: C. Scribner's Sons, 1936.
W8300 (ASU WCU ETSU BC UNCA)
The Thomas Wolfe Reader. Edited, with an introduction and notes, by C. Hugh Holman. New York: Scribner, 1962.
W8310 (ASU WCU WWC ETSU BC UNCA)
Thomas Wolfe's Letters to His Mother, Julia Elizabeth Wolfe. Edited with an introduction by John Sakally Terry. New York: C. Scribner's Sons, 1943.
W8320 (UNCA ASU BC)
Thomas Wolfe's Purdue Speech: Writing and Living. Edited from the dictated and rev. typescript, with an introduction and notes, by William Braswell and Leslie A. Field. West Lafayette, Ind.: Purdue Univ. Studies, 1964.
W8330 (ASU ETSU BC UNCA)
To Rupert Brooke. Paris: Lecram Press for R. J. Picard, 1948.
W8340 (ASU)
The Web and the Rock. New York: Harper and Brothers, 1939.
W8350 (UNCA ASU WCU BC)
The Web and the Rock. New York: Sun Dial, 1940.
W8360 (WWC ETSU)
A Western Journal: A Daily Log of the Great Parks Trip, June 20-July 2, 1928. Pittsburgh: Univ. of Pittsburgh Press, 1951.
W8370 (UNCA ASU WCU ETSU BC)
The Years of Wandering in Many Lands and Cities. New York: S. S. Boesen, 1949.
W8380 (ASU BC)
You Can't Go Home Again. New York: Harper and Brothers, 1940.
W8390 (ASU WWC WCU ETSU BC UNCA)
The Correspondence of Thomas Wolfe and Homer Andrew Watt. Edited by Oscar Cargill and Thomas Clark Pollock. New York: New York Univ. Press, 1954.
W8400 (ASU WCU ETSU)

Wolfe, Thomas Clayton see **Wolfe, Thomas**

Wolverton, John B., Jr. "A Study in Student Perceptions of the Person(s) Who Is Performing the Counseling Function at Watauga High School." Master's thesis. Appalachian State Univ., 1971.
W8420 (ASU)

Womack, James J. The Civil War Diary of Capt. J. J. Womack. n.p.: n.p., n.d.
W8430

Womack, John Walter, Jr. ed. Hale, William Thomas Early History of Warren County. McMinnville, Tenn.: Standard Print. Co., 1930.
H480 (ASU BC ETSU)

Womack, Walter McMinnville at a Milestone, 1810-1960. A Momento of the Sesquicentennial Year of McMinnville, Tennessee, 1960, 1958. McMinnville, Tenn.: Standard Pub. Co., 1960.
W8440 (ASU ETSU BC)

Womble, Walter L. Love in the Mists. Raleigh, N. C.: Edwards and Broughton, 1892. A very interesting story about the revenuers and the moonshiners.
W8450

Women's Society of Christian Service Cooking Favorites of Brucetown. Brucetown, Va.: The service, n.d.
W8460 (ASU)

Wonnacott, Ronald Johnston Manuf. Cost and the Comp. Advantage of U. S. Regions. Minneapolis: Univ. of Minn., 1963.
W8470

Wonser, C. H. Shearin, A. E. Soil Survey, Pickens County, South Carolina. Washington: U. S. Department of Agriculture, Bureau of Plant Industry, Soils, and Agricultural Engineering, 1943.
S2570

Wood, Clement The Life of a Man: A Biography of John R. Brinkley. Kansas City: Goshorn Pub. Co., 1934.
W8480 (ASU)

Wood, Frances Elizabeth Great Smoky Mountains, Everglades, Mammoth Cave: With Hot Springs, Platt, Virgin Islands, Abraham Lincoln Birthplace. Our National Parks. Chicago: Follett Pub. Co., 1964.
W8490 (ETSU BC)

Wood, George W. Report of Mr. Wood's Visit to the Choctaw and Cherokee Missions, 1855. Boston: T. R. Marvin, 1855.
W8500

Wood, Gordon H., Jr. Systematic Jointing in Western Part of Anthracite Region of Eastern Pennsylvania. Bulletin, 1271-D. Contributions to General Geology. Washington: U. S. Geological Survey, 1969.
W8510

Wood, Gordon Reid A List of Words from Tennessee. Report of a recent project of collecting by Frederick G. Cassidy. The secretary's report. American Dialect Society, Pub. no. 29. University: Univ. of Alabama Press, 1958.
W8520 (ASU)
Vocabulary Change; a Study of Variation in Regional Words in Eight of the Southern States. Carbondale: Southern Illinois Univ. Press, 1971.
W8530 (BC)

Wood, Harriette The Kentucky Mountaineer: A Study of Four Counties in Southeastern Kentucky. Chapel Hill: U. N. C., 1930.
W8540
"The Kentucky Mountaineer: A Study of Four Counties in Southeastern Kentucky." Microfilm. Master's thesis. Univ. of North Carolina, 1930.
W8550 (ASU)
The Need for Guidance Programs in Privately Supported Mountain Schools. Richmond: Southern Woman's Educational Alliance, 1933.
W8560 (BC)

Wood, James Thomas comp. Some of Our Families Ancestors and the Genealogy of Some of Their Descendants. Roanoke, Va.: n.p., n.d.
W8570

Wood, Joe B. "The Determination of a Prediction Equation for Algebra I at Elizabethton High School Utilizing Selected Variables." Master's thesis. East Tennessee State Univ., 1967.
W8580 (ETSU)

Wood, Katherine Hill Laney, Francis Baker Bibliography of North Carolina Geology, Mineralogy, and Geography, with a List of Maps. Raleigh: E. M. Uzzell and Co., 1909.
L390 (ASU LMC WWC ETSU)

Wood, Mayme Parrott Drifting Down Holston River Way, 1756-1966. Marysville, Tenn.: n.p., 1966.
W8590 (BC)
Hitch Hiking Along the Holston River from 1792-1962. Gatlinburg, Tenn.: n.p., 1964.
W8600
Shunem Church and Cemetery Speak: A Living Memorial to Those Who Sleep Here, 1824-1965. Gatlinburg: Brazos, 1965.
W8610

Wood, Ralph V. Wood, Virginia S. 1805 Georgia Land Lottery. Cambridge, Mass.: Greenewood Press, 1964.
W8670 (ASU BC)

Wood, Robert E. Heroes of the War of 1812 for Whom Kentucky Counties are Named. n.p.: n.p., n.d.
W8620

Wood, Robert S. Pleasure Packing, How to Backpack in Comfort. n.p.: n.p., n.d.
W8630

Wood, Rosa Aubrey Banjo and Pistols, a Tale of the Blue Ridge. Illustrated by Maginel Wright Barney. New York: R. M. McBride and Co., 1929.
W8640 (ASU BC)

Wood, Violet So Sure of Life. New York: Friendship Press, 1950.
W8650 (BC)
So Sure of Life. Illustrated by Oscar Grimley. New York: Friendship Press, 1951.
W8660 (LMC)

Wood, Virginia S. 1805 Georgia Land Lottery. Cambridge, Mass.: Greenewood Press, 1964.
W8670 (ASU BC)

Wood, Warren Representative Authors of West Virginia. Ravenswood, W. Va.: Worth While Book Co., 1926.
W8680

Wood, William W. Culture and Personality Aspects of the Pentecostal Holiness Religion. The Hague: Mouton, 1965.
W8690 (ASU)

Woodall, Thomas E. Design for Action, Community Problem Solving in Disadvantaged Communities. W. Va. Univ.: n.p., 1969.
W8700

Woodard, Clement Manly A Word-List from Virginia and North Carolina. Publication, no. 6. Greensboro, N. C.: American Dialect Society, 1946.
W8710 (ASU)

Woodard, Thomas H. Summary of Data on Temperature of Streams in North Carolina, 1943-67: Quality of Surface Waters of North Carolina. U. S. Geological Survey Water-supply Paper, no. 1895-A. Washington: Govt. Print. Off., 1970.
W8720 (LMC)

Woodbridge, Hensley C. Jesse and Jane Stuart: A Bibliography. Murray, Ky.: Murray State Univ., 1969.
W8730

Woodbridge, Hensley Charles Jesse Stuart: A Bibliography. With essays by Roland Carter and others. Harrogate, Tenn.: Lincoln Memorial Univ. Press, 1960.
W8740 (WCU BC)
Jesse Stuart; a Bibliography for May, 1960-May, 1965. "Reprinted from The Register of The Ky. Hist. Society, vol. 63, no. 4, October, 1965." n.p.: n.p., 1965.
W8750 (BC)

Woodford, Bessie Van Dyke Somebody, a Play in 4 Acts. New York: Fortuny's, 1937.
W8760 (BC)

Woodhouse, Betty Frost "Legislative Control of the Tennessee Valley Authority." Master's thesis. Louisiana State Univ., 1945.
W8770

Woodmason, Charles The Carolina Backcountry on the Eve of the Revolution: The Journal and Other Writings of Charles Woodmason, Anglican Itinerant. Edited with an introduction by Richard J. Hooker. Published for the Institute of Early American History and Culture at Williamsburg, Va. Chapel Hill: Univ. of North Carolina Press, 1953.
W8780 (ASU LMC BC)

Woodruff, W. W. and others Power Transmission. In the Standard Handbook for Electrical Engineers. 9th ed. New York: McGraw-Hill Book Co., 1957.
W8790

Woods, Edgar Albemarle County in Virginia: Giving Some Account of What It Was by Nature, of What It Was Made by Man, and of Some of the Men Who Made It. 1901. Reprint. Bridgewater, Va.: C. J. Carrier, 1964.
W8800
History of Albemarle County, Virginia Giving Some Account of What It Was by Nature, and What It Was Made by Man and Some of the Men Who Made It. Harrisonburg, Va.: C. J. Carrier, 1972.
W8810
One Branch of the Woodses. Charlottesville, Va.: Prout, the Printer, 1894.
W8820

Woods, Rev. Neander M. The Woods-McAfee Memorial containing an account of John Woods and James McAfee of Ireland and Their Descendants in America. Louisville, Ky.: Courier Journal Job Print. Co., 1905.
W8830

Woods, Robert E. Heroes of the War of 1812 for Whom Kentucky Counties are Named. n.p.: n.p., n.d. Address . . . at the state meeting of the Daughters of 1812 . . . Louisville, Ky.
W8840 (BC)

Woodside, Robert Edward "The Educational Development of Avery County." Master's thesis. Appalachian State Teachers College, 1952.
W8850 (ASU)

Woodson, Carter Godwin Freedom and Slavery in Appalachian America. Huntington, W. Va.: Appalachian Movement Press, 1973.
W8860

Woodson, Henry Morton comp. Historical Genealogy of the Woodsons and Their Connections. Columbia, Mo.: E. W. Stephens Pub. Co., 1915.
W8870

Woodson, Marshall S. "An Economic Survey of Oconee County." Master's thesis. Univ. of South Carolina, 1923.
W8880

Woodsworth, Robert Bell comp. Descendants of Robert and John Poage. Genealogy based on the manuscript collection of Professor Andrew Woods Williamson, Henry Marlyn Williamson and John Guy Bishop, Vol. 2. Staunton, Va.: McClure Print. Co., 1954.
W8890

Woodward, Grace Steele The Cherokees. Civilization of the American Indian Series, 65. Norman: Univ. of Oklahoma Press, 1963.
W8900 (ASU WCU LMC ETSU UNCA BC)

The Cherokees. 1963. Reprint. Norman: Univ. of Oklahoma Press, 1969.
W8910 (ASU LMC)

Woodward, Herbert P. McCue, John Bruce Limestones of West Virginia. Parkersburg, W. Va.: Scholl Print. Co., 1939.
M960 (ASU ETSU)

Woodward, Herbert Preston Cambrian System of West Virginia. With Comments on Older Rocks and Igneous Dikes. Reports, vol. 20. Morgantown: West Virginia Geological Survey, 1949.
W8920 (ETSU)

Devonian System of West Virginia. Reports, vol. 15. Morgantown: West Virginia Geological Survey, 1943.
W8930 (ETSU)

Ordovician System of West Virginia. Reports, vol. 21. Morgantown: West Virginia Geological Survey, 1951.
W8940 (ETSU)

Outline of the Geology and Mineral Resources of Russell County, Virginia. Bulletin, 49, County Series, no. 2. University: Virginia Geological Survey, 1938.
W8950 (ETSU)

Woodward, Herbert Preston ed. A Symposium on the Sandhill Deep Well, Wood County, West Virginia. Including papers presented at the joint meeting of the Appalachian Geological Society and Pittsburgh Geological Society, at Blackwater Falls Lodge, Tucker County, West Virginia, October 11-12, 1956. Paul H. Price and Ralph L. Miller, cochairmen. Report of Investigations, no. 18. Morgantown: West Virginia Geological Survey, 1959.
W8960 (ETSU)

Woodward, J. Fletch Fletch Woodward, His Fights with Those Bad, Bad Town Boys. McMinnville: n.p., 1878.
W8970

Woodworth, Robert Bell A History of the Presbytery of Winchester (Synod of Virginia): Its Rise and Growth, Ecclesiastical Relations, Institutions, Agencies, Churches and Ministers, 1719-1945. Based on official documents. Staunton, Va.: McClure Print. Co., 1947.
W8980 (ASU BC)

Woodworth, Robert Bell and others A History of the Presbyterian Church in Winchester, Virginia, 1780-1949. Based on official Documents. Winchester, Va.: Pifer Print. Co., 1950.
W8990 (BC)

Woody, Robert H. ed. Crittenden, Charles Christopher ed. 100 Years, 100 Men: 1871-1971. Raleigh, N. C.: Edwards and Broughton, 1971.
C8830 (ASU)

Woody, Virginia "The Reading Diagnosis and Remediation of Five Groups of Eighth Grade Students at John S. Battle High School in Washington County, Virginia." Master's thesis. East Tennessee State Univ., 1964.
W9000 (ETSU)

Woofter, Thomas Jackson Seven Lean Years. By T. J. Woofter, Jr. and Ellen Winston. Chapel Hill: Univ. of North Carolina Press, 1939.
W9010 (BC)

Wooldridge, J. ed. Rule, William ed. Standard History of Knoxville, Tennessee, with Full Outline of the Natural Advantages, Early Settlement, Territorial Government, Indian Troubles and General and Particular History of the City Down to the Present Time. Chicago: Lewis, 1900.
R4280

Woolqon, Constance Fenimore Rodman the Keeper: Southern Sketches. American Short Story Series, vol. 87. New York: Garrett Press, 1969.
W9060 (WCU ASU)

Woolsey, Elmo Murray Moving On. Bristol, Tenn.: n.p., 1954. Autobiographical sketch of the life of an East Tennessee lawyer.
W9020 (ASU)

Woolson, Constance Fenimore For the Major: A Novelette. New York: Harper and Brothers, 1883.
W9030 (ASU WCU ETSU BC)

Horace Chase. New York: Harper and Brothers, 1894. Partially set in Appalachia.
W9040 (ASU WCU BC)

Horace Chase. 1894. Reprint. Upper Saddle River, N. J.: Literature House, 1970. Partially set in Appalachia.
W9050 (ETSU)

Woolum, Leonard Franklin "History and Partial Evaluation of In-service Education in Harlan County, Kentucky." Ed. D. Diss. Univ. of Maryland, 1960.
W9070

Woolwine, Thomas Lee In the Valley of the Shadows. New York: Doubleday, Page and Co., 1909. A typical feud tale set in Tennessee.
W9080 (BC)

Wooten, Bobbie "A Comparative Study of the Achievement in Science of the Fifth and Sixth Grade Pupils in Bristol, Tennessee, Schools, 1953-57." Master's thesis. East Tennessee State College, 1957.
W9090 (ETSU)

Wooten, John M. comp. Scrapbook History of Polk County, Tennessee. n.p.: n.p., 1927-39. Microfilm copy at Tennessee State Library and Archives.
W9100

Wooten, John Morgan Centennial of the First Presbyterian Church, United States, in Cleveland, Tennessee, 1837-1937. Cleveland: The author, 1937.
W9110

A History of Bradley County. With the cooperation of the Tennessee Historical Commission. n.p.: Bradley County Post 81, 1949.
W9120 (ETSU)

Red Clay Council Ground, 1832-1838; Last Capital of the Cherokee Nation East of the Mississippi River. Cleveland: n.p., 1935.
W9130

Red Clay in History. Cleveland: n.p., 1935.
W9140

Wooten, Samuel R. "A History of Richmond Hill Law School." Master's thesis. Appalachian State Teachers College, Boone, 1963.
W9150

Wootton, Clara They Have Topped the Mountain. Frankfort, Ky.: Blue Grass Press, 1960.
W9160 (ASU)

Work Conference on Curriculum and Teaching in Depressed Urban Areas, 1962 Education in Depressed Areas. n.p.: Teachers College, Columbia University, 1963.
W9170

Work Projects Administration Guide to the manuscript collections in the archives of the N. C. Historical Commission. Raleigh: N. C. Historical Commission, 1942.
W9180 (LMC)

Guide to the Manuscripts in the Southern Historical Collection of the University of North Carolina. Chapel Hill: UNC Press, 1941.
W9190 (LMC)

Workshop on Methods of Working with Limited Resource Farmers Muscle Shoals, Ala.: 1972 Proceedings. Muscle Shoals, Ala.: Tennessee Valley Authority, National Fertilizer Development Center, 1972.
W9200 (BC)

Muscle Shoals, Ala.: Proceedings. n.p.: Tennessee Valley Authority, National Fertilizer Development Center, 1972.
W9210

Workshop on Problems of Chronically Depressed Areas Papers. Asheville, N. C., 1965. ("API Series," no. 19.) Raleigh: Agricultural Policy Institute, North Carolina State Univ., 1965.
W9220

Worrell, Anne Lowry Early Marriages, Wills and Some Revolutionary War Records, Botetourt County, Va. Hillsville, Va.: Carroll Pub. Co., 1958.
W9250

Early Marriages, Wills and Some Revolutionary War Records:, Botetourt County, Va. Baltimore, Md: n.p., n.d.
W9260

Our Mountain Men: Their Early Court Records in Southwest Virginia. Baltimore: Genealogical Pub. Co., 1962.
W9270 (BC)

Over the Mountain Men. Baltimore: n.p., n.d.
W9280

Worrell, Anne Lowry comp. A Brief of Wills and Marriages in Montgomery and Fincastle Counties, 1773-1831. n.p.: n.p., 1932.
W9230

A Brief of Wills and Marriages in Montgomery and Fincastle Counties, 1773-1831. 2nd ed. 1959. n.p.: n.p., 1932. Marriages are arranged alphabetically by males. Some errors due to copying and printing but a valuable guide to what records are available at the Courthouse in Christiansburg.
W9240

Worsham, John H. One of Jackson's Foot Cavalry: His Experience and What He Saw During the War, 1861-1865, Including a History of "F Company," Richmond, Va., 21st Regiment Virginia Infantry, Second Brigade, Jackson's Division, Second Corps. New York: A. N. Neale Pub. Co., 1912.
W9290 (ASU)

Worst, Edward Francis Foot-Power Loom Weaving. 2nd ed. enl. Milwaukee, Wisc.: Bruce Pub. Co., 1920.
W9300 (BC)

Foot-Power Loom Weaving. 3rd ed. enl. Milwaukee, Wisc.: The Bruce Pub. Co., 1924.
W9310 (BC)

How to Weave Linens. Milwaukee, Wisc.: The Bruce Pub. Co., 1926.
W9320 (BC)

Worthington, Paul Clayton Davis, Arthur Kyle, Jr. ed. More Traditional Ballads of Virginia: Collected with the Cooperation of Members of the Virginia Folklore Society. Chapel Hill: Univ. of North Carolina Press, 1960.
D790 (ASU FC BC LMC)

Wouk, Herman Youngblood Hawke. Garden City, N. J.: Doubleday, 1962. A novel about a young literary lion from the Southern Mountains: Appears to be roughly on the life of Thomas Wolfe.
W9330 (ASU ETSU BC)

Woulfe, Patrick ed. SLOINNANCE SAEDEAL IR SALL: Irish Names and Surnames. Collected and edited with explanatory and historical notes. 1923. Reprint. Baltimore: Genealogical Pub. Co., 1969.
W9340 (ASU)

Wray, Esther comp. Old-time Recipes from the Nu-Wray Inn, Burnsville, N. C. 3rd ed. Revised by Rush T. Wray. n.p.: n.p., n.d.
W9350 (LMC)

Wren, Christopher A Study of North Appalachian Indian Pottery. Wyoming Historical and Geological Society. Wilkes-Barre, Pa.: Yordy, 1914.
W9360 (LMC BC)

Wright, Anna M. Rose Hungry Hollow. New York: Friendship Press, 1951.
W9370 (BC)

Wright, Elizabeth C. Lichen Tufts, from the Alleghenies. New York: M. Doolady, 1860.
W9380 (BC)

Wright, Elizabeth Mary Tea Rustic Speech and Folklore. 1913. Reprint. Detroit: Gale Research Co., 1968.
W9390 (ASU)

Wright, Frank J. The Older Appalachians of the South. n.p.: Louis Ginsberg, 1932.
W9400

Wright, Harold Bell The Shepherd of the Hills. 1907. Reprint. New York: Grosset and Dunlap, 1961.
W9410 (ASU)

Wright, James B. Great Smoky Mountains National Park: Statement of Jas. B. Wright. Elicited by the Park Investigation Committee. Nashville: The author, 1929.
W9420 (LMC)

Wright, Jane Garland "A Study of the Mathematics Background of 2250 Dropouts from Tennessee High Schools, 1965-1966." Master's thesis. East Tennessee State Univ., 1966.
W9430 (ETSU)

Wright, Junius P. "The Extracurricular Activities of Teachers of Greenville County, South Carolina." Master's thesis. Furman Univ., 1952.
W9440

Wright, Katherine O. Christmas at Thunder Gap. New York: Arrowhead Books, 1954. Stereotypical mountain fiction.
W9450 (BC)

Wright, Louis B. ed. Strachey, William The History of Travel Into Virginia Britania (1612). London: Hakluyt Society, 1953.
S7730 (ASU)

Wright, Louis Booker Culture on the Moving Frontier. Harper Torchbooks. The Academy Library, TB 1053. New York: Harper, 1961.
W9460 (ASU)

Wright, Lyle H. American Fiction, 1774-1850: A . . . Bibliography. Rev. ed. San Marino, Calif.: Huntington Library, 1948.
W9470 (BC)

Wright, Marcus Joseph Tennessee in the War, 1861-1865: List of Military Organizations and Officers from Tennessee (Confederate and Union). New York: A. Lee Pub. Co., 1908.
W9480 (BC)

William Blount, 1749-1800. Washington: E. J. Gray, 1884.
W9490 (ETSU)

Wright, Muriel Hazel Springplace: Moravian Mission and the War Family of the Cherokee Nation. From the genealogical notes of Miss Clara Alice Ward and other sources. Guthrie, Okla.: Co-operative Pub. Co., 1940.
W9500 (MHC)

Wright, Richardson Little Hawkers and Walkers in Early America: Strolling Peddlers, Preachers, Lawyers, Doctors, Players, and Others, from the Beginning to the Civil War. By Richardson Wright . . . with 68 illustrations from mold sources. Philadelphia: J. B. Lippincott Co., 1927.
W9510

Hawkers and Walkers in Early America: Strolling Peddlers, Preachers, Lawyers, Doctors, Players and Others, from the Beginning to the Civil War. 1927. Reprint. American Classics. New York: F. Ungar Pub. Co., 1965.
W9520 (ASU)

Wright, Wade H. History of the Georgia Power Company; 1855-1956. Atlanta: Georgia Power Co., 1957.
W9530 (BC)

Wright, Watkins Eppes Home to the Hills. New York: Arcadia House, 1944.
W9540

Home to the Hills. New York: Arcadia House, 1944.
W9550

Wright, William Troy Devil John Wright of the Cumberlands. Pounds, Va.: W. T. Wright, 1932.
W9560 (BC)

Writers' Program, Kentucky In the Land of Breathitt. American Guide Series, 1941. Reprint. Northport, N. Y.: Bacon, Percy & Daggett, 1964.
W9570 (ASU)

In the Land of Breathitt. Compiled by Workers of the Writers' Program of the Work Projects Administration in the State of Ky. Northport, N. Y.: Bacon, Percy & Daggett, 1941.
W9580 (BC)

Kentucky: A Guide to the Bluegrass State. American Guide Series, 1939. Reprint. New York: Hastings House, 1947.
W9590 (ASU LMC)

Writers' Program, North Carolina Bundle of Troubles, and Other Tarheel Tales. Edited by W. C. Hendricks, illustrated by Hilda Ogburn. Publications. Durham, N. C.: Duke Univ. Press, 1943.
W9600 (WWC ASU LMC)

How They Began — The Story of North Carolina County, Town, and Other Place Names. Sponsored by North Carolina Department of Conservation and Development. New York: Harlan Pubs., 1941.
W9610 (ASU)

North Carolina, a Guide to the Old North State. American Guide Series. Chapel Hill: Univ. of North Carolina Press, 1939.
W9620 (ASU)

The North Carolina Guide. Edited by Blackwell P. Robinson. Chapel Hill: Univ. of North Carolina Press, 1955.
W9630 (ASU)

Writers' Program, South Carolina South Carolina Folk Tales: Stories of Animals and Supernatural Beings. Univ. of South Carolina Bulletin. Columbia: South Carolina Educational Association, 1941. Scant mention of counties.
W9640 (LMC)

South Carolina: A Guide to the Palmetto State. American Guide Series. New York: Oxford Univ. Press, 1941.
W9650 (ASU BC)

Writers' Program, Tennessee God Bless the Devil. Chapel Hill: The Univ. of North Carolina Press, 1940.
W9660 (BC)

Tennessee, a Guide to the State. New York: Viking Press, 1939.
W9670 (ASU)

Tennessee: A Guide to the State. American Guide Series. New York: Hastings House, 1949.
W9680 (ASU LMC)

Writers' Program, Virginia Roanoke, Story of County and City. Sponsored by the School Board of Roanoke City and the School Board of Roanoke County. American Guide Series. Roanoke, Va.: Stone Print. and Manufacturing Co., 1941.
W9690 (ASU BC)

Virginia: A Guide to the Old Dominion. New York: Oxford Univ. Press, 1964.
W9700 (BC)

Virginia: A Guide to the Old Dominion. American Guide Series, 1940. Reprint. New York: Oxford Univ. Press, 1964.
W9710 (ASU)

Virginia: The Old Dominion in Pictures. New York: Fleming Pub. Co., 1941.
W9720 (BC)

Writers' Program, West Virginia The Bulltown Country. Folk Studies, no. 10. Charleston, W. Va.: The program, 1940.
W9730 (ASU BC)

Plant Life of Braxton County, Number 8 Plant Ecology. Charleston, W. Va.: The program, 1940.
W9740 (ASU)

The Smoke Hole and Its People. Folk Studies, no. 3. Huntington: The program, n.d.
W9750 (BC)

Of Stars and Bars. Charleston, W. Va.: The program, 1940.
W9760 (BC)

West Virginia: A Guide to the Mountain State. Sponsored by the Conservation Commission of West Virginia. American Guide Series. New York: Oxford Univ. Press, 1941.
W9770 (ASU BC WWC ETSU)

Wrobel, Sylvia Isaac Shelby Kentucky's First Governor and Hero of Three Wars. Danville, Ky.: The Cumberland Press, 1974.
W9780

Wulfeck, Dorothy Ford ed. Hines, Lois Davidson Lynch Families of the Southern States. n.p.: Dorothy Ford Wulfeck privately printed, 1966.
H5590

Wust, Klaus Folk Art in Stone, Southwest Virginia. Edinburg, Va.: Shenandoah History, 1970.
W9790 (ASU ETSU BC)

Virginia Fraktur. Penmanship as Folk Art. Edinburg, Va.: Shenandoah History, 1972.
W9800

Virginia Germans. Charlottesville: Univ. Press, 1969. Well documented.
W9810

Wartburg: Dream and Reality of the New Germany in Tennessee. 31st Report, Society for the History of the Germans in Maryland. Baltimore: J. H. Furst, 1963.
W9820

Wyant, Edwards The Effects of Migration of the Labor Force. W. Va. Univ.: n.p., 1966.
W9830

Wyatt, Lucile Rebecca Douglass Wyatt Family Records. Richmond, Va.: Dietz Press, 1957.
W9840

Wyatt, Pearl Spitzer Wyatt Family. Richmond, Va.: n.p., 1962.
W9850

Wylie, John Cook ed. Preliminary Checklist for Abingdon, 1807-1876. Virginia Imprint Series no. 1. Richmond, Va.: State Library, 1946.
W9860

Wyman, Loraine comp. Twenty Kentucky Mountain Songs. The melodies collected and piano accompaniments added by Howard Brockway. Boston: Oliver Ditson Co., 1920.
W9880 (ASU BC)

Wyman, Loraine ed. Lonesome Tune, Folk Songs from the Kentucky Mountains. Pianoforte accompaniment by Howard Brockway. New York: H. W. Gray Co., 1916.
W9870 (ASU BC)

Wyoming County Advisory Committee for Library Service Wyoming County on the Alert: A Socio-Economic Survey by Wyoming County Advisory Committee for Library Service and West Virginia Library Commission. Charleston: The service, 1964.
W9890

Wysor, Rufus Johnson Boyhood Days in Southwest Virginia. New York: Vantage Press, 1961.
W9900 (BC)

Yadkin County (North Carolina) Record Book Yadkinville: James Williams, 1939.
Y10

Yancey County Teacher Training Department History and Geography of Yancey County. Burnsville: Edwards Print. Co., 1930.
Y20

Yancey, Rosa Faulkner Lynchburg and Its Neighbors. Richmond: J. W. Fergusson and Sons, 1935.
Y30 (ASU)

Yancey, William H. The Gate Is Down; A Novel of The Alabama Hills. New York: Exposition, 1956. A novel of the Alabama hills.
Y40

Yandle, Elizabeth Lewis A Critical Analysis of the Development Tasks of an Upper-elementary Class in Area 2 of the Greenville County-city School System and the Patterns of Direction Attempted for Better Group Action. Master's thesis. Appalachian State Teachers College, 1958.
Y50 (ASU)

Yates, Elizabeth Brave Interval. New York: Coward-McCann, 1952.
Y60 (BC)

Yates, Ernest K. Elder, Joe A. Soil Survey, Marion County, Tennessee. Washington: Govt. Print. Off., 1958.
E1490

Yates, Harry Orbell The Nantucket Pine Moth: A Literature Review. U. S. Forest Service Station Paper, no. 115. Asheville: Southeastern Forest Experiment Station, 1960.
Y70 (WCU)

Yates, Richard Edwin The Confederacy and Zeb Vance. Confederate Centennial Studies, no. 8. Tuscaloosa, Ala.: Confederate Pub. Co., 1958.
Y80 (ASU WCU UNCA)

Yeager, Barbara ed. Stories From the Hills Charleston, W. Va.: Morris Harvey College Publications, 1970-, annual.
S7630

Stories from the Hills, 1971. Charleston, W. Va.: Morris Harvey College Publications, 1971. A collection of choice stories from the mountains selected from items submitted to Morris Harvey's annual literary festival.
Y90 (LMC)

Yearick, L. G. Bacon, Samuel Rankin Soil Survey, Montour and Northumberland Counties, Pennsylvania. Washington: Govt. Print. Off., 1955.
B90

Yelsew, Jean pseud. see Smith, J. Wesley

Yoder, Don Pennsylvania Spirituals. Lancaster, Pa.: Pennsylvania Folklore Society, 1961.
Y100 (ASU)

Yoder, Don ed. Boyer, Walter E. Songs along the Mahantongo: Pennsylvania Dutch Folk-songs. Hatboro, Pa.: Folklore Associates, 1964.
B6050 (ASU)

Yoder, Gerald Bacon, Samuel Rankin Soil Survey, Union County, Pennsylvania. Washington: U. S. Department of Agriculture, Bureau of Plant Industry, Soils, and Agricultural Engineering, 1946.
B100

Yoder, Julian Clifton The Economic Geography of Watauga County, North Carolina. Boone, N. C.: n.p., 1941.
Y110 (ASU)

"North Carolina: A Geographic Study." Ph. D. Diss. Univ. of North Carolina, 1950.
Y120 (LMC)

Yoho, James G. Pomeroy, Kenneth Brownridge North Carolina Lands: Ownership, Use, and Management of Forest and Related Lands. Washington: American Forestry Assoc., 1964.
P3470 (ASU LMC BC WCU UNCA)

York, Alvin C. Sergeant York: His Own Life Story and War Diary. Edited by Tom Skeyhill. Garden City, N. Y.: Doubleday, 1928. The story of a mountain man who became America's favorite hero of World War I.
Y130 (LMC BC)

Yost, Doyle A. Thoughts from the Hills. Tazewell, Va.: privately printed, 1965. A book of poetry, dealing with various topics.
Y140

Youmans, E. Grant Aging Patterns in a Rural and an Urban Area of Kentucky. Bulletin no. 681. Lexington: Kentucky Agricultural Experiment Station, Univ. of Kentucky, March, 1963.
Y150

The Educational Attainment and Future Plans of Kentucky Rural Youths. Lexington: Kentucky Agricultural Experiment Station, 1959.
Y160

Information on School Dropouts. KAES Miscellaneous Publication no. 252. Mimeographed. Lexington: Kentucky Agricultural Experiment Station, Department of Rural Sociology, University of Kentucky, January, 1962.
Y170

Leisure-Time Activities of Older Persons in Selected Rural and Urban Areas of Kentucky. Progress Report no. 115. Lexington: Kentucky Agricultural Experiment Station, Univ. of Kentucky, March, 1962.
Y180

Older Rural Americans: A Sociological Perspective. Lexington: Univ. of Kentucky Press, 1967.
Y190 (BC)

The Rural School Dropout: A Ten-Year Follow-Up Study of Eastern Kentucky Youth. Bulletin of the Bureau of School Service, vol. xxxvi, no. 1. Lexington: Univ. of Kentucky, September, 1963.
Y200

Socio-Economic Problems of Older Persons in Casey County, Kentucky. Progress Report no. 88. Lexington: Kentucky Agricultural Experiment Station, Univ. of Kentucky, March, 1960.
Y210

Young, Bennett H. The Prehistoric Men of Kentucky. Louisville: J. P. Morton and Co., 1910. An account written by a famous confederate hero.
Y220 (BC)

Young, Bennett Henderson The Prehistoric Men of Kentucky; a History of What Is Known of Their Lives and Habits, Together with a Description of Their Implements and Other Relics and of the Tumuli Which Have Earned from Them the Designation of Mound Builders; a Paper Prepared to Commemorate the Silver Anniversary of the Filson Club, by Colonel Bennett H. Young. Louisville, Ky.: J. P. Morton and Co., 1910.
Y230

Young, D. C. ed. History of the First Presbyterian Church, Sweetwater, Tennessee, 1860-1960. Knoxville: n.p., n.d.
Y240

Young, Harry F. "History of Education in Wayne County, Kentucky." Master's thesis. Univ. of Kentucky, 1927.
Y250

Young, Harry P. Veatch, Jethro O. Soil Survey of Blair County, Pennsylvania. Washington: U. S. Department of Agriculture, Bureau of Soils, 1917.
V490

Young, Jacob Autobiography of a Pioneer: Or, The Nativity, Experience, Travels, and Ministerial Labors of Rev. Jacob Young, with Incidents, Observations, and Reflections. Cincinnati: L. Swormstedt and A. Poe, 1857.
Y260 (BC)

Young, James Oliver A Baptist Looks Back: The Origin and Early History of Roan Mountain Baptist Association, Now Mitchell Baptist Association. Boone, N. C.: The author, 1968.
Y270 (ASU WCU LMC BC)

Young, R. S. Hack, John Tilton Intrenched Meanders of the North Fork of the Shenandoah River, Virginia. Washington: Govt. Print. Off., 1959.
H100

Young, Raymond "An Analysis of the Sources and Expenditures of Internal Funds in the High Schools of Carter County, Tennessee." Master's thesis. East Tennessee State College, 1957.
Y280 (ETSU)

Young, Willie Pauline comp. Abstracts of the Old Ninety-Six and Abbeville District Wills and Bonds, as on File in the Abbeville, South Carolina, Courthouse. 1950. Reprint. Abbeville, S. C.: n.p., 1969.
Y290 (ASU)

Young, Zachary Taylor Boone Logan's Letters to the Sentinel-Democrat (Mount Sterling, Kentucky) Pertaining to the Rowan County Feud and Other Matters. n.p.: n.p., n.d.
Y300 (BC)

Yount, John The Trapper's Last Shot. New York: Random House, 1973.
Y310

Wolf at the Door. New York: Random House, 1967.
Y320 (ASU)

Yowell, Claude Lindsay A History of Madison County, Virginia. Strasburg, Va.: Shenandoah Pub. House, 1926.
Y330 (BC)

Zandarski, Joseph Robert "Problems in the Anthracite Industry with Special Reference to Marketing." Ph. D. Diss. Univ. of Pittsburgh, 1964.
Z10

Zanolli, Stelvid W. "The Coal Miner in a Large Scale, Highly Mechanized, Highly Integrated Bituminous Coal Mining Plant." Master's thesis. Univ. of Pittsburgh, 1948.
Z20

Zanotti, Victor W. "Market Structure Analysis of the West Virginia Peach Industry." Master's thesis. West Virginia Univ., 1967.
Z30

Zappone, C. R., Jr. McLendon, Willie E. Soil Survey of Coffee County, Tennessee. Washington: U. S. Department of Agriculture, Bureau of Soils, 1910.
M2030

Zeigler, Wilbur Gleason The Heart of the Alleghenies: Or, Western North Carolina. Comprising Its Topography, History, Resources, People, Narratives, Incidents, and Pictures of Travel, Adventures in Hunting and Fishing and Legends of Its Wildernesses. Raleigh, N. C.: A. Williams and Co.; Cleveland: W. W. Williams, 1883.
Z40 (ASU LMC WCU BC ETSU)

Zeitner, June Culp Appalachian Mineral and Gem Trails. 1st ed. San Diego, Calif.: Lapidary Journal, 1968.
Z50 (ASU WCU LMC BC)

Zeller, Frederick A. Economic Development in West Virginia. Morgantown: West Virginia Univ., Office of Research and Development, 1968.
Z60

Problems of Community Action in Appalachia. Morgantown: West Virginia Univ., Appalachian Center, Office of Research and Development, 1968.
Z70

Zeller, Frederick Anthony Manpower Development in Appalachia: An Approach to Unemployment. Based on papers from a conference held at West Virginia University, 1966, sponsored by the Institute for Labor Studies, West Virginia University, and the AFL-CIO Appalachian Council. Praeger Special Studies in U. S. Economic and Social Development. New York: Praeger, 1968.
Z80 (UNCA ASU LMC ETSU)

Zen, E-an ed. Studies of Appalachian Geology: Northern and Maritime New York: Interscience Publishers, 1968.
S8800 (ASU ETSU UNCA)

Ziegler, Martin L. "Social Legislation for the Protection of Coal Miners in Pennsylvania." Master's thesis. Pennsylvania State College, 1947.
Z90

Zinn, Jack The Battle of Rich Mountain. Parsons, W. Va.: McClain Print. Co., 1971.
Z100 (ASU BC)

R. E. Lee's Cheat Mountain Campaign. Parsons, W. Va.: McClain Print. Co., 1974.
Z110 (ASU)

Zinn, William Davidson The Story of Woodbine Farm. Buckhannon, W. Va.: K. Reger, 1931.
Z120 (BC)

Zirkle, Gordon J. Zirkle Family in America, Germany to America. vol. 1. Sponsored by the Zerkel-Zirkle-Circle Family Committee, Mt. Jackson, Virginia. New Market: Henkel Press, 1971.
Z130

Zopf, Paul E. North Carolina, a Demographic Profile. Chapel Hill, N. C.: Carolina Population Center, 1965.
Z140 (ASU LMC)

Zubovic, Peter Distribution of Minor Elements in Coals of Appalachian Region. Bulletin, 1117-C. Washington: U. S. Geological Survey, 1966.
Z150

Zugsmith, Leane The Summer Soldier. New York: Random House, 1938.
Z160 (ETSU)

Zukofsky, Louis Found Objects. Georgetown, Ky.: H. B. Chapin, 1962.
Z170 (BC)

Zumstein, William C. "A Study of School Transportation, Morgan Co., Tenn." Master's thesis. Univ. of Tenn., 1953.
Z180

Zwartendyk, Jan "Economic Aspects of Surface Subsidence Resulting from Underground Mineral Exploitation." Ph. D. Diss. Pennsylvania State Univ., 1971.
Z190

SUBJECT INDEX

ABOLITION — APP.
Address to the People of West Virginia: Shewing That Slavery Is Injurious to the Public Welfare, and That It May Be Gradually Abolished, Without Detriment to the Rights and Interests of Slaveholders.
R4260 (ASU BC)
ABSENTEE OWNERSHIP — APP.
Home Mission Investments.
L630 (LMC)
ACID MINE DRAINAGE
Message from the President of the United States Transmitting the Appalachian Regional Commission's Report, Acid Mine Drainage in Appalachia, Pursuant to the Provisions of Section 302 (b) of the Appalachian Regional Development Act.
A210 (ASU)
Evaluation of Pollution Abatement Techniques Applicable to Lost Creek and Brown's Creek Watershed, West Virginia.
A220 (ASU)
Stream Quality in Appalachia as Related to Coal-mine Drainage, 1965.
B3570 (LMC BC ASU)
Stream Quality in Appalachia as Related to Coal-mine Drainage.
B3571
Mine Drainage Abstracts, a Bibliography.
B4270 (ASU)
Kentucky Law on Water.
C4790
Mine Drainage Abstracts: A Bibliography.
C5200 (ASU)
"Macroinvertebrate Community Structure as an Indicator of Acid Mine Pollution."
D2470
E2000
Determination of Estimated Mean Mine Water, Quantity and Quality from Imperfect Data and Historical Records.
E2050 (ASU)
Handbook of Pollution Control Costs in Mine Drainage Management.
M6470
ACID MINE DRAINAGE — APP.
I100 (ASU)
I110 (ASU)
I120 (ASU)
I130 (ASU)
ACID MINE DRAINAGE — KY.
Influences of Strip Mining on the Hydrologic Environment of Parts of Beaver Creek Basin, Kentucky, 1955-59.
C5930 (BC)
ACID MINE DRAINAGE — MD.
Western Maryland Mine Drainage Survey, 1962-65.
H7110
ACID MINE DRAINAGE — W. VA.
I920
AGED
Status of the Aging in Kanawha County.
A2560
The Older West Virginian.
W3270
Aging Patterns in a Rural and an Urban Area of Kentucky.
Y150
Leisure-Time Activities of Older Persons in Selected Rural and Urban Areas of Kentucky.
Y180
Older Rural Americans: A Sociological Perspective.
Y190 (BC)
Socio-Economic Problems of Older Persons in Casey County, Kentucky.
Y210
AGED — APP.
Economic Provisions for Old Age of Rural Families in Five Southern States.
B170
AGED — ECONOMIC CONDITIONS
"An Economic Study of Old Age Pensions with Special Reference to Seven Upper East Tennessee Counties."
G760
AGED — W. VA.
"A Survey of the Status of the Retired School Teacher in West Virginia."
B7670
Health, Welfare, and Housing Needs of the Aged in Berkeley County, West Virginia.
S1320
. . .and Live Forever.
S4920 (ASU)
AGRICULTURE
Soil Survey, Hamblen County, Tennessee.
A10 (ASU)
Let Us Now Praise Famous Men.
A730 (BC ASU WCU)
Let Us Now Praise Famous Men.
A740 (ETSU)
Let Us Now Praise Famous Men.
A750 (WCU)
Soil Survey: Dawson, Lumpkin, and White Counties, Georgia.
A850
The Present and Projected Agricultural Economy of the Appalachian Region of Alabama.
A860 (ASU)
A Rural Community in Time of War: The Valley Community in Rabun County, Georgia.
A1340 (BC)
An Economic Analysis of Farming in Overton County, Tennessee.
A1830 (ETSU)
How the Swiss Farmers Operate on the Cumberland Plateau.
A1860
Significant Changes in Agriculture of Cumberland County, Tennessee.
A1870
"The Geography of Christmas Tree Production and Marketing in Anglo-America: With Special Attention to Twelve Counties in Western Pennsylvania."
A2460
Traveling Conference of the Department of Agriculture in the Southern Appalachian Region, Oct. 30-Nov. 4, 1939.
A4430
Ways of Making Southern Mountain Farms More Productive.
A4840. (ASU BC)
"An Economic Analysis of Farming in Overton County, Tennessee."
A5340
Soil Survey of Marion County, Alabama.
A5870
Soil Survey of Overton County, Tennessee.
A5880
Soil Survey, McMinn County, Tennessee.
B80
Soil Survey, Montour and Northumberland Counties, Pennsylvania.
B90
Soil Survey, Union County, Pennsylvania.
B100
Two Supply Cooperatives Serving Low-income Farmers: A Preliminary Analysis in Appalachia.
B310
Characteristics of Families on Small Farms.
B2000
Characteristics of the United States Population by Farm and Nonfarm Origin.
B2240
Soil Survey, Cocke County, Tennessee.
B2650
Soil Resources of Johnson City, Tennessee.
B4200 (ETSU)
Wintering Beef Cattle in the Appalachian Region.
B4350
Soil Survey, Colbert County, Alabama.
B6130
Soil Survey, Elmore County, Alabama.
B6140
Soil Survey, Gordon County, Georgia.
B6290
Soil Survey, Alleghany County, North Carolina.
B6530
Soil Survey, Banks and Stevens Counties, Georgia.
B6760
Soil Survey, Carroll and Haralson Counties, Georgia.
B6940
The Family Group in a Kentucky Mountain Farming Community.
B7180
Soil Survey of Alleghany County, North Carolina.
B8670 (ASU)
Soil Survey of Alleghany County.
B8680
Soil Survey of Washington County, Maryland.
B8690
Soil Survey of Indiana County, Pennsylvania.
B8700
Soil Survey of Limestone County, Alabama.
B8710
Soil Survey of Madison County, Alabama.
B8720
Soil Survey of Randolph County, Alabama.
B8730
Soil Survey of Rockcastle County, Kentucky
B8740
Soil Survey of St. Clair County, Alabama.
B8750
Soil Survey, Oconee County, South Carolina.
B9600
Soil Survey, Pickens County, South Carolina.
B9610
Soil Survey, Sparfanburg County, South Carolina.
C510
Soil Survey of Chilton County, Alabama.
C1130
Soil Survey, Rappahannock County, Virginia.
C1710
Soil Survey, Chambers County, Alabama.
C1730
Soil Survey, Fulton County, Pennsylvania.
C4090
Land Utilization in Laurel County, Kentucky.
C4820 (BC)
Soil Survey of Caldwell County, North Carolina.
C5330
An Economic Survey of the Appalachian Region, with Special Reference to Agriculture.
C6100 (ETSU WCU LMC ASU)
Soil Survey, Fayette County, Alabama.
C7730
Adjustments of Rural Resources Use and Characteristics to Economic Growth.
H4490 (ASU)
Soil Survey of Wyoming County, Pennsylvania.
H4620
"Single and Multi-region Intersectoral Plows Analysis: An Examination of the Rows-only Approach with Applications to the Tennessee Economy."
L2130
Soil Survey of Etowah County, Alabama.
L4070
Soil Survey of Coffee County, Tennessee.
M2030
Soil Survey of Franklin County, Georgia.
M2040
Soil Survey of Oconee County, South Carolina.
M2060
The Rural Land Use of Washington County, Tennessee.
M2970
Soil Survey of Meigs County, Ohio.
M4930
Soil Survey, Hall County, Georgia.
M5850 (ASU)
Soil Survey, Towns County, Georgia.
M5860
Soil Survey, Union County, Georgia.
M5870
Soil Survey: DeKalb County, Tennessee.
M6440
Employment Opportunities and Usable Agricultural Skills in Non-Farm Agricultural Occupations in Appalachia.
M7410
"The Agricultural Needs of Claiborne County, Tennessee."
N1500
Home and Farm Ownership.
N1740 (LMC)
"Land Utilization in Roane County, Tennessee."
P450
Economic Land Classification of Clarke Co., Va.
P720
Soil Survey, Preston County, West Virginia.
P820
"An Analysis of the Effects of Federal Farm Programs on Incomes of Appalachian Farmers."
P1040 (LMC)
Soil Survey, Transylvania County, North Carolina.
P2130
Yancey County, North Carolina.
P2140

AGRICULTURE

Soil Survey of Belmont County, Ohio.
P2620

Soil Survey: Fannin County, Georgia.
P2630

Resources of the Southern Fields and Forests, Medical, Economical, and Agricultural. Being Also a Medical Botany of the Confederate States.
P3590 (LMC BC)

The Colony Bernstadt in Laurel County, Kentucky.
S920

Soil Survey, Pickens County, South Carolina.
S2570

Soil Survey of Wayne County, Pennsylvania.
S3430

"Evaluation of Alternative Income Opportunities For Farm Operations in Macon County, North Carolina."
S3720 (LMC)

Soil Survey of Blount County, Alabama.
S5180

Soil Survey of Colbert County, Alabama.
S5190

Soil Survey of Garrett County, Maryland.
S5320

Soil Survey, Clinton County, Pennsylvania.
S7080

Change in Agricultural and Economic Trends in North Carolina; Information by Area Development Associations and Counties.
S7530

Soil Survey of Franklin County, Alabama.
S8120

Soil Survey of Shelby County, Alabama.
S8130

Soil Survey of Cherokee County, Alabama.
S8140

Soil Survey, Roane County, Tennessee.
S9440

Soil Survey of Winston County, Alabama.
S9450

Soil Survey of Meigs County, Tennessee.
S9570

Soil Survey, De Kalb County, Alabama.
S9670

Soil Survey, Jackson County, Alabama.
S9680

Soil Survey, Madison County, Alabama.
S9690

Food at the Grass Roots; the Nation's Stake in Soil Minerals.
T4460

The Folk-lore of Plants.
T7720 (ASU)

Family Chicken Flock for Appalachia.
U140

Growing Vegetables in Appalachian Region.
U150

Appraisal of ARA Program to Date and Its Relationship to Economic Opportunity and Appalachia Programs, Address by William L. Batt, Jr., Administrator, Area Redevelopment Administration, Department of Commerce, before Association of State Planning and Development Agencies, Washington, D. C., May 26, 1964.
U170

Soil Survey, Bath County, Kentucky.
W2360

Soil Survey, Elliott County, Kentucky.
W2390

Certain Econ-Aspects of Agriculture in Jackson Co. Soil Conservation Area.
W2450

Soil Survey, Douglas County, Georgia.
W2760

Valley of Tomorrow: The TVA and Agriculture.
W2840 (ASU LMC WCU ETSU BC)

Bulletin.
W3130 (BC)
W3140 (ETSU)

An Informal Series Covering Agric. Econ., in Its Broadest Sense.
W4530

Soils of the Appalachian Mountain and Plateau Province.
W5860

Seven Lean Years.
W9010 (BC)

Muscle Shoals, Ala.: 1972 Proceedings.
W9200 (BC)

Muscle Shoals, Ala.: Proceedings.
W9210

Papers.
W9220

The Story of Woodbine Farm.
Z120 (BC)

AGRICULTURE — ALA.

Soil Survey, Marshall County, Alabama.
F4090

Soil Survey, Calhoun County, Alabama.
H2360

Soil Survey, Limestone County, Alabama.
H3380

Soil Survey of Calhoun County, Alabama.
H8540

The German Settlement in Cullman County, Alabama: An Agricultural Island in the Cotton Belt.
K2980 (BC)

Soil Survey of Cleburne County, Alabama.
L2170

Soil Survey of Lawrence County, Alabama.
L2180

Soil Survey, Cullman County, Alabama.
M2450

Soil Survey of Talladega County, Alabama.
M6700

Opportunities for and Limitations of Social and Economic Adjustments in an Alabama Rural County.
N1190

Soil Survey of Fayette County, Alabama.
O700

Soil Survey, Randolph County, Alabama.
P320

Soil Survey of Morgan County, Alabama.
P590

Soil Survey: Franklin County, Alabama.
S2860

Soil Survey, Lawrence County, Alabama.
S2870

Soil Survey, Morgan County, Alabama.
S2880

Soil Survey of Chambers County, Alabama.
S4760

Soil Survey of Jefferson County, Alabama.
S4770

Soil Survey of Clay County, Alabama.
T410

Soil Survey of Coosa County, Alabama.
T430

Soil Survey of Bibb County, Alabama.
T7660

Soil Survey of Cullman County, Alabama.
T7670

Cumberland Plateau and Mountains and Southern Appalachian Ridges and Valley of Alabama, Georgia, and Tennessee.
U3930

Soil Survey of Walker County, Alabama.
V500

Soil Survey of Jackson County, Alabama.
W200

Soil Survey of Marshall County, Alabama.
W210

Soil Survey of Putnam County, Tennessee.
W220

Soil Survey of Tuscaloosa County, Alabama.
W7820

AGRICULTURE — APP.

Farming: A Hand Book.
B3250 (WCU ASU)

Development and Application of a Level-of-living Scale for White, Open Country Families, Both Farm and Non-farm in the Southeast.
G2190

History of Agriculture in the Southern United States to 1860.
G3380 (BC MHC)

"Possum Ridge Farmers: A Study in Cultural Change."
H6120 (ASU)

Soil: Its Influence on the History of the United States, with Special Reference to Migration and the Scientific Study of Local History.
H8170 (ASU)

Appalachia: Problems and Solutions.
J1240 (ASU)

Social Changes and Their Implications for Southern Agriculture.
K280

Appalachian Resource Development Project, Submitted to the Kellogg Foundation.
K1390

The Legal Status of the Tenant Farmer in the Southeast.
M3040 (LMC)

"Optimum Farm Organizations for a Portion of the Appalachian Plateau."
N610

"An Analysis of the Effects of Federal Farm Programs on Incomes of Appalachian Farmers."
P1000

Towards Solving the Low-income Problem of Small Farmers in the Appalachian Area.
P1060 (LMC)

Some Postwar Rural Trends in Kentucky, North Carolina, Tennessee, Virginia, and West Virginia.
R3080

Tenn. Valley Land and Its Changing Use.
S150

"The Relationship of the Economic Production of Farmers of the Southern Appalachian Region to Certain Social Factors."
S6200 (ASU)

Evaluation of Forestry Opportunities on Farms in the Beech River Watershed.
T2620

Fertilizer Science and the American Farmer — the Research and Education Programs of the Tennessee Valley Authority.
T2680

Fertilizer Science and the American Farmer — the Research and Education Programs of the Tennessee Valley Authority.
T2690

Systematic Farm Planning in Relation to Water Resources at Parker Branch Pilot Tributary Watershed.
T3590

Census of Agriculture for the 125 Tennessee Valley Watershed Counties.
T4140

Report of the Project on Research in Agriculture and Industrial Development in the Tennessee Valley Region.
T4300

Fertilizer Trends.
T4340

Southern Bulk Blending Conference, Jan. 21-23, 1963.
T4350

Bulk-Blending — An Innovation in Fertilizer Marketing.
T4360

Do Fertilizer Education and Services Pay?
T4380

Fertilizer Summary Data.
T4390

Fertilizer Summary Data.
T4400

Fertilizer, One Key to Better Land Use. Summary of Distributor Demonstration Program for TVA Fertilizers, Fiscal Year 1955.
T4410

Fertilizer Trends.
T4420

Fertilizer Trends; the Scope of TVA's Fertilizer Activities.
T4430

Fertilizer Trends; the Scope of TVA's Fertilizer Activities.
T4440

Fertilizer Trends; the Scope of TVA's Fertilizer Activities.
T4450

Interpreting Results of Irrigation Experiments; a Progress Report.
T4480

Plant Nutrient Consumption by States and Geographic Areas.
T4500

Problems and Suggested Programs for Low-Income Farmers with Special Reference to the Tennessee Valley.
T4510

Problems of Underemployed Rural People.
T4520

AGRICULTURE — APP.

Progress Through Cooperative Research on Fertilizer Evaluations; a Report of TVA Soils and Fertilizer Research Branch for the Period July 1957 Through June 1960.
T4530

Report.
T4540

Research Contributes to More Efficient Use of Fertilizers. A Report of Progress of the Soils and Fertilizers, Fertilizer Research Branch.
T4550

Test-Demonstration Farms and the Spread of Improved Farm Practices in Southwest Virginia.
T4560

U. S. Plant Nutrient Consumption.
T4570

Use of Linear Programming Technique to Compute Least-Cost Bulk-Blended Fertilizers.
T4580

Comparative Data on Farm Income and Employment, 1929-51.
T5170

Differentials in Farm Income and Employment in the Tennessee Valley Region Counties.
T5180

Agricultural-Industrial Survey of Hamblen County, Tennessee.
T5670

Report of the Secretary of Agriculture on the Southern Appalachian and White Mountain Watersheds. Commercial Importance, Area, Condition, Advisability of the Purchase for National Forests, and Probable Cost.
U2540 (BC)

Appalachian land stabilization and conservation program, program results from inception through Dec. 31, 1968.
U2565

Crop Production Practices, Labor, Power, and Materials, by Operation: Sec. 3, Appalachian, Southeast, and Mississippi Delta.
U2570

1967 Regional Summary of Fruit Tree Surveys, Selected Appalachian States.
U2580

An economic survey of the Appalachian Region, with special reference to Agriculture.
U2600

Suggestions for Planning and Zoning in Appalachia.
U2610 (LMC)

Ways of Making Southern Mountain Farms More Productive. Farm Practices That Increase Crop Yield in Ky. and Tenn.
U2620

AGRICULTURE — GA.

Soil Survey of Bartow County, Georgia.
F3680

Soil Survey, Cherokee, Gilmer, and Pickens Counties, Georgia.
J2710

"Some Economic Aspects of the Changes in Towns County Agriculture during the Period, 1934-1950."
L280

Soil Survey of Carroll County, Georgia.
L2160

Soil Survey of Floyd County, Georgia.
L3230

Soil Survey of Jackson County, Georgia.
L3240

Soil Survey of Jackson County, Georgia.
L3250

Soil Survey of Madison County, Georgia.
L3260

Soil Survey of Polk County, Georgia.
L3270

Soil Survey of Rabun County, Georgia.
L3280

Soil Survey: Dawson, Lumpkin, and White Counties, Georgia.
M1720

Soil Survey of Walker County, Georgia.
M2070

Soil Survey of Chattooga County, Georgia.
M3030

Soil Survey, Forsyth County, Georgia.
R3180

Soil Survey, Habersham County, Georgia.
R3190

Soil Survey: Gwinnett County, Georgia.
T330

Soil Survey, Catoosa County, Georgia.
T400

Soil Survey, Dade County, Georgia.
T440

Optimum Farm Organizations and Area Production Patterns for the Upper Hiwassee Watershed Area.
W7870

AGRICULTURE — KY.

Soil Survey, Adair County, Kentucky.
A4710

Farm Practices That Increase Crop Yields in Kentucky and Tennessee.
A4830 (BC)

Labor Supply and Farm Production on Eastern Kentucky Farms.
B5270

The Farm Family in a Kentucky Mountain Neighborhood.
B7190

Social Security and the Farmer in Kentucky.
C4000

. . . Land Utilization in Laurel County, Kentucky.
C4810 (ASU)

Part-time Farming in Eastern Kentucky.
G160

Rural Manpower in Eastern Kentucky: A Study of Under-Employment among Rural Workers in Economic Area Eight.
G170

Utilization of Rural Manpower in Eastern Kentucky.
G180

Soil Survey of Madison County, Kentucky.
G4090

"Factors That Influence Young Couples to Stay on the Farm in Adair County, Kentucky: Some Social and Economic Factors That Influence Young Couples to Stay on the Farm in a Low-income County in Kentucky."
H1710

Soil Survey, Jefferson County, West Virginia.
H3490

A General Picture of Commercial Agriculture in Eastern Kentucky.
J700

Circular. No. 1-.
K920

Farm Population Changes in Eastern Kentucky.
K930

Tables Showing Components of Population Change and Percent Due to Net Migration for State Economic Areas, Metropolitan Areas, and Counties, Southern Appalachians, 1950-1960.
K940

Soil Survey of Garrard County, Kentucky.
K1640

Reconnaissance Soil Survey, Fourteen Counties in Eastern Kentucky.
M1140

Farm Management and Family Incomes in Eastern Kentucky.
N920

"The Social and Economic Structure of Kentucky Agriculture, 1850-1860."
T9470

Soil Survey, Bath County, Kentucky.
W2370

Soil Survey, Elliott County, Kentucky.
W2380

Family Living in Knott County, Kentucky.
W6530 (BC)

AGRICULTURE — MD.

Soil Survey of Allegany County, Maryland.
B7610

Soil Survey, Washington County, Maryland.
M4270

AGRICULTURE — N. C.

Agricultural Developments in North Carolina, 1783-1860.
C2070 (LMC)

Soil Survey of Caldwell County, North Carolina.
C5340

Soil Survey, Yadkin County, North Carolina.
C9840

Soil Survey, Stokes County, North Carolina.
D1260 (ASU)

Soil Survey of Surry County, North Carolina.
D1270

Soil Survey of Watauga County, North Carolina.
D1280 (ASU)

Soil Survey of Macon County.
D1960

Soil Survey of Macon County, North Carolina.
D1970

Soil Survey, Wood and Wirt Counties, West Virginia.
E1870

Papers.
F180

Soil Survey, Buncombe County, North Carolina.
G2380

Soil Survey, Graham County, North Carolina.
G2390

Soil Survey, Haywood County, North Carolina.
G2400

Soil Survey, Jackson County, North Carolina.
G2410

Soil Survey, Macon County, North Carolina.
G2420

Soil Survey, Madison County, North Carolina.
G2430

Soil Survey of Ashe County, North Carolina.
H2170

Memories of 4-H.
H2600 (ASU)

Soil Survey of Gaston County, North Carolina.
H4190 (ASU)

Soil Survey of Henderson County, North Carolina.
H4200

Soil Survey of Transylvania County, North Carolina.
H4210

Soil Survey of Transylvania County.
H4220

Soil Survey of Cherokee County, North Carolina.
J2860 (ASU)

Soil Survey of Davie County, North Carolina.
J2870

Soil Survey of Haywood County, North Carolina.
J2880

Soil Survey of Rutherford County, North Carolina.
J2910

Soil Survey of Wilkes County, North Carolina.
J2950

Soil Survey of Transylvania County, North Carolina.
K2300

Soil Survey of the Asheville, North Carolina, Area.
L620

Soil Survey of Burke County.
L1430

Soil Survey of Burke County, North Carolina.
L1440

Soil Survey, Yadkin County, North Carolina.
L1450

Soil Survey, Watauga County, North Carolina.
L1670

"The Asheville Basin of North Carolina: A Study in Highland Agricultural Land Use."
L3690 (LMC ASU)

"The County Farm Life Schools of North Carolina."
M1930 (ASU)

North Carolina and Its Resources.
N1810 (ASU BC UNCA)

North Carolina: Land of Opportunity.
N1820 (LMC)

Soil Survey of Buncombe County, North Carolina.
P2060

Soil Survey, Cherokee County, North Carolina.
P2070

Soil Survey, Clay County, North Carolina.
P2080

Soil Survey, Henderson County, North Carolina.
P2100

Soil Survey, Mitchell County, North Carolina.
P2110

Soil Survey, Swain County, North Carolina.
P2120

The Tobacco Kingdom: Plantation, Market, and Factory in Virginia and North Carolina, 1800-1860.
R2650 (ASU)

Soil Survey, Avery County, North Carolina.
R3290

Soil Survey, Watauga County, North Carolina.
U3940

Soil Survey of Cleveland County, North Carolina.
V40

AGRICULTURE — N. C.

The Leguminous Plants of North Carolina.
W6090 (LMC)

"The History of the Soil Conservation Service in Watauga County, North Carolina."
W6700 (ASU)

AGRICULTURE — N. Y.

Economic Study of Land Utilization in Chautaugua County, New York.
J2750

Economic Study of Land Utilization in Otsego County, New York.
J2760

AGRICULTURE — OHIO

Soil Survey, Scioto County, Ohio.
C6780

Subsequent Movement of Kentucky Hill Families Relocated as Farm Laborers in Ohio.
M3050 (ASU)

Soil Survey, Athens County, Ohio.
P530

Soil Survey of Vinton County, Ohio.
P540

Soil Survey, Ross County, Ohio.
P2430

Soil Survey of Washington County, Ohio.
P2670

Soil Survey of Adams County, Ohio.
T390

Soil Survey: Clermont County, Ohio.
T420

AGRICULTURE — PA.

"Agriculture Production in Pennsylvania."
C3610

Soil Survey of Mercer County, Pennsylvania.
D1600

Soil Survey of Cambria County, Pennsylvania.
D1880

Soil Survey, Carbon County, Pennsylvania.
F1180

The Low-Income Farmer in a Changing Society.
F1540

"Equating Timber and Wildlife Values and Returns to the Farm Resource Base in Sullivan County, Pennsylvania."
G200

Soil Survey, Potter County Pennsylvania.
G2530

Soil Survey, Mercer County, Pennsylvania.
G4060

"Equating Timber and Wildlife Values and Returns to the Farm Resources Base in Sullivan County, Pennsylvania."
H3970

Soil Survey of Tioga County, Pennsylvania.
H4610

Soil Survey, Huntingdon County, Pennsylvania.
H5260

"An Economic Analysis of Idle Farm Land, Potter County, Pennsylvania, 1953."
J530

"Agriculture Development in the Pittsburgh District."
K2080

Soil Survey, Fayette County, Pennsylvania.
K3020

"Agricultural Regions of Clarion County, Pennsylvania."
L1250

"Socioeconomic Factors Which May Affect Part Time Farmer Education in Butler County, Pennsylvania."
L3310

"The Identification and Analysis of Agricultural Occupations in Seventeen Pennsylvania Counties."
M1430

Soil Survey of Bedford County, Pennsylvania.
M3130

Soil Survey of the Lock Haven, Pennsylvania, Area.
M3680

Soil Survey of the Lock Haven, Pennsylvania, Area.
M3690

Soil Survey of Centre County, Pennsylvania.
M6660

Soil Survey, Columbia County, Pennsylvania.
P460

Soil Survey of Greene County, Pennsylvania.
P2090

"A History of Land Subsistence and Its Consequences Caused by the Mining of Anthracite Coal in Luzerne County, Pennsylvania."
R2870

Reconnaissance Soil Survey of Northeastern Pennsylvania.
S2470

"A Study of Buyers on the Allegheny County Farmer's Market, Pittsburgh, Pennsylvania, 1946."
S6450

Soil Survey, Lycoming County, Pennsylvania.
S7120

Soil Survey, Westmoreland County, Pennsylvania.
T500

Soil Survey of Blair County, Pennsylvania.
V490

Reconnaissance Soil Survey of Northwestern Pennsylvania.
W6120

AGRICULTURE — S. C.

Soil Survey of Cherokee County, South Carolina.
D3230

Soil Survey, Cherokee County, South Carolina.
J2670

Farm Business Study of the Six Mile Area of Pickens County, 1940.
K2120 (ASU)

Soil Survey of Spartanburg County, South Carolina.
L790

Soil Survey of the Campobello Area, South Carolina.
M3020

South Carolina: A Handbook.
S5580 (LMC)

Soil Survey of Greenville County, South Carolina.
W1480

AGRICULTURE — TENN.

Farm Practices That Increase Crop Yields in Kentucky and Tennessee.
A4830 (BC)

Soil Survey, Claiborne County, Tennessee.
A5560 (ASU)

An Economic Survey of the Upper Cumberland Area with a Special Reference to Agriculture.
B110 (ASU)

Better Farming Practices through Rural Community Organization.
B5330

Neighborhoods and Communities of Cumberland County, Tennessee.
B5370

Changes in Tennessee Agriculture by Counties, 1954-64.
B5420

Selected Population and Agricultural Statistics for Tennessee Counties.
C4870 (ASU)

Bibliography of Tennessee Geology, Soils, Drainage, Forestry, etc. with Subject Index.
C5440 (LMC ETSU)

Minimum Land Requirements for Specified Levels of Farm Income in the Eastern Highland Rim of Tennessee.
E30

Manpower and Employment Trends in Tennessee.
E650

Soil Survey, Blount County, Tennessee.
E1470

Soil Survey, Loudon County, Tennessee.
E1480

Soil Survey, Marion County, Tennessee.
E1490

Soil Survey, Washington County, Tennessee.
E1500

Soil Survey, Bradley County, Tennessee
F2470

Soil Survey, Franklin County, Tennessee
F2480

"Rural Land Use in Franklin County, Tennessee."
G630

Soil Survey, Rhea County, Tennessee.
H3390

"Economic Progress and Resource Adjustments of Rural Households is the Upper East Tennessee Valley."
H4500 (ASU)

"Significant Factors Influencing Quality and Success of Supervised Farming Programs of Vocational Agriculture Students in Seven Schools of East Tennessee."
H5650

Soil Survey, Cumberland County, Tennessee.
H7800

Soil Survey, Grainger County, Tennessee.
H7810

Soil Survey, Putnam County, Tennessee.
J130

Soil Survey, Warren County, Tennessee.
J140

The Grasses of Tennessee: Including Cereals and Forage Plants.
K1900 (BC ASU LMC)

Tennessee: Its Agricultural and Mineral Wealth, With an Appendix Showing the Extent, Value and Accessibility of its Ores, With Analyses of the Same.
K1920 (ASU LMC)

The German-Swiss in Franklin County, Tennessee: A Study of the Significance of Cultural Considerations in Farming Enterprises.
K2990 (ASU BC)

"The Impact of TVA on Agriculture."
L1320

"A Study of the Working Relationships of the Agriculture Extension Service and the Vocational Agriculture Program in East Tennessee."
L1750

Types of Farming in Tennessee.
L1930

Soil Survey, Coffee County, Tennessee.
L3660

Soil Survey of Grainger County, Tennessee.
M2050

Types of Farming in Tennessee.
M3710 (ASU)

The Cumberland Plateau in Tennessee.
M4140

Soil Survey, Sullivan County, Tennessee.
M4370

"The Farmers Home Administration and Agricultural Poverty in Tennessee."
M6450

Soil Survey, Jefferson County, Tennessee.
M6630

Soil Survey of the Greenville Area, Tennessee.
M6680

"Agricultural and Social Aspects of the Swiss Settlement in Grundy County, Tennessee."
N600

Soil Survey, Johnson County, Tennessee.
O270 (BC ASU)

Soil Survey, Sevier County, Tennessee.
O280
P3810

Expected Returns from Selected Specialized Farming Systems in the Northern Highland Rim Area of Tennessee.
R460 (ASU)

Production and Marketing of Hatching Eggs in Tennessee.
R510

Soil Survey, Hamilton County, Tennessee.
R3100

Soil Survey, Knox County, Tennessee.
R3110

Bob Taylor and the Agrarian Revolt in Tennessee.
R3230

Soil Survey of Jackson County, Tennessee.
R3560

Soil Survey of Jackson County, Tennessee.
R3570

Soil Survey, Carter County, Tennessee.
R4220

Soil Survey, Norris Area, Tennessee.
R4230

"Relation of Land Base Quality to the Agricultural Economy of Knox County, Tennessee."
R4320

"An Interpretation of the Distribution of Crops and Livestock in East Tennessee as Reported by the 1950 Census."
S1420 (ETSU)

"A Curriculum in Agricultural Education for Two Consolidated High Schools in Washington County, Tennessee."
S4220 (ETSU)

AGRICULTURE — TENN.

A Brief Historical, Statistical and Descriptive Review of East Tennessee, United States of America: Developing Its Immense Agricultural, Mining and Manufacturing Advantages, with Remarks to Emigrants. Accompanied with a Map & Lithographed Sketch of a Tennessee Farm, Mansion House, and Buildings.
S4800

An Inventory of Land and Its Use in the Tennessee Valley.
S5100

Tenn. Valley Land and Its Changing Use.
S5400

"Agricultural Changes in the TVA Area, 1930-1945."
S7740

Agricultural Trends in Tennessee: A Record of Crop and Livestock Statistics, 1866-1947.
T990 (ETSU)

Makers of Millions, Not for Themselves But for You: Stories of Tennesseans whose Accomplishments for Agriculture Brought Renown to Their State and Caused an Appreciating and Benefited Public to Propose Their Admission to the Tennessee Agricultural Hall of Fame.
T1000 (ASU)

Mineral and Agricultural Resources of the Portion of Tennessee Along the Cincinnati Southern and Knoxville and Ohio Railroads.
T1010 (ASU)

Division of Geology Bulletin.
T1020

Tennessee Resources — Agriculture, Forestry, and Minerals.
T1720 (ETSU)

Valley of Tomorrow, the TVA and Agriculture.
T2230

Changing Agricultural of the Tennessee Valley.
T4370

Agricultural-Industrial Survey of Anderson County, Tennessee.
T5570

Agricultural-Industrial Survey of Bledsoe County.
T5580

Agricultural-Industrial Survey of Carter County.
T5590

Agricultural-Industrial Survey of Cocke County.
T5600

Agricultural-Industrial Survey of Coffee County.
T5610

Agricultural-Industrial Survey of Cumberland County.
T5620

Agricultural-Industrial Survey of Fentress County.
T5630

Agricultural-Industrial Survey of Franklin County, Tennessee.
T5640

Agricultural-Industrial Survey of Grainger County.
T5650

Agricultural-Industrial Survey of Greene County, Tennessee.
T5660

Agricultural-Industrial Survey of Johnson County, Tennessee.
T5680

Agricultural-Industrial Survey of Loudon County, Tennessee.
T5690

Agricultural-Industrial Survey of McMinn County, Tennessee.
T5700

Agricultural-Industrial Survey of Marion County, Tennessee.
T5710

Agricultural-Industrial Survey of Meigs County, Tennessee.
T5720

Agricultural-Industrial Survey of Monroe County, Tennessee.
T5730

Agricultural-Industrial Survey of Morgan County, Tennessee.
T5740

Agricultural-Industrial Survey of Polk County, Tennessee.
T5750

Agricultural-Industrial Survey of Rhea County.
T5760

Agricultural-Industrial Survey of Sevier County.
T5770

Agricultural-Industrial Survey of Sullivan County.
T5780

Agricultural-Industrial Survey of Washington County, Tennessee.
T5790

Agricultural-Industrial Survey of White County.
T5800

Agricultural-Industrial Survey of Unicoi County.
T5810

Soil Survey of Blount County, Tenn.
U870 (BC)

Soil Survey of Bradley Co., Tenn.
U880 (BC)

Soil Survey of Carter Co., Tenn.
U890

Soil Survey of Claiborne Co., Tenn.
U900 (BC)

Soil Survey of Cumberland Co., Tenn.
U910 (BC)

Soil Survey of Cumberland Co., Tenn.
U920

Soil Survey of Grainger Co., Tenn.
U930 (BC)

Soil Survey of Grainger Co., Tenn.
U940

Soil Survey of Hamblen Co., Tenn.
U950 (BC)

Soil Survey of Hamilton Co., Tenn.
U960 (BC)

Soil Survey of Hamilton Co., Tenn.
U970

Soil Survey of Jefferson Co., Tenn.
U980 (BC)

Soil Survey of Jefferson Co., Tenn.
U990

Soil Survey of Johnson Co., Tenn.
U1000 (BC)

Soil Survey of Johnson Co., Tenn.
U1010

Soil Survey of Knox Co., Tenn.
U1020 (BC)

Soil Survey of Knox Co., Tenn.
U1030

Soil Survey of Marion Co., Tenn.
U1040

Soil Survey of Marion Co., Tenn.
U1050 (BC)

Soil Survey of McMinn Co., Tenn.
U1060 (BC)

Soil Survey of Norris Area, Tenn.
U1070

Soil Survey of Norris Area, Tenn.
U1080 (BC)

Soil Survey of Rhea Co., Tenn.
U1090 (BC)

Soil Survey of Rhea Co., Tenn.
U1100

Soil Survey of Roane Co., Tenn.
U1110 (BC)

Soil Survey of Roane Co., Tenn.
U1120

Soil Survey of Sevier Co., Tenn.
U1130 (BC)

Soil Survey of Sevier Co., Tenn.
U1140

Soil Survey of Sullivan Co., Tenn.
U1150 (BC)

Soil Survey of Sullivan Co., Tennessee.
U1160

Soil Survey of Washington Co., Tennessee.
U1170 (BC)

Watershed Work Plan for Little Bigby Creek Watershed, Maury County, Tennessee. Report of the Soil Conservation Service, Department of Agriculture, in Accordance with Public Law 83-566, April, 1971.
U2470

Cumberland Plateau and Mountains and Southern Appalachian Ridges and Valley of Alabama, Georgia, and Tennessee.
U3930

Soil Survey of Meigs County, Tenn.
W970

Soil Survey of the Pikeville Area, Tennessee.
W6130

AGRICULTURE — TENN., EASTERN

Increasing Incomes Through Farm Adjustments in the Red Soil Area, Eastern Highland Rim of Tennessee.
A5350 (ASU)

AGRICULTURE — VA.

Soils of the Shenandoah River Terrace: Revision of Certain Soils in the Albemarle Area, Virginia.
B2980

The Present and Projected Agricultural Economy of the Appalachian Region of Alabama.
B4440 (ASU)

Soil Survey of the Leesburg, Virginia, Area.
C1770

Soil Survey, Culpeper County, Virginia.
C5730

Soil Survey, Albemarle County, Virginia.
D1940

Soil Survey of Grayson County, Virginia.
D1950

Soil Survey of Frederick County, Virginia.
D2180

Virginia Rural Youth Adjustments.
G410

Virginia's Marginal Population — A Study in Rural Poverty.
G420 (BC)

Soil Survey of Augusta County, Virginia.
J2850

Soil Survey, Lee County, Virginia.
J2890

Soil Survey of Rockbridge County, Virginia.
J2900

Soil Survey, Scott County, Virginia.
J2920

Soil Survey, Smyth County, Virginia.
J2930

Soil Survey, Washington County, Virginia.
J2940

Soil Survey of the Albemarle Area, Virginia.
M6640

Soil Survey of the Bedford Area, Virginia.
M6650

Farmer Cooperation in Southwest Virginia.
M7500 (ASU)

"An Evaluation of the Impact of the Vocational Education Act of 1963 on Agricultural Education in the Blue Ridge Area of Southwestern Virginia."
N950 (ETSU)
N1410

Soil Survey, Russell County, Virginia.
O100 (BC)

"Shifts in Land Use in the Appalachian Region of Virginia."
O550 (LMC ASU)

Economic Land Classification of Carroll County, Virginia.
P710

"Those Who Enroll for Vocational Agriculture in West Virginia, Considering Certain Scholastic Achievements and Some Background Factors."
P960

Soil Survey, Wise County, Virginia.
P2210

Historical Study of Prices Received by Producers of Farm Products in Virginia, 1801-1927.
P2320 (LMC)

Soil Survey, Fauquier County, Virginia.
P2420

Soil Survey, Bland County, Virginia.
P3640

Soil Survey, Loudoun County, Virginia.
P3650

Soil Survey, Tazewell County, Virginia.
P3660

The Tobacco Kingdom: Plantation, Market, and Factory in Virginia and North Carolina, 1800-1860.
R2650 (ASU)

Soil Survey, Carroll County, Virginia.
T8040
V550

Study of the Organization and Management of Farmers in Grayson County, Va.
V560

Bulletin.
V680 (BC)

AGRICULTURE — VA.
Virginia: A Geographical and Political Summary, Embracing a Description of the State, Its Geology, Soils, Minerals and Climate; Its Animal and Vegetable Productions; Manufacturing and Commercial Facilities; Religious and Educational Advantages; Internal Improvements, and Form of Government.
V700 (BC)
Virginia.
V740 (BC)
AGRICULTURE — W. VA.
"The Granger and Populist Movements in West Virginia, 1873-1914."
B1380
The West Virginia State Grange: The First Century, 1873-1973.
B1390
Soil Survey, Barbour County, West Virginia.
B3440
Soil Survey, Marshall County, West Virginia.
B3450
Rural Underemployment and Land Use in a Marginal Agricultural Area of West Virginia.
B6150
Soil Survey of the Middlebourne Area, West Virginia.
C60
Soil Survey of the Wheeling Area, West Virginia.
C70
Proceedings.
C6400
Some Effects of Price and Income Support Programs on Marginal Farms.
E2320
Soil Survey of Mercer County, West Virginia.
G2300
Soil Survey, Berkeley County, West Virginia.
G2770
Soil Survey, Greenbrier County, West Virginia.
G2780
Soil Survey, Jackson and Mason Counties, West Virginia.
G2790
Soil Survey, Monroe County, West Virginia.
G2800
Soil Survey of Upshur County, West Virginia.
G4100
Soil Survey of Fayette County, West Virginia.
K1630
Soil Survey of Monroe County, West Virginia.
K1650
Soil Survey of Summers County, West Virginia.
K1660
"Effects of Urbanization on Vocational Agriculture in Jackson County, West Virginia."
K1690
Soil Survey of Barbour and Upshur Counties, West Virginia.
L690
Soil Survey of Boone County, West Virginia.
L700
Soil Survey of Braxton and Clay Counties, West Virginia.
L710
Soil Survey of Jefferson, Berkeley, and Morgan Counties, West Virginia.
L720
Soil Survey of Kanawha County, West Virginia.
L730
Soil Survey of Lewis and Gilmer Counties, West Virginia.
L740
Soil Survey of Logan and Mingo Counties, West Virginia.
L750
Soil Survey of McDowell and Wyoming Counties, West Virginia.
L760
Soil Survey of Preston County, West Virginia.
L770
Soil Survey of Raleigh County, West Virginia.
L780
Soil Survey of the Huntington Area, West Virginia.
L800
Soil Survey of the Point Pleasant, West Virginia, Area.
L810
Soil Survey of the Spencer, West Virginia, Area.
L820
Vocational Agricultural Instruction for Adult Farmer Classes in Preston County.
L2730
Soil Survey, Tucker County, Part of Northern Randolph County, West Virginia.
L3540
L3740
"Socioeconomic Characteristics of Young Farmers Enrolled in Vocational Agriculture Classes in West Virginia."
M1500
"Some Employment Opportunities of the Vocational Agriculture Trainees of Gilmer County."
M4020
Soil Survey of the Parkersburg Area, West Virginia.
M4920
Soil Survey of Clarksburg Area, West Virginia.
M6670
Soil Survey of the Morgantown, West Virginia Area.
M6690
Soil Survey of Webster County, West Virginia.
M6710
Towards Solving the Low-Income Problem of Small Farmers in the Appalachian Area.
P1010
Economic Utilization of Marginal Lands in Nicholas and Webster Counties, West Virginia.
P1540
Soil Survey of Grant and Mineral Counties, West Virginia.
P2640
Soil Survey of Nicholas County, West Virginia.
P2650
Soil Survey of Tucker County, West Virginia.
P2660
The Learning Experiences of Youth Groups: A Study of 4-H Clubs in Barbour County, West Virginia.
S3790
Soil Survey, Greenbrier County, West Virginia.
V580
Soil Survey of Hampshire County, West Virginia.
W6420
Soil Survey of Hardy and Pendleton Counties, West Virginia.
W6430
Soil Survey of Pocahontas County, West Virginia.
W6440
Soil Survey of Randolph County, West Virginia.
W6450
"Market Structure Analysis of the West Virginia Peach Industry."
Z30
ALA. — DESCRIPTION AND TRAVEL
Mary Gordon Duffee's Sketches of Alabama.
B7420
Stars Fell on Alabama.
C1290 (BC)
C8050
ALA. — HISTORY
Early History of Huntsville, Alabama, 1804-1870.
B3420 (ASU BC)
The History of Marshall County, Alabama.
D3920 (ASU BC)
School at Speedwell.
E1120
Speedwell Sketches.
E1130 (ASU BC)
Annals of Northwest Alabama.
E1660
Annals of Northwest Alabama Vol. III; Including a Reprint of the 1856 Nelson F. Smith's History of Pickens County, Alabama.
E1670
Horse and Buggy Days on Hatchet Creek.
G450 (ASU BC)
H5990
L310
History of Fayette County, Alabama.
N750 (ASU BC)
The Coosa River Valley from DeSoto to Hydroelectric Power.
R1660 (ASU)
Cherokee Country History, 1836-1956.
S7280 (ASU BC)
Early Settlers of Alabama.
S8750
The Free State of Winston: A History of Winston County, Alabama.
T8340 (ASU)
ALLEGHENY RIVER
The Allegheny.
W1620 (BC)
"The Allegheny-Monongahela Flood Control Program and Its Benefits to Metropolitan Pittsburgh."
W7330
AM. REVOLUTION
Western Lands and the American Revolution.
A120
Western Lands and the American Revolution.
A130 (FC BC ASU)
D520 (ASU)
D540
The German Allied Troops in the North American War of Independence, 1776-1783.
E1220 (ASU)
The Cymry of '76: Or, Welshmen and Their Descendants of the American Revolution.
J2270 (ASU)
L2760
Known Military Dead During the American Revolutionary War, 1775-1783.
P2350 (ASU)
Records of the Revolutionary War.
S60 (ASU)
Revolutionary pensioners; a transcript of the pension list of the United States for 1813.
U3910 (ASU)
Revolutionary Pensioners of 1818.
U4070
Road to Revolution; Virginia's Rebels from Bacon to Jefferson, 1676-1776.
W880
The Carolina Backcountry on the Eve of the Revolution: The Journal and Other Writings of Charles Woodmason, Anglican Itinerant.
W8780 (ASU LMC BC)
Our Mountain Men: Their Early Court Records in Southwest Virginia.
W9270 (BC)
AM. REVOLUTION — ALA.
Revolutionary Soldiers in Alabama: Being a List of Names, Compiled from Authentic Sources, of Soldiers of the American Revolution, Who Resided in the State of Alabama.
O990 (ASU)
AM. REVOLUTION — APP.
Daniel Morgan, Ranger of the Revolution.
C310 (BC)
C2620
Hessian Soldiers in the American Revolution: Records of Their Marriages and Baptisms of Children in America Performed by the Rev. G. C. Coster, 1776-1783, Chaplain of Two Hessian Regiments.
D2190 (ASU)
The Colonial Cavalier: Or, Southern Life Before the Revolution.
G2640 (LMC)
Historical Register of Officers of the Continental Army During the War of the Revolution, April, 1775 to December, 1783.
H4340 (ASU)
I140
I150
R1440
The Winning of the West.
R3700 (ASU)
AM. REVOLUTION — BATTLES — KINGS MTN.
One Heroic Hour at Kings Mountain.
A1240 (BC LMC ASU)
One Heroic Hour at Kings Mountain, October 7, 1780.
A1250
The Overmountain Men: Early Tennessee History, 1760-1780.
A1260 (BC ETSU)
The Overmountain Men: Early Tennessee History, 1760-1795.
A1270 (ASU LMC FC)
Commanders at King's Mountain.
B250
King's Mountain, an Epic of Revolution: With Historical and Biographical Sketches, and Illustrations.
C1380 (BC)

AM. REVOLUTION — CAMPAIGNS AND BATTLES — KING'S MTN.

Kings Mountain and Its Heroes.
D3300

King's Mountain and Its Heroes: History of the Battle of King's Mountain.
D3310 (LMC)

King's Mountain and Its Heroes: History of the Battle of King's Mountain, October 7th, 1780, and the Events Which Led to It.
D3320 (BC ASU)

King's Mountain and Its Heroes: History of the Battle of King's Mountain, October 7th, 1780, and the Events Which Led to It.
D3330

King's Mountain and Its Heroes: History of the Battle of King's Mountain, October 7th, 1780, and the Events Which Led to It.
D3340 (ASU LMC)

King's Mountain and Its Heroes: History of the Battle of King's Mountain, October 7th, 1780, and the Events Which Led to It.
D3350

AM. REVOLUTION — EARLY DECLARATIONS

Proceedings of the County Committees, 1774-1776, The Committees of Safety of Westmoreland and Fincastle.
H3320

The First Rebel; Being a Lost Chapter of Our History on a True Narrative of America's First Uprising Against English Military Authority and An Account of the First Fighting Between Armed Colonists and British Regulars. Together with a Biography of Colonel James Smith. . .
S9460 (BC)

AM. REVOLUTION — EARLY INDEPENDENCE MOVEMENTS

A Seed-bed of the Republic, a Study of the Pioneers in the Upper (Southern) Valley of Virginia.
S7600 (FC BC)

A Seed-bed of the Republic: A Study of the Pioneers in the Upper (Southern) Valley of Virginia.
S7610 (ASU)

AM. REVOLUTION — KY.

Estill County, Kentucky, Record of Abstracts of Pension Papers of Revolutionary Soldiers, War of 1812 and Indian Wars. . . .
B9050

AM. REVOLUTION — MD.

History of Cumberland (Maryland), From the Time of the Indian Town, Caiuctucus, in 1728, Up to the Present Day, Embracing an Account of Washington's First Campaign, and the Battle of Fort Necessity, Together with a History of Braddock's Expedition.
L3700 (ASU)

AM. REVOLUTION — N. C.

Abstract of Pensions of North Carolina Soldiers of the Revolution, War of 1812, and Indian Wars.
B9030 (ASU)

Interesting Revolutionary Incidents: And Sketches of Character, Chiefly in the "Old North State."
C1840 (ASU)

Revolutionary Incidents: And Sketches of Character, Chiefly in the "Old North State."
C1850 (ASU)

Revolutionary Leaders of North Carolina.
C6760 (ASU LMC)

Revolutionary Leaders of North Carolina.
C6770 (WWC)

The Descendants of Claiborne Howard, Soldier of the American Revolution.
C6840 (ASU)

Roster of Soldiers from North Carolina in the American Revolution, with an Appendix Containing a Collection of Miscellaneous Records.
D530 (ASU)

The Loyalists in North Carolina during the Revolution.
D1800 (ASU LMC)

Revolutionary Service of Col. John Walker & Family and Memoirs of Hon. Felix Walker.
G4160 (BC)

A Defence of the Revolutionary History of the State of North Carolina from the Aspersions of Mr. Jefferson.
J2430 (ASU BC)

Memoirs of the American Revolution, So Far as It Is Related to the States of North and South Carolina, and Georgia.
M8330 (ASU)

The Regulators in North Carolina: A Documentary History, 1759-1776.
P4030 (ASU)

North Carolina in the American Revolution.
R450 (ASU LMC)

North Carolina. 1780-81. Being a History of the Invasion of the Carolinas by the British Army Under Lord Cornwallis in 1780-81, with the Particular Design of Showing the Part Borne by North Carolina in That Struggle for Liberty and Independence, and to Correct Some of the Errors of History in Regard to That State and Its People.
S900 (ASU LMC)

Prelude to Yorktown: The Southern Campaign of Nathanael Greene, 1780-1781.
T9180 (ASU)

The Kings Mountain Men: The Story of the Battle, with Sketches of the American Soldiers Who Took Part.
W5490 (ASU)

The King's Mountain Men, the Story of the Battle, with Sketches of the American Soldiers Who Took Part.
W5500 (BC)

AM. REVOLUTION — N. C. — APP. REGION

North Carolina in the Revolutionary War.
R4390 (ASU LMC)

AM. REVOLUTION — PA.

Fort Duquesne and Fort Pitt. Early Names of Pittsburgh Streets.
D550 (ASU)

History of Cumberland (Maryland), From the Time of the Indian Town, Caiuctucus, in 1728, Up to the Present Day, Embracing an Account of Washington's First Campaign, and the Battle of Fort Necessity, Together with a History of Braddock's Expedition.
L3700 (ASU)

AM. REVOLUTION — PRISONERS

American Prisoners of the Revolution.
D70 (ASU)

AM. REVOLUTION — S. C.

Some Heroes of the American Revolution.
B260

A Brief Description of the Battle of King's Mountain, "The Turning Point of the American Revolution," Fought in York County, S. C. October 7, 1780. Together with the Brief Accounts of Previous Celebrations, Illustrations Showing the Battlefield and Monuments and Interesting Data Concerning 150th Anniversary Celebration To Be Held on the Battleground October 7, 1930.
C2890

Kings Mountain and Its Heroes.
D3300

King's Mountain and Its Heroes: History of the Battle of King's Mountain.
D3310 (LMC)

King's Mountain and Its Heroes: History of the Battle of King's Mountain, October 7th, 1780, and the Events Which Led to It.
D3320 (BC ASU)

King's Mountain and Its Heroes: History of the Battle of King's Mountain, October 7th, 1780, and the Events Which Led to It.
D3330

King's Mountain and Its Heroes: History of the Battle of King's Mountain, October 7th, 1780, and the Events Which Led to It.
D3340 (ASU LMC)

King's Mountain and Its Heroes: History of the Battle of King's Mountain, October 7th, 1780, and the Events Which Led to It.
D3350

Memoirs of the American Revolution, from Its Commencement to the Year 1776, Inclusive: As Relating to the State of South Carolina. And Occasionally Refering to the States of North Carolina and Georgia.
D3390 (ASU)

South Carolinians in the Revolution.
E2180 (ASU)

Colonial and Revolutionary History of Upper South Carolina, Embracing for the Most Part the Primitive and Colonial History of the Territory Comprising the Original County of Spartanburg with a General Review of the Entire Military Operations in the Upper Portion of South Carolina and Portions of North Carolina.
L320 (ASU WCU LMC BC)

Colonial and Revolutionary History of Upper South Carolina.
L330 (LMC)

The History of South Carolina in the Revolution, 1775-1780.
M900 (ASU)

Memoirs of the American Revolution, So Far as It Is Related to the States of North and South Carolina, and Georgia.
M8330 (ASU)

Copy of the Original Index Book, Showing the Revolutionary Claims Filed in South Carolina Between August, 20, 1783, and August 31, 1786.
R1590 (ASU)

Historical Statements Concerning the Battle of Kings Mountain and the Battle of the Cowpens, South Carolina.
U330 (ASU)

Calendar of the Tennessee and King's Mountain Papers of the Draper Collection of Manuscripts.
W7850 (LMC)

AM. REVOLUTION — S. C. — CAMPAIGNS AND BATTLES — KINGS MTN.

The Kings Mountain Men: The Story of the Battle, with Sketches of the American Soldiers Who Took Part.
W5490 (ASU)

The King's Mountain Men, the Story of the Battle, with Sketches of the American Soldiers Who Took Part.
W5500 (BC)

AM. REVOLUTION — TENN.

Some Tennessee Heroes of the Revolution; Compiled from Pension Statements.
A4790

Commanders at King's Mountain.
B250

Some Heroes of the American Revolution.
B260

"The Life and Times of Isaac Shelby."
B2380

The Over Mountain Men: Some Passages from a Page of Neglected History.
B9010

A Brief Description of the Battle of King's Mountain, "The Turning Point of the American Revolution," Fought in York County, S. C. October 7, 1780. Together with the Brief Accounts of Previous Celebrations, Illustrations Showing the Battlefield and Monuments and Interesting Data Concerning 150th Anniversary Celebration To Be Held on the Battleground October 7, 1930.
C2890

Notes on the War in the South; with Biographical Sketches of the Lives of Montgomery, Jackson, Sevier, the Late Governor Claiborne, and Others.
C4190

Beloved Landmarks of Loudon County, Tennessee.
D560 (BC)

Benton County, Tennessee, Marriages, 1832-1957.
D570 (ASU)

Kings Mountain and Its Heroes.
D3300

King's Mountain and Its Heroes: History of the Battle of King's Mountain.
D3310 (LMC)

King's Mountain and Its Heroes: History of the Battle of King's Mountain, October 7th, 1780, and the Events Which Led to It.
D3320 (BC ASU)

King's Mountain and Its Heroes: History of the Battle of King's Mountain, October 7th, 1780, and the Events Which Led to It.
D3330

King's Mountain and Its Heroes: History of the Battle of King's Mountain, October 7th, 1780, and the Events Which Led to It.
D3340 (ASU LMC)

AM. REVOLUTION — TENN.
King's Mountain and Its Heroes: History of the Battle of King's Mountain, October 7th, 1780, and the Events Which Led to It.
D3350
The Rear-guard of the Revolution.
G1790 (BC LMC)
Tales of the Revolution, by a Young Gentleman of Tennessee.
R280
Tennessee's Part in the Revolution: Address at Valley Forge, at the Presentation of the Tennessee State Flag and Inauguration of Tennessee Sunday, April 24, 1927.
T9930
The Kings Mountain Men: The Story of the Battle, with Sketches of the American Soldiers Who Took Part.
W5490 (ASU)
The King's Mountain Men, the Story of the Battle, with Sketches of the American Soldiers Who Took Part.
W5500 (BC)
Tennessee During the Revolutionary War.
W6840 (ASU BC)
AM. REVOLUTION — TENN. — SOURCES
C230
AM. REVOLUTION — VA.
Revolutionary War Records: Vol. I, Virginia.
B7690
Revolutionary War Records: Vol. I, Virginia. Virginia Army and Navy Forces with Bounty Land Warrants for Virginia Military Scrip: From Federal and State Archives.
B7700 (ASU)
Virginia Soldiers of 1776.
B8590
Virginia Colonial Militia, 1651-1776.
C9310
Virginia Colonial Militia, 1651-1776.
C9320 (ASU)
Virginia Revolutionary Pension Applications.
D2960
List of the Colonial Soldiers of Virginia.
E710 (ASU)
The Revolution in Virginia.
E730 (LMC FC)
Separation of Church and State in Virginia; A Study in the Development of the Revolution.
E740
Historical Register of Virginians in the Revolution.
G5020 (ASU)
Loyalism in Virginia: Chapters in the Economic History of the Revolution.
H2570 (ASU LMC)
The Valley of Virginia in the American Revolution, 1763-1789.
H3160 (ASU BC FC)
Virginia Militia in the Revolutionary War: McAllister's Data.
M100 (ASU)
West Virginia Revolutionary Ancestors Whose Services Were Non-military and Whose Names, Therefore, Do Not Appear in Revolutionary Indexes of Soldiers and Sailors.
R870 (ASU)
Amherst County, Virginia, in the Revolution: Including Extracts from the "Lost Order Book", 1773-1782.
S9530 (ASU)
The Kings Mountain Men: The Story of the Battle, with Sketches of the American Soldiers Who Took Part.
W5490 (ASU)
The King's Mountain Men, the Story of the Battle, with Sketches of the American Soldiers Who Took Part.
W5500 (BC)
Virginia Revolutionary Land Bounty Warrants.
W7460
Catalogue of Revolutionary Soldiers and Sailors of the Commonwealth of Va.; to Whom Land Bounty Warrants were Granted. . . .
W7470 (BC)
Catalogue of Revolutionary Soldiers and Sailors of the Commonwealth of Virginia to Whom Land Bounty Warrants Were Granted by Virginia for Military Services in the War for Independence.
W7480 (ASU)

ANTHROPOLOGY — APP.
Morphologic and Systematic Relationships of Some Middle Ordovician Ostracoda.
K3120 (ETSU)
ANTHROPOLOGY — KY.
Ancient Life in Kentucky: A Brief Presentation of the Paleontological Succession in Kentucky Coupled with a Systematic Outline of the Archaeology of the Commonwealth.
F3850 (ASU BC)
Ancient Life in Kentucky: A Brief Presentation of the Paleontological Succession in Kentucky Coupled with a Systematic Outline of the Archaeology of the Commonwealth.
F3860 (WCU MHC BC)
ANTHROPOLOGY — VA.
The Virginia Indians in the Seventeenth Century.
W7040 (ASU)
APP.
Growing Up Country.
A5800 (BC ASU LMC)
APP. CITIES — ABINGDON, VA.
Publications of the Historical Society of Washington County, Virginia.
H5960
Historical Sketch of Sinking Spring Presbyterian Church of Abingdon, Virginia.
S7070
Preliminary Checklist for Abingdon, 1807-1876.
W9860
APP. CITIES — ANDERSON, S. C.
"An Enrollment Projection for the Estes Elementary School, Anderson, S. C."
C5740 (WCU)
APP. CITIES — ANDREWS, N. C.
Population and economy of Andrews, N. C.
W4910
APP. CITIES — ASHEVILLE, N. C.
Asheville and Land of the Sky.
A1590 (BC ASU WCU LMC MHC)
Asheville and Vicinity. "Where the Snowbirds Nest."
A5150 (BC ASU)
City Directory.
A5160
Asheville — Live and Invest in the Land of the Sky.
A5170 (ASU)
In the Land of the Sky, for Your Year-round Home.
A5180 (ASU)
Asheville Handbook: A Condensed Summary of Important Facts and Figures.
A5190 (LMC)
Community Action for Social Redevelopment in Asheville and Buncombe County.
A5200 (WWC)
A Population and Economic Analysis of the Asheville Metropolitan Area and the Western North Carolina That It Serves.
A5210 (BC)
B3670 (WCU)
A Spire in the Mountains: The Story of 176 Years of a Church and a Town Growing Together, 1794-1969.
B4430 (ASU ETSU UNCA)
Early Days: All Souls' Church and Biltmore Village.
B5970
After the Good Gay Times: Asheville — Summer of '35; A Season with F. Scott Fitzgerald.
B9430
Glimpses of a Land of Beauty.
C400
The Thought at Midnight: The Story of the Asheville Normal.
C500 (LMC)
A Survey of the Public Libraries of Asheville and Buncombe County, North Carolina.
C2730 (LMC ETSU ASU)
Fishers of Men: A Charge to the Clergy of the Jurisdiction of Asheville, by the Bishop of North Carolina.
C3790 (WCU)
C9110 (UNCA)
D2500 (UNCA)
"The Land of the Sky."
G3470
In the Land of the Sky, Grove Park Inn.
G4460 (ASU)

Asheville, Western North Carolina, Nature's Trundle-Bed of Recuperation for Tourist and Health-beds.
H4370
Good Victuals from the Mountains.
H6980
Soil Survey of the Asheville, North Carolina, Area.
L620
L2840
Battle of Asheville.
M720 (ASU LMC UNCA)
Asheville, in Land of the Sky.
M4740 (ASU WCU LMC WWC UNCA)
Area Manpower Review: Asheville Standard Metropolitan Statistical Area — Buncombe County.
N2240 (ASU WWC)
Two City Managers in Asheville, North Carolina: Politics, Administration and Policy Formulation.
P4740 (UNCA)
An Emission Survey and Ambient Air Quality Data of Buncombe, Haywood, Henderson Counties and the City of Asheville.
R1330 (WCU)
Photogravures.
R3590 (BC)
Souvenir of Asheville or the Sky-land.
S590 (ASU WCU BC)
Asheville and Buncombe County.
S5480 (WCU BC)
Sixty-four Selected Views of Western North Carolina, "The Land of the Sky, America's Beauty Spot".
S5810 (ASU)
The Image of Asheville.
T5210 (LMC)
Floods on French Broad and Swannanoa Rivers, in Vicinity of Asheville, North Carolina.
T7040
Fifty-eight Years in Asheville.
W2030 (UNCA)
APP. CITIES — ASHLAND, KY.
A History of Ashland, Kentucky, 1786 to 1954.
A5220 (ASU BC)
The Fire Clays and Fire Clay Industries of the Olive Hill and Ashland Districts of Northeastern Kentucky.
C8780 (BC)
Oil Domes of Ashland.
J1180
The Exception; The Story of the Ashland Oil and Refining Co.
S1450
APP. CITIES — BECKLEY, W. VA.
Brief History of Beckley, West Virginia.
B2500 (ASU)
Beckley, U.S.A.
W930 (BC)
APP. CITIES — BEREA, KY.
U4140
APP. CITIES — BIRMINGHAM, ALA.
Early Days in Birmingham.
B4210 (BC)
This Is Birmingham.
H4670 (BC)
Water Supply of the Birmingham Area, Alabama.
R3340
APP. CITIES — BLACKSBURG, VA.
A Social Study of the Blacksburg Community.
G390 (ASU)
APP. CITIES — BLOWING ROCK, N. C.
The Lenoir-Blowing Rock Wonderland.
L1760 (ASU)
APP. CITIES — BLUEFIELD, VA. AND W. VA.
Follow-up Study of MDTA E. and D. Project at Bluefield State College.
H6290
APP. CITIES — BOONE, N. C.
Code.
B5430 (ASU)
Land Development Plan.
B5440 (BC ASU)
Land Development Plan.
B5450
The Population and Economy of Boone, North Carolina.
C3600 (LMC ASU)
"A Study of Visually-handicapped Children in the Eighth Grade of Boone High School."
D1160 (ASU)

APP. CITIES — BOONE, N. C.

The First Baptist Church at Boone, North Carolina: A History.
E1260 (ASU LMC)

"A Study of the Motor Ability of a Selected Number of Boys at the Appalachian Elementary School During the 1959-1960 School Year."
K2840 (ASU)

This is Our Town: Boone, N. C.
L1200 (LMC ASU)

Zoning Ordinance: Boone, N. C.
N2190 (LMC ASU)

"A Study of the Needs, Growth, and Development of the Presbyterian Church of Boone, N. C."
P230 (ASU)

"An Investigation of the Arithmetical Disabilities of Beginning Ninth Grade Pupils in Appalachian High School."
S3590 (ASU)

APP. CITIES — BRISTOL, TENN.

"A Study of the Intramural Sports Program in George W. Vance Junior High School, Bristol, Tennessee."
B1770 (ETSU)

Course of Study for Elementary Schools, Bristol, Tennessee, Grades 1-6.
B6700

New Course of Study; A Teachers Guide for the Elementary Schools of Bristol, Tennessee . . .
B6710 (ETSU)

"A Study of the Reactions of a Representative Group of Students toward Guidance Received While Attending Bristol, Tennessee, High School, 1958-59."
C4260 (ETSU)

"A Proposed Nongraded Primary Organization for Central School: Bristol, Tennessee."
D1750 (ETSU)

"Educational Facilities and Economic Development of Bristol, 1930-1950."
H6520 (ETSU)

"The Home Visitation Program of the Bristol, Tennessee, Schools, 1948-1969."
H8650 (ETSU)

"An Evaluation of the Changes in Reading Achievement Effected by a Federal Project in the Bristol, Tennessee, Elementary Schools."
H8830 (ETSU)

"A Study of the Drop-outs from the Bristol, Tennessee, School Systems in Grades 8-12 from 1946 to 1951."
J1950

"An Analysis of the Relationship of Religious Commitment and Alienation Among High School Students of Bristol, Tennessee."
K1620 (ETSU)

"An Industrial and Commercial History of the Tri-cities in Tennessee."
L1070

Double Destiny: The Story of Bristol, Tennessee-Virginia.
L3670 (LMC ETSU)

Double Destiny: The Story of Bristol, Tennessee-Virginia.
L3680 (ASU)

A Golden Book of the History and Tradition of Bristol, Tennessee, High School, 1915-1965.
M3450 (ETSU)

"A Search for a Meaningful Program in Mathematics for the Slow Learner in the Seventh Grade in the Bristol, Tennessee, City Schools."
M6200 (ETSU)

"A Proposed Individualized Primary Mathematics Program for Holston Heights Elementary School, Bristol, Tennessee."
M8290 (ETSU)

"What the Patrons of the Elementary School of Bristol, Tennessee, Think About Their Schools."
M9300 (ETSU)

The Story of Bristol.
P4450 (ETSU ASU)

"The Social, Economic, Cultural, Religious and Family Educational Backgrounds of Recent Dropouts from Bristol, Tennessee, High School."
S4340 (ETSU)

"A Study of the Factors Which Might Affect Achievements in Reading in the First Grade of Anderson School, Bristol, Tennessee."
T750 (ETSU)

"The History of the First Presbyterian Church of Bristol, Tennessee."
V150 (ETSU)

"A Comparative Study of the Achievement in Science of the Fifth and Sixth Grade Pupils in Bristol, Tennessee, Schools, 1953-57."
W9090 (ETSU)

APP. CITIES — BRISTOL, TENN. AND VA.

"A Study of the Effect of Participation in Football on the Grades of Students at Bristol, Tennessee, High School."
A1420 (ETSU)

APP. CITIES — BRISTOL, VA.

"Merger of Local Government: Case Study, Washington County and Bristol, Virginia, 1971."
C9830 (ETSU)

"The Role of the Bristol, Virginia, Elementary School Principals in Classroom Visitation."
E1630 (ETSU)

"Evaluation of Reading in the Bristol, Virginia, Schools with a Suggested Corrective Program."
F3230 (ETSU)

"Suburban Opposition to Annexation: Case Study Bristol, Virginia, 1972."
G750 (ETSU)

Bristol-Kingsport Metropolitan Area Projections and Economic Base Analysis.
G4220

"A Comparison of Special Characteristics of College Bound Seniors and Non-college Seniors from Virginia High School, Bristol, Virginia."
H830 (ETSU)

"Educational Facilities and Economic Development of Bristol, 1930-1950."
H6510

"The Third-grade Social Studies Program in Bristol, Virginia, 1969-70."
K2680 (ETSU)

Double Destiny: The Story of Bristol, Tennessee-Virginia.
L3670 (LMC ETSU)

Double Destiny: The Story of Bristol, Tennessee-Virginia.
L3680 (ASU)

"Evaluation of the Collection of the Solid Waste in Bristol, Virginia, with a Consideration for the Proposed Annexation Area."
M2460 (ETSU)

The Story of Bristol.
P4450 (ETSU ASU)

"A Study of the Economically and Educationally Deprived Students of Bristol, Virginia, Junior High School."
Q120 (ETSU)

"A Consultative Conference in Science for Elementary Teachers in Bristol, Virginia, 1955-56."
V70 (ETSU)

Projections and Economic Base Analysis: Bristol-Kingsport Metropolitan Area Including the City of Bristol, Virginia, and the Counties of Washington, Virginia, and Sullivan, Tennessee.
V820

Labor Supply Survey of Bristol, Virginia-Tennessee.
V860 (ETSU)

APP. CITIES — BRISTOL, VA. AND TENN.

The City of Bristol, Virginia-Tennessee, Its Interests and Industries; Compiled under the Auspices of the Board of Trade. Also a Series of Comprehensive Sketches of Representative Business Enterprises.
I990

APP. CITIES — BRYSON CITY, N. C.

Floods on the Tuckaseigee River and Deep Creek in Vicinity of Bryson City, North Carolina.
T2750

APP. CITIES — CALHOUN, GA.

Climb the Hills of Gordon: Stories of Gordon County and Calhoun, Georgia.
R1180 (LMC ASU BC)

APP. CITIES — CARTERSVILLE, GA.

Geology and Mineral Deposits of the Cartersville District, Georgia.
K1700

APP. CITIES — CHARLESTON, W. VA.

Survey of Governmental and Voluntary Health, Welfare and Recreation Services in Greater Kanawha Valley. (Community Services Report.)
C4170

One Hundred Years: An Anthology — Charleston Jewry.
M5270 (ASU)

Charleston 175.
M7580 (ASU)

APP. CITIES — CHARLOTTESVILLE, VA.

Pursuits of War: The People of Charlottesville and Albemarle County, Virginia, in the Second World War.
A970 (ASU)

APP. CITIES — CHATTANOOGA, TENN.

Guide Book of Chattanooga and Vicinity.
A1620

History of the First Presbyterian Church of Chattanooga.
A4750

The History of Hamilton County and Chattanooga, Tennessee.
A4760 (ETSU BC ASU)

Guide Book to Lookout Mountain and a Brief Account of Battles Fought near Chattanooga, Tennessee.
B580

Pioneers of Old Frontiers.
B7270 (ETSU)

"Municipal Ownership of Public Utilities in Chattanooga, Tennessee."
B7940
C2630

Chattanooga, Industrial Center of the South.
C3520
C3530 (BC)

"The Negroes of Chattanooga, Tennessee."
C7830

"Coordination of Anti-poverty Programs in Chattanooga."
D1250

Storming of the Gateway: Chattanooga, 1863.
D3170 (WCU BC ASU)

Helen Exum's Chattanooga Cook Book.
E2460 (ASU)

Guide to Chattanooga, Lookout Mountain and Chickamauga National Military Park.
F600

The Chattanooga Country, 1540-1951: From Tomahawks to TVA.
G2950 (ASU LMC MHC ETSU BC)

The Chattanooga Country, 1540-1962: From Tomahawks to TVA.
G2960 (WCU)

Men and Vision: The Secret of Yesterday's Success, the Formula for Tomorrow's. A Brief History of the Chattanooga Medicine Company.
G4630 (ETSU)

Physiography of the Chattanooga District in Tenn., Georgia, and Ala. 1899.
H3870

Chattanooga.
J290

An Honorable Titan: A Biographical Study of Adolph S. Ochs.
J1750

"The Incidence of Social Diseases among Negroes in Chattanooga, Tennessee, and the Educational Implications."
J2310

"The Chattanooga Region as a Plant Site for the Nylon Industry."
K2090 (ETSU)

"The Influence of Geography on the Growth of Chattanooga Industries."
L1420

Chattanooga and Her Battlefields.
M1650

Standard History of Chattanooga, Tennessee, with Full Outline of the Early Settlement, Pioneer Life, Indian History and General and Particular History of the City to the Close of the Year 1910.
M1660

Chattanooga: Its History and Geography.
M2310 (BC ETSU)

Chattanooga, The Mountain City.
M9120 (BC)

APP. CITIES — CHATTANOOGA, TENN.
"Civil War Anecdotes and Legends of Chattanooga."
N710
The Chickamauga and Chattanooga Campaign and Battle-fields. A Chronological Historic Guide, August 16-November 25, 1863.
N2870
Chattanooga and Hamilton County, Tennessee.
O20
O670
Chattanooga, Tennessee; Hamilton County, and Lookout Mountain. An Epitome of Chattanooga from Her Early Days Down to the Present; Hamilton County, Its Soil, Climate, Area, Population, Wealth, etc.
P170
P570
The Circuit Rider and Those Who Followed. Sketches of Methodist Churches Organized before 1860 in the Chattanooga Area with Special Reference to Centenary.
P1160
Evaluation of the East Ridge High School, Chattanooga, Tennessee; Completed by the visiting Committee March 5-9, 1962. . . .
S5690
Evaluative study made in Chattanooga High School, Chattanooga, Tennessee; completed by Visiting Committee March 12-16, 1950.
S5700
A Study of the Chattanooga Labor Market Area.
T1170 (ETSU)
Chattanooga Flood Control Problem.
T2380
Floods on North Chickamauga, Mountain, and Lookout Creeks, in Vicinity of Chattanooga, Tennessee.
T7110
Chattanooga, Its History and Growth.
W300
This is Chattanooga.
W320
Historic City, Chattanooga; Containing Views and Descriptive Matter of Historic Points of Interest, Scenery, Pictures of Old and New Buildings, Leading Men, etc., All Artistically and Pleasingly Intermingled.
W2160

APP. CITIES — CLARKSBURG, W. VA.
"A Study of the Factors Influencing Job-satisfaction among Factory Workers of Clarksburg, West Virginia, and Coal Miners of Morgantown, West Virginia."
M4720
Soil Survey of Clarksburg Area, West Virginia.
M6670
"Transportation and Trade Areas; Analysis of Morgantown, Fairmont, and Clarksburg."
S330 (ASU)

APP. CITIES — CLEVELAND, TENN.
Guest's Guide; Points of Interest in Cleveland.
B8790
City and County with a Future: Cleveland, Bradley County, Tennessee.
C4980
Health and Sanitation Needs and Resources, Bradley County, Tennessee.
T9400

APP. CITIES — CLINTON, TENN.
One Hundred Years: A Story of the First Baptist Church, Clinton, Tennessee.
W2000

APP. CITIES — CORBIN, KY.
I340

APP. CITIES — DALTON, GA.
Official History of Whitfield County, Georgia.
W5710 (BC)

APP. CITIES — DANVILLE, VA.
The Story of Danville.
H190 (ASU)

APP. CITIES — ELIZABETHTON, TENN.
"An Overview of Special Education Services in the Elizabethton City School with Emphasis on the Homebound Program."
B2310 (ETSU)
"An Investigation of the Readability of Textbooks Used in the Intermediate Grades in the Elizabethton, Tennessee, School System."
B6670 (ETSU)
"A Seventh Grade Homeroom Guidance Experiment at Elizabethton Junior High School, Elizabethton, Tennessee."
B7330 (ETSU)
"A Survey of the Occupational Information Needs of the Ninth Graders of the Elizabethton High School, Elizabethton, Tennessee."
C2790 (ETSU)
"Art Handbook for Elementary Teachers of Elizabethton City Schools, Elizabethton, Tennessee."
C9900 (ETSU)
Helping Our Children Grow.
E1560 (ETSU)
"A Study of Vocational Education at the Elizabethton, Tennessee, Area Vocational-Technical School."
F2950 (ETSU)
"Team Teaching at Douglas School, Elizabethton, Carter County, Tennessee."
H3310 (ETSU)
"A Survey of Reading Readiness and Reading Achievement of City Kindergarten and Non-kindergarten Children in the First Grades in Elizabethton, Tennessee."
H3780 (ETSU)
"The Social and Economic Effects Produced upon Small Towns by Rapid Industrialization."
H6740
"A Guidance Program for Elizabethton High School."
L30 (ETSU)
"A Determination of Ambient Air Concentrations of Sulfur Dioxide in Elizabethton, Tennessee."
M2480 (ETSU)
"An Analysis of the Errors in Word Recognition Made by Pupils of One Section Each of the Second Through Sixth Grades of Lynn Avenue School, 1956-57, in Elizabethton, Tennessee."
M6380 (ETSU)
"A Program for Mentally Retarded, Elizabethton City Schools."
P2890 (ETSU)
"A Reading Improvement Program Developed by a Classroom Teacher for a Selected Seventh-grade Group at Elizabethton Junior High School."
R1850 (ETSU)
"An Analysis of Youth Centers for White Youth in Three Tennessee Cities: Johnson City, Elizabethton and Kingsport."
R3720 (ETSU)
"The History and Educational Influence of Douglas School, Elizabethton, Tennessee, 1900-1965."
S2550 (ETSU)
"Diagnosis and Remediation of Difficulties in Arithmetic in Fifth Grade at West Side School, Elizabethton, Tennessee, 1956-57."
S5240 (ETSU)
Floods on Watauga and Doe Rivers in Vicinity of Elizabethton, Tennessee.
T2760

APP. CITIES — ERWIN, TENN.
"The Diagnosis and Remediation of Difficulties in Arithmetical Skills of a Seventh-grade Class at Rock Creek School in Erwin, Tennessee."
H5270 (ETSU)

APP. CITIES — FAIRMONT, W. VA.
Economic Stability and Growth Potential, Fairmont, W. Va.
H2230
"Transportation and Trade Areas; Analysis of Morgantown, Fairmont, and Clarksburg."
S330 (ASU)

APP. CITIES — FLORENCE, ALA.
A History of Florence, Alabama, with 1850 Census of Lauderdale County.
G430 (ASU)
Report of Industrial Survey of Florence, Alabama, and Muscle Shoals District.
L3050 (ASU)
Floods on the Tennessee River and Cypress and Cox Creeks in Vicinity of Florence, Alabama.
T7270

APP. CITIES — GATLINBURG, TENN.
Gatlinburg, Gateway to the Great Smokies.
F2230
Gatlinburg and the Great Smokies.
P4970

APP. CITIES — GREENEVILLE, TENN.
Historic Greeneville, Tennessee. A City among the Mountains.
A1530
Resources and Enterprises of Upper East Tennessee: Johnson City, Jonesboro, Greenville, Rogersville, Morristown, Watauga, Tennessee. Franklin, Territory South of the Ohio.
E2040 (ETSU)
The Economy of Greeneville, Tennessee; a Study of the Information and Data Related to the Greeneville, Tennessee, Economic Community.
H6730
P70
Greeneville's Government; a Study of the Organization and Administration of the Government of Greeneville, Tennessee.
U4110

APP. CITIES — GREENVILLE, S. C.
"A Study of Special Services in the Schools of Greenville County, South Carolina."
B1500
Greenville's Big Idea.
G3870 (ETSU)
Botanical Gardening in Greenville.
S300 (BC ASU)
Sixteenth South Carolina Regiment, CSA, From Greenville, S. C.
T610 (ASU)
Schools for a Growing Democracy.
T8720 (ETSU)
A Critical Analysis of the Develgpmental Tasks of an Upper-elementary Class in Area 2 of the Greenville County-city School System and the Patterns of Direction Attempted for Better Group Action.
Y50 (ASU)

APP. CITIES — GREENVILLE, TENN.
Lest We Forget.
D3770 (BC)
Bridging the Gap. A Guide to Early Greenville, South Carolina.
E620 (ASU)
"A Study of a Group of Drop-outs of the Greenville High School."
H2520
"An Investigation of the Reading Interest of the Junior High School Students in Greenville, Tennessee."
M6070
Soil Survey of the Greenville Area, Tennessee.
M6680

APP. CITIES — HAGERSTOWN, MD.
Jonathan Hager, Founder of Hagerstown, Maryland.
M6230
The History of Washington County, Maryland, from the Earliest Settlements to the Present Time, Including a History of Hagerstown.
W6870 (ASU)

APP. CITIES — HARLAN, KY.
I380
Harlan County, Existing Land Use Analysis. Harlan-Harlan County Major Thoroughfare Plan.
K1150
Population-Economic Study, Harlan-Harlan County, Kentucky.
K1170

APP. CITIES — HARPER'S FERRY, W. VA.
Harper's Ferry in Pictures.
R2690 (ASU WCU)

APP. CITIES — HARRISBURG, PA.
Annals, Comprising Memoirs, Incidents and Statistics of Harrisburg, from the Period of Its First Settlement.
M7540 (ASU)

APP. CITIES — HARRISONBURG, VA.
My Recollections of Rocktown, Now Known as Harrisonburg.
C1460 (ASU BC)
Historic Harrisonburg.
W1760 (ASU BC)

APP. CITIES — HAZARD, KY.
Industrial Resources, Hazard, Kentucky.
H4090
I390
The Story of Hazard, Kentucky.
P2940 (BC)

APP. CITIES — HENDERSONVILLE, N. C.
B4820

APP. CITIES — HENDERSONVILLE, N. C.
Minutes and Records, Feb., 1917-Dec. 25, 1960.
H4570 (WCU)
A Study of the Hendersonville Central Business District.
H4580 (LMC)
Hendersonville in Civil War Times.
H8100
S190
APP. CITIES — HICKORY, N. C.
Clinard Looks Back, a Compilation of Short Stories Covering Early Days in Hickory.
C5060 (ASU LMC)
APP. CITIES — HINDMAN, KY.
I400
APP. CITIES — HUNTINGTON, W. VA.
Huntington's Park System and Recreational Facilities.
H8490
Soil Survey of the Huntington Area, West Virginia.
L800
The First Methodist Episcopal Church, Huntington, West Virginia.
N670 (ASU)
Huntington (West Virginia) Through Seventy Five Years.
W470
APP. CITIES — HUNTSVILLE, ALA.
Rocket City U. S. A. from Huntsville, Alabama to the Moon.
B3140
Early History of Huntsville, Alabama, 1804-1870.
B3420 (ASU BC)
"The Social Backgrounds of Scientists and Engineers in Oak Ridge, Tennessee, and Huntsville, Alabama."
D4130
The Pictorial History of Huntsville, 1805-1865.
H10 (BC)
Impact of the war on the Huntsville Area, Madison County, Alabama; working notebook for use by local groups studying recent economic developments and formulating plans for the post-war period.
U1400
APP. CITIES — HYDEN, KY.
I410
APP. CITIES — JACKSON, KY.
I430
APP. CITIES — JEFFERSON CITY, TENN.
An Educational Study of Jefferson County, Tennessee.
C1650
APP. CITIES — JOHNSON CITY
"A Comparison of Intelligence in Students with Mixed and Lateral Dominance in Johnson City Vocational Schools."
C5460 (ETSU)
"A Comparison of Intelligence in Students with Mixed and Lateral Dominance in Johnson City Vocational Schools."
C5460 (ETSU)
APP. CITIES — JOHNSON CITY, TENN.
"History of the Schools of Johnson City, Tennessee, 1868-1950."
A4550 (ETSU)
"The Establishment of a Remedial Reading Program at Columbus Powell Elementary School, Johnson City, Tennessee, School Year, 1966-1967."
B1340 (ETSU)
Soil Resources of Johnson City, Tennessee.
B4200 (ETSU)
"The Applicability of the Industrial Arts Curriculum Project, Construction to the New Junior High Schools in Johnson City."
B7720 (ETSU)
"The Predictive Value of the Metropolitan Readiness Tests for First Grade Achievement for Selected Groups of Children in the Johnson City, Tennessee, Public Schools."
B9270 (ETSU)
"An Evaluation of the Remedial Speech Program in the Johnson City Schools."
C7330 (ETSU)
"A Proposed Social Studies Curriculum for the Schools of Johnson City, Tennessee."
C7560 (ETSU)
"A Comparative Analysis of Three Evaluation Procedures Used with Kindergarten Pupils at Southside Elementary School, Johnson City, Tennessee."
C9230 (ETSU)
"Formative Years of Johnson City, Tennessee, 1885-1890: A Social History."
D210 (ETSU)
"A Proposed Course of Study in Electronics for Johnson City Vocational School's Evening Program."
E1840 (ETSU)
Resources and Enterprises of Upper East Tennessee: Johnson City, Jonesboro, Greenville, Rogersville, Morristown, Watauga, Tennessee. Franklin, Territory South of the Ohio.
E2040 (ETSU)
A Brief History of Johnson City, Tennessee.
E2250 (ETSU)
"Enriching the Curriculum of South Side School, Johnson City, Tennessee, by Parent Participation."
F1910 (ETSU)
"Effect of Consolidation on Johnson County School, Johnson City, Tennessee."
G330 (ETSU)
"Annexation: A Case Study of Supporting and Opposing Factions in Johnson City, Tennessee."
G1940 (ETSU)
"A Study of Glass and Paper Recycling in Johnson City, Tennessee."
G4860 (ETSU)
"The Use of the Case Method in the Study of Juvenile Delinquency in Johnson City."
H230 (ETSU)
"Development of a Course in Fractions for Johnson City Vocational School."
H4970 (ETSU)
Johnson City, Tennessee, Population and Economic Base Study.
H5390
"A Five-year Study of an Educable Mentally Retarded Class in Keystone School, Johnson City, Tennessee."
H7430 (ETSU)
"A Multilevel Approach to Reading for One Section of a Sixth Grade Class in Keystone Elementary School Year, 1965-1966."
J680 (ETSU)
Industrial Advantages of the Johnson City Area.
J1340 (ETSU)
The Wataugan Annual.
J1360 (ETSU)
Annual Report . . . for Fiscal Year Ended June 30, 1944-.
J1370 (ETSU)
Annual Report . . . for Fiscal Year Ended June 30, 1944-.
J1380 (ETSU)
Code.
J1390 (ETSU)
The Code of the City of Johnson City, Tennessee: The Chart and the General Ordinances of the City, Published by Order of the Board of Commissioners.
J1400 (ETSU)
Zoning Ordinance for the City of Johnson City, Tennessee.
J1410 (ETSU)
Map of Johnson City, Washington County, Tennessee.
J1420 (ETSU)
Newsletter.
J1430 (ETSU)
Directory of First Methodist Church, November 1, 1950. . .
J1440 (ETSU)
Evaluation Report, North Junior High School, Johnson City, Tennessee.
J1450 (ETSU)
Washington County-Johnson City Civil Defense Operational Survival Plan.
J1460 (ETSU)
Manual for Receiving and Processing Instructional Materials.
J1470 (ETSU)
Johnson City Shopping Center District Regulations.
J1480 (ETSU)
Johnson City, Tennessee: Population and Economic Base Study.
J1490 (ETSU)
Johnson City's Community Facilities.
J1500 (ETSU)
Land Use Analysis.
J1510 (ETSU)
Land Use Plan.
J1520 (ETSU)
Neighborhood Analyses.
J1530 (ETSU)
Subdivision Regulations of Johnson City Regional Planning Commission.
J1540 (ETSU)
Evaluative Study of South Junior High School, Johnson City, Tennessee; Completed by the Visiting Committee March 15-18, 1965. . .
J1560 (ETSU)
Evaluative Study Made in Science Hill High School, Johnson City, Tennessee . . . March 4-8, 1951.
J1570 (ETSU)
Report.
J1590 (ETSU)
"A Survey of the Problems of Freshmen Student Nurses at Memorial Hospital and a Proposed Guidance Program."
J1650 (ETSU)
"An Industrial and Commercial History of the Tri-cities in Tennessee."
L1070
"An Analysis of Particulate Pollution in Johnson City and Rural Washington County, Tennessee."
L1400 (ETSU)
"A Study to Determine the Major Causes of Withdrawal from Science Hill High School During the 1965-1966 School Year."
L2820 (ETSU)
100th Anniversary History and Directory, 1871-1971, First Christian Church, Johnson City, Tennessee.
M650
Brief Chronological History of Johnson City, Tennessee and Three Suggested Historical Tours of the Johnson City Area.
M660 (BC LMC ETSU ASU)
"A Comparative Analysis of the Results of the Kraus-Weber Test for Minimum Muscular Fitness in Four of the Elementary Schools of Johnson City, Tennessee."
M1290
"A Follow-up Study of the 1959-1963 Graduates of Langston High School, Johnson City, Tennessee."
M1890 (ETSU)
"A Study of Problems of Junior High School Students of Johnson City, Tennessee."
M4220 (ETSU)
"Geographic Factors Affecting Manufacturers of Durable Goods in Johnson City, Tennessee."
M6030 (ETSU)
"An Experimental Program in Grouping for Third Grade at Fairmont School, Johnson City, Tennessee."
M6430 (ETSU)
"The Effects of a Physical Education Program on the Motor Skills of Selected Severely Retarded Children in Johnson City, Tennessee."
M7120 (ETSU)
"A Program of Folk Songs Used to Enrich and Implement the Social Studies Program in Grades Four, Five and Six at North Side School, Johnson City, Tennessee."
M7380 (ETSU)
"Materials for Teaching Social Studies in a Selected Fifth Grade at Asbury School, Johnson City, Tennessee, 1956-57."
M9090 (ETSU)
"An Improved Language Arts Program for a Selected Third Grade at Henry Johnson School in Johnson City, Tennessee."
O830 (ETSU)
"A Comparison of Parents and Teachers Viewpoints Relative to Teacher Competencies in Johnson City, Tennessee."
O980
"A Study of Two Areas for Future Supermarket Location in Johnson City, Tennessee."
P670 (ETSU)

APP. CITIES — JOHNSON CITY, TENN.

"A Study of the Physical Education Program at the Junior High School, Johnson City, Tennessee."
P1110 (ETSU)

"A Speech Improvement Program in Kindergarten of the Johnson City, Tennessee, Public School System."
P1560 (ETSU)

"An Analysis of Youth Centers for White Youth in Three Tennessee Cities: Johnson City, Elizabethton and Kingsport."
R3720 (ETSU)

Parking Program, Central Business District, Johnson City, Tennessee.
S5130 (ETSU)

Traffic and Parking, Johnson City, Tennessee.
S5140 (ETSU)

Johnson City Transportation Study: Major Route Plan. Traffic Operation Study and Parking Study.
T1220 (ETSU)

"An Attitudinal Study of Sunday Closing Laws in Johnson City, Tennessee: A Contribution to the "Interest-group" (Conflict) Model of Law."
T7830 (ETSU)

Illustrated Johnson City, Tennessee.
W1960 (ETSU)

"An Analysis of Problems of Eight and Ninth Grade Students in the Junior High School of Johnson City, Tennessee."
W6110 (ETSU)

History of Johnson City and Its Environs.
W6760 (ASU LMC ETSU BC)

History of Johnson City and Its Environs.
W6770 (ETSU)

APP. CITIES — JOHNSTOWN, PA.

The Potential for Human Resources and Economic Growth in a Declining Local Community; A Socioeconomic Study of the Johnstown, Penn. Economy.
L2000

APP. CITIES — JONESBORO, TENN.

Resources and Enterprises of Upper East Tennessee: Johnson City, Jonesboro, Greenville, Rogersville, Morristown, Watauga, Tennessee. Franklin, Territory South of the Ohio.
E2040 (ETSU)

APP. CITIES — KINGSPORT, TENN.

"Vocational Preferences of Eighth Grade Students at Ross N. Robinson Junior High School, Kingsport, TENNESSEE."
A1540 (ETSU)

Wings Over Kingsport, No. 2: Tennessee's Planned City & Its Industries as Viewed from the Sky in 1938 and 1963.
A1980 (ETSU)

"A Study of Book Losses During the Period 1965-1969 in the Dobyns-Bennett High School Materials Center, Kingsport, Tennessee."
B2920 (ETSU)

"A Brief Survey of Industrial Plants in Kingsport, Tennessee, with Emphasis on the Geographic Location of the Industrial Worker."
B7860 (ETSU)

"A Brief Survey of Industrial Plants in Kingsport, Tennessee with Emphasis on the Geographic Location of the Industrial Worker."
B7870

"Differences between Negro and Caucasian Students at John Sevier Junior High School, Kingsport, Tennessee."
C2810 (ETSU)

Back Home. Kingsport, Tennessee.
C4470 (BC ASU)

"Social and Economic History of Kingsport before 1908."
C7840 (ETSU)

"A Study of the Word Recognition Abilities in the Fourth and Sixth Grades of Douglass School, 1957-58, in Kingsport, Tennessee."
C8150 (ETSU)

"Educational and Vocational Choices of the 1960 Graduates of Dobyns-Bennett High School, Kingsport, Tennessee."
C9210 (ETSU)

"A Descriptive Study of the Science Fair at Robinson Junior High School, Kingsport, Tennessee, and in Orange County, Florida, for 1960-1962."
C9780 (ETSU)

"The Effect of Team Teaching on Academic Achievement, John Sevier Junior High School, Kingsport, Tennessee."
D4330 (ETSU)

"The Reading Habits of 200 Adults in Kingsport, Tennessee."
E990

Bristol-Kingsport Metropolitan Area Projections and Economic Base Analysis.
G4220

Kingsport, Tennessee — a Modern American City Developed through Industry.
H150

"An Improved Language Arts Program for a Selected Third Grade at Thomas Jefferson School, Kingsport, Tennessee."
H650 (ETSU)

"A Study of Some Problems of Eighth Grade Students of John Sevier Junior High School, Kingsport, Tennessee."
I840 (ETSU)

"A Survey of Programs Offered for the Academically Talented Students at Dobyns-Bennett High School, Kingsport, Tennessee, and the Resulting Implications for the School Library."
K210 (ETSU)

Kingsport Book of Type Faces.
K2510 (ETSU)

New Dimensions in Mathematics for the Elementary Schools in Kingsport, Tennessee.
K2540 (ETSU)

Kingsport, the Planned Industrial City.
K2550 (ETSU)

Kingsport, Tennessee, a Modern American City — Developed through Industry.
K2560 (LMC ETSU)

Kingsport, the Planned Industrial City.
K2570 (ETSU ASU)

"A Study of the Use of Periodicals Received by the Dobyns-Bennett Senior High School Materials Center, Kingsport, Tennessee."
K3110 (ETSU)

"An Experimental Study of the Effect of an Individualized Reading Program on Third, Fourth, and Fifth Grade Students in the Thomas Jefferson School, Kingsport, Tennessee."
K3170 (ETSU)

"An Industrial and Commercial History of the Tri-cities in Tennessee."
L1070

A Survey of Social Services in the Greater Kingsport Area.
L1210 (ETSU)

"Development of a Comprehension Skills Program for the Primary Educable Mentally Retarded Class in Kingsport, Tennessee."
L1470 (ETSU)

"A Study of the Influence of Certain Personal and Other Factors on the Number of Observed Unsafe Acts and Injuries Sustained by Employees of Kingsport Power Company."
L2590 (ETSU)

Kingsport: A Romance of Industry.
L3290 (BC ASU ETSU)

"A Team Teaching Approach to Reading in the Fourth Grade at Dickson Elementary School in Kingsport, Tennessee, 1964-1965."
M3760 (ETSU)

"An Individualized Reading Program for a Fifth Grade Group of Students at Andrew Johnson School, Kingsport, Tennessee."
M5420 (ETSU)

"A Study of Ninth-grade Science Students in Phase Two at John Sevier Junior High School, Kingsport, Tennessee, 1967-1968."
M7690 (ETSU)

"City-county Separation in Tennessee, a Case Study of Kingsport and Sullivan County."
N970

"Teaching Exceptional Children in the Fifth Grade of Lincoln Elementary School — Kingsport, Tennessee."
P350 (ETSU)

The Kingsport Strike.
P2440 (ASU LMC BC)

Kingsport, City of Industries, Schools, Churches and Homes.
P3080

Kingsport, the Planned Industrial City.
P3090

The Battle of Kingsport.
R320 (ASU ETSU)

"Business Education in the Kingsport Area High Schools: An Evaluation of Their Business Graduates."
R1030 (ETSU)

"Specific Techniques Used to Improve the Reading of Three Groups of Children in the Eighth Grade at Robinson Jr. High School in Kingsport, Tennessee."
R3210 (ETSU)

"An Analysis of Youth Centers for White Youth in Three Tennessee Cities: Johnson City, Elizabethton and Kingsport."
R3720 (ETSU)

"Socio-economic Status of Teachers in Kingsport, Tennessee, 1968-1969."
S1530 (ETSU)

"The Teaching of French, Grades 3-6, Lincoln School, Kingsport, Tennessee, 1965-1966."
S4930 (ETSU)

Kingsport, Tennessee: Historical Map of Long Island of the Holston.
S6300

City Manager Government in Kingsport.
S7520

Projections and Economic Base Analysis: Bristol-Kingsport Metropolitan Area Including the City of Bristol, Virginia, and the Counties of Washington, Virginia, and Sullivan, Tennessee.
V820

"The Planning of Art Facilities for Dobyns-Bennett High School, Kingsport, Tennessee."
W7030 (ETSU)

"The Symphony Orchestra of Kingsport, Tennessee."
W7400 (ETSU)

"An Occupational Survey of Selected Industries in the Kingsport Area of Sullivan County, Tennessee."
W7770 (ETSU)

APP. CITIES — KNOXVILLE, TENN.

Memorial of the Rev. James Park.
B20

Men of Affairs in Knoxville.
B620

"Politics of Innovation."
B670

"A Bibliographical Checklist of Knoxville and Memphis Imprints, 1867-1876 with an Introductory Essay on the Knoxville and Memphis Press."
B890

"The Cost of Administering Criminal Justice in Memphis and Knoxville, Tennessee."
B2810

He That Serveth; Twenty-five Years' Adventures in Christian Ministry, George Creswell and Second Church.
B2900

Annual Handbook of Knoxville, Tennessee, for the Year 1892. A Concise Statement of the Financial, Commercial and Manufacturing Interests of This City; Its Climate, and the Magnificent Scenery of Its Surroundings; Its Mineral, Marble and Timber Interests, as well as a Complete Memoranda of the Laws of Tennessee, and Other Matters of Interest to Homeseekers and Capitalists.
B6380

Recollections of the East Tennessee Campaign, Battle of Campbell Station, 16th Nov., 1863: Siege of Knoxville, 17th Nov.-5th Dec., 1863.
B6420

Joshua William Caldwell. A Memorial Volume, Containing His Biography, Writings and Addresses.
C120
C2640

"History of the Hamilton National Bank of Knoxville."
C2930

"History of the Knoxville Iron Company."
C4500

Knoxville.
C8680 (ASU ETSU BC)

APP. CITIES — KNOXVILLE, TENN.
A Social Study of the Colored Population of Knoxville, Tennessee.
D1100
"The Net Direct Economic Effect of the University of Tennessee on the City of Knoxville and on Knox County Resulting from the Expansion of the Knoxville Campus since 1962."
D1560
"Factors Influencing the Development of the Broadway Shopping Center at Knoxville, Tennessee."
D2710
"Manufacturing in the West Central Knoxville Area."
D2950
The French Broad-Holston Country: A History of Knox County, Tennessee.
E150 (ASU BC)
A Church Census of the 134 Churches in the City of Knoxville, Tennessee as of Date January 31, 1925.
E870
"A History of the First Baptist Church of Knoxville, Tennessee."
E1230
The Founding of Knoxville.
F1720 (ETSU)
Memoirs.
F2420
The First Exposition of Conservation and its Builders; an Official History of the National Conservation Exposition, Held at Knoxville, Tenn. in 1913 and of its Forerunner, the Appalachian Expositions of 1910-1911, Embracing a Review of the Conservation Movement in the U. S. from its Inception the Present Time.
G2550
Souvenir History of Knoxville.
G2560 (BC)
Souvenir History of Knoxville, the Marble City and Great Jobbing Market. Its Importance as a Manufacturing Center. . . .
G2570
The City of Knoxville, Tennessee and Vicinity and Their Resources.
G3060
G3460
"The Reaction of Presbyterian Ministers in the Knoxville Area to Specific Questions Concerning Ministerial Counseling."
G4380
"City-county Consolidation Attempts in Nashville and Knoxville, Tennessee."
G4600
The Economy of Metropolitan Knoxville. A Study Focused on the Economic Base and Potentials of Knoxville and Knox County.
H1260 (ETSU)
Men of Affairs in Knoxville.
H1500
"The History of Transportation Advertising, 1850-1956, and a Study of Its Importance in Knoxville, Tennessee."
H5550
H5710
H5970
H6020
H6990
Knoxville: Commercial and Industrial Survey of Knoxville, Tennessee.
H7330
Historical Discourse of St. John's Church, Knoxville, Tennessee.
H8270
"A Geographical Survey of Knoxville, Tennessee."
H8810
The Battle of Fort Sanders. An Address Delivered November 28th, 1814 . . . at the Unveiling and Dedication of the Monument Erected by the Knoxville Chapter, United Daughters of the Confederacy, to the Memory of the Confederate Soldiers Who Lost Their Lives during the Siege of Knoxville, Tennessee, November 29, 1863.
K820
Knoxville as an Iron Center.
K1910
K2890 (ETSU)
The Knoxville Area Diet Manual.
K2900 (ETSU)
K2920
Governments in Knox County.
L210 (ETSU)
"Federal Centralization versus Local Values: A Case Study of Federal-Local Relations in the Knoxville-Knox County Community Action Committee."
L3480
"A History of the Webb School of Knoxville, Tennessee."
L3560
Knoxville-Knox County Consolidation and the County and City School Systems.
M510
History of Forestdale Evangelical United Brethren Church.
M1060
History of the First Presbyterian Church in Knoxville, Tennessee.
M2300
M3180
"A History of Knoxville Journalism."
M4170
Proposed Metropolitan Government Charter for Knoxville and Knox County, Tennessee, 1959.
M5220
Staub School. A Brief History of Its First Fifty Years' Service to the Community.
M7610
History of the First Presbyterian Church in Knoxville, Tennessee.
P200
"A Corporate History of Knoxville, Tennessee, before 1860."
P1950
"The Influence of the Baptist Church on Knoxville Government."
P2580
Personal Recollections of the Occupation of East Tennessee and the Defense of Knoxville.
P3300
P4710
P4730
Knoxville, Past, Present and Future.
R1420
"A History of Municipal Government in Knoxville since 1911."
R2050
Standard History of Knoxville, Tennessee, with Full Outline of the Natural Advantages, Early Settlement, Territorial Government, Indian Troubles and General and Particular History of the City Down to the Present Time.
R4280
S180
"The Reading Interests of Students as Revealed in a Study of an Individualized Reading Program at Pond Gap School, Knoxville, Tennessee."
S850
A History of 100 Years of St. Johns Episcopal Church in Knoxville, Tenn.
S2100
Divided Loyalties: Fort Sanders and the Civil War in East Tennessee.
S2110 (BC ETSU)
Seventy-Five Years: Shannondale Presbyterian Church, Knoxville, Tennessee, 1886-1961.
S2240
Centennial Celebration of Island Home Baptist Church, Knoxville, Tennessee, October 2, 1960 - December 11, 1960.
S3080
"An Accounting Study of the Educational Progress of Knoxville Negro Pupils Over a Sixteen-year Period."
S4590
"The Economic Impact of the University of Tennessee upon Metropolitan Knoxville."
S4810
S5350
Letters from the Slave States.
S7470
"The Public Career of Joseph Alexander Mabry."
T590
The Cost of Distributing Power, Knoxville, Tennessee.
T2490
Knoxville and Vicinity, Tennessee. 1953.
T3000
Bert Vincent's Strolling, Being Sort of a Side-Glance at the Little Odds and Ends of Life in These Parts.
V630
The Best Stories of Bert Vincent, ed. Willard Yarbrough.
V640
More of the Best Stories of Bert Vincent.
V650
"The Marble Industry of the Knoxville Area."
W640
Tombstone Inscriptions and Death Records, Calvary Cemetery, Knoxville, Tennessee, 1869-1967.
W1640 (ETSU)
Art Work of Knoxville, with Sketch of Knoxville.
W5530
Knoxville Negro.
W7100

APP. CITIES — LENOIR CITY, TENN.
Floods on Tennessee River, Little Tennessee River, and Town and Muddy Creeks in Vicinity of Lenoir City, Tennessee.
T7290

APP. CITIES — LENOIR, N. C.
The Lenoir-Blowing Rock Wonderland.
L1760 (ASU)

APP. CITIES — LOGAN, W. VA.
"A Follow-up of 1952 Graduates of Logan High School, Logan, West Virginia."
O850

APP. CITIES — LYNCHBURG, VA.
A History of Lynchburg's Pioneer Quakers and Their Meeting House, 1754-1936.
B7110 (ASU)
Sketches and Recollections of Lynchburg, by the Oldest Inhabitant.
C10 (ASU)
Historic and Heroic Lynchburg.
H980 (ASU)
Bulletin of the Virginia State Library: Index to Mrs. Cabell's "Sketches and Recollections of Lynchburg."
H6460 (ASU)
Lynchburg in Old Virginia, the City of Industry and Opportunity.
L4080 (ASU)
S120
Lynchburg and Its Neighbors.
Y30 (ASU)

APP. CITIES — MCMINNVILLE, TENN.
McMinnville at a Milestone, 1810-1960. A Momento of the Sesquicentennial Year of McMinnville, Tennessee, 1960, 1958.
W8440 (ASU ETSU BC)

APP. CITIES — MANCHESTER, KY.
I530

APP. CITIES — MARION, N. C.
"Eliminations from the Class of 1950 in the Marion High School."
E1610 (ASU)
F1110

APP. CITIES — MARION, VA.
Hello Towns.
A2400 (ASU)
Hello Towns.
A2410 (LMC ASU)

APP. CITIES — MARYVILLE, TENN.
The History of New Providence Church, Maryville, Tennessee.
B1530
"The Social and Economic History of Maryville since 1890."
B1920
History of New Providence Presbyterian Church, Maryville, Tennessee, 1786-1921.
M2530 (ETSU)

APP. CITIES — MIDDLESBORO, KY.
I550
Middlesboro and Before Middlesboro Was.
S4330
Just the Little Story of Cumberland Gap.
V450

APP. CITIES — MOREHEAD, KY.
I570

APP. CITIES — MORGANTON, N. C.
Historical Sketch of Grace Church, Morganton, North Carolina.
S7620 (ASU)
Geology and Ground-water of the Morganton Area, North Carolina.
S9090 (WCU)

APP. CITIES — MORGANTOWN, W. VA.
Morgantown Disciples: A History of the First Christian Church of Morgantown, West Virginia.
C7410 (ASU)
"A Study of the Factors Influencing Job-satisfaction among Factory Workers of Clarksburg, West Virginia, and Coal Miners of Morgantown, West Virginia."
M4720
Soil Survey of the Morgantown, West Virginia Area.
M6690
"Transportation and Trade Areas; Analysis of Morgantown, Fairmont, and Clarksburg."
S330 (ASU)
"Contacts of Negroes and Whites in Morgantown."
W6380

APP. CITIES — MORRISTOWN, TENN.
History of Morristown, 1787-1936.
B6890
Resources and Enterprises of Upper East Tennessee: Johnson City, Jonesboro, Greenville, Rogersville, Morristown, Watauga, Tennessee. Franklin, Territory South of the Ohio.
E2040 (ETSU)
Morristown Centennial, 1855-1955.
M7960
Centennial Souvenir Program, 1855-1955: An Historical Pageant of Davy Crockett's Home Town, "Arrows to Atoms."
M7970 (ETSU)
A Century of Service: The Story of First Methodist Church, Morristown, Tennessee, 1852-1952.
M7980 (ETSU)
The Itakha Annual.
M7990 (ETSU)
"A Political History of Morristown and Hamblen County, Tennessee."
P1100
"The Attitudes of Students and Parents Toward the Division of Morristown, Tenn., High School."
P2600 (ETSU)
"The Development of a Middle School Program for the Morristown City School System, Morristown, Tennessee."
T760 (ETSU)
"A Study of Pupil Achievement in the Nongraded John F. Hay Elementary School in Morristown, Tennessee."
W6680 (ETSU)

APP. CITIES — NEWPORT, TENN.
Newport.
G2240

APP. CITIES — NORTH WILKESBORO, N. C.
Public Improvement Program and Capital Improvement Budget.
N2810 (LMC)

APP. CITIES — OAK RIDGE, TENN.
"The Social Backgrounds of Scientists and Engineers in Oak Ridge, Tennessee, and Huntsville, Alabama."
D4130
The Oak Ridge Story: The Saga of a People Who Share in History.
R3280 (ASU WCU BC)
Report to the Atomic Energy Commission on the Master Plan, Oak Ridge, Tennessee.
S4000 (ASU)

APP. CITIES — PAINTSVILLE, KY.
A Short History of Paintsville and Johnson County.
W2720 (ASU BC)

APP. CITIES — PARKERSBURG, W. VA.
Ground-water Conditions along the Ohio Valley at Parkersburg, West Virginia.
J520 (ETSU)
The Parkersburg Story.
U130 (ASU)

APP. CITIES — PIKEVILLE, KY.
I630
Pikeville, Kentucky, Neighborhood Analysis.
K1160

APP. CITIES — PITTSBURGH, PA.
"Some Factors That Have Influenced the Location of the Electric Power Plants in the Greater Pittsburgh Area."
C4040
Fort Duquesne and Fort Pitt. Early Names of Pittsburgh Streets.
D550 (ASU)
"Agriculture Development in the Pittsburgh District."
K2080
Pittsburg: The Story of an American City.
L3460 (ASU)
Employment Trends in the Pittsburgh Metropolitan Area.
P3180
"The Economic Position of Railroad Commuter Service in the Pittsburgh District — Its History, Present and Future.
S1190

APP. CITIES — PRESTONBURG, KY.
I660
Industrial Resources, Prestonburg, Kentucky.
P4460
Historic Floyd, 1890-1950.
S690

APP. CITIES — RADFORD, VA.
Lovely Mount Tavern: The Birth of a City, and Something of the Early New River Settlers.
H7700

APP. CITIES — RICHMOND, KY.
A Glimpse at Historic Madison County and Richmond, Kentucky.
D3000 (BC)
Glimpses of Historic Madison County, Ky.
D3010
I230
I680

APP. CITIES — ROANOKE, VA.
A History of Roanoke.
B1310 (FC)
Home Reminiscences of John Randolph, of Roanoke.
B5650 (ASU)
Folk-songs of Roanoke and the Albemarle.
C3300 (ASU)
Comprehensive City Plan, Roanoke.
C4180
The Geology of the Region Between Roanoke and Winchester in the Appalachian Valley of Western Virginia.
C7120
Presbyterian Churches of Roanoke, Virginia.
H6220 (ASU BC)
Randolph of Roanoke: A Political Fantastic.
J1760 (ASU)
Kegley's Virginia Frontier: The Beginning of the Southwest. The Roanoke of Colonial Days, 1740-1783.
K470 (ASU ETSU FC BC)
R2610
Roanoke, Story of County and City.
W9690 (ASU BC)

APP. CITIES — ROGERSVILLE, TENN.
Resources and Enterprises of Upper East Tennessee: Johnson City, Jonesboro, Greenville, Rogersville, Morristown, Watauga, Tennessee. Franklin, Territory South of the Ohio.
E2040 (ETSU)
"An Economic and Educational Survey of Rogersville Community."
L3210
The Fiftieth Anniversary of the Rogersville Synodical College.
P190

APP. CITIES — ROME, GA.
A History of Rome and Floyd County, State of Georgia, United States of America, Including Numerous Incidents of More Than Local Interest from 1540-1922.
B1940 (BC ASU)
A History of Rome and Floyd County, State of Georgia, United States of America, Including Numerous Incidents of More Than Local Interest from 1540-1922.
B1950 (LMC MHC)

APP. CITIES — STAUNTON, VA.
It Happened around Staunton in Virginia.
C4880 (ASU)
D2510 (ASU)
The First Presbyterian Church, Staunton, Virginia.
H6390 (ASU BC)

APP. CITIES — STEUBENVILLE, OHIO
Water Resources of the Wheeling-Steubenville Area, West Virginia and Ohio.
S4960

APP. CITIES — STRASBURG, VA.
The Story of Strasburg.
C20 (ASU)
Strasburg, Virginia and the Keister Family.
K540

APP. CITIES — SWEETWATER, TENN.
History of the First Presbyterian Church, Sweetwater, Tennessee, 1860-1960.
Y240

APP. CITIES — VA.
Dates of Origin of Virginia Counties and Municipalities.
W2250

APP. CITIES — WAYNESVILLE, N. C.
Centennial of Haywood County and Its County Seat Waynesville, N. C., 1808-1908.
A1710
C9110 (UNCA)

APP. CITIES — WHEELING, W. VA.
When Men and Mountains Meet.
A3500
Soil Survey of the Wheeling Area, West Virginia.
C70
Principio to Wheeling.
M4590 (BC)
"A Study of Commercial Banking in Two Economically Depressed Cities: Youngstown, Ohio, and Wheeling, West Virginia, 1951-1967."
N1010
Wheeling: A West Virginia Place Name of Indian Origin.
N1470 (ASU)
Water Resources of the Wheeling-Steubenville Area, West Virginia and Ohio.
S4960

APP. CITIES — WHITESBURG, KY.
I230

APP. CITIES — WILKESBORO, N. C.
North Wilkesboro, Wilkes County, N. C.: Key to the Blue Ridge Parkway.
N2800 (ASU LMC)

APP. CITIES — WILLIAMSBURG, KY.
I230

APP. CITIES — WINCHESTER, KY.
Kentucky Mayor: The Humor and Philosophy of John Edwin Garner.
C2610 (BC)

APP. CITIES — WINCHESTER, VA.
You Are Greater Than You Know.
A5550 (BC)
The Geology of the Region Between Roanoke and Winchester in the Appalachian Valley of Western Virginia.
C7120
This Heritage.
E1410
Announcement.
E2060 (ASU)
Winchester, Virginia, and Its Beginnings, 1743-1814: From Its Founding by Colonel James Wood to the Close of the Life of His Son, Brigadier General and Governor James Wood. With the Publication for the first Time of Valuable Manuscripts, relics of their long Tenure of Public offices.
G3800 (ASU BC)
The Story of Winchester in Virginia, the Oldest Town in the Shenandoah Valley.
M8140 (ASU BC ETSU WCU)
The Churches of Winchester, Virginia: A Brief History of Those Established Prior to 1825.
Q60
George Washington and Winchester, Virginia 1748-1758; A Decade of Preparation for Responsibilities to Come.
Q70 (ASU)
The Schools of Winchester, Virginia.
Q80
The Story of One Hundred Old Homes in Winchester, Virginia.
Q90
The Streets of Winchester, Virginia: The Origin and Significance of Their Names.
Q100
What I Know about Winchester: Recollections of William Greenway Russell, 1800-1891.
R4410 (ASU BC)
Diaries, Letters and Recollections of the War Between the States.
W7580

APP. CITIES — WINCHESTER, VA.
2200 Gravestone Inscriptions from Winchester and Frederick County, Virginia (Death Dates Range from 1700's to Early 1900's).
W7600 (ASU)
Souvenir.
W7610 (ASU)
The Code of the City of Winchester, Virginia, 1947. The Charter of the City and the General Ordinances of the City, Enacted as a Whole May 6, 1947, Effective May 6, 1947.
W7630 (ASU)
APP. CITIES — WYTHEVILLE, VA.
Industrial Survey, Wytheville, Virginia.
H8250 (ASU)
APP. COUNTIES
. . . County Government and Administration in the Tennessee Valley States.
T2500
County Government and Administration in the Tennessee Valley States.
T4280
APP. COUNTIES — ALA. — BIBB CO.
"A Historical Analysis of Student Drop-outs in the Negro Schools for Bibb County, Alabama."
M4620
Soil Survey of Bibb County, Alabama.
T7660
APP. COUNTIES — ALA. — BLOUNT CO.
"The Status of the Negro Teachers in Blount, Cullman, DeKalb, and Marshall Counties, Alabama 1952-53."
J2260
Report on the Coal Measures of the Plateau Region of Alabama.
M230 (BC)
Soil Survey of Blount County, Alabama.
S5180
APP. COUNTIES — ALA. — CALHOUN CO.
Surface Water Resources of Calhoun County, Alabama.
H2240 (ETSU)
Soil Survey, Calhoun County, Alabama.
H2360
Soil Survey of Calhoun County, Alabama.
H8540
Lower Piedmont Country.
N1210 (ASU BC ETSU LMC WCU)
Possum Trot, Rural Community, South.
N1220 (ASU BC WCU)
Geology and Ground-Water Resources of Calhoun County, Alabama: An Interim Report.
W820 (ETSU)
Geology and Ground-Water Resources of Calhoun County, Alabama.
W830 (ETSU)
APP. COUNTIES — ALA. — CHAMBERS CO.
Soil Survey, Chambers County, Alabama.
C1730
Soil Survey of Chambers County, Alabama.
S4760
APP. COUNTIES — ALA. — CHEROKEE CO.
Geology and Ground-water Resources of Cherokee County, Alabama: A Reconnaissance.
C2530 (ETSU)
An Inventory of Human and Physical Resources of Cherokee, Dekalb, Jackson, and Marshall Counties, Alabama.
K1590 (ASU)
"The Educational Progress of the Negro Schools in Cherokee County, Alabama, from 1930-1950."
S6640
Cherokee Country History, 1836-1956.
S7280 (ASU BC)
Soil Survey of Cherokee County, Alabama.
S8140
APP. COUNTIES — ALA. — CHILTON CO.
Soil Survey of Chilton County, Alabama.
C1130
APP. COUNTIES — ALA. — CLAY CO.
Resource and Beneficiation Studies of Copperbearing Pyrite Ore, Pyriton, Clay County, Alabama.
L240 (ETSU)
Geology and Mineral Resources of Clay County, with Special Reference to the Graphite Industry.
P4770 (ETSU)
Soil Survey of Clay County, Alabama.
T410
APP. COUNTIES — ALA. — CLEBURNE CO.
Soil Survey of Cleburne County, Alabama.
L2170
Report on Stone Hill Copper Mines and Works, Cleburne County, Alabama.
R3960 (ASU)
APP. COUNTIES — ALA. — COLBERT CO.
Soil Survey, Colbert County, Alabama.
B6130
Geology and Ground-water Resources of Colbert County, Alabama.
H2870 (ETSU)
Interim Report on Ground-water Study in Colbert County, Alabama.
H2880 (ETSU)
Springs in Colbert and Lauderdale Counties, Alabama.
H2890 (ETSU)
Two Hundred Years at Muscle Shoals Being an Authentic History of Colbert County, 1700-1900.
L1590
Soil Survey of Colbert County, Alabama.
S5190
APP. COUNTIES — ALA. — COOSA CO.
Soil Survey of Coosa County, Alabama.
T430
APP. COUNTIES — ALA. — CULLMAN CO.
"The Status of the Negro Teachers in Blount, Cullman, DeKalb, and Marshall Counties, Alabama 1952-53."
J2260
The German Settlement in Cullman County, Alabama: An Agricultural Island in the Cotton Belt.
K2980 (BC)
Soil Survey, Cullman County, Alabama.
M2450
Soil Survey of Cullman County, Alabama.
T7670
APP. COUNTIES — ALA. — DE KALB CO.
Soil Survey, De Kalb County, Alabama.
S9670
"The Status of the Negro Teachers in Blount, Cullman, DeKalb, and Marshall Counties, Alabama 1952-53."
J2260
An Inventory of Human and Physical Resources of Cherokee, Dekalb, Jackson, and Marshall Counties, Alabama.
K1590 (ASU)
L310
APP. COUNTIES — ALA. — ELMORE CO.
Soil Survey, Elmore County, Alabama.
B6140
APP. COUNTIES — ALA. — ETOWAH CO.
Ground-water Resources of Etowah County, Alabama: A Reconnaissance.
C2540 (ETSU)
H5990
Soil Survey of Etowah County, Alabama.
L4070
APP. COUNTIES — ALA. — FAYETTE CO.
Soil Survey, Fayette County, Alabama.
C7730
Stratigraphy and Structure of Outcropping Pre-Selma Coastal Plain Beds of Fayette and Lamar Counties, Alabama.
D3400 (ASU)
History of Fayette County, Alabama.
N750 (ASU BC)
Opportunities for and Limitations of Social and Economic Adjustments in an Alabama Rural County.
N1190
Soil Survey of Fayette County, Alabama.
O700
APP. COUNTIES — ALA. — FRANKLIN CO.
Russellville Brown Iron Ore District, Franklin County, Alabama.
B8470 (ETSU)
Geology and Ground-water Resources of Franklin County, Alabama: A Reconnaissance.
P1150 (ETSU)
Soil Survey: Franklin County, Alabama.
S2860
Soil Survey of Franklin County, Alabama.
S8120
APP. COUNTIES — ALA. — JACKSON CO.
An Inventory of Human and Physical Resources of Cherokee, Dekalb, Jackson, and Marshall Counties, Alabama.
K1590 (ASU)
Sequatchie: A Story of the Southern Cumberlands.
R540 (ASU)
Soil Survey, Jackson County, Alabama.
S9680
Soil Survey of Jackson County, Alabama.
W200
APP. COUNTIES — ALA. — JEFFERSON CO.
"A Study of Administrative and Supervisory Practices of Principals in the Public School System of Jefferson County, Alabama."
C5520
Sketches of Alabama, Being an Account of the Journey from Tuscaloosa to Blount Springs through Jefferson County on the Old Stage Roads, Now First Published in Book Form.
D3700 (ASU)
"Factors Contributing to the Educational Development of the Negro Schools in the Jefferson County (Alabama) School System, 1945-51."
G1950
"Factors Affecting the Health and Educational Growth of Elementary Pupils in Three Selected Schools of Jefferson County, Alabama."
M1920
"A Study of the Changes in the Educational Levels of the Negro Teachers in Jefferson County, Alabama, 1930-50."
M6280
Soil Survey of Jefferson County, Alabama.
S4770
"A Survey of School Library Facilities and Services in Four Selected High Schools in Jefferson County, Alabama."
W6410
APP. COUNTIES — ALA. — LAUDERDALE CO.
A History of Florence, Alabama, with 1850 Census of Lauderdale County.
G430 (ASU)
Springs in Colbert and Lauderdale Counties, Alabama.
H2890 (ETSU)
APP. COUNTIES — ALA. — LAWRENCE CO.
Health Development Plan — 1969, Morgan, Lawrence, Limestone Counties, Alabama.
A930 (ASU)
Health Development Plan — 1970, Morgan, Lawrence, Limestone Counties.
A940 (ASU)
Regional Health Demonstration Project, Phase 2, Morgan, Lawrence, Limestone Counties, Ala.
A950 (ASU)
Soil Survey of Lawrence County, Alabama.
L2180
Soil Survey, Lawrence County, Alabama.
S2870
APP. COUNTIES — ALA. — LIMESTONE CO.
Health Development Plan — 1969, Morgan, Lawrence, Limestone Counties, Alabama.
A930 (ASU)
Health Development Plan — 1970, Morgan, Lawrence, Limestone Counties.
A940 (ASU)
Regional Health Demonstration Project, Phase 2, Morgan, Lawrence, Limestone Counties, Ala.
A950 (ASU)
Soil Survey of Limestone County, Alabama.
B8710
Soil Survey, Limestone County, Alabama.
H3380
General Geology and Ground-water Resources of Limestone County, Alabama: A Reconnaissance.
M2170 (ETSU)
APP. COUNTIES — ALA. — MADISON CO.
Soil Survey of Madison County, Alabama.
B8720
Geology and Ground-water Resources of Madison County, Alabama.
M2890 (ETSU)
Sequatchie: A Story of the Southern Cumberlands.
R540 (ASU)
Gound-water Levels in Madison County, Alabama, July 1956 to July 1959.
S420 (ETSU)

APP. COUNTIES — ALA. — MADISON CO.
Soil Survey, Madison County, Alabama.
S9690
APP. COUNTIES — ALA. — MARION CO.
Soil Survey of Marion County, Alabama.
A5870 ()
History of Marion County, Alabama.
M3220
APP. COUNTIES — ALA. — MARSHALL CO.
The History of Marshall County, Alabama.
D3920 (ASU BC)
Soil Survey, Marshall County, Alabama.
F4090
"The Status of the Negro Teachers in Blount, Cullman, DeKalb, and Marshall Counties, Alabama 1952-53."
J2260
An Inventory of Human and Physical Resources of Cherokee, Dekalb, Jackson, and Marshall Counties, Alabama.
K1590 (ASU)
Ground Water in Marshall County, Alabama: A Reconnaissance.
S430 (ASU ETSU)
Soil Survey of Marshall County, Alabama.
W210
APP. COUNTIES — ALA. — MORGAN CO.
Health Development Plan — 1969, Morgan, Lawrence, Limestone Counties, Alabama.
A930 (ASU)
Health Development Plan — 1970, Morgan, Lawrence, Limestone Counties.
A940 (ASU)
Regional Health Demonstration Project, Phase 2, Morgan, Lawrence, Limestone Counties, Ala.
A950 (ASU)
Geology and Ground-water Resources of Morgan County, Alabama.
D2750 (ETSU)
Interim Report on the Geology and Groundwater Resources of Morgan County, Alabama.
D2770 (ETSU)
Soil Survey of Morgan County, Alabama.
P590
Soil Survey, Morgan County, Alabama.
S2880
APP. COUNTIES — ALA. — PICKENS CO.
Annals of Northwest Alabama.
E1660
Annals of Northwest Alabama Vol. III; Including a Reprint of the 1856 Nelson F. Smith's History of Pickens County, Alabama.
E1670
APP. COUNTIES — ALA. — RANDOLPH CO.
Soil Survey of Randolph County, Alabama.
B8730
Soil Survey, Randolph County, Alabama.
P320
APP. COUNTIES — ALA. — SHELBY CO.
Soil Survey of Shelby County, Alabama.
S8130
APP. COUNTIES — ALA. — ST. CLAIR CO.
Soil Survey of St. Clair County, Alabama.
B8750
"A Study of the Progress of Negro Education in Saint Clair County, Alabama."
C1750
Geology and Coal Resources of the Northeast Part of the Coosa Coal Field, St. Clair County, Alabama.
R3930 (ETSU)
APP. COUNTIES — ALA. — TALLADEGA CO.
The Gold Log Mine, Talladega County, Alabama.
B1870
Availability of Ground Water in Talladega County, Alabama: A Reconnaissance.
C2520 (ETSU)
"What Progress in Health Has Been Made among the Negro Youths of the Elementary School Age for the Past Ten Years in Talladega County, Alabama."
C9500
Soil Survey of Talladega County, Alabama.
M6700
APP. COUNTIES — ALA. — TALLAPOOSA CO.
Battle of Horseshoe Bend in Tallapoosa County, Alabama, March 27, 1814.
B6390 (BC)
APP. COUNTIES — ALA. — TALLEDEGA CO.
"A Study of the Causes of Drop-outs and Irregular Attendance among Boys in the Four Negro High Schools of Talledega County, Alabama."
G2040
The Talc Deposits of Talledega County, Alabama.
M2320 (BC ETSU)
APP. COUNTIES — ALA. — TUSCALOOSA CO.
"A Survey of the Library Facilities in the Negro Schools of Tuscaloosa County, Alabama."
D2540
"A Comparative Study of School Dropouts from 1945-50 in Holt Junior High School and Jaylorville Junior High School, Tuscaloosa County, Alabama."
H2210
Geology and Ground-water Resources of Tuscaloosa County, Alabama.
M5760 (ETSU)
Ground-water in the Vicinity of Bryce State Hospital, Tuscaloosa County, Alabama.
M5770 (ETSU)
Ground-water Resources and Geology of Tuscaloosa County, Alabama.
P1030 (ETSU)
Soil Survey of Tuscaloosa County, Alabama.
W7820
APP. COUNTIES — ALA. — WALKER CO.
Soil Survey of Walker County, Alabama.
V500
APP. COUNTIES — ALA. — WINSTON CO.
Soil Survey of Winston County, Alabama.
S9450
The Free State of Winston: A History of Winston County, Alabama.
T8340 (ASU)
APP. COUNTIES — GA. — BANKS CO.
Soil Survey, Banks and Stevens Counties, Georgia.
B6760
APP. COUNTIES — GA. — BARTOW CO.
The History of Bartow County, Formerly Cass.
C1150 (ASU)
The History of Bartow County, Formerly Cass.
C9800 (BC ASU)
Soil Survey of Bartow County, Georgia.
F3680
Geology and Mineral Deposits of the Cartersville District, Georgia.
K1700
Rebecca Latimer Felton, Nine Stormy Decades.
T110 (ASU)
The Bauxite Deposits of Floyd, Bartow, and Polk Counties of Northwest Georgia.
W5630
APP. COUNTIES — GA. — CARROLL CO.
Georgia's Last Frontier: The Development of Carroll County.
B5310 (ASU LMC BC)
Soil Survey, Carroll and Haralson Counties, Georgia.
B6940
Soil Survey of Carroll County, Georgia.
L2160
APP. COUNTIES — GA. — CATOOSA CO.
Geology and Ground-water Resources of Catoosa County, Georgia.
C8710 (ETSU)
Official History of Catoosa County, Georgia, 1853-1953.
M1070 (ASU LMC BC)
Soil Survey, Catoosa County, Georgia.
T400
APP. COUNTIES — GA. — CHATTOOGA CO.
Geology and Ground-water Resources of the Paleozoic Rock Area, Chattooga County, Georgia.
C8720 (ETSU)
Soil Survey of Chattooga County, Georgia.
M3030
APP. COUNTIES — GA. — CHEROKEE CO.
Soil Survey, Cherokee, Gilmer, and Pickens Counties, Georgia.
J2710
The History of Cherokee County.
M3300 (BC)
APP. COUNTIES — GA. — DADE CO.
Geology and Ground-water Resources of Dade County, Georgia.
C9070 (ETSU)
Soil Survey, Dade County, Georgia.
T440
APP. COUNTIES — GA. — DAWSON CO.
Soil Survey: Dawson, Lumpkin, and White Counties, Georgia.
A850
Soil Survey: Dawson, Lumpkin, and White Counties, Georgia.
M1720
Geology and Ground-water Resources of Crystalline Rocks, Dawson County, Georgia.
S2010 (ASU ETSU)
APP. COUNTIES — GA. — DOUGLAS CO.
Soil Survey, Douglas County, Georgia.
W2760
APP. COUNTIES — GA. — FANNIN CO.
Soil Survey: Fannin County, Georgia.
P2630
Forest Inventory Statistics for Fannin County, Georgia.
T4680
APP. COUNTIES — GA. — FLOYD CO.
A History of Rome and Floyd County, State of Georgia, United States of America, Including Numerous Incidents of More Than Local Interest from 1540-1922.
B1940 (BC ASU)
A History of Rome and Floyd County, State of Georgia, United States of America, Including Numerous Incidents of More Than Local Interest from 1540-1922.
B1950 (LMC MHC)
"A Study of Voluntary Withdrawals from McHenry and Five Feeder Schools in Floyd County, Georgia."
G1180
Cave Spring and Van's Valley.
H2930 (LMC)
"A Study of the Relationship Existing Between Amount of Education Completed by White and Negro Head of Households in Floyd County."
H4240
Soil Survey of Floyd County, Georgia.
L3230
Marriage Record "A', Floyd County, Georgia, 1834-1848.
M3120 (ASU)
The Bauxite Deposits of Floyd, Bartow, and Polk Counties of Northwest Georgia.
W5630
APP. COUNTIES — GA. — FORSYTH CO.
Soil Survey, Forsyth County, Georgia.
R3180
APP. COUNTIES — GA. — FRANKLIN CO.
Soil Survey of Franklin County, Georgia.
M2040
APP. COUNTIES — GA. — GILMER CO.
Soil Survey, Cherokee, Gilmer, and Pickens Counties, Georgia.
J2710
The Annals of Upper Georgia Centered in Gilmer County.
W740 (ASU LMC)
APP. COUNTIES — GA. — GORDON CO.
"History of Education in Gordon County, Georgia."
B2930
Soil Survey, Gordon County, Georgia.
B6290
Climb the Hills of Gordon: Stories of Gordon County and Calhoun, Georgia.
R1180 (LMC ASU BC)
"A Description of Government in Gordon, Clark and Paulding Counties, Georgia."
R3520
APP. COUNTIES — GA. — GWINNETT CO.
Soil Survey: Gwinnett County, Georgia.
T330
APP. COUNTIES — GA. — HABERSHAM CO.
The Hills of Habersham.
C4050 (ASU LMC BC)
The Hills of Habersham.
C4060
Seventy Years in Clarksville Baptist Church.
C4070 (ASU)
Exploration for Mineral Deposits in Habersham County, Georgia.
H8580
Exploration for Mineral Deposits in Habersham County, Georgia.
H8590 (LMC)
Habersham County, Georgia, Genealogical Records.
K2100 (ASU)

APP. COUNTIES — GA. — HABERSHAM CO.
Soil Survey, Habersham County, Georgia.
R3190
U4230
APP. COUNTIES — GA. — HALL CO.
Hall County, Georgia, 1819-1839, Marriages.
M2490 (ASU)
Tombstone Inscriptions of Hall County, Georgia.
M2500 (ASU)
Soil Survey, Hall County, Georgia.
M5850 (ASU)
APP. COUNTIES — GA. — HARALSON CO.
Soil Survey, Carroll and Haralson Counties, Georgia.
B6940
APP. COUNTIES — GA. — JACKSON CO.
Soil Survey of Jackson County, Georgia.
L3240
Soil Survey of Jackson County, Georgia.
L3250
APP. COUNTIES — GA. — LUMPKIN CO.
Soil Survey: Dawson, Lumpkin, and White Counties, Georgia.
A850
Soil Survey: Dawson, Lumpkin, and White Counties, Georgia.
M1720
Observations from a Peak in Lumpkin.
T9110 (BC ASU)
APP. COUNTIES — GA. — MADISON CO.
Soil Survey of Madison County, Georgia.
L3260
APP. COUNTIES — GA. — MURRAY CO.
My Life and Travels.
B6340 (ASU)
Geology and Mineral Resources of the Northwest Quarter of the Cohutta Mountain Quadrangle.
S220 (ETSU)
History of Murray County.
S3210
History of Murray County.
S3220 (ASU)
Genealogical History of Original Murray County.
W5650
Springplace: Moravian Mission and the War Family of the Cherokee Nation.
W9500 (MHC)
APP. COUNTIES — GA. — PAULDING CO.
"A Description of Government in Gordon, Clark and Paulding Counties, Georgia."
R3520
APP. COUNTIES — GA. — PICKENS CO.
Soil Survey, Cherokee, Gilmer, and Pickens Counties, Georgia.
J2710
"An Investigation of Elementary Guidance in Pickens County."
K700 (ASU)
History of Pickens Co.
T320 (ASU)
APP. COUNTIES — GA. — POLK CO.
Soil Survey of Polk County, Georgia.
L3270
"Improving School Attendance in Six White Elementary Schools in Polk County, Georgia."
M7680
The Bauxite Deposits of Floyd, Bartow, and Polk Counties of Northwest Georgia.
W5630
APP. COUNTIES — GA. — RABUN CO.
A Rural Community in Time of War: The Valley Community in Rabun County, Georgia.
A1340 (BC)
Rabun County, Georgia, Records.
K2110 (ASU)
Sketches of Rabun County History, 1819-1948.
R2390 (BC ASU LMC)
Soil Survey of Rabun County, Georgia.
L3280
APP. COUNTIES — GA. — STEPHENS CO.
Soil Survey, Banks and Stephens Counties, Georgia.
B6760
APP. COUNTIES — GA. — TOWNS CO.
"Some Economic Aspects of the Changes in Towns County Agriculture during the Period, 1934-1950."
L280
"Initiating the Rural Library Program in Towns and Union Counties, Georgia."
L3710
Soil Survey, Towns County, Georgia.
M5860
Forest Inventory Statistics for Towns County, Georgia.
T4700
APP. COUNTIES — GA. — UNION CO.
"Initiating the Rural Library Program in Towns and Union Counties, Georgia."
L3710
Soil Survey, Union County, Georgia.
M5870
Forest Inventory Statistics for Union County, Georgia.
T4710
APP. COUNTIES — GA. — WALKER CO.
Geology and Ground-water Resources of Walker County, Georgia.
C8730 (ETSU)
"A History of the Development of Schools for Negroes in Walker County, Georgia."
J170
Soil Survey of Walker County, Georgia.
M2070
History of Walker Co., Ga.
S450 (ASU BC)
History of Walker County, Georgia.
S460 (ASU)
Forest Inventory Statistics for Walker County, Georgia.
T4720
APP. COUNTIES — GA. — WHITE CO.
Soil Survey: Dawson, Lumpkin, and White Counties, Georgia.
A850
Exploration for Mineral Deposits in White County, Georgia.
H8600 (LMC)
Soil Survey: Dawson, Lumpkin, and White Counties, Georgia.
M1720
History of the Public Schools of White County, Georgia 1870 Thru 1938.
S3450 (BC)
APP. COUNTIES — GA. — WHITFIELD CO.
Forest Inventory Statistics for Whitfield County, Georgia.
T4730
Official History of Whitfield County, Georgia.
W5710 (BC)
APP. COUNTIES — KY.
The Social Dimensions of Kentucky Counties: Data and Rankings of the State's 120 Counties on Each of 81 Characteristics.
S9360
APP. COUNTIES — KY. — ADAIR CO.
"Factors That Influence Young Couples to Stay on the Farm in Adair County, Kentucky: Some Social and Economic Factors That Influence Young Couples to Stay on the Farm in a Low-income County in Kentucky."
H1710
APP. COUNTIES — KY. — BATH CO.
I250
A History of Bath County, Kentucky.
R2020 (BC)
An Historical Sketch of Springfield Presbyterian Church, Bath County, Kentucky.
S360 (BC)
Soil Survey, Bath County, Kentucky.
W2360
Soil Survey, Bath County, Kentucky.
W2370
APP. COUNTIES — KY. — BELL CO.
The Unfolding of a Century.
B2750
Memorial Records of Josh Bell County, Kentucky (Adjoining Historical Cumberland Gap, Tennessee), Family Bible Records Given to the United States Census Taken in 1870.
B9080 (BC)
United States Census of Bell County, Kentucky, 1880: Which are Family Bible Records as Given the Census Taker on That Date.
B9100 (BC)
United States Census of Bell Co., Ky., 1890.
B9110
Geological Map of the Balkan Quadrangle, Bell and Harlan Counties, Kentucky.
F3450 (BC)
History of Bell County, Kentucky.
F4030 (BC)
I260
"Factors Influencing Political Behavior in Bell, Clay, Knox, and Whitley Counties."
J450 (ASU)
APP. COUNTIES — KY. — BOYD CO.
"The Economic History of Boyd County, Kentucky."
G1160 (ASU)
"The History of Education of Boyd County, Kentucky."
J200
APP. COUNTIES — KY. — BREATHITT CO.
"Political Behavior in Breathitt, Knott, Perry and Leslie Counties, Kentucky."
C5990
Breathitt: A Guide to the Feud Country.
F460
Coals of the North Fork of the Ky. River in Perry and Portions of Breathitt & Knott Co. Ky.
H6150
Memories.
N1270 (BC)
Bloody Breathitt.
N1280 (BC)
The Story of Jackson City (Breathitt County).
P2950 (BC)
"History of Education in Breathitt County, Kentucky."
R1960
Methodism in Jackson and Breathitt County, Kentucky.
S6170
"Recollections of Breathitt."
T9350 (BC)
In the Land of Breathitt.
W9570 (ASU)
In the Land of Breathitt.
W9580 (BC)
APP. COUNTIES — KY. — CARTER CO.
A Survey of Low-Cost Housing in Carter County, Kentucky.
L2850 (ASU)
"History of Education in Carter County, Kentucky."
Q50
No More Muffled Hoofbeats.
R2600 (ASU)
APP. COUNTIES — KY. — CASEY CO.
Geology of a New Oil Pool in Casey Co., Ky.
J1040
Geology of the Nimtonville Dome in Casey Co., Ky.
J1150
The Bastins of Casey, Lincoln, and Pulaski County, Kentucky.
R80 (BC)
The Blacks of Casey and Pulaski County, Kentucky, and of Kansas.
R90 (BC)
The Carmans of Casey County, Kentucky.
R100
The men, women, events, institutions, and lore of Casey Co., Kentucky.
W1490 (BC)
APP. COUNTIES — KY. — CLARK CO.
Bibliography of Clark Co., Kentucky.
J830
Geology of Clark Co., Ky.
J1050
Geology of the Mica Dome in Clark Co., Ky.
J1140
APP. COUNTIES — KY. — CLAY CO.
"Factors Influencing Political Behavior in Bell, Clay, Knox, and Whitley Counties."
J450 (ASU)
Surname Index to the 1850 Federal Population Census of Kentucky.
M1240
Pioneer Families of Clay County, Kentucky.
M7600 (ASU BC)
APP. COUNTIES — KY. — CLINTON CO.
A Lighthouse in the Wilderness.
G540 (BC)
Surname Index to the 1850 Federal Population Census of Kentucky.
M1240
APP. COUNTIES — KY. — CUMBERLAND CO.
Geology of Cumberland Co., Kentucky.
J1070

APP. COUNTIES — KY. — CUMBERLAND CO.

Awakening. Of Cumberland County on the Last Fifty Years.
L950 (ASU BC)

Surname Index to the 1850 Federal Population Census of Kentucky.
M1240

History of Cumberland County.
W2750 (ASU BC)

APP. COUNTIES — KY. — ELLIOTT CO.

Peridotite of Elliott County, Kentucky.
D2420
H5700

Bibliography of Elliott Co., Ky.
J840

Soil Survey, Elliott County, Kentucky.
W2380

Soil Survey, Elliott County, Kentucky.
W2390

APP. COUNTIES — KY. — ESTILL CO.

Estill County, Kentucky, Record of Abstracts of Pension Papers of Revolutionary Soldiers, War of 1812 and Indian Wars. . . .
B9050

The Irvine Oil Field, Estill County, Kentucky.
S2480

APP. COUNTIES — KY. — FLOYD CO.

"A Study of Pupil Withdrawal in Ten Secondary Schools of Floyd, Knott, Letcher, and Pike Counties through the School Year of 1932-33."
C7190

Poverty, Politics, and Health Care: An Appalachian Experience.
C8060 (ASU)

"History of Education of Floyd County, Kentucky."
F3120

Bibliography of Floyd Co., Ky.
J850

Historic Floyd, 1890-1950.
S690

Mountain Kinsmen Ride; a Story of the James Family.
S720

APP. COUNTIES — KY. — GARRARD CO.

History of Garrard County, Kentucky, and Its Churches.
C260 (BC)

Soil Survey of Garrard County, Kentucky.
K1640

Historical Sketches of Lancaster and Garrard County, 1796-1924.
K2610

APP. COUNTIES — KY. — GREEN CO.

Surname Index to the 1850 Federal Population Census of Kentucky.
M1250

APP. COUNTIES — KY. — GREENUP CO.

History of Greenup County, Kentucky.
B3580 (BC)

A Supplementary Edition of a History of Greenup County.
B3590 (ASU BC)
I370

Surname Index to the 1850 Federal Population Census of Kentucky.
M1250

APP. COUNTIES — KY. — HARLAN CO.

History Records of Harlan County, Kentucky, People.
B9070 (BC)

A History of Harlan County.
C6340 (BC)

The Shame That Is Kentucky's! The Story of the Harlan Mine War.
C7610 (ASU)

Geological Map of the Balkan Quadrangle, Bell and Harlan Counties, Kentucky.
F3450 (BC)

Harlan County Schools Have Problems.
H2310 (ASU)

"A New Deal for Harlan: The Roosevelt Labor Policies in a Kentucky Coal Field, 1931-1939."
H5120 (BC)

Harlan County, Existing Land Use Analysis. Harlan-Harlan County Major Thoroughfare Plan.
K1150

Population-Economic Study, Harlan-Harlan County, Kentucky.
K1170

"School Attendance in Harlan County, Kentucky, 1948-1954."
L2940

"History of Education in Harlan County, Kentucky."
M840

Geologic Map of Part of the Rose Hill Quadrangle, Harlan County, Kentucky.
M4380 (ASU)

Harlan County, Kentucky.
M5360 (BC)

Bulletin of the Bureau of School Service, Vol. XX, no. 2.
P4820

At Home in the Hills: Glimpses of Harlan County, Kentucky, through the Media of the Linoleum Block and the Woodcut.
S6130 (LMC BC)

"Coal and Conflict: The U.M.W.A. in Harlan County, 1931-1939."
T690 (BC ASU)

Hell in Harlan.
T8760 (WCU)
T8850 (BC)

"History and Partial Evaluation of In-service Education in Harlan County, Kentucky."
W9070

The Kentucky Mountaineer: A Study of Four Counties in Southeastern Kentucky.
W8540

"The Kentucky Mountaineer: A Study of Four Counties in Southeastern Kentucky."
W8550 (ASU)

APP. COUNTIES — KY. — JACKSON CO.

"History of Education in Jackson County, Kentucky."
C1230
I440

Geologic Map of the McKee Quadrangle, Jackson and Owsley Counties, Ky.
W2310 (BC)

APP. COUNTIES — KY. — JOHNSON CO.

Johnson County, Kentucky: A History of the County, and Genealogy of Its People up to the Year 1927.
H860 (ASU BC)

Neighborhood Standing and Population Changes in Johnson and Robertson Counties.
O1080

A Short History of Paintsville and Johnson County.
W2720 (ASU BC)

Attitudes Toward Rural Migration and Family Life in Johnson and Robertson Counties, Kentucky, 1941.
W6690

APP. COUNTIES — KY. — KNOTT CO.

"Political Behavior in Breathitt, Knott, Perry and Leslie Counties, Kentucky."
C5990

"A Study of Pupil Withdrawal in Ten Secondary Schools of Floyd, Knott, Letcher, and Pike Counties through the School Year of 1932-33."
C7190

Forestry in the Economic Life of Knott County, Kentucky.
C8430

Coals of the North Fork of the Ky. River in Perry and Portions of Breathitt & Knott Co. Ky.
H6150
I450

Family Incomes and Land Utilization in Knott County, Kentucky.
N900

Family Incomes and Land Utilization in Knott County, Kentucky.
N910

Community and Neighborhood Groupings in Knott County, Kentucky.
O1050

Family Living in Knott County, Kentucky.
W6530 (BC)

APP. COUNTIES — KY. — KNOX CO.

A Selective Description of a Knox County Mountain Neighborhood.
C40

A Survey of the Legal Environment of Knox County, Kentucky.
C2590

History of Knox County, Kentucky (1674-1941).
D1580 (BC)

Selected Demographic Studies, Knox Co., Ky.
E800

"The Economic History of Knox County."
H7600

"Factors Influencing Political Behavior in Bell, Clay, Knox, and Whitley Counties."
J450 (ASU)

Bibliography of Knox Co., Ky.
J860

Geology and Coal of Stinking Creek.
J1020

APP. COUNTIES — KY. — LAUREL CO.

. . . Land Utilization in Laurel County, Kentucky.
C4810 (ASU)

Land Utilization in Laurel County, Kentucky.
C4820 (BC)

History of Coal Mining in Laurel County, Kentucky, 1920-1944.
M8160

The Colony Bernstadt in Laurel County, Kentucky.
S920
S1910

"History of Education in Laurel County, Kentucky."
T600

APP. COUNTIES — KY. — LAWRENCE CO.

"History of Education of Lawrence County, Kentucky."
E1590

Bibliography of Lawrence Co., Ky.
J870

APP. COUNTIES — KY. — LEE CO.

I470

APP. COUNTIES — KY. — LESLIE CO.

The Kentucky Mountaineer: A Study of Four Counties in Southeastern Kentucky.
W8540

"The Kentucky Mountaineer: A Study of Four Counties in Southeastern Kentucky."
W8550 (ASU)

Of Bolder Men (A History of Leslie County).
B6540 (BC)

"Political Behavior in Breathitt, Knott, Perry and Leslie Counties, Kentucky."
C5990

Sugar Creek Resettlement Area, Leslie County, Kentucky. A Report of a Conference on Planned Relocation, New Housing and Local Employment in Eastern Kentucky, 1966.
G1040

Existing Land Use Analysis, Leslie County, Kentucky.
K1140

"A comparison of Some Aspects of Family Life Between Two Areas of Leslie Co., Kentucky."
Q110

"Income and Health in Remote Rural Areas: A Study of Four Hundred Families in Leslie County, Kentucky."
W6350

Income and Health in Remote Rural Areas; a Study of 400 Families in Leslie County, Ky.
W6360 (BC)

APP. COUNTIES — KY. — LETCHER CO.

History of Letcher Co., Ky., Its Political and Economic Growth and Development.
B5740

"A Study of Pupil Withdrawal in Ten Secondary Schools of Floyd, Knott, Letcher, and Pike Counties through the School Year of 1932-33."
C7190

"History of Education in Letcher County, Kentucky."
R190

Geologic Map of the Whitesburg Quadrangle, Kentucky-Virginia, and Part of the Flat Gap Quadrangle, Letcher County, Ky.
R1910

"History of Education in Letcher County, Kentucky."
R3660

The Kentucky Mountaineer: A Study of Four Counties in Southeastern Kentucky.
W8540

"The Kentucky Mountaineer: A Study of Four Counties in Southeastern Kentucky."
W8550 (ASU)

APP. COUNTIES — KY. — LEWIS CO.

History of Lewis County, Kentucky.
R50

APP. COUNTIES — KY. — LINCOLN CO.
Early Lincoln County History.
D3990 (ASU BC)
The Bastins of Casey, Lincoln, and Pulaski County, Kentucky.
R80 (BC)
Geologic Map of the Stanford Quadrangle, Boyle and Lincoln Counties, Kentucky.
S2520
APP. COUNTIES — KY. — LOGAN CO.
Facts About the Two Armed Marches on Logan.
S9400 (ASU BC)
The Incomparable Don Chafin.
S9410 (BC ASU)
APP. COUNTIES — KY. — MADISON CO.
The Meaning of the Past for the Future.
C4760 (BC)
A Glimpse at Historic Madison County and Richmond, Kentucky.
D3000 (BC)
Glimpses of Historic Madison County, Ky.
D3010
Soil Survey of Madison County, Kentucky.
G4090
Bibliography of Madison Co., Ky.
J890
Lion of White Hall: The Life of Cassius M. Clay.
S4400 (MHC)
U4140
APP. COUNTIES — KY. — MAGOFFIN CO.
"History of Education of Magoffin County, Kentucky."
B220
APP. COUNTIES — KY. — MENIFEE CO.
Bibliography of Menifee Co., Ky.
J900
APP. COUNTIES — KY. — MONROE CO.
William Ballard: A Genealogical Record of His Descendants in Monroe County.
B870 (BC)
APP. COUNTIES — KY. — MONTGOMERY CO.
Where Bluegrass and Mountains Meet: A Community Profile of Mt. Sterling and Montgomery County, Kentucky.
B8490
History of Methodism in Montgomery County.
S520 (ASU)
APP. COUNTIES — KY. — MORGAN CO.
A Brief History of Our Early Life and Morgan County, Kentucky.
B7140 (BC)
Selections from Morgan County History: Sesquicentennial Volume.
S6420 (ASU)
APP. COUNTIES — KY. — OWLSEY CO.
"History of Education in Owsley County, Kentucky."
G10 (BC)
Notes from the History of Education in Owsley County.
G20
"History of Education in Owsley County, Kentucky."
S20
Geologic Map of the McKee Quadrangle, Jackson and Owsley Counties, Ky.
W2310 (BC)
APP. COUNTIES — KY. — PERRY CO.
"Political Behavior in Breathitt, Knott, Perry and Leslie Counties, Kentucky."
C5990
History of Perry County, Ky.
D490
History of Perry County, Kentucky.
D500 (BC)
Coals of the North Fork of the Ky. River in Perry and Portions of Breathitt & Knott Co. Ky.
H6150
Articles of Impeachment Against John A. Duff, Surveyor of Perry Co.
K1230
The Coal Fields of Perry Co., Ky.
V60
The Kentucky Mountaineer: A Study of Four Counties in Southeastern Kentucky.
W8540
"The Kentucky Mountaineer: A Study of Four Counties in Southeastern Kentucky."
W8550 (ASU)

APP. COUNTIES — KY. — PIKE CO.
"A Study of Pupil Withdrawal in Ten Secondary Schools of Floyd, Knott, Letcher, and Pike Counties through the School Year of 1932-33."
C7190
"History of Education in Pike County Kentucky."
C8750
Coal Deposits of Pike County, Kentucky.
H8370
"A Study of the Opinions of the Various Classes of People Toward Pike County's Medical Facilities."
J2960
Environmental Study of Logan, McDowell, and Mingo Counties, West Virginia and Pike County, Kentucky.
U2680 (ASU)
Coal deposits of Pike Co., Ky.
U3120
APP. COUNTIES — KY. — POWELL CO.
"Land Use in Powell County, Kentucky."
D1900
I650
Bibliography of Powell Co., Ky.
J910
Geology of Powell Co., Ky.
J1080
Geology of the Area Around Powell Co., Ky.
J1090
Rural Family Health in a Selected County in Kentucky.
M4000
APP. COUNTIES — KY. — PULASKI CO.
I670
Bibliography of Pulaski Co., Ky.
J920
The Bastins of Casey, Lincoln, and Pulaski County, Kentucky.
R80 (BC)
The Blacks of Casey and Pulaski County, Kentucky, and of Kansas.
R90 (BC)
A History of Pulaski Co., Kentucky.
T810
A History of Pulaski County, Kentucky.
T8550
APP. COUNTIES — KY. — ROCKCASTLE CO.
Soil Survey of Rockcastle County, Kentucky
B8740
I230
I690
"History of Education in Rockcastle, Kentucky."
N2840 (BC)
APP. COUNTIES — KY. — ROWAN CO.
Boone Logan's Letters to the Sentinel-Democrat (Mount Sterling, Kentucky) Pertaining to the Rowan County Feud and Other Matters.
Y300 (BC)
APP. COUNTIES — KY. — RUSSELL CO.
I230
I700
APP. COUNTIES — KY. — WAYNE CO.
The Double Head Academy.
C2600 (BC)
Glimpses of Historical Wayne County, Kentucky.
E960 (ASU BC)
A Century of Wayne County, Kentucky, 1800-1900.
J1300 (ASU BC)
Reconnaissance of Oil and Gas Fields in Wayne and McCreary Counties, Kentucky.
M8590
"History of Education in Wayne County, Kentucky."
Y250
APP. COUNTIES — KY. — WHITLEY CO.
"Factors Influencing Political Behavior in Bell, Clay, Knox, and Whitley Counties."
J450 (ASU)
A History of Jellico, Tennessee, Containing Historical Information on Campbell County, Tennessee and Whitley County, Kentucky.
S3330
History of the Family Snyder (Schneider) (Snider).
S5310
APP. COUNTIES — KY. — WOLFE CO.
Early and Modern History of Wolfe County.
W8035 (ASU BC)

APP. COUNTIES — LAWRENCE CO.
Geology and Ground-water Resources of Lawrence County, Alabama: A Reconnaissance.
H3030 (ETSU)
APP. COUNTIES — MD. — ALLEGANY CO.
Soil Survey of Allegany County, Maryland.
B7610
History of Western Maryland: Being a History of Frederick, Montgomery, Carroll, Washington, Allegany, and Garrett Counties from the Earliest Period to the Present Day. Including Biographical Sketches of Their Representative Men.
S840 (ASU)
The Water Resources of Allegany and Washington Counties.
S4170 (ETSU)
History of Allegany County, Maryland.
T7870 (ASU)
Fact Sheet on Appalachian Maryland — Garrett, Allegany, and Washington Counties.
M3880
Allegany County.
M3900 (ETSU)
APP. COUNTIES — MD. — CUMBERLAND CO.
History of Cumberland (Maryland), From the Time of the Indian Town, Caiuctucus, in 1728, Up to the Present Day, Embracing an Account of Washington's First Campaign, and the Battle of Fort Necessity, Together with a History of Braddock's Expedition.
L3700 (ASU)
APP. COUNTIES — MD. — FREDERICK CO.
Rural Social Organization of Frederick County, Maryland.
G4250
APP. COUNTIES — MD. — GARRETT CO.
Geology and Water Resources of Garrett County.
A2230 (ETSU)
Fact Sheet on Appalachian Maryland — Garrett, Allegany, and Washington Counties.
M3880
Soil Survey of Garrett County, Maryland.
S5320
Taming the Savage River.
T130 (ASU BC)
APP. COUNTIES — MD. — WASHINGTON CO.
Soil Survey of Washington County, Maryland.
B8690
Fact Sheet on Appalachian Maryland — Garrett, Allegany, and Washington Counties.
M3880
Occupational Outlook for Washington County.
M3890
The Physical Features of Washington County.
M3910 (ETSU)
Soil Survey, Washington County, Maryland.
M4270
History of Western Maryland: Being a History of Frederick, Montgomery, Carroll, Washington, Allegany, and Garrett Counties from the Earliest Period to the Present Day. Including Biographical Sketches of Their Representative Men.
S840 (ASU)
The Water Resources of Allegany and Washington Counties.
S4170 (ETSU)
The History of Washington County, Maryland, from the Earliest Settlements to the Present Time, Including a History of Hagerstown.
W6870 (ASU)
APP. COUNTIES — N. C.
N1680 (ASU LMC)
The Formation of the North Carolina Counties, 1663-1943.
N1840 (WWC)
Sawmills and Lumber Production for 26 Counties in Western North Carolina, 1959.
N1960
North Carolina Basic County Data.
N2620 (LMC)
County Government in North Carolina.
N2680 (WWC ASU LMC)
Story of the Counties of North Carolina, with Other Data.
O530 (ASU)
Buncombe to Mecklenburg: Speculation Lands.
P860

APP. COUNTIES — N. C. — ALEXANDER CO.
Historical Sketches of Alexander County.
C9160
"A Study of the Educational Facilities of the Public Schools of Alexander County, North Carolina."
L1800
Dr. John McLeod Oxford, 1841-1928; A Sketch of His Life.
O1030 (ASU)
Alexander County's Confederates.
P3110
Prologue: a History of Alexander County, North Carolina.
P3130
Facts and Events of the Watts Family.
W1600 (ASU)
A History of Alexander County, North Carolina.
W5640
APP. COUNTIES — N. C. — ALLEGHANY CO.
A1730
Soil Survey, Alleghany County, North Carolina.
B6530
Soil Survey of Alleghany County, North Carolina.
B8670 (ASU)
Soil Survey of Alleghany County.
B8680
Measuring Unemployment in Small Rural Labor Areas: Report on a Household Survey Conducted in Alleghany County, N. C., 1969.
N2260
History of Alleghany County.
T8320
Alleghany, Ashe, Watauga Planning Project for Handicapped Children, ESEA Title III.
W1360 (WCU)
APP. COUNTIES — N. C. — ASHE CO.
Ashe County: A History.
F1520 (ASU WCU)
Soil Survey of Ashe County, North Carolina.
H2170
"Educational Development of Ashe County."
H8640
"Coordination of Physical Education and Community Recreation in Ashe, Avery, and Watauga Counties."
Q170 (ASU)
Alleghany, Ashe, Watauga Planning Project for Handicapped Children, ESEA Title III.
W1360 (WCU)
APP. COUNTIES — N. C. — AVERY CO.
"A Study of the Cranberry Ore Belt."
B5750 (ASU)
History of Avery County, North Carolina.
C7170 (ASU LMC WCU BC)
The War Trails of the Blue Ridge, Containing an Authentic Description of the Battle of King's Mountain, the Incidents Leading up to and the Echoes of the Aftermath of This Epochal Engagement, and Other Stories Whose Scenes Are Laid in the Blue Ridge.
D3760 (BC ASU LMC)
Smaller Communities Program: Manpower Resources Report — Avery County.
N2250 (WCU)
Characteristics of Households in Areas Served by the W. A. M. Y.
N2290 (ASU)
"Coordination of Physical Education and Community Recreation in Ashe, Avery, and Watauga Counties."
Q170 (ASU)
Soil Survey, Avery County, North Carolina.
R3290
"The Economic Impact of Recreation Resort Development on the Local Economy: A Case Study of Avery County, North Carolina."
R3580 (LMC)
A Profile of Community Problems: Watauga, Avery, Mitchell, Yancey Counties.
W710
"The Educational Development of Avery County."
W8850 (ASU)
APP. COUNTIES — N. C. — BUNCOMBE CO.
Community Action for Social Redevelopment in Asheville and Buncombe County.
A5200 (WWC)
B8390 (BC)
List of the Birds of Buncombe County, North Carolina.
C80 (ASU LMC)
A Survey of the Public Libraries of Asheville and Buncombe County, North Carolina.
C2730 (LMC ETSU ASU)
Prelude to Planning in Buncombe County, North Carolina.
C6230 (WWC)
"Developing a Core Plan in the Seventh and Eighth Grades at Candler Elementary School."
C6940 (WCU)
C9110 (UNCA)
Buncombe County, North Carolina, Grantee Deed Index.
D2370
Buncombe County, North Carolina, Grantor Deed Index.
D2380
Historical Facts Concerning Buncombe County Government.
D2390 (WCU LMC)
D2500 (UNCA)
Soil Survey, Buncombe County, North Carolina.
G2380
Irrigation Arrangements in Buncombe County, North County, North Carolina; a Report of an Irrigation Survey in Buncombe County, Conducted in the Summer of 1962.
M3650 (LMC)
Education in Buncombe County, 1793-1965.
M5900
Buncombe County, Economic and Social.
M8190
Buncombe County: Economic and Social.
M8200 (ASU BC LMC)
Land Development Plan for Black Mountain, N. C.
N2050 (WCU)
Area Manpower Review: Asheville Standard Metropolitan Statistical Area — Buncombe County.
N2240 (ASU WWC)
Buncombe County: Economic and Social.
N2670 (ASU)
Soil Survey of Buncombe County, North Carolina.
P2060
Dry Ridge: Some of Its History, Some of Its People.
P2830 (LMC ASU)
An Emission Survey and Ambient Air Quality Data of Buncombe, Haywood, Henderson Counties and the City of Asheville.
R1330 (WCU)
Public School Education in Buncombe County, 1935-1969.
R2640 (WCU)
Asheville and Buncombe County.
S5480 (WCU BC)
A History of Buncombe County, North Carolina.
S5500 (ASU WCU LMC BC)
Medicine in Buncombe County Down to 1885, Historical and Biographical Sketches.
T880
Forest Inventory Statistics for Buncombe County, North Carolina.
T2780
Parker Branch; an Experiment in Appalachian Agriculture, 1953-1962.
T3170
Flood of August 24-25, 1961: Upper French Broad River Basin.
T6940
APP. COUNTIES — N. C. — BURKE CO.
History of the Presbyterian Churches at Quaker Meadows and Morganton, from the Year 1780 to 1913.
A5720
Idle Comments.
A5730
Supplement to Annotated Bibliography of Burke County Resource Materials, 1969.
B8650 (ASU)
Sketches of Burke County.
C480 (ASU)
Sketches of Burke County.
C490
The Waldenses of Burke County.
C8560 (ASU WCU LMC)
"An Archaeological Survey of the Upper Catawba River Valley."
K390
Soil Survey of Burke County.
L1430
Soil Survey of Burke County, North Carolina.
L1440
Community Facilities Plan and Public Improvements Program: Glen Alpine, North Carolina.
N2030 (WCU)
Community Facilities Plan & Public Improvements Program: Valdese, North Carolina.
N2040 (WCU)
Land Use Survey & Analysis and Land Development Plan: Glen Alpine, North Carolina.
N2100 (WCU)
Land Use Survey and Analysis and Land Development Plan: Valdese, North Carolina.
N2110 (WCU)
Neighborhood Analysis: Valdese, North Carolina.
N2130 (ASU WCU)
Population and Economy: Valdese, North Carolina.
N2160 (WCU)
The Burke County Gold Rush.
P3540 (LMC)
Subdivision Regulations, Valdese, N. C., Adopted April 3, 1967.
V30 (LMC)
Sketches of the Pioneers in Burke County History.
W690
The Waldenses of Valdese.
W1580 (LMC WCU)
APP. COUNTIES — N. C. — CALDWELL CO.
Here Will I Dwell: The Story ofCaldwell County.
A1400 (ASU WCU BC)
Caldwell County, North Carolina Geography Supplement.
A2490 (ASU)
Caldwell County, North Carolina in the Great War of 1861-1865.
C4650
Soil Survey of Caldwell County.
C5330
Soil Survey of Caldwell County, North Carolina.
C5340
"A Study of School Leavers at the Patterson School for Boys, Caldwell County, North Carolina."
F900 (ASU)
Echoes of Happy Valley: Letters and Diaries, Family Life in the South, Civil War History.
H5190 (ASU LMC BC)
Happy Valley, History and Genealogy.
H5200 (ASU)
The World of My Childhood.
I970 (ASU LMC)
"The Growth and Development of Education in Caldwell County."
S800 (ASU)
Annals of Caldwell County.
S1470
"The History of Patterson School, Caldwell County, North Carolina."
S6000 (ASU)
APP. COUNTIES — N. C. — CATAWBA CO.
"The History of Lutheran Elementary Education in Catawba County."
T30
History of Concordia College, Conover, North Carolina.
V1330 (ASU)
APP. COUNTIES — N. C. — CHEROKEE CO.
Ducktown Back in Raht's Time.
B1120 (BC ASU WCU ETSU)
The Cherokee Indians and Those Who Came After, Notes for a History of Cherokee County, North Carolina, 1835-1860.
B7000 (ASU)
"A History of the Public Library in Murphy, N.C."
C6930
"Locating and Providing for Murphy High School's Bright Pupils."
C7620 (WCU)
Geology and Ground-water Resources of the Murphy Area, North Carolina.
D2760 (WCU)
Our Heritage, the People of Cherokee County, North Carolina, 1540-1955.
F3170 (ASU WCU BC)
Soil Survey of Cherokee County, North Carolina.
J2860 (ASU)
"Community Use of School Resources in Cherokee County, North Carolina, as Compared with a National Trend."
O900

APP. COUNTIES — N. C. — CHEROKEE CO.

Soil Survey, Cherokee County, North Carolina.
P2070

"A Survey of Educational Facilities in Cherokee County, North Carolina."
T8060 (ASU)

Population and economy of Andrews, N. C.
W4910

Today and Tomorrow, Murphy, North Carolina.
W4930 (LMC)

APP. COUNTIES — N. C. — CLAY CO.

Clay County, 1861-1961; Commemorating the One Hundredth Anniversary of the Creating of Clay County, North Carolina.
C4780

Preliminary Report on Corundum Deposits in the Buck Creek Peridotite, Clay County, North Carolina.
H170 (ASU)

Land-use in Clay County.
H7050 (LMC)

Little Church of the Valley (Moss Baptist Church), in the Shadow of the Potrock.
M8250

Soil Survey, Clay County, North Carolina.
P2080

APP. COUNTIES — N. C. — CLEVELAND CO.

History of the First Baptist Church of Kings Mountain, N. C.
B4310

Lengthened Shadows: A History of Gardner-Webb College, 1907-1956.
D1590 (ASU)

"A Critical Study of Negro Education in Cleveland County, North Carolina, from 1944 to 1954."
F2250 (ASU)

History of First Baptist Church of Shelby, North Carolina.
H1390

"An Analysis of the Types of Retardation in the Elementary Departments of Fine Negro Union Schools in Rural Cleveland County."
L3200
P3240

Cleveland County, North Carolina, Marriages, 1851-1868.
R220

Soil Survey of Cleveland County, North Carolina.
V40

The Living Past of Cleveland County, a History.
W1950 (ASU)

APP. COUNTIES — N. C. — DAVIE CO.

Soil Survey of Davie County, North Carolina.
J2870

APP. COUNTIES — N. C. — GASTON CO.

The County of Gaston: Two Centuries of a North Carolina Region.
C7260 (LMC ASU BC)

APP. COUNTIES — N. C. — GRAHAM CO.

The Village of Five Lives: The Fontana of the Great Smoky Mountains.
B5960 (ASU BC LMC WCU)

Our Heritage, the People of Cherokee County, North Carolina, 1540-1955.
F3170 (ASU WCU BC)

Soil Survey, Graham County, North Carolina.
G2390
G3120 (ASU LMC)

APP. COUNTIES — N. C. — HAYWOOD CO.

The Annals of Haywood County, North Carolina: Historical, Sociological, Bibliographical, and Genealogical.
A1700 (ASU WCU BC)

Centennial of Haywood County and Its County Seat Waynesville, N. C., 1808-1908.
A1710

The 1916 Pictorial Story of Haywood County.
C1330 (WCU)
C9110 (UNCA)

Soil Survey, Haywood County, North Carolina.
G2400

Acceptance of Voluntary Health Insurance in Four Rural Communities of Haywood County, North Carolina.
H3790

Land Use Plan, Haywood County, N. C.
H4020 (LMC)

Certain Mounds in Haywood County, North Carolina.
H5140 (ASU)

Soil Survey of Haywood County, North Carolina.
J2880

The Early History of Haywood County.
M4830 (LMC WCU)

Finis and Farewell.
M4840 (ASU BC LMC WCU)

Great Smoky Mountain Stories and Sun over Ol' Starlin.
M4850 (LMC WCU)

Haywood's Heritage and Finest Hour.
M4860 (ASU BC WCU)

The Middle History of Haywood County, with Story Supplement.
M4880 (BC LMC WCU)

Mountain People, Mountain Times.
M4890 (BC LMC WCU)

"A History of Haywood County."
R1250 (ASU)

An Emission Survey and Ambient Air Quality Data of Buncombe, Haywood, Henderson Counties and the City of Asheville.
R1330 (WCU)

The economy of Haywood County.
W4900

APP. COUNTIES — N. C. — HENDERSON CO.

Early Sketch of St. John in the Wilderness and Flat Rock, North Carolina.
A1910 (ASU)

Along the Ridges.
B380 (ASU LMC)
C9110 (UNCA)

Crossties Over Saluda.
G1280

Crossties through Carolina.
G1290 (ASU LMC MHC)

Soil Survey of Henderson County, North Carolina.
H4200

Calvary Church Episcopal, where City and County Meet to Worship God; A Historical Sketch of Calvary Episcopal Church.
J660

"Geology of the Bat Cave and Fuitland Quadrangles and the Origin of the Henderson Gneiss, Western North Carolina."
L1720

Historic Flat Rock: Where the Old South Lingers.
M3370 (ASU LMC BC)

Irrigation Arrangements in Henderson County, North Carolina; a Report of an Irrigation Survey in Henderson County, Conducted in the Summer of 1962.
M3660 (LMC)

Historical Sketch of Flat Rock.
M5040 (ASU)

An Historical Sketch of Flat Rock . . .
M5050 (ASU)

A Condensed History of Flat Rock (the Little Charleston of the Mountains).
P880 (ASU WCU LMC)

The Kingdom of the Happy Land.
P890 (ASU LMC)

St. James Episcopal Church: Book of Memory, 1843-1950.
P910 (ASU)

The Story of Henderson County.
P940 (ASU WCU LMC)

The Story of Henderson County.
P950

Pearson's Falls Glen: Its Story, Its Flora, Its Birds.
P1420 (WWC)

Soil Survey, Henderson County, North Carolina.
P2100

Postmarks: A History of Henderson County, North Carolina, 1787-1968.
R580 (BC ASU ETSU LMC)

An Emission Survey and Ambient Air Quality Data of Buncombe, Haywood, Henderson Counties and the City of Asheville.
R1330 (WCU)
S190

Flood of August 24-25, 1961: Upper French Broad River Basin.
T6940

Population and economy of Henderson County.
W4920 (LMC)

APP. COUNTIES — N. C. — JACKSON CO.

"Social and Economic Conditions in Jackson County During the Depression."
A780 (WCU)

"The Utilization of Community Resources in the Elementary Public Schools of Jackson County."
A810 (WCU)

Master Plan for Recreation and Parks: Jackson County, North Carolina.
G300 (WCU)

Soil Survey, Jackson County, North Carolina.
G2410

A History of Dillsboro, North Carolina.
G3390 (WCU)

Panorama of Progress: Jackson County Centennial.
H7780

Outdoor Recreation Potential Appraisal.
J30 (WCU)

Jackson County: Operational Survival Plan.
N1790 (WCU)

Jackson County Public Schools, 1853-1954.
N2230 (WCU)
P150 (WCU)

APP. COUNTIES — N. C. — LINCOLN CO.

The German Settlers in Lincoln County and Western North Carolina.
N1240 (LMC)

Annals of Lincoln County, North Carolina: Containing Interesting and Authentic Facts of Lincoln County History through the Years 1749 to 1937.
S2960 (ASU)

APP. COUNTIES — N. C. — MCDOWELL CO.

"An Archaeological Survey of the Upper Catawba River Valley."
K400

APP. COUNTIES — N. C. — MACON CO.

Soil Survey of Macon County.
D1960

Soil Survey of Macon County, North Carolina.
D1970

Soil Survey, Macon County, North Carolina.
G2420

Favorite Recipes.
M2640
S160

"Evaluation of Alternative Income Opportunities For Farm Operations in Macon County, North Carolina."
S3720 (LMC)

A Brief History of Macon County, North Carolina.
S4430

APP. COUNTIES — N. C. — MADISON CO.

Soil Survey, Madison County, North Carolina.
G2430

Land Potential Study: Madison County, North Carolina.
N2080 (WCU)

Population and Economy: Marshall, N.C.
N2150 (ASU WCU)

Geology and Mineral Resources of the Hot Springs Window, Madison County, North Carolina.
O800 (ASU WCU ETSU)

A Demonstration of Watershed Protective Logging, Mars Hill Municipal Watershed, Madison County, North Carolina.
T4640

The Kingdom of Madison, a Southern Mountain Fastness and Its People.
W2560 (ASU LMC WWC WCU MHC BC)

APP. COUNTIES — N. C. — MITCHELL CO.
B690 (LMC BC)

"Study of Factors Causing Potential Drop-outs to Remain in the Mitchell County, North Carolina, High Schools."
I810

"A Study of Serum Protein Variation in Peromyscus Maniculatus Nubiterrae Rhoads at Six Attitudinal Habitats on Roan Mountain, Carter County, Tennessee, and Mitchell County, North Carolina."
M880 (ETSU)

Discovering Mitchell County, 1939-40: A Cooperative Study Made by the Teachers and Pupils of Mitchell County.
M6290 (ASU)

Gift from the Hills: Miss Lucy Morgan's Story of Her Unique Penland School.
M7620 (ASU BC ETSU FC WCU WWC)

Gift from the Hills: Miss Lucy Morgan's Story of Unique Penland School.
M7630

APP. COUNTIES — N. C. — MITCHELL CO.
Characteristics of Households in Areas Served by the W. A. M. Y.
N2290 (ASU)
Soil Survey, Mitchell County, North Carolina.
P2110
Discovering Mitchell County.
T780
A Profile of Community Problems: Watauga, Avery, Mitchell, Yancey Counties.
W710
APP. COUNTIES — N. C. — POLK CO.
50 Years Ago Around Saluda, N. C.
P10
Polk County Centennial: Souvenir Historical Booklet.
P3350
Know Our County: People, Places, and Facts. A Survey of Polk County in Western North Carolina.
T9540 (WCU)
Proposed Development Plan, Tryon, N. C., Central Business District.
T9550 (LMC)
T9560
APP. COUNTIES — N. C. — RUTHERFORD CO.
Rutherford County, North Carolina, Abstracts of Wills, 1779-1822.
D890 (ASU)
Bechtler's Gold.
F3180
Abstracts of Deeds, Rutherford County, North Carolina, Volumes A-D.
G3570
Centennial History of Pleasant Grove Methodist Church, 1838-1938.
G4110 (ASU BC)
History of Old Tryon and Rutherford Counties, North Carolina, 1730-1936.
G4130 (ASU BC WCU)
History of Rutherford County, 1937-1951.
G4140 (WCU LMC BC)
Public Officials of Rutherford County, N. C. 1779-1934: With Introductory Sketches of Orgin and Development of Various County Offices, and Public and Local Laws Governing Same.
G4150 (ASU BC)
"The Background, Education, and Experience of Teachers in Rutherford County, N. C."
H3840
Soil Survey of Rutherford County, North Carolina.
J2910
A Program for the Improvement of Instruction in Spelling in the High Schools of Rutherford County.
N520 (ASU)
Buncombe to Mecklenburg: Speculation Lands.
P860
Rutherford County: Economic and Social.
P4590 (ASU)
R4430 (ASU)
"The Development of Negro Education in Rutherford County, North Carolina."
T9510
A Country Doctor in the South Mountains.
W1000 (ASU LMC MHC BC)
Rutherford County and Its Hospital.
W1010 (BC)
APP. COUNTIES — N. C. — STOKES CO.
Soil Survey, Stokes County, North Carolina.
D1260 (ASU)
APP. COUNTIES — N. C. — SURRY CO.
Soil Survey of Surry County, North Carolina.
D1270
History of Surry County, or, Annals of Northwest North Carolina.
H6680 (LMC ASU WCU BC)
History of Surry County, or, Annals of Northwest North Carolina.
H6690
Fisher's River Scenes.
T60 (ASU)
Fisher's River (North Carolina) Scenes and Characters by "Skitt Who Was Raised Thar."
T70 (ETSU BC)
APP. COUNTIES — N. C. — SWAIN CO.
"Youth Involvement in Swain County."
P1370 (LMC)
Soil Survey, Swain County, North Carolina.
P2120
A National Park in the Great Smoky Mountains.
S9380
"Education in Swain County, North Carolina."
T8100
Swain County: Early History and Educational Development.
T8110 (ASU WCU LMC)
APP. COUNTIES — N. C. — TRANSYLVANIA CO.
A2870
"An Inquiry into Present Practices in Guidance in Transylvania County High Schools."
B8170 (ASU)
C9110 (UNCA)
"Beginnings: A History of the Founding of Churches in Transylvania County, 1795-1865."
G700 (WCU)
Soil Survey of Transylvania County, North Carolina.
H4210
Soil Survey of Transylvania County.
H4220
"An Archaeological Survey of Transylvania County, North Carolina."
H6490 (WCU)
Soil Survey of Transylvania County, North Carolina.
K2300
Irrigation Arrangements in Transylvania County, North Carolina; a Report of an Irrigation Survey in Transylvania County, Conducted in the Summer of 1962.
M3670 (LMC)
Digest of Information About Transylvania County, North Carolina, Containing Information of General Interest to Commercial and Industrial Businesses.
M5010 (WCU)
Community Facilities Plan. Brevard, N. C.
N1980
Community Facilities Plan: Brevard, N. C.
N2020
Neighborhood Analysis: Brevard, N. C.
N2120 (LMC WCU ASU)
Soil Survey, Transylvania County, North Carolina.
P2130
1861-1961, Transylvania County Centennial: Historical Souvenir Program.
T9170
APP. COUNTIES — N. C. — WATAUGA CO.
A History of Watauga County, North Carolina. With Sketches of Prominent Families.
A4990 (ASU LMC)
"Twenty-five Common Mosses of Watauga County, North Carolina."
B140 (ASU)
"The Growth and Development of Education in Watauga County."
B3720 (ASU)
"A Study of the Music Education Program of Watauga County."
B7980 (ASU)
"Industrial Waste and Human Sewage Pollution within the New River Drainage Basin of Watauga County."
C1490 (ASU)
William West Skiles: A Sketch of Missionary Life at Valle Crucis in Western North Carolina, 1842-1862.
C7210 (ASU WCU BC)
Soil Survey of Watauga County, North Carolina.
D1280 (ASU)
"The History of Banking in Watauga County, North Carolina."
E20 (ASU)
"Dealing with Problem Children in the Mabel Elementary School."
E1860 (ASU)
"A Survey of Public Education in Watauga County, North Carolina."
G2120 (ASU)
A Disastrous Flood, a True and Fascinating Story.
G3780 (ASU LMC)
"The Hepatic Flora of Watauga County, North Carolina."
H5220 (ASU)
"Negro Life in Watauga County."
H7310 (ASU)
"Folk Songs of Watauga."
K3000
Handbook of Watauga County.
L1190 (ASU LMC)
Soil Survey, Watauga County, North Carolina.
L1670
A Study of Farm Families and Their Level of Living Income Patterns in Watauga County, North Carolina.
M250 (ASU)
Sketches of Early Watauga.
M1340 (ASU)
Beech Mountain Folk-Songs and Ballads.
M4260
"A Study of Folklore in Watauga County, North Carolina."
M5600 (LMC)
Watauga County Reception and Care Plan.
N1720 (ASU)
Watauga County Records: Bonds, Court Records, Estates Records, Land Records, Military and Pension Records, Tax and Fiscal Records and Wills.
N1900 (ASU)
Land Development Plan: Boone, North Carolina.
N2060 (WCU ASU)
Watauga County Land Development Plan.
N2180 (ASU)
Characteristics of Households in Areas Served by the W. A. M. Y.
N2290 (ASU)
Sketches of Early Watauga.
P3460
"Coordination of Physical Education and Community Recreation in Ashe, Avery, and Watauga Counties."
Q170 (ASU)
"The Development of Secondary Education in Watauga County, North Carolina."
S6560
A Profile of Community Problems: Watauga, Avery, Mitchell, Yancey Counties.
W710
W1100 (ASU)
W1110 (ASU)
W1120 (ASU)
W1130 (ASU)
W1140 (ASU)
W1150 (ASU)
W1160 (ASU)
W1170 (ASU)
W1180 (ASU)
W1190 (ASU)
W1200 (ASU)
W1210 (ASU)
W1220 (ASU)
W1230 (ASU)
W1240 (ASU)
W1250 (ASU)
W1260 (ASU)
W1270 (ASU)
W1280 (ASU)
W1290 (ASU)
W1300 (ASU)
W1310 (ASU)
W1320 (ASU)
W1330 (ASU)
W1340 (ASU)
W1350 (ASU)
Alleghany, Ashe, Watauga Planning Project for Handicapped Children, ESEA Title III.
W1360 (WCU)
Daniel Boone Wagon Train.
W5670 (ASU)
History of Watauga County: A Souvenir of Watauga Centennial.
W5680 (ASU WCU LMC ETSU)
"The History of the Soil Conservation Service in Watauga County, North Carolina."
W6700 (ASU)
"A Study in Student Perceptions of the Person(s) Who Is Performing the Counseling Function at Watauga High School."
W8420 (ASU)
The Economic Geography of Watauga County, North Carolina.
Y110 (ASU)
APP. COUNTIES — N. C. — WILKES CO.
Deed Book B-1 Wilkes County, North Carolina.
A150
Land Entry Book, Wilkes County, North Carolina, 1778-1781.
A160 (ASU)
Deed Book A-1 Wilkes County, North Carolina.
A170

APP. COUNTIES — N. C. — WILKES CO.
"A History and Development of Education in Wilkes County, North Carolina."
A1660
1850 Census: Wilkes County, North Carolina.
C3570 (ASU)
"A History of Traphill Institute, Wilkes County, North Carolina."
C4440 (ASU)
"A History of Mountain View School, Wilkes County, North Carolina."
C4450 (ASU)
Historical Sketches of Wilkes County.
C9130 (ASU)
"The Growth of a Community Centered Curriculum at Wilkes Central High School, 1952-1960."
D3820 (ASU)
Will Books, Wilkes County, North Carolina.
G770
The Land of Wilkes.
H3930 (ASU WCU LMC BC)
Echoes of Happy Valley: Letters and Diaries, Family Life in the South, Civil War History.
H5190 (ASU LMC BC)
Happy Valley, History and Genealogy.
H5200 (ASU)
"A History of Negro Education in Wilkes County, North Carolina."
I820
Soil Survey of Wilkes County, North Carolina.
J2950
The Country Youth: Autobiography of B. B. McGee.
M1380 (ASU)
Historical Address . . . in Celebration of the Founding of Beaver Creek Baptist Church, Wilkes County.
M2430
The North Carolina Census of Wilkes County, 1787.
N1860 (ASU)
Land Potential Study & Land Development Plan: Wilkes County, North Carolina.
N2090 (ASU WCU)
Public Facilities Plan: Wilkes County, North Carolina.
N2170 (ASU WCU)
Zoning Ordinance of the W. Kerr Scott Reservoir Area, Wilkes County, N. C.
N2200 (ASU)
Zoning Ordinance: Wilkes County, North Carolina.
N2210 (ASU WCU)
North Wilkesboro, Wilkes County, N. C.: Key to the Blue Ridge Parkway.
N2800 (ASU LMC)
Biography of James Patton.
P830
The Ballad of Tom Dula: The Documented Story Behind the Murder of Laura Foster and the Trials and Execution of Tom Dula.
W3030 (ASU BC)
Identifying and Organizing for Individual Needs: An Evaluation.
W6270 (WCU ASU)

APP. COUNTIES — N. C. — YADKIN CO.
Soil Survey, Yadkin County, North Carolina.
C9840
The Red Strings Baseball Team of Yadkin County, N. C., 1896-1902.
D4000
Soil Survey, Yadkin County, North Carolina.
L1450
An Illustrated History of Yadkin County, 1850-1965.
R4440 (ASU)
"A History of Richmond Hill Law School."
W9150
Y10

APP. COUNTIES — N. C. — YANCEY CO.
In the Shadow of Big Bald: About the Appalachians and Their People.
A1230 (ETSU)
"A History of Yancey Collegiate Institute."
H8440 (ASU)
Land Development Plan: Burnsville, N. C.
N2070 (WCU)
Characteristics of Households in Areas Served by the W. A. M. Y.
N2290 (ASU)
Roan Mountain.
P1190 (LMC)
Yancey County, North Carolina.
P2140
History and Geography of Yancey County.
T790 (ASU)
"The Drop-Out Problem in Harris High School, Spruce Pine, North Carolina."
T8050 (ASU)
A Profile of Community Problems: Watauga, Avery, Mitchell, Yancey Counties.
W710
History and Geography of Yancey County.
Y20

APP. COUNTIES — N. Y. — CHAUTAUQUA CO.
Economic Study of Land Utilization in Chautauqua County, New York.
J2750

APP. COUNTIES — N. Y. — OTSEGO CO.
Economic Study of Land Utilization in Otsego County, New York.
J2760

APP. COUNTIES — N. Y. — SCHUYLER CO.
Economic Study of Land Utilization in Schuyler County, N. Y.
D410
"The Pisgah Culture and Its Place in the Prehistory of the Southern Appalachians."
D2090 (ASU WWC WCU)

APP. COUNTIES — OHIO — ADAMS CO.
Soil Survey of Adams County, Ohio.
T390

APP. COUNTIES — OHIO — ATHENS CO.
Soil Survey, Athens County, Ohio.
P530

APP. COUNTIES — OHIO — BELMONT CO.
G4350
Soil Survey of Belmont County, Ohio.
P2620

APP. COUNTIES — OHIO — CLERMONT CO.
Soil Survey: Clermont County, Ohio.
T420

APP. COUNTIES — OHIO — GUERNSEY CO.
G4350
The Impact of Water Resources Development upon Local Rural Communities: Adjustment Factors to Rapid Change.
N80

APP. COUNTIES — OHIO — HARRISON CO.
G4350

APP. COUNTIES — OHIO — MEIGS CO.
Soil Survey of Meigs County, Ohio.
M4930

APP. COUNTIES — OHIO — ROSS CO.
Soil Survey, Ross County, Ohio.
P2430

APP. COUNTIES — OHIO — SCIOTO CO.
Soil Survey, Scioto County, Ohio.
C6780

APP. COUNTIES — OHIO — VINTON CO.
Soil Survey of Vinton County, Ohio.
P540

APP. COUNTIES — OHIO — WASHINGTON CO.
Soil Survey of Washington County, Ohio.
P2670

APP. COUNTIES — PA. — ALLEGHENY CO.
More Allegheny Episodes: Legends and Traditions, Old and New.
S3130

APP. COUNTIES — PA. — BEDFORD CO.
Soil Survey of Bedford County, Pennsylvania.
M3130

APP. COUNTIES — PA. — BUTLER CO.
"Socioeconomic Factors Which May Affect Part Time Farmer Education in Butler County, Pennsylvania."
L3310

APP. COUNTIES — PA. — CAMBRIA CO.
Soil Survey of Cambria County, Pennsylvania.
D1880

APP. COUNTIES — PA. — CAMERON CO.
A Regional Economic Study of Cameron County, Pennsylvania.
G2050 (ASU)

APP. COUNTIES — PA. — CARBON CO.
Soil Survey, Carbon County, Pennsylvania.
F1180
Overall Economic Development Program for the Counties of Carbon, Lackawanna, Luzerne, Monroe, Pike, Schuylkill, Wayne, in the Northeastern Pennsylvania Economic Development District.
P1820 (ASU)

APP. COUNTIES — PA. — CENTRE CO.
Soil Survey of Center County, Pennsylvania.
M6660

APP. COUNTIES — PA. — CENTRE CO.
Index to History of Northumberland, Huntingdon, Mifflin, Centre, Union, Columbia, Juniata, and Clinton Counties, Pennsylvania.
L3370 (ASU)
"Measurement of Personal Wealth in Centre County, Pennsylvania."
M1600
Penn's Grandest Cavern: The History, Legends and Description of Penn's Cave in Centre County, Pennsylvania.
S3140

APP. COUNTIES — PA. — CLARION CO.
"Bituminous Coal Open Pit Mining in Clarion County, Pennsylvania."
J180
"Agricultural Regions of Clarion County, Pennsylvania."
L1250

APP. COUNTIES — PA. — CLINTON CO.
The Impact of Interchange Development on the Economy of Clinton County.
G210
Index to History of Northumberland, Huntingdon, Mifflin, Centre, Union, Columbia, Juniata, and Clinton Counties, Pennsylvania.
L3370 (ASU)
Soil Survey, Clinton County, Pennsylvania.
S7080
An Economic Survey of Clinton Co., Pa.
W840

APP. COUNTIES — PA. — COLUMBIA CO.
Index to History of Northumberland, Huntingdon, Mifflin, Centre, Union, Columbia, Juniata, and Clinton Counties, Pennsylvania.
L3370 (ASU)
Soil Survey, Columbia County, Pennsylvania.
P460

APP. COUNTIES — PA. — FAYETTE CO.
Soil Survey, Fayette County, Pennsylvania.
K3020
Fayette County, Pennsylvania; An Economic Survey.
S670

APP. COUNTIES — PA. — FULTON CO.
Soil Survey, Fulton County, Pennsylvania.
C4090

APP. COUNTIES — PA. — GREENE CO.
Pioneer History of Greene County, Pennsylvania.
E2340 (ASU)
Waynesburg, Prosperous and Beautiful, a Souvenir Pictorial Story of the Biggest and Best Little City in Pennsylvania. . . .
H5280
Soil Survey of Greene County, Pennsylvania.
P2090

APP. COUNTIES — PA. — HUNTINGDON CO.
Soil Survey, Huntingdon County, Pennsylvania.
H5260
Index to History of Northumberland, Huntingdon, Mifflin, Centre, Union, Columbia, Juniata, and Clinton Counties, Pennsylvania.
L3370 (ASU)

APP. COUNTIES — PA. — INDIANA CO.
Soil Survey of Indiana County, Pennsylvania.
B8700
An Economic Survey of Indiana County, Pennsylvania.
S640

APP. COUNTIES — PA. — JUNIATA CO.
Index to History of Northumberland, Huntingdon, Mifflin, Centre, Union, Columbia, Juniata, and Clinton Counties, Pennsylvania.
L3370 (ASU)

APP. COUNTIES — PA. — JUNIATA CO.
Juniata Memories: Legends Collected in Central Pennsylvania.
S3120

APP. COUNTIES — PA. — LACKAWANNA CO.
Overall Economic Development Program for the Counties of Carbon, Lackawanna, Luzerne, Monroe, Pike, Schuylkill, Wayne, in the Northeastern Pennsylvania Economic Development District.
P1820 (ASU)

APP. COUNTIES — PA. — LUZERNE CO.
Overall Economic Development Program for the Counties of Carbon, Lackawanna, Luzerne, Monroe, Pike, Schuylkill, Wayne, in the Northeastern Pennsylvania Economic Development District.
P1820 (ASU)
"A History of Land Subsistence and Its Consequences Caused by the Mining of Anthracite Coal in Luzerne County, Pennsylvania."
R2870
APP. COUNTIES — PA. — LYCOMING CO.
Soil Survey, Lycoming County, Pennsylvania.
S7120
APP. COUNTIES — PA. — MCKEAN CO.
A Community Attack on Chronic Unemployment: Hazleton, Pennsylvania, a Case Study.
F700
APP. COUNTIES — PA. — MERCER CO.
Soil Survey of Mercer County, Pennsylvania.
D1600
Soil Survey, Mercer County, Pennsylvania.
G4060
APP. COUNTIES — PA. — MIFFLIN CO.
Index to History of Northumberland, Huntingdon, Mifflin, Centre, Union, Columbia, Juniata, and Clinton Counties, Pennsylvania.
L3370 (ASU)
APP. COUNTIES — PA. — MONROE CO.
Overall Economic Development Program for the Counties of Carbon, Lackawanna, Luzerne, Monroe, Pike, Schuylkill, Wayne, in the Northeastern Pennsylvania Economic Development District.
P1820 (ASU)
Capability of Local Government in the Stroudsburg Area, Monroe County.
P1850 (ASU)
APP. COUNTIES — PA. — MONTGOMERY CO.
History of Montgomery County with the Schuylkill Valley: Containing Sketches of all the Townships, Boroughs and Villages, in Said Limits, from the Earliest Period to the Present Time. With an Account of the Indians, the Swedes, and Other Early Settlers, and the Local Events of the Revolution: Besides Notices of the Progress of Population, Improvements, and Manufactures.
B8230 (ASU)
APP. COUNTIES — PA. — MONTOUR CO.
Soil Survey, Montour and Northumberland Counties, Pennsylvania.
B90
APP. COUNTIES — PA. — NORTHUMBERLAND CO.
Soil Survey, Montour and Northumberland Counties, Pennsylvania.
B90
Wills and Administrations of Northumberland County.
F1160
Early Assessment Records: Union County and Northumberland County.
L3360 (ASU)
Index to History of Northumberland, Huntingdon, Mifflin, Centre, Union, Columbia, Juniata, and Clinton Counties, Pennsylvania.
L3370 (ASU)
An Economic Survey of Northumberland County, Pennsylvania.
S650
APP. COUNTIES — PA. — PENDLETON CO.
The Igneous Rocks of Pendleton County, West Virginia.
G380 (ETSU)
APP. COUNTIES — PA. — PENNSYLVANIA CO.
Index to History of Northumberland, Huntingdon, Mifflin, Centre, Union, Columbia, Juniata, and Clinton Counties, Pennsylvania.
L3370 (ASU)
APP. COUNTIES — PA. — PIKE CO.
Overall Economic Development Program for the Counties of Carbon, Lackawanna, Luzerne, Monroe, Pike, Schuylkill, Wayne, in the Northeastern Pennsylvania Economic Development District.
P1820 (ASU)
APP. COUNTIES — PA. — POTTER CO.
Soil Survey, Potter County Pennsylvania.
G2530
"An Economic Analysis of Idle Farm Land, Potter County, Pennsylvania, 1953."
J530
APP. COUNTIES — PA. — SCHUYLKILL CO.
Overall Economic Development Program for the Counties of Carbon, Lackawanna, Luzerne, Monroe, Pike, Schuylkill, Wayne, in the Northeastern Pennsylvania Economic Development District.
P1820 (ASU)
APP. COUNTIES — PA. — SNYDER CO.
Probate and Orphans Court Records of Snyder County, Pennsylvania.
F1150
APP. COUNTIES — PA. — SULLIVAN CO.
The Economic Structure of Sullivan County, Pennsylvania.
G190 (ASU)
"Equating Timber and Wildlife Values and Returns to the Farm Resource Base in Sullivan County, Pennsylvania."
G200
"Equating Timber and Wildlife Values and Returns to the Farm Resources Base in Sullivan County, Pennsylvania."
H3970
APP. COUNTIES — PA. — TIOGA CO.
Soil Survey of Tioga County, Pennsylvania.
H4610
APP. COUNTIES — PA. — UNION CO.
Soil Survey, Union County, Pennsylvania.
B100
Early Assessment Records: Union County and Northumberland County.
L3360 (ASU)
Index to History of Northumberland, Huntingdon, Mifflin, Centre, Union, Columbia, Juniata, and Clinton Counties, Pennsylvania.
L3370 (ASU)
Tombstone Inscriptions of Union County, Pennsylvania.
L3380 (ASU)
Union County, Pennsylvania, 1865-1965.
L3390 (ASU)
APP. COUNTIES — PA. — VENANGO CO.
An Economic Survey of Venango County, Pennsylvania.
S660
APP. COUNTIES — PA. — WASHINGTON CO.
History of the Mount Prospect Graveyard and Cemetery, in Mount Pleasant Township, Washington County, Pennsylvania.
W5300
APP. COUNTIES — PA. — WAYNE CO.
Overall Economic Development Program for the Counties of Carbon, Lackawanna, Luzerne, Monroe, Pike, Schuylkill, Wayne, in the Northeastern Pennsylvania Economic Development District.
P1820 (ASU)
Soil Survey of Wayne County, Pennsylvania.
S3430
APP. COUNTIES — PA. — WESTMORELAND CO.
Soil Survey, Westmoreland County, Pennsylvania.
T500
APP. COUNTIES — PA. — WYOMING CO.
Soil Survey of Wyoming County, Pennsylvania.
H4620
APP. COUNTIES — S. C. — ANDERSON CO.
Survey of Unemployment Compensation Beneficiaries in Anderson, Greenville, Spartanburg Counties, South Carolina.
C4940
APP. COUNTIES — S. C. — CHEROKEE CO.
Soil Survey of Cherokee County, South Carolina.
D3230
Soil Survey, Cherokee County, South Carolina.
J2670
APP. COUNTIES — S. C. — GREENVILLE CO.
Survey of Unemployment Compensation Beneficiaries in Anderson, Greenville, Spartanburg Counties, South Carolina.
C4940
Greenville County, Economic and Social.
G4870
Greenville County, Economic and Social.
G4880
"The Scope of Religious Education in the Secondary Schools of Greenville County, South Carolina."
H460
An Analysis of School District Organization in Greenville County, South Carolina.
M8550
The Kingdom of the Happy Land.
P890 (ASU LMC)
"Teachers Attitudes Toward Their Profession in Greenville County, South Carolina."
T570
APP. COUNTIES — S. C. — OCONEE CO.
Soil Survey, Oconee County, South Carolina.
B9600
"Educational Development of Oconee County, South Carolina."
E1880
Soil Survey of Oconee County, South Carolina.
M2060
"An Economic Survey of Oconee County."
W8880
APP. COUNTIES — S. C. — PICKENS CO.
It Happened in Pickens County.
M1310 (ASU BC)
Soil Survey, Pickens County, South Carolina.
B9610
Farm Business Study of the Six Mile Area of Pickens County, 1940.
K2120 (ASU)
Soil Survey, Pickens County, South Carolina.
S2570
APP. COUNTIES — S. C. — SPARTANBURG CO.
Soil Survey, Spartanburg County, South Carolina.
C510
Survey of Unemployment Compensation Beneficiaries in Anderson, Greenville, Spartanburg Counties, South Carolina.
C4940
History of Spartanburg County: Embracing an Account of Many Important Events, and Biographical Sketches of Statesmen, Divines and Other Public Men.
L340 (ASU BC)
Soil Survey of Spartanburg County, South Carolina.
L790
Soil Survey of the Campobello Area, South Carolina.
M3020
APP. COUNTIES — SOURCES
Consolidated Bibliography of County Histories in Fifty States in 1961, Consolidated 1935-1961.
P2340 (ASU)
APP. COUNTIES — SOUTHEASTERN STATES
Statistical Atlas of Southern Counties Listing and Analysis of Socio-economic Indices of 1104 Southern Counties.
J1330 (ASU LMC MHC BC)
APP. COUNTIES — TENN.
P4720
Tennessee County Inventory.
T980 (ETSU)
T1370
Population and Labor Force Characteristics of Tennessee Counties.
T1800
Crosstie Industry Facts for the Tennessee Valley Counties.
T5280
APP. COUNTIES — TENN. — ANDERSON CO.
The Children of the South.
A2310
Geological Report: Coal Creek Mining and Manufacturing Company of Tennessee.
B6190
Petitions of Anderson County Tennessee.
C9940 (ASU)
Coal Creek Rebellion.
F1770 (ASU)
"An Educational Survey of Coal Creek Community, Anderson County, Tennessee."
H2990
Inventory of the County Archives of Tennessee: Anderson County.
H5800
H5980
Clinton, Tennessee: A Tentative Description and Analysis of the School Desegregation Crisis.
H6470
"A Study of School Transportation, Anderson County, Tennessee."
I950

APP. COUNTIES — TENN. — ANDERSON CO.

A Report of Student Internships in Resource Development, & Legal Services Development.
O10

Soil Survey, Norris Area, Tennessee.
R4230

"A History of Anderson County, Tennessee."
S1670

Private Acts of Anderson County, 1801-1956.
T1570

Agricultural-Industrial Survey of Anderson County, Tennessee.
T5570

One Hundred Years: A Story of the First Baptist Church, Clinton, Tennessee.
W2000

APP. COUNTIES — TENN. — BLEDSOE CO.
B3760
B3900
B3990

"An Educational and Economic Survey of Bledsoe County, Tennessee."
B7060

Educational, Economic and Community Survey, Bledsoe County.
B7070

A Report on Coal Lands Lying in Bledsoe County.
G4800

Sequatchie Valley, a Historical Sketch.
H5170

The Southern Tennessee Coal Field Included in Bledsoe, Cumberland, Franklin, Grundy, Rhea, Sequatchie, Van Buren, Warren, and White Counties.
N580 (ETSU)

Sequatchie: A Story of the Southern Cumberlands.
R540 (ASU)

"A History of Bledsoe County, Tennessee: 1807-1957."
R3350

"Pikeville, Market Center of the Upper Sequatchie Valley."
S1430

"Inventory of Bledsoe County Records."
T1840

Agricultural-Industrial Survey of Bledsoe County.
T5580

Soil Survey of the Pikeville Area, Tennessee.
W6130

APP. COUNTIES — TENN. — BLOUNT CO.

"The Social and Economic History of Maryville since 1890."
B1920
B3770

History of Blount County, Tennessee, From War Trail to Landing Strip, 1795-1955.
B9130 (ASU ETSU BC)

Soil Survey, Blount County, Tennessee.
E1470
E2270

"A Study of School Transportation, Blount County, Tennessee."
H2330

"A Study of the Physical Plants of Blount County High Schools."
H4160

Inventory of the County Archives of Tennessee: Blount County.
H5810

History of the Chilhowee Baptist Association.
H7020

"An Educational, Economic, and Community Survey of Blount County, Tennessee."
H7540

An Economic Survey of Blount County, Tennessee, a Study of Resources and Industrial Potentials.
H8720

"Social Survey of Blount County, Tennessee."
M3940

"A Geographical Survey of Blount County, Tennessee."
R2560

Report of the Survey of the Schools of Blount County, Tennessee, for School Year, 1934-1935.
T1130 (ETSU)

"Inventory of Blount County Records."
T1850

"The Achievement of Selected Economically Deprived Secondary School Male Athletes as Related to Non-athletes in Blount County, Tennessee, Schools."
W7220 (ETSU)

APP. COUNTIES — TENN. — BRADLEY CO.
B3780
B3960

Guest's Guide; Points of Interest in Cleveland.
B8790

Bradley County, Tennessee.
C4970

City and County with a Future: Cleveland, Bradley County, Tennessee.
C4980

Red Clay and Rattlesnake Springs: A History of the Cherokee Indians of Bradley County, Tennessee.
C7530 (ASU LMC MHC BC)

Soil Survey, Bradley County, Tennessee
F2470

"A Study of School Transportation, Bradley County, Tennessee."
H1420

An Album of Historical Memories. Chatata-Tasso, Bradley County, Tennessee, 1830-1961.
H2190

Inventory of the County Archives of Tennessee: Bradley County.
H5820

History of the Rebellion in Bradley County, East Tennessee.
H8520

"History of the Development of Negro Public Schools in Bradley County, Tennessee, 1931-1951."
M3580

"Church Organization in Bradley County, Tennessee, in 1950."
P2860

"An Educational Study of Bradley County, Tennessee."
R3830

Historical Cemetery Records of Bradley County, Tennessee.
R3840 (ETSU)

"A History of Bradley County, Tennessee, to 1861."
S4190

Geology, Mineral Resources, and Ground Water of the Cleveland Area, Tennessee.
S9710 (ETSU)

Bradley County Schools Survey Report.
T1080

Health and Sanitation Needs and Resources, Bradley County, Tennessee.
T9400

Centennial of the First Presbyterian Church, United States, in Cleveland, Tennessee, 1837-1937.
W9110

A History of Bradley County.
W9120 (ETSU)

APP. COUNTIES — TENN. — CAMPBELL CO.
C561

"An Administrative and Educational Survey of the Schools of Campbell County, Tennessee."
H3370

"The Development of Public Education in Campbell County, Tennessee."
R2240

The Land of the Lake: A History of Campbell County, Tennessee.
R2250

A History of Jellico, Tennessee, Containing Historical Information on Campbell County, Tennessee and Whitley County, Kentucky.
S3330

"An Economic, Social and Educational Survey of Campbell County, Tennessee."
S4690

"Job Retraining under the Area Development Act: The Campbell, Claiborne Counties (Tennessee) Case."
S5420

Campbell County School Survey.
T1090

A Study of the Community of La Follette, Tenn.
T2050

APP. COUNTIES — TENN. — CARTER CO.

"An Overview of Special Education Services in the Elizabethton City School with Emphasis on the Homebound Program."
B2310 (ETSU)
B3790
B3860
B4010
C1661

"A Study of the Language Arts Program in Grade One of the Carter County School System with Some Suggestions for the Improvement of the Program."
C2050 (ETSU)

"A Study to Present the Status of Industrial Arts in the Five White Carter County, Tennessee, High Schools."
C4540 (ETSU)

"An Analysis of the Industrial Potential of Carter County, Tennessee."
C9180 (ETSU)

Early History of Carter County.
E90

"A Study of the Title I Reading Program During the 1966-68 School Years in Carter County, Tennessee."
E1850 (ETSU)
E2330 (ETSU)

"A Survey of Special Education Services in Washington, Carter and Sullivan Counties, Tennessee."
G4010

"A Survey of the Flowering Plants and Ferns on the Forge Hill, Carter County, Tennessee."
G4290 (ETSU)

"A Study of the Program of Vocational Rehabilitation in Carter County, Tennessee."
G4300

"A Study of the Physical Education Programs of the High Schools in Carter County, Tennessee."
H2150 (ETSU)

"Team Teaching at Douglas School, Elizabethton, Carter County, Tennessee."
H3310 (ETSU)

"The Social and Economic Effects Produced upon Small Towns by Rapid Industrialization."
H6740

"A Survey of ESEA Title 1 Equipment and Its Extended Usage in Carter County, Tennessee."
J2400 (ETSU)

"Carter County's Greatest Need in the Homebound Program of Services for Exceptional Children, 1952-54."
K2660 (ETSU)

"A Study of Serum Protein Variation in Peromyscus Maniculatus Nubiterrae Rhoads at Six Attitudinal Habitats on Roan Mountain, Carter County, Tennessee, and Mitchell County, North Carolina."
M880 (ETSU)

Early History of Carter County, 1760-1861.
M5160 (ASU ETSU LMC)

"An Educational Survey of Carter County, Tennessee."
M7460

"A Simplified Library Program for the Elementary Schools of Carter County, Tennessee."
M8320 (ETSU)

"A History of the Iron Industry in Carter County to 1860."
N270 (ETSU)

"A Survey of the Vascular Plants of the Sinking Creek Area of Carter County, Tennessee."
P1240 (ETSU)

"A Sampling of the Folklore of Carter County, Tennessee."
P2220

"An Analysis of Faculty and Administrative Attitudes Toward Teacher Corps Interns in Carter County, Tennessee."
R1430 (ETSU)

"A Proposed Health Instruction Program for Upper Elementary Grades Adaptable to Carter County."
R1730 (ETSU)

Soil Survey, Carter County, Tennessee.
R4220

History of the Thirteenth Regiment, Tennessee Volunteer Cavalry, U. S. A., Including a Narrative of the Bridge Burning: The Carter County Rebellion, and the Loyalty, Heroism and Suffering of the Union Men and Women of Carter and Johnson Counties, Tennessee, During the Civil War.
S1460 (ASU LMC)

APP. COUNTIES — TENN. — CARTER CO.

"A Study of Debt History in Carter County, Tennessee, 1892-1952."
S2380

"The Use of Locational Analysis in the Determination of School Sites: A Case Example, Carter County, Tennessee."
S7310 (ETSU)

"What Citizens of Carter County Know about Their Schools."
S7700 (ETSU)

"The Influence of Community Pressure Groups on School Principals in Carter County."
S7840 (ETSU)

"Determining the Most Effective Method by Which the Children in Each of Three Groups in the First Grade at South Side School, Carter County, Tennessee, Learn to Recognize Words."
T470 (ETSU)

"A Tentative Health Instruction Program for the Secondary Schools of Carter County, Tennessee."
T480 (ETSU)

"Inventory of Carter County Records."
T1860

Agricultural-Industrial Survey of Carter County.
T5590

Industrial Site Survey of Carter County, Sullivan County, and Washington County.
U4160

"A Comparison of Sources and Expenditures of the Funds Raised by the Schools and Organizations in Carter County with the School Budget of 1960-61."
W6550 (ETSU)

"A Survey of Co-curricular Programs in the Five High Schools of Carter County, Tennessee."
W7440 (ETSU)

"An Analysis of the Sources and Expenditures of Internal Funds in the High Schools of Carter County, Tennessee."
Y280 (ETSU)

APP. COUNTIES — TENN. — CLAIBORNE CO.

Soil Survey, Claiborne County, Tennessee.
A5560 (ASU)

"A Study of the Development of Special Education in Claiborne County."
B200 (ETSU)

"Appraisal of Vocational Education in Agriculture in Claiborne County by Business and Professional Leaders."
B6460
C9420

"The Study of the Four High Schools in Claiborne County, Tennessee."
D1010

Minutes of Davis Creek Church, 1897-1907.
E1100

A Doctor's Pilgrimage.
H1070

The Changing Economy of Claiborne County, Tennessee.
H2580

The Surrender of Cumberland Gap.
M1350

"The Agricultural Needs of Claiborne County, Tennessee."
N1500

"Job Retraining under the Area Development Act: The Campbell, Claiborne Counties (Tennessee) Case."
S5420

Just the Little Story of Cumberland Gap.
V450

APP. COUNTIES — TENN. — CLAY CO.

"Farm Taxation and County Government in Overton, Clay and Pickett Counties, Tennessee."
P3930

"Historical Sketches of Clay County, Tennessee."
S7550

APP. COUNTIES — TENN. — COCKE CO.

Soil Survey, Cocke County, Tennessee.
B2650
C5401

Newport.
G2240

"Cocke County Ballads and Songs."
H3650 (ASU)

"A History of the Secondary Schools of Cocke County, Tennessee."
K2810

Over the Misty Blue Hills: The Story of Cocke County, Tennessee.
O200

"Negro Education in Cocke County."
R180
S3860

Geology and Barite Deposits of the Del Rio District, Cocke County, Tennessee.
T1280 (ETSU)

Agricultural-Industrial Survey of Cocke County.
T5600

"A Study of the Ability of Cocke County to Support Its Schools."
V670

APP. COUNTIES — TENN. — COFFEE CO.

B3800
B3840

History of Coffee County, Tennessee.
E2430

The Excavation and Interpretation of the Old Stone Fort, Coffee County, Tennessee.
F310 (ASU)

Soil Survey, Coffee County, Tennessee.
L3660

Soil Survey of Coffee County, Tennessee.
M2030

Coffee County from Arrowheads to Rockets: A History of Coffee County, Tennessee.
M3590

Coffee County from Arrowheads to Rockets; a History of Coffee County, Tennessee.
M3810

Coffee County: From Arrowheads to Rockets. A History of Coffee County, Tennessee.
M3820 (ETSU)

"Inventory of Coffee County Records."
T1870

Agricultural-Industrial Survey of Coffee County.
T5610

APP. COUNTIES — TENN. — CUMBERLAND CO.

Significant Changes in Agriculture of Cumberland County, Tennessee.
A1870

Significant Changes in Agriculture of Cumberland County, Tennessee.
A1880

Local Leadership in Rural Communities of Cumberland County, Tennessee.
B5360

Neighborhoods and Communities of Cumberland County, Tennessee.
B5370

A Brief History of the First Congregational Church, Crossville, Tennessee, 1887-1962.
B6850

Cumberland County's First Hundred Years.
B8340 (LMC)

Crossville.
C7150

History of Pleasant Hill; a History of Pleasant Hill Academy and Who's Who of Alumni.
D2680 (BC)

"Economic Set-up of the Cumberland Homesteads, Crossville, Tennessee."
F1450

Tales of the Civil War Era.
H3290

Soil Survey, Cumberland County, Tennessee.
H7800

Cumberland County's First Hundred Years.
K3210 (ASU ETSU LMC BC)

"Physiography of the Grassy Cove District, Cumberland County, Tennessee."
L360 (LMC)

Social Relationships and Institutions in Seven Rural Communities. United States Farm Security Administration Social Research Report no. 18.
L3420

Standards of Living of the Residents of Seven Rural Resettlement Communities.
L3440

"An Analysis of the New Deal Subsistence Homesteads Program in Cumberland County, Tennessee."
M7210

The Southern Tennessee Coal Field Included in Bledsoe, Cumberland, Franklin, Grundy, Rhea, Sequatchie, Van Buren, Warren, and White Counties.
N580 (ETSU)

"Inventory of Cumberland County Records."
T1880

Agricultural-Industrial Survey of Cumberland County.
T5620

Ground Water Resources and Geology of Cumberland County, Tennessee.
W7340 (LMC)

APP. COUNTIES — TENN. — DEKALB CO.

B3810

History of DeKalb County, Tennessee.
H490

History of DeKalb County, Tennessee.
H500 (ASU BC)

Love's Valley.
L3650

"Name Index to (Hale's) History of DeKalb County, Tennessee."
M3290

Soil Survey: DeKalb County, Tennessee.
M6440

"Inventory of DeKalb County Records."
T1890

APP. COUNTIES — TENN. — FENTRESS CO.

B3820
B3940
B3950

Seventh Census of the United States, 1850: Fentress County, Tennessee, Free Population Schedules.
C1390 (ASU)

True Stories of Jamestown and Its Environs.
H510

Davy Crockett and Others in Fentress County Who Have Given the County a Prominent Place in History.
H6400 (ETSU BC)

History of Fentress County, Tennessee, the Old Home of Mark Twain's Ancestors.
H6410

Mark Twain's Obedstown and Knobs of Tennessee; a History of Jamestown and Fentress County, Tennessee.
H6420

One Hundred Years in the Cumberland Mountains along the Continental Line.
H6430 (ETSU ASU)

"The Labor Struggle at Wilder, Tennessee."
P2280 (ASU)

Agricultural-Industrial Survey of Fentress County.
T5630

APP. COUNTIES — TENN. — FRANKLIN CO.

B3830

Seventh Census of the United States, 1850: Franklin County, Tennessee, Free Population Schedules.
C1400 (ASU)

"History of Private Educational Institutions of Franklin County, Tennessee."
F1060

Soil Survey, Franklin County, Tennessee
F2480

"Rural Land Use in Franklin County, Tennessee."
G630

Confederate Action in Franklin County, Tennessee.
H1580

"Sewanee a Unique Community."
H5460

"A History of Higher Education in Franklin County, Tennessee."
H8390

"A History of St. Andrew's School."
K740

The German-Swiss in Franklin County, Tennessee: A Study of the Significance of Cultural Considerations in Farming Enterprises.
K2990 (ASU BC)

"Churvallic's Chronicle of Franklin County, Tennessee."
M1830

The Southern Tennessee Coal Field Included in Bledsoe, Cumberland, Franklin, Grundy, Rhea, Sequatchie, Van Buren, Warren, and White Counties.
N580 (ETSU)

"An Economic, Educational, and Social Survey of Franklin County, Tennessee."
R570 (ASU)

"A Brief History of Franklin County, Tennessee."
R1840

Focus on Franklin County.
R3460

"Inventory of Franklin County Records."
T1900

APP. COUNTIES — TENN. — FRANKLIN CO.
Agricultural-Industrial Survey of Franklin County, Tennessee.
T5640
"Development of the Health Program for Negroes in Franklin County, Tennessee from 1940-1953."
W5820
APP. COUNTIES — TENN. — GRAINGER CO.
G3170
Soil Survey, Grainger County, Tennessee.
H7810
"A Study of the School Transportation Problem in Grainger County, Tennessee."
J2700
Tenn. Grainger Co., Marriage Bonds and Licenses.
K810
Soil Survey of Grainger County, Tennessee.
M2050
"A Study of the Reorganization of the Attendance Centers of the Grainger County School System."
N830
O320
Grainger County Schools Survey Report.
T1100
Agricultural-Industrial Survey of Grainger County.
T5650
APP. COUNTIES — TENN. — GREENE CO.
Neighbor against Neighbor, Brother against Brother; Greene County in the Civil War.
H3850
APP. COUNTIES — TENN. — GREENE CO.
Kirchen Buch (Church Book) Register, 1815-1828. St. James Lutheran Church, Greene County, Tennessee.
B8600
Soil Survey, Greene County, Tennessee.
E1150
F3630
G3720 (ETSU)
The Economy of Greeneville, Tennessee; a Study of the Information and Data Related to the Greeneville, Tennessee, Economic Community.
H6730
"The Status of Public Relations Activities in the Secondary Schools of Greene County, Tennessee."
M8440
P70
"Geographic Factors in the Land Use of Green County, Tennessee."
P390
Greene County, Tennessee: Early Marriage Bonds, 1782-1820.
P2380
Greene County Cemeteries, from Earliest Dates to 1970-1971.
R1640 (ASU ETSU)
"A Study of Parent-child Relationships in Greene County, Tennessee."
R1720 (ETSU)
A Report of the Survey of the Finances and Management of Greene County, Tennessee.
T2130 (ETSU)
Agricultural-Industrial Survey of Greene County, Tennessee.
T5660
Greeneville's Government; a Study of the Organization and Administration of the Government of Greeneville, Tennessee.
U4110
APP. COUNTIES — TENN. — GRUNDY CO.
Grundy County, Tennessee, Relief in a Coal Mining Community.
A1850
"Public Welfare and Related Problems in Grundy County, Tennessee."
A2180
Sketch of Beersheba Springs: and: Chickamuga Trace.
B3030
B3800
B3840
"An Educational Survey of the Elementary Schools of Grundy County, Tennessee."
M240
"Development of the Coal Industry of Grundy County, Tennessee."
M620
The Southern Tennessee Coal Field Included in Bledsoe, Cumberland, Franklin, Grundy, Rhea, Sequatchie, Van Buren, Warren, and White Counties.
N580 (ETSU)
"Agricultural and Social Aspects of the Swiss Settlement in Grundy County, Tennessee."
N600
"Inventory of Grundy County Records."
T1910
APP. COUNTIES — TENN. — HAMBLEN CO.
Soil Survey, Hamblen County, Tennessee.
A10 (ASU)
History of Morristown, 1787-1936.
B6890
Diary of Kate Livingston, 1859-1868.
C140
The Herbert Walters Story.
H5420
"Migration Patterns of Residents in a High In-Migration County, Hamblen County, Tennessee."
H7610
"A Political History of Morristown and Hamblen County, Tennessee."
P1100
Historic Hamblen, 1870-1970.
R4210
"The Relationship between Reading Capacity and Reading Achievement of One Hundred and Twenty-three Third Grade Children of Morrison and Hamblen County, Tennessee."
S4940
Agricultural-Industrial Survey of Hamblen County, Tennessee.
T5670
APP. COUNTIES — TENN. — HAMILTON CO.
Hamilton County Confederate Soldiers.
A4740
The History of Hamilton County and Chattanooga, Tennessee.
A4760 (ETSU BC ASU)
A4980
Guide Book to Lookout Mountain and a Brief Account of Battles Fought near Chattanooga, Tennessee.
B580
"An Analysis of Curriculum Offerings, Changes and Trends in Five Selected Hamilton County High Schools."
B610 (ETSU)
In Retrospect: Reminiscencies (sic) and Observations of a Hamilton County, Tennessee, Retired Teacher.
B2580
B3850
C2630
The Centenary of Sts. Peter and Paul's Parish, Chattanooga, Tenn. The Story of the First One Hundred Years of the Catholic Church in Hamilton County.
C3540
"The Negroes of Chattanooga, Tennessee."
C7830
The Hamilton County Course of Study.
H1100 (ETSU)
Directory of Churches, Missions, and Religious Institutions of Tennessee, no. 33. Hamilton County.
H5760
Inventory of the County Archives of Tennessee: Hamilton County, Tennessee.
H5830
"Civil War Anecdotes and Legends of Chattanooga."
N710
The Chickamauga and Chattanooga Campaign and Battle-fields. A Chronological Historic Guide, August 16-November 25, 1863.
N2870
Chattanooga and Hamilton County, Tennessee.
O20
Chattanooga, Tennessee; Hamilton County, and Lookout Mountain. An Epitome of Chattanooga from Her Early Days Down to the Present; Hamilton County, Its Soil, Climate, Area, Population, Wealth, etc.
P170
P570
Signal Mountain and Walden's Ridge.
P600
History of Summertown, Walden's Ridge, Tennessee.
P610
So Firm a Foundation.
P640
Sequatchie: A Story of the Southern Cumberlands.
R540 (ASU)
Soil Survey, Hamilton County, Tennessee.
R3100
"Recreational Habits of Rural Youth in Selected Communities of Hamilton County, Tennessee."
S990
Hamilton County, Economic and Social: A Laboratory Study in the Department of Agricultural Economics Under the Direction of Professor C. E. Allred.
S6910
A Report of the Survey of the Management and Finances of the Government of Hamilton County.
T2160 (ETSU)
Chattanooga, Its History and Growth.
W300
The Chickamauga Dam and Its Environs.
W310
This is Chattanooga.
W320
Historic City, Chattanooga; Containing Views and Descriptive Matter of Historic Points of Interest, Scenery, Pictures of Old and New Buildings, Leading Men, etc., All Artistically and Pleasingly Intermingled.
W2160
APP. COUNTIES — TENN. — HANCOCK CO.
"The Melungeons of Newman's Ridge."
B1440 (ETSU ASU)
Report.
H1410 (ETSU)
"A Study of Public School Finance in Hancock County, Tennessee."
L2920
"A Study of Pupil Transportation in Hancock, Tennessee."
W6510
APP. COUNTIES — TENN. — HAWKINS CO.
A Sermon, Delivered on September 8th, 1813. . .
A2290
"The Melungeons of Newman's Ridge."
B1440 (ETSU ASU)
"A History of Education in Hawkins County with Special Reference to Rock Hill School."
C7250
"A Study of Seven School Communities of Hawkins County, Tennessee."
D1110
"What the Patrons of Hawkins County Schools Think about Their Schools."
D4320 (ETSU)
F1090
"A Study of Reorganization of Attendance Centers in Hawkins County, Tennessee."
J1940
"A Guidance Program for the Schools of Hawkins County."
M3240
The Fiftieth Anniversary of the Rogersville Synodical College.
P190
"A Study of School Transportation, Hawkins County, Tennessee."
R170
Stratigraphic Section at Lee Valley, Hawkins County, Tennessee.
R3400 (ETSU)
"Written Board of Education Policies for Hawkins County, Tennessee."
S5270 (ETSU)
"A Study of a Possible Plan for Further School Consolidation in Hawkins County."
S6620 (ETSU)
"A Study of High Schools in Hawkins County, Tennessee."
V80
W7920
APP. COUNTIES — TENN. — JACKSON CO.
"Early History of Jackson County, Tennessee."
D3360
"History of the Development of Education prior to 1900 in Jackson County, Tennessee."
H300

APP. COUNTIES — TENN. — JACKSON CO.

"An Educational Economic, and Community Survey of Jackson County, Tennessee."
O950

Soil Survey of Jackson County, Tennessee.
R3560

Soil Survey of Jackson County, Tennessee.
R3570

"History of Educational Development in Jackson County, Tennessee, 1800 to 1950."
S4550

APP. COUNTIES — TENN. — JEFFERSON CO.

An Educational Study of Jefferson County, Tennessee.
C1650

"The Zinc Industry of Jefferson County, Tennessee."
C7750

"Secession and Civil War in Jefferson County, Tennessee, 1860-1865."
K2200 (ETSU)

Historical Records of East Tennessee. Jefferson County, Dandridge Edition. 2 vols.
M1480

"A History of Education in Jefferson County, Tennessee."
M2950

Soil Survey, Jefferson County, Tennessee.
M6630

Jefferson County Survey Report.
T1120

The Romance of a Sesquicentennial, The Dumplin Creek Baptist Church of Christ, Jefferson County, Tennessee, Organized 1797.
T8910 (BC)

Shunem Church and Cemetery Speak: A Living Memorial to Those Who Sleep Here, 1824-1965.
W8610

APP. COUNTIES — TENN. — JOHNSON CO.

"The Natural Vegetation of Johnson County, Tennessee, Past and Present."
B1110 (ETSU)
B3790
B3860
B4010

Story of Captain Jesse Cox of Johnson Co., Tennessee.
C5720

"A Survey of the Guidance Services Available in the Elementary Schools of Johnson County, Tennessee."
C8040 (ETSU)

"Effect of Consolidation on Johnson County School, Johnson City, Tennessee."
G330 (ETSU)

The Donnelly-Barry-Butler Families and Their Kin-folks of Johnson Co., Tennessee.
N290

Leonard Shoun and his Wife Barbara Slemp Shoun of Johnson Co., Tennessee.
N300

The McQueen Family of Johnson Co., Tennessee.
N310

Wills Family of Johnson County, Tennessee.
N320

Soil Survey, Johnson County, Tennessee.
O270 (BC ASU)

History of the Thirteenth Regiment, Tennessee Volunteer Cavalry, U. S. A., Including a Narrative of the Bridge Burning: The Carter County Rebellion, and the Loyalty, Heroism and Suffering of the Union Men and Women of Carter and Johnson Counties, Tennessee, During the Civil War.
S1460 (ASU LMC)

"A Study of the Program of Pupil Transportation in Johnson County, Tennessee."
S7680 (ETSU)

Agricultural-Industrial Survey of Johnson County, Tennessee.
T5680

APP. COUNTIES — TENN. — KNOX CO.

"The Office of Knox County Sheriff: An Administrative Study."
B660

"Politics of Innovation."
B670

"The Cost of Administering Criminal Justice in Memphis and Knoxville, Tennessee."
B2810

He That Serveth; Twenty-five Years' Adventures in Christian Ministry, George Creswell and Second Church.
B2900
B3870

Recollections of the East Tennessee Campaign, Battle of Campbell Station, 16th Nov., 1863: Siege of Knoxville, 17th Nov.-5th Dec., 1863.
B6420

Brief Historical Sketch of the Village of Bearden.
C8740

Knox County, Tenn., Marriage Records.
D380 (ETSU)

A Social Study of the Colored Population of Knoxville, Tennessee.
D1100

"Impact of World War II on Juvenile Delinquency in Knox County, Tennessee."
D1380

"The Net Direct Economic Effect of the University of Tennessee on the City of Knoxville and on Knox County Resulting from the Expansion of the Knoxville Campus since 1962."
D1560

The French Broad-Holston Country: A History of Knox County, Tennessee.
E150 (ASU BC)

"A History of the First Baptist Church of Knoxville, Tennessee."
E1230

"Available Material in Knox County for Enriching the Teaching of Tennessee History."
F190 (ETSU)

Gemini.
G1840

Bench and Bar of Knox County, Tennessee.
G3580 (BC)

"A Study of Underachieving Academically Talented Students in a Knox County School."
G4420

Community Historical Sketches in Knox County, Tennessee: Corryton — Harbison's Cross Roads — Smithwood.
H5230

Historic Treasure Spots of Knox County, Tennessee.
H5240 (ETSU BC)

The John Adair Section of Knox County, Tennessee.
H5250

"The History of Transportation Advertising, 1850-1956, and a Study of Its Importance in Knoxville, Tennessee."
H5550
H5710

Directory of Churches, Missions, and Religious Institutions of Tennessee, no. 47. Knox County.
H5770

Inventory of the County Archives of Tennessee: Knox County.
H5840

Transcription of the County Archives of Tennessee: Minutes of the County Court of Knox County (Book No. 0") 1792-95.
H5910 (ASU)

"The Status and Problems of the Ministry in Knox County."
H8320

The Knox County Missionary Baptists 1786-1945.
J1880
K2860

Governments in Knox County.
L210 (ETSU)

Some Sketches from My Life, Written for My 80th Birthday, May 1, 1910.
L840

"Federal Centralization versus Local Values: A Case Study of Federal-Local Relations in the Knoxville-Knox County Community Action Committee."
L3480

Knoxville-Knox County Consolidation and the County and City School Systems.
M510

Proposed Metropolitan Government Charter for Knoxville and Knox County, Tennessee, 1959.
M5220

The Knox County Economic Opportunity Council Anti-Poverty Arts and Crafts.
M9080
O330
O470

Thomas Hope of Tennessee, 1757-1820, House Carpenter and Joiner.
P120

History of the First Presbyterian Church in Knoxville, Tennessee.
P200

Personal Recollections of the Occupation of East Tennessee and the Defense of Knoxville.
P3300

"The History and Development of Education in Knox County, Tennessee."
P4120

Diary of a Sit-in.
P4750 (WCU ETSU)

History of Lebanon Presbyterian Church, "In the Fork," Five Miles East of Knoxville.
R270

Knoxville, Past, Present and Future.
R1420

"A History of Municipal Government in Knoxville since 1911."
R2050

Soil Survey, Knox County, Tennessee.
R3110

The French Broad-Holston Country: A History of Knox County, Tennessee.
R3940 (LMC BC)

The French Broad-Holston Country: A History of Knox County, Tennessee.
R3950 (ETSU)

Standard History of Knoxville, Tennessee, with Full Outline of the Natural Advantages, Early Settlement, Territorial Government, Indian Troubles and General and Particular History of the City Down to the Present Time.
R4280

"Relation of Land Base Quality to the Agricultural Economy of Knox County, Tennessee."
R4320

Historical Forts and Houses in Knoxville and Nearby Vicinity.
R4450

"The Reading Interests of Students as Revealed in a Study of an Individualized Reading Program at Pond Gap School, Knoxville, Tennessee."
S850

Divided Loyalties: Fort Sanders and the Civil War in East Tennessee.
S2110 (BC ETSU)

Centennial Celebration of Island Home Baptist Church, Knoxville, Tennessee, October 2, 1960 - December 11, 1960.
S3080

"The Public Career of Andrew Jackson Graves."
S6140

"The Economic Status of Knox County Teachers."
S6530

"Marble Deposits and Marble Industry of the Knoxville Area."
T870

A Report of the Survey of the Finances and Management of the Government of Knox County, Tennessee.
T2140 (ETSU)

"The Marble Industry of the Knoxville Area."
W640

Abstract of Wills, 1792-1835.
W1630

Tombstone Inscriptions and Death Records, Calvary Cemetery, Knoxville, Tennessee, 1869-1967.
W1640 (ETSU)

Art Work of Knoxville, with Sketch of Knoxville.
W5530

Memoirs.
F2420

APP. COUNTIES — TENN. — LOUDON CO.
B3880
B3930

Beloved Landmarks of Loudon County, Tennessee.
D560 (BC)

Soil Survey, Loudon County, Tennessee.
E1480

Inventory of the County Archives of Tennessee: Loudon County.
H5850

"Inventory of Loudon County Records."
T1920

APP. COUNTIES — TENN. — LOUDON CO.
Agricultural-Industrial Survey of Loudon County, Tennessee.
T5690
APP. COUNTIES — TENN. — MCMINN CO.
A5300
Soil Survey, McMinn County, Tennessee.
B80
"A Study of McMinn County High School as Determined by Its Graduates."
B3050
B3910
Marriage Records of McMinn County, Tennessee, 1820-1870.
B5990 (ASU BC)
Population Schedule of U. S. Census of 1850 for McMinn County, Tennessee.
B6020 (ASU)
Wills and Estate Records of McMinn County, Tennessee, 1820-1870.
B6030 (ASU BC)
"The McMinn County, Tennessee, Election of August 1, 1946."
B6410 (ASU)
E40
"A Study of Teacher and Parent Opinion of McMinn County High School, Athens, Tennessee."
G4590
"A Study of the Practices and Techniques Used by Principals and Teachers in the McMinn County Schools to Improve School Attendance."
H2590
"A Study of the School Buildings of McMinn County."
H8060
"A History of Education in McMinn County, Tennessee."
P4090
Recollections of Hearsays of Athens, Fifty Years and Beyond.
S2370
"Inventory of McMinn County Records."
T1930
Agricultural-Industrial Survey of McMinn County, Tennessee.
T5700
A Guidance Program for McMinn County High School.
W2300
APP. COUNTIES — TENN. — MACON CO.
"Folklore of Macon County, Tennessee."
B900
B3890
APP. COUNTIES — TENN. — MARION CO.
B3760
B3900
B3990
My Life and Travels.
B6340 (ASU)
Soil Survey, Marion County, Tennessee.
E1490
"A Study of Certain Phases of the Educational and Economic Conditions of Marion County, Tennessee."
G370
Sequatchie Valley, a Historical Sketch.
H5170
"A History of Marion County."
L2630
Public Administration Study: Marion County, Tennessee.
M3210
M3230
Sequatchie: A Story of the Southern Cumberlands.
R540 (ASU)
S5590
"Inventory of Marion County Records."
T1940
Agricultural-Industrial Survey of Marion County, Tennessee.
T5710
APP. COUNTIES — TENN. — MEIGS CO.
Rhea and Meigs Counties (Tennessee) in the Confederate War.
A1680 (ASU BC)
B3920
B3970
Sequatchie: A Story of the Southern Cumberlands.
R540 (ASU)

Soil Survey of Meigs County, Tennessee.
S9570
"Inventory of Meigs County Records."
T1950
Agricultural-Industrial Survey of Meigs County, Tennessee.
T5720
Soil Survey of Meigs County, Tenn.
W970
APP. COUNTIES — TENN. — MONROE CO.
B3880
B3930
Monroe County Records, 1820-1870.
B6000
Monroe County, Tennessee: Records, 1820-1870.
B6010 (ASU BC)
History of Sweetwater Valley.
L1770
"Early Days in Monroe County, Tennessee."
R590
"An Educational and Economic Survey of Monroe County, Tennessee."
S6550
"Local Ability to Support Education in Monroe County, Tennessee."
S7750
Forest Conditions in Monroe County, Tennessee.
T4590
Agricultural-Industrial Survey of Monroe County, Tennessee.
T5730
"The Sequent Occupance of Tellico Plains, Tennessee."
V50
"The Development of Education in Monroe County, Tennessee."
V480
An Economic Survey of Monroe County, Conducted by the Bureau of Business Research, College of Business Administration, Penn. State Univ. in Cooperation with Pocono Mountains Chamber of Commerce, Stroudsburg, Pa.
W850
History of the First Presbyterian Church, Sweetwater, Tennessee, 1860-1960.
Y240
APP. COUNTIES — TENN. — MORGAN CO.
"German and Swiss Colonization in Morgan County, Tennessee."
C7160 (ASU)
A History of Morgan County, Tennessee.
F3280 (ASU BC)
"A Study of Preparatory to Cooperative Development of Board of Education Policies for Morgan County, Tennessee."
H8220
"A Geographical Survey of Morgan County, Tennessee."
J2570
Deer Lodge, Tennessee, Its Little-Known History.
S6440
Agricultural-Industrial Survey of Morgan County, Tennessee.
T5740
"A Study of Secondary Schools of Morgan County."
W7450
Wartburg: Dream and Reality of the New Germany in Tennessee.
W9820
"A Study of School Transportation, Morgan Co., Tenn."
Z180
APP. COUNTIES — TENN. — OVERTON CO.
An Economic Analysis of Farming in Overton County, Tennessee.
A1830 (ETSU)
Social Factors Associated with Land Class in Overton County, Tennessee.
A1890
Soil Survey of Overton County, Tennessee.
A5880
B3820
B3940
B3950
Geology and Oil Possibilities of the Northern Part of Overton County, Tennessee, and of Adjoining Parts of Clay, Pickett and Fentress Counties.
B9490 (ETSU)

"Songs and Ballads Sung in Overton County, Tennessee a Collection."
C8310
A History of the First Methodist Church in Livingston, Tennessee, Established 1836.
E1510
Overton County Address of Albert V. Goodpasture Delivered at Livingston, Tennessee, July 4, 1876.
G2590
Overton County Address of Albert V. Goodpasture Delivered at Livingston, Tennessee, July 4, 1876.
G2600
"The Development of a Plan for Parent Education for the Speech Handicapped Children in Overton County, Tennessee."
G2760
"A Study of Rural Cooperative Organizations in Overton County, Tennessee."
H3460
"Fifty Years Ago, a History of Overton County, Tennessee, Around the Year 1850."
M6360
"Farm Taxation and County Government in Overton, Clay and Pickett Counties, Tennessee."
P3930
"Standard of Living and Migration of 136 Farm Families in Overton County, Tennessee."
S8910
"A History of Livingston Academy from 1909 through 1947."
W5280
Tennessee Genealogical Records: Overton County.
W5770 (BC)
APP. COUNTIES — TENN. — OVERTON, TENN.
"An Economic Analysis of Farming in Overton County, Tennessee."
A5340
APP. COUNTIES — TENN. — PICKETT CO.
B3820
B3940
B3950
Seventy Years in the Cumberlands.
H6920
History of Pickett Co., Tenn.
H7940
Pioneer Families of Pickett County, Tennessee.
H7950
Geology of Pickett Co., Tenn.
J1070
"Pupil Transportation in Pickett County, Tennessee."
M3590
"An Analysis of the Possibilities for Local Support of Education in Pickett County, Tennessee."
M6270
"Farm Taxation and County Government in Overton, Clay and Pickett Counties, Tennessee."
P3930
"An Educational and Economic Survey of Pickett County, Tennessee."
S310
"A Social and Economic Survey of Pickett County."
S4460
APP. COUNTIES — TENN. — POLK CO.
Ducktown Back in Raht's Time.
B1120 (BC ASU WCU ETSU)
B3780
B3960
"Development of Education in Polk County, Tennessee."
B4480
Autobiography and Sermons.
C1950
"J. D. Clemmer's Scrapbooks, 1884-1934."
C4930
"The Good Government League and Polk County Politics, 1946-1965."
L1740
"A Brief History of the First Baptist Church (Ocoee Baptist Church), Benton, Tennessee, 1836-1959."
L2480
"The Ocoee Lodge no. 212, F & A. M., Benton, Tennessee."
L2490
"Some Aspects of Polk County Politics."
L2500

APP. COUNTIES — TENN. — POLK CO.
Echoes from the Foothills.
L2930
Sketches of Polk County History.
P900 (ASU WCU LMC)
Studies in Polk County History.
P3360 (ASU BC)
"A Study of Pupil Transportation in Polk County, Tennessee."
S1810
S8810 (ETSU)
"Inventory of Polk County Records."
T1960
Agricultural-Industrial Survey of Polk County, Tennessee.
T5750
A Confederate History of Polk County, Tennessee, 1860-1866.
W6390
"A History of Polk County."
W6960
Scrapbook History of Polk County, Tennessee.
W9100
APP. COUNTIES — TENN. — PUTNAM CO.
"A History of the Library Resources of Putnam County, Tennessee."
B8180
Recollections of a Long Life.
G4260
"A History and Educational Survey of Putnam County, Tennessee."
H3470
Soil Survey, Putnam County, Tennessee.
J130
A History of Putnam County.
M370
"An Analysis of Putnam County's Ability to Support Education Based on a Study and Comparison of Assessed Value to Real Value of Property."
N860
Soil Survey of Putnam County, Tennessee.
W220
Cookeville in Retrospect.
W5850
APP. COUNTIES — TENN. — RHEA CO.
Rhea and Meigs Counties (Tennessee) in the Confederate War.
A1680 (ASU BC)
B3920
B3970
Records of Rhea: A Condensed County History.
C960 (ASU BC)
Old Grandview: Grandview Normal Institute, Grandview, Tennessee, 1884-1919: A History.
G3210
"The Development of Education in Rhea County, Tennessee."
G4990
Soil Survey, Rhea County, Tennessee.
H3390
The Southern Tennessee Coal Field Included in Bledsoe, Cumberland, Franklin, Grundy, Rhea, Sequatchie, Van Buren, Warren, and White Counties.
N580 (ETSU)
Sequatchie: A Story of the Southern Cumberlands.
R540 (ASU)
R1790
Spring City High School, 1912-1962, Golden Anniversary Celebration, May 12, 1962.
S6360
"Inventory of Rhea County Records."
T1970
Agricultural-Industrial Survey of Rhea County.
T5760
APP. COUNTIES — TENN. — ROANE CO.
"A Follow-up Study of Graduates of Roane County High School, 1946-55."
A2540
A Church Called Bethel.
B910
"Fort Southwest Point, Tennessee: The Development of a Frontier Post, 1792-1807."
B920
"A Study of School Transportation, Roane County, Tennessee."
B3610
B3980
Historical Review, Rockwood's Centennial Year, 1868-1968.
B8780
"History of Roane County, Tennessee, 1860-1870."
F2450
Tennessee Records of Roane County Marriage Records, 1801-1838.
H5900 (ETSU)
"The Development of Education in Roane County, Tennessee."
L80
Roane County, Tennessee: Abstracts of Estate Book "A" 1801-1824.
M450 (ASU)
"Rockwood: A Prototype of the New South."
M7360
"Land Utilization in Roane County, Tennessee."
P450
"A History of Roane County to 1860."
P2820
Scenes and Information about Rockwood, Tennessee, in the Heart of the Great Tennessee Valley Development.
S2040
"Rural Leadership in Roane County, Tennessee."
S4880
"Rural Leadership in Roane County, Tennessee."
S7480 (ASU)
Soil Survey, Roane County, Tennessee.
S9440
"Inventory of Roane County Records."
T1980
Pioneers of Roane County, Tennessee, 1801-1830.
T8400 (ETSU)
T9890
The History of Roane County, Tennessee, 1801-1870.
W2690
The History of Roane County, Tennessee, 1801-1870.
W2700 (ASU LMC ETSU BC)
"The Development of a Statement of Written Policies for the Roane County Tennessee Board of Education."
W6670
APP. COUNTIES — TENN. — SCOTT CO.
"Geographic Factors Influencing the Development of Scott County, Tennessee."
B8630
"A Study of Scott County, Tennessee, and Oneida Independent School District Finances."
C9100
"Educational, Economic and Community Survey of Scott County, Tennessee."
P1630
"What the Eighth Grade Patrons of Scott County Think about Their Schools."
R3200
County Scott and Its Mountain Folk.
S390 (ASU LMC WCU BC)
"A History of Education in Scott County, Tennessee."
S2070
Samuel Roberts: A Welsh Colonizer in Civil War Tennessee.
S2850 (ASU)
"A Study of Pupil Transportation in Scott County, Tennessee."
S8160
"Big South Fork, Cumberland River (Kentucky-Tennessee), Interagency Field Task Group Report."
U220
APP. COUNTIES — TENN. — SEQUATCHIE CO.
B3760
B3900
B3990
Sequatchie Valley, a Historical Sketch.
H5170
Sequatchie County: History and Development.
L1100
"The Sequatchie Valley, Tennessee, a Study in Land Utilization."
M3770
The Southern Tennessee Coal Field Included in Bledsoe, Cumberland, Franklin, Grundy, Rhea, Sequatchie, Van Buren, Warren, and White Counties.
N580 (ETSU)
Sequatchie: A Story of the Southern Cumberlands.
R540 (ASU)
"Inventory of Sequatchie County Records."
T1990
APP. COUNTIES — TENN. — SEVIER CO.
The White-Caps: A History of the Organization in Sevier County.
C9240
The White-Caps: A History of the Organization in Sevier County.
C9250
The White-Caps: A History of the Organization in Sevier County.
C9260
Facts about Sevier County.
D3720
Descendants of East Tennessee Pioneers.
E1190 (ASU)
Gatlinburg, Gateway to the Great Smokies.
F2230
"Handicrafts in Sevier County, Tennessee."
H6180 (ASU)
Sevier County, Tennessee.
M2160
History of Sevier County, Tennessee.
M4300
"A Study of Living Conditions in the Pittman Center Community, 1934-1935."
M4400
Soil Survey, Sevier County, Tennessee.
O280
Gatlinburg and the Great Smokies.
P4970
"A Study of Financing a Program for Education in Sevier County, Tennessee."
S4370
A Proposed Plan for Development: Sevier County, Tennessee.
T1690
Agricultural-Industrial Survey of Sevier County.
T5770
APP. COUNTIES — TENN. — SMITH CO.
B4000
Smith County History.
B5670
Handbook of Smith County.
B8620
The County of Smith.
G2340
"Inventory of Smith County Records."
T2000
APP. COUNTIES — TENN. — SULLIVAN CO.
Tennessee Soldiers in the Revolution: A Roster of Soldiers Living During the Revolutionary War in the Counties of Washington and Sullivan.
A1630 (ETSU)
Effects of Industrial Development on Rural Life in Sullivan County, Tennessee.
A1840
"The History of Educational Development in Sullivan County, Tennessee."
A2320
"Local History Stories for the Third Grade Washington and Sullivan Counties, Tennessee."
B1180 (ETSU)
Population Schedule of the United States Census of 1850 for Sullivan County, Tennessee.
B8610 (ETSU)
"Changes in Social and Economic Status of the People in Sullivan County for a Thirty Year Period."
C3390 (ASU)
Back Home. Kingsport, Tennessee.
C4470 (BC ASU)
"Joseph Ketron and His Kingsley Seminary, Sullivan County, Tennessee."
F3690 (ASU)
"A Survey of Special Education Services in Washington, Carter and Sullivan Counties, Tennessee."
G4010
Inventory of the County Archives of Tennessee: Sullivan County.
H5870
Summary of Special Legislation Relating to the Government of Sullivan County.
H5890
"Educational Facilities and Economic Development of Bristol, 1930-1950."
H6510
"The Social and Economic Effects Produced upon Small Towns by Rapid Industrialization."
H7650

APP. COUNTIES — TENN. — SULLIVAN CO.

"What Citizens of Sullivan County Know about Their Schools."
K2290

Soil Survey, Sullivan County, Tennessee.
M4370

The New Bethel Sesquicentennial 1782-1932.
N660

"City-county Separation in Tennessee, a Case Study of Kingsport and Sullivan County."
N970

"A Follow-up Study of Attitudes of Sullivan County High School Seniors toward the Church."
P360

Kingsport, City of Industries, Schools, Churches and Homes.
P3080

Personal and Professional Reminiscences of an Old Lawyer.
P3160

Historical Sketches of the Holston Valleys.
P4440 (ASU WCU LMC ETSU BC)

Story of Rotherwood, from the Autobiography of Rev. Frederick A. Ross.
R3790

Memoirs.
S4750 (ETSU)

Historic Sullivan: A History of Sullivan County, Tennessee, with Brief Biographies of the Makers of History.
T650 (ASU ETSU BC)

Historic Sullivan: A History of Sullivan County, Tennessee, With Brief Biographies of the Makers of History.
T660 (ASU)

Historic Sullivan: A History of Sullivan County, Tennessee, With Brief Biographies of the Makers of History.
T670

Agricultural-Industrial Survey of Sullivan County.
T5780

"A Survey of Library Services in the County Schools of Sullivan County, Tennessee."
T7840 (ETSU)

Industrial Site Survey of Carter County, Sullivan County, and Washington County.
U4160

Projections and Economic Base Analysis: Bristol-Kingsport Metropolitan Area Including the City of Bristol, Virginia, and the Counties of Washington, Virginia, and Sullivan, Tennessee.
V820

"Diagnosis and Remediation of Reading and Personality Problems of a Second Level First Grade at Valley Pike School, Sullivan County, Tennessee."
W7540

APP. COUNTIES — TENN. — TAZEWELL CO.

"A Study of Absenteeism in the Tazewell County One Room Negro Elementary Schools."
H6630

APP. COUNTIES — TENN. — UNICOI CO.

The Wonders of the Unakas in Unicoi County.
A1280 (ETSU ASU LMC)

"An Educational History of Unicoi County, Tennessee."
B1280
B3790
B3860
B4010

"A Program for Developing Mental and Emotional Health in Third-grade Children at Love Street School, Erwin, Tennessee."
B4990 (ETSU)

"The Distribution and Relative Abundance of Some Immature Aquatic Insects in Red Fork Creek, Unicoi County, Tennessee."
C5810 (ETSU)

"Written Board of Education Policies for Unicoi County, Tennessee."
E2370 (ETSU)

"Small Mammals of Washington and Unicoi Counties, Tennessee."
G1390 (ETSU)

The Valley of the Long Hunters.
M4160 (ASU LMC ETSU BC)

"School Transportation Costs in Unicoi County: A Comparison of Publicly-owned and Privately-owned Systems."
M5790 (ETSU)

"The Opinions of Certain Groups Toward Teaching the Bible in Unicoi County High School."
N2910 (ETSU)

"A Vegetational Analysis of the Rattlesnake Ridge Area of Unaka Mountain, Unicoi County, Tennessee."
P1130 (ETSU)

"Unicoi County Court: 1876-1918."
P4110 (ETSU)

Geology and Mineral Deposits of Bumpass Cove, Unicoi and Washington Counties, Tennessee.
R3390 (ETSU)

Agricultural-Industrial Survey of Unicoi County.
T5810

"An Analysis of the Homebound Program for Exceptional Children in Unicoi County."
T8260 (ETSU)

"An Educational Survey of Unicoi County, Tennessee."
T8440

Overall Economic Development Program for Unicoi County, Tennessee.
U120 (ETSU)

"A Survey of Reading Achievement of First Grade Pupils in Unicoi County."
W8020 (ETSU)

APP. COUNTIES — TENN. — UNION CO.

In the Shadow of Big Bald: About the Appalachians and Their People.
A1230 (ETSU)

"The Diagnosis and Remediation of Comprehensive Skills of a Sixth-grade Class at Rock Creek School in Erwin, Tennessee."
B230 (ETSU)
S9130

"A Geographic Appraisal of Union County, Tennessee."
T8300

APP. COUNTIES — TENN. — VAN BUREN CO.

B4020

The Southern Tennessee Coal Field Included in Bledsoe, Cumberland, Franklin, Grundy, Rhea, Sequatchie, Van Buren, Warren, and White Counties.
N580 (ETSU)

"Inventory of Van Buren County Records."
T2010

APP. COUNTIES — TENN. — WARREN CO.

B4020
B4030

My Grandfather's Diary of the War.
C4350

"A Historical Survey of Education in Warren County, Tennessee."
G4360

This Is My Story.
G4450

Early History of Warren County.
H480 (ASU BC ETSU)

History of Mt. Zion Methodist Episcopal Church 4, South of Mount Zion, Warren County, Tenn., 1809-1930.
H5470

Soil Survey, Warren County, Tennessee.
J140

Warren County, Its Organization, Scenery, Resources and Representative Men.
K1930
M3320 (ASU)

"A Survey to Determine the Need of Trade and Industrial Education in Warren County, Tennessee."
M4250

The Southern Tennessee Coal Field Included in Bledsoe, Cumberland, Franklin, Grundy, Rhea, Sequatchie, Van Buren, Warren, and White Counties.
N580 (ETSU)
P3580

The Life of John H. Savage: Citizen, Soldier, Lawyer, Congressman.
S540 (LMC)

"Inventory of Warren County Records."
T2020

The Civil War Diary of Capt. J. J. Womack.
W8430

Fletch Woodward, His Fights with Those Bad, Bad Town Boys.
W8970

APP. COUNTIES — TENN. — WASHINGTON CO.

Tennessee Soldiers in the Revolution: A Roster of Soldiers Living During the Revolutionary War in the Counties of Washington and Sullivan.
A1630 (ETSU)

"An Evaluation of the Physical Education Programs in the High Schools in the Washington County School System."
A2330 (ETSU)

"History of the Schools of Johnson City, Tennessee, 1868-1950."
A4550 (ETSU)

"Local History Stories for the Third Grade Washington and Sullivan Counties, Tennessee."
B1180 (ETSU)

"Some Phases of the Social and Economic History of Washington County, Tennessee, 1865-1917."
B6220

"Some Phases of the Social and Economic History of Washington County, Tennessee, 1865-1917."
B6230 (ETSU)

"Washington County Court: The Government of a Tennessee Frontier Community."
B7470

"The Attitudes of a Selected Group of Community Leaders Concerning Consolidation of Five Rural Elementary Schools in Washington County, Tennessee."
B8330 (ETSU)

"A Survey of the Reading Interests of Sixth-grade Pupils in Washington County, Tennessee."
C3980 (ETSU)

"A Study of Health Instruction in Selected High Schools in Washington County, Tennessee."
D900 (ETSU)

"A Proposed Curriculum for Consolidated High Schools in Washington County, Tennessee."
E10 (ETSU)

Soil Survey, Washington County, Tennessee.
E1500

"A Transitional English Program for Crockett High School, Washington County, Tennessee."
F620 (ETSU)

"A Survey of Selected Characteristics of the Washington County, Tennessee, School Teacher."
F910 (ETSU)

"Washington County Court, 1796-1836."
F920 (ETSU)

"Some Phases of the Social and Economic History of Jonesboro, Tennessee, prior to the Civil War."
F960

"Job Opportunities for High School Graduates in the Manufacturing Industries in Washington County, Tennessee."
F3620 (ETSU)

"Small Mammals of Washington and Unicoi Counties, Tennessee."
G1390 (ETSU)

Marriage Record of Washington County, Tennessee, 1787-1840.
G3190 (ETSU)

Marriage Records of Washington County, Tennessee, 1787-1840.
G3200 (ASU)

"A Survey of Special Education Services in Washington, Carter and Sullivan Counties, Tennessee."
G4010

"A Nutrition Survey of Some Eleventh Grade Students in Washington County, Tennessee."
H410 (ETSU)

"Long-lots in Washington County, Tennessee, with Reference to Past and Present Land-holding Shapes."
H1230 (ETSU)

Directory of Churches, Missions, and Religious Institutions of Tennessee, no. 90. Washington County.
H5780

Annual Report . . . for Fiscal Year Ended June 30, 1944-.
J1370 (ETSU)

Code.
J1390 (ETSU)

APP. COUNTIES — TENN. — WASHINGTON CO.

The Code of the City of Johnson City, Tennessee: The Chart and the General Ordinances of the City, Published by Order of the Board of Commissioners.
J1400 (ETSU)

Map of Johnson City, Washington County, Tennessee.
J1420 (ETSU)

Newsletter.
J1430 (ETSU)

Report.
J1590 (ETSU)

"Problems of Beginning Teachers in Washington County, Tennessee."
K370 (ETSU)

"The Enriched Curriculum as a Means of Meeting the Emotional and Social Needs of First Grade Children in Washington County."
K1800 (ETSU)

"Some Problems Concerning the Relations of Administrators and Beginning Teachers in the Washington County School System, 1955-1956."
K1820 (ETSU)

"Some Factors Affecting School Attendance as a Family Problem, as Revealed by a Comparison of Two Groups of Families in Washington County, Tennessee, 1951-1952."
L350 (ETSU)

"A Distributive Education Program for Washington County, Tennessee, High Schools Based on an Occupational Survey of the County."
L590 (ETSU)

"An Analysis of Particulate Pollution in Johnson City and Rural Washington County, Tennessee."
L1400 (ETSU)

Washington County, Tennessee, Records.
M680 (ETSU ASU)

Washington County, Tennessee, Records, Transcribed by Mary Hardin McCown. Vol. 1, Washington County Lists of Taxables, 1778-1801, ed. Nancy E. Jones Stickley and Inez Burns.
M690

"Human Resources Available to the Schools of Washington County, Tennessee."
M2020 (ETSU)

The Rural Land Use of Washington County, Tennessee.
M2970

"A Comparison of Socio-economic Status and Art Interest of Two Sixth Grade Groups in Washington County, Tennessee."
M5550 (ETSU)

"Some Factors Affecting Retardation in the Six High Schools of Washington County."
M6580 (ETSU)

"A Study of Some Differentiating Characteristics of Dropouts and Graduates of Lamar and Jonesboro High Schools."
P1650 (ETSU)

"The Factors Affecting Absenteeism in the Sixth, Seventh, and Eighth Grades at Barnes Elementary School, Washington County, Tennessee."
P2360 (ETSU)

"A Comparative Study of the Relationship Between ACT Composite Scores and GPA of Washington County Students at East Tennessee State University, 1965-66."
P3940 (ETSU)

"A Role Definition of Secondary School Assistant Principals in Washington County, Virginia."
R2880 (ETSU)

Geology and Mineral Deposits of Bumpass Cove, Unicoi and Washington Counties, Tennessee.
R3390 (ETSU)

"Trends and Needs of the Washington County, Tennessee, Schools, 1948-1966."
S2790 (ETSU)

"A Curriculum in Agricultural Education for Two Consolidated High Schools in Washington County, Tennessee."
S4220 (ETSU)

"A Comparative Study of Twenty-five Children Who Attended Project Head Start and Twenty-five Children Who Did Not: Paired at the First-grade Level in the Jonesboro Elementary School, Jonesboro, Tennessee, 1965-1966."
S4290 (ETSU)

Washington County, Tennessee, Marriages and Wills.
S4640 (ETSU)

Reminiscences of an Old-Timer.
S5050

"The Status of Eighth Grade Social Science in Washington County, Tennessee, 1960-61."
S7640 (ETSU)

Washington County, Tenn., 1830 Federal Census.
S7900 (ASU)

Washington County Survey Report.
T1140 (ETSU)

"Inventory of Washington County Records."
T2030

A Report of the Survey of the Finances and Management of the Government of Washington County, Tennessee.
T2150 (ETSU)

Agricultural-Industrial Survey of Washington County, Tennessee.
T5790

"The History of the First Baptist Church of Jonesboro, Tennessee."
T7860 (ETSU)

Industrial Site Survey of Carter County, Sullivan County, and Washington County.
U4160

"An Ecological Study of Some Small Mammals of Horse Cove, Washington County, Tennessee."
W6610 (ETSU)

APP. COUNTIES — TENN. — WHITE CO.

B4020
B4040

Freemasonry in Pioneer Times, White County.
C6260

"An Educational, Economic and Community Survey of White County, Tennessee."
F2440

"A Survey of the Causes of Absences in the Public School System of White County and Sparta, Tennessee."
G2350

The Southern Tennessee Coal Field Included in Bledsoe, Cumberland, Franklin, Grundy, Rhea, Sequatchie, Van Buren, Warren, and White Counties.
N580 (ETSU)

"Economic History of White County, Tennessee."
P4100

History of White County.
S1500
S5920

"Inventory of White County Records."
T2040

Agricultural-Industrial Survey of White County.
T5800

"Legends and Stories of White County, Tennessee."
W6460

APP. COUNTIES — VA.

Our County Origins.
H1210 (FC)

Personal Income Estimates for Virginia Counties and Cities, 1955.
L270

Dates of Origin of Virginia Counties and Municipalities.
W2250

APP. COUNTIES — VA. — ALBEMARLE CO.

Thomas Jefferson and the University of Virginia.
A410 (ASU)

Pursuits of War: The People of Charlottesville and Albemarle County, Virginia, in the Second World War.
A970 (ASU)

Soils of the Shenandoah River Terrace: Revision of Certain Soils in the Albemarle Area, Virginia.
B2980

Evidence of Indian Occupancy in Albemarle County, Virginia.
B9340 (BC)

Folk-songs of Roanoke and the Albemarle.
C3300 (ASU)

Soil Survey, Albemarle County, Virginia.
D1940

An Economic and Social Survey of Albemarle County.
G740
M2750 (ASU)

The Albemarle of Other Days.
R550 (LMC ASU)

Albemarle County in Virginia: Giving Some Account of What It Was by Nature, of What It Was Made by Man, and of Some of the Men Who Made It.
W8800

APP. COUNTIES — VA. — ALLEGHANY CO.

Alleghany County, Virginia: Its Resources and Industries.
C8080 (BC)

A Centennial History of Alleghany County, Virginia.
M8040 (BC)

A Centennial History of Alleghany County, Virginia.
M8050 (ASU)

An Economic and Social Survey of Alleghany County.
W290 (ASU BC)

APP. COUNTIES — VA. — AMHERST CO.

Virginia Wills Before 1799: A Complete Abstract Register of All Names Mentioned in Over Six Hundred Recorded Wills.
C4910 (ETSU)

Occurrence and Origin of the Titanium Deposits of Nelson and Amherst Counties, Virginia.
R3800

Amherst County, Virginia, in the Revolution: Including Extracts from the "Lost Order Book", 1773-1782.
S9530 (ASU)

Marriage Records of Amherst County, Virginia, 1815-1821, and Subscription for Building St. Mark's Church, Amherst Co., Virginia.
S9540 (ASU)

Marriage Bonds and Other Marriage Records of Amherst County, Virginia, 1763-1800.
S9550 (ASU)

APP. COUNTIES — VA. — AUGUSTA CO.

Chronicles of the Scotch-Irish Settlement in Virginia.
A5480 (ASU)

Chronicles of the Scotch-Irish Settlement in Virginia, Extracted from the Original Court Records of Augusta County, 1745-1800.
A5490 (ASU)

First Marriage Records of Augusta County, Virginia, 1785-1813.
A5500 (ASU)

Early History of Staunton and Beverley Manor in Augusta County, Virginia.
A5510 (ASU BC)

An Economic and Social Survey of Augusta County.
C2110 (ASU BC)

The James Stewart Family of Early Augusta County, Virginia, and Descendants, 1740-1960.
D2130 (ASU)
D2510 (ASU)

Augusta County, Virginia, in the History of the U. S.
D3950 (BC)
F1100

Settlers by the Long Grey Trail, Some Pioneers to Old Augusta County, Virginia, and Their Descendants, of the Family of Harrison and Allied Lines.
H3070 (ASU BC)

"Augusta County, Virginia: A Study of Patterns."
H7960 (LMC)

"Augusta County, Virginia: A Study of Patterns."
H7970 (ASU)

Soil Survey of Augusta County, Virginia.
J2850

Manganese Deposits of the Lyndhurst-Vesuvius District, Augusta and Rockbridge Counties, Virginia.
K2760

Economic Land Classification of Augusta Co., Virginia.
P690

History of Augusta County, Virginia.
P2490 (ASU)

Augusta Parish, Virginia, 1738-1780.
R4250 (ASU BC)

APP. COUNTIES — VA. — AUGUSTA CO.
Manganese deposits of the Lyndhurst-Vesuvius district, Augusta & Rockbridge Co., Va., 1943.
U3230
Annals of Augusta County, Virginia, 1726-1871.
W20
Annals of Augusta County, Virginia, with Reminiscences and a Diary of the War, 1861-1865, and a Chapter on Reconstruction.
W30 (LMC BC ASU)
The Tinkling Spring, Headwater of Freedom: A Study of the Church and Her People, 1732-1952.
W7320 (ASU BC)
APP. COUNTIES — VA. — BARBOUR CO.
Soil Survey of Barbour and Upshur Counties, West Virginia.
L690
APP. COUNTIES — VA. — BATH CO.
"An Inspection of Standardized Test Results in the Schools of Bath County, Virginia."
G140 (ETSU)
The Valley Road.
I770 (ASU BC FC)
A Brief History of Bath County, Virginia.
M60 (ASU)
Historical Sketches of Virginia, Hot Springs, Warm Sulphur Springs and Bath County.
M90 (BC)
Annals of Bath County, Virginia.
M8020 (BC)
Annals of Bath County, Virginia.
M8030 (ASU)
APP. COUNTIES — VA. — BEDFORD CO.
Our Kin.
A230
An Economic and Social Survey of Bedford Co., Va.
A480 (ASU)
Cumberland parish, Lunenburg County, Virginia, 1746-1816. Vestry book, 1746-1816.
B2770 (ASU)
Virginia Wills Before 1799: A Complete Abstract Register of All Names Mentioned in Over Six Hundred Recorded Wills.
C4910 (ETSU)
Marriage Bonds of Bedford County, Virginia 1755-1800.
D1810 (ASU FC)
Methodism in Bedford County; a Study Made by William B. Jones with Recommendations by C. Ralph Arthur.
J2660 (FC)
"A Study Designed for the Attitudes of the Negro Teachers of Bedford County, Virginia Toward In-Service Teacher Education."
M3140
History of Bedford County, Virginia.
P270 (FC)
Classification of Land Ownership in Bedford Co., Virginia.
P680
Abstracts of Bedford County, Virginia Wills, Inventories and Accounts 1754-1787.
W5900 (FC)
APP. COUNTIES — VA. — BLAND CO.
History of Bland County (Virginia).
B4570 (ASU BC)
Industrial Survey, Bland County, Virginia.
H8240
New River Tithables, 1770-73.
K510
Tax List of Montgomery County, Virginia, 1782.
K520
Soil Survey, Bland County, Virginia.
P3640
Manganese deposits of the Flat Top & Round Mtn district, Bland & Giles Co., Va., 1944.
U3240
APP. COUNTIES — VA. — BOTETOURT CO.
Botetourt County, Virginia, 1820 Census.
A1060
Botetourt County, Virginia, 1820 Census.
B1560
An Economic and Social Survey of Botetourt County."
C5600
William Cross of Botetourt County, Virginia and His Descendants, 1733-1932.
C9080
Botetourt County, Virginia, 1850 Census.
J690
The Descendants of John Little of Botetourt and Rockbridge Counties, Virginia.
L4150
Economic Land Classification of Botetourt Co., Virginia.
P700
Industrial Sites and Economic Data, Botetourt County, Virginia.
V780
Early Marriages, Wills and Some Revolutionary War Records, Botetourt County, Va.
W9250
APP. COUNTIES — VA. — BRADFORD CO.
Sketches and Recollections of Lynchburg, by the Oldest Inhabitant.
C10 (ASU)
APP. COUNTIES — VA. — BUCHANAN CO.
The Man from Buchanan.
B8810
Industrial Survey. Blacksburg, Va.
H8230
Geology and Coal Resources of Buchanan Co., Va.
V950
APP. COUNTIES — VA. — CARROLL CO.
Carroll County, Virginia, 1850 Census.
A1070
Carroll County, Virginia, 1860 Census.
A1080
Carroll County, Virginia, 1870 Census.
A1090
Industrial Survey. Blacksburg, Va.
H8230
New River Tithables, 1770-73.
K510
Tax List of Montgomery County, Virginia, 1782.
K520
Economic Land Classification of Carroll County, Virginia.
P710
Soil Survey, Carroll County, Virginia.
T8040
APP. COUNTIES — VA. — CLARKE CO.
Clarke County, 1836-1936.
C3940 (ASU)
History of Clarke County, Virginia, and Its Connection with the War between the States, with Illustrations of Colonial Homes and of Confederate Officers.
G2330 (BC ASU LMC)
Frederick Parrish, Virginia, 1744-1780.
M4760 (BC)
History of the Lower Shenandoah Valley: Counties of Frederick, Berkeley, Jefferson, and Clarke.
N1490 (ASU BC)
Economic Land Classification of Clarke Co., Va.
P720
An Economic and Social Survey of Clarke County.
W900
APP. COUNTIES — VA. — CRAIG CO.
Industrial Survey. Blacksburg, Va.
H8230
APP. COUNTIES — VA. — CULPEPER CO.
Soil Survey, Culpeper County, Virginia.
C5730
Confederate History of Culpeper County.
C240
Genealogical and Historical Notes on Culpeper County, Virginia.
G3650 (ASU)
Economic Land Classification of Culpeper Co., Va.
P730
A History of St. Mark's Parish, Culpeper County, Va., With Notes of Old Churches and Old Families and Illustrations of the Manners and Customs of the Olden Time.
S4150 (ASU)
The Knights of the Golden Horseshoe from the History of St. Mark's Parish.
S4160
APP. COUNTIES — VA. — DICKENSON CO.
"Meet Virginia's Baby"; a Brief Pictorial History of Dickenson County.
D2100 (BC ASU)
The Geology and Coal Resources of Dickenson County, Virginia.
G1340 (ETSU)
Industrial Survey. Blacksburg, Va.
H8230
M4970
Dickenson County in War Time; a Community History.
S9150
Folk Games from Frying Pan Creek in Dickenson County, Virginia.
S9160
Meet Virginia's Baby.
S9190
Meet Virginia's Baby: A Brief Pictorial History of Dickenson County, Virginia, from Its Formation in 1880 to 1955, with Stress on Pioneer Background.
S9200 (ASU LMC BC)
Some Sandy Basin Characters.
S9250
Tall Tales of the Devils Apron.
S9270 (LMC BC FC)
APP. COUNTIES — VA. — DICKENSON CO.
A Short History of Extreme Southwest Virginia.
A530 (ASU LMC)
APP. COUNTIES — VA. — DICKENSON CO.
The Geology and Coal Resources of Dickinson Co., Va.
V970
APP. COUNTIES — VA. — FAUQUIER
Fauquier County, Virginia, Tombstone Inscriptions.
B480 (ASU)
Northern Virginia Heritage; a Pictorial Compilation of the Historic Sites and Homes in the Counties of Arlington, Fairfax, Loudoun, Fauquier, Prince William and Stafford, and the Cities of Alexandria and Fredericksburg, by Eleanor Lee Templeman and Nan Netherton.
T860 (BC)
Early Fauquier County, Virginia, Marriage Bonds, 1759-1854.
C3250 (ASU)
Fauquier County Va., 1759-1959.
F350 (ASU)
Water Powered Mills of Fauquier County Virginia.
M6400 (ASU)
Soil Survey, Fauquier County, Virginia.
P2420
Boyhood Memories of Fauquier.
S4950 (ASU)
APP. COUNTIES — VA. — FLOYD CO.
Floyd County, Virginia, 1840 Census.
A1100
Floyd County, Virginia, 1850 Census.
A1110
Geology and Mineral Resources of Floyd County of the Blue Ridge Upland, Southwestern Virginia.
D2340 (ETSU)
Industrial Survey. Blacksburg, Va.
H8230
Tax List of Montgomery County, Virginia, 1782.
K520
APP. COUNTIES — VA. — FRANKLIN CO.
Franklin County, Virginia, 1820 Census.
A1120
Cumberland parish, Lunenburg County, Virginia, 1746-1816. Vestry book, 1746-1816.
B2770 (ASU)
I180 (FC)
An Old Virginia Court: Being a Transcript of the Records of the First Court of Franklin County, Virginia, 1786-1789, with Biographies of the Justices and Stories of Famous Cases.
V730 (ASU ETSU)
Franklin County, Virginia, a History.
W7720 (ASU BC FC)
Marriage Bonds of Franklin County, Virginia, 1786-1858, Transcribed from the Original Records.
W7740 (ASU BC)
Pioneer Families of Franklin County, Virginia.
W7750 (ASU BC FC)
APP. COUNTIES — VA. — FREDERICK CO.
Frederick County, Virginia, Marriages, 1771-1825.
D990 (ASU ETSU)
Soil Survey of Frederick County, Virginia.
D2180

APP. COUNTIES — VA. — FREDERICK CO.

Hopewell Friends History, 1734-1934, Frederick County, Virginia: Records of Hopewell Monthly Meetings and Meetings Reporting to Hopewell.
J2200 (ASU)

Abstracts of Wills, Inventories, and Administrations Accounts of Frederick County, Virginia.
K2370

History of the Lower Shenandoah Valley: Counties of Frederick, Berkeley, Jefferson, and Clarke.
N1490 (ASU BC)

An Economic and Social Survey of Frederick County.
P2840 (ASU LMC)

Civil War Battles in Winchester and Frederick County, Virginia, 1861-1865.
W7570 (BC ASU LMC)

Diaries, Letters and Recollections of the War Between the States.
W7580

Gravestone Inscriptions: From 61 Graveyards in Frederick County and the Counties That Were Once a Part of Frederick County and Includes the Inscriptions from the "Old Lutheran and German Reform Graves" in Mt. Hebron Cemetery.
W7590 (ASU)

2200 Gravestone Inscriptions from Winchester and Frederick County, Virginia (Death Dates Range from 1700's to Early 1900's).
W7600 (ASU)

Souvenir.
W7610 (ASU)

APP. COUNTIES — VA. — GILES CO.

B4050

Giles County, 1806-1956, a Brief History.
F3350

A Givens-Hall Family History from Pre-Revolutionary Times to 1970. . .
G1930

Giles County, 1806-1956.
G2440

Listen to the Mockingbird.
H7680

Listen to the Mockingbird; The Life and Times of a Pioneer Virginia Family.
H7690

Industrial Survey. Blacksburg, Va.
H8230

New River Tithables, 1770-73.
K510

Tax List of Montgomery County, Virginia, 1782.
K520

Marble Prospects in Giles County, Virginia, with a section on Petrography of Marbles by Arthur A. Pegan.
M4240

Edward Morgan 1751-1884, Pioneer Minister in Southwest, Virginia.
M7490

An Economic and Social Survey of Giles County.
S5250

Manganese deposits of the Flat Top & Round Mtn district, Bland & Giles Co., Va., 1944.
U3240

Marble Prospects in Giles Co., Va.
V1000

APP. COUNTIES — VA. — GRAYSON CO.

Grayson County, Virginia, Census of 1820, 1830, 1840, 1850.
A1130

Grayson County Deed Books 1, 2, 3, 4.
A1140

Index to Grayson County Deed Books 1-9, Grantee.
A1150

Index to Grayson County Deed Books 1-9, Grantor.
A1160

Personal Property Tax Lists, Grayson County.
A1190

Soil Survey of Grayson County, Virginia.
D1950

Industrial Survey. Blacksburg, Va.
H8230

New River Tithables, 1770-73.
K510

Tax List of Montgomery County, Virginia, 1782.
K520

Pioneer Settlers of Grayson County, Virginia.
N2940 (ASU)

Economic Land Classification of Grayson Co., Va.
P740

Study of the Organization and Management of Farmers in Grayson County, Va.
V560

A List of Lands and Lots Returned as Delinquent, in Grayson County, Va.
V690 (BC)

APP. COUNTIES — VA. — GREENE CO.

Economic Land Classification of Greene Co., Va.
P750

APP. COUNTIES — VA. — HANCOCK CO.

History of Hancock Co., Va. and W. Va.
W2470 (BC)

APP. COUNTIES — VA. — HARRISONBURG CO.

Men of Mark and Representative Citizens of Harrisonburg and Rockingham County, Virginia.
W1810 (ASU BC)

APP. COUNTIES — VA. — HIGHLAND CO.

1850 Census of Highland County, Virginia.
M4190

A Handbook of Highland County, and a Supplement to Pendleton and Highland History.
M8060

A History of Highland County, Virginia.
M8070 (ASU BC)

A History of Highland County, Virginia.
M8080 (ASU)

APP. COUNTIES — VA. — LEE CO.

A Short History of Extreme Southwest Virginia.
A530 (ASU LMC)

Early Records of Lee County, Virginia.
C2130

Tombstone Inscriptions of Lee County, Virginia.
C2140 (BC)

The Geology and Coal Resources of the Coal-bearing Portion of Lee County, Virginia.
G1350 (LMC ETSU)

"A Study for a Guidance Program at Jonesville High School, Jonesville, Virginia."
H3500 (ETSU)

Industrial Survey. Blacksburg, Va.
H8230
I730

Soil Survey, Lee County, Virginia.
J2890

Geology and Oil Resources of the Jonesville District, Lee County, Virginia.
M5960

Southwest Virginia: Lee, Scott, Wise Counties, Summary of Resources.
T3500 (ASU BC)

Southwest Virginia, Lee, Scott, Wise Counties; Summary of Resources.
T3510

APP. COUNTIES — VA. — LEWIS CO.

H6030

APP. COUNTIES — VA. — LOUDOUN CO.

Soil Survey of the Leesburg, Virginia, Area.
C1770

Virginia Wills Before 1799: A Complete Abstract Register of All Names Mentioned in Over Six Hundred Recorded Wills.
C4910 (ETSU)

History and Comprehensive Description of Loudoun County, Virginia.
H4110 (ASU BC)

Memoirs of Samuel M. Janney; Late of Lincoln, Loudoun Co., Va.
J390

Loudoun Co., Virginia, Marriage bonds, 1762-1850.
J750 (ASU)

Ground-water Supplies in Shale and Sandstone in Fairfax, Loudoun, and Prince William Counties, Virginia.
J2150

Loudoun County and the Civil War: A History and Guide.
L3600

Legends of Loudoun Valley.
N870 (ASU)

Loudoun Valley Legends.
N880 (BC)

Economic Land Classification of Loudoun Co., Va.
P760
P3210

Soil Survey, Loudoun County, Virginia.
P3650

Loudoun County, Virginia, Past and Present.
S250 (ASU)

Northern Virginia Heritage; a Pictorial Compilation of the Historic Sites and Homes in the Counties of Arlington, Fairfax, Loudoun, Fauquier, Prince William and Stafford, and the Cities of Alexandria and Fredericksburg, by Eleanor Lee Templeman and Nan Netherton.
T860 (BC)

Geology of the Leesburg Quadrangle, Virginia.
T8800 (ETSU)

Legends of Loudoun: An Account of the History and Homes of a Border County of Virginia's Northern Neck.
W6560 (ASU BC)

APP. COUNTIES — VA. — MADISON CO.

History of the Hebron Lutheran Church, Madison Co., Va.
H7890 (BC)

The Proceedings of a Special Conference Held in Madison County, Virginia, in the Lutheran Congregation of Said County, on the 14th Day of September, 1817, and the Subsequent Days.
L4030 (ASU)

A History of Madison County, Virginia.
Y330 (BC)

APP. COUNTIES — VA. — MONTGOMERY CO.

Montgomery County, Virginia, 1820 and 1830 Census.
A1170
B4050

The Montgomery County Story, 1776-1957.
C9360 (ASU)

Listen to the Mockingbird.
H7680

Listen to the Mockingbird; The Life and Times of a Pioneer Virginia Family.
H7690

Industrial Survey. Blacksburg, Va.
H8230

New River Tithables, 1770-73.
K510

Births in Court Records of Montgomery County, Virginia, 1853-1871.
L3860

Indian Massacres in Montgomery County, 1775-1776; Drapers Meadow Massacre Retold. Also, Fort Vause and Its Traditions.
P1670

1810 Montgomery County Census.
R1510

Montgomery County, Virginia Circa 1790.
S1100

A Brief of Wills and Marriages in Montgomery and Fincastle Counties, 1773-1831.
W9230

A Brief of Wills and Marriages in Montgomery and Fincastle Counties, 1773-1831.
W9240

APP. COUNTIES — VA. — NELSON CO.

Colonial History of Nelson County, 1734-1807.
C5620 (ASU)

Occurrence and Origin of the Titanium Deposits of Nelson and Amherst Counties, Virginia.
R3800

APP. COUNTIES — VA. — PAGE CO.

Old Homes of Page County, Virginia.
K1580

APP. COUNTIES — VA. — PATRICK CO.

Marriages of Patrick County, 1791-1850.
A430

Patrick County, Virginia Census, 1820, 1830, 1840, 1850.
A1180

Cumberland parish, Lunenburg County, Virginia, 1746-1816. Vestry book, 1746-1816.
B2770 (ASU)

An Economic and Social Survey of Patrick County.
C6680 (BC)

APP. COUNTIES — VA. — PULASKI CO.

Pulaski County, Virginia, 1840 Census.
A1200

Early History of Snowville.
A1790
B4050

A Way of Life in Virginia at the Turn of the Century.
F250

APP. COUNTIES — VA. — PULASKI CO.
Economic Land Classification of Pulaski County.
G1190
Listen to the Mockingbird.
H7680
Listen to the Mockingbird; The Life and Times of a Pioneer Virginia Family.
H7690
Industrial Survey. Blacksburg, Va.
H8230
New River Tithables, 1770-73.
K510
Tax List of Montgomery County, Virginia, 1782.
K520
Edward Morgan 1751-1884, Pioneer Minister in Southwest, Virginia.
M7490

APP. COUNTIES — VA. — RAPPAHANNOCK CO.
Soil Survey, Rappahannock County, Virginia.
C1710
Wills of Rappahannock Co., Va., 1656-1692.
S9560 (ASU BC)
The History of the Town of Washington, Virginia, "The First Washington of All."
B130 (BC)

APP. COUNTIES — VA. — ROANOKE CO.
B4050
Fort Lewis: A Community in Transition.
H7440 (FC)
Fort Lewis: A Community in Transition.
H7450
Fort Lewis: A Community in Transition.
H7460
History of Roanoke Co.
J10 (BC)
R2610
An Economic and Social Survey of Roanoke County.
S7130
Roanoke, Story of County and City.
W9690 (ASU BC)

APP. COUNTIES — VA. — ROCKBRIDGE CO.
Virginia Wills Before 1799: A Complete Abstract Register of All Names Mentioned in Over Six Hundred Recorded Wills.
C4910 (ETSU)
Clifton Forge, Virginia: Scenic, Busy, Friendly.
C7580 (FC)
A History of Methodism in Rockbridge County, Virginia.
C9810 (BC)
Standards of Living in Six Virginia Counties.
D640
A Curiosity in Chancery.
D660
The Reverend Samuel Houston.
D2310 (BC)
Soil Survey of Rockbridge County, Virginia.
J2900
Manganese Deposits of the Lyndhurst-Vesuvius District, Augusta and Rockbridge Counties, Virginia.
K2760
The Descendants of John Little of Botetourt and Rockbridge Counties, Virginia.
L4150
Historical Significance of Rockbridge County, Virginia.
M460 (BC)
A History of Rockbridge County, Virginia.
M8110 (ASU BC WCU)
Rockbridge County, Virginia.
T8890
Manganese deposits of the Lyndhurst-Vesuvius district, Augusta & Rockbridge Co., Va., 1943.
U3230

APP. COUNTIES — VA. — ROCKINGHAM CO.
Civil War Action in Rockingham County, Virginia, 1861-1865.
R3370 (ASU LMC)
Atlas of Rockingham County, Virginia.
S3200 (ASU)
A History of the Town of Dayton, Virginia.
S3760 (ASU BC)
Old Tenth Legion Marriages; Marriages in Rockingham Co., Va. from 1778 to 1816.
S7990
Tenth Legion Tithables, Rockingham Division, Rockingham County, Virginia, Tithables for 1792.
S8010
Old Houses in Rockingham County, 1750-1850.
T7610 (ASU WCU)
A History of Rockingham County, Virginia.
W1780 (ASU BC)
Men of Mark and Representative Citizens of Harrisonburg and Rockingham County, Virginia.
W1810 (ASU BC)
Virginia Valley Records: Genealogical and Historical Materials of Rockingham County, Virginia, and Related Regions.
W1860 (ASU BC)

APP. COUNTIES — VA. — RUSSELL CO.
A Short History of Extreme Southwest Virginia.
A530 (ASU LMC)
Russell County, Virginia Personal Property and Land Tax List . . .
A980
The Seventh Population Census of the United States for Russell County, Virginia, 1850.
B790 (BC ASU)
Castle's Woods 1769-1799, Frontier Virginia Settlement.
H250
Castle's Woods: Frontier Virginia Settlement, 1779-1799.
H260
Industrial Survey. Blacksburg, Va.
H8230
Soil Survey, Russell County, Virginia.
O100 (BC)
Russell County.
P4150
Elk Garden Tales.
P4160
Russell County, Virginia's Bluegrass Empire.
P4180 (ASU)
Russell Co., Va. Census of 1820.
S9230
An Economic and Social Survey of Russell County.
T300 (BC)
V550
Russell Co. in Retrospect.
W240 (BC)
Outline of the Geology and Mineral Resources of Russell County, Virginia.
W8950 (ETSU)

APP. COUNTIES — VA. — SCOTT CO.
Encomium for Scott County, Virginia.
A500
A Short History of Extreme Southwest Virginia.
A530 (ASU LMC)
History of Scott County, Virginia.
A580 (LMC FC ASU BC)
History of Scott County, Virginia.
A590
Scott County, Virginia, Census, 1820 and 1830.
A1210
The Early Grove Gas Field, Scott and Washington Counties, Virginia.
A5710 (ETSU)
Scott County, Virginia: U. S. Census, 1850.
B780 (BC ASU)
Oil and Gas Possibilities at Early Grove, Scott County, Virginia.
B9520 (ETSU)
"A Study of the Problems of Sixth Grade Students in Selected Schools of Scott County, Virginia."
D400
The Geology and Mineral Resources of Wise County and the Coal-bearing Portion of Scott County, Virginia.
E670 (FTSU ASU)
Industrial Survey. Blacksburg, Va.
H8230
I730
Soil Survey, Scott County, Virginia.
J2920
Southwest Virginia: Lee, Scott, Wise Counties, Summary of Resources.
T3500 (ASU BC)
Southwest Virginia, Lee, Scott, Wise Counties; Summary of Resources.
T3510
Geology and Mineral Resources of Wise Co. and Coal Bearing Portions of Scott Co., Va. with a Chapter on the Forest of Wise Co.
V980

APP. COUNTIES — VA. — SHENANDOAH CO.
Shenandoah County, Virginia, Marriage Bonds, 1772-1850.
A5080 (ASU ETSU)
Ground Water in the Ordovician Rocks near Woodstock, Virginia.
H660
A Brief History of New Market and Vicinity. The Battle of New Market Centennial, May 15, 1864-1964.
H5340 (ASU)
Economic Land Classification of Shenandoah County, Va.
P770
S7650
A History of Shenandoah County, Virginia.
W1790 (ASU BC)
A History of Shenandoah County, Virginia (1969)
W1800

APP. COUNTIES — VA. — SMYTH CO.
B4050
H2110
Industrial Survey. Blacksburg, Va.
H8230
Soil Survey, Smyth County, Virginia.
J2930
Tax List of Montgomery County, Virginia, 1782.
K520
Economic Land Classification of Smyth Co., Va.
P780
Smyth County Families and History.
P4320
Handbook of Smyth County, Virginia.
S2620
Smyth County History and Traditions.
W7240 (ASU BC)

APP. COUNTIES — VA. — TAZEWELL CO.
History of the Settlement and Indian Wars of Tazewell County, Virginia.
B3530 (FC ASU)
History of the Settlement and Indian Wars of Tazewell County, Va. with added material compiled by J. Allen Neal.
B3540
The Captives of Abb's Valley.
B7151
The Captives of Abb's Valley, a Legend of Frontier Life.
B7152 (ASU)
Annals of Tazewell County, Virginia from 1800 to 1922.
H2400 (BC ASU)
The Geology and Coal Resources of the Coal-bearing Portion of Tazewell County, Virginia.
H2510 (ETSU)
Industrial Survey. Blacksburg, Va.
H8230
Tax List of Montgomery County, Virginia, 1782.
K520
Memoirs of Burkes Garden and Tazewell County.
L2580
History of Tazewell County and Southwest Virginia 1748-1920.
P1690 (ASU ETSU LMC)
Soil Survey, Tazewell County, Virginia.
P3660
Archives of the Pioneers of Tazewell County.
S1080
The Forests of Tazewell County, Virginia.
S1210
Industrial Sites and Economic Data.
V770 (BC)
The Geology and Coal Resources of the Coal-Bearing Portion of Tazewell Co., Va.
V960

APP. COUNTIES — VA. — WARREN CO.
An Economic and Social Survey of Warren County.
H520 (ASU)
"School Desegregation in Warren County, Virginia, During 1958-1960; A Study in the Mobilization of Restraints."
L2050
An Economic and Social Survey of Warren Co.
V1240 (BC ASU)

APP. COUNTIES — VA. — WARREN CO.
Observance, Battle of Front Royal Virginia, May 19-20, 1962.
W920 (LMC)
APP. COUNTIES — VA. — WASHINGTON CO.
A Short History of Extreme Southwest Virginia.
A530 (ASU LMC)
The Early Grove Gas Field, Scott and Washington Counties, Virginia.
A5710 (ETSU)
Ancestry, Life and Family of Col. William Edmiston of Washington County.
C5710
"An Evaluation of the Elementary School Libraries in Washington County, Virginia."
C6510 (ETSU)
"Merger of Local Government: Case Study, Washington County and Bristol, Virginia, 1971."
C9830 (ETSU)
An Economic and Social Survey of Washington County.
D3830 (ASU BC)
Virginia Colonial Abstracts Vol. XXXIV, Washington County Marriage Register, 1782-1820.
F1420
Emory and Henry's Contribution to the Development of Democracy.
F3010
"The Design and Preparation of a Proposal for Federal Aid for the Education of Children from Low Income Families in Damascus Elementary School, Washington County, Virginia."
H5380 (ETSU)
Publications of the Historical Society of Washington County, Virginia.
H5960
Industrial Survey. Blacksburg, Va.
H8230
79 Families of Washington County.
J2840
Soil Survey, Washington County, Virginia.
J2940
High on a Windy Hill.
M520 (ASU)
"A Comparative Study of Twenty Business Trainees of the Gate City, Virginia, MDTA Program with Twenty Business Graduates of the Washington County, Virginia, Technical School."
S6460 (ETSU)
History of Southwest Virginia, 1746-1786, Washington County, 1777-1870.
S9060 (ASU BC ETSU)
History of Southwest Virginia, 1746-1786, Washington County, 1777-1870.
S9070 (ASU LMC FC ETSU)
History of Southwest Virginia, 1746-1786, Washington County, 1777-1870.
S9080 (ASU ETSU)
Projections and Economic Base Analysis: Bristol-Kingsport Metropolitan Area Including the City of Bristol, Virginia, and the Counties of Washington, Virginia, and Sullivan, Tennessee.
V820
Publications.
W1070 (ASU LMC ETSU)
"The Reading Diagnosis and Remediation of Five Groups of Eighth Grade Students at John S. Battle High School in Washington County, Virginia."
W9000 (ETSU)
APP. COUNTIES — VA. — WISE CO.
A Short History of Extreme Southwest Virginia.
A530 (ASU LMC)
The Story of Wise County, Virginia.
A540 (BC ASU)
Wise County Geography Supplement.
A570 (BC)
When the Trains Came to Norton, Wise County, in Old Virginia in 1891.
A5330 (BC ASU)
Community Relationships.
B9260 (BC)
The Geology and Mineral Resources of Wise County and the Coal-bearing Portion of Scott County, Virginia.
E670 (ETSU ASU)
"A Descriptive Study of Patients Accepted for Service During a Three-month Period at Psychiatric Service Clinic in Norton, Virginia."
G530
Industrial Survey. Blacksburg, Va.
H8230
A Narrative History of Wise County, Virginia.
J1310 (LMC ASU)
An Economic and Social Survey of Wise County.
K790 (ASU BC)
The Life and Times of a Mountaineer Game Warden.
O740
Soil Survey, Wise County, Virginia.
P2210
Southwest Virginia: Lee, Scott, Wise Counties, Summary of Resources.
T3500 (ASU BC)
Southwest Virginia, Lee, Scott, Wise Counties; Summary of Resources.
T3510
Geology and Mineral Resources of Wise Co. and Coal Bearing Portions of Scott Co., Va. with a Chapter on the Forest of Wise Co.
V980
APP. COUNTIES — VA. — WYTHE CO.
Wythe County, Virginia, Census, 1810, 1820, 1830, 1840.
A1220
A Baumgardner Family in America.
B2110
B4050
The Copenhaver Family of Wythe County.
C1030
Standards of Living in Six Virginia Counties.
D640
The Lutheran Church in Virginia, 1717-1962.
E1420 (FC)
Sermons and Essays.
F1590
Pioneers of the Virginia Bluegrass (And Their Descendants).
G2830
H2110
Industrial Survey. Blacksburg, Va.
H8230
St. John's Evangelical Lutheran Church, Wythe County, Virginia, Its Pastors and Their Records 1800-1924.
K460
New River Tithables, 1770-73.
K510
Tax List of Montgomery County, Virginia, 1782.
K520
Sanders Saga.
M530
Southwest Virginia Historical Records, Census of 1810, Wytheville, Wythe County edition.
M1490
Economic and Social Aspects of Negro Slavery in Wythe County, Virginia, 1790-1860.
M9210
Economic Land Classification of Wythe Co., Va.
P790
Wythe County Chapters.
P4330 (ASU)
1800 Tax Lists and Abstracts of Deeds (1796-1800) of Wythe County, Virginia.
S1090
Historical Facts About Churches of Wythe County.
W5790
The Iron Industry of Wythe County from 1792.
W5800 (ASU BC)
Virginia Germans.
W9810
APP. COUNTIES — W. VA. — BARBOUR CO.
Soil Survey, Barbour County, West Virginia.
B3440
Oil and Gas Report on Barbour and Upshur Counties, West Virginia.
H3600 (ETSU)
The History of Barbour County, West Virginia, from Its Earliest Exploration and Settlement to the Present Time.
M4510 (ASU ETSU)
Barbour and Upshur Counties and Western Portion of Randolph County.
R1260 (ASU ETSU)
The Learning Experiences of Youth Groups: A Study of 4-H Clubs in Barbour County, West Virginia.
S3790
Barbour and Upshur Counties. . . .
W3640 (ETSU)
APP. COUNTIES — W. VA. — BERKELEY CO.
Alee's History of Martensburg and Berkeley Company, West Virginia.
A1310
Ground-water Features of Berkeley and Jefferson Counties, West Virginia.
B3560 (ETSU)
Berkeley County, U. S. A.: A Bicentennial History of a Virginia and West Virginia County, 1772-1972.
D2810 (ASU BC)
Soil Survey, Berkeley County, West Virginia.
G2770
Jefferson, Berkeley, and Morgan Counties.
G4280 (ETSU)
Marriage Records of Berkeley County, Virginia, for the Period of 1781-1854, Located at Berkeley County Court House, Martinsburg, West Virginia.
K440 (ETSU)
Soil Survey of Jefferson, Berkeley, and Morgan Counties, West Virginia.
L720
Health, Welfare, and Housing Needs of the Aged in Berkeley County, West Virginia.
S1320
Jefferson, Berkeley, and Morgan Counties.
W3740 (ETSU)
APP. COUNTIES — W. VA. — BOONE CO.
Soil Survey of Boone County, West Virginia.
L700
"A Survey of Boone County (West Virginia) School Buildings."
S350
Boone County Household Survey.
W3490
APP. COUNTIES — W. VA. — BRAXTON CO.
Braxton County, Virginia (Now West Virginia) Marriage Book 1.
A5390 (ASU)
Industrial and Commercial Potentials and Site and Project Analysis in Braxton, Clay and Nicholas Counties, West Virginia.
D1930
Oil and Gas Report on Braxton and Clay Counties, West Virginia.
H3610 (ETSU)
Braxton and Clay Counties.
H4700 (ASU)
Soil Survey of Braxton and Clay Counties, West Virginia.
L710
History of Braxton County and Central West Virginia.
S9320 (ASU BC)
Plant Life of Braxton County, Number 8 Plant Ecology.
W9740 (ASU)
APP. COUNTIES — W. VA. — BROOKE CO.
History of the Pan-handle.
N820 (BC)
APP. COUNTIES — W. VA. — CABELL CO.
Cabell, Wayne and Lincoln Counties.
K3180 (ETSU ASU)
Soil Survey of the Huntington Area, West Virginia.
L800
Cabell, Wayne and Lincoln Counties.
W3660 (ETSU)
APP. COUNTIES — W. VA. — CALHOUN CO.
Wirt, Roane and Calhoun Counties.
H4720 (ETSU)
Wirt, Roane and Calhoun Counties.
W3930 (ETSU)
APP. COUNTIES — W. VA. — CLAY CO.
Industrial and Commercial Potentials and Site and Project Analysis in Braxton, Clay and Nicholas Counties, West Virginia.
D1930
Oil and Gas Report on Braxton and Clay Counties, West Virginia.
H3610 (ETSU)
Braxton and Clay Counties.
H4700 (ASU)
Soil Survey of Braxton and Clay Counties, West Virginia.
L710

APP. COUNTIES — W. VA. — DODDRIDGE CO.
Doddridge County, Virginia (Now West Virginia) Marriage Book 1: Being a Record of the First Marriage in That County Created in 1845 from Parts of Tyler, Harrison, Lewis, and Ritchie Counties.
A5400 (ASU)
The Incentive Approach to State School Administration: Change in Two Pilot Centers, Mason County, West Virginia, and Doddridge County, West Virginia, 1959-60.
B3640
Oil and Gas Report and Map of Doddridge and Harrison Counties, West Virginia.
H3550 (ETSU)
Oil and Gas Report and Map of Doddridge and Harrison Counties, West Virginia.
W3800 (ETSU)
APP. COUNTIES — W. VA. — FAYETTE CO.
"A Study of Homeschool Contacts and Attitudes toward Participation in Lincoln School, Kingsport, Tennessee."
A600 (ETSU)
Rural Development Problems and Prospects in Fayette, Raleigh, and Summers Counties, West Virginia.
A4640
Survey for Library Development in Fayette and Raleigh Counties, West Virginia.
B8370 (BC)
History of Oak Hill, West Virginia.
D2900
Fayette County.
H4710 (ETSU)
Soil Survey of Fayette County, West Virginia.
K1630
History of Fayette County, West Virginia.
P2310 (ASU)
Fayette County.
W3700 (ETSU)
APP. COUNTIES — W. VA. — GILMER CO.
Oil and Gas Report and Map of Lewis and Gilmer Counties, West Virginia.
H3560 (ETSU)
Soil Survey of Lewis and Gilmer Counties, West Virginia.
L740
"Some Employment Opportunities of the Vocational Agriculture Trainees of Gilmer County."
M4020
APP. COUNTIES — W. VA. — GRANT CO.
History of Grant and Hardy Counties, West Virginia.
J2810 (ASU)
Soil Survey of Grant and Mineral Counties, West Virginia.
P2640
Mineral and Grant Counties.
R1290 (ASU ETSU)
Mineral and Grant Counties.
W3780 (ETSU)
APP. COUNTIES — W. VA. — GREENBRIER CO.
"Land Use in Greenbrier County, West Virginia."
W5110 (BC)
Greenbrier Pioneers and Their Homes.
D1420
Soil Survey, Greenbrier County, West Virginia.
G2780
G3690
The Journal of the Greenbrier Historical Society.
G3700 (ASU)
Greenbrier County.
P4530 (LMC ETSU)
Soil Survey, Greenbrier County, West Virginia.
V580
Greenbrier County.
W3720 (ETSU)
School-community Improvement, a Report of the Greenbrier County Program.
W7360 (ASU WCU)
APP. COUNTIES — W. VA. — HAMPSHIRE CO.
History of Hampshire County, West Virginia, from Its Earliest Settlement to the Present.
M4520
History of Hampshire County, West Virginia, from Its Earliest Settlement to the Present.
M4530 (ASU)
Capon Valley.
P4850 (BC)
Early Records, Hampshire County Virginia, Now West Virginia, Including at the Start Most of Known Va. Aside from Augusta District.
S130 (BC ASU)
Hampshire and Hardy Counties.
T8670 (ETSU)
Hampshire and Hardy Counties.
W3730 (ETSU)
Soil Survey of Hampshire County, West Virginia.
W6420
APP. COUNTIES — W. VA. — HANCOCK CO.
History of the Pan-handle.
N820 (BC)
History of Hancock Co., Va. and W. Va.
W2470 (BC)
APP. COUNTIES — W. VA. — HARDY CO.
History of Grant and Hardy Counties, West Virginia.
J2810 (ASU)
History of Hardy County of the Borderland.
M6820 (ASU BC)
Hampshire and Hardy Counties.
T8670 (ETSU)
Hampshire and Hardy Counties.
W3730 (ETSU)
Soil Survey of Hardy and Pendleton Counties, West Virginia.
W6430
APP. COUNTIES — W. VA. — HARRISON CO.
The Shawnee Trail Program: An Historical Pageant Presented at Clarksburg, W. Va., June 13, and 15, 1923.
C6240 (BC)
History of Harrison County, West Virginia.
D970 (BC ASU)
Oil and Gas Report and Map of Doddridge and Harrison Counties, West Virginia.
H3550 (ETSU)
History of Harrison County.
H3960 (ASU)
"Social and Economic Implications of Strip Mining in Harrison County, W. Va."
H5440
"Analysis and Projection of Population and School Enrollment in Harrison County."
H6340
Ground-water Resources of Harrison County, West Virginia.
N20 (ETSU)
Oil and Gas Report and Map of Doddridge and Harrison Counties, West Virginia.
W3800 (ETSU)
APP. COUNTIES — W. VA. — JACKSON CO.
"Current and Future Needs for Vocational Education in Jackson County, West Virginia."
C9770
Soil Survey, Jackson and Mason Counties, West Virginia.
G2790
"Effects of Urbanization on Vocational Agriculture in Jackson County, West Virginia."
K1690
History of First Settlers of Cow Run.
K2480
Washington's Woods: A History of Ravenswood and Jackson County, West Virginia.
M7090 (ASU)
The Slaughter of the PfostGreen Family of Jackson County, West Virginia.
M7940 (ASU)
Oil and Gas Report on Jackson, Mason, and Putnam Counties, West Virginia.
O940 (ETSU)
APP. COUNTIES — W. VA. — JEFFERSON CO.
The Story of Smithfield, Jefferson County, West Virginia.
B1900
Ground-water Features of Berkeley and Jefferson Counties, West Virginia.
B3560 (ETSU)
A History of Jefferson County, West Virginia.
B9360 (ASU BC)
Historic Harpers Ferry in Jefferson Co., W. Va.
F20 (BC)
Military Operations in Jefferson County, Virginia and West Virginia, 1861-1865.
F200
Jefferson, Berkeley, and Morgan Counties.
G4280 (ETSU)
Soil Survey, Jefferson County, West Virginia.
H3490
Military Operations in Jefferson Co., Virginia and West Virginia, 1961-65.
J490 (ASU)
Soil Survey of Jefferson, Berkeley, and Morgan Counties, West Virginia.
L720
M5490
Jefferson, Berkeley, and Morgan Counties.
W3740 (ETSU)
APP. COUNTIES — W. VA. — KANAWHA CO.
Status of the Aging in Kanawha County.
A2560
The Characteristics and Attitudes of Juvenile Delinquents of Kanawha County, West Virginia.
A2590
Action for Appalachian Youth: A Demonstration Program for Kanawha County Youth under the Auspices and Direction of the President's Committee on Juvenile Delinquency and Youth Crime.
C3370 (ASU)
The Kanawha Spectator.
D1630
Water Resources of Kanawha County, West Virginia.
D2830 (ETSU)
Oil and Gas Report on Kanawha County, West Virginia.
H3620 (ETSU)
Soil Survey of Kanawha County, West Virginia.
L730
APP. COUNTIES — W. VA. — LEWIS CO.
Oil and Gas Report and Map of Lewis and Gilmer Counties, West Virginia.
H3560 (ETSU)
Soil Survey of Lewis and Gilmer Counties, West Virginia.
L740
APP. COUNTIES — W. VA. — LINCOLN CO.
Cabell, Wayne and Lincoln Counties.
K3180 (ETSU ASU)
Cabell, Wayne and Lincoln Counties.
W3660 (ETSU)
APP. COUNTIES — W. VA. — LOGAN CO.
"A Study of the Status of the Elementary Principal of Logan County, West Virginia."
C8320
Soil Survey of Logan and Mingo Counties, West Virginia.
L750
"History of Education in Logan County, West Virginia."
M1050
The Logan Coal Field of West Virginia: A Brief History.
T8470 (ASU ETSU WCU)
Environmental Study of Logan, McDowell, and Mingo Counties, West Virginia and Pike County, Kentucky.
U2680 (ASU)
Logan and Mingo County.
W3760 (BC)
"Development of the Bituminous Coal Mining Industry in Logan County, West Virginia."
W5400
APP. COUNTIES — W. VA. — MCDOWELL CO.
McDowell County, West Virginia, Library Survey.
B8360 (BC)
"History of Education in McDowell County, West Virginia."
F3310
Wyoming and McDowell Counties.
H4730 (ETSU)
Soil Survey of McDowell and Wyoming Counties, West Virginia.
L760
"Chief Causes of Non-attendance in the Schools of McDowell County, West Virginia."
M8170
Environmental Study of Logan, McDowell, and Mingo Counties, West Virginia and Pike County, Kentucky.
U2680 (ASU)
Wyoming and McDowell Counties.
W3940 (ETSU)
APP. COUNTIES — W. VA. — MARION CO.
"Superstitions about Food and Health among Negro Girls in Elementary and Secondary Schools in Marion County, West Virginia."
B4600
Marion County in the Making.
F60 (BC)

APP. COUNTIES — W. VA. — MARION CO.
Oil and Gas Report and Map of Monongalia, Marion, and Taylor Counties, West Virginia.
H3580 (ETSU)
"History of Education of Marion County, West Virginia."
H5570
Now and Long Ago, a History of the Marion County Area.
L3610 (ASU)
Oil and Gas Report and Map of Monongalia, Marion, and Taylor Counties, West Virginia.
W3820 (ETSU)

APP. COUNTIES — W. VA. — MARSHALL CO.
Soil Survey, Marshall County, West Virginia.
B3450
Oil and Gas Report and Map of Marshall, Wetzel, and Tyler Counties, West Virginia.
H3570 (ETSU)
History of the Pan-handle.
N820 (BC)
History of Marshall County, from Forest to Hill. A Story of the Early Settlement and Development of Marshall County, W. Va., with Incidents of Early Life and Roster of Soldiers of the Several Wars, with Other Matters of Interest.
P3970 (BC ASU)
Oil and Gas Report and Map of Marshall, Wetzel, and Tyler Counties, West Virginia.
W3810 (ETSU)

APP. COUNTIES — W. VA. — MASON CO.
The Incentive Approach to State School Administration: Change in Two Pilot Centers, Mason County, West Virginia, and Doddridge County, West Virginia, 1959-60.
B3640
"A Proposed Program of Public Relations for the Schools of Mason County, West Virginia."
D2320
Soil Survey, Jackson and Mason Counties, West Virginia.
G2790
Soil Survey of the Point Pleasant, West Virginia, Area.
L810
Pioneers of Mason County, West Virginia.
M970
Oil and Gas Report on Jackson, Mason, and Putnam Counties, West Virginia.
O940 (ETSU)
Ground Water in Mason and Putnam Counties, West Virginia.
W7050 (ETSU)

APP. COUNTIES — W. VA. — MERCER CO.
Soil Survey of Mercer County, West Virginia.
G2300
The Story of Mercer County.
M640 (BC ASU)
Mercer, Monroe, and Summers Counties.
R1280 (ASU ETSU)
Mercer, Monroe, and Summers Counties.
W3770 (ETSU)

APP. COUNTIES — W. VA. — MINERAL CO.
Soil Survey of Grant and Mineral Counties, West Virginia.
P2640
Mineral and Grant Counties.
R1290 (ASU ETSU)
Mineral and Grant Counties.
W3780 (ETSU)

APP. COUNTIES — W. VA. — MINGO CO.
"A Case Study of Mingo County Economic Opportunity Commission: The Use of Title II of the Economic Opportunity Act of 1964 in a Rural County in West Virginia."
B1300
Soil Survey of Logan and Mingo Counties, West Virginia.
L750
"They'll Cut Off Your Project": A Mingo County Chronicle.
P2230 (ASU MHC WCU WWC)
Environmental Study of Logan, McDowell, and Mingo Counties, West Virginia and Pike County, Kentucky.
U2680 (ASU)
ARA Field Report, Opportunities for Economic Development in Mingo County, W. Va.
U2690
Logan and Mingo County.
W3760 (BC)

APP. COUNTIES — W. VA. — MONONGALIA CO.
"An Investigation of Some Needs for Expansion of Vocational Education in Monongalia, Preston and Taylor Counties, West Virginia."
H3020
"Some Aspects of the Coal Mining Industry in Monongalia County, West Virginia."
B5640
Ground-water Resources of Monongalia County, West Virginia.
C1280 (ETSU)
The Monongalia Story, a Bicentennial History.
C7400
Oil and Gas Report and Map of Monongalia, Marion, and Taylor Counties, West Virginia.
H3580 (ETSU)
The 175th Anniversary of the Formation of Monongalia County, West Virginia, and Other Relative Historical Data.
M6480 (ASU)
"A Survey of the Attitudes of Women in Monongalia County, West Virginia, toward the Use of Contraceptives."
S9720
Oil and Gas Report and Map of Monongalia, Marion, and Taylor Counties, West Virginia.
W3820 (ETSU)

APP. COUNTIES — W. VA. — MONROE CO.
Soil Survey, Monroe County, West Virginia.
G2800
Soil Survey of Monroe County, West Virginia.
K1650
A History of Monroe County, W. Va.
M8090 (BC)
Mercer, Monroe, and Summers Counties.
R1280 (ASU ETSU)
Mercer, Monroe, and Summers Counties.
W3770 (ETSU)

APP. COUNTIES — W. VA. — MORGAN CO.
Jefferson, Berkeley, and Morgan Counties.
G4280 (ETSU)
Soil Survey of Jefferson, Berkeley, and Morgan Counties, West Virginia.
L720
Jefferson, Berkeley, and Morgan Counties.
W3740 (ETSU)

APP. COUNTIES — W. VA. — NICHOLAS CO.
History of Nicholas County, West Virginia.
B7430 (ASU BC)
Industrial and Commercial Potentials and Site and Project Analysis in Braxton, Clay and Nicholas Counties, West Virginia.
D1930
Archeological Survey of Nicholas County, West Virginia.
M2250 (ASU)
Economic Utilization of Marginal Lands in Nicholas and Webster Counties, West Virginia.
P1540
Soil Survey of Nicholas County, West Virginia.
P2650
Nicholas County.
R1300 (ASU ETSU)
Forest-Land Utilization in Nicholas and Webster Co., W. Va.
W2460
Nicholas County.
W3790 (ETSU)

APP. COUNTIES — W. VA. — OHIO CO.
Occurrence and Availability of Ground Water in Ohio County, West Virginia.
R3330 (ETSU)

APP. COUNTIES — W. VA. — PARKERSBURG CO.
Soil Survey of the Parkersburg Area, West Virginia.
M4920

APP. COUNTIES — W. VA. — PENDLETON CO.
The Hammers and Allied Families.
B5050 (BC)
A History of Franklin, the County Seat of Pendleton County, West Virginia.
B5060 (BC)
Twixt North and South.
C250 (ASU)
A History of Pendleton County, W. Va.
M8100 (ASU BC)
Pendleton County.
T8680 (ETSU)
Pendleton County.
W3840 (BC)
Soil Survey of Hardy and Pendleton Counties, West Virginia.
W6430

APP. COUNTIES — W. VA. — PLEASANTS CO.
Pleasants County, West Virginia, Register of Deaths, 1853 — 1873.
A5410 (ASU)
Oil and Gas Report and Map of Pleasants, Wood, and Ritchie Counties, West Virginia.
H3590 (ETSU)
A Proposed Regional Library for Wood, Pleasants, Tyler, and Wetzel Counties.
M5710
County Reports and Maps.
W3690 (BC)
Oil and Gas Report and Map of Pleasants, Wood and Ritchie Counties, West Virginia.
W3830 (ETSU)

APP. COUNTIES — W. VA. — POCAHONTAS CO.
The McNeel Family Records: Descendants of Pioneer John McNeel and Martha Davis of Pocahontas County, West Virginia, 1765-1967.
E830 (ASU)
Pocahontas County Cooking Yesterday and Today.
E850
Tales of Pocahontas County.
M2380
Pocahontas County.
P4550 (ETSU)
Historical Sketches of Pocahontas County, West Virginia.
P4630 (BC ASU)
Pocahontas County.
W3850 (BC)
Soil Survey of Pocahontas County, West Virginia.
W6440

APP. COUNTIES — W. VA. — PRESTON CO.
Community Schools in Action.
C4220 (ASU)
"An Investigation of Some Needs for Expansion of Vocational Education in Monongalia, Preston and Taylor Counties, West Virginia."
H3020
A Survey of Attitudes and Opinions of Preston County Voters.
H6360
Soil Survey of Preston County, West Virginia.
L770
Vocational Agricultural Instruction for Adult Farmer Classes in Preston County.
L2730
Soil Survey, Preston County, West Virginia.
P820
Christopher Call's Family of Preston County, West Virginia 1741-1973.
S3740
History of Preston County (West Virginia).
W6210 (ASU)
History of Preston County (West Virginia).
W6220 (ASU BC)

APP. COUNTIES — W. VA. — PUTNAM CO.
Biological and Archaeological Analysis of Bones from a 17th Century Indian Village (46 PU 31), Putnam County, West Virginia.
G4810 (ASU)
Oil and Gas Report on Jackson, Mason, and Putnam Counties, West Virginia.
O940 (ETSU)
Ground Water in Mason and Putnam Counties, West Virginia.
W7050 (ETSU)

APP. COUNTIES — W. VA. — RALEIGH CO.
"A Study of Homeschool Contacts and Attitudes toward Participation in Lincoln School, Kingsport, Tennessee."
A600 (ETSU)
Rural Development Problems and Prospects in Fayette, Raleigh, and Summers Counties, West Virginia.
A4640
Survey for Library Development in Fayette and Raleigh Counties, West Virginia.
B8370 (BC)
"Cost of Operating the Schools in Raleigh County, West Virginia, from 1940-50."
C8360
Soil Survey of Raleigh County, West Virginia.
L780

APP. COUNTIES — W. VA. — RANDOLPH CO.
A History of Randolph County, West Virginia, from Its Earliest Settlement to the Present Time.
B5580 (BC)
The Blackwater Chronicle; A Narrative of an Expedition into the Land of Canaan.
K750 (BC ASU)
Soil Survey, Tucker County, Part of Northern Randolph County, West Virginia.
L3540
The History of Randolph County, West Virginia, from Its Earliest Settlement to the Present, Embracing Records of All the Leading Families, Reminiscences and Traditions.
M4540 (ASU)
The Sinks of Gandy Creek.
P4270 (ASU BC WCU)
Barbour and Upshur Counties and Western Portion of Randolph County.
R1260 (ASU ETSU)
The Cheat Mountain Coal Field of Randolph County, West Virginia.
R1270 (ASU ETSU)
Randolph County.
R1310 (ASU ETSU)
Virginia Illustrated: Containing a Visit to the Virginian Canaan, and the Adventures of Porte Crayon and His Cousins.
S8110 (ASU BC)
Randolph County.
W3860 (ETSU)
Soil Survey of Randolph County, West Virginia.
W6450

APP. COUNTIES — W. VA. — RITCHIE CO.
Ritchie County, Virginia (now West Virginia) Marriages 1843 — 1853: Minister's Returns — With Notes on the Ancestry and Birth Place of Some of the Earliest Settlers.
A5420 (ASU)
Oil and Gas Report and Map of Pleasants, Wood, and Ritchie Counties, West Virginia.
H3590 (ETSU)
County Reports and Maps.
W3690 (BC)
Oil and Gas Report and Map of Pleasants, Wood and Ritchie Counties, West Virginia.
W3830 (ETSU)

APP. COUNTIES — W. VA. — ROANE CO.
History of Roane County, West Virginia, from the Time of Its Exploration to A. D. 1927.
B4250 (ASU BC)
A Social and Economic Survey of the Spencer Soil Conservation Area.
C7540
Wirt, Roane and Calhoun Counties.
H4720 (ETSU)
Soil Survey of the Spencer, West Virginia, Area.
L820
Wirt, Roane and Calhoun Counties.
W3930 (ETSU)

APP. COUNTIES — W. VA. — SUMMERS CO.
Rural Development Problems and Prospects in Fayette, Raleigh, and Summers Counties, West Virginia.
A4640
Soil Survey of Summers County, West Virginia.
K1660
History of Summers County from the Earliest Settlement to the Present Time.
M5780 (ASU)
Mercer, Monroe, and Summers Counties.
R1280 (ASU ETSU)
Mercer, Monroe, and Summers Counties.
W3770 (ETSU)

APP. COUNTIES — W. VA. — TAYLOR CO.
"An Investigation of Some Needs for Expansion of Vocational Education in Monongalia, Preston and Taylor Counties, West Virginia."
H3020
Oil and Gas Report\and Map of Monongalia, Marion, and Taylor Counties, West Virginia.
H3580 (ETSU)
The Need for a New Perspective of the School Plant and School Organization in Taylor County.
H6350
Oil and Gas Report and Map of Monongalia, Marion, and Taylor Counties, West Virginia.
W3820 (ETSU)

APP. COUNTIES — W. VA. — TUCKER CO.
History of Tucker County, West Virginia.
F100 (LMC ASU BC)
An Economic Profile of Tucker County, West Virginia.
L3490 (ASU)
Soil Survey, Tucker County, Part of Northern Randolph County, West Virginia.
L3540
History of Tucker County, West Virginia.
M4490
History of Tucker County, West Virginia, from the Earliest Explorations and Settlements to the Present Time: With Biographical Sketches of More Than Two Hundred and Fifty of the Leading Men, and a Full Appendix of Official and Electional History. Also, an Account of the Rivers, Forests and Caves of the County.
M4550 (ASU)
Soil Survey of Tucker County, West Virginia.
P2660
Tucker County.
R1320 (ASU LMC ETSU)
Blackwater Country.
S4860 (ASU WCU MHC BC)
Tucker County.
W3910 (ETSU)

APP. COUNTIES — W. VA. — TYLER CO.
Tyler County, Virginia (Now West Virginia) Marriages, 1815 — 1852.
A5430 (ASU)
"The Educational Development of Tyler County, West Virginia."
C5310
Oil and Gas Report and Map of Marshall, Wetzel, and Tyler Counties, West Virginia.
H3570 (ETSU)
A Proposed Regional Library for Wood, Pleasants, Tyler, and Wetzel Counties.
M5710
Oil and Gas Report and Map of Marshall, Wetzel, and Tyler Counties, West Virginia.
W3810 (ETSU)

APP. COUNTIES — W. VA. — UPSHUR CO.
Soil Survey of Upshur County, West Virginia.
G4100
Oil and Gas Report on Barbour and Upshur Counties, West Virginia.
H3600 (ETSU)
Upshur Brothers of the Blue and the Gray.
H7230 (ASU)
Soil Survey of Barbour and Upshur Counties, West Virginia.
L690
Barbour and Upshur Counties and Western Portion of Randolph County.
R1260 (ASU ETSU)
Overall Economic Development Program for Upshur County, West Virginia.
U4180
Barbour and Upshur Counties. . . .
W3640 (ETSU)

APP. COUNTIES — W. VA. — WAYNE CO.
A Short History of the Wayne Methodist Church.
B3470
Cabell, Wayne and Lincoln Counties.
K3180 (ETSU ASU)
Soil Survey of the Huntington Area, West Virginia.
L800
The Impact of Water Resources Development upon Local Rural Communities: Adjustment Factors to Rapid Change.
N80
History of Wayne County, West Virginia.
T630 (ASU)
Cabell, Wayne and Lincoln Counties.
W3660 (ETSU)

APP. COUNTIES — W. VA. — WEBSTER CO.
Annals of Webster County, West Virginia.
M5990
Soil Survey of Webster County, West Virginia.
M6710
Economic Utilization of Marginal Lands in Nicholas and Webster Counties, West Virginia.
P1540
Forest-Land Utilization in Nicholas and Webster Co., W. Va.
W2460

APP. COUNTIES — W. VA. — WETZEL CO.
Oil and Gas Report and Map of Marshall, Wetzel, and Tyler Counties, West Virginia.
H3570 (ETSU)
History of Wetzel County, West Virginia.
M1280 (BC)
A Proposed Regional Library for Wood, Pleasants, Tyler, and Wetzel Counties.
M5710
Oil and Gas Report and Map of Marshall, Wetzel, and Tyler Counties, West Virginia.
W3810 (ETSU)

APP. COUNTIES — W. VA. — WIRT CO.
Soil Survey, Wood and Wirt Counties, West Virginia.
E1870
Wirt, Roane and Calhoun Counties.
H4720 (ETSU)
Warning in Appalachia: A Study of Wirt County, West Virginia.
R1110 (BC ASU WCU LMC MHC)
Wirt, Roane and Calhoun Counties.
W3930 (ETSU)

APP. COUNTIES — W. VA. — WOOD CO.
The Story of Washington Bottom, Wood County, West Virginia.
B2510 (BC)
Soil Survey, Wood and Wirt Counties, West Virginia.
E1870
Oil and Gas Report and Map of Pleasants, Wood, and Ritchie Counties, West Virginia.
H3590 (ETSU)
A Proposed Regional Library for Wood, Pleasants, Tyler, and Wetzel Counties.
M5710
County Reports and Maps.
W3690 (BC)
Oil and Gas Report and Map of Pleasants, Wood and Ritchie Counties, West Virginia.
W3830 (ETSU)
A Symposium on the Sandhill Deep Well, Wood County, West Virginia.
W8960 (ETSU)

APP. COUNTIES — W. VA. — WYOMING CO.
Reference Book of Wyoming County History.
B5800 (ASU BC LMC)
"A History of Education in Wyoming County, West Virginia."
C7040
Wyoming and McDowell Counties.
H4730 (ETSU)
Soil Survey of McDowell and Wyoming Counties, West Virginia.
L760
"Excess Levies and School Bond Issues in Wyoming County (West Virginia) from 1933-1951."
M7570
"A Study of Students Dropping Out of Wyoming County, West Virginia, High Schools for the 1950-51 School Term."
S7250
Wyoming and McDowell Counties.
W3940 (ETSU)
Wyoming County on the Alert: A Socio-Economic Survey by Wyoming County Advisory Committee for Library Service and West Virginia Library Commission.
W9890

APP. CULTURE
People's Cultural Heritage in Appalachia.
W2950
This Proud Land.
W3040

APP. — DESCRIPTION AND TRAVEL
Journal of a Tour in the Unsettled Parts of North America, in 1796 and 1797.
B350
The Unsettled Parts of North America in 1796 and 1797.
B360
Journal of a Tour in the Unsettled Parts of North America in 1796 and 1797.
B370
Reisen durch die Vereinigten Staaten und Ober-Canada.
B6820
Travels in the New South: A Bibliography.
C4620

APP. — DESCRIPTION AND TRAVEL

Travels in the Old South: A Bibliography.
C4630

Discovering the Appalachians: What to Look for from the Past in the Present along America's Eastern Frontier.
C6670 (ASU WCU MHC ETSU LMC WWC UNCA BC)

Five Years in the Alleghenies.
C9090 (ASU BC)

A Southerner Discovers the South.
D180 (ASU BC FC)

Highlights and Travels of a Southern Highlander.
D4170 (ASU)

Journal.
F70 (LMC ETSU ASU)

Roaming the Eastern Mountains.
F140 (ASU BC)

Seeing the Sunny South.
F150 (ASU LMC BC)

Journal of Jos. W. Fawcett.
F390 (ASU)

Excursion through the Slave States, from Washington on the Potomac to the Frontier of Mexico; with Sketches of Popular Manners and Geological Notices.
F430 (ASU LMC)

These are our Lives; as Told by the People and Written by Members of the Federal Writers' Project of the Works Progress Administration in North Carolina, Tennessee, and Georgia.
F440 (FC ASU)

Our Native Land: Or, Glances at American Scenery and Places, with Sketches of Life and Adventure.
F710 (ASU)

Bubbling Waters.
F1070 (ASU LMC BC)

The Poetry of Traveling in the United States.
G1680 (LMC BC)

My Southern Friends.
G1770 (BC WCU)
G4680

Skylines and Horizons.
H5160 (ASU LMC BC)

Letters from North America Written During a Tour in the United States and Canada.
H6200

A Winter in the West.
H6240

A Photographic Documentary of the Blue Ridge Mountains.
J480 (LMC)

Highways and Byways of the South.
J1580 (BC LMC)

The Blue Ridge Parkway Guide.
L3470 (LMC ASU)

The Southern Poor-white from Lubberland to Tobacco Road.
M1690 (ASU)

The Southern Poor-white from Lubberland to Tobacco Road.
M1700 (LMC)

Retrospect of Western Travel.
M3800

Frederick Law Olmsted: A Critic of the Old South.
M6260

A Thousand-Mile Walk to the Gulf.
M8470

Wilderness Adventure.
P30 (ASU)

Journey into America.
P1410 (WCU)

Southern Accent: From Uncle Remus to Oak Ridge.
P3370 (LMC WWC BC)

A Narrative of the Visit to the American Churches, by the Deputation from the Congregational Union of England and Wales.
R1010

The Discoveries of John Lederer.
R2330 (ASU LMC)

Where Time Stood Still: A Portrait of Appalachia.
R2710 (ASU UNCA BC WCU MHC ETSU FC LMC WWC)

Sketches of History, Life, and Manners in the United States. By a Traveller.
R4150

Travels in the Confederation, 1783-1784.
S1060 (ASU)

A Short Description of the Tennessee Government, or The Territory of the United States South of the River Ohio, to Accompany and Explain a Map of That Country.
S4500 (BC ASU)

The Old South Illustrated.
S8060 (ASU BC)

The Tennessee Valley Region: Important Features and Recent Trends.
T5330

Trade and Travel Around the Southern Appalachians Before 1830.
T9520 (ASU LMC)

On Horseback: A Tour in Virginia, North Carolina and Tennessee. With Notes of Travel in Mexico and California.
W860 (BC)

On Horseback: A Tour in Virginia, North Carolina, and Tennessee. With Notes of Travel in Mexico and California.
W870 (ASU WCU LMC)

APP. — EARLY EXPLORATION

Journal of a Tour in the Unsettled Parts of North America, in 1796 and 1797.
B350

The Unsettled Parts of North America in 1796 and 1797.
B360

Journal of a Tour in the Unsettled Parts of North America in 1796 and 1797.
B370

Logan. The Last of the Race of Shikellemus, Chief of the Cayuga Nation. A Dramatic Piece. To Which Is Added, the Dialogue of the Backwoodsman and the Dandy, First Recited at the Buffaloe Seminary. July the 1st 1821.
D2650 (ASU BC)

A Canoe Voyage up the Minnay Sotor; with an Account of the Lead and Copper Deposits in Wisconsin; of the Gold Region in the Cherokee Country: and Sketches of Popular Manners.
F410

A Canoe Voyage up the Minnay Sotor; with an Account of the Lead and Copper Deposits in Wisconsin; of the Gold Region in the Cherokee Country: and Sketches of Popular Manners.
F420

Letters from North America Written During a Tour in the United States and Canada.
H6200

A Topographical Description of the Western Territory of North America.
I70

A Topographical Description of the Western Territory of North America.
I80 (LMC ETSU BC)

A Topographical Description of the Western Territory of North America.
I90 (LMC)

The Appalachian Indian Frontier: The Edmond Atkin Report and Plan of 1755.
J240

Indians of the Southern Colonial Frontier; The Edmond (Edmund) Atkin Report and Plan of 1755.
J250

The Transylvania Colony.
L1910 (BC ASU)

Lost Heritage.
S510 (LMC)

Lieutenant Henry Timberlake's Memoirs 1756-1765.
W6830

APP. — EARLY EXPLORATIONS

Travels in the New South: A Bibliography.
C4620

Travels in the Old South: A Bibliography.
C4630

Journal.
F70 (LMC ETSU ASU)

The Great South: A Record of Journeys.
K2250 (LMC)

The Great South: A Record of Journeys in Louisiana, Texas, the Indian Territory, Missouri, Arkansas, Mississippi, Alabama, Georgia, Florida, South Carolina, North Carolina, Kentucky, Tennessee, Virginia, West Virginia, and Maryland.
K2260 (ASU BC)

APP. — FEDERAL PROGRAMS AND AID

The Industrialization of Southern Rural Areas: A Study of Industry and Federal Assistance in Small Towns with Recommendations for Future Policy.
A180

"A Study of Effect of Government Aid and Other Factors on the Economic Development of Three Selected Areas in Georgia."
A340

Appalachian Alabama: Development Plan — 1970.
A870 (ASU)

Health Development Plan — 1969, Morgan, Lawrence, Limestone Counties, Alabama.
A930 (ASU)

Health Development Plan — 1970, Morgan, Lawrence, Limestone Counties.
A940 (ASU)

Regional Health Demonstration Project, Phase 2, Morgan, Lawrence, Limestone Counties, Ala.
A950 (ASU)

The Appalachian Regional Development Bill. S3, Sen. Randolph; H.R. 4, Rep. Fallon.
A2130 (UNCA)

An Analysis of the Vista Program and Appalachian Volunteers, Inc.
A2190
A2650 (ASU MHC LMC)

Papers.
A3050

Appalachian Regional Commission.
A3100 (ETSU MHC ASU)

Meeting, May 8, 1961, the White House.
A3160
A3370 (ASU)

Annual Report.
A3550

Appalachia: A Report, 1964.
A3560 (LMC ASU WCU ETSU)

Appalachia: An Economic Report — 1970. Trends in Employment, Income and Population.
A3570 (ASU)

The Appalachian Experiment, 1965-1970.
A3620 (ASU)

Appalachian North Carolina Youth Development Project, Final Report.
A3640 (ASU)

At Transition: Executive Director's Semiannual Administrative and Economic Report, July 1-December 31, 1968.
A3680 (ASU)

"Measurement of the Economic Impact of Public Investment of Regional Economic Growth in Appalachia."
B3220

Experiment in Regional Federalism: Implementation of the Appalachian Regional Development Act of 1965 in Georgia, North Carolina, and Tennessee.
C1300

Status of West Virginia in the Economic Opportunity Program under Public Law 88-452.
C1310

A Poverty Program and the Public Schools.
C2260

An Evaluation of the Appalachian Volunteers.
C5870 (BC)

Status of West Virginia in the Economic Opportunity Program Under Public Law 88-452.
C8540
C8810 (ASU WCU BC)

"Coordination of Anti-poverty Programs in Chattanooga."
D1250

A Decade of Action for Progress in Kentucky.
E520 (ASU)

Program 60, 1960-70; a Decade of Action for Progress in Eastern Kentucky.
E530 (BC)

APP. — FEDERAL PROGRAMS AND AID

"A Study of the Title I Reading Program During the 1966-68 School Years in Carter County, Tennessee."
E1850 (ETSU)

A Guide to Resources for Anti-poverty Programs: A Selected Bibliography.
F500 (ASU)

"Public Policy for Depressed Areas with Special Reference to North Carolina."
F1630

"The Appalachian Experiment: Growth or Development."
F3730

"Impact of a Federal Grant-in-aid Program on an Economically Depressed, Rural State: A Case Study of Mental Health Programs in West Virginia."
G1050

The Economic Needs of Neighborhood Youth Corps Enrollees. Final Report.
G2540
G4780

"An Analysis and Evaluation of the OEO National Antipoverty Planning Process."
H930

A Review of the Appalachian Regional Commission Program.
H1690 (ASU)

"The Design and Preparation of a Proposal for Federal Aid for the Education of Children from Low Income Families in Damascus Elementary School, Washington County, Virginia."
H5380 (ETSU)

"Federal Payments in Lieu of Taxation with Emphasis on the Program of the Tennessee Valley Authority."
H7650

War on Poverty.
H8300
I860

Action Programs for Eastern Kentucky: Final Report of the Kentucky Flood Rehabilitation Study.
K1060 (BC ASU)

Federal Aid in Kentucky.
K1190

Community Action in Appalachia: An Appraisal of the "War on Poverty" in a Rural Setting of Southeastern Kentucky.
K1380

Government Against Poverty.
K1680

"Governmental Assistance to Industrial Development in West Virginia."
K1870

Scouting the War on Poverty: Social Reform Politics in the Kennedy Administration.
K2740

"A Study of the Blue Ridge Job Corps Center."
L830 (ETSU)

Federal Aid to Depressed Areas — An Evaluation of the Area Redevelopment Association.
L2010 (BC)

The Great Society's Poor Law, a New Approach to Poverty.
L2020

Programs in Aid of the Poor.
L2030

Programs in Aid of the Poor for the 1970's.
L2040

"An Administrative History of Public Programs for Dependent Children in North Carolina, Virginia, Tennessee, and Kentucky, 1900-1942."
L2740

"Centralization-decentralization in a Context of Intergovernmental Relations: A Study of Selected Federal Projects in Appalachia."
M1010

"The Appalachian Regional Development Act of 1965."
M2900

"The State Development Planning Process: Implementation of the Appalachian Regional Development Act of 1965 in West Virginia."
P850

"An Analysis of the Effects of Federal Farm Programs on Incomes of Appalachian Farmers."
P1000

"An Analysis of the Effects of Federal Farm Programs on Incomes of Appalachian Farmers."
P1040 (LMC)

Pennsylvania Appalachian Development Plan.
P1870 (ASU WCU)

Pennsylvania Appalachian Development Plan: Revision for 1970.
P1880 (ASU)

"The Relation of the Hot Lunch Program to the Progress of Pupils in the Deep Water School, West Virginia."
P2030

"They'll Cut Off Your Project": A Mingo County Chronicle.
P2230 (ASU MHC WCU WWC)

Appalachia.
P4340 (ASU)

"Public Information and the Community Action Programs of the War on Poverty: The First Three Years."
R3320

The Appalachian Regional Development Program.
R3900 (ASU)

Regional Planning: The Appalachian Experience.
R3910 (ASU WCU WWC LMC)

"The Appalachian Regional Commission: Selected Aspects of Institutions and Processes and Their Relationship to Natural and Human Resources Development."
S40

Report on the School Sponsored Program, Appalachian Area.
S550

Preparation of Plans and Specifications for Pollution Abatement Activities in Cherry Creek Watershed, Maryland.
S3850 (ASU)

"An Overview of Federal Programs and Their Impacts on Appalachia."
S7690

Tennessee Appalachian Development Plan, 1969-1970.
T1600 (ASU)

Appalachian Regional Development Act, 1965-; Rationale and Model for Application in Tennessee.
T1770

Report on First Year's Activities in the Appalachian Development Program.
T1780 (LMC)

Is the Tennessee Valley Favored in Federal Expenditures?
T2970 (BC)

"Southern Appalachian State Newspapers' Treatment of the Antipoverty and Appalachia Acts."
T8020

"Why Aid Doesn't Help: Organizing for Community Economic Development in Central Appalachia."
T9690

Appalachian Regional Development Act of 1965.
U1670

Appalachian Regional Development Act, 1967.
U1680

Consideration of H. R. 11946. Report to Accompany H. Res. 861, Aug. 20, 1964.
U1960

Appalachian Regional Development Act of 1964. Hearings before the Ad Hoc Subcommittee on Appalachian Regional Development of the Committee on Public Works on H. R. 11065 and H. R. 11066, May 5-June 11, 1964, to Provide Public Works and Economic Development Programs and the Planning and Coordination Needed to Assist in the Development of the Appalachian Region.
U1970

Appalachian Regional Development Act of 1964: Report to Accompany H. R. 11946, July 31, 1964.
U1980

Appalachian Regional Development Act of 1965: Report to Accompany S. 3, February 17, 1965.
U1990

Appalachian Regional Development Act of 1964. Report Together with Minority Views to Accompany S. 2782, Aug. 13, 1964.
U2000

Appalachian Regional Development Act of 1964. Hearings on S. 2782, a Bill to Provide Public Works and Economic Development Programs and the Planning Coordination Needed to Assist in the Development of the Appalachian Region, June 22-26, 1964.
U2010

Section-by-section Analysis of H. R. 11065 and H. R.. 11066: Appalachian Regional Development Act of 1964 as Submitted in Draft to the Committee, April 29, 1964.
U2020

Proposed Appropriation for Appalachian Regional Commission, Fiscal Year 1965. Sept. 29, 1964.
U2030

War on Poverty: The Economic Opportunity Act of 1964. A Compilation of Materials Relevant to S. 2642, Prepared for the Select Subcommittee, July 23, 1964.
U2040

Authorizing Printing of Additional Copies of Hearings by Committee on Public Works on Appalachian Regional Development Act of 1965. Report from Committee on House Administration to Accompany H. Res. 724. June 2, 1966.
U2050

Authorizing Printing of Additional Copies of Committee Print 1 of Committee on Public Works on Section-by-section Analysis of H. R. 4, Appalachian Regional Development Act of 1965, and Difference between H. R. 4 (89th Cong.), and H. R. 11946 (88th Cong.) as Reported to House of Representatives and S. 2782 (88th Cong.) as Passed by Senate. Report from Committee on House Administration to Accompany H. Res. 722. June 2, 1966.
U2060

Supplemental Estimates of Appropriations for Various Agencies for Fiscal Year 1965 to Finance Appalachian Regional Development Act of 1965. Mar. 15, 1965.
U2070

Examination of the War on Poverty Program. Hearings before the Subcommittee on the War on Poverty Program, April 12-30, 1965.
U2100

Appalachian Regional Development Act of 1965: Report to Accompany S. 3.
U2110 (ETSU)

Highlights of Appalachian Regional Development Act of 1965, Mar. 10, 1965.
U2120

Section-by-section Analysis of H. R. 4: Appalachian Regional Development Act of 1965, and Differences between H. R. 4 (89th Congress) and H. R. 11946 (88th Congress), as Reported to the House of Representatives, and S. 2782 (88th Congress) as Passed by the Senate.
U2130

Appalachian Regional Development Act of 1965. Hearings on H. R. 4 and S. 3, February 3-5, 1965.
U2140

Authorizing Printing for Use of Committee on Public Works of Additional Copies of Its Hearings on Appalachian Regional Development Act of 1965 (S.3). Report from Committee on Rules and Administration to Accompany S. Res. 208. Feb. 16, 1966.
U2150

Appalachian Regional Development Act of 1965. Hearings on S. 3, January 19 and 21, 1965.
U2170

Appalachian Regional Development Act of 1965: Report, Together with Individual Views, to Accompany S. 3, January 27, 1965.
U2180

Appalachian Regional Development Act, 1965, Communication from President of United States Transmitting Recommendation that Congress Extend Appalachian Regional Development Act of 1965. Jan. 23, 1967.
U2190

Appalachian Regional Development Act Amendments of 1967. Conference Report to Accompany S. 602. Sept. 26, 1967.
U2200

APP. FEDERAL PROGRAMS AND AID

Appalachian Regional Development Act Amendments of 1967, and Amendments to Public Works and Economic Development Act of 1965.
U2210

Appalachian Regional Development Act, 1967. Hearings on H. R. 4446 and Related Bills, May 9-July 12, 1967.
U2220 (ASU ETSU)

Revising and Extending Appalachian Regional Development Act of 1965, and Amending Title 5 to Public Works and Economic Development Act of 1965. Report Together with Supplemental Views, to Accompany S. 602. April 6, 1967.
U2260

Appalachian Regional Development Act Amendments of 1967 Hearings on S. 602, Jan. 24-Feb. 3, 1967.
U2270 (ASU)

Appalachian and Regional Action Planning Commissions. Report.
U2310

Independent Offices and Department of Housing and Urban Development Appropriations for Fiscal Year 1970.
U2320

Regional Economic Development Legislation. Extension and Revision of Appalachian Regional Development Act of 1965, as Amended, and of Titles 1-5 of Public Works and Economic Development Act of 1965, as Amended.
U2370

Public Works Acceleration Act. Public Works and Economic Development Act, Appalachian Regional Development Act Extensions. Conference Report to Accompany S. 575, June 2, 1971.
U2380

Public Works Acceleration Act. Public Works and Economic Development Act, and Appalachian Regional Development Act Extensions Report with Minority and supplemental Views, 92d Congress, 1st session, on H. R. 5376, March 29, 1971.
U2390

Public Works and Economic Development Act and Appalachian Regional Development Act Extensions. Report to Accompany H. R. 9922, July 21, 1971.
U2400

Appalachian Regional Development Act Amendments of 1971. Hearings on H. R. 5376 and Related Bills, March 15-17, 1971.
U2410

Public Works Acceleration Act. Public Works and Economic Development Act, and Appalachian Regional Development Act Extensions. Conference Report to Accompany S. 575, June 1, 1971.
U2420

Appalachian Regional Development Act Amendments of 1971. Report Together with Individual Views to Accompany S. 575, March 9, 1971.
U2450

Public Works and Economic Development Act and Appalachian Regional Development Act Extensions. Report to Accompany S. 2317, July 20, 1971.
U2460

Appalachian Regional Development Act of 1971. Hearings on S. 575, February 8-10, 1971.
U2480

Economic Development, Project Activity Supplement.
U2700

VISTA Services Urban Ghetto, Rural America, Appalachia, Migrant Worker, American Indian, Mentally Handicapped, Job Corps.
U3780

War on Poverty Projects, March 31, 1965.
U3790

War on Poverty Projects, April 30, 1965.
U3800

American Imprints Inventory.
U4090

Guide to civilian organizations . . .
U4100

Federal Grants-in-Aid; a Comprehensive Analysis of Federal Grants-in-Aid to All the States, with a Detailed Analysis of Programs in Effect in Each City and County of Virginia.
V710 (BC)

VISTA: Challenge in Poverty.
W5910

APP. — FEDERAL PROGRAMS AND AID — COOPERATIVE ASSOCIATIONS

Two Supply Cooperatives Serving Low-income Farmers: A Preliminary Analysis in Appalachia.
B310

APP. — FEDERAL PROGRAMS AND AID — TENNESSEE VALLEY AUTHORITY

. . . A Compilation of the More Important Congressional Acts, Treaties, Presidential Messages, Judicial Decisions, and Official Reports and Documents Having to do with the Control, Conservation, and Utilization of Water Resources.
T5090

APP. — HISTORY

A3410 (ASU)

Oral History for the Local Historical Society, American Assoc. for State and Local History.
B2070

Appalachian People's History Book.
C9220 (ASU FC WCU ETSU)

An Appalachian Reader.
D3240 (WCU MHC FC BC ASU)

The Appalachian South: An Historical Bibliography.
D3250

An Outline History of Appalachian America.
D3270 (BC ASU)

The Underside of American History: Other Readings Since 1865.
F3140

The South in American History.
H5090 (LMC FC)

Stories of the South, Old and New.
H5180 (ASU BC WWC)
I160 (ASU)

Drums Along the Antietam.
S930 (MHC ASU)

John Wesley North and the Reform Frontier.
S7580

"Lincoln's Carpetbagger, J. W. North."
S7590
T20

The Blount Journal, 1790-1796: The Proceedings of Government Over the Territory of the United States of America, South of the River Ohio.
T7620 (ASU)

Blue Ridge Country.
T7900 (FC WWC ETSU BC ASU)

Blue Ridge Country.
T7910 (ASU WCU LMC)
T9160 (BC)

Letter from the Secretary of War in reply to the resolution of the House of Representatives of the 23d ultimo, respecting the interference of any officer or agent of the Government with the Cherokee Indians in the formation of a government for the regulation of their own internal affairs.
U4040

Huntington (West Virginia) Through Seventy Five Years.
W470

The Journal of Major George Washington.
W1080

The Log Cabin in America: From Pioneer Days to the Present.
W2880 (ASU WCU BC)

APP. — HISTORY — SOURCES

A Guide for Field Workers in Folklore.
G2360 (BC ASU)

APP. — KY.

Appalachian Regional Commission.
A3060 (ASU MHC)

APP. — LABOR FORCE

General Agreement Between the Tennessee Valley Authority and the Tennessee Valley Trades and Labor Council.
T2830

Development of Salary Policy Employee Panel (Documentation).
T6790

Documentation of TVA Apprenticeship Program.
T6800

The Labor Force Characteristics of Women in Low-Income Rural Areas of the South.
T7630

Bituminous Coal Mining: Labor Market Developments.
U1210

APP. MOUNTAINEERS

A2170 (ASU BC)
A2790 (ASU)

APP. MTNS.

A2800
A2830 (ETSU BC)

Appalachian Wilderness.
B2330

The Appalachians.
B6960 (ASU WCU LMC MHC FC WWC ETSU BC FC UNCA)

The Southern Highlander and His Homeland.
C640 (ASU ETSU WWC BC)

The Southern Highlander and His Homeland.
C650 (LMC MHC WCU FC)

The Southern Highlander and His Homeland.
C660

Exploring the Mountains of North Carolina.
C1250 (MHC)

The Southern Appalachian Heritage.
C2041

My Appalachia: A Reminiscence.
C2380 (ASU LMC MHC ETSU WCU FC WWC BC UNCA)

Discovering the Appalachians: What to Look for from the Past in the Present along America's Eastern Frontier.
C6670 (ASU WCU MHC ETSU LMC WWC UNCA BC)

Culture in the South.
C7760 (ASU LMC MHC BC)

Mass Meeting Study of the Appalachian South.
C7870

Appalachian Volunteer Reader.
D3260 (BC)

An Outline History of Appalachian America.
D3270 (BC ASU)

The Appalachian Mountain Log Book.
E1200

Roaming the Eastern Mountains.
F140 (ASU BC)

Provinical America, 1690-1740.
G3740

The Gatherers: The Gospel among the Highlanders.
G4610 (ASU LMC)

The Southern Appalachians.
H3880

The Southern Appalachians.
H3890 (ASU BC)

Folk-songs from the Southern Highlands.
H4790 (ASU LMC MHC ETSU BC)

Songs Sung in the Southern Appalachians.
H4800 (BC)

Still More Ballads and Folk-songs from the Southern Highlands.
H4810

The First West.
H4820 (ASU WCU MHC ETSU BC)

"Southern Mountain Folk Songs for American Schools."
H6440 (ASU)

Marthy Lou's Kiverlid.
H8780

"Marthy Lou's Kiverlid," a Sketch of Mountain Life.
H8790 (ASU)

"Marthy Lou's Kiverlid," a Sketch of Mountain Life.
H8800 (ASU)

Look to the Mountain Top.
I10

Easy to Follow Directions on How to Get Lost in the Land of the Sky.
J580 (WCU)

Appalachian Rivers.
J1610

Stream Sculpture on the Atlantic Slope: A Study in the Evolution of Appalachian Rivers.
J1630 (ASU LMC ETSU)

Topography and Geology of the Southern Appalachians.
K560

Our Southern Highlanders.
K1490 (ETSU BC ASU)

APP. MTNS.
Our Southern Highlanders: Narrative of Adventure in the Southern Appalachians and a Study of the Life Among the Mountaineers.
K1500 (BC ASU)
Our Southern Highlanders: Narrative of Adventure in the Southern Appalachians and a Study of the Life Among the Mountaineers.
K1510 (ASU WCU LMC)
Our Southern Highlanders: Narrative of Adventure in the Southern Appalachians and a Study of the Life Among the Mountaineers.
K1520 (ASU)
Our Southern Highlanders: A Narrative of Adventure in the Southern Appalachians and a Study of Life Among the Mountaineers.
K1530 (WWC)
Our Southern Highlanders: A Narrative of Adventure in the Southern Appalachians and a Study of the Life Among the Mountaineers.
K1540 (FC)
A Way of Life, Our Home in the Southern Appalachians.
K2520 (BC ETSU)
Adventures in the Wilds of the United States and British American Provinces.
L550 (LMC)
Letters from the Allegheny Mountains.
L560 (LMC ASU BC)
The Relation of the Southern Appalachian Mountains to Inland Water Navigation.
L1650 (BC ASU)
The Relation of the Southern Appalachian Mountains to the Development of Water Power.
L1660 (ASU BC)
L2770 (ASU MHC)
Clasping Hands with Generations Past.
L2960
Standards of Living in Four Southern Appalachian Mountain Counties. Farm Security Administration Social Research Report, no. 10.
L3430 (LMC ASU BC)
"Self-concepts of Appalachian Children: A Comparative Study of Economically Poor and Economically Disadvantaged Children Using the Piers-Harris Self-concept Inventory."
L3510 (LMC ASU)
"Inside Down Under Australia and New Zealand Development Characteristics Compared to West Virginia as a Part of the Appalachian Highlands, U. S. A."
L3920
Official Data on Western North Carolina's 223 Highest Mountain Peaks.
M770 (WCU)
The Southern Poor-white from Lubberland to Tobacco Road.
M1690 (ASU)
The Southern Poor-white from Lubberland to Tobacco Road.
M1700 (LMC)
Berryman Brown of Roanoke County, Virginia and Clinton Dade and Ozark Counties, Missouri.
M3720
Over the Blue Wall.
M4290 (BC ASU LMC ETSU WCU)
The Spirit of the Mountains.
M5440 (ASU BC WCU)
"The Appalachia of Wilma Dykeman's Fiction."
M7340
N2790 (MHC ASU)
American Regionalism.
O240
Southern Regions of the United States.
O250 (BC LMC MHC WWC)
The Way of the South: Toward the Regional Balance of America.
O260 (ASU LMC BC)
A Journey in the Back Country.
O580 (ASU LMC)
A Journey in the Back Country.
O590 (LMC)
A Journey in the Back Country.
O600 (BC LMC)
A Catalogue of the South.
O1040 (ASU)
My Mountains, My People.
P410 (ASU WWC UNCA)
Mountain Bred.
P420 (ASU LMC MHC WCU WWC)
Roaming the Mountains with John Parris.
P430 (ASU WCU LMC MHC ETSU WWC)
These Storied Mountains.
P440 (ASU ETSU MHC WCU WWC)
Life and Labor in the Old South.
P2690 (LMC BC FC)
Rural Southern Appalachia and Mass Society, and Overview.
P2780 (ASU LMC)
Appalachian Wilderness: The Great Smoky Mountains.
P3600 (UNCA BC ASU WCU ETSU)
Appalachian Wilderness: The Great Smoky Mountains.
P3610 (ASU BC)
The Southern Appalachian Region: Hitherto Untold Stories.
R1770 (ASU LMC)
Sense of Discovery: The Mountain.
R2700 (ASU LMC BC WCU)
Where Time Stood Still: A Portrait of Appalachia.
R2710 (ASU UNCA BC WCU MHC ETSU FC LMC WWC)
Sense of Discovery: The Mountain.
R3060 (ASU LMC WCU BC)
The Hill Billies.
R4110 (ASU BC)
Blue Ridge Breezes.
R4120 (LMC FC WCU BC)
Blue Ridge Breezes.
R4130 (ASU BC)
"A Strange Land and Peculiar People: The Discovery of Appalachia, 1870-1920."
S2250 (ASU LMC)
The South Old and New.
S3580 (BC)
The Mountaineer, A New Edition.
S6110
Echoes of a Passing Era (Down Memories Lane).
S7030 (LMC BC)
Regionalism and Beyond: Essays of Randall Stewart.
S7340 (ASU)
Mainstreams of Mountain Thought; Attitudes of Selected Figures in the Heart of the Appalachian South.
T730 (ASU)
The Highlanders of the South.
T8330 (ASU ETSU BC LMC)
Appalachia: The Mountains, the Place, and the People.
T8920 (ASU LMC MHC BC ETSU)
A World of Green Hills: Observation of Nature and Human Nature in the Blue Ridge.
T8980 (ASU LMC BC)
Appalachian Data Book.
U160 (UNCA)
Message From the President of the United States Transmitting a Report of the Secretary of Agriculture in Relation to the Forests, Rivers, and Mountains of the Southern Appalachian Region.
U2510 (UNCA ASU ETSU)
Appalachia — Rebirth of a Region.
U2900 (ETSU)
Highland Heritage: The Southern Mountains and the Nation.
W5380
The Heart of the Alleghenies: Or, Western North Carolina. Comprising Its Topography, History, Resources, People, Narratives, Incidents, and Pictures of Travel, Adventures in Hunting and Fishing and Legends of Its Wildernesses.
Z40 (ASU LMC WCU BC ETSU)

APP. MTNS. — ALA.
Man on a Mountain.
B1290 (BC)
Geography of the Great Appalachian Valley of Alabama.
G2090 (BC ASU)

APP. MTNS. — ALTITUDE
Dictionary of Altitude in the U. S.
G260

APP. MTNS. — DESCRIPTION AND TRAVEL
C8050
Camping Around the Appalachian Mountains.
C8470 (ASU)
Southern Appalachian Region.
I880
Appalachia Meets the Potomac.
I900
Travels to the West of the Allegheny Mountains. . .
M5330 (ASU BC)
"Westerners at Home: Comments of French and British Travelers on life in the West, 1800-1840."
P110
The Great Smokies and the Blue Ridge: The Story of the Southern Appalachians.
P1500 (WCU ASU LMC ETSU MHC WWC)

APP. MTNS. — DESCRIPTION AND TRAVEL — EARLY TRAVELLERS
The History of Travel Into Virginia Britania (1612).
S7730 (ASU)

APP. MTNS. — EARLY TRAVELLERS ACCOUNTS
Final Report of the United States De Soto Expedition Commission.
S9480

APP. MTNS. — GA.
Highlights of the Economy of the Georgia Mountains Area.
G1010 (BC ASU)
"An Experimental and Field Study of North Georgia Mountaineers."
J2440 (ASU)
Factors Influencing Recent Industrial Growth in Northeastern Georgia.
N2820 (ASU)
Highlights of the Economy of the Georgia Mountains Area.
W5510

APP. MTNS. — HISTORY
Gone Are the Days: An Illustrated History of the Old South.
K130 (MHC)

APP. MTNS. — KY.
Geography of the Mountains of Eastern Kentucky.
D960 (BC ASU)
The Feuds in the Cumberland Mountains.
H7630
Yearbook.
K1320
The Land of Saddle-bags: A Study of the Mountain People of Appalachia.
R130 (BC ASU ETSU WWC)
The Land of Saddle-bags: A Study of the Mountain People of Appalachia.
R140 (LMC MHC WCU)
Saddlebag Folk: The Way of Life in the Kentucky Mountains.
R160 (BC ASU LMC ETSU)

APP. MTNS. — ME.
The Length and Breadth of Maine.
A5450

APP. MTNS. — MT. MITCHELL
Mount Mitchell and Dr. Elisha Mitchell.
W2040

APP. MTNS. — N. C.
Our Carolina Highlanders.
B6370 (ASU WCU)
Measurements of the Black Mountains.
C5070
Mitchell's Peak and Dr. Mitchell.
C8420 (ASU LMC)
Measurements of Points in North Carolina and Tennessee.
G5000
Notes on the Geography of the Mountain District of Western North Carolina.
G5010
A Preliminary Check-list of the Ligneous Flora of the Highland Region, North Carolina.
H2050 (ASU)
Southern Appalachian Highlanders of Western North Carolina.
H7240
The Southern Highlands Mountain Resources Management Plan.
N2480
"Folklore of the North Carolina Mountaineers."
P240

APP. MTNS. — OHIO
A Plan for Development of Ohio Appalachia.
H8530 (ASU)

APP. MTNS. — RECREATION AND TOURISM
Camping Around the Appalachian Mountains.
C8470 (ASU)
APP. MTNS. — S. C.
A History of the Upper Country of South Carolina.
L3070 (LMC BC)
A History of the Upper Country of South Carolina: From the Earliest Periods to the Close of the War of Independence.
L3080 (ASU WCU LMC)
APP. MTNS. — SOUTHERN
A Photographic Documentary of the Blue Ridge Mountains.
J480 (LMC)
APP. MTNS. — TENN.
Measurements of Points in North Carolina and Tennessee.
G5000
K2920
APP. MTNS. — UNAKA MTNS.
In the Shadow of Big Bald: About the Appalachians and Their People.
A1230 (ETSU)
The Wonders of the Unakas in Unicoi County.
A1280 (ETSU ASU LMC)
APP. MTNS. — VA.
G4770
The Shenandoah Valley and Virginia, 1861 to 1865: A War Study.
K620 (ASU BC)
APP. MTNS. — VT. — WHITE MTNS.
A Bibliography of the White Mountain.
B3020
APP. MTNS. — W. VA.
"West Virginia's Appalachia Participation."
S6160
APP. — N. C.
Appalachian Regional Commission.
A3070 (ASU MHC)
APP. — N. Y.
New York State Appalachian Development Plan; A Twenty Year Plan for the Fourteen Counties of the New York Appalachian Region.
N700
APP. — OHIO
Ohio Appalachia Regional Community Study.
P2590 (ASU)
APP. PEOPLE
A2170 (ASU BC)
A Search for Appalachian People.
A5600
Appalachians Speak Up.
B3350 (BC)
Resources and People in East Kentucky: Problems and Potentials of a Lagging Economy.
B5790 (ASU WCU LMC ETSU BC)
Annihilating the Hillbilly: The Appalachians' Struggle with America's Institutions.
B6350
Our Carolina Highlanders.
B6370 (ASU WCU)
"The Mountain People of the South: A Sociological Study."
B7130 (WCU)
"The Evolution of Southern Appalachian Culture as Evidenced in Folklore."
B8850 (ETSU)
"A Classification of Mountain Whites."
C930
The Southern Appalachian Heritage.
C2041
"The Southern Poor Whites 1800-1869, with Particular Reference to Kentucky and Tennessee."
C6490 (ASU)
The Southern Highlands: An Inquiry into Their Needs, and Qualifications Desired in Church, Educational, and Social Service Workers in the Mountain Country.
C7960 (BC ASU)
The Mountain People in Eastern Kentucky.
D2110
"A Population Study of the Appalachian Members of the Freshman Class at Morehead (Kentucky) State University, 1967-1968."
D3090
Our Land Too.
D3890 (ASU BC WCU)
The Appalachian Mountain Log Book.
E1200
"South Appalachian Mississippian."
F610 (WCU BC)
Grandfather's Land: We Are Mountain People.
F1310 (WCU)
The Gatherers: The Gospel among the Highlanders.
G4610 (ASU LMC)
Southern Forests and Southern People.
H1650 (LMC)
Mountain People, Mountain Crafts.
H7320 (ASU)
H7880
Poverty, Rural Poverty and Minority Groups Living in Rural Poverty, an Annotated Bibliography.
I870
Hillbilly Women.
K20 (ASU BC UNCA)
Our Southern Highlanders.
K1490 (ETSU BC ASU)
Our Southern Highlanders: Narrative of Adventure in the Southern Appalachians and a Study of the Life Among the Mountaineers.
K1500 (BC ASU)
Our Southern Highlanders: Narrative of Adventure in the Southern Appalachians and a Study of the Life Among the Mountaineers.
K1510 (ASU WCU LMC)
Our Southern Highlanders: Narrative of Adventure in the Southern Appalachians and a Study of the Life Among the Mountaineers.
K1520 (ASU)
Our Southern Highlanders: A Narrative of Adventure in the Southern Appalachians and a Study of Life Among the Mountaineers.
K1530 (WWC)
Our Southern Highlanders: A Narrative of Adventure in the Southern Appalachians and a Study of the Life Among the Mountaineers.
K1540 (FC)
"Southern White Laborers in Chicago's West Side."
K1940 (ASU)
A Way of Life, Our Home in the Southern Appalachians.
K2520 (BC ETSU)
"A Rorschach Comparison of Adult Male Personality in Big Cove, Cherokee, North Carolina, and 'Henry's Branch', Kentucky."
K3440
Adventures in the Wilds of the United States and British American Provinces.
L550 (LMC)
Letters from the Allegheny Mountains.
L560 (LMC ASU BC)
People of Coal Town.
L600 (ASU BC WWC WCU)
People of Coal Town.
L610 (LMC)
"The Southern Mountaineer in Fiction."
L2220 (ASU)
L2770 (ASU MHC)
Clasping Hands with Generations Past.
L2960
"Self-concepts of Appalachian Children: A Comparative Study of Economically Poor and Economically Disadvantaged Children Using the Piers-Harris Self-concept Inventory."
L3510 (LMC ASU)
"Inside Down Under Australia and New Zealand Development Characteristics Compared to West Virginia as a Part of the Appalachian Highlands, U. S. A."
L3920
Nativism in Kentucky in 1860.
M1370 (ASU)
The Southern Poor-white from Lubberland to Tobacco Road.
M1690 (ASU)
The Southern Poor-white from Lubberland to Tobacco Road.
M1700 (LMC)
Berryman Brown of Roanoke County, Virginia and Clinton Dade and Ozark Counties, Missouri.
M3720
List of References on the Mountain Whites.
M5260
The Frontier Mind: A Cultural Analysis of the Kentucky Frontiersman.
M6830 (ASU BC ETSU UNCA)
The Frontier Mind.
M6840 (ASU WCU)
The Frontier Mind: A Cultural Analysis of the Kentucky Frontiersman.
M6850
Southern Character Sketches.
M7190 (ASU WCU)
"Aesthetic Attitudes and Values of Selected Appalachian Youths."
M7800
Down to Earth-People of Appalachia.
M9100
The Influence of the Physiographic Features of Western North Carolina on the Settlement and Development of the Region.
N1400 (ASU)
Dry Ridge: Some of Its History, Some of Its People.
P2830 (LMC ASU)
The Southern Highlanders of America.
P3670 (BC ASU)
The Hill Billies.
R4110 (ASU BC)
"A Strange Land and Peculiar People: The Discovery of Appalachia, 1870-1920."
S2250 (ASU LMC)
Cabins in the Laurel.
S2810 (ASU MHC LMC WCU ETSU WWC BC FC UNCA)
Cabins in the Laurel.
S2820 (FC ASU)
Hollow Folk.
S2940 (BC LMC ETSU WWC)
Hollow Folk.
S2950 (ASU)
Down by the Riverside.
S4440
The Men of the Mountains: The Story of the Southern Mountaineer and His Kin of the Piedmont. With an Account of Some of the Agencies of Progress among Them.
S5970 (ASU ETSU LMC)
The Mountaineer, A New Edition.
S6110
Mainstreams of Mountain Thought; Attitudes of Selected Figures in the Heart of the Appalachian South.
T730 (ASU)
Blue Ridge Country.
T7900 (FC WWC ETSU BC ASU)
Blue Ridge Country.
T7910 (ASU WCU LMC)
The Highlanders of the South.
T8330 (ASU ETSU BC LMC)
Appalachia: The Mountains, the Place, and the People.
T8920 (ASU LMC MHC BC ETSU)
A World of Green Hills: Observation of Nature and Human Nature in the Blue Ridge.
T8980 (ASU LMC BC)
The Appalachian Photographs of Doris Ulmann. Remembrance by John Jacob Niles.
U40 (ASU LMC ETSU FC MHC WCU WWC BC)
References on the Mountaineers of the Southern Appalachians.
U2520
V1320 (BC)
A Right Good People.
W940 (ASU)
Pioneers of Destiny: The Romance of the Appalachian People.
W1930 (LMC BC)
Students in Appalachia.
W1970 (ETSU)
Yesterday's People: Life in Contemporary Appalachia.
W2490 (UNCA ASU WCU MHC LMC ETSU WWC FC BC)
Romantic Appalachia; Or Poverty Pays If You Aren't Poor.
W2980
Sketches of Our Mountain Pioneers.
W3080 (BC)
The Older West Virginian.
W3270
Highland Heritage: The Southern Mountains and the Nation.
W5380
The Southern Mountaineers.
W7520 (ASU ETSU MHC WWC BC)
The Southern Mountaineers.
W7530 (ASU LMC)

APP. PEOPLE
The Kentucky Mountaineer: A Study of Four Counties in Southeastern Kentucky.
W8540
"The Kentucky Mountaineer: A Study of Four Counties in Southeastern Kentucky."
W8550 (ASU)
The Older Appalachians of the South.
W9400
Virginia Germans.
W9810
Wartburg: Dream and Reality of the New Germany in Tennessee.
W9820
The Heart of the Alleghenies: Or, Western North Carolina. Comprising Its Topography, History, Resources, People, Narratives, Incidents, and Pictures of Travel, Adventures in Hunting and Fishing and Legends of Its Wildernesses.
Z40 (ASU LMC WCU BC ETSU)
Zirkle Family in America, Germany to America.
Z130
APP. PEOPLE — CHILDREN
Children of Appalachia.
S3270 (ASU ETSU MHC BC)
APP. PEOPLE — GA.
"An Experimental and Field Study of North Georgia Mountaineers."
J2440 (ASU)
APP. PEOPLE — KY.
History Records of Harlan County, Kentucky, People.
B9070 (BC)
The Kentucky Highlanders from a Native Mountaineers Viewpoint.
C6140 (BC ASU)
Employment Problems of the Eastern Kentucky Mountain People.
F1990
The Southern Mountaineer.
F2890
The Mountain People of Kentucky. An Account of Present Conditions with the Attitude of the People toward Improvement.
H1490 (ASU BC)
An Experimental Study of the East Kentucky Mountaineers: A Study in Heredity and Environment.
H5680 (ETSU BC ASU)
"The Settlement of the Kentucky Appalachian Highlands."
M480 (ASU BC)
Life Among the Hills and Mountains of Kentucky.
T8080 (ASU BC)
APP. PEOPLE — N. C.
Interdisciplinary Cultural Heritage Program.
B8640 (WCU)
Southern Appalachian Highlanders of Western North Carolina.
H7240
APP. PEOPLE — VA.
"The Mountain People of Virginia: Their Nature and Their Needs."
D160 (ASU)
"The Mountain People of Virginia: Their Nature and Their Needs."
D170 (ASU)
The Southern Mountaineer.
F2890
P1080
APP. PEOPLE — W. VA.
Teacher's Manual for West Virginia: The State and Its People.
R1980
West Virginia: The State and Its People.
R1990 (ASU)
APP. REGIONAL COMMISSION
The Appalachian Regional Commission, Educational Advisory Committee Interim Report.
A1690
A2650 (ASU MHC LMC)
Code.
A3710 (WCU ASU)
Current Regional Reports.
A3720
Guidelines for Funding Appalachian Projects, Development Districts, and Research.
A3740 (ASU)
Guidelines for Funding Appalachian Projects, Development Districts and Research.
A3750 (ASU)
New Directions: Executive Director's Semi-annual Report, January 1-June 30, 1971.
A3770
Report.
A3800 (ETSU ASU WCU BC)
Summary Report.
A3850 (ASU)
Appalachian — Education for Tomorrow.
A3910 (ASU)
Interim Report.
A3930 (ASU LMC BC)
Experiment in Regional Federalism: Implementation of the Appalachian Regional Development Act of 1965 in Georgia, North Carolina, and Tennessee.
C1300
C8810 (ASU WCU BC)
A Review of the Appalachian Regional Commission Program.
H1690 (ASU)
I100 (ASU)
I110 (ASU)
I120 (ASU)
I130 (ASU)
Guidelines for an Appalachian Airport System.
M2980
Catalog of ARC Section 302B Research and Demonstration Projects.
O310 (ASU)
Appalachia.
P4340 (ASU)
Program Budgeting for Planners; A Case Study of Appalachia With Projections Through 1985.
R4040
"The Appalachian Regional Commission: Selected Aspects of Institutions and Processes and Their Relationship to Natural and Human Resources Development."
S40
A Report to the Area-Redevelopment Administration; U. S. Department of Commerce on a Model for an Appalachian Regional Commission.
S9790
Tennessee Appalachian Development Plan, 1969-1970.
T1600 (ASU)
Appalachian Regional Development Act, 1965-; Rationale and Model for Application in Tennessee.
T1770
Report on First Year's Activities in the Appalachian Development Program.
T1780 (LMC)
"Southern Appalachian State Newspapers' Treatment of the Antipoverty and Appalachia Acts."
T8020
Appalachian Regional Development Act, 1967.
U1650
Appalachian Regional Development Act of 1965.
U1670
Appalachian Regional Development Act, 1967.
U1680
Consideration of H. R. 11946. Report to Accompany H. Res. 861, Aug. 20, 1964.
U1960
Appalachian Regional Development Act of 1964. Hearings before the Ad Hoc Subcommittee on Appalachian Regional Development of the Committee on Public Works on H. R. 11065 and H. R. 11066, May 5-June 11, 1964, to Provide Public Works and Economic Development Programs and the Planning and Coordination Needed to Assist in the Development of the Appalachian Region.
U1970
Appalachian Regional Development Act of 1964: Report to Accompany H. R. 11946, July 31, 1964.
U1980
Appalachian Regional Development Act of 1965: Report to Accompany S. 3, February 17, 1965.
U1990
Appalachian Regional Development Act of 1964. Report Together with Minority Views to Accompany S. 2782, Aug. 13, 1964.
U2000
Appalachian Regional Development Act of 1964. Hearings on S. 2782, a Bill to Provide Public Works and Economic Development Programs and the Planning Coordination Needed to Assist in the Development of the Appalachian Region, June 22-26, 1964.
U2010
Section-by-section Analysis of H. R. 11065 and H. R. 11066: Appalachian Regional Development Act of 1964 as Submitted in Draft to the Committee, April 29, 1964.
U2020
Proposed Appropriation for Appalachian Regional Commission, Fiscal Year 1965. Sept. 29, 1964.
U2030
War on Poverty: The Economic Opportunity Act of 1964. A Compilation of Materials Relevant to S. 2642, Prepared for the Select Subcommittee, July 23, 1964.
U2040
Authorizing Printing of Additional Copies of Hearings by Committee on Public Works on Appalachian Regional Development Act of 1965. Report from Committee on House Administration to Accompany H. Res. 724. June 2, 1966.
U2050
Authorizing Printing of Additional Copies of Committee Print 1 of Committee on Public Works on Section-by-section Analysis of H. R. 4, Appalachian Regional Development Act of 1965, and Difference between H. R. 4 (89th Cong.), and H. R. 11946 (88th Cong.) as Reported to House of Representatives and S. 2782 (88th Cong.) as Passed by Senate. Report from Committee on House Administration to Accompany H. Res. 722. June 2, 1966.
U2060
Supplemental Estimates of Appropriations for Various Agencies for Fiscal Year 1965 to Finance Appalachian Regional Development Act of 1965. Mar. 15, 1965.
U2070
Examination of the War on Poverty Program. Hearings before the Subcommittee on the War on Poverty Program, April 12-30, 1965.
U2100
Appalachian Regional Development Act of 1965: Report to Accompany S. 3.
U2110 (ETSU)
Highlights of Appalachian Regional Development Act of 1965, Mar. 10, 1965.
U2120
Section-by-section Analysis of H. R. 4: Appalachian Regional Development Act of 1965, and Differences between H. R. 4 (89th Congress) and H. R. 11946 (88th Congress), as Reported to the House of Representatives, and S. 2782 (88th Congress) as Passed by the Senate.
U2130
Appalachian Regional Development Act of 1965. Hearings on H. R. 4 and S. 3, February 3-5, 1965.
U2140
Authorizing Printing for Use of Committee on Public Works of Additional Copies of Its Hearings on Appalachian Regional Development Act of 1965 (S.3). Report from Committee on Rules and Administration to Accompany S. Res. 208. Feb. 16, 1966.
U2150
Appalachian Regional Development Act of 1965. Hearings on S. 3, January 19 and 21, 1965.
U2170
Appalachian Regional Development Act of 1965: Report, Together with Individual Views, to Accompany S. 3, January 27, 1965.
U2180
Appalachian Regional Development Act, 1965, Communication from President of United States Transmitting Recommendation that Congress Extend Appalachian Regional Development Act of 1965. Jan. 23, 1967.
U2190
Appalachian Regional Development Act Amendments of 1967. Conference Report to Accompany S. 602. Sept. 26, 1967.
U2200

APP. REGIONAL COMMISSION

Appalachian Regional Development Act Amendments of 1967, and Amendments to Public Works and Economic Development Act of 1965.
U2210

Appalachian Regional Development Act, 1967. Hearings on H. R. 4446 and Related Bills, May 9-July 12, 1967.
U2220 (ASU ETSU)

Nomination of Joe W. Fleming II to be Federal Co-chairman of the Appalachian Regional Commission Hearing, Feb. 7, 1967.
U2240

Nomination of Meriwether Lewis Clark Tyler to be Alternate Federal Co-chairman of the Appalachian Regional Commission. Hearing, March 21, 1968.
U2250

Revising and Extending Appalachian Regional Development Act of 1965, and Amending Title 5 to Public Works and Economic Development Act of 1965. Report Together with Supplemental Views, to Accompany S. 602. April 6, 1967.
U2260

Appalachian Regional Development Act Amendments of 1967 Hearings on S. 602, Jan. 24-Feb. 3, 1967.
U2270 (ASU)

Appalachian and Regional Action Planning Commissions. Report.
U2310

Nominations of Federal Cochairmen of Regional Economic Development Commissions. Hearing on Nominations of John B. Waters, Jr., to be Federal Cochairman of the Appalachian Regional Commission, W. Donald Brewer to be Federal Cochairman of the Four Corners Regional Commission, G. Fred Steele to be Federal Cochairman of the Coastal Plains Regional Commission, Stewart Lamprey to be Federal Cochairman of the New England Regional Commission, and E. L. Stewart to be Federal Cochairman of the Ozarks Regional Commission, March 25, 1969.
U2350

Nomination of Orville H. Lerch for Alternative Cochairman, Appalachian Regional Commission. Hearing, July 15, 1969.
U2360

Regional Economic Development Legislation. Extension and Revision of Appalachian Regional Development Act of 1965, as Amended, and of Titles 1-5 of Public Works and Economic Development Act of 1965, as Amended.
U2370

Public Works Acceleration Act. Public Works and Economic Development Act, Appalachian Regional Development Act Extensions. Conference Report to Accompany S. 575, June 2, 1971.
U2380

Public Works Acceleration Act. Public Works and Economic Development Act, and Appalachian Regional Development Act Extensions Report with Minority and supplemental Views, 92d Congress, 1st session, on H. R. 5376, March 29, 1971.
U2390

Public Works and Economic Development Act and Appalachian Regional Development Act Extensions. Report to Accompany H. R. 9922, July 21, 1971.
U2400

Appalachian Regional Development Act Amendments of 1971. Hearings on H. R. 5376 and Related Bills, March 15-17, 1971.
U2410

Public Works Acceleration Act. Public Works and Economic Development Act, and Appalachian Regional Development Act Extensions. Conference Report to Accompany S. 575, June 1, 1971.
U2420

Appalachian Regional Development Act Amendments of 1971. Report Together with Individual Views to Accompany S. 575, March 9, 1971.
U2450

Public Works and Economic Development Act and Appalachian Regional Development Act Extensions. Report to Accompany S. 2317, July 20, 1971.
U2460

Appalachian Regional Development Act of 1971. Hearings on S. 575, February 8-10, 1971.
U2480

Economic Development, Project Activity Supplement.
U2700

Highway Program Shows Limited Progress toward Increasing Accessibility to and through Appalachia: Report to the Congress on the Appalachian Regional Commission by the Comptroller General of the United States.
U3060

Appalachian Region as Designated by the Appalachian Regional Commission, 1965.
U3090

Examination of the War on Poverty Program.
U3440

Poverty in the United States.
U3450

An act to provide public work and economic development programs and the planning and coordination needed to assist in development of the Appalachian Region.
U3460

An act to provide public work & economic development programs & the planning & coordination needed to assist in development of the App. Region.
U3470

H. R. 10090, Act Making Appropriations for Public Works for Water and Power Development, Including Corps of Engineers, Civil, Bureau of Reclamation, Bonneville Power Administration, and Other Power Agencies of Department of Interior, Appalachian Regional Commission, Federal Power Commission, Tennessee Valley Authority, Atomic Energy Commission, and Related Independent Agencies and Commissions for Fiscal Year 1972, and for Other Purposes.
U3510

H. R. 15586, Act Making Appropriations for Public Works for Water and Power Development, Including Corps of Engineers — Civil, Bureau of Reclamation, Bonneville Power Administration, and Other Power Agencies of the Department of Interior, Appalachian Regional Development Programs, Federal Power Commission, Tennessee Valley Authority, Atomic Energy Commission, and Related Independent Agencies and Commissions for Fiscal Year 1973, and for Other Purposes. Approved August 25, 1972.
U3520

S. 3, Act to Provide Public Works and Economic Development Programs and Planning and Coordination Needed to Assist in Development of Appalachian Region. Approved Mar. 9, 1965.
U3530 (ETSU)

S. 602, Act to Revise and extend Appalachian Regional Development Act of 1965, and to Amend Public Works and Economic Development Act of 1965. Approved October 11, 1967.
U3550

S. 2317, Act to Extend Public Works and Economic Development Act of 1965 and Appalachian Regional Development Act of 1965. Approved Aug. 5, 1971.
U3560 (ETSU)

Should the Federal Government Establish a National Program of Public Work for the Unemployed? Selected Excerpts and References Relating to the National College Debate Topic, 1964-65.
U3610

A Nation Aroused, 1st Annual Report.
U3760

Poverty Program Information, as of January 1, 1966.
U3770

War on Poverty Projects, March 31, 1965.
U3790

War on Poverty Projects, April 30, 1965. .
U3800

Strengthening Labor's Role in the War on Poverty: Labor Leadership for Community Action in Appalachia. Report of CAP 66-9205 to the Office of E. O.
U3810

Strengthening labor's role in the War on Poverty: labor leadership training for community action in Appalachia; a report of CAP 66-9205 to the Office of Economic Opportunity, by Frederick A. Zeller, Project Director; Robert W. Miller, Associate Project Director.
U3820

Recreation Potential in the Appalachian Highlands: A Market Analysis.
U4220 (ASU)

APP. TRAIL

Walking in the Clouds.
A380 (ETSU ASU)

The Appalachian Trail.
A4120

The Appalachian Trail: A Mountain Footpath — A National Scenic Trail.
A4130 (LMC ETSU)

The Appalachian Trail.
A4140 (ETSU)

The Appalachian Trail: A Footpath Through the Wilderness for More Than 2,000 Miles from Katahdin in Maine to Springer Mountain in Georgia.
A4150 (ASU)

The Appalachian Trail: A Mountain Footpath, a National Scenic Trail.
A4160 (ASU)

Appalachian Trail Conference, Undertaking the Appalachian Trail (A Mountain Foot-path from Maine to Georgia. . . .
A4170 (ASU)

Guide to the Appalachian Trail in Central and Southwestern Virginia.
A4180 (BC LMC ASU)

Guide to the Appalachian Trail in the Great Smokies, the Nantahalas, and Georgia.
A4190 (LMC BC)

Guide to the Appalachian Trail in the Great Smokies, the Nantahalas, and Georgia.
A4200 (ASU BC)

Guide to the Appalachian Trail in the Great Smokies, the Nantahalas, and Georgia.
A4210 (ASU)

Guide to the Appalachian Trail in the Southern Appalachians.
A4250 (ASU BC)

Guide to the Appalachian Trail in the Southern Appalachians.
A4260 (ASU)

Guide to the Appalachian Trail in the Southern Appalachians.
A4270 (ASU)

Guide to the Appalachian Trail in Tennessee and North Carolina, Cherokee, Pisgah, and the Great Smokies.
A4280 (LMC)

Guide to the Appalachian Trail in Tennessee and North Carolina: Cherokee, Pisgah, and Great Smokies.
A4290

Guide to the Appalachian Trail in Tennessee and North Carolina, Cherokee, Pisgah, and Great Smokies.
A4300 (ETSU)

Guide to the Appalachian Trail in Tennessee and North Carolina, Cherokee, Pisgah, and Great Smokies.
A4310 (ASU)

Guide to the Southern Appalachians. The Appalachian Trail from Virginia-Tennessee Line to Mt. Oglethorpe, Ga.
A4320 (ASU BC)

Plans for an Appalachian Trail Lean-to. . .
A4330 (ASU)

Suggestions for Appalachian Trail Users.
A4340

Suggestions for Appalachian Trail Users.
A4350

Suggestions for Appalachian Trail Users.
A4360

Trail Manual for the Appalachian Trail.
A4370 (ASU)

Trail Manual for the Appalachian Trail.
A4380

Trail Manual for the Appalachian Trail.
A4390 (ASU)

APP. TRAIL
Trail Manual for Appalachian Trail.
A4400
Trail Manual for the Appalachian Trail.
A4410
Arnold Guyot's Notes on the Geography of the Mountain District of Western North Carolina.
A5740
Campfires Along the Appalachian Trail.
B650 (ASU LMC WCU BC)
The Appalachian Trail.
F1200 (BC ASU FC WWC ETSU MHC)
Appalachian Hiker: Adventure of a Lifetime.
G520 (BC ASU WCU ETSU)
G4650
G4660
G4670
G4680
G4690
G4700
G4710
G4720
G4730
G4740
G4750
G4760
Guide to the Appalachian Trail in Pennsylvania: From the Maryland Line to the Delaware Water Gap---222.4 Miles.
K1860 (ETSU)
Guide to the Appalachian Trail in New York and New Jersey.
N680 (ASU)
Guide to Paths in the Blue Ridge: The Appalachian Trail and Side Trails in Southern Pennsylvania, Maryland, and Virginia.
P3820 (ASU)
Guide to Paths in the Blue Ridge: The Appalachian Trail and Side Trails in Southern Pennsylvania, Maryland, and Virginia.
P3830 (ASU)
Guide to the Appalachian Trail and Side Trails in the Shenandoah National Park.
P3840 (ETSU)
Guide to the Appalachian Trail: From the Susquehanna River to the Shenandoah National Park.
P3850 (WCU ETSU LMC)
Guide to the Appalachian Trail in Central and Southwestern Virginia.
P3860
Guide to the Appalachian Trail: Susquehanna River to the Shenandoah National Park.
P3870
Guide to Trails in the Shenandoah National Park: The Appalachian Trail and Side Trails.
P3880
Hiking, Camping, Mountaineering and Trailclearing Equipment.
P3890 (ASU)
The Appalachian Trail; Wilderness on the Doorstep.
S9300 (ASU)
The Appalachian Trail: Wilderness on the Doorstep.
S9310 (ASU WCU LMC ETSU FC WWC UNCA BC)
The Appalachian Trail. Hearing on S. 622, September 16, 1965.
U2160 (LMC)
Nationwide System of Trails. Hearings before the Committee on S. 827, March 15 and 16, 1967.
U2230 (LMC)

APP. TRAIL — ME.
Guide to the Appalachian Trail in Maine. . .
A4220
Guide to the Appalachian Trail in Maine; the Route of the Appalachian Trail in Maine. . .
A4230
Guide to the Appalachian Trail in Maine. . .
A4240

APP. — VA.
Appalachian Regional Commission.
A3090 (ASU MHC)

APP. — VOLUNTEERS
Papers.
A3050

APPALACHIA REGIONAL DEVELOPMENT ACT
"The State Development Planning Process: Implementation of the Appalachian Regional Development Act of 1965 in West Virginia."
P850

APPALACHIAN REGIONAL COMMISSION
The Appalachian Regional Development Program.
R3900 (ASU)

ARCHAEOLOGIST — TENN.
Ten Years of the Tennessee Archaeologist: Selected Subjects.
T930 (ETSU)

ARCHAEOLOGY
The Mound Builders.
A1820 (BC)
A Bibliography of Kentucky Archaeology.
B5810 -
"The Pisgah Culture and Its Place in the Prehistory of the Southern Appalachians."
D2090 (ASU WWC WCU)
Hiwassee Island, an Archaeological Account of Four Tennessee Indian Peoples.
L2270 (ETSU ASU WCU LMC BC)
Tribes That Slumber: Indians of the Tennessee Region.
L2300 (ETSU)
An Archeological Survey of Rickwick Basin in the Adjacent Portions of the States of Alabama, Mississippi, and Tennessee.
W2070
The Adena People, no. 2.
W2080 (MHC)
An Archaeological Survey of Guntersville Basin on the Tennessee River in Northern Alabama.
W2090 (LMC BC)
An Archaeological Survey of the Norris Basin in Eastern Tennessee.
W2100 (BC)
Indian Knoll.
W2110
The Prehistoric Men of Kentucky.
Y220 (BC)

ARCHAEOLOGY — APP.
Prehistoric Races of the United States of America.
F2330 (ASU)
Archaeology of Eastern United States.
G4190 (WCU)
Annual Report of the Secretary of the Smithsonian Institution, 1879-80.
U380
Anthropological Papers.
U390 (BC)
Bulletin.
U400 (WCU)
Fifth Annual Report of the Bureau of Ethnology to the Secretary of the Smithsonian Institution, 1883-84.
U410 (ASU)
Index to Bulletins 1-100 of the Bureau of American Ethnology; with index to Contributions to North American ethnology.
U420 (WCU)
Reports.
U430 (BC)
Seventh annual report of the Bureau of Ethnology to the secretary of the Smithsonian Institution, 1885-86.
U440 (ASU)

ARCHAEOLOGY — GA.
The Cherokee Nation: Fort Mountain, Vann House, Chester Inns, New Echota.
A1550 (ASU BC)
Short Contributions to the Geology, Geography, and Archaeology of Georgia.
G920 (ETSU)
The Paleozoic Group: The Geology of Ten Counties of Northwestern Georgia.
G1020 (BC ASU)
P2550

ARCHAEOLOGY — MD.
Cetothere Skeletons from the Miocene Choptank Formation of Maryland and Virginia.
K610 (ETSU)

ARCHAEOLOGY — N. C.
Certain Mounds in Haywood County, North Carolina.
H5140 (ASU)
"An Archaeological Survey of Transylvania County, North Carolina."
H6490 (WCU)

ARCHAEOLOGY — TENN.
Pre-historic Man in Tennessee. The Problem Solved. A Centennial Booklet.
B4650
"Archaeological Investigations in the Tims Ford Reservation, Tennessee, 1966."
F300 (ETSU)
The Excavation and Interpretation of the Old Stone Fort, Coffee County, Tennessee.
F310 (ASU)
Excavations in Nickajack Reservoir: Season I.
F320 (ETSU)
The Old Stone Fort: Exploring an Archaeological Mystery.
F330 (ASU LMC BC)
Archaeological Investigations in the Tellico Reservoir: Interim Report, 1970.
G2110 (ASU ETSU)
Cherokee and Earlier Remains on Upper Tennessee River.
H2610 (BC LMC)
Explorations of the Aboriginal Remains of Tennessee.
J2420 (ASU BC)
Annotations Pertaining to Prehistoric Research in Tennessee.
L2240
Eva, an Archaic Site.
L2250 (BC ASU WCU ETSU)
The First Tennesseans; an Interpretation of Tennessee Prehistory.
L2260
The Prehistory of the Chickamauga Basin in Tennessee, a Preview.
L2280
Tribes That Slumber: Indian Times in the Tennessee Region.
L2290 (ASU LMC WCU MHC BC)
Aboriginal Sites on Tennessee River.
M7080
T920 (ETSU)
The Antiquities of Tennessee and the Adjacent States, and the State of Aboriginal Society in the Scale of Civilization Represented by Them.
T8460 (LMC ASU)

ARCHAEOLOGY — VA.
Evidence of Indian Occupancy in Albemarle County, Virginia.
B9340 (BC)
An Archaeological Survey of Southwest Virginia.
H6560 (ASU WCU ETSU BC)
Cetothere Skeletons from the Miocene Choptank Formation of Maryland and Virginia.
K610 (ETSU)

ARCHAEOLOGY — W. VA.
Second Preliminary Report: The St. Albans Site, Kanawha County, West Virginia, 1964-1968.
B7540 (ASU)
A Guide to the Common Fossils Plants of W. Va.
G1640
Plant Fossils of West Virginia.
G1650 (BC ETSU)
West Virginia Geology, Archaeology, and Pedology: A Bibliography and Index.
G1660 (BC ETSU)
Biological and Archaeological Analysis of Bones from a 17th Century Indian Village (46 PU 31), Putnam County, West Virginia.
G4810 (ASU)
Archaeological Excavations on Virginius Island, Harpers Ferry National Historic Park, 1966-1968.
H1570
Archeological Survey of the Rowlesburg Reservoir Area, West Virginia.
J720 (ASU)
Selected Archeological and Historical Sites in West Virginia; Preliminary Plan for Development.
W5170

ARCHEOLOGY
COPENA: A Tennessee Valley Middle Woodland Culture.
W670

ARCHEOLOGY — APP.
The Mound-Builders; a Reconstruction of the Life of a Prehistoric American Race, through Exploration and Interpretation of Their Earth Mounds, Their Burials, and Their Cultural Remains.
S3050

ARCHEOLOGY — APP.
"The Cherokees Probably Mound Builders."
T7780
ARCHEOLOGY — GA.
Exploration of the Etowah Site in Georgia.
M7370 (ASU)
ARCHEOLOGY — KY.
Conceptions of Kentucky Prehistory: A Case Study in the History of Archeology.
S1220 (ASU BC)
ARCHEOLOGY — N. C.
Peachtree Mound and Village Site, Cherokee County, North Carolina.
S2000 (ASU LMC UNCA)
ARCHEOLOGY — TENN.
Archaeological Investigations in the Tellico Reservoir, Tennessee, 1967-1968: An Interim Report.
S230 (ASU)
ARCHEOLOGY — W. VA.
Archeological Survey of Nicholas County, West Virginia.
M2250 (ASU)
Excavation of the Murad Mound, Kanawha County, West Virginia, and an Analysis of Kanawha Valley Mounds.
M2260 (ASU)
Introduction to West Virginia Archeology.
M2270 (ASU)
Introduction to West Virginia Archeology.
M2280
Part 1: The Living Flora of West Virginia. Part 2: The Fossil Flora of West Virginia.
M6100 (ETSU)
Moundsville's Mammoth Mound.
N1450
P4280 (ETSU)
The Mound-Builders; a Reconstruction of the Life of a Prehistoric American Race, through Exploration and Interpretation of Their Earth Mounds, Their Burials, and Their Cultural Remains.
S3050
ARCHITECTURE — APP.
Wilderness Homes.
K720
ARCHITECTURE — KY.
Kentucky's Covered Bridges.
B6330
ARCHITECTURE — VA.
Architecture in Virginia: An Official Guide to Four Centuries of Building in the Old Dominion.
O710 (ASU)
ARCHITECTURE — W. VA.
Covered Bridges of West Virginia, Past and Present.
A5620 (ASU BC)
ARCHIVES
Guide to Civil War Records in the N. C. State Archives.
N2590
Guide to Private Manuscript Collections in the North Carolina State Archives.
N2600 (ASU)
ART
From the Appalachians: A Portfolio of Drawings and Paintings.
C1530 (ASU BC)
The Collectors: Dr. Claribel and Miss Etta Cone.
P3400 (ASU)
Rexrode Art: Sketches from the Hills of West Virginia.
R1630 (ASU)
ART — APP.
"Aesthetic Attitudes and Values of Selected Appalachian Youths."
M7800
ARTS AND CRAFTS
A2750
Shuttlecraft Book of American Handweaving.
A5460 (BC)
American Patchwork Quilts.
B70 (ASU)
The Art of Hooked-rug Making.
B1880 (LMC)
The Art of Blacksmithing.
B2290 (ASU)
The Moravian Potters in North Carolina.
B4290 (LMC)
American Folk Painting.
B4330 (ASU)
The Story of a Homespun Web.
B4780 (BC)
Kentucky Coverlets.
B5660 (BC)
Homespun Handicrafts.
B5710 (BC)
The Wooden Tower.
C2510
The Magic of Spinning.
C2940 (ASU WCU)
Basketry.
C4020 (ASU WCU)
Common Clay.
C7980 (LMC ASU WCU)
Encouraging American Craftsmen.
C7990 (WCU LMC ASU)
Encouraging American Handcrafts: What Role in Economic Development?
C8000 (LMC)
Pottery Workshop: A Study in the Making of Pottery from Idea to Finished Form.
C8010 (WCU)
"Glass Production Processes of the Kanawha Valley Area."
C8070 (ASU)
The Dye-Pot.
D680
A Handweaver's Pattern Book.
D1290 (ASU BC)
A Handweaver's Source Book; A Selection of 224 Patterns from the Laura M. Allen Collection.
D1300
Pennsylvania German Home Weaving.
D1310
Artisans of the Appalachians.
D4040 (ASU WCU LMC MHC WWC BC)
Handicrafts of the Southern Highlands: With an Account of the Rural Handicraft Movement in the United States and Suggestions for the Wider Use of Handicrafts in Adult Education and in Recreation.
E560 (ASU WCU LMC MHC WWC ETSU BC)
References on the Handicrafts of the Southern Highlands.
E1000 (BC)
References on the Mountaineers of the Southern Appalachians.
E1010
References on the Mountaineers of the Southern Appalachians.
E1020 (BC ETSU LMC ASU)
Handspinning: Art and Technique.
F90 (LMC)
Old Patchwork Quilts and the Women Who Made Them.
F1040 (BC)
The Story of the Penland Weavers.
F1880 (ASU BC)
Pattern in the Material Folk Culture of the Eastern United States.
G2080 (ASU BC WCU LMC FC)
Complete Guide to Hand Spinning, Teasing, Carding, Spinning.
G3280 (ASU)
Patchwork for Beginners.
G3660 (ASU)
The Romance of the Patchwork Quilt in America: In Three Parts.
H590 (ASU BC)
Mountain People, Mountain Crafts.
H7320 (ASU)
The Standard Book of Quilt Making and Collecting.
I30 (ASU BC)
Weaving as a Hobby.
I40 (BC ASU)
Loom-fixing and Weaving; A Book for All Who Are Interested in Such Matters.
I1010
Indian Basketry.
J340
Vegetable Dyeing: 151 Color Recipes for Dyeing Yarns and Fabrics with Natural Materials.
L1880 (ASU)
One Hundred and One Patchwork Patterns: Quilt Name Stories, Cutting Designs, Material Suggestions, Yardage Estimates, Definite Instructions for Every Step of Quilt Making.
M1880 (ASU WCU BC)
The Knox County Economic Opportunity Council Anti-Poverty Arts and Crafts.
M9080
Inkle.
N390
Potential Earning Power of Southern Mountaineer Handicraft.
N1020 (BC)
Artistry in Quilts.
N2470 (ASU)
Potential Earning Power of Southern Mountaineer Handicrafts.
N2990
A Book of Handwoven Coverlits.
O60 (BC)
O680 (ASU)
Catalog.
P1720 (ETSU)
Seat Weaving.
P2250
American Quilts and Coverlets; A History of a Charming Native Art.
P2390
How to Make Whirligigs and Whimmy Diddles and Other American Folkcraft Objects.
P2450
Dictionary of Weaves; a Collection of All Weaves from Four to Nine Harness.
P3770 (BC)
American Potters and Pottery.
R230 (BC)
Mountain Artisans: An Exhibit of Patchwork and Quilting, Appalachia.
R1820 (BC)
The Shenandoah Pottery.
R1890 (ASU BC)
Dyes from Plants.
R3170 (ASU)
America's Quilts and Coverlets.
S70 (ASU)
America's Quilts and Coverlets.
S80 (ASU)
American Folk Toys: 85 American Folk Toys and How to Make Them.
S1000 (ASU)
Old Fashioned Quilts.
S2060
The Origins and Characteristics of Folk Art in West Virginia.
S2450
Introducing Quilting.
S3180 (ASU)
Arts and Crafts of the Shenandoah Valley.
S4610 (ASU BC FC)
Confrontation with the Arts: The Arts in Education — What? For Whom? How? A Symposium Held at Western Carolina University, March 6-7, 1969.
S5230 (ASU WCU)
Vanishing Crafts and Their Craftsmen.
S6940 (ASU)
A Weavin' Woman.
S7110 (LMC)
Apple and Doughhead Dollmaking: Clothes Patterns Included.
T520 (WCU)
Crafts in the Southern Highlands.
W1980
Quilts: Their Story and How to Make Them.
W2130 (ASU)
Quilts: Their Story and How to Make Them.
W2140 (BC)
How to Make Cornhusk Dolls.
W2810
Foot-Power Loom Weaving.
W9300 (BC)
Foot-Power Loom Weaving.
W9310 (BC)
How to Weave Linens.
W9320 (BC)
A Study of North Appalachian Indian Pottery.
W9360 (LMC BC)
ARTS AND CRAFTS — APP.
C2040 (ASU)
C8350 (WCU ASU)
Mountain Homespun.
G2610 (ASU WCU LMC MHC ETSU BC ~~WWC~~)
The Southern Mountains, a Collection of Drawings.
H6970 (ASU BC)
A Handbook and Resource Guide for New Craft Groups.
H8040
The Mountain Artisans Quilting Book.
L2060 (BC ASU LMC)

ARTS AND CRAFTS — APP.
Four-Harness Huck.
N380
The Arts Workshop of Rural America: A Study of the Rural Arts Program of the Agricultural Extension Service.
P630 (LMC)
Home Industries and Domestic Weavings.
W5100
ARTS AND CRAFTS — CARVING
Whittling and Woodcarving.
T160 (ASU)
ARTS AND CRAFTS — CHEROKEE
The Golden Book of Indian Crafts and Lore.
H8380 (MHC)
Arts and Crafts of the Cherokee.
L1600 (UNCA ASU WCU LMC ETSU BC)
. . . Decorative Art and Basketry of the Cherokee.
S6100 (ASU)
ARTS AND CRAFTS — GA.
"Georgia Jug Makers: A History of Southern Folk Pottery."
B9190
ARTS AND CRAFTS — GUILDS
Crafts in the Southern Highlands.
S5750 (BC ASU)
Crafts in the Southern Highlands.
S5760
ARTS AND CRAFTS — INDIAN
Sun Circles and Human Hands: The Southeastern Indians Art and Industries.
F3830 (ASU MHC WCU BC)
Aboriginal Pottery of the Eastern United States.
H6890
Handbook of Aboriginal American Antiquities.
H6900 (LMC)
ARTS AND CRAFTS — KY.
The Development of Kentucky's Handicraft Industry.
E2380
ARTS AND CRAFTS — N. C.
Traditional Pottery in North Carolina by Bob Conway.
C6810
The Arts and Crafts in North Carolina, 1699-1840.
C8380 (ASU LMC MHC BC)
Jugtown Pottery: History and Design.
C8600 (ASU LMC MHC BC)
The Silversmiths of North Carolina.
C9980 (ASU)
The Arts in North Carolina, 1967.
N1660 (LMC)
North Carolina Museum of History, Raleigh.
N2010 (ASU)
ARTS AND CRAFTS — TENN.
"Art Handbook for Elementary Teachers of Elizabethton City Schools, Elizabethton, Tennessee."
C9900 (ETSU)
KIOSK.
T9260 (ETSU)
"The Planning of Art Facilities for Dobyns-Bennett High School, Kingsport, Tennessee."
W7030 (ETSU)
ARTS AND CRAFTS — VA.
The Silversmiths of Virginia.
C9990 (FC BC)
KIOSK.
T9260 (ETSU)
ARTS AND CRAFTS — W. VA.
Economic Impact of the Mountain State Art and Craft Fair, Ripley, West Virginia, 1964.
H50
Mountain Heritage.
M4410
Mountain Heritage, Mountain State Art and Craft Fair Cedar Lakes.
M4420
"The Revival of the Folk Arts in West Virginia."
R420 (ASU LMC)
ARTS — APP.
Discovery, Expression, Communication: An Arts Approach to the Problems of Appalachia.
F510
ARTS — CRAFTS
"Handicrafts in Sevier County, Tennessee."
H6180 (ASU)
BANKING — N. C.
"The History of Banking in Watauga County, North Carolina."
E20 (ASU)
"The History of Banking in Watauga County, North Carolina."
E20 (ASU)
BANKS AND BANKING
Pioneers of Old Frontiers.
B7270 (ETSU)
"A Study of Commercial Banking in Two Economically Depressed Cities: Youngstown, Ohio, and Wheeling, West Virginia, 1951-1967."
N1010
North Carolina County Data.
W10
BANKS AND BANKING — TENN.
"History of the Hamilton National Bank of Knoxville."
C2930
BIBLIOGRAPHIES
Guide to Manuscripts and Archives in the West Virginia Collection.
W4620 (ASU ETSU BC)
Jesse and Jane Stuart: A Bibliography.
W8730
Jesse Stuart: A Bibliography.
W8740 (WCU BC)
Jesse Stuart; a Bibliography for May, 1960-May, 1965.
W8750 (BC)
BIBLIOGRAPHIES — N. C.
Guide to the Manuscripts in the Southern Historical Collection of the University of North Carolina.
W9190 (LMC)
BIBLIOGRAPHY
Some Tennessee Rarities.
A1640 (ASU)
Tennessee Books: A Preliminary Guide.
A1650 (LMC)
A2760 (BC)
A2860 (ASU ETSU LMC MHC WWC BC)
Resources of the Appalachian Library and Culture Center, an Annotated Listing of Books, Recordings and Other Media.
A3240
Literature List, June, 1972.
A3310 (ASU BC)
A3400 (BC ETSU ASU)
A Bibliography of Research Studies Produced with Appalachian Regional Development Program Funds.
A3690
A Select Bibliography on High Risk Education for Appalachian Youth: Programs and Practices.
A3820
The American Indian: A Bibliography.
A4071
An Indexed Bibliography of the Tennessee Valley Authority.
B2020
1924 Works of Fiction by Southern Appalachian Authors, Or with Southern Appalachian Settings: Mountain Fiction from Addington to Zugsmith.
B3080 (ASU MHC ETSU BC)
Farm Migration, 1940-1945: An Annotated Bibliography.
B3180
B3490 (BC)
B3500 (ASU)
Mine Drainage Abstracts, a Bibliography.
B4270 (ASU)
The Southern Mountaineer in Literature, an Annotated Bibliography.
B5040 (ETSU ASU LMC BC FC UNCA)
Bibliography of Georgia Authors, 1949-1965.
B5320 (BC ASU)
A Bibliography of Kentucky Archaeology.
B5810
West Virginia Authors: A Bio-bibliography.
B6480
West Virginia Authors: A Bibliography.
B6490 (BC)
North Carolina Fiction, 1958-1971: An Annotated Bibliography.
B6720 (ASU)
A Descriptive Bibliography of West Virginia Ornithology.
B6900 (BC)
A Bibliography of Dissertations in Geography, 1901-1969.
B7460 (LMC)
Kentucky Authors, a History of Kentucky Literature.
B7480 (ASU BC)
The George Pullen Jackson Collection of Southern Hymnody: A Bibliography.
C280 (BC)
Southern Literary Culture: A Bibliography of Master's and Doctor's Theses.
C1120 (ASU LMC)
Bibliography of Virginia History Since 1865.
C1190 (BC FC)
John Griswold White Collection.
C4990
Resources of the Appalachian Library and Culture Center: An Annotated Listing of Books.
C5000 (WCU ASU)
Mine Drainage Abstracts: A Bibliography.
C5200 (ASU)
Bibliography of Tennessee Geology, Soils, Drainage, Forestry, etc. with Subject Index.
C5440 (LMC ETSU)
A Bibliography of Kentucky History.
C5770 (ASU LMC)
An Index of State Geological Survey Publications Issued in Series.
C7380 (LMC)
1973-1974 Bibliography of the Appalachian South: Books, Records, Pamphlets, Magazines, and Films.
C7880 (ASU ETSU)
A Selection of Books, Magazines and Records on the Appalachian South.
C7900 (MHC ASU)
Annotated Bibliography of Georgia Geology Through 1959.
C8500 (ETSU)
Sociological Aspects of Poverty, a Bibliography.
C9380
The Southeast in Early Maps with an Annotated Check List of Printed and Manuscript Regional and Local Maps of Southeastern North America during the Colonial Period.
C9470 (ASU LMC)
List of Books and Related Materials About Virginia for use of Schools.
C9490
Andrew Johnson, 1808-1875. Chronology-Documents-Bibliographical Aids.
D2200 (ASU)
Regimental Publications and Personal Narratives of the Civil War. A Checklist.
D2970 (LMC)
A Little More Light on Andrew Johnson.
D4010
"An Annotated Bibliography of Books by Southwest Virginia Authors."
D4120 (ETSU ASU)
Southern Appalachian Books: An Annotated, Selected Bibliography.
D4280 (WWC BC)
Subject Index to Films Available at the Audio-Visual Center.
E380 (ETSU)
Catalog of Films and Filmstrips, by Subject (and) by Title.
E410 (ETSU)
Catalog of films, by Subject (and) by Title.
E420 (ETSU)
Catalog of Filmstrips, by Subject (and) by Title.
E430 (ETSU)
Resources: Recordings and Cassettes.
E440 (ETSU)
Film Catalog.
E450 (ETSU)
Bibliography; the Eastern Band of Cherokee Indians.
E490
References on the Handicrafts of the Southern Highlands.
E1000 (BC)
References on the Mountaineers of the Southern Appalachians.
E1010
References on the Mountaineers of the Southern Appalachians.
E1020 (BC ETSU LMC ASU)
A Bibliography of Appalachian Children's and Young People's Books.
E1170
Andrew Johnson, President of the United States: His Life and Speeches.
F2340 (ASU)

BIBLIOGRAPHY

A Bibliography for the T.V.A. Program.
F2990

Surface Mined Areas: Control and Reclamation of Environmental Damage; a Bibliography.
F3090 (ASU)

A Guide to Manuscripts relating to the American Indian in the library of the American Philosophical Society.
F3190 (ASU MHC)

A Revised Bibliography of Strip Mine Reclamation.
F3840 (ASU)

The Papers of Andrew Johnson.
G3100

A Bibliography of North American Folklore and Folksong.
H4010 (ASU WWC)

Bibliography for the Study of American Folk Songs with Many Titles from Other Lands.
H4780

Annotated Bibliography on Slope Stability of Strip Mine Soil Banks.
H6250 (ASU)

Bibliography of Maryland Water Resources Data.
H8180

Bibliography of Clark Co., Kentucky.
J830

Bibliography of Elliott Co., Ky.
J840

Bibliography of Floyd Co., Ky.
J850

Bibliography of Knox Co., Ky.
J860

Bibliography of Lawrence Co., Ky.
J870

Bibliography of Licking River Valley in Ky.
J880

Bibliography of Madison Co., Ky.
J890

Bibliography of Menifee Co., Ky.
J900

Bibliography of Powell Co., Ky.
J910

Bibliography of Pulaski Co., Ky.
J920

Bibliography of the Big Sandy Valley.
J930

Bibliography of the Cumberland River Valley.
J940

A Bibliography of the Mineral Resources of Kentucky.
J950

Bibliography of the Green River Valley.
J1120

Thomas Wolfe: A Checklist.
J1670 (ASU)

Of Time and Thomas Wolfe: A Bibliography with a Character Index of His Works.
J1680 (ASU UNCA)

Southern Fiction Prior to 1860: An Attempt at a First Hand Bibliography.
J1820 (ASU)

Southern Fiction Prior to 1860: An Attempt at a First-hand Bibliography.
J1830 (MHC)

North Carolina Fiction, 1734-1957: An Annotated Bibliography.
J2210 (ASU MHC)

Bibliography of Coal in Kentucky.
K1410

Folksingers and Folksongs in America: A Handbook of Biography, Bibliography, and Discography.
L890 (ASU WWC BC)
L2770 (ASU MHC)

American Folk Songs and Folklore: A Regional Bibliography.
L3110

Bibliography of the Virginia Indians.
M320 (FC)

A Bibliography for the Great Smoky Mountains.
M730

List of References on the Mountain Whites.
M5260

Bibliography of the Eastern Band of Cherokee Indians.
M5280

A List of Magazines, Journals, Small Presses, Newspapers, etc. of Interest to Students of Appalachia.
M5820

Published Works of Cratis Williams.
M5840 (ASU BC)
M6140

Daniel Boone.
M6160 (ASU BC ETSU)

The Coal Industry in America: A Bibliography and Guide to Studies.
M8610 (ASU BC)

Index to the Press of the Kanawha Valley, 1855-1865.
M8620 (BC)

Index to West Virginiana.
M8630 (ASU BC)

The Southern Mountaineer: A Bibliography and Guide to Studies.
M8650 (ASU BC)

Strip Mining, an Annotated Bibliography.
M8660 (ASU BC)
N90 (ASU)

Bibliography on Appalachia: A Guide to Studies Dealing with Appalachia in General and Including Rural and Urban Working Class Attitudes Toward Change.
N420 (ASU BC ETSU LMC WCU MHC)

Bibliography on Appalachia: A Guide to Studies Dealing with Appalachia in General and Including Rural and Urban Working Class Attitudes Toward Change.
N430 (ASU)

The American Indian: A Bibliography.
N1580

A Cumulative Author and Subject Index Covering Material in N. C. Publications. . . .
N2430 (ASU UNCA)

Guide to Private Manuscript Collections in the North Carolina State Archives.
N2600 (ASU)

Books on the Southern Mountain Area That Contain Certain Religions or Sections on Religion, 1947-55.
N2900 (BC)

Appalachia's People, Problems, Alternatives.
P1970 (BC ASU)

Appalachia's People, Problems, Alternatives; an Introductory Social Science Reader.
P1980 (BC ASU)

Consolidated Bibliography of County Histories in Fifty States in 1961, Consolidated 1935-1961.
P2340 (ASU)

North Carolina County Histories: A Bibliography.
P3980 (MHC)

North Carolina County Histories: A Bibliography.
P3990 (ASU)

North Carolina Fiction 1734-1957: An Annotated Bibliography.
P4000 (ASU MHC)

North Carolina: A Students' Guide to Localized History.
P4020 (LMC WCU)

A Selective Music Bibliography from the Period 1663-1763.
P4800 (LMC)

The George Pullen Jackson Collection of Southern Hymnody: A Bibliography.
R1600

"A Bibliographic Center in the West Virginia Region: An Analysis of Present Needs and Future Directions."
R1690 (ASU)

Forests and Forestry in West Virginia, a Bibliography.
R1700

Kentucky Literature 1784-1963.
R2170 (BC)

Annotated Geological Bibliography of Virginia.
R2890 (ETSU)

Andrew Jackson, 1767-1845: Chronology, Documents, Bibliographical Aids.
S2510

W. Va. Civil War Literature.
S2670

Guide to the Study of West Virginia History.
S3000

West Virginia Civil War Literature; An Annotated Bibliography.
S3040

A Bibliography of the Zoology of Tennessee and Tennessee Valley Region.
S3190 (ASU BC)

Tennessee History, a Bibliography.
S5070 (ASU)

North Carolina Local History: A Select Bibliography.
S7200 (ASU)

A Bibliography for the TVA Program.
T2340 (ASU BC LMC)

A Bibliography for the TVA Program.
T2350 (ASU)

A Bibliography for the TVA Program.
T2360 (LMC)

Benefit-Cost Analysis for Water Resource Projects: A Selected Annotated Bibliography.
T5100

Benefit-Cost Analysis for Water Resource Projects; a Selected Annotated Bibliography.
T5110

. . . A Bibliography of the Tennessee Valley Authority.
T5880

A Bibliography for the TVA Program.
T5890

Flood Damage Prevention; an Indexed Bibliography.
T5920

Flood Damage Prevention; an Indexed Bibliography.
T5940

Flood Damage Prevention; an Indexed Bibliography.
T5950

. . . An Indexed Bibliography of the Tennessee Valley Authority, Compiled by Harry C. Bauer, Technical Librarian.
T5980

. . . A Selected List of Books, Theses, and Pamphlets on TVA, Compiled by Ernest I. Miller, Reference Librarian.
T6020

. . . A Selected List of Books and Pamphlets on TVA. January 1, 1945.
T6030

. . . A Selected List of Books, Theses, and Pamphlets on TVA.
T6040

. . . A Selected List of Books, Theses, and Pamphlets on TVA.
T6050

The TVA Program; a Bibliography of Selected Readings, Prepared by the Training and Educational Relations Staff of the Personnel Dept. and the Staff of the Technical Library.
T6060

The TVA Program; a Bibliography of Selected Readings, Compiled by Bernard L. Foy, Technical Librarian.
T6070

The TVA Program; a Bibliography of Selected Readings, Compiled by Bernard L. Foy, Technical Librarian.
T6080

TVA, Symbol of Valley Resource Development; a Digest and Selected Bibliography of Information.
T6090

TVA as a Symbol of Resource Development in Many Countries; a Digest and Selected Bibliography of Information.
T6100

Analytical Index of Chemical Engineering Publications Patents and Reports.
T6120

A Bibliography for the TVA Program.
T6890

Flood Damage Prevention; An Indexed Bibliography.
T6900

The Kentucky Novel.
T8240 (ASU)

Official Publications of the Colony and State of North Carolina, 1749-1939, a Bibliography.
T8430 (ASU LMC)

Poverty in the U. S. During the Sixties, a Bibliography.
T8860 (BC)

An Annotated Bibliography of Water Resource Papers Pertaining to West Virginia.
T9570
V1100 (LMC)

A Bibliography of Virginia, Part 1.
V1180

A List of Books and Other Sources of Information Regarding Coal and Coal Products.
W70

BIBLIOGRAPHY

John Eston Cooke: A Critical Biography.
W420

A Selective Bibliography of Writings on Poverty in the United States.
W1030

"The Paradox of the Mountains: A Study of the Influences on Thomas Wolfe."
W2440 (LMC)

Short Title Check-list of West Virginia State Publications. 1947/48-.
W3340 (ETSU)

West Virginia Graduate Research Studies in Education, 1894-1965: A Bibliographical Listing.
W6050 (ETSU)

A Selected Bibliography: The Southern Mountaineer in Fact and Fiction.
W6480 (ASU MHC)

American Fiction, 1774-1850: A . . . Bibliography.
W9470 (BC)

Preliminary Checklist for Abingdon, 1807-1876.
W9860

The Nantucket Pine Moth: A Literature Review.
Y70 (WCU)

BIBLIOGRAPHY — APP.

Directory.
C7950 (ASU)

The Appalachian South: An Historical Bibliography.
D3250

Bibliography for Appalachian Studies.
K1710

Resources for the Study of Appalachia: A Bibliography.
M8220

From Bishop Percy (1765) to John Jacob Niles (1974): 340 Books of Ballads and Songs in the Berea College Collection.
P2150 (BC ASU)

Mountain Fiction From Addington to Zugsmith: 924 Works of Fiction by Southern Appalachian Authors, Or With Southern Appalachian Settings.
P2160

A Shelf List of More than 760 Works of Fiction.
P2170

BIBLIOGRAPHY — APP. MTNS.

The Southern Highlands: A selected Bibliography.
C850

BIBLIOGRAPHY — COAL

Annotated Bibliography on Industrial Concentration and Firm Diversification in the Bitumonous Coal Industry with Special Reference to the Southeastern United States, 1950-1970.
G1270

BIBLIOGRAPHY — KY.

Historical Collections of Kentucky.
C6010

BIBLIOGRAPHY — N. C.

Supplement to Annotated Bibliography of Burke County Resource Materials, 1969.
B8650 (ASU)

Bibliography of North Carolina Geology, Mineralogy, and Geography, with a List of Maps.
L390 (ASU LMC WWC ETSU)

A Bibliography of North Carolina, 1589-1955.
T8420 (LMC UNCA ASU)

Guide to the manuscript collections in the archives of the N. C. Historical Commission.
W9180 (LMC)

BIBLIOGRAPHY — PNEUMOCONIOSIS

"A literature Survey of the Effects and Controls of Pneumoconiosis."
C100

BIBLIOGRAPHY — TENN.

"A Bibliographical Checklist of Knoxville and Memphis Imprints, 1867-1876 with an Introductory Essay on the Knoxville and Memphis Press."
B890

Annotated Bibliography of the Geology of Tennessee Through December, 1950.
W7130 (ETSU)

Annotated Bibliography of the Geology of Tennessee, January, 1951, Through December, 1960.
W7140 (ETSU)

BIBLIOGRAPHY — W. VA.

A Bibliography of West Virginia.
D1060

West Virginia Geology, Archaeology, and Pedology: A Bibliography and Index.
G1660 (BC ETSU)

Bibliography and Index of West Virginia Geology and Natural Resources to July 1, 1937.
L3870 (ETSU)

West Virginia Imprints, 1790-1863.
N1460

BIG SANDY RIVER

The Big Sandy Valley: A History of the People and Country from the Earliest Settlement to the Present Time.
E1890 (ASU)

Bibliography of the Big Sandy Valley.
J930

The Big Sandy Valley: A Regional History Prior to the Year 1850.
J960 (ASU BC)

The Big Sandy Valley: A Regional History Prior to the Year 1850.
J970 (MHC)
P90

Big Sandy.
T7890 (ASU BC)

Bulletin. Surface and Water Supply of Va. New, Big Sandy, and Tenn. River Basins, 1942-1950.
V750 (BC)

BIOGRAPHY

Daniel Boone, Pioneer of Kentucky.
A30 (ASU)

Daniel Boone, Pioneer of Kentucky.
A40 (ETSU)

Daniel Boone, the Pioneer of Kentucky.
A50 (ASU BC)

David Crockett: His Life and Adventures.
A60 (ASU ETSU)

Heroes of the Alamo: Accounts and Documents.
A260 (ETSU)

Thomas Wolfe, Carolina Student: A Brief Biography.
A360 (ASU WCU)

Thomas Wolfe: Carolina Student; A Brief Biography.
A370 (ASU WCU)

Thomas Jefferson and the University of Virginia.
A410 (ASU)

Pen and Politics: The Autobiography of a Working Writer.
A1370 (ASU)

Tom Dooley.
A1410 (ASU LMC)

Thomas A. R. Nelson of East Tennessee.
A1450 (ASU LMC BC)

John L. Lewis: An Unauthorized Biography.
A1470 (WCU BC)

History of the Campaign of General T. J. (Stonewall) Jackson in the Shenandoah Valley of Virginia from Nov. 4, 1861, to June 17, 1862.
A1480 (ASU)

Crockett's Life.
A1510 (ETSU)

David Crockett; Scout, Small Boy, Pilgrim, Mountaineer, Soldier, Bearhunter, and Congressman, Defender of the Alamo.
A1520 (BC)

Memoirs of J. Sidna Allen, Being a True Narrative of His Life and Early Manhood, the History of the Allen Family, What Happened at Hillsville and His Life at the Penitentiary.
A1560 (LMC ASU)

Philip Pendelton Cooke.
A1580 (BC)

Dropped Stitches in Tennessee History.
A1770 (ASU BC)

Notable Men of Tennessee: Personal and Genealogical with Portraits.
A1780 (ASU)

Lewis Wetzel: Indian Fighter. The Life and Times of a Frontier Hero.
A1810 (ASU BC)

West Virginia: Stories and Biographies.
A2060

Sergeant York: Reluctant Hero.
A2520 (ETSU)

"Willis Duke Weatherford: An Interpretation of His Work in Race Relations, 1906-1946."
A2630 (ASU BC)

Early Life and Letters of General Thomas J. Jackson, "Stonewall" Jackson.
A4860 (ASU)

Thomas Jefferson and Education in a Republic.
A4970 (ETSU)

Journal and Letters.
A5060 (ASU BC WWC)

A Methodist Saint.
A5070 (ASU)

Biographical History of North Carolina from Colonial Times to the Present.
A5100 (WWC)

Bob and Alf Taylor: Their Lives and Lectures. The Story of Senator Robert Love Taylor and Governor Alfred Alexander Taylor. Followed by the Most Famous of Their Lectures and Speeches, Including "The Fiddle and the Bow" and "Yankee Doodle" and "Dixie".
A5470 (BC)

You Are Greater Than You Know.
A5550 (BC)

A Biography of Thomas Wolfe.
A5570 (ASU WCU)

Daniel Boone.
A5700 (ETSU BC)

Idle Comments.
A5730

Nancy Hanks, the Destined Mother of a President: The Factual Story of a Pioneer Family as Revealed in an Exhaustive Study of Ancestral History.
B10 (ASU)

Life and Speeches of President Andrew Johnson. Embracing His Early History, Political Career, Speeches, Proclamations, etc. With a Sketch of the Secession Movement, and His Course in Relation Thereto; Also His Policy as President of the United States.
B50

The Autobiography of Waldron Bailey.
B390 (ASU LMC BC)

"Maryland's Reaction to Andrew Johnson, 1865-1868."
B450

Daniel Boone.
B500 (ASU FC ETSU UNCA BC)

Daniel Boone.
B510 (ASU WCU)

Daniel Boone.
B520 (ASU MH)

Fighting Frontiersman, the Life of Daniel Boone.
B530

Fighting Frontiersman, the Life of Daniel Boone.
B540 (ASU BC)

Master of the Wilderness: Daniel Boone.
B550

Men of Affairs in Knoxville.
B620

Party Leaders: Sketches of Thomas Jefferson, Alex'r Hamilton, Andrew Jackson, Henry Clay, John Randolph, of Roanoke, Including Notices of Many Other Distinguished American Statesmen.
B710 (ASU)

Red Trails and White.
B770 (BC)

Back to the Mountains, Autobiography.
B950 (BC)

Abraham Lincoln, Kentucky Mountaineer: An Address Delivered before the Faculty and Students of Berea College, Berea, Kentucky, Thursday, March 8, 1923.
B1570 (ASU BC)

The Autobiography of William E. Barton.
B1580 (BC)

Cherokee Messenger.
B1790 (ASU)

Cherokee Messenger.
B1800 (BC ASU WCU)

The Life of Andrew Jackson.
B1830

The Life of Andrew Jackson.
B1840

The Life of Andrew Jackson.
B1850

"Andrew Johnson and the Patronage."
B2090

"Inconsistent Men of Principle: Future Liberal Republicans and the Johnson Administration."
B2100

BIOGRAPHY

The Critical Year: A Study of Andrew Johnson and Reconstruction.
B2260

The Critical Year: A Study of Andrew Johnson and Reconstruction.
B2270

The Critical Year: A Study of Andrew Johnson and Reconstruction.
B2280

Davy Crockett.
B2320 (ETSU)

"The Life and Times of Isaac Shelby."
B2380

"Life and Literary Contributions of Luther Foster Addington, a Southwest Virginia Writer and Educator.
B2910

Jennie Wiley, Pioneer: The True Story of a Virginia Frontier Heroine.
B3000 (ASU)

"Andrew Johnson, Governor of Tennessee, 1853-1857."
B3040

"The Post-presidential Career of Andrew Johnson."
B3480
B3760
B3770
B3780
B3790
B3800
B3810
B3820
B3830
B3840
B3850
B3860
B3870
B3880
B3890
B3900
B3910
B3920
B3930
B3940
B3950
B3960
B3970
B3980
B3990
B4000
B4010
B4020
B4030
B4040

Davy Crockett, Frontier Hero; the Truth as He Told It, the Legend as Friends Built It.
B4490

Religion in Shoes.
B4540 (BC)

Gift from the Hills.
B4880 (ASU LMC)

James W. Davis, North Carolina Surgeon.
B4890 (ASU BC MHC)

Mountain Doctor.
B4900 (ASU BC WCU LMC MHC WWC)

The Border Boy.
B4991

The Border Boy and How He Became the Great Pioneer of the West; a Life of Daniel Boone.
B5000 (BC)

Daniel Boone, and the Hunters of Kentucky.
B5010 (ASU)

Daniel Boone, and the Hunters of Kentucky.
B5020 (LMC)

Daniel Boone, and the Hunters of Kentucky.
B5030 (ETSU)

Home Reminiscences of John Randolph, of Roanoke.
B5650 (ASU)

Simon Girty, the White Savage.
B5940 (ASU)

Andrew Johnson: A Life in Pursuit of the Right Course, 1808-1875. The Seventeenth President of the United States.
B6120 (ASU)

Border Fights and Fighters.
B6240 (BC)

My Life and Travels.
B6340 (ASU)

Thomas Wolfe
B6800 (ASU WCU)

Nisi Prius.
B6990 (ASU BC)

Daniel Boone: The Opening of the Wilderness.
B7240 (ASU BC)

Blanford Barnard Dougherty, a Man to Match His Mountains.
B7350 (ASU)

Daniel Boone and the Wilderness Road.
B7570 (ASU BC)

Daniel Boone and the Wilderness Road.
B7580 (ETSU)

Life of General Houston, 1793-1863.
B7590

The Life of Morris Purdy Shawkey.
B8240 (ASU BC)

History of Andrew Jackson: Pioneer, Patriot, Soldier, Politician, President.
B8320 (ASU)

The Man from Buchanan.
B8810

This Was My Valley.
B8980 (ASU WCU LMC WWC UNCA)

Old Jube: A Biography of Jubat A. Early from West Point in the 1830's to the Battles of Chancellorsville, Lynchburg, Winchester, and a Wealth of Other Data on the Civil War.
B9370

History of the Girty's Being a Concise Account of the Girty Brothers.
B9420 (BC)

Martha Berry: The Sunday Lady of Possum Trot.
B9550 (ASU LMC WWC BC)

Martha Berry: The Sunday Lady of Possum Trot.
B9560 (LMC)

Joshua William Caldwell. A Memorial Volume, Containing His Biography, Writings and Addresses.
C120

Diary of Kate Livingston, 1859-1868.
C140

Donald McElroy, Scotch Irishman.
C220 (ASU BC)

Daniel Morgan, Ranger of the Revolution.
C310 (BC)

David Lowry Swain, Governor and University President.
C430 (ASU WCU LMC)

Governor Vance: A Life for Young People.
C440 (ASU WCU WWC)

Governor Vance, a Life for Young People.
C450 (LMC)

The Life and Work of John Charles Campbell, September 15, 1868-May 2, 1919.
C840 (WWC BC)

My Beloved Zebulon. The correspondence of Zebulon Baird Vance and Harriett Neivell Espy.
C1090 (ASU)

The Life and Times of C. G. Memmings.
C1160 (ETSU)

The Saint of the Wilderness.
C1430 (ASU)

"Administrations of John Sevier."
C1660

Autobiography of Peter Cartwright, the Backwoods Preacher.
C1810 (BC)

Mary N. Murfree.
C1890 (ASU)

"The Administration of Governor Andrew Johnson 1853-1857."
C1960

The Genesis of Lincoln: Truth is Stranger than Fiction.
C2080 (LMC)

Truth is Stranger than Fiction: Or, the True Genesis of a Wonderful Man.
C2090 (ASU)

The Public Career of David Crockett.
C2150

Dark Hills to Westward: The Saga of Jennie Wiley.
C2200 (ASU WCU LMC MHC ETSU BC)

The High Cost of Writing.
C2370 (BC)
C2640

"The Struggle between President Johnson and the Congress over Reconstruction."
C2660

Stonewall Jackson.
C2780 (ASU)

Early Biography, Travels and Adventures of Rev. James Champlin, Who Was Born Blind; with a Description of the Different Countries through Which He Has Traveled in America, and of the Different Institutions, etc., Visited by Him; Also an Appendix, Which Contains Extracts from Addresses Delivered by Him upon Several Occasions.
C2840

Just a Country Lawyer; a Biography of Senator Sam Ervin.
C4210 (ASU BC)

Cherokee Chief: The Life of John Ross.
C4380 (LMC ETSU)

The Life of Cassius Marcellus Clay. Memoirs, Writings, and Speeches, Showing His Conduct in the Overthrow of American Slavery, the Salvation of the Union, and the Restoration of the Autonomy of the States.
C4750 (MHC BC)

Rock of Chickamauga, the Life of General George H. Thomas.
C4850 (ASU)

Selections from the Speeches and Writings of Hon. Thomas L. Clingman, of North Carolina. With Additions and Explanatory Notes.
C5080 (ASU BC)

Wilderness Road.
C5140 (ASU)

Wilderness Road.
C5150 (BC)

The Life and Adventures of Wilburn Waters, the Famous Hunter and Trapper of White Top Mountain.
C5230 (BC)

Wilburn Waters History 1812-1879.
C5240

Sequoya.
C5350 (WCU ETSU BC)

Sequoya.
C5360 (ASU)

Simon Kenton.
C5390 (ASU)

Johnny Park Talks of Thomas Wolfe.
C5430 (ASU LMC)

Abraham Lincoln: A North Carolinian.
C5530 (ASU)

The Eugenics of President Abraham Lincoln: His German-Scotch Ancestry Irrefutably Established from Recently Discovered Documents.
C5540 (ASU)

Story of Captain Jesse Cox of Johnson Co., Tennessee.
C5720

As I See It.
C6530 (ASU)

Fire from the Flint: The Amazing Careers of Thomas Dixon.
C6860 (BC ASU)

Thomas Dixon: His Books and His Career.
C6870

The Family and Early Life of Stonewall Jackson.
C6900 (ASU)

Stonewall Jackson.
C7000 (ASU BC)

Stonewall Jackson and the Old Stonewall Brigade.
C7010 (ASU BC)

"Isaac Shelby, 1750-1796."
C7030

Simon Kenton, the Scout: A Tale of Frontier Life During the Revolution.
C7390 (BC)

A Mountain Trail: To the Schoolroom, the Editor's Chair, the Lawyer's Office, and the Governorship of West Virginia.
C7570 (ASU BC)

William G. Brownlow, Fighting Parson of the Southern Highlands.
C7810 (ASU WCU BC)

William G. Brownlow: Fighting Parson of the Southern Highlands.
C7820 (ETSU)

Sergeant York and His People.
C8110 (WWC ETSU BC)

Wheels on the Mountains.
C8340 (ASU LMC WCU BC)

Mitchell's Peak and Dr. Mitchell.
C8420 (ASU LMC)

BIOGRAPHY

An Account of Col. Crockett's Tour to the North and Down East, in the Year of Our Lord One Thousand Eight Hundred and Thirty-four. His Object Being to Examine the Grand Manufacturing Establishments of the Country; and Also to Find Out the Condition of Its Literature and Morals, the Extent of Its Commerce, and the Practical Operation of "The Experiment." Written by Himself.
C8860

An Account of Col. Crockett's Tour to the North and Down East, in the Year of Our Lord One Thousand Eight Hundred and Thirty-four. His Object Being to Examine the Grand Manufacturing Establishment of the Country; and Also to Find Out the Condition of Its Literature and Morals, the Extent of Its Commerce, and the Practical Operation of "The Experiment." Written by Himself.
C8870

An Account of Col. Crockett's Tour to the North and Down East, in the Year of Our Lord One Thousand Eight Hundred and Thirty-four. His Objective Being to Examine the Grand Manufacturing Establishments of the Country; and Also to Find Out the Condition of Its Literature and Morals, the Extent of Its Commerce, and the Practical Operation of "The Experiment." Written by Himself.
C8880

The Adventures of Davy Crockett: Told Mostly by Himself.
C8890 (ASU)

The Adventures of Davy Crockett, Told Mostly by Himself.
C8900

The Autobiography of David Crockett.
C8910 (ETSU)

The Autobiography of David Crockett.
C8920

The Crockett Almanacks. Nashville Series, 1835-1838.
C8930

The Crockett Tavern and Pioneer Museum.
C8940

Davy Crockett's Own Story as Written by Himself; the Autobiography of America's Great Folk Hero.
C8950

Life of Col. Crockett, Written by Himself.
C8960 (ETSU)

Life of David Crockett.
C8970 (ETSU)

Life of David Crockett.
C8980 (ETSU)

Life of David Crockett, the Original Humorist and Irrepressible Backwoodsman: Comprising His Early History; His Bear Hunting and Other Adventures. His Services in the Creek War. His Electioneering Speeches and Career in Congress. With His Triumphal Tour Through the Northern States, and Services in the Texas War. To Which Is Added an Account of His Glorious Death at the Alamo while Fighting in Defence of Texan Independence.
C8990 (ASU)

Life of David Crockett, the Original Humorist and Irrepressible Backwoodsman, Comprising His Early History: His Bear Hunting and Other Adventures, His Services in the Creek War. His Electioneering Speeches and Career in Congress. With His Triumphal Tour Through the Northern States and Services in the Texan War. To Which Is Added an Account of His Glorious Death at the Alamo while Fighting in Defence of Texan Independence.
C9000 (ASU BC)

Life of David Crockett, the Original Humorist and Irrepressible Backwoodsman: Comprising His Early History; His Bear Hunting and Other Adventures; His Services in the Creek War; His Electioneering Speeches and Career in Congress with His Triumphal Tour Through the Northern States, and Services in the Texan War. To Which Is Added an Account of His Glorious Death at the Alamo while Fighting in Defence of Texan Independence. . .
C9010 (ASU)

A Narrative of the Life of David Crockett of the State of Tennessee.
C9020 (ASU)

A Narrative of the Life of David Crockett of the State of Tennessee.
C9030 (ASU MHC)

A Narrative of the Life of David Crockett of the State of Tennessee.
C9040

A Narrative of the Life of David Crockett, Written by Himself.
C9050 (ETSU)

The Real Book about Daniel Boone.
C9790 (BC)

Thomas Wolfe: October Recollections.
D200 (ASU)

Daniel Boone.
D460 (MHC ETSU UNCA)

Daniel Boone.
D470 (ASU)

The Man Who Moved a Mountain.
D620 (ASU FC BC)

Jeb Stuart, the Last Cavalier.
D870 (ASU)

They Called Him Stonewall: A Life of Lt. General T. J. Jackson, C. S. A.
D880 (ASU BC)

Chronicle of the Cavaliers: A Life of the Virginia Novelist, Dr. William A. Caruthers.
D950 (WCU ASU)

The Mountain Preacher.
D1070 (BC)

Legacy of Love.
D1130

Shepherd Monroe Dugger: A Critical Biography.
D1370 (LMC ASU)

Wilderness Wife: The Story of Rebecca Bryan Boone.
D1620 (ASU MHC WCU BC)

Push the Button: The Chronicle of a Professor's Wife.
D2020 (ASU)

The Impeachment and Trial of Andrew Johnson, Seventeenth President of the United States; a History.
D2030

The Impeachment and Trial of Andrew Johnson, Seventeenth President of the United States; a History.
D2040

Andrew Johnson, 1808-1875. Chronology-Documents-Bibliographical Aids.
D2200 (ASU)

The Reverend Samuel Houston.
D2310 (BC)

"Some Phases of the Congressional Career of Andrew Johnson."
D2630

Pardon and Amnesty under Lincoln and Johnson; the Restoration of the Confederates to Their Rights and Privileges, 1861-1898.
D3030

Davy Crockett: American Comic Legend.
D3060 (ASU)

Life of Zebulon B. Vance.
D3160 (ASU LMC BC)

Pioneer Life in Kentucky, 1785-1800.
D3210 (ASU ETSU BC)

Pioneer Life in Kentucky, a Series of Reminiscential Letters from Daniel Drake . . . to His Children.
D3220 (ASU)

A Winner on Satin's Doorstep.
D3370 (BC)

John Sevier: Pioneer of the Old Southwest.
D3450

John Sevier: Pioneer of the Old Southwest.
D3460

John Sevier: Pioneer of the Old Southwest.
D3470 (ASU LMC BC)

Life of S. Miller Willis
D3960 (BC)

A Little More Light on Andrew Johnson.
D4010

John Filson, the First Historian of Kentucky: An Account of His Life and Writings.
D4100 (LMC)

Prophet of Plenty: The First Ninety Years of W. D. Weatherford.
D4250 (ASU WCU LMC MHC ETSU FC WWC BC)

Seeds of Southern Change: The Life of Will Alexander.
D4270 (WWC WCU MHC ETSU)
E80 (ETSU)

John Ross and the Cherokee Indians.
E580 (ASU)

John Ross and the Cherokee Indians.
E590 (ASU)

John Ross and the Cherokee Indians.
E600 (ASU BC)

Harriette Arrow.
E770 (BC)

The Life of Rev. David Brainerd, Chiefly Extracted from His Diary, Somewhat Abridged, Embracing, in the Chronological Order, Brainerds Public Journal.
E1070 (LMC)

Thirty-eight years in the Parsonage: The Fruitful Career of the Reverend Opie Eldridge in the Methodist Ministry of Rural and Urban West Virginia-Perceptively Recounted by His Wife and Fellow Worker.
E1580 (ASU)

Sam Houston.
E1730

The Life and Times of Col. Daniel Boone, Hunter, Soldier, and Pioneer.
E1780 (ETSU BC FC ASU WCU LMC)

The Life and Times of Col. Daniel Boone, the Hunter of Kentucky, with Sketches of His Contemporaries: Narrative of St. Clair's Defeat. Mrs. Merrill's Adventures, etc.
E1790 (ASU BC)

Life of Colonel David Crockett: Comprising His Adventures as Backwoodsman and Hunter; His Services as Soldier and Scout in the Creek War; His Electioneering Canvasses; His Career as Congressman; His Tour through the Northern States; and His Services and Death in the Texan War of Independence. To Which Are Added, Sketches of General Sam Houston, General Santa Anna, Rezin P. and Colonel James Bowie.
E1800 (ASU)

"Dr. J. G. M. Ramsey of East Tennessee: A Career of Public Service."
E2260

"David Crockett: An Interpretation."
E2350

Nolichucky Jack.
F130 (ASU LMC ETSU)

The Man on Horseback; a Story of Life Among W. Va. Hills.
F220 (BC)

The Saga of the Country Doctor Among the W. Va. Hills.
F230 (BC)

Old Bill Williams, Mountain Man.
F380 (ASU)

Autobiography of John G. Fee, Berea, Kentucky.
F520 (ASU BC)

Country Life in Georgia in the Days of My Youth.
F570

Mother Jones, the Miners' Angel: A Portrait.
F740 (ASU MHC)

The Adventures of Colonel Daniel Boone, formerly a Hunter: Containing a Narrative of the Wars of Kentucky, with the Discovery, Purchase, and Settlement of Kentucky, and the Piankashaw Council, 1784, and Territory of North American Indians, and the Rights Land in Kentucky.
F850 (BC ASU LMC)

Kentucky and the Adventures of Col. Daniel Boone.
F890

Thomas Wolfe as I Knew Him, and Other Essays.
F1210 (BC ASU UNCA WCU)

BIOGRAPHY

The Origin, Rise and Downfall of the State of Franklin under Her First and Only Governor, John Sevier.
F1320

Campaigns of the Army of Northern Virginia, Including the Jackson Valley Campaign, 1861-1865.
F1490 (ASU)

Biographical Memoir of Daniel Boone, the First Settler of Kentucky: Interspersed with Incidents in the Early Annals of the Country.
F1560 (ASU BC)

Biographical Memoir of Daniel Boone, the First Settler of Kentucky: Interspersed with Incidents in the Early Annals of the Country.
F1570 (ETSU WCU)

The Life and Adventures of Daniel Boone, the First Settler of Kentucky.
F1580 (ETSU)

Biographical Genealogies of the Virginia-Kentucky Floyd Families, with Notes of Some Collateral Branches.
F1640 (ASU)

The Alderson story; my Life as a Political Prisoner.
F1650

A Narrative of the Life of David Crockett of the State of Tennessee.
F1730

Sketches of North Carolina, Historical and Biographical, Illustrative of the Principles of a Portion of Her Early Settlers.
F1790 (ASU LMC)

Sketches of North Carolina, Historical and Biographical, Illustrative of the Principles of a Portion of Her Early Settlers.
F1800 (MHC BC)

Sketches of Virginia Historical and Biographical.
F1820

Sketches of Virginia Historical and Biographical.
F1830

Sketches of Virginia: Historical and Biographical, First Series.
F1840 (LMC UNCA)

Daniel Boone, Backwoodsman.
F1860

Davy Crockett.
F1870 (ETSU)

This is My Story: This is My Song.
F1900 (BC)

Sequoyah.
F2080 (BC UNCA WCU ETSU)

Sequoyah.
F2090 (ASU)

Sequoyah.
F2100 (ASU LMC)

Impeached: The President Who Almost Lost His Job.
F2260

Se-quo-yah; the American Cadmus and Modern Moses. A Complete Biography of the Greatest of Redmen, around Whose Wonderful Life Has Been Woven the Manners, Customs and Beliefs of the Early Cherokees, Together with a Recital of Their Wrongs and Wonderful Progress toward Civilization.
F2280

Se-quo-yah; the American Cadmus and Modern Moses. A Complete Biography of the Greatest of Redmen, around Whose Wonderful Life Has Been Woven the Manners, Customs and Beliefs of the Early Cherokees, Together with a Recital of their Wrongs and Wonderful Progress toward Civilization.
F2290

Se-quo-yah; the American Cadmus and Modern Moses. A Complete Biography of the Greatest of Redmen, around Whose Wonderful Life Has Been Woven the Manners, Customs and Beliefs of the Early Cherokees, Together with a Recital of Their Wrongs and Wonderful Progress toward Civilization.
F2300

Andrew Johnson, President of the United States: His Life and Speeches.
F2340 (ASU)

Capt. John Fowler of Virginia and Kentucky; Patriot, Soldier, Pioneer, Statesman, Land Baron, and Civic Leader.
F2430 (BC)

The Crockett Family and Connecting Lines.
F3240

Davy Crockett and the Crockett Family.
F3250

Notable Southern Families. The Doak Family.
F3260

Sam Houston, the Great Designer.
F3340

For the Mountains, an Autobiography.
F3570 (ASU LMC BC)

The Pioneer: A Biography.
F3590 (BC)

Tennessee Centennial Poem. A Synopsis of the History of Tennessee from Its Earliest Settlement on Watauga to the Present Time, with Short Biographies of Her Most Prominent Men.
F3610 (ASU)

Strange Experience: The Autobiography of a Hexenmeister.
G240 (LMC)

A Grain of Mustard.
G310

Green Power, the Successful Way of A. G. Gaston.
G560

"Fact and Fiction in the Early Biographies of David Crockett."
G580

The Yankee from Tennessee.
G1090 (ASU ETSU BC)

A Little Better Than Plumb: The Biography of a House.
G1380 (BC ASU ETSU)

I Went to Pit College.
G1590

The Advance-Guard of Western Civilization.
G1730

John Sevier as a Commonwealth-builder. A Sequel to The Rear-guard of the Revolution.
G1750 (ASU WCU LMC BC)

Gemini.
G1840
G2620 (ASU BC)

My Mother's Story.
G2750 (BC)

Rachel Jackson: Tennessee Girl.
G2920 (BC LMC ETSU)

The Papers of Andrew Johnson.
G3100

The Faith of Billy Graham.
G3150 (WCU)

The Quotable Billy Graham.
G3160 (WCU)

The Great Iron Wheel: Or, Republicanism Backwards and Christianity Reversed.
G3310 (ASU)

One Woman's Life. The Steppings of Faith. Edna Gray's Story.
G3330 (ASU BC)

Aunt Molly Jackson Memorial Issue.
G3490

Defender of the Constitution: Andrew Johnson.
G3600

Sparks from a Blacklog.
G3620

When I Was a Boy.
G3850 (ASU)

Sam Houston with the Cherokees, 1829-1833.
G3990 (ASU WCU MHC)

Revolutionary Service of Col. John Walker & Family and Memoirs of Hon. Felix Walker.
G4160 (BC)

Recollections of a Long Life.
G4260

The Gospel of the Lilies.
G4620 (BC)

Daniel Boone.
G4890 (ASU BC)

The Blue Hen's Chick: A Life in Context.
G4960 (WCU)

Daniel Boone. Some Facts and Incidents Not Hitherto Published. His Ten or Twelve Years' Residence in Kanawha County, Near Charleston, West Virginia.
H340 (ASU BC)

Autobiography of "Old Claib Jones."
H370

"Cry Aloud and Spare Not; the Formative Years of Brownlow's WHIG, 1839-1841."
H530

Andrew Johnson: Military Governor of Tennessee.
H600 (BC ASU)

Andrew Johnson: Military Governor of Tennessee.
H610 (BC ASU)

Autobiography of "Old Claib Jones."
H720

"Andrew Johnson, the Radicals, and the Negro, 1865-1866."
H970

A Doctor's Pilgrimage.
H1070

Life of Andrew Johnson, Seventeenth President of the United States.
H1160

Aunt Bet, the Story of a Long Life: A Memoir of Elizabeth S. W. Taylor.
H1340 (ASU BC LMC)

Hill-Billy Bill; a Biography of Hon. J. Will Taylor of Tennessee.
H1660 (BC)

Lawyer's Lawyer; the Life of John W. Davis.
H1750 (ASU BC)
H2110

Abraham Lincoln and the Cumberland Gap.
H2250 (ASU ETSU)

Witness to an Epoch: Personal Inventory of the Experiences and Impressions of a Man of Varied Interests.
H2300 (LMC)

My Book and Heart.
H2730 (ASU BC)

My Son.
H2740 (ASU BC)

The Life of Daniel Boone, the Founder of the State of Kentucky.
H3190 (ASU)

Life of Daniel Boone, the Great Western Hunter and Pioneer, Comprising an Account of His Early History, His Daring and Remarkable Career as the First Settler of Kentucky. To Which is Added His Autobiography Complete as Dictated by Himself.
H3200 (WCU BC ETSU)

Life of Daniel Boone, the Great Western Hunter and Pioneer, Comprising an Account of His Early History, His Daring and Remarkable Career as the First Settler of Kentucky. To Which Is Added His Autobiography Complete as Dictated by Himself.
H3210 (ASU BC ETSU)

"Ananias Davisson: Southern Tune Book Compiler (1780-1857)."
H3230

Stories of Hatfield, the Pioneer.
H3430

Stories of Hatfield, the Pioneer; embracing a detailed account of His Experience in the Wilderness of East Tennessee, Kentucky, and Southern Indiana.
H3440 (BC)

The Hatfields.
H3450 (ASU)

Junaluska at the Battle of Horse Shoe Bend: True Story of the Cherokee Chief.
H3710 (LMC)

Adventures of Daniel Boone, the Kentucky Rifleman.
H3720 (BC)

"Andrew Johnson's Reputation: A Study of Changing Interpretations."
H3990

Bill Haywood's Book: The Autobiography of William D. Haywood.
H4080 (ASU WCU)

Andrew Jackson and Early Tennessee History.
H4330

Boone of the Wilderness: A Tale of Pioneer Adventures and Achievement in "The Dark and Bloody Ground."
H4460 (ASU BC)

Stonewall Jackson and the American Civil War.
H4480 (ASU BC)

"Nolichucky Jack." (Gov. John Sevier.) Lecture of Wm. A. Henderson, to the Board of Trade of the City of Knoxville, January 7th, 1873.
H4560

Appalachian Shepherd: A Story of Religion in the Southern Appalachians.
H4590 (BC ASU LMC ETSU FC WWC)
H4940 (BC ASU)

BIOGRAPHY

Struggle in the Coal Fields. The Autobiography of Fred Mooney, Secretary-Treasurer, District 17, United Mine Workers of America.
H5070 (ASU)

Dr. J. G. Ramsey: Autobiography and Letters.
H5080 (ASU LMC)

Tales of a Frontier Preacher.
H5330

Daniel Boone: The Pioneer of Kentucky.
H5400

Life and Adventures of Daniel Boone, the Pioneer of Kentucky.
H5410 (ASU BC)

The Herbert Walters Story.
H5420

Nancy Hanks, the Story of Abe Lincoln's Mother.
H6040

In Quiet Ways: George H. Mead, the Man and the Company.
H6210 (LMC)

Andrew Jackson and North Carolina Politics.
H6330 (LMC)

Davy Crockett and Others in Fentress County Who Have Given the County a Prominent Place in History.
H6400 (ETSU BC)

Morgan and His Raiders: A Biography of the Confederate General.
H6530

Thomas Wolfe.
H6760 (ASU UNCA)

Three Modes of Modern Southern Fiction: Ellen Glasgow, William Faulkner, Thomas Wolfe.
H6770 (ASU MHC)

The World of Thomas Wolfe.
H6780 (ASU WCU MHC UNCA)

Pen and Politics, the Autobiography of a Working Writer.
H6790

The Unwanted Boy: The Autobiography of Governor Ben W. Hooper.
H7040 (ASU BC)

Boone's Wilderness Road.
H7870 (ETSU BC)

Whom the Lord Loveth; the Story of James A. Huff.
H8000 (BC)

The Memoirs of Cordell Hull.
H8190 (ASU)

Sketches of Western North Carolina, Historical and Biographical, Illustrating Principally the Revolutionary Period of Mecklenburg, Rowan, Lincoln, and Adjoining Counties.
H8420 (ASU BC WCU)

Sketches of Western North Carolina, Historical and Biographical, Illustrating Principally the Revolutionary Period of Mecklenburg, Rowan, Lincoln and Adjoining Counties, Accompanied with Miscellaneous Information, Much of It Never Before Published.
H8430 (ASU LMC ETSU)

"Gentlemen, I ain't a-goin'."
H8660
I170

A Biographical Sketch on the Life of the Late Captain Michael Cresap.
J210

Six Feet Six, the Heroic Story of Sam Houston.
J300 (ASU)

The Raven, a Biography of Sam Houston.
J360

Memoirs of Samuel M. Janney; Late of Lincoln, Loudoun Co., Va.
J390

Life and Public Services of General Andrew Jackson.
J650

The Boone Narrative.
J980 (LMC)

Daniel Boone in Kentucky.
J1010

The Violent Years.
J1260 (BC)

Speeches of Andrew Johnson, President of the United States.
J1280

Speeches of Andrew Johnson, President of the United States.
J1290 (ASU)

An Honorable Titan: A Biographical Study of Adolph S. Ochs.
J1750

Randolph of Roanoke: A Political Fantastic.
J1760 (ASU)

John Henry: Track Down a Negro Legend.
J1780

Autobiography of "Old Claib Jones."
J2390

Life of Andrew Johnson; Seventeenth President of the United States.
J2410

Autobiography of Mother Jones.
J2500 (BC LMC ASU WCU MHC)

Thoughts of Mother Jones: Compiled from Her Writings and Speeches.
J2510 (WCU)

My Colorful Days.
J2530

Uncle Sandy.
J2580 (ASU)

Simon Girty, the Outlaw.
J2610

The Road I Came.
J2730

Cecil Sharp: His Life and Work.
K230 (BC ASU LMC)

Biographical Record of Daniel and Mary (Jackson) Williams — Early Kentucky Pioneers, 1752-1898.
K590 (ASU)

Simon Kenton: His Life and Period.
K890 (ASU)

Parson of the Hills.
K1790

"Return Jonathan Meigs, Cherokee Indian Agent, 1801-1823."
K2070

Jinny and Jim.
K2150 (ASU)

The Wild Rose of Cherokee, or Nancy Ward, "The Pocahontas of the West." A Story of the Early Exploration, Occupancy, and Settlement of the State of Tennessee. A Romance Founded on and Interwoven With History.
K2270 (LMC BC)

The Wild Rose of Cherokee: Or, Nancy Ward, "The Pocahontas of the West", a Story of the Early Exploration, Occupancy and Settlement of the State of Tennessee. A Romance, Founded on and Interwoven with History.
K2280 (BC ASU)

Dr. William George Bagby: A Study of Virginia Literature 1850-1880.
K2310

Dr. George William Bagby: A Study of Virginia Literature, 1850-1880.
K2320 (ASU)

They Tried to Crucify Me; or, the Smokescreen of the Cumberlands.
L430

"Blanford Barnard Dougherty: Mountain Educator."
L490 (ASU)

Blanford Barnard Dougherty, Mountain Educator.
L500 (ASU)

Some Sketches from My Life, Written for My 80th Birthday, May 1, 1910.
L840

Folksingers and Folksongs in America: A Handbook of Biography, Bibliography, and Discography.
L890 (ASU WWC BC)
L1220

The Autobiography of Joseph LeConte.
L1270 (BC ASU LMC)

My Appalachia: Pipestem State Park Today and Yesterday.
L1370 (ASU BC ETSU LMC)

Memoir of the Rev. Jesse Lee. With Extracts From His Journals.
L1380 (ASU FC)

"Jesse Stuart: Kentucky's Chronicler-poet."
L1690

Experiences of a Circuit Rider.
L1870

The Journals of David E. Lilienthal.
L2440

Ralph McGill, Editor and Publisher.
L3100 (ASU)

Andrew Johnson: President on Trial.
L3120 (MHC ASU BC)

Love's Valley.
L3650

A Diary with Reminiscences of the War and Refugee Life in the Shenandoah Valley, 1860-1865.
M1110 (ASU LMC)

Thomas Wolfe.
M1270 (ASU WCU UNCA)

Daniel Boone.
M1670 (ETSU)

Belonging: A Nostalgic Look at Appalachia.
M1840 (LMC)

Andrew Johnson and Reconstruction.
M1940 (ASU)

Simon Kenton as Soldier, Scout, and Citizen: An Address Delivered Wednesday, August 19, 1936 at the Blue Licks Battlefield State Park, Robertson County, Kentucky on the Occasion of the Celebration of the Battle of the Blue Licks and Commemoration of the Centenary of the Death of General Simon Kenton.
M1970

The Great Wildcatter.
M2870 (ASU BC)

Ralph McGill, Reporter.
M3500

Ralph McGill, Reporter.
M3600

A Minister in the Tennessee Valley for Sixty Seven Years.
M3640

Daniel Boone.
M3750 (ASU)

James Harrod of Kentucky.
M3980 (ASU)

Daniel Boone: Wilderness Trailblazer.
M4010 (ASU ETSU)

William Blount.
M4180 (BC ETSU)

Major General Thomas Maley Harris, A Member of the Military Commission That Tried the President Abraham Lincoln Assassination Conspirators, and Roster of the 10th West Virginia Volunteer Infantry Regiment, 1861-1865.
M4200 (ASU BC)

General James Robertson, Father of Tennessee.
M4360 (ETSU ASU)

Daniel Boone in North Carolina.
M4450 (ASU LMC WCU BC)

On the Trail of Daniel Boone in North Carolina.
M4460 (ASU)

History of Tucker County, West Virginia, from the Earliest Explorations and Settlements to the Present Time: With Biographical Sketches of More Than Two Hundred and Fifty of the Leading Men, and a Full Appendix of Official and Electional History. Also, an Account of the Rivers, Forests and Caves of the County.
M4550 (ASU)

R. A. Sentelle, Educator, Preacher, Public Servant.
M4900 (LMC)

Eliza Ross; or, Illustrated Guide of Lookout Mountain.
M4910

Life and Adventures of Lewis Wetzel.
M5290 (BC)

Man from the Valley: Memoirs of a 20th-Century Virginian.
M5620 (ASU)

The Age of Hate: Andrew Johnson and the Radicals.
M6120 (ASU)

Daniel Boone.
M6160 (ASU BC ETSU)

Jonathan Hager, Founder of Hagerstown, Maryland.
M6230

"A Study of the Life and Works of Jesse Stuart."
M6250 (ASU)

Diary of a Geological Tour by Dr. Elisha Mitchell in 1827 and 1828.
M6300 (ASU BC LMC)

Struggle in the Coal Fields: The Autobiography of Fred Mooney.
M6720 (ASU BC WCU)

John Fox, Jr.: Personal and Family Letters and Papers.
M7110

BIOGRAPHY

Daniel Boone.
M7330
Edward Morgan 1751-1884, Pioneer Minister in Southwest, Virginia.
M7490
A History and Genealogy of the Family of Col. Morgan the First White Settler of the State of West Virginia.
M7530 (ASU)
The Real David Crockett: A Short, Authentic, Illustrated, History of Tennessee's Famous Hunter, Frontiersman, Soldier, Legislator, Statesman, Patriot, and Hero of the Alamo, Colonel David Crockett.
M7930
The Story of Daniel Boone.
M8130 (ASU BC)
Thomas Wolfe.
M8540 (ASU UNCA)
Angel of Appalachia: Martha Berry.
M9280 (ASU MHC)
The Zollie Tree.
M9310 (BC)
Andrew Johnson: Congress and Reconstruction.
N100
Leonard Shoun and his Wife Barbara Slemp Shoun of Johnson Co., Tennessee.
N300
"The Life and Works of Lamar Stringfield, 1897-1959."
N480 (ASU WCU)
Memories.
N1270 (BC)
N2460 (LMC)
The Marble Man's Wife, Thomas Wolfe's Mother.
N2880 (ASU WCU BC UNCA)
Thomas Wolfe, a Biography.
N2930 (BC ASU WCU UNCA)
The Forgotten Pioneer: The Life of Davy Crockett.
N2980 (ASU ETSU)
Bishop on Horseback.
N3040 (BC)
"Doctor Thomas Walker (1715-1794): Explorer, Physician, Surveyor, and Planter of Virginia and Kentucky."
N3050 (BC)
Thomas, Rock of Chickamauga.
O190 (ASU)
Agee.
O450 (WCU)
O690
"Andrew Johnson's Veto of the First Reconstruction Act."
O860
Dr. John McLeod Oxford, 1841-1928; A Sketch of His Life.
O1030 (ASU)
Thomas Hope of Tennessee, 1757-1820, House Carpenter and Joiner.
P120
Charles Egbert Craddock.
P340 (ASU)
Turnpikes and Dirt Roads.
P380
P470
Autobiography of Mother Jones.
P520 (ASU)
Biography of James Patton.
P830
Life of Lucius B. Compton.
P970
John Howard Payne to His Countrymen.
P1120 (WCU)
"Life of John Sevier."
P2190
My Head's High From Proudness.
P2270 (ASU)
Memoir of John Howe Peyton, in the Sketches of His Contemporaries, Together with Some of His Public and Private Letters, etc., Also a Sketch of Ann M. Peyton.
P2500 (ASU)
Martha Berry.
P2530
Samuel Davies: Apostle of Dissent in Colonial Virginia.
P2930 (ASU)
The Collectors: Dr. Claribel and Miss Etta Cone.
P3400 (ASU)
Trial of Andrew Johnson, President of the United States, before the Senate of the United States, on Impeachment by the House of Representatives for High Crimes and Misdemeanors.
P3570
Benjamin Hawkins, Indian Agent.
P3910
Thomas Wolfe, a Bibliography.
P4420 (BC ASU)
Without Script or Purse: Or, The Mountain Evangelist.
P4640 (BC)
George Washington and Winchester, Virginia 1748-1758; A Decade of Preparation for Responsibilities to Come.
Q70 (ASU)
"An Inquiry into the Life of Jesse Stuart as Related to His Literary Development and a Critical Study of His Works."
R210 (ASU)
Autobiography and Letters.
R260 (ASU BC)
The Story of My Life: Or, More Than a Half Century as I Have Lived It and Seen It Lived.
R440 (BC LMC)
"The Life and Career of General James Robertson."
R480
Life and Times of Andrew Johnson, Seventeenth President of the United States.
R700
The Courageous Commoner, a Biography of Andrew Johnson.
R930 (BC)
"The Ross-Watie Conflict: Factionalism in the Cherokee Nation, 1839-1865."
R1060
My Life Story.
R1070 (BC)
A Country Doctor Goes to Town.
R1200 (ASU)
George Washington Harris.
R2190 (BC)
William Gilmore Simms.
R2280 (BC)
Bob Taylor and the Agrarian Revolt in Tennessee.
R3230
Daniel Boone.
R3610 (BC)
How to Be Successful.
R3740
"Jesse Stuart: Pioneer Writer of the Kentucky Hills."
R3750 (ASU)
Story of Rotherwood, from the Autobiography of Rev. Frederick A. Ross.
R3790
Davy Crockett.
R4010 (ETSU BC)
Davy Crockett.
R4020 (ASU)
Andrew Johnson — Presidential Scapegoat.
R4160 (BC)
Thomas Wolfe; a Collection of Critical Essays.
R4180 (UNCA)
Thomas Wolfe: The Weather of His Youth.
R4190 (UNCA ASU WCU BC)
Francis Asbury.
R4240 (ASU WWC BC)
John Ross, Chief of an Eagle Race.
R4330 (ASU)
"William Holland Thomas, White Chief of the North Carolina Cherokees."
R4380
Thomas Wolfe.
R4530 (UNCA)
Life and Public Service of Andrew Johnson.
S530
The Life of John H. Savage: Citizen, Soldier, Lawyer, Congressman.
S540 (LMC)
Four Men of the Cumberlands: Big Ed Hall, Devil John Wright, Dr. M. B. Taylor, Bad Talt Hall.
S680 (ASU BC)
The Life of Daniel Boone in Picture and Story.
S760
Cathedrals in the Wilderness.
S860 (BC)
A Memoir of Hugh Lawson White, Judge of the Supreme Court of Tennessee, Member of the Senate of the United States, Etc., Etc.
S1440 (ASU BC)
Frederick Henry Koch: Pioneer Playmaker. A Brief Biography.
S1780 (LMC)
In Lincoln's Footsteps; the Life of Andrew Johnson.
S2020
Daniel Boone, Pioneer.
S2120 (ASU)
"The Autobiography of David Crockett: An Annotated Edition."
S2140 (ASU)
David Crockett, the Man and the Legend.
S2150 (ASU ETSU BC)
Yankee Thunder: The Legendary Life of Davy Crockett.
S2260 (ASU ETSU)
Andrew Jackson, 1767-1845: Chronology, Documents, Bibliographical Aids.
S2510
Samuel Roberts: A Welsh Colonizer in Civil War Tennessee.
S2850 (ASU)
Zebulon Vance, Tarheel Spokesman.
S3100 (ASU)
Zebulon Vance, Tarheel Spokesman.
S3110 (LMC)
John Uri Lloyd: His Life and Works, 1849-1936.
S3440
S3860
Sergeant York, His Own Life Story and War Diary.
S3870 (ASU ETSU LMC)
Sergeant York, Last of the Long Hunters.
S3880 (ASU BC)
Lion of White Hall: The Life of Cassius M. Clay.
S4400 (MHC)
Down by the Riverside.
S4440
The Daniel Boone Story.
S4540 (BC)
Nathan Goff, Jr., a Biography: With Some Account of Guy Despard Goff and Brazilla Carroll Reece.
S4710 (ASU)
Memoirs.
S4750 (ETSU)
"Emerson Etheridge as a Candidate in the Tennessee Gubernatorial Election of 1867."
S5060
Charles Lewis Cocke, Founder of Hollins College.
S5200
Daniel Boone.
S6010
"Elizabeth M. Roberts: A Biographical and Critical Study."
S6050 (ASU)
A Man in His Time.
S6290 (ASU)
Biographies of Southwest Virginians.
S6310
Davy Crockett.
S6320
Davy Crockett.
S6330 (WWC)
Spurrier With the Wildcats and Moonshiners.
S6390 (ASU BC)
A Rough Road in a Good Land.
S6580 (ASU)
A Colorful Career of a Miraculous Mountaineer: A Glimpse into the Life of a Remarkable Character.
S6700 (ASU)
The First President Johnson: The Three Lives of the Seventeenth President of the United States of America.
S6770
Anvil of Adversity: Biography of Furniture Pioneer.
S7140 (ASU WCU BC)
Daniel Boone, Boy Hunter.
S7160 (ETSU)
Daniel Boone, Boy Hunter.
S7170 (ASU)
A Touch of Charisma; a History of the 4-H Club Program in West Virginia.
S7240
The Biography of Eld. Barton Warren Stone, Written by Himself.
S7510 (ASU)

BIOGRAPHY

The Life of Jacob Gruder.
S7970 (BC)
Andrew Johnson; a Study in Courage.
S8170 (ASU)
Beyond Dark Hills: A Personal Story.
S8260 (ASU LMC)
Beyond Dark Hills: A Personal Story.
S8270 (ETSU WCU)
God's Oddling: The Story of Mick Stuart, My Father.
S8350 (ASU MHC WCU ETSU BC)
S8620
The Thread That Runs So True.
S8670 (ASU MHC LMC WCU WWC BC)
The Thread That Runs So True.
S8680 (ETSU UNCA)
To Teach, to Love.
S8700 (ASU MHC WWC UNCA ETSU BC)
The Year of My Rebirth.
S8720 (ASU ETSU BC)
Rimfire, His Life Story and Selections From His Own Writings. A Study of the Typical Mountaineer, Eli (Rimfire) Hamrick.
S8920 (ASU BC)
Recollections of an Old Man. Seventy Years in Dixie.
S8950
Borderland Confederate.
S9000
Richard D. B. Sutherland; An Early Leader of Education in Sandy Basin.
S9220
Jemima, Daughter of Daniel Boone.
S9340
The First Rebel; Being a Lost Chapter of Our History on a True Narrative of America's First Uprising Against English Military Authority and An Account of the First Fighting Between Armed Colonists and British Regulars. Together with a Biography of Colonel James Smith. . .
S9460 (BC)
The Rebel Raider, a Life of John Hunt Morgan.
S9700 (BC ASU)
Benjamin Logan, Kentucky Frontiersman.
T40 (WCU BC)
Rebecca Latimer Felton, Nine Stormy Decades.
T110 (ASU)
Kentucky Pioneer Women. Columbian Poems and Prose Sketches.
T150 (BC)
Andrew Johnson — Not Guilty.
T210
Life and Career of Senator Robert Love Taylor (Our Bob) by His Three Surviving Brothers.
T580 (ASU)
"The Public Career of Joseph Alexander Mabry."
T590
Memorial Addresses Delivered in the Senate and the House of Representatives of the United States.
T740 (ASU)
John Sevier, Citizen, Soldier, Legislator, Governor, Statesman.
T850 (ETSU)
Medicine in Buncombe County Down to 1885, Historical and Biographical Sketches.
T880
Commission Book, 1796-1801.
T1490 (ASU ETSU)
General Turner Ashby, the Centaur of the South: A Military Sketch.
T7760 (ASU)
The Sun Shines Bright.
T7960 (ASU WCU LMC ETSU BC)
The Traipsin' Woman.
T7970 (ASU WWC BC)
The First President Johnson: The Three Lives of the Seventeenth President of the United States of America.
T7990 (ASU)
Jeb Stuart.
T8090
Daniel Boone.
T8490 (ETSU BC)
Daniel Boone.
T8500 (ASU)
Frances Asbury, the Prophet of the Long Road.
T8730 (ASU)
The Heart of Asbury's Journal.
T8740
John Fox, Jr.
T8770
Biography of the State Officers and Members of the General Assembly of North Carolina, 1893, Other Interesting Facts.
T8840 (ASU LMC)
Colonel "Davey" Crockett.
T8960
Davy Crockett: Hero of the Alamo.
T9060 (ETSU)
Richard Hickman Menefee.
T9090 (BC)
William Gilmore Simms.
T9240 (ASU)
Zeb Vance: Champion of Personal Freedom.
T9640 (ASU WCU UNCA)
Thomas Wolfe.
T9750 (ASU WCU UNCA)
Life of General John Sevier.
T9790 (ASU)
My Beloved Zebulon; the Correspondence of Zebulon B. Vance and Harriett Newell Espy.
V100
Papers.
V110 (ASU LMC)
Daniel Boone, Backwoodsman: The Green Woods Were His Portion.
V390 (ASU WCU LMC MHC)
"Robert Jefferson Breckinridge as an Educational Administrator."
V460 (ETSU)
"Andrew Johnson and the National Union Movement."
W140
Terence V. Powderly, "Labor Mayor", Workingmen's Politics in Scranton, Pennsylvania, 1870-1884.
W360
John Eston Cooke: A Critical Biography.
W420
The Enigma of Thomas Wolfe: Biographical and Critical Selections.
W570 (ASU WCU)
Thomas Wolfe: An Introduction and Interpretation.
W630 (UNCA ASU WCU BC)
My Grandfather, My Grandchildren, and Me: An Autobiography of Charles W. Wampler.
W700 (ASU)
Andrew Jackson, Symbol for an Age.
W750 (ASU)
Lincoln's Parentage Childhood.
W960
The Life and Labors of Archibald McLean.
W990 (BC)
A Country Doctor in the South Mountains.
W1000 (ASU LMC MHC BC)
Six nights in a Block house.
W1520 (BC)
Men of Mark and Representative Citizens of Harrisonburg and Rockingham County, Virginia.
W1810 (ASU BC)
Sidney Lanier at Rockingham Springs.
W1840 (BC)
Mount Mitchell and Dr. Elisha Mitchell.
W2040
Benjamin Helm Bristow, Border State Politician.
W2060 (BC)
Alvin C. York, Young Marksman.
W2190 (ETSU)
Shadows on the Wall: The Life and Works of Howard Weeden.
W2220 (BC)
Twenty Years on Horseback.
W2240 (BC)
The Weiser Family.
W2400
"Andrew Johnson, Senator from Tennessee, 1857-1862."
W2770
Labor's Defiant Lady: The Story of Mother Jones.
W2850 (ASU)
Robert Rharin: Biography of a Mountain Abolitionist.
W2970 (LMC)
The Ballad of Tom Dula: The Documented Story Behind the Murder of Laura Foster and the Trials and Execution of Tom Dula.
W3030 (ASU BC)
Alexander Campbell and Natural Religion.
W3100 (BC)
W4870 (ASU)
Doctor Woman of the Cumberlands: The Autobiography of May Cravath Wharton, M. D.
W5020 (ASU LMC WWC BC)
Doctor Woman of the Cumberlands; the Autobiography of May Cravath Wharton, M. D.
W5030 (LMC WCU)
Thomas Wolfe and His Family.
W5040 (ASU WCU BC UNCA)
White Squaw: The True Story of Jennie Wiley.
W5050 (ASU ETSU)
White Squaw: The True Story of Jennie Wiley.
W5060 (MHC)
Historical Sketches of North Carolina from 1584 to 1851.
W5130 (ASU LMC)
Historical Sketches of North Carolina from 1584 to 1851 Compiled from Original Records, Official Documents, and Traditional Statements, with Biographical Sketches of Her Distinguished Statesmen, Jurists, Lawyers, Soldiers, Divines, etc.
W5140 (LMC BC)
Reminiscences and Memoirs of North Carolina and Eminent North Carolinians.
W5150 (UNCA BC ASU)
A History of the Life of Amos Owens, the Noted Blockader, of Cherry Mountain, North Carolina.
W5520 (LMC)
Daniel Boone: Wilderness Scout.
W5580 (ETSU ASU BC)
Daniel Boone; Wilderness Scout.
W5590 (BC)
Daniel Boone, Wilderness Scout.
W5600 (ETSU)
Daniel Boone: Wilderness Scout. The Life Story and True Adventure of the Great Hunter, Long Knife, Who First Blazed the Wilderness Trail Through the Indians Country to Kentucky.
W5610 (ASU)
Sam Davis, Hero of the Confederacy, 1842-1863, Coleman's Scouts.
W5760
David Lilienthal, Public Servant in a Power Age.
W5830 (BC)
Life and Times of Judge Caleb Wallace, Some Time a Justice of the Court of Appeals of the State of Ky.
W5870 (BC)
Daniel Boone: Taming the Wilds.
W6280 (BC)
John Sevier, Son of Tennessee.
W6300 (ETSU)
John Sevier, Son of Tennessee.
W6310 (LMC)
"Davis and Elkins of West Virginia: Businessmen in Politics."
W6620
William Tatham, Wataugan.
W6850 (ETSU ASU WCU BC)
A History of Windy Cove Church, Millboro Springs, Virginia, 1929-1949.
W7660 (ASU)
Andrew Johnson, Plebian and Patriot.
W7830 (ASU)
Mine Eyes Have Seen: A Woman Doctor's Saga.
W7970 (WWC BC)
The Life of a Man: A Biography of John R. Brinkley.
W8480 (ASU)
So Sure of Life.
W8650 (BC)
Fletch Woodward, His Fights with Those Bad, Bad Town Boys.
W8970
They Have Topped the Mountain.
W9160 (ASU)
The Shepherd of the Hills.
W9410 (ASU)
William Blount, 1749-1800.
W9490 (ETSU)
Devil John Wright of the Cumberlands.
W9560 (BC)
Isaac Shelby Kentucky's First Governor and Hero of Three Wars.
W9780
Boyhood Days in Southwest Virginia.
W9900 (BC)
The Confederacy and Zeb Vance.
Y80 (ASU WCU UNCA)

BIOGRAPHY

Sergeant York: His Own Life Story and War Diary.
Y130 (LMC BC)

Autobiography of a Pioneer: Or, The Nativity, Experience, Travels, and Ministerial Labors of Rev. Jacob Young, with Incidents, Observations, and Reflections.
Y260 (BC)

BIOGRAPHY — GA.

Historical Collections of Georgia: Containing the Most Interesting Facts, Traditions, Biographical Sketches, Anecdotes, etc., Relating to Its History and Antiquities, from Its First Settlement to the Present Time.
W5410 (ASU BC)

BIOGRAPHY — N. C.

100 Years, 100 Men: 1871-1971.
C8830 (ASU)

Tar Heels Track the Century: Andrew Johnson, Z. B. Vance, M. W. Ransom, C. B. Aycock, O. Henry, J. B. Duke, W. H. Page, F. M. Simmons, Josephus Daniels, Thomas Wolfe.
E900 (WCU ETSU ASU)

Builders of the Old North State: Selected Sketches.
H4060 (LMC)

The Tribe of Jacob: The Descendants of the Reverend Jacob Weaver of Reems Creek, North Carolina, 1786-1868, and Elizabeth Siler Weaver.
W2010

BIOGRAPHY — VA.

Men and Events: Chapters of Virginia History.
G2670 (LMC)

My Life's History.
K450

My Memoirs and Autobiography.
K501
V1110 (BC)

BIOLOGY

Appalachian Wilderness.
B2330

Follow the Butterfly Stream.
B5910 (ASU)

Military and Genealogical Records of the Famous Indian Woman; Nancy Ward. . . .
B9090

Sense of Discovery: The Mountain.
R2700 (ASU LMC BC WCU)

Sense of Discovery: The Mountain.
R3060 (ASU LMC WCU BC)

BIOLOGY — APP.

Studies of the Codling Moth in the Central Appalachian Region.
B6920

The Litter Arthropod Community in a Southern Appalachian Hardwood Forest: Numbers, Biomass and Mineral Element Content.
G1850

Geomorphology and Forest Ecology of the Mountain Region in the Central Appalachians.
H90

The Discoveries of John Lederer.
R2330 (ASU LMC)

The Effects of Acid Mine Drainage on Aquatic Insects.
R2630 (ASU)

North With the Spring: A Naturalist's Record of a 17,000 Mile Journey With the North-American Spring.
T800 (ASU LMC)

BIOLOGY — N. C.

Carolina Landscape Plants.
H540 (LMC)

Amphibians and Reptiles of Great Smoky Mountains National Park.
H8160 (UNCA ASU LMC WCU BC)

Hidden Valley of the Smokies.
H8690

Hidden Valley of the Smokies: With a Naturalist in the Great Smoky Mountains.
H8700 (ASU LMC MHC WWC BC WCU ETSU)

"An Ecological Survey of Flat Rock Mountain."
S3600 (ASU)

A Manual of the Fresh-Water Algae in North Carolina.
W5740 (LMC)

BIOLOGY — N. C. — WATAUGA CO.

A Survey of Monogenetic Trematodes from the Gills of Salmo Gairdneri, Salverinus Fontinalis, and Salmo Trutta in Watauga County, North Carolina.
A4620

BIOLOGY — TENN.

"The Distribution and Relative Abundance of Some Immature Aquatic Insects in Red Fork Creek, Unicoi County, Tennessee."
C5810 (ETSU)

"Small Mammals of Washington and Unicoi Counties, Tennessee."
G1390 (ETSU)

Amphibians and Reptiles of Great Smoky Mountains National Park.
H8160 (UNCA ASU LMC WCU BC)

"A Study of Serum Protein Variation in Peromyscus Maniculatus Nubiterrae Rhoads at Six Attitudinal Habitats on Roan Mountain, Carter County, Tennessee, and Mitchell County, North Carolina."
M880 (ETSU)

"Distribution of Tardigrades on Roan Mountain, Tennessee - North Carolina."
N510

A Bibliography of the Zoology of Tennessee and Tennessee Valley Region.
S3190 (ASU BC)

Annual Report of the State Entomologist and Plant Pathologist.
T940 (ETSU)

BIRTH CONTROL

Contraception and Fertility in the Southern Appalachians.
B2550 (BC ASU)

"Contraception and Fertility in the Southern Appalachians."
B2560

Contraception and Fertility in the Southern Appalachians.
B2570 (LMC)

The Bedroom of the Poor.
B6880

Appalachian Fertility Decline: A Demographic and Sociological Analysis.
D1660 (ASU WCU LMC ETSU BC UNCA)

Fertility Data for the Southern Appalachian Region.
D1670

"Human Fertility in the Southern Appalachian Region: Some Demographic and Sociological Aspects."
D1680 (ASU)

Too Many People, Too Little Love.
D4300

Changing Patterns of Fertility in Tennessee, 1960-1970.
E1940

"A Survey of the Attitudes of Women in Monongalia County, West Virginia, toward the Use of Contraceptives."
S9720

BIRTH CONTROL — APP.

"Mothers of the South: A Population Study of Native White Women of Childbearing Age of the Southeast."
H240

BIRTH CONTROL — KY.

"Metropolitan Dominance and the Diffusion of Human Fertility Patterns, Kentucky, 1939-65."
K3340

Projected Kentucky Population Growth by Age, Sex, and Color Groups: 1960 to 1970.
K3350

BIRTH CONTROL — TENN.

"Exploratory Study of the Views toward Birth Control Services."
C7100

BLUE RIDGE MOUNTAINS

The Mountain Angels: Trials of the Mountaineers of the Blue Ridge and Shenandoah Valley.
B2410 (BC ASU LMC)

"Fan-like Features and Related Periglacial Phenomena of the Southern Blue Ridge."
M5310 (WCU)

BLUE RIDGE PARKWAY

The Blue Ridge Parkway: Accommodations and Services.
B4800 (ETSU)
B4810

The Blue Ridge Parkway.
J2220 (BC ASU LMC WCU WWC FC ETSU)

"The Blue Ridge Parkway: Origins and Early Development."
J2230
J2820 (ETSU LMC)

"The Campaign for a National Park in Western North Carolina, 1885-1940."
L540 (WCU)

Pigeon Cove and Vicinity.
L1820

The Blue Ridge Parkway Guide.
L3470 (LMC ASU)

The Blue Ridge Parkway Guide.
L3520 (BC LMC ASU WCU)

North Wilkesboro, Wilkes County, N. C.: Key to the Blue Ridge Parkway.
N2800 (ASU LMC)

The Collectors: Dr. Claribel and Miss Etta Cone.
P3400 (ASU)

Camper's and Hiker's Guide to the Blue Ridge Parkway.
R3240 (ASU LMC ETSU FC WCU BC)

BLUE RIDGE PARKWAY — VA.

The Blue Ridge: Man and Nature in Shenandoah National Park and Blue Ridge Parkway.
W6260 (WCU LMC)

BOOK — W. VA.

West Virginia Imprints, 1790-1863.
N1460

BOTANY

Shade Trees for North Carolina.
A5140 (ASU LMC)

Identifying Southern Forest Types on Aerial Photographs.
A5780 (WCU)

"The Natural Vegetation of Johnson County, Tennessee, Past and Present."
B1110 (ETSU)

Diary of a Journey through the Carolinas, Georgia, and Florida, 1765-66.
B1700 (ASU BC)

Travels.
B1710 (LMC)

The Travels of William Bartram.
B1720 (WCU)

The Travels of William Bartram.
B1730 (ASU)

Travels through North Carolina and South Carolina, Georgia, East and West Florida.
B1740 (ASU)

Deterioration of Chestnut in the Southern Appalachians.
B2130

Appalachian Wilderness.
B2330

Flowering Trees and Shrubs.
B3680

The Natural History of North Carolina.
B6600 (ASU BC LMC)

The Appalachians.
B6960 (ASU WCU LMC MHC FC WWC ETSU BC FC UNCA)

The Life of the Mountains.
B6970 (BC)
C2000 (ETSU UNCA BC)

"A Survey of the Vascular Plants of the Sinking Creek Area of Carter County, Tennessee."
P1240 (ETSU)

Sense of Discovery: The Mountain.
R2700 (ASU LMC BC WCU)

Sense of Discovery: The Mountain.
R3060 (ASU LMC WCU BC)

Dyes from Plants.
R3170 (ASU)

Lost Heritage.
S510 (LMC)

William Bartram's Venture into the Cherokee Country, 1775.
S7010 (LMC WCU)

The Natural Gardens of North Carolina, with Keys and Descriptions of the Herbaceous Wild Flowers Found Therein.
W2640 (ASU WWC)

The Natural Gardens of North Carolina, with Keys and Descriptions of the Herbaceous Wild Flowers Found Therein.
W2650 (ASU ETSU LMC)

The Remarkable Flora of the Great Smoky Mountains.
W2660

BOTANY
Flowers of the Mountain Country. 1975 Deals with Some of the More Representative of Both Conspicuous and Inconspicuous Types.
W2780
Plant Life of Braxton County, Number 8 Plant Ecology.
W9740 (ASU)
BOTANY — APP.
Tennessee Valley Wildlife: An Outlook for the Year 2000.
E1920
"A Geographic Approach to a Vegetation Problem: The Case of the Southern Appalachian Grassy Balds."
G1060 (BC ASU)
"Vegetation of the Grassy Balds of the Great Smoky Mountains."
G1300
Flowers of the South, Native and Exotic.
G3840 (ASU BC)
Wild Flowers of the Alleghenies.
H2490 (BC)
Manna: Foods of the Frontier.
H2850 (ASU WCU)
American Medicinal Barks.
H4640 (ASU)
Plants of the Caloosa Experimental Range.
H5540 (WCU)
The Distributional History of the Biota of the Southern Appalachians.
H6940
Ginseng, Its Cultivation, Harvesting, Marketing and Market Value: With a Short Account of Its History and Botany.
K70 (WWC)
The Old Naturalist's Notebook: Wild Flowers of the Appalachian.
L670 (UNCA ASU)
A Southern Garden: A Handbook for the Middle South.
L900 (ASU)
The Discoveries of John Lederer.
L1280 (LMC)
The Discoveries of John Lederer, in Three Several Marches From Virginia, to the West of Carolina, and Other Parts of the Continent: Begun in March 1669, and Ended in September 1670.
L1290 (ASU FC BC)
The Discoveries of John Lederer, with Unpublished Letters By and About Lederer to Governor John Winthrop, Jr.
L1300 (ASU WCU ETSU)
Memoirs of Burkes Garden and Tazewell County.
L2580
Silvical Characteristics of Sweetgum.
M3790 (WCU)
Travels to the West of the Allegheny Mountains . . .
M5330 (ASU BC)
Decorative Plants of Appalachia: A Source of Income.
N530 (ASU ETSU LMC)
Wilderness Adventure.
P30 (ASU)
The Discoveries of John Lederer.
R2330 (ASU LMC)
Ferns in the Southeastern States. Descriptions of the Fern Plants Growing Naturally in the States South of the Virginia-Kentucky State Line and East of the Mississippi River.
S4300 (ASU BC)
Manual of the Southeastern Flora; Being Descriptions of the Seed Plants Growing in Florida, Alabama, Mississippi, Eastern Louisiana, Tennessee, North Carolina, South Carolina and Georgia.
S4310
Common Seed Plants of the Mid-Appalachian Region.
S7820 (ASU BC)
Trees, Shrubs, and Woody Vines of Great Smoky Mountains National Park.
S8870 (ASU WCU LMC WWC UNCA)
Trees, Shrubs, and Woody Vines of Great Smoky Mountains National Park.
S8880
North With the Spring: A Naturalist's Record of a 17,000 Mile Journey With the North-American Spring.
T800 (ASU LMC)
Rhododendrons in America.
V440 (ASU)
Trees and Shrubs for the Southeast.
W6000 (BC)
Ferns of Ky; with Full-page Etchings and Wood Cuts.
W6950 (BC)
BOTANY — GA.
Ferns of Georgia.
M2550 (LMC)
BOTANY — KY.
John Filson, the First Historian of Kentucky: An Account of His Life and Writings.
D4100 (LMC)
A Guide to the Wildflowers and Ferns of Kentucky.
W5000 (ASU ETSU WCU BC WWC)
Trees and Shrubs of Kentucky.
W5010 (BC)
BOTANY — N. C.
"Twenty-five Common Mosses of Watauga County, North Carolina."
B140 (ASU)
The Grasses of North Carolina.
B4740 (ASU BC LMC WWC)
The Boletaceae of North Carolina.
C5650 (ASU WWC)
The Trees of North Carolina.
C5660 (ASU)
Botany: Containing a Catalogue of the Indigenous and Naturalized Plants of the State.
C9910 (LMC ASU)
The Shrubs and Woody Vines of North Carolina.
C9920 (LMC)
A Preliminary Check-list of the Ligneous Flora of the Highland Region, North Carolina.
H2050 (ASU)
North Carolina Drug Plants of Commercial Value.
H2130 (ASU LMC UNCA)
Poisonous Plants of North Carolina.
H2140 (LMC)
Mushrooms of the Great Smokies: A Field Guide to Some Mushrooms and Their Relatives.
H5050 (ASU WHC LMC UNCA BC WWC)
"The Hepatic Flora of Watauga County, North Carolina."
H5220 (ASU)
Hidden Valley of the Smokies.
H8690
Hidden Valley of the Smokies: With a Naturalist in the Great Smoky Mountains.
H8700 (ASU LMC MHC WWC BC WCU ETSU)
The Flora of North Carolina from Ranunculaceae to Salviniaceae.
H8770 (LMC)
Wild Flowers of North Carolina.
J3020 (ASU LMC WWC ETSU)
The Flora of North Carolina from Ranunculaceae to Salviniaceae.
J3390 (ASU)
A New Voyage to Carolina.
L1000 (LMC ETSU)
A New Voyage to Carolina.
L1010 (UNCA)
"Vascular Flora of the Sim's Pond Area."
L2890 (ASU)
Drug Plants of Western North Carolina.
M2740 (WCU ASU)
An Appalachian Valley.
M3840 (ASU)
An Appalachian Valley.
M3840 (ASU)
"The Phytoecology of Boone Fork Sphagnum Bog."
M7350 (ASU)
Silvical Characteristics of Bitternut Hickory.
N540 (WCU)
Silvical Characteristics of the Commercial Hickories.
N550 (WCU)
Silvical Characteristics of Mockernut Hickory.
N560 (WCU)
Silvical Characteristics of Shagbark Hickory.
N570 (WCU)
The Shrubs and Woody Vines of North Carolina.
N1970 (ASU)
Atlas of the Vascular Flora of the Carolinas.
R10 (LMC WWC)
Guide to the Vascular Flora of the Carolinas, with Distribution in the Southeastern States.
R20 (LMC WWC)
Manual of the Vascular Flora of the Carolinas.
R30 (ETSU LMC WWC)
"An Ecological Survey of Flat Rock Mountain."
S3600 (ASU)
A Manual of the Fresh-Water Algae in North Carolina.
W5740 (LMC)
BOTANY — S. C.
Wild Flowers in South Carolina.
B1910 (ASU LMC)
Atlas of the Vascular Flora of the Carolinas.
R10 (LMC WWC)
Guide to the Vascular Flora of the Carolinas, with Distribution in the Southeastern States.
R20 (LMC WWC)
Manual of the Vascular Flora of the Carolinas.
R30 (ETSU LMC WWC)
Botanical Gardening in Greenville.
S300 (BC ASU)
BOTANY — TENN.
List of Tennessee Certified Nurseries Collectors of Native Wild Plants and Nursery Dealers for the Season 1967-1968.
B7680 (LMC)
The Flora of Tennessee and a Philosophy of Botany, Respectfully Dedicated to the Citizens of Tennessee.
G600
The Medicinal Plants of Tennessee Exhibiting Their Commercial Value, with an Analytical Key, Descriptions in Aid of Their Recognition, and Notes Relating to Their Distribution, Time and Mode of Collection, and Preparation for the Drug Market.
G610
The Tennessee Flora: With Special Reference to the Flora of Nashville. Phaenogams and Vascular Crytogams.
G620
"A Survey of the Flowering Plants and Ferns on the Forge Hill, Carter County, Tennessee."
G4290 (ETSU)
Dr. Augustin Gattinger: The Pioneer Botanist of Tennessee.
H940
Some Mushrooms of Eastern Tennessee. I. Amanitas.
H5060 (ASU)
The Grasses of Tennessee: Including Cereals and Forage Plants.
K1900 (BC ASU LMC)
"A Vegetational Analysis of the Rattlesnake Ridge Area of Unaka Mountain, Unicoi County, Tennessee."
P1130 (ETSU)
Summer Key to Tennessee Trees.
S2220 (ASU LMC BC)
Ferns of Tennessee, with the Fern Allies Excluded.
S2460 (WWC)
Annual Report of the State Entomologist and Plant Pathologist.
T940 (ETSU)
"Some Tennessee Trees — a Simple, Illustrated Key."
T1070
BOTANY — VA.
Pilgrim at Tinker Creek.
D2400 (BC ASU)
Pilgrim at Tinker Creek.
D2410 (ASU)
John Banister and His Natural History of Virginia, 1678-1692.
E2420 (LMC)
BOTANY — W. VA.
A History of Botany in West Virginia.
B5470 (ASU ETSU WCU BC)
West Virginia Trees.
B6870 (ASU WCU)
Plant Life of West Virginia.
C7420 (ETSU)
Vegetation of West Virginia.
C7440 (ASU LMC BC)
A Compilation of the Edible Wild Plants of W. Va.
G1630
A Guide to the Common Fossils Plants of W. Va.
G1640
Plant Fossils of West Virginia.
G1650 (BC ETSU)
West Virginia Geology, Archaeology, and Pedology: A Bibliography and Index.
G1660 (BC ETSU)

BOTANY — W. VA.
Spring Flora of Virginia.
H3300 (ASU BC LMC)
Part 1: The Living Flora of West Virginia. Part 2: The Fossil Flora of West Virginia.
M6100 (ETSU)
Flora of West Virginia.
S7830 (ASU)
CAMPING
Suggestions as to Outfit for Tramping and Camping.
A3290
On Wandering Wheels, Through Roadside Camps from Maine to Georgia in an Old Sedan Car.
G2730
Pleasure Packing, How to Backpack in Comfort.
W8630
CAMPING — APP.
Camping and Woodcraft: A Handbook for Vacation Campers and for Travelers in the Wilderness.
K1460 (ASU)
CATAWBA RIVER
"An Archaeological Survey of the Upper Catawba River Valley."
K390
"An Archaeological Survey of the Upper Catawba River Valley."
K400
CAVES AND CAVERNS
Geology of Luray Caverns, Virginia.
H80 (ETSU FC)
CAVES AND CAVERNS — APP.
Celebrated American Caverns.
H7550
Celebrated American Caverns, Especially Mammoth, Wyandot, and Luray.
H7560
CAVES AND CAVERNS — KY.
Mammoth Cave of Kentucky . . . with an Account of Colossal Cave.
H7570
Letcher County's Pine Mountain Caves.
J730 (BC)
Geology of the Mammoth Cave National Park Area. Rev. by Preston McGrain. Kentucky Geological Survey Series 10, Special publication 7. Revision of Series 9, Special publication 2.
L2910 (ETSU ASU)
Caverns of Virginia.
M1540 (LMC)
CAVES AND CAVERNS — PA.
Penn's Grandest Cavern: The History, Legends and Description of Penn's Cave in Centre County, Pennsylvania.
S3140
CAVES AND CAVERNS — TENN.
Caves of Tennessee.
B1450
CAVES AND CAVERNS — VA.
Exploring the Endless Caverns of New Market, Virginia.
A5260 (LMC)
The Flint Ridge Cave System, Mammoth Cave National Park, Kentucky.
C2580 (ASU BC)
The Endless Caverns of the Shenandoah Valley.
R1150 (BC)
CAVES AND CAVERNS — W. VA.
Caverns of West Virginia.
D710 (ETSU)
The Sinks of Gandy Creek.
P4270 (ASU BC WCU)
CHATTAHOOCHEE RIVER
Tourism Development in the Chattahoochee-Flint Area.
K430
CHEOAH RIVER
Floods on Cheoah River and Tributary Creeks in Vicinity of Robbinsville, North Carolina.
T6990
CHEROKEE LEGENDS
Younger Brother, a Cherokee Indian Tale.
S3575 (ETSU)
CHILD REARING
"Structural Analysis of Mothers' Attitudes toward Child Rearing in Four Communities in Appalachia."
N1310
CHILD WELFARE
Girl in the Rural Family.
M5950 (ASU BC)
Child Welfare in Kentucky: An Inquiry.
N130 (ASU BC)
CHILD WELFARE — APP.
From Mountain Cabin to Cotton Mill.
C610
Health and Nutrition in Disadvantaged Children.
C1700
Wages of Neglect.
C5910 (ASU)
The Child That Toileth Not: The Story of a Government Investigation.
D1320 (ASU BC)
Appalachia's Children: The Challenge of Mental Health.
L3400 (ASU WCU ETSU LMC MHC WWC BC)
"Self-concepts of Appalachian Children: A Comparative Study of Economically Poor and Economically Disadvantaged Children Using the Piers-Harris Self-concept Inventory."
L3510 (LMC ASU)
"Structural Analysis of Mothers' Attitudes toward Child Rearing in Four Communities in Appalachia."
N1310
Roots of Fertility.
P3340
Report on the School Sponsored Program, Appalachian Area.
S550
"Experimental Preschool Intervention in the Appalachian Home."
W6940
CHILD WELFARE — GA.
. . . Maternity and Infant Care in a Mountain County in Georgia.
S6750 (BC)
Bureau publication No. 120 Steete, Glenn. Maternity and infant care in a mountain county in Georgia.
U1600
CHILD WELFARE — KY.
Rural Child Care Project, 1968-1969 Research Evaluation.
A4530
Rural Child Care Project, 1969-1970 Research Evaluation. Final Report.
A4540
"A Report of a Summer Internship at Buckhorn Children's Center, Buckhorn, Kentucky."
A4680 (ASU)
Child Welfare in Kentucky.
C5110 (ASU)
"Child-rearing Practices in Mountain Country, Kentucky."
H4770 (LMC)
"An Administrative History of Public Programs for Dependent Children in North Carolina, Virginia, Tennessee, and Kentucky, 1900-1942."
L2740
The Nutrition and Care of Children in a Mountain County of Kentucky.
R3000
Children of Appalachia.
S3270 (ASU ETSU MHC BC)
The Nutrition and Care of Children in a Mountain County in Kentucky.
U1610
This Happened in the Hills of Kentucky.
V1300 (ASU LMC)
CHILD WELFARE — N. C.
Rural Children in Selected Counties of North Carolina.
B6180 (ASU BC LMC)
"An Administrative History of Public Programs for Dependent Children in North Carolina, Virginia, Tennessee, and Kentucky, 1900-1942."
L2740
CHILD WELFARE — TENN.
"An Administrative History of Public Programs for Dependent Children in North Carolina, Virginia, Tennessee, and Kentucky, 1900-1942."
L2740
"Development of Adoption Practices in East Tennessee."
M8430
"A Study of Parent-child Relationships in Greene County, Tennessee."
R1720 (ETSU)
"Community Concept of Juvenile Court Function in Knox County, Tennessee."
S3460
Report to the Governor and Members of the General Assembly (81st) State of Tennessee.
T960 (ETSU)
Report to Honorable Frank G. Clement, Governor, and Members of the 80th General Assembly, State of Tennessee.
T970 (ETSU)
Tennessee's Children and Youth.
T1760 (ETSU)
CHILD WELFARE — VA.
"An Administrative History of Public Programs for Dependent Children in North Carolina, Virginia, Tennessee, and Kentucky, 1900-1942."
L2740
CHILD WELFARE — W. VA.
Our Troubled Children.
K110
The Welfare of Children in Bituminous Coal Mining Communities in West Virginia.
M1530 (ASU)
The 1965 Head Start Psychological Screening Program; Final Report on the Data Analysis Conducted Under a Contract Between the West Virginia Office of Economic Opportunity and West Virginia University.
S810 (ASU)
Opportunities for Improving Administration of Federal Program of Aid to Educationally Deprived Children in West Virginia, Office of Education, Department of Health, Education, and Welfare.
U3070
CHILDREN AND YOUTH
Youth Action and Youth Issues in Appalachia: A Report.
A3980 (ASU)
This Happened in the Hills of Kentucky.
V1300 (ASU LMC)
CHILDREN AND YOUTH — KY.
Dropouts and Jobs: The Report of the Kentucky Conference on Youth, August 22-23, 1963.
K1000
Youth Education and the Economic Opportunity Act of 1964: Some Indications of Need for Broad-based School and Community Action Programs for Kentucky Youth with Implications for Federal Assistance Programs.
K1100
CHILDREN AND YOUTH — N. C. — 4-H CLUBS
Memories of 4-H.
H2600 (ASU)
CHILDREN AND YOUTH — TENN.
Tennessee's Children and Youth.
T1760 (ETSU)
CHILDREN AND YOUTH — VA.
Virginia Rural Youth Adjustments.
G410
The Youth of the Old Dominion.
H7100 (ASU)
CHILDREN AND YOUTH — W. VA.
Our Troubled Children.
K110
CHILDREN AND YOUTH — W. VA. — COAL CAMPS
Youth Recreation in the Coal Mining Towns of West Virginia.
H6590
CHRISTMAS CUSTOMS
Once Upon a Christmas.
B8190
Ten Christmas Carols from the Southern Appalachian Mountains.
N1130 (ASU BC)
Ancient English Christmas Carols.
R2200 (FC)
American Folk Songs for Christmas.
S1700 (ASU)
CHRISTMAS CUSTOMS — APP.
The Southern Christmas Book: The Full Story from Earliest Times to Present. People, Customs, Conviviality, Carols, Cooking.
K150 (MHC)
Colonial Holiday Treats, Special Recipes.
S2690 (ASU BC)

CHRISTMAS CUSTOMS — TENN.
Christmas at Grinder's Switch.
P1230 (LMC)
CHRISTMAS CUSTOMS — VA.
Christmas in the Mountains, Southwest Virginia Christmas Customs and Their Origins.
D1040 (ASU BC FC)
CIVIL WAR
Political Reconstruction in Tennessee.
A1430
Political Reconstruction in Tennessee.
A1440 (BC ASU)
Rhea and Meigs Counties (Tennessee) in the Confederate War.
A1680 (ASU BC)
The Stonewall Brigade Band.
B6590 (ASU BC)
Annals of Augusta County, Virginia, with Reminiscences and a Diary of the War, 1861-1865, and a Chapter on Reconstruction.
W30 (LMC BC ASU)
Harpers Ferry, Prize of War.
W2540 (ASU)
The Civil War Diary of Capt. J. J. Womack.
W8430
One of Jackson's Foot Cavalry: His Experience and What He Saw During the War, 1861-1865, Including a History of "F Company," Richmond, Va., 21st Regiment Virginia Infantry, Second Brigade, Jackson's Division, Second Corps.
W9290 (ASU)
Tennessee in the War, 1861-1865: List of Military Organizations and Officers from Tennessee (Confederate and Union).
W9480 (BC)
Of Stars and Bars.
W9760 (BC)
The Confederacy and Zeb Vance.
Y80 (ASU WCU UNCA)
CIVIL WAR — ALA.
Arbitrary Arrests in the South: Or, Scenes From the Experiences of an Alabama Unionist.
T7650 (WCU)
The Free State of Winston: A History of Winston County, Alabama.
T8340 (ASU)
CIVIL WAR — APP.
B1990
The Army of the Cumberland.
C4140
A History of the Eleventh New Hampshire Regiment, Volunteer Infantry in the Rebellion War, 1861-65. . . Chapter V-VII.
C5570
Army of the Heartland: The Army of Tennessee, 1861-1862.
C6660 (LMC ASU)
Through the South with a Union Soldier.
D1870
Regimental Publications and Personal Narratives of the Civil War. A Checklist.
D2970 (LMC)
The Secession Movement, 1860-1861.
D3840
The Secession Movement, 1860-1861.
D3850
The Secession Movement, 1860-1861.
D3860
The Seccession Movement, 1860-1861.
D3870
Confederate Military History: A Library of Confederate States History.
E2290 (ASU)
Manual of Instruction for the Volunteers and Militia of the Confederate States.
G1600 (LMC)
Among the Pines: Or, South in Secession-time.
G1740 (WCU MHC)
The Little Fork Rangers: A Sketch of Company "D," Fourth Virginia Cavalry.
H140 (ASU)
The Diary of a Confederate Soldier: James E. Hall.
H760 (ASU)
Stonewall Jackson and the American Civil War.
H4480 (ASU BC)
Bethel to Sharpsbury.
H5360 (ASU LMC)
A Narrative of Service With the Third Wisconsin Infantry.
H5610 (ASU)
The Army of Tennessee: A Military History.
H7200 (ASU)
Invisible Empire: The Story of the Ku Klux Klan, 1866-1871.
H7210
Invisible Empire: The Story of the Ku Klux Klan, 1866-1871.
H7211
Invisible Empire: The Story of the Ku Klux Klan, 1866-1871.
H7212
Invisible Empire: The Story of the Ku Klux Klan, 1866-1871.
H7213
Invisible Empire: The Story of the Ku Klux Klan, 1866-1871.
H7214
Narrative of Military Operations, Directed, During the Late War Between the States.
J2050 (ASU)
The Campaigns of Lieut.-Gen. N. B. Forrest, and of Forrest's Cavalry.
J2740 (ASU)
Norman Holt: A Story of the Army of the Cumberland.
K2240 (BC ASU)
History of the Fifteenth Pennsylvania Volunteer Cavalry: Which Was Recruited and Known as the Anderson Cavalry in the Rebellion of 1861-1865.
K2630 (LMC)
Bedford Forrest and His Critter Company.
L4120 (ASU)
The Life and Campaigns of Major General J. E. B. Stuart, Commander of the Calvary of the Army of Northern Virginia.
M390
History of the Thirty-fifth Regiment Massachusetts Volunteers, 1862-1865.
M4060
History of the Thirty-sixth Regiment Massachusetts Volunteers, 1862-1865.
M4070 (ASU)
Sparks from the Camp Fire: Or, Tales of the Old Veterans, A Photograph of Our Old Life.
M8010 (LMC)
A Small Boy's Recollections of the Civil War (War Between the States)
R3130 (ASU)
A Small Boy's Recollections of the Civil War.
R3140
The Winning of the West.
R3700 (ASU)
The Olive Branch of Peace and Good Will to Men: Anti-war History of the Brethren and Mennonites, the Peace People of the South, During the Civil War, 1861-1865.
S440 (ASU)
From Chattanooga to Petersburg Under Generals Grant and Butler: A Contribution to the History of the War, and a Personal Vindication.
S5170 (ASU)
Disloyalty in the Confederacy.
T350 (BC LMC)
History of the 112th Regiment of Illinois Volunteer Infantry, in the Great War of the Rebellion, 1862-1865.
T8140 (ASU)
History of the Army of the Cumberland, Its Organization, Campaigns, and Battles; Written at the Request of Maj.-Gen. George H. Thomas, Chiefly from his Private Military Journal and Official and Other Documents Furnished by Him.
V300
Stoneman's Last Raid.
V360
Stoneman's Last Raid.
V370 (ASU LMC WCU)
Western North Carolina Since the Civil War.
V380 (ASU WWC ETSU)
CIVIL WAR — APP. — GUERILLA WARFARE
The Confederate Horsemen.
K2730
CIVIL WAR — APP. MTNS.
The Debt of Our Country to the American Highlanders During the War.
R4510
Jeb Stuart.
T8090
CIVIL WAR — APP. — RAIDERS
Spies of the Confederacy.
B560
Morgan and His Raiders: A Biography of the Confederate General.
H6530
The Confederate Horsemen.
K2730
CIVIL WAR — BATTLEFIELDS — GA.
Dedication of the Chickamauga and Chattanooga National Military Park, September 18-20, 1895. Report of the Joint Committee to Represent the Congress at the Dedication of the . . .
B6080 (ASU)
The National Military Park, Chickamauga-Chattanooga. An Historical Guide.
B6090
CIVIL WAR — BATTLEFIELDS — TENN.
Dedication of the Chickamauga and Chattanooga National Military Park, September 18-20, 1895. Report of the Joint Committee to Represent the Congress at the Dedication of the . . .
B6080 (ASU)
The National Military Park, Chickamauga-Chattanooga. An Historical Guide.
B6090
CIVIL WAR — BATTLEFIELDS — TENN. AND GA.
The National Military Park, Chickamauga-Chattanooga: An Historical Guide, with Maps and Illustrations.
B6100 (ASU BC)
CIVIL WAR — CAMPAIGNS AND BATTLES — CHATTANOOGA
Report of a Board of Army Officers upon the Claim of Maj. Gen. William Farrar Smith, U. S. V., That He, and Not General Rosecrans, Originated the Plan for the Relief of Chattanooga in October, 1863.
B6950 (ASU)
CIVIL WAR — CAMPAIGNS AND BATTLES — CHATTANOOGA AND CHICKAMAUGA
Chattanooga and Chickamauga, Reprint of Gen. H. V. Boynton's Letters to the Cincinnati Commercial Gazette, August, 1888.
B6070 (ASU BC)
CIVIL WAR — CAMPAIGNS AND BATTLES — CHICKAMAUGA
Rock of Chickamauga, the Life of General George H. Thomas.
C4850 (ASU)
Thomas, Rock of Chickamauga.
O190 (ASU)
CIVIL WAR — CAMPAIGNS AND BATTLES — SHENANDOAH VALLEY
Conquest of a Valley.
B6570
CIVIL WAR — CAMPAIGNS AND BATTLES — SHENANDOAH VALLEY CAMPAIGN
History of the Campaign of General T. J. (Stonewall) Jackson in the Shenandoah Valley of Virginia from Nov. 4, 1861, to June 17, 1862.
A1480 (ASU)
CIVIL WAR — COLEMAN SCOUTS AND OTHER RAIDERS
Stoneman's Last Raid.
V360
Stoneman's Last Raid.
V370 (ASU LMC WCU)
CIVIL WAR — GA.
Guide to Chattanooga, Lookout Mountain and Chickamauga National Military Park.
F600
The Truth about Chickamauga.
G3050 (ASU)
K830
Battles of Chattanooga and Vicinity.
L4090
Chickamauga and Chattanooga National Military Park with Narratives of the Battles of Chickamauga, Lookout Mountain and Missionary Ridge.
L4100
"The Ordeal of Command: Bragg before Chickamauga."
M2540

CIVIL WAR — GA.
The Chickamauga and Chattanooga Campaign and Battle-fields. A Chronological Historic Guide, August 16-November 25, 1863.
N2870
O670
Wild Train; the Story of Andrews Raiders.
O720
The Civil War Battles of Chickamauga and Chattanooga.
R3490
Chickamauga and Chattanooga Battlefields; Chickamauga and Chattanooga National Military Park, Georgia-Tennessee.
S8960
Chickamauga: Bloody Battle in the West.
T9610 (ASU MHC)
CIVIL WAR — GA. — BATTLEFIELDS
Pennsylvania at Chickamauga and Chattanooga: Ceremonies at the Dedication of the Monuments Erected by the Commonwealth of Pennsylvania to Mark the Positions of the Pennsylvania Commands Engaged in the Battles.
S4090 (ASU)
CIVIL WAR — GA. — RAIDERS
The Andrews Raid; or, The Great Locomotive Chase, April 12, 1862.
E2090
CIVIL WAR — GA. — RAIDS
Daring and Suffering: A History of the Andrews Railroad Raid into Georgia in 1862.
P3140 (ASU WCU)
The Great Locomotive Chase: A History of the Andrews Railroad into Georgia in 1862.
P3150 (ETSU)
CIVIL WAR — HISTORY
Making a State, Formation of West Virginia.
S1940
CIVIL WAR — KY.
Kentuckians, C. S. A.
B2530 (ASU)
The Civil War and Readjustment in Kentucky.
C7780 (BC)
Josie M. Davidson, Her Life and Work, by Herself.
D670 (BC)
Old Cane Springs; a Story of the War Between the States in Madison County, Kentucky.
D3020 (BC)
No More Muffled Hoofbeats.
R2600 (ASU)
The Borderland in the Civil War.
S4570
Cumberland Gap.
S7180
The Wild Riders of the First Kentucky Cavalry. A History of the Regiment in the First Great War of the Rebellion. 1861-1865.
T280 (ASU)
CIVIL WAR — KY. — RAIDERS
The Patriots and Guerrillas of East Tennessee and Kentucky. The Suffering of the Patriots. Also the Experience of the Author as an Officer in the Union Army. Including Sketches of Noted Guerrillas and Distinguished Patriots.
B6510
CIVIL WAR — N. C.
The Civil War in North Carolina.
B1460 (UNCA ASU LMC)
Caldwell County, North Carolina in the Great War of 1861-1865.
C4650
Histories of the Several Regiments and Battalions from North Carolina in the Great War, 1861-65.
C4660 (LMC)
The Catawba Soldier of the Civil War. A Sketch of Every Soldier from Catawba County, North Carolina, with the Photograph, Biographical Sketch, and Reminiscence of Many of Them, Together with a sketch of Catawba County from 1860 to 1911.
H270 (ASU)
Reminiscences of Caldwell County, N. C., in the Great War of 1861-65.
H2530
Echoes of Happy Valley: Letters and Diaries, Family Life in the South, Civil War History.
H5190 (ASU LMC BC)
"The Forgotten Sons: North Carolinans in the Union Army."
H5210 (ASU)
Index to Moore's Roster of North Carolina Troops in the War Between the States.
H5740 (ASU)
Hendersonville in Civil War Times.
H8100
Battle of Asheville.
M720 (ASU LMC UNCA)
North Carolina Troops, 1861-1865, a Roster.
M2990 (ASU LMC)
Keepers of Memories: Biographical Sketches of Confederate Widows Living in North Carolina, 1961-1965, Plus Other Related Features.
M3390 (MHC)
Roster of North Carolina Troops: In the War Between the States.
M7320 (LMC)
Guide to Civil War Records in the N. C. State Archives.
N2590
Alexander County's Confederates.
P3110
The Raid, East Tennessee, Western N. Carolina, Southwest Virginia.
R330 (ASU)
The Secession Movement in North Carolina.
S3770 (LMC)
Recollections of a Confederate Staff Officer.
S5530 (LMC)
Front Rank.
T9620 (LMC)
Zeb Vance: Champion of Personal Freedom.
T9640 (ASU WCU UNCA)
Special Schedules Enumerating Union Veterans and Widows of Union Veterans of the Civil War, North Carolina.
U840 (ASU)
My Beloved Zebulon; the Correspondence of Zebulon B. Vance and Harriett Newell Espy.
V100
Papers.
V110 (ASU LMC)
CIVIL WAR — RAIDERS
Thee Bold Cavaliers. Morgan's 2nd Kentucky Cavalry Raiders.
B7080
History of Morgan's Cavalry.
D3780
History of Morgan's Cavalry.
D3790
History of Morgan's Cavalry.
D3800
On Jordan's Stormy Banks: A Novel of Sam Davis, the Confederate Scout.
R4080
Yankee Cavalrymen: Through the Civil War with the Ninth Pennsylvania Cavalry.
R4090
Morgan and His Captors.
S1890 (ASU)
The Rebel Raider, a Life of John Hunt Morgan.
S9700 (BC ASU)
CIVIL WAR — RAIDERS — TENN.
Story of Sam Davis.
R3680
CIVIL WAR — RAIDS
Wild Train: The Story of the Andrews Raiders.
O730 (ASU ETSU)
CIVIL WAR — S. C.
B1980
South Carolina Goes to War, 1860-1865.
C2550 (ASU)
Sixteenth South Carolina Regiment, CSA, From Greenville, S. C.
T610 (ASU)
CIVIL WAR — TENN.
The Attack upon and Defense of Fort Sanders, Knoxville, Tennessee, November 29, 1863.
A4700 (ASU)
Hamilton County Confederate Soldiers.
A4740
Guide Book to Lookout Mountain and a Brief Account of Battles Fought near Chattanooga, Tennessee.
B580
The Dedication of the Chickamauga and Chattanooga National Park. Address of Gen. Wm. B. Bate, One of the Speakers Appointed by the Secretary of War for the Above Occasion, Delivered on September 20, 1895.
B1890
The Testimony of a Refugee from East Tennessee.
B5120 (ASU)
Recollections of the East Tennessee Campaign, Battle of Campbell Station, 16th Nov., 1863: Siege of Knoxville, 17th Nov.-5th Dec., 1863.
B6420
Report of a Board of Army Officers upon the Claim of Maj. Gen. William Farrar Smith, U. S. V., That He, and Not General Rosecrans, Originated the Plan for the Relief of Chattanooga in October, 1863.
B6950 (ASU)
Sketches of the Rise, Progress, and Decline of Secession: with a Narrative of Personal Adventure among the Rebels.
B7530 (ASU)
Fiddles in the Cumberlands.
B9020 (ASU BC)
The Attitude of Tennesseans toward the Union.
C780 (BC ASU)
Tennessee and the Union, 1847-1861.
C790
"Tennessee's Attitude toward Secession."
C800
History of the First Regiment of Tennessee Volunteer Cavalry in the Great War of the Rebellion: With the Armies of the Ohio and Cumberland, under Generals Morgan, Rosecrans, Thomas, Stanley and Wilson, 1862-1865.
C1760 (LMC)
My Grandfather's Diary of the War.
C4350
"Tennessee: A Reluctant Seceder, 1847-1861."
C4460
Story of Captain Jesse Cox of Johnson Co., Tennessee.
C5720
Storming of the Gateway: Chattanooga, 1863.
D3170 (WCU BC ASU)
The Andrews Raid; or, The Great Locomotive Chase, April 12, 1862.
E2090
Account of the Fund for the Relief of East Tennessee; with a Complete List of Contributors.
E2390
Guide to Chattanooga, Lookout Mountain and Chickamauga National Military Park.
F600
The Secession and Reconstruction of Tennessee. . .
F720 (ASU LMC)
The Chattanooga Campaign, with Especial Reference to Wisconsin's Participation Therein.
F1300 (ASU BC)
The Truth about Chickamauga.
G3050 (ASU)
Andrew Johnson: Military Governor of Tennessee.
H600 (BC ASU)
Andrew Johnson: Military Governor of Tennessee.
H610 (BC ASU)
Confederate Action in Franklin County, Tennessee.
H1580
Tales of the Civil War Era.
H3290
Neighbor against Neighbor, Brother against Brother; Greene County in the Civil War.
H3850
"The Tennessee Conservatives and Secession, 1847-61."
H4750
Tennessee's War: 1861-1865, Described by Participants.
H7220 (BC ASU)
"Political Activities of the Republican Party in the State of Tennessee, 1860-1870."
H7760
The Loyal Mountaineers of Tennessee.
H8280 (ASU BC LMC)
History of the Rebellion in Bradley County, East Tennessee.
H8520

CIVIL WAR — TENN.

The Battle of Fort Sanders. An Address Delivered November 28th, 1814 . . . at the Unveiling and Dedication of the Monument Erected by the Knoxville Chapter, United Daughters of the Confederacy, to the Memory of the Confederate Soldiers Who Lost Their Lives during the Siege of Knoxville, Tennessee, November 29, 1863.
K820

"Secession and Civil War in Jefferson County, Tennessee, 1860-1865."
K2200 (ETSU)

"Sectionalism in East Tennessee, 1796 to 1861."
L50

Vanquished Volunteers: East Tennessee Sectionalism From Statehood to Secession.
L60 (LMC ETSU BC)

Some Sketches from My Life, Written for My 80th Birthday, May 1, 1910.
L840

The Military Annals of Tennessee: Confederate. First Series. Embracing a Review of Military Operations with Regimental Histories and Memorial Rolls Compiled from Original and Official Sources.
L2570 (LMC)

Battles of Chattanooga and Vicinity.
L4090

Chickamauga and Chattanooga National Military Park with Narratives of the Battles of Chickamauga, Lookout Mountain and Missionary Ridge.
L4100

The Surrender of Cumberland Gap.
M1350

Chattanooga and Her Battlefields.
M1650

"The Ordeal of Command: Bragg before Chickamauga."
M2540

"Civil War Anecdotes and Legends of Chattanooga."
N710

The Chickamauga and Chattanooga Campaign and Battle-fields. A Chronological Historic Guide, August 16-November 25, 1863.
N2870
O670
P470

"The Secession Movement in Tennessee."
P510

Unionism and Reconstruction in Tennessee, 1860-1869.
P840 (ASU WCU)

Personal Recollections of the Occupation of East Tennessee and the Defense of Knoxville.
P3300

"The Republican Party in East Tennessee, 1865-1900."
Q130

The Battle of Kingsport.
R320 (ASU ETSU)

The Raid, East Tennessee, Western N. Carolina, Southwest Virginia.
R330 (ASU)

The Vicksburg Campaign, and the Battles about Chattanooga under the Command of General U. S. Grant in 1862-63; an Historical Review.
R1140

East Tennessee in the War of the Rebellion. And Read at the Stated Meeting of December 3, 1902.
R1170 (ASU)

With Thomas in Tennessee.
R3220

The Civil War Battles of Chickamauga and Chattanooga.
R3490

Story of Sam Davis.
R3680

History of the Thirteenth Regiment, Tennessee Volunteer Cavalry, U. S. A., Including a Narrative of the Bridge Burning: The Carter County Rebellion, and the Loyalty, Heroism and Suffering of the Union Men and Women of Carter and Johnson Counties, Tennessee, During the Civil War.
S1460 (ASU LMC)

Samuel Roberts: A Welsh Colonizer in Civil War Tennessee.
S2850 (ASU)

Report of the Proceedings.
S5370 (LMC)

Cumberland Gap.
S7180

East Tennessee, Chickamauga, Chattanooga.
S7350 (ASU)

Chickamauga and Chattanooga Battlefields; Chickamauga and Chattanooga National Military Park, Georgia-Tennessee.
S8960

Mission Ridge and Lookout Mountain, With Pictures of Life in Camp and Field.
T450 (ASU)

Relief for East Tennessee.
T640 (BC)

East Tennessee and the Civil War.
T820 (ASU)

East Tennessee and the Civil War.
T830 (ETSU)

East Tennessee and the Civil War.
T840 (ASU ETSU)

Tennesseans in the Civil War: A Military History of Confederate and Union Units with Available Rosters of Personnel.
T950 (ASU)

Chickamauga: Bloody Battle in the West.
T9610 (ASU MHC)

Lookout, the Story of a Mountain.
W340 (LMC BC)

"Co. Aytch," Maury Grays, First Tennessee Regiment: Or, A Side Show of the Big Show.
W1470 (ASU)

"Unconventional Warfare in East Tennessee, 1861-1865."
W5200

Sam Davis, Hero of the Confederacy, 1842-1863, Coleman's Scouts.
W5760

War Memoranda: Cheat River to the Tennessee, 1861-1862.
W5920 (BC)

A Confederate History of Polk County, Tennessee, 1860-1866.
W6390

CIVIL WAR — TENN. — BATTLEFIELDS

Pennsylvania at Chickamauga and Chattanooga: Ceremonies at the Dedication of the Monuments Erected by the Commonwealth of Pennsylvania to Mark the Positions of the Pennsylvania Commands Engaged in the Battles.
S4090 (ASU)

CIVIL WAR — TENN. — FT. SANDERS

Divided Loyalties: Fort Sanders and the Civil War in East Tennessee.
S2110 (BC ETSU)

CIVIL WAR — TENN. — RAIDERS

When Yesterday Was Today.
B4610

The Patriots and Guerrillas of East Tennessee and Kentucky. The Suffering of the Patriots. Also the Experience of the Author as an Officer in the Union Army. Including Sketches of Noted Guerrillas and Distinguished Patriots.
B6510

"Special Warfare in Middle Tennessee and Surrounding Areas, 1861-62."
D150

Thrilling Adventures of Daniel Ellis, the Great Union Guide of East Tennessee, for a Period of Nearly Four Years During the Great Southern Rebellion.
E1750 (ASU LMC BC)

Thrilling Adventures of Daniel Ellis, the Great Union Guide of East Tennessee, for a Period of Nearly Four Years during the Great Southern Rebellion. Written by Himself. Containing a Short Biography of the Author.
E1760

Full Many a Name; the Story of Sam Davis, Scout and Spy, C. S. A.
F3080

Champ Ferguson: A Sketch of the War in East Tennessee Detailing Some of the Awful Murders on the Border and Describing One of the Leading Spirits of the Rebellion.
H390

Champ Ferguson, Confederate Guerilla.
S1900

CIVIL WAR — TENN. — RAIDS

"The Coleman Scouts."
P3120

CIVIL WAR — VA.

"The Civil War in Western Virginia: The Decisive Campaigns of 1861."
B4970

Conquest of a Valley.
B6570

Old Jube: A Biography of Jubat A. Early from West Point in the 1830's to the Battles of Chancellorsville, Lynchburg, Winchester, and a Wealth of Other Data on the Civil War.
B9370

Confederate History of Culpeper County.
C240

Stonewall Jackson.
C2780 (ASU)

Stonewall Jackson.
C7000 (ASU BC)

Stonewall Jackson and the Old Stonewall Brigade.
C7010 (ASU BC)

The V. M. I. New Market Cadets. Biographical Sketches of All Members of the Virginia Military Institute Corps of Cadets Who Fought in The Battle of New Market, May 15, 1864.
C8030 (ASU)

The Montgomery County Story, 1776-1957.
C9360 (ASU)

Jeb Stuart, the Last Cavalier.
D870 (ASU)

They Called Him Stonewall: A Life of Lt. General T. J. Jackson, C. S. A.
D880 (ASU BC)

Campaign of 1864 in the Valley of Virginia and the Expedition to Lynchburg.
D4030

The Political History of Virginia During the Reconstruction.
E720

Military Operations in Jefferson County, Virginia and West Virginia, 1861-1865.
F200

Campaigns of the Army of Northern Virginia, Including the Jackson Valley Campaign, 1861-1865.
F1490 (ASU)

Fredericksburg, Virginia. Its Homes and History, the Battlefields and the Rappahannock Valley.
G2650

The Little Fork Rangers: A Sketch of Company "D," Fourth Virginia Cavalry.
H140 (ASU)

Four Valiant Years in the Lower Shenandoah Valley 1861-1865.
H400 (ASU)

The Rending of Virginia; a History.
H700 (BC)

The Two Virginias: Gensis of Old and New; a Romance of American History; State Sovereignty, Phantom of a Stupendous Folly.
H710 (BC)
H3120 (ASU)

A Brief History of New Market and Vicinity. The Battle of New Market Centennial, May 15, 1864-1964.
H5340 (ASU)

Life and Campaigns of George B. McClellan, Major-General U. S. Army.
H5510 (ASU)

The Shenandoah Valley and Virginia, 1861 to 1865: A War Study.
K620 (ASU BC)

History of the Fifteenth Pennsylvania Volunteer Cavalry: Which Was Recruited and Known as the Anderson Cavalry in the Rebellion of 1861-1865.
K2630 (LMC)

Loudoun County and the Civil War: A History and Guide.
L3600

Sketch of Captain Thompson McAllister, Co. A, 27th Virginia Regiment.
M50 (ASU)

Report on the Organization and Campaigns of the Army of the Potomac: To Which Is Added an Account of the Campaign in Western Virginia, with Plans of Battlefields.
M380 (ETSU)

CIVIL WAR — VA.

A Diary with Reminiscences of the War and Refugee Life in the Shenandoah Valley, 1860-1865.
M1110 (ASU LMC)

Virginia's Attitude Toward Slavery and Secession.
M8570 (FC LMC)

Cole's Cavalry: or, Three Years in the Saddle in the Shenandoah Valley.
N730 (ASU)

Turnpikes and Dirt Roads.
P380

A Narrative of the Campaign in the Valley of the Shenandoah in 1861.
P800 (ASU)

The Shenandoah in 1864.
P3480 (BC)

The Raid, East Tennessee, Western N. Carolina, Southwest Virginia.
R330 (ASU)

The Vicksburg Campaign, and the Battles about Chattanooga under the Command of General U. S. Grant in 1862-63; an Historical Review.
R1140

Civil War Action in Rockingham County, Virginia, 1861-1865.
R3370 (ASU LMC)

Sheridan in the Shenandoah: Jubal Early's Nemesis.
S6410 (ASU)

Borderland Confederate.
S9000

General Turner Ashby, the Centaur of the South: A Military Sketch.
T7760 (ASU)

Jeb Stuart.
T8090

The New Market Campaign, May, 1864.
T9770 (ASU)

Observance, Battle of Front Royal Virginia, May 19-20, 1962.
W920 (LMC)

War Memoranda: Cheat River to the Tennessee, 1861-1862.
W5920 (BC)

An Inside View of the Formation of the State of West Virginia, with Character Sketches of the Pioneers in that Movement.
W6370 (BC)

Civil War Battles in Winchester and Frederick County, Virginia, 1861-1865.
W7570 (BC ASU LMC)

Diaries, Letters and Recollections of the War Between the States.
W7580

The Military History of the Virginia Military Institute from 1839 to 1865.
W7880 (ASU)

CIVIL WAR — VA. — SHENANDOAH VALLEY

Early Life and Letters of General Thomas J. Jackson, "Stonewall" Jackson.
A4860 (ASU)

CIVIL WAR — W. VA.

The Strange Story of Harper's Ferry, with Legends of the Surrounding Country.
B1520 (BC)

The Guns of Harpers Ferry.
B7390 (ASU BC)

Twixt North and South.
C250 (ASU)

"A House Divided: A Study of Statehood Politics and the Copperhead Movement in West Virginia During the Civil War."
C9860

A House Divided: A Study of Statehood Politics and the Copperhead Movement in West Virginia.
C9870 (WCU ETSU ASU BC)

Berkeley County, U. S. A.: A Bicentennial History of a Virginia and West Virginia County, 1772-1972.
D2810 (ASU BC)

Historic Harpers Ferry in Jefferson Co., W. Va.
F20 (BC)

Military Operations in Jefferson County, Virginia and West Virginia, 1861-1865.
F200

Dear Annie: A Collection of Letters, 1860-1886.
F3640 (ASU)

The Rending of Virginia; a History.
H700 (BC)

The Two Virginias: Gensis of Old and New; a Romance of American History; State Sovereignty, Phantom of a Stupendous Folly.
H710 (BC)

Archaeological Excavations on Virginius Island, Harpers Ferry National Historic Park, 1966-1968.
H1570

Upshur Brothers of the Blue and the Gray.
H7230 (ASU)

Military Operations in Jefferson Co., Virginia and West Virginia, 1961-65.
J490 (ASU)

Thunder at Harper's Ferry.
K570 (ASU)

Loyal W. Va. from 1861 to 1865.
L420

The Geology of Watoga and Droop Mountain Battlefield State Parks, West Virginia.
L3910 (ETSU)

Major General Thomas Maley Harris, A Member of the Military Commission That Tried the President Abraham Lincoln Assassination Conspirators, and Roster of the 10th West Virginia Volunteer Infantry Regiment, 1861-1865.
M4200 (ASU BC)

A Banner in the Hills: West Virginia's Statehood.
M7140 (ASU BC WCU)

"West Virginia and the Civil War, 1861-1863."
M7150

Harper's Ferry in Pictures.
R2690 (ASU WCU)

W. Va. Civil War Literature.
S2670

West Virginia Civil War Literature.
S3030

Battle of Point Pleasant . . .
S3640

The Borderland in the Civil War.
S4570

Borderland Confederate.
S9000

War Memoranda: Cheat River to the Tennessee, 1861-1862.
W5920 (BC)

An Inside View of the Formation of the State of West Virginia, with Character Sketches of the Pioneers in that Movement.
W6370 (BC)

The Battle of Rich Mountain.
Z100 (ASU BC)

R. E. Lee's Cheat Mountain Campaign.
Z110 (ASU)

CLINCH RIVER

Frontier Forts along the Clinch, Powell and Holston.
H1130 (BC)

Clinch-Powell Valley; Summary of Resources.
T2420

Floods on Clinch River, in Vicinity of Clinton, Tennessee.
T7000

COAL INDUSTRY

Work, Safety, and Life Style Among Southern Appalachian Coal Miners: A Survey of the Men of Standard Mines.
A1970 (ASU)

ACI Bulletin.
A2880

ACI experimental 30-day coal consumption forecast. December 1948-April 1949.
A2890

Analysis of Potential Market for ACI Coals in the Production of Gas and Coke.
A2900

Coal-weather Forecast.
A2910

Design Trends in Boiler Installations in the Pulp & Paper Industry of the South.
A2920

Forecast.
A2930

Fuel Engineering Data.
A2940

Fuels and Hydro Power Used in the Production of Electricity for Public Use in the United States (1933 through 1936).
A2950

Heating Season Weather, 1948-49 Heating Season.
A2960

How to Compare the Heating Values and Costs of Coal, Fuel Oil and Gas.
A2970

Industrial Coal-burning Equipment.
A2980

Miscellaneous Publications.
A2990

Residential Heating, Equipment, and Fuel Consumption; Study and Comparison by States, 1940 and 1948.
A3000

Southern High-volatile Coals.
A3010

Proceedings of the Fuel Engineering Conference
A3020

Proceedings: General Index of Fuel Engineering Conferences, First Through Twenty-sixth, 1934-1940.
A3030

Bituminous Coal Wages, Profits and Productivity.
B40

Picking Poverty's Pocket.
B1150

Coal and Coal Mining in West Virginia.
B1200

The Negro in the Bituminous Coal Mining Industry.
B1400 (WCU BC MHC)

"A Study of the Minnesota Multiphasic Personality Inventory and Its Use in Identification of Acceptable Mine Foremen."
B2870

Report of the Economic Growth of Oak Hill, Correlated With the History of King Coal-Fayette County's First Major Industry.
B3010

Conspiracy in Coal.
B3360
B3490 (BC)

The Molly Maguires.
B3690 (ASU WCU BC)

Mine Drainage Abstracts, a Bibliography.
B4270 (ASU)

"The Econometric Forecasting of National Rail Car Requirements for Bituminous Coal."
B5410

Survey of Opportunities to Stimulate Coal Utilization.
B5510

Special Report on an Evaluation of Mine Scaling.
B6250 (ASU)

Underground Riches: The Story of Mining.
B8310 (ASU)

Medical Care in Selected Areas of the Appalachian Bituminous Coal Fields.
B8500

"A Literature Survey of the Effects and Controls of Pneumoconiosis."
C100

Night Comes to the Cumberlands: Biography of a Depressed Area.
C2230 (ASU MHC WCU ETSU FC UNCA)

Night Comes to the Cumberlands: A Biography of a Depressed Area.
C2240 (LMC)

"The Demand for Coal for Power Generation in the Tennessee Valley and the Impact of Changing Demand Patterns on a Supplying Coal Field."
C3360

Waste Disposal Costs at Two Coal Mines in Kentucky and Alabama.
D240

"Earnings, Health, Safety, and Welfare of Bituminous Coal Miners Since the Encouragement of Mechanization by the United Mine Workers of America."
D610

"A Study of Fatal Roof Fall Accidents in Bituminous Coal Mines."
D3110 (LMC)

"A Study of the Literature on Accidents in Coal Mines of the United States with Comparisons of the Records in Other Coal-producing Countries."
D3640

"Government in an Eastern Kentucky Coal Field County."
D3690 (ASU)

"A Validation Study of a Psychological Test Battery for Selection of Joy Ripper-type Continuous Miner Operators."
D4090

COAL INDUSTRY

Coal Through the Ages.
E610 (BC)

"Economic Consequences of the Seven-hour Day and Wage Changes in the Bituminous Coal Industry."
F1220

Wage Rates and Working Time in the Bituminous Coal Industry, 1912-1922.
F1230 (BC)

Seventy Years in the Coal Mines.
F3050 (BC)

"Industrial Retardation and Economic Growth: A Case Study of Secular and Structural Change in the United States, 1920-1960."
F3430

The Pioneer: A Biography.
F3590 (BC)

"Coal Mining Safety: National Solutions in the Progressive Period."
G3090

Only a Miner: Studies in Recorded Coal Mining Songs.
G3500 (ASU LMC MHC WCU BC)

"Recorded American Coal Mining Songs."
G3510

Coal and Coal Mines.
G3760 (BC)

Coal and Coal Mines.
G3770 (ASU)

"The Economic Effects of Collective Bargaining in Bituminous Coal Mining."
G3860

"The United Mine Workers of America and the Non-Union Coal Fields."
H5620

Slope Stability of Coal Strip Mine Spoil Banks.
H6260 (ASU)

Research, Education and Mine Personnel Safety in W. Va.
H6550 (BC)

Coal Mine Health and Safety; the Case of West Virginia.
M110 (BC)

Coal Mining Health and Safety in West Virginia.
M120

The Resources of the Coal Field of the Upper Kanawha, with a Sketch of the Iron Belt of Virginia, Setting Forth Some of Their Markets and Means of Development.
M4470 (ASU)

"Economics of the Southern Smokeless Coals."
M5150

"The United Mine Workers: A Study of How Trade Union Policy Relates to Technological Change."
M6000
M6140
M6150 (BC)

Postwar Changes in the Export Markets for American Coal: A Study in the Industry Response to Variations in Foreign Demand.
M6210 (ASU)

Theory and Practice of Mine Ventilation.
M6610

Struggle in the Coal Fields: The Autobiography of Fred Mooney.
M6720 (ASU BC WCU)

"Attitude of Coal Miners toward Union and Coal Industry."
M7730 (ASU)

The Plight of the Bituminous Coal Miner.
M7790 (ASU BC)

History of Coal Mining in Laurel County, Kentucky, 1920-1944.
M8160

"An Evaluation of the Pension Plans in the Anthracite Coal Industry."
M8450

The Coal Industry in America: A Bibliography and Guide to Studies.
M8610 (ASU BC)

Papers and Proceedings.
N160

Anthracite: An Instance of Natural Resource Monopoly.
N350 (ASU LMC)

The Southern Tennessee Coal Field Included in Bledsoe, Cumberland, Franklin, Grundy, Rhea, Sequatchie, Van Buren, Warren, and White Counties.
N580 (ETSU)

The Story of American Coals.
N980 (BC)

The Coal Miner's Struggle in Eastern Kentucky.
N3020 (ASU)

Peabody Atlas.
P1140 (BC)

"The Growth and Overdevelopment of the Kentucky Coal Industry, 1912-1929."
P1210 (ASU)

Operation Scarlift, the After-Effects of Over 100 Years of Coal Mining In Pennsylvania and Current Programs to Combat Them.
P1800

The Rock Dust Remedy for Coal Mine Explosions; An Open Letter to the Operators in the 27th Bituminous District of Pennsylvania.
P2810

The Population and Employment Outlook for the Anthracite Region of Pennsylvania.
R1560

The Coal Trade, a Compendium of Valuable Information Relative to Coal Production, Prices, Transportation, etc., at Home and Abroad.
S580 (BC)

Cloud by Day: The Story of Coal and Coke People.
S2830 (ASU LMC BC)

Mobility of Chemical Workers in a Coal Mining Area.
S5450

Coal, The Curse and the Key: Overall Economic Development Program for the Southern West Virginia Economic Development District.
S5890

"A Sociological Analysis of Ecology, Structure and Processes in a Virginia Coal Mining Community."
S8080

Facts About the Two Armed Marches on Logan.
S9400 (ASU BC)

Hours and earnings in anthracite and bituminous coal mining.
U1390

Mining and Mineral Operations in the United States; a Visitor's Guide.
U1480

Federal Coal Mine Health and Safety Act of 1969. Report Together with Minority, Supplemental, and Separate Views from the Committee to Accompany H. R. 13950, October 13, 1969.
U2280

Legislative History: Federal Coal Mine Health and Safety Act.
U2290

Coal Mine Health and Safety. Hearings before the Subcommittee on H. R. 4047, H. R. 4295, and H. R. 7976, March 4-May 1, 1969.
U2300

Federal Coal Mine Health and Safety Act of 1969. Report from the Committee Together with Individual Views to Accompany S. 2917, September 17, 1969.
U2330

Coal Mine Health and Safety. Hearings before the Subcommittee on S. 355, S. 467, S. 1094, S. 1178, S. 1300, and S. 1907, February 27-May 2, 1969.
U2340

A List of Books and Other Sources of Information Regarding Coal and Coal Products.
W70

Labor Revolt in Alabama: The Great Strike of 1894.
W770 (WCU BC)

"The Economics of the Transportation of Ohio Coal."
W890

W. Va. Coal Facts, 1971.
W3250

Proceedings.
W3260 (BC)

Work Stoppages and the Grievance Procedure in the Appalachian Coal Industry.
W4690 (ASU)

Work Stoppages and the Grievance Procedure in the Appalachian Coal Industry.
W4710 (ASU)

Newsletter.
W4945 (BC)

Systematic Jointing in Western Part of Anthracite Region of Eastern Pennsylvania.
W8510

COAL INDUSTRY — ALA.

The Story of Coal and Iron in Alabama.
A4650 (ASU)

Report on the Coal Measures of the Plateau Region of Alabama.
M230 (BC)

Report on the Calaba Coal Field.
S6400

Report on the Plateau Coal Field of Alabama.
T6590

Report on the Reserves of Coal in a Part of the Warrier Coal Field of Alabama.
T6600

COAL INDUSTRY — APP.

Fighting for Survival: The Bootleg Coal Industry.
A350 (ASU)

The Economic Impact of Public Policy on the Appalachian Coal Industry and the Regional Economy.
A3730 (ASU)

Manpower Report for the Appalachian Coal Industry.
A3760 (ASU)

Medical-Hospital Problems in the Bituminous Coal Mining Areas.
B8510

Froth Floatation Washability Data of Various Appalachian Coals Using Timed Release Analysis Technique.
C2570

Report on the Mining Methods and Appliances Used in Anthracite Coal Fields.
C2850 (BC)
C5170 (BC)

Practical Kinks for Coal Mining Men.
C5180 (BC)

Successful Solutions to Everyday Coal Mining Problems.
C5190 (BC)
C5210 (BC)

"Collective Bargaining in the Bituminous Coal Industry."
C5380 (ASU)

History of the Consolidated Coal Company.
C6790

Survey of Sulfur Reduction in Appalachian Coals by Stage Crushing.
D1920

"Habitat-economy-society, a Frame of Reference Applied to Southern Appalachian Coal Country."
G1130

Those Black Diamond Men: A Tale of the Anthrax Valley.
G1140 (BC ASU)

Annotated Bibliography on Industrial Concentration and Firm Diversification in the Bitumonous Coal Industry with Special Reference to the Southeastern United States, 1950-1970.
G1270

"The Coal Buying Policies: Effects on Prices and Method of Mining in Supplying States."
H3150

"The Coal Miner's Insurrections, 1891-1892."
H8740 (ASU)

"A "New Deal" for Soft Coal: The Attempted Revitalization of the Bituminous Coal Industry under the New Deal."
J1840

"Bituminous Coal Strip Mines; Some Financing Considerations."
K580

Look at Mine-timber Market in the Appalachian Bituminous Coal Region.
K2930

"The Price of Coal: A Study of the Policies of the National Coal Board."
L3300

Miner's Wages and the Cost of Coal: An Inquiry into the Wages System in the Bituminous Coal Industry.
L3790

"The Competitive Position of Bituminous Coal in the Utility Markets of the Northeast."
L3800

Coal and Unionism: A History of the American Coal Miners Unions.
M1120 (BC ASU)

COAL INDUSTRY — APP.
The Coal Regions of America.
M1360
"The Decline of Anthracite, 1913-1955."
M5320
Trees Above the Coal Below.
N3000
Demonstration of Safety Plugging of Oil Wells Penetrating Appalachian Coal Mines.
R1480
"The Economics of the Coal Industry."
R2370
"Union Economic Politics and Union Discipline in the Bituminous Wage Dispute of 1949-1950."
R4030 (ASU)
A History of the Coal Miners of the United States.
R4140 (BC)
"United States Bituminous Coal Markets — Trends Since 1920, and Prospects to 1975."
S10
Facts about Strip Mining.
S560
Benefit/Cost Approach to Decision Making: The Dilemma with Coal Production.
S970 (ASU)
Statement on Benefit/Cost Evaluation of Strip Mining in Appalachia.
S980 (ASU)
The Issues Related to Surface Mining; a Summary Review, with Selected Readings.
S3300 (WCU)
S8050
Statistics of Coal. The Geographical and Geological Distribution of Mineral Combustibles or Fossils Fuel, Including, Also, Notices and Localities of the Various Mineral Bituminous Substances, Employed in Arts and Manufactures...Embracing, From Official Reports of the Great Coal-Producing Countries, the Respective Amounts of Their Production, Consumption and Commercial Distribution, in All Parts of the World; Together With Their Prices, Tariffs, Duties and International Regulations...
T710 (BC)
Comparison of Coal-Fired and Nuclear Power Plants for the TVA System.
T6620
Petroleum and Coal; the Keys to the Future.
T7740 (BC)
"Coal Country: The Rise of the Southern Smokeless Coal Industry and Its Effect on Area Development."
T7980
Black Diamonds.
T8000 (ASU)
Significant Trends in the West Virginia Coal Industry, 1900-1957.
T8230 (ASU)
Strip Mining for Coal.
T8870 (BC)
Bituminous Coal Mining: Labor Market Developments.
U1210
List of publications, Bureau of Mines.
U1430
List of publications, Bureau of Mines.
U1440
List of publications, Bureau of Mines.
U1450
Miners' Circular.
U1460
Miners' Circular.
U1470
A medical survey of the bituminous-coal industry.
U1620
Conditions in the Coal Fields of Penn., W. Va., and Ohio.
U1760
Unemployment problems.
U1800
Hearings before the Special Subcommittee on Coal Research on Establishment of Research and Development Program or the Coal Industry.
U1940
Study of the Strip and Surface Mining in Appalachia; an Interim Report to the Appalachian Regional Commission.
U2820 (BC)
Surface Mining and our Environment; a Special Report to the Nation.
U2830 (BC)
A Medical Survey of the Bituminous-coal Industry.
U2850 (LMC)
One Sunset a Week, the Story of a Coal Miner . . . .
V510 (ASU)
The Kentucky Mountains, Transportation and Commerce, 1750-1911: A Study in the Economic History of a Coal Field.
V530 (ASU WCU BC)
The Northern Appalachian Coal Field.
W5340
Levels. Coal Analyses.
W5460 (ETSU)
"Development and Operation of the Welfare and Retirement Fund in the Bituminous Coal Industry."
W5620
The American Miners Association: A Record of the Origin of Coal Miners' Unions in the United States.
W5970 (ASU)
The Miners' Case and the Public Interest: A Documented Chronology.
W5980
Preventing Fatal Explosions in Coal Mines: A Study of Recent Major Disasters in the United States as Accompaniments of Technological Change.
W5990
"Disorganization and Delinquency in Three Coal Communities."
W6860 (ASU)
Current and Proposed Regulations and Legislation on Air Pollution Concerning the Appalachian Coal Industry.
W7190
"Problems in the Anthracite Industry with Special Reference to Marketing."
Z10
"The Coal Miner in a Large Scale, Highly Mechanized, Highly Integrated Bituminous Coal Mining Plant."
Z20

COAL INDUSTRY — APP. MTNS.
Manual of Coal and Its Topography.
L1890

COAL INDUSTRY — FOLK SONGS
Coal Dust on the Fiddle: Songs and Stories of the Bituminous Industry.
K3050 (ASU LMC WCU BC)
Minstrels of the Mine Patch: Songs and Stories of the Anthracite Industry.
K3060 (ASU LMC MHC BC)

COAL INDUSTRY — KY.
A Study of the Eastern Industrial Coal Market.
B5500
Geology of the Big Stone Gap Coal Field of Virginia and Kentucky.
C760 (BC)
Night Comes to the Cumberlands: A Biography of a Depressed Area.
C2220 (WWC BC FC)
"The Influence of Coal in the Big Sandy Valley."
C3230 (ASU)
Coal Workers' Pneumoconiosis: Workmen's Compensation Treatment and Its Prevention in Kentucky.
C3550 (ASU)
The Shame That Is Kentucky's! The Story of the Harlan Mine War.
C7610 (ASU)
Geology and Coal Resources of the Cannel City Quadrangle, Kentucky.
E2020
"Twentieth Century Development of the Coal Mining Industry in Eastern Kentucky and Its Influence upon the Political Behavior of This Area."
F3420 (ASU)
Coals of the North Fork of the Ky. River in Perry and Portions of Breathitt & Knott Co. Ky.
H6150
"External Diseconomies of Bituminous Coal Surface Mining — A Case Study of Eastern Kentucky, 1960-1967."
H7590
Coal Deposits of Pike County, Kentucky.
H8370
I740
A Bibliography of the Mineral Resources of Kentucky.
J950
The Coal Industry in Kentucky.
J990
The Coal Industry in Kentucky.
J1000
Economic Data on Eastern Kentucky Coal Fields.
K910
Annual Report, 1885-1919.
K1110
Directory of Kentucky Mineral Operators.
K1120
Strip Mining in Kentucky.
K1130 (BC ASU)
Strip Mining.
K1290
Coal Mining Reference Book.
K1300
Proceedings.
K1310
Bibliography of Coal in Kentucky.
K1410
Silver Fleece, a Tale of the Swift Mines of Old Kentucky.
K1890 (LMC BC)
Economic Data on Eastern Kentucky Coal Field.
L1260
The Superfluous People of Hazard, Kentucky.
P1220
"Social Effects of the Mining Industry in Eastern Kentucky."
S400 (ASU)
"A Study of Woodworking Industry of the Eastern Mountains and Coal Field Region of Kentucky."
S1330
Application of Current Utilization Research to the Kentucky Coal Industry.
S5930
The Economic Viability of the Small Underground Coal Mine. . . .
S5940
Coal Resources of the Russell Fork Basin in Kentucky and Virginia.
S7540
The Incomparable Don Chafin.
S9410 (BC ASU)
"Bloody" Harlan, 1931-1938; an Appalachian Coal County in the Thirties.
T170
"Coal and Conflict: The U.M.W.A. in Harlan County, 1931-1939."
T690 (BC ASU)
Coal Reserves in Portions of Butler, Edmonson, Grayson, Muhlenberg, Ohio, and Warren Counties, Kentucky.
T2430
The Coal Fields of Perry Co., Ky.
V60

COAL INDUSTRY — LABOR FORCE
Labor Costs in the Bituminous Coal Industry.
N740

COAL INDUSTRY — MD.
The Best-dressed Miners: Life and Labor in the Maryland Coal Region, 1835-1910.
H3270 (ASU)
"The Coal Miners of Western Maryland."
H3280

COAL INDUSTRY — OHIO
Coal Reserves of the Pittsburgh (No. 8) Bed in Belmont County, Ohio.
B3310 (ASU)
Economic Geology of the Summerfield and Woodsfield Quadrangles, Ohio, with Descriptions of Coal and Other Mineral Resources, Except Oil and Gas.
C6320
Stratigraphy of the Bituminous Coal Field of Pennsylvania, Ohio, and West Virginia.
W5470

COAL INDUSTRY — PA.
The Molly Maguires. The Origin, Growth, and Character of the Organization.
D2010 (ASU WCU)
Buried Black Treasure: The Story of Pennsylvania Anthracite.
F760 (ASU)
"Bituminous Coal Open Pit Mining in Clarion County, Pennsylvania."
J180

COAL INDUSTRY — PA.
"Measuring Productivity in Coal Mining: A Case Study of Multiple Input Measurement at the County Level in Pennsylvania."
J310
"The Use and Interchangeability of Fuels in Pennsylvania."
J470
Lament for the Molly Maquires.
L2080
Coal in Pennsylvania, Recent Developments and Prospects.
P1830
Bituminous Coal Fields in Pennsylvania.
P1840
"A History of Land Subsistence and Its Consequences Caused by the Mining of Anthracite Coal in Luzerne County, Pennsylvania."
R2870
Anthracite Coal Communities.
R3070 (BC)
"A Quantitative Description and Analysis of the Growth of the Pennsylvania Anthracite Coal Industry, 1820 to 1865."
S780
The Economic Importance of the Coal Industry to Pennsylvania.
S910
Stratigraphy of the Bituminous Coal Field of Pennsylvania, Ohio, and West Virginia.
W5470
"Social Legislation for the Protection of Coal Miners in Pennsylvania."
Z90

COAL INDUSTRY — TECHNOLOGY
"A Recursive Programing Model of Resource Allocation and Technological Change in the United States Bituminous Coal Industry."
T10

COAL INDUSTRY — TENN.
Geological Report: Coal Creek Mining and Manufacturing Company of Tennessee.
B6190
Coals in the Area between Bon Air and Clifty, Tennessee.
B9460
Coal Losses of Tennessee.
F1850 (ETSU)
The Northern Tennessee Coal Field.
G2140 (ETSU)
"Tennessee Coal Mining and Marketing Trends."
H8570 (ETSU)
The Coal Industry of Tennessee.
L4010 (ETSU)
The Coal Reserves of Tennessee.
L4020 (ETSU)
"Development of the Coal Industry of Grundy County, Tennessee."
M620
Study on the Coal Industry.
T1460 (ASU)

COAL INDUSTRY — TENN. — EDUCATION
"Training for Coal Miners in Cooperation with the Public Schools of Tennessee."
B180

COAL INDUSTRY — VA.
Geology of the Big Stone Gap Coal Field of Virginia and Kentucky.
C760 (BC)
The Valley Coal Fields of Virginia.
C770 (ETSU)
"The Changing Economic Position of Southwest Virginia as Affected by the Coal Industry."
C1450 (ETSU)
Coal: Southwest Virginia's Source of Misery.
C7850
The Geology and Coal Resources of Dickenson County, Virginia.
G1340 (ETSU)
The Geology and Coal Resources of the Coal-bearing Portion of Lee County, Virginia.
G1350 (LMC ETSU)
The Geology and Coal Resources of the Coal-bearing Portion of Tazewell County, Virginia.
H2510 (ETSU)
New River Cripple Creek Mineral Region of Virginia.
M940
The Resources of the Coal Field of the Upper Kanawha, with a Sketch of the Iron Belt of Virginia, Setting Forth Some of Their Markets and Means of Development.
M4480
Coal, Southwest Virginia's Source of Misery.
O760 (ASU)
Coal Resources of the Russell Fork Basin in Kentucky and Virginia.
S7540
S8040 (ASU)
Geology and Coal Resources of Buchanan Co., Va.
V950
The Geology and Coal Resources of the Coal-Bearing Portion of Tazewell Co., Va.
V960
Geology and Mineral Resources of Wise Co. and Coal Bearing Portions of Scott Co., Va. with a Chapter on the Forest of Wise Co.
V980

COAL INDUSTRY — W. VA.
"A History of the Labor Movement in West Virginia."
A2610
The Pittston Mentality: Manslaughter on Buffalo Creek.
B3380
"Some Aspects of the Coal Mining Industry in Monongalia County, West Virginia."
B5640
The Myles Job Mine — A Study of Benefits and Costs of Surface Mining for Coal in Northern West Virginia.
B6780
Coal Company Scrip.
C210 (ASU)
Character of Coal in the Thomas Bed near Harrison, West Virginia.
C750
The Smokeless Coal Fields of West Virginia.
C1010 (LMC)
History of West Virginia Coal Industry.
C6550 (ASU BC)
"The Mine War on Cabin Creek and Paint Creek, West Virginia, in 1912-1913."
C8590 (ASU)
West Virginia's Buffalo Creek Flood: A Study of the Hydrology and Engineering Geology.
D720
Coals and Coke of W. Va.; a Handbook of the Coals and Cokes of the Great Kanawha, New River, Flat Top, and Adjacent Coal Districts in W. Va.
E1210 (BC)
The Igneous Rocks of Pendleton County, West Virginia.
G380 (ETSU)
"Cultural and Historical Geography of Mining Settlements in the Pocahontas Coal Fields of Southern West Virginia, 1880 to 1930."
G1620
Coal and Coal Mining in West Virginia.
H3510 (ASU BC ETSU)
"The Pattern of Settlements in the Southern and Middle Anthracite Region of Pennsylvania."
K220
"The Negro Miner in West Virginia."
L130
The New-Kanawha River and the Mind War of West Virginia.
M630 (BC)
The Welfare of Children in Bituminous Coal Mining Communities in West Virginia.
M1530 (ASU)
"Coal Consolidation: Profile of the Fairmont Field of Northern West Virginia, 1852-1903."
M4090
Paint Creek Miner.
P660
The Cheat Mountain Coal Field of Randolph County, West Virginia.
R1270 (ASU ETSU)
Some Churches of Coal Mining Communities of West Virginia.
R2010
The Story of Glen Rogers, W. Va.
S1050 (BC)
Human Crisis in the Kingdom of Coal.
S5020
"Grievance Settlement in Coal Mining."
S5440
New Small Business in a Redevelopment Coal Area in West Virginia.
S7330
The Changing Markets for West Virginia Coal 1951-1963.
T8200
The Logan Coal Field of West Virginia: A Brief History.
T8470 (ASU ETSU WCU)
W. Va. Coal Fields.
U1750
Characteristics of Minable Coals of West Virginia.
W3670 (ETSU)
"Development of the Bituminous Coal Mining Industry in Logan County, West Virginia."
W5400
Levels Above Tide. True Meridians. Report on Coal.
W5450 (ETSU)
Stratigraphy of the Bituminous Coal Field of Pennsylvania, Ohio, and West Virginia.
W5470
Supplementary Coal Report.
W5480 (ETSU)

COAL INDUSTRY — W. VA. — ANTHRACITE
The Smokeless Coal Fields of West Virginia: A Brief History.
T140 (BC ETSU ASU WCU)

COAL INDUSTRY — W. VA. — LABOR FORCE
"A Survey of Labor Requirements in Northern West Virginia Coal Mines in 1957."
B7960

COAL MARKET
"Anthracite Coal: A Study in Advanced Industrial Decline."
B680
A Study of the Eastern Industrial Coal Market.
B5500
Survey of Opportunities to Stimulate Coal Utilization.
B5510
Coal: Energy and Crisis.
C2680
From Mine to Market: The History of Coal Transportation on the Norfolk and Western Railway.
L220 (ASU BC)
"The Norfolk and Western Railroad, 1881-1896: A Study in Coal Transportation."
L230

COAL MARKET — APP.
"Bituminous Coal Strip Mines; Some Financing Considerations."
K580
Black Land, the Way of Life in the Coal Fields.
K3030
"The Price of Coal: A Study of the Policies of the National Coal Board."
L3300
Miner's Wages and the Cost of Coal: An Inquiry into the Wages System in the Bituminous Coal Industry.
L3790
"The Competitive Position of Bituminous Coal in the Utility Markets of the Northeast."
L3800
"Problems in the Anthracite Industry with Special Reference to Marketing."
Z10

COAL MARKET — KY.
Economic Data on Eastern Kentucky Coal Fields.
K910
Annual Report, 1885-1919.
K1110
Coal Mining Reference Book.
K1300
Proceedings.
K1310

COAL MARKET — PA.
Buried Black Treasure: The Story of Pennsylvania Anthracite.
F760 (ASU)
"Measuring Productivity in Coal Mining: A Case Study of Multiple Input Measurement at the County Level in Pennsylvania."
J310

COAL MARKET — W. VA.
"Coal Consolidation: Profile of the Fairmont Field of Northern West Virginia, 1852-1903."
M4080

COAL MINES AND MINERS
Death in the Dark.
A420 (BC ASU)

COAL MINES AND MINERS

"Factors Affecting Social Participation in Coal Communities."
A800 (ASU)

Grundy County, Tennessee; Relief in a Coal Mining Community.
A1850

Work, Safety, and Life Style Among Southern Appalachian Coal Miners. A Survey of the Men of Standard Mines.
A1930

Work, Safety, and Life Style Among Southern Appalachian Coal Miners: A Survey of the Men of Standard Mines.
A1970 (ASU)

The Kentucky Miner's Struggle: The Record of a Year of Lawless Violence. The Only Complete Picture of Events Briefly Told.
A2090 (ASU)

Life in a West Virginia Coal Field.
A2100

Coal Mine Modernization Year Book.
A2160

Facts about the Bituminous Coal Industry.
A4450

The Abram Creek-Stony River Coal Field, Northeastern West Virginia.
A5230

Geology and Mineral Resources of Part of the Cumberland Gap Coal Field, Kentucky.
A5240 (ASU)

A Key to Mine Ventilation.
A5360 (BC)

"The Anthracite Mine Workers, 1869-1897: A Functional Approach to Labor History."
A5520 (ASU)

The Strip Mining of America: An Analysis of Surface Coal Mining and the Environment.
A5590 (ASU)

"The Economics of Strip Coal Mining."
A5820 (ASU)

Bituminous Coal Wages, Profits and Productivity.
B40

"Training for Coal Miners in Cooperation with the Public Schools of Tennessee."
B180

"Anthracite Coal: A Study in Advanced Industrial Decline."
B680

"The Southern Appalachian Coal Community: An Explorative Study."
B820 (ASU)

Coal and Coal Mining in West Virginia.
B1200

The Negro in the Bituminous Coal Mining Industry.
B1400 (WCU BC MHC)

"A Study of the Minnesota Multiphasic Personality Inventory and Its Use in Identification of Acceptable Mine Foremen."
B2870

Coal Reserves of the Pittsburgh (No. 8) Bed in Belmont County, Ohio.
B3310 (ASU)

The Hurricane Creek Massacre: An Inquiry into the Circumstances Surrounding the Deaths of Thirty-eight Men in a Coal Mine Explosion.
B3370 (ASU BC LMC WCU MHC)

Camerton Slope, a Story of Mining Life.
B4240 (ASU BC)

Special Report on an Evaluation of Mine Scaling.
B6250 (ASU)

"A Survey of Labor Requirements in Northern West Virginia Coal Mines in 1957."
B7960

Underground Riches: The Story of Mining.
B8310 (ASU)

Character of Coal in the Thomas Bed near Harrison, West Virginia.
C750

The Smokeless Coal Fields of West Virginia.
C1010 (LMC)

Report on the Mining Methods and Appliances Used in Anthracite Coal Fields.
C2850 (BC)

Practical Kinks for Coal Mining Men.
C5180 (BC)

Successful Solutions to Everyday Coal Mining Problems.
C5190 (BC)

Men and Coal.
C5790 (ASU BC)

Men and Coal.
C5800 (MHC WCU)

History of the Consolidated Coal Company.
C6790

Coal: Southwest Virginia's Source of Misery.
C7850

"Earnings, Health, Safety, and Welfare of Bituminous Coal Miners Since the Encouragement of Mechanization by the United Mine Workers of America."
D610

Notable Mine Disasters of Fayette County, West Virginia.
D2880 (BC)

"The Public School in the Mining Community."
D3100

"A Study of Fatal Roof Fall Accidents in Bituminous Coal Mines."
D3110 (LMC)

"A Study of the Literature on Accidents in Coal Mines of the United States with Comparisons of the Records in Other Coal-producing Countries."
D3640

"A Validation Study of a Psychological Test Battery for Selection of Joy Ripper-type Continuous Miner Operators."
D4090

Coal Through the Ages.
E610 (BC)

Geology and Coal Resources of the Cannel City Quadrangle, Kentucky.
E2020

Mother Jones, the Miners' Angel: A Portrait.
F740 (ASU MHC)

"Economic Consequences of the Seven-hour Day and Wage Changes in the Bituminous Coal Industry."
F1220

Wage Rates and Working Time in the Bituminous Coal Industry, 1912-1922.
F1230 (BC)

Coal Creek Rebellion.
F1770 (ASU)

Seventy Years in the Coal Mines.
F3050 (BC)

"Segregation Patterns in a Coal Camp."
F3220 (ASU)

"Industrial Retardation and Economic Growth: A Case Study of Secular and Structural Change in the United States, 1920-1960."
F3430

"Coal Mining Safety: National Solutions in the Progressive Period."
G3090

Coal and Coal Mines.
G3760 (BC)

Coal and Coal Mines.
G3770 (ASU)

The Road from West Virginia.
H2120 (ASU BC LMC)

"A New Deal for Harlan: The Roosevelt Labor Policies in a Kentucky Coal Field, 1931-1939."
H5120 (BC)

"The United Mine Workers of America and the Non-Union Coal Fields."
H5620

Annotated Bibliography on Slope Stability of Strip Mine Soil Banks.
H6250 (ASU)

"The Coal Miner's Insurrections, 1891-1892."
H8740 (ASU)

"The Pattern of Settlements in the Southern and Middle Anthracite Region of Pennsylvania."
K220

People of Coal Town.
L600 (ASU BC WWC WCU)

People of Coal Town.
L610 (LMC)

"Social Behavior under Conditions of Extreme Stress: A Study of Miners Entrapped by a Coal Mine Disaster."
L3820

The Coal Reserves of Tennessee.
L4020 (ETSU)

Coal Mine Health and Safety; the Case of West Virginia.
M110 (BC)

Coal Mining Health and Safety in West Virginia.
M120

"A Study of the Factors Influencing Job-satisfaction among Factory Workers of Clarksburg, West Virginia, and Coal Miners of Morgantown, West Virginia."
M4720

"Economics of the Southern Smokeless Coals."
M5150

"Characteristics of Mining and Nonmining Psychiatric Patients."
M5630
M6140

Handbook of Pollution Control Costs in Mine Drainage Management.
M6470

Theory and Practice of Mine Ventilation.
M6610

"Attitude of Coal Miners toward Union and Coal Industry."
M7730 (ASU)

The Plight of the Bituminous Coal Miner.
M7790 (ASU BC)

"The Coal Camp: A Pattern of Limited Community Life."
M7860 (ASU)

History of Coal Mining in Laurel County, Kentucky, 1920-1944.
M8160

Papers and Proceedings.
N160

The Story of American Coals.
N980 (BC)

Peabody Atlas.
P1140 (BC)

"Anxiety in Coal Miners."
R1680

Human Crisis in the Kingdom of Coal.
S5010 (ASU BC)

"A Recursive Programing Model of Resource Allocation and Technological Change in the United States Bituminous Coal Industry."
T10

The Smokeless Coal Fields of West Virginia: A Brief History.
T140 (BC ETSU ASU WCU)

Hours and earnings in anthracite and bituminous coal mining.
U1390

Story about Fighting Mine Fires in Abandoned Coal Workings, Mine Fire Control Project in Appalachia.
U1490

Coal deposits of Pike Co., Ky.
U3120

A List of Books and Other Sources of Information Regarding Coal and Coal Products.
W70

Labor Revolt in Alabama: The Great Strike of 1894.
W770 (WCU BC)

Labor Baron, a Portrait of John L. Lewis.
W2170 (BC)

Labor's Defiant Lady: The Story of Mother Jones.
W2850 (ASU)

W. Va. Coal Facts, 1971.
W3250

Proceedings.
W3260 (BC)

Fayette County.
W3700 (ETSU)

Newsletter.
W4945 (BC)

COAL MINES AND MINERS — ALA.

Waste Disposal Costs at Two Coal Mines in Kentucky and Alabama.
D240

Report on the Plateau Coal Field of Alabama.
T6590

COAL MINES AND MINERS — APP.

Fighting for Survival: The Bootleg Coal Industry.
A350 (ASU)

Coal: Energy and Crisis.
C2680

Schools in the Bituminous Coal Regions of the Appalachian Mountains.
D1610

Those Black Diamond Men: A Tale of the Anthrax Valley.
G1140 (BC ASU)

"The Economic Effects of Collective Bargaining in Bituminous Coal Mining."
G3860

COAL MINES AND MINERS — APP.
"The Coal Buying Policies: Effects on Prices and Method of Mining in Supplying States."
H3150
"A "New Deal" for Soft Coal: The Attempted Revitalization of the Bituminous Coal Industry under the New Deal."
J1840
Autobiography of Mother Jones.
J2500 (BC LMC ASU WCU MHC)
Thoughts of Mother Jones: Compiled from Her Writings and Speeches.
J2510 (WCU)
"Bituminous Coal Strip Mines; Some Financing Considerations."
K580
An Analysis of Appalachian State Coal Mine Health and Safety and Workmen's Compensation Programs: Recommendations for Improvement.
K880 (ASU)
Look at Mine-timber Market in the Appalachian Bituminous Coal Region.
K2930
Black Land, the Way of Life in the Coal Fields.
K3030
Pneumoconiosis in Appalachian Bituminous Coal Miners.
L140 (ASU)
Lament for the Molly Maquires.
L2080
"Occupational Roles and Family Roles: A Study of Coal Mining Families in the Southern Appalachians."
L2150
"Coal Miners and Religion."
L2950
Men in Crisis: A Study of a Mine Disaster.
L3810
Legal Problems of Coal Mine Reclamation: Study in Maryland, Ohio, Pennsylvania, and West Virginia.
M3930 (BC)
"The Decline of Anthracite, 1913-1955."
M5320
"The Economics of the Coal Industry."
R2370
"Union Economic Politics and Union Discipline in the Bituminous Wage Dispute of 1949-1950."
R4030 (ASU)
A History of the Coal Miners of the United States.
R4140 (BC)
An Appraisal of Coal Strip Mining.
T2270 (BC)
"Coal Country: The Rise of the Southern Smokeless Coal Industry and Its Effect on Area Development."
T7980
Black Diamonds.
T8000 (ASU)
Significant Trends in the West Virginia Coal Industry, 1900-1957.
T8230 (ASU)
Story of Operation Backfill, Mine Subsidence Project in Appalachia.
U1500
A medical survey of the bituminous-coal industry.
U1620
Consumer Protection and Environmental Health Service
U2750
One Sunset a Week, the Story of a Coal Miner . . . .
V510 (ASU)
The Northern Appalachian Coal Field.
W5340
Levels. Coal Analyses.
W5460 (ETSU)
"Development and Operation of the Welfare and Retirement Fund in the Bituminous Coal Industry."
W5620
The American Miners Association: A Record of the Origin of Coal Miners' Unions in the United States.
W5970 (ASU)
The Miners' Case and the Public Interest: A Documented Chronology.
W5980
Preventing Fatal Explosions in Coal Mines: A Study of Recent Major Disasters in the United States as Accompaniments of Technological Change.
W5990
"Disorganization and Delinquency in Three Coal Communities."
W6860 (ASU)
"Problems in the Anthracite Industry with Special Reference to Marketing."
Z10
"The Coal Miner in a Large Scale, Highly Mechanized, Highly Integrated Bituminous Coal Mining Plant."
Z20

COAL MINES AND MINERS — KY.
"The Influence of Coal in the Big Sandy Valley."
C3230 (ASU)
Coal Workers' Pneumoconiosis: Workmen's Compensation Treatment and it's Prevention in Kentucky.
C3550 (ASU)
Waste Disposal Costs at Two Coal Mines in Kentucky and Alabama.
D240
D2840
"Twentieth Century Development of the Coal Mining Industry in Eastern Kentucky and Its Influence upon the Political Behavior of This Area."
F3420 (ASU)
"External Diseconomies of Bituminous Coal Surface Mining — A Case Study of Eastern Kentucky, 1960-1967."
H7590
Coal Deposits of Pike County, Kentucky.
H8370
Bibliography of the Big Sandy Valley.
J930
The Coal Industry in Kentucky.
J990
The Coal Industry in Kentucky.
J1000
Economic Data on Eastern Kentucky Coal Fields.
K910
Annual Report, 1885-1919.
K1110
Directory of Kentucky Mineral Operators.
K1120
Strip Mining in Kentucky.
K1130 (BC ASU)
Coal Mining Reference Book.
K1300
Proceedings.
K1310
Bibliography of Coal in Kentucky.
K1410
Silver Fleece, a Tale of the Swift Mines of Old Kentucky.
K1890 (LMC BC)
Economic Data on Eastern Kentucky Coal Field.
L1260
Harlan Miners Speak: Report on Terrorism in the Kentucky Coal Fields.
N140 (ASU BC)
Harlan Miners Speak: Report on Terrorism in the Kentucky Coal Fields.
N150 (ASU LMC WCU)
The Coal Miner's Struggle in Eastern Kentucky.
N3020 (ASU)
The Superfluous People of Hazard, Kentucky.
P1220
"Social Effects of the Mining Industry in Eastern Kentucky."
S400 (ASU)
Coal Reserves in Portions of Butler, Edmonson, Grayson, Muhlenberg, Ohio, and Warren Counties, Kentucky.
T2430
Hell in Harlan.
T8760 (WCU)
The Coal Fields of Perry Co., Ky.
V60

COAL MINES AND MINERS — MD.
The Best-dressed Miners: Life and Labor in the Maryland Coal Region, 1835-1910.
H3270 (ASU)
"The Coal Miners of Western Maryland."
H3280

COAL MINES AND MINERS — PA.
The Molly Maguires. The Origin, Growth, and Character of the Organization.
D2010 (ASU WCU)
Buried Black Treasure: The Story of Pennsylvania Anthracite.
F760 (ASU)
"Bituminous Coal Open Pit Mining in Clarion County, Pennsylvania."
J180
"Measuring Productivity in Coal Mining: A Case Study of Multiple Input Measurement at the County Level in Pennsylvania."
J310
Black Rock: Mining Folklore of the Pennsylvania Dutch.
K3040 (ASU)
The Molly Maguires and the Detectives.
P3030
Cloud by Day: The Story of Coal and Coke People.
S2830 (ASU LMC BC)
"Social Legislation for the Protection of Coal Miners in Pennsylvania."
Z90

COAL MINES AND MINERS — TENN.
The Northern Tennessee Coal Field.
G2140 (ETSU)
"Tennessee Coal Mining and Marketing Trends."
H8570 (ETSU)
The Coal Industry of Tennessee.
L4010 (ETSU)
Study on the Coal Industry.
T1460 (ASU)

COAL MINES AND MINERS — VA.
The Geology and Coal Resources of the Coal-bearing Portion of Tazewell County, Virginia.
H2510 (ETSU)
The Resources of the Coal Field of the Upper Kanawha, with a Sketch of the Iron Belt of Virginia, Setting Forth Some of Their Markets and Means of Development.
M4480
Coal, Southwest Virginia's Source of Misery.
O760 (ASU)
The Geology and Coal Resources of Dickenson Co., Va.
V970

COAL MINES AND MINERS — VA. AND KY.
Geology of the Big Stone Gap Coal Field of Virginia and Kentucky.
C760 (BC)

COAL MINES AND MINERS — W. VA.
The Myles Job Mine — A Study of Benefits and Costs of Surface Mining for Coal in Northern West Virginia.
B6780
Coals and Coke of W. Va.; a Handbook of the Coals and Cokes of the Great Kanawha, New River, Flat Top, and Adjacent Coal Districts in W. Va.
E1210 (BC)
"Cultural and Historical Geography of Mining Settlements in the Pocahontas Coal Fields of Southern West Virginia, 1880 to 1930."
G1620
Coal and Coal Mining in West Virginia.
H3510 (ASU BC ETSU)
John Henry: An American Legend.
K350
"The Negro Miner in West Virginia."
L130
Civil War in West Virginia: A Story of the Industrial Conflict in the Coal Mines.
L380 (ASU BC)
"Coal Consolidation: Profile of the Fairmont Field of Northern West Virginia, 1852-1903."
M4080
Paint Creek Miner.
P660
Coaltown Revisited: An Appalachian Notebook.
P2330 (ASU LMC ETSU WCU WWC BC)
The Story of Glen Rogers, W. Va.
S1050 (BC)
Human Crisis in the Kingdom of Coal.
S5020
Climate, Weather and Coal Mine Explosions; with a Meteorological Review of the Farmington Disaster.
W2230
"Development of the Bituminous Coal Mining Industry in Logan County, West Virginia."
W5400

COAL MINES AND MINERS — W. VA.
"A Cross-Validation Study of a Mining Foreman Selection He Devised from the Minnesota Multiphasic Personality Inventory."
W6230
COAL MINES AND MINING
Questions and Answers for American Mine Examinations.
T340 (BC)
COAL MINES AND MINING — APP.
P3200
COAL MINES — MINERS
Coal Company Scrip.
C210 (ASU)
COAL MINING
The Potomac and Roaring Creek Coal Fields in West Virginia.
W2260
COAL MINING AND MINERS
Wage Chronology: Bituminous Coal Mines, 1933/66-.
U1410
Bulletin 1.
U1420
COAL MINING — PA.
A Description of the George Korson Folklore Archive.
C7460 (ASU)
COLLEGES AND UNIVERSITIES
ELOJO (The Eye).
A1920 (ASU)
The Story of Montreat from Its Beginning, 1897-1947.
A2340 (ASU WCU LMC)
B4340 (ASU)
Blanford Barnard Dougherty, a Man to Match His Mountains.
B7350 (ASU)
A Report of Student Internships in Resource Development, & Legal Services Development.
O10
COLLEGES AND UNIVERSITIES — ALA. — BIRMINGHAM SOUTHERN COLLEGE
A History of Birmingham-Southern College, 1856-1931.
P2290
COLLEGES AND UNIVERSITIES — APP.
Survey of Environmental Education Programs in Colleges and Universities in the Appalachian Region.
A3860 (ASU)
"The Student Population in the Institutions of Higher Education in the Southern Appalachian Region, 1933-1958."
B9530 (BETSU)
The Future of the Church and Independent Schools in our Southern Highlands.
C630 (ASU)
Southern Highland Schools Maintained by Denominational and Independent Agencies.
C860 (ASU)
How to Pay for College, a Complete Guide to Scholarships, Loans and Self-help Opportunities in the Appalachian South.
C7860 (MHC ASU BC)
COLLEGES AND UNIVERSITIES — APP. — FRONTIER
Washington College: A Study of an Attempt to Provide Higher Education in Eastern Tennessee.
C1420 (ETSU BC)
COLLEGES AND UNIVERSITIES — BOONE — APPALACHIAN STATE UNIV.
"A Comparative Analysis of Student Teaching Programs in the Elementary Schools at Appalachian State Teachers College."
B4640 (ASU)
COLLEGES AND UNIVERSITIES — GA. — BERRY COLLEGE
Martha Berry: The Sunday Lady of Possum Trot.
B9550 (ASU LMC WWC BC)
Martha Berry: The Sunday Lady of Possum Trot.
B9560 (LMC)
Angel of Appalachia: Martha Berry.
M9280 (ASU MHC)
Martha Berry.
P2530
S5770
COLLEGES AND UNIVERSITIES — KY. — ALICE LLOYD COLLEGE
Stay on, Stranger: An Extraordinary Story of the Kentucky Mountains.
D4110 (ASU LMC WWC BC)
COLLEGES AND UNIVERSITIES — KY. — BEREA COLLEGE
"Willis Duke Weatherford: An Interpretation of His Work in Race Relations, 1906-1946."
A2630 (ASU BC)
Berea College, Kentucky, An Interesting History.
B3060 (ASU)
"Educational Values of the Berea College Labor Program."
B4910 (ASU)
The Impact of Berea College on Student Characteristics.
B4920 (BC)
Oration before Students and Historical Class of Berea College, Berea, Ky., Oct. 16, 1895.
C4770 (BC)
Prophet of Plenty: The First Ninety Years of W. D. Weatherford.
D4250 (ASU WCU LMC MHC ETSU FC WWC BC)
Berea College, Ky.
F50
Autobiography of John G. Fee, Berea, Kentucky.
F520 (ASU BC)
Berea College from Servitude to Service, Being the Old South Lectures on the History and Work of the Negro.
F3560 (BC)
For the Mountains, an Autobiography.
F3570 (ASU LMC BC)
Cooking with Hougen.
H7370 (ASU)
Look No Further.
H7380 (ASU)
More Hougen Favorites.
H7390 (ASU)
Berea College: The Telescope and the Spade.
H8710 (ASU)
The Forgotten Region.
M1990 (BC)
Flickering Light.
M7470 (BC WWC)
The Fruit of This Tree: The Story of a Great American College and Its Contribution to the Education of a Changing World.
M7480 (ASU BC)
Berea's First Century, 1855-1955.
P1510 (ASU LMC)
Nurses in Time.
P1520
Memoirs of Berea.
R2090 (BC)
A Charge to Keep; Narratives and Episodes Devoted to the Women Who Helped Build a Place for Worship and for Learning on the Berea Ridge.
R2290 (BC)
Birth of Berea College; a Story of Providence.
R3500 (BC ASU)
Birth of Berea College: A Story of Providence.
R3510 (MHC)
COLLEGES AND UNIVERSITIES — KY. — CUMBERLAND COLLEGE
T9140 (BC)
COLLEGES AND UNIVERSITIES — KY. — EASTERN KENTUCKY STATE COLLEGE
Five Decades of Progress: Eastern Kentucky State College, 1906-1957. Eastern Kentucky.
D2990 (ASU)
Five Decades of Progress.
K1210
COLLEGES AND UNIVERSITIES — KY. — HIGHLAND COLLEGE
Edward O. Guerrant: Apostle to the Southern Highlanders.
M40 (LMC BC ASU)
COLLEGES AND UNIVERSITIES — KY. — MOREHEAD STATE UNIV.
"A Population Study of the Appalachian Members of the Freshman Class at Morehead (Kentucky) State University, 1967-1968."
D3090
COLLEGES AND UNIVERSITIES — KY. — STUART ROBINSON COLLEGE
Edward O. Guerrant: Apostle to the Southern Highlanders.
M40 (LMC BC ASU)
COLLEGES AND UNIVERSITIES — KY. — WITHERSPOON COLLEGE
Buckhorn: The Story of a Christian Enterprise on Squabble Creek in the Mountains of Kentucky.
B8250 (BC)
Edward O. Guerrant: Apostle to the Southern Highlanders.
M40 (LMC BC ASU)
COLLEGES AND UNIVERSITIES — N. C.
A2810 (ASU)
A3370 (ASU)
Appalachian North Carolina Youth Development Project, Final Report.
A3640 (ASU)
The Asheville Archive, College of the City of Asheville, N. C.
N1780
Educational Guide: Technical Institutes/Community Colleges.
N1910 (LMC)
R1830 (ASU)
COLLEGES AND UNIVERSITIES — N. C. — APPALACHIAN STATE UNIV.
"A Study of the Needs for an Audio-Visual Education Center at Appalachian State Teachers College."
B8270 (ASU)
"An Examination of the Leisure Activities and Recreational Interests of Students, and Available Equipment and Facilities at Appalachian State Teachers College."
C580 (ASU)
"Extent of Sexual Knowledge, Accumulation of Sexual Information, and Sex Education Attitudes of Undergraduate Students at Appalachian State University."
C5090 (ASU)
"A Study of the Applied Psychology Classes for Sophomores and Juniors at Appalachian State Teachers College."
D1120 (ASU)
"A Study to Identify Some Personality Characteristics of Freshmen Academic Underachievers at Appalachian State University."
D1790 (ASU)
A Comprehensive Study of the Academic Characteristics and Success Patterns of North Carolina Community College Transfer Students and Native Students of Appalachian State University.
E700
"A Survey of the Study Habits of the Freshman Class of 1959-1960 at Appalachian State Teachers College."
H7080 (ASU)
"The Effect of the Physical Activity Program on the Strength Development of Freshmen at Appalachian State Teachers College."
J610 (ASU)
"A Study of Reasons Why Freshmen Drop Out of Appalachian State Teachers College."
J1270 (ASU)
"Treatment of Pupil Misbehavior by Textbooks Used in Undergraduate Education Courses at Appalachian State Teachers College."
J2790 (ASU)
"A Historical Study of the Relationship Between the Watauga Democrat and Appalachian State Teachers College."
K90 (ASU)
K1740 (ASU)
"Blanford Barnard Dougherty: Mountain Educator."
L490 (ASU)
Blanford Barnard Dougherty, Mountain Educator.
L500 (ASU)
"A Critical Study of the Physical Education Undergraduate Curriculum at Appalachian State Teachers College."
L3930 (ASU)
"A Survey of Recreational Music Activities Available to the General College Student in Georgia, North Carolina, South Carolina and Tennessee."
M4340 (ASU)
Faculty Publications.
N1540 (BC ASU LMC ETSU)
Folk Arts Workshop.
N1550 (ASU)
Singing Light.
N1560
College Bulletin.
N1570 (ASU)
Dedication: B. B. Dougherty Administration Building.
N1590 (ASU)

COLLEGES AND UNIVERSITIES — N. C. — APPALACHIAN STATE UNIV.

Institutional Self-study for the Southern Association of Colleges and Schools.
N1600 (ASU)

President's Annual Report to the Board of Trustees for the Year Ending June 30, 1969.
N1610 (ASU)

A Proposal for the Institution of Programs Leading to the Bachelor of Arts and the Bachelor of Science Degrees Not Requiring Professional Preparation for Teaching at Appalachian State Teachers College.
N1630 (ASU)

A Self-evaluation Report Submitted to the National Council for Accreditation of Teacher Education.
N1640 (ASU)

A Self Study Report Submitted to the Southern Association of Colleges and Schools.
N1650 (ASU)

"An Evaluation of the Library Proficiencies of Freshmen at Appalachian State Teachers College, 1953-54."
O1020 (ASU)
R1460 (ASU)

"Problem Analysis Study of Selected Freshmen Students at Appalachian State Teachers College."
R3540 (ASU)

"A Comparative Study of Certain Personality Traits Between Female Physical Education Majors and Non-Majors at Appalachian State University."
T7640 (ASU)
V570 (ASU)

"A Comparative Study of Changes in Selected Personality Variables in Guidance and Counseling Majors as Compared with Reading Majors at Appalachian State University, 1967-68 Academic Year."
V600 (ASU)

"A Study of the Freshmen Placement Tests Given at Appalachian State Teachers College as a Basis for Determining Their Effective Use as a Screening Device."
W4990 (ASU)

"A Comparative Study of Tendencies and Motivational Factors of Students from Various Academic Departments Who Vandalize Library Materials at Appalachian State University."
W6570 (ASU)

COLLEGES AND UNIVERSITIES — N. C. — APPALACHIAN STATE UNIV. — WATAUGA CO.

The Impact of Appalachain State University on the Economy of Watauga County.
E1600 (ASU)

COLLEGES AND UNIVERSITIES — N. C. — ASHEVILLE-BUNCOMBE TECHNICAL INSTITUTE

A Five Year Follow-up Study of Graduates of Asheville-Buncombe Technical Institute, 1966-67 through 1970-71.
J1690 (ASU)

COLLEGES AND UNIVERSITIES — N. C. — BLACK MOUNTAIN COLLEGE

"Willis Duke Weatherford: An Interpretation of His Work in Race Relations, 1906-1946."
A2630 (ASU BC)

"Theory and Practice in the Black Mountain Poets Duncan, Olson, and Creeley."
D600 (WCU)

The Black Mountain Book.
D1350

Black Mountain: An Exploration in Community.
D3650 (ASU WWC BC)

COLLEGES AND UNIVERSITIES — N. C. — BLUE RIDGE TECH.

"An Investigation of Instructors' and Students' Philosophy of Education with Student Evaluations of Instructors at Blue Ridge Technical Institute During the First Year of Operation."
B5570 (ASU)

COLLEGES AND UNIVERSITIES — N. C. — CATAWBA COLLEGE

History of Catawba College, Formerly Located at Newton, Now at Salisbury, N. C.
L1830 (ASU)

COLLEGES AND UNIVERSITIES — N. C. — COMMUNITY COLLEGES

A Comprehensive Study of the Academic Characteristics and Success Patterns of North Carolina Community College Transfer Students and Native Students of Appalachian State University.
E700

COLLEGES AND UNIVERSITIES — N. C. — CONCORDIA COLLEGE

History of Concordia College, Conover, North Carolina.
V1330 (ASU)

COLLEGES AND UNIVERSITIES — N. C. — CULLOWHEE STATE NORMAL SCHOOL

The Spirit of Western North Carolina: A Pageant.
B4190 (WCU LMC)

COLLEGES AND UNIVERSITIES — N. C. — GARDNER-WEBB COLLEGE

Lengthened Shadows: A History of Gardner-Webb College, 1907-1956.
D1590 (ASU)

COLLEGES AND UNIVERSITIES — N. C. — LEES-MCRAE COLLEGE

Report on Its Institutional Self-study for the Commission on Colleges and Universities, Southern Association, 1962-63.
L1480 (LMC)

COLLEGES AND UNIVERSITIES — N. C. — MARS HILL COLLEGE

Outlines of History of French Broad Association and Mars Hill College . . . 1807 to 1907.
A2220

From These Stones: Mars Hill College, 1856-1968.
M2080 (LMC WCU WWC)

From These Stones: Mars Hill College, the First Hundred Years.
M2090 (ASU WCU BC)

CRISIS: Addresses Delivered at the Spring Symposium, Mars Hill College, 1967, 1968.
U70 (WCU)

COLLEGES AND UNIVERSITIES — N. C. — UNIV. OF NORTH CAROLINA AT ASHEVILLE
I60 (BC UNCA)

COLLEGES AND UNIVERSITIES — N. C. — WESTERN CAROLINA UNIV.

The History of Western Carolina College: The Progress of an Idea.
B4160 (BC ASU LMC WCU)

The Superior and Gifted Student Project at Cullowhee, Western Carolina College.
B4300 (WCU)

The Legal Problems of the Appalachian Area in the Immediate Region of Western North Carolina.
B5530 (LMC)

The Cullowhee Conference on Training in Biomathematics: An International Conference Held at Western Carolina College, Cullowhee, North Carolina, August 14-18, 1961.
C6460 (WCU)

"A Curriculum Analysis of the Undergraduate Professional Preparation Program in Health and Physical Education at Western Carolina University."
H8500 (WCU)

Report to State Evaluation Committee on Western Carolina University by the Visitation Committee Oct. 1821, 1964.
N1990 (ASU WCU)

A Faculty Handbook of Western Carolina University.
N2700 (WCU)

A Report on Studies and Investigations Dealing with a Prospective Expanded Program of Service by Western Carolina Univ.
N2720 (WCU)

Teacher Education Programs: A Self-study Report to Division of Professional Services, State Department of Public Instruction.
N2730 (WCU ASU)

Views.
N2740 (ASU WCU)

College Preparatory Program for Visually Impaired Students: A Cooperative Program Between the North Carolina Commission for the Blind and Western Carolina University.
N2750 (WCU)

Institutional Self Study Report, 1963.
N2760 (WCU)

Teacher Education Report to National Council for Accreditation of Teacher Education.
N2770 (WCU)

Horizon 1980: Report of the Special Committee "Which Way From Here" Appointed by President Paul A. Reid, Sept. 3, 1965.
N2780 (WCU)

"A Follow-up of the Fifth Year Graduates of the Department of Administration and School Personnel."
S9330 (WCU)

Address by Secretary of Commerce Luther H. Hodges, Prepared for Delivery at Western Carolina College Commencement, Cullowhee, North Carolina, May 24, 1964.
U2730

COLLEGES AND UNIVERSITIES — PA.

A Description of the George Korson Folklore Archive.
C7460 (ASU)

COLLEGES AND UNIVERSITIES — PA. — PITTSBURG COLLEGE

I Went to Pit College.
G1590

COLLEGES AND UNIVERSITIES — S. C. — FURMAN COLLEGE

The Furman Bulletin, New Series.
F4000

COLLEGES AND UNIVERSITIES — S. C. — FURMAN UNIV.

Furman University, a History.
D220 (WCU)

COLLEGES AND UNIVERSITIES — TENN.

A Study of the Work of the Land-Grant Colleges in the Tennessee Valley Area in Cooperation with the Tennessee Valley Authority.
B800

"A Proposed Central Supply, Storage, and Technicians' Work Area for the Industrial Education Department of East Tennessee State University."
B3400 (ETSU)

"An Analysis of the Relationship Between the Anxiety Level and the Academic Performance of Freshmen at East Tennessee State University for the Year 1965."
R3860 (ETSU)

"A Follow-up of Industrial Arts Graduates of East Tennessee State College from 1930 to 1953."
S2630 (ETSU)

"A Survey of Comprehension Weaknesses of 417 East Tennessee State University Freshmen."
S3280 (ETSU)

"The Economic Impact of the University of Tennessee upon Metropolitan Knoxville."
S4810

COLLEGES AND UNIVERSITIES — TENN. — CARSON-NEWMAN COLLEGE

An Educational Study of Jefferson County, Tennessee.
C1650

"A History of Carson-Newman College."
H910 (WCU)

COLLEGES AND UNIVERSITIES — TENN. — CUMBERLAND UNIV.

History of Cumberland University, 1842-1935.
B5280 (ASU)

COLLEGES AND UNIVERSITIES — TENN. — EAST TENN. UNIV.
O490 (ETSU)

COLLEGES AND UNIVERSITIES — TENN. — EAST TENNESSEE STATE, KINGSPORT UNIV. CENTER

"An Assessment of Why Part-time Under-graduates Are Enrolled at the Kingsport University Center."
G3340 (ETSU)

COLLEGES AND UNIVERSITIES — TENN. — EAST TENNESSEE STATE UNIV.
B7900 (ETSU)

History of the East Tennessee State College.
B8830 (ETSU)

East Tennessee State University Football Statistics, 1920-1970.
B8840 (ETSU)

The Buccaneer, 1937-.
E170

Bulletin.
E180 (ETSU)

Scrap Book.
E190 (ETSU)

COLLEGES AND UNIVERSITIES — TENN. — EAST TENNESSEE STATE UNIV.
Teacher Preparation Programs, East Tennessee State College.
E210 (ETSU)
Alumni Quarterly.
E220 (ETSU)
Master Booklist.
E230 (ETSU)
The Dean Says.
E240 (ETSU)
Report.
E250 (ETSU)
Manual on Thesis Writing.
E260 (ETSU)
Abstracts of Theses Done at East Tennessee State College, Graduate School, by Candidates for the Master of Arts Degree during 1950-.
E270 (ETSU)
Complete List of Master's Theses in the Graduate School . . . For Degrees Awarded, Through August 1960-.
E280
Complete List of Master's Theses in the Graduate School . . . For Degrees Awarded, Through August 1960-.
E290 (ETSU)
Audio-visual Materials at East Tennessee State College in the Teaching Aids Laboratory: Films, Filmstrips, Disc Recordings, Tape Recordings, Framed Pictures.
E300 (ETSU)
Educational Films and Filmstrips; East Tennessee State College Collection. . . .
E310 (ETSU)
Library handbook. . . .
E320 (ETSU)
Report.
E330 (ETSU)
Bulletin.
E340 (ETSU)
The Role and Scope of East Tennessee State University, a Report Submitted to the Tennessee Higher Education Commission, June 1968.
E360 (ETSU)
The ETSU Journalist.
E390 (ETSU)
East Tennessee State University Track and Field School Records, Together with ETSU Field Records for College Meets.
E400 (ETSU)
Newsletter.
E460 (ETSU)
"A Proposed Master of Arts in Teaching Program for East Tennessee State University."
F3650 (ETSU)
Research in the Language Arts at East Tennessee State College.
G1330 (ETSU)
"Professional Characteristics of the Master's Degree Graduates of East Tennessee State University."
H3350 (ETSU)
"An Analysis of Occupational Conditions in Selected Shops and Laboratories at East Tennessee State University."
H3680 (ETSU)
"A Proposed Course in Ceramics for the Fine Arts Department of East Tennessee State College."
H3980 (ETSU)
"A Follow-up Study of Graduates in Industrial Technology at East Tennessee State University, 1962 Through 1967."
H8820 (ETSU)
Curriculum for the Observation and Practice School.
J1350 (ETSU)
"A Study of the Effect of Participation in Athletics on the Grades of Students at East Tennessee State College."
M7920 (ETSU)
"A Study of Noise Levels at the College of Health Building in East Tennessee State University."
P2680 (ETSU)
Curriculum Improvement Conference.
T1310 (ETSU)
Instructional Leadership Conference, June 25-July 13, 1951.
T1320 (ETSU)
Curriculum for the Observation and Practice School.
T1330 (ETSU)
Bulletin.
T1340 (ETSU)
The Role and Scope of East Tennessee State University.
T1350 (ETSU)
T1360 (ETSU)
East Tennessee University 1840-1879.
T2200
W1380 (ETSU)
"An Analysis and Basis for Curriculum Revision Concerning the Drafting Program at East Tennessee State University."
W5880 (ETSU)
W5940 (ETSU)
"A Study of Cooperative Education in Relation to the Industrial Technology Program of East Tennessee State University."
W7020 (ETSU)

COLLEGES AND UNIVERSITIES — TENN. — EAST TENNESSEE STATE UNIV., KINGSPORT CENTER
"A Projection for the Future Needs and Potentials of the Kingsport Center of East Tennessee State University."
P3050 (ETSU)

COLLEGES AND UNIVERSITIES — TENN. — EAST TENNESSEE STATE UNIV. LIBRARY
"A Program of Visual Instruction for Use in Teaching the Location of Major Resources in the East Tennessee State University Library."
L1030 (ETSU)

COLLEGES AND UNIVERSITIES — TENN. — KINGSLEY SEMINARY
"Joseph Ketron and His Kingsley Seminary, Sullivan County, Tennessee."
F3690 (ASU)

COLLEGES AND UNIVERSITIES — TENN. — LINCOLN MEMORIAL UNIV.
Abraham Lincoln and the Cumberland Gap.
H2250 (ASU ETSU)
A Boy Finds a College.
K2140
The Living Memorial to Lincoln.
L2530
Lincoln Memorial University. "Sine Qua Non." Why It Is, Why It Should Be, Why It Must Be, Why It Is America's Hope.
L2551 (BC)
The Living Memorial to Lincoln.
L2552 (BC)

COLLEGES AND UNIVERSITIES — TENN. — MARYVILLE COLLEGE
Maryville College: A History of 150 Years, 1819-1969.
L3020 (ETSU WWC ASU)
A Century of Maryville College, 1819-1919, a Story of Altruism.
W7490 (ASU BC)
Chronicles of Maryville College: A Story of Altruism.
W7500 (ASU ETSU BC)
Isaac Anderson, Founder and First President of Maryville College.
W7510 (BC)

COLLEGES AND UNIVERSITIES — TENN. — ROGERSVILLE SYNODICAL COLLEGE
The Fiftieth Anniversary of the Rogersville Synodical College.
P190

COLLEGES AND UNIVERSITIES — TENN. — SHARP COLLEGE
Dr. Z. C. Graves and the Mary Sharp College, 1850-1896.
M3850

COLLEGES AND UNIVERSITIES — TENN. — TENNESSEE WESLEYAN COLLEGE
A History of Tennessee Wesleyan College.
M3730
A History of Tennessee Wesleyan College, 1857-1957.
M3740 (WCU ASU)

COLLEGES AND UNIVERSITIES — TENN. — UNIV. OF CHATTANOOGA
The University of Chattanooga: Sixty Years.
G2970 (ASU WCU ETSU BC)

COLLEGES AND UNIVERSITIES — TENN. — UNIV. OF TENNESSEE
"The Net Direct Economic Effect of the University of Tennessee on the City of Knoxville and on Knox County Resulting from the Expansion of the Knoxville Campus since 1962."
D1560
Blount College and East Tennessee College, 1794-1840: The First Predecessors of the University of Tennessee.
F1700 (ETSU)
East Tennessee University, 1840-1879, Predecessor of the University of Tennessee.
F1710 (ASU)
Calvin Morgan McClung Historical Collection.
L4040
Blount College and the Univ. of Tennessee.
S410 (ASU BC ETSU)
The University of Tennessee Sesqui-Centennial, 1794-1944.
T2170 (ASU)

COLLEGES AND UNIVERSITIES — UNIV. OF VIRGINIA
Thomas Jefferson and the University of Virginia.
A410 (ASU)

COLLEGES AND UNIVERSITIES — VA.
Announcement.
E2060 (ASU)

COLLEGES AND UNIVERSITIES — VA. — BLUEFIELD STATE COLLEGE
Follow-up Study of MDTA E. and D. Project at Bluefield State College.
H6290

COLLEGES AND UNIVERSITIES — VA. — EMORY AND HENRY COLLEGE
Emory and Henry's Contribution to the Development of Democracy.
F3010
The History of the Emory and Henry College Library, 1839-1954.
O840
Increase in Excellence, a History of Emory and Henry College.
S7190 (ASU BC)

COLLEGES AND UNIVERSITIES — VA. — FERRUM COLLEGE
"A History of Ferrum College — The First Fifty Years, 1913-1963."
A5840 (ASU)
Address by Secretary of Commerce Luther H. Hodges, Prepared for Delivery at 50th Anniversary Observance, Ferrum Junior College, Ferrum, Virginia, May 15, 1964.
U2720

COLLEGES AND UNIVERSITIES — VA. — HOLLINS COLLEGE
Hollins College; an Illustrated History.
N990
Charles Lewis Cocke, Founder of Hollins College.
S5200
Hollins College, 1842-1942; an Historical Sketch, Being an Account of the Principal Developments in the One-Hundred-Year History of Hollins College.
V610 (BC)

COLLEGES AND UNIVERSITIES — VA. — MARTHA WASHINGTON COLLEGE
Three Quarters of a Century at Martha Washington College.
C9880 (ASU)

COLLEGES AND UNIVERSITIES — VA. — ROANOKE COLLEGE
Songs and Fantasies.
B5490
The First Hundred Years of Roanoke College, 1842-1952.
E1430

COLLEGES AND UNIVERSITIES — VA. — UNIV. OF VA.
Songs of the University of Virginia.
W7070 (ASU)

COLLEGES AND UNIVERSITIES — VA. — UNIV. OF VIRGINIA
Pursuits of War: The People of Charlottesville and Albemarle County, Virginia, in the Second World War.
A970 (ASU)

COLLEGES AND UNIVERSITIES — VA. — VIRGINIA MILITARY INSTITUTE

The V. M. I. New Market Cadets. Biographical Sketches of All Members of the Virginia Military Institute Corps of Cadets Who Fought in The Battle of New Market, May 15, 1864.
C8030 (ASU)

Official Register, 1910-1911.
V1120 (ASU)

The Military History of the Virginia Military Institute from 1839 to 1865.
W7880 (ASU)

COLLEGES AND UNIVERSITIES — VA. — VIRGINIA POLYTECHNIC INSTITUTE AND STATE UNIV.

The First 100 Years: A History of Virginia Polytechnic Institute and State University.
K2620

COLLEGES AND UNIVERSITIES — W. VA.

Approaches to University Extension Work with the Rural Disadvantaged: Description and Analysis of a Pilot Effort.
M5970
P4830

COLLEGES AND UNIVERSITIES — W. VA. — DAVIS AND ELKINS COLLEGE

D750 (BC)

COLLEGES AND UNIVERSITIES — W. VA. — MARSHALL COLLEGE

The Life of Morris Purdy Shawkey.
B8240 (ASU BC)

One Hundred Years of Marshall College.
M3420 (BC)

COLLEGES AND UNIVERSITIES — W. VA. — MORRIS HARVEY COLLEGE

Where there is Faith; The Morris Harvey College Story, 1888-1970.
K3190

COLLEGES AND UNIVERSITIES — W. VA. — SALEM COLLEGE

The Light of the Hills: A History of Salem College.
B5260

COLLEGES AND UNIVERSITIES — W. VA. — SHEPHERD COLLEGE

A History of Shepherd College, Shepherdstown, West Virginia.
S4210 (ASU BC)

COLLEGES AND UNIVERSITIES — W. VA. — WEST VIRGINIA UNIV.

"West Virginia Higher Education Long-range Enrollment and Operating Budget Projections."
D3970

"Worker Education in West Virginia: A Study in Union-University Cooperation."
R3670 (ASU)

"Food Habits of a Sample of University High School Students."
W5660

COLLEGES AND UNIVERSITIES — W. VA. — WEST VIRGINIA WESLEYAN COLLEGE

West Virginia Wesleyan College, First 50 Years, 1890-1940.
H3640

COLLEGES AND UNIVERSITIES — W. VA. — WHEELING COLLEGE

Selected Archeological and Historical Sites in West Virginia; Preliminary Plan for Development.
W5170

COLLEGES AND UNIVERSITIES — WESTERN CAROLINA UNIV.

"The Attitudes of Freshmen Female Students Toward Physical Education at Western Carolina University."
B7830 (WCU)

COMMUNITY DEVELOPMENT

Suggestion for Planning and Zoning in Appalachia.
S5410

City Manager Government in Kingsport.
S7520

COMMUNITY DEVELOPMENT — W. VA.

Guiding Principles for Rural Development in West Virginia.
S7290

COMMUNITY PLANNING

A Selective Description of a Knox County Mountain Neighborhood.
C40

Changes in the Rural Southern Appalachian Community.
P2720 (ASU)

Change in Rural Appalachia: Implications for Action Programs.
P2750 (FC LMC WCU ETSU ASU BC)

COMMUNITY PLANNING AND ORGANIZATION

"Conservation Projects by Community Organizations in Tennessee and Other Southeastern States."
B300

A Study of Potential State and Local Programs to Stimulate Low- and Moderate-income Housing Construction in Ohio Appalachia. Supplement.
B1930 (ASU)

A Framework for Community Economic Planning Based on the Integration of an Input-output Model and a Linear Programming Model.
B1960

The Community Development Process: The Rediscovery of Local Initiative.
B3550

"Geographic Factors Influencing the Development of Scott County, Tennessee."
B8630
C3530 (BC)

Comprehensive City Plan, Roanoke.
C4180

"The Development of a Management Evaluation System for Community Action Agencies."
C7340

Region Building: Community Development Lessons from the Tennessee Valley.
D40 (ASU)

Community Analysis and Program Planning, Big Caney Valley, Kentucky.
M5940

Guidance in a Rural-Indust. Comm., Harlan Co., a Ky. Coal Mining District, Plans.
W720

An Evaluation of the Impact of the Community Action Program Upon Poverty Conditions in McDowell Co.
W4580

Design for Action, Community Problem Solving in Disadvantaged Communities.
W8700

COMMUNITY PLANNING AND ORGANIZATION — APP.

Tennessee Valley Country: Rural Government in the Hill Country of Alabama.
B5600

"The Community Action Movement in North Carolina."
F1620 (LMC)

Regional Development and Planning: A Reader.
F3320 (ASU)

Community Action in Appalachia: An Appraisal of the "War on Poverty" in a Rural Setting of Southeastern Kentucky.
K1380

"The Development of a Community Water Supply to Serve a Rural Area of Southern Appalachia."
L2640 (ETSU)

Problems of Community Action in Appalachia.
Z70

COMMUNITY PLANNING AND ORGANIZATION — KY.

Communication and Mountain Development: A Summary Report Two East Kentucky Studies.
B5780

Non-federal Aid for Community Development Projects in Kentucky.
G480

Commonwealth and Community: The Kentucky Program of State Assistance for Community Improvement.
K1010

Harlan County, Existing Land Use Analysis. Harlan-Harlan County Major Thoroughfare Plan.
K1150

COMMUNITY PLANNING AND ORGANIZATION — N. C.

Code.
B5430 (ASU)

Land Development Plan.
B5440 (BC ASU)

Land Development Plan.
B5450

Planning for Flood Damage Prevention at Clyde, N. C.
C5160 (LMC)

Prelude to Planning in Buncombe County, North Carolina.
C6230 (WWC)

Master Plan for Recreation and Parks: Jackson County, North Carolina.
G300 (WCU)

Land Use Plan, Haywood County, N. C.
H4020 (LMC)

A Study of the Hendersonville Central Business District.
H4580 (LMC)

"Community Resources of Tryon, North Carolina."
H6960 (WCU)

Community Facilities Plan. Brevard, N. C.
N1980

COMMUNITY PLANNING AND ORGANIZATION — PA.

A Community Organizes for Action: A Case Study of the Mon-Yough Region in Pennsylvania.
A5770

COMMUNITY PLANNING AND ORGANIZATION — TENN.

Better Farming Practices through Rural Community Organization.
B5330

Better Homemaking Practices through Rural Community Organization.
B5340

Local Leadership in Rural Communities of Cumberland County, Tennessee.
B5360

Neighborhoods and Communities of Cumberland County, Tennessee.
B5370

Selective Participation of Farmers and Their Wives in Rural Organization.
B5380

Educational, Economic and Community Survey, Bledsoe County.
B7070

"An Analysis of the Industrial Potential of Carter County, Tennessee."
C9180 (ETSU)

Report.
H1410 (ETSU)

"A Study of Rural Cooperative Organizations in Overton County, Tennessee."
H3460

"The Lenoir City Company, and Attempt in Community Development."
H3770

Johnson City, Tennessee, Population and Economic Base Study.
H5390

Kingsport, the Planned Industrial City.
K2550 (ETSU)

Kingsport, Tennessee, a Modern American City — Developed through Industry.
K2560 (LMC ETSU)

Kingsport, the Planned Industrial City.
K2570 (ETSU ASU)

"Federal Centralization versus Local Values: A Case Study of Federal-Local Relations in the Knoxville-Knox County Community Action Committee."
L3480

COMMUNITY PLANNING AND ORGANIZATION — VA.

Community Relationships.
B9260 (BC)

COMMUNITY PLANNING AND ORGANIZATION — W. VA.

Survey of Governmental and Voluntary Health, Welfare and Recreation Services in Greater Kanawha Valley. (Community Services Report.)
C4170

Professional Overall Economic Development for Fayette Co., West Virginia.
F400

COMMUNITY PLANNING — APP.

Modernization and Diffusion of Innovations in a Rural Appalachia County; General Systems Analysis.
S3710 (BC)

COMMUNITY PLANNING — KY.

The Superfluous People of Hazard, Kentucky.
P1220

COMMUNITY PLANNING — KY. — BEREA
Land Use Plan for the City of Berea, Ky.
B3120 (BC)
Public Improvements for the City of Berea, Ky.
B3130 (BC)
COMMUNITY PLANNING — N. C.
Community Facilities Plan: Brevard, N. C.
N2020
Community Facilities Plan and Public Improvements Program: Glen Alpine, North Carolina.
N2030 (WCU)
Community Facilities Plan & Public Improvements Program: Valdese, North Carolina.
N2040 (WCU)
Land Development Plan for Black Mountain, N. C.
N2050 (WCU)
Land Development Plan: Boone, North Carolina.
N2060 (WCU ASU)
Land Development Plan: Burnsville, N. C.
N2070 (WCU)
Land Potential Study: Madison County, North Carolina.
N2080 (WCU)
Land Potential Study & Land Development Plan: Wilkes County, North Carolina.
N2090 (ASU WCU)
Land Use Survey & Analysis and Land Development Plan: Glen Alpine, North Carolina.
N2100 (WCU)
Land Use Survey and Analysis and Land Development Plan: Valdese, North Carolina.
N2110 (WCU)
Neighborhood Analysis: Brevard, N. C.
N2120 (LMC WCU ASU)
Neighborhood Analysis: Valdese, North Carolina.
N2130 (ASU WCU)
Public Facilities Plan: Wilkes County, North Carolina.
N2170 (ASU WCU)
Watauga County Land Development Plan.
N2180 (ASU)
Zoning Ordinance: Boone, N. C.
N2190 (LMC ASU)
Zoning Ordinance of the W. Kerr Scott Reservoir Area, Wilkes County, N. C.
N2200 (ASU)
Zoning Ordinance: Wilkes County, North Carolina.
N2210 (ASU WCU)
"Community Appearance Commissions in North Carolina."
S3170 (ASU)
Western North Carolina Associated Communities.
S3610 (WCU)
Population and Economy: Sylva, N. C.
S9750 (LMC)
Today and Tomorrow, Murphy, North Carolina.
W4930 (LMC)
COMMUNITY PLANNING — TENN.
"A Study of Two Areas for Future Supermarket Location in Johnson City, Tennessee."
P670 (ETSU)
Decatur Story.
S2680
Flood Problems and Their Solution Through Urban Planning Programs.
S3360
Johnson City Transportation Study: Major Route Plan. Traffic Operation Study and Parking Study.
T1220 (ETSU)
Flood Problems and Their Solution Through Urban Planning Programs.
T1630
Local Planning in Tennessee, 1956-57.
T1640
Policy Conclusions, Problems and Opportunities.
T1670
Historic District Plan: Jonesborough, Tennessee.
T1750
COMMUNITY PLANNING — W. VA.
Elk Garden, West Virginia: A Reconnaissance Survey of a Problem Town.
P3710
CONSERVATION
Soil Survey, Hamblen County, Tennessee.
A10 (ASU)
A2640 (ASU)
A2670 (ASU)
Annual Report.
A3260
Voices from Earth, a Collection of Writings on Environment.
A4500 (ASU)
"The Economics of Strip Coal Mining."
A5820 (ASU)
Surface Mining — Extent and Economic Importance, Impact on Natural Resources, and Proposals for Reclamation of Mined-lands: Proceedings.
C6440 (ASU)
Proceedings.
F1780 (WCU)
Surface Mined Areas: Control and Reclamation of Environmental Damage; a Bibliography.
F3090 (ASU)
Denudation and Erosion in the Southern Appalachian Region and the Monongahela Basin.
G2130 (ASU ETSU)
Natural Resource Special Districts in Appalachia: Review of Enabling Laws.
H1330
Conservation of Wildlife and Forests in Tennessee.
H4120 (ETSU BC)
Conservation of Wildlife and Forests in Tennessee.
H4130
Slope Stability of Coal Strip Mine Spoil Banks.
H6260 (ASU)
J2770
The Earthman Story, Starring Shenandoah Skyline.
L180 (BC ASU MHC)
The Diligent Destroyers.
L1090 (ASU WCU)
Footprints in the Soil and Reflections on the Water: Conservation in West Virginia.
O570 (ASU)
"Community Appearance Commissions in North Carolina."
S3170 (ASU)
The Issues Related to Surface Mining; a Summary Review, with Selected Readings.
S3300 (WCU)
CONSERVATION — APP.
Conservation: An American Story of Conflict and Accomplishment.
C8240
Hunting and Conservation: The Book of the Boone and Crockett Club.
G4310 (ETSU)
Conservation Fight from Theodore Roosevelt to the Tennessee Valley Authority.
K2330
CONSERVATION — KY.
The Long-legged House.
B3260 (ASU MHC WCU BC)
The Unforseen Wilderness: An Essay on Kentucky's Red River Gorge.
B3300 (ASU BC LMC)
Influences of Strip Mining on the Hydrologic Environment of Parts of Beaver Creek Basin, Kentucky, 1955-59.
C5930 (BC)
CONSERVATION — N. C.
"A Ecological Survey of Flat Rock Mountain."
S3600 (ASU)
CONSERVATION — PA.
Conservation Law and Administration: A Case Study of Law and Resource Use in Pennsylvania.
S1170
CONSERVATION — TENN.
"Conservation Projects by Community Organizations in Tennessee and Other Southeastern States."
B300
The First Exposition of Conservation and its Builders; an Official History of the National Conservation Exposition, Held at Knoxville, Tenn. in 1913 and of its Forerunner, the Appalachian Expositions of 1910-1911, Embracing a Review of the Conservation Movement in the U. S. from its Inception the Present Time.
G2550
Rescued Earth, a Study of the Public Administration of Natural Resources in Tennessee.
G3820 (ASU LMC ETSU)
"A Study of Glass and Paper Recycling in Johnson City, Tennessee."
G4860 (ETSU)
COOKERY
Kirsty's Secrets: A Yearly Round of Scottish Fare.
A1380 (ASU)
Kentucky Living Cookbook. Bicentennial Edition.
A4580 ()
Rebecca Boone Cook Book.
B1250 (ASU)
Cherokee Cooklore: Preparing Cherokee Foods.
C3870 (ASU LMC MHC WCU)
To Make My Bread.
C3890
Cumberland Cook Book.
N1520
Colonial Kitchen Herbs and Remedies: Garden and Kitchen Secrets from Early America.
S2700 (ASU LMC)
Pioneer Comforts and Kitchen Remedies. Old Timey Highland Secrets from the Blue Ridge and Great Smoky Mountains.
S2730 (MHC ASU BC WCU)
Pioneer Cookbook, Favorite Campfire and Kitchen Recipes from Early America.
S2740 (ASU BC)
Southern Appalachian Mountain Cookbook: Rare Time-tested Recipes from the Blue Ridge and Great Smoky Mountains.
S2770 (ASU LMC BC)
Shenandoah Valley Cooking; Recipes and Kitchen Lore.
S4630 (FC)
Favorite Recipes of the John C. Campbell Folk School.
T8750 (BC WCU ASU)
Cooking Favorites of Brucetown.
W8460 (ASU)
Old-time Recipes from the Nu-Wray Inn, Burnsville, N. C.
W9350 (LMC)
COOKERY — APP.
Mountain Makin's in the Smokies: A Cookbook.
G3430 (LMC)
Manna: Foods of the Frontier.
H2850 (ASU WCU)
H5520
Cooking with Hougen.
H7370 (ASU)
Look No Further.
H7380 (ASU)
More Hougen Favorites.
H7390 (ASU)
Smoky Mountain Magic; a Superb View of Treasured Recipes.
J2830 (LMC)
Favorite Recipes.
M2640
Queen of Appalachia Cook Book.
P3230
Granny's Hillbilly Cookbook.
R4470 (ASU BC)
Tennessee Cookbook, More Than 300 Tasty Tennessee Recipes.
R4540 (ASU)
Colonial Holiday Treats, Special Recipes.
S2690 (ASU BC)
Colonial Treasure Cookbook.
S2710 (ASU)
Hillbilly Cookin' by the Tates.
T290 (ASU)
COOKERY — APP. MTNS.
Old Timey Recipes.
C6690 (ASU LMC BC)
Old Timey Recipes.
C6700 (WCU BC)
Old Timey Recipes.
C6710 (LMC)
COOKERY — GA.
Boilin' n Bakin' in Boogar Hollow.
H850 (BC ASU)
COOKERY — GREAT SMOKY MOUNTAINS
Smoky Mountain Magic; a Superb View of Treasured Recipes.
J2830 (LMC)
COOKERY — KY.
What's Cooking in Kentucky?
H3920 (ASU BC WCU)
COOKERY — N. C.
Good Victuals from the Mountains.
H6980
The Webster Cookbook.
R1800
Good Cooking in Asheville.
T9370

COOKERY — TENN.
Helen Exum's Chattanooga Cook Book.
E2460 (ASU)
Favorite Recipes: A Collection of Favorite Recipes of Home Demonstration Club Women of Washington County.
W1060 (ETSU)
COOKERY — VA.
Jonesville Cook Book.
J2690
COOKERY — W. VA.
Pocahontas County Cooking Yesterday and Today.
E850 ()
Adventures in Good Living.
H8330 (ASU BC)
COOSA RIVER
The Coosa River Valley from DeSoto to Hydroelectric Power.
R1660 (ASU)
Report on Coosa River System, Georgia-Alabama.
U3900
COUNCIL OF THE SOUTHERN MTNS.
Seeking a People Partnership: Eleven Speeches.
A5830 (ASU LMC MHC WCU BC)
Mass Meeting Study of the Appalachian South.
C7870
CRAFTS
Highland Highlights.
S5765 (BC)
CRIME
A Winner on Satin's Doorstep.
D3370 (BC)
Dead and Gone: Classic Crimes of North Carolina.
W2530 (LMC BC)
CRIME — KY.
The Hanging of "Bad Tom" Smith and the Events Leading to his Hanging.
H3860 (BC)
Delinquency in Kentucky.
K990
They Tried to Crucify Me; or, the Smokescreen of the Cumberlands.
L430
My Own Story: An Account of the Conditions in Kentucky Leading to the Assassination of William Goobel, Who Was Declared Governor of the State, and My Indictment and Conviction on the Charge of Complicity in His Murder.
P4060 (ASU)
CRIME — N. C.
Tom Dooley.
A1410 (ASU LMC)
"Community Correlates of Crime and Law Enforcement Activities in Northwestern North Carolina."
H6160 (ASU)
CRIME — N. C., WESTERN
Toward a Safer Society: Five Year Proposal.
N2830 (ASU LMC)
CRIME — TENN.
The White-Caps: A History of the Organization in Sevier County.
C9240
The White-Caps: A History of the Organization in Sevier County.
C9250
The White-Caps: A History of the Organization in Sevier County.
C9260
CRIME — VA.
Was Rev. J. R. Moffett Murdered? Clark vs. Commonwealth, D. M. No. 43Z, from the Corporation Court of the City of Danville.
C4490 (ASU)
The Courthouse Tragedy at Hillsville, Va.
G320 (ASU)
"Gentlemen, I ain't a-goin'."
H8660
The Allen Outlaws: A Complete History of Their Lives and Exploits, Concluding with the Hillsville Courthouse Tragedy.
J320 (ASU BC)
Crimes, Criminals and Characters of the Cumberlands and Southwest Virginia.
S8900
T9250 (BC)
CRIME — W. VA.
The Characteristics and Attitudes of Juvenile Delinquents of Kanawha County.
A2550
The Characteristics and Attitudes of Juvenile Delinquents of Kanawha County, West Virginia.
A2590
The Alderson story; my Life as a Political Prisoner.
F1650
CULLASAJA RIVER
Floods on Little Tennessee River, Cullasaja River, and Cartoogechave Creek in Vicinity of Franklin, North Carolina.
T7090
CUMBERLAND RIVER
Steamboatin' on the Cumberland.
D3120 (BC ASU ETSU)
Bibliography of the Cumberland River Valley.
J940
The Cumberland.
M190 (LMC)
The Cumberland Plateau in Tennessee.
M4140
"Two Resettlement Communities on the Cumberland Plateau."
M6600
Adventures along the Cumberland.
O160 (BC)
On the Watauga and the Cumberland.
S5300 (LMC)
Stream Pollution Control In The Upper Cumberland River Basin, 1965.
T1230
The Lower Cumberland Region: A Study of Its Population, Economic Base and Potential.
T2100 (ETSU)
The Upper Cumberland Economy.
T2110 (ETSU)
Stream Pollution Control in the Upper Cumberland River Basin, 1964.
T2120 (ETSU)
. . . Report on the Physiographic, Economic, and Other Relationships Between the Tennessee and Cumberland Rivers and Between Their Drainage Areas. Message from the President of the United States, Transmitting Report Entitled "The Physiographic, Economic, and Other Relationships Between the Tennessee and Cumberland Rivers and Between Their Drainage Areas" . . .
T3380
"Big South Fork, Cumberland River (Kentucky-Tennessee), Interagency Field Task Group Report."
U220
Big South Fork, Cumberland River, Kentucky and Tennessee.
U230 (ETSU)
Big South Fork, Cumberland River, Kentucky and Tennessee.
U240
DAIRY INDUSTRY — APP.
Cheesemaking Brings Prosperity to Farmers of Southern Mountains.
D2600 (ASU)
DAIRY INDUSTRY — N. C.
An Economic Adjustment Study of Dairy Farms in Western North Carolina.
D2780 (LMC)
DAIRY INDUSTRY — TENN.
"Economic Levels of Forage and Grain Production on Dairy Farms in East Tennessee."
S4520
DAVIDSON RIVER
Floods on French Broad and Davidson Rivers and King, Nicholson, and Tucker Creeks in Vicinity of Brevard, North Carolina.
T7030
DEMOGRAPHY
"Appalachian Fertility Levels and the Role of Interpersonal Relations."
B160
Characteristics of the United States Population by Farm and Nonfarm Origin.
B2240
Recent Population Trends in the United States with Emphasis on Rural Areas.
B2250
Contraception and Fertility in the Southern Appalachians.
B2550 (BC ASU)
"Contraception and Fertility in the Southern Appalachians."
B2560
Contraception and Fertility in the Southern Appalachians.
B2570 (LMC)
Mobility of Rural Population.
B2600
People and Resources in Eastern Kentucky.
B2610
Rural People in the City: A Study of the Socio-economic Status of 297 Families in Lexington, Kentucky.
B2620
Urban Adjustments of Rural Migrants.
B2630
Number of Inhabitants of the Southern Appalachians, 1900-1957.
B2680
Farm Population: Net Migration from the Rural Farm Population, 1940-1950.
B5720
Net Migration of the Population, 1950-1960 by Age, Sex and Color.
B5730
The Bedroom of the Poor.
B6880
The Changing Kentucky Population: A Summary of Population Data for Counties.
B7170
Rural Population Changes in Five Kentucky Mountain Districts, 1943-1946.
B7200
Southern Appalachian Population Change, 1960-1970: A First Look at the 1970 Census.
B7220 (BC)
Comparative Economic Growth Measures — Population and Personal Income Estimates for Tennessee Counties, 1950 Through 1962.
C7590
Appalachian Fertility Decline: A Demographic and Sociological Analysis.
D1660 (ASU WCU LMC ETSU BC UNCA)
Fertility Data for the Southern Appalachian Region.
D1670
"Human Fertility in the Southern Appalachian Region: Some Demographic and Sociological Aspects."
D1680 (ASU)
Selected Demographic Studies, Knox Co., Ky.
E800
Changing Patterns of Fertility in Tennessee, 1960-1970.
E1940
"The Drain of Talent out of Kentucky."
H2790
Johnson City, Tennessee, Population and Economic Base Study.
H5390
Rural Population Density in the Southern Appalachians.
M3350 (ASU)
The Appalachian Region: A Preliminary Analysis of Economic and Population Trends in an Eleven State Problem Area.
M3860 (BC)
Fertility Rates and Migration of Kentucky's Population, 1920-1940.
O1060 (ASU)
"Occupance Formation Concept: A Case Study of the Asheville Basin."
P1990 (LMC)
"Comparative Study of Related Health Fertility Attitudes and Behavior of Families Residing in a Poverty Area."
S6190
Tennessee Manpower: Current Trend and Future Projections.
T1200
Census of Population: 1960. The Eighteenth Decennial Census of the United States.
U460
Fifteenth Census of the United States: 1930.
U470 (BC)
"The Sequent Occupance of Tellico Plains, Tennessee."
V50
North Carolina, a Demographic Profile.
Z140 (ASU LMC)
DEMOGRAPHY — ALA.
Income and Population in Alabama.
H3750 (ASU)

DEMOGRAPHY — APP.
Basic Population Data for the Southern Appalachians by State, Economic Area, and Metropolitan Area.
B7160
"An Analysis of the Spatial Structure of Manufacturing in the Appalachian Region Between 1950-1960."
F3740 (ASU)
The Appalachian Region: A Preliminary Analysis of Economic and Population Trends in an Eleven State Problem Area.
G4440
"Mothers of the South: A Population Study of Native White Women of Childbearing Age of the Southeast."
H240
Basic Population Data for the Southern Appalachians.
K1420
Selected Rural Counties in Appalachia.
U860
Human Geography of the South: A Study in Regional Resources and Human Adequacy.
V90 (ASU LMC WWC MHC)
DEMOGRAPHY — KY.
"Household and Family Composition in Selected Rural Areas of Eleven Kentucky Counties."
B5950
Health and Demography in Kentucky.
F2000 (LMC BC)
Population Growth in Kentucky, 1820-1960.
H5530
"Metropolitan Dominance and the Diffusion of Human Fertility Patterns, Kentucky, 1939-65."
K3340
Projected Kentucky Population Growth by Age, Sex, and Color Groups: 1960 to 1970.
K3350
Migration Within Kentucky.
M3990
Mobility and Fertility Rates of Rural Families in Johnson County, Kentucky, 1918-1941.
S6020
DEMOGRAPHY — N. C.
1980 Population Projections for North Carolina Counties, with 1950, 1960 and 1970 Population by Age Groups.
P2240
Population Schedules, North Carolina.
U610 (ASU)
DEMOGRAPHY — RURAL
"An Economic Analysis of Fertility Differentials Among Rural Farm Communities in United States in 1960."
A2250
DEMOGRAPHY — TENN.
Migration and Level of Living in the Tennessee Valley.
F1680
Population Changes in Tennessee since 1930.
L1940
DEMOGRAPHY — VA.
Exploring Virginia's Human Resources.
H8120 (ASU BC)
DEMOGRAPHY — W. VA.
West Virginia and Her Population.
M8240
Selected Demographic Aspects of the West Virginia Economy, 1950-1975: Estimates and Projections of Migration and Population.
P4880 (ETSU BC)
DEPRESSION, THE
Let Us Now Praise Famous Men.
A730 (BC ASU WCU)
Let Us Now Praise Famous Men.
A740 (ETSU)
Let Us Now Praise Famous Men.
A750 (WCU)
"Social and Economic Conditions in Jackson County During the Depression."
A780 (WCU)
DESCRIPTION AND TRAVEL
Hitch Hiking Along the Holston River from 1792-1962.
W8600
DESCRIPTION AND TRAVEL — KY.
Cumberland Falls, Kentucky.
N1360
DESEGREGATION
The Children of the South.
A2310
DEVELOPMENT
Seeking More Effective Means to Overcome Poverty: Proceedings.
A2680 (ASU LMC)
The Emerging Pattern of Appalachian Regional Development.
A2720
Appalachian Highlands Recreation Study, Phase I, Inventory and Analysis.
A3630 (ASU)
A Bibliography of Research Studies Produced with Appalachian Regional Development Program Funds.
A3690
Capitalizing on New Development Opportunities along the Baltimore-Cincinnati Appalachian Development Highway: A Staff Recommendation.
A3700 (ASU)
State and Regional Development Plans in Appalachia.
A3830 (ASU)
The Possibilities of a Maple Sugar Industry in Western North Carolina.
A5130 (ASU LMC)
"The Regional Growth Points in Economic Development; A Comparison of West Virginia and West Pakistan."
B2660
Economic Development in the Ohio River Valley Region.
B6280
Statewide Development Planning for West Virginia — A Prospectus for Implementation Under Provisions of Section 701 of the Housing Act of 1954.
D4140
A Decade of Action for Progress in Kentucky.
E520 (ASU)
Program 60, 1960-70; a Decade of Action for Progress in Eastern Kentucky.
E530 (BC)
Annual Report for 1964.
E540
"The Effects of Environment on Public Planning: The Case of Appalachian Planning in Tennessee."
G470 (LMC)
The Development Index for 60 Counties in Central Appalachia.
G2890 (ASU BC)
Proceedings.
G2980 (ASU BC)
An Urban Development Program for the Big Sandy Area.
S6260 (ASU)
Federal Grants-in-Aid; a Comprehensive Analysis of Federal Grants-in-Aid to All the States, with a Detailed Analysis of Programs in Effect in Each City and County of Virginia.
V710 (BC)
DEVELOPMENT — APP.
Preliminary Analysis for Development of Central Appalachia, Kentucky, Tennessee, Virginia, West Virginia.
A3780
C1180
Report.
C6370
Education for Economic Development — The South's Education and Employment Prospects for the Future.
C7970
"Local Government Social Overhead Expenditures and Economic Growth in the Appalachian Region."
D2450
Regional Development and Planning: A Reader.
F3320 (ASU)
"The Appalachian Experiment: Growth or Development."
F3730
Exurban Development in Selected Areas of the Appalachian Mountains.
J1790
Private Outdoor Recreation Enterprises in Rural Appalachia.
J1800
"Measuring and Analyzing the Impact of Employment Generation Benefits of a Public Water Resource Development Project in Appalachia."
K2050
A Preliminary Analysis for an Economic Development Plan for the Appalachian Region.
L2860
Appalachian Development: The Long-run View.
M5370 (LMC)
Appalachian Future, the Economic Challenge.
M5380
Joint Reports.
N240
Appalachia: A Case Study of Regional Business Development.
O430
"The State Development Planning Process: Implementation of the Appalachian Regional Development Act of 1965 in West Virginia."
P850
Institute of Regional Development of the Southeast.
T2210
Rural Recreation Enterprises for Profit: An Aid to Rural Areas Development.
U2550
Regional Economic Development in the United States.
U2710
Appalachia — Rebirth of a Region.
U2900 (ETSU)
DEVELOPMENT — APP. — N. C.
Updated Investment Guidelines for North Carolina Appalachian Region 1971 to 1975, and A Plan for Public Investment in Appalachian North Carolina, Fiscal 1971.
A3880
DEVELOPMENT — APP. — N. Y.
Abstract of the New York State Appalachian Program: A Development Plan.
A3530
A Report on the Identification of Areas of Potential Growth in the Appalachian Region of New York State and a General Development Philosophy for the Region.
A3810
DEVELOPMENT — GA.
Developing Georgia, a Statistical Study.
G900
Tourism Development in the Chattahoochee-Flint Area.
K430
DEVELOPMENT — KY.
Communication and Mountain Development: A Summary Report Two East Kentucky Studies.
B5780
Non-federal Aid for Community Development Projects in Kentucky.
G480
"Economic Development of Areas Contiguous to Multipurpose Reservoirs: The Kentucky-Tennessee Experience."
H2220 (BC)
DEVELOPMENT — N. C.
Overall Economic Development Program for Avery County.
A5790 (LMC)
"The Economic Impact of Recreation Resort Development on the Local Economy: A Case Study of Avery County, North Carolina."
R3580 (LMC)
DEVELOPMENT — OHIO
A Plan for Development of Ohio Appalachia.
H8530 (ASU)
DEVELOPMENT — OHIO — APP. REGION
A Development Program for the Ohio Valley Region.
O380
DEVELOPMENT — PA.
Preliminary Over-all Economic Development Program for the North-western Pennsylvania Redevelopment Area.
K300
Overall Economic Development Program for the Counties of Carbon, Lackawanna, Luzerne, Monroe, Pike, Schuylkill, Wayne, in the Northeastern Pennsylvania Economic Development District.
P1820 (ASU)
Pennsylvania Appalachian Development Plan.
P1870 (ASU WCU)

DEVELOPMENT — PA.

Pennsylvania Appalachian Development Plan: Revision for 1970.
P1880 (ASU)

A Rationale for Public Investment in Appalachia Pennsylvania: An Interim Statement.
P1890

DEVELOPMENT — TENN.

E780 (ASU)

Report.
H1410 (ETSU)

"Economic Development of Areas Contiguous to Multipurpose Reservoirs: The Kentucky-Tennessee Experience."
H2220 (BC)

"The Lenoir City Company, an Attempt in Community Development."
H3770

Tennessee Appalachian Development Plan, 1969-1970.
T1600 (ASU)

Comprehensive Plan for Development: Kentucky Reservoir Region.
T1610 (ETSU)

Melton Hill Reservoir, Comprehensive Plan for Land Use Development.
T1650

A Proposed Plan for Development: Sevier County, Tennessee.
T1690

Appalachian Regional Development Act, 1965-; Rationale and Model for Application in Tennessee.
T1770

Report on First Year's Activities in the Appalachian Development Program.
T1780 (LMC)

Overall Economic Development Program for Unicoi County, Tennessee.
U120 (ETSU)

A Technical Assistance Program for the Upper Cumberlands of Tennessee.
W170

DEVELOPMENT — VA.

Development Potentials For Kentucky Counties With Related Statistics
F3770

"Shifts in Land Use in the Appalachian Region of Virginia."
O550 (LMC ASU)

DEVELOPMENT — VA. — SOUTHWEST

Southwest Virginia and Shenandoah Valley. An Inquiry into the Causes of the Rapid Growth and Wonderful Development of Southwest Virginia and Shenandoah Valley, with a History of the Norfolk and Western and Shenandoah Valley Railroads.
B7650 (ASU BC FC)

DEVELOPMENT — W. VA.

Semi-Centennial History of West Virginia. With Special Articles on Development and Resources.
C300 (ASU ETSU BC)

"The Transformation of the Tug and Guyandot Valleys: Economic Development and Social Change in West Virginia, 1888-1921."
C9390

Professional Overall Economic Development for Fayette Co., West Virginia.
F400

West Virginia Housing. A Consultant's Report to the Governor's Task Force on Housing and the West Virginia State Development Plan.
G30

The Contributions of Local Subsidies to the Economic Development of West Virginia, 1956-1966.
H330 (ASU)

Economic Stability and Growth Potential, Fairmont, W. Va.
H2230

Overall Economic Development Program.
L2120

"Inside Down Under Australia and New Zealand Development Characteristics Compared to West Virginia as a Part of the Appalachian Highlands, U. S. A."
L3920

Stimulating Regional Economic Development. An Interindustry Analysis of West Virginia Economy.
M5400

A Development Program for the Ohio Valley Region.
O380

"The State Development Planning Process: Implementation of the Appalachian Regional Development Act of 1965 in West Virginia."
P850
P4700 (BC)

ARA Field Report, Opportunities for Economic Development in Mingo County, W. Va.
U2690

Overall Economic Development Program for Upshur County, West Virginia.
U4180

Functional Program Planning for the State of W. Va.
W3370

Experimental Rural Area Program.
W3430

State Legislation Governing Planning and Land — Use Control and the Value of Planning and Controls in Fostering Highway Detection and Economic Development with Particular Reference to W. Va. and Bordering States.
W4550

Professional Development Lectures.
W4590 (ASU)

Man and His Community, A 100th Anniversary Symposium.
W4640

Information Series.
W4650

Public Affairs Series.
W4660

Research Report.
W4670

Research Series.
W4680 (BC)

Bulletin Series.
W4740

Conference Papers Series.
W4750 (BC)

Information Series.
W4760 (BC)

Public Affairs Series.
W4770 (BC)

Public Affairs Series.
W4780

Research Report.
W4790 (BC)

Research Series.
W4800

West Virginia Business Dev. Opportunities.
W4810

Economic Development in West Virginia.
Z60

DIALECTS

Word-lists from the South.
A2120 (ASU)

Dictionary of Americanisms. A glossary of Words and Phrases Usually Regarded as Peculiar to the United States.
B1550 (ASU)

"Study of a Dialect Employed by the People of the Kentucky Mountains and Presented through a Group of Original Short Stories."
B5760 (ASU)

Proverbs, and How to Collect Them.
B7850 (ASU)

A Method for Collecting Dialect.
C1990 (ASU)

"Mountain Dialect in North Georgia."
C5840 (ETSU ASU)

The Mountain Preacher.
D1070 (BC)

"A Lexicographical Study of the Vocabulary of Greenup County, Kentucky, Set Forth in Jesse Stuart's "Beyond Dark Hills"."
D2210 (ASU)

Bits of Mountain Speech Gathered Between 1910 and 1965 along the Mountains Bordering North Carolina and Tennessee.
F970 (ASU)

Language and Culture.
G2100 (ASU BC)

Word-book of Virginia Folk-speech.
G3520 (ASU LMC BC)

Word-book of Virginia Folk-speech.
G3530 (ETSU)

Mountain Speech in the Great Smokies.
H770 (BC)

Sayings from Old Smoky, Some Traditional Phrases, Expressions, and Sentences Heard in the Great Smoky Mountains and Nearby Areas: An Introduction to a Southern Mountain Dialect.
H800 (ASU BC LMC MHC)

Smoky Mountain Folks and Their Lore.
H810 (BC ASU WCU LMC MHC)

Smoky Mountain Folks and Their Lore.
H820 (ETSU)

Dialect Tales.
M1210 (BC ASU ETSU)

Folk-etymology, a Dictionary of Verbal Corruptions or Words Perverted in Form or Meaning by False Derivation or Mistaken Analogy.
P100 (ASU)

"Bituminous Coal Mining Vocabulary of the Eastern United States: A Pilot Study in the Collecting of Geographically Distributed Occupational Vocabulary."
P4390

"A Dialect Survey of the Appalachian Region."
Q10 (LMC ASU)

A Dialect Survey of the Appalachian Region.
Q20 (BC)

English Archaisms in Pennsylvania German.
R1020 (ASU)

Popular Folk Dictionary of Ozarks Talk.
T8030 (ASU)

The Dialect of the Southern Highlands.
W2330 (BC)

Instructions to Collectors of Dialect.
W7230 (ASU)

DIALECTS — APP.

"Southern Appalachian Non-standard Speech in Conflict with the Standard English of the Classroom."
B280 (ETSU)

A Survey of Speech Education in Selected North Carolina High Schools.
E1250 (ASU)

The Phonetics of Great Smoky Mountain Speech.
G790 (ASU ETSU)

The Phonetics of Great Smoky Mountain Speech.
H780

The Word-Book of a Backwoodsman.
N360

The Idiom of the People.
S2350 (ASU BC)

DIALECTS — APP. — VA.

A Glossary of Virginia Words.
N1250 (ASU)

DIALECTS — KY.

Parlance of Kentucky Backwoods.
C3740 (BC)

DIALECTS — MTNS. — N. C.

Tarheel Talk: An Historical Study of the English Language in North Carolina to 1860.
E1550 (ASU LMC MHC ETSU)

DIALECTS — N. C.

"The Dialect of the Southern Highlander as Recorded in North Carolina Novels."
E980 (ASU)

DISASTERS

Shinnston tornado.
F1020

DISASTERS — N. C.

Watauga County Reception and Care Plan.
N1720 (ASU)

Jackson County: Operational Survival Plan.
N1790 (WCU)

DISASTERS — VA.

"Debris Avalanching as a Natural Hazard in the Southern Appalachians: A Case Study of the Davis Creek Watershed, Virginia."
K3370 (ETSU)

DISASTERS — W. VA.

Death at Buffalo Creek: The 1972 West Virginia Flood Disaster.
N2970 (BC LMC ASU)

Buffalo Creek (W. Va.) Disaster, 1972. Hearings before the Subcommittee. 2 pts.
U2430

Climate, Weather and Coal Mine Explosions; with a Meteorological Review of the Farmington Disaster.
W2230

DOE RIVER

Floods on Watauga and Doe Rivers in Vicinity of Elizabethton, Tennessee.
T2760

DRAMA
Agee on Film: Five Film Scripts.
A640 (BC ASU)
Agee on Film: Reviews and Comments.
A650 (ASU)
Among the Highlanders Yesterday and Today. (A PAGEANT OF Western North Carolina.)
B4150 (ASU WCU)
The Spirit of Western North Carolina: A Pageant.
B4190 (WCU LMC)
Roseanna McCoy: Final Screenplay.
C5940
Hunger: A Tragedy of North Carolina Farm Folk.
D120
Lords and Lovers, and Other Dramas.
D300 (ASU BC)
The Mortal Gods, and Other Plays.
D310 (UNCA WCU)
Semiranis, and Other Plays.
D330 (BC)
Look Homeward, Angel: A Play Based on the Novel by Thomas Wolfe.
F3410 (ASU BC)
Mountain Pageant of Historic Tableaux and Symbolic Figures: The Story of a People Lost in the Appalachians for Nearly Two Hundred Years.
G1220 (LMC)
Wilderness Road; a Parable for Modern Times.
G3630
Wilderness Road: A Symphonic Outdoor Drama.
G3640 (WCU BC ASU)
Thickety Bush: A Drama in Three Acts.
H5100 (WCU WWC)
Moonshine; a One Act Play.
H7090 (BC)
Scrapbooks, 1954- .
H7180 (ASU)
Hell-bent for Heaven, a Play in Three Acts.
H8070 (ASU LMC ETSU BC)
Ruint; a Folk Comedy in Four Acts.
H8080
Unto These Hills: A Drama of the Cherokee.
H8460 (ASU MHC ETSU)
Kentucky Mountain Fantasies: Three Short Plays for an Appalachian Theatre.
M1760 (ASU BC)
Kentucky Mountain Fantasies: Three Short Plays for an Appalachian Theatre.
M1770 (LMC)
All the Way Home.
M8180 (ASU BC)
Folk Ballads for Young Actors.
N1080 (ASU BC)
Folk Carols for Young Actors.
N1090 (ASU)
P70
The Wander Weed.
P1490
Appalachia, My Sorrow: A Play for Voice.
P1750 (ASU)
Melungeons: The Vanishing Colony of Newman's Ridge.
P4500 (ETSU)
Dark of the Moon.
R2100 (ASU WCU)
Dark of the Moon.
R2110 (ASU)
Dark of the Moon.
R2120 (LMC MHC)
Dark of the Moon.
R2130 (ETSU)
Frederick Henry Koch: Pioneer Playmaker. A Brief Biography.
S1780 (LMC)
S7630
The Hill Between; a Folk Play in Three Acts.
V1340
Moonshine and Honeysuckle; a Play in Three Acts.
V1350
Sun-up; a Play in Three Acts.
V1360 (ETSU ASU)
Sun-up: A Play in Three Acts.
V1370 (ASU LMC)
Mannerhouse, a Play in a Prologue and Three Acts.
W8210 (ASU WCU ETSU BC)
The Mountains: A Play in One Act. The Mountains: A Drama in Three Acts and a Prologue.
W8220 (ASU WCU ETSU LMC MHC BC UNCA)
Somebody, a Play in 4 Acts.
W8760 (BC)

DRAMA — CHEROKEE
Cherokee Dance and Drama.
S6090 (ASU WCU ETSU BC)

DRAMA — KY.
The Theatre in Early Kentucky, 1790-1820.
H5490 (BC)

DRAMA — N. C.
Unto These Hills: A Drama of the Cherokee People.
C3650 (WCU ASU)
Carolina Folk-Plays.
K2950 (ASU BC)
Carolina Folk-plays.
K2960 (LMC)

DULCIMER
Four and Twenty Songs for the Mountain Dulcimer.
M2520 (ASU BC)
The Dulcimer Book, Being a Book about the Three-stringed Appalachian Dulcimer, Including Some Ways of Tuning and Playing: Some Recollections in Its Local History in Perry and Knott Counties, Kentucky. Some Observations on the Probable Origins of the Instrument in the Old Countries of Europe: And with Words and Music for Some Sixteen Songs from the Ritchie Family of Kentucky.
R2430 (ASU BC ETSU LMC WCU)
The Dulcimer Book, Being a Book about the Three-stringed Appalachian Dulcimer, Including Some Ways of Tuning and Playing: Some Recollections in Its Local History in Perry and Knott Counties, Kentucky. Some Observations on the Probable Origins of the Instrument in the Old Countries of Europe: With Plentiful Photographic Illustrations and Drawings. And with Words and Music for Some Sixteen Songs from the Ritchie Family of Kentucky.
R2440 (ASU)

DULCIMERS
Making an Appalachian Dulcimer.
B290 (LMC BC)
The Hammered Dulcimer — How to Make and Play It.
M6330
The Mountain Dulcimer.
M6340
Teach Yourself Appalachian Dulcimer.
P1270
The Plucked Dulcimer of the Southern Mountains.
P4910 (ASU BC)
The Plucked Dulcimer and How to Play It.
P4920 (WCU ASU BC)
The Plucked Dulcimer and How to Play It.
P4930 (ASU LMC MHC)
A bibliography of hammered and plucked (Appalachian or mountain) dulcimers and related instruments.
U3620
Appalachian Dulcimer Plans.
W540

ECONOMIC CONDITION — COAL CAMPS
Wage Rates and Working Time in the Bituminous Coal Industry, 1912-1922.
F1230 (BC)

ECONOMIC CONDITIONS
Let Us Now Praise Famous Men.
A730 (BC ASU WCU)
Let Us Now Praise Famous Men.
A740 (ETSU)
Let Us Now Praise Famous Men.
A750 (WCU)
"Social and Economic Conditions in Jackson County During the Depression."
A780 (WCU)
Seeking More Effective Means to Overcome Poverty: Proceedings.
A2680 (ASU LMC)
"Migration and Economic Opportunity in Tennessee Counties, 1940-1950."
B2420
Development Opportunities in Kentucky: Final Report.
B6270
"Association of Selected Socio-economic Characteristics with Net Migration from Three Kentucky Economic Areas, 1920-1950."
B6440
An Economic and Social Survey of Botetourt County."
C5600
"Socioeconomic Characteristics of Young Farmers Enrolled in Vocational Agriculture Classes in West Virginia."
M1500
"Economics of the Southern Smokeless Coals."
M5150
"The Decline of Anthracite, 1913-1955."
M5320
Postwar Changes in the Export Markets for American Coal: A Study in the Industry Response to Variations in Foreign Demand.
M6210 (ASU)
The Economic Impact of TVA.
M7230
A Review of the Literature Pertaining to Appalachia; Stressing Attitudes to Social Change and Religious and Educational Orientations; A Working Paper for the Boards of Christian Education of the United Presbyterian Church in the U. S.
N450 (BC)
Economic Development of the Upper French Broad Area: Summary of Needs and Opportunities, Resources, the Regional Economy.
N2690 (ASU)
Resources of the Southern Fields and Forests, Medical, Economical, and Agricultural. Being Also a Medical Botany of the Confederate States.
P3590 (LMC BC)
Education, Migration and Economic Life Chances of Male Entrants to the Labor Force from a Low Income Rural Area.
S1240 (ASU)
Economic and Social Problems and Conditions of the Southern Appalachians.
U2490
Proceedings.
W3260 (BC)
Utilizing a College's Resources to Provide Technical Assistance to Business Firms in Southern West Virginia: A Report on the Concord College Center for Economic Action, July 1, 1963, Through June 30, 1966.
W3290
An Economic Atlas for West Virginia.
W3350
Economic Profiles of West Virginia Counties.
W3360
West Virginia Economic Outlook, 1967-1972.
W3380
W. Va. Redevelopment Plan for Webster County.
W3400
West Virginia Economic Outlook 1965-1966.
W3410
The West Virginia Geological and Economic Survey: Its Accomplishments and Outlook.
W3920 (ETSU)
W4460
Population and economy of Andrews, N. C.
W4910
Population and economy of Henderson County.
W4920 (LMC)

ECONOMIC CONDITIONS — ALA.
The Present and Projected Agricultural Economy of the Appalachian Region of Alabama.
B4440 (ASU)
Income and Population in Alabama.
H3750 (ASU)
Opportunities for and Limitations of Social and Economic Adjustments in an Alabama Rural County.
N1190

ECONOMIC CONDITIONS AND POLICIES — KY.
The Structure of the Kentucky Economy: An Input-output Study.
B1230

ECONOMIC CONDITIONS — APP.
Factors Associated with the Adjustment of Families in Three Low-Income Counties of North Carolina.
A460 (ASU)
"Factors Associated with the Adjustment of Families in Three Low Income Counties of North Carolina."
A470

ECONOMIC CONDITIONS — APP.

An Economic and Social Survey of Bedford Co., Va.
A480 (ASU)

The Present and Projected Agricultural Economy of the Appalachian Region of Alabama.
A860 (ASU)

The Appalachian Regional Development Bill. S3, Sen. Randolph; H.R. 4, Rep. Fallon.
A2130 (UNCA)
A2660 (BC)
A2681
A2682 (ASU)
A2683 (ASU)
A2790 (ASU)
A3120 (ETSU)

Meeting, May 8, 1961, the White House.
A3160

Report of the Appalachian Institute Committee to the Conference of Appalachian Governors and the President's Appalachian Regional Commission.
A3200 (BC ASU)

Appalachia: A Report, 1964.
A3560 (LMC ASU WCU ETSU)

Appalachia: An Economic Report — 1970. Trends in Employment, Income and Population.
A3570 (ASU)

Appalachia — An Economic Report: Trends in Employment, Income and Population.
A3580 (WCU ASU ETSU)

Appalachia — An Economic Report: Trends in Employment, Income and Population. Supplement.
A3590 (ASU)

Appalachian Data Book.
A3600 (ASU ETSU BC)

Appalachian Data Book.
A3610 (MHC BC ETSU ASU)

The Appalachian Region: A Statistical Appendix of Comparative Socioeconomic Indicators.
A3650 (MHC ASU)

The Economic Impact of Public Policy on the Appalachian Coal Industry and the Regional Economy.
A3730 (ASU)

A Summary Economic Report: Appalachian Region.
A3840 (ASU)

Employment and Underemployment of Rural People in the Appalachian Area.
A4630

Picking Poverty's Pocket.
B1150

A Bibliographic Guide to the Economic Regions of the United States.
B3210

"Measurement of the Economic Impact of Public Investment of Regional Economic Growth in Appalachia."
B3220

Economic Subregions of the United States.
B5100

History of Letcher Co., Ky., Its Political and Economic Growth and Development.
B5740

Voices from the Mountain.
C1210 (ASU)

Poverty and Affluence in Appalachia.
C2190

"The Relation of Level of Living to Selected Additional Characteristics of Central Appalachia Rural Families."
C2920 (ASU)

Migrants, Sharecroppers, Mountaineers.
C5890 (BC ASU)

An Economic Survey of the Appalachian Region, with Special Reference to Agriculture.
C6100 (ETSU WCU LMC ASU)

Methods for Estimating Income Payments in Counties; a Technical Supplement to County Income Estimates for Seven Southeastern States.
C7300

Education for Economic Development — The South's Education and Employment Prospects for the Future.
C7970

"Local Government Social Overhead Expenditures and Economic Growth in the Appalachian Region."
D2450

Our Land Too.
D3890 (ASU BC WCU)

A Profile and Economic Impact Analysis of Four Cumberland Gap Counties.
E1390

Apprenticeship and Economic Change.
F120

The Southern Appalachian Region: A Survey.
F2010

Economic Base Study and Survey of Basic Services.
F2210

"An Input-output Model Incorporating Impact Analysis to Evaluate the Resources and Economy of a Rural Appalachian Community."
G220

"Association of Selected Economic Factors with Net Migration Rates in the Southern Appalachian Region, 1935-1937."
G870

"Habitat-economy-society, a Frame of Reference Applied to Southern Appalachian Coal Country."
G1130

Underemployment Concept, Way to Measure Need for Economic Development in Appalachia.
G1260

Appalachia in Transition.
G2150 (ASU WCU LMC MHC ETSU FC BC)

Development and Application of a Level-of-living Scale for White, Open Country Families, Both Farm and Non-farm in the Southeast.
G2190

The Economic Needs of Neighborhood Youth Corps Enrollees. Final Report.
G2540

Proceedings.
G2980 (ASU BC)

Economic and Social Problems and Conditions of the Southern Appalachians.
G3370

The Appalachian Region: A Preliminary Analysis of Economic and Population Trends in an Eleven State Problem Area.
G4440

"Economic Development of Areas Contiguous to Multipurpose Reservoirs: The Kentucky-Tennessee Experience."
H2220 (BC)

"Migration, Mobility and Social Participation."
J1230

Appalachia: Problems and Solutions.
J1240 (ASU)

Mountain Families in Poverty.
J1600

Hillbilly Women.
K20 (ASU BC UNCA)

How People Get Power: Organizing Oppressed Communities Get Action.
K40 (WCU ASU)

State Planning and Economic Development in the South.
L1850

"Economic Development in Appalachia."
L1990 (BC ASU)

A Planner's Reference Guide Relating to Socioeconomic Factors Within Appalachia as Applied to Public Education.
L2620 (ETSU)

Project Economic Study of the Ohio River Basin.
L2800

A Preliminary Analysis for an Economic Development Plan for the Appalachian Region.
L2860

Standards of Living in Four Southern Appalachian Mountain Counties. Farm Security Administration Social Research Report, no. 10.
L3430 (LMC ASU BC)

"Self-concepts of Appalachian Children: A Comparative Study of Economically Poor and Economically Disadvantaged Children Using the Piers-Harris Self-concept Inventory."
L3510 (LMC ASU)

The Geographic Basis of American Economic Life.
M310 (ASU)

Income and Employment in the Southeast: A Study of Cyclical Behavior.
M1440 (ASU BC)

The South in Continuity and Change.
M1910 (BC FC)

The Appalachian Region: A Preliminary Analysis of Economic and Population Trends in an Eleven State Problem Area.
M3860 (BC)

Appalachian Development: The Long-run View.
M5370 (LMC)

Appalachian Future, the Economic Challenge.
M5380

Stimulating Regional Economic Development with an Input-Output Model.
M5390

Pockets of Hope: Studies of Land and People.
M8690

Down to Earth-People of Appalachia.
M9100

Business and Economic Problems in Appalachia.
M9150 (ASU LMC)

The Political Economy of Appalachia; A Case Study in Regional Integration.
N780 (BC WWC ASU ETSU MHC WCU)
N2920

Potential Earning Power of Southern Mountaineer Handicrafts.
N2990

Appalachia: A Case Study of Regional Business Development.
O430

"An Analysis of the Effects of Federal Farm Programs on Incomes of Appalachian Farmers."
P1040 (LMC)

Towards Solving the Low-income Problem of Small Farmers in the Appalachian Area.
P1060 (LMC)

Appalachian Regional Data Book, 1964.
P3190

Family Income and Related Characteristics Among Low-Income Counties and States.
R40

"The Economics of the Coal Industry."
R2370

Some Postwar Rural Trends in Kentucky, North Carolina, Tennessee, Virginia, and West Virginia.
R3080

"United States Bituminous Coal Markets — Trends Since 1920, and Prospects to 1975."
S10

"Transport Improvement and the Appalachian Barrier: A Case Study in Economic Innovation."
S50 (ASU)

An Economic Survey of Indiana County, Pennsylvania.
S640

What's Next?
S1720 (ASU)

Poverty as a Public Issue.
S1800 (BC)

The Southern Appalachian Region; A Survey.
S5670 (BC ASU UNCA FC)

The Southern Appalachian Region.
S5680 (ASU ETSU FC LMC MHC WCU WWC BC)

"A Definition of the Economic Subregions of Appalachia Using Factor Analysis."
S6270

Recollections of an Old Man. Seventy Years in Dixie.
S8950

The Hollow.
S9110 (WWC ASU LMC ETSU BC)

Navigation and Economic Growth: Tennessee River Experience; a Report.
T3100

Report.
T4220

Social and Economic Characteristics of Six Tennessee Valley Reservoir Areas.
T4330 (BC)

The Tennessee Valley Region: Highlights of Growth and Change; Historical Perspectives, Recent Trends.
T5200

The Tennessee Valley Region: Important Features and Recent Trends.
T5330

ECONOMIC CONDITIONS — APP.

"Why Aid Doesn't Help: Organizing for Community Economic Development in Central Appalachia."
T9690

Economic and Social Problems and Conditions of the Southern Appalachians.
U360 (ASU)

Economic and Social Problems and Conditions of the Southern Appalachians.
U370

Regional Economic Development in the United States.
U2710

Economic Development Acts: Pt. 1, Public Law 90-103, Title 1, Appalachian Regional Development Act Amendments of 1967, Title 2, Amendments to Public Works and Economic Development Act of 1965. Pt. 1, Section-by-section Analysis of Title 1, Appalachian Regional Development Act of 1967, Appalachian Regional Development Act of 1965, as Amended, Pt. 3, Section-by-section Analysis of Title 2 Amendments to Public Works and Economic Development Act of 1965, Public Works and Economic Development Act of 1965, as Amended.
U3480

Economic Development Programs under the Jurisdiction of the Committee of Public Works, Pt. 1, 1971 Amendments to Public Works and Economic Development Act of 1965 and Appalachian Regional Development Act of 1965. Pt. 2, Public Works and Economic Development Act of 1965, as Amended. Pt. 3, Appalachian Regional Development Act of 1965 as Amended, December, 1971, 92nd Congress.
U3490

H. R. 8947, Act Making Appropriations for Public Works for Water and Power Development, Including Corps of Engineers — Civil, Bureau of Reclamation, Bonneville Power Administration and Other Power Agencies of the Department of Interior, Appalachian Regional Development Programs, Federal Power Commission, Tennessee Valley Authority, Atomic Energy Commission, and Related Independent Agencies and Commissions for Fiscal Year Ending June 30, 1974, and for Other Purposes. Approved August 16, 1973.
U3500

Recreation Potential in the Appalachian Highlands: A Market Analysis.
U4220 (ASU)

Planning for the South, an Inquiry into the Economics of Regionalism.
V420 (ASU)

Projections and Economic Base Analysis: Bristol-Kingsport Metropolitan Area Including the City of Bristol, Virginia, and the Counties of Washington, Virginia, and Sullivan, Tennessee.
V820

"The Structure and Polarization of Economic Activity in the Appalachian Region."
V1280 (LMC)

West Virginia — An Economic Profile.
W480

Appalachia in the Sixties: Decade of Reawakening.
W550 (ASU LMC WWC WCU MHC ETSU BC UNCA)

An Economic Survey of Clinton Co., Pa.
W840

An Economic Survey of Monroe County, Conducted by the Bureau of Business Research, College of Business Administration, Penn. State Univ. in Cooperation with Pocono Mountains Chamber of Commerce, Stroudsburg, Pa.
W850

"The Economics of the Transportation of Ohio Coal."
W890

An Economic and Social Survey of Clarke County.
W900

The Economics of Poverty, an American Paradox.
W2350

Retail Trading Areas in W. Va.
W3230

W. Va. Personal Income and Retail Sales by Counties, 1948-1965.
W3240

W. Va. Coal Facts, 1971.
W3250

Geology and Economic Resources of the Ohio River Valley in West Virginia.
W3710 (ETSU)

The Condition and Prospects of the West Virginia Economy.
W4000

Status of West Virginia in the Economic Opportunity Program under Public Law 88-452.
W4010

West Virginia: Economic Profile.
W4100

The economy of Haywood County.
W4900

"Reservoir Impacts on Economic Activity, Land Use and Land Values in Appalachia."
W5220

"Socio-cultural Factors and Economic Development in West Central Appalachia."
W6060

"Economic Aspects of Surface Subsidence Resulting from Underground Mineral Exploitation."
Z190

ECONOMIC CONDITIONS — APP. — COLONIALISM

Anthracite: An Instance of Natural Resource Monopoly.
N350 (ASU LMC)

ECONOMIC CONDITIONS — APP. — TENN.

An Economic Analysis of Farming in Overton County, Tennessee.
A1830 (ETSU)

ECONOMIC CONDITIONS — ASHEVILLE

A Population and Economic Analysis of the Asheville Metropolitan Area and the Western North Carolina That It Serves.
A5210 (BC)

ECONOMIC CONDITIONS — COAL CAMPS

"Economic Consequences of the Seven-hour Day and Wage Changes in the Bituminous Coal Industry."
F1220

ECONOMIC CONDITIONS — COAL INDUSTRY

"Industrial Retardation and Economic Growth: A Case Study of Secular and Structural Change in the United States, 1920-1960."
F3430

"The Coal Buying Policies: Effects on Prices and Method of Mining in Supplying States."
H3150

ECONOMIC CONDITIONS — GA.

"A Study of Effect of Government Aid and Other Factors on the Economic Development of Three Selected Areas in Georgia."
A340

The Economic Development of the Northeast Georgia Commission Area Through Use of Forest Products and Water Resources.
B7120 (ASU ETSU)

Highlights of the Economy of the Georgia Mountains Area.
G1010 (BC ASU)

"Some Economic Aspects of the Changes in Towns County Agriculture during the Period, 1934-1950."
L280

Statistics of the State of Georgia.
W5420 (BC)

Highlights of the Economy of the Georgia Mountains Area.
W5510

ECONOMIC CONDITIONS — KY.

Resources and People in East Kentucky: Problems and Potentials of a Lagging Economy.
B5790 (ASU WCU LMC ETSU BC)

"Sociocultural Differences among Three Areas in Kentucky."
B6110

"The Influence of Coal in the Big Sandy Valley."
C3230 (ASU)

Capital Resources in the Central Appalachian Region.
C3560 (ASU ETSU)

Poverty, Politics, and Health Care: An Appalachian Experience.
C8060 (ASU)

Population Estimates for Kentucky Counties and Economic Area, July 1, 1958.
D250 (ASU)

"The State Employment Service in Appalachian Kentucky."
E1160

Kentucky Employment Trends from 1951 to 1963 with Projections to 1965-1975.
F3780

Kentucky Employment Trends from 1951 to 1963, with Projections to 1965-75.
F3790

"The Economic History of Boyd County, Kentucky."
G1160 (ASU)

"The Economic History of Knox County."
H7600

Economic Data on Eastern Kentucky Coal Fields.
K910

Eastern Kentucky Economic Atlas.
K1070

Population-Economic Study, Harlan-Harlan County, Kentucky.
K1170

Development Potentials for Kentucky Counties with Related Statistics.
K1360 (ASU)

"Development of Procedures for Quantifying and Assessing the Economic Well-being of Rural Areas."
K2710

A Survey of Low-Cost Housing in Carter County, Kentucky.
L2850 (ASU)

Family Incomes and Land Utilization in Knott County, Kentucky.
N900

Family Incomes and Land Utilization in Knott County, Kentucky.
N910

Farm Management and Family Incomes in Eastern Kentucky.
N920
N2920

"The Growth and Overdevelopment of the Kentucky Coal Industry, 1912-1929."
P1210 (ASU)

In the East Kentucky Hills.
Q160 (ASU WCU ETSU LMC)

Economic Impact of Secondary Road Improvements.
S8150

Life Among the Hills and Mountains of Kentucky.
T8080 (ASU BC)

"The Social and Economic Structure of Kentucky Agriculture, 1850-1860."
T9470

"The Economic and Cultural Development of Eastern Kentucky from 1900 to the Present."
W1540 (ASU)

ECONOMIC CONDITIONS — KY. — COAL INDUSTRY

"External Diseconomies of Bituminous Coal Surface Mining — A Case Study of Eastern Kentucky, 1960-1967."
H7590

ECONOMIC CONDITIONS — N. C.

Overall Economic Development Program for Avery County.
A5790 (LMC)
B8390 (BC)

The Population and Economy of Boone, North Carolina.
C3600 (LMC ASU)

Travel Industry in North Carolina. An Economic Survey.
C7320

An Economic Adjustment Study of Dairy Farms in Western North Carolina.
D2780 (LMC)
E780 (ASU)

Economy of Western North Carolina.
H1040

The Economy of Western North Carolina.
H1270 (LMC UNCA)

Investment Guidelines for the North Carolina Appalachian Region.
H1280 (WCU WWC ASU)

Investment Guidelines for the North Carolina Appalachian Region.
H1290 (WWC)

ECONOMIC CONDITIONS — N. C.
Manpower Education in the North Carolina Appalachian Region.
H1300 (ASU WWC LMC)
Manpower Education in the North Carolina Appalachian Region.
H1310 (LMC ASU WWC)
North Carolina: An Economic and Social Profile.
H6070 (LMC BC)
North Carolina, Economic and Social.
H6080 (WWC LMC BC UNCA)
Blue Ridge: An Appalachian Community in Transition.
K180 (ASU WCU FC ETSU BC)
Report of the Geographical Survey of North Carolina: Physical Geography, Resume, Economical Geology.
K1670 (LMC ASU)
A Study of Farm Families and Their Level of Living Income Patterns in Watauga County, North Carolina.
M250 (ASU)
Buncombe County, Economic and Social.
M8190
Buncombe County: Economic and Social.
M8200 (ASU BC LMC)
Personal Income Statistics for North Carolina Counties, 1949-1959.
N2140
Population and Economy: Marshall, N.C.
N2150 (ASU WCU)
Population and Economy: Valdese, North Carolina.
N2160 (WCU)
The Dimensions of Poverty in North Carolina.
N2300 (ASU)
Altitudes in North Carolina.
N2310 (ASU LMC WCU)
Biennial Report of the State Geologist: 1919-1920.
N2330 (ASU LMC)
North Carolina Manual 1874-19.
N2560 (ASU LMC)
Buncombe County: Economic and Social.
N2670 (ASU)
Rutherford County: Economic and Social.
P4590 (ASU)
Change in Agricultural and Economic Trends in North Carolina; Information by Area Development Associations and Counties.
S7530
U4150

ECONOMIC CONDITIONS — N. Y.
Economic Study of Land Utilization in Schuyler County, N. Y.
D410

ECONOMIC CONDITIONS — OHIO
"Economic Inventory and Value Added Estimates of the Natural Resources of a Watershed Region Located in the Appalachian Highland Area of Ohio."
D3630
"Analysis of Costs and Benefits from Commuting for Employment among Core and Satellite Communities in the Appalachian Region of Ohio."
E2360
"A Study of Commercial Banking in Two Economically Depressed Cities: Youngstown, Ohio, and Wheeling, West Virginia, 1951-1967."
N1010

ECONOMIC CONDITIONS — PA.
"A Study of the Need for Curricular Changes in Secondary Schools in an Economically Distressed Area of Pennsylvania."
B9170
"A Preliminary Economic Evaluation of the Corey Creek Watershed."
D50
The Economic Structure of Sullivan County, Pennsylvania.
G190 (ASU)
A Regional Economic Study of Cameron County, Pennsylvania.
G2050 (ASU)
Readings in Pennsylvania Economic Growth.
G2310
"Labor Market Adjustments in a Depressed Area."
G2740
"An Economic Analysis of Idle Farm Land, Potter County, Pennsylvania, 1953."
J530
"Minimum Wages in Pennsylvania."
K530
The Potential for Human Resources and Economic Growth in a Declining Local Community; A Socioeconomic Study of the Johnstown, Penn. Economy.
L2000
"Measurement of Personal Wealth in Centre County, Pennsylvania."
M1600
An Economic Background for Regional Planning in the Anthracite Counties.
P1860
An Economic Survey of Northumberland County, Pennsylvania.
S650
An Economic Survey of Venango County, Pennsylvania.
S660
Fayette County, Pennsylvania; An Economic Survey.
S670
"The Economic Structure and Growth of the Pennsylvania Economy: 1956-1966."
S4510

ECONOMIC CONDITIONS — S. C.
Selected South Carolina Economic Data.
C6500
Greenville County, Economic and Social.
G4870
Greenville County, Economic and Social.
G4880
"An Economic Survey of Oconee County."
W8880

ECONOMIC CONDITIONS — TENN.
"The Social and Economic History of Maryville since 1890."
B1920
"Some Phases of the Social and Economic History of Washington County, Tennessee, 1865-1917."
B6220
"Some Phases of the Social and Economic History of Washington County, Tennessee, 1865-1917."
B6230 (ETSU)
"An Educational and Economic Survey of Bledsoe County, Tennessee."
B7060
Educational, Economic and Community Survey, Bledsoe County.
B7070
Dimensions of Change in East Tennessee, Tennessee, the South, and the Nation: A Comparative Analysis.
B7310 (ASU ETSU LMC WCU)
Measurements of Poverty in East Tennessee.
B7320 (ASU BC ETSU LMC)
"Geographic Factors Influencing the Development of Scott County, Tennessee."
B8630
"The Identification and Evaluation of Factors Affecting Economic Growth in the Tennessee Valley Region, 1950-1960."
C3340
"Changes in Social and Economic Status of the People in Sullivan County for a Thirty Year Period."
C3390 (ASU)
Comparative Economic Growth Measures — Population and Personal Income Estimates for Tennessee Counties, 1950 Through 1962.
C7590
"Social and Economic History of Kingsport before 1908."
C7840 (ETSU)
"A Study of the Reading Abilities of the Economically Deprived Students in the Fourth, Fifth, and Sixth Grades at Stratton Elementary School."
D2520 (ETSU)
"Factors Influencing the Development of the Broadway Shopping Center at Knoxville, Tennessee."
D2710
Minimum Land Requirements for Specified Levels of Farm Income in the Eastern Highland Rim of Tennessee.
E30
E780 (ASU)
Social and Economic Trends in Tennessee and Their Implications for Education.
F2530 (ETSU)
The Spatial Structure of Economic Development in the Tennessee Valley.
F3330 (BC)
"A Study of Certain Phases of the Educational and Economic Conditions of Marion County, Tennessee."
G370
The City of Knoxville, Tennessee and Vicinity and Their Resources.
G3060
The Economy of Metropolitan Knoxville. A Study Focused on the Economic Base and Potentials of Knoxville and Knox County.
H1260 (ETSU)
The Changing Economy of Claiborne County, Tennessee.
H2580
Adjustments of Rural Resources Use and Characteristics to Economic Growth.
H4490 (ASU)
"Economic Progress and Resource Adjustments of Rural Households is the Upper East Tennessee Valley."
H4500 (ASU)
Johnson City, Tennessee, Population and Economic Base Study.
H5390
"Educational Facilities and Economic Development of Bristol, 1930-1950."
H6510
"Educational Facilities and Economic Development of Bristol, 1930-1950."
H6520 (ETSU)
The Economy of Greeneville, Tennessee; a Study of the Information and Data Related to the Greeneville, Tennessee, Economic Community.
H6730
"An Educational, Economic, and Community Survey of Blount County, Tennessee."
H7540
The TVA and Economic Security in the South.
H7660 (ASU WCU LMC)
An Economic Survey of Blount County, Tennessee, a Study of Resources and Industrial Potentials.
H8720
Annual Report . . . for Fiscal Year Ended June 30, 1944-.
J1380 (ETSU)
Johnson City, Tennessee: Population and Economic Base Study.
J1490 (ETSU)
"An Economic and Educational Survey of Rogersville Community."
L3210
"The Tennessee Political System: The Relationship of the Socioeconomic Environment to Political Processes and Policy Outputs."
M870
Human Resources in the Economy of the Upper French Broad Area.
M4310 (LMC)
"Socio-Economic Readjustment of Farm Families Displaced by the TVA Land Purchase in the Norris Area."
N1000
"The First Hundred Days of the New Deal in Upper East Tennessee."
O210 (ETSU)
"Economic History of White County, Tennessee."
P4100
"An Economic, Educational, and Social Survey of Franklin County, Tennessee."
R570 (ASU)
"Relation of Land Base Quality to the Agricultural Economy of Knox County, Tennessee."
R4320
The Economic Geography of Tennessee.
S1600
"A Study of Debt History in Carter County, Tennessee, 1892-1952."
S2380
"The Social, Economic, Cultural, Religious and Family Educational Backgrounds of Recent Dropouts from Bristol, Tennessee, High School."
S4340 (ETSU)

ECONOMIC CONDITIONS — TENN.

"An Economic, Social and Educational Survey of Campbell County, Tennessee."
S4690

"The Economic Status of Knox County Teachers."
S6530

"An Educational and Economic Survey of Monroe County, Tennessee."
S6550

Hamilton County, Economic and Social: A Laboratory Study in the Department of Agricultural Economics Under the Direction of Professor C. E. Allred.
S6910

"Standard of Living and Migration of 136 Farm Families in Overton County, Tennessee."
S8910

Tennessee — Its Resources and Economy — The Tennessee Economy — Vol. I.
T1210

An Economic Survey of the Tri-Counties Region of Upper East Tennessee.
T1620 (ETSU)

Southeast Tennessee Region Profile and Policies.
T2090

The Lower Cumberland Region: A Study of Its Population, Economic Base and Potential.
T2100 (ETSU)

The Upper Cumberland Economy.
T2110 (ETSU)

Summary of Resources.
T3550

Problems and Suggested Programs for Low-Income Farmers with Special Reference to the Tennessee Valley.
T4510

Overall Economic Development Program for Unicoi County, Tennessee.
U120 (ETSU)

Tennessee: Its Growth and Progress.
W5570 (BC)

The Incidence of Poverty — Social and Economic Conditions in Tennessee.
W6600

ECONOMIC CONDITIONS — TENNESSEE VALLEY AUTHORITY

TVA: The First Twenty Years. A Staff Report.
T3790 (ASU WCU LMC)

Defense Expansion in the Tennessee Valley Region.
T5820

ECONOMIC CONDITIONS — VA.

Economic History of Virginia in the Seventeenth Century.
B7620 (BC FC)

Institutional History of Virginia in the Seventeenth Century: An Inquiry into the Religious, Moral, Educational, Legal, Military, and Political Condition of the People Based on Original and Contemporaneous Records.
B7630 (ETSU)

"The Changing Economic Position of Southwest Virginia as Affected by the Coal Industry."
C1450 (ETSU)

An Economic and Social Survey of Augusta County.
C2110 (ASU BC)

An Economic and Social Survey of Patrick County.
C6680 (BC)

Standards of Living in Six Virginia Counties.
D640

The Rise and Fall of Alderson, West Virginia.
D2590 (ASU BC)

An Economic and Social Survey of Washington County.
D3830 (ASU BC)

An Economic and Social Survey of Albemarle County.
G740

Economic Land Classification of Pulaski County.
G1190

An Economic and Social Survey of Warren County.
H520 (ASU)

An Economic and Social Survey of Wise County.
K790 (ASU BC)

Economic and Social Aspects of Negro Slavery in Wythe County, Virginia, 1790-1860.
M9210

An Economic and Social Survey of Frederick County.
P2840 (ASU LMC)

"A Study of the Economically and Educationally Deprived Students of Bristol, Virginia, Junior High School."
Q120 (ETSU)

An Economic and Social Survey of Giles County.
S5250

An Economic and Social Survey of Roanoke County.
S7130

An Economic and Social Survey of Russell County.
T300 (BC)

Lebanon, A Virginia Community.
T310

An Economic and Social Survey of Virginia Counties.
U4120 (FC)
V550

Industrial Sites and Economic Data.
V770 (BC)

Industrial Sites and Economic Data, Botetourt County, Virginia.
V780

Economic Data.
V810 (BC)
V850 (BC)

Virginia, Economic and Civic.
V1160 (BC)

Report.
V1170 (BC)

Travel in Virginia, Its Economic Significance.
V1200

An Economic and Social Survey of Warren Co.
V1240 (BC ASU)

An Economic and Social Survey of Alleghany County.
W290 (ASU BC)

ECONOMIC CONDITIONS — W. VA.

Centennial Field Trip.
A5290 (ETSU)

Coal and Coal Mining in West Virginia.
B1200

"The Regional Growth Points in Economic Development; A Comparison of West Virginia and West Pakistan."
B2660

Report of the Economic Growth of Oak Hill, Correlated With the History of King Coal-Fayette County's First Major Industry.
B3010

"An Input-output Analysis of the Upper South Branch Valley of West Virginia."
B3630

"Productive Capacity and Economic Growth in West Virginia."
B7090

Status of West Virginia in the Economic Opportunity Program under Public Law 88-452.
C1310

Economic Structure of West Virginia.
C2560

The Structure of the West Virginia Economy, 1965: A Preliminary Report.
C3020 (LMC)

A Forecast of the Economy of West Virginia and the Effect on Certain Operations of the Chesapeake and Potomac Telephone Company of West Virginia, 1961-1970.
C3770

"A Regional Linear Programming Model of the West Virginia Economy."
C5370

Proceedings.
C6400

A Social and Economic Survey of the Spencer Soil Conservation Area.
C7540

"The Transformation of the Tug and Guyandot Valleys: Economic Development and Social Change in West Virginia, 1888-1921."
C9390

Annual Report for 1964.
E540

Some Effects of Price and Income Support Programs on Marginal Farms.
E2320

Economic Impact of the Mountain State Art and Craft Fair, Ripley, West Virginia, 1964.
H50

The Contributions of Local Subsidies to the Economic Development of West Virginia, 1956-1966.
H330 (ASU)

Development of an Economic/Environmental Plan for Dents Run Watershed, West Virginia.
H950 (ASU)

Economic Stability and Growth Potential, Fairmont, W. Va.
H2230

"Social and Economic Implications of Strip Mining in Harrison County, W. Va."
H5440

Overall Economic Development Program.
L2120

Personal Income in West Virginia Counties by Type and Magnitude, 1960-1963: A Pilot Study.
L2410 (ASU)
L3740

The Geology of Watoga and Droop Mountain Battlefield State Parks, West Virginia.
L3910 (ETSU)

West Virginia Budgeting: Problems and Possibilities.
M5180

Stimulating Regional Economic Development. An Interindustry Analysis of West Virginia Economy.
M5400

The Structure of the West Virginia Economy in 1975, a Preliminary Forecast.
M5410

Approaches to University Extension Work with the Rural Disadvantaged: Description and Analysis of a Pilot Effort.
M5970

"A Comparison of the Personal and Economic Characteristics of the Mobile and Immobile."
M6040

"Mass Media Use Patterns and Interests Among West Virginia Rural Non-farm Families of Low Socio-economic Status."
M8530

"A Study of Commercial Banking in Two Economically Depressed Cities: Youngstown, Ohio, and Wheeling, West Virginia, 1951-1967."
N1010

Towards Solving the Low-Income Problem of Small Farmers in the Appalachian Area.
P1010

Selected Demographic Aspects of the West Virginia Economy, 1950-1975: Estimates and Projections of Migration and Population.
P4880 (ETSU BC)

Warning in Appalachia: A Study of Wirt County, West Virginia.
R1110 (BC ASU WCU LMC MHC)

"The Relationship Between the Structure of the Transportation Network and the Economic Development of West Virginia."
S2170
S3690 (UNCA)

A Case Study of Six Central West Virginia Counties of the Interrelationships of Factors Leading to Persistence of Low Incomes and Unemployment with Corrective Suggestions.
S7460

Opportunities for Economic Development in Mingo County, West Virginia.
U190

ARA Field Report, Opportunities for Economic Development in Mingo County, W. Va.
U2690

Overall Economic Development Program for Upshur County, West Virginia.
U4180
W4440
W4450

Business and Economic Studies.
W4490 (BC)

Economic Development Series, no. 1.
W4520 (BC)

An Informal Series Covering Agric. Econ., in Its Broadest Sense.
W4530

Economic Development in West Virginia.
Z60

ECONOMIC CONDITIONS — W. VA. — TUCKER CO.

An Economic Profile of Tucker County, West Virginia.
L3490 (ASU)

ECONOMIC MODELS
A Demonstration Program in Rural Housing: An Area-wide Housing Organization in the Northwest Local Development District.
A4880
A Decade of Action for Progress in Kentucky.
E520 (ASU)
Program 60, 1960-70; a Decade of Action for Progress in Eastern Kentucky.
E530 (BC)
Annual Report for 1964.
E540
ECONOMIC MODELS — APP.
Appalachia, Rebirth of a Nation.
B3170
"An Input-output Model Incorporating Impact Analysis to Evaluate the Resources and Economy of a Rural Appalachian Community."
G220
ECONOMIC MODELS — KY.
"An Application of the Leontief Regional Model: An Input-output Analysis for Eastern Kentucky."
B490
ECONOMIC MODELS — W. VA.
"Transportation and Trade Areas; Analysis of Morgantown, Fairmont, and Clarksburg."
S330 (ASU)
ECONOMIC PROBLEMS — APP.
"Related Aspects of the Social and Economic Problems, Cultural Transitions and Educational System of Rural Appalachia: An Analysis Based on the Concept of Scale."
R2220 (BC)
EDUCATION
Thomas Jefferson and the University of Virginia.
A410 (ASU)
"Kentucky State Aid and the Educationally Disadvantaged Child."
A1390
"A Study of the Effect of Participation in Football on the Grades of Students at Bristol, Tennessee, High School."
A1420 (ETSU)
"A History and Development of Education in Wilkes County, North Carolina."
A1660
The Children of the South.
A2310
Federal Programs for Young Children.
A3890 (ASU ETSU)
Status of Secondary Vocational Education in Appalachia.
A3950 (ASU LMC)
The Appalachian School. . .
A4040
The Appalachian School Department of Fireside Industries.
A4050
Appalachian School Summer Camp.
A4060
"Student Involvement in the Policies of a Junior High School Library — An Experiment."
B340 (ETSU)
The Story of the McGuffeys.
R4270 (ASU BC)
Education, Migration and Economic Life Chances of Male Entrants to the Labor Force from a Low Income Rural Area.
S1240 (ASU)
Bulletin.
U3830
Bulletin.
W3420 (BC)
An Administrative Survey of the Public Schools of Boone County, West Va.
W4360 (BC)
Pilot Project, App. Center, W. Va. Univ., Youhger Youth Science Camp, Aug. 2-7, 1964.
W4540
Seminar and Conference Reports and Proceedings Series.
W4600 (ASU)
Journal of Education.
W4860
"The Reading Diagnosis and Remediation of Five Groups of Eighth Grade Students at John S. Battle High School in Washington County, Virginia."
W9000 (ETSU)
"History and Partial Evaluation of In-service Education in Harlan County, Kentucky."
W9070
"A Comparative Study of the Achievement in Science of the Fifth and Sixth Grade Pupils in Bristol, Tennessee, Schools, 1953-57."
W9090 (ETSU)
"A Study of School Transportation, Morgan Co., Tenn."
Z180
EDUCATION — ALA.
Public Education in Alabama.
A900 (ASU)
"A Study of the Progress of Negro Education in Saint Clair County, Alabama."
C1750
"A Study of Administrative and Supervisory Practices of Principals in the Public School System of Jefferson County, Alabama."
C5520
"What Progress in Health Has Been Made among the Negro Youths of the Elementary School Age for the Past Ten Years in Talladega County, Alabama."
C9500
School at Speedwell.
E1120
Speedwell Sketches.
E1130 (ASU BC)
"Factors Contributing to the Educational Development of the Negro Schools in the Jefferson County (Alabama) School System, 1945-51."
G1950
"A Study of the Causes of Drop-outs and Irregular Attendance among Boys in the Four Negro High Schools of Talledega County, Alabama."
G2040
"A Comparative Study of School Dropouts from 1945-50 in Holt Junior High School and Jaylorville Junior High School, Tuscaloosa County, Alabama."
H2210
"The Status of the Negro Teachers in Blount, Cullman, DeKalb, and Marshall Counties, Alabama 1952-53."
J2260
"Factors Affecting the Health and Educational Growth of Elementary Pupils in Three Selected Schools of Jefferson County, Alabama."
M1920
"A Historical Analysis of Student Drop-outs in the Negro Schools for Bibb County, Alabama."
M4620
"A Study of the Changes in the Educational Levels of the Negro Teachers in Jefferson County, Alabama, 1930-50."
M6280
"The Educational Progress of the Negro Schools in Cherokee County, Alabama, from 1930-1950."
S6640
EDUCATION — APP.
Cooperative Action on the Educational Problems of Appalachia.
A190
Research for Better Schools: A Federal Projects Workshop for Educational Programs in Tennessee and Appalachia.
A200
Directions for Educational Development in Appalachia; Report of an Educational Needs and Feasibility Study Involving the Appalachian Areas of Six States.
A2710 (ASU)
Quality education for Appalachia: A prospectus proposing the establishment of a regional educational laboratory.
A2730 (FC)
A2770 (ASU)
Quality Education for Appalachia: A Prospectus Proposing the Establishment of a Regional Education Laboratory.
A2780 (FC)
A Select Bibliography on High Risk Education for Appalachian Youth: Programs and Practices.
A3820
Survey of Environmental Education Programs in Colleges and Universities in the Appalachian Region.
A3860 (ASU)
Appalachian — Education for Tomorrow.
A3910 (ASU)
Preliminary Report.
A3940
Summary and Recommendations to the Appalachian Regional Commission: Report I.
A3960 (ASU)
Characteristics of High School Seniors as Related to Subsequent College Attendance.
B150
"Southern Appalachian Non-standard Speech in Conflict with the Standard English of the Classroom."
B280 (ETSU)
"From Existence to Essence; A Conceptual Model for an Appalachian Studies Curriculum."
B3340
Compensatory Education for Cultural Deprivation.
B4760
Annihilating the Hillbilly: The Appalachians' Struggle with America's Institutions.
B6350
The Future of the Church and Independent Schools in our Southern Highlands.
C630 (ASU)
Directions for Education Development in Appalachia: Report of an Educational Need and Feasibility Study Involving the Appalachian Areas of Six States.
C810 (BC ASU)
Adjustment to Rural Industrial Change with Special Reference to Mountain Areas.
C820
Southern Highland Schools Maintained by Denominational and Independent Agencies.
C860 (ASU)
The Double Head Academy.
C2600 (BC)
Dead End School.
C5860 (ASU)
"Study of Industrial Arts Education in Public Secondary Schools of the Southern Appalachian Region."
C5970
Proceedings.
C6480 (ASU)
How to Pay for College, a Complete Guide to Scholarships, Loans and Self-help Opportunities in the Appalachian South.
C7860 (MHC ASU BC)
Age-grade School Progress of Farm and Nonfarm Youth:
C8130
"The Curriculum of the Senior High School: A Survey of Offerings, Changes and Current Trends in the Southern Appalachian Region."
C8230
Appalachian People's History Book.
C9220 (ASU FC WCU ETSU)
Universal Education in the South.
D10 (WWC BC)
"Public School Enrollment Prediction for the Southern Appalachian Region."
D1740
Impacts of Educational Change Efforts in Appalachia.
D2910 (ETSU)
An Appalachian Reader.
D3240 (WCU MHC FC BC ASU)
Appalachian Volunteer Reader.
D3260 (BC)
"A Study of Public School Finance in the Southern Appalachian Region."
D4310
E920
Appalachia, Education for Tomorrow.
E930
The Status of Secondary Vocational Education in Appalachia.
E940
E2100
"The Professional Status of Teachers in the Southern Appalachian Region."
E2400
Discovery, Expression, Communication: An Arts Approach to the Problems of Appalachia.
F510

EDUCATION — APP.

A Statistical Study of the Public Schools of the Southern Appalachian Mountains.
F3540 (ASU BC)

Education in the Southern Mountains.
G640 (ASU BC)

Good References on Educational Problems of the Southern Highlands.
G650

"Health, Education, and Income as Correlates of Demand for Hospital Care in the Southern Mountains."
G1100

Appalachian Students and Guidance.
H1670 (ASU BC WCU MHC ETSU)

The Road from West Virginia.
H2120 (ASU BC LMC)

Schoolhouses in the Foothills.
H2370

Hooky Cop Saga: Frustrations and Rewards of an Attendance Officer in Appalachia.
H3260 (ASU BC)

The Educational Needs of Appalachia.
H6580

"School Ain't No Way . . ." Appalachian Consciousness.
I20 (ASU LMC MHC WCU BC)

"A Preliminary Edition of a Reading Test For Use With Disadvantaged Children in the Primary Grades of the Southern Appalachian Region."
J2300 (ETSU)

"High-interest, Low-vocabulary Original Prose and Poetry for Teenagers in Southern Appalachia."
K1610 (ETSU)

Settlement Institutions in Southern Appalachia.
K3130

"A Study of the Academic Achievement of Kindergarten and Non-kindergarten Children in a Rural School in Appalachia."
L1310 (ETSU)

Technical-Vocational Education and the Community College.
L1610

Children of the Cumberland.
L2100 (BC ASU LMC WCU WWC)

Children of the Cumberland.
L2110 (ASU)

A Planner's Reference Guide Relating to Socioeconomic Factors Within Appalachia as Applied to Public Education.
L2620 (ETSU)

Teachers in Appalachia.
L2810 (ASU ETSU MHC)

"The Social and Educational Aspects of the Tennessee Valley Authority."
M2630

Dropout Proneness in Appalachia.
M6180 (ASU)

Dropout Proneness in Appalachia.
M6190 (ETSU)

Analysis of Attitudes Relative to Education in the Appalachian Region.
N40 (ASU ETSU)

The Mountains Are Moving. Sixth NEA National Conference on Human Rights in Education. Equality of Educational Opportunity for Children of Appalachia.
N190 (ASU)

Conference Report: Equality of Educational Opportunity for Children of Appalachia.
N230 (ASU)

A Review of the Literature Pertaining to Appalachia; Stressing Attitudes to Social Change and Religious and Educational Orientations; A Working Paper for the Boards of Christian Education of the United Presbyterian Church in the U. S.
N450 (BC)

Appalachian Schools — A Case of Consistency.
O360 (ASU)

"A Study of the Factors Affecting the Holding Power of High Schools in a Certain Mountainous Rural County."
O890

Appalachia: Realities of Deprivation.
P60
Q40

Education in Appalachia as Depicted in Major Periodicals.
R290

"Related Aspects of the Social and Economic Problems, Cultural Transitions and Educational System of Rural Appalachia: An Analysis Based on the Concept of Scale."
R2220 (BC)

Southern Mountain Schools Maintained by Denominational and Independent Agencies.
R4400 (LMC)

Adult Education, a part of a Total Educational Program. A Description of the Educational and Training Program of the Tennessee Valley Authority.
S1560

Adult Education, a Part of a Total Educational Program. A Description of the Educational and Training Program of the Tennessee Valley Authority.
S1570 (ASU)

With Reference to Appalachia.
S1590 (ASU)

"An Analysis and Evaluation of High School Sociology as Taught in Southern Appalachia."
S1840 (ETSU)

Southern Schools: Progress and Problems.
S5710 (WWC)

Educational Conditions in the Southern Appalachians.
S5720

Report on Appalachian Culture Preschool Curriculum Project.
S6600 (ASU)

"An Assessment of the Characteristics, Education, and Training of Public School Superintendents in Southern Appalachia and in West Virginia."
T490

Bulletin.
U1190 (BC)

Bulletin.
U1200 (BC)

"A Survey of the Church and Independent Schools and Colleges of the Southern Appalachians."
W500

Alleghany, Ashe, Watauga Planning Project for Handicapped Children, ESEA Title III.
W1360 (WCU)

"A Study of the Cooperative Vocational Education Program at Boones Creek High School."
W1430 (ETSU)

Teacher Education in Service.
W1890 (BC)

Educational Opportunities in the Appalachian Mountains.
W1900 (ASU LMC WWC BC)

The Goals of Higher Education.
W1910 (BC)

Students in Appalachia.
W1970 (ETSU)

My Country School Diary.
W2120 (BC)

A Guidance Program for McMinn County High School.
W2300

"School Failure in Relation to Delinquency, Scott County, Tennessee."
W3090

Look into These Hills.
W3190

Utilizing a College's Resources to Provide Technical Assistance to Business Firms in Southern West Virginia: A Report on the Concord College Center for Economic Action, July 1, 1963, Through June 30, 1966.
W3290

"A History of Livingston Academy from 1909 through 1947."
W5280

"Experimental Preschool Intervention in the Appalachian Home."
W6940

The Need for Guidance Programs in Privately Supported Mountain Schools.
W8560 (BC)

Education in Depressed Areas.
W9170

A Critical Analysis of the Developmental Tasks of an Upper-elementary Class in Area 2 of the Greenville County-city School System and the Patterns of Direction Attempted for Better Group Action.
Y50 (ASU)

EDUCATION — APP. — COAL CAMPS

Schools in the Bituminous Coal Regions of the Appalachian Mountains.
D1610

EDUCATION — APP. MIGRANTS

E2450 (ASU)

EDUCATION — APPALACHIAN STUDIES

Appalachia, Resource Unit.
O540 (ASU)

EDUCATION — CHEROKEE NATION

TSVLVKI SQCLVLV: A Cherokee Spelling Book.
B9450

EDUCATION — COAL CAMP

"The Public School in the Mining Community."
D3100

EDUCATION — GA.

"History of Education in Gordon County, Georgia."
B2930

"A Study of Voluntary Withdrawals from McHenry and Five Feeder Schools in Floyd County, Georgia."
G1180

"A Study of the Relationship Existing Between Amount of Education Completed by White and Negro Head of Households in Floyd County."
H4240

"An Investigation of Elementary Guidance in Pickens County."
K700 (ASU)

"Improving School Attendance in Six White Elementary Schools in Polk County, Georgia."
M7680

History of the Public Schools of White County, Georgia 1870 Thru 1938.
S3450 (BC)

EDUCATION — INDIANS

Textbooks and the American Indian.
H4760 (MHC)

EDUCATION — KY.

Final Report.
A2820

"A Report of a Summer Internship at Buckhorn Children's Center, Buckhorn, Kentucky."
A4680 (ASU)

"History of Education of Magoffin County, Kentucky."
B220

"The Kentucky Council on Public Higher Education."
B1190

Report, 1953-1957.
B3110 (BC ETSU)

"Teenage Dating Behavior in Two Eastern Kentucky High Schools."
B4730

Sociocultural Differences Among Three Areas in Kentucky, as Determinants of Educational and Occupational Aspirants and Expectations of Rural Youth.
B5090 (BC)

"History of Education in Jackson County, Kentucky."
C1230

"Music in Four Kentucky Mountain Settlement Schools."
C2820 (LMC BC)

"An Evaluation of the Community Service or Continuing Education Project: Developing and Stimulating Recreation in Six Counties of Eastern Kentucky."
C2910

Proceedings.
C6480 (ASU)

"A Study of Pupil Withdrawal in Ten Secondary Schools of Floyd, Knott, Letcher, and Pike Counties through the School Year of 1932-33."
C7190

"History of Education in Pike County Kentucky."
C8750

"Economic Education in Kentucky Public Secondary Schools."
C9200

"The Public School in the Mining Community."
D3100

Stay on, Stranger: An Extraordinary Story of the Kentucky Mountains.
D4110 (ASU LMC WWC BC)

EDUCATION — KY.

"History of Education of Lawrence County, Kentucky."
E1590

"History of Education of Floyd County, Kentucky."
F3120

"History of Education in Owsley County, Kentucky."
G10 (BC)

Notes from the History of Education in Owsley County.
G20

"A History of Religious Education in the Kentucky Mountains."
G4230 (ASU)

Out of Time and Tide: The Evolution of Education in Kentucky (the Beginnings Through the 1930's).
H120 (ETSU)

Early School Leaders in Kentucky.
H130

"Tales of the Mountains" A Complete Directory of the Eastern Kentucky Coalfields with Extracts from the Geological Reports, Forestry, Oil Development, Education, Superstitions, and Religion of the Mountains.
H730

Harlan County Schools Have Problems.
H2310 (ASU)

Emphasizing Values in Five Kentucky Schools.
H3180 (ASU)

"The History of Education of Boyd County, Kentucky."
J200

"A Proposed Certification Plan for Kentucky Teachers Through Credentials, a Complete Investigation and a Comprehensive Examination in Major Fields."
J800 (LMC BC)

"Environmental School Sanitation of an Eastern Kentucky County."
J2650

Dropouts and Jobs: The Report of the Kentucky Conference on Youth, August 22-23, 1963.
K1000
K1040 (ETSU ASU)

Educational Attainment of the Adult Population in the Forty-four County Appalachian Region of Kentucky.
K1080 (ASU)

History of Education in Kentucky.
K1090 (ETSU ASU)

Youth Education and the Economic Opportunity Act of 1964: Some Indications of Need for Broad-based School and Community Action Programs for Kentucky Youth with Implications for Federal Assistance Programs.
K1100

Five Decades of Progress.
K1210

Moonlight School Courses of Study.
K1270

"School Attendance in Harlan County, Kentucky, 1948-1954."
L2940

"History of Education in Harlan County, Kentucky."
M840

The Gates Open Slowly: A History of Education in Kentucky.
M2560 (BC LMC)

"A Method of Measuring the Financial Ability of Kentucky School Districts to Support an Educational Program."
M6090

Carter County, Kentucky; A Study of an Unconscionable Combination of Politics and Education.
N180

"History of Education in Rockcastle, Kentucky."
N2840 (BC)
P3020

Bulletin of the Bureau of School Service, Vol. XX, no. 2.
P4820

"History of Education in Carter County, Kentucky."
Q50

"History of Education in Letcher County, Kentucky."
R190

"History of Education in Breathitt County, Kentucky."
R1960

"History of Education in Letcher County, Kentucky."
R3660

"History of Education in Owsley County, Kentucky."
S20

Moonlight Schools for the Emancipation of Adult Illiterates.
S7270 (BC)

"History of Education in Laurel County, Kentucky."
T600

A Study of Private Secondary Schools in Southeastern Kentucky.
W650

Some Appalachian Short Stories: A Bibliography.
W1590

Teacher Education in Service.
W1890 (BC)

The Educational Attainment and Future Plans of Kentucky Rural Youths.
Y160

Information on School Dropouts.
Y170

The Rural School Dropout: A Ten-Year Follow-Up Study of Eastern Kentucky Youth.
Y200

"History of Education in Wayne County, Kentucky."
Y250

EDUCATION — KY. — APP. COUNTIES

Evidence of Inequality of Educational Opportunity in Kentucky Mountain Counties.
B3100 (BC)

EDUCATION — KY. — SETTLEMENT SCHOOLS

"Social Value of Settlement Schools in the Kentucky Mountains."
J460 (ASU)

EDUCATION — N. C.

"The Utilization of Community Resources in the Elementary Public Schools of Jackson County."
A810 (WCU)
A3370 (ASU)

Appalachian North Carolina Youth Development Project, Final Report.
A3640 (ASU)

Extracts from the Diary of Benjamin Elberfield Atkins: A Teacher of the Old School, 1848-1909.
A5320 (LMC)

"A Study of the Causative Factors for Reading RETARDATION IN THE Eighth Grade in the Parkway School."
B1350 (ASU)

"The Growth and Development of Education in Watauga County."
B3720 (ASU)

The History of Western Carolina College: The Progress of an Idea.
B4160 (BC ASU LMC WCU)

The Superior and Gifted Student Project at Cullowhee, Western Carolina College.
B4300 (WCU)

"A Comparative Analysis of Student Teaching Programs in the Elementary Schools at Appalachian State Teachers College."
B4640 (ASU)
B4820

"An Investigation of Instructors' and Students' Philosophy of Education with Student Evaluations of Instructors at Blue Ridge Technical Institute During the First Year of Operation."
B5570 (ASU)

"The Attitudes of Freshmen Female Students Toward Physical Education at Western Carolina University."
B7830 (WCU)

"A Study of the Music Education Program of Watauga County."
B7980 (ASU)

"An Inquiry into Present Practices in Guidance in Transylvania County High Schools."
B8170 (ASU)

"A Survey of the Reading Materials Found in the Homes of the Fourth and Seventh Grade Students of the Elementary Demonstration School, Boone, North Carolina."
B8280 (ASU)

The Thought at Midnight: The Story of the Asheville Normal.
C500 (LMC)

"A Survey of the Guidance Programs in North Carolina Junior Colleges."
C4370 (ASU)

"A History of Traphill Institute, Wilkes County, North Carolina."
C4440 (ASU)

"A History of Mountain View School, Wilkes County, North Carolina."
C4450 (ASU)

"A Study of the Mill Schools of North Carolina."
C6850

"Developing a Core Plan in the Seventh and Eighth Grades at Candler Elementary School."
C6940 (WCU)

The Beginnings of Public Education in North Carolina: A Documentary History, 1790-1840.
C7070 (LMC BC)

North Carolina Schools and Academies, 1790-1840: A Documentary History.
C7080 (LMC WWC)

"Locating and Providing for Murphy High School's Bright Pupils."
C7620 (WCU)

"A Study of the Applied Psychology Classes for Sophomores and Juniors at Appalachian State Teachers College."
D1120 (ASU)

"A Study of Visually-handicapped Children in the Eighth Grade of Boone High School."
D1160 (ASU)

"A Study to Identify Some Personality Characteristics of Freshmen Academic Underachievers at Appalachian State University."
D1790 (ASU)

Higher Education in North Carolina before 1860. A Reflection Book.
D3280 (LMC)

"The Growth of a Community Centered Curriculum at Wilkes Central High School, 1952-1960."
D3820 (ASU)

A Comprehensive Study of the Academic Characteristics and Success Patterns of North Carolina Community College Transfer Students and Native Students of Appalachian State University.
E700

A Survey of Speech Education in Selected North Carolina High Schools.
E1250 (ASU)

"Eliminations from the Class of 1950 in the Marion High School."
E1610 (ASU)

"Dealing with Problem Children in the Mabel Elementary School."
E1860 (ASU)

"A Study of School Leavers at the Patterson School for Boys, Caldwell County, North Carolina."
F900 (ASU)

"A Critical Study of Negro Education in Cleveland County, North Carolina, from 1944 to 1954."
F2250 (ASU)

"A Survey of Public Education in Watauga County, North Carolina."
G2120 (ASU)

Church-state Relationships in Education in North Carolina since 1776.
G2220 (LMC)

"The Background, Education, and Experience of Teachers In Rutherford County, N. C."
H3840

"A Survey of the Study Habits of the Freshman Class of 1959-1960 at Appalachian State Teachers College."
H7080 (ASU)

"A History of Yancey Collegiate Institute."
H8440 (ASU)

"Educational Development of Ashe County."
H8640

"Study of Factors Causing Potential Drop-outs to Remain in the Mitchell County, North Carolina, High Schools."
I810

EDUCATION — N. C.

"A History of Negro Education in Wilkes County, North Carolina."
I820

A Five Year Follow-up Study of Graduates of Asheville-Buncombe Technical Institute, 1966-67 through 1970-71.
J1690 (ASU)

"A Study of the Changing Role of the Music Specialist in the North Carolina Elementary Schools, 1950-1957."
K2060 (ASU)

"A Study of the Motor Ability of a Selected Number of Boys at the Appalachian Elementary School During the 1959-1960 School Year."
K2840 (ASU)

"A Study of the Educational Facilities of the Public Schools of Alexander County, North Carolina."
L1800

"An Analysis of the Types of Retardation in the Elementary Departments of Five Negro Union Schools in Rural Cleveland County."
L3200

"The County Farm Life Schools of North Carolina."
M1930 (ASU)

Education in Buncombe County, 1793-1965.
M5900

Gift from the Hills: Miss Lucy Morgan's Story of Her Unique Penland School.
M7620 (ASU BC ETSU FC WCU WWC)

Gift from the Hills: Miss Lucy Morgan's Story of Unique Penland School.
M7630

"A Study of the Factors Influencing the Election of Home Economics at Clyde A. Erwin High School."
M7650 (WCU)

A Program for the Improvement of Instruction in Spelling in the High Schools of Rutherford County.
N520 (ASU)

Higher Education in North Carolina, 1969-71: Report.
N1710 (LMC ASU)

Jackson County Public Schools, 1853-1954.
N2230 (WCU)

Report: Education in North Carolina, Today and Tomorrow.
N2610 (LMC BC)

College Preparatory Program for Visually Impaired Students: A Cooperative Program Between the North Carolina Commission for the Blind and Western Carolina University.
N2750 (WCU)

"Community Use of School Resources in Cherokee County, North Carolina, as Compared with a National Trend."
O900

Catalog.
P1720 (ETSU)

Public School Education in Buncombe County, 1935-1969.
R2640 (WCU)

"The Growth and Development of Education in Caldwell County."
S800 (ASU)

"An Investigation of the Arithmetical Disabilities of Beginning Ninth Grade Pupils in Appalachian High School."
S3590 (ASU)

Confrontation with the Arts: The Arts in Education — What? For Whom? How? A Symposium Held at Western Carolina University, March 6-7, 1969.
S5230 (ASU WCU)

"The History of Patterson School, Caldwell County, North Carolina."
S6000 (ASU)

"The Development of Secondary Education in Watauga County, North Carolina."
S6560

"A Follow-up of the Fifth Year Graduates of the Department of Administration and School Personnel."
S9330 (WCU)

"The Drop-Out Problem in Harris High School, Spruce Pine, North Carolina."
T8050 (ASU)

"A Survey of Educational Facilities in Cherokee County, North Carolina."
T8060 (ASU)

"Education in Swain County, North Carolina."
T8100

Swain County: Early History and Educational Development.
T8110 (ASU WCU LMC)

"The Development of Negro Education in Rutherford County, North Carolina."
T9510

"A Comparative Study of Changes in Selected Personality Variables in Guidance and Counseling Majors as Compared with Reading Majors at Appalachian State University, 1967-68 Academic Year."
V600 (ASU)

Identifying and Organizing for Individual Needs: An Evaluation.
W6270 (WCU ASU)

"A Study in Student Perceptions of the Person(s) Who Is Performing the Counseling Function at Watauga High School."
W8420 (ASU)

"The Educational Development of Avery County."
W8850 (ASU)

"A History of Richmond Hill Law School."
W9150

EDUCATION — N. C. — BURKE CO.

Interdisciplinary Cultural Heritage Program.
B8640 (WCU)

EDUCATION — OHIO

A Study of Ohio Appalachian and Non-Appalachian Public Secondary School Teacher's Attitudes Towards Selected Aspects of Training and Experience.
H4350

EDUCATION — PA.

Educational Attainment among Pennsylvania Rural Youth.
B8200

"A Study of the Need for Curricular Changes in Secondary Schools in an Economically Distressed Area of Pennsylvania."
B9170

"Socioeconomic Factors Which May Affect Part Time Farmer Education in Butler County, Pennsylvania."
L3310

EDUCATION — PRESCHOOL

The Appalachia Preschool Education: A Home-oriented Approach.
A2690

The Appalachia Preschool Education Program.
A2700

Evaluation Report: Early Childhood Education Program, 1969-1970 Field Test.
A2740

Federal Programs for Young Children.
A3890 (ASU ETSU)

Programs for Infants and Young Children.
A3900 (ASU ETSU)

Early Childhood Education for Appalachia.
A3920 (ASU)

EDUCATION — S. C.

"A Study of Special Services in the Schools of Greenville County, South Carolina."
B1500

Human Gold from Southern Hills, Not a Novel But a Romance of Facts.
C350 (BC)

"An Enrollment Projection for the Estes Elementary School, Anderson, S. C."
C5740 (WCU)

A History of Reidville Private High Schools, Reidville, South Carolina.
E1620 (ASU)

"Educational Development of Oconee County, South Carolina."
E1880

"The Scope of Religious Education in the Secondary Schools of Greenville County, South Carolina."
H460

An Analysis of School District Organization in Greenville County, South Carolina.
M8550

"Teachers Attitudes Toward Their Profession in Greenville County, South Carolina."
T570

Schools for a Growing Democracy.
T8720 (ETSU)

"A Study of Relevant Community Resources for Elementary Classes (Grade 4-6) in Walhalla, S. C."
W7290 (WCU)

"The Extracurricular Activities of Teachers of Greenville County, South Carolina."
W9440

EDUCATION — TENN.

Research for Better Schools: A Federal Projects Workshop for Educational Programs in Tennessee and Appalachia.
A200

"The Effort and Ability of Grainger County to Support Its Schools."
A250 (ASU)

"A Study of Homeschool Contacts and Attitudes toward Participation in Lincoln School, Kingsport, Tennessee."
A600 (ETSU)

"Disciplinary Beliefs and Practices of Selected East Tennessee High School Principals."
A840

"A Study of the Effect of Participation in Co-curricular Activities on Grades of Male Students at Science Hill High School."
A1300 (ETSU)

"Vocational Preferences of Eighth Grade Students at Ross N. Robinson Junior High School, Kingsport, TENNESSEE,
A1540 (ETSU)

"The History of Educational Development in Sullivan County, Tennessee."
A2320

"An Evaluation of the Physical Education Programs in the High Schools in the Washington County School System."
A2330 (ETSU)

"A Follow-up Study of Graduates of Roane County High School, 1946-55."
A2540

"History of the Schools of Johnson City, Tennessee, 1868-1950."
A4550 (ETSU)

"Training for Coal Miners in Cooperation with the Public Schools of Tennessee."
B180

"A Study of the Development of Special Education in Claiborne County."
B200 (ETSU)

"The Diagnosis and Remediation of Comprehensive Skills of a Sixth-grade Class at Rock Creek School in Erwin, Tennessee."
B230 (ETSU)

"An Analysis of Curriculum Offerings, Changes and Trends in Five Selected Hamilton County High Schools."
B610 (ETSU)

"Local History Stories for the Third Grade Washington and Sullivan Counties, Tennessee."
B1180 (ETSU)

"An Educational History of Unicoi County, Tennessee."
B1280

"The Establishment of a Remedial Reading Program at Columbus Powell Elementary School, Johnson City, Tennessee, School Year, 1966-1967."
B1340 (ETSU)

"A Study of the Intramural Sports Program in George W. Vance Junior High School, Bristol, Tennessee."
B1770 (ETSU)

"An Overview of Special Education Services in the Elizabethton City School with Emphasis on the Homebound Program."
B2310 (ETSU)

In Retrospect: Reminiscencies (sic) and Observations of a Hamilton County, Tennessee, Retired Teacher.
B2580

"A Study of McMinn County High School as Determined by Its Graduates."
B3050

"A Proposed Central Supply, Storage, and Technicians' Work Area for the Industrial Education Department of East Tennessee State University."
B3400 (ETSU)

"A Study of School Transportation, Roane County, Tennessee."
B3610

EDUCATION — TENN.

"A Contract Plan of Teaching Fifth Grade at Jefferson Elementary School in Kingsport, Tennessee."
B4320 (ETSU)

"Development of Education in Polk County, Tennessee."
B4480

"A Survey of the Elementary School Libraries in Washington County, Tennessee."
B4560 (ETSU)

"A Program for Developing Mental and Emotional Health in Third-grade Children at Love Street School, Erwin, Tennessee."
B4990 (ETSU)

"The Development of a Prediction Equation for Geometry at Holston Valley High School, Bristol, Tennessee."
B5690 (ETSU)

"A Study of the Trends and Guidelines of Inservice Education Programs in the Carter County Public School System, Carter County, Tennessee."
B6300 (ETSU)

"Appraisal of Vocational Education in Agriculture in Claiborne County by Business and Professional Leaders."
B6460

"An Investigation of the Readability of Textbooks Used in the Intermediate Grades in the Elizabethton, Tennessee, School System."
B6670 (ETSU)

Course of Study for Elementary Schools, Bristol, Tennessee, Grades 1-6.
B6700

New Course of Study; A Teachers Guide for the Elementary Schools of Bristol, Tennessee . . .
B6710 (ETSU)

"An Investigation of the Administrative Duties and Responsibilities of Selected Assistant Principals in Upper East Tennessee."
B6840 (ETSU)

"An Educational and Economic Survey of Bledsoe County, Tennessee."
B7060

"A Seventh Grade Homeroom Guidance Experiment at Elizabethton Junior High School, Elizabethton, Tennessee."
B7330 (ETSU)

"History of Boone's Creek School, 1851-1958."
B7710

"The Applicability of the Industrial Arts Curriculum Project, Construction to the New Junior High Schools in Johnson City."
B7720 (ETSU)

"The Attitudes of a Selected Group of Community Leaders Concerning Consolidation of Five Rural Elementary Schools in Washington County, Tennessee."
B8330 (ETSU)

"A Study of the Media Center in the Individualized Instructional Program of Jefferson Elementary School in Kingsport, Tennessee."
B8580 (ETSU)

"The Predictive Value of the Metropolitan Readiness Tests for First Grade Achievement for Selected Groups of Children in the Johnson City, Tennessee, Public Schools."
B9270 (ETSU)

"An Individualized Reading Program for Students in Grades 4-7 at Hayter's Gap Elementary School, Fall 1970."
C700 (ETSU)

"An Investigation of the Exceptional Child in the Negro Secondary Schools of East Tennessee."
C1860

"A Study of the Language Arts Program in Grade One of the Carter County School System with Some Suggestions for the Improvement of the Program."
C2050 (ETSU)

"A Survey of the Occupational Information Needs of the Ninth Graders of the Elizabethton High School, Elizabethton, Tennessee."
C2790 (ETSU)

"Differences between Negro and Caucasian Students at John Sevier Junior High School, Kingsport, Tennessee."
C2810 (ETSU)

"A Follow-up Study of Twenty-four Dropouts and Twenty-four High School Graduates: Paired at the Seventh Grade Level, North Junior High School, Johnson City, Tennessee, 1953-1962."
C3910 (ETSU)

"A Survey of the Reading Interests of Sixth-grade Pupils in Washington County, Tennessee."
C3980 (ETSU)

"A Study of the Reactions of a Representative Group of Students toward Guidance Received While Attending Bristol, Tennessee, High School, 1958-59."
C4260 (ETSU)

Echo in My Soul.
C4530 (BC)

"A Study to Present the Status of Industrial Arts in the Five White Carter County, Tennessee, High Schools."
C4540 (ETSU)

"Variance in the Theory and Practice of Attendance Workers in Selected East Tennessee Systems."
C5320

"A Comparison of Intelligence in Students with Mixed and Lateral Dominance in Johnson City Vocational Schools."
C5460 (ETSU)

"A Comparison of Intelligence in Students with Mixed and Lateral Dominance in Johnson City Vocational Schools."
C5460 (ETSU)

"A History of Education in Hawkins County with Special Reference to Rock Hill School."
C7250

"An Evaluation of the Remedial Speech Program in the Johnson City Schools."
C7330 (ETSU)

"A Proposed Social Studies Curriculum for the Schools of Johnson City, Tennessee."
C7560 (ETSU)

"A Survey of the Guidance Services Available in the Elementary Schools of Johnson County, Tennessee."
C8040 (ETSU)

"A Study of the Word Recognition Abilities in the Fourth and Sixth Grades of Douglass School, 1957-58, in Kingsport, Tennessee."
C8150 (ETSU)

"A Study of Scott County, Tennessee, and Oneida Independent School District Finances."
C9100

"Educational and Vocational Choices of the 1960 Graduates of Dobyns-Bennett High School, Kingsport, Tennessee."
C9210 (ETSU)

"A Comparative Analysis of Three Evaluation Procedures Used with Kindergarten Pupils at Southside Elementary School, Johnson City, Tennessee."
C9230 (ETSU)

"A Descriptive Study of the Science Fair at Robinson Junior High School, Kingsport, Tennessee, and in Orange County, Florida, for 1960-1962."
C9780 (ETSU)

"Some Types of County and City Library Services to Schools in Tennessee."
C9890 (ETSU)

"Art Handbook for Elementary Teachers of Elizabethton City Schools, Elizabethton, Tennessee."
C9900 (ETSU)

"A Study of Health Instruction in Selected High Schools in Washington County, Tennessee."
D900 (ETSU)

"A Study of the Vocational Guidance Now Provided to Non-college Bound Students in East Tennessee High Schools."
D920

"The Study of the Four High Schools in Claiborne County, Tennessee."
D1010

"A Study of Seven School Communities of Hawkins County, Tennessee."
D1110

"Problem of the Public School Principals in East Tennessee."
D1170 (ETSU)

"A Proposed Nongraded Primary Organization for Central School: Bristol, Tennessee."
D1750 (ETSU)

"The Qualifications and Instructional Program of 100 Elementary Geography Teachers in Northeast Tennessee."
D2460

"A Study of the Reading Abilities of the Economically Deprived Students in the Fourth, Fifth, and Sixth Grades at Stratton Elementary School."
D2520 (ETSU)

History of Pleasant Hill; a History of Pleasant Hill Academy and Who's Who of Alumni.
D2680 (BC)

"Public Education in Tennessee during the Reconstruction Period."
D4060

"What the Patrons of Hawkins County Schools Think about Their Schools."
D4320 (ETSU)

"The Effect of Team Teaching on Academic Achievement, John Sevier Junior High School, Kingsport, Tennessee."
D4330 (ETSU)

"A Proposed Curriculum for Consolidated High Schools in Washington County, Tennessee."
E10 (ETSU)

Research Bulletin.
E70 (ETSU)

Teacher Preparation Programs.
E200 (ETSU)

Teacher Preparation Programs, East Tennessee State College.
E210 (ETSU)

Audio-visual Materials at East Tennessee State College in the Teaching Aids Laboratory: Films, Filmstrips, Disc Recordings, Tape Recordings, Framed Pictures.
E300 (ETSU)

Report.
E330 (ETSU)

The Role and Scope of East Tennessee State University, a Report Submitted to the Tennessee Higher Education Commission, June 1968.
E360 (ETSU)

"An Analysis of Educational Qualifications and Methods of Selection of School Board Members in the First Congressional District of Tennessee."
E820 (ETSU)

"The Reading Habits of 200 Adults in Kingsport, Tennessee."
E990

"An Assessment of Needs and Guidelines for Development of an Industrial Ceramics Program."
E1440 (ETSU)

Helping Our Children Grow.
E1560 (ETSU)

"The Personal Characteristics, Social Background, and Academic Achievements of Forty Non-Promoted Pupils at Kennburg School."
E1690 (ETSU)

"A Proposed Course of Study in Electronics for Johnson City Vocational School's Evening Program."
E1840 (ETSU)

"A Study of the Title I Reading Program During the 1966-68 School Years in Carter County, Tennessee."
E1850 (ETSU)

"A Comparison of Certain Factors Related to Dropouts and Potential Dropouts in South Junior High School."
E2280 (ETSU)
E2330 (ETSU)

"Written Board of Education Policies for Unicoi County, Tennessee."
E2370 (ETSU)

"A Transitional English Program for Crockett High School, Washington County, Tennessee."
F620 (ETSU)

"A Survey of Selected Characteristics of the Washington County, Tennessee, School Teacher."
F910 (ETSU)

"History of Private Educational Institutions of Franklin County, Tennessee."
F1060

"Enriching the Curriculum of South Side School, Johnson City, Tennessee, by Parent Participation."
F1910 (ETSU)

EDUCATION — TENN.

Social and Economic Trends in Tennessee and Their Implications for Education.
F2530 (ETSU)

"A Study of Vocational Education at the Elizabethton, Tennessee, Area Vocational-Technical School."
F2950 (ETSU)

"A Program of Library Instruction for the Ninth Grade Pupils at Jonesboro High School."
F3030 (ETSU)

"A Critical Analysis of the Counselor's Role in Blountville Junior High School."
F3110 (ETSU)
F3630

"A Proposed Master of Arts in Teaching Program for East Tennessee State University."
F3650 (ETSU)

A Study of the Physical Education Problems as Found In Negro Schools in East Tennessee."
F3710

"Effect of Consolidation on Johnson County School, Johnson City, Tennessee."
G330 (ETSU)

"A Study of Certain Phases of the Educational and Economic Conditions of Marion County, Tennessee."
G370

"An Investigation of the Factors Causing Absenteeism at Blountville High School."
G2270 (ETSU)

"A Survey of the Causes of Absences in the Public School System of White County and Sparta, Tennessee."
G2350

"The Development of a Plan for Parent Education for the Speech Handicapped Children in Overton County, Tennessee."
G2760

Old Grandview: Grandview Normal Institute, Grandview, Tennessee, 1884-1919: A History.
G3210

"An Assessment of Why Part-time Under-graduates Are Enrolled at the Kingsport University Center."
G3340 (ETSU)
G3720 (ETSU)

"An Inservice Program to Promote the Use of the John S. Battle High School Media Center Based on a Study of Faculty Attitudes Toward the Use of Instructional Materials and the Media Services Rendered."
G3960 (ETSU)

"A Historical Survey of Education in Warren County, Tennessee."
G4360

"A Study of Special Classes for Educable Mentally Handicapped Children."
G4400 (ETSU)

"A Proposed Method of Instruction Based on the British Infant and Primary Schools for First and Second Year Students at East Side Elementary School."
G4410 (ETSU)

"A Study of Underachieving Academically Talented Students in a Knox County School."
G4420

"A Study of Teacher and Parent Opinion of McMinn County High School, Athens, Tennessee."
G4590

"An Identification of Social-personal Problems in Two Selected Junior High Schools: Implications for Guidance Services."
G4820

"The Development of Education in Rhea County, Tennessee."
G4990

"History of the Development of Education prior to 1900 in Jackson County, Tennessee."
H300

"A Nutrition Survey of Some Eleventh Grade Students in Washington County, Tennessee."
H410 (ETSU)

"An Improved Language Arts Program for a Selected Third Grade at Thomas Jefferson School, Kingsport, Tennessee."
H650 (ETSU)

The Hamilton County Course of Study.
H1100 (ETSU)

"Proposed Curriculum for Sequential Concept Development in Language Arts for Upper East Tennessee Exemplary Kindergarten Project."
H1380 (ETSU)

"A Study of the Physical Education Programs of the High Schools in Carter County, Tennessee."
H2150 (ETSU)

"A Study of a Group of Drop-outs of the Greenville High School."
H2520

"A Study of the Practices and Techniques Used by Principals and Teachers in the McMinn County Schools to Improve School Attendance."
H2590

Education for an Age of Power: The TVA Poses a Problem.
H3170 (ASU)

"Team Teaching at Douglas School, Elizabethton, Carter County, Tennessee."
H3310 (ETSU)

"Professional Characteristics of the Master's Degree Graduates of East Tennessee State University."
H3350 (ETSU)

"An Administrative and Educational Survey of the Schools of Campbell County, Tennessee."
H3370

"A History and Educational Survey of Putnam County, Tennessee."
H3470

"A Study of an Enriched Language Arts Program for Third Grade Students at Fairmont School."
H3690 (ETSU)

"A Survey of Reading Readiness and Reading Achievement of City Kindergarten and Non-kindergarten Children in the First Grades in Elizabethton, Tennessee."
H3780 (ETSU)

"A Proposed Course in Ceramics for the Fine Arts Department of East Tennessee State College."
H3980 (ETSU)

"A Study of the Physical Plants of Blount County High Schools."
H4160

"The Use of Inquiry Learning in Teaching Early Tennessee History."
H5010 (ETSU)

"The Diagnosis and Remediation of Difficulties in Arithmetical Skills of a Seventh-grade Class at Rock Creek School in Erwin, Tennessee."
H5270 (ETSU)

"Significant Factors Influencing Quality and Success of Supervised Farming Programs of Vocational Agriculture Students in Seven Schools of East Tennessee."
H5650
H6020

Clinton, Tennessee: A Tentative Description and Analysis of the School Desegregation Crisis.
H6470

"A Survey of the Qualification of Some Teachers of the Educable Mentally Retarded in East Tennessee."
H6480 (ETSU)

"Educational Facilities and Economic Development of Bristol, 1930-1950."
H6510

"Educational Facilities and Economic Development of Bristol, 1930-1950."
H6520 (ETSU)

"A Study of Absenteeism in the Tazewell County One Room Negro Elementary Schools."
H6630

The Struggle for a State System of Public Schools in Tennessee, 1903-1936.
H6910 (ETSU)

"A Five-year Study of an Educable Mentally Retarded Class in Keystone School, Johnson City, Tennessee."
H7430 (ETSU)

"A Language Arts Program for a Fourth Grade of Culturally Deprived Pupils."
H7500 (ETSU)

"An Educational, Economic, and Community Survey of Blount County, Tennessee."
H7540

"A Study of the Use of Student Library Assistants in the Secondary Schools of East Tennessee."
H7620
H7770 (ETSU)

"A Study of the School Buildings of McMinn County."
H8060

"A Study of Preparatory to Cooperative Development of Board of Education Policies for Morgan County, Tennessee."
H8220

"Learning Opportunities in Science in Six Public Schools in Upper East Tennessee."
H8340 (ETSU)

"A History of Higher Education in Franklin County, Tennessee."
H8390

"Trends in the Social Studies in Eighty Tennessee High Schools, 1931-1952."
H8550

"An Evaluation of the Changes in Reading Achievement Effected by a Federal Project in the Bristol, Tennessee, Elementary Schools."
H8830 (ETSU)

"A Study of Some Problems of Eighth Grade Students of John Sevier Junior High School, Kingsport, Tennessee."
I840 (ETSU)

"A Study of School Transportation, Anderson County, Tennessee."
I950

"A Study of the Procedures Used for the Recruitment, Selection, and Assignment of Professional Personnel in Six Selected East Tennessee School Systems."
J330 (ETSU)

Educational and Vocational Goals of Rural Youth and Their Parents in Tennessee.
J540 (ASU)

"The History of Watauga Academy of Butler, Tennessee."
J630 (ASU)

"A Multilevel Approach to Reading for One Section of a Sixth Grade Class in Keystone Elementary School Year, 1965-1966."
J680 (ETSU)

Curriculum for the Observation and Practice School.
J1350 (ETSU)

The Wataugan Annual.
J1360 (ETSU)

Evaluation Report, North Junior High School, Johnson City, Tennessee.
J1450 (ETSU)

Manual for Receiving and Processing Instructional Materials.
J1470 (ETSU)

To the Top with the Toppers; the History of Science Hill High School Football, 1920-1970, with Official Team and Individual Statistics.
J1550 (ETSU)

Evaluative Study of South Junior High School, Johnson City, Tennessee; Completed by the Visiting Committee March 15-18, 1965. . .
J1560 (ETSU)

Evaluative Study Made in Science Hill High School, Johnson City, Tennessee . . . March 4-8, 1951.
J1570 (ETSU)

"A Survey of the Problems of Freshmen Student Nurses at Memorial Hospital and a Proposed Guidance Program."
J1650 (ETSU)

"A Study of Reorganization of Attendance Centers in Hawkins County, Tennessee."
J1940

"A Study of the Drop-outs from the Bristol, Tennessee, School Systems in Grades 8-12 from 1946 to 1951."
J1950

"A Survey of ESEA Title 1 Equipment and Its Extended Usage in Carter County, Tennessee."
J2400 (ETSU)

Evaluative Study; Made in Jonesboro High School, Jonesboro, Tennessee . . . Completed by the Visiting Committee April 8-11, 1957. . .
J2680 (ETSU)

EDUCATION — TENN.

"A Study of the School Transportation Problem in Grainger County, Tennessee."
J2700

"A Survey of Programs Offered for the Academically Talented Students at Dobyns-Bennett High School, Kingsport, Tennessee, and the Resulting Implications for the School Library."
K210 (ETSU)

"Problems of Beginning Teachers in Washington County, Tennessee."
K370 (ETSU)

"A History of St. Andrew's School."
K740

"An Analysis of the Relationship of Religious Commitment and Alienation Among High School Students of Bristol, Tennessee."
K1620 (ETSU)

"The Enriched Curriculum as a Means of Meeting the Emotional and Social Needs of First Grade Children in Washington County."
K1800 (ETSU)

"Some Problems Concerning the Relations of Administrators and Beginning Teachers in the Washington County School System, 1955-1956."
K1820 (ETSU)

"What Citizens of Sullivan County Know about Their Schools."
K2290

"Flexible Scheduling in Secondary Schools."
K2530 (ETSU)

New Dimensions in Mathematics for the Elementary Schools in Kingsport, Tennessee.
K2540 (ETSU)

"Carter County's Greatest Need in the Homebound Program of Services for Exceptional Children, 1952-54."
K2660 (ETSU)

"A History of the Secondary Schools of Cocke County, Tennessee."
K2810
K2890 (ETSU)

The Other Children: A Seatwork Activities Bulletin.
K2910 (ETSU)

"A Study of the Use of Periodicals Received by the Dobyns-Bennett Senior High School Materials Center, Kingsport, Tennessee."
K3110 (ETSU)

"An Experimental Study of the Effect of an Individualized Reading Program on Third, Fourth, and Fifth Grade Students in the Thomas Jefferson School, Kingsport, Tennessee."
K3170 (ETSU)

"A Guidance Program for Elizabethton High School."
L30 (ETSU)

"A Survey of Physical Education Programs for Educable Mentally Retarded Students in Tennessee Public Elementary Schools."
L40 (ETSU)

"The Development of Education in Roane County, Tennessee."
L80

"Some Factors Affecting School Attendance as a Family Problem, as Revealed by a Comparison of Two Groups of Families in Washington County, Tennessee, 1951-1952."
L350 (ETSU)

"A Distributive Education Program for Washington County, Tennessee, High Schools Based on an Occupational Survey of the County."
L590 (ETSU)

"Flexible Scheduling in Secondary Schools."
L960 (ETSU)

"Development of a Comprehension Skills Program for the Primary Educable Mentally Retarded Class in Kingsport, Tennessee."
L1470 (ETSU)

"A Study of the Working Relationships of the Agriculture Extension Service and the Vocational Agriculture Program in East Tennessee."
L1750

"The Status of Geography Teaching in the Schools of Carter County, Tennessee."
L2140 (ETSU)

"A Study to Determine the Major Causes of Withdrawal from Science Hill High School During the 1965-1966 School Year."
L2820 (ETSU)

"A Comparison of Tennessee's Revenue Potential, Utilization, Tax Burden, and Educational Effort with Selected States."
L2870 (ETSU)

"A Study of Public School Finance in Hancock County, Tennessee."
L2920

Echoes from the Foothills.
L2930

"An Economic and Educational Survey of Rogersville Community."
L3210

"A History of the Webb School of Knoxville, Tennessee."
L3560

"A Survey of Guidance Activities in the Public Secondary Schools of Tennessee."
L3620 (ETSU)

"The Reactions of the Students of the Jonesboro, Tennessee, Middle School to Newbery Book Award Winners."
L3720 (ETSU)

"An Educational Survey of the Elementary Schools of Grundy County, Tennessee."
M240

Knoxville-Knox County Consolidation and the County and City School Systems.
M510

"A Survey of Industrial Arts Students at Dobyns-Bennett High School, 1950-1955."
M590 (ETSU)

"A Study of the Status of Rural Teachers in East Tennessee."
M980 (ETSU)

"A Comparative Analysis of the Results of the Kraus-Weber Test for Minimum Muscular Fitness in Four of the Elementary Schools of Johnson City, Tennessee."
M1290

"A Follow-up Study of the 1959-1963 Graduates of Langston High School, Johnson City, Tennessee."
M1890 (ETSU)

"Human Resources Available to the Schools of Washington County, Tennessee."
M2020 (ETSU)

"A Follow-up Study of the Physics Students at Science Hill High School from 1944-1955."
M2470 (ETSU)

"A Study of the Effect of Individualization on Achievement in Language Arts at North Side Elementary School."
M2850 (ETSU)

"A History of Education in Jefferson County, Tennessee."
M2950

Public Administration Study: Marion County, Tennessee.
M3210

"A Guidance Program for the Schools of Hawkins County."
M3240

A Golden Book of the History and Tradition of Bristol, Tennessee, High School, 1915-1965.
M3450 (ETSU)

"History of the Development of Negro Public Schools in Bradley County, Tennessee, 1931-1951."
M3580

"Pupil Transportation in Pickett County, Tennessee."
M3590

"A Team Teaching Approach to Reading in the Fourth Grade at Dickson Elementary School in Kingsport, Tennessee, 1964-1965."
M3760 (ETSU)

Dr. Z. C. Graves and the Mary Sharp College, 1850-1896.
M3850

"A Survey of the Training and Experience of Secondary Principals in Five Upper East Tennessee Counties."
M3960 (ETSU)

"A Study of Problems of Junior High School Students of Johnson City, Tennessee."
M4220 (ETSU)

"A Study of Living Conditions in the Pittman Center Community, 1934-1935."
M4400

Higher Education in Tennessee.
M5140 (ETSU)

"An Individualized Reading Program for a Fifth Grade Group of Students at Andrew Johnson School, Kingsport, Tennessee."
M5420 (ETSU)

"A Comparison of Socio-economic Status and Art Interest of Two Sixth Grade Groups in Washington County, Tennessee."
M5550 (ETSU)

"School Transportation Costs in Unicoi County: A Comparison of Publicly-owned and Privately-owned Systems."
M5790 (ETSU)

"An Investigation of the Reading Interest of the Junior High School Students in Greenville, Tennessee."
M6070

"A Search for a Meaningful Program in Mathematics for the Slow Learner in the Seventh Grade in the Bristol, Tennessee, City Schools."
M6200 (ETSU)

"An Analysis of the Possibilities for Local Support of Education in Pickett County, Tennessee."
M6270

"An Analysis of the Errors in Word Recognition Made by Pupils of One Section Each of the Second Through Sixth Grades of Lynn Avenue School, 1956-57, in Elizabethton, Tennessee."
M6380 (ETSU)

"An Experimental Program in Grouping for Third Grade at Fairmont School, Johnson City, Tennessee."
M6430 (ETSU)

"Some Factors Affecting Retardation in the Six High Schools of Washington County."
M6580 (ETSU)

"The Effects of a Physical Education Program on the Motor Skills of Selected Severely Retarded Children in Johnson City, Tennessee."
M7120 (ETSU)

"A Program of Folk Songs Used to Enrich and Implement the Social Studies Program in Grades Four, Five and Six at North Side School, Johnson City, Tennessee."
M7380 (ETSU)

"An Educational Survey of Carter County, Tennessee."
M7460

Staub School. A Brief History of Its First Fifty Years' Service to the Community.
M7610

"A Study of Ninth-grade Science Students in Phase Two at John Sevier Junior High School, Kingsport, Tennessee, 1967-1968."
M7690 (ETSU)

The Itakha Annual.
M7990 (ETSU)

"A Proposed Individualized Primary Mathematics Program for Holston Heights Elementary School, Bristol, Tennessee."
M8290 (ETSU)

"A Simplified Library Program for the Elementary Schools of Carter County, Tennessee."
M8320 (ETSU)

"The Status of Public Relations Activities in the Secondary Schools of Greene County, Tennessee."
M8440

"Materials for Teaching Social Studies in a Selected Fifth Grade at Asbury School, Johnson City, Tennessee, 1956-57."
M9090 (ETSU)

Schoolhouse in the Foothills.
M9110 (ASU BC ETSU WWC)

"What the Patrons of the Elementary School of Bristol, Tennessee, Think About Their Schools."
M9300 (ETSU)

"A Study of the Reorganization of the Attendance Centers of the Grainger County School System."
N830

"An Analysis of Putnam County's Ability to Support Education Based on a Study and Comparison of Assessed Value to Real Value of Property."
N860

EDUCATION — TENN.

"The Opinions of Certain Groups Toward Teaching the Bible in Unicoi County High School."
N2910 (ETSU)

"An Improved Language Arts Program for a Selected Third Grade at Henry Johnson School in Johnson City, Tennessee."
O830 (ETSU)

"A Comparison of Parents and Teachers Viewpoints Relative to Teacher Competencies in Johnson City, Tennessee."
O980

The Fiftieth Anniversary of the Rogersville Synodical College.
P190

"Teaching Exceptional Children in the Fifth Grade of Lincoln Elementary School — Kingsport, Tennessee."
P350 (ETSU)

"Teacher Education in Tennessee."
P480 (ETSU)

"A Study of the Physical Education Program at the Junior High School, Johnson City, Tennessee."
P1110 (ETSU)

"A Speech Improvement Program in Kindergarten of the Johnson City, Tennessee, Public School System."
P1560 (ETSU)

"Educational, Economic and Community Survey of Scott County, Tennessee."
P1630

"A Study of Some Differentiating Characteristics of Dropouts and Graduates of Lamar and Jonesboro High Schools."
P1650 (ETSU)

"The Factors Affecting Absenteeism in the Sixth, Seventh, and Eighth Grades at Barnes Elementary School, Washington County, Tennessee."
P2360 (ETSU)

"The Attitudes of Students and Parents Toward the Division of Morristown, Tenn., High School."
P2600 (ETSU)

"A Program for Mentally Retarded, Elizabethton City Schools."
P2890 (ETSU)

"A Study of Academic Achievement of Band Students and Non-band Students, Blountville High School (1964-1967)."
P3070 (ETSU)

"A Comparative Study of the Relationship Between ACT Composite Scores and GPA of Washington County Students at East Tennessee State University, 1965-66."
P3940 (ETSU)

"A History of Education in McMinn County, Tennessee."
P4090

"The History and Development of Education in Knox County, Tennessee."
P4120

"Coordination of Physical Education and Community Recreation in Ashe, Avery, and Watauga Counties."
Q170 (ASU)

"A Study of School Transportation, Hawkins County, Tennessee."
R170

"Negro Education in Cocke County."
R180

"Guidance in the Selection of Elective Courses for the Students of Tennessee High School."
R520 (ETSU)

"An Economic, Educational, and Social Survey of Franklin County, Tennessee."
R570 (ASU)

"Business Education in the Kingsport Area High Schools: An Evaluation of Their Business Graduates."
R1030 (ETSU)

"An Analysis of Faculty and Administrative Attitudes Toward Teacher Corps Interns in Carter County, Tennessee."
R1430 (ETSU)

"A Proposed Health Instruction Program for Upper Elementary Grades Adaptable to Carter County."
R1730 (ETSU)

"A Reading Improvement Program Developed by a Classroom Teacher for a Selected Seventh-grade Group at Elizabethton Junior High School."
R1850 (ETSU)

"The Development of Public Education in Campbell County, Tennessee."
R2240

"A Role Definition of Secondary School Assistant Principals in Washington County, Virginia."
R2880 (ETSU)

"What the Eighth Grade Patrons of Scott County Think about Their Schools."
R3200

"Specific Techniques Used to Improve the Reading of Three Groups of Children in the Eighth Grade at Robinson Jr. High School in Kingsport, Tennessee."
R3210 (ETSU)

Light from Many Candles: A History of Pioneer Women in Education in Tennessee.
R3550 (ETSU)

"A Survey of Vocabulary Weaknesses of 417 Freshmen at East Tennessee State University."
R3710 (ETSU)

"An Educational Study of Bradley County, Tennessee."
R3830

"An Analysis of the Relationship Between the Anxiety Level and the Academic Performance of Freshmen at East Tennessee State University for the Year 1965."
R3860 (ETSU)

"The Reading Interests of Students as Revealed in a Study of an Individualized Reading Program at Pond Gap School, Knoxville, Tennessee."
S850

"Socio-economic Status of Teachers in Kingsport, Tennessee, 1968-1969."
S1530 (ETSU)

"A Study of the Attitudes Toward Modern Mathematics of Secondary Mathematics Teachers in Upper East Tennessee."
S1550 (ETSU)

Adult Education, a part of a Total Educational Program. A Description of the Educational and Training Program of the Tennessee Valley Authority.
S1560

Adult Education, a Part of a Total Educational Program. A Description of the Educational and Training Program of the Tennessee Valley Authority.
S1570 (ASU)

Elementary Education in Two Communities of the Tennessee Valley: A Description of the Wilson Dam and Gilbertsville Schools.
S1580 (ETSU)

"A Study of Pupil Transportation in Polk County, Tennessee."
S1810

"A History of Education in Scott County, Tennessee."
S2070

"The History and Educational Influence of Douglas School, Elizabethton, Tennessee, 1900-1965."
S2550 (ETSU)

"A Follow-up of Industrial Arts Graduates of East Tennessee State College from 1930 to 1953."
S2630 (ETSU)

"Trends and Needs of the Washington County, Tennessee, Schools, 1948-1966."
S2790 (ETSU)

"A Survey of Comprehension Weaknesses of 417 East Tennessee State University Freshmen."
S3280 (ETSU)

"A Curriculum in Agricultural Education for Two Consolidated High Schools in Washington County, Tennessee."
S4220 (ETSU)

"A Comparative Study of Twenty-five Children Who Attended Project Head Start and Twenty-five Children Who Did Not: Paired at the First-grade Level in the Jonesboro Elementary School, Jonesboro, Tennessee, 1965-1966."
S4290 (ETSU)

"The Social, Economic, Cultural, Religious and Family Educational Backgrounds of Recent Dropouts from Bristol, Tennessee, High School."
S4340 (ETSU)

"A Study of Financing a Program for Education in Sevier County, Tennessee."
S4370

"History of Educational Development in Jackson County, Tennessee, 1800 to 1950."
S4550

"An Accounting Study of the Educational Progress of Knoxville Negro Pupils Over a Sixteen-year Period."
S4590

"An Economic, Social and Educational Survey of Campbell County, Tennessee."
S4690

"The Teaching of French, Grades 3-6, Lincoln School, Kingsport, Tennessee, 1965-1966."
S4930 (ETSU)

"The Relationship between Reading Capacity and Reading Achievement of One Hundred and Twenty-three Third Grade Children of Morrison and Hamblen County, Tennessee."
S4940

Level of Education and Estimated Rate of School Dropout in the Tennessee Valley.
S5110 (ASU)

"Diagnosis and Remediation of Difficulties in Arithmetic in Fifth Grade at West Side School, Elizabethton, Tennessee, 1956-57."
S5240 (ETSU)

"Written Board of Education Policies for Hawkins County, Tennessee."
S5270 (ETSU)

Evaluation of the East Ridge High School, Chattanooga, Tennessee; Completed by the visiting Committee March 5-9, 1962. . . .
S5690

Evaluative study made in Chattanooga High School, Chattanooga, Tennessee; completed by Visiting Committee March 12-16, 1950.
S5700

"A Study of Readiness Needs of the First Grade Children at Henry Johnson School, 1952-1953."
S6430 (ETSU)

"An Educational and Economic Survey of Monroe County, Tennessee."
S6550

"A Study of a Possible Plan for Further School Consolidation in Hawkins County."
S6620 (ETSU)

"A Study of Twenty Superior Students at Ketron High School."
S6630 (ETSU)

"The Use of Locational Analysis in the Determination of School Sites: A Case Example, Carter County, Tennessee."
S7310 (ETSU)

"The Status of Eighth Grade Social Science in Washington County, Tennessee, 1960-61."
S7640 (ETSU)

"What Citizens of Carter County Know about Their Schools."
S7700 (ETSU)

"Local Ability to Support Education in Monroe County, Tennessee."
S7750

"The Influence of Community Pressure Groups on School Principals in Carter County."
S7840 (ETSU)

"A Study of Pupil Transportation in Scott County, Tennessee."
S8160

"Determining the Most Effective Method by Which the Children in Each of Three Groups in the First Grade at South Side School, Carter County, Tennessee, Learn to Recognize Words."
T470 (ETSU)

"A Tentative Health Instruction Program for the Secondary Schools of Carter County, Tennessee."
T480 (ETSU)

"A Survey of Innovative Practices in East Tennessee Secondary Schools."
T550 (ETSU)

"A Study of the Factors Which Might Affect Achievements in Reading in the First Grade of Anderson School, Bristol, Tennessee."
T750 (ETSU)

EDUCATION — TENN.

"The Development of a Middle School Program for the Morristown City School System, Morristown, Tennessee."
T760 (ETSU)

Campbell County School Survey.
T1090

Grainger County Schools Survey Report.
T1100

A Guide for Developing and Evaluating Language Arts Courses of Study, Grades 1-12.
T1110 (ETSU)

Jefferson County Survey Report.
T1120

Report of the Survey of the Schools of Blount County, Tennessee, for School Year, 1934-1935.
T1130 (ETSU)

Washington County Survey Report.
T1140 (ETSU)

Curriculum Improvement Conference.
T1310 (ETSU)

Curriculum for the Observation and Practice School.
T1330 (ETSU)

Public Education in Tennessee, Grades 1-12: A Report to the Education Survey Subcommittee.
T1430

Directory of Member Schools.
T1810 (ETSU)

Highlander Folk School Audio Collection.
T2070 (ETSU)

Highlander Folk School Manuscript Records Collection, 1932-1966.
T2080 (LMC)

"A Study of the Effects of the Elementary-Secondary Education Act of 1965 Upon Education at Greendale Elementary School."
T7680 (ETSU)

"An Analysis of the Homebound Program for Exceptional Children in Unicoi County."
T8260 (ETSU)

"An Educational Survey of Unicoi County, Tennessee."
T8440

"An Analysis of the Continuing Consultant Program and the Development of a Profile of Schools in the Tennessee Appalachia Educational Cooperative."
T8810

D-Days at Dayton: Reflections on the Scopes Trial.
T8900 (ASU BC)

"The Driving Habits and Experiences of One Hundred Graduates of Tennessee High School, Bristol."
T9430 (ETSU)

"A Study of High Schools in Hawkins County, Tennessee."
V80

"Robert Jefferson Breckinridge as an Educational Administrator."
V460 (ETSU)

"The Development of Education in Monroe County, Tennessee."
V480

"A Study of the Ability of Cocke County to Support Its Schools."
V670

"Characteristics of School Board Members of Selected Upper East Tennessee School Districts."
W260 (ETSU)

Torchlights to the Cherokee: The Brainerd Mission.
W350 (ASU ETSU BC)

"An Educational Survey of Grundy County, Tennessee."
W450

"A Proposal for the Two-Dimensional Design Course at Virginia Intermont College, Bristol, Virginia."
W760 (ETSU)

Bulletin.
W1040 (BC)

School Board Policies.
W1050 (ETSU)

"A Study of the Cooperative Vocational Education Program at Boones Creek High School."
W1430 (ETSU)

"A Study of Selected Fifth Grade Children in Lincoln School, Kingsport, Tennessee."
W1460 (ETSU)

"The Library in the Literature Program at Daniel Boone High School, Washington County, Tennessee."
W1530 (ETSU)

Development of the Tennessee State Educational Organization, 1796-1929.
W5550 (ETSU BC)

"A Comparative Study of the Science Achievement of Fifth and Sixth Grades in Bristol, Tennessee, 1958-1962."
W5780 (ETSU)

"An Analysis of Problems of Eighth and Ninth Grade Students in the Junior High School of Johnson City, Tennessee."
W6110 (ETSU)

"Language Experience Approach to Remedial Reading: Fourth Grade, Dunbar School, 1965-66."
W6200 (ETSU)

"A Comparison of Sources and Expenditures of the Funds Raised by the Schools and Organizations in Carter County with the School Budget of 1960-61."
W6550 (ETSU)

"A Study of Pupil Achievement in the Nongraded John F. Hay Elementary School in Morristown, Tennessee."
W6680 (ETSU)

"A Study of Cooperative Education in Relation to the Industrial Technology Program of East Tennessee State University."
W7020 (ETSU)

"The Planning of Art Facilities for Dobyns-Bennett High School, Kingsport, Tennessee."
W7030 (ETSU)

"The Achievement of Selected Economically Deprived Secondary School Male Athletes as Related to Non-athletes in Blount County, Tennessee, Schools."
W7220 (ETSU)

"A Survey of Co-curricular Programs in the Five High Schools of Carter County, Tennessee."
W7440 (ETSU)

"A Study of Secondary Schools of Morgan County."
W7450

A Century of Maryville College, 1819-1919, a Story of Altruism.
W7490 (ASU BC)

"Diagnosis and Remediation of Reading and Personality Problems of a Second Level First Grade at Valley Pike School, Sullivan County, Tennessee."
W7540

"A Survey of Reading Achievement of First Grade Pupils in Unicoi County."
W8020 (ETSU)

"The Determination of a Predition Equation for Algebra I at Elizabethton High School Utilizing Selected Variables."
W8580 (ETSU)

"A Study of the Mathematics Background of 2250 Dropouts from Tennessee High Schools, 1965-1966."
W9430 (ETSU)

"An Analysis of the Sources and Expenditures of Internal Funds in the High Schools of Carter County, Tennessee."
Y280 (ETSU)

EDUCATION — TENN. — WASHINGTON CO. — ACADEMY

Washington College: A Study of an Attempt to Provide Higher Education in Eastern Tennessee.
C1420 (ETSU BC)

EDUCATION — VA.

Thomas Jefferson and Education in a Republic.
A4970 (ETSU)

The Church, the State, and Education in Virginia.
B2820 (MHC)

Vocational and Educational Goals of Rural Youth in Virginia.
B4220

Highlights of Vocational and Educational Goals of Rural Youth in Virginia.
B4850

"Guidelines for the Cooperating Teachers in Bristol, Virginia, High School."
B5480 (ETSU)

"A Study of a Small School in the Mountains of Virginia."
B5820

"An Evaluation of the Elementary School Libraries in Washington County, Virginia."
C6510 (ETSU)

List of Books and Related Materials About Virginia for use of Schools.
C9490

Three Quarters of a Century at Martha Washington College.
C9880 (ASU)

Hornbook of Virginia History.
D130

"A Study of the Problems of Sixth Grade Students in Selected Schools of Scott County, Virginia."
D400

"The Role of the Bristol, Virginia, Elementary School Principals in Classroom Visitation."
E1630 (ETSU)

Announcement.
E2060 (ASU)

"A Discriminative Study of Trends and Innovations: Modern Educational Concepts and Their Application to the Norton, Virginia, City Schools."
F810 (ETSU)

"Evaluation of Reading in the Bristol, Virginia, Schools with a Suggested Corrective Program."
F3230 (ETSU)

A Study of Library Services in Some Southwest Virginia Schools."
F3720 (ETSU)

"An Inspection of Standardized Test Results in the Schools of Bath County, Virginia."
G140 (ETSU)

"A Comparison of Special Characteristics of College Bound Seniors and Non-college Seniors from Virginia High School, Bristol, Virginia."
H830 (ETSU)

"A Study for a Guidance Program at Jonesville High School, Jonesville, Virginia."
H3500 (ETSU)

A History of Education in Virginia.
H4260 (ETSU FC)

A Curriculum Study in a Mountain District.
H4530 (ASU ETSU BC)

"The Third-grade Social Studies Program in Bristol, Virginia, 1969-70."
K2680 (ETSU)

"A Study Designed for the Attitudes of the Negro Teachers of Bedford County, Virginia Toward In-Service Teacher Education."
M3140

"An Evaluation of the Impact of the Vocational Education Act of 1963 on Agricultural Education in the Blue Ridge Area of Southwestern Virginia."
N950 (ETSU)

"A Study of the Factors Affecting the Holding Power of High Schools in a Certain Mountainous Rural County."
O890

"Those Who Enroll for Vocational Agriculture in West Virginia, Considering Certain Scholastic Achievements and Some Background Factors."
P960
P1080

The Schools of Winchester, Virginia.
Q80

"A Study of the Economically and Educationally Deprived Students of Bristol, Virginia, Junior High School."
Q120 (ETSU)

Charles Lewis Cocke, Founder of Hollins College.
S5200

Richard D. B. Sutherland; An Early Leader of Education in Sandy Basin.
S9220

"A Consultative Conference in Science for Elementary Teachers in Bristol, Virginia, 1955-56."
V70 (ETSU)

Hollins College, 1842-1942; an Historical Sketch, Being an Account of the Principal Developments in the One-Hundred-Year History of Hollins College.
V610 (BC)

EDUCATION — VA.

Virginia: A Geographical and Political Summary, Embracing a Description of the State, Its Geology, Soils, Minerals and Climate; Its Animal and Vegetable Productions; Manufacturing and Commercial Facilities; Religious and Educational Advantages; Internal Improvements, and Form of Government.
V700 (BC)

The Military History of the Virginia Military Institute from 1839 to 1865.
W7880 (ASU)

EDUCATION — VA. — TECHNICAL

"A Comparative Study of Twenty Business Trainees of the Gate City, Virginia, MDTA Program with Twenty Business Graduates of the Washington County, Virginia, Technical School."
S6460 (ETSU)

EDUCATION — W. VA.

"Leisure Time Interests and Activities of Girls in High School."
A2270

Handbook of Appalachian Materials.
A2300

"The Pattern and Nature of the Informal and Formal Institutional Contacts Participated in by Residents of New Hill."
B1270

The Incentive Approach to State School Administration: Change in Two Pilot Centers, Mason County, West Virginia, and Doddridge County, West Virginia, 1959-60.
B3640

"Superstitions about Food and Health among Negro Girls in Elementary and Secondary Schools in Marion County, West Virginia."
B4600

"The Status of the Secondary School Principal of West Virginia During the Years 1935-36."
B5220

"A Survey of the Status of the Retired School Teacher in West Virginia."
B7670

"Legislative Politics and the Public Schools in West Virginia, 1933-1958: A Twenty-five Year History."
C1900 (ASU BC)

Education in Anttal West Virginia, 1910-1975.
C3000 (ASU)

Community Schools in Action.
C4220 (ASU)

"Attitudes toward Education and the Schools in a Rural Industrialized County."
C5010

"The Educational Development of Tyler County, West Virginia."
C5310

"Food Habits of a Selected Group of Pupils in the Wellsbury High School, West Virginia."
C6920

"A History of Education in Wyoming County, West Virginia."
C7040

"A Study of the Status of the Elementary Principal of Logan County, West Virginia."
C8320

"Cost of Operating the Schools in Raleigh County, West Virginia, from 1940-50."
C8360

"Current and Future Needs for Vocational Education in Jackson County, West Virginia."
C9770

"Problem Survey of the Elementary and High School at Crum, West Virginia."
D1360

"A Proposed Program of Public Relations for the Schools of Mason County, West Virginia."
D2320

"Adult Basic Education: A Study of the Backgrounds, Characteristics, Aspirations, and Attitudes of Undereducated Adults in West Virginia."
D2530

"West Virginia Higher Education Long-range Enrollment and Operating Budget Projections."
D3970

"The Status of School Board Members of West Virginia."
D4080

E950

"History of Education in McDowell County, West Virginia."
F3310

"The Leisure Time Activities and Interests of the Boys of Spencer High School."
H280

"History of Education of Marion County, West Virginia."
H5570

"Analysis and Projection of Population and School Enrollment in Harrison County."
H6340

The Need for a New Perspective of the School Plant and School Organization in Taylor County.
H6350

"A Proposed Course of Study for General Shop in the John Sevier Junior High School."
H6370 (ETSU)

Research, Education and Mine Personnel Safety in W. Va.
H6550 (BC)

"Editorial Attitudes of West Virginia Newspapers toward School and Education."
K1830

Vocational Agricultural Instruction for Adult Farmer Classes in Preston County.
L2730

"A Survey of Withdrawals from Mullins High School in 1954-1958."
L3410

"An Analysis of Achievement, Motivational, and Perceptual Variables Between High School Seniors Who Do and Do Not Attend College."
M130

"History of Education in Logan County, West Virginia."
M1050

"Socioeconomic Characteristics of Young Farmers Enrolled in Vocational Agriculture Classes in West Virginia."
M1500

In West Virginia, It Is Working: One Teacher Education Center in Action.
M2690 (WCU BC ASU)

"A Study of the Status of the Elementary School Principal of West Virginia."
M5110

"A Survey of the Public Relations Programs of West Virginia High Schools."
M5590

"Community Uses of Public School Buildings in West Virginia."
M6570

"Excess Levies and School Bond Issues in Wyoming County (West Virginia) from 1933-1951."
M7570

"Chief Causes of Non-attendance in the Schools of McDowell County, West Virginia."
M8170

West Virginia Conference to Explore Ways in which Space Science and Technology Might be Applied to the Development of West Virginia's Industry and Educational Institutions, 1964.
N10

"A Follow-up of 1952 Graduates of Logan High School, Logan, West Virginia."
O850

"The Relation of the Hot Lunch Program to the Progress of Pupils in the Deep Water School, West Virginia."
P2030

Improving County School Systems in West Virginia, The School Bond Issues and Its Management.
P2760

The School Law of West Virginia.
P4040 (ASU)

Educational Renaissance in Appalachia; an Evaluation.
P4940

Development of Tele-lecture and Associated Media Systems for the Improvement of Nursing Education in West Virginia.
P4950

Project Era: A Three Year Study of a Follow Through Program. A Longitudinal Study of the Monongalia County Follow Through Program.
P4960

"Factors Influencing Social Status, Social Participation in the Elementary School of Crum, West Virginia."
R200

"A Survey of Boone County (West Virginia) School Buildings."
S350

The 1965 Head Start Psychological Screening Program; Final Report on the Data Analysis Conducted Under a Contract Between the West Virginia Office of Economic Opportunity and West Virginia University.
S810 (ASU)

"Why Pupils Drop Out of School Before Finishing the Grades in the Rural Schools of West Virginia."
S2160

The Learning Experiences of Youth Groups: A Study of 4-H Clubs in Barbour County, West Virginia.
S3790

Rural Industrialization: A Case Study in Educational Values and Attitudes.
S3810 (ASU)

A History of Shepherd College, Shepherdstown, West Virginia.
S4210 (ASU BC)

History of Summersville Normal School, Summersville, West Virginia, 1893-1914.
S4530 (ASU)

"A Study of Students Dropping Out of Wyoming County, West Virginia, High Schools for the 1950-51 School Term."
S7250

The Effects of School Bus Transportation upon the Achievement of Students in Calhoun County, High School.
S8820

Public Higher Education in West Virginia.
S9120 (ASU)

"An Assessment of the Characteristics, Education, and Training of Public School Superintendents in Southern Appalachia and in West Virginia."
T490

Training Program for Auxiliary Health and Education Personnel in Nine Counties of Southern West Virginia.
T9150 (ASU)

Opportunities for Improving Administration of Federal Program of Aid to Educationally Deprived Children in West Virginia, Office of Education, Department of Health, Education, and Welfare.
U3070

Biennial Report.
W3540 (ETSU)

History of Education in West Virginia.
W3550 (ASU)

Year Book.
W3620 (ETSU)

The School Law of West Virginia.
W4130 (BC)

The School Law of West Virginia.
W4140 (BC)

School Laws of West Virginia.
W4150 (ETSU)

The School Law of West Va. and Opinions of the Attorney-General and Decisions of the State Superintendent of Free Schools.
W4160 (BC)

A Survey of the Educational Programs of the West Virginia Public Schools.
W4170 (BC)

A Survey of the Educational Programs of the W. Va. Public Schools.
W4180

A Digest of a Report of a Survey of Public Education in the State of West Virginia.
W4190 (BC)

A New Plan for the Allocation of State Aid for Schools; Report by the Joint Committee on Gov. and Finance and the Commission on Interstate Cooperation.
W4200

A Study of State Institutions of Higher Education.
W4210 (BC)

EDUCATION — W. VA.
Survey of Education in West Virginia.
W4310 (ETSU)
Reference Manual of Occupational Information Materials.
W4320
A Catalog of Educational Change in West Virginia.
W4330 (BC)
History of Education in West Virginia.
W4340 (BC)
The History of Education in W. Va.
W4350 (BC)
Superintendent of Free Schools Biennial Report of the State Superintendent of Free Schools of West Va.
W4370
Biennial Report of the State Superintendent of Free Schools of West Virginia.
W4430 (ETSU)
The History of Education in West Va.
W4470 (BC)
Publications of the Faculty and Staff, West Va. University, 1960-1969.
W4500 (BC)
Annual Report of the Board of Governors . . . 1st — July 1, 1972/Oct. 1, 1932.
W4510 (BC)
Approaches to University Extension Work with the Rural Disadvantaged: Description and Analysis of a Pilot Effort.
W4730 (ASU)
West Virginia Graduate Research Studies in Education, 1894-1965: A Bibliographical Listing.
W6050 (ETSU)
School-community Improvement, a Report of the Greenbrier County Program.
W7360 (ASU WCU)

EDUCATION — W. VA. — HISTORY
A History of Education in West Virginia, from Early Colonial Times to 1949.
A2000 (ASU)

ELECTIONS — APP.
"Presidential Voting Patterns in Appalachia: An Analysis of the Relationship Between Turnout, Partisan Change, and Selected Socioeconomic Variables."
R2520

ELECTIONS — KY.
"Population Trends and Other Factors Influencing the Voting Habits of the Cumberland Valley Region of Southeast Kentucky."
R1210
Presidential Politics in Kentucky, 1824-1948: A Compilation of Election Statistics and an Analysis of Political Behavior.
S2230 (LMC)

ELECTRIC POWER
Fuels and Hydro Power Used in the Production of Electricity for Public Use in the United States (1933 through 1936).
A2950
"Struggle for Power: The Relations between the Tennessee Valley Authority and the Private Power Industry, 1933-1939.
B2990
All Down the Valley.
B3620 (BC ASU WCU LMC)
"Municipal Ownership of Public Utilities in Chattanooga, Tennessee."
B7940
"The Demand for Coal for Power Generation in the Tennessee Valley and the Impact of Changing Demand Patterns on a Supplying Coal Field."
C3360
"Some Factors That Have Influenced the Location of the Electric Power Plants in the Greater Pittsburgh Area."
C4040
Power Supply in the Development of the Region.
C4230
Sparks at the Grassroots; Municipal Distribution of TVA Electricity in Tennessee.
H6090
Sparks at the Grassroots, Municipal Distributions of TVA Electricity in Tennessee.
H6100 (ASU WCU LMC BC)
"Prelude to TVA: The Wadsworth-Kahn Bill, 1919-1921."
P3550
The Tennessee Valley Authority: A Case Study in the Economics of Multiple Purpose Stream Planning.
R470 (ASU BC UNCA)
"An Economic Analysis of Competition Between the Tennessee Valley Authority and Private Power."
S1880
Proceedings.
S5650
Annual Report of the Distributors of TVA Power, 1937-Date.
T2260
The Cherokee Project, a Comprehensive Report on the Planning, Design, Construction, and Initial Operations of the Cherokee Project.
T2400
The Colbert Steam Plant; a Report on the Planning, Design, Construction, Costs, and First Power Operations of the Initial Four-Unit Plant.
T2440
Comparison of Coal-Fired and Nuclear Power Plants for the TVA System.
T2450
The Douglas Project; a Comprehensive Report on the Planning, Design, Construction, and Initial Operations of the Douglas Project.
T2540
. . . Drawings for the Chickamauga Project. . . .
T2550
Electrical Demonstration Branch Electricity in Dairying.
T2580
Municipalities (Electric Departments Only) and Cooperatives Purchasing Power from Tennessee Valley Authority. Financial Statements for the Fiscal Year Ended June 30, 1940; a Report from the Comptroller to the Directors of Tennessee Valley Authority.
T3060
The Paradise Steam Plant; a Report on the Planning, Design, Construction, Costs, and First Power Operations of the Initial Two-Unit Plant.
T3160
Power Annual Report. 1960-.
T3240
. . . A Technical Review of the Chickamauga Project . . .
T3610
. . . A Technical Review of the Norris Project.
T3640
. . . A Technical Review of the Wheeler Project.
T3660
The Tellico Project of the TVA.
T3670
TVA Electricity Rates, A Statement of Facts.
T3770
TVA's Influence on Electric Rates.
T3830
TVA Power, 1966.
T3850
TVA's Influence on Electric Rates.
T3950
The Upper Holston Projects: Watauga, South Holston, Boone, and Fort Patrick Henry; a Comprehensive Report on the Planning, Design, Construction, Initial Operations, and Costs of Four Hydro Projects in the Holston Basin at the Eastern Tip of Tennessee.
T4040
Pumps and Plumbing for the Farmstead.
T4210
. . . Statistical Bulletin no. 1.
T4270
Drawings for the Boone Project by Tennessee Valley Authority, Divisions of Engineering and Construction.
T6270
Drawings for the Fontana Project.
T6300
Drawings for the Fort Loudoun Project by the Tennessee Valley Authority, Divisions of Engineering and Construction.
T6310
Drawings for the Hiwassee Project.
T6320
Drawings for the Johnsonville Steam Plant.
T6330
Drawings for the Ocoee no. 3 Project.
T6350
Drawings for the Watauga and Wilbur Projects.
T6380
Engineering Data.
T6420
The Kingston Steam Plant; a Report on the Planning, Design, Construction, Costs, and First Power Operations.
T6500
Transmission System of Tennessee Valley Authority.
T6560
Electricity Sales Statistics, Monthly Report no. 1.
T6570
Industrial Development in the TVA Area During 1962.
T6580
Report on the Plateau Coal Field of Alabama.
T6590
Report on the Reserves of Coal in a Part of the Warrier Coal Field of Alabama.
T6600
Electricity and Your Farm; a Manual for Instruction on the Practical Uses and Application of Electricity in Rural Areas.
T6610
Comparison of Coal-Fired and Nuclear Power Plants for the TVA System.
T6620
Rate Reductions by the Distributors of TVA Power.
T6640
Rate Reductions by the Distributors of TVA Power.
T6650
TWA Power. 1953-.
T6660
TVA Power and Taxes.
T6670
Industrial Development in the TVA Area, 1955-Date.
T6690
Electricity Sales Statistics.
T6700
All-Electric Schools . . . in the Tennessee Valley.
T6720
Underground Residential Distribution.
T7570
Necessity for a Load Building Program.
W2900
Problems on a Large Power System with Large Generating Units.
W2910
David Lilienthal, Public Servant in a Power Age.
W5830 (BC)
"An Economic Evaluation of the Power Program of the Tennessee Valley Authority."
W6920
History of the Georgia Power Company; 1855-1956.
W9530 (BC)

ELECTRIC POWER — APP.
To Bankers Trust Company and F.N.B. Close, Trustees; Trust Deed.
A3430
Profitable Boat Manufacturing Opportunities in Virginia. Introductory Report to Boat Manufacturers.
A3460
Safety Hand Book.
A3470
United States of America, on the Relation of Oscar L. Chapman, Secretary of the Interior, Petitioner v. Federal Power Commission, Virginia Electric and Power Company, et al. Virginia REA Association, et al. On Writs of Certiorari to the United States Court of Appeals for the Fourth Circuit. Brief for Appalachian Electric Power Company, Intervenor.
A3490
Report.
A3510
Public Organization of Electric Power: Conditions, Policies, and Program.
B2030
The Relation of the Southern Appalachian Mountains to the Development of Water Power.
L1660 (ASU BC)
The Hiwassee Valley Projects.
T2880
How Cheap Electricity Pays Its Way. TVA.
T2890

ELECTRIC POWER — APP.
. . . Hydraulic Data Activities of the Tennessee Valley Authority . . .
T2900
. . . Investment of the Tennessee Valley Authority in Wilson, Norris, and Wheeler Projects. Letter from the Chairman of the Board of the Tennessee Valley Authority Transmitting a Report on the Investment and the Allocation of the Investment of the Authority in the Wilson, Norris, and Wheeler-Projects, Pursuant to Section 14 of the Tennessee Valley Authority Act of 1933 . . .
T2960
Municipal and Cooperative Distributors of TVA Power; Annual Report.
T3050
Norris Dam . . .
T3120
. . . The Norris Project, A Comprehensive Report on the Planning, Design, Construction, and Initial Operations of the Tennessee Valley Authority's First Water Control Project . . .
T3130
Survey of Electrical Appliances in the Homes and Farms of the TVA Area.
T3570
Land Acquisition in TVA. An Analysis of TVA Land Acquisition, Land Management, and Family Relocation Procedures as They Could Relate to the Missouri Valley Development. Statements Presented Before the Select Subcommittee on Real Property Acquisition of the Committee on Public Works.
T5150
Boone Project, Hydraulic Model Studies.
T5520
Fontana Project Hydraulic Model Studies.
T5540
Tennessee and Cumberland Valley Reservoirs Level Storage Tables and Profile Storage Charts.
T5560
The Colbert Steam Plant; a Report on the Planning, Design, Construction, Costs, and First Power Operations of the Initial Four-Unit Plant.
T6240
ELECTRIC POWER — N. C.
The Dissent of Commissioner Thomas R. Eller, Jr., in the Nantahala Power and Light Company Transfer Case.
E1640 (WCU)
Directory of Electric Agencies Serving Rural North Carolina.
N2530 (LMC)
ELECTRIC POWER — TENN.
Electricity on Farms and in Rural Homes in the East Tennessee Valley.
B5350
Should We Have More TVA's?
D230
"A Study of the Influence of Certain Personal and Other Factors on the Number of Observed Unsafe Acts and Injuries Sustained by Employees of Kingsport Power Company."
L2590 (ETSU)
"A Study of Factors Related to the Entrophication of Boone Reservoir, Tennessee."
L3640 (ETSU)
Towers of Power Back Industrial Opportunities in Tennessee, First Public Power State.
T1740
God's Valley: People and Power Along the Tennessee River.
W5840 (ASU WWC BC)
ELECTRIC POWER — VA.
Hydro-electric Power in the Southwest of Virginia.
A3440
Order of Business for Real Estate and Rights of Way.
A3450
Appalachian Power Company and the American Electric Power System.
A3520
ELECTRIC POWER — VA. — REUSENS STATION
The Story of the Reusens hydro-electric station, tracing its development over a thirty-year period 1903-1931.
A3480
ELECTRIC POWER — W. VA.
Order of Business for Real Estate and Rights of Way.
A3450
When Men and Mountains Meet.
A3500
ELK RIVER
Elk River Watershed; Summary of Resources.
T2590
Floods on Elk River and Norris Creek, in Vicinity of Fayetteville, Tennessee.
T7010
Floods on Elk River in Vicinity of Fayetteville, Tennessee.
T7020
EMIGRATION
Ireland and the American Emigration, 1850-1900.
S1140 (ASU)
EMPLOYMENT AND UNEMPLOYMENT
Manpower Study of Appalachian Alabama.
A960
A2682 (ASU)
A2683 (ASU)
Appalachia — An Economic Report: Trends in Employment, Income and Population.
A3580 (WCU ASU ETSU)
Appalachia — An Economic Report: Trends in Employment, Income and Population. Supplement.
A3590 (ASU)
Growth in Employment by County, 1940-1950 and 1950-1960.
A5090
In Aid of the Unemployed.
B2490
Labor Force Participation in the Pittsburgh Standard Metropolitan Area.
B3320
Labor Supply and Farm Production on Eastern Kentucky Farms.
B5270
Resources and People in East Kentucky: Problems and Potentials of a Lagging Economy.
B5790 (ASU WCU LMC ETSU BC)
Rural Underemployment and Land Use in a Marginal Agricultural Area of West Virginia.
B6150
The Changing Kentucky Population: A Summary of Population Data for Counties.
B7170
Employment Problems of the Eastern Kentucky Mountain People.
F1990
Manpower Education in the North Carolina Appalachian Region.
H1320 (ASU)
"The Efficacy of the Labor Migration with Special Emphasis on Depressed Areas."
M4710
Employment Opportunities and Usable Agricultural Skills in Non-Farm Agricultural Occupations in Appalachia.
M7410
Migration into and out of Depressed Areas.
M8460
State Population, Net Migration, Labor Force and Industry Employment Trends to 1975.
N250
P4720
Education, Migration and Economic Life Chances of Male Entrants to the Labor Force from a Low Income Rural Area.
S1240 (ASU)
Career Placement and Economic Life Chances of Young Men from Eastern Kentucky.
S1250 (ASU)
Human Crisis in the Kingdom of Coal.
S5010 (ASU BC)
Employment, Unemployment, and Low Incomes in Appalachia.
U2590
EMPLOYMENT AND UNEMPLOYMENT — APP.
A2681
Manpower Report for the Appalachian Coal Industry.
A3760 (ASU)
Employment and Underemployment of Rural People in the Appalachian Area.
A4630
The Southern Highlands, an Inquiry into their Needs, and Qualifications Desired in Service Workers in the Mountain Country.
C6360
Report of Social Welfare Manpower Project for Appalachia, July 15, 1969 to August 31, 1970.
C7890 (ASU BC)
The Southern Highlands: An Inquiry into Their Needs, and Qualifications Desired in Church, Educational, and Social Service Workers in the Mountain Country.
C7960 (BC ASU)
"Regional Labor Markets and Migration: An Analysis of Gross Migration in the United States, 1955-1960."
F10
Growth and Labor Characteristics of Manufacturing Industries.
F1600
Employment in Appalachia: Trends and Prospects.
F3750 (ASU)
Employment, Unemployment, and Low Incomes in Appalachia.
F3760 (LMC ASU)
Migration and Changes in the Quality of the Labor Force.
G670 (ETSU)
Underemployment Concept, Way to Measure Need for Economic Development in Appalachia.
G1260
Report of a Social Welfare Manpower Project for Appalachia, July 15, 1969 to August 31, 1990.
H6300 (BC ASU)
"Measuring and Analyzing the Impact of Employment Generation Benefits of a Public Water Resource Development Project in Appalachia."
K2050
A Report of the Findings of a Demonstration Retraining Project for Long Term Unemployed Persons in a Rural Appalachian Mountain Area.
M3150 (ASU)
Economic Redevelopment Research: Population, Labor Force and Unemployment in Chronically Depressed Areas.
S1730
Problems of Underemployed Rural People.
T4520
Differentials in Farm Income and Employment in the Tennessee Valley Region Counties.
T5180
Manufacturing Employment in the Tennessee Valley Region.
T5300
The Labor Force Characteristics of Women in Low-Income Rural Areas of the South.
T7630
Family Characteristics of the Long-term Unemployed: A Report on a Study of Claimants under the Temporary Extended Unemployment Compensation Program, 1961-1962.
U1180
Causes of Unemployment in Coal and Other Specified Industries. Report Pursuant to S. Res. 274 with Supplemental View of Mr. Taft.
U1930
Manpower Development in Appalachia: An Approach to Unemployment.
Z80 (UNCA ASU LMC ETSU)
EMPLOYMENT AND UNEMPLOYMENT — KY.
Application for Community Organizing Program in the Four Counties of the Upper Kentucky River Area Development Council.
A3040
Structure of Employment in the Area Development Districts of Kentucky, 1960-1970: Analysis and Implications.
C1500
Population Estimates for Kentucky Counties and Economic Area, July 1, 1958.
D250 (ASU)
"The State Employment Service in Appalachian Kentucky."
E1160
Kentucky Employment Trends from 1951 to 1963 with Projections to 1965-1975.
F3780
Kentucky Employment Trends from 1951 to 1963, with Projections to 1965-75.
F3790
Rural Manpower in Eastern Kentucky: A Study of Under-Employment among Rural Workers in Economic Area Eight.
G170

EMPLOYMENT AND UNEMPLOYMENT — KY.
Utilization of Rural Manpower in Eastern Kentucky.
G180
Sugar Creek Resettlement Area, Leslie County, Kentucky. A Report of a Conference on Planned Relocation, New Housing and Local Employment in Eastern Kenucky, 1966.
G1040
Utilization of Rural Manpower in Eastern Kentucky.
K950
Dropouts and Jobs: The Report of the Kentucky Conference on Youth, August 22-23, 1963.
K1000
Analysis of Manufacturing Employment Trends in Kentucky Counties, 1960-64, and Their Economic Significance.
K1340
Analysis of Occupational Trends in Kentucky from 1950 to 1960, with Projections to 1975.
K1350
EMPLOYMENT AND UNEMPLOYMENT — MD.
Employment and Underemployment in Rural People: Low Income Groups in Arkansas, Maryland, and West Virginia.
L1860
Occupational Outlook for Washington County.
M3890
EMPLOYMENT AND UNEMPLOYMENT — N. C.
Papers.
C6410
Area Manpower Review: Asheville Standard Metropolitan Statistical Area — Buncombe County.
N2240 (ASU WWC)
Smaller Communities Program: Manpower Resources Report — Avery County.
N2250 (WCU)
Measuring Unemployment in Small Rural Labor Areas: Report on a Household Survey Conducted in Alleghany County, N. C., 1969.
N2260
EMPLOYMENT AND UNEMPLOYMENT — OHIO
"The Occupational Adaptation of a Selected Group of Eastern Kentuckians in Southern Ohio."
C9190
"Analysis of Costs and Benefits from Commuting for Employment among Core and Satellite Communities in the Appalachian Region of Ohio."
E2360
Employment, Income and Resources of Rural Families of Southeastern Ohio.
S7230
EMPLOYMENT AND UNEMPLOYMENT — PA.
Available for Work: The Pennsylvania Unemployment Compensation Interpretation.
B7550
A Community Attack on Chronic Unemployment: Hazleton, Pennsylvania, a Case Study.
F700
"Labor Market Adjustments in a Depressed Area."
G2740
"The Non-attainment of Adolescents' Occupational Aspirations: A Longitudinal Study of Rural Pennsylvania Males."
K3450
Employment Trends in the Pittsburgh Metropolitan Area.
P3180
Availability for Employment of Rural People in the Upper Monongahela Valley.
P3700
The Population and Employment Outlook for the Anthracite Region of Pennsylvania.
R1560
EMPLOYMENT AND UNEMPLOYMENT — S. C.
Survey of Unemployment Compensation Beneficiaries in Anderson, Greenville, Spartanburg Counties, South Carolina.
C4940
EMPLOYMENT AND UNEMPLOYMENT — TENN.
Manpower and Employment Trends in Tennessee.
E650
"Job Opportunities for High School Graduates in the Manufacturing Industries in Washington County, Tennessee."
F3620 (ETSU)
A Study of the Chattanooga Labor Market Area.
T1170 (ETSU)
Population and Labor Force Characteristics of Tennessee Counties.
T1180
Tennessee Employment Statistics, 1939-1964.
T1190
Tennessee Manpower: Current Trend and Future Projections.
T1200
Migration and Industrial Development in Tennessee.
T1420
Population, Labor Force, and Employment Projections and Interpretations.
T1680
Population and Labor Force Characteristics of Tennessee Counties.
T1800
EMPLOYMENT AND UNEMPLOYMENT — VA.
Redevelopment Manpower Report for the Norton-Big Stone Gap Area.
V890 (ASU)
EMPLOYMENT AND UNEMPLOYMENT — W. VA.
A5690
Job Development for the Hard-to-employ.
F680 (ETSU)
"A Case Study of the Effects of Automation on Employment in a West Virginia Continuous Process Industry."
F930
Employment Changes in West Virginia, 1948-1958.
F1250 (ASU)
The Unemployed in West Virginia.
G680 (ASU)
The Labor Force in West Virginia — A Study of Its Growth and Characteristics.
H1440
Employment Security in West Virginia.
H3940
Employment and Underemployment in Rural People: Low Income Groups in Arkansas, Maryland, and West Virginia.
L1860
"The Problems of Unemployment in a Depressed Area."
M3490
"Some Employment Opportunities of the Vocational Agriculture Trainees of Gilmer County."
M4020
Employment and Underemployment of Rural People in the Upper Monongahela Valley, West Virginia.
M5230
"Occupational Status and Reasons for Leaving the State of West Virginia."
P3100
A Case Study of Six Central West Virginia Counties of the Interrelationships of Factors Leading to Persistence of Low Incomes and Unemployment with Corrective Suggestions.
S7460
ENGINEERING
Development of the Tennessee River Waterway.
B4710
E2000
The Douglas Project; a Comprehensive Report on the Planning, Design, Construction, and Initial Operations of the Douglas Project.
T2540
. . . Drawings for the Chickamauga Project. . . .
T2550
. . . Drawings for the Guntersville Project. . . .
T2560
Engineering Geology and Mineral Resources of the Tennessee Valley Authority Region.
T2600
. . . Engineering Geology of the Tennessee River System. . . .
T2610
Facts About Major TVA Dams.
T2640
Facts About TVA Steam Plants.
T2670
The Fontana Project: A Comprehensive Report on the Planning, Design, Construction, and Initial Operations of the Fontana Project.
T2770 (WCU)
The Fort Loudoun Project; a Comprehensive Report on the Planning, Design, Construction, and Initial Operations of the Fort Loudoun Project.
T2820
General Outline of Chemical Engineering Activities.
T2840
The Guntersville Project. A Comprehensive Report on the Planning, Design, Construction, and Initial Operations of the Guntersville Project . . .
T2860 (BC)
. . . Investment of the Tennessee Valley Authority in Wilson, Norris, and Wheeler Projects. Letter from the Chairman of the Board of the Tennessee Valley Authority Transmitting a Report on the Investment and the Allocation of the Investment of the Authority in the Wilson, Norris, and Wheeler-Projects, Pursuant to Section 14 of the Tennessee Valley Authority Act of 1933 . . .
T2960
The Johnsonville Steam Plant; a Comprehensive Report on the Planning, Design, Construction, Costs, and First Power Operations of the Initial Six-Unit Plant.
T2980
. . . The Norris Project, A Comprehensive Report on the Planning, Design, Construction, and Initial Operations of the Tennessee Valley Authority's First Water Control Project . . .
T3130
Surveying, Mapping and Related Engineering.
T3580
. . . The Wheeler Project, A Comprehensive Report on the Planning, Design, Construction, and Initial Operations of the Wheeler Project . . .
T4090
Engineering Data.
T5240
Measurements of the Structural Behavior at Fontana Dam.
T5250
Measurements of the Structural Behavior of Norris and Hiwassee Dams.
T5260
The Colbert Steam Plant; a Report on the Planning, Design, Construction, Costs, and First Power Operations of the Initial Four-Unit Plant.
T6240
Construction Plant for TVA Projects.
T6250
Drawings for the Boone Project by Tennessee Valley Authority, Divisions of Engineering and Construction.
T6270
Drawings for the Chatuge and Nottely Projects by the Tennessee Valley Authority, Engineering and Construction Departments.
T6280
Drawings for the Cherokee Project by the Tennessee Valley Authority, Engineering and Construction Departments.
T6290
Drawings for the Fontana Project.
T6300
Drawings for the Fort Loudoun Project by the Tennessee Valley Authority, Divisions of Engineering and Construction.
T6310
Drawings for the Hiwassee Project.
T6320
Drawings for the Johnsonville Steam Plant.
T6330
Drawings for the Kentucky Project.
T6340
Drawings for the Ocoee no. 3 Project.
T6350
Drawings for the South Holston Project.
T6370
Drawings for the Watauga and Wilbur Projects.
T6380
Drawings for the Watts Bar Project.
T6390
. . . Drawings for the Wheeler Project . . .
T6400
Engineering Data.
T6410

ENGINEERING
Measurements of the Structural Behavior at Fontana Dam.
T6440
Measurements of the Structural Behavior of Norris and Hiwassee Dams.
T6450
. . . Plans and Specifications for the Norris Dam .. .
T6470
Plans and Specifications for the Norris Dam.
T6480
The Bull Run Steam Plant; a Report on the Planning, Design, Construction, costs, and First Power Operations of the Initial One-Unit Plant.
T6490
The Melton Hill Project; a Report on the Planning, Design, Construction, Initial Operations, and Costs.
T6510
The Paradise Steam Plant; a Report on the Planning, Design, Construction, Costs, and First Power Operations of the Initial Two-Unit Plant.
T6520
Research in the Fields of Civil Engineering, Mechanical Engineering, Instrumentation. 1965/66-.
T6530
TVA and Engineering: Electrical, Civil, Mechanical, Chemical, Architectural, Nuclear, Fuels.
T6860
Hydraulic Model Investigations of Lock Filling and Emptying Systems.
T7410
Maps and Surveys.
T7450
ENGINEERING — APP.
Draft Paper Discussing the Background of the Problems in Appalachia.
C6450
Engineering and the Future of Appalachia.
K160
Analytical Index of Chemical Engineering Publications Patents and Reports.
T6120
Preparation of Research and Engineering Reports.
T6210
Drawings for the Appalachian Project.
T6260
ENGINEERING — VA.
Bulletin.
V1150 (BC)
ENGLISH
Scotch-Irish and English Proverbs and Sayings of the West Branch Valley of Central Pennsylvania.
S3150 (ASU)
ENVIRONMENT
Voices from Earth, a Collection of Writings on Environment.
A4500 (ASU)
ENVIRONMENT — TENN.
"The Effects of Environment on Public Planning: The Case of Appalachian Planning in Tennessee."
G470 (LMC)
ETHNIC GROUP — VA.
White, Red, and Black: The Seventeenth-century Virginian.
C8570 (ETSU)
ETHNIC GROUPS
The Melungeons (Their Origin and Kin).
B760 (ASU LMC WCU FC BC)
British Family Names: Their Origin and Meaning with Lists of Scandinavian, Frisian, Anglo-Saxon and Norman Names.
B1060 (ASU)
"The Melungeons of Newman's Ridge."
B1440 (ETSU ASU)
Documents, Chiefly Unpublished, Relating to the Huguenot Emigration to Virginia and to the Settlement at Manakintown, with an Appendix of Genealogies, Presenting Data of the Fontaine, Maury, Dupuy, Trabue, Marys, Chastain, Cooke, and Other Families.
B6770 (ASU)
Race Elements in the White Population of North Carolina.
C6750 (ASU BC)
A Historical Account of the Settlements of Scotch Highlanders in America Prior to the Peace of 1783: Together with Notices of Highland Regiments and Biographical Sketches.
M2010 (ASU)
The Highland Scots of North Carolina.
M5240 (LMC BC)
The Highland Scots of North Carolina, 1732-1776.
M5250 (ASU LMC WWC)
The German Settlers in Lincoln County and Western North Carolina.
N1240 (LMC)
The Colony Bernstadt in Laurel County, Kentucky.
S920
The Scotch-Irish in History as Master Builders of Empires, States, Churches, Schools and Civilization.
S2500 (ASU BC)
Scotch-Irish and English Proverbs and Sayings of the West Branch Valley of Central Pennsylvania.
S3150 (ASU)
Charn Cuimhne to Our Scots of North Carolina.
S4650 (ASU)
North Carolina Palatine-Germans (Futch Family).
S4660 (ASU)
Memorials of the Huguenot's in America, with Special Reference to Their Emigration to Pennsylvania.
S6590 (ASU)
Pennsylvania German Pioneers: A Publication of the Original Lists of Arrivals in the Port of Philadelphia from 1727 to 1808.
S7790 (ASU)
Pennsylvania German Pioneers: A Publication of the Original Lists of Arrivals in the Port of Philadelphia from 1727 to 1808.
S7800 (ASU)
Poor Whites of the South.
W4950
ETHNIC GROUPS — ALA. — GERMAN
The German Settlement in Cullman County, Alabama: An Agricultural Island in the Cotton Belt.
K2980 (BC)
ETHNIC GROUPS — APP.
Ethnology in Folklore.
G2450 (ASU)
ETHNIC GROUPS — APP. — IRISH
Scotch and Irish Seeds in American Soil: The Early History of the Scotch and Irish Churches, and Their Relations to the Presbyterian Church of America.
C8450 (BC)
ETHNIC GROUPS — APP. — SCOTCH
Scotch and Irish Seeds in American Soil: The Early History of the Scotch and Irish Churches, and Their Relations to the Presbyterian Church of America.
C8450 (BC)
ETHNIC GROUPS — APP. — SCOTCH-IRISH
Mountain Spirits, a Chronicle of Corn Whiskey from King James Ulster Plantation to America's Appalachians and the Moonshine Life.
D20 (BC ASU)
The Scotch-Irish: Or, the Scot in North Britain, North Ireland, and North America.
H1520 (ASU BC)
The Scotch-Irish: Or, The Scot in North Britain, North Ireland, and North America.
H1530 (ASU BC)
ETHNIC GROUPS — DUTCH
Surnames in the United States Census of 1790; an Analysis of National Origins of the Population.
A2110
The Dutch and Quaker Colonies in America.
F1280 (ASU)
A Collection of Upwards of Thirty Thousand Names of German, Swiss, Dutch, French, and Other Immigrants in Pennsylvania from 1727 to 1776.
R4300 (ASU)
ETHNIC GROUPS — ENGLISH
Emigrants from England, 1773-1776.
F2370 (ASU)
ETHNIC GROUPS — FRENCH
The French Blood in America.
F2240 (ASU)
A Collection of Upwards of Thirty Thousand Names of German, Swiss, Dutch, French, and Other Immigrants in Pennsylvania from 1727 to 1776.
R4300 (ASU)
ETHNIC GROUPS — FRENCH HUGUENOT
Huguenot Pedigrees.
L660 (ASU)
Family Names of Huguenot Refugees to America.
L1060 (ASU)
ETHNIC GROUPS — GERMAN
German Element in the United States.
F370
German New River Settlement, Virginia.
H4270 (ASU FC)
"The German Swiss Settlers at Gruetli, Tennessee."
J150 (ASU)
Early Eighteenth Century Palatine Emigration: A British Government Redemptioner Project to Manufacture Naval Stores.
K2820 (ASU)
The German and Swiss Settlements of Colonial Pennsylvania: A Study of the So-called Pennsylvania Dutch.
K3380 (ASU)
History of Daniel's Evangelical Lutheran & Reformed Churches, Lincoln Co., N. C.
N1200
A Collection of Upwards of Thirty Thousand Names of German, Swiss, Dutch, French, and Other Immigrants in Pennsylvania from 1727 to 1776.
R4300 (ASU)
History of the German Element in Virginia.
S1180
The Pennsylvania Germans of the Shenandoah Valley.
S4620 (ASU)
Lists of Germans From the Palatinate Who Came to England in 1709.
T9270 (ASU)
Virginia's First German Colony.
V350 (ASU FC)
German Element of the Shenandoah Valley of Virginia.
W1740 (BC)
The German Element of the Shenandoah Valley of Virginia.
W1750 (ASU)
Gravestone Inscriptions: From 61 Graveyards in Frederick County and the Counties That Were Once a Part of Frederick County and Includes the Inscriptions from the "Old Lutheran and German Reform Graves" in Mt. Hebron Cemetery.
W7590 (ASU)
Virginia Germans.
W9810
Wartburg: Dream and Reality of the New Germany in Tennessee.
W9820
Zirkle Family in America, Germany to America.
Z130
ETHNIC GROUPS — GERMAN — SWISS
The German-Swiss in Franklin County, Tennessee: A Study of the Significance of Cultural Considerations in Farming Enterprises.
K2990 (ASU BC)
ETHNIC GROUPS — GERMANS
Surnames in the United States Census of 1790; an Analysis of National Origins of the Population.
A2110
History of the German Settlements and of the Lutheran Church in North and South Carolina, from the Earliest Period of the Colonization of the Dutch, German and Swiss Settlers to the Close of the First Half of the Recent Century.
B3200 (ASU)
Emigrants From the Palatinate to the American Colonies in the 18th Century.
K3200 (ASU)
ETHNIC GROUPS — IRISH
Surnames in the United States Census of 1790; an Analysis of National Origins of the Population.
A2110
A History of the Irish Settlers in North America, from the Earliest Period to the Census of 1850.
M1450 (ASU)

ETHNIC GROUPS — IRISH
A Guide to Irish Surnames.
M2130 (ASU)
More Irish Families.
M2140 (ASU)
Supplement to Irish Families.
M2150 (ASU)
Corpus Genealogiarum Hiberniae.
O140 (ASU)
The Irish in America: Immigration, Land, Probate, Administrations, Birth, Marriage, and Burial Records of the Irish in America in and about the Eighteenth Century.
O150 (ASU)
Ireland and the American Emigration, 1850-1900.
S1140 (ASU)
ETHNIC GROUPS — N. C. — ITALIAN
The Waldenses of Burke County.
C8560 (ASU WCU LMC)
ETHNIC GROUPS — NEGROES
Free Negro Labor and Property Holding in Virginia, 1830-1860.
J160 (ETSU)
"A History of the Development of Schools for Negroes in Walker County, Georgia."
J170
ETHNIC GROUPS — PA.
"They Walk These Hills: A Study of Social Solidarity among the Racially-mixed People of the Ramapo Mountains."
C5590 (ASU)
ETHNIC GROUPS — SCOTCH-IRISH
Chronicles of the Scotch-Irish Settlement in Virginia.
A5480 (ASU)
Chronicles of the Scotch-Irish Settlement in Virginia, Extracted from the Original Court Records of Augusta County, 1745-1800.
A5490 (ASU)
Scotch Irish Pioneers in Ulster and America.
B5170 (ASU)
Donald McElroy, Scotch Irishman.
C220 (ASU BC)
Chronicles of the Scotch-Irish Settlement in Virginia.
C2740 (BC ASU)
Chronicles of Scotch-Irish Settlement in Virginia.
C2750
Scotch-Irish Settlers in the Valley of Virginia.
C3960 (BC)
Ulster Emigration to Colonial America, 1718-1775.
D2240 (ASU)
The Scotch-Irish in America.
F1920
The Scotch-Irish in America.
F1930 (ASU)
The Scotch-Irish in Northern Ireland and in the American Colonies.
G2030 (ASU)
The Scotch-Irish: A Social History.
L2400 (ASU BC)
ETHNIC GROUPS — SCOTCH-IRISH — PA.
Scotch-Irish of Colonial Pennsylvania.
D2870
The Scotch-Irish of Colonial Pennsylvania.
D3880
ETHNIC GROUPS — SCOTS
The Clans, Septs and Regiments of the Scottish Highlands.
A330 (ASU)
Emigrants from Scotland to America, 1774-1775.
C410 (ASU)
Old Scottish Customs, Local and General.
G4980 (ASU)
ETHNIC GROUPS — SWISS
How the Swiss Farmers Operate on the Cumberland Plateau.
A1860
Lists of Swiss Emigrants in the Eighteenth Century to the American Colonies.
F360 (ASU)
"The German Swiss Settlers at Gruetli, Tennessee."
J150 (ASU)
The German and Swiss Settlements of Colonial Pennsylvania: A Study of the So-called Pennsylvania Dutch.
K3380 (ASU)
"Agricultural and Social Aspects of the Swiss Settlement in Grundy County, Tennessee."
N600

A Collection of Upwards of Thirty Thousand Names of German, Swiss, Dutch, French, and Other Immigrants in Pennsylvania from 1727 to 1776.
R4300 (ASU)
ETHNIC GROUPS — TENN.
Briefe aus den Vereinigten Staaten von Nord-amerika in die Heimath, mit besonderer Rucksicht auf deutsche Auswanderer.
B2080
"German and Swiss Colonization in Morgan County, Tennessee."
C7160 (ASU)
ETHNIC GROUPS — WELSH
Surnames in the United States Census of 1790; an Analysis of National Origins of the Population.
A2110
Welsh Settlement of Pennsylvania.
B7450 (ASU)
Merion in the Welsh Tract, With Sketches of the Townships of Haverford and Padner.
G2170 (ASU)
The Cymry of '76: Or, Welshmen and Their Descendants of the American Revolution.
J2270 (ASU)
ETHNIC GROUPS — WELSH — PA.
Welsh Founders of Pennsylvania.
G2180 (ASU)
FAIRS AND FESTIVALS
Premium List and Prospectus.
A3110 (LMC)
FAMILIES AND FAMILY LIFE
Characteristics of Families on Small Farms.
B2000
"Needs and Interests in Family Relationships of a Selected Group of West Virginia Eighth and Ninth Grade Pupils, 1948-1949."
B7020
The Farm Family in a Kentucky Mountain Neighborhood.
B7190
Legacy of Love.
D1130
Southern Appalachian Migration.
D1410
Living Conditions and Population Migration in Four Appalachian Counties.
D2790
We Live with the Wheel Chair.
E860 (ASU)
Report of a Workshop on the Southern Mountaineer in Cincinnati.
G4210 (ASU)
Rural Social Organization of Frederick County, Maryland.
G4250
Socio-cultural Adaptation of Newcomers to Cities in the Piedmont Industrial Crescent.
G4850
Family Ties, Migration, and Transitional Adjustment of Young Men from Eastern Kentucky.
S1260
Research Design, Field Work Procedures, and Data Collection Problems in a Follow-Up Study of Young Men from Eastern Kentucky.
S1280
A Profile of the Appalachian Family.
W2480
FAMILIES AND FAMILY LIFE — APP.
"Analysis of the Values and Value Systems Reported by Students, The General Public, and Educators in a Selected Appalachian Public School District."
B9390
"The Relation of Level of Living to Selected Additional Characteristics of Central Appalachia Rural Families."
C2920 (ASU)
Church and Family in Modern Rural Appalachia.
C4860 (ASU)
From the Freedom of the Mountains to the Hurly-burly City.
C6050
Our Changing Rural Society — Perspectives and Trends.
C7350
"Alienation Among Low-income People in Appalachia."
C9170 (LMC ASU)

Appalachian Fertility Deline: A Demographic and Sociological Analysis.
D1660 (ASU WCU LMC ETSU BC UNCA)
Fertility Data for the Southern Appalachian Region.
D1670
"Human Fertility in the Southern Appalachian Region: Some Demographic and Sociological Aspects."
D1680 (ASU)
The Longest Mile.
G710 (ASU WCU LMC ETSU FC BC WWC)
"Possum Ridge Farmers: A Study in Cultural Change."
H6120 (ASU)
Low-income Life Styles.
I930
"Occupational Roles and Family Roles: A Study of Coal Mining Families in the Southern Appalachians."
L2150
Clasping Hands with Generations Past.
L2960
"Structural Analysis of Mothers' Attitudes toward Child Rearing in Four Communities in Appalachia."
N1310
West Virginians in Their Own State and In Cleveland, Ohio.
P2800 (ASU)
"A Comparative Analysis of the Felt Need Pattern of the Personality Structure in Rural Appalachia and Suburban America."
S3400 (ETSU)
The Girl in the Rural Family.
T9740 (ASU)
FAMILIES AND FAMILY LIFE — CHEROKEE
"Behavioral Premises in the Culture of Conservative Eastern Cherokee Indians."
G3260 (ASU)
FAMILIES AND FAMILY LIFE — KY.
"Household and Family Composition in Selected Rural Areas of Eleven Kentucky Counties."
B5950
The Family Group in a Kentucky Mountain Farming Community.
B7180
"A Population Study of the Appalachian Members of the Freshman Class at Morehead (Kentucky) State University, 1967-1968."
D3090
"Patterns of Response to Rural Medical Practice and Rural Life in Eastern Kentucky."
E2030
The Integration of Locality Groups in an Eastern Kentucky County.
H1550
"Child-rearing Practices in Mountain Country, Kentucky."
H4770 (LMC)
An Experimental Study of the East Kentucky Mountaineers: A Study in Heredity and Environment.
H5680 (ETSU BC ASU)
Participation in Organized Activities in Selected Kentucky Localities.
K250
"A comparison of Some Aspects of Family Life Between Two Areas of Leslie Co., Kentucky."
Q110
Attitudes Toward Rural Migration and Family Life in Johnson and Robertson Counties, Kentucky, 1941.
W6690
FAMILIES AND FAMILY LIFE — N. C.
"Social Interaction and Kinship in Big Cove Community, Cherokee, N. C."
D1020 (ASU)
"Social Interaction and Kinship in Big Cove Community, Cherokee, N. C."
D1030 (ASU)
"Social Organization and Community Solidarity in Painttown, Cherokee, North Carolina."
G280 (ETSU ASU)
"A Cultural Study of a Mountain Community in Western North Carolina."
H3240 (ASU)
"A Cultural Study of Mountain Community in Western North Carolina."
H3250 (ASU)

FAMILIES AND FAMILY LIFE — N. C.
Characteristics of Households in Areas Served by the W. A. M. Y.
N2290 (ASU)
FAMILIES AND FAMILY LIFE — TENN.
"The Personal Characteristics, Social Background, and Academic Achievements of Forty Non-Promoted Pupils at Kennburg School."
E1690 (ETSU)
FAMILIES AND FAMILY LIFE — W. VA.
"Segration Patterns in a Coal Camp."
F3220 (ASU)
"French Creek Community."
L2600 (ASU)
FAMILIES — FAMILY LIFE
"Social Structural Factors Influencing the Urbanization of Appalachian Hill Emigrants in an Urban Ghetto."
H2090
FAMILY LIFE — TENN.
"A Study of Parent-child Relationships in Greene County, Tennessee."
R1720 (ETSU)
FERTILITY
"Comparative Study of Related Health Fertility Attitudes and Behavior of Families Residing in a Poverty Area."
S6190
FEUDS
Pioneers of Eastern Kentucky, Their Feuds and Settlements.
C2180 (ASU)
Breathitt: A Guide to the Feud Country.
F460
The Mountain Massacre.
P210 (ASU)
Four Men of the Cumberlands: Big Ed Hall, Devil John Wright, Dr. M. B. Taylor, Bad Talt Hall.
S680 (ASU BC)
"Recollections of Breathitt."
T9350 (BC)
Banjo and Pistols, a Tale of the Blue Ridge.
W8640 (ASU BC)
Boone Logan's Letters to the Sentinel-Democrat (Mount Sterling, Kentucky) Pertaining to the Rowan County Feud and Other Matters.
Y300 (BC)
FEUDS — APP.
The Pine Ridge Feud.
E2300
FEUDS — KY.
The Crucible, A Tale of the Kentucky Feuds.
B9140 (ASU LMC WWC BC)
Stories of the Kentucky Feuds.
C5250
Stories of Kentucky Feuds.
C5260 (ASU LMC)
Roseanna McCoy: Final Screenplay.
C5940
The Hatfield-McCoy Feud Reader.
D2890 (ASU BC)
"Two Famous Kentucky Feuds and Their Causes."
H2860
"Two Famous Kentucky Feuds and Their Causes."
H3000 (ASU)
"Two Famous Kentucky Feuds and Their Causes."
H3010 (ASU)
The Hatfields.
H3450 (ASU)
The True Story of the Hatfield and McCoy Feud.
H3480 (BC)
The Hanging of "Bad Tom" Smith and the Events Leading to his Hanging.
H3860 (BC)
The Feuds in the Cumberland Mountains.
H7630
The Hatfields and the McCoys.
J2620 (BC ASU LMC WCU WWC)
The Hatfield-McCoy Feud.
L1040
The Hatfield-McCoy Vendetta.
L1050
"The Rise of Education and the Decline of Feudal Tendencies in the Tug River Valley of West Virginia and Kentucky in Relation to the Hatfield and McCoy Feud."
M780 (ASU)
Kentucky's Famous Feuds and Tragedies.
M9230

History of the Feuds of the Mountain Parts of Eastern Kentucky, Lives of Noah and John Reynolds.
R1710 (ASU LMC BC)
The Devil's Brigade: The Story of the Hatfield-McCoy Feud.
S6280 (ASU WCU BC)
The True Facts about the Famous Hatfield-McCoy Feud.
S9430 (ASU BC)
A History of the Feud Between the Hill and Evans Parties of Garrard County, Ky.
T8190 (ASU BC)
FEUDS — VA.
Memoirs of J. Sidna Allen, Being a True Narrative of His Life and Early Manhood, the History of the Allen Family, What Happened at Hillsville and His Life at the Penitentiary.
A1560 (LMC ASU)
The Inside Story of the World Famous Courtroom Tragedy.
C7060 (BC)
The Courthouse Tragedy at Hillsville, Va.
G320 (ASU)
"Gentlemen, I ain't a-goin'."
H8660
The Allen Outlaws: A Complete History of Their Lives and Exploits, Concluding with the Hillsville Courthouse Tragedy.
J320 (ASU BC)
The Allen Gang.
R1670 (LMC BC ASU)
T9250 (BC)
FICTION
Moonshine: Being Appalachia's Arabian Nights.
A70 (ASU LMC)
The Leaf Against the Sky.
A610 (ASU WCU BC)
The Collected Short Prose of James Agee.
A670 (ASU WCU ETSU BC)
A Death in the Family.
A680 (ETSU BC WWC ASU)
A Death in the Family.
A690 (WCU)
Four Early Stories.
A700 (ETSU BC)
The Morning Watch.
A760 (BC ASU WCU)
American Nabob.
A1360 (BC)
The Road to Carolina.
A1491 (WWC BC)
Aftermath; The Bride of the Mistletoe; A Cathedral Singer; The Choir Invisible; The Doctor's Christmas Eve. . . ; The Emblems of Fidelity; Flute and Violin, and Other Kentucky Tales and Romances; The Heroine in Bronze; A Kentucky Cardinal; The Kentucky Warbler; The Landmark; The Last Christmas Tree; The Mettle of the Pasture; The Reign of Law: A Tale of the Hemp Fields; and Summer in Arcady: A Tale of Nature.
A1570
The White Feather.
A1600 (BC ASU)
Beyond Desire.
A2370 (ASU)
Death in the Woods and Other Stories.
A2390
Kit Brandon: A Portrait.
A2420 (ASU ETSU BC)
Kill 1, Kill 2.
A2480 (BC ASU)
Sharp-Eye; or the Scout's Revenge.
A2570
The Potters O'Skunk Hollow.
A2620 (BC ASU)
This Day and Time.
A4720 (ASU)
This Day and Time.
A4730 (BC ETSU ASU)
'Mongst the Hills of Kentucky.
A4810 (ASU)
Aunt Malissa's Memory Jug: Original Folk Stories.
A4850 (BC)
The Dollmaker.
A4900 (ETSU BC ASU WCU LMC MHC WWC)
Hunter's Horn.
A4920 (BC ASU ETSU WCU LMC MHC WWC)

Kentucky Trace: A Novel of the American Revolution.
A4930
Mountain Path.
A4940 (ASU WCU MHC ETSU UNCA BC LMC)
Heart of the Blue Ridge.
B400 (ASU WCU LMC BC)
Heart of the Blue Ridge.
B410 (ETSU)
June Gold.
B420 (WCU)
When the Cock Crows.
B430 (WCU)
The Circle's End.
B440
The Master of L'Etrange
B590
Cis Martin: Or, The Furriners in the Tennessee Mountains.
B640 (ASU BC)
Alas Lucinda!
B720
The Long Way Through.
B860 (BC)
The End of the Day.
B960 (ASU)
The Little Hills.
B980
The Little Hills.
B990 (ASU)
I Took My Love to the Country.
B1020 (ASU)
In the Virginias, Stories and Sketches.
B1050 (ASU BC WCU)
The Ferry Maid of the Chattahoochee: A story for Girls.
B1240 (ASU)
Time Lay Asleep.
B1260 (BC)
Behind the Blue Ridge: A Homely Narrative.
B1410 (BC ASU)
Behind the Blue Ridge. A Homely Narrative. . .
B1411 (ASU)
Big Laurel.
B1540 (BC ASU LMC)
A Hero in Homespun. A Tale of the Loyal South.
B1590 (BC ASU)
A Hero in Homespun. A Tale of the Loyal South.
B1600
Life in the Hills of Kentucky.
B1610 (ASU ETSU LMC BC)
Pine Knot.
B1620 (BC)
Pine Knot. A Story of Kentucky Life.
B1630 (ASU)
Sim Galloway's Daughter.
B1640 (BC)
Sim Galloway's Daughter-in-Law.
B1650
A Tale of the Cumberland Mountains. The Wind-up of the Big Meetin' on No Business.
B1660 (BC ASU)
The Truth about the Trouble at Roundstone.
B1670
Truth about the Trouble at Roundstone.
B1680 (BC ASU)
Wind-up of the Big Meetin' on No Business.
B1690 (BC)
After the Goat Man.
B2371
The Oracle of Moccasin Bend: A Story of Lookout Mountain.
B2520 (ASU BC)
Strange Lady.
B2670 (BC)
Sunday Shoes.
B2710 (BC ASU)
Floreen: Or the Story of Mitchell.
B2720
Fish on the Steeple.
B2760 (ASU)
The Bride of the Wilderness.
B2940 (BC)
Ella Barnwell.
B2950 (BC)
The Phantom of the Forest: A Tale of the Dark and Bloody Ground.
B2960 (ASU BC)
One-string Fiddle.
B3230 (LMC)
The Memory of Old Jack.
B3270 (ASU)

FICTION
A Place on Earth.
B3280 (ASU LMC BC)
A Place on Earth.
B3290 (ASU WCU)
The Gentle Insurrection, and Other Stories.
B3410 (LMC)
Joe, A Civil War Novel of the Blue Ridge.
B3710
Blue Moon Over Cashier's Valley.
B3750
The Hawks of Hawk Hollow.
B4080 (BC)
The Hawks of Hawk Hollow.
B4090
The Path to Snowbird Mountain.
B4130 (ETSU)
Act of Darkness.
B4230 (ASU)
Mixed Harvest.
B4370 (ASU BC)
Of Men and a Mighty Mountain.
B4380 (ASU WCU BC)
Riders of the Flood.
B4390 (ASU BC)
Sawdust in Your Eyes.
B4400 (ASU WCU BC)
Shadows Slant North.
B4690 (ASU)
Alexandriana.
B4870 (ASU BC WCU LMC)
Jack Crews.
B5070
The Bleeding Hills of West Virginia.
B5080 (BC ASU)
Tennessee Outpost.
B5200
Black Blood in Kentucky.
B5210 (BC)
Trail to Oklahoma.
B5400 (ASU)
Andrew Trayton: A Novel of Modern Life.
B5550 (ASU)
His Friend Miss McFairlane.
B5560 (BC ASU)
All the Dark Places.
B5590 (BC ASU)
Tall in the Sight of God.
B5680 (ASU LMC BC)
Drums.
B5870 (MHC)
Drums.
B5880 (LMC ETSU)
Long Hunt.
B5890 (ASU BC ETSU LMC)
Marching On.
B5900 (ASU BC ETSU WWC)
The Call of the Mountains.
B6060 (BC)
The Three-Headed Angel.
B6160 (ASU BC)
Sketches from Old Virginia.
B6170 (BC)
Daughter of the Stars.
B6580
An Earthy Paragon.
B6730 (ASU)
Bound in Shallows.
B6740
A Broken Bondage.
B7340
Mary Gordon Duffee's Sketches of Alabama.
B7420
Below the James, a Plantation Sketch.
B7660 (ASU)
1860-1865. A Romance of the Valley of Virginia.
B7770 (ASU BC)
The Batle Cry.
B8000 (ASU BC LMC)
The Call of the Cumberlands.
B8010 (ASU WCU LMC BC)
The Code of the Mountains.
B8020 (ASU WCU LMC BC)
Destiny.
B8030 (ASU BC)
Flight to the Hills.
B8040 (ASU BC)
Hazard of the Hills.
B8050 (ASU)
Iron Will.
B8060 (ASU BC)
The Key to Yesterday.
B8070 (ASU BC)
Marked Men.
B8080
Mountain Justice: A Tale of the Cumberlands.
B8090 (ASU LMC BC)
A Pagan of the Hills.
B8100 (BC)
A Pagan of the Hills.
B8110 (ASU)
The Portal of Dreams.
B8120
The Roof Tree.
B8130 (LMC BC ASU)
The Rouge's Badge.
B8140
The Tempering.
B8150 (ASU BC)
When "Bear Cat" Went Dry.
B8160 (ASU WCU BC)
Valley of Power.
B8290 (LMC WCU BC ASU)
Long Discovery.
B8560
To the Bright and Shining Sun.
B8660 (ASU LMC BC)
The Minstrel of the Mountains.
B8820 (BC)
Everywhere I Roam.
B8860 (ASU WCU ETSU BC)
The Four Lives of Mundy Tolliver.
B8870 (ASU WCU ETSU BC)
Rooster Crows for Day.
B8880 (ETSU)
In Connection with The De Willoughby Claim.
B8910 (ASU WCU LMC ETSU BC)
Jarl's Daughter: and Other Novelettes.
B8920 (ASU ETSU)
Louisiana.
B8930 (ASU BC)
Louisiana. The Pretty Sister of Jose'.
B8940 (ASU LMC WCU)
Surly Tim, and Other Stories.
B8950 (ASU BC)
Surly Tim, and Other Stories.
B8960 (WCU BC)
Surly Tim, and Other Stories.
B8970 (ASU LMC ETSU)
Gap o' the Mountains.
B8990
Still Water.
B9230 (ASU)
The Delectable Mountains.
B9240 (LMC ASU)
Satan's Rock.
B9250 (LMC BC)
Goose Creek Folks: A Story of the Kentucky Mountains.
B9320 (ETSU BC)
The Summer of the Swans.
B9540
Tale of the Elk.
B9640
The Butterfly.
C30 (ASU WCU LMC ETSU BC)
There Was Time.
C110
The Balance Wheel.
C180 (ASU BC)
The Balance Wheel.
C190 (WCU)
There Was a Time.
C200 (ASU BC)
Unto the Hills. A story of the Blue Ridge Mountains.
C330
Saul.
C340 (ASU)
June of the Hills: The Junaluska Prize Novel, a Story of the Southern Mountains with Lake Junaluska, N. C., as the Center of Action.
C360 (ASU WCU LMC BC)
Survival.
C570 (BC)
Swing Old Adam.
C690
Cloud-walking.
C710 (ASU WWC BC)
Cloud-walking.
C720 (LMC ETSU WCU BC)
Folks Do Get Born.
C730 (BC)
Tales from the Cloud Walking Country.
C740 (ASU WCU LMC MHC ETSU BC)
Big End of the Horn.
C1020 (LMC)
On Skidd's Branch, a Tale of the Kentucky Mountains.
C1080 (ASU BC)
Look to the Mountain.
C1100 (LMC)
The Saint of the Wilderness.
C1430 (ASU)
Peanut.
C1540
The Boy Scouts in the Blue Ridge: Or Marooned Among the Moonshiners.
C1690 (ASU LMC BC)
North Carolina Sketches: Phases of Life Where the Galax Grows.
C1720 (ASU WCU LMC BC)
The Knights of the Golden Horse-shoe: A Traditionary Tale of the Cocked Hat Gentry in the Old Dominion.
C1870 (WCU ETSU BC)
The Knights of the Horseshoe.
C1880
Otha.
C2010 (ASU BC)
Sapphira and the Slave Girl.
C2060 (ASU ETSU)
The Senator from Slaughter County.
C2250 (ASU BC)
The Wooden Tower.
C2510
The Breed and the Pasture.
C2770 (ASU)
The Eagle's Mate.
C2950 (ASU LMC BC)
The Eagle's Mate.
C2960
Mountain Madness.
C2970 (ASU BC)
Mountain Madness.
C2980
The Under Trail.
C2990
Clue of the Faded Dress.
C3030 (ASU BC)
Eagle Cliff.
C3040 (WWC ASU)
Glen Hazard.
C3050 (ASU LMC BC)
The Happy Mountain.
C3060 (ASU BC)
The Happy Mountain.
C3070 (LMC WCU ETSU WWC)
Homeplace.
C3080 (ASU BC ETSU LMC WCU WWC)
Mystery of the Broken Key.
C3090 (WWC)
Rogue's March.
C3100 (ASU WCU LMC BC)
The Weather Tree.
C3110 (ETSU ASU WCU LMC BC)
The Weather Tree.
C3120 (WWC)
Wild Cat Ridge.
C3130 (LMC BC)
Wild Cat Ridge.
C3140
Clue of the Faded Dress.
C3150
Eagle Cliff.
C3160
Flood in Glen Hazard.
C3170 (ASU)
Girls of Glen Hazard.
C3180
Marsh Island Mystery.
C3190
Mystery of the Missing Car.
C3200
Rogues on Red Hill.
C3210
Timber Train.
C3220
Dagon.
C3260 (ASU LMC)
The Gaudy Place.
C3270 (ASU)
The Inkling.
C3280 (ASU LMC)
It Is Time, Lord.
C3290 (ASU)
Scott Burton in the Blue Ridge.
C3810

FICTION

The Crossing.
C4100 (ASU LMC ETSU BC)
The Crossing.
C4110 (WCU)
Sourwood Tales: Stories.
C4310 (ASU)
Captain Paul, the Kentucky Moonshiner; or, the Boy Spy of the Mountains.
C4340
The Strength of the Hills: A Story of Andrew Jackson, and of the Pioneers of Tennessee.
C4390 (LMC WWC BC)
The Strangers Were There: Selected Stories.
C4830 (BC)
One-Fourth of Kentucky. Eleven Stories on the Mountains.
C5120 • (BC ASU)
Bypaths in Dixie: Folk Tales of the South.
C5410 (ASU BC)
The Master of the Hills: A Tale of the Georgia Mountains.
C5420 (ASU BC)
The Glass House, a Novel.
C5490 (BC ASU)
A Son of the Mountains.
C5630
The Common Problem.
C5820
Free Forester: A Novel of Pioneer Kentucky.
C6080 (ASU LMC WCU BC)
A Moonshiner's Folly, and Other Stories.
C6250 (BC)
The Man Thou Gavest.
C6270 (ASU BC)
The Shield of Silence.
C6280 (ASU BC)
A Son of the Hills.
C6290 (ASU WCU BC)
The Mountain Murder.
C6560 (ASU BC)
The Power and the Glory.
C6950 (BC)
Fairfax: Or, the Master of Greenway Court. A Chronicle of the Valley of the Shenandoah.
C6960 (BC ASU)
The Last of the Foresters: Of Humors on the Border. A Story of the Old Virginia Frontier.
C6970 (ASU BC)
Leather Stocking and Silk.
C6980 (BC)
Mohun: Or, The Last Days of Lee and His Paladins. Final Memoirs of a Staff Officer Serving in Virginia.
C6990 (ASU WCU BC)
C7020 (ASU WCU BC)
Farewell the Hills: A Novel of the Eastern Cherokees.
C7520 (ASU LMC)
An American Story-book. Short Stories from Studies of Life in Southwestern Pennsylvania.
C8090 (ASU)
Southwestern Pennsylvania in Song and Story.
C8100
The Legionaries; a Story of the Great Raid.
C8200
A Mockingbird Sang at Chickamauga: A Tale of Embattled Chattanooga.
C8270 (ASU WCU WWC)
Peace at Bowling Green.
C8280 (ASU BC)
Reunion at Chattanooga.
C8290
The Singing Hills.
C8410 (ASU WCU BC)
Smoke on the Mountain.
C8460 (LMC)
Second Awakening.
C8550 (BC)
In Beaver Cove and Elsewhere.
C8790 (ASU BC)
The Entwined Lives of Miss Gabrielle Austin, Daughter of the Late Rev. Ellis C. Austin, and of Redmond, the Outlaw Leader of the North Carolina "Moonshiners".
C8840 (BC)
Spurrier with the Wildcats and Moonshiners.
C9370 (ASU BC)
Marmaduke of Tennessee.
C9480 (ASU BC)
The Affair at the Boat Landing.
C9510 (ASU BC)
The Bancock Murder Case.
C9520
The Cane-patch Mystery.
. C9530 (ASU BC)
Death at "the Bottoms."
C9540
Death Haunts the Dark Lane.
C9550 (ASU)
Death Rides a Sorrel Horse.
C9560 (ASU BC)
Death Visits the Apple Hole.
C9570 (ASU)
The Great Yant Mystery.
C9580
The Hunter is the Hunted.
C9590 (ASU BC)
The Killer Watches the Manhunt.
C9600
The Manse at Barren Rocks.
C9610 (ASU BC)
Murder at Deer Lick.
C9620 (BC)
Murder at the Schoolhouse.
C9630
Murder Before Midnight.
C9640 (ASU BC)
Murder Without Weapons.
C9650 (ASU BC)
One Man Must Die.
C9660 (ASU BC)
Singing Mountains.
C9670 (ASU BC)
Skeleton in the Closet.
C9680 (ASU BC)
Strait is the Gait.
C9690
The Strange Death of Manny Square.
C9700 (BC)
Strange Return.
C9710 (ASU BC)
Who Killed Pretty Becky Low?
C9720 (ASU BC)
Swing Your Mountain Gal, Sketches of Life in the Southern Highlands.
C9950 (ASU WCU LMC MHC BC)
The Hickory Grew Tall.
C9970
The Trail of the Gray Dragoon.
D100 (ASU)
The West Virginian.
D110 (BC)
The Girl in Checks: Or, The Mystery of the Mountain Cabin.
D140 (ASU BC)
Call Home the Heart.
D260 (ASU BC)
From My Highest Hill; Carolina Mountain Folks.
D270 (ASU WCU BC UNCA)
Highland Annals.
D280 (ASU WCU LMC ETSU UNCA BC)
Innocent Bigamy, and Other Stories.
D290 (ASU WCU LMC BC)
The Spotted Hawk.
D340 (ASU WCU BC UNCA)
A Stone Came Rolling.
D350 (ASU BC WCU LMC)
A Stone Came Rolling.
D360
The Melting of Molly.
D730 (ASU)
Over Paradise Ridge: A Romance.
D740 (ASU BC)
Beulah Land.
D1000 (ASU BC WCU)
Kent Hampden.
D1180 (BC ASU)
Silhouettes of American Life.
D1200 (ETSU ASU)
Silhouettes of American Life.
D1210 (ASU BC ETSU)
Waiting for the Verdict.
D1220
Separated by Mountains.
D1230 (ASU)
Three Steps.
D1340 (BC ASU)
Dunbar's Cove.
D1450 (ASU WCU BC)
Dunbar's Cove.
D1460 (ASU)
The Insolent Breed.
D1470 (ASU BC)
Walk Through the Valley.
D1480 (ASU BC)
Skull Mountain.
D1500
Juny: Or, Only One Girl's Story. A Romance of the Society Crust — Upper and Under.
D1720 (ASU)
The Wilderness Brigade.
D1780
Ludlow on the Kanawha.
D1840 (ASU BC)
Deliverance.
D2150 (ASU WCU)
Deliverance.
D2160 (ASU)
Reuben Dalton, Preacher: A Sequel to "The Story of Marthy."
D2260
The Story of Marthy.
D2270
The Black Hood.
D2550 (ASU)
The Clansman: An Historical Romance of the Ku Klux Klan.
D2560 (ASU)
The Traitor: A Story of the Fall of the Invisible Empire.
D2570 (ASU)
The Traitor: A Story of the Fall of the Invisible Empire.
D2580 (ETSU)
Rosy.
D2700
Flames of the Blue Ridge.
D2980 (ASU LMC BC)
Adventures of a Young Man.
D3070 (ASU)
Adventures of a Young Man.
D3080
The Great Yant Mystery.
D3410
A Taste for Violence.
D3420
At the Foot of No-man.
D3490 (BC)
Cinch, and Other Stories: Tales of Tennessee.
D3500 (ASU ETSU BC)
Harum-scarum Joe.
D3510 (ASU)
The Heart of Old Hickory and Other Stories of Tennessee.
D3520 (ASU BC)
The Heart of Old Hickory, and Other Stories of Tennessee.
D3530 (ETSU WWC BC ASU)
Hero-chums.
D3540 (ASU BC)
The Island of Beautiful Things: A Romance of the South.
D3550 (ASU BC)
A Moonshiner's Son.
D3560 (ASU)
A Moonshiner's Son.
D3570 (WCU LMC BC)
Rare Old Chums.
D3580 (ASU BC)
The Sunny Side of the Cumberland: A Story of the Mountains.
D3590 (ETSU BC)
The Valley Path.
D3600 (ASU BC)
The Balsam Groves of the Grandfather Mountain: A Tale of the Western North Carolina Mountains. Together with information relating to the section and its hotels, also a table showing the height of important mountains, etc.
D3730 (ASU WCU LMC BC)
The Balsam Groves of the Grandfather Mountain.
D3740
The Heart of Happy Hollow.
D3900
Samanthy Billins of Hangin' Dog.
D3910
The Prophet of Little Cane Creek.
D4150
The Prophet of Little Cane Creek.
D4160 (WCU) •
Before I Sleep.
D4180 (BC)

FICTION

Look to This Day.
D4230 (ASU LMC MHC WWC ETSU)
Return the Innocent Earth.
D4260 (ASU WWC MHC ETSU BC)
The Tall Woman.
D4290 (ASU LMC MHC WWC ETSU BC)
Timothy Corn Stories; as Told by Uncle Dave Arnold of Knobley Farm.
E660
Earthenware, a Group of Stories.
E880 (ASU)
Red, White and Black: Twelve Stories of the South.
E890 (ASU BC)
Tales of the Blue Ridge.
E970 (LMC ASU BC)
The Marbeau Cousins.
E1040 (ASU BC)
Two Runaways, and Other Stories.
E1050 (ASU BC)
The Log Meeting-house, and the McIlhanys.
E1060 (ASU)
Camp Venture; a Story of the Virginia Mountains.
E1270 (ETSU ASU)
Irene of the Mountains; a Romance of old Virgina.
E1280 (ASU BC)
A Man of Honor.
E1290 (ASU BC)
The Journey of August King.
E1320 (ASU WCU LMC BC)
The Land Breakers.
E1330 (ASU BC)
The Land Breakers.
E1340 (ASU WCU LMC MHC ETSU BC)
Lion on the Hearth.
E1350 (ASU WCU LMC BC)
Move Over, Mountain.
E1360 (ASU WCU LMC BC)
The Road.
E1370 (ASU WCU LMC ETSU BC)
Time of Drums: A Novel.
E1380 (ASU WCU LMC MHC BC)
Echoes from the Hills, A Novel.
E1460 (ETSU BC)
Wendy's Halloween Ride: Witch Shadows.
E1540 (LMC)
The Durket Sperret.
E1700 (ASU)
An Incident, and Other Happenings.
E1710 (WCU BC)
Jerry, a Novel.
E1720 (LMC BC)
The Last Trail.
E1770
Logan the Mingo; a Story of the Frontier.
E1810
Kentucky Stories.
E1820
Tang of the South Stories.
E1830
A Girl of the Blue Ridge.
E2120 (ASU)
The Girl of the Blue Ridge.
E2130 (BC ASU LMC)
The Mountain Girl.
E2140 (ASU LMC BC)
When the Gates Lift up Their Heads: A Story of the Seventies.
E2150 (ASU)
Tennessee Mountaineers in Type: A Collection of Stories.
E2240 (ASU BC)
Nolichucky Jack.
F130 (ASU LMC ETSU)
Power: A Novel.
F270 (ASU BC)
The Tall Hunter.
F280 (ASU BC)
Laurel, a Novel.
F550 (ASU)
Christopher Laird.
F580
Stormy Present.
F770 (ASU BC)
A Cry of Angels.
F820 (ASU)
The Forest Cavalier: A Romance of America's First Frontier and of Bacon's Rebellion.
F1400 (ASU BC)
While Rivers Flow.
F1440 (ASU BC)
I'll Walk to the Mountain.
F1940 (ASU)
The Liberation of Lord Byron Jones.
F1950 (ASU WCU ETSU BC)
Mountains of Gilead, a Novel.
F1960 (BC ASU ETSU)
Burn Forever.
F1970 (ASU BC)
Trail of Tears.
F2150 (WCU BC)
God in the Straw Pen, a Novel.
F2160 (ASU WCU BC)
Stone Dougherty.
F2180 (BC)
Blue-grass and Rhododendron: Out-doors in Old Kentucky.
F2540 (ASU BC)
Blue-grass and Rhododendron: Out-doors in Old Kentucky.
F2550 (LMC)
Christmas Eve on Lonesome.
F2560 (WWC)
Christmas Eve on Lonesome and Other Stories.
F2570 (BC ASU WCU LMC ETSU)
Christmas Eve on Lonesome, "Hell-fer-sartin," and Other Stories.
F2580 (MHC BC)
Crittenden: A Kentucky Story of Love and War.
F2590 (ASU WCU LMC BMC BC)
A Cumberland Vendetta.
F2600
A Cumberland Vendetta: A Novel.
F2610 (ASU)
A Cumberland Vendetta and Other Stories.
F2620 (ETSU BC)
A Cumberland Vendetta, and Other Stories.
F2630 (WCU)
Erskine Dale, Pioneer.
F2640 (ASU LMC ETSU)
The Heart of the Hills.
F2650 (ASU WCU LMC ETSU BC)
"Hell-fer-sartain" and Other Stories.
F2660 (LMC ETSU BC)
Hell for Sartain and Other Stories.
F2670 (ASU)
"Hell for Sartain" and Other Stories.
F2680 (ASU)
"Hell fer Sartain" and Other Stories.
F2690 (ASU)
In Happy Valley.
F2700 (ASU LMC ETSU)
The Kentuckians.
F2710
The Kentuckians: A Knight of the Cumberland.
F2720 (ASU WCU LMC ETSU)
The Kentuckians: A Knight of the Cumberland.
F2730 (WWC)
A Knight of the Cumberland.
F2740 (ASU LMC ETSU BC)
The Kentuckians: A Novel.
F2750 (WCU BC)
The Little Shepherd of Kingdom Come.
F2760 (WCU UNCA BC)
The Little Shepherd of Kingdom Come.
F2770 (LMC)
The Little Shepherd of Kingdom Come.
F2780 (MHC)
The Little Shepherd of Kingdom Come.
F2790
The Little Shepherd of Kingdom Come.
F2800 (ASU)
The Little Shepherd of Kingdom Come.
F2810 (ASU ETSU)
A Mountain Europa.
F2820
A Mountain Europa.
F2830
A Mountain Europa.
F2840 (ASU BC)
A Mountain Europa. A Cumberland Vendetta. The Last Stetson.
F2850 (WCU ETSU MHC BC)
A Mountain Europa. A Cumberland Vendetta. The Last Stetson.
F2860 (LMC)
A Mountain Europa. A Cumberland Vendetta. The Last Stetson.
F2870 (LMC)
A Purple Rhododendron and Other Stories.
F2880 (ASU ETSU BC)
The Trail of the Lonesome Pine.
F2900
The Trail of the Lonesome Pine.
F2910 (ASU WCU LMC MHC BC)
The Trail of the Lonesome Pine.
F2920 (WCU)
The Trail of the Lonesome Pine.
F2930 (ETSU)
The Trail of the Lonesome Pine.
F2940 (WCU)
In the Path of the Storm.
F3070 (ASU BC LMC)
Ballad of Calamity Creek.
F3360 (ASU BC)
The Glass Window; a Story of the Kentucky Mountains.
F3890
The Glass Window: A Story of the Quare Woman.
F3900 (ASU LMC BC)
The Lonesome Road.
F3910 (WWC)
Lonesome Road.
F3920
The Lonesome Road.
F3930 (ASU LMC)
Mothering on Perilous.
F3940 (ASU BC)
Mothering on Perilous.
F3950
The Quare Women.
F3960 (BC WWC)
Quare Women.
F3970
The Quare Women: A Story of the Kentucky Mountains.
F3980 (ASU LMC BC)
Sight to the Blind: A Story.
F3990 (ASU LMC BC)
Tomorrow Achieved, a Novel.
F4010 (ASU BC)
Hill Man.
G510 (BC)
Shenandoah; or The Horizon's Bar. A Story of the War.
G730
The Only Nancy. A Tale of the Kentucky Mountains.
G850
The Cumberland Rifles.
G1070 (ASU BC)
Franklin, America's "Lost State."
G1080 (ASU ETSU)
The Yankee from Tennessee.
G1090 (ASU ETSU BC)
The Light on the Hill: A Romance of the Southern Mountains.
G1200 (BC ASU LMC)
Mammy's Reminiscences, and Other Sketches.
G1210 (ASU BC)
Old Andy, the Moonshiner.
G1230 (LMC ASU BC)
Uncle Sam.
G1240 (ASU BC LMC)
Harbin's Ridge.
G1370 (BC ASU WCU LMC WWC)
40 Acres and No Mule.
G1400 (ETSU BC)
40 Acres and No Mule.
G1410 (ASU WWC)
The Believers.
G1420 (BC ASU WCU ETSU)
The Enduring Hills.
G1430 (BC ASU WCU LMC WWC)
The Enduring Hills.
G1440 (WCU)
The Great Adventure: A Novel.
G1450 (BC ASU ETSU)
Hannah Fowler.
G1460 (ASU WCU ETSU BC)
The Kentuckians.
G1470 (BC ASU WCU MHC LMC)
The Land Beyond the Mountains.
G1480 (BC ASU WCU)
Miss Willie.
G1490 (BC)
Miss Willie.
G1500 (BC WWC)
Miss Willie.
G1510 (LMC)
The Plum Thicket.
G1520
Run Me a River.
G1530 (BC ASU ETSU)

FICTION

Savanna.
G1540 (ASU BC WCU)
Six-Horse Hitch: A Novel.
G1560 (ASU BC)
Tara's Healing.
G1570 (ASU WWC BC)
Tara's Healing.
G1580
Beyond the Bluegrass; A Kentucky Novel.
G1610
Bugles at the Border.
G1670 (ASU WCU BC)
A Mountain-White Heroine.
G1760
On the Border.
G1780 (ASU WCU BC)
All Cats Are Gray.
G1900 (BC ASU LMC)
The Devil Takes a Hill Town.
G1910 (ASU BC)
The Doctor's Pills Are Stardust.
G1920 (ASU BC)
Barren Ground.
G1970
Barren Ground.
G1980 (MHC)
Barren Ground.
G1990 (ASU)
The Battle-ground.
G2000 (ETSU)
The Battle-ground.
G2010 (ASU)
Vein of Iron.
G2020 (ASU MHC ETSU)
The Lily of Carlisle: a Story of the Days of Cromwell and Blake. The Parson of the S. Fork; a Story of W. Va. Hills.
G2280
The Forest of the South.
G2690 (ASU BC WWC)
Green Centuries.
G2700
Green Centuries.
G2710 (WCU BC)
Dark Moon of March.
G2990 (ASU BC)
Mountain Born.
G3000 (WWC BC ASU)
Mountain Born.
G3010 (ASU)
Old Hell.
G3020 (ASU WCU BC)
Old Hell.
G3030
Stories of the Foot-hills.
G3140 (ASU)
A Kentucky Chronicle.
G3360
And Scatter the Proud.
G3590 (ASU LMC WWC BC)
Honeysuckle Hill; a Hillbilly Makes the Grade.
G3610
The Blind Brother: A Story of the Pennsylvania Coal Mines.
G3750 (ASU BC)
Nance; a Story of Kentucky Feuds.
G3830
A Little Leaven.
G4050 (WCU ASU)
The Barefoot Man.
G4500 (ASU WCU MHC BC)
A Dream of Kings.
G4510 (LMC WWC BC ASU)
Fools' Parade.
G4520 (ASU LMC)
The Night of the Hunter.
G4530 (ASU WCU BC)
Shadow of My Brother.
G4540 (WCU BC ASU)
A Tree Full of Stars.
G4550
Twelve Tales of Suspense and the Supernatural.
G4560 (LMC BC)
The Voices of Glory.
G4570 (BC ASU WCU LMC)
The Watchman.
G4580
The Last Valley.
H20 (BC ASU LMC MHC)
Look Away, Look Away: A Novel.
H30 (ASU WCU)
A Mountain Exile: The Story of a Kentucky Feud.
H180
Up Creek and Down Creek.
H640 (WCU LMC BC)
Daughter of the Elm. A Tale of Western Virginia Before the War.
H670
Daughter of the Elm: A Tale of Western Virginia before the War.
H680 (LMC BC)
Daughter of the Elm: A Tale of Western Virginia before the War.
H690 (ASU)
The Harpe's Head.
H740 (BC)
Tales of the Border.
H750 (WCU BC)
Give Us This Valley.
H1000 (BC ASU)
Give Us This Valley.
H1010
The Parson's Proxy.
H1170 (BC)
Zeb Harkins.
H1190
Fifty Roads to Town, a Novel.
H1350 (ASU BC)
The Homecoming: A Novel about Spencer's Mountain.
H1360 (BC FC ASU LMC WWC ETSU)
Menace on the Mountain.
H1430 (BC ASU LMC WCU)
The Gods and One.
H1590 (ASU BC)
The Hills Step Lightly.
H1600 (ASU ETSU BC)
Look Back with Love: A Recollection of the Blue Ridge.
H1610 (ASU WCU LMC MHC ETSU FC WWC BC)
Roseanna McCoy.
H1620 (BC ASU)
Thursday April.
H1630 (WCU ASU)
Thursday April.
H1640
Rites of Summer.
H1700 (ASU BC)
Abner Daniel.
H1760 (ASU)
Abner Daniel.
H1770
Ann Boyd.
H1780 (ETSU)
Ann Boyd.
H1790
Ann Boyd: A Novel.
H1800 (ASU BC)
The Cottage of Delight: A Novel.
H1810 (ASU BC)
The Desired Woman.
H1820
The Desired Woman.
H1830 (ASU BC)
The Divine Event.
H1840 (ASU BC)
Dixie Hart.
H1850 (ASU BC)
The Georgians: A Novel.
H1860 (ASU BC)
Gilbert Neal: A Novel.
H1870 (ASU BC)
The Hills of Refuge: A Novel.
H1880 (ASU BC)
The Inner Law: A Novel.
H1890 (ASU ETSU BC)
Jane Dawson: A Novel.
H1900 (ASU)
The New Clarion.
H1920
The New Clarion.
H1930 (ASU BC)
Northern Georgia Sketches.
H1940 (ASU WCU LMC)
Northern Georgia Sketches.
H1950 (ETSU)
Paul Rundel: A Novel.
H1960 (ASU BC)
Pole Baker.
H1970
Pole Baker: A Novel.
H1980 (ASU LMC BC)
The Redemption of Kenneth Galt.
H1990 (BC)
The Redemption of Kenneth Galt.
H2000
Second Choice.
H2010 (ASU BC)
Second Choice.
H2020 (ETSU)
The Triumph: A Novel.
H2030 (ASU BC)
Westerfelt.
H2040
Dan Georgen of the Divided House.
H2380 (ASU LMC)
Hearthstones, a Novel of the Roanoke River Country in North Carolina.
H2630 (WCU)
Janey Jeems.
H2640 (ASU WCU BC)
A Circuit Rider's Widow.
H2660 (ASU WCU BC)
A Circuit Rider's Wife.
H2670 (ASU BC LMC WCU)
The Co-citizens.
H2680 (ASU BC)
Eve's Second Husband.
H2690 (ASU)
Flapper Anne.
H2700 (ASU)
The Happy Pilgrimage.
H2710 (ASU BC)
In Search of a Husband.
H2720 (ASU)
The Recording Angel.
H2750 (ASU BC)
Sunlight Patch.
H2760 (BC)
High Times and Hard Times: Sketches and Tales.
H2800 (ASU BC)
Sut Lovingood.
H2820 (ASU)
Sut Lovingood. Yarns Spun by a "Nat'ral Born Durn'd Fool." Warped and Wove for Public Wear.
H2830 (ASU BC ETSU)
Sut Lovingood's Yarns.
H2840 (ASU WWC)
Balaam and His Master, and Other Sketches and Stories.
H2940 (WCU)
Mingo.
H2960 (WCU)
Mingo and Other Sketches.
H2970 (WWC)
Mingo and Other Sketches in Black and White.
H2980 (WCU)
Social Types in Southern Prose Fiction.
H3040
A Son of the Old Dominion.
H3050
The Fear and the Guilt.
H3090
Heat Lightening.
H3100 (ASU)
The Mating Call.
H3110
Patterns of Wolfpen.
H3400
The Hawk's Done Gone.
H3660
The Hawk's Done Gone And Other Stories.
H3670 (ASU BC WCU LMC WWC)
Moonshine Strategy, and Other Stories.
H3740 (BC)
The Bellamy Case.
H3800 (ASU)
The Hidden Women.
H3810 (BC)
The Winning Clue.
H3820 (ASU BC)
Borderland Echoes, a W. Va. Story.
H3950 (BC ASU)
The Lattiner Legend.
H4280 (LMC BC)
Daisy's Fanny.
H4360 (BC)
Nitchey Tilley.
H4390
Nitchey Tilley, a Novel.
H4400 (ASU BC)
A Long, Long Day for November.
H4550 (ASU)

FICTION

Deep River.
H4660 (ASU BC)
King's Mountain.
H4740 (ASU BC)
True to the Old Flag: A Tale of the American War of Independence.
H4870 (ASU)
The Limestone Tree.
H4900 (ASU WCU BC)
Mountain Blood, a Novel.
H4910 (ASU BC)
Tol'able David.
H4920 (BC)
Hills, Hollers and Hickory Flats.
H5110 (BC)
Angel.
H5150 (ASU ETSU BC)
Stories of the South, Old and New.
H5180 (ASU BC WWC)
The White Rocks; or The Robbers Den; a Tragedy of the Mountains.
H5350 (BC)
The Master of the Red Buck and the Bay Doe: A Story of Whig and Tory Warfare in North Carolina in 1781-83.
H5500 (LMC)
My Rappahannock Storybook.
H6060 (BC ASU)
Lindy Loyd, a Tale of the Mountains.
H6280 (BC ASU)
The Dark Mountains.
H6310 (BC)
A Walk to the River.
H6320 (WCU)
Rose Mather.
H6880
Azure-Lure: A Romance of the Mountains.
H6950
Some Adventures of Capt. Simon Suggs.
H7060 (ASU)
Lonesome Valley.
H7250 (ASU LMC BC ETSU)
The Blue Balloon, a Tale of the Shenandoah Valley.
H7270
The Pike.
H7340 (LMC BC WCU)
The Way Out, a Story of the Cumberland Today.
H7400 (ASU BC)
A Handful of Stars!
H7470 (ASU MHC BC)
Pleasure Piece.
H7480 (ASU BC)
Before the Sun Goes Down.
H7580 (ASU)
Payne Hollow.
H7820
The Claybrooks.
H7920 (ASU WCU BC)
In All Its Glory.
H8020
Aunt Zona's Web.
H8050 (ASU LMC)
Missa Appalachia.
H8480
The Mountains Redeemed; the Romance of the Mountains, a True Story of Life and Love in Southwest Virginia, Interwoven with an Exposition of her Mountain Life and the Weird Religion of the Mountains, Embracing Scores of Humorous, Ridiculous, Laughable, and Tragic Stories, Episodes, and Incidents and the Religious, Moral, Educational, Industrial and Political Redemption of the Mountains.
H8560
Yesterday's Rain.
H8680 (ASU LMC WCU BC)
Chimney Rock Anthology.
I50
Light as the Morning.
I790 (ETSU BC ASU)
Milbry.
I800 (LMC BC)
Gold in the Blue Ridge: The True Story of the Beale Treasure.
I850 (ASU LMC)
The Mountain.
J190 (LMC BC)
Delilah's Mountain.
J280 (ETSU ASU WCU BC)
The Little Seeds of Christmas and Other Stories.
J710 (WWC)
Kentucky Days.
J760 (ETSU)
Melee; or Woman in Command.
J780 (BC)
Georgina's Service Stars.
J1980 (WCU)
In League with Israel; a Tale of the Chattanooga Conference.
J1990
The Little Colonel's Knight Comes Riding.
J2000 (ASU BC)
Audrey.
J2070 (ASU BC WCU ETSU)
Cease Firing.
J2080 (ASU WWC BC)
The Great Valley.
J2090 (ASU BC)
Hagar.
J2100 (WCU)
Hunting Shirt.
J2110 (BC ASU WWC ETSU)
Lewis Rand.
J2120 (ASU BC ETSU WCU)
The Long Roll.
J2130 (ASU WWC)
Sir Mortimer, a Novel.
J2140 (ASU BC)
Mr. Absalom Billingslea, and Other Georgia Folk.
J2160 (WCU)
The Secret Shot, or the Rivals of Misty Mount, A Romance of the Old North State.
J2190
Chattanooga.
J2240
A Buried Land, a Novel.
J2460 (BC ASU LMC WCU ETSU)
An Exile.
J2470 (BC ASU WCU ETSU)
Forest of the Night.
J2480 (BC ASU LMC ETSU)
The Innocent.
J2490 (ASU LMC WCU ETSU BC)
Shirley.
J2550
The Ghost of the Gugan.
J2970 (BC)
The Gallant Mrs. Stonewall: A Novel Based on the Lives of General and Mrs. Stonewall Jackson.
K120 (MHC)
Highland Mills.
K320
Yankee Revenooer.
K340 (ASU LMC)
Kildares of Storm.
K630
The Mansion House.
K640 (ASU BC)
Mixed Company.
K650
Horse-shoe Robinson.
K760 (WCU ASU)
Horse-shoe Robinson: A Tale of the Tory Ascendency.
K770 (ETSU)
Horse-shoe Robinson: A Tale of the Tory Ascendency in South Carolina, in 1780.
K780 (MHC BC)
The Trail of the Three Notched Road.
K1600 (BC)
The Prodigal Judge.
K1720 (BC ASU LMC WCU)
Mountain Stories.
K1880
Norman Holt: A Story of the Army of the Cumberland.
K2240 (BC ASU)
Cabin in the Valley.
K2390
Forgotten Valleys.
K2400
A New Home — Who'll Follow? or, Glimpses at Western Life.
K2640
Where the Star Still Shines.
K2650 (LMC)
A Young Volunteer With Old Hickory.
K2750 (ASU BC)
Little Benders.
K2870 (BC ASU WCU)
The Cabin in the Cotton.
K3250 (ASU BC)
Darker Grows the Valley.
K3260 (ASU LMC ETSU BC)
The Mountain Singer.
K3270 (BC ASU)
My Heart's in the Hills.
K3280 (ASU BC)
The Rider on the Bronze Horse.
K3290
The Smouldering Fire.
K3300
Summer Gold.
K3310 (BC)
Their Ancient Grudge.
K3320 (ASU ETSU BC)
Three Brothers and Seven Daddies.
K3330 (ASU LMC BC)
The Brown Mountain Lights.
L90 (ASU LMC)
Along Came the Other Girl; a Story of Love and Adventure in Pre-Revolutionary Virginia.
L200
Night March.
L250 (ASU BC WCU)
No Bugles Tonight.
L260 (ASU)
Hill-billy.
L370 (ASU BC)
Tiger-lilies: A Novel.
L520 (ASU)
Tiger-lilies: A Novel.
L530 (ASU ETSU)
Rider on the Mountains.
L570
Shoot for a Mule.
L580
The Twelfth Juror.
L640 (BC ASU)
Our Cousin Veronica; or, Scenes and Adventurers over the Blue Ridge.
L680
Walk a Rocky Road.
L910 (LMC)
Leonora, A Tale of the Great Smokies.
L1020
The Hatfield-McCoy Feud.
L1040
Big Nick: The Story of a Remarkable Black Bear.
L1080 (ASU BC)
A Virginia Feud: The Story of a Mountain Lassie.
L1340 (ASU BC)
Stoke of Brier Hill.
L1490 (BC)
The Moonshine War.
L1810 (LMC)
When Men Grew Tall: Or, The Story of Andrew Jackson.
L2070 (ASU)
Cry to the Hills.
L2090 (BC LMC ASU)
New Hope; or, The Rescue. A Tale of the Great Kanawha.
L2190 (ASU)
Young Kate; or, The Rescue. A Tale of the Great Kanawha.
L2200
The Great Forest.
L2470 (LMC)
Reaching for Reality.
L2510 (BC)
The First Shearing.
L2550 (ASU)
Heathen Valley.
L2680 (ASU LMC WCU)
Slowly, By Thy Hand Unfurled.
L2690 (ASU)
The Sorrows of Frederick: A Play.
L2700 (ASU)
A Maid of the Kentucky Hills.
L2780 (ASU)
Stones for Bread.
L2790 (BC)
Felix Moses, the Beloved Jew of Stringtown on the Pike. Illustrated by J. Augustus Knapp.
L2970 (ASU BC)
Our Willie: A Folklore Story of the Gunpowder Creek and Hills, Boone County, Kentucky.
L2980 (ASU WCU)
Red Head.
L2990 (BC ASU WCU LMC ETSU)

FICTION

Stringtown on the Pike: A Tale of Northernmost Kentucky.
L3000 (BC LMC ETSU ASU WCU)
Warwick of the Knobs: A Story of Stringtown County, Kentucky.
L3010 (ASU LMC WCU ETSU)
L3220
Georgia Scenes.
L3320 (ASU)
Georgia Scenes: Characters, Incidents, etc., in the First Half Century of the Republic.
L3330 (ASU)
Georgia Scenes: Characters, Incidents, etc., in the First Half Century of the Republic.
L3340 (ASU)
Tennessee Sketches.
L3450 (ASU ETSU BC)
L3550
To Make My Bread.
L3960 (ASU BC)
The Law of Hemlock Mountain.
L4000 (BC ASU)
The Long Night
L4130 (ASU)
The Velvet Horn.
L4140 (ASU WCU ETSU BC)
Romance of the Cumberlands.
M20 (LMC BC ASU)
Planting the Wilderness: Or, The Pioneer Boys: A Story of Frontier Life.
M170 (BC)
Other Fires: The Story of Tsali.
M180 (WWC BC)
Appalachian Gothic.
M270 (ASU)
Child of God.
M280 (ASU)
The Orchard Keeper.
M290 (ASU WCU LMC ETSU BC)
Outer Dark.
M300 (ASU LMC ETSU BC)
Burkett's Lock.
M410 (ASU)
Jean Montioth.
M420 (ASU)
Oblivion: An Episode.
M430 (ETSU BC)
Bone and Striffen.
M440 (ASU)
Big as Life.
M800 (LMC BC ASU)
The Secret Doorways.
M810
Black Top.
M1020 (WCU BC ASU)
On Silver Creek Knob.
M1021 (BC)
Strength of the Hills.
M1030 (BC)
The Red Debt.
M1130 (BC)
Dialect Tales.
M1210 (BC ASU ETSU)
Juletty: A Story of Old Kentucky.
M1300 (ASU BC)
Journey Proud.
M1460 (ASU)
For Which the First Was Made.
M1510
Judith of the Cumberlands.
M1560 (ASU)
The Sword in the Mountains.
M1570 (ASU BC)
The Sword in the Mountains.
M1580
The Wiving of Lance Cleaverage.
M1590 (BC)
In Kentucky with Daniel Boone.
M1730 (ASU)
Tall Tales of the Kentucky Mountains.
M1780 (ASU WCU LMC BC)
Captain Jack, the Scout: Or, the Indian Wars about Old Fort Duquesne, an Historical Novel.
M1950 (ASU BC)
Old Fort Duquesne: Or, Captain Jack, the Scout. An Historical Novel with Copious Notes.
M1960 (ASU)
"The Southern Highlands in Prose Fiction."
M2100 (ASU WCU)
Tyrone of Kentucky.
M2200 (WCU)
Journey Cake.
M2220 (BC)
Juba's New Moon.
M2230 (ASU WCU BC)
"Glory" of the Hills.
M2350 (BC)
The Last Forest; Tales of the Allegheny Woods.
M2370
Storm Center.
M2510 (BC)
Hushed Were the Hills.
M2570 (ASU LMC ETSU MHC WCU BC)
The Scout of the Buckongehanon: An Historical Romance of the Western Virginia Border, 1764-1782.
M2580 (ASU WCU BC)
Bijou, A Novel.
M2650
Cassandra Singing: A Novel.
M2660 (ASU BC)
Fiction Into Film: A Walk in the Spring Rain.
M2710 (ASU)
Weep for the Dawn.
M2770 (ASU WCU BC)
The Holcombes. A Story of Virginia Homelife.
M2790 (ASU BC)
Sons of Vengeance.
M2960 (BC ASU)
The Crowning Event and Other Stories.
M3070 (ASU)
A Mountain Code and Other Stories.
M3080 (ASU)
Kentucky Kate; or, The Moonshiners' League.
M3110
The Coming of Rain.
M3260 (WCU ETSU BC)
That Far Paradise.
M3270 (BC)
Kentucky Jane.
M3280
Vestige of Valor.
M3310 (BC)
Sequoyah: Leader of the Cherokees.
M3340 (ASU LMC BC)
Old Hickory's Prisoner: A Tale of the Second War for Independence.
M3400 (ASU)
Christy.
M3410 (ASU LMC MHC ETSU WCU WWC BC)
In Old Kentucky.
M3430 (ETSU BC ASU)
Julia Gwynn.
M3470 (WCU BC)
Little Squire Jim.
M3480 (ETSU BC)
Hang My Wreath.
M4050 (ASU)
Jonathan Fish and His Neighbors.
M4560 (BC)
Cousin to Human.
M4610 (ASU)
On Indian Trails with Daniel Boone.
M4780 (ETSU)
On Indian Trails with Daniel Boone.
M4790 (ETSU)
The Story of Andrew Jackson.
M4800 (ASU BC)
The Story of Davy Crockett.
M4810 (ASU BC ETSU WCU)
The Parson's Mountaineers.
M4940 (BC)
The Valley People.
M4950 (BC)
Call of the Mountain.
M4980 (ASU)
Will West.
M5200
Bethel.
M5500 (ASU BC LMC)
Daintie's Cruel Rivals.
M5510 (BC)
Lynette's Wedding.
M5520 (BC)
The Pearl and the Ruby.
M5530 (BC)
Lamb in His Bosom.
M5560 (ASU WWC)
Lamb in His Bosom.
M5570 (ASU)
The Red Swan's Neck: A Tale of the North Carolina Mountains.
M5580
The Edge of the Woods.
M5650 (ASU)
Tenants of the House.
M5660 (WCU BC)
After the Glory.
M5680 (ASU BC ETSU)
Hawk in the Wind.
M5690 (ASU BC)
Horns of Capricorn.
M5700 (BC ETSU WCU WWC)
Sharon.
M5720 (ASU)
Slow Dies the Thunder.
M5730 (ASU BC ETSU)
The Sound of Chariots: A Novel of John Sevier and the State of Franklin.
M5740 (ASU BC ETSU WCU)
Splendor of Eagles.
M5750
Be Ye Begger or King.
M6080
Love in the Backwoods.
M6350 (BC)
Deep Channel.
M6490 (ASU)
In Calvert's Valley.
M6500
Linda.
M6510 (ASU BC)
The Poet, Miss Kate and I.
M6520 (ASU BC)
The Sowing of Alderson Cree.
M6530 (ASU BC)
Uncle Sam of Freedom Ridge.
M6540 (BC)
Up Eel River.
M6550 (ASU BC LMC WCU)
Long Meadows.
M6620 (ASU)
Blacktop.
M6880 (ASU)
The Girl of the Listening Heart.
M6920
Laborers Together.
M6980
Ordered Steps.
M7000
Silver Creek's Camp Jolly.
M7010 (ASU)
Strength of the Hills.
M7030 (ASU)
These, My People.
M7040
Like a River Flowing.
M7180 (ASU)
The Bishop of Cottontown: A Story of the Southern Cotton Mills.
M7250 (ASU BC)
Hearts of Hickory: A Story of Andrew Jackson and the War of 1812.
M7260 (ASU BC WCU)
Hearts of Hickory: A Story of Andrew Jackson and the War of 1812.
M7270 (ETSU)
Jack Ballington, Forester.
M7280 (ASU)
A Summer Hymnal, a Romance of Tennessee.
M7300 (ASU BC ETSU)
Rain on the Just.
M7420 (ASU)
Again the River.
M7670 (ASU LMC)
First Blood.
M7740 (BC)
Stephen.
M7760 (ASU)
Opie Read, American Humorist, 1852-1939.
M7830 (BC WCU)
Chilhowee Boys.
M7950 (ASU)
Land of the Laurel: A Story of the Alleghanies.
M8120 (ASU BC ETSU)
Winning or Losing? A Story of the West Virginia Hills.
M8150 (BC)
The Rock Was Free.
M8260
The Shadow of the Potrock.
M8270
Push Boat.
M8300 (ASU)
The Boy from Hollow Hut.
M8560 (BC)

FICTION

Almetta of Gabriel's Run.
M8710 (BC)
The Amulet: A Novel.
M8720 (ASU BC)
The Bushwhackers, and Other Stories.
M8730 (ASU BC LMC)
The Bushwhackers, and Other Stories.
M8740 (ASU ETSU)
The Despot of Broomsedge Cove.
M8750 (ASU BC ETSU LMC)
Down the Ravine, a Story.
M8760 (ASU BC ETSU LMC)
The Frontiersmen.
M8770 (ASU BC WCU)
His Vanished Star.
M8780 (ASU BC ETSU LMC)
In the Clouds, a Story.
M8790 (ASU BC ETSU LMC)
In the "Stranger People's" Country: A Novel.
M8800 (ASU BC ETSU LMC)
In the Tennessee Mountains.
M8810 (LMC)
In the Tennessee Mountains.
M8820 (ASU BC)
In the Tennessee Mountains.
M8830 (ASU BC)
In the Tennessee Mountains.
M8840 (LMC)
In the Tennessee Mountains.
M8850 (ASU LMC)
In the Tennessee Mountains.
M8860 (ETSU LMC)
In the Tennessee Mountains.
M8870 (WCU)
In the Tennessee Mountains.
M8880 (LMC MHC)
The Juggler.
M8890 (ASU BC ETSU LMC)
The Mystery of Witch-Face Mountain and Other Stories.
M8900 (ASU BC ETSU LMC)
The Mystery of Witch-Face Mountain, and Other Stories.
M8910 (WCU)
The Ordeal: A Mountain Romance of Tennessee.
M8920 (ASU BC ETSU)
The Phantoms of the Foot-bridge, and Other Stories.
M8930 (ASU BC ETSU WCU)
The Prophet of the Great Smoky Mountains.
M8940 (ASU BC)
The Prophet of the Great Smoky Mountains.
M8950 (ASU BC LMC WCU)
The Prophet of the Great Smoky Mountains.
M8960 (ETSU WCU WWC)
The Raid of the Guerilla, and Other Stories.
M8970 (ASU WWC)
The Raid of the Guerilla, and Other Stories.
M8980 (ETSU WCU)
A Spectre of Power.
M8990 (ASU BC WCU)
The Storm Centre: A Novel.
M9000 (ASU LMC)
The Story of Keedon Bluffs.
M9010 (ASU BC ETSU LMC)
The Story of Old Fort Loudon.
M9020 (ASU BC)
The Story of Old Fort Loudon.
M9030 (WCU)
Where the Battle Was Fought: A Novel.
M9040 (ASU)
The Windfall.
M9050 (ASU BC)
The Young Mountaineers: Short Stories.
M9060 (ASU BC WCU ETSU)
Black Fury.
M9200 (BC)
Backwoods Teacher.
N500 (ASU)
The Cavalier of Tennessee.
N940 (ASU BC)
Send Me An Angel.
N1140 (ASU)
Woman with a Sword: The Biographical Novel of Anna Ella Carroll of Maryland.
N1290 (ASU BC WCU)
The Lure of the Hills: A Tale of Life in the Mountains of Kentucky.
N1390 (BC ASU)
Divine Right's Trip: A Folktale.
N1420 (ASU)
Chattooga Griffin.
N1440 (LMC BC ASU)
All the Kingdoms of Earth, a Novel.
N1480 (BC ASU WCU)
The Days of Daniel Boone.
N2850 (ETSU)
The Days of Daniel Boone: A Romance of the "Dark and Bloody Ground".
N2860 (LMC ASU BC)
Aunt Jane of Kentucky.
O40 (ASU)
Aunt Jane of Kentucky.
O50 (WCU)
The Land of Long Ago.
O70 (BC WCU ASU)
To Love and to Cherish.
O80 (BC)
Sally Ann's Experience.
O90 (ASU BC)
Ginsey Kreider.
O110 (ASU)
The Anxious Seat.
O130 (BC)
Moonshine.
O290
Hand in Hand Through the Happy Valley.
O300
Winespring Mountain.
O340 (BC ASU)
Death on the Mountain.
O350
At Top of Tobin.
O610 (BC LMC)
Mountain Magic for Rosy.
O820
Home Is Where the Heart Is.
P20
With Sun in Our Blood.
P40 (ASU)
Red Rock: A Chronicle of Reconstruction.
P50 (ASU)
A Maid of the Mountains.
P80
Mountain Mating.
P280 (BC ASU WCU LMC MHC)
Two Boys in the Blue Ridge.
P310 (ASU)
The Mountaineer Detective. A Thrilling Tale of the Moonshiners.
P620 (ASU)
"Har Lampkins"; A Narrative of Mountain Life, On the Borders of the Two Virginians.
P810
Short Stories and Legends of the Mountains.
P930
Christmas at Grinder's Switch.
P1230 (LMC)
The Double Standard.
P1280
Up Country. A Story of the Vanguard.
P1430 (ASU)
Annie Laurie and Azalea.
P1440
Azalea's Silver Web.
P1450
Azalea: The Story of a Girl in the Blue Ridge Mountains.
P1460 (ASU WCU)
A Mountain Woman.
P1470 (ASU)
Tibb's Flooders.
P1530
Alabama Sketches.
P1550 (ASU)
Witch in the Mill.
P1580 (ASU LMC FC)
Red Belts.
P1660 (ASU WCU BC)
Corona of the Nantahalas, A Romance.
P1680
The History of Rome Hanks and Kindred Matters.
P1740 (ASU)
The Young Mrs. Blennerhasset: A Novel of Early Days in West Virginia.
P2010
My Head's High From Proudness.
P2270 (ASU)
Rain on the Mountain.
P2470
Blennerhassett: Or, The Degrees of Fate. A Romance Founded Upon Events in American History.
P2850 (ASU WCU WWC BC)
The Witch of Turner's Bald.*
P2900 (ASU)
The Daughter of the Smokies.
P2910 (ASU)
How Old Man Corn Held Possession.
P3220
The Trouble at Pinelands: A Detective Story.
P3270
"A Tale of the Ragged Mountains" in The Complete Works of Edgar Allan Poe.
P3280 (ASU ETSU)
Beautiful Upon the Mountains, the Story of a Kentucky Missionary.
P3290 (ASU)
Paul Judson: A Story of the Kentucky Mountains.
P3390
The Cudgel.
P3450
Against Human Nature.
P3490 (BC ASU)
Dally.
P3500 (BC ASU)
In Buncombe County.
P3510 (BC ASU LMC WCU)
The Red-bridge Neighborhood, A Novel.
P3520 (LMC BC)
The Common Problem.
P3690
The Complete Works of C. Henry.
P3720
Dwellers in the Hills.
P3780
The Mountain Schoolteacher.
P3790 (ASU BC)
Uncle Abner, Master of Mysteries.
P3800 (ASU BC)
North Carolina Fiction 1734-1957: An Annotated Bibliography.
P4000 (ASU MHC)
In the Shadow of the Cumberlands; a Story of Kentucky Mountain Life.
P4070
Elk Garden Tales.
P4160
Land of Canaan. Plain Tales from the Mountains of West Virginia.
P4250 (ETSU BC)
Land of Canaan: Plain Tales from the Mountains of West Virginia.
P4260 (ASU)
The Slate-picker: Story of a Boy's Life in the Coal Mines.
P4300 (WCU BC)
Paths of Glory.
P4430
Dear Teacher.
P4470 (BC)
Larning.
P4480
My Lady Lee.
P4490 (BC)
The Double Man.
P4810
John Gamp: Or, Coves and Cliffs of the Cumberlands.
P4870 (LMC BC)
April Is the Cruelest Month.
Q150 (BC)
Visiting the Sin: A Tale of Mountain Life in Kentucky and Tennessee.
R690 (BC ASU)
The Captain's Romance, or, Tales of the Backwoods.
R720 (ASU BC)
The Jucklins: A Novel.
R730 (BC ASU WCU ETSU)
Odd Folks.
R740 (BC ASU WCU)
Old Lim Jucklin.
R750 (ETSU)
The Starbucks: A New Novel.
R760 (ASU BC)
A Tennessee Judge: A Novel.
R770 (ASU ETSU)
The Waters of Caney Fork: A Romance of Tennessee.
R780 (ASU ETSU)
The Wives of the Prophet: A Novel.
R790 (ASU)
Partisan Rate; or, A Stirring Story of the Battle of Mill Springs.
R910

FICTION

Better a Dinner of Herbs.
R950 (ASU)
The Hawk and the Sun.
R970
The Morningside of the Hill.
R1090 (BC)
A Whimsical Collection.
R1190
Remembrance Way.
R1350 (ASU)
"Old Limber": Or, The Tale of the Taylors.
R1930 (ASU)
A Mountain Idyll.
R1950 (WCU BC ASU)
Tallulah and Jocassee, or, Romances of Southern Landscape, and Other Tales.
R2030
Snakes and the Devil.
R2140
From Cedar Mountain: A Collection of Stories from the Large American Novel, Cedar Mountain.
R2160 (ASU)
The Grandfathers.
R2180
The Road to Wildcat: A Tale of Southern Mountaineering.
R2360 (BC ASU LMC)
Tanis, the Sang-Digger.
R2570
The Mountain Journey.
R2720 (ASU)
Black Is My Truelove's Hair.
R2730 (ASU LMC ETSU WCU BC)
A Buried Treasure.
R2740 (ASU LMC WCU ETSU)
The Great Meadow.
R2750 (ASU LMC ETSU BC WWC)
The Haunted Mirror.
R2760
The Haunted Mirror; Stories.
R2770
He Sent Forth a Raven.
R2780 (ASU)
He Sent Forth a Raven.
R2790 (ETSU)
My Heart and My Flesh, a Novel.
R2800 (ASU ETSU WCU)
Not by Strange Gods; Stories.
R2810
The Time of Man.
R2830 (ETSU LMC WCU WWC BC)
The Time of Man, a Novel.
R2840 (WCU)
The Time of Man, a Novel.
R2850 (ASU)
The Man from Smiling Pass: Or, The Honorable Abe Blount.
R3250 (ASU BC)
"Smiles," a Rose of the Cumberlands.
R3260 (ASU WCU BC)
Smiling Pass: Being a Further Account of the Career of "Smiles," a Rose of the Cumberlands.
R3270 (ASU)
Daniel Boone: Or, The Pioneers of Kentucky.
R3300 (BC)
Daddy's Pearl and Other Stories.
R3420 (BC)
How Jack Went to College.
R3430 (BC)
Biny's Choice.
R3440 (BC)
Sarepty's Schoolin'; the Tale of a Mountain Maid Who Hungered for Knowledge.
R3450 (BC)
Adventures of Elder Triptolemus Tub.
R3470 (WCU)
Birthright.
R3530 (ASU)
Impassioned Foothills.
R3640
Love's Tapestry.
R3650
Jackson Mahaffey, a Novel.
R3850 (ASU)
Black Earth.
R4060 (ASU)
Stormy Road.
R4070
Bright Angel Trail.
R4100 (ASU)
A Quaker Scout.
R4290
Paths of Glory: A Simple Tale of a Faring Bride, Elizabeth, Sister of Patrick Henry.
R4350 (ASU)
Snakes and the Devil.
R4360 (LMC)
A Pagan of the Alleghanies.
R4480 (ASU BC)
Told in the Hills.
R4490
The Lost Country: A Novel.
S200 (ASU BC)
These Are My People.
S260 (ASU)
The Wheel of Earth.
S280 (ASU WCU BC)
The Wizard's Child.
S290 (ASU WCU LMC)
Hill-bred Barton's Code, a Western Story.
S320 (ASU BC)
Tenn. Boy.
S570 (BC ASU)
Cradle Valley.
S620 (BC ASU)
Brick Without Straw, a Story of Kentucky Mountain Life.
S630 (ASU BC)
Let the Spring Come.
S940 (ETSU BC ASU)
Betty Zane, Heroine of Fort Henry.
S1010 (ASU)
The Selfish and the Strong.
S1200
Witch Perkins.
S1390 (BC)
Hillbilly Doctor.
S1750 (ASU BC)
Never No More, a Novel.
S1760 (ASU WCU BC)
Red Clay Country.
S1790 (ASU)
Fight Night on a Sweet Saturday, a Novel.
S1950 (ASU WCU BC)
Know Nothing.
S1960 (ASU WCU)
O Beulah Land, a Novel.
S1970 (ASU LMC WCU)
O Beulah Land.
S1980 (WWC)
Gold or Guilt.
S2800 (ASU)
Hacey Miller: A Novel.
S2890 (BC LMC ASU)
Stand like Men.
S2900 (BC)
The Way to Fort Pillow: A Novel.
S2910 (LMC ASU BC WCU ETSU)
Daisy's Fanny.
S2920
Charlemont: Or, the Pride of the Village. A Tale of Kentucky.
S3470 (ASU)
Charlemont: Or, The Pride of the Village, a Tale of Kentucky.
S3480 (ETSU)
Guy Rivers: A Tale of Georgia.
S3490
Guy Rivers: A Tale of Georgia.
S3500 (ASU BC)
Guy Rivers: A Tale of Georgia.
S3510 (ASU ETSU)
The Scout: Or, The Black Riders of Congaree.
S3520 (ASU WCU ETSU)
Voltmeier, or The Mountain Men: A Tale of the Old North State.
S3530 (ASU)
The Wigwam and the Cabin.
S3540 (ASU)
The Wigwam and the Cabin. Life in America.
S3550 (WCU LMC)
Woodcraft: Or, Hawks About the Dovecote A Story of the South at the Close of the Revolution.
S3560 (ASU WCU ETSU)
The Writings of William Gilmore Simms, Centennial Edition.
S3570 (ASU)
Memo. to Timothy Sheldon.
S3680 (ASU)
King Coal.
S3700 (ETSU)
Disturb Not Our Dreams.
S3890 (ASU BC)
O Careless Love.
S3900 (ASU)
Hawk's Nest.
S3920 (BC ASU)
Heaven Came So Near.
S3930 (ASU LMC BC)
Hill Doctor.
S3940 (ASU WCU BC)
Hill Lawyer.
S3950 (BC LMC)
Hill Lawyer.
S3960 (ASU)
I Will Lift Up Mine Eyes.
S3970 (BC ASU)
I Will Lift Up Mine Eyes.
S3980 (LMC)
River Rising!
S3990 (ASU LMC)
Becky Landers; Frontier Warrior.
S4030 (BC)
Silent Scott, Frontier Scout.
S4070
Silent Scott, Frontier Scout.
S4080 (WWC BC)
Drought, and Other North Carolina Yarns.
S4560 (LMC ASU)
The Mountaineers: Or, Bottled Sunshine for Blue Mondays.
S4850 (ASU BC)
Call of the Big Eastatoe.
S4890 (LMC ASU)
A Tar-Heel Baron.
S4900 (ASU WCU BC)
A Tar-Heel Baron.
S4910 (ASU)
The Lost Children of the Allegheníes.
S5150 (ASU)
A Multitude of Men.
S5160 (BC)
Fisher's River Scenes, Reproduced from the Original.
S5290 (LMC WCU ASU BC)
Fallen Pride; or the Mountain Girl's Love.
S5900 (BC)
The Prince of Darkness, a Romance of the Blue Ridge.
S5910
The Sheriff of the Beech Fork: A Story of Kentucky.
S5980 (ASU BC)
The Old Mill on the Withrose.
S5990 (BC)
Junaluskie, the Cherokee; a Story of the War.
S6180
Toppy and the Circuit Rider.
S6350
This Time Next Year.
S6480 (ASU BC)
Fred Fearnot in West Virginia.
S6540
Ghost Stories from the Southern Mountains.
S6570 (ASU)
The Old Wilderness Road: An American Journey.
S6830 (WCU BC ETSU)
The Story of Daniel Boone.
S6860 (ASU BC)
They Had a Glory.
S7210 (ASU BC)
Rainbow Road.
S7220 (ASU BC)
River of Earth.
S7400 (BC ASU UNCA)
River of Earth.
S7410 (LMC ETSU)
River of Earth.
S7420 (WCU)
Sentimental Calendar, Being Twelve Funny Stories.
S7450 (ASU WCU)
Years of Harvest, Poems and Tales from the Smoky Foothills, 1924-1964.
S7500 (BC LMC WCU)
S7630
Eoneguski, or the Cherokee Chief: A Tale of Past Wars, by an American.
S7770
Eoneguski: Or, the Cherokee Chief (1839).
S7780 (ASU LMC MHC WCU BC)
With Boone on the Frontier, or The Pioneer Boys of Old Kentucky.
S7810

FICTION
Pride of Possession.
S7860 (ASU)
Droner's Gold.
S7870
Bright Metal.
S7910 (ASU LMC ETSU)
The Sound Wagon.
S7920 (ASU)
The Store.
S7930 (ASU)
Teeftallow.
S7940 (ASU WCU ETSU)
Unfinished Cathedral.
S7950 (ASU)
The Starlight of the Hills; A Romance of the Kentucky Mountains.
S8090
Behind the Great Smokies.
S8100 (ASU)
Passerman's Hollow.
S8190 (BC ASU)
Yellowhawk.
S8210 (BC ASU)
Clearing in the Sky and Other Stories.
S8280 (ETSU ASU)
Come Back to the Farm.
S8290 (ASU LMC MHC WCU ETSU FC BC)
Come, Gentle Spring.
S8300 (ASU LMC MHC WCU ETSU BC UNCA)
Come to My Tomorrowland.
S8310 (LMC ASU WCU MHC ETSU BC)
Daughter of the Legend.
S8320 (ASU MHC LMC WCU WWC ETSU BC UNCA)
Foretaste of Glory.
S8340 (ASU WCU BC)
The Good Spirit of Laurel Ridge.
S8360 (ASU ETSU BC)
Head o' W-Hollow.
S8380 (ASU)
Head o' W-Hollow.
S8390 (WCU ETSU)
Hie to the Hunters.
S8400 (ASU WCU LMC MHC ETSU BC)
A Jesse Stuart Harvest.
S8430 (FC BC ASU)
A Jesse Stuart Reader: Stories and Poems.
S8440 (ASU WCU BC ETSU)
Men of the Mountains.
S8490 (ASU WWC BC)
Mongrel Mettle, the Autobiography of a Dog.
S8500 (LMC WCU UNCA ETSU BC)
Mr. Gallion's School.
S8510 (ASU WCU MHC LMC WWC ETSU BC UNCA)
My Land Has a Voice.
S8520 (ASU MHC WCU LMC WWC ETSU FC UNCA)
Plowshare in Heaven: Stories.
S8550 (ASU WCU MHC WWC ETSU BC)
The Rightful Owner.
S8580 (ASU LMC ETSU BC)
The Rightful Owner.
S8590 (WCU)
Save Every Lamb.
S8600 (ASU WCU MHC ETSU BC)
Tales from the Plum Grove Hills.
S8630 (ASU FC ETSU)
Taps for Private Tussie.
S8640 (ETSU BC)
Taps for Private Tussie.
S8650 (ASU WCU LMC MHC UNCA)
32 Votes before Breakfast: Politics at the Grass Roots, as Seen in Short Stories.
S8660 (ASU BC)
Tim, a Story.
S8690 (ASU LMC BC ETSU)
Trees of Heaven.
S8710 (ASU WCU WWC ETSU BC)
Kentucky Story, a Collection of Short Stories.
S9030 (ASU BC)
Tall Tales of the Devils Apron.
S9270 (LMC BC FC)
My Kentucky Cousins.
S9760 (ASU BC)
Carolina Humor: Sketches.
T50 (ASU)
Bloody Ground: A Cycle of the Southern Hills.
T260 (ASU LMC BC ETSU)
Some Trust in Chariots.
T270 (ASU LMC BC ETSU)
The Singing Hills.
T7850 (ASU)
Brave Heart Elizabeth; a Story of the Ohio Frontier.
T8120 (ASU BC)
At Love's Extremes.
T8270 (BC)
Stories of the Cherokee Hills.
T8280 (BC WCU)
Oic-? Science Fiction.
T8350 (ASU)
The Witch's Castle.
T8390 (ASU)
My "Budie" and I.
T8410 (ASU)
Barbara's Vagaries.
T8560 (WCU BC)
Bonny Kate. A Novel.
T8580 (ASU)
His Victory.
T8590
The Land of the Sky; or Adventures in Mountain By-Ways.
T8600
"The Land of the Sky": Or, Adventures in Mountain By-Ways.
T8610 (LMC)
The Land of the Sky: Or, Adventures in Mountain By-Ways.
T8620 (LMC)
"The Land of the Sky": Or, Adventures in Mountain Byways.
T8630
A Little Maid of Arcady.
T8640
A Summer Idyl.
T8650
Bricks Without Straw: A Novel.
T9010 (WCU BC ETSU)
A Fool's Errand, by One of the Fools: The Famous Romance of American History.
T9020 (WCU BC)
A Fool's Errand: A Novel of the South During Reconstruction.
T9030 (WWC)
The Invisible Empire: A Concise Review of the Epoch, With Many Thrilling Personal Narratives and Startling Facts of Life at the South, Never Before Narrated for the General Reader, All Fully Authenticated.
T9040 (WCU)
A Royal Gentleman: A Novel.
T9050 (WCU)
Katy of Catoctin: Or, The Chain-Breakers, a National Romance.
T9070 (ASU WCU BC WCU)
In the Nantahalas: A Novel.
T9100 (LMC BC ASU WCU)
Tanis, the Sang-Digger.
T9440 (ASU)
Virginia of Virginia: A Story.
T9450 (LMC)
Cudjo's Cave.
T9490 (ASU ETSU)
Legion of the Lost Mine; Stories of the Cumberland.
T9500
The Partisan Leader.
T9580
The Partisan Leader.
T9650 (ASU)
The Partisan Leader.
T9660 (ETSU)
Son of the Valley.
T9720 (ASU ETSU)
Stories and Verse of West Virginia.
T9780
Acres of Beauty.
T9860
Voyage; an Anthology of Selected Stories by Mary Lavin, Rhys Davies, James Hanley and Others.
V20
The Captive Witch.
V210 (ASU)
Our Country Then: Tales of Our First Frontier.
V260 (ASU)
The Trembling Earth.
V270 (ASU)
The Shadow of Hampton Mead.
V340
This Green Thicket World.
V660 (ASU)
Wiley Buck and Other Stories.
W130 (LMC)
Beckoning Ridge.
W190 (ASU)
Tennessee Tales.
W280 (ASU LMC ETSU BC)
The Cave.
W980 (ETSU BC)
The Green Arch.
W1020
Hang My Wreath.
W2020
Mountain Feud.
W2590 (ASU MHC BC)
Mystery at Bear Paw Gap.
W2600 (ASU)
The South Fork Rangers.
W2610 (MHC)
The Specter of Bear Paw Gap.
W2620 (WCU BC)
Who Fears the Devil?
W2630 (LMC)
Rain on the Mountain.
W2860 (BC)
Appalachian Dawn.
W3020 (ASU LMC WCU)
Time Was.
W3060 (ASU LMC)
Gentlemen, Hush!
W5180 (BC ETSU)
Kentucky Stand.
W5190 (ASU LMC ETSU WCU BC)
Mark Ellis, or Unsolved Problems: A Story for the Present Day.
W5240 (ASU)
The Rural School Teacher: Or, A Double West Virginia Love Story.
W5330 (BC)
Mr. G. Strings Along.
W6160 (LMC)
Sim Greene and Tom the Tinker's Men.
W6190 (BC)
Cale.
W6340 (ASU)
Hostile Valley.
W6400 (ASU)
Greenbones.
W6880 (ASU)
Walk Egypt.
W6890 (ASU WCU LMC BC)
Saint Elmo, a Novel.
W7080 (ASU)
A Speckled Bird.
W7090 (ASU)
Our Bed Is Green.
W7160
The Grandfather and the Globe.
W7180 (ASU LMC WWC BC)
The Hill Billy Kid.
W7210 (BC)
Fidelity Folks.
W7250 (WWC)
The Valley of Time.
W7270 (LMC)
The Happy Years.
W7420
The Nine Brides and Granny Hite.
W7430 (ASU BC)
The Lost Trail: A Story of the Kentucky Mountains.
W7550 (BC)
Diomed: The Life, Travels, and Observations of a Dog.
W7900 (ASU)
Look Homeward, Angel; a Story of the Buried Life.
W8140 (MHC BC UNCA)
Look Homeward, Angel: A Story of the Buried Life.
W8150 (WWC)
Look Homeward, Angel: A Story of the Buried Life.
W8160 (WCU)
Look Homeward, Angel: A Story of the Buried Life.
W8170 (WCU)
Look Homeward, Angel: A Story of the Buried Life.
W8180 (LMC WCU MHC ETSU)
The Lost Boy.
W8190 (BC)

FICTION
Of Time and the River: A Legend of Man's Hunger in His Youth.
W8240 (ASU WCU BC UNCA WWC)
Of Time and the River: A Legend of Man's Hunger in His Youth.
W8250 (ETSU)
You Can't Go Home Again.
W8390 (ASU WWC WCU ETSU BC UNCA)
Love in the Mists.
W8450
For the Major: A Novelette.
W9030 (ASU WCU ETSU BC)
Horace Chase.
W9040 (ASU WCU BC)
Horace Chase.
W9050 (ETSU)
Rodman the Keeper: Southern Sketches.
W9060 (WCU ASU)
In the Valley of the Shadows.
W9080 (BC)
Youngblood Hawke.
W9330 (ASU ETSU BC)
Hungry Hollow.
W9370 (BC)
Christmas at Thunder Gap.
W9450 (BC)
Home to the Hills.
W9540
Home to the Hills.
W9550
Bundle of Troubles, and Other Tarheel Tales.
W9600 (WWC ASU LMC)
The Gate Is Down; A Novel of The Alabama Hills.
Y40
Brave Interval.
Y60 (BC)
Stories from the Hills, 1971.
Y90 (LMC)
The Trapper's Last Shot.
Y310
Wolf at the Door.
Y320 (ASU)
The Summer Soldier.
Z160 (ETSU)
Bitter Sweet, A Mountain Story.
2600 (LMC)

FICTION — APP.
Mountain Fiction From Addington to Zugsmith: 924 Works of Fiction by Southern Appalachian Authors, Or With Southern Appalachian Settings.
P2160
A Shelf List of More than 760 Works of Fiction.
P2170
Deep in the Hearts of Men.
W520 (BC)
The Woodcarver of Olympus.
W530 (ASU)

FICTION — APP. MTNS.
Yours for the Asking.
A20 (ASU BC)

FICTION — JUVENILE
The Little Fiddler of Laurel Cove.
A520 (ASU BC)
Sugar in the Gourd.
A550
Tip Off to Win.
A560 (BC)
My Rose Valley.
A5580 (ASU)
Geraldine the Sightseeing Cow.
B850 (ASU LMC BC)
The Witch and Cinderella, The Boom-cat Kid and other stories.
B970 (ASU)
Some Snow for Christmas.
B2730 (BC ASU)
Mountain Boy.
B2830 (LMC)
Snow.
B2840 (ASU)
The Two Worlds of Davy Blount.
B2850 (ASU BC)
Yaller-Eye.
B2860
Caleb's Luck.
B2880
B3660 (BC ASU)
Trouble on Old Smoky.
B4630 (ETSU)
How Davy Crockett Got a Bearskin Coat.
B4680 (ETSU)
Renfroe's Christmas.
B8410
Beanie.
C1510 (ASU WWC BC)
The Christmas Kitten.
C1520 (MHC)
The Picnic Bear.
C1550 (ASU)
Runaway Pony.
C1560 (ASU MHC BC)
Tough Enough.
C1570 (ASU MHC WWC BC)
Tough Enough and Sassy.
C1580 (ASU LMC BC)
Tough Enough's Indians.
C1590 (ASU LMC ETSU)
Tough Enough's Pony.
C1600 (ASU MHC LMC BC)
Tough Enough's Trip.
C1610 (ASU MHC LMC BC)
Tough Enough's Trip.
C1620 (WWC)
Barrie and Daughter.
C2270
Barrie and Daughter.
C2280 (ASU ETSU)
The Best-loved Doll.
C2290 (ETSU)
A Certain Small Shepherd.
C2300 (ASU LMC WWC ETSU)
Contrary Jenkins.
C2320 (ASU MHC ETSU BC)
Did You Carry the Flag Today, Charley?
C2330 (ASU LMC MHC ETSU WWC BC)
The Far-off Land.
C2340 (LMC WCU ASU)
Happy Little Family.
C2350 (ASU LMC ETSU BC)
Higgins and the Great Big Scare.
C2360 (ETSU)
A Pocketful of Cricket.
C2390 (ASU WWC LMC WCU ETSU)
Saturday Cousins.
C2400 (ASU LMC BC)
Saturday Cousins.
C2410 (ETSU)
Schoolhouse in the Woods.
C2420 (ASU LMC WCU ETSU BC)
Schoolroom in the Parlor.
C2430 (ASU LMC WCU)
Schoolroom in the Parlor.
C2440 (ETSU)
Susan Cornish.
C2450 (WCU ETSU BC)
Susan Cornish.
C2460 (ASU LMC)
Time for Lisa.
C2470
Tree of Freedom.
C2480 (ASU LMC BC)
Tree of Freedom.
C2490 (ETSU)
Up and Down the River.
C2500 (ASU LMC WCU ETSU BC)
Bear Weather.
C2670 (BC ASU)
Freeman.
C2690 (ASU LMC BC)
John Henry McCoy.
C2700 (ASU LMC MHC BC)
Roy in the Mountains.
C4200 (ASU)
The Champion of Sourwood Mountain.
C4270 (LMC BC ASU)
Goodbye Kate.
C4280 (ASU BC)
A Long Row to Hoe.
C4290 (ASU BC)
The Mooneyed Hound.
C4300 (BC ASU)
Lazar and Boone Stop Strip Mining Bully to Save Apple Valley and Buttermilk Creek.
C4510 (ASU)
Where the Lilies Bloom.
C4840 (BC ASU)
Down Tumbledown Mountain.
C5270 (LMC)
Old Whirlwind.
C5280 (ETSU)
This Snake is Good.
C7280 (ASU)
Johnnie Mountain.
C8390 (WWC)
Big Doin's on Razorback Ridge.
C8610 (ETSU ASU)
Down Down the Mountain.
C8620 (ASU MHC BC)
Johnny and His Mule.
C8630 (ETSU ASU)
Beneath the Hill.
C9850
Howard McPhlinn. A Story for Boys.
D2250
The Court-martial of Daniel Boone: A Novel.
E750 (ASU BC)
A Bibliography of Appalachian Children's and Young People's Books.
E1170
The Secret of the Simple Code.
F340
Cynthia of Bee Tree Hollow.
F2490 (ETSU ASU)
Lona of Hollybrush Creek.
F2500 (ASU)
Mountain Girl.
F2510 (ETSU BC ASU)
Mountain Girl Comes Home.
F2520 (ASU BC)
The Moon of the Bears.
G860 (ETSU)
The Whispering Fairy: Constructive Stories for Children.
G1250 (LMC)
Sal-o-quah; or, Boy-life Among the Cherokees.
G2900
. . . Sal-o-quah; or, Boy-life Among the Cherokees.
G2910
Sweet Opossum Valley.
G2930 (ASU WWC BC)
Those Plummer Children.
G2940 (ETSU)
I Want to Be Coal Miner.
G3710
Angeline Doin' Society.
G3910 (BC)
Angeline Hittin' on High.
G3920 (BC)
Angeline of the Hill Country.
G3930 (ASU WCU BC)
Angeline Steppin' Out.
G3940 (BC)
Big Sky.
G4950 (WCU WWC BC)
The Here to Yonder Girl.
H630 (ASU BC)
The Hillbillys, a Book for Children.
H2340 (ASU)
Malinda of the Blue Ridge.
H2390 (ASU LMC)
Smoke on Old Thunderhead.
H2780 (ASU BC LMC)
The Boy Troopers Among the Wild Mountaineers.
H3900 (BC)
Dan'l Boone Kissed Me.
H6930 (ASU)
Pink Puppy.
H7000 (ASU)
The History Limb.
H7830 (BC ASU)
Lost on Hawk Mountain.
J1850 (ASU)
Big Log Mountain.
J3030 (LMC ASU)
Children of the Great Smoky Mountains.
J3040 (WCU ETSU)
Children of the Great Smoky Mountains.
J3050 (ASU LMC MHC)
Eben and the Rattlesnake.
J3070 (ETSU)
Here Comes Mary Ellen.
J3080 (ETSU)
Holidays in No-End Hollow.
J3090
Holidays in No-End Hollow.
J3100 (BC ETSU)
Honey Jane.
J3110 (ETSU)
House in No-End Hollow.
J3120 (ETSU WWC ASU)
Hurrah for Jerry Jake.
J3130 (ETSU)
It happened in No-End Hollow.
J3140

FICTION — JUVENILE
Jerry Jake Carries On.
J3150 (ETSU ASU)
Jumping Johnny Outwits Skedaddle.
J3160
Lester and His Hound Pup.
J3170 (ASU LMC)
Lizzie.
J3180 (ETSU ASU)
Luck for Little Lihu.
J3190 (ETSU ASU)
Lucky Penny.
J3200 (ETSU ASU)
The Mail Wagon Mystery.
J3210 (ASU WWC ETSU)
New Boy in School.
J3220 (LMC MHC WCU ASU)
A New Home for Billy.
J3230 (LMC ASU)
The Other Side of the Mountain.
J3240 (ASU LMC WCU)
Peter Pocket and His Pickle Pup.
J3260 (ETSU)
Sammy.
J3270 (ETSU ASU)
Smoky Mountain Sampler: Stories.
J3280 (ASU LMC MHC)
Step Along and Jerry Jake.
J3290 (ETSU ASU)
Surprise for Perky Pup.
J3300
Surprise for Peter Pocket.
J3310 (ASU LMC)
Tales from Near-side and Far.
J3320
Tale of a Pig.
J3330 (LMC ASU)
Then Came Mr. Billy Barker.
J3340 (ASU LMC WCU)
Toby Has a Dog.
J3350 (ETSU)
Use Your Head, Hildy.
J3360 (ASU LMC ETSU)
Winds a Blowing.
J3370 (ASU LMC)
You're Sure Silly, Billy.
J3380 (ASU)
Cherokee Boy.
K1750 (ASU BC)
Escape to Witch Mountain.
K1760 (ASU)
The Forgotten Door.
K1770
With Daniel Boone on the Caroliny Trail.
K1780 (ASU LMC WCU ETSU BC)
Snakehunter.
K2190 (ASU LMC)
Up the Big Mountain.
K2940
Blue Ridge Billy.
L1780 (ASU LMC MHC BC WCU ETSU)
Coal Camp Girl.
L1790 (WCU ETSU BC)
Gertrude's Pocket.
M5460 (ASU BC LMC ETSU)
Hoagie's Rifle-Gun.
M5470 (ASU BC LMC)
As by Fire.
M6860 (ASU)
Autumn on Breezy Hill.
M6870 (ASU)
Dan and Jack Find a Pal.
M6890 (ASU)
Doctor Happy.
M6900 (ASU)
Eyes Unto the Hills.
M6910 (ASU)
The Healing Hills.
M6930 (ASU)
The Jolly J's Have a Reunion.
M6940 (ASU)
The Jolly J's Make Decisions.
M6950 (ASU)
The Jolly J's of Silver Creek.
M6960 (ASU)
Joy Shop Stories.
M6970 (ASU)
On Silver Creek Knob.
M6990 (ASU BC)
Spring on Breezy Hill.
M7020 (ASU)
The Touch of Polly Tucker.
M7050 (ASU)
The Triplets Go to Camp.
M7060
"Selected Children's Fiction with a Contemporary Setting in the Mountains of Kentucky and North Carolina."
M7880 (ASU)
The Boy Spies at the Defense of Fort Henry, a Story of Wheeling Creek in 1777.
O910 (ASU BC)
Hannah of Kentucky, a Story of the Wilderness Road.
O920 (ASU BC)
Let's Be Early Settlers with Daniel Boone.
P180 (ASU ETSU)
Davy Crockett, Young Rifleman.
P330 (ETSU)
Snifty.
P4510
Jud.
R660 (ASU)
Up from Appalachia.
R670 (ASU LMC MHC ETSU)
The Only Nancy.
R3150 (LMC ASU)
Journey Cake, Ho!
S600 (ASU)
Zuska of the Burning Hills.
S1630 (BC ASU)
A Sight of Everything.
S5280 (ASU)
Stories of W. Va. for Boys & Girls.
S5560
The Secret of Fiery Gorge.
S6760 (ASU)
Daniel Boone's Echo.
S6780 (ASU BC)
The Far Frontier.
S6790 (BC)
Flaming Arrows.
S6800 (WCU BC)
John Sevier, Boy Pioneer.
S6810 (BC)
The Lone Hunt.
S6820 (BC)
Over-Mountain Boy.
S6840
The Perilous Road.
S6850
Tomahawks and Trouble.
S6870 (BC)
Triple Trouble for Hound Dog Zip.
S6880
Wilderness Journey.
S6890 (ASU WCU BC)
Winter Danger.
S6900 (WCU BC)
Witch of the Cumberlands.
S7040
Moccasin Tracks.
S7880 (ASU)
Andy Finds a Way.
S8230 (ASU BC)
The Beatinest Boy.
S8250 (ASU LMC ETSU WWC WCU MHC)
Dawn of Remembered Spring.
S8330 (ASU WCU LMC ETSU)
Huey, the Engineer.
S8420
Old Ben.
S8530 (ASU LMC ETSU BC)
A Penny's Worth of Character.
S8540 (ASU LMC MHC WCU ETSU BC)
Red Mule.
S8560 (ASU LMC MHC ETSU BC)
A Ride with Huey, the Engineer.
S8570 (ASU LMC ETSU BC)
Stories by Jesse Stuart.
S8610 (ASU LMC WCU BC)
Scouting with Daniel Boone.
T8830 (ASU LMC BC)
Cherokee.
T9120 (LMC BC WCU MHC)
Highpockets.
T9710 (ASU)
The Fiddler of High Lonesome.
T9730 (LMC ASU WCU)
Gena of the Appalachians.
W490 (BC ASU ETSU)
Betsy Dowdy's Ride.
W2180
Battle at Bear Paw Gap.
W2500 (ASU)
Battle for King's Mountain.
W2510 (ASU LMC)
Clash on the Catawba.
W2520 (ASU)
Lights over Skeleton Ridge.
W2570
The Master of Scare Hollow.
W2580 (ASU WCU BC)
Danger down River.
W3010 (ASU LMC)
This Boy Cody.
W7370 (ASU ETSU)
This Boy Cody and His Friends.
W7380 (ASU ETSU)
Tip of the Toe.
W8010 (LMC)

FICTION — JUVENILE — CIVIL WAR
The Rock of Chickamauga: A Story of the Western Crisis.
A1940 (ASU BC)
The Sword of Antietam: A Story of the Nation's Crisis.
A1950 (ASU)

FICTION — JUVENILE — KY.
The Young Trailers: A Story of Early Kentucky.
A1960 (ASU WCU BC)

FICTION — KY.
Oldfield: A Kentucky Tale of the Last Century.
B1000 (ASU BC WCU)
"Tales of the Mountains" A Complete Directory of the Eastern Kentucky Coalfields with Extracts from the Geological Reports, Forestry, Oil Development, Education, Superstitions, and Religion of the Mountains.
H730

FICTION — N. C.
The Carolinians.
B1510 (ASU WWC)
"The Dialect of the Southern Highlander as Recorded in North Carolina Novels."
E980 (ASU)

FICTION — WILDLIFE — ELK
Appalachian Elk.
B2540 (ASU)

FIRE PROTECTION — N. C.
Organization of Co-operative Forest Fire Protective Areas in North Carolina.
H6850 (ASU)

FLOODS AND FLOOD CONTROL
The Pittston Mentality: Manslaughter on Buffalo Creek.
B3380
West Virginia's Buffalo Creek Flood: A Study of the Hydrology and Engineering Geology.
D720
A Disastrous Flood, a True and Fascinating Story.
G3780 (ASU LMC)
Action Programs for Eastern Kentucky: Final Report of the Kentucky Flood Rehabilitation Study.
K1060 (BC ASU)
Planning for Flood Damage Prevention.
M7200
The Floods of July 1916: How the Southern Railway Organization Met an Emergency.
S5850 (ASU LMC)
Chattanooga Flood Control Problem.
T2380
Floods on the Tuckaseigee River and Deep Creek in Vicinity of Bryson City, North Carolina.
T2750
Operation of TVA Reservoirs, Annual 1963.
T3140
Preliminary Report: Floods on Scott Creek in Vicinity of Sylva, North Carolina.
T3250
A Program for Reducing the National Flood Damage Potential.
T3270
Program for Reducing the National Flood Damage Potential.
T3280
TVA Flood Control.
T3810
TVA Flood Control; New Concepts.
T3820
TVA; A River Controlled.
T3870
TVA Tames the River.
T3890
To Keep the Water in the Rivers and the Soil on the Land . . .
T3990

FLOODS AND FLOOD CONTROL

. . . Value of Flood Height Reduction from TVA Reservoirs to the Alluvial Valley of the Lower Mississippi River . . .
T4070

Drawings for the Kentucky Project.
T6340

Flood Damage Prevention; An Indexed Bibliography.
T6900

Boone Project Hydraulic Model Studies.
T6920

. . . Flood Control for Upper French Broad River and Tributaries; a Preliminary Report.
T6930

Flood of August 24-25, 1961: Upper French Broad River Basin.
T6940

Flood on Piney River, November 18-19, 1957, in Vicinity of Spring City, Tennessee.
T6950

Floods of March 1963 in Tennessee River Basin.
T6960

Floods on Beaver Creek, in Vicinity of Bristol, Virginia-Tennessee.
T6970

Floods on Brush Creek in Vicinity of Johnson City, Tennessee.
T6980

Floods on Cheoah River and Tributary Creeks in Vicinity of Robbinsville, North Carolina.
T6990

Floods on Clinch River, in Vicinity of Clinton, Tennessee.
T7000

Floods on Elk River and Norris Creek, in Vicinity of Fayetteville, Tennessee.
T7010

Floods on Elk River in Vicinity of Fayetteville, Tennessee.
T7020

Floods on French Broad and Davidson Rivers and King, Nicholson, and Tucker Creeks in Vicinity of Brevard, North Carolina.
T7030

Floods on French Broad and Swannanoa Rivers, in Vicinity of Asheville, North Carolina.
T7040

Floods on French Broad River and Spring Creek in Vicinity of Hot Springs, North Carolina.
T7050

Floods on French Broad River in the Vicinity of Marshall, N. C.
T7060

Floods on Hiwassee River, Valley River, and Peachtree Creek in Vicinity of Murphy, N C.
T7070

Floods on Little Pigeon and West Fork Little Pigeon in the Vicinity of Sevierville, Tenn.
T7080

Floods on Little Tennessee River, Cullasaja River, and Cartoogechave Creek in Vicinity of Franklin, North Carolina.
T7090

Floods on Nolichucky River and North and South Indian Creeks in Vicinity of Erwin, Tennessee.
T7100

Floods on North Chickamauga, Mountain, and Lookout Creeks, in Vicinity of Chattanooga, Tennessee.
T7110

Floods on North Toe River and Beaver and Grassy Creeks in Vicinity of Spruce Pine, North Carolina.
T7120

Floods on Oconaluftee and Tuckaseigee Rivers and Soco Creek in Vicinity of Cherokee, North Carolina.
T7130

Floods on Oostanaula Creek, in Vicinity of Athens, Tennessee.
T7140

Floods on Oostanaula Creek in Vicinity of Athens, Tenn.
T7150

Floods on Powell River and South Fork Powell River in Vicinity of Big Stone Gap, Virginia.
T7160

Floods on Powell River and South Fork Powell River in Vicinity of Big Stone Gap, Virginia.
T7170

Floods on Reedy Creek in Vicinity of Kingsport, Tennessee.
T7180

Floods on Richland Creek and Tributary Streams in Vicinity of Waynesville and Hazelwood, North Carolina.
T7190

Floods on Rock Creek, West Fork and North Fork, in Vicinity of Tullahoma, Tennessee.
T7200

Floods on South Mouse Creek in Vicinity of Cleveland, Tennessee.
T7210

Floods on Streams in Vicinity of Newport, Tennessee.
T7220

Floods on Streams in Vicinity of Paris, Tennessee.
T7230

Floods on Swannanoa River and Beetree Creek in Vicinity of Swannanoa, North Carolina.
T7240

Floods on Swannanoa River and Flat Creek in Vicinity of Black Mountain and Montreat, North Carolina.
T7250

Floods on Tennessee River and Battle Creek, in Vicinity of South Pittsburg and Richard City, Tennessee.
T7260

Floods on the Tennessee River and Cypress and Cox Creeks in Vicinity of Florence, Alabama.
T7270

Floods on Tennessee River in Vicinity of Tri-Counties Alabama (Lawrence, Limestone, Morgan.)
T7280

Floods on Tennessee River, Little Tennessee River, and Town and Muddy Creeks in Vicinity of Lenoir City, Tennessee.
T7290

Floods on Toccoa-Ocoee River and Fightingtown Creek, in Vicinity of McCaysville, Ga. — Copperhill, Tenn.
T7300

Floods on Valley River, Tatham Creek, and Junaluska Creek in Vicinity of Andrews, North Carolina.
T7310

Floods on Yellow Creek in Vicinity of Burnsville, Mississippi.
T7320

Hydraulic Model Investigations of Lock Filling and Emptying Systems.
T7410

Reforestation and Erosion Control Influences Upon the Hydrology of the Pine Tree Branch Watershed 1941 to 1960.
T7500

Floods in Youghiogheny and Kiskiminetas River Basins, Pennsylvania and Maryland, Frequency and Magnitude.
U3140

The Tennessee River Basin.
U3870

FLOODS AND FLOOD CONTROL — APP.

The Floods of March, 1936, Part 3, Potomac, James, and Upper Ohio Rivers.
G4470

Floods of Ohio and Mississippi Rivers, January-February, 1937.
G4480

The Ohio River Basin.
I890

Flood Problems and Management in the Tennessee River Basin.
T2730

Floods and Flood Control.
T2740

Floods on Watauga and Doe Rivers in Vicinity of Elizabethton, Tennessee.
T2760

Flood Damage Prevention; an Indexed Bibliography.
T5920

Flood Damage Prevention; an Indexed Bibliography.
T5930

Flood Damage Prevention; an Indexed Bibliography.
T5940

Flood Damage Prevention; an Indexed Bibliography.
T5950

Flood Damage Prevention; an Indexed Bibliography.
T5960

Drainage Modifications in Southeastern Ohio and Adjacent Parts of West Virginia and Kentucky.
T8660

FLOODS AND FLOOD CONTROL — KY.

Flood of July 5, 1939, in Eastern Kentucky.
S1070

FLOODS AND FLOOD CONTROL — N. C.

Flood Damage Prevention in North Carolina.
H4250 (LMC)

Floods on Small Streams in North Carolina: Probable Magnitude and Frequency.
H5630 (LMC)

FLOODS AND FLOOD CONTROL — PA.

"The Allegheny-Monongahela Flood Control Program and Its Benefits to Metropolitan Pittsburgh."
W7330

FLOODS AND FLOOD CONTROL — TENN.

Floods in Tennessee; Magnitude and Frequency.
J620

Planning for Flood Damage Prevention.
L2390

Flood Problems and Their Solution Through Urban Planning Programs.
S3360

Flood Problems and Their Solution Through Urban Planning Programs.
T1630

. . . The Chickamauga Project, a Comprehensive Report on the Planning, Design, Construction, and Initial Operations of the Chickamauga Project. . . .
T2410

Flood on Piney River, November 18-19, 1957 in the Vicinity of Spring City, Tenn.
T5530

FLOODS AND FLOOD CONTROL — VA.

"Debris Avalanching as a Natural Hazard in the Southern Appalachians: A Case Study of the Davis Creek Watershed, Virginia."
K3370 (ETSU)

FLOODS AND FLOOD CONTROL — W. VA.

Disaster on Buffalo Creek, 1972; Report of the Citizen's Commission Investigation.
C4160 (BC ASU WCU)

Flood of August 4-5, 1943, in Central West Virginia, with a Summary of Flood Stages and Discharges in West Virginia.
E2160 (ASU)

The Ohio Valley Flood of March-April, 1913, Including Comparisons with Some Earlier Floods.
H7290

Death at Buffalo Creek: The 1972 West Virginia Flood Disaster.
N2970 (BC LMC ASU)

FLOODS — APP.

Cost Study of Pumping Versus Flowing Oil Production from Appalachian Waterfloods.
R3970

FLOODS — W. VA.

Relation of Geology to Drainage, Floods, and Landslides in the Petersburg Area, West Virginia.
S8030 (ETSU)

FOLK ART

How to Make Whirligigs and Whimmy Diddles and Other American Folkcraft Objects.
P2450

America's Folk Art.
P3410 (ASU)

American Folk Toys: 85 American Folk Toys and How to Make Them.
S1000 (ASU)

The Origins and Characteristics of Folk Art in West Virginia.
S2450

Arts and Crafts of the Shenandoah Valley.
S4610 (ASU BC FC)

Vanishing Crafts and Their Craftsmen.
S6940 (ASU)

Apple and Doughhead Dollmaking: Clothes Patterns Included.
T520 (WCU)

FOLK ART — PA.

Sketches and Chronicles: The Reflections of a Nineteenth Century Pennsylvania German Folk Artist.
M5910 (FC)

FOLK ART — VA.
Folk Art in Stone, Southwest Virginia.
W9790 (ASU ETSU BC)
Virginia Fraktur. Penmanship as Folk Art.
W9800
FOLK ART — W. VA.
"The Revival of the Folk Arts in West Virginia."
R420 (ASU LMC)
FOLK ARTS
American Folk Painting.
B4330 (ASU)
Pattern in the Material Folk Culture of the Eastern United States.
G2080 (ASU BC WCU LMC FC)
Vegetable Dyeing: 151 Color Recipes for Dyeing Yarns and Fabrics with Natural Materials.
L1880 (ASU)
FOLK ARTS — APP.
"Chairmaking in Appalachia: A Study in Style and Creative Imagination in American Folk Art."
J2520 (ASU)
FOLK CUSTOMS
Early Ballads, Illustrative of History, Traditions, and Customs: Also Ballads and Songs of the Peasantry of England, Taken Down from Oral Recitation and Transcribed from Private Manuscripts, Rare Broadsides, and Scarce Publications.
B2800 (ASU)
Reminiscences and Traditions of Western North Carolina.
D700
Folk Dances of Tennessee; Folk Customs and Old Play Party Games of the Caney Fork Valley.
M1190 (ASU)
FOLK DANCE — CHEROKEE
Cherokee Dance and Drama.
S6090 (ASU WCU ETSU BC)
FOLK DANCES
Favorite Folk Dance Tunes.
B3070 (ASU BC)
The Games of Children, Their Origin and History.
B3390 (ASU)
The American Play-party Song.
B5610 (ASU)
Handy Square-Dance Book.
C7230 (WCU ASU)
The Folk Dance Book for Elementary Schools, Class Room, Playground, and Gymnasium.
C8510 (BC)
And Promenade All.
E1400
Smoky Mountain Square Dances.
H4630 (ASU)
Folk Dances of Tennessee; Folk Customs and Old Play Party Games of the Caney Fork Valley.
M1190 (ASU)
Swing Your Partners: A Guide to Modern Country Dancing.
M2680
Kentucky Mountain Square Dancing Running Set.
M4350 (ASU)
Everybody Square Dances: In the Southern Appalachians: The Story of Folk Dancing and Mountain Music as Enjoyed by Natives and Visitors in the Southern Highlands.
M8510 (ASU WCU)
Kentucky Mountain Square Dancing.
N70 (ASU BC LMC)
Folk Arts Workshop.
N1550 (ASU)
Dances of Our Pioneers.
R4460 (ASU BC)
The Country Dance Book.
S2280 (ASU BC)
Circle Left! Folk Play of the Kentucky Mountains.
S3840 (ASU LMC BC)
The Appalachian Square Dance.
S4680 (ASU MHC LMC WCU BC)
Folk Games from Frying Pan Creek in Dickenson County, Virginia.
S9160
Folk Dancing in America.
W180 (BC)
English Folk Song and Dance.
W6580
Sing and Dance: Folk Songs and Dances Including American Play-party Games.
W7280 (BC)

FOLK DANCES — APP.
Bascom Lamar Lunsford, "Minstrel of the Appalachians." His Ballads and His Folk Songs, His Mountain Square Dancing.
G1810 (ASU UNCA WCU LMC WWC MHC)
Folk Dancing.
K3160 (FC ASU)
It's Fun to Square Dance: Southern Appalachian Calls and Figures.
L3980
FOLK DANCES — KY.
A Gatherin'; Ky. Lore of Mt. Music, Songs, and Dances.
K2830
Renfro Valley; Then and Now.
L160
FOLK LIFE
The Scamps of Bucksnort: Memories of a Nineteenth-century Childhood in Rural Tennessee.
P140 (ASU)
Manners, Customs, and Observances: Their Origins and Signification.
W110 (ASU)
FOLK MEDICINE
Medicine in Virginia in the Seventeenth Century.
B4660
Southern Home Remedies.
C3920 (BC ASU)
Herbs: Their Culture and Uses.
C4700 (LMC)
Old Timey Recipes.
C6690 (ASU LMC BC)
Old Timey Recipes.
C6700 (WCU BC)
Old Timey Recipes.
C6710 (LMC)
The Medicinal Plants of Tennessee Exhibiting Their Commercial Value, with an Analytical Key, Descriptions in Aid of Their Recognition, and Notes Relating to Their Distribution, Time and Mode of Collection, and Preparation for the Drug Market.
G610
North Carolina Drug Plants of Commercial Value.
H2130 (ASU LMC UNCA)
Ginseng and Other Medicinal Plants; a Book of Valuable Information for Growers as well as Collectors of Medicinal Roots, Barks, Leaves, etc.
H2160
Southern Home Remedies.
H2650 (ASU LMC)
Index of Plants of North Carolina With Reputed Medicinal Uses.
J230 (WWC)
Colonial Kitchen Herbs and Remedies: Garden and Kitchen Secrets from Early America.
S2700 (ASU LMC)
Pioneer Beauty Secrets: Old and New Cosmetics from the Kitchen, Garden and Insect Control.
S2720 (ASU LMC)
Pioneer Comforts and Kitchen Remedies. Old Timey Highland Secrets from the Blue Ridge and Great Smoky Mountains.
S2730 (MHC ASU BC WCU)
An Occult Remedy Manuscript from Pendleton County, West Virginia.
S7300
The Folk-lore of Plants.
T7720 (ASU)
Kentucky Superstitions.
T7790 (ASU BC)
Grannies's Remedies.
T8010 (ASU)
Natural and Folk Remedies.
W40 (ASU LMC WCU BC)
Nature's Pantry; 100 Wild Edible Plants Alphabetically Listed, Each with Full Description, Food Preparation and Folk Medicinal Properties.
W7170 (BC)
FOLK MEDICINE — APP.
American Medicinal Barks.
H4640 (ASU)
American Medicinal Leaves and Herbs.
H4650 (ASU)
Ginseng, Its Cultivation, Harvesting, Marketing and Market Value: With a Short Account of Its History and Botany.
K70 (WWC)

Guide to Medicinal Plants of Appalachia.
K3230 (BC)
A Guide to Medicinal Plants of Appalachia.
K3240 (ASU ETSU LMC)
FOLK MEDICINE — CHEROKEE
Notebook of a Cherokee Shaman.
K2000 (WCU ETSU UNCA ASU)
The Cherokee Physician . . . As Given by Richard Foreman.
M2830
The Sacred Formulas of the Cherokees.
M6790 (WCU ASU)
The Swimmer Manuscript, Cherokee Sacred Formulas and Medicinal Prescriptions.
M6800 (ETSU)
FOLK MEDICINE — N. C.
Drug Plants of Western North Carolina.
M2740 (WCU ASU)
Medicine in Buncombe County Down to 1885, Historical and Biographical Sketches.
T880
FOLK MUSIC
The Old-time Fiddler's Repertory: 245 Traditional Tunes.
C3950 (ASU BC)
FOLK SCHOOLS
B4770 (BC)
The First 40 Years: John C. Campbell Folk School.
M2440 (ASU LMC MHC BC)
Gift from the Hills: Miss Lucy Morgan's Story of Her Unique Penland School.
M7620 (ASU BC ETSU FC WCU WWC)
Gift from the Hills: Miss Lucy Morgan's Story of Unique Penland School.
M7630
FOLK SCHOOLS — HIGHLANDER
Unearthing Seeds of Fire: The Idea of Highlander.
A390
Annual Report.
H5300
The Story of an Educational Center for Working People.
H5310
FOLK SCHOOLS — J. C. CAMPBELL
The John C. Campbell Folk School, 1925-1952.
B7490
FOLK SCHOOLS — PENLAND
The Story of the Penland Weavers.
F1880 (ASU BC)
FOLK SCHOOLS — TENN.
Or We'll All Hang Separately: The Highlander Idea.
B4700 (LMC WWC ETSU BC)
Echo in My Soul.
C4530 (BC)
Highlander Folk School Audio Collection.
T2070 (ETSU)
Highlander Folk School Manuscript Records Collection, 1932-1966.
T2080 (LMC)
FOLK SONG
Letters on Scottish Ballads from Professor Child to William Walter.
C3840 (ASU)
FOLK SONGS
Anglo-American Folksong Style.
A140 (ASU BC)
Death in the Dark.
A420 (BC ASU)
A History of the Musical Careers of Dewitt "Snuffy" Jenkins, Banjoist, and Homer "Pappy" Sherrill, Fiddler.
A790 (LMC)
The Ballad Book.
A1750 (BC)
The Story of American Folk Song.
A2200 (ASU BC)
Songs of Freedom.
A3330
Old English Ballads and Folk Songs.
A4660
Songs from the Carolina Hills.
A4670
"The Melodic and Rhythmic Characteristics of the Traditional Ballad Variants Found in the Southern Appalachians."
A4690 (ASU)
A Century of Ballads.
A5270 (ASU)

FOLK SONGS

English Folk-songs Collected, Arranged, and Provided with Symphonies and Accompaniments for the Pianoforte.
B1470 (ASU)

Hill Country Tunes: Instrumental Folk Music of Southwestern Pennsylvania.
B2150 (LMC)

Early Ballads, Illustrative of History, Traditions, and Customs: Also Ballads and Songs of the Peasantry of England, Taken Down from Oral Recitation and Transcribed from Private Manuscripts, Rare Broadsides, and Scarce Publications.
B2800 (ASU)

Singa Hipsy Doodle, and Other Folk Songs of West Virginia.
B4980 (ASU ETSU BC)

Songs along the Mahantongo: Pennsylvania Dutch Folk-songs.
B6050 (ASU)

Singing Carr and Other Song-ballads of the Cumberlands.
B6210 (ASU BC)

The Ballad Mongers: Rise of the Modern Folk Song.
B6310 (BC)

The Folk-carol of England.
B6560 (BC)

The Traditional Tunes of the Child Ballads.
B6830 (ASU BC)

Gleanings of Scarce Old Ballads, With Explanatory Notes.
B7920 (ASU)

The Minstrel of the Mountains.
B8820 (BC)

The Technique and Variation in an American Fiddle Tune.
B8890

Collection of Folklore: Folksongs.
B9290 (ASU LMC WCU ETSU BC)

Collection of Folklore: Folksongs II.
B9300 (ASU LMC ETSU BC)

ETSU Collection of Folklore; Folksongs.
B9310 (LMC)

Folk Songs of Central West Virginia.
B9330 (ASU WCU LMC BC)

East Tennessee and Western Virginia Mountain Ballads (The Last Stand of American Pioneer Civilization).
C370 (ASU BC)

English Folk Songs from the Southern Appalachians, Comprising 122 Songs and Ballads, and 323 Tunes.
C830 (ASU LMC WWC BC)

Folk-songs of Roanoke and the Albemarle.
C3300 (ASU)

American Folk Tales and Songs, and Other Examples of English-American Tradition as Preserved in the Appalachian Mountains and Elsewhere in the United States.
C3400 (ASU WCU LMC BC)

American Folk Tales and Songs, and Other Examples of English-American Tradition as Preserved in the Appalachian Mountains and Elsewhere in the United States.
C3410 (WWC)

Hullabaloo, and Other Singing Folk Games.
C3430 (WCU WWC BC)

Old Songs and Singing Games.
C3470 (ASU WCU BC)

Old Songs and Singing Games.
C3480 (LMC)

Singing Games and Playparty Games.
C3490 (ASU MHC BC)

The English and Scottish Popular Ballads.
C3820 (ASU)

The English and Scottish Popular Ballads.
C3830 (BC)

The British Traditional Ballad in North America.
C5500 (ASU FC)
C5920 (ETSU ASU LMC BC)

Folksongs of the Southern United States.
C6130 (ASU WCU MHC LMC WWC BC FC)

Songs of All Time.
C7240 (WCU)

Songs of All Time.
C7910 (ASU ETSU LMC BC)

Southwestern Pennsylvania in Song and Story.
C8100

Folk-songs of the South.
C8160 (ETSU BC FC)

Folk-songs of the South.
C8170 (ASU WCU LMC MHC ETSU)

"Songs and Ballads Sung in Overton County, Tennessee a Collection."
C8310

"Ballad Characteristics in Modern Popular Country Music."
C8580 (ETSU)

Traditional Tales of the English and Scottish Peasantry.
C9730

Traditional Tales of the English and Scottish Peasantry, Vol. I.
C9740

Traditional Tales of the English and Scottish Peasantry, Vol. II.
C9750

Folksongs of Virginia.
D760 (ASU)

Folk-songs of Virginia, a Descriptive Index and Classification of Material.
D770 (ASU LMC FC BC)

Folk-songs of Virginia, a Descriptive Index and Classification of Material.
D780 (ETSU)

More Traditional Ballads of Virginia: Collected with the Cooperation of Members of the Virginia Folklore Society.
D790 (ASU FC BC LMC)

Traditional Ballads of Virginia.
D800

Traditional Ballads of Virginia.
D801 (ASU)

Traditional Ballads of Virginia: Collected Under the Auspices of the Virginia Folk-lore Society.
D810 (LMC FC BC)

Traditional Ballads of Virginia: Collected Under the Auspices of the Virginia Folklore Society.
D820 (WCU ETSU ASU)

A Valley and a Song; the Story of the Shenandoah River.
D1150 (BC ASU)

The Oxford Book of Carols.
D1520 (LMC)

The American Folk Scene; Dimensions of the Folksong Revival.
D1910 (BC)

The Frank C. Brown Collection of North Carolina.
D3810 (ASU WCU LMC MHC BC WWC ETSU)

Anthology of American Folk Music.
D4020 (ASU BC)

Folklore on the American Land.
E1970 (ASU BC MHC)

The HodgePodge Book, An Almanac of American Folklore.
E1980
F80 (ASU)

Folk-songs, Chanteys and Singing Games.
F210 (ASU LMC BC)

John Henry and His Hammer.
F560
F1690 (ASU BC WCU WWC LMC ETSU FC)

Scraps of Songs and Southern Scenes: A Collection of Humorous and Pathetic Poems and Descriptive Sketches of Plantation Life in the Backwoods of Georgia.
F1760 (ASU)

A Literary History of the Popular Ballad.
F2400 (BC ASU)

Mountain Ballads.
F3210 (BC)

Ballads of the Kentucky Highland.
F4020 (ASU LMC ETSU BC)

The Face of Folk Music.
G90 (ASU)

"The Heritage and Folk Music of Cades Cove, Tennessee."
G230 (LMC)

West Virginia Lyrics.
G1870 (ASU)

Songs of Hill and MOUNTAIN Folk, Ballads, Historical Songs, Folk Songs.
G2060 (BC ASU)

Folksongs and Their Makers.
G2070 (ASU MHC BC)

Aunt Molly Jackson Memorial Issue.
G3490

Only a Miner: Studies in Recorded Coal Mining Songs.
G3500 (ASU LMC MHC WCU BC)

"Recorded American Coal Mining Songs."
G3510

"An Edited Collection of Beech Mountain Folksongs."
G3680 (ETSU)

American Folksongs of Protest.
G3880

Old English Ballads.
G4900 (BC)

Smoky Mountain Folks and Their Lore.
H810 (BC ASU WCU LMC MHC)

Smoky Mountain Folks and Their Lore.
H820 (ETSU)

The Book of British Ballads.
H890 (BC)

American Folk Legend.
H1450

Middletown Valley in Song and Story.
H1740 (BC)

"Ananias Davisson: Southern Tune Book Compiler (1780-1857)."
H3230

"Cocke County Ballads and Songs."
H3650 (ASU)

A Bibliography of North American Folklore and Folksong.
H4010 (ASU WWC)

Bundle of Troubles, and Other Tarheel Tales.
H4600

Bibliography for the Study of American Folk Songs with Many Titles from Other Lands.
H4780

Folk-songs from the Southern Highlands.
H4790 (ASU LMC MHC ETSU BC)

Songs Sung in the Southern Appalachians.
H4800 (BC)

Still More Ballads and Folk-songs from the Southern Highlands.
H4810

"Southern Mountain Folk Songs for American Schools."
H6440 (ASU)

Sing to Me of Heaven: A Study of Folk and Early American Materials in Three Old Harp Books.
H7170 (ASU BC)

Sweet Rivers of Song: A Book of Traditional Songs From the Southern Appalachian Mountain Region.
J370 (ASU MHC WCU BC)

Tuning and Playing the Appalachian Dulcimer.
J570 (WCU)

Popular British Ballads, Ancient and Modern.
J1930

Peddler's Pack.
J3250 (ETSU ASU)

Tale of a Pig.
J3330 (LMC ASU)

"The Carter Family: A Reflection of Changes in Society."
K10 (WCU)

Cecil Sharp: His Life and Work.
K230 (BC ASU LMC)
K1850 (ETSU)

Country and Bluegrass Dobro.
K2220 (WCU)

A Folk Song Chapbook.
K2580 (LMC)

Hi! Ho! The Rattlin' Hog and other Folk Songs for Group Singing.
L450

The Swapping Boy.
L460 (ASU)

Jim Along, Josie; a Collection of Folk Songs and Singing Games for Young Children.
L470 (ASU)

American Balladry from British Broadsides: A Guide for Students and Collectors of Traditional Song.
L920 (BC ASU)

Native American Balladry, a Descriptive Study and a Bibliographical Syllabus.
L930 (FC)

The Ballad Book.
L1130 (ASU)
L2830 (BC ASU ETSU)

A Peddlar's Pack of Ballads and Songs.
L3090 (ASU BC)

FOLK SONGS

Hard Hitting Songs for Hard Hit People: American Folk Songs of the Depression and the Labor Movement of the 1930's.
L3140 (BC ASU MHC LMC)
American Ballads and Folk Songs.
L3160 (LMC BC FC)
American Ballads and Folk Songs.
L3170 (WCU ASU)
Folk Song U. S. A., the 111 Best American Ballads.
L3180 (WCU FC ASU)
Our Singing Country: A Second Volume of American Ballads and Folk Songs.
L3190 (WCU BC)
Folk Songs on Records.
L3950 (ASU)
30 and 1 Folksongs from the Southern Mountains.
L3990 (ASU BC)
Ancient Ballads and Songs, Chiefly from Tradition, Manuscripts, and Scarce Works.
L4060 (ASU)
Hillbilly Records and Tune Transcriptions.
M990
Some Child Ballads on Hillbilly Records.
M1000
Folk Dances of Tennessee; Folk Customs and Old Play Party Games of the Caney Fork Valley.
M1190 (ASU)
Songs of the Old Camp Ground.
M1220 (BC ASU)
Melodies and Mountaineers.
M2240 (ASU)
Four and Twenty Songs for the Mountain Dulcimer.
M2520 (ASU BC)
A New Book of Old Ballads.
M2840
Country Music U. S. A.: A Fifty-year History.
M2910 (FC ASU)
Songs and Ballads of the Southern People, 1861-1865.
M7130 (ASU)
"A Program of Folk Songs Used to Enrich and Implement the Social Studies Program in Grades Four, Five and Six at North Side School, Johnson City, Tennessee."
M7380 (ETSU)
Living with Ballads.
M8480 (ASU FC)
Ballads, Folk Songs and Folk Tales from West Virginia.
M9170 (ASU BC)
"The Life and Works of Lamar Stringfield, 1897-1959."
N480 (ASU WCU)
An Introduction to Folk Music in the United States.
N620 (BC)
Games and Songs of American Children, Collected and Compared.
N760 (ASU BC)
A Book of Old Ballads.
N840 (BC)
A Book of Old Ballads.
N850
The Ballad Book.
N1030 (ASU BC FC LMC MHC)
The Ballad Book.
N1040 (ASU ETSU)
The Ballad Book.
N1050 (ASU WCU)
Ballads, Carols, and Tragic Legends from the Southern Appalachian Mountains.
N1060 (ASU ETSU LMC)
Ballads, Lovesongs, and Tragic Legends from the Southern Appalachian Mountains.
N1070 (ASU)
Folk Ballads for Young Actors.
N1080 (ASU BC)
Folk Carols for Young Actors.
N1090 (ASU)
More Songs of the Hill-folk: Ten Ballads and Tragic Legends from Kentucky, Virginia, Tennessee, North Carolina, and Georgia.
N1100 (ASU ETSU)
Seven Kentucky Mountain Tunes.
N1110 (BC)
Songs of the Hill-folk: Twelve Ballads from Kentucky, Virginia, and North Carolina.
N1120 (ASU BC ETSU LMC)
Ten Christmas Carols from the Southern Appalachian Mountains.
N1130 (ASU BC)
The Guitar Songbook.
N1260
The Lady Angeline: A Lay of the Appalachians.
N1300 (BC)
Folk Arts Workshop.
N1550 (ASU)
Mountain Songs of North Carolina.
N3030
Something to Sing About.
O460 (BC)
The Bothy Songs & Ballads of Aberdeen, Banff & Moray, Angus and the Mearns.
O770 (ASU)
Ramblin' Boy, and Other Songs.
P1090 (ASU)
A Selective Music Bibliography from the Period 1663-1763.
P4800 (LMC)
The Foggy Dew; More English Folk Songs from the Hammond and Gardiner Manuscripts.
P4890 (ASU)
Go Tell Aunt Rhody.
Q30 (ASU)
Grass Roots Harmony.
R120 (LMC)
Mountain Ballads for Social Singing.
R150 (BC)
Gordon Ballads.
R920 (ASU)
"The Cyclone of Rye Cove: The Event, the Folklore, the Song."
R1040 (ETSU)
American Mountain Songs.
R2060 (ETSU BC ASU)
American Mountain Songs.
R2070 (ASU ETSU WCU BC)
Ancient English Christmas Carols.
R2200 (FC)
A Singer and Her Songs.
R2230 (BC)
Apple Seeds and Soda Straws: Some Love Charms and Legends.
R2400 (ASU)
Celebration of Life, Her Songs, Her Poems.
R2410 (ASU)
Celebration of Life: Her Songs, Her Poems.
R2420 (LMC)
The Dulcimer Book, Being a Book about the Three-stringed Appalachian Dulcimer, Including Some Ways of Tuning and Playing: Some Recollections in Its Local History in Perry and Knott Counties, Kentucky. Some Observations on the Probable Origins of the Instrument in the Old Countries of Europe: And with Words and Music for Some Sixteen Songs from the Ritchie Family of Kentucky.
R2430 (ASU BC ETSU LMC WCU)
The Dulcimer Book, Being a Book about the Three-stringed Appalachian Dulcimer, Including Some Ways of Tuning and Playing: Some Recollections in Its Local History in Perry and Knott Counties, Kentucky. Some Observations on the Probable Origins of the Instrument in the Old Countries of Europe: With Plentiful Photographic Illustrations and Drawings. And with Words and Music for Some Sixteen Songs from the Ritchie Family of Kentucky.
R2440 (ASU)
Folk Songs of the Southern Appalachian As Sung by Jean Ritchie.
R2450 (WWC)
Folk Songs of the Southern Appalachians; As Sung by Jean Ritchie.
R2460 (LMC WWC ETSU)
A Garland of Mountain Song: Songs from the Repertoire of the Ritchie Family of Viper, Kentucky.
R2470 (ASU WWC)
The Folksongs of Virginia.
R3780 (FC)
The American Songbag.
S270 (FC)
A Song Catcher in Southern Mountains: American Folk Songs of British Ancestry.
S730 (ASU WCU ETSU WWC BC)
A Song Catcher in Southern Mountains: American Folk Songs of British Ancestry.
S740 (ASU LMC ETSU)
English Song Book.
S1410
The Incomplete Folksinger.
S1690
American Folk Songs for Christmas.
S1700 (ASU)
American-English Folk Songs, Collected in the Southern Appalachians.
S2270 (ASU)
Eighty English Folk Songs from the Southern Appalachians.
S2300 (WCU ASU BC ETSU)
English Folk Songs from the Southern Appalachians.
S2320 (ASU WWC FC)
English Folk Songs from the Southern Appalachians.
S2330 (ETSU)
English Folk Songs from the Southern Appalachians.
S2340 (ASU WCU LMC MHC)
Nursery Songs from the Appalachian Mountains.
S2360 (ASU BC LMC)
British Ballads in the Cumberland Mountains.
S2580
A Syllabus of Kentucky Folk-Songs.
S2590
Folk Songs of the Blue Ridge Mountains: 50 Traditional Songs as Sung by the People of the Blue Ridge Mountains Country.
S2640 (ASU ETSU LMC MHC WCU BC)
The Country Music Story: A Picture History of Country and Western Music.
S2780 (ASU WCU)
The Music Lover's Handbook.
S3290 (ASU)
Beginning the Folk Guitar, an Instructional Manual.
S3380 (ASU)
Folk Blues: 110 American Folk Blues.
S3390 (ASU)
American Anthology of Old-world Ballads.
S4980 (ASU)
South Carolina Ballads: With a Study of the Traditional Ballad Today.
S4990 (ASU BC)
The Traditional Ballad and Its South Carolina Survivals.
S5000 (LMC)
S5520 (ASU)
Read 'Em and Weep: The Songs You Forgot to Remember.
S5950 (ASU)
The Cherokee in Romance, Tragedy, and Song in the Great Smokies.
S8020 (ETSU)
S9580
Folk-style Autoharp; an Instruction Method for Playing the Autoharp and Accompanying Folk Songs.
T360 (ASU)
Ballad Makin' in the Mountains of Kentucky.
T7880 (ASU WCU LMC ETSU BC)
Devil's Ditties, Being Stories of the Kentucky Mountain People, Told by Jean Thomas, With the Songs They Sing.
T7920 (ASU BC)
The Singin' Fiddler of Lost Hope Hollow.
T7930 (LMC ASU ETSU BC)
The Singin' Gatherin': Tunes From the Southern Appalachians.
T7940 (UNCA BC ETSU ASU)
The Singin' Gatherin': Tunes From the Southern Appalachians.
T7950 (LMC BC)
The Sun Shines Bright.
T7960 (ASU WCU LMC ETSU BC)
Folk Music in America.
V180
The Songs of Doc Watson.
W1510 (ASU WCU)
The Ballad Tree, a Study of British and American Ballads, Their Folklore, Verse and Music, Together with Sixty Traditional Ballads and Their Tunes.
W2710 (BC)
Southern Mountain Folk Traditions: And the Folksong "Stars" Syndrome.
W2990 (ASU LMC)
The W. Va. Centennial Book of One Hundred Songs: 1863-1963; Patriotic Songs, Folk Songs, and Hymns.
W3220 (BC)

FOLK SONGS
New Race of Song Sparrows from the Appalachian Region.
W4960
Mountain Songs of North Carolina.
W4970 (BC)
Smoky Mountain Ballads.
W4980
The Billy Edd Wheeler Song Book.
W5070 (WWC)
Anglo-American Folksong Scholarship Since 1898.
W6250 (BC)
English Folk Song and Dance.
W6580
Lonesome Tune, Folk Songs from the Kentucky Mountains.
W9870 (ASU BC)
Twenty Kentucky Mountain Songs.
W9880 (ASU BC)
Pennsylvania Spirituals.
Y100 (ASU)

FOLK SONGS — APP.
Vagabond Songs and Ballads of Scotland.
F1980 (ASU)
Bascom Lamar Lunsford, "Minstrel of the Appalachians." His Ballads and His Folk Songs, His Mountain Square Dancing.
G1810 (ASU UNCA WCU LMC WWC MHC)
Hillbilly Ballads.
H2450
Ballad Books and Ballad Men: Raids and Rescues in Britain, America, and the Scandinavian North Since 1800.
H8670 (ASU BC)
Songs of the Workers to Fan the Flames of Discontent.
I750 (ASU)
Wake and Sing: A Miniature Anthology of the Music of Appalachian America.
J380 (WWC BC ASU)
Tuning and Playing the Appalachian Dulcimer.
J550 (ASU LMC)
Tuning and Playing the Appalachian Dulcimer.
J560 (BC)
Songs from the Hills.
J2320 (WCU)
Peculiarities of the Appalachian Mountaineers: A Summary of Legends, Traditions, Signs, and Superstitions That Are Almost Forgotten.
J2540 (BC ASU LMC WCU ETSU MHC)
"Folk Songs of Watauga."
K3000
Coal Dust on the Fiddle: Songs and Stories of the Bituminous Industry.
K3050 (ASU LMC WCU BC)
Minstrels of the Mine Patch: Songs and Stories of the Anthracite Industry.
K3060 (ASU LMC MHC BC)
Appalachian Fiddle.
K3140
Folksingers and Folksongs in America.
L880 (BC)
Folksingers and Folksongs in America: A Handbook of Biography, Bibliography, and Discography.
L890 (ASU WWC BC)
The Ballad Book.
L1140 (WCU)
American Folk Songs and Folklore: A Regional Bibliography.
L3110
The Folk Songs of North America, in the English Language. Melodies and guitar chords transcribed by Peggy Seeger with one-hundred piano arrangements by Matyas Seiber and Don Banks. Illustrated by Michael Leonard. Editorial assistant Shirley Collins.
L3130 (WCU ASU)
Adventures of a Ballad Hunter.
L3150 (ASU BC)
A Collection of Highland Vocal Airs.
M1160 (ASU)
Beech Mountain Folk-Songs and Ballads.
M4260
From Bishop Percy (1765) to John Jacob Niles (1974): 340 Books of Ballads and Songs in the Berea College Collection.
P2150 (BC ASU)
Jean Ritchie's Swapping Song Book.
R2480 (ASU WCU)
Singing Family of the Cumberlands.
R2490 (ASU MHC WWC BC)
Singing Family of the Cumberlands.
R2500 (ASU WCU LMC)
The Swapping Song Book.
R2510 (BC ASU LMC)
Folk Songs from the Southern Appalachians.
S2290 (ASU BC)
English Folk Songs from the Southern Appalachians, Comprising 273 Songs and Ballads with 968 Tunes, Including 39 Tunes Contributed by Olive Dame Campbell.
S2310 (ASU)
Twenty-Five Great Folk Songs.
W5090 (BC)
Kentucky Mountain Folk-Songs.
W5160
Sing and Dance: Folk Songs and Dances Including American Play-party Games.
W7280 (BC)
Folklore in the English and Scottish Ballads.
W7560 (ASU FC)
English and Scottish Popular Ballads.
W7930 (BC)

FOLK SONGS — BRITISH
Gleanings of Scotch, English, and Irish: Scarce Old Ballads, Chiefly Tragical and Historical. Many of Them Connected with the Localities of Aberdeenshire.
B7930 (ASU)

FOLK SONGS — CHEROKEE
Walk in Your Soul: Love Incantations of the Oklahoma Cherokees.
K2030 (LMC)

FOLK SONGS — ENGLISH
A History of English Balladry, and Other Studies.
B7840 (ASU)

FOLK SONGS — KY.
Kentucky Mountain Melodies.
J770
A Gatherin'; Ky. Lore of Mt. Music, Songs, and Dances.
K2830
Renfro Valley; Then and Now.
L160
Folk-songs of the Kentucky Mountains.
M1520 (ASU WCU BC)
Twenty-five Kentucky Folk Ballads.
S8990 (BC)
"Ballads and Songs of Eastern Kentucky."
W6470

FOLK SONGS — PA.
Two Penny Ballads and Four Dollar Whiskey: A Pennsylvania Folklore Miscellany.
G2370
Pennsylvania Songs and Legends.
K3070

FOLK SONGS — RELIGIOUS
"Folk-hymns of the Southland."
S5080 (WCU)
S9580

FOLK SONGS — S. C.
Folk Song in South Carolina.
J2780 (WCU)

FOLK SONGS — SCOTTISH
Ancient Ballads and Songs of the North of Scotland.
B7910 (ASU)

FOLK SONGS — TENN.
"A Collection of Ballads and Songs from East Tennessee."
A2280 (LMC)
Folk Dances of Tennessee; Old Play Party Games of the Caney Fork Valley.
M1200 (BC ASU)
Bulletin.
T1380 (ETSU)

FOLK SONGS — W. VA.
Traditional Ballads and Folk-songs Mainly from West Virginia.
C8180 (ASU WCU ETSU BC)
The West Virginia Centennial Book of One Hundred Songs, 1863-1963; Patriotic Songs, Folk Songs and Hymns.
G100
Paint Creek Miner.
P660

FOLK TALES — N. C.
High Lands.
R1760 (ASU LMC WCU)

FOLK TALES — TENN.
Governor Bob Taylor's Tales.
R1920

FOLK TALES — W. VA.
John Henry: An American Legend.
K350

FOLKLIFE
The Southern Appalachian Heritage.
C2041
Survivals in Belief Among the Celts.
H4470
From Laurel Hill to Siler's Bog.
T7600 (ETSU)
The Foxfire Book: Hog Dressing; Log Cabin Building; Mountain Crafts and Foods; Planting by the Signs; Snake Lore, Hunting Tales, Faith Healing; Moonshining; and Other Affairs of Plain Living.
W6020 (FC ASU BC)
Foxfire 2: Ghost Stories, Spring Wild Plant Foods, Spinning and Weaving, Midwifing, Burial Customs, Corn Shuckin's, Wagon Making and More Affairs of Plain Living.
W6030 (FC ASU BC)
Foxfire 3: Animal Care, Banjos and Dulcimers, Hide Tanning, Summer and Fall Wildplant Foods, Butter Churns, Ginseng, and Still More Affairs of Plain Living.
W6040 (ASU)
America's Vanishing Folkways.
W7200 (MHC)
The Smoke Hole and Its People.
W9750 (BC)

FOLKLIFE — KY.
In the East Kentucky Hills.
Q160 (ASU WCU ETSU LMC)

FOLKLORE
Appalachia Revisited: How People Lived Fifty Years Ago.
A400 (ETSU BC ASU WCU FC LMC)
Witch, Warlock, and Magician: Historical Sketches of Magic and Witchcraft in England and Scotland.
A490 (ASU)
Indian Stories of Virginia's Last Frontier.
A510
Tom Dooley.
A1410 (ASU LMC)
West Virginia: Stories and Biographies.
A2060
Aunt Malissa's Memory Jug: Original Folk Stories.
A4850 (BC)
The Devil in Britain and America.
A5280 (ASU)
"An Empirical Study of the Application of the Folk-urban Typology to the Classification of Social Systems."
A5540 (ASU)
Along the Ridges.
B380 (ASU LMC)
"Folklore of Macon County, Tennessee."
B900
I Hear America Singing.
B1320 (BC)
The Folk-lore Manual.
B1820 (ASU)
Early Ballads, Illustrative of History, Traditions, and Customs: Also Ballads and Songs of the Peasantry of England, Taken Down from Oral Recitation and Transcribed from Private Manuscripts, Rare Broadsides, and Scarce Publications.
B2800 (ASU)
"Superstitions about Food and Health among Negro Girls in Elementary and Secondary Schools in Marion County, West Virginia."
B4600
The Voice of the Folk: Folklore and American Literary Theory.
B4840 (FC)
Singa Hipsy Doodle, and Other Folk Songs of West Virginia.
B4980 (ASU ETSU BC)
The Counting-Out Rhymes of Children: Their Antiquity, Origin, and Wide Distribution, A Study in Folk-lore.
B5190 (ASU)
A Treasury of American Folklore: Stories, Ballads, and Traditions of the People.
B5620 (ASU FC)
A Treasury of Southern Folklore: Stories, Ballads, Traditions and Folkways.
B5630 (WWC BC FC ETSU WCU)
The Mystery of the Wizard Clip.
B7030 (ASU)

FOLKLORE

Hill Doctor, Tells in Story and Ballads, Tales of the Appalachians.
B7750
Proverbs, and How to Collect Them.
B7850 (ASU)
"The Evolution of Southern Appalachian Culture as Evidenced in Folklore."
B8850 (ETSU)
Collection of Folklore: Folksongs.
B9290 (ASU LMC WCU ETSU BC)
Collection of Folklore: Folksongs II.
B9300 (ASU LMC ETSU BC)
ETSU Collection of Folklore; Folksongs.
B9310 (LMC)
Country Style: An Anthology of Hillbilly Humor.
B9630 (LMC)
Superstitions of the Highlands and Islands of Scotland.
C680
Cloud-walking.
C710 (ASU WWC BC)
Cloud-walking.
C720 (LMC ETSU WCU BC)
Tales from the Cloud Walking Country.
C740 (ASU WCU LMC MHC ETSU BC)
The Southern Appalachian Heritage.
C2041
Popular Rhymes of Scotland.
C2800 (ASU)
John Henry, a Folklore Study.
C3310
John Henry: A Folklore Study.
C3320
American Folk Tales and Songs, and Other Examples of English-American Tradition as Preserved in the Appalachian Mountains and Elsewhere in the United States.
C3400 (ASU WCU LMC BC)
American Folk Tales and Songs, and Other Examples of English-American Tradition as Preserved in the Appalachian Mountains and Elsewhere in the United States.
C3410 (WWC)
Grandfather Tales: American-English Folk Tales.
C3420 (ASU WCU LMC MHC WWC ETSU BC FC)
Jack and the Three Sillies.
C3440 (ASU LMC MHC WCU BC)
The Jack Tales.
C3450 (ASU LMC MHC WWC WCU ETSU BC)
The Jack Tales.
C3460
Wicked John and the Devil.
C3500 (WCU BC)
The English and Scottish Popular Ballads.
C3820 (ASU)
The English and Scottish Popular Ballads.
C3830 (BC)
Letters on Scottish Ballads from Professor Child to William Walter.
C3840 (ASU)
Ring-tailed Roarers: Tall Tales of the American Frontier, 1830-60.
C3900 (ASU)
Blue Ridge Facts and Legends.
C4360 (ASU LMC)
Uncle Bud Long: The Birth of a Kentucky Folk Legend.
C4670 (ASU)
Proverb, Proverbial Phrases and Proverbial Comparisons in the Writings of Jesse Stuart.
C4690
John Griswold White Collection.
C4990
Bypaths in Dixie: Folk Tales of the South.
C5410 (ASU BC)
The British Traditional Ballad in North America.
C5500 (ASU FC)
A Description of the George Korson Folklore Archive.
C7460 (ASU)
The Whang Doddle; Folk Tales from the Carolinas.
C7690 (BC)
An Introduction to Folk-lore.
C8190 (ASU)
Tall Tales from the High Hills, and Other Stories.
C8640 (ASU LMC MHC WCU BC)
Witchcraft in North Carolina.
C9120 (LMC)
Traditional Tales of the English and Scottish Peasantry.
C9730
Traditional Tales of the English and Scottish Peasantry, Vol. I.
C9740
Traditional Tales of the English and Scottish Peasantry, Vol. II.
C9750
Swing Your Mountain Gal, Sketches of Life in the Southern Highlands.
C9950 (ASU WCU LMC MHC BC)
Reminiscences and Traditions of Western North Carolina.
D700
Folksongs of Virginia.
D760 (ASU)
Folk-songs of Virginia, a Descriptive Index and Classification of Material.
D770 (ASU LMC FC BC)
Folk-songs of Virginia, a Descriptive Index and Classification of Material.
D780 (ETSU)
More Traditional Ballads of Virginia: Collected with the Cooperation of Members of the Virginia Folklore Society.
D790 (ASU FC BC LMC)
Traditional Ballads of Virginia.
D800
Traditional Ballads of Virginia.
D801 (ASU)
Traditional Ballads of Virginia: Collected Under the Auspices of the Virginia Folk-lore Society.
D810 (LMC FC BC)
Traditional Ballads of Virginia: Collected Under the Auspices of the Virginia Folklore Society.
D820 (WCU ETSU ASU)
'Pon my Honor, Hit's the Truth; Tall Tales from the Mountains.
D1050 (BC)
Bloody Ground.
D1400 (ASU LMC BC)
A Treasury of American Superstition.
D1770
America in Legend: Folklore from the Colonial Period to the Present.
D3040 (FC)
Davy Crockett: American Comic Legend.
D3060 (ASU)
The Frank C. Brown Collection of North Carolina.
D3810 (ASU WCU LMC MHC BC WWC ETSU)
Carolina Mountain Breezes.
E630 (ASU)
Tales of the Blue Ridge.
E970 (LMC ASU BC)
Gravel in My Shoe.
E1090 (ASU WCU LHC MHC ETSU BC)
Wendy's Halloween Ride: Witch Shadows.
E1540 (LMC)
Folklore on the American Land.
E1970 (ASU BC MHC)
The HodgePodge Book, An Almanac of American Folklore.
E1980
The Nonsense Book of Riddles, Rhymes, Tongue Twisters, Puzzles and Jokes from American Folklore.
E1990 (ASU BC)
Old Bill Williams, Mountain Man.
F380 (ASU)
John Henry and His Hammer.
F560
That's Why They Call It . . . the Names and Lore of the Great Smokies.
F1000 (WCU ETSU BC ASU)
That's Why They Call It . . . the Names and Lore of the Great Smokies.
F1010 (ASU LMC)
F2960 (ASU ETSU BC)
F2970 (ASU WWC MHC ETSU BC FC)
F2980 (WWC ASU BC FC)
"The Heritage and Folk Music of Cades Cove, Tennessee."
G230 (LMC)
The Courthouse Tragedy at Hillsville, Va.
G320 (ASU)
West Virginia Lyrics.
G1870 (ASU)
A Guide for Field Workers in Folklore.
G2360 (BC ASU)
Essays on the Superstitions of the Higlanders of Scotland.
G3220
Highland Folk Ways.
G3250 (ASU)
Word-book of Virginia Folk-speech.
G3520 (ASU LMC BC)
Word-book of Virginia Folk-speech.
G3530 (ETSU)
The Blue Hen's Chick: A Life in Context.
G4960 (WCU)
Old Scottish Customs, Local and General.
G4980 (ASU)
Mountain Speech in the Great Smokies.
H770 (BC)
Smoky Mountain Folks and Their Lore.
H810 (BC ASU WCU LMC MHC)
Smoky Mountain Folks and Their Lore.
H820 (ETSU)
American Folk Legend.
H1450
Middletown Valley in Song and Story.
H1740 (BC)
The Devil's Tramping Ground, and Other North Carolina Mystery Stories.
H2070 (ASU LMC MHC BC)
Tar Heel Ghosts.
H2080 (ASU BC LMC MHC ETSU)
Times Gone By.
H2420
High Times and Hard Times: Sketches and Tales.
H2800 (ASU BC)
Sut Lovingood.
H2820 (ASU)
Sut Lovingood. Yarns Spun by a "Nat'ral Born Durn'd Fool." Warped and Wove for Public Wear.
H2830 (ASU BC ETSU)
Sut Lovingood's Yarns.
H2840 (ASU WWC)
Highland Halloween.
H4000 (LMC)
A Bibliography of North American Folklore and Folksong.
H4010 (ASU WWC)
Survivals in Belief Among the Celts.
H4470
Bundle of Troubles, and Other Tarheel Tales.
H4600
The Proverbs of Scotland.
H5690 (ASU)
Down a Dusty Road.
H7640 (BC ASU)
Aunt Zona's Web.
H8050 (ASU LMC)
Walking Bear of Silvermine Mountain.
J810
How and Why: Stories in Carolina Folklore.
J1710 (WCU)
Witches and Demons in History and Folklore.
J1740 (LMC)
John Henry: Track Down a Negro Legend.
J1780
Welsh Legends and Folk-Tales.
J2330 (ASU)
The Complete Peddler's Pack: Games, Songs, Rhymes, and Riddles from Mountain Folklore.
J3060 (ASU WCU LMC MHC WWC ETSU FC)
Peddler's Pack.
J3250 (ETSU ASU)
Folklore of the Teeth.
K170 (ASU)
Moonshine: Its History and Folklore.
K600 (BC ASU LMC WCU MHC)
K1220 (ASU ETSU BC)
K1850 (ETSU)
American Balladry from British Broadsides: A Guide for Students and Collectors of Traditional Song.
L920 (BC ASU)
Native American Balladry, a Descriptive Study and a Bibliographical Syllabus.
L930 (FC)
A Guide for Collectors of Oral Traditions.
L1150
God Had a Dog: Folklore of the Dog.
L1160 (ASU)
How the People Sang the Mountains Up: How and Why Stories.
L1170 (ASU)

FOLKLORE

The Rainbow Book of American Folk Tales and Legends.
L1180 (ASU FC)
Virginia Ghosts.
L1410 (FC ASU BC)
Legends of the Ohio Valley.
M2180 (BC ASU)
Let's Set a Spell.
M2880 (ASU)
Tall Tales from Old Smoky.
M4210 (ASU LMC BC ETSU)
"A Study of Folklore in Watauga County, North Carolina."
M5600 (LMC)
News from Pigeon Roost.
M5640 (ASU)
Published Works of Cratis Williams.
M5840 (ASU BC)
"Investigation of the Regional English of Unicoi County, Tennessee."
M6020
Up Eel River.
M6550 (ASU BC LMC WCU)
Pioneer Superstitions; Old-timey Signs and Sayings.
M7170 (ASU BC)
Southern Character Sketches.
M7190 (ASU WCU)
Stories My Father Told Us.
M7510 (ASU)
Ghost Tales of the Uwharries.
M7520 (ASU WCU)
Folklore of the Blue Ridge Mountains and Early Settlers.
M7870
Salt O'Life.
M9130 (ASU BC LMC WCU)
Ballads, Folk Songs and Folk Tales from West Virginia.
M9170 (ASU BC)
Green Hills of Magic, West Virginia Folk Tales from Europe.
M9180 (ASU BC LMC WCU)
The Telltale Lilac Bush, and Other West Virginia Ghost Tales.
M9190 (ASU BC ETSU LMC WCU)
Lower Piedmont Country.
N1210 (ASU BC ETSU LMC WCU)
Folk Arts Workshop.
N1550 (ASU)
N2270 (BC ASU ETSU MHC)
The Scamps of Bucksnort: Memories of a Nineteenth-century Childhood in Rural Tennessee.
P140 (ASU)
My Mountains, My People.
P410 (ASU WWC UNCA)
Roaming the Mountains with John Parris.
P430 (ASU WCU LMC MHC ETSU WWC)
These Storied Mountains.
P440 (ASU ETSU MHC WCU WWC)
"A Sampling of the Folklore of Carter County, Tennessee."
P2220
Barefoot in Boogar Hollow; Yesterday's Sayings to Live by Today.
P4080 (BC LMC ASU)
Funeral Customs, Their Origin and Development.
P4840 (ASU)
Hills, Hollers and Hickory Flats.
R70
Bygone Beliefs, Being a Series of Excursions in the Byways of Thought.
R890 (ASU)
Gordon Ballads.
R920 (ASU)
"The Cyclone of Rye Cove: The Event, the Folklore, the Song."
R1040 (ETSU)
Tales from Cabin Creek.
R1390 (ASU)
"Sketches and Legends of Upper East Tennessee."
R1780 (LMC ASU)
"Old Limber": Or, The Tale of the Taylors.
R1930 (ASU)
Apple Seeds and Soda Straws: Some Love Charms and Legends.
R2400 (ASU)
Celebration of Life, Her Songs, Her Poems.
R2410 (ASU)
Celebration of Life: Her Songs, Her Poems.
R2420 (LMC)
The Tales and Songs of the Couch Family.
R2900
Folk Tales of the Southern Mountains.
R2910 (ASU MHC)
I Bought Me a Dog, and Other Folktales from the Southern Mountains.
R2920 (ASU WCU LMC MHC ETSU BC)
Nippy and the Yankee Doodle, and More Folk Tales from the Southern Mountains.
R2930 (ASU LMC ETSU BC)
Old Greasybeard: Tales from the Cumberland Gap.
R2940 (ASU WCU ETSU LMC WWC MHC BC FC)
Sang Branch Settler, Folksongs and Tales of a Kentucky Mountain Family.
R2950 (ASU)
South from Hell-fer-Sartin: Kentucky Mountain Folk Tales.
R2960 (ASU WCU MHC BC)
South from Hell-fer-Sartin: Kentucky Mountain Folk Tales.
R2970 (LMC MHC ETSU WWC)
South from Hell-fer-Sartin: Kentucky Mountain Folk Tales.
R2980 (ETSU)
Up Cutshin and Down Greasy: Folkways of a Kentucky Family.
R2990 (ASU WCU LMC ETSU BC UNCA)
Told in the Hills.
R4490
Stories of W. Va. for Boys and Girls.
S500
Wildflowers of Kentucky.
S2130 (BC)
Juniata Memories: Legends Collected in Central Pennsylvania.
S3120
More Allegheny Episodes: Legends and Traditions, Old and New.
S3130
Myths & Legends of Our Own Land.
S4020 (ASU)
Drought, and Other North Carolina Yarns.
S4560 (LMC ASU)
The Mountaineers: Or, Bottled Sunshine for Blue Mondays.
S4850 (ASU BC)
Stories of W. Va. for Boys & Girls.
S5560
S5730 (ASU BC)
Ghost Stories from the Southern Mountains.
S6570 (ASU)
History of the Cherokee Indians and Their Legends and Folk Lore.
S6680 (ASU LMC)
Echoes From the Hills: Tall Tales From Tennessee.
S7020 (LMC BC)
Years of Harvest, Poems and Tales from the Smoky Foothills, 1924-1964.
S7500 (BC LMC WCU)
The Cherokee in Romance, Tragedy, and Song in the Great Smokies.
S8020 (ETSU)
Folk Games from Frying Pan Creek in Dickenson County, Virginia.
S9160
Tall Tales of the Devils Apron.
S9270 (LMC BC FC)
Carolina Humor: Sketches.
T50 (ASU)
Dictionary of American Folklore.
T100 (ASU)
A Collection of Irish Riddles.
T380 (FC)
From Laurel Hill to Siler's Bog.
T7600 (ETSU)
The Folk-lore of Plants.
T7720 (ASU)
Kentucky Superstitions.
T7790 (ASU BC)
Big Sandy.
T7890 (ASU BC)
Blue Ridge Country.
T7900 (FC WWC ETSU BC ASU)
Blue Ridge Country.
T7910 (ASU WCU LMC)
Devil's Ditties, Being Stories of the Kentucky Mountain People, Told by Jean Thomas, With the Songs They Sing.
T7920 (ASU BC)
A Treasury of American Folk Humor; a Rare Collection of Laughter, Tall Tales, Jests and Other Gems of Merriment of the American People.
T8570 (FC)
Pioneer Proverbs; Wit and Wisdom From Early America.
T9830
American Folk Legends; a Symposium.
U10 (FC)
Folklore of the North American Indians.
U30 (LMC)
U4210 (ASU LMC)
Bert Vincent's Strolling, Being Sort of a Side-Glance at the Little Odds and Ends of Life in These Parts.
V630
The Best Stories of Bert Vincent, ed. Willard Yarbrough.
V640
More of the Best Stories of Bert Vincent.
V650
Manners, Customs, and Observances: Their Origins and Signification.
W110 (ASU)
Tennessee Tales.
W280 (ASU LMC ETSU BC)
West of Suez.
W510 (ASU BC)
A Right Good People.
W940 (ASU)
W3630 (BC)
New Race of Song Sparrows from the Appalachian Region.
W4960
The Foxfire Book: Hog Dressing; Log Cabin Building; Mountain Crafts and Foods; Planting by the Signs; Snake Lore, Hunting Tales, Faith Healing; Moonshining; and Other Affairs of Plain Living.
W6020 (FC ASU BC)
Foxfire 2: Ghost Stories, Spring Wild Plant Foods, Spinning and Weaving, Midwifing, Burial Customs, Corn Shuckin's, Wagon Making and More Affairs of Plain Living.
W6030 (FC ASU BC)
Foxfire 3: Animal Care, Banjos and Dulcimers, Hide Tanning, Summer and Fall Wildplant Foods, Butter Churns, Ginseng, and Still More Affairs of Plain Living.
W6040 (ASU)
All Good Times.
W7800 (BC)
Hit Haint the Fish.
W7810 (LMC BC)
South Carolina Folk Tales: Stories of Animals and Supernatural Beings.
W9640 (LMC)
God Bless the Devil.
W9660 (BC)
The Bulltown Country.
W9730 (ASU BC)
The Smoke Hole and Its People.
W9750 (BC)
Buying the Wind: Regional Folklore in the United States.
3050 (ASU WWC LMC BC)

FOLKLORE — ALA.

Horse and Buggy Days on Hatchet Creek.
G450 (ASU BC)

FOLKLORE — APP.

Ethnology in Folklore.
G2450 (ASU)
Riddles from the Cumberland Valley.
G4970 (ASU)
Peculiarities of the Appalachian Mountaineers: A Summary of Legends, Traditions, Signs, and Superstitions That Are Almost Forgotten.
J2540 (BC ASU LMC WCU ETSU MHC)
Jack and Jill Go Up a Hill.
J2800 (ASU)
The Origins of Popular Superstitions and Customs.
K2850 (ASU)
American Folk Songs and Folklore: A Regional Bibliography.
L3110
Beech Mountain Folk-Songs and Ballads.
M4260
Recollections of Hearsays of Athens, Fifty Years and Beyond.
S2370
T20

FOLKLORE — APP.
"The Folklore of the Cumberlands as Reflected in the Writings of Jesse Stuart."
W1090
Folklore in the English and Scottish Ballads.
W7560 (ASU FC)
FOLKLORE — CHEROKEE
Chronicles of Wolftown: Social Documents of the North Carolina Cherokees, 1850-1862.
K1960 (WCU ASU)
Friends of Thunder, Folktales of the Oklahoma Cherokees.
K1980 (ASU)
Run Toward the Nightland: Magic of the Oklahoma Cherokees.
K2010 (LMC MHC)
FOLKLORE — GA.
Boilin' n Bakin' in Boogar Hollow.
H850 (BC ASU)
Uncle Sandy.
J2580 (ASU)
A Treasury of Georgia Folk-lore.
K1950 (BC ASU MHC ETSU)
Historical Collections of Georgia: Containing the Most Interesting Facts, Traditions, Biographical Sketches, Anecdotes, etc., Relating to Its History and Antiquities, from Its First Settlement to the Present Time.
W5410 (ASU BC)
FOLKLORE — INDIAN
Indian Stories of Virginia's Last Frontier.
A510
FOLKLORE — KY.
Folk Ways and Customs of Old Kentucky.
C6060 (ASU BC)
Clever Country: Kentucky Mountain Trails.
G290 (LMC BC)
"Tales of the Mountains" A Complete Directory of the Eastern Kentucky Coalfields with Extracts from the Geological Reports, Forestry, Oil Development, Education, Superstitions, and Religion of the Mountains.
H730
A Gatherin'; Ky. Lore of Mt. Music, Songs, and Dances.
K2830
Folklore of the Mammoth Cave Region.
W7260 (BC)
FOLKLORE — N. C.
Gateway to North Carolina Folklore.
B3430
C5920 (ETSU ASU LMC BC)
North Carolina Mountain Folklore and Miscellany.
C7180 (MHC ASU LMC BC)
Grandfather's Tales of North Carolina History.
C8650 (ASU WCU LMC MHC BC UNCA)
Home on the Yadkin.
F660 (ASU BC)
How and Why Stories in Carolina Folklore.
J1720 (LMC)
The Brown Mountain Lights.
L90 (ASU LMC)
Great Smoky Mountain Stories and Sun over Ol' Starlin.
M4850 (LMC WCU)
Mountain Yarns, Legends, and Lore.
M8500 (ASU LMC)
Folklore Studies in Honor of Arthur Palmer Hudson.
N2280 (ASU LMC)
"Folklore of the North Carolina Mountaineers."
P240
Hemlock Twigs and Balsam Sprigs.
P250 (ASU)
Mountain Bred.
P420 (ASU LMC MHC WCU WWC)
Cherokee Indian Lore and Smoky Mountain Stories.
S3340 (ASU BC)
Cherokee Indian Lore and Smoky Mountains Stories.
S3350 (ETSU)
FOLKLORE — PA.
Two Penny Ballads and Four Dollar Whiskey: A Pennsylvania Folklore Miscellany.
G2370
Pennsylvania Songs and Legends.
K3070
Scotch-Irish and English Proverbs and Sayings of the West Branch Valley of Central Pennsylvania.
S3150 (ASU)
South Mountain Sketches, Folk Tales, and Legends Collected in the Mountains of Southern Pennsylvania.
S3160 (ASU)
The Pennsylvania Germans of the Shenandoah Valley.
S4620 (ASU)
FOLKLORE — TENN.
"A Collection of Ballads and Songs from East Tennessee."
A2280 (LMC)
"Folklore in White County, Tennessee."
D2940
Governor Bob Taylor's Tales.
R1920
Bulletin.
T1380 (ETSU)
FOLKLORE — VA.
Sugar in the Gourd.
A550
Legends of Virginia.
C1170 (LMC)
The Pennsylvania Germans of the Shenandoah Valley.
S4620 (ASU)
Legends of the Skyline Drive and the Great Valley of Virginia.
W7000 (ASU WCU LMC BC)
Legends of the Skyline Drive and the Great Valley of Va.
W7010 (BC)
FOLKLORE — W. VA.
Moccasin Tracks, and Other Imprints.
D2730 (BC)
Moccasin Tracks and Other Imprints.
D2740 (ASU)
Timothy Corn Stories; as Told by Uncle Dave Arnold of Knobley Farm.
E660
John Henry: An American Legend.
K350
The Burning Springs, and Other Tales of the Little Kanawha.
L1360 (ASU BC)
My Appalachia: Pipestem State Park Today and Yesterday.
L1370 (ASU BC ETSU LMC)
Tales and Lore of the Mountaineer.
P4620 (BC)
West Virginia, Her Land, Her People, Her Traditions, Her Resources.
R4200 (BC)
FOLKS SONGS — APP.
Favorite Mountain Ballads and Old Time Songs.
K2130
FOLKSONGS — VA.
The Folksongs of Virginia: A Checklist of the WPA Holdings, Alderman Library University of Virginia.
V1230 (ETSU ASU LMC)
FOLKTALES
Go Tell Aunt Rhody.
Q30 (ASU)
From Laurel Hill to Siler's Bog.
T7600 (ETSU)
American Folk Legends; a Symposium.
U10 (FC)
U4210 (ASU LMC)
The Ballad Tree, a Study of British and American Ballads, Their Folklore, Verse and Music, Together with Sixty Traditional Ballads and Their Tunes.
W2710 (BC)
"Legends and Stories of White County, Tennessee."
W6460
All Good Times.
W7800 (BC)
Hit Haint the Fish.
W7810 (LMC BC)
South Carolina Folk Tales: Stories of Animals and Supernatural Beings.
W9640 (LMC)
God Bless the Devil.
W9660 (BC)
The Bulltown Country.
W9730 (ASU BC)
FOLKTALES — TENN.
Bulletin.
T1380 (ETSU)
FOLKWAYS
Appalachia Revisited: How People Lived Fifty Years Ago.
A400 (ETSU BC ASU WCU FC LMC)
In the Shadow of Big Bald: About the Appalachians and Their People.
A1230 (ETSU)
F2970 (ASU WWC MHC ETSU BC FC)
F2980 (WWC ASU BC FC)
"The Heritage and Folk Music of Cades Cove, Tennessee."
G230 (LMC)
Highland Folk Ways.
G3250 (ASU)
"A Cultural Study of a Mountain Community in Western North Carolina."
H3240 (ASU)
"A Cultural Study of Mountain Community in Western North Carolina."
H3250 (ASU)
Highland Halloween.
H4000 (LMC)
The Complete Peddler's Pack: Games, Songs, Rhymes, and Riddles from Mountain Folklore.
J3060 (ASU WCU LMC MHC WWC ETSU FC)
Moonshine: Its History and Folklore.
K600 (BC ASU LMC WCU MHC)
Walker Fox Hounds.
W440 (BC)
America's Vanishing Folkways.
W7200 (MHC)
FOLKWAYS — APP.
Peculiarities of the Appalachian Mountaineers: A Summary of Legends, Traditions, Signs, and Superstitions That Are Almost Forgotten.
J2540 (BC ASU LMC WCU ETSU MHC)
FOLKWAYS — GA.
F2960 (ASU ETSU BC)
Uncle Sandy.
J2580 (ASU)
FOLKWAYS — KY.
A Gatherin'; Ky. Lore of Mt. Music, Songs, and Dances.
K2830
FOLKWAYS — N. C.
Times Gone By.
H2420
A Brief History of Macon County, North Carolina.
S4430
FOLKWAYS — TENN.
Bulletin.
T1380 (ETSU)
FOLKWAYS — W. VA.
West Virginia, Her Land, Her People, Her Traditions, Her Resources.
R4200 (BC)
FOREST AND FOREST PRODUCTS
"A Cost Analysis of Methods of Salvaging Logging Residue in Appalachia."
T8930
A Scenic Guide to the Monogahela National Forest.
W2430 (LMC ASU WCU BC)
FORESTRY
Forest Fires and Area Burned, State and Private Lands, Tennessee Valley, 1934-1958.
A5030
Biltmore Forest: The Property of Mr. George W. Vanderbilt, and Account of its Treatment, and the Results of the First Year's Work.
P2970 (LMC UNCA ASU)
Resources of the Southern Fields and Forests, Medical, Economical, and Agricultural. Being Also a Medical Botany of the Confederate States.
P3590 (LMC BC)
A forest industry processing and marketing complex for eastern Kentucky.
U180 (BC)
FORESTRY AND FOREST PRODUCTS
"Marketing of Lumber Produced by Sawmills in Pennsylvania."
A1800
Government Land Acquisition: A Summary of Land Acquisition by Federal, State and Local Governments up to 1964.
A2140 (LMC)

FORESTRY AND FOREST PRODUCTS

"The Geography of Christmas Tree Production and Marketing in Anglo-America: With Special Attention to Twelve Counties in Western Pennsylvania."
A2460

A Method of Appraising Pine Sawtimber in South Carolina.
A2470 (WCU)

Appalachian Oak in Fine Furniture.
A3170 (ASU)

Official Grading Rules for Eastern Hemlock Lumber: Conforming to American Lumber Standards Effective November 10, 1950.
A3180

Appalachia's Forest Resources: Timber.
A3670

Shade Trees for North Carolina.
A5140 (ASU LMC)

Identifying Southern Forest Types on Aerial Photographs.
A5780 (WCU)

The Southern Appalachian Forests.
A5850 (ASU BC LMC ETSU)

Appalachian Scale Shelter.
B1360

Effect of Competition on Survival and Height Growth of Red Oak Seedlings.
B2440 (WCU)

Seed Production in Southern Appalachian Oak Stands.
B2450

Yield of Unthinned Yellow-poplar.
B2460 (WCU)

Lessons in Appalachian Forestry.
B2970

Selected Opportunities for Wood Industries Development in West Virginia Through Application of Forest Products Laboratory Research.
B3330

Forestry and Wood Industries.
B6860 (ETSU)

Lumbering on the Cumberland: A Romance Taken from Life.
B7010 (BC)

The Economic Development of the Northeast Georgia Commission Area Through Use of Forest Products and Water Resources.
B7120 (ASU ETSU)

Publications of the Southeastern Forest Station, 1921-1958.
B7230 (WCU)

Value Growth of Pine Pulpwood on the George Walton Experimental Forest.
C3350 (WCU)

Tumult on the Mountains: Lumbering in West Virginia, 1770-1920.
C4710 (ASU LMC WCU MHC BC)

Silvical Characteristics of Slash Pine.
C7200 (WCU)

The Comp'ny: The Story of the Surry, Sussex and Southampton Railway and the Surry Lumber Company.
C8850 (ASU LMC BC)

Air-drying Practices in Central Appalachians.
C9820

Trees of the South.
G3550 (ASU BC)

Conservation of Wildlife and Forests in Tennessee.
H4120 (ETSU BC)

Conservation of Wildlife and Forests in Tennessee.
H4130

In Quiet Ways: George H. Mead, the Man and the Company.
H6210 (LMC)

Proceedings of Second Annual Convention of the North Carolina Forestry Association Held at Raleigh, North Carolina, February 21, 1912.
H6860 (ASU)

"The Effect of Basal Wounding By Forest Fires on the Diameter Growth of Some Southern Appalachian Hardwoods."
J590

Erosion Control on Logging Roads in the Appalachians.
K2970 (ASU LMC)

Products from Hickory Bolts.
L1630 (WCU)

Evaluation of Timber Development Organization.
M1080 (ASU WCU)

Silvical Characteristics of Sweetgum.
M3790 (WCU)

Hydraulic Spray Applications of Insecticides for the Control of Slash Pine Cone and Seed Insects.
M5120 (WCU)
M5190 (ASU)

Silvical Characteristics of Bitternut Hickory.
N540 (WCU)

Silvical Characteristics of the Commercial Hickories.
N550 (WCU)

Silvical Characteristics of Mockernut Hickory.
N560 (WCU)

Silvical Characteristics of Shagbark Hickory.
N570 (WCU)

American Heartwood.
P1400 (WCU)

Breaking New Ground.
P2980 (LMC BC)

Timber Trees and Forests of North Carolina.
P2990 (UNCA ASU WCU LMC)

Gifford Pinchot: Private and Public Forester.
P3040 (WCU LMC)

The Biltmore Story: Recollections of the Beginning of Forestry in the United States.
S880 (ASU WCU BC)

Issues by the U. S. Southern Forest Experiment Station in cooperation with the Southern Pulpwood Conservation Association.
S5820 (WCU)

Stamper Tract Prescribed Burn.
T510 (WCU)

Forest Products Industry Notes, no. 1.
T2790 (BC)

The Changing Sawmill Industry; a Status Report on 58 Circular Sawmills in the Tennessee Valley, 1950-1960.
T4610

Fish and Wildlife in the Tennessee Valley.
T4670

Forest Inventory Statistics for Whitfield County, Georgia.
T4730

Forest Resources and Industries in the Tennessee Valley.
T4740 (ETSU)

Forest Resources of the Beech River Watershed.
T4750

Forest Resource Trends in the Tennessee Valley.
T4970

Operations Guide for TVA Forest Nurseries.
T5000

Quality-Control in Circular Sawmill Operation . . .
T5020

Report: A Record of Activities and Accomplishments.
T5040

Influences of Reforestation and Erosion Control Upon the Hydrology of the Pine Tree Branch Watershed 1941 to 1950.
T5550

Forest Cover Improvement Influences Upon Hydrologic Characteristics of White Hollow Watershed, 1935-1958.
T7340

Influences of Reforestation and Erosion Control Upon the Hydrology of the Pine Tree Branch Watershed 1941 to 1950.
T7430

Reforestation and Erosion Control Influences Upon the Hydrology of the Pine Tree Branch Watershed 1941 to 1960.
T7500

Growth of Appalachian Hardwoods as Affected by Site and Residual Stand Density.
T9310

Printing as Senate Document Information Relative to the Timber Resources and National Forests of West Virginia. Report from the committee on Rules and Administration to Accompany S. Res. 137, June 14, 1961.
U1950

Nantahala National Forest, Georgia, North Carolina, South Carolina.
U2920 (WCU)

National Forests of the Southern Appalachians.
U2930

National Forests of the Southern Appalachians. Help Banish Fire from our Appalachian Forests.
U2940

Special Forest Products for Profit, Self-Help Suggestions for Rural Areas Development.
U2980

Timber in North Carolina.
U2990 (WCU)

Watauga Lake recreation areas, Cherokee National Forest, Tennessee.
U3000

Annual Report and Program.
U3020 (BC)

Annual Report and Program.
U3040

Joyce Kilmer Memorial Forest in the Nantahala National Forest.
U3050

The Southern Appalachian Forest.
U3370

The Forest Products Marketing Laboratory at Princeton, West Virginia, Research Facility of the Northeastern Forest Experiment Station.
U3750

Forest Survey Release.
U3980

Improvements at Coweeta.
U3990

Research Information Digest; Recent Publications of the Southeastern Forest Experiment Station.
U4000

1963 Research at the Southeastern Forest Experiment Station.
U4010 (WCU)

Geology and Mineral Resources of Wise Co. and Coal Bearing Portions of Scott Co., Va. with a Chapter on the Forest of Wise Co.
V980

Method for Determining Public Fire Control Expenditures for Private Lands.
V1310

Technique for Hand Planting of Forest Trees on Southern Appalachians.
W160

Forest-Land Utilization in Nicholas and Webster Co., W. Va.
W2460
W3140 (ETSU)

Common Forest Trees of West Virginia: How to Know Them.
W3570 (ASU)

Forest Trees of West Virginia.
W3580

The Nantucket Pine Moth: A Literature Review.
Y70 (WCU)

FORESTRY AND FOREST PRODUCTS — ALA.

Pine Pulpmill Possibilities, North Alabama.
T4840

FORESTRY AND FOREST PRODUCTS — APP.

Cubic-foot Volume Tables for Yellow-poplar in the South Appalachians.
B2430

Farm Woodland Management in Southern Appalachians, 8-Year Summary.
C880

Forest Service Log Grades for Southern Pine.
C890 (WCU)

A Guide to Grading Features in Southern Pine Logs and Trees.
C900 (WCU)

Ten Years of Experimental Farm Woodland Management in the Southern Appalachians.
C910 (WCU)

Tree Grades Give Accurate Estimate of Second-Growth Yellow Poplar Values.
C920 (WCU)
C2020 (ETSU)

Trees of the Southeastern States, Including Virginia, North Carolina, South Carolina, Tennessee, Georgia, and Northern Florida.
C5670 (ASU BC)

Construction-grade Plywood from Grade 3 Appalachian Oak.
C8330

Profits from Pruning Appalachian White Pine.
C9440

Intensive Cleaning Increases Sapling Growth and Browse Production in Southern Appalachians.
D1730

Site Index Curves for Natural Stands of White Pine in the Southern Appalachians.
D2930

Evaluating Appalachian Woods for Highway Posts.
D3200

FORESTRY AND FOREST PRODUCTS — APP.

"The Economic Problems of Forestry in the Appalachian Region."
D3670

The Economic Problems of Forestry in the Appalachian Region.
D3680 (ASU LMC BC)

Insects Affecting Seed Production of Slash and Longleaf Pines: Their Identification and Biological Annotation.
E640 (WCU)

The Southern Appalachian Forest Reserve.
E1740
F2130

Chestnut Oak in the Southern Appalachians.
F2320 (ASU)

Timber Growing and Logging Practice in the Southern Appalachian Region.
F3580 (BC ASU)

Forced Air Drying of Southern Pine Lumber.
G70 (WCU)

Physical Suitability of Appalachian Hardwood Sawlogs for Sawed Timbers.
G440

The Litter Arthropod Community in a Southern Appalachian Hardwood Forest: Numbers, Biomass and Mineral Element Content.
G1850

Denudation and Erosion in the Southern Appalachian Region and the Monongehela Basin.
G2130 (ASU ETSU)

Characteristics of Factory-grade Hardwood Logs Delivered to Appalachian Sawmills.
G2290

Chestnut Blight in the Southern Appalachians.
G3300

White Oak in the Southern Appalachians.
G3480 (ASU)

Operations Guide for TVA Forest Nurseries.
G4080

Geomorphology and Forest Ecology of the Mountain Region in the Central Appalachians.
H90

"The Location Decision for Primary Wood-using Industries in the Northern Appalachians."
H200

Location Decision for Wood-using Industries in Northern Appalachians.
H210

Waning Hardwood Supply and the Appalachian Forests.
H920

A Revised Shortleaf Pine Bibliography.
H1470 (WCU)

Silvical Characteristics of Southern Red Oak.
H1480 (WCU)

Southern Forests and Southern People.
H1650 (LMC)

Spacing-environmental Relationships in a Slash Pine Plantation.
H2480 (WCU)

Rainfall Interception by Hardwood Forest Litter in Southern Appalachians.
H4410 (WCU)

Decay in Merchantable Oak, Yellow Poplar, and Basswood in the Appalachian Region.
H4880

Grading and Measuring Hickory Trees, Logs, and Products.
H4950 (WCU)

Diseases in Southeastern Forest Nurseries and Their Control.
H6170 (WCU)

This Fascinating Lumber Business.
H7190 (ASU)

Fertilization of Young Slash Pine in a Cultivated Plantation.
H8110 (WCU)

The Anthracite Forest Region, a Problem Area.
I760 (ASU)

Timber Stand Improvement in the Southern Appalachian Region.
J600

Look at Mine-timber Market in the Appalachian Bituminous Coal Region.
K2930

The Economic Development of the Furniture Industry of the South and Its Future Dependence Upon Forestry.
K3080 (LMC)

The Olustee Arboretum Performance of 67 Species of Forest Trees.
K3150 (WCU)

Wind Directions for Prescribed Burning in Southeastern United States.
K3360 (WCU)

Appalachian Hardwoods for Pallets, Laboratory Evaluation.
K3430

Marketing West Virginia Lumber to Manufacturers in Other States.
L2540

Silvical Characteristics of Shumard Oak.
L3580 (WCU)

"Industrial Organization of the Appalachian Hardwood Lumber Using Industry."
L4110

Regeneration After Clearcutting in the Southern Appalachians.
M1390 (LMC)

Regeneration in Southern Appalachian Oak Stands.
M1400

A Guide to Forestry Activities in North Carolina, South Carolina, and Tennessee.
M4390 (ETSU LMC)

Tree Planting in the Central Piedmont, and Southern Appalachian Region. U. S. Department of Agriculture Farmers' Bulletin, no. 1994.
M6130 (WCU)
N210

Trees Above the Coal Below.
N3000

Early Survival and Growth of Planted Northern Red Oak in Southern Appalachians.
O630

Practical Forestry in the Southern Appalachians.
P4520
P4700 (BC)

Silvical Characteristics of Yellow-poplar.
R1490 (WCU)

Silvical Characteristics of White Basswood.
R1500 (WCU)

The Romance of Appalachian Hardwood Lumber: 1890 — Fifty Years of Service — 1940.
R2550 (BC ASU WCU LMC)

Heart Rots of Appalachian Hardwoods.
R3890

Birth of Forestry in America, Biltmore Forest School, 1898-1913.
S890 (ASU)

Exploratory Studies on Chemical Control of Unwanted Hardwoods in Southern Appalachians.
S4240

"Variation in Wood Specific Gravity of Yellow-poplar (Liriodendron tulipifera L.) and Its Relationship to Environmental Conditions in the Southern Appalachians."
S4260 (LMC)

A White Pine Provenance Study in the Southern Appalachians.
S4270 (WCU)

White Pine Provenance Study in the Southern Appalachians.
S4280 (ASU)

Cubic-foot Volume Table and Point-sampling Factors for White Pine Plantations in Southern Appalachians.
S4320

Epicormic Branching on 8 Species of Appalachian Hardwoods.
S4730

Cumulated Index for Proceedings of the Society of American Foresters, Volumes 1-11, May 1905-1916. Forestry Quarterly, Volumes 1-14.
S5360 (ASU)

Nails and Spikes in Hickory.
S7090 (WCU)

Circular Slide Rule for Calculating Wood Moisture Content.
T220 (WCU)

A Comparison of Increment Core Sampling Methods For Estimating Tree Specific Gravity.
T230 (WCU)

Wood Density Surveys of the Minor Species of Yellow Pine in the Eastern United States: Pt. I — Spruce Pine (Pinus Glabra Walt.).
T250 (WCU)

Evaluation of Forestry Opportunities on Farms in the Beech River Watershed.
T2620

Forests and Human Welfare.
T2800

Forestry Bulletin, no. 1.
T2810 (BC)

Initial Forest Management in the Tennessee Valley.
T2930

Plant Trees — Grow Jobs; Reforest 7 States in 7 Years.
T3230 (ASU)

Annual Report, 1963.
T4600

Comparative Data for Additional Hardwood Pulp and Paper Mills in the Tennessee Valley.
T4620

Comparative Results of Circular Sawmill Surveys in the Tennessee Valley, 1950 and 1955.
T4630

Development of Forests — Fish — Wildlife in the Tennessee Valley.
T4650

Evaluation of Forestry Opportunities on Farms in the Beech River Watershed.
T4660 (ETSU)

Hardwood-Logging Methods and Costs in the Tennessee Valley.
T4770

Hardwood Utilization Centers: Their Potential for the Tennessee Valley.
T4780 (ASU)

Influence of Woodland and Owner Characteristics of Forest Management.
T4790

Laminated Lumber From Low-Grade Hardwoods by the Continuous Glue Press Process.
T4800

Operations Manual for TVA Forest Nurseries.
T4830

Private Forest Management in the Tennessee Valley.
T4850

Publications Available for General Distribution.
T4860

Status of the Forest Resource in the Tennessee Valley — 1950.
T4870

TVA and Forestry.
T4890

TVA and Forestry.
T4900

TVA and Forestry.
T4910

Twenty Years of Fire Records for State and Private Forest Lands in the Tennessee Valley.
T4920

Why Invest in Forest Land? Some Forest Owners Give Their Answers.
T4930

Annual Report.
T4940

Design and Operation of Open-Tank Timber Treating Plants.
T4950

Farm Forestry Planning Through Linear Programming.
T4960

Guide to Selection of Superior Loblolly, Shortleaf and Virginia Pine in the Tennessee Valley.
T4980

Inventorying Forest Properties; Suggested Standard Procedure and Specifications for Use in the Tennessee Valley.
T4990

Private Forest Management Trends in the Tennessee Valley.
T5010

Reforestation Estimates for the Tennessee Valley.
T5030

Sawmill Facts; First Step Toward Good Management.
T5050

A Survey of Pulpwood Dealers in the Tennessee Valley . . .
T5060

TVA Fish and Game Activities.
T5070

Utilizing Pine Sawmill Residue for Pulp Chips.
T5080

FORESTRY AND FOREST PRODUCTS — APP.
Crosstie Industry Facts for the Tennessee Valley Counties.
T5280
Statistical Summary of Forest-Products Industries in the Tennessee Valley.
T5290
An Appraisal of Methods for Salvaging Small Sawmill Residues in the Southeast.
T8780 (WCU)
Appraisal of Early Reproduction After Cutting in Northern Appalachian Hardwood Stands.
T9290
Diameter Increase in Second-Growth Appalachian Hardwood Stands, Comparison of Species.
T9300
Regeneration of Central Appalachian Hardwoods with Emphasis on the Effects of Site Quality and Harvesting Practice.
T9320
Reproduction 7 Years After Seed-Tree Harvest Cutting in Appalachian Hardwoods.
T9330
What Happens to Living Cull Trees Left After Heavy Cutting in Mixed Hardwood Stands?
T9340
Report of the Secretary of Agriculture on the Southern Appalachian and White Mountain Watersheds. Commercial Importance, Area, Condition, Advisability of the Purchase for National Forests, and Probable Cost.
U2540 (BC)
Purchase of Land under the Weeks Law in the Southern Appalachian and White Mountains.
U2960
Purchase of Land under the Weeks Law in the Southern Appalachian and White Mountains.
U2970
Measures for Stand Improvement in Southern Appalachian Forests with List of Selected References.
U3010
Southern Appalachian White Pine Plantations, Site, Volume, and Yield.
V620 (WCU)
Costs and Returns for Hardwood Lumber Production in Appalachian Region of Kentucky and Ohio.
W5260

FORESTRY AND FOREST PRODUCTS — GA.
Forest Inventory Statistics for Fannin County, Georgia.
T4680
Forest Inventory Statistics for Towns County, Georgia.
T4700
Forest Inventory Statistics for Union County, Georgia.
T4710
Forest Inventory Statistics for Walker County, Georgia.
T4720
North Georgia Forest Industry Outlook.
T4820

FORESTRY AND FOREST PRODUCTS — KY.
Forestry in the Economic Life of Knott County, Kentucky.
C8430
"Tales of the Mountains" A Complete Directory of the Eastern Kentucky Coalfields with Extracts from the Geological Reports, Forestry, Oil Development, Education, Superstitions, and Religion of the Mountains.
H730
A Look at Kentucky's Lumber Industry.
H4960 (BC)
Sawmill Practices and Problems in Appalachian Hill Country of Ohio and Kentucky.
M350
Value Added by Sawmilling in Appalachian Hill Country of Ohio and Kentucky.
M360
A Forest Industry Processing and Marketing Complex for Eastern Kentucky.
M1090 (LMC)
Progress Report on a Study of Forest Conditions in Kentucky.
U2950 (BC)
Strip Mining Reclamation in Appalachia.
U3030

FORESTRY AND FOREST PRODUCTS — N. C.
The Trees of North Carolina.
C5660 (ASU)
The Woods and Timbers of North Carolina.
H440 (ASU LMC)
Woods and Timbers of North Carolina.
H450 (BC)
Common Forest Trees of North Carolina: How to Know Them. A Pocket Manual.
H6820 (LMC)
Common Forest Trees of North Carolina: How to Know Them. A Pocket Manual.
H6830 (LMC ASU)
Forest Conditions in Western North Carolina.
H6840 (ASU WCU LMC UNCA)
Organization of Co-operative Forest Fire Protective Areas in North Carolina.
H6850 (ASU)
Silvical Characteristics of Cherrybark Oak.
L3570 (WCU)
Silvical Characteristics of Swamp Chestnut Oak.
L3590 (WCU)
N200 (WCU)
Common Forest Trees of North Carolina, How to Know Them.
N1930 (ASU UNCA)
Sawmills and Lumber Production for 26 Counties in Western North Carolina, 1959.
N1960
Report of the State Geologist and Director. 1891-92 - 1923-24.
N2340 (ASU UNCA)
North Carolina Lands: Ownership, Use, and Management of Forest and Related Lands.
P3470 (ASU LMC BC WCU UNCA)
Report on an Examination of a Forest Tract in Western North Carolina.
R1050 (ASU LMC)
Tests on Direct Seeding of Oak in Piedmont and Southern Appalachians of North Carolina.
S4250 (WCU)
Forest Inventory Statistics for Buncombe County, North Carolina.
T2780
A Demonstration of Watershed Protective Logging, Mars Hill Municipal Watershed, Madison County, North Carolina.
T4640
Report on an Examination of a Forest Tract in Western North Carolina.
U2530
Growing Christmas Trees in North Carolina.
W5720 (WCU)

FORESTRY AND FOREST PRODUCTS — OHIO
Ten Years of Strip-mine Forestation Research in Ohio.
F1050
Sawmill Practices and Problems in Appalachian Hill Country of Ohio and Kentucky.
M350
Value Added by Sawmilling in Appalachian Hill Country of Ohio and Kentucky.
M360
Forestry Accomplishments in Southeastern Ohio under the U. S. Agricultural Conservation Program, 1957-64.
M5060

FORESTRY AND FOREST PRODUCTS — PA.
"Marketing Forest Products in Pennsylvania; a study of Marketing Practices and Pricing Processes at the Farm level for Forest Products in Pennsylvania 1949-1951."
C1630
The Timber Resources of Pennsylvania.
F640 (ASU)
"Pennsylvania Markets for Primary Forest Products."
F3060
"Equating Timber and Wildlife Values and Returns to the Farm Resource Base in Sullivan County, Pennsylvania."
G200
"Equating Timber and Wildlife Values and Returns to the Farm Resources Base in Sullivan County, Pennsylvania."
H3970
Opportunities for Forest-Based Industries in Pennsylvania: A Manual for the Development of Pennsylvania's Wood Using Industries.
H7160
"An Analysis of the Christmas Tree Industry in Pennsylvania."
K2690
Forestry Returns Evaluated for Uneven-aged Management in Two Appalachian Woodlots.
M340
"Forest Products Marketing from Public Lands in Pennsylvania."
S1130
"Promotion of the Recreational Use of State Forests, with Special Reference to Pennsylvania."
S1480

FORESTRY AND FOREST PRODUCTS — APP.
Suitability of Appalachian Woods for Sanitary Tissue and Toweling.
F2140

FORESTRY AND FOREST PRODUCTS — TENN.
Tennessee Timber Trees.
B270
"Wood Production Investment Opportunities on the Cumberland Plateau in Tennessee: A Regional Economic Analysis."
B460
Preliminary Study of Forest Conditions in Tennessee.
H880 (ETSU)
Common Forest Trees of Tennessee: How to Know Them, a Pocket Manual.
J2280 (LMC)
"Radial Growth and Wood Density of White Pine in Relation to Coal-Derived Environmental Pollutants."
L870
Changing Sawmill Industry; a Status Report on 58 Circular Sawmills in the Tennessee Valley, 1950-60.
L1620
Common Forest Trees of Tennessee, How to Know Them; a Pocket Manual.
M2700
The Economics of Using Low-Quality Hardwoods for Producing Charcoal in Tennessee.
M3700
Harvesting Pine Pulpwood in the Tennessee Valley.
S1040
Initial Forest Management in the Tennessee Valley.
S1770
Summer Key to Tennessee Trees.
S2220 (ASU LMC BC)
Forest Trees and Forest Facts of Tennessee.
T1060 (ETSU)
"Some Tennessee Trees — a Simple, Illustrated Key."
T1070
The Horseshoe Properties Forest Management Demonstration.
T1240
Tennessee Resources — Agriculture, Forestry, and Minerals.
T1720 (ETSU)
Forest Conditions in Monroe County, Tennessee.
T4590
Forest Inventory Statistics — Holston River Tributary Area, East Tennessee and Southwest Virginia.
T4690
Forest Industries in Appalachian Counties of Tennessee.
V410

FORESTRY AND FOREST PRODUCTS — VA.
Virginia Forest Resources and Industries.
C8440 (LMC)
Forest Recreation: Estimated and Predictions in the North River Area, George Washington National Forest, Virginia.
C9960
Common Forest Trees of Virginia: A Pocket Manual Describing Their Most Important Characteristics.
J2290 (BC LMC)
Virginia's Timber, 1966.
K2780 (LMC)
The Forests of the Valley Coal Fields of Virginia.
P1570
The Forests of Tazewell County, Virginia.
S1210
Forest Inventory Statistics — Holston River Tributary Area, East Tennessee and Southwest Virginia.
T4690
Bulletin.
V900 (BC)

FORESTRY AND FOREST PRODUCTS — W. VA.
Call of the Mountains.
B2640 (BC ASU)
Freight Rates of West Virginia Wood Products.
C950 (ASU)
C6220
The Timber Resources of West Virginia.
F630 (ASU)
Tree Diameter, Poor Indicator of Age in West Virginia Hardwoods.
G1150
A Manual of West Virginia's Wood-using Industries, with Directory.
G3110 (ASU)
An Analysis of Some Selected Characteristics of Cabin Vacationists in West Virginia State Parks and Forests in 1961.
H40 (ASU)
The Manufacture of Hardwood Dimension Stock in West Virginia, a Feasibility Study.
H60 (ASU)
Prospects and Problems for the Manufacture of Laminated Timber in West Virginia.
H1030
The Effect of Workmen's Compensation on the Logging and Sawmilling Industries in the Northeast.
H6380
Fifty Year History of the Monongahela National Forest.
M1870
Timber Inventory and Wood Manufacturing Opportunities in the Northern and Central West Virginia Region.
M6460
Haven in the Hardwood: The History of Pickens, West Virginia.
N460 (ASU)
Marketing of Lumber Through Retail Outlets in W. Va.
N470
Forests and Forestry in West Virginia, a Bibliography.
R1700
FORESTS AND FORESTRY
Early Reproduction After Seed-tree Harvest Cuttings in Appalachian Hardwoods.
W2790
Seasonal Moisture Fluctuations in Four Species of Pocosin Vegetation.
W2800 (WCU)
FORESTS AND FORESTRY PRODUCTS
The Relation of Growth to Stand Density in Natural Loblolly Pine Stands.
W2820 (WCU)
Silvical Characteristics of Loblolly Pine.
W2830 (WCU)
FORESTS, NATIONAL
Whose Woods These Are: The Story of the National Forests.
F3490 (MHC)
The Forest Service and Appalachia.
K30 (ASU)
FORESTS — NATURAL
A Scenic Guide to the Monongahela National Forest.
W2430 (LMC ASU WCU BC)
4-H CLUBS
A Touch of Charisma; a History of the 4-H Club Program in West Virginia.
S7240
FRENCH BROAD RIVER
The French Broad.
D4210 (WWC BC)
The French Broad.
D4220 (ASU ETSU WCU LMC MHC BC)
E780 (ASU)
Human Resources in the Economy of the Upper French Broad Area.
M4310 (LMC)
Economic Development of the Upper French Broad Area: Summary of Needs and Opportunities, Resources, the Regional Economy.
N2690 (ASU)
Economic Development of the Upper French Broad Area by North Carolina State and the Tennessee Valley Authority.
T2570 (LMC)
. . . Flood Control for Upper French Broad River and Tributaries; a Preliminary Report.
T6930
Flood of August 24-25, 1961: Upper French Broad River Basin.
T6940
Floods on French Broad and Davidson Rivers and King, Nicholson, and Tucker Creeks in Vicinity of Brevard, North Carolina.
T7030
Floods on French Broad and Swannanoa Rivers, in Vicinity of Asheville, North Carolina.
T7040
Floods on French Broad River and Spring Creek in Vicinity of Hot Springs, North Carolina.
T7050
Floods on French Broad River in the Vicinity of Marshall, N. C.
T7060
FRENCH HUGUENOTS
Memorials of the Huguenot's in America, with Special Reference to Their Emigration to Pennsylvania.
S6590 (ASU)
FRENCH-BROAD RIVER
The French-Broad Holston Country: A History of Knox County, Tennessee.
R3940 (LMC BC)
The French Broad-Holston Country: A History of Knox County, Tennessee.
R3950 (ETSU)
FRONTIER AND PIONEER LFFE — APP.
The Southern Frontier, 1670-1732.
C8520 (WCU BC)
FRONTIER AND PIONEER LIFE
Daniel Boone, Pioneer of Kentucky.
A30 (ASU)
Daniel Boone, Pioneer of Kentucky.
A40 (ETSU)
Daniel Boone, the Pioneer of Kentucky.
A50 (ASU BC)
David Crockett: His Life and Adventures.
A60 (ASU ETSU)
From Frontier to Plantation in Tennessee.
A80 (WWC BC)
From Frontier to Plantation in Tennessee: A Study in Frontier Democracy.
A90 (ASU LMC)
Three Virginia Frontiers.
A100 (ETSU BC)
Three Virginia Frontiers.
A110 (ASU WCU)
Western Lands and the American Revolution.
A120
Western Lands and the American Revolution.
A130 (FC BC ASU)
Land Entry Book, Wilkes County, North Carolina, 1778-1781.
A160 (ASU)
Heroes of the Alamo: Accounts and Documents.
A260 (ETSU)
The Story of Wise County, Virginia.
A540 (BC ASU)
New Governments West of the Alleghenies Before 1780.
A1010 (BC)
John Stuart and the Southern Colonial Frontier.
A1040
John Stuart and the Southern Colonial Frontier: A Study of Indian Relations, War, Trade, and Land Problems in the Southern Wilderness, 1754-1775.
A1050 (ASU BC FC WCU)
The Overmountain Men: Early Tennessee History, 1760-1780.
A1260 (BC ETSU)
The Overmountain Men: Early Tennessee History, 1760-1795.
A1270 (ASU LMC FC)
Lewis Wetzel: Indian Fighter. The Life and Times of a Frontier Hero.
A1810 (ASU BC)
The First Explorations of the Trans-Allegheny Region by the Virginians, 1650-1674.
A1990 (ASU BC)
The Ocoee District, South East Tennessee in the United States of America, Especially the Hundred Thousand Acres, and the Gold Region, with a Sketch of the Character of the People Who Inhabit East Tennessee Generally.
A2450
The Appalachian Indian Frontier. The Edmond Atkin Report and Plan of 1755.
A5310 (ASU BC WCU LMC ETSU)
Chronicles of the Scotch-Irish Settlement in Virginia.
A5480 (ASU)
Chronicles of the Scotch-Irish Settlement in Virginia, Extracted from the Original Court Records of Augusta County, 1745-1800.
A5490 (ASU)
Daniel Boone.
A5700 (ETSU BC)
The Ohio Company of Virginia and the Westward Movement, 1748-1792.
B330 (BC)
Daniel Boone.
B500 (ASU FC ETSU UNCA BC)
Daniel Boone.
B510 (ASU WCU)
Daniel Boone.
B520 (ASU MH)
Fighting Frontiersman, the Life of Daniel Boone.
B530
Fighting Frontiersman, the Life of Daniel Boone.
B540 (ASU BC)
Master of the Wilderness: Daniel Boone.
B550
"Fort Southwest Point, Tennessee: The Development of a Frontier Post, 1792-1807."
B920
Valley of Democracy: The Frontier Versus the Plantation in the Ohio Valley, 1755-1818.
B1370 (BC)
The Peopling of Virginia.
B2350 (ASU)
The Peopling of Virginia.
B2360 (FC)
Jennie Wiley, Pioneer: The True Story of a Virginia Frontier Heroine.
B3000 (ASU)
Davy Crockett, Frontier Hero; the Truth as He Told It, the Legend as Friends Built It.
B4490
Scotch Irish Pioneers in Ulster and America.
B5170 (ASU)
Georgia's Last Frontier: The Development of Carroll County.
B5310 (ASU LMC BC)
Border Fights and Fighters.
B6240 (BC)
Virginia Settlers and English Adventurers: Abstracts of Wills, 1484-1798, and Legal Proceedings, Relating to Early Virginia Families.
B6620 (ASU)
The Captives of Abb's Valley.
B7151
The Captives of Abb's Valley, a Legend of Frontier Life.
B7152 (ASU)
Daniel Boone: The Opening of the Wilderness.
B7240 (ASU BC)
Pioneers of Old Frontiers.
B7270 (ETSU)
Early Maps of the Ohio Valley.
B7290 (BC)
Daniel Boone and the Wilderness Road.
B7580 (ETSU)
Heritage of the Trans-Allegheny Pioneers: Or, Resources of Central West Virginia.
B7640 (ASU BC)
Sketches of Tennessee's Pioneer Baptist Preachers.
B9000 (WCU)
The Upper Tennessee.
C970 (BC)
North Carolina Land Grants in Tennessee, 1778-1791.
C1800 (ETSU BC ASU)
The Appalachian Frontier: America's First Surge Westward.
C1820 (ASU WCU LMC MHC WWC ETSU BC UNCA)
The Southern Frontier.
C1830 (WCU)
Famous Frontiersmen, Pioneers and Scouts: The Vanguards of American Civilization.
C2170 (BC)
Dark Hills to Westward: The Saga of Jennie Wiley.
C2200 (ASU WCU LMC MHC ETSU BC)
Simon Kenton, the Scout: A Tale of Frontier Life During the Revolution.
C7390 (BC)

FRONTIER AND PIONEER LIFE
The Log Meeting-house, and the McIlhanys.
E1060 (ASU)
The Life and Times of Col. Daniel Boone, Hunter, Soldier, and Pioneer.
E1780 (ETSU BC FC ASU WCU LMC)
"David Crockett: An Interpretation."
E2350
Old Bill Williams, Mountain Man.
F380 (ASU)
The Adventures of Colonel Daniel Boone, formerly a Hunter: Containing a Narrative of the Wars of Kentucky, with the Discovery, Purchase, and Settlement of Kentucky, and the Piankashaw Council, 1784, and Territory of North American Indians, and the Rights Land in Kentucky.
F850 (BC ASU LMC)
The Discovery, Settlement, and Present State of Kentucky.
F880 (ASU)
Kentucky and the Adventures of Col. Daniel Boone.
F890
Daniel Boone, Backwoodsman.
F1860
Davy Crockett.
F1870 (ETSU)
Wilderness Road; a Parable for Modern Times.
G3630
Wilderness Road: A Symphonic Outdoor Drama.
G3640 (WCU BC ASU)
Trans-Allegheny Pioneers.
H350 (ASU)
Trans-Allegheny Pioneers. . . .
H360 (ETSU)
Trans-Allegheny Pioneers: Historical Sketches of the First White Settlements West of the Alleghenies 1784 and After. Wonderful Experiences of Hardships and Heroism of Those Who First Braved the Dangers of the Inhospitable Wilderness, and the Savage Tribes That Then Inhabited It.
H380 (ASU BC)
Autobiography of "Old Claib Jones."
H720
The Life of Daniel Boone, the Founder of the State of Kentucky.
H3190 (ASU)
Life of Daniel Boone, the Great Western Hunter and Pioneer, Comprising an Account of His Early History, His Daring and Remarkable Career as the First Settler of Kentucky. To Which is Added His Autobiography Complete as Dictated by Himself.
H3200 (WCU BC ETSU)
Life of Daniel Boone, the Great Western Hunter and Pioneer, Comprising an Account of His Early History, His Daring and Remarkable Career as the First Settler of Kentucky. To Which Is Added His Autobiography Complete as Dictated by Himself.
H3210 (ASU BC ETSU)
Stories of Hatfield, the Pioneer.
H3430
Stories of Hatfield, the Pioneer; embracing a detailed account of His Experience in the Wilderness of East Tennessee, Kentucky, and Southern Indiana.
H3440 (BC)
Adventures of Daniel Boone, the Kentucky Rifleman.
H3720 (BC)
Borderland Echoes, a W. Va. Story.
H3950 (BC ASU)
The First West.
H4820 (ASU WCU MHC ETSU BC)
Daniel Boone: The Pioneer of Kentucky.
H5400
Life and Adventures of Daniel Boone, the Pioneer of Kentucky.
H5410 (ASU BC)
Boone's Wilderness Road.
H7870 (ETSU BC)
Six Feet Six, the Heroic Story of Sam Houston.
J300 (ASU)
The Raven, a Biography of Sam Houston.
J360
The Frontier Camp Meeting.
J1320 (WWC)
Kegley's Virginia Frontier: The Beginning of the Southwest. The Roanoke of Colonial Days, 1740-1783.
K470 (ASU ETSU FC BC)
L1220
Cumberland Gap and Trails West.
M200 (BC)
Sketches of Western Adventure: Containing an Account of the Most Interesting Incidents Connected with the Settlement of the West, from 1755 to 1794.
M470 (ETSU BC)
Travels in the American Colonies.
M5090 (ASU BC)
Life and Adventures of Lewis Wetzel.
M5290 (BC)
Protestants and Pioneers; Individualism and Conformity on the American Frontier.
M6370
Folklore of the Blue Ridge Mountains and Early Settlers.
M7870
The Story of Daniel Boone.
M8130 (ASU BC)
Some Early Emigrants to America, Also, Early Emigrants to America from Liverpool, abstracted by Reginal Sharpe France.
N930 (ASU)
The Forgotten Pioneer: The Life of Davy Crockett.
N2980 (ASU ETSU)
"Doctor Thomas Walker (1715-1794): Explorer, Physician, Surveyor, and Planter of Virginia and Kentucky."
N3050 (BC)
A History of the United States Indian Factory System, 1795-1822.
P1200
Frontier Mission: A History of Religion West of the Southern Appalachians to 1861.
P3740 (BC WWC)
Pioneer Presbyterianism in Tennessee; Addresses Delivered at the Tennessee Exposition on Presbyterian Day, Oct. 28, 1897.
P4310 (ASU)
Cathedrals in the Wilderness.
S860 (BC)
Daniel Boone, Pioneer.
S2120 (ASU)
The Daniel Boone Story.
S4540 (BC)
The Wilderness Road: a Description of the Routes of Travel by Which the Pioneers and Early Settlers First Came to Kentucky.
S6120 (ASU FC LMC BC)
Daniel Boone, Boy Hunter.
S7160 (ETSU)
Daniel Boone, Boy Hunter.
S7170 (ASU)
A Sketch of the Cherokee and Choctaw Indians.
S8740
Meet Virginia's Baby: A Brief Pictorial History of Dickenson County, Virginia, from Its Formation in 1880 to 1955, with Stress on Pioneer Background.
S9200 (ASU LMC BC)
Jemima, Daughter of Daniel Boone.
S9340
Religion in Colonial America.
S9630 (MHC FC)
Religion in the Development of American Culture, 1795-1840.
S9640 (ASU)
Benjamin Logan, Kentucky Frontiersman.
T40 (WCU BC)
Daniel Boone.
T8490 (ETSU BC)
Daniel Boone.
T8500 (ASU)
Withers Chronicles of Border Warfare.
T8540
A Company of Heroes.
V220
Forth to the Wilderness: The First American Frontier, 1754-1774.
V240 (ASU)
Men of the Western Waters; a Second Look at the First Americans.
V250
Daniel Boone, Backwoodsman: The Green Woods Were His Portion.
V390 (ASU WCU LMC MHC)
The Log Cabin in America: From Pioneer Days to the Present.
W2880 (ASU WCU BC)
Sketches of Our Mountain Pioneers.
W3080 (BC)
Daniel Boone: Wilderness Scout.
W5580 (ETSU ASU BC)
Daniel Boone; Wilderness Scout.
W5590 (BC)
Daniel Boone, Wilderness Scout.
W5600 (ETSU)
Daniel Boone: Wilderness Scout. The Life Story and True Adventure of the Great Hunter, Long Knife, Who First Blazed the Wilderness Trail Through the Indian Country to Kentucky.
W5610 (ASU)
Daniel Boone: Taming the Wilds.
W6280 (BC)
John Sevier, Son of Tennessee.
W6300 (ETSU)
John Sevier, Son of Tennessee.
W6310 (LMC)
History of the Lost State of Franklin.
W6790

FRONTIER AND PIONEER LIFE — ALA.
Early Settlers of Alabama.
S480 (ASU BC)

FRONTIER AND PIONEER LIFE — APP.
The Rampaging Frontier: Manners and Humors of Pioneer Days in the South and Middle West.
C4590 (ASU)
The Rampaging Frontier: Manners and Humors of Pioneer Days in the South and Middle West.
C4600 (WWC)
The Life and Adventures of Wilburn Waters, the Famous Hunter and Trapper of White Top Mountain.
C5230 (BC)
Wilburn Waters History 1812-1879.
C5240
The Southern Frontier, 1670-1732.
C8530 (ASU LMC FC)
The Dixie Frontier, a Social History of the Southern Frontier from the First Transmontane Beginnings to the Civil War.
D2080 (ASU MHC)
The Frontiersmen.
E760
The Life and Times of Col. Daniel Boone, the Hunter of Kentucky, with Sketches of His Contemporaries: Narrative of St. Clair's Defeat. Mrs. Merrill's Adventures, etc.
E1790 (ASU BC)
Life of Colonel David Crockett: Comprising His Adventures as Backwoodsman and Hunter; His Services as Soldier and Scout in the Creek War; His Electioneering Canvasses; His Career as Congressman; His Tour through the Northern States; and His Services and Death in the Texan War of Independence. To Which Are Added, Sketches of General Sam Houston, General Santa Anna, Rezin P. and Colonel James Bowie.
E1800 (ASU)
Woman on the American Frontier.
F2460
The Colonial Cavalier: Or, Southern Life Before the Revolution.
G2640 (LMC)
The Wilderness Trail: Or, The Ventures and Adventures of the Pennsylvania Traders on the Allegheny Path, with Some New Annals of the Old West, and the Records of Some Strong Men and Some Bad Ones.
H1540 (ASU BC)
The Conquest of the Old Southwest: The Romantic Story of the Early Pioneers into Virginia, the Carolinas, Tennessee, and Kentucky, 1740-1790.
H4420 (ASU WCU LMC BC)
H4940 (BC ASU)
Tales of a Frontier Preacher.
H5330
The Appalachian Indian Frontier: The Edmond Atkin Report and Plan of 1755.
J240
Indians of the Southern Colonial Frontier; The Edmond (Edmund) Atkin Report and Plan of 1755.
J250

FRONTIER AND PIONEER LIFE — APP.

The Violent Years.
J1260 (BC)

Simon Girty, the Outlaw.
J2610

Colonial and Revolutionary History of Upper South Carolina, Embracing for the Most Part the Primitive and Colonial History of the Territory Comprising the Original County of Spartanburg with a General Review of the Entire Military Operations in the Upper Portion of South Carolina and Portions of North Carolina.
L320 (ASU WCU LMC BC)

Colonial and Revolutionary History of Upper South Carolina.
L330 (LMC)

Cherokees and Pioneers.
M220 (ASU LMC)

The American Indian Frontier.
M2110 (ASU)

The Mitchell-Doak Group.
M6320

The Influence of the Physiographic Features of Western North Carolina on the Settlement and Development of the Region.
N1400 (ASU)

Daughters of the Country: The Women of the Fur Traders and Mountain Men.
O660 (WCU)

History of the American Frontier, 1763-1893.
P1070 (ASU BC)

The Allegheny Frontier: West Virginia Beginnings, 1730-1830.
R1970 (ASU WCU LMC ETSU MHC WWC BC FC UNCA)

"Frontier West Virginia: Some Aspects of Its Political, Social, and Economic Development."
R2000 (ASU)

The Winning of the West.
R3700 (ASU)

In the Ranks of Old Hickory, When with the Western Riflemen in Defense Against from Within and Without, Young and Old of All Degrees United Under Andrew Jackson to Make the Republic's Borders Safe.
S30 (ETSU ASU BC)

The Scotch-Irish in History as Master Builders of Empires, States, Churches, Schools and Civilization.
S2500 (ASU BC)

Pioneers of the Old Southwest.
S4040 (LMC)

Pioneers of the Old Southwest: A Chronicle of the Dark and Bloody Ground.
S4050 (ASU)

Pioneers of the Old Southwest: A Chronicle of the Dark and Bloody Ground.
S4060 (ETSU)

Colonists in Bondage: White Servitude and Convict Labor in America, 1607-1776.
S4410 (ASU)

Colonists in Bondage: White Servitude and Convict Labor in America, 1607-1776.
S4420 (ASU)

Documentary History of Dunmore's War, 1774.
T8510

Frontier Defense on Upper Ohio, 1777-1778.
T8520

Revolution on the Upper Ohio, 1775-1777.
T8530

Conquering the Wilderness: Or, New Pictorial History of the Life and Times of the Pioneer Heroes and Heroines of America.
T9380 (ASU BC)

Trade and Travel Around the Southern Appalachians Before 1830.
T9520 (ASU LMC)

The Frontier in American History.
T9800 (MHC)

The Frontier in American History.
T9810 (ASU)

Rise of the New West, 1819-1829.
T9820

The Voice of the Old Frontier.
V10

Backwoods America.
W7110 (ASU LMC BC)

The Westward Movement.
W7790 (BC)

The Westward Movement: A Book of Readings on Our Changing Frontiers.
W8000 (ASU)

FRONTIER AND PIONEER LIFE — GA.

Sketches of Some of the First Settlers of Upper Georgia, of the Cherokees, and the Author.
G1700 (ASU BC LMC)

Sketches of Some of the First Settlers of Upper Georgia, of the Cherokees, and the Author.
G1710 (ETSU)

FRONTIER AND PIONEER LIFE — KY.

Daniel Boone and the Wilderness Road.
B7570 (ASU BC)

Family History Records of Dr. Thomas Walker, First Explorer of Kentucky.
B9040

Pioneers of Eastern Kentucky, Their Feuds and Settlements.
C2180 (ASU)

Kentucky; The Pioneer State of the West.
C3750

A History of Kentucky.
C4550 (ASU BC)

Simon Kenton, Kentucky Scout.
C4610 (BC)

Wilderness Road.
C5140 (ASU)

Wilderness Road.
C5150 (BC)

Eastern Kentucky Papers: The Founding of Harman's Station, with an Account of the Indian Captivity of Mrs. Jennie Wiley and the Exploration and Settlement of the Big Sandy Valley in the Virginia's and Kentucky. To Which Is Affixed a Brief Account of the Connelley Family and Some of Its Collateral and Related Families in America.
C6640 (ASU)

The Founding of Harman's Station and the Wiley Captivity.
C6650 (BC ASU)

History of Pioneer Kentucky.
C7700 (LMC BC ASU)

Pioneer Life in Kentucky, 1785-1800.
D3210 (ASU ETSU BC)

Pioneer Life in Kentucky, a Series of Reminiscential Letters from Daniel Drake . . . to His Children.
D3220 (ASU)

The Discovery and Settlement of Kentucky.
F860 (LMC ETSU BC)

The Discovery, Settlement, and Present State of Kentucky.
F870 (UNCA)

Biographical Memoir of Daniel Boone, the First Settler of Kentucky: Interspersed with Incidents in the Early Annals of the Country.
F1560 (ASU BC)

Biographical Memoir of Daniel Boone, the First Settler of Kentucky: Interspersed with Incidents in the Early Annals of the Country.
F1570 (ETSU WCU)

The Life and Adventures of Daniel Boone, the First Settler of Kentucky.
F1580 (ETSU)

Boone's Wilderness Road.
H5320

Autobiography of "Old Claib Jones."
J2390

Biographical Record of Daniel and Mary (Jackson) Williams — Early Kentucky Pioneers, 1752-1898.
K590 (ASU)

Pioneer Families of Eastern and Southeastern Kentucky.
K3100 (ASU BC)

The Cumberland.
M190 (LMC)

"The Settlement of the Kentucky Appalachian Highlands."
M480 (ASU BC)

James Harrod of Kentucky.
M3980 (ASU)

The Frontier Mind: A Cultural Analysis of the Kentucky Frontiersman.
M6830 (ASU BC ETSU UNCA)

The Frontier Mind.
M6840 (ASU WCU)

The Frontier Mind: A Cultural Analysis of the Kentucky Frontiersman.
M6850

Pioneer Families of Clay County, Kentucky.
M7600 (ASU BC)

Adventures along the Cumberland.
O160 (BC)

Boonesborough: Its Founding, Pioneer Struggles, Indian Experiences, Transylvania Days and Revolutionary Annals.
R340 (BC ASU LMC)

Boonesborough: Its Founding, Pioneer Struggles, Indian Experiences, Transylvania Days and Revolutionary Annals.
R350 (ASU WCU ETSU)

Petitions of the Early Inhabitants of Kentucky to the General Assembly of Virginia, 1769.
R3160

Kentucky's Last Frontier.
S700 (MHC BC)

Kentucky's Last Frontier.
S710 (ASU LMC)

Kentucky: A Pioneer Commonwealth.
S2190 (LMC BC ASU)

Kentucky: A Pioneer Commonwealth.
S2200 (WWC)

Kentucky; a Pioneer Commonwealth.
S2210

Kentucky Pioneer Women. Columbian Poems and Prose Sketches.
T150 (BC)

FRONTIER AND PIONEER LIFE — KY. AND TENN.

Flowering of the Cumberland.
A4910 (FC BC UNCA WWC ASU WCU LMC MHC)

FRONTIER AND PIONEER LIFE — MD.

Western Maryland Pioneers: Marriages, Early Settlers, Births and Deaths with Location.
C2870 (ASU)

FRONTIER AND PIONEER LIFE — N. C.

The Settlement of North Carolina.
C470 (ASU BC)

The Carolina Indian Frontier.
C7470 (ASU WCU)

Colonial North Carolina in the Eighteenth Century: A Study in Historical Geography.
M5130 (UNCA LMC)

Carolina Cradle: Settlement of the Northwest Carolina Frontier, 1747-1762.
R310 (BC LMC ASU)

Early Settlement of Western North Carolina.
S5490

FRONTIER AND PIONEER LIFE — PA.

A Journal of a Surveying Trip into Western Pennsylvania under Andrew Ellicott in the Year 1795.
B8570 (BC)

Notes on the Settlement and Indian Wars of the Western Parts of Virginia and Pennsylvania from 1763 to 1783. Together with a Review of the State of Society and Manners of the First Settlers of the Western Country. With a memoir of the author by his daughter, Narcissa Doddridge. Republished.
D2660 (ASU BC FC)

Notes on the Settlements and Indian of the Western Parts of Virginia and Pennsylvania from 1763 to 1783, Inclusive.
D2670 (ETSU BC)

The German and Swiss Settlements of Colonial Pennsylvania: A Study of the So-called Pennsylvania Dutch.
K3380 (ASU)

FRONTIER AND PIONEER LIFE — TENN.

The Attack upon and Defense of Fort Sanders, Knoxville, Tennessee, November 29, 1863.
A4700 (ASU)

Old Tales Retold: Or, Perils and Adventures of Tennessee Pioneers.
B5250 (ASU LMC BC)

"Washington County Court: The Government of a Tennessee Frontier Community."
B7470

History of Blount County, Tennessee, From War Trail to Landing Strip, 1795-1955.
B9130 (ASU ETSU BC)

"Isaac Shelby, 1750-1796."
C7030

"Theodore Roosevelt, Franklin Historian."
D910

Descendants of East Tennessee Pioneers.
E1190 (ASU)

A Narrative of the Life of David Crockett of the State of Tennessee.
F1730

Make Way for the Great.
F2170 (ETSU BC)

FRONTIER AND PIONEER LIFE — TENN.

The Backward Trail; Stories of the Indians and Tennessee Pioneers.
H470

Tennessee, a History, 1673-1932.
H1060 (LMC)

Frontier Forts along the Clinch, Powell and Holston.
H1130 (BC)

The First American Frontier: Civil and Political History of the State of Tennessee from Its Earliest Settlement up to the Year 1796.
H4040 (LMC)

The Natural and Aboriginal History of Tennessee, up to the First Settlements Therein by the White People in the Year 1768.
H4050 (ASU ETSU BC)

Pioneer Families of Pickett County, Tennessee.
H7950

Historic Fort Loudoun.
K680

Historic Fort Loudoun.
K690

The Cumberland.
M190 (LMC)

Signal Mountain and Walden's Ridge.
P600

"Early North Carolina Migrations into the Tennessee Country, 1768-1782: A Study in Historical Demography."
P990

Davy Crockett.
R4010 (ETSU BC)

Davy Crockett.
R4020 (ASU)

Pioneers of Roane County, Tennessee, 1801-1830.
T8400 (ETSU)

History of the Lost State of Franklin.
W6780 (ASU MHC BC)

History of the Lost State of Franklin.
W6800 (LMC WCU ETSU ASU)

History of the Lost State of Franklin.
W6810 (ETSU)

History of the Lost State of Franklin.
W6820

FRONTIER AND PIONEER LIFE — TENN. AND KY.

Seedtime on the Cumberland.
A4950 (ETSU FC ASU WCU BC LMC MHC WWC)

FRONTIER AND PIONEER LIFE — VA.

Economic History of Virginia in the Seventeenth Century.
B7620 (BC FC)

Frontiers Along the Upper Roanoke River, 1740-1776.
C4920

The Life and Adventures of Wilburn Waters, Early History of Southwest Virginia.
C5220

Notes on the Settlement and Indian Wars of the Western Parts of Virginia and Pennsylvania from 1763 to 1783. Together with a Review of the State of Society and Manners of the First Settlers of the Western Country. With a memoir of the author by his daughter, Narcissa Doddridge. Republished.
D2660 (ASU BC FC)

Notes on the Settlements and Indian of the Western Parts of Virginia and Pennsylvania from 1763 to 1783, Inclusive.
D2670 (ETSU BC)

Old Virginia and Her Neighbours.
F1290 (ASU MHC)

Capt. John Fowler of Virginia and Kentucky; Patriot, Soldier, Pioneer, Statesman, Land Baron, and Civic Leader.
F2430 (BC)

Fauquier during the Proprietorship: A Chronicle of the Colonization and Organization of a Northern Neck County.
G4390 (ASU)

Castle's Woods 1769-1799, Frontier Virginia Settlement.
H250

Castle's Woods: Frontier Virginia Settlement, 1779-1799.
H260

Historical Sketches of Southwest Virginia.
H5950

The Blackwater Chronicle; A Narrative of an Expedition into the Land of Canaan.
K750 (BC ASU)

The Virginia Frontier, 1754-1763.
K3010 (ASU BC)

Pioneer Settlers of Grayson County, Virginia.
N2940 (ASU)

The Adventures of My Grandfather.
P2480 (ASU)

Massanutten, Settled by the Pennsylvania Pilgrim, 1726: The First White Settlement in the Shenandoah Valley.
S7980 (ASU BC)

Memoir of Indian Wars, and Other Occurrences.
S8730 (ASU)

List of the Colonial Soldiers of Virginia.
V1190 (ASU)

FRONTIER AND PIONEER LIFE — W. VA.

Annals of Blackwater and the Land of Canaan, 1746-1880.
B7380 (ASU BC)

Simon Kenton, Kentucky Scout.
C4610 (BC)

West Virginia Reader, Stories of Early Days.
C6610 (ASU ETSU)

George Michael Bedinger: A Kentucky Pioneer.
D80 (ASU)

Heritage of a Pioneer, Being the Story of William (English Bill Doddridge) Dodrill and His Wife, Rebecca (Lewis) Daugherty, Their Family, the Times in Which They Lived, and a Genealogy.
D2720 (ASU)

The Trail of the Dead Years. . .
D3660

The McNeel Family Records: Descendants of Pioneer John McNeel and Martha Davis of Pocahontas County, West Virginia, 1765-1967.
E830 (ASU)

Pioneer West Virginia.
H8090 (ASU)

Simon Kenton: His Life and Period.
K890 (ASU)

Pioneers of Mason County, West Virginia.
M970

The Border Settlements of Northwestern Virginia from 1768-1795.
M2590 (BC)

West Virginia Surnames, the Pioneers.
M6390 (ASU)

"Helvetia, West Virginia: A Study of Pioneer Development and Community Survival in Appalachia."
P490

"Helvetia, West Virginia: A Study of Pioneer Development and Community Survival in the Appalachia."
P500

Chronicles of Border Warfare; or, A History of the Settlement by the Whites, of Northwestern Va., and . . . .
W7940 (BC)

Chronicles of Border Warfare; or, A History of the Settlement by the Whites, of Northwestern Virginia, and of the Indian Wars and Massacres, in That Section of the State.
W7950 (ASU ETSU WCU BC)

Chronicles of Border Warfare: or, A History of the Settlement by the Whites, of Northwestern Virginia, and of the Indian Wars and Massacres, in That Section of the State.
W7960 (ASU UNCA)

FRUIT INDUSTRY

Annual Report.
A2840

Apple Handling and Packing in the Appalachian Area.
B9210

"The Nature of Competition among Apple Processors in the Appalachian Area."
E2310

FRUIT INDUSTRY — APP.

Elements of Success in Marketing Appalachian Apples.
G4320

"Farm-level Demand Analysis of the Appalachian Fresh Apple Industry."
M5920

Costs of Marketing Appalachian Apples.
P3950

Transportation of Apples in the Appalachian Belt, 1952-53.
S5260

FRUIT INDUSTRY — N. C.

Blueberries, Production Guide for North Carolina.
B6930 (LMC)

Smoky Mountain Wines.
M2820 (ASU)

Production, Marketing, and Prices of North Carolina Apples, 1947-1963.
P550 (LMC)

FRUIT INDUSTRY — TENN.

"The Strawberry Industry of the Hilly and Mountainous Regions of Tennessee."
H5450 (ASU)

FRUIT INDUSTRY — W. VA.

"Market Structure Analysis of the West Virginia Peach Industry."
Z30

FURNITURE

The Story of Two Chairs.
S1360 (BC)

FURNITURE INDUSTRY

Appalachian Oak in Fine Furniture.
A3170 (ASU)

The Economic Development of the Furniture Industry of the South and Its Future Dependence Upon Forestry.
K3080 (LMC)

Anvil of Adversity: Biography of Furniture Pioneer.
S7140 (ASU WCU BC)

Furniture Industry Expansion in the Tennessee Valley.
T4760

"Early History of the North Carolina Furniture Industry, 1880-1921."
T7800

FURNITURE INDUSTRY — APP.

Prospects and Problems for the Manufacture of Laminated Timber in West Virginia.
H1030

"Industrial Organization of the Appalachian Hardwood Lumber Using Industry."
L4110

FURNITURE INDUSTRY — N. C.

Sixty Years of Progress in the Making of Fine Furniture, 1903-1963.
D3440 (ASU LMC)

GA. — DESCRIPTION AND TRAVEL

Scraps of Songs and Southern Scenes: A Collection of Humorous and Pathetic Poems and Descriptive Sketches of Plantation Life in the Backwoods of Georgia.
F1760 (ASU)

Georgia: A Guide to Its Towns and Countryside.
G880 (MHC)

GA. — HISTORY

Who Discovered America? The Amazing Story of Madoc.
A4800

The History of Bartow County, Formerly Cass.
C1150 (ASU)

The Hills of Habersham.
C4050 (ASU LMC BC)

The Hills of Habersham.
C4060

Auraria: The Story of a Georgia Gold-Mining Town.
C7770 (ASU BC)

A List of the Early Settlers of Georgia.
C7790 (ASU)

A Short History of Georgia.
C7800 (LMC BC ASU)

The History of Bartow County, Formerly Cass.
C9800 (BC ASU)

Country Life in Georgia in the Days of My Youth.
F570

The Paleozoic Group: The Geology of Ten Counties of Northwestern Georgia.
G1020 (BC ASU)

Sketches of Some of the First Settlers of Upper Georgia, of the Cherokees, and the Author.
G1700 (ASU BC LMC)

Sketches of Some of the First Settlers of Upper Georgia, of the Cherokees, and the Author.
G1710 (ETSU)

The History of Cherokee County.
M3300 (BC)

Wild Train: The Story of the Andrews Raiders.
O730 (ASU ETSU)

The Coosa River Valley from DeSoto to Hydroelectric Power.
R1660 (ASU)

Sketches of Rabun County History, 1819-1948.
R2390 (BC ASU LMC)

GA. — HISTORY
History of Walker Co., Ga.
S450 (ASU BC)
History of Walker County, Georgia.
S460 (ASU)
History of Murray County.
S3210
History of Murray County.
S3220 (ASU)
Georgia and the Union in 1850.
S3230 (MHC)
The Story of Georgia and the Georgia People, 1732 to 1860.
S4700 (ASU FC BC)
A Rough Road in a Good Land.
S6580 (ASU)
History of Pickens Co.
T320 (ASU)
Opinion of the Supreme Court of the U. S. at the Jan. Term, 1832.
U4030
The Annals of Upper Georgia Centered in Gilmer County.
W740 (ASU LMC)
Yesterday in the Hills.
W1450 (ASU LMC ETSU BC)
Historical Collections of Georgia: Containing the Most Interesting Facts, Traditions, Biographical Sketches, Anecdotes, etc., Relating to Its History and Antiquities, from Its First Settlement to the Present Time.
W5410 (ASU BC)
Statistics of the State of Georgia.
W5420 (BC)
1805 Georgia Land Lottery.
W8670 (ASU BC)
Springplace: Moravian Mission and the War Family of the Cherokee Nation.
W9500 (MHC)
History of the Georgia Power Company; 1855-1956.
W9530 (BC)

GAMES
The Games of Children, Their Origin and History.
B3390 (ASU)
The Counting-Out Rhymes of Children: Their Antiquity, Origin, and Wide Distribution, A Study in Folk-lore.
B5190 (ASU)
The American Play-party Song.
B5610 (ASU)
East Tennessee State University Football Statistics, 1920-1970.
B8840 (ETSU)
Popular Rhymes of Scotland.
C2800 (ASU)
Hullabaloo, and Other Singing Folk Games.
C3430 (WCU WWC BC)
Old Songs and Singing Games.
C3470 (ASU WCU BC)
Old Songs and Singing Games.
C3480 (LMC)
Singing Games and Playparty Games.
C3490 (ASU MHC BC)
Games of the North American Indians. 24th Annual Report of the Bureau of American Ethnology to the Secretary of the Smithsonian Institute.
C9400 (LMC)
And Promenade All.
E1400
Folk-songs, Chanteys and Singing Games.
F210 (ASU LMC BC)
Folk Dances of Tennessee; Folk Customs and Old Play Party Games of the Caney Fork Valley.
M1190 (ASU)
Folk Dances of Tennessee; Old Play Party Games of the Caney Fork Valley.
M1200 (BC ASU)
Games and Songs of American Children, Collected and Compared.
N760 (ASU BC)
Circle Left! Folk Play of the Kentucky Mountains.
S3840 (ASU LMC BC)
Folk Games from Frying Pan Creek in Dickenson County, Virginia.
S9160
The Witchery of Archery.
T8290 (ASU)

GENEALOGY
Montgomery County, Virginia, 1820 and 1830 Census.
A1170
Peter Angle, 1754-1968, and Related Families: Wills, Lee, Mooreman.
A2530
Wiseman Family.
C3240 (LMC)
The German Allied Troops in the North American War of Independence, 1776-1783.
E1220 (ASU)
Fairbairn's Book of Crests of the Families of Great Britain and Ireland.
F40 (ASU)
The Dutch and Quaker Colonies in America.
F1280 (ASU)
The Hagey Families in America and the Dulaney Family.
H220
In Search of British Ancestry.
H1110
They Went Thataway.
H1240
Founding in America of the Hamrick (Hamerick) Family by Hans George Hamerick in the Year 1731 at the Port of Philadelphia, Pa.
H1400 (ASU)
Ohio Valley Genealogies, Relating Chiefly to Families in Harrison, Belmont and Jefferson Counties, Ohio, and Washington, Westmoreland, and Fayette Counties, Pennsylvania.
H1510 (ASU BC)
The Atlantic Migration, 1607-1860: A History of the Continuing Settlement of the United States.
H1680 (ASU)
Kerfoot, Kearfoot and Allied Families in America.
K330
McNair, McNear, and McNeir Genealogies.
M2340 (ASU)
A History and Genealogy of the Family of Col. Morgan the First White Settler of the State of West Virginia.
M7530 (ASU)
N2350
John R. Rohrbach (Rohrabaugh) 1728-1821: Descendants and Marriage Connections.
R3730 (ASU)
The Scherer Family of Montgomery County, Illinois.
S380 (ASU)
Links That Bind.
S1370 (ASU)
The Harris Genealogy.
S1540 (ASU)
The Squires of Springfield.
S6380 (ASU)
My Grandfather, My Grandchildren, and Me: An Autobiography of Charles W. Wampler.
W700 (ASU)
Lincoln's Parentage Childhood.
W960
Genealogical Gleanings in England: Abstracts of Wills Relating to Early American Families, with Genealogical Notes and Pedigrees Constructed from the Wills and from Other Records.
W1420 (ASU)
Virginia Valley Records.
W1710
Virginia Valley Records: Genealogical and Historical Materials of Rockingham County, Virginia, and Related Regions.
W1860 (ASU BC)
The Tribe of Jacob: The Descendants of the Reverend Jacob Weaver of Reems Creek, North Carolina, 1786-1868, and Elizabeth Siler Weaver.
W2010
The Big Wells Family.
W2740 (BC)
One Branch of the Woodses.
W8820
The Woods-McAfee Memorial containing an account of John Woods and James McAfee of Ireland and Their Descendants in America.
W8830
Zirkle Family in America, Germany to America.
Z130

GENEALOGY — W. VA.
Genealogy of Thomas Hall, His Children and Grandchildren.
H900 (ASU)

GENEALOGY — ALA.
Old Speedwell Families.
E1110
Early Settlers of Alabama.
S480 (ASU BC)
Genealogy of the Tankersley Family in the United States.
T180 (ASU)

GENEALOGY — ALA. — SOURCES
A880 (ASU)
Alabama Census Returns, 1820: And an Abstract of Federal Census of Alabama, 1830.
A890 (ASU)
First Marriage Records, 1838-1850, Barbour County, Alabama.
F1660 (ASU)
Marriage Records, 1850, Barbour County, Alabama.
F1670 (ASU)
Revolutionary Soldiers in Alabama: Being a List of Names, Compiled from Authentic Sources, of Soldiers of the American Revolution, Who Resided in the State of Alabama.
O990 (ASU)
Early Settlers of Alabama.
S8750

GENEALOGY — APP.
Genealogy of the Deckard Family.
D1570
A Genealogical Cross Index of the Four Volumes of the Genealogical Dictionary of James Savage.
D2060 (ASU)
The Furches Folks.
F3870 (ASU)
A Genealogical Resume of "The Furches Folks."
F3880 (ASU)
The Hamrick Generation, Being a Genealogy of the Hamrick Family.
J2600 (ASU)
History of Henry McWhorter Family of New Jersey and West Virginia.
M2600 (ASU)
The Moss Family: William Paul Moss, Thaddeus Augustus Moss, Amanda Holden Moss, Howell Moss, Crestus Howell Moss, Henry Moss, Their Families and Progenitors.
M8280 (ASU)
The McKnight Families and Their Descendants: Also the Wallace and Alexander Families.
P1170 (ASU)
The McKnight Family and Their Descendants, Also the Wallaces, Alexander and English Families.
P1180 (ASU)
David Rawson Ancestors and Descendants.
S5460 (ASU)
Lists of Germans From the Palatinate Who Came to England in 1709.
T9270 (ASU)
Trogdon Family History.
T9420 (ASU)
The Tuley Family Memoirs; an Historical, Biographical and Genealogical Story of the Tuleys and the Floyd Family Connection in Virginia, Kentucky, and Indiana.
T9700
Revolutionary pensioners; a transcript of the pension list of the United States for 1813.
U3910 (ASU)
The Pension List of 1818-1819.
U4050
Pensioners of Revolutionary War Struck off the roll; with an added index to States.
U4060 (ASU)
Revolutionary Pensioners of 1818.
U4070
Wilder and Some Connecting (Especially Some Ware) Families in Southeast United States of America.
W6170
Historical Genealogy of the Woodsons and Their Connections.
W8870
Descendants of Robert and John Poage.
W8890

GENEALOGY — APP. — SOURCES
Hessian Soldiers in the American Revolution: Records of Their Marriages and Baptisms of Children in America Performed by the Rev. G. C. Coster, 1776-1783, Chaplain of Two Hessian Regiments.
D2190 (ASU)

GENEALOGY — APP. — SOURCES

Colonial Families of the Southern States of America: A History and Genealogy of Colonial Families Who Settled in the Colonies Prior to the Revolution.
H2200 (ASU)

Huguenot Pedigrees.
L660 (ASU)

Look Back Into Your Mighty Ancestors.
L1640

List of Emigrants to America from Liverpool, 1697-1707. Transcribed by Elizabeth French.
L2900 (ASU)

SLOINNANCE SAEDEAL IR SALL: Irish Names and Surnames.
W9340 (ASU)

GENEALOGY — CHEROKEE

Military and Genealogical Records of the Famous Indian Woman; Nancy Ward. . . .
B9090

Old Cherokee Families: "Old Families and Their Genealogy" . . . with a Comprehensive Index.
H5430

Old Cherokee Families: Old Families and Their Genealogy.
S6690 (WCU MHC)

GENEALOGY — GA.

Georgia's Roster of the Revolution.
G890 (ASU)

David Morgan (ca. 1779-1857) and His Descendants.
M7560

History of Walker County, Georgia.
S460 (ASU)

Genealogy of the Tankersley Family in the United States.
T180 (ASU)

Index to the 1830 Census of Georgia.
U660 (ASU)

GENEALOGY — GA. — SOURCES

A List of the Early Settlers of Georgia.
C7790 (ASU)

Historical Collections of the Georgia Chapters.
D480 (ASU)

Wilkes County.
D650 (ASU)
G930 (ASU)

The Third and Fourth or 1820 and 1821 Land Lotteries of Georgia.
G940 (ASU)

Index to United States Census of Georgia for 1820.
G950 (ASU)

Century of Columbia County, Georgia, Wills, 1790-1890.
G970 (ASU)

Columbia County, Georgia, Early Court Records.
G980 (ASU)

Columbia County, Georgia: Early Marriage Records.
G990 (ASU)

600 Revolutionary Soldiers Living in Georgia in 1827-8.
H7520 (ASU)

Habersham County, Georgia, Genealogical Records.
K2100 (ASU)

Rabun County, Georgia, Records.
K2110 (ASU)

Index to the Headright and Bounty Grants of Georgia, 1759-1909.
L3830 (ASU)

The Second or 1807 Land Lottery of Georgia.
L3840 (ASU)

Roster of Revolutionary Soldiers in Georgia.
M210 (ASU)

Hall County, Georgia, 1819-1839, Marriages.
M2490 (ASU)

Tombstone Inscriptions of Hall County, Georgia.
M2500 (ASU)

Marriage Record "A', Floyd County, Georgia, 1834-1848.
M3120 (ASU)
R1550 (ASU)

1832 Cherokee Land Lottery: Index to Revolutionary Soldiers, Their Widows and Orphans Who Were Fortunate Drawers.
R2150 (ASU WCU)

History of Walker Co., Ga.
S450 (ASU BC)

The Cherokee Land Lottery.
S4820 (LMC ETSU ASU BC)

The Cherokee Land Lottery.
S4830 (ETSU)

The Cherokee Land Lottery, Containing a Numerical List of the Names of the Fortunate Drawers in Said Lottery, With an Engraved Map of Each District.
S4840 (ASU WCU BC)

Genealogical History of Original Murray County.
W5650

GENEALOGY — KY.

The Brashear Story: A Family History, Containing a Partial Account of a Family That Has Been in America for Well over Three Hundred Years.
B30 (BC)

Record of the Coe Family and Descendants from 1596-1856.
C5470 (BC)

Larsh Creech and Joseph Wynn Family Tree.
D1510 (BC)

The Meechor Engle Family History and Genealogy.
E2010 (BC)

Biographical Genealogies of the Virginia-Kentucky Floyd Families, with Notes of Some Collateral Branches.
F1640 (ASU)

History of the Fuson Family.
F4040 (BC)

Historic Families of Kentucky, with Special Reference to Stocks Immediately Derived from the Valley of Virginia.
G3670 (ASU MHC BC)

Johnson County, Kentucky: A History of the County, and Genealogy of Its People up to the Year 1927.
H860 (ASU BC)

The Hatfields.
H3450 (ASU)

Genealogy of Hollon and Related Families.
H6500

Genealogy of Hollon and Related Families.
H6700

Genealogy of Hollon and Related Families: Early Settlers of Eastern Ky. and Their Descendants.
H6710

Descendants of Isham Lane.
L1110

Irvins, Doaks, Logans and McCampbells of Virginia and Kentucky.
M7810

"General" John Norwood and Related Lines.
N2890 (ASU)

The Bastins of Casey, Lincoln, and Pulaski County, Kentucky.
R80 (BC)

The Blacks of Casey and Pulaski County, Kentucky, and of Kansas.
R90 (BC)

The Carmans of Casey County, Kentucky.
R100

The Ragles of Pennsylvania, Virginia, Kentucky, and Kansas.
R110

The History of the Pepper Family in America and Allied Lines.
R650

Mountain Kinsmen Ride; a Story of the James Family.
S720

History of the Family Snyder (Schneider) (Snider).
S5310

The Boone Family; a Genealogical History of the Descendants of George and Mary Boone Who Came to America in 1717, Containing Many Unpublished Bits of Early Kentucky History. . . .
S6340 (ASU)

Genealogy of the Tankersley Family in the United States.
T180 (ASU)

The A. K. Wilson Family: Abraham Key Wilson and Mary Jane Wilson, Their Descendants and Their Ancestors.
W7410 (BC)

GENEALOGY — KY. — SOURCES

Kentucky Records. Early Wills and Marriages Copied from Court House Records by Regents, Historians and the State Historian. Old Bible Records and Tombstone Inscriptions. Records from Barren, Bath, Bourbon Counties.
A4570 (BC ASU)

William Ballard: A Genealogical Record of His Descendants in Monroe County.
B870 (BC)

Estill County, Kentucky, Record of Abstracts of Pension Papers of Revolutionary Soldiers, War of 1812 and Indian Wars. . . .
B9050

Hensley Family Records and Allied Families.
B9060

United States Census of Bell County, Kentucky, 1880: Which are Family Bible Records as Given the Census Taker on That Date.
B9100 (BC)

United States Census of Bell Co., Ky., 1890.
B9110

Kentucky Marriages, 1797-1865.
C5020 (BC)

Notes on Kentucky Veterans of the War of 1812.
C5030 (BC)

"Second Census" of Kentucky, 1800: A Private Compiled and Published Enumeration of Tax Payers Appearing in the 79 Manuscript Volumes Extant of Tax Lists of the 42 Counties of Kentucky in Existence in 1800.
C5040 (ASU BC)

George Michael Bedinger: A Kentucky Pioneer.
D80 (ASU)

Historic Sketches of the Edwards and Todd Families and Their Descendants, 1523-1895.
E1030 (ASU)

Polish Pioneers of Virginia and Kentucky with Notes on Genealogy of the Sadowski Family.
H310 (BC)

Kentucky Soldiers of the War of 1812.
K900 (ASU)
K960

Kentucky Marriages, 1797-1865.
K1260 (ASU BC)

Abstract of Early Kentucky Wills and Inventories, Copied From Original and Recorded Wills and Inventories.
K2360 (BC ASU)

Early Families of Eastern and Southeastern Kentucky and Their Descendants.
K3090 (ASU)

Pioneer Families of Eastern and Southeastern Kentucky.
K3100 (ASU BC)

Kentucky Pioneer and Court Records: Abstracts of Early Wills, Deeds, and Marriages from Court Houses and Records of Old Bibles, Churches, Grave Yards and Cemeteries.
M30 (ASU)

Genealogies of the Lewis and Kindred Families.
M70

Surname Index to the 1850 Federal Population Census of Kentucky.
M1240

Surname Index to the 1850 Federal Population Census of Kentucky.
M1250

The McKees of Virginia and Kentucky.
M1820
M5030 (ASU)

Pioneer Families of Clay County, Kentucky.
M7600 (ASU BC)

Kentucky in the War of 1812.
Q190 (ASU MHC)

Talley's Kentucky Papers.
T80 (BC)

Talley's Northeastern Kentucky Papers.
T90

Kentucky Soldiers of the War of 1812.
W6150

GENEALOGY — MD.

The Douglas Register, Being a Detailed Record of Births, Marriages, and Deaths, Together with Other Interesting Notes, as Kept by the Rev. William Douglas from 1750 to 1797; an Index of Goochland Wills Notes on the French-Huguenot Refugees Who Lived in Manakin-town.
D3150 (ASU)

GENEALOGY — MD.

Heads of Families at the First Census of the United States Taken in the Year 1790: Maryland.
U530 (ASU)

A Census of Pensioners for Revolutionary or Military Services, with Their Names, Ages, and Places of Residence, as Returned by the Marshals of the Several Judicial Districts, under the Act for Taking the Sixth Census in 1840.
U680 (ASU)

GENEALOGY — MD. — SOURCES

Western Maryland Pioneers: Marriages, Early Settlers, Births and Deaths with Location.
C2870 (ASU)

Index of Maryland Colonial Wills, 1634-1777, in the Hall of Records, Annapolis, Maryland.
M2800 (ASU)

Magruder's Maryland Colonial Abstracts: Wills, Accounts and Inventories, 1772-1777.
M2810 (ASU)

An Index of the Source Records of Maryland: Genealogical, Bibliographical, Historical.
P560 (ASU)

GENEALOGY — N. C.

The Hortons of Western North Carolina.
B1210 ()

A History of William Taylor and Sarah Jones and their Descendants.
B7780 (UNCA)

The Genealogy of James Caldwell and his Descendants, 1750-1968: With the Intermarried Families of Campbell, Drum, Grice, Jones, Reep, Setzer, Styles, and Williams.
C170 (ASU)

Rev. John Craig, 1709-1774, his Descendants and Allied Families.
C8400 ()

North Carolina Genealogical Reference: Research Guide for All Genealogists Both Amateur and Professional.
D3380 (ASU LMC)

Happy Valley, History and Genealogy.
H5200 (ASU)

Our Kin.
H6270

David Morgan (ca. 1779-1857) and His Descendants.
M7560

Smathers from Yadkin Valley to Pigeon River: Smathers and Agner Families.
P920 (ASU)

The Brays of Fisher River.
R1000 (ASU)

Charn Cuimhne to Our Scots of North Carolina.
S4650 (ASU)

North Carolina Palatine-Germans (Futch Family).
S4660 (ASU)

The Family of Hoge — Genealogy.
T9900

Heads of Families at the First Census of the United States Taken in the Year 1790: North Carolina.
U540 (ASU)

Heads of Families at the First Census of the United States Taken in the Year 1790: North Carolina.
U550 (LMC)

Heads of Families at the First Census of the United States taken in the Year 1790: North Carolina.
U560 (ASU UNCA)

Population Schedules, North Carolina.
U620 (ASU)

Population Schedules, North Carolina.
U630 (ASU)

Population Schedules, North Carolina.
U640 (ASU)

Population Schedules, North Carolina.
U670 (ASU)

Population Schedules, North Carolina.
U690 (ASU)

Population Schedules, North Carolina.
U720 (ASU)

Population Schedules, North Carolina.
U790 (ASU)

Population Schedules, North Carolina.
U800 (ASU)

Index to the 1880 Population Schedules, North Carolina.
U810 (ASU)

Population Schedules, North Carolina.
U820 (ASU)

Eastern Band of Cherokees of North Carolina.
U830 (WCU)

Special Schedules Enumerating Union Veterans and Widows of Union Veterans of the Civil War, North Carolina.
U840 (ASU)

History of Watauga County: A Souvenir of Watauga Centennial.
W5680 (ASU WCU LMC ETSU)

GENEALOGY — N. C. — SOURCES

Deed Book B-1 Wilkes County, North Carolina.
A150

Adams, Caruthers, Clancy, Neely and Townsend Descendants Composing the Adams, Legerton, Wakefield, Brockmann and Other Twentieth Century Families of the Carolinas.
B6790 (BC)

The Genealogy of Marion-Davis Families.
B8400 (ASU)

Marriage Bonds of Tryon and Lincoln Counties, North Carolina.
B9570

Marriage Bonds of Tryon and Lincoln Counties, North Carolina.
B9580 (ASU)

Marriage Bonds of Tryon and Lincoln Counties, North Carolina.
B9590

1850 Census: Wilkes County, North Carolina.
C3570 (ASU)

North and South Carolina Marriage Records.
C4900

The Descendants of Claiborne Howard, Soldier of the American Revolution.
C6840 (ASU)

Rutherford County, North Carolina, Abstracts of Wills, 1779-1822.
D890 (ASU)

Buncombe County, North Carolina, Grantee Deed Index.
D2370

Buncombe County, North Carolina, Grantor Deed Index.
D2380

Will Books, Wilkes County, North Carolina.
G770

Abstracts of Deeds, Rutherford County, North Carolina, Volumes A-D.
G3570

Public Officials of Rutherford County, N. C. 1779-1934: With Introductory Sketches of Origin and Development of Various County Offices, and Public and Local Laws Governing Same.
G4150 (ASU BC)

The Land of Wilkes.
H3930 (ASU WCU LMC BC)

"The Forgotten Sons: North Carolinans in the Union Army."
H5210 (ASU)

Index to North Carolina Wills, 1663-1900.
J1960 (ASU)

The North Carolinian . . . A Quarterly Journal of Genealogy and History.
J1970 (ASU)

North Carolina Census Records, 1784-1900.
M1640

North Carolina Troops, 1861-1865, a Roster.
M2990 (ASU LMC)

Records of Emigrants from England and Scotland to North Carolina, 1774-1775.
N810 (ASU)

Watauga County Records: Bonds, Court Records, Estates Records, Land Records, Military and Pension Records, Tax and Fiscal Records and Wills.
N1900 (ASU)
N2400 (ASU)

Abstract of North Carolina Wills, Compiled from Original and Recorded Wills in the Office of the Secretary of State by J. Bryan Grimes, Secretary of State.
N2540 (ASU BC)

North Carolina Wills and Inventories, Copied from Original and Recorded Wills and Inventories in the Office of the Secretary of State by J. Bryan Grimes.
N2570 (ASU)

An Abstract of North Carolina Wills from about 1760 to about 1800.
O510 (BC ASU)

An Abstract of North Carolina Wills from about 1760 to about 1800.
O520 (BC ASU)

Carolina Cradle: Settlement of the Northwest Carolina Frontier, 1747-1762.
R310 (BC LMC ASU)

Index and Digest to Hathaway's North Carolina Historical and Genealogical Register, with Genealogical Notes and Annotations.
R600 (ASU)

Index and Digest to Hathaway's North Carolina Historical and Genealogical Register.
R610 (ASU)

The Lost Tribes of North Carolina. Where Did They Come from? Where Did They Go?
R620 (ASU)

Ray's Index and Digest to Hathaway's North Carolina Historical and Genealogical Register.
R630

State Census of North Carolina 1784-1787.
R1340
R4430 (ASU)

Daniel Boone Wagon Train.
W5670 (ASU)

GENEALOGY — PA.

Pennsylvania Genealogies: Chiefly Scotch Irish and German.
E1310 (ASU)

An Index to the Will Books and Interstate Records of Lancaster County, Pennsylvania, 1729-1850, with an Historical Sketch and Classified Bibliography.
F3800 (ASU)

Genealogy of the Mickley Family of America.
M5350

Rohrback Genealogy.
R3600

Umberger Family Chart.
U50

The Umberger (Umbarger) Family Chart.
U60

Heads of Families at the First Census of the United States Taken in the Year 1790: Pennsylvania.
U570 (ASU)

GENEALOGY — PA. — SOURCES

Names of Foreigners Who Took the Oath of Allegiance to the Province and State of Pennsylvania, 1727. 1775, with the Foreign Arrivals, 1786-1808.
E1300 (ASU)

Historic Background and Annals of the Swiss and German Pioneer Settlers of Southeastern Pennsylvania, and of Their Remote Ancestors from the Middle of the Dark Ages down to the Time of the Revolutionary War.
E2220 (ASU)

Central Pennsylvania Marriages, 1700-1896.
F1130 (ASU)

Central Pennsylvania Marriages, 1700-1896.
F1140 (ASU)

Probate and Orphans Court Records of Snyder County, Pennsylvania.
F1150

Wills and Administrations of Northumberland County.
F1160

William Penn and the Dutch Quaker Migration to Pennsylvania.
H8200 (ASU)

Persons Naturalized in the Province in Pennsylvania, 1740-1773.
L2650 (ASU)

Record of Pennsylvania Marriages, Prior to 1810.
L2660 (ASU)

Record of Pennsylvania Marriages, Prior to 1810.
L2670 (ASU)

Early Assessment Records: Union County and Northumberland County.
L3360 (ASU)

Tombstone Inscriptions of Union County, Pennsylvania.
L3380 (ASU)

Immigration of the Irish Quakers into Pennsylvania 1682-1750: With Their Early History in Ireland.
M9250 (ASU)

Irish Quaker Arrivals to Pennsylvania, 1682-1750: List of Certificates of Removal from Ireland, Received at the Monthly Meetings of Friends in Pennsylvania, 1682-1750.
M9260 (ASU)

GENEALOGY — PA. — SOURCES

Muster Rolls of the Pennsylvania Volunteers in the War of 1812-1814.
P1790 (ASU)

Record of Indentures of Individuals Bound Out As Apprentices, Servants and of German and other Redemptioneers in the Office of the Mayor of Philadelphia.
P2540
R830 (ASU)

The Pennsylvania Germans of the Shenandoah Valley.
S4620 (ASU)

Names of Persons Who Took the Oath of Allegiance to the State of Pennsylvania between the Years 1788 and 1789 with a History of the "Test Laws" of Pennsylvania.
W4820 (ASU)

History of the Mount Prospect Graveyard and Cemetery, in Mount Pleasant Township, Washington County, Pennsylvania.
W5300

GENEALOGY — S. C.

The Sineath Family and Affiliated Family Lineages.
B2040 (ASU)

Hunting Your Ancestors in South Carolina: A Guide for Amateur Genealogists.
F3130 (ASU)

The Huguenots of Colonial South Carolina.
H5660 (ASU)

1880 Census of Horry County, South Carolina.
H7260 (ASU)

Heads of Families at the First Census of the United States Taken in the Year 1790: South Carolina.
U590 (ASU)

Heads of Families at the First Census of the United States Taken in the Year 1790: South Carolina.
U600 (ASU LMC)

GENEALOGY — S. C. — SOURCES

North and South Carolina Marriage Records.
C4900

Bridging the Gap. A Guide to Early Greenville, South Carolina.
E620 (ASU)

Indexes to the Country Wills of South Carolina.
H7510 (ASU)

A Compilation of the Original Lists of Protestant Immigrants to South Carolina, 1763-1773.
R1580 (ASU)

Copy of the Original Index Book, Showing the Revolutionary Claims Filed in South Carolina Between August, 20, 1783, and August 31, 1786.
R1590 (ASU)

GENEALOGY — SOURCES

Land Entry Book, Wilkes County, North Carolina, 1778-1781.
A160 (ASU)

Deed Book A-1 Wilkes County, North Carolina.
A170

Tennessee Records.
A240 (ASU)

The Clans, Septs and Regiments of the Scottish Highlands.
A330 (ASU)

Marriages of Patrick County, 1791-1850.
A430

Russell County, Virginia Personal Property and Land Tax List . . .
A980

Carroll County, Virginia, 1850 Census.
A1070

Carroll County, Virginia, 1870 Census.
A1090

Floyd County, Virginia, 1840 Census.
A1100

Franklin County, Virginia, 1820 Census.
A1120

Grayson County, Virginia, Census of 1820, 1830, 1840, 1850.
A1130

Grayson County Deed Books 1, 2, 3, 4.
A1140

Index to Grayson County Deed Books 1-9, Grantee.
A1150

Index to Grayson County Deed Books 1-9, Grantor.
A1160

Patrick County, Virginia Census, 1820, 1830, 1840, 1850.
A1180

Personal Property Tax Lists, Grayson County.
A1190

Pulaski County, Virginia, 1840 Census.
A1200

Scott County, Virginia, Census, 1820 and 1830.
A1210

Wythe County, Virginia, Census, 1810, 1820, 1830, 1840.
A1220

Notable Men of Tennessee: Personal and Genealogical with Portraits.
A1780 (ASU)

The Allred Family in America.
A1900 (ASU)
A2070 (ASU)

Surnames in the United States Census of 1790; an Analysis of National Origins of the Population.
A2110

Notable Southern Families.
A4770 (ASU ETSU)

The Sevier Family.
A4780 (BC)

Shenandoah County, Virginia, Marriage Bonds, 1772-1850.
A5080 (ASU ETSU)

Doddridge County, Virginia (Now West Virginia) Marriage Book 1: Being a Record of the First Marriage in That County Created in 1845 from Parts of Tyler, Harrison, Lewis, and Ritchie Counties.
A5400 (ASU)

Pleasants County, West Virginia, Register of Deaths, 1853 — 1873.
A5410 (ASU)

Ritchie County, Virginia (now West Virginia) Marriages 1843 — 1853: Minister's Returns — With Notes on the Ancestry and Birth Place of Some of the Earliest Settlers.
A5420 (ASU)

Tyler County, Virginia (Now West Virginia) Marriages, 1815 — 1852.
A5430 (ASU)

First Marriage Records of Augusta County, Virginia, 1785-1813.
A5500 (ASU)

History of the Huguenot Emigration to America.
B470 (FC)

First Settlers of South Carolina, 1670-1680.
B700 (ASU)

The Dickenson Families of England and America.
B740

Scott County, Virginia: U. S. Census, 1850.
B780 (BC ASU)

The Seventh Population Census of the United States for Russell County, Virginia, 1850.
B790 (BC ASU)

The Planters of the Commonwealth. A Study of the Emigrants and Emigration in Colonial Times. To Which Are Added Lists of Passengers to Boston and to the Bay Colony: The Ships Which Brought Them, Their English Homes and the Places of Their Settlement in Massachusetts, 1620-1640.
B930 (ASU)

Topographical Dictionary of 2885 English Emigrants to New England, 1620-1650.
B940 (ASU)

British Family Names: Their Origin and Meaning with Lists of Scandinavian, Frisian, Anglo-Saxon and Norman Names.
B1060 (ASU)

A Dictionary of English and Welsh Surnames, with Special American Instances.
B1130 (ASU)

Family Names and Their Story.
B1140 (ASU)

Kentuckians, C. S. A.
B2530 (ASU)

History of the German Settlements and of the Lutheran Church in North and South Carolina, from the Earliest Period of the Colonization of the Dutch, German and Swiss Settlers to the Close of the First Half of the Recent Century.
B3200 (ASU)

Colonial Surry.
B4940 (ASU BC)

Historical Southern Families.
B4950 (ASU)

Southside Virginia Families.
B4960 (ASU)

Marriage Notices, 1785-1794, for the Whole United States, Copied from the Massachusetts Centinel and the Columbian Centinel.
B5160 (ASU)

Immigrants to New England, 1700-1775.
B5180 (ASU)

Bristol and America, a Record of the First Settlers in the Colonies of North America, 1654-1685, Including the Names with Places of Origin of More than 10,000 Servants to Foreign Plantations Who Sailed from the Port of Bristol to Virginia, Maryland, and Other Parts of the Atlantic Coast, and Also to the West Indies from 1654 to 1685.
B6680 (ASU)

Memorial Records of Josh Bell County, Kentucky (Adjoining Historical Cumberland Gap, Tennessee), Family Bible Records Given to the United States Census Taken in 1870.
B9080 (BC)

History of Blount County, Tennessee, From War Trail to Landing Strip, 1795-1955.
B9130 (ASU ETSU BC)

Emigrants from Scotland to America, 1774-1775.
C410 (ASU)

Tracing Your Ancestors.
C420 (ASU)
C2620

Checklist of Historical Records Survey Publications: Bibliography of Research Projects Reports.
C3850 (ASU)

A General Index to a Census of Pensioners for the Revolutionary or Military Service 1840.
C4080 (ASU)

American Marriage Records before 1699.
C4890 (ASU)

Crozier's General Armory: A Registry of American Families Entitled to Coat Armor.
C9270 (ASU)

A Key to Southern Pedigrees, Being a Comprehensive Guide to the Colonial Ancestry of Families in the States of Virginia, Maryland, Georgia, North Carolina, South Carolina, Kentucky, Tennessee, West Virginia and Alabama.
C9300 (ASU)

American Prisoners of the Revolution.
D70 (ASU)
D540

The Handy Book for Genealogists.
E2410 (ASU)

A History of Surnames of the British Isles: A Concise Account of the Origin, Evolution, Etymology, and Legal Status.
E2440 (ASU)

Lists of Swiss Emigrants in the Eighteenth Century to the American Colonies.
F360 (ASU)

German Element in the United States.
F370

The French Blood in America.
F2240 (ASU)

Emigrants from England, 1773-1776.
F2370 (ASU)

A List of Emigrant Ministers to America, 1690-1811.
F2380 (ASU)

Lost Links: New Recordings of Old Data from Many States.
F3040 (ASU)

An Introduction to the Use of the Public Records.
G110 (ASU)
G790

Wills and Where to Find Them.
G1170 (ASU)

Naturalizations of Foreign Protestants in the American and West Indian Colonies, (Pursuant to Statute 13 George 2, c. 7).
G1880 (ASU)

The Scotch-Irish in Northern Ireland and in the American Colonies.
G2030 (ASU)

A List of Some American Genealogies Which Have Been Printed in Book Form.
G2160 (ASU)

Merion in the Welsh Tract, With Sketches of the Townships of Haverford and Padner.
G2170 (ASU)

GENEALOGY — SOURCES

Tracing your Civil War Ancestor.
G4370 (ASU)

Homes of Family Names in Great Britain.
G4930 (ASU)

In Search of Scottish Ancestry
H1120 (ASU)

Surnames of the United Kingdom: A Concise Etymological Dictionary.
H3060 (ASU)
H4170

First Census of Kentucky, 1790.
H4320 (ASU BC UNCA)

Historical Register of Officers of the Continental Army During the War of the Revolution, April, 1775 to December, 1783.
H4340 (ASU)

Encyclopedia of American Quaker genealogy.
H5640 (ASU)

The Original Lists of Persons of Quality, Emigrants, Religious Exiles, Political Rebels, Serving Men Sold for a Term of Years, Apprentices, Children Stolen, Maidens Pressed, and Others, Who Went from Great Britain to the American Plantations, 1600-1700.
H7360 (ASU BC)
I140
I150
I160 (ASU)

Genealogy As Pastime and Profession.
J260 (ASU)

Index to Genealogical Periodicals.
J270 (ASU)

Lineage Book of the National Society of Daughters of American Colonists.
J640

The Cymry of '76: Or, Welshmen and Their Descendants of the American Revolution.
J2270 (ASU)

Your Family Tree.
J2720 (ASU)

A List of Emigrants from England to America, 1718-1759.
K80 (ASU)

A Bibliography of Ship Passenger Lists, 1538-1825: Being a Guide to Published Lists of Early Immigrants to North America.
L290 (ASU)

Family Names of Huguenot Refugees to America.
L1060 (ASU)
L2760

English Surnames. An Essay on Family Nomenclature, Historical, Etymological, and Humorous.
L3730 (ASU)

The Welcome Claimants Proved, Disproved and Doubtful with an Account of Their Descendants.
M890 (ASU)

A History of the Irish Settlers in North America, from the Earliest Period to the Census of 1850.
M1450 (ASU)

A Guide to Irish Surnames.
M2130 (ASU)

More Irish Families.
M2140 (ASU)

Supplement to Irish Families.
M2150 (ASU)

Special Report on Surnames in Ireland. Together with Varieties and Synonyms of Surnames and Christian Names in Ireland.
M4230 (ASU)
M4820

Abstracts of the Wills of the State of South Carolina, 1740-1760.
M7070 (ASU)

Roster of North Carolina Troops: In the War Between the States.
M7320 (LMC)

Folklore of the Blue Ridge Mountains and Early Settlers.
M7870

Quaker Arrivals at Philadelphia, 1682-1750: Being a List of Certificates of Removal Received at Philadelphia Monthly Meeting of Friends.
M9270 (ASU)

Maryland Revolutionary Records: Data Obtained from 3,050 Pension Claims and Bounty Land Applications, Including 1,000 Marriages of Maryland Soldiers and a List of 1,200 Proved Services of Soldiers and Patriots of Other States.
N770 (ASU)

Some Early Emigrants to America, Also, Early Emigrants to America from Liverpool, abstracted by Reginal Sharpe France.
N930 (ASU)

State Census of North Carolina, 1784-1787.
N1880 (ASU)

State Census of North Carolina, 1784-1787.
N1890 (ASU)

Abstract of North Carolina Wills, Compiled from Original and Recorded Wills in the Office of the Secretary of State by J. Bryan Grimes.
N2550 (ASU BC)

Corpus Genealogiarum Hiberniae.
O140 (ASU)

The Irish in America: Immigration, Land, Probate, Administrations, Birth, Marriage, and Burial Records of the Irish in America in and about the Eighteenth Century.
O150 (ASU)
P1910
P1920
P1930
P1940

Known Military Dead During the American Revolutionary War, 1775-1783.
P2350 (ASU)

Greene County, Tennessee: Early Marriage Bonds, 1782-1820.
P2380
P3580

Revolutionary Soldiers in Kentucky, Containing a Roll of the Officers of Virginia Line Who Received Land Bounties: A Roll of the Revolutionary Pensioners in Kentucky. A List of the Illinois Regiment Who Served Under George Rogers Clark in the Northwest Campaign, Also a Roster of the Virginia Navy.
Q210 (ASU BC)
R1440

Greene County Cemeteries, from Earliest Dates to 1970-1971.
R1640 (ASU ETSU)

A Collection of Upwards of Thirty Thousand Names of German, Swiss, Dutch, French, and Other Immigrants in Pennsylvania from 1727 to 1776.
R4300 (ASU)

Records of the Revolutionary War.
S60 (ASU)

Pioneer Blood.
S170 (ASU)

Archives of the Pioneers of Tazewell County.
S1080

1800 Tax Lists and Abstracts of Deeds (1796-1800) of Wythe County, Virginia.
S1090

Montgomery County, Virginia Circa 1790.
S1100

Ireland and the American Emigration, 1850-1900.
S1140 (ASU)

Passengers and Ships Prior to 1684.
S2840 (ASU)

American Colonists in English Records: A Guide to Direct References in Authentic Records, Passenger Lists Not in "Hotten".
S2980 (ASU)

True and Authentic Register of Persons Still Living, by God's Grace, Who in the Year 1709, under the Wonderful Providence of the Lord, Journeyed from Germany to America or New World, and There Seek Their Piece of Bread at Various Places, Reported with Joy to All Admirers, Especially to Their Families and Close Friends.
S3410 (ASU)

The Early Settlers of Maryland: An Index to Names of Immigrants Compiled from Records of Land Patents, 1633-1680, in the Hall of Records, Annapolis, Maryland.
S4100 (ASU)

A History of St. Mark's Parish, Culpeper County, Va., With Notes of Old Churches and Old Families and Illustrations of the Manners and Customs of the Olden Time.
S4150 (ASU)

Colonists in Bondage: White Servitude and Convict Labor in America, 1607-1776.
S4410 (ASU)

Colonists in Bondage: White Servitude and Convict Labor in America, 1607-1776.
S4420 (ASU)

White Servitude in Colonial South Carolina.
S5090 (ASU)

Memorials of the Huguenot's in America, with Special Reference to Their Emigration to Pennsylvania.
S6590 (ASU)

Pennsylvania German Pioneers: A Publication of the Original Lists of Arrivals in the Port of Philadelphia from 1727 to 1808.
S7790 (ASU)

Pennsylvania German Pioneers: A Publication of the Original Lists of Arrivals in the Port of Philadelphia from 1727 to 1808.
S7800 (ASU)

Rejected or Suspended Applications for Revolutionary War Pensions.
U2840 (ASU)

The Abridged Compendium of American Genealogy: First Families of America, a Genealogical Encyclopedia of the United States.
V1250 (ASU)

Immigrant Ancestors: A List of 2,500 Immigrants to America Before 1750.
V1260 (ASU)

Immigrants to America Before 1750: An Alphabetical List of Immigrants to the Colonies Before 1750, Compiled from Official and Other Records.
V1270 (ASU)

Tombstone Inscriptions and Death Records, Calvary Cemetery, Knoxville, Tennessee, 1869-1967.
W1640 (ETSU)

Abstracts of the Old Ninety-Six and Abbeville District Wills and Bonds, as on File in the Abbeville, South Carolina, Courthouse.
Y290 (ASU)

GENEALOGY — SOURCES — APP.

Draper Families in America.
A2260 (ASU)

GENEALOGY — SOURCES — GA.

Columbia County, Georgia, Early Court Records.
B600 (ASU)

GENEALOGY — SOURCES — N. C.

The Annals of Haywood County, North Carolina: Historical, Sociological, Bibliographical, and Genealogical.
A1700 (ASU WCU BC)

Abstract of Pensions of North Carolina Soldiers of the Revolution, War of 1812, and Indian Wars.
B9030 (ASU)

GENEALOGY — SOURCES — PA.

Welsh Founders of Pennsylvania.
G2180 (ASU)

GENEALOGY — SOURCES — TENN.

Tennessee Soldiers in the Revolution: A Roster of Soldiers Living During the Revolutionary War in the Counties of Washington and Sullivan.
A1630 (ETSU)

GENEALOGY — TENN.

Ayres Kin and Kin to Kin.
A5860

The Family Chronicle and Kinship Book of Maclin, Clack, Cocke, Carter, Taylor, Cross, Gordon and Other Related American Lineages.
B5240 (ASU ETSU)

Bowens of Virginia and Tennessee; Descendants of John Bowen and Lily McIlhaney.
G3070

Marriage Record of Washington County, Tennessee, 1787-1840.
G3190 (ETSU)

Marriage Records of Washington County, Tennessee, 1787-1840.
G3200 (ASU)

"The Settlement Pattern of Upper East Tennessee."
H3910 (ETSU)

GENEALOGY — TENN.

Tennessee Records of Roane County Marriage Records, 1801-1838.
H5900 (ETSU)

The Massengills, Massengales and Variants 1472-1931.
M4100

The Donnelly-Barry-Butler Families and Their Kin-folks of Johnson Co., Tennessee.
N290

Leonard Shoun and his Wife Barbara Slemp Shoun of Johnson Co., Tennessee.
N300

The McQueen Family of Johnson Co., Tennessee.
N310

Wills Family of Johnson County, Tennessee.
N320

Neel-Dickson Genealogy.
N370

Historical Sketches of Campbell, Pilcher and Kindred Families.
P2960

Tennessee Cousins: A History of Tennessee People.
R640 (BC ASU WCU)

Sevier Family History, with the Collected Letters of Gen. John Sevier, First Governor of Tennessee and 28 Collateral Family Lineages.
S2030 (ASU ETSU MHC BC)

Guide to the Use of Genealogical Materials in the Tenn. State Library and Archives.
T1830

United States census 1850 for Knox County, Tennessee.
U520

1830 Census, Tennessee.
U650 (ASU ETSU)

Coffee County, Tennessee, 1850 Census.
U700 (ETSU)

Fentress County, Tennessee, Free Population Schedules.
U710 (ASU)

Population Schedule of the U. S. Census of 1850 (Seventh Census) for McMinn County, Tennessee.
U730 (ASU)

Population Schedule of the United States Census of 1850 (Seventh Census) for Warren County, Tennessee.
U740 (ETSU)

Tennessee Population Schedule of the United States Census of 1850, Meigs County.
U770 (ASU)

United States Census 1850 for Knox County, Tennessee.
U780 (ETSU)

Tennessee Genealogical Records: Overton County.
W5770 (BC)

Know Your Ancesters: A Guide to Genealogical Research.
W6520 (ASU)

GENEALOGY — TENN. — SOURCES

Marriage Records of McMinn County, Tennessee, 1820-1870.
B5990 (ASU BC)

Monroe County Records, 1820-1870.
B6000

Monroe County, Tennessee: Records, 1820-1870.
B6010 (ASU BC)

Population Schedule of U. S. Census of 1850 for McMinn County, Tennessee.
B6020 (ASU)

Wills and Estate Records of McMinn County, Tennessee, 1820-1870.
B6030 (ASU BC)

Abstracts of Death and Obituary Notices Gathered from Herald-Tribune, Jonesboro, Tennessee.
B9160 (ETSU)
C561

Seventh Census of the United States, 1850: Fentress County, Tennessee, Free Population Schedules.
C1390 (ASU)

Seventh Census of the United States, 1850: Franklin County, Tennessee, Free Population Schedules.
C1400 (ASU)
C1661

Carter of Tennessee, Including the Taylors: Descendants of Colonel John Carter of Tennessee.
C1670 (ETSU)
C5401

Population Schedule of the U. S. Census of 1850 (Seventh Census) for Sevier County, Tennessee.
C8690 (ETSU BC)

Tennessee Marriage Records.
C8700 (ETSU)

Early East Tennessee Tax Lists.
C9930 (ASU)

D. C. Armond Family in America.
D370

Knox County, Tenn., Marriage Records.
D380 (ETSU)

Benton County, Tennessee, Marriages, 1832-1957.
D570 (ASU)

East Tennessee Kinsman.
D1330

Index to Marriages 1792-1900.
E100

Marriages 1795-1865.
E110

Marriages 1796-1837.
E120

Marriages 1796-1850.
E130

"The Connection" in East Tennessee.
E1180 (ASU BC)

Descendants of East Tennessee Pioneers.
E1190 (ASU)

The Crockett Family and Connecting Lines.
F3240

Davy Crockett and the Crockett Family.
F3250

Notable Southern Families. The Doak Family.
F3260

Tombstone Inscriptions and Death Records, Calvary. Macedonia Cemetery, Knoxville, Tennessee, 1851-1967. Baptismal Records, 1846-1870, Immaculate Conception Church, Knoxville, Tennessee.
G3080 (ETSU)
G3170

Duck River Valley in Tennessee and Its Pioneers.
J220 (ASU)

History and Genealogy, Dudley, 1406-1956 and McWane, 1796-1956.
K490

. . . History (and) Genealogy, Kegley, 1760-1959 and Grubb, 1743-1959.
K500

Tenn. Grainger Co., Marriage Bonds and Licenses.
K810

The Military Annals of Tennessee: Confederate. First Series. Embracing a Review of Military Operations with Regimental Histories and Memorial Rolls Compiled from Original and Official Sources.
L2570 (LMC)

Washington County, Tennessee, Records.
M680 (ETSU ASU)

Washington County, Tennessee, Records, Transcribed by Mary Hardin McCown. Vol. 1, Washington County Lists of Taxables, 1778-1801, ed. Nancy E. Jones Stickley and Inez Burns.
M690

Sevier County, Tennessee.
M2160
M3230
M3320 (ASU)
R1790

Historical Cemetery Records of Bradley County, Tennessee.
R3840 (ETSU)

1830 Census, East Tennessee.
S3750

Washington County, Tennessee, Marriages and Wills.
S4640 (ETSU)

Washington County, Tenn., 1830 Federal Census.
S7900 (ASU)
T1370

Pioneers of Roane County, Tennessee, 1801-1830.
T8400 (ETSU)

Whitfield History and Genealogy of Tennessee.
W5730 (ASU)

GENEALOGY — VA.

Our Kin.
A230

Links With the Past.
A1000

Botetourt County, Virginia, 1820 Census.
A1060

Floyd County, Virginia, 1850 Census.
A1110

Skillern Family History and Genealogy.
A4510

Archer and Silvester Families.
A4560

Braxton County, Virginia (Now West Virginia) Marriage Book 1.
A5390 (ASU)

March of the Sages.
B750

A Baumgardner Family in America.
B2110

Known Descendants of Edward Blakemore, Junior, of Lancaster Co. Virginia.
B4550

Shenandoah Valley Pioneers and Their Descendants: A History of Frederick County, Virginia, from Its Formation in 1738 to 1908.
C1780 (ASU BC)

Kettenring Family.
C2160

Records of the Myers, Hays and Mordecai Families, 1707-1913.
C5580

Ancestry, Life and Family of Col. William Edmiston of Washington County.
C5710

The Robert Coleman Family, from Virginia to Texas, 1652-1965.
C5750 (ASU)

The Cornett Family.
C7550

Virginia Heraldica, Being a Registry of Virginia Gentry Entitled to Coat Armor with Genealogical Notes of the Families.
C9330 (ASU)

Dickerson and Walden Families.
D2120 (ASU)

The James Stewart Family of Early Augusta County, Virginia, and Descendants, 1740-1960.
D2130 (ASU)

Old Oxford and Her Families.
D2300

Genealogical Serendipity.
D2820

Twelve Generations of Farleys.
F170

Biographical Genealogies of the Virginia-Kentucky Floyd Families, with Notes of Some Collateral Branches.
F1640 (ASU)

Foulke Family, one branch descended from James Ffookes.
F2390

Capt. John Fowler of Virginia and Kentucky; Patriot, Soldier, Pioneer, Statesman, Land Baron, and Civic Leader.
F2430 (BC)

Crabtrees of Southwest Virginia.
F3440

Our Garst Family in America.
G500

The Groseclose Family History.
G2820

Pioneers of the Virginia Bluegrass (And Their Descendants).
G2830

Bowens of Virginia and Tennessee; Descendants of John Bowen and Lily McIlhaney.
G3070

The McGavock Family. A Genealogical History of James McGavock and His Descendants from 1760-1903.
G3410 (ASU)

McGavock Family, a Genealogical History of James McGavock and his Descendants, 1760-1903.
G3420

Genealogical and Historical Notes on Culpepper County, Virginia.
G3650 (ASU)

GENEALOGY — VA.

Historic Families of Kentucky, with Special Reference to Stocks Immediately Derived from the Valley of Virginia.
G3670 (ASU MHC BC)

Historical Register of Virginians in the Revolution.
G5020 (ASU)

A History of Damascus.
H840

Harman Genealogy (Southern Branch), with Biographical Sketches, 1700-1924.
H2410

Lindamood Family History.
H2550

Settlers by the Long Grey Trail, Some Pioneers to Old Augusta County, Virginia, and Their Descendants, of the Family of Harrison and Allied Lines.
H3070 (ASU BC)

Virginia Genealogies: A Genealogy of the Glassell Family of Scotland and Virginia, Also of the Families of Ball, Brown, Bryan, Conway, Daniel, Ewell, Holladay, Lewis, Littlepage, Nioncure, Peyton, Robinson, Scott, Taylor, Wallace and Others of Virginia and Maryland.
H3830 (ASU)

German New River Settlement, Virginia.
H4270 (ASU FC)

Lynch Families of the Southern States.
H5590

Genealogy of Matthias Hoffer (Huffard) and his Descendants in the United States of America.
H6230

Genealogy of Matthias Hoffer (Huffard) and his Descendants in the United States of America.
H6231

Holmes Family History.
H6870

Hopkins of Virginia and Related Families.
H7120

Leftwich-Turner Families of Virginia and Their Connections.
H7130

Listen to the Mockingbird.
H7680

Listen to the Mockingbird; The Life and Times of a Pioneer Virginia Family.
H7690

History of the Descendants of John Hottel.
H7910

Huddleston Family Tables.
H7930

Pittsylvania County, Virginia Abstracts of Wills, 1768-1800.
H8140

Supplement to the History of the Dodson-Dotson Family of Southwest Virginia.
L3850 (ASU)

Gordon Kinship.
M150

Marriage Records of Kanawha County, West Virginia 1816-1850.
M490

The Massengills, Massengales and Variants 1472-1931.
M4100

The Ferns and Fern Allies of Virginia.
M4120 (LMC)

1850 Census of Highland County, Virginia.
M4190

The Descendants of Capt. Thomas Carter.
M5880

David Morgan (ca. 1779-1857) and His Descendants.
M7560

Irvins, Doaks, Logans and McCampbells of Virginia and Kentucky.
M7810

The Beaver Pond Neals of Virginia.
N280

Neel-Dickson Genealogy.
N370

The First Virginia Nuckolls and Kindred.
N2950

Woods Wallace, Cousin Clues.
P2400

Descendants of Samuel Bachman and wife Rachel Owen.
P2710

Seven Pierce Families.
P2870

Blacks and Other Families.
P3680 (ASU)

Smyth County Families and History.
P4320

Wythe County Chapters.
P4330 (ASU)
P4380

Allied Families of Read, Corbin, Luttrell, Bywaters. Starting from Culpeper County, Virginia, Their Descendants Are Now Planted in Every State Westward to the Pacific. My Wife's Kin.
P4650 (ASU)

This An' That.
P4680

The Ragles of Pennsylvania, Virginia, Kentucky, and Kansas.
R110

1810 Montgomery County Census.
R1510

Emera Altizer and His Descendants.
R3090

McChesneys of Virginia.
S1150

Pioneers and Their Coat of Arms of Floyd County: Genealogies of Prominent Early Settlers of the Blue Ridge Plateau of Virginia.
S2650 (ASU FC)

A History of Bristol Parish, Va.; With Genealogies of Families Connected Therewith, and Historical Illustrations.
S4140 (ASU BC)

Descendants of Samuel Miller, John Detrick, John and Mary Snell of Rockingham County, Virginia.
S4600

From the Alps to the Appalachians (Neff Families).
S4740

David Rawson: Ancestors and Descendants, 1636-1974.
S5470

Peter Stephens and Some of his Descendants, 1690-1935.
S6960

Stephens Family Genealogies.
S6970

Genealogy of the Tankersley Family in the United States.
T180 (ASU)

Virginia Wills and Administrations, 1632-1800: An Index of Wills Recorded in Local Courts of Virginia, 1632-1800, and of Administrations of Estates Shown by Inventories of the Estates of Intestates Recorded in Will (and Other) Books of Local Courts, 1632-1800.
T8950 (ASU BC)

Southwest Virginia Families.
T9280

The Letters and Times of the Tylers.
T9920 (ASU)

Umberger Family Chart.
U50

The Umberger (Umbarger) Family Chart.
U60

Heads of Families at the First Census of the United States Taken in the Year 1790: Records of the State Enumerations, 1782 to 1785, Virginia.
U580 (ASU LMC)

The Seventh Population Census of the U. S. for Russell County, Va., 1850.
U750

The Seventh Population Census of the United States for Russell County, Virginia, 1850.
U760

Partial History of the Vaught Family.
V470

The McClanahans.
W5430

The Bradfords of Virginia in the Revolutionary War, and Their Kin.
W5540 (ASU)

Willis Family of Virginia.
W6990

Michael Miller Family.
W7670

The Wine Family in America, Section 3.
W7680

Christian Wine Family.
W7690

Wise's Digested Index and Genealogical Guide to Bishop Meade's Old Churches, Ministers and Families of Virginia.
W7890

Some of Our Families Ancestors and the Genealogy of Some of Their Descendants.
W8570

A Brief of Wills and Marriages in Montgomery and Fincastle Counties, 1773-1831.
W9230

A Brief of Wills and Marriages in Montgomery and Fincastle Counties, 1773-1831.
W9240

Early Marriages, Wills and Some Revolutionary War Records, Botetourt County, Va.
W9250

Wyatt Family Records.
W9840

Wyatt Family.
W9850

GENEALOGY — VA. — SOURCES

History of Five Southern Families.
A990

Carroll County, Virginia, 1860 Census.
A1080

Early Southwest Virginia Families.
A1760

Fauquier County, Virginia, Tombstone Inscriptions.
B480 (ASU)

The Ball Family of Southwest Virginia: A Genealogy of Some of the Descendants of Moses Ball of Fairfax County.
B810 (ASU)

Botetourt County, Virginia, 1820 Census.
B1560

Lunenburg County, Virginia wills, 1746-1825.
B2790 (ASU)

James and Rachel Holmes Scott.
B2890

The Irvines and Their Kin.
B5920

Virginia Settlers and English Adventurers: Abstracts of Wills, 1484-1798, and Legal Proceedings, Relating to Early Virginia Families.
B6620 (ASU)

Documents, Chiefly Unpublished, Relating to the Huguenot Emigration to Virginia and to the Settlement at Manakintown, with an Appendix of Genealogies, Presenting Data of the Fontaine, Maury, Dupuy, Trabue, Marys, Chastain, Cooke, and Other Families.
B6770 (ASU)

Virginia Genealogies: A Trial List of Printed Books and Pamphlets.
B7410 (ASU)

Revolutionary War Records: Vol. I, Virginia.
B7690

Revolutionary War Records: Vol. I, Virginia. Virginia Army and Navy Forces with Bounty Land Warrants for Virginia Military Scrip: From Federal and State Archives.
B7700 (ASU)

Virginia Soldiers of 1776.
B8590

Virginia Genealogies and County Records.
B9120

A History of Our Cain Family of Virginia, Alabama and Tennessee.
C50 (FC)

Confederate History of Culpeper County.
C240

The Copenhaver Family of Wythe County.
C1030

The Descendants of Joseph Samson Hounshell and Mandana Hedrick.
C1040

The Hounshell Family of Southwest Virginia.
C1050

Rosenbaum Family.
C1060

Rosenbaum-Rosenbalm Family of Southwest Virginia.
C1070

Shenandoah Valley Pioneers and Their Descendants: A History of Frederick County, Virginia, from Its Formation in 1738 to 1908.
C1790 (ASU ETSU)

GENEALOGY — VA. — SOURCES

Personal Names in Hening's "Statutes at Large of Virginia" and Shepherd's Continuation.
C1940 (ASU)

Early Records of Lee County, Virginia.
C2130

Tombstone Inscriptions of Lee County, Virginia.
C2140 (BC)

Chronicles of the Scotch-Irish Settlement in Virginia.
C2740 (BC ASU)

Chronicles of Scotch-Irish Settlement in Virginia.
C2750

Early Fauquier County, Virginia, Marriage Bonds, 1759-1854.
C3250 (ASU)

Scotch-Irish Settlers in the Valley of Virginia.
C3960 (BC)

Virginia Wills Before 1799: A Complete Abstract Register of All Names Mentioned in Over Six Hundred Recorded Wills.
C4910 (ETSU)

Genealogy of the Cloyd, Basye and Tapp Families in America.
C5130
C6070

Index to 1810 Virginia Census.
C8760

Early Virginia Marriages.
C9280 (ASU)

Early Virginia Marriages.
C9290 (ASU)

Virginia Colonial Militia, 1651-1776.
C9310

Virginia Colonial Militia, 1651-1776.
C9320 (ASU)

The Montgomery County Story, 1776-1957.
C9360 (ASU)

The Darsts of Virginia: A Chronicle of Ten Generations in the Old Dominion.
D420

The Darter-Tarter Family.
D430

Roster of the Virginia Daughters of the American Revolution.
D510

Frederick County, Virginia, Marriages, 1771-1825.
D990 (ASU ETSU)

Marriage Bonds of Bedford County, Virginia 1755-1800.
D1810 (ASU FC)

Virginia Revolutionary Pension Applications.
D2960

Campbell Chronicles and Family Sketches, Embracing the History of Campbell County, Virginia, 1782-1926.
E60 (ASU BC)

List of the Colonial Soldiers of Virginia.
E710 (ASU)

The Revolution in Virginia.
E730 (LMC FC)

Marriage Records, 1749-1840, Cumberland County, Virginia.
E1680 (ASU)
F1100

Virginia Colonial Abstracts Vol. XXXIV, Washington County Marriage Register, 1782-1820.
F1420

Virginia Tax Payers, 1782-87: Other Than Those Published by the United States Census Bureau.
F2360 (ASU)

A Givens-Hall Family History from Pre-Revolutionary Times to 1970. . .
G1930

The Durst and Darst Families of America, with Discussions of Some Forty Related Families.
G1960

Life of Jefferson Dillard Goodpasture with Genealogy of the Family of James Goodpasture by his Sons.
G2580

Early Virginia Immigrants, 1623-1666.
G3900 (ASU FC)

Polish Pioneers of Virginia and Kentucky with Notes on Genealogy of the Sadowski Family.
H310 (BC)

Virginia Ancestors and Adventurers.
H1250
H2110

Hennen's Choice: A Compilation of the Descendents of Matthew Hennen (1752-1839).
H4680 (ASU)

Encyclopedia of American Quaker Genealogy.
H4830
I180 (FC)

Loudoun Co., Virginia, Marriage bonds, 1762-1850.
J750 (ASU)

William Johnston of Isle of Wight County, Virginia, and His Descendants, 1648-1964: A Genealogical Study of One Branch of the Family in the South.
J2010 (ASU)

79 Families of Washington County.
J2840

History and Genealogy, Dudley, 1406-1956 and McWane, 1796-1956.
K490

. . . History (and) Genealogy, Kegley, 1760-1959 and Grubb, 1743-1959.
K500

New River Tithables, 1770-73.
K510

Tax List of Montgomery County, Virginia, 1782.
K520

Strasburg, Virginia and the Keister Family.
K540

Burk(e) Family of Southwest Virginia in Valley.
K660

Betsy's Descendants. The Descendants of Thomas Jefferson Duff and his wife Ann Elizabeth (Betsy) Spraker Ketron.
K670

Abstracts of Wills, Inventories, and Administrations Accounts of Frederick County, Virginia.
K2370

Old Sherry, Portrait of a Virginia Family (Wysors).
K2720

Births in Court Records of Montgomery County, Virginia, 1853-1871.
L3860

Genealogies of the Lewis and Kindred Families.
M70

Virginia Militia in the Revolutionary War: McAllister's Data.
M100 (ASU)

High on a Windy Hill.
M520 (ASU)

Sanders Saga.
M530

Who Am I? A Brief Sketch of the McConnell and Related Families in Southwest Virginia.
M540 (ASU)

Journals of the Council of the State of Virginia.
M1680

Some Virginia Families Being Genealogies of the Kinney, Stribling, Trout, McIlhany, Milton, Rogers, Tate, Snickers, Taylor, McCormick, and other Families of Virginia.
M1710 (ASU)

The McKees of Virginia and Kentucky.
M1820
M3330

The Massengills, Massengales and Variants 1472-1931.
M4110

Old Churches, Ministers and Families of Virginia.
M4750

Old Churches, Ministers, and Families of Virginia.
M4770 (ASU)

Supplement to 1810 Census of Virginia.
S1110

The Knights of the Golden Horseshoe from the History of St. Mark's Parish.
S4160

The Pennsylvania Germans of the Shenandoah Valley.
S4620 (ASU)

Some Emigrants to Virginia.
S6510 (ASU)

Some Emigrants to Virginia.
S6520 (ASU)

Old Tenth Legion Marriages; Marriages in Rockingham Co., Va. from 1778 to 1816.
S7990

Russell Co., Va. Census of 1820.
S9230

Early Osbornes and Alleys, With Notes on Allied Families.
S9350 (BC)

Amherst County, Virginia, in the Revolution: Including Extracts from the "Lost Order Book", 1773-1782.
S9530 (ASU)

Marriage Records of Amherst County, Virginia, 1815-1821, and Subscription for Building St. Mark's Church, Amherst Co., Virginia.
S9540 (ASU)

Marriage Bonds and Other Marriage Records of Amherst County, Virginia, 1763-1800.
S9550 (ASU)

Wills of Rappahannock Co., Va., 1656-1692.
S9560 (ASU BC)

List of the Colonial Soldiers of Virginia.
V1190 (ASU)

Abstracts of Bedford County, Virginia Wills, Inventories and Accounts 1754-1787.
W5900 (FC)

The Tinkling Spring, Headwater of Freedom: A Study of the Church and Her People, 1732-1952.
W7320 (ASU BC)

Virginia Revolutionary Land Bounty Warrants.
W7460

Catalogue of Revolutionary Soldiers and Sailors of the Commonwealth of Va.; to Whom Land Bounty Warrants were Granted. . . .
W7470 (BC)

Catalogue of Revolutionary Soldiers and Sailors of the Commonwealth of Virginia to Whom Land Bounty Warrants Were Granted by Virginia for Military Services in the War for Independence.
W7480 (ASU)

Gravestone Inscriptions: From 61 Graveyards in Frederick County and the Counties That Were Once a Part of Frederick County and Includes the Inscriptions from the "Old Lutheran and German Reform Graves" in Mt. Hebron Cemetery.
W7590 (ASU)

2200 Gravestone Inscriptions from Winchester and Frederick County, Virginia (Death Dates Range from 1700's to Early 1900's).
W7600 (ASU)

Marriage Bonds of Franklin County, Virginia, 1786-1858, Transcribed from the Original Records.
W7740 (ASU BC)

Pioneer Families of Franklin County, Virginia.
W7750 (ASU BC FC)

GENEALOGY — W. VA.

Heritage of a Pioneer, Being the Story of William (English Bill Doddridge) Dodrill and His Wife, Rebecca (Lewis) Daugherty, Their Family, the Times in Which They Lived, and a Genealogy.
D2720 (ASU)

The Trail of the Dead Years. . .
D3660

Holt-Bennett Family History.
E50 (ASU)

The Parr Family: Allied Families — Holden, Hutchinson, Moore, Jolly, Franks, Sheets, et al.
F1460 (ASU)

Marriage Records of Kanawha County, West Virginia 1816-1850.
M490

Genealogy of the Musick Family and Some Kindred Lines.
M9160

Capon Valley.
P4850 (BC)

History of the Cross Creek Graveyard and Cross Creek Cemetery. Originally compiled in 1894 by James Simpson, revised and prepared for publication by Alvin D. White.
S3620

History of the Cross Creek Graveyard and Cross Creek Cemetery.
S3630

Christopher Call's Family of Preston County, West Virginia 1741-1973.
S3740

David Rawson: Ancestors and Descendants, 1636-1974.
S5470

Trimble Families of America.
T9360

GENEALOGY — W. VA. — SOURCES
The Hammers and Allied Families.
B5050 (BC)
The McNeel Family Records: Descendants of Pioneer John McNeel and Martha Davis of Pocahontas County, West Virginia, 1765-1967.
E830 (ASU)
West Virginia Estate Settlements (1753-1850).
J2170 (ASU)
Marriage Records of Berkeley County, Virginia, for the Period of 1781-1854, Located at Berkeley County Court House, Martinsburg, West Virginia.
K440 (ETSU)
The Soldiery of West Virginia in the French and Indian War, Lord Dunmore's War, The Whiskey Insurrection, The Second War with England, The War with Mexico, and Addenda Relating to West Virginians in the Civil War.
L2370 (ASU)
Genealogical History of the Descendants of Machir of Scotland.
M2610 (ASU)
The Somerville Family and Descendants, 1789-1963.
M2620 (ASU)
West Virginia Surnames, the Pioneers.
M6390 (ASU)
O480 (ASU)
West Virginia Revolutionary Ancestors Whose Services Were Non-military and Whose Names, Therefore, Do Not Appear in Revolutionary Indexes of Soldiers and Sailors.
R870 (ASU)

GEOGRAPHY
A Bibliography of Dissertations in Geography, 1901-1969.
B7460 (LMC)
A Cartographic Summary of United States Census Data, 1930, Tennessee Valley and Surrounding Area by Land Classification Section, Land Planning and Housing Division, Tennessee Valley Authority.
T5840
The Potomac and Roaring Creek Coal Fields in West Virginia.
W2260
How They Began — The Story of North Carolina County, Town, and Other Place Names.
W9610 (ASU)
History and Geography of Yancey County.
Y20
The Economic Geography of Watauga County, North Carolina.
Y110 (ASU)
"North Carolina: A Geographic Study."
Y120 (LMC)

GEOGRAPHY — ALA.
Geography of the Great Appalachian Valley of Alabama.
G2090 (BC ASU)
Atlas of Alabama.
L2520

GEOGRAPHY — APP.
The Southeast in Early Maps with an Annotated Check List of Printed and Manuscript Regional and Local Maps of Southeastern North America during the Colonial Period.
C9470 (ASU LMC)
Studies of Appalachian Geology: Central and Southern.
F1170 (ASU LMC ETSU)
Dictionary of Altitude in the U. S.
G260
"A Geographic Approach to a Vegetation Problem: The Case of the Southern Appalachian Grassy Balds."
G1060 (BC ASU)
Appalachian Mountain Elevations.
R900 (ASU LMC ETSU WCU)
Ice Storms in the Southern Appalachian Mountains.
R1810
American History and Its Geographic Conditions.
S1850 (BC)
American History and Its Geographic Conditions.
S1860 (ASU MHC)
Potassium-Argon Geochronology of the Brevard Fault, Southern Appalachians.
S7570
North With the Spring: A Naturalist's Record of a 17,000 Mile Journey With the North-American Spring.
T800 (ASU LMC)
Surveying, Mapping and Related Engineering.
T3580
Atlas of the Tennessee Valley Region.
T5830
The Three Major Physical Divisions of the Upper Tennessee Basin.
T5870
How Topographic Maps are Made.
T7380
How Topographic Maps Are Made.
T7390
Arnold Guyot, First to Measure the Peaks of the Appalachians.
U2880 (BC)
Appalachian Region as Designated by the Appalachian Regional Commission, 1965.
U3090

GEOGRAPHY — APP. MTNS.
Appalachian Tectonics.
C4640 (ASU ETSU LMC WCU)

GEOGRAPHY — BOUNDARIES
Four Steps West.
S240 (ETSU ASU)

GEOGRAPHY — CHEROKEE NATION
Map of the Cherokee County, 1837.
D1530

GEOGRAPHY — GA.
"Geographic Analysis of Single Dwelling Settlement in Northeast Georgia."
B5110 (LMC BC ASU)
C5050
Short Contributions to the Geology, Geography, and Archaeology of Georgia.
G920 (ETSU)
Stratigraphy, Structure, Mineral Resources of the Mineral Bluff Quadrangle, Georgia.
H8630 (ETSU)

GEOGRAPHY — KY.
The Geography of the Kentucky Knobs.
B9200 (BC)
Geography of the Mountains of Eastern Kentucky.
D960 (BC ASU)
Abraham Lincoln and the Cumberland Gap.
H2250 (ASU ETSU)
Eastern Kentucky Economic Atlas.
K1070

GEOGRAPHY — MD.
The Fry and Jefferson Map of Virginia and Maryland.
F3600 (FC)
An Outline of the Maryland Boundary Disputes and Related Events.
M7900 (ASU)

GEOGRAPHY — N. C.
Caldwell County, North Carolina Geography Supplement.
A2490 (ASU)
The Influences of Geography Upon Early North Carolina.
C460 (ASU LMC WWC)
Measurements of the Black Mountains.
C5070
North Carolina in Maps.
C9460 (ASU WCU)
Report of the Geographical Survey of North Carolina: Physical Geography, Resume, Economical Geology.
K1670 (LMC ASU)
Bibliography of North Carolina Geology, Mineralogy, and Geography, with a List of Maps.
L390 (ASU LMC WWC ETSU)
North Carolina Geography: A Study of How We Live in North Carolina.
L1710 (LMC ASU)
Atlas of North Carolina.
L3350 (ASU LMC UNCA)
"The Asheville Basin of North Carolina: A Study in Highland Agricultural Land Use."
L3690 (LMC ASU)
The Influence of the Physiographic Features of Western North Carolina on the Settlement and Development of the Region.
N1400 (ASU)
. . . Altitudes in North Carolina, comp. by the North Carolina Geological and Economic Survey.
N2320 (ASU UNCA)
Maps of North Carolina Congressional Districts, 1789-1960, and State Senatorial Districts and Apportionment of State Representatives, 1776-1960.
S340 (BC WWC)
A New Geography of North Carolina.
S2390 (ASU LMC BC UNCA)
History and Geography of Yancey County.
T790 (ASU)
Soil Maps. Cleveland County, Caldwell County, and Lincoln County.
U3340
Soil Surveys Alleghany County, Gaston County, Transylvania County.
U3360
"The Climatology of the Southern Blue Ridge Mountains."
W5320 (LMC)

GEOGRAPHY — N. C. — GAZETTEER
The North Carolina Gazetteer.
P4010 (BC ASU LMC MHC UNCA)

GEOGRAPHY — N. C., WESTERN
Arnold Guyot's Notes on the Geography of the Mountain District of Western North Carolina.
A5740

GEOGRAPHY — OHIO
O400

GEOGRAPHY — PA.
"The Economic Geography of the State Industry in Eastern Pennsylvania."
C1260
"A Geographical Analysis of the Rail Freight Shipments of Pennsylvania."
G1110

GEOGRAPHY — TENN.
Hand-Book to the Sequatchie Valley.
B5830
"Geographic Factors Influencing the Development of Scott County, Tennessee."
B8630
"Oak Ridge, Tennessee: A Geographic Study."
C1910
"The Valley of East Tennessee: The Adjustment of Industry to Natural Environment."
C1920 (LMC)
C9420
"The Qualifications and Instructional Program of 100 Elementary Geography Teachers in Northeast Tennessee."
D2460
"The Boones Creek Community, Some Geographical Aspects."
E2070 (ETSU)
"Geographic Factors Influencing the Manufactural Industries of Upper East Tennessee."
E2080 (LMC)
Geologic Map of Tennessee.
H2060 (ETSU)
Abraham Lincoln and the Cumberland Gap.
H2250 (ASU ETSU)
"A Geographical Survey of Knoxville, Tennessee."
H8810
"Physiography of the Grassy Cove District, Cumberland County, Tennessee."
L360 (LMC)
A Brief Geography of Tennessee.
L860 (ASU)
"The Influence of Geography on the Growth of Chattanooga Industries."
L1420
"The Status of Geography Teaching in the Schools of Carter County, Tennessee."
L2140 (ETSU)
Eastin Morris' Tennessee Gazetteer, 1834, and Matthew Rhea's Map of the State of Tennessee, 1832.
M7770 (ASU)
The Tennessee Gazetteer, or Topographical Dictionary: Containing a Description of the Several Counties, Towns, Etc.
M7780 (ASU BC)
"Geographic Factors in the Land Use of Green County, Tennessee."
P390
"A Geographical Survey of Blount County, Tennessee."
R2560
The Economic Geography of Tennessee.
S1600
Division of Geology Bulletin.
T1020

GEOGRAPHY — TENN.
"A Geographic Appraisal of Union County, Tennessee."
T8300
"The Resources of the Cumberland Plateau as Exemplified by Cumberland County, Tennessee: A Geographic Analysis."
W2050
GEOGRAPHY — VA.
Wise County Geography Supplement.
A570 (BC)
The Earthquake History of Virginia, 1900-1970.
B5140
The Fry and Jefferson Map of Virginia and Maryland.
F3600 (FC)
The Earthquake History of Virginia, 1774 to 1900.
H7140
History of Saltville, Virginia.
K870
The Fairfax Line, a Profile in History and Geography.
M7890 (ASU)
Wappatomaka: A Survey of the History and Geography of the South Branch Valley.
M7910 (ASU)
N260
Virginia: A Geographical and Political Summary, Embracing a Description of the State, Its Geology, Soils, Minerals and Climate; Its Animal and Vegetable Productions; Manufacturing and Commercial Facilities; Religious and Educational Advantages; Internal Improvements, and Form of Government.
V700 (BC)
GEOGRAPHY — VA. — ROCKINGHAM CO.
Atlas of Rockingham County, Virginia.
S3200 (ASU)
GEOGRAPHY — W. VA.
A Gazetteer of West Virginia.
G270 (BC ASU)
"Cultural and Historical Geography of Mining Settlements in the Pocahontas Coal Fields of Southern West Virginia, 1880 to 1930."
G1620
The Geography of West Virginia.
K840
West Va. Place Names.
K850
The Fairfax Line, a Profile in History and Geography.
M7890 (ASU)
An Outline of the Maryland Boundary Disputes and Related Events.
M7900 (ASU)
Wappatomaka: A Survey of the History and Geography of the South Branch Valley.
M7910 (ASU)
O400
Indexed County and Railroad Pocket Map and Shipper's Guide of West Virginia.
R390 (BC)
West Virginia: A Book of Geography, History, and Industry.
S2530 (WCU)
Climate, Weather and Coal Mine Explosions; with a Meteorological Review of the Farmington Disaster.
W2230
W4380 (BC)
GEOLOGY
Report.
A910 (BC)
The Chattanooga Black Shale, a Possible Future Source of Uranium.
A1320 (ETSU)
Geology and Water Resources of Garrett County.
A2230 (ETSU)
Bulletin.
A3130 (ASU ETSU LMC)
The Abram Creek-Stony River Coal Field, Northeastern West Virginia.
A5230
Geology and Mineral Resources of Part of the Cumberland Gap Coal Field, Kentucky.
A5240 (ASU)
Deposits of Brown Iron Ores (Brown Hematite) in Western North Carolina.
B2170 (ASU LMC WCU UNCA)
The Appalachians.
B6960 (ASU WCU LMC MHC FC WWC ETSU BC FC UNCA)
The Life of the Mountains.
B6970 (BC)
B8380
Asheville Folio, North Carolina — Tennessee.
U3100 (WCU)
Geology of Big Stone Gap.
U3150
The Potomac and Roaring Creek Coal Fields in West Virginia.
W2260
Barbour and Upshur Counties. . . .
W3640 (ETSU)
Bulletin.
W3650 (ETSU)
Cabell, Wayne and Lincoln Counties.
W3660 (ETSU)
County Report, no. 1. 1911.
W3680 (ETSU)
County Reports and Maps.
W3690 (BC)
Fayette County.
W3700 (ETSU)
Geology and Economic Resources of the Ohio River Valley in West Virginia.
W3710 (ETSU)
Greenbrier County.
W3720 (ETSU)
Hampshire and Hardy Counties.
W3730 (ETSU)
Jefferson, Berkeley, and Morgan Counties.
W3740 (ETSU)
Log of Appalachian Geological Society Field Trip.
W3750 (ETSU)
Logan and Mingo County.
W3760 (BC)
Mercer, Monroe, and Summers Counties.
W3770 (ETSU)
Mineral and Grant Counties.
W3780 (ETSU)
Nicholas County.
W3790 (ETSU)
Oil and Gas Report and Map of Doddridge and Harrison Counties, West Virginia.
W3800 (ETSU)
Oil and Gas Report and Map of Marshall, Wetzel, and Tyler Counties, West Virginia.
W3810 (ETSU)
Oil and Gas Report and Map of Monongalia, Marion, and Taylor Counties, West Virginia.
W3820 (ETSU)
Oil and Gas Report and Map of Pleasants, Wood and Ritchie Counties, West Virginia.
W3830 (ETSU)
Pendleton County.
W3840 (BC)
Pocahontas County.
W3850 (BC)
Randolph County.
W3860 (ETSU)
Report of Investigations.
W3870 (ETSU)
Reports.
W3880 (ETSU)
Salt Brines of West Virginia.
W3890 (ETSU)
State Park Series. Bulletin.
W3900 (ETSU)
Tucker County.
W3910 (ETSU)
The West Virginia Geological and Economic Survey: Its Accomplishments and Outlook.
W3920 (ETSU)
Wirt, Roane and Calhoun Counties.
W3930 (ETSU)
Wyoming and McDowell Counties.
W3940 (ETSU)
Lower Pennsylvanian Species of Mariopteris, Eremopteris, Diplothmema, and Aneimities from the Appalachian Region.
W5370
Cambrian System of West Virginia. With Comments on Older Rocks and Ingneous Dikes.
W8920 (ETSU)
Devonian System of West Virginia.
W8930 (ETSU)
Ordovician System of West Virginia.
W8940 (ETSU)
Outline of the Geology and Mineral Resources of Russell County, Virginia.
W8950 (ETSU)
Distribution of Minor Elements in Coals of Appalachian Region.
Z150
GEOLOGY — ALA.
A4080 (ETSU)
Iron Ore in the Red Mountain Formation in Greasy Cove, Alabama.
B8420
Preliminary Report on the Red Iron Ores of East Tennessee, Northeast Alabama, and Northwest Georgia.
B8430
Availability of Ground Water in Talladega County, Alabama: A Reconnaissance.
C2520 (ETSU)
Geology and Ground-water Resources of Cherokee County, Alabama: A Reconnaissance.
C2530 (ETSU)
Ground-water Resources of Etowah County, Alabama: A Reconnaissance.
C2540 (ETSU)
Geology and Ground-water Resources of Morgan County, Alabama.
D2750 (ETSU)
Interim Report on the Geology and Groundwater Resources of Morgan County, Alabama.
D2770 (ETSU)
Stratigraphy and Structure of Outcropping Pre-Selma Coastal Plain Beds of Fayette and Lamar Counties, Alabama.
D3400 (ASU)
Stratigraphy and Uranium Content of the Chattanooga Shale in Northeastern Alabama, Northwestern Georgia, and Eastern Tennessee.
G2210
Surface Water Resources of Calhoun County, Alabama.
H2240 (ETSU)
. . . Natural Resources of the Tenn. Valley Region in Alabama.
H2540 (BC)
Geology and Ground-water Resources of Colbert County, Alabama.
H2870 (ETSU)
Interim Report on Ground-water Study in Colbert County, Alabama.
H2880 (ETSU)
Springs in Colbert and Lauderdale Counties, Alabama.
H2890 (ETSU)
Geology and Ground-water Resources of Lawrence County, Alabama: A Reconnaissance.
H3030 (ETSU)
Physiography of the Chattanooga District in Tenn., Georgia, and Ala. 1899.
H3870
Physical Divisions of Northern Alabama.
J2180 (ETSU)
An Inventory of Human and Physical Resources of Cherokee, Dekalb, Jackson, and Marshall Counties, Alabama.
K1590 (ASU)
Atlas of Alabama.
L2520
Report on the Coal Measures of the Plateau Region of Alabama.
M230 (BC)
General Geology and Ground-water Resources of Limestone County, Alabama: A Reconnaissance.
M2170 (ETSU)
Geology and Ground-water Resources of Madison County, Alabama.
M2890 (ETSU)
Stratigraphy of the Chickamauga Supergroup in Its Type Area.
M5480 (ETSU)
Geology and Ground-water Resources of Tuscaloosa County, Alabama.
M5760 (ETSU)
Ground-water in the Vicinity of Bryce State Hospital, Tuscaloosa County, Alabama.
M5770 (ETSU)
Ground-water Resources and Geology of Tuscaloosa County, Alabama.
P1030 (ETSU)
Geology and Ground-water Resources of Franklin County, Alabama: A Reconnaissance.
P1150 (ETSU)

GEOLOGY — ALA.

Building Sandstones of Northern Alabama.
P1710 (ETSU)

Iron Making in Alabama.
P2700 (ASU)

Surface Water in Tuscaloosa County, Alabama.
P2880 (ETSU)

Geology and Mineral Resources of Clay County, with Special Reference to the Graphite Industry.
P4770 (ETSU)

Geology and Coal Resources of the Northeast Part of the Coosa Coal Field, St. Clair County, Alabama.
R3930 (ETSU)

Report on the Calaba Coal Field.
S6400

Geology and Ground-Water Resources of Calhoun County, Alabama: An Interim Report.
W820 (ETSU)

Geology and Ground-Water Resources of Calhoun County, Alabama.
W830 (ETSU)

GEOLOGY — APP.

Appalachian Basin Ordovician Symposium: Papers Read at the Meeting of the Pittsburgh Geological Society at Pittsburgh, Pa., May 16, 1947, and Published in the Bulletin of the American Assn. of Petroleum Geologists, Aug. 1948.
A2850 (BC)

Fall Meeting of the Appalachian Geological Society and the Pittsburgh Geological Society with the Cooperation of the West Virginia Geological Survey, October 11-12, 1957, at Blackwater Falls State Park: Log of Field Trip.
A3140 (ETSU)

Silurian Stratigraphy: Central Appalachian Basin.
A3150 (ASU)

Appalachian Structures: Origin, Evolution and Possible Potential for New Exploration Frontiers.
A4090

An Index of State Geological Survey Publications Issued in Series.
C7380 (LMC)

Studies of Appalachian Geology: Central and Southern.
F1170 (ASU LMC ETSU)

Uranium in the Appalachian Mobile Belt.
G50 (LMC)

Dictionary of Altitude in the U. S.
G260

The Geology and Coal Resources of Dickenson County, Virginia.
G1340 (ETSU)

Reconnaissance of Some Gold and Tin Deposits of the Southern Appalachians.
G3290

Geomorphology and Forest Ecology of the Mountain Region in the Central Appalachians.
H90

Geology of Oil and Gas.
H3520 (ETSU)

Appalachian Connate Water.
H4290 (ETSU)

Raw Materials for Lightweight Aggregate in Appalachian Region, Alabama and Georgia.
H6610

Shales for Lightweight Aggregate in Appalachian Region, Kentucky and Tennessee.
H6620

Photogeologic Techniques Applied to the Mapping of Rock Joints.
H7410 (ETSU)

Mercury and Other Trace Elements in Sphalerite and Wallrocks from Central Kentucky, Tennessee, and Appalachian Zinc Districts.
J2250

Topography and Geology of the Southern Appalachians.
K560

Morphologic and Systematic Relationships of Some Middle Ordovician Ostracoda.
K3120 (ETSU)

Cabell, Wayne and Lincoln Counties.
K3180 (ETSU ASU)

"Fan-like Features and Related Periglacial Phenomena of the Southern Blue Ridge."
M5310 (WCU)

O790

Tectonics and Cambrianordovician Stratigraphy in the Central Appalachians of Pennsylvania.
P3170 (ETSU)

Appalachian Mountain Elevations.
R900 (ASU LMC ETSU WCU)

Ice Storms in the Southern Appalachian Mountains.
R1810

The Texture of Mississippian, Upper Devonian, and Lower Pennsylvanian Sandstones in the Appalachian Basin.
R2530

The Texture of Paleozoic Sandstones and Sandy Limestones in the Appalachian Basin.
R2540

The Tectonics of the Appalachians.
R3410 (LMC ETSU WWC)

Origin of the Copper Deposits of the Ducktown Type in the Southern Appalachian Region.
R3810 (ETSU ASU)

Rotary Coring of Appalachian Area Oil-producing Formations with Mud or Air.
R3990

Electrical and Hydraulic Flow Properties of Appalachian Petroleum Reservoir Rocks.
S610

Densities and Porosities of Core Samples from Wells in Appalachian Oilfields.
S4130

Potassium-Argon Geochronology of the Brevard Fault, Southern Appalachians.
S7570
S8790 (ETSU WWC ASU)
S8800 (ASU ETSU UNCA)

North With the Spring: A Naturalist's Record of a 17,000 Mile Journey With the North-American Spring.
T800 (ASU LMC)

Engineering Geology and Mineral Resources of the Tennessee Valley Authority Region.
T2600

Arnold Guyot, First to Measure the Peaks of the Appalachians.
U2880 (BC)

The Mechanics of Appalachian Structure.
W6970

The Northern Appalachians.
W6980 (BC)

GEOLOGY — APP. MTNS.

Appalachian Tectonics.
C4640 (ASU ETSU LMC WCU)

Manual of Coal and Its Topography.
L1890

GEOLOGY — GA.

Georgia's Fabulous Treasure Hoards: A Compendium for Rockhounds, Prospectors, and Various Seekers of Gold, Silver, Diamonds, etc., with Known and Historic Locations, . . .
A2500 (MHC)

Geology of the Tate Quadrangle.
B2200 (ETSU)

Preliminary Report on the Red Iron Ores of East Tennessee, Northeast Alabama, and Northwest Georgia.
B8430

Annotated Bibliography of Georgia Geology Through 1959.
C8500 (ETSU)

Geology and Ground-water Resources of Catoosa County, Georgia.
C8710 (ETSU)

Geology and Ground-water Resources of the Paleozoic Rock Area, Chattooga County, Georgia.
C8720 (ETSU)

Geology and Ground-water Resources of Walker County, Georgia.
C8730 (ETSU)

Geology of the Crystalline Rocks of Georgia.
C8770 (ETSU)

Geology and Ground-water Resources of Dade County, Georgia.
C9070 (ETSU)

The Romance of Georgia Marble.
D90 (ASU BC)

Publications on the Geology and Mineral Resources of Georgia.
G910 (ETSU)

Short Contributions to the Geology, Geography, and Archaeology of Georgia.
G920 (ETSU)

The Paleozoic Group: The Geology of Ten Counties of Northwestern Georgia.
G1020 (BC ASU)

Stratigraphy and Uranium Content of the Chattanooga Shale in Northeastern Alabama, Northwestern Georgia, and Eastern Tennessee.
G2210

Field Excursion: Stone Mountain — Lithonia District.
G3270 (ETSU)

Physiography of the Chattanooga District in Tenn., Georgia, and Ala. 1899.
H3870

Geology of the Stone Mountain-Lithonia District, Georgia.
H5000 (ETSU)

Forsterite Olivine Deposits of North Carolina and Georgia.
H8400 (ETSU WCU)

Field Excursion: Ocoee Metasediments: North Central Georgia and Southeast Tennessee.
H8610 (ETSU)

The Geology and Mineralogy of Graves Mountain, Georgia.
H8620 (ETSU)

Stratigraphy, Structure, Mineral Resources of the Mineral Bluff Quadrangle, Georgia.
H8630 (ETSU)

Geology and Mineral Deposits of the Cartersville District, Georgia.
K1700

Stratigraphy of the Chickamauga Supergroup in Its Type Area.
M5480 (ETSU)

Subsurface "Basement" Rocks of Georgia.
M6110 (ETSU ASU)

Geology and Mineral Resources of the Dalton Quadrangle, Georgia-Tennessee.
M8680 (ASU ETSU)

Field Excursion: The Georgia Marble District.
P4050 (ETSU)

Geology and Mineral Resources of the Northwest Quarter of the Cohutta Mountain Quadrangle.
S220 (ETSU)

Geology and Ground-water Resources of Crystalline Rocks, Dawson County, Georgia.
S2010 (ASU ETSU)

The Geology of the Sand Lookout Mountain Area, Northwest Georgia.
S8970 (ETSU)

The Bauxite Deposits of Floyd, Bartow, and Polk Counties of Northwest Georgia.
W5630

GEOLOGY — GA., NORTHERN

Zonation of the Middle and Upper Ordovician Strata in Northwestern Georgia.
A1500 (ETSU)

GEOLOGY — KY.

Geology and Ground-water Resources of the Paintsville Area, Kentucky.
B630 (ASU)

The Unforseen Wilderness: An Essay on Kentucky's Red River Gorge.
B3300 (ASU BC LMC)

The Geography of the Kentucky Knobs.
B9200 (BC)

Geology of the Big Stone Gap Coal Field of Virginia and Kentucky.
C760 (BC)

The Fire Clays and Fire Clay Industries of the Olive Hill and Ashland Districts of Northeastern Kentucky.
C8780 (BC)

Geography of the Mountains of Eastern Kentucky.
D960 (BC ASU)

Geologic-Map of the Adult Quadrangle, Northeastern Kentucky.
D1710

Age of Bedford Shale, Berea Sandstone, and Sunbury Shale in the Appalachian and Michigan Basins, Pennsylvania, Ohio, and Michigan.
D2050

Peridotite of Elliott County, Kentucky.
D2420

Geology and Coal Resources of the Cannel City Quadrangle, Kentucky.
E2020

The Genealogy about Mills Springs, Monticello Quadrangle, Kentucky.
F3020 (BC)

GEOLOGY — KY.

Regional Subsurface Stratigraphy of the Cambrian and Ordovician in Kentucky and Vicinity.
F3200 (ETSU)

Geological Map of the Balkan Quadrangle, Bell and Harlan Counties, Kentucky.
F3450 (BC)

Ancient Life in Kentucky: A Brief Presentation of the Paleontological Succession in Kentucky Coupled with a Systematic Outline of the Archaeology of the Commonwealth.
F3850 (ASU BC)

Ancient Life in Kentucky: A Brief Presentation of the Paleontological Succession in Kentucky Coupled with a Systematic Outline of the Archaeology of the Commonwealth.
F3860 (WCU MHC BC)

Itinerary: Some Stratigraphic and Structural Features of the Middlesboro Basin.
G830 (ETSU)

Selected Features of the Kentucky Fluorspar District and the Barkley Dam Site.
G840 (ETSU)

"Tales of the Mountains" A Complete Directory of the Eastern Kentucky Coalfields with Extracts from the Geological Reports, Forestry, Oil Development, Education, Superstitions, and Religion of the Mountains.
H730

Stratigraphy and Paleoecology of the Saluda Formation (Cincinnation) in Indiana, Ohio, and Kentucky.
H3420 (ETSU)

Coals of the North Fork of the Ky. River in Perry and Portions of Breathitt & Knott Co. Ky.
H6150

The Anthracite Forest Region, a Problem Area.
I760 (ASU)

Geology and Coal of Stinking Creek.
J1020

The Geology and Mineral Resources of Kentucky: A Brief Description of the Physiography, Stratigraphy, Areal and Structural Geology, and Mineral Resources of Each of the Counties Comprising the Commonwealth.
J1030 (ETSU)

Geology of a New Oil Pool in Casey Co., Ky.
J1040

Geology of Clark Co., Ky.
J1050

Geology of Cumberland Co., Kentucky.
J1070

Geology of Powell Co., Ky.
J1080

Geology of the Area Around Powell Co., Ky.
J1090

Geology of the Glencairn and Pine Ridge Faults.
J1100

Geology of the Goose Creek Dome.
J1110

Geology of the Meadow Anticline.
J1130

Geology of the Mica Dome in Clark Co., Ky.
J1140

Geology of the Nimtonville Dome in Casey Co., Ky.
J1150

. . . Geological Map of Kentucky. Presented in Colors, Showing Oil, Gas, Coal, Fluorspar, and Asphalt Fields; and Other Mineral Resources and Geologic Data Including Faults, Folds, Sections, Elevations, and Physiographic Divisions of the Commonwealth.
K1250

Soil Survey of Garrard County, Kentucky.
K1640

Geologic Map of the Maulden Quadrangle, Southeastern Kentucky.
L1390

The Pleistocene of Northern Kentucky, a Regional Reconnaissance Study of the Physical Effects of Glaciation Within the Commonwealth.
L1980 (ETSU)

Geology of the Mammoth Cave National Park Area. Rev. by Preston McGrain. Kentucky Geological Survey Series 10, Special publication 7. Revision of Series 9, Special publication 2.
L2910 (ETSU ASU)

Geologic Map of the Sardis Quadrangle, Northwestern Kentucky.
M1230 (BC)

Some Old Chester Problems — Correlations Along the Eastern Belt of Outcrop.
M1330 (ETSU)

Geologic Map of Part of the Rose Hill Quadrangle, Harlan County, Kentucky.
M4380 (ASU)

The Menifee Gas Field and the Ragland Oil Field, Kentucky.
M8580

Reconnaissance of Oil and Gas Fields in Wayne and McCreary Counties, Kentucky.
M8590

Geology of the Bedford Shale and Berea Sandstone in the Appalachian Basin.
P2000

Economic Geology of the Kenova Quadrangle, Kentucky, Ohio, and West Virginia.
P2510

Geology and Ground-water Resources of the Prestonburg Quadrangle, Kentucky.
P4600

The Silurian Formations of East-central Kentucky and Adjacent Ohio.
R1620 (ETSU)

Geologic Map of the Jenkins West Quadrangle, Kentucky-Virginia.
R1900

Geologic Map of the Whitesburg Quadrangle, Kentucky-Virginia, and Part of the Flat Gap Quadrangle, Letcher County, Ky.
R1910

The Irvine Oil Field, Estill County, Kentucky.
S2480

Geologic Map of the Stanford Quadrangle, Boyle and Lincoln Counties, Kentucky.
S2520

Geologic Map of the Evarts Quadrangle and Part of the Hubbard Springs Quadrangle, Southeastern Kentucky and Virginia.
T770 (BC)

Oil Shales of Kentucky.
T7710

Coal deposits of Pike Co., Ky.
U3120

Geology and Mineral Resources of part of the Cumberland Gap coal field, Ky., 1906.
U3170

Geology and ground water resources in the Paintsville area, Ky. 1955, Surface water of the U. S. 1953; Cumberland and Tenn. River Basin.
U3420

Geologic Map of the McKee Quadrangle, Jackson and Owsley Counties, Ky.
W2310 (BC)

Geological Map of Paint Lick Quadrangle.
W2320 (BC)

Geology and Oil and Gas Possibilities of Upper Mississippian Rocks of Southwestern Virginia, Southern West Virginia, and Eastern Kentucky.
W7060 (ASU)

GEOLOGY — MD.

Brachipoda of the Keyser Limestone (Silurian-Devonian) of Maryland and Adjacent Areas.
B5700 (ETSU)

Soil Survey of Allegany County, Maryland.
B7610

Microtectonics Along the Western Edge of the Blue Ridge, Maryland and Virginia.
C5100 (LMC)

Structure of Devonian Strata along Allegheny Front from Corriganville, Maryland, to Spruce Knob, West Virginia.
D1830 (ETSU)

Cetothere Skeletons from the Miocene Choptank Formation of Maryland and Virginia.
K610 (ETSU)

The Physical Features of Washington County.
M3910 (ETSU)

Eocene Stratigraphy and Foraminifera of the Aquia Formation.
S3060 (ETSU)

GEOLOGY — N. C.

General Features of the Brown Hematite Ores of Western North Carolina.
B2180 (ASU)

General Features of the Magnetite Ores of Western North Carolina and Eastern Tennessee.
B2190 (UNCA ASU)

The Kaolins of North Carolina.
B2210 (WCU)

Magnetic Iron Ores of East Tennessee and Western North Carolina.
B2220 (UNCA)

An Introduction to the Topography, Geology, and Mineral Resources of North Carolina.
B6750 (ETSU)

Geology of the Blowing Rock Quadrangle, N. C.
B7790

Geology of the Grandfather Mountain Window and vicinity, North Carolina and Tennessee.
B7800 (ASU)

Geology of the Linville Quadrangle, North Carolina-Tennessee: A Preliminary Report.
B7810 (LMC)

Mineral Resources of the Grandfather Mountain Window and Vicinity, North Carolina.
B7820 (ASU)

The Story of the Geologic Making of North Carolina.
B7890 (LMC UNCA)

Feldspar Deposits of the Bryson City District, North Carolina.
C390 (ASU WCU)

Mineral Localities of North Carolina.
C6520 (ASU)

Botany: Containing a Catalogue of the Indigenous and Naturalized Plants of the State.
C9910 (LMC ASU)

The Shrubs and Woody Vines of North Carolina.
C9920 (LMC)

Geology and Ground-water Resources of the Murphy Area, North Carolina.
D2760 (WCU)

The Mineral Industry in North Carolina from 1918-1923.
D3290 (LMC)

The Geomorphic History of the New Kanawha River System.
F3300 (ETSU)

Surface Water Supply of the New-Kanawha River Basin, West Virginia, and North Carolina.
G4490

Measurements of Points in North Carolina and Tennessee.
G5000

Geology of the Eastern Great Smoky Mountains, North Carolina and Tennessee.
H160 (LMC ASU)

Preliminary Report on Corundum Deposits in the Buck Creek Peridotite, Clay County, North Carolina.
H170 (ASU)

In the Coal and Iron Counties of North Carolina.
H420 (LMC WCU)

In the Coal and Iron Counties of North Carolina.
H430 (BC ASU)

Forsterite Olivine Deposits of North Carolina and Georgia.
H8400 (ETSU WCU)

Halloysite Deposits of Western North Carolina.
H8410 (ETSU WCU)

Tin Resources of the King's Mountain District, North Carolina and South Carolina.
K550

Bibliography of North Carolina Geology, Mineralogy, and Geography, with a List of Maps.
L390 (ASU LMC WWC ETSU)

The Geology and Ore Deposits of the Virgilina District of Virginia and North Carolina.
L400 (ETSU ASU)

The Gold Hill Mining District of North Carolina.
L410 (LMC ETSU)

"Geology of the Bat Cave and Fuitland Quadrangles and the Origin of the Henderson Gneiss, Western North Carolina."
L1720

Corundum and the Basic Magnesian Rocks of Western North Carolina.
L2210 (WCU)

Limestones and Marls of North Carolina.
L3630 (ASU LMC WCU)

Reconnaissance of the Ground-water Resources in the Waynesville Area, North Carolina.
M3380 (LMC WCU)

Diary of a Geological Tour by Dr. Elisha Mitchell in 1827 and 1828.
M6300 (ASU BC LMC)

GEOLOGY — N. C.

Chromite Deposits of North Carolina: Geology and Mining.
N1920

Altitudes in North Carolina.
N2310 (ASU LMC WCU)

. . . Altitudes in North Carolina, comp. by the North Carolina Geological and Economic Survey.
N2320 (ASU UNCA)

Biennial Report of the State Geologist: 1919-1920.
N2330 (ASU LMC)

Report of the State Geologist and Director. 1891-92 - 1923-24.
N2340 (ASU UNCA)

Mica Deposits of the Franklin-Sylva District, North Carolina.
O640 (ASU WCU ETSU)

Pegmatites of the Cashiers and Zirconia Districts, North Carolina.
O650 (ETSU ASU)
O790

Geology and Mineral Resources of the Hot Springs Window, Madison County, North Carolina.
O800 (ASU WCU ETSU)

Residual Kaolin Deposits of the Spruce Pine District, North Carolina.
P260 (ETSU)

A Memoir of the Rev. Elisha Mitchell, D. D., Late Professor of Chemistry, Mineralogy and Geology in the University of North Carolina: Together with the Tributes of Respect to His Memory, by Various Public Meetings and Literary Associations, and the Addresses Delivered at the Re-interment of His Remains.
P2570 (ASU LMC)

Geology of the Linville Falls Quadrangle, North Carolina.
R1100 (ASU)

North Carolina: Its Geology and Mineral Resources.
S8760 (LMC WWC ETSU UNCA)

Pyrophyllite Deposits in North Carolina.
S8770 (ETSU)

Geology and Ground-water of the Morganton Area, North Carolina.
S9090 (WCU)

"Gold Mining in North Carolina: 1799-1860."
S9290 (WCU)

The Magnetic Iron Ore of East Tennessee and Western North Carolina.
T1150

Geology of the Spruce Pine District: Avery, Mitchell, and Yancey Counties, North Carolina.
U3130 (ASU)

Cranberry Folio, North Carolina — Tennessee.
U3130 (WCU)

Greenville Folio, Tennessee — North Carolina.
U3200 (WCU)

Knoxville Folio, Tennessee — North Carolina.
U3220 (WCU)

Mount Mitchell Folio, North Carolina — Tennessee.
U3260 (WCU)

Nantahala Folio, North Carolina — Tennessee.
U3270 (WCU)

Pisgah Folio, North Carolina — South Carolina.
U3300 (WCU)

Roan Mountain Folio, Tennessee — North Carolina.
U3330 (WCU)

Soil Survey of the Mt. Mitchell Area.
U3350

GEOLOGY — OHIO

Economic Geology of the Summerfield and Woodsfield Quadrangles, Ohio, with Descriptions of Coal and Other Mineral Resources, Except Oil and Gas.
C6320

Structure of the Berea Oil Sand in the Summerfield Quadrangle, Guernsey, Noble, and Monroe Counties, Ohio.
C6330

Age of Bedford Shale, Berea Sandstone, and Sunbury Shale in the Appalachian and Michigan Basins, Pennsylvania, Ohio, and Michigan.
D2050

Geology of Oil and Gas Fields in Steubenville, Burgettstown, and Claysville Quadrangles, Ohio, W. Va., and Pa.
G4340
G4350

Stratigraphy and Paleoecology of the Saluda Formation (Cincinnation) in Indiana, Ohio, and Kentucky.
H3420 (ETSU)

Economic Geology of the Kenova Quadrangle, Kentucky, Ohio, and West Virginia.
P2510

Stratigraphy of the Bituminous Coal Field of Pennsylvania, Ohio, and West Virginia.
W5470

GEOLOGY — PA.

Age of Bedford Shale, Berea Sandstone, and Sunbury Shale in the Appalachian and Michigan Basins, Pennsylvania, Ohio, and Michigan.
D2050

Geology of Oil and Gas Fields in Steubenville, Burgettstown, and Claysville Quadrangles, Ohio, W. Va., and Pa.
G4340

Geologic Map of Southwest Pennsylvania.
P1900

Tectonics and Cambrianordovician Stratigraphy in the Central Appalachians of Pennsylvania.
P3170 (ETSU)

Laboratory Investigation of In Situ Combustion Process for Recovering Pennsylvania Grade Crude Oil.
S7100

Stratigraphy of the Bituminous Coal Field of Pennsylvania, Ohio, and West Virginia.
W5470

GEOLOGY — S. C.

Tin Resources of the King's Mountain District, North Carolina and South Carolina.
K550

Pisgah Folio, North Carolina — South Carolina.
U3300 (WCU)

GEOLOGY — TENN.

General Features of the Magnetite Ores of Western North Carolina and Eastern Tennessee.
B2190 (UNCA ASU)

Magnetic Iron Ores of East Tennessee and Western North Carolina.
B2220 (UNCA)

Summary of the Mineral Resources of Tennessee.
B5540 (ETSU)

Geological Report: Coal Creek Mining and Manufacturing Company of Tennessee.
B6190

Stratigraphy of the Mascot-Jefferson City Zinc District, Tennessee.
B6610

Geology of the Linville Quadrangle, North Carolina-Tennessee: A Preliminary Report.
B7810 (LMC)

The Red Iron Ores of East Tennessee.
B8440 (BC)

Coals in the Area between Bon Air and Clifty, Tennessee.
B9460

Geology and Mineral Resources of the Crossville Quadrangle, Tennessee.
B9480 (ETSU)

Geology and Oil Possibilities of the Northern Part of Overton County, Tennessee, and of Adjoining Parts of Clay, Pickett and Fentress Counties.
B9490 (ETSU)

Bibliography of Tennessee Geology, Soils, Drainage, Forestry, etc. with Subject Index.
C5440 (LMC ETSU)

Geology and Ore Deposits of the Ducktown Mining District, Tennessee.
E1960 (ASU BC)

Stratigraphy and Uranium Content of the Chattanooga Shale in Northeastern Alabama, Northwestern Georgia, and Eastern Tennessee.
G2210

Measurements of Points in North Carolina and Tennessee.
G5000

Geology of the Eastern Great Smoky Mountains, North Carolina and Tennessee.
H160 (LMC ASU)

Geology of the Richardson Cove and Jones Cove Quadrangles, Tennessee.
H1220 (LMC)

Geologic Map of Tennessee.
H2060 (ETSU)

Physiography of the Chattanooga District in Tenn., Georgia, and Ala. 1899.
H3870

Limestone and Dolomite Resources of Tennessee.
H5040 (ETSU)

Ceramic Evaluation of Clays and Shales of East Tennessee.
H6600 (ETSU)

Field Excursion: Ocoee Metasediments: North Central Georgia and Southeast Tennessee.
H8610 (ETSU)

Geology of Pickett Co., Tenn.
J1070

Techniques Used in Mine-water Problems of the East Tennessee Zinc District.
K860 (ASU)

Tennessee: Its Agricultural and Mineral Wealth, With an Appendix Showing the Extent, Value and Accessibility of its Ores, With Analyses of the Same.
K1920 (ASU LMC)

Geology and Manganese Deposits of Northeastern Tennessee.
K2410 (ETSU)

Geology of Northeasternmost Tennessee with a Section on the Description of the Basement Rocks by Warren Hamilton.
K2420 (ETSU)

Geology of the Central Great Smoky Mountains, Tennessee.
K2430 (ASU LMC)

Geology of the Great Smoky Mountains National Park, Tennessee and North Carolina.
K2450 (ETSU)

The Coal Industry of Tennessee.
L4010 (ETSU)

Tuscaloosa Formation in Tennessee.
M3190 (ETSU)

Stratigraphy of the Chickamauga Supergroup in Its Type Area.
M5480 (ETSU)

Mineral Resources of the Waynesboro Quadrangle, Tennessee.
M6220 (ETSU)

Geology and Mineral Resources of the Dalton Quadrangle, Georgia-Tennessee.
M8680 (ASU ETSU)

The Southern Tennessee Coal Field Included in Bledsoe, Cumberland, Franklin, Grundy, Rhea, Sequatchie, Van Buren, Warren, and White Counties.
N580 (ETSU)

Geology of the Western Great Smoky Mountains, Tennessee.
N630 (ASU LMC)

Middle Ordovician Rocks of the Tellico-Sevier Belt, Eastern Tennessee.
N640

Geology of the Mascot-Jefferson City Zinc District, Tennessee.
O220 (ETSU)

Geology of the Buffalo Mountain-Cherokee Mountain Area, Northeastern Tennessee.
O780 (ETSU ASU)

Oil and Gas Report on Jackson, Mason, and Putnam Counties, West Virginia.
O940 (ETSU)
P160 (ETSU)

Lower Middle Ordovician of Southwest Virginia and Northeast Tennessee.
P4760 (ETSU)

Upper Cambrian Trilobite Faunas of Northeastern Tennessee.
R500 (LMC)

Manganese Resources of East Tennessee.
R1380 (ETSU)

Geologic Map of East Tennessee.
R3380 (ETSU)

Geology and Mineral Deposits of Bumpass Cove, Unicoi and Washington Counties, Tennessee.
R3390 (ETSU)

Stratigraphic Section at Lee Valley, Hawkins County, Tennessee.
R3400 (ETSU)

Soil Survey of Jackson County, Tennessee.
R3570

The Elements of the Geology of Tennessee.
S90 (ASU LMC BC)

GEOLOGY — TENN.

Geological Reconnaissance of the State, Tennessee.
S100 (ASU)

Geology of Tennessee.
S110 (ETSU)

Zinc Deposits of East Tennessee.
S1640 (LMC)

The Phosphate Resources of Tennessee.
S5030 (ETSU)

The Cumberland Plateau Overthrust and Geology of the Crab Orchard Mountains Area, Tennessee.
S6720 (ETSU)

Pennsylvanian Rocks of the Southern Appalachians.
S6730 (ETSU)

Manganese Deposits of East Tennessee.
S7660

Soil Survey of Meigs County, Tennessee.
S9570

Geology, Mineral Resources, and Ground Water of the Cleveland Area, Tennessee.
S9710 (ETSU)

Division of Geology Bulletin.
T1020

The Magnetic Iron Ore of East Tennessee and Western North Carolina.
T1150

Administrative Report of State Geological Survey, 1910-1923-1924.
T1250 (ETSU)

Bulletin.
T1260 (ETSU)

Geologic Maps and Mineral Resources Summary.
T1270 (ETSU)

Geology and Barite Deposits of the Del Rio District, Cocke County, Tennessee.
T1280 (ETSU)

Knoxville and Vicinity, Tennessee. 1953.
T3000

Cranberry Folio, North Carolina — Tennessee.
U3130 (WCU)

Geology & ore deposits of the Ducktown mining district, Tenn., 1926.
U3180

Greenville Folio, Tennessee — North Carolina.
U3200 (WCU)

Knoxville Folio, Tennessee — North Carolina.
U3220 (WCU)

Mount Mitchell Folio, North Carolina — Tennessee.
U3260 (WCU)

Nantahala Folio, North Carolina — Tennessee.
U3270 (WCU)

Roan Mountain Folio, Tennessee — North Carolina.
U3330 (WCU)

Annotated Bibliography of the Geology of Tennessee Through December, 1950.
W7130 (ETSU)

Annotated Bibliography of the Geology of Tennessee, January, 1951, Through December, 1960.
W7140 (ETSU)

Guidebook to Geology Along Tennessee Highways.
W7150 (ETSU)

Ground Water Resources and Geology of Cumberland County, Tennessee.
W7340 (LMC)

GEOLOGY — TENN., EAST

Preliminary Report on the Red Iron Ores of East Tennessee, Northeast Alabama, and Northwest Georgia.
B8430

GEOLOGY — VA.

Geology of the Lexington Quadrangle, Virginia.
B3510 (ETSU ASU)

The Earthquake History of Virginia, 1900-1970.
B5140

Resources of South-west Virginia, Showing the Mineral Deposits of Iron, Coal, Zinc, Copper and Lead. Also, the Staples of the Various Counties, Methods of Transportation Access, etc.
B5840 (ASU BC)

Southwest Virginia and Contiguous Territory: Mineral Resources and Railway Facilities, Statistics, Information, Markets for Coke, Fuel, Ores, etc.
B5850 (BC)

Geology of the Clinchport Quadrangle, Virginia.
B6500 (ETSU)

Geology and Mineral Resources of the Lynchburg Quadrangle, Virginia.
B7440 (ETSU)

Fensters in the Cumberland Overthrust Block in Southwestern Virginia.
B9470 (ETSU)

Geology of the Appalachian Valley in Virginia.
B9500 (ETSU ASU)

Geologic Map of the Appalachian Valley of Virginia with Explanatory Text.
B9510 (ETSU)

Geology of the Big Stone Gap Coal Field of Virginia and Kentucky.
C760 (BC)

The Valley Coal Fields of Virginia.
C770 (ETSU)

Sedimentary Studies in the Middle River Drainage Basin of the Shenandoah Valley of Virginia.
C1480 (ASU)

Microtectonics Along the Western Edge of the Blue Ridge, Maryland and Virginia.
C5100 (LMC)

Geology of the Draper Mountain Area, Virginia.
C7110 (ETSU)

The Geology of the Region Between Roanoke and Winchester in the Appalachian Valley of Western Virginia.
C7120

Journal of a Tour through the United States and Canada, Made during the Years 1937-38.
D440

Bits of History and Legends Around and About the Natural Bridge of Virginia, 1730-1950.
D1080 (ASU)

Bits of History and Legends around and about the Natural Bridge of Virginia from 1730-1950.
D1090 (BC)

Geology and Mineral Resources of Floyd County of the Blue Ridge Upland, Southwestern Virginia.
D2340 (ETSU)

Geology and Virginia.
D2350 (ETSU)

Virginia Mineral Localities.
D2360 (ETSU)

The Geology and Mineral Resources of Wise County and the Coal-bearing Portion of Scott County, Virginia.
E670 (ETSU ASU)

The Geomorphic History of the New Kanawha River System.
F3300 (ETSU)

The Geology and Coal Resources of the Coal-bearing Portion of Lee County, Virginia.
G1350 (LMC ETSU)
G4770

Geology of Luray Caverns, Virginia.
H80 (ETSU FC)

Intrenched Meanders of the North Fork of the Shenandoah River, Virginia.
H100

Ground Water in the Ordovician Rocks near Woodstock, Virginia.
H660

The Geology and Coal Resources of the Coal-bearing Portion of Tazewell County, Virginia.
H2510 (ETSU)

Possibilities for Manganese Ore on Certain Undeveloped Tracts in the Shenandoah Valley, Virginia.
H5130

The Earthquake History of Virginia, 1774 to 1900.
H7140

Oil and Gas Wells Drilled in Southwestern Virginia before 1950.
H7900 (ASU)

Ground-water Supplies in Shale and Sandstone in Fairfax, Loudoun, and Prince William Counties, Virginia.
J2150

Cetothere Skeletons from the Miocene Choptank Formation of Maryland and Virginia.
K610 (ETSU)

Geology of the Elkton Area, Virginia.
K2440

Manganese Deposits of the Elkton Area, Virginia.
K2460

Manganese Deposits of the Lyndhurst-Vesuvius District, Augusta and Rockbridge Counties, Virginia.
K2760

Manganese Deposits of the Sweet Springs District, West Virginia and Virginia.
L70

The Geology and Ore Deposits of the Virgilina District of Virginia and North Carolina.
L400 (ETSU ASU)

Caverns of Virginia.
M1540 (LMC)

Triassic Formations of the Danville Basin.
M5300 (ETSU)
N260

Lower Middle Ordovician of Southwest Virginia and Northeast Tennessee.
P4760 (ETSU)

The Endless Caverns of the Shenandoah Valley.
R1150 (BC)

The Natural Bridge of Virginia and Its Environs.
R1160

Annotated Geological Bibliography of Virginia.
R2890 (ETSU)

Occurrence and Origin of the Titanium Deposits of Nelson and Amherst Counties, Virginia.
R3800

Manganese and Quartzite Deposits in the Lick Mountain Region of Wythe Co.
S6710

Phosphate Deposits in Southwestern Virginia.
S7670

Geologic Map of the Evarts Quadrangle and Part of the Hubbard Springs Quadrangle, Southeastern Kentucky and Virginia.
T770 (BC)

Geology of the Leesburg Quadrangle, Virginia.
T8800 (ETSU)

The Natural Bridge and Its Historical Surroundings.
T8880 (ASU FC BC)

Manganese deposits of the Lyndhurst-Vesuvius district, Augusta & Rockbridge Co., Va., 1943.
U3230

Manganese deposits of the Flat Top & Round Mtn district, Bland & Giles Co., Va., 1944.
U3240

Oil & gas wells drilled in southwest Va., before 1950.
U3280

Possibilities for Manganese ore or certain undeveloped tracks in Shenandoah Valley, Va., 1918.
U3310

Virginia: A Geographical and Political Summary, Embracing a Description of the State, Its Geology, Soils, Minerals and Climate; Its Animal and Vegetable Productions; Manufacturing and Commercial Facilities; Religious and Educational Advantages; Internal Improvements, and Form of Government.
V700 (BC)

Bulletin.
V910

The Clay and Shales of Va. West of the Blue Ridge.
V920

Fensters in the Cumberland Over Thrust in Southwest Va.
V940

Geology and Coal Resources of Buchanan Co., Va.
V950

The Geology and Coal Resources of the Coal-Bearing Portion of Tazewell Co., Va.
V960

The Geology and Coal Resources of Dickenson Co., Va.
V970

Geology and Mineral Resources of Wise Co. and Coal Bearing Portions of Scott Co., Va. with a Chapter on the Forest of Wise Co.
V980

Guidebook, Field Conference of Pennsylvania Geologists, Virginia — 1938.
V990 (ETSU)

Reprint Series.
V1020 (ETSU)

GEOLOGY — VA.
Geology and Oil and Gas Possibilities of Upper Mississippian Rocks of Southwestern Virginia, Southern West Virginia, and Eastern Kentucky.
W7060 (ASU)
GEOLOGY — VA. — WILLIAMSVILLE QUADRANGLE
Geology of the Williamsville Quadrangle, Virginia.
B3520 (ETSU)
GEOLOGY — W. VA.
Sandstones of West Virginia.
A4610 (ETSU)
Centennial Field Trip.
A5290 (ETSU)
Coal and Coal Mining in West Virginia.
B1200
Wood County Deep Well. Well Log, Sample, and Core Description.
B2160 (ETSU)
Ground-water Features of Berkeley and Jefferson Counties, West Virginia.
B3560 (ETSU)
Second Preliminary Report: The St. Albans Site, Kanawha County, West Virginia, 1964-1968.
B7540 (ASU)
Annual Field Trip of the Appalachian and Pittsburgh Geological Societies in the Great Valley in West Virginia.
B8530 (ETSU)
Soil Survey of the Middlebourne Area, West Virginia.
C60
Soil Survey of the Wheeling Area, West Virginia.
C70
Character of Coal in the Thomas Bed near Harrison, West Virginia.
C750
Grand Appalachian Field Excursion.
C7130 (BC)
Caverns of West Virginia.
D710 (ETSU)
West Virginia's Buffalo Creek Flood: A Study of the Hydrology and Engineering Geology.
D720
Stratigraphy of Onesquethaw Stage of Devonian in West Virginia and Bordering States.
D1820 (ETSU)
Structure of Devonian Strata along Allegheny Front from Corriganville, Maryland, to Spruce Knob, West Virginia.
D1830 (ETSU)
Water Resources of Kanawha County, West Virginia.
D2830 (ETSU)
Surface Water Supply of West Virginia.
E2170 (ETSU)
Publications of West Virginia Geological Survey.
E2190 (ASU)
A Subsurface Study of the Greenbrier Limestone in West Virginia.
F1610 (ETSU ASU)
The Geomorphic History of the New Kanawha River System.
F3300 (ETSU)
A Gazetteer of West Virginia.
G270 (BC ASU)
The Igneous Rocks of Pendleton County, West Virginia.
G380 (ETSU)
Iron Ores, Salt and Sandstones.
G4270 (ETSU)
Geology of Oil and Gas Fields in Steubenville, Burgettstown, and Claysville Quadrangles, Ohio, W. Va., and Pa.
G4340
Surface Water Supply of the New-Kanawha River Basin, West Virginia, and North Carolina.
G4490
Oil and Gas Report and Map of Doddridge and Harrison Counties, West Virginia.
H3550 (ETSU)
Oil and Gas Report and Map of Lewis and Gilmer Counties, West Virginia.
H3560 (ETSU)
Oil and Gas Report and Map of Marshall, Wetzel, and Tyler Counties, West Virginia.
H3570 (ETSU)
Oil and Gas Report and Map of Monongalia, Marion, and Taylor Counties, West Virginia.
H3580 (ETSU)
Oil and Gas Report on Braxton and Clay Counties, West Virginia.
H3610 (ETSU)
Oil and Gas Report on Kanawha County, West Virginia.
H3620 (ETSU)
West Virginia's Oil and Gas Lubricants and Fuels.
H3630 (ETSU)
Germanium in Coals of West Virginia.
H4140 (ETSU)
Permeability, Porosity, Oil, and Water Content of Natural Gas Reservoirs, Kanawha-Jackson and Campbells Creek Oriskany Fields.
H4150 (ETSU)
Braxton and Clay Counties.
H4700 (ASU)
Wirt, Roane and Calhoun Counties.
H4720 (ETSU)
Wyoming and McDowell Counties.
H4730 (ETSU)
Photogeologic Techniques Applied to the Mapping of Rock Joints.
H7410 (ETSU)
Spectrographic Chemical Analysis.
H8470 (ETSU)
Earth Science, A Handbook on the Geology of West Virginia.
J400
Soil Survey of Fayette County, West Virginia.
K1630
Soil Survey of Monroe County, West Virginia.
K1650
Soil Survey of Summers County, West Virginia.
K1660
Manganese Deposits of the Sweet Springs District, West Virginia and Virginia.
L70
Bibliography and Index of West Virginia Geology and Natural Resources to July 1, 1937.
L3870 (ETSU)
The Geology of Cacapon State Park, West Virginia.
L3880 (ETSU)
The Geology of Hawks Nest State Park, West Virginia.
L3890 (ETSU)
The Geology of Lost River State Park, West Virginia.
L3900 (ETSU)
The Geology of Watoga and Droop Mountain Battlefield State Parks, West Virginia.
L3910 (ETSU)
Clays of West Virginia.
M950 (ETSU)
Limestones of West Virginia.
M960 (ASU ETSU)
Dolomite Zone at Base of Greenbrier Limestone (Big Lime).
M3520 (ETSU)
Petrology and Correlation of Deep-well Sections in West Virginia and Adjacent States.
M3530 (ETSU)
Well-sample Records.
M3570 (ETSU)
Part 1: The Living Flora of West Virginia. Part 2: The Fossil Flora of West Virginia.
M6100 (ETSU)
Economic Geology of the Kenova Quadrangle, Kentucky, Ohio, and West Virginia.
P2510
P4280 (ETSU)
Greenbrier County.
P4530 (LMC ETSU)
Pocahontas County.
P4550 (ETSU)
Salt Brines of West Virginia.
P4560 (ETSU)
Springs of West Virginia.
P4570 (ETSU)
Barbour and Upshur Counties and Western Portion of Randolph County.
R1260 (ASU ETSU)
Mercer, Monroe, and Summers Counties.
R1280 (ASU ETSU)
Mineral and Grant Counties.
R1290 (ASU ETSU)
Nicholas County.
R1300 (ASU ETSU)
Randolph County.
R1310 (ASU ETSU)
Tucker County.
R1320 (ASU LMC ETSU)
A Pressure Chamber for the Impregnation of Porous Rock Specimens.
R1520 (ETSU)
A Simple Technique for the Determination of Weight Per Cent of Calcite and Dolomite in Carbonate Rocks.
R1530 (ETSU)
Relation of Geology to Drainage, Floods, and Landslides in the Petersburg Area, West Virginia.
S8030 (ETSU)
High-alumina Clays of West Virginia.
T120 (ETSU)
Hampshire and Hardy Counties.
T8670 (ETSU)
Pendleton County.
T8680 (ETSU)
Deep-well Records.
T9670 (ETSU)
Summarized Records of Deep Wells.
T9680 (ETSU)
Levels Above Tide. True Meridians. Report on Coal.
W5450 (ETSU)
Levels. Coal Analyses.
W5460 (ETSU)
Stratigraphy of the Bituminous Coal Field of Pennsylvania, Ohio, and West Virginia.
W5470
Supplementary Coal Report.
W5480 (ETSU)
Geology and Oil and Gas Possibilities of Upper Mississippian Rocks of Southwestern Virginia, Southern West Virginia, and Eastern Kentucky.
W7060 (ASU)
GEORGIA — HISTORY
Official History of Catoosa County, Georgia, 1853-1953.
M1070 (ASU LMC BC)
GERMANS
The German Settlers in Lincoln County and Western North Carolina.
N1240 (LMC)
Pennsylvania German Pioneers: A Publication of the Original Lists of Arrivals in the Port of Philadelphia from 1727 to 1808.
S7790 (ASU)
Pennsylvania German Pioneers: A Publication of the Original Lists of Arrivals in the Port of Philadelphia from 1727 to 1808.
S7800 (ASU)
GERMANS — PA.
The Pennsylvania Germans of the Shenandoah Valley.
S4620 (ASU)
GERMANS (PALATINE)
North Carolina Palatine-Germans (Futch Family).
S4660 (ASU)
GLASS INDUSTRY — W. VA.
The Pressed and Blown Glassware Industry.
S4180 (ASU)
GRANDFATHER MOUNTAIN
"An Avifaunal Strip Census on Grandfather Mountain."
A1460 (ASU)
GRANTS AND RECORDS — TENN.
North Carolina Land Grants in Tennessee, 1778-1791.
C1800 (ETSU BC ASU)
GREAT SMOKY MOUNTAINS
Walking in the Clouds.
A380 (ETSU ASU)
Mt. LeConte.
A440 (LMC ETSU)
Mt. LeConte.
A450 (WCU ASU)
Land of High Horizons.
B5770 (ASU WCU LMC BC ETSU)
The Village of Five Lives: The Fontana of the Great Smoky Mountains.
B5960 (ASU BC LMC WCU)
Smoky Mountain Country.
C320 (ASU WCU LMC ETSU BC)
Birth of a National Park in the Great Smoky Mountains: An Unprecedented Crusade which Created, as a Gift of the People, the Nation's Most Popular Park.
C520 (ASU ETSU WCU MHC WWC BC)

GREAT SMOKY MOUNTAINS
Birth of a National Park in the Great Smoky Mountains; an Unprecedented Crusade Which Created, as a Gift of the People, the Nation's Most Popular Park.
C530
Great Smoky Mountains Wildflowers.
C540 (LMC WCU ETSU)
Great Smoky Mountains Wildflowers.
C550 (ASU LMC WCU WWC BC)
Great Smoky Mountains Wildflowers.
C560 (ETSU BC)
Wild Flowers of the Great Smokies and Surrounding Area, a Pictorial Guide.
C2120 (ASU UNCA)
Song of Life in the Smokies.
C7670 (LMC)
Song of Life in the Smokies: Stories of Mine Own People and Sketches of Life as It Was Lived in the Mountains Before the Park Took Over.
C7680 (ETSU)
Great Smokies: Wonderland for Boys and Girls.
D2230 (ASU)
That's Why They Call It . . . the Names and Lore of the Great Smokies.
F1000 (WCU ETSU BC ASU)
That's Why They Call It . . . the Names and Lore of the Great Smokies.
F1010 (ASU LMC)
The Cherokee and His Smoky Mountain Legends.
F1340 (ASU ETSU BC)
Jessie's Children.
F2120 (LMC)
Gatlinburg, Gateway to the Great Smokies.
F2230
Strangers in High Places: The Story of the Great Smoky Mountains.
F3470 (ASU WCU LMC MHC FC ETSU BC)
Hunting and Fishing in the Great Smokies.
G550 (BC UNCA ASU WCU LMC)
The Phonetics of Great Smoky Mountain Speech.
G790 (ASU ETSU)
"Vegetation of the Grassy Balds of the Great Smoky Mountains."
G1300
G3450 (ASU)
G4640 (ASU)
Geology of the Eastern Great Smoky Mountains, North Carolina and Tennessee.
H160 (LMC ASU)
The Phonetics of Great Smoky Mountain Speech.
H780
Sayings from Old Smoky, Some Traditional Phrases, Expressions, and Sentences Heard in the Great Smoky Mountains and Nearby Areas: An Introduction to a Southern Mountain Dialect.
H800 (ASU BC LMC MHC)
Twenty Years of Hunting and Fishing in the Great Smoky Mountains.
H3850
Smoky Mountain Square Dances.
H4630 (ASU)
Mushrooms of the Great Smokies: A Field Guide to Some Mushrooms and Their Relatives.
H5050 (ASU WHC LMC UNCA BC WWC)
Your National Parks: Great Smoky Mountains.
H7790 (ETSU)
Amphibians and Reptiles of Great Smoky Mountains National Park.
H8160 (UNCA ASU LMC WCU BC)
Twenty Years of Hunting and Fishing in the Great Smoky Mountains.
H8360
"Regional English of the Former Inhabitants of Cades Cove in the Great Smoky Mountains."
J2450
The Complete Peddler's Pack: Games, Songs, Rhymes, and Riddles from Mountain Folklore.
J3060 (ASU WCU LMC MHC WWC ETSU FC)
Geology of the Central Great Smoky Mountains, Tennessee.
K2430 (ASU LMC)
Geology of the Great Smoky Mountains National Park, Tennessee and North Carolina.
K2450 (ETSU)
L300 (UNCA ASU)
"The Campaign for a National Park in Western North Carolina, 1885-1940."
L540 (WCU)
Mammals of the Great Smoky Mountains National Park.
L2710 (WCU WWC ASU LMC)
Mammals of Great Smoky Mountains National Park.
L2720 (BC)
A Bibliography for the Great Smoky Mountains.
M730
A Brief History of the Great Smoky Mountains National Park Movement in North Carolina.
M740
Guide to the Great Smoky Mountains National Park.
M760 (WCU)
Fishing in the Great Smoky Mountains National Park and Adjacent Waters.
M3090
The Lure of the Great Smokies.
M4030
The Lure of the Great Smokies.
M4040 (ASU LMC WCU ETSU WWC BC)
Tall Tales from Old Smoky.
M4210 (ASU LMC BC ETSU)
Valhalla in the Smokies.
M4580 (ETSU ASU BC)
Great Smoky Mountain Stories and Sun over Ol' Starlin.
M4850 (LMC WCU)
Hiker's Guide to the Smokies.
M9070 (ASU LMC WCU)
Appalachian Wilderness: The Great Smoky Mountains.
P3600 (UNCA BC ASU WCU ETSU)
Appalachian Wilderness: The Great Smoky Mountains.
P3610 (ASU BC)
Gatlinburg and the Great Smokies.
P4970
The Great Smoky Mountains National Park.
R560 (ASU)
In the Arms of the Mountain: An Intimate Journal of the Great Smokies.
S1710 (ASU WCU LMC ETSU BC)
Great Smoky Mountains National Park, North Carolina and Tennessee.
S8840 (ASU LMC WCU ETSU)
Trees, Shrubs, and Woody Vines of Great Smoky Mountains National Park.
S8870 (ASU WCU LMC WWC UNCA)
Trees, Shrubs, and Woody Vines of Great Smoky Mountains National Park.
S8880
A National Park in the Great Smoky Mountains.
S9380
Joint Legislative Committee Report on the Great Smoky Mountains and Other Areas for a National or State Park.
T1400
The Great Smoky Mountains.
T8360 (ASU WCU LMC WWC UNCA)
The Great Smoky Mountains.
T8370 (WCU LMC BC ETSU)
The Great Smoky Mountains.
T8380 (ETSU)
Cherokee Landmarks Around the Great Smokies.
W6100 (LMC)

GREAT SMOKY MOUNTAINS — DESCRIPTION AND TRAVEL
Roamin' with the Roamin' Men of the Smoky Mountains.
O30 (ASU LMC BC)

GREAT SMOKY MOUNTAINS NATIONAL PARK
N2790 (MHC ASU)

GREEN RIVER
Bibliography of the Green River Valley.
J1120

GUNS — KENTUCKY RIFLES
Thoughts on the Kentucky Rifle in its Golden Age.
K2210 (ASU)

GUNS — KY. RIFLES
Recreating the Kentucky Rifle.
B7990 (ASU BC)

GUNS — LONG RIFLES — KY.
The Kentucky Rifle: A Study of the Origin and Development of a Purely American Type of Firearm, Together with Accurate Historical Data Concerning Early Colonial Gunsmiths and Profusely Illustrated with Photographic Reproduction of Their Finest Work.
D2430 (LMC BC)
The Kentucky Rifle.
D2440 (ASU MHC BC)

GUNS — LONGRIFLES
Longrifles of North Carolina.
B4280 (ASU LMC BC)
Recreating the Kentucky Rifle.
B7990 (ASU BC)
The Pennsylvania-Kentucky Rifle.
K240 (BC LMC ASU)

GUYANDOT RIVER
"The Transformation of the Tug and Guyandot Valleys: Economic Development and Social Change in West Virginia, 1888-1921."
C9390

HANDICRAFTS
Natural Dyes and Home Dyeing.
A620 (BC ASU WCU)
A2750
"Some Recent Contributions of the Cherokee Indians of North Carolina to the Crafts of the Southern Highlands."
A4820 (ASU ETSU)
Shuttlecraft Book of American Handweaving.
A5460 (BC)
American Patchwork Quilts.
B70 (ASU)
The Art of Hooked-rug Making.
B1880 (LMC)
The Moravian Potters in North Carolina.
B4290 (LMC)
Kentucky Coverlets.
B5660 (BC)
Homespun Handicrafts.
B5710 (BC)
The Magic of Spinning.
C2940 (ASU WCU)
Basketry.
C4020 (ASU WCU)
Common Clay.
C7980 (LMC ASU WCU)
Encouraging American Craftsmen.
C7990 (WCU LMC ASU)
Encouraging American Handcrafts: What Role in Economic Development?
C8000 (LMC)
Pottery Workshop: A Study in the Making of Pottery from Idea to Finished Form.
C8010 (WCU)
"Glass Production Processes of the Kanawha Valley Area."
C8070 (ASU)
The Dye-Pot.
D680
A Handweaver's Pattern Book.
D1290 (ASU BC)
A Handweaver's Source Book; A Selection of 224 Patterns from the Laura M. Allen Collection.
D1300
Pennsylvania German Home Weaving.
D1310
Artisans of the Appalachians.
D4040 (ASU WCU LMC MHC WWC BC)
Handicrafts of the Southern Highlands: With an Account of the Rural Handicraft Movement in the United States and Suggestions for the Wider Use of Handicrafts in Adult Education and in Recreation.
E560 (ASU WCU LMC MHC WWC ETSU BC)
References on the Handicrafts of the Southern Highlands.
E1000 (BC)
References on the Mountaineers of the Southern Appalachians.
E1010
References on the Mountaineers of the Southern Appalachians.
E1020 (BC ETSU LMC ASU)
Handspinning: Art and Technique.
F90 (LMC)
Old Patchwork Quilts and the Women Who Made Them.
F1040 (BC)
The Story of the Penland Weavers.
F1880 (ASU BC)

HANDICRAFTS
Pattern in the Material Folk Culture of the Eastern United States.
G2080 (ASU BC WCU LMC FC)
Complete Guide to Hand Spinning, Teasing, Carding, Spinning.
G3280 (ASU)
Patchwork for Beginners.
G3660 (ASU)
The Romance of the Patchwork Quilt in America: In Three Parts.
H590 (ASU BC)
Mountain People, Mountain Crafts.
H7320 (ASU)
The Standard Book of Quilt Making and Collecting.
I30 (ASU BC)
Weaving as a Hobby.
I40 (BC ASU)
Loom-fixing and Weaving; A Book for All Who Are Interested in Such Matters.
I1010
Indian Basketry.
J340
One Hundred and One Patchwork Patterns: Quilt Name Stories, Cutting Designs, Material Suggestions, Yardage Estimates, Definite Instructions for Every Step of Quilt Making.
M1880 (ASU WCU BC)
Gift from the Hills: Miss Lucy Morgan's Story of Her Unique Penland School.
M7620 (ASU BC ETSU FC WCU WWC)
The Knox County Economic Opportunity Council Anti-Poverty Arts and Crafts.
M9080
Inkle.
N390
Potential Earning Power of Southern Mountaineer Handicraft.
N1020 (BC)
Artistry in Quilts.
N2470 (ASU)
Potential Earning Power of Southern Mountaineer Handicrafts.
N2990
A Book of Handwoven Coverlits.
O60 (BC)
O680 (ASU)
Catalog.
P1720 (ETSU)
Seat Weaving.
P2250
American Quilts and Coverlets; A History of a Charming Native Art.
P2390
How to Make Whirligigs and Whimmy Diddles and Other American Folkcraft Objects.
P2450
Dictionary of Weaves; a Collection of All Weaves from Four to Nine Harness.
P3770 (BC)
American Potters and Pottery.
R230 (BC)
Mountain Artisans: An Exhibit of Patchwork and Quilting, Appalachia.
R1820 (BC)
The Shenandoah Pottery.
R1890 (ASU BC)
Dyes from Plants.
R3170 (ASU)
America's Quilts and Coverlets.
S70 (ASU)
America's Quilts and Coverlets.
S80 (ASU)
Old Fashioned Quilts.
S2060
The Origins and Characteristics of Folk Art in West Virginia.
S2450
Introducing Quilting.
S3180 (ASU)
Arts and Crafts of the Shenandoah Valley.
S4610 (ASU BC FC)
Confrontation with the Arts: The Arts in Education — What? For Whom? How? A Symposium Held at Western Carolina University, March 6-7, 1969.
S5230 (ASU WCU)
Crafts in the Southern Highlands.
S5750 (BC ASU)
Crafts in the Southern Highlands.
S5760
Vanishing Crafts and Their Craftsmen.
S6940 (ASU)
A Weavin' Woman.
S7110 (LMC)
Whittling and Woodcarving.
T160 (ASU)
Apple and Doughhead Dollmaking: Clothes Patterns Included.
T520 (WCU)
Crafts in the Southern Highlands.
W1980

HANDICRAFTS — APP.
C8350 (WCU ASU)
Mountain Homespun.
G2610 (ASU WCU LMC MHC ETSU BC WWC)
A Handbook and Resource Guide for New Craft Groups.
H8040
"Chairmaking in Appalachia: A Study in Style and Creative Imagination in American Folk Art."
J2520 (ASU)
Four-Harness Huck.
N380
The Golden Age of Homespun.
V400 (ASU)
Home Industries and Domestic Weavings.
W5100

HANDICRAFTS — CHEROKEE
. . . Decorative Art and Basketry of the Cherokee.
S6100 (ASU)

HANDICRAFTS — GA.
"Georgia Jug Makers: A History of Southern Folk Pottery."
B9190
The Foxfire Book: Hog Dressing; Log Cabin Building; Mountain Crafts and Foods; Planting by the Signs; Snake Lore, Hunting Tales, Faith Healing; Moonshining; and Other Affairs of Plain Living.
W6020 (FC ASU BC)
Foxfire 2: Ghost Stories, Spring Wild Plant Foods, Spinning and Weaving, Midwifing, Burial Customs, Corn Shuckin's, Wagon Making and More Affairs of Plain Living.
W6030 (FC ASU BC)
Foxfire 3: Animal Care, Banjos and Dulcimers, Hide Tanning, Summer and Fall Wildplant Foods, Butter Churns, Ginseng, and Still More Affairs of Plain Living.
W6040 (ASU)

HANDICRAFTS — INDIAN
Sun Circles and Human Hands: The Southeastern Indians Art and Industries.
F3830 (ASU MHC WCU BC)

HANDICRAFTS — KY.
The Development of Kentucky's Handicraft Industry.
E2380

HANDICRAFTS — N. C.
The Arts and Crafts in North Carolina, 1699-1840.
C8380 (ASU LMC MHC BC)
Jugtown Pottery: History and Design.
C8600 (ASU LMC MHC BC)
Gift from the Hills: Miss Lucy Morgan's Story of Unique Penland School.
M7630
North Carolina Museum of History, Raleigh.
N2010 (ASU)

HANDICRAFTS — TENN.
"Handicrafts in Sevier County, Tennessee."
H6180 (ASU)

HANDICRAFTS — W. VA.
Economic Impact of the Mountain State Art and Craft Fair, Ripley, West Virginia, 1964.
H50
Mountain Heritage.
M4410
Mountain Heritage, Mountain State Art and Craft Fair Cedar Lakes.
M4420
"The Revival of the Folk Arts in West Virginia."
R420 (ASU LMC)

HEALTH
"Tuberculosis in Eastern Kentucky."
A820 (ASU)
Health Development Plan — 1969, Morgan, Lawrence, Limestone Counties, Alabama.
A930 (ASU)
Health Development Plan — 1970, Morgan, Lawrence, Limestone Counties.
A940 (ASU)
Regional Health Demonstration Project, Phase 2, Morgan, Lawrence, Limestone Counties, Ala.
A950 (ASU)
A2770 (ASU)
Immunization Cooperation in Southwest Virginia.
B60
Wide Neighborhoods: A Story of the Frontier Nursing Service.
B6450 (ASU BC LMC MHC WCU WWC)
"A Literature Survey of the Effects and Controls of Pneumoconiosis."
C100
Health and Nutrition in Disadvantaged Children.
C1700
Southern Home Remedies.
C3920 (BC ASU)
Coal Mine Health and Safety; the Case of West Virginia.
M110 (BC)
Coal Mining Health and Safety in West Virginia.
M120
Resources of the Southern Fields and Forests, Medical, Economical, and Agricultural. Being Also a Medical Botany of the Confederate States.
P3590 (LMC BC)
"Anxiety in Coal Miners."
R1680
The Nutrition and Care of Children in a Mountain County of Kentucky.
R3000
Federal Coal Mine Health and Safety Act of 1969. Report Together with Minority, Supplemental, and Separate Views from the Committee to Accompany H. R. 13950, October 13, 1969.
U2280
Legislative History: Federal Coal Mine Health and Safety Act.
U2290
Coal Mine Health and Safety. Hearings before the Subcommittee on H. R. 4047, H. R. 4295, and H. R. 7976, March 4-May 1, 1969.
U2300
Federal Coal Mine Health and Safety Act of 1969. Report from the Committee Together with Individual Views to Accompany S. 2917, September 17, 1969.
U2330
Coal Mine Health and Safety. Hearings before the Subcommittee on S. 355, S. 467, S. 1094, S. 1178, S. 1300, and S. 1907, February 27-May 2, 1969.
U2340
Malaria Control on Impounded Water.
U3880

HEALTH — APP.
A2770 (ASU)
Report to the Appalachian Regional Commission.
A3970 (ASU)
A Model Rural Non-profit Health Care System.
A4000 (ASU)
C4150 (WCU)
Health Care Services and Facilities in the Southern Appalachian Region.
C7930 (BC)
Health Careers in the Appalachian South.
C7940 (BC)
Bubbling Waters.
F1070 (ASU LMC BC)
"Health, Education, and Income as Correlates of Demand for Hospital Care in the Southern Mountains."
G1100
Health and Health Services in the Southern Appalachians, a Source Book.
H1090 (ASU ETSU)
Southern Home Remedies.
H2650 (AASU LMC)
The Case Against Hunger: A Demand for a National Policy.
H6670
An Analysis of Appalachian State Coal Mine Health and Safety and Workmen's Compensation Programs: Recommendations for Improvement.
K880 (ASU)

HEALTH — APP.
Pneumoconiosis in Appalachian Bituminous Coal Miners.
L140 (ASU)
"Severity of Malocclusion Found in Children of Appalachian Heritage Compared with Children of Non-Appalachian Heritage."
M3250
Appalachian Regional Hospitals.
N1430
Appalachia: Realities of Deprivation.
P60
Nurses on Horseback.
P3530 (ASU ETSU LMC BC WWC)
We Made Peace with Polio.
R3310 (ASU)
R4310 (ASU BC)
S3860
Society and Health in a Mountain Community: A Working Paper.
S4720 (ASU)
Health Development Plan — 1970.
S5570 (ASU)
Health & Health Service in the Southern Appalachians, a Source Book.
S5660
"Comparative Study of Related Health Fertility Attitudes and Behavior of Families Residing in a Poverty Area."
S6190
Patterns of Adaptation in a Changing Mountain Community; Stress and Health.
S7060 (BC)
Trachoma in Eastern Kentucky.
S8780
. . . Community Health and Safety Series no. 1.
T5340
Malaria and Its Control in the Tennessee Valley.
T5360
Malaria and Its Control in the Tennessee Valley.
T5370
Malaria Control: 1. How the Community Can Help. An Office of War Information Reprint of the Tennessee Valley Authority Booklet.
T5380
Malaria, the Story of an Individual Problem and a Community Problem.
T5400
Prediction of Stream Reaeration Rates.
T5410
Quality of Water in Chickamauga Reservoir.
T5420
Report.
T5430
Significant Developments in TVA's Malaria Control Program Through 1947.
T5440
Surface Water Quality in the Chestuee Creek Watershed.
T5480
TVA; the Health of a Region.
T5500
Annual Report. 1969/70-.
T6540
Report to Council of the Southern Mountains on Health Care Services and Facilities in the Southern Appalachian Region.
T9850 (ETSU)
A medical survey of the bituminous-coal industry.
U1620
Consumer Protection and Environmental Health Service
U2750
A Medical Survey of the Bituminous-coal Industry.
U2850 (LMC)
Alleghany, Ashe, Watauga Planning Project for Handicapped Children, ESEA Title III.
W1360 (WCU)
Newsletter.
W4945 (BC)
Doctor Woman of the Cumberlands: The Autobiography of May Cravath Wharton, M. D.
W5020 (ASU LMC WWC BC)
Doctor Woman of the Cumberlands; the Autobiography of May Cravath Wharton, M. D.
W5030 (LMC WCU)
Frontier Nurse: Mary Breckenridge.
W6290 (ASU LMC BC)
"Income and Health in Remote Rural Areas: A Study of Four Hundred Families in Leslie County, Kentucky."
W6350
Mine Eyes Have Seen: A Woman Doctor's Saga.
W7970 (WWC BC)

HEALTH — APP. — COAL FIELDS
Medical Care in Selected Areas of the Appalachian Bituminous Coal Fields.
B8500
Medical-Hospital Problems in the Bituminous Coal Mining Areas.
B8510

HEALTH — APP. — HOSPITALS
Evolution of a Model Rural Non-profit Health Care System, 1963-1973.
A3990 (ASU)

HEALTH — CHEROKEE
The Cherokee Physician . . . As Given by Richard Foreman.
M2830

HEALTH — COAL CAMPS
"Earnings, Health, Safety, and Welfare of Bituminous Coal Miners Since the Encouragement of Mechanization by the United Mine Workers of America."
D610

HEALTH EDUCATION
Health Development Plan — 1969, Morgan, Lawrence, Limestone Counties, Alabama.
A930 (ASU)
Health Development Plan — 1970, Morgan, Lawrence, Limestone Counties.
A940 (ASU)
Regional Health Demonstration Project, Phase 2, Morgan, Lawrence, Limestone Counties, Ala.
A950 (ASU)
Immunization Cooperation in Southwest Virginia.
B60

HEALTH EDUCATION — GA.
Use of Health Care Services and Enrollment in Voluntary Health Insurance in Habersham County, Georgia, 1957.
B2690

HEALTH — GA.
Use of Health Care Services and Enrollment in Voluntary Health Insurance in Habersham County, Georgia, 1957.
B2690
Basic Health Needs and Resources in the Upper Hiwassee Development Association Area.
S5880 (WCU)
. . . Maternity and Infant Care in a Mountain County in Georgia.
S6750 (BC)
Bureau publication No. 120 Steete, Glenn. Maternity and infant care in a mountain county in Georgia.
U1600
U4230

HEALTH — KY.
Coal Workers' Pneumoconisosis: Workmen's Compensation Treatment and Its Prevention in Kentucky.
C3550 (ASU)
Trends in the Number and Distribution of Medical Doctors in Kentucky.
C4010
Child Welfare in Kentucky.
C5110 (ASU)
Poverty, Politics, and Health Care: An Appalachian Experience.
C8060 (ASU)
"Patterns of Response to Rural Medical Practice and Rural Life in Eastern Kentucky."
E2030
Health and Demography in Kentucky.
F2000 (LMC BC)
Quarterly Bulletin.
F3500 (ASU BC)
Thirty Years Onward. Frontier N. S., 1925-1955.
F3510 (BC ASU)
Today, Yesterday and Tomorrow.
F3520 (BC)
"Environmental School Sanitation of an Eastern Kentucky County."
J2650
"A Study of the Opinions of the Various Classes of People Toward Pike County's Medical Facilities."
J2960
Rural Family Health in a Selected County in Kentucky.
M4000
Nurses in Time.
P1520
Annual Report.
P2920 (BC)
"A Cultural Comparison of Schizophrenia in Mountain Rural and Metropolitan Kentucky."
Q140
Southeastern Kentucky Regional Health Demonstration Project.
S5610 (ASU)
Southeastern Kentucky Regional Health Demonstration Project.
S5620 (ASU)
Health Development Plan for Year, 1968-69.
S5630 (ASU)
Southeastern Kentucky Regional Health Demonstration Project. Health Development Plan for Year 1969-70.
S5640 (ASU)
Trachoma in Eastern Kentucky.
S8780
The Nutrition and Care of Children in a Mountain County in Kentucky.
U1610
Income and Health in Remote Rural Areas; a Study of 400 Families in Leslie County, Ky.
W6360 (BC)
The Frontier Nursing Service.
W7780 (BC)

HEALTH — MIDWIVES
Folks Do Get Born.
C730 (BC)

HEALTH — N. C.
Acceptance of Voluntary Health Insurance in Four Rural Communities of Haywood County, North Carolina.
H3790
Asheville, Western North Carolina, Nature's Trundle-Bed of Recuperation for Tourist and Health-beds.
H4370
Miracle in the Mountains.
K140 (ASU LMC MHC WCU WWC FC BC)
"Social Change, Adaptive Problems, and Health in a Mountain Community."
K190 (LMC ASU)
Biennial report.
N1690 (ASU LMC)
A History of the North Carolina State Board of Health, 1877-1925.
N1700 (LMC)
Watauga County Reception and Care Plan.
N1720 (ASU)
Jackson County: Operational Survival Plan.
N1790 (WCU)
Biennial Report.
N2580 (LMC)
A Country Doctor Goes to Town.
R1200 (ASU)
Miracle in the Hills.
S4230 (ASU WCU LMC WWC BC)
Medicine in Buncombe County Down to 1885, Historical and Biographical Sketches.
T880
Rates study for water supply and sewage disposal at Cherokee Indian Agency, Cherokee, North Carolina.
U1250
Report on water and sewerage facilities at Cherokee and Soco Valley, North Carolina.
U1260
A Country Doctor in the South Mountains.
W1000 (ASU LMC MHC BC)
Rutherford County and Its Hospital.
W1010 (BC)

HEALTH — OHIO — APP. REGION
Ohio Appalachia Health Development Plan, 1970.
O440 (ASU)

HEALTH — SPAS
The Mineral Springs of Virginia.
B8760
The Mineral Springs of Western Virginia: with Remarks on Their Use, and The Diseases to Which They are Applicable.
B8770
The Valley Road.
I770 (ASU BC FC)

HEALTH — SPAS
Historical Sketches of Virginia, Hot Springs, Warm Sulphur Springs and Bath County.
M90 (BC)
HEALTH SPAS — APP.
Bubbling Waters.
F1070 (ASU LMC BC)
HEALTH SPAS — VA.
The Springs of Virginia: Life, Love and Death at the Waters, 1775-1900.
R1470 (ASU FC)
HEALTH SPAS — W. VA.
The White Sulfur Springs: The Traditions, History, and Social Life of the Greenbriar, White Sulfur Springs.
M610 (ASU BC)
White Sulphur Springs, a Brief History.
T700 (ASU)
HEALTH — TENN.
"A Study of Health Instruction in Selected High Schools in Washington County, Tennessee."
D900 (ETSU)
The Medicinal Plants of Tennessee Exhibiting Their Commercial Value, with an Analytical Key, Descriptions in Aid of Their Recognition, and Notes Relating to Their Distribution, Time and Mode of Collection, and Preparation for the Drug Market.
G610
A Doctor's Pilgrimage.
H1070
"A Survey of the Problems of Freshmen Student Nurses at Memorial Hospital and a Proposed Guidance Program."
J1650 (ETSU)
The Knoxville Area Diet Manual.
K2900 (ETSU)
"A Proposed Health Instruction Program for Upper Elementary Grades Adaptable to Carter County."
R1730 (ETSU)
Basic Health Needs and Resources in the Upper Hiwassee Development Association Area.
S5880 (WCU)
"A Tentative Health Instruction Program for the Secondary Schools of Carter County, Tennessee."
T480 (ETSU)
Health and Sanitation Needs and Resources, Bradley County, Tennessee.
T9400
"Development of the Health Program for Negroes in Franklin County, Tennessee from 1940-1953."
W5820
HEALTH — TENNESSEE VALLEY AUTHORITY
Malaria Control in the Tennessee Valley.
T5390
HEALTH — VA.
Medicine in Virginia in the Seventeenth Century.
B4660
The Mineral Springs of Virginia.
B8760
The Mineral Springs of Western Virginia: with Remarks on Their Use, and The Diseases to Which They are Applicable.
B8770
A Country Doctor Goes to Town.
R1200 (ASU)
Hollow Folk.
S2940 (BC LMC ETSU WWC)
Hollow Folk.
S2950 (ASU)
HEALTH — W. VA.
A Half-Century of Nursing in West Virginia: The History of the West Virginia State Nurses' Association 1907-1957.
B5230 (ASU)
The Annals of Pharmacy in West Virginia.
C6880 (ASU)
"Food Habits of a Selected Group of Pupils in the Wellsbury High School, West Virginia."
C6920
The Saga of the Country Doctor Among the W. Va. Hills.
F230 (BC)
Health, Welfare, and Housing Needs of the Aged in Berkeley County, West Virginia.
S1320
Training Program for Auxiliary Health and Education Personnel in Nine Counties of Southern West Virginia.
T9150 (ASU)
Early Teachers in W. Va. Univ. School of Medicine, 1869-1922.
V330
Report.
W3560 (BC)
"Food Habits of a Sample of University High School Students."
W5660
"Food Habits of the Pupils in Monongahela and Dunbar (West Virginia) High School Whose Parents are Engaged in Coal Mining."
W6500
HIGHWAYS
C1180
Evaluating Appalachian Woods for Highway Posts.
D3200
Highway Accessibility Study for the Appalachian Development Highway System.
P4400
Highway Transportation and Appalachian Development: The Impact and Costs of the Appalachian Development Highway System
P4410 (ETSU LMS ASU)
Economic Impact of Secondary Road Improvements.
S8150
Johnson City Transportation Study: Major Route Plan. Traffic Operation Study and Parking Study.
T1220 (ETSU)
Study on Automobile Junk Yard and Highway Beautification 1964; A Final Report.
T1450
HIGHWAYS — APP.
The Appalachian Thruway Study.
R4420
"The Economic Effects of the Original Section of the Pennsylvania Turnpike on Adjacent Areas."
S2560
Appalachian Highway Corridor D-E Impact Study. Final Report.
S9140
Highway Program Shows Limited Progress toward Increasing Accessibility to and through Appalachia: Report to the Congress on the Appalachian Regional Commission by the Comptroller General of the United States.
U3060
HIGHWAYS — APP. DEVELOPMENT HIGHWAY SYSTEM
"A Plan Formulation Methodology for the Appalachian Development Highway System."
M140
HIGHWAYS — GA.
A Preliminary Major Highway Plan, A Part of the Georgia Mountains Region Development Program.
T9130
HIGHWAYS — KY.
Boone's Wilderness Road.
H5320
Remarks by Lawrence Jones, Deputy Federal Highway Administrator.
U1570
HIGHWAYS — PA.
The Impact of Interchange Development on the Economy of Clinton County.
G210
HIGHWAYS — TENN.
Tenn. Historical Markers.
T1510
HIGHWAYS — VA.
New Roads in Old Virginia.
R3920 (LMC)
V1050 (BC)
HIGHWAYS — W. VA.
The Impact of Highway Beautification on the Outdoor Advertising Industry in West Virginia.
C1680
"The Economic Impact of Highway Beautification on the Outdoor Advertising Industry in West Virginia."
S9280
Public Facility Location Determinations and Impact of New Highway Investment on Accessibility Changes in a Specified Subregion of W. Va.
V310
Annual Report.
W4400 (BC)
General Highway Maps.
W4410 (BC)
West Virginia Historic and Scenic Highway Markers.
W4420 (BC)
"Cost Estimating Model for Identifying Gross Dollar Needs for West Virginia Highways."
W5810
HIKING
Mt. LeConte.
A440 (LMC ETSU)
Mt. LeConte.
A450 (WCU ASU)
A2640 (ASU)
A2670 (ASU)
Annual Report.
A3260
Suggestions as to Outfit for Tramping and Camping.
A3290
The Appalachian Trail.
A4120
The Appalachian Trail: A Mountain Footpath — A National Scenic Trail.
A4130 (LMC ETSU)
The Appalachian Trail.
A4140 (ETSU)
The Appalachian Trail: A Footpath Through the Wilderness for More Than 2,000 Miles from Katahdin in Maine to Springer Mountain in Georgia.
A4150 (ASU)
The Appalachian Trail: A Mountain Footpath, a National Scenic Trail.
A4160 (ASU)
Appalachian Trail Conference, Undertaking the Appalachian Trail (A Mountain Foot-path from Maine to Georgia. . . .
A4170 (ASU)
Guide to the Appalachian Trail in Central and Southwestern Virginia.
A4180 (BC LMC ASU)
Guide to the Appalachian Trail in the Great Smokies, the Nantahalas, and Georgia.
A4190 (LMC BC)
Guide to the Appalachian Trail in the Great Smokies, the Nantahalas, and Georgia.
A4200 (ASU BC)
Guide to the Appalachian Trail in the Great Smokies, the Nantahalas, and Georgia.
A4210 (ASU)
Guide to the Appalachian Trail in Maine. . .
A4220
Guide to the Appalachian Trail in Maine; the Route of the Appalachian Trail in Maine. . .
A4230
Guide to the Appalachian Trail in Maine. . .
A4240
Guide to the Appalachian Trail in the Southern Appalachians.
A4250 (ASU BC)
Guide to the Appalachian Trail in the Southern Appalachians.
A4260 (ASU)
Guide to the Appalachian Trail in the Southern Appalachians.
A4270 (ASU)
Guide to the Appalachian Trail in Tennessee and North Carolina, Cherokee, Pisgah, and the Great Smokies.
A4280 (LMC)
Guide to the Appalachian Trail in Tennessee and North Carolina: Cherokee, Pisgah, and Great Smokies.
A4290
Guide to the Appalachian Trail in Tennessee and North Carolina, Cherokee, Pisgah, and Great Smokies.
A4300 (ETSU)
Guide to the Appalachian Trail in Tennessee and North Carolina, Cherokee, Pisgah, and Great Smokies.
A4310 (ASU)
Guide to the Southern Appalachians. The Appalachian Trail from Virginia-Tennessee Line to Mt. Oglethorpe, Ga.
A4320 (ASU BC)
Plans for an Appalachian Trail Lean-to. . .
A4330 (ASU)
Suggestions for Appalachian Trail Users.
A4340
Suggestions for Appalachian Trail Users.
A4350

HIKING
Suggestions for Appalachian Trail Users.
A4360
Trail Manual for the Appalachian Trail.
A4370 (ASU)
Trail Manual for the Appalachian Trail.
A4380
Trail Manual for the Appalachian Trail.
A4390 (ASU)
Trail Manual for Appalachian Trail.
A4400
Trail Manual for the Appalachian Trail.
A4410
Campfires Along the Appalachian Trail.
B650 (ASU LMC WCU BC)
The Blue Ridge Boys; Narrations of Early Actual Mountain Experiences and Humorous Anecdotes of the Shenandoah National Park Section.
B2400 (BC)
C1000 (BC)
Outdoors in the Cumberlands.
C9450 (BC)
Jessie's Children.
F2120 (LMC)
Appalachian Hiker: Adventure of a Lifetime.
G520 (BC ASU WCU ETSU)
G4650
G4660
G4670
G4680
G4690
G4700
G4710
G4720
G4730
G4740
G4750
G4760
Hiker's Guide to the Smokies.
M9070 (ASU LMC WCU)
Guide to the Appalachian Trail in New York and New Jersey.
N680 (ASU)
Roamin' with the Roamin' Men of the Smoky Mountains.
O30 (ASU LMC BC)
Guide to Paths in the Blue Ridge: The Appalachian Trail and Side Trails in Southern Pennsylvania, Maryland, and Virginia.
P3820 (ASU)
Guide to Paths in the Blue Ridge: The Appalachian Trail and Side Trails in Southern Pennsylvania, Maryland, and Virginia.
P3830 (ASU)
Guide to the Appalachian Trail and Side Trails in the Shenandoah National Park.
P3840 (ETSU)
Guide to the Appalachian Trail: From the Susquehanna River to the Shenandoah National Park.
P3850 (WCU ETSU LMC)
Guide to the Appalachian Trail in Central and Southwestern Virginia.
P3860
Guide to the Appalachian Trail: Susquehanna River to the Shenandoah National Park.
P3870
Guide to Trails in the Shenandoah National Park: The Appalachian Trail and Side Trails.
P3880
Hiking, Camping, Mountaineering and Trailclearing Equipment.
P3890 (ASU)
The Backpacker. A Pocket-size Manual Which Deals with All Aspects of Backpacking. Covers Equipment, Food, Getting Organized for Your Trip, and Takes the Reader on a Sample Trip Through the Mountains.
S140
Hiker's Guide.
S5430 (ASU)
The Appalachian Trail: Wilderness on the Doorstep.
S9310 (ASU WCU LMC ETSU FC WWC UNCA BC)

HISTORIC HOMES
Historic Homes of the South-west Mountains, Virginia.
M4730 (ASU BC ETSU LMC)

HISTORIC HOMES — N. C.
The Early Architecture of North Carolina: A Pictorial Survey.
J2030 (ASU MHC LMC)
Sketches of Early Watauga.
M1340 (ASU)

HISTORIC HOMES — TENN.
Landmarks of Tennessee History.
A1290
Historical Forts and Houses in Knoxville and Nearby Vicinity.
R4450

HISTORIC HOMES — VA.
Colonial History of Nelson County, 1734-1807.
C5620 (ASU)
Old Virginia Houses.
F240 (FC)
Fredericksburg, Virginia. Its Homes and History, the Battlefields and the Rappahanrock Valley.
G2650
Old Homes of Page County, Virginia.
K1580
Architecture in Virginia: An Official Guide to Four Centuries of Building in the Old Dominion.
O710 (ASU)
The Story of One Hundred Old Homes in Winchester, Virginia.
Q90
Old Houses in Rockingham County, 1750-1850.
T7610 (ASU WCU)
State Historical Markers of Virginia.
V720
Legends of Loudoun: An Account of the History and Homes of a Border County of Virginia's Northern Neck.
W6560 (ASU BC)

HISTORIC HOMES — W. VA.
Greenbrier Pioneers and Their Homes.
D1420
Lewisburg Landmarks.
D1430 (ASU BC)
Pioneers and Their Homes on Upper Kanawha.
D1440 (ASU BC)
Our House.
E840 (ASU)
The Washington Homes of Jefferson County, West Virginia.
F30 (WCU)

HISTORY
West of Suez.
W510 (ASU BC)
Freedom on the Mountains.
W2930
People's Cultural Heritage in Appalachia.
W2950
Freedom and Slavery in Appalachian America.
W8860

HISTORY — ALA.
History of Marion County, Alabama.
M3220

HISTORY — CIVIL WAR
The End of an Era.
W7910 (BC)

HISTORY — KY.
Family History Records of Dr. Thomas Walker, First Explorer of Kentucky.
B9040

HISTORY — MD.
Copy of a Correspondence Between Governor Thomas, of Maryland, and Governor Tazewell, of Virginia, in Relation to the Unsettled Divisional Boundary Lines Between the Two States.
M3920 (ASU)

HISTORY — N. C., WESTERN
Regional Sketches.
N2710 (WCU)

HISTORY — VA.
Copy of a Correspondence Between Governor Thomas, of Maryland, and Governor Tazewell, of Virginia, in Relation to the Unsettled Divisional Boundary Lines Between the Two States.
M3920 (ASU)
V1100 (LMC)

HISTORY — W. VA.
"The Negro in West Virginia Before 1900."
S2610

HIWASSEE RIVER
Economic Base Study and Survey of Basic Services for the Hiwassee River Watershed Development Association.
F2220 (BC)
Lower Hiwassee Valley; Summary of Resources.
T3020
Floods on Hiwassee River, Valley River, and Peachtree Creek in Vicinity of Murphy, N C.
T7070

HOLSTON RIVER
Report of the Conference, 2D Kingsport, Tennessee, 1962.
C6390
Frontier Forts along the Clinch, Powell and Holston.
H1130 (BC)
Historical Sketches of the Holston Valleys.
P4440 (ASU WCU LMC ETSU BC)
The French-Broad Holston Country: A History of Knox County, Tennessee.
R3940 (LMC BC)
The French Broad-Holston Country: A History of Knox County, Tennessee.
R3950 (ETSU)
Kingsport, Tennessee: Historical Map of Long Island of the Holston.
S6300
Forest Inventory Statistics — Holston River Tributary Area, East Tennessee and Southwest Virginia.
T4690
Hitch Hiking Along the Holston River from 1792-1962.
W8600

HOME ECONOMICS — APP.
Appalachian Resource Development Project, Submitted to the Kellogg Foundation.
K1390

HOME ECONOMICS — KY.
I860

HOME ECONOMICS — W. VA.
Adventures in Good Living.
H8330 (ASU BC)

HOSPITALS — APP.
Appalachian Regional Hospitals.
N1430

HOUSING
"Tuberculosis in Eastern Kentucky."
A820 (ASU)
A Study of Potential State and Local Programs to Stimulate Low- and Moderate-income Housing Construction in Ohio Appalachia. Supplement.
B1930 (ASU)
Status of Rural Housing in the United States.
B4120
Sugar Creek Resettlement Area, Leslie County, Kentucky. A Report of a Conference on Planned Relocation, New Housing and Local Employment in Eastern Kenucky, 1966.
G1040
The Rural Land Classification Program; a Summary of Techniques and Uses Submitted by G. Donald Hudson, Chief, Land Classification Section, Division of Land Planning and Housing, Tennessee Valley Authority.
T5860
Homes for Mountaineers.
W4020
Homes for Mountaineers.
W4030

HOUSING — APP.
H7490
A Summary of a Study of Potential State and Local Programs to Stimulate Low and Moderate-income Housing Construction in Ohio Appalachia.
O370 (ASU)
Quality of Rural and Urban Housing in the Appalachian Region.
P1050 (LMC)
Selected Rural Counties in Appalachia.
U850
Appalachian Housing Assistance.
U2760

HOUSING — GA.
"Geographic Analysis of Single Dwelling Settlement in Northeast Georgia."
B5110 (LMC BC ASU)

HOUSING — KY.

Recent Home Construction in Two Appalachian Counties.
F790

A Survey of Low-Cost Housing in Carter County, Kentucky.
L2850 (ASU)

Kentucky Housing Fund: A Housing Proposal for the Commonwealth of Kentucky. Prospectus and Final Report to the Appalachian Regional Commission.
U4190

HOUSING — N. C.

A Demonstration Program in Rural Housing: An Area-wide Housing Organization in the Northwest Local Development District.
A4880

Tri-county Housing: A Multi-county Response to Housing Problems.
A4890

HOUSING — PA.

Housing Conditions in Rural Pennsylvania.
W7760

HOUSING — TENN.

The Tennessee River Valley; a Case Study.
G3320

Houses at Norris, Tennessee; a Review of Costs.
T5850

HOUSING — W. VA.

West Virginia Housing. A Consultant's Report to the Governor's Task Force on Housing and the West Virginia State Development Plan.
G30
H7490

West Virginia Housing, Considerations for Planning and Programming.
M1860

Economic Analysis and Feasibility Study of Proposed Transient Facilities at East River Mountain, Mercer County, West Virginia.
R810

Health, Welfare, and Housing Needs of the Aged in Berkeley County, West Virginia.
S1320

West Virginia Housing Development Fund: A Housing Proposal for the State of West Virginia. Prospectus and Final Report.
U4200

HUMOR

Kentucky Mayor: The Humor and Philosophy of John Edwin Garner.
C2610 (BC)

Ring-tailed Roarers: Tall Tales of the American Frontier, 1830-60.
C3900 (ASU)

Gunpowder Creek Philosophy.
C4800 (BC)

The Adventures of Davy Crockett: Told Mostly by Himself.
C8890 (ASU)

The Adventures of Davy Crockett, Told Mostly by Himself.
C8900

Davy Crockett's Own Story as Written by Himself; the Autobiography of America's Great Folk Hero.
C8950

Life of David Crockett, the Original Humorist and Irrepressible Backwoodsman, Comprising His Early History: His Bear Hunting and Other Adventures, His Services in the Creek War. His Electioneering Speeches and Career in Congress. With His Triumphal Tour Through the Northern States and Services in the Texan War. To Which Is Added an Account of His Glorious Death at the Alamo while Fighting in Defence of Texan Independence.
C9000 (ASU BC)

The Sayings of Davy Crockett in His Own Language.
C9060 (ASU)

'Pon my Honor, Hit's the Truth; Tall Tales from the Mountains.
D1050 (BC)

The Mountain Preacher.
D1070 (BC)

Davy Crockett: American Comic Legend.
D3060 (ASU)

Tales of the Blue Ridge.
E970 (LMC ASU BC)

Gravel in My Shoe.
E1090 (ASU WCU LHC MHC ETSU BC)

School at Speedwell.
E1120

Speedwell Sketches.
E1130 (ASU BC)

The Nonsense Book of Riddles, Rhymes, Tongue Twisters, Puzzles and Jokes from American Folklore.
E1990 (ASU BC)

Scraps of Songs and Southern Scenes: A Collection of Humorous and Pathetic Poems and Descriptive Sketches of Plantation Life in the Backwoods of Georgia.
F1760 (ASU)

Autobiography of "Old Claib Jones."
H720

High Times and Hard Times: Sketches and Tales.
H2800 (ASU BC)

Sut Lovingood.
H2820 (ASU)

Sut Lovingood. Yarns Spun by a "Nat'ral Born Durn'd Fool." Warped and Wove for Public Wear.
H2830 (ASU BC ETSU)

Sut Lovingood's Yarns.
H2840 (ASU WWC)

Limericks and Lyrics from My Rhododendron Thicket.
H4230 (ASU)

Some Adventures of Capt. Simon Suggs.
H7060 (ASU)

Aunt Zona's Web.
H8050 (ASU LMC)

Southeastern Broadsides Before 1877.
H8290 (ASU)

Laughter and Tears in the Mountains.
L3780 (ASU BC)

Humor among These Hills.
R530 (ASU LMC MHC WCU)

Born of the Mountains.
R1740 (ASU WCU LMC)

George Washington Harris.
R2190 (BC)

Nippy and the Yankee Doodle, and More Folk Tales from the Southern Mountains.
R2930 (ASU LMC ETSU BC)

Old Greasybeard: Tales from the Cumberland Gap.
R2940 (ASU WCU ETSU LMC WWC MHC BC FC)

Sang Branch Settler, Folksongs and Tales of a Kentucky Mountain Family.
R2950 (ASU)

American Humor: Study of the National Character.
R4000 (MHC)

Pioneer Proverbs: Wit and Wisdom from Early America.
S2750 (ASU WCU)

Bill Arp (pseud.) So Called, a Side Show of the Southern Side of the Civil War.
S4470 (ASU)

Bill Arp: From the Uncivil War to Date, 1861-1903.
S4480 (ASU)

The Mountaineers: Or, Bottled Sunshine for Blue Mondays.
S4850 (ASU BC)

Fisher's River Scenes, Reproduced from the Original.
S5290 (LMC WCU ASU BC)

Senator Sam Ervin's Best Stories.
S6950 (WCU BC ASU)

Nubbins From Fodderstack Ridge.
S6980 (ASU)

Echoes From the Hills: Tall Tales From Tennessee.
S7020 (LMC BC)

Way Down Yonder on Troublesome Creek: Appalachian Riddles and Rusties.
S7430 (BC ASU)

Sentimental Calendar, Being Twelve Funny Stories.
S7450 (ASU WCU)

Tall Tales of the Devils Apron.
S9270 (LMC BC FC)

Carolina Humor: Sketches.
T50 (ASU)

Fisher's River Scenes.
T60 (ASU)

Fisher's River (North Carolina) Scenes and Characters by "Skitt Who Was Raised Thar."
T70 (ETSU BC)

A Treasury of American Folk Humor; a Rare Collection of Laughter, Tall Tales, Jests and Other Gems of Merriment of the American People.
T8570 (FC)

Tennessee Tales.
W280 (ASU LMC ETSU BC)

Incidents and Anecdotes.
W5270 (LMC)

Historical Collections of Georgia: Containing the Most Interesting Facts, Traditions, Biographical Sketches, Anecdotes, etc., Relating to Its History and Antiquities, from Its First Settlement to the Present Time.
W5410 (ASU BC)

All Good Times.
W7800 (BC)

Hit Haint the Fish.
W7810 (LMC BC)

HUMOR — APP.

Chuckles to Brighten the Day.
K480

Frankly Speaking: A Concoction of Humorous, Serious, and Satirical Verses.
W60 (ASU)

HUMOR — GA.

Bill Arp's Peace Papers.
S4490 (ASU)

HUMOR — MTN.

Wiley Buck and Other Stories.
W130 (LMC)

HYMNS

And They All Sang Hallelujah, Plainfolk Camp-meeting Religion, 1800-1845.
B7560 (ASU)

The George Pullen Jackson Collection of Southern Hymnody: A Bibliography.
C280 (BC)

"The Singing School and Shape Note Tradition: Residuals in 20th Century American Hymnody."
C3590 (WCU)

West Virginia Gems: Songs for the Revival and Social Prayer Meeting.
D2280

"The Music of American Revivalism."
D3180 (WCU)

"The Sacred Harp Tradition of the South: Its Origin and Evolution.
E1650 (WCU)

"Shape Note Hymnody in the Shenandoah Valley, 1816-1860."
E2230 (WCU)

James D. Vaughan, Music Publisher, Lawrenceberg, Tennessee, 1912-1964.
F1470 (WCU)

The West Virginia Centennial Book of One Hundred Songs, 1863-1963; Patriotic Songs, Folk Songs and Hymns.
G100

"A Study of the Gospel Song."
G2320 (WCU)

Cherokee Hymns.
G3980 (ASU)

The Musical Million: A Study and Analysis of the Periodical Promoting Music Reading through Shape Notes in North America from 1870 to 1914.
H870 (WCU)

"Ananias Davisson: Southern Tune Book Compiler (1780-1857)."
H3230

Sing to Me of Heaven: A Study of Folk and Early American Materials in Three Old Harp Books.
H7170 (ASU BC)

The George Pullen Jackson Collection of Southern Hymnody: A Bibliography.
R1600

The Southern Harmony.
W400 (WCU)

The Southern Harmony Songbook . . . .
W410 (BC)

The Sacred Harp.
W5310 (WCU ASU)

INCOME

A2681
A2682 (ASU)
A2683 (ASU)

Labor in the Industrial South: A Survey of Wages and Living Conditions in Three Major Industries of the New Industrial South.
B3150 (LMC)

INCOME
Kentucky Income Payments by Counties, 1939, 1947, 1950 and 1951.
M9330
Career Placement and Economic Life Chances of Young Men from Eastern Kentucky.
S1250 (ASU)
Hours and earnings in anthracite and bituminous coal mining.
U1390
Employment, Unemployment, and Low Incomes in Appalachia.
U2590
INCOME — ALA.
Personal Income in Alabama Counties since 1939.
H3760 (ASU)
Area Wage Survey: The Birmingham, Alabama, Metropolitan Area.
U1320
Area Wage Survey: The Huntsville, Alabama, metropolitan area.
U1360
INCOME — APP.
Income and Wages in the South.
H4300 (LMC)
Standards of Living in Four Southern Appalachian Mountain Counties. Farm Security Administration Social Research Report, no. 10.
L3430 (LMC ASU BC)
Miner's Wages and the Cost of Coal: An Inquiry into the Wages System in the Bituminous Coal Industry.
L3790
Income and Employment in the Southeast: A Study of Cyclical Behavior.
M1440 (ASU BC)
Differentials in Farm Income and Employment in the Tennessee Valley Region Counties.
T5180
Wage Chronology: Bituminous Coal Mines, 1933/66-.
U1410
Standards of Living in Four Southern Appalachian Mountain Counties.
U2560 (BC)
"Income and Health in Remote Rural Areas: A Study of Four Hundred Families in Leslie County, Kentucky."
W6350
INCOME — GA.
Area Wage Survey: The Chattanooga, Tennessee-Georgia, Metropolitan Area.
U1340
INCOME — KY.
"Distribution of Income Payments to Individuals in Kentucky Counties by Amount, by Type, and by Size: 1950."
J1860
Income in Kentucky: County Distributions by Amount, by Type, and by Size.
J1870 (LMC BC)
Income and Health in Remote Rural Areas; a Study of 400 Families in Leslie County, Ky.
W6360 (BC)
INCOME — KY. — APP. REGION
Kentucky Personal Income, 1961.
S370
INCOME — MD.
Employment and Underemployment in Rural People: Low Income Groups in Arkansas, Maryland, and West Virginia.
L1860
INCOME — N. C.
Personal Income Statistics for North Carolina Counties, 1949-1959.
N2140
"A Comparative Analysis of Per Capita Income and Related Factors in North Carolina Counties and the United States for Selected Years From 1939 to 1954."
T9530
INCOME — OHIO — APP. COUNTIES
Employment, Income and Resources of Rural Families of Southeastern Ohio.
S7230
INCOME — PA.
"Measurement of Personal Wealth in Centre County, Pennsylvania."
M1600
Area Wage Survey: The Pittsburgh, Pennsylvania, Metropolitan Area.
U1370
Area Wage Survey: The Scranton, Pennsylvania, Metropolitan Area.
U1380
INCOME — S. C.
Area Wage Survey: The Greenville, South Carolina, Metropolitan Area.
U1350
INCOME — TENN.
Income Differences of Rural People in the Upper East Tennessee Valley.
H4510 (ASU)
Resources and Incomes of Rural Upper East Tennessee People, a Progress Report of a Study of the Economic Status and Opportunities of Rural People.
H4520 (ASU BC)
Standards of Living of the Residents of Seven Rural Resettlement Communities.
L3440
Income Levels in the Upper Tennessee Valley: A Comparative Analysis.
T4470
Problems and Suggested Programs for Low-Income Farmers with Special Reference to the Tennessee Valley.
T4510
Area Wage Survey: The Chattanooga, Tennessee-Georgia, Metropolitan Area.
U1340
INCOME — VA.
Personal Income Estimates for Virginia Counties and Cities, 1955.
L270
Personal income estimates for Virginia counties and cities, 1957 and 1958, by John Littlepage Lancaster.
V1220 (BC)
INCOME — W. VA.
Employment and Underemployment in Rural People: Low Income Groups in Arkansas, Maryland, and West Virginia.
L1860
Personal Income in West Virginia Counties by Type and Magnitude, 1960-1963: A Pilot Study.
L2410 (ASU)
L3740
Towards Solving the Low-Income Problem of Small Farmers in the Appalachian Area.
P1010
A Case Study of Six Central West Virginia Counties of the Interrelationships of Factors Leading to Persistence of Low Incomes and Unemployment with Corrective Suggestions.
S7460
Area Wage Survey: The Charleston, West Virginia, Metropolitan Area.
U1330
INDIAN — LEGENDS
John Rattling-Gourd of Big Cove: A Collection of Cherokee Indian Legends.
B2740 (ASU WCU LMC WWC)
The Path to Snowbird Mountain.
B4130 (ETSU)
A Legend of Oconaluftee.
B6650 (ASU)
Indian Legends and Poems.
C1200 (ASU)
Ocona of the Cherokee Hills.
C7140 (ASU LMC MHC)
The Story of Lake Junaluska.
C9340 (BC)
The Cherokee and His Smoky Mountain Legends.
F1340 (ASU ETSU BC)
Indian Story and Song from North America.
F1510 (FC)
The Backward Trail; Stories of the Indians and Tennessee Pioneers.
H470
Legends and Lore, Southern Indians, Flowers, Holidays.
H2270 (ASU)
Origin of the Brown Mountain Light in North Carolina.
M3160 (ASU)
Chilhowee, a Legend of the Great Smoky Mountains.
M4500 (LMC BC)
Cherokee Animal Tales.
M6740 (ASU)
Myths of the Cherokee.
M6750 (ASU LMC)
Myths of the Cherokee.
M6760 (ASU BC WCU)
Myths of the Cherokee.
M6770 (ASU ETSU WWC)
Myths of the Cherokee and Sacred Formulas of the Cherokee.
M6780 (ASU LMC)
The Sacred Formulas of the Cherokees.
M6790 (WCU ASU)
Cherokee Indian Lore and Smoky Mountain Stories.
S3340 (ASU BC)
Cherokee Indian Lore and Smoky Mountains Stories.
S3350 (ETSU)
The Indian's Curse; a Legend of the Cherokees.
S5510 (UNCA ASU)
Princess Aracoma, Beautiful Story of the Comely Daughter of Chief Cornstalk, Great Sachem of the Shawnee Tribe of Indians Who Was Born Near Point Pleasant, Married a "Pale-face", Migrated to the Guyan Valley and There Met a Tragic Fate at the Hands of the White Man.
S9420 (ASU)
INDIAN LEGENDS — CHEROKEE
Indian Tales of North America: An Anthology for the Adult Reader.
C5510 (ASU)
Forgotten Trails.
G3790
Cherokee Legends and Myths: Appendix to "Junaluska."
H3700 (LMC)
INDIAN WARS
List of the Colonial Soldiers of Virginia.
V1190 (ASU)
INDIANS — ALLEGHENY
Indian Blood.
O620 (ASU)
INDIANS — APP.
The American Indian: A Bibliography.
A4071 ()
The Southern Indians: The Story of the Civilized Tribes Before Removal.
C7710 (ASU WCU BC)
The Southern Indians: The Story of the Civilized Tribes Before Removal.
C7720 (LMC)
The Southern Frontier, 1670-1732.
C8520 (WCU BC)
The Southern Frontier, 1670-1732.
C8530 (ASU LMC FC)
N90 (ASU)
Early History of the Creek Indians and Their Neighbor.
S9470 (LMC)
A Study of North Appalachian Indian Pottery.
W9360 (LMC BC)
INDIANS — APP. REGION
The Appalachian Indian Frontier. The Edmond Atkin Report and Plan of 1755.
A5310 (ASU BC WCU LMC ETSU)
INDIANS — CAPTIVES
Red Trails and White.
B770 (BC)
Jennie Wiley, Pioneer: The True Story of a Virginia Frontier Heroine.
B3000 (ASU)
The Captives of Abb's Valley.
B7151
The Captives of Abb's Valley, a Legend of Frontier Life.
B7152 (ASU)
Dark Hills to Westward: The Saga of Jennie Wiley.
C2200 (ASU WCU LMC MHC ETSU BC)
Eastern Kentucky Papers: The Founding of Harman's Station, with an Account of the Indian Captivity of Mrs. Jennie Wiley and the Exploration and Settlement of the Big Sandy Valley in the Virginia's and Kentucky. To Which Is Affixed a Brief Account of the Connelley Family and Some of Its Collateral and Related Families in America.
C6640 (ASU)
The Founding of Harman's Station and the Wiley Captivity.
C6650 (BC ASU)
Escape From Indian Captivity. The Story of Mary Draper Ingles and Son Thomas Ingles.
S6740

INDIANS — CAPTIVES
The Kinnan Massacre.
S8930 (ASU BC)
Held Captive by Indians: Selected Narratives, 1642-1836.
V160 (ASU MHC)
White Squaw: The True Story of Jennie Wiley.
W5050 (ASU ETSU)
White Squaw: The True Story of Jennie Wiley.
W5060 (MHC)
INDIANS — CATAWBA
Adair's History of the American Indians.
A270 (BC FC ASU LMC)
Adair's History of the American Indians.
A280 (WCU)
History of the American Indians.
A290 (ETSU)
The History of the American Indians: Particularly Those Nations Adjoining to the Mississippi, East and West Florida. . .
A300 (LMC)
John Stuart and the Southern Colonial Frontier.
A1040
John Stuart and the Southern Colonial Frontier: A Study of Indian Relations, War, Trade, and Land Problems in the Southern Wilderness, 1754-1775.
A1050 (ASU BC FC WCU)
American Indians Dispossessed: Fraud in Land Cessions Forced Upon the Tribes.
B4860 (ASU)
The Catawba Indians: The People of the River.
B7100 (ASU)
Indians of the Southeast: Then and Now.
B9220 (BC)
Games of the North American Indians. 24th Annual Report of the Bureau of American Ethnology to the Secretary of the Smithsonian Institute.
C9400 (LMC)
Indians of North America.
D3480 (ASU)
An Essay towards an Indian Bibliography: Being a Catalog of Books Relating to the History, Antiquities, Languages, Customs, Religion, Wars, Literature, and Origin of the American Indians, in the Library of Thomas W. Field.
F800 (LMC BC)
Indian Story and Song from North America.
F1510 (FC)
A Guide to Manuscripts relating to the American Indian in the library of the American Philosophical Society.
F3190 (ASU MHC)
Southeastern Indians: Life Portraits: A Catalogue of Pictures, 1564-1860.
F3820 (MHC BC)
Sun Circles and Human Hands: The Southeastern Indians Art and Industries.
F3830 (ASU MHC WCU BC)
Textbooks and the American Indian.
H4760 (MHC)
The Book of Indians.
H6660 (ASU MHC)
Aboriginal Pottery of the Eastern United States.
H6890
The Catawba Nation.
H7980 (LMC)
The Appalachian Indian Frontier: The Edmond Atkin Report and Plan of 1755.
J240
Indians of the Southern Colonial Frontier; The Edmond (Edmund) Atkin Report and Plan of 1755.
J250
Traditions of the North American Indians.
J2380 (LMC)
Red Carolinians.
M6050 (ASU BC WCU)
Red Carolinians.
M6060 (LMC)
The Aboriginal Population of America North of Mexico.
M6730
Indian Trails of the Southeast.
M9240 (ASU FC LMC)
North Carolina Indians.
R370 (WCU)
The North Carolina Indians.
R380 (ASU LMC BC)
The American Indian in North Carolina.
R2310 (WCU)
The American Indian in North Carolina.
R2320 (ASU WCU LMC ETSU UNCA BC)
Indians in North Carolina.
S5600 (ASU WCU MHC BC UNCA)
Catawba Texts.
S6080 (LMC BC)
INDIANS — CATAWHA
Cry of the Thunderbird: The American Indian's Own Story.
H1080 (MHC)
INDIANS — CAYUGA
Logan. The Last of the Race of Shikellemus, Chief of the Cayuga Nation. A Dramatic Piece. To Which Is Added, the Dialogue of the Backwoodsman and the Dandy, First Recited at the Buffaloe Seminary. July the 1st 1821.
D2650 (ASU BC)
INDIANS — CHEROKEE
Adair's History of the American Indians.
A270 (BC FC ASU LMC)
Adair's History of the American Indians.
A280 (WCU)
History of the American Indians.
A290 (ETSU)
The History of the American Indians: Particularly Those Nations Adjoining to the Mississippi, East and West Florida. . .
A300 (LMC)
John Stuart and the Southern Colonial Frontier.
A1040
John Stuart and the Southern Colonial Frontier: A Study of Indian Relations, War, Trade, and Land Problems in the Southern Wilderness, 1754-1775.
A1050 (ASU BC FC WCU)
The Cherokee Nation: Fort Mountain, Vann House, Chester Inns, New Echota.
A1550 (ASU BC)
The Annals of Haywood County, North Carolina: Historical, Sociological, Bibliographical, and Genealogical.
A1700 (ASU WCU BC)
Memoir of Catherine Brown, a Christian Indian of the Cherokee Nation.
A2350 (ASU BC)
Memoir of Catharine Brown, a Christian Indian of the Cherokee Nation.
A2360
A Description of Hiwassee Old Town.
A2440
"Some Recent Contributions of the Cherokee Indians of North Carolina to the Crafts of the Southern Highlands."
A4820 (ASU ETSU)
Stories from an Indian Cave: The Cherokee Cave Builders.
B190 (ASU ETSU WCU)
Cherokee Messenger.
B1790 (ASU)
Cherokee Messenger.
B1800 (BC ASU WCU)
Cherokee Messenger.
B1810 (ASU)
Land of the North Carolina Cherokees.
B2010 (ASU MHC ETSU)
Only the Names Remain: The Cherokees and the Trail of Tears.
B2300 (ASU BC WCU ETSU)
John Rattling-Gourd of Big Cove: A Collection of Cherokee Indian Legends.
B2740 (ASU WCU LMC WWC)
"Protestant Missionaries to the American Indians, 1789 to 1862."
B3160
The Path to Snowbird Mountain.
B4130 (ETSU)
Tell Them They Lie.
B4140 (ASU LMC)
The Cherokee: Indians of the Mountains.
B4720 (ASU BC WCU LMC)
American Indians Dispossessed: Fraud in Land Cessions Forced Upon the Tribes.
B4860 (ASU)
A Legend of Oconaluftee.
B6650 (ASU)
The Cherokee Indians and Those Who Came After, Notes for a History of Cherokee County, North Carolina, 1835-1860.
B7000 (ASU)
Old Frontiers: The Story of the Cherokee Indians from Earliest Times to the Date of their Removal to the West, 1838.
B7250 (ASU BC ETSU LMC WCU)
Old Frontiers: The Story of the Cherokee Indians from Earliest Times to the Date of Their Removal to the West, 1838.
B7260
Military and Genealogical Records of the Famous Indian Woman; Nancy Ward. . . .
B9090
Indians of the Southeast: Then and Now.
B9220 (BC)
TSVLVKI SQCLVLV: A Cherokee Spelling Book.
B9450
My Friends, the Cherokees.
C1140 (MHC)
Indian Legends and Poems.
C1200 (ASU)
C3630 (ASU)
Oconaluftee Indian Village.
C3640 (ASU)
These Are My People.
C3660
Constitution and Laws of the Cherokee Nation.
C3680 (ASU)
C3710 (ASU)
C3720 (ASU)
C3730 (MHC ASU)
Cherokee Cooklore: Preparing Cherokee Foods.
C3870 (ASU LMC MHC WCU)
Cherokee Words with Pictures.
C3880 (ASU LMC BC)
To Make My Bread.
C3890
Cherokee Chief: The Life of John Ross.
C4380 (LMC ETSU)
Sequoya.
C5350 (WCU ETSU BC)
Sequoya.
C5360 (ASU)
Ocona of the Cherokee Hills.
C7140 (ASU LMC MHC)
The Carolina Indian Frontier.
C7470 (ASU WCU)
The Cherokee Frontier: Conflict and Survival, 1740-62.
C7480 (LMC WCU BC UNA ASU UNCA)
The Cherokee Frontier; Conflict and Survival, 1740-62.
C7490 (WCU)
The Cherokee Frontier: Conflict and Survival, 1740-62.
C7500 (ASU)
Red Clay and Rattlesnake Springs: A History of the Cherokee Indians of Bradley County, Tennessee.
C7530 (ASU LMC MHC BC)
The Southern Indians: The Story of the Civilized Tribes Before Removal.
C7710 (ASU WCU BC)
The Southern Indians: The Story of the Civilized Tribes Before Removal.
C7720 (LMC)
Story of the Cherokee Indians, and the Trail of Tears, Battle of Cabin Creek, Alloting of Lands: Personal Interviews of Famous People.
C9140 (MHC WCU)
"Missionary Activities among the Cherokee Indians, 1757-1838."
C9150
Games of the North American Indians. 24th Annual Report of the Bureau of American Ethnology to the Secretary of the Smithsonian Institute.
C9400 (LMC)
"Social Interaction and Kinship in Big Cove Community, Cherokee, N. C."
D1020 (ASU)
"Social Interaction and Kinship in Big Cove Community, Cherokee, N. C."
D1030 (ASU)
Map of the Cherokee County, 1837.
D1530
"The Indian Boundary Line in the Southern District of British North America, 1763-1779."
D1890
The Indian Boundary in the Southern Colonies, 1763-1775.
D2000 (ASU WCU LMC BC)
"The Judicial History of the Cherokee Nation from 1721 to 1835."
D2220
Eastern Band of Cherokees in North Carolina.
D2860

INDIANS — CHEROKEE

Indians of North America.
D3480 (ASU)
Romance of the Siamese twins, a Thrilling Story of a Cherokee Indian Family.
D3750
The War Trails of the Blue Ridge, Containing an Authentic Description of the Battle of King's Mountain, the Incidents Leading up to and the Echoes of the Aftermath of This Epochal Engagement, and Other Stories Whose Scenes Are Laid in the Blue Ridge.
D3760 (BC ASU LMC)
Bibliography; the Eastern Band of Cherokee Indians.
E490
E500 (ASU)
E510 (ASU)
"A History of the Cherokee Indians, 1763-1776."
E570 (ASU)
John Ross and the Cherokee Indians.
E580 (ASU)
John Ross and the Cherokee Indians.
E590 (ASU)
John Ross and the Cherokee Indians.
E600 (ASU BC)
Social Anthropology of North American Tribes.
E1240
A Canoe Voyage up the Minnay Sotor; with an Account of the Lead and Copper Deposits in Wisconsin; of the Gold Region in the Cherokee Country: and Sketches of Popular Manners.
F410
A Canoe Voyage up the Minnay Sotor; with an Account of the Lead and Copper Deposits in Wisconsin; of the Gold Region in the Cherokee Country: and Sketches of Popular Manners.
F420
An Essay towards an Indian Bibliography: Being a Catalog of Books Relating to the History, Antiquities, Languages, Customs, Religion, Wars, Literature, and Origin of the American Indians, in the Library of Thomas W. Field.
F800 (LMC BC)
The Removal of the Cherokee Nation: Manifest Destiny or National Dishonor?
F840 (WCU UNCA FC)
The Cherokee.
F1330 (BC)
The Cherokee and His Smoky Mountain Legends.
F1340 (ASU ETSU BC)
The Cherokees, 1540-1937.
F1350 (ASU UNCA)
The Cherokees.
F1360
The Cherokee Removal, 1838: An Entire Indian Nation Is Forced Out of Its Homeland.
F1430 (ASU BC WCU ETSU)
Sketch of the Life of Elder Humphrey, Baptist Missionary to the Cherokee Indians.
F1480
Indian Story and Song from North America.
F1510 (FC)
Indian Women Chiefs.
F2020 (MHC ASU)
Indians Abroad, 1493-1938.
F2030
The Five Civilized Tribes.
F2040 (WCU BC)
The Five Civilized Tribes.
F2050
The Five Civilized Tribes.
F2060
Indian Removal: The Emigration of the Five Civilized Tribes of Indians.
F2070 (ASU BC LMC WCU)
Sequoyah.
F2080 (BC UNCA WCU ETSU)
Sequoyah.
F2090 (ASU)
Sequoyah.
F2100 (ASU LMC)
Reminiscences of Travel in Cherokee Lands. An Address Delivered before the Ladies' Missionary Society of the Ithaca, New York, Congregational Church, 1898.
F2270
Se-quo-yah; the American Cadmus and Modern Moses. A Complete Biography of the Greatest of Redmen, around Whose Wonderful Life Has Been Woven the Manners, Customs and Beliefs of the Early Cherokees, Together with a Recital of Their Wrongs and Wonderful Progress toward Civilization.
F2280
Se-quo-yah; the American Cadmus and Modern Moses. A Complete Biography of the Greatest of Redmen, around Whose Wonderful Life Has Been Woven the Manners, Customs and Beliefs of the Early Cherokees, Together with a Recital of their Wrongs and Wonderful Progress toward Civilization.
F2290
Se-quo-yah; the American Cadmus and Modern Moses. A Complete Biography of the Greatest of Redmen, around Whose Wonderful Life Has Been Woven the Manners, Customs and Beliefs of the Early Cherokees, Together with a Recital of Their Wrongs and Wonderful Progress toward Civilization.
F2300
Story of the Cherokee Bible. An Address, with Additional and Explanatory Notes, Delivered before the Meeting of the Ladies' Missionary Society of the First Congregational Church, Ithaca, N. Y., Feb. 5, 1897.
F2310
A Guide to Manuscripts relating to the American Indian in the library of the American Philosophical Society.
F3190 (ASU MHC)
Southeastern Indians: Life Portraits: A Catalogue of Pictures, 1564-1860.
F3820 (MHC BC)
Sun Circles and Human Hands: The Southeastern Indians Art and Industries.
F3830 (ASU MHC WCU BC)
Priest and Warriors: Social Structures for Cherokee Politics in the 18th Century.
G720 (ASU ETSU BC)
The Eastern Cherokees.
G1320
Sketches of Some of the First Settlers of Upper Georgia, of the Cherokees, and the Author.
G1700 (ASU BC LMC)
Sketches of Some of the First Settlers of Upper Georgia, of the Cherokees, and the Author.
G1710 (ETSU)
Forgotten Trails.
G3790
"Change in Attitude toward the Indian As the Frontier Line Advanced."
G3950
Cherokee Hymns.
G3980 (ASU)
Sam Houston with the Cherokees, 1829-1833.
G3990 (ASU WCU MHC)
Starr's History of the Cherokee Indians.
G4000 (BC ASU)
Indians of Today.
G4070 (MHC)
The Backward Trail; Stories of the Indians and Tennessee Pioneers.
H470
Fort Loudoun on the Little Tennessee.
H1050 (ASU)
Cry of the Thunderbird: The American Indian's Own Story.
H1080 (MHC)
An Album of Historical Memories. Chatata-Tasso, Bradley County, Tennessee, 1830-1961.
H2190
Legends and Lore, Southern Indians, Flowers, Holidays.
H2270 (ASU)
Cherokee and Earlier Remains on Upper Tennessee River.
H2610 (BC LMC)
Cave Spring and Van's Valley.
H2930 (LMC)
Map of the Cherokee Territory.
H3130
Cherokee Legends and Myths: Appendix to "Junaluska."
H3700 (LMC)
Junaluska at the Battle of Horse Shoe Bend: True Story of the Cherokee Chief.
H3710 (LMC)
Textbooks and the American Indian.
H4760 (MHC)
Old Cherokee Families: "Old Families and Their Genealogy" . . . with a Comprehensive Index.
H5430
"The Tribal Voice of a People in Transition."
H6570
The Book of Indians.
H6660 (ASU MHC)
Aboriginal Pottery of the Eastern United States.
H6890
Expansion and American Indian Policy, 1783-1812.
H7280
The Golden Book of Indian Crafts and Lore.
H8380 (MHC)
George Hunter's Map of the Cherokee Country and the Paths Thereto in 1730.
H8450 (WCU)
Unto These Hills: A Drama of the Cherokee.
H8460 (ASU MHC ETSU)
Look to the Mountain Top.
I10
I190 (WCU)
Cherokees.
I980 (MHC)
The Appalachian Indian Frontier: The Edmond Atkin Report and Plan of 1755.
J240
Indians of the Southern Colonial Frontier; The Edmond (Edmund) Atkin Report and Plan of 1755.
J250
Indian Basketry.
J340
Traditions of the North American Indians.
J2380 (LMC)
Historic Fort Loudoun.
K680
Historic Fort Loudoun.
K690
The Cherokees of the Smoky Mountains.
K1470 (WCU ASU)
The Cherokees of the Smoky Mountains: A Little Band That Has Stood Against the White Tide for Three Hundred Years.
K1480 (ASU MHC UNCA)
The Wahnenauhi Manuscripts: Historical Sketches of the Cherokees, Together with Some of Their Customs, Traditions, and Superstitions.
K1810 (WCU)
Chronicles of Wolftown: Social Documents of the North Carolina Cherokees, 1850-1862.
K1960 (WCU ASU)
Eastern Cherokee Folktales: Reconstructed from the Field Notes of Frans M. Olbrechts.
K1970 (WCU ASU)
Friends of Thunder, Folktales of the Oklahoma Cherokees.
K1980 (ASU)
New Echota Letters: Contributions of Samuel A. Worcester to the Cherokee Phoenix.
K1990 (WCU LMC MHC ASU)
Notebook of a Cherokee Shaman.
K2000 (WCU ETSU UNCA ASU)
Run Toward the Nightland: Magic of the Oklahoma Cherokees.
K2010 (LMC MHC)
The Shadow of the Sequoyah: Social Documents of the Cherokees, 1862-1964.
K2020 (BC ASU WCU LMC ETSU)
Walk in Your Soul: Love Incantations of the Oklahoma Cherokees.
K2030 (LMC)
"Return Jonathan Meigs, Cherokee Indian Agent, 1801-1823."
K2070
The Wild Rose of Cherokee, or Nancy Ward, "The Pocahontas of the West." A Story of the Early Exploration, Occupancy, and Settlement of the State of Tennessee. A Romance Founded on and Interwoven With History.
K2270 (LMC BC)

INDIANS — CHEROKEE

The Wild Rose of Cherokee: Or, Nancy Ward, "The Pocahontas of the West", a Story of the Early Exploration, Occupancy and Settlement of the State of Tennessee. A Romance, Founded on and Interwoven with History.
K2280 (BC ASU)

A Study of Judicial Procedures on the Cherokee Indian Reservation.
K2670 (LMC ASU)

The "Principal People", 1960: A Study of Cultural and Social Groups of the Eastern Cherokee.
K3420 (WCU)

History of North Carolina, Containing the Exact Description and Natural History of That Country, Together with the Present State Thereof, and a Journal of a Thousand Miles Traveled Through Several Nations of Indians, Giving a Particular Account of Their Customs, Manners, Etc., Etc.
L970 (LMC MHC BC)

History of North Carolina, Containing the Exact Description and Natural History of that Country, Together with the Present State Thereof, and a Journal of a Thousand Miles Traveled through Several Nations of Indians, Giving a Particular Account of Their Customs, Manners, Etc., Etc.
L980 (UNCA)

History of North Carolina, Containing the Exact Description and Natural History of That Country, Together with the Present State Thereof and a Journal of a Thousand Miles Traveled Through Several Nations of Indians, Giving Particular Account of Their Customs, Manners, Etc.
L990 (WWC ASU)

A New Voyage to Carolina.
L1000 (LMC ETSU)

A New Voyage to Carolina.
L1010 (UNCA)

Annotations Pertaining to Prehistoric Research in Tennessee.
L2240

American State Papers. Indian Affairs.
L3750

Indian Legends.
L4050 (LMC)

Other Fires: The Story of Tsali.
M180 (WWC BC)

Cherokees and Pioneers.
M220 (ASU LMC)

History of Baptist Indian Missions: Embracing Remarks of the Former and Present Condition of the Aboriginal Tribes. Their Settlement Within the Indian Territory, and Their Future Prospects.
M790 (WCU)

Documents Relating to Indian Affairs, 1754-1756.
M1260 (LMC)

The Keowee River and Cherokee Background.
M1320 (BC)

Cherokee and Creek Indians. Returns a Property Left in Tennessee and Georgia, 1838.
M1470

Memoirs, Official and Personal; with Sketches of Travels among the Northern and Southern Indians; Embracing a War Excursion, and Descriptions of Scenes along the Western Borders.
M1850

The American Indian Frontier.
M2110 (ASU)

The Cherokee Physician . . . As Given by Richard Foreman.
M2830

Cherokees of the Old South: A People in Transition.
M2920 (UNCA ASU WCU LMC BC ETSU)

The Early Nineteenth Century Missionaries in the Cherokee Country.
M2930

"A Social History of the Eastern Cherokee Indians from the Revolution to the Removal."
M2940 (WCU ASU)

"Imperial Regulation of American Indian Affairs 1763-1774."
M3460
M5020 (ASU)

Bibliography of the Eastern Band of Cherokee Indians.
M5280

Red Carolinians.
M6050 (ASU BC WCU)

Red Carolinians.
M6060 (LMC)

The American Indian on the New Trail: The Red Man of the United States and the Christian Gospel.
M6410 (ASU)

The Aboriginal Population of America North of Mexico.
M6730

Cherokee Animal Tales.
M6740 (ASU)

Myths of the Cherokee.
M6750 (ASU LMC)

Myths of the Cherokee.
M6760 (ASU BC WCU)

Myths of the Cherokee.
M6770 (ASU ETSU WWC)

Myths of the Cherokee and Sacred Formulas of the Cherokee.
M6780 (ASU LMC)

The Sacred Formulas of the Cherokees.
M6790 (WCU ASU)

The Swimmer Manuscript, Cherokee Sacred Formulas and Medicinal Prescriptions.
M6800 (ETSU)

Indian Trails of the Southeast.
M9240 (ASU FC LMC)

The American Indian: A Bibliography.
N1580

Southern Indians in the American Revolution.
O230 (ASU)

The Cherokee Story.
P400 (UNCA ASU WCU ETSU)

John Howard Payne to His Countrymen.
P1120 (WCU)

A History of the United States Indian Factory System, 1795-1822.
P1200

Red Men of Fire, a History of the Cherokee Indians.
P1610 (LMC MHC)

Benjamin Hawkins, Indian Agent.
P3910

American Indian Policy in the Formative Years, the Indian Trade and Intercourse Acts, 1780-1834.
P4780 (BC ASU)

North Carolina Indians.
R370 (WCU)

The North Carolina Indians.
R380 (ASU LMC BC)

"The Ross-Watie Conflict: Factionalism in the Cherokee Nation, 1839-1865."
R1060

A Law of Blood: The Primitive Law of the Cherokee Nation.
R1410 (LMC BC UNCA)

Cherokee and Creek.
R1750 (ASU LMC)

The American Indian in North Carolina.
R2310 (WCU)

The American Indian in North Carolina.
R2320 (ASU WCU LMC ETSU UNCA BC)

Indian Territory.
R3880 (ASU)

"The Cherokee Nation of Indians." Fifth Annual Report of the Bureau of Ethnology to the Secretary of the Smithsonian Institution, 1883-84.
R4170 (UNCA ASU)

John Ross, Chief of an Eagle Race.
R4330 (ASU)

"William Holland Thomas, White Chief of the North Carolina Cherokees."
R4380

In the Ranks of Old Hickory, When with the Western Riflemen in Defense Against from Within and Without, Young and Old of All Degrees United Under Andrew Jackson to Make the Republic's Borders Safe.
S30 (ETSU ASU BC)

Select Speeches of John Sergeant, of Pennsylvania (1818-1828).
S1930 (ASU)

Peachtree Mound and Village Site, Cherokee County, North Carolina.
S2000 (ASU LMC UNCA)

Cherokee Fun and Learn Book Play and Color as You Learn About the Cherokee Indian People.
S2420 (ASU)

The Cherokees, Past and Present: An Authentic Guide of the Cherokee People.
S2430 (ASU BC WWC)

The British Administration of the Southern Indians, 1756-1783.
S2490

Cherokee Indian Lore and Smoky Mountain Stories.
S3340 (ASU BC)

Cherokee Indian Lore and Smoky Mountains Stories.
S3350 (ETSU)

Younger Brother, a Cherokee Indian Tale.
S3575 (ETSU)

The Story of the Cherokees.
S5210

The Indian's Curse; a Legend of the Cherokees.
S5510 (UNCA ASU)

Indians in North Carolina.
S5600 (ASU WCU MHC BC UNCA)
S5790 (ASU)

Cherokee Dance and Drama.
S6090 (ASU WCU ETSU BC)

A Faithful History of the Cherokee Tribe of Indians from the Period of Our First Intercourse with Them, Down to the Present Time. The Reasons and Considerations Which Produced a Separation of the Tribe at an Early Period; Organizing a Nation East and a Nation West of the Mississippi River. With a Full Exposition of the Causes Which Led to Their Subsequent Division into Three Parties, and Involved Them in Their Present Deplorable Condition, and of the Nature and Extent of Their Present Claims.
S6490

The Cherokee Nation.
S6610 (ASU LMC ETSU BC)

Cherokees "West," 1794-1839.
S6650

Early History of the Cherokees: Embracing Aboriginal Customs, Religion, Laws, Folklore and Civilization.
S6660

History of the Cherokee Indians.
S6670 (ASU BC ETSU WCU)

History of the Cherokee Indians and Their Legends and Folk Lore.
S6680 (ASU LMC)

Old Cherokee Families: Old Families and Their Genealogy.
S6690 (WCU MHC)

William Bartram's Venture into the Cherokee Country, 1775.
S7010 (LMC WCU)

Eoneguski, or the Cherokee Chief: A Tale of Past Wars, by an American.
S7770

Eoneguski: Or, the Cherokee Chief (1839).
S7780 (ASU LMC MHC WCU BC)

A Sketch of the Cherokee and Choctaw Indians.
S8740

The Indians of the Southeastern United States.
S9490 (BC)

The Indians of the Southeastern United States.
S9500 (ASU)

The Indians of the Southeastern United States.
S9510 (LMC WCU)

The Indian Tribes of North America.
S9520 (FC)

Papers.
S9770 (ETSU WCU BC)

The Cherokees and the Great Smoky Mountains.
T620 (LMC)

Cherokee Collection.
T2060 (LMC WCU ETSU)

Explanation of the Fund Held in Trust By the United States For the North Carolina Cherokees.
T8070 (ASU)

Lieut. Henry Timberlake's Memoirs, 1756-1765.
T8690 (BC ETSU)

Lieut. Henry Timberlake's Memoirs, 1756-1765, With Annotation, Introduction and Index.
T8700 (ASU WCU LMC)

Memoirs, 1756-1765.
T8710 (ETSU ASU WCU)
T9190

INDIANS — CHEROKEE

Look to the Mountaintop.
U20

Folklore of the North American Indians.
U30 (LMC)

Cherokee Legends and the Trail of Tears.
U80 (ASU LMC MHC WCU)

Legends of the Ancient Cherokee.
U90

The Story of the Cherokee People.
U100 (ASU LMC MHC BC)

The Story of the Cherokee People.
U110 (WCU)

Eastern Band of Cherokees of North Carolina.
U830 (WCU)

Census Roll, 1835, of the Cherokee Indians East of the Mississippi.
U1220 (ETSU)

Rates study for water supply and sewage disposal at Cherokee Indian Agency, Cherokee, North Carolina.
U1250

Report on water and sewerage facilities at Cherokee and Soco Valley, North Carolina.
U1260

Letters Received by the Office of Indian Affairs, 1824-81: Cherokee Reserves, 1828-1850.
U1270 (WCU)

Letters Received by the Office of Indian Affairs, 1824-81: Cherokee Emigration, 1828-1854.
U1280 (WCU)

Letters Received by the Office of Indian Affairs, 1824-81: Cherokee Agency (East), 1824-36.
U1290 (WCU)

Letters Received by the Office of Indian Affairs, 1824-81: Southern Superintendency, 1851-1856.
U1300 (WCU)

Records of the Cherokee Indian Agency in Tennessee, 1801-1835.
U1310 (WCU)

Indians, Cherokees.
U1660

Speeches on the Passage of the Bill for the Removal of the Indians, Delivered in the Congress of the U. S., April and May, 1830.
U1820 (ETSU)

Cherokee Indians.
U1830

The Eastern Cherokees: A Census of the Cherokee Nation in North Carolina, Tennessee, Alabama, and Georgia in 1851.
U2770

Opinion of the Supreme Court of the U. S. at the Jan. Term, 1832.
U4030

Letter from the Secretary of War in reply to the resolution of the House of Representatives of the 23d ultimo, respecting the interference of any officer or agent of the Government with the Cherokee Indians in the formation of a government for the regulation of their own internal affairs.
U4040

The Earth Speaks.
U4130 (ASU)

Held Captive by Indians: Selected Narratives, 1642-1836.
V160 (ASU MHC)

Indian Oratory: Famous Speeches by Noted Indian Chief-tains.
V190 (LMC)

Disinherited: The Lost Birthright of the American Indian.
V230 (ASU MHC UNCA)

Cry of the Eagle: History and Legends of the Cherokee Indians and Their Buried Treasures.
W50 (ASU WCU BC)

Indian Battles, Murders, Sieges and Forays in the South-west.
W230

Torchlights to the Cherokee: The Brainerd Mission.
W350 (ASU ETSU BC)

A Political History of the Cherokee Nation, 1838-1907.
W780 (ASU LMC)

Cherokee Landmarks Around the Great Smokies.
W6100 (LMC)

Cherokee Tragedy: The Story of the Ridge Family and the Decimation of a People.
W6330 (ASU WCU LMC BC UNCA)

Lieutenant Henry Timberlake's Memoirs 1756-1765.
W6830

Report of Mr. Wood's Visit to the Choctaw and Cherokee Missions, 1855.
W8500

The Cherokees.
W8900 (ASU WCU LMC ETSU UNCA BC)

The Cherokees.
W8910 (ASU LMC)

Red Clay Council Ground, 1832-1838; Last Capital of the Cherokee Nation East of the Mississippi River.
W9130

Red Clay in History.
W9140

Springplace: Moravian Mission and the War Family of the Cherokee Nation.
W9500 (MHC)

INDIANS — CHEROKEE — BIBLE

Cherokee Indian New Testament.
S1920 (LMC ASU)

INDIANS — CHEROKEE — EASTERN

The Eastern Cherokees: A Census of the Cherokee Nation in North Carolina, Tennessee, Alabama, and Georgia in 1851.
S3320 (BC ASU)

INDIANS — CHEROKEE — GOVERNMENT RELATIONS

Imperial Management of Indian Affairs in the South 1756-1775.
A1030

"The Relations of the Cherokee Indians with the English in America Prior to 1763."
B7950 (ASU)
C3670 (ASU)

Memorial of the Cherokee Indians Residing in North Carolina. Paying the Payment of Their Claims, Agreeably to the 8th and 12th Articles of the Treaty of 1835.
C3690 (ASU)

Reply of the Southern Cherokees to the Memorial of Certain Delegates from the Cherokee Nation. Together with the Message of John Ross, Ex-chief of the Cherokees, and Proceedings of the Council of the "Loyal Cherokees," Relative to the Alliance with the So-called Confederate States.
C3700

"Benjamin Hawkins, Indian Agent from 1796-1817."
C5480

Auraria: The Story of a Georgia Gold-Mining Town.
C7770 (ASU BC)

Eastern Cherokees of North Carolina; a Collection of Eight Reports and Memorials.
E480

"Government Patronage of Indian Missions."
E1140

"A History, of the Cherokee Indians of the Tennessee Region from 1783-1794."
F3550 (ASU)

"Indian Affairs in the Southern Department, 1763-1785."
G1890

"The Southern Indians as a Factor in the Relations of Spain and the U. S., 1783-1795."
H5020

"Return Jonathan Meigs, Cherokee Indian Agent, 1801-1823."
K2070

Memoirs, Official and Personal; with Sketches of Travels among the Northern and Southern Indians; Embracing a War Excursion, and Descriptions of Scenes along the Western Borders.
M1850

"Imperial Regulation of American Indian Affairs 1763-1774."
M3460

Cherokee Lands, Report.
N2360

The Cherokee Indians, with Special Reference to Their Relations with the United States Government.
P290 (ETSU ASU WCU LMC)

"Relations of the United States Government with the Cherokee Tribe."
P300

Seeds of Extinction: Jeffersonian Philanthropy and the American Indian.
S2600 (MHC)
T9190

Look to the Mountaintop.
U20

Disinherited: The Lost Birthright of the American Indian.
V230 (WCU ETSU MHC UNCA)

INDIANS — CHEROKEE — HISTORY

Cherokee Landmarks Around the Great Smokies.
W6100 (LMC)

INDIANS — CHEROKEE — LAND TREATIES

"James Robertson: Frontiersman."
B570

INDIANS — CHEROKEE — LANGUAGE AND PRINTING

Cherokee Bible.
A2080 (ASU)

INDIANS — CHEROKEE — LAWS

Compiled Laws of the Cherokee Nation, Published by Authority of the General Council.
A310

Compiled Laws of the Cherokee Nation, Published by Authority of the General Council.
A320

"The Development of Law and Legal Institutions among the Cherokees."
B880

INDIANS — CHEROKEE — LEGENDS

History of the Cherokee Indians and Their Legends and Folk Lore.
S6680 (ASU LMC)

Cry of the Eagle: History and Legends of the Cherokee Indians and Their Buried Treasures.
W50 (ASU WCU BC)

INDIANS — CHEROKEE — LITERATURE

The Cherokee in Romance, Tragedy, and Song in the Great Smokies.
S8020 (ETSU)

INDIANS — CHEROKEE — MISSIONS

History of the Moravian Missions Among Southern Indian Tribes of the United States.
S1230 (BC UNCA)

INDIANS — CHEROKEE — N. C.

Unto These Hills: A Drama of the Cherokee People.
C3650 (WCU ASU)

Tribal Enrollment of the Eastern Band of Cherokee Indians, Cherokee, North Carolina.
T8130 (LMC WCU)

INDIANS — CHEROKEE — POLITICS

Cherokee Cavaliers: Forty Years of Cherokee History as Told in the Correspondence of the Ridge — Watie — Boudinot Family.
D60 (ASU WCU LMC BC)

Priest and Warriors: Social Structures for Cherokee Politics in the 18th Century.
G720 (ASU ETSU BC)

"Behavioral Premises in the Culture of Conservative Eastern Cherokee Indians."
G3260 (ASU)

INDIANS — CHEROKEE — PREHISTORIC

The Cherokees in Pre-Columbian Times.
T7770 (BC LMC)

"The Cherokees Probably Mound Builders."
T7780

INDIANS — CHEROKEE — REMOVAL

Yunini's Story of the Trail of Tears.
B1490 (ETSU)

The Removal of the Cherokee Indians from Georgia.
L3970 (ASU LMC BC)

INDIANS — CHEROKEES

Cherokees at the Crossroads.
G4840 (ASU BC WCU LMC WWC ETSU)

INDIANS — CHEROKEES — N. C.

The Cherokees of North Carolina.
G1310

INDIANS — CHOCTAW

A Sketch of the Cherokee and Choctaw Indians.
S8740

INDIANS — COLONIAL GOVERNMENT

The British Administration of the Southern Indians, 1756-1783.
S2490

INDIANS — CREEK

John Stuart and the Southern Colonial Frontier.
A1040

INDIANS — CREEK
John Stuart and the Southern Colonial Frontier: A Study of Indian Relations, War, Trade, and Land Problems in the Southern Wilderness, 1754-1775.
A1050 (ASU BC FC WCU)
American Indians Dispossessed: Fraud in Land Cessions Forced Upon the Tribes.
B4860 (ASU)
Battle of Horseshoe Bend in Tallapoosa County, Alabama, March 27, 1814.
B6390 (BC)
Indians of the Southeast: Then and Now.
B9220 (BC)
The Creek Frontier, 1540-1783.
C7510 (ASU BC)
The Southern Indians: The Story of the Civilized Tribes Before Removal.
C7710 (ASU WCU BC)
The Southern Indians: The Story of the Civilized Tribes Before Removal.
C7720 (LMC)
Laws of the Creek Nation.
C8660 (ASU)
Cherokee and Creek Indians. Returns a Property Left in Tennessee and Georgia, 1838.
M1470
The Aboriginal Population of America North of Mexico.
M6730
Indian Trails of the Southeast.
M9240 (ASU FC LMC)
Cherokee and Creek.
R1750 (ASU LMC)

INDIANS — GA.
Report.
U1640

INDIANS — LEGENDS
Indian Stories of Virginia's Last Frontier.
A510
Look to the Mountain Top.
I10
The Tuscaroras: Mythology, Medicine, Culture.
J1730 (ASU LMC)
Indian Legends.
L4050 (LMC)
Cherokee Legends and the Trail of Tears.
U80 (ASU LMC MHC WCU)
Legends of the Ancient Cherokee.
U90
The Earth Speaks.
U4130 (ASU)

INDIANS — MIGRATION
Tribal Migrations East of the Mississippi.
B9350 (ASU BC)

INDIANS — MINGO
History of the Battle of Point Pleasant.
L2340 (BC ASU)

INDIANS — MOHAWK
Held Captive by Indians: Selected Narratives, 1642-1836.
V160 (ASU MHC)

INDIANS — N. C.
The Carolina Indian Frontier.
C7470 (ASU WCU)
Indian Wars In North Carolina, 1663-1763.
L1330 (ASU LMC ETSU WWC BC UNCA)
Indians of North Carolina.
U1230 (ASU)
Indians of North Carolina.
U1240 (ASU)

INDIANS — N. C. — CATAWBA
Catawba Frontier, 1775-1781: Memories of Pensioners.
L1120 (ASU BC)

INDIANS — OTTAWA
History of the Battle of Point Pleasant.
L2340 (BC ASU)

INDIANS — POLITICS
"A History of the Cherokee Indians, 1763-1776."
E570 (ASU)

INDIANS — PREHISTORY
Evidence of Indian Occupancy in Albemarle County, Virginia.
B9340 (BC)

INDIANS — S. C.
The Carolina Indian Frontier.
C7470 (ASU WCU)

INDIANS — SHAWNEE
The Shawnee Trail Program: An Historical Pageant Presented at Clarksburg, W. Va., June 13, and 15, 1923.
C6240 (BC)
Games of the North American Indians. 24th Annual Report of the Bureau of American Ethnology to the Secretary of the Smithsonian Institute.
C9400 (LMC)
Indians of North America.
D3480 (ASU)
An Essay towards an Indian Bibliography: Being a Catalog of Books Relating to the History, Antiquities, Languages, Customs, Religion, Wars, Literature, and Origin of the American Indians, in the Library of Thomas W. Field.
F800 (LMC BC)
Indian Story and Song from North America.
F1510 (FC)
A Guide to Manuscripts relating to the American Indian in the library of the American Philosophical Society.
F3190 (ASU MHC)
Southeastern Indians: Life Portraits: A Catalogue of Pictures, 1564-1860.
F3820 (MHC BC)
Sun Circles and Human Hands: The Southeastern Indians Art and Industries.
F3830 (ASU MHC WCU BC)
Cry of the Thunderbird: The American Indian's Own Story.
H1080 (MHC)
Textbooks and the American Indian.
H4760 (MHC)
The Book of Indians.
H6660 (ASU MHC)
Aboriginal Pottery of the Eastern United States.
H6890
The Appalachian Indian Frontier: The Edmond Atkin Report and Plan of 1755.
J240
Indians of the Southern Colonial Frontier; The Edmond (Edmund) Atkin Report and Plan of 1755.
J250
Traditions of the North American Indians.
J2380 (LMC)
History of the Battle of Point Pleasant.
L2340 (BC ASU)
The Aboriginal Population of America North of Mexico.
M6730
Held Captive by Indians: Selected Narratives, 1642-1836.
V160 (ASU MHC)

INDIANS — SOUTHERN
Southern Indians in the American Revolution.
O230 (ASU)

INDIANS — TENN.
Explorations of the Aboriginal Remains of Tennessee.
J2420 (ASU BC)
Tribes That Slumber: Indian Times in the Tennessee Region.
L2290 (ASU LMC WCU MHC BC)

INDIANS — TENN. — PREHISTORY
The Antiquities of Tennessee and the Adjacent States, and the State of Aboriginal Society in the Scale of Civilization Represented by Them.
T8460 (LMC ASU)

INDIANS — TUSCARORA
An Essay towards an Indian Bibliography: Being a Catalog of Books Relating to the History, Antiquities, Languages, Customs, Religion, Wars, Literature, and Origin of the American Indians, in the Library of Thomas W. Field.
F800 (LMC BC)
Indian Story and Song from North America.
F1510 (FC)
A Guide to Manuscripts relating to the American Indian in the library of the American Philosophical Society.
F3190 (ASU MHC)
Southeastern Indians: Life Portraits: A Catalogue of Pictures, 1564-1860.
F3820 (MHC BC)
Sun Circles and Human Hands: The Southeastern Indians Art and Industries.
F3830 (ASU MHC WCU BC)
Cry of the Thunderbird: The American Indian's Own Story.
H1080 (MHC)
Textbooks and the American Indian.
H4760 (MHC)
The Book of Indians.
H6660 (ASU MHC)
Aboriginal Pottery of the Eastern United States.
H6890
The Appalachian Indian Frontier: The Edmond Atkin Report and Plan of 1755.
J240
Indians of the Southern Colonial Frontier; The Edmond (Edmund) Atkin Report and Plan of 1755.
J250
Traditions of the North American Indians.
J2380 (LMC)

INDIANS — TUSCARORAS
The Tuscaroras: Mythology, Medicine, Culture.
J1730 (ASU LMC)

INDIANS — VA.
History of the Settlement and Indian Wars of Tazewell County, Virginia.
B3530 (FC ASU)
History of the Settlement and Indian Wars of Tazewell County, Va. with added material compiled by J. Allen Neal.
B3540
Bibliography of the Virginia Indians.
M320 (FC)
Indians in Seventeenth Century Virginia.
M330 (ASU)

INDIANS — WARS
Indian Wars In North Carolina, 1663-1763.
L1330 (ASU LMC ETSU WWC BC UNCA)
The Sword of the Republic: The United States Army on the Frontier, 1783-1846.
P4790 (ASU)
In the Ranks of Old Hickory, When with the Western Riflemen in Defense Against from Within and Without, Young and Old of All Degrees United Under Andrew Jackson to Make the Republic's Borders Safe.
S30 (ETSU ASU BC)
Memoir of Indian Wars, and Other Occurrences.
S8730 (ASU)
Documentary History of Dunmore's War, 1774.
T8510
Frontier Defense on Upper Ohio, 1777-1778.
T8520
Revolution on the Upper Ohio, 1775-1777.
T8530
Withers Chronicles of Border Warfare.
T8540
Lieutenant Henry Timberlake's Memoirs 1756-1765.
W6830
Chronicles of Border Warfare; or, A History of the Settlement by the Whites, of Northwestern Va., and . . . .
W7940 (BC)
Chronicles of Border Warfare; or, A History of the Settlement by the Whites, of Northwestern Virginia, and of the Indian Wars and Massacres, in That Section of the State.
W7950 (ASU ETSU WCU BC)
Chronicles of Border Warfare: or, A History of the Settlement by the Whites, of Northwestern Virginia, and of the Indian Wars and Massacres, in That Section of the State.
W7960 (ASU UNCA)

INDIANS — WARS — TENN.
Historic Fort Loudoun.
K680
Historic Fort Loudoun.
K690

INDUSTRY
Industrial Water Supplies of the Tennessee Valley Region.
T7420
Information Sources for Locating Industrial Prospects.
U210

INDUSTRY — ALA.
Report of Industrial Survey of Florence, Alabama, and Muscle Shoals District.
L3050 (ASU)

INDUSTRY — ALA.
Muscle Shoals: A Plan for the Use of the United States Properties on the Tennessee River by Private Industry for the Manufacture of Fertilizers and Other Useful Products.
M9140 (BC)
Area Wage Survey: The Birmingham, Alabama, Metropolitan Area.
U1320
Area Wage Survey: The Huntsville, Alabama, metropolitan area.
U1360

INDUSTRY — APP.
The Industrialization of Southern Rural Areas: A Study of Industry and Federal Assistance in Small Towns with Recommendations for Future Policy.
A180
A2660 (BC)
Labor in the Industrial South: A Survey of Wages and Living Conditions in Three Major Industries of the New Industrial South.
B3150 (LMC)
Adjustment to Rural Industrial Change with Special Reference to Mountain Areas.
C820
Industrial Location Research Studies.
F110 (ASU WCU)
Growth and Labor Characteristics of Manufacturing Industries.
F1600
"The Appalachian Experiment: Growth or Development."
F3730
"The Location Decision for Primary Wood-using Industries in the Northern Appalachians."
H200
Location Decision for Wood-using Industries in Northern Appalachians.
H210
"The Short-run Supply of Industrial Labour in Four Rural Areas of the Southeast, 1949-1964."
H6050
I120 (ASU)
Statement of Conditions 1930.
I220
The Economic Development of the Furniture Industry of the South and Its Future Dependence Upon Forestry.
K3080 (LMC)
Business and Economic Problems in Appalachia.
M9150 (ASU LMC)
State Population, Net Migration, Labor Force and Industry Employment Trends to 1975.
N250
Potential Earning Power of Southern Mountaineer Handicrafts.
N2990
The Machine Age in the Hills.
R3870 (ASU LMC BC WWC ETSU)
Tenn. Valley Land and Its Changing Use.
S150
The Spatial Concentration of Industry in Appalachia: An Analysis of the Potential for Import Substitution.
S490 (ASU ETSU)
Modernization and Diffusion of Innovations in a Rural Appalachia County; General Systems Analysis.
S3710 (BC)
Industrial Development in the TVA Area During 1965.
T2920
River Traffic and Industrial Growth.
T3420
TVA River Traffic and Industrial Growth.
T3880
Report of the Project on Research in Agriculture and Industrial Development in the Tennessee Valley Region.
T4300
Local Government Services and Industrial Development in the Southeast.
T5190
Manufacturing Employment in the Tennessee Valley Region.
T5300
Manufacturing Structure and Change in the Tennessee Valley Region, 1959-1963.
T5310
Agricultural-Industrial Survey of Hamblen County, Tennessee.
T5670
Industrial Development in the TVA Area During 1962.
T6580
Industrial Development in the TVA Area. 1958-.
T6710
Water Used by Appalachian Manufacturers, 1964.
U1580
Water used by Appalachian Manufacturers, 1964.
U1590
Recreation Potential in the Appalachian Highlands: A Market Analysis.
U4220 (ASU)
"The Industrial Development Policy of the Tennessee Valley Authority for the Period 1933-1950."
W6590
Manuf. Cost and the Comp. Advantage of U. S. Regions.
W8470

INDUSTRY — APP. — OIL AND GAS
Geology of Oil and Gas.
H3520 (ETSU)
Catalog of Oil and Gas Wells in Well Sample Repository on August 1, 1959.
L1950

INDUSTRY — ATOMIC — TENN.
"Oak Ridge, Tennessee: A Geographic Study."
C1910

INDUSTRY — GA.
Factors Influencing Recent Industrial Growth in Northeastern Georgia.
N2820 (ASU)
Area Wage Survey: The Chattanooga, Tennessee-Georgia, Metropolitan Area.
U1340
Highlights of the Economy of the Georgia Mountains Area.
W5510

INDUSTRY — GA. — MINERAL
Field Excursion: Ocoee Metasediments: North Central Georgia and Southeast Tennessee.
H8610 (ETSU)

INDUSTRY — KY.
The Structure of the Kentucky Economy: An Input-output Study.
B1230
"Tales of the Mountains" A Complete Directory of the Eastern Kentucky Coalfields with Extracts from the Geological Reports, Forestry, Oil Development, Education, Superstitions, and Religion of the Mountains.
H730
Industrial Resources, Hazard, Kentucky.
H4090
I230
I240
I250
I260
I270
I280
I290
I300
I310
I320
I330
I340
I350
I360
I370
I380
I390
I400
I410
I420
I430
I440
I450
I460
I470
I480
I490
I500
I510
I520
I530
I540
I550
I560
I570
I580
I590
I600
I610
I620
I630
I640
I660
I670
I680
I690
I700
I710
I720
Industrial Resources: Northern Kentucky.
K1020 (ASU)
Resources for Industry.
K1030 (ASU)
Analysis of Manufacturing Employment Trends in Kentucky Counties, 1960-64, and Their Economic Significance.
K1340
Analysis of Occupational Trends in Kentucky from 1950 to 1960, with Projections to 1975.
K1350
Development Potentials for Kentucky Counties with Related Statistics.
K1360 (ASU)
Industrial Resources, Prestonburg, Kentucky.
P4460
Life Among the Hills and Mountains of Kentucky.
T8080 (ASU BC)

INDUSTRY — KY. — LUMBER
A Look at Kentucky's Lumber Industry.
H4960 (BC)

INDUSTRY — KY. — OIL AND GAS
One More River to Cross.
G820 (BC)
"Tales of the Mountains" A Complete Directory of the Eastern Kentucky Coalfields with Extracts from the Geological Reports, Forestry, Oil Development, Education, Superstitions, and Religion of the Mountains.
H730
I740
Natural Gas in Eastern Ky.
J1170
Oil Domes of Ashland.
J1180
The Rose Hill Oil Pool.
J1210

INDUSTRY — LOCATION
Annotated Bibliography on Industrial Concentration and Firm Diversification in the Bitumonous Coal Industry with Special Reference to the Southeastern United States, 1950-1970.
G1270

INDUSTRY — LOCATION — TENN.
Wings Over Kingsport, No. 2: Tennessee's Planned City & Its Industries as Viewed from the Sky in 1938 and 1963.
A1980 (ETSU)
"A Brief Survey of Industrial Plants in Kingsport, Tennessee, with Emphasis on the Geographic Location of the Industrial Worker."
B7860 (ETSU)

INDUSTRY — LUMBER — VA.
The Golden Anniversary Dinner, February 24, 1940, in Honor of William McClellan Ritter, Founder of W. M. Ritter Lumber Company.
B2780 (WCU)

INDUSTRY — N. C.
The Possibilities of a Maple Sugar Industry in Western North Carolina.
A5130 (ASU LMC)
The Industrial Development Program of North Carolina, 1954 to 1962, with Projections to 1970.
B4450
Digest of Information About Transylvania County, North Carolina, Containing Information of General Interest to Commercial and Industrial Businesses.
M5010 (WCU)
Contemporary Industrial Processes.
N1730 (LMC)
Directory of Services Available to Industry from the State of North Carolina.
N1800 (UNCA)
Sawmills and Lumber Production for 26 Counties in Western North Carolina, 1959.
N1960
The Mining Industry in North Carolina.
N2220 (ASU UNCA ETSU LMC)

INDUSTRY — N. C.
"Early History of the North Carolina Furniture Industry, 1880-1921."
T7800
From the Cotton Field to the Cotton Mill: A Study of the Industrial Transition in North Carolina.
T8180 (LMC)
Industrial Water Use in North Carolina.
W430
Growing Christmas Trees in North Carolina.
W5720 (WCU)
INDUSTRY — N. C. — APP.
N1530 (LMC ASU UNCA)
INDUSTRY — OHIO
"The Location and Distribution of the Glass Industry of Ohio, Pennsylvania, and West Virginia."
W2290
INDUSTRY — OHIO — OIL AND GAS
Geology of Oil and Gas Fields in Steubenville, Burgettstown, and Claysville Quadrangles, Ohio, W. Va., and Pa.
G4340
G4350
INDUSTRY — OIL AND GAS — OHIO
Structure of the Berea Oil Sand in the Summerfield Quadrangle, Guernsey, Noble, and Monroe Counties, Ohio.
C6330
INDUSTRY — OIL AND GAS — PA.
"The Economics of Oil Refining in the Pennsylvania Area."
B1750
The Great Oildarado; the Gaudy and Turbulent Years of the First Oil Rush: Pennsylvania, 1859-1880.
D2850
INDUSTRY — PA.
"An Analysis of the Industrial Potential of Johnstown, Pennsylvania."
H1730
I200
"An Analysis of the Christmas Tree Industry in Pennsylvania."
K2690
"Basic Industrial Resources of the Altoona, Pennsylvania, Area."
S5040
Area Wage Survey: The Pittsburgh, Pennsylvania, Metropolitan Area.
U1370
Area Wage Survey: The Scranton, Pennsylvania, Metropolitan Area.
U1380
Steeltown, an Industrial Case History of the Conflict between Progress and Security.
W250
"The Location and Distribution of the Glass Industry of Ohio, Pennsylvania, and West Virginia."
W2290
INDUSTRY — PA. — DAIRY
"Analysis of the Market Structure of the Fluid Milk Industry in Pennsylvania."
D1850
INDUSTRY — PA. — OIL AND GAS
"Application of Unitization to the Pennsylvania Crude Oil Industry."
D2290
The Wonder of the Nineteenth Century, Rock Oil in Pennsylvania and Elsewhere.
G130 (ASU)
Geology of Oil and Gas Fields in Steubenville, Burgettstown, and Claysville Quadrangles, Ohio, W. Va., and Pa.
G4340
"The Use and Interchangeability of Fuels in Pennsylvania."
J470
INDUSTRY — S. C.
I210
Area Wage Survey: The Greenville, South Carolina, Metropolitan Area.
U1350
INDUSTRY — TENN.
Effects of Industrial Development on Rural Life in Sullivan County, Tennessee.
A1840
"A Brief Survey of Industrial Plants in Kingsport, Tennessee with Emphasis on the Geographic Location of the Industrial Worker."
B7870
"The Valley of East Tennessee: The Adjustment of Industry to Natural Environment."
C1920 (LMC)
Chattanooga, Industrial Center of the South.
C3520
"History of the Knoxville Iron Company."
C4500
"An Analysis of the Industrial Potential of Carter County, Tennessee."
C9180 (ETSU)
"Geographic Factors Influencing the Manufactural Industries of Upper East Tennessee."
E2080 (LMC)
"Industrial Parks in East Tennessee: Characteristics and Effectiveness in Attracting Manufacturing."
G2470
Souvenir History of Knoxville.
G2560 (BC)
Souvenir History of Knoxville, the Marble City and Great Jobbing Market. Its Importance as a Manufacturing Center. . . .
G2570
G3460
Men and Vision: The Secret of Yesterday's Success, the Formula for Tomorrow's. A Brief History of the Chattanooga Medicine Company.
G4630 (ETSU)
Kingsport, Tennessee — a Modern American City Developed through Industry.
H150
"The Social and Economic Effects Produced upon Small Towns by Rapid Industrialization."
H6740
Knoxville: Commercial and Industrial Survey of Knoxville, Tennessee.
H7330
"The Social and Economic Effects Produced upon Small Towns by Rapid Industrialization."
H7650
An Economic Survey of Blount County, Tennessee, a Study of Resources and Industrial Potentials.
H8720
Migration and Industrial Development in Tennessee.
H8730
The City of Bristol, Virginia-Tennessee, Its Interests and Industries; Compiled under the Auspices of the Board of Trade. Also a Series of Comprehensive Sketches of Representative Business Enterprises.
I990
Industrial Advantages of the Johnson City Area.
J1340 (ETSU)
Knoxville as an Iron Center.
K1910
"The Chattanooga Region as a Plant Site for the Nylon Industry."
K2090 (ETSU)
Kingsport, the Planned Industrial City.
K2550 (ETSU)
Kingsport, Tennessee, a Modern American City — Developed through Industry.
K2560 (LMC ETSU)
Kingsport, the Planned Industrial City.
K2570 (ETSU ASU)
"An Industrial and Commercial History of the Tri-cities in Tennessee."
L1070
"The Influence of Geography on the Growth of Chattanooga Industries."
L1420
Kingsport: A Romance of Industry.
L3290 (BC ASU ETSU)
O320
P570
Migration and Industrial Development in Tennessee.
T1420
Towers of Power Back Industrial Opportunities in Tennessee, First Public Power State.
T1740
Agricultural-Industrial Survey of Anderson County, Tennessee.
T5570
Agricultural-Industrial Survey of Bledsoe County.
T5580
Agricultural-Industrial Survey of Carter County.
T5590
Agricultural-Industrial Survey of Cocke County.
T5600
Agricultural-Industrial Survey of Coffee County.
T5610
Agricultural-Industrial Survey of Cumberland County.
T5620
Agricultural-Industrial Survey of Fentress County.
T5630
Agricultural-Industrial Survey of Franklin County, Tennessee.
T5640
Agricultural-Industrial Survey of Grainger County.
T5650
Agricultural-Industrial Survey of Greene County, Tennessee.
T5660
Agricultural-Industrial Survey of Johnson County, Tennessee.
T5680
Agricultural-Industrial Survey of Loudon County, Tennessee.
T5690
Agricultural-Industrial Survey of McMinn County, Tennessee.
T5700
Agricultural-Industrial Survey of Marion County, Tennessee.
T5710
Agricultural-Industrial Survey of Meigs County, Tennessee.
T5720
Agricultural-Industrial Survey of Monroe County, Tennessee.
T5730
Agricultural-Industrial Survey of Morgan County, Tennessee.
T5740
Agricultural-Industrial Survey of Polk County, Tennessee.
T5750
Agricultural-Industrial Survey of Rhea County.
T5760
Agricultural-Industrial Survey of Sevier County.
T5770
Agricultural-Industrial Survey of Sullivan County.
T5780
Agricultural-Industrial Survey of Washington County, Tennessee.
T5790
Agricultural-Industrial Survey of White County.
T5800
Agricultural-Industrial Survey of Unicoi County.
T5810
Defense Expansion in the Tennessee Valley Region.
T5820
Area Wage Survey: The Chattanooga, Tennessee-Georgia, Metropolitan Area.
U1340
Industrial Site Survey of Carter County, Sullivan County, and Washington County.
U4160
"The Marble Industry of the Knoxville Area."
W640
W1390 (ETSU)
Tennessee: Its Growth and Progress.
W5570 (BC)
Industrial Resources of Tennessee.
W5750 (ETSU)
INDUSTRY — TENN. — MINERAL
Field Excursion: Ocoee Metasediments: North Central Georgia and Southeast Tennessee.
H8610 (ETSU)
INDUSTRY — TENN. — OIL AND GAS
Geology and Oil Possibilities of the Northern Part of Overton County, Tennessee, and of Adjoining Parts of Clay, Pickett and Fentress Counties.
B9490 (ETSU)
INDUSTRY — TENN. — PUBLISHING CO.
Kingsport Book of Type Faces.
K2510 (ETSU)
INDUSTRY — VA.
Alleghany County, Virginia: Its Resources and Industries.
C8080 (BC)
Industrial Survey, Bland County, Virginia.
H8240
Industrial Survey, Wytheville, Virginia.
H8250 (ASU)
I730
Lynchburg in Old Virginia, the City of Industry and Opportunity.
L4080 (ASU)

INDUSTRY — VA.
N1410
Industrial Sites and Economic Data.
V770 (BC)
Industrial Sites and Economic Data, Botetourt County, Virginia.
V780
Manufacturing Plants in Va. Established Since 1940, Listed by Counties and Independent Cities.
V790
Economic Data.
V810 (BC)
INDUSTRY — VA. — GAS AND OIL
The Early Grove Gas Field, Scott and Washington Counties, Virginia.
A5710 (ETSU)
INDUSTRY — VA. — OIL AND GAS
Oil and Gas Possibilities at Early Grove, Scott County, Virginia.
B9520 (ETSU)
Oil and Gas Wells Drilled in Southwestern Virginia before 1950.
H7900 (ASU)
INDUSTRY — W. VA.
Call of the Mountains.
B2640 (BC ASU)
The Impact of Highway Beautification on the Outdoor Advertising Industry in West Virginia.
C1680
Industrial and Commercial Potentials and Site and Project Analysis in Braxton, Clay and Nicholas Counties, West Virginia.
D1930
West Virginia: Its Farms and Forest, Mines and Oil Wells, with a Glimpse of Its Scenery, a Photograph of Its Population, and an Exhibit of Its Industrial Statistics.
D2690 (BC)
"A Case Study of the Effects of Automation on Employment in a West Virginia Continuous Process Industry."
F930
Employment Changes in West Virginia, 1948-1958.
F1250 (ASU)
Grant's West Virginia Illustrated.
G3230
Current and Proposed Regulations and Legislation on Water Pollution Concerning Appalachian Industries.
H6540
"Compulsory and Flexible Retirement Policies and Practices; An Analysis of West Virginia Industrial Patterns."
J1640
"Water Data for Industrial Site Development, Monongahela Valley, West Virginia."
K360
"Governmental Assistance to Industrial Development in West Virginia."
K1870
"Characteristics of Mobile Workers in a Rural Industrialized Community."
K2600
"Types, Quantities and Destinations of West Virginia's Manufactured Exports, an Exploratory Study."
L850
"A Study of the Factors Influencing Job-satisfaction among Factory Workers of Clarksburg, West Virginia, and Coal Miners of Morgantown, West Virginia."
M4720
West Virginia Conference to Explore Ways in which Space Science and Technology Might be Applied to the Development of West Virginia's Industry and Educational Institutions, 1964.
N10
Thomas, West Virginia: History, Progress, and Development, 1906.
N3010 (ASU)
How to Be Successful.
R3740
West Virginia and the Captains of Industry: State Politics and the Origins of Modern Appalachia, 1880-1913.
S1620
West Virginia: A Book of Geography, History, and Industry.
S2530 (WCU)
West Virginia, in History, Life, Literature and Industry.
S2540
S3690 (UNCA)
Rural Industrialization: A Case Study in Educational Values and Attitudes.
S3810 (ASU)
Nathan Goff, Jr., a Biography: With Some Account of Guy Despard Goff and Brazilla Carroll Reece.
S4710 (ASU)
Factors Influencing Plant Location in West Virginia, 1945-1956.
T8210
Labor Market Areas for Manufacturing Plants in West Virginia.
T8220
Area Wage Survey: The Charleston, West Virginia, Metropolitan Area.
U1330
"The Location and Distribution of the Glass Industry of Ohio, Pennsylvania, and West Virginia."
W2290
West Virginia Manufacturing Directory, 1962.
W3390 (BC)
W4380 (BC)
"The Resources and Industries of the New River Drainage Basin in West Virginia."
W7990
INDUSTRY — W. VA. — CHEMICALS
Spectrographic Chemical Analysis.
H8470 (ETSU)
INDUSTRY — W. VA. — GLASS
"Glass Production Processes of the Kanawha Valley Area."
C8070 (ASU)
"A Study of the Effects of Foreign Imports on the Hand-blown and Hand-pressed Glass Industry in the United States, Especially in Ohio, Pennsylvania, and West Virginia from 1948-1958."
H4690
INDUSTRY — W. VA. — LUMBER
The Comp'ny: The Story of the Surry, Sussex and Southampton Railway and the Surry Lumber Company.
C8850 (ASU LMC BC)
INDUSTRY — W. VA. — OIL AND GAS
The Newburg of West Virginia.
C1240
The Igneous Rocks of Pendleton County, West Virginia.
G380 (ETSU)
Geology of Oil and Gas Fields in Steubenville, Burgettstown, and Claysville Quadrangles, Ohio, W. Va., and Pa.
G4340
Oil and Gas in Southern West Virginia.
H3530 (ETSU)
Oil and Gas in West Virginia.
H3540 (ETSU)
Oil and Gas Report and Map of Doddridge and Harrison Counties, West Virginia.
H3550 (ETSU)
Oil and Gas Report and Map of Lewis and Gilmer Counties, West Virginia.
H3560 (ETSU)
Oil and Gas Report and Map of Marshall, Wetzel, and Tyler Counties, West Virginia.
H3570 (ETSU)
Oil and Gas Report and Map of Monongalia, Marion, and Taylor Counties, West Virginia.
H3580 (ETSU)
Oil and Gas Report and Map of Pleasants, Wood, and Ritchie Counties, West Virginia.
H3590 (ETSU)
Oil and Gas Report on Barbour and Upshur Counties, West Virginia.
H3600 (ETSU)
Oil and Gas Report on Braxton and Clay Counties, West Virginia.
H3610 (ETSU)
Oil and Gas Report on Kanawha County, West Virginia.
H3620 (ETSU)
West Virginia's Oil and Gas Lubricants and Fuels.
H3630 (ETSU)
Permeability, Porosity, Oil, and Water Content of Natural Gas Reservoirs, Kanawha-Jackson and Campbells Creek Oriskany Fields.
H4150 (ETSU)
INTEGRATION — W. VA.
"Integration in West Virginia Since 1954."
J1920 (ASU)
INTELLIGENCE AND APTITUDE — APP.
"A Comparative Study of the Relationship Between ACT Composite Scores and GPA of Washington County Students at East Tennessee State University, 1965-66."
P3940 (ETSU)
IRISH
Corpus Genealogiarum Hiberniae.
O140 (ASU)
The Irish in America: Immigration, Land, Probate, Administrations, Birth, Marriage, and Burial Records of the Irish in America in and about the Eighteenth Century.
O150 (ASU)
Ireland and the American Emigration, 1850-1900.
S1140 (ASU)
IRON INDUSTRY — ALA.
The Story of Coal and Iron in Alabama.
A4650 (ASU)
JAMES RIVER
Industrial Limestones and Dolomites in Va.: James River District West of the Blue Ridge.
E910
The Floods of March, 1936, Part 3, Potomac, James, and Upper Ohio Rivers.
G4470
JUVENILE DELINQUENCY
Delinquency in Kentucky.
K990
JUVENILE DELINQUENCY — APP.
Rural Youth in Crises: Facts, Myths, and Social Change.
B8480
Helping Youth: A Study of Six Community Organization Programs.
G4430
JUVENILE DELINQUENCY — N. C.
The Use of Hostile Verbs by Male Committed Youthful Offenders.
P2040 (ASU)
JUVENILE DELINQUENCY — TENN.
"Impact of World War II on Juvenile Delinquency in Knox County, Tennessee."
D1380
"The Use of the Case Method in the Study of Juvenile Delinquency in Johnson City."
H230 (ETSU)
"Community Concept of Juvenile Court Function in Knox County, Tennessee."
S3460
Report to the Governor and Members of the General Assembly (81st) State of Tennessee.
T960 (ETSU)
Report to Honorable Frank G. Clement, Governor, and Members of the 80th General Assembly, State of Tennessee.
T970 (ETSU)
JUVENILE DELINQUENCY — W. VA.
The Characteristics and Attitudes of Juvenile Delinquents of Kanawha County.
A2550
Action for Appalachian Youth: A Demonstration Program for Kanawha County Youth under the Auspices and Direction of the President's Committee on Juvenile Delinquency and Youth Crime.
C3370 (ASU)
Our Troubled Children.
K110
JUVENILE DELINQUINCY — W. VA.
The Characteristics and Attitudes of Juvenile Delinquents of Kanawha County, West Virginia.
A2590
KANAWHA RIVER
Pioneers and Their Homes on Upper Kanawha.
D1440 (ASU BC)
The Geomorphic History of the New Kanawha River System.
F3300 (ETSU)
Surface Water Supply of the New-Kanawha River Basin, West Virginia, and North Carolina.
G4490
Kanawha River: Comprehensive Basin Study.
K100 (ASU)
The New-Kanawha River and the Mind War of West Virginia.
M630 (BC)
KENTUCKY RIVER
P90

KENTUCKY RIVER
. . . The Kentucky River Navigation.
V540
KEOWEE RIVER
The Keowee River and Cherokee Background.
M1320 (BC)
KY. — DESCRIPTION AND TRAVEL
Peter Pilgrim: Or, A Rambler's Recollections.
B4100 (ASU)
The Slave States of America.
B8260
My Old Kentucky Home.
B9400 (BC)
History of Cavelier de LaSalle, 1643-1687; Explorations in the Valleys of the Ohio, Illinois and Mississippi, taken from his Letters, Reports to King Louis XIV, also the Reports of Several of his Associates, Official Acts and Contemporaneous Documents,
C3800
Kentucky: Land of Contrast.
C4580 (LMC ASU WCU BC UNCA)
Kentucky: A Pictorial History.
C5780 (ASU)
Unto the Hills; Glimpses of Berea's Outdoors.
C7600
Kentucky through Thick and Thin.
E1450
Kentucky: A Guide to the Blue Grass State.
F470
Jenny Wiley Country.
H580
Kentucky and Tennessee, Twin Centers of Interest.
H2260 (ASU BC)
Down a Dusty Road.
H7640 (BC ASU)
From the Prairies to the Mountains; Memories Especially of Illinois and Eastern Kentucky.
H8310
Stories of Hatfield the Pioneer . . . His Experiences in the Wilderness of East Tennessee, Kentucky and South Indiana.
I830
A Tour Downstream.
J1220
Comin' Through the Gap.
P2460
Kentucky on the March.
S770 (ASU BC)
The Kentucky Story.
V280
W5210 (BC)
KY. — EARLY EXPLORATION
First Explorations of Kentucky Doctor Thomas Walker's Journal, of an Exploration of Kentucky in 1750, Being the First Record of a White Man's Visit to the Interior of that Territory . . . Also Colonel Christopher Gist's Journal, of a Tour through Ohio and Kentucky in 1751. . .
J2060
The Wilderness Road.
K2160 (BC WCU WWC ETSU)
The Wilderness Road.
K2170
The Wilderness Road.
K2180 (ASU LMC)
A Description of Kentucky in North America: To Which Are Prefixed Miscellaneous Observations Respecting the United States.
T8990 (ASU LMC)
The Western Country in 1793: Reports on Kentucky and Virginia.
T9000 (ASU BC ETSU)
Journal of an Exploration in the Spring of the Year 1750.
W380
Kentucky's First House; the Journal of Dr. Thomas Walker.
W390
KY. — HISTORY
Daniel Boone, Pioneer of Kentucky.
A30 (ASU)
Daniel Boone, Pioneer of Kentucky.
A40 (ETSU)
Daniel Boone, the Pioneer of Kentucky.
A50 (ASU BC)
The History of Kentucky, from Its Earliest Settlement to the Present Time.
A5020 (BC WCU)
Fighting Frontiersman, the Life of Daniel Boone.
B530
Fighting Frontiersman, the Life of Daniel Boone.
B540 (ASU BC)
Master of the Wilderness: Daniel Boone.
B550
Kentucky: A History of the State.
B1970
The Unfolding of a Century.
B2750
History of Greenup County, Kentucky.
B3580 (BC)
A Supplementary Edition of a History of Greenup County.
B3590 (ASU BC)
Dark and Bloodied Ground.
B5150 (ASU)
The Patriots and Guerrillas of East Tennessee and Kentucky. The Suffering of the Patriots. Also the Experience of the Author as an Officer in the Union Army. Including Sketches of Noted Guerrillas and Distinguished Patriots.
B6510
Of Bolder Men (A History of Leslie County).
B6540 (BC)
In the Foothills of the Cumberland; a History of Eastern Kentucky.
B7150 (BC)
Daniel Boone and the Wilderness Road.
B7580 (ETSU)
History Records of Harlan County, Kentucky, People.
B9070 (BC)
A History of the Commonwealth of Kentucky.
B9410 (ASU LMC MHC WCU BC)
Kentucky; The Pioneer State of the West.
C3750
A History of Kentucky.
C4550 (ASU BC)
Kentucky: Land of Contrast.
C4580 (LMC ASU WCU BC UNCA)
The Meaning of the Past for the Future.
C4760 (BC)
A Bibliography of Kentucky History.
C5770 (ASU LMC)
Historical Collections of Kentucky.
C6010
Eastern Kentucky Papers: The Founding of Harman's Station, with an Account of the Indian Captivity of Mrs. Jennie Wiley and the Exploration and Settlement of the Big Sandy Valley in the Virginia's and Kentucky. To Which Is Affixed a Brief Account of the Connelley Family and Some of Its Collateral and Related Families in America.
C6640 (ASU)
The Founding of Harman's Station and the Wiley Captivity.
C6650 (BC ASU)
History of Pioneer Kentucky.
C7700 (LMC BC ASU)
The Civil War and Readjustment in Kentucky.
C7780 (BC)
The Real Book about Daniel Boone.
C9790 (BC)
History of Perry County, Ky.
D490
History of Perry County, Kentucky.
D500 (BC)
History of Knox County, Kentucky (1674-1941).
D1580 (BC)
Wilderness Wife: The Story of Rebecca Bryan Boone.
D1620 (ASU MHC WCU BC)
John Filson, the First Historian of Kentucky: An Account of His Life and Writings.
D4100 (LMC)
The Border States: Kentucky, North Carolina, Tennessee, Virginia, West Virginia.
D4190 (BC ASU LMC WWC ETSU)
Glimpses of Historical Wayne County, Kentucky.
E960 (ASU BC)
The Big Sandy Valley: A History of the People and Country from the Earliest Settlement to the Present Time.
E1890 (ASU)
Breathitt: A Guide to the Feud Country.
F460
The Discovery and Settlement of Kentucky.
F860 (LMC ETSU BC)
The Discovery, Settlement, and Present State of Kentucky.
F870 (UNCA)
The Discovery, Settlement, and Present State of Kentucky.
F880 (ASU)
History of Bell County, Kentucky.
F4030 (BC)
Notes from the History of Education in Owsley County.
G20
Clever Country: Kentucky Mountain Trails.
G290 (LMC BC)
Newspaper History of a Town: A History of Danville, Kentucky.
G4200 (ASU)
Autobiography of "Old Claib Jones."
H370
The Hatfields.
H3450 (ASU)
The True Story of the Hatfield and McCoy Feud.
H3480 (BC)
The Transylvania Company and the Founding of Henderson, Ky.
H4450 (ASU)
Boone of the Wilderness: A Tale of Pioneer Adventures and Achievement in "The Dark and Bloody Ground."
H4460 (ASU BC)
The Theatre in Early Kentucky, 1790-1820.
H5490 (BC)
H5700
"The Economic History of Knox County."
H7600
The Big Sandy Valley: A Regional History Prior to the Year 1850.
J960 (ASU BC)
The Big Sandy Valley: A Regional History Prior to the Year 1850.
J970 (MHC)
The Boone Narrative.
J980 (LMC)
Daniel Boone in Kentucky.
J1010
A Century of Wayne County, Kentucky, 1800-1900.
J1300 (ASU BC)
First Explorations of Kentucky Doctor Thomas Walker's Journal, of an Exploration of Kentucky in 1750, Being the First Record of a White Man's Visit to the Interior of that Territory . . . Also Colonel Christopher Gist's Journal, of a Tour through Ohio and Kentucky in 1751. . .
J2060
Biographical Record of Daniel and Mary (Jackson) Williams — Early Kentucky Pioneers, 1752-1898.
K590 (ASU)
Historical Sketches of Lancaster and Garrard County, 1796-1924.
K2610
Sketches of Western Adventure: Containing an Account of the Most Interesting Incidents Connected with the Settlement of the West, from 1755 to 1794.
M470 (ETSU BC)
Old Kentucky Country.
M2190 (ASU LMC WWC BC UNCA)
The History of Kentucky.
M3440 (MHC BC)
Harlan County, Kentucky.
M5360 (BC)
An Address in Commemoration of the First Settlement of Kentucky.
M7390
The Story of Daniel Boone.
M8130 (ASU BC)
"Doctor Thomas Walker (1715-1794): Explorer, Physician, Surveyor, and Planter of Virginia and Kentucky."
N3050 (BC)
My Own Story: An Account of the Conditions in Kentucky Leading to the Assassination of William Goobel, Who Was Declared Governor of the State, and My Indictment and Conviction on the Charge of Complicity in His Murder.
P4060 (ASU)
The Wilderness Road to Kentucky.
P4900
The Life and Times of Hon. Humphrey Marshall.
Q200 (LMC BC MHC)
A History of Bath County, Kentucky.
R2020 (BC)

KY. — HISTORY
No More Muffled Hoofbeats.
R2600 (ASU)
Petitions of the Early Inhabitants of Kentucky to the General Assembly of Virginia, 1769.
R3160
Historic Floyd, 1890-1950.
S690
Kentucky on the March.
S770 (ASU BC)
Flood of July 5, 1939, in Eastern Kentucky.
S1070
S1910
Kentucky: A Pioneer Commonwealth.
S2190 (LMC BC ASU)
Kentucky: A Pioneer Commonwealth.
S2200 (WWC)
Kentucky; a Pioneer Commonwealth.
S2210
A History of Jellico, Tennessee, Containing Historical Information on Campbell County, Tennessee and Whitley County, Kentucky.
S3330
The Daniel Boone Story.
S4540 (BC)
Selections from Morgan County History: Sesquicentennial Volume.
S6420 (ASU)
Talley's Kentucky Papers.
T80 (BC)
Talley's Northeastern Kentucky Papers.
T90
The Register of the Kentucky Historical Society.
T200 (BC)
The Wild Riders of the First Kentucky Cavalry. A History of the Regiment in the First Great War of the Rebellion. 1861-1865.
T280 (ASU)
A History of Pulaski Co., Kentucky.
T810
Big Sandy.
T7890 (ASU BC)
Kentucky Tradition.
T8250 (ASU)
A History of Pulaski County, Kentucky.
T8550
A Description of Kentucky in North America: To Which Are Prefixed Miscellaneous Observations Respecting the United States.
T8990 (ASU LMC)
The Western Country in 1793: Reports on Kentucky and Virginia.
T9000 (ASU BC ETSU)
The Kentucky Story.
V280
Kentucky's First House; the Journal of Dr. Thomas Walker.
W390
Kentucky Resolutions of 1798.
W810 (BC)
The men, women, events, institutions, and lore of Casey Co., Kentucky.
W1490 (BC)
The Partisan Spirit: Kentucky Politics, 1779-1792.
W1500 (WWC BC)
Chronicles of a Kentucky Settlement.
W1610 (BC)
A Short History of Paintsville and Johnson County.
W2720 (ASU BC)
History of Cumberland County.
W2750 (ASU BC)
Kentucky Soldiers of the War of 1812.
W6150
History of Ravenna, Kentucky.
W6910 (BC)
Early and Modern History of Wolfe County.
W8035 (ASU BC)
Heroes of the War of 1812 for Whom Kentucky Counties are Named.
W8620
Heroes of the War of 1812 for Whom Kentucky Counties are Named.
W8840 (BC)
Isaac Shelby Kentucky's First Governor and Hero of Three Wars.
W9780

KY. — HISTORY — ORAL
The Saga of Coe Ridge: A Study in Oral History.
M6560 (ASU BC ETSU LMC WCU WWC)

KY. — RECREATION AND TOURISM
Comin' Through the Gap.
P2460

KY. RIVERS
The Kentucky.
C4560 (WWC WCU UNCA)
The Kentucky.
C4570 (ASU UNCA BC)
A Kentucky Riverlands Development Program.
G570

LABOR FORCE
The Effects of Migration of the Labor Force.
W9830

LABOR FORCE — APP.
Migration and Changes in the Quality of the Labor Force.
G670 (ETSU)
State Population, Net Migration, Labor Force and Industry Employment Trends to 1975.
N250

LABOR FORCE — COAL INDUSTRY
The Best-dressed Miners: Life and Labor in the Maryland Coal Region, 1835-1910.
H3270 (ASU)

LABOR FORCE — TENN.
Labor Supply Survey of Bristol, Virginia-Tennessee.
V860 (ETSU)

LABOR FORCE — VA.
Labor Supply Survey of Bristol, Virginia-Tennessee.
V860 (ETSU)
Labor Supply Survey of New River Valley.
V870 (ASU)
Labor Supply Survey of Northern Shenandoah Valley.
V880 (ASU)
Redevelopment Manpower Report for the Norton-Big Stone Gap Area.
V890 (ASU)

LABOR MARKET — TENN.
A Study of the Chattanooga Labor Market Area.
T1170 (ETSU)

LABOR RELATIONS
Labor Relations in the Fairmont, West Virginia, Bituminous Coal Field.
E1950 (ASU)
"The Economic Effects of Collective Bargaining in Bituminous Coal Mining."
G3860
"Cooperation-conflict in Labor Management: A Study of Contrasting Cases (Women's Garment Industry and Bituminous Coal Industry)."
H110
Work Stoppages and the Grievance Procedure in the Appalachian Coal Industry.
W4700

LABOR RELATIONS — ALA.
Labor Revolt in Alabama: The Great Strike of 1894.
W770 (WCU BC)

LABOR RELATIONS — APP.
American Folksongs of Protest.
G3880
TVA Labor Relations Policy at Work; Successful Cooperation Between Public Power and Organized Labor in the Public Interest.
K2350
Articles of Agreement . . . Negotiated December 5, 1950. Revisions Through February 4, 1955.
T2290
TVA Labor Relations, 1933-1953.
T6870

LABOR RELATIONS — N. C.
"The Textile Strikes in Marion, North Carolina, 1929: A Challenge to the New South."
H6450 (ETSU)

LABOR RELATIONS — TENN.
Labor and TVA; Collective Bargaining Under Government Operation of a Public Utility and an Analysis of the Benefits to All the People of the Integrated Development of a River Basin.
T1560
Articles of Agreement Between the Tennessee Valley Authority and the Salary Policy Employee Panel. Negotiated December 5, 1950.
T2280

LABOR RELATIONS — TENNESSEE VALLEY AUTHORITY
Tennessee Valley Authority Program: The Role of the States and Their Political Subdivisions.
T5320

LABOR RELATIONS — W. VA.
"The West Virginia Labor Federation and the West Virginia Legislature, 1957-1961."
B8350
"The Labor Movement in West Virginia, 1900-1948."
P3730

LABOR UNIONS
Thoughts of Mother Jones; Compiled from her Writings and Speeches.
A5810
The Molly Maguires.
B6810 (ASU WCU)
Men and Coal.
C5790 (ASU BC)
F80 (ASU)
Mother Jones, the Miners' Angel: A Portrait.
F740 (ASU MHC)
The Corrupt Kingdom: The Rise and Fall of the United Mine Workers.
F1030
"Economic Consequences of the Seven-hour Day and Wage Changes in the Bituminous Coal Industry."
F1220
Wage Rates and Working Time in the Bituminous Coal Industry, 1912-1922.
F1230 (BC)
I Went to Pit College.
G1590
H2320
Bill Haywood's Book: The Autobiography of William D. Haywood.
H4080 (ASU WCU)
Struggle in the Coal Fields. The Autobiography of Fred Mooney, Secretary-Treasurer, District 17, United Mine Workers of America.
H5070 (ASU)
"The United Mine Workers of America and the Non-Union Coal Fields."
H5620
Death and the Mines: Rebellion and Murder in the United Mine Workers.
H8260 (ASU BC LMC WCU)
"The United Mine Workers: A Study of How Trade Union Policy Relates to Technological Change."
M6000
Struggle in the Coal Fields: The Autobiography of Fred Mooney.
M6720 (ASU BC WCU)
"Attitude of Coal Miners toward Union and Coal Industry."
M7730 (ASU)
The Coal Miner's Struggle in Eastern Kentucky.
N3020 (ASU)
Autobiography of Mother Jones.
P520 (ASU)
"The Labor Struggle at Wilder, Tennessee."
P2280 (ASU)
The Kingsport Strike.
P2440 (ASU LMC BC)
"A Study of the United Mine Workers of America Welfare and Retirement Fund."
S1400
Human Crisis in the Kingdom of Coal.
S5010 (ASU BC)
"Grievance Settlement in Coal Mining."
S5440
Facts About the Two Armed Marches on Logan.
S9400 (ASU BC)
The Incomparable Don Chafin.
S9410 (BC ASU)
"Bloody" Harlan, 1931-1938; an Appalachian Coal County in the Thirties.
T170

LABOR UNIONS — APP.
The Kentucky Miner's Struggle: The Record of a Year of Lawless Violence. The Only Complete Picture of Events Briefly Told.
A2090 (ASU)
"A History of the Labor Movement in West Virginia."
A2610
Proceedings, October 12-14, 1964.
A4110

LABOR UNIONS — APP.
"Strikes in the Southern West Virginia Coal Fields, 1912-1922."
B1040 (ASU)
B4750 (BC)
Labor's Untold Story.
B6040 (ASU)
"Collective Bargaining in the Bituminous Coal Industry."
C5380 (ASU)
Men and Coal.
C5800 (MHC WCU)
The Molly Maguires. The Origin, Growth, and Character of the Organization.
D2010 (ASU WCU)
"The Economic Effects of Collective Bargaining in Bituminous Coal Mining."
G3860
"Cooperation-conflict in Labor Management: A Study of Contrasting Cases (Women's Garment Industry and Bituminous Coal Industry)."
H110
"The Coal Miner's Insurrections, 1891-1892."
H8740 (ASU)
Autobiography of Mother Jones.
J2500 (BC LMC ASU WCU MHC)
Thoughts of Mother Jones: Compiled from Her Writings and Speeches.
J2510 (WCU)
"A Study of a Labor Unions of the Textile Industry in the Southern Appalachian Piedmont."
K2230 (ETSU)
Bloodletting in Appalachia: The Story of West Virginia's Four Major Mine Wars and Other Thrilling Incidents of Its Coal Fields.
L1350 (ASU WCU LMC BC MHC)
Lament for the Molly Maquires.
L2080
Hard Hitting Songs for Hard Hit People: American Folk Songs of the Depression and the Labor Movement of the 1930's.
L3140 (BC ASU MHC LMC)
"Union Economic Politics and Union Discipline in the Bituminous Wage Dispute of 1949-1950."
R4030 (ASU)
"An Analysis of Federative Patterns in Social Organization with a Field Study of the Council of Southern Mountain Workers."
S1510 (BC)
S5520 (ASU)
"Coal and Conflict: The U.M.W.A. in Harlan County, 1931-1939."
T690 (BC ASU)
The Logan Coal Field of West Virginia: A Brief History.
T8470 (ASU ETSU WCU)
Hell in Harlan.
T8760 (WCU)
Labor Baron, a Portrait of John L. Lewis.
W2170 (BC)
The American Miners Association: A Record of the Origin of Coal Miners' Unions in the United States.
W5970 (ASU)
The Miners' Case and the Public Interest: A Documented Chronology.
W5980

LABOR UNIONS — KY.
The Shame That Is Kentucky's! The Story of the Harlan Mine War.
C7610 (ASU)
D2840
"A New Deal for Harlan: The Roosevelt Labor Policies in a Kentucky Coal Field, 1931-1939."
H5120 (BC)

LABOR UNIONS — N. C.
Welfare Work in Mill Villages, the Story of Extra-mill Activities in North Carolina.
H4990 (WWC)
"The Textile Strikes in Marion, North Carolina, 1929: A Challenge to the New South."
H6450 (ETSU)
Millhand and Preachers, a Study of Gastonia.
P3560 (MHC)

LABOR UNIONS — PA.
The Molly Maguire Riots: Industrial Conflict in the Pennsylvania Coal Region.
C5760 (WCU ASU)

LABOR UNIONS — TENN.
"The Negro and Organized Labor as Voting Blocs in Tennessee, 1960-1964."
D2070

LABOR UNIONS — UMW
"The Anthracite Mine Workers, 1869-1897: A Functional Approach to Labor History."
A5520 (ASU)
From the Molly Maguires to the United Mine Workers: The Social Ecology of an Industrial Union, 1869-1997.
A5530 (WCU BC)

LABOR UNIONS — W. VA.
The Socialist and Labor Star, Huntington, West Virginia, 1912-1915.
C7370 (ASU BC)
"The Mine War on Cabin Creek and Paint Creek, West Virginia, in 1912-1913."
C8590 (ASU)
Labor Relations in the Fairmont, West Virginia, Bituminous Coal Field.
E1950 (ASU)
From Humble Beginnings; West Virginia State Federation of Labor, 1903-1957.
H2770 (BC)
Civil War in West Virginia: A Story of the Industrial Conflict in the Coal Mines.
L380 (ASU BC)
"The Labor Movement in West Virginia, 1900-1948."
P3730
"Worker Education in West Virginia: A Study in Union-University Cooperation."
R3670 (ASU)

LAND CLASSIFICATION AND USE
Land Use Plan for the City of Berea, Ky.
B3120 (BC)
Land Development Plan.
B5450
Land Use Plan, Haywood County, N. C.
H4020 (LMC)
The Diligent Destroyers.
L1090 (ASU WCU)

LAND CLASSIFICATION AND USE — KY.
Land Utilization in Laurel County, Kentucky.
C4820 (BC)
Existing Land Use Analysis, Leslie County, Kentucky.
K1140
Harlan County, Existing Land Use Analysis. Harlan-Harlan County Major Thoroughfare Plan.
K1150
Pikeville, Kentucky, Neighborhood Analysis.
K1160

LAND CLASSIFICATION AND USE — N. C.
Land-use in Clay County.
H7050 (LMC)

LAND CLASSIFICATION AND USE — N. Y.
Economic Study of Land Utilization in Schuyler County, N. Y.
D410
Economic Study of Land Utilization in Chautauqua County, New York.
J2750
Economic Study of Land Utilization in Otsego County, New York.
J2760

LAND CLASSIFICATION AND USE — TENN.
Minimum Land Requirements for Specified Levels of Farm Income in the Eastern Highland Rim of Tennessee.
E30
"Rural Land Use in Franklin County, Tennessee."
G630
Land Use Analysis.
J1510 (ETSU)
Land Use Plan.
J1520 (ETSU)

LAND CLASSIFICATION AND USE — VA.
Economic Land Classification of Pulaski County.
G1190

LAND CLASSIFICATION AND USE — W. VA.
Rural Underemployment and Land Use in a Marginal Agricultural Area of West Virginia.
B6150

LAND GRANTS AND LOTTERIES — GA.
Index to the Headright and Bounty Grants of Georgia, 1759-1909.
L3830 (ASU)
The Second or 1807 Land Lottery of Georgia.
L3840 (ASU)

LAND GRANTS AND RECORDS
Two Years of Harriman, Tennessee. Established by the East Tennessee Land Company, February 26, 1890.
E160 (ASU BC)
L2760
Cavaliers and Pioneers: Abstracts of Virginia Land Patents and Grants, 1623-1666.
N2960 (ASU)

LAND GRANTS AND RECORDS — GA.
The Third and Fourth or 1820 and 1821 Land Lotteries of Georgia.
G940 (ASU)
Genealogical History of Original Murray County.
W5650
1805 Georgia Land Lottery.
W8670 (ASU BC)

LAND GRANTS AND RECORDS — INDIANS
"James Robertson: Frontiersman."
B570

LAND GRANTS AND RECORDS — KY.
The Transylvania Company and the Founding of Henderson, Ky.
H4450 (ASU)
The Kentucky Land Grants: A Systematic Index to the Land Grants Recorded in the State Land Office at Frankfort, Kentucky, 1782-1924.
J1160 (ASU)
Old Kentucky Entries and Deeds. A Complex Index to All of the Earliest Land Entries, Military Warrants, Deeds and Wills of the Commonwealth of Kentucky.
J1190 (ASU MHC)
A Calendar of the Warrants for Land in Kentucky Granted for Service in the French and Indian War.
K1280 (BC ASU)

LAND GRANTS AND RECORDS — N. C.
Land Entry Book, Wilkes County, North Carolina, 1778-1781.
A160 (ASU)
Deed Book A-1 Wilkes County, North Carolina.
A170
Buncombe County, North Carolina, Grantee Deed Index.
D2370
Buncombe County, North Carolina, Grantor Deed Index.
D2380
Abstracts of Deeds, Rutherford County, North Carolina, Volumes A-D.
G3570
The History of Land Titles in Western North Carolina: With Supplement.
S4360 (ASU LMC WCU UNCA)

LAND GRANTS AND RECORDS — TENN.
Rugby, Tennessee, Being Some Account of the Settlement Founded on the Cumberland Plateau by the Board of Aid to Land Ownership, Ltd.
H8130 (LMC BC)

LAND GRANTS AND RECORDS — VA.
Abstract of Land Grant Surveys, 1761-1791.
K310 (ASU)
Virginia Revolutionary Land Bounty Warrants.
W7460
Catalogue of Revolutionary Soldiers and Sailors of the Commonwealth of Va.; to Whom Land Bounty Warrants were Granted. . . .
W7470 (BC)
Catalogue of Revolutionary Soldiers and Sailors of the Commonwealth of Virginia to Whom Land Bounty Warrants Were Granted by Virginia for Military Services in the War for Independence.
W7480 (ASU)

LAND GRANTS AND RECORDS — W. VA.
Indexes to Land Grants in West Virginia.
S3660 (ASU)

LAND GRANTS — N. C.
L2750 (WCU ASU)

LAND GRANTS — TENN.
L2750 (WCU ASU)

LAND LOTTERIES
L2760
1805 Georgia Land Lottery.
W8670 (ASU BC)

LAND LOTTERIES — GA.
The Third and Fourth or 1820 and 1821 Land Lotteries of Georgia.
G940 (ASU)

LAND LOTTERIES — N. C.
L2750 (WCU ASU)
LAND LOTTERIES — TENN.
"Long-lots in Washington County, Tennessee, with Reference to Past and Present Land-holding Shapes."
H1230 (ETSU)
L2750 (WCU ASU)
LAND OWNERSHIP
Social Factors Associated with Land Class in Overton County, Tennessee.
A1890
Government Land Acquisition: A Summary of Land Acquisition by Federal, State and Local Governments up to 1964.
A2140 (LMC)
"James Robertson: Frontiersman."
B570
Rights-of-Way for Removal of Natural Resources From West Virginia Land: An Examination of Existing Applicable Law and of Possible Changes Therein.
B7300 (ASU)
General James Robertson, Father of Tennessee.
M4360 (ETSU ASU)
Home and Farm Ownership.
N1740 (LMC)
Cavaliers and Pioneers: Abstracts of Virginia Land Patents and Grants, 1623-1666.
N2960 (ASU)
Classification of Land Ownership in Bedford Co., Virginia.
P680
LAND OWNERSHIP — APP.
The Southern Appalachian Forests.
A5850 (ASU BC LMC ETSU)
The Transylvania Colony.
L1910 (BC ASU)
Biography of James Patton.
P830
Influence of Woodland and Owner Characteristics of Forest Management.
T4790
Purchase of Land under the Weeks Law in the Southern Appalachian and White Mountains.
U2960
Purchase of Land under the Weeks Law in the Southern Appalachian and White Mountains.
U2970
LAND OWNERSHIP — APPALACHIAN POWER CO.
Order of Business for Real Estate and Rights of Way.
A3450
LAND OWNERSHIP — COLONIALISM — APP.
A4470 (ASU)
LAND OWNERSHIP — GA.
Cherokee and Creek Indians. Returns a Property Left in Tennessee and Georgia, 1838.
M1470
LAND OWNERSHIP — GOVT.
Managing 10,000 Miles of Shoreline.
C670
LAND OWNERSHIP — KY.
The Kentucky Land Grants: A Systematic Index to the Land Grants Recorded in the State Land Office at Frankfort, Kentucky, 1782-1924.
J1160 (ASU)
Old Kentucky Entries and Deeds. A Complex Index to All of the Earliest Land Entries, Military Warrants, Deeds and Wills of the Commonwealth of Kentucky.
J1190 (ASU MHC)
A Calendar of the Warrants for Land in Kentucky Granted for Service in the French and Indian War.
K1280 (BC ASU)
Appalachian Kentucky, an Exploited Region.
L440 (ETSU)
Petitions of the Early Inhabitants of Kentucky to the General Assembly of Virginia, 1769.
R3160
LAND OWNERSHIP — LEGATION
United States of America, on the Relation of Oscar L. Chapman, Secretary of the Interior, Petitioner v. Federal Power Commission, Virginia Electric and Power Company, et al. Virginia REA Association, et al. On Writs of Certiorari to the United States Court of Appeals for the Fourth Circuit. Brief for Appalachian Electric Power Company, Intervenor.
A3490
LAND OWNERSHIP — LOTTERIES
1832 Cherokee Land Lottery: Index to Revolutionary Soldiers, Their Widows and Orphans Who Were Fortunate Drawers.
R2150 (ASU WCU)
The Cherokee Land Lottery.
S4820 (LMC ETSU ASU BC)
The Cherokee Land Lottery.
S4830 (ETSU)
The Cherokee Land Lottery, Containing a Numerical List of the Names of the Fortunate Drawers in Said Lottery, With an Engraved Map of Each District.
S4840 (ASU WCU BC)
LAND OWNERSHIP — N. C.
Deed Book B-1 Wilkes County, North Carolina.
A150
Land Entry Book, Wilkes County, North Carolina, 1778-1781.
A160 (ASU)
Deed Book A-1 Wilkes County, North Carolina.
A170
C3670 (ASU)
Cherokee Lands, Report.
N2360
North Carolina Lands: Ownership, Use, and Management of Forest and Related Lands.
P3470 (ASU LMC BC WCU UNCA)
The History of Land Titles in Western North Carolina: With Supplement.
S4360 (ASU LMC WCU UNCA)
LAND OWNERSHIP — TENN.
North Carolina Land Grants in Tennessee, 1778-1791.
C1800 (ETSU BC ASU)
Two Years of Harriman, Tennessee. Established by the East Tennessee Land Company, February 26, 1890.
E160 (ASU BC)
"Long-lots in Washington County, Tennessee, with Reference to Past and Present Land-holding Shapes."
H1230 (ETSU)
"The Settlement Pattern of Upper East Tennessee."
H3910 (ETSU)
Rugby, Tennessee, Being Some Account of the Settlement Founded on the Cumberland Plateau by the Board of Aid to Land Ownership, Ltd.
H8130 (LMC BC)
Cherokee and Creek Indians. Returns a Property Left in Tennessee and Georgia, 1838.
M1470
LAND OWNERSHIP — VA.
Virginia Baron: The Story of Thomas, 6th Lord Fairfax.
B7400 (ASU BC)
Washington's Western Lands.
C6910 (ASU)
Free Negro Labor and Property Holding in Virginia, 1830-1860.
J160 (ETSU)
LAND OWNERSHIP — W. VA.
Indexes to Land Grants in West Virginia.
S3660 (ASU)
Surveying Rural Property Boundary Lines in West Virginia: A Guide For Surveyors, Attorneys, Landowners, and Others.
S3730 (LMC)
LAND USE
A2870
Land Development Plan.
B5440 (BC ASU)
The Rural Land Use of Washington County, Tennessee.
M2970
"Shifts in Land Use in the Appalachian Region of Virginia."
O550 (LMC ASU)
Footprints in the Soil and Reflections on the Water: Conservation in West Virginia.
O570 (ASU)
"Land Utilization in Roane County, Tennessee."
P450
Economic Land Classification of Clarke Co., Va.
P720
Tenn. Valley Land and Its Changing Use.
S5400
LAND USE — APP.
Conservation: An American Story of Conflict and Accomplishment.
C8240
Planning a Tourist Recreation Region for the Age of Leisure. Printed by Planning and Land Use Education Program, Appalachian State Univ., 1974.
N890 (ASU)
"Socio-Economic Readjustment of Farm Families Displaced by the TVA Land Purchase in the Norris Area."
N1000
Tenn. Valley Land and Its Changing Use.
S150
An Inventory of Land and Its Use in the Tennessee Valley.
S5100
Fifty Inches of Rain. A Story of Land and Water Conservation.
T2700 (BC)
The Land Between the Lakes; A Demonstration in Recreation Resource Development; Revised Concept Statement.
T3010
Recreational Development of the Southern Highlands Region; A Study of the Use and Control of Scenic and Recreational Resources.
T4290 (LMC)
The Scenic Resources of the Tennessee Valley; A Descriptive and Pictorial Inventory.
T4310
Land Acquisition in TVA. An Analysis of TVA Land Acquisition, Land Management, and Family Relocation Procedures as They Could Relate to the Missouri Valley Development. Statements Presented Before the Select Subcommittee on Real Property Acquisition of the Committee on Public Works.
T5150
Atlas of the Tennessee Valley Region.
T5830
Inundation & erosion in the Appalachian region.
U3210
"Reservoir Impacts on Economic Activity, Land Use and Land Values in Appalachia."
W5220
"Economic Aspects of Surface Subsidence Resulting from Underground Mineral Exploitation."
Z190
LAND USE — KY.
"Land Use in Powell County, Kentucky."
D1900
Family Incomes and Land Utilization in Knott County, Kentucky.
N900
Family Incomes and Land Utilization in Knott County, Kentucky.
N910
LAND USE — N. C.
"The Asheville Basin of North Carolina: A Study in Highland Agricultural Land Use."
L3690 (LMC ASU)
Planning a Tourist Recreation Region for the Age of Leisure. Printed by Planning and Land Use Education Program, Appalachian State Univ., 1974.
N890 (ASU)
Proceedings of the Third Annual Workshop on the Third Annual Workshop on the Planning and Utilization of Leisure Resources, March 18-19.
N1620 (ASU)
Community Facilities Plan & Public Improvements Program: Valdese, North Carolina.
N2040 (WCU)
Land Development Plan for Black Mountain, N. C.
N2050 (WCU)
Land Development Plan: Boone, North Carolina.
N2060 (WCU ASU)
Land Development Plan: Burnsville, N. C.
N2070 (WCU)
Land Potential Study: Madison County, North Carolina.
N2080 (WCU)
Land Potential Study & Land Development Plan: Wilkes County, North Carolina.
N2090 (ASU WCU)
Land Use Survey and Analysis and Land Development Plan: Valdese, North Carolina.
N2110 (WCU)
Watauga County Land Development Plan.
N2180 (ASU)
Zoning Ordinance: Boone, N. C.
N2190 (LMC ASU)

LAND USE — N. C.
Zoning Ordinance of the W. Kerr Scott Reservoir Area, Wilkes County, N. C.
N2200 (ASU)
Zoning Ordinance: Wilkes County, North Carolina.
N2210 (ASU WCU)
The Southern Highlands Mountain Resources Management Plan.
N2480
LAND USE — PA.
Operation Scarlift, the After-Effects of Over 100 Years of Coal Mining In Pennsylvania and Current Programs to Combat Them.
P1800
Conservation Law and Administration: A Case Study of Law and Resource Use in Pennsylvania.
S1170
LAND USE — TENN.
"The Sequatchie Valley, Tennessee, a Study in Land Utilization."
M3770
"Geographic Factors in the Land Use of Green County, Tennessee."
P390
Melton Hill Reservoir, Comprehensive Plan for Land Use Development.
T1650
Reservoir Shore Line Development in Tennessee; a Study of Problems and Opportunities.
T1700
Multiple-Use of Norris Watershed.
T4810
Pickwick Landing Dam on the Tennessee River.
T6460
LAND USE — VA.
Economic Land Classification of Augusta Co., Virginia.
P690
Economic Land Classification of Botetourt Co., Virginia.
P700
Economic Land Classification of Culpeper Co., Va.
P730
Economic Land Classification of Grayson Co., Va.
P740
Economic Land Classification of Greene Co., Va.
P750
Economic Land Classification of Loudoun Co., Va.
P760
Economic Land Classification of Shenandoah County, Va.
P770
Economic Land Classification of Smyth Co., Va.
P780
Economic Land Classification of Wythe Co., Va.
P790
LAND USE — W. VA.
"Land Use in Greenbriar County, West Virginia."
W5110 (BC)
LAW — APP.
. . . Injunctions in Cases Involving Acts of Congress. Letter from the Chairman of the Tennessee Valley Authority Transmitting, in Response to Senate Resolution no. 82, Certain Information Concerning Injunctions or Judgments Issued or Rendered by Federal Courts Since March 4, 1933, in Cases Involving Acts of Congress. . . .
T2940
Current and Proposed Regulations and Legislation on Air Pollution Concerning the Appalachian Coal Industry.
W7190
LAW ENFORCEMENT
The Incomparable Don Chafin.
S9410 (BC ASU)
LAW ENFORCEMENT — APP.
W5350 (BC)
LAW ENFORCEMENT — TENN.
"The Office of Knox County Sheriff: An Administrative Study."
B660
LAW — KY.
Richard Hickman Menefee.
T9090 (BC)
Life and Times of Judge Caleb Wallace, Some Time a Justice of the Court of Appeals of the State of Ky.
W5870 (BC)
LAW — PA.
"Social Legislation for the Protection of Coal Miners in Pennsylvania."
Z90
LAW — TENN.
Personal and Professional Reminiscences of an Old Lawyer.
P3160
History of Codification in Tennessee.
W6750 (ETSU)
LAW — TENNESSEE VALLEY AUTHORITY
. . . A Compilation of the More Important Congressional Acts, Treaties, Presidential Messages, Judicial Decisions, and Official Reports and Documents Having to do with the Control, Conservation, and Utilization of Water Resources.
T5090
Congressional Hearings, Reports, and Documents Relating to TVA. 1933-.
T5910
LAW — VA.
An Old Virginia Court: Being a Transcript of the Records of the First Court of Franklin County, Virginia, 1786-1789, with Biographies of the Justices and Stories of Famous Cases.
V730 (ASU ETSU)
LAW — W. VA.
Acts of the Legislature of West Virginia at Its First Session, Commencing June 20th, 1863.
W4120 (BC)
The School Law of West Virginia.
W4130 (BC)
The School Law of West Virginia.
W4140 (BC)
School Laws of West Virginia.
W4150 (ETSU)
The School Law of West Va. and Opinions of the Attorney-General and Decisions of the State Superintendent of Free Schools.
W4160 (BC)
LAWS
Constitution and Laws of the Cherokee Nation.
C3680 (ASU)
LAWS — APP.
Natural Resource Special Districts in Appalachia: Review of Enabling Laws.
H1330
LAWS — CHEROKEE
"The Judicial History of the Cherokee Nation from 1721 to 1835."
D2220
L940
A Law of Blood: The Primitive Law of the Cherokee Nation.
R1410 (LMC BC UNCA)
LAWS — KY.
Nisi Prius.
B6990 (ASU BC)
Kentucky Law on Water.
C4790
Lawyer's Lawyer; the Life of John W. Davis.
H1750 (ASU BC)
The County Courts in Antebellum Kentucky.
I940 (BC WWC)
LAWS — MD.
Maryland Water Law: Water Laws and Legal Principles Affecting the Use of Water in Maryland.
G120
LAWS — N. C.
"Community Correlates of Crime and Law Enforcement Activities in Northwestern North Carolina."
H6160 (ASU)
North Carolina County Legislation Index: A Complete Listing of the Local or Special Acts Passed by the General Assembly for Each County, 1669-1961.
N2440 (LMC)
LAWS — RECONSTRUCTION — KU KLUX KLAN
Invisible Empire: The Story of the Ku Klux Klan, 1866-1871.
H7210
Invisible Empire: The Story of the Ku Klux Klan, 1866-1871.
H7211
Invisible Empire: The Story of the Ku Klux Klan, 1866-1871.
H7212
Invisible Empire: The Story of the Ku Klux Klan, 1866-1871.
H7213
Invisible Empire: The Story of the Ku Klux Klan, 1866-1871.
H7214
LAWS — TENN.
"Washington County Court, 1796-1836."
F920 (ETSU)
Six Days or Forever? Tennessee v. John Thomas Scopes.
G1830 (ASU BC)
Bench and Bar of Knox County, Tennessee.
G3580 (BC)
Private Acts of Anderson County, 1801-1956.
T1570
"An Attitudinal Study of Sunday Closing Laws in Johnson City, Tennessee: A Contribution to the "Interest-group" (Conflict) Model of Law."
T7830 (ETSU)
LAWS — TENN. — EVOLUTION
Center of the Storm: Memoirs of John T. Scopes.
R1340 (ASU WCU)
The World's Most Famous Court Trial, Tennessee Evolution Case: A Complete Stenographic Report of the Famous Court Test of the Tennessee Anti-evolution Act, at Dayton, July 10 to 21, 1925, Including Speeches and Arguments of Attorneys.
R1350 (ASU BC)
LAWS — VA.
The Compacts of Virginia.
C6800 (FC)
The Inside Story of the World Famous Courtroom Tragedy.
C7060 (BC)
Virginia Court Records in Southwestern Pennsylvania. Records of the District of West Augusta and Ohio and Yohogania Counties, Virginia, 1775-1780.
C9350
A Curiosity in Chancery.
D660
The Code of Virginia: With the Declaration of Independence and Constitution of the U. S.: And the Declaration of Rights and Constitution of Virginia.
V1090 (LMC)
LAWS — W. VA.
The Lawmaking Process in West Virginia: A Study in Legislative Ethics.
C5560 (LMC)
Issues of Constitutional Revision in West Virginia.
D930
West Virginia State and Local Government.
D940 (ETSU BC)
LEGAL SERVICE — KY.
They Tried to Crucify Me; or, the Smokescreen of the Cumberlands.
L430
LEGAL SERVICES
Appalachian Research and Defense Fund Public Interest Report.
A4010
B4750 (BC)
Rights-of-Way for Removal of Natural Resources From West Virginia Land: An Examination of Existing Applicable Law and of Possible Changes Therein.
B7300 (ASU)
A Survey of the Legal Environment of Knox County, Kentucky.
C2590
The Traipsin' Woman.
T7970 (ASU WWC BC)
LEGAL SERVICES — APP.
Papers and Proceedings of Appalachian Legal Services Conference, Knoxville, Tenn., July 24-26, 1969.
A3230 (BC)
The Legal Problems of the Appalachian Area in the Immediate Region of Western North Carolina.
B5530 (LMC)
Directory.
C7950 (ASU)
The Legal Status of the Tenant Farmer in the Southeast.
M3040 (LMC)

LEGAL SERVICES — APP.
Legal Problems of Coal Mine Reclamation: Study in Maryland, Ohio, Pennsylvania, and West Virginia.
M3930 (BC)
LEGAL SERVICES — CHEROKEE
A Study of Judicial Procedures on the Cherokee Indian Reservation.
K2670 (LMC ASU)
LEGAL SERVICES — N. C.
North Carolina County Legislation Index: A Complete Listing of the Local or Special Acts Passed by the General Assembly for Each County, 1669-1961.
N2440 (LMC)
LEGAL SERVICES — OHIO
Comparative State Strip Mining and Reclamation Laws.
O390
LEGAL SERVICES — PA.
Available for Work: The Pennsylvania Unemployment Compensation Interpretation.
B7550
Conservation Law and Administration: A Case Study of Law and Resource Use in Pennsylvania.
S1170
LEGAL SERVICES — TENN.
Sketches of the Bench and Bar of Tennessee.
C130 (ASU)
"Unicoi County Court: 1876-1918."
P4110 (ETSU)
"Community Concept of Juvenile Court Function in Knox County, Tennessee."
S3460
LEGAL SERVICES — VA.
P4690
LEGAL SERVICES — W. VA.
"The West Virginia Labor Federation and the West Virginia Legislature, 1957-1961."
B8350
The Lawmaking Process in West Virginia: A Study in Legislative Ethics.
C5560 (LMC)
The Recollections of Fifty Years of West Virginia.
M600 (BC ASU)
LIBRARIES
A2760 (BC)
"Student Involvement in the Policies of a Junior High School Library — An Experiment."
B340 (ETSU)
Library Services in West Virginia, Present and Proposed.
B4670 (ASU)
"A History of the Library Resources of Putnam County, Tennessee."
B8180
Libraries in North Carolina.
N2450 (WWC)
The Development of a Bibliographic Center in the West Virginia Region: Final Report, 1966.
W4610 (ASU)
Guide to Manuscripts and Archives in the West Virginia Collection.
W4620 (ASU ETSU BC)
LIBRARIES — ALA.
"A Survey of the Library Facilities in the Negro Schools of Tuscaloosa County, Alabama."
D2540
"A Survey of School Library Facilities and Services in Four Selected High Schools in Jefferson County, Alabama."
W6410
LIBRARIES — APP.
Resources of the Appalachian Library and Culture Center, an Annotated Listing of Books, Recordings and Other Media.
A3240
Libraries of the South — A Report on Developments, 1930-1935.
B1160
The Library in the TVA Adult Education Program.
C2880 (ETSU)
County Library Service in the South.
W7390 (BC)
LIBRARIES — GA.
"Initiating the Rural Library Program in Towns and Union Counties, Georgia."
L3710
LIBRARIES — KY.
"Book Extension Services in Eastern Kentucky."
B2230 (ASU)
From Bishop Percy (1765) to John Jacob Niles (1974): 340 Books of Ballads and Songs in the Berea College Collection.
P2150 (BC ASU)
Mountain Fiction From Addington to Zugsmith: 924 Works of Fiction by Southern Appalachian Authors, Or With Southern Appalachian Settings.
P2160
A Shelf List of More than 760 Works of Fiction.
P2170
"A Plan for Regional Library Development in Eastern Kentucky."
P3920
Kentucky Public Library Inventory and Projected Needs.
S6240
LIBRARIES — N. C.
A Survey of the Public Libraries of Asheville and Buncombe County, North Carolina.
C2730 (LMC ETSU ASU)
"A History of the Public Library in Murphy, N. C."
C6930
The Asheville Archive, College of the City of Asheville, N. C.
N1780
"An Evaluation of the Library Proficiencies of Freshmen at Appalachian State Teachers College, 1953-54."
O1020 (ASU)
S5780 (MHC)
Union List of Periodicals in Libraries of Western North Carolina Library Association.
W4880 (ASU)
Union List of Periodicals in Libraries of Western North Carolina.
W4890 (LMC)
"A Comparative Study of Tendencies and Motivational Factors of Students from Various Academic Departments Who Vandalize Library Materials at Appalachian State University."
W6570 (ASU)
Guide to the Manuscripts in the Southern Historical Collection of the University of North Carolina.
W9190 (LMC)
LIBRARIES — PA.
A Description of the George Korson Folklore Archine.
C7460 (ASU)
LIBRARIES — TENN.
"A Study of Book Losses During the Period 1965-1969 in the Dobyns-Bennett High School Materials Center, Kingsport, Tennessee."
B2920 (ETSU)
"A Survey of the Elementary School Libraries in Washington County, Tennessee."
B4560 (ETSU)
"Some Types of County and City Library Services to Schools in Tennessee."
C9890 (ETSU)
Library handbook. . . .
E320 (ETSU)
"Available Material in Knox County for Enriching the Teaching of Tennessee History."
F190 (ETSU)
"A Program of Library Instruction for the Ninth Grade Pupils at Jonesboro High School."
F3030 (ETSU)
Guide to Depositories of Manuscript Collection in Tennessee.
H5790 (ETSU)
List of Tennessee Imprints, 1793-1840, in Tennessee Libraries.
H5880 (ETSU)
"A Study of the Use of Student Library Assistants in the Secondary Schools of East Tennessee."
H7620
"A Program of Visual Instruction for Use in Teaching the Location of Major Resources in the East Tennessee State University Library."
L1030 (ETSU)
Calvin Morgan McClung Historical Collection.
L4040
"A Simplified Library Program for the Elementary Schools of Carter County, Tennessee."
M8320 (ETSU)
Public Library Service Study: Final Report.
T1440
T1590 (ETSU)
University of Tennessee Library Lectures.
T2240 (ASU)
. . . A Bibliography of the Tennessee Valley Authority.
T5880
A Bibliography for the TVA Program.
T5890
. . . A Chronology of the Tennessee Valley Authority.
T5900
"A Survey of Library Services in the County Schools of Sullivan County, Tennessee."
T7840 (ETSU)
LIBRARIES — VA.
"An Evaluation of the Elementary School Libraries in Washington County, Virginia."
C6510 (ETSU)
A Study of Library Services in Some Southwest Virginia Schools."
F3720 (ETSU)
LIBRARIES — W. VA.
McDowell County, West Virginia, Library Survey.
B8360 (BC)
Survey for Library Development in Fayette and Raleigh Counties, West Virginia.
B8370 (BC)
A Proposed Regional Library for Wood, Pleasants, Tyler, and Wetzel Counties.
M5710
W4220 (ETSU)
Wyoming County on the Alert: A Socio-Economic Survey by Wyoming County Advisory Committee for Library Service and West Virginia Library Commission.
W9890
LICKING RIVER
Bibliography of Licking River Valley in Ky.
J880
Interim Study report on Upper Licking River Basin, Kentucky.
U290 (BC)
LITERATURE
Thomas Wolfe, Carolina Student: A Brief Biography.
A360 (ASU WCU)
Thomas Wolfe: Carolina Student; A Brief Biography.
A370 (ASU WCU)
Encomium for Scott County, Virginia.
A500
Agee on Film: Five Film Scripts.
A640 (BC ASU)
Agee on Film: Reviews and Comments.
A650 (ASU)
The Collected Poems of James Agee.
A660 (ASU WCU ETSU BC)
The Collected Short Prose of James Agee.
A670 (ASU WCU ETSU BC)
A Death in the Family.
A680 (ETSU BC WWC ASU)
A Death in the Family.
A690 (WCU)
Four Early Stories.
A700 (ETSU BC)
Letters of James Agee to Father Flye.
A710 (BC ETSU ASU)
Letters of James Agee to Father Flye.
A720
The Morning Watch.
A760 (BC ASU WCU)
Permit Me Voyage.
A770 (ETSU)
Philip Pendelton Cooke.
A1580 (BC)
The Buck Fever Papers.
A2380 (ASU)
Death in the Woods and Other Stories.
A2390
Hello Towns.
A2400 (ASU)
Hello Towns.
A2410 (LMC ASU)
Kit Brandon: A Portrait.
A2420 (ASU ETSU BC)
Letters; Selected and Edited with an Introduction and Notes by Howard Mumford Jones, in association with Walter B. Rideout.
A2430 (BC ASU)

LITERATURE
The Dollmaker.
A4900 (ETSU BC ASU WCU LMC MHC WWC)
A Biography of Thomas Wolfe.
A5570 (ASU WCU)
The Autobiography of Waldron Bailey.
B390 (ASU LMC BC)
Voices from Vale and Hill.
B730 (BC)
A Barbecue Toast.
B840 (ASU)
Southern Writers: Biographical and Critical.
B1780
John Esten Cooke, Virginian.
B2390
"Life and Literary Contributions of Luther Foster Addington, a Southwest Virginia Writer and Educator.
B2910
1924 Works of Fiction by Southern Appalachian Authors, Or with Southern Appalachian Settings: Mountain Fiction from Addington to Zugsmith.
B3080 (ASU MHC ETSU BC)
Afterglow: A Collection of Short Stories and Poems.
B4360 (ASU BC)
"Jesse Stuart and His Work: A Critical Study."
B4460 (ASU BC)
Jesse Stuart: His Life and Works.
B4470 (ASU BC)
Native American Humor (1800-1900).
B4500 (MHC BC)
Stray Leaves from the Hillside.
B4590
The Voice of the Folk: Folklore and American Literary Theory.
B4840 (FC)
The Southern Mountaineer in Literature, an Annotated Bibliography.
B5040 (ETSU ASU LMC BC FC UNCA)
"Study of a Dialect Employed by the People of the Kentucky Mountains and Presented through a Group of Original Short Stories."
B5760 (ASU)
West Virginia Authors: A Bibliography.
B6490 (BC)
Thomas Wolfe
B6800 (ASU WCU)
After the Good Gay Times: Asheville — Summer of '35; A Season with F. Scott Fitzgerald.
B9430
Country Style: An Anthology of Hillbilly Humor.
B9630 (LMC)
Sketches of the Bench and Bar of Tennessee.
C130 (ASU)
Elizabeth Madox Roberts, American Novelist.
C590 (BC)
Southern Literary Culture: A Bibliography of Master's and Doctor's Theses.
C1120 (ASU LMC)
Mountain Lyrics and Sketches.
C1370 (WCU)
Mary N. Murfree.
C1890 (ASU)
Fugitive Lyrics of John Heiskell Booton.
C1980
The Southern Appalachian Heritage.
C2041
The High Cost of Writing.
C2370 (BC)
The Wooden Tower.
C2510
A World of Books.
C2720 (BC)
The Lost World of Thomas Wolfe, Thomas Wolfe Home.
C2830 (LMC MHC ASU)
Carolina Country Reader.
C2900 (WCU)
"The Social and Economic Aspects of the Novels of Jesse Stuart."
C3330 (ASU)
Lazar and Boone Stop Strip Mining Bully to Save Apple Valley and Buttermilk Creek.
C4510 (ASU)
Jesse Stuart's Kentucky.
C4680 (ASU WCU LMC MHC BC)
Proverb, Proverbial Phrases and Proverbial Comparisons in the Writings of Jesse Stuart.
C4690
Southern Season.
C4730 (ASU)
Clinard Looks Back, a Compilation of Short Stories Covering Early Days in Hickory.
C5060 (ASU LMC)
Johnny Park Talks of Thomas Wolfe.
C5430 (ASU LMC)
"A Study of the Black Mountain Poets."
C6150 (WCU)
Best of Hillbilly: A Prize Collection of 100-proof Writings from Jim Comstock's West Virginia Hillbilly.
C6300 (ASU MHC WCU LMC BC)
Thomas Dixon: His Books and His Career.
C6870
An American Story-book. Short Stories from Studies of Life in Southwestern Pennsylvania.
C8090 (ASU)
Southwestern Pennsylvania in Song and Story.
C8100
Hunger: A Tragedy of North Carolina Farm Folk.
D120
Thomas Wolfe: October Recollections.
D200 (ASU)
Chronicle of the Cavaliers: A Life of the Virginia Novelist, Dr. William A. Caruthers.
D950 (WCU ASU)
'Pon my Honor, Hit's the Truth; Tall Tales from the Mountains.
D1050 (BC)
Silhouettes of American Life.
D1200 (ETSU ASU)
Silhouettes of American Life.
D1210 (ASU BC ETSU)
Waiting for the Verdict.
D1220
Shepherd Monroe Dugger: A Critical Biography.
D1370 (LMC ASU)
"A Lexicographical Study of the Vocabulary of Greenup County, Kentucky, Set Forth in Jesse Stuart's "Beyond Dark Hills"."
D2210 (ASU)
Dipped in Sky; a Study of Percy MacKaye's "Kentucky Mountain Cycle."
D2800 (BC)
Davy Crockett: American Comic Legend.
D3060 (ASU)
Dubose Heyward: The Southern as Artist.
D4050
John Filson, the First Historian of Kentucky: An Account of His Life and Writings.
D4100 (LMC)
Harriette Arnow.
E770 (BC)
A Bibliography of Appalachian Children's and Young People's Books.
E1170
E1570
John Henry and His Hammer.
F560
Springboard to Optimism Versus Majoring in the Minors: A Dozen Books in One.
F670 (ASU)
Thomas Wolfe: Three Decades of Criticism.
F780 (ASU WCU BC UNCA)
Thomas Wolfe as I Knew Him, and Other Essays.
F1210 (BC ASU UNCA WCU)
Provincial Types in American Fiction.
F1270 (ASU)
Jesse Stuart.
F2350 (ASU LMC WCU BC)
Look Homeward, Angel: A Play Based on the Novel by Thomas Wolfe.
F3410 (ASU BC)
F3460 (ASU BC)
Southern Life in Southern Literature.
F3810
G1000 (MHC)
Thomas Wolfe and the Glass of Time.
G1030 (ETSU ASU)
Around Our House.
G1360 (BC)
A Little Better Than Plumb: The Biography of a House.
G1380 (BC ASU ETSU)
Stories of the Foot-hills.
G3140 (ASU)
The Portable Sherwood Anderson.
G3970
Essays on North Carolina History.
G4120 (ASU LMC)
Look Back with Love: A Recollection of the Blue Ridge.
H1610 (ASU WCU LMC MHC ETSU FC WWC BC)
Middletown Valley in Song and Story.
H1740 (BC)
My Book and Heart.
H2730 (ASU BC)
High Times and Hard Times: Sketches and Tales.
H2800 (ASU BC)
The Lovingood Papers.
H2810
Sut Lovingood.
H2820 (ASU)
Sut Lovingood. Yarns Spun by a "Nat'ral Born Durn'd Fool." Warped and Wove for Public Wear.
H2830 (ASU BC ETSU)
Sut Lovingood's Yarns.
H2840 (ASU WWC)
"Charles Egbert Craddock as an Interpreter of Mountain Life."
H2900
"Charles Egbert Craddock as an Interpreter of Mountain Life."
H2910 (ASU)
"The Southern Mountaineer in American Fiction, 1824-1910."
H2920 (ASU ETSU)
Balaam and His Master, and Other Sketches and Stories.
H2940 (WCU)
Joel Chandler Harris, Editor and Essayist: Miscellaneous Literary, Political and Social Writings.
H2950 (WCU)
The Frontier in American Literature.
H4100
My Rappahannock Storybook.
H6060 (BC ASU)
The Ballad of Tall Tom Wolfe.
H6190 (ASU)
History of Fentress County, Tennessee, the Old Home of Mark Twain's Ancestors.
H6410
Mark Twain's Obedstown and Knobs of Tennessee; a History of Jamestown and Fentress County, Tennessee.
H6420
Bulletin of the Virginia State Library: Index to Mrs. Cabell's "Sketches and Recollections of Lynchburg."
H6460 (ASU)
A History of Southern Literature.
H6640
Thomas Wolfe.
H6760 (ASU UNCA)
Three Modes of Modern Southern Fiction: Ellen Glasgow, William Faulkner, Thomas Wolfe.
H6770 (ASU MHC)
The World of Thomas Wolfe.
H6780 (ASU WCU MHC UNCA)
Some Adventures of Capt. Simon Suggs.
H7060 (ASU)
Chimney Rock Anthology.
I50
"Elements of Local Color in the Prose Fiction of Jesse Stuart."
J740 (ASU)
Kentucky Days.
J760 (ETSU)
Walking Bear of Silvermine Mountain.
J810
Thomas Wolfe: A Checklist.
J1670 (ASU)
Of Time and Thomas Wolfe: A Bibliography with a Character Index of His Works.
J1680 (ASU UNCA)
Southern Fiction Prior to 1860: An Attempt at a First Hand Bibliography.
J1820 (ASU)
Southern Fiction Prior to 1860: An Attempt at a First-hand Bibliography.
J1830 (MHC)
The Art of Thomas Wolfe.
J1890 (ASU WCU)
Thomas Wolfe: A Critical Study.
J1900 (ASU WCU BC)
North Carolina Fiction, 1734-1957: An Annotated Bibliography.
J2210 (ASU MHC)

LITERATURE

The Window of Memory: The Literary Career of Thomas Wolfe.
K800 (BC UNCA ASU WCU)
K1440

The Centennial Edition of the Works of Sidney Lanier.
L510 (MHC)

"The Literary Career of Jesse Stuart."
L1230 (ASU)

"Jesse Stuart: Kentucky's Chronicler-poet."
L1690

"The Southern Mountaineer in Fiction."
L2220 (ASU)

Cheap and Contented Labor; the Picture of a Southern Mill Town in 1929.
L2230

Fiction Fights the Civil War: An Unfinished Chapter in the Literary History of the American People.
L2880 (ASU)

"The Reactions of the Students of the Jonesboro, Tennessee, Middle School to Newbery Book Award Winners."
L3720 (ETSU)

Laughter and Tears in the Mountains.
L3780 (ASU BC)

Tom Wolfe's "Dixieland."
M830 (ASU WCU)

Dialect Tales.
M1210 (BC ASU ETSU)

Thomas Wolfe.
M1270 (ASU WCU UNCA)

Belonging: A Nostalgic Look at Appalachia.
M1840 (LMC)

"The Southern Highlands in Prose Fiction."
M2100 (ASU WCU)

Rediscoveries: Informal Essays in Which Well-known Novelists Rediscover Neglected Works of Fiction by One of Their Favorite Authors.
M2670 (ASU)

Human Migration: A Guide to Migration Literature in English, 1955-1962.
M3000

Southern Literature from 1579-1895.
M3100

Tall Tales from Old Smoky.
M4210 (ASU LMC BC ETSU)

Kentucky Moonshine.
M4440

"North Georgia Life in the Fiction of Will N. Harben."
M5080

Sketches of Life in North Carolina.
M5340

"A Study of the Life and Works of Jesse Stuart."
M6250 (ASU)

"An Intimate Study of Mary Noailles Murfree, Charles Egbert Craddock."
M6810 (ASU)

John Fox, Jr.: Personal and Family Letters and Papers.
M7110

Southern Character Sketches.
M7190 (ASU WCU)

"The Appalachia of Wilma Dykeman's Fiction."
M7340

Stories My Father Told Us.
M7510 (ASU)

Opie Read, American Humorist, 1852-1939.
M7830 (BC WCU)

"Selected Children's Fiction with a Contemporary Setting in the Mountains of Kentucky and North Carolina."
M7880 (ASU)

Thomas Wolfe.
M8540 (ASU UNCA)

Salt O'Life.
M9130 (ASU BC LMC WCU)

The Marble Man's Wife, Thomas Wolfe's Mother.
N2880 (ASU WCU BC UNCA)

Thomas Wolfe, a Biography.
N2930 (BC ASU WCU UNCA)

Agee.
O450 (WCU)

"A Study and Contrast of the Kentucky Mountaineer and the Bluegrass Aristocrat in the Works of John Fox, Jr."
O880 (ASU)

Charles Egbert Craddock.
P340 (ASU)

Queer Books.
P1290 (ASU LMC)

The Dark Hills of Jesse Stuart: A Consideration of Symbolism and Vision in the Novels of Jesse Stuart.
P1770 (LMC)

Reflections of Jesse Stuart on a Land of Many Moods.
P2200 (BC ASU WCU LMC MHC)

Thomas Wolfe at Washington Square.
P3440 (WCU ASU)

"They Are a Curious and Most Native Stock." The Southern Mountaineer in the Short-story."
P3630 (ASU)

North Carolina Fiction 1734-1957: An Annotated Bibliography.
P4000 (ASU MHC)

Thomas Wolfe, a Bibliography.
P4420 (BC ASU)

"The Southern Poor White in Fiction."
P4860

"An Inquiry into the Life of Jesse Stuart as Related to His Literary Development and a Critical Study of His Works."
R210 (ASU)

Randolph-Macon Prose and Verse, a Collection of Undergraduate Writings.
R430 (ASU)

Without Shelter: The Early Career of Ellen Glasgow.
R490 (ASU)

Thomas Wolfe: Memoir of a Friendship.
R710 (ASU WCU UNCA)

"An Examination of the Negro Character in Selected Fiction by White East Tennessee Writers."
R850 (ETSU)

The Merrill Studies in Look Homeward, Angel.
R1220 (ASU WCU)

Thomas Wolfe's Albatross: Race and Nationality in America.
R1230 (BC ASU WCU UNCA)

Thomas Wolfe and the Glass of Time.
R1240 (ETSU ASU WCU BC)

Charles Egbert Craddock and die Amerikanische Short Story.
R1370

Born of the Mountains.
R1740 (ASU WCU LMC)

The Southern Appalachian Region: Hitherto Untold Stories.
R1770 (ASU LMC)

"Sketches and Legends of Upper East Tennessee."
R1780 (LMC ASU)

Tallulah and Jocassee, or, Romances of Southern Landscape, and Other Tales.
R2030

Kentucky Literature 1784-1963.
R2170 (BC)

George Washington Harris.
R2190 (BC)

William Gilmore Simms.
R2280 (BC)

Sketches of Rabun County History, 1819-1948.
R2390 (BC ASU LMC)

"Jesse Stuart: Pioneer Writer of the Kentucky Hills."
R3750 (ASU)

Herald to Chaos: The Novels of Elizabeth Madox Roberts.
R4050 (ASU BC)

Thomas Wolfe; a Collection of Critical Essays.
R4180 (UNCA)

Thomas Wolfe: The Weather of His Youth.
R4190 (UNCA ASU WCU BC)

The Story of the McGuffeys.
R4270 (ASU BC)

Told in the Hills.
R4490

Thomas Wolfe.
R4530 (UNCA)

West Virginia, in History, Life, Literature and Industry.
S2540

West Virginia Civil War Literature.
S3030

Celluloid Muse: A Critical Study of James Agee.
S3310

The Folk of Southern Fiction.
S3830 (ASU)

Thomas Wolfe: Ulysses and Narcissus.
S5340 (ASU)

North Carolina Writers.
S6030 (LMC)

North Carolina Writers.
S6040 (LMC)

"Elizabeth M. Roberts: A Biographical and Critical Study."
S6050 (ASU)

Regionalism and Beyond: Essays of Randall Stewart.
S7340 (ASU)

"The Hillfolk Tradition and Images of the Hillfolk in American Fiction Since 1926."
S7560 (LMC BC)

The Cherokee in Romance, Tragedy, and Song in the Great Smokies.
S8020 (ETSU)

The Land beyond the River.
S8460 (LMC MHC WCU ETSU BC)

"Jesse Stuart and the Short Story."
T370 (ASU)

Lectures and Best Literary Productions of Bob Taylor.
T460 (ASU)

"The Short Stories of Jesse Stuart."
T540 (ASU)

Echoes: Centennial and Other Notable Speeches, Lectures, and Stories.
T720 (ASU)

The Kentucky Novel.
T8240 (ASU)

A Treasury of American Folk Humor; a Rare Collection of Laughter, Tall Tales, Jests and Other Gems of Merriment of the American People.
T8570 (FC)

John Fox, Jr.
T8770

Kentucky in American Letters, 1784-1912.
T9080 (ASU BC)
T9140 (BC)

William Gilmore Simms.
T9240 (ASU)

"Charles Egbert Craddock and the Southern Mountains and Mountaineers."
T9480 (ASU)

Thomas Wolfe.
T9750 (ASU WCU UNCA)
T9870

Bert Vincent's Strolling, Being Sort of a Side-Glance at the Little Odds and Ends of Life in These Parts.
V630

The Best Stories of Bert Vincent, ed. Willard Yarbrough.
V640

More of the Best Stories of Bert Vincent.
V650
W1380 (ETSU)

Thomas Wolfe's Characters: Portraits from Life.
W1440 (ASU WCU BC UNCA)

The Shenandoah Valley in History and Literature.
W1830 (ASU)

Wind Before Rain.
W1990 (ASU LMC BC)

"The Paradox of the Mountains: A Study of the Influences on Thomas Wolfe."
W2440 (LMC)

Poor Whites of the South.
W4950

Smoky Mountain Ballads.
W4980

Thomas Wolfe and His Family.
W5040 (ASU WCU BC UNCA)

Incidents and Anecdotes.
W5270 (LMC)

From the Mountain.
W5440 (ASU BC)
W5930 (BC)

A Selected Bibliography: The Southern Mountaineer in Fact and Fiction.
W6480 (ASU MHC)

"The Southern Mountaineer in Fact and Fiction."
W6490 (ASU MHC ETSU WWC BC)

"James Still: An Inquiry into the Intrinsic Value of the Works of a Regional Writer."
W7700 (LMC)

Thomas Wolfe's Letters to His Mother.
W8040 (ASU WCU)

The Correspondence of Thomas Wolfe and Homer Andrew Watt.
W8050 (UNCA ASU BC)

LITERATURE
The Face of a Nation: Poetical Passages from the Writings of Thomas Wolfe.
W8060 (ASU WCU BC ETSU)
From Death to Morning.
W8070 (ASU WCU LMC MHC BC UNCA ETSU)
The Hills Beyond.
W8080 (WWC)
The Hills Beyond.
W8090 (ASU WCU MHC ETSU BC)
The Hills Beyond.
W8100 (UNCA ASU)
Letters.
W8110 (UNCA)
The Letters of Thomas Wolfe.
W8120 (ASU WCU ETSU BC)
The Letters of Thomas Wolfe to His Mother.
W8130 (UNCA ASU WCU ETSU BC)
The Lost Boy.
W8190 (BC)
The Lost World of Thomas Wolfe.
W8200 (ASU WCU ETSU BC UNCA)
The Notebooks of Thomas Wolfe.
W8230 (UNCA BC WCU ETSU ASU)
Of Time and the River: A Legend of Man's Hunger in His Youth.
W8240 (ASU WCU BC UNCA WWC)
Of Time and the River: A Legend of Man's Hunger in His Youth.
W8250 (ETSU)
The Portable Thomas Wolfe.
W8260 (WCU ETSU)
Short Novels.
W8270 (UNCA ASU WCU WWC ETSU)
The Story of a Novel.
W8300 (ASU WCU ETSU BC UNCA)
The Thomas Wolfe Reader.
W8310 (ASU WCU WWC ETSU BC UNCA)
Thomas Wolfe's Letters to His Mother, Julia Elizabeth Wolfe.
W8320 (UNCA ASU BC)
Thomas Wolfe's Purdue Speech: Writing and Living.
W8330 (ASU ETSU BC UNCA)
To Rupert Brooke.
W8340 (ASU)
The Web and the Rock.
W8350 (UNCA ASU WCU BC)
The Web and the Rock.
W8360 (WWC ETSU)
A Western Journal: A Daily Log of the Great Parks Trip, June 20-July 2, 1928.
W8370 (UNCA ASU WCU ETSU BC)
The Years of Wandering in Many Lands and Cities.
W8380 (ASU BC)
You Can't Go Home Again.
W8390 (ASU WWC WCU ETSU BC UNCA)
The Correspondence of Thomas Wolfe and Homer Andrew Watt.
W8400 (ASU WCU ETSU)
LITERATURE — ALA.
Mary Gordon Duffee's Sketches of Alabama.
B7420
LITERATURE — APP.
Hill Doctor, Tells in Story and Ballads, Tales of the Appalachians.
B7750
The Literary Tradition of the Southern Mountaineer, 1824-1900.
C5950 (ETSU ASU)
Nineteenth Century Fiction of the Southern Appalachians.
C5960
Descriptive List of Novels and Tales Dealing with American Country Life.
G4330
Literary Profiles of the Southern States: A Manual for Schools and Clubs.
H2280 (ASU)
William Gilmore Simms: Realistic Romancer.
J410
"High-interest, Low-vocabulary Original Prose and Poetry for Teenagers in Southern Appalachia."
K1610 (ETSU)
"The Regionalist Movement in the Cumberland."
L1680 (ASU)
Great Smoky Mountain Stories and Sun over Ol' Starlin.
M4850 (LMC WCU)
Mountain Fiction From Addington to Zugsmith: 924 Works of Fiction by Southern Appalachian Authors, Or With Southern Appalachian Settings.
P2160
A Shelf List of More than 760 Works of Fiction.
P2170
Federal Writer's Project. Historical Records Survey.
U4080
"Folk Elements in the Fiction of James Still."
W270 (ASU)
Tennessee Tales.
W280 (ASU LMC ETSU BC)
The Enigma of Thomas Wolfe: Biographical and Critical Selections.
W570 (ASU WCU)
Literary North Carolina.
W580 (ASU BC)
North Carolina in the Short Story.
W610 (LMC BC)
Thomas Wolfe: An Introduction and Interpretation.
W630 (UNCA ASU WCU BC)
With Pen and Camera Thru the "Land of the Sky": Western North Carolina and the Asheville Plateau.
W790 (ASU)
"The Library in the Literature Program at Daniel Boone High School, Washington County, Tennessee."
W1530 (ETSU)
Some Appalachian Short Stories: A Bibliography.
W1590
LITERATURE — CHEROKEE
Cherokee Indian Lore and Smoky Mountain Stories.
S3340 (ASU BC)
Cherokee Indian Lore and Smoky Mountains Stories.
S3350 (ETSU)
LITERATURE — JUVENILE
Stories from an Indian Cave: The Cherokee Cave Builders.
B190 (ASU ETSU WCU)
Grandfather Tales: American-English Folk Tales.
C3420 (ASU WCU LMC MHC WWC ETSU BC FC)
Jack and the Three Sillies.
C3440 (ASU LMC MHC WCU BC)
The Jack Tales.
C3450 (ASU LMC MHC WWC WCU ETSU BC)
The Jack Tales.
C3460
Wicked John and the Devil.
C3500 (WCU BC)
"An Analysis of the Social Life and Customs of the Southern Appalachians as Reflected in Selected Children's Books."
D2610 (ASU)
"An Analysis of the Social Life and Customs of the Southern Appalachians as Reflected in Selected Children's Books."
D2620 (ASU)
Easter Story.
E1530 (LMC)
Daniel Boone.
M3750 (ASU)
Sissy, She's Coming Sunday.
M4150
Cain.
M4630
Call of the Hills.
M4640
Child of the Hills.
M4650
Echoes from the Hills.
M4660
Epic of Creation.
M4670
Philosophy of the Hills.
M4680
Ramble in the Hills.
M4690
The Return to the Hills.
M4700
Go Tell Aunt Rhody.
Q30 (ASU)
Sense of Discovery: The Mountain.
R2700 (ASU LMC BC WCU)
Sense of Discovery: The Mountain.
R3060 (ASU LMC WCU BC)
Stories of W. Va. for Boys and Girls.
S500
Way Down Yonder on Troublesome Creek: Appalachian Riddles and Rusties.
S7430 (BC ASU)
LITERATURE — KY.
Kentucky Authors, a History of Kentucky Literature.
B7480 (ASU BC)
LITERATURE — N. C.
North Carolina Fiction, 1958-1971: An Annotated Bibliography.
B6720 (ASU)
"The Dialect of the Southern Highlander as Recorded in North Carolina Novels."
E980 (ASU)
Literary and Historical Activities of North Carolina, 1900-1905.
N2390 (LMC WWC ASU)
Regional Sketches.
N2710 (WCU)
The Pen and Plate Club of Asheville, North Carolina. 1904-1929.
P1640 (ASU)
The North Carolina Miscellany.
W590 (LMC ASU)
Short Stories from the Old North State.
W620 (ASU LMC WWC)
LITERATURE — VA.
Anthology '67.
B6690
Legends of Virginia.
C1170 (LMC)
"An Annotated Bibliography of Books by Southwest Virginia Authors."
D4120 (ETSU ASU)
Dr. William George Bagby: A Study of Virginian Literature 1850-1880.
K2310
Dr. George William Bagby: A Study of Virginia Literature, 1850-1880.
K2320 (ASU)
V1070 (BC)
LITERATURE — W. VA.
West Virginia Authors: A Bio-bibliography.
B6480
LITERATURE — W. VA. — EDUCATIONAL
Handbook of Appalachian Materials.
A2300
LITTLE PIGEON RIVER
Floods on Little Pigeon and West Fork Little Pigeon in the Vicinity of Sevierville, Tenn.
T7080
LITTLE SANDY RIVER
Ohio River Basin, Grayson reservoir, Little Sandy River, Kentucky design memorandum no. 3A preliminary master plan.
U300 (BC)
LITTLE TENNESSEE RIVER
Fort Loudoun on the Little Tennessee.
H1050 (ASU)
Floods on Little Tennessee River, Cullasaja River, and Cartoogechave Creek in Vicinity of Franklin, North Carolina.
T7090
Floods on Tennessee River, Little Tennessee River, and Town and Muddy Creeks in Vicinity of Lenoir City, Tennessee.
T7290
Upper Little Tennessee River Region: Summary of Resources.
T9880 (WWC)
LIVESTOCK
Family Chicken Flock for Appalachia.
U140
LIVESTOCK — APP.
Relative Merits of Producing Creep-fed, Feeder, and Lot-Fattened Clones in the Appalachian Region.
M500
LIVESTOCK INDUSTRY
Wintering Beef Cattle in the Appalachian Region.
B4350
LIVESTOCK INDUSTRY — APP.
Livestock Auction Markets in the Appalachian Area: Methods and Facilities.
B6400

MAXIMS
Smoky Mountain Folks and Their Lore.
H820 (ETSU)
The Proverbs of Scotland.
H5690 (ASU)
Aunt Zona's Web.
H8050 (ASU LMC)
Southeastern Broadsides Before 1877.
H8290 (ASU)
Barefoot in Boogar Hollow; Yesterday's Saying's to Live by Today.
P4080 (BC LMC ASU)
Hills, Hollers and Hickory Flats.
R70
Born of the Mountains.
R1740 (ASU WCU LMC)
How to Be Successful.
R3740
Pioneer Proverbs: Wit and Wisdom from Early America.
S2750 (ASU WCU)
Pioneer Superstitions: Old-timey Signs and Sayings.
S2760 (ASU LMC WCU)
More Allegheny Episodes: Legends and Traditions, Old and New.
S3130
Scotch-Irish and English Proverbs and Sayings of the West Branch Valley of Central Pennsylvania.
S3150 (ASU)
Bill Arp (pseud.) So Called, a Side Show of the Southern Side of the Civil War.
S4470 (ASU)
Bill Arp: From the Uncivil War to Date, 1861-1903.
S4480 (ASU)
Bill Arp's Peace Papers.
S4490 (ASU)
Nubbins From Fodderstack Ridge.
S6980 (ASU)
Kentucky Superstitions.
T7790 (ASU BC)
Grannies's Remedies.
T8010 (ASU)
Popular Folk Dictionary of Ozarks Talk.
T8030 (ASU)
Pioneer Proverbs; Wit and Wisdom From Early America.
T9830
Incidents and Anecdotes.
W5270 (LMC)
All Good Times.
W7800 (BC)
Hit Haint the Fish.
W7810 (LMC BC)
MD. — HISTORY
Inventory of the County and Town Archives of Maryland.
H5720 (ASU)
Jonathan Hager, Founder of Hagerstown, Maryland.
M6230
An Outline of the Maryland Boundary Disputes and Related Events.
M7900 (ASU)
History of Allegany County, Maryland.
T7870 (ASU)
The History of Washington County, Maryland, from the Earliest Settlements to the Present Time, Including a History of Hagerstown.
W6870 (ASU)
MD. — HISTORY — WESTERN REGION
History of Western Maryland.
S830 (ETSU)
History of Western Maryland: Being a History of Frederick, Montgomery, Carroll, Washington, Allegany, and Garrett Counties from the Earliest Period to the Present Day. Including Biographical Sketches of Their Representative Men.
S840 (ASU)
MEDIA
Fiction Into Film: A Walk in the Spring Rain.
M2710 (ASU)
MEDIA — W. VA.
"An Historical Study of the Growth of Commercial Television in West Virginia."
M2120
"Mass Media Use Patterns and Interests Among West Virginia Rural Non-farm Families of Low Socio-economic Status."
M8530

MEDICINAL PLANTS
Index of Plants of North Carolina With Reputed Medicinal Uses.
J230 (WWC)
Nature's Pantry; 100 Wild Edible Plants Alphabetically Listed, Each with Full Description, Food Preparation and Folk Medicinal Properties.
W7170 (BC)
MEDICINAL PLANTS AND HERBS
Drug Plants of Western North Carolina.
M2740 (WCU ASU)
MEDICINAL PLANTS — APP.
Guide to Medicinal Plants of Appalachia.
K3230 (BC)
A Guide to Medicinal Plants of Appalachia.
K3240 (ASU ETSU LMC)
MELUNGEONS
The Melungeons (Their Origin and Kin).
B760 (ASU LMC WCU FC BC)
"The Melungeons of Newman's Ridge."
B1440 (ETSU ASU)
Melungeons: The Vanishing Colony of Newman's Ridge.
P4500 (ETSU)
MENTAL HEALTH
M5070
A Selective Bibliography of Writings on Poverty in the United States.
U3650
Mental Health in Appalachia: Problems and Prospects in the Central Highlands.
U3660 (LMC)
Mental Health in Appalachia. A Report of a Conference in Bethesda, Md., July 13-14, 1964.
U3670
Mental Health in Appalachia, Problems and Prospects in the Central Highlands.
U3890
MENTAL HEALTH — APP.
Appalachia's Children: The Challenge of Mental Health.
L3400 (ASU WCU ETSU LMC MHC WWC BC)
"Characteristics of Mining and Nonmining Psychiatric Patients."
M5630
MENTAL HEALTH — KY.
"A Cultural Comparison of Schizophrenia in Mountain Rural and Metropolitan Kentucky."
Q140
MENTAL HEALTH — VA.
"A Descriptive Study of Patients Accepted for Service During a Three-month Period at Psychiatric Service Clinic in Norton, Virginia."
G530
MENTAL HEALTH — W. VA.
"Impact of a Federal Grant-in-aid Program on an Economically Depressed, Rural State: A Case Study of Mental Health Programs in West Virginia."
G1050
METAL WORKING INDUSTRIES
The Resources of the Coal Field of the Upper Kanawha, with a Sketch of the Iron Belt of Virginia, Setting Forth Some of Their Markets and Means of Development.
M4480
Principio to Wheeling.
M4590 (BC)
METAL WORKING INDUSTRIES — APP.
A History of Production in the Iron and Steel Industry in the Southern Appalachian States.
D2640
METAL WORKING INDUSTRIES — N. C.
The Silversmiths of North Carolina.
C9980 (ASU)
METAL WORKING INDUSTRIES — OHIO
"Employment Opportunities and Training Needs for Technicians in the Metalworking Manufacturing Industries of the Central Ohio Valley with Projections through 1975."
L1500
METAL WORKING INDUSTRIES — TENN.
"A History of the Iron Industry in Carter County to 1860."
N270 (ETSU)
METAL WORKING INDUSTRIES — VA.
The Silversmiths of Virginia.
C9990 (FC BC)

METAL WORKING INDUSTRY
Iron Ore in the Red Mountain Formation in Greasy Cove, Alabama.
B8420
Preliminary Report on the Red Iron Ores of East Tennessee, Northeast Alabama, and Northwest Georgia.
B8430
"History of the Knoxville Iron Company."
C4500
The Pioneer: A Biography.
F3590 (BC)
The Resources of the Coal Field of the Upper Kanawha, with a Sketch of the Iron Belt of Virginia, Setting Forth Some of Their Markets and Means of Development.
M4470 (ASU)
METAL WORKING INDUSTRY — ALA. — IRON
Iron Ore Outcrops of the Red Mountain Formation in Northeast Alabama.
B8450 (ETSU)
Iron Ores, Fuels, and Fluxes of the Birmingham District, Alabama.
B8460
Russellville Brown Iron Ore District, Franklin County, Alabama.
B8470 (ETSU)
METAL WORKING INDUSTRY — KY.
Red River Iron Works.
J1200
METAL WORKING INDUSTRY — PA.
Pennsylvania's Iron and Steel Industry.
B3730 (ASU)
Pennsylvania Iron Manufacture in the Eighteenth Century.
B3740
Life in the Iron Mills: Or, The Korl Woman.
D1190 (ASU)
METAL WORKING INDUSTRY — TENN.
"History of the Tennessee Coal, Iron, and Railroad Company, 1852-1907."
F3700
"The Development of the Iron Industry in East Tennessee."
H5030 (ASU)
Knoxville as an Iron Center.
K1910
METAL WORKING INDUSTRY — TENN. — IRON
The Red Iron Ores of East Tennessee.
B8440 (BC)
METAL WORKING INDUSTRY — VA.
Virginia Iron Manufacture In the Slave Era.
B7600
MIGRATION
The Industrialization of Southern Rural Areas: A Study of Industry and Federal Assistance in Small Towns with Recommendations for Future Policy.
A180
"Southern Whites in Detroit."
A830
"A Follow-up Study of Graduates of Roane County High School, 1946-55."
A2540
Growth in Employment by County, 1940-1950 and 1950-1960.
A5090
In the Midst of Plenty: The Poor in America.
B120 (BC)
Migration of Farm People: An Annotated Bibliography, 1946-1960.
B1010
"Migration and Economic Opportunity in Tennessee Counties, 1940-1950."
B2420
Mobility of Rural Population.
B2600
Rural People in the City: A Study of the Socio-economic Status of 297 Families in Lexington, Kentucky.
B2620
Urban Adjustments of Rural Migrants.
B2630
Farm Migration, 1940-1945: An Annotated Bibliography.
B3180
Farm Population: Net Migration from the Rural Farm Population, 1940-1950.
B5720
Net Migration of the Population, 1950-1960 by Age, Sex and Color.
B5730

MIGRATION

Detroit's Southern Whites and the Store Front Church.
B5860

Rural Population Changes in Five Kentucky Mountain Districts, 1943-1946.
B7200

Southern Appalachian Population Change, 1960-1970: A First Look at the 1970 Census.
B7220 (BC)

"The Migration of Workers from Tennessee to Michigan."
B7970 (ASU)

Net Migration for Southern Counties, 1940-1950 and 1950-1960.
B8540

Probability Projections of Rates of Net Migration for Southern Counties and Other Applications of Markov Chains.
B8550

From Mountain Cabin to Cotton Mill.
C610

Report of a Workshop on the Southern Mountaineer in Cincinnati, April 29, 1954.
C4120 (ASU BC)

Selected Population and Agricultural Statistics for Tennessee Counties.
C4870 (ASU)

Children of Crisis.
C5850 (WCU ASU)

The South Goes North.
C5900 (ASU BC)

From the Freedom of the Mountains to the Hurly-burly City.
C6050

"Population Migration in the State of Tennessee."
C6120

Southern Appalachian Migrant on Public Aid in Cook County.
C6820 (ASU)

A Study of Families from the Southern Appalachian Region Receiving Public Assistance.
C6830 (ASU)

Our Changing Rural Society — Perspectives and Trends.
C7350

"The Occupational Adaptation of a Selected Group of Eastern Kentuckians in Southern Ohio."
C9190

"Religious Concerns of Southern Appalachian Migrants in a North Central City."
C9760

Southern Appalachian Migration.
D1410

Is Out-migration from Appalachia Declining?
D1690 (ASU)

The Population of Kentucky: Changes in the Number of Inhabitants, 1950-1960.
D1700

Ulster Emigration to Colonial America, 1718-1775.
D2240 (ASU)

"Farm-nonfarm Migration in the Southeast: A Costs-returns Analysis."
D2330

Living Conditions and Population Migration in Four Appalachian Counties.
D2790

Manpower and Employment Trends in Tennessee.
E650

Selected Demographic Studies, Knox Co., Ky.
E800
E2450 (ASU)

Up Here and Down Home: Appalachians in Cities.
F2410 (ASU)

"Recent Migration into Chicago."
F3150

Recent Migration into Chicago.
F3160

Uptown: Poor Whites in Chicago.
G1860 (ASU BC)

Adolescent Behavior in Urban Areas: A Bibliographic Review and Discussion of the Literature.
G2850

Understanding Children of Poverty.
G2860 (WCU BC)

Report of a Workshop on the Southern Mountaineer in Cincinnati.
G4210 (ASU)

Socio-cultural Adaptation of Newcomers to Cities in the Piedmont Industrial Crescent.
G4850

"Drain of Talent out of Georgia and South Carolina."
H1560 (ASU)

"Social Structural Factors Influencing the Urbanization of Appalachian Hill Emigrants in an Urban Ghetto."
H2090

"Social and Cultural Links in the Urban and Occupational Adjustment of Southern Appalachian Migrants."
H2430

"The Drain of Talent out of Kentucky."
H2790

Urban Adjustments of Rural Migrants: A Study of 297 Families in Lexington, Kentucky, 1942.
H4310

"Possum Ridge Farmers: A Study in Cultural Change."
H6120 (ASU)

"Migration Patterns of Residents in a High In-Migration County, Hamblen County, Tennessee."
H7610

Exploring Virginia's Human Resources.
H8120 (ASU BC)

Soil: Its Influence on the History of the United States, with Special Reference to Migration and the Scientific Study of Local History.
H8170 (ASU)

Migration and Industrial Development in Tennessee.
H8730

"Migration, Mobility and Social Participation."
J1230

Poverty Programs and Social Mobility.
K290

Farm Population Changes in Eastern Kentucky.
K930

Tables Showing Components of Population Change and Percent Due to Net Migration for State Economic Areas, Metropolitan Areas, and Counties, Southern Appalachians, 1950-1960.
K940

Basic Population Data for the Southern Appalachians.
K1420

"Effects of Urbanization on Vocational Agriculture in Jackson County, West Virginia."
K1690

"Southern White Laborers in Chicago's West Side."
K1940 (ASU)

"Characteristics of Mobile Workers in a Rural Industrialized Community."
K2600

The People of Tennessee: A Study of Population Trends.
K2880 (BC ASU WCU)

Appalachians in Cleveland.
K3400 (LMC ASU)

The Drain of Talent Out of the Virginias.
L110

A Further Note on the Drain of Talent Out of the Virginias.
L120

Population Changes in Tennessee since 1930.
L1940

Human Migration: A Guide to Migration Literature in English, 1955-1962.
M3000

Subsequent Movement of Kentucky Hill Families Relocated as Farm Laborers in Ohio.
M3050 (ASU)

The Appalachian Region: A Preliminary Analysis of Economic and Population Trends in an Eleven State Problem Area.
M3860 (BC)

"The Efficacy of the Labor Migration with Special Emphasis on Depressed Areas."
M4710

"A Comparison of the Personal and Economic Characteristics of the Mobile and Immobile."
M6040

Migration into and out of Depressed Areas.
M8460

State Population, Net Migration, Labor Force and Industry Employment Trends to 1975.
N250

Fertility Rates and Migration of Kentucky's Population, 1920-1940.
O1060 (ASU)

Migration and Occupational Adjustment of West Virginians in the City.
P2770

Selected Social and Sociopsychological Characteristics of West Virginians in Their Own State and in Cleveland, Ohio.
P2790 (ETSU)

"Occupational Status and Reasons for Leaving the State of West Virginia."
P3100

When Cultures Meet.
P3620 (BC ASU)

Selected Demographic Aspects of the West Virginia Economy, 1950-1975: Estimates and Projections of Migration and Population.
P4880 (ETSU BC)
R1860

"Immigrants from the Appalachian Region to the City of Columbus, Ohio: A Case Study."
R2210 (BC)

The Southern Appalachian Migrant.
R3690

A Human Relations Study — The Southern White In-Migrant.
S950

Education, Migration and Economic Life Chances of Male Entrants to the Labor Force from a Low Income Rural Area.
S1240 (ASU)

Career Placement and Economic Life Chances of Young Men from Eastern Kentucky.
S1250 (ASU)

Family Ties, Migration, and Transitional Adjustment of Young Men from Eastern Kentucky.
S1260

Mountain Families in Transition: A Case Study of Appalachian Migration.
S1270 (ASU WCU LMC ETSU WWC BC UNCA)

Research Design, Field Work Procedures, and Data Collection Problems in a Follow-Up Study of Young Men from Eastern Kentucky.
S1280

Social Structure of the Contact Situation, Rural Appalachia and Urban America.
S1290

Sociocultural Origins and Migration Patterns of Young Men from Eastern Kentucky.
S1310

The Cleveland Southern In-Migrant Study; an Overview.
S2440

"A Comparative Analysis of the Felt Need Pattern of the Personality Structure in Rural Appalachia and Suburban America."
S3400 (ETSU)

"Migration and Adjustment Experiences of Rural Migrant Workers in Indianapolis."
S4580

Movement of Labor Between Farm and Non Farm Sectors and Multiple Jobholding by Farm Operators in the Tennessee Valley.
S5120

Mobility of Chemical Workers in a Coal Mining Area.
S5450

"Migration from Kentucky: A Study of Intervening Opportunities."
S8070 (ASU)

"Standard of Living and Migration of 136 Farm Families in Overton County, Tennessee."
S8910

Population and Labor Force Characteristics of Tennessee Counties.
T1800

The Effects of Migration of the Labor Force.
W9830

MIGRATION — APP.

"Regional Labor Markets and Migration: An Analysis of Gross Migration in the United States, 1955-1960."
F10

Economic Effects of Internal Migration: An Exploratory Study, Substantive Report.
F1240

Migration and Changes in the Quality of the Labor Force.
G670 (ETSU)

MIGRATION — APP.
"Association of Selected Economic Factors with Net Migration Rates in the Southern Appalachian Region, 1935-1937."
G870
The Appalachian Region: A Preliminary Analysis of Economic and Population Trends in an Eleven State Problem Area.
G4440
"The Drain of Talent Out of North Carolina and Tennessee."
M3010 (ASU)
The Myth of the Appalachian Brain Drain: A Case Study of West Virginia.
R680 (BC ASU WCU)
Living Conditions and Population Migration in Four Appalachian Counties.
U2500 (BC)
Internal Migration in the United States 1958 to 1964: A List of References.
W6080
"Socio-economic Status and Formal Social Participation of Rural Migrant Families in Pittsburgh."
W7650

MIGRATION — KY.
An Urban Development Program for the Big Sandy Area.
A3870
"Association of Selected Socio-economic Characteristics with Net Migration from Three Kentucky Economic Areas, 1920-1950."
B6440
Population Estimates for Kentucky Counties and Economic Area, July 1, 1958.
D250 (ASU)
Population Growth in Kentucky, 1820-1960.
H5530
Migration Within Kentucky.
M3990
Natural Increase and Migration of Kentucky's Population, 1920-1935.
O1070 (ASU)
"Population Trends and Other Factors Influencing the Voting Habits of the Cumberland Valley Region of Southeast Kentucky."
R1210
Mobility and Fertility Rates of Rural Families in Johnson County, Kentucky, 1918-1941.
S6020
Attitudes Toward Rural Migration and Family Life in Johnson and Robertson Counties, Kentucky, 1941.
W6690

MIGRATION — OHIO
"Analysis of Costs and Benefits from Commuting for Employment among Core and Satellite Communities in the Appalachian Region of Ohio."
E2360

MIGRATION — PA.
"Socio-economic Status and Formal Social Participation of Rural Migrant Families in Pittsburgh."
W7650

MIGRATION — PSYCHOLOGICAL EFFECTS
"Social-psychological Adjustment of Kentucky Mountain Migrants in Urbanized Industrial Areas of Southern Ohio."
S1740 (ASU)

MIGRATION — TENN.
Migration and Level of Living in the Tennessee Valley.
F1680
"Mobility and Economic Progress in the Tennessee Valley Region: 1957-65."
L1840
"Socio-Economic Readjustment of Farm Families Displaced by the TVA Land Purchase in the Norris Area."
N1000
Migration and Industrial Development in Tennessee.
T1420
Population, Labor Force, and Employment Projections and Interpretations.
T1680

MIGRATION — W. VA.
The West Virginia Handbook and Immigrant's Guide.
D1540
"Patterns of Development and Net Migration, 1960-1970: A Study of West Virginia Counties."
D1760
Economic Effects of Internal Migration: An Exploratory Study, Substantive Report.
F1240
Employment Changes in West Virginia, 1948-1958.
F1250 (ASU)
Population Changes in West Virginia 1900-1950.
S3800

MINE DISASTERS
"Social Behavior under Conditions of Extreme Stress: A Study of Miners Entrapped by a Coal Mine Disaster."
L3820
The Rock Dust Remedy for Coal Mine Explosions; An Open Letter to the Operators in the 27th Bituminous District of Pennsylvania.
P2810
Human Crisis in the Kingdom of Coal.
S5010 (ASU BC)

MINE DISASTERS — APP.
Men in Crisis: A Study of a Mine Disaster.
L3810
Preventing Fatal Explosions in Coal Mines: A Study of Recent Major Disasters in the United States as Accompaniments of Technological Change.
W5990

MINE INDUSTRY
Wyoming and McDowell Counties.
W3940 (ETSU)

MINE SAFETY
Work, Safety, and Life Style Among Southern Appalachian Coal Miners. A Survey of the Men of Standard Mines.
A1930
Work, Safety, and Life Style Among Southern Appalachian Coal Miners: A Survey of the Men of Standard Mines.
A1970 (ASU)
A Key to Mine Ventilation.
A5360 (BC)
Conspiracy in Coal.
B3360
The Hurricane Creek Massacre: An Inquiry into the Circumstances Surrounding the Deaths of Thirty-eight Men in a Coal Mine Explosion.
B3370 (ASU BC LMC WCU MHC)
Report on the Mining Methods and Appliances Used in Anthracite Coal Fields.
C2850 (BC)
Coal Workers' Pneumoconisosis: Workmen's Compensation Treatment and It's Prevention in Kentucky.
C3550 (ASU)
Successful Solutions to Everyday Coal Mining Problems.
C5190 (BC)
"Earnings, Health, Safety, and Welfare of Bituminous Coal Miners Since the Encouragement of Mechanization by the United Mine Workers of America."
D610
Notable Mine Disasters of Fayette County, West Virginia.
D2880 (BC)
"A Study of Fatal Roof Fall Accidents in Bituminous Coal Mines."
D3110 (LMC)
"A Study of the Literature on Accidents in Coal Mines of the United States with Comparisons of the Records in Other Coal-producing Countries."
D3640
"A Validation Study of a Psychological Test Battery for Selection of Joy Ripper-type Continuous Miner Operators."
D4090
"Economic Consequences of the Seven-hour Day and Wage Changes in the Bituminous Coal Industry."
F1220
Wage Rates and Working Time in the Bituminous Coal Industry, 1912-1922.
F1230 (BC)
"Twentieth Century Development of the Coal Mining Industry in Eastern Kentucky and Its Influence upon the Political Behavior of This Area."
F3420 (ASU)
"Coal Mining Safety: National Solutions in the Progressive Period."
G3090
Research, Education and Mine Personnel Safety in W. Va.
H6550 (BC)
Coal Mine Health and Safety; the Case of West Virginia.
M110 (BC)
Coal Mining Health and Safety in West Virginia.
M120
Theory and Practice of Mine Ventilation.
M6610
Papers and Proceedings.
N160
Demonstration of Safety Plugging of Oil Wells Penetrating Appalachian Coal Mines.
R1480
"A Recursive Programing Model of Resource Allocation and Technological Change in the United States Bituminous Coal Industry."
T10
Questions and Answers for American Mine Examinations.
T340 (BC)
Federal Coal Mine Health and Safety Act of 1969. Report Together with Minority, Supplemental, and Separate Views from the Committee to Accompany H. R. 13950, October 13, 1969.
U2280
Legislative History: Federal Coal Mine Health and Safety Act.
U2290
Coal Mine Health and Safety. Hearings before the Subcommittee on H. R. 4047, H. R. 4295, and H. R. 7976, March 4-May 1, 1969.
U2300
Federal Coal Mine Health and Safety Act of 1969. Report from the Committee Together with Individual Views to Accompany S. 2917, September 17, 1969.
U2330
Coal Mine Health and Safety. Hearings before the Subcommittee on S. 355, S. 467, S. 1094, S. 1178, S. 1300, and S. 1907, February 27-May 2, 1969.
U2340

MINE SAFETY — APP.
An Analysis of Appalachian State Coal Mine Health and Safety and Workmen's Compensation Programs: Recommendations for Improvement.
K880 (ASU)

MINE WARS
The Kentucky Miner's Struggle: The Record of a Year of Lawless Violence. The Only Complete Picture of Events Briefly Told.
A2090 (ASU)
"A History of the Labor Movement in West Virginia."
A2610
From the Molly Maguires to the United Mine Workers: The Social Ecology of an Industrial Union, 1869-1997.
A5530 (WCU BC)
Thoughts of Mother Jones; Compiled from her Writings and Speeches.
A5810
The Molly Maguires.
B3690 (ASU WCU BC)
B4750 (BC)
Labor's Untold Story.
B6040 (ASU)
The Molly Maguires.
B6810 (ASU WCU)
Notable Mine Disasters of Fayette County, West Virginia.
D2880 (BC)
Mother Jones, the Miners' Angel: A Portrait.
F740 (ASU MHC)
Coal Creek Rebellion.
F1770 (ASU)
"Cooperation-conflict in Labor Management: A Study of Contrasting Cases (Women's Garment Industry and Bituminous Coal Industry)."
H110
H2320

MINE WARS
Struggle in the Coal Fields. The Autobiography of Fred Mooney, Secretary-Treasurer, District 17, United Mine Workers of America.
H5070 (ASU)
Autobiography of Mother Jones.
P520 (ASU)
Human Crisis in the Kingdom of Coal.
S5010 (ASU BC)
Facts About the Two Armed Marches on Logan.
S9400 (ASU BC)
The Incomparable Don Chafin.
S9410 (BC ASU)
"Bloody" Harlan, 1931-1938; an Appalachian Coal County in the Thirties.
T170
MINE WARS — APP.
"The Coal Miner's Insurrections, 1891-1892."
H8740 (ASU)
S5520 (ASU)
The Logan Coal Field of West Virginia: A Brief History.
T8470 (ASU ETSU WCU)
MINE WARS — KY.
The Shame That Is Kentucky's! The Story of the Harlan Mine War.
C7610 (ASU)
Harlan Miners Speak: Report on Terrorism in the Kentucky Coal Fields.
N140 (ASU BC)
Harlan Miners Speak: Report on Terrorism in the Kentucky Coal Fields.
N150 (ASU LMC WCU)
"Coal and Conflict: The U.M.W.A. in Harlan County, 1931-1939."
T690 (BC ASU)
Hell in Harlan.
T8760 (WCU)
MINE WARS — PA.
The Molly Maguire Riots: Industrial Conflict in the Pennsylvania Coal Region.
C5760 (WCU ASU)
The Molly Maguires and the Detectives.
P3030
MINE WARS — TENN.
"The Labor Struggle at Wilder, Tennessee."
P2280 (ASU)
MINE WARS — W. VA.
"Strikes in the Southern West Virginia Coal Fields, 1912-1922."
B1040 (ASU)
"The Mine War on Cabin Creek and Paint Creek, West Virginia, in 1912-1913."
C8590 (ASU)
Labor Relations in the Fairmont, West Virginia, Bituminous Coal Field.
E1950 (ASU)
Civil War in West Virginia: A Story of the Industrial Conflict in the Coal Mines.
L380 (ASU BC)
Bloodletting in Appalachia: The Story of West Virginia's Four Major Mine Wars and Other Thrilling Incidents of Its Coal Fields.
L1350 (ASU WCU LMC BC MHC)
The New-Kanawha River and the Mine War of West Virginia.
M630 (BC)
Paint Creek Miner.
P660
"The Labor Movement in West Virginia, 1900-1948."
P3730
MINERAL
TVA's Coal-Buying Program.
T3940
MINERAL RESOURCES
Soil Survey: Dawson, Lumpkin, and White Counties, Georgia.
A850
Report.
A910 (BC)
Deposits of Brown Iron Ores (Brown Hematite) in Western North Carolina.
B2170 (ASU LMC WCU UNCA)
"A Study of the Cranberry Ore Belt."
B5750 (ASU)
Preliminary Report on the Red Iron Ores of East Tennessee, Northeast Alabama, and Northwest Georgia.
B8430
The Red Iron Ores of East Tennessee.
B8440 (BC)
Russellville Brown Iron Ore District, Franklin County, Alabama.
B8470 (ETSU)
The Carolina Gold Rush.
R2660 (ASU MHC ETSU)
North Carolina: Its Geology and Mineral Resources.
S8760 (LMC WWC ETSU UNCA)
Mineral Resources of the Appalachian Region: A Compilation of Information on the Mineral Resources, Mineral Industry, and Geology of the Appalachian Region.
U3250 (ASU LMC ETSU)
Cabell, Wayne and Lincoln Counties.
W3660 (ETSU)
Oil and Gas Report and Map of Doddridge and Harrison Counties, West Virginia.
W3800 (ETSU)
Oil and Gas Report and Map of Marshall, Wetzel, and Tyler Counties, West Virginia.
W3810 (ETSU)
Oil and Gas Report and Map of Monongalia, Marion, and Taylor Counties, West Virginia.
W3820 (ETSU)
Oil and Gas Report and Map of Pleasants, Wood and Ritchie Counties, West Virginia.
W3830 (ETSU)
Pendleton County.
W3840 (BC)
Randolph County.
W3860 (ETSU)
Wyoming and McDowell Counties.
W3940 (ETSU)
Outline of the Geology and Mineral Resources of Russell County, Virginia.
W8950 (ETSU)
MINERAL RESOURCES — ALA.
Iron Ore in the Red Mountain Formation in Greasy Cove, Alabama.
B8420
Iron Ore Outcrops of the Red Mountain Formation in Northeast Alabama.
B8450 (ETSU)
Iron Ores, Fuels, and Fluxes of the Birmingham District, Alabama.
B8460
Stratigraphy and Uranium Content of the Chattanooga Shale in Northeastern Alabama, Northwestern Georgia, and Eastern Tennessee.
G2210
Raw Materials for Lightweight Aggregate in Appalachian Region, Alabama and Georgia.
H6610
Report on the Coal Measures of the Plateau Region of Alabama.
M230 (BC)
Building Sandstones of Northern Alabama.
P1710 (ETSU)
Iron Making in Alabama.
P2700 (ASU)
Geology and Mineral Resources of Clay County, with Special Reference to the Graphite Industry.
P4770 (ETSU)
Report on Stone Hill Copper Mines and Works, Cleburne County, Alabama.
R3960 (ASU)
MINERAL RESOURCES — ALA. — COAL
Geology and Coal Resources of the Northeast Part of the Coosa Coal Field, St. Clair County, Alabama.
R3930 (ETSU)
MINERAL RESOURCES — ALA. — COPPER
Resource and Beneficiation Studies of Copperbearing Pyrite Ore, Pyriton, Clay County, Alabama.
L240 (ETSU)
MINERAL RESOURCES — ALA. — GOLD
The Gold Log Mine, Talladega County, Alabama.
B1870
MINERAL RESOURCES — ALA. — TALC
The Talc Deposits of Talledega County, Alabama.
M2320 (BC ETSU)
MINERAL RESOURCES — APP.
Survey of Sulfur Reduction in Appalachian Coals by Stage Crushing.
D1920
Uranium in the Appalachian Mobile Belt.
G50 (LMC)
Reconnaissance of Some Gold and Tin Deposits of the Southern Appalachians.
G3290
Mercury and Other Trace Elements in Sphalerite and Wallrocks from Central Kentucky, Tennessee, and Appalachian Zinc Districts.
J2250
The Ore Knob Copper Deposit, North Carolina, and Other Massive Sulfide Deposits of the Appalachians.
K2590 (LMC)
The Coal Regions of America.
M1360
Origin of the Copper Deposits of the Ducktown Type in the Southern Appalachian Region.
R3810 (ETSU ASU)
Proceedings.
S9780 (ASU BC)
Engineering Geology and Mineral Resources of the Tennessee Valley Authority Region.
T2600
Agglomeration of Phosphate Fines for Furnace Use.
T6110
Origin of the Cooper Deposits of the Ducktown Type in the Southern Appalachian Region.
U2800 (ASU)
Greenbrier County.
W3720 (ETSU)
Jefferson, Berkeley, and Morgan Counties.
W3740 (ETSU)
The Northern Appalachian Coal Field.
W5340
Appalachian Mineral and Gem Trails.
Z50 (ASU WCU LMC BC)
Distribution of Minor Elements in Coals of Appalachian Region.
Z150
MINERAL RESOURCES — APP. — GOLD
Gold Mining in North Carolina and Adjacent South Appalachian Regions.
N1160 (ASU WCU LMC)
MINERAL RESOURCES — COPPER
Copper Deposits of the Appalachian States.
W2210
MINERAL RESOURCES — COPPER — TENN.
Geology & ore deposits of the Ducktown mining district, Tenn., 1926.
U3180
MINERAL RESOURCES — GA.
Georgia's Fabulous Treasure Hoards: A Compendium for Rockhounds, Prospectors, and Various Seekers of Gold, Silver, Diamonds, etc., with Known and Historic Locations, . . .
A2500 (MHC)
Geology of the Tate Quadrangle.
B2200 (ETSU)
The Romance of Georgia Marble.
D90 (ASU BC)
Publications on the Geology and Mineral Resources of Georgia.
G910 (ETSU)
Stratigraphy and Uranium Content of the Chattanooga Shale in Northeastern Alabama, Northwestern Georgia, and Eastern Tennessee.
G2210
Raw Materials for Lightweight Aggregate in Appalachian Region, Alabama and Georgia.
H6610
Forsterite Olivine Deposits of North Carolina and Georgia.
H8400 (ETSU WCU)
Exploration for Mineral Deposits in Habersham County, Georgia.
H8580
Exploration for Mineral Deposits in Habersham County, Georgia.
H8590 (LMC)
Exploration for Mineral Deposits in White County, Georgia.
H8600 (LMC)
The Geology and Mineralogy of Graves Mountain, Georgia.
H8620 (ETSU)
Stratigraphy, Structure, Mineral Resources of the Mineral Bluff Quadrangle, Georgia.
H8630 (ETSU)
Geology and Mineral Deposits of the Cartersville District, Georgia.
K1700
Geology and Mineral Resources of the Dalton Quadrangle, Georgia-Tennessee.
M8680 (ASU ETSU)

MINERAL RESOURCES — GA.
Geology and Mineral Resources of the Northwest Quarter of the Cohutta Mountain Quadrangle.
S220 (ETSU)
The Georgia Mountains: A View of Its Resources, Problems, and Potentials.
S1120 (ASU LMC)
The Geology of the Sand Lookout Mountain Area, Northwest Georgia.
S8970 (ETSU)
MINERAL RESOURCES — GA. — BAUXITE
The Bauxite Deposits of Floyd, Bartow, and Polk Counties of Northwest Georgia.
W5630
MINERAL RESOURCES — GA. — GOLD
Auraria: The Story of a Georgia Gold-Mining Town.
C7770 (ASU BC)
MINERAL RESOURCES — KY.
The Fire Clays and Fire Clay Industries of the Olive Hill and Ashland Districts of Northeastern Kentucky.
C8780 (BC)
Peridotite of Elliott County, Kentucky.
D2420
Lost Silver Mines and Buried Treasures of Kentucky.
H4860 (BC)
Coals of the North Fork of the Ky. River in Perry and Portions of Breathitt & Knott Co. Ky.
H6150
Shales for Lightweight Aggregate in Appalachian Region, Kentucky and Tennessee.
H6620
Coal Deposits of Pike County, Kentucky.
H8370
A Bibliography of the Mineral Resources of Kentucky.
J950
Red River Iron Works.
J1200
Directory of Kentucky Mineral Operators.
K1120
. . . Geological Map of Kentucky. Presented in Colors, Showing Oil, Gas, Coal, Fluorspar, and Asphalt Fields; and Other Mineral Resources and Geologic Data Including Faults, Folds, Sections, Elevations, and Physiographic Divisions of the Commonwealth.
K1250
Geology of the Bedford Shale and Berea Sandstone in the Appalachian Basin.
P2000
Coal Resources of the Russell Fork Basin in Kentucky and Virginia.
S7540
Geology and Mineral Resources of part of the Cumberland Gap coal field, Ky., 1906.
U3170
MINERAL RESOURCES — MD.
Brachipoda of the Keyser Limestone (Silurian-Devonian) of Maryland and Adjacent Areas.
B5700 (ETSU)
Alleghany County.
M3900 (ETSU)
MINERAL RESOURCES — N. C.
General Features of the Brown Hematite Ores of Western North Carolina.
B2180 (ASU)
General Features of the Magnetite Ores of Western North Carolina and Eastern Tennessee.
B2190 (UNCA ASU)
An Introduction to the Topography, Geology, and Mineral Resources of North Carolina.
B6750 (ETSU)
Feldspar Deposits of the Bryson City District, North Carolina.
C390 (ASU WCU)
Mineral Localities of North Carolina.
C6520 (ASU)
The Mineral Industry in North Carolina from 1918-1923.
D3290 (LMC)
E1910
Bechtler's Gold.
F3180
The Minerals and Mineral Localities of North Carolina.
G800 (ASU)
In the Coal and Iron Counties of North Carolina.
H420 (LMC WCU)
In the Coal and Iron Counties of North Carolina.
H430 (BC ASU)
Forsterite Olivine Deposits of North Carolina and Georgia.
H8400 (ETSU WCU)
Halloysite Deposits of Western North Carolina.
H8410 (ETSU WCU)
History of the Gems Found in North Carolina.
K3410 (LMC)
Bibliography of North Carolina Geology, Mineralogy, and Geography, with a List of Maps.
L390 (ASU LMC WWC ETSU)
The Geology and Ore Deposits of the Virgilina District of Virginia and North Carolina.
L400 (ETSU ASU)
Quartz Crystal Deposits of Southwestern Virginia and Western North Carolina.
M5170
A Directory of the Principal Mineral Producers of North Carolina.
N1940 (ASU ETSU)
The Mining Industry in North Carolina.
N2220 (ASU UNCA ETSU LMC)
Altitudes in North Carolina.
N2310 (ASU LMC WCU)
Biennial Report of the State Geologist: 1919-1920.
N2330 (ASU LMC)
Residual Kaolin Deposits of the Spruce Pine District, North Carolina.
P260 (ETSU)
Zircon, Monazite and Other Minerals Used in Production of Chemical Compounds Employed in the Manufacture of Lighting Apparatus.
P4190 (LMC)
Talc and Pyrophyllite Deposits in North Carolina.
P4200 (ASU)
Corundum and the Peridotites of Western North Carolina.
P4220 (ASU WCU LMC)
The Tin Deposits of the Carolinas.
P4230 (WCU)
Clay Deposits and Clay Industry in North Carolina, a Preliminary Report.
R2300 (WCU)
Pyrophyllite Deposits in North Carolina.
S8770 (ETSU)
"Gold Mining in North Carolina: 1799-1860."
S9290 (WCU)
MINERAL RESOURCES — N. C. — CHROMITE
Chromite Deposits of North Carolina: Geology and Mining.
N1920
MINERAL RESOURCES — N. C. — COPPER
The Ore Knob Copper Deposit, North Carolina, and Other Massive Sulfide Deposits of the Appalachians.
K2590 (LMC)
MINERAL RESOURCES — N. C. — CORUNDUM
Corundum and the Basic Magnesian Rocks of Western North Carolina.
L2210 (WCU)
MINERAL RESOURCES — N. C. — GOLD
The Gold Hill Mining District of North Carolina.
L410 (LMC ETSU)
Gold Deposits of North Carolina.
N1150 (LMC)
The Burke County Gold Rush.
P3540 (LMC)
MINERAL RESOURCES — N. C. — IRON ORE
. . . Iron Ores of North Carolina; A Preliminary Report.
N1170 (ASU UNCA)
MINERAL RESOURCES — N. C. — LIMESTONE
Limestones and Marls of North Carolina.
L3630 (ASU LMC WCU)
MINERAL RESOURCES — N. C. — MICA
Mica Deposits of the Blue Ridge in North Carolina.
L1920 (LMC)
MINERAL RESOURCES — N. C. — MONAZITE
Monazite, and Monazite Deposits in North Carolina.
N1180 (WCU)
MINERAL RESOURCES — N. C. — TIN
Tin Resources of the King's Mountain District, North Carolina and South Carolina.
K550
MINERAL RESOURCES — OHIO
Economic Geology of the Summerfield and Woodsfield Quadrangles, Ohio, with Descriptions of Coal and Other Mineral Resources, Except Oil and Gas.
C6320
MINERAL RESOURCES — OIL
Cable-tool Coring with Oil-base Mud in Appalachian Oilfields.
W2870
MINERAL RESOURCES — PA.
"The Economic Geography of the State Industry in Eastern Pennsylvania."
C1260
Bituminous Coal Fields in Pennsylvania.
P1840
MINERAL RESOURCES — S. C. — TIN
Tin Resources of the King's Mountain District, North Carolina and South Carolina.
K550
MINERAL RESOURCES — SALT
Salt Brines of West Virginia.
W3890 (ETSU)
MINERAL RESOURCES — TENN.
The Chattanooga Black Shale, a Possible Future Source of Uranium.
A1320 (ETSU)
Outline Introduction to the Mineral Resources of Tennessee.
A5250 (ETSU)
General Features of the Magnetite Ores of Western North Carolina and Eastern Tennessee.
B2190 (UNCA ASU)
Summary of the Mineral Resources of Tennessee.
B5540 (ETSU)
Stratigraphy of the Mascot-Jefferson City Zinc District, Tennessee.
B6610
Geology and Mineral Resources of the Crossville Quadrangle, Tennessee.
B9480 (ETSU)
Geology and Ore Deposits of the Ducktown Mining District, Tennessee.
E1960 (ASU BC)
Coal Losses of Tennessee.
F1850 (ETSU)
The Northern Tennessee Coal Field.
G2140 (ETSU)
Stratigraphy and Uranium Content of the Chattanooga Shale in Northeastern Alabama, Northwestern Georgia, and Eastern Tennessee.
G2210
Marble Deposits of East Tennessee: Occurrence and Distribution.
G2680 (LMC)
"The Development of the Iron Industry in East Tennessee."
H5030 (ASU)
Limestone and Dolomite Resources of Tennessee.
H5040 (ETSU)
Ceramic Evaluation of Clays and Shales of East Tennessee.
H6600 (ETSU)
Shales for Lightweight Aggregate in Appalachian Region, Kentucky and Tennessee.
H6620
Knoxville as an Iron Center.
K1910
Tennessee: Its Agricultural and Mineral Wealth, With an Appendix Showing the Extent, Value and Accessibility of its Ores, With Analyses of the Same.
K1920 (ASU LMC)
Mineral Resources of the Waynesboro Quadrangle, Tennessee.
M6220 (ETSU)
Geology and Mineral Resources of the Dalton Quadrangle, Georgia-Tennessee.
M8680 (ASU ETSU)
Manganese Resources of East Tennessee.
R1380 (ETSU)
Geology and Mineral Deposits of Bumpass Cove, Unicoi and Washington Counties, Tennessee.
R3390 (ETSU)
Zinc Deposits of East Tennessee.
S1640 (LMC)
The Phosphate Resources of Tennessee.
S5030 (ETSU)
Manganese Deposits of East Tennessee.
S7660

MINERAL RESOURCES — TENN.
Geology, Mineral Resources, and Ground Water of the Cleveland Area, Tennessee.
S9710 (ETSU)
"Marble Deposits and Marble Industry of the Knoxville Area."
T870
T910 (LMC)
Mineral and Agricultural Resources of the Portion of Tennessee Along the Cincinnati Southern and Knoxville and Ohio Railroads.
T1010 (ASU)
Division of Geology Bulletin.
T1020
Geologic Maps and Mineral Resources Summary.
T1270 (ETSU)
Report on Mineral Resources of Tenn.
T1290
Tennessee Resources — Agriculture, Forestry, and Minerals.
T1720 (ETSU)
MINERAL RESOURCES — TENN. — COAL
The Coal Reserves of Tennessee.
L4020 (ETSU)
MINERAL RESOURCES — TENN. — COPPER
The Deposits of Copper — Ores at Ducktown Tenn.
K710
MINERAL RESOURCES — TENN. — JEFFERSON CO.
"The Zinc Industry of Jefferson County, Tennessee."
C7750
MINERAL RESOURCES — TENN. — MANGANESE
Geology and Manganese Deposits of Northeastern Tennessee.
K2410 (ETSU)
MINERAL RESOURCES — TENN. — ZINC
Techniques Used in Mine-water Problems of the East Tennessee Zinc District.
K860 (ASU)
MINERAL RESOURCES — TITANIUM — VA.
Titanium deposits of Nelson and Amherst Co., in Va.
U3390
MINERAL RESOURCES — VA.
The Cement Resources of Virginia, West of the Blue Ridge.
B1860 (ASU)
Resources of South-west Virginia, Showing the Mineral Deposits of Iron, Coal, Zinc, Copper and Lead. Also, the Staples of the Various Counties, Methods of Transportation Access, etc.
B5840 (ASU BC)
Southwest Virginia and Contiguous Territory: Mineral Resources and Railway Facilities, Statistics, Information, Markets for Coke, Fuel, Ores, etc.
B5850 (BC)
Geology and Mineral Resources of the Lynchburg Quadrangle, Virginia.
B7440 (ETSU)
Virginia Iron Manufacture In the Slave Era.
B7600
Geology and Mineral Resources of Floyd County of the Blue Ridge Upland, Southwestern Virginia.
D2340 (ETSU)
Virginia Mineral Localities.
D2360 (ETSU)
The Geology and Mineral Resources of Wise County and the Coal-bearing Portion of Scott County, Virginia.
E670 (ETSU ASU)
Industrial Limestones and Dolomites in Va.: James River District West of the Blue Ridge.
E910
Possibilities for Manganese Ore on Certain Undeveloped Tracts in the Shenandoah Valley, Virginia.
H5130
The Geology and Ore Deposits of the Virgilina District of Virginia and North Carolina.
L400 (ETSU ASU)
Directory of the Mineral Industry in Virginia, 1966.
L1960
The Mineral Wealth of Virginia Tributary to the Lines of the Norfolk and Western and Shenandoah Valley Railroad Companies.
M930 (BC)
New River Cripple Creek Mineral Region of Virginia.
M940
Outline of the Mineral Resources of Virginia.
M1550 (LMC)
Marble Prospects in Giles County, Virginia, with a section on Petrography of Marbles by Arthur A. Pegan.
M4240
The Resources of the Coal Field of the Upper Kanawha, with a Sketch of the Iron Belt of Virginia, Setting Forth Some of Their Markets and Means of Development.
M4470 (ASU)
Quartz Crystal Deposits of Southwestern Virginia and Western North Carolina.
M5170
Triassic Formations of the Danville Basin.
M5300 (ETSU)
Report.
M8340
Manganese and Quartzite Deposits in the Lick Mountain Region of Wythe Co.
S6710
Coal Resources of the Russell Fork Basin in Kentucky and Virginia.
S7540
Phosphate Deposits in Southwestern Virginia.
S7670
Bulletin.
V830 (BC)
The Clay and Shales of Va. West of the Blue Ridge.
V920
Marble Prospects in Giles Co., Va.
V1000
Zinc and Lead Region of Southwestern Va.
V1030
V1130 (BC)
. . . Mineral Resources of Virginia.
W1560 (LMC)
MINERAL RESOURCES — VA. — IRON
The Iron Industry of Wythe County from 1792.
W5800 (ASU BC)
MINERAL RESOURCES — VA. — MANGANESE
Manganese Deposits of the Elkton Area, Virginia.
K2460
Manganese Deposits of the Sweet Springs District, West Virginia and Virginia.
L70
MINERAL RESOURCES — W. VA.
Some Low-alumina Quartzitic Sandstones in West Virginia: A Preliminary Report.
C3620 (ETSU)
A Subsurface Study of the Greenbrier Limestone in West Virginia.
F1610 (ETSU ASU)
Iron Ores, Salt and Sandstones.
G4270 (ETSU)
Germanium in Coals of West Virginia.
H4140 (ETSU)
Lithification of Sandstones in West Virginia.
H4180 (ETSU)
"Coal Consolidation: Profile of the Fairmont Field of Northern West Virginia, 1852-1903."
M4090
The Resources of the Coal Field of the Upper Kanawha, with a Sketch of the Iron Belt of Virginia, Setting Forth Some of Their Markets and Means of Development.
M4470 (ASU)
Salt Brines of West Virginia.
P4560 (ETSU)
The Cheat Mountain Coal Field of Randolph County, West Virginia.
R1270 (ASU ETSU)
Resources of the Upper South Branch Valley, West Virginia.
S6470
High-alumina Clays of West Virginia.
T120 (ETSU)
Fayette County.
W3700 (ETSU)
MINERAL RESOURCES — W. VA. — COAL
Levels Above Tide. True Meridians. Report on Coal.
W5450 (ETSU)
Supplementary Coal Report.
W5480 (ETSU)
MINERAL RESOURCES — W. VA. — LIMESTONE
Dolomite Zone at Base of Greenbrier Limestone (Big Lime).
M3520 (ETSU)
Possibility of Shaft Mining of Greenbrier Limestone.
M3540 (ETSU)
MINERAL RESOURCES — W. VA. — MANGANESE
Manganese Deposits of the Sweet Springs District, West Virginia and Virginia.
L70
MINERAL RESOURCES — W. VA. — ROCK SALT
Rock Salt Deposits of West Virginia.
M3550 (ETSU)
MINERAL RESOURCES — W. VA. — SULPHATE
Sulphate Minerals in West Virginia.
M3560 (ETSU)
MINING INDUSTRIES — ALA. — GRAPHITE
Geology and Mineral Resources of Clay County, with Special Reference to the Graphite Industry.
P4770 (ETSU)
MINING INDUSTRIES — ALA. — SANDSTONE
Building Sandstones of Northern Alabama.
P1710 (ETSU)
MINING INDUSTRIES — APP. — COPPER
Origin of the Copper Deposits of the Ducktown Type in the Southern Appalachian Region.
R3810 (ETSU ASU)
MINING INDUSTRIES — COPPER — SOUTHERN APP.
Origin of Copper deposits S. Appal. Region.
U3290
MINING INDUSTRIES — GA. — MARBLE
Geology of the Tate Quadrangle.
B2200 (ETSU)
The Romance of Georgia Marble.
D90 (ASU BC)
MINING INDUSTRIES — KY. — SHALE AND SANDSTONE
Geology of the Bedford Shale and Berea Sandstone in the Appalachian Basin.
P2000
MINING INDUSTRIES — N. C.
The Mineral Industry in North Carolina from 1918-1923.
D3290 (LMC)
Zircon, Monazite and Other Minerals Used in Production of Chemical Compounds Employed in the Manufacture of Lighting Apparatus.
P4190 (LMC)
Corundum and the Peridotites of Western North Carolina.
P4220 (ASU WCU LMC)
The Tin Deposits of the Carolinas.
P4230 (WCU)
MINING INDUSTRIES — N. C. — CLAY
Clay Deposits and Clay Industry in North Carolina, a Preliminary Report.
R2300 (WCU)
MINING INDUSTRIES — N. C. — GOLD
The Carolina Gold Rush.
R2660 (ASU MHC ETSU)
"Gold Mining in North Carolina: 1799-1860."
S9290 (WCU)
MINING INDUSTRIES — N. C. — IRON ORE
Deposits of Brown Iron Ores (Brown Hematite) in Western North Carolina.
B2170 (ASU LMC WCU UNCA)
General Features of the Brown Hematite Ores of Western North Carolina.
B2180 (ASU)
MINING INDUSTRIES — N. C. — KAOLIN
The Kaolins of North Carolina.
B2210 (WCU)
Residual Kaolin Deposits of the Spruce Pine District, North Carolina.
P260 (ETSU)
MINING INDUSTRIES — N. C. — MAGNETITE
General Features of the Magnetite Ores of Western North Carolina and Eastern Tennessee.
B2190 (UNCA ASU)
MINING INDUSTRIES — N. C. — PYROPHYLLITE
Pyrophyllite Deposits in North Carolina.
S8770 (ETSU)
MINING INDUSTRIES — N. C. — QUARTZ
Quartz Crystal Deposits of Southwestern Virginia and Western North Carolina.
M5170
MINING INDUSTRIES — N. C. — TALC
Talc and Pyrophyllite Deposits in North Carolina.
P4200 (ASU)
MINING INDUSTRIES — TENN. — MANGANESE
Manganese Resources of East Tennessee.
R1380 (ETSU)

MINING INDUSTRIES — TENN. — MANGANESE
Manganese Deposits of East Tennessee.
S7660
MINING INDUSTRIES — TENN. — MARBLE
Marble Deposits of East Tennessee: Occurrence and Distribution.
G2680 (LMC)
MINING INDUSTRIES — TENN. — PHOSPHATE
The Phosphate Resources of Tennessee.
S5030 (ETSU)
MINING INDUSTRIES — TENN. — ZINC
Zinc Deposits of East Tennessee.
S1640 (LMC)
MINING INDUSTRIES — VA. — PHOSPHATE
Phosphate Deposits in Southwestern Virginia.
S7670
MINING INDUSTRIES — VA. — QUARTZ
Quartz Crystal Deposits of Southwestern Virginia and Western North Carolina.
M5170
Manganese and Quartzite Deposits in the Lick Mountain Region of Wythe Co.
S6710
MINING INDUSTRIES — W. VA.
A Pressure Chamber for the Impregnation of Porous Rock Specimens.
R1520 (ETSU)
A Simple Technique for the Determination of Weight Per Cent of Calcite and Dolomite in Carbonate Rocks.
R1530 (ETSU)
MINING INDUSTRIES — W. VA. — CLAYS
High-alumina Clays of West Virginia.
T120 (ETSU)
MINING INDUSTRIES — W. VA. — LIMESTONE
A Subsurface Study of the Greenbrier Limestone in West Virginia.
F1610 (ETSU ASU)
MINING INDUSTRIES — W. VA. — SALT
Salt Brines of West Virginia.
P4560 (ETSU)
MINING INDUSTRY
Mineral Resources of the Appalachian Region: A Compilation of Information on the Mineral Resources, Mineral Industry, and Geology of the Appalachian Region.
U3250 (ASU LMC ETSU)
Acid Mine Drainage in Appalachia.
U3430 (ASU)
Labor Baron, a Portrait of John L. Lewis.
W2170 (BC)
Proceedings.
W4240
MINING INDUSTRY — ALA. — COPPER
Report on Stone Hill Copper Mines and Works, Cleburne County, Alabama.
R3960 (ASU)
MINING INDUSTRY — ALA. — IRON
Iron Making in Alabama.
P2700 (ASU)
MINING INDUSTRY — APP.
Copper Deposits of the Appalachian States.
W2210
"Economic Aspects of Surface Subsidence Resulting from Underground Mineral Exploitation."
Z190
MINING INDUSTRY — APP. — COPPER
O790
Origin of the Copper Deposits of the Ducktown Type in the Southern Appalachian Region.
U2800 (ASU)
MINING INDUSTRY — APP. — GEMS
Appalachian Mineral and Gem Trails.
Z50 (ASU WCU LMC BC)
MINING INDUSTRY — APP. — SANDSTONE
Age of Bedford Shale, Berea Sandstone, and Sunbury Shale in the Appalachian and Michigan Basins, Pennsylvania, Ohio, and Michigan.
D2050
MINING INDUSTRY — APP. — SHALE
Age of Bedford Shale, Berea Sandstone, and Sunbury Shale in the Appalachian and Michigan Basins, Pennsylvania, Ohio, and Michigan.
D2050
Stratigraphy and Uranium Content of the Chattanooga Shale in Northeastern Alabama, Northwestern Georgia, and Eastern Tennessee.
G2210
MINING INDUSTRY — APP. — URANIUM
Uranium in the Appalachian Mobile Belt.
G50 (LMC)
Stratigraphy and Uranium Content of the Chattanooga Shale in Northeastern Alabama, Northwestern Georgia, and Eastern Tennessee.
G2210
MINING INDUSTRY — COAL
The Geology and Mineral Resources of Wise County and the Coal-bearing Portion of Scott County, Virginia.
E670 (ETSU ASU)
MINING INDUSTRY — GA.
Exploration for Mineral Deposits in Habersham County, Georgia.
H8580
Exploration for Mineral Deposits in White County, Georgia.
H8600 (LMC)
MINING INDUSTRY — GA. — GOLD
Auraria: The Story of a Georgia Gold-Mining Town.
C7770 (ASU BC)
MINING INDUSTRY — GA. — OLIVINE
Forsterite Olivine Deposits of North Carolina and Georgia.
H8400 (ETSU WCU)
MINING INDUSTRY — GA. — TALC
Geology and Mineral Resources of the Northwest Quarter of the Cohutta Mountain Quadrangle.
S220 (ETSU)
MINING INDUSTRY — IRON — VA.
The Resources of the Coal Field of the Upper Kanawha, with a Sketch of the Iron Belt of Virginia, Setting Forth Some of Their Markets and Means of Development.
M4480
MINING INDUSTRY — KY. — COAL
Geology and Coal Resources of the Cannel City Quadrangle, Kentucky.
E2020
MINING INDUSTRY — KY. — SHALE
Shales for Lightweight Aggregate in Appalachian Region, Kentucky and Tennessee.
H6620
MINING INDUSTRY — MARBLE
Field Excursion: The Georgia Marble District.
P4050 (ETSU)
MINING INDUSTRY — MD. — LIMESTONE
Brachipoda of the Keyser Limestone (Silurian-Devonian) of Maryland and Adjacent Areas.
B5700 (ETSU)
MINING INDUSTRY — N. C.
The Minerals and Mineral Localities of North Carolina.
G800 (ASU)
Preliminary Report on Corundum Deposits in the Buck Creek Peridotite, Clay County, North Carolina.
H170 (ASU)
The Mining Industry in North Carolina.
N2220 (ASU UNCA ETSU LMC)
MINING INDUSTRY — N. C. — COAL
In the Coal and Iron Counties of North Carolina.
H420 (LMC WCU)
In the Coal and Iron Counties of North Carolina.
H430 (BC ASU)
MINING INDUSTRY — N. C. — COPPER
O790
MINING INDUSTRY — N. C. — FELDSPAR
Feldspar Deposits of the Bryson City District, North Carolina.
C390 (ASU WCU)
MINING INDUSTRY — N. C. — GEMS
E1910
MINING INDUSTRY — N. C. — GOLD
Bechtler's Gold.
F3180
MINING INDUSTRY — N. C. — HALLOYSITE
Halloysite Deposits of Western North Carolina.
H8410 (ETSU WCU)
MINING INDUSTRY — N. C. — IRON
In the Coal and Iron Counties of North Carolina.
H420 (LMC WCU)
In the Coal and Iron Counties of North Carolina.
H430 (BC ASU)
MINING INDUSTRY — N. C. — IRON ORE
"A Study of the Cranberry Ore Belt."
B5750 (ASU)
MINING INDUSTRY — N. C. — MICA
Mica Deposits of the Franklin-Sylva District, North Carolina.
O640 (ASU WCU ETSU)
MINING INDUSTRY — N. C. — OLIVINE
Forsterite Olivine Deposits of North Carolina and Georgia.
H8400 (ETSU WCU)
MINING INDUSTRY — N. C. — PEGMATITES
Pegmatites of the Cashiers and Zirconia Districts, North Carolina.
O650 (ETSU ASU)
MINING INDUSTRY — PA. — SLATE
"The Economic Geography of the State Industry in Eastern Pennsylvania."
C1260
MINING INDUSTRY — TALC
Talc Deposits of the Murphy Marble Belt.
V290 (WCU)
MINING INDUSTRY — TENN. — CLAY
Ceramic Evaluation of Clays and Shales of East Tennessee.
H6600 (ETSU)
MINING INDUSTRY — TENN. — COPPER
Geology and Ore Deposits of the Ducktown Mining District, Tennessee.
E1960 (ASU BC)
MINING INDUSTRY — TENN. — DOLOMITE
Limestone and Dolomite Resources of Tennessee.
H5040 (ETSU)
MINING INDUSTRY — TENN. — LIMESTONE
Limestone and Dolomite Resources of Tennessee.
H5040 (ETSU)
MINING INDUSTRY — TENN. — SHALE
Ceramic Evaluation of Clays and Shales of East Tennessee.
H6600 (ETSU)
Shales for Lightweight Aggregate in Appalachian Region, Kentucky and Tennessee.
H6620
MINING INDUSTRY — TENN. — ZINC
Stratigraphy of the Mascot-Jefferson City Zinc District, Tennessee.
B6610
"The Zinc Industry of Jefferson County, Tennessee."
C7750
Geology of the Mascot-Jefferson City Zinc District, Tennessee.
O220 (ETSU)
MINING INDUSTRY — VA. — COAL
Coal, Southwest Virginia's Source of Misery.
O760 (ASU)
MINING INDUSTRY — VA. — COKE AND COAL
Southwest Virginia and Contiguous Territory: Mineral Resources and Railway Facilities, Statistics, Information, Markets for Coke, Fuel, Ores, etc.
B5850 (BC)
MINING INDUSTRY — VA. — DOLOMITES
Industrial Limestones and Dolomites in Va.: James River District West of the Blue Ridge.
E910
MINING INDUSTRY — VA. — IRON
The Iron Industry of Wythe County from 1792.
W5800 (ASU BC)
MINING INDUSTRY — VA. — IRON, COAL, ZINC, COPPER AND LEAD
Resources of South-west Virginia, Showing the Mineral Deposits of Iron, Coal, Zinc, Copper and Lead. Also, the Staples of the Various Counties, Methods of Transportation Access, etc.
B5840 (ASU BC)
MINING INDUSTRY — VA. — LEAD
Zinc and Lead Region of Southwestern Va.
V1030
Lead and Zinc Deposits in Virginia.
W1550
MINING INDUSTRY — VA. — LIMESTONES
Industrial Limestones and Dolomites in Va.: James River District West of the Blue Ridge.
E910
MINING INDUSTRY — VA. — MARBLE
Marble Prospects in Giles Co., Va.
V1000
MINING INDUSTRY — VA. — ZINC
Zinc and Lead Region of Southwestern Va.
V1030
Lead and Zinc Deposits in Virginia.
W1550

MINING INDUSTRY — W. VA. — IRON AND STEEL
Principio to Wheeling.
M4590 (BC)
MINING INDUSTRY — W. VA. — IRON, SALE AND SANDSTONE
Iron Ores, Salt and Sandstones.
G4270 (ETSU)
MINING INDUSTRY — W. VA — SANDSTONE
Some Low-alumina Quartzitic Sandstones in West Virginia: A Preliminary Report.
C3620 (ETSU)
Lithification of Sandstones in West Virginia.
H4180 (ETSU)
MINING INTERESTS — TENN. — MARBLE
"Marble Deposits and Marble Industry of the Knoxville Area."
T870
MINING INUDSTRY — VA. — MANGANESE
Possibilities for Manganese Ore on Certain Undeveloped Tracts in the Shenandoah Valley, Virginia.
H5130
MINING RESOURCES — APP. — GOLD
Reconnaissance of Some Gold and Tin Deposits of the Southern Appalachians.
G3290
MINING RESOURCES — APP. — TIN
Reconnaissance of Some Gold and Tin Deposits of the Southern Appalachians.
G3290
MINING — ROCK SALT
Rock Salt Deposits of West Virginia.
M3550 (ETSU)
MISSION AND MISSIONARIES — ALA.
Angels in the Mountains.
S7720
MISSION SCHOOLS
History of the Methodist Episcopal Church, South.
A1350 (ASU)
The West Virginia Hills: A Study of the Work of the Presbyterian Church in the United States in the Synod of West Virginia.
A1670 (ASU)
Minutes, 1834-1852.
A2150 (WCU)
Memoir of Catherine Brown, a Christian Indian of the Cherokee Nation.
A2350 (ASU BC)
Memoir of Catharine Brown, a Christian Indian of the Cherokee Nation.
A2360
Appalachian Mountain Community Center under the Auspices of the Protestant Episcopal Church. . .
A3300
The Appalachian School. . .
A4040
The Appalachian School Department of Fireside Industries.
A4050
Appalachian School Summer Camp.
A4060
"Protestant Missionaries to the American Indians, 1789 to 1862."
B3160
Buckhorn: The Story of a Christian Enterprise on Squabble Creek in the Mountains of Kentucky.
B8250 (BC)
Future of the Church and Independent Schools in Our Southern Highlands.
C620 (BC)
The Future of the Church and Independent Schools in our Southern Highlands.
C630 (ASU)
Southern Highland Schools Maintained by Denominational and Independent Agencies.
C860 (ASU)
Southern Mountain Schools Maintained by Denominational and Independent Agencies.
C870
The Double Head Academy.
C2600 (BC)
"Music in Four Kentucky Mountain Settlement Schools."
C2820 (LMC BC)
Directory of Appalachian Mission Enterprises.
C6190 (BC)
Stuart Robinson School and Its Work.
C7220 (BC)
Stay on, Stranger: An Extraordinary Story of the Kentucky Mountains.
D4110 (ASU LMC WWC BC)
Announcement.
E2060 (ASU)
Berea College, Ky.
F50
A Mountain School: A Study Made by the Southern Woman's Educational Alliance and Kennarock Training School.
H3410 (WWC BC)
Religion in the Highlands: Native Churches and Missionary Enterprises in the Southern Appalachian Area.
H7030 (WWC ASU BC)
Edward O. Guerrant: Apostle to the Southern Highlanders.
M40 (LMC BC ASU)
Faith Victorious in the Kentucky Mountains.
M550 (BC)
Faith Victorious in the Kentucky Mountains.
M560
Hitherto and Henceforth in the Kentucky Mountains.
M570 (BC)
The Pauline Ministry in the Kentucky Mountains: Or, A Brief Account of the Kentucky Mountain Holiness Association.
M580 (ASU LMC BC)
History of Baptist Indian Missions: Embracing Remarks of the Former and Present Condition of the Aboriginal Tribes. Their Settlement Within the Indian Territory, and Their Future Prospects.
M790 (WCU)
The Forgotten Region.
M1990 (BC)
"Unfinished Tasks" of the Southern Presbyterian church.
M2290
The Gates Open Slowly: A History of Education in Kentucky.
M2560 (BC LMC)
M5020 (ASU)
The American Indian on the New Trail: The Red Man of the United States and the Christian Gospel.
M6410 (ASU)
"A History of the Early Baptist Missions Among the Five Civilized Tribes."
M6420 (WCU)
The South To-day.
M7220 (LMC)
At Our Own Door: A Study of Home Missions with Special Reference to the South and West.
M7840 (BC LMC)
The Romance of Home Missions.
M7850 (ASU LMC)
M8360
"Them Missionary Women;" or Work in the Southern Mountains.
M9290
O690
Call of the Home Land; A Study of Home Missions.
P2560
Findings of the Pine Mountain Guidance Institute.
P3000 (BC)
Pine Mountain Bulletin.
P3010 (BC)
The Southern Highlanders of America.
P3670 (BC ASU)
Without Script or Purse: Or, The Mountain Evangelist.
P4640 (BC)
A Sketch of Missionary Life at Valle Crucis in Western North Carolina, 1842-1862.
S4010 (LMC)
Torchlights to the Cherokee: The Brainerd Mission.
W350 (ASU ETSU BC)
In the Land of Mudholes and Mountains; a Story of Three Years' Missionary Work in the Cumberland Mountains.
W2340 (BC)
Springplace: Moravian Mission and the War Family of the Cherokee Nation.
W9500 (MHC)
MISSION SCHOOLS — APP.
Heroine of the Missionary Enterprize.
E810 (BC)
The Church's Mission to the Mountaineers of the South.
H8150
Settlement Institutions in Southern Appalachia.
K3130
Home Mission Investments.
L630 (LMC)
Southern Mountain Schools Maintained by Denominational and Independent Agencies.
R4400 (LMC)
Experiences in Mountain Mission Work.
S4970 (ASU WWC)
Presbyterian Missions in the Southern United States.
T8150 (LMC)
MISSION SCHOOLS — GA.
The Rabun Industrial School and Mountain Extension Work Among the Mountain Whites.
R2380
MISSION SCHOOLS — N. C.
Mission Work among the Mountain Whites in Asheville Presbytery, North Carolina.
C940 (BC)
Miracle in the Mountains.
K140 (ASU LMC MHC WCU WWC FC BC)
Gift from the Hills: Miss Lucy Morgan's Story of Her Unique Penland School.
M7620 (ASU BC ETSU FC WCU WWC)
Gift from the Hills: Miss Lucy Morgan's Story of Unique Penland School.
M7630
O930
Miracle in the Hills.
S4230 (ASU WCU LMC WWC BC)
MISSIONS AND MISSIONARIES
Minutes, 1834-1852.
A2150 (WCU)
Memoir of Catherine Brown, a Christian Indian of the Cherokee Nation.
A2350 (ASU BC)
Memoir of Catharine Brown, a Christian Indian of the Cherokee Nation.
A2360
Appalachian Mountain Community Center under the Auspices of the Protestant Episcopal Church. . .
A3300
Cherokee Messenger.
B1790 (ASU)
Cherokee Messenger.
B1800 (BC ASU WCU)
"Protestant Missionaries to the American Indians, 1789 to 1862."
B3160
Utopia in the Hills. Story of Valeria Home.
B5300
Buckhorn: The Story of a Christian Enterprise on Squabble Creek in the Mountains of Kentucky.
B8250 (BC)
Future of the Church and Independent Schools in Our Southern Highlands.
C620 (BC)
Southern Mountain Schools Maintained by Denominational and Independent Agencies.
C870
Keepers of the Poor.
C1340 (ASU LMC)
Proceedings: A United Approach to Fulfilling the Church's Mission in Appalachia.
C6210 (ASU WCU)
Stuart Robinson School and Its Work.
C7220 (BC)
"Government Patronage of Indian Missions."
E1140
Story of the Cherokee Bible. An Address, with Additional and Explanatory Notes, Delivered before the Meeting of the Ladies' Missionary Society of the First Congregational Church, Ithaca, N. Y., Feb. 5, 1897.
F2310
The Gatherers: The Gospel among the Highlanders.
G4610 (ASU LMC)
The Gospel of the Lilies.
G4620 (BC)
Ministry to the Southern Mountaineer.
H1200
The Mountain People of Kentucky. An Account of Present Conditions with the Attitude of the People toward Improvement.
H1490 (ASU BC)

MISSIONS AND MISSIONARIES

A Mountain School: A Study Made by the Southern Woman's Educational Alliance and Kennarock Training School.
H3410 (WWC BC)

Religion in the Highlands: Native Churches and Missionary Enterprises in the Southern Appalachian Area.
H7030 (WWC ASU BC)

Faith Victorious in the Kentucky Mountains.
M550 (BC)

Faith Victorious in the Kentucky Mountains.
M560

Hitherto and Henceforth in the Kentucky Mountains.
M570 (BC)

The Pauline Ministry in the Kentucky Mountains: Or, A Brief Account of the Kentucky Mountain Holiness Association.
M580 (ASU LMC BC)

History of Baptist Indian Missions: Embracing Remarks of the Former and Present Condition of the Aboriginal Tribes. Their Settlement Within the Indian Territory, and Their Future Prospects.
M790 (WCU)

The Forgotten Region.
M1990 (BC)

"Unfinished Tasks" of the Southern Presbyterian Church.
M2290

The Early Nineteenth Century Missionaries in the Cherokee Country.
M2930

"A History of the Early Baptist Missions Among the Five Civilized Tribes."
M6420 (WCU)

The South To-day.
M7220 (LMC)

At Our Own Door: A Study of Home Missions with Special Reference to the South and West.
M7840 (BC LMC)

The Romance of Home Missions.
M7850 (ASU LMC)

"Them Missionary Women;" or Work in the Southern Mountains.
M9290

Call of the Home Land; A Study of Home Missions.
P2560

The Southern Highlanders of America.
P3670 (BC ASU)

Without Script or Purse: Or, The Mountain Evangelist.
P4640 (BC)

A Sketch of Missionary Life at Valle Crucis in Western North Carolina, 1842-1862.
S4010 (LMC)

Torchlights to the Cherokee: The Brainerd Mission.
W350 (ASU ETSU BC)

In the Land of Mudholes and Mountains; a Story of Three Years' Missionary Work in the Cumberland Mountains.
W2340 (BC)

Report of Mr. Wood's Visit to the Choctaw and Cherokee Missions, 1855.
W8500

MISSIONS AND MISSIONARIES — APP.

Directory of Appalachian Mission Enterprises.
C6190 (BC)

Highways and Byways of Appalachia: A Study of the Work of the Synod of Appalachia of the Presbyterian Church in the United States.
C8370 (ASU LMC BC)

The Protestant Church as a Social Institution.
D3130

Christian Reconstruction in the South.
D3140

Unfinished Business of the Presbyterian Church in America.
E550 (ASU)

Heroine of the Missionary Enterprise.
E810 (BC)

The Life of Rev. David Brainerd, Chiefly Extracted from His Diary, Somewhat Abridged, Embracing, in the Chronological Order, Brainerds Public Journal.
E1070 (LMC)

Bringing in the Sheaves; Gleanings from Harvest Fields in Ohio, Ky., and W. Va.
F530

The Church's Distinctive Challenge in Southern Appalachia.
G1120 (BC)

The Church's Mission to the Mountaineers of the South.
H8150

Home Mission Investments.
L630 (LMC)

Life of Lucius B. Compton.
P970

Experiences in Mountain Mission Work.
S4970 (ASU WWC)

Presbyterian Missions in the Southern United States.
T8150 (LMC)

Presbyterians in the South.
T8160 (WWC BC)

The Life and Labors of Archibald McLean.
W990 (BC)

A Round Robin, the Southern Highlands and Highlanders.
W5290 (BC)

A Century of Faith.
W5360 (BC)

MISSIONS AND MISSIONARIES — CHEROKEE

Reminiscences of Travel in Cherokee Lands. An Address Delivered before the Ladies' Missionary Society of the Ithaca, New York, Congregational Church, 1898.
F2270

Elias Boudinot, Cherokee, and His America.
G60 (ASU BC UNCA)

MISSIONS AND MISSIONARIES — CHEROKEE NATION

"Missionary Activities among the Cherokee Indians, 1757-1838."
C9150

MISSIONS AND MISSIONARIES — GA.

Sketch of the Life of Elder Humphrey, Baptist Missionary to the Cherokee Indians.
F1480

The Moravians in Georgia, 1735-1740.
F3370 (ASU)
M5020 (ASU)

MISSIONS AND MISSIONARIES — KY.

F3270 (BC)

"A History of Religious Education in the Kentucky Mountains."
G4230 (ASU)

MISSIONS AND MISSIONARIES — N. C.

Mission Work among the Mountain Whites in Asheville Presbytery, North Carolina.
C940 (BC)

William West Skiles: A Sketch of Missionary Life at Valle Crucis in Western North Carolina, 1842-1862.
C7210 (ASU WCU BC)

The Story of a Mountain Missionary: Rev. James Floyd Fletcher, 1858-1946.
F1500 (ASU)

A History of the Ashe County, North Carolina, and New River, Virginia, Baptist Associations.
F1530 (ASU)

Records of the Moravians in North Carolina.
F3380 (ASU LMC MHC)

Annual Report.
M6240 (LMC)
O930

MISSIONS AND MISSIONARIES — TENN.

Sketch of the Life of Elder Humphrey, Baptist Missionary to the Cherokee Indians.
F1480

MISSIONS AND MISSIONARIES — VA.

Mission.
F3100 (ASU LMC BC)

MISSIONS AND MISSIONARIES — W. VA.

Human Crisis in the Kingdom of Coal.
S5020

MISSISSIPPI RIVER

. . . Value of Flood Height Reduction from TVA Reservoirs to the Alluvial Valley of the Lower Mississippi River . . .
T4070

MOLLY MAGUIRES

The Molly Maguires.
B3690 (ASU WCU BC)

MONONGAHELA RIVER

The Monongahela.
B4260 (BC)

Denudation and Erosion in the Southern Appalachian Region and the Monongehela Basin.
G2130 (ASU ETSU)

Employment and Underemployment of Rural People in the Upper Monongahela Valley, West Virginia.
M5230

Handbook of Pollution Control Costs in Mine Drainage Management.
M6470

Water Pollution Control In the Monongahela River Basin.
P1810

Availability for Employment of Rural People in the Upper Monongahela Valley.
P3700

Priority Determination Procedure for the Selection of Pollution Abatement Projects in the Monongahela River Basin.
R2590 (ASU)

"The Allegheny-Monongahela Flood Control Program and Its Benefits to Metropolitan Pittsburgh."
W7330

MOONSHINE — APP.

Mountain Spirits, a Chronicle of Corn Whiskey from King James Ulster Plantation to America's Appalachians and the Moonshine Life.
D20 (BC ASU)

MOONSHINING

Moonshine: Being Appalachia's Arabian Nights.
A70 (ASU LMC)

The 20,000,000,000 a Year Racket of Bootleggers and Liquor-stamp Counterfeiters in Several Southeastern States Is Here Detailed by One of the Men Who Broke It Up.
A4590

No Place for Revenuers.
A4600 (BC LMC)

After the Mountaineers.
A5370 (BC)

Mac Day, Crusader; A Story of the Fight for Americanism.
B8800 (BC)

The Second Oldest Profession: An Informal History of Moonshining in America.
C1440 (ASU BC)

Spurrier with the Wildcats and Moonshiners.
C9370 (ASU BC)

Moonshine: Its History and Folklore.
K600 (BC ASU LMC WCU MHC)

Spurrier With the Wildcats and Moonshiners.
S6390 (ASU BC)

A History of the Life of Amos Owens, the Noted Blockader, of Cherry Mountain, North Carolina.
W5520 (LMC)

MOONSHINING — APP.

The Incredible Moonshine Menace.
L2420 (ASU)

Moonshine: Public Enemy.
L2430 (ASU)

MOONSHINING — N. C.

Prohibition in North Carolina, 1715-1945.
W5700 (LMC)

MOONSHINING — VA.

The Life and Times of a Mountaineer Game Warden.
O740

MOUNTAINEERING

Roamin' with the Roamin' Men of the Smoky Mountains.
O30 (ASU LMC BC)

MTN. PEOPLE

My Southern Friends.
G1770 (BC WCU)

"A Study and Contrast of the Kentucky Mountaineer and the Bluegrass Aristocrat in the Works of John Fox, Jr."
O880 (ASU)

MTN. PEOPLE — ALA.

Angels in the Mountains.
S7720

MTN. PEOPLE — GA.

The Foxfire Book: Hog Dressing; Log Cabin Building; Mountain Crafts and Foods; Planting by the Signs; Snake Lore, Hunting Tales, Faith Healing; Moonshining; and Other Affairs of Plain Living.
W6020 (FC ASU BC)

MTN. PEOPLE — GA.

Foxfire 2: Ghost Stories, Spring Wild Plant Foods, Spinning and Weaving, Midwifing, Burial Customs, Corn Shuckin's, Wagon Making and More Affairs of Plain Living.
W6030 (FC ASU BC)

Foxfire 3: Animal Care, Banjos and Dulcimers, Hide Tanning, Summer and Fall Wildplant Foods, Butter Churns, Ginseng, and Still More Affairs of Plain Living.
W6040 (ASU)

MTN. PEOPLE — VA.

The Blue Ridge: Man and Nature in Shenandoah National Park and Blue Ridge Parkway.
W6260 (WCU LMC)

MUSIC

Country-Western Music and the Urban Hillbilly.
W6240 (ASU)

Playing Lead Dulcimer.
W6320 (ASU)

MUSIC AND MUSICAL INSTRUMENTS

Anglo-American Folksong Style.
A140 (ASU BC)

Death in the Dark.
A420 (BC ASU)

A History of the Musical Careers of Dewitt "Snuffy" Jenkins, Banjoist, and Homer "Pappy" Sherrill, Fiddler.
A790 (LMC)

The Ballad Book.
A1750 (BC)

The Story of American Folk Song.
A2200 (ASU BC)

"A Collection of Ballads and Songs from East Tennessee."
A2280 (LMC)

Songs of Freedom.
A3330

Old English Ballads and Folk Songs.
A4660

Songs from the Carolina Hills.
A4670

"The Melodic and Rhythmic Characteristics of the Traditional Ballad Variants Found in the Southern Appalachians."
A4690 (ASU)

A Century of Ballads.
A5270 (ASU)

Making an Appalachian Dulcimer.
B290 (LMC BC)

English Folk-songs Collected, Arranged, and Provided with Symphonies and Accompaniments for the Pianoforte.
B1470 (ASU)

Hill Country Tunes: Instrumental Folk Music of Southwestern Pennsylvania.
B2150 (LMC)

The Sweet Songster, a Collection of the Most Popular and Approved Songs, Hymns and Ballads.
B3650 (ASU BC WCU)
B4830 (ETSU)

Singa Hipsy Doodle, and Other Folk Songs of West Virginia.
B4980 (ASU ETSU BC)

Singing Carr and Other Song-ballads of the Cumberlands.
B6210 (ASU BC)

The Ballad Mongers: Rise of the Modern Folk Song.
B6310 (BC)

The Folk-carol of England.
B6560 (BC)

The Stonewall Brigade Band.
B6590 (ASU BC)

The Traditional Tunes of the Child Ballads.
B6830 (ASU BC)

The Encyclopedia of Country and Western Music.
B7280 (WCU)

A History of English Balladry, and Other Studies.
B7840 (ASU)

Ancient Ballads and Songs of the North of Scotland.
B7910 (ASU)

"A Study of the Music Education Program of Watauga County."
B7980 (ASU)

The Minstrel of the Mountains.
B8820 (BC)

The Technique and Variation in an American Fiddle Tune.
B8890

The George Pullen Jackson Collection of Southern Hymnody: A Bibliography.
C280 (BC)

East Tennessee and Western Virginia Mountain Ballads (The Last Stand of American Pioneer Civilization).
C370 (ASU BC)

English Folk Songs from the Southern Appalachians, Comprising 122 Songs and Ballads, and 323 Tunes.
C830 (ASU LMC WWC BC)

"The Singing School and Shape Note Tradition: Residuals in 20th Century American Hymnody."
C3590 (WCU)

The Old-time Fiddler's Repertory: 245 Traditional Tunes.
C3950 (ASU BC)

"Ballad Characteristics in Modern Popular Country Music."
C8580 (ETSU)

The American Folk Scene; Dimensions of the Folksong Revival.
D1910 (BC)

"The Music of American Revivalism."
D3180 (WCU)

Anthology of American Folk Music.
D4020 (ASU BC)

"Shape Note Hymnody in the Shenandoah Valley, 1816-1860."
E2230 (WCU)

James D. Vaughan, Music Publisher, Lawrenceberg, Tennessee, 1912-1964.
F1470 (WCU)
F1690 (ASU BC WCU WWC LMC ETSU FC)

A Literary History of the Popular Ballad.
F2400 (BC ASU)

Ballads of the Kentucky Highland.
F4020 (ASU LMC ETSU BC)

The Face of Folk Music.
G90 (ASU)

A History and Encyclopedia of Country, Western, and Gospel Music.
G810 (ASU)

Songs of Hill and MOUNTAIN Folk, Ballads, Historical Songs, Folk Songs.
G2060 (BC ASU)

Folksongs and Their Makers.
G2070 (ASU MHC BC)

Only a Miner: Studies in Recorded Coal Mining Songs.
G3500 (ASU LMC MHC WCU BC)

"Recorded American Coal Mining Songs."
G3510

"An Edited Collection of Beech Mountain Folksongs."
G3680 (ETSU)

Hillbilly Ballads.
H2450

"Ananias Davisson: Southern Tune Book Compiler (1780-1857)."
H3230

Sing to Me of Heaven: A Study of Folk and Early American Materials in Three Old Harp Books.
H7170 (ASU BC)

Another Sheaf of White Spirituals.
J40 (ASU LMC)

Down-east Spirituals, and Others: Three Hundred Songs Supplementary to the Author's Spiritual Folk-songs of Early America.
J50 (ASU)

Spiritual Folk-songs of Early America: Two Hundred and Fifty Tunes and Texts with an Introduction and Notes.
J60 (ASU)

Spiritual Folk-songs of Early America: Two Hundred and Fifty Tunes and Texts with an Introduction and Notes.
J70 (ASU WCU LMC BC)

The Story of The Sacred Harp, 1844-1944, a Book of Religious Folk Songs as an American Institution.
J80 (LMC WCU MHC BC ASU)

White and Negro Spirituals, Their Life Span and Kinship, Tracing 200 Years of Untrammeled Song Making and Singing Among Our Country Folk, with 116 Songs as Sung by Both Races.
J90 (ASU BC)

White Spirituals in the Southern Uplands.
J100

White Spirituals in the Southern Uplands: The Story of the Fascola Folk, Their Songs, Singings, and "Buckwheat Notes".
J110 (ASU BC WCU ETSU LMC MHC)

White Spirituals in the Southern Uplands: The Story of the Fasola Folk, Their Songs, Singings, and "Buckwheat Notes".
J120 (ETSU WWC)

Sweet Rivers of Song: A Book of Traditional Songs From the Southern Appalachian Mountain Region.
J370 (ASU MHC WCU BC)

Wake and Sing: A Miniature Anthology of the Music of Appalachian America.
J380 (WWC BC ASU)

Tuning and Playing the Appalachian Dulcimer.
J550 (ASU LMC)

Tuning and Playing the Appalachian Dulcimer.
J560 (BC)

Tuning and Playing the Appalachian Dulcimer.
J570 (WCU)

Kentucky Mountain Melodies.
J770

Popular British Ballads, Ancient and Modern.
J1930

Songs from the Hills.
J2320 (WCU)

"The Carter Family: A Reflection of Changes in Society."
K10 (WCU)

Cecil Sharp: His Life and Work.
K230 (BC ASU LMC)
K1220 (ASU ETSU BC)

"A Study of the Changing Role of the Music Specialist in the North Carolina Elementary Schools, 1950-1957."
K2060 (ASU)

Country and Bluegrass Dobro.
K2220 (WCU)

A Folk Song Chapbook.
K2580 (LMC)

Folksingers and Folksongs in America.
L880 (BC)
L2830 (BC ASU ETSU)

A Peddlar's Pack of Ballads and Songs.
L3090 (ASU BC)

The Folk Songs of North America, in the English Language. Melodies and guitar chords transcribed by Peggy Seeger with one-hundred piano arrangements by Matyas Seiber and Don Banks. Illustrated by Michael Leonard. Editorial assistant Shirley Collins.
L3130 (WCU ASU)

The Social Harp.
M1040 (ASU BC)

Melodies and Mountaineers.
M2240 (ASU)

Four and Twenty Songs for the Mountain Dulcimer.
M2520 (ASU BC)

Country Music U. S. A.: A Fifty-year History.
M2910 (FC ASU)

Beech Mountain Folk-Songs and Ballads.
M4260

"A Survey of Recreational Music Activities Available to the General College Student in Georgia, North Carolina, South Carolina and Tennessee."
M4340 (ASU)

The Hammered Dulcimer — How to Make and Play It.
M6330

The Mountain Dulcimer.
M6340

You're Only Human Once.
M7160 (ASU)

"The Life and Works of Lamar Stringfield, 1897-1959."
N480 (ASU WCU)

An Introduction to Folk Music in the United States.
N620 (BC)

The Ballad Book.
N1030 (ASU BC FC LMC MHC)

The Ballad Book.
N1040 (ASU ETSU)

The Ballad Book.
N1050 (ASU WCU)

Ballads, Carols, and Tragic Legends from the Southern Appalachian Mountains.
N1060 (ASU ETSU LMC)

MUSIC AND MUSICAL INSTRUMENTS

Ballads, Lovesongs, and Tragic Legends from the Southern Appalachian Mountains.
N1070 (ASU)

More Songs of the Hill-folk: Ten Ballads and Tragic Legends from Kentucky, Virginia, Tennessee, North Carolina, and Georgia.
N1100 (ASU ETSU)

Seven Kentucky Mountain Tunes.
N1110 (BC)

Songs of the Hill-folk: Twelve Ballads from Kentucky, Virginia, and North Carolina.
N1120 (ASU BC ETSU LMC)

Ten Christmas Carols from the Southern Appalachian Mountains.
N1130 (ASU BC)

The Guitar Songbook.
N1260

Mountain Songs of North Carolina.
N3030

Something to Sing About.
O460 (BC)
O500

Teach Yourself Appalachian Dulcimer.
P1270

"A Study of Academic Achievement of Band Students and Non-band Students, Blountville High School (1964-1967)."
P3070 (ETSU)

A Selective Music Bibliography from the Period 1663-1763.
P4800 (LMC)

The Foggy Dew; More English Folk Songs from the Hammond and Gardiner Manuscripts.
P4890 (ASU)

The Plucked Dulcimer of the Southern Mountains.
P4910 (ASU BC)

The Plucked Dulcimer and How to Play It.
P4920 (WCU ASU BC)

The Plucked Dulcimer and How to Play It.
P4930 (ASU LMC MHC)

Go Tell Aunt Rhody.
Q30 (ASU)

Grass Roots Harmony.
R120 (LMC)

Mountain Ballads for Social Singing.
R150 (BC)

American Mountain Songs.
R2060 (ETSU BC ASU)

American Mountain Songs.
R2070 (ASU ETSU WCU BC)

The Dulcimer Book, Being a Book about the Three-stringed Appalachian Dulcimer, Including Some Ways of Tuning and Playing: Some Recollections in Its Local History in Perry and Knott Counties, Kentucky. Some Observations on the Probable Origins of the Instrument in the Old Countries of Europe: And with Words and Music for Some Sixteen Songs from the Ritchie Family of Kentucky.
R2430 (ASU BC ETSU LMC WCU)

The Dulcimer Book, Being a Book about the Three-stringed Appalachian Dulcimer, Including Some Ways of Tuning and Playing: Some Recollections in Its Local History in Perry and Knott Counties, Kentucky. Some Observations on the Probable Origins of the Instrument in the Old Countries of Europe: With Plentiful Photographic Illustrations and Drawings. And with Words and Music for Some Sixteen Songs from the Ritchie Family of Kentucky.
R2440 (ASU)

Folk Songs of the Southern Appalachian As Sung by Jean Ritchie.
R2450 (WWC)

Folk Songs of the Southern Appalachians; As Sung by Jean Ritchie.
R2460 (LMC WWC ETSU)

A Garland of Mountain Song: Songs from the Repertoire of the Ritchie Family of Viper, Kentucky.
R2470 (ASU WWC)

Jean Ritchie's Swapping Song Book.
R2480 (ASU WCU)

Singing Family of the Cumberlands.
R2490 (ASU MHC WWC BC)

Singing Family of the Cumberlands.
R2500 (ASU WCU LMC)

The Swapping Song Book.
R2510 (BC ASU LMC)

Old-time Mountain Banjo: An Instruction Method for Playing the Old-time Five-string Mountain Banjo Based on the Styles of Traditional Banjo-pickers.
R3760 (WCU ASU BC)

The American Songbag.
S270 (FC)

A Song Catcher in Southern Mountains: American Folk Songs of British Ancestry.
S730 (ASU WCU ETSU WWC BC)

A Song Catcher in Southern Mountains: American Folk Songs of British Ancestry.
S740 (ASU LMC ETSU)

English Song Book.
S1410

Earl Scruggs and the 5-string Banjo.
S1490 (WCU BC)

How to Play the 5-String Banjo: A Manual for Beginners.
S1680 (ASU LMC)

The Incomplete Folksinger.
S1690

American-English Folk Songs, Collected in the Southern Appalachians.
S2270 (ASU)

Folk Songs from the Southern Appalachians.
S2290 (ASU BC)

Eighty English Folk Songs from the Southern Appalachians.
S2300 (WCU ASU BC ETSU)

English Folk Songs from the Southern Appalachians, Comprising 273 Songs and Ballads with 968 Tunes, Including 39 Tunes Contributed by Olive Dame Campbell.
S2310 (ASU)

English Folk Songs from the Southern Appalachians.
S2320 (ASU WWC FC)

English Folk Songs from the Southern Appalachians.
S2330 (ETSU)

English Folk Songs from the Southern Appalachians.
S2340 (ASU WCU LMC MHC)

Nursery Songs from the Appalachian Mountains.
S2360 (ASU BC LMC)

British Ballads in the Cumberland Mountains.
S2580

A Syllabus of Kentucky Folk-Songs.
S2590

Folk Songs of the Blue Ridge Mountains: 50 Traditional Songs as Sung by the People of the Blue Ridge Mountains Country.
S2640 (ASU ETSU LMC MHC WCU BC)

The Country Music Story: A Picture History of Country and Western Music.
S2780 (ASU WCU)

The Music Lover's Handbook.
S3290 (ASU)

Beginning the Folk Guitar, an Instructional Manual.
S3380 (ASU)

Folk Blues: 110 American Folk Blues.
S3390 (ASU)

American Anthology of Old-world Ballads.
S4980 (ASU)

South Carolina Ballads: With a Study of the Traditional Ballad Today.
S4990 (ASU BC)

The Traditional Ballad and Its South Carolina Survivals.
S5000 (LMC)

Twenty-five Kentucky Folk Ballads.
S8990 (BC)

Folk-style Autoharp; an Instruction Method for Playing the Autoharp and Accompanying Folk Songs.
T360 (ASU)

The Fiddle Book: The Comprehensive Book on American Folk Music, Fiddlin, and Fiddle Styles Including More Than 150 Traditional Fiddle Tunes Compiled From Country Fiddlers.
T7690 (ASU)

Ballad Makin' in the Mountains of Kentucky.
T7880 (ASU WCU LMC ETSU BC)

The Singin' Gatherin': Tunes From the Southern Appalachians.
T7940 (UNCA BC ETSU ASU)

The Singin' Gatherin': Tunes From the Southern Appalachians.
T7950 (LMC BC)

The Sun Shines Bright.
T7960 (ASU WCU LMC ETSU BC)

Check-list of Recorded Songs.
U3580

A bibliography of hammered and plucked (Appalachian or mountain) dulcimers and related instruments.
U3620

Folk Music in America.
V180

The Folksongs of Virginia: A Checklist of the WPA Holdings, Alderman Library University of Virginia.
V1230 (ETSU ASU LMC)

The Southern Harmony.
W400 (WCU)

The Southern Harmony Songbook . . . .
W410 (BC)

The Songs of Doc Watson.
W1510 (ASU WCU)

"A Suggested Plan for Developing a More Effective Community Music Program in Johnson City."
W2200 (ETSU)

The Golden Song Book.
W2890 (BC)

Southern Mountain Folk Traditions: And the Folksong "Stars" Syndrome.
W2990 (ASU LMC)

"The Songs of the Mountaineers."
W3110 (ASU)

The W. Va. Centennial Book of One Hundred Songs: 1863-1963; Patriotic Songs, Folk Songs, and Hymns.
W3220 (BC)

Mountain Songs of North Carolina.
W4970 (BC)

The Billy Edd Wheeler Song Book.
W5070 (WWC)

Kentucky Mountain Folk-Songs.
W5160

The Sacred Harp.
W5310 (WCU ASU)

Anglo-American Folksong Scholarship Since 1898.
W6250 (BC)

Pennsylvania Spirituals.
Y100 (ASU)

MUSIC AND MUSICAL INSTRUMENTS — APP.

"The Sacred Harp Tradition of the South: Its Origin and Evolution.
E1650 (WCU)

Vagabond Songs and Ballads of Scotland.
F1980 (ASU)

The Musical Million: A Study and Analysis of the Periodical Promoting Music Reading through Shape Notes in North America from 1870 to 1914.
H870 (WCU)

"Southern Mountain Folk Songs for American Schools."
H6440 (ASU)

Ballad Books and Ballad Men: Raids and Rescues in Britain, America, and the Scandinavian North Since 1800.
H8670 (ASU BC)

Favorite Mountain Ballads and Old Time Songs.
K2130

Appalachian Fiddle.
K3140

Appalachian Dulcimer Plans.
W540

New Race of Song Sparrows from the Appalachian Region.
W4960

Twenty-Five Great Folk Songs.
W5090 (BC)

Folklore in the English and Scottish Ballads.
W7560 (ASU FC)

MUSIC AND MUSICAL INSTRUMENTS — KY.

A Gatherin'; Ky. Lore of Mt. Music, Songs, and Dances.
K2830

MUSIC AND MUSICAL INSTRUMENTS — TENN.

"The Symphony Orchestra of Kingsport, Tennessee."
W7400 (ETSU)

MUSIC AND MUSICAL INSTRUMENTS — VA.

A Brief History of the Musical Movement or Stream, Which was Started in Mountain Valley (Now Singers Glen, Va.) in the Early Part of the Nineteenth Century by Joseph Funk.
F1380 (ASU FC)

N. C. — DESCRIPTION AND TRAVEL
North Carolina Sketches and Places.
A1610 (ASU)
These Friendly Mountains.
B7880 (ASU)
The Slave States of America.
B8260
This Was My Valley.
B8980 (ASU WCU LMC WWC UNCA)
Smoky Mountain Country.
C320 (ASU WCU LMC ETSU BC)
Shopping Round the Mountains.
C380
Glimpses of a Land of Beauty.
C400
Exploring the Mountains of North Carolina.
C1250 (MHC)
C1320 (ASU)
The Best from Almar Farm in Western North Carolina.
C1360 (LMC ASU)
C6030 (LMC)
Mountain Scenery: The Scenery of the Mountains of Western North Carolina and Western South Carolina.
C6090 (ASU WCU)
Exploring the Mountains of North Carolina.
C7450 (ASU LMC SCU WCU)
Song of Life in the Smokies.
C7670 (LMC)
Song of Life in the Smokies: Stories of Mine Own People and Sketches of Life as It Was Lived in the Mountains Before the Park Took Over.
C7680 (ETSU)
Tar Heels.
D190 (LMC BC)
Reminiscences and Traditions of Western North Carolina.
D700
Land of Waterfalls: A Portfolio of Exclusive Lithographs Suitable for Framing.
D1860 (WCU)
The War Trails of the Blue Ridge, Containing an Authentic Description of the Battle of King's Mountain, the Incidents Leading up to and the Echoes of the Aftermath of This Epochal Engagement, and Other Stories Whose Scenes Are Laid in the Blue Ridge.
D3760 (BC ASU LMC)
Carolina Mountain Breezes.
E630 (ASU)
. . . North Carolina, a Guide to the Old North State.
F450 (WWC ASU UNCA)
Sketches of North Carolina, Historical and Biographical, Illustrative of the Principles of a Portion of Her Early Settlers.
F1790 (ASU LMC)
Sketches of North Carolina, Historical and Biographical, Illustrative of the Principles of a Portion of Her Early Settlers.
F1800 (MHC BC)
Down Home.
G2250 (ASU)
Azure-lure, a Romance of the Mountains: Souvenir of Asheville and Western North Carolina.
G3350 (ASU BC WCU LMC WWC UNCA)
"The Land of the Sky."
G3470
Western North Carolina Sketches.
G4180 (ASU BC WCU LMC MHC)
Notes on the Geography of the Mountain District of Western North Carolina.
G5010
Souvenir Views of the Beautiful Blowing Rock Region.
H2180
Five Months in the Old North State.
H6720 (ASU BC)
The World of My Childhood.
I970 (ASU LMC)
Outdoor Recreation Potential Appraisal.
J30 (WCU)
Easy to Follow Directions on How to Get Lost in the Land of the Sky.
J580 (WCU)
L300 (UNCA ASU)
A New Voyage to Carolina.
L1000 (LMC ETSU)
A New Voyage to Carolina.
L1010 (UNCA)
Lindsey's Guidebook to Western North Carolina.
L2560
An Appalachian Valley.
M3840 (ASU)
An Appalachian Valley.
M3840 (ASU)
Asheville, in Land of the Sky.
M4740 (ASU WCU LMC WWC UNCA)
Land o' the Sky; History, Stories, Sketches.
M4870 (ASU BC LMC WCU UNCA)
Digest of Information About Transylvania County, North Carolina, Containing Information of General Interest to Commercial and Industrial Businesses.
M5010 (WCU)
The Carolina Mountains.
M7710 (ASU BC LMC MHC WCU WWC)
The Carolina Mountains.
M7720 (UNCA)
Scenic Western North Carolina, a Vacation Guide to the Highlands.
M8520 (ASU)
A Sketch of North Carolina.
N1830 (ASU LMC)
North Carolina: A Good Place to Live. . . .
N1950 (UNCA)
N2790 (MHC ASU)
Journey into America.
P1410 (WCU)
Western North Carolina Facts, Figures, Photographs.
P4210 (LMC WCU)
High Lands.
R1760 (ASU LMC WCU)
The Face of North Carolina.
R2670 (ASU LMC UNCA)
The Goodliest Land — North Carolina.
R2680 (ASU LMC)
Souvenir of Asheville or the Sky-land.
S590 (ASU WCU BC)
North Carolina: A Description by Counties.
S2400 (LMC)
Tar on My Heels, a Press Agent's Notebook.
S2410 (ASU LMC BC)
Sixty-four Selected Views of Western North Carolina, "The Land of the Sky, America's Beauty Spot".
S5810 (ASU)
Camping on Mount Mitchell, Information Regarding Good Places for Summer Camps in United States Forests in North Carolina.
S5830 (ASU)
The Land of the Sky, Western North Carolina.
S5860 (LMC)
North Carolina by North Carolinians: A Photographic Exhibition Sponsored By the North Carolina Arts Council: The People, Places and Things of One State as Seen by the People Who Know It Best — Those Who Live Here.
S6370 (LMC)
Great Smoky Mountains National Park, North Carolina and Tennessee.
S8840 (ASU LMC WCU ETSU)
The Heart of the Alleghenies: Or, Western North Carolina. Comprising Its Topography, History, Resources, People, Narratives, Incidents, and Pictures of Travel, Adventures in Hunting and Fishing and Legends of Its Wildernesses.
Z40 (ASU LMC WCU BC ETSU)

N. C. — EARLY EXPLORATION
The Natural History of North Carolina.
B6600 (ASU BC LMC)
History of North Carolina, Containing the Exact Description and Natural History of That Country, Together with the Present State Thereof, and a Journal of a Thousand Miles Traveled Through Several Nations of Indians, Giving a Particular Account of Their Customs, Manners, Etc., Etc.
L970 (LMC MHC BC)
History of North Carolina, Containing the Exact Description and Natural History of that Country, Together with the Present State Thereof, and a Journal of a Thousand Miles Traveled through Several Nations of Indians, Giving a Particular Account of Their Customs, Manners, Etc., Etc.
L980 (UNCA)
History of North Carolina, Containing the Exact Description and Natural History of That Country, Together with the Present State Thereof and a Journal of a Thousand Miles Traveled Through Several Nations of Indians, Giving Particular Account of Their Customs, Manners, Etc.
L990 (WWC ASU)
The Discoveries of John Lederer.
L1280 (LMC)
The Discoveries of John Lederer, in Three Several Marches From Virginia, to the West of Carolina, and Other Parts of the Continent: Begun in March 1669, and Ended in September 1670.
L1290 (ASU FC BC)
The Discoveries of John Lederer, with Unpublished Letters By and About Lederer to Governor John Winthrop, Jr.
L1300 (ASU WCU ETSU)
Early Settlement of Western North Carolina.
S5490

N. C. — HISTORY
A1730
A History of Watauga County, North Carolina. With Sketches of Prominent Families.
A4990 (ASU LMC)
Western North Carolina: A History (from 1730 to 1913).
A5000 (BC ASU UNCA WCU LMC WWC)
Western North Carolina; a History, 1730-1913.
A5010 (ETSU ASU LMC)
History of North Carolina.
A5110 (BC LMC ASU)
History of North Carolina.
A5120 (WWC UNCA)
The Cherokee Indians and Those Who Came After, Notes for a History of Cherokee County, North Carolina, 1835-1860.
B7000 (ASU)
Histories of the Dividing Line Betwixt Virginia and North Carolina.
B9620 (BC FC)
Governor Vance: A Life for Young People.
C440 (ASU WCU WWC)
Governor Vance, a Life for Young People.
C450 (LMC)
Sketches of Burke County.
C480 (ASU)
Sketches of Burke County.
C490
C1320 (ASU)
North Carolina from Its Glorious Past to the Present.
C1350 (ASU)
North Carolina Land Grants in Tennessee, 1778-1791.
C1800 (ETSU BC ASU)
The Genesis of Lincoln: Truth is Stranger than Fiction.
C2080 (LMC)
Truth is Stranger than Fiction: Or, the True Genesis of a Wonderful Man.
C2090 (ASU)
Clay County, 1861-1961; Commemorating the One Hundredth Anniversary of the Creating of Clay County, North Carolina.
C4780
History of North Carolina.
C6720 (LMC)
Makers of North Carolina History.
C6730 (LMC)
North Carolina: Rebuilding an Ancient Commonwealth, 1584-1925.
C6740 (UNCA BC LMC)
Race Elements in the White Population of North Carolina.
C6750 (ASU BC)
Revolutionary Leaders of North Carolina.
C6760 (ASU LMC)
Revolutionary Leaders of North Carolina.
C6770 (WWC)
History of Avery County, North Carolina.
C7170 (ASU LMC WCU BC)
"Appalachian North Carolina: A Political Study, 1860-1889."
C7740
Foot Prints on The Sands of Time, A History of South-western Virginia and North-western North Carolina.
C8140 (ASU LMC)

N. C. — HISTORY

North Carolina Governors, 1585-1958: Brief Sketches.
C8300 (LMC BC)
Grandfather's Tales of North Carolina History.
C8650 (ASU WCU LMC MHC BC UNCA)
North Carolina Newspapers before 1790.
C8820 (LMC)
100 Years, 100 Men: 1871-1971.
C8830 (ASU)
Historical Sketches of Wilkes County.
C9130 (ASU)
Tar Heels.
D190 (LMC BC)
The Border States: Kentucky, North Carolina, Tennessee, Virginia, West Virginia.
D4190 (BC ASU LMC WWC ETSU)
Home on the Yadkin.
F660 (ASU BC)
Sketches of North Carolina, Historical and Biographical, Illustrative of the Principles of a Portion of Her Early Settlers.
F1790 (ASU LMC)
Sketches of North Carolina, Historical and Biographical, Illustrative of the Principles of a Portion of Her Early Settlers.
F1800 (MHC BC)
Our Heritage, the People of Cherokee County, North Carolina, 1540-1955.
F3170 (ASU WCU BC)
Preachers, Pedagogues and Politicians: The Evolution Controversy in North Carolina, 1920-1927.
G590 (WCU WWC)
Will Books, Wilkes County, North Carolina.
G770
G3120 (ASU LMC)
A History of Dillsboro, North Carolina.
G3390 (WCU)
Essays on North Carolina History.
G4120 (ASU LMC)
History of Old Tryon and Rutherford Counties, North Carolina, 1730-1936.
G4130 (ASU BC WCU)
History of Rutherford County, 1937-1951.
G4140 (WCU LMC BC)
Public Officials of Rutherford County, N. C. 1779-1934: With Introductory Sketches of Origin and Development of Various County Offices, and Public and Local Laws Governing Same.
G4150 (ASU BC)
Western North Carolina Sketches.
G4180 (ASU BC WCU LMC MHC)
History of North Carolina.
H3730 (LMC MHC)
Builders of the Old North State: Selected Sketches.
H4060 (LMC)
North Carolina: The Old North State and the New.
H4440 (UNCA LMC)
"The Forgotten Sons: North Carolinans in the Union Army."
H5210 (ASU)
Young People's History of North Carolina.
H5370 (LMC WWC)
The Historical Records of North Carolina.
H5730 (ASU LMC BC)
Introduction to the County Records of North Carolina, Including the General Introduction to the Historical Records of North Carolina.
H5750 (ASU)
H6010 (MHC)
History of Surry County, or, Annals of Northwest North Carolina.
H6680 (LMC ASU WCU BC)
History of Surry County, or, Annals of Northwest North Carolina.
H6690
Southern Appalachian Highlanders of Western North Carolina.
H7240
Panorama of Progress: Jackson County Centennial.
H7780
Sketches of Western North Carolina, Historical and Biographical, Illustrating Principally the Revolutionary Period of Mecklenburg, Rowan, Lincoln, and Adjoining Counties.
H8420 (ASU BC WCU)
Sketches of Western North Carolina, Historical and Biographical, Illustrating Principally the Revolutionary Period of Mecklenburg, Rowan, Lincoln and Adjoining Counties, Accompanied with Miscellaneous Information, Much of It Never Before Published.
H8430 (ASU LMC ETSU)
For History's Sake: The Preservation and Publication of North Carolina History, 1663-1903.
J2340 (BC LMC ASU MHC)
North Carolina's Local Records Program.
J2350 (ASU)
History of North Carolina, Containing the Exact Description and Natural History of That Country, Together with the Present State Thereof, and a Journal of a Thousand Miles Traveled Through Several Nations of Indians, Giving a Particular Account of Their Customs, Manners, Etc., Etc.
L970 (LMC MHC BC)
History of North Carolina, Containing the Exact Description and Natural History of that Country, Together with the Present State Thereof, and a Journal of a Thousand Miles Traveled through Several Nations of Indians, Giving a Particular Account of Their Customs, Manners, Etc., Etc.
L980 (UNCA)
History of North Carolina, Containing the Exact Description and Natural History of That Country, Together with the Present State Thereof and a Journal of a Thousand Miles Traveled Through Several Nations of Indians, Giving Particular Account of Their Customs, Manners, Etc.
L990 (WWC ASU)
A Guide to the Study and Reading of North Carolina History.
L1520 (LMC)
A Guide to the Study and Reading of North Carolina History.
L1530 (UNCA ASU)
A Guide to the Study and Reading of North Carolina History.
L1540 (LMC)
History of North Carolina.
L1550 (BC LMC UNCA)
North Carolina History Told by Contemporaries.
L1560 (BC LMC WWC)
North Carolina, the History of a Southern State.
L1570 (UNCA WWC)
North Carolina, the History of a Southern State.
L1580 (BC FC ASU LMC)
In the Red Hills: A Story of the Carolina Country.
M260 (ASU)
The Early History of Haywood County.
M4830 (LMC WCU)
Historical Sketch of Flat Rock.
M5040 (ASU)
An Historical Sketch of Flat Rock . . .
M5050 (ASU)
Fading Hi-lights Relating to the Birth and Growth of the Swannanoa Valley in Western North Carolina, 1845-1960.
M6310 (ASU)
History of North Carolina: From the Earliest Discoveries to the Present Time.
M7310 (LMC)
Western North Carolina: A History.
M8210 (ASU)
The Influence of the Physiographic Features of Western North Carolina on the Settlement and Development of the Region.
N1400 (ASU)
The Formation of the North Carolina Counties, 1663-1943.
N1840 (WWC)
Guide to North Carolina Historical Highway Markers.
N1850 (ASU)
The North Carolina Census of Wilkes County, 1787.
N1860 (ASU)
State Census of North Carolina, 1784-1787.
N1880 (ASU)
State Census of North Carolina, 1784-1787.
N1890 (ASU)
Watauga County Records: Bonds, Court Records, Estates Records, Land Records, Military and Pension Records, Tax and Fiscal Records and Wills.
N1900 (ASU)
N2380 (ASU UNCA)
Literary and Historical Activities of North Carolina, 1900-1905.
N2390 (LMC WWC ASU)
N2400 (ASU)
N2410
N2460 (LMC)
North Carolina Manual 1874-19.
N2560 (ASU LMC)
Guide to Civil War Records in the N. C. State Archives.
N2590
50 Years Ago Around Saluda, N. C.
P10
P150 (WCU)
Buncombe to Mecklenburg: Speculation Lands.
P860
A Condensed History of Flat Rock (the Little Charleston of the Mountains).
P880 (ASU WCU LMC)
The Story of Henderson County.
P940 (ASU WCU LMC)
The Story of Henderson County.
P950
Historical and Literary Activities in North Carolina, 1900-1905.
P1590 (LMC)
The Pen and Plate Club of Asheville, North Carolina. 1904-1929.
P1640 (ASU)
Dry Ridge: Some of Its History, Some of Its People.
P2830 (LMC ASU)
Alexander County's Confederates.
P3110
Prologue: a History of Alexander County, North Carolina.
P3130
Polk County Centennial: Souvenir Historical Booklet.
P3350
Sketches of Early Watauga.
P3460
North Carolina County Histories: A Bibliography.
P3980 (MHC)
North Carolina County Histories: A Bibliography.
P3990 (ASU)
North Carolina: A Students' Guide to Localized History.
P4020 (LMC WCU)
A History of Catawba County.
P4360
Postmarks: A History of Henderson County, North Carolina, 1787-1968.
R580 (BC ASU ETSU LMC)
Ray's Index and Digest to Hathaway's North Carolina Historical and Genealogical Register.
R630
An Illustrated History of Yadkin County, 1850-1965.
R4440 (ASU)
Annals of Lincoln County, North Carolina: Containing Interesting and Authentic Facts of Lincoln County History through the Years 1749 to 1937.
S2960 (ASU)
Zebulon Vance, Tarheel Spokesman.
S3100 (ASU)
Zebulon Vance, Tarheel Spokesman.
S3110 (LMC)
Historical Sketches of Churches in the Diocese of Western North Carolina Episcopal Church.
S3370 (LMC WCU BC)
A History of Buncombe County, North Carolina.
S5500 (ASU WCU LMC BC)
North Carolina Local History: A Select Bibliography.
S7200 (ASU)
Notes on the History of Western North Carolina.
S7440 (WCU)
Discovering Mitchell County.
T780
History and Geography of Yancey County.
T790 (ASU)
Medicine in Buncombe County Down to 1885, Historical and Biographical Sketches.
T880

N. C. — HISTORY
Swain County: Early History and Educational Development.
T8110 (ASU WCU LMC)
History of Alleghany County.
T8320
A Bibliography of North Carolina, 1589-1955.
T8420 (LMC UNCA ASU)
Official Publications of the Colony and State of North Carolina, 1749-1939, a Bibliography.
T8430 (ASU LMC)
1861-1961, Transylvania County Centennial: Historical Souvenir Program.
T9170
Western North Carolina Since the Civil War.
V380 (ASU WWC ETSU)
Sketches of the Pioneers in Burke County History.
W690
"A Historical Study of the ET&WNC Narrow Gauge Railroad."
W730 (ASU)
With Pen and Camera Thro the "Land of the Sky": Western North Carolina and the Asheville Plateau.
W790 (ASU)
The Waldenses of Valdese.
W1580 (LMC WCU)
Facts and Events of the Watts Family.
W1600 (ASU)
North Carolina Roads and Their Builders.
W1870 (ASU LMC)
The Living Past of Cleveland County, a History.
W1950 (ASU)
Fifty-eight Years in Asheville.
W2030 (UNCA)
. . . Church and State in North Carolina.
W2270 (BC)
The Religious Development in the Province of North Carolina.
W2280 (LMC WWC UNCA)
The Ballad of Tom Dula: The Documented Story Behind the Murder of Laura Foster and the Trials and Execution of Tom Dula.
W3030 (ASU BC)
W4870 (ASU)
Historical Sketches of North Carolina, from 1584 to 1851.
W5120 (UNCA)
Historical Sketches of North Carolina from 1584 to 1851.
W5130 (ASU LMC)
Historical Sketches of North Carolina from 1584 to 1851 Compiled from Original Records, Official Documents, and Traditional Statements, with Biographical Sketches of Her Distinguished Statesmen, Jurists, Lawyers, Soldiers, Divines, etc.
W5140 (LMC BC)
Reminiscences and Memoirs of North Carolina and Eminent North Carolinians.
W5150 (UNCA BC ASU)
A History of Alexander County, North Carolina.
W5640
Daniel Boone Wagon Train.
W5670 (ASU)
History of Watauga County: A Souvenir of Watauga Centennial.
W5680 (ASU WCU LMC ETSU)
Local History — How to Find and Write It.
W5690 (ASU)
The North Carolina Historical Almanack, Being a Collection of Notable Events That Have Befallen People and Places in Our Great State.
W6070 (ASU BC)
The History of North Carolina.
W6930 (ASU LMC BC)
The Carolina Backcountry on the Eve of the Revolution: The Journal and Other Writings of Charles Woodmason, Anglican Itinerant.
W8780 (ASU LMC BC)
History and Geography of Yancey County.
Y20

N. C. — HISTORY — CHEROKEE
E500 (ASU)

N. C. — HISTORY — HAYWOOD CO.
The Annals of Haywood County, North Carolina: Historical, Sociological, Bibliographical, and Genealogical.
A1700 (ASU WCU BC)

N. C. — HISTORY — STORIES
North Carolina History Stories.
A1720 (LMC MHC)

N. C. — HISTORY — WESTERN COUNTIES
Random Thoughts and the Musings of a Mountaineer.
A1740 (BC ASU WCU LMC ETSU)

N. C. — RECREATION AND TOURISM
Oconaluftee Indian Village.
C3640 (ASU)
C3720 (ASU)
Camping on Mount Mitchell, Information Regarding Good Places for Summer Camps in United States Forests in North Carolina.
S5830 (ASU)
The Land of the Sky, Western North Carolina.
S5860 (LMC)

N. C. RIVERS
Canoeing White Water: A Guide Book to the Rivers of Virginia and Eastern West Virginia, The Great Smoky Mountain Area.
C1740 (LMC)

NANTAHALA RIVER
The Dissent of Commissioner Thomas R. Eller, Jr., in the Nantahala Power and Light Company Transfer Case.
E1640 (WCU)

NATIONAL RESOURCES — KY.
Natural Resources of Kentucky.
K1050 (ETSU ASU)

NATURAL HISTORY
Spring Notes From Tennessee.
T8970 (LMC BC)

NATURAL RESOURCES
Soil Survey: Dawson, Lumpkin, and White Counties, Georgia.
A850
Report.
A910 (BC)
Appalachian Basin Ordovician Symposium: Papers Read at the Meeting of the Pittsburgh Geological Society at Pittsburgh, Pa., May 16, 1947, and Published in the Bulletin of the American Assn. of Petroleum Geologists, Aug. 1948.
A2850 (BC)
People and Resources in Eastern Kentucky.
B2610
The Life of the Mountains.
B6970 (BC)
Smoky Mountain Country.
C320 (ASU WCU LMC ETSU BC)
Geologic Bulletin no. 1-10.
T7360
Pocahontas County.
W3850 (BC)
Resources of West Virginia.
W4300 (BC)
W4460

NATURAL RESOURCES — ALA.
. . . Natural Resources of the Tenn. Valley Region in Alabama.
H2540 (BC)
Report on the Plateau Coal Field of Alabama.
T6590
Report on the Reserves of Coal in a Part of the Warrier Coal Field of Alabama.
T6600

NATURAL RESOURCES — APP.
Voices from Earth, a Collection of Writings on Environment.
A4500 (ASU)
Rich Land, Poor Land; A Study of Waste in the Natural Resources of America.
C3510
"An Input-output Model Incorporating Impact Analysis to Evaluate the Resources and Economy of a Rural Appalachian Community."
G220
Natural Resource Special Districts in Appalachia: Review of Enabling Laws.
H1330
Appalachian Resource Development Project, Submitted to the Kellogg Foundation.
K1390
Anthracite: An Instance of Natural Resource Monopoly.
N350 (ASU LMC)
Summary of Resources Tributary Area Development Program.
T3560
Recreational Development of the Southern Highlands Region; A Study of the Use and Control of Scenic and Recreational Resources.
T4290 (LMC)
The Scenic Resources of the Tennessee Valley; A Descriptive and Pictorial Inventory.
T4310
Fish and Wildlife, Valuable Natural Resources.
T5270
TVA as a Symbol of Resource Development in Many Countries.
T6910
Southern Highlands Mountain Resources Management Plan, Vols. I and II.
T9390
Message From the President of the United States Transmitting a Report of the Secretary of Agriculture in Relation to the Forests, Rivers, and Mountains of the Southern Appalachian Region.
U2510 (UNCA ASU ETSU)
Development of Water Resources in Appalachia.
U2670 (ASU)

NATURAL RESOURCES — GA.
The Georgia Mountains: A View of Its Resources, Problems, and Potentials.
S1120 (ASU LMC)

NATURAL RESOURCES — KY.
Geology and Mineral Resources of Part of the Cumberland Gap Coal Field, Kentucky.
A5240 (ASU)
Resources for Industry.
K1030 (ASU)
K1450 (ETSU ASU)
Appalachian Kentucky, an Exploited Region.
L440 (ETSU)
Management of Kentucky Natural Resources.
L1900
Life Among the Hills and Mountains of Kentucky.
T8080 (ASU BC)

NATURAL RESOURCES — N. C.
The Possibilities of a Maple Sugar Industry in Western North Carolina.
A5130 (ASU LMC)
"Community Resources of Tryon, North Carolina."
H6960 (WCU)
North Carolina: Resources, Advantages, and Opportunities.
N1750 (LMC ASU)
Chromite Deposits of North Carolina: Geology and Mining.
N1920
The Mining Industry in North Carolina.
N2220 (ASU UNCA ETSU LMC)
Report of the State Geologist and Director. 1891-92 - 1923-24.
N2340 (ASU UNCA)
The Southern Highlands Mountain Resources Management Plan.
N2480
N2500
N2650 (ASU UNCA)
Ecological Effects of Hot Water Discharge by an Electric Power Generating Plant.
N2660 (ASU UNCA)
Economic Development of the Upper French Broad Area: Summary of Needs and Opportunities, Resources, the Regional Economy.
N2690 (ASU)

NATURAL RESOURCES — N. Y. — APP. REGION
The Appalachian Region of New York State: An Atlas of Natural and Cultural Resources.
N690 (ETSU)

NATURAL RESOURCES — OHIO
"Economic Inventory and Value Added Estimates of the Natural Resources of a Watershed Region Located in the Appalachian Highland Area of Ohio."
D3630

NATURAL RESOURCES — PA.
"The Economics of Oil Refining in the Pennsylvania Area."
B1750
"Basic Industrial Resources of the Altoona, Pennsylvania, Area."
S5040

NATURAL RESOURCES — S. C.
South Carolina's Natural Resources: A Study in Public Administration.
L650 (ASU)

NATURAL RESOURCES — TENN.
Outline Introduction to the Mineral Resources of Tennessee.
A5250 (ETSU)
The City of Knoxville, Tennessee and Vicinity and Their Resources.
G3060
Rescued Earth, a Study of the Public Administration of Natural Resources in Tennessee.
G3820 (ASU LMC ETSU)
Adjustments of Rural Resources Use and Characteristics to Economic Growth.
H4490 (ASU)
"Economic Progress and Resource Adjustments of Rural Households is the Upper East Tennessee Valley."
H4500 (ASU)
Resources and Incomes of Rural Upper East Tennessee People, a Progress Report of a Study of the Economic Status and Opportunities of Rural People.
H4520 (ASU BC)
An Economic Survey of Blount County, Tennessee, a Study of Resources and Industrial Potentials.
H8720
Geology of the Mascot-Jefferson City Zinc District, Tennessee.
O220 (ETSU)
Soil and Sky; the Development and Use of Tennessee Valley Resources.
S470
Tennessee — Its Resources and Economy — The Tennessee Economy — Vol. I.
T1210
Resource Inventory and Analysis of Tennessee Appalachia.
T1710 (ETSU)
Tennessee Resources — Agriculture, Forestry, and Minerals.
T1720 (ETSU)
Clinch-Powell Valley; Summary of Resources.
T2420
Sequatchie Valley; Summary of Resources.
T3470
Summary of Resources.
T3550
Upper Little Tennessee River Region: Summary of Resources.
T9880 (WWC)

NATURAL RESOURCES — TVA LAKES
Applications of the Common Mooring: Fundamental Principles in the Utilization of Resources.
A630

NATURAL RESOURCES — VA.
The Early Grove Gas Field, Scott and Washington Counties, Virginia.
A5710 (ETSU)
The Cement Resources of Virginia, West of the Blue Ridge.
B1860 (ASU)
Alleghany County, Virginia: Its Resources and Industries.
C8080 (BC)
Southwest Virginia: Lee, Scott, Wise Counties, Summary of Resources.
T3500 (ASU BC)
Virginia: A Geographical and Political Summary, Embracing a Description of the State, Its Geology, Soils, Minerals and Climate; Its Animal and Vegetable Productions; Manufacturing and Commercial Facilities; Religious and Educational Advantages; Internal Improvements, and Form of Government.
V700 (BC)

NATURAL RESOURCES — W. VA.
The Abram Creek-Stony River Coal Field, Northeastern West Virginia.
A5230
Coal and Coal Mining in West Virginia.
B1200
"Productive Capacity and Economic Growth in West Virginia."
B7090
Rights-of-Way for Removal of Natural Resources From West Virginia Land: An Examination of Existing Applicable Law and of Possible Changes Therein.
B7300 (ASU)
West Virginia: Its Farms and Forest, Mines and Oil Wells, with a Glimpse of Its Scenery, a Photograph of Its Population, and an Exhibit of Its Industrial Statistics.
D2690 (BC)
Grant's West Virginia Illustrated.
G3230
Bibliography and Index of West Virginia Geology and Natural Resources to July 1, 1937.
L3870 (ETSU)
Footprints in the Soil and Reflections on the Water: Conservation in West Virginia.
O570 (ASU)
West Virginia, Her Land, Her People, Her Traditions, Her Resources.
R4200 (BC)
Resources of the Upper South Branch Valley, West Virginia.
S6470
The Mountain State.
S9010
Natural Resources of West Virginia, the Mountain State.
U2790 (ASU)
Natural Resources of West Virginia, the Mountain State.
U2860
Resources of West Virginia.
W3180
"The Resources and Industries of the New River Drainage Basin in West Virginia."
W7990

NATURAL RESOURCES — W. VA. REGIONAL
Semi-Centennial History of West Virginia. With Special Articles on Development and Resources.
C300 (ASU ETSU BC)

NAUGLE, JOHN MARK
Virginia Tax Payers, 1782-87: Other Than Those Published by the United States Census Bureau.
F2360 (ASU)

NAVIGATION
River Traffic and Industrial Growth.
T3440

NEGROES
"What Progress in Health Has Been Made among the Negro Youths of the Elementary School Age for the Past Ten Years in Talladega County, Alabama."
C9500
"The Development of Negro Education in Rutherford County, North Carolina."
T9510
W3200 (ETSU)
A Survey of Negroes Employed by the State of West Virginia.
W4080

NEGROES — ALA.
"A Study of the Progress of Negro Education in Saint Clair County, Alabama."
C1750
"A Survey of the Library Facilities in the Negro Schools of Tuscaloosa County, Alabama."
D2540
"Factors Contributing to the Educational Development of the Negro Schools in the Jefferson County (Alabama) School System, 1945-51."
G1950
"A Study of the Causes of Drop-outs and Irregular Attendance among Boys in the Four Negro High Schools of Talledega County, Alabama."
G2040
"The Status of the Negro Teachers in Blount, Cullman, DeKalb, and Marshall Counties, Alabama 1952-53."
J2260
"A Historical Analysis of Student Drop-outs in the Negro Schools for Bibb County, Alabama."
M4620
"The Educational Progress of the Negro Schools in Cherokee County, Alabama, from 1930-1950."
S6640
Arbitrary Arrests in the South: Or, Scenes From the Experiences of an Alabama Unionist.
T7650 (WCU)

NEGROES — APP.
My Life and Travels.
B6340 (ASU)
Ought American Slavery to be Perpetuated? A Debate between Rev. W. G. Brownlow and Rev. A. Pryne. Held at Philadelphia, September, 1858.
B7520 (ASU BC)
Berea College from Servitude to Service, Being the Old South Lectures on the History and Work of the Negro.
F3560 (BC)
"Negro Life in a Rural Community."
K2380
Facilitative and Inhibitive Factors in Training Program Recruitment Among Rural Negroes.
M3360

NEGROES — GA.
"A Study of the Relationship Existing Between Amount of Education Completed by White and Negro Head of Households in Floyd County."
H4240
"A History of the Development of Schools for Negroes in Walker County, Georgia."
J170

NEGROES — KY.
Kentucky's Black Heritage.
K980 (BC ETSU)
The Saga of Coe Ridge: A Study in Oral History.
M6560 (ASU BC ETSU LMC WCU WWC)

NEGROES — N. C.
"A Critical Study of Negro Education in Cleveland County, North Carolina, from 1944 to 1954."
F2250 (ASU)
"Negro Life in Watauga County."
H7310 (ASU)
"A History of Negro Education in Wilkes County, North Carolina."
I820
The Negro in North Carolina, 1876-1894.
L3060 (LMC)
"An Analysis of the Types of Retardation in the Elementary Departments of Fine Negro Union Schools in Rural Cleveland County."
L3200

NEGROES — TENN.
"The Negro in East Tennessee."
B210 (ASU)
Three Generations: The Story of a Colored Family of Eastern Tennessee.
C1110 (ASU LMC BC)
"An Investigation of the Exceptional Child in the Negro Secondary Schools of East Tennessee."
C1860
"Differences between Negro and Caucasian Students at John Sevier Junior High School, Kingsport, Tennessee."
C2810 (ETSU)
"The Negroes of Chattanooga, Tennessee."
C7830
A Social Study of the Colored Population of Knoxville, Tennessee.
D1100
"The Negro and Organized Labor as Voting Blocs in Tennessee, 1960-1964."
D2070
The Emancipator.
E1900 (ASU)
A Study of the Physical Education Problems as Found In Negro Schools in East Tennessee."
F3710
Gemini.
G1840
"History of the Development of Negro Public Schools in Bradley County, Tennessee, 1931-1951."
M3580
The Negro in Tennessee, 1790-1865.
P650 (LMC)
"Negro Education in Cocke County."
R180
"An Examination of the Negro Character in Selected Fiction by White East Tennessee Writers."
R850 (ETSU)
"An Accounting Study of the Educational Progress of Knoxville Negro Pupils Over a Sixteen-year Period."
S4590
Letters from the Slave States.
S7470

NEGROES — TENN.

"Development of the Health Program for Negroes in Franklin County, Tennessee from 1940-1953."
W5820

Knoxville Negro.
W7100

NEGROES — VA.

Virginia Iron Manufacture In the Slave Era.
B7600

Carry Me Back: Slavery and Servitude in Seventeenth Century Virginia.
C7270 (MHC FC ASU)

Free Negro Labor and Property Holding in Virginia, 1830-1860.
J160 (ETSU)

"School Desegregation in Warren County, Virginia, During 1958-1960; A Study in the Mobilization of Restraints."
L2050

"A Study Designed for the Attitudes of the Negro Teachers of Bedford County, Virginia Toward In-Service Teacher Education."
M3140

Economic and Social Aspects of Negro Slavery in Wythe County, Virginia, 1790-1860.
M9210

The Free Negro in Virginia, 1619-1865.
R4370 (ETSU FC)

NEGROES — W. VA.

Report of C. F. Hopson, M. D., Director, Bureau of Negro Welfare and Statistics of the State of West Virginia to Governor Clarence W. Meadows, 1945-46.
H7150 (ASU)

John Henry: Track Down a Negro Legend.
J1780

"Integration in West Virginia Since 1954."
J1920 (ASU)

"The Negro Miner in West Virginia."
L130

"The Negro in West Virginia Before 1900."
S2610

"Contacts of Negroes and Whites in Morgantown."
W6380

NEW RIVER

"Land Utilization in the New and Watauga River Basins of North Carolina."
B3700 (LMC)

"Industrial Waste and Human Sewage Pollution within the New River Drainage Basin of Watauga County."
C1490 (ASU)

The Geomorphic History of the New Kanawha River System.
F3300 (ETSU)

Surface Water Supply of the New-Kanawha River Basin, West Virginia, and North Carolina.
G4490

German New River Settlement, Virginia.
H4270 (ASU FC)

Lovely Mount Tavern: The Birth of a City, and Something of the Early New River Settlers.
H7700

A History of Middle New River Settlements and Contiguous Territory.
J2020 (ASU FC)

Kanawha River: Comprehensive Basin Study.
K100 (ASU)

The New-Kanawha River and the Mind War of West Virginia.
M630 (BC)

New River Cripple Creek Mineral Region of Virginia.
M940

Bulletin. Surface and Water Supply of Va. New, Big Sandy, and Tenn. River Basins, 1942-1950.
V750 (BC)

New River Basin Comprehensive Water Resources Plan.
V840

"The Resources and Industries of the New River Drainage Basin in West Virginia."
W7990

NEWSPAPERS

Pen and Politics: The Autobiography of a Working Writer.
A1370 (ASU)

The Buck Fever Papers.
A2380 (ASU)

"Dan Tompkins: Mountain Editor."
A5610 (WCU)

Gunpowder Creek Philosophy.
C4800 (BC)

Best of Hillbilly: A Prize Collection of 100-proof Writings from Jim Comstock's West Virginia Hillbilly.
C6300 (ASU MHC WCU LMC BC)

The Socialist and Labor Star, Huntington, West Virginia, 1912-1915.
C7370 (ASU BC)

Observations from a Peak in Lumpkin: Or, the Writings of W. Ba. Townsend, Editor, The Dahlonega Nugget.
D1490 (ASU)

The Kanawha Spectator.
D1630

The ETSU Journalist.
E390 (ETSU)

Newsletter.
E460 (ETSU)

Southeastern Broadsides Before 1877.
H8290 (ASU)

Ralph McGill, Editor and Publisher.
L3100 (ASU)
M2730

Ralph McGill, Reporter.
M3500

Ralph McGill, Reporter.
M3600

News from Pigeon Roost.
M5640 (ASU)

A List of Magazines, Journals, Small Presses, Newspapers, etc. of Interest to Students of Appalachia.
M5820

Index to the Press of the Kanawha Valley, 1855-1865.
M8620 (BC)

Editors Make War: Southern Newspapers in the Secession Crisis.
R1650

Religious News Press in Appalachia, 1971. A Directory of News Periodicals of . . . all Members of the Commission on Religion in Appalachia. . .
S4120 (ASU BC)

Bill Arp (pseud.) So Called, a Side Show of the Southern Side of the Civil War.
S4470 (ASU)

Bill Arp: From the Uncivil War to Date, 1861-1903.
S4480 (ASU)

Bill Arp's Peace Papers.
S4490 (ASU)

A Man in His Time.
S6290 (ASU)

"The Public Career of Joseph Alexander Mabry."
T590

"Southern Appalachian State Newspapers' Treatment of the Antipoverty and Appalachia Acts."
T8020

Observations from a Peak in Lumpkin.
T9110 (BC ASU)

Bert Vincent's Strolling, Being Sort of a Side-Glance at the Little Odds and Ends of Life in These Parts.
V630

The Best Stories of Bert Vincent, ed. Willard Yarbrough.
V640

More of the Best Stories of Bert Vincent.
V650

NEWSPAPERS — APP.

Catalogue, Southern Newspaper Library. . . .
S5800

NEWSPAPERS — CHEROKEE
C3710 (ASU)

New Echota Letters: Contributions of Samuel A. Worcester to the Cherokee Phoenix.
K1990 (WCU LMC MHC ASU)

NEWSPAPERS — KY.

Newspaper History of a Town: A History of Danville, Kentucky.
G4200 (ASU)

"Survey and Sociological Study of 25 Weekly Newspapers in Eastern Kentucky."
W660 (ASU)

NEWSPAPERS — N. C.

North Carolina Newspapers before 1790.
C8820 (LMC)

Union List of North Carolina Newspapers, 1751-1900.
J2360 (LMC)

My Affair with a Weekly.
J2640 (ASU LMC MHC BC)

"A Historical Study of the Relationship Between the Watauga Democrat and Appalachian State Teachers College."
K90 (ASU)

NEWSPAPERS — TENN.

An Honorable Titan: A Biographical Study of Adolph S. Ochs.
J1750

"A History of Knoxville Journalism."
M4170

NEWSPAPERS — VA.

A Checklist of Southwest Virginia Newspapers, 1800-1974.
J1660

NEWSPAPERS — W. VA.

"Editorial Attitudes of West Virginia Newspapers toward School and Education."
K1830

NOLICHUCKY RIVER

Floods on Nolichucky River and North and South Indian Creeks in Vicinity of Erwin, Tennessee.
T7100

NORTH CAROLINA RIVER

High and Low Flows and Flow Duration at Stream Gages in North Carolina in Tennessee River Basin.
T7370

NORTH CHICKAMAUGA RIVER

Floods on North Chickamauga, Mountain, and Lookout Creeks, in Vicinity of Chattanooga, Tennessee.
T7110

NORTH TOE RIVER

Floods on North Toe River and Beaver and Grassy Creeks in Vicinity of Spruce Pine, North Carolina.
T7120

NURSING

Quarterly Bulletin.
F3500 (ASU BC)

Thirty Years Onward. Frontier N. S., 1925-1955.
F3510 (BC ASU)

Today, Yesterday and Tomorrow.
F3520 (BC)

Development of Tele-lecture and Associated Media Systems for the Improvement of Nursing Education in West Virginia.
P4950

NURSING — APP.

Frontier Nurse: Mary Breckenridge.
W6290 (ASU LMC BC)

NURSING — KY.

The Frontier Nursing Service.
W7780 (BC)

NURSING — W. VA.

A Half-Century of Nursing in West Virginia: The History of the West Virginia State Nurses' Association 1907-1957.
B5230 (ASU)

NUTRITION

"Tuberculosis in Eastern Kentucky."
A820 (ASU)

"Food Habits of a Selected Group of Pupils in the Wellsbury High School, West Virginia."
C6920

NUTRITION — TENN.

"A Nutrition Survey of Some Eleventh Grade Students in Washington County, Tennessee."
H410 (ETSU)

OCCUPATIONAL VOCABULARY

"Bituminous Coal Mining Vocabulary of the Eastern United States: A Pilot Study in the Collecting of Geographically Distributed Occupational Vocabulary."
P4390

OCONALUFTEE RIVER

Floods on Oconaluftee and Tuckaseigee Rivers and Soco Creek in Vicinity of Cherokee, North Carolina.
T7130

OHIO RIVER

"The Economic Aspects of the Water Pollution Abatement Program in the Ohio River Valley."
B6260

OHIO RIVER
Economic Development in the Ohio River Valley Region.
B6280
Early Maps of the Ohio Valley.
B7290 (BC)
Sycamore Shores.
F1080 (ASU)
The Floods of March, 1936, Part 3, Potomac, James, and Upper Ohio Rivers.
G4470
Floods of Ohio and Mississippi Rivers, January-February, 1937.
G4480
The Ohio Valley Flood of March-April, 1913, Including Comparisons with Some Earlier Floods.
H7290
The Ohio River Basin.
I890
Ground-water Conditions along the Ohio Valley at Parkersburg, West Virginia.
J520 (ETSU)
A Tour Downstream.
J1220
Project Economic Study of the Ohio River Basin.
L2800
Blennerhassett Island in Romance and Tragedy; the Authentic Story of Blennerhassett Island, with the Burr Episode Entwined about it; the Romance and Mystery of the Blannerhassetts; Burr under Footlights and Shadows; Tragedy of Theodosia Burr.
L3770
Locust Bloom.
M3970 (BC)
A Development Program for the Ohio Valley Region.
O380
O400
Ohio River Basin: Comprehensive Survey, Main Report.
O410 (ASU)
O420

OIL AND GAS INDUSTRIES — APP.
Demonstration of Safety Plugging of Oil Wells Penetrating Appalachian Coal Mines.
R1480
Cost Study of Pumping Versus Flowing Oil Production from Appalachian Waterfloods.
R3970
Lithologic Descriptions of Appalachian Area Oil-producing Formations.
R3980
Rotary Coring of Appalachian Area Oil-producing Formations with Mud or Air.
R3990
Electrical and Hydraulic Flow Properties of Appalachian Petroleum Reservoir Rocks.
S610
Densities and Porosities of Core Samples from Wells in Appalachian Oilfields.
S4130

OIL AND GAS INDUSTRIES — KY.
Blazer and Ashland Oil; a Study in Management.
M4130
The Menifee Gas Field and the Ragland Oil Field, Kentucky.
M8580
Reconnaissance of Oil and Gas Fields in Wayne and McCreary Counties, Kentucky.
M8590
P90
The Exception; The Story of the Ashland Oil and Refining Co.
S1450
The Irvine Oil Field, Estill County, Kentucky.
S2480

OIL AND GAS INDUSTRIES — OHIO
"Taxation and Assessment of Coal, Gas and Oil with Special Reference to Western Pennsylvania, Eastern Ohio and Northern West Virginia."
R1940

OIL AND GAS INDUSTRIES — PA.
Pennsylvania's Oil Industry.
M5610
"Taxation and Assessment of Coal, Gas and Oil with Special Reference to Western Pennsylvania, Eastern Ohio and Northern West Virginia."
R1940
Laboratory Investigation of In Situ Combustion Process for Recovering Pennsylvania Grade Crude Oil.
S7100

OIL AND GAS INDUSTRIES — VA.
Geology and Oil Resources of the Jonesville District, Lee County, Virginia.
M5960
Geology and Mineral Resources of Wise Co. and Coal Bearing Portions of Scott Co., Va. with a Chapter on the Forest of Wise Co.
V980
Oil and Gas Possibilities at Early Grove, in Scott Co., Va.
V1010

OIL AND GAS INDUSTRIES — W. VA.
The Great Wildcatter.
M2870 (ASU BC)
Petrology and Correlation of Deep-well Sections in West Virginia and Adjacent States.
M3530 (ETSU)
Physical and Chemical Properties of Natural Gas of West Virginia.
P4540 (ETSU)
"Taxation and Assessment of Coal, Gas and Oil with Special Reference to Western Pennsylvania, Eastern Ohio and Northern West Virginia."
R1940

OIL AND GAS INDUSTRY
Oil and Gas Report and Map of Pleasants, Wood and Ritchie Counties, West Virginia.
W3830 (ETSU)
Pendleton County.
W3840 (BC)
Pocahontas County.
W3850 (BC)

OIL AND GAS INDUSTRY — APP.
Petroleum and Coal; the Keys to the Future.
T7740 (BC)

OIL AND GAS INDUSTRY — KY.
Oil Shales of Kentucky.
T7710
Geology and Oil and Gas Possibilities of Upper Mississippian Rocks of Southwestern Virginia, Southern West Virginia, and Eastern Kentucky.
W7060 (ASU)

OIL AND GAS INDUSTRY — VA.
Oil & gas wells drilled in southwest Va., before 1950.
U3280
Geology and Oil and Gas Possibilities of Upper Mississippian Rocks of Southwestern Virginia, Southern West Virginia, and Eastern Kentucky.
W7060 (ASU)

OIL AND GAS INDUSTRY — W. VA.
History of the Oil and Gas Industry in West Virginia.
T7730 (ASU BC)
Deep-well Records.
T9670 (ETSU)
Summarized Records of Deep Wells.
T9680 (ETSU)
Oil and Gas Report and Map of Doddridge and Harrison Counties, West Virginia.
W3800 (ETSU)
Oil and Gas Report and Map of Marshall, Wetzel, and Tyler Counties, West Virginia.
W3810 (ETSU)
Oil and Gas Report and Map of Monongalia, Marion, and Taylor Counties, West Virginia.
W3820 (ETSU)
Geology and Oil and Gas Possibilities of Upper Mississippian Rocks of Southwestern Virginia, Southern West Virginia, and Eastern Kentucky.
W7060 (ASU)

ORNITHOLOGY
"An Avifaunal Strip Census on Grandfather Mountain."
A1460 (ASU)
A4520 (BC)
A Descriptive Bibliography of West Virginia Ornithology.
B6900 (BC)
Birds of the South: Permanent and Winter Birds Commonly Found in Gardens, Fields, and Woods.
G3540 (ASU BC UNCA)
Birds of West Virginia, Their Economic Value and Aesthetic Beauty.
J2040 (ASU)
Our Southern Birds.
M5430 (ASU BC)
Birds of North Carolina.
P1380 (WWC)
Birds of North Carolina.
P1390 (ASU WWC)
Notes on the Birds of Great Smoky Mountains National Park.
S8850 (ASU WCU LMC WWC UNCA BC)
Notes on the Birds of Great Smoky Mountains National Park.
S8860 (UNCA)
Spring Notes From Tennessee.
T8970 (LMC BC)
Birds of West Virginia.
W4390 (BC)

ORNITHOLOGY — APP.
Birds of Southern Appalachians.
C2760

ORNITHOLOGY — GA.
Birds of Georgia: A Preliminary Check-list and Bibliography of Georgia Ornithology.
G3730 (ASU)

ORNITHOLOGY — KY.
Kentucky Birds: A Finding Guide.
B1100 (ASU)
K970 (ASU WCU)

ORNITHOLOGY — N. C.
List of the Birds of Buncombe County, North Carolina.
C80 (ASU LMC)
Ornithology of North Carolina: A List of the Birds of N. C. with Notes on Each Species.
S5220 (LMC)
Birds of the Smokies.
S8830 (LMC)

ORNITHOLOGY — N. C., WESTERN
The Mammals and Summer Birds of Western North Carolina.
O120

ORNITHOLOGY — TENN.
A Distributional List of the Birds of Tennessee.
G250
Birds of Knox County.
H7730
Birds of the Smokies.
S8830 (LMC)

ORNITHOLOGY — VA.
The Birds of Virginia.
B240 (ASU)

ORNITHOLOGY — W. VA.
List of the Birds Found in West Virginia.
B6910

PA. — DESCRIPTION AND TRAVEL
Pen Pictures of Early Western Pennsylvania.
H2560 (ASU)
Waynesburg, Prosperous and Beautiful, a Souvenir Pictorial Story of the Biggest and Best Little City in Pennsylvania. . . .
H5280
A Traveler's Guide to Historic Western Pennsylvania.
M8490 (ASU)
The Monongahela of Old: Or, Historical Sketches of South-Western Pennsylvania to the Year 1800.
V520 (ASU)

PA. — HISTORY
Index to Hungerford and Ellis' History of Susquehanna and Juniata Valleys.
C2860 (ASU)
Southwestern Pennsylvania in Song and Story.
C8100
Historic Background and Annals of the Swiss and German Pioneer Settlers of Southeastern Pennsylvania, and of Their Remote Ancestors from the Middle of the Dark Ages down to the Time of the Revolutionary War.
E2220 (ASU)
Early Western Pennsylvania Politics.
F650
Drums Along the Antietam.
S930 (MHC ASU)
More Allegheny Episodes: Legends and Traditions, Old and New.
S3130

PA. — HISTORY

South Mountain Sketches, Folk Tales, and Legends Collected in the Mountains of Southern Pennsylvania.
S3160 (ASU)

The Monongahela of Old: Or, Historical Sketches of South-Western Pennsylvania to the Year 1800.
V520 (ASU)

Names of Persons Who Took the Oath of Allegiance to the State of Pennsylvania between the Years 1888 and 1789 with a History of the "Test Laws" of Pennsylvania.
W4820 (ASU)

PARKS, NATIONAL

The Appalachian National Parks; an Analysis of Work Accomplished, November 1899 up to Aug. 30, 1901.
A3340

Southern Pictures and Pencilings: Official Organ of the Appalachian National Park Association.
A3350

The Life of the Mountains.
B6970 (BC)

Birth of a National Park in the Great Smoky Mountains: An Unprecedented Crusade which Created, as a Gift of the People, the Nation's Most Popular Park.
C520 (ASU ETSU WCU MHC WWC BC)

Birth of a National Park in the Great Smoky Mountains; an Unprecedented Crusade Which Created, as a Gift of the People, the Nation's Most Popular Park.
C530

Song of Life in the Smokies.
C7670 (LMC)

Song of Life in the Smokies: Stories of Mine Own People and Sketches of Life as It Was Lived in the Mountains Before the Park Took Over.
C7680 (ETSU)

Jessie's Children.
F2120 (LMC)
G3450 (ASU)

Romance of the National Parks.
J350 (ASU)

"Regional English of the Former Inhabitants of Cades Cove in the Great Smoky Mountains."
J2450

Scenic and Historic Old Virginia and Eastern National Parks.
K2790 (WCU)

The Earthman Story, Starring Shenandoah Skyline.
L180 (BC ASU MHC)
L300 (UNCA ASU)

"The Campaign for a National Park in Western North Carolina, 1885-1940."
L540 (WCU)

Pigeon Cove and Vicinity.
L1820

The Blue Ridge Parkway Guide.
L3520 (BC LMC ASU WCU)

The Lure of the Great Smokies.
M4030

The Lure of the Great Smokies.
M4040 (ASU LMC WCU ETSU WWC BC)

Appalachian Wilderness: The Great Smoky Mountains.
P3600 (UNCA BC ASU WCU ETSU)

Appalachian Wilderness: The Great Smoky Mountains.
P3610 (ASU BC)

A National Park in the Great Smoky Mountains.
S9380

Joint Legislative Committee Report on the Great Smoky Mountains and Other Areas for a National or State Park.
T1400

Preliminary report of investigations upon forest of Southern Appalachian region.
U1860

The Timber Resources of W. Va.
U1880

Printing as Senate Document Information Relative to the Timber Resources and National Forests of West Virginia. Report from the committee on Rules and Administration to Accompany S. Res. 137, June 14, 1961.
U1950

Establishment of Mount Rogers National Recreation Area in Virginia.
U2080

Establishment of Spruce Knob-Seneca Rocks National Recreation Area in West Virginia. Report from the Committee to Accompany H. R. 10330, August 31, 1965.
U2090

Shenandoah and Other National Parks; Letter from Sec'y of Interior Transmitting Information as to Boundaries and Areas of Shenandoah and Other National Parks.
U2890

S. 7, Act to Provide for the Establishment of Spruce Knob-Seneca Rocks National Recreation Area in West Virginia, and for Other Purposes. Approved September 28, 1965.
U3540

Appalachian National Scenic Trail.
U3690

Great Smoky Mountains, Everglades, Mammoth Cave: With Hot Springs, Platt, Virgin Islands, Abraham Lincoln Birthplace.
W8490 (ETSU BC)

Great Smoky Mountains National Park: Statement of Jas. B. Wright.
W9420 (LMC)

PARKS, NATIONAL — APP.

Final Report of the Southern Appalachian National Park Commission to the Secretary of the Interior, June 30, 1931.
U4020 (ASU)

PARKS, NATIONAL — APPALACHIA

Our Country's National Parks.
M5000 (ASU)

Our National Parks.
R3620 (ASU LMC BC)

PARKS, NATIONAL — CHICKAMAUGA AND CHATTANOOGA MILITARY
O670

PARKS, NATIONAL — CHICKAMAUGA AND CHATTANOOGA NATIONAL MILITARY PARK

Chickamauga and Chattanooga Battlefields; Chickamauga and Chattanooga National Military Park, Georgia-Tennessee.
S8960

PARKS, NATIONAL — CIVIL WAR — TENN.

Eliza Ross; or, Illustrated Guide of Lookout Mountain.
M4910

PARKS, NATIONAL — CUMBERLAND GAP

A Profile and Economic Impact Analysis of Four Cumberland Gap Counties.
E1390

PARKS, NATIONAL — GA.
K830

Chickamauga-Chattanooga National Military Park. Tennessee. Georgia.
U3700

PARKS, NATIONAL — GREAT SMOKY MOUNTAINS

Walking in the Clouds.
A380 (ETSU ASU)

Land of High Horizons.
B5770 (ASU WCU LMC BC ETSU)

Great Smokies: Wonderland for Boys and Girls.
D2230 (ASU)

Strangers in High Places: The Story of the Great Smoky Mountains.
F3470 (ASU WCU LMC MHC FC ETSU BC)

Your National Parks: Great Smoky Mountains.
H7790 (ETSU)

Amphibians and Reptiles of Great Smoky Mountains National Park.
H8160 (UNCA ASU LMC WCU BC)

A Bibliography for the Great Smoky Mountains.
M730

A Brief History of the Great Smoky Mountains National Park Movement in North Carolina.
M740

Guide to the Great Smoky Mountains National Park.
M760 (WCU)

Fishing in the Great Smoky Mountains National Park and Adjacent Waters.
M3090

Complete Report (of the Commission Created to Establish a National Park in the Great Smoky Mountains) Submitted to Governor Clyde R. Hoey, Dec. 31, 1939.
N2490 (LMC WCU)

The Great Smoky Mountains National Park.
R560 (ASU)

"History of the Great Smoky Mountains National Park."
S5330

The Smokies Guide.
S6990 (BC ASU WCU)

The Smokies Guide.
S7000 (LMC)

Great Smoky Mountains National Park, North Carolina and Tennessee.
S8840 (ASU LMC WCU ETSU)

Trees, Shrubs, and Woody Vines of Great Smoky Mountains National Park.
S8870 (ASU WCU LMC WWC UNCA)

Trees, Shrubs, and Woody Vines of Great Smoky Mountains National Park.
S8880

The Great Smoky Mountains.
T8360 (ASU WCU LMC WWC UNCA)

The Great Smoky Mountains.
T8370 (WCU LMC BC ETSU)

The Great Smoky Mountains.
T8380 (ETSU)

PARKS, NATIONAL — KENNESAW MOUNTAIN BATTLEFIELD

The Road Past Kennesaw: The Atlanta Campaign of 1864.
M2330

PARKS, NATIONAL — KY.

The Allegheny Parkway, West Virginia, Virginia, Kentucky: Report to the Congress of the U. S.
U3680

PARKS, NATIONAL — MAMMOTH CAVE NATIONAL PARK

The Flint Ridge Cave System, Mammoth Cave National Park, Kentucky.
C2580 (ASU BC)

PARKS, NATIONAL — MAMMOUTH CAVE

Geology of the Mammoth Cave National Park Area. Rev. by Preston McGrain. Kentucky Geological Survey Series 10, Special publication 7. Revision of Series 9, Special publication 2.
L2910 (ETSU ASU)

PARKS, NATIONAL — N. C.

Mammals of the Great Smoky Mountains National Park.
L2710 (WCU WWC ASU LMC)

Mammals of Great Smoky Mountains National Park.
L2720 (BC)

Chickamauga-Chattanooga National Military Park. Tennessee. Georgia.
U3700

Great Smoky Mountains National Park. North Carolina-Tennessee. The Land and its People.
U3720

Great Smoky Mountains National Park. North Carolina-Tennessee. The Land and its People.
U3730

PARKS, NATIONAL — S. C.
K2500

PARKS, NATIONAL — SHENANDOAH

The Blue Ridge Boys; Narrations of Early Actual Mountain Experiences and Humorous Anecdotes of the Shenandoah National Park Section.
B2400 (BC)

The Shenandoah National Park Travelogue; an Official Illustrated Guide Book for the First Great Nat'l Park of the East.
H5560

Skyland: The Heart of the Shenandoah National Park.
P3420 (FC BC ASU WCU)

Guide to the Appalachian Trail and Side Trails in the Shenandoah National Park.
P3840 (ETSU)

Guide to the Appalachian Trail: Susquehanna River to the Shenandoah National Park.
P3870

Guide to Trails in the Shenandoah National Park: The Appalachian Trail and Side Trails.
P3880

PARKS, NATIONAL — SHENANDOAH
The Blue Ridge: Man and Nature in Shenandoah National Park and Blue Ridge Parkway.
W6260 (WCU LMC)
PARKS, NATIONAL — TENN.
Landmarks of Tennessee History.
A1290
Mammals of the Great Smoky Mountains National Park.
L2710 (WCU WWC ASU LMC)
Mammals of Great Smoky Mountains National Park.
L2720 (BC)
Great Smoky Mountains National Park. North Carolina-Tennessee. The Land and its People.
U3720
Great Smoky Mountains National Park. North Carolina-Tennessee. The Land and its People.
U3730
PARKS, NATIONAL — TENN. AND GA.
The National Military Park, Chickamauga-Chattanooga: An Historical Guide, with Maps and Illustrations.
B6100 (ASU BC)
PARKS, NATIONAL — VA.
The Allegheny Parkway, West Virginia, Virginia, Kentucky: Report to the Congress of the U. S.
U3680
Feasibility Study for Development of a New River Gorge National Parkway Virginia and West Virginia.
U3710
PARKS, NATIONAL — W. VA.
The Allegheny Parkway, West Virginia, Virginia, Kentucky: Report to the Congress of the U. S.
U3680
Feasibility Study for Development of a New River Gorge National Parkway Virginia and West Virginia.
U3710
PENSIONS
The Effect of Workmen's Compensation on the Logging and Sawmilling Industries in the Northeast.
H6380
PENSIONS — N. C.
Workmen's Compensation in North Carolina, 1929-1940.
K380 (LMC)
PERIODICALS
A2640 (ASU)
A2650 (ASU MHC LMC)
A2670 (ASU)
A2770 (ASU)
A2800
A2810 (ASU)
A2830 (ETSU BC)
ACI Bulletin.
A2880
Forecast.
A2930
A3120 (ETSU)
Bulletin.
A3130 (ASU ETSU LMC)
A3190 (ETSU ASU BC)
A3210
A3220 (ASU ETSU BC)
A3250 (BC)
Appalachia.
A3270
Appalachia Bulletin.
A3280
Literature List, June, 1972.
A3310 (ASU BC)
Pamphlets.
A3320 (ASU BC)
A3360 (ASU BC)
A3380 (ASU ETSU BC)
A3390
A3400 (BC ETSU ASU)
A3420
Current Regional Reports.
A3720
Newsletter.
A4020 (BC)
A4030 (ASU ETSU BC)
A4070 (ASU ETSU MHC BC)
Twigs.
A4100 (ASU)
A4420 (ASU)
Newsletter.
B3090 (BC ASU)
B4340 (ASU)
B4770 (BC)
B5460 (BC)
Publications of the Southeastern Forest Station, 1921-1958.
B7230 (WCU)
B8380
The 1916 Pictorial Story of Haywood County.
C1330 (WCU)
C2000 (ETSU UNCA BC)
C3530 (BC)
C5170 (BC)
C5210 (BC)
Best of Hillbilly: A Prize Collection of 100-proof Writings from Jim Comstock's West Virginia Hillbilly.
C6300 (ASU MHC WCU LMC BC)
The Socialist and Labor Star, Huntington, West Virginia, 1912-1915.
C7370 (ASU BC)
An Index of State Geological Survey Publications Issued in Series.
C7380 (LMC)
C9410 (BC)
D520 (ASU)
D750 (BC)
Observations from a Peak in Lumpkin: Or, the Writings of W. Ba. Townsend, Editor, The Dahlonega Nugget.
D1490 (ASU)
The Kanawha Spectator.
D1630
D2480 (ETSU)
D2490 (ASU)
Research Bulletin.
E70 (ETSU)
Publications. . . .
E140 (ASU WCU ETSU BC)
Bulletin.
E180 (ETSU)
Scrap Book.
E190 (ETSU)
Alumni Quarterly.
E220 (ETSU)
Master Booklist.
E230 (ETSU)
The Dean Says.
E240 (ETSU)
Educational Films and Filmstrips; East Tennessee State College Collection. . . .
E310 (ETSU)
Bulletin.
E340 (ETSU)
The ETSU Journalist.
E390 (ETSU)
Newsletter.
E460 (ETSU)
E680 (ETSU)
E690
E920
E1570
The Emancipator.
E1900 (ASU)
Proceedings.
F1780 (WCU)
F2960 (ASU ETSU BC)
F3460 (ASU BC)
Quarterly Bulletin.
F3500 (ASU BC)
The Furman Bulletin, New Series.
F4000
G1000 (MHC)
Checklist of Southern Periodicals to 1861.
G1720 (LMC)
"Cry Aloud and Spare Not; the Formative Years of Brownlow's WHIG, 1839-1841."
H530
The Lovingood Papers.
H2810
Historical Sketches of Southwest Virginia.
H5950
I60 (BC UNCA)
I740
Index to Genealogical Periodicals.
J270 (ASU)
J2770
Circular. No. 1-.
K920
K960
Travel in Kentucky.
K1200
K1220 (ASU ETSU BC)
Proceedings.
K1310
K1330
K1440
K1850 (ETSU)
"A Study of the Use of Periodicals Received by the Dobyns-Bennett Senior High School Materials Center, Kingsport, Tennessee."
K3110 (ETSU)
The Blue Ridge Parkway Guide.
L3470 (LMC ASU)
The Blue Ridge Parkway Guide.
L3520 (BC LMC ASU WCU)
M2730
M2750 (ASU)
A List of Magazines, Journals, Small Presses, Newspapers, etc. of Interest to Students of Appalachia.
M5820
M6150 (BC)
Bulletin of Applied Linguistics.
M7400
M8350
M8360
M8370 (ASU ETSU MHC BC)
M8380 (ASU BC ETSU)
M8390
M8400
M8410
M8420
N790 (ASU)
N800 (ASU BC ETSU)
Faculty Publications.
N1540 (BC ASU LMC ETSU)
College Bulletin.
N1570 (ASU)
N2270 (BC ASU ETSU MHC)
N2350
N2400 (ASU)
N2410
N2420 (BC ASU)
A Cumulative Author and Subject Index Covering Material in N. C. Publications. . . .
N2430 (ASU UNCA)
Our Mountain Work.
N2520
North Carolina Manual 1874-19.
N2560 (ASU LMC)
O490 (ETSU)
O500
O750
A Catalogue of the South.
O1040 (ASU)
P1960 (ASU BC)
Appalachia's People, Problems, Alternatives.
P1970 (BC ASU)
Appalachia's People, Problems, Alternatives; an Introductory Social Science Reader.
P1980 (BC ASU)
Pine Mountain Bulletin.
P3010 (BC)
P3020
Bay Leaves.
P3330 (ASU)
Studies in Polk County History.
P3360 (ASU BC)
P3900 (BC)
Education in Appalachia as Depicted in Major Periodicals.
R290
Magazine of History — Biography.
R410
R840 (ASU)
R1570 (ASU)
Journal.
R2620 (BC ETSU)
Proceedings of the Rockbridge Historical Society.
R3360 (BC ASU)
Religious News Press in Appalachia, 1971. A Directory of News Periodicals of . . . all Members of the Commission on Religion in Appalachia. . .
S4120 (ASU BC)
Proceedings.
S5650
S5730 (ASU BC)
Highland Highlights.
S5765 (BC)
S5770
S5780 (MHC)

PERIODICALS
S8810 (ETSU)
T20
Bulletin. no. 1-.
T890 (BC)
Rural Research Series. Monograph no. 1-.
T900
Annual Report of the State Entomologist and Plant Pathologist.
T940 (ETSU)
T1790
Drirectory of Member Schools.
T1810 (ETSU)
Tennessee Blue Book.
T1820 (LMC)
. . . Chemical Engineering Report, no. 1.
T2390
Forestry Bulletin, no. 1.
T2810 (BC)
Financial Statements for the Fiscal Years Ended June 20, 1938-Date.
T4250
Municipalities (Electric Departments Only) and Cooperatives, Purchasing Power from Tennessee Valley Authority. Financial Statements for the Fiscal Years Ended June 30, 1938-Date.
T4260
Chemical Engineering Bulletins.
T6130
Chemical Engineering Reports.
T6140
T9140 (BC)
T9160 (BC)
T9870
Annual Report and Program.
U3020 (BC)
V430
V570 (ASU)
Bulletin.
V680 (BC)
Bulletin.
V830 (BC)
Bulletin.
V900 (BC)
V1110 (BC)
V1130 (BC)
Bulletin.
V1150 (BC)
The University of Virginia Record . . . .
V1210 (BC)
V1320 (BC)
W1380 (ETSU)
W1390 (ETSU)
Community Planning Newsletter.
W3280
W3300 (BC)
W3630 (BC)
West Virginia Heritage.
W4040 (ASU BC)
W4050 (BC)
W4070 (UNCA ETSU)
W4250 (BC)
Business and Economic Studies.
W4490 (BC)
W4630 (ETSU BC ASU)
From the Mountain.
W5440 (ASU BC)
W5930 (BC)
PERIODICALS — APP.
Readings About Appalachia: A Guide to Pamphlets and Periodicals.
K50
PERIODICALS — N. C.
Union List of North Carolina Newspapers, 1751-1900.
J2360 (LMC)
Union List of Periodicals in Libraries of Western North Carolina Library Association.
W4880 (ASU)
Union List of Periodicals in Libraries of Western North Carolina.
W4890 (LMC)
PERIODICALS — VA.
A Checklist of Southwest Virginia Newspapers, 1800-1974.
J1660
PIGEON RIVER
Planning for Flood Damage Prevention at Clyde, N. C.
C5160 (LMC)
N2650 (ASU UNCA)
Ecological Effects of Hot Water Discharge by an Electric Power Generating Plant.
N2660 (ASU UNCA)
Smathers from Yadkin Valley to Pigeon River: Smathers and Agner Families.
P920 (ASU)
POETRY
The Collected Poems of James Agee.
A660 (ASU WCU ETSU BC)
Permit Me Voyage.
A770 (ETSU)
Wedding of the Waters.
A2240 (BC)
A3420
The Grace of the Bough.
A5630 (ASU BC)
Green of a Hundred Springs.
A5640 (ASU BC)
Love-vine.
A5650 (ASU BC)
Meadow-rue.
A5660 (ASU BC)
No Stranger to the Earth.
A5670 (ASU BC)
With Thorn and Stone.
A5680 (ASU BC)
Laments of an Egotist.
B830
Trammel Fork Creek.
B1220 (BC)
I Hear America Singing.
B1320 (BC)
Sunset Views: A Book of Verses.
B1330 (ASU)
The Mountain Pine.
B1430 (BC)
Kentucky, Yesterday and Today.
B2050 (LMC BC)
Listening Hills.
B2060 (BC)
From the Heart.
B2470
Men "Pro and Con."
B2480
Echoes from the Cumberlands, Being Made from His Poems Written During the Last Thirty Years.
B3460 (ASU BC)
Level Paths: New Songs by the Layman.
B4170 (WCU ASU)
Lyrics of a Layman.
B4180 (WCU)
Afterglow: A Collection of Short Stories and Poems.
B4360 (ASU BC)
Of Life and Love and Things.
B4510 (ASU BC)
Stray Leaves from the Hillside.
B4590
Whispering Pines.
B5290 (ASU)
Old Christmas, and Other Kentucky Tales in Verse.
B6200 (BC)
Kentucky Harvest.
B6320 (BC LMC)
Mountain State Gleanings.
B6470 (BC)
I Sing of Appalachia: Poems.
B6520 (ASU BC)
The Mountain Muse: Comprising the Adventures of Daniel Boone. And, The Power of Virtuous and Refined Beauty.
B7760 (ASU BC)
Blue Ridge Magic and Other Poems.
C90 (ASU)
Mountain Lyrics and Sketches.
C1370 (WCU)
Fugitive Lyrics of John Heiskell Booton.
C1980
Come Along.
C2310 (ASU WCU ETSU BC)
The Wooden Tower.
C2510
Lines and Points.
C2710 (BC)
The Whistling Wind and Other Poems.
C3010 (BC)
The Simple Things and Other Poems.
C3580 (LMC)
The Mountain Bard: A Series of Original Poems.
C3970 (BC)
Rouse with the Dawn.
C4030 (ASU)
Back Home. Kingsport, Tennessee.
C4470 (BC ASU)
The Mountaineers, and Other Poems.
C4520 (BC)
Southern Season.
C4730 (ASU)
Poems for Her.
C4740
Kinfolks: Kentucky Mountain Rhymes.
C5300 (ASU BC)
The Hill Way Home: Poems from the Appalachian Highlands, Including "A House in the Country, II."
C5610 (LMC BC)
Cumberland Gap, and Other Poems.
C5680 (BC)
My Land — My People.
C5690 (BC)
Kentucky Cargo.
C5700 (BC)
The Land of the Sky, an Idyl.
C5830 (LMC ASU)
A Song of the Alleghenies.
C5980
Plenteous Heritage.
C6020 (BC)
The Bubble.
C6110
"A Study of the Black Mountain Poets."
C6150 (WCU)
Froissart Ballads, and Other Poems.
C7050 (BC)
Poems From a Land of Hills.
C7090 (ASU LMC)
Barefoot in the Smokies.
C7630 (LMC)
Lamp in the Cabin: Poems of the Smokies.
C7640 (BC)
Poems of Paradise.
C7650 (BC)
Poems of the Smokies.
C7660 (LMC)
Poverty Poems.
C8210 (BC)
Path, Flower, and Other Verses.
D320 (ASU BC)
"Theory and Practice in the Black Mountain Poets Duncan, Olson, and Creeley."
D600 (WCU)
The Kingdom Gained and Other Poems.
D980 (BC)
The Girl of Luna's Creek.
D1390 (BC)
A Rosary of the Ridges.
D1980 (ASU)
Buckdancer's Choice: Poems by James Dickey.
D2140 (ASU)
Poems, 1957-1967.
D2170 (ASU)
Smiles and Tears.
D2920 (ASU)
Lays of Life from the Southern Appalachians.
D3190 (ASU LMC)
Appalachia, My Land.
D3430
Foothills: Poems.
D3980 (BC)
E690
Mountain Laurel.
E1930 (LMC ETSU BC)
Wanetka, and Other Poems.
E2200 (ASU)
The Philosophy of a Partriarch.
F260 (ASU BC)
Springboard to Optimism Versus Majoring in the Minors: A Dozen Books in One.
F670 (ASU)
F3460 (ASU BC)
Tennessee Centennial Poem. A Synopsis of the History of Tennessee from Its Earliest Settlement on Watauga to the Present Time, with Short Biographies of Her Most Prominent Men.
F3610 (ASU)
The Angel in the Cloud: With Memoir and Portrait of the Author, and Additional Poems.
F3660 (ASU)
The Angel in the Cloud.
F3670 (ASU)

POETRY
I Chant the Mountains.
F4050 (BC)
Just from Kentucky.
F4060 (BC)
The Pinnacle and Other Kentucky Mountain Poems.
F4070 (ASU BC)
The Strange Shape.
F4080 (BC)
This is My Country: A Book of Poetry.
G150 (ASU)
For All the Lost and Lonely.
G340 (LMC ASU WCU)
Sketchbook from Hell.
G350 (WCU)
When Men and Mountains Meet.
G360 (WCU LMC MHC ASU)
Unto the Hills.
G2200 (ASU)
Cabin Fever.
G2230
Mountain Dooryards.
G2500 (ASU LMC MHC BC)
The Whistle and the Wind.
G2510 (ASU LMC MHC BC)
My Sunrise.
H560 (BC)
Three Score Years and Ten.
H570 (ETSU)
Abel Anders.
H1460 (BC)
Songs of the Woods Poet.
H2100 (ASU BC)
Slow Creek.
H2440 (ASU)
Rhymes of a Mountaineer.
H2460 (ASU)
Rhymes of a Mountaineer; the Best of Roy Lee Harmon.
H2470 (BC)
Hill Saga.
H2500
Limericks and Lyrics from My Rhododendron Thicket.
H4230 (ASU)
Lonesome Water.
H4380 (BC)
Windsongs.
H4540 (ASU)
The Ballad of Tall Tom Wolfe.
H6190 (ASU)
H7880
Songs of the Cumberlands.
H7990 (BC)
My Poetry Book.
H8010 (ASU)
Come Up the Valley: Ballads and Poems.
H8210 (ASU BC WWC)
Down in West Virginia and Other Poems.
H8510
Chimney Rock Anthology.
I50
Back Home and Other Poems. Being a Collection of Poems.
J420 (LMC)
Occoneechee, the Maid of the Mystic Lake.
J430 (ASU WCU)
Occoneechee, the Maid of the Mystic Lake.
J440 (UNCA LMC)
Mountain Rhythms: Or, Poems of a Mountaineer.
J670 (ASU)
My Kentucky; Plain Verse of a Mountain Man from Old Kentucky.
J790 (BC)
A Man and a Woman and God.
J2980 (BC)
Take Time to Stroll.
J2990
Tears and Laughter and Other Poems.
J3000
This Way Lies Peace.
J3010
Songs of the Open Air and Other Poems.
K730 (BC)
Haiku and Tanka.
L1460 (ASU)
Echoes from the Foothills.
L2930
On a High Hill.
L3500 (ASU)
The Tempter's Harvest.
M700
Till the Frost.
M710
The Tempter's Harvest.
M850
Till the Frost.
M860 (ASU BC)
The Gobbler of God: A Poem of the Southern Appalachians.
M1750 (LMC WCU BC)
Plumed Depths.
M1810
The Bronze Hunter.
M2210
Melodies and Mountaineers.
M2240 (ASU)
From a Dark Mountain, Lyrics from the Production of Louise McNeill's Premiere Reading.
M2390 (ASU)
Gauley Mountain.
M2400 (ASU LMC BC)
Mountain White.
M2410
Paradox Hill from Appalachia to Lunar Shore.
M2420 (ASU)
Green Autumn.
M2860 (BC)
Locust Bloom.
M3970 (BC)
Kentucky Moonshine.
M4440
Chilhowee, a Legend of the Great Smoky Mountains.
M4500 (LMC BC)
Mountain Echoes, a Book of Poetic Reflections.
M4570 (ASU)
Halfway Up the Sky.
M5100
Strains from a Dulcimore.
M5450 (BC)
As Once I Passed This Way.
M5540
The Wind Southerly.
M5670
Copperhead Cane, Poems.
M5800 (ASU BC)
Dialogue with a Dead Man.
M5810 (ASU BC)
The More Things Change, the More They Stay the Same.
M5830 (ASU BC LMC)
The Hills and Home.
M5930 (ASU)
Versatile Verse.
M7430 (ASU)
Zirconia Poems.
M7660 (LMC)
The Selected Poetry and Prose of John T. Napier.
N60 (ASU BC)
The Lady Angeline: A Lay of the Appalachians.
N1300 (BC)
Lincoln and Twenty Other Poems.
N1320 (BC)
Tip Sams of Kentucky.
N1330 (BC)
Tip Sams Again.
N1330 (BC)
The Valleys of Parnassus; A Selection From the Poetry of J. T. Cotton Noe.
N1350
Cumberland Falls, Kentucky.
N1360
A Time for Poetry: An Anthology.
N2510 (LMC)
The Quiet Hills.
O180 (BC)
A Collection of Poems.
O870
Fruitful Year.
P220 (ETSU)
The Backwoodsman.
P980
Castle Gates (a Book of Poems) Through Which the Knowing Ones Are Admitted into Some of My Castles in Spain.
P1300 (ASU)
Early Harvest: The First Experimental Poems of a Self-taught Farm Boy.
P1310 (ASU)
Fifty Acres, and Other Poems.
P1320 (ASU)
My Fingers and My Toes.
P1330 (ASU LMC)
Pearson's Poems.
P1340 (ASU)
Plowed Ground, Humorous and Dialect Poems.
P1350 (ASU)
Selected Poems.
P1360 (ASU LMC)
April Poems.
P1760
Scenes from a Southern Road.
P1780 (LMC ASU)
Tomorrow's People, a Storm in Harlan, Kentucky.
P2410 (LMC)
Poems From the Hills, 1971.
P3250 (ASU BC)
P3310
P3320
Bay Leaves.
P3330 (ASU)
Clinch Mountain Gems.
P4130
Country Voices.
P4140
Exploring with Verses.
P4170 (LMC)
The Unfortunate Mountain Girl: A Collection of Miscellanies in Prose and Verse.
P4240 (LMC)
Sing. O Mountaineer!
P4610 (BC ASU LMC)
A Bit O' Sunshine.
P4660
This An' That.
P4680
The Tree in the Far Pasture.
R60 (ASU)
Hills, Hollers and Hickory Flats.
R70
Randolph-Macon Prose and Verse, a Collection of Undergraduate Writings.
R430 (ASU)
Humor among These Hills.
R530 (ASU LMC MHC WCU)
The Wagoner of the Alleghanies: A Poem of the Days of Seventy-six.
R800 (BC)
Tapestry of Time.
R820
The Call of the Smokies.
R860 (BC LMC WCU)
Gordon Ballads.
R920 (ASU)
Ballad of the Bones.
R940
Bow Down in Jericho.
R960
The Season of Flesh.
R980 (LMC BC)
A Song of Joy, and Other Poems.
R990
Songs of the Hills.
R1080 (ASU)
The Green Bough.
R1120 (BC)
Lyrics of Life and the Great Outdoors.
R1130 (BC)
R1860
Spirit Happy.
R2340
Celebration of Life, Her Songs, Her Poems.
R2410 (ASU)
Celebration of Life: Her Songs, Her Poems.
R2420 (LMC)
Song in the Meadow: Poems.
R2820 (ASU)
Tellico Blue.
S750 (BC)
S1610 (BC)
The Banner Floats on and Other Poems.
S1650 (ASU)
Noon Shouts.
S1660 (ASU)
Hungering for the Hills and Other Poems.
S2970
Fire on the Mountain.
S3240 (ASU WCU)
Night Is Always Kind.
S3250 (ASU WCU)
Red Leaf Carols.
S3260 (ASU WCU LMC)
Backside of Heaven: Selected Verse From Bystander in the Smoky Mountain Times.
S5540 (WCU BC UNCA)

POETRY
Falling Sky.
S5550 (WCU)
The Feudalist.
S6060 (BC)
River Island.
S6070 (BC)
The Untoward Hills.
S7260 (BC)
Hounds on the Mountain.
S7360 (ETSU BC)
Hounds on the Mountain.
S7370 (ASU)
Hounds on the Mountain.
S7380 (WWC)
On Troublesome Creek.
S7390 (ASU UNCA)
Years of Harvest, Poems and Tales from the Smoky Foothills, 1924-1964.
S7500 (BC LMC WCU)
Eyes of the Mole.
S8180 (BC)
A Year's Harvest.
S8200 (BC)
Album of Destiny.
S8220 (LMC WCU ETSU)
Autumn Lovesong: A Celebration of Love's Fulfillment.
S8240 (ETSU ASU)
Dawn of Remembered Spring.
S8330 (ASU WCU LMC ETSU)
Harvest of Youth.
S8370 (ASU WCU LMC ETSU BC)
Hold April: New Poems.
S8410 (ASU WCU LMC ETSU BC)
A Jesse Stuart Harvest.
S8430 (FC BC ASU)
A Jesse Stuart Reader: Stories and Poems.
S8440 (ASU WCU BC ETSU)
Kentucky Is My Land. Poems.
S8450 (ASU ETSU BC)
Man with a Bull-tongue Plow.
S8470 (ASU WCU BC UNCA)
Man With a Bull-tongue Plow.
S8480 (WCU ETSU ASU)
Someone Else; Sixteen Poems About Other Children.
S9040
Poisoned Ivy.
S9100
In Lonesome Cove.
S9170 (ASU)
In Lonesome Cove: Poems from TVA-land.
S9180 (ASU)
The Sunken Star.
S9260 (BC)
Kentucky Pioneer Women. Columbian Poems and Prose Sketches.
T150 (BC)
T1790
Echoes from the Kentucky Hills.
T7810
The Blue Ridge Parkway: A Poem.
T8790 (WCU)
T8850 (BC)
The Crystal Prison.
T9200 (BC)
The Silver Chain.
T9210 (BC)
Thorns and Thistledown.
T9220 (BC)
Wind in the Reed.
T9230 (BC)
Stories and Verse of West Virginia.
T9780
Cat Claws and Tree Bark.
T9840 (ASU)
The Brown Thrush; Anthology of Verse by Negro Students, Talladega College, Tougaloo College.
V1380 (BC)
Frankly Speaking: A Concoction of Humorous, Serious, and Satirical Verses.
W60 (ASU)
Looking Back.
W560 (BC)
North Carolina Poetry.
W600 (LMC BC)
Vale of Shenandoah and Other Poems.
W680 (ASU)
A Paraphrase of Seven Days.
W910 (BC)
Hill Country Poems.
W2150 (ASU LMC BC)
Clods of Southern Earth.
W2920 (BC)
O Mountaineers! A Collection of Poems.
W2940 (ASU BC)
The Road Is Rocky: A Collection of Poems.
W2960 (LMC BC)
A Time for Anger: Poems Selected from. . . .
W3000 (ASU LMC)
Up Ego!
W3070 (ASU)
For Crossing Wide Waters.
W4830 (BC)
Give a Man Courage.
W4840 (BC)
Song of a Woods Colt: Poetry.
W5080 (LMC ASU MHC BC)
Blues and Roots, Rue and Bluets: A Garland for the Appalachians.
W6640 (ASU LMC BC)
An Ear in Bartram's Tree: Selected Poems, 1957-1967.
W6650 (LMC BC)
The Loco Logodaedalist in Situ: Selected Poems, 1968-70.
W6660 (LMC)
W7640 (BC)
Crest on the Wave.
W8030 (BC)
A Stone, a Leaf, a Door: Poems.
W8280 (ETSU)
A Stone, a Leaf, a Door: Poems by Thomas Wolfe.
W8290 (UNCA ASU WCU BC)
Lichen Tufts, from the Alleghanies.
W9380 (BC)
Thoughts from the Hills.
Y140
Found Objects.
Z170 (BC)

POETRY — GA.
Stone Mountain: Or, the Lay of the Gray Minstrel. An Epic Poem in Twenty-four Parts, Commemorative of the South's Confederate, Pre-Historic, Colonial, Revolutionary, and World War Days, to Which Are Added a Number of Other Poems, Patriotic, Humorous, and Occasional, Besides a Few Prose Selections.
K2800 (ASU)

POETRY — N. C.
Stories and Poems From the Old North State.
L1240 (LMC)

POLITICS — APP.
"Appalachian North Carolina: A Political Study, 1860-1889."
C7740
Authentic History of Ku Klux Klan, 1865-1877.
D1240 (LMC)
"Local Government Social Overhead Expenditures and Economic Growth in the Appalachian Region."
D2450
The Secession Movement, 1860-1861.
D3840
The Secession Movement, 1860-1861.
D3850
The Secession Movement, 1860-1861.
D3860
The Seccession Movement, 1860-1861.
D3870
"Political Attitudes of the Poor — An Inquiry into Their Position on a Liberal-Conservative Continuum."
E1520
Politics in the Border States.
F590 (UNCA ASU)
Why the Solid South? or, Reconstruction and its Results.
H4890 (ASU)
"Political Socialization in Appalachia: An Inquiry into the Process of Political Learning in an American Sub-Culture."
H5670
How People Get Power: Organizing Oppressed Communities Get Action.
K40 (WCU ASU)
Who Speaks for Appalachia 1972?
K60 (ASU)
"The Regionalist Movement in the Cumberland."
L1680 (ASU)
The Political Economy of Appalachia; A Case Study in Regional Integration.
N780 (BC WWC ASU ETSU MHC WCU)
The Union League of America: Political Activities in Tennessee, the Carolinas, and Virginia, 1865-1870.
O1010
"Presidential Voting Patterns in Appalachia: An Analysis of the Relationship Between Turnout, Partisan Change, and Selected Socioeconomic Variables."
R2520
John Wesley North and the Reform Frontier.
S7580
"Lincoln's Carpetbagger, J. W. North."
S7590
The Blount Journal, 1790-1796: The Proceedings of Government Over the Territory of the United States of America, South of the River Ohio.
T7620 (ASU)

POLITICS — APP. — REPUBLICANISM
"Mountain Republicanism, 1876-1900."
M1900

POLITICS — CHEROKEE
Cherokee Tragedy: The Story of the Ridge Family and the Decimation of a People.
W6330 (ASU WCU LMC BC UNCA)

POLITICS — CIVIL WAR — VA.
Virginia's Attitude Toward Slavery and Secession.
M8570 (FC LMC)

POLITICS — GA.
"A Description of Government in Gordon, Clark and Paulding Counties, Georgia."
R3520
Rebecca Latimer Felton, Nine Stormy Decades.
T110 (ASU)
Government in Georgia.
U480 (LMC)

POLITICS — KY.
"The Mountains and the Blue Grass: A Comparative Study of County Officials in Kentucky."
B8300
A Survey of the Legal Environment of Knox County, Kentucky.
C2590
Kentucky Mayor: The Humor and Philosophy of John Edwin Garner.
C2610 (BC)
"Political Behavior in Breathitt, Knott, Perry and Leslie Counties, Kentucky."
C5990
Poverty, Politics, and Health Care: An Appalachian Experience.
C8060 (ASU)
Josie M. Davidson, Her Life and Work, by Herself.
D670 (BC)
"Government in an Eastern Kentucky Coal Field County."
D3690 (ASU)
"Twentieth Century Development of the Coal Mining Industry in Eastern Kentucky and Its Influence upon the Political Behavior of This Area."
F3420 (ASU)
"A New Deal for Harlan: The Roosevelt Labor Policies in a Kentucky Coal Field, 1931-1939."
H5120 (BC)
"Factors Influencing Political Behavior in Bell, Clay, Knox, and Whitley Counties."
J450 (ASU)
Kentucky Politics.
J820 (ASU BC)
Articles of Impeachment Against John A. Duff, Surveyor of Perry Co.
K1230
Hearings Held at Pikeville.
K1240
Nativism in Kentucky in 1860.
M1370 (ASU)
The Life and Times of Hon. Humphrey Marshall.
Q200 (LMC BC MHC)
"Population Trends and Other Factors Influencing the Voting Habits of the Cumberland Valley Region of Southeast Kentucky."
R1210
"Kentucky Politics and Society: 1919-1932."
S2080 (BC)

POLITICS — KY.
Presidential Politics in Kentucky, 1824-1948: A Compilation of Election Statistics and an Analysis of Political Behavior.
S2230 (LMC)
Lion of White Hall: The Life of Cassius M. Clay.
S4400 (MHC)
"The Public Career of Andrew Jackson Graves."
S6140
"Bloody" Harlan, 1931-1938; an Appalachian Coal County in the Thirties.
T170
Government in Kentucky.
U490 (LMC)
The Partisan Spirit: Kentucky Politics, 1779-1792.
W1500 (WWC BC)
Benjamin Helm Bristow, Border State Politician.
W2060 (BC)
POLITICS — N. C.
Selections from the Speeches and Writings of Hon. Thomas L. Clingman, of North Carolina. With Additions and Explanatory Notes.
C5080 (ASU BC)
"Appalachian North Carolina: A Political Study, 1860-1889."
C7740
North Carolina Governors, 1585-1958: Brief Sketches.
C8300 (LMC BC)
Historical Facts Concerning Buncombe County Government.
D2390 (WCU LMC)
Life of Zebulon B. Vance.
D3160 (ASU LMC BC)
North Carolina Politics: An Introduction.
F1410 (LMC)
"Public Policy for Depressed Areas with Special Reference to North Carolina."
F1630
Preachers, Pedagogues and Politicians: The Evolution Controversy in North Carolina, 1920-1927.
G590 (WCU WWC)
Jeffersonian Democracy in North Carolina, 1789-1816.
G1800 (LMC)
Party Politics in North Carolina, 1835-1960.
H1140 (LMC)
Andrew Jackson and North Carolina Politics.
H6330 (LMC)
Handbook of Watauga County.
L1190 (ASU LMC)
This is Our Town: Boone, N. C.
L1200 (LMC ASU)
State Reconstruction Studies.
N1760 (LMC ASU)
County Government in North Carolina.
N2680 (WWC ASU LMC)
"Political Leadership and Social Structure in a Rural County."
R1870 (ASU)
"The Republican Party of North Carolina: 1900 to 1916."
R3630
Maps of North Carolina Congressional Districts, 1789-1960, and State Senatorial Districts and Apportionment of State Representatives, 1776-1960.
S340 (BC WWC)
Zebulon Vance, Tarheel Spokesman.
S3100 (ASU)
Zebulon Vance, Tarheel Spokesman.
S3110 (LMC)
The Secession Movement in North Carolina.
S3770 (LMC)
Biography of the State Officers and Members of the General Assembly of North Carolina, 1893, Other Interesting Facts.
T8840 (ASU LMC)
Zeb Vance: Champion of Personal Freedom.
T9640 (ASU WCU UNCA)
Government in North Carolina.
U500 (LMC)
Memorial addresses on the life and character of Zebulon Baird Vance.
U1840 (UNCA)
Statue of Zebulon Baird Vance, Erected Statuary Hall of the United States Capitol by the State of North Carolina.
U1910 (ASU WCU)
My Beloved Zebulon; the Correspondence of Zebulon B. Vance and Harriett Newell Espy.
V100
Papers.
V110 (ASU LMC)
Repeal of Civil Service Law. Speech of Hon. Zebulon B. Vance of North Carolina, Delivered in the United States Senate, Wednesday, March 31, 1886.
V120 (ASU)
The Scattered Nation.
V130 (ASU WCU)
The Tariff and the Farmers: Speech of Hon. Z. B. Vance, of North Carolina, on the McKinley Tariff Bill in the Senate of the United States, 1890.

County Government and Administration in North Carolina.
W80 (LMC BC)
Federalism in North Carolina.
W120 (LMC)
The People Govern North Carolina.
W950 (WWC)
POLITICS — N. C. — BOUNDARY DISPUTES
North Carolina Boundary Disputes Involving Her Southern Line.
S3820 (ASU LMC)
POLITICS — PA.
Early Western Pennsylvania Politics.
F650
Capability of Local Government in the Stroudsburg Area, Monroe County.
P1850 (ASU)
POLITICS — S. C.
The Life and Times of C. G. Memmings.
C1160 (ETSU)
Sectionalism and Representation in South Carolina.
S820 (ASU BC)
POLITICS — TENN.
Political Reconstruction in Tennessee.
A1430
Political Reconstruction in Tennessee.
A1440 (BC ASU)
Life and Speeches of President Andrew Johnson. Embracing His Early History, Political Career, Speeches, Proclamations, etc. With a Sketch of the Secession Movement, and His Course in Relation Thereto; Also His Policy as President of the United States.
B50
"James Robertson: Frontiersman."
B570
"The Office of Knox County Sheriff: An Administrative Study."
B660
"Politics of Innovation."
B670
"The Socialist Party in West Virginia from 1898 to 1920: A Study in Working Class Radicalism."
B1170
The Carpet-bagger in Tennessee.
B1760
The Life of Andrew Jackson.
B1830
The Life of Andrew Jackson.
B1840
The Life of Andrew Jackson.
B1850
"The Cost of Administering Criminal Justice in Memphis and Knoxville, Tennessee."
B2810
"Andrew Johnson, Governor of Tennessee, 1853-1857."
B3040
B3760
B3770
B3780
B3790
B3800
B3810
B3820
B3830
B3840
B3850
B3860
B3870
B3880
B3890
B3900
B3910
B3920
B3930
B3940
B3950
B3960
B3970
B3980
B3990
B4000
B4010
B4020
B4030
B4040
"The McMinn County, Tennessee, Election of August 1, 1946."
B6410 (ASU)
"Washington County Court: The Government of a Tennessee Frontier Community."
B7470
The Great Iron Wheel Examined: Or, Its False Spokes Extracted, and an Exhibition of Elder Graves, Its Builder.
B7500 (ASU)
"The Financing of Reconstruction in Tennessee."
B9280
The Duck's Back: A Report on Certain Phases of the Socialistic Experiments Conducted by the Federal Government in Tennessee Valley.
C160 (BC)
The Attitude of Tennesseans toward the Union. -.
C780 (BC ASU)
Tennessee and the Union, 1847-1861.
C790
"Tennessee's Attitude toward Secession."
C800
"Administrations of John Sevier."
C1660
"The Administration of Governor Andrew Johnson 1853-1857."
C1960
The Public Career of David Crockett.
C2150
"Tennessee: A Reluctant Seceder, 1847-1861."
C4460
Petitions of Anderson County Tennessee.
C9940 (ASU)
The Impeachment and Trial of Andrew Johnson, Seventeenth President of the United States; a History.
D2030
The Impeachment and Trial of Andrew Johnson, Seventeenth President of the United States; a History.
D2040
"Some Phases of the Congressional Career of Andrew Johnson."
D2630
"An Analysis of Educational Qualifications and Methods of Selection of School Board Members in the First Congressional District of Tennessee."
E820 (ETSU)
"Written Board of Education Policies for Unicoi County, Tennessee."
E2370 (ETSU)
Account of the Fund for the Relief of East Tennessee; with a Complete List of Contributors.
E2390
The Secession and Reconstruction of Tennessee. . . .
F720 (ASU LMC)
The Origin, Rise and Downfall of the State of Franklin under Her First and Only Governor, John Sevier.
F1320
Intergovernment Relations in the Tennessee Valley.
G2720
The Great Iron Wheel: Or, Republicanism Backwards and Christianity Reversed.
G3310 (ASU)
Bench and Bar of Knox County, Tennessee.
G3580 (BC)
Government in Tennessee.
G3810 (BC LMC)
Old Times in Tennessee, with Historical, Personal, and Political Scraps and Sketches.
G4790 (ASU)
"Cry Aloud and Spare Not; the Formative Years of Brownlow's WHIG, 1839-1841."
H530

POLITICS — TENN.

Andrew Johnson: Military Governor of Tennessee.
H600 (BC ASU)

Andrew Johnson: Military Governor of Tennessee.
H610 (BC ASU)

"Andrew Johnson, the Radicals, and the Negro, 1865-1866."
H970

Hill-Billy Bill; a Biography of Hon. J. Will Taylor of Tennessee.
H1660 (BC)

"Andrew Johnson's Reputation: A Study of Changing Interpretations."
H3990

The Civil and Political History of the State of Tennessee, from Its Earliest Settlement up to the Year 1796: Including the Boundaries of the State.
H4030 (ASU WCU LMC MHC BC)

The First American Frontier: Civil and Political History of the State of Tennessee from Its Earliest Settlement up to the Year 1796.
H4040 (LMC)

The Natural and Aboriginal History of Tennessee, up to the First Settlements Therein by the White People in the Year 1768.
H4050 (ASU ETSU BC)

"The Tennessee Conservatives and Secession, 1847-61."
H4750

Structure of County Government in Tennessee.
H6800

The Unwanted Boy: The Autobiography of Governor Ben W. Hooper.
H7040 (ASU BC)

"Political Activities of the Republican Party in the State of Tennessee, 1860-1870."
H7760
I170

Prohibition and Politics: Turbulent Decades in Tennessee, 1885-1920.
I960 (ASU LMC)

Life of Andrew Johnson; Seventeenth President of the United States.
J2410

Legislative History of Muscle Shoals.
K2340

"Sectionalism in East Tennessee, 1796 to 1861."
L50

Vanquished Volunteers: East Tennessee Sectionalism From Statehood to Secession.
L60 (LMC ETSU BC)

Governments in Knox County.
L210 (ETSU)

A Survey of Social Services in the Greater Kingsport Area.
L1210 (ETSU)

"The Good Government League and Polk County Politics, 1946-1965."
L1740

"Some Aspects of Polk County Politics."
L2500

"The Politics of Legislative Reapportionment in Tennessee, 1962."
L3040

"The Tennessee Political System: The Relationship of the Socioeconomic Environment to Political Processes and Policy Outputs."
M870

Unionism and Reconstruction in Tennessee, 1860-1869.
P840 (ASU WCU)

"The Republican Party in East Tennessee, 1865-1900."
Q130

Governor Bob Taylor's Tales.
R1920

"Old Limber": Or, The Tale of the Taylors.
R1930 (ASU)

Bob Taylor and the Agrarian Revolt in Tennessee.
R3230

"County Government in Tennessee."
S3650 (BC)

"Emerson Etheridge as a Candidate in the Tennessee Gubernatorial Election of 1867."
S5060

"A Study of Local Sources of Local Government Agencies in Twenty-three Selected Tennessee Counties."
S7760

Lectures and Best Literary Productions of Bob Taylor.
T460 (ASU)

Echoes: Centennial and Other Notable Speeches, Lectures, and Stories.
T720 (ASU)

Memorial Addresses Delivered in the Senate and the House of Representatives of the United States.
T740 (ASU)

House Journal, 1861-62, of the First Session of the Thirty-Fourth General Assembly of the State of Tennessee, Which Convened at Nashville, on the First Monday in October, A. D. 1861, and Adjourned in Memphis, March 20, 1862.
T1410 (ASU)

Messages of the Governors of Tennessee.
T1470 (ASU)

Commission Book, 1796-1801.
T1490 (ASU ETSU)

The Blount Journal, 1790-1796.
T1500

Three Pioneer Tennessee Documents: Donelson's Journal, Cumberland Compact, Minutes of Cumberland Court.
T1530 (ASU)

A Report of the Survey of the Finances and Management of Greene County, Tennessee.
T2130 (ETSU)

A Report of the Survey of the Finances and Management of the Government of Knox County, Tennessee.
T2140 (ETSU)

A Report of the Survey of the Finances and Management of the Government of Washington County, Tennessee.
T2150 (ETSU)

A Report of the Survey of the Management and Finances of the Government of Hamilton County.
T2160 (ETSU)

The Blount Journal, 1790-1796: The Proceedings of Government Over the Territory of the United States of America, South of the River Ohio.
T7620 (ASU)

The First President Johnson: The Three Lives of the Seventeenth President of the United States of America.
T7990 (ASU)

Walter P. Brownlow.
U1890

Robert Love Taylor.
U1900

Memorial Services Held in the House of Representatives of the United States, Together with Remarks Presented in Eulogy of James Willis Taylor, Late Representative from Tennessee.
U1920 (ASU)

"Andrew Johnson and the National Union Movement."
W140

Andrew Johnson, Plebian and Patriot.
W7830 (ASU)

POLITICS — TENN. — RECONSTRUCTION

"Some Social and Economic Phases of Reconstruction in East Tennessee, 1864-1869."
C600

Disunion and Restoration in Tennessee....
N330

Disunion and Restoration in Tennessee....
N340

POLITICS — VA.

County Government in Virginia.
B8520

The Man from Buchanan.
B8810

A Curiosity in Chancery.
D660

The Political History of Virginia During the Reconstruction.
E720

Separation of Church and State in Virginia; A Study in the Development of the Revolution.
E740

Randolph of Roanoke: A Political Fantastic.
J1760 (ASU)

Political History of Appalachian Virginia 1776-1927.
P1700 (ASU WCU ETSU LMC)

Government in Virginia.
U510 (LMC)

Road to Revolution; Virginia's Rebels from Bacon to Jefferson, 1676-1776.
W880

POLITICS — W. VA.

The Makers of West Virginia and Their Work.
A2020

"The Granger and Populist Movements in West Virginia, 1873-1914."
B1380

The West Virginia State Grange: The First Century, 1873-1973.
B1390

"Legislative Politics and the Public Schools in West Virginia, 1933-1958: A Twenty-five Year History."
C1900 (ASU BC)

The Lawmaking Process in West Virginia: A Study in Legislative Ethics.
C5560 (LMC)

Pa and Ma and Mister Kennedy.
C6310 (ASU BC)

Uncle Amos, Politician.
C6570 (ASU BC)

"A House Divided: A Study of Statehood Politics and the Copperhead Movement in West Virginia During the Civil War."
C9860

A House Divided: A Study of Statehood Politics and the Copperhead Movement in West Virginia.
C9870 (WCU ETSU ASU BC)

Issues of Constitutional Revision in West Virginia.
D930

West Virginia State and Local Government.
D940 (ETSU BC)

The Primary that Made a President: West Virginia, 1960.
E2110 (ASU)

The History and Government of West Virginia.
F290 (BC)

The Alderson Story; my Life as a Political Prisoner.
F1650

The West Virginia Establishment.
H2350 (ASU)

A Survey of Attitudes and Opinions of Preston County Voters.
H6360

"West Virginia Politics: A Socio-Cultural Analysis of Political Participation."
J1770

West Virginia and its Government.
L190

Loyal W. Va. from 1861 to 1865.
L420

"The West Virginia Statehouse Democratic Machine; Structure, Function and Process."
L480

"The Temperance Movement in West Virginia."
L3030 ·

West Virginia Governors.
M7590

Forty Years Mountain Politics, 1930-1970.
P2260 (ASU LMC MHC WCU)

Coaltown Revisited: An Appalachian Notebook.
P2330 (ASU LMC ETSU WCU WWC BC)

West Virginia and the Captains of Industry: State Politics and the Origins of Modern Appalachia, 1880-1913.
S1620
W3160 (ETSU ASU)

Debates and Proceedings.
W3310 (BC)

State Papers and Public Addresses.
W3950

State papers and public addresses of Clarence Watson Meadows.
W3960

State Papers and Public Addresses of Homer Adams Holt, Twentieth Governor of West Virginia, January 18, 1937 to January 13, 1941.
W3970

State Papers and Public Addresses of Okey L. Patterson, E. Rosalind Carroll Funk.
W3980

State Papers and Public Addresses of William C. Marland, Twenty-Fourth Governor of the State of West Virginia, 1953-1957.
W3990

Manual of the state of West Virginia.
W4290 (BC)

POLITICS — W. VA.
An Inside View of the Formation of the State of West Virginia, with Character Sketches of the Pioneers in that Movement.
W6370 (BC)
"Davis and Elkins of West Virginia: Businessmen in Politics."
W6620
POLLUTION
Proceedings.
A4440
Waste Disposal Costs at Two Coal Mines in Kentucky and Alabama.
D240
POLLUTION — APP.
Full-Scale Study of Dispersion of Stack Gases; a Summary Report.
T5350
Current and Proposed Regulations and Legislation on Air Pollution Concerning the Appalachian Coal Industry.
W7190
POLLUTION — APP. — COAL INDUSTRY
Survey of Sulfur Reduction in Appalachian Coals by Stage Crushing.
D1920
POLLUTION — KY.
The Long-legged House.
B3260 (ASU MHC WCU BC)
Management of Kentucky Natural Resources.
L1900
POLLUTION — N. C.
An Emission Survey and Ambient Air Quality Data of Buncombe, Haywood, Henderson Counties and the City of Asheville.
R1330 (WCU)
POLLUTION — TENN.
"An Analysis of Particulate Pollution in Johnson City and Rural Washington County, Tennessee."
L1400 (ETSU)
"A Determination of Ambient Air Concentrations of Sulfur Dioxide in Elizabethton, Tennessee."
M2480 (ETSU)
POLLUTION — W. VA.
Kanawha Valley Air Pollution Study.
U3640
POPULATION
A2681
A2682 (ASU)
A2683 (ASU)
Appalachia — An Economic Report: Trends in Employment, Income and Population.
A3580 (WCU ASU ETSU)
Appalachia — An Economic Report: Trends in Employment, Income and Population. Supplement.
A3590 (ASU)
Appalachian Data Book.
A3600 (ASU ETSU BC)
Appalachian Data Book.
A3610 (MHC BC ETSU ASU)
A Population and Economic Analysis of the Asheville Metropolitan Area and the Western North Carolina That It Serves.
A5210 (BC)
"Appalachian Fertility Levels and the Role of Interpersonal Relations."
B160
Characteristics of the United States Population by Farm and Nonfarm Origin.
B2240
Recent Population Trends in the United States with Emphasis on Rural Areas.
B2250
The Peopling of Virginia.
B2350 (ASU)
The Peopling of Virginia.
B2360 (FC)
People and Resources in Eastern Kentucky.
B2610
Number of Inhabitants of the Southern Appalachians, 1900-1957.
B2680
Changes in Tennessee Agriculture by Counties, 1954-64.
B5420
Farm Population: Net Migration from the Rural Farm Population, 1940-1950.
B5720
Net Migration of the Population, 1950-1960 by Age, Sex and Color.
B5730
"Household and Family Composition in Selected Rural Areas of Eleven Kentucky Counties."
B5950
The Bedroom of the Poor.
B6880
Basic Population Data for the Southern Appalachians by State, Economic Area, and Metropolitan Area.
B7160
The Changing Kentucky Population: A Summary of Population Data for Counties.
B7170
Rural Population Changes in Five Kentucky Mountain Districts, 1943-1946.
B7200
Southern Appalachian Population Change, 1960-1970: A First Look at the 1970 Census.
B7220 (BC)
Appalachian Fertility Decline: A Demographic and Sociological Analysis.
D1660 (ASU WCU LMC ETSU BC UNCA)
Fertility Data for the Southern Appalachian Region.
D1670
"Human Fertility in the Southern Appalachian Region: Some Demographic and Sociological Aspects."
D1680 (ASU)
The Population of Kentucky: Changes in the Number of Inhabitants, 1950-1960.
D1700
"A Population Study of the Appalachian Members of the Freshman Class at Morehead (Kentucky) State University, 1967-1968."
D3090
Selected Demographic Studies, Knox Co., Ky.
E800
Changing Patterns of Fertility in Tennessee, 1960-1970.
E1940
Johnson City, Tennessee, Population and Economic Base Study.
H5390
Rural Population Density in the Southern Appalachians.
M3350 (ASU)
The Appalachian Region: A Preliminary Analysis of Economic and Population Trends in an Eleven State Problem Area.
M3860 (BC)
Fertility Rates and Migration of Kentucky's Population, 1920-1940.
O1060 (ASU)
"Occupance Formation Concept: A Case Study of the Asheville Basin."
P1990 (LMC)
P4720
The Population and Employment Outlook for the Anthracite Region of Pennsylvania.
R1560
Economic Redevelopment Research: Population, Labor Force and Unemployment in Chronically Depressed Areas.
S1730
"Comparative Study of Related Health Fertility Attitudes and Behavior of Families Residing in a Poverty Area."
S6190
"A Survey of the Attitudes of Women in Monongalia County, West Virginia, toward the Use of Contraceptives."
S9720
Tennessee Manpower: Current Trend and Future Projections.
T1200
Census of Population: 1960. The Eighteenth Decennial Census of the United States.
U460
Fifteenth Census of the United States: 1930.
U470 (BC)
POPULATION — ALA.
Income and Population in Alabama.
H3750 (ASU)
POPULATION — APP.
Our Changing Rural Society — Perspectives and Trends.
C7350
The Appalachian Region: A Preliminary Analysis of Economic and Population Trends in an Eleven State Problem Area.
G4440
"Mothers of the South: A Population Study of Native White Women of Childbearing Age of the Southeast."
H240
Exurban Development in Selected Areas of the Appalachian Mountains.
J1790
Basic Population Data for the Southern Appalachians.
K1420
Warning in Appalachia: A Study of Wirt County, West Virginia.
R1110 (BC ASU WCU LMC MHC)
Selected Rural Counties in Appalachia.
U850
Selected Rural Counties in Appalachia.
U860
POPULATION — FERTILITY DIFFERENTIALS
"An Economic Analysis of Fertility Differentials Among Rural Farm Communities in United States in 1960."
A2250
Contraception and Fertility in the Southern Appalachians.
B2550 (BC ASU)
"Contraception and Fertility in the Southern Appalachians."
B2560
Contraception and Fertility in the Southern Appalachians.
B2570 (LMC)
POPULATION — GA.
Index to the 1830 Census of Georgia.
U660 (ASU)
POPULATION — INDIANS — CHEROKEE
Tribal Enrollment of the Eastern Band of Cherokee Indians, Cherokee, North Carolina.
T8130 (LMC WCU)
POPULATION — KY.
An Urban Development Program for the Big Sandy Area.
A3870
Population Estimates for Kentucky Counties and Economic Area, July 1, 1958.
D250 (ASU)
"The Drain of Talent out of Kentucky."
H2790
Population Growth in Kentucky, 1820-1960.
H5530
Farm Population Changes in Eastern Kentucky.
K930
Tables Showing Components of Population Change and Percent Due to Net Migration for State Economic Areas, Metropolitan Areas, and Counties, Southern Appalachians, 1950-1960.
K940
Utilization of Rural Manpower in Eastern Kentucky.
K950
Resources for Industry.
K1030 (ASU)
Population-Economic Study, Harlan-Harlan County, Kentucky.
K1170
"Metropolitan Dominance and the Diffusion of Human Fertility Patterns, Kentucky, 1939-65."
K3340
Projected Kentucky Population Growth by Age, Sex, and Color Groups: 1960 to 1970.
K3350
Natural Increase and Migration of Kentucky's Population, 1920-1935.
O1070 (ASU)
Neighborhood Standing and Population Changes in Johnson and Robertson Counties.
O1080
The Superfluous People of Hazard, Kentucky.
P1220
"Population Trends and Other Factors Influencing the Voting Habits of the Cumberland Valley Region of Southeast Kentucky."
R1210
Ohio River Valley Population: Trends and Projections, 1930-1970.
S7850

POPULATION — MD.

Heads of Families at the First Census of the United States Taken in the Year 1790: Maryland.
U530 (ASU)

A Census of Pensioners for Revolutionary or Military Services, with Their Names, Ages, and Places of Residence, as Returned by the Marshals of the Several Judicial Districts, under the Act for Taking the Sixth Census in 1840.
U680 (ASU)

POPULATION — N. C.

The Population and Economy of Boone, North Carolina.
C3600 (LMC ASU)

Race Elements in the White Population of North Carolina.
C6750 (ASU BC)

Population and Economy: Marshall, N.C.
N2150 (ASU WCU)

Population and Economy: Valdese, North Carolina.
N2160 (WCU)

1980 Population Projections for North Carolina Counties, with 1950, 1960 and 1970 Population by Age Groups.
P2240

Heads of Families at the First Census of the United States Taken in the Year 1790: North Carolina.
U540 (ASU)

Heads of Families at the First Census of the United States Taken in the Year 1790: North Carolina.
U550 (LMC)

Heads of Families at the First Census of the United States taken in the Year 1790: North Carolina.
U560 (ASU UNCA)

Population Schedules, North Carolina.
U610 (ASU)

Population Schedules, North Carolina.
U620 (ASU)

Population Schedules, North Carolina.
U630 (ASU)

Population Schedules, North Carolina.
U640 (ASU)

Population Schedules, North Carolina.
U670 (ASU)

Population Schedules, North Carolina.
U690 (ASU)

Population Schedules, North Carolina.
U720 (ASU)

Population Schedules, North Carolina.
U790 (ASU)

Population Schedules, North Carolina.
U800 (ASU)

Index to the 1880 Population Schedules, North Carolina.
U810 (ASU)

Population Schedules, North Carolina.
U820 (ASU)

Eastern Band of Cherokees of North Carolina.
U830 (WCU)

Special Schedules Enumerating Union Veterans and Widows of Union Veterans of the Civil War, North Carolina.
U840 (ASU)

POPULATION — PA.

Heads of Families at the First Census of the United States Taken in the Year 1790: Pennsylvania.
U570 (ASU)

POPULATION — S. C.

Heads of Families at the First Census of the United States Taken in the Year 1790: South Carolina.
U590 (ASU)

Heads of Families at the First Census of the United States Taken in the Year 1790: South Carolina.
U600 (ASU LMC)

POPULATION — TENN.

Population Schedule of U. S. Census of 1850 for McMinn County, Tennessee.
B6020 (ASU)

Population Schedule of the United States Census of 1850 for Sullivan County, Tennessee.
B8610 (ETSU)

Selected Population and Agricultural Statistics for Tennessee Counties.
C4870 (ASU)

"Population Migration in the State of Tennessee."
C6120

Comparative Economic Growth Measures — Population and Personal Income Estimates for Tennessee Counties, 1950 Through 1962.
C7590

Johnson City, Tennessee: Population and Economic Base Study.
J1490 (ETSU)

Neighborhood Analyses.
J1530 (ETSU)

The People of Tennessee: A Study of Population Trends.
K2880 (BC ASU WCU)

Population Changes in Tennessee since 1930.
L1940

Human Resources in the Economy of the Upper French Broad Area.
M4310 (LMC)

Population and Labor Force Characteristics of Tennessee Counties.
T1180

Population, Labor Force, and Employment Projections and Interpretations.
T1680

Population and Labor Force Characteristics of Tennessee Counties.
T1800

The Lower Cumberland Region: A Study of Its Population, Economic Base and Potential.
T2100 (ETSU)

United States census 1850 for Knox County, Tennessee.
U520

1830 Census, Tennessee.
U650 (ASU ETSU)

Coffee County, Tennessee, 1850 Census.
U700 (ETSU)

Fentress County, Tennessee, Free Population Schedules.
U710 (ASU)

Population Schedule of the U. S. Census of 1850 (Seventh Census) for McMinn County, Tennessee.
U730 (ASU)

Population Schedule of the United States Census of 1850 (Seventh Census) for Warren County, Tennessee.
U740 (ETSU)

Tennessee Population Schedule of the United States Census of 1850, Meigs County.
U770 (ASU)

United States Census 1850 for Knox County, Tennessee.
U780 (ETSU)

POPULATION — VA.

Index to 1810 Virginia Census.
C8760

Exploring Virginia's Human Resources.
H8120 (ASU BC)

Personal Income Estimates for Virginia Counties and Cities, 1955.
L270

Heads of Families at the First Census of the United States Taken in the Year 1790: Records of the State Enumerations, 1782 to 1785, Virginia.
U580 (ASU LMC)

The Seventh Population Census of the U. S. for Russell County, Va., 1850.
U750

The Seventh Population Census of the United States for Russell County, Virginia, 1850.
U760

POPULATION — W. VA.

West Virginia: Its Farms and Forest, Mines and Oil Wells, with a Glimpse of Its Scenery, a Photograph of Its Population, and an Exhibit of Its Industrial Statistics.
D2690 (BC)

"The Pattern of Settlements in the Southern and Middle Anthracite Region of Pennsylvania."
K220

West Virginia and Her Population.
M8240

Population Changes in West Virginia 1900-1950.
S3800

POTOMAC RIVER

The Floods of March, 1936, Part 3, Potomac, James, and Upper Ohio Rivers.
G4470

The Potomac.
G4940 (FC)

Appalachia Meets the Potomac.
1900

Potomac River Basin Directory.
1910

The Potomac Naturalist: The Natural History of the Headwaters of the Historic Potomac.
S4870 (ASU BC)

Potomac River Basin Report: Summary.
U310

The Nation's River. Official Report on the Potomac from the Department, with Recommendations for Action by the Federal Interdepartmental Task Force on the Potomac.
U2780

Potomac Valley, Model of Scenic and Recreational Values: A Preliminary Report of the Joint Federal-State Planning Team on Landscape and Recreation, Potomac Valley.
U2810

POTTERY

The Moravian Potters in North Carolina.
B4290 (LMC)

Common Clay.
C7980 (LMC ASU WCU)

Pottery Workshop: A Study in the Making of Pottery from Idea to Finished Form.
C8010 (WCU)

The Fire Clays and Fire Clay Industries of the Olive Hill and Ashland Districts of Northeastern Kentucky.
C8780 (BC)

Handicrafts of the Southern Highlands: With an Account of the Rural Handicraft Movement in the United States and Suggestions for the Wider Use of Handicrafts in Adult Education and in Recreation.
E560 (ASU WCU LMC MHC WWC ETSU BC)

"An Assessment of Needs and Guidelines for Development of an Industrial Ceramics Program."
E1440 (ETSU)

Aboriginal Pottery of the Eastern United States.
H6890

American Potters and Pottery.
R230 (BC)

The Shenandoah Pottery.
R1890 (ASU BC)

Clay Deposits and Clay Industry in North Carolina, a Preliminary Report.
R2300 (WCU)

POTTERY — GA.

"Georgia Jug Makers: A History of Southern Folk Pottery."
B9190

POTTERY — N. C.

Traditional Pottery in North Carolina by Bob Conway.
C6810

POVERTY

Factors Associated with the Adjustment of Families in Three Low-Income Counties of North Carolina.
A460 (ASU)

"Factors Associated with the Adjustment of Families in Three Low Income Counties of North Carolina."
A470

"Tuberculosis in Eastern Kentucky."
A820 (ASU)

"Kentucky State Aid and the Educationally Disadvantaged Child."
A1390

Grundy County, Tennessee, Relief in a Coal Mining Community.
A1850

"Public Welfare and Related Problems in Grundy County, Tennessee."
A2180

Seeking More Effective Means to Overcome Poverty: Proceedings.
A2680 (ASU LMC)

In the Midst of Plenty: The Poor in America.
B120 (BC)

"A Case Study of Mingo County Economic Opportunity Commission: The Use of Title II of the Economic Opportunity Act of 1964 in a Rural County in West Virginia."
B1300

POVERTY

The Future of American Poverty, Some Basic Issues in Evaluating Alternative Anti-poverty Measures.
B3240

Poverty in Areas of the United States.
B4060

White Americans in Rural Poverty.
B4070 (ASU)

"Toward a Theory of Training People for the War on Poverty — A Qualitative Comparative Study of Three Antipoverty Training Centers."
B4530

Health and Nutrition in Disadvantaged Children.
C1700

Night Comes to the Cumberlands: Biography of a Depressed Area.
C2230 (ASU MHC WCU ETSU FC UNCA)

Night Comes to the Cumberlands: A Biography of a Depressed Area.
C2240 (LMC)

Sociological Aspects of Poverty, a Bibliography.
C9380

"The Depressed Area Controversy; A Study in the Politics of American Business."
D690 (ASU)

Living Conditions and Population Migration in Four Appalachian Counties.
D2790

A Winner on Satin's Doorstep.
D3370 (BC)

Too Many People, Too Little Love.
D4300

"Political Attitudes of the Poor — An Inquiry into Their Position on a Liberal-Conservative Continuum."
E1520

Employment, Unemployment, and Low Incomes in Appalachia.
F3760 (LMC ASU)

The Great Society's Poor Law, a New Approach to Poverty.
L2020

"The Efficacy of the Labor Migration with Special Emphasis on Depressed Areas."
M4710

Appalachia: Realities of Deprivation.
P60

"The Relation of the Hot Lunch Program to the Progress of Pupils in the Deep Water School, West Virginia."
P2030

Poverty Amid Plenty: The American Paradox.
P4350 (MHC)

Blaming the Victim.
R4500 (WCU BC ASU)

"The Culture of Poverty — A Study of the Value-orientation Preferences of the Chronically Impoverished."
S1030

Human Crisis in the Kingdom of Coal.
S5010 (ASU BC)

"Southern Appalachian State Newspapers' Treatment of the Antipoverty and Appalachia Acts."
T8020

Poverty in the U. S. During the Sixties, a Bibliography.
T8860 (BC)

Examination of the War on Poverty Program.
U3440

Poverty in the United States.
U3450

The people left behind; a report by the President's National Advisory Commission on Rural Poverty.
U3630

A Selective Bibliography of Writings on Poverty in the United States.
U3650

War on Poverty Projects, March 31, 1965.
U3790

War on Poverty Projects, April 30, 1965.
U3800

Rural Poverty in the United States.
U3850

A Selective Bibliography of Writings on Poverty in the United States.
W1030

The Economics of Poverty, an American Paradox.
W2350

"Characteristics of Low Income Rural Families Related to Expenditure and Consumption Patterns: An Analysis of Rural Poverty for Public Program Purposes."
W2410

The Story of Why and How the Leah Weiss Relief Kitchen Became a Landmark in Cincinnati.
W2420 (BC)

Poverty Amid Affluence: Papers.
W4560 (ETSU WCU BC)

An Evaluation of the Impact of the Community Action Program Upon Poverty Conditions in McDowell Co.
W4580

The Landscape of Rural Poverty: Corn Bread and Creek Water.
W7120 (BC)

Design for Action, Community Problem Solving in Disadvantaged Communities.
W8700

Papers.
W9220

POVERTY — APP.

Poverty and Affluence in Appalachia.
C2190

Growing Up Poor: An Over-view and Analysis of Child-rearing and Family Life Patterns Associated with Poverty.
C3860

Summary.
C6350

Poverty and Deprivation in the United States: The Plight of Two-fifths of a Nation.
C6380

Poverty in Plenty.
C6430

Poverty Poems.
C8210 (BC)

Breakthrough to the Great Society.
C8250
E2100

A Guide to Resources for Anti-poverty Programs: A Selected Bibliography.
F500 (ASU)

Poverty in America.
F690

Poverty and Affluence.
F1260

"Health, Education, and Income as Correlates of Demand for Hospital Care in the Southern Mountains."
G1100

The American Serfs.
G2480 (ASU)

The American Serfs.
G2490 (WCU)

Understanding Children of Poverty.
G2860 (WCU BC)

The Other America: Poverty in the United States.
H2620 (MHC BC)

The Case Against Hunger: A Demand for a National Policy.
H6670

War on Poverty.
H8300

Low-income Life Styles.
I930

Mountain Families in Poverty.
J1600

"A Preliminary Edition of a Reading Test For Use With Disadvantaged Children in the Primary Grades of the Southern Appalachian Region."
J2300 (ETSU)

My Colorful Days.
J2530

Seeking More Effective Means to Overcome Poverty.
K200 (ASU)

Poverty Programs and Social Mobility.
K290

Government Against Poverty.
K1680

Poverty and Deprivation in the United States.
K1840

Scouting the War on Poverty: Social Reform Politics in the Kennedy Administration.
K2740

Federal Aid to Depressed Areas — An Evaluation of the Area Redevelopment Association.
L2010 (BC)

Programs in Aid of the Poor.
L2030

Programs in Aid of the Poor for the 1970's.
L2040

Poverty — Its Roots and the Future.
L3940

The Geographic Basis of American Economic Life.
M310 (ASU)

Poverty in the Affluent Society.
M4990

A Summary of a Study of Potential State and Local Programs to Stimulate Low and Moderate-income Housing Construction in Ohio Appalachia.
O370 (ASU)

Roots of Fertility.
P3340

"Public Information and the Community Action Programs of the War on Poverty: The First Three Years."
R3320

Poverty as a Public Issue.
S1800 (BC)

"Training the Poor: A Benefit-cost Analysis of Vocational Instruction in the United States Antipoverty Program."
S2050

Hungry Children: Special Report.
S5870 (ETSU)

Poverty in the Nonmetropolitan South.
T7820 (WWC)

Romantic Appalachia; Or Poverty Pays If You Aren't Poor.
W2980

VISTA: Challenge in Poverty.
W5910

POVERTY — KY.

Night Comes to the Cumberlands: A Biography of a Depressed Area.
C2220 (WWC BC FC)

Poverty, Politics, and Health Care: An Appalachian Experience.
C8060 (ASU)

"Factors That Influence Young Couples to Stay on the Farm in Adair County, Kentucky: Some Social and Economic Factors That Influence Young Couples to Stay on the Farm in a Low-income County in Kentucky."
H1710

Poverty, Rural Poverty and Minority Groups Living in Rural Poverty, an Annotated Bibliography.
I870

Federal Aid in Kentucky.
K1190

Community Action in Appalachia: An Appraisal of the "War on Poverty" in a Rural Setting of Southeastern Kentucky.
K1380

Forms and Scope of Poverty in Kentucky.
R300

POVERTY — N. C.

The Dimensions of Poverty in North Carolina.
B6980

The Dimensions of Poverty in North Carolina.
N2300 (ASU)

POVERTY — PA.

The Low-Income Farmer in a Changing Society.
F1540

POVERTY — RURAL

Economic Provisions for Old Age of Rural Families in Five Southern States.
B170

POVERTY — TENN.

Measurements of Poverty in East Tennessee.
B7320 (ASU BC ETSU LMC)

"Coordination of Anti-poverty Programs in Chattanooga."
D1250

Migration and Level of Living in the Tennessee Valley.
F1680

"The Design and Preparation of a Proposal for Federal Aid for the Education of Children from Low Income Families in Damascus Elementary School, Washington County, Virginia."
H5380 (ETSU)

"The Farmers Home Administration and Agricultural Poverty in Tennessee."
M6450

The Incidence of Poverty — Social and Economic Conditions in Tennessee.
W6600

POVERTY — VA.
The Challenge: Motivating the Poor.
F730
Virginia's Marginal Population — A Study in Rural Poverty.
G420 (BC)
POVERTY — W. VA.
Approaches to University Extension Work with the Rural Disadvantaged: Description and Analysis of a Pilot Effort.
M5970
"A Comparison of the Personal and Economic Characteristics of the Mobile and Immobile."
M6040
POWELL RIVER
Frontier Forts along the Clinch, Powell and Holston.
H1130 (BC)
Clinch-Powell Valley; Summary of Resources.
T2420
PROVERBS
Pioneer Proverbs; Wit and Wisdom From Early America.
T9830
PSYCHOLOGICAL EFFECTS — MIGRATION
"A Comparative Analysis of the Felt Need Pattern of the Personality Structure in Rural Appalachia and Suburban America."
S3400 (ETSU)
PSYCHOLOGICAL EFFECTS — POVERTY
"A Comparative Analysis of the Felt Need Pattern of the Personality Structure in Rural Appalachia and Suburban America."
S3400 (ETSU)
PUBLIC HEALTH — APP.
R4310 (ASU BC)
PUBLIC HEALTH — N. C.
Biennial report.
N1690 (ASU LMC)
A History of the North Carolina State Board of Health, 1877-1925.
N1700 (LMC)
PUBLIC — N. C.
Biennial Report.
N2580 (LMC)
PUBLIC SCHOOLS
Standards for Schoolhouse Construction Approved by the State Board of Education.
W3320 (ETSU)
PUBLIC WELFARE
Grundy County, Tennessee, Relief in a Coal Mining Community.
A1850
"Public Welfare and Related Problems in Grundy County, Tennessee."
A2180
Southern Appalachian Migrant on Public Aid in Cook County.
C6820 (ASU)
A Study of Families from the Southern Appalachian Region Receiving Public Assistance.
C6830 (ASU)
Welfare Work in Mill Villages, the Story of Extra-mill Activities in North Carolina.
H4990 (WWC)
Muscle Shoals and the Public Welfare.
O960
PUBLIC WELFARE — APP.
Low-income Life Styles.
I930
PUBLIC WELFARE — KY.
I860
PUBLIC WELFARE — N. C.
Research and Regional Welfare.
C5640 (ASU)
D2500 (UNCA)
"Public Policy for Depressed Areas with Special Reference to North Carolina."
F1630
PUBLIC WELFARE — W. VA.
Digest of Programs Containing Federal Funds in W. Va.
W3530
PUBLIC WORKS
Public Improvements for the City of Berea, Ky.
B3130 (BC)
The North Carolina Chain Gang: A Study of County Convict Road Work.
S6920 (LMC)
The North Carolina Chain Gang: A Study of County Convict Road Work.
S6930 (WWC)

QUILTING
American Patchwork Quilts.
B70 (ASU)
Kentucky Coverlets.
B5660 (BC)
Old Patchwork Quilts and the Women Who Made Them.
F1040 (BC)
Patchwork for Beginners.
G3660 (ASU)
The Romance of the Patchwork Quilt in America: In Three Parts.
H590 (ASU BC)
The Standard Book of Quilt Making and Collecting.
I30 (ASU BC)
The Mountain Artisans Quilting Book.
L2060 (BC ASU LMC)
One Hundred and One Patchwork Patterns: Quilt Name Stories, Cutting Designs, Material Suggestions, Yardage Estimates, Definite Instructions for Every Step of Quilt Making.
M1880 (ASU WCU BC)
North Carolina Museum of History, Raleigh.
N2010 (ASU)
Artistry in Quilts.
N2470 (ASU)
O680 (ASU)
American Quilts and Coverlets; A History of a Charming Native Art.
P2390
Mountain Artisans: An Exhibit of Patchwork and Quilting, Appalachia.
R1820 (BC)
America's Quilts and Coverlets.
S70 (ASU)
America's Quilts and Coverlets.
S80 (ASU)
Old Fashioned Quilts.
S2060
Introducing Quilting.
S3180 (ASU)
Quilts: Their Story and How to Make Them.
W2130 (ASU)
Quilts: Their Story and How to Make Them.
W2140 (BC)
RACE RELATIONS
The Children of the South.
A2310
The Negro in the Bituminous Coal Mining Industry.
B1400 (WCU BC MHC)
Neither Black nor White.
D4240 (ASU WWC ETSU BC)
RACE RELATIONS — ALA.
"A Study of the Progress of Negro Education in Saint Clair County, Alabama."
C1750
"Factors Contributing to the Educational Development of the Negro Schools in the Jefferson County (Alabama) School System, 1945-51."
G1950
"A Study of the Causes of Drop-outs and Irregular Attendance among Boys in the Four Negro High Schools of Talledega County, Alabama."
G2040
"A Study of the Changes in the Educational Levels of the Negro Teachers in Jefferson County, Alabama, 1930-50."
M6280
RACE RELATIONS — APP.
Authentic History of Ku Klux Klan, 1865-1877.
D1240 (LMC)
Berea College from Servitude to Service, Being the Old South Lectures on the History and Work of the Negro.
F3560 (BC)
"Negro Life in a Rural Community."
K2380
RACE RELATIONS — KY.
Kentucky's Black Heritage.
K980 (BC ETSU)
RACE RELATIONS — N. C.
"A History of Negro Education in Wilkes County, North Carolina."
I820
The Negro in North Carolina, 1876-1894.
L3060 (LMC)

"An Analysis of the Types of Retardation in the Elementary Departments of Fine Negro Union Schools in Rural Cleveland County."
L3200
Equal Protection of the Laws in North Carolina.
U1630 (LMC)
RACE RELATIONS — TENN.
"The Negro in East Tennessee."
B210 (ASU)
Three Generations: The Story of a Colored Family of Eastern Tennessee.
C1110 (ASU LMC BC)
Echo in My Soul.
C4530 (BC)
The Emancipator.
E1900 (ASU)
Gemini.
G1840
Clinton, Tennessee: A Tentative Description and Analysis of the School Desegregation Crisis.
H6470
Diary of a Sit-in.
P4750 (WCU ETSU)
RACE RELATIONS — VA.
"School Desegregation in Warren County, Virginia, During 1958-1960; A Study in the Mobilization of Restraints."
L2050
RACE RELATIONS — W. VA.
"Segration Patterns in a Coal Camp."
F3220 (ASU)
"The Negro Miner in West Virginia."
L130
"The Negro in West Virginia Before 1900."
S2610
RAPPAHANNOCK RIVER
My Rappahannock Storybook.
H6060 (BC ASU)
Fredericksburg, Virginia. Its Homes and History, the Battlefields and the Rappahanrock Valley.
G2650
READING
"The Reading Habits of 200 Adults in Kingsport, Tennessee."
E990
RECLAMATION
A Revised Bibliography of Strip Mine Reclamation.
F3840 (ASU)
Operation Scarlift, the After-Effects of Over 100 Years of Coal Mining In Pennsylvania and Current Programs to Combat Them.
P1800
RECLAMATION — KY.
Surface Mining and Reclamation in Kentucky.
K1180
Strip Mining.
K1290
RECLAMATION — OHIO
Comparative State Strip Mining and Reclamation Laws.
O390
RECREATION
Applications of the Common Mooring: Fundamental Principles in the Utilization of Resources.
A630
"A Study of the Effect of Participation in Football on the Grades of Students at Bristol, Tennessee, High School."
A1420 (ETSU)
"Leisure Time Interests and Activities of Girls in High School."
A2270
"An Evaluation of the Physical Education Programs in the High Schools in the Washington County School System."
A2330 (ETSU)
"An Examination of the Leisure Activities and Recreational Interests of Students, and Available Equipment and Facilities at Appalachian State Teachers College."
C580 (ASU)
Managing 10,000 Miles of Shoreline.
C670
"An Evaluation of the Community Service or Continuing Education Project: Developing and Stimulating Recreation in Six Counties of Eastern Kentucky."
C2910

RECREATION
The Effect of Modern Dance Upon Strength and Flexibility in Selected College Students.
P2610 (ASU)
"Coordination of Physical Education and Community Recreation in Ashe, Avery, and Watauga Counties."
Q170 (ASU)
"Recreational Habits of Rural Youth in Selected Communities of Hamilton County, Tennessee."
S990
Extent of Recreation Development and Use of TVA Lakes and Actual Lake Frontage Property.
T2630
Fish and Fishing, Fort Loudoun Reservoir.
T2720
The Witchery of Archery.
T8290 (ASU)

RECREATION AND TOURISM
The Appalachian National Parks; an Analysis of Work Accomplished, November 1899 up to Aug. 30, 1901.
A3340
Southern Pictures and Pencilings: Official Organ of the Appalachian National Park Association.
A3350
Appalachian Highlands Recreation Study, Phase I, Inventory and Analysis.
A3630 (ASU)
"A Study of the Intramural Sports Program in George W. Vance Junior High School, Bristol, Tennessee."
B1770 (ETSU)
The Travel Industry in North Carolina.
B2370 (LMC)
Income Opportunities for Rural Families from Outdoor Recreation Enterprises.
B4110
C1000 (BC)
Canoeing White Water: A Guide Book to the Rivers of Virginia and Eastern West Virginia, The Great Smoky Mountain Area.
C1740 (LMC)
Games of the North American Indians. 24th Annual Report of the Bureau of American Ethnology to the Secretary of the Smithsonian Institute.
C9400 (LMC)
Hiker's Guide.
S5430 (ASU)
Outdoor Recreation for a Growing Nation; TVA's Experience With Man-Made Reservoirs.
T3150
Recreation Areas on TVA Lakes.
T3320
Recreation Areas on TVA Lakes.
T3330
. . . Recreation Development of the Tennessee River System.
T3340
Recreation & Tourism Develop. Through Federal Programs.
U200
Watauga Lake recreation areas, Cherokee National Forest, Tennessee.
U3000
Report, V. 2: Ten Rivers in America's Future.
U3860
W. Va. in color.
W3210 (BC)
Wonderful West Virginia.
W3590
State Park Series. Bulletin.
W3900 (ETSU)
West Virginia Highway Markers, Historic, Prehistoric, Scenic, Geologic.
W4060 (ASU)
Scenery: "Land of the Sky."
W4940 (BC)

RECREATION AND TOURISM — ALA.
Stars Fell on Alabama.
C1290 (BC)
Tourist and Recreation Potential: Lewis Smith Lake (Cullman, Walker and Winston Counties, Alabama).
U1540 (LMC)

RECREATION AND TOURISM — APP.
The Southern Highlands, an Inquiry into their Needs, and Qualifications Desired in Service Workers in the Mountain Country.
C6360
D2490 (ASU)
Roaming the Eastern Mountains.
F140 (ASU BC)
Seeing the Sunny South.
F150 (ASU LMC BC)
Bubbling Waters.
F1070 (ASU LMC BC)
"Economic Development of Areas Contiguous to Multipurpose Reservoirs: The Kentucky-Tennessee Experience."
H2220 (BC)
Romance of the National Parks.
J350 (ASU)
Private Outdoor Recreation Enterprises in Rural Appalachia.
J1800
Camping and Woodcraft: A Handbook for Vacation Campers and for Travelers in the Wilderness.
K1460 (ASU)
Recreation as an Industry in Appalachia.
N120 (ASU WCU)
Planning a Tourist Recreation Region for the Age of Leisure. Printed by Planning and Land Use Education Program, Appalachian State Univ., 1974.
N890 (ASU)
Tennessee Valley, a Recreation Domain.
N1230
Recreation Impact on Southern Appalachian Campgrounds and Picnic Sites.
R2350 (WCU)
Tenn. Valley Land and Its Changing Use.
S150
A Geographical Analysis of Selected Ski Resorts in the Southeastern United States.
T2190 (ASU)
The Land Between the Lakes; A Demonstration in Recreation Resource Development; Revised Concept Statement.
T3010
Non-Urban Outdoor Recreation, an Analysis of Its Functions, Forms, and Types of Areas.
T3110
Recreational Development of the Southern Highlands Region, A Study of the Use and Control of Scenic and Recreational Resources.
T3350 (ASU)
Recreational Development of the Southern Highlands Region; A Study of the Use and Control of Scenic and Recreational Resources.
T4290 (LMC)
Social and Economic Characteristics of Six Tennessee Valley Reservoir Areas.
T4330 (BC)
Recreation Maps — Tennessee Valley Lakes.
T7490
A Report on Outdoor Recreation Demand, Supply, and Needs in Appalachia.
U1510
National parks in southern Appalachian Mountains.
U1710
Appalachian Mountains.
U1850
Preliminary report of investigations upon forest of Southern Appalachian region.
U1860
Rural Recreation Enterprises for Profit: An Aid to Rural Areas Development.
U2550
Potomac Valley, Model of Scenic and Recreational Values: A Preliminary Report of the Joint Federal-State Planning Team on Landscape and Recreation, Potomac Valley.
U2810
Recreation Potential in the Appalachian Highlands: A Market Analysis.
U4220 (ASU)

RECREATION AND TOURISM — GA.
Highlights of the Economy of the Georgia Mountains Area.
G1010 (BC ASU)
The Georgia Travel Industry, 1960-1963.
K410
A Study of Out-of-State Requests for Travel Information from the State of Georgia.
K420
Tourism Development in the Chattahoochee-Flint Area.
K430
The Georgia Mountains: A View of Its Resources, Problems, and Potentials.
S1120 (ASU LMC)
Highlights of the Economy of the Georgia Mountains Area.
W5510

RECREATION AND TOURISM — KY.
Tourist and Recreation Facility Survey of Nine Counties in Southeastern Kentucky.
H6810
Travel in Kentucky.
K1200
Kentucky Tourist Preferences.
K1370
Tour. & Recreation Potential E. Ky.
U1520
Kentucky: A Guide to the Bluegrass State.
W9590 (ASU LMC)

RECREATION AND TOURISM — MD.
Blue Ridge Voyages: One and Two Day River Cruises. Pennsylvania, Maryland, Virginia, West Virginia.
C7360 (LMC)

RECREATION AND TOURISM — N. C.
The Village of Five Lives: The Fontana of the Great Smoky Mountains.
B5960 (ASU BC LMC WCU)
Glimpses of a Land of Beauty.
C400
Exploring the Mountains of North Carolina.
C1250 (MHC)
C6030 (LMC)
Travel Industry in North Carolina. An Economic Survey.
C7320
Master Plan for Recreation and Parks: Jackson County, North Carolina.
G300 (WCU)
Souvenir Views of the Beautiful Blowing Rock Region.
H2180
Outdoor Recreation Potential Appraisal.
J30 (WCU)
The Lenoir-Blowing Rock Wonderland.
L1760 (ASU)
Valhalla in the Smokies.
M4580 (ETSU ASU BC)
Scenic Western North Carolina, a Vacation Guide to the Highlands.
M8520 (ASU)
Planning a Tourist Recreation Region for the Age of Leisure. Printed by Planning and Land Use Education Program, Appalachian State Univ., 1974.
N890 (ASU)
Proceedings of the Third Annual Workshop on the Third Annual Workshop on the Planning and Utilization of Leisure Resources, March 18-19.
N1620 (ASU)
Road Maps and Tour Book of Western North Carolina.
N2370 (BC ASU LMC)
Pearson's Falls Glen: Its Story, Its Flora, Its Birds.
P1420 (WWC)
Western North Carolina Facts, Figures, Photographs.
P4210 (LMC WCU)
"The Economic Impact of Recreation Resort Development on the Local Economy: A Case Study of Avery County, North Carolina."
R3580 (LMC)
Tourist and Recreation Potential: Western North Carolina.
U1560
North Carolina, a Guide to the Old North State.
W9620 (ASU)
The North Carolina Guide.
W9630 (ASU)

RECREATION AND TOURISM — PA.
Blue Ridge Voyages: One and Two Day River Cruises. Pennsylvania, Maryland, Virginia, West Virginia.
C7360 (LMC)
A Traveler's Guide to Historic Western Pennsylvania.
M8490 (ASU)
"Promotion of the Recreational Use of State Forests, with Special Reference to Pennsylvania."
S1480

RECREATION AND TOURISM — S. C.
South Carolina: A Guide to the Palmetto State.
W9650 (ASU BC)
RECREATION AND TOURISM — TENN.
Estimating Tennessee's Tourist Business.
C7290 (ASU)
Tourists and the Travel Service and Transportation Business in Tennessee, 1948 to 1961, Inclusive, an Economic Analysis.
C7310
C9420
Outdoors in the Cumberlands.
C9450 (BC)
D2480 (ETSU)
The Story of Gatlinburg.
G4040
G4640 (ASU)
"Diversions in East Tennessee, 1920-25."
G4830 (ETSU)
People's Shorelines. Address before Tennessee Public Power Association, Nashville, Tennessee, April 15-18, 1958.
H7740
Planning for Recreation Use of Impounded Waters — TVA Experience.
H7750
Chattanooga.
J290
Valhalla in the Smokies.
M4580 (ETSU ASU BC)
Eliza Ross; or, Illustrated Guide of Lookout Mountain.
M4910
"Resources for Physical Recreation in the Tennessee Valley Authority Region."
M4960
"A Study of the Effect of Participation in Athletics on the Grades of Students at East Tennessee State College."
M7920 (ETSU)
Multiple-use on Norris Watershed.
N1510
Recreation Grows Up in the Tennessee Valley.
O560
Tourist and Recreation Potential: Upper Cumberland Lakes Area of Tennessee (Clay, Dekalb, Jackson, Overton, Pickett, Smith, and Warren Counties).
U1550
An Appraisal of Potentials for Outdoor Recreational Development in Fort Worth.
U3920
Tennessee, a Guide to the State.
W9670 (ASU)
Tennessee: A Guide to the State.
W9680 (ASU LMC)
RECREATION AND TOURISM — VA.
Blue Ridge Voyages: One and Two Day River Cruises. Pennsylvania, Maryland, Virginia, West Virginia.
C7360 (LMC)
Bits of History and Legends Around and About the Natural Bridge of Virginia, 1730-1950.
D1080 (ASU)
Bits of History and Legends around and about the Natural Bridge of Virginia from 1730-1950.
D1090 (BC)
D2480 (ETSU)
N260
The Shenandoah and Its Byways.
S7150 (ASU BC)
The Natural Bridge and Its Historical Surroundings.
T8880 (ASU FC BC)
Establishment of Mount Rogers National Recreation Area in Virginia.
U2080
Va's Common Wealth, a Study at Va.'s Outdoor Recreation Resources.
V1140
Travel in Virginia, Its Economic Significance.
V1200
Scenic and Historical Guide to the Shenandoah Valley.
W1680
Scenic and Historical Guide to the Shenandoah Valley: A Handbook of Useful Information for Tourists and Students.
W1820 (WCU)
Roanoke, Story of County and City.
W9690 (ASU BC)
Virginia: A Guide to the Old Dominion.
W9700 (BC)
Virginia: A Guide to the Old Dominion.
W9710 (ASU)
Virginia: The Old Dominion in Pictures.
W9720 (BC)
RECREATION AND TOURISM — W. VA.
Blue Ridge Voyages: One and Two Day River Cruises. Pennsylvania, Maryland, Virginia, West Virginia.
C7360 (LMC)
An Analysis of Some Selected Characteristics of Cabin Vacationists in West Virginia State Parks and Forests in 1961.
H40 (ASU)
West Virginia Travel and Tourism Study — The Potential Market.
H70
Youth Recreation in the Coal Mining Towns of West Virginia.
H6590
Huntington's Park System and Recreational Facilities.
H8490
"West Virginia's Program of State Publicity."
I1020
Outdoor Recreation Potential in West Virginia's Eastern Panhandle.
M7820
West Virginia Travel and Tourism Study: An Evaluation.
S960
Tourist and Recreation Potential: Eastern Panhandle Area, West Virginia (Grant, Hardy, Hampshire, Mineral, and Morgan Counties).
U1530
Establishment of Spruce Knob-Seneca Rocks National Recreation Area in West Virginia. Report from the Committee to Accompany H. R. 10330, August 31, 1965.
U2090
S. 7, Act to Provide for the Establishment of Spruce Knob-Seneca Rocks National Recreation Area in West Virginia, and for Other Purposes. Approved September 28, 1965.
U3540
West Virginia: A Guide to the Mountain State.
W9770 (ASU BC WWC ETSU)
RECREATION AND TRAVEL — N. C.
Proceedings.
F1780 (WCU)
RECREATION — APP.
Annual Report, 1958 and 1959.
T5220
Fish and Wildlife, Valuable Natural Resources.
T5270
RECREATION — N. C.
The Red Strings Baseball Team of Yadkin County, N. C., 1896-1902.
D4000
RECREATION — TENN.
East Tennessee State University Basketball Press Guide. --.
E350 (ETSU)
East Tennessee State University Track and Field School Records, Together with ETSU Field Records for College Meets.
E400 (ETSU)
RECREATION — TOURISM — TENN.
Guide to the Summer Resorts and Watering Places of East Tennessee.
E470
RECREATION — W. VA.
Wild Water West Virginia: A Paddler's Guide to the White Water Rivers of the Mountain State.
B9180 (ASU BC)
"The Leisure Time Activities and Interests of the Boys of Spencer High School."
H280
RED RIVER
The Unforseen Wilderness: An Essay on Kentucky's Red River Gorge.
B3300 (ASU BC LMC)
Fishes of the Red River Drainage, Eastern Kentucky.
B6360
RED RIVERS
Red River Iron Works.
J1200
REGIONAL DEVELOPMENT
. . . The Wheeler Project, A Comprehensive Report on the Planning, Design, Construction, and Initial Operations of the Wheeler Project . . .
T4090
Major Freight Terminals on the Tennessee River Waterway.
T7440
REGIONAL DEVELOPMENT — ALA.
The Guntersville Project. A Comprehensive Report on the Planning, Design, Construction, and Initial Operations of the Guntersville Project . . .
T2860 (BC)
REGIONAL DEVELOPMENT — APP.
"Why Aid Doesn't Help: Organizing for Community Economic Development in Central Appalachia."
T9690
REGIONAL DEVELOPMENT — KY.
Development Potentials for Kentucky Counties with Related Statistics.
K1360 (ASU)
New Towns for the Appalachian Regions: A Case Study Located in Eastern Kentucky.
K1400
REGIONAL DEVELOPMENT — N. C.
E780 (ASU)
U4150
REGIONAL PLANNING
"A Study of Effect of Government Aid and Other Factors on the Economic Development of Three Selected Areas in Georgia."
A340
A2660 (BC)
The Emerging Pattern of Appalachian Regional Development.
A2720
Appalachian Highlands Recreation Study, Phase I, Inventory and Analysis.
A3630 (ASU)
A Bibliography of Research Studies Produced with Appalachian Regional Development Program Funds.
A3690
Capitalizing on New Development Opportunities along the Baltimore-Cincinnati Appalachian Development Highway: A Staff Recommendation.
A3700 (ASU)
State and Regional Development Plans in Appalachia.
A3830 (ASU)
Rural Development Problems and Prospects in Fayette, Raleigh, and Summers Counties, West Virginia.
A4640
Community Action for Social Redevelopment in Asheville and Buncombe County.
A5200 (WWC)
The Industrial Development Program of North Carolina, 1954 to 1962, with Projections to 1970.
B4450
Region Building: Community Development Lessons from the Tennessee Valley.
D40 (ASU)
Annual Report for 1964.
E540
New York State Appalachian Development Plan; A Twenty Year Plan for the Fourteen Counties of the New York Appalachian Region.
N700
The Political Economy of Appalachia; A Case Study in Regional Integration.
N780 (BC WWC ASU ETSU MHC WCU)
The Spatial Concentration of Industry in Appalachia: An Analysis of the Potential for Import Substitution.
S490 (ASU ETSU)
Suggestion for Planning and Zoning in Appalachia.
S5410
Charleston, W. Va.: Dept. of Planning, Commerce, Research Div.
W4230
Horizon Committee on Capital and Finance — Capital and Finance for Development.
W4260
Horizon Committee on Human Resources. The Development of W. Va.'s Human Resources.
W4270

REGIONAL PLANNING
Horizon Committee on Natural Resources. The Development of W. Va.'s Natural Resources.
W4280
REGIONAL PLANNING — ALA.
Appalachian Alabama: Development Plan — 1970.
A870 (ASU)
REGIONAL PLANNING — APP.
A2771 (ASU)
Appalachian Research Reports.
A3660 (ASU WCU)
Preliminary Analysis for Development of Central Appalachia, Kentucky, Tennessee, Virginia, West Virginia.
A3780
Summary.
C6350
Report.
C6370
Papers.
C6470 (ASU)
"The Depressed Area Controversy; A Study in the Politics of American Business."
D690 (ASU)
"Local Government Social Overhead Expenditures and Economic Growth in the Appalachian Region."
D2450
Regional Development and Planning: A Reader.
F3320 (ASU)
"The Effects of Environment on Public Planning: The Case of Appalachian Planning in Tennessee."
G470 (LMC)
Underemployment Concept, Way to Measure Need for Economic Development in Appalachia.
G1260
The Development Index for 60 Counties in Central Appalachia.
G2890 (ASU BC)
Proceedings.
G2980 (ASU BC)
Seeking More Effective Means to Overcome Poverty.
K200 (ASU)
"Measuring and Analyzing the Impact of Employment Generation Benefits of a Public Water Resource Development Project in Appalachia."
K2050
State Planning and Economic Development in the South.
L1850
Joint Reports.
N240
Appalachia: A Case Study of Regional Business Development.
O430
"The State Development Planning Process: Implementation of the Appalachian Regional Development Act of 1965 in West Virginia."
P850
Guidelines for an Appalachian Airport System.
P2050 (ASU WCU)
Program Budgeting for Planners; A Case Study of Appalachia With Projections Through 1985.
R4040
"The Appalachian Regional Commission: Selected Aspects of Institutions and Processes and Their Relationship to Natural and Human Resources Development."
S40
Economic Redevelopment Research: Population, Labor Force and Unemployment in Chronically Depressed Areas.
S1730
"George W. Norris and the Concept of a Planned Region."
S4350
A Model for Sequencing Public Investment Programs and Allocating Multiprogram Benefits.
S6250
Southern Highlands Mountain Resources Management Plan, Vols. I and II.
T9390
Planning for the South, an Inquiry into the Economics of Regionalism.
V420 (ASU)
REGIONAL PLANNING — APP. — N. C.
Updated Investment Guidelines for North Carolina Appalachian Region 1971 to 1975, and A Plan for Public Investment in Appalachian North Carolina, Fiscal 1971.
A3880
REGIONAL PLANNING — APP. — N. Y.
Abstract of the New York State Appalachian Program: A Development Plan.
A3530
A Report on the Identification of Areas of Potential Growth in the Appalachian Region of New York State and a General Development Philosophy for the Region.
A3810
REGIONAL PLANNING — GA.
The Economic Development of the Northeast Georgia Commission Area Through Use of Forest Products and Water Resources.
B7120 (ASU ETSU)
A Preliminary Major Highway Plan, A Part of the Georgia Mountains Region Development Program.
T9130
REGIONAL PLANNING — KY.
"An Application of the Leontief Regional Model: An Input-output Analysis for Eastern Kentucky."
B490
Communication and Mountain Development: A Summary Report Two East Kentucky Studies.
B5780
Proceedings. The Planning Concept.
C6420
A Decade of Action for Progress in Kentucky.
E520 (ASU)
Commonwealth of Kentucky Planning Inventory.
S6210
Commonwealth of Kentucky Program Planning Communication & Coordination (P2C2): A Preliminary System Design.
S6220
Goals, Objectives, and Policies.
S6230
Kentucky Public Library Inventory and Projected Needs.
S6240
An Urban Development Program for the Big Sandy Area.
S6260 (ASU)
REGIONAL PLANNING — N. C.
Overall Economic Development Program for Avery County.
A5790 (LMC)
Water Resource Needs for Selected Development Corridors in Appalachian North Carolina.
N2630 (ASU)
Today and Tomorrow, Murphy, North Carolina.
W4930 (LMC)
REGIONAL PLANNING — PA.
Preliminary Over-all Economic Development Program for the North-western Pennsylvania Redevelopment Area.
K300
An Economic Background for Regional Planning in the Anthracite Counties.
P1860
A Rationale for Public Investment in Appalachia Pennsylvania: An Interim Statement.
P1890
REGIONAL PLANNING — TENN.
Report.
H1410 (ETSU)
Johnson City Shopping Center District Regulations.
J1480 (ETSU)
Johnson City, Tennessee: Population and Economic Base Study.
J1490 (ETSU)
Johnson City's Community Facilities.
J1500 (ETSU)
Land Use Analysis.
J1510 (ETSU)
Land Use Plan.
J1520 (ETSU)
Neighborhood Analyses.
J1530 (ETSU)
Subdivision Regulations of Johnson City Regional Planning Commission.
J1540 (ETSU)
Organization for Watershed Planning in the Public Interest.
L3760
Soil and Sky; the Development and Use of Tennessee Valley Resources.
S470
Tennessee Appalachian Development Plan, 1969-1970.
T1600 (ASU)
Policy Conclusions, Problems and Opportunities.
T1670
REGIONAL PLANNING — VA.
Development Potentials For Kentucky Counties With Related Statistics
F3770
REGIONAL PLANNING — W. VA.
"A Regional Linear Programming Model of the West Virginia Economy."
C5370
Status of West Virginia in the Economic Opportunity Program Under Public Law 88-452.
C8540
C8810 (ASU WCU BC)
"The Transformation of the Tug and Guyandot Valleys: Economic Development and Social Change in West Virginia, 1888-1921."
C9390
"Patterns of Development and Net Migration, 1960-1970: A Study of West Virginia Counties."
D1760
Statewide Development Planning for West Virginia — A Prospectus for Implementation Under Provisions of Section 701 of the Housing Act of 1954.
D4140
Program 60, 1960-70; a Decade of Action for Progress in Eastern Kentucky.
E530 (BC)
Professional Overall Economic Development for Fayette Co., West Virginia.
F400
West Virginia Housing. A Consultant's Report to the Governor's Task Force on Housing and the West Virginia State Development Plan.
G30
Economic Stability and Growth Potential, Fairmont, W. Va.
H2230
"Governmental Assistance to Industrial Development in West Virginia."
K1870
"The State Development Planning Process: Implementation of the Appalachian Regional Development Act of 1965 in West Virginia."
P850
Coal, The Curse and the Key: Overall Economic Development Program for the Southern West Virginia Economic Development District.
S5890
Guiding Principles for Rural Development in West Virginia.
S7290
Economic Development in West Virginia.
Z60
RELIGION AND RELIGIOUS BODIES — TENN.
"The Status and Problems of the Ministry in Knox County."
H8320
RELIGION AND RELIGIOUS BODIES
Religion in Shoes.
B4540 (BC)
The Great Revival, 1787-1805: The Origins of the Southern Evangelical Mind.
B5130 (ASU BC)
"Religious Concerns of Southern Appalachian Migrants in a North Central City."
C9760
"The Music of American Revivalism."
D3180 (WCU)
H5980
"Unfinished Tasks" of the Southern Presbyterian church.
M2290
O480 (ASU)
Frontier Mission: A History of Religion West of the Southern Appalachians to 1861.
P3740 (BC WWC)
Torchlights to the Cherokee: The Brainerd Mission.
W350 (ASU ETSU BC)
History of the Church of the Redeemer, Shelby, N. C., 1858-1958.
W460

RELIGION AND RELIGIOUS BODIES

Life and Religion in Southern Appalachia, an Interpretation of Selected Data from the Southern Appalachian Studies.
W1920 (ASU MHC WCU LMC ETSU WWC BC UNCA)

Religion in the Appalachian Mountains: A Symposium.
W1940 (ASU BC)

One Hundred Years: A Story of the First Baptist Church, Clinton, Tennessee.
W2000

Twenty Years on Horseback.
W2240 (BC)

. . . Church and State in North Carolina.
W2270 (BC)

The Religious Development in the Province of North Carolina.
W2280 (LMC WWC UNCA)

In the Land of Mudholes and Mountains; a Story of Three Years' Missionary Work in the Cumberland Mountains.
W2340 (BC)

Alexander Campbell and Natural Religion.
W3100 (BC)

Hills of Home.
W7730

Shunem Church and Cemetery Speak: A Living Memorial to Those Who Sleep Here, 1824-1965.
W8610

Culture and Personality Aspects of the Pentecostal Holiness Religion.
W8690 (ASU)

A History of the Presbytery of Winchester (Synod of Virginia): Its Rise and Growth, Ecclesiastical Relations, Institutions, Agencies, Churches and Ministers, 1719-1945.
W8980 (ASU BC)

Centennial of the First Presbyterian Church, United States, in Cleveland, Tennessee, 1837-1937.
W9110

The Shepherd of the Hills.
W9410 (ASU)

Springplace: Moravian Mission and the War Family of the Cherokee Nation.
W9500 (MHC)

Pennsylvania Spirituals.
Y100 (ASU)

History of the First Presbyterian Church, Sweetwater, Tennessee, 1860-1960.
Y240

Autobiography of a Pioneer: Or, The Nativity, Experience, Travels, and Ministerial Labors of Rev. Jacob Young, with Incidents, Observations, and Reflections.
Y260 (BC)

A Baptist Looks Back: The Origin and Early History of Roan Mountain Baptist Association, Now Mitchell Baptist Association.
Y270 (ASU WCU LMC BC)

RELIGION AND RELIGIOUS BODIES — ALABAMA — CUMBERLAND PRESBYTERIAN

Historical Contributions.
C9430

RELIGION AND RELIGIOUS BODIES — APP.

A5440 (BC)

Church Life in the Rural South: A Study of the Opportunity of Protestantism Based Upon Data From Seventy Counties.
B7740 (ASU BC)

The Failure and the Hope: Essays of Southern Churchmen.
C980 (WCU ASU BC)

Up to Our Steeples in Politics.
C990 (WCU BC)

The Small Sects in America.
C4420 (ASU)

The Small Sects in America.
C4430

Church and Family in Modern Rural Appalachia.
C4860 (ASU)

The Great Revival in the West, 1797-1805.
C4950

The Great Revival in the West, 1797-1805.
C4960 (ASU)

The Thrones of the Apostles, a Study of the Pentecostal Phenomena.
C5550 (BC)

CORA: Our Christian Commitment in Appalachia.
C6180

Directory of Appalachian Mission Enterprises.
C6190 (BC)

Proceedings: A United Approach to Fulfilling the Church's Mission in Appalachia.
C6210 (ASU WCU)

The Mountain Preacher.
D1070 (BC)

The Protestant Church as a Social Institution.
D3130

Christian Reconstruction in the South.
D3140

Life of S. Miller Willis
D3960 (BC)

A Church Census of the 134 Churches in the City of Knoxville, Tennessee as of Date January 31, 1925.
E870

A List of Emigrant Ministers to America, 1690-1811.
F2380 (ASU)

How Churches Fight Poverty, 60 Successful Local Projects.
G3890 (ASU LMC WCU)

Memoirs of the Life and Gospel Labours of Stephen Grellet.
G4030 (ASU)

The Gatherers: The Gospel among the Highlanders.
G4610 (ASU LMC)

The Gospel of the Lilies.
G4620 (BC)

"Sectarianism and Social Participation: A Study of the Relationship between Religious Attitudes and Involvement in Voluntary Organizations in Seventy-two Churches in the Southern Appalachian Mountains."
H3220 (LMC)

Appalachian Shepherd: A Story of Religion in the Southern Appalachians.
H4590 (BC ASU LMC ETSU FC WWC)

Tales of a Frontier Preacher.
H5330

Southern Churches in Crisis.
H5480 (WCU WWC)

Religion in the Highlands: Native Churches and Missionary Enterprises in the Southern Appalachian Area.
H7030 (WWC ASU BC)

The Church's Mission to the Mountaineers of the South.
H8150

"Religious Beliefs and Social Status: A Study of the Relationships between Religious Beliefs and Social Status Levels in Sixty-one Churches of the Southern Appalachian Mountains."
J20 (ASU)

The Frontier Camp Meeting.
J1320 (WWC)

The Commission on Religion in Appalachia, Inc.; a Case Study.
J1620 (BC ASU)

Sermons, Wise and Witty: By Rev. Sam P. Jones, the Mountain Evangelist.
J2590 (ASU)

"Religiosity as Related to Social Factors and Modes of Social Institutional Behavior in the Southern Appalachian Region."
K2040 (LMC ASU)

"Fundamentalism and Selected Social Factors in the Southern Appalachian Region."
L170 (ASU)

"Coal Miners and Religion."
L2950

Protestants and Pioneers; Individualism and Conformity on the American Frontier.
M6370

"A History of the Early Baptist Missions Among the Five Civilized Tribes."
M6420 (WCU)

A Comparison of Religious Groupings in Appalachia.
N440 (ASU)

A Review of the Literature Pertaining to Appalachia; Stressing Attitudes to Social Change and Religious and Educational Orientations; A Working Paper for the Boards of Christian Education of the United Presbyterian Church in the U. S.
N450 (BC)

Books on the Southern Mountain Area That Contain Certain Religions or Sections on Religion, 1947-55.
N2900 (BC)

Life of Lucius B. Compton.
P970

The Presbyterian Church in the Old Southwest, 1778-1838.
P3750 (BC LMC)

Religious Strife on the Southern Frontier.
P3760 (ASU LMC BC)

Without Script or Purse: Or, The Mountain Evangelist.
P4640 (BC)

Atlas of the Church in Appalachia, Administrative Units and Boundaries.
Q180 (ASU)
R1450 (BC)

Cane Ridge Meeting-house. To Which Is Appended the Autobiography of B. W. Stone and a Sketch of David Purviance.
R3480 (BC ASU)

The Art of the American Folk Preacher.
R3770 (BC)

Cathedrals in the Wilderness.
S860 (BC)

Anvil to the Pulpit.
S2090 (BC)

Religion in the Development of American Culture, 1795-1840.
S9640 (ASU)

Revivalism in America.
S9650

Voices from Cane Ridge.
T8310 (BC)
V430

The Southern Mountaineers.
W7520 (ASU ETSU MHC WWC BC)

The Southern Mountaineers.
W7530 (ASU LMC)

RELIGION AND RELIGIOUS BODIES — APP. — BAPTIST

"The Rhetoric of Immediacy: Baptist and Methodist Preaching on the Trans-Appalachian Frontier.
B9440 (ASU BC)

"Social Factors Affecting Selected Southern Baptist Churches in the Southern Appalachian Region of the United States."
D1550 (WCU ASU)

Authority and Power in the Free Church Tradition: A Social Case Study of the American Baptist Convention.
H3080

Oak and Laurel.
W7980 (ASU BC)

RELIGION AND RELIGIOUS BODIES — APP. — BAPTISTS

Encylopedia of Southern Baptists.
C8220 (ASU)

The Baptists, a Collection of Source Material, General Introduction by Shirley Jackson Chase. Religion on the American Frontier, 1783-1840.
S9590 (ASU BC)

A Century of Faith.
W5360 (BC)

RELIGION AND RELIGIOUS BODIES — APP. — CATHOLICISM

Catholicity in the Carolinas and Georgia: Leaves of Its History.
O170 (BC ASU WCU LMC)

RELIGION AND RELIGIOUS BODIES — APP. — CHURCH OF CHRIST

Churches and Church Membership in the United States ("Series B," Nos. 1-4; "Series C," Nos. 32-35, 37-38, 40-43.)
N170

The Biography of Eld. Barton Warren Stone, Written by Himself.
S7510 (ASU)

RELIGION AND RELIGIOUS BODIES — APP. — CIRCUIT RIDERS

The Dramatic Story of Early American Methodism.
M3950 (ASU)

Francis Asbury.
R4240 (ASU WWC BC)

RELIGION AND RELIGIOUS BODIES — APP. — COLONIAL PERIOD

Religion in Colonial America.
S9630 (MHC FC)

RELIGION AND RELIGIOUS BODIES — APP. — CONGREGATIONAL
A Narrative of the Visit to the American Churches, by the Deputation from the Congregational Union of England and Wales.
R1010
RELIGION AND RELIGIOUS BODIES — APP. — CUMBERLAND PRESBYTERIAN
Cumberland: The Story of a Name.
G660 (BC)
Sparks from a Backlog.
G3620
History of the Cumberland Presbyterian Church.
M1170 (ASU BC)
History of the Cumberland Presbyterian Church.
M1180 (ASU)
RELIGION AND RELIGIOUS BODIES — APP. — CUMBERLAND PRESBYTERIAN CHURCH
The Old Log House, a History and Defense of the Cumberland Presbyterian Church.
B4520 (ASU)
RELIGION AND RELIGIOUS BODIES — APP. — DISCIPLES OF CHRIST
Religion Follows the Frontier; a History of the Disciples of Christ.
G490 (BC)
RELIGION AND RELIGIOUS BODIES — APP. — METHODISM
Personal Memoirs.
B5930 (BC)
The Journals and Letters of Francis Asbury.
C4400
Highlights and Travels of a Southern Highlander.
D4170 (ASU)
The Circuit Rider Dismounts: A Social History of Southern Methodism, 1865-1900.
F160 (ASU BC)
A Pocket Full of Change: Methodist Ministries in the New Appalachia.
J2630
Memoir of the Rev. Jesse Lee. With Extracts From His Journals.
L1380 (ASU FC)
Experiences of a Circuit Rider.
L1870
The Dramatic Story of Early American Methodism.
M3950 (ASU)
Will Makes a Way.
N1380 (BC)
Francis Asbury.
R4240 (ASU WWC BC)
Methodism in American History.
S9600 (BC FC)
The Methodists, a Collection of Source Materials. Religion on the American Frontier, 1783-1840.
S9610 (ASU)
Frances Asbury, the Prophet of the Long Road.
T8730 (ASU)
The Heart of Asbury's Journal.
T8740
RELIGION AND RELIGIOUS BODIES — APP. — METHODIST
"The Rhetoric of Immediacy: Baptist and Methodist Preaching on the Trans-Appalachian Frontier.
B9440 (ASU BC)
The Log Meeting-house, and the McIlhanys.
E1060 (ASU)
RELIGION AND RELIGIOUS BODIES — APP. — METHODISTS
Bishop on Horseback.
N3040 (BC)
RELIGION AND RELIGIOUS BODIES — APP. — MISSIONS
The Church's Distinctive Challenge in Southern Appalachia.
G1120 (BC)
RELIGION AND RELIGIOUS BODIES — APP. — MORAVIAN
A Brief History of the Moravian Church.
S210 (ASU)
History of the Moravian Missions Among Southern Indian Tribes of the United States.
S1230 (BC UNCA)
RELIGION AND RELIGIOUS BODIES — APP. — MORAVIAN CHURCH
History of the Moravian Church: The Renewed Unitas Fratrum, 1722-1957.
H1150 (ASU)

RELIGION AND RELIGIOUS BODIES — APP. — PRESBYTERIAN
Mission Work among the Mountain Whites in Asheville Presbytery, North Carolina.
C940 (BC)
Unfinished Business of the Presbyterian Church in America.
E550 (ASU)
The Appalachian Presbyterian: Some Rural-Urban Differences, a Preliminary Report.
N410 (ASU BC MHC)
Call of the Home Land; A Study of Home Missions.
P2560
Experiences in Mountain Mission Work.
S4970 (ASU WWC)
The Presbyterians, a Collection of Source Materials. Religion on the American Frontier, 1783-1840.
S9620 (ASU BC)
Presbyterian Missions in the Southern United States.
T8150 (LMC)
Presbyterians in the South.
T8160 (WWC BC)
Life of Elder John Smith.
W6630 (BC)
RELIGION AND RELIGIOUS BODIES — APP. — PRESBYTERIAN CHURCH
Highways and Byways of Appalachia: A Study of the Work of the Synod of Appalachia of the Presbyterian Church in the United States.
C8370 (ASU LMC BC)
Scotch and Irish Seeds in American Soil: The Early History of the Scotch and Irish Churches, and Their Relations to the Presbyterian Church of America.
C8450 (BC)
Origin and Doctrines of the Cumberland Presbyterian Church.
C8800
RELIGION AND RELIGIOUS BODIES — APP. — PROTESTANT EPISCOPAL
The Church in the Confederate States: A History of the Protestant Episcopal Church in the Confederate States.
C3780 (LMC)
RELIGION AND RELIGIOUS BODIES — APP. — PROTESTANTISM
Southern White Protestantism in the Twentieth Century.
B320
RELIGION AND RELIGIOUS BODIES — APP. — QUAKER
The Dutch and Quaker Colonies in America.
F1280 (ASU)
RELIGION AND RELIGIOUS BODIES — APP. — REVIVALS
And They All Sang Hallelujah, Plainfolk Camp-meeting Religion, 1800-1845.
B7560 (ASU)
Primitive Traits in Religious Revivals.
D590
RELIGION AND RELIGIOUS BODIES — APP. — SNAKE HANDLERS
Snake Handlers: God-Fearers? or, Fanatics?
P1620
RELIGION AND RELIGIOUS BODIES — APP. — SNAKE HANDLING CULTS
Tests of Faith.
H6650 (ASU BC)
They Shall Take Up Serpents: Psychology of the Southern Snake-handling Cult.
L10 (BC ASU WCU WWC)
They Shall Take Up Serpents: Psychology of the Southern Snake-handling Cult.
L20 (ASU)
RELIGION AND RELIGIOUS BODIES — CHEROKEE
C3730 (MHC ASU)
RELIGION AND RELIGIOUS BODIES — CHEROKEE NATION
"Missionary Activities among the Cherokee Indians, 1757-1838."
C9150
Elias Boudinot, Cherokee, and His America.
G60 (ASU BC UNCA)
RELIGION AND RELIGIOUS BODIES — CUMBERLAND — PRESBYTERIAN
A People Called Cumberland Presbyterians.
B1480 (BC ASU)

RELIGION AND RELIGIOUS BODIES — GA.
Religion and the State in Georgia in the Eighteenth Century.
S7960 (WCU)
RELIGION AND RELIGIOUS BODIES — GA. — BAPTIST
Seventy Years in Clarksville Baptist Church.
C4070 (ASU)
RELIGION AND RELIGIOUS BODIES — GA. — MORAVIANS
The Moravians in Georgia, 1735-1740.
F3370 (ASU)
RELIGION AND RELIGIOUS BODIES — KY.
"The Interrelationships of Organized Religion and Certain Other Community Subsystems in Five Selected Counties of Kentucky with Implications for Educational Administration."
B2340
History of Garrard County, Kentucky, and Its Churches.
C260 (BC)
A Story of Four Churches and Reminiscences of Poosey Ridge in Madison County, Kentucky.
C270 (BC)
"Sect Religion and Social Change in an Isolated Rural Community of Southern Appalachia, with Case Story, "Fruit of the Land"."
C5290 (ASU)
"A History of Religious Education in the Kentucky Mountains."
G4230 (ASU)
Religious Organization in Kentucky.
K260
Rural Churches in Kentucky, 1947.
K270
Faith Victorious in the Kentucky Mountains.
M550 (BC)
Faith Victorious in the Kentucky Mountains.
M560
Hitherto and Henceforth in the Kentucky Mountains.
M570 (BC)
The Pauline Ministry in the Kentucky Mountains: Or, A Brief Account of the Kentucky Mountain Holiness Association.
M580 (ASU LMC BC)
A Charge to Keep; Narratives and Episodes Devoted to the Women Who Helped Build a Place for Worship and for Learning on the Berea Ridge.
R2290 (BC)
RELIGION AND RELIGIOUS BODIES — KY. — BAPTIST
A Lighthouse in the Wilderness.
G540 (BC)
"The Traveling Church": An Account of the Baptist Exodus from Virginia to Kentucky in 1781, under the Leadership of Rev. Lewis Craig and Capt. William Ellis.
R360 (BC)
RELIGION AND RELIGIOUS BODIES — KY. — CHRISTIAN CHURCH
The Disciples in Kentucky.
F2200 (BC)
RELIGION AND RELIGIOUS BODIES — KY. — HOLINESS CHURCH
T9410
RELIGION AND RELIGIOUS BODIES — KY. — METHODISM
History of the First Methodist Church Prestonsburg, Ky.
M4600
History of Methodism in Montgomery County.
S520 (ASU)
Methodism in Jackson and Breathitt County, Kentucky.
S6170
RELIGION AND RELIGIOUS BODIES — KY. — METHODIST
A History of Methodism in Kentucky.
A4870 (BC)
RELIGION AND RELIGIOUS BODIES — KY. — METHODIST EPISCOPAL
K1330
Western Cavaliers, Embracing the History of the Methodist Episcopal Church in Kentucky from 1832 to 1844.
R880 (ASU)
RELIGION AND RELIGIOUS BODIES — KY. — PRESBYTERIAN
Stuart Robinson School and Its Work.
C7220 (BC)

RELIGION AND RELIGIOUS BODIES — KY. — PRESBYTERIAN
An Historical Sketch of Springfield Presbyterian Church, Bath County, Kentucky.
S360 (BC)
RELIGION AND RELIGIOUS BODIES — KY. — PRESBYTERIAN CHURCH
F3270 (BC)
RELIGION AND RELIGIOUS BODIES — METHODISM — CIRCUIT RIDERS
Francis Asbury in North Carolina.
A5040 (ASU)
Journal of Rev. Francis Asbury, Bishop of the Methodist Episcopal Church.
A5050 (BC)
Journal and Letters.
A5060 (ASU BC WWC)
A Methodist Saint.
A5070 (ASU)
RELIGION AND RELIGIOUS BODIES — METHODIST EPISCOPAL
History of the Methodist Episcopal Church, South.
A1350 (ASU)
RELIGION AND RELIGIOUS BODIES — METHODIST-EPISCOPAL CHURCH — W. VA.
The West Virginia Pulpit of the Methodist-Episcopal Church.
A5380 (BC)
RELIGION AND RELIGIOUS BODIES — MIGRANTS
Detroit's Southern Whites and the Store Front Church.
B5860
RELIGION AND RELIGIOUS BODIES — MIGRANTS — CHURCH OF THE ADVENT
Ministry to the Southern Mountaineer.
H1200
RELIGION AND RELIGIOUS BODIES — N. C.
Early Days: All Souls' Church and Biltmore Village.
B5970
Fishers of Men: A Charge to the Clergy of the Jurisdiction of Asheville, by the Bishop of North Carolina.
C3790 (WCU)
"Beginnings: A History of the Founding of Churches in Transylvania County, 1795-1865."
G700 (WCU)
Church-state Relationships in Education in North Carolina since 1776.
G2220 (LMC)
Parson of the Hills.
K1790
The Goodly Heritage: A History of St. Phillips Church of Brevard, N. C., and of St. Pauls in the Diocese of Western Carolina.
M910 (WCU BC)
Annual Report.
M6240 (LMC)
The Country Church in North Carolina: A Study of the Country Church of North Carolina in Relation to the Material Progress of the State.
O810 (ASU WCU LMC WWC)
Millhand and Preachers, a Study of Gastonia.
P3560 (MHC)
Historical Sketch of Grace Church, Morganton, North Carolina.
S7620 (ASU)
"The History of Lutheran Elementary Education in Catawba County."
T30
North Carolina Disciples of Christ.
W800 (BC)
RELIGION AND RELIGIOUS BODIES — N. C. — BAPTIST
History of the First Baptist Church of Kings Mountain, N. C.
B4310
The First Baptist Church at Boone, North Carolina: A History.
E1260 (ASU LMC)
The Story of a Mountain Missionary: Rev. James Floyd Fletcher, 1858-1946.
F1500 (ASU)
A History of the Ashe County, North Carolina, and New River, Virginia, Baptist Associations.
F1530 (ASU)
The First Baptist Church of Forest City, N. C.
F2110 (BC)
Abstract of Reddies River Church Membership.
G4020
History of First Baptist Church of Shelby, North Carolina.
H1390
Minutes and Records, Feb., 1917-Dec. 25, 1960.
H4570 (WCU)
Historical Address . . . in Celebration of the Founding of Beaver Creek Baptist Church, Wilkes County.
M2430
Tuckaseigee Minutes, 1829-1857.
N1670 (WCU)
"A Baptist People and the Events Leading to the Formation of the Three Forks Association."
P1730 (ASU)
P3240
Minutes. Three Fork Baptist Church, 1790-1895.
T8450 (ASU)
RELIGION AND RELIGIOUS BODIES — N. C. — BAPTISTS
Outlines of History of French Broad Association and Mars Hill College . . . 1807 to 1907.
A2220
A History of North Carolina Baptists, 1727-1932.
H8030 (LMC)
Day Book, Sept., 1907-Aug. 24, 1909.
R2260 (WCU)
Minutes, 1909-1931.
R2270 (WCU)
RELIGION AND RELIGIOUS BODIES — N. C. — CATHOLIC
C2100 (LMC)
RELIGION AND RELIGIOUS BODIES — N. C. — CATHOLICISM
The Trials of a Mind in the Progress to Catholicism: A Letter to His Old Friends.
I1000 (LMC)
RELIGION AND RELIGIOUS BODIES — N. C. — EPISCOPAL
Early Sketch of St. John in the Wilderness and Flat Rock, North Carolina.
A1910 (ASU)
William West Skiles: A Sketch of Missionary Life at Valle Crucis in Western North Carolina, 1842-1862.
C7210 (ASU WCU BC)
Pictorial History of the Episcopal Church in North Carolina, 1701-1964.
D3930 (LMC)
Calvary Church Episcopal, where City and County Meet to Worship God; A Historical Sketch of Calvary Episcopal Church.
J660
St. James Episcopal Church: Book of Memory, 1843-1950.
P910 (ASU)
S160
S190
Historical Sketches of Churches in the Diocese of Western North Carolina Episcopal Church.
S3370 (LMC WCU BC)
A Sketch of Missionary Life at Valle Crucis in Western North Carolina, 1842-1862.
S4010 (LMC)
RELIGION AND RELIGIOUS BODIES — N. C. — EPISCOPAL CHURCH
Lives of the Bishops of North Carolina from the Establishment of the Episcopate in that State down to the Division of the Diocese.
H4070 (LMC)
RELIGION AND RELIGIOUS BODIES — N. C. — LUTHERAN
History of Daniel's Evangelical Lutheran & Reformed Churches, Lincoln Co., N. C.
N1200
RELIGION AND RELIGIOUS BODIES — N. C. — METHODISM
Early Methodism in the Carolinas.
C3930 (ASU BC)
Methodism in Western North Carolina.
C4410 (ASU WCU LMC MHC)
Centennial History of Pleasant Grove Methodist Church, 1838-1938.
G4110 (ASU BC)
G4170 (BC)
Little Church of the Valley (Moss Baptist Church), in the Shadow of the Potrock.
M8250
RELIGION AND RELIGIOUS BODIES — N. C. — METHODIST
The Story of Lake Junaluska.
C9340 (BC)
RELIGION AND RELIGIOUS BODIES — N. C. — METHODIST EPISCOPAL
Journal of the Western North Carolina Annual Conference . . . 1890-.
M5210 (WCU)
RELIGION AND RELIGIOUS BODIES — N. C. — MORAVIAN CHURCH
Records of the Moravians in North Carolina.
H1180 (ASU)
RELIGION AND RELIGIOUS BODIES — N. C. — MORAVIANS
Records of the Moravians in North Carolina.
F3380 (ASU LMC MHC)
The Road to Salem.
F3390 (ASU LMC)
Some Moravian Heroes.
F3400 (ASU)
The Moravians in North Carolina.
R1360 (ASU LMC)
RELIGION AND RELIGIOUS BODIES — N. C. — PRESBYTERIAN
The Story of Montreat from Its Beginning, 1897-1947.
A2340 (ASU WCU LMC)
History of the Presbyterian Churches at Quaker Meadows and Morganton, from the Year 1780 to 1913.
A5720
A Spire in the Mountains: The Story of 176 Years of a Church and a Town Growing Together, 1794-1969.
B4430 (ASU ETSU UNCA)
F1110
If Ye Know These Things: The Presbyterian Task in North Carolina.
H7010 (LMC)
Recollections and Observations During a Ministry in the North Carolina Conference, Methodist Episcopal Church, South, of Forty-three Years.
N110 (ASU)
Our Mountain Work.
N2520
O930
"A Study of the Needs, Growth, and Development of the Presbyterian Church of Boone, N. C."
P230 (ASU)
RELIGION AND RELIGIOUS BODIES — N. C. — PRESBYTERIAN AND REFORMED
The Historical Foundation and Its Treasures.
S6150
RELIGION AND RELIGIOUS BODIES — N. C. — PRESBYTERIAN CHURCH
The First Presbyterian Church, Asheville, North Carolina, 1794-1951.
M750
RELIGION AND RELIGIOUS BODIES — N. C. — PROTESTANT EPISCOPAL CHURCH
Appalachian Mountain Community Center under the Auspices of the Protestant Episcopal Church. . .
A3300
RELIGION AND RELIGIOUS BODIES — N. C. — QUAKERISM
I Have Called You Friends: The Story of Quakerism in North Carolina.
A2580 (ASU)
RELIGION AND RELIGIOUS BODIES — OHIO — METHODIST
Keepers of the Poor.
C1340 (ASU LMC)
RELIGION AND RELIGIOUS BODIES — PA.
Participation in the Rural Church.
H7350
RELIGION AND RELIGIOUS BODIES — PA. — METHODISM
Methodism in Western Pennsylvania, 1784-1968.
S4380 (ASU)
The Story of Methodism in the Pittsburgh Region.
S4390 (ASU)
RELIGION AND RELIGIOUS BODIES — PA. — PALATINE
Palatine Church Visitations, 1609.
G780 (ASU)
RELIGION AND RELIGIOUS BODIES — PRESBYTERIAN — APP.
A Search for Appalachian People.
A5600
RELIGION AND RELIGIOUS BODIES — PRESBYTERIAN CHURCH
Edward O. Guerrant: Apostle to the Southern Highlanders.
M40 (LMC BC ASU)

RELIGION AND RELIGIOUS BODIES — QUAKER CHURCH

A History of Lynchburg's Pioneer Quakers and Their Meeting House, 1754-1936.
B7110 (ASU)

RELIGION AND RELIGIOUS BODIES — S. C. — METHODISM

Early Methodism in the Carolinas.
C3930 (ASU BC)

The History of Methodism in South Carolina.
S3090 (ASU BC)

RELIGION AND RELIGIOUS BODIES — TENN.

Fire in the Hills, the Story of Parson Frakes and the Henderson Settlement.
F1190 (ASU LMC BC)

Directory of Churches, Missions, and Religious Institutions of Tennessee, no. 33. Hamilton County.
H5760

Directory of Churches, Missions, and Religious Institutions of Tennessee, no. 47. Knox County.
H5770

Directory of Churches, Missions, and Religious Institutions of Tennessee, no. 90. Washington County.
H5780

Whom the Lord Loveth; the Story of James A. Huff.
H8000 (BC)

"An Analysis of the Relationship of Religious Commitment and Alienation Among High School Students of Bristol, Tennessee."
K1620 (ETSU)

History of Forestdale Evangelical United Brethren Church.
M1060

"The Rural Church and Organized Community Activity, a Study of Church-community Relations in Two East Tennessee Communities."
M4430

"A Follow-up Study of Attitudes of Sullivan County High School Seniors toward the Church."
P360

"Church Organization in Bradley County, Tennessee, in 1950."
P2860

RELIGION AND RELIGIOUS BODIES — TENN. — BAPTIST

"The Nolichucky Baptist Association of East Tennessee, 1828-1871."
B7050 (ETSU)

Sketches of Tennessee's Pioneer Baptist Preachers.
B9000 (WCU)

Lest We Forget.
D3770 (BC)
F1090

History of Meridian Baptist Church. Old Sevierville Pike, Knoxville, Tennessee: Church Directory and Church Roll in Celebration of the Seventy-sixth Anniversary.
H1020

History of the Chilhowee Baptist Association.
H7020

"A Brief History of the First Baptist Church (Ocoee Baptist Church), Benton, Tennessee, 1836-1959."
L2480

"The Influence of the Baptist Church on Knoxville Government."
P2580

Centennial Celebration of Island Home Baptist Church, Knoxville, Tennessee, October 2, 1960 - December 11, 1960.
S3080

"The History of the First Baptist Church of Jonesboro, Tennessee."
T7860 (ETSU)

The Romance of a Sesquicentennial, The Dumplin Creek Baptist Church of Christ, Jefferson County, Tennessee, Organized 1797.
T8910 (BC)

The Baptists of Tennessee.
W6710 (ASU)

RELIGION AND RELIGIOUS BODIES — TENN. — BAPTISTS

"The Baptists of Tennessee: With Particular Attention to the Primitive Baptist of East Tennessee."
E1080 (LMC)

"A History of the First Baptist Church of Knoxville, Tennessee."
E1230

History of the Baptists of Tennessee.
H290 (WCU)

The Knox County Missionary Baptists 1786-1945.
J1880

Early Tennessee Baptists, 1769-1832.
T680 (ASU)

RELIGION AND RELIGIOUS BODIES — TENN. — CAMP MEETINGS

Songs of the Old Camp Ground.
M1220 (BC ASU)

RELIGION AND RELIGIOUS BODIES — TENN. — CATHOLIC

The Centenary of St. Peter and St. Paul's Parish; Chattanooga, Tennessee. The Story of the First 100 Years of the Catholic Church in Hamilton County.
F1390

RELIGION AND RELIGIOUS BODIES — TENN. — CATHOLIC CHURCH

The Centenary of Sts. Peter and Paul's Parish, Chattanooga, Tenn. The Story of the First One Hundred Years of the Catholic Church in Hamilton County.
C3540

RELIGION AND RELIGIOUS BODIES — TENN. — CHRISTIAN CHURCH

100th Anniversary History and Directory, 1871-1971, First Christian Church, Johnson City, Tennessee.
M650

RELIGION AND RELIGIOUS BODIES — TENN. — CONGREGATIONAL CHURCH

A Brief History of the First Congregational Church, Crossville, Tennessee, 1887-1962.
B6850

RELIGION AND RELIGIOUS BODIES — TENN., EASTERN

The Great Iron Wheel Examined: Or, Its False Spokes Extracted, and an Exhibition of Elder Graves, Its Builder.
B7500 (ASU)

RELIGION AND RELIGIOUS BODIES — TENN. — EPISCOPAL

Historical Discourse of St. John's Church, Knoxville, Tennessee.
H8270
S180

A History of 100 Years of St. Johns Episcopal Church in Knoxville, Tenn.
S2100

Christ Church, Episcopal, Rugby, Tennessee, a Short History.
W5950 (BC)

RELIGION AND RELIGIOUS BODIES — TENN. — JEFFERSON CO.

"A Study of the Development of Organized Religion in Jefferson County, Tennessee (1785-1950)."
C5450

RELIGION AND RELIGIOUS BODIES — TENN. — LUTHERAN

Kirchen Buch (Church Book) Register, 1815-1828. St. James Lutheran Church, Greene County, Tennessee.
B8600

History of The Lutheran Church in Virginia and East Tennessee.
C1970 (ASU BC FC)

RELIGION AND RELIGIOUS BODIES — TENN. — METHODISM

He That Serveth; Twenty-five Years' Adventures in Christian Ministry, George Creswell and Second Church.
B2900

A History of Mars Hill Presbyterian Church, Athens, Tenn. 1823-1973.
B5980 (ASU)

A History of the First Methodist Church in Livingston, Tennessee, Established 1836.
E1510

A Minister in the Tennessee Valley.
M3610 (BC)

Church Street Methodists, Children of Francis Asbury: A History of Church Street Methodist Church. Knoxville, Tennessee, 1816-1947.
M3620

Methodism in Holston.
M3630

A Minister in the Tennessee Valley for Sixty Seven Years.
M3640

A Century of Service: The Story of First Methodist Church, Morristown, Tennessee, 1852-1952.
M7980 (ETSU)

The Circuit Rider and Those Who Followed. Sketches of Methodist Churches Organized before 1860 in the Chattanooga Area with Special Reference to Centenary.
P1160

The Story of My Life: Or, More Than a Half Century as I Have Lived It and Seen It Lived.
R440 (BC LMC)

Reminiscences and Sketches.
S4450 (ASU)

RELIGION AND RELIGIOUS BODIES — TENN. — METHODIST
C2630

Early Biography, Travels and Adventures of Rev. James Champlin, Who Was Born Blind; with a Description of the Different Countries through Which He Has Traveled in America, and of the Different Institutions, etc., Visited by Him; Also an Appendix, Which Contains Extracts from Addresses Delivered by Him upon Several Occasions.
C2840

Directory of First Methodist Church, November 1, 1950. . .
J1440 (ETSU)
M3500

From Sunrise to Sunset, Reminiscence of Bristol, Tennessee.
R2080 (BC)

RELIGION AND RELIGIOUS BODIES — TENN. — METHODIST EPISCOPAL

The Great Iron Wheel: Or, Republicanism Backwards and Christianity Reversed.
G3310 (ASU)

History of Mt. Zion Methodist Episcopal Church 4, South of Mount Zion, Warren County, Tenn., 1809-1930.
H5470

RELIGION AND RELIGIOUS BODIES — TENN. — PRESBYTERIAN

History of the First Presbyterian Church of Chattanooga.
A4750

Memorial of the Rev. James Park.
B20

A Church Called Bethel.
B910

The History of New Providence Church, Maryville, Tennessee.
B1530

Her Walls before Thee Stand: History of the Second Presbyterian Church, 1818-1968.
B6660

Helps to the Study of Presbyterianism. . . .
B7510
C2640
C2650

William G. Brownlow, Fighting Parson of the Southern Highlands.
C7810 (ASU WCU BC)

William G. Brownlow: Fighting Parson of the Southern Highlands.
C7820 (ETSU)
E2270

"The Reaction of Presbyterian Ministers in the Knoxville Area to Specific Questions Concerning Ministerial Counseling."
G4380

"A History of the First Presbyterian Church of Jonesboro, Tennessee."
H3340 (ETSU)

A History of Concord Presbyterian Church, Concord, Tennessee.
H3360
H6990

History of the First Presbyterian Church in Knoxville, Tennessee.
M2300

History of New Providence Presbyterian Church, Maryville, Tennessee, 1786-1921.
M2530 (ETSU)

History and Times of Mars Hill Presbyterian Church, 1823-1923.
N50

The New Bethel Sesquicentennial 1782-1932.
N660

RELIGION AND RELIGIOUS BODIES — TENN. — PRESBYTERIAN
O470
History of the First Presbyterian Church in Knoxville, Tennessee.
P200
Pioneer Presbyterianism in Tennessee; Addresses Delivered at the Tennessee Exposition on Presbyterian Day, Oct. 28, 1897.
P4310 (ASU)
History of Lebanon Presbyterian Church, "In the Fork," Five Miles East of Knoxville.
R270
Seventy-Five Years: Shannondale Presbyterian Church, Knoxville, Tennessee, 1886-1961.
S2240
"The History of the First Presbyterian Church of Bristol, Tennessee."
V150 (ETSU)
RELIGION AND RELIGIOUS BODIES — TENN. — PRESBYTERIAN CHURCH
History of the Cumberland Presbyterian Church.
M1100
RELIGION AND RELIGIOUS BODIES — VA.
Cumberland Parish, Lunenburg County, Virginia, 1746-1816. Vestry book, 1746-1816.
B2770 (ASU)
The Church, the State, and Education in Virginia.
B2820 (MHC)
Parish Lines, Diocese of Southwestern Virginia.
C5400 (ETSU)
Sermons and Essays.
F1590
The Virginia Rural Church and Related Influences, 1900-1950.
G400
M3330
Old Churches, Ministers and Families of Virginia.
M4750
Frederick Parrish, Virginia, 1744-1780.
M4760 (BC)
Old Churches, Ministers, and Families of Virginia.
M4770 (ASU)
The Churches of Winchester, Virginia: A Brief History of Those Established Prior to 1825.
Q60
Marriage Records of Amherst County, Virginia, 1815-1821, and Subscription for Building St. Mark's Church, Amherst Co., Virginia.
S9540 (ASU)
History of the Augusta Church, from 1737 to 1900.
V200 (ASU)
Wise's Digested Index and Genealogical Guide to Bishop Meade's Old Churches, Ministers and Families of Virginia.
W7890
RELIGION AND RELIGIOUS BODIES — VA. — BAPTIST
History of Long Branch Baptist Church, Fauquier County, Virginia.
G2840
Regular Primitive Baptist Washington District Association.
S9210
The Struggle for Religious Freedom in Virginia by the Baptists.
T7750 (ASU)
RELIGION AND RELIGIOUS BODIES — VA. — BAPTISTS
The Baptists of Virginia, 1699-1926.
R4520 (BC)
History of the Rise and Progress of the Baptists in Virginia.
S1870 (LMC BC)
Virginia Baptist Ministers, Fourth Series.
T530 (LMC)
Virginia Baptist Ministers.
T560 (ASU)
RELIGION AND RELIGIOUS BODIES — VA. — BAPTISTS, PRIMITIVE
Sand Lick Primitive Baptist Church; The First Hundred Years, 1837-1937.
S9240
RELIGION AND RELIGIOUS BODIES — VA. — LUTHERAN
History of The Lutheran Church in Virginia and East Tennessee.
C1970 (ASU BC FC)
History of the Hebron Lutheran Church, Madison Co., Va.
H7890 (BC)

The Proceedings of a Special Conference Held in Madison County, Virginia, in the Lutheran Congregation of Said County, on the 14th Day of September, 1817, and the Subsequent Days.
L4030 (ASU)
RELIGION AND RELIGIOUS BODIES — VA. — LUTHERAN CHURCH
This Heritage.
E1410
The Lutheran Church in Virginia, 1717-1962.
E1420 (FC)
St. John's Evangelical Lutheran Church, Wythe County, Virginia, Its Pastors and Their Records 1800-1924.
K460
RELIGION AND RELIGIOUS BODIES — VA. — MENNONITE
History of Mennonites in Virginia.
B7730 (ASU BC FC)
RELIGION AND RELIGIOUS BODIES — VA. — METHODISM
Story of the Life of Robert Sayers Sheffey.
B1080 (BC)
A History of Methodism in Rockbridge County, Virginia.
C9810 (BC)
The Reverend Samuel Houston.
D2310 (BC)
H6030
Methodism in Bedford County; a Study Made by William B. Jones with Recommendations by C. Ralph Arthur.
J2660 (FC)
His New Creation; a History of Greene Memorial Methodist Church (1859-1959), from Methodism's Earliest Days in the Roanoke Valley.
R1610 (FC)
RELIGION AND RELIGIOUS BODIES — VA. — METHODIST
The Man Who Moved a Mountain.
D620 (ASU FC BC)
Edward Morgan 1751-1884, Pioneer Minister in Southwest, Virginia.
M7490
RELIGION AND RELIGIOUS BODIES — VA. — METHODIST EPISCOPAL
Foot-prints of an Itinerant.
G80
RELIGION AND RELIGIOUS BODIES — VA. — PRESBYTERIAN
The Planting of the Presbyterian Church in Northern Virginia, Prior to the Organization of Winchester Presbytery, December 4, 1794.
G3130 (ASU BC LMC)
Presbyterian Churches of Roanoke, Virginia.
H6220 (ASU BC)
The First Presbyterian Church, Staunton, Virginia.
H6390 (ASU BC)
Samuel Davies: Apostle of Dissent in Colonial Virginia.
P2930 (ASU)
Historical Sketch of Sinking Spring Presbyterian Church of Abingdon, Virginia.
S7070
The Lexington Presbytery Heritage.
W7300 (BC)
The Tinkling Spring, Headwater of Freedom: A Study of the Church and Her People, 1732-1952.
W7320 (ASU BC)
A History of Windy Cove Church, Millboro Springs, Virginia, 1929-1949.
W7660 (ASU)
RELIGION AND RELIGIOUS BODIES — VA. — PROTESTANT EPISCOPAL
Mission.
F3100 (ASU LMC BC)
RELIGION AND RELIGIOUS BODIES — VA. — QUAKERS
Encyclopedia of American Quaker Genealogy.
H4830
RELIGION AND RELIGIOUS BODIES — VA. — SOCIETY OF FRIENDS
Memoirs of Samuel M. Janney; Late of Lincoln, Loudoun Co., Va.
J390

Hopewell Friends History, 1734-1934, Frederick County, Virginia: Records of Hopewell Monthly Meetings and Meetings Reporting to Hopewell.
J2200 (ASU)
RELIGION AND RELIGIOUS BODIES — W. VA.
Autobiography of Peter Cartwright, the Backwoods Preacher.
C1810 (BC)
The White Pole Meeting House, Hillsboro, West Virginia.
J1700 (ASU BC)
"The Temperance Movement in West Virginia."
L3030
Religion in an Appalachian State.
P2740
Some Churches of Coal Mining Communities of West Virginia.
R2010
RELIGION AND RELIGIOUS BODIES — W. VA. — BAPTIST
Diamond Jubilee. Fifth Avenue Baptist Church.
F830
Souvenir of the 125th Anniversary of the Greenbriar Baptist Church (1781-1906), Alderson, West Virginia.
M7550 (ASU)
A Charge to Keep; History of the First Baptist Church of Kenova, West Virginia.
M7750 (ASU)
RELIGION AND RELIGIOUS BODIES — W. VA. — CHRISTIAN CHURCH
Morgantown Disciples: A History of the First Christian Church of Morgantown, West Virginia.
C7410 (ASU)
The Christian Church (Disciples of Christ) in West Virginia.
C8490 (BC)
RELIGION AND RELIGIOUS BODIES — W. VA. — JEWS
West Virginia Jewry: Origins and History, 1850-1958.
S3070 (ASU LMC)
RELIGION AND RELIGIOUS BODIES — W. VA. — JUDAISM
One Hundred Years: An Anthology — Charleston Jewry.
M5270 (ASU)
RELIGION AND RELIGIOUS BODIES — W. VA. — METHODISM
The Methodist Temple of Beckley, West Virginia: A History of Seventy-five Years of Active Organization, 1891-1966.
A2210 (ASU)
Through the Years: A History of Methodism in Kingwood, West Virginia.
B2590 (ASU)
A Brief History of the Athens Methodist Church (1848-1942).
B2700
A Short History of the Wayne Methodist Church.
B3470
Christ Church Methodist, a Historical Sketch, 1804-1961.
C6890 (ASU)
Thirty-eight years in the Parsonage: The Fruitful Career of the Reverend Opie Eldridge in the Methodist Ministry of Rural and Urban West Virginia-Perceptively Recounted by His Wife and Fellow Worker.
E1580 (ASU)
One Hundred Years of Methodism, the History of St. John's Methodist Church, New Martinsville, W. Va.
F1370
A History of the First Methodist Church.
G2260
History of Methodism in the South Branch Valley.
H320
History of Methodism in the South Branch Valley.
H990 (BC)
H6000
M3170
Holston Methodism. From Its Origin to the Present Time.
P4580 (BC ASU)
RELIGION AND RELIGIOUS BODIES — W. VA. — METHODISTS
The First Methodist Episcopal Church, Huntington, West Virginia.
N670 (ASU)

RELIGION AND RELIGIOUS BODIES — W. VA. — PRESBYTERIAN
The West Virginia Hills: A Study of the Work of the Presbyterian Church in the United States in the Synod of West Virginia.
A1670 (ASU)
The Presbyterian Church at Philippi, West Virginia.
G3240
History of the Presbytery of Kanawha, 1895-1956.
M8000 (ASU)
French Creek Presbyterian Church: A Memorial to the 150 Years of Service of the French Creek Presbyterian Church.
P3060 (ASU)
RELIGION AND RELIGIOUS BODIES — W. VA. — PROTESTANT EPISCOPAL
A History and Record of the Protestant Episcopal Church in the Diocese of West Virginia.
P2300
RELIGION AND RELIGIOUS BODIES — W. VA. — REVIVALS
West Virginia Gems: Songs for the Revival and Social Prayer Meeting.
D2280
RELIGION AND RELIGIOUS BODIES — W. VA. — SEVENTH DAY BAPTISTS
A History of Seventh Day Baptist in West Virginia Including the Woodbridgetown and Salemville Churches in Pennsylvania and the Shrewbury Church in New Jersey.
R400 (BC)
RELIGION AND RELIGIOUS BODIES — W. VA. — UNITED BRETHREN IN CHRIST
Rise and Progress of the Church of the United Brethren in Christ of West Virginia.
H4840
The Rise and Progress of the United Brethren in Christ in West Virginia.
H4850 (BC ASU)
RELIGION AND RELIGIOUS EDUCATION — S. C.
"The Scope of Religious Education in the Secondary Schools of Greenville County, South Carolina."
H460
RELIGION AND RELIGIOUS BODIES
A History of the Presbyterian Church in Winchester, Virginia, 1780-1949.
W8990 (BC)
RERECLAMATION
Surface Mined Areas: Control and Reclamation of Environmental Damage; a Bibliography.
F3090 (ASU)
RESORTS — APP.
Recreation Potential in the Appalachian Highlands: A Market Analysis.
U4220 (ASU)
RESORTS — TENN.
Whittle Springs Hotel and Golf and Country Club.
W6900
RESORTS — VA.
The Springs of Virginia: Life, Love and Death at the Waters, 1775-1900.
R1470 (ASU FC)
Va's Common Wealth, a Study at Va.'s Outdoor Recreation Resources.
V1140
REVENUERS
The 20,000,000,000 a Year Racket of Bootleggers and Liquor-stamp Counterfeiters in Several Southeastern States Is Here Detailed by One of the Men Who Broke It Up.
A4590
No Place for Revenuers.
A4600 (BC LMC)
After the Mountaineers.
A5370 (BC)
Mac Day, Crusader; A Story of the Fight for Americanism.
B8800 (BC)
Spurrier With the Wildcats and Moonshiners.
S6390 (ASU BC)
RIVERS
Appalachian Rivers.
J1610
Stream Sculpture on the Atlantic Slope: A Study in the Evolution of Appalachian Rivers.
J1630 (ASU LMC ETSU)
The Relation of the Southern Appalachian Mountains to Inland Water Navigation.
L1650 (BC ASU)
M5190 (ASU)
RIVERS — ALLEGHENY
The Allegheny.
W1620 (BC)
"The Allegheny-Monongahela Flood Control Program and Its Benefits to Metropolitan Pittsburgh."
W7330
RIVERS — BIG SANDY
The Big Sandy Valley: A History of the People and Country from the Earliest Settlement to the Present Time.
E1890 (ASU)
Bibliography of the Big Sandy Valley.
J930
The Big Sandy Valley: A Regional History Prior to the Year 1850.
J960 (ASU BC)
The Big Sandy Valley: A Regional History Prior to the Year 1850.
J970 (MHC)
P90
Big Sandy.
T7890 (ASU BC)
Bulletin. Surface and Water Supply of Va. New, Big Sandy, and Tenn. River Basins, 1942-1950.
V750 (BC)
RIVERS — CATAWBA
"An Archaeological Survey of the Upper Catawba River Valley."
K390
"An Archaeological Survey of the Upper Catawba River Valley."
K400
RIVERS — CHATTAHOOCHEE
Tourism Development in the Chattahoochee-Flint Area.
K430
RIVERS — CHEOAH
Floods on Cheoah River and Tributary Creeks in Vicinity of Robbinsville, North Carolina.
T6990
RIVERS — CLINCH
Frontier Forts along the Clinch, Powell and Holston.
H1130 (BC)
Clinch-Powell Valley; Summary of Resources.
T2420
Floods on Clinch River, in Vicinity of Clinton, Tennessee.
T7000
RIVERS — COOSA
The Coosa River Valley from DeSoto to Hydroelectric Power.
R1660 (ASU)
Report on Coosa River System, Georgia-Alabama.
U3900
RIVERS — CULLASAJA
Floods on Little Tennessee River, Cullasaja River, and Cartoogechave Creek in Vicinity of Franklin, North Carolina.
T7090
RIVERS — CUMBERLAND
Steamboatin' on the Cumberland.
D3120 (BC ASU ETSU)
Bibliography of the Cumberland River Valley.
J940
The Cumberland.
M190 (LMC)
The Cumberland Plateau in Tennessee.
M4140
"Two Resettlement Communities on the Cumberland Plateau."
M6600
Adventures along the Cumberland.
O160 (BC)
On the Watauga and the Cumberland.
S5300 (LMC)
Stream Pollution Control In The Upper Cumberland River Basin, 1965.
T1230
The Lower Cumberland Region: A Study of Its Population, Economic Base and Potential.
T2100 (ETSU)
The Upper Cumberland Economy.
T2110 (ETSU)
Stream Pollution Control in the Upper Cumberland River Basin, 1964.
T2120 (ETSU)
. . . Report on the Physiographic, Economic, and Other Relationships Between the Tennessee and Cumberland Rivers and Between Their Drainage Areas. Message from the President of the United States, Transmitting Report Entitled "The Physiographic, Economic, and Other Relationships Between the Tennessee and Cumberland Rivers and Between Their Drainage Areas" . . .
T3380
"Big South Fork, Cumberland River (Kentucky-Tennessee), Interagency Field Task Group Report."
U220
Big South Fork, Cumberland River, Kentucky and Tennessee.
U230 (ETSU)
Big South Fork, Cumberland River, Kentucky and Tennessee.
U240
RIVERS — DAVIDSON
Floods on French Broad and Davidson Rivers and King, Nicholson, and Tucker Creeks in Vicinity of Brevard, North Carolina.
T7030
RIVERS — DOE
Floods on Watauga and Doe Rivers in Vicinity of Elizabethton, Tennessee.
T2760
RIVERS — ELK
Elk River Watershed; Summary of Resources.
T2590
Floods on Elk River and Norris Creek, in Vicinity of Fayetteville, Tennessee.
T7010
Floods on Elk River in Vicinity of Fayetteville, Tennessee.
T7020
RIVERS — FRENCH BROAD
The French Broad.
D4210 (WWC BC)
The French Broad.
D4220 (ASU ETSU WCU LMC MHC BC)
E780 (ASU)
Human Resources in the Economy of the Upper French Broad Area.
M4310 (LMC)
Economic Development of the Upper French Broad Area: Summary of Needs and Opportunities, Resources, the Regional Economy.
N2690 (ASU)
Economic Development of the Upper French Broad Area by North Carolina State and the Tennessee Valley Authority.
T2570 (LMC)
. . . Flood Control for Upper French Broad River and Tributaries; a Preliminary Report.
T6930
Floods on French Broad and Davidson Rivers and King, Nicholson, and Tucker Creeks in Vicinity of Brevard, North Carolina.
T7030
Floods on French Broad and Swannanoa Rivers, in Vicinity of Asheville, North Carolina.
T7040
Floods on French Broad River and Spring Creek in Vicinity of Hot Springs, North Carolina.
T7050
Floods on French Broad River in the Vicinity of Marshall, N. C.
T7060
RIVERS — FRENCH-BROAD
The French-Broad Holston Country: A History of Knox County, Tennessee.
R3940 (LMC BC)
The French Broad-Holston Country: A History of Knox County, Tennessee.
R3950 (ETSU)
RIVERS — GREEN
Bibliography of the Green River Valley.
J1120
RIVERS — GUYANDOT
"The Transformation of the Tug and Guyandot Valleys: Economic Development and Social Change in West Virginia, 1888-1921."
C9390
RIVERS — HIWASSEE
Economic Base Study and Survey of Basic Services for the Hiwassee River Watershed Development Association.
F2220 (BC)

RIVERS — HIWASSEE
Lower Hiwassee Valley; Summary of Resources.
T3020
Floods on Hiwassee River, Valley River, and Peachtree Creek in Vicinity of Murphy, N C.
T7070
RIVERS — HOLSTON
Report of the Conference, 2D Kingsport, Tennessee, 1962.
C6390
Frontier Forts along the Clinch, Powell and Holston.
H1130 (BC)
Historical Sketches of the Holston Valleys.
P4440 (ASU WCU LMC ETSU BC)
The French Broad-Holston Country: A History of Knox County, Tennessee.
R3940 (LMC BC)
The French Broad-Holston County: A History of Knox County, Tennessee.
R3950 (ETSU)
Kingsport, Tennessee: Historical Map of Long Island of the Holston.
S6300
Forest Inventory Statistics — Holston River Tributary Area, East Tennessee and Southwest Virginia.
T4690
Hitch Hiking Along the Holston River from 1792-1962.
W8600
RIVERS — JAMES
Industrial Limestones and Dolomites in Va.: James River District West of the Blue Ridge.
E910
The Floods of March, 1936, Part 3, Potomac, James, and Upper Ohio Rivers.
G4470
RIVERS — KANAWHA
Pioneers and Their Homes on Upper Kanawha.
D1440 (ASU BC)
The Geomorphic History of the New Kanawha River System.
F3300 (ETSU)
Surface Water Supply of the New-Kanawha River Basin, West Virginia, and North Carolina.
G4490
Kanawha River: Comprehensive Basin Study.
K100 (ASU)
The New-Kanawha River and the Mind War of West Virginia.
M630 (BC)
RIVERS — KENTUCKY
P90
. . . The Kentucky River Navigation.
V540
RIVERS — KEOWEE
The Keowee River and Cherokee Background.
M1320 (BC)
RIVERS — KY.
The Kentucky.
C4560 (WWC WCU UNCA)
The Kentucky.
C4570 (ASU UNCA BC)
A Kentucky Riverlands Development Program.
G570
RIVERS — LICKING
Bibliography of Licking River Valley in Ky.
J880
Interim Study Report on Upper Licking River Basin, Kentucky.
U290 (BC)
RIVERS — LITTLE PIGEON
Floods on Little Pigeon and West Fork Little Pigeon in the Vicinity of Sevierville, Tenn.
T7080
RIVERS — LITTLE SANDY
Ohio River Basin, Grayson Reservoir, Little Sandy River, Kentucky design memorandum no. 3A preliminary master plan.
U300 (BC)
RIVERS — LITTLE TENNESSEE
Fort Loudoun on the Little Tennessee.
H1050 (ASU)
Floods on Little Tennessee River, Cullasaja River, and Cartoogechave Creek in Vicinity of Franklin, North Carolina.
T7090
Floods on Tennessee River, Little Tennessee River, and Town and Muddy Creeks in Vicinity of Lenoir City, Tennessee.
T7290

Upper Little Tennessee River Region: Summary of Resources.
T9880 (WWC)
RIVERS — LOST
The Geology of Lost River State Park, West Virginia.
L3900 (ETSU)
RIVERS — MISSISSIPPI
. . . Value of Flood Height Reduction from TVA Reservoirs to the Alluvial Valley of the Lower Mississippi River . . .
T4070
RIVERS — MONONGAHELA
The Monongahela.
B4260 (BC)
Denudation and Erosion in the Southern Appalachian Region and the Monongehela Basin.
G2130 (ASU ETSU)
Employment and Underemployment of Rural People in the Upper Monongahela Valley, West Virginia.
M5230
Handbook of Pollution Control Costs in Mine Drainage Management.
M6470
Water Pollution Control In the Monongahela River Basin.
P1810
Availability for Employment of Rural People in the Upper Monongahela Valley.
P3700
Priority Determination Procedure for the Selection of Pollution Abatement Projects in the Monongahela River Basin.
R2590 (ASU)
"The Allegheny-Monongahela Flood Control Program and Its Benefits to Metropolitan Pittsburgh."
W7330
RIVERS — N. C.
Canoeing White Water: A Guide Book to the Rivers of Virginia and Eastern West Virginia, The Great Smoky Mountain Area.
C1740 (LMC)
RIVERS — N. C. — FRENCH BROAD
Flood of August 24-25, 1961: Upper French Broad River Basin.
T6940
RIVERS — NANTAHALA
The Dissent of Commissioner Thomas R. Eller, Jr., in the Nantahala Power and Light Company Transfer Case.
E1640 (WCU)
RIVERS — NEW
"Land Utilization in the New and Watauga River Basins of North Carolina."
B3700 (LMC)
"Industrial Waste and Human Sewage Pollution within the New River Drainage Basin of Watauga County."
C1490 (ASU)
The Geomorphic History of the New Kanawha River System.
F3300 (ETSU)
Surface Water Supply of the New-Kanawha River Basin, West Virginia, and North Carolina.
G4490
German New River Settlement, Virginia.
H4270 (ASU FC)
Lovely Mount Tavern: The Birth of a City, and Something of the Early New River Settlers.
H7700
A History of Middle New River Settlements and Contiguous Territory.
J2020 (ASU FC)
Kanawha River: Comprehensive Basin Study.
K100 (ASU)
The New-Kanawha River and the Mind War of West Virginia.
M630 (BC)
New River Cripple Creek Mineral Region of Virginia.
M940
Bulletin. Surface and Water Supply of Va. New, Big Sandy, and Tenn. River Basins, 1942-1950.
V750 (BC)
New River Basin Comprehensive Water Resources Plan.
V840

"The Resources and Industries of the New River Drainage Basin in West Virginia."
W7990
RIVERS — NOLICHUCKY
Floods on Nolichucky River and North and South Indian Creeks in Vicinity of Erwin, Tennessee.
T7100
RIVERS — NORTH CAROLINA
High and Low Flows and Flow Duration at Stream Gages in North Carolina in Tennessee River Basin.
T7370
RIVERS — NORTH CHICKAMAUGA
Floods on North Chickamauga, Mountain, and Lookout Creeks, in Vicinity of Chattanooga, Tennessee.
T7110
RIVERS — NORTH TOE
Floods on North Toe River and Beaver and Grassy Creeks in Vicinity of Spruce Pine, North Carolina.
T7120
RIVERS — OCONALUFTEE
Floods on Oconaluftee and Tuckaseigee Rivers and Soco Creek in Vicinity of Cherokee, North Carolina.
T7130
RIVERS — OHIO
"The Economic Aspects of the Water Pollution Abatement Program in the Ohio River Valley."
B6260
Economic Development in the Ohio River Valley Region.
B6280
Early Maps of the Ohio Valley.
B7290 (BC)
Sycamore Shores.
F1080 (ASU)
The Floods of March, 1936, Part 3, Potomac, James, and Upper Ohio Rivers.
G4470
Floods of Ohio and Mississippi Rivers, January-February, 1937.
G4480
The Ohio Valley Flood of March-April, 1913, Including Comparisons with Some Earlier Floods.
H7290
The Ohio River Basin.
I890
Ground-water Conditions along the Ohio Valley at Parkersburg, West Virginia.
J520 (ETSU)
A Tour Downstream.
J1220
Project Economic Study of the Ohio River Basin.
L2800
Blennerhassett Island in Romance and Tragedy; the Authentic Story of Blennerhassett Island, with the Burr Episode Entwined about it; the Romance and Mystery of the Blannerhassetts; Burr under Footlights and Shadows; Tragedy of Theodosia Burr.
L3770
Locust Bloom.
M3970 (BC)
A Development Program for the Ohio Valley Region.
O380
O400
Ohio River Basin: Comprehensive Survey, Main Report.
O410 (ASU)
O420
RIVERS — PIGEON
Planning for Flood Damage Prevention at Clyde, N. C.
C5160 (LMC)
N2650 (ASU UNCA)
Ecological Effects of Hot Water Discharge by an Electric Power Generating Plant.
N2660 (ASU UNCA)
Smathers from Yadkin Valley to Pigeon River: Smathers and Agner Families.
P920 (ASU)
RIVERS — POTOMAC
The Floods of March, 1936, Part 3, Potomac, James, and Upper Ohio Rivers.
G4470
The Potomac.
G4940 (FC)

RIVERS — POTOMAC
Appalachia Meets the Potomac.
I900
Potomac River Basin Directory.
I910
The Potomac Naturalist: The Natural History of the Headwaters of the Historic Potomac.
S4870 (ASU BC)
Potomac River Basin Report: Summary.
U310
The Nation's River. Official Report on the Potomac from the Department, with Recommendations for Action by the Federal Interdepartmental Task Force on the Potomac.
U2780
Potomac Valley, Model of Scenic and Recreational Values: A Preliminary Report of the Joint Federal-State Planning Team on Landscape and Recreation, Potomac Valley.
U2810
RIVERS — POWELL
Frontier Forts along the Clinch, Powell and Holston.
H1130 (BC)
Clinch-Powell Valley; Summary of Resources.
T2420
RIVERS — RAPPAHANNOCK
My Rappahannock Storybook.
H6060 (BC ASU)
RIVERS — RAPPAHANROCK
Fredericksburg, Virginia. Its Homes and History, the Battlefields and the Rappahanrock Valley.
G2650
RIVERS — RED
The Unforseen Wilderness: An Essay on Kentucky's Red River Gorge.
B3300 (ASU BC LMC)
Fishes of the Red River Drainage, Eastern Kentucky.
B6360
Red River Iron Works.
J1200
RIVERS — ROCKFISH
Old Bethesda at the Head of Rockfish.
B9380 (LMC)
RIVERS — SAVAGE
Taming the Savage River.
T130 (ASU BC)
RIVERS — SHENANDOAH
Sedimentary Studies in the Middle River Drainage Basin of the Shenandoah Valley of Virginia.
C1480 (ASU)
The Shenandoah.
D1140 (ASU BC FC)
A Valley and a Song; the Story of the Shenandoah River.
D1150 (BC ASU)
In the Picturesque Shenandoah Valley.
G2660 (ASU BC)
The Wonderful Shenandoah Valley.
G3400
Intrenched Meanders of the North Fork of the Shenandoah River, Virginia.
H100
To the Shenandoah and Beyond: The Chronicle of a Leisurely Journey through the Uplands of Virginia and Tennessee, Sketching Their Scenery, Noting Their Legends, Portraying Social and Material Progress, and Explaining Routes of Travel.
I780
RIVERS — SWANNANOA
Floods on French Broad and Swannanoa Rivers, in Vicinity of Asheville, North Carolina.
T7040
Floods on Swannanoa River and Beetree Creek in Vicinity of Swannanoa, North Carolina.
T7240
Floods on Swannanoa River and Flat Creek in Vicinity of Black Mountain and Montreat, North Carolina.
T7250
RIVERS — TENN.
A History of Navigation on the Tennessee River System: An Interpretation of the Economic Influence of This River System on the Tennessee Valley.
A1490
Development of the Tennessee River Waterway.
B4710
The Upper Tennessee.
C970 (BC)
The Tennessee. Rivers of America.
D630 (ASU WCU LMC MHC UNCA BC)
"Tennessee River Navigation; Government and Private Enterprise Since 1932."
D3620
The Tennessee River Valley; a Case Study.
G3320
"The Agricultural, Cooperative and Rural Electrification Activities of the Tennessee Valley Authority, and the Work of the Farm Credit Administration in the Tennessee River Basin."
H6110
The Taming of the Tennessee: Continued Study Units in Geographic Backgrounds.
L1510
Surveys of the Tennessee River.
M3200
Aboriginal Sites on Tennessee River.
M7080
Muscle Shoals: A Plan for the Use of the United States Properties on the Tennessee River by Private Industry for the Manufacture of Fertilizers and Other Useful Products.
M9140 (BC)
The Tennessee River Basin.
U3870
RIVERS — TENNESSEE
R1540
One River — Seven States: TVA-State Relations in the Development of the Tennessee River.
R2860 (ASU WCU LMC BC)
The French-Broad Holston Country: A History of Knox County, Tennessee.
R3940 (LMC BC)
The French Broad-Holston County: A History of Knox County, Tennessee.
R3950 (ETSU)
The Tennessee River Gorge, Its Scenic Preservation; a Report to the 1961 General Assembly.
T1730
One River, Seven States.
T2220
Atlas Finding List of the Tennessee Valley Region. The Tennessee Valley Area and Adjacent Districts in Alabama, Arkansas, Georgia, Illinois, Kentucky, Mississippi, Missouri, North Carolina, South Carolina, Tennessee, Virginia and West Virginia.
T2300
Atlas of the Tennessee Valley Region. pt. 1.
T2310
Chattanooga Flood Control Problem.
T2380
. . . Engineering Geology of the Tennessee River System. . . .
T2610
Flood Problems and Management in the Tennessee River Basin.
T2730
A History of Navigation of the Tennessee River System; an Interpretation of the Economic Influence of this River System on the Tennessee Valley. Message From the President of the United States Transmitting a Survey Entitled "A History of Navigation on the Tennessee River and Its Tributaries."
T2870 (BC ASU)
Navigation and Economic Growth: Tennessee River Experience; a Report.
T3100
Pickwick Landing Dam on the Tennessee River. Tennessee Valley Authority, Engineering and Construction Departments.
T3200
. . . Report on the Physiographic, Economic, and Other Relationships Between the Tennessee and Cumberland Rivers and Between Their Drainage Areas. Message from the President of the United States, Transmitting Report Entitled "The Physiographic, Economic, and Other Relationships Between the Tennessee and Cumberland Rivers and Between Their Drainage Areas" . . .
T3380
Report to the Congress on the Unified Development of the Tennessee River System.
T3400 (ASU)
River Traffic and Industrial Growth.
T3430
River Traffic and Industrial Growth.
T3450
Tennessee River Navigation.
T3690
The Tennessee River Navigation System; History, Development, and Operation.
T3700
The Tennessee River Waterway.
T3710
TVA and the River.
T3750
Cheaper Transportation via the Tennessee River.
T4170
Major Freight Terminals on the Tennessee River Waterway.
T5120
Navigation Charts, Tennessee River Waterway, Paducah, Kentucky to Knoxville, Tennessee; Showing Underwater Conditions, Navigation Channels and Aids and Adjacent Shore Planimetry.
T5130
The Tennessee River Navigation System: History, Development, and Operation.
T5140
The Tennessee Valley Region: Important Features and Recent Trends.
T5330
Stream Sanitation in the Tennessee Valley.
T5450
Studies of the Pollution of the Tennessee River System.
T5460
Studies of the Pollution of the Tennessee River System.
T5470
Pickwick Landing Dam on the Tennessee River.
T6460
Floods of March 1963 in Tennessee River Basin.
T6960
Floods on Tennessee River and Battle Creek, in Vicinity of South Pittsburg and Richard City, Tennessee.
T7260
Floods on the Tennessee River and Cypress and Cox Creeks in Vicinity of Florence, Alabama.
T7270
Floods on Tennessee River in Vicinity of Tri-Counties Alabama (Lawrence, Limestone, Morgan.)
T7280
Floods on Tennessee River, Little Tennessee River, and Town and Muddy Creeks in Vicinity of Lenoir City, Tennessee.
T7290
Floods on Toccoa-Ocoee River and Fightingtown Creek, in Vicinity of McCaysville, Ga. — Copperhill, Tenn.
T7300
Report on Review of Allocations of Costs of the Multiple-Purpose Water Control System in the Tennessee River Basin, as Determined by the Tennessee Valley Authority and Approved by the President Under the Provisions of the TVA Act of 1933 as Amended.
U2910
God's Valley: People and Power Along the Tennessee River.
W5840 (ASU WWC BC)
Dawn of Tennessee Valley and Tennessee History.
W6720 (ASU LMC BC)
RIVERS — TUCKASEEGEE
Planning for Flood Damage Prevention at Clyde, N. C.
C5160 (LMC)
RIVERS — TUCKASEIGEE
Tuckaseigee Minutes, 1829-1857.
N1670 (WCU)
Floods on the Tuckaseigee River and Deep Creek in Vicinity of Bryson City, North Carolina.
T2750
Floods on Oconaluftee and Tuckaseigee Rivers and Soco Creek in Vicinity of Cherokee, North Carolina.
T7130
RIVERS — TUG
"The Transformation of the Tug and Guyandot Valleys: Economic Development and Social Change in West Virginia, 1888-1921."
C9390

RIVERS — TUG
"The Rise of Education and the Decline of Feudal Tendencies in the Tug River Valley of West Virginia and Kentucky in Relation to the Hatfield and McCoy Feud."
M780 (ASU)
RIVERS — UPPER DUCK
Upper Duck River Valley; Summary of Resources.
T4020
RIVERS — VA.
Canoeing White Water: A Guide Book to the Rivers of Virginia and Eastern West Virginia, The Great Smoky Mountain Area.
C1740 (LMC)
Bulletin. Surface and Water Supply of Va. New, Big Sandy, and Tenn. River Basins, 1942-1950.
V750 (BC)
RIVERS — VALLEY
Floods on Hiwassee River, Valley River, and Peachtree Creek in Vicinity of Murphy, N C.
T7070
RIVERS — W. VA.
Canoeing White Water: A Guide Book to the Rivers of Virginia and Eastern West Virginia, The Great Smoky Mountain Area.
C1740 (LMC)
Indexed County and Railroad Pocket Map and Shipper's Guide of West Virginia.
R390 (BC)
RIVERS — WATAUGA
"Land Utilization in the New and Watauga River Basins of North Carolina."
B3700 (LMC)
The Watauga River Basin: A Survey of Existing Pollution in the Watauga River Basin Together with Recommended Classification of Its Waters, 1960-1962.
N2640 (ASU)
On the Watauga and the Cumberland.
S5300 (LMC)
Floods on Watauga and Doe Rivers in Vicinity of Elizabethton, Tennessee.
T2760
RIVERS — WEST FORD
I920
RIVERS — YADKIN
Smathers from Yadkin Valley to Pigeon River: Smathers and Agner Families.
P920 (ASU)
ROADS
C1180
Highway Accessibility Study for the Appalachian Development Highway System.
P4400
Highway Transportation and Appalachian Development: The Impact and Costs of the Appalachian Development Highway System
P4410 (ETSU LMS ASU)
The North Carolina Chain Gang: A Study of County Convict Road Work.
S6920 (LMC)
The North Carolina Chain Gang: A Study of County Convict Road Work.
S6930 (WWC)
North Carolina Roads and Their Builders.
W1870 (ASU LMC)
ROADS — APP.
New Roads in Old Virginia.
R3920 (LMC)
The Appalachian Thruway Study.
R4420
"The Economic Effects of the Original Section of the Pennsylvania Turnpike on Adjacent Areas."
S2560
Economic Impact of Secondary Road Improvements.
S8150
ROADS — APP. DEVELOPMENT HIGHWAY SYSTEM
"A Plan Formulation Methodology for the Appalachian Development Highway System."
M140
ROADS — KY.
Old Roads in Kentucky.
B7040 (ASU BC)
Boone's Wilderness Road.
H7870 (ETSU BC)
ROADS — LOGGING
Configuration of Appalachian Logging Roads.
B2120
Erosion Control on Logging Roads in the Appalachians.
K2970 (ASU LMC)
ROADS — N. C.
The War Trails of the Blue Ridge, Containing an Authentic Description of the Battle of King's Mountain, the Incidents Leading up to and the Echoes of the Aftermath of This Epochal Engagement, and Other Stories Whose Scenes Are Laid in the Blue Ridge.
D3760 (BC ASU LMC)
Road Maps and Tour Book of Western North Carolina.
N2370 (BC ASU LMC)
ROADS — THE WILDERNESS
Daniel Boone and the Wilderness Road.
B7570 (ASU BC)
Daniel Boone and the Wilderness Road.
B7580 (ETSU)
ROADS — TURNPIKES
The Valley Turnpike, Winchester to Staunton, and Other Roads.
W1850 (ASU BC)
ROADS — VA.
Braddock's Road Through the Virginia Colony.
H7420 (ASU)
ROADS — WESTWARD MOVEMENT
Cumberland Gap and Trails West.
M200 (BC)
ROADS, WILDERNESS
The Wilderness Road to Kentucky.
P4900
The Wilderness Road: a Description of the Routes of Travel by Which the Pioneers and Early Settlers First Came to Kentucky.
S6120 (ASU FC LMC BC)
ROANOKE RIVER
Frontiers Along the Upper Roanoke River, 1740-1776.
C4920
ROCKFISH RIVER
Old Bethesda at the Head of Rockfish.
B9380 (LMC)
ROOTS AND HERBS
Natural Dyes and Home Dyeing.
A620 (BC ASU WCU)
Medicine in Virginia in the Seventeenth Century.
B4660
Herbs: Their Culture and Uses.
C4700 (LMC)
The Dye-Pot.
D680
The Medicinal Plants of Tennessee Exhibiting Their Commercial Value, with an Analytical Key, Descriptions in Aid of Their Recognition, and Notes Relating to Their Distribution, Time and Mode of Collection, and Preparation for the Drug Market.
G610
North Carolina Drug Plants of Commercial Value.
H2130 (ASU LMC UNCA)
Ginseng and Other Medicinal Plants; a Book of Valuable Information for Growers as well as Collectors of Medicinal Roots, Barks, Leaves, etc.
H2160
Index of Plants of North Carolina With Reputed Medicinal Uses.
J230 (WWC)
Guide to Medicinal Plants of Appalachia.
K3230 (BC)
A Guide to Medicinal Plants of Appalachia.
K3240 (ASU ETSU LMC)
Vegetable Dyeing: 151 Color Recipes for Dyeing Yarns and Fabrics with Natural Materials.
L1880 (ASU)
Dyes from Plants.
R3170 (ASU)
Colonial Kitchen Herbs and Remedies: Garden and Kitchen Secrets from Early America.
S2700 (ASU LMC)
Pioneer Comforts and Kitchen Remedies. Old Timey Highland Secrets from the Blue Ridge and Great Smoky Mountains.
S2730 (MHC ASU BC WCU)
Grannies's Remedies.
T8010 (ASU)
ROOTS AND HERBS — APP.
Southern Home Remedies.
H2650 (AASU LMC)
American Medicinal Leaves and Herbs.
H4650 (ASU)
Ginseng, Its Cultivation, Harvesting, Marketing and Market Value: With a Short Account of Its History and Botany.
K70 (WWC)
Drug Plants of Western North Carolina.
M2740 (WCU ASU)
RURAL DEVELOPMENT
Development Opportunities in Kentucky: Final Report.
B6270
S. C. — DESCRIPTION AND TRAVEL
The History of Travelors Rest.
G2520 (ASU)
A New Voyage to Carolina.
L1000 (LMC ETSU)
A New Voyage to Carolina.
L1010 (UNCA)
S. C. — HISTORY
Historical Collections of South Carolina.
C1470 (ASU)
Bridging the Gap. A Guide to Early Greenville, South Carolina.
E620 (ASU)
Colonial and Revolutionary History of Upper South Carolina, Embracing for the Most Part the Primitive and Colonial History of the Territory Comprising the Original County of Spartanburg with a General Review of the Entire Military Operations in the Upper Portion of South Carolina and Portions of North Carolina.
L320 (ASU WCU LMC BC)
Colonial and Revolutionary History of Upper South Carolina.
L330 (LMC)
History of Spartanburg County: Embracing an Account of Many Important Events, and Biographical Sketches of Statesmen, Divines and Other Public Men.
L340 (ASU BC)
A History of the Upper Country of South Carolina.
L3070 (LMC BC)
A History of the Upper Country of South Carolina: From the Earliest Periods to the Close of the War of Independence.
L3080 (ASU WCU LMC)
In the Red Hills: A Story of the Carolina Country.
M260 (ASU)
A Sketch of the History of South Carolina to the Close of the Proprietary Government by the Revolution of 1719.
R2580 (ASU)
The History of Methodism in South Carolina.
S3090 (ASU BC)
SAVAGE RIVER
Taming the Savage River.
T130 (ASU BC)
SCHOOL ATTENDANCE
"Eliminations from the Class of 1950 in the Marion High School."
E1610 (ASU)
SCOTCH-IRISH
Surnames in the United States Census of 1790; an Analysis of National Origins of the Population.
A2110
Chronicles of Scotch-Irish Settlement in Virginia.
C2750
Scotch-Irish Settlers in the Valley of Virginia.
C3960 (BC)
Ulster Emigration to Colonial America, 1718-1775.
D2240 (ASU)
The Scotch-Irish in Northern Ireland and in the American Colonies.
G2030 (ASU)
The Scotch-Irish: Or, the Scot in North Britain, North Ireland, and North America.
H1520 (ASU BC)
The Scotch-Irish: Or, The Scot in North Britain, North Ireland, and North America.
H1530 (ASU BC)
Scotch-Irish and English Proverbs and Sayings of the West Branch Valley of Central Pennsylvania.
S3150 (ASU)
SCOTCH-IRISH — APP.
The Scotch-Irish in America.
F1920
The Scotch-Irish in America.
F1930 (ASU)

SCOTCH-IRISH — APP.
The Scotch-Irish in History as Master Builders of Empires, States, Churches, Schools and Civilization.
S2500 (ASU BC)
SCOTS
Surnames in the United States Census of 1790; an Analysis of National Origins of the Population.
A2110
A Historical Account of the Settlements of Scotch Highlanders in America Prior to the Peace of 1783: Together with Notices of Highland Regiments and Biographical Sketches.
M2010 (ASU)
The Highland Scots of North Carolina.
M5240 (LMC BC)
The Highland Scots of North Carolina, 1732-1776.
M5250 (ASU LMC WWC)
Charn Cuimhne to Our Scots of North Carolina.
S4650 (ASU)
SHENANDOAH RIVER
Sedimentary Studies in the Middle River Drainage Basin of the Shenandoah Valley of Virginia.
C1480 (ASU)
The Shenandoah.
D1140 (ASU BC FC)
A Valley and a Song; the Story of the Shenandoah River.
D1150 (BC ASU)
In the Picturesque Shenandoah Valley.
G2660 (ASU BC)
The Wonderful Shenandoah Valley.
G3400
Intrenched Meanders of the North Fork of the Shenandoah River, Virginia.
H100
To the Shenandoah and Beyond: The Chronicle of a Leisurely Journey through the Uplands of Virginia and Tennessee, Sketching Their Scenery, Noting Their Legends, Portraying Social and Material Progress, and Explaining Routes of Travel.
I780
SHENANDOAH VALLEY — HISTORY — CIVIL WAR
History of the Campaign of General T. J. (Stonewall) Jackson in the Shenandoah Valley of Virginia from Nov. 4, 1861, to June 17, 1862.
A1480 (ASU)
SOCIAL CONDITIONS — N. C.
Rutherford County: Economic and Social.
P4590 (ASU)
SOCIAL INSURANCE
"An Evaluation of the Pension Plans in the Anthracite Coal Industry."
M8450
SOCIAL INSURANCE — APP.
An Analysis of Appalachian State Coal Mine Health and Safety and Workmen's Compensation Programs: Recommendations for Improvement.
K880 (ASU)
SOCIAL INSURANCE — COAL INDUSTRY
"Development and Operation of the Welfare and Retirement Fund in the Bituminous Coal Industry."
W5620
SOCIAL INSURANCE — W. VA.
"A Study of the United Mine Workers of America Welfare and Retirement Fund."
S1400
SOCIAL LIFE AND CUSTOMS
Pioneers of Destiny: The Romance of the Appalachian People.
W1930 (LMC BC)
"Characteristics of Low Income Rural Families Related to Expenditure and Consumption Patterns: An Analysis of Rural Poverty for Public Program Purposes."
W2410
The Story of Why and How the Leah Weiss Relief Kitchen Became a Landmark in Cincinnati.
W2420 (BC)
A Profile of the Appalachian Family.
W2480
The Kingdom of Madison, a Southern Mountain Fastness and Its People.
W2560 (ASU LMC WWC WCU MHC BC)
Boyhood Days in Southwest Virginia.
W9900 (BC)
Aging Patterns in a Rural and an Urban Area of Kentucky.
Y150
Leisure-Time Activities of Older Persons in Selected Rural and Urban Areas of Kentucky.
Y180
Older Rural Americans: A Sociological Perspective.
Y190 (BC)
Socio-Economic Problems of Older Persons in Casey County, Kentucky.
Y210
SOCIAL LIFE AND CUSTOMS — PA.
Life in the Iron Mills: Or, The Korl Woman.
D1190 (ASU)
SOCIAL PROBLEMS
Seven Lean Years.
W9010 (BC)
SOCIAL STRUCTURE AND CONDITIONS
Appalachia Revisited: How People Lived Fifty Years Ago.
A400 (ETSU BC ASU WCU FC LMC)
Let Us Now Praise Famous Men.
A730 (BC ASU WCU)
Let Us Now Praise Famous Men.
A740 (ETSU)
Let Us Now Praise Famous Men.
A750 (WCU)
"Social and Economic Conditions in Jackson County During the Depression."
A780 (WCU)
"Factors Affecting Social Participation in Coal Communities."
A800 (ASU)
"Kentucky State Aid and the Educationally Disadvantaged Child."
A1390
Social Factors Associated with Land Class in Overton County, Tennessee.
A1890
Life in a West Virginia Coal Field.
A2100
"The Southern Appalachian Coal Community: An Explorative Study."
B820 (ASU)
"The Social and Economic History of Maryville since 1890."
B1920
"The Interrelationships of Organized Religion and Certain Other Community Subsystems in Five Selected Counties of Kentucky with Implications for Educational Administration."
B2340
In Retrospect: Reminiscencies (sic) and Observations of a Hamilton County, Tennessee, Retired Teacher.
B2580
Appalachians Speak Up.
B3350 (BC)
Camerton Slope, a Story of Mining Life.
B4240 (ASU BC)
Sociocultural Differences Among Three Areas in Kentucky, as Determinants of Educational and Occupational Aspirants and Expectations of Rural Youth.
B5090 (BC)
"Association of Selected Socio-economic Characteristics with Net Migration from Three Kentucky Economic Areas, 1920-1950."
B6440
Factors Related to Changes in Social Participation in a Pennsylvania Rural Community.
B8220
"The Evolution of Southern Appalachian Culture as Evidenced in Folklore."
B8850 (ETSU)
"The Mountain People of Virginia: Their Nature and Their Needs."
D170 (ASU)
"Social Structural Factors Influencing the Urbanization of Appalachian Hill Emigrants in an Urban Ghetto."
H2090
"The Enriched Curriculum as a Means of Meeting the Emotional and Social Needs of First Grade Children in Washington County."
K1800 (ETSU)
Social Relationships and Institutions in Seven Rural Communities. United States Farm Security Administration Social Research Report no. 18.
L3420
"Socioeconomic Characteristics of Young Farmers Enrolled in Vocational Agriculture Classes in West Virginia."
M1500
The Southern Poor-White from Lubberland to Tobacco Road.
M1690 (ASU)
The Southern Poor-white from Lubberland to Tobacco Road.
M1700 (LMC)
The South in Continuity and Change.
M1910 (BC FC)
Sketches of Life in North Carolina.
M5340
The Spirit of the Mountains.
M5440 (ASU BC WCU)
"Three Appalachian Communities: Cultural Differentials as They Affect Levels of Living and Population Pressure."
M6590 (ASU)
A Review of the Literature Pertaining to Appalachia; Stressing Attitudes to Social Change and Religious and Educational Orientations; A Working Paper for the Boards of Christian Education of the United Presbyterian Church in the U. S.
N450 (BC)
"Educational, Economic and Community Survey of Scott County, Tennessee."
P1630
Changes in the Rural Southern Appalachian Community.
P2720 (ASU)
Change in Rural Appalachia: Implications for Action Programs.
P2750 (FC LMC WCU ETSU ASU BC)
Rural Southern Appalachia and Mass Society, and Overview.
P2780 (ASU LMC)
An Economic and Social Survey of Frederick County.
P2840 (ASU LMC)
"Immigrants from the Appalachian Region to the City of Columbus, Ohio: A Case Study."
R2210 (BC)
Mountain Families in Transition: A Case Study of Appalachian Migration.
S1270 (ASU WCU LMC ETSU WWC BC UNCA)
Sociocultural Origins and Migration Patterns of Young Men from Eastern Kentucky.
S1310
"Social-psychological Adjustment of Kentucky Mountain Migrants in Urbanized Industrial Areas of Southern Ohio."
S1740 (ASU)
"Kentucky Politics and Society: 1919-1932."
S2080 (BC)
Cabins in the Laurel.
S2810 (ASU MHC LMC WCU ETSU WWC BC FC UNCA)
Cabins in the Laurel.
S2820 (FC ASU)
Hollow Folk.
S2940 (BC LMC ETSU WWC)
Hollow Folk.
S2950 (ASU)
"An Economic, Social and Educational Survey of Campbell County, Tennessee."
S4690
Hamilton County, Economic and Social: A Laboratory Study in the Department of Agricultural Economics Under the Direction of Professor C. E. Allred.
S6910
Shiloh: A Mountain Community.
S7050 (ASU ETSU FC LMC UNCA WCU WWC BC)
Patterns of Adaptation in a Changing Mountain Community; Stress and Health.
S7060 (BC)
Fisher's River Scenes.
T60 (ASU)
An Economic and Social Survey of Russell County.
T300 (BC)
Lebanon, A Virginia Community.
T310

SOCIAL STRUCTURE AND CONDITIONS

The Traipsin' Woman.
T7970 (ASU WWC BC)

Economic and Social Problems and Conditions of the Southern Appalachians.
U2490

Manners, Customs, and Observances: Their Origins and Signification.
W110 (ASU)

A Profile of Community Problems: Watauga, Avery, Mitchell, Yancey Counties.
W710

An Economic and Social Survey of Clarke County.
W900

The Silent Riders.
W1570 (BC)

Life and Religion in Southern Appalachia, an Interpretation of Selected Data from the Southern Appalachian Studies.
W1920 (ASU MHC WCU LMC ETSU WWC BC UNCA)

Pioneers of Destiny: The Romance of the Appalachian People.
W1930 (LMC BC)

"Characteristics of Low Income Rural Families Related to Expenditure and Consumption Patterns: An Analysis of Rural Poverty for Public Program Purposes."
W2410

A Profile of the Appalachian Family.
W2480

The Kingdom of Madison, a Southern Mountain Fastness and Its People.
W2560 (ASU LMC WWC WCU MHC BC)

Culture on the Moving Frontier.
W9460 (ASU)

Hawkers and Walkers in Early America: Strolling Peddlers, Preachers, Lawyers, Doctors, Players and Others, from the Beginning to the Civil War.
W9520 (ASU)

The Smoke Hole and Its People.
W9750 (BC)

Socio-Economic Problems of Older Persons in Casey County, Kentucky.
Y210

SOCIAL STRUCTURE AND CONDITIONS — ALA.

"The Social Backgrounds of Scientists and Engineers in Oak Ridge, Tennessee, and Huntsville, Alabama."
D4130

Lower Piedmont Country.
N1210 (ASU BC ETSU LMC WCU)

Possum Trot, Rural Community, South.
N1220 (ASU BC WCU)

SOCIAL STRUCTURE AND CONDITIONS — APP.

Factors Associated with the Adjustment of Families in Three Low-Income Counties of North Carolina.
A460 (ASU)

"Factors Associated with the Adjustment of Families in Three Low Income Counties of North Carolina."
A470

An Economic and Social Survey of Bedford Co., Va.
A480 (ASU)
A2790 (ASU)

Appalachian Data Book.
A3600 (ASU ETSU BC)

Appalachian Data Book.
A3610 (MHC BC ETSU ASU)

The Appalachian Region: A Statistical Appendix of Comparative Socioeconomic Indicators.
A3650 (MHC ASU)

"An Empirical Study of the Application of the Folk-urban Typology to the Classification of Social Systems."
A5540 (ASU)

"The Mountain People of the South: A Sociological Study."
B7130 (WCU)

"Analysis of the Values and Value Systems Reported by Students, The General Public, and Educators in a Selected Appalachian Public School District."
B9390

Voices from the Mountain.
C1210 (ASU)

The Southern Appalachian Heritage.
C2041

"The Relation of Level of Living to Selected Additional Characteristics of Central Appalachia Rural Families."
C2920 (ASU)

The Rampaging Frontier: Manners and Humors of Pioneer Days in the South and Middle West.
C4590 (ASU)

The Rampaging Frontier: Manners and Humors of Pioneer Days in the South and Middle West.
C4600 (WWC)

Children of Crisis.
C5850 (WCU ASU)

Farewell to the South.
C5880 (ASU WCU)

Report of Social Welfare Manpower Project for Appalachia, July 15, 1969 to August 31, 1970.
C7890 (ASU BC)

Five Years in the Alleghenies.
C9090 (ASU BC)

"Alienation Among Low-income People in Appalachia."
C9170 (LMC ASU)

Swing Your Mountain Gal, Sketches of Life in the Southern Highlands.
C9950 (ASU WCU LMC MHC BC)

"Some Correlates of Alienation Among Southern Appalachians."
D450 (ASU)

The Mountain Preacher.
D1070 (BC)

"Social Factors Affecting Selected Southern Baptist Churches in the Southern Appalachian Region of the United States."
D1550 (WCU ASU)

The Dixie Frontier, a Social History of the Southern Frontier from the First Transmontane Beginnings to the Civil War.
D2080 (ASU MHC)

"An Analysis of the Social Life and Customs of the Southern Appalachians as Reflected in Selected Children's Books."
D2610 (ASU)

"An Analysis of the Social Life and Customs of the Southern Appalachians as Reflected in Selected Children's Books."
D2620 (ASU)

The Southern Appalachian Region: A Survey.
F2010

The Southern Mountaineer.
F2890

The Longest Mile.
G710 (ASU WCU LMC ETSU FC BC WWC)

"Habitat-economy-society, a Frame of Reference Applied to Southern Appalachian Coal Country."
G1130

Appalachia in Transition.
G2150 (ASU WCU LMC MHC ETSU FC BC)

Economic and Social Problems and Conditions of the Southern Appalachians.
G3370

"Social and Cultural Links in the Urban and Occupational Adjustment of Southern Appalachian Migrants."
H2430

"Sectarianism and Social Participation: A Study of the Relationship between Religious Attitudes and Involvement in Voluntary Organizations in Seventy-two Churches in the Southern Appalachian Mountains."
H3220 (LMC)

"Political Socialization in Appalachia: An Inquiry into the Process of Political Learning in an American Sub-Culture."
H5670

"Possum Ridge Farmers: A Study in Cultural Change."
H6120 (ASU)

"Migration, Mobility and Social Participation."
J1230

My Colorful Days.
J2530

"The Carter Family: A Reflection of Changes in Society."
K10 (WCU)

Hillbilly Women.
K20 (ASU BC UNCA)

How People Get Power: Organizing Oppressed Communities Get Action.
K40 (WCU ASU)

Poverty Programs and Social Mobility.
K290

"Religiosity as Related to Social Factors and Modes of Social Institutional Behavior in the Southern Appalachian Region."
K2040 (LMC ASU)

Black Land, the Way of Life in the Coal Fields.
K3030

"Fundamentalism and Selected Social Factors in the Southern Appalachian Region."
L170 (ASU)

People of Coal Town.
L600 (ASU BC WWC WCU)

People of Coal Town.
L610 (LMC)

Children of the Cumberland.
L2100 (BC ASU LMC WCU WWC)

Children of the Cumberland.
L2110 (ASU)

A Planner's Reference Guide Relating to Socioeconomic Factors Within Appalachia as Applied to Public Education.
L2620 (ETSU)

Clasping Hands with Generations Past.
L2960

"Social Behavior under Conditions of Extreme Stress: A Study of Miners Entrapped by a Coal Mine Disaster."
L3820

"The Social and Educational Aspects of the Tennessee Valley Authority."
M2630

Experience-worlds of Mountain People: Institutional Efficiency in Appalachian Village and Hinterland Communities.
M4320 (ETSU WWC BC)

Experience-worlds of Mountain People: Institutional Efficiency in Appalachian Village and Hinterland Communities.
M4330 (ASU)

Girl in the Rural Family.
M5950 (ASU BC)

A Thousand-Mile Walk to the Gulf.
M8470

The Rural Society in Transition.
N590 (ASU)

Little Smoky Ridge: The Natural History of a Southern Appalachian Neighborhood.
P1250 (ASU WCU LMC MHC ETSU WWC FC UNCA)

"Some Aspects of Culture Change in A Mountain Neighborhood of East Tennessee."
P1260 (ASU)

West Virginians in Their Own State and In Cleveland, Ohio.
P2800 (ASU)

Roots of Fertility.
P3340

When Cultures Meet.
P3620 (BC ASU)

"Related Aspects of the Social and Economic Problems, Cultural Transitions and Educational System of Rural Appalachia: An Analysis Based on the Concept of Scale."
R2220 (BC)

Blue Ridge Breezes.
R4120 (LMC FC WCU BC)

Blue Ridge Breezes.
R4130 (ASU BC)

A Human Relations Study — The Southern White In-Migrant.
S950

"The Culture of Poverty — A Study of the Value-orientation Preferences of the Chronically Impoverished."
S1030

Social Structure of the Contact Situation, Rural Appalachia and Urban America.
S1290

Sociocultural Factors in the Career. Aspirations and Plans of Rural Kentucky High School Seniors.
S1300

Background in Tennessee.
S1380 (ASU)

"An Analysis of Federative Patterns in Social Organization with a Field Study of the Council of Southern Mountain Workers."
S1510 (BC)

The Cleveland Southern In-Migrant Study; an Overview.
S2440

SOCIAL STRUCTURE AND CONDITIONS — APP.
The Development of Attitudes.
S2930
Society and Health in a Mountain Community: A Working Paper.
S4720 (ASU)
The Southern Appalachian Region; A Survey.
S5670 (BC ASU UNCA FC)
The Southern Appalachian Region.
S5680 (ASU ETSU FC LMC MHC WCU WWC BC)
"The Relationship of the Economic Production of Farmers of the Southern Appalachian Region to Certain Social Factors."
S6200 (ASU)
"An Overview of Federal Programs and Their Impacts on Appalachia."
S7690
Recollections of an Old Man. Seventy Years in Dixie.
S8950
The Hollow.
S9110 (WWC ASU LMC ETSU BC)
From Laurel Hill to Siler's Bog.
T7600 (ETSU)
Life Among the Hills and Mountains of Kentucky.
T8080 (ASU BC)
The Highlanders of the South.
T8330 (ASU ETSU BC LMC)
Appalachia: The Mountains, the Place, and the People.
T8920 (ASU LMC MHC BC ETSU)
Economic and Social Problems and Conditions of the Southern Appalachians.
U360 (ASU)
Economic and Social Problems and Conditions of the Southern Appalachians.
U370
Standards of Living in Four Southern Appalachian Mountain Counties.
U2560 (BC)
Appalachia in the Sixties: Decade of Reawakening.
W550 (ASU LMC WWC WCU MHC ETSU BC UNCA)
Yesterday's People: Life in Contemporary Appalachia.
W2490 (UNCA ASU WCU MHC LMC ETSU WWC FC BC)
Doctor Woman of the Cumberlands: The Autobiography of May Cravath Wharton, M. D.
W5020 (ASU LMC WWC BC)
Doctor Woman of the Cumberlands; the Autobiography of May Cravath Wharton, M. D.
W5030 (LMC WCU)
Highland Heritage: The Southern Mountains and the Nation.
W5380
"Socio-cultural Factors and Economic Development in West Central Appalachia."
W6060
"Disorganization and Delinquency in Three Coal Communities."
W6860 (ASU)
The Southern Mountaineers.
W7520 (ASU ETSU MHC WWC BC)
The Southern Mountaineers.
W7530 (ASU LMC)

SOCIAL STRUCTURE AND CONDITIONS — CHEROKEE
Social Anthropology of North American Tribes.
E1240

SOCIAL STRUCTURE AND CONDITIONS — COAL CAMPS
The Plight of the Bituminous Coal Miner.
M7790 (ASU BC)
"The Coal Camp: A Pattern of Limited Community Life."
M7860 (ASU)
Anthracite Coal Communities.
R3070 (BC)

SOCIAL STRUCTURE AND CONDITIONS — GA.
"An Experimental and Field Study of North Georgia Mountaineers."
J2440 (ASU)
Statistics of the State of Georgia.
W5420 (BC)

SOCIAL STRUCTURE AND CONDITIONS — KY.
"Teenage Dating Behavior in Two Eastern Kentucky High Schools."
B4730
"Sociocultural Differences among Three Areas in Kentucky."
B6110
"The Social Organization of an Isolated Kentucky Mountain Neighborhood."
B7210 (ASU)
A Selective Description of a Knox County Mountain Neighborhood.
C40
Informal Social Participation in Five Kentucky Counties.
C3990
"Sect Religion and Social Change in an Isolated Rural Community of Southern Appalachia, with Case Story, "Fruit of the Land"."
C5290 (ASU)
Bloody Ground.
D1400 (ASU LMC BC)
The Mountain People in Eastern Kentucky.
D2110
A Winner on Satin's Doorstep.
D3370 (BC)
Stinking Creek.
F750 (ASU WCU LMC ETSU WWC BC FC UNCA)
The Mountain People of Kentucky. An Account of Present Conditions with the Attitude of the People toward Improvement.
H1490 (ASU BC)
The Integration of Locality Groups in an Eastern Kentucky County.
H1550
An Experimental Study of the East Kentucky Mountaineers: A Study in Heredity and Environment.
H5680 (ETSU BC ASU)
Participation in Organized Activities in Selected Kentucky Localities.
K250
"A Rorschach Comparison of Adult Male Personality in Big Cove, Cherokee, North Carolina, and "Henry's Branch', Kentucky."
K3440
Community and Neighborhood Groupings in Knott County, Kentucky.
O1050
Neighborhood Standing and Population Changes in Johnson and Robertson Counties.
O1080
Elites and Change in the Kentucky Mountains.
P3260 (ASU MHC WCU BC)
"A Comparison of Some Aspects of Family Life Between Two Areas of Leslie Co., Kentucky."
Q110
In the East Kentucky Hills.
Q160 (ASU WCU ETSU LMC)
The Land of Saddle-bags: A Study of the Mountain People of Appalachia.
R130 (BC ASU ETSU WWC)
The Land of Saddle-bags: A Study of the Mountain People of Appalachia.
R140 (LMC MHC WCU)
Saddlebag Folk: The Way of Life in the Kentucky Mountains.
R160 (BC ASU LMC ETSU)
"Social Effects of the Mining Industry in Eastern Kentucky."
S400 (ASU)
Children of Appalachia.
S3270 (ASU ETSU MHC BC)
The Social Dimensions of Kentucky Counties: Data and Rankings of the State's 120 Counties on Each of 81 Characteristics.
S9360
The Singin' Gatherin': Tunes From the Southern Appalachians.
T7940 (UNCA BC ETSU ASU)
The Singin' Gatherin': Tunes From the Southern Appalachians.
T7950 (LMC BC)
"The Social and Economic Structure of Kentucky Agriculture, 1850-1860."
T9470
"The Economic and Cultural Development of Eastern Kentucky from 1900 to the Present."
W1540 (ASU)

SOCIAL STRUCTURE AND CONDITIONS — MD.
Rural Social Organization of Frederick County, Maryland.
G4250

SOCIAL STRUCTURE AND CONDITIONS — N. C.
Along the Ridges.
B380 (ASU LMC)
B8390 (BC)
"Weaverton — A Study of Culture and Personality in a Southern Mill Town."
C3380
Reminiscences and Traditions of Western North Carolina.
D700
"Social Organization and Community Solidarity in Painttown, Cherokee, North Carolina."
G280 (ETSU ASU)
Socio-cultural Adaptation of Newcomers to Cities in the Piedmont Industrial Crescent.
G4850
"A Cultural Study of a Mountain Community in Western North Carolina."
H3240 (ASU)
"A Cultural Study of Mountain Community in Western North Carolina."
H3250 (ASU)
North Carolina: An Economic and Social Profile.
H6070 (LMC BC)
North Carolina, Economic and Social.
H6080 (WWC LMC BC UNCA)
Blue Ridge: An Appalachian Community in Transition.
K180 (ASU WCU FC ETSU BC)
"Social Change, Adaptive Problems, and Health in a Mountain Community."
K190 (LMC ASU)
"A Rorschach Comparison of Adult Male Personality in Big Cove, Cherokee, North Carolina, and "Henry's Branch', Kentucky."
K3440
Buncombe County, Economic and Social.
M8190
Buncombe County: Economic and Social.
M8200 (ASU BC LMC)
Characteristics of Households in Areas Served by the W. A. M. Y.
N2290 (ASU)
North Carolina Manual 1874-19.
N2560 (ASU LMC)
Buncombe County: Economic and Social.
N2670 (ASU)
High Lands.
R1760 (ASU LMC WCU)
"Political Leadership and Social Structure in a Rural County."
R1870 (ASU)
The Hills o' Ca'liny.
S5960 (ASU LMC)
Fisher's River (North Carolina) Scenes and Characters by "Skitt Who Was Raised Thar."
T70 (ETSU BC)

SOCIAL STRUCTURE AND CONDITIONS — N. C. — WESTERN COUNTIES
Community Life in Western North Carolina.
S5840 (ASU)

SOCIAL STRUCTURE AND CONDITIONS — PA.
Formal Participation Patterns in a Central Pennsylvania Rural Community.
B8210
"They Walk These Hills: A Study of Social Solidarity among the Racially-mixed People of the Ramapo Mountains."
C5590 (ASU)
Social Stratification in a Pennsylvania Rural Community.
D3940
Forces Influencing Rural Life.
J1250
Steeltown, an Industrial Case History of the Conflict between Progress and Security.
W250

SOCIAL STRUCTURE AND CONDITIONS — S. C.
Greenville County, Economic and Social.
G4870
Greenville County, Economic and Social.
G4880
Social Problems of South Carolina.
W6540 (LMC)

SOCIAL STRUCTURE AND CONDITIONS — TENN.
"Some Phases of the Social and Economic History of Washington County, Tennessee, 1865-1917."
B6220

SOCIAL STRUCTURE AND CONDITIONS — TENN.

"Some Phases of the Social and Economic History of Washington County, Tennessee, 1865-1917."
B6230 (ETSU)

Dimensions of Change in East Tennessee, Tennessee, the South, and the Nation: A Comparative Analysis.
B7310 (ASU ETSU LMC WCU)

"Changes in Social and Economic Status of the People in Sullivan County for a Thirty Year Period."
C3390 (ASU)

The Tennessee Yeomen, 1840-1860.
C4320 (ASU ETSU)

The Tennessee Yeomen, 1840-1860.
C4330 (LMC)

"Social and Economic History of Kingsport before 1908."
C7840 (ETSU)

Land of Hope: The Way of Life in the Tennessee Valley.
C8260 (WWC ASU)

"Formative Years of Johnson City, Tennessee, 1885-1890: A Social History."
D210 (ETSU)

A Social Study of the Colored Population of Knoxville, Tennessee.
D1100

"The Social Backgrounds of Scientists and Engineers in Oak Ridge, Tennessee, and Huntsville, Alabama."
D4130

"The Personal Characteristics, Social Background, and Academic Achievements of Forty Non-Promoted Pupils at Kennburg School."
E1690 (ETSU)

Social and Economic Trends in Tennessee and Their Implications for Education.
F2530 (ETSU)

"Sewanee a Unique Community."
H5460

"The Social and Economic Effects Produced upon Small Towns by Rapid Industrialization."
H7650

"The Tennessee Political System: The Relationship of the Socioeconomic Environment to Political Processes and Policy Outputs."
M870

"Social Survey of Blount County, Tennessee."
M3940

Neighbor and Kin: Life in a Tennessee Ridge Community.
M4280 (ASU WCU LMC BC WWC FC UNCA)

"A Study of Living Conditions in the Pittman Center Community, 1934-1935."
M4400

"The Rural Church and Organized Community Activity, a Study of Church-community Relations in Two East Tennessee Communities."
M4430

"Two Resettlement Communities on the Cumberland Plateau."
M6600

"Socio-Economic Readjustment of Farm Families Displaced by the TVA Land Purchase in the Norris Area."
N1000
O330

"Some Aspects of Culture Change in A Mountain Neighborhood of East Tennessee."
P1260 (ASU)

"An Economic, Educational, and Social Survey of Franklin County, Tennessee."
R570 (ASU)

"The Social, Economic, Cultural, Religious and Family Educational Backgrounds of Recent Dropouts from Bristol, Tennessee, High School."
S4340 (ETSU)

"Rural Leadership in Roane County, Tennessee."
S4880
S5350

"Rural Leadership in Roane County, Tennessee."
S7480 (ASU)

"A Study of Local Sources of Local Government Agencies in Twenty-three Selected Tennessee Counties."
S7760

The Incidence of Poverty — Social and Economic Conditions in Tennessee.
W6600

SOCIAL STRUCTURE AND CONDITIONS — VA.

Institutional History of Virginia in the Seventeenth Century: An Inquiry into the Religious, Moral, Educational, Legal, Military, and Political Condition of the People Based on Original and Contemporaneous Records.
B7630 (ETSU)

An Economic and Social Survey of Augusta County.
C2110 (ASU BC)

An Economic and Social Survey of Botetourt County."
C5600

An Economic and Social Survey of Patrick County.
C6680 (BC)

"The Mountain People of Virginia: Their Nature and Their Needs."
D160 (ASU)

An Economic and Social Survey of Washington County.
D3830 (ASU BC)

A Social Study of the Blacksburg Community.
G390 (ASU)

An Economic and Social Survey of Albemarle County.
G740

An Economic and Social Survey of Warren County.
H520 (ASU)

"Augusta County, Virginia: A Study of Patterns."
H7960 (LMC)

"Augusta County, Virginia: A Study of Patterns."
H7970 (ASU)

An Economic and Social Survey of Wise County.
K790 (ASU BC)

The Springs of Virginia: Life, Love and Death at the Waters, 1775-1900.
R1470 (ASU FC)

An Economic and Social Survey of Giles County.
S5250

An Economic and Social Survey of Roanoke County.
S7130

"A Sociological Analysis of Ecology, Structure and Processes in a Virginia Coal Mining Community."
S8080

An Economic and Social Survey of Virginia Counties.
U4120 (FC)

Virginia, Economic and Civic.
V1160 (BC)

An Economic and Social Survey of Warren Co.
V1240 (BC ASU)

An Economic and Social Survey of Alleghany County.
W290 (ASU BC)

SOCIAL STRUCTURE AND CONDITIONS — W. VA.

Work, Safety, and Life Style Among Southern Appalachian Coal Miners: A Survey of the Men of Standard Mines.
A1970 (ASU)

Salesman of Appalachia.
A4960

"The Pattern and Nature of the Informal and Formal Institutional Contacts Participated in by Residents of New Hill."
B1270

"Needs and Interests in Family Relationships of a Selected Group of West Virginia Eighth and Ninth Grade Pupils, 1948-1949."
B7020

A Social and Economic Survey of the Spencer Soil Conservation Area.
C7540

"The Status of School Board Members of West Virginia."
D4080

Daybreak on Cranberry Ridge.
F540 (ASU)

"Segration Patterns in a Coal Camp."
F3220 (ASU)

"Cultural and Historical Geography of Mining Settlements in the Pocahontas Coal Fields of Southern West Virginia, 1880 to 1930."
G1620

"Social and Economic Implications of Strip Mining in Harrison County, W. Va."
H5440

"French Creek Community."
L2600 (ASU)

"The Temperance Movement in West Virginia."
L3030

"Community Uses of Public School Buildings in West Virginia."
M6570

"Mass Media Use Patterns and Interests Among West Virginia Rural Non-farm Families of Low Socio-economic Status."
M8530

Community Size and Social Attributes in West Virginia.
P2730 (WCU ASU)

Migration and Occupational Adjustment of West Virginians in the City.
P2770

"Factors Influencing Social Status, Social Participation in the Elementary School of Crum, West Virginia."
R200

County Study Data Book: Measures of Social Change in West Virginia.
S3780

SOCIAL STRUCTURE AND CONDITIONS — W. VA. — COAL CAMPS

Human Crisis in the Kingdom of Coal.
S5020

SOCIAL STRUCTURE — CONDITIONS

Coal Company Scrip.
C210 (ASU)

SOCIAL STRUCTURE — CONDITIONS — APP.

Migrants, Sharecroppers, Mountaineers.
C5890 (BC ASU)

SOCIAL STRUCTURES AND CONDITIONS

Child Welfare in Kentucky: An Inquiry.
N130 (ASU BC)

Economic and Social Problems and Conditions of the Southern Appalachians.
U340 (ETSU ASU BC)

Economic and Social Problems and Conditions of the Southern Appalachians.
U350 (ASU ETSU WCU WWC)

Hawkers and Walkers in Early America: Strolling Peddlers, Preachers, Lawyers, Doctors, Players, and Others, from the Beginning to the Civil War.
W9510

SOCIAL STRUCTURES AND CONDITIONS — INDIANS — CHEROKEE

Priest and Warriors: Social Structures for Cherokee Politics in the 18th Century.
G720 (ASU ETSU BC)

SOCIAL STRUCTURES AND CONDITIONS — TENN.

"The First Hundred Days of the New Deal in Upper East Tennessee."
O210 (ETSU)

SPEECH — APP.

Hillbilly Dictionary, and Enlightening Collection of Mountain Expressions.
W1880 (ASU)

SPEECH — MTN.

Word-lists from the South.
A2120 (ASU)

"Southern Appalachian Non-standard Speech in Conflict with the Standard English of the Classroom."
B280 (ETSU)

Dictionary of Americanisms. A Glossary of Words and Phrases Usually Regarded as Peculiar to the United States.
B1550 (ASU)

A Method for Collecting Dialect.
C1990 (ASU)

"Mountain Dialect in North Georgia."
C5840 (ETSU ASU)

"A Lexicographical Study of the Vocabulary of Greenup County, Kentucky, Set Forth in Jesse Stuart's "Beyond Dark Hills"."
D2210 (ASU)

"The Dialect of the Southern Highlander as Recorded in North Carolina Novels."
E980 (ASU)

Bits of Mountain Speech Gathered Between 1910 and 1965 along the Mountains Bordering North Carolina and Tennessee.
F970 (ASU)

Word-book of Virginia Folk-speech.
G3520 (ASU LMC BC)

Word-book of Virginia Folk-speech.
G3530 (ETSU)

Mountain Speech in the Great Smokies.
H770 (BC)

SPEECH, MTN.
Sayings from Old Smoky, Some Traditional Phrases, Expressions, and Sentences Heard in the Great Smoky Mountains and Nearby Areas: An Introduction to a Southern Mountain Dialect.
H800 (ASU BC LMC MHC)
Smoky Mountain Folks and Their Lore.
H810 (BC ASU WCU LMC MHC)
Smoky Mountain Folks and Their Lore.
H820 (ETSU)
"High-interest, Low-vocabulary Original Prose and Poetry for Teenagers in Southern Appalachia."
K1610 (ETSU)
Published Works of Cratis Williams.
M5840 (ASU BC)
"Investigation of the Regional English of Unicoi County, Tennessee."
M6020
The Word-Book of a Backwoodsman.
N360
A Glossary of Virginia Words.
N1250 (ASU)
Folk-etymology, a Dictionary of Verbal Corruptions or Words Perverted in Form or Meaning by False Derivation or Mistaken Analogy.
P100 (ASU)
Southern Accent: From Uncle Remus to Oak Ridge.
P3370 (LMC WWC BC)
"A Dialect Survey of the Appalachian Region."
Q10 (LMC ASU)
A Dialect Survey of the Appalachian Region.
Q20 (BC)
English Archaisms in Pennsylvania German.
R1020 (ASU)
The Idiom of the People.
S2350 (ASU BC)
Development and Learning of Language and Speech: A Brief Synopsis.
T7590 (ETSU)
Popular Folk Dictionary of Ozarks Talk.
T8030 (ASU)
Instructions to Collectors of Dialect.
W7230 (ASU)
A List of Words from Tennessee.
W8520 (ASU)
Vocabulary Change; a Study of Variation in Regional Words in Eight of the Southern States.
W8530 (BC)
A Word-List from Virginia and North Carolina.
W8710 (ASU)
Rustic Speech and Folklore.
W9390 (ASU)

SPEECH, MTN. — APP.
The Phonetics of Great Smoky Mountain Speech.
G790 (ASU ETSU)
Language and Culture.
G2100 (ASU BC)
The Phonetics of Great Smoky Mountain Speech.
H780
"Regional English of the Former Inhabitants of Cades Cove in the Great Smoky Mountains."
J2450

SPEECH, MTN. — KY.
Parlance of Kentucky Backwoods.
C3740 (BC)

SPEECH, MTN. — N. C.
A Survey of Speech Education in Selected North Carolina High Schools.
E1250 (ASU)
Tarheel Talk: An Historical Study of the English Language in North Carolina to 1860.
E1550 (ASU LMC MHC ETSU)

STATE GOVERNMENT — W. VA.
West Virginia State and Local Government.
D940 (ETSU BC)

STRIP MINING
The Strip Mining of America: An Analysis of Surface Coal Mining and the Environment.
A5590 (ASU)
"The Economics of Strip Coal Mining."
A5820 (ASU)
Night Comes to the Cumberlands: Biography of a Depressed Area.
C2230 (ASU MHC WCU ETSU FC UNCA)
Lazar and Boone Stop Strip Mining Bully to Save Apple Valley and Buttermilk Creek.
C4510 (ASU)
Annotated Bibliography on Slope Stability of Strip Mine Soil Banks.
H6250 (ASU)
Slope Stability of Coal Strip Mine Soil Banks.
H6260 (ASU)
Strip Mining, an Annotated Bibliography.
M8660 (ASU BC)
The Issues Related to Surface Mining; a Summary Review, with Selected Readings.
S3300 (WCU)

STRIP MINING — APP.
Strip Mining in Appalachia.
C6200
Surface Mining — Extent and Economic Importance, Impact on Natural Resources, and Proposals for Reclamation of Mined-lands: Proceedings.
C6440 (ASU)
We Will Stop the Bulldozers.
C7920
A Revised Bibliography of Strip Mine Reclamation.
F3840 (ASU)
"Bituminous Coal Strip Mines; Some Financing Considerations."
K580
Strip Mining and the Three E's.
M7240 (ASU)
Facts about Strip Mining.
S560
Benefit/Cost Approach to Decision Making: The Dilemma with Coal Production.
S970 (ASU)
Statement on Benefit/Cost Evaluation of Strip Mining in Appalachia.
S980 (ASU)
An Appraisal of Coal Strip Mining.
T2270 (BC)
Strip Mining for Coal.
T8870 (BC)
Study of the Strip and Surface Mining in Appalachia; an Interim Report to the Appalachian Regional Commission.
U2820 (BC)
Surface Mining and our Environment; a Special Report to the Nation.
U2830 (BC)

STRIP MINING — KY.
The Long-legged House.
B3260 (ASU MHC WCU BC)
Influences of Strip Mining on the Hydrologic Environment of Parts of Beaver Creek Basin, Kentucky, 1955-59.
C5930 (BC)
Proceedings. The Planning Concept.
C6420
"External Diseconomies of Bituminous Coal Surface Mining — A Case Study of Eastern Kentucky, 1960-1967."
H7590
Strip Mining in Kentucky.
K1130 (BC ASU)
Surface Mining and Reclamation in Kentucky.
K1180
Strip Mining.
K1290
Description of the Physical Environment and of Strip-mining Operations in Parts of the Beaver Creek Basin, Kentucky.
M9220
Strip Mining Reclamation in Appalachia.
U3030
"Study of Thought Relating to Strip Mining in the Commonwealth of Kentucky."
W2730

STRIP MINING — OHIO
Comparative State Strip Mining and Reclamation Laws.
O390

STRIP MINING — VA.
S8040 (ASU)

STRIP MINING — W. VA.
Current and Proposed Regulations and Legislation on Water Pollution Concerning Appalachian Industries.
H6540

STRIP-MINING
Night Comes to the Cumberlands: A Biography of a Depressed Area.
C2240 (LMC)
My Appalachia: A Reminiscence.
C2380 (ASU LMC MHC ETSU WCU FC WWC BC UNCA)
Beneath the Hill.
C9850
Surface Mined Areas: Control and Reclamation of Environmental Damage; a Bibliography.
F3090 (ASU)

STRIP-MINING — APP.
My Land is Dying.
C2210 (ASU MHC LMC WCU ETSU BC)
Night Comes to the Cumberlands: A Biography of a Depressed Area.
C2220 (WWC BC FC)
S8050

STRIP-MINING — OHIO
Ten Years of Strip-mine Forestation Research in Ohio.
F1050

SUPERSTITION
Witchcraft in North Carolina.
C9120 (LMC)
Wendy's Halloween Ride: Witch Shadows.
E1540 (LMC)
How and Why: Stories in Carolina Folklore.
J1710 (WCU)
How and Why Stories in Carolina Folklore.
J1720 (LMC)
Folklore of the Teeth.
K170 (ASU)

SUPERSTITIONS
Witch, Warlock, and Magician: Historical Sketches of Magic and Witchcraft in England and Scotland.
A490 (ASU)
The Devil in Britain and America.
A5280 (ASU)
"Superstitions about Food and Health among Negro Girls in Elementary and Secondary Schools in Marion County, West Virginia."
B4600
Superstitions of the Highlands and Islands of Scotland.
C680
A Treasury of American Superstition.
D1770
The Frank C. Brown Collection of North Carolina.
D3810 (ASU WCU LMC MHC BC WWC ETSU)
Gravel in My Shoe.
E1090 (ASU WCU LHC MHC ETSU BC)
Essays on the Superstitions of the Highlanders of Scotland.
G3220
Tar Heel Ghosts.
H2080 (ASU BC LMC MHC ETSU)
Highland Halloween.
H4000 (LMC)
Survivals in Belief Among the Celts.
H4470
Bundle of Troubles, and Other Tarheel Tales.
H4600
Witches and Demons in History and Folklore.
J1740 (LMC)
Virginia Ghosts.
L1410 (FC ASU BC)
Weathergoose-wool.
M1800 (ASU LMC BC)
An Epitome of the Superstitions of the Highlanders of Scotland.
M2000
Origin of the Brown Mountain Light in North Carolina.
M3160 (ASU)
Pioneer Superstitions; Old-timey Signs and Sayings.
M7170 (ASU BC)
Ghost Tales of the Uwharries.
M7520 (ASU WCU)
The Telltale Lilac Bush, and Other West Virginia Ghost Tales.
M9190 (ASU BC ETSU LMC WCU)
Witches' Potions and Spells.
P1020 (ASU)
Ghosts of the Carolinas.
R3010 (ASU LMC MHC BC)
Ghosts of the Carolinas.
R3020 (ASU)
An Illustrated Guide to Ghosts and Mysterious Occurrences in the Old North State.
R3030 (ASU LMC)
This Haunted Land.
R3040 (ASU MHC BC)
This Haunted Land.
R3050 (LMC)

SUPERSTITIONS
Pioneer Superstitions: Old-timey Signs and Sayings.
S2760 (ASU LMC WCU)
Ghost Stories from the Southern Mountains.
S6570 (ASU)
An Occult Remedy Manuscript from Pendleton County, West Virginia.
S7300
Tall Tales of the Devils Apron.
S9270 (LMC BC FC)
Kentucky Superstitions.
T7790 (ASU BC)
The Witchery of Archery.
T8290 (ASU)
The Foxfire Book: Hog Dressing; Log Cabin Building; Mountain Crafts and Foods; Planting by the Signs; Snake Lore, Hunting Tales, Faith Healing; Moonshining; and Other Affairs of Plain Living.
W6020 (FC ASU BC)
Foxfire 3: Animal Care, Banjos and Dulcimers, Hide Tanning, Summer and Fall Wildplant Foods, Butter Churns, Ginseng, and Still More Affairs of Plain Living.
W6040 (ASU)
SUPERSTITIONS — APP.
"A Geographic Approach to a Vegetation Problem: The Case of the Southern Appalachian Grassy Balds."
G1060 (BC ASU)
Peculiarities of the Appalachian Mountaineers: A Summary of Legends, Traditions, Signs, and Superstitions That Are Almost Forgotten.
J2540 (BC ASU LMC WCU ETSU MHC)
The Origins of Popular Superstitions and Customs.
K2850 (ASU)
Ghost Stories and Legends of the Mountains.
P870
SUPERSTITIONS — GA.
Foxfire 2: Ghost Stories, Spring Wild Plant Foods, Spinning and Weaving, Midwifing, Burial Customs, Corn Shuckin's, Wagon Making and More Affairs of Plain Living.
W6030 (FC ASU BC)
SUPERSTITIONS — N. C.
The Shape of Fear, and Other Ghostly Tales.
P1480 (WCU)
SUPERSTITIONS — W. VA.
The Mystery of the Wizard Clip.
B7030 (ASU)
SWANNANOA RIVER
Floods on French Broad and Swannanoa Rivers, in Vicinity of Asheville, North Carolina.
T7040
Floods on Swannanoa River and Beetree Creek in Vicinity of Swannanoa, North Carolina.
T7240
Floods on Swannanoa River and Flat Creek in Vicinity of Black Mountain and Montreat, North Carolina.
T7250
SWISS
The Colony Bernstadt in Laurel County, Kentucky.
S920
TAXATION
TVA Power and Taxes.
T6680
TAXATION — APP.
The Impact of State and Local Taxes in North Carolina and the Southeastern States.
C1220 (LMC)
TAXATION — KY.
"Second Census" of Kentucky, 1800: A Private Compiled and Published Enumeration of Tax Payers Appearing in the 79 Manuscript Volumes Extant of Tax Lists of the 42 Counties of Kentucky in Existence in 1800.
C5040 (ASU BC)
"A Method of Measuring the Financial Ability of Kentucky School Districts to Support an Educational Program."
M6090
TAXATION — N. C.
The Impact of State and Local Taxes in North Carolina and the Southeastern States.
C1220 (LMC)
Studies in Taxation.
N1770 (LMC)
TAXATION — TENN.
Early East Tennessee Tax Lists.
C9930 (ASU)
"A Study of Public School Finance in Hancock County, Tennessee."
L2920
"An Analysis of Putnam County's Ability to Support Education Based on a Study and Comparison of Assessed Value to Real Value of Property."
N860
"Farm Taxation and County Government in Overton, Clay and Pickett Counties, Tennessee."
P3930
A Report of the Survey of the Finances and Management of Greene County, Tennessee.
T2130 (ETSU)
A Report of the Survey of the Finances and Management of the Government of Knox County, Tennessee.
T2140 (ETSU)
A Report of the Survey of the Finances and Management of the Government of Washington County, Tennessee.
T2150 (ETSU)
A Report of the Survey of the Management and Finances of the Government of Hamilton County.
T2160 (ETSU)
TAXATION — TENNESSEE VALLEY AUTHORITY
. . . Payments in Lieu of Taxes, a Selected List of References, January 2, 1946.
T5990
TAXATION — VA.
Virginia Tax Payers, 1782-87: Other Than Those Published by the United States Census Bureau.
F2360 (ASU)
Tax List of Montgomery County, Virginia, 1782.
K520
Tenth Legion Tithables, Rockingham Division, Rockingham County, Virginia, Tithables for 1792.
S8010
TAXATION — W. VA.
The Tax Problem in West Virginia.
N220
Biennial Report.
W4480 (BC)
TENN. — DESCRIPTION AND TRAVEL
Peter Pilgrim: Or, A Rambler's Recollections.
B4100 (ASU)
Hand-Book to the Sequatchie Valley.
B5830
The Slave States of America.
B8260
Handbook of Smith County.
B8620
Guest's Guide; Points of Interest in Cleveland.
B8790
Tennessee Hill Folk.
C4480 (ASU MHC LMC WCU ETSU BC)
Song of Life in the Smokies.
C7670 (LMC)
Song of Life in the Smokies: Stories of Mine Own People and Sketches of Life as It Was Lived in the Mountains Before the Park Took Over.
C7680 (ETSU)
C8050
Guide to the Summer Resorts and Watering Places of East Tennessee.
E470
Tennessee: A Guide to the State.
F480
The Story of Gatlinburg.
G4040
G4640 (ASU)
Kentucky and Tennessee, Twin Centers of Interest.
H2260 (ASU BC)
Tennessee and Virginia, the Mountain Empire.
H2290 (ETSU)
Songs of the Cumberlands.
H7990 (BC)
To the Shenandoah and Beyond: The Chronicle of a Leisurely Journey through the Uplands of Virginia and Tennessee, Sketching Their Scenery, Noting Their Legends, Portraying Social and Material Progress, and Explaining Routes of Travel.
I780
Stories of Hatfield the Pioneer . . . His Experiences in the Wilderness of East Tennessee, Kentucky and South Indiana.
I830
Chattanooga.
J290
A Short Description of the Tennessee Government, or The Territory of the United States South of the River Ohio, to Accompany and Explain a Map of That Country.
S4500 (BC ASU)
A Brief Historical Statistical and Descriptive Review of East Tennessee, United States of America: Developing Its Immense Agricultural, Mining and Manufacturing Advantages, with Remarks to Emigrants. Accompanied with a Map & Lithographed Sketch of a Tennessee Farm, Mansion House, and Buildings.
S4800
On the Watauga and the Cumberland.
S5300 (LMC)
Great Smoky Mountains National Park, North Carolina and Tennessee.
S8840 (ASU LMC WCU ETSU)
Tennessee: A Guide to the State.
T1030 (MHC)
The Tennessee Scene.
T1050
The Valley of East Tennessee.
T1160
Atlas of the Tennessee Valley Region. pt. 1.
T2310
Spring Notes From Tennessee.
T8970 (LMC BC)
Bert Vincent's Strolling, Being Sort of a Side-Glance at the Little Odds and Ends of Life in These Parts.
V630
The Best Stories of Bert Vincent, ed. Willard Yarbrough.
V640
More of the Best Stories of Bert Vincent.
V650
TENN. — EARLY EXPLORATION
The Ocoee District, South East Tennessee in the United States of America, Especially the Hundred Thousand Acres, and the Gold Region, with a Sketch of the Character of the People Who Inhabit East Tennessee Generally.
A2450
The Wilderness Road.
K2160 (BC WCU WWC ETSU)
The Wilderness Road.
K2170
The Wilderness Road.
K2180 (ASU LMC)
The Valley of the Long Hunters.
M4160 (ASU LMC ETSU BC)
"Early North Carolina Migrations into the Tennessee Country, 1768-1782: A Study in Historical Demography."
P990
Early Travels in the Tennessee County, 1540-1800.
W6730 (ETSU)
Early Travels in the Tennessee Country, 1540-1800: With Introductions, Annotations and Index.
W6740 (ASU LMC BC)
TENN. — GEOLOGY
T910 (LMC)
TENN. — HISTORIC HOMES
The Blount Mansion, Built 1792.
B4790
TENN. — HISTORY
David Crockett: His Life and Adventures.
A60 (ASU ETSU)
From Frontier to Plantation in Tennessee.
A80 (WWC BC)
From Frontier to Plantation in Tennessee: A Study in Frontier Democracy.
A90 (ASU LMC)
Tennessee Records.
A240 (ASU)
State of Franklin.
A1020
One Heroic Hour at Kings Mountain.
A1240 (BC LMC ASU)
One Heroic Hour at Kings Mountain, October 7, 1780.
A1250
The Overmountain Men: Early Tennessee History, 1760-1780.
A1260 (BC ETSU)

TENN. — HISTORY

The Overmountain Men: Early Tennessee History, 1760-1795.
A1270 (ASU LMC FC)
Landmarks of Tennessee History.
A1290
A History of Navigation on the Tennessee River System: An Interpretation of the Economic Influence of This River System on the Tennessee Valley.
A1490
Dropped Stitches in Tennessee History.
A1770 (ASU BC)
The Ocoee District, South East Tennessee in the United States of America, Especially the Hundred Thousand Acres, and the Gold Region, with a Sketch of the Character of the People Who Inhabit East Tennessee Generally.
A2450
The History of Hamilton County and Chattanooga, Tennessee.
A4760 (ETSU BC ASU)
Who Discovered America? The Amazing Story of Madoc.
A4800
Life and Speeches of President Andrew Johnson. Embracing His Early History, Political Career, Speeches, Proclamations, etc. With a Sketch of the Secession Movement, and His Course in Relation Thereto; Also His Policy as President of the United States.
B50
"James Robertson: Frontiersman."
B570
Lost State of Franklin.
B1030 (ETSU)
Ducktown Back in Raht's Time.
B1120 (BC ASU WCU ETSU)
"Local History Stories for the Third Grade Washington and Sullivan Counties, Tennessee."
B1180 (ETSU)
The Carpet-bagger in Tennessee.
B1760
"Andrew Johnson and the Patronage."
B2090
"Inconsistent Men of Principle: Future Liberal Republicans and the Johnson Administration."
B2100
"The Life and Times of Isaac Shelby."
B2380
Sketch of Beersheba Springs: and: Chickamuga Trace.
B3030
"The Post-presidential Career of Andrew Johnson."
B3480
"Development of Railroad Transportation in East Tennessee during the Reconstruction Period."
B3600
When Yesterday Was Today.
B4610
Life As It Is: Or, Matters and Things in General.
B6430 (ASU BC ETSU)
The Patriots and Guerrillas of East Tennessee and Kentucky. The Suffering of the Patriots. Also the Experience of the Author as an Officer in the Union Army. Including Sketches of Noted Guerrillas and Distinguished Patriots.
B6510
Sketches of the Rise, Progress, and Decline of Secession: with a Narrative of Personal Adventure among the Rebels.
B7530 (ASU)
Life of General Houston, 1793-1863.
B7590
Cumberland County's First Hundred Years.
B8340 (LMC)
Handbook of Smith County.
B8620
Historical Review, Rockwood's Centennial Year, 1868-1968.
B8780
The Over Mountain Men: Some Passages from a Page of Neglected History.
B9010
Fiddles in the Cumberlands.
B9020 (ASU BC)
"Some Social and Economic Phases of Reconstruction in East Tennessee, 1864-1869."
C600
Records of Rhea: A Condensed County History.
C960 (ASU BC)
Three Generations: The Story of a Colored Family of Eastern Tennessee.
C1110 (ASU LMC BC)
Seventh Census of the United States, 1850: Fentress County, Tennessee, Free Population Schedules.
C1390 (ASU)
Seventh Census of the United States, 1850: Franklin County, Tennessee, Free Population Schedules.
C1400 (ASU)
History of Tennessee.
C1410
"Administrations of John Sevier."
C1660
North Carolina Land Grants in Tennessee, 1778-1791.
C1800 (ETSU BC ASU)
Autobiography and Sermons.
C1950
The Tennessee Yeomen, 1840-1860.
C4320 (ASU ETSU)
The Tennessee Yeomen, 1840-1860.
C4330 (LMC)
"A Study of the Development of Organized Religion in Jefferson County, Tennessee (1785-1950)."
C5450
C6170
Red Clay and Rattlesnake Springs: A History of the Cherokee Indians of Bradley County, Tennessee.
C7530 (ASU LMC MHC BC)
Arrows to Atoms, The Story of East Tennessee.
C8670 (ASU LMC ETSU BC)
Brief Historical Sketch of the Village of Bearden.
C8740
C9420
"Formative Years of Johnson City, Tennessee, 1885-1890: A Social History."
D210 (ETSU)
Beloved Landmarks of Loudon County, Tennessee.
D560 (BC)
"Theodore Roosevelt, Franklin Historian."
D910
John Sevier: Pioneer of the Old Southwest.
D3450
John Sevier: Pioneer of the Old Southwest.
D3460
John Sevier: Pioneer of the Old Southwest.
D3470 (ASU LMC BC)
Facts about Sevier County.
D3720
The Border States: Kentucky, North Carolina, Tennessee, Virginia, West Virginia.
D4190 (BC ASU LMC WWC ETSU)
E40
E80 (ETSU)
Early History of Carter County.
E90
Index to Marriages 1792-1900.
E100
Publications. . . .
E140 (ASU WCU ETSU BC)
The French Broad-Holston Country: A History of Knox County, Tennessee.
E150 (ASU BC)
E680 (ETSU)
"The Connection" in East Tennessee.
E1180 (ASU BC)
Thrilling Adventures of Daniel Ellis, the Great Union Guide of East Tennessee, for a Period of Nearly Four Years During the Great Southern Rebellion.
E1750 (ASU LMC BC)
Thrilling Adventures of Daniel Ellis, the Great Union Guide of East Tennessee, for a Period of Nearly Four Years during the Great Southern Rebellion. Written by Himself. Containing a Short Biography of the Author.
E1760
Resources and Enterprises of Upper East Tennessee: Johnson City, Jonesboro, Greenville, Rogersville, Morristown, Watauga, Tennessee. Franklin, Territory South of the Ohio.
E2040 (ETSU)
A Brief History of Johnson City, Tennessee.
E2250 (ETSU)
"Dr. J. G. M. Ramsey of East Tennessee: A Career of Public Service."
E2260
History of Coffee County, Tennessee.
E2430
"Available Material in Knox County for Enriching the Teaching of Tennessee History."
F190 (ETSU)
Jonesborough: The First Century of Tennessee's First Town.
F980 (ETSU ASU BC)
Jonesborough: The First Century of Tennessee's First Town.
F990 (ASU)
"Economic Set-up of the Cumberland Homesteads, Crossville, Tennessee."
F1450
The Founding of Knoxville.
F1720 (ETSU)
Sectionalism and Internal Improvements in Tennessee, 1796-1845.
F1740 (WWC ASU)
Tennessee; a Short History (by) Stanley J. Folmsbee, Robert E. Corlew and Enloch L. Mitchell.
F1750 (LMC ASU BC)
Make Way for the Great.
F2170 (ETSU BC)
Memoirs.
F2420
A History of Morgan County, Tennessee.
F3280 (ASU BC)
The Advance-Guard of Western Civilization.
G1730
John Sevier as a Commonwealth-builder. A Sequel to The Rear-guard of the Revolution.
G1750 (ASU WCU LMC BC)
The Rear-guard of the Revolution.
G1790 (BC LMC)
The County of Smith.
G2340
G2620 (ASU BC)
This Is My Story.
G4450
Old Times in Tennessee, with Historical, Personal, and Political Scraps and Sketches.
G4790 (ASU)
"Diversions in East Tennessee, 1920-25."
G4830 (ETSU)
Early History of Warren County.
H480 (ASU BC ETSU)
History of DeKalb County, Tennessee.
H490
History of DeKalb County, Tennessee.
H500 (ASU BC)
True Stories of Jamestown and Its Environs.
H510
Fort Loudoun on the Little Tennessee.
H1050 (ASU)
Tennessee, a History, 1673-1932.
H1060 (LMC)
Frontier Forts along the Clinch, Powell and Holston.
H1130 (BC)
An Album of Historical Memories. Chatata-Tasso, Bradley County, Tennessee, 1830-1961.
H2190
Tennessee and Virginia, the Mountain Empire.
H2290 (ETSU)
Witness to an Epoch: Personal Inventory of the Experiences and Impressions of a Man of Varied Interests.
H2300 (LMC)
"A History and Educational Survey of Putnam County, Tennessee."
H3470
The Civil and Political History of the State of Tennessee, from Its Earliest Settlement up to the Year 1796: Including the Boundaries of the State.
H4030 (ASU WCU LMC MHC BC)
The First American Frontier: Civil and Political History of the State of Tennessee from Its Earliest Settlement up to the Year 1796.
H4040 (LMC)
The Natural and Aboriginal History of Tennessee, up to the First Settlements Therein by the White People in the Year 1768.
H4050 (ASU ETSU BC)
Andrew Jackson and Early Tennessee History.
H4330

TENN. — HISTORY

"Nolichucky Jack." (Gov. John Sevier.) Lecture of Wm. A. Henderson, to the Board of Trade of the City of Knoxville, January 7th, 1873.
H4560

William Tatham and the Culture of Tobacco: Including a Facsimile Reprint of an Historical and Practical Essay on the Culture and Commerce of Tobacco by William Tatham.
H4930

"The Use of Inquiry Learning in Teaching Early Tennessee History."
H5010 (ETSU)

Dr. J. G. Ramsey: Autobiography and Letters.
H5080 (ASU LMC)

Sequatchie Valley, a Historical Sketch.
H5170

Community Historical Sketches in Knox County, Tennessee: Corryton — Harbison's Cross Roads — Smithwood.
H5230

Historic Treasure Spots of Knox County, Tennessee.
H5240 (ETSU BC)

The John Adair Section of Knox County, Tennessee.
H5250

The Herbert Walters Story.
H5420

Guide to Depositories of Manuscript Collection in Tennessee.
H5790 (ETSU)

Inventory of the County Archives of Tennessee: Anderson County.
H5800

Inventory of the County Archives of Tennessee: Blount County.
H5810

Inventory of the County Archives of Tennessee: Bradley County.
H5820

Inventory of the County Archives of Tennessee: Hamilton County, Tennessee.
H5830

Inventory of the County Archives of Tennessee: Knox County.
H5840

Inventory of the County Archives of Tennessee: Loudon County.
H5850

Inventory of the County Archives of Tennessee.
H5860 (ETSU)

Inventory of the County Archives of Tennessee: Sullivan County.
H5870

Summary of Special Legislation Relating to the Government of Sullivan County.
H5890

Tennessee Records of Roane County Marriage Records, 1801-1838.
H5900 (ETSU)

Transcription of the County Archives of Tennessee: Minutes of the County Court of Knox County (Book No. 0") 1792-95.
H5910 (ASU)

History of Fentress County, Tennessee, the Old Home of Mark Twain's Ancestors.
H6410

One Hundred Years in the Cumberland Mountains along the Continental Line.
H6430 (ETSU ASU)

Seventy Years in the Cumberlands.
H6920

The Army of Tennessee: A Military History.
H7200 (ASU)

History of Pickett Co., Tenn.
H7940
I170

Prohibition and Politics: Turbulent Decades in Tennessee, 1885-1920.
I960 (ASU LMC)

"The German Swiss Settlers at Gruetli, Tennessee."
J150 (ASU)

Duck River Valley in Tennessee and Its Pioneers.
J220 (ASU)

Historic Fort Loudoun.
K680

Historic Fort Loudoun.
K690

"A History of St. Andrew's School."
K740

Warren County, Its Organization, Scenery, Resources and Representative Men.
K1930

The Wild Rose of Cherokee, or Nancy Ward, "The Pocahontas of the West." A Story of the Early Exploration, Occupancy, and Settlement of the State of Tennessee. A Romance Founded on and Interwoven With History.
K2270 (LMC BC)

The Wild Rose of Cherokee: Or, Nancy Ward, "The Pocahontas of the West", a Story of the Early Exploration, Occupancy and Settlement of the State of Tennessee. A Romance, Founded on and Interwoven with History.
K2280 (BC ASU)

Cumberland County's First Hundred Years.
K3210 (ASU ETSU LMC BC)

Vanquished Volunteers: East Tennessee Sectionalism From Statehood to Secession.
L60 (LMC ETSU BC)

History of Sweetwater Valley.
L1770

"A Brief History of the First Baptist Church (Ocoee Baptist Church), Benton, Tennessee, 1836-1959."
L2480

Love's Valley.
L3650

Double Destiny: The Story of Bristol, Tennessee-Virginia.
L3670 (LMC ETSU)

Double Destiny: The Story of Bristol, Tennessee-Virginia.
L3680 (ASU)

Calvin Morgan McClung Historical Collection.
L4040

More Landmarks of Tennessee History.
M160 (ASU LMC)

Brief Chronological History of Johnson City, Tennessee and Three Suggested Historical Tours of the Johnson City Area.
M660 (BC LMC ETSU ASU)

The Surrender of Cumberland Gap.
M1350

A History of Tennessee from 1663 to 1905.
M1410 (ASU BC)

A History of Tennessee from 1663 to 1930.
M1420 (ASU)

Standard History of Chattanooga, Tennessee, with Full Outline of the Early Settlement, Pioneer Life, Indian History and General and Particular History of the City to the Close of the Year 1910.
M1660

"Name Index to (Hale's) History of DeKalb County, Tennessee."
M3290

Coffee County: From Arrowheads to Rockets. A History of Coffee County, Tennessee.
M3820 (ETSU)

William Blount.
M4180 (BC ETSU)

History of Sevier County, Tennessee.
M4300

Eliza Ross; or, Illustrated Guide of Lookout Mountain.
M4910

The Mitchell-Doak Group.
M6320

"Fifty Years Ago, a History of Overton County, Tennessee, Around the Year 1850."
M6360

Morristown Centennial, 1855-1955.
M7960

Centennial Souvenir Program, 1855-1955: An Historical Pageant of Davy Crockett's Home Town, "Arrows to Atoms."
M7970 (ETSU)

"Civil War Anecdotes and Legends of Chattanooga."
N710

Chattanooga and Hamilton County, Tennessee.
O20

Over the Misty Blue Hills: The Story of Cocke County, Tennessee.
O200

"The First Hundred Days of the New Deal in Upper East Tennessee."
O210 (ETSU)
O320
O330

"An Educational Economic, and Community Survey of Jackson County, Tennessee."
O950

Thomas Hope of Tennessee, 1757-1820, House Carpenter and Joiner.
P120

The Story of Tennessee.
P370 (LMC)

History of Tennessee: The Making of a State.
P2520 (ASU LMC BC)

"A History of Roane County to 1860."
P2820

Personal Recollections of the Occupation of East Tennessee and the Defense of Knoxville.
P3300

Studies in Polk County History.
P3360 (ASU BC)

Historical Sketches of the Holston Valleys.
P4440 (ASU WCU LMC ETSU BC)
P4730

Diary of a Sit-in.
P4750 (WCU ETSU)

The Annals of Tennessee to the End of the Eighteenth Century: Comprising Its Settlement, as the Watauga Association, from 1769 to 1777. A Part of North Carolina, from 1777 to 1784: The State of Franklin, from 1784-1788. A Part of North Carolina, from 1788-1790: The Territory of the U. States, South of the Ohio, from 1790 to 1796. The State of Tennessee, from 1796 to 1800.
R240 (ASU BC)

The Annals of Tennessee to the End of the Eighteenth Century: Comprising Its Settlement, as the Watauga Association, from 1769 to 1777. A Part of North Carolina, from 1777 to 1784: The State of Franklin, from 1784-1788. A Part of North Carolina, from 1788-1790: The Territory of the U. States, South of the Ohio, from 1790 to 1796. The State of Tennessee, from 1796 to 1800.
R250 (ASU LMC WCU)

Autobiography and Letters.
R260 (ASU BC)

"The Life and Career of General James Robertson."
R480

"Early Days in Monroe County, Tennessee."
R590

Tennessee Cousins: A History of Tennessee People.
R640 (BC ASU WCU)

Life and Times of Andrew Johnson, Seventeenth President of the United States.
R700

The Courageous Commoner, a Biography of Andrew Johnson.
R930 (BC)

Center of the Storm: Memoirs of John T. Scopes.
R1340 (ASU WCU)

The World's Most Famous Court Trial, Tennessee Evolution Case: A Complete Stenographic Report of the Famous Court Test of the Tennessee Anti-evolution Act, at Dayton, July 10 to 21, 1925, Including Speeches and Arguments of Attorneys.
R1350 (ASU BC)

"A Brief History of Franklin County, Tennessee."
R1840

"A History of Bledsoe County, Tennessee: 1807-1957."
R3350

Focus on Franklin County.
R3460

Story of Rotherwood, from the Autobiography of Rev. Frederick A. Ross.
R3790

History of the Impeachment of Andrew Johnson, President of the United States, by the House of Representatives, and His Trial by the Senate, for High Crimes and Misdemeanors in Office, 1868.
R3820 (ASU)

On Jordan's Stormy Banks: A Novel of Sam Davis, the Confederate Scout.
R4080

Yankee Cavalrymen: Through the Civil War with the Ninth Pennsylvania Cavalry.
R4090

TENN. — HISTORY

Standard History of Knoxville, Tennessee, with Full Outline of the Natural Advantages, Early Settlement, Territorial Government, Indian Troubles and General and Particular History of the City Down to the Present Time.
R4280

Historical Forts and Houses in Knoxville and Nearby Vicinity.
R4450

"An Educational and Economic Survey of Pickett County, Tennessee."
S310

County Scott and Its Mountain Folk.
S390 (ASU LMC WCU BC)

Life and Public Service of Andrew Johnson.
S530

The Life of John H. Savage: Citizen, Soldier, Lawyer, Congressman.
S540 (LMC)

Background in Tennessee.
S1380 (ASU)

A Memoir of Hugh Lawson White, Judge of the Supreme Court of Tennessee, Member of the Senate of the United States, Etc., Etc.
S1440 (ASU BC)

History of White County.
S1500

Tennessee Printers, 1791-1945: A Review of Printing History from Roulstone's First Press to Printers of the Present.
S1520 (ASU BC)

"A History of Anderson County, Tennessee."
S1670

Champ Ferguson, Confederate Guerilla.
S1900

Recollections of Hearsays of Athens, Fifty Years and Beyond.
S2370

Andrew Jackson, 1767-1845: Chronology, Documents, Bibliographical Aids.
S2510

Decatur Story.
S2680

A History of Jellico, Tennessee, Containing Historical Information on Campbell County, Tennessee and Whitley County, Kentucky.
S3330

1830 Census, East Tennessee.
S3750

"A History of Bradley County, Tennessee, to 1861."
S4190

Reminiscences and Sketches.
S4450 (ASU)

"A Social and Economic Survey of Pickett County."
S4460

A Brief Historical Statistical and Descriptive Review of East Tennessee, United States of America: Developing Its Immense Agricultural, Mining and Manufacturing Advantages, with Remarks to Emigrants. Accompanied with a Map & Lithographed Sketch of a Tennessee Farm, Mansion House, and Buildings.
S4800

Reminiscences of an Old-Timer.
S5050

Tennessee History, a Bibliography.
S5070 (ASU)
S5590
S5920

The First President Johnson: The Three Lives of the Seventeenth President of the United States of America.
S6770

"Historical Sketches of Clay County, Tennessee."
S7550

John Wesley North and the Reform Frontier.
S7580

Andrew Johnson; a Study in Courage.
S8170 (ASU)
S8810 (ETSU)

Recollections of an Old Man. Seventy Years in Dixie.
S8950
S9130

Andrew Johnson — Not Guilty.
T210

Historic Sullivan: A History of Sullivan County, Tennessee, with Brief Biographies of the Makers of History.
T650 (ASU ETSU BC)

Historic Sullivan: A History of Sullivan County, Tennessee, With Brief Biographies of the Makers of History.
T660 (ASU)

Historic Sullivan: A History of Sullivan County, Tennessee, With Brief Biographies of the Makers of History.
T670

East Tennessee and the Civil War.
T820 (ASU)

East Tennessee and the Civil War.
T830 (ETSU)

East Tennessee and the Civil War.
T840 (ASU ETSU)

John Sevier, Citizen, Soldier, Legislator, Governor, Statesman.
T850 (ETSU)

Tennesseans in the Civil War: A Military History of Confederate and Union Units with Available Rosters of Personnel.
T950 (ASU)

Bradley County Schools Survey Report.
T1080

The Valley of East Tennessee.
T1160

House Journal, 1861-62, of the First Session of the Thirty-Fourth General Assembly of the State of Tennessee, Which Convened at Nashville, on the First Monday in October, A. D. 1861, and Adjourned in Memphis, March 20, 1862.
T1410 (ASU)

Messages of the Governors of Tennessee.
T1470 (ASU)

Commission Book, 1796-1801.
T1490 (ASU ETSU)

The Blount Journal, 1790-1796.
T1500

Tenn. Historical Markers.
T1510

Tennessee Old and New. Sesquicentennial. 1796-1946.
T1520 (ASU LMC)

Three Pioneer Tennessee Documents: Donelson's Journal, Cumberland Compact, Minutes of Cumberland Court.
T1530 (ASU)

Landmarks of Tennessee History.
T1540
T1550

Historic District Plan: Jonesborough, Tennessee.
T1750

"Inventory of Bledsoe County Records."
T1840

"Inventory of Blount County Records."
T1850

"Inventory of Carter County Records."
T1860

"Inventory of Coffee County Records."
T1870

"Inventory of Cumberland County Records."
T1880

"Inventory of DeKalb County Records."
T1890

"Inventory of Franklin County Records."
T1900

"Inventory of Grundy County Records."
T1910

"Inventory of Loudon County Records."
T1920

"Inventory of McMinn County Records."
T1930

"Inventory of Marion County Records."
T1940

"Inventory of Meigs County Records."
T1950

"Inventory of Polk County Records."
T1960

"Inventory of Rhea County Records."
T1970

"Inventory of Roane County Records."
T1980

"Inventory of Sequatchie County Records."
T1990

"Inventory of Smith County Records."
T2000

"Inventory of Van Buren County Records."
T2010

"Inventory of Warren County Records."
T2020

"Inventory of Washington County Records."
T2030

"Inventory of White County Records."
T2040

The University of Tennessee Sesqui-Centennial, 1794-1944.
T2170 (ASU)

The Blount Journal, 1790-1796: The Proceedings of Government Over the Territory of the United States of America, South of the River Ohio.
T7620 (ASU)

Pioneers of Roane County, Tennessee, 1801-1830.
T8400 (ETSU)

D-Days at Dayton: Reflections on the Scopes Trial.
T8900 (ASU BC)

Life of General John Sevier.
T9790 (ASU)

"Andrew Johnson and the National Union Movement."
W140

Indian Battles, Murders, Sieges and Forays in the South-west.
W230

Chattanooga, Its History and Growth.
W300

The Chickamauga Dam and Its Environs.
W310

This is Chattanooga.
W320

Lookout, the Story of a Mountain.
W340 (LMC BC)

Torchlights to the Cherokee: The Brainerd Mission.
W350 (ASU ETSU BC)

"The Marble Industry of the Knoxville Area."
W640

"A Historical Study of the ET&WNC Narrow Gauge Railroad."
W730 (ASU)

Andrew Jackson, Symbol for an Age.
W750 (ASU)

Watauga: "The Dangerous Example." The Story of Sycamore Shoals.
W1370 (ETSU)

"Co. Aytch," Maury Grays, First Tennessee Regiment: Or, A Side Show of the Big Show.
W1470 (ASU)

Historic City, Chattanooga; Containing Views and Descriptive Matter of Historic Points of Interest, Scenery, Pictures of Old and New Buildings, Leading Men, etc., All Artistically and Pleasingly Intermingled.
W2160

The History of Roane County, Tennessee, 1801-1870.
W2690

The History of Roane County, Tennessee, 1801-1870.
W2700 (ASU LMC ETSU BC)

"Andrew Johnson, Senator from Tennessee, 1857-1862."
W2770

Tennessee: Its Growth and Progress.
W5570 (BC)

John Sevier, Son of Tennessee.
W6300 (ETSU)

John Sevier, Son of Tennessee.
W6310 (LMC)

"Legends and Stories of White County, Tennessee."
W6460

Dawn of Tennessee Valley and Tennessee History.
W6720 (ASU LMC BC)

Early Travels in the Tennessee County, 1540-1800.
W6730 (ETSU)

Early Travels in the Tennessee Country, 1540-1800: With Introductions, Annotations and Index.
W6740 (ASU LMC BC)

History of the Lost State of Franklin.
W6780 (ASU MHC BC)

History of the Lost State of Franklin.
W6790

History of the Lost State of Franklin.
W6800 (LMC WCU ETSU ASU)

History of the Lost State of Franklin.
W6810 (ETSU)

TENN. — HISTORY

History of the Lost State of Franklin.
W6820

Tennessee During the Revolutionary War.
W6840 (ASU BC)

William Tatham, Wataugan.
W6850 (ETSU ASU WCU BC)

Calendar of the Tennessee and King's Mountain Papers of the Draper Collection of Manuscripts.
W7850 (LMC)
W7920

McMinnville at a Milestone, 1810-1960. A Momento of the Sesquicentennial Year of McMinnville, Tennessee, 1960, 1958.
W8440 (ASU ETSU BC)

Drifting Down Holston River Way, 1756-1966.
W8590 (BC)

"Legislative Control of the Tennessee Valley Authority."
W8770

Scrapbook History of Polk County, Tennessee.
W9100

Centennial of the First Presbyterian Church, United States, in Cleveland, Tennessee, 1837-1937.
W9110

A History of Bradley County.
W9120 (ETSU)

Red Clay Council Ground, 1832-1838; Last Capital of the Cherokee Nation East of the Mississippi River.
W9130

Red Clay in History.
W9140

William Blount, 1749-1800.
W9490 (ETSU)

Wartburg: Dream and Reality of the New Germany in Tennessee.
W9820

History of the First Presbyterian Church, Sweetwater, Tennessee, 1860-1960.
Y240

TENN. — HISTORY — CIVIL WAR

Guide Book to Lookout Mountain and a Brief Account of Battles Fought near Chattanooga, Tennessee.
B580

TENN. — HISTORY — EARLY TRAVEL ACCOUNTS

History Excursions into Tennessee, Its Early Heritage.
S7490 (LMC)

TENN. — HISTORY — EVOLUTION TRIAL

The Scopes Trial: The State of Tennessee v. John Thomas Scopes.
S1990 (ASU)

TENN. — HISTORY — FRANKLIN, STATE OF

"The Life and Times of Isaac Shelby."
B2380

TENN. — HISTORY — WATAUGA ASSOCIATION

Tennessee: The Dangerous Example; Watauga to 1849.
C150 (BC)

TENN. — LABOR FORCE

Population and Labor Force Characteristics of Tennessee Counties.
T1180

Tennessee Employment Statistics, 1939-1964.
T1190

Tennessee Manpower: Current Trend and Future Projections.
T1200

Manufacturing Employment in the Tennessee Valley Region.
T5300

TENN. RIVER

A History of Navigation on the Tennessee River System: An Interpretation of the Economic Influence of This River System on the Tennessee Valley.
A1490

The Upper Tennessee.
C970 (BC)

The Taming of the Tennessee: Continued Study Units in Geographic Backgrounds.
L1510

Surveys of the Tennessee River.
M3200

Aboriginal Sites on Tennessee River.
M7080

Muscle Shoals: A Plan for the Use of the United States Properties on the Tennessee River by Private Industry for the Manufacture of Fertilizers and Other Useful Products.
M9140 (BC)

The Tennessee River Basin.
U3870

TENN. RIVERS

Development of the Tennessee River Waterway.
B4710

The Tennessee. Rivers of America.
D630 (ASU WCU LMC MHC UNCA BC)

"Tennessee River Navigation; Government and Private Enterprise Since 1932."
D3620

The Tennessee River Valley; a Case Study.
G3320

"The Agricultural, Cooperative and Rural Electrification Activities of the Tennessee Valley Authority, and the Work of the Farm Credit Administration in the Tennessee River Basin."
H6110

TENNESSEE RIVER

R1540

One River — Seven States: TVA-State Relations in the Development of the Tennessee River.
R2860 (ASU WCU LMC BC)

The French-Broad Holston Country: A History of Knox County, Tennessee.
R3940 (LMC BC)

The French Broad-Holston Country: A History of Knox County, Tennessee.
R3950 (ETSU)

The Tennessee River Gorge, Its Scenic Preservation; a Report to the 1961 General Assembly.
T1730

One River, Seven States.
T2220

Atlas Finding List of the Tennessee Valley Region. The Tennessee Valley Area and Adjacent Districts in Alabama, Arkansas, Georgia, Illinois, Kentucky, Mississippi, Missouri, North Carolina, South Carolina, Tennessee, Virginia and West Virginia.
T2300

Atlas of the Tennessee Valley Region. pt. 1.
T2310

Chattanooga Flood Control Problem.
T2380

. . . Engineering Geology of the Tennessee River System. . . .
T2610

Flood Problems and Management in the Tennessee River Basin.
T2730

A History of Navigation of the Tennessee River System; an Interpretation of the Economic Influence of this River System on the Tennessee Valley. Message From the President of the United States Transmitting a Survey Entitled "A History of Navigation on the Tennessee River and Its Tributaries."
T2870 (BC ASU)

Navigation and Economic Growth: Tennessee River Experience; a Report.
T3100

Pickwick Landing Dam on the Tennessee River. Tennessee Valley Authority, Engineering and Construction Departments.
T3200

. . . Report on the Physiographic, Economic, and Other Relationships Between the Tennessee and Cumberland Rivers and Between Their Drainage Areas. Message from the President of the United States, Transmitting Report Entitled "The Physiographic, Economic, and Other Relationships Between the Tennessee and Cumberland Rivers and Between Their Drainage Areas" . . .
T3380

Report to the Congress on the Unified Development of the Tennessee River System.
T3400 (ASU)

River Traffic and Industrial Growth.
T3430

River Traffic and Industrial Growth.
T3450

Tennessee River Navigation.
T3690

The Tennessee River Navigation System; History, Development, and Operation.
T3700

The Tennessee River Waterway.
T3710

TVA and the River.
T3750

Cheaper Transportation via the Tennessee River.
T4170

Major Freight Terminals on the Tennessee River Waterway.
T5120

Navigation Charts, Tennessee River Waterway, Paducah, Kentucky to Knoxville, Tennessee; Showing Underwater Conditions, Navigation Channels and Aids and Adjacent Shore Planimetry.
T5130

The Tennessee River Navigation System: History, Development, and Operation.
T5140

The Tennessee Valley Region: Important Features and Recent Trends.
T5330

Stream Sanitation in the Tennessee Valley.
T5450

Studies of the Pollution of the Tennessee River System.
T5460

Studies of the Pollution of the Tennessee River System.
T5470

Pickwick Landing Dam on the Tennessee River.
T6460

Floods of March 1963 in Tennessee River Basin.
T6960

Floods on Tennessee River and Battle Creek, in Vicinity of South Pittsburg and Richard City, Tennessee.
T7260

Floods on the Tennessee River and Cypress and Cox Creeks in Vicinity of Florence, Alabama.
T7270

Floods on Tennessee River in Vicinity of Tri-Counties Alabama (Lawrence, Limestone, Morgan.)
T7280

Floods on Tennessee River, Little Tennessee River, and Town and Muddy Creeks in Vicinity of Lenoir City, Tennessee.
T7290

Floods on Toccoa-Ocoee River and Fightingtown Creek, in Vicinity of McCaysville, Ga. — Cooperhill, Tenn.
T7300

Report on Review of Allocations of Costs of the Multiple-Purpose Water Control System in the Tennessee River Basin, as Determined by the Tennessee Valley Authority and Approved by the President Under the Provisions of the TVA Act of 1933 as Amended.
U2910

God's Valley: People and Power Along the Tennessee River.
W5840 (ASU WWC BC)

Dawn of Tennessee Valley and Tennessee History.
W6720 (ASU LMC BC)

TENNESSEE VALLEY AUTHORITY

Applications of the Common Mooring: Fundamental Principles in the Utilization of Resources.
A630

Owners and Tenants of Small Farms in the Life of a Selected Community: A Cultural Analysis.
A1330

Forest Fires and Area Burned, State and Private Lands, Tennessee Valley, 1934-1958.
A5030

Experiment in Management: Personnel Decentralization in the Tennessee Valley Authority.
A5750

Experiment in Management: Personnel Decentralization in the Tennessee Valley Authority.
A5760 (ASU LMC)

A Study of the Work of the Land-Grant Colleges in the Tennessee Valley Area in Cooperation with the Tennessee Valley Authority.
B800

TENNESSEE VALLEY AUTHORITY

An Indexed Bibliography of the Tennessee Valley Authority.
B2020
Public Organization of Electric Power: Conditions, Policies, and Program.
B2030
"Struggle for Power: The Relations between the Tennessee Valley Authority and the Private Power Industry, 1933-1939.
B2990
All Down the Valley.
B3620 (BC ASU WCU LMC)
A Watershed Development Program for the TVA.
B4420
Electricity on Farms and in Rural Homes in the East Tennessee Valley.
B5350
Tennessee Valley Country: Rural Government in the Hill Country of Alabama.
B5600
"Family Removal of the Tennessee Valley."
B7360
The Duck's Back: A Report on Certain Phases of the Socialistic Experiments Conducted by the Federal Government in Tennessee Valley.
C160 (BC)
Managing 10,000 Miles of Shoreline.
C670
The Upper Tennessee.
C970 (BC)
Personnel Policy in a Public Agency: The TVA Experience.
C1930
The Library in the TVA Adult Education Program.
C2880 (ETSU)
"The Identification and Evaluation of Factors Affecting Economic Growth in the Tennessee Valley Region, 1950-1960."
C3340
"The Demand for Coal for Power Generation in the Tennessee Valley and the Impact of Changing Demand Patterns on a Supplying Coal Field."
C3360
Rich Land, Poor Land; A Study of Waste in the Natural Resources of America.
C3510
"TVA — A Critique of a Regional Plan."
C4130
Power Supply in the Development of the Region.
C4230
The TVA: An Approach to the Development of a Region.
C4240 (ASU WWC BC)
The TVA: An Approach to the Development of a Region.
C4250
The Facts About Muscle Shoals.
C4720 (LMC)
Uncle Sam's Billion-dollar Baby, a Taxpayer Looks at the TVA.
C6000 (ASU UNCA)
Estimating Tennessee's Tourist Business.
C7290 (ASU)
Land of Hope: The Way of Life in the Tennessee Valley.
C8260 (WWC ASU)
Region Building: Community Development Lessons from the Tennessee Valley.
D40 (ASU)
Should We Have More TVA's?
D230
High Dams and Slack Water: TVA Rebuilds a River.
D3610 (ASU WCU LMC BC)
"Tennessee River Navigation; Government and Private Enterprise Since 1932."
D3620
The Valley and Its People, a Portrait of TVA.
D3710 (ASU LMC BC)
Upon Its Own Resources: Conservation and State Administration.
D4070
E790 (ASU LMC WCU BC UNCA)
Tennessee Valley Wildlife: An Outlook for the Year 2000.
E1920
Fish and Fishing in TVA Impoundments.
E2210
Excavations in Nickajack Reservoir: Season I.
F320 (ETSU)
T. V. A. Lessons for International Application.
F940
The T. V. A. Lessons for International Application.
F950
A Bibliography for the T.V.A. Program.
F2990
The TVA Program: A Bibliography.
F3000
The Spatial Structure of Economic Development in the Tennessee Valley.
F3330 (BC)
"The Tennessee Valley Authority and Its Relation to Private Enterprise."
G40
Archaeological Investigations in the Tellico Reservoir: Interim Report, 1970.
G2110 (ASU ETSU)
Intergovernment Relations in the Tennessee Valley.
G2720
"An Analysis of the Tennessee Valley Authority."
G2810
The Tennessee River Valley; a Case Study.
G3320
An Analysis of the Real Cost of TVA Power. Original and Supplemental Reports.
G3560
Rescued Earth, a Study of the Public Administration of Natural Resources in Tennessee.
G3820 (ASU LMC ETSU)
Operations Guide for TVA Forest Nurseries.
G4080
Story of TVA.
G4910
The Story of TVA.
G4920
"The Tennessee Valley Authority: An Examination of Its Historical Background and of Some of the Major Controversies in Which It Has Been Involved."
H550
"Economic Development of Areas Contiguous to Multipurpose Reservoirs: The Kentucky-Tennessee Experience."
H2220 (BC)
. . . Natural Resources of the Tenn. Valley Region in Alabama.
H2540 (BC)
Education for an Age of Power: The TVA Poses a Problem.
H3170 (ASU)
Sparks at the Grassroots; Municipal Distribution of TVA Electricity in Tennessee.
H6090
Sparks at the Grassroots, Municipal Distributions of TVA Electricity in Tennessee.
H6100 (ASU WCU LMC BC)
"The Agricultural, Cooperative and Rural Electrification Activities of the Tennessee Valley Authority, and the Work of the Farm Credit Administration in the Tennessee River Basin."
H6110
The Tennessee Valley Authority: A National Experiment in Regionalism.
H6130 (LMC BC)
The Tennessee Valley Authority: A National Experiment in Regionalism.
H6140 (ASU)
"Tennessee Valley Authority Legislation."
H7300
"TVA, a Study in Policy Formation."
H7530
"Federal Payments in Lieu of Taxation with Emphasis on the Program of the Tennessee Valley Authority."
H7650
The TVA and Economic Security in the South.
H7660 (ASU WCU LMC)
Authority in the TVA Land.
H7670 (ASU LMC BC)
People's Shorelines. Address before Tennessee Public Power Association, Nashville, Tennessee, April 15-18, 1958.
H7740
Planning for Recreation Use of Impounded Waters — TVA Experience.
H7750
Origins of the TVA; the Muscle Shoals Controversy, 1920-1932.
H7840
Origins of the TVA; The Muscle Shoals Controversy, 1920-1932.
H7850 (ASU LMC WCU)
Origins of the TVA; the Muscle Shoals Controversy, 1920-1932.
H7860
TVA, Adventure in Planning.
H8750
TVA, Adventure in Planning.
H8760
Floods in Tennessee; Magnitude and Frequency.
J620
A Foreigner Looks at the TVA.
K1730 (BC ASU WWC)
Conservation Fight from Theodore Roosevelt to the Tennessee Valley Authority.
K2330
Legislative History of Muscle Shoals.
K2340
TVA Labor Relations Policy at Work; Successful Cooperation Between Public Power and Organized Labor in the Public Interest.
K2350
"Influence of Reservoir Projects on Land Values."
K3220
Budget Administration in the Tennessee Valley Authority.
K3390
The Building of TVA, an Illustrated History.
K3460 (ASU WCU LMC BC)
"Tennessee Valley Authority 1933 to 1960: An Investigation of Progress."
L100
"The Impact of TVA on Agriculture."
L1320
The Taming of the Tennessee: Continued Study Units in Geographic Backgrounds.
L1510
Two Hundred Years at Muscle Shoals Being an Authentic History of Colbert County, 1700-1900.
L1590
Changing Sawmill Industry; a Status Report on 58 Circular Sawmills in the Tennessee Valley, 1950-60.
L1620
"Mobility and Economic Progress in the Tennessee Valley Region: 1957-65."
L1840
Planning for Flood Damage Prevention.
L2390
The Journals of David E. Lilienthal.
L2440
TVA: Democracy on the March.
L2450 (BC WCU LMC MHC)
TVA: Democracy on the March.
L2460 (ASU MHC WWC BC UNCA)
"An Evaluation of the Tennessee Valley Authority Manpower Training and Development Demonstration Project."
L3530 (ASU BC)
"A Study of Factors Related to the Entrophication of Boone Reservoir, Tennessee."
L3640 (ETSU)
Organization for Watershed Planning in the Public Interest.
L3760
TVA and the Power Fight.
M920 (LMC BC)
Morgan vs. Lilienthal: The Feud within the TVA.
M1610
"TVA and the Power Fight, 1933-1939."
M1620
"The Social and Educational Aspects of the Tennessee Valley Authority."
M2630
"Senator Kenneth D. McKellar and the Tennessee Valley Authority, 1933-1944."
M3060
"The Sequatchie Valley, Tennessee, a Study in Land Utilization."
M3770
The First Twenty Years.
M3780
Effectiveness of Apprentice Training in the Tennessee Valley Authority.
M3830
"Resources for Physical Recreation in the Tennessee Valley Authority Region."
M4960
The Economic Impact of TVA.
M7230

TENNESSEE VALLEY AUTHORITY

Log of the TVA.
M7440
The Making of the TVA.
M7450
Finding His World: The Story of Arthur E. Morgan.
M7640
Valley of Vision: The TVA Years.
M8700 (ASU BC)
Muscle Shoals: A Plan for the Use of the United States Properties on the Tennessee River by Private Industry for the Manufacture of Fertilizers and Other Useful Products.
M9140 (BC)
Financial and Operating Characteristics of the Municipal and Cooperative Distributors of T.V.A. Power.
N650
"Socio-Economic Readjustment of Farm Families Displaced by the TVA Land Purchase in the Norris Area."
N1000
Tennessee Valley, a Recreation Domain.
N1230
Muscle Shoals and the Public Welfare.
O960
The Tennessee Valley Authority.
O970
Tennessee Valley Authority's Bull Run Steam Plant.
P130
Big Dam Foolishness; the Problem of Modern Flood Control and Water Storage.
P2370
"Prelude to TVA: The Wadsworth-Kahn Bill, 1919-1921."
P3550
The Tennessee Valley Authority, a Study in Public Administration.
P4670 (BC ASU WCU)
The Tennessee Valley Authority: A Case Study in the Economics of Multiple Purpose Stream Planning.
R470 (ASU BC UNCA)
R1540
The Coosa River Valley from DeSoto to Hydroelectric Power.
R1660 (ASU)
One River — Seven States: TVA-State Relations in the Development of the Tennessee River.
R2860 (ASU WCU LMC BC)
The TVA Idea.
R4340 (BC)
Tenn. Valley Land and Its Changing Use.
S150
Soil and Sky; the Development and Use of Tennessee Valley Resources.
S470
Harvesting Pine Pulpwood in the Tennessee Valley.
S1040
Adult Education, a Part of a Total Educational Program. A Description of the Educational and Training Program of the Tennessee Valley Authority.
S1560
Adult Education, a Part of a Total Educational Program. A Description of the Educational and Training Program of the Tennessee Valley Authority.
S1570 (ASU)
Elementary Education in Two Communities of the Tennessee Valley: A Description of the Wilson Dam and Gilbertsville Schools.
S1580 (ETSU)
Initial Forest Management in the Tennessee Valley.
S1770
TVA and the Grass Roots.
S1820 (WWC BC)
TVA and the Grass Roots: A Study in the Sociology of Formal of Organization.
S1830 (ASU LMC MHC UNCA)
"An Economic Analysis of Competition Between the Tennessee Valley Authority and Private Power."
S1880
Scenes and Information about Rockwood, Tennessee, in the Heart of the Great Tennessee Valley Development.
S2040
"What Lessons India Can Learn from the Tennessee Valley Authority."
S2180
Decatur Story.
S2680
A Bibliography of the Zoology of Tennessee and Tennessee Valley Region.
S3190 (ASU BC)
Flood Problems and Their Solution Through Urban Planning Programs.
S3360
"George W. Norris and the Concept of a Planned Region."
S4350
The Politics of Conservation.
S4670
Financial Control System of the Tennessee Valley Authority. Revised ed. Federal Fiscal Series. Study no. 1.
S5390
"Agricultural Changes in the TVA Area, 1930-1945."
S7740
"Tennessee Municipalities and TVA Power."
S9660
Tennessee Fishing Waters, Featuring TVA Lakes.
T1040
A Report to the President of the United States on the Tennessee Valley Authority, October 8, 1953.
T1480
Labor and TVA; Collective Bargaining Under Government Operation of a Public Utility and an Analysis of the Benefits to All the People of the Integrated Development of a River Basin.
T1560
A Plan for Development-Nicka Jack Reservoir Area.
T1660 (ASU LMC)
Reservoir Shore Line Development in Tennessee; a Study of Problems and Opportunities.
T1700
The Tennessee River Gorge, Its Scenic Preservation; a Report to the 1961 General Assembly.
T1730
Towers of Power Back Industrial Opportunities in Tennessee, First Public Power State.
T1740
One River, Seven States.
T2220
Valley of Tomorrow, the TVA and Agriculture.
T2230
Annual Report. 1935-.
T2250 (ASU WCU LMC BC)
Annual Report of the Distributors of TVA Power, 1937-Date.
T2260
An Appraisal of Coal Strip Mining.
T2270 (BC)
Articles of Agreement Between the Tennessee Valley Authority and the Salary Policy Employee Panel. Negotiated December 5, 1950.
T2280
Articles of Agreement . . . Negotiated December 5, 1950. Revisions Through February 4, 1955.
T2290
Atlas Finding List of the Tennessee Valley Region. The Tennessee Valley Area and Adjacent Districts in Alabama, Arkansas, Georgia, Illinois, Kentucky, Mississippi, Missouri, North Carolina, South Carolina, Tennessee, Virginia and West Virginia.
T2300
Atlas of the Tennessee Valley Region. pt. 1.
T2310
Basic Data on TVA and Its Revenue Bond Financing.
T2320 (ASU)
Bear Creek Watershed, Summary of Resources.
T2330
A Bibliography for the TVA Program.
T2340 (ASU BC LMC)
A Bibliography for the TVA Program.
T2350 (ASU)
A Bibliography for the TVA Program.
T2360 (LMC)
The Bull Run Steam Plant; a Report on the Planning, Design, Construction, Costs, and First Power Operations of the Initial One-Unit Plant.
T2370
Chattanooga Flood Control Problem.
T2380
. . . Chemical Engineering Report, no. 1.
T2390
The Cherokee Project, a Comprehensive Report on the Planning, Design, Construction, and Initial Operations of the Cherokee Project.
T2400
. . . The Chickamauga Project, a Comprehensive Report on the Planning, Design, Construction, and Initial Operations of the Chickamauga Project. . . .
T2410
The Colbert Steam Plant; a Report on the Planning, Design, Construction, Costs, and First Power Operations of the Initial Four-Unit Plant.
T2440
Comparison of Coal-Fired and Nuclear Power Plants for the TVA System.
T2450
. . . A Compilation of the More Important Congressional Acts, Treaties, Presidential Messages, Judicial Decisions, and Official Reports and Documents Having to do with the Control Conservation, and Utilization of Water Resources.
T2460
. . . Communication from Tennessee Valley Authority.
T2470
Concrete Production and Control, Tennessee Valley Authority Projects.
T2480
The Cost of Distributing Power, Knoxville, Tennessee.
T2490
. . . County Government and Administration in the Tennessee Valley States.
T2500
Design of TVA Projects.
T2510
Development of the Tennessee Valley.
T2520
The Development of the Tennessee Valley.
T2530
The Douglas Project; a Comprehensive Report on the Planning, Design, Construction, and Initial Operations of the Douglas Project.
T2540
. . . Drawings for the Chickamauga Project. . . .
T2550
. . . Drawings for the Guntersville Project. . . .
T2560
Economic Development of the Upper French Broad Area by North Carolina State and the Tennessee Valley Authority.
T2570 (LMC)
Electrical Demonstration Branch Electricity in Dairying.
T2580
Elk River Watershed; Summary of Resources.
T2590
Engineering Geology and Mineral Resources of the Tennessee Valley Authority Region.
T2600
. . . Engineering Geology of the Tennessee River System. . . .
T2610
Extent of Recreation Development and Use of TVA Lakes and Actual Lake Frontage Property.
T2630
Facts About Major TVA Dams.
T2640
Facts About TVA Operations.
T2650
Facts About TVA Operations.
T2660
Facts About TVA Steam Plants.
T2670
Fertilizer Science and the American Farmer — the Research and Education Programs of the Tennessee Valley Authority.
T2680
Fertilizer Science and the American Farmer — the Research and Education Programs of the Tennessee Valley Authority.
T2690

TENNESSEE VALLEY AUTHORITY

Fifty Inches of Rain. A Story of Land and Water Conservation.
T2700 (BC)

. . . Financial Statements. . . .
T2710

Flood Problems and Management in the Tennessee River Basin.
T2730

Floods and Flood Control.
T2740

Floods on the Tuckaseigee River and Deep Creek in Vicinity of Bryson City, North Carolina.
T2750

Floods on Watauga and Doe Rivers in Vicinity of Elizabethton, Tennessee.
T2760

Forest Inventory Statistics for Buncombe County, North Carolina.
T2780

Forest Products Industry Notes, no. 1.
T2790 (BC)

Forests and Human Welfare.
T2800

Forestry Bulletin, no. 1.
T2810 (BC)

The Fort Loudoun Project; a Comprehensive Report on the Planning, Design, Construction, and Initial Operations of the Fort Loudoun Project.
T2820

General Agreement Between the Tennessee Valley Authority and the Tennessee Valley Trades and Labor Council.
T2830

General Outline of Chemical Engineering Activities.
T2840

Geology and Foundation Treatment, Tennessee Valley Authority Projects.
T2850 (ETSU)

The Guntersville Project. A Comprehensive Report on the Planning, Design, Construction, and Initial Operations of the Guntersville Project . . .
T2860 (BC)

A History of Navigation of the Tennessee River System; an Interpretation of the Economic Influence of this River System on the Tennessee Valley. Message From the President of the United States Transmitting a Survey Entitled "A History of Navigation on the Tennessee River and Its Tributaries."
T2870 (BC ASU)

The Hiwassee Valley Projects.
T2880

How Cheap Electricity Pays Its Way. TVA.
T2890

. . . Hydraulic Data Activities of the Tennessee Valley Authority . . .
T2900

Hydrology of Small Watersheds in Relation to Various Crop Covers and Soil Characteristics. A Pictorial Brochure. Cooperative Research Project in Western North Carolina.
T2910

Industrial Development in the TVA Area During 1965.
T2920

Initial Forest Management in the Tennessee Valley.
T2930

. . . Injunctions in Cases Involving Acts of Congress. Letter from the Chairman of the Tennessee Valley Authority Transmitting, in Response to Senate Resolution no. 82, Certain Information Concerning Injunctions or Judgments Issued or Rendered by Federal Courts Since March 4, 1933, in Cases Involving Acts of Congress. . . .
T2940

Interterritorial Freight Rate Problem of the United States.
T2950

. . . Investment of the Tennessee Valley Authority in Wilson, Norris, and Wheeler Projects. Letter from the Chairman of the Board of the Tennessee Valley Authority Transmitting a Report on the Investment and the Allocation of the Investment of the Authority in the Wilson, Norris, and Wheeler-Projects, Pursuant to Section 14 of the Tennessee Valley Authority Act of 1933 . . .
T2960

Is the Tennessee Valley Favored in Federal Expenditures?
T2970 (BC)

The Johnsonville Steam Plant; a Comprehensive Report on the Planning, Design, Construction, Costs, and First Power Operations of the Initial Six-Unit Plant.
T2980

The Kentucky Project; a Comprehensive Report on the Planning, Design, Construction and Initial Operations of the Kentucky Project.
T2990

Knoxville and Vicinity, Tennessee. 1953.
T3000

Lower Hiwassee Valley; Summary of Resources.
T3020

Management Services Report. no. 1-.
T3030

The Melton Hill Project; a Report on the Planning, Design, Construction, Initial Operations, and Costs.
T3040

Municipal and Cooperative Distributors of TVA Power; Annual Report.
T3050

Municipalities (Electric Departments Only) and Cooperatives Purchasing Power from Tennessee Valley Authority. Financial Statements for the Fiscal Year Ended June 30, 1940; a Report from the Comptroller to the Directors of Tennessee Valley Authority.
T3060

Nature's Constant Gift, a Report on the Water Resource of the Tennessee Valley.
T3070 (BC ASU)

Nature's Constant Gift; a Report on the Water Resource of the Tennessee Valley.
T3080

Nature's Constant Gift; a Report on the Water Resource of the Tennessee Valley.
T3090

Navigation and Economic Growth: Tennessee River Experience; a Report.
T3100

Non-Urban Outdoor Recreation, an Analysis of Its Functions, Forms, and Types of Areas.
T3110

Norris Dam . . .
T3120

. . . The Norris Project, A Comprehensive Report on the Planning, Design, Construction, and Initial Operations of the Tennessee Valley Authority's First Water Control Project . . .
T3130

Operation of TVA Reservoirs, Annual 1963.
T3140

Outdoor Recreation for a Growing Nation; TVA's Experience With Man-Made Reservoirs.
T3150

The Paradise Steam Plant; a Report on the Planning, Design, Construction, Costs, and First Power Operations of the Initial Two-Unit Plant.
T3160

Parker Branch; an Experiment in Appalachian Agriculture, 1953-1962.
T3170

Parker Branch Research Watershed; Project Report, 1953-1962.
T3180

Personnel Administration in TVA; the Experience of 14 Years.
T3190

Pickwick Landing Dam on the Tennessee River. Tennessee Valley Authority, Engineering and Construction Departments.
T3200

. . . The Pickwick Landing Project, a Comprehensive Report on the Planning, Design, Construction, and Initial Operations of the Pickwick Landing Project . . .
T3210

. . . Plant Nutrient Losses in the Tennessee River System.
T3220

Plant Trees — Grow Jobs; Reforest 7 States in 7 Years.
T3230 (ASU)

Power Annual Report. 1960-.
T3240

Preliminary Report: Floods on Scott Creek in Vicinity of Sylva, North Carolina.
T3250

Profile of a Region; Some Characteristics and General Trends, Tennessee Valley States.
T3260

A Program for Reducing the National Flood Damage Potential.
T3270

Program for Reducing the National Flood Damage Potential.
T3280

Progress in Seven States. TVA Now.
T3290

Progress in the Valley, TVA, 1947.
T3300

A Quality Environment in the Tennessee Valley.
T3310

Recreation Areas on TVA Lakes.
T3320

Recreation Areas on TVA Lakes.
T3330

. . . Recreation Development of the Tennessee River System.
T3340

Recreational Development of the Southern Highlands Region, A Study of the Use and Control of Scenic and Recreational Resources.
T3350 (ASU)

. . . Regionalized Freight Rates: Barrier to National Productiveness. Message from the President of the United States, Transmitting a Report of the Tennessee Valley Authority Entitled "Regionalized Freight Rates: Barrier to National Productiveness". . .
T3360

Report.
T3370

. . . Report on the Physiographic, Economic, and Other Relationships Between the Tennessee and Cumberland Rivers and Between Their Drainage Areas. Message from the President of the United States, Transmitting Report Entitled "The Physiographic, Economic, and Other Relationships Between the Tennessee and Cumberland Rivers and Between Their Drainage Areas" . . .
T3380

Report on Scientific Research Projects.
T3390

Report to the Congress on the Unified Development of the Tennessee River System.
T3400 (ASU)

Report to the Nation from the Tennessee Valley Authority on Its First Twenty-Five Years.
T3410

River Traffic and Industrial Growth.
T3420

River Traffic and Industrial Growth.
T3430

River Traffic and Industrial Growth.
T3440

River Traffic and Industrial Growth.
T3450

Sequatchie Valley; Summary of Resources.
T3470

Short History of the Tennessee Valley Authority, 1933-1963.
T3480

Soil . . . People, and Fertilizer Technology.
T3490

Southwest Virginia, Lee, Scott, Wise Counties; Summary of Resources.
T3510

. . . Statistical Bulletin no. 1-.
T3520

TENNESSEE VALLEY AUTHORITY

A Study of Methods Used in Measurement and Analysis of Sediment Loads in Streams. Planned and Conducted Jointly by Tennessee Valley Authority, Corps of Engineers, Department of Agriculture, Geological Survey, Bureau of Reclamation, Indian Service, and Iowa Institute of Hydraulic Research. Report no. 1-.
T3530

A Study of Methods Used in Measurement and Analysis of Sediment Loads in Streams, Planned and Conducted Jointly by Tennessee Valley Authority.
T3540

Survey of Electrical Appliances in the Homes and Farms of the TVA Area.
T3570

Systematic Farm Planning in Relation to Water Resources at Parker Branch Pilot Tributary Watershed.
T3590

. . . Technical Report no. 1.
T3600

. . . A Technical Review of the Chickamauga Project . . .
T3610

. . . A Technical Review of the Guntersville Project.
T3620

. . . A Technical Review of the Hiwassee Project . . .
T3630

. . . A Technical Review of the Norris Project.
T3640

. . . A Technical Review of the Pickwick Landing Project . . .
T3650

. . . A Technical Review of the Wheeler Project.
T3660

The Tellico Project of the TVA.
T3670

Tennessee River History.
T3680

Tennessee River Navigation.
T3690

The Tennessee River Navigation System; History, Development, and Operation.
T3700

The Tennessee River Waterway.
T3710

The Tennessee Valley Authority.
T3720

Tennessee Valley Authority.
T3730

Tennessee Valley Authority, 1933-1937.
T3740

TVA and the River.
T3750

TVA dams; the Twenty Major Dams Built by the Tennessee Valley Authority and Wilson Dam.
T3760

TVA Electricity Rates, A Statement of Facts.
T3770

Tennessee Valley Authority Facts Book; Norris, Wheeler and Wilson Projects . . .
T3780

TVA: The First Twenty Years. A Staff Report.
T3790 (ASU WCU LMC)

TVA: The First Twenty Years; A Staff Report.
T3800 (UNCA)

TVA Flood Control.
T3810

TVA Flood Control; New Concepts.
T3820

TVA's Influence on Electric Rates.
T3830

TVA — a National Asset.
T3840

TVA Power, 1966.
T3850

TVA Power — 1963/64.
T3860

TVA; A River Controlled.
T3870

TVA River Traffic and Industrial Growth.
T3880

TVA Tames the River.
T3890

TVA Today, 1965.
T3900

TVA 25th Anniversary; Progress Thru Resource Development, A Report to the Nation from the Tennessee Valley Authority on Its First Twenty-Five Years, 1933-1958.
T3910

TVA, Its Work and Accomplishments.
T3920

TVA, The Valley of Light, 1933-1963.
T3930

TVA's Coal-Buying Program.
T3940

TVA's Influence on Electric Rates.
T3950

General Agreement . . . and Supplementary Schedules.
T3960

Tennessee Valley Authority Act, May 18, 1933 with Amendments.
T3961

The Tennessee Valley Region; Population Changes, 1950-1955.
T3970

Tennessee Valley Resources; Their Development and Use.
T3980

To Keep the Water in the Rivers and the Soil on the Land . . .
T3990

Tributary Area Development Activities; Selected List of Reports and Publications. 1963.
T4000

Tributary Area Development in the Tennessee Valley.
T4010

Upper Duck River Valley; Summary of Resources.
T4020

Upper Hiwassee Valley: Summary of Resources.
T4030

The Upper Holston Projects: Watauga, South Holston, Boone, and Fort Patrick Henry; a Comprehensive Report on the Planning, Design, Construction, Initial Operations, and Costs of Four Hydro Projects in the Holston Basin at the Eastern Tip of Tennessee.
T4040

The Valley is Paying off, TVA 1949.
T4050

Valley With a Future, TVA in the Sixties.
T4060

. . . Value of Flood Height Reduction from TVA Reservoirs to the Alluvial Valley of the Lower Mississippi River . . .
T4070

. . . The Wheeler Project, A Comprehensive Report on the Planning, Design, Construction, and Initial Operations of the Wheeler Project . . .
T4090

Working With Areas of Special Need, With Examples From the Beech River Watershed.
T4100

Working with Areas of Special Need, with Examples from the Beech River Watershed.
T4110

Working with TVA.
T4120

The Yellow Creek Port Project.
T4130

Census of Agriculture for the 125 Tennessee Valley Watershed Counties.
T4140

Teamwork: the Cooperative Program of the Tennessee Valley Trades and Labor Council and the Tennessee Valley Authority.
T4150

Goals of the Cooperative Program.
T4160

Cheaper Transportation via the Tennessee River.
T4170

Commerce Series.
T4180

Electric Poultry Equipment for the Farm.
T4190

. . . The Initial Phase of Public-Use Terminal Development at Chattanooga, Tennessee.
T4200

Pumps and Plumbing for the Farmstead.
T4210

Report.
T4220

Rural Electrification; Lessons for Boys' Groups.
T4230

. . . Supplemental Phases of the Interterritorial Freight Rate Problem of the United States.
T4240

Financial Statements for the Fiscal Years Ended June 20, 1938-Date.
T4250

Municipalities (Electric Departments Only) and Cooperatives, Purchasing Power from Tennessee Valley Authority. Financial Statements for the Fiscal Years Ended June 30, 1938-Date.
T4260

. . . Statistical Bulletin no. 1.
T4270

County Government and Administration in the Tennessee Valley States.
T4280

Recreational Development of the Southern Highlands Region; A Study of the Use and Control of Scenic and Recreational Resources.
T4290 (LMC)

Report of the Project on Research in Agriculture and Industrial Development in the Tennessee Valley Region.
T4300

TVA Demountable Houses for Defense Workers; a Report.
T4320

Social and Economic Characteristics of Six Tennessee Valley Reservoir Areas.
T4330 (BC)

Fertilizer Trends.
T4340

Southern Bulk Blending Conference, Jan. 21-23, 1963.
T4350

Bulk-Blending — An Innovation in Fertilizer Marketing.
T4360

Changing Agricultural of the Tennessee Valley.
T4370

Do Fertilizer Education and Services Pay?
T4380

Fertilizer Summary Data.
T4390

Fertilizer Summary Data.
T4400

Fertilizer, One Key to Better Land Use. Summary of Distributor Demonstration Program for TVA Fertilizers, Fiscal Year 1955.
T4410

Fertilizer Trends.
T4420

Fertilizer Trends; the Scope of TVA's Fertilizer Activities.
T4430

Fertilizer Trends; the Scope of TVA's Fertilizer Activities.
T4440

Fertilizer Trends; the Scope of TVA's Fertilizer Activities.
T4450

Food at the Grass Roots; the Nation's Stake in Soil Minerals.
T4460

Income Levels in the Upper Tennessee Valley: A Comparative Analysis.
T4470

Interpreting Results of Irrigation Experiments; a Progress Report.
T4480

The Occurrence of Drought in the Tennessee Valley.
T4490

Plant Nutrient Consumption by States and Geographic Areas.
T4500

Problems and Suggested Programs for Low-Income Farmers with Special Reference to the Tennessee Valley.
T4510

Problems of Underemployed Rural People.
T4520

Progress Through Cooperative Research on Fertilizer Evaluations; a Report of TVA Soils and Fertilizer Research Branch for the Period July 1957 Through June 1960.
T4530

Report.
T4540

TENNESSEE VALLEY AUTHORITY

Research Contributes to More Efficient Use of Fertilizers. A Report of Progress of the Soils and Fertilizers, Fertilizer Research Branch.
T4550

Test-Demonstration Farms and the Spread of Improved Farm Practices in Southwest Virginia.
T4560

U. S. Plant Nutrient Consumption.
T4570

Use of Linear Programming Technique to Compute Least-Cost Bulk-Blended Fertilizers.
T4580

Annual Report, 1963.
T4600

The Changing Sawmill Industry; a Status Report on 58 Circular Sawmills in the Tennessee Valley, 1950-1960.
T4610

Comparative Data for Additional Hardwood Pulp and Paper Mills in the Tennessee Valley.
T4620

Comparative Results of Circular Sawmill Surveys in the Tennessee Valley, 1950 and 1955.
T4630

A Demonstration of Watershed Protective Logging, Mars Hill Municipal Watershed, Madison County, North Carolina.
T4640

Development of Forests — Fish — Wildlife in the Tennessee Valley.
T4650

Evaluation of Forestry Opportunities on Farms in the Beech River Watershed.
T4660 (ETSU)

Fish and Wildlife in the Tennessee Valley.
T4670

Forest Inventory Statistics for Fannin County, Georgia.
T4680

Forest Inventory Statistics — Holston River Tributary Area, East Tennessee and Southwest Virginia.
T4690

Forest Inventory Statistics for Towns County, Georgia.
T4700

Forest Inventory Statistics for Union County, Georgia.
T4710

Forest Inventory Statistics for Walker County, Georgia.
T4720

Forest Inventory Statistics for Whitfield County, Georgia.
T4730

Forest Resources and Industries in the Tennessee Valley.
T4740 (ETSU)

Forest Resources of the Beech River Watershed.
T4750

Furniture Industry Expansion in the Tennessee Valley.
T4760

Hardwood-Logging Methods and Costs in the Tennessee Valley.
T4770

Hardwood Utilization Centers: Their Potential for the Tennessee Valley.
T4780 (ASU)

Influence of Woodland and Owner Characteristics of Forest Management.
T4790

Laminated Lumber From Low-Grade Hardwoods by the Continuous Glue Press Process.
T4800

Multiple-Use of Norris Watershed.
T4810

North Georgia Forest Industry Outlook.
T4820

Operations Manual for TVA Forest Nurseries.
T4830

Pine Pulpmill Possibilities, North Alabama.
T4840

Private Forest Management in the Tennessee Valley.
T4850

Publications Available for General Distribution.
T4860

Status of the Forest Resource in the Tennessee Valley — 1950.
T4870

TVA and Forestry.
T4890

TVA and Forestry.
T4900

TVA and Forestry.
T4910

Twenty Years of Fire Records for State and Private Forest Lands in the Tennessee Valley.
T4920

Why Invest in Forest Land? Some Forest Owners Give Their Answers.
T4930

Annual Report.
T4940

Design and Operation of Open-Tank Timber Treating Plants.
T4950

Farm Forestry Planning Through Linear Programming.
T4960

Forest Resource Trends in the Tennessee Valley.
T4970

Guide to Selection of Superior Loblolly, Shortleaf and Virginia Pine in the Tennessee Valley.
T4980

Inventorying Forest Properties; Suggested Standard Procedure and Specifications for Use in the Tennessee Valley.
T4990

Operations Guide for TVA Forest Nurseries.
T5000

Private Forest Management Trends in the Tennessee Valley.
T5010

Quality-Control in Circular Sawmill Operation . . .
T5020

Reforestation Estimates for the Tennessee Valley.
T5030

Report: A Record of Activities and Accomplishments.
T5040

Sawmill Facts; First Step Toward Good Management.
T5050

A Survey of Pulpwood Dealers in the Tennessee Valley . . .
T5060

TVA Fish and Game Activities.
T5070

Utilizing Pine Sawmill Residue for Pulp Chips.
T5080

. . . A Compilation of the More Important Congressional Acts, Treaties, Presidential Messages, Judicial Decisions, and Official Reports and Documents Having to do with the Control, Conservation, and Utilization of Water Resources.
T5090

Benefit-Cost Analysis for Water Resource Projects; a Selected Annotated Bibliography.
T5110

Major Freight Terminals on the Tennessee River Waterway.
T5120

Navigation Charts, Tennessee River Waterway, Paducah, Kentucky to Knoxville, Tennessee; Showing Underwater Conditions, Navigation Channels and Aids and Adjacent Shore Planimetry.
T5130

The Tennessee River Navigation System: History, Development, and Operation.
T5140

Land Acquisition in TVA. An Analysis of TVA Land Acquisition, Land Management, and Family Relocation Procedures as They Could Relate to the Missouri Valley Development. Statements Presented Before the Select Subcommittee on Real Property Acquisition of the Committee on Public Works.
T5150

The Barge Grain Case — Its Significance to the Tennessee Valley and the Southeast.
T5160

Comparative Data on Farm Income and Employment, 1929-51.
T5170

Local Government Services and Industrial Development in the Southeast.
T5190

The Tennessee Valley Region: Highlights of Growth and Change; Historical Perspectives, Recent Trends.
T5200

The Image of Asheville.
T5210 (LMC)

Annual Report, 1958 and 1959.
T5220

Public Grounds Maintenance Handbook.
T5230

Engineering Data.
T5240

Measurements of the Structural Behavior at Fontana Dam.
T5250

Measurements of the Structural Behavior of Norris and Hiwassee Dams.
T5260

Crosstie Industry Facts for the Tennessee Valley Counties.
T5280

Statistical Summary of Forest-Products Industries in the Tennessee Valley.
T5290

Manufacturing Employment in the Tennessee Valley Region.
T5300

Manufacturing Structure and Change in the Tennessee Valley Region, 1959-1963.
T5310

Tennessee Valley Authority Program: The Role of the States and Their Political Subdivisions.
T5320

The Tennessee Valley Region: Important Features and Recent Trends.
T5330

. . . Community Health and Safety Series no. 1.
T5340

Full-Scale Study of Dispersion of Stack Gases; a Summary Report.
T5350

Malaria and Its Control in the Tennessee Valley.
T5360

Malaria and Its Control in the Tennessee Valley.
T5370

Malaria Control: 1. How the Community Can Help. An Office of War Information Reprint of the Tennessee Valley Authority Booklet.
T5380

Malaria Control in the Tennessee Valley.
T5390

Malaria, the Story of an Individual Problem and a Community Problem.
T5400

Prediction of Stream Reaeration Rates.
T5410

Quality of Water in Chickamauga Reservoir.
T5420

Report.
T5430

Significant Developments in TVA's Malaria Control Program Through 1947.
T5440

Stream Sanitation in the Tennessee Valley.
T5450

Studies of the Pollution of the Tennessee River System.
T5460

Studies of the Pollution of the Tennessee River System.
T5470

Surface Water Quality in the Chestuee Creek Watershed.
T5480

Surface Water Quality in the Chestuee Creek Watershed.
T5490

TVA; the Health of a Region.
T5500

Vector Control and Water Resource Development — The Experience of TVA.
T5510

Boone Project, Hydraulic Model Studies.
T5520

Fontana Project Hydraulic Model Studies.
T5540

Influences of Reforestation and Erosion Control Upon the Hydrology of the Pine Tree Branch Watershed 1941 to 1950.
T5550

Tennessee and Cumberland Valley Reservoirs Level Storage Tables and Profile Storage Charts.
T5560

TENNESSEE VALLEY AUTHORITY

Agricultural-Industrial Survey of Anderson County, Tennessee.
T5570
Agricultural-Industrial Survey of Bledsoe County.
T5580
Agricultural-Industrial Survey of Carter County.
T5590
Agricultural-Industrial Survey of Cocke County.
T5600
Agricultural-Industrial Survey of Coffee County.
T5610
Agricultural-Industrial Survey of Cumberland County.
T5620
Agricultural-Industrial Survey of Fentress County.
T5630
Agricultural-Industrial Survey of Franklin County, Tennessee.
T5640
Agricultural-Industrial Survey of Grainger County.
T5650
Agricultural-Industrial Survey of Greene County, Tennessee.
T5660
Agricultural-Industrial Survey of Hamblen County, Tennessee.
T5670
Agricultural-Industrial Survey of Johnson County, Tennessee.
T5680
Agricultural-Industrial Survey of Loudon County, Tennessee.
T5690
Agricultural-Industrial Survey of McMinn County, Tennessee.
T5700
Agricultural-Industrial Survey of Marion County, Tennessee.
T5710
Agricultural-Industrial Survey of Meigs County, Tennessee.
T5720
Agricultural-Industrial Survey of Monroe County, Tennessee.
T5730
Agricultural-Industrial Survey of Morgan County, Tennessee.
T5740
Agricultural-Industrial Survey of Polk County, Tennessee.
T5750
Agricultural-Industrial Survey of Rhea County.
T5760
Agricultural-Industrial Survey of Sevier County.
T5770
Agricultural-Industrial Survey of Sullivan County.
T5780
Agricultural-Industrial Survey of Unicoi County.
T5810
Agricultural-Industrial Survey of Washington County, Tennessee.
T5790
Agricultural-Industrial Survey of White County.
T5800
Defense Expansion in the Tennessee Valley Region.
T5820
Atlas of the Tennessee Valley Region.
T5830
A Cartographic Summary of United States Census Data, 1930, Tennessee Valley and Surrounding Area by Land Classification Section, Land Planning and Housing Division, Tennessee Valley Authority.
T5840
Houses at Norris, Tennessee; a Review of Costs.
T5850
The Rural Land Classification Program; a Summary of Techniques and Uses Submitted by G. Donald Hudson, Chief, Land Classification Section, Division of Land Planning and Housing, Tennessee Valley Authority.
T5860
The Three Major Physical Divisions of the Upper Tennessee Basin.
T5870
. . . A Bibliography of the Tennessee Valley Authority.
T5880
A Bibliography for the TVA Program.
T5890
. . . A Chronology of the Tennessee Valley Authority.
T5900
Congressional Hearings, Reports, and Documents Relating to TVA. 1933-.
T5910
Flood Damage Prevention; an Indexed Bibliography.
T5960
. . . Government Corporations, a Selected List of References, September 15, 1945.
T5970
. . . An Indexed Bibliography of the Tennessee Valley Authority, Compiled by Harry C. Bauer, Technical Librarian.
T5980
. . . Payments in Lieu of Taxes, a Selected List of References, January 2, 1946.
T5990
Personnel Administration in TVA; a Selected List of References.
T6000
. . . Regional Authority Developments, a Selected List of References, Including Legislative Bills Introduced in Congress, 1933-1945.
T6010
. . . A Selected List of Books, Theses, and Pamphlets on TVA, Compiled by Ernest I. Miller, Reference Librarian.
T6020
. . . A Selected List of Books and Pamphlets on TVA. January 1, 1945.
T6030
. . . A Selected List of Books, Theses, and Pamphlets on TVA.
T6040
. . . A Selected List of Books, Theses, and Pamphlets on TVA.
T6050
The TVA Program; a Bibliography of Selected Readings, Prepared by the Training and Educational Relations Staff of the Personnel Dept. and the Staff of the Technical Library.
T6060
The TVA Program; a Bibliography of Selected Readings, Compiled by Bernard L. Foy, Technical Librarian.
T6070
The TVA Program; a Bibliography of Selected Readings, Compiled by Bernard L. Foy, Technical Librarian.
T6080
TVA, Symbol of Valley Resource Development; a Digest and Selected Bibliography of Information.
T6090
TVA as a Symbol of Resource Development in Many Countries; a Digest and Selected Bibliography of Information.
T6100
Agglomeration of Phosphate Fines for Furnace Use.
T6110
Analytical Index of Chemical Engineering Publications Patents and Reports.
T6120
Chemical Engineering Bulletins.
T6130
Chemical Engineering Reports.
T6140
Development of Processes for Production of Calcium Metaphosphate Fertilizer.
T6150
Development of Processes for Production of Concentrated Superphosphate.
T6160
Development of Processes for Production of Fused Tricalcium Phosphate.
T6170
Development of Processes and Equipment for Production of Phosphoric Acid.
T6180
General Outline of Chemical Engineering Activities.
T6190
Phosphorus; Properties of the Element and Some of Its Compounds.
T6200
Preparation of Research and Engineering Reports.
T6210
Production of Elemental Phosphorus by the Electric — Furnace Method.
T6220
TVA Chemical Plant and National Defense.
T6230
The Colbert Steam Plant; a Report on the Planning, Design, Construction, Costs, and First Power Operations of the Initial Four-Unit Plant.
T6240
Construction Plant for TVA Projects.
T6250
Drawings for the Appalachian Project.
T6260
Drawings for the Boone Project by Tennessee Valley Authority, Divisions of Engineering and Construction.
T6270
Drawings for the Chatuge and Nottely Projects by the Tennessee Valley Authority, Engineering and Construction Departments.
T6280
Drawings for the Cherokee Project by the Tennessee Valley Authority, Engineering and Construction Departments.
T6290
Drawings for the Fontana Project.
T6300
Drawings for the Fort Loudoun Project by the Tennessee Valley Authority, Divisions of Engineering and Construction.
T6310
Drawings for the Hiwassee Project.
T6320
Drawings for the Johnsonville Steam Plant.
T6330
Drawings for the Kentucky Project.
T6340
Drawings for the Ocoee no. 3 Project.
T6350
. . . Drawings for the Pickwick Landing Project . . .
T6360
Drawings for the South Holston Project.
T6370
Drawings for the Watauga and Wilbur Projects.
T6380
Drawings for the Watts Bar Project.
T6390
. . . Drawings for the Wheeler Project . . .
T6400
Engineering Data.
T6410
Engineering Data.
T6420
Instructions for Scale Checking Aerial Photographs.
T6430
Measurements of the Structural Behavior at Fontana Dam.
T6440
Measurements of the Structural Behavior of Norris and Hiwassee Dams.
T6450
Pickwick Landing Dam on the Tennessee River.
T6460
. . . Plans and Specifications for the Norris Dam . . .
T6470
Plans and Specifications for the Norris Dam.
T6480
The Bull Run Steam Plant; a Report on the Planning, Design, Construction, costs, and First Power Operations of the Initial One-Unit Plant.
T6490
The Kingston Steam Plant; a Report on the Planning, Design, Construction, Costs, and First Power Operations.
T6500
The Melton Hill Project; a Report on the Planning, Design, Construction, Initial Operations, and Costs.
T6510
The Paradise Steam Plant; a Report on the Planning, Design, Construction, Costs, and First Power Operations of the Initial Two-Unit Plant.
T6520
Research in the Fields of Civil Engineering, Mechanical Engineering, Instrumentation. 1965/66-.
T6530
Annual Report. 1969/70-.
T6540

TENNESSEE VALLEY AUTHORITY

Transmission System of Tennessee Valley Authority.
T6560
Electricity Sales Statistics, Monthly Report no. 1.
T6570
Industrial Development in the TVA Area During 1962.
T6580
Report on the Plateau Coal Field of Alabama.
T6590
Report on the Reserves of Coal in a Part of the Warrier Coal Field of Alabama.
T6600
Electricity and Your Farm; a Manual for Instruction on the Practical Uses and Application of Electricity in Rural Areas.
T6610
Comparison of Coal-Fired and Nuclear Power Plants for the TVA System.
T6620
Fire Protection Manual.
T6630
Rate Reductions by the Distributors of TVA Power.
T6640
Rate Reductions by the Distributors of TVA Power.
T6650
TWA Power. 1953-.
T6660
TVA Power and Taxes.
T6670
TVA Power and Taxes.
T6680
Industrial Development in the TVA Area, 1955-Date.
T6690
Electricity Sales Statistics.
T6700
Industrial Development in the TVA Area. 1958-.
T6710
File Audit Handbook.
T6730
File Operation Handbook.
T6740
Records Management in TVA.
T6750
Records Retention and Disposal Handbook.
T6760
Secretarial Handbook.
T6770
Administration and Standards of Apprenticeship of the Tennessee Valley Authority.
T6780
Development of Salary Policy Employee Panel (Documentation).
T6790
Documentation of TVA Apprenticeship Program.
T6800
Effectiveness of Apprentice Training in TVA.
T6810
Group Participation in Personnel Administration in the Tennessee Valley Authority.
T6820
Management Guide for Handling Grievances of Employees, Represented by the Salary Policy Employee Panel.
T6830
Report.
T6840
TVA Employment Policy and Methods for Salary Policy Jobs.
T6850
TVA and Engineering: Electrical, Civil, Mechanical, Chemical, Architectural, Nuclear, Fuels.
T6860
TVA Labor Relations, 1933-1953.
T6870
Valley of Opportunity; Tennessee Valley Authority, 1963-1964.
T6880
A Bibliography for the TVA Program.
T6890
TVA as a Symbol of Resource Development in Many Countries.
T6910
Boone Project Hydraulic Model Studies.
T6920
. . . Flood Control for Upper French Broad River and Tributaries; a Preliminary Report.
T6930
Flood on Piney River, November 18-19, 1957, in Vicinity of Spring City, Tennessee.
T6950
Floods of March 1963 in Tennessee River Basin.
T6960
Floods on Beaver Creek, in Vicinity of Bristol, Virginia-Tennessee.
T6970
Floods on Brush Creek in Vicinity of Johnson City, Tennessee.
T6980
Floods on Cheoah River and Tributary Creeks in Vicinity of Robbinsville, North Carolina.
T6990
Floods on Clinch River, in Vicinity of Clinton, Tennessee.
T7000
Floods on Elk River and Norris Creek, in Vicinity of Fayetteville, Tennessee.
T7010
Floods on Elk River in Vicinity of Fayetteville, Tennessee.
T7020
Floods on French Broad and Davidson Rivers and King, Nicholson, and Tucker Creeks in Vicinity of Brevard, North Carolina.
T7030
Floods on French Broad and Swannanoa Rivers, in Vicinity of Asheville, North Carolina.
T7040
Floods on French Broad River and Spring Creek in Vicinity of Hot Springs, North Carolina.
T7050
Floods on French Broad River in the Vicinity of Marshall, N. C.
T7060
Floods on Hiwassee River, Valley River, and Peachtree Creek in Vicinity of Murphy, N.C.
T7070
Floods on Little Pigeon and West Fork Little Pigeon in the Vicinity of Sevierville, Tenn.
T7080
Floods on Little Tennessee River, Cullasaja River, and Cartoogechave Creek in Vicinity of Franklin, North Carolina.
T7090
Floods on Nolichucky River and North and South Indian Creeks in Vicinity of Erwin, Tennessee.
T7100
Floods on North Chickamauga, Mountain, and Lookout Creeks, in Vicinity of Chattanooga, Tennessee.
T7110
Floods on North Toe River and Beaver and Grassy Creeks in Vicinity of Spruce Pine, North Carolina.
T7120
Floods on Oconaluftee and Tuckaseigee Rivers and Soco Creek in Vicinity of Cherokee, North Carolina.
T7130
Floods on Oostanaula Creek, in Vicinity of Athens, Tennessee.
T7140
Floods on Oostanaula Creek in Vicinity of Athens, Tenn.
T7150
Floods on Powell River and South Fork Powell River in Vicinity of Big Stone Gap, Virginia.
T7160
Floods on Powell River and South Fork Powell River in Vicinity of Big Stone Gap, Virginia.
T7170
Floods on Reedy Creek in Vicinity of Kingsport, Tennessee.
T7180
Floods on Richland Creek and Tributary Streams in Vicinity of Waynesville and Hazelwood, North Carolina.
T7190
Floods on Rock Creek, West Fork and North Fork, in Vicinity of Tullahoma, Tennessee.
T7200
Floods on South Mouse Creek in Vicinity of Cleveland, Tennessee.
T7210
Floods on Streams in Vicinity of Newport, Tennessee.
T7220
Floods on Streams in Vicinity of Paris, Tennessee.
T7230
Floods on Swannanoa River and Beetree Creek in Vicinity of Swannanoa, North Carolina.
T7240
Floods on Swannanoa River and Flat Creek in Vicinity of Black Mountain and Montreat, North Carolina.
T7250
Floods on Tennessee River and Battle Creek, in Vicinity of South Pittsburg and Richard City, Tennessee.
T7260
Floods on the Tennessee River and Cypress and Cox Creeks in Vicinity of Florence, Alabama.
T7270
Floods on Tennessee River in Vicinity of Tri-Counties Alabama (Lawrence, Limestone, Morgan.)
T7280
Floods on Tennessee River, Little Tennessee River, and Town and Muddy Creeks in Vicinity of Lenoir City, Tennessee.
T7290
Floods on Toccoa-Ocoee River and Fightingtown Creek, in Vicinity of McCaysville, Ga. — Copperhill, Tenn.
T7300
Floods on Valley River, Tatham Creek, and Junaluska Creek in Vicinity of Andrews, North Carolina.
T7310
Floods on Yellow Creek in Vicinity of Burnsville, Mississippi.
T7320
Geologic Bulletin no. 1-10.
T7360
How Topographic Maps are Made.
T7380
How Topographic Maps Are Made.
T7390
. . . Hydraulic Data Activities of the Tennessee Valley Authority . . .
T7400
Industrial Water Supplies of the Tennessee Valley Region.
T7420
Maps and Surveys.
T7450
Navigation Charts Tennessee River Reservoirs: Paducah, Kentucky to Knoxville, Tennessee, Showing Underwater Conditions, Navigation Channels and Aids and Adjacent Shore Planimetry.
T7470
Precipitation in Tennessee River Basin Annual.
T7480
Recreation Maps — Tennessee Valley Lakes.
T7490
Reforestation and Erosion Control Influences Upon the Hydrology of the Pine Tree Branch Watershed 1941 to 1960.
T7500
Report on Initial Phases, Chestuee Watershed Project.
T7510
. . . Technical Monography . . . no. 1.
T7520
An Analysis of the Parker Branch Watershed Project, 1953 Through 1959: A Progress Report.
T7540
Bear Creek Watershed; Summary of Resources.
T7550
Clinch-Powell Valley; Summary of Resources.
T7560
Answers to Questions That Are Frequently Asked About TVA.
T7580
"Kenneth D. McKellar and the Politics of the Tennessee Valley Authority, 1941-1946."
T7700
Economics of Watershed Planning Sponsored by the Southeast Land Tenure Research Committee, the Farm Foundation, and the Tennessee Valley Authority.
T8820
Report on Apprentice Training Program of the Tennessee Valley Authority.
U450
Tennessee Valley Authority Financing.
U1690
Tennessee Valley Authority.
U1700

TENNESSEE VALLEY AUTHORITY
Investigation of the Tennessee Valley Authority.
U1720
Investigation of the TVA.
U1730
Labor-Management Relations in TVA.
U1740
Amending the TVA Act.
U1770
Revenue Bond Financing by TVA.
U1780
Tennessee Valley Authority Financing.
U1790
Water Resources Activities in the United States.
U1810
Report on Review of Allocations of Costs of the Multiple-Purpose Water Control System in the Tennessee River Basin, as Determined by the Tennessee Valley Authority and Approved by the President Under the Provisions of the TVA Act of 1933 as Amended.
U2910
Report on the Audit of Tennessee Valley Authority.
U3080
Tennessee Valley Authority Act: Public no. 17-73d Congress, 1st Session (H. R. 5081) May 18, 1933, 48 Stat. 58 . . . as Amended by Public Resolution, no. 88-76th Congress, 3d Session (H. J. Res. 544) June 26, 1940.
U3570
Valley Authorities.
U3600
Scientific Information Activities of Federal Agencies: Tennessee Valley Authority.
U3740
Muscle Shoals Development Message from the President of the U. S. Transmitting a Request for Legislation to Create a Tennessee Valley Authority.
U3840
The Tennessee River Basin.
U3870
Malaria Control on Impounded Water.
U3880
"The Tennessee Valley Authority: Administrative Development of the Last Two Decades, 1940-1960."
V590
TVA Revenue Bond Financing Presented by the Board of Directors, Tennessee Valley Authority.
V1290
Method for Determining Public Fire Control Expenditures for Private Lands.
V1310
TVA Power System.
W100
The Chickamauga Dam and Its Environs.
W310
"The TVA Tributary Area Development Program."
W2670
The TVA Tributary Area Development Program.
W2680 (LMC BC)
Valley of Tomorrow: The TVA and Agriculture.
W2840 (ASU LMC WCU ETSU BC)
Necessity for a Load Building Program.
W2900
Problems on a Large Power System with Large Generating Units.
W2910
America's Greatest Dam, Muscle Shoals, Alabama: Description and Pictorial Illustration of Muscle Shoals.
W4815 (ASU)
David Lilienthal, Public Servant in a Power Age.
W5830 (BC)
God's Valley: People and Power Along the Tennessee River.
W5840 (ASU WWC BC)
Waterfowl on the Tennessee River Impoundments.
W5960
"The Industrial Development Policy of the Tennessee Valley Authority for the Period 1933-1950."
W6590
"An Economic Evaluation of the Power Program of the Tennessee Valley Authority."
W6920
"The Genesis of TVA."
W7710
"Legislative Control of the Tennessee Valley Authority."
W8770
Power Transmission.
W8790
Muscle Shoals, Ala.: 1972 Proceedings.
W9200 (BC)
Muscle Shoals, Ala.: Proceedings.
W9210

TEXTILE INDUSTRY
From Mountain Cabin to Cotton Mill.
C610
Some Southern Cotton Mill Workers and Their Villages.
R1880 (WWC ASU)
From the Cotton Field to the Cotton Mill: A Study of the Industrial Transition in North Carolina.
T8180 (LMC)

TEXTILE INDUSTRY AND WORKERS
Faces We See.
B1420 (ASU BC LMC)
Labor in the Southern Cotton Mills.
B4620
The Child That Toileth Not: The Story of a Government Investigation.
D1320 (ASU BC)
Human Relations in the Industrial Southeast, a Study of the Textile Industry.
G1690 (BC)
The Road from West Virginia.
H2120 (ASU BC LMC)
Passing of the Mill Village.
H4980
Southern Mill Hills, a Study of Social and Economic Forces in Certain Textile Mill Villages.
M1150 (ASU WWC)
Millways of Kent.
M7700

TEXTILE INDUSTRY AND WORKERS — APP.
Highland Mills.
K320
"A Study of a Labor Unions of the Textile Industry in the Southern Appalachian Piedmont."
K2230 (ETSU)
The Cotton Textile Industry of the Southern Appalachian Piedmont.
L1700 (BC ASU ETSU)
Cheap and Contented Labor; the Picture of a Southern Mill Town in 1929.
L2230

TEXTILE INDUSTRY AND WORKERS — N. C.
"Weaverton — A Study of Culture and Personality in a Southern Mill Town."
C3380
"A Study of the Mill Schools of North Carolina."
C6850
A Study of Water Pollution Control in the Textile Industry of North Carolina.
G3180 (LMC)
Welfare Work in Mill Villages, the Story of Extra-mill Activities in North Carolina.
H4990 (WWC)
H5290 (ASU)
"The Textile Strikes in Marion, North Carolina, 1929: A Challenge to the New South."
H6450 (ETSU)
Millhand and Preachers, a Study of Gastonia.
P3560 (MHC)

TEXTILE INDUSTRY — N. C.
The County of Gaston: Two Centuries of a North Carolina Region.
C7260 (LMC ASU BC)

TEXTILE INDUSTRY — TENN.
W1390 (ETSU)

TOBACCO
William Tatham and the Culture of Tobacco: Including a Facsimile Reprint of an Historical and Practical Essay on the Culture and Commerce of Tobacco by William Tatham.
H4930

TOURIST INDUSTRY
Scenery: "Land of the Sky."
W4940 (BC)

TOURIST INDUSTRY — APP.
A Geographical Analysis of Selected Ski Resorts in the Southeastern United States.
T2190 (ASU)

TOURIST INDUSTRY — GA.
The Georgia Travel Industry, 1960-1963.
K410
A Study of Out-of-State Requests for Travel Information from the State of Georgia.
K420
Tourism Development in the Chattahoochee-Flint Area.
K430

TOURIST INDUSTRY — KY.
Travel in Kentucky.
K1200
Kentucky Tourist Preferences.
K1370

TOURIST INDUSTRY — N. C.
The Lenoir-Blowing Rock Wonderland.
L1760 (ASU)

TOURIST INDUSTRY — TENN.
Eliza Ross; or, Illustrated Guide of Lookout Mountain.
M4910

TOURISTS AND TOURISM
Hitch Hiking Along the Holston River from 1792-1962.
W8600

TRANSPORTATION
Economic Impact of Secondary Road Improvements.
S8150
Interterritorial Freight Rate Problem of the United States.
T2950
. . . Regionalized Freight Rates: Barrier to National Productiveness. Message from the President of the United States, Transmitting a Report of the Tennessee Valley Authority Entitled "Regionalized Freight Rates: Barrier to National Productiveness". . .
T3360
River Traffic and Industrial Growth.
T3440
Tennessee River Navigation.
T3690
The Tennessee River Navigation System; History, Development, and Operation.
T3700
The Tennessee River Waterway.
T3710
TVA River Traffic and Industrial Growth.
T3880
Major Freight Terminals on the Tennessee River Waterway.
T7440

TRANSPORTATION — APP.
Guidelines for an Appalachian Airport System.
M2980
"Transportation Investment and Depressed Regions: The Case of Appalachia."
M8670 (ASU LMC)
Guidelines for an Appalachian Airport System.
P2050 (ASU WCU)
"Transport Improvement and the Appalachian Barrier: A Case Study in Economic Innovation."
S50 (ASU)
"The Relationship Between the Structure of the Transportation Network and the Economic Development of West Virginia."
S2170
Transportation of Apples in the Appalachian Belt, 1952-53.
S5260
Appalachian Airports. Hearing on Development of Regional Airports for Purpose of Improving Transportation and Passenger Safety, March 2, 1971.
U2440

TRANSPORTATION — APP. EXPLORATION
A Journal of a Surveying Trip into Western Pennsylvania under Andrew Ellicott in the Year 1795.
B8570 (BC)
C9420
The Transylvania Colony.
L1910 (BC ASU)

TRANSPORTATION — APP. — RAILROADS
From Trail to Railway through the Appalachians.
B6630 (ASU BC LMC)
From Trail to Railway through the Appalachians.
B6640 (ETSU MHC)
The Life and Times of C. G. Memmings.
C1160 (ETSU)
History of the Louisville and Nashville Railroad.
K2700

TRANSPORTATION — APP. — RAILROADS

The Lima Shays on the Greenbrier, Cheat and Elk Railroad Co.
N400 (ASU)

Extra South.
R1400 (ASU)

The Railroads of the South, 1865-1900: A Study in Finance and Control.
S7710 (LMC BC)

Crosstie Industry Facts for the Tennessee Valley Counties.
T5280

TRANSPORTATION — APP. SETTLEMENT

Boonesborough: Its Founding, Pioneer Struggles, Indian Experiences, Transylvania Days and Revolutionary Annals.
R340 (BC ASU LMC)

Boonesborough: Its Founding, Pioneer Struggles, Indian Experiences, Transylvania Days and Revolutionary Annals.
R350 (ASU WCU ETSU)

Watauga: "The Dangerous Example." The Story of Sycamore Shoals.
W1370 (ETSU)

TRANSPORTATION — APP. SETTLEMENTS

Daniel Boone, Pioneer of Kentucky.
A30 (ASU)

Daniel Boone, Pioneer of Kentucky.
A40 (ETSU)

Daniel Boone, the Pioneer of Kentucky.
A50 (ASU BC)

David Crockett: His Life and Adventures.
A60 (ASU ETSU)

From Frontier to Plantation in Tennessee.
A80 (WWC BC)

From Frontier to Plantation in Tennessee: A Study in Frontier Democracy.
A90 (ASU LMC)

Three Virginia Frontiers.
A100 (ETSU BC)

Three Virginia Frontiers.
A110 (ASU WCU)

New Governments West of the Alleghenies Before 1780.
A1010 (BC)

State of Franklin.
A1020

John Stuart and the Southern Colonial Frontier: A Study of Indian Relations, War, Trade, and Land Problems in the Southern Wilderness, 1754-1775.
A1050 (ASU BC FC WCU)

The Overmountain Men: Early Tennessee History, 1760-1780.
A1260 (BC ETSU)

The Overmountain Men: Early Tennessee History, 1760-1795.
A1270 (ASU LMC FC)

The First Explorations of the Trans-Allegheny Region by the Virginians, 1650-1674.
A1990 (ASU BC)

The Ohio Company of Virginia and the Westward Movement, 1748-1792.
B330 (BC)

The Peopling of Virginia.
B2350 (ASU)

The Peopling of Virginia.
B2360 (FC)

Welsh Settlement of Pennsylvania.
B7450 (ASU)

Heritage of the Trans-Allegheny Pioneers: Or, Resources of Central West Virginia.
B7640 (ASU BC)

"The Rhetoric of Immediacy: Baptist and Methodist Preaching on the Trans-Appalachian Frontier.
B9440 (ASU BC)

The Appalachian Frontier: America's First Surge Westward.
C1820 (ASU WCU LMC MHC WWC ETSU BC UNCA)

The Southern Frontier.
C1830 (WCU)

Pioneers of Eastern Kentucky, Their Feuds and Settlements.
C2180 (ASU)

"Isaac Shelby, 1750-1796."
C7030

Virginia Court Records in Southwestern Pennsylvania. Records of the District of West Augusta and Ohio and Yohogania Counties, Virginia, 1775-1780.
C9350

"Theodore Roosevelt, Franklin Historian."
D910

History of the Early Settlement and Indian Wars of Western Virginia: Embracing an Account of the Various Expeditions in the West, Previous to 1795. Also, Biographical Sketches of Distinguished Actors in Our Border Wars.
D1640 (ASU BC)

History of the Early Settlement and Indian Wars of Western Virginia: Embracing an Account of the Various Expeditions in the West Previous to 1795. Also, Biographical Sketches of Co. Ebenezer Zane. . . and other Distinguished Actors in our Border Wars.
D1650 (ASU LMC FC)

The Indian Boundary in the Southern Colonies, 1763-1775.
D2000 (ASU WCU LMC BC)

The Dixie Frontier, a Social History of the Southern Frontier from the First Transmontane Beginnings to the Civil War.
D2080 (ASU MHC)

The Log Meeting-house, and the McIlhanys.
E1060 (ASU)

Resources and Enterprises of Upper East Tennessee: Johnson City, Jonesboro, Greenville, Rogersville, Morristown, Watauga, Tennessee. Franklin, Territory South of the Ohio.
E2040 (ETSU)

Provinical America, 1690-1740.
G3740

Trans-Allegheny Pioneers.
H350 (ASU)

Trans-Allegheny Pioneers. . . .
H360 (ETSU)

Trans-Allegheny Pioneers: Historical Sketches of the First White Settlements West of the Alleghenies 1784 and After. Wonderful Experiences of Hardships and Heroism of Those Who First Braved the Dangers of the Inhospitable Wilderness, and the Savage Tribes That Then Inhabited It.
H380 (ASU BC)

The Conquest of the Old Southwest: The Romantic Story of the Early Pioneers into Virginia, the Carolinas, Tennessee, and Kentucky, 1740-1790.
H4420 (ASU WCU LMC BC)

William Tatham and the Culture of Tobacco: Including a Facsimile Reprint of an Historical and Practical Essay on the Culture and Commerce of Tobacco by William Tatham.
H4930

Early Eighteenth Century Palatine Emigration: A British Government Redemptioner Project to Manufacture Naval Stores.
K2820 (ASU)

The Virginia Frontier, 1754-1763.
K3010 (ASU BC)

Emigrants From the Palatinate to the American Colonies in the 18th Century.
K3200 (ASU)

The Border Settlements of Northwestern Virginia from 1768-1795.
M2590 (BC)

Over the Blue Wall.
M4290 (BC ASU LMC ETSU WCU)

Frontier Mission: A History of Religion West of the Southern Appalachians to 1861.
P3740 (BC WWC)

The Winning of the West.
R3700 (ASU)

Six nights in a Block house.
W1520 (BC)

Chronicles of a Kentucky Settlement.
W1610 (BC)

The Bowmans, a Pioneering Family in Virginia, Kentucky and the Northwest Territory.
W1730 (ASU BC)

Early Travels in the Tennessee County, 1540-1800.
W6730 (ETSU)

Early Travels in the Tennessee Country, 1540-1800: With Introductions, Annotations and Index.
W6740 (ASU LMC BC)

History of the Lost State of Franklin.
W6780 (ASU MHC BC)

History of the Lost State of Franklin.
W6790

History of the Lost State of Franklin.
W6800 (LMC WCU ETSU ASU)

History of the Lost State of Franklin.
W6810 (ETSU)

History of the Lost State of Franklin.
W6820

TRANSPORTATION — APP. SETTLEMENTS — PA.

Notes on the Settlement and Indian Wars of the Western Parts of Virginia and Pennsylvania from 1763 to 1783. Together with a Review of the State of Society and Manners of the First Settlers of the Western Country. With a memoir of the author by his daughter, Narcissa Doddridge. Republished.
D2660 (ASU BC FC)

Notes on the Settlements and Indian of the Western Parts of Virginia and Pennsylvania from 1763 to 1783, Inclusive.
D2670 (ETSU BC)

TRANSPORTATION — APP. SETTLEMENTS — TENN.
C2650

Early History of Carter County.
E90

Two Years of Harriman, Tennessee. Established by the East Tennessee Land Company, February 26, 1890.
E160 (ASU BC)

"The Settlement Pattern of Upper East Tennessee."
H3910 (ETSU)

The First American Frontier: Civil and Political History of the State of Tennessee from Its Earliest Settlement up to the Year 1796.
H4040 (LMC)

The Natural and Aboriginal History of Tennessee, up to the First Settlements Therein by the White People in the Year 1768.
H4050 (ASU ETSU BC)

TRANSPORTATION — APP. SETTLEMENTS — VA.

Virginia Baron: The Story of Thomas, 6th Lord Fairfax.
B7400 (ASU BC)

Frederick County, Virginia, Marriages, 1771-1825.
D990 (ASU ETSU)

Notes on the Settlement and Indian Wars of the Western Parts of Virginia and Pennsylvania from 1763 to 1783. Together with a Review of the State of Society and Manners of the First Settlers of the Western Country. With a memoir of the author by his daughter, Narcissa Doddridge. Republished.
D2660 (ASU BC FC)

Notes on the Settlements and Indian of the Western Parts of Virginia and Pennsylvania from 1763 to 1783, Inclusive.
D2670 (ETSU BC)

Virginia Beyond the Blue Ridge; a Pictorial Survey of Western Virginia.
G3040 (ASU)

Braddock's Road Through the Virginia Colony.
H7420 (ASU)

James Patton and the Appalachian Colonists.
J1910 (ASU)

TRANSPORTATION — GA. — RAILROADS

Wild Train; the Story of Andrews Raiders.
O720

Daring and Suffering: A History of the Andrews Railroad Raid into Georgia in 1862.
P3140 (ASU WCU)

The Great Locomotive Chase: A History of the Andrews Railroad into Georgia in 1862.
P3150 (ETSU)

TRANSPORTATION — KY.

The Kentucky Mountains, Transportation and Commerce, 1750-1911: A Study in the Economic History of a Coal Field.
V530 (ASU WCU BC)

TRANSPORTATION — KY. — RAILROADS

Ghost Railroads of Kentucky.
S8980 (BC)

TRANSPORTATION — N. C. — RAILROADS

Some Facts Concerning the Appalachian and Western North Carolina Railroad.
A4460 (ASU)

Crossties Over Saluda.
G1280

Crossties through Carolina.
G1290 (ASU LMC MHC)

"A Historical Study of the ET&WNC Narrow Gauge Railroad."
W730 (ASU)

TRANSPORTATION — N. C. — RAILROADS
Scenery: "Land of the Sky."
W4940 (BC)
TRANSPORTATION — N. C. — ROADS
North Carolina Roads and Their Builders.
W1870 (ASU LMC)
TRANSPORTATION — OHIO
"The Economics of the Transportation of Ohio Coal."
W890
TRANSPORTATION — PA. — RAILROADS
"The Econometric Forecasting of National Rail Car Requirements for Bituminous Coal."
B5410
"A Geographical Analysis of the Rail Freight Shipments of Pennsylvania."
G1110
TRANSPORTATION — RAILROADS
John Henry, a Folklore Study.
C3310
John Henry: A Folklore Study.
C3320
Views of Chesapeake and Ohio Railroad Scenery.
C3760 (BC)
Blue Ridge Trolley. The Hagerstown and Frederick Railway.
H3330 (ASU)
Peabody Atlas.
P1140 (BC)
Slow Train to Yesterday, a Last Glance at the Local.
R3120 (ASU LMC BC)
"The Economic Position of Railroad Commuter Service in the Pittsburgh District — Its History, Present and Future.
S1190
Seasoning and Preservative Treatment of Hickory Crossties.
T240 (WCU)
Mineral and Agricultural Resources of the Portion of Tennessee Along the Cincinnati Southern and Knoxville and Ohio Railroads.
T1010 (ASU)
TRANSPORTATION — RAILROADS — APP.
Tweetsie, the Blue Ridge Sidewinder.
S870 (ASU LMC BC)
TRANSPORTATION — RIVERS
. . . Supplemental Phases of the Interterritorial Freight Rate Problem of the United States.
T4240
TRANSPORTATION — SCHOOL BUSES
The Effects of School Bus Transportation upon the Achievement of Students in Calhoun County, High School.
S8820
TRANSPORTATION — TENN.
Tourists and the Travel Service and Transportation Business in Tennessee, 1948 to 1961, Inclusive, an Economic Analysis.
C7310
"The History of Transportation Advertising, 1850-1956, and a Study of Its Importance in Knoxville, Tennessee."
H5550
"A Study of School Transportation, Hawkins County, Tennessee."
R170
"A Study of Pupil Transportation in Hancock, Tennessee."
W6510
TRANSPORTATION — TENN. — RAILROADS
"Development of Railroad Transportation in East Tennessee during the Reconstruction Period."
B3600
Guide to the Summer Resorts and Watering Places of East Tennessee.
E470
"History of the Tennessee Coal, Iron, and Railroad Company, 1852-1907."
F3700
"A Historical Study of the ET&WNC Narrow Gauge Railroad."
W730 (ASU)
TRANSPORTATION — TENN. — RIVERS
. . . The Initial Phase of Public-Use Terminal Development at Chattanooga, Tennessee.
T4200
TRANSPORTATION — TENN. — SCHOOL BUS
"A Study of School Transportation, Roane County, Tennessee."
B3610
"A Study of School Transportation, Morgan Co., Tenn."
Z180
TRANSPORTATION — TENN. — SCHOOL BUSES
"A Study of School Transportation, Bradley County, Tennessee."
H1420
"A Study of School Transportation, Blount County, Tennessee."
H2330
"A Study of School Transportation, Anderson County, Tennessee."
I950
"A Study of the School Transportation Problem in Grainger County, Tennessee."
J2700
"Pupil Transportation in Pickett County, Tennessee."
M3590
"A Study of Pupil Transportation in Polk County, Tennessee."
S1810
"A Study of the Program of Pupil Transportation in Johnson County, Tennessee."
S7680 (ETSU)
TRANSPORTATION — VA.
N1410
TRANSPORTATION — VA. — RAILROADS
When the Trains Came to Norton, Wise County, in Old Virginia in 1891.
A5330 (BC ASU)
Southwest Virginia and Contiguous Territory: Mineral Resources and Railway Facilities, Statistics, Information, Markets for Coke, Fuel, Ores, etc.
B5850 (BC)
From Mine to Market: The History of Coal Transportation on the Norfolk and Western Railway.
L220 (ASU BC)
"The Norfolk and Western Railroad, 1881-1896: A Study in Coal Transportation."
L230
The Mineral Wealth of Virginia Tributary to the Lines of the Norfolk and Western and Shenandoah Valley Railroad Companies.
M930 (BC)
Claudius Crozet: His Story of the Four Tunnels in the Blue Ridge Region of Virginia.
N490 (BC)
TRANSPORTATION — VA. — ROADS
The Valley Turnpike, Winchester to Staunton, and Other Roads.
W1850 (ASU BC)
TRANSPORTATION — W. VA.
Wheels on the Mountains.
C8340 (ASU LMC WCU BC)
"Types, Quantities and Destinations of West Virginia's Manufactured Exports, an Exploratory Study."
L850
Indexed County and Railroad Pocket Map and Shipper's Guide of West Virginia.
R390 (BC)
"Transportation and Trade Areas; Analysis of Morgantown, Fairmont, and Clarksburg."
S330 (ASU)
TRANSPORTATION — W. VA. — AIR
Twenty Feet from Glory: From the Land of Ford to the Land of Canaan.
G2630 (ASU BC)
TRANSPORTATION — W. VA. — RAILROADS
Your Train Ride through History: An Authentic History of the Town of Cass and the Great Lumber Empire Which Gave Rise to Your Ride on the Cass Scenic Railroad.
B4410 (ASU BC)
Freight Rates of West Virginia Wood Products.
C950 (ASU)
The Comp'ny: The Story of the Surry, Sussex and Southampton Railway and the Surry Lumber Company.
C8850 (ASU LMC BC)
TRANSPORTATION — W. VA. — SCHOOL BUSES
"Pupil Transportation in W. Va., 1934-55."
S9730
TUCKASEEGEE RIVER
Planning for Flood Damage Prevention at Clyde, N. C.
C5160 (LMC)
TUCKASEIGEE RIVER
Tuckaseigee Minutes, 1829-1857.
N1670 (WCU)
Floods on the Tuckaseigee River and Deep Creek in Vicinity of Bryson City, North Carolina.
T2750
Floods on Oconaluftee and Tuckaseigee Rivers and Soco Creek in Vicinity of Cherokee, North Carolina.
T7130
TUG RIVER
"The Transformation of the Tug and Guyandot Valleys: Economic Development and Social Change in West Virginia, 1888-1921."
C9390
"The Rise of Education and the Decline of Feudal Tendencies in the Tug River Valley of West Virginia and Kentucky in Relation to the Hatfield and McCoy Feud."
M780 (ASU)
UNITED MINE WORKERS
Men and Coal.
C5790 (ASU BC)
Men and Coal.
C5800 (MHC WCU)
"The United Mine Workers: A Study of How Trade Union Policy Relates to Technological Change."
M6000
"Attitude of Coal Miners toward Union and Coal Industry."
M7730 (ASU)
Coaltown Revisited: An Appalachian Notebook.
P2330 (ASU LMC ETSU WCU WWC BC)
UNITED MINE WORKERS OF AMERICA
The Kentucky Miner's Struggle: The Record of a Year of Lawless Violence. The Only Complete Picture of Events Briefly Told.
A2090 (ASU)
Labor's Untold Story.
B6040 (ASU)
The Corrupt Kingdom: The Rise and Fall of the United Mine Workers.
F1030
"Economic Consequences of the Seven-hour Day and Wage Changes in the Bituminous Coal Industry."
F1220
Wage Rates and Working Time in the Bituminous Coal Industry, 1912-1922.
F1230 (BC)
Coal Creek Rebellion.
F1770 (ASU)
"Coal Mining Safety: National Solutions in the Progressive Period."
G3090
"The Economic Effects of Collective Bargaining in Bituminous Coal Mining."
G3860
H2320
Struggle in the Coal Fields. The Autobiography of Fred Mooney, Secretary-Treasurer, District 17, United Mine Workers of America.
H5070 (ASU)
"The United Mine Workers of America and the Non-Union Coal Fields."
H5620
Death and the Mines: Rebellion and Murder in the United Mine Workers.
H8260 (ASU BC LMC WCU)
Autobiography of Mother Jones.
J2500 (BC LMC ASU WCU MHC)
Thoughts of Mother Jones: Compiled from Her Writings and Speeches.
J2510 (WCU)
Hearings Held at Pikeville.
K1240
Coal and Unionism: A History of the American Coal Miners Unions.
M1120 (BC ASU)
"A Study of the United Mine Workers of America Welfare and Retirement Fund."
S1400
"Coal and Conflict: The U.M.W.A. in Harlan County, 1931-1939."
T690 (BC ASU)
Hell in Harlan.
T8760 (WCU)
The American Miners Association: A Record of the Origin of Coal Miners' Unions in the United States.
W5970 (ASU)
The Miners' Case and the Public Interest: A Documented Chronology.
W5980

UPPER DUCK RIVER
Upper Duck River Valley; Summary of Resources.
T4020
VA. — DESCRIPTION AND TRAVEL
Travels of a Frenchman in Maryland and Virginia with a Description of Philadelphia and Baltimore, in 1791: Or, Travels in the Interior of the United States, to Bath, Winchester, in the Valley of the Shenandoah, etc., During the Summer of 1791.
B2140
Reise sr. Hoheit des Herzogs Bernhard zu Sachsen-Weimar-Eisenach durch Nord-Amerika in den Jahren 1825 und 1826.
B3190
The Discovery of New Brittaine.
B4580 (ASU BC)
The Mineral Springs of Virginia.
B8760
The Mineral Springs of Western Virginia: with Remarks on Their Use, and The Diseases to Which They are Applicable.
B8770
Travels in America. The Poetry of Pope. Two Lectures Delivered to the Leeds Mechanics' Institution and Literary Society, December 5th and 6th, 1850.
C1270
My Recollections of Rocktown, Now Known as Harrisonburg.
C1460 (ASU BC)
Clifton Forge, Virginia.
C1640
It Happened around Staunton in Virginia.
C4880 (ASU)
Clifton Forge, Virginia: Scenic, Busy, Friendly.
C7580 (FC)
C8050
Journal of a Tour through the United States and Canada, Made during the Years 1937-38.
D440
Bits of History and Legends Around and About the Natural Bridge of Virginia, 1730-1950.
D1080 (ASU)
Bits of History and Legends around and about the Natural Bridge of Virginia from 1730-1950.
D1090 (BC)
Virginia: A Guide to the Old Dominion.
F490
Sketches of Virginia.
F1810
Sketches of Virginia Historical and Biographical.
F1820
Sketches of Virginia Historical and Biographical.
F1830
Sketches of Virginia: Historical and Biographical, First Series.
F1840 (LMC UNCA)
What Is It About Virginia?
F3290
Virginia.
F3480 (ASU)
In the Picturesque Shenandoah Valley.
G2660 (ASU BC)
Virginia at Mid-century.
G2870 (FC BC)
Virginia in our Century.
G2880 (BC FC)
Virginia Beyond the Blue Ridge; a Pictorial Survey of Western Virginia.
G3040 (ASU)
The Wonderful Shenandoah Valley.
G3400
G4650
Twelve Virginia Counties Where Western Migration Began.
G5030
Tennessee and Virginia, the Mountain Empire.
H2290 (ETSU)
History and Comprehensive Description of Loudoun County, Virginia.
H4110 (ASU BC)
To the Shenandoah and Beyond: The Chronicle of a Leisurely Journey through the Uplands of Virginia and Tennessee, Sketching Their Scenery, Noting Their Legends, Portraying Social and Material Progress, and Explaining Routes of Travel.
I780
A Photographic Documentary of the Blue Ridge Mountains.
J480 (LMC)
Notes on the State of Virginia.
J500 (ASU)
Notes on the State of Virginia.
J510 (FC)
The Present State of Virginia; from Whence Is Inferred a Short View of Maryland and North Carolina.
J2370 (FC)
Scenic and Historic Old Virginia and Eastern National Parks.
K2790 (WCU)
Historical Sketches of Virginia.
M80
A Virginian Village, and Other Papers: Together with Some Autobiographical Notes.
N30 (WCU)
Letters Descriptive of the Virginia Springs: the Roads Leading Thereto and the Doings Thereat.
N960
P1080
The Virginia Tourist. Sketches of the Springs and Mountains of Virginia: Containing an Exposition of Fields for the Tourist in Virginia, Natural Beauties and Wonders of the State: Also Accounts of Its Mineral Springs. And a Medical Guide to the Use of the Waters, Etc., Etc.
P3380 (ASU BC)
Handbook of Smyth County, Virginia.
S2620
S4110 (ASU)
Virginia Illustrated: Containing a Visit to the Virginian Canaan, and the Adventures of Porte Crayon and His Cousins.
S8110 (ASU BC)
Virginia: A Geographical and Political Summary, Embracing a Description of the State, Its Geology, Soils, Minerals and Climate; Its Animal and Vegetable Productions; Manufacturing and Commercial Facilities; Religious and Educational Advantages; Internal Improvements, and Form of Government.
V700 (BC)
Virginia.
V740 (BC)
V1040
A Bird's Eye View of the Shenandoah Valley with Map.
W1650
VA. — DESCRIPTION AND TRAVEL — SHENANDOAH VALLEY
The Shenandoah and Its Byways.
S7150 (ASU BC)
VA. — EARLY EXPLORATION
The Discovery of New Brittaine.
B4580 (ASU BC)
James Patton and the Appalachian Colonists.
J1910 (ASU)
A History of Middle New River Settlements and Contiguous Territory.
J2020 (ASU FC)
The Blackwater Chronicle; A Narrative of an Expedition into the Land of Canaan.
K750 (BC ASU)
The Discoveries of John Lederer.
L1280 (LMC)
The Discoveries of John Lederer, in Three Several Marches From Virginia, to the West of Carolina, and Other Parts of the Continent: Begun in March 1669, and Ended in September 1670.
L1290 (ASU FC BC)
The Discoveries of John Lederer, with Unpublished Letters By and About Lederer to Governor John Winthrop, Jr.
L1300 (ASU WCU ETSU)
P4380
The Western Country in 1793: Reports on Kentucky and Virginia.
T9000 (ASU BC ETSU)
Doctor Walker's Diary of Exploration, 1750; with Will Subjoined.
W370 (BC)
Journal of an Exploration in the Spring of the Year 1750.
W380
VA. — GENEALOGY — SOURCES
William Cross of Botetourt County, Virginia and His Descendants, 1733-1932.
C9080
VA. — GEOGRAPHY
Virginia Place Names: Derivations, Historical Uses.
H1720 (ASU BC FC)
Old Place Names.
P2020
VA. — HISTORY
Three Virginia Frontiers.
A100 (ETSU BC)
Three Virginia Frontiers.
A110 (ASU WCU)
Western Lands and the American Revolution.
A120
Western Lands and the American Revolution.
A130 (FC BC ASU)
A Short History of Extreme Southwest Virginia.
A530 (ASU LMC)
The Story of Wise County, Virginia.
A540 (BC ASU)
History of Scott County, Virginia.
A580 (LMC FC ASU BC)
History of Scott County, Virginia.
A590
History of the Campaign of General T. J. (Stonewall) Jackson in the Shenandoah Valley of Virginia from Nov. 4, 1861, to June 17, 1862.
A1480 (ASU)
Early History of Snowville.
A1790
The First Explorations of the Trans-Allegheny Region by the Virginians, 1650-1674.
A1990 (ASU BC)
Sectionalism in Virginia from 1776-1861.
A2030
Virginia, the Old Dominion.
A2510 (FC BC)
Early History of Staunton and Beverley Manor in Augusta County, Virginia.
A5510 (ASU BC)
History of Bland County (Virginia).
B4570 (ASU BC)
The Discovery of New Brittaine.
B4580 (ASU BC)
Gleanings of Virginia History.
B5390
Economic History of Virginia in the Seventeenth Century.
B7620 (BC FC)
Southwest Virginia and Shenandoah Valley. An Inquiry into the Causes of the Rapid Growth and Wonderful Development of Southwest Virginia and Shenandoah Valley, with a History of the Norfolk and Western and Shenandoah Valley Railroads.
B7650 (ASU BC FC)
Histories of the Dividing Line Betwixt Virginia and North Carolina.
B9620 (BC FC)
Bibliography of Virginia History Since 1865.
C1190 (BC FC)
Clifton Forge, Virginia.
C1640
Clarke County, 1836-1936.
C3940 (ASU)
The Life and Adventures of Wilburn Waters, Early History of Southwest Virginia.
C5220
The Compacts of Virginia.
C6800 (FC)
Stonewall Jackson.
C7000 (ASU BC)
Stonewall Jackson and the Old Stonewall Brigade.
C7010 (ASU BC)
Carry Me Back: Slavery and Servitude in Seventeenth Century Virginia.
C7270 (MHC FC ASU)
History of Shenandoah Valley.
C8020
Foot Prints on The Sands of Time, A History of South-western Virginia and North-western North Carolina.
C8140 (ASU LMC)
White, Red, and Black: The Seventeenth-century Virginian.
C8570 (ETSU)
Index to 1810 Virginia Census.
C8760

VA. — HISTORY

Early Virginia Marriages.
C9280 (ASU)
Early Virginia Marriages.
C9290 (ASU)
Virginia Colonial Militia, 1651-1776.
C9310
Virginia Colonial Militia, 1651-1776.
C9320 (ASU)
Virginia Heraldica, Being a Registry of Virginia Gentry Entitled to Coat Armor with Genealogical Notes of the Families.
C9330 (ASU)
Virginia Court Records in Southwestern Pennsylvania. Records of the District of West Augusta and Ohio and Yohogania Counties, Virginia, 1775-1780.
C9350
The Montgomery County Story, 1776-1957.
C9360 (ASU)
List of Books and Related Materials About Virginia for Use of Schools.
C9490
Virginia, The New Dominion.
D30 (FC BC)
Hornbook of Virginia History.
D130
Frederick County, Virginia, Marriages, 1771-1825.
D990 (ASU ETSU)
Bits of History and Legends Around and About the Natural Bridge of Virginia, 1730-1950.
D1080 (ASU)
Bits of History and Legends around and about the Natural Bridge of Virginia from 1730-1950.
D1090 (BC)
The Shenandoah.
D1140 (ASU BC FC)
A Valley and a Song; the Story of the Shenandoah River.
D1150 (BC ASU)
History of the Early Settlement and Indian Wars of Western Virginia: Embracing an Account of the Various Expeditions in the West, Previous to 1795. Also, Biographical Sketches of Distinguished Actors in Our Border Wars.
D1640 (ASU BC)
History of the Early Settlement and Indian Wars of Western Virginia: Embracing an Account of the Various Expeditions in the West Previous to 1795. Also, Biographical Sketches of Co. Ebenezer Zane. . . and other Distinguished Actors in our Border Wars.
D1650 (ASU LMC FC)
Augusta County, Virginia, in the History of the U. S.
D3950 (BC)
The Border States: Kentucky, North Carolina, Tennessee, Virginia, West Virginia.
D4190 (BC ASU LMC WWC ETSU)
A Way of Life in Virginia at the Turn of the Century.
F250
Fauquier County Va., 1759-1959.
F350 (ASU)
Old Virginia and Her Neighbours.
F1290 (ASU MHC)
Sketches of Virginia.
F1810
Sketches of Virginia Historical and Biographical.
F1820
Sketches of Virginia Historical and Biographical.
F1830
Sketches of Virginia: Historical and Biographical, First Series.
F1840 (LMC UNCA)
What Is It About Virginia?
F3290
Giles County, 1806-1956, a Brief History.
F3350
Giles County, 1806-1956.
G2440
Fredericksburg, Virginia. Its Homes and History, the Battlefields and the Rappahanrock Valley.
G2650
In the Picturesque Shenandoah Valley.
G2660 (ASU BC)
Men and Events: Chapters of Virginia History.
G2670 (LMC)
Virginia Beyond the Blue Ridge; a Pictorial Survey of Western Virginia.
G3040 (ASU)
Genealogical and Historical Notes on Culpeper County, Virginia.
G3650 (ASU)
Winchester, Virginia, and Its Beginnings, 1743-1814: From Its Founding by Colonel James Wood to the Close of the Life of His Son, Brigadier General and Governor James Wood. With the Publication for the first Time of Valuable Manuscripts, relics of their long Tenure of Public offices.
G3800 (ASU BC)
Twelve Virginia Counties Where Western Migration Began.
G5030
The Rending of Virginia; a History.
H700 (BC)
The Two Virginias: Genesis of Old and New; a Romance of American History; State Sovereignty, Phantom of a Stupendous Folly.
H710 (BC)
A History of Damascus.
H840
Historic and Heroic Lynchburg.
H980 (ASU)
Virginia Place Names: Derivations, Historical Uses.
H1720 (ASU BC FC)
Tennessee and Virginia, the Mountain Empire.
H2290 (ETSU)
Annals of Tazewell County, Virginia from 1800 to 1922.
H2400 (BC ASU)
The Valley of Virginia in the American Revolution, 1763-1789.
H3160 (ASU BC FC)
History and Comprehensive Description of Loudoun County, Virginia.
H4110 (ASU BC)
Dr. Thomas Walker and The Loyal Company of Virginia.
H4430
Historical Sketches of Southwest Virginia.
H5950
Bulletin of the Virginia State Library: Index to Mrs. Cabell's "Sketches and Recollections of Lynchburg."
H6460 (ASU)
An Archaeological Survey of Southwest Virginia.
H6560 (ASU WCU ETSU BC)
The Earthquake History of Virginia, 1774 to 1900.
H7140
Fort Lewis: A Community in Transition.
H7450
Fort Lewis: A Community in Transition.
H7460
Listen to the Mockingbird.
H7680
Listen to the Mockingbird; The Life and Times of a Pioneer Virginia Family.
H7690
Lovely Mount Tavern: The Birth of a City, and Something of the Early New River Settlers.
H7700
Historical Collections of Virginia . . .
H7710
Historical Collections of Virginia.
H7720
A Narrative History of Wise County, Virginia.
J1310 (LMC ASU)
James Patton and the Appalachian Colonists.
J1910 (ASU)
A History of Middle New River Settlements and Contiguous Territory.
J2020 (ASU FC)
The Present State of Virginia; from Whence Is Inferred a Short View of Maryland and North Carolina.
J2370 (FC)
Kegley's Virginia Frontier: The Beginning of the Southwest. The Roanoke of Colonial Days, 1740-1783.
K470 (ASU ETSU FC BC)
History of Saltville, Virginia.
K870
A History of the Valley of Virginia.
K1550 (ASU BC)
History of the Valley of Virginia.
K1560
History of the Valley of Virginia.
K1570
Scenic and Historic Old Virginia and Eastern National Parks.
K2790 (WCU)
The Virginia Frontier, 1754-1763.
K3010 (ASU BC)
Double Destiny: The Story of Bristol, Tennessee-Virginia.
L3670 (LMC ETSU)
Double Destiny: The Story of Bristol, Tennessee-Virginia.
L3680 (ASU)
The Washington Randophs and Their Friends: Extracts from the Diary of a Lady of Old Virginia, Selected and Edited by T. M.
M10 (ASU)
A Brief History of Bath County, Virginia.
M60 (ASU)
Historical Sketches of Virginia.
M80
Southwest Virginia Historical Records, Census of 1810, Wytheville, Wythe County edition.
M1490
The Border Settlements of Northwestern Virginia from 1768-1795.
M2590 (BC)
M2750 (ASU)
History of Virginia, for the Use of Schools.
M2780 (LMC)
Historic Homes of the South-west Mountains, Virginia.
M4730 (ASU BC ETSU LMC)
M4970
Man from the Valley: Memoirs of a 20th-Century Virginian.
M5620 (ASU)
The Fairfax Line, a Profile in History and Geography.
M7890 (ASU)
Wappatomaka: A Survey of the History and Geography of the South Branch Valley.
M7910 (ASU)
Annals of Bath County, Virginia.
M8020 (BC)
Annals of Bath County, Virginia.
M8030 (ASU)
A Centennial History of Alleghany County, Virginia.
M8040 (BC)
A Centennial History of Alleghany County, Virginia.
M8050 (ASU)
A Handbook of Highland County, and a Supplement to Pendleton and Highland History.
M8060
A History of Highland County, Virginia.
M8070 (ASU BC)
A History of Highland County, Virginia.
M8080 (ASU)
History of the Lower Shenandoah Valley: Counties of Frederick, Berkeley, Jefferson, and Clarke.
N1490 (ASU BC)
"Doctor Thomas Walker (1715-1794): Explorer, Physician, Surveyor, and Planter of Virginia and Kentucky."
N3050 (BC)
History of Bedford County, Virginia.
P270 (FC)
P1080
Old Place Names.
P2020
Memoir of John Howe Peyton, in the Sketches of His Contemporaries, Together with Some of His Public and Private Letters, etc., Also a Sketch of Ann M. Peyton.
P2500 (ASU)
P3210
The Virginia Tourist. Sketches of the Springs and Mountains of Virginia: Containing an Exposition of Fields for the Tourist in Virginia, Natural Beauties and Wonders of the State: Also Accounts of Its Mineral Springs. And a Medical Guide to the Use of the Waters, Etc., Etc.
P3380 (ASU BC)
Russell County, Virginia's Bluegrass Empire.
P4180 (ASU)
P4380

VA. — HISTORY
George Washington and Winchester, Virginia 1748-1758; A Decade of Preparation for Responsibilities to Come.
Q70 (ASU)
The Albemarle of Other Days.
R550 (LMC ASU)
What I Know about Winchester: Recollections of William Greenway Russell, 1800-1891.
R4410 (ASU BC)
S120
Early Records, Hampshire County Virginia, Now West Virginia, Including at the Start Most of Known Va. Aside from Augusta District.
S130 (BC ASU)
Loudoun County, Virginia, Past and Present.
S250 (ASU)
Drums Along the Antietam.
S930 (MHC ASU)
History of the German Element in Virginia.
S1180
Handbook of Smyth County, Virginia.
S2620
A History of the Town of Dayton, Virginia.
S3760 (ASU BC)
A History of Bristol Parish, Va.; With Genealogies of Families Connected Therewith, and Historical Illustrations.
S4140 (ASU BC)
Addresses of Famous Southwestern Virginians.
S4200
Boyhood Memories of Fauquier.
S4950 (ASU)
The Story of Virginia's First Century.
S6500 (LMC)
Escape From Indian Captivity. The Story of Mary Draper Ingles and Son Thomas Ingles.
S6740
Massanutten, Settled by the Pennsylvania Pilgrim, 1726: The First White Settlement in the Shenandoah Valley.
S7980 (ASU BC)
Old Tenth Legion Marriages; Marriages in Rockingham Co., Va. from 1778 to 1816.
S7990
Recollections of an Old Man. Seventy Years in Dixie.
S8950
Annals of Southwest Virginia, 1769-1800.
S9050 (ASU BC FC ETSU)
History of Southwest Virginia, 1746-1786, Washington County, 1777-1870.
S9060 (ASU BC ETSU)
History of Southwest Virginia, 1746-1786, Washington County, 1777-1870.
S9070 (ASU LMC FC ETSU)
History of Southwest Virginia, 1746-1786, Washington County, 1777-1870.
S9080 (ASU ETSU)
Dickenson County in War Time; a Community History.
S9150
Meet Virginia's Baby.
S9190
Meet Virginia's Baby: A Brief Pictorial History of Dickenson County, Virginia, from Its Formation in 1880 to 1955, with Stress on Pioneer Background.
S9200 (ASU LMC BC)
Regular Primitive Baptist Washington District Association.
S9210
Some Sandy Basin Characters.
S9250
Amherst County, Virginia, in the Revolution: Including Extracts from the "Lost Order Book", 1773-1782.
S9530 (ASU)
Northern Virginia Heritage; a Pictorial Compilation of the Historic Sites and Homes in the Counties of Arlington, Fairfax, Loudoun, Fauquier, Prince William and Stafford, and the Cities of Alexandria and Fredericksburg, by Eleanor Lee Templeman and Nan Netherton.
T860 (BC)
Documentary History of Dunmore's War, 1774.
T8510
Withers Chronicles of Border Warfare.
T8540
Rockbridge County, Virginia.
T8890
Hallowed Heritage: The Life of Virginia.
T8940 (FC BC)
The Western Country in 1793: Reports on Kentucky and Virginia.
T9000 (ASU BC ETSU)
The Valley of Shenandoah; Or, Memoirs of the Graysons.
T9590
The Valley of Shenandoah: Or, Memoirs of the Graysons.
T9600 (ASU ETSU WWC)
Men of Mark in Virginia.
T9910
The Letters and Times of the Tylers.
T9920 (ASU)
Virginia's First German Colony.
V350 (ASU FC)
Virginia: A Geographical and Political Summary, Embracing a Description of the State, Its Geology, Soils, Minerals and Climate; Its Animal and Vegetable Productions; Manufacturing and Commercial Facilities; Religious and Educational Advantages; Internal Improvements, and Form of Government.
V700 (BC)
State Historical Markers of Virginia.
V720
An Old Virginia Court: Being a Transcript of the Records of the First Court of Franklin County, Virginia, 1786-1789, with Biographies of the Justices and Stories of Famous Cases.
V730 (ASU ETSU)
A Hornbook of Virginia History.
V760 (ASU)
V1040
V1060
V1070 (BC)
V1110 (BC)
Annals of Augusta County, Virginia, 1726-1871.
W20
Annals of Augusta County, Virginia, with Reminiscences and a Diary of the War, 1861-1865, and a Chapter on Reconstruction.
W30 (LMC BC ASU)
Russell Co. in Retrospect.
W240 (BC)
Observance, Battle of Front Royal Virginia, May 19-20, 1962.
W920 (LMC)
Facts and Fiction in Virginia History.
W1660
Scenic and Historical Guide to the Shenandoah Valley.
W1680
Twenty-Five Chapters on the Shenandoah Valley.
W1700 (BC)
Virginia Valley Records.
W1710
German Element of the Shenandoah Valley of Virginia.
W1740 (BC)
The German Element of the Shenandoah Valley of Virginia.
W1750 (ASU)
A History of Rockingham County, Virginia.
W1780 (ASU BC)
A History of Shenandoah County, Virginia.
W1790 (ASU BC)
A History of Shenandoah County, Virginia (1969)
W1800
Scenic and Historical Guide to the Shenandoah Valley: A Handbook of Useful Information for Tourists and Students.
W1820 (WCU)
The Shenandoah Valley in History and Literature.
W1830 (ASU)
Virginia Valley Records: Genealogical and Historical Materials of Rockingham County, Virginia, and Related Regions.
W1860 (ASU BC)
History of Hancock Co., Va. and W. Va.
W2470 (BC)
Papa's Diary.
W5560 (BC)
Historical Facts About Churches of Wythe County.
W5790
Abstracts of Bedford County, Virginia Wills, Inventories and Accounts 1754-1787.
W5900 (FC)
Legends of Loudoun: An Account of the History and Homes of a Border County of Virginia's Northern Neck.
W6560 (ASU BC)
Smythe County History and Traditions.
W7240 (ASU BC)
Diaries, Letters and Recollections of the War Between the States.
W7580
Gravestone Inscriptions: From 61 Graveyards in Frederick County and the Counties That Were Once a Part of Frederick County and Includes the Inscriptions from the "Old Lutheran and German Reform Graves" in Mt. Hebron Cemetery.
W7590 (ASU)
2200 Gravestone Inscriptions from Winchester and Frederick County, Virginia (Death Dates Range from 1700's to Early 1900's).
W7600 (ASU)
Souvenir.
W7610 (ASU)
Annual Papers.
W7620 (ASU)
Franklin County, Virginia, a History.
W7720 (ASU BC FC)
Albemarle County in Virginia: Giving Some Account of What It Was by Nature, of What It Was Made by Man, and of Some of the Men Who Made It.
W8800
A History of the Presbytery of Winchester (Synod of Virginia): Its Rise and Growth, Ecclesiastical Relations, Institutions, Agencies, Churches and Ministers, 1719-1945.
W8980 (ASU BC)
A History of the Presbyterian Church in Winchester, Virginia, 1780-1949.
W8990 (BC)
Our Mountain Men: Their Early Court Records in Southwest Virginia.
W9270 (BC)
One of Jackson's Foot Cavalry: His Experience and What He Saw During the War, 1861-1865, Including a History of "F Company," Richmond, Va., 21st Regiment Virginia Infantry, Second Brigade, Jackson's Division, Second Corps.
W9290 (ASU)
Virginia Germans.
W9810
A History of Madison County, Virginia.
Y330 (BC)

VA. — HISTORY — APP. COUNTIES
Political History of Appalachian Virginia 1776-1927.
P1700 (ASU WCU ETSU LMC)

VA. — HISTORY — COLONIAL PERIOD
Fauquier during the Proprietorship: A Chronicle of the Colonization and Organization of a Northern Neck County.
G4390 (ASU)
The Transition in Virginia from Colony to Commonwealth. Studies in History, Economics and Public Law, No. 96.
L2610 (LMC)

VA. — HISTORY, WESTERN REGION
History of Tazewell County and Southwest Virginia 1748-1920.
P1690 (ASU ETSU LMC)

VA. — LABOR FORCE
Exploring Virginia's Human Resources.
H8120 (ASU BC)

VA. — POLITICS
Notes on the State of Virginia.
J500 (ASU)
Notes on the State of Virginia.
J510 (FC)

VA. — RECREATION AND TOURISM
The Virginia Tourist. Sketches of the Springs and Mountains of Virginia: Containing an Exposition of Fields for the Tourist in Virginia, Natural Beauties and Wonders of the State: Also Accounts of Its Mineral Springs. And a Medical Guide to the Use of the Waters, Etc., Etc.
P3380 (ASU BC)
Guide to the Appalachian Trail in Central and Southwestern Virginia.
P3860

VA. RIVER
Bulletin. Surface and Water Supply of Va. New, Big Sandy, and Tenn. River Basins, 1942-1950.
V750 (BC)
VA. RIVERS
Canoeing White Water: A Guide Book to the Rivers of Virginia and Eastern West Virginia, The Great Smoky Mountain Area.
C1740 (LMC)
VALLEY RIVER
Floods on Hiwassee River, Valley River, and Peachtree Creek in Vicinity of Murphy, N C.
T7070
VISTA VOLUNTEERS
An Analysis of the Vista Program and Appalachian Volunteers, Inc.
A2190
VOCATIONAL TRAINING AND RETRAINING
Status of Secondary Vocational Education in Appalachia.
A3950 (ASU LMC)
Vocational and Educational Goals of Rural Youth in Virginia.
B4220
"The Non-attainment of Adolescents' Occupational Aspirations: A Longitudinal Study of Rural Pennsylvania Males."
K3450
Vocational Rehabilitation Needs and Resources in Eastern Kentucky.
S7890
VOCATIONAL TRAINING AND RETRAINING — APP.
"Study of Industrial Arts Education in Public Secondary Schools of the Southern Appalachian Region."
C5970
Proceedings.
C6480 (ASU)
Apprenticeship and Economic Change.
F120
Retraining the Work Force, an Analysis of Current Experience.
H7070
Statement of Conditions 1930.
I220
"Employment Opportunities and Training Needs for Technicians in the Metalworking Manufacturing Industries of the Central Ohio Valley with Projections through 1975."
L1500
Technical-Vocational Education and the Community College.
L1610
A Report of the Findings of a Demonstration Retraining Project for Long Term Unemployed Persons in a Rural Appalachian Mountain Area.
M3150 (ASU)
"Training the Poor: A Benefit-cost Analysis of Vocational Instruction in the United States Antipoverty Program."
S2050
VOCATIONAL TRAINING AND RETRAINING — N. C.
Manpower Education in the North Carolina Appalachian Region.
H1320 (ASU)
VOCATIONAL TRAINING AND RETRAINING — TENN.
"A Comparison of Intelligence in Students with Mixed and Lateral Dominance in Johnson City Vocational Schools."
C5460 (ETSU)
"Educational and Vocational Choices of the 1960 Graduates of Dobyns-Bennett High School, Kingsport, Tennessee."
C9210 (ETSU)
"A Study of the Vocational Guidance Now Provided to Non-college Bound Students in East Tennessee High Schools."
D920
"An Assessment of Needs and Guidelines for Development of an Industrial Ceramics Program."
E1440 (ETSU)
"A Proposed Course of Study in Electronics for Johnson City Vocational School's Evening Program."
E1840 (ETSU)
"A Study of Vocational Education at the Elizabethton, Tennessee, Area Vocational-Technical School."
F2950 (ETSU)
"A Study of the Program of Vocational Rehabilitation in Carter County, Tennessee."
G4300
"Development of a Course in Fractions for Johnson City Vocational School."
H4970 (ETSU)
Educational and Vocational Goals of Rural Youth and Their Parents in Tennessee.
J540 (ASU)
"A Study of the Blue Ridge Job Corps Center."
L830 (ETSU)
"A Study of the Working Relationships of the Agriculture Extension Service and the Vocational Agriculture Program in East Tennessee."
L1750
"An Evaluation of the Tennessee Valley Authority Manpower Training and Development Demonstration Project."
L3530 (ASU BC)
"A Survey to Determine the Need of Trade and Industrial Education in Warren County, Tennessee."
M4250
"Job Retraining under the Area Development Act: The Campbell, Claiborne Counties (Tennessee) Case."
S5420
Report on Apprentice Training Program of the Tennessee Valley Authority.
U450
A Technical Assistance Program for the Upper Cumberlands of Tennessee.
W170
VOCATIONAL TRAINING AND RETRAINING — VA.
Highlights of Vocational and Educational Goals of Rural Youth in Virginia.
B4850
"An Evaluation of the Impact of the Vocational Education Act of 1963 on Agricultural Education in the Blue Ridge Area of Southwestern Virginia."
N950 (ETSU)
VOCATIONAL TRAINING AND RETRAINING — W. VA.
"Current and Future Needs for Vocational Education in Jackson County, West Virginia."
C9770
Job Development for the Hard-to-employ.
F680 (ETSU)
"Employer Reaction to Retraining in the Clarksburg, West Virginia Labor Market Area."
H620
"An Investigation of Some Needs for Expansion of Vocational Education in Monongalia, Preston and Taylor Counties, West Virginia."
H3020
Outcomes of Vocational Retraining in West Virginia.
P3430
VOCATIONAL TRAINING — TENN.
"A Comparison of Intelligence in Students with Mixed and Lateral Dominance in Johnson City Vocational Schools."
C5460 (ETSU)
W. VA. — DESCRIPTION AND TRAVEL
When Men and Mountains Meet.
A3500
History of Cavelier de LaSalle, 1643-1687; Explorations in the Valleys of the Ohio, Illinois and Mississippi, taken from his Letters, Reports to King Louis XIV, also the Reports of Several of his Associates, Official Acts and Contemporaneous Documents,
C3800
Grant's West Virginia Illustrated.
G3230
An Analysis of Some Selected Characteristics of Cabin Vacationists in West Virginia State Parks and Forests in 1961.
H40 (ASU)
West Virginia Travel and Tourism Study — The Potential Market.
H70
Fayette County.
H4710 (ETSU)
"West Virginia's Program of State Publicity."
I1020
Locust Bloom.
M3970 (BC)
From Baltimore to Charleston.
S790
Blackwater Country.
S4860 (ASU WCU MHC BC)
White Sulphur Springs, a Brief History.
T700 (ASU)
W. VA. — HISTORIC HOMES
The Washingtons and Their Colonial Homes in W. Va.
T8480 (BC)
W. VA. — HISTORY
Alee's History of Martensburg and Berkeley Company, West Virginia.
A1310
A History of West Virginia. . .
A2010 (BC WCU)
The Makers of West Virginia and Their Work.
A2020
Sectionalism in Virginia from 1776-1861.
A2030
West Virginia, the Mountain State.
A2040 (ASU ETSU BC)
West Virginia, the Mountain State.
A2050 (ASU WCU ETSU)
West Virginia: Stories and Biographies.
A2060
"A History of the Labor Movement in West Virginia."
A2610
Salesman of Appalachia.
A4960
"The Socialist Party in West Virginia from 1898 to 1920: A Study in Working Class Radicalism."
B1170
The Story of Smithfield, Jefferson County, West Virginia.
B1900
The Story of Washington Bottom, Wood County, West Virginia.
B2510 (BC)
Call of the Mountains.
B2640 (BC ASU)
History of Roane County, West Virginia, from the Time of Its Exploration to A. D. 1927.
B4250 (ASU BC)
A History of Franklin, the County Seat of Pendleton County, West Virginia.
B5060 (BC)
A History of Randolph County, West Virginia, from Its Earliest Settlement to the Present Time.
B5580 (BC)
Reference Book of Wyoming County History.
B5800 (ASU BC LMC)
Annals of Blackwater and the Land of Canaan, 1746-1880.
B7380 (ASU BC)
History of Nicholas County, West Virginia.
B7430 (ASU BC)
A History of Jefferson County, West Virginia.
B9360 (ASU BC)
Twixt North and South.
C250 (ASU)
History of West Virginia: Old and New, in One Volume.
C290 (LMC BC)
Semi-Centennial History of West Virginia. With Special Articles on Development and Resources.
C300 (ASU ETSU BC)
The Thirty-fifth State: Documentary History of Virginia.
C6160 (ASU LMC BC)
Beacon Lights of West Virginia History.
C6540 (BC)
West Virginia: Brief History of the Mountain State.
C6580 (ASU BC)
The West Virginia Encyclopedia.
C6590 (LMC BC)
West Virginia History.
C6600
West Virginia Reader, Stories of Early Days.
C6610 (ASU ETSU)
West Virginia, Yesterday and Today.
C6620 (BC)

W. VA. — HISTORY

West Virginia, Yesterday and Today.
C6630 (ASU)
The Monongalia Story, a Bicentennial History.
C7400
A Mountain Trail: To the Schoolroom, the Editor's Chair, the Lawyer's Office, and the Governorship of West Virginia.
C7570 (ASU BC)
Wheels on the Mountains.
C8340 (ASU LMC WCU BC)
"A House Divided: A Study of Statehood Politics and the Copperhead Movement in West Virginia During the Civil War."
C9860
A House Divided: A Study of Statehood Politics and the Copperhead Movement in West Virginia.
C9870 (WCU ETSU ASU BC)
History of Harrison County, West Virginia.
D970 (BC ASU)
A Bibliography of West Virginia.
D1060
Greenbrier Pioneers and Their Homes.
D1420
Lewisburg Landmarks.
D1430 (ASU BC)
Pioneers and Their Homes on Upper Kanawha.
D1440 (ASU BC)
The West Virginia Handbook and Immigrant's Guide.
D1540
Heritage of a Pioneer, Being the Story of William (English Bill Doddridge) Dodrill and His Wife, Rebecca (Lewis) Daugherty, Their Family, the Times in Which They Lived, and a Genealogy.
D2720 (ASU)
Moccasin Tracks, and Other Imprints.
D2730 (BC)
Moccasin Tracks and Other Imprints.
D2740 (ASU)
History of Oak Hill, West Virginia.
D2900
The Trail of the Dead Years. . .
D3660
Historic Harpers Ferry in Jefferson Co., W. Va.
F20 (BC)
Marion County in the Making.
F60 (BC)
History of Tucker County, West Virginia.
F100 (LMC ASU BC)
The History and Government of West Virginia.
F290 (BC)
History of Worthington, West Virginia, and Surrounding Communities.
F2190 (ASU)
The Geomorphic History of the New Kanawha River System.
F3300 (ETSU)
Twenty Feet from Glory: From the Land of Ford to the Land of Canaan.
G2630 (ASU BC)
G3690
When I Was a Boy.
G3850 (ASU)
Daniel Boone. Some Facts and Incidents Not Hitherto Published. His Ten or Twelve Years' Residence in Kanawha County, Near Charleston, West Virginia.
H340 (ASU BC)
The Rending of Virginia; a History.
H700 (BC)
The Two Virginias: Genesis of Old and New; a Romance of American History; State Sovereignty, Phantom of a Stupendous Folly.
H710 (BC)
Archaeological Excavations on Virginius Island, Harpers Ferry National Historic Park, 1966-1968.
H1570
History of Harrison County.
H3960 (ASU)
Fayette County.
H4710 (ETSU)
The White Rocks; or The Robbers Den; a Tragedy of the Mountains.
H5350 (BC)
Historical Records Survey of County Archives of West Virginia.
H5920
A Check List of West Virginia Imprints, 1791-1830.
H5930 (ETSU BC)
W. Va. Co. Formations and Boundary Changes.
H5940 (BC)
Upshur Brothers of the Blue and the Gray.
H7230 (ASU)
Pioneer West Virginia.
H8090 (ASU)
"West Virginia's Program of State Publicity."
I1020
A Biographical Sketch on the Life of the Late Captain Michael Cresap.
J210
The Violent Years.
J1260 (BC)
History of Grant and Hardy Counties, West Virginia.
J2810 (ASU)
Thunder at Harper's Ferry.
K570 (ASU)
History of First Settlers of Cow Run.
K2480
West Virginia and its Government.
L190
First Biennial Report of the Department of Archives and History of the State of West Virginia.
L2310 (ASU)
History and Government of West Virginia.
L2320 (ASU)
History and Government of West Virginia.
L2330 (WCU)
History of the Battle of Point Pleasant.
L2340 (BC ASU)
History of West Virginia
L2350 (BC ASU)
How West Virginia was Made. Proceedings of the First Convention of the People of North-western Virginia at Wheeling, May 13, 14 and 15, 1861, and the Journal of the Second Convention of the People of Northwestern Virginia at Wheeling, which Assembled, June 11th 1861.
L2360 (ASU)
Third Biennial Report of the Department of Archives and History of the State of West Virginia.
L2380 (ASU)
The Recollections of Fifty Years of West Virginia.
M600 (BC ASU)
The Disruption of Virginia.
M1630 (BC ASU ETSU)
Legends of the Ohio Valley.
M2180 (BC ASU)
Tales of Pocahontas County.
M2380
The Border Settlements of Northwestern Virginia from 1768-1795.
M2590 (BC)
History of Tucker County, West Virginia.
M4490
The History of Barbour County, West Virginia, from Its Earliest Exploration and Settlement to the Present Time.
M4510 (ASU ETSU)
History of Hampshire County, West Virginia, from Its Earliest Settlement to the Present.
M4520
History of Hampshire County, West Virginia, from Its Earliest Settlement to the Present.
M4530 (ASU)
The History of Randolph County, West Virginia, from Its Earliest Settlement to the Present, Embracing Records of All the Leading Families, Reminiscences and Traditions.
M4540 (ASU)
History of Tucker County, West Virginia, from the Earliest Explorations and Settlements to the Present Time: With Biographical Sketches of More Than Two Hundred and Fifty of the Leading Men, and a Full Appendix of Official and Electional History. Also, an Account of the Rivers, Forests and Caves of the County.
M4550 (ASU)
Life and Adventures of Lewis Wetzel.
M5290 (BC)
M5490
History of Summers County from the Earliest Settlement to the Present Time.
M5780 (ASU)
Annals of Webster County, West Virginia.
M5990
West Virginia and Its People.
M6010
West Virginia Surnames, the Pioneers.
M6390 (ASU)
The 175th Anniversary of the Formation of Monongalia County, West Virginia, and Other Relative Historical Data.
M6480 (ASU)
History of Hardy County of the Borderland.
M6820 (ASU BC)
Washington's Woods: A History of Ravenswood and Jackson County, West Virginia.
M7090 (ASU)
A Banner in the Hills: West Virginia's Statehood.
M7140 (ASU BC WCU)
"West Virginia and the Civil War, 1861-1863."
M7150
The Fairfax Line, a Profile in History and Geography.
M7890 (ASU)
An Outline of the Maryland Boundary Disputes and Related Events.
M7900 (ASU)
Wappatomaka: A Survey of the History and Geography of the South Branch Valley.
M7910 (ASU)
A History of Pendleton County, W. Va.
M8100 (ASU BC)
History of Davis and Canaan Valley.
M8310 (ASU)
Virginia's Attitude Toward Slavery and Secession.
M8570 (FC LMC)
Index to West Virginiana.
M8630 (ASU BC)
Myers' History of West Virginia.
M9320 (BC)
Thomas, West Virginia: History, Progress, and Development, 1906.
N3010 (ASU)
Easton-Avery Community History, 1963.
O1000 (ASU)
"Helvetia, West Virginia: A Study of Pioneer Development and Community Survival in the Appalachia."
P500
History of Fayette County, West Virginia.
P2310 (ASU)
"The Labor Movement in West Virginia, 1900-1948."
P3730
Teacher's Manual for West Virginia: The State and Its People.
R1980
West Virginia: The State and Its People.
R1990 (ASU)
"Frontier West Virginia: Some Aspects of Its Political, Social, and Economic Development."
R2000 (ASU)
West Virginia, Her Land, Her People, Her Traditions, Her Resources.
R4200 (BC)
Address to the People of West Virginia: Shewing That Slavery Is Injurious to the Public Welfare, and That It May Be Gradually Abolished, Without Detriment to the Rights and Interests of Slaveholders.
R4260 (ASU BC)
Early Records, Hampshire County Virginia, Now West Virginia, Including at the Start Most of Known Va. Aside from Augusta District.
S130 (BC ASU)
Stories of W. Va. for Boys and Girls.
S500
Making a State, Formation of West Virginia.
S1940
West Virginia: A Book of Geography, History, and Industry.
S2530 (WCU)
West Virginia, in History, Life, Literature and Industry.
S2540
Milestones of West Virginia History...Some Events of Importance in the Development of the Mountain State.
S2660
Guide to the Study of West Virginia History.
S3000
Guide to the Study of West Virginia History.
S3010 (BC)

W. VA. — HISTORY
Milestones of West Virginia History: Some Events of Importance in the Development of the Mountain State.
S3020 (ASU)
West Virginia Civil War Literature.
S3030
West Virginia Jewry: Origins and History, 1850-1958.
S3070 (ASU LMC)
History of the Cross Creek Graveyard and Cross Creek Cemetery.
S3630
Indexes to Land Grants in West Virginia.
S3660 (ASU)
Making a State; Formation of West Virginia, Including Maps, Illustrations, Plats, Grants and the Acts of the Virginia Assembly and the Legislature of West Virginia Creating the Counties.
S3670 (BC)
Nathan Goff, Jr., a Biography: With Some Account of Guy Despard Goff and Brazilla Carroll Reece.
S4710 (ASU)
Stories of W. Va. for Boys & Girls.
S5560
The Kinnan Massacre.
S8930 (ASU BC)
West Virginia in the Civil War.
S8940 (ASU BC)
Borderland Confederate.
S9000
The Mountain State.
S9010
Pages from the Past.
S9020 (BC)
History of Braxton County and Central West Virginia.
S9320 (ASU BC)
Proud Heritage of West Virginia.
S9740
History of Wayne County, West Virginia.
T630 (ASU)
The Washingtons and Their Colonial Homes in W. Va.
T8480 (BC)
West Virginia, the Centennial of Statehood, 1863-1963.
U3590 (ETSU)
Historic Homes of Northern Virginia and the Eastern Panhandle of West Virginia.
W1770 (ASU)
History of Hancock Co., Va. and W. Va.
W2470 (BC)
Biennial Report.
W3330 (BC)
Short Title Check-list of West Virginia State Publications. 1947/48-.
W3340 (ETSU)
History of Education in West Virginia.
W3550 (ASU)
State Papers and Public Addresses.
W3950
State papers and public addresses of Clarence Watson Meadows.
W3960
State Papers and Public Addresses of Homer Adams Holt, Twentieth Governor of West Virginia, January 18, 1937 to January 13, 1941.
W3970
State Papers and Public Addresses of Okey L. Patterson, E. Rosalind Carroll Funk.
W3980
State Papers and Public Addresses of William C. Marland, Twenty-Fourth Governor of the State of West Virginia, 1953-1957.
W3990
West Virginia Highway Markers, Historic, Prehistoric, Scenic, Geologic.
W4060 (ASU)
W4070 (UNCA ETSU)
W4090 (BC)
Report of the Archives of the Division of Documents.
W4570 (BC)
Selected Archeological and Historical Sites in West Virginia; Preliminary Plan for Development.
W5170
History of Preston County (West Virginia).
W6210 (ASU)
History of Preston County (West Virginia).
W6220 (ASU BC)
An Inside View of the Formation of the State of West Virginia, with Character Sketches of the Pioneers in that Movement.
W6370 (BC)
Chronicles of Border Warfare; or, A History of the Settlement by the Whites, of Northwestern Va., and . . . .
W7940 (BC)
Chronicles of Border Warfare; or, A History of the Settlement by the Whites, of Northwestern Virginia, and of the Indian Wars and Massacres, in That Section of the State.
W7950 (ASU ETSU WCU BC)
Chronicles of Border Warfare: or, A History of the Settlement by the Whites, of Northwestern Virginia, and of the Indian Wars and Massacres, in That Section of the State.
W7960 (ASU UNCA)
Acts of the Legislature of West Virginia at Its First Session, Commencing June 20th, 1863.
W4120 (BC)

W. VA. — HISTORY — CIVIL WAR
West Virginia Civil War Literature; An Annotated Bibliography.
S3040

W. VA. — LABOR FORCE
Labor Market Areas for Manufacturing Plants in West Virginia.
T8220
Manpower Requirement of Training Needs.
W3440
A Study of the Manpower Resources of Braxton, Clay, Lewis, Nicholas, Upshur, and Webster Counties.
W3450
W. Va. Labor Force.
W3460
West Virginia Labor Force.
W3470
Work Force, Employment, Unemployment, 1958.
W3480
Labor Supply Survey.
W3500
Personal and Economic Characteristics of the Insured Unemployed.
W3510
West Central West Virginia Area Manpower Requirements Survey to 1972.
W3520
W4110 (BC)

W. VA. — POLITICS
A Mountain Trail: To the Schoolroom, the Editor's Chair, the Lawyer's Office, and the Governorship of West Virginia.
C7570 (ASU BC)

W. VA. — RECREATION AND TOURISM
From Baltimore to Charleston.
S790

W. VA. — RESORTS
White Sulphur Springs, a Brief History.
T700 (ASU)

W. VA. RIVER
Indexed County and Railroad Pocket Map and Shipper's Guide of West Virginia.
R390 (BC)

W. VA. RIVERS
Canoeing White Water: A Guide Book to the Rivers of Virginia and Eastern West Virginia, The Great Smoky Mountain Area.
C1740 (LMC)

WAGES AND SALARIES — PA.
"Minimum Wages in Pennsylvania."
K530

WAGES AND SALARIES — W. VA.
Wage Differentials in West Virginia.
G690

WAGES — APP.
Miner's Wages and the Cost of Coal: An Inquiry into the Wages System in the Bituminous Coal Industry.
L3790

WAR — WORLD WAR 1
Sergeant York, His Own Life Story and War Diary.
S3870 (ASU ETSU LMC)
Sergeant York, Last of the Long Hunters.
S3880 (ASU BC)

WARS — APP.
The Winning of the West.
R3700 (ASU)

WARS — COLONIAL
Yearbook of the Society of Colonial Wars in the Commonwealth of Kentucky.
S5380 (ETSU)

WARS — FRENCH
Lieut. Henry Timberlake's Memoirs, 1756-1765.
T8690 (BC ETSU)
Lieut. Henry Timberlake's Memoirs, 1756-1765, With Annotation, Introduction and Index.
T8700 (ASU WCU LMC)
Memoirs, 1756-1765.
T8710 (ETSU ASU WCU)

WARS — INDIAN
"Fort Southwest Point, Tennessee: The Development of a Frontier Post, 1792-1807."
B920
Abstract of Pensions of North Carolina Soldiers of the Revolution, War of 1812, and Indian Wars.
B9030 (ASU)
Estill County, Kentucky, Record of Abstracts of Pension Papers of Revolutionary Soldiers, War of 1812 and Indian Wars. . . .
B9050
Kentucky Pioneers and Their Descendants.
D580 (ASU BC)
History of the Early Settlement and Indian Wars of Western Virginia: Embracing an Account of the Various Expeditions in the West, Previous to 1795. Also, Biographical Sketches of Distinguished Actors in Our Border Wars.
D1640 (ASU BC)
History of the Early Settlement and Indian Wars of Western Virginia: Embracing an Account of the Various Expeditions in the West Previous to 1795. Also, Biographical Sketches of Co. Ebenezer Zane. . . and other Distinguished Actors in our Border Wars.
D1650 (ASU LMC FC)
Notes on the Settlement and Indian Wars of the Western Parts of Virginia and Pennsylvania from 1763 to 1783. Together with a Review of the State of Society and Manners of the First Settlers of the Western Country. With a memoir of the author by his daughter, Narcissa Doddridge. Republished.
D2660 (ASU BC FC)
Notes on the Settlements and Indian of the Western Parts of Virginia and Pennsylvania from 1763 to 1783, Inclusive.
D2670 (ETSU BC)
Border Wars of the West.
F3530 (BC)
Fort Loudoun on the Little Tennessee.
H1050 (ASU)
Annals of Tazewell County, Virginia from 1800 to 1922.
H2400 (BC ASU)
The Winning of the West.
R3700 (ASU)
In the Ranks of Old Hickory, When with the Western Riflemen in Defense Against from Within and Without, Young and Old of All Degrees United Under Andrew Jackson to Make the Republic's Borders Safe.
S30 (ETSU ASU BC)
Lieut. Henry Timberlake's Memoirs, 1756-1765.
T8690 (BC ETSU)
Lieut. Henry Timberlake's Memoirs, 1756-1765, With Annotation, Introduction and Index.
T8700 (ASU WCU LMC)
Memoirs, 1756-1765.
T8710 (ETSU ASU WCU)

WARS — INDIANS
History of the Battle of Point Pleasant.
L2340 (BC ASU)
Memoir of Indian Wars, and Other Occurrences.
S8730 (ASU)

WARS — VA.
Virginia War Agencies Selective Draft and Volunteers.
D830
Virginia War History in Newspaper Clippings.
D840
Virginia War Letters and Diaries and Editorials.
D850

WARS — VA.
Virginians of Distinguished Service in World War.
D860
WARS — VA. — INDIAN
History of the Settlement and Indian Wars of Tazewell County, Virginia.
B3530 (FC ASU)
History of the Settlement and Indian Wars of Tazewell County, Va. with added material compiled by J. Allen Neal.
B3540
WARS — W. VA.
The Soldiery of West Virginia in the French and Indian War, Lord Dunmore's War, The Whiskey Insurrection, The Second War with England, The War with Mexico, and Addenda Relating to West Virginians in the Civil War.
L2370 (ASU)
WARS — WAR OF 1812
Notes on Kentucky Veterans of the War of 1812.
C5030 (BC)
A Journal Containing an Accurate and Interesting Account of the Hardships, Suffering, Battles, Defeat, and Captivity of Those Heroic Kentucky Volunteers and Regulars, Commanded by General Winchester, in the Years 1812-13. Also, Two Narratives by Men That Were Wounded in the Battles on the River Raisen, and Taken Captive by the Indians.
D390 (ASU BC)
Junaluska at the Battle of Horse Shoe Bend: True Story of the Cherokee Chief.
H3710 (LMC)
Kentucky Soldiers of the War of 1812.
K900 (ASU)
Kentucky Soldiers of the War of 1812.
W6150
Heroes of the War of 1812 for Whom Kentucky Counties are Named.
W8840 (BC)
WARS — WAR OF 1812 — N. C.
Frustrated Patriots: North Carolina and the War of 1812.
L1730 (MHC)
WARS — WAR OF 1812 — TENN.
Soldiers of the War of 1812 Buried in Tennessee.
M670 (ASU)
WARS — WORLD WAR 1
Sergeant York and His People.
C8110 (WWC ETSU BC)
Virginians of Distinguished Service in World War.
D860
K2860
Dickenson County in War Time; a Community History.
S9150
W7920
Sergeant York: His Own Life Story and War Diary.
Y130 (LMC BC)
WARS — WORLD WAR 2
Pursuits of War: The People of Charlottesville and Albemarle County, Virginia, in the Second World War.
A970 (ASU)
A Rural Community in Time of War: The Valley Community in Rabun County, Georgia.
A1340 (BC)
Sergeant York: Reluctant Hero.
A2520 (ETSU)
Crossville.
C7150
"Impact of World War II on Juvenile Delinquency in Knox County, Tennessee."
D1380
Selective Service in North Carolina in World War II.
K2470 (LMC)
WATAUGA RIVER
"Land Utilization in the New and Watauga River Basins of North Carolina."
B3700 (LMC)
The Watauga River Basin: A Survey of Existing Pollution in the Watauga River Basin Together with Recommended Classification of Its Waters, 1960-1962.
N2640 (ASU)
On the Watauga and the Cumberland.
S5300 (LMC)
Floods on Watauga and Doe Rivers in Vicinity of Elizabethton, Tennessee.
T2760
WATER POLLUTION
Message from the President of the United States Transmitting the Appalachian Regional Commission's Report, Acid Mine Drainage in Appalachia, Pursuant to the Provisions of Section 302 (b) of the Appalachian Regional Development Act.
A210 (ASU)
Evaluation of Pollution Abatement Techniques Applicable to Lost Creek and Brown's Creek Watershed, West Virginia.
A220 (ASU)
A Program for Simulation of Acid Mine Drainage in a River Basin.
A3790 (ASU)
Proceedings.
A4440
Stream Quality in Appalachia as Related to Coal-mine Drainage, 1965.
B3570 (LMC BC ASU)
Stream Quality in Appalachia as Related to Coal-mine Drainage.
B3571
Effects of Surface Mining on Fish and Wildlife in Appalachia, Special Report.
B4930
"The Economic Aspects of the Water Pollution Abatement Program in the Ohio River Valley."
B6260
Sedimentary Studies in the Middle River Drainage Basin of the Shenandoah Valley of Virginia.
C1480 (ASU)
"Industrial Waste and Human Sewage Pollution within the New River Drainage Basin of Watauga County."
C1490 (ASU)
Mine Drainage Abstracts: A Bibliography.
C5200 (ASU)
"Macroinvertebrate Community Structure as an Indicator of Acid Mine Pollution."
D2470
E2000
Determination of Estimated Mean Mine Water, Quantity and Quality from Imperfect Data and Historical Records.
E2050 (ASU)
M6140
Handbook of Pollution Control Costs in Mine Drainage Management.
M6470
Water Pollution Control In the Monongahela River Basin.
P1810
The Effects of Acid Mine Drainage on Aquatic Insects.
R2630 (ASU)
WATER POLLUTION — APP.
Acid Mine Drainage in Appalachia.
A3540 (ASU BC)
Froth Floatation Washability Data of Various Appalachian Coals Using Timed Release Analysis Technique.
C2570
I100 (ASU)
I110 (ASU)
I120 (ASU)
I130 (ASU)
The Ohio River Basin.
I890
Legal Problems of Coal Mine Reclamation: Study in Maryland, Ohio, Pennsylvania, and West Virginia.
M3930 (BC)
Prediction of Stream Reaeration Rates.
T5410
Quality of Water in Chickamauga Reservoir.
T5420
Stream Sanitation in the Tennessee Valley.
T5450
Studies of the Pollution of the Tennessee River System.
T5460
Studies of the Pollution of the Tennessee River System.
T5470
Surface Water Quality in the Chestuee Creek Watershed.
T5480
Surface Water Quality in the Chestuee Creek Watershed.
T5490
Drainage Modifications in Southeastern Ohio and Adjacent Parts of West Virginia and Kentucky.
T8660
WATER POLLUTION — KY.
Kentucky Law on Water.
C4790
Influences of Strip Mining on the Hydrologic Environment of Parts of Beaver Creek Basin, Kentucky, 1955-59.
C5930 (BC)
Proceedings. The Planning Concept.
C6420
Public and Industrial Water Supplies of the Jackson Purchase Region, Kentucky.
P4290
WATER POLLUTION — MD.
Maryland Water Law: Water Laws and Legal Principles Affecting the Use of Water in Maryland.
G120
Western Maryland Mine Drainage Survey, 1962-65.
H7110
Preparation of Plans and Specifications for Pollution Abatement Activities in Cherry Creek Watershed, Maryland.
S3850 (ASU)
WATER POLLUTION — N. C.
A Study of Water Pollution Control in the Textile Industry of North Carolina.
G3180 (LMC)
The Watauga River Basin: A Survey of Existing Pollution in the Watauga River Basin Together with Recommended Classification of Its Waters, 1960-1962.
N2640 (ASU)
N2650 (ASU UNCA)
Ecological Effects of Hot Water Discharge by an Electric Power Generating Plant.
N2660 (ASU UNCA)
Summary of Data on Chemical Quality of Streams of North Carolina, 1943-67: Quality of Surface Waters of North Carolina.
W6140 (LMC)
WATER POLLUTION — OHIO
Ohio River Basin: Comprehensive Survey, Main Report.
O410 (ASU)
WATER POLLUTION — PA.
Drainage Evolution in the Appalachians of Pennsylvania.
T8170 (ETSU)
WATER POLLUTION — TENN.
Report of the Conference, 2D Kingsport, Tennessee, 1962.
C6390
"Fish Fauna Diversity as an Indication of Pollution Stress in Streams."
H5600 (ETSU)
Techniques Used in Mine-water Problems of the East Tennessee Zinc District.
K860 (ASU)
"Mercury Pollution in Fish in Boone Reservoir, Tennessee."
M5980 (ETSU)
Stream Pollution Control In The Upper Cumberland River Basin, 1965.
T1230
Stream Pollution Control in the Upper Cumberland River Basin, 1964.
T2120 (ETSU)
WATER POLLUTION — VA.
Report of the Conference, 2D Kingsport, Tennessee, 1962.
C6390
WATER POLLUTION — W. VA.
Fluvial Sediment in the Salem Fork Watershed, West Virginia.
F1550
Current and Proposed Regulations and Legislation on Water Pollution Concerning Appalachian Industries.
H6540
Ground-water Conditions along the Ohio Valley at Parkersburg, West Virginia.
J520 (ETSU)

WATER POLLUTION — W. VA.

Priority Determination Procedure for the Selection of Pollution Abatement Projects in the Monongahela River Basin.
R2590 (ASU)

WATER POWER — TENN.

Organization for Watershed Planning in the Public Interest.
L3760

WATER RESOURCES

"A Watershed Development Program for the TVA.
B4420

Water Use by Appalachian Manufacturers, 1964.
B6550

The Economic Development of the Northeast Georgia Commission Area Through Use of Forest Products and Water Resources.
B7120 (ASU ETSU)

Ground-water Resources of Monongalia County, West Virginia.
C1280 (ETSU)

Maryland's Role in Water Resources Development: A Study.
C8480

Irrigation Arrangements in Buncombe County, North County, North Carolina; a Report of an Irrigation Survey in Buncombe County, Conducted in the Summer of 1962.
M3650 (LMC)
M5190 (ASU)

Ohio River Basin: Comprehensive Survey, Main Report.
O410 (ASU)

Surface Water in Tuscaloosa County, Alabama.
P2880 (ETSU)

Ground Water in Marshall County, Alabama: A Reconnaissance.
S430 (ASU ETSU)

Bear Creek Watershed, Summary of Resources.
T2330

Tennessee River History.
T3680

Tennessee River Navigation.
T3690

The Tennessee River Navigation System; History, Development, and Operation.
T3700

The Tennessee River Waterway.
T3710

TVA Dams; the Twenty Major Dams Built by the Tennessee Valley Authority and Wilson Dam.
T3760

TVA 25th Anniversary; Progress Thru Resource Development, A Report to the Nation from the Tennessee Valley Authority on Its First Twenty-Five Years, 1933-1958.
T3910

Upper Duck River Valley; Summary of Resources.
T4020

Upper Hiwassee Valley: Summary of Resources.
T4030

Working With Areas of Special Need, With Examples From the Beech River Watershed.
T4100

The Yellow Creek Port Project.
T4130

. . . Hydraulic Data Activities of the Tennessee Valley Authority . . .
T7400

Industrial Water Supplies of the Tennessee Valley Region.
T7420

Influences of Reforestation and Erosion Control Upon the Hydrology of the Pine Tree Branch Watershed 1941 to 1950.
T7430

Maps and Surveys.
T7450

Report on Initial Phases, Chestuee Watershed Project.
T7510

Water supply paper, no. 1.
U3400

The Ohio River Basin Except the Cumberland and Tennessee River Basins.
U3410

H. R. 10090, Act Making Appropriations for Public Works for Water and Power Development, Including Corps of Engineers, Civil, Bureau of Reclamation, Bonneville Power Administration, and Other Power Agencies of Department of Interior, Appalachian Regional Commission, Federal Power Commission, Tennessee Valley Authority, Atomic Energy Commission, and Related Independent Agencies and Commissions for Fiscal Year 1972, and for Other Purposes.
U3510

H. R. 15586, Act Making Appropriations for Public Works for Water and Power Development, Including Corps of Engineers — Civil, Bureau of Reclamation, Bonneville Power Administration, and Other Power Agencies of the Department of Interior, Appalachian Regional Development Programs, Federal Power Commission, Tennessee Valley Authority, Atomic Energy Commission, and Related Independent Agencies and Commissions for Fiscal Year 1973, and for Other Purposes. Approved August 25, 1972.
U3520

Report, V. 2: Ten Rivers in America's Future.
U3860

A Design for a W. Va. Water Resources Plan.
W3610

Summary of Data on Temperature of Streams in North Carolina, 1943-67: Quality of Surface Waters of North Carolina.
W8720 (LMC)

A Symposium on the Sandhill Deep Well, Wood County, West Virginia.
W8960 (ETSU)

WATER RESOURCES — ALA.

Availability of Ground Water in Talladega County, Alabama: A Reconnaissance.
C2520 (ETSU)

Geology and Ground-water Resources of Cherokee County, Alabama: A Reconnaissance.
C2530 (ETSU)

Ground-water Resources of Etowah County, Alabama: A Reconnaissance.
C2540 (ETSU)

Geology and Ground-water Resources of Morgan County, Alabama.
D2750 (ETSU)

Interim Report on the Geology and Groundwater Resources of Morgan County, Alabama.
D2770 (ETSU)

Surface Water Resources of Calhoun County, Alabama.
H2240 (ETSU)

Geology and Ground-water Resources of Colbert County, Alabama.
H2870 (ETSU)

Interim Report on Ground-water Study in Colbert County, Alabama.
H2880 (ETSU)

Springs in Colbert and Lauderdale Counties, Alabama.
H2890 (ETSU)

Geology and Ground-water Resources of Lawrence County, Alabama: A Reconnaissance.
H3030 (ETSU)

Report of Industrial Survey of Florence, Alabama, and Muscle Shoals District.
L3050 (ASU)

General Geology and Ground-water Resources of Limestone County, Alabama: A Reconnaissance.
M2170 (ETSU)

Geology and Ground-water Resources of Madison County, Alabama.
M2890 (ETSU)

Geology and Ground-water Resources of Tuscaloosa County, Alabama.
M5760 (ETSU)

Ground-water in the Vicinity of Bryce State Hospital, Tuscaloosa County, Alabama.
M5770 (ETSU)

Ground-water Resources and Geology of Tuscaloosa County, Alabama.
P1030 (ETSU)

Geology and Ground-water Resources of Franklin County, Alabama: A Reconnaissance.
P1150 (ETSU)

Water Supply of the Birmingham Area, Alabama.
R3340

Gound-water Levels in Madison County, Alabama, July 1956 to July 1959.
S420 (ETSU)

Watershed Work plan.
U3950

Ground Water in the Vicinity of Bryce Hospital, Negro Colony, Tuscaloosa County, Alabama.
W150 (ETSU)

Geology and Ground-Water Resources of Calhoun County, Alabama: An Interim Report.
W820 (ETSU)

Geology and Ground-Water Resources of Calhoun County, Alabama.
W830 (ETSU)

WATER RESOURCES — APP.

Appalachian Water: Maryland, Virginia, West Virginia, Kentucky, North Carolina, Tennessee, Alabama, Georgia, South Carolina, and Florida.
B8900 (LMC)

Papers.
C6470 (ASU)

Appalachian Connate Water.
H4290 (ETSU)

Rainfall Interception by Hardwood Forest Litter in Southern Appalachians.
H4410 (WCU)

The Ohio River Basin.
I890

Appalachia Meets the Potomac.
I900

Potomac River Basin Directory.
I910

Kanawha River: Comprehensive Basin Study.
K100 (ASU)

"Measuring and Analyzing the Impact of Employment Generation Benefits of a Public Water Resource Development Project in Appalachia."
K2050

The Relation of the Southern Appalachian Mountains to Inland Water Navigation.
L1650 (BC ASU)

The Relation of the Southern Appalachian Mountains to the Development of Water Power.
L1660 (ASU BC)

"The Development of a Community Water Supply to Serve a Rural Area of Southern Appalachia."
L2640 (ETSU)

North Carolina Water Plan Progress Report, Chapter 44; the Appalachian Region in North Carolina.
N2000 (ASU)

Deforestation Effects on Soil Moisture, Streamflow, and Water Balance in Central Appalachians.
P580

Hydrography of the Southern Appalachian Region.
P4370

Water Resources of the Appalachian Region, Pa. to Ala.
S1020

Atlas Finding List of the Tennessee Valley Region. The Tennessee Valley Area and Adjacent Districts in Alabama, Arkansas, Georgia, Illinois, Kentucky, Mississippi, Missouri, North Carolina, South Carolina, Tennessee, Virginia and West Virginia.
T2300

Elk River Watershed; Summary of Resources.
T2590

Fifty Inches of Rain. A Story of Land and Water Conservation.
T2700 (BC)

Hydrology of Small Watersheds in Relation to Various Crop Covers and Soil Characteristics. A Pictorial Brochure. Cooperative Research Project in Western North Carolina.
T2910

Nature's Constant Gift, a Report on the Water Resource of the Tennessee Valley.
T3070 (BC ASU)

Nature's Constant Gift; a Report on the Water Resource of the Tennessee Valley.
T3080

WATER RESOURCES — APP.

Nature's Constant Gift; a Report on the Water Resource of the Tennessee Valley.
T3090

Recreation Areas on TVA Lakes.
T3320

Summary of Resources Tributary Area Development Program.
T3560

Systematic Farm Planning in Relation to Water Resources at Parker Branch Pilot Tributary Watershed.
T3590

Tributary Area Development Activities; Selected List of Reports and Publications. 1963.
T4000

Tributary Area Development in the Tennessee Valley.
T4010

Working with Areas of Special Need, with Examples from the Beech River Watershed.
T4110

Social and Economic Characteristics of Six Tennessee Valley Reservoir Areas.
T4330 (BC)

The Occurrence of Drought in the Tennessee Valley.
T4490

Evaluation of Forestry Opportunities on Farms in the Beech River Watershed.
T4660 (ETSU)

Benefit-Cost Analysis for Water Resource Projects: A Selected Annotated Bibliography.
T5100

Benefit-Cost Analysis for Water Resource Projects; a Selected Annotated Bibliography.
T5110

Major Freight Terminals on the Tennessee River Waterway.
T5120

Navigation Charts, Tennessee River Waterway, Paducah, Kentucky to Knoxville, Tennessee; Showing Underwater Conditions, Navigation Channels and Aids and Adjacent Shore Planimetry.
T5130

The Tennessee River Navigation System: History, Development, and Operation.
T5140

Annual Report, 1958 and 1959.
T5220

Quality of Water in Chickamauga Reservoir.
T5420

Stream Sanitation in the Tennessee Valley.
T5450

Studies of the Pollution of the Tennessee River System.
T5460

Studies of the Pollution of the Tennessee River System.
T5470 .

Surface Water Quality in the Chestuee Creek Watershed.
T5490

Vector Control and Water Resource Development — The Experience of TVA.
T5510

Flood on Piney River, November 18-19, 1957 in the Vicinity of Spring City, Tenn.
T5530

Forest Cover Improvement Influences Upon Hydrologic Characteristics of White Hollow Watershed, 1935-1958.
T7340

High and Low Flows and Flow Duration at Stream Gages in North Carolina in Tennessee River Basin.
T7370

Major Freight Terminals on the Tennessee River Waterway.
T7440

Navigation Charts: Tennessee River.
T7460

Navigation Charts Tennessee River Reservoirs: Paducah, Kentucky to Knoxville, Tennessee, Showing Underwater Conditions, Navigation Channels and Aids and Adjacent Shore Planimetry.
T7470

Precipitation in Tennessee River Basin Annual.
T7480

An Analysis of the Parker Branch Watershed Project, 1953 Through 1959: A Progress Report.
T7540

Bear Creek Watershed; Summary of Resources.
T7550

Clinch-Powell Valley; Summary of Resources.
T7560

Drainage Modifications in Southeastern Ohio and Adjacent Parts of West Virginia and Kentucky.
T8660

Economics of Watershed Planning Sponsored by the Southeast Land Tenure Research Committee, the Farm Foundation, and the Tennessee Valley Authority.
T8820

Big South Fork, Cumberland River, Kentucky and Tennessee.
U230 (ETSU)

Dev. of Water Resources in Appalachia.
U250

Development of Water Resources in Appalachia: Report of the Secretary of the Army.
U260

Ohio River Basin, Grayson Reservoir, Little Sandy River, Kentucky design memorandum no. 3A preliminary master plan.
U300 (BC)

Water Resources Dev. by the U. S. Army Corps of Engineers.
U320

Water used by Appalachian Manufacturers, 1964.
U1590

Report of the Secretary of Agriculture on the Southern Appalachian and White Mountain Watersheds. Commercial Importance, Area, Condition, Advisability of the Purchase for National Forests, and Probable Cost.
U2540 (BC)

Development of Water Resources in Appalachia.
U2670 (ASU)

H. R. 8947, Act Making Appropriations for Public Works for Water and Power Development, Including Corps of Engineers — Civil, Bureau of Reclamation, Bonneville Power Administration and Other Power Agencies of the Department of Interior, Appalachian Regional Development Programs, Federal Power Commission, Tennessee Valley Authority, Atomic Energy Commission, and Related Independent Agencies and Commissions for Fiscal Year Ending June 30, 1974, and for Other Purposes. Approved August 16, 1973.
U3500

Minutes of the Meeting.
W1400 (ETSU LMC)

Minutes of the Meeting.
W1410 (ETSU)

WATER RESOURCES — GA.

Geology and Ground-water Resources of Catoosa County, Georgia.
C8710 (ETSU)

Geology and Ground-water Resources of the Paleozoic Rock Area, Chattooga County, Georgia.
C8720 (ETSU)

Geology and Ground-water Resources of Walker County, Georgia.
C8730 (ETSU)

Geology and Ground-water Resources of Dade County, Georgia.
C9070 (ETSU)

Economic Base Study and Survey of Basic Services for the Hiwassee River Watershed Development Association.
F2220 (BC)

The Georgia Mountains: A View of Its Resources, Problems, and Potentials.
S1120 (ASU LMC)

Geology and Ground-water Resources of Crystalline Rocks, Dawson County, Georgia.
S2010 (ASU ETSU)

Optimum Farm Organizations and Area Production Patterns for the Upper Hiwassee Watershed Area.
W7870

WATER RESOURCES — KENTUCKY

Interim Study report on Upper Licking River Basin, Kentucky.
U290 (BC)

WATER RESOURCES — KY.

Geology and Ground-water Resources of the Paintsville Area, Kentucky.
B630 (ASU)

Resources for Industry.
K1030 (ASU)
K1430

Public and Industrial Water Supplies of the Jackson Purchase Region, Kentucky.
P4290

Geology and Ground-water Resources of the Prestonburg Quadrangle, Kentucky.
P4600

Flood of July 5, 1939, in Eastern Kentucky.
S1070

Chemical character of surface waters of Kentucky, 1949-1951.
U3110

Geology and ground water resources in the Paintsville area, Ky. 1955, Surface water of the U. S. 1953; Cumberland and Tenn. River Basin.
U3420

WATER RESOURCES — MD.

Maryland Water Law: Water Laws and Legal Principles Affecting the Use of Water in Maryland.
G120

Bibliography of Maryland Water Resources Data.
H8180

Allegany County.
M3900 (ETSU)

The Water Resources of Allegany and Washington Counties.
S4170 (ETSU)

WATER RESOURCES — N. C.

Geology and Ground-water Resources of the Murphy Area, North Carolina.
D2760 (WCU)

Surface Water Supply of the New-Kanawha River Basin, West Virginia, and North Carolina.
G4490

Reconnaissance of the Ground-water Resources in the Waynesville Area, North Carolina.
M3380 (LMC WCU)

Irrigation Arrangements in Henderson County, North Carolina; a Report of an Irrigation Survey in Henderson County, Conducted in the Summer of 1962.
M3660 (LMC)

Irrigation Arrangements in Transylvania County, North Carolina; a Report of an Irrigation Survey in Transylvania County, Conducted in the Summer of 1962.
M3670 (LMC)

North Carolina Water Plan Progress Report, Chapter 44; the Appalachian Region in North Carolina.
N2000 (ASU)

Water Resource Needs for Selected Development Corridors in Appalachian North Carolina.
N2630 (ASU)
N2650 (ASU UNCA)

Ecological Effects of Hot Water Discharge by an Electric Power Generating Plant.
N2660 (ASU UNCA)

Economic Development of the Upper French Broad Area: Summary of Needs and Opportunities, Resources, the Regional Economy.
N2690 (ASU)

Papers on the Waterpower in North Carolina, a Preliminary Report.
S9390 (LMC)

A Demonstration of Watershed Protective Logging, Mars Hill Municipal Watershed, Madison County, North Carolina.
T4640

Flood plain information Lenoir, North Carolina; Lower Creek, Blair Fork, Long Branch.
U270

Flood plain information, Morganton, North Carolina.
U280

Geology & ground water resources in the Paintsville Area, Ky., 1955.
U3160

Industrial Water Use in North Carolina.
W430

Summary of Data on Chemical Quality of Streams of North Carolina, 1943-67: Quality of Surface Waters of North Carolina.
W6140 (LMC)

WATER RESOURCES — OHIO
"Economic Inventory and Value Added Estimates of the Natural Resources of a Watershed Region Located in the Appalachian Highland Area of Ohio."
D3630
Water Resources of the Wheeling-Steubenville Area, West Virginia and Ohio.
S4960
WATER RESOURCES — PA.
"A Preliminary Economic Evaluation of the Corey Creek Watershed."
D50
Drainage Evolution in the Appalachians of Pennsylvania.
T8170 (ETSU)
WATER RESOURCES — S. C.
Watershed Work Plan . . . Eighteen Mile Creek Watershed, Pickens and Anderson Counties, South Carolina.
U3960
WATER RESOURCES — TENN.
Legislative History of Muscle Shoals.
K2340
Water Resources of Tennessee: Being A Compilation of Existing Data Pertaining to the Surface Waters of Tennessee and Their Utilization.
K2490 (LMC)
"A Study of Factors Related to the Entrophication of Boone Reservoir, Tennessee."
L3640 (ETSU)
Ground-water Resources of the Cumberland Plateau in Tennessee.
N720 (BC)
Geology, Mineral Resources, and Ground Water of the Cleveland Area, Tennessee.
S9710 (ETSU)
Interagency Report on Water Resource Activities in Tennessee.
T1300
Tennessee's Water Resources and Related Lands.
T1580
Comprehensive Plan for Development: Kentucky Reservoir Region.
T1610 (ETSU)
A Plan for Development-Nicka Jack Reservoir Area.
T1660 (ASU LMC)
Reservoir Shore Line Development in Tennessee; a Study of Problems and Opportunities.
T1700
Clinch-Powell Valley; Summary of Resources.
T2420
Upper Little Tennessee River Region: Summary of Resources.
T9880 (WWC)
Surface water of the U. S. 1953; Cumberland and Tenn. River Basin.
U3310 (U)
Geology and ground water resources in the Paintsville area, Ky. 1955, Surface water of the U. S. 1953; Cumberland and Tenn. River Basin.
U3420
Ground Water Resources and Geology of Cumberland County, Tennessee.
W7340 (LMC)
Summary of Ground Water Data for Tennessee, Through May 1971.
W7350 (LMC)
WATER RESOURCES — VA.
Springs of Virginia.
C6040
Ground Water in the Ordovician Rocks near Woodstock, Virginia.
H660
Ground-water Supplies in Shale and Sandstone in Fairfax, Loudoun, and Prince William Counties, Virginia.
J2150
Water Resources of Virginia.
M1740
Bulletin. Surface and Water Supply of Va. New, Big Sandy, and Tenn. River Basins, 1942-1950.
V750 (BC)
New River Basin Comprehensive Water Resources Plan.
V840
WATER RESOURCES — W. VA.
Wood County Deep Well. Well Log, Sample, and Core Description.
B2160 (ETSU)
Wild Water West Virginia: A Paddler's Guide to the White Water Rivers of the Mountain State.
B9180 (ASU BC)
Water Resources of Kanawha County, West Virginia.
D2830 (ETSU)
Surface Water Supply of West Virginia.
E2170 (ETSU)
Fluvial Sediment in the Salem Fork Watershed, West Virginia.
F1550
Surface Water Supply of the New-Kanawha River Basin, West Virginia, and North Carolina.
G4490
Development of an Economic/Environmental Plan for Dents Run Watershed, West Virginia.
H950 (ASU)
Ground-water Conditions along the Ohio Valley at Parkersburg, West Virginia.
J520 (ETSU)
"Water Data for Industrial Site Development, Monongahela Valley, West Virginia."
K360
Ground-water Resources of Harrison County, West Virginia.
N20 (ETSU)
The Impact of Water Resources Development upon Local Rural Communities: Adjustment Factors to Rapid Change.
N80
Footprints in the Soil and Reflections on the Water: Conservation in West Virginia.
O570 (ASU)
Springs of West Virginia.
P4570 (ETSU)
Occurrence and Availability of Ground Water in Ohio County, West Virginia.
R3330 (ETSU)
Water Resources of the Wheeling-Steubenville Area, West Virginia and Ohio.
S4960
An Annotated Bibliography of Water Resource Papers Pertaining to West Virginia.
T9570
Watershed Work Plan; Mill Creek Watershed, Jackson and Roane Counties, West Virginia.
U3970 (ASU)
Ground Water in Mason and Putnam Counties, West Virginia.
W7050 (ETSU)
WEAVING
Shuttlecraft Book of American Handweaving.
A5460 (BC)
The Story of a Homespun Web.
B4780 (BC)
Kentucky Coverlets.
B5660 (BC)
Homespun Handicrafts.
B5710 (BC)
A Handweaver's Pattern Book.
D1290 (ASU BC)
A Handweaver's Source Book; A Selection of 224 Patterns from the Laura M. Allen Collection.
D1300
Pennsylvania German Home Weaving.
D1310
Handicrafts of the Southern Highlands: With an Account of the Rural Handicraft Movement in the United States and Suggestions for the Wider Use of Handicrafts in Adult Education and in Recreation.
E560 (ASU WCU LMC MHC WWC ETSU BC)
The Story of the Penland Weavers.
F1880 (ASU BC)
Marthy Lou's Kiverlid.
H8780
"Marthy Lou's Kiverlid," a Sketch of Mountain Life.
H8790 (ASU)
"Marthy Lou's Kiverlid," a Sketch of Mountain Life.
H8800 (ASU)
Weaving as a Hobby.
I40 (BC ASU)
Loom-fixing and Weaving; A Book for All Who Are Interested in Such Matters.
I1010
Four-Harness Huck.
N380
Inkle.
N390
A Book of Handwoven Coverlits.
O60 (BC)
Dictionary of Weaves; a Collection of All Weaves from Four to Nine Harness.
P3770 (BC)
A Weavin' Woman.
S7110 (LMC)
WEAVING — APP.
Mountain Homespun.
G2610 (ASU WCU LMC MHC ETSU BC WWC)
The Golden Age of Homespun.
V400 (ASU)
Home Industries and Domestic Weavings.
W5100
WELL DRILLING — W. VA.
Well-sample Records.
M3570 (ETSU)
WEST FORD RIVER
I920
WEST VIRGINIA — DESCRIPTION AND TRAVEL — PERIODICALS
Wonderful West Virginia.
W3600 (ETSU ASU)
WILDFLOWERS
Flowering Trees and Shrubs.
B3680
List of Tennessee Certified Nurseries Collectors of Native Wild Plants and Nursery Dealers for the Season 1967-1968.
B7680 (LMC)
Great Smoky Mountains Wildflowers.
C540 (LMC WCU ETSU)
Great Smoky Mountains Wildflowers.
C550 (ASU LMC WCU WWC BC)
Great Smoky Mountains Wildflowers.
C560 (ETSU BC)
Wild Flowers of the Great Smokies and Surrounding Area, a Pictorial Guide.
C2120 (ASU UNCA)
Wildflowers of Kentucky.
S2130 (BC)
WILDFLOWERS — APP.
Wild Flowers of the Alleghenies.
H2490 (BC)
Ferns of Ky; with Full-page Etchings and Wood Cuts.
W6950 (BC)
WILDFLOWERS — APP. MTNS.
The Old Naturalist's Notebook: Wild Flowers of the Appalachian.
L670 (UNCA ASU)
Wildflowers in Color.
S8890 (ASU ETSU UNCA)
WILDFLOWERS — KY.
A Guide to the Wildflowers and Ferns of Kentucky.
W5000 (ASU ETSU WCU BC WWC)
WILDFLOWERS — N. C.
"The Hepatic Flora of Watauga County, North Carolina."
H5220 (ASU)
Wild Flowers of North Carolina.
J3020 (ASU LMC WWC ETSU)
The Flora of North Carolina from Ranunculaceae to Salviniaceae.
J3390 (ASU)
WILDFLOWERS — TENN.
Tennessee Wildflowers.
S9370
WILDFLOWERS — W. VA.
Spring Wild Flowers.
C7430 (BC)
WILDLIFE
Effects of Surface Mining on Fish and Wildlife in Appalachia, Special Report.
B4930
The Appalachians.
B6960 (ASU WCU LMC MHC FC WWC ETSU BC FC UNCA)
The Life of the Mountains.
B6970 (BC)
Fish and Fishing in TVA Impoundments.
E2210
Hunting and Fishing in the Great Smokies.
G550 (BC UNCA ASU WCU LMC)
Conservation of Wildlife and Forests in Tennessee.
H4120 (ETSU BC)

WILDLIFE
Conservation of Wildlife and Forests in Tennessee.
H4130
"Fish Fauna Diversity as an Indication of Pollution Stress in Streams."
H5600 (ETSU)
J2770
Mammals of the Great Smoky Mountains National Park.
L2710 (WCU WWC ASU LMC)
Mammals of Great Smoky Mountains National Park.
L2720 (BC)
Fishing in the Great Smoky Mountains National Park and Adjacent Waters.
M3090
"Mercury Pollution in Fish in Boone Reservoir, Tennessee."
M5980 (ETSU)
The Life and Times of a Mountaineer Game Warden.
O740
Fish and Fishing, Fort Loudoun Reservoir.
T2720
Forest Reservations and Protection of Game Committee.
U1870

WILDLIFE — APP.
Tennessee Valley Wildlife: An Outlook for the Year 2000.
E1920
Hunting and Conservation: The Book of the Boone and Crockett Club.
G4310 (ETSU)
Atlas of Southern Forest Game.
H960 (ASU)
Twenty Years of Hunting and Fishing in the Great Smoky Mountains.
H3850
Twenty Years of Hunting and Fishing in the Great Smoky Mountains.
H8360
"A Historical Study of the European Wild Boar in North Carolina."
J2560 (ASU)
Big Nick: The Story of a Remarkable Black Bear.
L1080 (ASU BC)
Wilderness Adventure.
P30 (ASU)
Annual Report, 1963.
T4600
Development of Forests — Fish — Wildlife in the Tennessee Valley.
T4650
Fish and Wildlife in the Tennessee Valley.
T4670
Annual Report.
T4940
Farm Forestry Planning Through Linear Programming.
T4960
Fish and Wildlife, Valuable Natural Resources.
T5270

WILDLIFE — KY.
Amphibians and Reptiles of Kentucky.
B1090 (BC ASU LMC WCU)
Fishes of the Red River Drainage, Eastern Kentucky.
B6360
K970 (ASU WCU)
What Kentuckians Ought to Know about the State Game and Fish Commission . . . .
W90 (BC)

WILDLIFE — N. C.
Our Wildlife Neighbors: Important Game Mammals, Fur Bearers, Upland Game Birds and Fish of North Carolina.
B1070 (LMC)
A Catalog of the Inland Fishing Waters in North Carolina.
F1120 (LMC)
The Fishes of North Carolina.
S4780 (LMC)
North Carolina Geological and Economic Survey. The Fishes of North Carolina.
S4790
Tar Heel Wildlife.
W6180 (LMC)

WILDLIFE — N. C., WESTERN
The Mammals and Summer Birds of Western North Carolina.
O120

WILDLIFE — PA.
"Equating Timber and Wildlife Values and Returns to the Farm Resource Base in Sullivan County, Pennsylvania."
G200
"Equating Timber and Wildlife Values and Returns to the Farm Resources Base in Sullivan County, Pennsylvania."
H3970

WILDLIFE — TENN.
The Flora of Tennessee and a Philosophy of Botany, Respectfully Dedicated to the Citizens of Tennessee.
G600
TVA Lakes as a Fishery and Wildlife Asset.
M5890
Multiple-use on Norris Watershed.
N1510
Statewide Wildlife Survey of Tennessee, a Study of the Land, Wildlife, Farmer, Hunter and Trapper; Final Report of Work Accomplished with Federal Aid to Wildlife Restoration Funds Under Pittman-Robertson Project no. W-16-R.
S1160
Amphibians and Reptiles of Tennessee.
T1390 (ASU)
An Appraisal of Potentials for Outdoor Recreational Development in Fort Worth.
U3920
As the Indians Left It: The Story of the Chattanooga Audubon Society and Its Elise Chapin Wildlife Sanctuary.
W330 (ASU MHC)
Waterfowl on the Tennessee River Impoundments.
W5960
"An Ecological Study of Some Small Mammals of Horse Cove, Washington County, Tennessee."
W6610 (ETSU)

WILDLIFE — VA.
Pilgrim at Tinker Creek.
D2400 (BC ASU)
Pilgrim at Tinker Creek.
D2410 (ASU)
The Blue Ridge: Man and Nature in Shenandoah National Park and Blue Ridge Parkway.
W6260 (WCU LMC)

WOODWORKING INDUSTRIES — APP.
"Industrial Organization of the Appalachian Hardwood Lumber Using Industry."
L4110

WOODWORKING INDUSTRIES — N. C.
Seasoning and Preservative Treatment of Hickory Crossties.
T240 (WCU)

WOODWORKING INDUSTRIES — W. VA.
A Manual of West Virginia's Wood-using Industries, with Directory.
G3110 (ASU)

WOODWORKING INDUSTRY — APP.
This Fascinating Lumber Business.
H7190 (ASU)
"Chairmaking in Appalachia: A Study in Style and Creative Imagination in American Folk Art."
J2520 (ASU)

WOODWORKING INDUSTRY — KY.
"A Study of Woodworking Industry of the Eastern Mountains and Coal Field Region of Kentucky."
S1330

WOODWORKING INDUSTRY — MARKETING
Marketing West Virginia Lumber to Manufacturers in Other States.
L2540

WOODWORKING INDUSTRY — PA.
Opportunities for Forest-Based Industries in Pennsylvania: A Manual for the Development of Pennsylvania's Wood Using Industries.
H7160

WOODWORKING INDUSTRY — TENN.
Changing Sawmill Industry; a Status Report on 58 Circular Sawmills in the Tennessee Valley, 1950-60.
L1620

WOODWORKING INDUSTRY — W. VA.
The Effect of Workmen's Compensation on the Logging and Sawmilling Industries in the Northeast.
H6380

WYSOR, PAUL S.
Characteristics of Factory-grade Hardwood Logs Delivered to Appalachian Sawmills.
G2290

YADKIN RIVER
Smathers from Yadkin Valley to Pigeon River: Smathers and Agner Families.
P920 (ASU)

FILMOGRAPHY OF SOUTHERN APPALACHIA

(including Videotapes)

Compiled by
Dr. Robert J. Higgs
Department of English
East Tennessee State University
with the assistance of
Nick Smith
and
Katherine Honour

FILMS

Introduction

The purpose of this work is to make available information on a variety of films and video tapes on Appalachian studies. This filmography is by no means complete, but it can be of value to the Appalachian researcher as a starting point. Subjects covered include history, music, folklore, arts and crafts, religion, festivals, and the environment.

The material is divided into three sections:

I) A collection of 16mm movies and documentaries listed in alphabetical order. Each listing is provided with information concerning length, color or black and white, a description, awards when given, and distributor. An addendum of 16mm films by source brings the filmography up to date of publication and follows the earlier alphabetical listing.

II) A complete listing of all film distributors with their addresses.

III) A section on video tapes with name and address of distributors at the end of each listing.

No attempt has been made to evaluate the quality of the films and video tapes either in terms of technique or content.

I—16mm Films

1. All the Way Home B&W 103min 16mm 1963
A father dies in an auto accident—but life goes on. The somber theme is handled with restraint and awareness in a story laid in Knoxville, Tennessee in 1915 as seen through the eyes of a boy—from his first bewilderment through a final realization. Poignant blend of nostalgia and sorrow. Based on the novel by James Agee, *A Death in the Family*.
Distributor—Films Incorporated

2. The American Square Dance B&W 11min 16mm 1947
Relates the Square Dance to social dancing, teaches the positions of the dancers in relation to the calls, and defines terms. Includes the swing, allemande, grand right and left, promenade, promenade the outside ring, right and left through and back, two ladies chain and back, four hands up and half around, and do-si-do.
Distributor—Coronet Instructional Films

3. Andrew Jackson B&W 18min 16mm 1951
Portrays major events in the life of Andrew Jackson, the symbol of the common man. Depicts experiences of his boyhood, military career, and presidential years.
Distributor—Encyclopaedia Britannica Educational Corporation

4. Andrew Johnson B&W 48min 16mm 1966
Discusses the man who opposed the secession of his own State of Tennessee and was the lone southerner to remain in the United States Senate. From the Profiles in Courage series.
Distributor—IQ Films

5. Appalachia: Rich Land, Poor People B&W 59min 16mm 1969
"Discusses the poverty and problems of Appalachia, explaining that the land is rich with coal, yet its residents are denied adequate food, housing, and medical care."
Distributor—Indiana Univ. A-V Center

6. Applachian Adventure Color 22min 16mm
Details man's use of rocks for vast construction projects such as highways and flood control reservations. Shows how men and machines, working day and night, accomplish these gigantic tasks. Includes scenes of famous old buildings and landmarks built out of rock.
Distributor—Modern Talking Picture Service

7. Appalachian Genesis Color 30min 16mm 1970
"Youth of Appalachia talking about coal mining, education, health facilities, recreation, job opportunities, and politics."
Distributor—Appalshop

8. Appalachian Genesis Color 30min 16mm 1971
Appalachian Youth discuss coal mining, the educational system, job opportunities, recreation, health facilities, politics and poverty in this documentary; hailed as one of the most comprehensive statements on Appalachian youth today. Contracted by the Appalachian Regional Commission, this film touches all the vital issues in Appalachia today.
Awards: University of Tennessee Film Festival
Distributor—Appalshop

9. Appalachian Heritage Color 51min 16mm 1968
Documents the severe economic and social depression of Appalachia fed by illiteracy, cultural isolation, exploitation, and the destruction of the land by coal companies. Shows the conditions which have forced two million mountain people to leave their land for the core areas of the industrial cities of the north and examines the relationship of the migration to the urban crisis.
Distributor—Embassy Picture Corporation

10. Appalachian Highlands, The 14min 16mm 1967
Pictures the Appalachian Highlands which stretch from northeastern Canada to southern Alabama and are characterized by an extensive mountain system. Describes the revitalization of the region's resources—traditionally used for light manufacturing, cash crop farming and mining. Through conservation, public works projects and new industry. Shows the impact of this growth on the people and the economy. From the North American regions series No. 2.
Distributor—Coronet Films

11. Appalachian Music Color 20min 16mm
Features the balladeering of John Jacob Niles, whose style harks back to that of the folk singer of early American colonial days and Elizabethan England. Explains that Niles has spent most of his life treading the back roads of America, gathering the folk songs of whites and blacks and has also written songs himself which capture the folk idiom of America. From the Music of America Series.
Distributor—Great Plains Instructional TV Library

12. Appalachian Spring B&W 32min 16mm 1959
A ballet interpretation of a folk tale about the wedding day of a young couple living in the Appalachian wilderness during the pioneer period in America.
Distributor—Rembrandt Film Library

13. Appalachian Trail B&W 11min 16mm 1951
Released for public educational use through U.S. Office of Education, 1952.

14. Appalachian Woodcrafters, The Color 13min 16mm 1970
Shows artisans of the Appalachian region of southeastern United States in their homes and workshops, working with their families and apprentices as they create their handicrafts. Features chairs, bowls, clocks, guns, dulcimers, and inlaid wood panel pictures. Concentrates on the artist's pride and respect each has for his work.
Distributor—Herbert Kline

15. Arrow and the Bow, the: Andrew Johnson B&W 20min 16mm 1964
Adapted from the 1953 Cavalcade of America TV program. Dramatizes the formative years of Andrew Johnson, when as an illiterate tailor's apprentice he meets his future wife, Eliza McCardle, who teaches him to read and write.
Distributors—Teaching Film Custodians

16. Ballad of Parker Branch Color 30min 16mm 1963
"Gives an account of a ten-year experiment in Appalachian agriculture and its results in terms of farm incomes and resource conservation."
Distributor—Tennessee Valley Authority

17. Before the Mountain Was Moved Color 59min 16mm 1970
Shows poor Appalachian land owners fighting to obtain a law controlling strip-mining, a process which has damaged their houses and farms, and desecrated the beauty of their mountains. Portrays their struggle within themselves and with the outside forces that oppose them.
Distributor—U.S. National A.V. Center

18. A Better West Virginia B&W 9min 16mm 1937
Shows WPA projects in West Virginia, including construction of an airport at Clarksburg, improvement of fish hatcheries, and relief and restoration work after flood of 1936.
Distributor—U.S. Work Projects Administration

19. Beyond These Hills Color 13min 16mm 1967
A government documentary on poverty and cultural life in Avery County, North Carolina.
Distributor—Office of Economic Opportunity

20. Birth of the Grand Ole Opry B&W 6min 1964
Re-enacts the first radio broadcast on Nov. 28, 1925 of the Grand Ole Opry.
Distributor—Don G. Cummings

21. Buffalo Creek 1972: An Act of God? B&W 30 min
February 26, 1972: A giant coal waste dam at the head of Logan Creek, West Virginia, burst, sweeping 130 million gallons of water down the crowded valley of Buffalo Creek. Aftermath: 124 people dead, 4,000 homeless; and the coal company responsible for the deadly dam shrugged its shoulders and called the massacre "an act of God." The resulting documentary covers the destruction and clean-up, interviews with survivors, the people's hearings, wildcat strikes in the Logan County mines, the demonstration at the Pittston Coal Company stockholders meeting, and an interview with the president of Pittston.
". . . footage of the survivors, intercut with callous statements from the governor of West Virginia and coal executives, is a powerful piece of muckraking on film."
Maureen Orth—*Newsweek*
Distributor—Appalshop

22. Candlemaking (3rd Ed.) Color 7min 1970
Uses an original folk ballad and photographs to tell of the hard work required to make a home on the frontier of pioneer America, and the process of making handdipped candles.
Distributor—Barr Films

23. The Captive B&W 28min
This film is about Herb Honnaker, who represents the thousands of coal miners who were displaced by the machine. He goes from part-time job to made-work programs to the city and back to part-time jobs trying to support a family. Produced by the National Council of Churches of Christ. Narrated by Jack Weller of the Presbyterian Church.
Distributor—Council of Southern Mountains

24. Catfish Man of the Woods Color 25min 1974
This film is a portrait of Clarence Gray, a fifth generation herb doctor whom people call Catfish Man of the Woods. He sells a mixture of roots and herbs called "bitters" for all types of ailments from rheumatism to heart trouble and which is acclaimed for its ability to make one lose weight. He is outspoken about his philosophy of life and comments freely about sex, religion, and the way of the woods.
Distributor—Appalshop

25. Chairmaker Color 20min 1974
Dewey Thompson is an 80 year old chairmaker who does everything by hand, he even chops down the tree. The film is about his simple lifestyle—getting up at 3 a.m. and whittling on his chairs until 10 p.m. A rough hewn rocking chair takes form under his experienced hands and well worn knife during the course of the film.
Distributor—Appalshop

26. Chimney Rock Park—In the Land of the Sky Color 14min 1959
Pictures the scenic beauty of Chimney Rock Park near Ashville, North Carolina. Shows scenes of Hickory Nut Falls and Gorge, Needles Eye and Lake Lure.
Distributor—Chimney Rock Park Service

27. Christmas in Appalachia B&W 29min 1965
Shows the meager holiday season Appalachia has, but the fact that poverty prevails year round is emphasized. Pictures the misery and discouragement of adults, the scant prospects of education for the children and the hovels and shacks that serve as homes.
Distributor—Carousel Films, Incorporated

28. Clinton and the Law Color 60min 1965
Shows the attempts of white citizen's councils to prevent the school officials of Clinton, Tennessee. Presents Kaspar of Washington, D.C., organizing opposition to the school board decision. (CBS)
Distributor—AFL-CIO

29. Clinton and the Law: A Study in Desegregation B&W 54min 1957
Reports on desegregation in Clinton, Tennessee, and on the community's reaction to the attack on Rev. Turner by a small group of anti-integrationists.
Distributor—Contemporary McGraw-Hill Text Films

30. Coal Miner: Frank Jackson B&W 12min 1971
Frank Jackson has been a coal miner since he was fifteen years old. In this portrait Jackson is seen in and around the mines, and through his words one understands what it's like to have spent a lifetime working in a hole in the ground. The music is Jean Ritchie's famous song, "Blue Diamond Mines," sung by Mike Kline.
"After listening to him talk about his years in the mines, you're not likely to forget the craggy face or mountain dialect or simple decency of Frank Jackson."

Gary Arnold: *The Washington Post*

Awards: Museum of Modern Art, Robert Flaherty Film Seminar 1973, Janus Theater, Temple University Anthropological and Documentary Film Conference.
Distributor—Appalshop

31. Come to the Fair Color 19min 1973
The scene is the Mountain State Art and Craft Fair held June 30–July 4, 1972, at Cedar Lakes, West Virginia. Mountain arts and crafts are made and exhibited by local artists and craftsmen.
Distributor—Doug Britton

32. Coon Branch Mountain B&W 13min 1971
"The story of the people in a small community of McDowell County, West Virginia, in their fight for a better educational system and a school bus for their children."
Distributor—Appalshop

33. Daniel Boone B&W 18min 1950
Studies the personality, traits, and experiences of the wilderness scout, Daniel Boone. Portrays Boone's youth, his activities in the French and Indian and Revolutionary Wars, his pioneering adventures in Kentucky and his final settlement in Missouri.
Distributor—Encyclopaedia Britannica Educational Corporation

34. Daniel Boone in America's Story B&W 16min 1968
Traces the life of Daniel Boone from North Carolina to Missouri. Shows his involvement with the settling of Kentucky.
Distributor—Coronet Films

35. Davy Crockett—King of the Wild Frontier Color 93min 1967
Presents the story of Davy Crockett.
Distributor—Walt Disney Productions

36. Davy Crockett, Indian Scout Color 71min
A thrill packed film on the early westward movement and Davy Crockett.
Distributor—Associated Instructional Materials

37. Depressed Area USA Color 14min 1961
Shows economic and educational problems of Appalachia. Emphasizes the effects of automation and strip-mining on employment and the exhaustion of farmland. Discuss federal aid and relief projects. Filmed in Clay County, Kentucky.
Distributor—Columbia Broadcasting System

38. Echoes From the Hills Color 51min 1970
Presents a picture of lifestyle and overall culture in Northern Georgia.
Distributor—WQXI-TV

39. End of an Old Song B&W 26min
Mountaineer Dillard Chandler is featured in this film about folk music of the North Carolina Mountains. Although he is illiterate, Chandler sings from memory the mountain songs his father taught him. His ballads, as well as others performed by his friends, provide a musical history of the area.
Distributor—Macmillan

40. Explore Kentucky Color 15min
Follows a family on a vacation in Kentucky State parks.
Distributor—Modern Talking Picture Series

41. The Feathered Warrior Color 20min 1973
The illegal sport of game cock fighting is documented in this film in which a fighter explains how he has managed to win over 65% of his fights—as he says, "not a very bad record." A slow motion close-up sequence during a fight shows the sweeping motion of the birds as each attempts to cut to victory.
Awards: Honorable Mention—Sinking Creek Film Celebration 1974
Distributor—Appalshop

42. A Feud in the Kentucky Hills B&W 15min 1912 (silent)
Presents the story of a feud between two Kentucky families, and the sacrifice by a young man of his own life to save those of his brother and girlfriend.
Distributor—Biograph Company

43. Five Days in Moorefield Color 29min 1972
Film portrait of a small town in the 1970's which focuses on its struggle to survive in a largely urban society. Interviews with the townspeople present differing ideas on the traditional values and morality of this small community.
Distributor—Reader's Digest Foundation and WITF-TV

44. Fixin' to Tell About Jack Color 25min 1974
Master of the art of storytelling, Ray Hicks is a mountain farmer with a genius for telling traditional folktales or "Jack Tales" each with specific detail and histories that have been passed on from generation to generation. In this film he tells the tales to a group of children in the traditional style.
Distributor—Appalshop

45. Folk Artist of the Blue Ridge Color 17min 1973
A study of the paintings of Harriet Turner showing changing seasons in the Virginia Mountains. Includes folk music and poetry.
Distributor—Colonial Williamsburg, Incorporated

46. Foxfire Color 21min
A film depicting the work of Eliot Wigginton and his folk studies group in Rabun Gap, Georgia. Scenes are shown of the Georgia mountain people at work during their daily lives.
Distributor—Contemporary McGraw-Hill Films

47. Frontier Women B&W 36min (silent) 1923
Tells the story of the Watauga Settlement in 1780. The men were at King's Mountain fighting Major Ferguson and the British when traders brought tales of an Indian attack. The women, however, refused to recall their men and carried on alone.
Distributor—Yale University Press Film Service

48. Geography of the Middle Atlantic States Color 11min 1953
Surveys the Middle Atlantic States of New York, New Jersey, Pennsylvania, Delaware, Maryland, and West Virginia. Includes scenes of the people, cities, key industries, and vast transportation networks of this densely populated area.
Distributor—Cornet Films

49. Grandfather of the Blue Ridge Color 15min 1960
A film of Grandfather Mountain and the area attractions about it.
Distributor—Hugh Morton

50. Greene Valley Grandparents B&W 10min
Greene Valley Grandparents is a documentary about retired mechanics, truck drivers, farmers, and housewives who work with the mentally retarded

children at Greene Valley Developmental Center.
The film follows grandparents dressing, feeding, and playing with their children. Since the program began in 1970, the children have begun to respond to their surroundings through the love of their foster grandparents. Throughout the film grandparents comment on what the program means to them and to the children.
Awards: Cine Golden Eagle Certificate, Chris Bronze Medal
Distributor—Judy Paiser and Gill Farris

51. The Heart 'O the Hills B&W 100min 1919 (silent)
Story of a Kentucky mountain girl who saves her mother's land from land sharks, becomes a night rider, avenges her father's death, and eventually marries her sweetheart.
Distributor—First National Exhibiters Circuit

52. The High Lonesome Sound B&W 30min 1963
"The many kinds of music enjoyed by the mountain people of eastern Kentucky, help them hold their lives and traditions together."
Distributor—Brandon Films

53. Hiking the Appalachian Trail B&W 12min
A hike by four scouts from Davenport Gap to Newfound Gap in Tennessee. From the World Outdoors Series, No. 11.
Distributor—Tennessee Game and Fish Commission

54. Holy Ghost People B&W 53min 1968
A report on the religious fervor of a small Pentecostal congregation in West Virginia whose fundamentalist philosophy encourages the Biblical teaching of speaking in tongues and handling serpents.
Distributors—Contemporary Films/McGraw-Hill

55. If elected . . . Color 56min 1972
Describes a state senate race in West Virginia focusing on candidate Warren R. McGraw. Filmed along the campaign trail, the movie concentrates on the candidate's problems, frustrations, and exhausting pace in his attempt to unseat an incumbent in the state legislature.
Distributor—Wayne Ewing

56. The Inheritance B&W 58min
An excellent, moving film which documents the historic struggles of America's working men and women to win the right of collective bargaining with management and to establish unions. The film covers labor history from the first great strikes of this century through contemporary labor struggles. The theme song is "Freedom Doesn't Come Like a Bird on a Wing," and it is used throughout the film to stress that "Every generation has to win it again."
Distributor—Council of the Southern Mountains

57. Inherit the Wind B&W 127min 1960
The film deals with a version of the famous Scopes Trial at Dayton, Tennessee in the Twenties. Highlights of this film are the great performances of Spencer Tracy as the fictionalized Clarence Darrow and of Frederic March as the fictionalized William Jennings Bryan. Based on the play by Robert E. Lee and Jerome Lawrence.
Distributor—United Artists/16

58. In the Good Old Fashion Way Color 30min 1973
The Old Regular Baptist Church is the oldest and one of the most unique churches in the mountains. This film shows the spirit and the faith of the people of this church, and the impact their religion has on their lives. Widespread only among mountain people, this religion is uniquely a product of the Appalachian culture. This film attempts to capture the feeling of the religion by following the people through various services and ceremonies while they explain their church as they see it.
Distributor—Appalshop

59. In Ya Blood B&W 20min 1971
The Appalshop's first dramatic film follows its main character, Randy, as he makes the difficult decision faced by all Appalachian youth—whether to stay in Appalachia or leave in search of a "better life." Randy's problem takes him into the coal mines of Eastern Kentucky where he decides to stay and work rather than to leave the region and go on to college.
Distributor—Appalshop

60. Judge Wooten and Coon-on-a-Log B&W 10min 1970
A Fourth of July coon-on-a-log contest serves as the background for this film portrait of Leslie County Kentucky's Judge George Wooten. His attitude typifies the easy-going mountaineer as he discusses life in the mountains through subjects ranging from tourism to moonshine.
Distributor—Appalshop

61. Kentucky Feud, The B&W 30min 1913 (silent)
A drama in which a wife who is falsely accused of unfaithfulness leaves home, taking her little girl with her. She leaves the child in the care of Kentucky mountaineers after she joins a traveling opera company.
Distributor—Warner Brothers

62. Kentucky Pioneers B&W 11min 1941
Follows pioneer families along Wilderness Road to Kentucky. Shows their schools, recreation and everyday tasks such as weaving, soap-making, cooking, carpentry, and candle-making.
Distributor—Encyclopaedia Britannica Educational Corporation

63. Kentucky Pioneers Color 26min 1969
Explains why the pioneers moved out to settle the frontier wilderness. Shows the type of community that existed among the pioneers and some of the hardships they endured.
Distributors—Encyclopaedia Britannica Educational Corporation

64. Kentucky Rifle Color 7min 1970
Discusses the pioneer's search for a new home on the frontier, explains the importance of his rifle, and describes the loading and firing sequence.
Distributor—Barr Films

65. The Kingdom Come School Color 20min 1973
The film follows the 22 pupils and their teacher Harding Ison as they work and play together during a typical day at the Kingdom Come School in Eastern Kentucky. The school has survived the years and the threat of consolidation because of the contemporary teaching methods employed by this teacher and the enthusiastic attitude of the pupils.
Distributor—Appalshop

66. Knoxville Where Lakes and Mountains Meet B&W 20min 1959
Depicts Knoxville, the Great Smoky Mountains National Park and points of interest around Knoxville.
Distributor—Knoxville Tennessee Chamber of Commerce

67. Life in a Coal-Mining Town Color 11min 1956
"Describes the small coal-mining town of David, Kentucky, and shows typical activities of a miner and his family."
Distributor—Coronet Instructional Films

68. Life, Liberty and the Pursuit of Coal Color 52min 1973
Narrated by ABC news correspondent Jim Kincaid, the film explores the economic and power politics of the coal industry and how they pervade the state of West Virginia and affect the lives of the people.
Distributor—ABC News and Xerox Films

69. Line Fork Falls and Caves B&W 10min 1970
One of Appalshop's earliest films, this film takes the crew into one of the local scenic spots to visit the caves and waterfalls of Line Fork, Kentucky. Once inside the cave the film depends largely on the soundtrack to explain the happenings inside. After losing their way more than once, the crew finally finds their way back out into the sunlight, and happily films themselves during their first try at making movies.
Distributor—Appalshop

70. Linda and Billy Ray from Appalachia Color 15min 1970
"Portrays the difficulties that an Appalachian family encounters in adapting to city living when lack of job opportunities forces them to move to Cincinnati."
Distributor—Encyclopaedia Britannica

71. Lonesome Valleys of Kentucky
This is a study of the mining communities of Eastern Kentucky and the people who no longer have a place in the system. Produced by WHAS-TV in Louisville, Kentucky.
Distributor—Council of the Southern Mountains

72. Look Up and Live Color 29min 1968
A film crew goes into the mountains of southwest Virginia and eastern Kentucky—"hard-core" Appalachia—and interviews a cross-section of local people who are victims of exploitation and are working for social, economic and political change. Issues dealt with are strip-mining, the coal industry, colonialism and welfare reform.
Distributor—CBS News

73. The Millstone Sewing Center Color 10min 1972
This documents the highly successful OEO project, the Millstone Sewing Center, during its most productive period. Before the film was finished, however, the center's funds were cut, a point that is made in the titles, not in the body of the film. The film speaks clearly, the value of the center comes across in the works of the seamstresses, who explain what the work and the center has meant to them.
"The New Left never produced a documentary with content as radically instructive as The *Millstone Sewing Center*"

Gary Arnold—*Washington Post*

Distributor—Appalshop

74. Morgan Sorghum Color 12min 1974
This film covers three craftsmen that were featured at the Morgan County (Kentucky) Sorghum Festival, a knifemaker, a broommaker, and a woman

who spins her own yarn on a spinning wheel. It details their work then follows them to the fair where their work is displayed.
Distributor—Appalshop

75. Mountain Farmer B&W 8min 1974
Lee Banks practices "What I guess you'd call old-time farming," tilling the soil with his horse and wooden plow, and using methods barely different from his ancestors. The film is a tribute to a true mountaineer—a strong independent man who finds joy in his work and harmony with the land.
Distributor—Appalshop

76. The Mountaineer's Honor B&W 15min 1909 (silent)
A story of love and honor in the Kentucky Hills.
Distributor—Biograph Company

77. The Mountains Are Smoking Color 27min 1962
A feature on the Great Smoky Mountains National Park.
Distributor—CCM Films, Inc.

78. Music Fair Color 20min 1973
Film depicts the First Annual Appalachian People's Music Fair held in High Knob, Va. on September 12 and 13, 1970. Five musical segments of jug band, bluegrass, blues, and two special numbers—a strip-mining epic and the tragicomic "Ballad of Big Josie"—are shown.
Distributor—Appalshop

79. Music Makers of the Blue Ridge B&W 48min 1966
Studies life in the eastern mountains by examining folk music and dance. Includes scenes of isolated areas in western North Carolina. Visits the friends of folksinger Bascom L. Lunsford.
Distributor—Indiana University A-V Center

80. Nature's Way Color 20min 1974
Many mountaineers still care for their own ailments with the help of herbs, home remedies, and Indian folklore: midwives are still in popular demand. This film shows several people as they explain their cures and remedies, and covers a midwife as she assists in the delivery of twins.
"Every young person should be exposed to the beauty of birth and I know of no better or more moving presentation."
Herb Kohl, author—*Open Classroom*
Awards: Honorable mention—Sinking Creek Film Celebration, 1974
Distributor—Appalshop

81. The Newcomers B&W 25min
This film tells the story of migrant families from the Southern Appalachians to Cincinnati, Ohio. It explores their background—the economy, religion, and cultural patterns—and follows them as they try to find jobs and housing in the city. Produced by the Board of Missions of the Methodist Church and directed by George Stoney.

82. Ohio River Color 14min 1967
Relates the history of the settlement of cities along the Ohio River and shows the steel, chemical, aluminum, and atomic energy plants that exist in the area today. Emphasizes efforts being made to solve problems of water pollution, flood control, and increasing traffic.
Distributor—Coronet Instructional Films

83. People of the Cumberland B&W 18min 1937
This film is a study of the Highlander Folk School at Monteagle Tennessee. Also portrayed are the people of the land about the school. Commentary is done by Erskine Caldwell and Davil Wolff.
Distributor—Brandon Films

84. Pioneer Journey Across the Appalachians Color and B&W 14min 1956
"A North Carolina family journeys westward across the Appalachians before the Revolutionary War."
Distributor—Coronet Instructional Films

85. Poverty in Rural America B&W 28½min 1965
Explores the causes of poverty in rural areas such as the Appalachian Region, the Deep South and the Southwest. It also shows examples of communities which have taken successful attempts to solve their problems. Projects at Buckhorn and Red Bird Valley in Kentucky and Hyters Gap in Virginia are visited.
Distributor—U.S. Department of Agriculture

86. The Ramsey Trade Fair Color 20min 1974
In Ramsey, a small community in the coalfields of Southwestern Virginia, people gather every Wednesday to do their trading. This film is a close look at the loving art of trading, and at the traders themselves. Ramsey Day is more of a social event than a business venture, people come to meet with each other, to hear music and preaching, and sometimes to buy, sell, and trade.
Distributor—Appalshop

87. Ravaged Earth Color (no time given)
Shows the rape of the land caused by Appalachian strip-mining.
Distributor—NBC-TV

88. The Ravaged Earth Color 27min 1970
Describes the strip-mined lands of Appalachia. Features Stewart Udall with a commentary on strip-mining.
Distributor—NBC Educational Enterprises.

89. Sergeant York B&W 13min 1941
A film based on hero Alvin York of World War I. How he came back to his hills, spurning the adulation of his nation.
Distributor—Brandon Films

90. Southern Highlands Attractions Color 25min 1965
Follows a family vacation through North Carolina, Virginia, and Tennessee. Features Barter Theater, Clingman's Dome, and Chimney Rock.
Distributor—Southern Highlands Attractions Association

91. Spring Comes to Vintroux
A film story of a pilot project in community development by county extension agents, children and adults in a by-passed West Virginia community in the Kanawha Valley. It tells the story of establishing the project, progressive accomplishments and the spontaneous response of families that live in the project area. Produced by C. Gregor Van Camp, assisted by Foster Mullenax, both from West Virginia University and by Joseph Tonkin, Federal Extension Service, Washington, D.C.
Distributor—Council of the Southern Mountains

92. Strip Mine Trip Color 12min 1962
"Shows fifteen miles of Kentucky land that has been devastated by strip mining. Includes the comments of mine operators and citizens about the stripping operations."
Distributor—Churchill Films

93. Stripmining in Appalachia B&W 25min 1973
A film about Appalachia's most controversial problem. *Stripmining in Appalachia* speaks with the voices of and for the powerless little man caught up in the jaws of a cancerous industrial process. The film speaks of the beauty of the mountains, the humanity of the people, and the attitudes of the stripmine operators. Aerial photography is used to enhance a local biologist's scientific explanation of what stripmining does to the land.
Distributor—Appalshop

94. The Stripping of Appalachia Color 30min
This is an excellent film by a British firm which shows the strip mining of the British land company, the American Association, in Claiborne and Campbell Counties in Tennessee.
"I think the film is good to educate people about strip mining with," said Elmer Rasnick, chairman of Citizens for Social and Economic Justice. "It has all points of view. They go from the people directly affected, to the mine site with the operator, and finally to England to talk with the landowners. I doubt if many of the people right there in Tennessee knew that the company that was doing all the stripping was from England . . . just letting the people know that is reason enough to show the film all around."
Distributor—Council of the Southern Mountains

95. The Struggle of Coon Branch Mountain B&W 13min 1972
In their efforts to better their children's education, the residents of this small West Virginia community find themselves face to face with an unfeeling and bureaucratic political structure. The film follows their fight for better roads and schools through the first community meeting, a march on the governors' office, to a partial victory and determination to continue their struggle.
Distributor—Appalshop

96. Tennessee Holiday Color 30min
Visits Tennessee and features the Cherokees, TVA, Oak Ridge and Cumberland Gap.
Distributor—Modern Talking Picture Service

97. Tennessee River Color 14min 1971
A survey of TVA and what it has meant to the river valley.
Distributor—BFA Educational Media

98. They Shall Take Up Serpents Color 17min 1972
A film done by two East Tennessee State University professors on a snake-handling cult in Newport, Tennessee. This group is the same one which was reported in the national media when two of its leaders died of strychnine poisoning. One of these two men is the film's main commentator.
Distributor—ETSU

99. This World is Not My Home B&W 30min
This film is a portrait of 78 year old Nimrod Workman, a retired coal miner and singer who writes and performs songs and traditional ballads. Nimrod reminisces about his life as a miner in the film, and also sings traditional Appalachian songs.
Distributor—Appalshop

100. Thomas Wolfe: Ghost, Come Back Again B&W 29min
Dr. Herman Harvey, professor at University of South Carolina, considers the relation between Wolfe's life and work. He uses a dramatization from *Look Homeward Angel* to illustrate the autobiographical nature of the work.
Distributor—University of South Carolina

101. Thunder Road B&W 92min 1958
A Korean war hero returns to help his father in the moonshine business. He is pressured by Federal agents, a rival racketeer, and a clinging girlfriend.
Distributor—United Artist/16

102. Tobacco Road B&W 84min 16mm 1947
The film version of Erskine Caldwell's novel. The story of a hill family in Georgia during the 1930's. Directed by John Ford.
Distributor—Brandon Films

103. Todd: Growing Up in Appalachia Color 14min 1971
Story of Todd, a boy of a poor Appalachian family who finds a purse full of food stamps. Reveals Todd's character by showing his actions upon seeing the owner's name in the purse. From the Many Americans Series.
Distributor—Learning Corporation of America

104. Tomorrow's People Color 25min 1973
This is a presentation of mountain music—a sight and sound experience of mountain culture without narration. A visual montage of old time photographs accompanies the dulcimer sequence, while the central portion of the film turns loose to the banjo and fiddle to render "Fox Chase" by Coy Morton. The film ends with a rousing square dance in a one room schoolhouse high on a mountaintop.
Distributor—Appalshop

105. Tradition Color 20min 1974
Moonshining is regarded as one of the strongest traditions in the mountains. Though the number steadily decreases, there are still mountaineers who "had rather make moonshine than go on welfare." In this film, a moonshiner tells what it's like to have been "sent up" four times for making liquor, while IRS agents relate tales of tracking down stills and arresting moonshiners.
Awards: Sinking Creek Film Celebration Honorable Mention 1974
Distributor—Appalshop

106. Trail of Tears B&W 100min
This film is a study of the removal of the Cherokee Indians from their mountain homeland in North Carolina, Tennessee and Georgia under the direction of Andrew Jackson. This film is narrated by Johnny Cash.
Distributor—NET Film Service

107. Trail of the Lonesome Pine Color 102 min 1936
Two feuding families in the primitive mountains of Virginia find their way of life threatened by the construction of a railroad. A moving and uncompromising climax concludes this film which is notable as the first outdoor film made in color.
Distributor—Universal/16

108. UMWA 1970: A House Divided B&W 15min 1971
This portrait of W.A. (Tony) Boyle, filmed two years before the rank and file UMW rejected him, records his speech at a Miners' rally. Intercut with scenes of dissident miners, the film contrasts Boyle's statements with those of the anti-Boyle faction to expose the weaknesses of the union under Boyle's leadership.
"A first rate film that captures the real spirit of rank and file coal miners fighting to clean up their union. It's the kind of film only people who lived with that struggle day in and day out could have made."
Don Stillman, Director of Publications
UNITED MINE WORKERS OF AMERICA

109. Valley of Darkness Color 18min 1970
Presents the employment problems of young West Virginia men who must work in the mines and risk black lung and cave-ins. Also shows the conflict between attempting to raise the children out of the coal camps and economic pressures brought to bear by the coal companies.
Distributor—NBC-TV

110. A Walk in the Spring Rain Color 100min
The story of a woman—the wife of a New York City professor, on sabbatical in the Tennessee mountains. She meets and falls in love with a giant of a country man. The film deals with the growth and maturing of their love amid the background of the Great Smoky Mountains. Ingrid Bergman and Anthony Quinn play the lead roles in this film—shot on location in Knoxville, Tennessee.
Distributor-Swank Motion Pictures, Inc.

111. West Virginia, Land for Relaxation Color 14min 1962
Portrays a trip through West Virginia, showing scenic, recreational, and historic features.
Distributor—Ellis Dungan Productions

112. Whitesburg Epic B&W 10min 1970
This film made in the spring of 1970, is a series of interviews on the streets of Whitesburg. Opinions on the war in Vietnam, Kent State, college unrest, the draft, and recreation are voiced by the residents of this small eastern Kentucky town. One of the *Appalshop's* earliest films, it speaks clearly about the problems faced by young people in Appalachia in the early seventies.
Distributor—Appalshop

113. The Wilderness Road B&W 23min 1953
Follows Daniel Boone and other pioneers who carved out the wilderness road from North Carolina to Kentucky. Describes their explorations, fight for independence, and settlement of the frontier country.
Distributor—Virginia Department of Education

114. Woodrow Cornett: Letcher County Butcher B&W 10min 1970
The film follows Woodrow Cornett as he goes through the intricate process of butchering a hog. Narrated by Frank Majority, with harmonica and humor, by Ashland Fouts, it is a portrait of a man and his work, and a look at the mountain custom of hog butchering performed by a master at the craft.
"WOODROW CORNETT: LETCHER CO. BUTCHER is a simply fascinating ten minute picture, the first one the workshop made, telling how one man makes a living butchering hogs and steer . . . I cannot convey in words how interesting this film is, made even more so by the harmonica musical background, performed by one old timer, Ashland Fouts, that gives to this documentary much meaning."
Awards: Sinking Creek Film Celebration 1972, UT Film Festival, Robert Flaherty Film Seminar 1973, D. W. Griffith Film Festival, Temple University Anthropological and Documentary Film Conference, Museum of Modern Art, Yale Film Society
Distributor—Appalshop

115. Young'uns Color 25min 1968
Examines the effects of rural poverty on a 16 year old boy, Paul Tabier, and his fatherless family. Their day to day struggles in Ohio's Appalachian area are eased by their deep religious convictions and their love of the land.
Distributor—Films, Inc.

Additional Films (16mm)

The following films are in addition to the list of 16 mm films provided above:

Appalachian State University Library

1. Appalachian Trail B&W 16mm 16min 1975
General film dealing with the geographical, social, and economic history of this area. Primary emphasis on historical background.

2. Basket Builder Color 16mm 12min 1974
Blue Ridge Films

3. Camping in the Smokies Color 29min 16mm
Produced by Ford Motor Company

4. Everlasting Hills Color 26min 16mm
The NNCDA is an organization of civic-minded North Carolinians from an eleven-county area of Northwest North Carolina. This film depicts advance-

ment in agriculture, industry, travel, recreation, and community development. Produced by Reynolds Tobacco Co.

5. Foxfire Color 26min 16mm 1973
Shows how a young teacher and his formerly disillusioned class wrote and created, as an integral part of English curriculum, a popular magazine dealing with ways of life and crafts of pioneer America still surviving in Appalachia. Produced by Appalshop.

6. In the Good Old-fashioned Way Color 20 min 16mm 1973
The old Regular Baptist Church is the oldest in the mountains. This film shows the spirit and faith of the people of this church, and the impact their religion has on their lives. Widespread only among mountain people, this religion in uniquely a product of the Appalachian culture. This film attempts to capture the feeling through various services and ceremonies while they explain their church as they see it. Produced by Appalshop.

7. Moonshine (Or Tradition) Color 20 min 16mm 1974
In this film, a moonshiner tells what it's like to have been sent up four times for making liquor while IRS agents relate tales of tracking down stills and arresting moonshiners.

8. Singing on the Mountain B&W 12 min 16mm 1958
Shows the actual singing on the mountain festival held in July of each year and preserves early Anglo-Saxon folk arts. Produced by Hugh Morton.

9. Tennessee Tweetsie B&W 7min 16mm
A ride on Watauga County's famed Tweetsie Railroad is the topic of this film. The Tweetsie station, detailed shots of the train and the Indian attack are included.

10. Variety Vacationland Color 15min 16mm
Depicts scenes in North Carolina that have value to tourists and natives from the standpoint of history and interest.

East Tennessee State University Instructional Materials Center All films made by Thomas G. Burton and Jack Schrader.

1. Alex Stewart: Cooper Color 13min 16mm 1973
Demonstration of constructing a churn by mountain craftsman Alex Stewart, from near Sneedville, Tennessee; commentary on use of non-powered tools and skills handed down in his family in making wooden containers such as buckets, barrels, etc.

2. Buna and Bertha Color 13min 16mm 1973
Performance of and commentary on Anglo-American ballads and songs by 86- and 92-year old mountain women, Buna Hicks of Beech Creek and Bertha Baird of Rominger in western North Carolina.

3. Edd Presnell: Dulcimer Maker Color 6min 16mm 1973
Demonstration of and commentary on constructing a dulcimer by mountain craftsman Edd Presnell, a native of Watauga County, North Carolina, who learned his craft from his father-in-law; brief performance on finished dulcimer by Mr. Presnell's wife Nettie.

4. A Film about Ray Hicks Color 19min 16mm 1974
Audio-visual portrait of mountain man Ray Hicks of Beech Mountain, North Carolina—his close ties to the land and his heritage; shows him and his family gathering herbs, reaping buckwheat, etc., living a century-old way of life at the same time modern influences begin to affect his children.

5. Gandy Dancers Color 14min 16mm 1973
Presentation of "gandy dancers," members of a railroad work crew laying crossties, spiking rails, and aligning track, synchronizing movements by traditional worksongs and chants, all of which have been made obsolete through mechanization.

6. "Ott" Blair: Sled Maker Color 5min 16mm 1973
Demonstration of and commentary on the mountain craft of building wooden farm sleds by Ott Blair, a native of Heaton, North Carolina; commentary includes his first selling of sleds and his attitudes toward economic self-sufficiency.

7. "They Shall Take up Serpents" Color 17min 16mm 1972
Documentary of religious service of the Holiness Church of God in Jesus Name, of Newport, Tennessee, in which serpents are handled and poison drunk; one participant is bitten and taken to the home of the assistant pastor, where the latter explains the congregation's beliefs.

Indiana University Audio Visual Center

1. And So They Live B&W 26min 16mm
Documents the tragic poverty of families in the southern mountains, the poor land, the lack of proper diet, inadequate housing, absence of sanitation, and the complete lack of adaptation of the school program to the local situation.

2. Audubon Color 58min 16mm
Traces the travels of John J. Audubon (1785–1851) who classified birds in America and Europe. Recounts Audubon's warning that many species of birds would become extinct when the forest was cut, and that he foresaw the depletion of wild bison in America.

3. Flatboatmen of the Frontier (Ohio Valley Farmers: 1790–1820) B&W 11min 16mm
Shows that the early settlers of the Ohio Valley were "farmer boatmen" through their dependence on the soil for livelihood and on the rivers for transportation. Includes the valley agricultural economy, frontier homes, and domestic activities, flatboat building and loading, the trip down-river to market, frontier personalities, speech, and music.

4. Geography of the Southern States Color 11min 16mm
Depicts the basic geographic elements of climate and soil in the southern states, as related to the human activities of history, invention, change, new methods, and new attitudes.

5. Hunger in America Color 51min 16mm
Presents evidence that 10,000,000 Americans go to bed hungry every night from "gut hunger" accompanied by malnutrition and starvation and not simply an unsatisfied appetite for delightful or exotic foods. Visits poor people in four areas: Spanish Americans in Texas, sharecroppers in Virginia, Navajo Indians in Arizona, and Negroes in Alabama.

6. Kentucky Pioneers B&W 11min 16mm
Follows two pioneer families along the difficult and dangerous Wilderness Road to the Kentucky frontier fort at Harrold's Station. Describes the hardships encountered in establishing a new home in the wilderness and recalls the courage and faith that helped overcome these hardships. Reenacts such representative activities as weaving, soap-making, cooking, candle-making, carpentry, cabin construction, schooling, and square dancing.

7. Kentucky Pioneers Color 26min 16mm
Presents the dangers and hardships encountered by a pioneer family settling in new territory as well as the sacrifices they had to make. Describes cooperation within and among families. Shows an Indian raid, a cabin being built, religious observations, and community gatherings.

8. Leaving Home Blues Color 51min 16mm
Interviews various high school students, parents, school administrators, and farmers to examine the characteristics and problems of rural migration to urban areas, focusing on North Carolina, Nebraska, and Texas. Emphasizes that the lack of employment opportunities in rural communities forces high school students to leave the area after graduation and stresses that the young people neither want to leave home and family nor have the needed skills to work in urban areas.

9. Preventing Coal Pneumoconiosis Through Engineering Controls Color 20min 16mm
Discusses the 1969 Coal Health and Safety Act and examines the research the United States Bureau of Mines is undertaking to try to control coal pneumoconiosis. Points out that this disease is the "killer of coal miners" and shows how tiny particles of coal collects in miners' lungs to prevent proper breathing.

10. The Ravaged Earth Color 24min 16mm
Utilizes interviews with Stewart Udall to point out the dangers and senselessness of strip mining—environmental waste, health damage, and property damage. Places the blame on man's irresponsibility, the inadequacy of regulatory legislation, and the power of the mining companies. Shows scenes of Appalachian land that has been permanently destroyed.

11. TVA and the Nation Color 20min 16mm
Portrays the development of the Tennessee Valley and describes the benefits accruing to the people of this valley and the entire nation from TVA. Conditions in the valley before TVA are pictured and the actions needed to raise the area's economy to that of the other regions of the nation are described. The various changes that took place in the valley are enumerated in detail.

United Artists

1. The Night of the Hunter B&W 90min 1955
A film about a psychopathic backwoods preacher in West Virginia who marries the widow of a bank robber in order to discover where the robber had hidden $10,000. Since the robber has told no one but his two small children, ages four and nine, where the money is, his widow is no help to the clerical lunatic. He murders her and then persecutes the children until he drives them forth into the world. The movie depicts the children's nightmarish flight. It is based on the novel by Davis Grubb, was directed by

Charles Laughton and stars Robert Mitchum, Shelly Winters and Miss Lillian Gish.

University of California Extension Media Center

1. How to Make Sorghum Molasses 20min 16mm
Step by step, visual study of some central West Virginia farmers making sorghum molasses, with short essay.

2. All Hand Work 15min 16mm
Portrait of West Virginia musician and craftsman Jenes Cottrell.

Western Kentucky University Division of Media Services

1. Traditional Quilting Color 30min 16mm
A program showing the patchwork quilt as an art form and as a skill being revived in Kentucky. It makes use of samples of artistic quilting gathered from homes in western Kentucky and from the Kentucky Museum. Traditional Kentucky quilters appear on the show.

2. Traditional Hand Tools Color 30min 16mm
A film describing some of the simple hand tools used by Kentucky pioneers. The film also reminds the viewer of the special skills and special lore that went with a pioneer economy. Old-time workmen demonstrate the broad ax and frow, and a modern collector demonstrates some items from his collection.

3. Long Rifle in Revival Color 30min 16mm
A program exploring some of the history of the "Kentucky" rifle. It then turns to the contemporary phenomenon of revival of the manufacture and use of this historic weapon. Gunsmiths and marksmen demonstrate the loading and firing operations.

4. Basketmaking Color 15min 16mm
A disappearing folk art is preserved for posterity in this unique presentation of the skilled handiwork of an elderly woman. Mrs. Frannie Alvey of Wax, Kentucky, demonstrates the steps in the making of a basket basically using only a piece of white oak timber and a pocket knife.

5. Kentucky Heritage in Jesse Stuart's Writing Color 30min 16mm
An exploration of portions of a Kentucky author's works reveal the use of traditional speech, crafts, beliefs, and customs as a basis for the regional author's art. The special emphasis is literary.

6. Folk Housing in Kentucky Color 30min 16mm
This discussion of some of the principal types of traditional structures found in southwestern Kentucky also has illustrations of houses and barns following basic folk architectural plans.

Most of the above films from Western Kentucky University are also available in video tape quadraplex, video tape 3/4" cassette, and video tape 1/2" EIAJ (B & W).

West Virginia University, Office of University Relations

1. Hey, Look at Me Color 12min 16mm
Shows West Virginia children participating in an experimental Head Start program in which they use inexpensive movie cameras to learn about the world around them.

2. Only a Beginning B&W 29min 16mm
Depicts the history of West Virginia University and in the process tells much about life in West Virginia from 1862 to 1967 when the 100th anniversary of WVU was observed.

West Virginia University—Carl Fleischauer Box 3216 Sabraton Sta., Morgantown, WV 26505

1. John Mitchel Hickman B&W 17min 16mm
A portrait of a bluegrass banjo player from Kentucky, residing in Columbus, Ohio, trying to find self-expression and a living wage from his music.

II—Film Distributors (16mm)

ABC News and Xerox Films
1330 Avenue of the Americas
New York, NY 10019

AFL-CIO Education Department
815 Sixteenth St., N.W.
Washington, DC 20006

Appalachian State University
Library—Appalachian Collection
Boone, NC 28607

Appalshop
P. O. Box 332
Whitesburg, KY 41858

Barr Films
P. O. Box 7-C
1029 N. Allen Ave.
Pasadena, CA 91104

BFA Educational Media
2211 Michigan Ave.
Santa Monica, CA 90404

Biograph Company
P. O. Box 109
Canaan, NY 12029

Brandon Films
200 West 57th St.
New York, NY 10019

Carousel Films
1501 Broadway
New York, NY 10036

CBS News
383 Madison Ave.
New York, NY 10017

Chimney Rock Park Service
Chimney Rock, NC 28720

Churchill Films
662 N. Robertson Blvd.
Los Angeles, CA 90069

Colonial Williamsburg, Inc.
Film Distribution Center
Goodwin Building, Box C
Williamsburg, VA 23185

Contemporary/McGraw-Hill Films
1221 Avenue of the Americas
New York, NY 10020

Coronet Films
65 E. South Water St.
Chicago, IL 60601

Council of the Southern Mountains Bookstore
C.P.O. 2307
Berea, KY 40403

Crowell, Collier Macmillan, Inc.
866 Third Ave.
New York, NY 10022

Walt Disney Productions
Educational Film Division
500 S. Buena Vista Ave.
Burbank, CA 91503

Don G. Cummings—Madison Project
Scientific Development Corporation
379 Main Street
Watertown, MA 02172

Ellis Dungan Productions 16
Box 726
Wheeling, WV 26003

East Tennessee State University
Instructional Materials Center
Johnson City, TN 37601

Embassy Pictures Corporation
1301 Avenue of the Americas
New York, NY 10019

Encyclopedia Britannica Educational Corporation
425 N. Michigan Ave.
Chicago, IL 60601

Films Incorporated
277 Pharr Rd., N.E.
Atlanta, GA 30305

First National Exhibitors Circuit
Madison Project
Weston Woods Studios
Weston, CT 06880

Great Plains Instructional TV Library
University of Nebraska
Lincoln, NB 68504

Indiana University
Audio Visual Center
Bloomington, IN 47401

IQ Films
689 Fifth Ave.
New York, NY 10022

Herbert Kline—Madison Project
Weston Woods Studios
Weston, CT 06880

Knoxville Chamber of Commerce
704 Gay Street, S.W.
Knoxville, TN 37901

Learning Corporation of America
711 Fifth Ave.
New York, NY 10022

Macmillan Publishing Company, Inc.
866 Third Ave.
New York, NY 10022

Modern Talking Picture Service
1212 Avenue of the Americas
New York, NY 10020

Hugh Morton
Linville, NC 28646

NBC Educational Enterprises and NBC-TV
30 Rockefeller Plaza
New York, NY 10020

NET Film Service
10 Columbus Circle
New York, NY 10019

Office of Economic Opportunity
Madison Project
Weston Woods Studios
Weston, CT 06880

Reader's Digest Association, Inc.
Pleasantville, NY 10570

Rembrandt Film Library
267 W. 25th St.
New York, NY 10001

Southern Highlands Attractions Association
P. O. Box 839
Wilmington, NC 28401

Swank Motion Pictures, Inc.
201 S. Jefferson Ave.
St. Louis, MO 63166

Teaching Films Custodians
25 W. 43rd St.
New York, NY 10036

Tennessee Game and Fish Commission
Box 9400
White's Creek Pike
Nashville, TN 37220

Tennessee Valley Authority
New Sprangle Building
Knoxville, TN 37901

United Artists Sixteen
729 Seventh Ave.
New York, NY 10019

U.S. Department of Agriculture
Photography Division
Office of Information
Washington, DC 20250

United States National Audio-Visual Center
National Archives and Records Service
Washington, DC 20408

U.S. Office of Education
Department of Health, Education and Welfare
Rockville, MD 20852

United States Works Progress Administration
Madison Project
Weston Woods Studios
Weston, CT 06880

Universal Sixteen
445 Park Ave.
New York, NY 10022

University of California
Extension Media Center
2223 Fulton St.
Berkeley, CA 94720

University of South Carolina
Columbia, SC 29208

Virginia Department of Education
Film Production Service
523 Main Street
Richmond, VA 23216

Warner Brothers Sixteen
666 Fifth Avenue
New York, NY 10019

West Virginia University
University Relations
Communications Building
Morgantown, WV 26506

Western Kentucky University
Division of Media Services
Academic Complex
Bowling Green, Kentucky 42101

WQXI-TV
Atlanta, GA 30301

Yale University Press
Film Service
New Haven, CT 06520

III—Videotapes

A. Appalachian State University

1. Appalachian Paradox 60min
A tape of Harry Caudill's address at Tennessee Technological University. A wide-ranging analysis of the economy, failures and possibilities in Central Appalachia. Caudill is author of *Night Comes to the Cumberlands* and *My Land Is Dying*, and is an attorney in Letcher County, Kentucky.

2. Bays Mountain Park—Introductory Tour 30min
Produced by the Bays Mountain Park Environmental Education Center in Kingsport, Tennessee, under the sponsorship of the Appalachian Regional Commission. An overview and tour showing the facilities of the Bays Mountain Park, from its nature trails to its animals and planetarium.

3. Cave Dwellers and Hill People 30min
Dave O'Neil of Scott County, Virginia, talks of mountain people who lived in caves and ridges, the melungeons, how he met John Fox, where the true Lonesome Pine is.

4. Dave O'Neil and Kate Sturgill 30min
Talk of what life was like early in the century. Kate sings songs she wrote about growing up. From Scott County, Virginia.

5. The Foxfire Project 60min
The founder of the Foxfire project in Rabun Gap, Georgia, and editor of the Foxfire book, *Eliot* Wiggenton, explains his project to the Appalachian Workshop at East Tennessee State University, accompanied by one of the Rabun Gap students.

6. History of Country Music Approximately 8 one hour tapes
A special series of eight tapes of Broadside SW Virginia from the Clinch Valley College seminar conducted by Helen Lewis and Joe Smiddy. Explores in depth traditional forms, ballads and other aspects of country music with such artists as Janette Carter, Ralph Stanley, Guy Caravan, John Boyd and others.

7. The Land of Conspiracy 30min
Warren Wright, past director of the Council of the Southern Mountains and one of the region's most articulate grass roots spokesmen, talks of the land conspiracy in Appalachia, and how the education of a professional class in Appalachia contributed to that conspiracy.

8. Living and Learning in Appalachia—Jesse Stuart 60min
One of Appalachia's most noted authors talks, in an address at Tennessee Technological University, of his life in the mountains.

9. Open Season on Game Wardens 30min
Dave O'Neil shares some more Scott County stories on law enforcement, game wardens, the prosecution of people for killing robins for food in the depression, feuds and violence.

10. Songs for Children 30min
Jack Wright and John McCutcheon sing traditional tunes, Guthrie tunes and other songs for children at Dungannon Elementary School in Southwest Virginia.

11. To Look Over the Land and Take Care of It 30min
If the mountains have a living folk hero, it is Uncle Dan Gibson of Knott County, Kentucky, who, at the age of 86, took his gun and stood on top of his mountain to successfully resist strip miners. His act was one nucleus that formed the Appalachian Group to Save the Lane and People—one of the strongest anti-stripping groups in the mountains. He talks of his experiences and the Appalachian Group while sitting on the front porch of his home and cradling his old 30-30 carbine for gentle emphasis.

12. The Union Struggle 60min
An edited overview of early union history in the mountains as told by the people who were involved. The tape includes some of the material from the Tillman Cadle, and Florence Reece tapes, along with tapes from Cabin Creek, West Virginia, including Mrs. Miller, the mother of Arnold Miller, Miners for Democracy candidate against Tony Boyle.

Appalachian State University
Library—Appalachian Collection
Boone, NC 28607

B. Broadside TV

I. General Tapes

1. Appalachian Workshop B&W 60min
A tape from a Highlander workshop with Jim Branscome, Florence Reece, George Tucker and others discussing the history and culture of the region. Tucker and Mrs. Reece sing several songs.

2. Black Midwife and Nurse B&W 30min
Aunt Minnie Conley of Carter County is a ninety-six year old lady who talks of her service to the mountain community delivering babies and offering other health services such as pre and post natal care. She talks of other health practices in her days as a midwife.

3. The Blackly School Situation B&W 27min
A woman of Letcher County, Kentucky, talks about the struggle to rebuild a local school after it was destroyed by fire. The film is a picture of education given by a native of Eastern Kentucky.

4. Brookside Strike B&W 60min
Hearings of inquiry into this extended strike at Evarts, Kentucky, set the scene along with interviews with people in the area to define the issues around the struggle for representation by the United Mine Workers union.

5. Cherokee-Choctaw Blood, and Damned English Too B&W 30min
Hop Watts of Putnam County, Tennessee, left the mountains to ride boxcars with the Woody Guthrie's of the 30's. He talks of his travels, of life in the mountains, and his views on racism, government, and education.

6. Food Co-op B&W 30min
A study of three community groups in the Tri-Cities of East Tennessee who have formed small grocery co-ops. They describe their co-ops and talk about their development.

7. Garbage: The Johnson City Situation B&W 43min 1976
This is a documentary of area landfills including state and local officials, rural community residents of the proposed landfill site, and people living near a sanitary landfill in a neighboring county. It represents an effort to document the problems surrounding the disposal of solid waste.

8. Hard Row to Hoe B&W 47min 1976
This is a documentary about the changing farm situation in East Tennessee. Because of the low margin of profit in small farming in East Tennessee and the increasing land values, East Tennessee is rapidly losing its farms. A look is taken at four different types of farmers and their farms.

9. Harlan Coal Miners' Strike B&W
This tape documents the early stages of the Harlan miners' strike supported by the new leadership of UMW president, Arnold Miller.

10. A Harlan Miner Speaks B&W 30min
A union organizer of the famous "Bloody Harlan" struggle during the 1920's and 1930's recalls incidents and his life during that period.

11. Hazel Dickens Sings B&W 30min
One of the mountain's fine musicians sings some of her well-known songs and hymns.

12. The Hyder Mine Disaster B&W 20min
The famous explosion at the Hyder Mine of the Finley Coal Company killed all but one man—A.T. Collins. He talks of the explosion, how he survived it, and then makes a brief and moving statement about life in the mines.

13. I would Have Gone Back B&W 30min
Thousands of young men face charges of desertion from military service. The reasons stem as often from the complexities of mountain people as they do from the complexities of military processes. Eddie Caudhill of Ft. Gay, West Virginia, tells of his own all too familiar journey from an E-5 wounded purple heart veteran of Vietnam to a deserter facing charges by the Army after confusion over medical treatment and red tape.

14. International Special Olympic Games B&W 20min
A delegation from Southwest Virginia is featured at the Fourth International Special Olympic Games on the campus of Central Michigan University at Mt. Pleasant, Michigan. The participants representing all fifty states and eight foreign countries are all mentally impaired and some are also physically handicapped. The games, which are sponsored by the Joseph P. Kennedy, Jr., Foundation, include swimming, track and field events, gym-

nastics, wheel chair events, and bowling. Interviews with Susan St. James and Tom Lucas point out the spirit and enthusiasm of hundreds of volunteer celebrities from around the world.

15. In These Hills B&W 30min
A brief view of mountain people and issues.

16. James Dickey—Readings B&W 30min
The noted author-poet reads some of his work and speaks during an appearance at the Virginia Highlands Festival in Abingdon, Virginia.

17. Jesse Stuart—Living and Learning in Appalachia. B&W 60min
An address by the writer at Tennessee Technological University.

18. Land Use—Mt. Rodgers Recreation Area B&W 30min
Development of additional national forest lands and a new lake by the U.S. Forest Service threatens residents of traditional mountain communities with loss of their land and way of life.

19. Little Men and Big Machines B&W 60min
Politics in Appalachia—an address by Harry Caudill at East Tennessee State University's Appalachian Workshop.

20. Midwife Nurse B&W 30min
A tape of a proposal by Kingsport, Tennessee, to have a clinic with trained midwife nurses.

21. A Mountain Has No Seed B&W 27min
A farmer of the Cumberland Mountains in Tennessee gives a statement about strip-mining and the destruction it has wrought.

22. Movin' on to Washington B&W 32min 1975
Broadside TV went to Washington, D.C., with 3,000 coal miners and 700 trucks from Wise, Virginia, in protest of strip mining legislation that would establish more stringent requirements for reclamation.

23. The New America Color 25min 1974
Doug Anderson and Dan McCrimmon, poets traveling with Artrain, spend some time in the Tri-Cities area of Tennessee conducting workshops in the writing of poetry. This tape shows them picking the guitar, singing and reading their own poetry as they meet with young people and help them with writing their own poetry.

24. Nimrod, Sarah and Jack B&W 30min
A fine informal collection of mountain music old and new.

25. Strip Mining in Germany B&W 30min
This tape shows strip mining and reclamation practices in Germany. Included are interviews with local people and strip miners (English dubbed over). This is an old copy with somewhat unstable edits but important content.

26. To Raise the Dead and Bury the Living—Strip Mining B&W 60min
This tape deals with the problem of strip mining in the mountains as told by the people of the mountains. Scenes of stripping and the words of mountain residents are mixed with the testimony taped from the People's Trial on Strip Mining held in Wise, Virginia. Some of the people on the tape are Uncle Dan Gibson, Bessie Smith, Arden Franklin, Warren Wright, Mark Shepard, and excerpts from a meeting with mountain people and TVA staff on the problem of stripping and land reclamation.

27. Tobacco Cutting B&W 30min
C. L. Perkins of Washington County, Tennessee, talks about the growth of tobacco, what to look for when it is ready to cut. He demonstrates cutting and shows how to hang tobacco for the curing process.

28. Tour of Historic Jonesboro B&W 53min 1974
Paul Fink, local historian, conducts a tour of Jonesboro, former capital of the lost state of Franklin and oldest town in Tennessee. He speaks of the architecture and historical significance of various public buildings, homes and churches.

29. Which Side Are You On? B&W 30min
Florence and Dan Reese fought to unionize the coal fields in the 1930's. They talk of their experiences, and Florence sings some of her own songs, including the famous "Which Side Are You On?" which she wrote to explain the union struggle.

30. The Wobblies B&W 60min
Utah Phillips, singer and member of the still active IWW, proves that neither Wobblies nor a Joe Hill song can ever die and talks of IWW history between songs.

II. SAVES Tapes
(Southern Appalachian Video Ethnography Series):

This series of videotapes includes documentaries dealing with various aspects of Southern mountain culture. Code numbers are given for those that have been catalogued by the system of the Human Relations Area Files. These tapes are available through Broadside TV.

1. Apple Butter Making (NN5/252/1) B&W 18 min 1975
Apple butter making is a traditional food preservation activity in the Southern Appalachians during the fall. This tape shows the process from the peeling of the apples to the canning of the finished product. The individuals shown are family members and neighbors of Phyllis Scalf, the videomaker.

2. Blue Ridge Folklife B&W 1975 50min
This event features old-time string bands and blues from the Piedmont and mountain sections of Virginia. Among the musicians participating were Uncle Homer Walker of Narrows, Virginia, and Daniel Womack, a blues-guitarist from the Virginia mountains. Uncle Homer's performance on the banjo is a rare example of traditional black banjo playing.

3. Broom-Maker (NN5/391/1) B&W 30 min 1974
This videotape of John Sizemore, a traditional mountain broom-maker, was recorded at an annual community festival held near Greeneville, Greene County, Tennessee. Aside from providing a clear view of the steps involved in the assembly of a short-handled mountain broom, John Sizemore's lively conversational style adds to the appeal of this tape.

4. Dreadful Memories (NN5/468/1) B&W 32min 1972
Sara Gunning and Tilman Caudle recount songs and stories of the struggle for unionization in the Harlan coal mines during the 1930's.

5. Ernest East (NN5/533/1) B&W 33min 1974
During the summer months, fiddle contests are held at many towns in the Blue Ridge counties of Virginia and North Carolina in the Southern Appalachians. One string band that has taken more than its share of prizes is headed up by Ernest East, a mill worker and fiddler from Pine Ridge, Surry County, North Carolina.

6. Fiddlin' Powers Family (NN5/533/4) B&W 58min 1974
Fiddlin' Powers and family, a mountain string band from Dungannon, Scott County, Virginia, were among the first Southern Appalachian folk musicians to make commercial recordings in the 1920's. On this tape, three of Fiddlin' Powers' daughters and a son-in-law perform on mandolin, guitar, banjo-guitar and autoharp, and discuss their family's musical tradition and instrumental styles with interviewer, George Reynolds.

7. Frank Duff, Farrier (NN5/326/1) B&W 30min 1973
Aside from illustrating the complete process of shoeing a horse, this tape also provides insight into a traditional craft that has survived in modern times as an adjunct to a popular form of recreation, horseback riding.

8. Ghost Stories—Kathryn Tucker Windham (NN1/538/1) B&W 20min 1974
Kathryn Tucker Windham of Selma, Alabama, is a former newspaper woman and author of several children's books dealing with Deep South ghost lore. Included are several short tales: "The Waverly Ghost," Waverly, Mississippi, "The Jumbo (Alabama) Ghost Light," and "The Ghost Collie."

9. Grandpa Jones at the A. P. Carter Store (NN5/545/2) B&W 50min 1975
The veteran country music performer, Grandpa Jones, his wife, Ramona, and their son, Mark, along with a young neighbor, Larry Lowe, perform before an enthusiastic audience at a community music center established by Janette Carter Kelly, daughter of Sarah and the late A. P. Carter. Along with songs, instrumental numbers and comedy routines, Grandpa performs a "bell dance" that indicates the early ties between professional country music and vaudeville. Members of the audience step-dance during instrumentals.

10. Home Crafts Day (NN5/545/1) B&W 25min 1974
Old-Timers' celebrations and crafts festivals are held in many Southern Appalachian communities, especially during the autumn, and they serve as a focal point for people interested in traditional music, dancing, crafts and subsistence techniques. This tape includes a variety of musical genres, ranging from folk revival topical songs to bluegrass and old-time banjo picking; clog dancing; demonstrations of apple cider pressing and sled-making; also interviews with a weaver and a corn shuck doll maker.

11. Instrument Maker (NN5/534/1) B&W 30min 1973
Mr. Blaine Green of Washington County, Tennessee is an old time fiddler and self-taught instrument maker who has produced a number of fiddles, guitars, and dulcimers. This tape includes discussion and exhibition of Mr. Green's instruments, along with several performances with local musicians.

12. Marshall Ward (NN5/538/1) B&W 53min 1973
Marshall Ward is a retired school teacher who is able to trace the storytelling tradition in his mountain family back to his great-grandparents' generation. Marshall Ward tells a Jack tale, a children's tale with a startling ending, a ghost tale and an "Irishman" or numbskull tale. He also provides information concerning his family background and his career as a storyteller.

13. Meadows of Dan Folk Festival (NN5/545/1) B&W 34 min 1974
This tape features the highlights of a folk festival sponsored by the Ruritan Club, at the Meadows of Dan School. Among the performers are Eunice McAlexander, a ballad singer from Meadows of Dan, Virginia, and Taylor and Stella Kimble from Laurel Fork, Virginia, who appear on the SAVES tape "Taylor and Stella Kimble."

14. Mike Seeger at the A. P. Carter Store B&W 50min 1976
Mike Seeger, brother of Pete Seeger, has a long standing reputation in old-time music. A former member of the New Lost City Ramblers, he is now traveling to universities and colleges and giving other performances like the one at the A. P. Carter Store. During these performances Mike shows the variety of instruments and styles that make up old-time music and also the humor that keeps the music alive.

15. The Morris Brothers at the A. P. Carter Store (NN5/545/5) B&W 50min 1975
Dave and John Morris of Ivydale, West Virginia, have been actively promoting mountain music as performers and festival organizers during the past decade. At a recent appearance at Janette Carter Kelly's community music center, they presented a lively program of traditional and modern songs, and several fiddle tunes which drew members of the audience out onto the floor to step-dance.

16. Mountain Weaver (NN5/286/1) B&W 28min 1973
Taft Greer of Mountain City, Johnson County, Tennessee, is a weaver of traditional mountain coverlets whose grandmother was mentioned in Allen H. Eaton's *Handicrafts of the Southern Highlands*. On this tape, he discusses and exhibits various materials involved in the steps leading up to setting up the loom, and also demonstrates the actual weaving process.

17. News from Pigeon Roost: Harvey Miller (NN5/18/2) B&W 52min 1975
Harvey J. Miller is a self-taught writer and sympathetic observer of life in the mountains of western North Carolina. Recently Eliot Wigginton compiled the best of Miller's articles in a special issue of *Foxfire* magazine. This tape, apart from its value as a general introduction to mountain folk culture, can be fruitfully employed in anthropology and folklore courses to illustrate the interaction between interviewer and informant in a field situation.

18. Nimrod Workman (NN5/18/1) B&W 49min 1973
Nimrod Workman is a 79 year old former coal miner from Mingo County, West Virginia, and one of the most remarkable performers in the Southern Appalachian region. In addition to performing traditional songs and ballads, he is also a song writer who adapts old and modern tunes to convey his own ideas and feelings about life in the mountains. In this tape he moves from anecdotes to songs and back again without any sense of self-consciousness or artificiality. Topics covered include coal-mining, the union struggle, black lung, herb gathering and the Hatfield-McCoy feud.

19. Parking Lot Pickin' and Fiddlin' Around B&W 55min 1975
Most work on fiddlers' conventions deals with the competition aspects that occur onstage and only briefly deals with the activities in campsites and parking lots. This tape deals solely with the spontaneous music and people that make up the heart of the large scale conventions.

20. Ralph Stanley Memorial Blue Grass Festival (NN5/545/3a-h) B&W 1974
In 1970, Ralph Stanley established an annual festival at his family's homestead in southwestern Virginia, dedicated to the memory of his late brother and singing partner, Carter. The fourth annual festival included many outstanding figures in the bluegrass field. Included in this series of tapes are:
Ralph Stanley (NN5/545/3a)
Bill Monroe (NN5/545/3b)
Don Reno & Bill Harrell (NN5/545/3c)
Country Gentlemen/Bill Clifton (NN5/545/3d)
Goins Brothers with Red Rector/James Monroe/Blue Denim (NN5/545/3e)
Bluegrass Alliance/Jones Brothers (NN5/545/3f)
Bluegrass Tarheels/Al Wood/Sloane Family/McClain Family (NN5/545/eg)
Marshall Dutton and the Good Timers/Lee Allen/Glenn Roberts and the Rolling Firestones (NN5/545/3h)

21. Renfro Valley (NN5/545/4) B&W 1974
In 1974, Mac Wiseman's bluegrass festival at Renfro Valley, Kentucky, was combined with a fiddle contest supported by prominent traditionalists in the commercial country music field and the Tennessee Valley Old Time Fiddlers Association. Mike Seeger was called upon to lead workshops including a number of well known early country music performers. Tapes in this series include:
Mike Seeger and Lonnie Glosson (NN5/545/4a)
Cliff Carlisle/Henry Gilbert (NN5/545/4b)
Chubby Wise and Mac Wiseman (NN5/545/4c)
Country Gentlemen (NN5/545/4d)
Bluegrass Drifters/Outdoor Plumbing Company (NN5/545/4e)

22. Roosevelt Presnell/Herb Gatherer B&W 55min 1975
Roosevelt Presnell is a farmer from Beech Creek, North Carolina, who has gathered, bought and sold herbs for over fifty years. This video tape traces Mr. Presnell's life history and focuses on his vast knowledge of herbs and their gathering. The tape demonstrates the gathering of herbs in the field and their preparation for sale and use. Some herbs featured are black cohash, spignet and ginseng.

23. Taft Greer: Weaving the Wall of Jericho B&W 50min 1975
This tape deals with the life of Taft Greer and his weaving. Besides giving his life history, it explains the whole process of dying wool from walnuts and herbs to weaving it into a bedspread to selling the finished product. Some of Taft's work is on exhibit at the Smithsonian Institute and his reputation is nationwide.

24. Taylor and Stella Kimble (NN5/533/3) B&W 32min 1974
Taylor and Stella Kimble of Laurel Fork in Carroll County, Virginia, were both born into music-loving families in 1892. Like many other old-time musicians, Taylor and Stella gave up their music for many years, but took it up again during the nation-wide revival of traditional string band and fiddle music that began to emerge in the early sixties. Since then, they have made numerous appearances at fiddle contests and folk festivals in Virginia and North Carolina.

25. "They Shall Take up Serpents" (NN5/787/788/1a) B&W 49min Fire and Serpent Handlers (NN5/787/788/1b) B&W 53min 1973
The handling of poisonous serpents is one of the most spectacular and controversial forms of religious expression to be found in the Pentecostal Churches of the Southern mountains. In 1973, the deaths of several members of the Church of God in Jesus' Name during its services brought about a confrontation with Tennessee courts and law enforcement agencies, and an influx of network newspeople gained the church instant national notoriety. The first tape in this series includes an interview with the assistant preacher of the church who provides a detailed insider's view of its belief system, segments of actual services, and a brief interview with a judge involved with the case. The second tape begins with further excerpts from services, including fire handling and concludes with a panel discussion with several ministers in Bluff City, Tennessee.

26. Third Annual Jonesboro Storytelling Festival B&W 1975
The Jonesboro Storytelling festival of 1975 features veteran storyteller Ray Hicks of Sugar Grove, North Carolina, and Doc McConnell of Rogersville, Tennessee. In addition to the traditional Jack tales, Ray tells of his first encounter with a witch, and Doc discusses various aspects of traditional mountain life.

27. Tommy Jarrell (NN5/533/2) B&W 32min 1974
Tommy Jarrell who was born about the turn of this century in Round Peak, North Carolina, was influenced by his father, Ben Jarrell, one of the finest fiddlers in the Blue Ridge Area, and a master claw-hammer banjo player, Charlie Lowe. Although this tape is primarily devoted to Tommy's fiddling, he is also a vigorous singer.

Broadside TV has all tapes in 1/2 inch reel to reel or 3/4 inch format. Contact Broadside about tapes listed and others in production, using code number when given.

Broadside TV
Elm and Millard
Johnson City, TN 37601
Phone: 926-8191

C. East Tennessee State University, Department of English

1. **Gathering of the Clans: Scottish Games B&W 30min**

2. **Marshall Ward: Jack Tale (Jack and the Heifer Hide) B&W 30min**

3. **Marshall Ward: Jack Tale (Continuation) B&W 30min**

4. **Ralph Nelson: Log Hewing B&W 30min**

5. **Ray Hicks: Herbs B&W 30min**

6. **Ray Hicks: Cradle Reaping B&W 30min**

7. **Stanley Hicks: Still Operation B&W 30min**

8. **Ray Hicks: Jack Tale; Marshall Ward; Riving Boards, Splitting Rails B&W 30min**

D. WSJK-TV, East Tennessee State University, East Tennessee State University—Department of English Johnson City, TN 37601

1. Appalachian Area Crafts Color 30min
A combination of three films by Professors Thomas G. Burton and Jack Schrader that feature Alex Stuart, Ott Blair and Edd Presnell.

2. Appalachian Museum Color 30min
An interview conducted by Professor Thomas G. Burton with John Rice Erwin, director of the Museum of Appalachia in Norris, Tennessee. The old fashioned ways of making shingles and molasses are shown.

3. The Appalachians B&W 30min
An interview with Cratis Williams.

4. A Film About Ray Hicks B&W 30min
Made by Professors Thomas G. Burton and Jack Schrader, it tells about the life of a mountain man who specializes in herbs, cradle reaping and Jack tales.

5. Interviews with Fred Wolfe B&W 30min
Professor David McClellan interviews Fred Wolfe, brother of writer Thomas Wolfe.

6. Interview with Jesse Stuart B&W 30min
This interview is conducted by Professors Ambrose Manning, Robert J. Higgs, and John Tallent.

7. John Fox, Jr. Color 30min
Professor Virginia David interviews Miss Glissee Martin, former postmistress and friend of novelist John Fox and his family. Miss Martin talks about Mr. Fox who wrote *Trail of the Lonesome Pine* and *The Little Shepherd of Kingdom Come.*

8. Kentucky Heritage B&W 30min
Three programs:
a. Basketmaking
b. Long Rifle in Revival
c. Traditional Hand Tools.

9. Interview with Mrs. Sherwood Anderson Color 30min
A discussion about Mrs. Anderson's husband, Sherwood Anderson, conducted by Professors Robert J. Higgs and Virginia David. It includes a tour of the Anderson country home, Ripshin, twenty miles from Marion, Virginia.

10. Tipton-Haynes Historical Farm B&W 30min
A guided tour through the buildings of the farm with information about its different owners and the events of historical importance which occurred there. It is located at Johnson City, Tennessee.

These 10 two-inch video tapes are in the permanent library of WSJK-TV. For borrowing contact:

Mr. Jerry Ruetz
WSJK-TV, East Tennessee State University
Johnson City, TN 37601

E. West Virginia University, Station WWVU-TV Morgantown, WV 26506

1. The West Virginia State Folk Festival 60min
A musical variety show from Glenville festival, featuring performances by older residents of the area.

2. Volcano 30min
A descriptive documentary about an old West Virginia oil field, one last working "continuous wire" oil well, and the 86 year old man who keeps it going.

The above two programs on videocassettes were produced by WWVU-TV and are distributed in non-broadcast form by:

The Public Television Library
475 L'Enfant Plaza SW
Washington, DC 20024

ABOUT THE AUTHOR

CHARLOTTE TANKSLEY ROSS is also known as the "Legend Lady." Ross has collected about 4,000 folk tales. She is a noted storyteller, folklorist and Appalachian State University communications adjunct professor. She has performed at the American Folklore Society, Smithsonian Institution Folklore Festival, Opryland and the Ulster (Ireland) Folklife Festival. In 1969, Ross was hired as the Appalachian Room's first Librarian. In 1976, Charlotte Ross published the *Bibliography of Southern Appalachia*. She is co-author of *From My Grandmother's Grandmother Unto Me* with her daughter Clarinda. She and her husband Carl Ross had two children: Clarinda and Tyler.

www.ingramcontent.com/pod-product-compliance
Lightning Source LLC
LaVergne TN
LVHW061235100826
845148LV00008B/960

* 9 7 8 1 4 6 9 6 4 2 1 3 0 *